[legit for
Judge to
use]

What do you think is the right way
for A Judge to Approach Statutory interpretation?

[tools of
statutory int]
TOOLS Textualists + Purposfulists use.

CASES AND MATERIALS ON
LEGISLATION AND REGULATION

STATUTES AND THE CREATION OF PUBLIC POLICY

Sixth Edition

■ ■ ■

William N. Eskridge Jr.
John A. Garver Professor of Jurisprudence
Yale University

James J. Brudney
Joseph Crowley Chair in Labor and Employment Law
Fordham University Law School

Josh Chafetz
Professor of Law
Cornell Law School

Philip P. Frickey
Late Alexander F. & May T. Morrison Professor of Law
University of California at Berkeley

Elizabeth Garrett
Late President, Cornell University and
Professor of Law, Cornell Law School

AMERICAN CASEBOOK SERIES®

WEST
ACADEMIC
PUBLISHING

American Casebook Series is a trademark registered in the U.S. Patent and Trademark Office.

ISBN: 978-1-68328-183-2

In Memory of Our Friends and Major Contributors to These Materials

Philip P. Frickey, 1953–2010

Elizabeth Garrett, 1963–2016

PREFACE TO THE SIXTH EDITION

The Sixth Edition expands and deepens our focus on how legislatures, agencies, and courts contribute to the creation of public policy. This edition includes new treatment of the Affordable Care Act, the Congressional Review Act, and other legislation. It covers recent executive orders and regulatory developments during the first years of the Trump Administration. And it incorporates decisions by the Supreme Court, lower federal courts, and state courts addressing *inter alia* political gerrymandering; bribery and extortion; pragmatic and other theoretical approaches to statutory interpretation; language, structural, and substantive policy canons; the uses and value of legislative background/context; the nondelegation doctrine; agency implementation under the APA; and the extent of judicial deference to agency interpretations of statutes or regulations.

The organization of the book's nine chapters has been slightly modified. Following an introductory chapter and three chapters examining legislative and political processes, chapter five addresses theories of statutory interpretation that had been covered in chapter six (incorporating almost all of former chapter six as well as some material from former chapter five). Chapters six and seven address doctrines of statutory interpretation, separately examining intrinsic and extrinsic dimensions (these were previously part of a single chapter seven). Chapters eight and nine deal with implementing statutes in the administrative state and judicial deference to agency interpretations, as in the fifth edition.

We are grateful for the suggestions and comments of many colleagues in preparing this new edition. While listing them inevitably risks omitting some who also deserve mention, we would single out Aaron-Andrew Bruhl, Abbe Gluck, Jennifer Gordon, Clare Huntington, Olati Johnson, Anita Krishnakumar, Joe Landau, Ethan Leib, Victoria Nourse, Kimani Paul-Emile, Nicholas Parrillo, Richard Re, Ed Rubin, Aaron Saiger, Kate Shaw, Matthew Stephenson, Peter Strauss, and Olivier Sylvain for helpful insights.

We thank Yale, Fordham, and Cornell law schools for generous research support. In preparing the Sixth Edition, we have benefitted from the contributions of outstanding research assistants: Geoff Block (Yale class of 2021); Elliot Fink (Fordham Class of 2020); Rebecca Guthrie (Fordham class of 2021); Taylor Hoogendoorn (Yale class of 2018); Alexandra Lichtenstein (Yale class of 2020) Patrick Sandman (Cornell class of 2018); and Amy Torres (Fordham Class of 2018).

Finally, we continue to benefit enormously from the talents and insights of our departed colleagues and friends, Phil Frickey and Beth Garrett. Phil's pathbreaking work starting from the First Edition remains foundational. Beth's insights into the legislative process have enriched the book since the Third Edition. We remain ever mindful of our debt to these brilliant and empathic scholars.

WILLIAM N. ESKRIDGE JR.
New Haven, Connecticut

JAMES J. BRUDNEY
New York, New York

JOSH CHAFETZ
Ithaca, New York

SUMMARY OF CONTENTS

TABLE OF CONTENTS

TABLE OF CASES

The principal cases are in bold type.

_____

CASES AND MATERIALS ON

LEGISLATION AND REGULATION

STATUTES AND THE CREATION OF PUBLIC POLICY

Sixth Edition

CHAPTER 1

AN INTRODUCTION TO STATUTES

■ ■ ■

We introduce the study of statutory interpretation through a case study, followed by descriptions of several theoretical frameworks for understanding that story. Section 1 of this chapter tells the story of the Civil Rights Act of 1964, Pub. L. No. 88–352, 78 Stat. 241 (codified as amended in scattered sections of 42 U.S.C.). We have chosen this law, in part, because it is a dramatic example of how statutes can and do make a significant difference in our society and our lives. The principles set forth in *Brown v. Board of Education*, 347 U.S. 483 (1954), would have been left largely unfulfilled were it not for the statute, which amplified and implemented the principles in ways that the Court was not able, or willing, to do. Also, the story of the law's enactment is itself a case study of the legislative process and of the unpredictable path followed by the official as well as private implementers of the statute.

The Civil Rights Act is also a useful starting point for a theoretical discussion of the legislative process in the United States. We offer three types of theories: pluralist theories, which focus on the role of social and economic groups in policymaking; public choice theories, which treat legislation as a transaction between buyers (interest groups) and sellers (legislators); and proceduralist theories, which emphasize the many obstacles a bill must pass through before it becomes a law. Each theory has a descriptive dimension (this is how the legislative process *does* work) and a normative dimension (this is how the legislative process *should* work).

In Section 2, we trace the dynamic interpretation of Title VII (the employment discrimination title) of the Civil Rights Act. We start with the implementation of the 1964 Act by the Equal Employment Opportunity Commission (EEOC). Although Congress purposely structured the EEOC as a weak agency, it developed important legal rules that gave teeth to the statutory scheme—more teeth than some of the law's supporters probably thought they were enacting into law. We also introduce you to theories of statutory interpretation through examination of an important case, *United Steelworkers v. Weber*, in which the Court interpreted the Act to allow voluntary affirmative action plans.

Today, the process by which a bill becomes a law has evolved. What was once considered "unorthodox lawmaking" has become the new normal. Section 3 introduces the student to this complicated, hyper-partisan legislative process through a case study of the Affordable Care Act of 2010. Just as the Civil Rights Act was the landmark statute of an earlier generation, so the Affordable Care Act aspires to be the landmark statute for the generation of today's students.

1. THE STORY OF THE CIVIL RIGHTS ACT OF 1964 AND THE CLASSIC PROCEDURES OF STATUTE-CREATION[1]

Brown v. Board of Education declared a great principle—non-discrimination and racial equality—but the principle did little to change the day-to-day lives of most African Americans in the 1950s. *Brown* applied only to public institutions, leaving private hotels, restaurants, swimming pools, and employers free to continue racially discriminatory practices. And the pace of desegregation even for public institutions (including schools) was slow. In the early 1960s, civil rights activists were no longer willing to wait. Demonstrations, sit-ins, and a March on Washington planned for August 1963 turned up the heat for congressional attention to still-segregated America.

On June 11, 1963, President John Kennedy addressed the country on national television and announced his intention to propose a comprehensive civil rights bill to address the burning issue, "whether all Americans are to be afforded equal rights and equal opportunities, whether we are going to treat our fellow Americans as we want to be treated." Although President Lincoln's Emancipation Proclamation (freeing the slaves) had been issued exactly one hundred years earlier, the descendants of those men and women "are not yet freed from the bonds of injustice. They are not yet freed from social and economic oppression. And this Nation, for all its hopes and all its boasts, will not be fully free until all its citizens are free."

OBSTACLES TO CIVIL RIGHTS LEGISLATION

Title II of the President's proposed legislation, the public accommodations provision, would guarantee equal access to all hotels, restaurants, places of amusement, and retail establishments. Title III covered school desegregation. It would give the federal government, particularly the Attorney General, greater authority to implement the *Brown* decision. Employment discrimination was treated in Title V of the President's bill, which expanded the powers of the Civil Rights Commission, and in Title VII, which would have established a Committee on Equal Employment to monitor the conduct of federal contractors. While not addressing private discrimination, the President reaffirmed his support for legislation addressing employment discrimination in the private sector. Finally, in Title VI, the President proposed that recipients of federal assistance be prohibited from discriminating on the basis of race. The events of 1963 suggested the need for such legislation. But there was good reason to doubt that the President's bill would ever become law.

---

[1]   The most informative source for our account of the 1964 Act was Charles Whalen & Barbara Whalen, *The Longest Debate: A Legislative History of the 1964 Civil Rights Act* (1985) (cited in text as "Whalens," with page numbers). Quotations from *The Longest Debate* are reprinted with the permission of Charles Whalen, Barbara Whalen, and the publisher, Seven Locks Press, Inc., P.O. Box 27, Cabin John, Maryland 20818. Other useful sources were Carl Brauer, *John F. Kennedy and the Second Reconstruction* (1977) ("Brauer"); Robert Caro, *The Passage of Power: The Years of Lyndon Johnson* (2012) ("Caro"); Hugh Davis Graham, *The Civil Rights Era: Origins and Development of National Policy, 1960–1972* (1990) ("Graham"); Cynthia Harrison, *On Account of Sex: The Politics of Women's Issues, 1945–1968* (1988) ("Harrison"); Neil MacNeil, *Dirksen: Portrait of a Public Man* (1970) ("MacNeil"); Merle Miller, *Lyndon: An Oral Biography* (1980) ("Miller"); Clay Risen, *The Bill of the Century: The Epic Battle for the Civil Rights Act* (2014) ("Risen"); Edward Schapsmeier & Frederick Schapsmeier, *Dirksen of Illinois: Senatorial Statesman* (1985) ("Schapsmeiers"); and Francis Vaas, *Title VII: Legislative History,* 7 B.C. Indus. & Com. L. Rev. 431 (1966) ("Vaas").

The Democratic Party enjoyed lopsided majorities in both chambers of Congress, but that was not good news for civil rights. Southern Democrats normally controlled as many as half of the party's votes in the Senate, and systematically killed civil rights bills through parliamentary maneuvers. In contrast, the Republicans—the Party of Lincoln—showed renewed interest in civil rights. In 1957, President Eisenhower introduced a civil rights bill—but a filibuster by Senate Democrats forced supporters to propose changes that made it an essentially toothless law. A similar presidential initiative in 1960 yielded a weak voting rights law, after Senate Democrats deleted school desegregation, employment, and housing discrimination provisions from the bill. Although 1960 GOP presidential candidate Richard Nixon had a strong civil rights record, his strategy was to peel away southern states from the Democrats. Although his record was mixed on civil rights, Senator John Kennedy, the Democrats' candidate, took stronger pro-civil rights stances and won the black vote.

Once he was President, Kennedy made no immediate move to introduce civil rights legislation. In November 1962, he issued the order prohibiting racial discrimination in federally financed housing, the same order he had, as a candidate in 1960, chastised Eisenhower for not issuing with a "stroke of his pen." It was not until he was faced with blatant defiance by Governors Ross Barnett (D-MS) and George Wallace (D-AL) that Kennedy, as Commander-in-Chief, used federal troops to enforce judicial desegregation orders. Vice-President Lyndon Johnson was not known as a force for civil rights either. In 1957, as Majority Leader, "LBJ" persuaded the Senate to pass the first civil rights statute since 1874—but liberals were disappointed that the law had virtually no legal effect.

The primary obstacle to civil rights legislation, however, was the gauntlet that a statute had to pass in order to become law. Over 90% of bills introduced in Congress die in the legislative labyrinth. Virtually all bills introduced in Congress are referred initially to a committee for consideration and cannot be voted on until the committee has reported them out.[2] Because a committee's chair controls the committee's staff and agenda, he or she has the power to effectively kill a bill by preventing the committee from considering it. In 1963–64, committee chairmanships had long been awarded on the basis of seniority—and many powerful chairs were Southern Democrats such as Senator James Eastland (D-MS), chair of the Senate Judiciary Committee, and Representative Howard "Judge" Smith (D-VA), chair of the House Rules Committee. In 1957, Smith stalled consideration of the civil rights bill simply by leaving Washington; he claimed that he needed to attend to his barn in Virginia that had recently burned down. Speaker of the House Sam Rayburn (D-TX) replied that he knew Smith was opposed to civil rights, but he never suspected that the Chairman would resort to arson.

Even if the civil rights bill were to survive the committee process, it faced a certain *filibuster* on the floor of the Senate. In 1963–64, Senate rules allowed unlimited debate of a question before voting, and civil rights opponents had

---

[2]   Current House Rule X, clause 1 and Senate Rule XXV, clause 1 identify the standing (permanent) committees in the two chambers and define the jurisdiction (area of exclusive authority) for each standing committee. House Rule XII, clause 2 and Senate Rule XVII, clause 3 govern referral to committees by the Speaker of the House and the Senate Majority Leader.

successfully used this tactic in 1957 and 1960 to prevent consideration of civil rights bills, allowing a vote only after they had exacted tremendous concessions from the bills' supporters. The only ways to break a filibuster were by permitting it to continue until the filibusterers were physically exhausted or by invoking *cloture* (a two-thirds vote to end discussion).[3] The former had been tried and had failed in 1957, while the latter had been successfully invoked only five times in the history of the Senate and never to end debate on a civil rights bill (Whalens 126).

PASSAGE IN THE HOUSE

The President's civil rights bill was introduced in both houses of Congress on June 19, 1963, but its supporters pushed for immediate consideration only in the House of Representatives. If they could develop a strong record and publicity for the bill in the House, supporters hoped that political momentum would improve the bill's chances in the Senate.

1.   *Writing a Bill the Hard Way—the Judiciary Committee.* House Speaker John McCormack (D-MA) referred H.R. 7152[4] to the House Judiciary Committee, which had jurisdiction over civil rights bills. Chairman Emanuel Celler (D-NY) referred the bill to Subcommittee No. 5. The Chairman referred the bill to this subcommittee, which normally handled antitrust matters, because it was dominated by civil rights advocates: its Chairman was Celler himself, the ranking Republican was William McCulloch (R-OH). Both were strong supporters of civil rights legislation—and the subcommittee had no senior southern member who could obstruct progress on a strong bill.

Celler scheduled subcommittee hearings to start before the Fourth of July recess. The free ride that the bill was expected to get through the subcommittee hit a snag with the first witness, Attorney General Robert Kennedy. The Attorney General was unaware that Representatives McCulloch and John Lindsay (R-NY) had introduced civil rights bills, and his failure to acknowledge their efforts was interpreted as a Democratic attempt to take partisan advantage of the civil rights issue. The Republican members of the subcommittee threatened to scuttle H.R. 7152 if it became a partisan measure. To repair the nascent bipartisan coalition, the Administration dispatched Assistant Attorney General Burke Marshall to negotiate a deal with McCulloch during the recess (Whalens 5–11).

Marshall found McCulloch supportive of civil rights but unwilling to allow the Democrats to hog the issue (particularly since the Democrats heading the Administration had undermined his own efforts in 1957 and 1960). Marshall brokered a deal whereby McCulloch pledged his support in exchange for the Administration's promise to publicize the initiative as bipartisan and not to allow the Senate to water down the bill, as it had done in 1957 (Whalens 10–14). This meant

---

3   Under current Senate Rule XXII, clause 2, cloture can be invoked in most cases by the vote of 60 of the 100 senators, but in 1963–64, Rule XXII provided for cloture of debate only by two-thirds of the senators voting on the question. Since important cloture votes could be expected to command all 100 senators, 67 votes were usually needed to close off debate. Even now, a two-thirds vote is required to end debate on any measure amending the Senate Rules, including the rule governing cloture.

4   Bills introduced in the House and Senate are assigned identifying numbers—"H.R. ___" and "S. ___"—just as cases filed in U.S. courts are assigned a docket number.

that McCulloch would be consulted on all changes to H.R. 7152 that the Administration wanted to accept after the bill passed the House.

During the congressional hearings, the civil rights proponents engaged in a campaign to build public support for H.R. 7152, which would culminate in the March on Washington in August, topped off by Dr. King's "I Have a Dream" speech. Some labor unions, such as Walter Reuther's United Auto Workers, lent their lobbying clout and grass-roots organization to the cause. Led by James Hamilton, the National Council of Churches lent its support, and an increasing number of rabbis, priests, and pastors lobbied for the bill; they would prove an important grass-roots lobbying force, especially in states where the impact of blacks and labor was minimal. In June and July, the Kennedy Administration helped recruit private support, although the President cautioned civil rights allies not to expect a really ambitious law, given all the obstacles to any legislation (Brauer 273–75).

By August 2, the subcommittee had held 22 days of hearings on H.R. 7152 and was ready to *mark up* the bill. A mark-up is a committee's drafting session where members consider amendments and rewrite bills. The Administration had asked Celler to stall final consideration on the bill until his tax reform proposal was voted out of the House Ways and Means Committee, where it had been languishing since January. The highly controversial tax cut was a cornerstone in the President's economic program, and Kennedy feared that Southerners on Ways and Means might use the bill as a target for retaliation if the civil rights bill cleared Subcommittee No. 5 first. Therefore, Celler delayed substantive mark-up of H.R. 7152 until September (Whalens 22–23). Meanwhile, public pressure for legislation mounted.[5]

On September 10, the Ways and Means Committee approved the tax bill, and Celler prepared for the mark-up of H.R. 7152. Deputy Attorney General Nicholas Katzenbach had written Celler a letter setting forth the "tactics" that the Administration expected him to follow, pursuant to its deal with McCulloch. But Celler chose to pursue a more aggressive approach. He remembered that the Senate had watered down the moderate civil rights bills passed by the House in 1957 and 1960. Why not start with a very strong bill this time, so that a compromise version would still be acceptable? Moreover, by publicly pushing a strong bill, Celler would be a hero to civil rights groups and would still be able to preserve his friendship with the conservatives by allowing them to score points with their constituents when the bill was inevitably weakened (Whalens 30–31).

Bill McCulloch watched in disbelief as Manny Celler and the liberal Democrats on the subcommittee proceeded to strengthen almost every title of the Administration's bill, betraying the President's agreement with the Republican leadership in the process. For example, Bob Kastenmeier (D-WI) offered an

---

[5]   On August 28, 1963, as Congress prepared to adjourn for the Labor Day recess, almost a quarter of a million people converged on Washington, D.C., in a peaceful demonstration for equal rights—the March on Washington for Jobs and Freedom (Martin 176–77). In his address to the crowd that afternoon, Dr. King argued that, one hundred years after the Emancipation Proclamation, African Americans were still not free. "One hundred years later, the life of the Negro is still sadly crippled by the manacles and the chains of discrimination. * * * One hundred years later, the Negro is still languishing in the corners of American society and finds himself an exile in his own land." Dr. King concluded: "I have a dream today that my four little children will one day live in a nation where they will not be judged by the color of their skin but by the content of their character. I have a dream today."

amendment to broaden Title II, the public accommodations provision, to include every private business—law firms, medical associations, and private schools—except rooming houses with five units or less (Whalens 34–35). On September 25, the subcommittee replaced H.R. 7152's weak equal employment provisions with a new title, embodied in a 30-page amendment offered by Peter Rodino (D-NJ). The new title would create an Equal Employment Opportunity Commission, with authority to investigate employment discrimination on account of race, religion, or national origin and to issue enforceable cease-and-desist orders (Vaas 435; Whalens 35).

On October 2, Subcommittee No. 5 reported the new H.R. 7152 to the full Judiciary Committee. Civil rights leaders, who had received virtually every provision they had lobbied for, called the bill a triumph. But McCulloch labeled the bill "a pail of garbage" with no chance of passage on the floor of the House (Whalens 38). Southern members of the Judiciary Committee who hoped to derail the bill apparently agreed, for they joined the liberals to vote H.R. 7152 as amended out of subcommittee.

Although a staunch supporter of civil rights legislation, House Minority Leader Charles Halleck (R-IN) resented the Democrats' partisan tactics. He told Deputy Attorney General Katzenbach and Speaker McCormack on October 8 that the Republicans would allow the strengthened bill to go to the House floor, where it would probably die—unless the liberal Democrats themselves cooperated in weakening the bill. The Administration agreed to the GOP proposal and browbeat Celler to go along (Whalens 42–44). On October 15, the Attorney General testified before the Committee to recommend weakening changes (Brauer 304). On October 22, the amendments were to be offered, the first by Roland Libonati (D-IL). At the last moment Libonati backed out, leaving the Republicans feeling betrayed again. A Republican member moved to report the subcommittee bill to the full House. The motion would have easily passed had Celler not adjourned the Committee for the day. The situation was a mess.

Administration officials met with Halleck and McCulloch to work out a compromise bill that would satisfy the Republicans (Whalens 52–53). The new bill reconciled a Republican redraft and the original Administration bill. The President and Republican leadership agreed that the compromise bill would be offered as a substitute for the subcommittee bill. All that remained was to defeat the motion to report out the unacceptable subcommittee version of H.R. 7152. Halleck and McCulloch agreed to provide seven Republican votes if the Democrats would provide ten votes. The President twisted arms and Celler invoked loyalty to party and the chairman to meet their quota (Whalens 59–64).

Now uneasy with Chairman Celler's ability to run the Judiciary Committee, the Administration prepared a "six-point script" for him to follow on October 29, describing precisely the manner in which to proceed. For once, events went as planned (Whalens 64–66). (1) A roll call vote was taken on the pending motion to report the subcommittee bill. Democratic members were called first, according to tradition, allowing Halleck and McCulloch to see if the Democrats could deliver their share of the votes to defeat the motion before having to commit themselves. Celler delivered ten Democratic votes, and the Republicans provided nine votes (more than promised) to defeat the motion. (2) Celler moved to strike all but the first sentence of the subcommittee bill and to insert the compromise bill as an amendment. (3) Celler and McCulloch explained the substitute, and Celler brushed aside a *point of order* challenge. (4) Once the compromise was read in its entirety, Representative Rodino moved the *previous question*, cutting off any debate on the proposed amendment. The Committee voted 20–12 in favor of the previous question. (5) The Judiciary Committee passed the compromise substitute by a vote of 20–14. (6) The Committee reported H.R. 7152 to the House.

Although civil rights leaders criticized the Administration for favoring cutbacks in the subcommittee substitute, the committee version was stronger than the Administration's original bill. For example, Title VII (equal employment) retained the main features of Rodino's substitute for the Administration's weak monitoring provisions, though the EEOC's adjudicatory powers were limited. The President praised the bill as "comprehensive and fair," and the Administration evenly distributed credit among Democrats and Republicans (Whalens 66).

2. *Surviving the Rules Committee.* On November 21, H.R. 7152 and the Judiciary Committee's report were conveyed to the Clerk of the House and then to the Rules Committee. Each bill reported out of committee passes through the Rules Committee, where a resolution (the *rule*) governing floor debate is prepared.[6] In addition to providing that high priority bills receive expedited consideration, the Rules Committee determines the amount of time to be allowed for debate, how the time for debate will be allocated, and the scope of permissible amendments.

The Rules Committee stage often constitutes a substantive consideration of the bill, and it presents an opportunity to derail a bill before the House itself has a chance to consider it. Unfortunately, the chairman of the Rules Committee, 80-year-old Howard ("Judge") Smith, had spent 33 years in the House killing or eviscerating progressive legislation in the areas of labor, public housing, education, medical care and, of course, civil rights.[7]

President Kennedy's assassination on November 22 meant that the task of getting H.R. 7152 through the Rules Committee fell to the new President, Lyndon Johnson. In an effort to seize the moral leadership of the nation, LBJ addressed a joint session of Congress soon after Kennedy's death: "[N]o memorial oration or eulogy could more eloquently honor President Kennedy's memory than the earliest possible passage of the civil rights bill for which he fought so long." Apparently,

---

[6]   Current House Rule XIII, clause 2 provides that all committee reports, including the views of the minority, shall be delivered to the Clerk for printing and reference to the proper *calendar* (described *infra*). Because House calendars contain many bills, and bills are to be considered in their order on the calendars, there is no assurance that the bill will be considered at all. The Rules Committee has the power to recommend a rule to expedite consideration of any bill—ahead of those previously placed on the calendars.

[7]   In an effort to curtail Judge Smith's ability to bury the Administration's progressive legislative agenda, President Kennedy had worked prior to the 1961 session with then-Speaker of the House, Sam Rayburn, to enlarge the Rules Committee from ten to fifteen members (ten Democrats and five Republicans). The appointment of five new committee members allowed Rayburn and the Administration to create an 8–7 liberal majority on the Rules Committee and to increase the control of party leaders over it. While the enlargement improved prospects for the President's legislative agenda, highly controversial bills—like civil rights proposals—still faced unfavorable odds in Judge Smith's lair (Harvey 15–16).

popular support for the bill was increasing—but with no effect on Judge Smith, who declined even to hold hearings on H.R. 7152.

There were three procedural options for dislodging Smith's stranglehold on H.R. 7152, and each was tried by the bill's supporters (Whalens 84–85). First, under House Rule XV, a petition signed by a majority of the House's members (218 when there are no vacancies) can remove any bill from committee, including the Rules Committee, after it has been in committee for 30 days. On December 9, Celler began circulating such a *discharge petition*, but McCulloch and Halleck refused to deliver the needed Republican signatures, on the ground that such a course was antithetical to the committee process (Whalens 84). Only a handful of discharge petitions have been successful in the last 50 years.

On December 11, the Republicans announced their intent to use a second device, *Calendar Wednesday*, to call up H.R. 7152. House Rule XXV allows the Speaker on each Wednesday to call the standing committees in alphabetical order to inquire whether the chairman wishes the House to consider any bill previously reported out of that committee. But with eleven committees coming alphabetically before the Judiciary Committee, including six chaired by Southerners, the bill's opponents could easily defeat the tactic by calling up other bills to exhaust the available time. To prevent an embarrassing display of intraparty divisions, the Democratic leadership simply adjourned the House before the Calendar Wednesday maneuver could be tried (Whalens 85).

The third mechanism was successful. House Rule XI permits any three members of a committee to request the chairman to call a meeting to consider a bill; if the meeting is not scheduled within three days, a majority of the committee may schedule one. With five liberal Democrats on the Rules Committee, three Republican votes were needed. The pivotal votes were controlled by Clarence Brown (R-OH), the ranking minority member on the Rules Committee (Whalens 85). Sharing the commitment to civil rights of his friend Bill McCulloch, Brown gently informed Judge Smith of his plans to lead a mutiny, so to head off a confrontation, Smith announced that hearings would begin on January 9, 1964 (Whalens 86).

Between January 9 and January 30, the House Rules Committee heard testimony from 40 different members of Congress (Vaas 438). No one expected the hearings to have any effect on the outcome, but they provided southern Democrats a forum for airing their opposition to the bill. On January 30, 1964, the Rules Committee approved House Resolution 616, governing debate on H.R. 7152, by a vote of 11–4 (Whalens 99). The bill had not only survived the Rules Committee, it had survived without a single amendment (Vaas 438).

3.   *Bipartisan House Victory*. The House of Representatives follows a six-step process in considering a bill called up from the floor. First, the House debates and votes on the bill's rule. If the rule is accepted, the body will resolve into the *Committee of the Whole House on the State of the Union*, which is simply the full House following simplified procedures for purposes of debate. Next, pursuant to the rule, members offer amendments, which are debated and then accepted or rejected by unrecorded votes. The members will then resume sitting formally as the House and, if requested by one-fifth of the members, take recorded votes on any accepted amendments. A

minority party member will be recognized to offer a motion to recommit the bill to committee. Finally, the House will vote on the bill, as amended by the Committee of the Whole (Whalens 101).

On January 31, 1964, Speaker John McCormack recognized a Rules Committee member to call up House Resolution 616 (the special rule) for immediate consideration. Under the rules of the House, debate on the resolution was limited to one hour, divided equally between each party. In a voice vote, the House approved the rule (Whalens 102–03). The House then resolved itself into the Committee of the Whole, and Speaker McCormack stepped down and handed the gavel to Eugene Keogh (D-NY), who assumed his position as Chairman of the Committee of the Whole.

The rule approved for H.R. 7152 specified that general debate would be limited to ten hours, divided equally between the two parties and between opponents and supporters, after which amendments would be offered, title by title, in accordance with *the five minute rule*. Under this rule, all speakers—the amendment's sponsor, its proponents, and its opponents—were limited to five minutes of remarks each. Furthermore, in exchange for the bill's supporters' pledge not to limit debate on any amendment, the bill's opponents agreed not to bog down the proceedings with redundant quorum calls. This was to be a battle, but it would be a genteel one (Whalens 108).

Celler and McCulloch delivered the opening statements. Manny Celler chose to describe the bill in broad dramatic terms:

> The legislation before you seeks only to honor the constitutional guarantees of equality under the law for all. It bestows no preferences on any one group; what it does is to place into balance the scales of justice so that the living force of our Constitution shall apply to all people, not only to those who by accident of birth were born with white skins.

Bill McCulloch discussed H.R. 7152 more simply, explaining the need for federal legislation and its validity under the Constitution. He argued that "this bill is comprehensive in scope, but moderate in application."

Southern Congressmen cast the bill in a different light. Edwin Willis (D-LA), for example, characterized the bill as "the most drastic and far-reaching proposal and grab for power ever to be reported out of a committee of Congress in the history of our Republic." Congressman Thomas Abernethy (D-MS) predicted that a civil rights law would precipitate a "counter-revolution that is bound to arise and continue to grow and grow and grow." After ten hours of such general debate, H.R. 7152 was ready to meet its ultimate test in the House—the amendment process on the floor.

McCulloch and Celler had prepared carefully for this stage of the process. They and other supporters had at hand a detailed manual created by the Justice Department. The manual, containing a section-by-section defense of the bill, responded to the opposing views expressed by the southern minority in the Judiciary Committee's report. The floor leaders had also assigned a member of the Judiciary Committee to each title with responsibility for becoming an expert on that particular area. Finally, there were eight Justice Department attorneys—one for each title of the bill—standing by for additional assistance (Whalens 103).

The amendment process began at noon on Monday, February 3, and continued, title-by-title and section-by-section, until 7:00 p.m. on February 10. Over the course of that week, 124 amendments were offered, debated, and voted on, but only 34 were accepted by the Committee of the Whole. Most were technical corrections, including 12 offered by Celler.

The most significant amendment expanded the scope of Title VII and was sponsored by none other than Judge Smith. Alice Paul and the National Women's Party had asked Judge Smith, a long-time ally and supporter of the Equal Rights Amendment, to offer an amendment protecting against workplace sex discrimination. On February 8, 1964, the Rules Committee Chairman proposed the addition of the word "sex" to Title VII's list of impermissible bases for employment decisions (Vaas 441–42; Whalens 115–16). Judge Smith explained that his amendment was necessary to "prevent discrimination against another minority group, the women," and that "it is indisputable fact that all throughout industry women are discriminated against in that just generally speaking they do not get as high compensation." He then read a letter from a female citizen complaining "that women currently outnumber men, that Congress and the President have made the situation worse by engaging in wars that further the imbalance, and that the imbalance prevents women from obtaining their 'right to happiness.'" According to the record, "Smith's comments evoked laughter, though he insisted that he was serious" (Osterman 412).

A mildly flustered Manny Celler opposed the amendment. While McCulloch sat on the sidelines, several liberal representatives joined Celler in ridiculing the amendment. The tone of good-ole-boy jocularity changed as 11 of the House's 12 female legislators rose to address Judge Smith's proposal. "I feel as a white woman when this bill has passed this House and the Senate and has been signed by the President that white women will be the last at the hiring gate," said Representative Martha W. Griffiths (D-MI). Representative Katharine Price Collier St. George (R-NY), joined Griffiths in favor of the amendment. "Why should women be denied equality of opportunity? Why should women be denied equal pay for equal work? That is all we are asking." Representatives Frances Bolton (R-OH), Catherine May (R-WA), and Edna Kelly (D-NY) also spoke in favor of the Smith Amendment. Opponents of the amendment responded that sex discrimination should have its own legislation, because of the physical differences between men and women; a letter from Esther Peterson, the head of the Women's Bureau in the Department of Labor, endorsed this approach. Ultimately, the Smith Amendment passed, 168–133. Although there was no roll-call vote, the amendment was apparently supported by southern opponents of the civil rights bill as well as many supporters of the bill, while many of the negative votes came from liberal supporters of the bill (Vaas 442).

At the close of amendments on February 10, the Committee of the Whole dissolved, John McCormack reclaimed the Speaker's chair, and the members resumed sitting as the House. Chairman Keogh reported H.R. 7152, as amended, back to the House, and the Speaker prepared to complete the final three steps in the process. It was 7:00 p.m., and few were interested in prolonging the affair. Attempts to obtain recorded votes on certain substantive amendments failed to receive sufficient support, and the motion to recommit the bill to the Judiciary Committee failed on a voice vote. Finally it was time for the vote—up or down—on H.R. 7152. When the roll call was over, there were 152 Democratic votes and 138 Republican votes in favor, 96 Democratic votes and 34 Republican votes against. The civil rights bill passed overwhelmingly, 290–130 (Whalens 120–21). Now it was on to the Senate.

PASSAGE IN THE SENATE

H.R. 7152 next had to face the Senate, the body that had diluted civil rights bills in 1957 and 1960. Senator Eastland's Judiciary Committee had essentially ignored the Senate version of the Administration's bill, holding only perfunctory hearings and calling only one witness: Attorney General Robert Kennedy.

In 1963–64, consideration of a typical bill in the Senate usually followed an eight-step process. (1) The bill was read for the first time. (2) If no objections were heard, the bill would immediately be read for the second time. (3) After the second reading, the bill was generally referred to committee, unless a majority voted to place the bill directly on the Senate calendar. (4) The next step was committee consideration where, as in the House, the bill could be amended or killed. (5) If the bill survived committee action, it was placed on the Senate calendar. (6) The supporters would then call up the bill for consideration, (7) and the actual debate of the bill would proceed, subject to the Senate's unlimited debate rules. (8) The final step was the third reading, followed by a vote on the bill, as amended by the committee and during floor debate (Whalens 131–32). The big obstacle to the civil rights bill, however, was the expected Southern filibuster.

1.   *The Longest Debate Begins.* H.R. 7152 arrived in the Senate from the House on Monday, February 17, 1964. On Majority Leader Mike Mansfield's motion, the bill was read for the first time. However, Mansfield objected to a second reading of the bill because he wanted to delay a filibuster until the Senate had completed work on the tax bill. Through a deft combination of flattery and budgetary logrolling, President Johnson had persuaded his old friend Senator Harry Byrd to move forward on the tax cut bill just before the civil rights bill arrived in the Senate (Caro 466–83, 552–57).

When the tax bill was completed on February 26, Mansfield called up the civil rights bill for its second reading. Mansfield then moved to have the bill placed directly on the Senate calendar, thereby bypassing the Judiciary Committee. Senator Richard Russell (D-GA), leader of the southern senators, objected and was joined by Minority Leader Everett Dirksen (R-IL). Although Dirksen shared Mansfield's concern about referring a civil rights bill to Eastland's committee, he felt that a bill of this importance deserved the full legislative history that only committee consideration could provide. Mansfield persuaded 20 Republicans to join him and was able to place H.R. 7152 on the Senate calendar (Whalens 132–35).

Mansfield delayed his next motion—to call up H.R. 7152 for debate—until after the Senate voted on a pending farm bill. This two-week hiatus provided an opportunity for the Senate leadership to organize for the coming battle. To lead the

Senate campaign, Mansfield selected Hubert Horatio Humphrey (D-MN), the Democrats' Senate Whip. An unabashed liberal, Humphrey also aspired to national office, and this was his opportunity to shine. The Republican floor manager was liberal Thomas Kuchel (R-CA), that party's Senate Whip. Dirksen appointed seven other Republicans to assist Kuchel (MacNeil 232). Senators Joseph Clark (D-PA) and Clifford Case (R-NJ) were the senators responsible for handling issues involving Title VII, the equal employment title (Vaas 445).

The liberals' lack of discipline had contributed to the success of the last two civil rights filibusters. President Johnson challenged Humphrey to keep the troops together this time. "You have this great opportunity now, Hubert, but you liberals will never deliver. You don't know the rules of the Senate, and your liberal friends will be off making speeches when they ought to be present. You've got a great opportunity here, but I'm afraid it's going to fall between the boards" (Miller 368). Humphrey organized a daily bipartisan newsletter, designed to inform members of the status of the debate, to refute arguments made on the floor by the bill's opponents, and to maintain a united front (Humphrey 86–87). The floor manager also set up a "quorum duty" system to ensure that there would always be sufficient senators on the floor to prevent the Southerners from adjourning the Senate. Finally, he scheduled regular strategy sessions with the bill's supporters (Humphrey 90).

On March 9, after the farm bill had been passed, Mansfield moved to make H.R. 7152 the pending business of the Senate, a motion he knew would draw a filibuster by the Southerners (Vaas 444).[8] For fourteen days the Senate debated this issue—not whether to pass H.R. 7152, but simply whether to consider the bill at all. Prior to moving for immediate consideration of the bill, Mansfield had met with the Southerners and had been assured that the filibuster on this preliminary issue would not last longer than four or five days. It became apparent, though, as debate dragged on, that the Southerners had merely been maneuvering to convince Mansfield not to call all-night sessions. On March 23, Humphrey kept the Senate in session until 10:15 p.m.—not all night, but long enough to give the filibusterers a taste of what was to come. The next day, supporters announced that they would object to the holding of any committee hearings before the Senate had finished with the civil rights bill. Southern opponents finally decided to allow a vote on Mansfield's motion. On March 26, 1964, the motion to take up H.R. 7152 passed 67–17, with only Southerners opposing (Whalens 146–47).

On March 30, 1964, the Senate began debate on the merits of H.R. 7152. Humphrey delivered the opening statement, treating the half-dozen senators present to a three and one-half hour speech. Tom Kuchel followed with an opening of a mere one and three-quarter hours (Whalens 150–51). Rather than let the Southerners monopolize debate, Humphrey and his team decided to take the offensive early, presenting a detailed, title-by-title defense of the bill over a period of twelve days.

---

[8]   Unlike the House, the Senate does not have a Rules Committee that recommends to the full chamber a rule allowing expedited consideration of important bills. Instead, the Majority Leader normally expedites consideration by negotiating a *unanimous consent agreement*, in which all interested senators agree to consider the bill on a stated date, sometimes with limitations on debate and amendments (like a House rule). But if even a single senator objects to this arrangement, it is nullified. Southern senators in 1964 were not going to agree readily to expedited consideration of the civil rights bill.

Senators were sent to appear on television and radio talk shows and were encouraged to send regular newsletters back to their constituents in an effort to maintain support for the bill in the press and public at large (Humphrey 89–90). Supporters of the civil rights bill emphasized the moral importance of the bill, attempting to elevate the issue above politics and appeal to a broad concept of justice (Humphrey 91–92).[9]

2. *Wooing the Wizard of Ooze.* Southern filibusterers dominated debate after early April and seemed capable of talking the year away. Could Humphrey and Kuchel muster the 67 votes needed to invoke cloture? A block of about 20 southern Democrats were certain to vote against cloture, and about 30 liberal Democrats and 12 liberal Republicans were equally certain to vote for it. To reach the 67 votes needed for cloture, Humphrey and Kuchel needed to win the votes of 25 senators from two groups: 21 conservative Republicans who were opposed to big government programs and 17 moderate Democrats from western and border states that had traditionally relied upon the filibuster to protect themselves from more populous states (Miller 370). Since 1917, when the procedure was formally codified in the Senate's standing rules, cloture had been invoked successfully only five times.

Although some conservative Republicans were willing to support cloture, the bill needed them to vote as a virtual block—which seemed unlikely unless the Minority Leader himself became an enthusiastic supporter of the bill. Although there were only 33 Republican senators, Everett Dirksen ruled the Senate along with Majority Leader Mike Mansfield (MacNeil 230–31). Dirksen had risen to his position of power on the strength of an oratorical prowess that combined flowery language with a throatily mellifluous voice, and an uncanny ability to turn the most difficult political situations into personal triumphs. The former earned him the sobriquet "Wizard of Ooze"; the latter, "Old Doctor Snake Oil" (Whalens 151).

Publicly, Dirksen struck a Delphic pose in his attitude toward the civil rights bill. When the Administration's bill was introduced in June 1963, Dirksen expressed doubts about either a public accommodations provision or a fair employment practices section (Humphrey 85), and as late as August he told representatives of the NAACP that a public accommodations title was not acceptable (MacNeil 223). The momentum created by House passage and increasing public support for the bill led him to soften his position—or perhaps to press for a bill he secretly supported all along. In early November he assured Katzenbach that a civil rights bill would make it to a vote in the Senate (Brauer 308). The bill's strong support from McCulloch and Halleck in the House put further pressure on Dirksen to play a leadership role—a role that Humphrey urged upon him. One of Humphrey's key strategies for collecting the support of GOP conservatives was to cast Dirksen in the starring role of this battle (Humphrey 85–86), and Dirksen's strategy was to play hard to get in public, so that when he did support the measure, with amendments, he would have credibility with his party's conservatives (Risen 198–200).

---

[9]   As a consequence, Humphrey realized that among all the groups lobbying for passage, the religious lobby would be crucial, because it reinforced the moral importance of the issue and provided a means of reaching senators not otherwise influenced by the labor and black lobbying efforts. Humphrey met with religious leaders and actively planned high-profile events to emphasize the interdenominational support for civil rights, including a silent, 24-hour vigil maintained by Protestant, Catholic, and Jewish seminarians on the Capitol grounds throughout the Senate debate (Humphrey 93–94).

By the time the filibuster began in earnest, Dirksen was likely to support some kind of strong civil rights bill. But his support carried a price tag—namely Dirksen's own conservative stamp on the final product (MacNeil 232–33). Initially, Dirksen proposed a package of 40 weakening amendments to Title VII (such as dropping the addition of "sex" to Title VII)—but he ran into immediate opposition from his party's influential liberals, including Senators George Aiken (VT), John Sherman Cooper (KY), Jacob Javits (NY), Tom Kuchel (CA), Leverett Saltonstall (MA), Hugh Scott (PA), and Margaret Chase Smith (ME). Senator Smith, one of only two women in the Senate, demanded that Dirksen not mess with the sex discrimination provision.

The liberals' opposition forced Dirksen to trim the package to ten. On April 16, Dirksen introduced his amendments, but did not seek a vote on the package (Whalens 159–64). On April 29, Dirksen met with Johnson and offered to deliver 22–25 Republican votes for cloture if the Administration would go along with weakening the bill. By one account, Johnson and Humphrey refused to compromise because they thought Dirksen had little choice but to support the civil rights bill (Whalens, 171–72). Another account, however, posits that Dirksen was in a stronger bargaining position. Through a series of meetings in early May with Mansfield, Humphrey, the Attorney General, and other senators, Dirksen agreed to a compromise that achieved much of what he wanted to gain for the small businesses that were his primary concern. Thus, he procured the Administration's support for provisions in the jobs title limiting the authority of the EEOC, protecting employers against government-required quota programs, and expanding employer defenses.[10]

On May 19, Dirksen presented his deal—the most he thought he could get the Democrats to go along with—to the Republican caucus (Risen 219–21). Just as his earlier amendments had been attacked by his party's liberals as going too far, Dirksen's latest proposal was attacked by some conservatives, led by crusty Senator Bourke Hickenlooper (R-IA), as not going nearly far enough. His response was to go public, with a *fait accompli* challenging his Republicans to follow their Minority Leader. Dirksen announced to stunned reporters that the time for action had arrived, that passage of the civil rights bill had become a moral imperative and that he was resolved to see it happen. Quoting Victor Hugo, Dirksen proclaimed, "No army is stronger than an idea whose time has come" (Whalens 185). He followed that proclamation with assiduous courting of his conservative colleagues—abetted by a dramatic assembly of 200 prominent clergy praying on the steps of the Supreme Court and by an editorial by former President Dwight Eisenhower urging a "responsible, forward-looking Republicanism" to support the bill (Risen 221–22).

On May 26, Dirksen presented Amendment No. 656 to the Senate, an amendment in the nature of a substitute for H.R. 7152, known as the "Mansfield-Dirksen Amendment" (Vaas 445).[11] Although liberal Democrats and Republicans

---

[10]   For sharply contrasting views as to the meaning and scope of the Dirksen amendments, compare Daniel Rodriguez & Barry Weingast, *The Positive Political Theory of Legislative History: New Perspectives on the 1964 Civil Rights Act and Its Interpretation*, 151 U. Pa. L. Rev. 1417 (2003), with Victoria Nourse, *Misunderstanding Congress: Statutory Interpretation, the Supermajoritarian Difficulty, and the Separation of Powers*, 99 Geo. L.J. 1119 (2011).

[11]   An *amendment in the nature of a substitute* proposes a whole new bill to replace the bill under consideration. We will briefly discuss the various kinds of amendments in the "Note on How a Bill Becomes a Federal Law," *infra*.

were ultimately satisfied that the anti-discrimination goal of the civil rights bill had not been significantly undermined (Whalens 188–89), the jobs title of the Mansfield-Dirksen substitute was somewhat more business-friendly and less regulatory than the earlier version of the bill (Rodriguez & Weingast 1487–96). Dirksen characteristically termed his bill "infinitely better than what came to us from the House" (Whalens 188), but Humphrey believed that he had kept his promise to Bill McCulloch not to support a bill that significantly diluted the protections of the House bill (Humphrey 85), probably in part because Dirksen's changes benefited small businesses that were important constituents for any midwestern Republican such as McCulloch.

With cloture now a tangible possibility, the bill's supporters spent the next two weeks stumping for votes. President Johnson twisted the arms of Howard Cannon (D-NV), whom Majority Leader Johnson had appointed to critical Senate committees, and J. Howard Edmondson (D-OK), whom LBJ had supported during the Democratic primary. While Johnson only stressed the principles in the bill, his personal involvement indicated that he was calling in markers (Whalens 187–88). Both senators would vote for cloture. A devastating earthquake had struck Alaska on March 27, and Johnson had responded promptly, making Air Force Two available to Senators Bartlett and Gruening (D-AK) and moving to free up $77.5 million in relief for the state. Although both senators had been considered questionable votes for cloture, the President's timely political favor pulled them into line (Whalens 200).

Mansfield and Humphrey concentrated on Democratic senators from the key western states, attempting to disrupt a traditional understanding between southern and western senators involving the exchange of votes on water projects for western votes against civil rights (Whalens 201). Meanwhile, Dirksen worked to pull in the 11 or more conservative Republicans he would need for cloture. In shifting H.R. 7152's focus toward federal intervention as a secondary, rather than primary, enforcement alternative, Dirksen argued to conservative colleagues from states with anti-discrimination laws that the federal legislation would have only a small incremental effect in their states. He complemented this approach by pointing to the Republican Party's heritage as the "Party of Lincoln." Conservatives were also influenced by the moral fervor of religious leaders who supported the bill. Finally, the effects of the filibuster itself were beginning to create pressure for cloture. The Senate had devoted twelve weeks to ducking the civil rights issue, and many senators were beginning to feel the embarrassment that came with public recognition of that fact (Whalens 202–03).

3. *Cloture and Victory in the Senate.* One by one, commitments fell into place. On June 7, before they were sure they had 67 votes, Mansfield and Dirksen moved for cloture: "We the undersigned Senators [27 Democrats, 11 Republicans], in accordance with the provisions of Rule XXII of the Standing Rules of the Senate, hereby move to bring to a close the debate on the bill * * *." On June 9, with lobbying for cloture right up to the last minute, the time came to vote. Mansfield explained the importance of the cloture motion and then listened as a weary Richard Russell denounced the bill as contrary to both the spirit and the letter of the Constitution. After an uncharacteristically brief statement by Humphrey, Dirksen rose to make the final speech. He introduced Senate Amendment No. 1052, a second substitute for

the entire bill to replace his earlier substitute amendment. Dirksen argued: "The time has come for equality of opportunity in sharing in government, in education, and in employment. It will not be stayed or denied."

The obligatory quorum call was a true formality on June 10, 1964: all 100 senators were present, including Clair Engle (D-CA), suffering from a brain tumor and unable to speak (Humphrey 91). The roll was called alphabetically by each senator's last name. Senator Engle cast his vote from his wheelchair by feebly lifting his left hand toward his eye. Surprising most observers, conservatives Carl Curtis (R-NH) and Bourke Hickenlooper (R-IA) voted for cloture. Another conservative, John Williams (R-DE), cast the 67th vote for cloture. Hubert Humphrey raised his arms over his head in jubilation (Whalens 199). The final vote was 71–29, four votes more than required.

After over 534 hours of continuous debate, spanning 58 days, the longest filibuster in the history of the Senate had been broken—the first time ever that cloture had been achieved on a civil rights bill. The final breakdown was 44 Democrats and 27 Republicans in favor and 23 Democrats and 6 Republicans against. Johnson and Humphrey had succeeded in capturing the votes of 19 of the 21 Democrats from western states, and Dirksen had convinced 16 of the 17 Republican senators from states with public accommodations and equal employment laws on the books (as well as eight of the ten senators from states with one or the other) to vote for cloture.

Even though cloture limited senators to 60 minutes of remarks—on both the bill and proposed amendments—the southern opponents of H.R. 7152 continued to delay the bill's progress. They attempted to bog down the proceedings by calling up countless amendments, even though they knew their proposals had no chance of adoption. They slowed things down further by insisting on long roll-call votes (including a record 34 in one day) on virtually every question (Schwartz 1091).[12] But they succeeded only in delaying the inevitable for another eight days (Vaas 446). In all, 115 different amendments were defeated, 106 on roll-call votes (Miller 371), with only two amendments of substance being accepted (Schwartz 1091).

On June 19, 1964—one year after President Kennedy had sent his civil rights bill to Congress—the Senate finally voted on H.R. 7152, having accepted the second Mansfield-Dirksen substitute two days earlier by an overwhelming 76–18 margin. The bill was read for the third time and the Clerk called the roll (Vaas 446). At 7:40 p.m., to the applause of the observers in the gallery, the Clerk of the Senate announced the final vote: 73–27 in favor of H.R. 7152, as amended by the Mansfield-Dirksen substitute. The bill received the support of 46 Democrats and 27 Republicans, including four senators who had opposed cloture. Twenty-one Democrats and six Republicans voted nay (Whalens 215).

---

[12] This phenomenon—the *post-cloture filibuster*—is made possible by the collegial Senate rules. During this period, absent a unanimous consent agreement, a Senator could propose any number of amendments, including those unrelated to the subject matter of the bill. (House Rule XVI, in contrast, limits amendments to those which are *germane* to the subject of the bill.) Moreover, any Senator could demand roll-call votes, not only on the amendments, but also on the normally routine motion to reconsider, and could seek repeated quorum calls. In 1979, the Senate amended Rule XXII, clause 2 to limit each Senator to calling up two amendments and to impose an overall 100-hour limit on post-cloture consideration.

Most important, the bill approved by the Senate was in substance almost as broad as the bill approved by the House in February (Miller 371). For example, of the 24 amendments to Title VII that were offered from the floor, only five were accepted. Even considering Dirksen's important changes, the title was not vastly weaker than the version delivered from the House in February.[13]

THE CIVIL RIGHTS BILL BECOMES LAW

A bill does not become a law unless both chambers of Congress agree to identical legislative language. Because the Senate had made a number of changes in H.R. 7152, it returned the bill to the House on June 27, 1964, together with a message asking for acquiescence in the Senate's changes. In a joint press release, Manny Celler and Bill McCulloch said that "none of the amendments do serious violence to the purpose of the bill. We are of a mind that a conference could fatally delay enactment of this measure" (Whalens 218). Celler and McCulloch knew that if the House refused to accept all of the Senate changes and a conference committee were called, the Senate conferees would be selected by Judiciary Chairman Eastland, guaranteeing further delay. Even if the conference committee did report out a bill, the Southerners would have another opportunity to filibuster in the Senate. On balance, the best strategy was simply to accept the Senate's changes (Whalens 218–19).

The revised H.R. 7152 returned to Judge Smith's Rules Committee. This time, with the national conventions of both parties approaching, supporters would tolerate no stalling by the Chairman. After a single day of hearings, the Rules Committee voted to report House Resolution 789, expressing the House's concurrence with the Senate's amendments to H.R. 7152. The Rules Committee also voted to limit debate to one hour prior to the final vote.

On July 2, the House took up consideration of House Resolution 789. Judge Smith spoke for 15 minutes, denouncing the Rules Committee's "exercise of raw, brutal power" in limiting debate to a single hour. But he conceded that "the bell has tolled. In a few minutes you will vote this monstrous instrument of oppression upon all of the American people." As he yielded the floor, Smith received applause from his southern colleagues and a handshake from Celler. Bill McCulloch, in his usual restrained manner, recommended approval of the Senate version of H.R. 7152 as a comprehensive, fair, and moderate statute. As he sat down, the House rose in a rare standing ovation. Finally, Manny Celler claimed the floor to use the remaining six minutes of the allotted hour. When he finished, the House rose once again in a standing ovation, this time led by Judge Smith (Whalens 224–26).

The House vote on House Resolution 789 was 289–126. After the House accepted the Senate bill, Speaker McCormack signed the official copy of H.R. 7152 and handed

---

[13]   See Rodriguez & Weingast, 1487–96. A new provision specified that preferential hiring practices to correct racial imbalances in the workforce (*affirmative action*) would not be required. The authority of the EEOC to sue in court was eliminated and replaced with a provision authorizing the Commission, when conciliation efforts failed, to refer a case to the Attorney General for possible civil suit or to authorize private suit. However, the reduction in EEOC authority was agreed to only in exchange for the inclusion of provisions allowing the courts to appoint attorneys to represent private Title VII plaintiffs and providing for an award of attorney's fees to successful plaintiffs. The new version also allowed local authorities to retain jurisdiction over cases for a short time, to attempt conciliation, before the EEOC could step in (Vaas 447–56).

it to the House Clerk for return to the Senate. When the bill arrived in the other chamber, business was suspended so that Carl Hayden, the Senate's President pro tempore, could place his signature alongside McCormack's. H.R. 7152, as amended, was now ready to be signed into law by the President. At 6:00 that evening, July 2, 1964, members of Congress and civil rights leaders arrived at the White House and, after brief remarks by President Johnson, witnessed the presidential signing of H.R. 7152 into law. H.R. 7152 had finally become "The Civil Rights Act of 1964."

Within days, Lyndon Johnson met with Nicholas Katzenbach, the new Attorney General, to discuss the President's plans for the next civil rights bill: "I want you to write me the goddamndest, toughest voting rights act that you can devise." As he had told Hubert Humphrey during the battle for the 1964 Act, "Yes, yes, Hubert, I want all of those other things—buses, restaurants, all of that—but the right to vote with no ifs, ands, or buts, that's the key. When the Negroes get that, they'll have every politician, north and south, east and west, kissing their ass, begging for their support" (Miller 371).[14] Johnson may have been overly optimistic (and typically crude), but he was astute enough to realize that the Civil Rights Act of 1964 was merely a start toward true equality and the end of discrimination.

NOTE ON HOW A BILL BECOMES A FEDERAL LAW[15]

The Civil Rights Act illuminates the important features of the federal legislative process. The Constitution and its amendments set forth the basic structure: laws will be enacted by elected representatives, not by the people directly or by some authoritarian person or group. "All legislative powers herein granted shall be vested in a Congress of the United States, which shall consist of a Senate and House of Representatives." U.S. Const. art. I, § 1. House members are "chosen every second Year by the People of the several states," *id.* art. I, § 2, and each state has two Senators, "elected by the people thereof," *id.* amend. XVII. Laws must be approved by two legislative chambers (the *bicameralism* requirement) and the chief executive (the *presentment* requirement). If the President signs it, the "Bill" is "Law"; if he returns it without signature, it is not law unless two-thirds majorities of each chamber vote to override his *veto*. *Id.* art. I, § 7. If the President does not sign or return the bill within ten days and the Congress remains in session, the bill becomes law as though he had signed it. If Congress adjourns during the ten-day period, the bill does not become law, and the President has *pocket vetoed* the proposal.

Each house adds further structure to its process through formal rules, interpretations of those rules, and custom and practice.[16] As the Story of the Civil Rights Act demonstrates, there are many such rules affecting legislation, including committee consideration, scheduling procedures, and Senate rules allowing filibusters. All of these

---

[14]   Johnson was successful. In 1965, Congress adopted a strong Voting Rights Act, which was reenacted in 1970, 1975, 1982, and 2006 and remains a major component of federal civil rights law.

[15]   Among the best scholarly sources on legislative procedures are Barbara Sinclair, *Unorthodox Lawmaking: New Legislative Processes in the U.S. Congress* (5th ed. 2017), as well as Burdett Loomis & Wendy Schiller, *The Contemporary Congress* (6th ed. 2016); Walter Oleszek et al., *Congressional Procedures and the Policy Process* (10th ed. 2016, 11th ed. forthcoming 2019); Gregory J. Wawro & Eric Schickler, *Filibuster: Obstruction and Lawmaking in the U.S. Senate* (2007).

[16]   The Senate has permanent rules that can be amended. See *Standing Rules of the Senate*, in *Senate Manual*, S. Doc. No. 112–1 (2011). The House adopts "new" rules in every Congress. See *Rules of the House of Representatives*, 116th Congress (Jan 3, 2019), for the current (2019–20) House Rules.

requirements are less durable than constitutional ones because, in most cases, they can be ignored by the leadership, or changed by a majority vote of the relevant house.

The discussion that follows focuses on the traditional or "textbook" federal legislative process, which is presented in Chart 1-1. (Note that the Chart starts in the House, where revenue bills must originate, but many other bills originate in the Senate.) State legislatures usually follow similar procedures. Section 3 will introduce "unorthodox lawmaking" that does not follow the textbook process depicted in Chart 1-1. See Barbara Sinclair, *Unorthodox Lawmaking* (5th ed. 2017).

[handwritten margin note: have (revenue Bills)]

Chart 1-1: How a Federal Bill Becomes a Law—Simplified Overview

[handwritten margin note: orthodox Law Making]

HOUSE OF REPRESENTATIVES

SENATE

Drafting of Bill or Resolution
(e.g., by legislative staff, government agency, interest group, academic)
↓
Introduction of Bill by Member
(revenue bills originate in House, see U.S. Const., art. I, § 7, cl. 1; customarily, appropriations bills do also)
↓
Referral to Standing Committee
↓
Committee Action
—can be referred to subcommittee
—hearings held on major bills
—committee resolution: take no action, defeat, accept or amend and report
↓
Major Calendars
—Union (appropriations and revenue)
—House (public)
—Discharge (extract bills from committee)
↓
Rules Committee (major bills)
(closed rules possible but generally modified open or open rules)
↓
Floor Action (passage or defeat)

Referred to standing committee
↓
Committee action (similar to House)
↓
Floor action (similar to House except that there is filibuster option in Senate; overriding filibuster requires 60 votes)
↓
CONFERENCE COMMITTEE
(if House and Senate pass differing versions, a conference committee can be created with members from each house; each House must agree to the conference report)
↓
BILL SIGNED BY SPEAKER AND VICE PRESIDENT
↓
PRESENTMENT TO PRESIDENT
(may sign, veto, or permit bill to become law without his/her signature; also possibility of "pocket veto" after adjournment)

1. *Introduction of Bills.* More than 200,000 bills are introduced in the 50 state legislatures each biennium, and around 10,000 in each Congress. Only legislators can

[handwritten note at bottom: 7 200k bills are introduced in 50 state leg every 2 years]

introduce bills, although in some states the governor is required to submit budget bills to the legislature. See, e.g., Ill. Const. art. VIII, § 2. The legislators themselves do not always come up with the ideas for major bills or draft them. The chief executive proposes or drafts much of the important legislation considered by the legislature. See Vasan Kesavan & Gregory Sidak, *The Legislator-in-Chief*, 44 Wm. & Mary L. Rev. 1, 48–55 (2002). As chief executive and head of one of the political parties, the President may be the country's chief law-initiator. For example, the Celler, Lindsay, and McCulloch civil rights bills went nowhere until President Kennedy publicized the issue; his Justice Department drafted the civil rights bill introduced in both the House and Senate in 1963. Private groups also present draft bills to members of the legislature or advise them about amendments to bills proposed by the executive. The NAACP, for example, probably helped draft the liberalizing amendments adopted by Subcommittee No. 5.

Whether legislation is enacted depends in large part on the nation's political agenda. John Kingdon defines *agenda* as "the list of subjects or problems to which governmental officials, and people outside of government closely associated with those officials, are paying some serious attention at any given time." Kingdon, *Agendas, Alternatives, and Public Policies* 3 (2d ed. 1995). Getting an issue on the agenda is a prerequisite to adopting a policy to address it. Kingdon identifies four aspects to policymaking: setting the agenda; specifying alternatives from which a policy choice is to be made; choosing among the alternatives; and implementing the decision. His work focuses on the first two processes and attempts to explain why some subjects and not others become salient to policymakers and the public, and why some alternatives receive serious consideration while others do not. With respect to the first, agenda setting, the President is the most influential political actor. "No other single actor in the political system has quite the capability of the president to set agendas in given policy areas for all who deal with those policies." *Id.* at 23. As suggested by our case study, the President has much more power to press an issue onto the legislative agenda than to determine the policy tradeoffs and compromises needed to pass the final legislation.

State legislators are often even more dependent upon the offices of state attorneys general and private groups to draft legislation than members of Congress are, because state legislators do not have the staff support enjoyed by federal lawmakers. The staff situation in state legislatures has improved somewhat in the last 35 years, however. Typically, states now provide full-time staff to individual legislators and additional staff during legislative sessions. Since 1979, the size of permanent state legislative staff has grown from around 27,000 persons to almost 31,700. See National Conference of State Legislatures, *Size of State Legislative Staff* (2015).

2. *Committee Consideration.* The presiding officer of the legislative chamber refers bills to standing committees. House Rule XII, clause 2 requires the Speaker to refer a bill to the committee(s) having jurisdiction over its subject matter. Clause 2 was amended in 1975 to give the Speaker the power to send parts of the same bill to more than one committee, to send the whole bill to more than one committee, and/or to create an "ad hoc committee" to consider a bill. In 1995, the House modified the process for referring legislation to committee by abolishing joint referrals and mandating instead that the Speaker designate a committee of "primary" jurisdiction upon initial referral. Senate Rule XVII and the rules in many state legislatures do not require referral of bills to the appropriate committees, but the practice is to do so.

Committee jurisdiction is akin to a property right over political issues, so lawmakers work hard to place important legislation within the jurisdiction of committees on which they serve. The parliamentarian, a relatively nonpartisan player, makes referral decisions using a "weight of the bill" test to assign a proposal to the committee or committees with the most compatible jurisdiction. Evolution in parliamentary practice tends to be incremental, resembling legal change in the courts.[17] Parliamentarians rely on congressional rules (a sort of *statutory jurisdiction*) and precedent (a sort of *common law jurisdiction*) to determine the appropriate referral. For example, congressional rules specify that tax legislation must be referred to the House Ways and Means and the Senate Finance Committees, but the rules provide only a partial list of all possible subject matter of federal legislation. When the rules are silent, the parliamentarian follows or reasons from past practice to make the referral. Politicians work to frame bills so they fall within jurisdictionally ambiguous areas and then to convince the parliamentarian to assign them to a committee on which the framers have influence.

The most important power of committees is the *power of negation*. In a typical Congress, fewer than one-sixth of the bills introduced survive committee consideration and actually make it to the floor of either chamber.[18] The key player is the chair of the committee. If the chair refuses to schedule hearings for a bill or refer the bill to subcommittee, or refers the bill to a hostile subcommittee, the bill will usually die—even if most of the committee members favor the bill. House Rule XI and Senate Rule XXVI permit a majority of the committee to compel the chair to place a bill on the agenda, as Representative Brown threatened to do in the House Rules Committee's consideration of the civil rights bill. This is a maneuver rarely threatened and almost never attempted. In addition, a majority of the House can bypass a committee by filing a *discharge petition* calling for a measure to be brought to the floor. This, too, is rarely a serious threat.

The committee process is also crucial for bills that have a good chance of being enacted. The committee can iron out difficulties and build a consensus in favor of the bill. The chair is again the critical person when a bill is actively considered. The committee or subcommittee chair schedules hearings, determines who will testify at the hearings, and asks most of the questions. Recall Representative Celler's power to manipulate both the committee and subcommittee consideration of the civil rights bill. The power of the committee chair has waned in recent years, as more power has been claimed by party organizations[19] and as recent Congresses have adopted rules diminishing the influence of chairs. For example, in 1995 as part of the Republicans' "Contract with America," the House voted to limit the terms of committee and subcommittee chairs (except for the chair of the Rules Committee) to "three consecutive Congresses" (i.e., six years) and abolished several subcommittees, thereby reducing the power of these positions and some of the more senior members of the body. This has been the rule when Republicans have controlled the House (1995–2007, 2011–19). When the Democrats have controlled the House, they have generally not imposed term limits.

---

[17]   See David King, *Turf Wars: How Congressional Committees Claim Jurisdiction* (1997).

[18]   See Steven Smith, Jason Roberts & Ryan Vander Wielen, *The American Congress* (7th ed. 2011).

[19]   Since the mid-1990s, more legislative work has been done in informal task forces or leadership committees, entirely controlled by the majority party and often followed by perfunctory or no formal hearings. Because these are not governed by open meeting rules, lobbyists and interest groups can have substantial influence. See Roger Davidson, *Building the Republican Regime: Leaders and Committees*, in *New Majority or Old Minority? The Impact of Republicans on Congress* 69, 79–80 (Nicol Rae & Colton Campbell eds., 1999).

Committees exercise great power, including the power to block measures the House majority would support. Nonetheless, committees serve essential functions in modern legislatures. First, they allow members to specialize and accumulate expertise in a substantive area. This *informational role* suggests that committees are part of an efficient congressional organization, particularly necessary in an increasingly complex world.[20] Members must monitor committees to ensure that they are faithful agents of the full body and that the information and recommendations they put forth are consistent with the wishes of the majority. As long as monitoring is less costly than developing expertise on all matters and allows members to detect divergence between committee activities and majority preferences, a committee structure is sensible.

Another theory of legislative organization, the *distributive theory*, describes committees as engines of *rent-seeking*, or the distribution of unjustified benefits to interest groups. Members partly self-select their committee assignments, so they seek appointment to committees with jurisdiction over areas about which they and their constituents have particularly intense preferences. At least some committees are composed of preference outliers.[21] In most cases, lawmakers specialize in areas that allow them to send benefits back to their constituents or to key special interests in order to improve their reelection chances. In other cases, they may seek committee assignments that allow them to capture personal benefits from interest groups. For example, the Senate Commerce Committee has wide jurisdiction over the telecommunications industry, full of wealthy interest groups willing to compensate their legislative friends.[22]

These two explanations for committees are not necessarily exclusive.[23] Members may be willing to invest time and resources in developing expertise and producing helpful information for the full body because they have special interest in the issues that fall within the jurisdiction of a particular committee. Given the hyperpartisan tilt of American politics, a third theory has gained currency: committees are primarily the *tools of the majority party*.[24] Majority-party committee members exclude members of the other party from decisionmaking and cooperate among themselves to further the majority party's collective goals. Those goals might be advanced by packing committees with party loyalists who can use their assignments to engage in rent-seeking for their districts that will enhance their odds for reelection. Or committees can be engines by which the majority party refines policy proposals that will satisfy or even expand its electoral base. Thus, committees during the Obama Administration were critical to developing the 2010

---

[20]   See Keith Krehbiel, *Information and Legislative Organization* (1991); Marco Battaglini et al., *The Informational Theory of Congressional Committees: An Experimental Analysis,* 113 Am. Pol. Sci. Rev. 55–76 (Feb. 2019); Arthur Lupia & Mathew McCubbins, *Who Controls? Information and the Structure of Legislative Decision Making,* 19 Legis. Studs. Q. 361 (1994).

[21]   See Kenneth Shepsle, *The Giant Jigsaw Puzzle: Democratic Committee Assignments in the Modern House* (1978); Barry Weingast & William Marshall, *The Industrial Organization of Congress; or, Why Legislatures, Like Firms, Are Not Organized as Markets,* 96 J. Pol. Econ. 132 (1988); Scott Adler, *Why Congressional Reforms Fail: Reelection and the House Committee System* (2002).

[22]   See also Christopher Deering & Steven Smith, *Committees in Congress* 63–77 (3d ed. 1997) (discussing committees in terms of their primary benefits to lawmakers and providing tripartite classification: constituency, policy, and influence committees).

[23]   See Forrest Maltzman, *Competing Principals: Committees, Parties, and the Organization of Congress* (1997) (offering a sophisticated theory of committee formation).

[24]   See Gary Cox & Mathew McCubbins, *Legislative Leviathan: Party Government in the House* (2d ed. 2007); Jeffrey Stonecash, ed., *New Directions in American Political Parties* (2010); Charles Tiefer, *The Polarized Congress: The Post-Traditional Procedure of Its Current Struggles* 2–5 (2016).

health care law, and those during the Trump Administration worked out the details of the 2017 tax cut package.

Once a committee marks up the bill and votes to send it to the full legislative chamber, the committee staff drafts a report on the bill that will be circulated to the other legislators. This is mandatory in both chambers of Congress (House Rule XIII; Senate Rule XXVI) and is the practice in many state legislatures as well. Committee reports in Congress set forth the procedural and substantive background of the reported bill, the exact language of the bill, and a section-by-section analysis of the bill. Such reports in state legislatures are often shorter, more general descriptions of reported bills; thus, they are often less helpful to interpreters than the more extensive federal legislative history.[25] Committee reports, or distillations of them prepared by party organizations, are frequently the only documents that most legislators and their staffs read before a vote is taken on the bill. Reports are not only the principal means of communicating committee decisions to the chamber, but they are also persuasive briefs setting forth the factual and policy reasons justifying the proposed legislation. Committee members dissenting from all or part of the report are entitled to set forth their views as well. Finally, provisions in several laws require committees to include certain information about bills in committee reports.

3.   *Scheduling Legislative Consideration.* Bills reported by committee are placed on a calendar of the legislative chamber. The U.S. House's calendar arrangement is especially complex. It has three primary calendars. The most important calendar is the *Union Calendar*, or the "Calendar of the Committee of the Whole House on the State of the Union." Virtually all bills are placed on this calendar. Second is the *House Calendar*, which now contains few bills, mostly special rules from the Rules Committee, changes in House rules, ethics resolutions, and some constitutional amendments. Third, private bills, such as those for the relief of individual noncitizens seeking to remain in the country, are placed on the *Private Calendar*. In addition, there are two calendars to which bills on the three main ones may move. The *Consent Calendar* consists of bills involving spending of less than $1 million on the Union or House Calendar that a member anticipates will be passed by unanimous consent. Minor bills on the Consent Calendar are considered by the House twice a month. The *Discharge Calendar* lists motions to discharge bills that are pending in committee. Additionally, bills may be called up and considered by the House under a process called *suspension of the rules*. Suspension of the rules allows the House, with the consent of the Speaker, to consider a bill in an expedited fashion with no amendments or motions, but it requires that the bill be passed by a two-thirds vote. The U.S. Senate has only two calendars, the *Calendar of General Orders* and the *Executive Calendar* for treaties and executive nominations.

Simply being on the appropriate calendar does not assure that the chamber will consider the bill. Salient or time-sensitive bills usually will be considered before other bills ahead of them on the calendar. In the House, major legislation moves to the floor from committees in two ways. Budget and appropriations bills are privileged matters and can be brought to the floor at virtually any time. For other major bills, and often for budget and appropriations bills when supporters want to structure deliberation in a particular way, the reporting committee will request a special order, or *rule*, from the Rules Committee to advance the bill for expedited floor consideration. The Rules

---

[25]   See, e.g., Eric Lane, *How to Read a Statute in New York: A Response to Judge Kaye and Some More*, 28 Hofstra L. Rev. 85, 118–19 (1999) (describing committee reports in New York).

Committee, which is essentially an arm of the majority party, then decides whether it will propose a rule for the bill (its refusal to grant a rule effectively kills the bill for that session); what kind of rule to grant (an *open rule* permitting amendments, a *closed rule* prohibiting all floor amendments, or a *modified closed rule* permitting specified floor amendments and structuring the order of their introduction); when a bill is to be considered; and how much time for debate. The full House votes on the proposed rule; such rules are almost always passed by party-line votes. Control of the legislative agenda, facilitated through the use of special rules, is an important tactical advantage that accrues to the majority party.[26]

There is no Rules Committee in the Senate, and expedited consideration is usually accomplished by *a unanimous consent agreement* (Senate Rule V). Like a House rule, a unanimous consent agreement is a roadmap for the bill's consideration: when it may be brought up, what amendments may be proposed, and how much time may be spent on it. Unlike a House rule, a Senate unanimous consent agreement must be acceptable to all senators; the objection of a single senator kills it. Recall that the civil rights bill languished for weeks in a pre-consideration filibuster, during which Southern senators objected to any expedition at all. Under current Senate rules, most bills are still susceptible to two filibuster threats: on the motion to proceed to consider the bill and on final passage.[27] Most filibusters now are virtual ones, which may explain the recent increase in threatened and actual filibusters. Members threaten to engage in extended debate, placing a *hold* on the bill until floor leaders can work out a compromise. For years, holds were largely anonymous, but their widespread use has prompted cries for reforms, and now the names of members blocking consideration of legislation or nominations are sometimes revealed.

In 2013, Senate Majority Leader Harry Reid (a Democrat) challenged the Senate filibuster-and-cloture rules as applied to confirmation of nominations to executive branch and lower court positions. Fifty-three Democratic senators voted to support his challenge, which set a new Senate precedent. In 2017, Majority Leader Mitch McConnell (a Republican) engaged in the same maneuver to allow majority votes for Supreme Court nominations.[28] As of 2019, the filibuster remains in place as a mechanism for a 41-senator minority to block most substantive legislation, but Washington insiders wonder how it will be eroded next. Change will not likely occur through a formal amendment to Senate Rule XXII (cloture), for that would require a two-thirds vote.

Most state legislatures use only a single calendar on which they list all pending bills ready for floor action. As in Congress, the order of listing is not a reliable indication of when the bill will actually be considered; priority items of consequence are mixed with unimportant bills. Oversimplifying a little, one can say that the actual order of consideration is determined in one of two ways, parallel to the two methods used in Congress. State legislatures with strong party caucus systems tend to have their agendas

---

[26]   Gary Cox & Mathew McCubbins, *Setting the Agenda: Responsible Party Government in the U.S. House of Representatives* (2005); Tiefer, *The Polarized Congress*, 52–83 (modern House), 84–111 (modern Senate).

[27]   See generally Gregory Koger, Filibustering: A Political History of Obstructionism in the House and Senate (2010); Gregory Wawro & Eric Schickler, Filibuster: Obstruction and Lawmaking in the U.S. Senate (2006). Some forms of budget legislation cannot be filibustered because the Senate has adopted strict time limits on the consideration of these important legislative vehicles. See Sarah Binder & Steven Smith, *Politics or Principle? Filibustering in the United States Senate* 192–94 (1997) (contrasting budget rules from traditional rules allowing filibuster).

[28]   Editorial Staff, Mitch McConnell Is Making the Senate's Minority Party Increasingly Powerless, Wash. Post, April 4, 2019.

set by the majority leader and/or the majority party caucus. State legislatures in which parties are weak typically vest agenda control in calendar committees, rules committees, or informal but less partisan mechanisms. In some states, the two methods effectively merge. For instance, where the presiding officer of the legislative chamber is also the chair of the rules committee, there is little functional difference between the two methods.

4. *Floor Consideration: Debate, Amendment, Voting.* Once a bill has been placed on the agenda by the relevant committee and advanced for consideration by the full legislative chamber, the process is mostly automatic. Most legislators routinely vote "yes," and the bill is passed. In the Senate, for example, dozens of routine bills are adopted through unanimous consent agreements read quickly at the end of a day's session. Consistent with the informational theory of legislative organization, the chamber as a whole usually ratifies the decisions and compromises reached in the smaller, more expert groups (committees). Of course, much important legislation, such as the Civil Rights Act, is controversial and has to run the further gauntlet of floor consideration. Three important aspects of congressional decisionmaking occur during such floor consideration: debate, amendment, and vote.

In the U.S. House and most state chambers, debate is severely limited by general or special rules. (Indeed, because many state legislatures still only meet for several months each year, there is simply not enough time for extended public debate on more than a few issues.) Even where debate is not formally limited, as in the U.S. Senate, it normally consists of "set" speeches read by members to virtually empty chambers (although many staffers and some lawmakers will watch the floor proceedings on closed circuit television) or of *colloquies*, rehearsed questions posed to the bill's sponsor in order to build a legislative record on some issue. Frequently, members of Congress simply submit statements for printing in the *Congressional Record*, and the statements are never uttered on the floor. The *Record* is supposed to identify such a statement by either a "bullet" (•) preceding it or by a different typeface.

Relatively few votes are altered by floor debates; instead members often use them to publish their positions, and sometimes to include in legislative history remarks supporting an interpretation of the proposal that they favor. Members may make floor speeches to publicize their positions or to pack the legislative history with remarks supporting an interpretation of the proposal that they favor. In the modern era of televised floor proceedings, members know that their constituents and lobbyists can monitor their activity and their positions. In addition, debate can be manipulated by organized minorities to delay passage of legislation that they oppose. For example, the filibuster used in the U.S. Senate enables a determined group of senators to kill a bill or force concessions from the majority by extended debate. Cloture (cutting off the debate) required a two-thirds vote of the Senators voting in 1964; under amended Senate Rule XXII, it now requires 60 votes except with respect to changes in the rules themselves.

Once they have been reported by committee, bills can be amended on "second reading," sometimes in the legislature sitting as a committee of the whole, or on "third reading" (just before the final up or down vote is taken on the bill). Amendment on third reading is rare and may require unanimous consent or some other special dispensation. Most legislative chambers do not follow the U.S. House practice of dissolving into a Committee of the Whole to consider amendments.

Major bills on controversial subjects will attract numerous proposed amendments. A first-degree amendment changing the text of the bill is a *perfecting amendment*, which can strike language, insert language, or do both. The reporting committee (through the chair or a sponsor) will sometimes propose perfecting amendments to correct minor problems with the bill or to attract more support for the bill through *saving amendments*. Perfecting amendments from the floor may include minor amendments addressed to a narrow problem with the bill; *riders*, or amendments seeking to add irrelevant matter to the bill (riders are prohibited by House Rule XVI and the rules of some state legislatures); and hostile amendments. Some floor amendments, called *killer amendments*, ostensibly strengthen the bill but are designed to antagonize the bill's more moderate supporters. Judge Smith's amendment adding "sex" to the list of impermissible bases for employment decisions prompted the opposition of floor leaders worried that expanding the legislation would prove fatal.

Amendments in the nature of a substitute seek to replace the entire bill, striking all after the enacting clause and inserting entirely new text. They can represent radically different approaches to the problem addressed by the bill, and adoption of such an amendment may spell the end of the bill either by ensuring its ultimate defeat or by impairing the operation of the bill, making passage useless. In other cases, the managers of the bill will propose an amendment in the nature of a substitute that reflects the results of negotiations on the proposal following committee action. Not to be confused with amendments in the nature of a substitute are *substitute amendments*. These are offered when another amendment is pending, and it changes part of the proposed amendment. This second-degree amendment can be minor—replacing only one word or phrase—or significant—proposing an entirely new text but in a way different from the pending amendment in the nature of a substitute. In the latter case, the amendment is both a substitute amendment and an amendment in the nature of a substitute.

Both opponents and proponents of legislation use amendments strategically, seeking to fill up the complex *amendment tree* to foreclose other changes in the bill or to obtain a special rule in the House that favors a particular sequence of voting on amendments. In some cases, bill managers will accept floor amendments in order to move debate forward and ensure final passage, but they do not intend to support the amendment in the conference committee. Lawmakers often observe that amendments can be "lost" in the Capitol building when conferees walk across the Rotunda to the other chamber to begin negotiations on the final legislation.

The vote on an amendment or a bill may be taken in one of four ways: voice vote, roll calls (increasingly by use of electronic devices), division of the house, and tellers. The first two methods do not leave a record of how each member of the legislative chamber voted, but division (where the yeas and nays rise to be counted) and tellers (where the yeas pass down the aisle to be counted, then the nays) permit observers to record how each member voted.[29] The number of votes needed to adopt an amendment or pass a bill is normally a majority of those voting in each house of Congress, assuming a quorum is present. Some state legislatures, in contrast, require the votes of a majority of the members elected; thus, members not wanting to commit themselves against a measure may help defeat it simply by staying away when the vote is taken. Two-thirds supermajorities are needed for Congress to propose a constitutional amendment, to override a presidential veto, to

---

[29] The U.S. House of Representatives uses all four methods, and the Senate uses all but tellers. One-fifth of a quorum may demand a roll-call vote in either chamber, except when the House committee of the whole is in session. Moreover, congressional rules can often require roll call votes on particular matters; for example, House Rule XX requires roll call votes on all tax rate increases and appropriations bills.

expel a member, or for the Senate to concur in a treaty. In states, supermajorities can be required to override gubernatorial vetoes, to pass emergency legislation or special appropriation bills, or to enact new tax legislation.

5.   *Conference Committees.* In the prevailing system of bicameral legislatures, there must be a "meeting of the minds" of the two legislative chambers to enact statutes. If the version passed by the U.S. House differs in any respect from that passed by the U.S. Senate, there is no enactment—unless one chamber recedes from its differences and joins the version of the other (as was the case for the Civil Rights Act). Sometimes the House and Senate send bills back and forth several times ("ping-ponging" the bill), acceding to part of the other chamber's alterations each time, in an effort to reconcile the two versions.

After both chambers have voted themselves into a state of disagreement, the last chamber to disagree may request a conference. The Speaker of the House and the Presiding Officer of the Senate formally appoint the conferees, but in practice the chair and ranking minority member of each relevant committee will submit a list of proposed conferees, who are then appointed. The objectives of the conferees are, first, to preserve the provisions most important to their respective chambers and, second, to achieve an overall result acceptable to a majority in each chamber. In Congress and most state legislatures, conferees are only authorized to consider matters about which the bills passed by the two chambers are in disagreement. Thus, they may not strike or amend any part of the bill that is identical in both versions, nor may they insert new matter not germane to the differences, nor may they expand any provision beyond that found in either version. In practice, because congressional conference committees do much of their work in private, it is difficult for other members, interest groups, and the public to monitor conferees' behavior. Lengthy omnibus bills that have been the product of long negotiations often emerge from conference with provisions never considered by either house or by any substantive committee. If the bill is nevertheless enacted, the rule against new provisions in conference is considered waived. When the conferees have reached agreement, they set forth their recommendations in a conference report, which will be printed in both chambers and will include a statement explaining the effect of the amendments or propositions agreed upon by the conferees on the measure.

After the conference committee reconciles the bills passed by the two chambers, the chamber that did not request the conference acts first on the "conference report," which is the bill created in conference. That chamber has three options—adopt the conference report, reject it, or recommit it to conference (which is tantamount to killing the bill). If the first chamber adopts the conference report, the conference committee is dissolved, and the other chamber is faced with a straight up-or-down vote on the reconciled bill. If the conference report is agreed to by both chambers, a copy of the bill is enrolled for presentment to the President or the Governor for signature.

6.   *Presentment for the Presidential or Gubernatorial Signature.* Under Article I, § 7 of the U.S. Constitution, once an enrolled bill is presented to the President, the President has ten days (not including Sundays) to sign it or veto it. If the President vetoes the bill, it is returned to Congress, where the veto can be overridden by two-thirds of those voting in each chamber. If the veto is overridden, the bill then becomes law without the President's signature. In most cases, if no action is taken within the constitutional ten-day period, the bill also becomes law without the President's signature. The exception to this last rule is that if Congress adjourns before the end of the ten-day period and the

President fails to sign the bill, it is killed by a *pocket veto*. Many major bills are passed in the waning days of each Congress, and so the President often has ample discretion to kill legislation without immediate congressional override.

The U.S. President must accept or reject the entire bill; if there are several provisions the President dislikes in the bill, the only formal option is to veto (or pocket veto) the entire bill. State Governors typically have more options, because they can veto individual provisions called *items* in bills presented to them. Congress attempted to delegate a similar power to the President in the Line Item Veto Act of 1996, Pub. L. No. 104–130, 110 Stat. 1200, codified at 2 U.S.C. §§ 691–692, but the Supreme Court struck down the federal act in *Clinton v. City of New York*, 524 U.S. 417 (1998).

NOTE ON THE IMPLICATIONS OF VETOGATES FOR PUBLIC LAW

Stop Here!

One way of thinking about the congressional lawmaking process is to see each step as a *vetogate*,[30] or a choke point in the process, a place where opponents can "veto" legislation even when it has majority support: (1) kill the bill in committee; (2) if committee approval cannot be avoided, stop the bill before full chamber consideration; (3) if full chamber consideration occurs, kill the bill there by filibustering it in the Senate, by amending it to death, or by outright defeating it on the chamber floor; (4) if one chamber has approved the bill, exploit the veto opportunities in the other chamber to prevent it from passing an identical measure; (5) if the other chamber produces a similar but not identical bill, amend or defeat it at the conference committee stage or in an interbranch summit; (6) if all else fails, persuade the President to veto it and then work against any congressional effort to override the veto.

Descriptively, the existence of vetogates means that determined minorities can often kill legislation or, in the alternative, maim legislation they cannot kill. Southern opponents of civil rights legislation were able to stop or to dilute such bills until 1964 because they controlled pivotal vetogates (the House Rules Committee, the Senate Judiciary Committee). The primary consequence of the vetogates structure is that it is harder to enact legislation than it would be under a parliamentary system, where laws can be adopted by majority vote in one elected chamber, and the chief executive is the head of the party controlling the chamber.

But vetogates do not mean that fewer laws will actually be adopted. Rather than killing a measure, a minority controlling a vetogate may extract concessions from the enacting coalition by a threat to stall it or change it significantly. This was the approach taken by Senator Dirksen. One would expect legislation under a vetogates model to involve more compromises, logrolls, and bundles than legislation under a parliamentary model. Logrolls involve deals to secure votes for Bill 1 by agreeing to support Bill 2 as well. Even though neither bill might have majority support, they might both be bundled into an "omnibus" statute that enjoys super-majority support.

One would also expect that vetogates would encourage legislators to delegate controversial questions to other decisionmakers. Most major federal statutes delegate extensive lawmaking authority to agencies, which are then trusted to make the hard

---

[30]   McNollgast (aka Mathew McCubbins, Roger Noll, and Barry Weingast), *Positive Canons: The Role of Legislative Bargains in Statutory Interpretation*, 80 Geo. L.J. 705–42 (1992); William Eskridge Jr., *Vetogates and American Public Law*, 31 J.L. Org. & Econ. 756–81 (2015); see also Keith Krehbiel, *Pivotal Politics: A Theory of U.S. Lawmaking* (1998); George Tsebelis, *Veto Players: How Political Institutions Work* (2002).

choices that legislators would like to avoid. The Note below introduces you to the text and structure of Title VII, the jobs provisions of the Civil Rights Act of 1964. Notice that Congress did not define "discriminate," the key term in the new law. To hold together the vetogate-generated super-majority of liberal Democrats and Republicans, border state and western Democrats, and farm state Republicans, the majority coalition was probably unable to agree on a definition of that term, and so left it to courts (in this case, not so much the weak agency) to fill in the details—a process we shall explore in Section 2 below. In turn, the judges or administrators who are the recipients of delegated authority will have greater policymaking discretion under our system, because the vetogates provide some insulation protecting policy entrepreneurship against legislative overrides.

NOTES ON PUBLIC CHOICE THEORIES OF LEGISLATION

While our process-oriented examination of the 1964 Act emphasized deliberative committees and legislators, national political parties, and presidential involvement, one could also approach the statute from the perspective of interest groups, which many scholars see as the driving force in American legislation.[31] Based on the theories of classical market economics, *public choice theorists* seek to explain the operation of the processes by which legislators are selected, take action and positions, and make collective decisions.[32] Public choice scholars treat politicians and voters as rational utility-maximizers operating in a competitive electoral market. One prominent aspect of public choice theory has been the creation of models treating the legislative process as a microeconomic system in which "actual political choices are determined by the efforts of individuals and groups to further their own interests." Gary Becker, *A Theory of Competition Among Pressure Groups for Political Influence*, 98 Q.J. Econ. 371, 371 (1983). "The basic assumption is that taxes, subsidies, regulations, and other political instruments are used to raise the welfare of more influential pressure groups." *Id.* at 373–74.

Public choice scholars model the legislative environment as a political market. Interest groups, and to a lesser extent the public, are the demanders of legislation. They send benefits to legislators, who can supply them with governmental largesse. Legislators can respond to demand by refusing to pass a bill, by avoiding a clear choice through delegation of broad decisionmaking authority to an agency in the executive branch, or by explicitly allocating tangible benefits. Inspired by the idea that political markets are analogous to economic markets, Hayes outlined the demand and supply patterns in *Lobbyists and Legislators: A Theory of Political Markets* (1981).

1. *Demand for Legislation by Organized Interest Groups.* Public choice theorists posit that the demand of legislation is driven by organized interest groups—which has generated an important literature on the circumstances under which political perspectives coalesce into interest groups. In *The Logic of Collective Action* (1965), Mancur Olson provided a theory to explain why some groups form and work to influence politics and why some do not. Legislation is a *public good*; once the state has decided to

---

[31]   E.g., Jeffrey Berry, *The New Liberalism: The Rising Power of Citizen Groups* (1999); Kay Lehman Schlozman & John Tierney, *Organized Interests and American Democracy* (1986); Elmer E. Schattschneider, *Politics, Pressures and the Tariff: A Study of Free Private Enterprise in Pressure Politics, as Shown in the 1929–1930 Revision of the Tariff* (1935).

[32]   In addition to Olson's book, other prominent works of public choice theory include James Buchanan & Gordon Tullock, *The Calculus of Consent* (1962); Anthony Downs, *An Economic Theory of Democracy* (1957); William Riker, *Liberalism Against Populism* (1982).

provide clean waterways or safe highways, for example, all in society will benefit. Yet any individual effort to pass such laws will have only an infinitesimal effect on the probability of its enactment. Therefore, a rational person will not participate in the political process at all, preferring instead to *free-ride* on the efforts of others. As long as the free-rider cannot be excluded from enjoying the public goods that legislation and the efforts of groups lobbying in favor of new laws provide, she will have no incentive to join the group or to expend time and resources. If all citizens follow this rational course, then none will work to influence her representative to pass legislation providing diffuse benefits to the public at large.

Olson's theory predicts, therefore, that groups will form most often when there are a few interested members. In that case, each member has a large enough stake in the sought-after law to justify its participation. Furthermore, in small groups, members can monitor the behavior of others, detect and punish shirking, and ensure collective action. In other cases, a group will form because one member will receive such a large fraction of the governmental benefit that it would work to obtain the legislation even if it had to internalize all the costs of political activity. Indeed, the interested party may expend significant resources forming an interest "group" as part of its political strategy. Under both of these scenarios of group formation, small groups have the advantage over larger ones, and they will work to obtain targeted benefits at the expense of the diffuse and unorganized public.

How serious is the problem of minority "rent-seeking" legislation? Some studies suggest that the problem may be less serious than Olson predicted. Empirical analyses have documented that large diffuse groups of citizens do form interest groups and do influence political outcomes.[33] Interest groups representing larger, more diffuse groups of citizens can exist and exercise influence even under Olson's model. For example, some groups formally organize for nonpolitical reasons and then turn to political activity as a *byproduct*. For these groups, the initial costs of organizing, often the greatest hurdle facing those who seek to influence governmental policies, have already been met. Examples include unions, farmers' cooperatives, and trade and business associations. Large groups can also form if they offer desirable *selective benefits* only to their members. Examples include the AARP, which offers excellent insurance supplements to Medicare, and the NRA, which offers members discounts on bullets.

The Internet offers new ways to overcome the free-rider problem, allowing large numbers of dispersed citizens to organize and exert political influence. Thus, the Internet facilitates the sharing of information, allows like-minded people to connect at lower cost, and reduces the cost of mobilizing like-minded people and institutions to act in political capacities.[34] Indeed, the Internet has fueled the most dynamic, generative period of political group activity and organization since the Progressive era. The Internet played a major role Barack Obama's 2008 and 2012 presidential races, and its influence is apparent in the green politics of global warming and other environmental issues. Twitter has been the communication mode of choice for Donald Trump's candidacy and

---

[33]   Frank Baumgartner, Jeffrey Berry, Marjorie Hojnacki, David Kimball & Beth Leech, *Lobbying and Policy Change: Who Wins, Who Loses, and Why* (2009); Jeffrey Berry & Clyde Wilcox, *The Interest Group Society* (6th ed. 2018); Paul Johnson, *Interest Group Recruiting: Finding Members and Keeping Them*, in *Interest Group Politics* 35 (Allan Cigler & Burdett Loomis eds., 5th ed. 1998).

[34]   See Bruce Bimber et al., *Technological Change and the Shifting Nature of Political Organization*, in *Handbook of Internet Politics* 72–85 (Andrew Chadwick & Philip Howard eds., 2009). For a skeptical view, see Mathew Hindman, *The Myth of the Digital Democracy* (2009).

presidency, and social media is central to the 2020 presidential race. Still, it remains to be seen how important the Internet will prove to be in the politics of ordinary legislation.

On the demand side for statutes, legislators are often faced with a myriad of interest groups on any given issue, and these groups may either agree (consensual pattern) or disagree (conflictual pattern) with each other. A consensual demand pattern is similar to a non-zero-sum situation, while a conflictual demand pattern is basically zero sum. If an issue is consensual, then everyone who is aware of and actively interested in the issue can come out a winner, while if it is conflictual, then the resolution of the conflict will necessarily result in immediately identifiable winners and losers. In a way, this dichotomy is unrealistic; in a world of limited resources, all policies are zero sum because someone, either now or later, has to pay for them. In the short run, however, government decisions can be relatively unconstrained by resource limitations if policymakers can push the costs onto an inattentive group or a group that does not vote in the next election. For example, government benefits funded through deficit financing places the costs on future generations of taxpayers, some of whom have not yet been born. See Daniel Shaviro, *Do Deficits Matter?* (1997). Living voters may be harmed by higher interest rates as the government competes for credit or by inflation if the government just prints more money, but those costs can be hard for citizens to trace back to particular legislative decisions. In these essentially consensual circumstances, interest groups may cooperate, making deals among themselves to obtain benefits at the expense of the general public.

In *Political Organizations* (1973), James Q. Wilson maintained that the degree and nature of interest group organization is determined by the perceived incidence of costs and benefits from a specified policy. Costs of a policy may be broadly *distributed*, such as a sales tax paid by all consumers, or may be *concentrated* on a small group, such as a license fee. Similarly, benefits may be widely distributed or shared by all, such as the benefits of national security, or they may be concentrated in the hands of a few, such as state subsidies to tobacco farmers. When Wilson's typology is combined with the insights of Olson's theory, a transactional theorist might surmise that because bills providing concentrated costs or benefits will affect smaller groups, they will *on average* stimulate more organizational activity than measures with distributed costs and benefits. Table 1-1 sets forth this model.

Each of these quadrants produces a particular kind of political climate. Quadrant I is best described as *majoritarian politics*. Although there is little group activity on either side, some large groups of citizens will weigh in both in favor of distributed benefits (for example, environmental groups will favor clean air legislation) and against distributed costs (deficit hawk groups). Quadrant II fits the model of *entrepreneurial politics*. Organized interests will form to derail the legislation; support is likely only if a policy entrepreneur is willing to push the proposal, rouse the public, and take the initiative in forming citizen groups offering purposive or solidary benefits to participants. *Client politics* describes the consensual interest group activity in Quadrant III, where logrolling dominates the essentially non-zero-sum game that interest groups play. Finally, Quadrant IV is the area of conflictual *interest group politics* where the process produces identifiable and short-term winners and losers, and both sides are organized and active.

Table 1-1
Taxonomy of Demand for Legislation Based on Benefits/Costs

I *Distributed benefits/distributed costs*	**II** *Distributed benefits/concentrated costs*
A general benefit-general taxation case that usually involves public goods. Little group activity on either side of most cases.	A general benefit-specific taxation case in which the majority imposes its will on the minority up to the capacity of the minority to pay. Opposition will tend to be well organized.
III *Concentrated benefits/distributed costs*	**IV** *Concentrated benefits/concentrated costs*
Tends to have strong interest group support and weak, if any, organized opposition because of the free-rider problem. The benefit to an individual of having the policy changed is simply too immaterial.	Results in continuous organized conflict over payment of benefits and distribution costs. A prime example is the NLRB and the conflicts between labor and management.

2. *Legislator Supply Patterns in Legislative Markets.* Public choice theorists tend to discount legislators' statements that they vote "for the public interest." Morris Fiorina, *Congress: Keystone of the Washington Establishment* (2d ed. 1989), and David Mayhew, *Congress: The Electoral Connection* (1974), posited that legislative behavior can best be explained by the assumption that the primary goal of legislators is to be reelected. Even legislators who ultimately want to enact particular policies that they believe benefit the country must remain in office to achieve their goals; thus, the electoral connection is a paramount concern. A large majority of legislators respond to this electoral incentive effectively and are reelected time after time.

How can a politician ensure that she will remain undefeated if her elected position demands that she take public stands on controversial issues? Fiorina has suggested that *abstention* (the legislator does not take sides) or *casework* (the legislator dollops out favors and regulatory interventions for constituents) can ameliorate the harmful effects of conflicting constituent demands. Other transactional theorists argue that the most effective response is for the legislator to act so that each of the conflicting groups will believe it has won something. Thus, the canny legislator will press conflicting groups to reach a compromise which the legislator will then support *or* to pass an ambiguous bill delegating policy responsibility to an agency. Public choice theorists maintain that agencies charged with regulating an industry tend to become "captured" by the interests they are supposed to be regulating.

Again, Wilson's typology may be useful. If a policy imposes concentrated costs, legislators will want to avoid responsibility as much as possible, perhaps by delegating the cost-imposition to a regulatory agency, such as the Environmental Protection Agency. The regulated interest may accept this outcome, hoping that its superior organization will allow it to capture the regulating agency and subvert the policy.[35] Even if the costs are distributed, such as in majoritarian politics, legislators may be wary of acting directly and decisively. Take, for example, the case of a clean air act funded through a general tax rate hike. The inattentive public is more likely to trace the immediate and somewhat costly increase in taxes back to lawmakers and vote against them than voters are apt to notice slight increases in air quality and to make the connection between cleaner air and a particular piece of legislation. In cases of concentrated benefits and distributed costs,

---

[35]   See Peter Aranson, Ernest Gellhorn, & Glen Robinson, *A Theory of Legislative Delegation*, 69 Cornell L. Rev. 1 (1982).

however, legislators may risk the wrath of the electorate to gain the gratitude of the attentive and organized public, particularly if they believe that the cost-bearers will remain unaware of the costs or can be deceived by public-regarding half-truths about the statutory purposes. Thus, in the arena of client politics, legislators often reward friendly interest groups with self-regulation or distributive benefits.

Table 1-2 illustrates the transactional supply model. Consider its relevance to our Story of the Civil Rights Act. Businesses required to change their hiring and promotion practices may have believed they were subject to concentrated costs. On the other hand, businesses in the South that wanted to expand their client base or expand their pool of potential workers may have preferred legislation that would allow them to integrate without violating ingrained racist norms in those regions. Most of the religious organizations favoring the bill were already organized; their political activity was a relatively cheap byproduct, given that the initial costs of organization had been defrayed and mechanisms of collecting financial support and harnessing human resources were well established. African Americans and other minority groups were relatively powerless in the South, but they had formed national organizations that had clout inside the Beltway and had become an important block of voters in presidential elections.

Table 1-2
Taxonomy of Supply of Legislation Based on Benefits/Costs

I *Distributed benefits/distributed costs*	**II** *Distributed benefits/concentrated costs*
Because there is no strong pressure from organized interests, legislature will favor no bill or symbolic action. Sometimes delegation to agency regulation will occur.	Because the proposal will be opposed by organized interests, the best legislative solution is to draft an ambiguous bill and delegate to agency regulation, so all sides can claim victory. Regulatory capture can result.
III *Concentrated benefits/distributed costs*	**IV** *Concentrated benefits/concentrated costs*
Because the costs can be allocated to an uninformed public, legislature will follow a policy of distribution of subsidies and power to the organized beneficiaries. Often self-regulation is the chosen policy.	Because any policy choice will incur the wrath of opposing interest groups, legislators will favor no bill or delegation to agency regulation.

3. *Implications and Critiques of a Transactional Model of Legislation: Madison's Nightmare?* The transactional model developed in Tables 1-1 and 1-2 suggests considerable pessimism regarding the results of imperfect political markets. On the one hand, the public sector will tend to spend too much money on statutes that concentrate benefits on special interests while distributing their costs to the general, and often unsuspecting, public. There is an obvious tendency to logroll in a specific benefit-general taxation scheme such as ours, because legislators can please important groups with tax subsidies, while avoiding blame for the overspending that results.

On the other hand, the public sector will tend to supply too few statutes that are likely to be public-regarding, namely, statutes that distribute benefits broadly (e.g., infrastructure programs, commercial codes, effective criminal laws). Legislators often have little interest in such statutes, because they do not as reliably generate votes in the next election. And even if the populace were appreciative of these statutes, it is possible that in many cases Congress would be unaware of the demand, because the free-rider problem precludes effective organization. This problem is particularly acute in Quadrant

II because a statute that provides distributed benefits through enacting concentrated costs will face strong and organized opposition that is likely to prevail over the shallow support that a policy entrepreneur can create. Some of these laws, notably federal criminal laws when violence and crime are salient for voters, may produce political payoffs attractive enough to encourage lawmakers to spend some time on these proposals and to pass legislation that is often primarily symbolic.

This taxonomy may suggest reforms that are likely to improve the legislative process because it helps to identify the equivalents of market failures. For example, if legislation in the majoritarian and entrepreneurial arenas tends to be more consistent with the public good but is underproduced because of interest group dynamics, reforms might emphasize empowering people whose interests are not well represented by organized groups. Alternatively, it might suggest that we should identify proxy groups with related interests that can serve as champions for the unorganized. Criminals are, for the most part, not well-organized politically, but lawyers are well-organized and usually serve as virtual representatives for the interests of those accused of crimes.

If we notice that inefficient, private-regarding legislation is less likely when interest group behavior is conflictual and not cooperative, we might seek to structure the legislative process to force interest groups to compete for limited resources. Structuring legislative processes so that losers are more clearly identified will make such legislation more difficult to pass.[36] It is also worth considering how changing technology may affect the dynamics of the transactional model. As noted above, the Internet may be a resource for consumers and other large and dispersed social groups to organize themselves into a more potent lobbying force. See generally Bruce Bimber, *Information and American Democracy: Technology in the Evolution of Power* (2003).

Like other economic models, public choice models of the legislative process have been charged with oversimplification of the political process and failure to recognize its institutional richness.[37] Study after study has documented that money and organization do not always translate into clout.[38] Instead, an interest group's influence depends upon the context. First, interest groups are more successful at blocking legislation than enacting a new policy. Groups defending the status quo need to prevail at only one stage in the convoluted legislative process, while proponents of new legislation must successfully navigate all of the procedural obstacles. In addition, cognitive psychology suggests that people work harder to preserve what they have than to gain a new benefit. Second, interest groups succeed more frequently on issues that are not salient to the larger public and that are perceived as narrow, technical, nonpartisan issues. Client

---

[36] See Elizabeth Garrett, *Rethinking the Structures of Decisionmaking in the Federal Budget Process*, 35 Harv. J. Legis. 387 (1998).

[37] E.g., Daniel Carpenter, *Reputation and Power: Organizational Image and Pharmaceutical Regulation at the FDA* (2010); Daniel Carpenter & David A. Moss, editors, *Preventing Regulatory Capture: Special Interest Influence and How to Limit It* (2014); Daniel Farber & Philip Frickey, *Law and Public Choice: A Critical Introduction* (1991); *The Rational Choice Controversy* (Jeffrey Friedman ed., 1996); Donald Green & Ian Shapiro, *Pathologies of Rational Choice Theory* (1994); Jerry Mashaw, *Greed, Chaos, and Governance: Using Public Choice To Improve Public Law* (1997); Colin Hay, *Theory, Stylized Heuristic or Self-Fulfilling Prophecy? The Status of Rational Choice Theory in Public Administration*, 82 Pub. Admin. 39 (2004); Symposium, *Getting Beyond Cynicism: New Theories of the Regulatory State*, 87 Cornell L. Rev. 267 (2002).

[38] See Baumgartner et al., *Lobbying and Policy Change*, 208–09, 223–24; Berry, *Interest Group Society*, 227–40; Schlozman & Tierney, *Organized Interests*, 314–15; Matthew R. Christiansen & William N. Eskridge Jr., *Congressional Overrides of Supreme Court Statutory Interpretation Decisions, 1967–2011*, 92 Tex. L. Rev. 1317 (2014).

politics is easier when it occurs outside the glare of publicity, and members are willing to trade support on minor issues in backroom deals.

Just as empirical studies have given us a more complex explanation than that provided by public choice theory for the demand side of legislation, case studies of Congress by institutional political scientists have questioned the public choice explanation for the supply side. Richard Fenno's classic case study, *Congressmen in Committees* (1973), argues that legislators are interested in more than simply being reelected, contrary to the assumptions of public choice theory. While reelection is certainly a powerful motivating factor and a necessary intermediate goal, legislators also want to have "status" within government and to make some positive contribution to what they consider good public policy. Especially when an issue involves moral questions and is publicly visible, the legislator's vote depends on something more than her calculations about reelection.[39] Recall the behavior of the legislators in our Story of the Civil Rights Act: Can it all be explained solely in terms of interest group influence, or were other factors at work? Even legislators committed to nothing higher than being reelected will anticipate reactions of their "inattentive" constituents, because a false move can be deployed by their opponents to transform constituents into "attentive" critics.[40]

Not only may public choice theory oversimplify legislator motivations, it may also misconceive the legislative process by viewing it statically and disregarding institutional changes that affect behavior. For example, political parties exercise pervasive influence over the operation of the legislative process, relative to committees and rank-and-file members, allowing lawmakers to coordinate their efforts more effectively and resist the urge to act in ways that benefit only narrow special interests or small constituencies. Relatedly, the President (head of one of the major parties) exercises a pervasive influence on the legislative process, as we have seen from Kennedy and Johnson to Obama and Trump.[41] As a unitary office backed by a more cohesive coalition than the multi-membered Congress, the Presidency is in a better position to develop coherent policies and, consequently, often initiates and propels controversial bills through the legislative labyrinth. As our nation's most visible public figure, the President is ideally situated to stimulate publicity about a public problem. As the chief of the executive branch, the President has access to an impressive brain trust (such as the Office of Management and Budget, the Treasury Department's Office of Tax Policy, and other prestigious executive branch entities), which can think creatively about a problem and draft proposed legislation.

Also modeling the dynamic nature of the legislative process, John Kingdon, in *Agenda, Alternatives, and Public Policies* (2d ed. 1995), de-emphasizes the role of interest groups and argues that public officials (the President, the Cabinet appointed by the President, Congress, as well as leaders of political parties) play the key roles in setting the nation's political agenda. The role of interest groups is usually to formulate and debate policy alternatives, a role they share with other less visible (but perhaps more public-regarding) participants, such as civil servants, academics and experts, the media, and legislative staff. Under Kingdon's model, Congress is an "organized anarchy," in which there is no linear process for identifying a problem, defining alternative solutions,

---

[39]   See also Keith Poole & Howard Rosenthal, *Congress: A Political-Economic History of Roll Call Voting* (1997) (finding ideology was largest influence on roll call voting behavior).

[40]   Douglas Arnold, *The Logic of Congressional Action* 5 (1990).

[41]   See, e.g., *The Presidency and the Political System* (Michael Nelson ed., 8th ed. 2006); Terry Moe & Scott Wilson, *Presidents and the Politics of Structure*, 57 Law & Contemp. Probs. 1 (Spring 1994).

and reaching a decision. Salient problems, possible solutions, and choice opportunities will coexist as separate "streams" in the "garbage can" (the system). Sometimes problems are resolved; sometimes they go away; sometimes the system despairs of solving them. The outcome depends on the "coupling of the streams": a problem becomes salient at the same time a solution becomes well-regarded and participants favoring the solution can seize the legislative process for that end. To change policy, groups must have more than just political clout; they must draw attention to their proposal when the political environment is receptive to it.

Another way of criticizing the static perspective is to question the public choice assumption that preferences are independent of and prior to political activity. To use economic terminology, public choice theorists tend to view preferences as *exogenous* rather than *endogenous*. This assumption is clearly unrealistic; we all know that participating in decisionmaking, whether in the political realm or elsewhere, significantly affects the way we think and feel about a particular issue.[42] As the members of Congress deliberated about the Civil Rights Act of 1964 and discussed their views with their colleagues and constituents, their conclusions about integration and racism surely developed and changed.

One can reject the public choice description of the legislative process in favor of one of the institutional political descriptions, yet still believe that some form of pluralism is and should be characteristic of our political system. But this normative vision has also become controversial. Typically, defenders of pluralism will now concede that interest group government sacrifices elements of fairness, rational policy, or other values but will argue that pluralism is justified by its facilitation of stability, moderation, and broad satisfaction with the political system. This may not be a persuasive justification for those who consider social justice more important than stability.[43] Furthermore, by defining "politics" as the relatively narrow conflict among professional groups, pluralism implicitly denies the existence or feasibility of other forms of political struggle as mechanisms to change existing institutions and to organize around broader lines of cleavage (such as class). Because most of the political activity under pluralism is by and among elites, pluralist democracy may tend to reinforce already-existing social and economic inequalities.[44]

NOTE ON TITLE VII OF THE CIVIL RIGHTS ACT OF 1964

The most complex, and most often litigated, portion of the Civil Rights Act has been Title VII, 78 Stat. 241, 253–66 (1964), codified as amended at 42 U.S.C. § 2000e *et seq.*, which prohibits job discrimination on the basis of race, sex, religion, or national origin. We shall now introduce you to the main provisions of the 1964 Act, before its amendments in 1972 and 1991. The prime directive of Title VII is found in § 703(a), 42 U.S.C. § 2000e–2(a):

It shall be an unlawful employment practice for an employer—

(1) to fail or refuse to hire or to discharge any individual, or otherwise to discriminate against any individual with respect to his compensation, terms,

[42] See Amartya Sen, *Behavior and the Concept of Preference*, 40 Economica 241 (1973).

[43] See, e.g., Stuart Hampshire, *Justice Is Conflict* (2000); Thomas Simon, *Democracy and Social Injustice: Law, Politics, and Philosophy* 151–71 (1995).

[44] See C. Wright Mills, *The Power Elite* (1959).

conditions, or privileges of employment, because of such individual's race, color, religion, sex, or national origin; or

(2) to limit, segregate, or classify his employees or applicants for employment in any way which would deprive or tend to deprive any individual of employment opportunities or otherwise adversely affect his status as an employee, because of such individual's race, color, religion, sex, or national origin.

Section 703(b)–(c), *id.* § 2000e–2(b)–(c), sets forth similar prohibitions of "unlawful employment practices" by employment agencies and labor organizations (unions). Section 703(d), *id.* § 2000e–2(d), applies the antidiscrimination principle specifically to apprenticeship or training programs.

The exact scope of this anti-discrimination rule (i.e., how broadly does the rule apply?) is provided by § 701's definitions of key terms. Thus "employer" is defined in § 701(b), *id.* § 2000e(b):

The term "employer" means a person engaged in an industry affecting commerce who has twenty-five or more employees for each working day in each of twenty or more calendar weeks in the current or preceding calendar year, and any agent of such a person, but such term does not include (1) the United States, a corporation wholly owned by the Government of the United States, an Indian tribe, or a State or political subdivision thereof, (2) a bona fide private membership club (other than a labor organization) which is exempt from taxation under section 501(c) of the Internal Revenue Code of 1954 * * *.

Section 701(h), *id.* § 2000e(h), defines "an industry affecting commerce" as "any activity, business, or industry in commerce or in which a labor dispute would hinder or obstruct commerce or the free flow of commerce and includes any activity or industry 'affecting commerce' within the meaning of the Labor-Management Reporting and Disclosure Act of 1959, and further includes any governmental industry, business, or activity." Section 701(g), *id.* § 2000e(g), defines "commerce" as "trade, traffic, commerce, transportation, transmission, or communication among the several States; or between a State and any place outside thereof; or within the District of Columbia, or a possession of the United States; or between points in the same State but through a point outside thereof." Section 701(i), *id.* § 2000e(i), defines "State" to include "a State of the United States, the District of Columbia, Puerto Rico, the Virgin Islands, American Samoa, Guam, Wake Island, the Canal Zone, and Outer Continental Shelf lands defined in the Outer Continental Shelf Lands Act." Definitions for "employment agency" and "labor organization" are set forth in § 701(c)–(e), *id.* § 2000e(c)–(e). There is no definition of "discriminate" or "discrimination" in Title VII.

There are various "exemptions" or "defenses" to the charge of unlawful employment practices under Title VII. Section 702, *id.* § 2000e–1, for example, exempts employment of aliens outside any State or employment of persons by religious groups from Title VII's application. But the main defenses are those which qualify the meaning of "unlawful employment practice" in § 703. Section 703(e), *id.* § 2000e–2(e), presents a defense for practices based on bona fide occupational qualifications:

Notwithstanding any other provision of this subchapter, (1) it shall not be an unlawful employment practice for an employer to hire and employ employees, for an employment agency to classify, or refer for employment any individual, for a labor organization to classify its membership or to classify or refer for employment any individual, or for an employer, labor organization, or joint labor-management committee controlling apprenticeship or other training or retraining programs to admit or employ any individual in any such program, on the basis of his religion, sex, or national origin in those certain instances where religion, sex, or national origin is a bona fide occupational qualification reasonably necessary to the normal operation of that particular business or enterprise, and (2) it shall not be an unlawful employment practice for a school, college, university, or other educational institution or institution of learning to hire and employ employees of a particular religion if such school, college, university, or other educational institution or institution of learning is, in whole or in substantial part, owned, supported, controlled, or managed by a particular religion or by a particular religious corporation, association, or society, or if the curriculum of such school, college, university, or other educational institution or institution of learning is directed toward the propagation of a particular religion.

Section 703(f)–(g), *id.* § 2000e–2(f)–(g), relates to employment decisions based upon Communist Party membership and national security reasons.

Section 703(h), id. § 2000e–2(h), protects employment decisions based upon "a bona fide seniority or merit system, * * * provided that such differences are not the result of an intention to discriminate because of race, color, religion, sex, or national origin, nor shall it be an unlawful employment practice for an employer to give and to act upon the results of any professionally developed ability test provided that such test, its administration or action upon the results is not designed, intended, or used to discriminate because of race, color, religion, sex or national origin." Section 703(i), *id.* § 2000e–2(i), stipulates Title VII's inapplicability "to any business or enterprise on or near an Indian reservation with respect to any publicly announced employment practice of such business or enterprise under which a preferential treatment is given to any individual because he is an Indian living on or near a reservation." Section 703(j), id. § 2000e–2(j), deals with affirmative action under Title VII:

Nothing contained in this subchapter shall be interpreted to require any employer, employment agency, labor organization, or joint labor-management committee subject to this subchapter to grant preferential treatment to any individual or to any group because of the race, color, religion, sex, or national origin of such individual or group on account of an imbalance which may exist with respect to the total number or percentage of persons of any race, color, religion, sex, or national origin employed by any employer, referred or classified for employment by any employment agency or labor organization, admitted to membership or classified by any labor organization, or admitted to, or employed in, any apprenticeship or other training program, in comparison with the total number or percentage of persons of such race, color, religion, sex, or national origin in any community, State, section, or other area, or in the available work force in any community, State, section, or other area.

Section 713(b)(1), *id.* § 2000e–12(b)(1), provides a defense to a person charged with violating Title VII "if he pleads and proves that the act or omission complained of was in good faith, in conformity with, and in reliance on any written interpretation or opinion of the Commission."

A person "claiming to be aggrieved" may not file suit herself, but should file a "charge" with the EEOC asserting violation of the substantive norms of Title VII, pursuant to § 706(a), *id.* § 2000e–5(a). (Note that § 706(b), (d) sets forth time requirements within which the charge must be filed with the EEOC; the schedule depends in part on whether the state has a remedy for the violation.) Once the aggrieved person has filed a timely charge, the EEOC determines whether there is "reasonable cause to believe that the charge is true," and if so it will try to eliminate the unlawful practice informally through "conference, conciliation, and persuasion" (§ 706(a)). If the EEOC is unable to obtain voluntary compliance with Title VII, it notifies the aggrieved person and informs her that she may bring a lawsuit in federal court within thirty days (§ 706(e), *id.* § 2000e–5(e)). To remedy an unlawful employment practice, a court may enjoin the practice and order "such affirmative action as may be appropriate, which may include reinstatement or hiring of employees, with or without back pay" (§ 706(g), *id.* § 2000e–5(g)).

PROBLEMS APPLYING TITLE VII

Problem 1-1. A Case of Disparate Racial Impact. Duke Power Company's electrical generating plant at Dan River Stream Station in Draper, North Carolina has ninety-five employees in 1966, including fourteen African Americans. Employees are divided into five departments: (1) Operations (responsible for the day-to-day operation of the plant's generating equipment); (2) Maintenance (fixing and maintaining equipment); (3) Laboratory and Testing (analysis of water and coal used in the plant's operation); (4) Coal Handling (unloading and handling coal); and (5) Labor (janitorial services). Workers in the Labor Department received the lowest hourly wage ($1.565), which was lower than any other department's minimum hourly wage ($1.705) and less than half the amount of other departments' maximum hourly wages ($3.18 to $3.65).

In 1955, Duke Power began requiring that every employee, except those in the Labor Department, had to have a high school diploma. The company also made the diploma a prerequisite for promotion of workers from the Labor Department into any of the others. Before 1955, the company's policy had been to limit African-American workers to the Labor Department. Under the 1955 policy, every African-American employee in the Dan River plant continued to work in Labor, and none was promoted. In 1965, when Title VII went into effect, the company instituted a new policy under which employees could be promoted out of Labor by passing one of two high school equivalency tests. Duke promoted Jesse Martin, a black man, from Labor to Coal Handling in 1966. Two other African-American workers were promoted in 1968. All had high school degrees.

After exhausting their administrative remedies with the EEOC, 13 of the 14 African-American employees at Dan River sued Duke Power for job discrimination in violation of Title VII. Six of the plaintiffs had no high school diplomas and were hired in Labor before 1955—when Duke had no high school diploma requirement for promotion but when it refused to promote African Americans as a matter of company policy. Four plaintiffs had no high school diplomas but were hired after the company instituted the diploma requirement in 1955. The plaintiffs sought an injunction requiring Duke to discontinue its diploma and testing requirements for promotion.

You are the General Counsel for Duke Power. The company wants to retain its diploma and testing requirements, and you believe that company policy is no longer to exclude African Americans from higher positions simply because of their race. Do the diploma and testing requirements violate Title VII? There is no precedent on this issue in the court system in early 1966, when the lawsuits are brought. You understand that the EEOC is going to issue guidelines requiring companies like Duke Power to justify policies that have a disparate impact on racial minorities. Should they make a difference in your advice to Duke Power?

Problem 1-2. Amending Title VII. You are still General Counsel for Duke Power, which in 1966 is concerned that its diploma-and-test policy will be rejected by the EEOC and the liberal Warren Court. Its concerns are shared by the Chamber of Commerce, the nation's premier association of small businesses and a potent lobbying group in Washington DC. Both Duke and the Chamber are interested in seeking legislation amending Title VII to insulate policies like Duke's from liability. You are in charge of this effort.

First, suggest statutory language that could be added to Title VII in order to confirm Duke's immunity from liability. *Second*, suggest a legislative strategy for passing this amendment through all the vetogates that are characteristic of the congressional process outlined above. (Assume that Congress in 1966 has pretty much the same key players as it had in 1964; the main exception is that Senator Humphrey is now Vice-President.) *Third*, figure out what obstacles might thwart the client's agenda and how those obstacles might be surmounted.

2. TITLE VII AS APPLIED: AN INTRODUCTION TO STATUTORY IMPLEMENTATION AND INTERPRETATION

The enactment of a statute is just the beginning, and not the end, of lawmaking, for the statute will invariably evolve as it is implemented, interpreted, and amended. See William Eskridge Jr., *Dynamic Statutory Interpretation* chs. 1–2 (1994). This section will introduce you to important themes of statutory implementation and will suggest that issues of legal theory and political theory are inextricably intertwined. The starting point for most statutory implementation and interpretation is agency action. As a case study of agency interpretation, we shall explore the EEOC's guidelines relating to employment policies having a disparate impact on employees based upon race (Part A). The EEOC's position ultimately prevailed with the Supreme Court—but the Supreme Court's decision raised new problems. The most notable is whether Title VII permits employers to engage in "affirmative action" to rectify underrepresentation of minority employees. Again, the EEOC tackled the issue first, and the Supreme Court followed the agency once again in the fascinating case of *Steelworkers v. Weber,* examined in Part B. Part C reveals that the Supreme Court's understanding of its own precedents has been just as dynamic as its reading of Title VII.

Judges and administrators are conventionally understood as "agents" of the legislature in matters of statutory interpretation, but that metaphor opens the door to larger institutional and even normative issues. And they are complicated by the fact that three different baselines for understanding the robustness of our political system are attractive to most public officials but often press them in different directions.

The Article I, § 7 structure and the expectations of the Framers rested upon *libertarian* assumptions: the default rules would be state common law, which allows people freedom to use their property, enter contracts, and form relationships as they choose; the constitutional vetogates, bicamercalism and presentment, would assure that there would be few federal statutes, and the ones that did pass would be modest adjustments to the libertarian status quo.[45] The appeal of libertarian values has not been extinguished by the modern regulatory state, though different groups entertain different priorities for "liberties" that are worth fighting for. Constitutional law reflects this variety, as Supreme Court decisions resting on "liberty" have run the gamut from property rights against regulatory takings to freedom of religion for closely-held corporations to marriage for lesbian and gay couples. An administrator or judge believing that fundamental liberties are being sacrificed by an aggressive application of an anti-discrimination law or a "no promo homo" law will tend to apply those statutes stingily.

Another normative theory of American politics is *pluralism*, which describes our polity as one where an array of different social, economic, and identity groups need to coexist peacefully and even to cooperate in common projects.[46] Political scientists such as David Truman and Robert Dahl maintain that pluralist politics is good for the country. A political environment with many groups actively competing will tend to produce moderate and well-considered policies. More important, policy adopted after receiving input from a variety of groups will enjoy a systemwide legitimacy and stability not possible for policies imposed by plebescites, agency directives, or judicial orders. "Because constant negotiations among different centers of power are necessary in order to make decisions, citizens and leaders will perfect the precious art of dealing peacefully with their conflicts, and not merely to the benefit of one partisan but to the mutual benefit of all the parties to a conflict." Robert Dahl, *Pluralist Democracy in the United States: Conflict and Consent* 24 (1967). For these thinkers, statutory implementation continues the dialectic among the relevant groups—but a dialectic that will evolve as groups change their perspectives and new groups enter the system.

Although the Framers created a libertarian structure and appreciated the inevitability of group behavior (what Madison called "factions," a more temporary alignment of citizens than that entailed in modern "interest groups"), they ultimately expected more out of government. *Federalist* Nos. 10 (Madison) & 78 (Hamilton). They expected government to solve collective action problems and advance the common good. *Civic republican* theories of politics understand law as problem-solving, legislation as deliberative, and statutory implementation as purposive.[47] To

---

[45]   *The Federalist* Nos. 73 & 78 (Hamilton); William Eskridge Jr. & John Ferejohn, *The Article I, Section 7 Game,* 70 Geo. L.J. 523 (1992). See also Nelson Polsby, *How Congress Evolves: Social Bases of Institutional Change* 147 (2004).

[46]   Robert Dahl, *A Preface to Democratic Theory* (1956); David Truman, *The Governmental Process* (1951). See also V.O. Key Jr., *Politics, Parties, and Pressure Groups* 9 (1958).

[47]   Henry Hart Jr. & Albert Sacks, *The Legal Process: Basic Problems in the Making and Application of Law* (William Eskridge Jr. & Philip Frickey eds., 1994); see also Amy Gutmann & Dennis Thompson, *Why Deliberative Democracy?* (2004); Philip Pettit, *Republicanism: A Theory of Freedom and Government* (1997); Michael Sandel, *Liberalism and the Limits of Justice* (2d ed. 1998); Symposium, *The Civic Republican Tradition,* 97 Yale L.J. 1043 (1988); Frank Michelman, *The Supreme Court, 1985 Term—Foreword: Traces of*

most law professors and students, this sounds like the "best" approach—who does not want to solve the nation's problems—but critics have warned that "deliberation" does not always prove to be public-regarding or legitimacy-enhancing and that purposive approaches to statutory implementation run the risk of unraveling statutory deals, undermining the rule of law, and creating social experiments that may be seriously counterproductive.[48]

In the abstract, it is hard to evaluate the various normative theories of American politics and how they should play out in statutory implementation. For this reason, we introduce you to a series of case studies in the implementation of Title VII to issues that were unknown or (more likely) buried during the drafting and debate over the Civil Rights Act.

A. AGENCY IMPLEMENTATION OF TITLE VII: DISPARATE IMPACT LIABILITY

1. Introduction to "Independent" and "Executive" Agencies

When Congress enacts a statute, a primary concern is how it will be administered. Some statutes, such as the Sherman Antitrust Act of 1890 as well as most criminal laws, vest administration in the judiciary. The Department of Justice or (in the case of antitrust) private enforcers bring lawsuits against alleged violators, with courts and juries as principal arbiters of whether the statute has been violated. More often, Congress vests primary administration in one or more agencies, with various powers and authorities to pursue the statutory goals. Agency enforcement has the advantages of creating expertise over time by administrators and of vesting authority in officials who will be more responsive to Congress. Chapter 8, § 1 introduces you to the large variety of agencies (including the EEOC) that Congress has created in the last 150 years.

In Title VII, Congress followed something of a hybrid approach. As the liberals like Humphrey wanted, Title VII created a new agency, the EEOC, which supporters expected would attract civil rights advocates who would work zealously and creatively to advance and elaborate on the statutory anti-discrimination norm. As conservatives like Dirksen wanted, however, the EEOC was not given authority to make legislative rules or deliver adjudicated orders having the force of law. In that respect, the EEOC was a weaker agency than the Interstate Commerce Commission ("ICC" created in 1887) or the Federal Communications Commission ("FCC" created in 1934), which had both rulemaking and adjudication authority. Because the EEOC did not have lawmaking authority under Title VII, a great deal of potential enforcement was left to private and sometimes public litigation in court.

Self-Government, 100 Harv. L. Rev. 4 (1986); Daniel Rodgers, *Republicanism: The Career of a Concept*, 79 J. Am. Hist. 11 (1992).

  [48] For critiques of republican or deliberative theories, see John Hibbing & Elizabeth Theiss-Morse, *Stealth Democracy: Americans' Beliefs About How Government Should Work* 191 (2002); Tom Tyler, *Why People Obey the Law* (rev. ed. 2006); Jeremy Waldron, *The Dignity of Legislation* (1999). See also Dennis Thompson, *Deliberative Democratic Theory and Empirical Political Science*, 2008 Ann. Rev. Pol. Sci. 497–520 (reviewing and answering some of the critiques).

Another kind of choice Congress made in 1964 was *not* to place the EEOC within the Department of Labor, where the Women's Bureau was located. Because the Secretary of Labor is appointed by the President and can be discharged by the President at any time, the Department of Labor is considered an *executive* department under the direct supervision of the White House. In contrast, the National Labor Relations Board ("NLRB" created in 1935), which adjudicates labor-management disputes is an *independent* agency outside of the Department of Labor. The EEOC is more like the NLRB and the FCC in this respect.

A potential advantage of an independent agency is that it may administer the law more neutrally, because its officials will not be subject to as much presidential and even partisan pressure. There are several possible indicia of functional independence possessed by the EEOC based on how Congress created the agency. One is its multi-member structure: there are five commissioners rather than simply one agency head. Another is its partisan balance: no more than three of the five may be members of the same political party. A third is fixed-term tenure: each commissioner is appointed to a five-year term. A fourth indicator is litigation authority: the EEOC General Counsel (appointed for a four-year term) is responsible for conducting litigation under specific provisions of Title VII. See Kirti Datla & Richard Revesz, *Deconstructing Independent Agencies (and Executive Agencies)*, 98 Cornell L. Rev. 769 (2013).

At the same time, the EEOC is Exhibit "A" for the proposition that a highly independent agency can also be a very weak agency. Moreover, the EEOC got off to a delayed start because President Johnson was slow to name commissioners and Congress was stingy in funding the agency. Notwithstanding these many obstacles, the EEOC's early history was one of innovation and some degree of regulatory achievement, to which we now turn.

2.   The Tools by Which Agencies "Regulate"

Recall Duke Power's diploma or testing requirement for promotion beyond its Labor Department (Problem 1-1). An employer that once explicitly discriminated because of race had, by 1965, abandoned de jure (as a matter of rule) segregation in its workforce. But Duke Power's workforce remained de facto (as a matter of practice) segregated even after Title VII took effect: almost all the black employees were relegated to the Labor Department, and almost all the white employees were in the better-paying departments of the company. Did this violate the statute?

On the one hand, the statute that was enacted in 1964 focused on intentional de jure discrimination: under § 703(a)(1), it was unlawful for Duke Power to set a race-based condition for employment opportunities—and in fact there was no such condition by 1965. What kept most blacks out of the better-paying jobs was the diploma or testing requirement, which was not explicitly race-based. On the other hand, the diploma or testing requirement had a dramatic race-based effect. It kept the black employees in the Labor Department and benefited white employees. The perpetuation of workplace segregation surely undermined the overall point of the statute. As President Johnson put it in 1965, Title VII's goal was "not just equality as a right and a theory but equality as a fact and equality as a result."[49]

From its first year in operation, key players in the EEOC believed that racial inequality in employment was the result of structural factors, not just intentional discrimination, and that the statutory mission was actual integration of workplaces.[50] Sonia Pressman of the General Counsel's Office argued that it would be impractical to expect direct evidence of discriminatory intent in most cases where workers of color continued to be absent. Just as litigants challenging racial discrimination in jury selection could rely on under-representation of minorities to prove an equal protection violation, Pressman argued that a claim of employment discrimination could be based upon the statistical under-representation of minorities in the workplace. Memorandum from Sonia Pressman to EEOC General Counsel Charles Duncan, "Use of Statistics in Title VII Proceedings" (May 31, 1966) (reprinted in the 2011 Documents Supplement for this casebook, 97–105).

The EEOC legal staff were candid about the tension between their views and the apparent compromises adopted in the 1964 statute, but they urged their approach as the most practical way to implement the statutory goal. By the end of the Johnson Administration, the EEOC Commissioners publicly interpreted the statute to bar employer practices "which prove to have a demonstrable racial effect." EEOC Commissioner Samuel Jackson, *EEOC vs. Discrimination, Inc.*, The Crisis, Jan. 1968, 16–17. Given the understanding EEOC's officials came to have about their statutory mission, namely, to discourage employment policies with discriminatory effects, how might the agency implement its understanding? Each agency has a mix of means by which it might seek to "enforce" its understanding of the statute, and the following note will explore the possibilities, as applied (or not) to the EEOC.

NOTE ON DIFFERENT AGENCY TOOLS FOR IMPLEMENTING STATUTES

Agencies always have a choice of instruments by which to seek compliance with statutes and to influence (and often dominate) the evolving interpretation of statutes.[51] We introduce here a continuum of mechanisms that agencies *might* use in order to implement their understanding of the statute they are charged with administering. Some of the mechanisms require authorization from Congress. The main reason the EEOC is considered a weak agency is that Congress vested it with few formal powers, and so the EEOC has had to rely on more informal mechanisms to press its vision for Title VII.

Substantive/Legislative Rulemaking. Substantive, or legislative, rules are like statutes, for they not only announce policy but give it legal force; typically, violations of substantive rules can be subject to sanctions. This is theoretically the most powerful tool

---

[49]   2 *Public Papers: Lyndon B. Johnson, 1965*, at 636 (1966) (June 1965 speech by President Johnson at Howard University). The story that follows is drawn from the records in the main cases and from recent archival research set forth in Hugh Davis Graham, *The Civil Rights Era: Origins and Development of National Policy, 1962–1971* (1990), supplemented by Neal Devins, *The Civil Rights Hydra*, 89 Mich. L. Rev. 1723 (1991).

[50]   See White House Conference on Equal Educational Opportunity (EEOC, 1965). Several key agency players published explanations and defenses of this approach. See EEOC Executive Director Herman Edelsberg, *Title VII of the Civil Rights Act: The First Year*, 19 N.Y.U. Conf. on Labor 289–295 (1967), and EEOC staff member Alfred Blumrosen, *Black Employment and the Law* (1971).

[51]   For useful analyses, see M. Elizabeth Magill, *Agency Choice of Policymaking Form*, 71 U. Chi. L. Rev. 1383 (2004); Peter Strauss, *The Rulemaking Continuum*, 41 Duke L. J. 1463 (1992).

for agency regulation, because legislative rules can set forth statutory requirements in greater detail and violators may be subject to direct sanctions. Under most circumstances, people and corporations want to avoid even the possibility of legal sanctions, and part of your job as a lawyer is to advise clients (whether the agency itself or a regulated entity) as to what "the law" (including agency rules) requires and what the penalties are for noncompliance. Thus, if the EEOC had been able to promulgate a legislative rule requiring employers like Duke Power to justify requirements having significant race-based effects, the EEOC could have supplemented the Title VII protections in an important way, for victims of "disparate impact" discrimination could have invoked the rule in proceedings before the EEOC or before a court.

The EEOC never issued such a disparate impact rule, because Congress has never vested the EEOC with substantive rulemaking authority to enforce Title VII, cf. 42 U.S.C. § 2000e–12(a) (granting the EEOC only authority to make rules for its internal process), though the EEOC does have substantive rulemaking authority in administering the Age Discrimination in Employment Act of 1967 and part of the Americans with Disabilities Act of 1990. Other agencies rely on rulemaking as their primary mode of regulation, especially the Environmental Protection Agency ("EPA"), as well as the Securities and Exchange Commission ("SEC"), the National Highway Traffic Safety Administration ("NHTSA"), and the Occupational Safety & Health Administration ("OSHA"). Because Congress has vested each of these agencies with legislative rulemaking authority, which each has deployed sometimes aggressively, they are considered to be more powerhouse agencies (i.e., more feared and respected) than the EEOC.

Even when Congress has delegated legislative rulemaking authority to an agency, this powerful tool has its limitations, examined in Chapter 8. Most important, the Administrative Procedure Act of 1946 ("APA") sets forth an arduous process for even "informal" rulemaking. In this process, the agency must publish notice of proposed rules in the Federal Register, 5 U.S.C. § 553(b), followed by the opportunity for interested persons to submit (usually written) comments on the proposed rules, 5 U.S.C. § 553(c), which may be followed by judicial review at the behest of affected persons or companies. *Id.* §§ 701–706. (The APA is excerpted in Appendix B to this casebook and is examined in detail in Chapter 8, § 2.)

Agency Adjudication. Agency enforcement through administrative adjudication, resulting in orders that either have the force of law or can be enforced judicially, also requires congressional authorization. An agency may charge a person or company with a statutory violation; if the administrative law judge finds culpability, she may direct sanctions. This is a retail approach (identifying particular lawbreakers) that might complement the wholesale approach of legislative rulemaking. Note that the possibility of adjudication is also a powerful regulatory tool: the agency can build a case against an apparent lawbreaker, present some or all of its evidence to its attorneys or officers, and usually exact an agreement between the agency and the lawbreaker where the latter agrees to some kind of restitution and commitment to not violate the statute again.

Again, there are limitations. For adjudication to be most effective, Congress must delegate the ability to issue adjudicative orders having the force of law to the agency. Persons complaining of job discrimination violating Title VII must seek resolution of their grievances from the EEOC, but the agency has no power to order employers to remedy policies or actions the agency believes to have violated the statute without going to court to seek enforcement. The EEOC offers aggrieved Title VII complainants the worst of both worlds: it imposes a burdensome procedure upon complainants, but without much hope that the agency procedure will motivate employers to remedy unlawful actions.

Although Congress has not delegated formal adjudication authority to the EEOC, it has done so for other important agencies, usually in tandem with a delegation of legislative rulemaking. The NLRB has adjudication authority, though it must go to court to enforce its orders. The Board also has rulemaking authority but has chosen to enforce the labor statute mainly through adjudication—a choice within the agency's discretion. In this respect, the NLRB is something of a relic from times past. In the 1950s, agency enforcement was primarily through adjudication, but since the 1970s it has been overwhelmingly through legislative rulemaking, especially by newer agencies such as the EPA, OSHA, and NHTSA. See Chapter 8, § 2.

Initiation of Litigation in Court. Agencies can bring their own lawsuits to enforce the statute they are charged with implementing if Congress has given them litigation authority. Cf. Office of Legal Counsel, *The Attorney General's Role as Chief Litigator for the United States,* 6 Op. O.L.C. 47, 48 (1982) (Attorney General has, by statute and custom, plenary authority over litigation by the United States, "absent clear legislative directives to the contrary"). The main advantage of this authority is that it gives the agency a path toward powerful judicial remedies—preliminary injunctions to preserve the status quo, injunctive relief (including structural injunctions), civil and possibly criminal monetary sanctions, and so forth. During the New Deal and Great Society eras, the Antitrust Division of the Department of Justice asserted a great deal of regulatory authority by bringing Sherman Act lawsuits against large companies or alliances of firms; even the threat of a lawsuit brought significant changes in the way whole industries did business. Since 1981, the Antitrust Division has been less regulatory, but has used its *amicus* brief power to continue to dominate the evolution of antitrust law.

The EEOC has authority to bring federal lawsuits against private employers to seek preliminary relief during an employment discrimination investigation or, more commonly, to remedy a probable discrimination that conciliation has been unable to remedy. Title VII § 706(f), 42 U.S.C. § 2000e–5(f); see also § 705(g)(6), 42 U.S.C. § 2000e–4(g)(6) (authorizing the EEOC to intervene in a lawsuit brought to enforce Title VII against nongovernmental employers). Pursuant to an executive order, the EEOC has authority to bring lawsuits to remedy a "pattern or practice" of statutory violations by private employers. *Id.* § 2000e–6. The Attorney General alone makes such decisions for lawsuits against public employers.

The main drawback to agency lawsuits is that they are an expensive way to enforce the statute. Like agency rulemaking and agency adjudication, this form of enforcement rests upon the old "command and control" model of government regulation and for some agencies on the less old, but even more controversial, "structural injunction" approach to regulation. These forms of regulation are "hard shoves"; economists are skeptical of hard shoves and tend to favor "gentle nudges." Dan Kahan, *Gentle Nudges vs. Hard Shoves: Solving the Sticky Norms Problem,* 67 U. Chi. L. Rev. 607 (2000). Nudges include government inducements or incentives for companies to engage in socially productive conduct, information about best practices that employers might follow, and default rules that can be contracted around (perhaps with some expense) if companies find them inefficient. Lawsuits are often a clunky way of nudging regulated parties, but the next three items in the regulatory toolkit will often be useful in that regard.

Informal Guidances, Policy Statements, etc. Agencies have a default authority to offer their opinion about what the law requires. Agencies do so through a broad range of mechanisms, including published guidances or policy statements, agency websites, speeches by agency heads or commissioners at public forums, media press releases, published answers to "frequently asked questions," and *amicus* briefs filed with the Supreme Court. (*Amicus* briefs almost always have to be submitted by the Solicitor General, who consults with the agency but is not bound by its interpretations of law.)

Without legislative rulemaking authority, the EEOC has relied extensively on these informal mechanisms for enforcing its understanding of Title VII. Many of its guidances have been pathbreaking. Shortly after Sonia Pressman's May 1966 memorandum, the EEOC issued Guidelines on Employment Testing Procedures that suggested legal problems with tests that had a demonstrated "adverse impact" upon racial minorities. In 1970, the EEOC promulgated detailed "Guidelines on Employee Selection Procedures," 35 Fed. Reg. 12333–36 (July 21, 1970) (2011 Documents Supplement 106–09), which argued that employer tests and other job prerequisites that had a significant disparate impact on different racial groups had to be justified by job-related criteria. Thus, not only would an employer violate Title VII by imposing diploma requirements only on black and not white employees (the old regime of de jure segregation), but an employer might *also* violate the statute by imposing diploma requirements that excluded most blacks from desirable jobs, unless the requirements were needed for a person to do the job well. In Problem 1-1, Duke Power's diploma or testing requirement for the job of Coal Handler was not *disparate treatment* discrimination—but it may have been *disparate impact* discrimination. (Did you really need a high school degree to be a Coal Handler?)

The 1970 guidelines did not have the force of law. The biggest problem with these informal mechanisms for statutory enforcement is that they carry no penalties for disobedience by the regulated parties. Why should a company follow EEOC guidelines? There are actually several reasons they might do so. One is that the guidelines tell the company what issues the EEOC actually might bring a lawsuit to enforce, and so the EEOC's litigation authority backs up its guidance. A company openly flouting the agency's guidelines is asking for trouble. Additionally, guidelines give the EEOC a first-mover advantage: the agency can canvass regulated firms as well as civil rights groups to come up with instructions that are well-linked to the statute and its goals, are easy to understand, and are reasonably comprehensive. They instantly become focal points for further discussion. Employees and their lawyers will plan complaints around such guidelines and firms will tend to avoid clashing with them.

Advice-Giving and Conciliation. Agencies spend a lot of time giving advice. The advice-giving function of an agency helps it enforce the statute, often in combination with public guidances and policy statements. The best example of this strategy is the Internal Revenue Service ("IRS"), which dispenses advice to millions of Americans through its instructions book mailed to taxpayers, its website, its telephone operators, and the local offices where IRS agents answer questions and help people with their taxes in the months before April 15 (the date on which most of us have to file our tax returns or request extensions). Although taxpayers have an incentive to minimize their income taxes, they form a remarkably cooperative relationship with the tax collector because of the IRS's advice-giving culture. Some have argued that tax compliance is as high as it is in the

United States for mostly normative reasons,[52] but our compliance also owes something to the agency's detailed advice to taxpayers. Most taxpayers pay their share of taxes more because they follow the agency's advice than because they fear a lawsuit or penalties.

Sonia Pressman's 1966 memorandum was developed partly in response to questions the EEOC was getting from employers wanting to know what their Title VII responsibilities were. After the EEOC suggested the invalidity of tests having a racially significant impact, the agency figured out what such a rule might look like through exchanges of letters with employers. For example, the Commission opined that requiring a sixth-grade education for a labor position was unlawful when it excluded many black workers from jobs they were perfectly qualified to fill.

Moreover, Congress vested the EEOC with conciliation authority: persons complaining of employer discrimination in violation of Title VII must file a "charge" with the EEOC, which in turn makes an evaluation of its merits and tries to persuade employers to rectify policies and actions that violate Title VII. Because the agency is not able to impose legal sanctions, the conciliation process is not coercive in the same way a lawsuit process would be. (In the latter, the defendant has an incentive to accommodate complainants who have plausible claims that might result in monetary liability or intrusive injunctions.) But the agency's forced dialogue with the employer's officials and supervisors can lead to some form of relief for the employee and altered personnel policies. For example, employers required to explain their policies will sometimes reconsider those policies in the face of an agency's questions and the complainant's story.

As is often true for regular individuals, companies may simply want to know what the law requires of them—and agency advice-giving is a potentially useful way to induce compliance in those cases. But if a firm or an individual believes that following the law is too expensive or distasteful, advice-giving or conciliation might be of little use. Put another way, the law often assumes the "bad person" standard: make rules that even bad, law-avoiding people will have to follow. Bad people/companies might listen attentively to agency advice and even solicit it (to see how secretive they have to be), but then they will ignore the advice, cheat, and make extra profits. The existence of even a few bad apples might trigger a cascade of disobedience, as persons or companies inclined to obey the law do not want the sucker's payoff.

On the other hand, the cascade might fall the other way, because of network power. See David Grewal, *Network Power: The Social Dynamics of Globalization* (2008). That is, bad actors might still obey the law articulated by agencies without sanctioning power, because other firms follow the law, internalize its norms, and exclude bad actors from the benefits of their networks on the basis of a reputation for not following norms. In other words, if an agency can tie its efforts into widespread social or economic networks, the impulse to conform to collective norms can do much of the enforcement. For example, after 1964 almost no company would openly admit to discriminating on the basis of race; the EEOC played little role in that overnight success, which owed its authority to the normative revolution led by the civil rights movement and the network power of the nondiscrimination idea. The EEOC proved very useful, however, in developing evidence that employers were still discriminating and bad numbers could reveal patterns of discrimination. It has taken decades for that idea to permeate American culture, but it

---

[52]   See Michael Wenzel, *Misperceptions of Social Norms About Tax Compliance: From Theory to Intervention*, 26 J. Econ. Psychol. 862 (2005) (providing an overview of academic explanations for tax compliance).

has done so. Even the worst firm today thinks twice before hiring that tenth white guy for an executive position filled by nine white guys.

Investigation, Information-Gathering and Promulgation, Publicity. Another tool available to agencies is informational. Congress often assigns agencies particular informational tasks, and agencies have broad discretion to gather and promulgate information they consider useful to the public. Many kinds of information have a regulatory value. For example, the EEOC gathers information about the race and sex composition of workforces, by state and by region; this information can be very useful to target companies that may be secretly or unconsciously discriminating, because their numbers will be out of line with aggregate numbers. Publishing this information has the further regulatory value of placing local employers on notice as to the "normal" numbers and encouraging concern if their numbers are not within the normal range.

Agencies can exercise power through promulgation of information, through their websites, informational booklets, and other forms of publicity. For example, the famous "food pyramid" suggesting a healthful balance of food groups for a day's meal, has shaped the thinking of two generations of Americans. (The federal government has recently abandoned the pyramid and has changed its mind about the most healthful balance of foods.) A powerful regulatory tool is *normalization,* where an institution simply promulgates a standard as normal and people follow that standard because they do not want to deviate from that norm. Federal agencies have no monopoly on normalizing strategies (think about church-supported and media-publicized norms), but by collecting data and publicizing trends, agencies can contribute powerfully to social normalization.

Finally, agencies can regulate by creating systematic arrays of regimes, through menus, for example. In family law and corporate law, to take two different areas, menus can be useful channeling devices even when people and companies are not required to follow the regimes listed in the menus.

PROBLEM APPLYING THE EEOC'S 1970 GUIDELINES

Problem 1-3. Disparate Racial Impact Revisited. Recall the Duke Power policy described in Problem 1-1. Assume that three categories of workers file unfair employment practice charges with the EEOC:

(a) Black employees with the company before 1955, who were disallowed from anything but the Labor Department until 1955 but did not have the diploma needed to advance;

(b) Black employees hired between 1955 and 1965, who were subject to the same diploma requirements as white employees but were generally unable to advance beyond the Labor Department because most black men in North Carolina did not receive high school diplomas from schools that remained segregated by race;

(c) Black employees hired after 1965, who were subject to the same diploma and testing requirements as white employees but whose education and testing lagged significantly behind white workers.

For which employees should the EEOC conclude that a violation of the statute has occurred? What legal analysis should the EEOC provide to Duke Power? What might motivate Duke Power to provide a remedy for one or more categories of workers? Think more broadly, and engage in the following thought experiment: If you were the Chair of the EEOC and wanted to entrench the disparate impact standard reflected in the 1970 Guidelines, what strategies might you follow?

3. Interaction of Agency Administration and Judicial Authority

That an agency administers a statute does not mean that courts are irrelevant, even when Congress has vested the agency with legislative rulemaking and adjudication authority. As we shall explore in Chapter 8, § 2, the APA subjects agency rules and orders to judicial review, mainly to determine whether they are consistent with the statute and are not "arbitrary and capricious." 5 U.S.C. § 706. More informal mechanisms of agency administration, such as guidances and conciliation, will be guided and may be trumped by judicial opinions. Because agency guidelines, opinion letters, press releases, and the like do not have the force of law, they are not binding authority on courts interpreting the statute. Indeed, Title VII vests ultimate interpretive authority in the federal judiciary.

On the other hand, might the agency's interpretation of a statute "inform" the court's determination of what the law requires with regard to an issue where the agency has considerable experience and deliberation? Judge John Minor Wisdom, for example, deferred to the EEOC's 1970 guidelines when his court ruled that seniority rules having a disparate impact upon racial minorities violated Title VII if they were not justified by business necessity. *Local 189, United Paper Makers,* 416 F.2d 980, 988–89 (5th Cir. 1969). Consider the following judgment by the Fourth Circuit in the Duke Power Case. (We shall give detailed attention to the issue of judicial deference to agency guidances as well as rules in Chapter 9.)

GRIGGS V. DUKE POWER COMPANY
United States Court of Appeals for the Fourth Circuit, 1970.
420 F.2d 1225.

BOREMAN, CIRCUIT JUDGE.

[Writing for the panel majority, Judge Boreman ruled that the claims of three of the Duke Power plaintiffs (described in Problem 1-3) were moot, because the plaintiffs had been promoted. Further, his opinion held that Duke's application of the diploma or testing requirement to six pre-1955 employees violated Title VII, because these employees had been treated differently from white employees of the same period. That is, prior to 1955, whites were sometimes hired or promoted into the other departments without high school diplomas. But Judge Boreman rejected the claims of four employees hired after 1955 and held that Duke's diploma or testing requirements were not discriminatory within the meaning of Title VII.]

Pointing out that it uses an intra-company promotion system to train its own employees for supervisory positions inside the company rather than hire supervisory personnel from outside, Duke claims that it initiated the high school education requirement, at least partially, so that it would have some reasonable assurance that its employees could advance into supervisory positions; further, that its educational and testing requirements are valid because they have a legitimate business purpose, and because the tests are professionally developed ability tests, as sanctioned under § 703(h) of the Act, 42 U.S.C. § 2000e–2(h).

* * * [I]t seems reasonably clear that this requirement did have a genuine business purpose and that the company initiated the policy with no intention to discriminate against Negro employees who might be hired after the adoption of the educational requirement. This conclusion would appear to be not merely supported, but actually compelled by the following facts:

> (1) Duke had long ago established the practice of training its own employees for supervisory positions rather than bringing in supervisory personnel from outside.

> (2) Duke instituted its educational requirement in 1955, nine years prior to the passage of the Civil Rights Act of 1964 and well before the civil rights movement had gathered enough momentum to indicate the inevitability of the passage of such an act.

> (3) Duke has, by plaintiffs' own admission, discontinued the use of discriminatory tactics in employment, promotions and transfers.

> (4) The company's expert witness, Dr. Moffie, testified that he had observed the Dan River operation * * * and he concluded that a high school education would provide the training, ability and judgment to perform tasks in the higher skilled classifications. This testimony is uncontroverted in the record.

> (5) When the educational requirement was adopted it adversely affected the advancement and transfer of white employees who were Watchmen [a miscellaneous category] or were in the Coal Handling Department as well as Negro employees in the Labor Department.

> (6) Duke has a policy of paying the major portion of the expenses incurred by an employee who secures a high school education or its equivalent. In fact, one of the plaintiffs recently obtained such equivalent, the company paying seventy-five percent of the cost.

[Having found the diploma requirement acceptable under Title VII, Judge Boreman then examined the testing requirement, which he found to be "professionally developed" and presumptively acceptable under § 703(h).]

The plaintiffs claim that tests must be *job-related* in order to be valid under § 703(h). The Equal Employment Opportunity Commission * * * supports plaintiffs' view. The EEOC has ruled that tests are unlawful "* * * in the absence of evidence that the tests are properly related to specific jobs and have been properly validated * * *." Decision of EEOC, December 2, 1966, reprinted in CCH Employment Practices Guide, ¶ 17,304.53. * * *

[Judge Boreman conceded that courts should give "great weight" to agency interpretations of statutes they administer, citing *Udall v. Tallman*, 380 U.S. 1, 15 (1965). But such interpretations are not binding on courts.] We cannot agree with plaintiffs' contention that such an interpretation by [the] EEOC should be upheld where, as here, it is clearly contrary to compelling legislative history * * *.

The amendment which incorporated the testing provision of § 703(h) was proposed in a modified form by Senator Tower, who was concerned about a then-recent finding by a hearing examiner for the Illinois Fair Employment Practices Commission in a case involving Motorola, Inc. The examiner had found that a pre-employment general intelligence test which Motorola had given to a Negro applicant for a job had denied the applicant an equal employment opportunity because Negroes were a culturally deprived or disadvantaged group. In proposing his original amendment, essentially the same as the version later unanimously accepted by the Senate, Senator Tower stated:

> "It [the amendment] is an effort to protect the system whereby employers give *general ability and intelligence tests to determine the trainability of prospective employees.* The amendment arises from my concern about what happened in the Motorola FEPC case * * *.

> *"If we should fail to adopt language of this kind, there could be an Equal Employment Opportunity Commission ruling which would in effect invalidate tests of various kinds of employees by both private business and Government to determine the professional competence or ability or trainability or suitability of a person to do a job."* (Emphasis added.) 110 Congressional Record 13492, June 11, 1964.

The discussion which ensued among members of the Senate reveals that proponents and opponents of the Act agreed that general intelligence and ability tests, if fairly administered and acted upon, were not invalidated by the Civil Rights Act of 1964. See 110 Congressional Record 13503–13505, June 11, 1964.

The "Clark-Case" interpretive memorandum pertaining to Title VII fortifies the conclusion that Congress did not intend to invalidate an employer's use of bona fide general intelligence and ability tests. It was stated in said memorandum:

> "There is no requirement in Title VII that employers abandon bona fide qualification tests *where, because of differences in background and education, members of some groups are able to perform better on these tests than members of other groups.* An employer may set his qualifications as high as he likes, he may test to determine which applicants have these qualifications, and he may hire, assign, and promote on the basis of test performance." (Emphasis added.) 110 Congressional Record 7213, April 8, 1964.

[When the Tower amendment was called up for a vote, Judge Boreman observed that Senator Humphrey urged its adoption, and it passed without dissent.]

Sobeloff, Circuit Judge [concurring in granting injunctive relief to the six pre-1955 employees and dissenting in refusing relief to the four post-1955 employees].

The pattern of racial discrimination in employment parallels that which we have witnessed in other areas. Overt bias, when prohibited, has oft-times been supplanted by more cunning devices designed to impart the appearance of neutrality, but to operate with the same invidious effect as before. Illustrative is the use of the Grandfather Clause in voter registration—a scheme that was condemned by the

Supreme Court without dissent over a half century ago. *Guinn v. United States*, 238 U.S. 347 (1915). Another illustration is the resort to pupil transfer plans to nullify rezoning which would otherwise serve to desegregate school districts. Again, the illusory even-handedness did not shield the artifice from attack; the Supreme Court unanimously repudiated the plan. *Goss v. Bd. of Education*, 373 U.S. 683 (1963). It is long-recognized constitutional doctrine that "sophisticated as well as simple-minded modes of discrimination" are prohibited. *Lane v. Wilson*, 307 U.S. 268, 275 (1938) (Frankfurter, J.). We should approach enforcement of the Civil Rights Act in much the same spirit. * * *

The statute is unambiguous. Overt racial discrimination in hiring and promotion is banned [by § 703(a)(1)]. So too, the statute [presumably § 703(a)(2)] interdicts practices that are fair in form but discriminatory in substance. Thus it has become well settled that "objective" or "neutral" standards that favor whites but do not serve business needs are indubitably unlawful employment practices. * * * For example, a requirement that all applicants for employment shall have attended a particular type of school would seem racially neutral. But what if it develops that the specified schools were open only to whites, and if, moreover, they taught nothing of particular significance to the employer's needs? No one can doubt that the requirement would be invalid. It is the position of the Equal Employment Opportunities Commission (EEOC) that educational or test requirements which are irrelevant to job qualifications and which put blacks at a disadvantage are similarly forbidden. * * *

Whites fare overwhelmingly better than blacks on all the criteria [imposed by Duke Power for promotion],[6] as evidenced by the relatively small promotion rate from the Labor Department since 1965. Therefore, the EEOC contends that use of the standards as conditions for transfer, unless they have significant relation to performance on the job, is improper. The requirements, to withstand attack, must be shown to appraise accurately those characteristics (and only those) necessary for the job or jobs an employee will be expected to perform. In other words, the standards must be "job-related."

[Judge Sobeloff urged deference to the EEOC interpretation of § 703(h). He further maintained that the EEOC's interpretation was not only "not unreasonable, but it makes eminent common sense," especially compared with Duke Power's lenient approach, which only required tests to be "professionally developed" to assure protection under the statutory exemption.] But, what is professionally developed for one purpose is not necessarily so for another. * * * [A] test that is adequately designed to determine academic ability, such as a college entrance examination, may be grossly wide of the mark when used in hiring a machine operator. * * * [M]y brethren's resolution of the issue contains a built-in invitation to evade the mandate

---

6   * * * *High School Education.* In North Carolina, census statistics show, as of 1960, while 34% of white males had completed high school, only 12% of Negro males had done so. On a gross level, then, use of the high school diploma requirement would favor whites by a ratio of approximately 3 to 1.

Standardized Tests. * * * Since for generations blacks have been afforded inadequate educational opportunities and have been culturally segregated from white society, it is no more surprising that their performance on "intelligence" tests is significantly different than whites' than it is that fewer blacks have high school diplomas. In one instance, for example, it was found that 58% of whites could pass a battery of standardized tests, as compared with only 6% of the blacks. Included among those tests were the Wonderlic and Bennett tests.

of the statute. To continue his discriminatory practices an employer need only choose any test that favors whites and is irrelevant to actual job qualifications. * * *

[Judge Sobeloff then examined the legislative response to *Motorola*.] That case went to the extreme of suggesting that standardized tests on which whites performed better than Negroes could never be used. The decision was generally taken to mean that such tests could never be justified *even if the needs of the business required them.*

Understandably, there was an outcry in Congress that Title VII might produce a *Motorola* decision. [Judge Sobeloff analyzed the language from the Clark-Case memorandum quoted above by Judge Boreman.] Read against the context of the *Motorola* controversy, the import of the Clark-Case statement plainly appears: employers were not to be prohibited from using tests that determine *qualifications.* "Qualification" implies qualification *for* something. A reasonable interpretation of what the Senators meant, in light of the events, was that nothing in the Act prevents employers from requiring that applicants be fit for the job. * * *

[Judge Sobeloff quoted Senator Tower's amendment as targeted only to protect tests "designed to determine or predict whether such individual is suitable or trainable with respect to his employment in the particular business or enterprise involved." 110 Cong. Rec. 13492 (1964) (text of original Tower amendment). Senators Humphrey and Case opposed the amendment as redundant, and Senator Case feared it was too broad: "If this amendment were enacted, it * * * would give an absolute right to an employer to state as a fact that he had given a test to all applicants, whether it was a good test or not, so long as it was professionally designed." *Id.* at 13504. The original Tower amendment was then defeated. *Id.* at 13724. Tower revised his amendment to render it acceptable to Humphrey and Case, and as revised the amendment passed.]

[Judge Sobeloff concluded that the EEOC interpretation, that employment tests must be job-related, was consistent with the legislative history. The District Court had found the tests not to be job-related, and Duke Power did not produce evidence showing that a high school education was necessary for jobs such as coal handling. He rejected Duke's argument that the tests were designed to identify future prospects rather than immediate promotion.] [T]he Company's criteria unfairly apply only to outsiders seeking entrance to the inside departments. This policy disadvantages those who were not favored with the lax criteria used for whites before 1955. * * * [T]his when juxtaposed with the history and racial composition of the Dan River plant, is itself sufficient to constitute a violation of Title VII. * * *

[While Duke's] practice does not constitute forthright racial discrimination, the policy disfavoring the outside employees has primary impact upon blacks. This effect is possible only because a history of overt bias caused the departments to become so imbalanced in the first place. The result is that in 1969, four years after the passage of Title VII, Dan River looks substantially like it did before 1965. The Labor Department is all black; the rest is virtually lily-white.

There no longer is room for doubt that a neutral superstructure built upon racial patterns that were discriminatorily erected in the past comes within the Title VII ban. * * *

A remedy for this kind of wrong is not without precedent. The "freezing" principle (more properly, the anti-freezing principle) developed by the Fifth Circuit in voting cases is analogous. In those cases a pattern and practice of discrimination excluded almost all eligible Negroes from the voting lists but enrolled the vast majority of whites. Faced with judicial attack, the authorities found that they could no longer avowedly employ discriminatory practices. They invented and put into effect instead new, unquestionably even-handed, but onerous voting requirements which had the effect of excluding new applicants of both races, but, as was to be expected, primarily affected Negroes, who in the main were the unlisted ones. [For this reason, the Fifth Circuit struck down the new rules, and the Supreme Court agreed. *Louisiana v. United States*, 380 U.S. 145 (1965).]

Title VII bars "freeze-outs" as well as pure discrimination, where the freeze is achieved by requirements that are arbitrary and have no real business justification. Thus Duke Power's discrimination against *all* those who did not benefit from the pre-1955 rule for whites operates as an illegal "freeze-out" of blacks from the inside departments.

NOTE ON GRIGGS AND BACKGROUND AGAINST WHICH STATUTES ARE READ

The NAACP Legal Defense & Education, Inc. Fund (the "Inc. Fund"), which represented the plaintiffs, appealed this decision's denial of relief for the post-1955 plaintiffs to the Supreme Court. Should defendant cross-appeal the Court's granting relief to the pre-1955 plaintiffs? Should the EEOC join in plaintiffs' appeal? How ought the Supreme Court rule on this issue?

As you ponder this last query, consider the issues that divided Judges Boreman and Sobeloff. Some are technical issues, such as how to read § 703(a), (h) and what to make of the legislative history of the Tower Amendment (§ 703(h)). Sympathetic to Judge Boreman's account, Daniel Rodriguez and Barry Weingast focus on the pivotal legislators—conservative Republicans who were needed to break the Senate filibuster— and claim that those members had a narrower vision of civil rights, namely, one focusing on equality of opportunity, with minimal "meddling" from the EEOC. They cite the history of the Tower Amendment as evidence that the liberal sponsors of Title VII needed the support of conservative Republicans and, for that reason, made a costly concession by ultimately going along with the Tower Amendment. See Rodriguez & Weingast, *The Positive Political Theory of Legislative History: New Perspectives on the 1964 Civil Rights Act and Its Interpretation*, 151 U. Pa. L. Rev. 1417, 1501–10 (2003).

Disputing this account is Victoria Nourse, *Misunderstanding Congress: Statutory Interpretation, the Supermajoritarian Difficulty, and the Separation of Powers*, 99 Geo. L.J. 1119 (2011). Nourse observes that Senator Tower, from segregated Texas, was *not* a possible vote for the civil rights bill, and so his statements about the proposed legislation are precisely the sort of cheap talk that interpreters should not rely on. Moreover, the Tower Amendment, ultimately accepted by the Senate, was a *post-cloture* amendment; in other words, it came *after* the pivotal legislators (especially Senator Dirksen) had signed onto the civil rights bill, with the changes reflected in the Mansfield-Dirksen substitute.

There are also larger issues that separate the two opinions, including different visions of racial justice, different degrees of deference to the EEOC, and different visions of the role of courts in implementing Title VII. Indeed, reading the legislative record may reflect different approaches. Nourse's account focuses on the majority coalition of liberal Democrats and moderate Republicans, whose project was racial integration of our country's segregated workforces. In contrast, Rodriguez and Weingast's account focuses on legislators they consider pivotal, such as the conservative Republicans whose votes were needed to break the Senate filibuster.[53]

NOTE ON THE EEOC, THE SOLICITOR GENERAL, AND THE SUPREME COURT'S DECISION IN GRIGGS V. DUKE POWER

The EEOC's rationale for an effects-based approach was that such an interpretation better served the statutory purpose. This position was shared by the Inc. Fund and other civil rights litigation groups. Directly encouraged by the EEOC, which filed helpful *amicus* briefs, civil rights litigation groups challenged employer testing and union seniority arrangements which had disproportionate and negative effects upon African Americans. These groups sometimes found a receptive audience in Eisenhower- and Johnson-appointed federal judges who were struggling with similar issues of racially discriminatory effects of arguably "neutral" state policies in the areas of education, voting, and jury selection. See, e.g., Judge Butzner's opinion in *Quarles v. Philip Morris, Inc.*, 279 F. Supp. 505 (E.D. Va. 1968), and Judge Wisdom's opinion in *Local 189, United Papermakers v. United States*, 416 F.2d 980 (5th Cir. 1969). Judge Soboloff, dissenting in *Griggs*, relied on *Quarles* and *Local 189* to argue for a results-oriented rather than merely an intent-focused inquiry in Title VII.

The Inc. Fund appealed its loss in *Griggs*, with the support of the EEOC and the Nixon Administration's Solicitor General, Erwin Griswold. To the surprise of many pundits, the Supreme Court not only unanimously reversed in *Griggs v. Duke Power Co.*, 401 U.S. 424 (1971), but it expanded upon Judge Soboloff's opinion. The Court held that a facially neutral employment practice that is not openly or intentionally discriminatory is nonetheless unlawful if it has the effect of excluding a group on the basis of race and without a strict showing of business necessity. Query: What provision of Title VII would such an employer be violating if it could not make a cogent showing of business necessity?

Although the Court reaffirmed the colorblindness of Title VII, its rationale stressed that "Congress directed the thrust of the Act to the *consequences* of employment practices." This appeared to be a recognition that, while § 703(a) speaks in terms of individuals, the problems addressed by Title VII might include institutionalized societal practices that systematically exclude minority groups from employment opportunities. The lower courts viewed the Supreme Court's decision in *Griggs* as a mandate to use Title VII to reform group employment practices in entire companies, based upon the disparate impact idea. *Cf.* Exec. Order No. 11,246 (1965) (2011 Documents Supp. 111–17) (imposing non-discrimination duties onto federal government contractors and their subcontractors, and thereby creating administrative pressure for those private firms to have more racially balanced workplaces).[54]

---

[53] See also James Brudney, *Intentionalism's Revival*, 44 San Diego L. Rev. 1001, 1022–24 (2007) (suggesting that ardent supporters such as the majority coalition may be more important than short-term pivotal participants when determining legislative intent, because the former group's continuity in leadership and oversight roles means that ardent legislators are more likely to follow closely how agencies and courts implement the statutory commands).

[54] As elaborated in 1970, Executive Order 11,246 required government contractors to establish "a set of specific and result-oriented procedures" to yield "equal employment opportunity." 35 Fed. Reg. 2586, 2587

Some commentators have criticized disparate impact liability as inconsistent with the original "deal" needed to get Title VII's protections through the vetogates, specifically, past the Senate filibuster. Assume that they are right. What, then, explains the Supreme Court's decision in *Griggs*? Judge Sobeloff's opinion suggests that an effects-based inquiry was needed to fulfill the statute's purpose. Congress in 1964 did not focus on the possibility that pre-1964 discrimination would have continuing effects, but once that became clear to the EEOC and the courts, they had a responsibility to apply the statute to new circumstances in a way that carried out the original purpose. One might understand such an approach as a *translation* of the statute, moving it away from its apparent textual mandates on the ground that a liberal reading is required to fulfill the statutory objectives. In other words, an interpretation that departs from the terms of the deal, as reflected in the text of the statute, is actually more faithful to legislative intent than a more literal interpretation. This sort of dynamic statutory interpretation is controversial, because it concedes the existence of discretionary power in the unelected judiciary. On the other hand, at least in theory, it requires judges to be the faithful and careful agents of the legislative drafters, modifying or enhancing statutory provisions only when necessary to avoid undermining legislative purpose and intent.

Another way of explaining *Griggs* is that the liberal EEOC and Supreme Court were moving statutory policy in a leftward direction away from original legislative intent. This can be expressed in the game-theoretic terms familiar to us from our study of institutional theories of the legislative process. *E.g.*, Lee Epstein & Jack Knight, *The Choices Justices Make* (1999). Strategic theories of institutional behavior emphasize the importance of all the players in the policymaking game, including the executive branch agencies that will implement the statute and the judges who will interpret it. If their preferences diverge from the legislature's, they may try to move policy closer to their ideal point, realizing that the Congress will monitor them and try to avert any substantial change in the outcome.

Thus, the experience the EEOC had with rooting out covert or even unconscious race discrimination gave that agency a more liberal viewpoint about how broadly Title VII ought to be applied than Senator Dirksen and Representative McCulloch might have had in 1964. Moreover, even if it were true that the 1964 Congress would have disapproved the result in *Griggs,* by 1971 Congress itself had changed in response to the evolving norms of the country. Especially after citizens of color gained greater access to the ballot box in the wake of the Voting Rights Act of 1965, Congress gradually shed its most ardent segregationists, who were replaced with pro-integration or neutral representatives. Overall, a Congress more sympathetic to actual workplace integration was a Congress that would have been okay with the EEOC's and the Supreme Court's approach in *Griggs*.

To be sure, any shift in legislative preferences between 1964 and 1971 was modest, and it is not clear that Congress in 1971 would have *enacted* a policy like *Griggs*. But here is where the third political dynamic comes into play: once the agency or a court has authoritatively and dynamically interpreted a statute, that interpretation prevails unless Congress can affirmatively *override* it. Matthew R. Christiansen & William N. Eskridge Jr., *Congressional Overrides of Supreme Court Statutory Interpretation Decisions, 1967–2011,* 92 Tex. L. Rev. 1317 (2014). But to override the interpretation, a proposal must surmount all the vetogates that the original enactment did. In 1972,

---

(1970). For a discussion of the role of executive orders to expand civil rights, perhaps beyond what Congress would enact, see Kenneth Mayer, *With the Stroke of a Pen: Executive Orders and Presidential Power* ch. 6 (2001).

Congress passed the Equal Employment Opportunity Act, 86 Stat. 103, increasing enforcement authority for the EEOC and otherwise broadening protections available under Title VII. The Court decided *Griggs* while the bill was being considered in committee. Both the House and Senate committee reports accompanying the 1972 Act discussed and expressly approved the holding and reasoning of *Griggs*. Each report cited *Griggs* to support its conclusion that, because employment discrimination—characterized "in terms of 'systems' and 'effects' rather than simply intentional wrongs"—was more complex and pervasive than had previously been believed, the EEOC needed broad and meaningful enforcement powers. See H.R. Rep. No. 238, 92d Cong., 1st Sess. 8–9, 20–22 (1971), reprinted in 1972 U.S.C.C.A.N. 2137, 2144–45, 2155–57; Sen. Rep. No. 415, 92d Cong., 1st Sess. 5 & n.1, 14–15 [14] (1971). Because those committees exercised gatekeeping power over issues on the legislative agenda, they had substantial ability to head off overrides of agency policies or judicial decisions, especially when they were supported by the majority party leadership, which was similarly liberal on civil rights issues and exerted great control over the congressional agenda and floor politics.

Under the foregoing analysis, the EEOC and the Supreme Court have a certain amount of slack in setting statutory policy—and in moving statutory policy away from original congressional deals. Note that under this analysis, the EEOC and the Court can be more strongly influenced by the preferences of members of the *current* Congress than they are by the preferences of the *enacting* Congress. This thought experiment reveals that the notion of legislative intent has a temporal element. Although many think of courts and executive branch officials as the agents of the enacting Congress, subsequent Congresses can exert substantial influence over policies even when (unlike the 1972 setting) they do not revisit the substantive statutory provisions, because they control the budget and have close connections with agency personnel with day-to-day oversight of federal programs. Indeed, one scholar has argued that enacting legislators may rationally prefer interpreters to track current legislative preferences, which he calls "enactable preferences," because that allows the enacting legislators to influence not only the legislation they pass, but also all legislation being interpreted while they are in office. Einer Elhauge, *Preference-Estimating Statutory Default Rules*, 102 Colum. L. Rev. 2027 (2002).

Under an analysis focused on strategy, however, *Griggs* itself might be subject to reinterpretation. After Justices Lewis Powell and William Rehnquist took their seats in 1972, the Burger Court became much more ambivalent about aggressively pressing for racial integration in schools as well as workplaces. In constitutional cases, where the Court is better protected against political overrides, the Burger Court rejected the *Griggs* approach and held that race-based or gender-based effects do not amount to unlawful discrimination, unless complainants can demonstrate a discriminatory "intent." See *Washington v. Davis*, 426 U.S. 229 (1976); *Personnel Administrator of Massachusetts v. Feeney*, 442 U.S. 256 (1979); see also Jeffrey Segal & Albert Cover, *Ideological Values and the Votes of U.S. Supreme Court Justices*, 83 Am. Pol. Sci. Rev. 557, 560 (1989) (Table 1). The Burger Court narrowed *Griggs* itself by tightening up the burden of proof for plaintiffs, but did not directly attack the decision—perhaps because the relevant congressional committees had embraced it in 1971, and Congress as a whole moved further to the left on civil rights issues in the 1970s. Any open retreat from *Griggs* would have generated immediate controversy because the civil rights community, the EEOC, and the gatekeeping (labor) committees would have mobilized for an override. In fact, this is precisely what happened when the Court retreated from *Griggs* by refusing to treat pregnancy discrimination as sex discrimination under Title VII: the Court suffered a firestorm of protest and was angrily overridden in 1978.[55]

B. THE NEXT BIG ISSUE: RACE-BASED AFFIRMATIVE ACTION

If you were counsel to a big company or a union in the 1970s, you would probably be concerned about the representation of people of color in your company's workforce. Under *Griggs*, your company or union might be subject to a disparate impact lawsuit if bad numbers were not justified. And if your company did business with the federal government, the Johnson and Nixon Administrations had implemented a policy under which such companies had to improve their numbers or lose their lucrative contracts. See Executive Order 11246, "Equal Employment Opportunity," (Sept. 24, 1965) (2011 Documents Supplement 111–17); "Affirmative Action Programs," 35 Fed. Reg. 2568 (Feb. 2, 1970) (2011 Documents Supplement 118–22). In short, companies faced the loss of government contracts and judicially imposed back-pay awards and quota systems if their hiring efforts did not produce concrete results. When Congress revisited Title VII in 1971–72, proposals to overturn the executive orders were advanced and rejected in both chambers (2011 Documents Supplement 123–28). At the same time, *Griggs* escaped controversy; the EEOC-Supreme Court approach to disparate impact liability was endorsed in the House committee report and not challenged on the floor as the executive orders were.

Consistent with *Griggs*, the Supreme Court encouraged companies to adopt their own plans to integrate their workforces. For example, in *Albemarle Paper Co. v. Moody*, 422 U.S. 405, 417–18 (1975), the Court approved broad EEOC guidelines seeking to provide the "spur or catalyst which causes employers and unions to self-examine and to self-evaluate their employment practices and to endeavor to eliminate, so far as possible, the last vestiges of an unfortunate and ignominious page in this country's history." See also *Franks v. Bowman Transp. Co.*, 424 U.S. 747, 778 (1976) (upholding retroactive award of seniority to African-American victims of discrimination and saying that "a collective bargaining agreement may go further, enhancing the seniority status of certain employees for purposes of furthering public policy interests beyond what is required by statute").

As a result of these developments, companies like Kaiser Aluminum and labor unions like the United Steelworkers had incentives to adopt their own preferential hiring programs, with the hope that they could avoid having one thrust upon them by a court. In *McDonald v. Santa Fe Trail Transp. Co.*, 427 U.S. 273 (1976), however, the Court held that Title VII prohibits racial discrimination against whites as well as blacks. The upshot of that case was that displaced white employees like Brian Weber had a colorable argument that voluntary affirmative action programs unlawfully discriminated against them as well—and that they had a cause of action under Title VII. That clash of different statutory purposes, different legally protected civil rights, and different Supreme Court signals generated the following case.

---

[55] The Pregnancy Discrimination Act of 1978, Pub. L. No. 95–555, 92 Stat. 2076 (1978), overriding *General Electric Co. v. Gilbert*, 429 U.S. 125 (1976); see William N. Eskridge Jr., *Reneging on History? Playing the Court/Congress/President Civil Rights Game*, 79 Calif. L. Rev. 613 (1991).

UNITED STEELWORKERS OF AMERICA V. WEBER

Supreme Court of the United States, 1979.
443 U.S. 193, 99 S.Ct. 2721, 61 L.Ed.2d 480.

MR. JUSTICE BRENNAN delivered the opinion of the Court. * * *

In 1974, petitioner United Steelworkers of America (USWA) and petitioner Kaiser Aluminum & Chemical Corp. (Kaiser) entered into a master collective-bargaining agreement covering terms and conditions of employment at 15 Kaiser plants. The agreement contained, *inter alia*, an affirmative action plan designed to eliminate conspicuous racial imbalances in Kaiser's then almost exclusively white craft-work forces. Black craft-hiring goals were set for each Kaiser plant equal to the percentage of blacks in the respective local labor forces. To enable plants to meet these goals, on-the-job training programs were established to teach unskilled production workers—black and white—the skills necessary to become craftworkers. The plan reserved for black employees 50% of the openings in these newly created in-plant training programs.

This case arose from the operation of the plan at Kaiser's plant in Gramercy, La. Until 1974, Kaiser hired as craftworkers for that plant only persons who had had prior craft experience. Because blacks had long been excluded from craft unions, few were able to present such credentials. As a consequence, prior to 1974 only 1.83% (5 out of 273) of the skilled craftworkers at the Gramercy plant were black, even though the work force in the Gramercy area was approximately 39% black.

[Kaiser adopted a training program, with the 50% quota, for its Gramercy plant. In 1974, it selected 13 employees, including 7 blacks. The most senior black worker selected into the program had less seniority than several white production workers whose bids for admission were rejected; one of those white employees, Brian Weber, brought a class action in federal court.]

The complaint alleged that the filling of craft trainee positions at the Gramercy plant pursuant to the affirmative action program had resulted in junior black employees' receiving training in preference to senior white employees, thus discriminating against respondent and other similarly situated white employees in violation of §§ 703(a) and (d) of Title VII [both quoted in our Note on Title VII, above]. The District Court held that the plan violated Title VII, entered a judgment in favor of the plaintiff class, and granted a permanent injunction prohibiting Kaiser and the USWA "from denying plaintiffs, Brian F. Weber and all other members of the class, access to on-the-job training programs on the basis of race." A divided panel of the Court of Appeals for the Fifth Circuit affirmed, holding that all employment preferences based upon race, including those preferences incidental to bona fide affirmative action plans, violated Title VII's prohibition against racial discrimination in employment. * * * We reverse.

We emphasize at the outset the narrowness of our inquiry. * * * [S]ince the Kaiser-USWA plan was adopted voluntarily, we are not concerned with what Title VII requires or with what a court might order to remedy a past proved violation of the Act. The only question before us is the narrow statutory issue of whether Title VII *forbids* private employers and unions from voluntarily agreeing upon bona fide affirmative action plans that accord racial preferences in the manner and for the purpose provided in the Kaiser-USWA plan. * * *

Respondent argues that Congress intended in Title VII to prohibit all race conscious affirmative action plans. Respondent's argument rests upon a literal interpretation of §§ 703(a) and (d) of the Act. Those sections make it unlawful to "discriminate * * * because of * * * race" in hiring and in the selection of apprentices for training programs. Since, the argument runs, *McDonald* settled that Title VII forbids discrimination against whites as well as blacks, and since the Kaiser-USWA affirmative action plan operates to discriminate against white employees solely because they are white, it follows that the Kaiser-USWA plan violates Title VII.

Respondent's argument is not without force. But it overlooks the significance of the fact that the Kaiser-USWA plan is an affirmative action plan voluntarily adopted by private parties to eliminate traditional patterns of racial segregation. In this context respondent's reliance upon a literal construction of §§ 703(a) and (d) and upon *McDonald* is misplaced. It is a "familiar rule, that a thing may be within the letter of the statute and yet not within the statute, because not within its spirit, nor within the intention of its makers." *Holy Trinity Church v. United States*, 143 U.S. 457, 459 (1892). The prohibition against racial discrimination in §§ 703(a) and (d) of Title VII must therefore be read against the background of the legislative history of Title VII and the historical context from which the Act arose. Examination of those sources makes clear that an interpretation of the sections that forbade all race-conscious affirmative action would "bring about an end completely at variance with the purpose of the statute" and must be rejected. *United States v. Public Utilities Comm'n*, 345 U.S. 295, 315 (1953).

Congress's primary concern in enacting the prohibition against racial discrimination in Title VII of the Civil Rights Act of 1964 was with "the plight of the Negro in our economy." 110 Cong. Rec. 6548 (1964) (remarks of Sen. Humphrey). Before 1964, blacks were largely relegated to "unskilled and semiskilled jobs." *Ibid.* (remarks of Sen. Humphrey); *id.*, at 7204 (remarks of Sen. Clark); *id.*, at 7379–7380 (remarks of Sen. Kennedy). Because of automation the number of such jobs was rapidly decreasing. As a consequence, "the relative position of the Negro worker [was] steadily worsening." * * *

Congress feared that the goals of the Civil Rights Act—the integration of blacks into the mainstream of American society—could not be achieved unless this trend were reversed. And Congress recognized that that would not be possible unless blacks were able to secure jobs "which have a future." *Id.*, at 7204 (remarks of Sen. Clark). See also *id.*, at 7379–7380 (remarks of Sen. Kennedy). As Senator Humphrey explained to the Senate:

> "What good does it do a Negro to be able to eat in a fine restaurant if he cannot afford to pay the bill? What good does it do him to be accepted in a hotel that is too expensive for his modest income? How can a Negro child be motivated to take full advantage of integrated educational facilities if he has no hope of getting a job where he can use that education?" *Id.*, at 6547.
> * * *

Accordingly, it was clear to Congress that "[t]he crux of the problem [was] to open employment opportunities for Negroes in occupations which have been traditionally closed to them," 110 Cong. Rec. 6548 (1964) (remarks of Sen. Humphrey), and it was to this problem that Title VII's prohibition against racial discrimination in employment was primarily addressed.

It plainly appears from the House Report accompanying the Civil Rights Act that Congress did not intend wholly to prohibit private and voluntary affirmative action efforts as one method of solving this problem. The Report provides:

"No bill can or should lay claim to eliminating all of the causes and consequences of racial and other types of discrimination against minorities. There is reason to believe, however, that national leadership provided by the enactment of Federal legislation dealing with the most troublesome problems *will create an atmosphere conducive to voluntary or local resolution of other forms of discrimination.*" H.R. Rep. No. 914, 88th Cong., 1st Sess., pt. 1, p. 18 (1963). (Emphasis supplied.) * * *

Given this legislative history, we cannot agree with respondent that Congress intended to prohibit the private sector from taking effective steps to accomplish the goal that Congress designed Title VII to achieve. * * * It would be ironic indeed if a law triggered by a Nation's concern over centuries of racial injustice and intended to improve the lot of those who had "been excluded from the American dream for so long," 110 Cong. Rec. 6552 (1964) (remarks of Sen. Humphrey), constituted the first legislative prohibition of all voluntary, private, race-conscious efforts to abolish traditional patterns of racial segregation and hierarchy.

Our conclusion is further reinforced by examination of the language and legislative history of § 703(j) of Title VII [quoted in our Note on Title VII]. Opponents of Title VII raised two related arguments against the bill. First, they argued that the Act would be interpreted to *require* employers with racially imbalanced work forces to grant preferential treatment to racial minorities in order to integrate. Second, they argued that employers with racially imbalanced work forces would grant preferential treatment to racial minorities, even if not required to do so by the Act. See 110 Cong. Rec. 8618–8619 (1964) (remarks of Sen. Sparkman). Had Congress meant to prohibit all race-conscious affirmative action, as respondent urges, it easily could have answered both objections by providing that Title VII would not require or *permit* racially preferential integration efforts. But Congress did not choose such a course. Rather, Congress added § 703(j) which addresses only the first objection. The section provides that nothing contained in Title VII "shall be interpreted to *require* any employer * * * to grant preferential treatment * * * to any group because of the race * * * of such * * * group on account of" a *de facto* racial imbalance in the employer's work force. The section does *not* state that "nothing in Title VII shall be interpreted to *permit*" voluntary affirmative efforts to correct racial imbalances. The natural inference is that Congress chose not to forbid all voluntary race-conscious affirmative action.

The reasons for this choice are evident from the legislative record. Title VII could not have been enacted into law without substantial support from legislators in both Houses who traditionally resisted federal regulation of private business. Those legislators demanded as a price for their support that "management prerogatives, and union freedoms * * * be left undisturbed to the greatest extent possible." H.R. Rep. No. 914, 88th Cong., 1st Sess., pt. 2, p. 29 (1963). Section 703(j) was proposed by Senator Dirksen to allay any fears that the Act might be interpreted in such a way as to upset this compromise. The section was designed to prevent § 703 of Title VII from being interpreted in such a way as to lead to undue "Federal Government interference with private businesses because of some Federal employee's ideas about racial balance or racial imbalance." 110 Cong. Rec. 14314 (1964) (remarks of Sen. Miller). See also *id.*, at 9881 (remarks of Sen. Allott); *id.*, at 10520 (remarks of Sen. Carlson); *id.*, at 11471 (remarks of Sen. Javits); *id.*, at 12817 (remarks of Sen. Dirksen). Clearly, a prohibition against all voluntary, race-conscious, affirmative action efforts would disserve these ends. Such a prohibition would augment the powers of the Federal Government and diminish traditional management prerogatives while at the same time impeding attainment of the ultimate statutory goals. In view of this legislative history and in view of Congress's desire to avoid undue federal regulation of private businesses, use of the word "require" rather than the phrase "require or permit" in § 703(j) fortifies the conclusion that Congress did not intend to limit traditional business freedom to such a degree as to prohibit all voluntary, race-conscious affirmative action.[7]

We therefore hold that Title VII's prohibition in §§ 703(a) and (d) against racial discrimination does not condemn all private, voluntary, race-conscious affirmative action plans. * * * [The Court held that the Kaiser plan was lawful under Title VII because both its purpose and effect were permissible: it was "designed to eliminate conspicuous racial imbalance in traditionally segregated job categories," and it did not unnecessarily trammel the interests of white employees, because no white employees lost their jobs, half of those trained in the program would be white, and it was a temporary measure slated to end when "the percentage of black skilled craftworkers in the Gramercy plant approximates the percentage of blacks in the local labor force."]

---

[7]   Respondent argues that our construction of § 703 conflicts with various remarks in the legislative record. See, *e.g.*, 110 Cong. Rec. 7213 (1964) (Sens. Clark and Case); *id.*, at 7218 (Sens. Clark and Case); *id.*, at 6549 (Sen. Humphrey); *id.*, at 8921 (Sen. Williams). We do not agree. In Senator Humphrey's words, these comments were intended as assurances that Title VII would not allow establishment of systems "to *maintain* racial balance in employment." *Id.*, at 11848 (emphasis added). They were not addressed to temporary, voluntary, affirmative action measures undertaken to eliminate manifest racial imbalance in traditionally segregated job categories. Moreover, the comments referred to by respondent all preceded the adoption of § 703(j), 42 U.S.C. § 2000e–2(j). After § 703(j) was adopted, congressional comments were all to the effect that employers would not be *required* to institute preferential quotas to avoid Title VII liability, see, *e.g.*, 110 Cong. Rec. 12819 (1964) (remarks of Sen. Dirksen); *id.*, at 13079–13080 (remarks of Sen. Clark); *id.*, at 15876 (remarks of Rep. Lindsay). There was no suggestion after the adoption of § 703(j) that wholly voluntary, race-conscious, affirmative action efforts would in themselves constitute a violation of Title VII. On the contrary, as Representative MacGregor told the House shortly before the final vote on Title VII:

"Important as the scope and extent of this bill is, it is also vitally important that all Americans understand what this bill does not cover.

"Your mail and mine, your contacts and mine with our constituents, indicates a great degree of misunderstanding about this bill. People complain about * * * preferential treatment or quotas in employment. There is a mistaken belief that Congress is legislating in these areas in this bill. When we drafted this bill we excluded these issues largely because the problems raised by these controversial questions are more properly handled at a governmental level closer to the American people and by communities and individuals themselves." 110 Cong. Rec. 15893 (1964).

MR. JUSTICE POWELL and MR. JUSTICE STEVENS took no part in the consideration or decision of these cases.

MR. JUSTICE BLACKMUN, concurring.

While I share some of the misgivings expressed in MR. JUSTICE REHNQUIST's dissent concerning the extent to which the legislative history of Title VII clearly supports the result the Court reaches today, I believe that additional considerations, practical and equitable, only partially perceived, if perceived at all, by the 88th Congress, support the conclusion reached by the Court today, and I therefore join its opinion as well as its judgment.

In his dissent from the decision of the United States Court of Appeals for the Fifth Circuit, Judge Wisdom pointed out that this litigation arises from a practical problem in the administration of Title VII. The broad prohibition against discrimination places the employer and the union on what he accurately described as a "high tightrope without a net beneath them." 563 F.2d 216, 230. If Title VII is read literally, on the one hand they face liability for past discrimination against blacks, and on the other they face liability to whites for any voluntary preferences adopted to mitigate the effects of prior discrimination against blacks.

In this litigation, Kaiser denies prior discrimination but concedes that its past hiring practices may be subject to question. Although the labor force in the Gramercy area was proximately 39% black, Kaiser's work force was less than 15% black, and its craftwork force was less than 2% black. Kaiser had made some effort to recruit black painters, carpenters, insulators, and other craftsmen, but it continued to insist that those hired have five years' prior industrial experience, a requirement that arguably was not sufficiently job related to justify under Title VII any discriminatory impact it may have had. * * * The parties dispute the extent to which black craftsmen were available in the local labor market. They agree, however, that after critical reviews from the Office of Federal Contract Compliance, Kaiser and the Steelworkers established the training program in question here and modeled it along the lines of a Title VII consent decree later entered for the steel industry. * * * Yet when they did this, respondent Weber sued, alleging that Title VII prohibited the program because it discriminated against him as a white person and it was not supported by a prior judicial finding of discrimination against blacks.

Respondent Weber's reading of Title VII, endorsed by the Court of Appeals, places voluntary compliance with Title VII in profound jeopardy. The only way for the employer and the union to keep their footing on the "tightrope" it creates would be to eschew all forms of voluntary affirmative action. Even a whisper of emphasis on minority recruiting would be forbidden. Because Congress intended to encourage private efforts to come into compliance with Title VII, see *Alexander v. Gardner-Denver Co.*, 415 U.S. 36, 44 (1974), Judge Wisdom concluded that employers and unions who had committed "arguable violations" of Title VII should be free to make reasonable responses without fear of liability to whites. Preferential hiring along the lines of the Kaiser program is a reasonable response for the employer, whether or not a court, on these facts, could order the same step as a remedy. The company is able to avoid identifying victims of past discrimination, and so avoids claims for backpay that would inevitably follow a response limited to such victims. If past victims should be benefited by the program, however, the company mitigates its liability to those persons. Also, to the extent that Title VII liability is predicated on the "disparate effect" of an employer's past hiring practices, the program makes it less likely that such an effect could be demonstrated. And the Court has recently held that work-force statistics resulting from private affirmative action were probative of benign intent in a "disparate treatment" case. *Furnco Construction Corp. v. Waters*, 438 U.S. 567 (1978).

The "arguable violation" theory has a number of advantages. It responds to a practical problem in the administration of Title VII not anticipated by Congress. It draws predictability from the outline of present law and closely effectuates the purpose of the Act. Both Kaiser and the United States urge its adoption here. Because I agree that it is the soundest way to approach this case, my preference would be to resolve this litigation by applying it and holding that Kaiser's craft training program meets the requirement that voluntary affirmative action be a reasonable response to an "arguable violation" of Title VII. * * *

MR. JUSTICE REHNQUIST, with whom THE CHIEF JUSTICE joins, dissenting.

In a very real sense, the Court's opinion is ahead of its time: it could more appropriately have been handed down five years from now, in 1984, a year coinciding with the title of a book from which the Court's opinion borrows, perhaps subconsciously, at least one idea. Orwell describes in his book a governmental official of Oceania, one of the three great world powers, denouncing the current enemy, Eurasia, to an assembled crowd:

> "It was almost impossible to listen to him without being first convinced and then maddened. * * * The speech had been proceeding for perhaps twenty minutes when a messenger hurried onto the platform and a scrap of paper was slipped into the speaker's hand. He unrolled and read it without pausing in his speech. Nothing altered in his voice or manner, or in the content of what he was saying, but suddenly the names were different. Without words said, a wave of understanding rippled through the crowd. Oceania was at war with Eastasia! * * * The banners and posters with which the square was decorated were all wrong! * * *

> "[T]he speaker had switched from one line to the other actually in mid-sentence, not only without a pause, but without even breaking the syntax."—G. Orwell, Nineteen Eighty-Four 181–182 (1949).

Today's decision represents an equally dramatic and equally unremarked switch in this Court's interpretation of Title VII. * * *

[II] Were Congress to act today specifically to prohibit the type of racial discrimination suffered by Weber, it would be hard pressed to draft language better tailored to the task than that found in § 703(d) of Title VII:

> "It shall be an unlawful employment practice for any employer, labor organization, or joint labor-management committee controlling apprenticeship or other training or retraining, including on-the-job training programs to discriminate against any individual because of his race, color, religion, sex, or national origin in admission to, or employment in, any

program established to provide apprenticeship or other training." 78 Stat. 256, 42 U.S.C. § 2000e–2(d).

Equally suited to the task would be § 703(a)(2), which makes it unlawful for an employer to classify his employees "in any way which would deprive or tend to deprive any individual of employment opportunities or otherwise adversely affect his status as an employee, because of such individual's race, color, religion, sex, or national origin." 78 Stat. 255, 42 U.S.C. § 2000e–2(a)(2).

Entirely consistent with these two express prohibitions is the language of § 703(j) of Title VII, which provides that the Act is not to be interpreted "to require any employer * * * to grant preferential treatment to any individual or to any group because of the race * * * of such individual or group" to correct a racial imbalance in the employer's work force. 42 U.S.C. § 2000e–2(j). Seizing on the word "require," the Court infers that Congress must have intended to "permit" this type of racial discrimination. Not only is this reading of § 703(j) outlandish in the light of the flat prohibitions of §§ 703(a) and (d), but also, as explained in Part III, it is totally belied by the Act's legislative history.

Quite simply, Kaiser's racially discriminatory admission quota is flatly prohibited by the plain language of Title VII. This normally dispositive fact, however, gives the Court only momentary pause. An "interpretation" of the statute upholding Weber's claim would, according to the Court, " 'bring about an end completely at variance with the purpose of the statute.' " To support this conclusion, the Court calls upon the "spirit" of the Act, which it divines from passages in Title VII's legislative history indicating that enactment of the statute was prompted by Congress's desire " 'to open employment opportunities for Negroes in occupations which [had] been traditionally closed to them.' " But the legislative history invoked by the Court to avoid the plain language of §§ 703(a) and (d) simply misses the point. To be sure, the reality of employment discrimination against Negroes provided the primary impetus for passage of Title VII. But this fact by no means supports the proposition that Congress intended to leave employers free to discriminate against white persons. In most cases, "[l]egislative history . . . is more vague than the statute we are called upon to interpret." [*United States v. Public Utilities Comm'n*, 345 U.S. 295, 320 (1953) (Jackson, J., concurring).] Here, however, the legislative history of Title VII is as clear as the language of §§ 703(a) and (d), and it irrefutably demonstrates that Congress meant precisely what it said in §§ 703(a) and (d)—that *no* racial discrimination in employment is permissible under Title VII, not even preferential treatment of minorities to correct racial imbalance.

[III] In undertaking to review the legislative history of Title VII, I am mindful that the topic hardly makes for light reading, but I am also fearful that nothing short of a thorough examination of the congressional debates will fully expose the magnitude of the Court's misinterpretation of Congress's intent.

[A] Introduced on the floor of the House of Representatives on June 20, 1963, the bill—H.R. 7152—that ultimately became the Civil Rights Act of 1964 contained no compulsory provisions directed at private discrimination in employment. The bill was promptly referred to the Committee on the Judiciary, where it was amended to include Title VII. With two exceptions, the bill reported by the House Judiciary

Committee contained §§ 703(a) and (d) as they were ultimately enacted. Amendments subsequently adopted on the House floor added § 703's prohibition against sex discrimination and § 703(d)'s coverage of "on-the-job training."

After noting that "[t]he purpose of [Title VII] is to eliminate * * * discrimination in employment based on race, color, religion, or national origin," the Judiciary Committee's Report simply paraphrased the provisions of Title VII without elaboration. H.R. Rep., pt. 1, p. 26. In a separate Minority Report, however, opponents of the measure on the Committee advanced a line of attack which was reiterated throughout the debates in both the House and Senate and which ultimately led to passage of § 703(j). Noting that the word "discrimination" was nowhere defined in H.R. 7152, the Minority Report charged that the absence from Title VII of any reference to "racial imbalance" was a "public relations" ruse and that "the administration intends to rely upon its own construction of 'discrimination' as including the lack of racial balance. . . ." H.R. Rep., pt. 1, pp. 67–68. To demonstrate how the bill would operate in practice, the Minority Report posited a number of hypothetical employment situations, concluding in each example that the employer "*may be forced to hire according to race*, to 'racially balance' those who work for him *in every job classification* or be in violation of Federal law." *Id.*, at 69 (emphasis in original).

When H.R. 7152 reached the House floor, the opening speech in support of its passage was delivered by Representative Celler, Chairman of the House Judiciary Committee and the Congressman responsible for introducing the legislation. A portion of that speech responded to criticism "seriously misrepresent[ing] what the bill would do and grossly distort[ing] its effects":

> "[T]he charge has been made that the Equal Employment Opportunity Commission to be established by title VII of the bill would have the power to prevent a business from employing and promoting the people it wished, and that a 'Federal inspector' could then order the hiring and promotion only of employees of certain races or religious groups. This description of the bill is entirely wrong. * * *

> "Even [a] court could not order that any preference be given to any particular race, religion or other group, but would be limited to ordering an end of discrimination. The statement that a Federal inspector could order the employment and promotion only of members of a specific racial or religious group is therefore patently erroneous. * * *

> "* * * The Bill would do no more than prevent * * * employers from discriminating against *or in favor* of workers because of their race, religion, or national origin.

> "It is likewise not true that the Equal Employment Opportunity Commission would have power to rectify existing 'racial or religious imbalance' in employment by requiring the hiring of certain people without regard to their qualifications simply because they are of a given race or religion. Only actual discrimination could be stopped." 110 Cong. Rec. 1518 (1964) (emphasis added).

Representative Celler's construction of Title VII was repeated by several other supporters during the House debate.

Thus, the battle lines were drawn early in the legislative struggle over Title VII, with opponents of the measure charging that agencies of the Federal Government such as the Equal Employment Opportunity Commission (EEOC), by interpreting the word "discrimination" to mean the existence of "racial imbalance," would "require" employers to grant preferential treatment to minorities, and supporters responding that the EEOC would be granted no such power and that, indeed, Title VII prohibits discrimination "in favor of workers because of their race." Supporters of H.R. 7152 in the House ultimately prevailed by a vote of 290 to 130, and the measure was sent to the Senate to begin what became the longest debate in that body's history.

[B]   The Senate debate was broken into three phases: the debate on sending the bill to Committee, the general debate on the bill prior to invocation of cloture, and the debate following cloture. * * *

Formal debate on the merits of H.R. 7152 began on March 30, 1964. Supporters of the bill in the Senate had made elaborate preparations for this second round. Senator Humphrey, the majority whip, and Senator Kuchel, the minority whip, were selected as the bipartisan floor managers on the entire civil rights bill. Responsibility for explaining and defending each important title of the bill was placed on bipartisan "captains." Senators Clark and Case were selected as the bipartisan captains responsible for Title VII. Vaas, Title VII: Legislative History, 7 B.C. Ind. & Com. L. Rev. 431, 444–445 (1966) (hereinafter Title VII: Legislative History).

In the opening speech of the formal Senate debate on the bill, Senator Humphrey addressed the main concern of Title VII's opponents, advising that not only does Title VII not require use of racial quotas, *it does not permit* their use. "The truth," stated the floor leader of the bill, "is that this title forbids discriminating against anyone on account of race. This is the simple and complete truth about title VII." 110 Cong. Rec. 6549 (1964). Senator Humphrey continued:

> "Contrary to the allegations of some opponents of this title, there is nothing in it that will give any power to the Commission or to any court to require hiring, firing, or promotion of employees in order to meet a racial 'quota' or to achieve a certain racial balance.

> "That bugaboo has been brought up a dozen times; but it is nonexistent. In fact, *the very opposite is true. Title VII prohibits discrimination.* In effect, it says that race, religion and national origin are not to be used as the basis for hiring and firing. Title VII is designed to encourage hiring on the basis of ability and qualifications, not race or religion." *Ibid.* (emphasis added).

At the close of his speech, Senator Humphrey returned briefly to the subject of employment quotas: "It is claimed that the bill would require racial quotas for all hiring, when in fact it provides that race shall not be a basis for making personnel decisions." *Id.*, at 6553. * * *

A few days later the Senate's attention focused exclusively on Title VII, as Senators Clark and Case rose to discuss the title of H.R. 7152 on which they shared floor "captain" responsibilities. In an interpretative memorandum submitted jointly to the Senate, Senators Clark and Case took pains to refute the opposition's charge that Title VII would result in preferential treatment for minorities. * * * Of particular relevance to the instant litigation were their observations regarding seniority rights. As if directing their comments at Brian Weber, the Senators said:

> "Title VII would have no effect on established seniority rights. Its effect is prospective and not retrospective. Thus, for example, if a business has been discriminating in the past and as a result has an all-white working force, when the title comes into effect the employer's obligation would be simply to fill future vacancies on a nondiscriminatory basis. He would not be obliged—*or indeed permitted*—to fire whites in order to hire Negroes, *or to prefer Negroes for future vacancies, or, once Negroes are hired, to give them special seniority rights at the expense of the white workers hired earlier." Id.*, at 7213 (emphasis added).

[In addition, Senator Kuchel made similar comments. Southern opponents of the bill were still not satisfied, though. Senator Robertson (D-VA) argued that the bill would mandate quotas. Senator Harrison Williams (D-NJ) responded:]

> "Those opposed to H.R. 7152 should realize that to hire a Negro solely because he is a Negro is racial discrimination, just as much as a 'white only' employment policy. Both forms of discrimination are prohibited by title VII of this bill. The language of that title simply states that race is not a qualification for employment. . . . Some people charge that H.R. 7152 favors the Negro, at the expense of the white majority. But how can the language of equality favor one race or one religion over another? Equality can have only one meaning, and that meaning is self-evident to reasonable men. Those who say that equality means favoritism do violence to common sense." *Id.*, at 8921. * * *

While the debate in the Senate raged, a bipartisan coalition under the leadership of Senators Dirksen, Mansfield, Humphrey, and Kuchel was working with House leaders and representatives of the Johnson administration on a number of amendments to H.R. 7152 designed to enhance its prospects of passage. The so-called "Dirksen-Mansfield" amendment was introduced on May 26 by Senator Dirksen as a substitute for the entire House-passed bill. The substitute bill, which ultimately became law, left unchanged the basic prohibitory language of §§ 703(a) and (d), as well as the remedial provisions in § 706(g). It added, however, several provisions defining and clarifying the scope of Title VII's substantive prohibitions. One of those clarifying amendments, § 703(j), was specifically directed at the opposition's concerns regarding racial balancing and preferential treatment of minorities, providing in pertinent part: "Nothing contained in [Title VII] shall be interpreted to require any employer . . . to grant preferential treatment to any individual or to any group because of the race . . . of such individual or group on account of" a racial imbalance in the employer's work force. 42 U.S.C. § 2000e–2(j). * * *

Contrary to the Court's analysis, the language of § 703(j) is precisely tailored to the objection voiced time and again by Title VII's opponents. Not once during the 83 days of debate in the Senate did a speaker, proponent or opponent, suggest that the bill would allow employers *voluntarily* to prefer racial minorities over white persons. In light of Title VII's flat prohibition on discrimination "against any individual . . . because of such individual's race," § 703(a), 42 U.S.C. § 2000e–2(a), such a contention would have been, in any event, too preposterous to warrant response. Indeed, speakers on both sides of the issue, as the legislative history makes clear, recognized that Title VII would tolerate no *voluntary* racial preference, whether in favor of blacks or whites. The complaint consistently voiced by the opponents was that Title VII, particularly the word "discrimination," would be *interpreted* by federal agencies such as the EEOC to *require* the correction of racial imbalance through the granting of preferential treatment to minorities. Verbal assurances that Title VII would not require—indeed, would not permit—preferential treatment of blacks having failed, supporters of H.R. 7152 responded by proposing an amendment carefully worded to meet, and put to rest, the opposition's charge. Indeed, unlike §§ 703(a) and (d), which are by their terms directed at entities—*e.g.*, employers, labor unions—whose actions are restricted by Title VII's prohibitions, the language of § 703(j) is specifically directed at entities—federal agencies and courts—charged with the responsibility of interpreting Title VII's provisions.

In light of the background and purpose of § 703(j), the irony of invoking the section to justify the result in this case is obvious. The Court's frequent references to the "voluntary" nature of Kaiser's racially discriminatory admission quota bear no relationship to the facts of this case. Kaiser and the Steelworkers acted under pressure from an agency of the Federal Government, the Office of Federal Contract Compliance, which found that minorities were being "underutilized" at Kaiser's plants. That is, Kaiser's work force was racially imbalanced. Bowing to that pressure, Kaiser instituted an admissions quota preferring blacks over whites, thus confirming that the fears of Title VII's opponents were well founded. Today, § 703(j), adopted to allay those fears, is invoked by the Court to uphold imposition of a racial quota under the very circumstances that the section was intended to prevent. * * *

[Justice Rehnquist also pointed to Senator Ervin's June 9 amendment to delete Title VII. Responding for the sponsors, Senator Clark emphasized that the bill "establishes no quotas." Senator Cotton (R-NH) offered an amendment to limit Title VII to firms having more than 100 employees. He opined that Title VII would forbid quotas. Although his amendment was defeated, Justice Rehnquist observed that the sponsors did not dispute the Cotton view.

[When cloture was invoked on June 10, 1964, debate was limited, but several post-cloture statements by the bill's supporters reinforced the earlier view that Title VII imposed no quotas. The substitute bill was passed June 19. In final form, the bill was passed by the House on July 2 and signed by the President the same day.]

[V] Our task in this case, like any other case involving the construction of a statute, is to give effect to the intent of Congress. To divine that intent, we traditionally look first to the words of the statute and, if they are unclear, then to the statute's legislative history. Finding the desired result hopelessly foreclosed by these conventional sources, the Court turns to a third source—the "spirit" of the Act. But close examination of what the Court proffers as the spirit of the Act reveals it as the spirit animating the present majority, not the 88th Congress. For if the spirit of the

Act eludes the cold words of the statute itself, it rings out with unmistakable clarity in the words of the elected representatives who made the Act law. It is *equality*. Senator Dirksen, I think, captured that spirit in a speech delivered on the floor of the Senate just moments before the bill was passed:

> "* * * [T]oday we come to grips finally with a bill that advances the enjoyment of living; but, more than that, it advances the equality of opportunity.

> "I do not emphasize the word 'equality' standing by itself. It means equality of opportunity in the field of education. It means equality of opportunity in the field of employment. It means equality of opportunity in the field of participation in the affairs of government * * *.

> "That is it.

> "Equality of opportunity, if we are going to talk about conscience, is the mass conscience of mankind that speaks in every generation, and it will continue to speak long after we are dead and gone." 110 Cong. Rec. 14510 (1964).

There is perhaps no device more destructive to the notion of equality than the *numerus clausus*—the quota. Whether described as "benign discrimination" or "affirmative action," the racial quota is nonetheless a creator of castes, a two-edged sword that must demean one in order to prefer another. In passing Title VII, Congress outlawed *all* racial discrimination, recognizing that no discrimination based on race is benign, that no action disadvantaging a person because of his color is affirmative. With today's holding, the Court introduces into Title VII a tolerance for the very evil that the law was intended to eradicate, without offering even a clue as to what the limits on that tolerance may be. We are told simply that Kaiser's racially discriminatory admission quota "falls on the permissible side of the line." By going not merely *beyond*, but directly *against* Title VII's language and legislative history, the Court has sown the wind. Later courts will face the impossible task of reaping the whirlwind.

NOTES ON WEBER AND MODES OF INTERPRETATION

The three opinions in this case present strikingly different normative visions of the Court's role in statutory interpretation. See William N. Eskridge Jr., *Dynamic Statutory Interpretation* 13–31, 35–44 (1994); Philip Frickey, *Wisdom on* Weber, 74 Tulane L. Rev. 1169 (2000). Each vision is beset with practical problems of evidence, however.

1. *Divining the "Intent" of Congress: Did the Court Invalidate the Original Legislative "Deal"?* One way to look at the role of the interpreter of a statute is to say that she is seeking the original intent of the author (the enacting Congress). Justices Brennan and Rehnquist both purported to perform this interpretive role, with four Justices agreeing with Justice Brennan and only the Chief Justice agreeing with Justice Rehnquist. Many of the commentators agree with Rehnquist that the Court "changed" the meaning of the statute by judicial fiat, and "[t]hat change goes to the roots of the bargain struck by the 88th Congress, and the roots of our color-blind aspiration." Bernard

Meltzer, *The* Weber *Case: The Judicial Abrogation of the Antidiscrimination Standard in Employment*, 47 U. Chi. L. Rev. 423, 456 (1980).[56] Do you agree?

Was Justice Rehnquist right to charge that Congress would have been "hard pressed" to have chosen language more clearly protecting Brian Weber than that of § 703(d), which makes it an unlawful practice for an employer "to discriminate against any individual because of his race * * * in admission to, or employment in, any program established to provide apprenticeship or other training"? What about the following:

> It shall be an unlawful employment practice for the employer * * * not to include any individual in any program established to provide apprenticeship or other training as a result of prohibited criteria, namely race * * *.

Did Justice Rehnquist overstate the clarity of § 703(d)?

Justice Rehnquist's dissent assumed, as many dictionaries say, that an employer *discriminates* on the basis of race if it makes a race-based *differentiation*. In a dictionary sense, it is a correct use of the term to say, "I discriminate against peaches," if I prefer pears to peaches. But that is not the way we usually use the word *discriminate*, which connotes an *invidious* differentiation. Consider the definition of *discriminate* found in a desk dictionary published in 1968, soon after Congress enacted Title VII. In this dictionary, the "prejudice" meaning is the first definition given. Is there a single "plain meaning" of "discriminate"? Are there other text-based arguments that Justice Rehnquist should have emphasized? Cf. Eskridge, *Dynamic Statutory Interpretation*, 42–43 (laying out arguments for Rehnquist's position based on the structure of § 703).

Perhaps it is not so clear that the "deal" described by Justice Rehnquist is inscribed in the language of the statute. For that reason, statutory interpreters often look to the legislative history to figure out the "intent" of Congress. As a rule, the most authoritative legislative history is the House and Senate committee reports, but Justice Rehnquist did not rely on them. Instead, like Justice Brennan, he relied on the colloquies between the bill's sponsors and the bill's opponents. Does this tell us anything about the "intent" of the 73 Senators and 290 Representatives who voted for the bill? Suppose that the statements of the sponsors are binding on everyone. Did anyone say: "We never want preferences for whites or blacks. By that we mean either governmentally required preferences, or preferences voluntarily agreed to by an employer or union to redress past discrimination." Did Justice Rehnquist discover such a "smoking gun" in the Clark-Case memorandum's passage that he claimed spoke directly to Brian Weber's situation?

Finally, note that most of Justice Rehnquist's evidence comes from legislative discussions *before* the final deal was reached, namely, the Mansfield-Dirksen substitute. Participants in the congressional process point out that anything that happens *before* the final deal is irrelevant if inconsistent with the final deal. The Mansfield-Dirksen substitute added § 703(j), which provides some support to Justice Brennan's position, and none to Justice Rehnquist's. To be sure, the latter would vehemently object that Senator Dirksen (a conservative Republican like Rehnquist) would *never* have read § 703(j) that way—but Rehnquist cited nothing to support his view, while Brennan cited Representative MacGregor (also a conservative Republican), who defended the

---

[56]   See also Nelson Lund, *The Law of Affirmative Action In and After the Civil Rights Act of 1991: Congress Invites Judicial Reform*, 6 Geo. Mason L. Rev. 87, 90–101 (1997); Daniel Rodriguez & Barry Weingast, *The Positive Political Theory of Legislative History: New Perspectives on the 1964 Civil Rights Act and Its Interpretation*, 151 U. Pa. L. Rev. 1417 (2003).

Mansfield-Dirksen substitute precisely along the give-business-discretion lines that Justice Brennan did. See Victoria Nourse, *A Decision Theory of Statutory Interpretation: Legislative History by the Rules*, 122 Yale L.J. 70, 104–09 (2012).

2. *Pitfalls of a Purpose-Oriented Interpretation.* Supporting the "spirit" approach taken by Justice Brennan, Burt Neuborne (ACLU counsel in *Weber*) argues:

> At best, the concept of legislative intent is discernible primarily by the judges who claim to have deciphered it. The truth of the matter is that a legislature, especially in the civil rights area, generally enacts a statute aimed at a broad philosophical concept—in this case, equality in employment. It does not and cannot foresee, much less resolve, the myriad questions which must arise whenever a broad philosophical proposition is applied to the protean complexity of everyday life * * *.

Neuborne, *Observations on* Weber, 54 N.Y.U. L. Rev. 546, 553 (1979). Is this a more realistic way of looking at the Civil Rights Act than Meltzer's specific bargain idea?

But who *was* right about the "spirit" of the Act? There is much to be said for Justice Rehnquist's position that when you read the committee report and the debate, you come away with the impression that the statute was mainly intended to eradicate racial criteria in hiring. Supporting Justice Brennan, Ronald Dworkin argues that the judge should interpret the statute to advance the policy that furnishes "the best political justification for the statute," because the "intent" of Congress on this issue is indeterminate. Dworkin, *How to Read the Civil Rights Act*, in *A Matter of Principle* 316, 327 (1985). Upon what model of the legislative process might this suggestion rest? Even if it is a valid approach, there seem to be two purposes in the Act—jobs for African Americans and creation of a color-blind society. How does the judge choose one politically coherent purpose over the other?

If we decide to interpret Title VII in light of its equal-results spirit, will encouraging unions and companies to set up their own affirmative action programs (effectively shifting the costs of past discrimination from themselves onto their white employees) really contribute to this purpose? For example, will the kind of "quota" programs approved in *Weber* undermine mainstream political support for Title VII? Would such programs "create incentives for employers to locate jobs away from black labor," so that they can avoid high black quotas? Edmund Kitch, *The Return of Color Consciousness to the Constitution:* Weber, Dayton, *and* Columbus, 1979 Sup. Ct. Rev. 1, 12–13. Indeed, in 1979 African-American unemployment was no less a problem than it had been in 1964.

Judge Wisdom's dissenting opinion in the court below recognized several purposes for the statute—integration, color-blindness, and flexible voluntary remedies—and concluded that the "arguable violation" approach best balanced these competing purposes. See Philip Frickey & William Eskridge Jr., *The Story of* Steelworkers v. Weber *(1979): Statutory Text, Spirit, and Practical Reasoning,* in *Statutory Interpretation Stories* 92, 112–14 (Eskridge, Frickey & Garrett eds., 2011). Yet only Justice Blackmun accepted that argument. Why did it not have more traction among the Court majority?

3. *Reading Statutes Dynamically.* Both Justices Brennan and Rehnquist purported to be interpreting the "will" of Congress on this issue as of 1964, when the statute was enacted. The implicit argument of each opinion is that on the day Title VII became law, this is the answer the interpreter as well as the representative would have given to the *Weber* question. Does that make sense to you? For purposes of statutory

interpretation, the *Weber* issue is so important because it represents a tension that did not really exist in the statute as enacted, as Justice Blackmun's concurring opinion suggests. In a functional sense, the Title VII of 1964 was not the same statute as the Title VII of 1979, not just because the statute was formally amended (in 1972), but also because the ongoing process of interpretation and elaboration altered the statute in response to evolving circumstances. *Griggs* as well as other decisions changed not only the statute, but the society on which the statute operated. For this reason, Justice Blackmun urged that the interpretation of Title VII reflect the unanticipated tension created by the ongoing application and interpretation process and permit the affirmative action plan in *Weber*. Upon what model of legislation was Justice Blackmun operating?

Two of us have argued that the most persuasive approach to *Weber* is Justice Blackmun's pragmatic appeal to current problems of statutory fairness and workability, not just the historical choices allegedly made in 1964.[57] The argument is that employment discrimination statutes start with gaps and ambiguities (including the precise meaning of "discriminate," a term that is not self-defining), which the EEOC and the Court had to interpret in light of factual settings they faced, and their interpretations went "beyond" Congress's original expectations. The gaps and ambiguities proliferated as the world changed—often in response to the statute and its applications—and offered more radical variations, including repeated fact patterns like *Weber*, where past discrimination continued to have present effects. Moreover, Title VII changed, often "against" the original legislative expectations, because the EEOC and the Court had their own values and "spin" on the statute, because the Congress with power to discipline these interpreters was the current rather than the enacting Congress (and the latter had a different spin on the statute than the former), and because the legal and social context changed over time. This is a *description* of what interpreters do with the statute. Do you find it *normatively* acceptable? Is it appropriate for the judiciary to undertake this task of updating the statute and filling gaps with new policies, or should Congress have the sole responsibility for amending old statutes to account for new social and economic developments? Does the answer change when the new conditions have resulted in large part from prior judicial opinions interpreting the act in unexpected ways?

Liberals have no monopoly on dynamic interpretation. The conservative Justices on the Burger Court had their own spin on affirmative action, and the cases after *Weber* were harder on affirmative action plans. See *Sheet Metal Workers v. EEOC*, 478 U.S. 421 (1986); *Local No. 93, Int'l Ass'n of Firefighters v. Cleveland*, 478 U.S. 501 (1986); *Local Union No. 1784 Firefighters v. Stotts*, 467 U.S. 561 (1984). The Supreme Court drifted further to the right when Justice Rehnquist became Chief Justice and yielded his seat to Judge Antonin Scalia, a devout foe of affirmative action. Would the new Court move Title VII policy in a more conservative direction?

An argument *against* such a move is *stare decisis*. That is, the Court is obliged to follow its own precedents, with a narrow exception: the precedent was wrongly decided *and* there is positive harm in continuing its error. Indeed, in statutory cases, the Court says it follows a super-strong form of *stare decisis*, where courts should leave correction of its own errors to Congress (see Chapter 5). Does this precept make sense to you? Should

---

[57]   See Eskridge, *Dynamic Statutory Interpretation*, 24–25; Philip Frickey, *From the Big Sleep to the Big Heat: The Revival of Theory in Statutory Interpretation*, 77 Minn. L. Rev. 241, 245–47, 259 (1992); Frickey & Eskridge, *Story of Weber*.

it save *Weber*? If you think it should save *Weber*, should it save precedents you think are very wrong?

Johnson v. Transportation Agency, Santa Clara County

480 U.S. 616, 107 S.Ct. 1442, 94 L.Ed.2d 613 (1987).

The Transportation Agency of Santa Clara County, California, promulgated an Affirmative Action Plan to remedy historic patterns of discrimination against women and minorities in some job categories. The Plan provided that, in making promotions to positions within a traditionally segregated job classification, in which women had been significantly underrepresented, the Agency was authorized to consider as one factor the sex of a qualified applicant. The Agency found women significantly underrepresented in its work force generally, and virtually unrepresented in the 238 Skilled Craft Worker positions. Pursuant to the Plan, the Agency promoted Diane Joyce to the position of road dispatcher in the Agency's Roads Division. Dispatchers assign road crews, equipment, and materials, and maintain records pertaining to road maintenance jobs. One of the applicants passed over was Paul Johnson, who had a slightly higher score than Joyce based upon his paper credentials and an oral interview. Johnson filed a complaint with the EEOC, and subsequently a federal lawsuit. The district court granted Johnson relief, based upon its finding that Johnson was more qualified for the position than Joyce, and that sex was the "determining factor" in Joyce's selection. The Ninth Circuit reversed.

Justice Brennan delivered the opinion of the Court, affirming the Ninth Circuit. He relied on *Weber*'s holding that race-based affirmative action was allowed under Title VII if needed to carry out the statutory objective of "break[ing] down old patterns of racial segregation and hierarchy." In footnote 7 of his opinion, Brennan opined that the requirements of *stare decisis* were particularly compelling here, because Congress made no move to override *Weber*. Relying on the Blackmun concurring opinion, Brennan characterized the *Weber* holding this way: "an employer seeking to justify the adoption of a plan need not point to its own prior discriminatory practices, nor even to evidence of an 'arguable violation' on its part. Rather, it need point only to a 'conspicuous . . . imbalance in traditionally segregated job categories.' "

Johnson's case was like Weber's under the Court's previous analysis. To begin with, Santa Clara was amply justified in finding a "manifest imbalance" in the relevant workforce that reflected underrepresentation of women in traditionally segregated job categories. "A manifest imbalance need not be such that it would support a prima facie case against the employer, as suggested in Justice O'Connor's concurrence, since we do not regard as identical the constraints of Title VII and the Federal Constitution on voluntarily adopted affirmative action plans. Application of the 'prima facie' standard in Title VII cases would be inconsistent with *Weber*'s focus on statistical imbalance, and could inappropriately create a significant disincentive for employers to adopt an affirmative action plan. A corporation concerned with maximizing return on investment, for instance, is hardly likely to adopt a plan if in order to do so it must compile evidence that could be used to subject it to a colorable Title VII suit."

"It is clear that the decision to hire Joyce was made pursuant to an Agency plan that directed that sex or race be taken into account for the purpose of remedying underrepresentation. * * * Specifically, 9 of the 10 Para-Professionals and 110 of the 145 Office and Clerical Workers were women. By contrast, women were only 2 of the 28 Officials and Administrators, 5 of the 58 Professionals, 12 of the 124 Technicians, none of the Skilled Craft Workers, and 1—who was Joyce—of the 110 Road Maintenance Workers. The Plan sought to remedy these imbalances."

The Court also considered whether the Agency's plan "unnecessarily trammeled the rights of male employees or created an absolute bar to their advancement." Unlike the quota plan in *Weber*, Santa Clara's plan disavowed quotas and "merely authorize[d] that consideration be given to affirmative action concerns when evaluating qualified applicants. As the Agency Director testified, the sex of Joyce was but one of numerous factors he took into account in arriving at his decision. The Plan thus resembles the 'Harvard Plan' approvingly noted by Justice Powell in *University of California Regents v. Bakke*, 438 U.S. 265, 316–319 (1978), which considers race [as a plus,] along with other criteria in determining admission to the college."

Justice Stevens joined the majority opinion and wrote a concurring statement that he would have joined the *Weber* dissenters in 1979. "In the *Bakke* case in 1978 and again in *Weber*, a majority of the Court interpreted the antidiscriminatory strategy of the statute in a fundamentally different way. * * * [T]he only problem for me is whether to adhere to an authoritative construction of the Act that is at odds with my understanding of the actual intent of the authors of the legislation. I conclude without hesitation that I must answer that question in the affirmative."

"*Bakke* and *Weber* have been decided and are now an important part of the fabric of our law. This consideration is sufficiently compelling for me to adhere to the basic construction of this legislation that the Court adopted in *Bakke* and in *Weber*. There is an undoubted public interest in 'stability and orderly development of the law.'"

Indeed, Stevens would have imposed fewer limits on voluntary affirmative action plans than the majority seemed to do. "Whether a voluntary decision of the kind made by respondent would ever be prohibited by Title VII is a question we need not answer until it is squarely presented. Given the interpretation of the statute the Court adopted in *Weber*, I see no reason why the employer has any duty, prior to granting a preference to a qualified minority employee, to determine whether his past conduct might constitute an arguable violation of Title VII. Indeed, in some instances the employer may find it more helpful to focus on the future. Instead of retroactively scrutinizing his own or society's possible exclusions of minorities in the past to determine the outer limits of a valid affirmative-action program—or indeed, any particular affirmative-action decision— in many cases the employer will find it more appropriate to consider other legitimate reasons to give preferences to members of underrepresented groups. Statutes enacted for the benefit of minority groups should not block these forward-looking considerations."

Justice O'Connor concurred only in the judgment allowing the Santa Clara plan's operation in Johnson's case. "In my view, the proper initial inquiry in evaluating the legality of an affirmative action plan by a public employer under Title VII is no different from that required by the Equal Protection Clause. In either case, consistent with the congressional intent to provide some measure of protection to the interests of the employer's nonminority employees, the employer must have had a firm basis for believing that remedial action was required. An employer would have such a firm basis if it can point to a statistical disparity sufficient to support a prima facie claim under Title VII by the employee beneficiaries of the affirmative action plan of a pattern or practice claim of discrimination." She found such a "firm basis" in the gross disparities between the number of women in other positions and their complete absence in the 238 skilled craft positions. She also emphasized that the agency's plan did not include quotas, which she opined would violate Title VII.

Justice White dissented and urged his colleagues to overrule *Weber* (an opinion he joined in 1979), because the Court's reinterpretation of it was "a perversion of Title VII."

Justice Scalia (joined by **Chief Justice Rehnquist** and, in part, by **Justice White**) dissented and would have overruled *Weber*. The earlier opinion blatantly ignored the statute's plain meaning, and the new opinion for the Court "today completes the process of converting this from a guarantee that race or sex will *not* be the basis for employment determinations, to a guarantee that it often *will*. Ever so subtly, without even alluding to the last obstacles preserved by earlier opinions that we now push out of our path, we effectively replace the goal of a discrimination-free society with the quite incompatible goal of proportionate representation by race and by sex in the workplace." Holy *1984*!

Justice Scalia also criticized the majority for extending *Weber* to public employers, which are subject to the constitutional limitations on affirmative action. (For reasons of procedural waiver, Justice Brennan's opinion did not rule on Johnson's constitutional challenge to the agency's program.) "It would be better, in my view, to acknowledge that case as fully applicable precedent, and to use the Fourteenth Amendment ramifications—which *Weber* did not address and which are implicated for the first time here—as the occasion for reconsidering and overruling it."

In note 7 of the majority opinion, **Justice Brennan** asserted that, since "Congress has not amended the statute to reject our construction, . . . we . . . may assume that our interpretation was correct." **Justice Scalia** was having none of this. "This assumption, which frequently haunts our opinions, should be put to rest. It is based, to begin with, on the patently false premise that the correctness of statutory construction is to be measured by what the current Congress desires, rather than by what the law as enacted meant. To make matters worse, it assays the current Congress's desires *with respect to the particular provision in isolation*, rather than (the way the provision was originally enacted) as part of a total legislative package containing many *quids pro quo*. Whereas the statute as originally proposed may have presented to the enacting Congress a question such as 'Should hospitals be required to provide medical care for indigent patients, with federal subsidies to offset the cost?,' the question theoretically asked of the later Congress, in order to establish the 'correctness' of a judicial interpretation that the statute provides no subsidies, is simply 'Should the medical care that hospitals are required to provide for indigent patients be federally subsidized?' Hardly the same question—and many of those legislators who accepted the subsidy provisions in order to gain the votes necessary for enactment of the care requirement would not vote for the subsidy in isolation, now that an unsubsidized care requirement is, thanks to the judicial opinion, safely on the books. But even accepting the flawed premise that the intent of the current Congress, with respect to the provision in isolation, is determinative, one must ignore rudimentary principles of political science to draw any conclusions regarding that intent from the *failure* to enact legislation. The 'complicated check on legislation,' The Federalist No. 62, p. 378 C. Rossiter ed. 1961), erected by our Constitution creates an inertia that makes it impossible to assert with any degree of assurance that congressional failure to act represents (1) approval of the status quo, as opposed to (2) inability to agree upon how to alter the status quo, (3) unawareness of the status quo, (4) indifference to the status quo, or even (5) political cowardice * * *. I think we should admit that vindication by congressional inaction is a canard."[58]

Justice Scalia announced several reasons why *stare decisis* ought not to save *Weber*. "First, this Court has applied the doctrine of *stare decisis* to civil rights statutes less rigorously than to other laws. See *Maine v. Thiboutot*, 448 U.S. 1, 33 (1980) (Powell, J., dissenting); *Monroe v. Pape*, [365 U.S. 167, 221–22 (1961)] (Frankfurter, J., dissenting in part). Second, * * * *Weber* was itself a dramatic departure from the Court's prior Title VII precedents, and can scarcely be said to be 'so consistent with the warp and woof of civil rights law as to be beyond question.' Third, *Weber* was decided a mere seven years ago, and has provided little guidance to persons seeking to conform their conduct to the law, beyond the proposition that Title VII does not mean what it says. Finally, 'even under the most stringent test for the propriety of overruling a statutory decision . . .— 'that it appear beyond doubt . . . that [the decision] misapprehended the meaning of the controlling provision,' *Weber* should be overruled."

Justice Scalia concluded with a flourish. "Today's decision does more, however, than merely reaffirm *Weber*, and more than merely extend it to public actors. It is impossible not to be aware that the practical effect of our holding is to accomplish *de facto* what the law—in language even plainer than that ignored in *Weber*, see 42 U.S.C. § 2000e–2(j)— forbids anyone from accomplishing *de jure*: in many contexts it effectively *requires* employers, public as well as private, to engage in intentional discrimination on the basis of race or sex. This Court's prior interpretations of Title VII, especially the decision in *Griggs*, subject employers to a potential Title VII suit whenever there is a noticeable imbalance in the representation of minorities or women in the employer's work force.* * * If, however, employers are free to discriminate through affirmative action, without fear of 'reverse discrimination' suits by their nonminority or male victims, they are offered a threshold defense against Title VII liability premised on numerical disparities. Thus, after today's decision the *failure* to engage in reverse discrimination is economic folly, and arguably a breach of duty to shareholders or taxpayers, wherever the cost of anticipated Title VII litigation exceeds the cost of hiring less capable (though still minimally capable) workers. (This situation is more likely to obtain, of course, with respect to the least skilled jobs—perversely creating an incentive to discriminate against precisely those members of the nonfavored groups *least* likely to have profited from societal discrimination in the past.) It is predictable, moreover, that this incentive will be greatly magnified by economic pressures brought to bear by government contracting agencies upon employers who refuse to discriminate in the fashion we have now approved. A statute designed to establish a color-blind and gender-blind workplace has thus been converted into a powerful engine of racism and sexism, not merely *permitting*

---

[58]   Justice Brennan responded to the "canard" point in footnote 7: "The fact that inaction may not always provide crystalline revelation, however, should not obscure the fact that it may be probative to varying degrees. *Weber*, for instance, was a widely-publicized decision that addressed a prominent issue of public debate. Legislative inattention thus is not a plausible explanation for Congressional inaction. Furthermore, Congress not only passed no contrary legislation in the wake of *Weber*, but not one legislator even proposed a bill to do so. The barriers of the legislative process therefore also seem a poor explanation for failure to act. By contrast, when Congress has been displeased with our interpretation of Title VII, it has not hesitated to amend the statute to tell us so. For instance, when Congress passed the Pregnancy Discrimination Act of 1978, 42 U.S.C. section 2000e(k), 'it unambiguously expressed its disapproval of both the holding and the reasoning of the Court in [*General Electric v. Gilbert*, 429 U.S. 125 (1976)].' *Newport News Shipbuilding & Dry Dock v. EEOC*, 462 U.S. 669, 678 (1983). Surely, it is appropriate to find some probative value in such radically different Congressional reactions to this Court's interpretations of the same statute."

intentional race- and sex-based discrimination, but often making it, through operation of the legal system, practically compelled.

"It is unlikely that today's result will be displeasing to politically elected officials, to whom it provides the means of quickly accommodating the demands of organized groups to achieve concrete, numerical improvement in the economic status of particular constituencies. Nor will it displease the world of corporate and governmental employers (many of whom have filed briefs as *amici* in the present case, all on the side of Santa Clara) for whom the cost of hiring less qualified workers is often substantially less—and infinitely more predictable—than the cost of litigating Title VII cases and of seeking to convince federal agencies by nonnumerical means that no discrimination exists. In fact, the only losers in the process are the Johnsons of the country, for whom Title VII has been not merely repealed but actually inverted. The irony is that these individuals— predominantly unknown, unaffluent, unorganized—suffer this injustice at the hands of a Court fond of thinking itself the champion of the politically impotent. I dissent."

NOTES ON JOHNSON

1.   *What Happened to* Weber? The debate in *Weber* is hardly recognizable in *Johnson*, not only because there are two new players (Justices O'Connor and Scalia), but also because the old players changed their positions. Justice White switched from the *Weber* majority to calling for its overruling; Justice Stevens switched from probable dissent from *Weber* (a case where he did not actually vote) to an aggressive approval of affirmative action; and Justice Powell joined the Brennan opinion that went much further than his opinion in *Regents of the University of California v. Bakke*, 438 U.S. 265 (1978). (Like Stevens, Powell did not vote in *Weber* but, according to an internal memorandum, leaned against the Brennan approach.) Almost as dramatic was Justice Brennan's new rationale for affirmative action, which ignored his *Weber* reasoning that Title VII was mainly aimed at bringing racial minorities into the workplace. Note, too, that the dissenting Justices in *Johnson* pretty much ignored the legislative history of the 1964 statute.

2.   *Congressional Acquiescence?* Footnote 7 of the Court's opinion was a classically dynamic move: whatever the original validity of *Weber* as implementing the intent or purpose of the 1964 Congress, it should not be reconsidered because Congress in the 1980s approved of the decision. Justice Scalia considered this argument a "canard," but the end of his opinion suggests why Justice Brennan may have been right. The powerful political forces inside the Beltway—labor unions, civil rights groups, and business interests—were satisfied with *Weber*, because it allowed them to advance their own goals (such as avoiding *Griggs* lawsuits) relatively cheaply, at least to them. The cost-payers were the diffuse group of blue-collar males like Paul Johnson and Brian Weber, unorganized and ill-represented on Capitol Hill. This point seems accurate, and it suggests that Congress in the 1980s was also happy with *Weber*. (By the way, hearings were held in 1981 on a constitutional amendment introduced in Congress to override *Weber* and other affirmative action cases; none of the political powerhouses showed up, demonstrating the absence of interest among the powerful lobbies to override *Weber*.)

Justice Scalia's main point was a normative one. He considered it objectionable for the Court to pay any attention to what goes on, or doesn't go on, in Congress short of formal bicameral approval mandated by Article I, § 7. As the heartfelt passage at the end of his dissent suggests that he had sympathy for the downtrodden, politically powerless, blue-collar white men who pay the price for affirmative action. Is this an appropriate factor to consider in statutory interpretation? Should statutory ambiguities be resolved *against* the more politically potent interests?

      3.   *The Court/Congress/President Civil Rights Game.* Recall that the blue-collar men whom Justice Scalia claims are politically "impotent" elected President Reagan twice, based upon a platform hostile to affirmative action—and Reagan delivered on his platform by appointing Rehnquist Chief Justice, elevating Scalia to the Court, and trying to elevate Judge Robert Bork to the Court (after *Johnson*). Although Bork was defeated, Reagan ended up appointing Judge Anthony Kennedy, a conservative on issues of race discrimination. Because Kennedy replaced Powell—Brennan's critical fifth vote in *Johnson*—the Court in 1988 was poised to shift civil rights policy rightward. Four Justices (Rehnquist, White, Scalia, Kennedy) were openly opposed to affirmative action, and one Justice (O'Connor) was skeptical. The Court had a great deal of room to maneuver, as a rightward shift in policy could be protected against congressional override by a presidential veto (by Reagan or his successor, George H.W. Bush).

C. THE COURT'S RETREAT FROM *GRIGGS*, CONGRESS'S RESPONSE, AND THE FATE OF AFFIRMATIVE ACTION

      The 1988–89 Term included several employment discrimination cases that bitterly divided the Court. The most important was *Wards Cove Packing Co. v. Atonio*, 490 U.S. 642 (1989), rejecting a Title VII claim against the operation of two salmon canneries in Alaska. Unskilled positions at the canneries were staffed almost entirely by racial minorities, while about half of the skilled office positions were filled by whites, usually hired through personal references. A cannery employee could not be promoted to an office position and ate and lived in separate areas from the office employees. Based upon this "plantation" set-up, the minority cannery employees sued Wards Cove for discriminating against them. The Ninth Circuit held that plaintiffs made out a *prima facie* case of disparate impact employment discrimination under *Griggs*. The Supreme Court reversed. The majority opinion was written by **Justice White** and was joined by Chief Justice Rehnquist and Justices O'Connor, Scalia, and Kennedy, none of whom had joined Justice Brennan's *Johnson* opinion.

      The majority held that the lower court's approach would impose excessive burdens on employers to get good numbers, and would encourage such employers to adopt quotas—actions in tension with § 703(j). Thus, a *prima facie* case of disparate impact discrimination could not be made out unless the plaintiffs demonstrated that the bad numbers were out of line with the number of "qualified" minority applicants for the positions in question. To make out a *prima facie* case, the plaintiffs would have to show that the poor minority representation among office workers was disproportionate to the percentage of qualified minority applicants for those positions.

      The Court remanded the case to the lower courts to reevaluate the disparate impact claim, but also set forth some guidelines for the lower courts to follow. Plaintiffs' burden of proof in disparate impact cases would now include the burden of identifying not only a statistical disparity in light of qualified applicants, but also the specific employment practice that caused the disparity. If plaintiffs were to succeed in establishing a prima facie disparate impact case, the Court further stated that the employer would have the burden of producing some evidence that the challenged practices were justified business practices. The burden of persuasion would remain with the plaintiffs. Dissenting were the four Justices remaining from the *Johnson* majority (Brennan, Marshall, Blackmun, and Stevens). The dissenters argued that the Court's opinion, especially its dicta about plaintiffs' burden of persuasion on the business justification defense, represented a striking departure from existing law and a partial renunciation of *Griggs.*

At about the same time it was deciding *Wards Cove* (June 5, 1989), the Supreme Court handed down five other decisions that gave narrow constructions to Title VII and related statutes. See *Martin v. Wilks,* 490 U.S. 755 (June 12, 1989) (allowing challenge to an affirmative action consent decree); *McLean Credit Union v. Patterson,* 491 U.S. 164 (June 15, 1989) (narrow interpretation of the Civil Rights Act of 1866) *Lorance v. AT & T Technologies,* 490 U.S. 900 (June 12, 1989) (narrow interpretation of Title VII's statute of limitations for challenging seniority plans); *Independent Federation of Flight Attendants v. Zipes,* 491 U.S. 754 (June 22, 1989) (narrow interpretation of Title VII's fee-shifting provision); *Price Waterhouse v. Hopkins,* 490 U.S. 228 (May 1, 1989) (recognizing gender-stereotyping as evidence of sex discrimination but imposing a high burden of proof in Title VII "mixed motive" cases). These decisions created a number of practical difficulties for litigants challenging discriminatory employment practices and signaled a determination by five Justices to close off the expansion of older civil rights statutes to help modern litigants (*Patterson*), to provide more procedural advantages for defendants in Title VII cases (*Wards Cove, Price Waterhouse, Lorance*), and, most important, to discourage employers from adopting affirmative action programs (*Wards Cove, Martin*). The Court earlier in the Term had struck down the Richmond municipal program for setting aside business for minority-owned enterprises in *City of Richmond v. J.A. Croson Co.,* 488 U.S. 469 (1989).

These six statutory job-discrimination decisions shocked the nation's civil rights community, which immediately sought to override them legislatively. On February 27, 1990, Senator Edward Kennedy (D-MA) and 33 co-sponsors introduced S. 2104, the Civil Rights Act of 1990. A similar House bill, H.R. 4000, was introduced by Representative Augustus Hawkins (D-CA) at the same time. The bill's purpose was "to respond to the Supreme Court's recent decisions by restoring the civil rights protections that were dramatically limited by those decisions." The substantive sections of the bill then amended Title VII and § 1981 to override one or more of the six offending Supreme Court cases, plus three earlier ones as well. The sponsors of the bill roundly condemned the Supreme Court's performance. "I believe the Supreme Court's recent rulings represent an effort to renege on history," said Senator James Jeffords (R-VT). 136 Cong. Rec. S1022 (daily ed. Feb. 7, 1990).

The George H.W. Bush Administration agreed that *Patterson* and *Lorance* should be overridden, but opposed the overrides of *Wards Cove* and *Martin v. Wilks* on the ground that the overrides as drafted encouraged employers to adopt racial quotas, in violation of § 703(j). See Letter from Attorney General Richard Thornburgh to Senator Kennedy, Apr. 3, 1990. The sponsors realized that they did not have enough votes to override a presidential veto, and the result was a series of negotiations to work out a compromise bill. Between June and October 1990, rotating groups representing liberal Democrats, moderate Republicans, and the Administration engaged in such negotiations—which continued after the Senate passed a revised bill on July 18 (by a vote of 65–34) and the House passed its own bill on August 3 (by a vote of 272–154), and after the submission of conference reports on September 26 and October 12.

The final conference bill made a number of changes in the controversial *Wards Cove* provision in a final effort to appease the White House and/or to obtain Republican support for the bill. Specifically, the bill included a more liberal definition of the business necessity defense in disparate impact cases, required that plaintiffs prove which employer practices caused the disparate impact alleged, confirmed that bad numbers alone do not violate Title VII, and reiterated that Title VII does not require quotas. 136 Cong. Rec. S15,327 (daily ed. Oct. 16, 1990) (statement of Sen. Kennedy). Nonetheless, the President vetoed the bill, and the Senate failed to override the veto by one vote (66–34).

On January 3, 1991, the bill that had come so close in 1990 was reintroduced as the Civil Rights and Women's Equity in Employment Act of 1991, H.R. 1, 102d Cong., 1st Sess. (1991). Not long after the bill reached the Senate floor, bipartisan negotiations yielded a new compromise bill, the Danforth-Kennedy substitute, S. 1745, which significantly rewrote the House bill, just as the Senate had done in 1990. On the *Wards Cove* issues, S. 1745 simplified the burdens of proof in disparate impact cases (by adding new § 703(k)(1)(A)), generally required that plaintiffs link specific employer practices to their claimed disparate impact (see new § 703(k)(1)(B)), and abandoned prior efforts to define "business necessity" and left the definition to pre-*Wards Cove* case law (see § 3(2) of the Act). Importantly, new § 703(k) represented a clear congressional ratification of *Griggs* in the text of the job discrimination law, but a ratification setting limits on disparate impact lawsuits. According to some inside-the-beltway accounts, at a meeting with President Bush in mid-October, several GOP senators told the President that they wanted to vote for a civil rights bill and would vote to override a veto. After the meeting, President Bush dramatically announced his support for broad override legislation, after a few more changes.

The final language of the bill (with much focus on § 703(k)) was hammered out during the week of October 21. During the Senate's debate upon the compromise bill, between October 25 and 30, numerous amendments were accepted and rejected and—perhaps not surprisingly, given the tools of interpretation used by the courts—a flurry of "interpretive statements" or "memoranda" were inserted into the Congressional Record to "explain" what the bill now "meant." Senator Jack Danforth (R-MO), a key architect of the compromise, offered his own interpretive memorandum, as well as the following wisdom, in response to attempts to amend the bill to forbid courts from using legislative history to interpret provisions of the 1991 Act (137 Cong. Rec. S15325 (daily ed. Oct. 29, 1991)):

> It is very common for Members of the Senate to try to affect the way in which a court will interpret a statute by putting things into the Congressional Record. * * * [A] court would be well advised to take with a large grain of salt floor debate and statements placed into the Congressional Record which purport to create an interpretation for the legislation that is before us. * * *

[A]ny judge who tries to make legislative history out of the free-for-all that takes place on the floor of the Senate is on very dangerous grounds.

The Senate passed S. 1745 on October 30, and the House passed it on November 7, 1991, in both cases by overwhelming margins (reflecting the new bipartisan consensus). The President signed the bill on November 21, 1991, as the "Civil Rights Act of 1991," Pub. L. No. 102–166, 105 Stat. 1071. See 1991 U.S. Code Cong. & Admin. News 768, for the President's signing statement.

PROBLEM ON THE CIVIL RIGHTS ACT OF 1991
AND AFFIRMATIVE ACTION

Problem 1-4. Weber Revisited. You are a law clerk to Justice Scalia in 2009. The Civil Rights Act of 1991 has been enacted, and a new race-based affirmative action case comes before the Supreme Court, where a city has rejected promotions of municipal firefighters awarded on the basis of professionally developed tests, allegedly because there were not enough Latino- and African-American candidates awarded promotions. Does Justice Scalia have any *legal* basis for overruling *Weber* in 2009? Does he have any *legal* basis for finding that Caucasian-American fire-fighters should have a Title VII claim for relief? Consider the text of the 1991 act. New § 703(m), added in 1991, says this:

(m) Except as otherwise provided in this title, an unlawful employment practice is established when the complaining party demonstrates that race, color, religion, sex, or national origin was a motivating factor for any employment practice, even though other factors also motivated the practice.

Should Justice Scalia rely on new § 703(m) as a reason to overrule *Weber*? Would it make a difference if you told him § 703(m) was added to override *Hopkins* and to provide a more plaintiff-friendly burden of proof in "mixed motive" cases?

Section 116 of the Civil Rights Act of 1991 said this: "Nothing in the amendments made by this title shall be construed to affect court-ordered remedies, affirmative action, or conciliation agreements, that are in accordance with the law." Jot down your answer and consider the most recent case.

Ricci v. DeStefano

557 U.S. 557 (2009).

In 2003, 118 New Haven firefighters took examinations to qualify for promotion to the rank of lieutenant or captain. The results would determine which firefighters would be considered for promotions during the next two years, and the order in which they would be considered. The City contracted with Industrial/Organizational Solutions, Inc. (IOS), a well-regarded job-testing firm for police and fire departments, to develop and administer the examinations. IOS representatives worked with officials and firefighters (including minority firefighters) within the department to develop written and oral tests that would be related to the job requirements and would be fair to all groups.

Seventy-seven candidates completed the lieutenant examination—43 persons of European ancestry, 19 of African ancestry, and 15 of Latino ancestry. Of those, 34 candidates passed—25 European Americans, 6 African Americans, and 3 Latino Americans. Eight lieutenant positions were vacant at the time of the examination; the top 10 candidates were eligible for an immediate promotion to lieutenant, and all were of

European ancestry. Subsequent vacancies would have allowed at least three African-American candidates to be considered for promotion to lieutenant. Forty-one candidates completed the captain examination—25 European Americans, 8 African Americans, and 8 Latino Americans. Of those, 22 candidates passed—16 European Americans, 3 African Americans, and 3 Latino Americans. Seven captain positions were vacant at the time of the examination; 9 candidates were eligible for an immediate promotion to captain—7 European Americans and 2 Latino Americans.

When the examination results showed that white candidates had outperformed minority candidates, Mayor DeStefano and other local politicians opened a public debate that turned rancorous. Some firefighters argued the tests should be discarded because the results showed the tests to be discriminatory. They threatened a discrimination lawsuit if the City made promotions based on the tests. Other firefighters said the exams were neutral, and they threatened a discrimination lawsuit if the City, relying on the statistical racial disparity, ignored the test results and denied promotions to the candidates who had performed well. In the end, New Haven threw out the examinations.

White and Latino firefighters who likely would have been promoted based on their test performances sued the City and some of its officials. They alleged that, by discarding the test results, the City and its officials discriminated against them based on their race, in violation of Title VII and the Equal Protection Clause. New Haven defended its actions, arguing that, if officials had certified the results, they could have faced liability under Title VII for adopting a practice that had a disparate impact on the minority firefighters.

The District Court granted summary judgment for New Haven, and the Second Circuit affirmed. Joined by Chief Justice Roberts and Justices Scalia, Thomas, and Alito, **Justice Kennedy**'s opinion for the Court ruled that "race-based action like the City's in this case is impermissible under Title VII unless the employer can demonstrate a strong basis in evidence that, had it not taken the action, it would have been liable under the disparate-impact statute. The respondents, we further determine, cannot meet that threshold standard. As a result, the City's action in discarding the tests was a violation of Title VII." Because New Haven's action violated Title VII, the Court did not reach the constitutional (equal protection) challenge.

Justice Kennedy's opinion rejected the firefighters' arguments that New Haven's disparate treatment of them (because of their white race) could not be justified by the threat of disparate impact lawsuits if the City had followed the test results. Reading the 1964 and 1991 Acts together, the Court held that an employer may adopt voluntary race-based remedies for apparent violations of the disparate impact provision of the 1991 Act, without violating the disparate treatment provision of the 1964 Act. The opinion also rejected the City's argument that a "good faith" belief that the tests violated the disparate impact provision would justify race-based remedies; such a lenient standard would, Justice Kennedy feared, open the door to a *de facto* quota system," inconsistent with the premises of § 703(j).

"In searching for a standard that strikes a more appropriate balance, we note that this Court has considered cases similar to this one, albeit in the context of the Equal Protection Clause of the Fourteenth Amendment. The Court has held that certain government actions to remedy past racial discrimination—actions that are themselves based on race—are constitutional only where there is a 'strong basis in evidence' that the remedial actions were necessary." *Richmond v. J.A. Croson Co.*, 488 U.S. 469, 500 (1989)

(O'Connor, J., for a majority), quoting *Wygant v. Jackson Bd. of Educ.,* 476 U.S. 267, 277 (1986) (Powell, J., for a plurality).

"The standard leaves ample room for employers' voluntary compliance efforts, which are essential to the statutory scheme and to Congress's efforts to eradicate workplace discrimination. And the standard appropriately constrains employers' discretion in making race-based decisions: It limits that discretion to cases in which there is a strong basis in evidence of disparate-impact liability, but it is not so restrictive that it allows employers to act only when there is a provable, actual violation." Was there a "strong basis in evidence" for New Haven to conclude that it would face disparate impact liability if it followed the test results? The disparate racial impact of the tests made out a *prima facie* case for liability under the 1991 Act, but Justice Kennedy ruled that the City had no "strong basis" to believe that its business necessity defense would not prevail in potential lawsuits.

Writing also for Justices Stevens, Souter, and Breyer, **Justice Ginsburg** dissented. She started with a broader context, namely, the long history of exclusion for African- and Latino-American citizens from municipal police and firefighting jobs, including near-total exclusion for most of New Haven's history. In light of this history of exclusion, especially in the officer ranks, New Haven had a great deal of discretion to question the results of a test that statistically favored persons of European descent. At public meetings (before the test results had been released), several observers claimed that the test had several questions not relevant to firefighting duties or command; others pointed out that some firefighters had earlier access to study materials than others did; one participant pointed out that a neighboring city had a racially imbalanced force until it abandoned the use of standardized tests such as this one. Experts told the City that a more problem-oriented approach would have been practical and would probably have had a less racially discriminatory impact.

"Congress [has] declared unambiguously that selection criteria operating to the disadvantage of minority group members can be retained only if justified by business necessity. In keeping with Congress's design, employers who reject such criteria due to reasonable doubts about their reliability can hardly be held to have engaged in discrimination 'because of' race. A reasonable endeavor to comply with the law and to ensure that qualified candidates of all races have a fair opportunity to compete is simply not what Congress meant to interdict. I would therefore hold that an employer who jettisons a selection device when its disproportionate racial impact becomes apparent does not violate Title VII's disparate-treatment bar automatically or at all, subject to this key condition: The employer must have good cause to believe the device would not withstand examination for business necessity."

Justice Ginsburg maintained that her approach was more consistent with the EEOC's longstanding guidance on remedial race-based affirmative action permissible under Title VII and with the Court's precedents, specifically *Johnson.* She also argued that equal protection precedents were of "limited utility" because the Equal Protection Clause does *not* regulate state rules that only have a disparate race-based impact; there is no equal protection parallel to either *Griggs* or to the 1991 Act's provision for disparate impact liability. Even under the Court's announced standard, Justice Ginsburg maintained that the City had a "strong basis in evidence" to question whether the IOS-developed test really met the business necessity requirement of the 1991 Act. So many questions were raised about the test, and the City had followed it simply because the union insisted on such a test.

Writing also for Justices Scalia and Thomas, **Justice Alito** wrote a concurring opinion responding to Justice Ginsburg's factual points. Justice Alito's understanding was that the City's *volte-face* was politically motivated. "Almost as soon as the City disclosed the racial makeup of the list of firefighters who scored the highest on the exam, the City administration was lobbied by an influential community leader to scrap the test results, and the City administration decided on that course of action before making any real assessment of the possibility of a disparate-impact violation. To achieve that end, the City administration concealed its internal decision but worked—as things turned out, successfully—to persuade the [review board] that acceptance of the test results would be illegal and would expose the City to disparate-impact liability. But in the event that the [review board] was not persuaded, the Mayor, wielding ultimate decisionmaking authority, was prepared to overrule the [board] immediately. Taking this view of the evidence, a reasonable jury could easily find that the City's real reason for scrapping the test results was not a concern about violating the disparate-impact provision of Title VII but a simple desire to please a politically important racial constituency."

Justice Ginsburg replied that she would be in favor of a remand to see precisely what various options a "reasonable" jury would have accepted. Moreover, Justice Alito's understanding of the decisionmaking ignored the fact that the reviewing board—an unelected, politically insulated group of experts—made the actual decision, and the Mayor did not. Finally, are all "political considerations" tantamount to race discrimination itself? "The real issue, then, is not whether the mayor and his staff were politically motivated; it is whether their attempt to score political points was legitimate (*i.e.,* nondiscriminatory). Were they seeking to exclude white firefighters from promotion (unlikely, as a fair test would undoubtedly result in the addition of white firefighters to the officer ranks), or did they realize, at least belatedly, that their tests could be toppled in a disparate-impact suit? In the latter case, there is no disparate-treatment violation. Justice Alito, I recognize, would disagree. In his view, an employer's action to avoid Title VII disparate-impact liability qualifies as a presumptively improper race-based employment decision. I reject that construction of Title VII. As I see it, when employers endeavor to avoid exposure to disparate-impact liability, they do not thereby encounter liability for disparate treatment."

NOTES ON THE NEW HAVEN FIREFIGHTERS CASE: WHAT IS THE STATUS OF WEBER?

1.   *Have* Weber *and* Johnson *Been Overruled?* At no point did Justice Kennedy cite *Weber*, and his opinion made only a perfunctory reference to *Johnson*. Has *Weber* been overruled? Has *Johnson* been overruled? If these statutory precedents have been overruled, what might be the *legal* justification? And why did the *Ricci* majority not mention that it was overruling these precedents?

2.   *What Is the Law Now?* Presumably, current Title VII law is the interpretation rendered by the Court majority in *Ricci*—but what is a "strong basis in evidence" for the existence of a *Griggs* violation? For example, would the *Ricci* Court have followed Justice O'Connor in *Johnson*, where she found that the employer had a "firm basis" for remedying prior discrimination? Recall that Justice Scalia (now part of the Court majority) rejected Justice O'Connor's reading of the record, in part because the District Court had found, as

a matter of fact, that there had been "no discrimination" against women in *Johnson*. How can the "strong basis in evidence" standard be administered? Should the EEOC issue a guidance along these lines? If so, what should it say?

3. *Continuing the Court/Congress/President Civil Rights Game.* Notice how *Ricci* reflects the dynamic potential of the law-implementation process. Soon after the 1964 Act was adopted, the EEOC and the Court pushed Title VII to the left through liberal construction of the disparate impact claim for relief. Congress rejected proposals to trim back Title VII in the 1972 Amendments, and *Weber-Johnson* confirmed the evolution of Title VII toward a more strongly integrationist stance than Congress had probably assumed in 1964. But the Supreme Court pushed the statute in a more conservative direction—and Congress pushed back with the 1991 Amendments. As *Ricci* dramatically illustrates, the 1989 Supreme Court decisions did not push Title VII back to 1964—nor did the 1991 Amendments push Title VII back to the heyday of liberal interpretation in the 1970s. Instead, Title VII's text represents a pretty detailed compromise between the Brennan-Ginsburg vision for workplace diversity and the Rehnquist-Scalia-Alito vision for employer color-blindness.

3. THE STORY OF THE AFFORDABLE CARE ACT OF 2010 AND "UNORTHODOX LAWMAKING"

In the last half-century, two of the greatest landmark statutes have been the Civil Rights Act of 1964, our focus in Section 1, and the Patient Protection and Affordable Care Act of 2010 ("ACA"), P.L. 111–148, 124 Stat. 119 (2010), our focus in this Section. As we shall see, the process by which the ACA was enacted was very different from the earlier process. The formal rules of the House and the Senate had not changed significantly between 1964 and 2010, but the operation of the congressional process was transformed by *hyperpartisan polarization*.

In 1964, both political parties were big tents, with liberal and conservative representatives. In the Senate, the most liberal Republican (Jacob Javits of New York) was to the left of most Democrats, and way to the left of conservative southern Democrats (like James Eastland of Mississippi), who were to the right of most Republicans. Since then, the two parties have become ideologically more homogeneous: the Democratic Party has become more monolithically liberal; the Republican Party has become more monolithically conservative. Richard Hasen, *End of the Dialogue? Political Polarization, the Supreme Court, and Congress*, 86 S. Cal. L. Rev. 205, 233–38 (2013). The most liberal Republican senator today (Susan Collins of Maine) is more conservative than the most conservative Democratic senator (Joe Manchin of West Virginia). The polarization of the political parties has fueled an increasingly bitter and contentious legislative process. Hyperpartisan polarization and the internal dynamics of each chamber as well as the ascendant presidency have combined to transform the federal lawmaking process into something quite different from the classic process reflected in Section 1.

The classic vetogates process diagrammed in Chart 1-1 above is no longer the norm for the congressional process of passing statutes—and has been supplanted by what Barbara Sinclair has called *unorthodox lawmaking*. Barbara Sinclair, *Unorthodox Lawmaking: New Legislative Processes in the U.S. Congress* (5th ed. 2017); see also Charles Tiefer, *The Polarized Congress: The Post-Traditional Process of Its Current Struggles* (2016); Abbe R. Gluck, Anne Joseph O'Connell & Rosa Po, *Unorthodox Lawmaking, Unorthodox Rulemaking*, 115 Colum. L. Rev. 1789 (2015). What was yesterday's "unorthodox" process is today's "new normal."[59] Consider several features of the new normal that are represented in the cited literature and that will be illustrated by our account of the ACA that follows:

Decline of Committees, Rise of Party Leaders. The biggest change has been the decline of the role of congressional committees and their chairs as the forum for drafting bills, working out enactable compromises, and managing the bills through the vetogates. As the parties have become more homogeneous, their leaders in the legislative and executive branches have assumed more centralized authority—and so the Speaker of the House, the Senate Majority Leader, and the President have increasingly assumed more of the responsibility for drafting bills, working out compromises, and managing the proposed legislation than was the case in the 1960s and 1970s. Gone, too, are the days when major legislation would be put together by single committees in the House and the Senate, with differences reconciled by a conference committee. In the new normal, many laws, and most major statutes, do not go through committee at all. In other cases, the Speaker or the Majority Leader refers legislation to several committees, either simultaneously or sequentially, and the party leaders become the primary authors for "blending" different bills into the bills that actually pass the respective chambers. Conference committees (long a source of power for committee chairs, who named the representatives) have virtually disappeared. Differences between House and Senate bills are resolved either by "ping-ponging," passing the bill back and forth between the chambers, or by "summits" of the political leaders.

The Pervasive Filibuster and Other Obstructive Tactics (Senate). In 1964, the filibuster was an obstructionist mechanism used mainly against civil rights legislation. Today, almost every bill of consequence (except most budget-related bills) is filibustered. In the 1960s, only 8% of the major measures considered by Congress were subject to what Sinclair calls "extended debate." By the 113th Congress (2013–14), the figure was 68%. In most of the modern "filibusters," there are no speeches; a senator merely signals she wants to filibuster, and the Majority Leader treats it as such. Cutting off debate by cloture requires only 60 senators (not two-thirds of those voting, as in 1964) but that means that major legislation needs 60 votes in the highly polarized Senate, an almost impossible goal for most proposals. Obstructionism has steadily increased in the last 20 years—and Congress has been gridlocked most of the time since the 1998 Clinton impeachment.[60] In addition to the filibuster, modes of obstruction include invocation of procedural requirements (such as reading the entire bill) and amendment marathons in committee or on the floor of the Senate.

The Hastert Rule and Tyranny of the Majority Caucus (House). Hyperpartisan polarization has had the opposite effect in the House: rather than drawing out the process of floor debate, as in the Senate, partisanship in the House has contributed

---

[59]   Joshua Chafetz, *Congress's Constitution: Legislative Authority and the Separation of Powers* 267–301 (2017); Chafetz, *Unprecedented? Judicial Confirmation Battles and the Search for a Usable Past*, 131 Harv. L. Rev. 96, 110–19 (2017).

[60]   Christiansen & Eskridge, *Congressional Overrides, 1967–2013*, at 1340–53 (override activity thrived in the 1990s, collapsed after 1998).

to a streamlined process, less floor debate, and much less bipartisan deliberation. Since the speakership of Dennis Hastert, GOP Speakers are not supposed to allow measures to come to the House floor unless a majority of its own caucus supports those measures. The "Hastert Rule" has created a new vetogate, operative only when the Republicans have a majority in the House (and when their Speaker feels like he has to invoke the Hastert Rule). When the Democrats control the House (2007–11, 2019 onward), their Speaker Nancy Pelosi has not adopted a Hastert Rule but has followed the Republican lead of excluding the minority party from any participation in important legislation. Thus, public committee "mark ups," when committee members of both parties would work up the final language of a bill, have given way to private sessions open only to the majority party.

Important Role of Budget Institutions and Processes. When Congress passed the Civil Rights Act, no one would have thought that its budget effects would have been relevant to the debate—although President Johnson paved the way for Senator Harry Byrd to acquiesce in the bill by slashing spending in the administration's budget. Today, almost all legislation is drafted in the shadow of the scoring system of the Congressional Budget Office (CBO).[61] That scoring system gained increasing importance with the enactment of PAYGO, which requires that any bill not increase the projected budget deficit as determined by the CBO. Even more important is the role of *reconciliation*. The Budget Act of 1974 created a process by which bills relating to the budget receive fast-track processes in both chambers and cannot be filibustered in the Senate. Reconciliation is, therefore, a desirable option if a proposal does not have the 60 senators needed for cloture, which is routine for substantive legislation under the new normal.

The Rise of Omnibus Legislation. A further consequence of ever-increasing polarization has been a steadily expanding use of *omnibus legislation* to bundle a variety of measures, often including budget measures, into one gigantic package. According to Sinclair, *Unorthodox Lawmaking,* 158, nothing major was accomplished through omnibus legislation in the 1960s, an average of 7% of major initiatives took that form in the 1970s, 13% in the 1980s, and between 1990 and 2014 an average of 11% of major measures were omnibus laws. The Reagan era (1981–89) saw many major proposals bundled into omnibus budget measures that escaped Senate filibusters and other vetogates, but the last generation has seen this approach for criminal law expansions and habeas cutbacks, welfare reform, and legislative responses to the financial crises of 2001–02 and 2008–09. These substantive (non-budget) omnibus bills included super-logrolls needed to secure super-majorities for measures that had broad popular support.

Massive and Variegated Delegation. Congress has long been known to delegate implementation authority to agencies, but the new normal has created delegations to an ever-increasing array of states, agencies, private actors, and quasi-private actors. State workforces have nearly tripled to 18 million employees, while the federal civil service largely has stayed constant at about 2 million. Often these delegations serve as workarounds to controversial issues—after all, civil servants are

---

[61]   Lisa Schultz Bressman & Abbe R. Gluck, *Statutory Interpretation from the Inside—An Empirical Study of Congressional Drafting, Delegation and the Canons: Part II,* 66 Stan. L. Rev. 725, 777–78 (2014).

much less exposed to political blowback than are duly elected legislative agents. Recent legislation commonly contains overlapping delegations to several federal agencies, joint or coordinated rulemaking authority, and delegations to state agencies, with requirements for coordination with federal agencies.[62]

* * *

The foregoing changes were in full bloom when Barack Obama took office as President in January 2009. Armed with a popular mandate, President Obama and his party controlled the Senate 58–42 (counting two Independents who caucused with the Democrats) and the House 256–179. The Democratic Party was committed to reform legislation to make decent health care affordable for the broad middle class, to bring in millions of uninsured Americans, and to end insurance practices such as exclusions for pre-existing injuries and conditions. Many liberals favored a "single-payer" system for all health insurance in the country, similar to Medicare for seniors or national health insurance regimes in Canada and Europe. Other Democrats favored a market-based solution: (1) imposing higher standards on private health insurance plans as well as a mandate for consumers to purchase insurance, (2) providing subsidies for families that could not afford decent insurance, and (3) expanding Medicaid coverage for poor persons and families. In 2006, GOP Governor Mitt Romney and the Democrat-controlled Massachusetts Legislature created a state plan that required all residents to secure health insurance, provided subsidies for some families, and expanded Medicaid for others. The national Democrats essentially adopted this approach and spent more than a year trying to get it through the hugely obstreperous congressional process. Our account below draws from the leading published sources for the Affordable Care Act of 2010 (ACA).[63]

AVOIDING THE MISTAKES OF THE PAST

As a presidential candidate, Senator Barack Obama started out relatively uninterested in massive health insurance reform, but in the course of the primary and election campaigns in 2008 became super-knowledgeable and increasingly committed to this issue. He and the congressional leadership believed that they had a strong electoral mandate to achieve what had eluded administrations from Roosevelt to Clinton: enacting a broad overhaul of health insurance. At the start of the process, in late 2008, there was relative consensus that the effort needed to avoid the mistakes of the past, especially the disastrous health care reform effort mounted in 1993 by the Clinton Administration (*Landmark* 16). First, the White House should not draft the bill. The President should assume a leadership role but should leave the details and the drafting to the House and Senate. Second, the enacting coalition should not emphasize the problems of the uninsured, and should not advertise the measure as redistributional or even humanitarian. Focus should be on the rising

---

[62]   Sean Farhang & Miranda Yaver, *Divided Government and the Fragmentation of American Law*, 59 Am. J. Pol. Sci. 401, 407–8 (2015); Jody Freeman & Jim Rossi, *Agency Coordination in Shared Regulatory Space*, 125 Harv. L. Rev. 1131, 1166–67 (2012).

[63]   Staff of the Washington Post, *Landmark: The Story of America's New Health Care Law—the Affordable Care Act—and What It Means for Us All* (2010); Sinclair, *Unorthodox Lawmaking*, 170–218 (5th ed. 2017) (ACA case study); John Cannan, *A Legislative History of the Affordable Care Act: How Legislative Procedure Shapes Legislative History*, 105 Law Library J. 131 (Spring 2013); Jonathan Cohn, *How They Did It: The Inside Account of Health Care Reform's Triumph*, The New Republic, June 10, 2010, at 14–25. Our account also draws from conversations and work we have done with Professors Abbe Gluck and Victoria Nourse.

costs that worry the middle class and companies and create a proposal that would make the system more efficient overall. (Everyone knew that there were massive inefficiencies in the system.)

Third, supporters needed to neutralize or even enlist potential opponents. In 1993–94, ClintonCare was torpedoed by the combined forces of the pharmaceutical industry, the hospitals, the insurance companies, and the Republican Party. From the very beginning, President Obama and many congressional leaders were committed to working hard to secure support, or at least neutrality, from these former opponents. Even before Obama's election, Billy Tauzin, representing the Pharmaceutical Research & Manufacturers of America (PhRMA), had been involved in a working group sponsored by Senator Edward Kennedy (D-MA), the chair of the Health, Education, Labor & Pensions (HELP) Committee and a longtime champion of liberalizing health insurance. As a GOP member of the House in 1994, Tauzin had worked with PhRMA to kill ClintonCare, but the drug companies were open to supporting a bill that poured more money into health care (and, therefore, fueled greater demand for drugs) but without imposing new regulations on the drug companies (Cohn 19).

Tauzin and PhRMA were also engaged in discussions with Tom Daschle, who would be in charge of health issues for the Obama transition. So too did Karen Ignagni, representing the America's Health Insurance Plans (AHIP), and Chip Kahn, representing the American Hospital Association (AHA). Both had led the opposition to ClintonCare, and Kahn had masterminded the "Harry and Louise" ads that turned public opinion against the earlier initiative. And both had engaged with Kennedy's "workhorse" team as well as the presidential transition. The Obama strategy was to disarm or even co-opt the powerful interests that had sunk the Clinton health insurance initiative (*Landmark* 16–19).

Given what we know about hyperpartisan polarization and the personal antipathy Republicans in Congress had toward the President, one might be surprised that the Democrats sought Republican support for an ambitious health care overhaul. But Kennedy's partner for reform was Senator Max Baucus, the Chair of the Finance Committee that would have to be involved in a measure that would have such large budget and tax effects. A moderate (some even thought conservative) Democrat from Montana, Baucus prided himself on bipartisanship. Given the Democrats' less-than-60 votes in the Senate, a health reform bill would need GOP votes to close off the filibuster promised by Senate Minority Leader Mitch McConnell (R-KY), the master of obstructionist tactics who was determined to frustrate any Obama initiative. For the better part of a year, Baucus engaged in negotiations with a "Gang of Six" senators—moderate Democrats Kent Conrad (ND), Jeff Bingaman (NM), and himself, plus Republicans Chuck Grassley (IA), Mike Enzi (WY), and Olympia Snowe (ME)—to find a bipartisan path toward a bill that could command 60 votes for cloture.

Obama himself was optimistic that a few Republicans could support a reform bill. On March 5, 2009, he hosted a White House forum of 150 representatives of stakeholder groups (including PhRMA, AHA, AHIP, major unions, corporate executives, consumer groups, and so on). The President made an effective pitch for reform, and the stakeholders were impressed that they had something from gain from cooperating, and much to lose. "If you don't get in the game * * * you're on the menu," one participant quipped (*Landmark* 17).

Fueling momentum for reform, the coalition for comprehensive health care also caught some lucky breaks in 2009. After a lengthy recount, comedian Al Franken ousted GOP Senator Norman Coleman in Minnesota, and the Democrats suddenly had 59 senators. They were up to 60 when long-time GOP Senator Arlen Specter (PA), a liberal increasingly out of step with his party, switched to the Democrats' caucus. These developments meant that health insurance reform would not need any Republican votes to pass, so long as the Democrats showed unaccustomed unity.

MULTIPLE COMMITTEES CRAFT OMNIBUS HEALTH CARE BILLS

At the White House forum, President Obama laid out his vision for universal health coverage at affordable prices. But he left the drafting and details to each chamber. The House and Senate proceeded along parallel tracks, but the drafting process worked very differently in the two chambers.

In the House, Speaker Nancy Pelosi (D-CA) played the central role from the very beginning. She controlled committee assignments and had installed allies as chairs in the relevant committees—Education and Labor (George Miller, D-CA), Energy and Commerce (Henry Waxman, D-CA), and Ways and Means (Charles Rangel, D-NY). In March, she charged the three chairs to harmonize their efforts and draft comprehensive legislation, along the lines set forth by the President. In June, the "three tenors" (as they were dubbed) circulated a discussion draft proposal for reform. It included provisions for a health insurance exchange, where consumers could shop for insurance; a public health insurance option that could compete with the private plans; an expansion of those covered by Medicaid; a mandate for individuals to either have insurance coverage or pay a fee (with hardship exemptions); and a mandate for employers to provide insurance or pay a contribution fee (with some exemptions).

The discussion draft circulated by the three tenors was the first public incarnation of health care legislation (Cannan 137). The strategy undergirding the draft, and all subsequent bills, was that the government was going to impose new requirements and regulations on health insurers, but in order for insurance companies to offer good plans at decent prices, the government had to ensure a greater supply of customers through the "individual mandate" (bringing many healthy young people into the market), through subsidies for working-class and other families, and through an expanded Medicaid program.

After additional hearings, the committee chairs and Pelosi on July 14 unveiled House Bill 3200, America's Affordable Health Choices Act. H.R. 3200 contained many of the provisions that had been in the earlier draft, along with a new surcharge on wealthy Americans to help pay for it. This bill was subsequently referred to the same three committees whose chairmen had already had a hand in drafting it. With all committee Republicans pledged to vote no, the chairs of each committee had to hold almost all their Democrats in order to secure positive votes. That was going to be more difficult after the CBO scored H.R. 3200 as running a $200 billion deficit, on top of the conceded costs (Cohn 21). The CBO score rattled the White House as well; Obama insisted that the overall price tag for the bill had to be less than $1 trillion.

Although he was a super-liberal, Waxman's committee contained a number of "Blue Dog Democrats," moderate-conservatives from rural districts, and they were adamant that the bill had to address the CBO cost concerns. Their spokesman Mike Ross (D-AR) gave Waxman a list of ten items that the Blue Dogs wanted, including lower spending in general and trimming back the proposed government-run plan (the public option) that would compete with the private plans. Without the Blue Dogs, Waxman did not have a committee majority, and so he, Pelosi, and White House Chief of Staff Rahm Emanuel took the intraparty negotiations seriously. A deal was reached at the end of July, and the committee voted for the scaled-back bill 31–28 (Sinclair 172–74). As a further concession to the Blue Dogs, the leadership agreed to postpone introduction of a House bill that reconciled the various committee bills until after the Senate committees had produced their bills.

The process in the Senate paralleled that followed in the House, with hearings and intraparty discussions. The staff of the HELP and Finance Committees coordinated very effectively to produce legislation that could be merged together into a single bill that could be brought to the floor (Cannan 144–45). With Ted Kennedy sidetracked by brain cancer, his friend Chris Dodd (D-CT) ran the HELP Committee effort, which produced its bill in early June. Under the draft bill, uninsured persons would be required to purchase insurance through state exchanges or make payments to the government. Subsidies would help many people purchase policies. There was no public option. The CBO score for the bill disappointed its supporters: the bill would cost $1 trillion but would decrease the uninsured by only 16 million. Back to the drawing board. A revised July 2 draft bill scaled back subsidies and included a public option that would be offered through the exchanges. CBO gave the new bill a better score on both cost and coverage. After an extensive committee mark-up, the HELP Committee voted for an Affordable Health Choices Act on July 15, 2009. It was not reported to the Senate until September.

Everyone was waiting for the Finance Committee and Max Baucus. In June, he worked with the White House to negotiate deals with the drug companies and the hospitals that would save $80 billion and $155 billion (respectively) for consumers and overall health care costs. He spent the rest of the summer trying to reach across the aisle, as he had done often in prior years, to cajole a Republican or two to support a bill. After he gave up on that quixotic effort, Baucus produced various draft bills in September—but they had a rocky reception from disappointed liberals and from conservatives who were emboldened by declining poll numbers for the Democrats' efforts. It was not until October 13 (after the all-important CBO score) that the Finance Committee reported S.B. 1796, the America's Healthy Future Act.

Under the Finance Committee's bill, there was a mandate that people obtain insurance, with subsidies for some and expanded Medicaid for the poor. Tax credits would be available to some employers to provide employee insurance. To pay for the expanded funding, the committee proposed a tax on plans with premiums above $8000 for individuals and $21,000 for families. Significantly, S.B. 1796 did not include a public option. Liberals had attempted to include one, but Baucus and the

Republicans had blocked them. The chair was dead set to achieve legislation but was sure that the public option could not muster 60 votes (Cannan 148).

PASSING A HEALTH CARE BILL IN THE HOUSE

After the Senate bills were reported, Speaker Pelosi and the House got back to work in October 2009. But the health care debate had been transformed on September 9, when the President had addressed a joint session of Congress and the nation in a major, beautifully articulated defense of health care reform. In the address, the President had insisted that health care reform's net cost should be around $900 billion over ten-year period—which CBO estimated could provide 30–35 million additional Americans health coverage. To help pay for the plan, the President picked up Senator John Kerry's suggestion that insurers (not customers) offering "Cadillac" health care plans would be taxed. These presidential pronouncements attracted Blue Dog support for the House and Senate proposals that had been developed that summer.

Obama also debunked some of the canards that the Republicans and Fox News had been spreading about the still-inchoate proposal. The biggest charge was that the plan would create "death panels" with authority to deny patients life-saving but expensive treatment. The President also dismissed as false the claim that the plan would subsidize coverage for illegal immigrants. Representative Joe Wilson, a brash young South Carolina Republican, shouted out, on national television, "You lie," a breach in decorum, reminiscent of Tea Party bullying during constituent meetings, that unified the Democrats more than anything the President said (Cohn 22).

On October 14, the three committee versions of H.R. 3200 were reported to the House's Union Calendar, where they died—because House leaders were working behind the scenes to "blend" the separate bills into one unified proposal. On October 29, 2009, the leadership introduced H.R. 3962, the Affordable Health Care for America Act. Like H.R. 3200, the new bill contained health exchanges, a public option, individual and employer mandates, Medicaid expansion, and a surcharge on those with high incomes. It also included the cost savings negotiated by the Blue Dogs in committee. Without going through any of the substantive committees, but with input from their chairs, the leadership moved H.R. 3962 to the floor through the Rules Committee.

Recall that in 1964 the Rules Committee had a deserved reputation for obstruction, but by 2009 it was an instrument of the House leadership. On November 2, the committee voted to recommend Resolution 903, a special rule with both procedural and substantive components. Resolution 903 included the traditional procedural road map for how H.R. 3962 would be considered on the House floor. It waived all points of order, set the time of debate for four hours, and called for a vote once debate was concluded. Like most Rules Committee resolutions under the new normal, House Resolution 903 allowed for debate and vote on only two amendments. One, from Representative Bart Stupak (D-MI), would prohibit any federal funding of abortion under the health care bill. The second essentially contained Republican health care proposals.

Why would the first female Speaker of the House and a dedicated pro-choice legislator like Nancy Pelosi allow the Stupak Amendment to come to a vote? An overwhelming majority of her caucus hated the amendment. Although she commanded 256 of the 435 voting representatives, Pelosi faced a daunting task of bringing 218 of them to vote for health care reform in the end. She could count on no Republicans, and numerous Blue Dog Democrats were likely no votes because of the daunting costs and the increasing unpopularity of the plans among voters. The U.S. Conference of Catholic Bishops (USCCB) had declared its opposition to any bill that would fund abortions, and Bart Stupak spoke for somewhere between 10 and 20 Democrats who would not vote for any bill that did not address the bishops' concerns. Pelosi needed some of those votes and called a meeting in her office of many of the women in the Democratic Party caucus for November 6. "We're standing on the brink of doing something great," she told them. "I'm not letting anything stand in the way of that." (*Landmark* 33.)

Most of the female representatives were strongly opposed to any further concessions, beyond the current bill's requirement that abortion benefits be segregated from everything else and paid separately. One of those objecting was Pelosi's ally, Louise Slaughter (D-NY), who was the chair of the Rules Committee. Several hours later, Pelosi met in the same conference room with Stupak and Richard Doerflinger, who represented the USCCB. Was there any room for compromise among the bishops and the Stupak Democrats? "I don't care what accounting gimmick you come up with," Doerflinger announced, the bishops were not budging from their demand that zero federal funds be used to pay for abortions, which the Church considered murder; Stupak stood with the bishops (*Landmark* 35). The Speaker was faced with the starkest of choices: the needs of women versus the needs of patients.

At 8 p.m. that night, Pelosi broke the bad news to her leadership team, including Slaughter, who had been stalling the Rules Committee vote. There were not 218 votes without some of the Stupak group, and that group was not open to negotiation. It was all or nothing, Pelosi declared. Conceding that Pelosi, as always, was on top of the vote counting, Diana DeGette (D-CO), the co-chair of the pro-Choice Caucus, was outraged that her caucus of 190 House members was "being held hostage by the bishops." As Slaughter noted, "all the women we were just throwing under the bus," a "betrayal of all the women that had fought for this for so long" (*Landmark* 37).

But the Speaker had spoken. Shortly after 11 p.m., Stupak, Doerflinger, and their associates presented the abortion amendment for the Rules Committee to add to Resolution 903. Louise Slaughter refused to attend the meeting of her own committee; she and two other women on the Rules Committee watched the vote on C-SPAN. The next day, Saturday, November 7, the House adopted Resolution 903 by a largely party-line vote, 242–187. With debate and amendments strictly limited, the Committee of the Whole immediately turned to the Stupak Amendment. With all the Republicans and 64 Democrats voting for the amendment, it was added to H.R. 3962 by a lopsided vote of 240–194. Then, the Republican substitute, which CBO had scored as not costly but not effective in providing insurance, went down 176–258.

On the evening of November 7, the House voted on the Affordable Health Care for America Act. The final vote was 220–215, with one Republican, Joseph Cao (R-LA), supporting the measure, as did 29 of the 53 Blue Dog Democrats. The bill passed the House only after a herculean effort by Speaker Pelosi, her committee chairs, and the White House. Yet an even heavier lift was ahead of the coalition: in the Senate, the Democrats could not afford to lose a single party member.

PASSING A HEALTH CARE BILL IN THE SENATE

While the House was moving steadily toward its vote on the Pelosi synthesis of its committee health care reform bills, Senate Majority Leader Reid was blending the two Senate committee bills and checking his draft bill with CBO, to make sure its cost and coverage met the goals announced by the President in his September 9 address. A champion amateur boxer, the pugnacious, savvy Harry Reid was more central than ever before to the success of health care reform, as Ted Kennedy had died in August, after struggling for a year with brain cancer. Kennedy had been the heart and soul of health care reform for more than a generation, and now Reid took up the mantle, even though he knew it would imperil his chances for reelection from Nevada voters in November 2010.

While abortion plagued Pelosi's efforts in the House, the public option proved tricky for Reid's efforts in the Senate. And, unlike Pelosi, Reid had no votes to spare: he needed to keep all 60 Democrats to break the filibusters Mitch McConnell was planning. Reid's core group—including Senators Dodd and Baucus, Nancy-Ann DeParle (the White House's top health policy adviser), Rahm Emanuel, and OMB Director Peter Orszag—had daily meetings with Democratic senators and, occasionally, with Olympia Snowe, the moderate Republican who flirted with a vote for health care reform but whose caucus was strongly discouraging her.

Reid's proposal was unveiled on November 18, 2009, after the CBO gave its imprimatur (with a cost estimate under $900 billion and coverage of 94% of the population). Compared with the House bill, Reid's proposed legislation included a tax on Cadillac health plans, had less restrictive provisions regarding abortion, and was less punitive to those who did not obtain insurance. Unlike the Finance Committee bill, Reid's synthesis contained a public option, with an opt-out provision for states that did not wish to participate. The public option was very popular within the Democrats' caucus, but at least four senators—Joe Lieberman (I-CT), Ben Nelson (D-NE), Mary Landrieu (D-LA), Blanche Lincoln (D-AR)—were adamantly opposed to this provision. Ultimately, they were all willing to vote for cloture on the Republicans' expected filibuster against the motion to debate the measure, but they privately warned Reid that they could not support the measure so long as it contained the public option, which the insurance industry strongly opposed.

The Reid proposal did not become a free-standing bill, nor did it go through one or both of the relevant committees. Instead, on November 21, the Majority Leader inserted it as an amendment to an existing bill, H.R. 3590, which would be the "shell" within which the 900+ page health care bill could be inserted. Reid's cloture motion, that would move the bill up for floor debate, passed on a party-line vote. At the end of the day, the Senate adjourned for the Thanksgiving break. After Thanksgiving, debate on H.R. 3590 proceeded, with a structure grounded in a series of unanimous consent agreements negotiated between Reid and McConnell (Cannan 155).

Most of the public debate and amendments were not deeply relevant to the fate of the health care bill. What was most relevant was whether Reid could pull his caucus together for a unanimous vote on the bill itself (thereby breaking the expected GOP filibuster). He offered state-specific concessions to Ben Nelson and Mary Landrieu—dubbed the "Cornhusker Kickback" and the "Louisiana Purchase" by critics—and constant cajoling for the fence-sitters.

On December 13, Lieberman announced that if the public option were not removed, he would kill the bill by voting with the Republicans against cloture. Not only did 52–55 senators in the caucus support the public option, but many strongly supported it. Reid felt he had no choice but to abandon it in return for Lieberman's support. In a contentious caucus meeting, Reid's colleagues fumed that "the turncoat" (the mavericky Lieberman had endorsed Republican John McCain for President in 2008) would hold the health care bill hostage, but Reid held firm (*Landmark* 45–47). A few days later, Reid nailed down the 60th vote, Ben Nelson, through the Cornhusker Kickback and a concession on abortion, whereby individual states could ban the sale of plans with abortion coverage in their exchanges.

On December 19, the Majority Leader offered Senate Amendment 3276, which was a synthesis of all the deals he had made to get to 60, including removal of the public option and insertion of the state option on abortion-inclusive plans. To start the clock running toward a final vote, Reid presented three successive cloture motions: one to close debate on the manager's amendment; one to close debate on his original amendment; and, finally, one on amended H.R. 3590 itself (Cannan 158).

Reid also proposed a series of amendments: (1) a requirement that the Finance Committee to report back on the bill in two days after enactment; (2) an amendment changing that deadline to one day; and (3) amendment changing the deadline to "immediately" (Cannan 158–69). These amendments had no substantive value but had the significant procedural effect of "filling the amendment tree," a tactic that prevented other amendments from being offered. With his/her priority to be recognized on the floor, the Majority Leader was filling the amendment tree to head off some of the Minority Leaders's expected obstructions.

With all 60 Democrats voting yes and all 40 Republicans no, Senate amendment 3276 was passed on December 22. In the Senate's first Christmas Eve session since 1895, Reid secured a final vote on H.R. 3590, as amended. With members chomping at the bit to return home of attend Christmas parties, the Senate reconvened at 6:45 a.m. on December 24, 2009. Vice-President Joe Biden (their longtime colleague) took his spot as presiding officer. Vicki Kennedy, Senator Kennedy's widow, sat in the gallery to witness a vote that her late husband had fought for until the end of his life. The vote went as expected, with all 60 Democrats and Independents voting yes. One of the final acts of housekeeping was to rename the bill the Patient Protection and Affordable Care Act.

After the vote, everyone raced to the airports, train station, or their local abodes—except for Chris Dodd. He drove across the river to Arlington Cemetery, where he visited the grave of his longtime friend, mentor, and ally, Ted Kennedy (*Landmark*, 48).

THE PRESIDENT RALLIES HIS PARTY: RECONCILIATION

For the first time that year, the Democrats at Christmas 2009 believed that the "ObamaCare" bill would actually become the law of the land. But there was one last hiccup. On January 19, 2010, Republican Scott Brown upset Attorney General Martha Coakley in the special election for Ted Kennedy's Senate seat. The Democrats were back to 59 senators—not enough to pass landmark legislation under the new normal, where any substantive legislation of consequence required 60 votes in the Senate.

Several advisers pressed an obvious suggestion under the premises of the new normal: Why not have the House pass the Senate bill, as is, and then add anything its members wanted through a budget reconciliation bill that could not be filibustered in the Senate? (Hedging their bets, the Democrats had inserted the right reconciliation instructions in the previous year's budget resolution.) Speaker Pelosi icily informed the White House that her caucus loathed the Senate bill, and she did not think she could sell it (*Landmark*, 49–52).

A former House member who appreciated Pelosi's point, Rahm Emanuel suggested that the administration scale back expectations with a smaller reform measure. The President vetoed this idea and insisted that his party press on, come what may, for the ambitious legislation they had envisioned. The White House would assume public leadership and would count on the canny political abilities of Pelosi and Reid to drag the ACA and a reconciliation bill across the finish line. And so that was the strategy.

In February and the first half of March 2010, Obama, Pelosi, and their lieutenants engaged in a non-stop campaign to persuade individual House members to vote for the Senate bill, without amendments. If the bill were amended in any way, it could not meet the requirements of Article I, § 7, that a measure could not be presented to the President unless passed in the same form by both chambers. Without 60 members in the Senate Democratic caucus, the Senate would not go along. One by one, jittery House members went along with the President's pleas, the Speaker's threats and inducements, lobbying by the hospitals and churches, and the many media stories of regular Americans denied decent care (*Landmark*, 52–62).

On Saturday, March 20, Barack Obama journeyed to the Capitol to meet with the House caucus. "Every once in a while a moment comes where you have a chance to vindicate all those best hopes that you had about yourself, about this country. This is one of those moments," he said with his accustomed eloquence (Sinclair 203). Harry Reid attended the caucus, to assure the House members that he had more than 51 senators committed to the reconciliation measure that the House Rules Committee had crafted from an earlier Budget Committee bill. He released a letter personally signed by more than 51 Senate Democrats to that effect (Sinclair 204). Even with strong substantive reservations, the caucus liberals, conservatives, and moderates alike were coming around.

As had been the case earlier, the final sticking point was abortion. The Catholic bishops and Stupak were adamant that the Senate abortion provision (states could opt out) was too weak, and everyone knew that a tougher provision could not be added through reconciliation, because it was not budget-related. But Representative John Dingell (D-MI), the longest serving House member and a longtime champion of health care reform, put it on the line to his Michigan protégé Stupak: you need to do this for me, your party, the people. Building on that, the President both privately and (the next day) publicly announced that he would sign an executive order making it clear that no federal funds would be used for abortions. Stupak signed on, and Pelosi had her majority.

On Sunday, March 21, 2010, the House convened to consider House Resolution 1203, Louise Slaughter's proposed rule to slate debate and a vote on *both* H.R. 3590, the Senate health care bill *and* H.R. 4872, the reconciliation bill that contained the House's health care fixes. The entire afternoon was consumed by Republican objections to the Rules Committee's process, and it was not until suppertime that the House voted 224–206 for Resolution 1203.

The substantive debate contrasted the Democrats' stories of middle- and working-class Americans who could no longer afford minimally decent health care, with Republicans' objections to growing the size of the federal government and to tyranny more generally. At the end of the debate, Minority Leader John Boehner (R-OH) proclaimed that this legislation "frightened" the American people and made them "angry." "Shame on this body," for passing this monstrosity, the perpetually tanned Boehner lectured. Speaker Nancy Pelosi compared the measure to social security and Medicare: it will make lives better for at least 32 million Americans. "This is an American proposal that honors the traditions of our country."

At 10:30 p.m., Representative John Spratt (D-SC) moved that the House agree to the Senate amendments, and the House did so, by a vote of 219–212. All the Republicans and 34 Democrats voted against the bill. The reconciliation bill passed a few hours later, 220–211. President Obama signed the health care bill on March 23, and the Senate on March 25 voted for the reconciliation bill, with amendments that were accepted by the House the same day. The President signed it into law on March 30, 2010. Seven months later, the Republicans swept the off-year elections and regained control of the House. Boehner replaced Pelosi as Speaker in 2011.

A PROBLEM WITH THE AFFORDABLE CARE ACT'S IMPLEMENTATION

Problem 1-5. An ObamaCare Drafting Glitch. The ACA delegated implementation authority to an array of federal agencies, especially the Internal Revenue Service and the Department of Health and Human Services, as well as to state agencies. The law required coordination among the various agencies, sometimes in creative and interesting ways. See Abbe R. Gluck, *Intrastatutory Federalism and Statutory Interpretation: State Implementation of Federal Law in Health Reform and Beyond*, 121 Yale L.J. 534, 576–94 (2011).

Drawn mostly from the HELP Committee's draft, the ACA's central operational mechanism was the "State Exchanges," where consumers who were not covered by employer plans or Medicare could purchase health care plans. The Act provides that "[e]ach State shall * * * establish an American Health Benefit Exchange * * * for the State." 42 U.S.C. § 18031. If a State chooses not to establish its own Exchange, the Act provides that the Secretary of Health and Human Services "shall * * * establish and operate such Exchange within the State." § 18041(c)(1). In the first year of the ACA's operation, most states did not establish their own Exchanges, and in all cases the Secretary established "such Exchanges" in those states. Even as late as 2016, only 16 States and the District of Columbia had established their own Exchanges; the other 34 States had elected to have HHS do so.

Consumers with low incomes were required to purchase qualified plans unless the costs would be too large a percentage of their incomes. Those low-income consumers who did not qualify for Medicare or Medicaid and who did not have an acceptable employer-provided health plan, however, were entitled to subsidies in the form of tax credits that would help them afford a plan offered under the Exchanges in their states. As amended by the ACA, § 36B of the Internal Revenue Code provides: "In the case of an applicable taxpayer, there shall be allowed as a credit against the tax imposed by this subtitle * * * an amount equal to the premium assistance credit amount." 26 U.S.C. § 36B(a). Section 36B then defines the term "premium assistance credit amount" as "the sum of the *premium assistance amounts* determined under paragraph (2) with respect to all *coverage months* of the taxpayer occurring during the taxable year." § 36B(b)(1) (emphasis added). Section 36B goes on to define the two italicized terms—"premium assistance amount" and "coverage month"—in part by referring to an insurance plan that is enrolled in through "an Exchange established by the State under [42 U.S.C. § 18031]." 26 U.S.C. § 36B(b)(2)(A), (c)(2)(A)(i).

Pursuant to its substantive rulemaking authority, the IRS had promulgated a rule that made subsidies available to taxpayers who had enrolled in both State and Federal Exchanges. 77 Fed. Reg. 30378 (2012). As relevant here, the IRS Rule provides that a taxpayer is eligible for a tax credit if he enrolled in an insurance plan through "an Exchange," 26 C.F.R. § 1.36B–2 (2013), which is defined as "an Exchange serving the individual market * * * regardless of whether the Exchange is established and operated by a State * * * or by HHS," 45 C.F.R. § 155.20.

After the ACA had been implemented and Exchanges had been created and were operating everywhere, ACA critic Michael Carvin noticed an issue that had escaped the attention of Congress during the ACA process, of the states during the implementation process, and perhaps of the IRS as well. By his reading, the ACA gave subsidies only to those taxpayers who had enrolled in insurance plans through an "Exchange[s] established by the State" under § 18031. Because taxpayers in 34 states enrolled in their plans through "Exchange[s] established by HHS," none of those taxpayers was eligible for subsidies.

Carvin filed a lawsuit on behalf of Virginia residents who did not want to purchase health care plans. They argued that the ACA did not require them to purchase such plans, because they would cost a large percentage of the plaintiffs' total income, and the ACA allowed such consumers to remain on the sidelines. The government's position was that these consumers were entitled to tax credits that would drive the cost below the exemptive threshold. Anticipating this argument, Carvin made the dramatic point that motivated his lawsuit. Because Virginia had not created a State Exchange, and HHS had created a Federal Exchange for Virginia consumers, none of the Virginia consumers was eligible for subsidies—or the subsidies they might theoretically be eligible for were zero (the "premium assistance amount" and "coverage month" were both defined by reference to an "Exchange established by the State").

This was an ingenious argument, but the district and circuit courts rejected Carvin's reading in *King v. Burwell,* 759 F.3d 358 (4th Cir. 2014). The Supreme Court took the Fourth Circuit's decision for review. What should the Justices do, as a matter of law? Some considerations you might ponder:

1. Carvin maintains that the ACA has a plain meaning that 100% supports his reading. If you represented the federal government (HHS and the IRS), how would you respond to that? Is there a plain meaning? Does plain meaning always end the judicial inquiry?

2. What role, if any, ought the statutory purpose to play in the Supreme Court's reading of the relevant provisions? How should the government characterize the statutory plan? How should Carvin characterize it, consistent with his reading of the statute? Consider the relevance of this fact: in 2014, approximately 87% of people who bought insurance on a Federal Exchange did so with tax credits, and virtually all of those people would become exempt under Carvin's argument. HHS, *Premium Affordability, Competition, and Choice in the Health Insurance Marketplace* 5 (2014). If you were the government, how would you weave this point into your argument?

3. Review our account of the ACA's arduous path toward enactment. Does this "legislative history" tell you anything useful about how to interpret the ACA in this case? Assume that a government lawyer claims that the original incarnation of § 18031 simply required all the states to establish Exchanges. Someone noticed that that would have been unconstitutional "commandeering" of state legislatures under *New York v. United States* (1995), and so the draft proposal was changed to something like its present form. If the government lawyer were right about that, how should Carvin respond?

4. The government will argue that the "whole act" assumes its reading, not Carvin's. After telling each State to establish an Exchange, § 18031 provides that all Exchanges "shall make available qualified health plans to qualified individuals." 42 U.S.C. § 18031(d)(2)(A). Section 18032 then defines the term "qualified individual" in part as an individual who "resides in the State that established the Exchange." § 18032(f)(1)(A). The government argues that if you interpret the phrase "the State that established the Exchange" Carvin's way, there would be *no* "qualified individuals" on federal Exchanges at all. Because the Act contemplates that there will be qualified individuals on *every* Exchange, e.g., § 18031(d)(2)(A), (e)(1)(B), Carvin's argument is inconsistent with the whole act, or with the statutory plan. How should Carvin respond to this argument?

5. The Supreme Court upheld the constitutionality of the ACA, including its individual mandate, in *National Federation of Independent Business v. Sebelius,* 567 U.S. 519 (2012), based on Congress's authority to tax and spend (a majority rejected the argument that Congress could enact the mandate under its authority to regulate interstate commerce). Does this constitutional decision have any relevance to the statutory issue in *King v. Burwell?*

6. If you were a Justice on the Supreme Court, how would you interpret the ACA as applied to the Carvin issue? You can check your reasoning with the arguments bruited about by the Justices in the case below. (No reading ahead until you have cast your vote!)

DAVID KING ET AL. v. SYLVIA BURWELL, SECRETARY OF HEALTH & HUMAN SERVICES, ET AL.

United States Supreme Court, 2015.
___ U.S. ___, 135 S.Ct. 2480, 192 L.Ed.2d 483.

[Excerpted in Chapter 9, § 2]

NOTE ON EVALUATING UNORTHODOX LAWMAKING

What is the neutral observer to make of the new normal? As a descriptive matter, it has reduced the role of committees and their deliberation; enhanced the role of party leaders in Congress and, especially, the role of the President in the legislative process; and has elevated omnibus legislation and reconciliation bills into central roles in federal lawmaking. Is this a good thing?

Barbara Sinclair, the leading expert, offers a dim view of the overall consequences. See Sinclair, *Unorthodox Lawmaking,* 256–74 (5th ed. 2017). She posits that, aspirationally, Congress's duties are to represent its constituents, to be responsive to popular opinion, and to engage in responsible policymaking. Often, Congress cannot satisfy all three criteria at the same time (e.g., the Clinton-era Don't Ask, Don't Tell Act and the Defense of Marriage Act), but Sinclair worries that unorthodox lawmaking tends to sacrifice all three values. In the House, unorthodox lawmaking has radically sacrificed representation, responsiveness, and responsible policymaking for expeditious decisionmaking. In the Senate, expedition is virtually dead, and the other three values seem diminished. The commanding role of the President is attractive to those Americans who like the current President—but ought to be disturbing to Americans who worry about separation of powers.

On the other hand, unorthodox lawmaking is, in part, a response to hyperpartisan polarization. Without unorthodox procedures, such as the closed rule in the House and reconciliation in the Senate, Congress would enact fewer statutes and would never address pressing problems. And when the stars align for Congress to pass a statute, unorthodox procedures enable unified government to move mountains. Finally, what Sinclair laments in terms of Congress's diminished representation, responsiveness, and policy responsibility might be matched by increased accountability of lawmaking more generally. To the extent that there is one political party in power (especially when the House, Senate, and Presidency are controlled by the same party, as they were in 2009–11 and 2017–19), that party is accountable for what Congress does or does not do. It is notable that hyperpartisan polarization has coincided with a long period of alternating party control of the House, Senate, and Presidency.

Consider other defects or virtues of unorthodox lawmaking—and think about what changes you would suggest for the procedures in Congress. For example, should the filibuster be retired?

A TRANSITIONAL NOTE

This chapter introduced you to the legislative lawmaking process, warts and all. The empirical generalizations and models of the political process presented in this chapter are worth considering as you study the rest of this book, especially statutory interpretation.

As you encounter the materials that follow, ask yourself the following questions: (1) What assumptions about the political process are animating the judicial behavior under consideration? Are those conceptions realistic? How would public law theory change, in a given situation, if the judicial understanding of the political process were altered? Should judges modify public law theory in light of what social scientists or public choice theorists suggest about the nature of the political process? (2) What role, if any, should be played by the understandings of the constitutional framers? Should Madisonian theory be rejected in light of modern circumstances? Or should the courts attempt to develop public law theory that would encourage the representative process to act more in accord with Madison's vision? (3) In the modern world of interest group politics, is the legislature a truly legitimate entity to make important public policies largely unchallenged by judicial review? Conversely, in the modern world in which the meaning of the federal Constitution has strayed far from the original intent of the framers, does a court have a legitimate basis for interfering with legislative outcomes? Does democracy simply mean that voters have periodic opportunities to replace representatives, or should it mean more than that—and if so, do courts have any role in promoting enhanced democracy?

Modern American public law is the result of a complex, contentious lawmaking partnership among legislatures, administrative agencies, the courts, and the citizenry. The remainder of this book continues the inquiry about how this law is made.

CHAPTER 2

REPRESENTATIONAL STRUCTURES

■ ■ ■

Public policy in a modern democratic state is not created directly by the people but by their representatives. Hanna Pitkin, in *The Concept of Representation* (1967), suggests several ways in which we might understand representation. First, a representative body may be viewed as *descriptive* of the larger group, a microcosm of the collective. John Adams, for example, argued that a legislature "should be an exact portrait, in miniature, of the people at large, as it should think, feel, reason and act like them." Letter to John Penn, in 4 *The Works of John Adams* 205 (1851). Descriptive theory retains a robust constituency today, particularly in thinking about the representation of minority groups.

Second, the representative may be viewed as the *agent* of the people who selected her. In the most extreme form, the representative's every action must be explicitly authorized by her constituency, but a moderate position would urge the representative to act as she thinks her constituents would have her act if the constituency were in her position and knew all that she knows. Pluralist theories of democracy today tend to rely on a moderate version of such an agency theory.

Third, the representative may be viewed as the *trustee* of the interests of her constituents, exercising her own conscientious judgment on issues. As Edmund Burke told his Bristol constituents shortly after being reelected a member of Parliament in 1774, a representative "betrays, instead of serving you, if he sacrifices [his judgment] to your opinion. * * * Parliament is a *deliberative* assembly of *one* nation, with *one* interest, that of the whole—where not local purposes, not local prejudices, ought to guide, but the general good, resulting from the general reason of the whole. You choose a member, indeed; but when you have chosen him, he is not a member of Bristol, but he is a member of *Parliament*." Speech to the Electors of Bristol (Nov. 3, 1774), in 2 *The Works of the Right Honorable Edmund Burke* 89, 95–96 (3d ed. 1869). Republican theories of government usually envision legislators as trustees charged with deliberating among themselves for the common good.

These three views of the representative are not mutually exclusive. Perhaps the ideal representative democracy would be one in which the legislative representatives broadly resemble the entire citizenry and thus naturally reflect the informed preferences of the majority, which happen to coincide with the best course of action for the society as a whole. In practice, however, these visions of representation often lead in different directions. In connection with the choice of representatives, descriptive theory could favor proportionate representation, in which each important segment of society is represented in the legislature; agency theory could favor frequent elections, so that the representative's votes could be periodically reviewed by her constituents; trusteeship theory could tend to eschew frequent elections and strict proportionality in favor of a system that would choose wise people and (perhaps) keep them in office for long periods of time.

Section 1 of this chapter explores the constitutional structures that shape the way we choose our legislative representatives. We outline the electoral structures laid out in the Constitution and then explore the further limitations that the Supreme Court has drawn from the constitutional norm of equal participation (a norm found in the Equal Protection Clause, the First Amendment, the Fifteenth Amendment, and elsewhere in the Constitution). Equality values include the principle of one person, one vote; a rule against racial vote dilution; and jurisprudence dealing with gerrymandering, the political manipulation of district lines to produce a particular electoral result.

In § 2, we introduce several ways in which the eligibility to serve as a representative is restricted. The first vehicle for discussion is the case involving Representative Adam Clayton Powell, whom the people kept reelecting notwithstanding serious accusations of misconduct. The Supreme Court in *Powell v. McCormack*, 395 U.S. 486 (1969), struck down the decision of the House of Representatives to exclude Powell. The Court's reasoning disallowing congressionally imposed qualifications in addition to those set forth in the Constitution served as the foundation for the Court's subsequent decision striking down state-imposed term limitations on federal lawmakers. We will discuss term limitations, which are a common feature of state legislatures and apply to most governors and to the President. Finally, we will focus on laws regulating candidate access to ballots because these laws significantly limit the choices voters can make on Election Day.

Section 3 examines the complex campaign finance system. Money has always been the lifeblood of elections, and how a polity regulates the use of money speaks loudly about its political self-image. Is money in politics "corrupting," and in what ways? How would each theory of representation provide a different answer to that question? Whatever the political theory of campaign finance, the First Amendment may be an impediment to extensive regulation of campaign finance, and this last part of the chapter introduces the debate within the First Amendment tradition.

1.   ELECTORAL STRUCTURES AND EQUALITY VALUES

The Constitution, in Article I, specifies the broad outlines of our national representative legislature, the Congress. "All legislative Powers herein granted shall be vested in a Congress of the United States, which shall consist of a Senate and House of Representatives." U.S. Const. Art. I, § 1. From the outset, House members have been elected for two-year terms and apportioned among the states according to their population. *Id.* § 2, cl. 1 & 3. In 1911, Congress fixed House membership at 435. An Act for the Apportionment of Representatives in Congress Among the Several States Under the Thirteenth Census, ch. 5, 37 Stat. 13, 13–14. The Constitution originally stated that each state would be represented by two senators elected to six-year terms by their state legislatures. U.S. Const. Art. I, § 3, cl. 1. The Seventeenth Amendment, ratified in 1913, now provides that senators are directly elected.

The Constitution also specifies the framework for congressional elections. "The Times, Places and Manner of holding Elections for Senators and Representatives, shall be prescribed in each State by the Legislature thereof; but the Congress may at any time by Law make or alter such Regulations." *Id.* Art. I, § 4, cl. 1. Congress has exercised this authority in 2 U.S.C. §§ 1–9, providing, *inter alia*, for the date of each regular election; the number, apportionment, and reapportionment of representatives; and the manner of filling vacancies. Persons qualified to vote for representatives "of the most numerous Branch of the State Legislature" are likewise qualified to vote for representatives and senators. U.S. Const. Art. I, § 2, cl. 1; *id.* amend. XVII, cl. 1. Pursuant to the authority of "[e]ach House [to] * * * Judge * * * the Elections, Returns and Qualifications of its own Members," *id.* Art. I, § 5, cl. 1, Congress has enacted a rather thorough code of provisions governing the resolution of contested elections. 2 U.S.C. §§ 381–396.

Every state has a bicameral legislative system with competing political parties except Nebraska, which has a nonpartisan unicameral legislature. The size of the state legislatures varies greatly.[1] For example, the lower house of the New Hampshire legislature contains 400 members, almost 17 times the number of its upper house. A member of the New Hampshire lower house represents around 3,300 people. In contrast, each of California's 80 members of its lower house represents a constituency about 140 times larger. Alaska has the smallest lower house, with 40 members. The number of members of the upper houses varies substantially as well, with Minnesota the largest with 67 and Alaska the smallest with 20.[2]

In most states, members of the upper house serve four-year terms; in 12 states such officeholders serve two-year terms. Lower-house members generally serve two-year terms, although in five states they serve four-year terms just like those states' senators. Fifteen states limit the number of terms their state legislators can serve (see § 2(B) of this chapter). Most states have annual rather than biennial legislative sessions, but in a majority of states the length of the session is limited, often to no more than 60 or 90 calendar days. Every state provides for special sessions: in 15 states, only the governor can call one, whereas in the other 35 states, either the governor or the legislature itself can.[3]

Since the mid-twentieth century, the composition of state and local legislatures, as well as of Congress, has been subject to various constitutional challenges, and the resulting jurisprudence has illuminated that the "right to vote" encompasses several different kinds of rights. Most basically, there is a right of *participation*. Outright

---

[1]   See Nat'l Conf. of State Legis., *2010 Constituents Per State Legislative District Table*, http://www.ncsl. org/research/about-state-legislatures/2010-constituents-per-state-legislative-district.aspx.

[2]   The size of the legislature is important for many reasons. It affects, among other things, the costs and difficulty of campaigning for office, the visibility and prestige of members, the difficulty of managing and administering the work of the legislature, and perhaps the degree to which a constituent feels represented. Yet policymakers and scholars have given relatively little attention to the relationship between state population and land area on the one hand and legislative size on the other.

[3]   For information on the makeup of state legislatures, see various websites provided by the National Conference of State Legislatures, such as http://www.ncsl.org/legislatures-elections/legisdata/number-of-legislators-and-length-of-terms.aspx (providing length of legislative terms for both houses), http://www.ncsl. org/research/about-state-legislatures/chart-of-term-limits-states.aspx (providing information on state legislative term limits), and http://www.ncsl.org/legislatures-elections/legislatures/legislative-session-length.aspx (providing length of legislative sessions).

exclusion from the vote—through such devices as the white primary, the poll tax, and durational residency requirements—is subject to searching judicial review.[4] The point of voting is to combine individual desires into a collective choice, however, so the right to participate, standing alone, is insufficient. Therefore, a second conception of the right to vote involves a right to a fair rule of *aggregation*. At its simplest level, this right encompasses the notion that legislators should represent roughly an equal number of persons, the so-called "one person, one vote" requirement. More complex controversies involving aggregation include how to draw districts of equal population so that distinctive communities of interest are not split among different districts or otherwise have their political power submerged. As this chapter will explain, this problem of the *vote dilution* of distinctive communities—whether they are racial minorities or the minority political party—has generated complex litigation and confusing judicial responses.[5]

Constitutional constraints on aggregation frequently attack the practice of gerrymandering, the drawing of electoral district lines for political advantage. Consider the following gerrymandering techniques. *Cracking* occurs when a geographically concentrated political or racial group that is large enough to constitute a dominant force in a district is broken up by district lines and dispersed throughout two or more districts. The group is therefore denied a realistic chance of being a majority in any of the districts. *Stacking* occurs when a large political or racial group is not split up, but rather is combined with and dominated by a larger opposition group that constitutes a supermajority. A classic example of stacking in the context of racial politics would be creating one large multimember district for the state legislature by combining two majority-black counties with four majority-white counties. *Packing* occurs when the majority finds itself unable completely to deny representation to a minority, but minimizes minority representation by concentrating the minority into as few districts as possible—for example, creating one 97% black district rather than two 60% black districts.

Although political or racial gerrymandering would usually be easier to accomplish if population equality among districts were not required, a requirement of population equality will not prevent any of these tactics. As you review the discussion that follows, consider whether the constitutional and statutory regulations of gerrymandering serve a coherent theory of representation or not.

---

[4]   See, e.g., *Terry v. Adams,* 345 U.S. 461 (1953) (invalidating white primary as violating the Fifteenth Amendment); *Harper v. Virginia State Bd. of Elections,* 383 U.S. 663 (1966) (invalidating poll tax as violating Equal Protection Clause); *Dunn v. Blumstein,* 405 U.S. 330 (1972) (invalidating one-year residency requirement under Equal Protection Clause).

[5]   Pamela Karlan also posits a third conception of voting rights, as an integral part of *governance*. In this sense, voting involves not simply selecting a particular legislator, but being satisfied with the overall composition and operation of the legislative body in question. See *The Rights to Vote: Some Pessimism About Formalism,* 71 Tex. L. Rev. 1705, 1716–19 (1993). Her thesis is that the Supreme Court's decisions on voting rights are doctrinally incoherent because they fail to differentiate among the three interconnected features of a "right to vote."

A. ONE PERSON, ONE VOTE: FORMAL EQUALITY IN REPRESENTATION

Numerical equality in representation (one person, one vote) now seems fundamental to our polity. For most of this country's history, however, districts of widely varying sizes were the norm. Federal courts were long uninterested in involving themselves in districting disputes, considering the issue a nonjusticiable "political question," unsuited to federal adjudication. The federal judicial reluctance to intervene in state and local legislative apportionment stemmed from concerns about federalism, from the notion that other government institutions were better suited to deal with essentially political issues, from the sense that no judicially administrable standard could be created to decide when there was too much population deviation across legislative districts, and from the concern that federal injunctions to remedy the problem would be too difficult to define and administer, inappropriately embroiling the federal courts in local and state politics. The most famous catchphrase capturing these concerns is found in Justice Frankfurter's plurality opinion in *Colegrove v. Green*, 328 U.S. 549, 556 (1946): "Courts ought not to enter this political thicket." But when demographic shifts after World War II exacerbated population disparities in local, state, and federal electoral districts, with booming urban and suburban areas greatly underrepresented and rural areas overrepresented, the Supreme Court changed direction (over the strident objection of Justice Frankfurter). *Baker v. Carr*, 369 U.S. 186 (1962), reversed the longstanding judicial avoidance and held that equal protection attacks on legislative apportionment are justiciable.

Baker remains the leading case on the contours of the political question doctrine. Justice Brennan's opinion for the Court reasoned that the doctrine stems from the separation of powers within the national government. The Court's survey of its precedents concluded that decisions finding nonjusticiable political questions did so for one or more of the following reasons:

> a textually demonstrable constitutional commitment of the issue to a coordinate political department; or a lack of judicially discoverable and manageable standards for resolving it; or the impossibility of deciding without an initial policy determination of a kind clearly for nonjudicial discretion; or the impossibility of a court's undertaking independent resolution without expressing lack of the respect due coordinate branches of government; or an unusual need for unquestioning adherence to a political decision already made; or the potentiality of embarrassment from multifarious pronouncements by various departments on one question.

Concluding that legislative apportionment did not raise any of those concerns, the Court held that it was justiciable.

Since *Baker*, the Court has developed equal representation rules for the U.S. House of Representatives and state legislatures. The national Senate flouts rules of formal equality, of course. The state with the smallest population has as many senators as the one with the largest population. And this inequality is particularly entrenched in the Constitution; Article V provides that no state can be deprived of its "equal Suffrage in the Senate" without its consent. In part this is the result of the historic compromise at the Convention of 1787: the small states, fearing domination by the large states, were given the Senate to make them more secure. See Gordon Wood, *The Creation of the American Republic 1776–1787*, 553–62 (rev. ed. 1998). In part, too, the Senate, with its six-year terms, larger geographic units of representation, and (until the ratification of the Seventeenth Amendment in 1913) appointment by state legislatures, reflects the Framers' desire that one body be insulated somewhat from "democratic" fluctuations, thus protecting property interests against "numbers." Under what theory of representation can this be justified?[6]

1. The House of Representatives

Article I, § 2 of the Constitution requires that the members of the House of Representatives be "chosen every second Year by the People of the several States" and "apportioned among the several States * * * according to their respective Numbers." The task of drawing congressional district lines is left to the state legislatures. In *Wesberry v. Sanders*, 376 U.S. 1 (1964), the Court struck down a Georgia congressional districting scheme in which some districts had more than twice the population of others, stating that Article I, § 2 requires that "as nearly as is practicable one [person's] vote in a congressional election is to be worth as much as another's." Does the Constitution's text support such a holding? Justice Harlan's dissent in *Wesberry* argued that before the Civil War the text of Art. I, § 2 specifically mandated inequality, for it excluded "Indians not taxed" from those counted for districting purposes and included only "three-fifths of all other Persons," that is, enslaved persons. Hence it was most improbable that this provision of the Constitution protects against disproportionate districts within a state, he argued.

After *Wesberry*, the Court was faced with a series of cases in which it defined and applied the one person, one vote standard. In these cases, the Court first inquired whether there was a statistical disparity between the largest and smallest districts, and then it required the plaintiffs to show that disparities could have been reduced or eliminated by a "good faith effort to draw districts of equal population." If plaintiffs carried that burden of persuasion, then the state bore a burden of justifying the remediable disparities by reference to a "legitimate state goal." Under this approach, the Court struck down almost all the deviations that it examined.[7]

In *Karcher v. Daggett*, 462 U.S. 725 (1983), the Court struck down the New Jersey legislature's reapportionment of the state's congressional districts in response to the 1980 census, even though the population of the largest and smallest districts differed by only 0.6984%. In a 5–4 vote, the Court rejected a *de minimis* exception to one person, one vote, swearing fidelity to "absolute population equality" as "the

---

[6] It has been suggested that the structure of the Senate systematically redistributes wealth from large population states to small ones and dilutes the influence of racial minorities in Congress. See Lynn Baker & Samuel Dinkin, *The Senate: An Institution Whose Time Has Gone?*, 13 J.L. & Pol. 21 (1997); Frances Lee & Bruce Oppenheimer, *Sizing Up the Senate: The Unequal Consequence of Equal Representation* (1999). For overviews of objections to Senate structure, see Sanford Levinson, *Our Undemocratic Constitution* 50–52 (2006); Suzanna Sherry, *Our Unconstitutional Senate*, in *Constitutional Stupidities, Constitutional Tragedies* 95 (William N. Eskridge, Jr. & Sanford Levinson eds., 1998).

[7] See, e.g., *Kirkpatrick v. Preisler*, 394 U.S. 526, 530–31 (1969) (striking down redistricting plan leaving deviation of 5.97% between most and least populous congressional districts); *White v. Weiser*, 412 U.S. 783 (1973) (striking down plan leaving deviation of 4.13%).

paramount objective." Applying the test described above, the Court concluded that the New Jersey plan failed under the first requirement because it could have achieved greater population equality "merely by shifting a handful of municipalities from one district to another." Nor did the state bear its burden of proving that the population variances were necessary to achieve some legitimate state objective, such as making districts compact, respecting municipal boundaries, preserving the cores of prior districts, or avoiding contests between incumbent representatives. The one justification presented by the state—the preservation of the voting strength of racial minority groups—was found to be factually unsupported.

Writing for four dissenters, Justice White argued that the Court's precedents did not require strict scrutiny of a "minuscule" deviation, and that good policy did not require such mathematical exactitude. The critical fifth vote in the case was that of Justice Stevens, who rejected the formalist approach of Justice Brennan's majority opinion and embraced a more functional approach. "In evaluating * * * challenges to districting plans * * * I would consider whether the plan has a significant adverse impact on an identifiable political group, whether the plan has objective indicia of irregularity, and then, whether the State is able to produce convincing evidence that the plan nevertheless serves neutral, legitimate interests of the community as a whole." (We shall return to Stevens' concurring opinion below, in § 1(C).) In response to Justices White and Stevens, Justice Brennan's opinion for the Court noted that exactitude in redistricting is now possible with the aid of computers, and that reality may explain why there was not a plethora of *Karcher* challenges after subsequent censuses.

Other issues have arisen, however. First, consider the obvious but difficult problem of allocating the seats in the House of Representatives. Allocating the 435 seats among 50 states of differing populations is made especially difficult because the Constitution guarantees each state at least one seat. The average size of a congressional district after the 1990 census was 572,466. The census found that Montana had 803,655 people, and under 2 U.S.C. § 2a(a), Montana was entitled to only one representative (it had two before the 1990 census), because its population was less than 150% the size of the average district. Montana complained that this "method of equal proportions" violates Article I, § 2: If Montana had retained its two districts, each would have varied from the average congressional district by − 170,638; with just one district, Montana varies from the average district by +231,189.[8] The District Court agreed that the principle of equal representation for equal numbers applied to intrastate districting in *Wesberry* should also be applied to interstate districting. Invoking *Baker v. Carr*, the Supreme Court rejected the government's argument on appeal that this was a nonjusticiable political question and reached the merits of Montana's claim. See *United States Dep't of Commerce v. Montana*, 503 U.S. 442 (1992). It unanimously upheld the apportionment, concluding that Congress had considered a variety of mathematical methods for House apportionment with the guidance of experts. Each method could be said to implement a norm of equal representation plausibly, but none could be said to be clearly superior based on simple equality principles. Thus, the mathematical precision required by

---

[8]   After the 2010 census, Montana remained the largest district in the country with 994,416 voters in its one district, compared to 710,767 voters in an average congressional district.

Wesberry for intrastate congressional districts could not be required in making interstate comparisons.

Second, the census method of asking persons to identify themselves and then having census counters attempt to enumerate any others obviously produces an undercount of the total number of persons. Racial minorities are probably the group most prone to undercounting under the usual method.[9] By the use of statistical sampling, demographers can make a good faith estimate of the undercount. Is the Secretary of Commerce required by equality principles to revise the census based on such statistical sampling? No, held the unanimous Court in *Wisconsin v. City of New York*, 517 U.S. 1 (1996). Applying a reasonableness standard, the Court deferred to the Secretary's decision to use traditional methods of census taking. But even if the Secretary is not required to use statistical sampling to modify the final census results, may the Secretary choose to do so if he or she wishes? The Clinton Administration attempted to change policy on this question and factor in statistical sampling for the 2000 census. In *Dep't of Commerce v. U.S. House of Representatives*, 525 U.S. 316 (1999) (see Chapter 6, Problem 6-3), the Court held by a 5–4 vote that the Census Act did not authorize the Secretary to use statistical sampling to modify the count obtained through traditional means. Although the decision turned on an interpretation of the federal statutes, such that presumably Congress could amend them to authorize or require statistical sampling, Justice Scalia, writing separately, suggested that statistically rooted revisions might even be unconstitutional as inconsistent with the Constitution's text (requiring an "actual Enumeration") and our longstanding tradition of how to conduct the census.[10]

In advance of the 2020 census, the Trump Administration announced its intention to add a citizenship question. Experts (including at the Census Bureau) predicted that this would lead millions of noncitizens to refuse to participate in the census, leading to a decrease in representation (among other things) for areas with large noncitizen populations. Indeed, it became clear that this decrease in representation was the actual (if unstated) motivation behind including the question. In *Department of Commerce v. New York*, 139 S.Ct. 2551 (2019), the Supreme Court, per Chief Justice Roberts, held that a citizenship question was permissible under both the Constitution and the Census Act. Moreover, the Administration's proffered rationale—that understanding the distribution of citizens was necessary for enforcing the Voting Rights Act—was a permissible one. However, the Court concluded that the record showed that the Administration's *rationale* was not its actual *reason* for including the question. The Court held that the Administrative Procedure Act requires that the reasons agencies give for their actions be genuine; accordingly, it affirmed the district court's remand of the issue to the agency. After

---

[9] See, e.g., Samuel Issacharoff & Allan Lichtman, *The Census Undercount and Minority Representation: The Constitutional Obligation of the States to Guarantee Equal Representation*, 13 Rev. Litig. 1 (1993); Nathaniel Persily, *The Law of the Census: How to Count, What to Count, Whom to Count, and Where to Count Them*, 32 Cardozo L. Rev. 755 (2011).

[10] Cf. *Utah v. Evans*, 536 U.S. 452 (2002), in which the Court held that the census technique of "hot-deck imputation"—whereby a housing unit with unknown population characteristics is assumed to have the same characteristics as its closest neighbor of the same type—may be used for purposes of apportionment of the House of Representatives. Justice O'Connor dissented on the ground that this technique was outlawed by the Census Act. Justice Thomas, joined by Justice Kennedy, dissented on constitutional grounds. Justice Scalia did not reach the merits, as he concluded that the appellants lacked standing.

initially declaring that it would try to come up with a new, permissible reason for keeping the citizenship question on the census, the Trump Administration eventually backed down and declared that the census would go forward without it. The Supreme Court's decision will be discussed in more detail in Chapter 8, § 3(C). For present purposes, it is simply worth contemplating the ways in which methods of counting can be politically manipulated in ways that affect the equality or inequality of representation.

2. State Legislatures

The Supreme Court in *Reynolds v. Sims*, 377 U.S. 533 (1964), held that apportionment in state legislatures must conform to the one person, one vote rule. The Court thereby reached the issue not considered in *Wesberry* (that holding rested upon Article I, § 2) and held that the Equal Protection Clause of the Fourteenth Amendment also ensures equality of representation. Chief Justice Warren's opinion for the Court reasoned:

> Legislators represent people, not trees or acres. Legislators are elected by voters, not farms or cities or economic interests. As long as ours is a representative form of government, * * * the right to elect legislators in a free and unimpaired fashion is a bedrock of our political system. It could hardly be gainsaid that a constitutional claim had been asserted by an allegation that certain otherwise qualified voters had been entirely prohibited from voting for members of their state legislature. And, if a State should provide that the votes of citizens in one part of the State should be given two times, or five times, or 10 times the weight of votes of citizens in another part of the State, it could hardly be contended that the right to vote of those residing in the disfavored areas had not been effectively diluted. * * * Of course, the effect of state legislative districting schemes which give the same number of representatives to unequal numbers of constituents is identical. * * *

> Logically, in a society ostensibly grounded on representative government, it would seem reasonable that a majority of the people of a State could elect a majority of that State's legislators. To conclude differently, and to sanction minority control of state legislative bodies, would appear to deny majority rights in a way that far surpasses any possible denial of minority rights that might otherwise be thought to result. * * *

Does this reasoning provide a better explanation for *Wesberry*? (Justice Clark's concurring opinion in *Wesberry* in fact relied on the Equal Protection Clause, as did Justice Stevens' concurring opinion in *Karcher*.) Under what theory of representation is this point of view operating?

The equal representation assured in state legislatures is both broader and narrower than that assured in the federal legislature. It is broader because the precept applies to both houses of bicameral state legislatures, and not just the lower house. Chief Justice Warren explained why the *Reynolds* Court found the analogy to the U.S. Senate (which flouts the equal representation precept) unpersuasive at the state level. The structure of congressional representation is "ingrained in our

Constitution" and arose "from [the] unique historical circumstances" of a group of states binding "themselves together under one national government." That rationale did not apply to the state legislatures themselves, in Warren's view. Moreover,

> The right of a citizen to equal representation and to have [his or her] vote weighted equally with those of all other citizens in the election of members of one house of a bicameral state legislature would amount to little if States could effectively submerge the equal-population principle in the apportionment of seats in the other house. * * * Deadlock between the two bodies might result in compromise and concession on some issues. But in all too many cases the more probable result would be frustration of the majority will through minority veto in the house not apportioned on a population basis[.]

Do you agree with this reasoning? Isn't the sort of "deadlock" suggested by the Chief Justice pretty much inherent in all the other blocking devices of legislatures, such as the committee system, expanded or unlimited debate, the amendment process, and so forth?

The equal representation guarantee for state legislatures is also narrower than that for the national legislature. Unlike apportionment of congressional districts under Article I, § 2, demonstrable population deviation among districts has been upheld in the context of state legislatures. For example, deviations under 10% have been routinely upheld.[11] Even an apportionment plan that contains a higher deviation may be upheld if it is deemed necessary to the achievement of legitimate state interests.[12] Why does the Court require near perfection for U.S. House seat apportionment, while only general approximation for state legislatures?

Relatedly, who exactly makes up the population that must be equalized? In *Reynolds*, Chief Justice Warren had contrasted the representation of people with that of "trees or acres." But do *all* people count for apportionment purposes, or may some be omitted? That is, does the Constitution require that *total population* be equalized, or does it allow—or even require—states to equalize some subset of their population? In the aftermath of *Reynolds*, states treated total population within the district as the number that needed to be equalized (although a few states then removed certain subpopulations—most commonly nonresident members of the military and inmates who were domiciled elsewhere prior to incarceration—from the total population to arrive at their apportionment base).

Evenwel v. Abbott

136 S.Ct. 1120 (2016).

In the wake of the 2010 census, Texas adopted a State Senate map in which the maximum total-population deviation was 8.04%, "safely within the presumptively permissible 10% range." However, "measured by a voter-population baseline—eligible voters or registered voters—the map's maximum population deviation exceed[ed] 40%,"

---

[11]   See *Connor v. Finch*, 431 U.S. 407 (1977); *White v. Regester*, 412 U.S. 755 (1973).
[12]   See, e.g., *Brown v. Thomson*, 462 U.S. 835 (1983) (5–4 decision upholding reapportionment of Wyoming's lower house that included the allocation of one of its 64 seats to the state's least populous county, which created an average deviation from population equality of 16% and a maximum deviation of 89%).

because nonvoting residents are not evenly distributed. For instance, districts with higher percentages of children, noncitizens, and disenfranchised felons correspondingly have fewer eligible voters. Those districts also tend to be more urban, to have a higher percentage of minority residents, and to vote for Democrats.

Two residents of State Senate districts with especially large eligible- and registered-voter populations filed suit, arguing that basing apportionment on total population violated the one-person, one-vote principle. A three-judge district court dismissed the complaint, and the plaintiffs appealed directly to the Supreme Court.

Three positions were advanced before the Court. Appellants argued that the Equal Protection Clause required the equalization of voter-eligible populations in legislative districts. Texas argued that states could use any population baseline of their choice, so long as the choice was rational and not invidiously discriminatory. And the United States, as *amicus curiae*, argued that the Court should find the use of total population permissible and stop there—that is, that it should not rule on Texas's claim that it could choose to use voter-eligible population if it wanted. Even though it urged the Court not to reach the question, the Solicitor General's brief strongly suggested that Texas's position was incorrect—in other words, that total population is the *only* permissible baseline.

Justice Ginsburg's decision for the Court took the position advocated by the United States, holding that "it is plainly permissible for jurisdictions to measure equalization by the total population of state and local legislative districts," and refraining from commenting on whether any other basis of apportionment might also be permissible.

Justice Ginsburg's opinion began by discussing constitutional history, noting that "the Framers confronted a question analogous to the one at issue here: On what basis should congressional districts be allocated to States? The Framers' solution, now known as the Great Compromise, was to provide each State the same number of seats in the Senate, and to allocate House seats based on States' total populations. * * * In other words, the basis of *representation* in the House was to include all inhabitants—although slaves were counted as only three-fifths of a person—even though States remained free to deny many of those inhabitants the right to participate in the selection of their representatives."

Turning from the Founding to Reconstruction, Justice Ginsburg noted the dilemma facing Republicans in Congress in the aftermath of the Thirteenth Amendment: the freedmen were now counted as full persons—five-fifths—for apportionment purposes, but the former slave states were highly unlikely to enfranchise the freedmen. The result would be that white Southerners would actually *gain* political power in the House of Representatives and the electoral college. Concern about this issue was at the forefront of the debates over what became the Fourteenth Amendment. Rejecting proposals by Thaddeus Stevens and other Radical Republicans that would have made eligible voters the basis of apportionment, § 2 of the Fourteenth Amendment "retained total population as the congressional apportionment base" but threatened to reduce that basis proportionately whenever a state disenfranchised any of its (adult, male, non-criminal) citizens.

Although both of these constitutional provisions dealt with how House seats would be allocated *to* states, Justice Ginsburg read their underlying logic as being applicable to the apportionment of legislative seats *within* states, as well: "It cannot be that the

Fourteenth Amendment calls for the apportionment of congressional districts based on total population, but simultaneously prohibits States from apportioning their own legislative districts on the same basis."

Justice Ginsburg argued that the Court's precedents supported this reading of history: "from *Reynolds* on, the Court has consistently looked to total-population figures when evaluating whether districting maps violate the Equal Protection Clause by deviating impermissibly from perfect population equality." And, finally, "[w]hat constitutional history and our prior decisions strongly suggest, settled practice confirms. Adopting voter-eligible apportionment as constitutional command would upset a well-functioning approach to districting that all 50 States and countless local jurisdictions have followed for decades, even centuries. Appellants have shown no reason for the Court to disturb this longstanding use of total population."

Concurring in the judgment, **Justice Thomas** argued that the Court had gone awry in *Wesberry* and *Reynolds*: "this Court has never provided a sound basis for the one-person, one-vote principle. * * * In my view, the majority has failed to provide a sound basis for the one-person, one-vote principle because no such basis exists. The Constitution does not prescribe any one basis for apportionment within States. It instead leaves States significant leeway in apportioning their own districts to equalize total population, to equalize eligible voters, or to promote any other principle consistent with a republican form of government. The majority should recognize the futility of choosing only one of these options. The Constitution leaves the choice to the people alone—not to this Court."

Justice Thomas did not read the Great Compromise as adopting a full-scale theory of representative apportionment; rather, the Framers "made difficult compromises on the apportionment of federal representation, and they did not prescribe any one theory of how States had to divide their legislatures." Instead, "the Framers understood [that] designing a government to fulfill the conflicting tasks of respecting the fundamental equality of persons while promoting the common good requires making incommensurable tradeoffs. For this reason, they did not attempt to restrict the States to one form of government.

"Instead, the Constitution broadly required that the States maintain a 'Republican Form of Government.' But the Framers otherwise left it to States to make tradeoffs and reconcile the competing goals.

"Republican governments promote the common good by placing power in the hands of the people, while curtailing the majority's ability to invade the minority's fundamental rights. The Framers recognized that there is no universal formula for accomplishing these goals." The Republican Guarantee Clause "prohibited [states] from having monarchies and aristocracies. * * * Beyond that, however, the Constitution left matters open for the people of the States to decide. The Constitution says nothing about what type of republican government the States must follow."

Justice Alito also concurred in the judgment. In his view, the Court's discussion of the constitutional formula for allocating House seats among states had no relevance to the question of the apportionment basis within states. In Alito's reading, the Great Compromise was "the outcome of a contest over raw political power" among the states, "not abstract political theory." Likewise, during Reconstruction, "it was power politics, not democratic theory, that carried the day." As a result, he argued, it is a mistake to attempt to induce some large-scale theory of representation from these provisions and then apply that theory to the context of intra-state apportionment: "It is impossible to draw any clear constitutional command from this complex history."

NOTES ON EVENWEL *AND* ONE-PERSON, ONE-VOTE

1. *One-Voter, One-Vote?* The Court's opinion in *Evenwel* holds that a state does not *have* to draw legislative districts with the aim of equalizing eligible voters, but it formally leaves open the question of whether a state could *choose* to do so. Nonetheless, Justice Ginsburg's reasoning might seem to suggest that any attempt by a state to do so would face a skeptical reaction by a majority of the justices. Recall that the Court's opinion begins by reasoning from the rules the Constitution provides in Article I and the Fourteenth Amendment for the allocation of districts to states, which must be done by total population. If districting within states is governed by the same principle as the allocation of districts to states, then it would seem to follow that districting within states, too, must be done with reference to total population. This likely explains why Justice Alito was at pains to reject the majority's historical reasoning.

Should states be permitted to district on the basis of anything other than total population? Why or why not? What underlying theories of representation would counsel for or against permitting other apportionment schemes? And what about the states that start with total population but then subtract groups like nonresident members of the military and nonresident prison inmates—are those deviations from strict total population permissible?

2. Justice Thomas argues in his concurrence that the Constitution does not embody any particular theory of representation more specific than the requirement that states have a "Republican Form of Government." Accordingly, he suggests that "the people" of each state have the right to choose the principle underlying their apportionment, so long as the principle does not render the state non-republican. But he leaves unaddressed the recursivity of his position: how are "the people" to choose? Presumably by electing representatives who will draw district maps. But this presupposes that the people are *already* divided into districts from which they can elect those representatives. Can Justice Thomas provide a response to this "turtles all the way down" problem?

B. RACE AND ELECTORAL STRUCTURES

Even under the regime of *Colegrove v. Green*, when the Supreme Court, led by Justice Frankfurter, generally refused to entertain claims concerning the distribution of political power, Frankfurter himself sometimes led the way in addressing claims that electoral structures were tainted by racial discrimination. *Gomillion v. Lightfoot*, 364 U.S. 339 (1960), involved an Alabama statute that allegedly altered the boundaries of the City of Tuskegee from the shape of a square to an irregular 28-sided figure, thereby removing from the city all but a few of its 400 African-American voters while not removing a single white voter or resident. Justice Frankfurter's unanimous opinion for the Court concluded that these allegations stated a Fifteenth Amendment claim. Unlike the *Colegrove* appellants, who "complained only of a dilution of the strength of their votes as a result of legislative inaction over a course of many years[, t]he petitioners here complain that affirmative legislative action deprives them of their votes and the consequent advantages that the ballot affords. When a legislature thus singles out a readily isolated segment of a racial minority for special discriminatory treatment, it violates the Fifteenth Amendment."

A separate problem from the formal equality of one person, one vote and from protection against intentional discrimination against racial minorities in drawing district lines is the tendency of majoritarian elections in the United States, by their very nature, to deprive minorities of "effective" voting strength. For example, even the most perfect numerical equality will often not yield districts where African Americans will have a good chance of election, especially if whites tend to vote *en bloc*, because of the winner-take-all character of elections and the geographic concentration of African-American voters in big states.

These concerns generated legal efforts to secure increased minority legislative representation.[13] The relevant constitutional provisions are the Equal Protection Clause of the Fourteenth Amendment and § 1 of the Fifteenth Amendment, which provides that "[t]he right of citizens of the United States to vote shall not be denied or abridged by the United States or by any State on account of race, color, or previous condition of servitude." The first cases we analyze in this part are constitutional cases. The protections against vote dilution in these cases have been supplemented by statutory protections in the Voting Rights Act of 1965, as amended. In more recent years, efforts to comply with the Voting Rights Act have sometimes produced a reverse dynamic, in which state legislatures have reapportioned seats with an eye toward ensuring minority representation through the use of "majority-minority" districts. The remainder of this part addresses these complex subjects.

1. The Constitutionality of At-Large Electoral Schemes

One way state and local governments historically gerrymandered electoral districts so as to minimize representation of African Americans and other minority groups was to elect all representatives "at large." If whites held a voting majority (perhaps one facilitated by other techniques of disfranchisement) and voted as a bloc, people of color could be denied any representation in the legislature. Consider the legitimacy of such practices under the various theories of representation (descriptive, agency, trustee). Now consider their constitutional legality. The following case provides an important starting point for current regulation.

City of Mobile v. Bolden

446 U.S. 55 (1980).

African-American citizens of Mobile, Alabama, challenged the constitutionality of at-large elections for the city commission. The at-large scheme had been adopted in 1911, when African Americans in Alabama were effectively disenfranchised by the state's 1901 constitution. Although African Americans made up about one-third of the city's population, none had ever been elected to the city commission. The lower courts invalidated the electoral scheme, but a plurality of the Supreme Court reversed, because

---

[13]   See generally *Quiet Revolution in the South* (Chandler Davidson & Bernard Grofman eds., 1994); Peyton McCrary, *How the Voting Rights Act Works: Implementation of a Civil Rights Policy, 1965–2005*, 57 S.C. L. Rev. 785 (2006); Richard Pildes, *The Politics of Race*, 108 Harv. L. Rev. 1359 (1995) (reviewing Davidson & Grofman).

the lower courts had not required a proper showing of discriminatory intent. The plurality decision, written by **Justice Stewart**, noted that a state action that "is racially neutral on its face violated the Fifteenth Amendment only if motivated by a discriminatory purpose." Similarly, the Court has recognized that multimember legislative districts may violate the Equal Protection Clause of the Fourteenth Amendment "if their purpose were invidiously to minimize or cancel out the voting potential of racial or ethnic minorities."

In reaching the conclusion that an invidious purpose is required to prevail, the plurality discussed *White v. Regester*, 412 U.S. 755 (1973), a case that had found that multimember legislative districts diluted the voting strength of discrete racial groups. In its holding that the political processes were not equally open to participation by African Americans and Mexican Americans in Texas, "the Court relied upon evidence in the record that included a long history of official discrimination against minorities as well as indifference to their needs and interests on the part of white elected officials. The Court also found in each county additional factors that restricted the access of minority groups to the political process. In one county, Negroes effectively were excluded from the process of slating candidates for the Democratic Party, while the plaintiffs in the other county were Mexican-Americans who 'suffer[ed] a cultural and language barrier' that made 'participation in community processes extremely difficult, particularly * * * with respect to the political life' of the county. * * * The Court stated the constitutional question in *White* to be whether the 'multimember districts [were] *being used invidiously* to cancel out or minimize the voting strength of racial groups,' strongly indicating that only a purposeful dilution of the plaintiffs' vote would offend the Equal Protection Clause."

Justice Stevens concurred in the judgment. He noted two kinds of fundamentally distinct cases: state action that inhibits a person's right to vote and state action that affects the political strength of various groups competing for leadership in a democracy. The first type of cases includes those challenging poll taxes or literacy tests that are used to deny people the right to vote. *Bolden* is not that type of case; instead, "this case draws into question a political structure that treats all individuals as equals but adversely affects the political strength of a racially identifiable group."

Justice Stevens argued that the same standards of review should be applied to any allegation of gerrymandering, whether aimed at racial minorities or other groups. "By definition, gerrymandering involves drawing district boundaries * * * in order to maximize the voting strength of those loyal to the dominant political faction and to minimize the strength of those opposed to it. In seeking the desired result, legislators necessarily make judgments about the probability that the members of certain identifiable groups, whether racial, ethnic, economic, or religious, will vote in the same way. * * * A prediction based on a racial characteristic is not necessarily more reliable than a prediction based on some other group characteristic. Nor, since a legislator's ultimate purpose in making the prediction is political in character, is it necessarily more invidious or benign than a prediction based on other group characteristics. In the line-drawing process, racial, religious, ethnic, and economic gerrymanders are all species of political gerrymanders."

Justice Stevens then reasoned that the proper test in these cases should focus "on the objective effects of the political decision rather than the subjective motivation of the decisionmaker." That standard means that "a political decision that affects group voting rights may be valid even if it can be proved that irrational or invidious factors have played some part in its enactment or retention. The standard for testing the acceptability of such a decision must take into account the fact that the responsibility for drawing political boundaries is generally committed to the legislative process and that the process inevitably involves a series of compromises among different group interests. * * * The standard cannot, therefore, be so strict that any evidence of a purpose to disadvantage a bloc of voters will justify a finding of 'invidious discrimination'; otherwise, the facts of political life would deny legislatures the right to perform the districting function. Accordingly, a political decision that is supported by valid and articulable justifications cannot be invalid simply because some participants in the decisionmaking process were motivated by a purpose to disadvantage a minority group." For Justice Stevens, the decision by Mobile fit this description: although supported by some in order to make it more difficult to elect African Americans, "I do not believe otherwise legitimate political choices can be invalidated simply because an irrational or invidious purpose played some role in the decisionmaking process."

Like Justice Stevens, **Justice Marshall**, in dissent, rejected the requirement of discriminatory intent as necessary to hold multimember districting unconstitutional. "*Reynolds v. Sims* and its progeny focused solely on the discriminatory *effects* of malapportionment. They recognize that, when population figures for the representational districts of a legislature are not similar, the votes of citizens in larger districts do not carry as much weight in the legislature as do votes cast by citizens in smaller districts. The equal protection problem attacked by the 'one person, one vote' principle is, then, one of vote dilution: under *Reynolds*, each citizen must have an 'equally effective voice' in the election of representatives. In the present cases, the alleged vote dilution, though caused by the combined effects of the electoral structure and social and historical factors rather than by unequal population distribution, is analytically the same concept: the unjustified abridgment of a fundamental right." Justice Marshall rejected the idea that the Constitution requires proportional representation and opined that for the Court to impose such a requirement would transform it into a "super-legislature." Instead, "[t]o prove unconstitutional vote dilution, the group is also required to carry the far more onerous burden of demonstrating that it has been effectively fenced out of the political process."

Marshall's dissent then went on to describe the situation in Mobile. "[N]o Negro had ever been elected to the Mobile City Commission, despite the fact that Negroes constitute about one-third of the electorate, and that the persistence of severe racial bloc voting made it highly unlikely that any Negro could be elected at large in the foreseeable future. * * * The plaintiffs convinced the District Court that Mobile Negroes were unable to use alternative avenues of political influence. They showed that Mobile Negroes still suffered pervasive present effects of massive historical, official and private discrimination, and that the City Commission had been quite unresponsive to the needs of the minority community. The City of Mobile has been guilty of such pervasive racial discrimination in hiring employees that extensive intervention by the Federal District Court has been required. Negroes are grossly underrepresented on city boards and committees. The city's distribution of public services is racially discriminatory. City officials and police were largely unmoved by Negro complaints about police brutality and a 'mock lynching.' "

Marshall concluded: "The Fifteenth Amendment cannot tolerate [a decision regarding electoral processes that has a discriminatory effect upon the minority's vote], even if made in good faith, because the Amendment grants racial minorities the full enjoyment of the right to vote, not simply protection against the unfairness of intentional vote dilution along racial lines."

NOTES ON BOLDEN AND CONSTITUTIONAL ATTACKS ON MINORITY VOTE DILUTION

1. *Discriminatory Intent. Bolden* says that legislative discrimination under the Fifteenth Amendment does not exist without proof of "intent" to discriminate. As the Court notes, a similar requirement of intentional legislative action was established for Fourteenth Amendment cases such as *Washington v. Davis*, 426 U.S. 229 (1976). These cases contemplate adjudication of legislative motivations. But how are the intentions of a multi-member body to be determined? Must they be the views of the majority of supporters of the action? The views of enough members to make the difference between passage and failure? Or something else? And how good will courts be at sussing out the actual motivations of legislators?

A related question is what motivations, exactly, should count as impermissible intent. Does the reduced representation of minority groups have to be the sole reason that legislators supported the plan? What if it is one reason among several? What if it is a foreseeable consequence of the plan but not actually the motivation for adopting it? Which of these standards should be used in determining whether there has been impermissible minority vote dilution under the Fifteenth Amendment?

2. *The Subsequent History of* Bolden. In 1982, the federal District Court on remand in *Bolden* held that the city's form of government had been adopted in 1911 for discriminatory purposes, even though African Americans were already disenfranchised at the time by the Alabama Constitution of 1901, because the 1911 scheme was "adopted in substantial part to reinforce the 1901 Constitution as a buttress against the possibility of black office holding." 542 F. Supp. 1050, 1075 (S.D. Ala. 1982). The parties settled the case soon after this decision. In a companion case involving the School Commission of Mobile County, the District Court also found that the adoption in 1876 of an at-large election plan for the school board was motivated by discriminatory animus. See *Brown v. Bd. of Sch. Comm'rs*, 542 F. Supp. 1078 (S.D. Ala. 1982).

While *Brown* was pending on appeal to the Eleventh Circuit, the Supreme Court in *Rogers v. Lodge*, 458 U.S. 613 (1982), upheld a lower court's finding that the system of at-large election of county commissioners of Burke County, Georgia, had been maintained for racially discriminatory purposes. Justice Powell, joined by Justice Rehnquist, protested in dissent that the evidence relied upon by the District Court—the presence of racial bloc voting, the failure of any African American to be elected despite the fact that African Americans made up a majority of the county's citizens, the present impact upon Burke County African Americans of past racial discrimination, and the county elected officials' unresponsiveness and insensitivity to the needs of African Americans—was no different in any relevant respect from that presented in *Bolden*, which in Justice Powell's view held that "this *kind* of evidence was not enough." Following *Rogers v. Lodge*, the Eleventh Circuit affirmed *Brown* in all respects, 706 F.2d 1103 (1983), and the Supreme Court summarily affirmed, 464 U.S. 1005 (1983). Do *Rogers* and *Brown* effectively nullify the thrust of *Bolden*?

2.   The Voting Rights Act and Racial Vote Dilution

Although the Fifteenth Amendment was ratified in 1870 and provides Congress the "power to enforce this article by appropriate legislation" (§ 2), it was not until 1965 that Congress took a major step toward protecting voting rights for African

Americans and other minorities. Finding that case-by-case litigation had failed to enforce compliance with the Amendment because it had proved to be too slow, too expensive, and too cumbersome, and because a decree outlawing a discriminatory device could easily be circumvented simply by adopting a different method of discrimination, Congress responded by passing the Voting Rights Act of 1965 (VRA), Pub. L. No. 89–110, 79 Stat. 437, *codified as amended at* 52 U.S.C. § 10101 *et seq.* Section 2 of the Act forbade any state or political subdivision of a state from using any "voting qualification or prerequisite to voting, or standard, practice or procedure * * * to deny or abridge the right of any citizen of the United States to vote on account of race or color." That provision applied nationwide, but did little to ameliorate the problems with case-by-case litigation.

Other provisions of the Act were meant to be responsive to those concerns. Section 4 of the VRA outlawed "any test or device" required in order to register to vote, such as literacy tests, which the Court had held not to be per se unconstitutional in *Lassiter v. Northampton County Bd. of Elections*, 360 U.S. 45 (1959). To prevent circumvention of the Act by the adoption of other discriminatory methods, § 5 of the Act provided that no change in voting qualifications or procedures could be implemented without the prior determination of either the attorney general or the United States District Court for the District of Columbia that the change "does not have the purpose and will not have the effect of denying or abridging the right to vote on account of race or color." These provisions of the 1965 Act did not apply nationwide: through its coverage formula in § 4(b), they reached only those jurisdictions that on November 1, 1964, (1) maintained any "test or device," and (2) had less than 50% of the voting-age population registered to vote or in which less than 50% of such persons voted in the presidential election of 1964. Although the coverage formula was written in these neutral terms, it was designed to have, and in fact had, the effect of bringing the Deep South within this "preclearance" regime.

The 1965 Act provided that its preclearance requirement would lapse in five years. In 1970, the Act was renewed for another five years, and in 1975 the Act was renewed for another seven years. In 1982, the Act was renewed again, this time with a 25-year sunset, as well as provisions allowing covered jurisdictions more opportunity to "bail out" of its coverage. In 2006, the Act was extended for another 25 years. Although the 2006 legislation passed by votes of 98–0 in the Senate and 390–33 in the House, there was considerable backroom grumbling from Southern legislators and their ideological allies chafing at its continuation of preclearance coverage and from a spectrum of legislators concerning the requirement of bilingual ballots.[14] The Act was substantially unchanged from the 1982 Act with the exception of an alteration to the standard for what constitutes discriminatory purpose and discriminatory effect. Congress effectively overturned *Reno v. Bossier Parish Sch. Bd.*, 528 U.S. 341 (2000), and made it clear that mere discriminatory purpose,

---

[14]   On the conflictual legislative history behind the seeming consensus, see Josh Chafetz, *Governing and Deciding Who Governs*, 2015 U. Chi. Legal F. 73, 98–103; Nathaniel Persily, *The Promise and Pitfalls of the New Voting Rights Act*, 117 Yale L.J. 174 (2007); James Tucker, *The Politics of Persuasion: Passage of the Voting Rights Reauthorization Act of 2006*, 33 J. Legis. 205 (2007). In addition, see generally, *The Future of the Voting Rights Act* (David Epstein, Richard Pildes, Rodolfo de al Garza & Sharyn O'Halloran eds., 2006); *Voting Rights Act Reauthorization of 2006: Perspectives on Democracy, Participation, and Power* (Ana Henderson ed., 2007); Michael Kang, *Race and Democratic Contestation*, 117 Yale L.J. 734 (2008).

regardless of the effect on minorities, is grounds for a denial of preclearance. Furthermore, by overturning *Georgia v. Ashcroft*, 539 U.S. 461 (2003), the Act required the denial of preclearance when the voting laws effectively diminished the ability of minorities to elect their preferred candidates.

Section 4's coverage formula, which was reenacted without change in 2006, was immediately criticized as being simultaneously overinclusive and underinclusive. For example, in states that do not have substantial histories of racial discrimination, such as Michigan and New Hampshire, certain jurisdictions were still covered. Jurisdictions in Ohio and Florida, where there had been more recent and well-publicized instances of serious voting rights violations, were not covered. The shortcomings of the coverage formula were acknowledged during the congressional debates on reenactment, but "[w]hat became clear throughout the reauthorization process was that a debate over the coverage formula would turn into a debate about the purpose and utility of section 5 itself. Such a debate likely would have led to the complete unraveling of the bill." Nathaniel Persily, *The Promise and Pitfalls of the New Voting Rights Act*, 117 Yale L.J. 174, 208–09 (2007). Moreover, the political concerns about partisan and regional backlash dissuaded Congress from changing the coverage criteria: Ohio and Florida are large and powerful, and the jurisdictions that would be targeted for coverage were controlled by Republicans whose votes were needed to ensure bipartisan support for the extension of the Act.

The question of the constitutionality of the coverage formula and the preclearance requirement was brought to the Supreme Court in the following case.

Shelby County v. Holder

570 U.S. 529 (2013).

Shelby County, Alabama, a covered jurisdiction, sued for a declaratory judgment on two grounds. First, both the coverage formula in § 4 and the preclearance provisions in § 5 were facially unconstitutional because they were no longer justified by current conditions in the covered jurisdictions. Second, Congress' decision to retain the decades-old coverage formula for another 25 years was not sufficiently supported by evidence of intentional discrimination in those states. The constitutional claim related to the structure of the federal government: the VRA, the petitioners argued, represents a "sharp depart[ure]" from the "basic principles" of our system in which states are allocated substantial (but not unlimited) authority to regulate elections and in which states enjoy equal "power, dignity and authority."

The 5–4 majority opinion, written by **Chief Justice Roberts**, emphasized that the VRA "imposes current burdens and must be justified by current needs." More sweepingly, the Court insisted that that Constitution contains "a fundamental principle of *equal* sovereignty among the States," any departure from which "requires a showing that a statute's disparate geographic coverage is sufficiently related to the problem that it targets." The VRA departed from that principle, applying preclearance to only nine states (plus a number of political subdivisions of other states). The Court thus viewed it as "extraordinary legislation otherwise unfamiliar to our federal system," requiring justification by "exceptional circumstances."

The Court believed that the coverage formula of the VRA satisfied that stringent test when it was first enacted because Congress limited its scope "to the geographic areas where immediate action seemed necessary" given the longstanding, pervasive, and systematic practices designed to deny black citizens the right to vote. The majority acknowledged that the significant improvement in African-American voter turnout and minority representation in the covered areas were no doubt "in large part *because of* the Voting Rights Act." Chief Justice Roberts then observed that, notwithstanding these improvements, "the Act has not eased the restrictions in § 5 or narrowed the scope of the coverage formula in § 4(b) along the way. Those extraordinary and unprecedented features were reauthorized—as if nothing had changed." In other words, in the majority's view, the current burdens on the covered states were no longer justified by current needs.

The majority acknowledged that Congress in 2006 had compiled an extensive record documenting intentional discrimination taking the form of "second-generation" barriers to equal representation—that is, vote dilution, rather than the "first-generation" barriers to ballot-casting that had existed in 1965. But the Court did not find that record sufficient to justify the scope of the coverage formula. "Viewing the preclearance requirements as targeting such efforts simply highlights the irrationality of continued reliance on the § 4 coverage formula, which is based on voting tests and access to the ballot, not vote dilution. We cannot pretend that we are reviewing an updated statute, or try our hand at updating the statute ourselves, based on the new record compiled by Congress. * * * [W]e are not ignoring the record; we are simply recognizing that it played no role in shaping the statutory formula before us today." The majority concluded: "If Congress had started from scratch in 2006, it plainly could not have enacted the present coverage formula. It would have been irrational for Congress to distinguish between states in such a fundamental way based on 40-year-old data, when today's statistics tell an entirely different story. And it would have been irrational to base coverage on the use of voting tests 40 years ago, when such tests have been illegal since that time."

Accordingly, the Court struck down § 4(b)'s coverage formula. It noted that its ruling did not affect the "permanent, nation-wide ban on racial discrimination found in § 2," nor did it rule on the constitutionality of § 5's preclearance requirement—although, of course, in the absence of the coverage formula, the preclearance requirement did not apply to any jurisdictions. The majority concluded: "Congress may draft another [coverage] formula based on current conditions. * * * Our country has changed, and while any racial discrimination in voting is too much, Congress must ensure that the legislation it passes to remedy that problem speaks to current conditions." Only **Justice Thomas** wrote separately that he would also have struck down § 5.

In her impassioned and lengthy dissent, **Justice Ginsburg** would have deferred to Congress' determination, "based on a voluminous record, that the scourge of discrimination was not yet extirpated." She argued that Congress, which passed the Act by overwhelming bipartisan margins in both houses, should be allowed to determine whether continuance of preclearance and the coverage formula "would facilitate completion of the impressive gains thus far made; and * * * would guard against backsliding." The dissent questioned the view of the federal system adopted by the majority, noting that the Civil War Amendments, at issue in voting rights cases, "authorized transformative new federal statutes designed to uproot all vestiges of unfreedom and inequality" and included "sweeping enforcement powers * * * to enact 'appropriate' legislation targeting state abuses." The dissent described the scrutiny it thought should be applied: "This Court has repeatedly reaffirmed Congress' prerogative to use any rational means in exercise of its power [to protect the right to vote]. And both precedent and logic dictate that the rational-means test should be easier to satisfy, and the burden on the statute's challenger should be higher, when what is at issue is the reauthorization of a remedy that the Court has previously affirmed, and that Congress has found, from contemporary evidence, to be working to advance the legislature's legitimate objective."

The dissenters were particularly dismayed that the Court would support a facial challenge by a county in Alabama, a state with a well-known history of intentional and often flagrant discrimination designed to discourage its African-American citizens from voting, including examples of purposeful discrimination that had supported recent successful legal challenges. The dissent accused the majority of "hubris" for allowing a facial challenge by a political subdivision that probably could not have succeeded in an as-applied challenge. Moreover, the Court erred "egregiously" in refusing to defer to Congress' judgment based on a record that the dissent viewed as "replete with examples of denial or abridgement of a paramount federal right." The dissent described the record as demonstrating a current need for the coverage formula, citing, among other evidence, the fact that covered jurisdictions saw a disproportionate number of § 2 lawsuits, which also had a greater chance of success, as well as greater racial polarization.

In conclusion, Justice Ginsburg wrote: "The Court appears to believe that the VRA's success in eliminating the specific devices extant in 1965 means that preclearance is no longer needed. With that belief, and the argument derived from it, history repeats itself. The same assumption—that the problem could be solved when particular methods of voting discrimination are identified and eliminated—was indulged and proved wrong repeatedly prior to the VRA's enactment. * * * In truth, the evolution of voting discrimination into more subtle second-generation barriers is powerful evidence that a remedy as effective as preclearance remains vital to protect minority voting rights and prevent backsliding. Beyond question, the VRA is no ordinary legislation. It is extraordinary because Congress embarked on a mission long delayed and of extraordinary importance: to realize the purpose and promise of the Fifteenth Amendment. For half a century, a concerted effort has been made to end racial discrimination in voting. Thanks to the Voting Rights Act, progress once the subject of a dream has been achieved and continues to be made."

NOTES ON SHELBY COUNTY AND THE FUTURE OF PRECLEARANCE

1. *Congress's (Lack of) Response.* It might seem that, by avoiding a decision on § 5, the Court left open the possibility that Congress could more appropriately tailor the coverage formula to current realities. How realistic is it, however, to expect that the current Congress will be able to respond to this judicial invitation? Remember the description of the 2006 legislative process to reauthorize the Act: testimony from scholars and others highlighted the possible constitutional problems that would likely arise if a 40-year-old coverage formula were reenacted unchanged. Richard Hasen, Shelby County *and the Illusion of Minimalism*, 22 Wm. & Mary Bill Rts. J. 713 (2014). The main reason for congressional reluctance to revisit the coverage formula was that any changes would likely affect the partisan balance, which in turn would make it harder to assemble the coalition necessary for passage. Samuel Issacharoff notes "that current voting controversies, unlike the concerns of racial exclusion under Jim Crow, are likely motivated by partisan zeal and emerge in contested partisan environments." *Beyond the Discrimination Model of Voting*, 127 Harv. L. Rev. 95, 100 (2013). He observes, for

example, that the likelihood that a state will adopt a restrictive voter identification law "turns on one variable: Republican control of the state legislature." *Id.* at 103.

Perhaps unsurprisingly, then, legislative attempts to pass a new coverage formula have been introduced in every Congress since *Shelby County* was decided, and they have failed each time.

2.   *Do the States Now Deserve Equal Dignity in the Arena of Voting Rights?* In oral argument, Chief Justice Roberts asked the Solicitor General: "Is it the government's submission that the citizens of the South are more racist than citizens of the North?" Certainly, the rejected coverage formula of the VRA "holds that the states with the worst histories of Jim Crow disenfranchisement from the middle part of the twentieth century remain, even today, under a cloud of suspicion that other states are not under. * * * Section 5 thus places the Southern states under a regime of regional federal oversight that is a faint echo, especially in its geographic outline, of Reconstruction itself." Joseph Fishkin, *The Dignity of the South*, 123 Yale L.J. Online 175, 178 (2013).

The sense that this particular petitioner, Shelby County, lies in a state that does not merit being treated with "equal dignity" as most other states in this realm motivated an extensive passage in Justice Ginsburg's dissent. Not only does Alabama have one of the highest rates of successful § 2 lawsuits against it in the nation, but it has also given rise to several successful Supreme Court cases concerning purposeful discrimination with respect to voting rights. Moreover, the dissent quoted extensively from an FBI investigation in 2010 that recorded "shocking" conversations among state legislators and their political allies filled with racial epithets and plans to adopt strategies to discourage African Americans from coming to the polls. Quoting the District Court judge who presided over the subsequent criminal trial, the dissent noted that "[r]acist sentiments * * * 'remain regrettably entrenched in the high echelons of state government.'" Fishkin observes in his essay that the Chief Justice would not likely be moved by such evidence because "[h]e was not asking whether the citizens of the South are, as a factual matter, 'more racist' than the citizens of the North. Rather, he was asking whether the United States was making a *claim* that would amount to an insult, a dignitary harm, to the South as a region and to its people." Fishkin, *supra*, at 191. How can we understand this notion of dignitary harm to states (and presumably their people), and how should it be balanced against the current harm of vote dilution? What role should history play here?

3.   *The Immediate Aftermath of* Shelby County *and the Possibility of "Bail In" Actions.* Within hours of the Court's decision, five states previously covered by § 5 announced plans to proceed with pending voter identification laws that many had argued would discourage particular racial groups of voters from coming to the polls. Two months after *Shelby County* was decided, the Department of Justice announced that it would invoke § 3 of the Voting Rights Act in an attempt to bring one of those states, Texas, back into the preclearance regime in two different cases: one arguing that the state had intentionally discriminated against Hispanics in the last redistricting process and the other challenging the state's strict voter ID law, which had been denied preclearance but which the state began enforcing after *Shelby County*. The § 3 "bail in" provision requires evidence of intentional racial discrimination in voting on the part of state actors. It also allows judges significant discretion to tailor the remedy; for example, the judge might require only certain types of changes in voting procedures to be precleared, and the judge also determines how long the jurisdiction will remain subject to preclearance.

Section 3 was a part of the original Voting Rights Act, but it has seldom been successfully invoked. Between the enactment of the Voting Rights Act in 1965 and the Supreme Court's decision in *Shelby County*, only eighteen jurisdictions were bailed into a preclearance regime. (These eighteen jurisdictions included two states—New Mexico and Arkansas—and sixteen counties, municipalities, school districts, and other smaller entities.) *See* Edward K. Olds, Note, *More Than "Rarely Used": A Post-*Shelby *Judicial Standard for Section 3 Preclearance*, 117 Colum. L. Rev. 2185, 2196–97 (2017). In the aftermath of *Shelby County*, there was some hope among voting-rights activists that § 3 would provide a useful mechanism for reinstating preclearance across many of the jurisdictions that had previously been covered by the § 4 coverage formula. The Department of Justice's initial invocation of § 3 against Texas partook of this optimism, but the Department switched sides in both Texas cases when the Trump Administration took office, and the challengers have not succeeded in convincing the courts to bail in the state in either case. Indeed, in the years since *Shelby County* wiped the preclearance slate clean, only two jurisdictions—the towns of Evergreen, Alabama (population: approximately 3900) and Pasadena, Texas (population: approximately 150,000)—have been bailed into a preclearance regime. *See* Olds, *supra*, at 2197. The high evidentiary bar for bailing in (i.e., the requirement of a showing of intentional discrimination), combined with the shift in outlook under the Trump Administration, seem thus far to be preventing its more widespread use.

In the aftermath of *Shelby County*, there was a marked uptick in voting restrictions, largely—although not exclusively—in states controlled by Republicans, who are thought to benefit politically from such restrictions. In advance of the 2016 elections, the Brennan Center noted that "17 states will have new voting restrictions in place for the first time in a presidential election. The new laws range from strict photo ID requirements to early voting cutbacks to registration restrictions."[15] Some of these new restrictions, as noted above, came in states that had previously been subject to preclearance; others were in states that had never been required to preclear their election laws. Challenges to these laws have relied on § 2 of the VRA and on the Fourteenth and Fifteenth Amendments.

Perhaps unsurprisingly, these new laws generated no small amount of litigation. Recall again the Texas voter ID litigation mentioned above. The *en banc* Fifth Circuit affirmed the trial court's finding that the voter ID law had an impermissible discriminatory effect under VRA § 2. *Veasey v. Abbott*, 830 F.3d 216 (5th Cir. 2016). While the case was on remand to the trial court, the state passed a new, somewhat less restrictive voter ID law, meant to be responsive to the courts' concerns. Reversing the district court, a Fifth Circuit panel allowed this revised voter ID law to go into effect. *Veasey v. Abbott*, 888 F.3d 792 (5th Cir. 2018).

By contrast, the Fourth Circuit struck down an omnibus North Carolina election law passed in the wake of *Shelby County* that was widely described as one of the toughest voting restriction laws in the nation. The law sought to impose voter ID requirements, reduce the number of early-voting days, eliminate same-day voter registration, eliminate the counting of certain ballots cast at the wrong precinct, and eliminate pre-registration of 16- and 17-year-olds. The court found that each of these was motivated by racially

---

[15] Brennan Ctr. for Justice, *Voting Restrictions in Place for the First Time in Presidential Election in 2016* (Apr. 4, 2016), http://www.brennancenter.org/sites/default/files/analysis/New_Restrictions_2016.pdf. These efforts have continued, albeit at a somewhat ameliorated pace, in the years since 2016. *See* Brennan Ctr. for Justice, *Voting Laws Roundup 2018* (Apr. 2, 2018), https://www.brennancenter.org/sites/default/files/analysis/04.02.18_Voting_Laws_Roundup_2018.pdf.

discriminatory intent in violation of the Voting Rights Act and the Equal Protection Clause, and it therefore ordered the district court to enjoin the challenged provisions of the law. *N.C. State Conf. of NAACP v. McCrory*, 831 F.3d 204 (4th Cir. 2016). The Supreme Court declined to hear the case, but the Chief Justice wrote separately to emphasize "our frequent admonition that '[t]he denial of a writ of certiorari imports no expression of opinion upon the merits of the case.'" *North Carolina v. N.C. State Conf. of NAACP*, 137 S.Ct. 1399 (2017).

Some states have also become significantly more aggressive about removing purportedly ineligible voters from the rolls.

Husted v. A. Philip Randolph Institute

138 S.Ct. 1833 (2018).

In the 1993 National Voter Registration Act (as amended by the 2002 Help America Vote Act), Congress forbade states from removing a voter from the rolls without prior notice. Specifically, unless a registrant had provided written notice that she had moved, the state could only remove her from the rolls if she failed to return a forwardable, preaddressed, postage-paid postcard that was mailed to her *and* she failed to vote during the period covering the next two general federal elections. 52 U.S.C. § 20507(d)(1)(B). The statutory "Failure to Vote Clause" also specified that a state program "shall not result in the removal of the name of any person from the official list of voters registered to vote in an election for Federal office by reason of the person's failure to vote, except that nothing in this paragraph may be construed to prohibit a State from using the procedures" specified above. *Id.* § 20507(b)(2).

Ohio had perhaps the most aggressive system in the nation for removing voters from its rolls. Under Ohio law, a registered voter who had "not engage[d] in any voter activity for a period of two consecutive years" would be sent the postcard. ("Voter activity" included voting in any election, signing a petition, filing a voter registration form, and updating a voting address with a state agency.)

Plaintiffs challenged the Ohio procedures on the grounds that they violated the Failure to Vote Clause. Specifically, they argued that Ohio "uses a person's failure to vote twice: once as the trigger for sending return cards and again as one of the requirements for removal." Thus, they argued, a person could be removed from the rolls "by reason of the person's failure to vote," in violation of the Clause.

Writing for a 5–4 majority, **Justice Alito** rejected this argument on the grounds that "the Failure-to-Vote Clause, both as originally enacted in the NVRA and as amended by HAVA, simply forbids the use of nonvoting as *the sole criterion* for removing a registrant, and Ohio does not use it that way. Instead, as permitted by subsection (d), Ohio removes registrants only if they have failed to vote *and* have failed to respond to a notice." On the Court's reading, "a State violates the Failure-to-Vote Clause only if it removes registrants for no reason other than their failure to vote." This is because "by reason of" in the Clause "denotes some form of causation," and the law knows only three types of causation: but-for, proximate, and sole. But the Clause cannot mean to refer to either but-for or proximate causation, because the federal statutory process for removal from the voting rolls expressly allows failure to vote to play *some* role in removing a voter from the rolls (i.e., failure to vote in two elections after having also failed to return the card.)

"By process of elimination, we are left with sole causation. This reading harmonizes the Failure-to-Vote Clause and subsection (d) because the latter provision does not authorize removal solely by reason of a person's failure to vote. Instead, subsection (d) authorizes removal only if a registrant also fails to mail back a return card." Since failure to vote was not the *sole* cause of removal from the rolls under the Ohio procedures, it did not run afoul of federal law.

In a concurring opinion, **Justice Thomas** argued that, in addition to the reasons laid out by the majority, "respondents' proposed interpretation of the National Voter Registration Act (NVRA) should also be rejected because it would raise significant constitutional concerns." In particular, citing his own dissent in *Arizona v. Inter Tribal Council of Arizona*, 570 U.S. 1, 29 (2013), he argued that "States have the exclusive authority to set voter qualifications and to determine whether those qualifications are satisfied." The respondents' arguments, if accepted, would "interfere with the State's 'authority to verify' that its qualifications are met 'in the way it deems necessary,' " and therefore would raise "serious constitutional problems." Invoking a version of the constitutional avoidance canon (see Chapter 6, § 3(B)), he argued that this was an additional reason to read the federal statutory provisions the way that the Court majority did.

Justice Breyer's dissent characterized the facts differently than did the majority: "Under [Ohio's p]rocess, a person's failure to vote is the sole basis on which the State identifies a registrant as a person whose address may have changed and the sole reason Ohio initiates a registered voter's removal." Accordingly, failure to vote is the reason for that voter's removal: "If the registrant had voted at any point, the registrant would not have been removed."

Justice Breyer rejected the majority's reliance on the intervening step of failure to return the postcard, on the grounds that, "In contrast to a *non*forwardable notice that is returned undeliverable, which tells the State that a registrant has likely moved, a *forwardable* notice [as federal law required the postcard to be] that elicits no response whatsoever tells the State close to nothing at all. That is because, as I shall discuss, most people who receive confirmation notices from the State simply do not send back the 'return card' attached to that mailing—whether they have moved or not." Because "the vast majority" of postcards sent received no response at all whether the intended recipient had moved or not, failure to respond to the postcard provided the state with no information about whether a voter had moved or not. In that case, Breyer argued, the *sole* reason for thinking that voter had moved, and therefore for removing her from the voting rolls, would be her failure to vote in the two elections after the postcard was sent. That, Breyer insisted, violated the Failure-to-Vote Clause.

Justice Sotomayor joined Justice Breyer's dissent, but also wrote separately "to emphasize how [Justice Breyer's] reading is bolstered by the essential purposes stated explicitly in the National Voter Registration Act * * * to increase the registration and enhance the participation of eligible voters in federal elections." Thus, "Congress crafted the NVRA with the understanding that, while States are required to make a 'reasonable effort' to remove ineligible voters from the registration lists, [52 U.S.C.] § 20507(a)(4), such removal programs must be developed in a manner that 'prevent[s] poor and illiterate voters from being caught in a purge system which will require them to needlessly re-register' and 'prevent[s] abuse which has a disparate impact on minority communities' [citing the Senate Report on the Act]." However, Ohio's process "reflects precisely the type of purge system that the NVRA was designed to prevent."

Relying on *amicus* briefs, Justice Sotomayor noted that, "low voter turnout rates, language-access problems, mail delivery issues, inflexible work schedules, and transportation issues, among other obstacles, make it more difficult for many minority, low-income, disabled, homeless, and veteran voters to cast a ballot or return a notice, rendering them particularly vulnerable to unwarranted removal" under Ohio's procedures. As a result, "It is unsurprising * * * that numerous *amici* report that [Ohio's process] has disproportionately affected minority, low-income, disabled, and veteran voters."

Justice Sotomayor concluded with an especially striking call for political organizing: "Communities that are disproportionately affected by unnecessarily harsh registration laws should not tolerate efforts to marginalize their influence in the political process, nor should allies who recognize blatant unfairness stand idly by. Today's decision forces these communities and their allies to be even more proactive and vigilant in holding their States accountable and working to dismantle the obstacles they face in exercising the fundamental right to vote."

The recordkeeping practices of many states, including Ohio, make it difficult to estimate how many registered voters who have not moved would be purged under a system like Ohio's. North Carolina's records, however, do make it possible to estimate for that state. Political scientists Michael Herron and Daniel Smith found that roughly 3% of registered North Carolina voters who had not moved had voted in 2008 but skipped the next three general elections. In other words, if North Carolina had Ohio's rules, these 3% of voters would have been purged *if* they also did not return the postcard.

Justice Breyer's dissent presented evidence that about 80% of Ohioans who were sent the postcard never responded. If the return rates in North Carolina were the same, that would mean that roughly 2.4% of all registered voters would have been purged, despite their not having moved. Moreover, about 28.5% of North Carolinians who voted in 2008 but not in 2010, 2012, or 2014 *did* vote in 2016. In other words, if North Carolina had Ohio's procedures, tens of thousands of eligible voters who sought to vote may have been purged from the rolls. Herron and Smith determined that, "If other states adopt Ohio's [procedures], our analysis suggests, millions of registered U.S. voters who are like Harmon [one of the plaintiffs in *Husted*] will be exposed to a purge."[16]

Of course, not all recent electoral reforms have been restrictive in character. Indeed, as the Brennan Center noted in 2018, "Broadly speaking, more pro-voter reforms are moving than anti-voter restrictions."[17] These reforms include provisions for automatic voter registration, pre-registration of 16- and 17-year-olds, expanded early voting opportunities, state-level voting rights acts, and more. *See generally* Joshua A. Douglas, *Vote for US: How to Take Back Our Elections and Change the Future of Voting* (2019).

Much like voting restrictions, voting expansions can have a partisan cast. Consider Virginia, where Democratic former Governor Terry McAuliffe circumvented the Republican-controlled state legislature and relied on an expansive understanding of his

[16]   Michael C. Herron & Daniel A. Smith, *If More States Start Using Ohio's System, How Many Voters Will Be Purged?*, Wash. Post Monkey Cage Blog, June 17, 2018, https://www.washingtonpost.com/news/monkey-cage/wp/2018/06/17/if-every-u-s-state-used-ohios-system-how-many-voters-would-be-purged/.

[17]   Brennan Ctr. for Justice, *Voting Laws Roundup 2018* (Apr. 2, 2018), https://www.brennancenter.org/sites/default/files/analysis/04.02.18_Voting_Laws_Roundup_2018.pdf.

clemency authority to restore voting rights to more than 200,000 convicted felons who had completed their sentences. Virginia is a swing state, and the move was widely understood to help Democrats. Republican leaders in the state legislature filed suit, arguing that McAuliffe had overstepped his authority. The state supreme court, by a vote of 4–3, struck down McAuliffe's initial executive order restoring voting rights en masse, holding that it was too broad an exercise of the clemency power. *Howell v. McAuliffe*, 788 S.E.2d 706 (Va. 2016). The governor then began issuing individual clemency orders to each of the former felons, and the state supreme court rejected Republican attempts to have McAuliffe held in contempt.[18] In the 2017 state legislative elections (in which approximately 42,000 ex-felons who had their right to vote restored by McAuliffe were registered to vote), Republicans lost fifteen seats in the House of Delegates, managing to retain control of the chamber by a bare 51–49 margin. In those elections, four seats were decided (all in the Republicans' favor) by fewer than 130 votes apiece. In the 94th district, the vote was a tie, with the Republican winning in a postelection random draw.[19] Small changes to the composition of the electorate in either direction can have outsized consequences! (In the 2017 election, Democrat Ralph Northam was elected to succeed the term-limited McAuliffe. Northam has continued his predecessor's program of restoring voting rights to ex-felons.)

4.   *Section 2 Protection Against Racial Vote Dilution.* African-American plaintiffs prevailed in *Rogers* and in *Bolden* on remand by satisfactorily proving that the at-large electoral schemes at issue in those cases had been adopted or maintained for discriminatory purposes. In the ordinary case, however, this burden of proof is hard to surmount: proof of discriminatory reasons for the adoption of an electoral scheme many years ago is usually unavailable because of the passage of time, and discriminatory maintenance of such a scheme cannot be shown without either overtly discriminatory actions or overwhelming circumstantial evidence. Moreover, to some extent the *Bolden* approach may ask the wrong question, for it is the present discriminatory impact of the electoral scheme, and not the motivations of present or past officials, that unfairly skews the political process.

The *Bolden* result in the Supreme Court triggered a firestorm of protest from civil rights advocates and members of Congress. A bipartisan coalition voted to amend the VRA in 1982 to override the *Bolden* decision. The operative provision is revised § 2 of the Act, 52 U.S.C. § 10301, which provides a permanent, nationwide ban on electoral procedures with discriminatory "results." In particular, the revised § 2 provides that it constitutes an unlawful denial or abridgment of the right to vote if members of a particular racial or language-minority group "have less opportunity than other members of the electorate to participate in the political process and to elect representatives of their choice." The section goes on to specify that, "The extent to which members of a protected class have been elected to office in the State or political subdivision is one circumstance which may be considered: *Provided*, That nothing in this section establishes a right to have members of a protected class elected in numbers equal to their proportion in the population."

---

[18]   Laura Vozzella, *Va. Supreme Court Finds McAuliffe Not in Contempt on Felon Voting Actions*, Wash. Post, Sept. 15, 2016, https://www.washingtonpost.com/local/virginia-politics/va-supreme-court-finds-mcauliffe-not-in-contempt-on-felon-voting-actions/2016/09/15/9dcfb504-7b7a-11e6-ac8e-cf8e0dd91dc7_story.html.

[19]   *See* Virginia House of Delegates Elections, 2017, Ballotpedia, https://ballotpedia.org/Virginia_House_of_Delegates_elections,_2017 (last updated Mar. 6, 2018).

The Senate committee report explaining the amendment to § 2 (S. Rep. 97–417, 97th Cong., 2d Sess. 28–29) cited these "typical factors," gleaned from pre-*Bolden* cases, as illustrative of the vote dilution Congress intended to outlaw by amending the statute:

1.   the extent of any history of official discrimination in the state or political subdivision that touched the right of the members of the minority group to register, to vote, or otherwise to participate in the democratic process;

2.   the extent to which voting in the elections of the state or political subdivision is racially polarized;

3.   the extent to which the state or political subdivision has used unusually large election districts, majority vote requirements, anti-single shot provisions, or other voting practices or procedures that may enhance the opportunity for discrimination against the minority group;

    * * *

5.   the extent to which members of the minority group in the state or political subdivision bear the effects of discrimination in such areas as education, employment and health, which hinder their ability to participate effectively in the political process;

6.   whether political campaigns have been characterized by overt or subtle racial appeals;

7.   the extent to which members of the minority group have been elected to public office in the jurisdiction.

Other factors mentioned in the Senate report were:

whether there is a significant lack of responsiveness on the part of elected officials to the particularized needs of the members of the minority group.

whether the policy underlying the state or political subdivision's use of such voting qualification, prerequisite to voting, or standard, practice or procedure is tenuous.

Thornburg v. Gingles

478 U.S. 30 (1986).

In this case, the Supreme Court construed the "totality of the circumstances" test of the revised § 2. **Justice Brennan**'s opinion for a five-justice majority concluded that the factors identified in the Senate report were probative, but neither comprehensive nor exclusive. For multimember districting to violate § 2, the Court held, three elements must be shown: (1) "[T]he minority group must be able to demonstrate that it is sufficiently large and geographically compact to constitute a majority in a single-member district." (2) "[T]he minority group must be able to show that it is politically cohesive." (3) "[T]he minority must be able to demonstrate that the white majority votes sufficiently as a bloc to enable it—in the absence of special circumstances, such as the minority candidate running unopposed—usually to defeat the minority's preferred candidate."

The Court "observe[d] that the usual predictability of the majority's success distinguishes structural dilution from the mere loss of an occasional election." Thus, "a pattern of racial bloc voting that extends over a period of time is more probative of a claim that a district experiences legally significant polarization than are the results of a single election." Moreover, "in a district where elections are shown usually to be polarized, the fact that racially polarized voting is not present in one or a few individual elections [or] the success of a minority candidate in a particular election does not necessarily prove" that § 2 has not been violated. The Court majority held that the occasional election of minority candidates does not, by itself, defeat a § 2 claim, but two Justices (Brennan and **White**) concluded that "persistent proportional representation" will do so unless the plaintiffs can show that this "sustained success does not accurately reflect the minority group's ability to elect its preferred representatives."

Justice O'Connor (writing also for **Chief Justice Burger** and **Justices Powell** and **Rehnquist**) concurred only in the judgment. Her opinion conceded that the 1982 Act overrode *Bolden*'s "intent" test and adopted the "results" test of *White v. Regester*, but she also noted that § 2 "unequivocally disclaims the creation of a right of proportional representation. This disclaimer was essential to the compromise that resulted in passage of the amendment," she argued, citing the views of Senator Dole in the Senate committee report. Note that in 1982 Dole was the Senate Majority Leader, and no bill opposed by the Republicans could have been enacted, either because they controlled the Senate or (most likely, given liberal Republican defections) because their opposition could sustain a presidential veto.

Justice O'Connor argued that the Court's approach would press enforcement of the VRA toward proportional representation. Consider her hypothetical: a 1,000-person town has an African-American population of 30%, concentrated in one section of town. If the town council has four members, the configuration of districts could determine the number of African-American councilmembers (assuming racial bloc voting). Single-member districts could yield results ranging from two African-American representatives (if two of the districts had 60% African Americans in each, while the other two districts had none) to none (if the 30% African-American vote were evenly distributed through all four districts). At-large elections would likely yield no minority representation. Justice O'Connor agreed that the last two options might be challenged under the 1982 Act but posed the question: if the Act prohibits minority "vote dilution," what would an "undiluted" minority representation look like? Would it be proportional representation, as the Court suggested, or a variety of results, including an all-white council whose members competed for the African-American vote and catered to minority group desires? Justice O'Connor argued for a more variegated approach than the relatively more bright-line approach adopted by the Court majority. She would have disallowed claims in three districts where African Americans had enjoyed some electoral success since the 1970s and would have reversed the trial court as to those three districts.[20]

---

[20]   In *Holder v. Hall*, 512 U.S. 874 (1994), the Court held that § 2 provides no basis for a claim of racial vote dilution based on changing the size of a legislative body (e.g., whether a commission is made up of a single member or multiple members). Justice Thomas, joined by Justice Scalia, concurred in the judgment in *Holder* and launched a full-scale attack upon *Gingles*, arguing that its test is inconsistent with the text of § 2 and encourages racial gerrymandering. Justices Thomas and Scalia would have overruled *Gingles* and held that § 2 applies only to claims of discriminatory denial of the ballot or discriminatory processing of ballots, and not to vote dilution claims. In *League of United Latin Am. Citizens v. Perry*, 548 U.S. 399 (2006), a fractured Court applied the *Gingles* factors and concluded that at least one redrawn Texas congressional district violated § 2 by diluting the voting power of the Latino community.

A VOTING RIGHTS ACT PROBLEM

Problem 2-1. After the 1990 census, the state of North Carolina gained an additional seat in the House of Representatives (up from 11 to 12). The racial composition of the state was 78% white, 20% black, 1% Indian, and 1% predominantly Asian. The African-American population was relatively dispersed through the state, constituting a majority in only five of the state's 100 counties (all located in the Coastal Plain in the eastern part of the state). As of 1992, no African American had been elected to the House from North Carolina in almost a century.

(a) Assume that North Carolina redistricted after the 1990 census by creating a new Republican district and strengthening incumbents in surrounding districts. (Even though Democrats controlled the legislature, there was a Republican governor, and population growth had been in Republican areas.) Under this configuration, 12 whites would be elected in 1992. What are the odds that North Carolina could be successfully sued for violating § 2 of the VRA, as amended in 1982 and as interpreted in *Gingles*?

(b) Assume that North Carolina redistricted after the 1990 census by creating a new "majority-minority" district (namely, a district where a majority of the population consists of racial minorities) in the Coastal Plain. If there were racial bloc voting, an African American would probably be elected in 1992. African-American plaintiffs challenge the plan under § 2, nonetheless. Their argument is that there should have been two rather than one majority-minority district and that a second district could have been created in the central part of the state by using boundary lines no more irregular than those found elsewhere. Does this lawsuit have a chance under § 2?

(c) North Carolina had 40 counties covered by § 5 of the VRA, and, until *Shelby County*, any redistricting had to be precleared by the Department of Justice or the D.C. district court. Assume that the Department of Justice insisted on two rather than one majority-minority district, for the reasons suggested in part (b) of this problem. The North Carolina General Assembly went along with the suggestion and created two such districts. The majority-minority districts are Districts 1 and 12. To create District 12, the legislature snaked the district lines along Interstate 85; the district passed through 10 counties, cutting most of them in half, as it also did many towns and cities. It was contiguous but only barely so. In the 1992 elections, eight Democrats and four Republicans were elected, with the Democrats picking up the extra seat. Two of the eight Democrats were African American—from districts 1 and 12.

Republicans challenged this plan on the ground that it was a partisan gerrymander designed to minimize their representation. Population growth occurred in GOP areas, yet the Democratic legislature captured the extra seat for themselves. In another lawsuit, white voters in the odd-shaped District 12 challenged the plan because it "diluted" their votes on racial grounds. Should either of these lawsuits succeed? Write down your answers, and then read on.

3. Redistricting Designed to Ensure Minority Representation

SHAW V. RENO

United States Supreme Court, 1993.
509 U.S. 630, 113 S.Ct. 2816, 125 L.Ed. 2d 511.

JUSTICE O'CONNOR delivered the opinion of the Court.

[The North Carolina General Assembly's reapportionment of the state's 12 seats in the federal House of Representatives based on the 1990 census included one majority-black congressional district. After the U.S. Attorney General objected to the plan pursuant to § 5 of the VRA, the General Assembly revised the plan and created a second majority-black district. Plaintiffs challenged the revised plan as involving an unconstitutional racial gerrymander.]

The first of the two majority-black districts contained in the revised plan, District 1, is somewhat hook shaped. Centered in the northeast portion of the State, it moves southward until it tapers to a narrow band; then, with finger-like extensions, it reaches far into the southern-most part of the State near the South Carolina border. District 1 has been compared to a "Rorschach ink-blot test" and a "bug splattered on a windshield."

The second majority-black district, District 12, is even more unusually shaped. It is approximately 160 miles long and, for much of its length, no wider than the I-85 corridor. It winds in snake-like fashion through tobacco country, financial centers, and manufacturing areas "until it gobbles in enough enclaves of black neighborhoods." Northbound and southbound drivers on I-85 sometimes find themselves in separate districts in one county, only to "trade" districts when they enter the next county. Of the 10 counties through which District 12 passes, five are cut into three different districts; even towns are divided. At one point the district remains contiguous only because it intersects at a single point with two other districts before crossing over them. * * *

[Appellants, five residents of Durham County, two of whom live in District 12 and three of whom live in neighboring District 2,] alleged that the General Assembly deliberately "create[d] two Congressional Districts in which a majority of black voters was concentrated arbitrarily—without regard to any other considerations, such as compactness, contiguousness, geographical boundaries, or political subdivisions" with the purpose "to create Congressional Districts along racial lines" and to assure the election of two black representatives to Congress. [The lower courts denied relief.]

[II(B)] * * * [A]ppellants' claim that the State engaged in unconstitutional racial gerrymandering * * * strikes a powerful historical chord: It is unsettling how closely the North Carolina plan resembles the most egregious racial gerrymanders of the past. [Earlier, the Court had described such past racial gerrymandering, citing *Gomillion v. Lightfoot* and Alabama's change in Tuskegee's boundaries "from a square to an uncouth twenty-eight-sided figure." Plaintiffs' complaint alleging that gerrymandering voters into districts that are "so extremely irregular" that they can only be understood as "an effort to segregate the races for purposes of voting" presents a claim for which relief can be granted under the Equal Protection Clause.]

[III(A)] * * * The * * * central purpose [of the Equal Protection Clause] is to prevent the States from purposefully discriminating between individuals on the basis of race. *Washington v. Davis*, 426 U.S. 229 (1976). Laws that explicitly distinguish between individuals on racial grounds fall within the core of that prohibition.

No inquiry into legislative purpose is necessary when the racial classification appears on the face of the statute. Express racial classifications are immediately suspect because, "[a]bsent searching judicial inquiry . . ., there is simply no way of determining what classifications are 'benign' or 'remedial' and what classifications are in fact motivated by illegitimate notions of racial inferiority or simple racial politics." *Richmond v. J.A. Croson Co.*, 488 U.S. 469, 493 (1989) (plurality opinion); *id.* (Scalia, J., concurring in the judgment).

Classifications of citizens solely on the basis of race "are by their very nature odious to a free people whose institutions are founded upon the doctrine of equality." *Hirabayashi v. United States*, 320 U.S. 81, 100 (1943). They threaten to stigmatize individuals by reason of their membership in a racial group and to incite racial hostility. Accordingly, we have held that the Fourteenth Amendment requires state legislation that expressly distinguishes among citizens because of their race to be narrowly tailored to further a compelling governmental interest.

These principles apply not only to legislation that contains explicit racial distinctions, but also to those "rare" statutes that, although race neutral, are, on their face, "unexplainable on grounds other than race." *Village of Arlington Heights v. Metropolitan Housing Development Corp.*, 429 U.S. 252, 266 (1977). * * *

[III(B)] Appellants contend that redistricting legislation that is so bizarre on its face that it is "unexplainable on grounds other than race" demands the same close scrutiny that we give other state laws that classify citizens by race. Our voting rights precedents support that conclusion.

[In *Guinn v. United States*, 238 U. S. 347 (1915), the Court found a Fifteenth Amendment violation when a state adopted a literacy requirement with a " 'grandfather clause' applicable to individuals and their lineal descendants" entitled to vote on January 1, 1866. Although facially neutral, the Court concluded that the law "was invalid because, on its face, it could not be explained on grounds other than race."]

The Court applied the same reasoning to the "uncouth twenty-eight-sided" municipal boundary line at issue in *Gomillion*. Although the statute that redrew the city limits of Tuskegee was race neutral on its face, plaintiffs alleged that its effect was impermissibly to remove from the city virtually all black voters and no white voters. The Court reasoned:

> "If these allegations upon a trial remained uncontradicted or unqualified, the conclusion would be irresistible, tantamount for all practical purposes to a mathematical demonstration, that the legislation is solely concerned with segregating white and colored voters by fencing Negro citizens out of town so as to deprive them of their pre-existing municipal vote." * * *

The Court extended the reasoning of *Gomillion* to congressional districting in *Wright v. Rockefeller*, 376 U.S. 52 (1964). At issue in *Wright* were four districts contained in a New York apportionment statute. The plaintiffs alleged that the statute excluded nonwhites from one district and concentrated them in the other three. Every member of the Court assumed that the plaintiffs' allegation that the statute "segregate[d] eligible voters by race and place of origin" stated a constitutional claim. The Justices disagreed only as to whether the plaintiffs had carried their burden of proof at trial. The dissenters thought the unusual shape of the district lines could "be explained only in racial terms." The majority, however, accepted the District Court's finding that the plaintiffs had failed to establish that the districts were in fact drawn on racial lines. Although the boundary lines were somewhat irregular, the majority reasoned, they were not so bizarre as to permit of no other conclusion. Indeed, because most of the nonwhite voters lived together in one area, it would have been difficult to construct voting districts without concentrations of nonwhite voters.

Wright illustrates the difficulty of determining from the face of a single-member districting plan that it purposefully distinguishes between voters on the basis of race. A reapportionment statute typically does not classify persons at all; it classifies tracts of land, or addresses. Moreover, redistricting differs from other kinds of state decisionmaking in that the legislature always is *aware* of race when it draws district lines, just as it is aware of age, economic status, religious and political persuasion, and a variety of other demographic factors. That sort of race consciousness does not lead inevitably to impermissible race discrimination. As *Wright* demonstrates, when members of a racial group live together in one community, a reapportionment plan that concentrates members of the group in one district and excludes them from others may reflect wholly legitimate purposes. The district lines may be drawn, for example, to provide for compact districts of contiguous territory, or to maintain the integrity of political subdivisions.

The difficulty of proof, of course, does not mean that a racial gerrymander, once established, should receive less scrutiny under the Equal Protection Clause than other state legislation classifying citizens by race. * * * In some exceptional cases, a reapportionment plan may be so highly irregular that, on its face, it rationally cannot be understood as anything other than an effort to "segregat[e] . . . voters" on the basis of race. *Gomillion. Gomillion*, in which a tortured municipal boundary line was drawn to exclude black voters, was such a case. So, too, would be a case in which a State concentrated a dispersed minority population in a single district by disregarding traditional districting principles such as compactness, contiguity, and respect for political subdivisions. We emphasize that these criteria are important not because they are constitutionally required—they are not—but because they are objective factors that may serve to defeat a claim that a district has been gerrymandered on racial lines.

Put differently, we believe that reapportionment is one area in which appearances do matter. A reapportionment plan that includes in one district individuals who belong to the same race, but who are otherwise widely separated by geographical and political boundaries, and who may have little in common with one another but the color of their skin, bears an uncomfortable resemblance to political apartheid. It reinforces the perception that members of the same racial group— regardless of their age, education, economic status, or the community in which they live—think alike, share the same political interests, and will prefer the same candidates at the polls. * * * By perpetuating such notions, a racial gerrymander may exacerbate the very patterns of racial bloc voting that majority-minority districting is sometimes said to counteract.

The message that such districting sends to elected representatives is equally pernicious. When a district obviously is created solely to effectuate the perceived common interests of one racial group, elected officials are more likely to believe that their primary obligation is to represent only the members of that group, rather than their constituency as a whole. This is altogether antithetical to our system of representative democracy. * * *

For these reasons, we conclude that a plaintiff challenging a reapportionment statute under the Equal Protection Clause may state a claim by alleging that the legislation, though race-neutral on its face, rationally cannot be understood as anything other than an effort to separate voters into different districts on the basis of race, and that the separation lacks sufficient justification. It is unnecessary for us to decide whether or how a reapportionment plan that, on its face, can be explained in nonracial terms successfully could be challenged. Thus, we express no view as to whether "the intentional creation of majority-minority districts, without more" always gives rise to an equal protection claim. * * *

[III(C)] The dissenters make two * * * arguments that cannot be reconciled with our precedents. First, they suggest that a racial gerrymander of the sort alleged here is functionally equivalent to gerrymanders for nonracial purposes, such as political gerrymanders. * * * But nothing in our case law compels the conclusion that racial and political gerrymanders are subject to precisely the same constitutional scrutiny. In fact, our country's long and persistent history of racial discrimination in voting— as well as our Fourteenth Amendment jurisprudence, which always has reserved the strictest scrutiny for discrimination on the basis of race—would seem to compel the opposite conclusion.

Second, Justice Stevens argues that racial gerrymandering poses no constitutional difficulties when district lines are drawn to favor the minority, rather than the majority. We have made clear, however, that equal protection analysis "is not dependent on the race of those burdened or benefited by a particular classification." *Croson.* * * *

[IV] Justice Souter contends that exacting scrutiny of racial gerrymanders under the Fourteenth Amendment is inappropriate because reapportionment "nearly always require[s] some consideration of race for legitimate reasons." "As long as members of racial groups have [a] commonality of interest" and "racial bloc voting takes place," he argues, "legislators will have to take race into account" in order to comply with the Voting Rights Act. Justice Souter's reasoning is flawed.

* * * That racial bloc voting or minority political cohesion may be found to exist in *some* cases, of course, is no reason to treat *all* racial gerrymanders differently from other kinds of racial classification. Justice Souter apparently views racial gerrymandering of the type presented here as a special category of "benign" racial discrimination that should be subject to relaxed judicial review. As we have said, however, the very reason that the Equal Protection Clause demands strict scrutiny

of all racial classifications is because without it, a court cannot determine whether or not the discrimination truly is "benign." Thus, if appellants' allegations of a racial gerrymander are not contradicted on remand, the District Court must determine whether the General Assembly's reapportionment plan satisfies strict scrutiny. We therefore consider what that level of scrutiny requires in the reapportionment context.

The state appellees suggest that a covered jurisdiction may have a compelling interest in creating majority-minority districts in order to comply with the Voting Rights Act. * * *

[For example,] the state appellees contend that the General Assembly's revised plan was necessary * * * to avoid dilution of black voting strength in violation of § 2, as construed in *Thornburg v. Gingles*. In *Gingles* the Court considered a multimember redistricting plan for the North Carolina State Legislature. The Court held that members of a racial minority group claiming § 2 vote dilution through the use of multimember districts must prove three threshold conditions: that the minority group "is sufficiently large and geographically compact to constitute a majority in a single-member district," that the minority group is "politically cohesive," and that "the white majority votes sufficiently as a bloc to enable it . . . usually to defeat the minority's preferred candidate." * * *

Appellants maintain that the General Assembly's revised plan could not have been required by § 2. They contend that the State's black population is too dispersed to support two geographically compact majority-black districts, as the bizarre shape of District 12 demonstrates, and that there is no evidence of black political cohesion. They also contend that recent black electoral successes demonstrate the willingness of white voters in North Carolina to vote for black candidates. Appellants point out that blacks currently hold the positions of State Auditor, Speaker of the North Carolina House of Representatives, and chair of the North Carolina State Board of Elections. They also point out that in 1990 a black candidate defeated a white opponent in the Democratic Party run-off for a United States Senate seat before being defeated narrowly by the Republican incumbent in the general election. Appellants further argue that if § 2 did require adoption of North Carolina's revised plan, § 2 is to that extent unconstitutional. These arguments were not developed below, and the issues remain open for consideration on remand.

* * *

[V]   Racial classifications of any sort pose the risk of lasting harm to our society. They reinforce the belief, held by too many for too much of our history, that individuals should be judged by the color of their skin. Racial classifications with respect to voting carry particular dangers. Racial gerrymandering, even for remedial purposes, may balkanize us into competing racial factions; it threatens to carry us further from the goal of a political system in which race no longer matters—a goal that the Fourteenth and Fifteenth Amendments embody, and to which the Nation continues to aspire. It is for these reasons that race-based districting by our state legislatures demands close judicial scrutiny.

In this case, the Attorney General suggested that North Carolina could have created a reasonably compact second majority-minority district in the south-central to southeastern part of the State. We express no view as to whether appellants successfully could have challenged such a district under the Fourteenth Amendment. * * * Today we hold only that appellants have stated a claim under the Equal Protection Clause by alleging that the North Carolina General Assembly adopted a reapportionment scheme so irrational on its face that it can be understood only as an effort to segregate voters into separate voting districts because of their race, and that the separation lacks sufficient justification. If the allegation of racial gerrymandering remains uncontradicted, the District Court further must determine whether the North Carolina plan is narrowly tailored to further a compelling governmental interest. * * *

JUSTICE WHITE, with whom JUSTICE BLACKMUN and JUSTICE STEVENS join, dissenting.

* * * [I(A)] The grounds for my disagreement with the majority are simply stated: Appellants have not presented a cognizable claim, because they have not alleged a cognizable injury. [Justice White asserted that in no prior voting case alleging unfair districting had relief been granted without a showing that the state action in question had both been intended to dilute the complaining group's power and had such a substantial discriminatory effect that the group was essentially "shut out of the political process." This requirement of substantial discriminatory impact was justified by "the nature of the redistricting process," which is inherently partisan and in which politically salient factors such as race are inevitably taken into account.]

[I]t strains credulity to suggest that North Carolina's purpose in creating a second majority-minority district was to discriminate against members of the majority group by "impair[ing] or burden[ing their] opportunity . . . to participate in the political process." The State has made no mystery of its intent, which was to respond to the Attorney General's objections by improving the minority group's prospects of electing a candidate of its choice. I doubt that this constitutes a discriminatory purpose as defined in the Court's equal protection cases—i.e., an intent to aggravate "the unequal distribution of electoral power." But even assuming that it does, there is no question that appellants have not alleged the requisite discriminatory effects. Whites constitute roughly 76 percent of the total population and 79 percent of the voting age population in North Carolina. Yet, under the State's plan, they still constitute a voting majority in 10 (or 83 percent) of the 12 congressional districts. Though they might be dissatisfied at the prospect of casting a vote for a losing candidate—a lot shared by many, including a disproportionate number of minority voters—surely they cannot complain of discriminatory treatment.

[I(B)] * * * As I understand the [majority's theory], a redistricting plan that uses race to "segregate" voters by drawing "uncouth" lines is harmful in a way that a plan that uses race to distribute voters differently is not, for the former "bears an uncomfortable resemblance to political apartheid." The distinction is untenable.

Racial gerrymanders come in various shades: At-large voting schemes; the fragmentation of a minority group among various districts "so that it is a majority in none," otherwise known as "cracking"; the "stacking" of "a large minority population concentration . . . with a larger white population"; and, finally, the "concentration of [minority voters] into districts where they constitute an excessive majority," also called "packing." In each instance, race is consciously utilized by the legislature for electoral purposes; in each instance, we have put the plaintiff challenging the district lines to the burden of demonstrating that the plan was meant to, and did in fact, exclude an identifiable racial group from participation in the political process.

Not so, apparently, when the districting "segregates" by drawing odd-shaped lines.[7] In that case, we are told, such proof no longer is needed. Instead, it is the *State* that must rebut the allegation that race was taken into account, a fact that, together with the legislators' consideration of ethnic, religious, and other group characteristics, I had thought we practically took for granted. Part of the explanation for the majority's approach has to do, perhaps, with the emotions stirred by words such as "segregation" and "political apartheid." But their loose and imprecise use by today's majority has, I fear, led it astray. The consideration of race in "segregation" cases is no different than in other race-conscious districting; from the standpoint of the affected groups, moreover, the line-drawings all act in similar fashion. A plan that "segregates" being functionally indistinguishable from any of the other varieties of gerrymandering, we should be consistent in what we require from a claimant: Proof of discriminatory purpose and effect.

The other part of the majority's explanation of its holding is related to its simultaneous discomfort and fascination with irregularly shaped districts. * * *

[While] district irregularities may provide strong indicia of a potential gerrymander, they do no more than that. * * * Given two districts drawn on similar, race-based grounds, the one does not become more injurious than the other simply by virtue of being snake-like * * *. The majority's contrary view is perplexing in light of its concession that "compactness or attractiveness has never been held to constitute an independent federal constitutional requirement for state legislative districts." It is shortsighted as well, for a regularly shaped district can just as effectively effectuate racially discriminatory gerrymandering as an odd-shaped one. * * *

Limited by its own terms to cases involving unusually-shaped districts, the Court's approach nonetheless will unnecessarily hinder to some extent a State's voluntary effort to ensure a modicum of minority representation. This will be true in areas where the minority population is geographically dispersed. It also will be true where the minority population is not scattered but, for reasons unrelated to race— for example, incumbency protection—the State would rather not create the majority-minority district in its most "obvious" location[.] * * *

---

[7]   I borrow the term "segregate" from the majority, but, given its historical connotation, believe that its use is ill-advised. Nor is it a particularly accurate description of what has occurred. The majority-minority district that is at the center of the controversy is, according to the State, 54.71% African-American. Even if racial distribution was a factor, no racial group can be said to have been "segregated"—i.e., "set apart" or "isolate[d]." Webster's Collegiate Dictionary 1063 (9th ed. 1983).

[III] * * * [T]he Court's discussion of the level of scrutiny it requires warrants a few comments. I have no doubt that a State's compliance with the Voting Rights Act clearly constitutes a compelling interest. * * *

The Court * * * warns that the State's redistricting effort must be "narrowly tailored" to further its interest in complying with the law. It is evident to me, however, that what North Carolina did was precisely tailored to meet the objection of the Attorney General to its prior plan. Hence, I see no need for a remand at all, even accepting the majority's basic approach to this case.

* * * To the extent that no other racial group is injured, remedying a Voting Rights Act violation does not involve preferential treatment. It involves, instead, an attempt to *equalize* treatment, and to provide minority voters with an effective voice in the political process. * * *

[The dissent of JUSTICE BLACKMUN is omitted.]

JUSTICE STEVENS, dissenting.

* * * [T]wo critical facts in this case are undisputed: first, the shape of District 12 is so bizarre that it must have been drawn for the purpose of either advantaging or disadvantaging a cognizable group of voters; and, second, regardless of that shape, it *was* drawn for the purpose of facilitating the election of a second black representative from North Carolina.

These unarguable facts, which the Court devotes most of its opinion to proving, give rise to three constitutional questions: Does the Constitution impose a requirement of contiguity or compactness on how the States may draw their electoral districts? Does the Equal Protection Clause prevent a State from drawing district boundaries for the purpose of facilitating the election of a member of an identifiable group of voters? And, finally, if the answer to the second question is generally "No," should it be different when the favored group is defined by race? * * *

The first question is easy. There is no independent constitutional requirement of compactness or contiguity, and the Court's opinion (despite its many references to the shape of District 12) does not suggest otherwise. The existence of bizarre and uncouth district boundaries is powerful evidence of an ulterior purpose behind the shaping of those boundaries—usually a purpose to advantage the political party in control of the districting process. Such evidence will always be useful in cases that lack other evidence of invidious intent. In this case, however, we know what the legislators' purpose was: The North Carolina Legislature drew District 12 to include a majority of African-American voters. Evidence of the district's shape is therefore convincing, but it is also cumulative, and, for our purposes, irrelevant.

As for the second question, I believe that the Equal Protection Clause is violated when the State creates * * * uncouth district boundaries * * * for the sole purpose of making it more difficult for members of a minority group to win an election. The duty to govern impartially is abused when a group with power over the electoral process defines electoral boundaries solely to enhance its own political strength at the expense of any weaker group. That duty, however, is not violated when the majority acts to facilitate the election of a member of a group that lacks such power because it remains underrepresented in the state legislature—whether that group is defined by political affiliation, by common economic interests, or by religious, ethnic, or racial characteristics. The difference between constitutional and unconstitutional gerrymanders has nothing to do with whether they are based on assumptions about the groups they affect, but whether their purpose is to enhance the power of the group in control of the districting process at the expense of any minority group, and thereby to strengthen the unequal distribution of electoral power. When an assumption that people in a particular minority group (whether they are defined by the political party, religion, ethnic group, or race to which they belong) will vote in a particular way is used to benefit that group, no constitutional violation occurs. Politicians have always relied on assumptions that people in particular groups are likely to vote in a particular way when they draw new district lines, and I cannot believe that anything in today's opinion will stop them from doing so in the future.

Finally, we must ask whether otherwise permissible redistricting to benefit an underrepresented minority group becomes impermissible when the minority group is defined by its race. The Court today answers this question in the affirmative, and its answer is wrong. If it is permissible to draw boundaries to provide adequate representation for rural voters, for union members, for Hasidic Jews, for Polish Americans, or for Republicans, it necessarily follows that it is permissible to do the same thing for members of the very minority group whose history in the United States gave birth to the Equal Protection Clause. A contrary conclusion could only be described as perverse.

JUSTICE SOUTER, dissenting.

[I]   * * * Unlike other contexts in which we have addressed the State's conscious use of race, see, e.g., *Croson* (city contracting), electoral districting calls for decisions that nearly always require some consideration of race for legitimate reasons where there is a racially mixed population. As long as members of racial groups have the commonality of interest implicit in our ability to talk about concepts like "minority voting strength," and "dilution of minority votes," cf. *Thornburg v. Gingles*, and as long as racial bloc voting takes place, legislators will have to take race into account in order to avoid dilution of minority voting strength in the districting plans they adopt. One need look no further than the Voting Rights Act to understand that this may be required * * *.

A second distinction between districting and most other governmental decisions in which race has figured is that those other decisions using racial criteria characteristically occur in circumstances in which the use of race to the advantage of one person is necessarily at the obvious expense of a member of a different race. Thus, for example, awarding government contracts on a racial basis excludes certain firms from competition on racial grounds. * * *

In districting, by contrast, the mere placement of an individual in one district instead of another denies no one a right or benefit provided to others. All citizens may register, vote, and be represented. In whatever district, the individual voter has a right to vote in each election, and the election will result in the voter's representation. As we have held, one's constitutional rights are not violated merely because the candidate one supports loses the election or because a group (including a racial group) to which one belongs winds up with a representative from outside that group. It is true, of course, that one's vote may be more or less effective depending on the interests of the other individuals who are in one's district, and our cases recognize the reality that members of the same race often have shared interests. "Dilution" thus refers to the effects of districting decisions not on an individual's political power viewed in isolation, but on the political power of a group. This is the reason that the placement of given voters in a given district, even on the basis of race, does not, without more, diminish the effectiveness of the individual as a voter.

[II] Our different approaches to equal protection in electoral districting and nondistricting cases reflect these differences. There is a characteristic coincidence of disadvantageous effect and illegitimate purpose associated with the State's use of race in those situations in which it has immediately triggered at least heightened scrutiny (which every Member of the Court to address the issue has agreed must be applied even to race-based classifications designed to serve some permissible state interest). Presumably because the legitimate consideration of race in a districting decision is usually inevitable under the Voting Rights Act when communities are racially mixed, however, and because, without more, it does not result in diminished political effectiveness for anyone, we have not taken the approach of applying the usual standard of such heightened "scrutiny" to race-based districting decisions. * * *

[III] The Court offers no adequate justification for treating the narrow category of bizarrely shaped district claims differently from other districting claims.[9] The only justification I can imagine would be the preservation of "sound districting principles" such as compactness and contiguity. But * * * as the Court acknowledges, we have held that such principles are not constitutionally required, with the consequence that their absence cannot justify the distinct constitutional regime put in place by the Court today. * * * I would not respond to the seeming egregiousness of the redistricting now before us by untethering the concept of racial gerrymander in such a case from the concept of harm exemplified by dilution. * * *

NOTES ON SHAW AND THE CONUNDRUM OF REPRESENTATION AND RACE

1. *What, Exactly, Did North Carolina Do Wrong?* Justice O'Connor creates a new cause of action: even if there is no dilution of the vote of a group nor any exclusion from the ballot, the Equal Protection Clause is violated if district lines are drawn with *too much* consideration of race and *not enough* consideration of traditional line-drawing practices. The opinion takes a sort of "Goldilocks" approach to the districting porridge—not too hot, not too cold, just right—that has bedeviled commentators and lower courts in trying to figure out how to apply it.[21] Her opinion is made all the more opaque by her

---

[9] The Court says its new cause of action is justified by what I understand to be some ingredients of stigmatic harm and by a "threa[t] . . . to our system of representative democracy," both caused by the mere adoption of a districting plan with the elements I have described in the text. To begin with, the complaint nowhere alleges any type of stigmatic harm. Putting that to one side, it seems utterly implausible to me to presume, as the Court does, that North Carolina's creation of this strangely-shaped majority-minority district "generates" within the white plaintiffs here anything comparable to "a feeling of inferiority as to their status in the community that may affect their hearts and minds in a way unlikely ever to be undone." *Brown v. Board of Education*, 347 U.S. 483 (1954). As for representative democracy, I have difficulty seeing how it is threatened (indeed why it is not, rather, enhanced) by districts that are not even alleged to dilute anyone's vote.

[21] Scholarship analyzing *Shaw* and its aftermath has become its own cottage industry. For a small sampling of some of the literature, see, in addition to other sources cited in these notes, J. Morgan Kousser,

apparent rejection of more judicially administrable approaches to intent (such as forbidding all consideration of race or allowing the consideration of race consistent with the purposes of the VRA) or to traditional districting practices (note that she does not hold that practices such as maintaining contiguity and compactness are constitutionally required).

Suggesting that only majority-majority districts with uncouth lines and excessive considerations of race are vulnerable raises a number of questions. Might not the intention to create a majority-minority district be just as clear to white voters even if that district has a more "couth" shape? If the basis of *Shaw* is stigmatization and dignitary harm, would not the white voters in that district be injured in much the same way as the plaintiffs in *Shaw*? If the basis of *Shaw* is the pernicious effects upon the political process of the elected representative being beholden to a racial group, aren't those effects the same regardless of whether the district's shape is couth or uncouth?

In the wake of *Shaw*, Richard Pildes and Richard Niemi wrote: "In resisting the use of race *in this specific way*, *Shaw* requires that redistricting continue to be understood— and, perhaps more important, perceived—as implicating multiple values. Public officials must maintain this commitment to value pluralism, even when they legitimately and intentionally take race into account." *Expressive Harms, "Bizarre Districts," and Voting Rights: Evaluating Election-District Appearances after* Shaw v. Reno, 92 Mich. L. Rev. 483, 501 (1993). If that is so, however, why does the Court emphasize "couthness"? Isn't that a pretty crude marker for value pluralism? Also, it appears that the "uncouthness" of District 12 was the result not only of the state's effort to create a majority-minority district, but also the Democrats' desire to protect their incumbents. In that event, it appears that race did not completely dominate the redistricting process. Pildes and Niemi draw from Niemi's earlier work quantifying criteria to determine relative compactness of districts (considering their geographic dispersion, perimeter, and population distribution). One finding of their study is that on a quantitative compactness scale, North Carolina's District 12 was the least compact district in the country. Would it have been preferable for the Court to adopt some statistical requirements for compactness, contiguity, and other factors, much like it has used the one person, one vote principle to implement geographical redistricting?

2. *Questions Left Open by* Shaw. A number of subsequent cases began to clear up some of the issues left open in *Shaw*.

(a) *Who may challenge majority-minority districting?* In *United States v. Hays*, 515 U.S. 737 (1995), the Court held that white Louisianans who did not live in the challenged majority-minority Louisiana district lacked standing to bring the case because they had not shown that they had been subjected to a racial classification. And in *Virginia House of Delegates v. Bethune-Hill*, 139 S.Ct. 1945 (2019), the Court held that, when the (Democratic) state attorney general declined to appeal a ruling that state legislative district lines were unconstitutionally racially gerrymandered, the (Republican-controlled) lower house of the state legislature lacked standing to appeal, either in its own right or on behalf of the state.

Colorblind Injustice: Minority Voting Rights and the Undoing of the Second Reconstruction 366–455 (1999); W. Mark Crain, *The Constitutionality of Race-Conscious Redistricting: An Empirical Analysis*, 30 J. Leg. Stud. 193 (2001); Heather Gerken, *Understanding the Right to an Undiluted Vote*, 114 Harv. L. Rev. 1663 (2001); Grant Hayden, *Resolving the Dilemma of Minority Representation*, 92 Cal. L. Rev. 1589 (2004); Daniel Lowenstein, *You Don't Have to Be Liberal to Hate the Racial Gerrymandering Cases*, 50 Stan. L. Rev. 779 (1998).

(b) *What is the nature of the harm involved?* Justice O'Connor, in her plurality opinion in *Bush v. Vera*, 517 U.S. 952 (1996), wrote that some majority-minority districts "cause constitutional harm insofar as they convey the message that political identity is, or should be, predominantly racial." She labeled this an "expressive harm," which Justice Souter, in dissent, defined as "one that 'results from the idea or attitudes expressed through a governmental action, rather than from the more tangible or material consequences the action brings about'" (quoting Pildes & Niemi, *supra*). Why is expressive harm, rather than more concrete harm, sufficient in this context to constitute a constitutional claim?

(c) *To be subject to challenge, must the challenged majority-minority district have a bizarre shape?* In *Miller v. Johnson*, 515 U.S. 900 (1995), Justice Kennedy's majority opinion for a Court that remained closely divided answered this question in the negative: "Shape is relevant not because bizarreness is a necessary element of the constitutional wrong or a threshold requirement of proof, but because it may be persuasive circumstantial evidence that race for its own sake, and not other districting principles, was the legislature's dominant and controlling rationale in drawing its district lines. The logical implication * * * is that parties may rely on evidence other than bizarreness to establish race-based districting."

In *Bethune-Hill v. Virginia State Board of Elections*, 137 S.Ct. 788 (2017), the Court, again per Justice Kennedy, rejected the argument that a plaintiff seeking to show that race predominated in the drawing of district lines must show an actual conflict between the adopted plan and traditional districting principles such as compactness. Kennedy argued that, "Race may predominate even when a reapportionment plan respects traditional principles, * * * if '[r]ace was the criterion that, in the State's view, could not be compromised,' and race-neutral considerations 'came into play only after the race-based decision had been made'" (quoting *Shaw v. Hunt*, 517 U.S. 899 (1996)). A misshapen district "may be persuasive circumstantial evidence tending to show racial predomination," but "there may be cases where challengers will be able to establish racial predominance in the absence of an actual conflict by presenting direct evidence of the legislative purpose and intent or other compelling circumstantial evidence."

(d) *If bizarre shape is not a requirement, what identifies presumptively unconstitutional majority-minority districts?* Recall the debate in *Shaw v. Reno* about how the consideration of demographics, including race, is an inherent part of the redistricting process. If, as *Miller* and *Bethune-Hill* held, there is no requirement of bizarre configuration, what stops the *Shaw v. Reno* cause of action from invalidating not only all majority-minority districts, but any district (regardless of demographics) that was designed in part because of racial considerations? *Miller* announced a potentially important qualification:

> The courts, in assessing the sufficiency of a challenge to a districting plan, must be sensitive to the complex interplay of forces that enter a legislature's redistricting calculus. Redistricting legislatures will, for example, almost always be aware of racial demographics; but it does not follow that race predominates in the redistricting process. *Shaw v. Reno*. The distinction between being aware of racial considerations and being motivated by them may be difficult to make. This evidentiary difficulty, together with the sensitive nature of redistricting and the presumption of good faith that must be accorded legislative enactments, requires courts to exercise extraordinary caution in

adjudicating claims that a state has drawn district lines on the basis of race. The plaintiff's burden is to show, either through circumstantial evidence of a district's shape and demographics or more direct evidence going to legislative purpose, that race was the predominant factor motivating the legislature's decision to place a significant number of voters within or without a particular district. To make this showing, a plaintiff must prove that the legislature subordinated traditional race-neutral districting principles, including but not limited to compactness, contiguity, respect for political subdivisions or communities defined by actual shared interests, to racial considerations. Where these or other race-neutral considerations are the basis for redistricting legislation, and are not subordinated to race, a state can "defeat a claim that a district has been gerrymandered on racial lines." *Shaw v. Reno.*

Is this consistent with the Court's general approach to proving discriminatory intent under the Equal Protection Clause (see notes following *Mobile v. Bolden, supra*)? Will it not require intensive case-by-case review of every majority-minority district? If, as is commonly asserted, redistricting involves a host of complex and interactive questions, including potentially hundreds of small decisions about precisely where to draw each little segment of the lines, is it likely that one "predominant" motive can be isolated after the fact? Moreover, if the harm in these cases concerns social messages and perceptions arising from redistricting lines, shouldn't liability turn on the public processes and outcomes (i.e., maps) of redistricting rather than whether, at the end of litigation some years later, a judge decides race was, or was not, the predominant motive? Consider Richard Pildes, *Principled Limitations on Racial and Partisan Redistricting*, 106 Yale L.J. 2505, 2540 (1997): "Judicial opinions in these cases, as well as editorial pages, reprint maps of the districts, not transcripts of political processes, for a reason. Social perceptions about the 'excessive' role of race are more likely attuned to objective characteristics of districts, such as their shapes, rather than the mysteries of intent."

(e) *How does the strict scrutiny analysis work in majority-minority districting cases?* As noted in *Shaw v. Reno* and subsequent cases, a finding that race predominated in drawing district lines does not resolve the case; it simply triggers strict scrutiny. How does that scrutiny play out in the majority-minority districting context? In a series of cases, the Court has "assumed" without deciding that compliance with the Voting Rights Act constitutes a compelling state interest for equal protection purposes. *Miller v. Johnson*; *Shaw v. Hunt*; *Bush v. Vera*; *Bethune-Hill v. Virginia State Board of Elections*; *Cooper v. Harris*, 137 S.Ct. 1455 (2017).

But the identification (or assumption) of a compelling state interest is only half of the strict scrutiny test. The other half is narrow tailoring. Here, the Court has taken a somewhat more lax approach than in other equal protection contexts. As Justice Breyer wrote for the Court in *Alabama Legislative Black Caucus v. Alabama*, 135 S.Ct. 1257 (2015), "the narrow tailoring requirement insists only that the legislature have a strong basis in evidence in support of the (race-based) choice that it has made. This standard * * * does not demand that a State's actions actually be necessary to achieve a compelling state interest in order to be constitutionally valid. And legislators may have a strong basis in evidence to use racial classifications in order to comply with a statute when they have *good reasons* to believe such use is required, even if a court does not find that the actions were necessary for statutory compliance" (internal citations and quotation marks omitted). The Court reiterated that formulation of the narrow tailoring prong in both *Bethune-Hill v. Virginia State Board of Elections* and *Cooper v. Harris*. In *Bethune-Hill*,

Justice Thomas complained in dissent that this "approach to narrow tailoring—deferring to a State's belief that it has good reasons to use race—is 'strict' in name only."

What it means for a state to have good reasons to believe that the VRA requires the use of race-based districting depends on which portion of the VRA is at issue. In cases arising before *Shelby County*, states asserted a compelling state interest in having their redistricting plans precleared by the Department of Justice under § 5 of the VRA. In *Miller*, the Court interpreted § 5 narrowly, asserting that it only authorizes DOJ to withhold preclearance when a redistricting plan constitutes a "retrogression" in minority voting power—that is, when it reduces minority voting strength relative to the appropriate benchmark year. Because the Georgia plan at issue in *Miller* did not constitute a retrogression, DOJ was wrong to deny it preclearance, and therefore there was not good reason to believe that failure to engage in race-based districting would lead to a failure to receive preclearance. The Court reiterated this holding with respect to § 5 in *Shaw v. Hunt* and in the plurality opinion in *Bush v. Vera*.

Alternatively, states may fear running afoul of VRA § 2's prohibition of vote dilution. Here, the Court turns to the three conditions for demonstrating § 2 vote dilution that it laid out in *Thornburg v. Gingles*: (1) the minority group must be large enough and compact enough to constitute a majority in a reasonably configured district; (2) the minority group must be politically cohesive; and (3) the district's white majority must vote sufficiently as a bloc so as usually to defeat the minority group's preferred candidate. In *Cooper v. Harris*, the Court held that, "If a State has good reason to think that all the '*Gingles* preconditions' are met, then so too it has good reason to believe that § 2 requires drawing a majority-minority district."

(f) *How large must the minority population be to be considered "sufficiently large and geographically compact to constitute a majority in a single-member district"?* In *Bartlett v. Strickland*, 556 U.S. 1 (2009), the minority voters argued that crossover majority voters could provide them the support they needed to elect their preferred candidate so they could attack a new districting plan that split African-American voters into two districts even though their numbers had fallen below 50% in the previous district. A plurality of the Court, led by Justice Kennedy, held that a party asserting a claim under § 2 must show that the minority population in the potential district is greater than 50%.

(g) *Nonjusticiability redux.* Recall that under the regime of *Colegrove v. Green*, federal courts were generally to stay out of "political thickets" involving state legislative apportionment—with an exception for cases involving intentional discrimination against racial minorities, who could invoke the specific protections of the Fifteenth Amendment (rather than merely the general protection of the Equal Protection Clause of the Fourteenth Amendment) and, at least in some cases, could plausibly claim that they had been singled out as identified individuals, not simply as members of a group (*Gomillion*). *Baker v. Carr* and *Reynolds v. Sims* changed all that—or did they? Could *Baker* and *Reynolds* simply be understood as allowing federal courts to hear state apportionment cases invoking equal protection only in the context where a simple, administrable standard—one person, one vote—was available? Contrast *Shaw v. Reno*'s allowance of race to be taken into account in ensuring minority representation so long as it is not taken into account too much. Should the Supreme Court's willingness to consider open-ended equality claims to state apportionment decisions be limited to unequal population claims (*Reynolds*) and race claims (*Gomillion* and *Shaw*)? What about apportionment designed to ensure the continued success of the political party currently in power, an even thicker political thicket and the topic of our next subsection?

C. POLITICAL GERRYMANDERING

In *Karcher v. Daggett*, 462 U.S. 725 (1983) (discussed above in § 1(A)(1)), the plaintiffs who challenged the New Jersey congressional districting argued not only that it violated the one person, one vote principle (the claim on which they won), but also that it was the product of an impermissible partisan gerrymander. In his concurrence, Justice Stevens, returning to themes from his concurrence in *City of Mobile v. Bolden* (see § 1(B)(1)), argued that the indications of a political gerrymander "certainly strengthen my conclusion that the New Jersey plan violates the Equal Protection Clause." *Karcher*, 462 U.S. at 762 (Stevens, J., concurring). He explained that, "In evaluating equal protection challenges to districting plans, just as in resolving such attacks on other forms of discriminatory action, I would consider whether the plan has a significant adverse impact on an identifiable political group, whether the plan has objective indicia of irregularity, and then, whether the State is able to produce convincing evidence that the plan nevertheless serves neutral, legitimate interests of the community as a whole." *Id.* at 751. In this case, the New Jersey map was sufficiently "uncouth" and "bizarre" as to "prompt an inquiry into the process that led to its adoption." *Id.* at 762–63. Conducting that inquiry, Stevens found that:

> The plan was sponsored by the leadership in the Democratic Party, which controlled both houses of the state legislature as well as the Governor's office, and was signed into law the day before the inauguration of a Republican Governor. The legislators never formally explained the guidelines used in formulating their plan or in selecting it over other available plans. Several [other plans] contained districts that were more nearly equal in population, more compact, and more consistent with subdivision boundaries[.] * * * [T]he record indicates that the decisionmaking process leading to adoption of the challenged plan was far from neutral. It was designed to increase the number of Democrats, and to decrease the number of Republicans, that New Jersey's voters would send to Congress in future years. * * *

Although only Justice Stevens would have relied on this rationale in *Karcher*, his colleagues would be forced to grapple with the question of partisan gerrymandering in the coming years.

In *Davis v. Bandemer*, 478 U.S. 109 (1986), six of the nine justices thought that claims that a partisan gerrymander violated the Equal Protection Clause were justiciable, but they could not agree on the standard to be applied in adjudicating those claims. Justice White's plurality opinion, joined by Justices Brennan, Marshall, and Blackmun, argued that "unconstitutional discrimination occurs only when the electoral system is arranged in a manner that will consistently degrade a voter's or a group of voters' influence on the political process as a whole." For those four justices, the evidence of a single election could not prove unconstitutional partisan gerrymandering, and they thus upheld the districts at issue. Justice Powell, joined in dissent by Justice Stevens, sought to apply a looser test. Relying on Justice Stevens' *Karcher* concurrence, Powell suggested that a number of criteria should be looked at as evidence of unconstitutional partisan gerrymandering, including the shapes of the districts, the extent to which the districts adhered to established political subdivision boundaries, and the legislative procedures by which the districts were created. Applying this test, Powell and Stevens would have struck down the districts at issue.

In an opinion concurring in the judgment, Justice O'Connor, joined by Chief Justice Burger and Justice Rehnquist, argued that challenges to partisan gerrymandering raised a nonjusticiable political question. Importantly, O'Connor suggested that no judicially manageable standard for resolving claims of unconstitutional partisan gerrymandering could be identified. (The fact that the six justices arguing for justiciability could not agree among themselves on what that standard might be undoubtedly lent some heft to this claim.)

Because six justices thought that partisan gerrymandering claims were justiciable, *Bandemer* fostered litigation in the lower courts. But because the plurality defined the cause of action so narrowly (as well as somewhat vaguely), virtually no redress for political gerrymandering resulted. In *Vieth v. Jubelirer*, 541 U.S. 267 (2004), the Court reconsidered *Bandemer*, but could reach no definitive conclusion: a four-justice plurality (Justice Scalia, joined by Chief Justice Rehnquist and Justices O'Connor and Thomas) would have held partisan gerrymandering claims nonjusticiable; four dissenters, writing three opinions (Justice Stevens; Justice Souter joined by Justice Ginsburg; and Justice Breyer) would have held them justiciable and applied different tests in evaluating them; and Justice Kennedy split the difference. In an opinion concurring in the judgment, Kennedy wrote that no one had yet presented judicially manageable standards for adjudicating partisan gerrymandering claims, but that did not mean that there were no such standards. "There are * * * weighty arguments for holding cases like these to be nonjusticiable; and those arguments may prevail in the long run. In my view, however, the arguments are not so compelling that they require us now to bar all future claims of injury from a partisan gerrymander. * * * That no [judicially manageable] standard has emerged in this case should not be taken to prove that none will emerge in the future. Where important rights are involved, the impossibility of full analytical satisfaction is reason to err on the side of caution."

For the remainder of Justice Kennedy's tenure, partisan gerrymandering cases remained in this limbo, with a majority of justices nominally committed to the proposition that they were or might be justiciable, but without ever identifying a standard that Kennedy considered judicially manageable. In *League of United Latin Am. Citizens v. Perry*, 548 U.S. 399 (2006) (*LULAC*), Kennedy again concluded that the appellants had not proffered a workable approach to political gerrymandering claims (they did, however win on a VRA § 2 claim). Justice Scalia, joined by Justice Thomas, reiterated that such claims should be nonjusticiable; Justice Stevens, joined by Justice Breyer, argued that the political gerrymander at issue was both justiciable and unconstitutional. The two new justices, Chief Justice Roberts and Justice Alito, agreed with Kennedy that no judicially manageable standard had been presented here and explicitly left open the question of whether partisan gerrymandering clams were justiciable at all, noting that the issue had not been argued in the case. Justice Souter, joined by Justice Ginsburg, treated the political gerrymandering claim as one that the Court had, for all practical purposes, ducked, as if it had determined that certiorari had been improvidently granted.

A little over a decade later, the Court ducked again. In *Gill v. Whitford*, 138 S.Ct. 1916 (2018), the Court held that the plaintiffs had failed to demonstrate that they had personal stakes in the outcome of the case and therefore had failed to demonstrate standing to challenge the districts. Per Chief Justice Roberts, the Court vacated the lower court's finding that Wisconsin's Republican gerrymander was unconstitutional and remanded to give the plaintiffs the opportunity to demonstrate standing by demonstrating that their votes had been diluted by the gerrymander. In *Benisek v. Lamone*, 138 S.Ct. 1942 (2018), a brief per curiam opinion issued the same day as *Gill*, the Court simply affirmed the lower court's denial of a preliminary injunction against Maryland's Democratic gerrymander, allowing the gerrymandered map to be used for the 2018 elections. Without reaching the underlying merits, the Court held that the trial court did not abuse its discretion in denying the injunction. At the end of the Term in which both of those cases were decided, Justice Kennedy retired and was replaced by Justice Kavanaugh.

RUCHO V. COMMON CAUSE
United States Supreme Court, 2019.
___ U.S. ___, 139 S.Ct. 2484, 204 L.Ed.2d 931.

CHIEF JUSTICE ROBERTS delivered the opinion of the Court [joined by JUSTICES THOMAS, ALITO, GORSUCH, and KAVANAUGH].

Voters and other plaintiffs in North Carolina and Maryland challenged their States' congressional districting maps as unconstitutional partisan gerrymanders. The North Carolina plaintiffs complained that the State's districting plan discriminated against Democrats; the Maryland plaintiffs complained that their State's plan discriminated against Republicans. * * * These cases require us to consider once again whether claims of excessive partisanship in districting are "justiciable"—that is, properly suited for resolution by the federal courts. This Court has not previously struck down a districting plan as an unconstitutional partisan gerrymander, and has struggled without success over the past several decades to discern judicially manageable standards for deciding such claims. The districting plans at issue here are highly partisan, by any measure. The question is whether the courts below appropriately exercised judicial power when they found them unconstitutional as well.

[I(A)] The first case [*Rucho v. Common Cause*] involves a challenge to the congressional redistricting plan enacted by the Republican-controlled North Carolina General Assembly in 2016. The Republican legislators leading the redistricting effort instructed their mapmaker to use political data to draw a map that would produce a congressional delegation of ten Republicans and three Democrats. As one of the two Republicans chairing the redistricting committee stated, "I think electing Republicans is better than electing Democrats. So I drew this map to help foster what I think is better for the country." He further explained that the map was drawn with the aim of electing ten Republicans and three Democrats because he did "not believe it [would be] possible to draw a map with 11 Republicans and 2 Democrats." One Democratic state senator objected that entrenching the 10–3 advantage for Republicans was not "fair, reasonable, [or] balanced" because, as recently as 2012, "Democratic congressional candidates had received more votes on a statewide basis than Republican candidates." The General Assembly was not swayed by that objection and approved the 2016 Plan by a party-line vote.

In November 2016, North Carolina conducted congressional elections using the 2016 Plan, and Republican candidates won 10 of the 13 congressional districts. In the 2018 elections, Republican candidates won nine congressional districts, while Democratic candidates won three. The Republican candidate narrowly prevailed in the remaining district, but the State Board of Elections called a new election after allegations of fraud. * * *

[I(B)] The second case before us is *Lamone v. Benisek*. In 2011, the Maryland Legislature—dominated by Democrats—undertook to redraw the lines of that State's eight congressional districts. The Governor at the time, Democrat Martin O'Malley, led the process. He appointed a redistricting committee to help redraw the map, and asked Congressman Steny Hoyer, who has described himself as a "serial gerrymanderer," to advise the committee. The Governor later testified that his aim was to "use the redistricting process to change the overall composition of Maryland's congressional delegation to 7 Democrats and 1 Republican by flipping" one district. "[A] decision was made to go for the Sixth," which had been held by a Republican for nearly two decades. To achieve the required equal population among districts, only about 10,000 residents needed to be removed from that district. The 2011 Plan accomplished that by moving roughly 360,000 voters out of the Sixth District and moving 350,000 new voters in. Overall, the Plan reduced the number of registered Republicans in the Sixth District by about 66,000 and increased the number of registered Democrats by about 24,000. The map was adopted by a party-line vote. It was used in the 2012 election and succeeded in flipping the Sixth District. A Democrat has held the seat ever since. * * *

[Plaintiffs in both jurisdictions sued, alleging that the districting plans violated equal protection, the First Amendment, and Article I. In both cases, the plaintiffs won before the district court.]

[II(A)] * * * The question here is whether there is an "appropriate role for the Federal Judiciary" in remedying the problem of partisan gerrymandering—whether such claims are claims of *legal* right, resolvable according to *legal* principles, or political questions that must find their resolution elsewhere.

[II(B)] Partisan gerrymandering is nothing new. Nor is frustration with it. The practice was known in the Colonies prior to Independence, and the Framers were familiar with it at the time of the drafting and ratification of the Constitution. During the very first congressional elections, George Washington and his Federalist allies accused Patrick Henry of trying to gerrymander Virginia's districts against their candidates—in particular James Madison, who ultimately prevailed over fellow future President James Monroe. * * *

In 1812, Governor of Massachusetts and future Vice President Elbridge Gerry notoriously approved congressional districts that the legislature had drawn to aid the Democratic-Republican Party. The moniker "gerrymander" was born when an outraged Federalist newspaper observed that one of the misshapen districts resembled a salamander. * * *

The Framers addressed the election of Representatives to Congress in the Elections Clause. Art. I, § 4, cl. 1. That provision assigns to state legislatures the power to prescribe the "Times, Places and Manner of holding Elections" for Members of Congress, while giving Congress the power to "make or alter" any such regulations. * * *

Congress has regularly exercised its Elections Clause power, including to address partisan gerrymandering. The Apportionment Act of 1842, which required single-member districts for the first time, specified that those districts be "composed of contiguous territory," Act of June 25, 1842, ch. 47, 5 Stat. 491, in "an attempt to forbid the practice of the gerrymander." Later statutes added requirements of compactness and equality of population. Act of Jan. 16, 1901, ch. 93, § 3, 31 Stat. 733; Act of Feb. 2, 1872, ch. 11, § 2, 17 Stat. 28. (Only the single member district requirement remains in place today. 2 U.S.C. § 2c.) Congress also used its Elections Clause power in 1870, enacting the first comprehensive federal statute dealing with elections as a way to enforce the Fifteenth Amendment. Force Act of 1870, ch. 114, 16 Stat. 140. Starting in the 1950s, Congress enacted a series of laws to protect the right to vote through measures such as the suspension of literacy tests and the prohibition of English-only elections. See, *e.g.*, 52 U.S.C. § 10101 *et seq.* [the Voting Rights Act].

Appellants suggest that, through the Elections Clause, the Framers set aside electoral issues such as the one before us as questions that only Congress can resolve. See *Baker*. We do not agree. In two areas—one-person, one-vote and racial gerrymandering—our cases have held that there is a role for the courts with respect to at least some issues that could arise from a State's drawing of congressional districts. See *Wesberry v. Sanders*; *Shaw v. Reno* (*Shaw I*). * * *

[II(C)] Courts have * * * been called upon to resolve a variety of questions surrounding districting. Early on, doubts were raised about the competence of the federal courts to resolve those questions. See *Wood v. Broom*; *Colegrove v. Green*. * * *

[The Court discussed the evolution of its one person, one vote jurisprudence and its racial gerrymandering jurisprudence, both of which are discussed earlier in this Chapter.]

Partisan gerrymandering claims have proved far more difficult to adjudicate. The basic reason is that, while it is illegal for a jurisdiction to depart from the one-person, one-vote rule, or to engage in racial discrimination in districting, "a jurisdiction may engage in constitutional political gerrymandering." *Hunt v. Cromartie*.

To hold that legislators cannot take partisan interests into account when drawing district lines would essentially countermand the Framers' decision to entrust districting to political entities. The "central problem" is not determining whether a jurisdiction has engaged in partisan gerrymandering. It is "determining when political gerrymandering has gone too far." *Vieth.* * * *

[The Court then summarized the line of cases from *Davis v. Bandemer* through *Gill.*]

As we summed up last Term in *Gill,* our "considerable efforts * * * leave unresolved whether . . . claims [of legal right] may be brought in cases involving allegations of partisan gerrymandering." Two "threshold questions" remained: standing, which we addressed in *Gill,* and "whether [such] claims are justiciable."

[III(A)] In considering whether partisan gerrymandering claims are justiciable, we are mindful of Justice Kennedy's counsel in *Vieth*: Any standard for resolving such claims must be grounded in a "limited and precise rationale" and be "clear, manageable, and politically neutral." An important reason for those careful constraints is that, as a Justice with extensive experience in state and local politics put it, "[t]he opportunity to control the drawing of electoral boundaries through the legislative process of apportionment is a critical and traditional part of politics in the United States." *Bandemer* (opinion of O'Connor, J.). An expansive standard requiring "the correction of all election district lines drawn for partisan reasons would commit federal and state courts to unprecedented intervention in the American political process," *Vieth* (opinion of Kennedy, J.).

As noted, the question is one of degree: How to "provid[e] a standard for deciding how much partisan dominance is too much." *LULAC* (opinion of Kennedy, J.). And it is vital in such circumstances that the Court act only in accord with especially clear standards: "With uncertain limits, intervening courts—even when proceeding with best intentions—would risk assuming political, not legal, responsibility for a process that often produces ill will and distrust." *Vieth* (opinion of Kennedy, J.). If federal courts are to "inject [themselves] into the most heated partisan issues" by adjudicating partisan gerrymandering claims, *Bandemer* (opinion of O'Connor, J.), they must be armed with a standard that can reliably differentiate unconstitutional from "constitutional political gerrymandering." *Cromartie.*

[III(B)] Partisan gerrymandering claims rest on an instinct that groups with a certain level of political support should enjoy a commensurate level of political power and influence. Explicitly or implicitly, a districting map is alleged to be unconstitutional because it makes it too difficult for one party to translate statewide support into seats in the legislature. But such a claim is based on a "norm that does not exist" in our electoral system—"statewide elections for representatives along party lines." *Bandemer* (opinion of O'Connor, J.).

Partisan gerrymandering claims invariably sound in a desire for proportional representation. As Justice O'Connor put it, such claims are based on "a conviction that the greater the departure from proportionality, the more suspect an apportionment plan becomes." "Our cases, however, clearly foreclose any claim that the Constitution requires proportional representation or that legislatures in reapportioning must draw district lines to come as near as possible to allocating seats to the contending parties in proportion to what their anticipated statewide vote will be."

The Founders certainly did not think proportional representation was required. For more than 50 years after ratification of the Constitution, many States elected their congressional representatives through at-large or "general ticket" elections. Such States typically sent single-party delegations to Congress. * * *

Unable to claim that the Constitution requires proportional representation outright, plaintiffs inevitably ask the courts to make their own political judgment about how much representation particular political parties *deserve*—based on the votes of their supporters—and to rearrange the challenged districts to achieve that end. But federal courts are not equipped to apportion political power as a matter of fairness, nor is there any basis for concluding that they were authorized to do so. As Justice Scalia put it for the plurality in *Vieth*:

> " 'Fairness' does not seem to us a judicially manageable standard. . . . Some criterion more solid and more demonstrably met than that seems to us necessary to enable the state legislatures to discern the limits of their districting discretion, to meaningfully constrain the discretion of the courts, and to win public acceptance for the courts' intrusion into a process that is the very foundation of democratic decisionmaking."

The initial difficulty in settling on a "clear, manageable and politically neutral" test for fairness is that it is not even clear what fairness looks like in this context. There is a large measure of "unfairness" in any winner-take-all system. Fairness may mean a greater number of competitive districts. Such a claim seeks to undo packing and cracking so that supporters of the disadvantaged party have a better shot at electing their preferred candidates. But making as many districts as possible more competitive could be a recipe for disaster for the disadvantaged party. As Justice White has pointed out, "[i]f all or most of the districts are competitive . . . even a narrow statewide preference for either party would produce an overwhelming majority for the winning party in the state legislature." *Bandemer* (plurality opinion).

On the other hand, perhaps the ultimate objective of a "fairer" share of seats in the congressional delegation is most readily achieved by yielding to the gravitational pull of proportionality and engaging in cracking and packing, to ensure each party its "appropriate" share of "safe" seats. Such an approach, however, comes at the expense of competitive districts and of individuals in districts allocated to the opposing party.

Or perhaps fairness should be measured by adherence to "traditional" districting criteria, such as maintaining political subdivisions, keeping communities of interest together, and protecting incumbents. But protecting incumbents, for example, enshrines a particular partisan distribution. And the "natural political geography" of a State—such as the fact that urban electoral districts are often dominated by one political party—can itself lead to inherently packed districts. As Justice Kennedy has explained, traditional criteria such as compactness and contiguity "cannot promise political neutrality when used as the basis for relief. Instead, it seems, a decision under these standards would unavoidably have significant political effect, whether intended or not." *Vieth* (opinion concurring in judgment).

Deciding among just these different visions of fairness (you can imagine many others) poses basic questions that are political, not legal. There are no legal standards discernible in the Constitution for making such judgments, let alone limited and precise standards that are clear, manageable, and politically neutral. Any judicial decision on what is "fair" in this context would be an "unmoored determination" of the sort characteristic of a political question beyond the competence of the federal courts.

And it is only after determining how to define fairness that you can even begin to answer the determinative question: "How much is too much?" At what point does permissible partisanship become unconstitutional? If compliance with traditional districting criteria is the fairness touchstone, for example, how much deviation from those criteria is constitutionally acceptable and how should mapdrawers prioritize competing criteria? Should a court "reverse gerrymander" other parts of a State to counteract "natural" gerrymandering caused, for example, by the urban concentration of one party? If a districting plan protected half of the incumbents but redistricted the rest into head to head races, would that be constitutional? A court would have to rank the relative importance of those traditional criteria and weigh how much deviation from each to allow.

If a court instead focused on the respective number of seats in the legislature, it would have to decide the ideal number of seats for each party and determine at what point deviation from that balance went too far. If a 5–3 allocation corresponds most closely to statewide vote totals, is a 6–2 allocation permissible, given that legislatures have the authority to engage in a certain degree of partisan gerrymandering? Which seats should be packed and which cracked? Or if the goal is as many competitive districts as possible, how close does the split need to be for the district to be considered competitive? Presumably not all districts could qualify, so how to choose? Even assuming the court knew which version of fairness to be looking for, there are no discernible and manageable standards for deciding whether there has been a violation. The questions are "unguided and ill suited to the development of judicial standards," *Vieth* (plurality opinion), and "results from one gerrymandering case to the next would likely be disparate and inconsistent," *id.* (opinion of Kennedy, J.).

Appellees contend that if we can adjudicate one-person, one-vote claims, we can also assess partisan gerrymandering claims. But the one-person, one-vote rule is relatively easy to administer as a matter of math. The same cannot be said of partisan gerrymandering claims, because the Constitution supplies no objective measure for assessing whether a districting map treats a political party fairly. It hardly follows from the principle that each person must have an equal say in the election of representatives that a person is entitled to have his political party achieve representation in some way commensurate to its share of statewide support.

More fundamentally, "vote dilution" in the one-person, one-vote cases refers to the idea that each vote must carry equal weight. In other words, each representative must be accountable to (approximately) the same number of constituents. That requirement does not extend to political parties. It does not mean that each party must be influential in proportion to its number of supporters. As we stated unanimously in *Gill*, "this Court is not responsible for vindicating generalized partisan preferences. The Court's constitutionally prescribed role is to vindicate the individual rights of the people appearing before it."

Nor do our racial gerrymandering cases provide an appropriate standard for assessing partisan gerrymandering. "[N]othing in our case law compels the conclusion that racial and political gerrymanders are subject to precisely the same constitutional scrutiny. In fact, our country's long and persistent history of racial discrimination in voting—as well as our Fourteenth Amendment jurisprudence, which always has reserved the strictest scrutiny for discrimination on the basis of race—would seem to compel the opposite conclusion." *Shaw I.* Unlike partisan gerrymandering claims, a racial gerrymandering claim does not ask for a fair share of political power and influence, with all the justiciability conundrums that entails. It asks instead for the elimination of a racial classification. A partisan gerrymandering claim cannot ask for the elimination of partisanship.

[IV] Appellees and the dissent propose a number of "tests" for evaluating partisan gerrymandering claims, but none meets the need for a limited and precise standard that is judicially discernible and manageable. And none provides a solid grounding for judges to take the extraordinary step of reallocating power and influence between political parties.

[IV(A)] The *Common Cause* District Court concluded that all but one of the districts in North Carolina's 2016 Plan violated the Equal Protection Clause by intentionally diluting the voting strength of Democrats. In reaching that result the court first required the plaintiffs to prove "that a legislative mapdrawer's predominant purpose in drawing the lines of a particular district was to 'subordinate adherents of one political party and entrench a rival party in power.'" The District Court next required a showing "that the dilution of the votes of supporters of a disfavored party in a particular district—by virtue of cracking or packing—is likely to persist in subsequent elections such that an elected representative from the favored party in the district will not feel a need to be responsive to constituents who support the disfavored party." Finally, after a prima facie showing of partisan vote dilution, the District Court shifted the burden to the defendants to prove that the discriminatory effects are "attributable to a legitimate state interest or other neutral explanation."

The District Court's "predominant intent" prong is borrowed from the racial gerrymandering context. In racial gerrymandering cases, we rely on a "predominant intent" inquiry to determine whether race was, in fact, the reason particular district boundaries were drawn the way they were. If district lines were drawn for the purpose of separating racial groups, then they are subject to strict scrutiny because "race-based decisionmaking is inherently suspect." *Miller.* But determining that lines were drawn on the basis of partisanship does not indicate that the districting was improper. A permissible intent—securing partisan advantage—does not become constitutionally impermissible, like racial discrimination, when that permissible intent "predominates."

The District Court tried to limit the reach of its test by requiring plaintiffs to show, in addition to predominant partisan intent, that vote dilution "is likely to persist" to such a degree that the elected representative will feel free to ignore the concerns of the supporters of the minority party. But "[t]o allow district courts to strike down apportionment plans on the basis of their prognostications as to the outcome of future elections . . . invites 'findings' on matters as to which neither judges nor anyone else can have any confidence." *Bandemer* (opinion of O'Connor, J.). And the test adopted by the *Common Cause* court requires a far more nuanced prediction than simply who would prevail in future political contests. Judges must forecast with unspecified certainty whether a prospective winner will have a margin of victory sufficient to permit him to ignore the supporters of his defeated opponent (whoever that may turn out to be). Judges not only have to pick the winner—they have to beat the point spread.

The appellees assure us that "the persistence of a party's advantage may be shown through sensitivity testing: probing how a plan would perform under other plausible electoral conditions." Experience proves that accurately predicting electoral outcomes is not so simple, either because the plans are based on flawed assumptions about voter preferences and behavior or because demographics and priorities change over time. In our two leading partisan gerrymandering cases themselves [*Bandemer* and *Vieth*], the predictions of durability proved to be dramatically wrong. * * *

Even the most sophisticated districting maps cannot reliably account for some of the reasons voters prefer one candidate over another, or why their preferences may change. Voters elect individual candidates in individual districts, and their selections depend on the issues that matter to them, the quality of the candidates, the tone of the candidates' campaigns, the performance of an incumbent, national events or local issues that drive voter turnout, and other considerations. Many voters split their tickets. Others never register with a political party, and vote for candidates from both major parties at different points during their lifetimes. For all of those reasons, asking judges to predict how a particular districting map will perform in future elections risks basing constitutional holdings on unstable ground outside judicial expertise.

It is hard to see what the District Court's third prong—providing the defendant an opportunity to show that the discriminatory effects were due to a "legitimate redistricting objective"—adds to the inquiry. The first prong already requires the plaintiff to prove that partisan advantage predominates. Asking whether a legitimate purpose other than partisanship was the motivation for a particular districting map just restates the question.

[IV(B)] The District Courts also found partisan gerrymandering claims justiciable under the First Amendment, coalescing around a basic three-part test: proof of intent to burden individuals based on their voting history or party affiliation; an actual burden on political speech or associational rights; and a causal link between the invidious intent and actual burden. Both District Courts concluded that the districting plans at issue violated the plaintiffs' First Amendment right to association. The District Court in North Carolina relied on testimony that, after the 2016 Plan was put in place, the plaintiffs faced "difficulty raising money, attracting candidates, and mobilizing voters to support the political causes and issues such Plaintiffs sought to advance." Similarly, the District Court in Maryland examined testimony that "revealed a lack of enthusiasm, indifference to voting, a sense of disenfranchisement, a sense of disconnection, and confusion," and concluded that

Republicans in the Sixth District "were burdened in fundraising, attracting volunteers, campaigning, and generating interest in voting." * * *

The plaintiffs' argument is that partisanship in districting should be regarded as simple discrimination against supporters of the opposing party on the basis of political viewpoint. Under that theory, any level of partisanship in districting would constitute an infringement of their First Amendment rights. But as the Court has explained, "[i]t would be idle . . . to contend that any political consideration taken into account in fashioning a reapportionment plan is sufficient to invalidate it." *Gaffney*. The First Amendment test simply describes the act of districting for partisan advantage. It provides no standard for determining when partisan activity goes too far.

As for actual burden, the slight anecdotal evidence found sufficient by the District Courts in these cases shows that this too is not a serious standard for separating constitutional from unconstitutional partisan gerrymandering. The District Courts relied on testimony about difficulty drumming up volunteers and enthusiasm. How much of a decline in voter engagement is enough to constitute a First Amendment burden? How many door knocks must go unanswered? How many petitions unsigned? How many calls for volunteers unheeded? * * *

These cases involve blatant examples of partisanship driving districting decisions. But the First Amendment analysis below offers no "clear" and "manageable" way of distinguishing permissible from impermissible partisan motivation. The *Common Cause* court embraced that conclusion, observing that "a judicially manageable framework for evaluating partisan gerrymandering claims need not distinguish an 'acceptable' level of partisan gerrymandering from 'excessive' partisan gerrymandering" because "the Constitution does not authorize state redistricting bodies to engage in such partisan gerrymandering." The decisions below prove the prediction of the *Vieth* plurality that "a First Amendment claim, if it were sustained, would render unlawful *all* consideration of political affiliation in districting," contrary to our established precedent.

[IV(C)] The dissent proposes using a State's own districting criteria as a neutral baseline from which to measure how extreme a partisan gerrymander is. The dissent would have us line up all the possible maps drawn using those criteria according to the partisan distribution they would produce. Distance from the "median" map would indicate whether a particular districting plan harms supporters of one party to an unconstitutional extent.

As an initial matter, it does not make sense to use criteria that will vary from State to State and year to year as the baseline for determining whether a gerrymander violates the Federal Constitution. The degree of partisan advantage that the Constitution tolerates should not turn on criteria offered by the gerrymanderers themselves. It is easy to imagine how different criteria could move the median map toward different partisan distributions. As a result, the same map could be constitutional or not depending solely on what the mapmakers said they set out to do. That possibility illustrates that the dissent's proposed constitutional test is indeterminate and arbitrary.

Even if we were to accept the dissent's proposed baseline, it would return us to "the original unanswerable question (How much political motivation and effect is too much?)." *Vieth* (plurality opinion). Would twenty percent away from the median map be okay? Forty percent? Sixty percent? Why or why not? (We appreciate that the dissent finds all the unanswerable questions annoying, but it seems a useful way to make the point.) The dissent's answer says it all: "This much is too much." That is not even trying to articulate a standard or rule.

The dissent argues that there are other instances in law where matters of degree are left to the courts. True enough. But those instances typically involve constitutional or statutory provisions or common law confining and guiding the exercise of judicial discretion. * * * Here, on the other hand, the Constitution provides no basis whatever to guide the exercise of judicial discretion. Common experience gives content to terms such as "substantial risk" or "substantial harm," but the same cannot be said of substantial deviation from a median map. There is no way to tell whether the prohibited deviation from that map should kick in at 25 percent or 75 percent or some other point. The only provision in the Constitution that specifically addresses the matter assigns it to the political branches. See Art. I, § 4, cl. 1.

[IV(D)] The North Carolina District Court further concluded that the 2016 Plan violated the Elections Clause and Article I, § 2. We are unconvinced by that novel approach. * * *

The District Court * * * asserted that partisan gerrymanders violate "the core principle of [our] republican government" preserved in Art. I, § 2, "namely, that the voters should choose their representatives, not the other way around." That seems like an objection more properly grounded in the Guarantee Clause of Article IV, § 4, which "guarantee[s] to every State in [the] Union a Republican Form of Government." This Court has several times concluded, however, that the Guarantee Clause does not provide the basis for a justiciable claim.

[V] Excessive partisanship in districting leads to results that reasonably seem unjust. But the fact that such gerrymandering is "incompatible with democratic principles," does not mean that the solution lies with the federal judiciary. We conclude that partisan gerrymandering claims present political questions beyond the reach of the federal courts. Federal judges have no license to reallocate political power between the two major political parties, with no plausible grant of authority in the Constitution, and no legal standards to limit and direct their decisions. "[J]udicial action must be governed by *standard*, by *rule*," and must be "principled, rational, and based upon reasoned distinctions" found in the Constitution or laws. *Vieth* (plurality opinion). Judicial review of partisan gerrymandering does not meet those basic requirements.

Today the dissent essentially embraces the argument that the Court unanimously rejected in *Gill*: "this Court *can* address the problem of partisan gerrymandering because it *must*." That is not the test of our authority under the Constitution; that document instead "confines the federal courts to a properly judicial role."

What the appellees and dissent seek is an unprecedented expansion of judicial power. We have never struck down a partisan gerrymander as unconstitutional—despite various requests over the past 45 years. The expansion of judicial authority would not be into just any area of controversy, but into one of the most intensely partisan aspects of American political life. That intervention would be unlimited in scope and duration—it would recur over and over again around the country with each new round of districting, for state as well as federal representatives. Consideration of the impact of today's ruling on democratic principles cannot ignore the effect of the unelected and politically unaccountable branch of the Federal Government assuming such an extraordinary and unprecedented role.

Our conclusion does not condone excessive partisan gerrymandering. Nor does our conclusion condemn complaints about districting to echo into a void. The States, for example, are actively addressing the issue on a number of fronts. In 2015, the Supreme Court of Florida struck down that State's congressional districting plan as a violation of the Fair Districts Amendment to the Florida Constitution. *League of Women Voters of Florida v. Detzner*, 172 So.3d 363 (2015). The dissent wonders why we can't do the same. The answer is that there is no "Fair Districts Amendment" to the Federal Constitution. Provisions in state statutes and state constitutions can provide standards and guidance for state courts to apply. (We do not understand how the dissent can maintain that a provision saying that no districting plan "shall be drawn with the intent to favor or disfavor a political party" provides little guidance on the question.) Indeed, numerous other States are restricting partisan considerations in districting through legislation. One way they are doing so is by placing power to draw electoral districts in the hands of independent commissions. For example, in November 2018, voters in Colorado and Michigan approved constitutional amendments creating multimember commissions that will be responsible in whole or in part for creating and approving district maps for congressional and state legislative districts. See Colo. Const., Art. V, §§ 44, 46; Mich. Const., Art. IV, § 6. Missouri is trying a different tack. Voters there overwhelmingly approved the creation of a new position—state demographer—to draw state legislative district lines. Mo. Const., Art. III, § 3.

Other States have mandated at least some of the traditional districting criteria for their mapmakers. Some have outright prohibited partisan favoritism in redistricting [citing provisions in Florida, Missouri, Iowa, and Delaware law].

As noted, the Framers gave Congress the power to do something about partisan gerrymandering in the Elections Clause. The first bill introduced in the 116th Congress would require States to create 15-member independent commissions to draw congressional districts and would establish certain redistricting criteria, including protection for communities of interest, and ban partisan gerrymandering. H. R. 1, 116th Cong., 1st Sess., §§ 2401, 2411 (2019).

Dozens of other bills have been introduced to limit reliance on political considerations in redistricting [citing examples]. * * *

We express no view on any of these pending proposals. We simply note that the avenue for reform established by the Framers, and used by Congress in the past, remains open.

* * *

No one can accuse this Court of having a crabbed view of the reach of its competence. But we have no commission to allocate political power and influence in the absence of a constitutional directive or legal standards to guide us in the exercise of such authority. "It is emphatically the province and duty of the judicial department to say what the law is." *Marbury v. Madison.* In this rare circumstance, that means our duty is to say "this is not law." * * *

JUSTICE KAGAN [joined by JUSTICES GINSBURG, BREYER, and SOTOMAYOR], dissenting.

For the first time ever, this Court refuses to remedy a constitutional violation because it thinks the task beyond judicial capabilities.

And not just any constitutional violation. The partisan gerrymanders in these cases deprived citizens of the most fundamental of their constitutional rights: the rights to participate equally in the political process, to join with others to advance political beliefs, and to choose their political representatives. In so doing, the partisan gerrymanders here debased and dishonored our democracy, turning upside-down the core American idea that all governmental power derives from the people. These gerrymanders enabled politicians to entrench themselves in office as against voters' preferences. They promoted partisanship above respect for the popular will. They encouraged a politics of polarization and dysfunction. If left unchecked, gerrymanders like the ones here may irreparably damage our system of government.

And checking them is *not* beyond the courts. The majority's abdication comes just when courts across the country, including those below, have coalesced around manageable judicial standards to resolve partisan gerrymandering claims. Those standards satisfy the majority's own benchmarks. They do not require—indeed, they do not permit—courts to rely on their own ideas of electoral fairness, whether proportional representation or any other. And they limit courts to correcting only egregious gerrymanders, so judges do not become omnipresent players in the political process. But yes, the standards used here do allow—as well they should—judicial intervention in the worst-of-the-worst cases of democratic subversion, causing blatant constitutional harms. In other words, they allow courts to undo partisan gerrymanders of the kind we face today from North Carolina and Maryland. In giving such gerrymanders a pass from judicial review, the majority goes tragically wrong.

[I] Maybe the majority errs in these cases because it pays so little attention to the constitutional harms at their core. After dutifully reciting each case's facts, the majority leaves them forever behind, instead immersing itself in everything that could conceivably go amiss if courts became involved. So it is necessary to fill in the gaps. To recount exactly what politicians in North Carolina and Maryland did to entrench their parties in political office, whatever the electorate might think. And to elaborate on the constitutional injury those politicians wreaked, to our democratic system and to individuals' rights. All that will help in considering whether courts confronting partisan gerrymandering claims are really so hamstrung—so unable to carry out their constitutional duties—as the majority thinks.

[I(A)] The plaintiffs here challenge two congressional districting plans—one adopted by Republicans in North Carolina and the other by Democrats in Maryland—as unconstitutional partisan gerrymanders. As I relate what happened in those two States, ask yourself: Is this how American democracy is supposed to work? * * *

[Here, Justice Kagan lays out in somewhat more detail the facts—the "grisly tale," in her words—described in Part I of the Court's opinion.]

[I(B)] Now back to the question I asked before: Is that how American democracy is supposed to work? I have yet to meet the person who thinks so.

"Governments," the Declaration of Independence states, "deriv[e] their just Powers from the Consent of the Governed." The Constitution begins: "We the People of the United States." The Gettysburg Address (almost) ends: "[G]overnment of the people, by the people, for the people." If there is a single idea that made our Nation (and that our Nation commended to the world), it is this one: The people are sovereign. The "power," James Madison wrote, "is in the people over the Government, and not in the Government over the people." 4 Annals of Cong. 934 (1794).

Free and fair and periodic elections are the key to that vision. The people get to choose their representatives. And then they get to decide, at regular intervals, whether to keep them. * * * Election day—next year, and two years later, and two years after that—is what links the people to their representatives, and gives the people their sovereign power. That day is the foundation of democratic governance.

And partisan gerrymandering can make it meaningless. At its most extreme—as in North Carolina and Maryland—the practice amounts to "rigging elections." *Vieth* (Kennedy, J., concurring in judgment). By drawing districts to maximize the power of some voters and minimize the power of others, a party in office at the right time can entrench itself there for a decade or more, no matter what the voters would prefer. Just ask the people of North Carolina and Maryland. The "core principle of republican government," this Court has recognized, is "that the voters should choose their representatives, not the other way around." *Arizona State Legislature v. Arizona Independent Redistricting Comm'n* [discussed later in this section]. Partisan gerrymandering turns it the other way around. By that mechanism, politicians can cherry-pick voters to ensure their reelection. And the power becomes, as Madison put it, "in the Government over the people." 4 Annals of Cong. 934.

The majority disputes none of this. I think it important to underscore that fact: The majority disputes none of what I have said (or will say) about how gerrymanders undermine democracy. Indeed, the majority concedes (really, how could it not?) that gerrymandering is "incompatible with democratic principles." And therefore what? That recognition would seem to demand a response. The majority offers two ideas that might qualify as such. One is that the political process can deal with the problem—a proposition so dubious on its face that I feel secure in delaying my answer for some time. The other is that political gerrymanders have always been with us. To its credit, the majority does not frame that point as an originalist constitutional argument. After all (as the majority rightly notes), racial and residential gerrymanders were also once with us, but the Court has done something about that fact. The majority's idea instead seems to be that if we have lived with partisan gerrymanders so long, we will survive.

That complacency has no cause. Yes, partisan gerrymandering goes back to the Republic's earliest days. (As does vociferous opposition to it.) But big data and modern technology—of just the kind that the mapmakers in North Carolina and Maryland used—make today's gerrymandering altogether different from the crude linedrawing of the past. Old-time efforts, based on little more than guesses, sometimes led to so-called dummymanders—gerrymanders that went spectacularly wrong. Not likely in today's world. * * *

The proof is in the 2010 pudding. That redistricting cycle produced some of the most extreme partisan gerrymanders in this country's history. I've already recounted the results from North Carolina and Maryland, and you'll hear even more about those. But the voters in those States were not the only ones to fall prey to such districting perversions. [Justice Kagan describes the 2010 Pennsylvania and Ohio gerrymanders.] * * * And gerrymanders will only get worse (or depending on your perspective, better) as time goes on—as data becomes ever more fine-grained and data analysis techniques continue to improve. What was possible with paper and pen—or even with Windows 95—doesn't hold a candle (or an LED bulb?) to what will become possible with developments like machine learning. And someplace along this road, "we the people" become sovereign no longer.

[I(C)] Partisan gerrymandering of the kind before us not only subverts democracy (as if that weren't bad enough). It violates individuals' constitutional rights as well. That statement is not the lonesome cry of a dissenting Justice. This Court has recognized extreme partisan gerrymandering as such a violation for many years.

Partisan gerrymandering operates through vote dilution—the devaluation of one citizen's vote as compared to others. A mapmaker draws district lines to "pack" and "crack" voters likely to support the disfavored party. He packs supermajorities of those voters into a relatively few districts, in numbers far greater than needed for their preferred candidates to prevail. Then he cracks the rest across many more districts, spreading them so thin that their candidates will not be able to win. Whether the person is packed or cracked, his vote carries less weight—has less consequence—than it would under a neutrally drawn (non-partisan) map. In short, the mapmaker has made some votes count for less, because they are likely to go for the other party.

That practice implicates the Fourteenth Amendment's Equal Protection Clause. The Fourteenth Amendment, we long ago recognized, "guarantees the opportunity for equal participation by all voters in the election" of legislators. *Reynolds v. Sims*. And that opportunity "can be denied by a debasement or dilution of the weight of a citizen's vote just as effectively as by wholly prohibiting the free exercise of the franchise." Based on that principle, this Court in its one-person-one-vote decisions prohibited creating districts with significantly different populations. A State could not, we explained, thus "dilut[e] the weight of votes because of place of residence." The constitutional injury in a partisan gerrymandering case is much the same, except that the dilution is based on party affiliation. In such a case, too, the districters have set out to reduce the weight of certain citizens' votes, and thereby deprive them of their capacity to "full[y] and effective[ly] participat[e] in the political process[ ]." As Justice Kennedy (in a controlling opinion) once hypothesized: If districters declared that they were drawing a map "so as most to burden [the votes of] Party X's" supporters, it would violate the Equal Protection Clause. *Vieth*. For (in the language of the one-person-one-vote decisions) it would infringe those voters' rights to "equal [electoral] participation." *Reynolds*.

And partisan gerrymandering implicates the First Amendment too. That Amendment gives its greatest protection to political beliefs, speech, and association. Yet partisan gerrymanders subject certain voters to "disfavored treatment"—again, counting their votes for less—precisely because of "their voting history [and] their expression of political views." *Vieth* (opinion of Kennedy, J.). And added to that strictly personal harm is an associational one. Representative democracy is "unimaginable without the ability of citizens to band together in [support of] candidates who espouse their political views." *California Democratic Party v. Jones*. By diluting the votes of certain citizens, the State frustrates their efforts to translate those affiliations into political effectiveness. In both those ways, partisan gerrymanders of the kind we confront here undermine the protections of "democracy embodied in the First Amendment."

Though different Justices have described the constitutional harm in diverse ways, nearly all have agreed on this much: Extreme partisan gerrymandering (as happened in North Carolina and Maryland) violates the Constitution [citing a number of opinions by different justices]. Once again, the majority never disagrees; it appears to accept the "principle that each person must have an equal say in the election of representatives." And indeed, without this settled and shared understanding that cases like these inflict constitutional injury, the question of whether there are judicially manageable standards for resolving them would never come up.

[II] So the only way to understand the majority's opinion is as follows: In the face of grievous harm to democratic governance and flagrant infringements on individuals' rights—in the face of escalating partisan manipulation whose compatibility with this Nation's values and law no one defends—the majority declines to provide any remedy. For the first time in this Nation's history, the majority declares that it can do nothing about an acknowledged constitutional violation because it has searched high and low and cannot find a workable legal standard to apply.

The majority gives two reasons for thinking that the adjudication of partisan gerrymandering claims is beyond judicial capabilities. First and foremost, the majority says, it cannot find a neutral baseline—one not based on contestable notions of political fairness—from which to measure injury. * * * And second, the majority argues that even after establishing a baseline, a court would have no way to answer "the determinative question: 'How much is too much?' " No "discernible and manageable" standard is available, the majority claims—and so courts could willy-nilly become embroiled in fixing every districting plan.

I'll give the majority this one—and important—thing: It identifies some dangers everyone should want to avoid. Judges should not be apportioning political power based on their own vision of electoral fairness, whether proportional representation or any other. And judges should not be striking down maps left, right, and center, on the view that every smidgen of politics is a smidgen too much. Respect for state legislative processes—and restraint in the exercise of judicial authority—counsels intervention in only egregious cases.

But in throwing up its hands, the majority misses something under its nose: What it says can't be done *has* been done. Over the past several years, federal courts across the country—including, but not exclusively, in the decisions below—have largely converged on a standard for adjudicating partisan gerrymandering claims (striking down both Democratic and Republican districting plans in the process). And that standard does what the majority says is impossible. The standard does not use any judge-made conception of electoral fairness—either proportional representation or any other; instead, it takes as its baseline a State's *own* criteria of fairness, apart from partisan gain. And by requiring plaintiffs to make difficult showings relating to both purpose and effects, the standard invalidates the most extreme, but only the most extreme, partisan gerrymanders. * * *

[II(A)] Start with the standard the lower courts used. The majority disaggregates the opinions below, distinguishing the one from the other and then chopping up each into "a number of 'tests.' " But in doing so, it fails to convey the decisions' most significant—and common—features. Both courts focused on the harm of vote dilution, though the North Carolina court mostly grounded its analysis in the Fourteenth Amendment and the Maryland court in the First. And both courts (like others around the country) used basically the same three-part test to decide whether the plaintiffs had made out a vote dilution claim. As many legal standards do, that test has three parts: (1) intent; (2) effects; and (3) causation. First, the plaintiffs challenging a districting plan must prove that state officials' "predominant purpose" in drawing a district's lines was to "entrench [their party] in power" by diluting the votes of citizens favoring its rival. Second, the plaintiffs must establish that the lines drawn in fact have the intended effect by "substantially" diluting their votes. And third, if the plaintiffs make those showings, the State must come up with a legitimate, non-partisan justification to save its map.[2] If you are a lawyer, you know that this test looks utterly ordinary. It is the sort of thing courts work with every day.

Turn now to the test's application. First, did the North Carolina and Maryland districters have the predominant purpose of entrenching their own party in power? Here, the two District Courts catalogued the overwhelming direct evidence that they did. * * *

The majority's response to the District Courts' purpose analysis is discomfiting. The majority does not contest the lower courts' findings; how could it? Instead, the majority says that state officials' intent to entrench their party in power is perfectly

---

[2]   Neither North Carolina nor Maryland offered much of an alternative explanation for the evidence that the plaintiffs put forward. Presumably, both States had trouble coming up with something. Like the majority, I therefore pass quickly over this part of the test.

"permissible," even when it is the predominant factor in drawing district lines. But that is wrong. True enough, that the intent to inject "political considerations" into districting may not raise any constitutional concerns. * * * But when political actors have a specific and predominant intent to entrench themselves in power by manipulating district lines, that goes too far. Consider again Justice Kennedy's hypothetical of mapmakers who set out to maximally burden (*i.e.,* make count for as little as possible) the votes going to a rival party. Does the majority really think that goal is permissible? But why even bother with hypotheticals? Just consider the purposes here. It cannot be permissible and thus irrelevant, as the majority claims, that state officials have as their purpose the kind of grotesquely gerrymandered map that, according to all this Court has ever said, violates the Constitution.

On to the second step of the analysis, where the plaintiffs must prove that the districting plan substantially dilutes their votes. The majority fails to discuss most of the evidence the District Courts relied on to find that the plaintiffs had done so. But that evidence—particularly from North Carolina—is the key to understanding both the problem these cases present and the solution to it they offer. The evidence reveals just how bad the two gerrymanders were (in case you had any doubts). And it shows how the same technologies and data that today facilitate extreme partisan gerrymanders also enable courts to discover them, by exposing just how much they dilute votes. See *Vieth* (opinion of Kennedy, J.) (predicting that development).

Consider the sort of evidence used in North Carolina first. There, the plaintiffs demonstrated the districting plan's effects mostly by relying on what might be called the "extreme outlier approach." (Here's a spoiler: the State's plan was one.) The approach—which also has recently been used in Michigan and Ohio litigation—begins by using advanced computing technology to randomly generate a large collection of districting plans that incorporate the State's physical and political geography and meet its declared districting criteria, *except for* partisan gain. For each of those maps, the method then uses actual precinct-level votes from past elections to determine a partisan outcome (*i.e.,* the number of Democratic and Republican seats that map produces). Suppose we now have 1,000 maps, each with a partisan outcome attached to it. We can line up those maps on a continuum—the most favorable to Republicans on one end, the most favorable to Democrats on the other. We can then find the median outcome—that is, the outcome smack dab in the center—in a world with no partisan manipulation. And we can see where the State's actual plan falls on the spectrum—at or near the median or way out on one of the tails? The further out on the tail, the more extreme the partisan distortion and the more significant the vote dilution. See generally Brief for Eric S. Lander as *Amicus Curiae* 7–22.

Using that approach, the North Carolina plaintiffs offered a boatload of alternative districting plans—all showing that the State's map was an out-out-out-outlier. One expert produced 3,000 maps, adhering in the way described above to the districting criteria that the North Carolina redistricting committee had used, other than partisan advantage. To calculate the partisan outcome of those maps, the expert also used the same election data (a composite of seven elections) that [the districting specialist hired by the North Carolina GOP] had employed when devising the North Carolina plan in the first instance. The results were, shall we say, striking. Every single one of the 3,000 maps would have produced at least one more Democratic House Member than the State's actual map, and 77% would have elected three or four more. A second expert obtained essentially the same results with maps conforming to more generic districting criteria (*e.g.,* compactness and contiguity of districts). Over 99% of that expert's 24,518 simulations would have led to the election of at least one more Democrat, and over 70% would have led to two or three more. Based on those and other findings, the District Court determined that the North Carolina plan substantially dilutes the plaintiffs' votes.[4]

Because the Maryland gerrymander involved just one district, the evidence in that case was far simpler—but no less powerful for that. You've heard some of the numbers before. The 2010 census required only a minimal change in the Sixth District's population—the subtraction of about 10,000 residents from more than 700,000. But instead of making a correspondingly minimal adjustment, Democratic officials reconfigured the entire district. They moved 360,000 residents out and another 350,000 in, while splitting some counties for the first time in almost two centuries. The upshot was a district with 66,000 fewer Republican voters and 24,000 more Democratic ones. In the old Sixth, 47% of registered voters were Republicans and only 36% Democrats. But in the new Sixth, 44% of registered voters were Democrats and only 33% Republicans. That reversal of the district's partisan composition translated into four consecutive Democratic victories, including in a wave election year for Republicans (2014). In what was once a party stronghold, Republicans now have little or no chance to elect their preferred candidate. The District Court thus found that the gerrymandered Maryland map substantially dilutes Republicans' votes.

The majority claims all these findings are mere "prognostications" about the future, in which no one "can have any confidence." But the courts below did not gaze into crystal balls, as the majority tries to suggest. Their findings about these gerrymanders' effects on voters—both in the past and predictably in the future—were evidence-based, data-based, statistics-based. Knowledge-based, one might say. The courts did what anyone would want a decisionmaker to do when so much hangs in the balance. They looked hard at the facts, and they went where the facts led them. They availed themselves of all the information that mapmakers (like Hofeller and Hawkins) and politicians (like Lewis and O'Malley) work so hard to amass and then use to make every districting decision. They refused to content themselves with unsupported and out-of-date musings about the unpredictability of the American voter. They did not bet America's future—as today the majority does—on the idea that maps constructed with so much expertise and care to make electoral outcomes impervious to voting would somehow or other come apart. They looked at the evidence—at the facts about how these districts operated—and they could reach only one conclusion. By substantially diluting the votes of citizens favoring their rivals,

---

4 The District Court also relied on actual election results (under both the new plan and the similar one preceding it) and on mathematical measurements of the new plan's "partisan asymmetry." Those calculations assess whether supporters of the two parties can translate their votes into representation with equal ease. See Stephanopoulos & McGhee, The Measure of a Metric, 70 Stan. L. Rev. 1503, 1505–1507 (2018). The court found that the new North Carolina plan led to extreme asymmetry, compared both to plans used in the rest of the country and to plans previously used in the State.

the politicians of one party had succeeded in entrenching themselves in office. They had beat democracy.

[II(B)] The majority's broadest claim, as I've noted, is that this is a price we must pay because judicial oversight of partisan gerrymandering cannot be "politically neutral" or "manageable." Courts, the majority argues, will have to choose among contested notions of electoral fairness. (Should they take as the ideal mode of districting proportional representation, many competitive seats, adherence to traditional districting criteria, or so forth?) And even once courts have chosen, the majority continues, they will have to decide "[h]ow much is too much?"—that is, how much deviation from the chosen "touchstone" to allow? In answering that question, the majority surmises, they will likely go far too far. So the whole thing is impossible, the majority concludes. To prove its point, the majority throws a bevy of question marks on the page. (I count nine in just two paragraphs.) But it never tries to analyze the serious question presented here—whether the kind of standard developed below falls prey to those objections, or instead allows for neutral and manageable oversight. The answer, as you've already heard enough to know, is the latter. That kind of oversight is not only possible; it's been done.

Consider neutrality first. Contrary to the majority's suggestion, the District Courts did not have to—and in fact did not—choose among competing visions of electoral fairness. That is because they did not try to compare the State's actual map to an "ideally fair" one (whether based on proportional representation or some other criterion). Instead, they looked at the difference between what the State did and what the State would have done if politicians hadn't been intent on partisan gain. Or put differently, the comparator (or baseline or touchstone) is the result not of a judge's philosophizing but of the State's own characteristics and judgments. The effects evidence in these cases accepted as a given the State's physical geography (*e.g.*, where does the Chesapeake run?) and political geography (*e.g.*, where do the Democrats live on top of each other?). So the courts did not, in the majority's words, try to "counteract 'natural' gerrymandering caused, for example, by the urban concentration of one party." Still more, the courts' analyses used the State's own criteria for electoral fairness—except for naked partisan gain. Under their approach, in other words, the State selected its own fairness baseline in the form of its other districting criteria. All the courts did was determine how far the State had gone off that track because of its politicians' effort to entrench themselves in office. * * *

So in North Carolina, for example, all the maps adhered to the traditional criteria of contiguity and compactness. But the comparator maps in another State would have incorporated different objectives—say, the emphasis Arizona places on competitive districts or the requirement Iowa imposes that counties remain whole. See Brief for Mathematicians et al. as *Amici Curiae* 19–20. The point is that the assemblage of maps, reflecting the characteristics and judgments of the State itself, creates a neutral baseline from which to assess whether partisanship has run amok. Extreme outlier as to what? As to the other maps the State could have produced given its unique political geography and its chosen districting criteria. *Not* as to the maps a judge, with his own view of electoral fairness, could have dreamed up. * * *

The majority's sole response misses the point. According to the majority, "it does not make sense to use" a State's own (non-partisan) districting criteria as the baseline from which to measure partisan gerrymandering because those criteria "will vary from State to State and year to year." But that is a virtue, not a vice—a feature, not a bug. Using the criteria the State itself has chosen at the relevant time prevents any judicial predilections from affecting the analysis—exactly what the majority claims it wants. At the same time, using those criteria enables a court to measure just what it should: the extent to which the pursuit of partisan advantage—by these legislators at this moment—has distorted the State's districting decisions. Sure, different non-partisan criteria could result, as the majority notes, in different partisan distributions to serve as the baseline. But that in itself raises no issue: Everyone agrees that state officials using non-partisan criteria (*e.g.,* must counties be kept together? should districts be compact?) have wide latitude in districting. The problem arises only when legislators or mapmakers substantially deviate from the baseline distribution by manipulating district lines for partisan gain. So once again, the majority's analysis falters because it equates the demand to eliminate partisan gerrymandering with a demand for a single partisan distribution—the one reflecting proportional representation. But those two demands are different, and only the former is at issue here.

The majority's "how much is too much" critique fares no better than its neutrality argument. How about the following for a first-cut answer: This much is too much. By any measure, a map that produces a greater partisan skew than any of 3,000 randomly generated maps (all with the State's political geography and districting criteria built in) reflects "too much" partisanship. Think about what I just said: The absolute worst of 3,001 possible maps. The *only one* that could produce a 10–3 partisan split even as Republicans got a bare majority of the statewide vote. And again: How much is too much? This much is too much: A map that without any evident non-partisan districting reason (to the contrary) shifted the composition of a district from 47% Republicans and 36% Democrats to 33% Republicans and 42% Democrats. A map that in 2011 was responsible for the largest partisan swing of a congressional district in the country. Even the majority acknowledges that "[t]hese cases involve blatant examples of partisanship driving districting decisions." If the majority had done nothing else, it could have set the line here. How much is too much? At the least, any gerrymanders as bad as these.

And if the majority thought that approach too case-specific, it could have used the lower courts' general standard—focusing on "predominant" purpose and "substantial" effects—without fear of indeterminacy. I do not take even the majority to claim that courts are incapable of investigating whether legislators mainly intended to seek partisan advantage. That is for good reason. Although purpose inquiries carry certain hazards (which courts must attend to), they are a common form of analysis in constitutional cases [citing cases from a number of different constitutional law doctrinal areas]. Those inquiries would be no harder here than in other contexts.

Nor is there any reason to doubt, as the majority does, the competence of courts to determine whether a district map "substantially" dilutes the votes of a rival party's supporters from the everything-but-partisanship baseline described above. (Most of the majority's difficulties here really come from its idea that ideal visions set the baseline. But that is double-counting—and, as already shown, wrong to boot.) As this Court recently noted, "the law is full of instances" where a judge's decision rests on "estimating rightly . . . some matter of degree"—including the "substantial[ity]" of risk or harm. The majority is wrong to think that these laws typically (let alone uniformly) further "confine[ ] and guide[ ]" judicial decisionmaking. They do not, either in themselves or through "statutory context." To the extent additional guidance has developed over the years (as under the Sherman Act), courts themselves have been its author—as they could be in this context too. And contrary to the majority's suggestion, courts all the time make judgments about the substantiality of harm without reducing them to particular percentages. If courts are no longer competent to do so, they will have to relinquish, well, substantial portions of their docket.

And the combined inquiry used in these cases set the bar high, so that courts could intervene in the worst partisan gerrymanders, but no others. Or to say the same thing, so that courts could intervene in the kind of extreme gerrymanders that nearly every Justice for decades has thought to violate the Constitution. * * *

The majority, in the end, fails to understand both the plaintiffs' claims and the decisions below. Everything in today's opinion assumes that these cases grew out of a "desire for proportional representation" or, more generally phrased, a "fair share of political power." And everything in it assumes that the courts below had to (and did) decide what that fair share would be. But that is not so. The plaintiffs objected to one specific practice—the extreme manipulation of district lines for partisan gain. Elimination of that practice could have led to proportional representation. Or it could have led to nothing close. What was left after the practice's removal could have been fair, or could have been unfair, by any number of measures. That was not the crux of this suit. The plaintiffs asked only that the courts bar politicians from entrenching themselves in power by diluting the votes of their rivals' supporters. And the courts, using neutral and manageable—and eminently legal—standards, provided that (and only that) relief. This Court should have cheered, not overturned, that restoration of the people's power to vote.

[III] This Court has long understood that it has a special responsibility to remedy violations of constitutional rights resulting from politicians' districting decisions. Over 50 years ago, we committed to providing judicial review in that sphere, recognizing as we established the one-person-one-vote rule that "our oath and our office require no less." *Reynolds.* Of course, our oath and our office require us to vindicate all constitutional rights. But the need for judicial review is at its most urgent in cases like these. "For here, politicians' incentives conflict with voters' interests, leaving citizens without any political remedy for their constitutional harms." *Gill* (Kagan, J., concurring). Those harms arise because politicians want to stay in office. No one can look to them for effective relief.

The majority disagrees, concluding its opinion with a paean to congressional bills limiting partisan gerrymanders. "Dozens of [those] bills have been introduced," the majority says. One was "introduced in 2005 and has been reintroduced in every Congress since." And might be reintroduced until the end of time. Because what all these *bills* have in common is that they are not *laws*. The politicians who benefit from partisan gerrymandering are unlikely to change partisan gerrymandering. And because those politicians maintain themselves in office through partisan gerrymandering, the chances for legislative reform are slight.

No worries, the majority says; it has another idea. The majority notes that voters themselves have recently approved ballot initiatives to put power over districting in the hands of independent commissions or other non-partisan actors. Some Members of the majority, of course, once thought such initiatives unconstitutional. See *Arizona State Legislature* (Roberts, C. J., dissenting). But put that aside. Fewer than half the States offer voters an opportunity to put initiatives to direct vote; in all the rest (including North Carolina and Maryland), voters are dependent on legislators to make electoral changes (which for all the reasons already given, they are unlikely to do). And even when voters have a mechanism they can work themselves, legislators often fight their efforts tooth and nail. Look at Missouri. There, the majority touts a voter-approved proposal to turn districting over to a state demographer. But before the demographer had drawn a single line, Members of the state legislature had introduced a bill to start undoing the change. See Mo. H. J. Res. 48, 100th Gen. Assembly, 1st Reg. Sess. (2019). I'd put better odds on that bill's passage than on all the congressional proposals the majority cites.

The majority's most perplexing "solution" is to look to state courts. * * * But what do those courts know that this Court does not? If they can develop and apply neutral and manageable standards to identify unconstitutional gerrymanders, why couldn't we?[6]

We could have, and we should have. The gerrymanders here—and they are typical of many—violated the constitutional rights of many hundreds of thousands of American citizens. Those voters (Republicans in the one case, Democrats in the other) did not have an equal opportunity to participate in the political process. Their votes counted for far less than they should have because of their partisan affiliation. When faced with such constitutional wrongs, courts must intervene: "It is emphatically the province and duty of the judicial department to say what the law is." *Marbury v. Madison.* That is what the courts below did. Their decisions are worth a read. They (and others that have recently remedied similar violations) are detailed, thorough, painstaking. They evaluated with immense care the factual evidence and legal arguments the parties presented. They used neutral and manageable and strict standards. They had not a shred of politics about them. Contra the majority, this *was* law. * * *

---

[6]   Contrary to the majority's suggestion, state courts do not typically have more specific "standards and guidance" to apply than federal courts have. The Pennsylvania Supreme Court based its gerrymandering decision on a constitutional clause providing only that "elections shall be free and equal" and no one shall "interfere to prevent the free exercise of the right of suffrage." And even the Florida "Free Districts Amendment," which the majority touts, says nothing more than that no districting plan "shall be drawn with the intent to favor or disfavor a political party." Fla. Const., Art. III, § 20(a). If the majority wants the kind of guidance that will keep courts from intervening too far in the political sphere, that Amendment does not provide it: The standard is in fact a good deal less exacting than the one the District Courts below applied. In any event, only a few States have a constitutional provision like Florida's, so the majority's state-court solution does not go far.

And gerrymandering is, as so many Justices have emphasized before, anti-democratic in the most profound sense. In our government, "all political power flows from the people." And that means, as Alexander Hamilton once said, "that the people should choose whom they please to govern them." 2 Debates on the Constitution 257 (J. Elliot ed. 1891). But in Maryland and North Carolina they cannot do so. In Maryland, election in and election out, there are 7 Democrats and 1 Republican in the congressional delegation. In North Carolina, however the political winds blow, there are 10 Republicans and 3 Democrats. Is it conceivable that someday voters will be able to break out of that prefabricated box? Sure. But everything possible has been done to make that hard. To create a world in which power does not flow from the people because they do not choose their governors.

Of all times to abandon the Court's duty to declare the law, this was not the one. The practices challenged in these cases imperil our system of government. Part of the Court's role in that system is to defend its foundations. None is more important than free and fair elections. With respect but deep sadness, I dissent.

NOTES ON JUDICIAL REVIEW OF POLITICAL GERRYMANDERING

1. *Coherence Across the Cases?* Precisely why is it that a majority of Justices are confident they can hear *Shaw v. Reno* sorts of cases, but not political gerrymandering cases? How persuasive is it to say that the difference is that race, unlike politics, is a constitutionally forbidden factor—when *Shaw* itself says that race may be taken into account in ensuring minority representation, so long as it is not taken into account too much? Why not say, similarly, that entrenching the current political majority may be taken into account, but not too much? Could it be the case that courts are better at figuring out when racial considerations have gone too far than when political considerations have? Or perhaps there is a stronger dignitary harm in the former situation—though that still leaves the question of how the courts draw the line. Is a more salient difference that the VRA requires state legislatures to consider race?

With judicial review of partisan gerrymanders now foreclosed, litigators looking to challenge such gerrymanders will have to raise other claims that *are* justiciable. Consider the possibility that some lower-court judges may be more willing to find violations of one person, one vote, or impermissible racial gerrymanders, where there is also an egregious partisan gerrymander.[22]

2. *Removing Politics Through Independent Redistricting Commissions?* As Chief Justice Roberts noted toward the end of his *Rucho* opinion, some states have created redistricting commissions in an attempt to remove state legislators from the process, thereby reducing legislative self-dealing. Currently, fourteen states utilize such a commission to draw state legislative districts. Of those fourteen, nine also provide for the

---

[22] On the political gerrymandering debate, see, e.g., Guy-Uriel Charles, *Democracy and Distortion*, 92 Cornell L. Rev. 601 (2007); Bernard Grofman & Gary King, *The Future of Partisan Symmetry as a Judicial Test for Partisan Gerrymandering after* LULAC v. Perry, 6 Election L.J. 2 (2007). For commentary seeking to place the partisan gerrymandering cases into this broader context of the judicial regulation of politics (e.g., one person, one vote; judicial regulation of political parties; campaign finance), see, e.g., James Gardner, *How to Do Things with Boundaries: Redistricting and the Construction of Politics*, 11 Election L.J. 399 (2012); Samuel Issacharoff & Pamela Karlan, *Where to Draw the Line?: Judicial Review of Political Gerrymanders*, 153 U. Pa. L. Rev. 541 (2004).

commission to draw congressional districts—although one of the nine states (Montana) currently has only a single congressional district.[23]

Although studies differ on the effects of independent districting commissions, one scholar summarizes the overall thrust as follows: "these bodies are less likely to produce democratic malfunctions than legislatures. Their district plans typically treat the major parties more symmetrically, exhibit higher levels of competitiveness, and improve voters' actual representation. To be sure, not all of the studies' findings are positive, but their overall orientation is indisputable. Gerrymandering does seem less prevalent when commissions are responsible for redistricting." Nicholas O. Stephanopoulos, *Arizona and Anti-Reform*, 2015 U. Chi. Legal F. 477, 495; *see also id.* at 499–500 (employing a new methodology and finding similar, if somewhat less clear-cut, results). However, a 2015 Supreme Court case nearly ended the experiment in independent commissions for congressional districting.

Arizona State Legislature v. Arizona Independent Redistricting Commission

135 S.Ct. 2652 (2015).

In a 2000 ballot initiative, Arizona voters adopted Proposition 106, which amended the state constitution to remove both state and congressional redistricting authority from the state legislature and vest it in the Arizona Independent Redistricting Commission, a five-member body. Out of a list of twenty-five members (ten Democrats, ten Republicans, and five who are members of neither major party) compiled by the state Commission on Appellate Court Appointments, the ranking majority and minority leaders of each house of the state legislature each choose one member of the Commission; those four members then choose a fifth member. The fifth member, who chairs the Commission, cannot be a member of either major party.

In 2012, the Commission finalized new congressional and state apportionment maps, based on the results of the 2010 census. Shortly thereafter, the Arizona State Legislature filed suit in federal court, arguing that the use of the Commission to draw congressional maps was unconstitutional, because the Constitution requires that, "The Times, Places and Manner of holding Elections for Senators and Representatives, shall be prescribed in each State by the Legislature thereof." The Legislature argued that the Commission was not "the Legislature" and therefore could not promulgate rules governing congressional elections. A three-judge district court ruled 2–1 in favor of the Commission, and the Legislature appealed to the Supreme Court.

Writing for a 5–4 majority, **Justice Ginsburg**, after holding that the Legislature did have standing to sue, argued that the word "legislature" has different meanings in different constitutional contexts. " '[T]he meaning of the word "legislature," used several times in the Federal Constitution, differs according to the connection in which it is employed, depend[ent] upon the character of the function which that body in each instance is called upon to exercise.' [quoting *Atlantic Cleaners & Dyers, Inc. v. United States,* 286 U.S. 427, 434 (1932).] Thus 'the Legislature' comprises the referendum and the Governor's veto in the context of regulating congressional elections. In the context of

---

[23]   Nat'l Conf. of State Legis., *Redistricting Commissions: State Legislative Plans* (Apr. 18, 2019), http:// www.ncsl.org/research/redistricting/2009-redistricting-commissions-table.aspx; Nat'l Conf. of State Legis., *Redistricting Commissions: Congressional Plans* (Apr. 18, 2019), http://www.ncsl.org/research/redistricting/ redistricting-commissions-congressional-plans.aspx.

ratifying constitutional amendments, by contrast, 'the Legislature' has a different identity, one that excludes the referendum and the Governor's veto [citing cases]."

"In sum, our precedent teaches that redistricting is a legislative function, to be performed in accordance with the State's prescriptions for lawmaking, which may include the referendum and the Governor's veto." Justice Ginsburg saw no reason to distinguish the ballot initiative from these other legislative mechanisms. If there was a constitutional problem, then, it did not stem from the fact that the Commission was created by ballot initiative.

But was there a problem with vesting districting decisions in an independent commission, regardless of how it was created? Relying on the "history and purpose" of the Elections Clause, Justice Ginsburg argued that there was not. Historically, she noted that the primary purpose of the Elections Clause "was to empower Congress to override state election rules, not to restrict the way States enact legislation." Moreover, American federalism encourages states to act as laboratories of democracy, including in how they structure their internal governance. The Arizona Constitution contains both the initiative power and the authorization for the Commission in its article defining the legislative power. Accordingly, the Court should read the Commission as simply exercising the legislative power in one substantive area: that of district-drawing. And, noting that the federal Constitution itself purports to derive its legitimacy from its promulgation by "We the People," "it would be perverse to interpret the term 'Legislature' in the Elections Clause so as to exclude lawmaking by the people, particularly where such lawmaking is intended to check legislators' ability to choose the district lines they run in, thereby advancing the prospect that Members of Congress will in fact be 'chosen . . . by the People of the several States.' " Accordingly, Court upheld the constitutionality of the independent districting commission in congressional elections.

Dissenting, **Chief Justice Roberts** focused on the distinction between state legislatures and the people of the states in the context of Senate elections: "Just over a century ago, Arizona became the second State in the Union to ratify the Seventeenth Amendment. That Amendment transferred power to choose United States Senators from 'the Legislature' of each State to 'the people thereof.' The Amendment resulted from an arduous, decades-long campaign in which reformers across the country worked hard to garner approval from Congress and three-quarters of the States."

"What chumps! Didn't they realize that all they had to do was interpret the constitutional term 'the Legislature' to mean 'the people'? The Court today performs just such a magic trick with the Elections Clause." Roberts insisted that the meaning of "the Legislature" at the Founding was clearly limited to the institutional lawmaking assembly of the state. Moreover, understanding the term the way the majority did led to inconsistencies within the Constitution: "The Constitution includes seventeen provisions referring to a State's 'Legislature.' Every one of those references is consistent with the understanding of a legislature as a representative body. More importantly, many of them are only consistent with an institutional legislature—and flatly incompatible with the majority's reading of 'the Legislature' to refer to the people as a whole."

Who has the better of this back-and-forth? Must the word "Legislature" mean the same thing every time it is used in the Constitution (as the Chief Justice asserts), or can its meaning be different in different contexts (as Justice Ginsburg claims)? Is it relevant whether or not independent commissions do a better job of producing fair and competitive elections? (And does the Chief Justice's discussion of independent commissions in *Rucho* indicate that he has changed his mind about their constitutionality?)

A final twist: in a separate challenge to the Arizona Commission's map of *state* legislative districts, a three-judge district court upheld a map with a total population deviation among districts of 8.8% (see § 1(A)(2) for a discussion of the scope of permissible deviations from absolute equality in state legislative districting). The map had been adopted by the Commission in a 3–2 vote, with both of the Republican members voting against it. The district court found that, "the population deviations were primarily a result of good-faith efforts to comply with the Voting Rights Act * * * even though partisanship played some role." Finding that this conclusion was supported by the record, the Supreme Court unanimously affirmed the district court's judgment. *Harris v. Arizona Independent Redistricting Commission*, 136 S.Ct. 1301 (2016).

Given the party-line vote in the Commission and the district court's determination (noted approvingly by the Supreme Court) that partisanship played some role in the drawing of legislative district lines, is it foolish to hope that politics can be removed from the districting process?

2. ELIGIBILITY TO SERVE IN THE LEGISLATURE

Shift your attention from the process of voting for legislators to the process of serving in the legislature. Theoretically, most citizens are eligible to serve in the legislature because state and federal laws place few substantive restrictions on service. Article I, § 2 only requires that members of the House of Representatives be at least 25 years of age, U.S. citizens for seven years or more, and inhabitants of the states from which they are elected. Article I, § 3 requires that senators be at least 30 years of age, U.S. citizens for nine years or more, and inhabitants of the states from which they are elected. What theory or concept of representation inspires these particular limitations? What requirements would you impose, based upon your preferred theory of representation?

Some extra-constitutional limitations on eligibility to serve in Congress have given rise to interesting constitutional litigation. We will first consider the case of Representative Adam Clayton Powell, in which Congress attempted to exclude Powell from the federal legislature notwithstanding his election to the position. We will then turn to the effort through popular initiatives to impose term limitations on federal lawmakers, an effort that was halted abruptly when the Supreme Court ruled such limitations unconstitutional. We will conclude with a less obvious way of restricting eligibility to serve in public office: state laws regulating access to the ballot. These laws, which are routinely upheld by courts, present the biggest hurdles to election. After all, we may all be eligible to serve in Congress, but our chances of election are close to nonexistent if our names never appear on the ballot.

A. CONGRESSIONALLY IMPOSED QUALIFICATIONS

Powell v. McCormack

395 U.S. 486, 89 S.Ct. 1944, 23 L.Ed.2d 491 (1969).

Adam Clayton Powell, Jr., was a civil rights activist and the first African-American to be elected to Congress from New York State. He was elected in 1944 to represent a

Harlem-based district, and he was repeatedly reelected thereafter. For his first decade in the House, he was one of only two African-American members, and he repeatedly clashed with segregationist Southern Democrats. (Powell himself was a Democrat.) By dining in, and inviting African-American constituents to join him in, the House restaurant, he challenged the unwritten ban on African-American representatives using Capitol facilities.

In 1961, he became chairman of the Education and Labor Committee, in which position he backed much of the social and civil rights legislation of the Kennedy and Johnson administrations. But he was also beginning to draw attention for other reasons. His trial for federal tax evasion ended with a hung jury in 1960, and in the early 1960s, he began to face mounting criticism for his frequent absences from Congress, for the number of trips he took abroad at taxpayer expense, and for irregularities in his management of the Education and Labor Committee's budget. After he was successfully sued for slander in 1963, he refused to pay the judgment, making him subject to arrest in New York State, and leading him to refrain from visiting his district so as to prevent his arrest.

During the 89th Congress (1965–1967), a House special subcommittee conducted an investigation into the financial management of the Education and Labor Committee, concluding that Powell had used Committee funds for personal benefit (in the form of both reimbursement for travel unrelated to his congressional duties and illegal salary payments to his wife). *See* H.R. Rep. No. 89–2349, at 6–7 (1967). No action was taken against Powell in the 89th Congress, and by the time of the subcommittee report, Powell had already been reelected for his twelfth term.

When the 90th Congress convened in January 1967, Powell was asked to step aside while the oath was administered to the other members-elect. After some debate, the House empaneled a select committee to determine Powell's eligibility to be seated. (The committee was chaired by Powell's fellow New York Democrat Rep. Emanuel Celler, who as Judiciary Committee chairman had been instrumental in pushing through the Civil Rights Act of 1964. *See* Chapter 1, § 1.) Powell appeared before the select committee once, but (on the advice of counsel) would testify only as to his age, citizenship, and residency. The committee found that Powell satisfied the Constitution's age, residency, and citizenship requirements. H.R. Rep. No. 90–27, at 22–24 (1967). However, relying on the House's Art. I, § 5, cl. 2 power to "punish its Members for disorderly Behaviour," the committee recommended that Powell be seated, but be censured, stripped of seniority, and fined $40,000, as punishment for both his financial improprieties as committee chair and his contempt of New York state courts in refusing to pay the judgment against him. *Id.* at 24–34.

The House, however, rejected a motion to bring the committee's resolution up for a vote. Instead, Rep. Thomas Bradford Curtis, a pro-civil-rights Republican from Missouri, offered an amendment to the resolution excluding Powell from his seat. On an inquiry from Rep. Celler, the Speaker ruled that the Curtis amendment would require only a majority vote to pass. 113 Cong. Rec. 5020 (1967). The amendment was ultimately adopted by a vote of 248 to 176, and the resolution as amended was adopted by a vote of 307 to 116. *Id.* at 5037–38. Powell was declared excluded from his seat, and the Governor of New York was notified that the seat was vacant.

Six weeks later, Powell won the special election to fill the vacancy created by his own exclusion, garnering 86% of the vote. However, he never sought to be sworn in to the 90th

Congress. In 1968, he was reelected to the 91st Congress, and he was seated in January 1969. (He was also fined $25,000 and denied seniority.) He and a number of his constituents also filed suit, seeking a declaratory judgment that his exclusion had been unconstitutional. In June 1969, the Supreme Court ruled in his favor.

Writing for an 8–1 majority, **Chief Justice Warren** focused on the constitutional distinction between *exclusion* and *expulsion*. Exclusion requires a bare majority, but is done pursuant to each house's ability to "Judge * * * the Elections, Returns and Qualifications of its own Members," while expulsion has no substantive limitations but requires "the Concurrence of two thirds." U.S. Const. art. I, § 5, cl. 1–2. The vote to exclude Powell (307 to 116) did pass the two-thirds bar, but the Court declined to read this exclusion vote as a constructive expulsion. To do so, Warren argued, "would require * * * speculation that the House would have voted to expel Powell had it been faced with that question. The Speaker ruled that the House was voting to exclude Powell, and we will not speculate what the result might have been if Powell had been seated and expulsion proceedings subsequently instituted." Perhaps some members voted strategically to exclude, knowing that the resolution would easily clear the majority bar with or without their votes, and they might have voted differently if they had thought their votes could be pivotal. Moreover, if the vote had been to expel, some members may have been swayed by a longstanding tradition that legislative houses did not expel members for actions taken in a previous Congress.

Relying on a historical analysis beginning with a 1553 exclusion from the House of Commons and continuing with the framing and adoption of the Constitution and post-ratification practice, the Court concluded that the House's power to judge Powell's "qualifications" was limited to those qualifications set forth in the Constitution (e.g., age, residency, and citizenship), and did not extend to a general power to *set* qualifications (such as good character) for membership. A contrary holding, Warren noted, "would effectively nullify the Convention's decision to require a two-thirds vote for expulsion."

Accordingly, the Court held that, "since Adam Clayton Powell, Jr., was duly elected by the voters of the 18th Congressional District of New York and was not ineligible to serve under any provision of the Constitution, the House was without power to exclude him from its membership."

Justice Douglas concurred to note that the question of whether Congress could add qualifications to those in the Constitution was really a question of whether the will of the voters would be respected. "Today we proclaim the constitutional principle of 'one man, one vote.' When that principle is followed and the electors choose a person who is repulsive to the Establishment in Congress, by what constitutional authority can that group of electors be disenfranchised?" He noted that this effect could be worked through the expulsion power, but this case "is not an expulsion case," and might well have turned out differently had it been one.

In a striking aside, Douglas also suggested that the exclusion of Powell had "racist overtones."

Justice Stewart dissented on the grounds that Powell's reelection had mooted the lawsuit.

Although Powell was reelected in 1968, his long absences from his district and the findings of misconduct finally caught up with him in 1970, when he lost the Democratic primary to Charles Rangel. Rangel went on to represent the district until 2017, when he retired, having faced allegations of ethical improprieties himself.

NOTES ON POWELL AND THE LEGISLATURE'S AUTHORITY TO REGULATE ITS MEMBERSHIP

1. *Policing the Boundaries.* The Court's opinion in *Powell* is careful to police the distinction between exclusion and expulsion. Exclusion has a lower procedural threshold (mere majority vote) because it is substantively specific: it must be for one of the constitutionally enumerated reasons. One can only be excluded as an exercise of the congressional houses' power to judge the elections, returns, and qualifications of members, and the qualifications are limited to those listed in constitutional text. Expulsion, on the other hand, has a very high procedural threshold: getting two-thirds of either chamber to agree on something is not easy. But the Constitution is silent as to what sorts of "disorderly Behaviour" would justify expulsion. The substance is left up to each chamber.

Powell holds that the House cannot expel under the guise of excluding—even in a situation where the vote to exclude cleared the two-thirds bar for expulsion. But the Court was also at pains to suggest that it would be much more deferential to congressional judgment so long as Congress stayed within the categories specified in the Constitution. Thus, citing *Baker v. Carr* (see § 1(A) of this chapter), Chief Justice Warren wrote that the House's power to judge qualifications "is at most a 'textually demonstrable commitment' to Congress to judge only the qualifications expressly set forth in the Constitution." In other words, a judgment *of* Powell's qualifications—say, that he was in fact under 25 years of age or not in fact a citizen of New York—might well be a nonjusticiable political question.

Likewise, in two footnotes, the majority went out of its way to "express no view on what limitations may exist on Congress' power to expel or otherwise punish a member." Justice Douglas's concurrence did in fact express a view on this question: "[I]f this were an expulsion case I would think that no justiciable controversy would be presented, the vote of the House being two-thirds or more."

One way to read *Powell*, then, is that the courts will "polic[e] the boundaries of congressional power," but "they [will] not stray[ ] inside those boundaries." Josh Chafetz, *Democracy's Privileged Few: Legislative Privilege and Democratic Norms in the British and American Constitutions* 56 (2007).

2. *Exclusion or Expulsion.* An institutional analysis provides support for the Court's refusal to equate a two-thirds vote to exclude Powell with a two-thirds vote to expel him. Understanding the order of voting illuminates the decision. The Committee that investigated the allegations against Powell recommended that he be seated and censured. After debate, the House rejected a motion that would have forced an immediate vote on the recommendation, thereby signaling that the Committee's proposal was in trouble. The resolution was then amended so that it required exclusion; that amendment passed by a simple majority of 248–176. In a pivotal ruling, the Chair determined that the final vote required to exclude Powell was also a simple majority; only expulsion required a two-thirds supermajority under the Constitution. Why was this ruling so important to the final vote margin? Think about the 59 members who supported passage of the amended resolution even though they had opposed the amendment itself. Had they been convinced to change their positions because of persuasive debate by their

colleagues? Probably not. These members likely voted strategically. They realized that the resolution of exclusion was going to pass because a simple majority had already voted in favor of it. Perhaps they voted as they did because they thought some punishment was appropriate and this resolution was the only option, or perhaps they did not want their votes to become controversial issues in their next reelection campaigns. The Supreme Court was entirely right, under this analysis, to refuse to equate the exclusion motion with a decision to expel, given the difference in the voting rule applied to each.

3.   *Exclusion and the First Amendment.* In *Bond v. Floyd*, 385 U.S. 116 (1966), the Supreme Court held that the Georgia House of Representatives had violated Julian Bond's First Amendment rights (as secured by the Due Process Clause of the Fourteenth Amendment) when it excluded him from membership, though he had been duly elected, because of his criticism of the Vietnam War and of the federal draft laws. Georgia argued that (1) the exclusion was proper because the Georgia Constitution requires representatives to take an oath pledging to support the constitutions of Georgia and the United States; (2) this requirement is clearly constitutional because the United States Constitution itself (Article VI, cl. 3) requires members of state legislatures to take an oath to support the federal Constitution; and (3) the state legislature has the power to determine whether a given representative can take the oath with sincerity. Georgia conceded that Bond stood ready to take the oath, but insisted on its legislature's right to withhold office because Bond's criticism of federal policy showed that he could not take the oath with sincerity.

The Court agreed that the Georgia oath requirement was constitutional, but held that neither Article VI, cl. 3, on its own force, nor the Georgia oath requirement in light of the First Amendment, can "authorize a majority of state legislators to test the sincerity with which another duly elected legislator can swear to uphold the Constitution. * * * [W]hile the State has an interest in requiring its legislators to swear to a belief in constitutional processes of government, surely the oath gives it no interest in limiting its legislators' capacity to discuss their views of local or national policy. The manifest function of the First Amendment in a representative government requires that legislators be given the widest latitude to express their views on issues of policy."

4.   *Exclusion and Race.* Both Powell and Bond were African-American legislators, and Justice Douglas adverted to the "racist overtones" of Powell's exclusion. During the debate on the exclusion, members who opposed the exclusion as unconstitutional noted that Congress had excluded members on the grounds of extra-constitutional qualifications only three times before "in rare instances of extreme political tension. * * * These deviations occurred in three categories of cases reflecting anti-Mormon[,] anti-Confederate[,] and antiradical * * * feeling." 113 Cong. Rec. 5023 (1967) (statement of Rep. Celler). Should these factors have led the Court to investigate the motives of the Georgia legislature in Bond's case or of Congress in Powell's? If so, what records should the Court have used to determine the legislature's motivation—only public records of deliberations or also affidavits from legislators detailing private conversations or internal reasoning? What about evidence of constituent communications and views that might have influenced the outcome?

PROBLEMS OF CONGRESSIONAL EXCLUSION AND EXPULSION

Problem 2-2. Representative Powell was reelected and seated before the Supreme Court's decision, and he was not later excluded from Congress. But assume that after

Powell's next reelection, the House had voted by a two-thirds majority to expel him. Powell then sued on the ground that his expulsion was racially motivated. Is that controversy justiciable? Has Powell stated a claim for which relief can be granted, if he can prove racially discriminatory intent? If Congress does not expel him but continues to deny him seniority, can he return to court to obtain an injunction restoring his status and placing him at the head of a subcommittee on which he is the most senior member? Or do matters of seniority and committee assignments present political questions that the courts should avoid?

   Problem 2-3. When Barack Obama became President of the United States, he left his Senate seat from Illinois vacant. State law allowed the Governor, Democrat Rod Blagojevich, to appoint the successor to serve until the 2010 election. It soon became apparent through federal wiretaps and other evidence that the Governor, who was already under investigation for corruption, was seeking favors from people he was considering for the position. As this controversy raged, Blagojevich announced that he would appoint Roland Burris, a Democrat who had been elected Illinois' first African-American State Comptroller and Attorney General. Soon there were allegations that Burris had discussed a *quid pro quo* with the venal Blagojevich, and his appointment became controversial. Although Burris received appointment papers from the Governor, the Illinois Secretary of State refused to sign them. When Burris arrived in Washington to take his seat, the Secretary of the Senate rejected his credentials because Senate Rule II, part of the Senate rules since 1884, requires that an appointment include the signatures of both the Governor and Secretary of State. Senate Majority Leader Harry Reid (D-Nev.) and the senior Senator from Illinois, Dick Durbin (D), declared that Burris should not be seated; Reid cited the Article I, § 5 provision making "[e]ach House * * * the Judge of the Elections, Returns and Qualifications of its own Members." Does *Powell v. McCormack* provide guidance as to the Senate's power in this case to scrutinize this appointment and possibly to refuse to seat Burris? What is the appropriate venue to determine Burris' suitability to serve, or is it sufficient that the sitting Governor appointed him, notwithstanding the circumstances of the appointment? To the extent that charges of corruption accompanied Blagojevich's decision, are there any facts that might support a decision by the Senate not to seat his appointee? To seat and then expel him by a two-thirds vote? *See* Akhil Reed Amar & Josh Chafetz, *How the Senate Can Stop Blagojevich*, Slate, Dec. 31, 2008, https://slate.com/news-and-politics/2008/12/how-the-senate-can-stop-blagojevich.html.

   In the end, Burris went to state court, which ruled that state law did not require the Secretary of State's signature for the appointment to be valid, and the Illinois Secretary of State signed a second document acknowledging the appointment to be legally valid. Accordingly, the Secretary of the Senate accepted his credentials, Democratic leadership dropped its objections to seating him, and Burris became a senator. He did not run for election in 2010 and, in a blow to the president, Republican Mark Kirk won Obama's old Senate seat, possibly aided by the scandal surrounding the Illinois Democratic Party. In 2011, former Governor Blagojevich was convicted of 18 counts of corruption and sentenced to a 14-year prison term.

B. QUALIFICATIONS IMPOSED BY STATES: TERM LIMITATIONS FOR FEDERAL LEGISLATORS

By the end of the 1994 elections, 22 states had amended their constitutions or passed legislation limiting the terms of office of their U.S. representatives and senators. Fourteen of these provisions were designed as ballot access measures, allowing long-term incumbents to run, but only as write-in candidates. We will discuss ballot access regulations, and the willingness of the courts to tolerate such restrictions, in Part C of this section. Term-limit advocates hoped to rid Congress of professional politicians in the belief that such lawmakers inevitably act in ways that are contrary to the public interest. They argued that replacing professional politicians with amateurs would weaken the power of special interests and eliminate unseemly, close relationships between elected officials and lobbyists.[24]

Most political scientists who study the issue, on the other hand, oppose term limits.[25] Some dispute that term limits will usher in the era of the citizen-legislator, noting that political careers remain possible with term limits, although a careerist will be forced to adopt a strategy of *progressive* political ambition by moving periodically to a new office or political job.[26] Many object to term limits because they will deprive legislatures of their most experienced members, thereby reducing the ability of Congress to pass legislation to deal with controversial or difficult problems. Moreover, because any expertise in legislating will only be useful for a very short time, they reduce the incentive for members to develop such expertise while they are in office, which in turn further degrades legislative capacity. Reduced legislator effectiveness also shifts the balance of power: numerous studies of term limits in state legislatures have shown that they shift power away from legislatures and toward governors, bureaucrats, and lobbyists.[27] Some opponents also argue that interest groups will continue to influence representatives disproportionately through campaign contributions. Moreover, term limits will provide special interests with an even more powerful tool for influence: post-service jobs for term-limited representatives. Finally, some point out that term limits take power away from voters: no matter how much they may want to reelect an incumbent, at some point they will be barred from doing so.

In 1995, the Supreme Court considered the constitutionality of state-imposed congressional term limits.

---

[24] See, e.g., George Will, *Restoration: Congress, Term Limits, and the Recovery of Deliberative Democracy* (1992) (arguing that term limits would enhance deliberation and representative democracy).

[25] For an overview of political scientists' views on term limits in the aftermath of their growth in the 1990s, see Bruce E. Cain & Marc A. Levin, *Term Limits*, 2 Ann. Rev. Pol. Sci. 163 (1999).

[26] *See* Elizabeth Garrett, *Term Limitations and the Myth of the Citizen-Legislator*, 81 Cornell L. Rev. 623 (1996).

[27] See John M. Carey et al., *The Effects of Term Limits on State Legislatures: A New Survey of the 50 States*, 31 Legis. Stud. Q. 105 (2006); Susan M. Miller et al., *Reexamining the Institutional Effects of Term Limits in U.S. State Legislatures*, 36 Legis. Stud. Q. 71 (2011); Gary Moncrief & Joel A. Thompson, *On the Outside Looking In: Lobbyists' Perspectives on the Effects of State Legislative Term Limits*, 1 State Pol. & Pol'y Q. 394 (2001); Marjorie Sarbaugh-Thompson, *Legislators and Administrators: Complex Relationships Complicated by Term Limits*, 35 Legis. Stud. Q. 57 (2010).

U.S. Term Limits, Inc. v. Thornton

514 U.S. 779 (1995).

In 1992, Arkansas voters adopted by ballot initiative an amendment to the state constitution prohibiting anyone who had served three or more terms in the House or two or more terms in the Senate from appearing on the ballot. **Justice Stevens'** opinion for the Court relied on *Powell v. McCormack* for the proposition that the qualifications for congressional service enumerated in the Constitution are " 'fixed,' at least in the sense that they may not be supplemented by Congress."

But here, it was not Congress seeking to add qualifications for service; it was a state. Does that make a difference? The Court held that it does not, for two reasons: "First, we conclude that the power to add qualifications is not within the 'original powers' of the States, and thus is not reserved to the States by the Tenth Amendment. Second, even if States possessed some original power in this area, we conclude that the Framers intended the Constitution to be the exclusive source of qualifications for Members of Congress, and that the Framers thereby 'divested' States of any power to add qualifications." Stevens also tied this holding to democratic theory: "Our conclusion that States lack the power to impose qualifications vindicates the same 'fundamental principle of our representative democracy' that we recognized in *Powell*, namely, that 'the people should choose whom they please to govern them.' "

Arkansas pointed out that it was not technically preventing anyone from being elected and therefore not imposing any qualifications for holding office—rather, it was imposing qualifications for appearing on the ballot, which it could do under its Art. I, § 4, cl. 1 power to prescribe the "Times, Places and Manner of holding Elections for Senators and Representatives." The Court rejected this argument because "[c]onstitutional rights would be of little value if they could be . . . indirectly denied. * * * In our view, [the Arkansas provision] is an indirect attempt to accomplish what the Constitution prohibits Arkansas from accomplishing directly. * * * [I]t cannot be seriously contended that the intent behind [the provision] is other than to prevent the election of incumbents. * * * In our view, an amendment with the avowed purpose and obvious effect of evading the requirements of the Qualifications Clauses by handicapping a class of candidates cannot stand. To argue otherwise is to suggest that the Framers spent significant time and energy in debating and crafting Clauses that could be easily evaded. More importantly, allowing States to evade the Qualifications Clauses by 'dress[ing] eligibility to stand for Congress in ballot access clothing' trivializes the basic principles of our democracy that underlie those Clauses. Petitioners' argument treats the Qualifications Clauses not as the embodiment of a grand principle, but rather as empty formalism" (internal quotation marks omitted).

Because this ballot access provision was effectively a term limit, and because term limits impose a qualification for serving in Congress beyond those listed in the Constitution, the Court struck it down.

In dissent, **Justice Thomas** took aim at the majority's invocation of democratic theory: "It is ironic that the Court bases today's decision on the right of the people to 'choose whom they please to govern them.' Under our Constitution, there is only one State whose people have the right to 'choose whom they please' to represent Arkansas in Congress. The Court holds, however, that neither the elected legislature of that State nor the people themselves (acting by ballot initiative) may prescribe any qualifications for those representatives. The majority therefore defends the right of the people of Arkansas to 'choose whom they please to govern them' by invalidating a provision that won nearly 60% of the votes cast in a direct election and that carried every congressional district in the State."

Contrary to the majority, Thomas insisted that "the people of Arkansas do enjoy 'reserved' powers over the selection of their representatives in Congress," and that the term limits at issue were simply an exercise of those reserved powers. For Thomas, the qualifications laid out in the Constitution imposed a sort of floor on each state, for the protection of the other states: "when the people of one State send immature, disloyal, or unknowledgeable representatives to Congress, they jeopardize not only their own interests but also the interests of the people of other States. Because Congress wields power over all the States, the people of each State need some guarantee that the legislators elected by the people of other States will meet minimum standards of competence. The Qualifications Clauses provide that guarantee: They list the requirements that the Framers considered essential to protect the competence of the National Legislature." But, "[i]f the people of a State decide that they would like their representatives to possess additional qualifications * * * they have done nothing to frustrate the policy behind the Qualifications Clauses."

For Thomas, the federalism dimension made this case entirely unlike *Powell*: "I agree with the majority that Congress has no power to prescribe qualifications for its own Members. This fact, however, does not show that the Qualifications Clauses contain a hidden exclusivity provision. The reason for Congress' incapacity is not that the Qualifications Clauses deprive Congress of the authority to set qualifications, but rather that nothing in the Constitution grants Congress this power. In the absence of such a grant, Congress may not act. But deciding whether the Constitution denies the qualification-setting power to the States and the people of the States requires a fundamentally different legal analysis."

And this distinction between state-imposed and congressionally imposed qualifications sounded in democratic theory: "One reason why the Framers decided not to let Congress prescribe the qualifications of its own Members was that incumbents could have used this power to perpetuate themselves or their ilk in office. As Madison pointed out at the Philadelphia Convention, Members of Congress would have an obvious conflict of interest if they could determine who may run against them. But neither the people of the States nor the state legislatures would labor under the same conflict of interest when prescribing qualifications for Members of Congress."

Finally, Thomas was far more sympathetic to Arkansas' claim that a ballot access provision is not the same as a term limit. Noting the advantages that incumbents enjoy in running for reelection, Thomas suggested that Arkansas' provision could be understood as "merely designed to level the playing field on which challengers compete with them."

NOTES ON U.S. TERM LIMITS AND SUBSEQUENT DEVELOPMENTS

1.   *Were the Voters Irrational?* At the same time that voters passed ballot initiatives imposing term limits on federal legislators, they also voted in most cases to return their senior incumbents to office. How can these seemingly inconsistent choices be reconciled? Einer Elhauge argues that this paradox disappears when we understand the collective-action problems that faced voters. "Incumbents by definition have more seniority than

challengers, and this seniority gives them more legislative clout. Any individual district that ousts its incumbent is thus penalized by a smaller share of legislative power and governmental benefits unless the other districts also oust their incumbents." *Are Term Limits Undemocratic?*, 64 U. Chi. L. Rev. 83, 85 (1997). Elhauge argues that voters might prefer less senior representatives with ideological views closer to theirs, but, on balance, voters will prefer a more influential representative, who can send her constituency a greater share of governmental benefits. If, however, voters can be sure that no district can vote for a more senior lawmaker because of term limits, the penalty for electing a challenger is reduced. In addition, term limits allow voters to get rid of the senior representatives from other districts, a result that cannot be obtained through regular voting. In some cases, the benefits of removing these lawmakers from office may exceed any costs to voters of losing the ability to elect their own incumbent to an unlimited number of terms.

Elhauge's explanation suggests why rational voters might simultaneously support term limits for all federal lawmakers and yet still vote for their own incumbent in the absence of such restrictions. It does not explain, however, why voters in a particular state would limit the terms of their representatives without an assurance that other states would also adopt term limitations. Again, however, voters may have been wiser than they appear at first glance. It is no coincidence that groups of states adopted term limits at the same time through a coordinated national effort led by a few organized interest groups. For example, 13 states adopted term limits in 1992. Some of the state constitutional amendments specified that the limitation would not go into effect until 21 or more states had also adopted limitations on the terms of federal lawmakers. Moreover, many of the provisions had delayed effective dates, allowing time for the states that moved quickly to repeal term limits if voters from other states declined to follow their lead.[28] Once a critical mass of states had adopted federal term limits, their representatives would command the votes to change congressional rules to weaken the power of the seniority system and reduce the relative advantage of longtime incumbents over junior members.

2.   *Limitations on State Officials.* Term limitations are common in state and local government. Fifteen states place term limits on state legislators, 36 states limit the number of terms their governors can serve, and many local officials face term limits after a few years of public service. These term limits can take a variety of forms: some are limits on consecutive years of service, while others are lifetime limits; some are quite strict (Virginia governors may not serve consecutive terms), while others are relatively lenient (in Louisiana, members of both the state senate and the state house can serve up to twelve consecutive years, with no lifetime limit, and those term limited out of one chamber are still eligible to run for the other).[29]

Although term limits on state legislators have been challenged as violating both state and federal constitutional requirements, they have generally been upheld. The leading case is *Legislature of the State of California v. Eu*, 816 P.2d 1309 (Cal. 1991), which balanced the interest of incumbents in retaining office and the interest of voters in

---

[28]   See John Carey, *Term Limits and Legislative Representation* 12–13 (1996) (detailing provisions of the state amendments).

[29]   For a breakdown of state legislative term limits, see Nat'l Conf. of State Legis., *The Term-Limited States* (Mar. 13, 2015), http://www.ncsl.org/research/about-state-legislatures/chart-of-term-limits-states.aspx. For a breakdown of gubernatorial term limits, see U.S. Term Limits, *Term Limits on Governor*, https://www.termlimits.com/governor_termlimits/.

having the choice of reelecting them against the state's interests in unclogging the political system and ending the incumbency advantage in elections. The court found that no fundamental rights had been critically burdened (voters have no "right" to vote for a particular candidate) and the state's interest was considerable.[30]

In some states, term limits have had very little effect on political dynamics because legislators did not tend to serve for long periods of time even when their terms were unlimited. In states like California, however, where legislatures were full of career politicians, term limits have caused significant, and sometimes complete, turnover, helped bring to power new leaders, and may have decreased the ability of legislators to pass controversial or significant laws. Some have suggested that term limits may be associated with demographic changes in legislatures, allowing more women and minorities to win seats. However, the most comprehensive study to date of term limits in state legislatures found that they had no appreciable effect on legislator wealth, religion, age, race, sex, or ideology.[31]

Supporters of term limits argued that elections would become more competitive because there would inevitably be more elections for open seats. Kousser reveals, however, that that has not occurred because "the increase in number of open seats has been outweighed by the decrease in the competitiveness of both open seats and races with incumbents." *Term Limits and State Legislatures*, in *Democracy in the States: Experiments in Election Reform* 117, 119 (Bruce Cain, Todd Donovan & Caroline Tolbert eds., 2008). Open-seat races now occur regularly, including in districts that are drawn to be dominated by one party, and strong challengers now wait until the incumbent is termed out, making the interim races less competitive. Moreover, a national survey of state legislators demonstrates that the growth of term limits has not ushered in the rise of the citizen-legislator. The overwhelming majority of lawmakers facing the end of their terms intend to run for another office, become a lobbyist, or vie for an appointed role. Only 18% of those in the lower house and 28% of those in the upper house plan to return to private life. *Id.* at 120–21.

Term limits' most significant effects are institutional ones. As noted above, term limits appear to weaken legislative party leaders and to strengthen the influence of governors, who, although term limited themselves, have access to more professional staff and the substantial resources of the executive branch. In several state legislatures, term limits have weakened the seniority norm and increased the involvement of junior members in key decisions. Term limits also seem to increase the influence of lobbyists, although this shift may be partially counterbalanced by lobbyists' need to establish relationships with new people and educate them about their issues.[32]

Some states with term limitations on state legislators subsequently witnessed efforts to roll back or repeal the limits. In February 2002, the Idaho legislature became

---

[30]   See also *Bates v. Jones*, 131 F.3d 843 (9th Cir. 1997) (en banc) (holding that voters could constitutionally adopt lifetime bans on incumbents after a limited period of service "as a means to promote democracy by opening up the political process and restoring competitive elections").

[31]   John M. Carey et al., *The Effects of Term Limits on State Legislatures: A New Survey of the 50 States*, 31 Legis. Stud. Q. 105, 113–16 (2006).

[32]   Alan Greenblatt, *The Truth About Term Limits*, Governing Mag., Jan. 2006, at 2; Thomas Little & Rick Farmer, *Legislative Leadership*, in *The Case of Term Limits* 55, 58–64 (Karl Kurtz, Bruce Cain & Richard Niemi eds., 2007). See also Christopher Mooney, *Lobbyists and Interest Groups*, in *Institutional Change in American Politics: The Case of Term Limits, supra*, at 119 (finding mixed evidence of increased influence of lobbyists in term-limited states but finding considerable effect on lobbyist behavior and legislator perceptions of lobbyists).

the first to repeal term limits, a reform that had been enacted nearly eight years earlier through a ballot initiative. The Governor vetoed the legislation on the ground that the "will of the voters * * * must be protected," but the legislature overrode his veto with a two-thirds vote in both houses. A study of the vote to overturn term limits reveals that support came primarily from Republican legislators, who wanted to retain their party's control over the legislature, and from representatives of rural areas.[33] Legislators from rural districts argued that term limits would deprive their constituents in sparsely populated areas of experienced leaders, particularly in local offices that are traditionally hard to fill. There was no significant reaction against the legislature's decision. A few incumbents were defeated in the 2002 primary elections, but it appears that other issues played a large role in those elections. A popular referendum to "repeal the repeal" and reinstate term limits ended in a narrow victory for anti-term-limits forces.

Only a few states with term limitations passed them in legislative form that would allow state legislators to repeal or modify them; in the other states, a popular vote would be required to repeal provisions in state constitutions imposing term limits on legislators. So far, voters have been unwilling to reject their decision to adopt legislative term limits. In 2012, California voters adopted Proposition 28, which reduced the total number of years allowed to a state legislator from 14 to 12 but allowed a legislator to serve that entire period in one house (rather than limiting a politician to three two-year terms in the state house and two four-year terms in the state senate). Legislators have also challenged term limits through litigation. Term limits adopted in 1992 in Wyoming were overturned in May 2004 by the state supreme court, which ruled in *Cathcart v. Meyer*, 88 P.3d 1050 (Wyo. 2004), that they should have been enacted as a constitutional amendment, not through a statutory ballot initiative. This holding substantially increased the obstacles for term-limit supporters in Wyoming because constitutional amendments must be first approved by two-thirds of each legislative house before they can be placed on the ballot.

3.   *Developments in Congress Since* U.S. Term Limits. The majority in *U.S. Term Limits* made clear that the adoption of federal term limits requires a constitutional amendment. Shortly after the decision, Congress considered such an amendment to impose 12-year limits on service in each house. Although the proposal received majority support, it lacked the two-thirds vote required for a constitutional amendment. (The Senate did not actually vote on the amendment because supporters lacked two votes to cut off a filibuster.)

There may, however, be other ways to approximate the effects of term limits. In 1995, as part of the Republican "Contract with America," the House of Representatives limited committee chairmanships to six years. The effect of the rule was significant. Four senior Republican members, including the Chair of the powerful Ways and Means Committee, retired in 2000 because they could not retain their chairmanships. In January 2002, the House eliminated the eight-year limit on holding the position as Speaker. Critics argue that these term limits make it more difficult for Congress to oversee the executive branch effectively, although defenders maintain that any loss is balanced by an increase in innovative ideas. Since 2000, the House has tended not to include term limits on committee chairs in the rules when Democrats control the body, and to reinstate them when Republicans return to power.

---

[33]   See Daniel Smith, *Overturning Term Limits: The Legislature's Own Private Idaho?*, 36 PS 215 (2003).

In recent years, the issue of term limits for members of Congress has again gained some traction, first because of the support of "Tea Party" Republicans and then when President Trump tied the issue to his "Drain the Swamp" mantra. Keith Larson has argued that this movement is not likely to succeed in convincing a supermajority of federal lawmakers to support a term-limit amendment because one of two necessary conditions for legislators to act against their electoral self-interest is not present. *Republican Revolutionaries and Tea Party Patriots: A Public Choice Analysis of Congressional Term Limits*, 86 St. John's L. Rev. 761 (2012). The two conditions he identifies as necessary to convince strategic lawmakers to apply term limits to themselves are, first, that the lawmakers are members "of an historically underrepresented ideological political faction," *id.* at 765, and, second, that voter dissatisfaction with Congress is strong. "[L]egislators will take public positions in favor of term limits to signal to voters that they are not part of the problem in Congress; rather, that they are attempting to fix the institution." *Id.* at 766. Although public opinion of Congress is currently very low, conservatives no longer suffer the sense of chronic underrepresentation given their recent power in Congress and the states. Thus, he concludes that this current push for federal term limits will be no more successful than the one in the mid-1990s. Are there any other conditions necessary or conducive for lawmaker support of a reform so distant from their interest in reelection? Can you imagine any scenario under which a term-limit constitutional amendment is sent to the states for ratification? If it were, what position would strategic state lawmakers likely take?

4. *Distinguishing Between Indirect Qualifications and Legitimate Ballot Access Provisions.* Remember that the Arkansas provision in *U.S. Term Limits* was phrased as a ballot access provision, denying a place on the ballot to lawmakers who had served a certain period of time in the House or Senate. The Court rejected the argument that the Arkansas amendment merely restricted incumbents' access to the ballot and found that it imposed an additional qualification on federal legislative offices. The Court looked to both the effect and the intent of the provision in reaching the conclusion that the state was trying to do indirectly what it was prohibited from doing directly. Although the Court indicated that empirical evidence was not required to determine the likely effect of a provision, it believed that the ballot restriction "will make it significantly more difficult for the barred candidate to win the election." It supported this conclusion with the following evidence: "[I]n over 1,300 Senate elections since the passage of the Seventeenth Amendment in 1913, only one has been won by a write-in candidate. In over 20,000 House elections since the turn of the century, only five have been won by write-in candidates."

Justice Thomas responded that these empirical data would not describe the state of affairs in a world with term limits. He argued that most write-in candidates in the past had been fringe candidates with virtually no name recognition or financial backing, while write-in candidates under the Arkansas amendment would be well-known incumbents. In the past, only twice had *incumbent* Congress members sought reelection as write-in candidates; one of them won with 83% of the vote, and the other managed a respectable showing of 23% support. Which prediction is likely to have been more accurate? Should the determination of the fate of such an amendment rest on this kind of empirical speculation?

In the *U.S. Term Limits* case, the Court relied on the state supreme court's finding that the intent of the amendment was to impose term limits on federal lawmakers. The opinion, therefore, says little about how a court is to discern the intent behind such a provision, particularly one that was enacted by hundreds of thousands of voters. The majority mentioned the initiative's preamble, which stated explicitly that "the people of Arkansas * * * herein limit the terms of elected officials." Also, the name of the primary group supporting the amendment and participating in the lawsuit—U.S. Term Limits, Inc.—led one judge on the state supreme court to conclude that the ballot access provision was actually a qualification. Are these legitimate ways to discern the intent of those enacting this provision? As the dissent noted, the preamble also evidenced a concern with entrenched incumbency that results in a system offering voters very little real choice among candidates. Given the electoral advantages that Justice Thomas lists in his dissent, ballot access limits may provide challengers—who lack the same access to the media, lists of donors and volunteers, and the ability to correspond with constituents using franked mail—a fair chance to unseat incumbents. Would an intent to level the political playing field be acceptable under the majority's test, allowing a court to uphold a provision similar to the Arkansas amendment as a permissible ballot access regulation?

Determining whether a law imposes qualifications on candidates or only restricts their access to the ballot is more than merely a matter of semantics. As we will see in the next section, the Court tends to apply less exacting constitutional tests to ballot access regulations, even though *U.S. Term Limits* suggests that imposing explicit qualifications on candidates for the federal legislature may not be relevantly different from restricting access to the ballot for certain categories of people.

C. BALLOT ACCESS PROVISIONS

Article I, § 4 of the Constitution, the Elections Clause, allows the states to regulate the "Times, Places and Manner of holding Elections for Senators and Representatives," although Congress can pass legislation to make or alter state electoral regulations. Before 1900, concerns about ballot access restrictions were nonexistent. There were no official ballots; instead, political parties provided voters with ballots listing only their candidates for office. Because party ballots were printed in distinctive colors, keeping one's vote secret was difficult, and voters were often bribed or intimidated into voting a particular way. Only with the adoption of the secret, uniform, and government-printed ballot did the question of ballot access become important for policymakers and the courts.[34] Ballot access implicates the interests of many players in the political system: voters, who realistically can only elect candidates who appear on the ballot; candidates; and political parties, the groups that largely determine who will be listed on the ballot.

Although states have the constitutional power to regulate elections, their authority is limited because restrictions implicate constitutional guarantees. Most obviously, ballot access laws affect the right to vote. In addition, laws that impair the right of minor-party or independent candidates to obtain a spot on the ballot undermine the right to associate for political purposes. Balanced against these constitutional concerns is the states' legitimate interest in regulating elections to reduce voter confusion, disorder, and fraud. The Court has applied a sliding-scale approach, calibrating the level of scrutiny to the burden imposed by the ballot access provision. In *Williams v. Rhodes*, 393 U.S. 23 (1968), the Court struck down a law requiring new political parties to obtain signatures equal to 15% of the ballots cast

---

[34]   See Marjorie Hershey, *Party Politics in America* 151 (15th ed. 2013).

in the last election and to file the petitions long before the election. It required that regulations imposing serious burdens on rights—in this case, essentially making it impossible for new parties to obtain ballot access—be narrowly tailored to achieve a compelling state interest. Laws that do not operate as prohibitions on access trigger less exacting scrutiny, allowing legitimate state regulatory interests to support reasonable and nondiscriminatory burdens. The choice of the standard of review— strict scrutiny versus some lesser scrutiny—often determines the outcome of the judicial analysis. See, e.g., *Lee v. Keith*, 463 F.3d 763 (7th Cir. 2006) (applying strict scrutiny to Illinois requirements that independent candidates file 323 days before the general election, the earliest filing deadline in the country, as well as meet stringent petition requirements, and holding statute unconstitutional); *Libertarian Party of Ohio v. Blackwell*, 462 F.3d 579 (6th Cir. 2006) (using strict scrutiny, invalidating Ohio deadlines for minor parties that required filing petitions more than a year before the general election).

Permissible state interests are linked to the Court's belief that "there must be a substantial regulation of elections if they are to be fair and honest and if some sort of order, rather than chaos, is to accompany the democratic processes." *Storer v. Brown*, 415 U.S. 724, 730 (1974). Consider the state interests identified in the following decision upholding a law that prohibits a candidate from appearing on the ballot as a candidate of more than one party. Such multiparty candidacies are called *fusion candidacies*. Is a ban on fusion candidacies designed to reduce voter confusion and protect the integrity of the electoral process, or is it a prohibition adopted by the two major parties to eliminate any threat from emerging political parties?

Timmons v. Twin Cities Area New Party

520 U.S. 351 (1997).

State Representative Andy Dawkins was running unopposed in the Democratic-Farmer-Labor (DFL) Party's primary. The Minnesota chapter of the national New Party also chose him as their candidate for the state legislature. Because Dawkins had already filed as a candidate for the DFL's nomination, local election officials refused to accept the New Party's nominating petition, citing state laws that prohibit fusion candidacies. The New Party sued, contending that the laws violate their members' associational rights under the federal Constitution. Although noting that the First Amendment "protects the right of citizens to associate and to form political parties for the advancement of common political goals and ideas," **Chief Justice Rehnquist** for the six-justice majority held that the antifusion law is a reasonable regulation of parties, elections, and ballots designed to reduce "election- and campaign-related disorder."

The Court reasoned that this burden on the New Party is a minor one. Although it cannot nominate the candidates of other parties, a political party "remains free to endorse whom it likes, to ally itself with others, to nominate candidates for office, and to spread its message to all who will listen." The state prohibition closes off one avenue of communication with the voters (i.e., the ballot), but "[b]allots serve primarily to elect candidates, not as forums for political expression." Because the burden on the New Party is slight, the state's interest in avoiding voter confusion and political chaos is sufficient to justify the law. As in previous ballot access cases, the majority did not require any empirical proof of voter confusion. Instead, it used the following worst-case scenario to support its conclusion that voters might be misled: "[M]embers of a major party could decide that a powerful way of 'sending a message' via the ballot would be for various factions of that party to nominate the major party's candidate as the candidate for the newly-formed 'No New Taxes,' 'Conserve Our Environment,' and 'Stop Crime Now' parties." Such tactics would transform the ballot "from a means of choosing candidates to a billboard for political advertising." This hypothetical implicated a second legitimate state interest: protecting the integrity of the electoral process and thus avoiding increased voter alienation and dissatisfaction.

Dissenting **Justice Stevens**, joined by **Justice Ginsburg**, thought fusion candidacies are "the best marriage of the virtues of minor party challenge to entrenched viewpoints and the political stability that the two-party system provides. * * * [They provide] a means by which voters with viewpoints not adequately represented by platforms of the two major parties can indicate to a particular candidate that—in addition to his support for the major party views—he should be responsive to the views of the minor party whose support for him was demonstrated where political parties demonstrate support—on the ballot." The majority, however, dismissed the argument that, without fusion-based alliances, minor parties would be unable to thrive, reasoning that the existence of benefits for minor parties does not mean that the state must permit fusion candidacies. "Many features of our political system—*e.g.*, single-member districts, 'first past the post' elections, and the high costs of campaigning—make it difficult for third parties to succeed in American politics. But the Constitution does not require States to permit fusion any more than it requires them to move to proportional-representation elections or public financing of campaigns."

Justice Stevens' dissent took particular issue with the majority's suggestion that the interest in maintaining a stable two-party system might be an acceptable state concern to justify ballot restrictions. "In most States, perhaps in all, there are two and only two major political parties. It is not surprising, therefore, that most States have enacted election laws that impose burdens on the development and growth of third parties. * * * The fact that the law was both intended to disadvantage minor parties and has had that effect is a matter that should weigh against, rather than in favor of, its constitutionality." He concluded: "It demeans the strength of the two-party system to assume that the major parties need to rely on laws that discriminate against independent voters and minor parties in order to preserve their positions of power. Indeed, it is a central theme of our jurisprudence that the entire electorate, which necessarily includes the members of major parties, will benefit from robust competition in ideas and governmental policies * * *."

NOTES ON TIMMONS AND THE IDEA OF A PARTISAN LOCKUP

1.   *Voter Confusion.* As in previous cases, the *Timmons* Court deferred to the state's allegation of voter confusion without requiring empirical proof. In *Munro v. Socialist Workers Party*, 479 U.S. 189, 195–96 (1986), the Court stated: "To require States to prove actual voter confusion, ballot overcrowding, or the presence of frivolous candidacies as a predicate to the imposition of reasonable ballot access restrictions would invariably lead to endless court battles over the sufficiency of the 'evidence' marshaled by a State to prove the predicate. Such a requirement would necessitate that a State's political system sustain some level of damage before the legislature could take corrective action. Legislatures, we think, should be permitted to respond to potential deficiencies in the electoral process with foresight rather than reactively, provided that the response is reasonable and does not significantly impinge on constitutionally protected rights."

Criticizing this kind of approach, Justice Stevens noted in *Timmons* that the only empirical data from a state with vibrant fusion politics, New York, revealed that the majority's "parade of horribles is fantastical."

Should courts require some showing that long ballots, fusion candidates, or multi-candidate races actually confuse voters rather than provide them with information or allow them more choices? With respect to fusion candidacies, is it not at least theoretically possible that the additional ballot information improves voters' ability to vote competently? Few voters are willing to invest significant time and energy to find and understand information about candidates for public office. Given their limited attention to political matters, most people vote on the basis of heuristic cues or shortcuts, such as party affiliation, that will allow them to vote in the same way that they would if they had full information about the candidates and their positions. These cues can allow them to vote competently even with limited information.[35] The strongest voting cues—party affiliation and incumbency—are usually apparent from the ballot; indeed, party affiliation is provided for most elections.

But the major-party cue may not sufficiently allow voters to distinguish among candidates. One result of a two-party system combined with single-member electoral districts is a convergence of the parties with respect to their positions on the issues.[36] Third-party endorsements, however, can provide a more particularized cue about a candidate's positions on the issues. Third parties that endorse candidates of major parties tend to be issue-oriented or ideologically driven; for example, knowing that the Republican candidate is supported by the Right-to-Life Party or the Libertarian Party reveals more completely her ideology than the Republican nomination alone. Can you make an argument that fusion candidacies actually help voters cast their ballots more competently, rather than add to their confusion?

Our discussion of ballot access rules demonstrates the profound importance of political parties in the organization of our electoral system. Political parties are challenging entities for the state to regulate. In a sense they organize government, and thus they are both the regulated and the regulators. They are fairly fragmented organizations, with local, state, and national organizations, and with arms in the government and outside it.[37]

2.   *The State Interest in Protecting the Two-Party System.* In some ballot access cases, the Court has accepted state claims that regulation was required to promote

[35]   See Elisabeth Gerber & Arthur Lupia, *Voter Competence in Direct Legislation Elections*, in *Citizen Competence and Democratic Institutions* 147 (Stephen Elkin & Karol Soltan eds., 1999); Christopher Elmendorf & David Schleicher, *Informing Consent: Voter Ignorance, Political Parties, and Election Law*, 2013 U. Ill. L. Rev. 363 (discussing ways to improve the partisan cue and voter competence).

[36]   See Jeffrey Berry & Clyde Wilcox, *The Interest Group Society* 64 (5th ed. 2009); Anthony Downs, *An Economic Theory of Democracy* 136 (1957). But see John Aldrich, *Why Parties? The Origin and Transformation of Political Parties in America* 169–74 (1995) (providing data to suggest that the public perceives parties as distinct and arguing that the "perception has a plausible basis"); Morris Fiorina, *Divided Government* 121–22 (2d ed. 1996) (suggesting that the two major parties are further apart ideologically than in the past, largely because of internal party politics).

[37]   See V.O. Key, Jr., *Politics, Parties, and Pressure Groups* 163–65 (5th ed. 1964) (differentiating among the party-in-government, the party-organization, and the party-in-the-electorate). For additional analysis of the regulation of political parties, see Samuel Issacharoff et al., *The Law of Democracy: Legal Structure of the Political Process*, chap. 4 (5th ed. 2016); David Ryden, *Representation in Crisis: The Constitution, Interest Groups, and Political Parties* (1996); Daniel Lowenstein, *Associational Rights of Major Political Parties: A Skeptical Inquiry*, 71 Tex. L. Rev. 1741 (1993); Symposium, *Law and Political Parties*, 100 Colum. L. Rev. 593–899 (2000).

political stability, to avoid splintered parties, and to restrain factionalism. This concern may be merely an interest in avoiding intraparty disputes by, for example, limiting the ability of people who have previously run in party primaries to appear on the ballot as independent candidates.[38] See *Storer v. Brown, supra.* Framed in this manner, the interest is not sufficient to support restrictions that are applied to independent candidates not recently associated with political parties. See *Anderson v. Celebrezze*, 460 U.S. 780 (1983). In *Clingman v. Beaver*, 544 U.S. 581 (2005), the Court upheld Oklahoma's law limiting participation in party primaries to only that party's members and independents, thereby forbidding, for example, a Republican from voting in the Libertarian Party's primary even if the Libertarian Party wished to open its primary fully. One of the state interests accepted to justify this law was the goal of preserving political parties as clearly identifiable groups with particular ideologies, and therefore ensuring that party affiliation sends a meaningful signal to voters who rely on party cue in casting ballots.

Increasingly, in cases such as *Timmons*, the Court is also willing to consider the state's interest in maintaining a stable, two-party electoral system. Even though he dissented in *Timmons*, Justice Souter agreed with the majority that "[i]f it could be shown that the disappearance of the two-party system would undermine" the state's interest in preserving a political system capable of governing effectively, it might justify certain restrictions. Unlike state interests tied to intraparty tension, this state interest can support broader ballot access regulations affecting independents, write-in candidates, and minor parties. In contrast, Stevens' dissent draws on *Williams v. Rhodes, supra*, in which the Court seemed dubious about the legitimacy of a state interest to protect the two-party system. Very clearly, the Court in *Williams* rejected the notion that laws could favor two particular parties, giving them a duopoly over ballot access. Instead, "[c]ompetition in ideas and governmental policies is at the core of our electoral process and of the First Amendment freedoms."

Several scholars have been sympathetic to Justice Stevens' concern in *Timmons* and have argued that courts should not apply very deferential review to ballot access provisions. Instead, they argue that the Court should be particularly aggressive in its review of such laws because they are enacted by incumbents who are members of established political parties and who are hostile to strong minor parties or independent candidacies.[39] Michael Klarman, for example, cites ballot access laws as examples of *legislative entrenchment* that foreclose for voters the option of expressing discontent with the two major parties. Incumbents have little to lose by passing restrictive ballot access laws because the laws themselves operate to keep candidates who might change the system off the ballot. *Majoritarian Judicial Review: The Entrenchment Problem*, 85 Geo. L.J. 491 (1997). These scholars not only do not accept protection of the current two-party system as a legitimate state interest, but they also argue that it should serve as a red flag to courts to view ballot access restrictions with great skepticism.[40]

---

[38]   For a sophisticated analysis of these "sore loser laws" and their effects on intraparty competition, see Michael Kang, *Sore Loser Laws and Democratic Contestation*, 99 Geo. L.J. 1013 (2011).

[39]   See, e.g., Richard Hasen, *Entrenching the Duopoly: Why the Supreme Court Should Not Allow the States to Protect the Democrats and Republicans from Political Competition*, 1997 Sup. Ct. Rev. 331; Samuel Issacharoff & Richard Pildes, *Politics as Markets: Partisan Lockups of the Democratic Process*, 50 Stan. L. Rev. 643 (1998).

[40]   But see David Dulio & James Thurber, *America's Two-Party System: Friend or Foe?*, 52 Admin. L. Rev. 769 (2000) (defending the ballot access cases from the perspective of "firm believers in the utility and value of the two-party system for American politics").

Under this *partisan lockup theory*, are many well-established features of our electoral system subject to constitutional attack? Many aspects of this system, including single-member districts and a simple plurality system, work to favor the development and entrenchment of two major parties.[41] Where should we draw the line between rigorous judicial scrutiny of laws that entrench the current political duopoly and more deferential review of choices made by the political branches? Are courts institutionally suited to draw such a line or to determine which laws fall on either side?[42]

3.   *The Other Side of the Balance: The First Amendment Rights Infringed by Ballot Access Restrictions.* Not only are courts willing to accept a variety of rationales as legitimate state interests justifying regulation, but they also tend to discount some of the interests of voters and political groups that are burdened by the restrictions. For example, the right to vote is viewed by the Court purely in instrumental terms. Similarly, as *Timmons* and the following case suggest, the Court has viewed the role of minor parties in our political system as a narrow one: to elect their own candidates. Is this an accurate vision of the influence of third parties?[43]

Munro v. Socialist Workers Party

479 U.S. 189 (1986).

The state of Washington used a blanket primary to select candidates for the general election.[44] There are three types of primaries: *closed*, in which only a voter who has declared her party affiliation can vote in the party's primary; *open*, in which a voter can participate in any party's primary, regardless of her partisan affiliation, but can vote in only one party's primary; and *blanket*, in which a voter not only does not have to declare a party affiliation, but may also vote in the primary of more than one party. In a blanket primary, for example, a voter can choose among Democrats for governor and then among Republicans for lieutenant governor. In Washington's system, minor-party candidates

---

[41]   See Maurice Duverger, *Political Parties: Their Organization and Activity in the Modern State* (1954) (classic formulation of this "true sociological law"); Gary Cox, *Making Votes Count: Strategic Coordination in the World's Electoral Systems* (1997) (evaluating Duverger's law).

[42]   See David Schleicher, *"Politics as Markets" Reconsidered: Natural Monopolies, Competitive Democratic Philosophy and Primary Ballot Access in American Elections*, 14 Sup. Ct. Econ. Rev. 163 (2006) (suggesting that the Supreme Court's ballot access line of cases has struck an appropriate balance between competing considerations).

[43]   See Steven Rosenstone, Roy Behr & Edward Lazarus, *Third Parties in America: Citizen Response to Major Party Failure* (2d ed. 1996).

[44]   Washington's blanket primary has since been ruled unconstitutional. *Democratic Party of Washington v. Reed*, 343 F.3d 1198 (9th Cir. 2003) (relying on *California Democratic Party v. Jones*, 530 U.S. 567 (2000), which struck down a California law enacted by popular vote to require blanket primaries on the ground that it interfered with associational rights of political parties, which had internal rules limiting participation in their primaries to members). The Supreme Court upheld the similar nonpartisan, or "top-two," primary that voters adopted to replace the blanket primary, but it left open the possibility of an as-applied challenge if the ballot design and text do not sufficiently alert voters that the party preference expressed by candidates is not the same as the parties endorsing those candidates. *Washington State Grange v. Washington State Republican Party*, 552 U.S. 442 (2008). The ballot provides a statement next to a candidate's name noting which party she prefers, or that she prefers no party, and a candidate is not limited to naming a qualified party. For example, in 2008, some candidates indicated a preference for the "Salmon Yoga Party," the "No Gas Taxes (R) Party," and similar labels, as well as the more traditional political parties. In the subsequent as-applied challenge, the appellate court ruled that the design of the ballot and other voter information materials made clear that a candidate's party preference was not an endorsement by the party and that there was no evidence of voter confusion. *Washington State Republican Party v. Washington State Grange*, 676 F.3d 784 (9th Cir. 2012). But see Mathew Manweller, *The Very Partisan Nonpartisan Top-Two Primary: Understanding What Voters Don't Understand*, 10 Election L.J. 255 (2011) (finding significant voter confusion about the relationship of candidates to parties in the Washington system). In June 2010, California adopted a similar top-two primary system through the initiative process.

could appear on the ballot for the general election only if they had been nominated at their parties' conventions and had received at least 1% of all the votes cast in the primary election. Before the ballot access law was adopted in 1977, minor-party candidates regularly appeared on the ballot (12 appeared in 1976); after the law was passed, only one in 12 minor-party candidates had qualified for the ballot for statewide office.

Dean Peoples was the nominee of the Socialist Workers Party, but received only nine one-hundredths of 1% of the total votes cast in the blanket primary. Accordingly, his name did not appear on the general ballot. Peoples, the party, and two voters argued that the ballot access law violated their rights under the First and Fourteenth Amendments. **Justice White** accepted as legitimate the state's interest in reducing ballot overcrowding and adopting reasonable regulations to ensure that candidates on the ballot had sufficient community support. Such regulations reduce voter confusion, avoid deception, and mitigate frustration of the democratic process. "We think that the State can properly reserve the general election ballot 'for major struggles,'" the Court wrote, citing *Storer*. The Court acknowledged that the restriction substantially burdened minor-party candidates and was a relatively greater burden than a requirement to gather signatures on a petition prior to the election, an alternative way of ensuring a modicum of support before a candidate appeared on the ballot. It noted, however, that in a blanket primary, minor-party candidates can campaign among the entire electoral pool to garner their 1%.

Although the majority realized that many minor parties only use a campaign as a platform to discuss issues, "[i]t can hardly be said that Washington's voters are denied freedom of association because they must channel their expressive activity into a campaign at the primary as opposed to the general election." Quoting *Storer*, the majority held that the foremost goal of the electoral process is "to winnow out and finally reject all but the chosen candidates." In dissent, **Justice Marshall** took vigorous exception to this cursory treatment of the associational rights of members of minor parties. "The minor party's often unconventional positions broaden political debate, expand the range of issues with which the electorate is concerned, and influence the positions of the majority, in some instances ultimately becoming majority positions. And its very existence provides an outlet for voters to express dissatisfaction with the candidates or platforms of the major parties." Marshall emphasized that minor parties' primary role is to affect political debate, not to elect their own candidates. To play a meaningful role in the process, minor-party candidates need to be included in the phase of the electoral process in which voters are most seriously considering their choices: the general election.

4.   *Ranked-Choice Voting*. In recent years, some voting-rights reformers have begun pushing for a ranked-choice voting system. Under such a system, for each office on the ballot, voters rank as many of the candidates as they want (i.e., first choice, second choice, etc.). If no candidate receives a majority of the first-choice votes, then the candidate with the fewest first-choice votes has her voters reassigned to their second choices. If there is still no candidate with a majority, then the candidate with the second-fewest first-choice votes has her voters reassigned to their second choices (unless their second choice has already been eliminated, in which case they get assigned to their third choice, and so on). The reassignment process continues until some candidate has a majority, at which point that candidate is declared the winner.

Proponents of ranked-choice voting argue that it allows voters to send a message by giving their first-choice vote to their favorite candidate, even if that candidate has very little chance of winning, while not having to worry that, by doing so, they are helping their least-favorite candidate win. For example, imagine that there are three candidates on the ballot: a Socialist, a Democrat, and a Republican. Without ranked-choice voting, a voter who most prefers the Socialist candidate may nevertheless vote for the Democrat, for fear that voting for the Socialist will help the Republican win. With ranked-choice voting, however, she can give the Socialist candidate her first-choice vote and the Democrat her second-choice vote, secure in the knowledge that, when the Socialist candidate is eliminated, her vote will be reallocated to the Democrat. Thus, proponents argue, ranked-choice voting allows for the expressive benefits of having third parties on the ballot (as Justice Marshall emphasized in his *Munro* dissent), while preventing some of the concerns animating the *Munro* majority.

Since 2000, a number of municipalities across the country have adopted ranked-choice voting.[45] Most prominently, the state of Maine adopted it in 2016 for use in all state and federal primary and general elections beginning in 2018. In the 2018 general election for Maine's Second Congressional District, the Republican incumbent, Bruce Poliquin, received a plurality of the first-choice votes (46.3%). Democratic challenger Jared Golden was close behind, with 45.6% of the first-choice votes. Two independent candidates split the remaining 8.1%. When the voters for the two independents were reallocated to their second-choice candidates, Golden won with 50.6% of the vote. Poliquin sued in federal court, arguing that ranked-choice voting exceeded the state's power to regulate elections and violated equal protection, due process, and the First Amendment. The district court was unconvinced by any of Poliquin's arguments. *Baber v. Dunlap*, 376 F. Supp. 3d 125 (D. Maine 2018). Jared Golden was seated in the 116th Congress.

Is ranked-choice voting a good idea? Would you like to see it spread more widely? Why or why not?

BALLOT ACCESS PROBLEMS

Problem 2-4. Hawaii's election law requires a candidate to participate in a new-party, established party, or nonpartisan primary election to obtain a position on the general election ballot. Primaries in Hawaii are open. The state does not allow write-in voting, and a voter who notified state officials that he intended to vote for a write-in candidate in the Democratic primary was told that such a vote would be ignored. The voter filed suit, claiming that the ban on write-in voting violates his freedom of expression and association under the First Amendment. How should this claim be analyzed? Also consider these facts about Hawaii's electoral system: its election laws date to the 1890s when Hawaii was still a monarchy. Hawaii is for all practical purposes a one-party Democratic state, so that the winner of the Democratic primary invariably wins the general election. The rules for new-party primaries and partisan primaries discourage independent voters or candidates from using these avenues to challenge the established political structure. A new political party can be organized through a petition drive to obtain signatures of 1% of registered voters; independents can run in a nonpartisan primary, but to advance to the general election, they need 10% of the total primary vote or votes equal to the minimum number required to nominate a partisan candidate to the general election ballot. The real disincentive to serious rivals to the Democratic candidates is the price voters pay for voting in a primary other than the Democratic. Since the Democratic primary essentially determines the winner, a voter who chooses to

---

[45]   For a list, see FairVote, *Where is Ranked Choice Voting Used?*, https://www.fairvote.org/rcv#where_is_ranked_choice_voting_used.

vote in another primary will have no effect on the outcome. As Samuel Issacharoff and Richard Pildes conclude: "[T]he cumulative structure of Hawaii's laws eviscerates any nascent resistance to the Democratic monopoly." *Politics as Markets: Partisan Lockups of the Democratic Process*, 50 Stan. L. Rev. 643, 671 (1998). After thinking about this problem, look at *Burdick v. Takushi*, 504 U.S. 428 (1992), for the Supreme Court's approach. See also *Clingman v. Beaver*, 544 U.S. 581, 607 (2005) (O'Connor, J., concurring in part and concurring in the judgment) (expressing concern that the statutory framework governing elections—particularly provisions affecting party registration and affiliation—as a whole might impermissibly burden voters, but noting that the question of the "*cumulative* burdens imposed by the *overall* scheme of electoral regulation upon the rights of voters and parties to associate" had not been properly raised).

Problem 2-5. The main problem identified by partisan lockup theorists is that, in the realm of election law, there is an inherent conflict of interest. This conflict leads to ballot access provisions favoring major parties and penalizing minor parties and independent candidates, to partisan gerrymandering, and, as we will see, to certain kinds of campaign finance and other ethics laws. Are courts the best way to guard against the self-interest of politicians in this arena? Some countries, including Australia, Canada, and the United Kingdom, rely on nonpartisan electoral administration entities to take the lead in regulating campaigns and elections. For example, the U.K.'s Electoral Commission supervises elections and oversees the regulatory structure, and it also provides reports and recommendations to Parliament on issues affecting campaign finance laws, districting, and political advertising. See Christopher Elmendorf, *Representation Reinforcement through Advisory Commissions: The Case of Election Law*, 80 N.Y.U. L. Rev. 1366 (2005) (describing these entities and proposing such a commission for the U.S.).

Could a nonpartisan, independent election commission work in the United States? What are the constitutional, political, and logistical challenges for such a reform? How successful have nonpartisan redistricting commissions been in drawing legislative district boundaries without undue political influence? What other solutions to partisan lockup, besides aggressive judicial review, are possible? See, e.g., Dennis Thompson, *Just Elections* 156–57 (2002) (discussing the appropriate role for direct democracy in decisions affecting the design of democratic institutions).

3. STRUCTURES OF CAMPAIGN FINANCE

Concerns about the influence of money in electoral outcomes are not new, and they have led to over a century of federal regulation. The Tillman Act of 1907, ch. 420, 34 Stat. 864, prohibited all corporations and national banks from making "money contribution[s]" in connection with federal elections. The prohibition was extended to *all* contributions by the Federal Corrupt Practices Act of 1925, ch. 368, 43 Stat. 1070 (later repealed). The Smith-Connally Act, ch. 144, 57 Stat. 163 (1943) (expired 1945), and then the Taft-Hartley Act, ch. 120, 61 Stat. 136 (1947), prohibited unions from making contributions in connection with federal elections. Because of the vagueness of these early laws, however, unions and corporations were able to make contributions virtually at will. Comprehensive reform was triggered by concern over the $60 million raised by President Nixon's 1972 reelection campaign. The discovery that some of this money was illegally diverted to finance the Watergate break-in stimulated passage of significant reform. The Federal Election Campaign

Act Amendments of 1974 (FECA), Pub. L. No. 93–443, 88 Stat. 1263, codified at 52 U.S.C. § 30101 *et seq.*, set limits on campaign contributions and expenditures in presidential and congressional election campaigns and established the Federal Election Commission (FEC) to administer and enforce the law.

Decades of experience with FECA demonstrated that serious challenges remained to effective federal campaign finance regulation, but Congress seemed unable to respond. The bankruptcy of Enron Corporation, an energy trading company, in late 2001, provided the momentum for reformers to get their proposal out of committee. Enron and its officers had contributed millions of dollars in largely unregulated money, and the company's collapse made these contributions and the political clout they might have bought more salient to voters and lawmakers. Primary Senate supporters John McCain (R-Ariz.) and Russ Feingold (D-Wisc.), together with their House counterparts Christopher Shays (R-Conn.) and Martin Meehan (D-Mass.), overcame all the procedural hurdles, and the Bipartisan Campaign Reform Act of 2002 (BCRA), Pub. L. No. 107–155, 116 Stat. 81, went into effect the day after the 2002 midterm elections. BCRA remains the primary law regulating federal campaigns, although some of its provisions have been struck down by the Supreme Court, just as occurred with FECA.

Some pluralist theorists object to stringent regulations of campaign finance. First, they argue that such regulation is counterproductive because money can be used to express political views that need to be heard and reflected by the representative. Indeed, the amount of the contribution can signal the intensity of those political views. Second, they view most regulation of money in politics as inconsistent with the Constitution. Whatever the outer limits of the First Amendment's Free Speech Clause, it is clear that at its core it protects "political speech." The Supreme Court has recognized "a profound national commitment to the principle that debate on public issues should be uninhibited, robust, and wide-open." *New York Times Co. v. Sullivan*, 376 U.S. 254, 270 (1964). Is political speech involved when someone contributes money to a candidate? The contribution helps the candidate spread her message, and thus perhaps amounts to "indirect speech," or speech by proxy. Is this different from the situation in which someone uses her money to engage in political speech independent of the candidate—for example, by directly purchasing an advertisement supporting the candidate or attacking her opponent? Which kind of expenditure poses the greater threat of corruption of the representational process? Does the answer to this question depend upon how "corruption" is defined?

Republican and critical theorists, on the other hand, tend to consider the political advantages of wealth in an unregulated political system to be corrupting in ways similar to outright bribery. "The American system is rooted in the assumption of political equality: 'one person, one vote.' But money, which candidates need to harvest votes, is not distributed equally. The substantial inequities of campaign financing have hindered the quest for political equality and have worried concerned Americans since the beginning of the twentieth century."[46] More skeptical observers of electoral politics respond to those who advocate far-reaching regulation with a

---

[46]   Herbert Alexander, *Financing Politics: Money, Elections, and Political Reform* 3 (4th ed. 1992).

pragmatic argument. They note that regulations and limitations merely change the form of the expenditure, diverting the money into unregulated channels and rendering campaign finance laws largely futile.[47]

We will begin our analysis of campaign finance by assessing FECA and the Supreme Court case that reshaped that law (*Buckley v. Valeo*, 424 U.S. 1 (1976) (per curiam)), and then BCRA and the first major Supreme Court case that left it largely intact (*McConnell v. Fed. Election Comm'n*, 540 U.S. 93 (2003)). After *McConnell*, a change in Supreme Court personnel shifted the judicial approach to campaign finance. We will accordingly next consider *Citizens United v. Fed. Election Comm'n*, 558 U.S. 310 (2010), which struck down key provisions of BCRA, and discuss the federal landscape in the wake of that decision. Finally, we will conclude by describing some key features of state regulatory systems, including public financing.

A. THE CONSTITUTIONAL FOUNDATION FOR REGULATING CAMPAIGNS

1. Providing the First Amendment Framework: *Buckley v. Valeo*

In *Buckley v. Valeo*, 424 U.S. 1 (1976) (per curiam), the Supreme Court addressed the constitutionality of the Federal Election Campaign Act (FECA) as amended in 1974 and Subtitle H of the Internal Revenue Code, which provides for the public financing of presidential elections. *Buckley* remains the foundational case in the constitutional jurisprudence affecting campaign finance laws, as well as other regulation of political speech and activity.

Perhaps the most important aspect of *Buckley* is the Court's decision to assess campaign regulation through the lens of the First Amendment, equating spending in campaigns with political expression and political association. The Court has never afforded these fundamental rights absolute protection but, under traditional First Amendment jurisprudence, has required the government to show a "compelling" or "sufficiently important" state interest, depending on the extent of the burden on expression, and to demonstrate that the regulation of political speech is "narrowly" or "closely" tailored to serve that interest. *Buckley* also identified the state interest that the Court continues to view as the primary justification for campaign regulation: the actuality and appearance of *quid pro quo* corruption. As it set forth in *Buckley*:

> To the extent that large contributions are given to secure a political *quid pro quo* from current and potential office holders, the integrity of our system of representative democracy is undermined. Although the scope of such pernicious practices can never be reliably ascertained, the deeply disturbing examples surfacing after the 1972 election demonstrate that the problem is not an illusory one.

> Of almost equal concern as the danger of actual *quid pro quo* arrangements is the impact of the appearance of corruption stemming from public

---

[47]   See, e.g., Samuel Issacharoff & Pamela Karlan, *The Hydraulics of Campaign Finance Reform*, 77 Tex. L. Rev. 1705 (1999).

awareness of the opportunities for abuse inherent in a regime of large individual financial contributions. * * *

Limitations on Political Contributions. FECA prohibited individuals and most groups from contributing more than $1,000 per candidate for each primary election, and more than $1,000 per candidate for each runoff or general election. In addition, individuals could not contribute more than a total of $25,000 per year. (These thresholds have since been increased and indexed for inflation; the aggregate limit on contributions was held unconstitutional in *McCutcheon v. Fed. Election Comm'n*, 572 U.S. 185 (2014).) Certain "political committees"—those registered as political committees with the FEC for not less than six months that have received contributions from more than 50 persons and, except for state political-party organizations, have contributed to five or more candidates for federal office—could contribute up to $5,000 to any candidate for federal office. (This threshold has not changed and is not indexed.) The Court in *Buckley* upheld these provisions. Although the Court stated that contribution limitations significantly interfered with the First Amendment right of political association, it found that these provisions passed constitutional muster because they limited "the actuality and appearance of corruption resulting from large * * * financial contributions."

Limitations on Political Expenditures. The Act also (a) limited expenditures by individuals and groups "relative to a clearly identified candidate during a calendar year" to $1,000, (b) limited spending by candidates from their personal or family funds, and (c) limited overall expenditures by candidates to differing amounts depending upon the federal office sought. The Court in *Buckley* struck down these provisions, establishing a bifurcated constitutional regime for contributions and expenditures that continues to shape regulatory policy today.[48] The Court first held that expenditure limits operated as a substantial restriction on First Amendment freedoms because "[a] restriction on the amount of money a person or group can spend on political communication during a campaign necessarily reduces the quantity of expression by restricting the number of issues discussed, the depth of their exploration and the size of the audience reached."

The Court determined that these restrictions were more severe than the limitations on contributions because "[a] contribution serves as a general expression of support for the candidate and his views, but does not communicate the underlying basis for the support. The quantity of communication by the contributor does not increase perceptibly with the size of his contribution, since the expression rests solely on the undifferentiated, symbolic act of contributing." In contrast, the Court said, "a primary effect of these expenditure limitations is to restrict the quantity of campaign speech by individuals, groups and candidates. The restrictions, while neutral as to the ideas expressed, limit political expression 'at the core of our electoral process and of the First Amendment freedoms.'" Accordingly, their "constitutionality * * * turns on whether the governmental interests advanced [to] support [them] satisfy the exacting scrutiny applicable to limitations on core First Amendment rights of political expression."

---

[48] See Kathleen Sullivan, *Against Campaign Finance Reform*, 1998 Utah L. Rev. 311 (noting the instability of a system that restricts the supply of money while leaving the demand for it unregulated).

The limitations on individual and group expenditures independent of a particular candidate did not survive this exacting scrutiny because, the Court held, they did not substantially serve the governmental interest in stemming actual or apparent corruption. Such expenditures are made independent of any candidates, alleviating the danger that expenditures will be given as a *quid pro quo* for improper commitments from the candidate. Furthermore, in response to the argument that the expenditure limitations serve a government interest "in equalizing the relative ability of individuals and groups to influence the outcome of elections," the Court stated:

> [T]he concept that government may restrict the speech of some elements of our society in order to enhance the relative voice of others is wholly foreign to the First Amendment, which was designed "to secure 'the widest possible dissemination of information from diverse and antagonistic sources,'" and "to assure unfettered interchange of ideas for the bringing about of political and social changes desired by the people." The First Amendment's protection against governmental abridgement of free expression cannot properly be made to depend on a person's financial ability to engage in public discussion.

Assuming that the only legitimate government purpose can be prevention of *quid pro quo* corruption or the appearance of corruption, is the Court's rationale persuasive? Isn't it more realistic to assume that candidates will be aware of independent expenditures and be grateful if they play a role in their electoral success? Certainly, in a world where direct contributions are limited but independent expenditures are not, wouldn't we expect groups wanting to influence lawmakers to take advantage of the unregulated route in order to circumvent the statute's limitations?

The limitations on expenditures from the funds of the candidate and the candidate's family were also inconsistent with the First Amendment. Most fundamentally, it is hard to see how a candidate spending on her own campaign could amount to *quid pro quo* corruption of that candidate. Moreover,

> [t]he * * * interest in equalizing the relative financial resources of candidates competing for elective office * * * provides the sole relevant rationale for [this] expenditure ceiling. That interest is clearly not sufficient to justify the provision's infringement of fundamental First Amendment rights. [T]he limitation may fail to promote financial equality among candidates. A candidate who spends less of his personal resources on his campaign may nonetheless outspend his rival as a result of more successful fundraising efforts. Indeed, a candidate's personal wealth may impede his efforts to persuade others that he needs their financial contributions or volunteer efforts to conduct an effective campaign.

Reporting and Disclosure Requirements. FECA required political committees to keep records of contributions and expenditures, including the names and addresses of contributors who gave them more than $10. Such committees were required to disclose to the FEC the source of every contribution of more than $100 and the payee and purpose of every expenditure of more than $100. (The current threshold for reporting is set at more than $200.) Moreover, the Act also mandated that individuals and groups, other than candidates and political committees, making contributions or expenditures exceeding $100 (now $250) "other than by contribution to a political committee or candidate" file reports with the Commission. The Court construed this disclosure requirement applying to independent political expenditures to reach only individuals and groups "when they make contributions earmarked for political purposes" and "when they make expenditures for communications that expressly advocate the election or defeat of a clearly identified candidate."

The Court in *Buckley* upheld these provisions. It noted that compelled disclosure, in itself, can seriously infringe on the privacy of association and belief guaranteed by the First Amendment, but held that the governmental interests sought to be advanced by the required disclosures were sufficiently important to outweigh the possibility of infringement of First Amendment rights. The Court identified these governmental interests:

> First, disclosure provides the electorate with information "as to where political campaign money comes from and how it is spent by the candidate" in order to aid the voters in evaluating those who seek federal office. * * *

> Second, disclosure requirements deter actual corruption and avoid the appearance of corruption by exposing large contributions and expenditures to the light of publicity. * * *

> Third, * * * recordkeeping, reporting, and disclosure requirements are an essential means of gathering the data necessary to detect violations of the contribution limitations described above.

In response to the contention that disclosure would infringe upon the First Amendment rights of contributors to minor parties and independent candidates, see *NAACP v. Alabama*, 357 U.S. 449 (1958) (disclosure required by state law of NAACP members is unconstitutional if it exposed those persons to physical or economic retaliation), the Court stated:

> [T]he damage done by disclosure to the associational interests of the minor parties and their members and to supporters of independents could be significant. These movements are less likely to have a sound financial base and thus are more vulnerable to falloffs in contributions. In some instances fears of reprisal may deter contributions to the point where the movement cannot survive. The public interest also suffers if that result comes to pass, for there is a consequent reduction in the free circulation of ideas both within and without the political arena.

> There could well be a case * * * where the threat to the exercise of First Amendment rights is so serious and the state interest furthered by disclosure so insubstantial that the Act's requirements cannot be constitutionally applied. But no appellant in this case has tendered record evidence of the sort proffered in *NAACP v. Alabama*. Instead, appellants primarily rely on "the clearly articulated fears of individuals, well experienced in the political process." At best they offer the testimony of several minor-party officials that one or two persons refused to make

contributions because of the possibility of disclosure. On this record, the substantial public interest in disclosure identified by the legislative history of this Act outweighs the harm generally alleged.

Public Financing of Presidential Election Campaigns. At the time of *Buckley*, Subtitle H of the Internal Revenue Code provided that taxpayers could authorize payment to a Presidential Election Campaign Fund of one dollar of their tax liability in the case of an individual return and two dollars in the case of a joint return. The Fund provides money to finance party nominating conventions, primary campaigns, and general election campaigns. In 1993, Congress raised the tax check-off amount to three dollars for single returns and six dollars for joint returns.

Subtitle H distinguishes among *major parties* (parties whose candidates for President in the most recent election received 25% or more of the popular vote), *minor parties* (parties whose candidates received at least 5% but less than 25% of the vote in the most recent election), and *new parties* (all others). With respect to expenses of general election campaigns, each major-party candidate is entitled to $20 million, adjusted for inflation, and is required to pledge not to incur expenses in excess of this amount and not to accept private contributions except to the extent that the public fund is insufficient to provide the full amount to which the candidate is entitled. In 2012, the major-party candidates each were eligible in the general election for $91.2 million in federal funds. Minor-party candidates, if they meet certain prerequisites, are entitled to a percentage of the amount available to major-party candidates; new-party candidates receive nothing. Subtitle H also created the Presidential Primary Matching Payment Account, which provides funds to candidates running in presidential primary elections who, *inter alia*, raise at least $5,000 in each of 20 states. Funds are provided through a matching formula based on the amount of private contributions received by the candidate. In return for federal money during the primaries, candidates must agree to abide by limitations applied to aggregate and state-by-state expenditures.

In recent years, this public financing system has become essentially irrelevant, as major candidates have opted out during both the primaries and the general elections, so as to avoid the expenditure limits that come with accepting public financing. Ironically, only because major candidates have opted out has the Presidential Election Campaign Fund managed to avoid insolvency, as the number of taxpayers participating in the check-off has declined.[49]

The Supreme Court in *Buckley* upheld the constitutionality of this system of partial public financing. The Court generally held that the important public interest in limiting "the improper influence of large private contributions" outweighed any First Amendment concerns, and that the distinctions among major parties, minor parties, and new parties did not violate the equal protection component of the Due Process Clause of the Fifth Amendment. Doesn't the Act, and the Supreme Court's

---

[49]   For discussion of the challenges facing the presidential system of public financing, see Task Force on Presidential Nomination Finance, Campaign Finance Institute, *Participation, Competition, Engagement: How to Revive and Improve Public Funding for Presidential Nomination Politics* (2003), http://www.cfinst.org/pdf/federal/president/TaskForce1_Fullreport.pdf. For a discussion of possible reforms, see John Green & Anthony Corrado, *The Impact of BCRA on Presidential Campaign Finance*, in *Life After Reform: When the Bipartisan Campaign Reform Act Meets Politics* 175, 180–86 (Michael Malbin ed., 2003).

decision upholding it, tend to ossify American politics by presumptively reinforcing the status quo? If the Court is correct that the First Amendment generally favors *more* variety, how could the Court justify such a heavy financial benefit to already-established political parties? Is this yet another instance of partisan lockup that we discussed in the context of ballot access laws?

———

As this description of *Buckley* reveals, the traditional justification for campaign finance regulation is connected to notions of corruption of the political system. Corruption, however, is an ambiguous term; it means different things to different people. Moreover, the extent and shape of regulation that one finds acceptable depends on one's vision of the corruption that must be combated. Let's think about various kinds of corruption that may occur in the election process and determine whether regulation should target each of them—and whether regulation can effectively control them.

Quid Pro Quo *Corruption.* The traditional justification for campaign finance regulation provided by the Court in *Buckley* is to combat *quid pro quo* corruption or the appearance of such arrangements. A system dominated by large contributions from wealthy individuals and interest groups clearly seeking influence, access, and favorable legislation appears corrupt to ordinary voters. This notion of corruption can be a rather limited one, focused on activity that appears virtually indistinguishable from bribery, or more expansive. In *Nixon v. Shrink Missouri Gov't PAC*, 528 U.S. 377, 389 (2000), the Court rejected an especially narrow notion. "In speaking [in *Buckley*] of 'improper influence' and 'opportunities for abuse' in addition to '*quid pro quo* arrangements,' we recognized a concern not confined to bribery of public officials, but extending to the broader threat from politicians too compliant with the wishes of large contributors." The Court worried that the "cynical assumption that large donors call the tune" jeopardizes public faith in the democratic system. *Id.* at 390. In recent years, the Roberts Court has embraced the narrower version of *quid pro quo* corruption—using contributions to secure political favors from individual politicians—and rejected a formulation of the corruption interest that aimed to limit "the appearance of mere influence or access" derived from large contributions. *McCutcheon*, 572 U.S. at 208 (plurality opinion).

Are the parameters of this more expansive notion of corruption clear? When is a lawmaker *too* compliant with the wishes of large donors, and when is the lawmaker merely representing constituents who supported her? Perhaps large contributions provide accurate signals of the intensity with which some constituents hold particular views. In a system where votes are equalized, campaign contributions and other electoral support can provide valuable information about the strength of voter preferences, certainly relevant information as lawmakers compromise and create policy. Theorists from a liberal tradition might be wary of the Court's apparent willingness to broaden its definition of *quid pro quo* corruption.

Bradley Smith (a professor who served as a commissioner on the FEC) attacks the *Buckley* formulation of political corruption on two grounds.[50] First, he points to

---

[50]	*Money Talks: Speech, Corruption, Equality, and Campaign Finance*, 86 Geo. L.J. 45, 58–59 (1997).

empirical studies suggesting that money seldom buys votes or particular outcomes. Rather, "the dominant forces in legislative voting [are] personal ideology, party affiliation and agenda, and constituency views." To the extent that money influences lawmaking, it affects the legislative agenda, the timing and subjects of lawmakers' speeches, and legislative drafting in the early stages. Second, Smith argues that "there are intuitive and logical reasons to believe that the problem [of *quid pro quo* corruption] is not as serious as it is made out to be. Most obviously, people who are attracted to electoral politics tend to have strong views on issues. Party support can be just as important to re-election efforts, if not more important, than private contributions. * * * And, of course, elected officials ultimately need votes, not cash." Are Smith's arguments persuasive? At the least, are they sufficient to encourage courts to demand persuasive empirical proof of the existence of *quid pro quo* corruption more subtle than outright bribery? Or does Smith ignore the corruption inherent in a system in which large donors can set the political agenda for the rest of us?

Finally, scholars who have attempted to discern whether adoption of campaign finance regulation actually causes voters to have more confidence in the integrity of the political system have generally found no effect on public perception. In *The Limits of Electoral Reform* (2013), Shaun Bowler and Todd Donovan compare public attitudes across U.S. states and among Western democracies and find virtually no impact of reforms on citizens' attitudes toward politics. They suggest several reasons for this null finding, including the possibility that politicians respond strategically to any reform and undermine real change. Moreover, reform may spark an unintended consequence of more public cynicism as better disclosure increases the awareness of the strong influence of money in politics. *Id.* at 94–95. Does this empirical result undermine *Buckley*'s state interest justifying regulation of campaign spending as combating the deleterious effects of the appearance of *quid pro quo* corruption on the public's confidence in our electoral system?

Increasing Voter Competence. Alternatively, a political system may be understood as corrupt if it systematically undermines voters' ability to vote competently. A competent voter is one who votes the same way on the basis of the limited information available to her as she would have voted if she had had complete information about candidates and their proposals.[51] Voters rely on numerous cues to improve their competence, including party affiliation and incumbency. Knowing who supports the candidate and with how much enthusiasm can also improve voter competence. Moreover, allowing all candidates—challengers and incumbents—the resources to participate in vigorous political debate may enrich the political environment for voters.

The *Buckley* Court identified such an interest as an important justification for FECA's disclosure system. That might be the most significant interest supporting disclosure in campaigns on ballot initiatives in which the threat of *quid pro quo* corruption is reduced. (See Chapter 4, § 1(B).) The kinds of regulation that would promote voter competence may turn on one's notion of what can realistically be

---

[51]   See Elisabeth Gerber & Arthur Lupia, *Voter Competence in Direct Legislation Elections*, in *Citizen Competence and Democratic Institutions* 147 (Stephen Elkin & Karol Soltan eds., 1999).

expected of voters. Daniel Ortiz identifies two groups of voters: engaged citizens and civic slackers. *The Democratic Paradox of Campaign Finance Reform*, 50 Stan. L. Rev. 893, 895 (1998). He argues that most democratic theory assumes that citizens are "engaged, informed voters who carefully reason through political arguments." Much of campaign finance reform, however, implicitly questions voters' ability or interest in spending the time required to develop civic virtue. Instead, most of us focus our attention on other aspects of life—our families, jobs, or leisure activities— and thus are susceptible to manipulation by slick advertisements funded by well-heeled interests and overflowing political coffers. To be successful, campaign finance reform efforts should be directed toward helping people make political decisions in light of their limited attention and scanty information. "[I]f reformers are to make their case, they must force us to recognize our civic failings. For only by recognizing our failings can we ever hope to grapple with and perhaps eventually overcome them." *Id.* at 914. What kind of information should be provided to civic slackers to improve their competence? What is the role of regulation in this process?

Electoral Competitiveness. Richard Briffault has argued that the Court should consider another important state interest in assessing the constitutionality of campaign finance restrictions. He contends that "[f]air and vigorous competition among candidates and parties is critical for the legitimacy of our elections and of the government those elections produce. Campaign finance law, in turn, can have a direct effect on the competitiveness of elections. In constructing a new campaign finance doctrine—or in revamping current doctrine—the Court should give greater weight to the effect of campaign finance rules on electoral competition." Nixon v. Shrink Missouri Government PAC: *The Beginning of the End of the* Buckley *Era?*, 85 Minn. L. Rev. 1729, 1731–32 (2001). If competitiveness were a compelling interest, what sort of regulation of campaign finance spending is permissible under the Constitution? What reform is best suited to improve electoral competition? How should courts measure the level of competition and determine what features of the regulatory landscape are hindering more robust competition?

At least some studies suggest that spending by political parties is an important factor contributing to competitive races, both in the context of open seats and, more importantly, in the context of candidates challenging entrenched incumbents.[52] Should the Court be especially leery of restrictions on expenditures by political parties? Or is it the province of the legislature to make the policy choices that will affect electoral competitiveness, at least in cases where reasonable people could disagree about the right answer? On the other hand, does the partisan lockup scholarship suggest that campaign finance regulation devised by incumbent politicians is more likely to work to their advantage than to herald the resurgence of competitiveness in legislative elections?

Equality Concerns and Corruption. Republican thinkers, along with many critical theorists, have argued that a system is corrupt if wealthy special interests

---

[52]   See, e.g., Gary Jacobson, *The Politics of Congressional Elections* 81–85 (8th ed. 2013). See also Richard Briffault, *The Political Parties and Campaign Finance Reform*, 100 Colum. L. Rev. 620, 661 (2000) (although favoring more stringent regulation of party campaign expenditures, acknowledging that parties "are more likely to support promising challengers. * * * Thus, far more than PAC money or donations by wealthy individuals, party money promotes the value of electoral competition.").

and individuals have more political influence solely because of their wealth.[53] Equal opportunity to influence political outcomes is undermined if that opportunity is tied to wealth and if economic resources are not equally distributed. This situation is even more disturbing because there is no reason to believe that the distribution of economic resources is related in any way to people's ability or desire to participate in the political realm. In other words, a poor voter and a rich one may have very intensely held and well-reasoned views, but only the latter will be able to affect the political agenda, participate in debate, and influence lawmakers. There is a "donor class" of people wealthy enough to contribute money to candidates and parties and thus obtain special access to policymakers that ordinary Americans are denied. See Spencer Overton, *The Donor Class: Campaign Finance, Democracy, and Participation*, 153 U. Pa. L. Rev. 73 (2004). Such a system is corrupt if political equality is an important democratic ideal.

Buckley rejected egalitarian justifications for campaign finance reform, holding clearly that "the concept that government may restrict the speech of some elements of our society in order to enhance the relative voice of others is wholly foreign to the First Amendment, which was designed 'to secure "the widest possible dissemination of information from diverse and antagonistic sources," ' and 'to assure unfettered interchange of ideas for the bringing about of political and social changes desired by the people.' " 424 U.S. at 48–49. *Buckley* was thus consistent with a libertarian notion of the First Amendment, a view that the Amendment protects only *negative liberty* because it only prohibits government intervention. Judge Guido Calabresi, among others, argues that the Supreme Court's jurisprudence is "impoverished" because it does not deal explicitly with egalitarian concerns, which are "at least as important as [*quid pro quo* corruption], and, perhaps, at the very heart of the problem."[54]

In *Austin v. Michigan Chamber of Commerce*, 494 U.S. 652 (1990), the Supreme Court seemed receptive to arguments based on egalitarian concerns. The Court upheld a Michigan law forbidding corporations from using their general treasury funds for independent expenditures in connection with state elections. Justice Marshall's opinion for the Court focused on the ways in which the law allows corporations to amass tremendous wealth and the potential unfairness of allowing those corporations to translate that wealth into political power:

> State law grants corporations special advantages—such as limited liability, perpetual life, and favorable treatment of the accumulation and distribution of assets—that enhance their ability to attract capital and to deploy their resources in ways that maximize the return on their shareholders' investments. These state-created advantages not only allow corporations to play a dominant role in the Nation's economy, but also permit them to use "resources amassed in the economic marketplace" to obtain "an unfair advantage in the political marketplace." *Federal Election Comm'n v.*

---

[53]   See Symposium: *Money, Politics, and Equality*, 77 Tex. L. Rev. 1603–2021 (1999); John Rawls, *The Idea of Public Reason Revisited*, 64 U. Chi. L. Rev. 765 (1997).

[54]   *Landell v. Sorrell*, 406 F.3d 159, 163 (2d Cir. 2005) (Calabresi, J., concurring in the denial of rehearing en banc), *rev'd sub nom.*, *Randall v. Sorrell*, 548 U.S. 230 (2006). See also Ronald Dworkin, *The Curse of American Politics*, N.Y. Rev. of Books, Oct. 17, 1996, at 19, 21 ("It is another premise of democracy that citizens must be able, as individuals, to participate on equal terms in both formal politics and in the informal cultural life that creates the moral environment of the community.").

Massachusetts Citizens for Life, 479 U.S. 238, 257 (1986) (*MCFL*). As the Court explained in *MCFL*, the political advantage of corporations is unfair because "[t]he resources in the treasury of a business corporation . . . are not an indication of popular support for the corporation's political ideas. They reflect instead the economically motivated decisions of investors and customers. The availability of these resources may make a corporation a formidable political presence, even though the power of the corporation may be no reflection of the power of its ideas."

For Marshall, this egalitarian concern was a kind of concern about corruption: "Michigan's regulation aims at a different type of corruption in the political arena: the corrosive and distorting effects of immense aggregations of wealth that are accumulated with the help of the corporate form and that have little or no correlation to the public's support for the corporation's political ideas."

Two dissents—one by Justice Scalia and the other by Justice Kennedy—decried the Court's decision as a legitimation of political censorship. Twenty years later, the Supreme Court overruled *Austin* in *Citizens United v. Fed. Election Comm'n*, 558 U.S. 310 (2010) (reproduced in § 3(B) below), a decision authored by Justice Kennedy and joined by Justice Scalia.

Arguably, the equality concern sounded in *Austin*'s majority opinion was relatively narrow and limited to the distortion of the political environment when money raised for business purposes has been spent for political expression. On the other hand, a broader reading of *Austin* might suggest that there is a compelling state interest in democratizing the political process and increasing public participation in campaigns. Justice Breyer has articulated a First Amendment principle of participatory self-government that could be seen as a way to include some element of equality concerns into campaign finance jurisprudence without expressly overruling *Buckley*. See *Active Liberty: Interpreting Our Democratic Constitution* 43–50 (2005). See also *McCutcheon*, 572 U.S. at 237 (Breyer, J., dissenting) ("Where enough money calls the tune, the general public will not be heard. * * * That is one reason why the Court has stressed the constitutional importance of Congress' concern that a few large donations not drown out the voices of the many.").

Beginning in earnest with Barack Obama's successful 2008 presidential campaign, the Internet has facilitated greater grassroots involvement in campaigns. This has taken the form of increased small-dollar fundraising as well as tools for organizing meetings, volunteer opportunities, and canvassing by a candidates's supporters. Recognizing this shift, some reform advocates began to reformulate campaign finance proposals with the goal of broadening still further the group of people participating in campaigns. For example, some have proposed an overhaul of the presidential public financing system so that small contributions would receive more generous matching funds (such as a match of three- or four-to-one for contributions of $200 or less) and candidates would not be subject to expenditure limits as long as they were spending funds raised from small donations. See Spencer Overton, *The Participation Interest*, 100 Geo. L.J. 1259, 1296–98 (2012) (discussing such systems used at the local level and linking them to a Breyer-like participation interest).

But other commentators have counseled that claims of a new era of the small donor may be overstated. Although small donors played an important role in Obama's success, he still received most of his sizable campaign war chest from wealthy individuals. In Obama's 2012 reelection campaign, 57.4% of the total individual contributions came from donors giving $200 or more. For his opponent, Mitt Romney, these large-contribution donors gave 73.4% of the total individual contributions.[55] In 2016, Donald Trump's victorious campaign received only 35.1% of its individual contributions from large-contribution donors (not counting the extent to which Trump self-financed his own campaign). By contrast, Hillary Clinton's losing campaign that year received 74% of its (much larger) pool of individual contributions from large-contribution donors.[56]

Are contribution and expenditure limitations the best way to ensure political equality in a world where financial resources are distributed unevenly? Even if they successfully reduce the amount of political spending by the wealthy, how can such regulations provide resources to the poor who wish to be politically active? Some theorists have suggested a more radical egalitarian reform: allowing people to spend only special money—"red-white-and-blue" dollars in Bruce Ackerman's proposal—for election-related activities.[57] All citizens would receive an equal amount of this special money; it could not be sold for green money, but it could be contributed to candidate campaigns, used to fund independent advertisements, or accumulated by PACs to signal the support of a group of voters for an idea or candidate. These proposals advocate a sort of public financing system, albeit a decentralized one in which the voters determine how to channel the money. Just as all citizens have an equal number of votes, so would they all have equal amounts of political resources to deploy. Of course, these proposals do not claim to impose absolute equality among citizens; there would remain inequality of talents, ability to communicate persuasively, appearance, and access to people with free time to volunteer. Perhaps in a world where financial resources were equalized, the distribution of these other qualities would become more important. Or, perhaps, inequality along these dimensions is less pernicious.

PROBLEM RELATING TO CAMPAIGN FINANCE PROPOSALS

Problem 2-6. Some scholars have argued that, instead of mandating disclosure of all campaign contributions, we should instead consider mandating that all contributions be anonymous. Ian Ayres & Jeremy Bulow, *The Donation Booth: Mandating Donor Anonymity to Disrupt the Market for Political Influence*, 50 Stan. L. Rev. 837 (1998). Just as the secret ballot makes it more difficult for candidates to buy votes, requiring anonymity of contributors would make it more difficult for candidates to sell access or influence. They suggest setting up blind trusts that would receive all campaign

---

[55] Ctr. for Responsive Pol., *2012 Presidential Race: Source of Funds* (May 3, 2013), https://www.opensecrets.org/pres12/sourceall.php.

[56] Ctr. for Responsive Pol., *Hillary Clinton* (Nov. 27, 2017), https://www.opensecrets.org/pres16/candidate?id=N00000019; Ctr. for Responsive Pol., *Donald Trump* (Nov. 27, 2017), https://www.opensecrets.org/pres16/candidate?id=N00023864.

[57] See Bruce Ackerman, *Crediting the Voters: A New Beginning for Campaign Finance*, 13 Am. Prospect 71 (1993). In addition, see Edward Foley, *Equal-Dollars-Per-Voter: A Constitutional Principle of Campaign Finance*, 94 Colum. L. Rev. 1204 (1994); Richard Hasen, *Clipping Coupons for Democracy: An Egalitarian/Public Choice Defense of Campaign Finance Vouchers*, 84 Cal. L. Rev. 1 (1996).

contributions. This structure would eliminate *quid pro quo* corruption because candidates would not know who had wanted to pay the price for beneficial legislation or official actions. In a world of anonymous donors, anyone could claim to have contributed to the blind trust, just as anyone can claim to have voted for a certain candidate. Is such a proposal constitutional? Is it sensible policy?

In *Voting with Dollars: A New Paradigm for Campaign Finance* (2002), Ian Ayres and Bruce Ackerman combine the proposal mandating anonymous private giving with the decentralized public financing plan described above. In this detailed, comprehensive proposal, each voter would receive 50 "Patriot dollars" that could be used only to support political campaigns. This influx of substantial public resources—directed by individual citizens to the candidates they support—would increase the overall resources spent on political activity, allow public funds to dominate private funds (they hope), and increase participation. They explain: "We refuse * * * to view the problem of campaign finance as if it represents the all-or-nothing choice of suppressing private contributions or leaving them unregulated. Our new paradigm uses anonymity to cleanse private giving of its worst abuses while allowing it to serve as a valuable supplementary support to the robust public debate fostered by billions of Patriot dollars allocated by millions of concerned citizens." *Id.* at 9. What are the likely effects of such a campaign finance system if adopted by a state or the federal government? Have the developments, both judicial and political, in the decade since Ayres and Ackerman put forward this proposal undermined its likelihood of meeting their goals or increased the urgency to consider a sweeping reform like this? Why has no jurisdiction considered a decentralized public financing program like this that allows citizens to channel public support to candidates, rather than directly subsidizing qualifying candidates? How would this proposal affect established political players such as major parties and incumbents? Are there other ways to expand the resources available to campaigns so that participation is broadened and the threat of undue influence by wealthy individuals, groups, and corporations is diluted?

2. The Experience After *Buckley* and the Need for Further Reform

Decades of experience with FECA demonstrated that serious challenges remained to effective campaign finance regulation. The Bipartisan Campaign Reform Act of 2002 (BCRA) sought to address these issues, so understanding them is fundamental to understanding BCRA and the jurisprudence that followed.

Political Action Committees. Political action committees (PACs) are not creatures of FECA, and the term does not appear in the Act, which uses instead "multicandidate political committee." Generally speaking, a PAC is a political committee, other than a political party, that receives contributions from more than 50 people and makes contributions to at least five candidates for federal office. PACs are required to register with and report information to the FEC. The 1976 amendments to FECA limited PAC contributions to a candidate to $5,000 per election and limited PAC contributions to a national committee of a political party to $15,000. By creating limitations that at the time were more generous than those applying to individuals, FECA encouraged the formation and growth of PACs. The first PAC was established in 1943 by a national labor union. In 1974, the number of registered PACs stood at 608; 10 years later, 4,009 were registered; and in 2018 there were 8,663 registered PACs. The largest category consists of corporate PACs: in 2018,

1,732 registered PACs were characterized as corporate, and they donated more total money to campaigns than labor or membership organizations.[58]

In the years immediately following *Buckley*, the issue of the influence of corporate and business PACs on the electoral process was the primary focus for reformers. For example, Judge J. Skelly Wright of the D.C. Circuit wrote in *Money and the Pollution of Politics: Is the First Amendment an Obstacle to Political Equality?*, 82 Colum. L. Rev. 609, 616, 618–19 (1982), that PACs have a malign effect on legislative policymaking: "When wealth of this magnitude is injected into the political bloodstream, the legislative process itself is affected. PAC contributions are given with a legislative purpose and it is a telling fact that they are most numerous in the more highly regulated industries, such as oil, transportation, utilities, drugs, health care, and government contracting. * * * Whatever the cause and effect relationship, studies of issue after issue demonstrate that a much higher percentage of legislators who voted with a PAC's position received money from the PAC in the previous campaign than those who voted the other way, and among the beneficiaries of PAC money those supporting the PAC position had received a substantially higher average contribution."

Empirical research, however, tends to show that PAC contributions influence legislative votes less than the legislator's personal philosophy, political party, and constituent views and interests.[59] Moreover, most of the money contributed to federal candidates comes from individuals, not PACs. One study of contributions to federal candidates in the 1999–2000 election cycle concluded that only around 22% of all money contributed to those campaigns could be considered special-interest money (e.g., from corporations, unions, other associations, or PACs). Stephen Ansolabehere, John de Figueiredo & James Snyder, Jr., *Why Is There So Little Money in U.S. Politics?*, 17 J. Econ. Persp. 105 (2003). Critics of PACs reply that PACs overwhelmingly contribute to incumbents, thereby further entrenching the status quo. In the 2012 election cycle, corporate PACs gave mainly to incumbents—with many, including those affiliated with energy, finance, health, and transportation, directing more than 85% of their funds to incumbents—and labor PACs sent 64% of their money to incumbents.[60]

Although they are often described as pernicious influences on the electoral process, PACs also empower individuals, who can increase their political influence

[58]   See Fed. Election Comm'n, *Summary of PAC Activity* (Apr. 7, 2017), https://transition.fec.gov/press/summaries/2018/tables/pac/PAC1_2018_24m.pdf; Fed. Election Comm'n, *Number of Federal PACs Increases* (March 9, 2009), https://www.fec.gov/updates/number-of-federal-pacs-increases/.

[59]   See, e.g., Stephen Bronars & John Lott, Jr., *Do Campaign Contributions Alter How a Politician Votes? Or, Do Donors Support Candidates Who Value the Same Things That They Do?*, 40 J.L. & Econ. 317 (1997). See also Jeffrey Milyo, David Primo & Timothy Groseclose, *Corporate PAC Campaign Contributions in Perspective*, 2 Bus. & Pol. 75 (2000) (arguing that corporate PAC contributions have little influence on policymakers and that other routes to influence, such as lobbying and soft-money contributions, are preferred by corporations); Note, *The Ass Atop the Castle: Competing Strategies for Using Campaign Donations to Influence Lawmaking*, 116 Harv. L. Rev. 2610, 2615–16 & n.24 (2003) (canvassing literature).

[60]   Ctr. for Responsive Pol., *PAC Dollars to Incumbents, Challengers, and Open Seat Candidates*, 2012 table, http://www.opensecrets.org/bigpicture/pac2cands.php?cycle=2012 & display=. See also Paul Herrnson & Stephanie Perry Curtis, *Financing the 2008 Congressional Elections*, in *Financing the 2008 Election* 166, 187 (David Magleby & Anthony Corrado eds., 2011) (corporate PACs directed 93% of their funds to House incumbents in 2008 elections); Randall Kroszner & Thomas Stratmann, *Corporate Campaign Contributions, Repeat Giving, and the Rewards to Legislator Reputation*, 48 J.L. & Econ. 41 (2005).

by working collectively. If various and diverse interests use this type of political organization to wield electoral influence, then PACs can be seen as a positive political force. For example, EMILY's List contributes money to female candidates and promotes a moderately feminist agenda. Critics of PACs argue that EMILY's List is notable because it is so rare; they maintain that corporate and business PACs exert a disproportionate influence compared to labor PACs or public-interest PACs. Opponents of further restrictions on PAC spending counter with a pragmatic argument, contending that any limitations will be easily circumvented. They point to the practice of *bundling*, in which individual contributions are presented as a group to a candidate in a way that makes it clear that the contributions were organized through a collective effort. Because the contributions are individual, the bundles of money do not count against the PAC contribution limit, although no single check can exceed the ceiling for individual contributions.

Until 2007, candidates were aware of the forces behind bundling and the interests that the contributions sought to advance, but they were not disclosed to the public unless the organizers voluntarily provided the information. As part of the Honest Leadership and Open Government Act of 2007, disclosure is required of any registered lobbyist providing bundled contributions to federal candidates or their committees that exceed $15,000 in any six-month period. Section 204, Pub. L. No. 110–81, 121 Stat. 735 (2007). The Act defines a bundled contribution as any contribution forwarded to the candidate by the person or any contribution "credited [by the candidate] to the person through records, designations, or other means of recognizing that a certain amount of money has been raised by the person."

Concerns about *stealth PACs* or *Section 527 organizations* (named for the section of the tax code under which such groups were organized) prompted a congressional response a few years before passage of the more comprehensive BCRA. In the late 1990s, political entrepreneurs began to use tax-exempt entities to evade campaign finance disclosure laws and contribution limitations. Section 527 organizations are nonprofit groups organized for the "function of influencing or attempting to influence the selection, nomination, election, or appointment of any individual to any Federal, State, or local public office." Internal Revenue Code § 527(e)(2). As is often the case in this area of unintended consequences, the drafters of Section 527 never envisioned its use as a blueprint for stealth PACs—instead, it was designed to protect most income of political parties from taxation.[61] In the summer of 2000, President Clinton signed a bill requiring Section 527 organizations to disclose their donors and their expenditures. Pub. L. No. 106–230, 114 Stat. 477 (2000). Within one month, nearly 5,000 organizations had filed disclosure forms with the IRS, which was then required to post the information on its website.

Soft Money. Money spent in connection with federal candidates, and therefore regulated by FECA, is hard money. *Soft money*, then, became the term used for any money left unregulated by FECA (although in 1990, the FEC required limited disclosure of soft-money expenditures). Soft money is spent on activities to benefit state candidates, to build infrastructure, and to fund voter mobilization programs,

[61]   See Donald Tobin, *Anonymous Speech and Section 527 of the Internal Revenue Code*, 37 Ga. L. Rev. 611, 623 (2003).

including direct-mail campaigns. Political parties also use soft money to fund issue advertisements that do not expressly advocate the election or defeat of a particular candidate. Although soft-money expenditures cannot be connected with a particular candidate, in fact they contribute significantly to the success of parties' nominees and are often intertwined with candidates' campaigns.

The use of soft money to evade federal restrictions, particularly in a presidential election in which candidates must comply with expenditure limitations in order to qualify for federal matching funds, increased substantially in the 1990s. The *McConnell* Court described the process through which parties and candidates exploited this loophole: "The evidence in the record shows that candidates and donors alike have in fact exploited the soft-money loophole, the former to increase their prospects of election and the latter to create debt on the part of officeholders, with the national parties serving as willing intermediaries. * * * Parties kept tallies of the amounts of soft money raised by each officeholder, and 'the amount of money a Member of Congress raise[d] for the national political committees often affect[ed] the amount the committees g[a]ve to assist the Member's campaign.' Donors often asked that their contributions be credited to particular candidates, and the parties obliged, irrespective of whether the funds were hard or soft. National party committees often teamed with individual candidates' campaign committees to create joint fundraising committees, which enabled the candidates to take advantage of the party's higher contribution limits while still allowing donors to give to their preferred candidate. Even when not participating directly in the fundraising, federal officeholders were well aware of the identities of the donors: National party committees would distribute lists of potential or actual donors, or donors themselves would report their generosity to officeholders." 540 U.S. at 146–47.

The pace of soft-money fundraising escalated immediately before passage of BCRA, so this phenomenon became a target of reformers. A study of the 1998 congressional elections revealed that soft money spent by party committees and raised from a few large donors played an important role in competitive congressional elections.[62] Soft-money expenditures in this midterm election were more than double the spending in 1994. From January 1999 through the end of November 2000, a time period that included a presidential campaign, the national party committees raised more than $487 million in soft money. Not surprisingly given these figures, reformers argued that soft-money donations directly resulted in favorable legislation for the groups providing funds. For example, Common Cause published a report linking large soft-money donations to particular tax breaks in the 1997 Budget Act. *Return on Investment: The Hidden Story of Soft Money, Corporate Welfare and the 1997 Budget & Tax Deal* (1997). Do such allegations provide support under any of the justifications described previously for laws regulating soft-money contributions?

Issue Advocacy. Adopting a narrow interpretation of FECA to avoid constitutional problems, the Court in *Buckley* upheld disclosure requirements only with respect to independent expenditures used for communications that expressly advocate the election or defeat of a clearly identified federal candidate. In a footnote,

---

[62] See *Outside Money: Soft Money and Issue Ads in Competitive 1998 Congressional Elections* (David Magleby & Marianne Holt eds., 1999).

the Court indicated that the following terms would meet the express advocacy test: "vote for," "elect," "support," "cast your ballot for," "Smith for Congress," "vote against," "defeat," or "reject." 424 U.S. at 44 n.52. Although the footnote does not state that using these words is the only way to meet the express advocacy test, they became known as the *magic words* distinguishing regulated communications from unregulated ones. See also *Fed. Election Comm'n v. Massachusetts Citizens for Life, Inc.*, 479 U.S. 238 (1986) (indicating some flexibility in the "magic words" formulation by noting that a communication of support "marginally less direct than 'Vote for Smith' does not change its essential nature"). The Court in *Buckley* rejected any test for express advocacy that would depend on the speaker's purpose or the audience's understanding because such a subjective test would chill political speech.

The absence of federal regulation after *Buckley* resulted in an explosion in the use of issue advocacy—political speech that did not meet the test for express advocacy but that often mentioned specific candidates or political parties. The Annenberg Public Policy Center estimated that political parties and various interest groups spent between $135 million and $150 million for issue ads in the 1996 election cycle. Deborah Beck, Paul Taylor, Jeffrey Stranger & Douglas Rivlin, *Issue Advocacy Advertising During the 1996 Campaign* (1997). Although issue advertisements were supposedly designed only to further the discussion of particular issues, the Annenberg Center found that nearly 87% mentioned a candidate for office by name and 59% of them pictured a candidate. Furthermore, issue ads appeared to be more negative in tone than other political advertising, perhaps because candidates tried to avoid being associated in the voters' minds with negative campaigning but understood how effective such communication could be. Of the issue ads, 41% were purely negative in tone, whereas only 24% of the advertisements directly paid for by presidential candidates criticized their opponents.

A Brennan Center for Justice study of more than 2,100 separate commercials run over 300,000 times in the top 75 media markets in the 1998 elections provided additional information about issue advertisements. Jonathan Krasno & Daniel Seltz, *Buying Time: Television Advertising in the 1998 Congressional Elections* (2000). Most (65%) issue ads were sponsored by political parties, rather than by interest groups, corporations, or labor unions. Perhaps surprisingly, candidate ads, which can include express advocacy, seldom used the magic words. Only 9% of candidate ads in the final week of the campaign included any of the magic words. This conclusion cast doubt on the efficacy of the magic words test as a way to separate express advocacy from other political communication. While none of the issue ads contained the key phrases required by *Buckley*'s footnote, 87% of them urged viewers to take some concrete action such as calling an elected official or candidate, although the ads rarely provided a phone number to assist motivated citizens. Just as with soft money, so-called "sham issue" ads became a focus for the authors of BCRA.

Finally, some of the issue ads were financed by groups designed to conceal their major donors. The Court in *McConnell v. Fed. Election Comm'n* noted two such examples: "'Citizens for Better Medicare,' for instance, was not a grassroots organization of citizens, as its name might suggest, but was instead a platform for an association of drug manufacturers. And 'Republicans for Clean Air,' which ran ads in the 2000 Republican Presidential primary, was actually an organization consisting of just two individuals—brothers who together spent $25 million on ads supporting their favored candidate." 540 U.S. at 128. This increased use of veiled political actors suggested the need for more effective disclosure, beyond even what had been adopted in 2000 aimed at Section 527 groups.

3. The Bipartisan Campaign Reform Act of 2002 and *McConnell v. Federal Election Commission*

The key provisions of the Bipartisan Campaign Reform Act of 2002, Pub. L. No. 107–155, 116 Stat. 81, include the following:

A Ban on Soft Money. The national committees of a political party can neither receive nor spend soft money. BCRA also prohibits federal-candidate-controlled PACs from raising or spending soft money. Local and state committees of political parties cannot spend soft money on federal election activities, although they can still spend such money solely to influence state or local races. "Federal election activity" is defined to include voter registration drives within 120 days of an election; get-out-the-vote drives conducted in connection with a federal election; any work by state or local campaign employees who spend more than 25% of their time on federal election activities; and advertisements specific to federal candidates. There is an exception to this ban that applies only to state and local party committees: they may use soft money to fund generic voter registration and get-out-the-vote drives that relate to federal elections, but they are limited to using contributions of no more than $10,000 per source.

A Ban on Candidate Solicitation of Soft Money. Federal office seekers and officeholders and their agents can neither solicit nor spend soft money. They may engage in soft-money fundraising efforts by nonprofit organizations for voter registration and get-out-the-vote drives, but they may only solicit up to $20,000 per individual and only from individuals.

Provisions Affecting Hard Money. The new law raised most of the hard-money limits, and it indexed for inflation the limits on individuals' contributions to candidates and national parties. The aggregate limit for an individual's contributions to candidates was raised from $25,000 to $37,500 per election cycle. Individuals could contribute $25,000 per year per national party committee, with an aggregate contribution limit of $20,000 to $57,500 per election cycle for donations to all national party committees, depending on how much money the individual contributes to PACs. (The aggregate contribution limits were ruled unconstitutional by the Supreme Court in *McCutcheon v. Fed. Election Comm'n*, 572 U.S. 185 (2014).) The limit on contributions that an individual can give to a federal candidate per election doubled to $2,000. Although BCRA would have allowed higher contribution limits to apply to candidates facing self-financed opponents who spend substantial amounts of their own money in their campaigns—a provision called the "millionaire opponent" provision—the Supreme Court struck this down as unconstitutional because it did not further the state's interest in deterring *quid pro quo* corruption. *Davis v. Fed. Election Comm'n*, 554 U.S. 724 (2008). The justification that the provision was required to "equalize the playing field" for candidates who were not personally wealthy was rejected as a revival of the equalization rationale rejected in *Buckley*.

Limitation on Expenditures for Electioneering Communications. The Act defines "electioneering communication" to include broadcast, cable, or satellite advertisements that refer to a clearly identified candidate; that are run within 30 days of a primary election or 60 days of a general election; and that are "targeted" in that they can be received by 50,000 or more persons in the congressional district or state where the election is being held. Political parties and candidates may spend only hard money to fund such advertisements. Corporations and unions were prohibited from funding such communication directly; instead, they were required to fund these broadcast advertisements through PACs that raise and use regulated hard money. This provision was challenged in *Citizens United v. Fed. Election Comm'n*, 558 U.S. 310 (2010), and we will consider its fate in the next section. Individuals and unincorporated entities can fund electioneering communication directly, but they must disclose within 24 hours the sources of contributions of $1,000 or more, once an aggregate of $10,000 has been spent.

Within hours of its passage, opponents of the law filed suit claiming that BCRA was facially unconstitutional in several respects. The case consolidated the challenges of nearly 80 plaintiffs, led by Senator Mitch McConnell (R-Ky.) and the National Rifle Association, and it generated 100,000 pages of evidence and testimony from more than 200 witnesses. A special District Court panel of three judges first heard the case. The judges issued four separate opinions totaling 744 pages of the *Federal Supplement*, striking down parts of BCRA, upholding others, and even rewriting a few. *McConnell v. Fed. Election Comm'n*, 251 F. Supp. 2d 176 (D.D.C. 2003) (three-judge panel). BCRA required the Supreme Court to review the case following a decision by the special panel, so the case immediately went to the Supreme Court, which expedited the process and held oral arguments in September before the regular term began. With the campaigns for the 2004 federal elections well under way, the Supreme Court issued its opinion on the constitutionality of BCRA, upholding virtually all of it and certainly all of its key provisions—at least for the time being.

McConnell v. Federal Election Commission

540 U.S. 93 (2003).

The majority opinion, written by **Justice Stevens** and **Justice O'Connor**, noted the problems that Congress hoped to solve by enacting BCRA: the increasing use of soft money and the explosion of issue ads. Section 323(a) is the main weapon used to regulate soft money; this section prohibits national party committees or their agents from soliciting, receiving, directing, or spending any soft-money contributions, thereby "tak[ing] national parties out of the soft-money business." Sections 201 and 203 are the provisions designed to more effectively regulate "electioneering communications," both increasing disclosure requirements and mandating the use of segregated funds by corporations and unions to fund that communication.

The Court first determined the appropriate First Amendment standard of review for Section 323, holding that a contribution limit that interferes with First Amendment rights is constitutional if it satisfies the "lesser demand" of being "closely drawn" to match a "sufficiently important interest." This test, rather than strict scrutiny, was used because "contribution limits, like other measures aimed at protecting the integrity of the process, tangibly benefit public participation in political debate. * * * The less rigorous standard of review we have applied to contribution limits (*Buckley*'s 'closely drawn' scrutiny) shows proper deference to Congress' ability to weigh competing constitutional interests in an area in which it enjoys particular expertise. It also provides Congress with sufficient room to anticipate and respond to concerns about circumvention of regulations designed to protect the integrity of the political process."

Applying this test, the majority believed combating *quid pro quo* corruption or its appearance provided ample justification for Congress' decision to close the soft-money loophole through § 323. "The evidence connects soft money to manipulations of the legislative calendar, leading to Congress' failure to enact, among other things, generic drug legislation, tort reform, and tobacco legislation. To claim that such actions do not change legislative outcomes surely misunderstands the legislative process. * * * More importantly, plaintiffs conceive of corruption too narrowly. * * * Many of the 'deeply disturbing examples' of corruption cited by this Court in *Buckley* to justify FECA's contribution limits were not episodes of vote buying, but evidence that various corporate interests had given substantial donations to gain access to high-level government officials. Even if that access did not secure actual influence, it certainly gave the 'appearance of such influence.' "

Justice Kennedy's dissent took vigorous issue with what he saw as an expansion of the traditional corruption rationale to include "any conduct that wins goodwill from or influences a Member of Congress. * * * [The majority] concludes that access, without more, proves influence is undue. Access, in the Court's view, has the same legal ramifications as actual or apparent corruption of officeholders. This new definition of corruption sweeps away all protections for speech that lie in its path. * * *Access in itself, however, shows only that in a general sense an officeholder favors someone or that someone has influence on the officeholder. There is no basis, in law or in fact, to say favoritism or influence in general is the same as corrupt favoritism or influence in particular." He went on: "Favoritism and influence are not, as the Government's theory suggests, avoidable in representative politics. It is in the nature of an elected representative to favor certain policies, and, by necessary corollary, to favor the voters and contributors who support those policies. It is well understood that a substantial and legitimate reason, if not the only reason, to cast a vote for, or to make a contribution to, one candidate over another is that the candidate will respond by producing those political outcomes the supporter favors. Democracy is premised on responsiveness."

Section 323(b) limits the ability of state and local parties to accept soft-money contributions, even though the congressional record contained little evidence that these entities presented the same problems for the federal campaign system. This was justified, the majority held, to prevent the possibility that political actors would circumvent the other provisions restricting soft money. "Having been taught the hard lesson of circumvention by the entire history of campaign finance regulation, Congress knew that soft-money donors would react to § 323(a) by scrambling to find another way to purchase influence. It was 'neither novel nor implausible,' *Nixon v. Shrink Missouri Gov't PAC*, 528 U.S. at 391, for Congress to conclude that political parties would react to § 323(a) by directing soft-money contributors to the state committees, and that federal candidates would be just as indebted to these contributors as they had been to those who had formerly contributed to the national parties." The Court concluded that it should defer to Congress' prediction of future political behavior, "particularly when, as here, those predictions are so firmly rooted in relevant history and common sense."

Justices Stevens and O'Connor next turned to the provisions aimed at issue ads. The parties challenging BCRA had interpreted *Buckley* as drawing "a constitutionally mandated line between express advocacy and so-called issue advocacy, and that speakers possess an inviolable First Amendment right to engage in the latter category of speech. * * * [However,] a plain reading of *Buckley* makes clear that the express advocacy limitation, in both the expenditure and the disclosure contexts, was the product of statutory interpretation rather than a constitutional command." The Court determined that no "rigid barrier" is required by the First Amendment between express advocacy and issue advocacy. "That notion cannot be squared with our longstanding recognition that the presence or absence of magic words cannot meaningfully distinguish electioneering speech from a true issue ad. Indeed, the unmistakable lesson from the record in this litigation, as all three judges on the District Court agreed, is that *Buckley*'s magic-words requirement is functionally meaningless." It concluded that the Act's definition of electioneering communication was not impermissibly vague, but clearly applied "(1) to a broadcast (2) clearly identifying a candidate for federal office, (3) aired within a specific time period, and (4) targeted to an identified audience of at least 50,000 viewers or listeners. These components are both easily understood and objectively determinable."

It then analyzed the various regulations applying to electioneering communication. First, BCRA imposed more sweeping disclosure requirements, all of which were upheld by the majority and most of the dissenting justices. The state interests articulated in *Buckley* relating to disclosure—providing the electorate with information, deterring actual corruption and avoiding any appearance thereof, and aiding in the enforcement of the more substantive electioneering restrictions—were relevant here. The Court was particularly concerned with the evidence that showed groups and individuals running ads while "hiding behind dubious and misleading names." The Court worried that public debate was significantly harmed when organizations producing political communications could avoid the scrutiny of voters. Finally, although the Court rejected the facial attack in this lawsuit, it allowed for the possibility of future lawsuits brought by organizations with credible evidence that their members had been exposed to "economic reprisals or physical threats as a result of the compelled disclosures."

Second, BCRA § 203 extended a segregated-fund requirement to include payments for any electioneering communication: corporations and unions could not use their general treasury funds to finance electioneering communication, but they could organize and administer segregated funds, or PACs, for that purpose. In its analysis, the Court noted that § 203 was not a "complete ban" on political expression, as those challenging it argued, because regulated entities could still use a segregated fund to pay for electioneering communication. With regard to the state interest justifying this regulation, the majority cited *Austin v. Michigan Chamber of Commerce*: "We have repeatedly sustained legislation aimed at 'the corrosive and distorting effects of immense aggregations of wealth that are accumulated with the help of the corporate form and that have little or no correlation to the public's support for the corporation's political ideas.'" The Court thus sustained § 203 because it regulated issue ads during a certain period of time that "are the functional equivalent of express advocacy * * * intended to influence the voters' decisions and [that] have that effect."

The majority concluded: "Many years ago we observed that '[t]o say that Congress is without power to pass appropriate legislation to safeguard . . . an election from the improper use of money to influence the result is to deny to the nation in a vital particular the power of self protection.' *Burroughs v. United States*, 290 U.S. [534,] 545 [1934]. We abide by that conviction in considering Congress' most recent effort to confine the ill effects of aggregated wealth on our political system. We are under no illusion that BCRA will be the last congressional statement on the matter. Money, like water, will always find an outlet. What problems will arise, and how Congress will respond, are concerns for another day."

In a separate opinion by **Chief Justice Rehnquist**, the Court held the challenge to the increased contribution limits, such as the increase from $1,000 to $2,000 in the amount that individuals could contribute to candidates per election cycle, to be nonjusticiable because the plaintiffs lacked standing to bring such a challenge. The Court struck down as unconstitutional the provision that prohibited minors from making contributions to candidates or political parties on the grounds that it violated their First Amendment rights.

Justice Scalia began his dissent: "This is a sad day for the freedom of speech. Who could have imagined that the same Court which, within the past four years, has sternly disapproved of restrictions upon such inconsequential forms of expression as virtual child pornography, tobacco advertising, dissemination of illegally intercepted communications, and sexually explicit cable programming, would smile with favor upon a law that cuts to the heart of what the First Amendment is meant to protect: the right to criticize the government." He alluded to a partisan lockup issue when he noted that, although the restrictions applied in an evenhanded way to all who ran for federal office, "[i]f *all* electioneering were evenhandedly prohibited, incumbents would have an enormous advantage. Likewise, if incumbents and challengers are limited to the same quantity of electioneering, incumbents are favored. * * * Beyond that, however, the present legislation *targets* for prohibition certain categories of campaign speech that are particularly harmful to incumbents. Is it accidental, do you think, that incumbents raise about three times as much 'hard money'—the sort of funding generally *not* restricted by this legislation—as do their challengers? * * * And is it mere happenstance, do you estimate, that national-party funding, which is severely limited by the Act, is more likely to assist cash-strapped challengers than flush-with-hard-money incumbents?"

Justice Scalia's main objection to the majority opinion concerned its view of corporations within the First Amendment jurisprudence of campaign finance, a view he traced to *Austin v. Michigan Chamber of Commerce*. "People who associate—who pool their financial resources—for purposes of economic enterprise overwhelmingly do so in the corporate form; and with increasing frequency, incorporation is chosen by those who associate to defend and promote particular ideas—such as the American Civil Liberties Union and the National Rifle Association, parties to these cases. Imagine, then, a government that wished to suppress nuclear power—or oil and gas exploration, or automobile manufacturing, or gun ownership, or civil liberties—and that had the power to prohibit corporate advertising against its proposals. To be sure, the individuals involved in, or benefited by, those industries, or interested in those causes, could (given enough time) form political action committees or other associations to make their case. But the organizational form in which those enterprises already *exist*, and in which they can most quickly and most effectively get their message across, is the corporate form. The First Amendment does not in my view permit the restriction of that political speech. And the same holds true for corporate electoral speech: A candidate should not be insulated from the most effective speech that the major participants in the economy and major incorporated interest groups can generate."

He also noted that disclosure statutes eliminated the risk that the political dialogue would be "distorted" by corporate spending because voters would know who is behind the speech. "The premise of the First Amendment is that the American people are neither sheep nor fools, and hence fully capable of considering both the substance of the speech presented to them and its proximate and ultimate source. If that premise is wrong, our democracy has a much greater problem to overcome than merely the influence of amassed wealth."

Justice Thomas argued that the appropriate standard of review is strict scrutiny, and that bribery laws and disclosure statutes would be less restrictive means of curtailing corruption. However, unlike all the other Justices, Justice Thomas would have invalidated BCRA's disclosure requirements because they allowed "the established right to anonymous speech to be stripped away based on the flimsiest of justifications." He rejected the notion that the interest of voters in knowing the source of political speech could support disclosure statutes because this interest was outweighed by the First Amendment right to engage in anonymous political speech.

Justice Kennedy's lengthy dissent took on the majority's reasoning with respect to § 203, the segregated-fund requirement imposed on corporations and unions that spend money on electioneering communication in the weeks before an election. He stated that he would have overruled *Austin*, rather than relying on it or "extending" it. He noted that the communications targeted by § 203 are "the ads speakers find most effective. Unlike express ads that leave nothing to the imagination, the record shows that issues ads are preferred by almost all candidates, even though politicians, unlike corporations, can lawfully broadcast express ads if they so choose." "The Government's use of the pejorative label [of 'sham issue' ad] should not obscure § 203's practical effect: It prohibits a mass communication technique favored in the modern political process for the very reason that it is the most potent." He also noted that that the burden on entities regulated by § 203 was not trivial. "These [segregated-fund] regulations are more than minor clerical requirements. Rather, they create major disincentives for speech, with the effect falling most heavily on smaller entities that often have the most difficulty bearing the costs of compliance."

Justice Kennedy next addressed the definition of "electioneering communication." He provided a hypothetical to prove his point: "[S]uppose a few Senators want to show their constituents in the logging industry how much they care about working families and propose a law, 60 days before the election, that would harm the environment by allowing logging in national forests. Under [BCRA], a nonprofit environmental group would be unable to run an ad referring to these Senators in their districts. The suggestion that the group could form and fund a PAC in the short time required for effective participation in the political debate is fanciful. * * * The group would want to refer to these Senators, either by name or by photograph, not necessarily because an election is at stake. * * * The ability to refer to candidates and officeholders is important because it allows the public to communicate with them on issues of common concern. [BCRA's] sweeping approach fails to take into account this significant free speech interest. Under any conventional definition of overbreadth, it fails to meet strict scrutiny standards. It forces electioneering communications sponsored by an environmental group to contend with faceless and nameless opponents and consign their broadcast * * * to a world where politicians who threaten the environment must be referred to as 'He Whose Name Cannot Be Spoken.'"

The Justice concluded his example: "We are supposed to find comfort in the knowledge that the ad is banned under § 203 only if it 'is targeted to the relevant electorate,' defined as communications that can be received by 50,000 or more persons in the candidate's district. This Orwellian criterion, however, is analogous to a law, unconstitutional under any known First Amendment theory, that would allow a speaker to say anything he chooses, so long as his intended audience could not hear him. A central purpose of issue ads is to urge the public to pay close attention to the candidate's platform on the featured issues. By banning broadcast in the very district where the candidate is standing for election, § 203 shields information at the heart of the First Amendment from precisely those citizens who most value the right to make a responsible judgment at the voting booth."

NOTE ON MCCONNELL V. FEDERAL ELECTION COMMISSION

Corruption and the Standard of Review. The Court in *McConnell* applies something like intermediate scrutiny to restrictions on campaign contributions, a less rigorous standard than the strict scrutiny to which expenditure limitations are subjected. In addition, the majority demonstrates a willingness to defer to Congress throughout its analysis. For example, it notes that Congress had enacted a comprehensive response to problems in the campaign fundraising system and thus judges should consider BCRA an integrated approach to regulation. The implication of this language is that judges should be hesitant to strike down part of the statute and leave other parts in place because such a piecemeal approach could lead to unintended consequences. The majority ends the main opinion by underscoring the primary role Congress plays in designing campaign finance laws and predicting that it will need to formulate new approaches as money begins to find new outlets.

McConnell also suggested that the "special access" to politicians that large contributions appear to buy counts as a legally cognizable form of corruption. As Richard Briffault writes: "Although the Court had previously made clear that corruption was not limited to outright vote-buying, the Court's language of undue influence had nonetheless focused on the effects of large contributions on government decision-making. By focusing on special access, *McConnell* reframed the corruption analysis from the consideration of the impact of contributions on formal decisions to their effect on the *opportunity to influence* government actions." McConnell v. FEC *and the Transformation of Campaign Finance Law*, 3 Election L.J. 147, 162–63 (2004). Much of Justice Kennedy's dissent argues against this expansion of the corruption rationale, contending that access to lawmakers is not inherently harmful but is instead an inevitable part of representative government. What do you think about this formulation of corruption? Does this state interest in preventing special access bought with large contributions, as the majority articulates it, have a limiting principle? What sorts of additional regulation of the electoral process would it support?

Problem 2-7. Remember the other state interests that have been put forth in the campaign finance context, although not all have been embraced by the Court: increasing voter competence, enhancing electoral competitiveness, equality concerns, and encouraging a more participatory democracy. Would the judicial analysis of BCRA's provisions be different if those state interests were considered as compelling or important? Would they support more aggressive regulation than Congress adopted in 2002?

The 2004 presidential and congressional campaigns were the first conducted under BCRA. Perhaps the biggest change was the increased importance of hard money both because of BCRA's soft-money restrictions and because of larger contribution limits for hard money. Thus, people who could bundle many $2,000 contributions from individuals were particularly important to candidates and political parties. Initially, the new emphasis on hard money was thought to provide a significant advantage to the Republican Party because it has a larger base of hard-money donors, many of whom could give amounts up to the new limits. Before enactment of BCRA, the two political parties were roughly equal in their ability to raise soft money, but the Republicans had always substantially outpaced the Democrats for hard money. As the 2004 election cycle developed, however, both parties were able to replace soft money with new hard money, and any Republican advantage was clearly not long-lived. Anthony Corrado found that "[b]y the end of the 2004 election, the national party committees had raised more money in hard dollars *alone* than they raised in hard and soft dollars *combined* in any previous election cycle." *Party Finance in the Wake of BCRA: An Overview*, in *The Election After Reform*, *supra*, at 19, 25.

With the closing of the soft-money spigot for political parties, 527 organizations, discussed above, became increasingly crucial political players in the 2004 elections. Although all PACs are also 527 organizations, not all 527s involved in politics at the federal level were considered PACs before BCRA and *McConnell*. These groups argued that, as long as they did not engage in express advocacy (as defined by the *Buckley* "magic words") and did not directly contribute to federal candidates' campaigns, they could raise unlimited amounts of soft money. Taking advantage of this loophole, federally active 527 groups spent approximately $424 million in the 2004 election cycle immediately following *McConnell*.[63] Most of the 527s with significant resources in 2004 supported the Democrats. Many of the 527s worked informally with the political parties: leading political consultants affiliated with parties in the past helped them raise money, and party officials signaled their support for certain 527s. See Stephen Weissman & Ruth Hassan, *BCRA and the 527 Groups*, in *The Election After Reform*, *supra*, at 79.

The *McConnell* opinions noted that evasion of BCRA was likely to center on the use of nonprofit organizations, which would include not only 527 organizations but also nonprofit organizations created under Sections 501(c)(3) and 501(c)(4) of the tax code. Chief Justice Rehnquist, in dissent, stated that "[n]onprofit organizations are currently able to accept, without disclosing [in the case of nonprofits other than 527 organizations], unlimited donations for voter registration, voter identification, and get-out-the-vote activities, and the record indicates that such organizations already receive large donations, sometimes in the millions of dollars, for these activities." Indeed, the next major campaign finance cases that reshaped the jurisprudential landscape focused on nonprofit corporations primarily engaged in political activity.

---

[63]   Michael Malbin, *Assessing the Bipartisan Campaign Reform Act*, in *The Election After Reform*, *supra*, at 1, 11.

B. THE ROBERTS COURT'S CHANGE OF COURSE:
CITIZENS UNITED V. FEDERAL ELECTION COMMISSION

Although *McConnell* left some questions open, it initially appeared that the issues would be resolved within the *Buckley/McConnell* framework and that the courts would be relatively deferential to legislative decisions regarding the appropriate regulation of campaign contributions. However, two changes in Supreme Court personnel unsettled the jurisprudential landscape. John Roberts replaced Chief Justice Rehnquist, and Samuel Alito replaced Justice Sandra Day O'Connor, one of the authors of the majority opinion in *McConnell*.

In 2007, Wisconsin Right to Life, Inc. (WRTL), a nonprofit ideological advocacy 501(c)(4) corporation, brought an as-applied challenge to BCRA's rules concerning electioneering communication.[64] During the 30-day period before Wisconsin's 2004 primary election, WRTL planned to run broadcast advertisements telling viewers to contact Senators Feingold and Kohl to urge them to oppose a filibuster of conservative judicial nominees. Because WRTL accepted some contributions from for-profit corporations and the ads it proposed to air met the requirements of § 203, BCRA required that WRTL set up a segregated fund and use that money to pay for the ads.

In *Fed. Election Comm'n v. Wisconsin Right to Life, Inc.*, 551 U.S. 449 (2007), a majority of the Court agreed with WRTL that BCRA was unconstitutional as applied to these ads. Chief Justice Roberts and Justice Alito noted that *McConnell* allowed regulation of issue ads under § 203 only when they are the "functional equivalent" of express advocacy. They held that "a court should find that an ad is the functional equivalent of express advocacy only if the ad is susceptible of no reasonable interpretation other than as an appeal to vote for or against a specific candidate." Noting that strict scrutiny demands that a "compelling state interest supports *each application* of a statute restricting speech," the Justices found that BCRA could not be applied in this instance because the concern about *quid pro quo* corruption was not implicated by "genuine" issue ads that are not the functional equivalent of express advocacy. Thus, WRTL could fund them directly with general treasury funds.

A few years later, *McConnell* came under even more serious attack. Citizens United, another ideological nonprofit that accepted a small amount of contributions from for-profit corporations, produced a 90-minute documentary called *Hillary: The Movie*, which it proposed to release on cable video-on-demand channels. The movie was a critical assessment of then-Senator Hillary Clinton (D-N.Y.) and her run for the presidency in 2008. The movie, as well as the ads produced to publicize it, seemed to trigger § 203's requirement that Citizens United use a segregated fund to produce the movie and the ads because all would have been aired within 30 days of the 2008 primary elections. Citizens United had funded the movie directly and thus faced civil and criminal penalties, so it brought an action for declaratory and injunctive relief, arguing that § 203, as well as BCRA's disclosure and disclaimer provisions applying

---

[64]　For an examination of the Roberts Court's use of as-applied challenges to determine broad questions of election law, see Nathaniel Persily & Jennifer Rosenberg, *Defacing Democracy?: The Changing Nature and Rising Importance of As-Applied Challenges in the Supreme Court's Recent Election Law Decisions*, 93 Minn. L. Rev. 1644 (2009).

to independent expenditures used for electioneering communications, were unconstitutional as applied to *Hillary* and the surrounding publicity for it.

After losing before a three-judge District Court panel, Citizens United appealed to the Supreme Court, which asked for a second round of arguments in an unusual September 2009 sitting. The Supreme Court had a new member: Justice Sonia Sotomayor had replaced Justice Souter. The reargument was also noteworthy because it was Solicitor General Elena Kagan's first appearance before the Court; less than a year later, she replaced retiring Justice Stevens. When the Court ordered reargument, it requested supplemental briefs addressing whether it should overrule *Austin v. Michigan Chamber of Commerce* and the part of *McConnell* dealing with the regulation of electioneering communication. It thus signaled a willingness to go beyond the as-applied challenge before it and revisit the holding of *McConnell* that § 203 was facially constitutional. (Note: Section 203 of BCRA amended 2 U.S.C. § 441b (subsequently transferred to 52 U.S.C. § 30118), which regulates corporate contributions and independent expenditures for express advocacy. Accordingly, the majority opinion in *Citizens United* refers to § 441b when it considers the regulation of corporate independent expenditures for electioneering communication.)

CITIZENS UNITED v. FEDERAL ELECTION COMMISSION
Supreme Court of the United States, 2010.
558 U.S. 310, 130 S.Ct. 876, 175 L.Ed.2d 753.

JUSTICE KENNEDY delivered the opinion of the Court, in which THE CHIEF JUSTICE, and JUSTICE SCALIA and JUSTICE ALITO, joined, in which JUSTICE THOMAS joined as to all but Part IV, and in which JUSTICES STEVENS, GINSBURG, BREYER, and SOTOMAYOR joined as to Part IV.

Federal law prohibits corporations and unions from using their general treasury funds to make independent expenditures for speech defined as an "electioneering communication" or for speech expressly advocating the election or defeat of a candidate. Limits on electioneering communications were upheld in *McConnell v. Federal Election Comm'n*. The holding of *McConnell* rested to a large extent on an earlier case, *Austin v. Michigan Chamber of Commerce*. *Austin* had held that political speech may be banned based on the speaker's corporate identity.

In this case we are asked to reconsider *Austin* and, in effect, *McConnell*. * * * [We] hold that *stare decisis* does not compel the continued acceptance of *Austin*. The Government may regulate corporate political speech through disclaimer and disclosure requirements, but it may not suppress that speech altogether. * * *

[The Court noted that federal law has long prohibited corporations and unions from using general treasury funds to make direct contributions to candidates or independent expenditures that expressly advocate the election or defeat of a federal candidate. The Court first considered several narrower ways in which it could have decided the case without overruling precedent or reaching the constitutional issues. For example, it had been argued that Citizens United might not meet the test in *WRTL* because *Hillary* should not be considered express advocacy or its functional equivalent; the test provided by *WRTL* was whether the communication is "susceptible of no reasonable interpretation other than as an appeal to vote for or against a specific candidate." But the Court concluded that *Hillary* was equivalent to express advocacy: "The movie, in essence, is a feature-length negative advertisement that urges viewers to vote against Senator Clinton for President." Thus, because it could not resolve the case on a narrower ground, the Court concluded that "full consideration of the continuing effect of the speech suppression upheld in *Austin*" was required.]

[II] * * * In the exercise of its judicial responsibility, it is necessary then for the Court to consider the facial validity of § 441b. Any other course of decision would prolong the substantial, nation-wide chilling effect caused by § 441b's prohibitions on corporate expenditures. * * *

[S]ubstantial time would be required to bring clarity to the application of the statutory provision on these points in order to avoid any chilling effect caused by some improper interpretation. It is well known that the public begins to concentrate on elections only in the weeks immediately before they are held. There are short timeframes in which speech can have influence. * * * A speaker's ability to engage in political speech that could have a chance of persuading voters is stifled if the speaker must first commence a protracted lawsuit. By the time the lawsuit concludes, the election will be over and the litigants in most cases will have neither the incentive nor, perhaps, the resources to carry on, even if they could establish that the case is not moot because the issue is "capable of repetition, yet evading review." Here, Citizens United decided to litigate its case to the end. Today, Citizens United finally learns, two years after the fact, whether it could have spoken during the 2008 Presidential primary—long after the opportunity to persuade primary voters has passed.

[An additional factor] is the primary importance of speech itself to the integrity of the election process. As additional rules are created for regulating political speech, any speech arguably within their reach is chilled. Campaign finance regulations now impose "unique and complex rules" on "71 distinct entities." Brief for Seven Former Chairmen of FEC et al. as *Amici Curiae* 11–12. These entities are subject to separate rules for 33 different types of political speech. The FEC has adopted 568 pages of regulations, 1,278 pages of explanations and justifications for those regulations, and 1,771 advisory opinions since 1975. In fact, after this Court in *WRTL* adopted an objective "appeal to vote" test for determining whether a communication was the functional equivalent of express advocacy, the FEC adopted a two-part, 11-factor balancing test to implement *WRTL*'s ruling.

This regulatory scheme may not be a prior restraint on speech in the strict sense of that term, for prospective speakers are not compelled by law to seek an advisory opinion from the FEC before the speech takes place. As a practical matter, however, given the complexity of the regulations and the deference courts show to administrative determinations, a speaker who wants to avoid threats of criminal liability and the heavy costs of defending against FEC enforcement must ask a governmental agency for prior permission to speak. * * *

The ongoing chill upon speech that is beyond all doubt protected makes it necessary in this case to invoke the earlier precedents that a statute which chills speech can and must be invalidated where its facial invalidity has been demonstrated. For these reasons we find it necessary to reconsider *Austin*.

[III] * * * The law before us is an outright ban [of political speech], backed by criminal sanctions. Section 441b makes it a felony for all corporations—including nonprofit advocacy corporations—either to expressly advocate the election or defeat of candidates or to broadcast electioneering communications within 30 days of a primary election and 60 days of a general election. Thus, the following acts would all be felonies under § 441b: The Sierra Club runs an ad, within the crucial phase of 60 days before the general election, that exhorts the public to disapprove of a Congressman who favors logging in national forests; the National Rifle Association publishes a book urging the public to vote for the challenger because the incumbent U.S. Senator supports a handgun ban; and the American Civil Liberties Union creates a Web site telling the public to vote for a Presidential candidate in light of that candidate's defense of free speech. These prohibitions are classic examples of censorship.

Section 441b is a ban on corporate speech notwithstanding the fact that a PAC created by a corporation can still speak. A PAC is a separate association from the corporation. So the PAC exemption from § 441b's expenditure ban does not allow corporations to speak. Even if a PAC could somehow allow a corporation to speak— and it does not—the option to form PACs does not alleviate the First Amendment problems with § 441b. PACs are burdensome alternatives; they are expensive to administer and subject to extensive regulations. * * *

Premised on mistrust of governmental power, the First Amendment stands against attempts to disfavor certain subjects or viewpoints. Prohibited, too, are restrictions distinguishing among different speakers, allowing speech by some but not others. As instruments to censor, these categories are interrelated: Speech restrictions based on the identity of the speaker are all too often simply a means to control content. * * *

[The Court cited a long line of precedents holding that corporations are protected by the First Amendment and that the protection extends to political speech. Nonetheless, direct contributions to candidates by corporations have been banned since the latter part of the 19th century, and in 1947 Congress prohibited independent expenditures in candidate elections by corporations and unions. After the Court in *Buckley* invalidated FECA's restriction on independent expenditures in federal elections, Congress enacted a prohibition on the use of the general treasury funds of corporations or unions for independent expenditures funding express advocacy. Subsequent Supreme Court cases dealt with corporate expenditures in state ballot measure campaigns. In *First Nat'l Bank of Boston v. Bellotti*, 435 U.S. 765 (1978), the Court struck down a state ban on the use of corporate treasury funds for such expenditures, resting on "the principle that the Government lacks the power to ban corporations from speaking." The next time the Court considered corporate political speech was in *Austin*. "To bypass *Buckley* and *Bellotti*, the *Austin* Court identified a new governmental interest in limiting political speech: an antidistortion interest."]

[III(B)] The Court is thus confronted with conflicting lines of precedent: a pre-*Austin* line that forbids restrictions on political speech based on the speaker's corporate identity and a post-*Austin* line that permits them. * * *

In its defense of the corporate-speech restrictions in § 441b, the Government notes the antidistortion rationale on which *Austin* and its progeny rest in part, yet it all but abandons reliance upon it. It argues instead that two other compelling interests support *Austin*'s holding that corporate expenditure restrictions are constitutional: an anticorruption interest, and a shareholder-protection interest. We consider the three points in turn.

* * * [First,] *Austin* sought to defend the antidistortion rationale as a means to prevent corporations from obtaining "an unfair advantage in the political marketplace" by using "resources amassed in the economic marketplace." But *Buckley* rejected the premise that the Government has an interest "in equalizing the relative ability of individuals and groups to influence the outcome of elections." * * * The rule that political speech cannot be limited based on a speaker's wealth is a necessary consequence of the premise that the First Amendment generally prohibits the suppression of political speech based on the speaker's identity. * * *

[The Court turned then to the argument that § 441b was designed to prevent corruption and its appearance. It relied on the analysis in *Buckley* that independent expenditures, not coordinated or arranged with a candidate, do not sufficiently implicate concerns about *quid pro quo* corruption to allow the restriction at issue in *Citizens United*. The majority definitively stated: "[W]e now conclude that independent expenditures, including those made by corporations, do not give rise to corruption or the appearance of corruption." Finally, it addressed the argument that corporate independent expenditures can be limited because of a state interest "in protecting dissenting shareholders from being compelled to fund corporate political speech."]

[With regard to this interest of shareholder protection,] the statute is both underinclusive and overinclusive. As to the first, if Congress had been seeking to protect dissenting shareholders, it would not have banned corporate speech in only certain media within 30 or 60 days before an election. A dissenting shareholder's interests would be implicated by speech in any media at any time. As to the second, the statute is overinclusive because it covers all corporations, including nonprofit corporations and for-profit corporations with only single shareholders. * * *

[III(C)] * * * For the reasons above, it must be concluded that *Austin* was not well reasoned. The Government defends *Austin*, relying almost entirely on "the quid pro quo interest, the corruption interest or the shareholder interest," and not *Austin*'s expressed antidistortion rationale. When neither party defends the reasoning of a precedent, the principle of adhering to that precedent through *stare decisis* is diminished. * * *

No serious reliance interests are at stake. As the Court stated in *Payne v. Tennessee,* 501 U.S. 808, 828 (1991), reliance interests are important considerations in property and contract cases, where parties may have acted in conformance with existing legal rules in order to conduct transactions. Here, though, parties have been prevented from acting—corporations have been banned from making independent expenditures. Legislatures may have enacted bans on corporate expenditures believing that those bans were constitutional. This is not a compelling interest for *stare decisis.* If it were, legislative acts could prevent us from overruling our own precedents, thereby interfering with our duty "to say what the law is." *Marbury v. Madison,* 5 U.S. 137, 1 Cranch 137, 177 (1803).

Due consideration leads to this conclusion: *Austin* should be and now is overruled. We return to the principle established in *Buckley* and *Bellotti* that the Government may not suppress political speech on the basis of the speaker's corporate identity. No sufficient governmental interest justifies limits on the political speech of nonprofit or for-profit corporations. * * *

Given our conclusion we are further required to overrule the part of *McConnell* that upheld BCRA § 203's extension of § 441b's restrictions on corporate independent expenditures. The *McConnell* Court relied on the antidistortion interest recognized in *Austin* to uphold a greater restriction on speech than the restriction upheld in *Austin,* and we have found this interest unconvincing and insufficient. This part of *McConnell* is now overruled.

[In Part IV, joined by all the Justices except Justice Thomas, the Court upheld BCRA's disclosure and disclaimer provisions as applied to *Hillary* and the ads for the movie. BCRA requires that electioneering communications funded by entities other than candidates include a disclaimer identifying the person or group responsible for the content of the communication, and that any entity spending more than $10,000 on electioneering communications within a calendar year must file a disclosure statement with the FEC. The Court found that disclosure served the compelling state interest of providing the electorate with the information necessary to evaluate the arguments and to avoid confusion about who is behind the communications. It approved of applying disclosure provisions to a wide array of political communication, not just express advocacy and its functional equivalent. It found that "the informational interest alone is sufficient to justify" applying BCRA's disclosure provisions to the movie and ads produced by Citizens United. It rejected Citizens United's argument that disclosure could subject its donors to threats or harassment because there was no such evidence of retaliation even though Citizens United had disclosed it donors publicly for years.]

[V] When word concerning the plot of the movie *Mr. Smith Goes to Washington* reached the circles of Government, some officials sought, by persuasion, to discourage its distribution. Under *Austin,* though, officials could have done more than discourage its distribution—they could have banned the film. After all, it, like *Hillary,* was speech funded by a corporation that was critical of Members of Congress. *Mr. Smith Goes to Washington* may be fiction and caricature; but fiction and caricature can be a powerful force. * * *

Some members of the public might consider *Hillary* to be insightful and instructive; some might find it to be neither high art nor a fair discussion on how to set the Nation's course; still others simply might suspend judgment on these points but decide to think more about issues and candidates. Those choices and assessments, however, are not for the Government to make. "The First Amendment underwrites the freedom to experiment and to create in the realm of thought and speech. Citizens must be free to use new forms, and new forums, for the expression of ideas. The civic discourse belongs to the people, and the Government may not prescribe the means used to conduct it." *McConnell* (opinion of KENNEDY, J.).

[The concurrences of CHIEF JUSTICE ROBERTS and JUSTICE SCALIA are omitted.]

JUSTICE STEVENS, with whom JUSTICE GINSBURG, JUSTICE BREYER, and JUSTICE SOTOMAYOR join, concurring in part [with respect to the disclosure provisions] and dissenting in part.

The real issue in this case concerns how, not if, the appellant may finance its electioneering. Citizens United is a wealthy nonprofit corporation that runs a political action committee (PAC) with millions of dollars in assets. Under the Bipartisan Campaign Reform Act of 2002 (BCRA), it could have used those assets to televise and promote *Hillary: The Movie* wherever and whenever it wanted to. It also could have spent unrestricted sums to broadcast *Hillary* at any time other than the 30 days before the last primary election. Neither Citizens United's nor any other corporation's speech has been "banned." All that the parties dispute is whether Citizens United had a right to use the funds in its general treasury to pay for broadcasts during the 30-day period. The notion that the First Amendment dictates an affirmative answer to that question is, in my judgment, profoundly misguided. Even more misguided is the notion that the Court must rewrite the law relating to campaign expenditures by *for-profit* corporations and unions to decide this case.

The basic premise underlying the Court's ruling is its iteration, and constant reiteration, of the proposition that the First Amendment bars regulatory distinctions based on a speaker's identity, including its "identity" as a corporation. * * *

In the context of election to public office, the distinction between corporate and human speakers is significant. Although they make enormous contributions to our society, corporations are not actually members of it. They cannot vote or run for office. Because they may be managed and controlled by nonresidents, their interests may conflict in fundamental respects with the interests of eligible voters. The financial resources, legal structure, and instrumental orientation of corporations raise legitimate concerns about their role in the electoral process. Our lawmakers have a compelling constitutional basis, if not also a democratic duty, to take measures designed to guard against the potentially deleterious effects of corporate spending in local and national races.

[The dissent takes strong issue with the decision of the Court to overrule its precedents, thereby deciding the case "on a basis relinquished below, not included in the questions presented to us by the litigants, and argued here only in response to the Court's invitation. * * * Our colleagues' suggestion that 'we are asked to reconsider *Austin* and, in effect, *McConnell*,' would be more accurate if rephrased to state that 'we have asked ourselves' to reconsider those cases."]

[II] * * * We have recognized that "*[s]tare decisis* has special force when legislators or citizens 'have acted in reliance on a previous decision, for in this instance overruling the decision would dislodge settled rights and expectations or require an extensive legislative response.'" *Hubbard v. United States*, 514 U.S. 695, 714 (1995). *Stare decisis* protects not only personal rights involving property or contract but also the ability of the elected branches to shape their laws in an effective and coherent fashion. Today's decision takes away a power that we have long permitted these branches to exercise. State legislatures have relied on their authority to regulate corporate electioneering, confirmed in *Austin*, for more than a century. The Federal Congress has relied on this authority for a comparable stretch of time, and it specifically relied on *Austin* throughout the years it spent developing and debating BCRA. The total record it compiled was *100,000 pages* long. Pulling out the rug beneath Congress after affirming the constitutionality of § 203 six years ago shows great disrespect for a coequal branch. * * *

[III] The novelty of the Court's procedural dereliction and its approach to *stare decisis* is matched by the novelty of its ruling on the merits. The ruling rests on several premises. First, the Court claims that *Austin* and *McConnell* have "banned" corporate speech. Second, it claims that the First Amendment precludes regulatory distinctions based on speaker identity, including the speaker's identity as a corporation. Third, it claims that *Austin* and *McConnell* were radical outliers in our First Amendment tradition and our campaign finance jurisprudence. Each of these claims is wrong.

The So-Called "Ban"

Pervading the Court's analysis is the ominous image of a "categorical ba[n]" on corporate speech. Indeed, the majority invokes the specter of a "ban" on nearly every page of its opinion. This characterization is highly misleading, and needs to be corrected.

* * * "The ability to form and administer separate segregated funds," we observed in *McConnell*, "has provided corporations and unions with a constitutionally sufficient opportunity to engage in express advocacy. That has been this Court's unanimous view."

* * * Administering a PAC entails some administrative burden, but so does complying with the disclaimer, disclosure, and reporting requirements that the Court today upholds, and no one has suggested that the burden is severe for a sophisticated for-profit corporation. To the extent the majority is worried about this issue, it is important to keep in mind that we have no record to show how substantial the burden really is, just the majority's own unsupported factfinding. * * *

So let us be clear: Neither *Austin* nor *McConnell* held or implied that corporations may be silenced; the FEC is not a "censor"; and in the years since these cases were decided, corporations have continued to play a major role in the national dialogue. Laws such as § 203 target a class of communications that is especially likely to corrupt the political process, that is at least one degree removed from the views of individual citizens, and that may not even reflect the views of those who pay for it. Such laws burden political speech, and that is always a serious matter, demanding careful scrutiny. But the majority's incessant talk of a "ban" aims at a straw man.

Identity-Based Distinctions

The second pillar of the Court's opinion is its assertion that "the Government cannot restrict political speech based on the speaker's . . . identity." * * * Like its paeans to unfettered discourse, the Court's denunciation of identity-based distinctions may have rhetorical appeal but it obscures reality. * * *

* * * As we have unanimously observed, legislatures are entitled to decide "that the special characteristics of the corporate structure require particularly careful regulation" in an electoral context. *Federal Election Commission v. National Right to Work Committee*, 459 U.S. 197, 209–10 (1982). Not only has the distinctive potential of corporations to corrupt the electoral process long been recognized, but * * * [c]ampaign finance distinctions based on corporate identity tend to be less worrisome, * * * because the "speakers" are not natural persons, much less members of our political community, and the governmental interests are of the highest order. * * *

Our First Amendment Tradition

A third fulcrum of the Court's opinion is the idea that *Austin* and *McConnell* are radical outliers, "aberration[s]," in our First Amendment tradition. The Court has it exactly backwards. It is today's holding that is the radical departure from what had been settled First Amendment law. * * *

By the time Congress passed FECA in 1971, the bar on corporate contributions and expenditures had become such an accepted part of federal campaign finance regulation that when a large number of plaintiffs, including several nonprofit corporations, challenged virtually every aspect of the Act in *Buckley,* no one even bothered to argue that the bar as such was unconstitutional. *Buckley* famously (or infamously) distinguished direct contributions from independent expenditures, but its silence on corporations only reinforced the understanding that corporate expenditures could be treated differently from individual expenditures. * * *

[IV] Having explained why this is not an appropriate case in which to revisit *Austin* and *McConnell* and why these decisions sit perfectly well with "First Amendment principles," I come at last to the interests that are at stake. The majority recognizes that *Austin* and *McConnell* may be defended on anticorruption, antidistortion, and shareholder protection rationales. * * *

The Anticorruption Interest

Undergirding the majority's approach to the merits is the claim that the only "sufficiently important governmental interest in preventing corruption or the appearance of corruption" is one that is "limited to *quid pro quo* corruption." This is the same "crabbed view of corruption" that was * * * squarely rejected by the Court in [*McConnell*]. * * *

Quid Pro Quo *Corruption*

* * * Even in the cases that have construed the anticorruption interest most narrowly, we have never suggested that such *quid pro quo* debts must take the form of outright vote buying or bribes, which have long been distinct crimes. Rather, they encompass the myriad ways in which outside parties may induce an officeholder to confer a legislative benefit in direct response to, or anticipation of, some outlay of money the parties have made or will make on behalf of the officeholder. * * * A

democracy cannot function effectively when its constituent members believe laws are being bought and sold. * * *

Austin *and Corporate Expenditures*

* * * The majority fails to appreciate that *Austin*'s antidistortion rationale is itself an anticorruption rationale, tied to the special concerns raised by corporations. Understood properly, "antidistortion" is simply a variant on the classic governmental interest in protecting against improper influences on officeholders that debilitate the democratic process. It is manifestly not just an "equalizing" ideal in disguise.

1. *Antidistortion*

* * * Corporate speech * * * is derivative speech, speech by proxy. A regulation such as BCRA § 203 may affect the way in which individuals disseminate certain messages through the corporate form, but it does not prevent anyone from speaking in his or her own voice. * * *

It is an interesting question "who" is even speaking when a business corporation places an advertisement that endorses or attacks a particular candidate. Presumably it is not the customers or employees, who typically have no say in such matters. It cannot realistically be said to be the shareholders, who tend to be far removed from the day-to-day decisions of the firm and whose political preferences may be opaque to management. Perhaps the officers or directors of the corporation have the best claim to be the ones speaking, except their fiduciary duties generally prohibit them from using corporate funds for personal ends. Some individuals associated with the corporation must make the decision to place the ad, but the idea that these individuals are thereby fostering their self-expression or cultivating their critical faculties is fanciful. It is entirely possible that the corporation's electoral message will *conflict* with their personal convictions. Take away the ability to use general treasury funds for some of those ads, and no one's autonomy, dignity, or political equality has been impinged upon in the least. * * *

* * * When citizens turn on their televisions and radios before an election and hear only corporate electioneering, they may lose faith in their capacity, as citizens, to influence public policy. A Government captured by corporate interests, they may come to believe, will be neither responsive to their needs nor willing to give their views a fair hearing. The predictable result is cynicism and disenchantment: an increased perception that large spenders "call the tune" and a reduced "willingness of voters to take part in democratic governance." *McConnell*. To the extent that corporations are allowed to exert undue influence in electoral races, the speech of the eventual winners of those races may also be chilled. Politicians who fear that a certain corporation can make or break their reelection chances may be cowed into silence about that corporation. * * * At the least, I stress again, a legislature is entitled to credit these concerns and to take tailored measures in response. * * *

2. *Shareholder Protection*

* * * Interwoven with *Austin*'s concern to protect the integrity of the electoral process is a concern to protect the rights of shareholders from a kind of coerced speech: electioneering expenditures that do not "reflec[t] [their] support." When corporations use general treasury funds to praise or attack a particular candidate for

office, it is the shareholders, as the residual claimants, who are effectively footing the bill. Those shareholders who disagree with the corporation's electoral message may find their financial investments being used to undermine their political convictions.

The PAC mechanism, by contrast, helps assure that those who pay for an electioneering communication actually support its content and that managers do not use general treasuries to advance personal agendas. * * *

[V] In a democratic society, the longstanding consensus on the need to limit corporate campaign spending should outweigh the wooden application of judge-made rules. The majority's rejection of this principle "elevate[s] corporations to a level of deference which has not been seen at least since the days when substantive due process was regularly used to invalidate regulatory legislation thought to unfairly impinge upon established economic interests." *Bellotti* (White, J., dissenting). At bottom, the Court's opinion is thus a rejection of the common sense of the American people, who have recognized a need to prevent corporations from undermining self-government since the founding, and who have fought against the distinctive corrupting potential of corporate electioneering since the days of Theodore Roosevelt. It is a strange time to repudiate that common sense. While American democracy is imperfect, few outside the majority of this Court would have thought its flaws included a dearth of corporate money in politics.

I would affirm the judgment of the District Court.

[The dissent by JUSTICE THOMAS, arguing that BCRA's disclosure provisions are unconstitutional, is omitted.]

NOTES ON CITIZENS UNITED AND ITS AFTERMATH

1. *The Corruption Interest After* Citizens United. The cases since *Buckley* have been remarkably inconsistent on what, exactly, counts as the sort of corruption that campaign finance regulation may combat. Recall that *Buckley* itself identified the problem as *quid-pro-quo* corruption, noting specifically the "the deeply disturbing examples surfacing after the 1972 election." That sentence was followed by a footnote noting that those 1972 abuses were discussed in the D.C. Circuit's opinion in the case. *Buckley v. Valeo*, 424 U.S. 1, 27 (1976) (per curiam). The cited pages of the circuit court's opinion, in turn, referred to things like "the revelation concerning the extensive contributions by dairy organizations to Nixon fund raisers, in order to gain a meeting with White House officials on price supports" and the testimony of executives in a range of industries that they "were motivated [to make large contributions to legislators] by the perception that this was necessary as a 'calling card, something that would get us in the door and make our point of view heard.'" *Buckley v. Valeo*, 519 F.2d 821, 839 nn.36–37 (D.C. Cir. 1975) (en banc) (per curiam). In *Buckley*, then, the purchasing of access would seem to count as a form of *quid pro quo* corruption.

Recall that, in *McConnell*, as well, the Court chastised the plaintiffs for "conceiv[ing] of corruption too narrowly," because "[m]any of the 'deeply disturbing examples' of corruption cited by this Court in *Buckley* to justify FECA's contribution limits were not episodes of vote buying, but evidence that various corporate interests had given substantial donations to gain access to high-level government officials." In his *McConnell* dissent, Justice Kennedy vigorously took issue with the notion of access as corruption, noting that "Democracy is premised on responsiveness." Kennedy subsequently cited his *McConnell* dissent extensively in his majority opinion in *Citizens United* in the process of determining, as a matter of law, that independent expenditures cannot give rise to the sorts of corruption (or the appearance thereof) sufficient to justify restrictions. In *McCutcheon v. Fed. Election Comm'n*, 572 U.S. 185 (2014) (plurality opinion of Roberts, C.J.), Chief Justice Roberts wrote as if this had been the Court's line all along: "In a series of cases over the past 40 years, we * * * have said that government regulation may not target the general gratitude a candidate may feel toward those who support him or his allies, or the political access such support may afford. 'Ingratiation and access . . . are not corruption.' " *Id.* at 192. *See also* Josh Chafetz, *Governing and Deciding Who Governs*, 2015 U. Chi. Legal F. 73, 76–78, 82–85 (tracing the Court's shifting conception of corruption, as well as its refusal to acknowledge that its conception was, in fact, shifting).

But there is another context in which the Roberts Court has operated with a very different conception of corruption: the judiciary. *Caperton v. A.T. Massey Coal Co.*, 556 U.S. 868 (2009), was argued only three weeks before *Citizens United* (although they were decided seven months apart, after *Citizens United* was re-argued). In *Caperton*, Justice Kennedy—who also authored *Citizens United*—held that due process required that an elected West Virginia Supreme Court justice recuse himself from a case in which the chairman of the corporate defendant had spent vast sums supporting that justice's election bid. Even though nearly all of the money was in the form of independent expenditures, Kennedy throughout referred to it as "campaign contributions." *See* James Sample, *Democracy at the Corner of First and Fourteenth: Judicial Campaign Spending and Equality*, 66 N.Y.U. Ann. Surv. Am. L. 727, 756–73 (2011) (coining the term "*Caperton* contribution"). And even though there was "no allegation of a *quid pro quo* agreement," *Caperton*, 556 U.S. at 886, the size of the contributions simply presented too much of a "risk" that the spending "engendered actual bias" to allow the justice to remain on the case. *Id.* at 885. As Laura Underkuffler has put it, *Caperton* embodies "the idea that we cannot trust—indeed, *cannot afford to trust*—individuals such as [the West Virginia justice] to act noncorruptly, whatever assurances they give and whatever the lack of evidence of instances of quid pro quo corruption there might be." Laura S. Underkuffler, *Captured by Evil: The Idea of Corruption in Law* 218–19 (2013).

Justice Kennedy denied that there was any tension between *Caperton* and *Citizens United*, writing in the latter that the two cases simply arose in different doctrinal areas. *Caperton* was a case about judicial recusal, not a case about whether a "litigant's political speech could be banned." *Citizens United v. Fed. Election Comm'n*, 558 U.S. 310, 360 (2010). But a subsequent case *did*, in fact, involve the banning of political speech. In *Williams-Yulee v. Florida Bar*, 135 S.Ct. 1656 (2015), the Court upheld a state judicial conduct rule forbidding candidates for judicial office from personally soliciting campaign contributions. Chief Justice Roberts, for the Court, wrote that, "Judges, charged with exercising strict neutrality and independence, cannot supplicate campaign donors without diminishing public confidence in judicial integrity." *Id.* at 1666. In other words, judicial integrity is compromised by a system in which donors appear to purchase influence or access, and this concern for judicial integrity justifies upholding a restriction on the electoral speech of judicial candidates, even though an identical restriction on the electoral speech of legislative or executive candidates would almost certainly be struck down.

One of us has argued that the differential conceptions of corruption in *Caperton* and *Williams-Yulee*, on the one hand, and *Citizens United*, on the other, serve the institutional interests of the judiciary by "suggest[ing] that the courts are different from mere elected politicians—after all, why else would they need to operate under a wholly different standard of corruption? Moreover, the fact that the Court *required* judges to operate under a stricter conception of corruption than it *allowed* legislative and executive officials to impose upon themselves not only held the courts out as different, but also held them up as better, nobler, purer, more ermined." Chafetz, *supra*, at 89. (Ermines were a traditional symbol of judicial rectitude because of a Renaissance myth that they would rather die than soil their pure white fur. They are also a kind of weasel.)

Is the author correct that different conceptions of corruption explain the outcomes in these cases? If so, is it appropriate to apply a different understanding of corruption to judges than to other governmental officials? Why or why not? This is a topic to which we will return in Chapter 3, § 1.

2. *What Counts as Evidence of Corruption?* Given the narrow conception of corruption put forward in *Citizens United* and *McCutcheon*, can campaign finance regulations for executive and legislative officials ever aim at something other than bribery-like behavior? If so, what sort of evidence would suffice to justify such regulations?

One state supreme court decided to press on this issue. Reading the outcome in *Citizens United* as depending on the nature of the evidence of corruption, the Montana Supreme Court determined that a more extensive evidentiary record, demonstrating a century-long history of electoral corruption, could support a state law limiting precisely the sort of spending that was at issue in *Citizens United*. In *Western Tradition P'ship, Inc. v. Attorney General*, 271 P.3d 1 (Mont. 2011), the court canvassed the history of state elections and allegations of improper behavior by corporate interests since the enactment of the state's campaign laws in the early twentieth century. It also relied on evidence that direct political spending by corporations could significantly affect the outcomes of current races because of the lower cost of campaigns in Montana relative to other states. It finally held that the administrative burdens of establishing separate political committees were relatively minimal. It therefore distinguished the case from *Citizens United* by finding that the differences in historical and modern contexts provided Montana a compelling state interest in requiring corporations to fund independent expenditures through separate political committees. The U.S. Supreme Court summarily reversed in a terse, one-paragraph decision. Indeed, the entirety of the Court's reasoning was contained in three sentences: "The question presented in this case is whether the holding of *Citizens United* applies to the Montana state law. There can be no serious doubt that it does. See U.S. Const., Art. VI, cl. 2 [the Supremacy Clause]. Montana's arguments in support of the judgment below either were already rejected in *Citizens United,* or fail to meaningfully distinguish that case." *Am. Tradition P'ship, Inc. v. Bullock*, 567 U.S. 516, 516–17 (2012) (per curiam).

In dissent, Justice Breyer, joined by three colleagues, argued both that *Citizens United* was wrongly decided and that, even if one accepted the *Citizens United* framework, the Montana Supreme Court's findings that conditions in Montana were different should at least be given serious consideration. Pamela Karlan has argued that the terseness with which the Court disposed of *Bullock* evinces a "deep distrust of democratic processes." Pamela S. Karlan, *The Supreme Court, 2011 Term—Foreword:*

Democracy and Disdain, 126 Harv. L. Rev. 1, 28 (2012); *see also id.* at 35–39. Do you agree?

3. *Regulation of Corporate Political Activity After* Citizens United. *Citizens United* considered only independent expenditures by corporations for electioneering communications; it did not change the longstanding rules requiring corporations to set up PACs to make contributions directly to federal candidates and political parties. Federal law includes a series of limitations on contributions made by corporate PACs, all of which still apply. For example, a PAC can contribute only $5,000 to a federal congressional candidate during an election cycle and only $15,000 to a political party per year. (These were not raised or indexed by BCRA, unlike many other limitations on campaign contributions.) The *Citizens United* Court attempted to distinguish contribution limits, calling them "an accepted means to prevent *quid pro quo* corruption," but opponents of campaign finance limitations immediately mounted challenges, arguing that the reasoning of the opinion could not be limited to independent expenditures.

A district court in Virginia was persuaded that there is no difference, and that the ban on direct corporate contributions to candidates is unconstitutional. *United States v. Danielczyk*, 791 F. Supp. 2d 513 (E.D. Va. 2011). Judge Cacheris ruled that "[t]aken seriously, *Citizens United* requires that corporations and individuals be afforded equal rights to political speech, unqualified. * * * [I]ndividuals and corporations must have equal rights to engage in *both* independent expenditures *and* direct contributions." He noted that corporations would be governed by the contribution limitations that restrict individuals, and so any contributions would be limited and disclosed. The appellate court reversed this decision, holding that nothing in Supreme Court jurisprudence signaled a change in the treatment of contributions made by corporations, 683 F.3d 611 (4th Cir. 2012). The Supreme Court declined to hear the case, 568 U.S. 1193 (2013) (denying cert.), leaving the prohibition on direct campaign contributions by corporations in place (for now).[65]

Citizens United was an ideological nonprofit, so political spending relating to candidates and political parties lay at the heart of its mission. In contrast, some—perhaps many—for-profit corporations are not eager to take advantage of the ability to use general treasury funds for independent expenditures. Traditionally, corporate managers have preferred to spend money on lobbying members of Congress rather than on campaign activity because they have viewed lobbying as a more successful and direct means of influencing policy and accomplishing a company's political objectives. See Samuel Issacharoff, *On Political Corruption*, 124 Harv. L. Rev. 118, 131–32 (2010). Some corporations have also found that taking political positions in a public way can cause backlash from consumers or employees. Following the Court's decision in *Citizens United*, Target donated $150,000 in 2010 to a conservative pro-business organization, which spent funds to pay for television ads in Minnesota supporting Republican gubernatorial candidate Tom Emmer, who opposed legal recognition of same-sex marriages. When Target's contribution was disclosed, the company came under fire from gay-rights groups,

---

[65] For a discussion of the tension between *Citizens United* and case law allowing restrictions on corporate contributions to candidates, see Richard Hasen, Citizens United *and the Illusion of Coherence*, 109 Mich. L. Rev. 581, 615–17 (2011).

whose calls for a nationwide boycott attracted media attention and hurt Target's image nationally.[66]

Which corporations do you expect will take advantage of the laxer rules governing independent expenditures? Is their spending likely to be of greater help to incumbents or to challengers? An early analysis of the effect of *Citizens United* on corporate spending during the 2010 and 2012 state legislative races found that the additional corporate spending tended to benefit Republican candidates more than Democrats, increasing by 4% overall the likelihood of a Republican victory. In some states, the impact was even greater: in eleven states, *Citizens United* was associated with a 7% or greater increase in the likelihood of a Republican victory, and in six states, it increased the Republicans' chances of winning by 10% or more. Tilman Klumpp, Hugo M. Mialon & Michael A. Williams, *The Business of American Democracy:* Citizens United, *Independent Spending, and Elections*, 59 J.L. & Econ. 1 (2016). It remains to be seen whether this partisan effect will fade over time.

With corporations now able to spend significantly more money on independent political expenditures, will businesses face pressure from legislators to play more active roles in federal campaigns? In an analysis of the corruption rationale in campaign finance cases published well before *Citizens United*, Professor David Strauss identified an element of extortion in a system "in which campaign contributions are freely exchanged for official action." Under these conditions, "there is a danger that representatives may coerce potential contributors, in effect extorting contributions by the threat that they will act against the contributor's interests." *Corruption, Equality, and Campaign Finance Reform*, 94 Colum. L. Rev. 1369, 1380 (1994). Are particular industries more likely to be the target of this manipulation by lawmakers seeking reelection? Is the possibility of such "extortion" reduced because *Citizens United* applies only to independent expenditures by corporations and unions, or can pressure still be applied? Is this kind of corruption likely to persuade the Supreme Court to uphold some restrictions on corporate political spending?

Some reform proposals that respond to *Citizens United* have centered on corporate law. For example, the Brennan Center for Justice proposed a Shareholder's Rights Act to require that shareholders vote at a public corporation's annual meeting to authorize the use of general treasury funds for political expenditures.[67] It would amend the Securities Exchange Act of 1934 to require periodic public disclosure of corporate political activities. If a public corporation made political expenditures without first obtaining shareholder approval, then the directors would be forced to repay the corporation, with interest. Several states began to consider similar changes in their corporate law codes. Is this a promising avenue for regulation of corporate political speech? For an intriguing proposal, see Lucian Bebchuk & Robert Jackson, *Corporate Political Speech: Who Decides?*, 124 Harv. L. Rev. 83 (2010) (arguing for different rules to govern corporate political speech decisions than other business decisions, including shareholder participation, oversight by independent directors, and disclosure).[68]

---

[66]   See Taren Kingser & Patrick Schmidt, *Business in the Bulls-Eye? Target Corp. and the Limits of Campaign Finance Disclosure*, 11 Election L.J. 21 (2012) (describing the Target situation and drawing conclusions about the efficacy of disclosure laws).

[67]   Ciara Torres-Spelliscy, *Corporate Campaign Spending: Giving Shareholders a Voice* 25–26 (2010).

[68]   These efforts may be strengthened by scholarship finding that politically connected firms have lower firm value and poor corporate governance quality. Ashley N. Newton & Vahap B. Uysal, *A Closer Look at Politically Connected Corporations: Evidence from* Citizens United, 45 Managerial Fin. 637 (2019).

4. *Developments Affecting Independent Expenditures and the Rise of "Super PACs."* The change ushered in by *Citizens United* receiving the most attention in recent elections is the rise of "Super PACs," nonprofit organizations that can receive unlimited amounts of money from donors to deploy in independent expenditures. As we have seen, Justice Kennedy's majority opinion held as a matter of law that independent expenditures do not give rise to corruption. This portion of his opinion may be more consequential for campaign finance regulation than the Court's decision to treat corporations like human beings with respect to independent expenditures. If such expenditures categorically cannot give rise to *quid pro quo* corruption, and that is the only acceptable state interest to justify regulation other than disclosure, then a great deal of the regulatory structure is open to challenge.

Not surprisingly, then, shortly after *Citizens United* the D.C. Circuit found no acceptable state interest in limiting contributions to entities making independent expenditures in federal campaigns. *SpeechNow.org v. Fed. Election Comm'n*, 599 F.3d 686 (D.C. Cir. 2010) (en banc). SpeechNow.org is an unincorporated nonprofit organization that promotes its view of the First Amendment in a variety of ways, including through advertisements supporting federal candidates who share its views and opposing those it believes are not sufficiently committed to the First Amendment. Donors wanted to contribute more than the $5,000 PAC limit to the nonprofit so that SpeechNow.org could produce ads attacking two incumbent lawmakers in the 2010 election cycle. Judge Sentelle wrote in a unanimous decision: "[B]ecause *Citizens United* holds that independent expenditures do not corrupt or give the appearance of corruption as a matter of law, then the government can have no anti-corruption interest in limiting contributions to independent expenditure-only organizations." *Id.* at 696. Consistent with *Citizens United*, the court allowed application of disclosure requirements and other administrative regulations to this organization. These rulings mean that independent-expenditure-only organizations are unconstrained by any limitations on contributions to them or any restrictions on their independent campaign expenditures advocating for the victory or defeat of federal candidates.

In response, the FEC released guidance on October 5, 2011, that freed independent PACs (those not associated with a company or union) from the $5,000 limit on individual contributions to them, including from corporations and unions.[69] If a PAC wishes to take advantage of this decision, it need not limit itself solely to independent expenditures, but it will have to maintain two accounts: one that can be used to make contributions to federal candidates and is subject to contribution limitations, and another that can be used solely for independent expenditures and is not subject to any limitations. These accounts join the independent-expenditure-only PACs that sprang up after *Citizens United* and first earned the title "Super PAC." As of March 2019, there are approximately 2,400 Super PACs in existence.[70]

Beginning with the 2010 congressional elections, the newly permissive regulatory environment for corporate spending has unleashed a torrent of money into the federal system, directed by ideological nonprofits and funded by wealthy Americans who can contribute unlimited amounts. In the 2012 election cycle, total independent expenditures

---

[69] Fed. Elec. Comm'n, FEC Statement on *Carey v. FEC*: Reporting Guidance for Political Committees that Maintain a Non-Contribution Account, Oct. 6, 2011, https://www.fec.gov/updates/fec-statement-on-carey-v-fec/.

[70] Ctr. for Responsive Pol., *Super PACs* (Mar. 26, 2019), https://www.opensecrets.org/pacs/superpacs.php.

in federal elections by entities other than party committees topped $1 billion; in the 2008 election cycle—the last presidential election cycle before *Citizens United*—such expenditures had been less than $150 million.[71] Many of the Super PACs, although formally independent, are run by political operatives with close ties to candidates and parties. Richard Briffault, *Super PACs*, 96 Minn. L. Rev. 1644, 1674–82 (2012). And although both ends of the political spectrum can and do take advantage of the Super PAC structure, conservative groups initially have been more successful in raising money through these vehicles. Of the ten groups spending the most on independent expenditures in the 2012 cycle, nine were tied to Republican candidates.[72]

The 2016 cycle was an interesting one from the perspective of spending. The total cost (including spending by both campaigns and outside groups) of the combined presidential and congressional elections was about 1.4% lower in inflation-adjusted terms than the cost of the 2012 elections. Congressional races continued to get more expensive, but the increase in their cost was more than offset by the presidential race, which, at a total cost of under $2.4 billion, was cheaper even in nominal terms than either the 2008 or 2012 presidential elections. Moreover, Hillary Clinton's losing campaign significantly outspent Donald Trump's victorious one, although Trump received nearly twice as much "free media" attention as Clinton did. One trend that did continue in 2016 was the growing importance of outside groups: while their spending made up 19% of the total cost of the 2012 elections, it grew to 24% of the total cost of the 2016 elections. And once again, that money went predominately to Republicans.[73]

The 2018 midterms continued the trend of increasingly expensive congressional races. It has been estimated that the 2018 elections cost a total of $5.7 billion, smashing the previous midterm record of $3.8 billion in 2014. Democrats outspent Republicans across the board, including by a total of $300 million in U.S. House races, which undoubtedly contributed to their gain of 40 seats and control of the chamber. Independent expenditures in 2018 topped $1 billion, the first time they had done so in a midterm election year.[74]

Some party leaders, especially in the Republican Party, have voiced concerns that the power of Super PACs to deploy vast sums of money may undermine larger party objectives.[75] Where ideological purity on a hot-button issue diverges from considerations of electability, for example, party leaders and some PAC leaders may not have aligned interests. What does this factionalism within major parties mean for elections, including primary elections? Did *Citizens United* weaken political parties in ways that will undermine governance at the federal level? How will parties evolve to account for this change in the campaign finance landscape?

---

[71]   Ctr. for Responsive Pol., *Total Outside Spending by Election Cycle, Excluding Party Committees*, https://www.opensecrets.org/outsidespending/cycle_tots.php (last viewed May 26, 2019).

[72]   Kevin Qualy & Derek Willis, *Election 2012: Independent Spending Totals*, N.Y. Times, http://elections.nytimes.com/2012/campaign-finance/independent-expenditures/totals (last viewed May 26, 2019).

[73]   Niv M. Sultan, Ctr. for Responsive Pol., *Election 2016: Trump's Free Media Helped Keep Cost Down, but Fewer Donors Provided More of the Cash* (Apr. 13, 2017), https://www.opensecrets.org/news/2017/04/election-2016-trump-fewer-donors-provided-more-of-the-cash/.

[74]   Ctr. for Responsive Pol., *Most Expensive Midterm Ever: Cost of 2018 Election Surpasses $5.7 Billion* (Feb. 6, 2019), https://www.opensecrets.org/news/2019/02/cost-of-2018-election-5pnt7bil/; Ctr. for Responsive Pol., *Total Outside Spending by Election Cycle, Excluding Party Committees*, https://www.opensecrets.org/outsidespending/cycle_tots.php (last viewed May 26, 2019).

[75]   *See* Eliza Newlin Carney, *Who Owns the GOP?*, Cong. Q., May 6, 2013, at 804.

Justice Stevens predicted in his dissent that political parties would be harmed by *Citizens United*: "By removing one of its central components, today's ruling makes a hash out of BCRA's 'delicate and interconnected regulatory scheme.' *McConnell*. Consider just one example of the distortions that will follow: Political parties are barred under BCRA from soliciting or spending 'soft money,' funds that are not subject to the statute's disclosure requirements or its source and amount limitations. Going forward, corporations and unions will be free to spend as much general treasury money as they wish on ads that support or attack specific candidates, whereas national parties will not be able to spend a dime of soft money on ads of any kind. The Court's ruling thus dramatically enhances the role of corporations and unions—and the narrow interests they represent—vis-à-vis the role of political parties—and the broad coalitions they represent—in determining who will hold public office." 558 U.S. at 412. Nathaniel Persily agreed that "political parties as institutions were probably the losers," but then wondered whether that would improve campaigns or affect them negatively. "[T]he extreme cohesiveness and polarization of the political parties might be countered by independent, non-party bases of support that influence candidates. At the same time (and more likely from my view), the decision might polarize the parties even further, because independent spenders tend to come from and support extreme positions."[76] Are the new developments in the regulatory landscape likely to harm political parties? And if so, would that be desirable or undesirable? *See also* Joseph Fishkin & Heather K. Gerken, *The Party's Over: McCutcheon, Shadow Parties, and the Future of the Party System*, 2014 Sup. Ct. Rev. 175 (arguing that nominally "independent" groups are really part of the parties "writ large," and that the real struggle is over who will have power *within* parties: the activist "party faithful" or the moneyed elite).

One change in the jurisprudential landscape after *Citizens United* was the Court's decision in 2014 to strike down aggregate limits on federal campaign contributions. *McCutcheon v. Fed. Election Comm'n*, 572 U.S. 185 (2014). The plurality opinion reasoned that, because aggregate limits did not directly combat the narrowed notion of *quid pro quo* corruption, they impermissibly burdened political speech. Even without an aggregate limit on all contributions, the limit on the amount that a donor can contribute to any particular candidate sufficiently protects against *quid pro quo* corruption and its appearance. To the extent that one donor might give the maximum contribution to many candidates and organizations in one political party and thus lead party leaders to appreciate that level of support, "[t]hat gratitude stems from the basic nature of the party system." Moreover, such contributions, all within the base limit to each candidate or organization, do not allow a donor to control a particular officeholder's official duties—the system has determined that contributions below the limit do not implicate *quid pro quo* corruption.

With the new opportunity for the wealthy to donate broadly to many candidates and committees supporting those candidates, will the influence of Super PACs be reduced? The Chief Justice in *McCutcheon* suggested it might: "The existing aggregate limits may in fact encourage the movement of money away from entities subject to disclosure. Because individuals' direct contributions are limited, would-be donors may turn to other avenues for political speech. * * * Individuals can, for example, contribute unlimited amounts to 501(c) organizations, which are not required to publicly disclose their donors. * * * Such organizations spent some $300 million on independent expenditures in the

---

[76]   Nathaniel Persily, Citizens United: *Qui Bono and Que Sera*, Balkinization blog (Jan. 25, 2010), http://balkin.blogspot.com/2010/01/citizens-united-qui-bono-and-que-sera.html.

2012 election cycle." After *McCutcheon*, the increased ability of donors to directly and substantially support a political party through its many committees, candidates, and subsidiaries may rejuvenate these flexible political actors, swinging the political pendulum back in their direction.

The role of corporations in politics, especially nonprofit corporations focused on influencing elections, will continue to be the subject of scrutiny and regulatory efforts as the post-*Citizens United* world evolves. In recent years, there has been a shift in the legal structure of nonprofit advocacy groups toward being organized under section 501(c)(4) of the tax code (for "social welfare organizations"), rather than 501(c)(3) (for public charities). As David Pozen explains the shift,

> Social-welfare organizations are also exempt from federal income tax, but they have fewer fiscal privileges. Donations to them are not deductible. Yet unlike public charities, they may lobby as much as they wish, and they may engage in partisan political work—from asking candidates to sign pledges to registering like-minded voters to endorsing specific pieces of legislation—as long as that work is not their "primary" purpose or activity (a requirement so hard to define and enforce that, in the words of one leading nonprofit tax scholar, it "virtually invites wholesale noncompliance"). Since [the summer of 2018], social-welfare organizations have also been allowed to withhold the names of their donors from the Internal Revenue Service.

David Pozen, *The Tax-Code Shift That's Changing Liberal Activism*, The Atlantic (Nov. 27, 2018), https://www.theatlantic.com/ideas/archive/2018/11/501c3-501c4-activists-and-tax-code/576364/. Moreover, under the 2017 Tax Cut and Jobs Act, Pub. L. No. 115–97, 131 Stat. 2054, the standard deduction for personal income taxes was raised, while itemized deductions were scaled back. The effect was to make itemizing deductions less beneficial and therefore less common—and only people who itemize can take advantage of tax deductions for donations to 501(c)(3) charities. For an increasing number of taxpayers, then, there's no benefit to donating to a 501(c)(3) over a 501(c)(4), while from the group's perspective, the latter form offers a great deal more flexibility and secrecy. As Pozen notes, this shift has the potential to significantly reshape the financial and legal architecture of political spending.

5.   *Challenges to Disclosure and the Rise of "Dark Money."* For many, after *Citizens United*, disclosure appears to be the least problematic form of regulation from a constitutional perspective (only Justice Thomas has objected to disclosure) and perhaps the only kind of law that is likely to work. Far-reaching disclosure statutes will raise constitutional issues; ironically, the more a law succeeds in revealing the identities of supporters and opponents, the more serious the constitutional concern. Disclosure certainly chills some kinds of political speech, especially when it links the speaker to disfavored groups or ideas, and some individuals and organizations may be less likely to participate in political debate if their involvement will be publicized. In other contexts, the Court has held that the First Amendment protects anonymous political speech. See *McIntyre v. Ohio Elections Comm'n*, 514 U.S. 334 (1995) (protecting a person's decision to remain anonymous while distributing campaign literature for issue-based election).

In *Buckley*, the Supreme Court held that FECA's provisions requiring the disclosure of contributors to a political group were constitutional on their face but might conceivably be unconstitutional as applied to a given group; *McConnell* echoed that with respect to BCRA. Given "the extensive body of state and federal legislation subjecting Communist

Party members to civil disability and criminal liability, * * * the history of governmental surveillance and harassment of Communist Party members, as well as * * * the desire of contributors to the [Communist Party] to remain anonymous," are disclosure requirements invalid as applied to the Communist Party?[77] What other kinds of groups could make the required showing to avoid disclosure?

Disclosure poses a practical problem as well. The more complex the reporting requirements, the more costly the burden placed on those who must provide information to the state. Moreover, this burden affects grassroots groups with few monetary resources and less access to consultants more severely than it does well-funded groups and sophisticated political players. See Dick Carpenter & Jeffrey Milyo, *The Public's Right to Know Versus Compelled Speech: What Does Social Science Research Tell Us About the Benefits and Costs of Campaign Finance Disclosure in Non-Candidate Elections?*, 40 Fordham Urb. L.J. 603 (2012) (identifying costs and burdens in ballot measure campaigns, some of which would also apply to groups active in candidate elections through independent expenditures). Although exemptions or reduced reporting requirements for small groups or individuals spending little money can reduce some of the burden, exemptions also increase the complexity of the regulatory regime.

Clearly, enhanced disclosure statutes are required for voters to have full information about the sources of funding in the post-*Citizens United* world. Although Section 527 groups are required to disclose their donors, more money is being injected into the federal political system anonymously now than in previous recent elections because of less rigorous disclosure requirements for other types of affiliated nonprofits and lax enforcement by federal regulatory bodies. Increasingly, political groups, including Super PACs, are using other nonprofit structures, such as the 501(c)(4) structure discussed above.

The organization of political groups can be stunningly complex, as one group may use various nonprofit structures to arrange its political activities to provide the most flexibility, the desired level of protection against disclosure, and the greatest ability to raise funds. A study by the Center for Responsive Politics concludes that 48.8% of non-party, independent political spending was fully publicly disclosed in 2010;[78] the rest has been called "dark money." The Center concluded that, in the 2012 federal elections, more than $310 million of campaign money was spent in ways that evaded disclosure, the vast majority from conservative groups. Since then, dark money spending appears to have declined, with less than $150 million in dark money spent in the 2018 elections.[79] But as one commentator has noted, this apparent decline may be misleading because it "doesn't include additional money funneled to other groups spending in elections or spent on political ads couched as issue advocacy and digital advertising that remains largely untouched by FEC disclosure requirements. Dark money has hardly waned. Instead, it has begun manifesting in new forms that are often harder to track and quantify. More than half of all 2018 election spending by outside groups, excluding party committees,

---

[77]   See *Fed. Election Comm'n v. Hall-Tyner Election Campaign Comm.*, 678 F.2d 416, 419 (2d Cir. 1982). See also *Brown v. Socialist Workers '74 Campaign Comm.*, 459 U.S. 87 (1982), in which the Court struck down an Ohio statute requiring disclosure of contributors.

[78]   See Ctr. for Responsive Pol., *Outside Spending by Disclosure, Excluding Party Committees*, http://www.opensecrets.org/outsidespending/disclosure.php (visited Jan. 29, 2012).

[79]   Thomas Edsall, *Dark Money Politics*, N.Y. Times, June 12, 2013; Ctr. for Responsive Pol., *Dark Money Basics* (Dec. 7, 2017), https://www.opensecrets.org/dark-money/basics.

was by groups that do not fully disclose their donors."[80] Even 527 organizations manage to evade or significantly delay disclosure by receiving contributions from nonprofits not subject to disclosure themselves or from corporations that do not disclose their owners or go out of business soon after the donation.

Inspired by the Court's strong affirmation of disclosure provisions, Democrats in the Senate and the House introduced the Democracy Is Strengthened by Casting Light On Spending in Elections (DISCLOSE) Act in 2010. The Act would have provided for enhanced disclosure provisions for nonprofit and for-profit corporations, as well as unions. These included requirements that a CEO or organization leader appear at the end of a broadcast advertisement to affirm that she "approves this message"; that the top five contributors to the organization be listed on the screen; and that groups inform their shareholders and members about political spending. It would also have banned spending by corporations with substantial foreign ownership or control, and political spending by government contractors and recipients of federal bailout funds for banks and other financial institutions. Are any of these provisions constitutionally problematic? What state interests justify the proposed regulations?

The DISCLOSE Act faced significant opposition in Congress, as members of both parties were concerned about its effect on various interest groups on whose support they counted. In the end, the bill narrowly passed the House but failed to secure the 60 votes necessary to invoke cloture in the Senate. But in the absence of meaningful federal action to shine the light on dark money, some states have adopted aggressive disclosure measures for political activity in state elections. For example, in October 2012, $11 million—perhaps the largest sum given in a statewide contest without its source being revealed—was injected into a California ballot measure campaign through a committee actively opposing the Governor's proposal to increase taxes and provide money for higher education. Another $4 million from a separate source was also sent to a California campaign committee from an out-of-state nonprofit. California's election law watchdog, the Fair Political Practices Commission (FPPC), worked to track down the donor behind the contribution, which was not subject to contribution limits because its support related to a ballot measure. The FPPC worked through layers of nonprofit organizations both in and outside the state, ultimately tracing the money to a Virginia-based nonprofit group, Americans for Job Security, associated with operatives who have been affiliated with the conservative Koch brothers.[81] In the end, California imposed a record $16 million in penalties on two California campaign committees and two Arizona nonprofits for failing to appropriately report their campaign activities. At the same time, the FPPC adopted new regulations designed to pierce the veil of the nonprofit form to determine the ultimate source behind funding being deployed in state elections; other states are enacting or considering enhanced disclosure statutes aimed at independent spending.[82]

---

[80] Anna Massoglia, Ctr. for Responsive Pol., *State of Money in Politics: Billion-Dollar 'Dark Money' Spending is Just the Tip of the Iceberg* (Feb. 21, 2019), https://www.opensecrets.org/news/2019/02/somp3-billion-dollar-dark-money-tip-of-the-iceberg/.

[81] Peter Stone, *California Officials Turn Up the Heat on Secretive "Dark Money" Groups*, Huffington Post, March 25, 2013; Chris Megerian & Anthony York, *California Probe of Campaign Donations Sheds Light on "Dark Money,"* L.A. Times, Nov. 3, 2013.

[82] See Elizabeth Garrett, *Campaign Finance in the Hybrid Realm of Recall Elections*, 97 Minn. L. Rev. 1654, 1696–97 (2013) (discussing California regulations and approaches to disclosure with respect to nonprofit groups); Matea Gold, Chris Megerian & Mark Barabak, *States Try to Tackle "Secret Money" in Politics*, L.A. Times, May 2, 2013 (describing efforts in Maryland and New York).

These developments at the state level are only part of the regulatory picture at the subnational level, our final topic in this chapter.

C. STATE REFORMS AND PUBLIC FINANCING

The past several decades have witnessed significant state activity regarding campaign finance. In 1980, 29 states placed no limits on individual contributions to candidates running for the state legislature; today, only eleven states place no limits on contributions.[83] Several states have adopted sweeping campaign finance reforms, often through ballot initiatives. State contribution limits can be significantly lower than the federal limits, with a few as low as $500 per candidate from an individual. See *Randall v. Sorrell*, 548 U.S. 230 (2006) (plurality opinion striking down very stringent statewide limits in Vermont). Some empirical studies suggest that the state reforms may fall victim to the hydraulic quality of political money. Evidence from Oregon, for example, indicates that, after the people passed a measure imposing a very low cap on contributions in statewide races, independent expenditures increased sharply in the next election.[84]

The other innovative state reform, largely a result of ballot initiatives, is public financing. Until recently, most state public financing systems had withstood significant judicial challenge; now their fate—at least as comprehensive systems designed to encourage robust participation by many serious candidates—is uncertain. Consistent with the presidential system upheld in *Buckley*, state public financing systems are all voluntary, providing public money to candidates who agree either not to accept any private money (see Me. Rev. Stat. Ann. tit. 21–A, § 1121 *et seq.*) or to abide by strict spending limits (see Vt. Stat. Ann. tit. 17, § 2853 *et seq.*).[85] In Maine, for, example, candidates qualify for public funds by raising seed money from voters making small contributions; this threshold ensures that recipients demonstrate a level of popular support.

The Arizona Citizens Clean Elections Act was adopted by initiative in 1998, and created a voluntary public financing system available to candidates for statewide office. Candidates who opt in to the system and receive public money must accept certain restrictions, such as limiting expenditures of their own funds to $500, participating in at least one public debate, and adhering to an expenditure cap (which differs according to the office sought). Publicly financed candidates receive a specified grant of money from the state and, under some circumstances, qualify for additional "matching funds." Payment of this additional grant of public money is triggered if the expenditures of a privately financed opponent, combined with independent expenditures in support of that privately financed opponent, exceed the initial public

---

[83] Nat'l Conf. of State Legis., *Campaign Contribution Limits: Overview* (June 28, 2017), http://www.ncsl.org/legislatures-elections/elections/campaign-contribution-limits-overview.aspx.

[84] See Eliza Newlin Carney, *Taking on the Fat Cats*, Nat'l J., Jan. 18, 1997, at 110. Oregon's stringent limits were struck down by the state supreme court in 1997. *Vannatta v. Keisling*, 931 P.2d 770, 773–74 (Or. 1997). See also David Schultz, *Money, Politics, and Campaign Finance Reform Law in the States* 20–21 (2002) (finding rise in soft-money and independent expenditures in some states with restrictions on individual contributions).

[85] See Elizabeth Daniel, *Subsidizing Political Campaigns: The Varieties and Values of Public Financing* (2000) (a report by the Brennan Center for Justice describing various kinds of public financing); Jason Frasco, Note, *Full Public Funding: An Effective and Legally Viable Model for Campaign Finance Reform in the States*, 92 Cornell L. Rev. 733 (2007) (describing laws and legal challenges).

grant to the publicly financed candidate. After that trigger, the state would provide the publicly financed candidate essentially a dollar-for-dollar match of the amount spent by her opponent. It was this matching funds provision that was ruled unconstitutional by the Supreme Court in the following case.

Arizona Free Enterprise Club's Freedom Club PAC v. Bennett

564 U.S. 721 (2011).

In a 5–4 decision written by **Chief Justice Roberts**, the Court held that the matching funds provision triggered by the expenditures relating to a privately financed candidate unconstitutionally burdened political speech without serving a compelling state interest. The plaintiffs were candidates who did not opt in to the public financing system and independent groups that wanted to support such candidates. In holding in favor of the plaintiffs' position, the Court found *Davis v. Fed. Election Comm'n*, 554 U.S. 724 (2008), the case striking down BCRA's "millionaire opponent" provision, to control the analysis. Although neither BCRA nor the Arizona law imposed a cap on any candidate's expenditures without her consent, both imposed a burden on certain kinds of spending by a privately financed candidate by offering her publicly financed opponent a substantial financial benefit. In the case of BCRA, the benefit was higher contribution limits for candidates facing opponents who spent significant personal resources; in the case of the Arizona law, the benefit was additional public money to candidates who were facing privately financed candidates spending over a certain threshold. The Court found the Arizona law especially problematic. With respect to BCRA, "[t]he candidate who benefited from the increased [contribution] limits still had to go out and raise the funds. He may or may not have been able to do so. * * * Here [in the Arizona law] the benefit to the publicly financed candidate is the direct and automatic release of public money. That is a far heavier burden than in *Davis*." There might even be a multiplier effect for the privately financed candidate facing several publicly financed opponents, all of whom would benefit from the additional subsidies.

Furthermore, the additional grant of public money could be triggered not only by the opponent's expenditures but also by the spending of independent groups to support that candidate. "That disparity in control—giving money directly to a publicly financed candidate, in response to independent expenditures that cannot be coordinated with the privately funded candidate—is a substantial advantage for the publicly financed candidate." Once the triggering amount of expenditures was reached, an independent group would be faced with a choice that the Court found unacceptable. "The group can either opt to change its message from one addressing the merits of the candidates to one addressing the merits of an issue, or refrain from speaking altogether." Taking these effects of the statute into account, the majority found a substantial burden on political speech that would reduce the amount of speech by privately funded candidates and groups supporting them.

The Court then turned to the state interest advanced to support the trigger mechanism and found a dispute as to whether it was the permissible interest of preventing *quid pro quo* corruption or the desire to equalize candidate resources and thereby level the political playing field. The Chief Justice was persuaded that the latter motive was the sole support for this aspect of Arizona's public financing statute. Not only did the provision operate explicitly to equalize resources, but the statutory section setting it out was titled "Equal funding of candidates." Since *Buckley*, the Court has rejected regulating campaign speech to serve an equalization rationale, and *Davis* warned that "[l]eveling electoral opportunities means making and implementing judgments about which strengths should be permitted to contribute to the outcome of an election." The Court concluded: "'Leveling the playing field' can sound like a good thing. But in a democracy, campaigning for office is not a game. It is a critically important form of speech."

Finally, the majority dismissed the argument that a corruption justification might be served by the trigger mechanism. First, burdening the candidate's expenditures of her own funds is completely unrelated to a concern about *quid pro quo* corruption because use of personal funds actually reduces the appearance of corruption by special interests. In *Citizens United*, the Court similarly held that independent expenditures cannot lead to corruption or the appearance of corruption, so burdening that speech could not be linked to the asserted state interest. Finally, the Court noted that Arizona has "ascetic" contribution limits of $840 for statewide candidates and $410 for legislative candidates. Combined with strict disclosure laws, these low contribution limits eliminate the threat of influence by large donors. Therefore, "it is hard to imagine what marginal corruption deterrence could be generated by the matching funds provision."

Justice Kagan issued a blistering dissent. She looked at the Arizona system as a comprehensive regulatory scheme, with the matching funds provision as a key component that ensured the willingness of candidates to opt in to public financing. "[C]andidates will choose to sign up only if the subsidy provided enables them to run competitive races." The state faces a dilemma in crafting a system that meets this essential goal: if the grant of public money is too low, no candidate will participate and the anticorruption interest that public financing serves generally will not be vindicated; if the subsidy is too high, the fiscal demands of the program may be unsustainable. The trigger provision that Arizona constructed solves that dilemma by allowing adjustments only in certain races, and it assures candidates considering public financing that they will not be placed in an untenable situation should they face a well-heeled opponent.

The dissent also took issue with the majority's characterization of the provision as restricting or burdening speech. "The law has quite the opposite effect: It subsidizes and so produces *more* political speech. * * * Except in a world gone topsy-turvy, additional campaign speech and electoral competition is not a First Amendment injury." Justice Kagan noted that all candidates are eligible to participate in public financing so the law does not discriminate against any particular set of ideas or ideological positions. No one is denied access to the state's subsidy unless she chooses not to participate in the system. "[W]hat petitioners demand is essentially a right to quash others' speech through the prohibition of a (universally available) subsidy program. Petitioners are able to convey their ideas without public financing—and they would prefer the field to themselves, so that they can speak free from response." In sharply worded language, the dissent observed that, after refusing the state's offer of public financing, the petitioners "are making a novel argument: that Arizona violated *their* First Amendment rights by disbursing funds to *other* speakers even though they could have received (but chose to spurn) the same financial assistance. Some people might call that *chutzpah*."

The majority and dissent fundamentally disagreed about whether to consider the matching funds provision separately from the rest of the regulatory structure. For the majority, the provision was assessed as a stand-alone feature of the law and therefore had only a marginal effect on reducing corruption. When viewed in isolation from the rest of the statute, the matching funds device seemed solely focused on providing equal resources for candidates, whether they opted in to the state system or chose to remain outside of it. For Justice Kagan, the provision was critical to the success of the Act: although serving as "no more than a disbursement mechanism * * * it is also the thing that makes the whole Clean Elections Act work." To the extent that there was ample evidence that a primary motivation for adopting the Clean Elections Act was to combat corruption and the influence of special interests in state politics, the entire Act could withstand First Amendment scrutiny.

The dissent concluded in the more deferential tone of the pre-*Citizens United* case law: "This case arose because Arizonans wanted their government to work on behalf of all the State's people. On the heels of a political scandal involving the near-routine purchase of legislators' votes, Arizonans passed a law designed to sever political candidates' dependence on large contributors. * * * The legislation that Arizona's voters enacted was the product of deep thought and care. It put into effect a public financing system that attracted large numbers of candidates at a sustainable cost to the State's taxpayers. The system discriminated against no ideas and prevented no speech. * * * No fundamental principle of our Constitution backs the Court's ruling; to the contrary, it is the law struck down today that fostered both the vigorous competition of ideas and its ultimate object—a government responsive to the will of the people."

The Chief Justice ended his majority opinion by limiting the breadth of the holding. "We do not today call into question the wisdom of public financing as a means of funding political candidacy. That is not our business." The Court reaffirmed its view in *Buckley* that public financing systems designed to serve the anticorruption rationale would be consistent with the First Amendment. Arizona went too far with its matching funds provision because it "inhibit[s] robust and wide-open political debate without sufficient justification." Thus, the fate of other state public financing systems that do not include the matching funds provision struck down by the Supreme Court was not determined by *Arizona Free Enterprise*. (Matching funds provisions in other states immediately suffered the fate of Arizona's. For example, the matching funds provision in Maine was declared unconstitutional by a stipulated agreement less than one month after *Arizona Free Enterprise* was issued.) After *Arizona Free Enterprise*, what mechanisms are still available to tailor the amount of any public subsidy to the features of a particular race to ensure that serious candidates will opt to participate at the outset and that competitive races will ensue?[86]

* * *

One question facing advocates of public financing is whether the reform has the intended effects on elections. Interestingly, a study of the effect of the trigger mechanism ruled unconstitutional in *Arizona Free Enterprise* had revealed that publicly financed candidates continued to feel at a disadvantage in campaigns. They were often forced into defensive positions, with their opponents withholding expenditures in excess of the threshold until the last days of the campaign, giving the subsidized candidates little time to deploy additional resources effectively. Had that part of the law remained in effect, it

---

[86] See Stephen Ansolabehere, Arizona Free Enterprise v. Bennett *and the Problem of Campaign Finance*, 2011 Sup. Ct. Rev. 39 (concluding that the only options after *Arizona Free Enterprise* and other Roberts Court cases are either full public financing or full private financing of elections); Nicholas Bamman, *Campaign Financing: Public Funding after* Bennett, 27 J.L. & Pol. 323 (2012) (providing some ideas for systems that could pass constitutional muster).

would have been interesting to see the effect of later expenditures of money on voter mobilization and other aspects of the campaign. Michael Miller, *Gaming Arizona: Public Money and Shifting Candidate Strategies*, 41 PS 527 (2008).

In 2010, the Government Accountability Office (GAO) released a study of the effects of full public financing in Maine and Arizona since 2000 (pre-*Arizona Free Enterprise*). *Campaign Finance Reform: Experiences of Two States That Offered Full Public Funding for Political Candidates* (2010). In both states, the GAO found that more candidates participated in public financing over time. In Maine, participating candidates were more likely to win, while in Arizona nonparticipating candidates were more successful. Differences might be a result of incumbency, partisan affiliation, or other characteristics not evident from the data. Changes in interest group participation and citizens' confidence in government after adoption of the Clean Elections Laws were not statistically significant, nor were measures of competition, except for a reduced margin of victory for winners, which might have been caused by other factors. Independent expenditures increased from 2000 to 2008 in both states, although that may have been influenced in Maine by a change in what counted as an independent expenditure.

Problem 2-8. You are a staff member of a state senator who seeks to adopt comprehensive campaign finance reform. In light of the Roberts Court precedents, provide your recommendation of the most aggressive legislation that is likely to withstand constitutional challenge. The senator has asked you to concentrate on the design of disclosure statutes; assessing the efficacy of contribution limits in the context of unlimited independent expenditures; and the promise, and challenges, of electioneering through the Internet and social media. Are there any provisions you would recommend that might give your boss—an incumbent in a relatively competitive district—pause as likely to make reelection more difficult? Even if she is willing to go forward because of her commitment to reform, such provisions could make legislative enactment unlikely. Would you recommend that the senator consider the avenue of direct democracy, assuming it is available in your state? We will return to this mechanism for reform in Chapter 4.

CHAPTER 3

STRUCTURES OF LEGISLATIVE DELIBERATION

■ ■ ■

Chapter 2 discussed different theories of representation, describing Hanna Pitkin's argument that representatives can be viewed in three different ways: as a microcosm of the larger electorate, as agents of the voters who elect them, or as trustees for the public interest. In this chapter, we consider the implications each theory might have for decisions that legislators make once elected.

In connection with the legislative deliberations of representatives, agency theorists suggest that the representative should mirror the views of her constituents, while trusteeship theorists direct the representative to use her judgment to advance the common good. Pitkin argues that the tension between these two views is largely a false one. First, a representative necessarily acts in a dual capacity most of the time: she is acting for her constituents, but on matters about which they have given little informed thought. Second, what the representative thinks is right and what the people want "normally * * * will coincide, and * * * when they fail to coincide there is a reason." The duty is to do what serves the "objective interest" of the people—so when the representative acts against the apparent desires of the constituents, she must be able to justify that action in terms of the long-range interests of society. Overall, Pitkin argues, representative government is most legitimate when it both promotes the public interest and responds to the people's desires over time.

Pitkin's general position that representative government should be broadly responsive to, but not specifically directed by, private preferences is widely accepted. Her more specific position, that representative government should sometimes seek to further the "public interest" and transform private preferences, is appealing to a republican vision of government. It seems consistent with Madison's argument in *Federalist 10* that, in an extensive republic, "the public voice, pronounced by the representatives of the people, will be more consonant to the public good than if pronounced by the people themselves, convened for the purpose." Nonetheless, the Madison-Pitkin position is subject to a pluralist critique. Much pluralist political theory questions whether there is such a thing as the "public interest" separate from aggregated private interests. Even if there is a public interest, how can it reliably be determined?

Both pluralist (agency) and republican (trusteeship) theorists emphasize the importance of legislative deliberation, although they view the process differently. Pluralism requires representatives to aggregate the preferences of various interests and work out compromises to satisfy as many interests as possible and perhaps also to satisfy the most intense preferences of each relevant group. To do this, the representatives must deliberate, both with their constituents and supporting groups, and with their colleagues in the legislature. Deliberation may help to solve some of the pathologies of majority rule (like cycling among policy alternatives), thereby allowing legislatures to reach rational and relatively stable outcomes. In republican theory, deliberation seeks out useful information and points of view that advance the collective understanding of common goals and that perhaps also transform the preferences of political citizens.

Both pluralist and republican theorists consider legislative deliberation illegitimate if it is corrupt. The theorists differ, however, in their view of what unacceptably warps the deliberative process, as we saw in the discussion of corruption and campaign finance reform in the previous chapter. Virtually everyone agrees that a deliberative process is corrupt if it is tainted by monetary bribes, physical coercion or threats, or other cheating by forces outside the legislature. Section 1 of this chapter explores issues associated with a relatively straightforward conception of corruption in the legislative process, especially as it relates to laws governing bribery, extortion, and conflicts of interest. As we will see, however, even uncontroversial notions of corruption become fuzzy when we move away from the obvious examples of bribery and extortion. In that regard, we turn to lobbying, which is expressly protected by the First Amendment but is also a possible source of corruption in the legislative process, at least according to republican theory. We also discuss the current legal regime regulating lobbying, a regime shaped since 1995 by the Lobbying Disclosure Act (LDA), Pub. L. 104–65, 109 Stat. 691 (codified at 2 U.S.C. §§ 1601–1607). In 2007, LDA was strengthened as part of a larger ethics reform effort in the wake of several corruption scandals involving members of Congress and lobbyists.

Section 2 sets forth some of the substantive constitutional rules designed to decrease interest group pressure on lawmakers and to impede legislative deal-making that often leads to omnibus legislation full of provisions that individually could garner only minority support. We will discuss the item vetoes provided to governors in most states and assess a federal law that purported to give a similar power to the President. This section also suggests some tensions between legislative immunities that are designed to preserve the independence of lawmakers and efforts to keep the legislative process free from bribery, extortion, and other forms of obvious and unhealthy corruption.

Finally, Section 3 identifies several constitutional rules requiring that particular processes be followed to enact laws. In a few cases, courts have required that some decisions be made by Congress, rather than other governmental institutions, because the legislature's institutional features better ensure the democratic pedigree of the decision. These mandates are not focused on the kind of corruption we have discussed in the preceding sections, but are designed to "improve" the legislative process. This material introduces an influential concept first articulated by a former justice of the Oregon Supreme Court: *due process of lawmaking*. Justice Hans Linde argued in *Due Process of Lawmaking*, 55 Neb. L. Rev. 197 (1976), that the legislative process should be designed to produce "rational lawmaking," which he described as follows: "It would obligate legislators to inform themselves in some fashion about the existing conditions on which the proposed law would operate, and about the likelihood that the proposal would in fact further the intended purpose. In order to weigh the anticipated benefits for some against the burdens the law would impose on others, legislators must inform themselves about those burdens. * * * The projections and assessments of conditions and consequences must presumably take some account of evidence, at least in committee sessions. * * * The committee must explain its factual and value premises to the full body. Surely there is no place for a vote on final passage by members who have never read even a summary of the bill, let alone a committee report or a resume of the factual documentation." *Id.* at 223–24. Can we devise procedures that facilitate due process of lawmaking, and should it be a constitutional principle that courts use to review statutes?

1. REGULATING DELIBERATION TO COMBAT "CORRUPTION"

Legal regulation of legislative corruption came relatively late to the Anglo-American tradition. There was a long history of "patronage" in the English Parliament, and when the House of Commons first began disciplining members for taking bribes in the 1660s and 1670s, some complained that they were improperly importing ethical standards for judges into the legislative sphere. *See* Josh Chafetz, *Congress's Constitution: Legislative Authority and the Separation of Powers* 235–37 (2017). Even then, it was the House itself that punished the legislators: Members of Parliament were not subject to criminal prosecution for bribery until 2010. Bribery Act, 2010, ch. 23, § 12(8) (U.K.). Likewise, in America, although laws from the earliest days of the Republic punished corruption by executive and judicial officers and employees, no statute governed congressional ethics until 1853. An Act to Prevent Frauds Upon the Treasury, ch. 81, 10 Stat. 170, 170–71. Even after that, the houses of Congress continued to exercise exclusive jurisdiction over their members for some time: no member was indicted for behavior directly tied to his congressional duties until the 1870s, and no member was convicted for such behavior until the early twentieth century. The first such convictions, of Senator Joseph Burton (R-Ks.) in 1904 and Senator John Mitchell (R-Or.) in 1905, were both accompanied by loud complaints that President Theodore Roosevelt was persecuting the senators because of policy disagreements. Chafetz, *supra*, at 247–53.

Today, corrupt legislators may be reined in by laws prohibiting bribery, extortion, and conflicts of interest—all of which have received considerable elaboration in recent years. What is properly prohibited under these categories? Consider the following conduct:

- Senator Doris Soaper agrees to support a bill exempting labor unions from certain tax liabilities in return for a promise by union leaders in her state that they will support her reelection bid. That support is likely to take the forms of: (1) explaining to their members that she is the "pro-union candidate," (2) organizing their members to canvass on her behalf, and (3) making donations from their unions' affiliated PACs to her campaign and paying for pro-Soaper "independent" advertisements.

- Senator Soaper and her husband attend a lavish cruise on the Potomac, hosted by the AFL-CIO. Pending labor legislation is discussed over drinks and a lobster dinner. The next day, Senator Soaper votes for a bill exempting labor unions from certain tax liabilities.

- Senator Soaper has established a legal defense fund to raise money to pay lawyers representing her in an investigation of her legislative activities related to the AFL-CIO's agenda. All the high-ranking officials of that union contribute $50,000 each to her fund, which is run by a group of her supporters.

Should any of this conduct be regulated? Prohibited?

This section will consider these broad questions. We shall proceed in three parts: Part A will examine laws prohibiting bribery and accepting gratuities. It will also examine federal law prohibiting extortion, including obtaining property under color of official right. Part B will set forth various conflict of interest rules prompted by concerns of legislative corruption. Part C will analyze legislation passed at the federal level to regulate the activity of lobbying, which is essential for a well-functioning democracy but sometimes seems to veer into the realm of corruption.

As you read these materials, consider whether it makes sense as a policy matter or as a constitutional matter to regulate political conduct as extensively as we do. Glenn Parker argues that the most effective mechanism to constrain corrupt behavior is a lawmaker's interest in maintaining a reputation for ethical behavior because, at least in the House, it increases the length of the lawmaker's career and enhances his chances of attractive post-elective employment. *Self-Policing in Politics: The Political Economy of Reputational Controls on Politicians* (2004). How do ethics codes benefit lawmakers who want to establish a reputation for trustworthiness? Are reputational controls sufficient given the temptations of elective office?

Moreover, remember that laws don't prosecute defendants or preside over trials: other government officials do. Should we be concerned about executive and judicial officials using anti-corruption statutes to target their political opponents in the legislature, as Senators Burton and Mitchell accused the Roosevelt administration (and compliant judges) of doing? If so, does this counsel a more restrictive role for the other branches in policing legislative corruption?

A. BRIBERY AND EXTORTION

Anti-bribery statutes might serve three different purposes: (1) to protect the integrity of the public servant's decisionmaking process, so that decisions are made to advance the public interest and not the decisionmaker's private agenda; (2) to avoid the appearance of unfairness and abuse of office; and (3) to assure equal access of all citizens to the services of public servants.[1] For such reasons, the United States and all the states have anti-bribery laws.

The federal bribery statute, 18 U.S.C. § 201(b)–(c), provides in part:

(b) Whoever—

(1) directly or indirectly, corruptly gives, offers or promises anything of value to any public official or person who has been selected to be a public

---

[1]   See John Noonan, Jr., *Bribes* 704 (1984); Beth Nolan, *Public Interest, Private Income: Conflicts and Control Limits on the Outside Income of Government Officials*, 87 Nw. U.L. Rev. 57, 71–80 (1992). For an analysis of the federal statute with citations to relevant case law, see Nicholas Jarcho & Neal Shechter, *Public Corruption*, 49 Am. Crim. L. Rev. 1107 (2012).

official, or offers or promises any public official or any person who has been selected to be a public official to give anything of value to any other person or entity, with intent—

(A) to influence any official act; or

(B) to influence such public official or person who has been selected to be a public official to commit or aid in committing, or collude in, or allow, any fraud * * * on the United States; or

(C) to induce such public official or such person who has been selected to be a public official to do or omit to do any act in violation of the lawful duty of such official or person;

(2) being a public official or person selected to be a public official, directly or indirectly, corruptly demands, seeks, receives, accepts, or agrees to receive or accept anything of value personally or for any other person or entity, in return for:

(A) being influenced in the performance of any official act;

(B) being influenced to commit or aid in committing, or to collude in, or allow, any fraud, or make opportunity for the commission of any fraud, on the United States; or

(C) being induced to do or omit to do any act in violation of the official duty of such official or person; * * *

shall be fined under this title or not more than three times the monetary equivalent of the thing of value, whichever is greater, or imprisoned for not more than fifteen years, or both, and may be disqualified from holding any office of honor, trust, or profit under the United States.

(c) Whoever—

(1) otherwise than as provided by law for the proper discharge of official duty—

(A) directly or indirectly, gives, offers, or promises anything of value to any public official, former public official, or person selected to be a public official, for or because of any official act performed or to be performed by such public official, former public official, or person selected to be a public official; or

(B) being a public official, former public official, or person selected to be a public official, otherwise than as provided by law for the proper discharge of official duty, directly or indirectly demands, seeks, receives, accepts, or agrees to receive or accept anything of value personally for or because of any official act performed or to be performed by such official or person; * * *

shall be fined under this title or imprisoned for not more than two years, or both.

"Public official" is defined in § 201(a)(1) as a "Member of Congress, Delegate, or Resident Commissioner, either before or after such official has qualified, or an officer or employee or person acting for or on behalf of the United States, or any department, agency or branch of Government thereof, including the District of Columbia, in any official function, under or by authority of any such department, agency, or branch of Government, or a juror." Section 201(a)(3) defines "official act" as any "decision or action on any question, matter, cause, suit, proceeding or controversy, which may at any time be pending, or which may by law be brought before any public official, in such official's official capacity, or in such official's place of trust or profit."

This federal statute covers conduct that state statutes traditionally have divided into categories of "bribery" (§ 201(b)) and "unlawful gratuities" (§ 201(c)). Section 201(b) has been interpreted to impose requirements similar to those of most state bribery statutes, namely, that a public official (1) obtains anything of value (2) in return for performing an official act, committing fraud on the U.S., or violating a lawful duty, and (3) the defendant public official or private person acted with "corrupt intent." The last element is the primary distinction between bribery and unlawful gratuity offenses. Payments to a public official for acts that would have occurred in any event are in most circumstances probably unlawful gratuities and not bribes. See *United States v. Campbell*, 684 F.2d 141 (D.C. Cir. 1982).

Section 201 and analogous state laws are phrased generally and might be interpreted to reach far beyond the prototype of bribery (the selling of one's legislative influence for money or material goods). How far should these statutes reach? Should they include Senator Soaper's agreement to support a bill exempting labor unions from certain tax liabilities in return for a promise by union leaders in her state that they will support her reelection bid? Should they cover contributions to the Senator's campaign, based upon the mutual expectation that Soaper will continue to support labor legislation?

Daniel Lowenstein, *Political Bribery and the Intermediate Theory of Politics*, 32 UCLA L. Rev. 784 (1985), argues that the answers to these questions typically depend upon one's definition of "corrupt intent," which in turn depends upon one's theory of politics. If you view a legislative representative as a trustee for the public good, you might be inclined to criminalize campaign contributions that carry a commitment by the legislator to vote in specified ways on future issues. On the other hand, if you view the legislator as nothing more than an agent for popular desires, you might want to limit bribery prosecutions to those cases in which the representative benefits personally (as, for example, by fattening her bank account or acquiring a new yacht). You might not want to prosecute those cases in which the representative is merely making political tradeoffs resulting in legislation that, on balance, serves the interests of her constituents. Obviously, most cases fall somewhere along the spectrum between clearly legitimate arrangements and patently corrupt deals—but where?

In light of this background, consider the following case, notes, and problem.

PEOPLE EX REL. DICKINSON V. VAN DE CARR

Supreme Court of New York, Appellate Division, First Department, 1903.
87 App. Div. 386, 84 N.Y.S. 461.

LAUGHLIN, J.

The relator is an alderman of the city of New York. He has been held to bail, and to appear at the Court of General Sessions, upon a charge of violating section 72 of the Penal Code, which relates to bribery[.] * * * The testimony showed that John McGaw Woodbury, the commissioner of street cleaning of the city of New York, wrote a letter to the relator on the 23d day of September, 1902, saying:

> "In reply to your letter of September 20th, I would say that the Department is so short of horses, particularly in the Borough of Brooklyn, that we have been very strict with the drivers during the warm weather to prevent any possibility of over-heating or damaging the stock. We are many behind our complement. Should, however, the Honorable Board grant me the moneys for new stock and plant, this would give employment to more drivers, and as the heavy season comes on, having made a note of your favorable recommendation, the case of Covino will be reconsidered."

—That on the 30th day of the same month the relator wrote and mailed a letter to Commissioner Woodbury in reply, saying:

> "If you will reinstate Antonio Covino, who I think was too severely punished by being dismissed from your Department, I will vote and otherwise help you to obtain the money needed for a new plant in Brooklyn."

And at this time there was pending in the board of aldermen a bill to authorize an issue of corporate stock "for new stock or plant for the Department of Street Cleaning, Borough of Brooklyn."

There is no question but that the magistrate has jurisdiction to inquire into a violation of section 72 of the Penal Code, and thereafter, upon proper proof, to hold a person to answer for the crime. The relator has not been convicted. He has been merely held to answer. We are therefore not concerned with the weight of evidence. Our inquiry is limited to whether there was any evidence tending to show his guilt. This is the single question presented by the appeal. Section 72 of the Penal Code provides as follows:

> "Officer Accepting Bribe. A judicial officer, a person who executes any of the functions of a public office not designated in titles VI and VII of this Code, or a person employed by or acting for the state, or for any public officer in the business of the state, who asks, receives, or agrees to receive a bribe, or any money, property, or value of any kind, or any promise or agreement therefor, upon any agreement or understanding that his vote, opinion, judgment, action, decision, or any other official proceeding, shall be influenced thereby, or that he will do or omit any act or proceeding, or in any way neglect or violate any official duty, is punishable by imprisonment for not more than ten years, or by a fine of not more than five thousand dollars, or both. A conviction also forfeits any office held by the offender, and forever disqualifies him from holding any public office under the state."

It will be observed that the clause, "asks, receives or agrees to receive a bribe, or any money, property, or value of any kind, or any promise or agreement therefor," is disjunctive. It first specifically includes certain officers who ask, receive, or agree to receive a bribe. In the absence of any statute defining a bribe, we must have recourse to the decisions and text-writers to determine what was embraced in that term at common law. Bribery was an indictable offense at common law, and, although in the early days it was limited to judicial officers and those engaged in the administration of justice, it was later extended to all public officers. It was variously defined as taking or offering an "undue reward" or a "reward" to influence official action. Bribery is defined in 4 Am. & Eng. Enc. of Law, p. 907, to be "the giving, offering, or receiving of anything of value, or any valuable service, intended to influence one in the discharge of legal duty." The cases of bribery that have been before the courts of this state, so far as brought to our attention, have related to the offering or giving of property or something of intrinsic value. The relator claims that, as no money or property was asked or agreed to be received by him to influence the official action of the street commissioner, he has not violated this statute. In view of the circumstances disclosed, his letter is open to the inference that he desired to obtain a political or other personal advantage from or by securing Covino's reinstatement in the public service, and that he took advantage of the known desire on the part of the street commissioner to obtain this appropriation of public moneys to improperly influence the action of the street commissioner on the application of Covino for reinstatement, by offering, in case that were done, to vote for and further the desired appropriation, and impliedly threatening in case of refusal to withhold his support therefrom. The interests of the public service require that public officers shall act honestly and fairly upon propositions laid before them for consideration, and shall neither be influenced by, nor receive pecuniary benefit from, their official acts, or enter into bargains with their fellow legislators or officers or with others for the giving or withholding of their votes, conditioned upon their receiving any valuable favor, political or otherwise, for themselves or for others. It was the duty of the relator to act fairly and honestly and according to his judgment upon the proposition of the street commissioner. It does not appear to have been the mandatory duty of the board of aldermen to favor the recommendation of Commissioner Woodbury. In these circumstances, it was the duty of the relator to favor or oppose the recommendation according to its merits or demerits. If, in his judgment, it should have been disapproved, he should have opposed it, and he should not bargain to vote for it upon obtaining an agreement from the street commissioner to reinstate Covino. It is quite as demoralizing to the public service, and as much against the spirit and intent of the statute, for a legislator or other public official to bargain to sell his vote or official action for a political or other favor or reward as for money. Either is a bribe, and they only differ in degree. Nor should he, by holding out this inducement, have tempted the commissioner to act favorably upon Covino's application for reinstatement. This was undue influence, and would be detrimental to the public service. In addition to the word "bribe" in section 72 of the Penal Code, other words are employed sufficiently broad to reach this case. It is a violation of the statute for a public officer to ask, receive, or agree to receive "property or value of any kind, or any promise or agreement therefor," upon any agreement or understanding that his vote or official action shall be influenced thereby. It is clear that words "value of any kind," as here used, are more comprehensive than "property." The benefit which the relator expected to receive from the reinstatement of his constituent would, we think, be embraced in the meaning of this clause, and would also constitute a bribe. We are therefore of the opinion that the facts tend to show that the relator has offended against the provisions of section 72 of the Penal Code, and that he was properly held to answer upon the charge.

It follows that the order should be affirmed. All concur.

NOTES ON BRIBERY PROSECUTIONS AND THEORIES OF REPRESENTATION

1.   *Is This Prosecution Supportable by Any Theory?* Wisconsin explicitly prohibits logrolling by legislators in a law that dates back to the Progressive Era. Section 13.05 of the Wisconsin statutes makes it a felony for a legislator to give, offer, or promise his or her vote on a bill "in consideration or upon condition that any other person elected to the same legislature will give or will promise or agree to give his or her vote or influence in favor of or against any other measure or proposition" in the legislature. Similarly, a lawmaker cannot promise to vote in a particular way on a bill in return for a promise by the governor to sign, veto, or line item veto any other legislation. Wisc. Stat., § 13.06. Wisconsin statutes further specify that these provisions shall not "be construed as prohibiting free discussion and deliberation upon any question pending before the legislature by members thereof, privately or publicly, nor as prohibiting agreements by members to support any single measure pending, on condition that certain changes be made in such measure, nor as prohibiting agreements to compromise conflicting provisions of different measures." *Id.* § 13.07.

On the other hand, a recent federal case has held that logrolling cannot give rise to a bribery conviction. Recall the circumstances described in Problem 2-3 in the previous chapter: After Barack Obama's election to the presidency, Illinois Governor Rod Blagojevich (a fellow Democrat) was entitled to appoint someone to Obama's vacated Senate seat. FBI wiretaps made clear that Blagojevich saw this as an opportunity for personal enrichment, initially offering to appoint Valerie Jarrett, a personal friend and political ally of Obama's. In exchange, Blagojevich demanded that Obama either appoint him to the Cabinet or persuade someone in the private sector to hire him at a high salary. When Obama declined, Blagojevich shopped the Senate seat around to other potential bidders. He was convicted on numerous counts of extortion, corrupt solicitation of funds, and wire fraud. Because he was not a "public official" under 18 U.S.C. § 201(a)(1) (which, recall, is limited to *federal* officials), he was not charged under the bribery statute; however, courts have interpreted the Hobbs Act's prohibition on extortion, 18 U.S.C. § 1951, to include taking a bribe. *Evans v. United States*, 504 U.S. 255, 260–69 (1992).

While affirming most of the convictions, the Seventh Circuit vacated those that may have been based on Blagojevich's attempts to trade the Senate seat for a Cabinet appointment for himself. Those, according to Judge Easterbrook, were just logrolling, which is "fundamentally unlike" bribery. The latter involves "a quid pro quo: a public official performs an official act (or promises to do so) in exchange for a private benefit, such as money." By contrast, logrolling "is the swap of one official act for another. Representative A agrees with Representative B to vote for milk price supports, if B agrees to vote for tighter controls on air pollution. A President appoints C as an ambassador, which Senator D asked the President to do, in exchange for D's promise to vote to confirm

E as a member of the National Labor Relations Board. Governance would hardly be possible without these accommodations, which allow each public official to achieve more of his principal objective while surrendering something about which he cares less, but the other politician cares more strongly. A proposal to appoint a particular person to one office (say, the Cabinet) in exchange for someone else's promise to appoint a different person to a different office (say, the Senate), is a common exercise in logrolling." Nor did it matter that here the proposer was seeking the position for himself: "It isn't clear to us that this is unusual." *United States v. Blagojevich*, 794 F.3d 729, 734–37 (7th Cir. 2015). Thus, unlike the *Van de Carr* court or the Wisconsin statutes, the Seventh Circuit held that logrolls—even logrolls intended to *personally* benefit at least one of the logrollers—cannot constitute bribery.

Consider *Van de Carr*, the Wisconsin statutes, and *Blagojevich* in light of the different theories of representation developed in this and the preceding chapter. The first two might seem to be consistent with a theory that considers the representative to be a trustee for the people, using her independent judgment to figure out what is best for the people. But even under a republican or trusteeship approach, shouldn't the representative be able to make deals with other officials, to ensure that her constituents receive needed services? Would *Van de Carr* and the Wisconsin law outlaw most forms of cooperative behavior to construct majority support for bills? Does the rationale of *Van de Carr* criminalize any voting or legislative action for strategic reasons and require that the representative always sincerely believe in the merits of the positions she takes? Can a legislature effectively work under such constraints? On the other hand, a republican might have no trouble condemning the *Blagojevich* decision, where no plausible public-interested rationale was on offer for the purported logroll. See generally Dennis Thompson, *Ethics in Congress: From Individual to Institutional Corruption* (1995) (arguing that a concern of modern ethics rules should be institutional corruption, where the gains are political rather than personal, the service offered by the lawmaker is procedurally improper, and the connection between gain and service damages either the legislature or the democratic process).

2. *The Sweep of* Van de Carr. This case may be a product of its times. It was written during a period in New York politics in which reformers in and out of government were working to eliminate rampant corruption and to break the power of party bosses. Leaders like Theodore Roosevelt came to national attention because of their efforts to clean up the sewers of local politics. Thus, Judge Laughlin may well have known about aspects of this case that made the political deal more dubious than it appears from the facts he gives, or he may have been a reform-minded judge hoping his opinion would get the attention of graft-addicted politicos.[2]

3. *The Connection Between an Unlawful Gratuity and the Official's Position.* The Supreme Court construed the unlawful gratuities portion of § 201 in a case that grew out of an independent prosecutor's investigation of President Bill Clinton's Secretary of Agriculture Mike Espy. *United States v. Sun-Diamond Growers of California*, 526 U.S. 398 (1999). Sun-Diamond Growers was a trade association for businesses that grew raisins, figs, walnuts, prunes, and hazelnuts. The independent prosecutor alleged that the association had given Espy tickets to the U.S. Open, luggage, meals, and a crystal

---

[2] For discussion of this era in New York and reform efforts, see Louis Eisenstein & Elliot Rosenberg, *A Stripe of Tammany's Tiger* (1966); Jerome Mushkat, *Tammany: The Evolution of a Political Machine, 1789–1865* (1971).

bowl, which had a total value of less than $6,000. The trade organization had several matters before the Secretary. For example, it wanted to be designated as a representative of "small-sized entities" so that it would continue to receive federal funds for overseas marketing plans for its members' commodities. It also wanted the Department of Agriculture to oppose plans by the Environmental Protection Agency to ban a particular kind of pesticide. The indictment of Sun-Diamond Growers described these matters, but it did not allege a direct nexus between them and the gratuities conferred on Espy. The government argued that it need not show a link to a particular official act, but only that the gratuity was motivated more generally by "the recipient's capacity to exercise governmental power or influence in the donor's favor." Justice Scalia's opinion for the Court rejected that interpretation, arguing that § 201(c)(1)(A)'s explicit provision that the gift be made "for or because of any official act" requires that some official act be identified and proved. Thus, the unlawful gratuity statute does not criminalize gifts given merely because the recipient holds a powerful office; instead, laws and ethics rules prohibiting or limiting gift giving to officials are designed to cover such situations. Scalia's opinion underscores the relationship among the laws regulating corruption: "[T]his regulation, and the numerous other regulations and statutes littering this field, demonstrate that this is an area where precisely targeted prohibitions are commonplace, and where more general prohibitions have been qualified by numerous exceptions. Given that reality, a statute in this field that can linguistically be interpreted to be either a meat axe or a scalpel should reasonably be taken to be the latter."

As a result of a 2016 case, Scalia's "scalpel" now cuts even more finely.

McDonnell v. United States

Supreme Court of the United States, 2016.
___ U.S. ___, 136 S.Ct. 2355, 195 L.Ed.2d 639.

CHIEF JUSTICE ROBERTS delivered the opinion of the [unanimous] Court.

In 2014, the Federal Government indicted former Virginia Governor Robert McDonnell and his wife, Maureen McDonnell, on bribery charges. The charges related to the acceptance by the McDonnells of $175,000 in loans, gifts, and other benefits from Virginia businessman Jonnie Williams, while Governor McDonnell was in office. Williams was the chief executive officer of Star Scientific, a Virginia-based company that had developed a nutritional supplement [called Anatabloc,] made from anatabine, a compound found in tobacco. Star Scientific hoped that Virginia's public universities would perform research studies on anatabine [which would aid the company in securing FDA approval for the supplement's use as an anti-inflammatory drug], and Williams wanted Governor McDonnell's assistance in obtaining those studies.

To convict the McDonnells of bribery, the Government was required to show that Governor McDonnell committed (or agreed to commit) an "official act" in exchange for the loans and gifts. The parties did not agree, however, on what counts as an "official act." The Government alleged in the indictment, and maintains on appeal, that Governor McDonnell committed at least five "official acts." Those acts included "arranging meetings" for Williams with other Virginia officials to discuss Star Scientific's product, "hosting" events for Star Scientific at the Governor's Mansion, and "contacting other government officials" concerning studies of anatabine. The

Government also argued more broadly that these activities constituted "official action" because they related to Virginia business development, a priority of Governor McDonnell's administration. Governor McDonnell contends that merely setting up a meeting, hosting an event, or contacting an official—without more—does not count as an "official act."

At trial, the District Court instructed the jury according to the Government's broad understanding of what constitutes an "official act," and the jury convicted both Governor and Mrs. McDonnell on the bribery charges. The Fourth Circuit affirmed Governor McDonnell's conviction, and we granted review to clarify the meaning of "official act."

[I(A)] * * * Governor McDonnell first met Williams in 2009, when Williams offered McDonnell transportation on his private airplane to assist with McDonnell's election campaign. Shortly after the election, Williams had dinner with Governor and Mrs. McDonnell at a restaurant in New York. The conversation turned to Mrs. McDonnell's search for a dress for the inauguration, which led Williams to offer to purchase a gown for her. Governor McDonnell's counsel later instructed Williams not to buy the dress, and Mrs. McDonnell told Williams that she would take a rain check.

In October 2010, Governor McDonnell and Williams met again on Williams's plane. During the flight, Williams told Governor McDonnell that he "needed his help" moving forward on the research studies at Virginia's public universities, and he asked to be introduced to the person that he "needed to talk to." Governor McDonnell agreed to introduce Williams to Dr. William Hazel, Virginia's Secretary of Health and Human Resources. Williams met with Dr. Hazel the following month, but the meeting was unfruitful; Dr. Hazel was skeptical of the science behind Anatabloc and did not assist Williams in obtaining the studies.

Six months later, Governor McDonnell's wife, Maureen McDonnell, offered to seat Williams next to the Governor at a political rally. Shortly before the event, Williams took Mrs. McDonnell on a shopping trip and bought her $20,000 worth of designer clothing. The McDonnells later had Williams over for dinner at the Governor's Mansion, where they discussed research studies on Anatabloc. Two days after that dinner, Williams had an article about Star Scientific's research e-mailed to Mrs. McDonnell, which she forwarded to her husband. Less than an hour later, Governor McDonnell texted his sister to discuss the financial situation of certain rental properties they owned in Virginia Beach. Governor McDonnell also e-mailed his daughter to ask about expenses for her upcoming wedding.

The next day, Williams returned to the Governor's Mansion for a meeting with Mrs. McDonnell. At the meeting, Mrs. McDonnell described the family's financial problems, including their struggling rental properties in Virginia Beach and their daughter's wedding expenses. Mrs. McDonnell, who had experience selling nutritional supplements, told Williams that she had a background in the area and could help him with Anatabloc. According to Williams, she explained that the "Governor says it's okay for me to help you and—but I need you to help me. I need you to help me with this financial situation." Mrs. McDonnell then asked Williams for a $50,000 loan, in addition to a $15,000 gift to help pay for her daughter's wedding, and Williams agreed. Williams testified that he called Governor McDonnell after the meeting and said, "I understand the financial problems and I'm willing to help. I just wanted to make sure that you knew about this." According to Williams, Governor McDonnell thanked him for his help. Governor McDonnell testified, in contrast, that he did not know about the loan at the time, and that when he learned of it he was upset that Mrs. McDonnell had requested the loan from Williams. Three days after the meeting between Williams and Mrs. McDonnell, Governor McDonnell directed his assistant to forward the article on Star Scientific to Dr. Hazel.

In June 2011, Williams sent Mrs. McDonnell's chief of staff a letter containing a proposed research protocol for the Anatabloc studies. The letter was addressed to Governor McDonnell, and it suggested that the Governor "use the attached protocol to initiate the 'Virginia Study' of Anatabloc at the Medical College of Virginia and the University of Virginia School of Medicine." Governor McDonnell gave the letter to Dr. Hazel. Williams testified at trial that he did not "recall any response" to the letter.

In July 2011, the McDonnell family visited Williams's vacation home for the weekend, and Governor McDonnell borrowed Williams's Ferrari while there. Shortly thereafter, Governor McDonnell asked Dr. Hazel to send an aide to a meeting with Williams and Mrs. McDonnell to discuss research studies on Anatabloc. The aide later testified that she did not feel pressured by Governor or Mrs. McDonnell to do "anything other than have the meeting," and that Williams did not ask anything of her at the meeting. After the meeting, the aide sent Williams a "polite blow-off" e-mail.

At a subsequent meeting at the Governor's Mansion, Mrs. McDonnell admired Williams's Rolex and mentioned that she wanted to get one for Governor McDonnell. Williams asked if Mrs. McDonnell wanted him to purchase a Rolex for the Governor, and Mrs. McDonnell responded, "Yes, that would be nice." Williams did so, and Mrs. McDonnell later gave the Rolex to Governor McDonnell as a Christmas present.

In August 2011, the McDonnells hosted a lunch event for Star Scientific at the Governor's Mansion. According to Williams, the purpose of the event was to launch Anatabloc. According to Governor McDonnell's gubernatorial counsel, however, it was just lunch. The guest list for the event included researchers at the University of Virginia and Virginia Commonwealth University. During the event, Star Scientific distributed free samples of Anatabloc, in addition to eight $25,000 checks that researchers could use in preparing grant proposals for studying Anatabloc. Governor McDonnell asked researchers at the event whether they thought "there was some scientific validity" to Anatabloc and "whether or not there was any reason to explore this further." He also asked whether this could "be something good for the Commonwealth, particularly as it relates to economy or job creation." When Williams asked Governor McDonnell whether he would support funding for the research studies, Governor McDonnell "very politely" replied, "I have limited decision-making power in this area."

In January 2012, Mrs. McDonnell asked Williams for an additional loan for the Virginia Beach rental properties, and Williams agreed. On February 3, Governor McDonnell followed up on that conversation by calling Williams to discuss a $50,000 loan. Several days later, Williams complained to Mrs. McDonnell that the Virginia universities were not returning Star Scientific's calls. She passed Williams's complaint on to the Governor. While Mrs. McDonnell was driving with Governor McDonnell, she also e-mailed Governor McDonnell's counsel, stating that the Governor "wants to know why nothing has developed" with the research studies after Williams had provided the eight $25,000 checks for preparing grant proposals, and that the Governor "wants to get this going" at the universities. According to Governor McDonnell, however, Mrs. McDonnell acted without his knowledge or permission, and he never made the statements she attributed to him.

On February 16, Governor McDonnell e-mailed Williams to check on the status of documents related to the $50,000 loan. A few minutes later, Governor McDonnell e-mailed his counsel stating, "Please see me about Anatabloc issues at VCU and UVA. Thanks." Governor McDonnell's counsel replied, "Will do. We need to be careful with this issue." The next day, Governor McDonnell's counsel called Star Scientific's lobbyist in order to "change the expectations" of Star Scientific regarding the involvement of the Governor's Office in the studies.

At the end of February, Governor McDonnell hosted a healthcare industry reception at the Governor's Mansion, which Williams attended. Mrs. McDonnell also invited a number of guests recommended by Williams, including researchers at the Virginia universities. Governor McDonnell was present, but did not mention Star Scientific, Williams, or Anatabloc during the event. That same day, Governor McDonnell and Williams spoke about the $50,000 loan, and Williams loaned the money to the McDonnells shortly thereafter.

In March 2012, Governor McDonnell met with Lisa Hicks-Thomas, the Virginia Secretary of Administration, and Sara Wilson, the Director of the Virginia Department of Human Resource Management. The purpose of the meeting was to discuss Virginia's health plan for state employees. At that time, Governor McDonnell was taking Anatabloc several times a day. He took a pill during the meeting, and told Hicks-Thomas and Wilson that the pills "were working well for him" and "would be good for" state employees. Hicks-Thomas recalled Governor McDonnell asking them to meet with a representative from Star Scientific; Wilson had no such recollection. After the discussion with Governor McDonnell, Hicks-Thomas and Wilson looked up Anatabloc on the Internet, but they did not set up a meeting with Star Scientific or conduct any other follow-up. It is undisputed that Virginia's health plan for state employees does not cover nutritional supplements such as Anatabloc.

In May 2012, Governor McDonnell requested an additional $20,000 loan, which Williams provided. Throughout this period, Williams also paid for several rounds of golf for Governor McDonnell and his children, took the McDonnells on a weekend trip, and gave $10,000 as a wedding gift to one of the McDonnells' daughters. In total, Williams gave the McDonnells over $175,000 in gifts and loans.

[I(B)] In January 2014, Governor McDonnell was indicted for accepting payments, loans, gifts, and other things of value from Williams and Star Scientific in exchange for "performing official actions on an as-needed basis, as opportunities arose, to legitimize, promote, and obtain research studies for Star Scientific's products." The charges against him comprised one count of conspiracy to commit honest services fraud, three counts of honest services fraud, one count of conspiracy to commit Hobbs Act extortion, six counts of Hobbs Act extortion, and two counts of making a false statement. See 18 U. S. C. §§ 1343, 1349 (honest services fraud); § 1951(a) (Hobbs Act extortion); § 1014 (false statement). Mrs. McDonnell was indicted on similar charges, plus obstructing official proceedings, based on her alleged involvement in the scheme. See § 1512(c)(2) (obstruction).

The theory underlying both the honest services fraud and Hobbs Act extortion charges was that Governor McDonnell had accepted bribes from Williams. See *Skilling v. United States*, 561 U. S. 358, 404 (2010) (construing honest services fraud to forbid "fraudulent schemes to deprive another of honest services through bribes or kickbacks"); *Evans v. United States*, 504 U. S. 255, 260, 269 (1992) (construing Hobbs Act extortion to include " 'taking a bribe' ").

The parties agreed that they would define honest services fraud with reference to the federal bribery statute, 18 U. S. C. § 201. That statute makes it a crime for "a public official or person selected to be a public official, directly or indirectly, corruptly" to demand, seek, receive, accept, or agree "to receive or accept anything of value" in return for being "influenced in the performance of any official act." § 201(b)(2). An "official act" is defined as "any decision or action on any question, matter, cause, suit, proceeding or controversy, which may at any time be pending, or which may by law be brought before any public official, in such official's official capacity, or in such official's place of trust or profit." § 201(a)(3). The parties also agreed that obtaining a "thing of value . . . knowing that the thing of value was given in return for official action" was an element of Hobbs Act extortion, and that they would use the definition of "official act" found in the federal bribery statute to define "official action" under the Hobbs Act. As a result of all this, the Government was required to prove that Governor McDonnell committed or agreed to commit an "official act" in exchange for the loans and gifts from Williams. See *Evans*, 504 U. S., at 268 ("the offense is completed at the time when the public official receives a payment in return for his agreement to perform specific official acts; fulfillment of the *quid pro quo* is not an element of the offense").

The Government alleged that Governor McDonnell had committed at least five "official acts":

(1) "arranging meetings for [Williams] with Virginia government officials, who were subordinates of the Governor, to discuss and promote Anatabloc";

(2) "hosting, and . . . attending, events at the Governor's Mansion designed to encourage Virginia university researchers to initiate studies of anatabine and to promote Star Scientific's products to doctors for referral to their patients";

(3) "contacting other government officials in the [Governor's Office] as part of an effort to encourage Virginia state research universities to initiate studies of anatabine";

(4) "promoting Star Scientific's products and facilitating its relationships with Virginia government officials by allowing [Williams] to invite individuals important to Star Scientific's business to exclusive events at the Governor's Mansion"; and

(5) "recommending that senior government officials in the [Governor's Office] meet with Star Scientific executives to discuss ways that the company's products could lower healthcare costs."

The case proceeded to a jury trial, which lasted five weeks. Pursuant to an immunity agreement, Williams testified that he had given the gifts and loans to the McDonnells to obtain the Governor's "help with the testing" of Anatabloc at Virginia's medical schools. Governor McDonnell acknowledged that he had requested loans and accepted gifts from Williams. He testified, however, that setting up meetings with government officials was something he did "literally thousands of times" as Governor, and that he did not expect his staff "to do anything other than to meet" with Williams.

Several state officials testified that they had discussed Anatabloc with Williams or Governor McDonnell, but had not taken any action to further the research studies. A UVA employee in the university research office, who had never spoken with the Governor about Anatabloc, testified that she wrote a pro/con list concerning research studies on Anatabloc. The first "pro" was the "[p]erception to Governor that UVA would like to work with local companies," and the first "con" was the "[p]olitical pressure from Governor and impact on future UVA requests from the Governor."

Following closing arguments, the District Court instructed the jury that to convict Governor McDonnell it must find that he agreed "to accept a thing of value in exchange for official action." The court described the five alleged "official acts" set forth in the indictment, which involved arranging meetings, hosting events, and contacting other government officials. The court then quoted the statutory definition of "official act," and—as the Government had requested—advised the jury that the term encompassed "acts that a public official customarily performs," including acts "in furtherance of longer-term goals" or "in a series of steps to exercise influence or achieve an end."

Governor McDonnell had requested the court to further instruct the jury that the "fact that an activity is a routine activity, or a 'settled practice,' of an office-holder does not alone make it an 'official act,'" and that "merely arranging a meeting, attending an event, hosting a reception, or making a speech are not, standing alone, 'official acts,' even if they are settled practices of the official," because they "are not decisions on matters pending before the government." He also asked the court to explain to the jury that an "official act" must intend to or "in fact influence a specific official decision the government actually makes—such as awarding a contract, hiring a government employee, issuing a license, passing a law, or implementing a regulation." The District Court declined to give Governor McDonnell's proposed instruction to the jury.

The jury convicted Governor McDonnell on the honest services fraud and Hobbs Act extortion charges, but acquitted him on the false statement charges. Mrs. McDonnell was also convicted on most of the charges against her. Although the Government requested a sentence of at least ten years for Governor McDonnell, the District Court sentenced him to two years in prison. Mrs. McDonnell received a one-year sentence.

[The district court denied Governor McDonnell's motion to vacate his convictions, and the Fourth Circuit affirmed.] * * * Mrs. McDonnell's separate appeal remains pending before the Court of Appeals.

[II] The issue in this case is the proper interpretation of the term "official act." Section 201(a)(3) defines an "official act" as "any decision or action on any question, matter, cause, suit, proceeding or controversy, which may at any time be pending, or which may by law be brought before any public official, in such official's official capacity, or in such official's place of trust or profit."

According to the Government, "Congress used intentionally broad language" in § 201(a)(3) to embrace "*any* decision or action, on *any* question or matter, that may at *any time* be pending, or which may by law be brought before *any* public official, in such official's official capacity." The Government concludes that the term "official act" therefore encompasses nearly any activity by a public official. In the Government's view, "official act" specifically includes arranging a meeting, contacting another public official, or hosting an event—without more—concerning any subject, including a broad policy issue such as Virginia economic development.

Governor McDonnell, in contrast, contends that statutory context compels a more circumscribed reading, limiting "official acts" to those acts that "direct[ ] a particular resolution of a specific governmental decision," or that pressure another official to do so. He also claims that "vague corruption laws" such as § 201 implicate serious constitutional concerns, militating "in favor of a narrow, cautious reading of these criminal statutes."

Taking into account the text of the statute, the precedent of this Court, and the constitutional concerns raised by Governor McDonnell, we reject the Government's reading of § 201(a)(3) and adopt a more bounded interpretation of "official act." Under that interpretation, setting up a meeting, calling another public official, or hosting an event does not, standing alone, qualify as an "official act."

[II(A)] The text of § 201(a)(3) sets forth two requirements for an "official act": First, the Government must identify a "question, matter, cause, suit, proceeding or controversy" that "may at any time be pending" or "may by law be brought" before a public official. Second, the Government must prove that the public official made a decision or took an action "on" that question, matter, cause, suit, proceeding, or controversy, or agreed to do so. The issue here is whether arranging a meeting, contacting another official, or hosting an event—without more—can be a "question, matter, cause, suit, proceeding or controversy," and if not, whether it can be a decision or action on a "question, matter, cause, suit, proceeding or controversy."

The first inquiry is whether a typical meeting, call, or event is itself a "question, matter, cause, suit, proceeding or controversy." The Government argues that nearly any activity by a public official qualifies as a question or matter—from workaday functions, such as the typical call, meeting, or event, to the broadest issues the government confronts, such as fostering economic development. We conclude, however, that the terms "question, matter, cause, suit, proceeding or controversy" do not sweep so broadly.

The last four words in that list—"cause," "suit," "proceeding," and "controversy"—connote a formal exercise of governmental power, such as a lawsuit, hearing, or administrative determination. [The Chief Justice cited several examples of the words' uses in that manner in statutes and Black's Law Dictionary.] Although it may be difficult to define the precise reach of those terms, it seems clear that a typical meeting, telephone call, or event arranged by a public official does not qualify as a "cause, suit, proceeding or controversy."

But what about a "question" or "matter"? A "question" could mean any "subject or aspect that is in dispute, open for discussion, or to be inquired into," and a "matter" any "subject" of "interest or relevance." Webster's Third New International Dictionary 1394, 1863 (1961). If those meanings were adopted, a typical meeting, call, or event would qualify as a "question" or "matter." A "question" may also be interpreted more narrowly, however, as "a subject or point of debate or a proposition being or to be voted on in a meeting," such as a question "before the senate." *Id.,* at 1863. Similarly, a "matter" may be limited to "a topic under active and usually serious or practical consideration," such as a matter that "will come before the committee." *Id.,* at 1394.

To choose between those competing definitions, we look to the context in which the words appear. Under the familiar interpretive canon *noscitur a sociis,* "a word is known by the company it keeps." [See the discussion of *noscitur a sociis* and its cousin, *ejusdem generis,* in Chapter 6, § 1(B).] While "not an inescapable rule," this canon "is often wisely applied where a word is capable of many meanings in order to avoid the giving of unintended breadth to the Acts of Congress." For example, in *Gustafson v. Alloyd Co.,* 513 U. S. 561 (1995), a statute defined the word "prospectus" as a "prospectus, notice, circular, advertisement, letter, or communication." *Id.,* at 573–574 (internal quotation marks omitted). We held that although the word "communication" could in the abstract mean any type of communication, "it is apparent that the list refers to documents of wide dissemination," and that inclusion "of the term 'communication' in that list suggests that it too refers to a public communication." *Id.,* at 575.

Applying that same approach here, we conclude that a "question" or "matter" must be similar in nature to a "cause, suit, proceeding or controversy." Because a typical meeting, call, or event arranged by a public official is not of the same stripe as a lawsuit before a court, a determination before an agency, or a hearing before a committee, it does not qualify as a "question" or "matter" under § 201(a)(3).

That more limited reading also comports with the presumption "that statutory language is not superfluous." [See the discussion of the presumption against surplusage in Chapter 6, § 2(B).] If "question" and "matter" were as unlimited in scope as the Government argues, the terms "cause, suit, proceeding or controversy" would serve no role in the statute—every "cause, suit, proceeding or controversy" would also be a "question" or "matter." Under a more confined interpretation, however, "question" and "matter" may be understood to refer to a formal exercise of governmental power that is similar in nature to a "cause, suit, proceeding or controversy," but that does not necessarily fall into one of those prescribed categories.

Because a typical meeting, call, or event is not itself a question or matter, the next step is to determine whether arranging a meeting, contacting another official, or hosting an event may qualify as a "decision or action" *on* a different question or matter. That requires us to first establish what counts as a question or matter in this case.

In addition to the requirements we have described, § 201(a)(3) states that the question or matter must be "pending" or "may by law be brought" before "any public official." "Pending" and "may by law be brought" suggest something that is relatively circumscribed—the kind of thing that can be put on an agenda, tracked for progress, and then checked off as complete. In particular, "may *by law* be brought" conveys something within the specific duties of an official's position—the function conferred by the authority of his office. The word "any" conveys that the matter may be pending either before the public official who is performing the official act, or before another public official.

The District Court, however, determined that the relevant matter in this case could be considered at a much higher level of generality as "Virginia business and economic development," or—as it was often put to the jury—"Bob's for Jobs" [the Governor's 2009 campaign slogan]. Economic development is not naturally described as a matter "pending" before a public official—or something that may be brought "by law" before him—any more than "justice" is pending or may be brought by law before a judge, or "national security" is pending or may be brought by law before an officer of the Armed Forces. Under § 201(a)(3), the pertinent "question, matter, cause, suit, proceeding or controversy" must be more focused and concrete.

For its part, the Fourth Circuit found at least three questions or matters at issue in this case: (1) "whether researchers at any of Virginia's state universities would initiate a study of Anatabloc"; (2) "whether the state-created Tobacco Indemnification and Community Revitalization Commission" would "allocate grant money for the study of anatabine"; and (3) "whether the health insurance plan for state employees in Virginia would include Anatabloc as a covered drug." We agree that those qualify as questions or matters under § 201(a)(3). Each is focused and concrete, and each involves a formal exercise of governmental power that is similar in nature to a lawsuit, administrative determination, or hearing.

The question remains whether—as the Government argues—merely setting up a meeting, hosting an event, or calling another official qualifies as a decision or action on any of those three questions or matters. Although the word "decision," and especially the word "action," could be read expansively to support the Government's view, our opinion in *United States v. Sun-Diamond Growers of Cal.*, 526 U.S. 398 (1999), rejects that interpretation.

In *Sun-Diamond*, the Court stated that it was not an "official act" under § 201 for the President to host a championship sports team at the White House, the Secretary of Education to visit a high school, or the Secretary of Agriculture to deliver a speech to "farmers concerning various matters of USDA policy." *Id.*, at 407. We recognized that "the Secretary of Agriculture *always* has before him or in prospect matters that affect farmers, just as the President always has before him or in prospect matters that affect college and professional sports, and the Secretary of

Education matters that affect high schools." *Ibid.* But we concluded that the existence of such pending matters was not enough to find that any action related to them constituted an "official act." *Ibid.* It was possible to avoid the "absurdities" of convicting individuals on corruption charges for engaging in such conduct, we explained, *"through the definition of that term,"* i.e., by adopting a more limited definition of "official acts." *Id.,* at 408.

It is apparent from *Sun-Diamond* that hosting an event, meeting with other officials, or speaking with interested parties is not, standing alone, a "decision or action" within the meaning of § 201(a)(3), even if the event, meeting, or speech is related to a pending question or matter. Instead, something more is required: § 201(a)(3) specifies that the public official must make a decision or take an action *on* that question or matter, or agree to do so.

For example, a decision or action to initiate a research study—or a decision or action on a qualifying step, such as narrowing down the list of potential research topics—would qualify as an "official act." A public official may also make a decision or take an action on a "question, matter, cause, suit, proceeding or controversy" by using his official position to exert pressure on *another* official to perform an "official act." In addition, if a public official uses his official position to provide advice to another official, knowing or intending that such advice will form the basis for an "official act" by another official, that too can qualify as a decision or action for purposes of § 201(a)(3).

Under this Court's precedents, a public official is not required to actually make a decision or take an action on a "question, matter, cause, suit, proceeding or controversy"; it is enough that the official agree to do so. The agreement need not be explicit, and the public official need not specify the means that he will use to perform his end of the bargain. Nor must the public official in fact intend to perform the "official act," so long as he agrees to do so. A jury could, for example, conclude that an agreement was reached if the evidence shows that the public official received a thing of value knowing that it was given with the expectation that the official would perform an "official act" in return. It is up to the jury, under the facts of the case, to determine whether the public official agreed to perform an "official act" at the time of the alleged *quid pro quo.* The jury may consider a broad range of pertinent evidence, including the nature of the transaction, to answer that question.

Setting up a meeting, hosting an event, or calling an official (or agreeing to do so) merely to talk about a research study or to gather additional information, however, does not qualify as a decision or action on the pending question of whether to initiate the study. Simply expressing support for the research study at a meeting, event, or call—or sending a subordinate to such a meeting, event, or call—similarly does not qualify as a decision or action on the study, as long as the public official does not intend to exert pressure on another official or provide advice, knowing or intending such advice to form the basis for an "official act." Otherwise, if every action somehow related to the research study were an "official act," the requirement that the public official make a decision or take an action on that study, or agree to do so, would be meaningless.

Of course, this is not to say that setting up a meeting, hosting an event, or making a phone call is always an innocent act, or is irrelevant, in cases like this one. If an official sets up a meeting, hosts an event, or makes a phone call on a question or matter that is or could be pending before another official, that could serve as evidence of an agreement to take an official act. A jury could conclude, for example, that the official was attempting to pressure or advise another official on a pending matter. And if the official agreed to exert that pressure or give that advice in exchange for a thing of value, that would be illegal.

* * * In sum, an "official act" is a decision or action on a "question, matter, cause, suit, proceeding or controversy." The "question, matter, cause, suit, proceeding or controversy" must involve a formal exercise of governmental power that is similar in nature to a lawsuit before a court, a determination before an agency, or a hearing before a committee. It must also be something specific and focused that is "pending" or "may by law be brought" before a public official. To qualify as an "official act," the public official must make a decision or take an action on that "question, matter, cause, suit, proceeding or controversy," or agree to do so. That decision or action may include using his official position to exert pressure on another official to perform an "official act," or to advise another official, knowing or intending that such advice will form the basis for an "official act" by another official. Setting up a meeting, talking to another official, or organizing an event (or agreeing to do so)—without more—does not fit that definition of "official act."

[II(B)] In addition to being inconsistent with both text and precedent, the Government's expansive interpretation of "official act" would raise significant constitutional concerns. Section 201 prohibits *quid pro quo* corruption—the exchange of a thing of value for an "official act." In the Government's view, nearly anything a public official accepts—from a campaign contribution to lunch—counts as a *quid*; and nearly anything a public official does—from arranging a meeting to inviting a guest to an event—counts as a *quo*.

But conscientious public officials arrange meetings for constituents, contact other officials on their behalf, and include them in events all the time. The basic compact underlying representative government *assumes* that public officials will hear from their constituents and act appropriately on their concerns—whether it is the union official worried about a plant closing or the homeowners who wonder why it took five days to restore power to their neighborhood after a storm. The Government's position could cast a pall of potential prosecution over these relationships if the union had given a campaign contribution in the past or the homeowners invited the official to join them on their annual outing to the ballgame. Officials might wonder whether they could respond to even the most commonplace requests for assistance, and citizens with legitimate concerns might shrink from participating in democratic discourse.

This concern is substantial. White House counsel who worked in every administration from that of President Reagan to President Obama warn that the Government's "breathtaking expansion of public-corruption law would likely chill federal officials' interactions with the people they serve and thus damage their ability effectively to perform their duties." Brief for Former Federal Officials as *Amici*

Curiae 6. Six former Virginia attorneys general—four Democrats and two Republicans—also filed an *amicus* brief in this Court echoing those concerns, as did 77 former state attorneys general from States other than Virginia—41 Democrats, 35 Republicans, and 1 independent. Brief for Former Virginia Attorneys General as *Amici Curiae* 1–2, 16; Brief for 77 Former State Attorneys General (Non-Virginia) as *Amici Curiae* 1–2.

None of this, of course, is to suggest that the facts of this case typify normal political interaction between public officials and their constituents. Far from it. But the Government's legal interpretation is not confined to cases involving extravagant gifts or large sums of money, and we cannot construe a criminal statute on the assumption that the Government will "use it responsibly." The Court in *Sun-Diamond* declined to rely on "the Government's discretion" to protect against overzealous prosecutions under § 201, concluding instead that "a statute in this field that can linguistically be interpreted to be either a meat axe or a scalpel should reasonably be taken to be the latter." 526 U.S., at 408, 412.

A related concern is that, under the Government's interpretation, the term "official act" is not defined "with sufficient definiteness that ordinary people can understand what conduct is prohibited," or "in a manner that does not encourage arbitrary and discriminatory enforcement." Under the " 'standardless sweep' " of the Government's reading, public officials could be subject to prosecution, without fair notice, for the most prosaic interactions. "Invoking so shapeless a provision to condemn someone to prison" for up to 15 years raises the serious concern that the provision "does not comport with the Constitution's guarantee of due process." Our more constrained interpretation of § 201(a)(3) avoids this "vagueness shoal."

The Government's position also raises significant federalism concerns. A State defines itself as a sovereign through "the structure of its government, and the character of those who exercise government authority." That includes the prerogative to regulate the permissible scope of interactions between state officials and their constituents. Here, where a more limited interpretation of "official act" is supported by both text and precedent, we decline to "construe the statute in a manner that leaves its outer boundaries ambiguous and involves the Federal Government in setting standards" of "good government for local and state officials."

[III. Because the jury instructions did not give an appropriately narrow definition of "official act," the Chief Justice concluded that the jury may have convicted McDonnell for conduct that fell outside the scope of the statute, properly understood. Accordingly, the Governor's convictions had to be vacated. However, the Court rejected McDonnell's arguments that the charges against him should be dismissed, instead remanding the case back to the Court of Appeals to determine whether there should be a new trial.]

* * *

There is no doubt that this case is distasteful; it may be worse than that. But our concern is not with tawdry tales of Ferraris, Rolexes, and ball gowns. It is instead with the broader legal implications of the Government's boundless interpretation of the federal bribery statute. A more limited interpretation of the term "official act" leaves ample room for prosecuting corruption, while comporting with the text of the statute and the precedent of this Court.

NOTES ON MCDONNELL

1. *Official Acts.* The Court's opinion necessarily relies upon a certain descriptive theory of how political power works. In particular, it seems to find a meaningful distinction between "formal exercise[s] of governmental power, such as a lawsuit, hearing, or administrative determination," on the one hand, and the sort of power that is exercised when, say, a governor strongly suggests that a subordinate state official consider doing something, on the other. Is this a sensible distinction? Much of a chief executive's job involves continuously engaging with the disparate components of the organization she oversees (whether it be a company, a state, or a country) in order to make sure that they're all on the same page and pursuing similar objectives. Frequently, that sort of coordination happens through conversations that never reach the level of formality of a "lawsuit, hearing, or administrative determination." Indeed, McDonnell testified that he set up meetings with other government officials "literally thousands of times"—which might suggest that setting up meetings is integral to the job of being governor.

Much of the focus of the "new governance" literature has been on the ways in which informal mechanisms of shared governance affect policy outcomes. In the words of one new governance scholar, "Governance is about managing networks." R.A.W. Rhodes, *The New Governance: Governing Without Government*, 44 Pol. Stud. 652, 658 (1996). In making introductions, forwarding communications, setting up meetings, and the like, wasn't McDonnell managing networks of state actors in a manner intended to achieve Williams' goals? If so, does it make any sense to say that McDonnell was not at the time engaging in "official acts"?

2. *Access as Corruption?, Redux.* Recall from the previous chapter that there has been a shift over time in whether the purchasing of access to public officials counts as the sort of corruption that can be addressed by campaign finance regulation. In *Buckley v. Valeo*, 424 U.S. 1 (1976), and *McConnell v. Federal Election Commission*, 540 U.S. 93 (2003), the Court suggested that the purchasing of access did count as corruption in the relevant sense. But in later cases like *Citizens United v. Federal Election Commission*, 558 U.S. 310 (2010), and *McCutcheon v. Federal Election Commission*, 572 U.S. 185 (2014), the Court argued that corruption had to consist of something more than the mere purchasing of access. (See Chapter 2, § 3(B).)

Admittedly, it arises in a very different doctrinal context—statutory interpretation of 18 U.S.C. § 201, as opposed to the First Amendment—but one way to think of *McDonnell* is as the post-election counterpart to *Citizens United* and *McCutcheon*. In both contexts, the Court looked skeptically at attempts to use law to limit the ability of individuals or entities to pay for access to public officials. In both contexts, the Court suggested, giving something in exchange for face-time with decisionmakers is just how politics works. Is this a descriptively accurate account of how politics works? Is it a self-fulfilling prophesy? If the Court continuously stymies attempts to thwart access-purchasing, then won't politics come to be increasingly defined by access-purchasing?

McDonnell has had far-reaching effects. As one news report noted, "within moments" of the decision's coming down, "defense lawyers from Illinois to New York were citing the unanimous ruling as grounds to challenge past and pending criminal corruption cases brought by the Justice Department."[3] Within a few months of the Court's decision, federal prosecutors announced that they would not seek to re-try either of the McDonnells. And in subsequent years, lower courts have relied on it in a number of high-profile corruption cases, including those vacating corruption convictions against the former Speaker of the New York State Assembly, *United States v. Silver*, 864 F.3d 102 (2d Cir. 2017) and the former Majority Leader of the New York State Senate, *United States v. Skelos*, 707 F. App'x. 733 (2d Cir. 2017), and granting habeas relief to former United States Representative William Jefferson on the grounds that most of the counts on which he was convicted came with flawed jury instructions under *McDonnell*, *United States v. Jefferson*, 289 F. Supp. 3d 717 (E.D. Va. 2017). Is it concerning that the *McDonnell* decision has led to freedom—or at least to a new trial or a reduced sentence—for so many public officials whose behavior (like McDonnell's) certainly seems to fit the common understanding of "corruption"?

B. CONFLICTS OF INTEREST

The criminal sanctions found in laws prohibiting bribery, unlawful gratuities, and extortion have not inspired complete confidence in politicians and the government in the wake of Watergate; ethics scandals that dogged the Clinton Administration; the successful prosecution of lobbyist Jack Abramoff for influence peddling, including bribing Rep. Bob Ney (R-Ohio); the resignation of House Majority Leader Tom DeLay (R-Tex.) in 2006 amid allegations of corruption; and other episodes that occur regularly. As a result, both state and federal legislatures have enacted statutes or adopted procedural rules designed to mitigate conflicts of interest, that is, any financial incentive that might affect a legislator's deliberations. As you review the various prescriptions and proscriptions, ask: Do the rules address important conflicts that would impair members' judgment or their ability to deliberate about the public good? Do the rules go further than necessary? Which rules could be most usefully pruned? Which strengthened?

The responses to the overall problem of conflicted interests have been twofold: the disinfectant of full disclosure of financial interests and the adoption of prophylactic rules to prevent even the potential for certain types of financial incentives to slant public deliberations. At the national level, Title I of the Ethics in Government Act of 1978, Pub. L. No. 95–521, 92 Stat. 1824 (codified as amended at 5 U.S.C. App. § 101 *et seq.*), sets forth comprehensive "Financial Disclosure Requirements of Federal Personnel." The requirements apply to Congress members, designated officers and employees of the legislative branch, and candidates seeking to become Congress members (§ 101(c), (f)). Members of Congress, as well as the designated officers and employees, must file on or before May 15 of each year "a full and complete statement" of income, gifts, honoraria, interests in property, liabilities owed to creditors, sales or exchanges of property or stocks, officership on corporate boards, and so forth (§ 102(a)). An exception from the reporting requirements is

---

[3]   Eric Lipton & Benjamin Weiser, *Decision Complicates Corruption Cases Against Officials from New York to Illinois*, N.Y. Times, June 28, 2016, at A14.

created in the Act for holdings of or the source of income from any holdings in "qualified blind trusts" (§ 102(f)).[4]

In addition to disclosure requirements, Congress has adopted various substantive prohibitions to head off potential conflicts of interest. The relevant provisions are a rich array of statutory and legislative rules, introduced in the discussion that follows.[5] It appears that the state's ability to regulate conflicts of interest is robust, and limited primarily by political will. In *Nevada Comm'n on Ethics v. Carrigan*, 564 U.S. 117 (2011), a legislator who failed to abstain from voting to approve a construction project that used his campaign manager as a paid consultant argued that the conflict of interest rule violated the First Amendment by burdening his freedom of expression. Writing for the Court, Justice Scalia upheld the law, holding first that a legislator's vote is "not personal to the legislator but belongs to the people; the legislator has no personal right to it." It is not a constitutionally protected expression of a particular political view, but rather a "commitment of his apportioned share of the legislature's power to the passage or defeat of a particular proposal" and could reflect various motivations from a deeply held personal view to the reflection of constituents' views to the influence of a major contributor. Because the state has the power to exclude a lawmaker with a conflict of interest from voting, a prohibition on advocating a position on the matter during the legislative session is also acceptable, as a reasonable time, place, and manner limitation. In the Court's view, such laws reflect a venerable and universal tradition of legislative recusal rules: virtually every state has such a rule; federal conflict of interest rules have applied to the federal judiciary since the founding; and Thomas Jefferson adopted such a rule when he was President of the Senate.

The rules governing members of Congress regulate the following:

1.   *Gifts Are Severely Limited.* The Ethics Reform Act of 1989, Pub. L. 101–194, 103 Stat. 1716, substantially amended federal law pertaining to gifts, bribes, honoraria, and other activities presenting potential conflicts of interest. In particular, it prohibits members of Congress from seeking or accepting "anything of value" from any person "whose interests may be substantially affected by the performance or nonperformance of the individual's official duties." 5 U.S.C. § 7353(a). The ethics offices of the House and Senate are empowered to devise reasonable exceptions to this rule. § 7353(b). Senate Rule XXXV and House Rule XXV, clause 5, set forth the gift rules of the respective chambers, which add further limitations on the receipt of gifts by members. These rules were substantially strengthened in 2007, largely as a response to corruption scandals involving high-profile lawmakers.

No member, employee, or officer of the House of Representatives or the Senate may accept gifts or meals from lobbyists unless they fit into certain exceptions, such

---

[4]   Candidates seeking to become members of Congress must file a similar report (with fewer disclosures) within 30 days of becoming a candidate or by May 15 of that year (whichever is later) and in every successive year until the election (§§ 101(d), 102(b)). See also Thomas Little & David Ogle, *The Legislative Branch of State Government: People, Process, and Politics* 113–14 (2006) (providing overview of ethics and conflict of interest rules and state-by-state descriptions); Alan Rosenthal, *The Decline of Representative Democracy: Process, Participation, and Power in State Legislatures* 94–100 (1998) (detailing ethics laws and codes in various states).

[5]   For a clear description of congressional ethics rules, see Robert F. Bauer & Rebecca H. Gordon, *Congressional Ethics: Gifts, Travel, and Outside Income*, in *The Lobbying Manual: A Complete Guide to Federal Lobbying Law and Practice* 107 (Rebecca H. Gordon & Thomas M. Susman eds., 5th ed. 2016).

as a meal that is served at a reception (sometimes called the "toothpick rule") or at a "widely attended" event on a particular issue that attracts many people other than just congressional aides. Furthermore, both chambers have adopted stringent restrictions on the kinds of travel for which private parties can reimburse members and their staff, and lobbyists are entirely banned from paying for member travel. Because Congress has now prohibited much of the travel, entertainment, and gifts previously allowed, the major arena excepted from regulation through ethics rules— campaign fundraisers in Washington and in a lawmaker's state or district—has become an increasingly important way for lobbyists to interact with legislators and their aides. In the past, congressional gift and travel rules were regularly evaded as lawmakers took advantage of loopholes; evasion is more difficult with the current rules but still occurs.[6]

One major change in the congressional gift rules occurred in 2007 when Congress amended the Lobbying Disclosure Act to require that lobbyists certify twice a year that no one covered in their disclosure filings (which may include other employees of the firm who engage in lobbying activities) has provided gifts or offered travel to senators or representatives that would violate the rules. Section 203 of the Honest Leadership and Open Government Act of 2007 (HLOGA), Pub. L. No. 110– 81, 121 Stat. 735, *codified at* 2 U.S.C. § 1604(d)(1)(G). Violations of this provision can be punished by up to $200,000 in fines and, for knowing and corrupt violations, up to five years in prison. Prior to this, House and Senate rules could only be enforced against members and staff, although gifts that were part of a scheme to bribe legislators could always form the basis of a criminal prosecution.

An Oregon Supreme Court case dealt with a First Amendment challenge to that state's gift restrictions. *Vannatta v. Oregon Gov't Ethics Comm'n*, 222 P.3d 1077 (Ore. 2009). A registered lobbyist attacked the gift ban and the restriction on the offering of gifts to lawmakers as an unconstitutional burden on expression protected by the First Amendment. The plaintiff argued that the law, by prohibiting gifts to lawmakers that exceeded $50 in value in a calendar year, banned "expenditures designed to facilitate dialogue and obtain goodwill with public officials." He also contended that the restrictions on communicating offers of gifts discriminated among speech on the basis of content and interfered with the constitutionally protected right to petition government for redress of grievances. The court rejected the attack on the provisions dealing with receipt of gifts because this action is not expressive conduct. Lawmakers and citizens, including lobbyists, can communicate and engage in the range of official conduct without also providing gifts to the public officials. It ruled, however, that the ban on offering gifts above the threshold did impermissibly burden speech and noted that the restrictions on offering gifts were not intended to curtail invidious behavior but were focused on the mere "utterance of an offer" without regard to its effects or intended behavior. Are the federal gift restrictions subject to similar First Amendment attack, either as political expression or as an intrinsic part of petitioning the government for policy change?

---

[6]   See Fredreka Schouten, *Despite Ethics Rules, Congress' Travel Junkets Creep Back Up*, USA Today, Nov. 1, 2011 (noting that travel is now funded by nonprofits, which is allowed by the rules).

2.   *Outside Earned Income Is Limited.* The Ethics Reform Act, as amended in 1990, provides that Congress members can have "outside earned income" no greater than 15% of level II of the executive pay schedule for each calendar year. 5 U.S.C. App. § 501(a)(1). Members may not serve in firms providing professional services with a fiduciary duty, receive compensation for practicing such a profession, serve on corporate boards of directors, or be paid for teaching (without the consent of the ethics body). *Id.* § 502(a). Senate Rule XXXVII(2) provides: "No Member * * * shall engage in any outside business or professional activity or employment for compensation which is inconsistent or in conflict with the conscientious performance of official duties." House Rule XXV(2) provides: "A Member * * * may not receive compensation for affiliating with or being employed by a firm, partnership, association, corporation, or other entity that provides professional services involving a fiduciary relationship except for the practice of medicine." These rules go beyond the statutory requirements and are enforceable by the chambers themselves.

3.   *Post-Employment Lobbying Is Restricted.* The number of former members who become highly compensated lobbyists continues to rankle the public, and there have been calls for reform to address the revolving door between government service and lobbying. As revised by the Ethics Reform Act, 18 U.S.C. § 207(e)(1) prohibits members of the House of Representatives, within a year of leaving office, from lobbying current members or employees of either House. In 2007, HLOGA extended the ban on lobbying that applies to former senators to two years. Unlike some of the other prohibitions, this one is found in the Criminal Code and is enforceable through criminal sanctions. Opponents of longer waiting periods argue that they make public service less attractive. It is too much, they contend, to ask that public servants not only forego large salaries while they work for Congress or the executive branch, but then also to expect them to refrain from using their expertise and skills for a substantial time after they leave government. See David Zaring, *Against Being Against the Revolving Door*, 2013 U. Ill. L. Rev. 507 (arguing that stints in the government and in the private sector can enhance the work done in both and foster citizen participation in government, but focusing mainly on law enforcement jobs).

Former lawmakers also enjoy perks that provide them special access to current legislators, including the use of the members' dining rooms and floor privileges. In the ethics reform bill that Congress enacted in 2007, these privileges were curtailed or eliminated for lawmakers-turned-lobbyists. For example, the Senate denied floor privileges, special parking spaces, and access to the Senate athletic facilities to former members who are currently registered lobbyists. Senate Rule XXIII.

4.   *Honoraria Are Banned.* The Ethics Reform Act of 1989, as amended at 5 U.S.C. App. §§ 501, 505, prohibits any member of Congress or any "officer or employee" of the federal government from "receiv[ing] any honorarium." In *United States v. Nat'l Treasury Emp. Union*, 513 U.S. 454 (1995), the Supreme Court, per Justice Stevens, held that this ban violated the First Amendment as applied to lower-level federal employees. (Examples included a postal employee who gave lectures on the Quaker religion, a NASA employee who lectured on African-American history, and an FDA employee who reviewed dance performances.) The Court balanced the interests of the employee in commenting on matters of public concern against the "undeniably powerful" governmental concern that "that federal officers not misuse

or appear to misuse power by accepting compensation for their unofficial and nonpolitical writing and speaking activities." Here, the Court found that the burden on the employees' speech was significant, while the governmental interest was slight: indeed, the government could cite no examples of lower-level federal employee misconduct relating to honoraria. In other words, a ban that made sense for certain high-level officials whose jobs involved both significant discretion and authority over wide swaths of policy made significantly less sense for other sorts of federal official. "[T]he Government has based its defense of the ban on abuses of honoraria by Members of Congress. Congress reasonably could assume that payments of honoraria to judges or high-ranking officials in the Executive Branch might generate a similar appearance of improper influence. Congress could not, however, reasonably extend that assumption to all [lower-level] federal employees * * *, an immense class of workers with negligible power to confer favors on those who might pay to hear them speak or to read their articles."

Chief Justice Rehnquist dissented, insisting that, "The theory underlying the Court's distinction—that [lower-level] federal employees * * * have negligible power to confer favors on those who might pay to hear them speak or to read their articles—is seriously flawed. Tax examiners, bank examiners, enforcement officials, or any number of federal employees have substantial power to confer favors."

CORRUPTION AND CONFLICT OF INTEREST PROBLEMS

Problem 3-1. Jack Abramoff was a registered lobbyist whose clients included numerous Indian tribes and Foxcom, an Israeli telecommunications start-up. He formed an unofficial business partnership with Michael Scanlon, who ran a lobbying and grassroots public relations firm. Among his many dubious business practices, Abramoff would refer clients to Scanlon's firm for grassroots and public relations services without revealing that he received 50% of the profits from these deals. Abramoff also requested that some clients pay a nonprofit he set up, the Capital Athletic Foundation, rather than his law firm, and he then used the money from the nonprofit to underwrite golf trips for himself and members of Congress. Abramoff had a particularly close relationship with Rep. Bob Ney (R-Ohio), in part because a former Ney staffer joined Abramoff's firm after he left government employment. Neil Volz, Ney's former Chief of Staff, acted as an intermediary between the lobbyist and the Congressman beginning just months after Volz left Capitol Hill.

Among the items of value given to Ney were all-expense-paid trips to the Super Bowl in Florida and golf courses in Scotland, numerous tickets to concerts and sporting events (including tickets to classical and rock concerts worth more than $1,100), tens of thousands of dollars of campaign contributions, and regular meals and drinks at Abramoff's restaurant. In return, Ney agreed to enter certain statements into the *Congressional Record* supporting Abramoff's clients or their positions; to use his position as Chair of the House Administration Committee to endorse Foxcom's bid to provide wireless telephone service to the House; and to work as the co-chair of the relevant conference committee to enact gaming legislation that would benefit Abramoff's tribal clients and to ensure that the government transferred property to a religious school founded by Abramoff. Ney also met with several of Abramoff's clients and promised them his help on matters or indicated to them that Abramoff was an effective lobbyist. Finally,

Ney contacted executive branch officials to influence decisions in ways that benefited Abramoff's clients.

What laws or ethical rules have each of these four men violated? Which particular acts violated which law or rule? Would Abramoff's payment for travel and gifts to Ney be treated differently from the campaign contributions that he provided to Ney? Should they be treated differently? How would each violation be punished? As you read through the Lobbying Disclosure Act, amended in the wake of the Abramoff scandal and discussed in the next subsection, consider how it might apply to these interactions and what it would require be disclosed.

Problem 3-2. Is it corrupt for a politician to break a promise made during a campaign? Take, for example, Representative Marty Meehan (D-Mass.), who in 1995 filed a letter with the clerk of the House of Representatives stating: "Should I be elected to serve more than two additional terms of office in the U.S. House of Representatives following the 104th Congress, by this letter I hereby resign and direct you to remove my name permanently from the Roll of Members." In other words, he purported to voluntarily term limit himself. (See Chapter 2, § 2(B) for a discussion of term limits.) When Meehan changed his mind and announced that he was running for the 107th Congress (an election he ultimately won), the Massachusetts Republican Party began to investigate legal remedies to enforce the resignation letter. Are there other ways to ensure that candidates tell the truth during campaigns?[7] Is this sort of behavior policed effectively by requiring members of Congress to stand for frequent reelection, thereby holding members accountable for their promises? Or is the electoral tie insufficient? Could it even be corrupt to break a campaign promise when everyone understands that campaign themes are often aspirational (or pandering), rather than realistic?

For that matter, is it corrupt to *make* a campaign promise? Suppose a candidate on the campaign trail promises to vote for (or against) some healthcare reform proposal (say, Medicare for all). Couldn't that be understood as a promise to perform an official act (i.e., the vote in the legislature) in exchange for a thing of value (i.e., a vote on election day)? If you don't consider making a campaign promise to be corrupt, why not? Is it important to treat some "things of value" differently than others? And, if so, what's the relevant distinction? For a case concerning whether a campaign promise made generally to all voters could itself be corrupt, see *Brown v. Hartlage*, 456 U.S. 45 (1982) (candidate who promised to accept a lower salary, a promise that violated state law, prosecuted under state corrupt practices act as the equivalent of a bribe; prosecution held unconstitutional under the First Amendment).

C. LOBBYING

The First Amendment to the U.S. Constitution provides that "Congress shall make no law * * * abridging the freedom of speech, or of the press; or the right of the people peaceably to assemble, and to petition the Government for a redress of grievances." The Speech Clause recognizes the general precept that speech, especially about political matters, presumptively cannot be limited by the government. The Petition Clause recognizes the general precept that legislative representatives in a democracy should be open to the viewpoints of their constituents,

---

[7]   See Saul Levmore, *Precommitment Politics*, 82 Va. L. Rev. 567 (1996) (presenting creative approaches to this question).

and the latter in turn should be encouraged to present their proposals and ideas to their representatives. But should "the people" be free to use any means to persuade their representatives to press their views in the legislature?

In the 19th century, lobbying was often thinly disguised bribery. But most modern lobbying is, at least formally, a rather ordinary affair. Almost all organized lobbying before Congress is aimed at getting the group's point of view across to the legislators and influencing legislative decisions.[8] H.R. Mahood, *Interest Groups in American National Politics: An Overview* 54 (2000), offers the following taxonomy of lobbying methods:

- *Direct Lobbying* is the presentation of a group's point of view by the lobbyist to the legislator or the staff. The most common means of direct lobbying are testimony at legislative hearings; contacting legislators by letter, phone, or email; presenting research results; submitting drafts of proposed legislation; and making contributions to legislators' reelection campaigns. Interest groups focus not only on the legislature but also on the executive branch, seeking to influence agency outcomes, the position the executive branch takes on legislation, and other decisions of implementation or agenda setting. Direct lobbying has also long included *social lobbying*, a less substantive and more controversial method of influence. Social interactions lay the groundwork for the future when the lobbyists and the interests they represent will seek access to the legislator and to influence policy outcomes. One variation of social lobbying is to offer legislators gifts, trips, or fees for speaking engagements. One can consider the involvement of lobbyists in raising campaign funds a form of social lobbying when it is not accompanied by any substantive discussion of the issues. Generally, social lobbying is on the decline, in large part because of the new gift, travel, and other conflict of interest rules discussed in the previous section.

- *Indirect Lobbying* involves efforts by interest groups and their lobbyists to stir up outside forces, primarily constituents, to bring pressure to bear. Increasingly, interest groups are using indirect methods, including "stealth campaigns with other organizations, alliances under positive-sounding names such as Citizens for Reform, or sponsorship of research studies or public opinion polls through independent organizations such as think tanks."[9] The most important kind of indirect lobbying is *grassroots lobbying* or "any type of action that attempts to influence inside-the-beltway inhabitants by influencing the attitudes or behavior of outside-the-beltway inhabitants."[10] An interest group stimulates constituent interest by mobilizing its own members, talking with media representatives to ensure that its point of view is presented favorably,

---

[8]   See John Wright, *Interest Groups and Congress: Lobbying, Contributions, and Influence* chap. 4 (2003); Richard Hasen, *Lobbying, Rent-Seeking, and the Constitution*, 64 Stan. L. Rev. 191, 219–25 (2012).

[9]   Darrell West & Burdett Loomis, *The Sound of Money: How Political Interests Get What They Want* 207 (1999). See also Mark Smith, *American Business and Political Power: Public Opinion, Elections, and Democracy* (2000).

[10]   Kenneth Goldstein, *Interest Groups, Lobbying, and Participation in America* 3 (1999).

conducting a public relations campaign to inspire letter writing, phone calls, and emails by constituents, and publicizing the legislator's voting record or "scorecard" on relevant votes.[11] Although there is concern that some of this activity produces "astroturf" (i.e., artificial grassroots) lobbying, thereby giving a misleading impression of the public's views, grassroots lobbying generally communicates substantive and relevant content about public opinion to policymakers and represents one of the most vibrant forms of mass political participation.

William Keefe & Morris Ogul, *The American Legislative Process: Congress and the States* 366–70 (10th ed. 2001), observe that interest groups and their lobbying techniques vary greatly as to effectiveness. Access (presenting the group's point of view) does not ensure success, and organization is not necessarily synonymous with clout. In fact, the term *access* can encompass a variety of concepts: "(1) convincing a policy maker to listen to arguments; (2) establishing a 'regular relationship' with a policy maker for the exchange of information; (3) becoming 'institutionalized' into the policy process, for example, acquiring formal representation on governing boards of agencies; and (4) gaining influence."[12] The most effective groups are those that have large, cohesive, and dispersed memberships, are considered prestigious, have skillful leaders who seem to have the support of the group's members and can rally them on an issue, and have a lot of money to spend. We would add other factors, such as the ability of the groups to form alliances and the value of the group in supplying information (including any monopoly it might have on information).[13]

Lobbyists can play a positive role in the legislative process by providing information to elected officials, who then can focus their energies, and those of their staff, on assessing the credibility of the information and on producing data about aspects of policy that may have escaped the notice of interest groups. Lobbyists produce three different but related kinds of information: information about the status and prospects of pending legislation; information about the electoral ramifications of the legislator's position on proposals; and analyses of the economic, social, and other substantive consequences of bills.[14] Although an interest group and its lobbyists will usually present arguments in a light most favorable to its position, lobbyists suffer reputational sanctions for lying, and competing interest groups have an incentive to point out the flaws and inaccuracies in their opponents' arguments. See Bruce Wolpe

---

[11]   See William Browne, *Lobbying the Public: All-Directional Advocacy*, in *Interest Group Politics* 343 (Allan Cigler & Burdett Loomis eds., 5th ed. 1998). See also Richard Davis, *The Web of Politics: The Internet's Impact on the American Political System* chap. 3 (1999) (analyzing electronic methods of grassroots lobbying and arguing that the new technology merely reinforces past patterns); Jonathan Zellner, Note, *Artificial Grassroots Advocacy and the Constitutionality of Legislative Identification and Control Measures*, 43 Conn. L. Rev. 357, 360–61 (2010) (describing "astroturf" lobbying and its increased use).

[12]   Wright, *supra,* at 77 (citing S.J. Makielski, *Pressure Politics in America* (1980)). See Lloyd Mayer, *What Is This "Lobbying" that We Are All So Worried About?*, 26 Yale L. & Pol'y Rev. 485, 534–39 (2008) (discussing factors that influence clout and access).

[13]   For a discussion of the factors, including access, that seem to allow interest groups to influence political outcomes, see Matt Grossmann, *The Not-So-Special Interests: Interest Groups, Public Representation, and American Governance* 86–90 (2012). On forming alliances, see Kevin Hula, *Lobbying Together: Interest Group Coalitions in Legislative Politics* (1999); on the role of interest groups in providing information and expertise, see Frank Baumgartner, Jeffrey Berry, Marie Hojnacki, David Kimball & Beth Leech, *Lobbying and Policy Change: Who Wins, Who Loses, and Why* 122–27 (2009).

[14]   See Wright, *supra,* at 88–89.

& Bertram Levine, *Lobbying Congress: How the System Works* 13–19 (2d ed. 1996) (including in the "Five Commandments" of lobbying "Tell the Truth" and "Spring No Surprises"). Thus, the information can be accurate and useful, and the government benefits because it has externalized some of its information costs.

Most lobbying activity consists of speech and written communications that are protected by the First Amendment. Very little lobbying involves clearly corrupt activity, and that sort of lobbying (or *influence peddling*) can probably be prosecuted under state or federal bribery, extortion, or gratuity statutes. Think back to the broad wording of § 201, the federal law criminalizing bribery and unlawful gratuities. What sorts of lobbying activities fall within the plain meaning of those provisions? How should courts distinguish corrupt attempts to influence legislators from ordinary politics? Is more regulation needed of behavior that is not quite corrupt but disturbing nonetheless? How would you describe that behavior?

Some pluralist theorists might oppose any additional regulation. Viewing government officials, and especially legislators, as the accommodators of interest group pressures who register the strength of the conflicting pressures and reach an appropriate middle position, pluralists might consider lobbying as simply part of the process itself.[15] This would suggest a relatively *laissez-faire* approach to the political process, although many pluralist thinkers would allow for at least some regulation. David Truman, for example, did not view legislators as utterly passive objects of interest group pressures, and he argued that there were certain basic "rules of the game" (mainly, to avoid the appearance of corruption that would undermine confidence in the legislature) that must be obeyed.[16]

The rules of the game advocated by Truman and others primarily involved disclosure of lobbying activities, because secrecy can allow corruption that the light of public scrutiny can destroy. One of the most influential early works indicting lobbying practices that seemed to thrive when sheltered from public scrutiny was Elmer Schattschneider's *Politics, Pressures and the Tariff* (1935). The study focused on the 1929 House and Senate hearings that crafted what was to become the notorious Smoot-Hawley Tariff of 1930. Schattschneider found that the deliberative process was essentially controlled by lobbyists for American businesses. "Indeed, the language of the hearings often was not what one might expect to find in communications between a sovereign state and its citizens, nor was it, in many instances, that of an inquiry by a governmental body into the merits of a public policy. It was, rather, in the style and manner of equals engaged in negotiation." *Id.* at 43–44. The most striking consequences were that Congress acted with skewed and often inaccurate information and that overall policy was therefore dramatically tilted.

At the same time Schattschneider's book was published, Senate hearings revealed similar patterns of conduct (misleading information, pressure, "inside" access) by public utility lobbyists. Responding to the Senate hearings, Senator Hugo Black (D-Ala.) championed lobbying reform in the mid-1930s. But the compromise

---

[15] See Earl Latham, *The Group Basis of Politics: A Study in Basing-Point Legislation* 35–36 (1952); Nelson Polsby, *Money Gains Access. So What?*, N.Y. Times, August 13, 1997, at A23.

[16] David Truman, *The Governmental Process: Political Interests and Public Opinion* 114–15, 159, 512 (1951).

bill that was crafted by a conference committee was rejected decisively by the House, defeated by a 3–1 majority. Lobbying reform was a dead issue in Congress for the next ten years, although Congress did enact the Foreign Agents Registration Act (FARA) in 1938 to expose Nazi propaganda efforts. FARA, as amended in 1966 and 1995, imposes substantial registration and disclosure obligations on representatives of a "foreign principal" before Congress, agencies, and the executive. 22 U.S.C. § 611 *et seq.*

The Joint Committee on the Organization of Congress proposed the Legislative Reorganization Act of 1946, which included a lobbying reform title as a minor part of its overall package of reforms.[17] Congressional consideration of the lobbying title was perfunctory, confused, and skeptical—but the whole package passed intact and became the Federal Regulation of Lobbying Act (FRLA), §§ 301–11, Pub. L. No. 79–601, 60 Stat. 812, 839–42. The FRLA was aimed primarily at disclosure of both contributions to a person who lobbied the Congress and the expenditures made by lobbyists. The Act clearly encompassed more than natural persons; it defined "person" to include not only individuals but also partnerships, committees, associations, corporations, and other organizations or groups. Because the bill had been cobbled together from past proposals and received little consideration during enactment, however, other aspects of its scope were not entirely clear.

Section 305 required that "[e]very person receiving any contributions or expending any money" for the principal purpose of influencing "directly or indirectly" the "passage or defeat of any legislation" must report the sources of contributions of $500 or greater and the recipients of expenditures of $10 or more. (The "principal purpose" language was not included in § 305, but was incorporated by a reference to § 307.) Section 307, which was labeled "Persons to Whom Applicable" and appeared to apply to the entire Act, described the class of persons regulated as "any person * * * who by himself, or through any agent or employee or other persons in any manner whatsoever, directly or indirectly, solicits, collects, or receives money or any other thing of value to be used principally to aid" in influencing "directly or indirectly" the "passage or defeat of any legislation." Thus, while § 305 seemed to include in the regulatory ambit anyone who spent money on lobbying, regardless of the source of that money, the provision that explicitly defined the group of people subject to disclosure limited the Act's effect only to those who received contributions from others that were then used for lobbying expenses. To make things more confusing, § 305 referred to § 307, but only to incorporate certain language regarding the purpose of actions, not specifically to include the limitation to persons receiving contributions.

In addition, § 308 of FRLA required that persons "engage[d] for pay or for any consideration for the purpose of attempting to influence the passage or defeat of any legislation by the Congress of the United States shall * * * register with the Clerk of the House of Representatives and the Secretary of the Senate." Violations of FRLA were punishable by a fine of up to $5,000 or imprisonment up to a year. The

---

[17]   See Belle Zeller, *American Government and Politics: The Federal Regulation of Lobbying Act*, 42 Am. Pol. Sci. Rev. 239 (1948) (providing detailed legislative history of Act).

constitutionality of FRLA was challenged in the following case, which remains the foundational case with respect to the constitutional validity of lobbying regulations.

UNITED STATES V. HARRISS
Supreme Court of the United States, 1954.
347 U.S. 612, 74 S.Ct. 808, 98 L. Ed. 989.

CHIEF JUSTICE WARREN delivered the opinion of the Court.

[The plaintiffs in this case were Robert Harriss, a commodity broker; Tom Linder, Commissioner of Agriculture for the State of Georgia; Ralph Moore, a trader of commodity futures; and the National Farm Committee (NFC), of which Harriss, Linder, and Moore were directors. Harriss funneled money to Moore ($50,000 in the last three months of 1946 alone), who would host dinners for members of Congress in the name of NFC and other farmer groups. It is not clear what subjects were discussed at these social gatherings. None of the individuals, nor NFC, registered or delivered reports under FRLA. The Justice Department secured indictments against Harriss for failure to report expenditure of his own money to influence legislation; Linder and Moore for seeking to influence Congress for pay without registering; and NFC for failing to report the solicitation and receipt of contributions to influence the enactment of legislation. The District Court judge dismissed the indictment against Harriss, Linder, Moore, and NFC, on the ground that FRLA as enacted was unconstitutional, a decision appealed to the Supreme Court.]

[I] The constitutional requirement of definiteness is violated by a criminal statute that fails to give a person of ordinary intelligence fair notice that his contemplated conduct is forbidden by the statute. The underlying principle is that no man shall be held criminally responsible for conduct which he could not reasonably understand to be proscribed. * * *

* * * The key section of the Lobbying Act is § 307, entitled "Persons to Whom Applicable." This section modifies the substantive provisions of the Act, including § 305 and § 308. In other words, unless a "person" falls within the category established by § 307, the disclosure requirements of § 305 and § 308 are inapplicable. Thus coverage under the Act is limited to those persons (except for the specified political committees) who solicit, collect, or receive contributions of money or other thing of value, and then only if "the principal purpose" of either the persons or the contributions is to aid in the accomplishment of the aims set forth in § 307(a) and (b). [These sections describe two purposes: "The passage or defeat of any legislation by the Congress of the United States" and "To influence, directly or indirectly, the passage or defeat of any legislation by the Congress of the United States."] In any event, the solicitation, collection, or receipt of money or other thing of value is a prerequisite to coverage under the Act.

The Government urges a much broader construction—namely, that under § 305 a person must report his expenditures to influence legislation even though he does not solicit, collect, or receive contributions as provided in § 307.[8] Such a construction,

------

[8] The Government's view is based on a variance between the language of § 307 and the language of § 305. Section 307 refers to any person who "solicits, collects, or receives" contributions; § 305, however, refers not only to "receiving any contributions" but also to "expending any money." It is apparently the Government's

we believe, would do violence to the title and language of § 307 as well as its legislative history. If the construction urged by the Government is to become law, that is for Congress to accomplish by further legislation.

We now turn to the alleged vagueness of the purposes set forth in § 307(a) and (b). As in *United States v. Rumely*, 345 U.S. 41 (1953), which involved the interpretation of similar language, we believe this language should be construed to refer only to "lobbying in its commonly accepted sense"—to direct communication with members of Congress on pending or proposed federal legislation. The legislative history of the Act makes clear that, at the very least, Congress sought disclosure of such direct pressures, exerted by the lobbyists themselves or through their hirelings or through an artificially stimulated letter campaign.[10] It is likewise clear that Congress would have intended the Act to operate on this narrower basis, even if a broader application to organizations seeking to propagandize the general public were not permissible.

There remains for our consideration the meaning of "the principal purpose" and "to be used principally to aid." The legislative history of the Act indicates that the term "principal" was adopted merely to exclude from the scope of § 307 those contributions and persons having only an "incidental" purpose of influencing legislation. Conversely, the "principal purpose" requirement does not exclude a contribution which in substantial part is to be used to influence legislation through direct communication with Congress or a person whose activities in substantial part are directed to influencing legislation through direct communication with Congress. If it were otherwise—if an organization, for example, were exempted because lobbying was only one of its main activities—the Act would in large measure be reduced to a mere exhortation against abuse of the legislative process. In construing

---

contention that § 307—since it makes no reference to expenditures—is inapplicable to the expenditure provisions of § 305. Section 307, however, limits the application of § 305 as a whole, not merely a part of it.

[10]   The Lobbying Act was enacted as Title III of the Legislative Reorganization Act of 1946, which was reported to Congress by the Joint Committee on the Organization of Congress. The Senate and House reports accompanying the bill were identical with respect to Title III. Both declared that the Lobbying Act applies "chiefly to three distinct classes of so-called lobbyists:

"First. Those who do not visit the Capitol but initiate propaganda from all over the country in the form of letters and telegrams, many of which have been based entirely upon misinformation as to facts. This class of persons and organizations will be required under the title, not to cease or curtail their activities in any respect, but merely to disclose the sources of their collections and the methods in which they are disbursed.

"Second. The second class of lobbyists are those who are employed to come to the Capitol under the false impression that they exert some powerful influence over Members of Congress. These individuals spend their time in Washington presumably exerting some mysterious influence with respect to the legislation in which their employers are interested, but carefully conceal from Members of Congress whom they happen to contact the purpose of their presence. The title in no wise prohibits or curtails their activities. It merely requires that they shall register and disclose the sources and purposes of their employment and the amount of their compensation.

"Third. There is a third class of entirely honest and respectable representatives of business, professional, and philanthropic organizations who come to Washington openly and frankly to express their views for or against legislation, many of whom serve a useful and perfectly legitimate purpose in expressing the views and interpretations of their employers with respect to legislation which concerns them. They will likewise be required to register and state their compensation and the sources of their employment."

S. Rep. No. 1400, 79th Cong., 2d Sess., p. 27; Committee Print, July 22, 1946, statement by Representative Monroney on Legislative Reorganization Act of 1946, 79th Cong., 2d Sess., pp. 32–33. See also the statement in the Senate by Senator La Follette, who was Chairman of the Joint Committee, at 92 Cong. Rec. 6367–6368.

the Act narrowly to avoid constitutional doubts, we must also avoid a construction that would seriously impair the effectiveness of the Act in coping with the problem it was designed to alleviate.

To summarize, therefore, there are three prerequisites to coverage under § 307: (1) the "person" must have solicited, collected, or received contributions; (2) one of the main purposes of such "person," or one of the main purposes of such contributions, must have been to influence the passage or defeat of legislation by Congress; (3) the intended method of accomplishing this purpose must have been through direct communication with members of Congress. And since § 307 modifies the substantive provisions of the Act, our construction of § 307 will of necessity also narrow the scope of § 305 and § 308, the substantive provisions underlying the information in this case. Thus § 305 is limited to those persons who are covered by § 307; and when so covered, they must report all contributions and expenditures having the purpose of attempting to influence legislation through direct communication with Congress. Similarly, § 308 is limited to those persons (with the stated exceptions) who are covered by § 307 and who, in addition, engage themselves for pay or for any other valuable consideration for the purpose of attempting to influence legislation through direct communication with Congress. Construed in this way, the Lobbying Act meets the constitutional requirement of definiteness.

[II] Thus construed, §§ 305 and 308 also do not violate the freedoms guaranteed by the First Amendment—freedom to speak, publish, and petition the Government.

Present-day legislative complexities are such that individual members of Congress cannot be expected to explore the myriad pressures to which they are regularly subjected. Yet full realization of the American ideal of government by elected representatives depends to no small extent on their ability to properly evaluate such pressures. Otherwise the voice of the people may all too easily be drowned out by the voice of special interest groups seeking favored treatment while masquerading as proponents of the public weal. This is the evil which the Lobbying Act was designed to help prevent.

Toward that end, Congress has not sought to prohibit these pressures. It has merely provided for a modicum of information from those who for hire attempt to influence legislation or who collect or spend funds for that purpose. It wants only to know who is being hired, who is putting up the money, and how much. * * *

The judgment below is reversed and the cause is remanded to the District Court for further proceedings not inconsistent with this opinion.

MR. JUSTICE DOUGLAS, with whom MR. JUSTICE BLACK concurs, dissenting. * * *

I am now convinced that the formula adopted to save this Act is too dangerous for use. It can easily ensnare people who have done no more than exercise their constitutional rights of speech, assembly, and press. * * *

It is contended that the Act plainly applies:

—to persons who pay others to present views to Congress either in committee hearings or by letters or other communications to Congress or Congressmen and

—to persons who spend money to induce others to communicate with Congress.

The Court adopts that view, with one minor limitation which the Court places on the Act—that only persons who solicit, collect, or receive money are included.

The difficulty is that the Act has to be rewritten and words actually added and subtracted to produce that result. * * *

What contributions might be used "principally to aid" in influencing "directly or indirectly, the passage or defeat" of any such measure by Congress? When is one retained for the purpose of influencing the "passage or defeat of any legislation"?

(1)   One who addresses a trade union for repeal of a labor law certainly hopes to influence legislation.

(2)   So does a manufacturers' association which runs ads in newspapers for a sales tax.

(3)   So does a farm group which undertakes to raise money for an educational program to be conducted in newspapers, magazines, and on radio and television, showing the need for revision of our attitude on world trade.

(4)   So does a group of oil companies which puts agents in the Nation's capital to sound the alarm at hostile legislation, to exert influence on Congressmen to defeat it, to work on the Hill for the passage of laws favorable to the oil interests.

(5)   So does a business, labor, farm, religious, social, racial, or other group which raises money to contact people with the request that they write their Congressman to get a law repealed or modified, to get a proposed law passed, or themselves to propose a law.

Are all of these activities covered by the Act? If one is included why are not the others? The Court apparently excludes the kind of activities listed in categories (1), (2), and (3) and includes part of the activities in (4) and (5)—those which entail contacts with the Congress.

There is, however, difficulty in that course, a difficulty which seems to me to be insuperable. I find no warrant in the Act for drawing the line, as the Court does, between "direct communication with Congress" and other pressures on Congress. The Act is as much concerned with one as with the other.

The words "direct communication with Congress" are not in the Act. Congress was concerned with the raising of money to aid in the passage or defeat of legislation, whatever tactics were used. But the Court not only strikes out one whole group of activities—to influence "indirectly"—but substitutes a new concept for the remaining group—to influence "directly." To influence "directly" the passage or defeat of legislation includes any number of methods—for example, nationwide radio, television or advertising programs promoting a particular measure, as well as the "buttonholing" of Congressmen. To include the latter while excluding the former is to rewrite the Act. * * *

[We have omitted the dissenting opinion of JUSTICE JACKSON, who believed that FRLA infringed on the Petition Clause of the First Amendment. "[O]ur constitutional system is to allow the greatest freedom of access to Congress, so that the people may press for their selfish interests, with Congress acting as arbiter of their demands and conflicts."]

NOTES ON THE AFTERMATH OF HARRISS

1. *The Court's Analysis.* The Court in *Harriss* essentially rewrote the statute in order to save its constitutionality. Was the Court on firm ground in reading § 307's "principal purpose" requirement into §§ 305 and 308? Where does the Court find the "direct communication" requirement? In its desire to trim back a "vague" statute, has the Court instead created a confusing one?

Consider whether the Court was doing the statute a "favor" by rewriting rather than just invalidating it. Justice Jackson thought not. Instead, he made an institutional argument for striking down the law, rather than redrafting it. "Congress has power to regulate lobbying for hire as a business or profession and to require such agents to disclose their principals, their activities, and their receipts. However, to reach the real evils of lobbying without cutting into the constitutional right of petition is a difficult and delicate task for which the Court's action today gives little guidance. I am in doubt whether the Act as construed does not permit applications which would abridge the right of petition, for which clear, safe and workable channels must be maintained. I think we should point out the defects and limitations which condemn this Act so clearly that the Court cannot sustain it as written, and leave its rewriting to Congress. After all, it is Congress that should know from experience both the good in the right of petition and the evils of professional lobbying." Is he right? Think about his observation again after you read about the aftermath of *Harriss*, and again later in this chapter when we turn to the concept of due process of lawmaking.

2. *The Impact of* Harriss. The Supreme Court's decision remanded *Harriss* to the lower court for further proceedings. The Justice Department not only abandoned the Harriss prosecutions (the last indictment, against Moore, was dropped on November 2, 1955), but essentially also abandoned any serious effort to enforce the statute, after having been fairly active between 1947 and 1954. Only a handful of indictments were returned under the Act after 1955, and the Justice Department testified in 1979 that the statute was a dead letter.

Congress itself expressed dissatisfaction with the statute as reconstructed. In the wake of the Watergate scandal and with a heightened sensitivity to ethics issues, the Senate Committee on Government Operations reported the following defects:

- Groups that used their own funds in an attempt to influence legislation were not required to register unless they solicited, collected, or received funds from others for that purpose.

- FRLA did not apply to organizations or individuals unless lobbying was their principal purpose. Due to the vagueness of the definition, many organizations did not register at all, concluding that lobbying was not their "principal purpose."

- FRLA did not clearly cover efforts by a lobbyist that did not involve direct contact with Congress. Thus, lobbyists who attempted to influence Congress by soliciting others to communicate with Congress did not report these grassroots lobbying efforts.

- FRLA did not clearly include lobbying communications with staff employees of Congress members.

- FRLA's reporting requirements were so vague and ambiguous that the lobbyists who did report often filed incomplete information or interpreted the requirements differently. Some groups considered more kinds of expenses to be related to lobbying than others. As a result, it was difficult to make a meaningful comparison between the reports filed by any two lobbyists.

See Senate Report No. 94–763 on S. 2477, 94th Cong., 2d Sess. (1976).

* * *

After years of dissatisfaction with FRLA and increasing public concern about lobbying excesses, Congress finally became serious about revising the lobbying laws when Senator Carl Levin (D-Mich.) held hearings on the topic in 1991 in the Senate Governmental Affairs Subcommittee on Oversight of Government Management. In 1993, both houses of Congress passed versions of a comprehensive lobbying disclosure bill. The conference committee managed to draft a compromise proposal, but opposition to the proposal had developed since floor consideration.

Most significantly, a coalition of interests had come together to oppose disclosure of grassroots lobbying. This coalition included a number of unusual political bedfellows, including the Christian Coalition and the American Civil Liberties Union. They argued that the reform proposal would violate the First Amendment by requiring them to open their membership lists to public scrutiny. Although the conference report passed the House, it was killed in the Senate by a filibuster led by the perennial opponent of campaign finance reform laws as well as this particular lobbying reform bill, Mitch McConnell (R-Ky.). In the next Congress, proponents dropped this controversial provision and made other concessions, and the Lobbying Disclosure Act of 1995 (LDA), Pub. L. No. 104–65, 109 Stat. 691, passed unanimously.

Lobbying and ethics reform became a salient issue again in the 110th Congress in the wake of several scandals involving lobbyists and members of Congress. For example, as part of the scandal involving lobbyist Jack Abramoff (detailed in Problem 3-1, *supra*), Representative Bob Ney (R-Ohio) pled guilty to conspiracy to defraud his constituents of their right to his honest service and making false statements about the items he received from Abramoff and others, among other things. Representative Randall "Duke" Cunningham (R-Calif.) pled guilty in 2005 to various charges stemming from his accepting at least $2.4 million in bribes. Cunningham, a member of the Defense Appropriations Subcommittee, provided a "menu" to defense contractors from which the contractor could determine how many millions of dollars in defense and intelligence contracts would be awarded to the contractor based upon the value of the bribe. Cunningham's dealings were more closely scrutinized, and eventually led to his arrest, when he sold his house to a defense contractor for substantially more than market value. Other bribes he admitted receiving included a used Rolls-Royce, antique furniture, jewelry, and money for his daughter's graduation party.

As with the 1995 LDA, original ethics reform proposals were more far reaching than the bill that ultimately passed, the Honest Leadership and Open Government Act of 2007 (HLOGA), Pub. L. No. 110–81, 121 Stat. 735. Again, for example, attempts to extend the Act's provisions to some grassroots lobbying were quickly abandoned after facing stiff opposition from many groups active in the legislative realm. The ultimate compromise was passed overwhelmingly by both houses (411–8 in the House and 83–14 in the Senate) in identical form to avoid a conference committee, and the Act was sent to the President just days before Congress left on its August break. With two former lawmakers serving prison time, others in trouble, and campaign promises of cleaning up Congress' act in danger of remaining unfulfilled, legislators did not want to return to their districts and states without having taken action on anti-corruption legislation.

The core of the LDA, as amended by HLOGA, remains registration and reporting requirements. Every lobbyist and organization employing lobbyists (except those meeting a de minimis exception) is required to register with the Secretary of the Senate and Clerk of the House of Representatives. The registration must, inter alia, identify the lobbyist's clients, as well as any other organization that both contributes more than $5000 per quarter to fund lobbying activities and "actively participates in the planning, supervision, or control of such lobbying activities." The registration must also include "the general issue areas in which the registrant expects to engage in lobbying activities on behalf of the client; and to the extent practicable, specific issues that have * * * already been addressed or are likely to be addressed in lobbying activities." The registration must also identify any lobbyists who have held certain executive or legislative branch positions in the last twenty years. 2 U.S.C. § 1603.

Lobbyists (or the organizations employing them) are also required to file quarterly reports with the Secretary of the Senate and the Clerk of the House. The reports are client-specific and must identify the client. For each "general issue area" for which the registrant lobbied for that client in the preceding quarter, the report must specify:

> (A) a list of the specific issues upon which a lobbyist employed by the registrant engaged in lobbying activities, including, to the maximum extent practicable, a list of bill numbers and references to specific executive branch actions;

> (B) a statement of the Houses of Congress and the Federal agencies contacted by lobbyists employed by the registrant on behalf of the client;

> (C) a list of the employees of the registrant who acted as lobbyists on behalf of the client; * * *

The report must also include "a good faith estimate" of the total amount of income from the client (or, in the case of registrants lobbying on their own behalf, of the total amount expended in connection with lobbying activities). 2 U.S.C. § 1604.

The Secretary of the Senate and Clerk of the House are directed to use the registration and reports to create "a publicly available list of all registered lobbyists, lobbying firms, and their clients" as well as to allow public access to registrations and reports, including "mak[ing] them available to the public over the Internet, without a fee or other access charge, in a searchable, sortable, and downloadable manner." Moreover, if they have warned a lobbyist or lobbying firm that it is out of compliance with the Act and the lobbyist or firm has not come into compliance, the Secretary and Clerk are empowered to make a referral to the U.S. Attorney for the District of Columbia. 2 U.S.C. § 1605.

Anyone who "knowingly" fails to remedy a defective filing after having been notified or otherwise fails to comply with the Act is subject a civil fine of up to $200,000. Anyone who "knowingly and corruptly fails to comply with any provision of this chapter shall be imprisoned for not more than 5 years or fined under title 18 [the title of the U.S. Code dealing with criminal penalties], or both." 2 U.S.C. § 1606.

Finally, but quite importantly, the Act defines sixteen of its terms. A few of the more important ones:

(2) CLIENT.—The term "client" means any person or entity that employs or retains another person for financial or other compensation to conduct lobbying activities on behalf of that person or entity. A person or entity whose employees act as lobbyists on its own behalf is both a client and an employer of such employees. In the case of a coalition or association that employs or retains other persons to conduct lobbying activities, the client is the coalition or association and not its individual members. * * *

(7) LOBBYING ACTIVITIES.—The term "lobbying activities" means lobbying contacts and efforts in support of such contacts, including preparation and planning activities, research and other background work that is intended, at the time it is performed, for use in contacts, and coordination with the lobbying activities of others.

(8) LOBBYING CONTACT.—

(A) DEFINITION.—The term "lobbying contact" means any oral or written communication (including an electronic communication) to a covered executive branch official or a covered legislative branch official that is made on behalf of a client with regard to—

(i)   the formulation, modification, or adoption of Federal legislation (including legislative proposals);

(ii) the formulation, modification, or adoption of a Federal rule, regulation, Executive order, or any other program, policy, or position of the United States Government;

(iii) the administration or execution of a Federal program or policy (including the negotiation, award, or administration of a Federal contract, grant, loan, permit, or license); or

(iv) the nomination or confirmation of a person for a position subject to confirmation by the Senate.

(B) EXCEPTIONS.—The term "lobbying contact" does not include a communication that is—

(i)   made by a public official acting in the public official's official capacity; * * *

(iii) made in a speech, article, publication or other material that is distributed and made available to the public, or through radio, television, cable television, or other medium of mass communication; * * *

(v)   a request for a meeting, a request for the status of an action, or any other similar administrative request, if the request does not include an attempt to influence a covered executive branch official or a covered legislative branch official; * * *

(xiv) a written comment filed in the course of a public proceeding or any other communication that is made on the record in a public proceeding;

(xv) a petition for agency action made in writing and required to be a matter of public record pursuant to established agency procedures;

(xvi) made on behalf of an individual with regard to that individual's benefits, employment, or other personal matters involving only that individual, except that this clause does not apply to any communication with—(I) a covered executive branch official, or (II) a covered legislative branch official (other than the individual's elected Members of Congress or employees who work under such Members' direct supervision), with respect to the formulation, modification, or adoption of private legislation for the relief of that individual;

(xvii) a disclosure by an individual that is protected under the amendments made by the Whistleblower Protection Act of 1989 [5 U.S.C. § 1211 *et seq.*], under the Inspector General Act of 1978 [5 U.S.C. App. § 1 *et seq.*] or under another provision of law;

(xviii) made by [a church, an association of churches, or a religious order]. * * *

(10) LOBBYIST.—The term "lobbyist" means any individual who is employed or retained by a client for financial or other compensation for services that include more than one lobbying contact, other than an individual whose lobbying activities constitute less than 20 percent of the time engaged in the services provided by such individual to that client over a 3-month period.

"Covered executive branch officials" include the president, vice president, and all senior executive branch officials. "Covered legislative branch officials" include all members of Congress and their staffers. 2. U.S.C. § 1602.

NOTES ON THE LOBBYING DISCLOSURE ACT[18]

1. *Lobbying Contacts and Lobbying Activities.* The Act distinguishes between *lobbying contacts* and *lobbying activities.* The Act's requirements are triggered when an individual makes a lobbying contact, which is a certain kind of communication to a covered official. Once such a contact has occurred, the individual must report on all her lobbying activities, which, among other things, include planning and preparing for the contact. An individual who makes such a contact is considered a lobbyist unless her lobbying activities constitute less than 20% of the services she provides a client during a three-month period. As you can see, the definitions of *lobbying contact, lobbying activities,* and *lobbyist* work together to determine when the Act's registration and disclosure provisions are triggered. In addition, it is clear that the definitions of these terms were drafted to address some of the problems in FRLA. For example, the 20% threshold provides a concrete way to determine whether someone's activities before the government are significant enough to make her a lobbyist. Furthermore, a communication need merely relate to legislation, executive branch rules, federal policies, nominations, and the

---

[18]   For a comprehensive explanation and analysis of LDA and HLOGA, as well as other rules applying to lobbyists at the federal level, see *The Lobbying Manual: A Complete Guide to Federal Lobbying Law and Practice* (Rebecca H. Gordon & Thomas M. Susman eds., 5th ed. 2016).

like; it need not be intended to influence the passage or defeat of legislation. Interestingly, the definition of *lobbying contact* depends in large part on a series of exceptions. Perhaps drafters believed it was easier to state what kinds of communication are *not* lobbying and thus sought to define the term accordingly. Do these interlocking definitions capture your intuitions about what should and should not be considered "lobbying"? What, if anything, should be covered that is not? And what, if anything, that is currently covered should be omitted?

Is LDA specific enough to withstand constitutional challenge, a case that would be governed by *Harriss*, as well as other First Amendment precedents in the realm of political speech? As in those cases, a court considering a challenge to the Act would apply strict scrutiny to this law that burdens fundamental political rights such as the right to petition the federal government and the right of free speech.

2.   *Effects of LDA.* LDA has been in effect since January 1, 1996, and significantly more information about lobbying at the federal level is now available to the press and the public. For example, more people and organizations are registering. Before 1996, the Government Accountability Office found that only 6,000 individuals and organizations had registered with Congress. As of 2017, the number of lobbyists registered with the Senate stood at 13,735, with 4,454 lobbying organizations filing. (Remember that a lobbying firm can file one registration listing all its employees.) These lobbyists represented a total of 17,134 clients.[19]

The Center for Responsive Politics reported that spending on federal lobbying in 2018 hit an all-time high of $3.46 billion. The top industries with regard to lobbying expenses were pharmaceutical businesses ($283 million), the insurance industry ($158 million), electronics manufacturing and equipment companies ($147 million), business associations ($142 million), oil and gas companies ($125 million), and electric utilities ($122 million). The Chamber of Commerce (and its affiliates) topped the list with respect to individual companies and trade organizations, shelling out nearly $95 million on federal lobbying in 2018. The second-highest spender, the National Association of Realtors, spent nearly $73 million.[20] Trade organizations representing corporate and business interests are extremely active in Washington, a phenomenon that merits study because membership in such organizations requires individual interests to cooperate and compromise. Participation in coalitions not only enhances the interests' clout on the Hill, but companies also participate to influence the trade organizations' positions so that they are consistent with their own interests.[21]

Three of the last four presidents have issued executive orders requiring administration appointees to take an "ethics pledge." Bill Clinton's pledge, Exec. Order No. 12834, 58 Fed. Reg. 5911 (Jan. 20, 1993), focused exclusively on post-government-service lobbying. It prohibited former officials from lobbying anyone in the agency in which they served (or the Executive Office of the President, if they served there) for five years after leaving the post. Barack Obama's pledge, Exec. Order No. 13490, 74 Fed. Reg.

---

[19]   U.S. Senate, *Data Summaries* (Sept. 30, 2017), https://www.senate.gov/legislative/Public_Disclosure/DataSummaries.htm.

[20]   Ctr. for Responsive Pol., *Lobbying Database: Overview* (2019), https://www.opensecrets.org/lobby/; Ctr. for Responsive Pol., *Lobbying Database: Top Industries, 2018*, https://www.opensecrets.org/lobby/top.php?showYear=2018&indexType=i; Ctr. for Responsive Pol., *Lobbying Database: Top Spenders, 2018*, https://www.opensecrets.org/lobby/top.php?showYear=2018&indexType=s.

[21]   Lee Drutman, *Trade Associations, the Collective Action Dilemma, and the Problem of Cohesion*, in *Interest Group Politics* 74 (Allen Cigler & Burdett Loomis eds., 8th ed. 2012).

4673 (Jan. 21, 2009), was more extensive. Like the Clinton order, it banned post-government-service lobbying: in particular, officials who left the administration were banned from lobbying the executive branch for the remainder of the Obama Administration. Unlike the Clinton order, the Obama order also focused on appointees' *pre*-government service employment: it forbade any appointee from participating in any matter involving former employers and clients for a period of two years; it forbade appointees who were registered lobbyists from participating in any matter on which they had lobbied within the last two years or "in any specific issue areas in which that particular matter falls"; and it forbade registered lobbyists from seeking employment with any executive branch agency that they had lobbied in the past two years. Donald Trump's pledge, Exec. Order No. 13770, 82 Fed. Reg. 9333 (Jan. 28, 2017), was largely patterned on the Obama order.[22]

Of course, having these pledges on the books is one thing; enforcing them is another. The Obama administration generally took a hard line, with the effect that lobbyists were largely kept out of the executive branch during his presidency. In a few instances, waivers were granted—including for a former Raytheon lobbyist to become Deputy Secretary of Defense and a former lobbyist for Goldman Sachs to become the Secretary of the Treasury's Chief of Staff—but the bad press surrounding these exceptions soon convinced the administration to grant even fewer, including with respect to people who came from the reform sector. The Trump administration, on the other hand, has been considerably laxer.[23]

One effect of the Obama-era rules, as well as of recurring anti-lobbyist public sentiment, has been a demand for formal methods of de-registering as a lobbyist. Previously, some would register even when they might not clearly meet the requirements or would continue to be registered after ceasing lobbying activities because there was no perceived disadvantage to registration and disclosure. Instead, people were counseled to register and remain registered when in doubt: better safe than sorry. As soon as the status of lobbyist resulted in concrete negative consequences, the Secretary of the Senate and the Clerk of the House—the officials responsible for the registration system—began to receive questions about de-registering. In June 2009, they released guidance about terminating registrations if a currently registered lobbyist "reasonably" expects that she will not be making lobbying contacts on behalf of a client at any time in the future, or if she has spent less than 20% of her time lobbying for a client in the previous quarter and expects to spend less than 20% of her time doing so in the next quarter.[24] Anecdotally, some observers have noted that many who might have been willing to register as lobbyists in the past have avoided that process and portray themselves as "senior advisors" on policy, giving rise to fears that increased regulation of lobbyists may have actually reduced transparency.

3.   *Increasing the Amount and Relevance of Disclosure.* The mandated public disclosure of registration and reports under LDA and HLOGA, including the requirement

---

[22]   For an excellent comparison of the three pledges, see Jacob R. Straus, Cong. Research Serv., R44974, *Ethics Pledges and Other Executive Branch Appointee Restrictions Since 1993: Historical Perspective, Current Practices, and Options for Change* 8–15, 18–25 (2017).

[23]   See Philip Bump, *Sustain the Swamp: Hundreds of Lobbyists Swim Through Trump's Administration*, Wash. Post (Mar. 8, 2019), https://www.washingtonpost.com/politics/2019/03/08/sustain-swamp-hundreds-lobbyists-swim-through-trumps-administration/.

[24]   See *Lobbying Disclosure Act Guidance* 28–29 (rev. Jan. 31, 2017), https://lobbyingdisclosure.house.gov/ldaguidance.pdf.

of publication online, has facilitated the use and dissemination of this information by media outlets and public interest groups. Indeed, much of the information about lobbyists and lobbying relayed above would have been considerably more difficult, if not impossible, to compile without the legally mandated disclosure regime.

HLOGA closed or reduced some of the loopholes in LDA's coverage, but did not eliminate all gaps. A crucial improvement made in 2007 was to lower LDA's thresholds for reporting and to require quarterly, rather than semiannual, reports on lobbying activities. Now lobbyists must disclose income from each client in increments of $10,000 (rather than $20,000 as required by the 1995 Act). Another major change in 2007 was the requirement that persons covered by LDA file reports detailing their campaign contributions and, on the other side of the campaign-finance equation, the requirement that federal candidates and political committees disclose contribution "bundling" by lobbyists (see Chapter 2, § 3(A)(2) for a discussion of bundling).

Before the 2007 amendments, LDA did not require that lobbyists reveal all the members of coalitions that hired them; only the names of organizational members that contributed more than $10,000 in a six-month period and that planned, supervised, or controlled, *in whole or in major part*, lobbying activities had to be listed in registration forms. Because interest groups work increasingly through coalitions to enhance their clout and broaden their base of support, this gap in the disclosure law was a target of reformers. HLOGA increased the disclosure relating to coalitions to include any organization that contributes more than $5,000 in any quarter and that "actively participates" in the planning, supervision, or control of lobbying activities. In other words, the organization need not be the major force behind the coalition; it will be disclosed as long as it is actively participating in the group. Balancing this more aggressive disclosure is language that protects individuals from disclosure and that allows a coalition to meet some of the disclosure requirements by posting information on its website.

4.   *Enforcing LDA.* Before the 2007 amendments, LDA was enforced through civil fines that could be calibrated up to $50,000 to reflect the "extent and gravity of the violation." (This was an approach different from the criminal sanctions in FRLA.) In the hearings on the 2007 Act, a House committee noted that there was substantial noncompliance with LDA's disclosure provisions, with more than 2,000 late submissions, failure to file certain forms by virtually all the top lobbying firms, and "almost 300 individuals, companies or associates [who] have lobbied without being registered." H.R. Rep. No. 110–161, 110th Cong., 1st Sess., at 10 (2007) (citing study by the Center for Public Integrity of activity since 1998). Firms realized that they could understate their expenses or fail to report certain lobbying contacts without much risk of a sanction. By 2005, the Department of Justice had pursued only thirteen cases out of the possible LDA violations referred to it by Congress. Six cases had been resolved; three resulted in total fines of $47,000.[25]

Accordingly, HLOGA increased the possible civil fines to $200,000 and authorized criminal prosecutions for knowing and corrupt violations of the Act. In criminal cases, offenders can be sentenced to up to five years in prison, as well as fined. In addition, the Attorney General is required to submit semiannual reports on the aggregate number of enforcement actions and the sentences imposed. Between 2009 and 2018, the U.S.

---

[25]   Kenneth Doyle, *Love It or Hate It, Lobbying, Ethics Bill Seen as Sea Change for Industry*, BNA Money & Politics Report (Aug. 20, 2007).

Attorney's Office for the District of Columbia received a total of 3798 referrals from the Secretary of the Senate and Clerk of the House for lobbyists' failure to properly file quarterly reports. Those referrals resulted in 2419 enforcement actions (which can include contacts aimed at bringing lobbyists into compliance).[26] Those enforcement actions seem to pay dividends, as a large percentage of the referrals quickly became compliant. Should we expect enforcement to be more vigorous after the increase of the penalties? What changes in behavior on the part of lobbyists and lawmakers are likely given the expansion of enforcement options?

5.   *Constitutional Objections to LDA.* The first challenge to LDA was brought in 2008 after HLOGA changed the rules affecting disclosure of members of a coalition engaged in lobbying. The provision at issue was 2 U.S.C. § 1603(b)(3), requiring any registrant under LDA to provide information about any organization (but not individuals) that contributes more than $5,000 to fund its lobbying activities and that "actively participates" in the "planning, supervision, or control" of the activities. The National Association of Manufacturers (NAM), the country's largest trade organization, challenged this provision under the First Amendment. NAM argued that disclosure of its organizational members would chill them from participating in the political process for fear of the consequences of such publicity. It also contended that the provisions were unconstitutionally vague.

The appellate court unanimously sustained the law against the attack in *Nat'l Ass'n of Mfrs. v. Taylor*, 582 F.3d 1 (D.C. Cir. 2009). In applying strict scrutiny, the court identified the compelling state interest behind the disclosure statute as revealing to the public the interests behind coalitions of organizations, including, but not limited to, so-called "stealth coalitions." It relied on the long line of cases affirming disclosure statutes in a variety of political contexts—lobbying and campaign-finance regulation—to demonstrate the legitimacy of the congressional objective of providing information to the public about the effect of paid lobbying on federal policy. It held that the provision was appropriately tailored to vindicate the government's interest in transparency. The court also found that LDA was not impermissibly vague; for example, other laws that did even more than require disclosure of political activity using a standard such as "actively participates" had been upheld. See, e.g., *U.S. Civil Service Comm'n v. Nat'l Ass'n of Letter Carriers*, 413 U.S. 548 (1973) (rejecting a similar attack on the Hatch Act, which bars federal employees from taking "an active part" in managing political campaigns). Moreover, LDA had been in effect since 1995 with no reported problems of registrants not understanding what constituted "lobbying activities."

The court also considered NAM's argument that, even if the provision is facially constitutional, it was nonetheless problematic as applied to NAM's members. The organization provided examples of some of the consequences its members feared from disclosure: "[M]ob violence has been directed at firms targeted by anti-globalization forces. * * * Firms that are identified as actively lobbying on issues relating to on-going litigation, e.g., asbestos, risk becoming litigation targets. Taking policy positions that are unpopular with some groups may lead to boycotts, shareholder suits, demands for political contributions or support, and other forms of harassment." There was, however, no evidence of the kind of serious harm or retaliation suffered by the members of the NAACP or the Socialist Workers Party that had led courts to exempt those organizations

---

[26]   Gov't Accountability Off., *2018 Lobbying Disclosure: Observations on Lobbyists' Compliance with Disclosure Requirements* 23–24 (Mar. 2019), https://www.gao.gov/assets/700/698103.pdf.

from disclosing their members in the campaign finance realm. See *NAACP v. Alabama*, 357 U.S. 449 (1958); *Brown v. Socialist Workers 74 Campaign Comm. (Ohio)*, 459 U.S. 87 (1982). Indeed, the court noted that NAM's website already identified more than 250 members, and none had produced evidence of adverse consequences from that publicity.

6.   *Further Federal Lobbying Reform Efforts.* Many believe that the federal law, even with the 2007 amendments, needs further refinement. The American Bar Association (ABA) embarked on an extensive effort to propose improvements to LDA, resulting in a January 2011 document, *Lobbying Law in the Spotlight: Challenges and Proposed Improvements: Report of the Task Force on Federal Lobbying Laws, Section of Administrative Law and Regulatory Practice, American Bar Association*, 63 Admin. L. Rev. 419 (2011). The ABA's House of Delegates recommended many of the improvements proposed by the task force, including:

- Refining the threshold that triggers the lobbying registration requirement, while also avoiding imposing unduly burdensome requirements on small entities. The Task Force recommended, for example, that a firm be required to register if employees make two or more lobbying contacts on behalf of a client and it expects to receive at least $3,000 as compensation for those activities during a quarter. This recommendation would eliminate the 20% threshold in the current law.

- Requiring LDA registrants to disclose lobbying support activities, including strategy, polling, coalition building, and public relations activities. Disclosure should include such activities performed by firms retained by the registrants. This recommendation would result in disclosure of some grassroots lobbying efforts but only by those entities required to register because of direct lobbying contacts; grassroots activities alone would not trigger registration.

- Requiring disclosure of all congressional offices and committees and federal agencies and offices contacted by lobbyists. **Query:** What is the optimal level of additional disclosure? Identifying a committee? A particular congressional office or agency subdivision? An individual staff member or agency bureaucrat? If congressional offices are identified whenever a member or key staff person meets with lobbyists from "the other side" (e.g., a conservative Republican House member or staffer meets with the AFL-CIO or Planned Parenthood; a liberal Democratic Senator or staffer meets with the Chamber of Commerce or the National Rifle Association), might this chill or prevent responsible efforts at information sharing and policy compromise? What constitutional issues might arise with more specific disclosure?

- Prohibiting registered lobbyists from lobbying a member of Congress for whom she engaged in fundraising in the past two years; from fundraising for a member of Congress whom she lobbied in the past two years; or making or soliciting a campaign contribution to a reelection committee for a member of Congress whom the lobbyist has approached for an earmark or narrow benefit. This proposal responded to the Task Force's recommendation that lobbying and campaign participation be separated to the extent possible.

- Transferring authority to enforce LDA to an appropriate administrative authority with sufficient power and resources to effectively enforce the Act. The Task Force suggested the Civil Division of the Department of Justice as a reasonable candidate for this responsibility.

LOBBYING DISCLOSURE ACT PROBLEMS

Problem 3-3. How would the amended LDA affect Robert Harriss, Tom Linder, and Ralph Moore, the people involved in the *Harriss* case? Who would be required to register under the Act, and what information would they be required to disclose? Does it matter if the conversations at the dinners with the members of Congress focused on a possible nominee for the Secretary of Agriculture, whose name had not yet been sent to the Senate for its advice and consent? What if those attending the dinners talked only generally about the country's agricultural policy, including the future of price supports? Would your answer change if the people that Linder and Moore entertained were congressional staff working on the House Appropriations Committee? What if they were high-level appointees in the Department of Commerce?

Problem 3-4. All states have enacted statutes requiring lobbying disclosure (with Pennsylvania being the last state to adopt such a law, in 2007), and the Center for Public Integrity found 47 states to have more effective lobbying-regulation laws than does the federal government.[27] Six states have a two-year waiting period affecting lawmakers who become lobbyists, and 19 states have a one-year ban to combat the problem of the revolving door. Twenty-seven states have independent agencies to oversee lobbying disclosure, with 18 states delegating that authority to the secretary of state. Like the federal government, 37 states include lobbying of the executive branch within the scope of their regulatory structure. Some state regulation goes beyond disclosure. Several states, including California, Kentucky, South Carolina, and Tennessee, prohibit lobbyists from making contributions to candidates for state offices; Alaska prohibits lobbyist contributions except to candidates in the district where the lobbyist votes; and other states prohibit any contributions while the legislature is in session (e.g., Arizona, Colorado, Connecticut, Iowa, Kansas, Louisiana, Maine, Minnesota, North Carolina, Oklahoma, Vermont, and Wisconsin).[28] Is this sort of prohibition constitutional? How would a court assess it? Compare *Preston v. Leake*, 660 F.3d 726 (4th Cir. 2011) (upholding North Carolina's ban on lobbyists contributing to state legislators, passed in 2006), with *Green Party of Connecticut v. Garfield*, 616 F.3d 189 (2d Cir. 2010) (striking down such a ban because of insufficient evidence of actual corruption, while sustaining a more targeted ban on contributions by state contractors). Finally, a few states adopt a more aggressive regulatory stance toward disclosure of grassroots lobbying than does the federal government, and some courts have upheld these laws against First Amendment challenge. Compare *Minn. State Ethical Practices Bd. v. Nat'l Rifle Ass'n of America*, 761 F.2d 509 (8th Cir. 1985) ("extensive letter-writing campaign for the purpose of influencing specific legislation" may be regulated as lobbying), with *New Jersey State Chamber of Commerce v. New Jersey Election Law Enforcement Comm'n*, 411 A.2d 168 (N.J. 1980) (reading *Harriss* limitations into ambiguous state statute). How would you analyze the

---

[27]   Leah Rush & David Jimenez, Ctr. for Pub. Integrity, *States Outpace Congress in Upgrading Lobbying Laws* (May 19, 2014), https://publicintegrity.org/state-politics/influence/hired-guns/states-outpace-congress-in-upgrading-lobbying-laws/ (analysis does not include the Pennsylvania law, 65 Pa.C.S.A. § 13A01 *et seq.*).

[28]   See Nat'l Conf. of State Legis., *Prohibited Donors* (Dec. 6, 2011), http://www.ncsl.org/legislatures-elections/elections/prohibited-donors.aspx.

constitutionality of these differing approaches? And constitutionality aside, are they wise policy?[29]

2. RULES STRUCTURING LEGISLATIVE DELIBERATION

At both the state and federal levels there are rules that structure and facilitate deliberation in the legislature. These rules are found in state and federal constitutions, in statutes, at common law, and in customs and regulations of specific legislative chambers. For analytical convenience, we shall organize our discussion around two kinds of rules: first, substantive constitutional requirements affecting legislation, primarily at the state level, including the single-subject rule and generality requirements; and, second, line item veto provisions that allow the executive to influence substance. We follow with an analysis of legislative immunities, which can affect the ability to enforce all the rules discussed in this chapter.

A. SUBSTANTIVE LIMITATIONS ON THE LEGISLATIVE PROCESS: SINGLE-SUBJECT RULES AND GENERALITY REQUIREMENTS

The federal and, even more frequently, state constitutions contain a variety of limitations on legislation and the legislative process. Some are substantive limits on the nature of legislation.[30] Generally, these substantive constitutional provisions at the state level are aimed at various forms of rent-seeking by private groups at the public's expense. Why do state constitutions seem more concerned about this problem than the U.S. Constitution seems to be? Perhaps part of the answer lies in the smaller geographic areas of the states relative to the entire United States. James Madison in *Federalist 10* argued that a benefit of a large country was the reduced likelihood that government would be captured by one faction. "[I]t is this circumstance [the greater extent of territory permitted by a representative government] principally which renders factious combinations less to be dreaded[.] * * * Extend the sphere, and you take in a greater variety of parties and interests; you make it less probable that a majority of the whole will have a common motive to invade the rights of other citizens; or if such a common motive exists, it will be more difficult for all who feel it to discover their own strength, and to act in unison with each other." Is Madison's argument persuasive? Can you think of other reasons why state constitutions might be more concerned with rent-seeking?

Interestingly, there have been proposals to import some of the state limitations into the federal sphere,[31] if not by constitutional amendment then by congressional

---

[29]   For an argument that regulation of grassroots lobbying is unconstitutional, see Jay Sekulow & Erik Zimmerman, *Weeding Them Out by the Roots: The Unconstitutionality of Regulating Grassroots Issue Advocacy*, 19 Stan. L. & Pol'y Rev. 164 (2008).

[30]   For a good analysis, see Robert Williams, *State Constitutional Limits on Legislative Procedure: Legislative Compliance and Judicial Enforcement*, 48 U. Pitt. L. Rev. 797 (1987).

[31]   See Brannon Denning & Brooks Smith, *Uneasy Riders: The Case for a Truth-in-Legislation Amendment*, 1999 Utah L. Rev. 957; Nancy Townsend, Comment, *Single Subject Restrictions as an Alternative*

rule. For example, the tax-law-writing committees in Congress adopted a policy in the late 1980s against *rifleshot provisions*, or tax provisions that benefit only one or a very few taxpayers. This was a self-imposed generality requirement of sorts.

Generality Requirements. Most state constitutions have provisions regulating the tendency of government to distribute benefits to special interests or private parties at the state's expense. See Adrian Vermeule, *Veil of Ignorance Rules in Constitutional Law*, 111 Yale L.J. 399, 411–15 (2001) (describing how constitutional provisions requiring generality adopted behind a "partial veil of ignorance" can dampen self-interested behavior). Such "anti-rent-seeking" provisions include the following:

1.   *Public Purpose Requirements.* Most state constitutions have general clauses requiring legislation (especially appropriations) to serve public rather than private purposes, and some state codes include general admonitions for courts to interpret statutes as though they were adopted for public rather than private purposes.[32] Theoretically (but usually not in practice) such provisions would require courts to invalidate rent-seeking legislation or to construe such legislation narrowly.

2.   *Rules Against Special Legislation.* Some state constitutions prohibit *special legislation*, others list subjects on which such legislation is not permitted, while others forbid special statutes when more general ones exist or might be drafted instead. Article 3, § 32 of the Pennsylvania Constitution combines these approaches, prohibiting special laws relating to specific subjects (for example, remission of fines, property tax exemptions, or labor regulations) or displacing general laws. Other state constitutions prohibit the government from making gifts, subsidies, or grants to private individuals.[33] Article IV, § 13 of the Illinois Constitution states: "The General Assembly shall pass no special or local law when a general law is or can be made applicable. Whether a general law is or can be made applicable shall be a matter for judicial determination." Courts have not often found that targeted laws are so narrow as to violate the constitutional prohibition against special legislation.[34]

---

to the Line-Item Veto, 1 Notre Dame J. L. Ethics & Pub. Pol'y 227 (1985) (both arguing for a single-subject requirement at the federal level).

[32]   See generally Dale F. Rubin, *Constitutional Aid Limitation Provisions and the Public Purpose Doctrine*, 12 St. Louis U. Pub. L. Rev. 143, 148–55 (1993) (describing the history of public purpose provisions). Such provisions are of course related to the "public use" requirements for taking private property that exist in every state constitution (save North Carolina) and the federal Constitution. See Donald Kochan, *"Public Use" and the Independent Judiciary: Condemnation in an Interest-Group Perspective*, 3 Tex. Rev. L. & Pol. 49, 51 n.5 (1998); U.S. Const. Amend. V.

[33]   The U.S. Constitution has no general prohibition or limitation on special legislation. During each Congress various *private bills* are enacted; one common type consists of a waiver of immigration requirements for particular individuals, and another common type allows compensation to persons whose claims against the federal government fall outside the scope of the Federal Tort Claims Act and other claims statutes. Although, theoretically, federal legislation that is special in character might violate the equal protection component of the Due Process Clause of the Fifth Amendment, we know of no case so holding. See generally Matthew Mantel, *Private Bills and Private Laws*, 99 Law Libr. J. 87 (2007) (providing short history of private bills and reasons for declining use); Note, *Private Bills in Congress*, 79 Harv. L. Rev. 1684 (1966). See also Bernadette Maguire, *Immigration: Public Legislation and Private Bills* (1997) (studying private bills in the immigration context through a series of case studies).

[34]   See, e.g., *Cutinello v. Whitley*, 641 N.E.2d 360 (Ill. 1994) (statute allowing specified counties to tax the retail sale of fuel does not violate special legislation provision of state constitution); *Village of Schaumburg v. Doyle*, 661 N.E.2d 496 (Ill. App. 1996) (amendment to Pesticide Act prohibiting regulation of pesticides by any political subdivisions except for counties and municipalities with populations of more than 2 million does not violate the state constitution's special legislation provision). See also Thomas Palisi, Comment, Town of

3. *Uniformity.* Many state constitutions require that laws (especially tax laws) be uniform. Compare U.S. Const. Art. I, § 8, cl. 1 (federal "Taxes, Duties, Imposts and Excises * * * shall be uniform throughout the United States") with *id.* Amend. XVI (allowing federal income tax without apportionment among the several states, overruling the Supreme Court's interpretation of § 8, cl. 1). State constitutions often require that state laws apply generally and uniformly across the state—an effort to prevent the legislature from providing special benefits to one region or locality. See, e.g., Wis. Const. Art. VIII, § 1 ("The rule of taxation shall be uniform but the legislature may empower cities, villages or towns to collect and return taxes on real estate located therein by optional methods."); N.J. Const. Art. VIII, § 1, cl. 1(a) ("Property shall be assessed for taxation under general laws and by uniform rules."); Pa. Const. Art. VIII, § 1 ("All taxes shall be uniform, upon the same class of subjects, within the territorial limits of the authority levying the tax, and shall be levied and collected under general laws.").[35]

Tax legislation is also increasingly the subject of state constitutional amendments, not all of which are substantive. Currently, sixteen states require supermajority votes to pass at least certain kinds of tax increases.[36] Additionally, several states have either a legislative or constitutional tax-limitation provision that requires the state to return to the taxpayers amounts of tax collected that exceed a certain threshold.[37] All these provisions are designed to make it harder for legislators and organized interests to construct special-interest tax breaks paid for by general tax revenues.

4. *The Single-Subject Rule.* Forty-one state constitutions have requirements that limit bills to one subject.[38] Under the majority of these provisions, the single subject of the bill must be expressed in its title. The requirement that the title explain what is in the bill historically predates the single-subject requirement; it apparently resulted from the notorious Yazoo Act of the Georgia Legislature in 1795.[39]

The major purpose of single-subject provisions is to minimize logrolling, derogatorily described by one court as the "practice of jumbling together in one act inconsistent subjects in order to force passage by uniting minorities with different

Secaucus v. Hudson County Board of Taxation: *An Analysis of the Special Legislation and Tax Uniformity Clauses of the New Jersey Constitution*, 47 Rutgers L. Rev. 1229 (1995).

[35] See also J. Anthony Coughlan, *Land Value Taxation and Constitutional Uniformity*, 7 Geo. Mason L. Rev. 261 (1999); Jack Stark, *The Uniformity Clause of the Wisconsin Constitution*, 76 Marq. L. Rev. 577 (1993).

[36] Nat'l Conf. of State Legis., *Supermajority Vote Requirements to Pass the Budget* (Nov. 9, 2018), http://www.ncsl.org/research/fiscal-policy/supermajority-vote-requirements-to-pass-the-budget635542510.aspx.

[37] Bert Waisanen, *State Tax and Expenditure Limits—2010*, http://www.ncsl.org/research/fiscal-policy/state-tax-and-expenditure-limits-2010.aspx.

[38] Nat'l Conf. of State Legis., *Single Subject Rules*, http://www.ncsl.org/legislatures-elections/elections/single-subject-rules.aspx (updated May 8, 2009). For the classic study, see Millard Ruud, *No Law Shall Embrace More than One Subject*, 42 Minn. L. Rev. 389 (1958).

[39] The Yazoo Act was titled "An act supplementary to an act for appropriating part of the unlocated territory of this state, for the payment of the late state troops, and for other purposes therein mentioned, and declaring the right of this state to the unappropriated territory thereof, for the protection and support of the frontiers of this state, and for other purposes." In fact, the Act ordered the sale of a considerable portion of state land to certain companies. Later, in 1796, the Georgia legislature passed a statute declaring the Yazoo Act null and void because of undue influence and fraud in its enactment. In *Fletcher v. Peck,* 10 U.S. (6 Cranch.) 87 (1810), the Supreme Court held that the 1796 Act could not divest title to land sold to an innocent purchaser under the earlier Act.

interests when the particular provisions could not pass on their own separate merits."[40] The fear is the following: proposals A, B, and C are bad measures, each benefiting a special interest and each favored by only a minority of legislators. Thus, none could be enacted as a stand-alone bill. But if the three factions can assemble a "Christmas tree" bill—i.e., a bill that, like a Christmas tree, is available for supporting each legislator's pet "ornament"—containing A, B, and C, a majority may well adopt the bill. This runs the risk of creating bad public policy and—if A, B, and C are spending proposals—state overspending.

Several states have single-subject and title requirements for popular initiatives. These provisions are justified not only on the ground that they reduce logrolling, but also that they reduce voter confusion that might arise with complicated and intricate legislative proposals. We will return to the single-subject requirement in the context of direct democracy in Chapter 4, § 1(B).

Consider the following case concerning the single-subject requirement for laws passed by a state legislature.

DEPARTMENT OF EDUCATION V. LEWIS
Supreme Court of Florida, 1982.
416 So.2d 455.

BOYD, JUSTICE.

House Bill No. 30-B was the general appropriations bill adopted by the 1981 Legislature[.] The appropriations for the Department of Education and the Commissioner of Education were prefaced by the following proviso:

> No funds appropriated herein shall be used to finance any state-supported public or private postsecondary educational institution that charters or gives official recognition or knowingly gives assistance to or provides meeting facilities for any group or organization that recommends or advocates sexual relations between persons not married to each other.

> Sexual relations means contact with sexual organs of one person by the body of another person for sexual gratification.

> Any postsecondary educational institution found in violation of this provision shall have all state funds withheld until that institution is again in compliance with the law.

> No state financial aid shall be given to students enrolled at any postsecondary educational institution located in Florida which is in violation of this provision. * * *

Article III, section 12, Florida Constitution, provides:

> Laws making appropriations for salaries of public officers and other current expenses of the state shall contain provisions on no other subject.

---

[40]   *State ex rel. Martin v. Zimmerman,* 289 N.W. 662, 664 (Wis. 1940); see *Simpson v. Tobin,* 367 N.W.2d 757, 767 (S.D. 1985).

This provision is a corollary of Article III, section 6, which requires that all laws be limited to a single subject and matters properly related to that subject. An extensive body of constitutional law teaches that the purpose of article III, section 6 is to ensure that every proposed enactment is considered with deliberation and on its own merits. A lawmaker must not be placed in the position of having to accept a repugnant provision in order to achieve adoption of a desired one.

Through a number of cases decided over many years this Court has attempted to make clear to the Legislature that under our constitutional plan for the lawful exercise of governmental powers an appropriations act is not the proper place for the enactment of general public policies on matters other than appropriations. In *Brown v. Firestone*, [382 So.2d 654 (Fla. 1980)], the Court said:

> * * * Provisions on substantive topics should not be ensconced in an appropriations bill in order to logroll or to circumvent the legislative process normally applicable to such action. Similarly, general appropriations bills should not be cluttered with extraneous matters which might cloud the legislative mind when it should be focused solely upon appropriations matters.

* * * *[Brown]* establish[ed] two principles[.] * * * First, if a provision in an appropriations bill changes existing law on any subject other than appropriations, it is invalid. Second, a qualification or restriction must directly and rationally relate to the purpose of the appropriation to which it applies. * * *

* * * The proviso [in question] attempts to make substantive policy on the governance of postsecondary educational institutions. Thus it amends a whole host of statutes pertaining to the operation of public colleges and universities and the regulation of private colleges and universities, [thereby failing the first test of *Brown*].

* * * The proviso is not directly and rationally related to the appropriation of state funds to postsecondary institutions and students. It is, rather, designed to further a legislative objective unrelated to such funding [and thereby fails the second test as well].

NOTES ON ENFORCEMENT OF STATE RESTRICTIONS ON LEGISLATION AND LEGISLATIVE PROCEDURES

1. *Enforcing the Single-Subject Rule.* State constitutions do not define what they mean by a "single subject" and "strict adherence to [the rule's] letter would seriously interfere with the practical business of legislation."[41] Thus, many state courts have articulated liberal tests that are easy for legislatures to meet. "[I]f, from the standpoint of legislative treatment, there is any reasonable basis for the grouping together in one 'act' of various matters, this court cannot say that such matters constitute more than one subject."[42] The remedy for a violation of the single-subject rule varies among the states. Some state constitutions explicitly provide the remedy: in Iowa, for example, the Constitution states that any provision that is not consistent with the subject of an act

[41] *Bernstein v. Comm'r of Public Safety*, 351 N.W.2d 24, 25 (Minn. App. 1984).
[42] *Dague v. Piper Aircraft Corp.*, 418 N.E.2d 207, 214–15 (Ind. 1981).

may be severed and declared void, while the rest of the provisions remain in effect. Iowa Const. Art. III, § 29. Where constitutions are silent, courts must determine whether to sever the offending provisions or to strike down the entire law because the unconstitutional procedure of enactment tainted the entire bill. Martha Dragich, *State Constitutional Restrictions on Legislative Procedure: Rethinking the Analysis of Original Purpose, Single Subject, and Clear Title Challenges*, 38 Harv. J. Legis. 103, 154–63 (2001), has argued that, in at least some cases in which the single-subject limitation has been contravened, severance is acceptable. On the other hand, if the goal of such provisions is to prevent logrolling, why should a court ever sever the provisions? If the concern animating the single-subject rule is that the various provisions of the statute could never have passed on their own, why not strike them all down and see which ones get repassed on their own?

Illinois has more aggressively enforced the single-subject requirement than most other states, and, in some instances, it has used the rule to throw out entire statutes, not just the offending provisions. In *Johnson v. Edgar*, No. 95 CH 12004 (Ill. Circ. Ct. May 7, 1996), *aff'd*, 680 N.E.2d 1372 (Ill. 1997), the Illinois Circuit Court was faced with a challenge to a crime bill. The bill had begun its legislative life as "An act in relation to prisoners' reimbursement to the Department of Corrections for the expenses incurred by their incarcerations," but by the end of House consideration it was known merely as "An act in relation to crime" because so many provisions had been added. These amendments included provisions dealing with pupil expulsion for bringing a weapon to school, competitive selection procedures on contracts in the State Public Defender's office, and permission for the Attorney General to bring a civil action against organizations engaging in international terrorism. By the end of the second conference committee, the proposal was "An act in relation to public safety" because it now included provisions dealing with fees for motor fuels, regulations for underground storage tanks, and exemptions for businesses from the wiretapping statute. (The judicial challenge to the bill was brought by opponents of this last provision.) The bill had grown from eight pages to 243 pages.

In striking the entire law down, the judge described some of the rationales justifying the constitutional rule: "This Act is a textbook case of the type of situation that Article IV of the Illinois Constitution was enacted to prevent—attaching an unpopular bill to a popular one to circumvent legislative input or scrutiny. Imagine the public rebuke that would be directed at a legislator who did not vote for a bill that sought to protect children from the horrid abuses at the hand of sex offenders [one of the many provisions in the Act]. At the same time these legislators are drafting in a measure in the very same Act that would allow employers to, in effect, eavesdrop on their own workforce. It is a reprehensible measure to ride a potentially unpassable piece of legislation [on] the backs of abused children." The court objected not only to the violation of the single-subject requirement, but also to the extensive revisions made by a conference committee without public hearings or deliberation. See also *People v. Olender*, 854 N.E.2d 593 (Ill. 2005) (striking down a law in its entirety and detailing how it grew from a bill amending three criminal laws to a more than 100-page act "in relation to government regulation").

The Illinois courts have sometimes pulled back, however, when the effect of invalidating a statute seems particularly disruptive. In *Arangold Corp. v. Zehnder,* 718 N.E.2d 191 (Ill. 1999), the Illinois Supreme Court found that an act implementing the fiscal year 1996 budget, and including provisions that began their legislative life as the Tobacco Products Tax Act, did not violate the single-subject rule. The supreme court held that all the provisions of the budget act, which amended more than 20 other laws, related to the implementation of the state's budget. Unlike *Johnson*, where the court rejected the legislature's attempt to unite disparate provisions under the rubric of "public safety," the challenged legislation in *Arangold* included "all the means reasonably necessary to accomplish" the purpose of implementing the state budget and thus covered only a single subject. The court held that all the provisions need not be related to each other, but only to the single subject identified by the legislature. Were the laws in *Johnson* and *Arangold* meaningfully different, or was it just the stakes of striking them down that were different? If the latter is the case, is this an argument for severability (i.e., keeping the budget statute but striking from it the tobacco provisions)?

In the more recent case of *Wirtz v. Quinn*, 953 N.E.2d 899 (Ill. 2011), the Illinois Supreme Court attempted to bridge *Johnson* and *Arangold*. The *Wirtz* court upheld Public Act 96–34, titled "An Act concerning revenue," against a single-subject-rule challenge. The Act contained provisions doing everything from legalizing and taxing video gambling to creating a pilot program for the purchase of lottery tickets online to increasing the sales taxes on candy, soft drinks, and beauty products to requiring quarterly audits of all state capital spending projects. Holding that the state is "not limited solely to the contents of the title of an act in offering a single subject rationale," the court agreed with the state that the single subject of the law was "capital projects," not revenue. And the act's substantive provisions "clearly are connected to capital projects in that they establish increased revenue sources to be deposited into the Capital Projects Fund. The few provisions that do not directly raise revenue are still related to the overall subject of the Act in that they help to implement the other provisions." Even if some of the money raised would go to non-capital projects, "it is not the function of this court to trace the origin and destination of every dollar amount cited in Public Act 96–34. Rather, our task is to decide whether Public Act 96–34, as a whole, is devoted to a single subject and, therefore, constitutional. In doing so, we bear in mind that the single subject rule is construed liberally and 'is not intended to handicap the legislature by requiring it to make unnecessarily restrictive laws.' "

In reconciling this result with *Johnson*, the *Wirtz* court focused on the legislative process: "Given that the single subject rule is intended to 'regulate[ ] the process by which legislation is enacted', it is useful to examine the legislative debates conducted by the General Assembly" (internal citation omitted). It emphasized the ways in which the bill in *Johnson* had grown through logrolling. In *Wirtz*, by contrast, "there are no 'smoking gun' provisions in Public Act 96–34 which clearly violate the intent and purpose of the single subject rule." Instead, the legislative debates were replete with examples of legislators talking about the bill as "a capital bill," or an "infrastructure" bill. The court thus read the legislative history to demonstrate that, "There is no evidence that any obviously unrelated provisions were 'tacked on' to the bill at a later time. Overall, the debate shows that the legislators were aware that they were voting on sources of funding for capital improvements to the state." Of course they had to strike compromises in doing so, but those were "legitimate compromise[s] on a bill which comprised a single subject. Indeed, there is a difference between impermissible logrolling and the normal compromise which is inherent in the legislative process." Is this focus on process a satisfactory way to reconcile the court's more aggressive use of the single-subject role in *Johnson* with its more permissive approach in *Arangold* and *Wirtz*?

2.   *Public Choice Arguments.* The insights of public choice theory suggest that more rigorous enforcement of the single-subject rule might well limit logrolling and help foster legislative deliberation. For example, consider how the proviso held unconstitutional in

Lewis might have been attached to the appropriations bill. What group was the likely target of the proviso in question? Are there not scenarios in which a conscientious legislator could get trapped into voting for the bill, proviso and all?

But public choice theory also might suggest the following normative argument for a narrow view of the single-subject rule: the overall satisfaction of groups with their political system might be enhanced if each group receives the legislation that it most intensely desires. Hence, even though proposals A, B, and C reflect minority preferences, the groups favoring them might have very strong preferences for those policies (e.g., anti-smoking regulations, anti-discrimination protections, and stricter penalties for drunk driving). In a simple majority-vote model, these groups could not satisfy their strongest preferences. With logrolling, the groups can express the intensity of their preferences by their willingness to vote for proposals that they would otherwise oppose, in exchange for the other groups' support for their favored proposals.[43] Furthermore, logrolling allows legislatures to assemble majority support for proposals and provides the necessary lubrication to allow multi-member bodies to overcome collective-action problems and enact laws.

Michael Gilbert adopts this approach—arguing that logrolling is often beneficial and a court cannot easily distinguish a "bad" logroll from a "good" one—to provide a procedurally based definition of "subject" for enforcement of the requirement. *Single Subject Rules and the Legislative Process*, 67 U. Pitt. L. Rev. 803 (2006). He contends that the more troublesome legislative phenomenon is the addition of riders, or unpopular substantive provisions attached to popular bills. Whereas logrolling leaves a majority of legislators better off through exchange, riders are a product of "manipulation of legislative procedures. Well-placed legislators can attach self-serving measures to otherwise popular bills, and they need not offer anything to the measures' opponents." Courts should therefore enforce the single-subject rule against riders but not against the product of legislative logrolls. How can a court distinguish one from the other? Gilbert suggests that any provisions added on the floor of the legislature are more likely to be logrolls; whereas provisions attached in committee are often riders. Courts should be less deferential when a bill is considered under a relatively closed rule on the floor, and "[i]n general, more floor debate should correspond to less judicial scrutiny." He advises courts to look carefully at legislative history, "voting records, political affiliation, and even poll data to hypothesize how legislators would vote on a truncated bill." Is this test realistic? Can courts differentiate between logrolls that should be encouraged and riders that reflect manipulation of the political process? Isn't this analysis especially challenging in the context of state legislatures, which produce less legislative history than the federal House or Senate? Is Gilbert's approach an improvement over the *Lewis* court's analysis?

3. *Substantive Legislation Through Riders to Appropriations Legislation*. As *Lewis* demonstrates, appropriations bills are popular targets for riders. Appropriations riders short-circuit the ordinary committee process because they emerge from a committee without primary jurisdiction over the substantive area, thereby depriving the legislature of the value of expert-committee deliberation. On the other hand, they can serve important legislature-empowering functions by logrolling executives—effectively forcing governors or presidents to agree to provisions they may not like (say, provisions limiting

---

[43] See James Buchanan & Gordon Tullock, *The Calculus of Consent: Logical Foundations of Constitutional Democracy* 131–45 (1962).

their power) so as to prevent lapses in appropriations.[44] Many states exempt appropriations measures from their single-subject rules, presumably so that omnibus budgets can be enacted. For jurisdictions having no single-subject rule for appropriations measures, courts may choose to introduce a limited version of the rule through statutory interpretation, in particular the interpretive canon that presumes against legislative amendment of substantive law through appropriations measures.[45] The leading federal case is *TVA v. Hill*, 437 U.S. 153 (1978), Chapter 5, § 2(C) (Endangered Species Act of 1973 required halting $100+ million dam whose construction threatened the endangered snail darter, notwithstanding continued post-1973 congressional appropriations for the dam and evidence that the appropriations committees knew of the Act and believed it inapplicable). The federal House and Senate also usually have internal rules that prohibit members from adding riders to appropriations bills, although these rules can be and frequently are waived or ignored without substantial political cost.

B. THE LINE ITEM VETO AND OTHER RULES TO ENFORCE BUDGET LIMITATIONS

Extensive logrolling in budgetary measures also raises concerns about government overspending and the attendant budget deficits. Unlike the U.S. Constitution, nearly all of the states have either constitutional or statutory balanced budget requirements.[46] Forty-four states also provide that the state governor may veto "items" in appropriations bills; a few of those states extend the power to all bills. In such states, the line item veto is often a complement to single-subject rules that may not apply to appropriations bills. In other words, the traditional veto coupled with a single-subject rule protects the governor from take-it-or-leave-it proposals in most contexts, and the line item veto empowers him to unravel such deals with respect to omnibus appropriations laws. For 39 states with item vetoes, the veto can be overridden only by supermajority votes (two-thirds of legislators present, two-thirds of legislators elected, or three-fifths of legislators elected); for the other states, an override requires only simple majorities or elected majorities in each legislative chamber.[47]

The main purpose of the item veto is to facilitate states' abilities to balance their budgets, but it also serves to ameliorate logrolling. In that regard, the item veto may be more effective than the single-subject rule because it is focused on where logrolling

---

[44]   See Josh Chafetz, *Congress's Constitution: Legislative Authority and the Separation of Powers* ch. 3 (2017) (discussing the ways in which legislatures can leverage the power of the purse to achieve policy changes in collateral areas).

[45]   See Sandra Beth Zellmer, *Sacrificing Legislative Integrity at the Altar of Appropriations Riders: A Constitutional Crisis*, 21 Harv. Envtl. L. Rev. 457 (1997). For a critique of the appropriations canon, see Mathew McCubbins & Daniel Rodriguez, *Canonical Construction and Statutory Revisionism: The Strange Case of the Appropriations Canon*, 14 J. Contemp. Legal Issues 669 (2005).

[46]   Nat'l Conf. of State Legis., *NCSL Fiscal Brief: State Balanced Budget Provisions* 2 (2010), http://www.ncsl.org/documents/fiscal/StateBalancedBudgetProvisions2010.pdf ("The National Conference of State Legislatures (NCSL) has traditionally reported that 49 states must balance their budgets, with Vermont being the exception. Other authorities add Wyoming and North Dakota as exceptions, and some authorities in Alaska contend that it does not have an explicit requirement for a balanced budget.").

[47]   *The Book of the States 2018* tbl. 3.16, at 69–72, *available at* http://knowledgecenter.csg.org/kc/system/files/3.16.2018_0.pdf. This source omits Delaware's legislative veto. See Del. Const. art. III, § 18, para. 3.

is most likely to occur, the appropriations process.[48] Moreover, some scholars have argued that spending constraints such as balanced budget rules will be ineffective in changing legislative behavior without the threat of third-party enforcement, a threat provided by an item veto.[49] In fact, most studies of the state item veto find that its availability does not push spending levels downward, although some studies indicate that it does allow the executive more influence over budgetary decisions. In other words, the final budget will reflect more of the governor's preferences if she wields the item veto weapon; thus, the tool affects the mix of spending programs and the relative power between the branches, rather than the level of spending.[50]

Maxwell Stearns argues that the item veto will necessarily change the kinds of deals legislators reach and the bargaining dynamics. *The Public Choice Case Against the Item Veto,* in *Public Choice and Public Law: Reading and Commentary* 11 (1997). Legislators will attempt to protect legislation from the governor's item veto through sophisticated drafting techniques and by reaching bargains with the governor. The latter strategy may actually increase the amount of spending if the price for the governor's forbearance is enactment of programs that she favors along with the legislative spending items. With respect to what Stearns calls *length bargains,* relatively unrelated riders added to proposals to attract majority support, a line item veto does not eliminate these deals; instead, it merely requires the executive's approval to assure bargainers that the item veto will not be used to eliminate goodies. In contrast, legislators can work unimpeded by the threat of an item veto to assemble majority support for bills by negotiating *substantive bargains* embedded in provisions to reduce any adverse effect on minority interests. Such changes do not produce new items and so are immune from the governor's item veto. Finally, legislative resistance to the item veto often kicks the issues into the courts, whose resolution will then affect subsequent interactions between the governor and the legislature in the veto game.

RUSH V. RAY
Supreme Court of Iowa, 1985.
362 N.W.2d 479.

SCHULTZ, JUSTICE.

[The Iowa General Assembly enacted five separate appropriation bills, each of which contained a provision that either provided "notwithstanding section eight point thirty-nine (8.39) of the Code, funds appropriated by this Act shall not be subject to transfer or expenditure for any purpose other than the purposes specified"

---

[48]   See Richard Briffault, *The Item Veto in State Courts,* 66 Temple L. Rev. 1171, 1178–79 (1993) (excellent article on item veto generally).

[49]   See, e.g., Lawrence Lessig, *Lessons from a Line Item Veto Law,* 47 Case W. Res. L. Rev. 1659 (1997).

[50]   For some of the best studies of the line item veto power in the states, see George Abney & Thomas Lauth, *The Line-Item Veto in the States: An Instrument for Fiscal Restraint or Partnership?,* 45 Pub. Admin. Rev. 372 (1985); James Dearden & Thomas Husted, *Do Governors Get What They Want?: An Alternative Examination of the Line-Item Veto,* 77 Pub. Choice 707 (1993); Rui de Figueiredo, Jr., *Budget Institutions and Political Insulation: Why States Adopt the Item Veto,* 87 J. Pub. Econ. 2677 (2003); Douglas Holtz-Eakin, *The Line Item Veto and Public Sector Budgets: Evidence from the States,* 36 J. Pub. Econ. 269 (1988); Joseph McCormack & Yaniv Reingewertz, *Politics, Partisanship and the Power to Veto: Does Gubernatorial Line-Item Veto Power Affect State Budgets?,* 50 Applied Econ. 3546 (2018); Glen Robinson, *Public Choice Speculations on the Item Veto,* 74 Va. L. Rev. 403 (1988).

or recited a phrase similar in language and content. Governor Robert D. Ray exercised his item veto power to excise the quoted and similar phrases from each act. The issue was whether the governor could properly use his item veto power to eliminate a provision in an appropriation bill that prohibits the expenditure or transfer of appropriated funds from one department of state government to another.]

The constitutional provision which gives the governor item veto authority provides in pertinent part:

> The governor may approve appropriation bills in whole or in part and may disapprove any item of an appropriation bill; and the part approved shall become a law. Any item of an appropriation bill disapproved by the governor shall be returned, . . . Any such item of an appropriation bill may be enacted into law notwithstanding the governor's objections, in the same manner as provided for other bills.

Iowa Const. Art. III, § 16 (1857, amended 1968).

Appellant [State Senator Robert Rush] asserts that the vetoed portions of these five acts are provisos or limitations, not items; thus, they were not subject to the governor's item veto power. On the other hand, the Governor asserts that the language stricken from the five appropriation bills constituted distinct, severable "items" within the meaning of article III, section 16 of the Iowa Constitution, that could be removed from the appropriation bills by the use of the item veto.

We have twice passed on the legality of the governor's exercise of the item veto power. * * * *Welden v. Ray*, 229 N.W.2d 706 (Iowa 1975); *State ex rel. Turner v. Iowa State Highway Commission*, 186 N.W.2d 141 (Iowa 1971). * * *

The problem presented in *Turner* arose when the legislature appropriated funds to the primary road fund, and the governor vetoed a portion of the bill that additionally prohibited removing certain established offices from their present location. When this item veto was challenged, we upheld the veto. We established certain principles to be used in interpreting the term "item" and distinguished items, which are subject to veto, from provisos or conditions inseparably connected to an appropriation, which are not subject to veto. We approved another court's statement that an "item" is "something that may be taken out of a bill without affecting its other purposes and provisions. It is something that can be lifted bodily from it rather than cut out. No damage can be done to the surrounding legislative tissue, nor should any scar tissue result therefrom." * * * While we surmised that the legislature may have intended to make the challenged language a limitation or proviso on the expenditure of funds, we held the act as drawn and enacted did not restrict the use of the appropriated funds for the purposes and uses referred to in the deleted language. We held the deleted language was an item rather than a qualification.

When the governor's authority to exercise his item veto power was challenged in *Welden*, we reached a different result than in *Turner*, holding that the attempted vetoes by the governor were beyond the scope of his constitutional power. The vetoed items in the appropriation bills provided limitations on how the money appropriated for each department was to be spent. Specifically, these provisions included limitations on the number of employees in a department, limitations on the percent of the appropriation that could be used for salaries, prohibition against construction of buildings, prohibition against spending beyond budget, and elimination of matching fund grants if the federal funds were discontinued—with the further provision that unused state matching funds would revert to the general fund. We held that these clauses were lawful qualifications upon the respective appropriations rather than separate, severable provisions.

In *Welden* we * * * quoted a New Mexico ruling that stated:

> The power of partial veto is the power to disapprove. This is a negative power, or a power to delete or destroy a part or item, and is not a positive power, or a power to alter, enlarge or increase the effect of the remaining parts or items. . . . Thus, a partial veto must be so exercised that it eliminates or destroys the whole of an item or part and does not distort the legislative intent, and in effect create legislation inconsistent with that enacted by the Legislature, by the careful striking of words, phrases, clauses or sentences.

([Q]uoting *State ex rel. Sego v. Kirkpatrick*, 86 N.M. 359, 524 P.2d 975 (1974)). * * * The message of these cases and others reviewed in *Welden* is that the governor's power is a negative one that does not allow him to legislate by striking qualifications in a manner which distorts legislative intent. Thus, he cannot strike a provision that would divert money appropriated by the legislature for one purpose so that it may be used for another. Finally, we held in *Welden* that the governor's veto of a legislatively-imposed qualification upon an appropriation must also include a veto of the appropriation.

In the present case the trial court determined that the vetoed portion of each appropriation bill did not change the basic purpose of the legislation; thus, the provision is properly considered a severable item rather than a legislatively-imposed condition. We agree with appellant's contention that "the effect of this veto was to make money from the treasury available for purposes not authorized by the legislation as it was originally written, contrary to the clear intent of the legislature." The Governor has used the item veto power affirmatively to create funds not authorized by the legislature. The vetoed language created conditions, restricting use of the money to the stated purpose. It is not severable, because upon excision of this language, the rest of the legislation is affected. The appropriated money is no longer required to be used only for the stated purpose; it could be used for other purposes. Thus, these are not items which are subject to veto.

This case is unlike *Turner* in which the deletion of directions concerning office changes had no effect on the appropriation of funds. We find it closer akin to *Welden* in which the governor had deleted provisions which dictated how and for what purposes the appropriated funds were to be expended. In the present case the legislature clearly limited the expenditure of the appropriated funds to specified purposes. The veto distorted the obvious legislative intent that the funds only be spent for the appropriated purposes and created additional ways the funds might be spent. This was use of the veto power to create rather than negate. We hold that the language vetoed constituted qualifications on the appropriations rather than separate items subject to veto. * * *

HARRIS, JUSTICE (dissenting [for three dissenting justices]).

The experience in other states shows that, at best, there tends to be a blurred line between an "item" (which can be vetoed from an appropriation bill) and a proviso or condition on how the funds are to be spent (which cannot). It does however seem clear that the line, no matter how blurred, is crossed when legislation (even if labeled a proviso or condition) is appended to an appropriation bill in violation of the single subject provision of a state constitution.

The cases recognize a difficulty faced by governors when presented with appropriation bills which have been infused with legislation, going beyond the appropriation, which impacts either on existing statutes or upon purely executive functions. Some governors are unprotected even by a single-subject constitutional provision. It is quite common to find provisions such as Art III, § 29 of the Iowa Constitution which provide that "every act shall embrace but one subject. . . ." Single subject provisions offer some protection but it is limited. If a provision is attached to an appropriation bill in violation of the single-subject provision the whole act could be challenged as void. But a governor is usually in a poor position to ask for an appropriation bill to be declared void. This would be the case when the government could not continue to function without the funds from the appropriation. Legislation attached by means of proviso or condition labels to crucial appropriation bills might thus become impervious to veto. The upshot was a liberal definition of an item, mentioned by the majority, which we adopted in *Turner*. We said: ". . . should the . . . [l]egislature attempt to coerce the [g]overnor into approving a lump sum appropriation by combining purposes and amount the court [will] interpret the term 'item' liberally to preserve the purpose of the item veto amendment." * * *

[Both *Turner* and *Welden* applied the "scar tissue" test, treating as vetoable "something that may be taken out of a bill without affecting its other purposes and provisions. It is something which can be lifted bodily from it rather than cut out. No damage can be done to the surrounding legislative tissue, nor should any scar tissue result therefrom." Senator Rush and the other plaintiffs object to that test.] But courts elsewhere commonly apply it. [Justice Harris cited decisions from nine other states.]

The majority recites, and seems to acknowledge the validity of, the "scar-tissue test," but does not follow it. Under the test the provisions in question here were proper subjects of item vetoes. Each appropriation was earmarked to a department of government which could use the funds only for the purpose specified by the legislature. The vetoes here in no way modified the legislative plan of how the department could use the funds. The vetoed provisions related only to funds which might remain unused. The power of the governor to transfer unused funds under section 8.39, acting after notice to and "review and comment by" appropriate legislative chairpersons, has been statutorily provided for more than forty years. All branches of Iowa government have become quite used to it. It is, to put it in simple terms, the way our state government works.

If the legislature were to pass an act calling for the repeal or suspension of section 8.39 the act would be subject to an executive veto. Under the scar tissue rule the governor should not be robbed of this veto power by the simple process of attaching the repeal or suspension of this existing statute to an appropriation bill. This is a textbook example of why we and states elsewhere adopted the scar tissue rule. The trial court should be affirmed.

NOTES ON DIFFERENT APPROACHES TO THE ITEM VETO

1. *Situating the Iowa Approach.* We have chosen this Iowa case in part because item vetoes have been rather frequently litigated in Iowa (see the next note) and in part because this approach is a fairly moderate one. Some state courts basically let the legislature define a vetoable "item," e.g., *Washington State Motorcycle Dealers Ass'n v. State*, 763 P.2d 442 (Wash. 1988). In his article *The Item Veto in State Court, supra*, Richard Briffault argues that these courts enable the legislature to evade the purposes of the item veto by clever drafting. On the other hand, Wisconsin courts have very expansively interpreted that state's item veto to allow the governor to veto words and phrases even when the veto completely changes the meaning of the statute. In *State ex rel. Wisconsin Senate v. Thompson*, 424 N.W.2d 385 (Wis. 1988), a divided court allowed the governor to veto word fragments, individual letters from words, and even individual digits from numbers as long as the resulting law made grammatical sense.[51] The reaction to this "Vanna White veto" was swift, with the voters in 1990 prohibiting the governor from deleting individual letters or numerical characters to change the intent of the legislature. Another referendum was passed by Wisconsin voters in 2008 to further limit the governor's line item veto, which had become known as the "Frankenstein veto" because he could still, through strategic editing, stitch two sentences together to form a new sentence with a different meaning. The new law prohibits the governor from creating "a new sentence by combining parts of 2 or more sentences," but still allows the governor the power to veto parts of appropriations bills. See Wis. Const. Art. V, § 10(1)(b)–(c).

The Iowa approach is an effort to find a middle way between approaches too deferential to the legislature and those too empowering of the governor. This approach seeks to limit item vetoes in a way that will not negate them altogether. It originates in the old "affirmative-negative" test that prevents the governor from creating "affirmative" or new legislation, e.g., *Colorado General Assembly v. Lamm*, 704 P.2d 1371, 1382–83 (Colo. 1985), but then elaborates upon that test. Does *Rush* create an appropriate balance (as the court thought), or does it open up the item veto to evasion (as the dissenters thought)?

2. *Subsequent Iowa Cases.* In *Colton v. Branstad*, 372 N.W.2d 184 (Iowa 1985), the court upheld an item veto of a condition attached to an appropriations bill that the court characterized as a *rider*, a non-germane attachment to the bill. What the court saw as a rider was language in the appropriation for the State Department of Health that directed the Department to relinquish authority over certain grants to the State Family Planning Council. "The Governor's constitutional power to veto bills of general legislation cannot be abridged by the careful placement of such measures in a general appropriation bill, thereby forcing the Governor to choose between approving unacceptable substantive legislation or vetoing 'items' of expenditure essential to the operation of government." Isn't this more in the spirit of the *Rush* dissent than of the majority opinion?

---

[51] See Mary Burke, Comment, *The Wisconsin Partial Veto: Past, Present and Future*, 1989 Wis. L. Rev. 1395; Winston Holliday, Jr., Comment, *Tipping the Balance of Power: A Critical Survey of the Gubernatorial Line Item Veto*, 50 S.C. L. Rev. 503 (1999) (focusing on Wisconsin, Iowa, and Virginia).

You might wonder, what is a *rider*? What is *non-germane* to an appropriations bill? Recall *Lewis*, the Florida single-subject rule case, which involved the court's attempt to distinguish "substantive" provisions from "appropriations." But is this distinction really so clear cut? After all, "Spend $X on higher education, *Provided* that no money be used to finance any educational institution that provides support to any organization that advocates sexual relations outside of marriage" (a stylized version of the Florida provisions at issue in *Lewis*) could be rewritten as "Spend $X on those institutions of higher education that don't provide support to any organization that advocates sexual relations outside of marriage." The first option above reads like an appropriation with a rider; the second reads like an appropriation full stop. More fundamentally, *all* appropriations involve a substantive policy decision about what to fund, and therefore what not to fund. Does this difficulty of distinguishing between an appropriation, a condition, and a rider suggest the wisdom of the court's approach in *Rush*? Or is there some principled way to distinguish among them?

ITEM VETO PROBLEMS

Problem 3-5. The governor of Iowa vetoes language attached to an appropriation for tourism and export trade promotion, which provided "as a condition, limitation, and qualification, any official Iowa trade delegation led by the governor which receives financial or other support from the appropriation in this subsection shall be represented by a bipartisan delegation." Under the Iowa precedents, could the governor veto this "condition"? Or was it really a "rider"? See *Welsh v. Branstad*, 470 N.W.2d 644 (Iowa 1991).

Problem 3-6. The legislature enacts a statewide sales tax of 6%. A clause in the bill sets a ceiling of $500 on the amount of tax that can be charged per product or service. The legislature apparently is concerned that the sales tax might discourage purchases of "big ticket" items, such as cars, boats, and appliances. The governor uses the item veto to delete the $500 ceiling, arguing that the state needs the revenue and that the exemption favors the wealthy, who purchase luxury goods. How would this exercise of the item veto be analyzed under the tests discussed above? How could the legislature draft the sales tax provision to insulate the ceiling from the item veto? See Antony Petrilla, *The Role of the Line-Item Veto in the Federal Balance of Power*, 31 Harv. J. Legis. 469, 501 (1994) (providing this example).

NOTES ON THE FEDERAL LINE ITEM VETO ACT

1.   *LIVA and* Clinton v. City of New York. In 1996, Congress passed the Line Item Veto Act (LIVA), Pub. L. 104–130, 110 Stat. 1200, which granted the President the power to cancel certain spending programs. Despite its name, the Act did not give the President the same kind of power enjoyed by governors. Governors can veto particular items in legislation while enacting only the rest of the bill into law; the vetoed items are never enacted. In contrast, before the President could exercise his power under the federal Act, he was required to sign, and thereby enact, the entirety of the bill containing provisions subject to the cancellation authority. He could then "cancel in whole—(1) any dollar amount of discretionary budget authority; (2) any item of new direct spending; or (3) any limited tax benefit" ("limited tax benefits" were defined as tax provisions benefitting a hundred or fewer entities). If the President canceled an item and Congress passed a new

law "disapproving" of that cancellation, the President could not use the cancellation authority on the disapproval bill. He could, of course, veto the disapproval bill.

In the first year the Act was effective, President Clinton canceled 82 items in 11 laws. Congress reinstated 38 of the provisions (all dealing with military construction projects) in a single bill passed over the President's veto. An Act Disapproving the cancellations transmitted by the President on October 6, 1997, regarding Public Law 105–45, Pub. L. No. 105–159, 112 Stat. 19 (1998). A court case challenging another cancellation resulted in a settlement that required the executive branch to spend the funds. In the end, the savings to the federal government amounted to less than $600 million over five years.

And then, in 1998, the Supreme Court invalidated LIVA in *Clinton v. City of New York*, 524 U.S. 417 (1998). Justice Stevens, for a six-justice majority, argued that these cancellations had allowed the President unilaterally to amend two acts of Congress by repealing a part of each. While the Constitution allows the President to veto an entire bill before signing it, he was not given the authority to enact parts and effectively repeal, after signing, other parts. "Familiar historical materials provide abundant support for the conclusion that the power to enact statutes may only 'be exercised in accord with a single, finely wrought and exhaustively considered, procedure.' * * * What has emerged in these cases from the President's exercise of his statutory cancellation powers, however, are truncated versions of two bills that passed both Houses of Congress. They are not the product of the 'finely wrought' procedure that the Framers designed." The cancellation authority differed in an important respect from other delegations of authority to the president: normally, in exercising delegated authority, the president is executing congressional policy. "In contrast, whenever the President cancels an item of new direct spending or a limited tax benefit he is rejecting the policy judgment made by Congress and relying on his own policy judgment."

In dissents, both Justice Scalia and Justice Breyer (note: two former administrative law professors) argued that the majority was simply confused. As Scalia put it, "The title of the Line Item Veto Act, which was perhaps designed to simplify for public comprehension, or perhaps merely to comply with the terms of a campaign pledge, has succeeded in faking out the Supreme Court." In fact, this was not a "veto" at all, but simply a run-of-the-mill delegation to the executive branch.

To see why, consider the following: Surely, Congress could pass a statute authorizing the President to spend "up to $X" on a given item. Indeed, the nation's very first appropriations statute authorized the expenditure of "sum[s] not exceeding" specified amounts in the four categories of spending that it contemplated. Appropriations Act, ch. 23, 1 Stat. 95, 95 (1789). If that's alright, then surely instead of repeating "up to" for each item of spending, Congress could simply write a section into an appropriations act reading, "Every dollar amount specified in this Act shall be understood to permit the president to spend any sum between $0 and that dollar amount for the specified purpose." And if Congress can delegate that authority, then presumably it would be kosher to delegate the lesser authority of forcing a president to choose *between* $0 or $X—that is, Congress could deny him the discretion to pick an amount in the middle. In other words, Congress could pretty clearly insert into any appropriations statute the following language: "Every dollar amount specified in this Act shall be understood to permit the president to spend either $0 or that dollar amount for the specified purpose." But if Congress could do that in an appropriations *act*, why could it not do the same for the entire U.S. *Code*? In other words, why couldn't there be a federal law reading, "Every dollar amount specified in any appropriations act shall be understood to permit the president to spend either $0 or that dollar amount for the specified purpose"? And that, of course (with some complications), is what LIVA said.

As Justice Breyer put it, "When the President 'canceled' the two appropriation measures now before us, he did not *repeal* any law nor did he *amend* any law. He simply *followed* the law, leaving the statutes, as they are literally written, intact." Moreover, as Breyer noted, the cancellation power was easy for Congress to take back: because the president had to sign the appropriations bill before he could cancel any items within it, Congress need only insert a provision into the bill saying that LIVA would not apply to that bill in order to prevent him from using the cancellation power on the appropriations in that bill.

2. *Is the Line Item Veto Act Dead?* On the day that the Court decided *Clinton v. City of New York*, members of Congress announced plans to re-establish the President's power in a constitutional form. Although some worked to draft and ratify a constitutional amendment giving the President a true line item veto, others in Congress hoped to find a less difficult path to success. One option is called *separate enrollment*. Using this procedure, Congress would divide an omnibus spending bill, formally enrolling each provision allocating funds to particular programs as a separate bill. The group of bills would be passed by Congress (probably using a procedure that would require only one vote to enact the bundle of bills). The President would then have the ability to use his constitutional veto to cancel as many of the programs as he wished; Congress would have the opportunity to override any veto with a supermajority vote. For example, rather than one bill with 950 sections, Congress would pass 950 bills, and the President would sign only the bills that provided money to programs he supported. Justice Breyer seemed to believe that separate enrollment is too unwieldy a procedure to work in the modern era; however, during the negotiations that led to the passage of LIVA, the Senate proposed separate enrollment as the best way to adopt a cancellation process that would survive constitutional review. Do you agree with the Senate's assessment? Are the political dynamics of separate enrollment different from those that resulted from LIVA? Would you expect members of Congress to be willing to pass as separate bills provisions that they had been willing to support as parts of one large bill? Does the state experience illustrated by *Rush v. Ray* suggest that Congress will divide omnibus bills in a way to minimize the effect of the President's veto?

In his 2006 State of the Union address, President Bush asked Congress to enact a new line item veto, but his proposal was different from the 1996 Act. He proposed an *expedited rescission* process whereby he would send cancellations to Congress, and Congress would be required, through internal rules, to consider his recommendations quickly and vote on them as a package without further amendment. In addition, the Senate would not be allowed to filibuster. This approach was considered by Congress in 1996, and it is generally considered to be constitutional because the decision not to spend money or enforce tax provisions is left to the Congress, albeit under streamlined procedures.[52] Both President Obama and President Trump have supported a similar expedited rescission process. How effective would expedited rescission be in reducing

---

[52]   See Elizabeth Garrett, *The Story of* Clinton v. City of New York: *Congress Can Take Care of Itself*, in *Administrative Law Stories* 47 (Peter Strauss ed., 2006) (providing legislative history of 1996 Act); Aaron-Andrew Bruhl, *The New Line Item Veto Proposal: This Time It's Constitutional (Mostly)*, 116 Yale L.J. Pocket Part 84 (2006) (discussing constitutionality of expedited rescission).

federal spending? Should Congress avoid using the words "line item veto" in the name of any bill it enacts? How binding are internal congressional procedures that purport to restrain congressional power to amend the President's proposal?

3.   *Federal Earmark Rules.* Earmarks, which received increased public scrutiny as a result of the lobbying scandals of the mid-2000s and notorious projects such as the "Bridge to Nowhere" in Alaska, are similar to the kinds of items that LIVA targeted or that governors excise from state bills through their line item veto powers. Rebecca Kysar defines the "elusive" concept of an earmark as "funds bestowed by Congress upon projects or programs by specifying a narrow location or recipient, or without a competitive allocation process." *Listening to Congress: Earmark Rules and Statutory Interpretation*, 94 Cornell L. Rev. 519, 534 (2009). Rule XXI of the House of Representatives defines "congressional earmark" in similar terms: "a provision or report language included primarily at the request of a Member * * * or Senator providing, authorizing, or recommending a specific amount of discretionary budget authority, credit authority, or other spending authority for a contract, loan, loan guarantee, grant, loan authority, or other expenditure with or to an entity, or targeted to a specific State, locality, or Congressional district, other than through a statutory or administrative formula-driven or competitive award process."

A House standing rule, first adopted in 2007, mandates disclosure of all earmarks as part of committee reports: "It shall not be in order to consider a bill or joint resolution reported by a committee unless the report includes a list of congressional earmarks, limited tax benefits, and limited tariff benefits in the bill or in the report (and the name of any Member * * * who submitted a request to the committee for each respective item included in such list) or a statement that the proposition contains no congressional earmarks, limited tax benefits, or limited tariff benefits." House Rule XXI, cl. 9(a)(1); see also Senate Rule XLIV (also initially adopted in 2007).

How (if at all) should courts review challenges brought against earmarks? Professor Kysar argues that, in cases of ambiguous text, "courts should construe narrowly, against special interests, statutory benefits that were not disclosed in accordance with the earmark disclosure rules but that would fall within the ambit of the rules if the statute were construed in the manner urged by the special interest." Kysar, *supra*, at 563. Do you see any problems with this approach? To what extent should courts defer to Congress' internal rules on what constitutes an earmark? Or on what constitutes adequate disclosure? See also Victoria Nourse, *A Decision Theory of Statutory Interpretation: Legislative History by the Rules*, 122 Yale L.J. 70 (2012) (arguing more broadly that interpreters should consider congressional rules when faced with ambiguous language). Kysar suggests that special-interest deals will often be concealed in more public-regarding terms. If this is true, how is a court to decide whether the text is ambiguous? And what approach should a court take if the statute is unambiguously a special-interest deal? We will return to some of these issues in the chapters on statutory interpretation, especially Chapters 5 and 6.

In addition to disclosure-oriented rules, Congress has adopted what amounts to a moratorium on earmarks since 2011. The House Republican majority agreed to an earmark ban; the Senate Appropriations Committee prohibited earmarks in appropriations bills; and President Obama threatened to veto any legislation including earmarks.[53] When Democrats retook the House in January 2019, they retained the ban,

---

[53]   Carl Hulse, *Senate Spending Panel Bans Earmarks for Two Years*, N.Y. Times, Feb. 2, 2011.

and Senate Republicans made the ban a permanent part of their caucus rules in 2019. Although this ban has been successful in reducing earmarks an estimated 98%,[54] there is evidence that members of Congress have been employing other methods to steer spending toward pet projects.[55]

Although critics of earmarks argue that they improperly direct government funds to special interests and result in wasteful spending, a growing number of members of Congress are seeking to bring them back.[56] Both Democratic and Republican members have argued that earmarks preserve congressional control over the appropriations process and appropriately help advance the interests of constituents. A number of scholars have supported the reintroduction of earmarks, both on the grounds that eliminating earmarks empowers the presidency vis-à-vis Congress more than it reduces spending and on the grounds that earmarks are an essential tool for congressional coalition building and dealmaking.[57] To what extent does how you view earmarks depend on your conception of the proper role of representatives laid out at the beginning of this chapter—as agents or trustees? To what extent does it depend on your view as to whether spending decisions are best made by legislators or bureaucrats?

C. LEGISLATIVE IMMUNITIES

1. Federal Protection for Members of Congress (Speech or Debate Clause)

Article I, § 6, clause 1 of the U.S. Constitution provides that "for any Speech or Debate in either House, [Members of Congress] shall not be questioned in any other place." The purpose of the clause was "to prevent intimidation [of legislators] by the executive and accountability before a possibly hostile judiciary." *United States v. Johnson*, 383 U.S. 169 (1966). "It insures that legislators are free to represent the interests of their constituents without fear that they will be later called to task in the courts for that representation." *Powell v. McCormack*, 395 U.S. 486 (1969). The clause encompasses speeches on the floor of Congress, voting on bills, conduct at committee hearings, preparation of committee reports, authorization of committee publications and their internal distribution, circulation of information to other members, and participation in committee investigations. *Eastland v. United States' Servicemen's Fund*, 421 U.S. 491 (1975); *Doe v. McMillan*, 412 U.S. 306 (1973); *Dombrowski v. Pfister*, 387 U.S. 82 (1967) (per curiam); see also Josh Chafetz,

---

[54]   *Outrageous Bills*, The Economist, Nov. 23, 2013, at 32.

[55]   Ron Nixon, *Congress Appears to Be Trying to Get Around Earmark Ban*, N.Y. Times, Feb. 5, 2012.

[56]   *See* Alexander Bolton, *Momentum for Earmarks Grows with Dem Majority*, The Hill (Jan. 23, 2019), https://thehill.com/homenews/house/426525-momentum-for-earmarks-grows-with-dem-majority;   Jennifer Shutt, *Earmarks Won't Be Back This Year, at Least in the House*, Roll Call (Mar. 1, 2019), https://www.rollcall.com/news/congress/earmarks-no-revival-house.

[57]   On the interbranch power dynamics point, see John Hudak, *Congress in 2019: Why the First Branch Should Bring Back Earmarks*, Brookings Inst. (Dec. 27, 2018), https://www.brookings.edu/blog/fixgov/2018/12/27/congress-in-2019-why-the-first-branch-should-bring-back-earmarks/.   On   the   coalition-building   and dealmaking point, see Diana Evans, *Greasing the Wheels: Using Pork Barrel Projects to Build Majority Coalitions in Congress* (2004); Mariano-Florentino Cuéllar, *Earmarking*, 49 Harv. J. on Legis. 249, 267–69 (2012); Frances E. Lee, *Geographic Politics in the U.S. House of Representatives: Coalition Building and Distribution of Benefits*, 47 Am. J. Pol. Sci. 714 (2003); Daniel B. Magleby & Molly E. Reynolds, *Putting the Breaks on Greased Wheels: The Politics of Weak Obstruction in the United States Senate*, 44 Cong. & the Presidency 344, 364 (2017).

Congress's Constitution: Legislative Authority and the Separation of Powers ch. 6 (2017) (discussing the history and functions of the Clause).

The Speech or Debate Clause is rooted in English history. In the sixteenth and seventeenth centuries, when Parliament was slowly wresting power from the Crown, the Tudor and Stuart monarchs would arrest Members of Parliament and question them about their legislative activities, trying to coerce them into changing their policies. Arguments about legislative free speech therefore became central to larger constitutional arguments about the respective roles of Crown and Parliament. American colonists tended to identify with the seventeenth-century Parliament in these debates, so it is unsurprising that the speech or debate privilege came to be codified in early republican state constitutions, the Articles of Confederation, and, finally, the U.S. Constitution. *See* Chafetz, *supra*, at 201–15.

There is a tension in the Speech or Debate Clause between the desire to protect the independence of the legislative process and the desire not to create congressional "super-citizens." *United States v. Brewster*, 408 U.S. 501, 516 (1972). Thus, defining the scope of the clause is crucial and subject to much discussion in the case law. The next case implicates at least two questions relevant to scope. First, what activities fall under the protection of the Speech or Debate Clause? The Court in *Brewster* distinguishes between acts that involve the legislative process per se and acts that are mere "legislative errands," such as constituent services and newsletters. Is this distinction realistic? Second, who besides members of Congress should receive the protection? Are legislative aides immunized and, if so, is the immunity co-extensive with that accorded to legislators?

GRAVEL V. UNITED STATES

Supreme Court of the United States, 1972.
408 U.S. 606, 92 S.Ct. 2614, 33 L.Ed.2d 583.

Opinion of the Court by MR. JUSTICE WHITE, announced by MR. JUSTICE BLACKMUN.

These cases arise out of the investigation by a federal grand jury into possible criminal conduct with respect to the release and publication of a classified Defense Department study entitled History of the United States Decision-Making Process on Viet Nam Policy. This document, popularly known as the Pentagon Papers, bore a Defense security classification of Top Secret-Sensitive. The crimes being investigated included the retention of public property or records with intent to convert (18 U.S.C. § 641), the gathering and transmitting of national defense information (18 U.S.C. § 793), the concealment or removal of public records or documents (18 U.S.C. § 2071), and conspiracy to commit such offenses and to defraud the United States (18 U.S.C. § 371).

Among the witnesses subpoenaed were Leonard S. Rodberg, an assistant to Senator Mike Gravel of Alaska and a resident fellow at the Institute of Policy Studies, and Howard Webber, Director of M.I.T. Press. Senator Gravel, as intervenor, filed motions to quash the subpoenas and to require the Government to specify the particular questions to be addressed to Rodberg. He asserted that requiring these witnesses to appear and testify would violate his privilege under the Speech or Debate Clause of the United States Constitution, Art. I, § 6, cl. 1.

It appeared that on the night of June 29, 1971, Senator Gravel, as Chairman of the Subcommittee on Buildings and Grounds of the Senate Public Works Committee, convened a meeting of the subcommittee and there read extensively from a copy of the Pentagon Papers. He then placed the entire 47 volumes of the study in the public record. Rodberg had been added to the Senator's staff earlier in the day and assisted Gravel in preparing for and conducting the hearing. Some weeks later there were press reports that Gravel had arranged for the papers to be published by Beacon Press, and that members of Gravel's staff had talked with Webber as editor of M.I.T. Press.

[The District Court overruled the motions to quash but prohibited the asking of certain questions. The Court of Appeals held that (a) neither the Senator nor his aide could be questioned about the subcommittee hearing because of the Speech or Debate Clause, (b) third parties could be questioned about the source of Gravel's information but not about his conduct at the hearing, and (c) republication with Beacon Press was protected by a common law immunity but not by the Speech or Debate Clause. Although agreeing with much of its analysis, the Supreme Court vacated the Court of Appeals opinion.]

[I] * * * [T]he United States strongly urges that because the Speech or Debate Clause confers a privilege only upon "Senators and Representatives," Rodberg himself has no valid claim to constitutional immunity from grand jury inquiry. * * * We agree with the Court of Appeals that for the purpose of construing the privilege a Member and his aide are to be "treated as one," or, as the District Court put it: the "Speech or Debate Clause prohibits inquiry into things done by Dr. Rodberg as the Senator's agent or assistant which would have been legislative acts, and therefore privileged, if performed by the Senator personally." Both courts recognized what the Senate of the United States urgently presses here: that it is literally impossible, in view of the complexities of the modern legislative process, with Congress almost constantly in session and matters of legislative concern constantly proliferating, for Members of Congress to perform their legislative tasks without the help of aides and assistants; that the day-to-day work of such aides is so critical to the Members' performance that they must be treated as the latter's alter egos; and that if they are not so recognized, the central role of the Speech or Debate Clause—to prevent intimidation of legislators by the Executive and accountability before a possibly hostile judiciary—will inevitably be diminished and frustrated. * * *

It is true that the Clause itself mentions only "Senators and Representatives," but prior cases have plainly not taken a literalistic approach in applying the privilege. The Clause also speaks only of "Speech or Debate," but the Court's consistent approach has been that to confine the protection of the Speech or Debate Clause to words spoken in debate would be an unacceptably narrow view. Committee reports, resolutions, and the act of voting are equally covered; "[i]n short, . . . things generally done in a session of the House by one of its members in relation to the business before it." *Kilbourn.* Rather than giving the clause a cramped construction, the Court has sought to implement its fundamental purpose of freeing the legislator from executive and judicial oversight that realistically threatens to control his conduct as a legislator. We have little doubt that we are neither exceeding our judicial powers nor mistakenly construing the Constitution by holding that the Speech or Debate Clause applies not only to a Member but also to his aides insofar as the conduct of the latter would be a protected legislative act if performed by the Member himself.

Nor can we agree with the United States that our conclusion is foreclosed by *Kilbourn*, *Dombrowski*, and *Powell*, where the speech or debate privilege was held unavailable to certain House and committee employees. Those cases do not hold that persons other than Members of Congress are beyond the protection of the Clause when they perform or aid in the performance of legislative acts. In *Kilbourn*, the Speech or Debate Clause protected House Members who had adopted a resolution authorizing Kilbourn's arrest; that act was clearly legislative in nature. But the resolution was subject to judicial review insofar as its execution impinged on a citizen's rights as it did there. That the House could with impunity order an unconstitutional arrest afforded no protection for those who made the arrest. * * *

Dombrowski v. Eastland is little different in principle. The Speech or Debate Clause there protected a Senator, who was also a subcommittee chairman, but not the subcommittee counsel. The record contained no evidence of the Senator's involvement in any activity that could result in liability, whereas the committee counsel was charged with conspiring with state officials to carry out an illegal seizure of records that the committee sought for its own proceedings. The committee counsel was deemed protected to some extent by legislative privilege, but it did not shield him from answering as yet unproved charges of conspiring to violate the constitutional rights of private parties. Unlawful conduct of this kind the Speech or Debate Clause simply did not immunize.

Powell v. McCormack reasserted judicial power to determine the validity of legislative actions impinging on individual rights—there the illegal exclusion of a representative-elect—and to afford relief against House aides seeking to implement the invalid resolutions. The Members themselves were dismissed from the case because shielded by the Speech or Debate Clause both from liability for their illegal legislative act and from having to defend themselves with respect to it. * * *

* * * The three cases reflect a decidedly jaundiced view towards extending the Clause so as to privilege illegal or unconstitutional conduct beyond that essential to foreclose executive control of legislative speech or debate and associated matters such as voting and committee reports and proceedings. In *Kilbourn*, the Sergeant-at-Arms was executing a legislative order, the issuance of which fell within the Speech or Debate Clause; in *Eastland*, the committee counsel was gathering information for a hearing; and in *Powell*, the Clerk and Doorkeeper were merely carrying out directions that were protected by the Speech or Debate Clause. In each case, protecting the rights of others may have to some extent frustrated a planned or completed legislative act; but relief could be afforded without proof of a legislative act or the motives or purposes underlying such an act. No threat to legislative independence was posed, and Speech or Debate Clause protection did not attach.

None of this, as we see it, involves distinguishing between a Senator and his personal aides with respect to legislative immunity. In *Kilbourn*-type situations, both aide and Member should be immune with respect to committee and House action leading to the illegal resolution. So, too, in *Eastland*, as in this litigation, senatorial aides should enjoy immunity for helping a Member conduct committee hearings. On the other hand, no prior case has held that Members of Congress would be immune if they executed an invalid resolution by themselves carrying out an illegal arrest, or if, in order to secure information for a hearing, themselves seized the property or invaded the privacy of a citizen. Neither they nor their aides should be immune from liability or questioning in such circumstances. * * *

[II] We are convinced also that the Court of Appeals correctly determined that Senator Gravel's alleged arrangement with Beacon Press to publish the Pentagon Papers was not protected speech or debate within the meaning of Art. I, § 6, cl. 1, of the Constitution.

Historically, the English legislative privilege was not viewed as protecting republication of an otherwise immune libel on the floor of the House. *Stockdale v. Hansard*, 9 Ad. & E., at 114, 112 Eng. Rep., at 1156 (1839), recognized that "[f]or speeches made in Parliament by a member to the prejudice of any other person, or hazardous to the public peace, that member enjoys complete impunity." But it was clearly stated that "if the calumnious or inflammatory speeches should be reported and published, the law will attach responsibility on the publisher." This was accepted in *Kilbourn v. Thompson* as a "sound statement of the legal effect of the Bill of Rights and of the parliamentary law of England" and as a reasonable basis for inferring "that the framers of the Constitution meant the same thing by the use of language borrowed from that source."

Prior cases have read the Speech or Debate Clause "broadly to effectuate its purposes," *Johnson*, and have included within its reach anything "generally done in a session of the House by one of its members in relation to the business before it." *Kilbourn*. Thus, voting by Members and committee reports are protected; and we recognize today * * * that a Member's conduct at legislative committee hearings, although subject to judicial review in various circumstances, as is legislation itself, may not be made the basis for a civil or criminal judgment against a Member because that conduct is within the "sphere of legitimate legislative activity."

But the Clause has not been extended beyond the legislative sphere. That Senators generally perform certain acts in their official capacity as Senators does not necessarily make all such acts legislative in nature. Members of Congress are constantly in touch with the Executive Branch of the Government and with administrative agencies—they may cajole, and exhort with respect to the administration of a federal statute—but such conduct, though generally done, is not protected legislative activity. *United States v. Johnson* decided at least this much. "No argument is made, nor do we think that it could be successfully contended, that the Speech or Debate Clause reaches conduct, such as was involved in the attempt to influence the Department of Justice, that is in no wise related to the due functioning of the legislative process."

Legislative acts are not all-encompassing. The heart of the Clause is speech or debate in either House. Insofar as the Clause is construed to reach other matters, they must be an integral part of the deliberative and communicative processes by which Members participate in committee and House proceedings with respect to the consideration and passage or rejection of proposed legislation or with respect to other matters which the Constitution places within the jurisdiction of either House. As the Court of Appeals put it, the courts have extended the privilege to matters beyond pure speech or debate in either House, but "only when necessary to prevent indirect impairment of such deliberations."

Here, private publication by Senator Gravel through the cooperation of Beacon Press was in no way essential to the deliberations of the Senate; nor does questioning as to private publication threaten the integrity or independence of the Senate by impermissibly exposing its deliberations to executive influence. The Senator had conducted his hearings; the record and any report that was forthcoming were available both to his committee and the Senate. Insofar as we are advised, neither Congress nor the full committee ordered or authorized the publication. We cannot but conclude that the Senator's arrangements with Beacon Press were not part and parcel of the legislative process. * * *

[III] Similar considerations lead us to disagree with the Court of Appeals insofar as it fashioned, tentatively at least, a nonconstitutional testimonial privilege protecting Rodberg from any questioning by the grand jury concerning the matter of republication of the Pentagon Papers. This privilege, thought to be similar to that protecting executive officials from liability for libel, see *Barr v. Matteo*, 360 U.S. 564 (1959), was considered advisable "[t]o the extent that a congressman has responsibility to inform his constituents. . . ." But we cannot carry a judicially fashioned privilege so far as to immunize criminal conduct proscribed by an Act of Congress or to frustrate the grand jury's inquiry into whether publication of these classified documents violated a federal criminal statute. The so-called executive privilege has never been applied to shield executive officers from prosecution for crime, the Court of Appeals was quite sure that third parties were neither immune from liability nor from testifying about the republication matter, and we perceive no basis for conferring a testimonial privilege on Rodberg as the Court of Appeals seemed to do.

[Part IV of the Court's opinion defined the appropriate remedial order in the case to allow the grand jury to interrogate Rodberg about the arrangements for republication of the papers and about "the source of obviously highly classified documents that came into the Senator's possession and are the basic subject matter of inquiry in this case, as long as no legislative act is implicated by the questions." The Court prohibited questions "(1) concerning the Senator's conduct, or the conduct of his aides, at the June 29, 1971, meeting of the subcommittee; (2) concerning the motives and purposes behind the Senator's conduct, or that of his aides, at that meeting; (3) concerning communications between the Senator and his aides during the term of their employment and related to said meeting or any other legislative act of the Senator; (4) except as it proves relevant to investigating possible third-party crime, concerning any act, in itself not criminal, performed by the Senator, or by his aides in the course of their employment, in preparation for the subcommittee hearing."]

MR. JUSTICE DOUGLAS, dissenting.

I would construe the Speech or Debate Clause to insulate Senator Gravel and his aides from inquiry concerning the Pentagon Papers, and Beacon Press from inquiry concerning publication of them, for that publication was but another way of informing the public as to what had gone on in the privacy of the Executive Branch concerning the conception and pursuit of the so-called "war" in Vietnam. Alternatively, I would hold that Beacon Press is protected by the First Amendment from prosecution or investigations for publishing or undertaking to publish the Pentagon Papers. * * *

As to Senator Gravel's efforts to publish the Subcommittee record's contents, wide dissemination of this material as an educational service is as much a part of the Speech or Debate Clause philosophy as mailing under a frank a Senator's or a Congressman's speech across the Nation. * * * "[I]t is the proper duty of a representative body to look diligently into every affair of government and to talk much about what it sees. . . . The informing function of Congress should be preferred even to its legislative function." W. Wilson, *Congressional Government* 303 (1885). "From the earliest times in its history, the Congress has assiduously performed an 'informing function.'" *Watkins v. United States*, 354 U.S. 178, 200 n.3. "Legislators have an obligation to take positions on controversial political questions so that their constituents can be fully informed by them." *Bond v. Floyd*, 356 U.S. 116, 136.

We said in *Johnson* that the Speech or Debate Clause established a "legislative privilege" that protected a member of Congress against prosecution "by an unfriendly executive and conviction by a hostile judiciary" in order, as Mr. Justice Harlan put it, to ensure "the independence of the legislature." That hostility emanates from every stage of the present proceedings. It emphasizes the need to construe the Speech or Debate Clause generously, not niggardly. If republication of a Senator's speech in a newspaper carries the privilege, as it doubtless does, then republication of the exhibits introduced at a hearing before Congress must also do so. That means that republication by Beacon Press is within the ambit of the Speech or Debate Clause and that the confidences of the Senator in arranging it are not subject to inquiry "in any other Place" than the Congress.

[We have omitted the dissenting opinion of MR. JUSTICE BRENNAN, with whom MR. JUSTICE DOUGLAS and MR. JUSTICE MARSHALL joined. These Justices agreed that the Speech and Debate Clause protects legislative aides but dissented from the Court's refusal to protect republication.]

NOTES ON THE SPEECH OR DEBATE CLAUSE AFTER GRAVEL

1. *Analytical Conundrums Presented by the Court's Decision.* Why should the Speech or Debate Clause be construed very liberally to include staff, but then narrowly to exclude republication? The Court distinguishes *Kilbourn*, *Eastland*, and *Powell* because the officials in those cases committed illegal acts, but wasn't Rodberg's alleged conspiracy to disclose classified documents equally illegal? And what about Gravel: could he be prosecuted for participating in a breach of national security?

In *Kilbourn v. Thompson*, 103 U.S. 168 (1881), the Supreme Court held that Thompson, the Sergeant-at-Arms of the House, was liable for his wrongful arrest of Kilbourn, who had refused to comply with a House subpoena *duces tecum*. Thompson made the arrest pursuant to the order of a House committee that was investigating Kilbourn's bankrupt company. The Court held that the members of the committee were protected by the Speech or Debate Clause for their actions and deliberation, but that the Sergeant-at-Arms was not for his actions. After *Gravel*, would the House Sergeant-at-Arms (a House staff member) still be liable? How can *Gravel* be reconciled with *Kilbourn*? And would the result in *Kilbourn* have been different if the wrongful arrest had been carried out by a member of Congress?

Gravel holds that the Speech or Debate Clause applies to Members of Congress and their aides who are their "alter egos." Is that a qualification of the Court's holding? If so, which staff qualify? All of them? The Sergeant-at-Arms in *Kilbourn*? How about the staff of the Government Accountability Office, who work for the Congress but are not the aides of any one member? Should they have the same immunity as someone on a member's personal staff? See *Campaign for Fiscal Equity v. New York*, 687 N.Y.S. 2d 227 (N.Y. Sup. Ct), *aff'd* 265 A.D. 2d 277 (N.Y. App. 1999) (interpreting parallel state constitutional provision as extending Speech or Debate Clause protection to employee of the State Education Department who assisted legislators in analyzing budget legislation).

2.   *Critiquing* Gravel*'s Republication Holding.* One of us has critiqued the *Gravel* republication holding on the grounds that it is both futile and unwise. First,

> It is hard to see this holding of the Court's as anything other than futile. After all, the release of classified information will almost always draw substantial public notice, and the *Congressional Record* and committee reports have long been widely available. Advances since Gravel's release of the *Pentagon Papers* in 1971, including the online availability of the *Congressional Record*, committee reports, and the entire C-SPAN video archive, mean that, even in the absence of a republication agreement, theretofore secret information released by members of Congress will be picked up, reported upon, and read by the public.

Josh Chafetz, *Congress's Constitution: Legislative Authority and the Separation of Powers* 218 (2017). More fundamentally, the Court's holding is unwise because it undermines a crucial function of the Speech or Debate Clause: allowing members of Congress to keep the public informed about what those in power are doing in their name. Indeed, across American history, many revelations like Gravel's "have come to be understood as deeply important and patriotic acts. Today, for instance, we rightly consider the release of the *Pentagon Papers* to be an important milestone in the checking of an imperial presidency at war. And despite the Nixon administration's hyperventilation at the time, their release did not harm American national interests (as distinct from the interests of the Nixon administration)," as both Nixon's solicitor general and later historians concur. *Id.* at 223 (internal footnote omitted). Indeed, such releases may serve a crucial separation-of-powers function:

> [T]he question of what [information] disclosures count as damaging depends crucially on a politically constructed understanding of our national security interests. * * * [T]he extant regime regulating disclosure of secret information— a cocktail of massive overclassification, the availability of draconian penalties, and the infrequency of actual enforcement actions—suits executive-branch

interests quite nicely. The regime allows high-level executive officials to control the public narrative and advance their own agendas by selectively releasing information without fear of prosecution by their own underlings. At the same time, the release of information by individuals working at cross-purposes to the administration * * * can be punished severely. This regime makes apparent a very important fact: *"secret" is a political category, not a natural one.* Facts in isolation do not cry out for secrecy; facts within a specific political context do. Treating "secrecy" as something that inheres in a piece of information itself simply privileges the actor who made the initial determination of secrecy. * * * In a context in which the executive makes the initial secrecy determinations (and is loath to declassify much of anything) and the courts are unwilling to accept improper classification as a defense, the Speech or Debate Clause gives members of Congress the authority to challenge the executive's construction of national security interests without having to worry about the threat of criminal sanctions. In a separation-of-powers scheme characterized by a multiplicity of legitimate power centers competing publicly with one another for public support, ensuring that members of Congress are able publicly to contest the executive's construction of national security interests is vital.

Importantly, this power to disclose information is centrally located in the public sphere. When Congress responsibly releases to the public information that the public wants, it enhances its own prestige and, hence, its power. It may simultaneously knock the president down a peg by showing the American people what he sought to withhold from them. The power to reveal information is a soft power, and, as such, its potency depends entirely on how well the member of Congress using it gauges public sentiment. A member releasing, say, the names of covert operatives would likely find her public standing diminished, not bolstered. But, as the aftermath of the release of the *Pentagon Papers* shows, a member who uses the power properly can enhance her own, and her branch's, stature, especially in relation to an executive branch that appears to be fighting to keep its own failures and misdeeds out of the public eye.

Id. at 224–25 (internal footnotes omitted). Do you agree with either or both of these critiques of the *Gravel* republication holding?

3.   *Whistleblowing Versus Blacklisting.* The dissenters appeal to the value of whistleblowing: Members of Congress ought to be able to "blow the whistle" on government skullduggery by exposing documents that reveal valuable information to the American people. Leaking classified documents has become a widely imitated practice on Capitol Hill, and in many instances the public finds the ventilation of state secrets informative and useful. On the other hand, republication of legislative reports may also chill freedom. During the Cold War, members of Congress sometimes made lavish allegations about the loyalty of Americans who criticized our government, and their accusations would be republished, often to the ruin of those accused. Two years before *Gravel*, Judge Gerhard Gesell enjoined the publication of a report of the Committee on Internal Security of the House of Representatives on the ground that it served no "legitimate" public purpose and was little more than an effort to "blacklist" and smear people who held different points of view from the conservative House Committee. *Hentoff v. Ichord*, 318 F. Supp. 1175 (D.D.C. 1970).

4. *Balancing Legislative Independence Against Individual Rights.* Sometimes, as in *Hentoff*, recognizing legislative immunity would mean denial of rights to citizens that otherwise would be enforced in a court of law. Chief Justice Burger forcefully described this difficulty: "The immunities of the Speech or Debate Clause were not written into the Constitution simply for the personal or private benefit of Members of Congress, but to protect the integrity of the legislative process by insuring the independence of individual legislators." *Brewster*, 408 U.S. at 507. The tension is presented by cases in which congressional staff seek to sue members of Congress for some form of employment discrimination. The Court of Appeals for the D.C. Circuit wrestled with this issue in several cases, and it initially ruled that members were insulated from liability only with respect to employees whose duties were integral to the legislative process. *Browning v. Clerk, U.S. House of Representatives*, 789 F.2d 923 (D.C. Cir 1986). Thus, a female manager of the House of Representatives' restaurant could sue representatives who oversaw food services in the House on the ground that she was fired because she was female. *Walker v. Jones*, 733 F.2d 923 (D.C. Cir. 1984). In *Fields v. Office of Eddie Bernice Johnson*, 459 F.3d 1 (D.C. Cir. 2006) (en banc), the D.C. Circuit rejected a broad reading of *Browning* and barred review only when the claim "question[s] the conduct of official Senate legislative business." *Id.* at 8 (relying on *Bastien v. Office of Sen. Ben Nighthorse Campbell*, 390 F.3d 1301 (10th Cir. 2004)). Therefore, the plaintiffs, one of whom was fired after telling a senator he needed heart surgery and the other after objecting to a hiring decision, could maintain their suits, although they might be hindered in presenting arguments that turned on the motivation behind any legislative acts.

The Congressional Accountability Act of 1995, P.L. 104–1, 109 Stat. 3, *codified at* 2 U.S.C. § 1301 *et seq.*, adds a new wrinkle to this aspect of Speech or Debate Clause jurisprudence. The Act allows congressional employees to sue their employing office for wrongful discharge, but it also states that the Act is not a waiver of the Speech or Debate Clause privileges of any member. Members of Congress are not personally liable under the act for damages; instead, awards are paid by a contingent fund of the United States.[58]

5. *Statements by a Member of Congress to a Congressional Ethics Committee.* Is a member of Congress immune for statements he or she makes to a Congressional Ethics Committee? The District of Columbia Circuit wrestled with this question in *In re Grand Jury Subpoenas*, 571 F.3d 1200 (D.C. Cir. 2009). The case arose out of a House Ethics Committee investigation into Rep. Tom Feeney's (R-Fla.) 2003 golf trip to Scotland, funded by infamous lobbyist Jack Abramoff (whom we have already encountered in our discussions of corruption, conflicts of interest, and lobbying). Although Feeney claimed he had embarked on a legitimate legislative fact-finding trip, the House Ethics Committee determined that he had violated House ethics rules, and he agreed to pay the cost of the trip to the U.S. Treasury. Judge Douglas Ginsburg, writing for the unanimous three-judge panel, held that the Government could not subpoena Feeney's statements to the House Ethics Committee. The court noted that, under D.C. Circuit precedent, the Speech or Debate Clause gives a member of Congress immunity when an ethics investigation is connected to an act that is claimed to have been performed in the legislative capacity. Inquiries into ethical violations for non-legislative activities,

[58] See Christina Deneka, *Congressional Anti-Accountability and the Separation of Powers: A Survey of the Congressional Accountability Act's Problems*, 52 Rutgers L. Rev. 855 (2000) (discussing structural concerns with the Act); James Brudney, *Congressional Accountability and Denial: Speech or Debate Clause and Conflict of Interest Challenges to Unionization of Congressional Employees*, 36 Harv. J. on Legis. 1 (1999); David Frederick, *Commentary on the Congressional Accountability Act of 1995: A Section-by-Section Analysis*, in *Lobbying the New Congress* (Thomas Susman & Barbara Timmer eds., 1995).

however, are not covered by the Speech or Debate Clause. The court held that, because Feeney claimed he was engaging in legislative factfinding when he traveled to Scotland, and the Ethics Committee was trying to resolve whether the trip was in fact for legislative or recreational purposes, the Government could not subpoena his statements to the Ethics Committee.

In a concurring opinion, then-Judge Kavanaugh criticized the D.C. Circuit's focus on the subject matter of the underlying congressional investigation. This approach, Judge Kavanaugh noted, "creates great uncertainty. After all, it can be quite difficult to determine whether an allegation of wrongdoing involves official or personal acts because the categories often overlap—for example, when a Member is alleged to have abused his or her official position for personal gain." Judge Kavanaugh contended that *all* statements by members of Congress to congressional ethics committees should be immune under the Speech or Debate Clause. Regardless of the subject of the investigation, "[a] Member's statement to a congressional ethics committee is speech in an official congressional proceeding."

Should Speech or Debate Clause protection hinge on whether conduct being examined by the Ethics Committee is characterized as personal or official? Should it matter whether the Ethics Committee or the member of Congress does the characterizing? For further discussion, see Case Note, *Constitutional Law—Speech or Debate Clause—D.C. Circuit Quashes Subpoena for Congressman's Testimony to the House Ethics Committee—*In re Grand Jury Subpoenas, *571 F.3d 1200 (D.C. Cir. 2009),* 123 Harv. L. Rev. 564 (2009).

SPEECH OR DEBATE CLAUSE PROBLEMS

Problem 3-7. Senator William Proxmire (D-Wis.) in the 1970s started a practice of awarding a "Golden Fleece of the Month Award" for egregiously wasteful governmental spending. The award went to federal agencies that funded projects that Proxmire felt accomplished little for their cost. The second such award, made in April 1975, went to the National Science Foundation and NASA for spending almost $500,000 to fund research by Ronald Hutchinson, a behavioral scientist who studied tension and aggressive behavior under conditions of stress. He studied the behavior of animals, focusing on their clenching of teeth when they were exposed to stressful stimuli.

Senator Proxmire found this wasteful and made the award to Hutchinson in a speech on the floor of the Senate, preceded by a press release to 275 members of the news media. The speech and release said:

> The funding of this nonsense makes me almost angry enough to scream and kick or even clench my jaws. It seems to me it is outrageous.

> Dr. Hutchinson's studies should make the taxpayers as well as his monkeys grind their teeth. In fact, the good doctor has made a fortune from his monkeys and in the process made a monkey out of the American taxpayer.

In May 1975 Proxmire referred to this Fleece Award and quoted the above language from his speech in a newsletter to approximately 100,000 constituents. Later in 1975, Proxmire appeared on a television interview program and repeated the charge of waste.

Hutchinson sues Proxmire and Morton Schwartz (the aide who researched the matter and worked on the speech) for defamation. Assuming that he has made out a claim under state law (and a claim that is permissible under the First Amendment), should the court accept Proxmire's defense under the Speech or Debate Clause to immunize him from liability for his speech on the Senate floor? What about his press release? Is the republication in the constituent newsletter immunized? If there is a difference in treatment, what is the justification? Does Schwartz have a good defense? See *Hutchinson v. Proxmire*, 443 U.S. 111 (1979). Assume that Schwartz called the agency after the award had been given to discover whether it had changed its decision or altered the way it dispensed federal money. During those phone calls with National Science Foundation staff, Schwartz made allegedly defamatory remarks about Dr. Hutchinson. Can he be sued, or is he protected under the Speech or Debate Clause? What if his calls had been prompted initially by a constituent concerned about the way the agencies awarded federal money? See *Chastain v. Sundquist*, 833 F.2d 311 (D.C. Cir. 1987) (allowing defamation suit against congressman relating to casework concerning the activities of attorneys in the Memphis Area Legal Services office).

Problem 3-8. The chairman of the Senate Judiciary Committee replaces his assistant committee counsel, Martin, with a comparably qualified woman, Marianne, based on the chairman's stated desire for more diversity in committee policymaking positions. When Martin asks whether his termination is due to poor performance, the chairman responds: "No, you have been doing a fine job. But I want a qualified woman in this position to develop a cross-section of perspectives among my inner circle of advisors. In addition, the Committee is facing a series of gender-related criminal and civil rights issues, and a woman's perspective will be valuable to me." Assuming arguendo that this personnel decision raises a red flag on sex discrimination, should the Senator's decision be protected under the Speech or Debate Clause? *See Davis v. Passman*, 442 U.S. 228 (1979) (declining to address the question because the circuit court had not done so); *id.* at 249–54 (noting views of four dissenting justices).

Problem 3-9. In the summer of 2013, Edward Snowden, a contract employee who had worked for the National Security Agency (NSA), leaked classified documents exposing the NSA's massive and longstanding surveillance program. In addition to igniting domestic and foreign outrage, the leaks led members of Congress to admit that they had known of the surveillance program for years but felt restricted from bringing it into the public light. Senators Ron Wyden (D-Ore.) and Mark Udall (D-Colo.), members of the Senate Intelligence Committee who had been briefed on the surveillance program at secret sessions, chose not to raise it on the Senate floor despite their grave concerns. In an August 2013 interview with *Rolling Stone* magazine, Senator Wyden stated that when he first learned of the surveillance in early 2007, he and one other senator wrote classified letters to senior officials urging them to disclose their interpretation that the 2001 Patriot Act authorized this level of data collection. Asked whether he regretted not having exposed the program well before the Snowden leaks, Senator Wyden stated that there are "very significant limits" on what a person can and cannot say, and "[i]f you want to play a watchdog role, you try to work within the rules."

Would the Speech or Debate Clause have protected Senator Wyden from prosecution for reading the classified material into the public record? Could such a public reading by a member of Congress on the Senate floor qualify as "treason," which the Constitution defines in relevant part (Art. III, Sec. 3) as "giving [enemies of the United States] aid and comfort"? *See Cramer v. United States*, 325 U.S. 1 (1945). What penalties might Senator

Wyden face from Congress itself? Are any such penalties relevant to whether he should be protected under the Speech or Debate Clause?[59]

SPEECH OR DEBATE AND BRIBERY PROSECUTIONS

Do prosecutions for corruption, like that in *Van de Carr* (§ 1(A) of this chapter), undermine the independence of the legislature? If so, the decision might trigger concern under the speech or debate provision of the applicable constitution. If there had been an applicable speech or debate clause, would it have counseled a different outcome in *Van de Carr*? Would the federal Speech or Debate Clause preclude such a prosecution under the federal bribery statute, 18 U.S.C. § 201? Consider the following case.

UNITED STATES V. HELSTOSKI

Supreme Court of the United States, 1979.
442 U.S. 477, 99 S.Ct. 2432, 61 L.Ed.2d 12.

MR. CHIEF JUSTICE BURGER delivered the opinion of the Court.

[Henry Helstoski, a former Member of the House of Representatives from New Jersey, was indicted under § 201 for receiving money from noncitizens in return for introducing private bills in Congress that would suspend the application of U.S. immigration laws so that they could remain in the United States. The lower courts ruled that the Government could not introduce "evidence of the performance of a past legislative act on the part of the defendant * * * derived from any source and for any purpose." The Government appealed this ruling, arguing that it was not required by the Speech or Debate Clause.]

The Court's holdings in *United States v. Johnson*, 383 U.S. 169 (1966), and *United States v. Brewster*, 408 U.S. 501 (1972), leave no doubt that evidence of a legislative act of a Member may not be introduced by the Government in a prosecution under § 201. In *Johnson* there had been extensive questioning of both Johnson, a former Congressman, and others about a speech which Johnson had delivered in the House of Representatives and the motive for the speech. The Court's conclusion was unequivocal:

> "We see no escape from the conclusion that such an intensive judicial inquiry, made in the course of a prosecution by the Executive Branch under a general conspiracy statute, violates the express language of the Constitution and the policies which underlie it."

In *Brewster*, we explained the holding of *Johnson* in this way:

> "*Johnson* thus stands as a unanimous holding that a Member of Congress may be prosecuted under a criminal statute provided that the Government's case does not rely on legislative acts or the motivation for legislative acts. A legislative act has consistently been defined as an act generally done in Congress in relation to the business before it. In sum, the Speech or Debate

59   See generally Josh Chafetz, *Congress's Constitution: Legislative Authority and the Separation of Powers* 220–25 (2017); Bruce Ackerman, *Breach or Debate,* Foreign Policy, August 1, 2013, https://foreignpolicy.com/2013/08/01/breach-or-debate/.

Clause prohibits inquiry only into those things generally said or done in the House or the Senate in the performance of official duties and into the motivation for those acts."

The Government, however, argues that exclusion of references to past legislative acts will make prosecutions more difficult because such references are essential to show the motive for taking money. In addition, the Government argues that the exclusion of references to past acts is not logically consistent. In its view, if jurors are told of promises to perform legislative acts they will infer that the acts were performed, thereby calling the acts themselves into question.

We do not accept the Government's arguments; without doubt the exclusion of such evidence will make prosecutions more difficult. Indeed, the Speech or Debate Clause was designed to preclude prosecution of Members for legislative acts. The Clause protects "against inquiry into acts that occur in the regular course of the legislative process and into the motivation for those acts." It "precludes any showing of how [a legislator] acted, voted, or decided." *Brewster.* Promises by a Member to perform an act in the future are not legislative acts. *Brewster* makes clear that the "compact" may be shown without impinging on the legislative function.

We therefore agree with the Court of Appeals that references to past legislative acts of a Member cannot be admitted without undermining the values protected by the Clause. We implied as much in *Brewster* when we explained: "To make a prima facie case under [the] indictment, the Government need not show any act of [Brewster] *subsequent* to the corrupt promise for payment, for it is taking the bribe, not performance of the illicit compact, that is a criminal act." A similar inference is appropriate from *Johnson* where we held that the Clause was violated by questions about motive addressed to others than Johnson himself. That holding would have been unnecessary if the Clause did not afford protection beyond legislative acts themselves.

MR. JUSTICE STEVENS misconstrues our holdings on the Speech or Debate Clause in urging: "The admissibility line should be based on the purpose of the offer rather than the specificity of the reference." The Speech or Debate Clause does not refer to the prosecutor's purpose in offering evidence. The Clause does not simply state, "No proof of a legislative act shall be offered"; the prohibition of the Clause is far broader. It provides that Members "shall not be questioned in any other Place." Indeed, as MR. JUSTICE STEVENS recognizes, the admission of evidence of legislative acts "may reveal [to the jury] some information about the performance of legislative acts and the legislator's motivation in conducting official duties." Revealing information as to a legislative act—speaking or debating—to a jury would subject a Member to being "questioned" in a place other than the House or Senate, thereby violating the explicit prohibition of the Speech or Debate Clause.

As to what restrictions the Clause places on the admission of evidence, our concern is not with the "specificity" of the reference. Instead, our concern is whether there is mention of a legislative act. To effectuate the intent of the Clause, the Court has construed it to protect other "legislative acts" such as utterances in committee hearings and reports. E.g., *Doe v. McMillan*, 412 U.S. 306 (1973). But it is clear from the language of the Clause that protection extends only to an act that has already been performed. A promise to deliver a speech, to vote, or to solicit other votes at some future date is not "speech or debate." Likewise, a promise to introduce a bill is not a legislative act. Thus, in light of the strictures of *Johnson* and *Brewster*, the District Court order prohibiting the introduction of evidence "of the performance of a past legislative act" was redundant.

[The Government also argued that the Speech or Debate Clause had been waived, either by (a) Helstoski's testimony before the grand jury in which he produced documentary evidence of his legislative acts or (b) the enactment of § 201 by Congress. The Court did not decide whether waiver was ever possible by the defendant, but held that any possible waiver would have to be an "explicit and unequivocal renunciation of the protection," which Helstoski's actions were not.]

The Speech or Debate Clause was designed neither to assure fair trials nor to avoid coercion. Rather, its purpose was to preserve the constitutional structure of separate, coequal, and independent branches of government. The English and American history of the privilege suggests that any lesser standard would risk intrusion by the Executive and the Judiciary into the sphere of protected legislative activities. The importance of the principle was recognized as early as 1808 in *Coffin v. Coffin*, 4 Mass. 1, 27, where the court said that the purpose of the principle was to secure to every member "*exemption* from prosecution, for every thing said or done by him, as a representative, in the exercise of the functions of that office."

This Court has reiterated the central importance of the Clause for preventing intrusion by Executive and Judiciary into the legislative sphere.

> [I]t is apparent from the history of the clause that the privilege was not born primarily of a desire to avoid private suits . . . but rather to prevent intimidation by the executive and accountability before a possibly hostile judiciary. * * *

> There is little doubt that the instigation of criminal charges against critical or disfavored legislators by the executive in a judicial forum was the chief fear prompting the long struggle for parliamentary privilege in England and, in the context of the American system of separation of powers, is the predominate thrust of the Speech or Debate Clause. *Johnson.* * * *

We recognize that an argument can be made from precedent and history that Congress, as a body, should not be free to strip individual Members of the protection guaranteed by the Clause from being "questioned" by the Executive in the courts. The controversy over the Alien and Sedition Acts reminds us how one political party in control of both the Legislative and the Executive Branches sought to use the courts to destroy political opponents.

The Supreme Judicial Court of Massachusetts noted in *Coffin* that "the privilege secured . . . is not so much the privilege of the house as an organized body, as of each individual member composing it, who is entitled to this privilege, *even against the declared will of the house.*" In a similar vein in *Brewster* we stated:

> "The immunities of the Speech or Debate Clause were not written into the Constitution simply for the personal or private benefit of Members of

Congress, but to protect the integrity of the legislative process *by insuring the independence of individual legislators.*"

We perceive no reason to undertake, in this case, consideration of the Clause in terms of separating the Members' rights from the rights of the body.

[*Affirmed.*]

MR. JUSTICE POWELL took no part in the consideration or decision of this case.

MR. JUSTICE STEVENS, with whom MR. JUSTICE STEWART joins, concurring in part and dissenting in part. * * *

In *Brewster*, the Court held that the Speech or Debate Clause did not bar prosecution of a former Senator for receiving money in return for being influenced in the performance of a legislative act. The Court read *Johnson* as allowing a prosecution of a Member of Congress so long as the Government's case does not rely on legislative acts or the motivation for such acts. It reasoned that Brewster was not being prosecuted for the performance of a legislative act, but rather for soliciting or agreeing to take money with knowledge that the donor intended to compensate him for an official act. Whether the Senator ever performed the official act was irrelevant.

As a practical matter, of course, it is clear that evidence relating to a legislator's motivation for accepting a bribe will also be probative of his intent in committing the official act for which the bribe was solicited or paid. Nonetheless, the Court made clear in *Brewster* that inquiries into the legislator's motivation in accepting payment are not barred by *Johnson*'s proscription against inquiry into legislative motivation. "[A]n inquiry into the purpose of a bribe," the *Brewster* Court held, " 'does not draw in question the legislative acts of the defendant member of Congress or his motives for performing them.' " Thus, so long as the Government's case does not depend upon the legislator's motivation in committing an official act, inquiries into his motivation in accepting a bribe—which obviously may be revealing as to both the existence of legislative acts and the motivation for them—are permissible under the Speech or Debate Clause, as interpreted in *Brewster*.

* * * Here, the Government is seeking to introduce written and testimonial evidence as to Helstoski's motivation in soliciting and accepting bribes. Some of this evidence makes reference to past or future legislative acts for which payment is being sought or given. Obviously, this evidence, to the extent it is probative of Helstoski's intent in accepting payment, is an important and legitimate part of the Government's case against the former Congressman. Whether or not he ever committed the legislative acts is wholly irrelevant to the Government's proof, and inquiry into that subject is prohibited by *Johnson* and *Brewster*. But the mere fact that legislative acts are mentioned does not, in my view, require that otherwise relevant and admissible evidence be excluded. * * * The admissibility line should be based on the purpose of the offer rather than the specificity of the reference. So long as the jury is instructed that it should not consider the references as proof of legislative acts, and so long as no inquiry is made with respect to the motivations for such acts, *Brewster* does not bar the introduction of evidence simply because reference is made to legislative acts.

Indeed, I think it important to emphasize that the majority today does not read *Brewster* to foreclose the introduction of any evidence making reference to legislative acts. The Court holds that evidence referring only to acts to be performed in the future may be admitted into evidence. The Court explains this holding by noting that a promise to perform a legislative act in the future is not itself a legislative act. But it is equally true that the solicitation of a bribe which contains a self-laudatory reference to past performance is not itself a legislative act. Whether the legislator refers to past or to future performance, his statement will be probative of his intent in accepting payment and, in either event, may incidentally shed light on the performance and motivation of legislative acts. The proper remedy, in my judgment, is not automatic inadmissibility for past references and automatic admissibility for future references. Rather, drawing on the language of the Constitution itself, the test should require the trial court to analyze the purpose of the prosecutor's questioning. If the evidentiary references to legislative acts are merely incidental to a proper purpose, the judge should admit the evidence and instruct the jury as to its limited relevance. The Constitution mandates that legislative acts "shall not be questioned"; it does not say they shall not be mentioned.

[The dissenting opinion of MR. JUSTICE BRENNAN has been omitted. The dissent argued that the indictment should have been dismissed. " '[P]roof of an agreement to be "influenced" in the performance of legislative acts is by definition an inquiry into their motives, whether or not the acts themselves or the circumstances surrounding them are questioned at trial.' " Quoting *Brewster*, 408 U.S. at 536 (Brennan, J., dissenting).]

NOTE ON BRIBERY PROSECUTIONS AFTER HELSTOSKI

In *United States v. Myers*, 635 F.2d 932 (2d Cir. 1980), former Congressman Myers (D-Pa.) argued that his indictment for bribery in violation of § 201 as part of the Abscam investigation was subject to dismissal under the Speech or Debate Clause because it required or contemplated that the prosecutor present evidence protected by the Clause. In rejecting this argument, the Second Circuit noted that the indictment alleged a *promise* to perform a legislative act (introduction of a private bill to allow foreign businessmen to remain in the United States), not the performance of the act. See also *United States v. Murphy*, 642 F.2d 699 (2d Cir. 1980), where the court stated that, under *Brewster*, acceptance of bribes in return for corrupt promises to take official action is not protected by the Clause. What objections might a pluralist raise to the claim that a promise to vote a certain way is not a legislative action?

In *United States v. Williams*, 644 F.2d 950 (2d Cir. 1981), the court held that the Speech or Debate Clause was not violated when the indicting grand jury was shown a videotape of defendant, former Senator Harrison Williams (D-N.J.), discussing a proposed immigration bill, because this discussion involved only possible future performance of legislative functions. And in *United States v. Myers, supra*, the Second Circuit rejected the contention of a co-defendant, former Congressman Frank Thompson (D-N.J.), that the trial court had erred in allowing into evidence proof of his private conversations on the floor of the House of Representatives in which he invited a second Congressman to join the ranks of those accepting bribes. The court said that "[o]ne would think that a Congressman, even when grasping for objections to a criminal conviction, would understand that the Speech or Debate Clause accords immunity to what is said on the House floor in the course of the legislative process, * * * not to whispered solicitations to commit a crime."

These cases reflect the difficulty of applying the Court's test for Speech or Debate Clause immunity to instances of allegedly corrupt behavior. Inquiry into the lawmaker's decision to accept a bribe, which seems to be allowed, may well shed light on the motives in performing any subsequent related legislative act. And how should courts treat self-laudatory references to past legislative acts designed to convince listeners to participate in the corrupt scheme? Under the Court's jurisprudence, these statements would probably be excluded from the courtroom, even though the accuracy of the statements is arguably not relevant to the prosecution. Should we worry that the clause is too expansive in its coverage, immunizing from prosecution corrupt politicians who should be held to answer for their perfidy? Or should we worry that it is too weak, allowing judges to poke their noses into even conversations on the floor of the legislature? Remember that the Clause protects a member only from questioning "in any other Place," thereby allowing the legislature the power to investigate and discipline its own members.

Problem 3-10. The House of Representatives was nearing a vote on the President's health reform proposal. The vote was going to be close, and the Republican Party leadership wanted to maintain party discipline to ensure passage. Representative Alex Noah, a Republican on the committee with jurisdiction over the bill, opposed the bill and announced his intention to vote no on the floor. A week before, Noah had announced that he was retiring from Congress, and his daughter Samantha had declared that she would run for her father's now-open seat in the next election.

On the floor of the House, during the voting period on the health care bill, the Speaker of the House told Noah that "a yes vote on this bill will help you and help your daughter because it will be a popular vote with the President and your Party." Minutes later, Noah was called off the floor into the cloakroom (a room right off the House floor where only representatives can enter and that has phones and comfortable chairs) to take a phone call from the Secretary of Health and Human Services. The Secretary told Noah that it was important that he end his distinguished career on a high note of support for the President. The Secretary added that he was sure Noah's expertise would be crucial to several blue-ribbon panels being established to study the challenges facing the health care system, and that he hoped the President would be in a position to nominate Noah for such positions after he retired. When Noah returned to the floor, the Republican Majority Leader told him that his state's Chamber of Commerce would like to raise $100,000 for Samantha's campaign, but that a no vote would probably discourage the Chamber from doing so. Representative Jane Skye, another Republican from Noah's state, told Noah on his way up to vote that if he voted no, she and other Republicans would make sure Samantha never came to Congress and that Samantha would be political "dead meat."

Noah voted no. Noah is willing to testify about the events in any criminal prosecutions that may be brought or in any other forum. What crimes may have been committed? What obstacles would stand in the way of any prosecutions? What arguments would you expect to be made by possible defendants? Are avenues available for an investigation into the events that Representative Noah has described other than criminal prosecutions in court?

One further wrinkle involves situations in which the member herself introduces evidence of legislative acts at trial, and those same acts are later the subject of government inquiry on rebuttal. In *United States v. Renzi*, 769 F.3d 731 (9th Cir. 2014), former Arizona Representative Richard Renzi was convicted of public corruption, insurance fraud, and racketeering, based on his having misappropriated his insurance company's client premiums to fund his congressional campaign. On appeal, Renzi argued that the district court had violated his Speech or Debate Clause protection when, after Renzi had introduced evidence of his legislative acts during the cross examination of a government witness, the court allowed the government to inquire about those same acts on rebuttal. The Ninth Circuit disagreed, holding that because the Congressman himself had introduced the evidence he could not then claim that the government witness was being "questioned" for purposes of the Clause. Notably, the appeals court distinguished its analysis from the Supreme Court's holding in *Helstoski* that any waiver of the Clause's protection would have to be "an explicit and unequivocal renunciation." The Ninth Circuit concluded that the discussion in *Helstoski* concerned whether a member of Congress can be said to have waived his Speech or Debate Clause privilege for trial after providing legislative act evidence in the grand jury; by contrast, "the limited rebuttal evidence at issue here [is] distinct from a waiver of the Speech or Debate privilege based on a willingness to testify before a grand jury." Is this distinction persuasive? The Ninth Circuit noted that it was joining the Second, Third, and D.C. Circuits in allowing such cross-examination on rebuttal. Do you think these circuits are correct when they circumscribe the meaning of "waiver" in *Helstoski*?

Problem 3-11. In 2006, the FBI conducted an investigation of bribery and other allegations concerning Rep. William Jefferson (D-La.). It was alleged that Jefferson used his position to influence some African nations to buy telecommunications equipment and services from a Louisiana-based firm in return for substantial cash and stock. One of his former staffers and the president of the firm pleaded guilty to bribing and conspiring to bribe the Congressman. Pursuant to a search warrant but without alerting congressional leadership, the FBI searched Jefferson's congressional office in Washington, D.C.—apparently the first time that federal law enforcement officials had searched the office of a representative or senator. The FBI seized computer hard drives and boxes of paper records, which it agreed to review using a "Filter Team" to remove any irrelevant documents or any material protected by the Speech or Debate Clause or any other privilege. (The FBI also searched Jefferson's home, where agents found $90,000 wrapped in aluminum foil and hidden in the freezer.) Lawmakers from both parties objected to the search as a violation of legislative privilege. Can congressional offices be searched consistent with the Speech or Debate Clause? Can law enforcement use the documents that agents find there? How would the case against Representative Jefferson be affected by the constitutional privilege and the cases interpreting it? See *United States v. Rayburn House Office Building*, 497 F.3d 654 (D.C. Cir. 2007) (holding that the execution of the search warrant violated the Speech or Debate Clause, that all privileged documents (originals and copies) must be returned, that the FBI officers who participated in the search cannot reveal contents of privileged documents or be involved in pending prosecution, but that non-privileged documents need not be returned). Jefferson was subsequently convicted on eleven counts of bribery, honest services wire fraud, money laundering, racketeering, and conspiracy. In the aftermath of *McDonnell* (see § 1(A) of this chapter), seven of the eleven convictions were vacated. *United States v. Jefferson*, 289 F. Supp. 3d 717 (E.D. Va. 2017).

2. State Protection of State Legislators (Speech or Debate Clauses in State Constitutions)

Forty-three state constitutions contain clauses similar to the U.S. Constitution's Speech or Debate Clause. State courts often interpret these clauses as having a similar meaning to the federal clause,[60] although the precise formulations in state constitutions vary.[61]

In *Iron v. Rhode Island Ethics Comm'n*, 973 A.2d 1124 (R.I. 2009), the Rhode Island Supreme Court held that the state's constitutional "speech in debate clause" prohibited the Rhode Island Ethics Commission from prosecuting Rhode Island State Senator William V. Irons for alleged violations of the Rhode Island Code of Ethics. The Ethics Commission accused Senator Irons of improperly participating in debate and voting on legislation impacting entities with which he had business ties. Neither party disputed that Senator Irons' allegedly improper activities were core legislative activities ordinarily covered by the speech in debate clause. However, the Ethics Commission, which was created by an amendment to the Rhode Island Constitution stating that "All elected and appointed officials * * * shall be subject to the code of ethics," argued that this more recent constitutional provision effected a "narrow repeal" of the Rhode Island Constitution's speech in debate clause. The state supreme court rejected the argument and held that the Ethics Commission can only investigate and prosecute legislators for non-core legislative activities. The court further noted that while the speech in debate clause is an absolute immunity, it does not protect: "speeches delivered outside the legislature; political activities of legislators; undertakings for constituents; assistance in securing government contracts; republication of defamatory material in press releases and newsletters; solicitation and acceptance of bribes; and criminal activities, even those committed to further legislative activity." For further discussion see James Mure, *Case Note, Speech in Debate Clause—The Rhode Island Supreme Court Refuses to Read an Implied Exception into the Speech in Debate Clause:* Irons v. Rhode Island Ethics Comm'n, 973 A.2d 1124 (R.I. 2009), 41 Rutgers L.J. 1099 (2010).

Recall the discussion of legislator personnel decisions in Problem 3-8, raising the question whether a U.S. Senator's decision to fire an aide based on gender should be protected under the Speech or Debate Clause. The scope of the Speech or Debate privilege for personnel decisions remains unresolved at the Supreme Court level. However, a Michigan appeals court recently addressed the matter, relying on the Court's decision in *Forrester v. White,* 484 U.S. 219 (1988), which had examined the personnel issue not for members of Congress but for judges. In *Cotton v. Banks,* 872 N.W.2d 1, 11–12 (Mich. Ct. App. 2015), a state representative's former driver claimed that he was fired for declining a romantic relationship with the legislator. Representative Brian Banks invoked absolute immunity from suit under the state constitution's speech or debate clause. The Michigan Court of Appeals relied on the "functional test" established in *Forrester* to determine whether the personnel decision was a legislative act—looking to the nature of the act being performed by

---

[60]   See, e.g., *Romer v. Colorado General Assembly*, 810 P.2d 215 (Colo. 1991); *People v. Ohrenstein*, 565 N.E.2d 493, 501 (N.Y. 1990); *Harristown Dev. Corp. v. Pa. Dep't of Gen. Serv.*, 580 A.2d 1174 (Pa. 1990).

[61]   For a survey of formulations, see Steven Huefner, *The Neglected Value of the Legislative Privilege in State Legislatures*, 45 Wm. & Mary L. Rev. 221, 236–37 (2003).

the legislator as opposed to the nature of the employee's duties. The court found that the act in question was administrative rather than legislative in nature, and declined to allow the asserted immunity.

Do you agree that personnel decisions should not be protected under the speech or debate privilege? All decisions or just some? If the latter, which ones? Should it matter that the privilege protecting legislators is written into constitutions (state and federal) whereas protection for judges' personnel decisions derives from common law? The Court in *Forrester* observed that because judges have very little freedom to delegate the performance of judicial acts to subordinates, judicial independence won't be unduly threatened if these subordinates are permitted to challenge termination decisions. Is the same observation about lack of staff delegation true with respect to performance of legislative acts? For fuller discussion of the arguments for and against Speech or Debate Clause coverage in the employment setting, see James Brudney, *Congressional Accountability and Denial: Speech or Debate Clause and Conflict of Interest Challenges to Unionization of Congressional Employees*, 36 Harv. J. on Legis. 1, 33–56 (1999).

3. Federal Protection of State Legislators

The Court addressed whether the policies of the Speech or Debate Clause protected state legislators in *United States v. Gillock*, 445 U.S. 360 (1980). In that case, a Tennessee state legislator was indicted on federal charges stemming from allegations that he had accepted money in return for using his office to block extradition of criminal defendants and for introducing legislation that would have enabled four persons to obtain electrician's licenses that they had been unable to obtain by way of examination. The District Court had granted Gillock's motion to suppress all evidence relating to his legislative activities, on the ground that the Federal Rules of Evidence should recognize a privilege to protect the integrity of the state legislative process. After the Court of Appeals affirmed, the Supreme Court reversed. The Court noted that the Speech or Debate Clause protects only federal legislators and rejected arguments that the policy considerations underlying the Speech or Debate Clause counsel recognition of a comparable evidentiary privilege for state legislators in federal prosecutions. The Court stated:

> Two interrelated rationales underlie the Speech or Debate Clause: first, the need to avoid intrusion by the Executive or Judiciary into the affairs of a coequal branch, and second, the desire to protect legislative independence. * * *
>
> The first rationale, resting solely on the separation of powers doctrine, gives no support to the grant of a privilege to state legislators in federal criminal prosecutions. * * * [I]n those areas where the Constitution grants the Federal Government the power to act, the Supremacy Clause dictates that federal enactments will prevail over competing state exercises of power. * * *
>
> [As to the second rationale,] we believe that recognition of an evidentiary privilege for state legislators for their legislative acts would impair the

legitimate interest of the Federal Government in enforcing its criminal statutes with only speculative benefit to the state legislative process.

Compare *Tenney v. Brandhove*, 341 U.S. 367 (1951) (recognizing a federal common law immunity for state legislators against civil lawsuits brought under § 1983 for violations of federal constitutional or statutory rights).

3. STRUCTURAL DUE PROCESS OF LAWMAKING

In an article proposing an alternative method of judicial review to replace the deferential rational basis review accorded to many statutes, former Justice of the Oregon Supreme Court Hans Linde articulated a theory of due process of lawmaking. *Due Process of Lawmaking*, 55 Neb. L. Rev. 197 (1976). He argued that the Due Process Clauses of the Constitution "instruct government itself to act by due process of law, not simply to legislate subject to later judicial second-guessing." *Id.* at 222. Legislative process should be designed, he argued, to produce "rational lawmaking," which he understood as requiring that legislators be well informed about legislative proposals before they vote on them; decisions by committees and on the floor be based on evidence about the problems in the status quo, the purpose of the bill, and the likely consequences of the new legal framework; and the committee's report provide full explanations to members.

Linde acknowledged that his description did not accurately depict reality, but he argued that courts should adopt methods of adjudication and statutory review designed to promote this type of lawmaking by legislative bodies. (Linde can thus be situated within the Legal Process tradition, which will be discussed further in Chapter 5, § 2.) Courts could work toward this objective by scrutinizing the rationale articulated by lawmakers to justify their choices of legislative ends and the means to reach those ends. For the most part, justices on the Supreme Court have declined to take up this more searching strategy of judicial review.

Recently, however, the Supreme Court has begun scrutinizing the legislative record for thoroughness in cases assessing the constitutionality of federal laws passed pursuant to Congress' authority to regulate interstate commerce and its authority to enforce the Reconstruction Amendments. In cases such as *Board of Trustees of the Univ. of Alabama v. Garrett*, 531 U.S. 356 (2001) (concerning the Americans with Disabilities Act), *United States v. Morrison*, 529 U.S. 598 (2000) (concerning the Violence Against Women Act), and *Shelby County v. Holder*, 570 U.S. 529 (2013) (concerning the Voting Rights Act), the Court has reviewed the state of the legislative record to determine whether the empirical basis on which Congress legislated was sufficient. In all three of those cases, the Court's review of the legislative record was in service of its determination that the statute at issue was (at least in part or as applied) unconstitutional. Perhaps unsurprisingly, many commentators have criticized this approach as an unacceptably intrusive encroachment on the prerogatives of the most politically accountable branch and as unsophisticated in its determination of what documents make up the legislative record. Ruth Colker and James Brudney, in their article *Dissing Congress*, argued that the Court "has treated the federal legislative process as akin to agency or lower court decisionmaking; in doing so, the Court has undermined Congress's ability to decide for itself how and whether to create a record in support of pending legislation." 100 Mich. L. Rev. 80, 83 (2001). Similarly, Philip Frickey and Steven Smith suggested that the Court has placed unrealistic record-developing obligations upon Congress and failed to respect that, in circumstances of political conflict, legislatures decide by majority vote rather than by consensual deliberation. See *Judicial Review, the Congressional Process, and the Federalism Cases: An Interdisciplinary Critique*, 111 Yale L.J. 1707 (2002).[62]

Linde himself was at least somewhat dubious about the merits of aggressive judicial scrutinizing of the legislative record. "Candor in giving reasons for a policy can be a mixed blessing. It may result in invalidating a policy for faulty premises even though it would be quite desirable if based on different reasons. * * * Pursued into the legislative process [past the context of administrative agencies], the hope for candor is more likely to produce hypocrisy. Recitals of findings and purposes are the task of anonymous draftsmen, committee staffs, and counsel for interested parties, not legislators. Such recitals will be an attempt to provide whatever, under prevailing case law, is expected to satisfy a court." Linde, *supra*, at 230–31.

Accordingly, Linde focused on the process of lawmaking, its rules and structural arrangements that are designed to facilitate reasoned deliberation and rational decisionmaking. Due process of lawmaking focuses in part on the "structures through which policies are both formed and applied." Laurence Tribe, *Structural Due Process*, 10 Harv. C.R.-C.L. L. Rev. 269, 269 (1975). This notion suggests that some kinds of actions should be taken only by entities with particular institutional features that enhance their special democratic legitimacy. After we assess requirements in the federal Constitution and in state constitutions setting forth procedural requirements for lawmaking, we will turn to *Hampton v. Mow Sun Wong*, 426 U.S. 88 (1976), where the Court adopted a due process of lawmaking approach.

A. FEDERAL STRUCTURAL DUE PROCESS

The Bicameralism and Presentment Requirements. Article I, § 7, cl. 2–3 of the U.S. Constitution provide that a bill becomes a law only if it is enacted in the same form by both the House and Senate, and then presented to the President. If the President vetoes the bill, the House and Senate can override the veto by a two-thirds vote in each chamber. State constitutions have similar provisions, with one exception (Nebraska only has one legislative chamber) and one interesting twist (most states allow their governors to veto specific items in some bills, discussed in § 2(B) of this chapter).

One justification for the bicameralism and presentment requirements is to ensure the sustained consideration of different points of view. In *Federalist 51*, James Madison defended the bicameralism requirement on the ground that it mandates consent of two bodies elected in different ways, representing different interests and electorates, and developing different internal customs. Moreover, requiring two

---

[62]   See also William Araiza, *Deference to Congressional Fact-Finding in Rights-Enforcing and Rights-Limiting Legislation*, 88 N.Y.U. L. Rev. 878 (2013) (providing factors to determine level of judicial deference in certain contexts); William Buzbee & Robert Schapiro, *Legislative Record Review*, 54 Stan. L. Rev. 87 (2001). But see John McGinnis & Charles Mulaney, *Judging Facts Like Law*, 25 Const. Comm. 69 (2008) (arguing for an independent judicial role in assessing "social fact-finding" by Congress).

heterogeneous bodies to agree on legislation helps to prevent the adoption of factious and partial laws. In *Federalist 62*, Madison argued that the Senate, with its longer terms and smaller membership, would serve as a cooling-off chamber, preventing the enactment of hasty legislation. Alexander Hamilton argued in *Federalist 73* that the executive veto is likewise "calculated to guard the community against the effects of faction, precipitancy, or of any impulse unfriendly to the public good, which may happen to influence a majority" of Congress.

Saul Levmore has offered a modern analysis of bicameralism in *Bicameralism: When Are Two Decisions Better than One?*, 12 Int'l Rev. L. & Econ. 145 (1992). He first considers the possibility that bicameralism reduces the "manipulative power of the agenda setter" because one cannot control outcomes as well in a bicameral system as in a unicameral process. Levmore concludes, however, that "only a very careful and difficult empirical inquiry would establish that a convener's power to influence committee and conference-committee membership does not offset the fact that bicameralism diminishes the convener's ability to manipulate the order in which alternative proposals are considered." *Id.* at 151. He acknowledges the Buchanan and Tullock argument that bicameralism protects the status quo by making it more difficult to enact legislation. Levmore argues that although supermajority voting requirements could achieve the same purpose, "supermajoritarianism [likely] encourages more wasteful rent-seeking and corruption than does bicameralism. The simple fact that in a bicameral system a proposal must be openly considered in two forums may work to expose misbehavior. And if the problems of corruption and inefficient rent-seeking are in part functions of a legislator's ability to promise and deliver results, then it is surely the case that with supermajoritarianism a legislator, or small group of legislators, is more likely to be in a position to block legislation on behalf of some interest group than is a legislator likely to be able to block or promote legislation in a bicameral system with simple-majority voting." *Id.* at 155.

Bicameralism on the federal level requires that two legislative institutions that are constituted in very different ways each have a say in the enactment of laws. These differences were more pronounced before passage of the Seventeenth Amendment, which ended the practice of having state legislatures select senators.[63] The most obvious remaining differences between the two institutions are the Senate's longer terms and unique apportionment scheme in which each state is equally represented. This latter feature of the Senate is doubly entrenched: Article V of the Constitution provides that "no State, without its Consent, shall be deprived of its equal Suffrage in the Senate."[64] In contrast, both houses of bicameral state legislatures are subject to the principle of one person, one vote, although courts may accept greater population deviations in state districting than in the context of districting for the House of Representatives. (See the discussion in Chapter 2, § 1(A).)

Frances Lee and Bruce Oppenheimer have raised several fairness concerns in their study of the Senate, *Sizing Up the Senate: The Unequal Consequences of Equal*

---

[63]   See Vikram Amar, *Indirect Effects of Direct Election: A Structural Examination of the Seventeenth Amendment*, 49 Vand. L. Rev. 1347 (1996).

[64]   For a critique of the Senate as an institution that violates the one person, one vote principle, see Lynn Baker & Samuel Dinkin, *The Senate: An Institution Whose Time Has Gone?*, 13 J. L. & Pol. 21 (1997); William Eskridge Jr., *The One Senator, One Vote Clause*, 12 Const. Comment. 159 (1995).

Representation (1999). They find first that state population "dramatically affects both the quantity of contact that constituents have with their senators and the perceived quality of those interactions." *Id.* at 12. Constituents from less populous states have more contact with their senators and are more likely to ask them for help with their problems, rather than just registering their opinion on some policy matter. This reality causes a disparity of access for both individuals and interest groups to influence members of Congress. Another troubling disparity that Lee and Oppenheimer link to the malapportionment of the Senate affects partisan control of the institution. "[E]qual representation of states often means that one political party wins Senate seats disproportionate to its share of the national popular vote, owing to its success in small-state elections." *Id.* at 226.[65] Small-state senators tend to spend more time pursuing particularized benefits for their constituents, whereas large-state senators spend relatively more time pursuing policy activism, which appeals more to the media and thus furthers their reelection goal in states where personal campaigning is logistically impossible.

One way that small-state senators enhance their ability to obtain benefits for their constituents is that they often cast the decisive votes on closely fought legislation. "[C]oalition leaders tend to seek out senators from small states to find needed votes and * * * these senators—who know that their demands are less costly and thus more likely to be accommodated—delay committing themselves to a side, expecting to be courted by coalition leaders." *Id.* at 14. Not surprisingly given their disproportionate influence in the Senate, small-state senators are able to force the Senate to adopt funding formulas in government programs that systematically favor small states and distribute resources away from populous ones. Lee and Oppenheimer find that neither the House nor the President exerts "sufficient influence to counterbalance the effects of equal representation of states in the Senate in distributive policymaking." *Id.* at 14–15.

What is the sanction if a bill is passed in violation of either the bicameralism or presentment requirements? The main check is institutional. The *enrolled bill* is signed by the presiding officers of the House and Senate; if it is then approved by the President, it is sent to the Secretary of State, who furnishes a correct copy to the Congressional Printer for publication in the Statutes at Large. What if a mistake is made? That was the argument in *Marshall Field & Co. v. Clark*, 143 U.S. 649 (1892). Because § 30 of the bill passed by both chambers of Congress was omitted from the enrolled bill, the appellants argued that the law was null and void. The Court agreed with the general proposition but still denied the relief requested, refusing to look at the extrinsic evidence offered by the appellants to question the enrolled bill:

> It is said that * * * it becomes possible for the Speaker of the House of Representatives and the President of the Senate to impose upon the people as a law a bill that was never passed by Congress. But this possibility is too remote to be seriously considered in the present inquiry. It suggests a deliberate conspiracy to which the presiding officers, the committees on enrolled bills and the clerks of the two houses must necessarily be parties,

---

[65]   But see Franco Mattei, *Senate Apportionment and Partisan Advantage: A Second Look*, 26 Legis. Stud. Q. 391 (2001) (finding smaller apportionment bias than Lee & Oppenheimer).

all acting with a common purpose to defeat an expression of the popular will in the mode prescribed by the Constitution. Judicial action based upon such a suggestion is forbidden by the respect due to a coordinate branch of the government. The evils that may result from the recognition of the principle that an enrolled act, in the custody of the Secretary of State, attested by the signatures of the presiding officers of the two houses of Congress, and the approval of the President, is conclusive evidence that it was passed by Congress, according to the forms of the Constitution, would be far less than those that would certainly result from a rule making the validity of Congressional enactments depend upon the manner in which the journals of the respective houses are kept by the subordinate officers charged with the duty of keeping them.

Later that same year, however, in *United States v. Ballin*, 144 U.S. 1 (1892), the Court examined the Journal of the House of Representatives to conclude that a quorum had been present when a bill was passed. Are *Field v. Clark* and *Ballin* consistent with one another? If not, which approach should prevail? Should differences in modern congressional recordkeeping impact the viability of this rule? In *Public Citizen v. United States Dist. Court for the Dist. of Columbia*, 486 F.3d 1342 (D.C. Cir. 2007), the D.C. Circuit applied the doctrine to dismiss a challenge to the Deficit Reduction Act of 2005. In that case, an apparent error by the Secretary of the Senate created a divergence between the versions of the bill passed by the two chambers, amounting to a difference of about $2 billion in Medicare spending. Holding that *Field v. Clark* clearly governed, the court declined to look behind the enrolled version of the bill.

But enrollment is not the end of the story. Most lawyers, judges, and other legal interpreters do not encounter statutes through the Statutes at Large. Instead, they turn to the United States Code, in which in-force statutory provisions are organized by subject matter. The codification process requires judgments about which provisions to include at all (only "general and permanent" provisions get codified), whether to include them in the main text of the Code or in notes, where to put them, whether they repeal or amend preexisting law, and so on. In the process, of course, statutes get torn apart and scattered across different sections of the Code. This process is carried out by the Office of Law Revision Counsel (OLRC), a nonpartisan office within Congress dedicated to codification. Making matters even more complicated, some titles of the U.S. Code (currently 27 of the 54 titles, but covering only about a quarter of the total words in the Code) have themselves been enacted by Congress into law—these titles are known as "positive law titles," and they can only be changed by explicit amendment by Congress. The opacity of this process raises both deep questions about what counts as "the law," as well as more practical questions like how to think about statutory interpretation canons like the whole act rule (see Chapter 6, § 2(A)) when most lawyers don't encounter statutory provisions in the context of the whole act. As Jarrod Shobe has put it in an important and eye-opening new account of the codification process (from which the information in this paragraph is drawn), "scholars and judges have an undertheorized understanding of what the Code is." *Codification and the Hidden Work of Congress*, 67 UCLA L. Rev.

(forthcoming 2019) (manuscript at 17), *available at* https://ssrn.com/abstract= 3361281.

Special Procedures for Revenue Measures. Article I, § 7, cl. 1 requires that "[a]ll Bills for raising Revenue shall originate in the House of Representatives." The purpose of this rule is to assure that the representatives "closest" to the people (House members, who are up for reelection every two years) bear responsibility for initiating measures (taxes) that have the greatest potential for oppressing the citizenry.[66] Some state constitutions have similar requirements.

The provision prompts several questions: what counts as a "Bill for raising Revenue"? When does a bill not "originate" in the House? If a bill does not so originate, but the House and Senate enact the bill and the President signs it, do we have a "law" under Article I, § 7? Consider the following case.

United States v. Munoz-Flores

495 U.S. 385 (1990).

Munoz-Flores challenged his fines pursuant to 18 U.S.C. § 3013, which required that anyone convicted of a federal crime pay a "special assessment" to be deposited into the Crime Victims Fund (see 34 U.S.C. § 20101). Munoz-Flores argued that the assessment was unconstitutional, because the statute was a revenue measure that had not originated in the House of Representatives. **Justice Marshall**'s opinion for the Court held that § 3013 did not violate the Origination Clause. In *Twin City Bank v. Nebeker*, 167 U.S. 196, 202 (1897), the Court had earlier ruled that "revenue bills are those that levy taxes in the strict sense of the word, and are not bills for other purposes which may incidentally create revenue." This meant that "a statute that creates a particular governmental program and that raises revenue to support that program, as opposed to a statute that raises revenue to support Government generally, is not a 'Bil[l] for raising Revenue' within the meaning of the Origination Clause." Although the statute provided that if the total income to the Fund from all sources exceeded $100 million in any one year, the excess would be deposited in the general fund of the Treasury, that happened only once, in fiscal year 1989. Any revenue for the general Treasury generated by § 3013 was thus found to be "incidenta[l]" to the purposes of the statute. In footnote 7, the Court reserved judgment on whether it would apply the *Nebeker* rule to a funded program that was entirely unrelated to the persons paying for the program.

Justice Stevens (joined by **Justice O'Connor**), concurring in the judgment, argued from the structure of Article I, § 7 that improperly "originated" bills become "law" so long as they are passed by both the House and Senate and presented to the President. Read Article I, § 7, which says that "[e]very" bill passed by both houses and presented to the President "shall become a Law." Also, compare the consequences of improper origination (no explicit consequence) with failure of bicameralism (no law) or presentment (also no law). Justice Stevens agreed with the Court that the Origination Clause is an important means by which the most popularly accountable institution (the House) is to monitor efforts to tax the people, but Stevens argued that the House itself—

------

[66]   See Michael Evans, *"A Source of Frequent and Obstinate Altercations": The History and Application of the Origination Clause*, Tax Notes, Nov. 29, 2004, at 1215; J. Michael Medina, *The Origination Clause in the American Constitution: A Comparative Survey*, 23 Tulsa L.J. 165 (1987).

rather than the Court—is in the best position to enforce and effectuate this goal. Indeed, the House has a procedure, known as the "blue slip," by which it returns to the Senate bills that, in the House's view, violate the Origination Clause.[67]

Justice Scalia concurred in the judgment as well. Relying on *Field v. Clark*, he argued that the Court cannot look behind the "enrolled bill" as it was presented to the President. The enrolled bill that became the Victims of Crime Act of 1984, Pub. L. No. 98–473, 98 Stat. 1837, 2170, bore the indication "H.J. Res. 648." The designation "H.J. Res." ("House Joint Resolution") conclusively attested that the legislation originated in the House.

ORIGINATION CLAUSE PROBLEMS

Problem 3-12. The Senate passes S. 93, which might fairly be characterized as a revenue bill. The House then passes a similar bill of its own, H.R. 617. The Senate requests a conference, and the bill that ultimately emerges is called H.R. 617, but its provisions are more like those in S. 93. The President signs the bill into law. Has the Origination Clause been violated? If so, what remedy (if any) is available?

Problem 3-13. The Patient Protection and Affordable Care Act (ACA), Pub. L. No. 111–148, 124 Stat. 119 (2010), contained an "individual mandate," requiring most Americans to maintain a minimal level of health insurance coverage or else make a "shared responsibility payment" to the federal Treasury. In *Nat'l Fed'n of Indep. Bus. v. Sebelius*, 567 U.S. 519 (2012), the Supreme Court held that the shared responsibility payments could not be upheld as an exercise of Congress's Commerce Clause powers, but *could* be sustained as an exercise of the power to levy taxes.

The bill that became the ACA was denominated H.R. 3590. But H.R. 3590, as it originally passed the House, was a bill to modify the first-time homebuyers tax credit for members of the armed forces. In the Senate, that bill became the vehicle for an "amendment in the nature of a substitute"—that is, an "amendment" that erases the entire operative text of a bill and replaces it with something entirely different. In this case, the "substitute" was what became the ACA.

Relying on this legislative history and on the Supreme Court's determination that the shared responsibility payment could only be justified as an exercise of Congress's taxing power, an individual subject to the payment files suit, alleging that this provision of the ACA violates the Origination Clause. How should a court rule? *See Sissel v. U.S. Dep't of Health & Human Servs.*, 760 F.3d 1 (D.C. Cir. 2014), *cert. denied*, 136 S.Ct. 925 (2016) (rejecting the challenge on the grounds that "after the Supreme Court's decision in *NFIB*, it is beyond dispute that the paramount aim of the Affordable Care Act is 'to increase the number of Americans covered by health insurance and decrease the cost of health care,' * * * not to raise revenue by means of the shared responsibility payment" and therefore declining to reach the question of whether the bill actually originated in the House or the Senate).

---

[67]   On the House blue slip procedure, see Josh Chafetz, *Congress's Constitution: Legislative Authority and the Separation of Powers* 32–33 (2017).

B. THE ENROLLED BILL RULE IN STATE CONSTITUTIONAL PRACTICE

State constitutions often include more procedural requirements for the enactment of laws than the relatively spare federal Constitution. Many state constitutions, for example, require that a bill be read a certain number of times before it can be passed and set specific time limits for legislative sessions. However, a bill that has been passed without receiving the requisite number of readings will not reveal that defect on its face; the same is true if, as is sometimes done, a bill has been passed after the legislature was supposed to have adjourned, but the legislative clock had been covered before the time for adjournment and the legislature pretended that time was standing still. How could one prove such a defect or any other violation of constitutionally prescribed procedures?

In many states, the enrolled bill rule severely restricts judicial review of legislative procedural errors. Just as on the federal level, an enrolled bill is a bill that purports to have passed both houses of the legislature and that has been signed by the presiding officers of both houses. In some states, the process of enrollment also involves the signature of the governor and filing with the secretary of state. Courts following the enrolled bill rule conclusively presume that the enrolled bill was validly enacted according to the prescribed procedures and refuse to entertain evidence purporting to demonstrate the contrary. One commentator has noted that:

> the rule has been supported by several theories. Traditionally the doctrine of separation of powers was the underlying support for the rule. Under this doctrine the courts are kept from being placed in the position of reviewing the work of a supposedly equal branch of government. Other practical considerations have been advanced in support of the rule. Certain defects are apparent on the face of the enrolled bill itself, but other judicial attacks on the status of legislation could undermine stability in the law and would confuse the trial of substantive issues. * * * Flagrant disregard for constitutional duties is better remedied by internal legislative procedures or by the electorate. The enrolled bill rule is further justified by the argument that legislative journals are subject to error and fraud, whereas enrollment includes "certification by the presiding officers . . . witnessed by other present members . . . [furnishing] adequate protection against the risk of error in the process of certification itself."

Elizabeth Cobb, Comment, *Judicial Review of the Legislative Enactment Process: Louisiana's "Journal Entry" Rule*, 41 La. L. Rev. 1187, 1190 (1981). Are these arguments persuasive? Consider the responsive argument of Linde in *Due Process of Lawmaking, supra*, at 243:

> Neither [respect for a co-equal branch nor evidentiary difficulties] keeps courts from insisting on [adherence to procedural rules] by executive officers or by local lawmakers, and those who oppose judicial review of faulty lawmaking on evidentiary grounds will equally oppose it on uncontested pleadings or stipulations. Fear of legislative resentment at judicial interference is not borne out by experience where procedural review exists, any more than it was after the Supreme Court told Congress that it had

used faulty procedure in unseating Representative Adam Clayton Powell. It is far more cause for resentment to invalidate the substance of a policy that the politically accountable branches and their constituents support than to invalidate a lawmaking procedure that can be repeated correctly, yet we take substantive judicial review for granted.

As Linde's analysis suggests, the enrolled bill rule at the state level has faced sustained academic attack, and many state courts have responded favorably. See the useful discussion in Robert Williams, *State Constitutional Limits on Legislative Procedure: Legislative Compliance and Judicial Enforcement*, 48 U. Pitt. L. Rev. 797 (1987). Some courts have adopted special exceptions to the rule. In many cases, these exceptions are based on evidence found in the journals of legislative proceedings that all state constitutions require state legislatures to keep. (Article I, § 5, cl. 3 of the U.S. Constitution similarly requires that "[e]ach House shall keep a Journal of its Proceedings, and from time to time publish the same.") State constitutions differ on the timing and manner of publication, the number of members necessary to have roll call votes recorded in the journal, and whether dissenting comments or protests must be recorded. Courts seeking to modify the enrolled bill rule have often relied on information found in these official journals. As explained in Cobb's comment, *supra*, at 1191–92:

> [Two] general categories have been delineated: 1) the "pure" journal entry rule, a conclusive presumption that the enrolled bill is valid only if it is in accordance with procedures recorded in the journal and the constitution; 2) the "affirmative contradiction" rule, a determination that the enrolled bill is valid unless the journals affirmatively show a statement that there has not been compliance with constitutional requirements * * *.

South Dakota, for example, finds the enrolled bill conclusive evidence of proper enactment, except when the asserted impropriety concerns a provision for which the constitution requires a journal entry. *Barnsdall Refining Corp. v. Welsh*, 269 N.W. 853 (S.D. 1936); cf. *Indep. Community Bankers Ass'n v. South Dakota*, 346 N.W.2d 737 (S.D. 1984) (reaffirming modified enrolled bill rule, over dissent arguing for abandonment of enrolled bill rule). For other examples of the journal entry rule, see *State v. Kaufman*, 430 So. 2d 904 (Fla. 1983); *People v. Dunigan*, 650 N.E.2d 1026 (Ill. 1995). See also *Fumo v. Pa. Public Utility Comm'n*, 719 A.2d 10 (Pa. Commw. Ct. 1998); *League of Women Voters of Pa. v. Commonwealth*, 692 A.2d 263 (Pa. Commw. Ct. 1996) (describing Pennsylvania's modified enrolled bill rule that allows courts some discretion when there is a clear violation of the state constitution).

Finally, some states follow an *extrinsic evidence rule*, in which they will entertain evidence beyond legislative journals. This rule was adopted in *D & W Auto Supply v. Dep't of Revenue*, 602 S.W.2d 420 (Ky. 1980), to invalidate a statute violating the constitution's requirement that appropriations measures be adopted by an absolute majority of the legislators in each chamber of the legislature. See also *Ass'n of Texas Prof. Educators v. Kirby*, 788 S.W.2d 827 (Tex. 1990) ("[W]hen the official legislative journals, testimony by the presiding officers of both houses, and stipulations of the attorney general acting in his official capacity conclusively show clerical error in the enrolled bill, an exception to the enrolled bill rule applies."). Even if commentators are generally right that extrinsic evidence should be considered, how far should courts carry that precept? Consider the problem of the legislature's "stopping the clock" and remaining in session past the time limit specified in the state constitution. In *State ex rel. Heck's Discount Ctrs. v. Winters*, 132 S.E.2d 374 (W. Va. 1963), the court concluded from the legislative journal and extrinsic evidence that the bill in question had been passed a few minutes into the early morning of March 10, 1963, when under the state constitution the legislative term had expired at midnight on March 9. The court noted the common legislative practice of "staying the hands of the clock to enable the Legislature to effect an adjournment apparently within the time fixed by the Constitution for the expiration of the term," and it concluded that "[d]oubtless it is a fact that the legislature of this state is not unique in having indulged in that practice." Nonetheless, the court held that when the legislative term expires the legislature "ceases to have the legislative power accorded to it while in lawful, constitutional session." Accordingly, it invalidated the legislation.

Consider the evidence in *Winters*. An affidavit by the clerk of the West Virginia House of Delegates stated that on March 9 "he was directed by the Speaker of the House of Delegates * * * to stop * * * the official clock of the House of Delegates," and that the legislation in question "was passed when the official clock was stopped at 11:28 P.M., but that the actual time was 12:15 or 12:18 A.M. March 10, 1963." The journal of the House contained comments such as these:

Mr. Nuzum. Mr. Watson, do you have a watch?

Mr. Watson. Yes, sir.

Mr. Nuzum. What time does your watch show?

Mr. Watson. I've got nine after one. * * *

Mr. Nuzum. Mr. Simonton, do you have a watch?

Mr. Simonton. Yes, sir.

Mr. Nuzum. What time does your watch show?

Mr. Simonton. My watch shows six after one. * * *

Mr. Nuzum. Mr. Myles, do you have a watch?

Mr. Myles. Yes, sir.

Mr. Nuzum. What time does your watch say?

Mr. Myles. I can't see it but the clock on the wall says four minutes till twelve on March 9, 1963.

Mr. Nuzum. You can't see your watch?

Mr. Myles. No, sir. It's covered up with my shirt sleeve.

If you were on a state supreme court, how would you react to this evidence? Can the enrolled bill rule be defended in these circumstances? See *Dillon v. King*, 529 P.2d 745 (N. Mex. 1974), where the court held prospectively that the enrolled bill rule would no longer be applied to an allegation that the bill under review was adopted after the legislative term had expired.

C. REQUIRING LAWMAKING BY THE MOST INSTITUTIONALLY COMPETENT BRANCH OF GOVERNMENT

The structures of lawmaking put in place by constitutions, statutes, and legislative rules are designed to ensure that legislatures discharge their responsibilities as the most democratically accountable governance entities in a rational and transparent way. Because of these features of institutional design, a due process of lawmaking perspective suggests that the legislature may be uniquely suited to make particular important decisions. Thus, perhaps some decisions made by administrative agencies should be subject to judicial invalidation and, in effect, remanded to the legislature (or perhaps the politically accountable chief executive) for reconsideration. Consider the following example of structural due process.

HAMPTON V. MOW SUN WONG
Supreme Court of the United States, 1976.
426 U.S. 88, 96 S.Ct. 1895, 48 L.Ed.2d 495.

JUSTICE STEVENS delivered the opinion of the Court.

[Respondents, five permanent resident aliens, had been denied employment by the General Services Administration, the Department of Health, Education, and Welfare, and the Postal Department. They filed this action challenging a Civil Service Commission rule barring noncitizens, including lawfully admitted resident aliens, from employment in the federal civil service on the ground that the rule violated the equal protection component of the Due Process Clause of the Fifth Amendment. Justice Stevens' opinion began with recognition of the "paramount federal power over immigration and naturalization," thereby distinguishing the case from *Sugarman v. Dougall*, 413 U.S. 634 (1973), in which the Court had invalidated a section of the New York civil service law providing that only U.S. citizens could hold permanent positions in the state's civil service.]

When the Federal Government asserts an overriding national interest as justification for a discriminatory rule which would violate the Equal Protection Clause if adopted by a State, due process requires that there be a legitimate basis for presuming that the rule was actually intended to serve that interest. If the agency which promulgates the rule has direct responsibility for fostering or protecting that interest, it may reasonably be presumed that the asserted interest was the actual predicate for the rule. That presumption would, of course, be fortified by an appropriate statement of reasons identifying the relevant interest. Alternatively, if the rule were expressly mandated by the Congress or the President, we might presume that any interest which might rationally be served by the rule did in fact give rise to its adoption.

In this case the petitioners have identified several interests which the Congress or the President might deem sufficient to justify the exclusion of noncitizens from the federal service. They argue, for example, that the broad exclusion may facilitate the President's negotiation of treaties with foreign powers by enabling him to offer employment opportunities to citizens of a given foreign country in exchange for reciprocal concessions—an offer he could not make if those aliens were already eligible for federal jobs. Alternatively, the petitioners argue that reserving the federal service for citizens provides an appropriate incentive to aliens to qualify for naturalization and thereby to participate more effectively in our society. They also point out that the citizenship requirement has been imposed in the United States with substantial consistency for over 100 years and accords with international law and the practice of most foreign countries. Finally, they correctly state that the need for undivided loyalty in certain sensitive positions clearly justifies a citizenship requirement in at least some parts of the federal service, and that the broad exclusion serves the valid administrative purpose of avoiding the trouble and expense of classifying those positions which properly belong in executive or sensitive categories.

The difficulty with all of these arguments except the last is that they do not identify any interest which can reasonably be assumed to have influenced the Civil Service Commission, the Postal Service, the General Services Administration, or the Department of Health, Education, and Welfare in the administration of their respective responsibilities or, specifically, in the decision to deny employment to the respondents in this litigation. We may assume with the petitioners that if the Congress or the President had expressly imposed the citizenship requirement, it would be justified by the national interest in providing an incentive for aliens to become naturalized, or possibly even as providing the President with an expendable token for treaty negotiating purposes; but we are not willing to presume that the Chairman of the Civil Service Commission, or any of the other original defendants, was deliberately fostering an interest so far removed from his normal responsibilities. Consequently, before evaluating the sufficiency of the asserted justification for the rule, it is important to know whether we are reviewing a policy decision made by Congress and the President or a question of personnel administration determined by the Civil Service Commission.

It is perfectly clear that neither the Congress nor the President has ever *required* the Civil Service Commission to adopt the citizenship requirement as a condition of eligibility for employment in the federal civil service. On the other hand, in view of the fact that the policy has been in effect since the Commission was created in 1883, it is fair to infer that both the Legislature and the Executive have been aware of the policy and have acquiesced in it. In order to decide whether such acquiescence should give the Commission rule the same support as an express statutory or Presidential command, it is appropriate to review the extent to which the policy has been given consideration by Congress or the President, and the nature of the authority specifically delegated to the Commission. * * *

[The Court concluded that the Commission had the statutory authority to retain or modify the citizenship requirement without further authorization from Congress or the President. But "[e]ven if this conclusion were doubtful," the Court added in a footnote, "in view of the consequences of the rule it would be appropriate to require a much more explicit directive from either Congress or the President before accepting the conclusion that the political branches of Government would consciously adopt a policy raising the constitutional questions presented by this rule." The Court then turned to the question of whether the rule was valid, assuming (without deciding) that Congress and the President have the constitutional power to impose the requirement that the Commission adopted.]

It is the business of the Civil Service Commission to adopt and enforce regulations which will best promote the efficiency of the federal civil service. That agency has no responsibility for foreign affairs, for treaty negotiations, for establishing immigration quotas or conditions of entry, or for naturalization policies. Indeed, it is not even within the responsibility of the Commission to be concerned with the economic consequences of permitting or prohibiting the participation by aliens in employment opportunities in different parts of the national market. On the contrary, the Commission performs a limited and specific function.

The only concern of the Civil Service Commission is the promotion of an efficient federal service. In general it is fair to assume that its goal would be best served by removing unnecessary restrictions on the eligibility of qualified applicants for employment. With only one exception, the interests which the petitioners have put forth as supporting the Commission regulation at issue in this case are not matters which are properly the business of the Commission. That one exception is the administrative desirability of having one simple rule excluding all noncitizens when it is manifest that citizenship is an appropriate and legitimate requirement for some important and sensitive positions. Arguably, therefore, administrative convenience may provide a rational basis for the general rule.

For several reasons that justification is unacceptable in this case. The Civil Service Commission, like other administrative agencies, has an obligation to perform its responsibilities with some degree of expertise, and to make known the reasons for its important decisions. There is nothing in the record before us, or in matter of which we may properly take judicial notice, to indicate that the Commission actually made any considered evaluation of the relative desirability of a simple exclusionary rule on the one hand, or the value to the service of enlarging the pool of eligible employees on the other. Nor can we reasonably infer that the administrative burden of establishing the job classifications for which citizenship is an appropriate requirement would be a particularly onerous task for an expert in personnel matters. * * * Of greater significance, however, is the quality of the interest at stake. Any fair balancing of the public interest in avoiding the wholesale deprivation of employment opportunities caused by the Commission's indiscriminate policy, as opposed to what may be nothing more than a hypothetical justification, requires rejection of the argument of administrative convenience in this case.

In sum, assuming without deciding that the national interests identified by the petitioners would adequately support an explicit determination by Congress or the President to exclude all noncitizens from the federal service, we conclude that those interests cannot provide an acceptable rationalization for such a determination by the Civil Service Commission. The impact of the rule on the millions of lawfully admitted resident aliens is precisely the same as the aggregate impact of comparable state rules which were invalidated by our decision in *Sugarman*. By broadly denying this class substantial opportunities for employment, the Civil Service Commission rule deprives its members of an aspect of liberty. Since these residents were admitted as a result of decisions made by the Congress and the President, implemented by the

Immigration and Naturalization Service acting under the Attorney General of the United States, due process requires that the decision to impose that deprivation of an important liberty be made either at a comparable level of government or, if it is to be permitted to be made by the Civil Service Commission, that it be justified by reasons which are properly the concern of that agency. We hold that § 338.101(a) of the Civil Service Commission Regulations has deprived these respondents of liberty without due process of law and is therefore invalid.

JUSTICE BRENNAN, with whom JUSTICE MARSHALL joins, concurring.

I join the Court's opinion with the understanding that there are reserved the equal protection questions that would be raised by congressional or Presidential enactment of a bar on employment of aliens by the Federal Government.

[The dissenting opinion of JUSTICE REHNQUIST, joined by CHIEF JUSTICE BURGER and JUSTICES WHITE and BLACKMUN, is omitted.]

NOTES ON MOW SUN WONG AND INSTITUTIONAL COMPETENCE

1. *The Aftermath of* Mow Sun Wong. Three months after the Supreme Court decided *Mow Sun Wong*, President Ford issued Executive Order 11935, which barred almost all noncitizens from employment in the federal civil service. In a letter to the Speaker of the House and the President of the Senate, President Ford stated that it was in the national interest to preserve the longstanding policy of exclusion, at least pending thorough reconsideration of the matter. He also stated that "a recognition of the specific constitutional authority vested in the Congress prompts me to urge that the Congress promptly address these issues." See 41 Fed. Reg. 37,303–04 (1976). The lower courts upheld the constitutionality of the order. See *Mow Sun Wong v. Hampton*, 435 F. Supp. 37 (N.D. Cal. 1977), aff'd, 626 F.2d 739 (9th Cir. 1980), cert. denied, 450 U.S. 959 (1981) (Justices Brennan, White, and Marshall voted to grant certiorari). Congress has never modified President Ford's order.

Did President Ford's action demonstrate that the Court's decision in *Mow Sun Wong* was futile? Alexander Aleinikoff has uncovered some internal government documents that shed light upon whether the Court's "remand for reconsideration" of the issue in *Mow Sun Wong* actually stimulated any thoughtful reconsideration. According to these documents, the impetus for President Ford's executive order came from the Civil Service Commission (CSC), which drafted the proposal to overturn the Court's decision. Several governmental departments, asked to comment on the proposal by the Office of Management and Budget (OMB), voiced support for the proposal without identifying any underlying reasons for their views; the U.S. Postal Service indicated that it had no difficulty with admitting resident aliens to nonsensitive and nonpolicymaking positions; the Department of Housing and Urban Development suggested a more narrowly drawn prohibition that would limit employment to resident aliens in nonpolicymaking positions; and the Department of State expressed doubts about the wisdom of a total prohibition. When the matter came before President Ford, accompanying it was a memorandum from the general counsel of the OMB that stated:

> * * * CSC suggested various reasons related to the national interest which might serve as justification for the issuance of [the] order. Agency comments, although generally favoring or having no objection to such an order, indicate that CSC's suggested justifications (*e.g.*, need for undivided loyalty; consistency

with the practices of foreign states) are more apparent than real. Further, the Postal Service advises that its recent practice of employing aliens in nonsensitive and nonpolicymaking positions has not presented any policy difficulties. Nevertheless, there is a widespread visceral feeling that Government jobs should be reserved for citizens, at least where there are qualified citizen-applicants.

The Department of Justice is of the opinion that the Congress, pursuant to its constitutional authority over immigration, has the authority to broadly prohibit aliens from employment in the competitive civil service. Although the Supreme Court left open the question whether the President could exclude aliens from the competitive service, there are Presidential concerns (*e.g.*, foreign policy) which would lend some support to Presidential order barring aliens from government employment. The Department of Justice concludes, based on the *Wong* decision, that an executive order barring aliens would probably be upheld by a divided Supreme Court.[68]

What do you make of this? Consider this view (which was written without the benefit of the internal documents noted above):

If the Court's goal in *Mow Sun Wong* was * * * to force either the executive or legislative branch to face up to the underlying policy questions and accept political responsibility for the rule, the goal was plainly not achieved. * * * The whole point of [President Ford's] order, as his letter makes clear, was to preserve the status quo pending congressional rethinking of the problem. * * * But Congress may well prefer to stay clear of the issue and allow the present policy to remain in operation by default. * * * [W]e are left precisely where we were before the decision in *Mow Sun Wong*: Aliens are still barred from employment in the civil service, although neither of the political branches has taken clear responsibility for the formulation of the policy.[69]

2. *The Precedential Value of* Mow Sun Wong. *Mow Sun Wong* and another case decided the same day were Justice Stevens' first opinions for the Supreme Court. It has been suggested that the other four Justices in the majority had voted to strike down the civil service regulation on the traditional equal protection ground that it discriminated against aliens, and that Stevens initially stood alone in proposing a due process of lawmaking solution to the case. The Chief Justice assigned the case to Justice Stevens, who wrote a proposed majority opinion in line with his personal views, and the other four Justices went along with it. See Bob Woodward & Scott Armstrong, *The Brethren: Inside the Supreme Court* 402 (1979). We do not know whether this is accurate, but assume for purposes of discussion that it is. Assume also that the other four Justices voted with Stevens at least in part to avoid friction over his first opinion (which is a plausible assumption, if the other assertions made above are accurate). Does this mean that *Mow Sun Wong* is of little precedential value? (Indeed, does it suggest some tension between the outcome in the case and the deliberative values on which the majority opinion rests?) So far as we can ascertain, *Mow Sun Wong* has never directly controlled the result in any subsequent Supreme Court decision, although it has been cited a number of times.

---

[68]   Memorandum from William N. Nichols, General Counsel, OMB, to Robert D. Linden, White House Chief Executive Clerk, Aug. 30, 1976 (on file in Gerald R. Ford Library, Ann Arbor, MI).

[69]   Gerald Rosberg, *The Protection of Aliens from Discriminatory Treatment by the National Government*, 1977 Sup. Ct. Rev. 275, 280–81.

3.   *Judicial Minimalism and Congressional Consideration of Constitutional Issues.* Cass Sunstein has described *Mow Sun Wong* as an example of judicial minimalism that reinforces democratic institutions. *One Case at a Time: Judicial Minimalism on the Supreme Court* (1999). For Sunstein, judicial minimalism consists of "saying no more than necessary to justify an outcome, and leaving as much as possible undecided." Among the "attractive features" of minimalism is that it "is likely to make judicial errors less frequent and (above all) less damaging. A court that leaves things open will not foreclose options in a way that may do a great deal of harm. * * * A court that decides relatively little will also reduce the risks that come from intervening in complex systems, where a single-shot intervention can have a range of unanticipated bad consequences. There is a relationship between judicial minimalism and democratic deliberation. Of course minimalist rulings increase the space for further reflection and debate at the local, state, and national levels, simply because they do not foreclose subsequent decisions." *Id.* at 3–4. Sunstein's work essentially updates the "passive virtues" philosophy of Alexander Bickel, most notably articulated in *The Least Dangerous Branch: The Supreme Court at the Bar of Politics* (1962). Sunstein argues that decisions like *Mow Sun Wong*, where the Court avoided deciding the constitutional issues presented, are "conspicuously" democracy-forcing because "the Court's judgment was expressly founded on the idea that publicly accountable bodies should make the decision that was challenged in the case." *Supra*, at 35. What do you think of this judicial strategy? Can we rely on legislators to take seriously an increased responsibility to consider constitutional issues?

4.   *The Major Questions Doctrine.* One candidate for a more recent equivalent to the *Mow Sun Wong* doctrine is the "major questions doctrine" in administrative law (discussed in more detail in Chapter 9, § 2(B)). In essence, that doctrine suggests that, for questions reaching a certain threshold level of importance (i.e., "major" questions), the courts will not apply the usual deferential standard of review of agencies' legal interpretation. In other words, instead of asking whether an agency's interpretation of a statute it administers is *reasonable*, see *Chevron U.S.A. v. Natural Resources Def. Council*, 467 U.S. 837 (1984), when dealing with a "major question," the court will ask whether the agency's interpretation was *right*. See *King v. Burwell*, 135 S.Ct. 2480, 2488–89 (2015) (reprinted in Chapter 7, § 2(A)). One might understand this doctrine as being similar to *Mow Sun Wong*: decisions should be made by the right decisionmaker, and administrative agencies are not the right entities to decide major policy questions.

But does the major questions doctrine have the minimalist virtues that Sunstein posited for *Mow Sun Wong*? Some scholars have argued that the doctrine does little more than empower judges to encode (generally deregulatory) substantive preferences into law. Lisa Heinzerling has noted that, in cases applying the doctrine, "the Court took interpretive power from an administrative agency, power that would normally have been the agency's due under *Chevron* * * * and kept it for itself. And * * * the Court's seizure of power aligned with its basic distrust of an active administrative state." Heinzerling notes that the doctrine also disempowers Congress, by "chang[ing] the ground rules of statutory interpretation after the other branches have acted, upsetting the reliance the other branches may have placed in the preexisting interpretive regime and yet not replacing that regime with stable and predictable rules that could foster reliance moving forward." *The Power Canons*, 58 Wm. & Mary L. Rev. 1933, 1937, 1999 (2017). Similarly, Josh Chafetz has noted that, "whether or not a particular question is 'major' is a political judgment, not a fact about the world. * * * [T]he 'majorness' of a question is necessarily a matter of (a) how that question is framed, and (b) what substantive values one understands as indicia of 'majorness,' [which means that] the major questions doctrine empowers whoever gets to make *those* (necessarily normative) determinations. * * * The major questions doctrine aggrandizes judges, who decide in any given case both how to frame the issue and how important that issue is." Josh Chafetz, *Gridlock?*, 130 Harv. L. Rev. F. 51, 55, 57 (2016).

These critiques should serve as a reminder that courts are not only *adjudicators* deciding how to allocate power, they are also *participants* and potential *recipients* of that power. Does this make you more skeptical of claims that they should be empowered to decide who the "right" decisionmaker in some context is? Or is this problem of assigning boundary-policing powers inevitable?

CHAPTER 4

DIRECT DEMOCRACY

■ ■ ■

No examination of lawmaking in the United States is complete without a discussion of the instruments of direct democracy: the initiative, the popular referendum, and the recall. Direct democracy is a consequential form of lawmaking in its own right; as of 2005, more than 70% of Americans lived in a state, locality, or both that provides access to the initiative (and the percentage has likely increased in the years since).[1] It also influences the behavior of elected and appointed officials, affects election results across the ballot, and elevates issues on the policy agenda. Understanding how direct democracy differs from representative processes also provides new insight into the latter, from lawmaking to agency implementation to judicial interpretation. In this chapter, we will first provide an overview of the tools of direct democracy, focusing particularly on the initiative. In § 2, we will discuss methods of statutory interpretation applied to laws adopted by the people. Finally, we will end with an assessment of the recall, which has gained new attention with high-profile recall efforts directed at state governors in the last two decades.

As you read these materials, ask yourself: is governance improved by some sort of *hybrid democracy* in which representative government operates alongside forms of popular lawmaking, rather than the relatively pure system of representative government that we have at the federal level? And, if it is a better system, what is the right mix of direct democracy and representative institutions? How do we ensure that both lead to accountability in government and effective policymaking?

1. OVERVIEW OF DIRECT DEMOCRACY

Doubts about the capacity of legislatures to address social problems, as well as fears that legislatures were often captured by powerful business interests and were subject to corruption, led the Populists (circa 1890) and their political successors, the Progressives, to propose a "return of the government to the people." The two major mechanisms they adopted to provide the people with lawmaking authority are the initiative and the referendum. In addition, a third device, recall, allows voters to remove elected officials from office before the expiration of their terms.

The *initiative* allows a certain percentage of the electorate to petition to have a proposed statute or state constitutional amendment put on the ballot for a vote of the electorate. There are two common forms. The *direct initiative* refers to the method in which the issue goes on the ballot automatically after the requisite signatures of voters are collected. In contrast, under the less prevalent format of the *indirect initiative*, after the collection of the requisite signatures, the proposed statute is submitted to the legislature, which is given a period of time to act on the measure. If

---

[1]   John Matsusaka, *Direct Democracy Works*, 19 J. Econ. Persp. 185, 185–86 (2005).

the legislature fails to pass the proposal, or if it adopts a significantly amended version, then the proposed statute in its original form is placed on the ballot, sometimes along with any legislatively approved variation.

The *referendum* is direct democracy from the other end of the telescope: a method whereby the electorate may approve or disapprove of a law proposed or already enacted by the legislature. One form, called the *popular referendum*, provides that, upon the collection of the requisite signatures, a law passed by the legislature is subject to approval or rejection by the electorate. Under the other form, referred to as the *legislative* or *submitted referendum*, the legislature places before the electorate a proposed law for approval or disapproval (a *binding legislative referendum*) or for the electorate's advice (an *advisory legislative referendum*).

The United States is one of the few major democracies not to have held a national referendum. However, 26 states provide for initiative, popular referendum, or both. Eighteen of those states have a constitutional initiative process, through which the people can directly initiate a constitutional change; 21 have a statutory initiative process; and 23 allow for popular referendum. A popular vote is required in every state except Delaware for adoption of constitutional amendments.[2] Moreover, state or local law often requires that certain questions—e.g., whether to issue bonds for construction of public facilities—must be submitted as referendums as well. From 1904, when the first statewide initiative appeared on Oregon's ballot, until 2019, there have been 2,609 statewide initiatives across the United States, with 1,079 (41%) being approved.[3] According to the *Initiative and Referendum Almanac*, "over 60% of all initiative activity has taken place in just six states—Arizona, California, Colorado, North Dakota, Oregon and Washington."[4]

Since the 1970s, when California passed the property-tax-cutting Proposition 13, ballot propositions have grown in importance and addressed such controversial subjects as tax or governmental spending limitations, same-sex marriage and civil unions, the death penalty, voting rights and election reforms, and educational policy (including charter schools and affirmative action). The 1990s saw the greatest number of initiatives on the ballot, with 382 proposed, and the first decade of the 21st century nearly matched that record with 374 initiatives.

The *recall* has a different relationship to representative government. Using this mechanism, a certain percentage of the electorate, by petition, may force the continued service of an elected official to be put to a vote. Nineteen states have statewide recall provisions;[5] recall is more frequently used on the local level in at

---

[2]   The Initiative and Referendum Institute (IRI) at the University of Southern California maintains a database of statewide initiatives and referendums and provides links to information by each state about its initiative process. See http://www.iandrinstitute.org/ballotwatch.cfm (for the Ballotwatch database) and http://www.iandrinstitute.org/states.cfm (for information on states and links). In addition, the National Conference of State Legislatures has developed extensive information on state-level direct democracy. See, e.g., *Initiative and Referendum States*, www.ncsl.org/legislatures-elections/elections/chart-of-the-initiative-states.aspx.

[3]   Initiative & Referendum Inst., *Overview of Initiative Use, 1900–2018*, at 1 (Jan. 2019), *available at* http://www.iandrinstitute.org/docs/IRI%20Initiative%20Use%20(1904-2018).pdf.

[4]   M. Dane Waters, *Initiative and Referendum Almanac* 7 (2003). Oregon has had the most initiatives on the ballot, with 363 through 2012, and California is a close second with 352 during the same time period.

[5]   Nat'l Conf. of State Legis., *Recall of State Officials* (Mar. 8, 2016), http://www.ncsl.org/legislatures-elections/elections/recall-of-state-officials.aspx.

least 29 states to target school board members, city councilmembers, and other local officials. Is recall a good way to "throw the bums out"? Or does it inhibit elected officials from adopting policies that are wise in the long run but painful in the short run? How does recall fit with your preferred conception of representation?

Direct democracy may be in tension with the conception of representative government embraced by the Framers of the American Constitution. The Constitution includes a provision requiring the United States to "guarantee to every State in this Union a Republican Form of Government." U.S. Const., art. IV, § 4. Challenges to direct democracy in the states on the theory that it is inconsistent with this provision have been held to be nonjusticiable political questions. See *Pacific States Tel. & Tel. Co. v. Oregon*, 223 U.S. 118 (1912).[6] Does it make a difference to the analysis that direct democracy always exists together with representative institutions? Does the Guarantee Clause suggest a constitutional reason to prefer methods of popular lawmaking that include some meaningful role for elected officials, such as the indirect initiative or the popular referendum?[7]

Think back to the discussion in Chapter 2, § 2(C), about theories of partisan lockup: the concern that elected officials will not pass certain reforms of the electoral system that voters might prefer because the changes are not in the self-interest of lawmakers. Could that theory provide an argument that representative government might actually work better if some avenues of direct lawmaking are incorporated?[8] The early proponents of direct democracy saw it as a way to circumvent state legislators and political parties that would block governance reforms like the direct primary and anti-corruption laws. Many modern initiatives deal with electoral reforms such as changes in the primary system, lobbying and campaign finance laws, term limits for legislators, and less partisan redistricting commissions. The evidence that states with hybrid democracy design their representative institutions differently than states without any form of direct democracy, however, is mixed. States with vibrant initiative processes are more likely, Caroline Tolbert has found, to have legislative term limits, tax and expenditure limitations, and supermajority voting requirements for tax increases.[9] Although Nathaniel Persily and Melissa Anderson determined that only the enactment of term limits would be "unimaginable" without the outlet of direct democracy, the presence of the initiative process has also influenced the adoption of public financing for legislative elections and redistricting

---

[6]   On the Guarantee Clause generally, see James Fischer, *Plebiscites, the Guaranty Clause, and the Role of the Judiciary*, 41 Santa Clara L. Rev. 973 (2001). For an argument that state courts should enforce the Guarantee Clause in the context of direct democracy, see Hans Linde, *Who Is Responsible for Republican Government?*, 65 U. Colo. L. Rev. 709, 710 (1994) ("[T]he Guarantee Clause precludes misuse of initiatives for * * * measures of popular passion or self-interest * * * [and the use] of initiatives to enact ordinary laws * * * in the form of constitutional text so as to insulate a law from change by elected lawmakers as well as from review of its constitutionality.").

[7]   For a proposal to reform the direct initiative process to provide opportunities for legislative involvement and to allow flexibility to amend the language of proposals before they are placed on the ballot, see Elizabeth Garrett & Mathew McCubbins, *The Dual Path Initiative Framework*, 80 S. Cal. L. Rev. 299 (2007).

[8]   See Dennis Thompson, *The Role of Theorists and Citizens in Just Elections: A Response to Professors Cain, Garrett, and Sabl,* 4 Election L.J. 153, 158–60 (2005).

[9]   *Changing Rules for State Legislatures: Direct Democracy and Governance Policies*, in *Citizens as Legislators: Direct Democracy in the United States* 171 (Shaun Bowler, Todd Donovan & Caroline Tolbert eds., 1998).

commissions.[10] In this vein, recall that the Arizona Independent Redistricting Commission (discussed in Chapter 2, § 1(C)) was created by ballot initiative. In upholding that arrangement, Justice Ginsburg remarked that, "it would be perverse to * * * exclude lawmaking by the people, particularly where such lawmaking is intended to check legislators' ability to choose the district lines they run in, thereby advancing the prospect that Members of Congress will in fact be 'chosen . . . by the People of the several States.'" *Arizona State Legislature v. Arizona Independent Redistricting Commission*, 135 S.Ct. 2652, 2675 (2015).

Is this too rosy a view of hybrid democracy? Critics argue that the ballot measures proposed and passed by the people tend to weaken representative institutions and undermine the ability of lawmakers to govern.[11] They point to term limits and tax limitations as examples. They contend that because people turn to initiatives out of frustration with their elected representatives, they will mostly enact legislation in the arena of electoral reform that reduces the power of elected officials. Certainly, there is some validity to this argument. Even the "good government" reforms, such as campaign finance legislation and nonpartisan redistricting commissions, work to reduce the discretion of elected officials. The issue is whether the policies adopted through popular means tend to reduce legislative discretion in ways that improve or harm representative institutions.

In addition, critics of direct democracy worry that initiatives are a tool for the majority of voters to enact laws that target ethnic, racial, and other minority groups. In such cases, those affected by the laws can turn to the courts to invalidate all or part of a statute or state constitutional amendment that violates federal constitutional protections. Courts do tend to be active in oversight of direct legislation. Between 1960 and 1999, for example, more than half (52%) of 163 statewide initiatives approved by voters in California, Oregon, Washington, and Colorado were challenged in court after the vote, and courts nullified, in part or in their entirety, more than half (55%) of those challenged, for a total invalidation rate of 28%.[12]

Even with this level of judicial review, however, direct democracy would be open to significant criticism if the evidence demonstrated a systematic tendency to enact discriminatory and oppressive legislation. As you remember from Chapter 1, § 2, Madison favored representative democracy and rejected direct democracy at the national level in part because of a concern that the latter process allows impassioned majorities to threaten the rights of minorities. Studies have come to mixed conclusions, but they do give rise to concerns. A 2002 study of all initiatives in California revealed that Latinos are more likely than other racial minorities to be

---

[10] *Regulating Democracy Through Democracy: The Use of Direct Legislation in Election Law Reform*, 78 S. Cal. L. Rev. 997 (2005). Matsusaka studied 14 different kinds of laws related to electoral reform and concluded that the initiative process has been essential only for legislative term limits. *Direct Democracy and Electoral Reform*, in *The Marketplace of Democracy: Electoral Competition and American Politics* 151 (Michael McDonald & John Samples eds., 2006).

[11] For a nuanced take, see Shaun Bowler & Todd Donovan, *Direct Democracy and Political Parties in America*, 12 Party Pol. 649 (2006) (finding that direct democracy weakened state political parties in the mid-twentieth century but that parties have subsequently adapted).

[12] Kenneth Miller, *The Davis Recall and the Courts*, 33 Am. Pol. Res. 135, 155–6 (2005) (some invalidations on grounds other than violation of federal constitutional guarantees).

targeted in anti-minority initiatives and are less likely than others to be on the winning side of initiatives targeting minority groups.[13] Other studies have found that gays and lesbians fare much better in the legislative process than in direct democracy. One study found that 71% of 143 ballot measures that would reduce their civil rights passed between 1972 and 2005.[14] Between November 2000 and May 2012, there were 32 state constitutional initiatives to deny marriage rights to lesbian and gay couples—and 31 of them prevailed, usually by more than 70% of the vote. Scholars have documented the ways these campaigns took advantage of the "politics of backlash." Advocates seeking to deny gays and lesbians marriage equality often engaged in rhetoric that stigmatized the minority group and caused the community to become less sympathetic to them.[15]

On the other hand, gay marriage supporters prevailed in popular referendums and initiatives in four states (Maine, Maryland, Minnesota, and Washington) in November 2012, electoral victories that were an important preface to the Supreme Court's decision striking down state discriminatory marriage laws and constitutional amendments in *Obergefell v. Hodges,* 135 S.Ct. 2584 (2015). And a number of successful 2018 ballot initiatives were friendly to the interests of minority groups, including a Florida initiative restoring voting rights to ex-felons, an initiative legalizing marijuana in Michigan, and one extending anti-discrimination protections to transgendered persons in Massachusetts.[16]

The issues raised by the increasing use of the popular initiative and referendum are many. In this section, we will discuss three of the most important ones for assessing the initiative process and crafting reform: the role of money in both ballot access and outcomes of initiative elections; the ability of voters to make decisions competently when they go to the polls and the importance of disclosure rules; and the interaction between direct democracy and representative institutions. As you read through these materials, keep in mind that one must evaluate the mechanisms of direct democracy by comparing them realistically to representative institutions. For example, money plays a role in both issue and candidate campaigns, and voters are often not fully informed about all the candidates on the ballot. Moreover, reforms of direct democracy might involve structures that include representative bodies in the process, and reforms of the legislative process might be possible because of the initiative process. Hybrid democracy allows opportunities for a wide array of responses to problems that arise in democratic structures.

---

[13]   Zoltan Hajnal, Elisabeth Gerber & Hugh Louch, *Minorities and Direct Legislation: Evidence from California Ballot Propositions*, 64 J. Pol. 154 (2002).

[14]   Donald Haider-Markel, Alana Querze & Kara Lindaman, *Lose, Win, or Draw? A Reexamination of Direct Democracy and Minority Rights*, 60 Pol. Res. Q. 304 (2007). See also Barbara Gamble, *Putting Civil Rights to a Popular Vote*, 41 Am. J. Pol. Sci. 245 (1997) (finding that voters passed three-quarters of initiatives limiting civil rights for minority groups, while only passing one-third of all popular initiatives).

[15]   Amy Stone, *Gay Rights at the Ballot Box* (2012); Todd Donovan, *Direct Democracy and Campaigns Against Minorities*, 97 Minn. L. Rev. 1730 (2013).

[16]   Stavros Agorakis & Ryan Mark, *Voters Had Say on Dozens of Issues on the Ballot, From Voting Rights for Felons to Redistricting to Marijuana*, Vox (Nov. 19, 2018), https://www.vox.com/a/midterms-2018/ballot-initiatives.

A. THE IMPORTANCE OF MONEY
IN DIRECT DEMOCRACY

Progressive-era reformers who advocated direct democracy characterized the initiative process as a way to take power away from special interests with disproportionate influence over elected officials and empower ordinary citizens to determine the direction of policy. The modern concern is that the initiative process is merely another avenue for the wealthy to influence public policy unduly. In just the 11 ballot-measure campaigns in California in 2012, groups and individuals spent more than $370 million, and in the campaign in 2008 surrounding Proposition 8 in that state—the referendum prohibiting same-sex marriage that was later ruled unconstitutional—both sides spent a total of $83 million, making it the most expensive race in that election other than the presidential contest.[17]

One substantial expense for initiative proponents is money spent to qualify a question for the ballot. It often requires hundreds of thousands of signatures to trigger a vote on a direct initiative or popular referendum. Well-funded interests have a great advantage at this stage because the Supreme Court has held that states may not prohibit them from paying petition circulators.[18] In California, circulating petitions can cost $2–$3 million per ballot proposition,[19] and, if they are paid enough, some firms will offer money-back guarantees ensuring a successful outcome. In short, money is a sufficient condition for ballot access. Even if the outcome of any vote on a ballot question mirrors the preference of the majority of voters, the dominance of money at the qualification stage means that groups with funds will determine which issues are placed before the people. As we discussed in Chapter 1, control of the political agenda is a valuable asset.

Although the Supreme Court has ruled out laws prohibiting paid petition circulators, states continue seeking to regulate this process. The following case involves a challenge to Colorado's law. Are these restrictions apt to reduce the role of money in the initiative process, while retaining it as an outlet for expression of the popular will, or is the statute mainly an attempt to muzzle direct democracy? Are there other ways to encourage true grassroots petition drives? Does the Internet provide a mechanism to gather signatures at a lower cost, and would turning to online petitions cause other problems? Consider as well what information should be provided to those asked to sign petitions at the beginning stages of the initiative process. Should they be informed of the interests bankrolling the petition drive, for example?

---

[17]   See MapLight, *California Ballot Measure Funding Tops $372 Million* (Nov. 6, 2012), http://maplight. org/content/73144; *Proposition 8: Who Gave in the Gay Marriage Battle?*, L.A. Times, http://projects.latimes. com/prop8/.

[18]   See *Meyer v. Grant*, 486 U.S. 414 (1988) (First Amendment violation to prohibit paid petition circulators).

[19]   See John Wildermuth, *Qualifying a California Ballot Measure to Become a 'Playground of Billionaires'*, S.F. Chron. (Jan. 2, 2019), https://www.sfchronicle.com/politics/article/Qualifying-a-California-ballot-measure-to-become-13501800.php.

Buckley v. American Constitutional Law Foundation

525 U.S. 182 (1999).

Colorado's statute controlling the initiative petition process included three provisions at issue in this case: petition circulators were required to be registered voters; circulators were required to wear name badges; and initiative backers had to report the names and addresses of paid circulators and how much each was paid. **Justice Ginsburg** began with the proposition that petition circulation is "core political speech" that involves "interactive communication concerning political change"; therefore, First Amendment protection is "at its zenith." On the other hand, citing the ballot access cases (Chapter 2, § 2(C)), she noted that states can regulate elections to avoid chaos and to ensure fairness. The Court concluded that "the First Amendment requires us to be vigilant in making * * * judgments [about the constitutionality of electoral regulations], to guard against undue hindrances to political conversations and the exchange of ideas."

The Court struck down the requirement that circulators be registered voters, noting that it burdened political speech by reducing the number of potential speakers, i.e., the number of people who could engage in discourse about initiatives as they gathered signatures. **Justice Thomas**, concurring, noted the "anecdotal evidence" that petition circulators do not actually engage in much political speech, working to gather as many signatures as possible as quickly as possible because often their pay is tied to the number of signatures. He concluded, however, that "the level of scrutiny cannot turn on the content or sophistication of a political message."

The Court acknowledged the argument, made by **Justice O'Connor** in dissent, that it is relatively easy for a circulator to register to vote and that this law is not a severe burden. However, it contended that some who wished to circulate petitions did not register as a form of protest against the system or because they were alienated from the political process. The state's primary justification for the provision, to police illegal activity among circulators, was adequately served by the requirement that signature gatherers be residents of the state, and it would be better served by requiring that circulators be eligible to vote, rather than actually registered. **Chief Justice Rehnquist** was scornful in his dissent on this point, noting that the majority held that "a State is constitutionally required to * * * allow those who make no effort to register to vote— political dropouts—and convicted drug dealers to engage in this electoral activity."

The majority also struck down the requirement that circulators wear name badges, which the state had justified as necessary to help it combat fraudulent practices by signature gatherers seeking to increase their compensation. The Court worried that those circulating petitions on unpopular issues might face harassment in face-to-face conversations with passersby; requiring them to provide their names would therefore chill political speech, especially because the badge required identification "at the precise moment when the circulator's interest in anonymity is greatest." See also *McIntyre v. Ohio Elections Comm'n*, 514 U.S. 334 (1995) (protecting right of leafleteer to distribute campaign literature anonymously).

The Court also trimmed the provisions requiring initiative proponents to provide information to the state. It struck down requirements that information specific to each circulator be provided (e.g., the name, address, and total amount paid), but it left unchanged the requirement that proponents report how much they paid circulators per signature, which effectively discloses the entire amount spent in the petition drive.

Justice Ginsburg was sympathetic to the notion that some disclosure was necessary as "a control or check on domination of the initiative process by affluent special interest groups" and to inform voters "of the source and amount of money spent" on ballot access.

In dissent, Justice O'Connor was willing to be much more deferential to the state's determination of what information it needed to regulate the electoral process effectively, particularly with regard to information disclosed to a state official rather than information disclosed during the signature-gathering stage to citizens in one-on-one discussions. She was not concerned that Colorado applied the more burdensome disclosure only to paid circulators because "the record suggests that paid circulators are more likely to commit fraud and gather false signatures than other circulators."

Query: The Court did not address the related issue of whether a badge could identify a circulator as either *PAID* or *VOLUNTEER* without also including a name, a provision currently included in several state systems, including Colorado's. Is that provision constitutional? Would it influence voter behavior?

––––––––––

Money also plays a role in the outcomes of ballot contests, but the picture here is more complicated than that of the influence of wealth in ballot access.[20] Studies suggest that money spent to defeat initiatives and referendums is more effective than money spent to pass them. In an early influential study, Daniel Lowenstein found that between 1968 and 1980 in California, in elections in which spending levels exceeded $250,000 and one side had a 2–1 spending advantage, opposition committees defeated 90% of the measures they opposed, and proponent committees won 64% of the time. *Campaign Spending and Ballot Propositions: Recent Experience, Public Choice Theory, and the First Amendment*, 29 UCLA L. Rev. 505 (1982). Subsequent studies have similarly found that money has a greater effect when spent to defeat an initiative, although increasingly sophisticated analyses of ballot campaigns may begin to reveal the influence of well-funded campaigns supporting ballot measures.[21] For example, Elisabeth Gerber has assessed whether spending by certain groups is particularly influential, finding that contributions from citizen groups have greater success in passing initiatives than do contributions from economic groups.[22]

The Supreme Court has consistently held that the First Amendment forbids states from limiting the amount of money spent or contributions made in support of or in opposition to a ballot measure because there is no possibility of *quid pro quo* corruption in the absence of candidates. See *Citizens Against Rent Control v. Berkeley*, 454 U.S. 290 (1981). Just as in the candidate-election context, the Court has been unwilling to accept egalitarian arguments to justify restrictions on spending in initiative contests. As more candidates take advantage of hybrid democracy and use initiatives to serve their own electoral and political goals, there are increasing

––––––––––

[20]   For discussion of the studies on the role of money in ballot campaigns, see Elizabeth Garrett & Elisabeth Gerber, *Money in the Initiative and Referendum Process: Evidence of Its Effects and Prospects for Reform*, in The Battle Over Citizen Lawmaking 73 (M. Dane Waters ed., 2001).

[21]   See Thomas Stratmann, *The Effectiveness of Money in Ballot Measure Campaigns*, 78 S. Cal. L. Rev. 1041 (2005).

[22]   See *The Populist Paradox: Interest Group Influence and the Promise of Direct Legislation* 101–20 (1999).

discussions of the possibility of limiting contributions to campaign committees in initiative campaigns that are controlled by candidates or elected officials.[23] In these cases, the traditional *quid pro quo* argument could arguably support contribution limits. If such restrictions are constitutional, are they desirable? Is it wise policy to restrict contributions to candidate-controlled ballot-measure committees if the courts won't allow restrictions on contributions to independent committees involved in the same election? How would you expect politicians to try to evade such regulations? We return to this question in the context of recalls later in this chapter.

B. VOTER COMPETENCE, VOTER CONFUSION, AND VOTING CUES

Whatever one concludes about the wisdom of a system with elements of direct democracy, it seems likely that the initiative process will endure in states that have it because voters like popular lawmaking. When asked what they thought about the initiative process in 2010, Californians had more trust in their fellow voters with respect to policymaking than in state elected officials (44% had at least a fair amount of trust in other voters compared to 33% in elected officials). Moreover, 66% of Californians were at least somewhat satisfied with the initiative process, although 42% of them supported unspecified "major changes" to the process.[24] One important question to ask in assessing whether those opinions are accurate—that is, whether the policies adopted at the voting booth are actually better than those formulated by legislators—is whether voters are sufficiently informed about the issues they are asked to decide.

If decisionmaking at the polls requires voters to be well versed in all the issues surrounding every contest, then very few voters will meet that standard. Of course, very few lawmakers casting their votes in a state legislature or Congress meet that standard for more than a handful of crucial bills. A more reasonable standard is voter competence. Voters are competent "if they cast the same votes they would have cast had they possessed all available knowledge about the policy consequences of their decision."[25] They need not have encyclopedic knowledge about every choice, but they need reliable shortcuts—voting cues or heuristics—that can allow them to vote in the same way that they would have with more complete information. Thinking back to the theories of politics discussed in Chapter 1, § 2, how would republican thinkers react to this notion of voter competence? Is it consistent with the ideal of civic virtue?

Scholars continue to work to determine which cues are helpful to voters, when they make a difference, and how to structure disclosure rules so that they provide information voters need at the time they can use it most effectively. In candidate elections, voters can use the strong voting cue of partisan affiliation, and they may also be able to use the cue of incumbency. But the information environment for ballot

---

[23]　See Richard Hasen, *Rethinking the Unconstitutionality of Contribution and Expenditures Limits in Ballot Measure Campaigns*, 78 S. Cal. L. Rev. 885 (2005); Hank Dempsey, Comment, *The "Overlooked Hermaphrodite" of Campaign Finance: Candidate-Controlled Ballot Measure Committees in California Politics*, 95 Cal. L. Rev. 123 (2007).

[24]　Mark Baldassare, Dean Bonner, Sonja Petek & Nicole Willcoxon (Public Policy Institute of California), *PPIC Statewide Survey: Californians and Their Government* 18–20 (Dec. 2010).

[25]　Elisabeth Gerber & Arthur Lupia, *Voter Competence in Direct Legislation Elections*, in *Citizen Competence and Democratic Institutions* 147, 149 (Stephen Elkin & Karol Soltan eds., 1999).

measures is much less rich; even though political parties and candidates now often associate themselves with one side or the other of an initiative, this information is not available on the ballot itself. Interestingly, the hybrid nature of democracy provides information to voters through the interaction of candidate and issue elections: candidates seek to use initiatives to demonstrate their commitment to certain issues, and the information environment surrounding ballot measures is enriched by the support or opposition of elected officials with a political "brand name."

Another helpful cue in direct democracy is knowing the groups—economic and ideological—that support and oppose an initiative. For example, in a study of voting on insurance-related ballot initiatives, Arthur Lupia compared voters who knew nothing about the initiatives' details but knew the insurance industry's preference, with voters who were "model citizens" in that they consistently gave correct answers to detailed questions about ballot measures. His study also included a third group who knew nothing about the ballot measures or the insurance industry's views. The first two groups of voters voted similarly, while the third group had completely different voting patterns. *Shortcuts versus Encyclopedias: Information and Voting Behavior in California Insurance Reform Elections*, 88 Am. Pol. Sci. Rev. 63 (1994). This finding suggests that, under certain circumstances, just knowing which group supports an initiative (or opposes it) may be enough to vote competently. Here, Californians could ascertain the economic interests of the insurance industry, determine if their interests differed from those companies, and vote accordingly.

More recent empirical work questions how often voters use such cues, however, finding relatively infrequent use of cues that could be effective heuristics in some ballot-measure campaigns.[26] These results reinforce the need to provide effective cues in ways that voters can access in appropriate campaigns. Some states send voters pamphlets with explanations of each ballot measure and arguments submitted by proponents and opponents (an example of which is included in Problem 4-5) but it is not clear whether voters use those regularly. It seems likely that information provided on the ballot itself at the crucial moment of voting might be more influential, and some states are considering reforms along these lines. There is also persuasive evidence that voters protect themselves when they are confused. The "defensive no" is the typical reaction by voters who are unsure about initiatives. See Shaun Bowler & Todd Donovan, *Demanding Choices: Opinion, Voting, and Direct Democracy* 47 (2000).

What information other than the identity of groups with political brand names, such as parties or politicians, might provide voters shortcuts to enable them to vote competently? Knowing who has provided the funding to support or oppose a ballot measure (including information like how much of the money came from out-of-state, how much came from small-dollar donors, etc.) might help voters understand the interests at play with respect to the measure. As you think about the kind of information most necessary for voter competence, consider also how to ensure that

---

[26]   See Craig Burnett, Elizabeth Garrett & Mathew McCubbins, *The Dilemma of Direct Democracy*, 9 Election L.J. 305 (2010); Craig Burnett & Mathew McCubbins, *When Common Wisdom Is Neither Common Nor Wisdom: Exploring Voters' Limited Use of Endorsements on Three Ballot Measures*, 97 Minn. L. Rev. 1557 (2013).

the information reaches citizens in a timely way, as well as how to structure the information so that they can use it. Does this interest in voter competence justify fairly aggressive disclosure laws about campaign spending in direct elections? What groups would you expect to try to avoid disclosure, and how would they do so? Could laws be drafted to pierce through such veiled political actors to discern the true parties in interest?

Disclosure Statutes in Direct Democracy. Generally, disclosure statutes in both candidate and ballot-measure elections have been upheld by courts as constitutional under the First Amendment. For example, in *First Nat'l Bank of Boston v. Belloti,* 435 U.S. 765 (1978), in which the Supreme Court struck down prohibitions on corporate expenditures in issue campaigns, the Court noted that "[i]dentification of the source of advertising may be required as a means of disclosure, so that people will be able to evaluate the arguments to which they are being subjected." *Id.* at 792 n.32. Similarly, when the Court struck down contribution limits in direct democracy, it observed that "[t]he integrity of the political system will be adequately protected if contributors are identified in a public filing revealing the amounts contributed; if it is thought wise, legislation can outlaw anonymous contributions." *Citizens Against Rent Control v. City of Berkeley,* 454 U.S. 290, 299–300 (1981). Disclosure statutes sometimes have gone too far to withstand the Court's "exacting scrutiny," such as the Ohio disclosure law that was applied to Mrs. McIntyre, who was disseminating anonymous leaflets in a campaign concerning a school board referendum. *McIntyre v. Ohio Elections Comm'n,* 514 U.S. 334 (1995). But *McIntyre* involved an ordinary citizen engaging in small-scale political speech; it has not generally been extended to laws requiring that information about political expenditures be reported to a government agency.

The growth of the Internet—together with the ease with which people can access information disclosed to state agencies and made available on public websites—may have changed the balance under the First Amendment, particularly when it comes to disclosure of the identity of people making relatively small contributions to a committee involved in a ballot-measure campaign. The issues have been raised clearly in two cases. First, in June 2010, the Supreme Court considered disclosure in the context of a request to reveal the names of those signing a petition regarding a ballot measure seeking to overturn a state law providing certain rights to same-sex couples.

Doe v. Reed

561 U.S. 186 (2010).

The Washington Public Records Act (PRA) requires disclosure of all public records, including referendum petitions. Petitions include the names and addresses of the people who sign them. In 2009, Protect Marriage Washington, a politically active nonprofit group organized to protect what it calls "traditional marriage," circulated a petition to overturn a state law that provided substantial rights to domestic partners. When the petition was turned in to the Secretary of State, several pro-gay-rights groups sought to obtain the documents under the PRA so they could post the names and addresses of signatories on websites. Protect Marriage Washington and individuals who signed the petition moved to enjoin the public release of the documents, claiming disclosure burdened their constitutional rights and chilled political speech.

The Supreme Court ruled that the PRA was not facially unconstitutional with respect to the disclosure of referendum petitions, but it left open the possibility of as-applied challenges in the future. Although eight members of the Court agreed with the judgment, there were seven opinions. The concurring opinions mainly provided views about the standard to be applied in any subsequent as-applied challenges raised by these plaintiffs or others concerned about the consequences of releasing referendum petitions. In the opinion for the Court, **Chief Justice Roberts** characterized signing a petition as an expression of a political view, thus implicating the First Amendment. He found that disclosure of petitions meets the "exacting scrutiny" required by the First Amendment because it assists state officials in discovering fraud and in verifying the accuracy of the signatures. The Secretary of State can only check a small fraction of signatures; disclosure "can help cure the inadequacies of the verification and canvassing process [and help] prevent certain types of petition fraud otherwise difficult to detect, such as outright forgery." He concluded that "[p]ublic disclosure also promotes transparency and accountability in the electoral process to an extent other measures cannot."

Although the Chief Justice acknowledged that these plaintiffs might be able to demonstrate a reasonable probability of threats, reprisals, and harassment—and thus avoid disclosure in this particular case—he rejected the argument that most ballot measures would give rise to such harm. He suggested that the subject matter of this measure was especially "controversial," in contrast to the typical fodder for direct democracy: tax policy, revenue and budget issues, property rights laws, and utility regulation. In his concurrence, **Justice Stevens** took issue with any distinction based on the subject matter of initiatives, noting that "[d]ebates about tax policy and regulation of private property can become just as heated as debates about domestic partnerships." And **Justice Thomas**, the only justice who dissented, argued that the nature of direct democracy, which operates as a "safety valve" for interests that have not succeeded in the legislature, means that many ballot measures will often be controversial.

Applying strict scrutiny to the PRA and finding it constitutionally objectionable as it affected referendum petitions, Justice Thomas argued that the state had many other, less burdensome approaches available to detect and combat fraud in the signature-gathering process. He characterized the Washington statute as a "blunderbuss approach," noting alternatives such as an electronic referendum database that could detect multiple references to a single voter and that could allow voters to search for their names to discover outright fraud. On the other side of the balance, he was concerned that as-applied challenges would not offer sufficient protection to petition signers. For example, if petition sponsors must seek an injunction before circulating petitions, how could they present sufficient evidence of a reasonable probability of threats, reprisals, and harassment? Do they have to wait until such retaliation occurs and then seek protection? Moreover, Thomas argued, "the state of technology today creates at least *some* probability that signers of every referendum will be subjected to threats, harassment, or reprisals if their personal information is disclosed."

Most of the other opinions focused on providing guidance for future as-applied challenges in the age of the Internet, and the justices disagreed about the showing that would be required for such a challenge to succeed. **Justice Alito** contended that First Amendment rights are appropriately protected only if an as-applied challenge could be brought "sufficiently far in advance" to avoid any political chill and "the showing necessary to obtain the exemption is not overly burdensome." Justice Alito went further to opine that the plaintiffs in *Doe v. Reed* had a strong case for an exemption. He rejected the notion that it was permissible to provide information to allow voters to contact signers and discuss the matter with them. In this case, the groups seeking names were intent on having "uncomfortable conversation[s]" with the supporters of the petition, so "disclosure becomes a means of facilitating harassment."

In contrast, **Justice Sotomayor** and **Justice Stevens** both wrote separately to underscore their views that the standard of proof to obtain a judicial exemption from disclosure should be rigorous. Disclosure is a long-accepted mechanism to protect the integrity of the electoral process; citizens signing petitions do so in public without a guarantee of confidentiality; and there is little, if any, evidence that disclosing the names of signers causes people to be less willing to sign a petition. Justice Sotomayor counseled that "courts * * * should be deeply skeptical of any assertion that the Constitution, which embraces political transparency, compels States to conceal the identity of persons who seek to participate in lawmaking through a state-created referendum process." Justice Stevens put it differently: for a successful as-applied challenge, "there would have to be a significant threat of harassment directed at those who sign the petition that cannot be mitigated by law enforcement measures."

Justice Scalia took a unique approach to the case, rejecting the initial conclusion that signing a petition implicated the First Amendment. His originalist approach included discussion of the history of voting in the U.S., which was not done by secret ballot until the late 19th century and was not justified then as a move compelled by the Constitution. He also noted that the initiative process grew out of town hall meetings and the right to petition the government for change, both of which occur in public. He viewed direct democracy as lawmaking, and "[t]he public nature of federal lawmaking is constitutionally required" by, among other things, Article I, § 5, cl. 3 of the Constitution, which mandates that each house of Congress keep and publish a Journal. He concluded: "There are laws against threats and intimidation; and harsh criticism, short of unlawful action, is a price our people have traditionally been willing to pay for self-governance. Requiring people to stand up in public for their political acts fosters civic courage, without which democracy is doomed."

The second case dealing with disclosure and the Internet presents the as-applied challenge that the Supreme Court left open in *Doe v. Reed*. It grew out of Proposition 8 in California, the 2008 ballot measure that amended the state constitution to deny marriage to same-sex couples and was later declared unconstitutional. After opponents of same-sex marriage won in a tight contest, supporters of same-sex marriage created a website that provided the names of the donors to the winning side, their addresses, the amount they contributed, and their occupations. The format through which the information was conveyed—a mash-up of Google maps and Prop 8 donor data posted by the Secretary of State—enabled people to easily check whether their neighbors, co-workers, and acquaintances had supported the controversial ballot measure. Gay-rights activists urged people who supported same-sex marriage to boycott businesses owned or run by those contributors.

In *ProtectMarriage.com v. Bowen*, 830 F. Supp. 2d 914 (E.D. Cal. 2011), several ballot committees that had been formed to support the passage of Prop 8, and thereby to end same-sex marriage, sought an exemption from the state's disclosure provisions. They alleged that, because personal information about donors was available on the Secretary of State's website, Prop 8 supporters and their businesses had been subject to threats, reprisals, and harassment. Among other allegations, they claimed that Fresno Mayor Alan Autry and a local pastor, both Prop 8 supporters, had received death threats. The plaintiffs also claimed that some supporters had been forced to resign from their jobs; others had property vandalized. Their arguments focused in particular on the $100 threshold for disclosure. ProtectMarriage.com contended that the state had no compelling interest in revealing personal information about individuals whose contributions were so small.

The District Court granted the Secretary of State's motion for summary judgment, affirming the constitutionality of the disclosure regime. The judge did not view the contributors to Prop 8 as facing the same threats that the Socialist Workers Party demonstrated with respect to its members in the case that exempted it from federal campaign disclosure laws. See *Brown v. Socialist Workers '74 Campaign Comm. (Ohio)*, 459 U.S. 87 (1982). The 60 members of the Socialist Workers Party experienced destruction of their property, hate mail and threatening phone calls, harassment by the police, and shots fired into the Party's offices. In contrast, the donors to Prop 8 are not part of a "fringe organization" out of step with the views of the majority. They were able to win in a statewide election, receiving more than seven million votes supporting their position. They did not face government persecution or widespread vilification; rather, they "sought to legislate a concept steeped in tradition and history." The judge noted that the decision in *Doe v. Reed* had not explicitly changed the threshold required to merit an exemption from disclosure, even though at least one of the concurring opinions (Justice Alito's) expressed a willingness to provide an exemption on the basis of a substantially lower showing of retaliation. Finally, while decrying any illegal actions taken against Prop 8 supporters, the court also noted that the First Amendment allows dissent through speech, debate, and even economic boycotts.

Perhaps the most difficult issue posed by this case is whether the state interest justifying disclosure of contributors in a ballot-measure campaign—the interest in providing important information to voters—is really implicated with regard to small donations of $100 by individuals. The judge described the state's informational interest in the language of voting cues. He concluded that voters "often base their decisions to vote for or against [a ballot measure] on cognitive cues such as the names of individuals supporting or opposing a measure." But can voters use the name of an individual donating $100 to a ballot committee as a credible voting cue? And if there is a chance that small donors may face some retaliation, even if it does not reach the level of harassment and threats faced by the Socialist Workers Party, won't that discourage some from participating in the political process? The threat of such political chill, made more serious by broad and immediate disclosure through user-friendly websites, might be sufficient to cause a court to question low disclosure thresholds that do not produce informational benefits.

However, the District Court judge in *ProtectMarriage.com* held that the $100 threshold in California is constitutionally permissible. He noted that to hold otherwise would draw into question "scores of statutes in which the legislature or the people have sought to draw similar lines." The judge also observed that only six states have higher thresholds and that laws range from no threshold to $300. While it may be constitutional to require disclosure of contributions to ballot measures or candidates as low as $100, is it good policy? What helpful information to voters does this level of detail provide? Does it threaten instead to deluge voters with so much information that they cannot distinguish credible voting cues from mere "noise"? As lawmakers consider the optimal design of a new disclosure regime, they should keep in mind that distinctions can be made between information provided to government regulators, justified by the need to enforce other campaign regulations, and information disseminated broadly. Thresholds triggering requirements that information be provided to regulators might reasonably be lower than those triggering wider disclosure. See Richard Briffault, *Campaign Finance Disclosure 2.0*, 9 Election L.J. 273 (2010).

What is the right standard for a court to apply when asked for an as-applied exemption from disclosure in cases like these? Think about the subsequent as-applied challenge to Washington's release of the names and addresses of petition signers. How would you analyze that case? For the lower court's analysis, see *Doe v. Reed*, 823 F. Supp. 2d 1195 (W.D. Wash. 2011), *appeal dismissed as moot*, 697 F.3d 1235 (9th Cir. 2012) (court allowed disclosure, relying on reasoning in *ProtectMarriage.com* about the nature of the group; holding that exemption from disclosure is available only to minor parties and fringe organizations; and finding no evidence of serious and widespread threats or harassment); see also *Doe v. Reed*, 132 S.Ct. 449 (2011) (Alito, J., dissenting from the denial of an application for an injunction during the appeal).

PROBLEM ON DISCLOSURE AND DIRECT DEMOCRACY

Problem 4-1. How would you design a disclosure statute to apply to campaigns for ballot measures? What information would you seek to disclose? How would you provide it to voters? How would you take account of technology, both in what is subject to disclosure and in how disclosure is made most effectively? How would you pierce the veils that political actors sometimes throw up to avoid disclosure by creating groups with innocuous-sounding names that mask the economic and ideological forces driving them?[27]

Single-Subject Rules. Some features of the initiative process are designed to reduce voter confusion. For example, some states restrict the subject matter of initiatives, prohibiting revenue or appropriations measures from being proposed through the initiative process.[28] Perhaps the most important such restriction is the single-subject rule that, as applied to ballot measures, is designed to ensure voters are presented with a proposal on a single subject that they can accept or reject. Of

---

[27]   For discussion of such tactics of evasion, see Elizabeth Garrett & Daniel Smith, *Veiled Political Actors and Campaign Disclosure Laws in Direct Democracy*, 4 Election L.J. 295 (2005).

[28]   See Waters, *supra*, at 18 (listing subject-matter restrictions).

course, ballot measures on one topic can be extremely complicated, just as an initiative that combines two straightforward proposals can be relatively easily understood. Thus, it is not clear that the single-subject rule is tailored appropriately to fit the objective. Another rationale given for the single-subject rule in direct democracy mirrors the justification offered in the legislative context discussed in Chapter 3, § 2(A): "The purpose of the single-subject requirement is to allow the citizens to vote on singular changes in our government that are identified in the proposal and to avoid voters having to accept parts of a proposal which they oppose in order to obtain a change which they support." *Fine v. Firestone*, 448 So. 2d 984, 993 (Fla. 1984).

The California Constitution has a single-subject rule specifically designed for direct democracy. It provides: "An initiative measure embracing more than one subject may not be submitted to the electors or have any effect." Cal. Const., art. II, § 8(d). The California Supreme Court has construed it identically with the state constitution's single-subject rule regarding legislation, applying to both a standard under which the rule is construed " 'liberally to uphold proper legislation, all parts of which are reasonably germane.' " *Perry v. Jordan*, 207 P.2d 47 (Cal. 1949) (quoting *Evans v. Superior Court of Los Angeles Cnty.*, 8 P.2d 467 (Cal. 1932)); see also *Briggs v. Brown*, 400 P.3d 29, 38–40 (Cal. 2017). Several justices have suggested, however, that a more stringent standard should apply in the context of direct democracy, under which the parts of an initiative must be "functionally related in furtherance of a common underlying purpose." *Schmitz v. Younger*, 577 P.2d 652 (Cal. 1978) (Manuel, J., dissenting). What policies support adoption of a stricter standard? Compare Marilyn Minger, Comment, *Putting the "Single" Back in the Single-Subject Rule: A Proposal for Initiative Reform in California*, 24 U.C. Davis L. Rev. 879 (1991) (proposing an amendment to encourage the court to engage in vigorous single-subject review), with Richard Hasen, *Ending Court Protection of Voters from the Initiative Process*, 116 Yale L.J. Pocket Part 115 (2006) (arguing that justifications for aggressive enforcement of the single-subject rule are unpersuasive and that the rule should be repealed).

An invigoration of the single-subject rule for ballot propositions seems to be occurring in some states. Florida has had a reputation for applying the single-subject rule aggressively; interestingly, the state is a relative newcomer to the initiative process, adopting it in 1968 for constitutional changes. Although deferential until the mid-1980s, Florida courts began to wield the single-subject rule so enthusiastically to strike down initiatives or keep them off the ballot that a 1994 ballot measure exempted initiatives limiting government revenues from the single-subject requirement.[29] A study by Daniel Lowenstein reveals that Florida is no longer the only state with a judiciary willing to enforce the single-subject rule aggressively in the context of initiatives. *Initiatives and the New Single Subject Rule*, 1 Election L.J. 35 (2002). Between 1998 and 1999, the supreme courts of California, Oregon, and Montana applied the single-subject doctrine "with surprising strictness," and Oklahoma, Missouri, and Colorado have inconsistently adopted a strict approach. Lowenstein notes that "even in states that have not so far been affected by the trend

---

[29]   See Philip Dubois & Floyd Feeney, *Lawmaking by Initiative: Issues, Options and Comparisons* 136–38 (1998).

toward restrictive review, the developments in the states reviewed above may provide a strong temptation to supreme court justices who are personally hostile to an initiative that comes before them." *Id.* at 44.

One challenge in the context of direct democracy, just as it was with traditional legislation, is the definition of a subject. Review the discussion of what constitutes a subject in Chapter 3, § 2(A). Should the inquiry be different when the people, rather than representative bodies, enact the law? Scholars have argued that the malleability of the tests allows judges to mask their political preferences in deciding cases they claim are determined on procedural grounds.[30] Robert Cooter and Michael Gilbert have developed a test to determine what constitutes a "subject" based on their conception of the democratic process. *A Theory of Direct Democracy and the Single Subject Rule*, 110 Colum. L. Rev. 687 (2010). They argue that the test should turn on whether voters have "sufficiently separable preferences" with respect to the two policy proposals—that is, whether they can decide how to vote on each without knowing whether the other will become law. A voter has insufficiently separable preferences when either the two are "strong complements, such that the voter only votes for one if she is certain also to get the other" or "strong substitutes, such that the voter only votes for one if she is certain not to get the other." *Id.* at 714. Consider this theory, as well as the judicially applied tests, as you work through the following problems. How is a court to determine what voters' preferences are and how closely related they are? Would such a test really avoid the problems that exist in the current system? For questions about the Cooter/Gilbert proposal, see Richard Hasen & John Matsusaka, *Some Skepticism about the "Separable Preferences" Approach to the Single Subject Rule: A Comment on Cooter & Gilbert*, 110 Colum. L. Rev. Sidebar 35 (2010).

PROBLEMS ON DIRECT DEMOCRACY AND THE SINGLE-SUBJECT RULE

Problem 4-2. Citizens in Florida petition to add the following to Article I, § 10 of the Florida Constitution:

> The state, political subdivisions of the state, municipalities or any other governmental entity shall not enact or adopt any law regarding discrimination against persons which creates, establishes or recognizes any right, privilege or protection for any person based upon any characteristic, trait, status, or condition other than race, color, sex, national origin, age, handicap, ethnic background, marital status, or familial status. * * *

Florida has a single-subject rule: Any revision to the Florida Constitution by initiative "shall embrace but one subject and matter directly connected therewith." The Florida Supreme Court has stated that the rule is "designed to insulate Florida's organic law from precipitous and cataclysmic change."

As is often done now, groups opposing this initiative bring suit to knock it off the ballot. Should the Florida Supreme Court hear such preliminary challenges? If so, how should it rule? See *In re Advisory Opinion to the Attorney General—Restricts Laws Related to Discrimination*, 632 So. 2d 1018 (Fla. 1994).

---

[30]   John Matsusaka & Richard Hasen, *Aggressive Enforcement of the Single Subject Rule*, 9 Election L.J. 399 (2010).

Problem 4-3. A proposed amendment to the Arizona state constitution provides:

To preserve and protect marriage in this state, only a union between one man and one woman shall be valid or recognized as a marriage by this state or its political subdivisions and no legal status for unmarried persons shall be created or recognized by this state or its political subdivisions that is similar to that of marriage.

Does this measure contain a single subject? Consider the formal argument that it (1) defines marriage, (2) prohibits same-sex marriages, (3) might prohibit civil unions and domestic partnerships, and (4) might even prohibit the state and its subdivisions from conferring any benefits upon persons in same-sex relationships, whether that status is recognized by law or not (e.g., it might prohibit the University of Arizona from extending health insurance coverage to partners of its employees). In addition, consider the functional argument that common sense and public opinion polls alike indicate that many voters who support (1) and (2) will not understand that (3) and (4) might also be involved—and at least a good number of them might oppose either or both (3) and (4) if they could vote separately on them. See *Arizona Together v. Brewer*, 214 Ariz. 118, 149 P.3d 742 (Ariz. 2007); see also *McConkey v. Van Hollen*, 326 Wis. 2d 1, 783 N.W. 2d 855 (Wisc. 2010) (more recent case, reaching similar result).

C. INTERACTION BETWEEN DIRECT DEMOCRACY AND REPRESENTATIVE INSTITUTIONS

Effect on the Lawmaking Agenda. The term "hybrid democracy" makes salient the reality that the presence of a robust initiative process affects the legislative branch in several ways. First, the presence of an initiative on the ballot will affect turnout generally, which in turn influences the results of candidate elections. Daniel Smith and Caroline Tolbert found that, in presidential elections, each ballot measure boosts turnout by half a percent, and in midterm elections, each ballot measure increases turnout by 1.2%.[31] Of course, turnout is not increased randomly; rather, the subject matter of the initiative motivates different groups of people to vote, and the shape of that turnout may determine who is elected to serve at the state and federal levels. The initiatives prohibiting same-sex marriage on the ballot in 11 states in 2004 certainly affected the outcome of Senate and other legislative races, and they may even have played a role in President George W. Bush's reelection by encouraging the turnout of conservative voters in Ohio, the key state for his victory.

Perhaps one of the most interesting findings by political scientists who focus on the interaction between the two sides of hybrid democracy is that the mere possibility of an initiative influences outcomes in the state legislature. Gerber describes the *indirect effect* of direct democracy, which she defines as political actors using initiatives to pressure state lawmakers to pass a new law. *The Populist Paradox: Interest Group Influence and the Promise of Direct Democracy* 23–28 (1999). Sometimes the pressure can be overt. For example, in 1998, Silicon Valley entrepreneur Reed Hastings led a group frustrated by the California Assembly's refusal to expand the charter school program. They believed that an entrenched

---

[31] *Educated by Initiative: The Effects of Direct Democracy on Citizens and Political Organizations in the American States* 42 (2004) (also finding that, at a certain point, each additional measure does not further increase turnout).

special interest, the teachers' union, was blocking meaningful reform through the traditional legislative process. Accordingly, they spent $3.5 million to pay petition circulators and obtained 1.2 million signatures for a proposal to institute their vision of charter schools, twice the number of required signatures. In addition, they threatened to spend another $12 million to pass the initiative. Hastings made it clear, however, that his group would halt the petition drive if representatives increased the number of charter schools and addressed other concerns. Within a short time, a compromise bill had passed the state legislature; once Governor Pete Wilson signed the bill, the initiative drive stopped.

Not all groups can enter into this sort of bargaining game with politicians. Under what conditions will such a threat be successful? Gerber identifies three conditions. First, "the group has sufficient resources to attract the legislature's attention." Second, "the group must have something legislators want," such as the ability to provide future campaign contributions. Third, "legislators must be electorally vulnerable."

Often the indirect influence of direct democracy is not as overt as in the charter schools example in California. For example, political scientists have found that legislative outcomes in states with the possibility of initiatives are different in meaningful ways from the outcomes in states without robust popular democracy. In *For the Many or the Few* (2004), John Matsusaka focuses his attention on fiscal policies. He finds that initiative states have lower overall spending by state and local governments; that spending in these states has shifted from the state to local governments; and that broad-based taxes in initiative states are reduced and replaced with more user fees. Using opinion polls, he determines that a majority of voters in those states favor such fiscal policies, leading him to conclude that, at least in this realm, direct democracy favors the majority, rather than special interests. Importantly, these policies are not all adopted through the initiative; rather, it is the pressure of the possibility of direct democracy that may be responsible for these systematic differences.[32] The existence of the initiative process may therefore empower the median voter in all policymaking realms, under some conditions. Of course, this may lead to other concerns, such as the tyranny of the majority undermining the rights of the minority.

In addition, political actors may turn to the initiative, or the threat of one, to enact policies that they cannot pass through the regular legislative channels. Former California Governor Arnold Schwarzenegger successfully wielded the threat of direct democracy early in his first term to pressure the legislature into adopting workers' compensation reform that had been stymied in the legislature, blocked by powerful interest groups representing labor.[33] In Minnesota, the structure of the ballot-

---

[32]   See also Elisabeth Gerber, *Legislative Response to the Threat of Popular Initiatives*, 40 Am. J. Pol. Sci. 99 (1996) (finding that parental consent laws in initiative states are closer to the median voter's preference than such laws in states without the initiative process); John Matsusaka & Nolan McCarty, *Political Resource Allocation: Benefits and Costs of Voter Initiatives*, 17 J.L. Econ. & Org. 413 (2001) (detailing conditions under which outcomes are closer to median voter's preference in initiative states). One study has even found that initiatives affect congressional voting behavior, particularly in the House. Joshua Huder, Jordan Ragusa & Daniel Smith, *Shirking the Initiative: The Effects of Statewide Ballot Measures on Congressional Roll Call Behavior*, 39 Am. Pol. Res. 582 (2011).

[33]   Elizabeth Garrett, *Democracy in the Wake of the California Recall*, 153 U. Pa. L. Rev. 239, 280 (2004).

measure process allows a majority of the legislature to propose a constitutional amendment for a vote of the people without any involvement by the Governor. Accordingly, in 2012 when the Republican-dominated legislature was blocked by the Democratic Governor from enacting a voter ID law, it bypassed the executive by placing the issue on the ballot (where it ultimately lost). The legislature also avoided having a Democratic Secretary of State provide a ballot title that might not have been as favorable as supporters desired by requiring particular wording for the title, and then defeating a judicial challenge to its end run around the regular process of titling and an examination of the accuracy of the title.[34]

Changing the "Political Process" by Initiative. Does a special problem arise when popular majorities use the mechanisms of direct democracy to change the lawmaking process going forward in a way that negatively impacts minority groups? Consider the following case.

Schuette v. Coalition to Defend Affirmative Action

572 U.S. 291 (2014).

After the Supreme Court upheld the University of Michigan Law School's use of race-based preferences in admissions, *Grutter v. Bollinger*, 539 U.S. 306 (2003), Michigan voters in 2006 adopted Proposal 2, which amended the state constitution to prohibit, *inter alia*, the use of race-based preferences in the admissions processes of the state's public universities. Supporters of racial preferences in admissions filed suit, arguing that Proposal 2 violated the "political process doctrine," as laid out in several previous decisions of the Court. In *Hunter v. Erickson*, 393 U.S. 385 (1969), the Court struck down an Akron initiative that amended the city charter to overturn a fair housing ordinance passed by the city council and to require that any future fair housing ordinance be approved by referendum. In *Washington v. Seattle School Dist. No. 1*, 458 U.S. 457 (1982), the Court struck down a Washington state initiative that prohibited the use of busing to desegregate schools. In both cases, the Court found an equal protection violation, not because of the policies ultimately adopted—Akron was not required to have a fair housing ordinance, nor was the Seattle school district required to bus students in order to integrate its schools—but rather because the initiative changed the level at which those decisions would be made in the future. The Akron City Council could no longer pass a fair housing ordinance without submitting it to a referendum, and school districts in Washington state would have to change the law statewide if they wanted to use busing to desegregate. It was this alteration of the political process, the Court held, that violated equal protection.

The plaintiffs in *Schuette* argued that Michigan's Proposal 2 was of the same character: the decision of whether to use racial preferences in admissions was no longer up to the elected board of each public university. Instead, proponents of such preferences would have to first amend the state constitution.

There was no opinion for the Court. **Justice Kennedy**'s plurality opinion, joined by **Chief Justice Roberts** and **Justice Alito**, noted that, "This case is not about how the debate about racial preferences should be resolved. It is about who may resolve it." Kennedy began by offering a narrow reading of *Hunter* and *Seattle* as cases "in which the

---

[34]   *Limmer v. Ritchie*, 819 N.W. 2d 622 (Minn. 2012) (see dissent by Justice Anderson describing the "end run" aspect of the legislative decision to propose the voter ID requirement as a constitutional amendment).

state action in question * * * had the serious risk, if not purpose, of causing specific injuries on account of race." It is true that *Seattle* contained broader language, suggesting that "any state action with a 'racial focus' that makes it 'more difficult for certain racial minorities than for other groups' to 'achieve legislation that is in their interest' is subject to strict scrutiny." But that broader reading, Kennedy argued, was based entirely on *dicta* and "must be rejected" for two reasons.

First, the broader reading of *Seattle* "has no principled limitation," because it is impossible to separate out those policies that are in the interest of minorities from those that are not: "Tax policy, housing subsidies, wage regulations, and even the naming of public schools, highways, and monuments are just a few examples of what could become a list of subjects that some organizations could insist should be beyond the power of voters to decide, or beyond the power of a legislature to decide when enacting limits on the power of local authorities or other governmental entities to address certain subjects." Second, by requiring as an initial step that a policy be classified as one that has a racial focus making it more difficult for minority groups to achieve legislation in their interest, the broad reading of *Seattle* necessitates an inquiry into how racial groups understand their interests, which constitutes a racial classification and is therefore "inherently suspect." Worse still, it risks "the creation of incentives for those who support or oppose certain policies to cast the debate in terms of racial advantage or disadvantage." Thus, for Justice Kennedy, the broad reading of *Seattle* would itself raise equal protection concerns.

And under the narrower reading, *Schuette* is distinguishable from *Hunter* and *Seattle*: "Here there was no infliction of a specific injury of the kind at issue" in those cases. Instead, "[w]hat is at stake here is not whether injury will be inflicted but whether government can be instructed not to follow a course that entails, first, the definition of racial categories and, second, the grant of favored status to persons in some racial categories and not others." That question is not governed by the *Hunter/Seattle* line of precedent, and extending those precedents to this case would cut against another important constitutional principle: "Our constitutional system embraces * * * the right of citizens to debate so they can learn and decide and then, through the political process, act in concert to try to shape the course of their own times and the course of a nation that must strive always to make freedom ever greater and more secure." In Justice Kennedy's view, that was what the voters of Michigan had done in passing Proposal 2.

Justice Scalia, joined by **Justice Thomas**, concurred in the judgment. He began by reiterating his longstanding claim that race-based preferences violate the Equal Protection Clause. Thus, for him, the case boiled down to "a frighteningly bizarre question: Does the Equal Protection Clause of the Fourteenth Amendment *forbid* what its text plainly *requires*? Needless to say (except that this case obliges us to say it), the question answers itself" in the negative.

Taking *Grutter* as given for the sake of argument, Justice Scalia argued that the plurality's attempt to distinguish *Hunter* and *Seattle* from the present case was unpersuasive: "In those cases, one level of government exercised borrowed authority over an apparently 'racial issue,' until a higher level of government called the loan. So too here. In those cases, we deemed the revocation an equal-protection violation *regardless* of whether it facially classified according to race or reflected an invidious purpose to discriminate," and the plaintiffs in this case sought the same determination. That, for Justice Scalia, was the problem: "Patently atextual, unadministrable, and contrary to our traditional equal-protection jurisprudence, *Hunter* and *Seattle* should be overruled," not "reinterpret[ed] * * * beyond recognition," as the plurality did.

Justice Sotomayor, in a dissent joined by **Justice Ginsburg**, agreed with Justice Scalia that the plurality mangled *Hunter* and *Seattle*, but she argued that they should have been applied to this case, not overruled. "[T]he majority of Michigan voters changed the rules in the middle of the game, reconfiguring the existing political process in Michigan in a manner that burdened racial minorities. * * * As a result of [Proposal 2], there are now two very different processes through which a Michigan citizen is permitted to influence the admissions policies of the State's universities: one for persons interested in race-sensitive admissions policies and one for everyone else. A citizen who is a University of Michigan alumnus, for instance, can advocate for an admissions policy that considers an applicant's legacy status by meeting individually with members of the Board of Regents to convince them of her views, by joining with other legacy parents to lobby the Board, or by voting for and supporting Board candidates who share her position. The same options are available to a citizen who wants the Board to adopt admissions policies that consider athleticism, geography, area of study, and so on. The one and only policy a Michigan citizen may not seek through this long-established process is a race-sensitive admissions policy that considers race in an individualized manner when it is clear that race-neutral alternatives are not adequate to achieve diversity. For that policy alone, the citizens of Michigan must undertake the daunting task of amending the State Constitution."

"Our precedents do not permit political restructurings that create one process for racial minorities and a separate, less burdensome process for everyone else." The political process doctrine enunciated in *Hunter* and *Seattle* "does not guarantee minority groups victory in the political process, [but] it does guarantee them meaningful and equal access to that process. It guarantees that the majority may not win by stacking the political process against minority groups permanently, forcing the minority alone to surmount unique obstacles in pursuit of its goals—here, educational diversity that cannot reasonably be accomplished through race-neutral measures."

For Justice Sotomayor, it was relatively clear-cut both that Proposal 2 "has a 'racial focus' " and that it "restructures the political process in Michigan in a manner that places unique burdens on racial minorities" by establishing "a distinct and more burdensome political process for the enactment of admissions plans that consider racial diversity."

(**Justice Breyer** concurred in the judgment on the idiosyncratic grounds that, because the elected university boards had in practice delegated admissions policy to "unelected faculty members and administrators," Proposal 2 simply "took decisionmaking authority away from these unelected actors and placed it in the hands of the voters." Accordingly, there was "no prior electoral process in which the minority participated" and therefore no diminution of the minority's ability to participate in the political process. And **Justice Kagan** did not participate in the case.)

NOTE ON SCHUETTE: SECOND-ORDER DIVERSITY

One way to understand the political process doctrine is in terms of what Heather Gerken has called "second-order diversity":

The idea I term "first-order diversity" fits the conventional understanding of diversity; it is the normative vision associated with statistical integration, the hope that democratic bodies will someday mirror the polity. The notion of "second-order diversity," [by contrast] posits that democracy sometimes benefits from having decisionmaking bodies that do not mirror the underlying population, but instead encompass a wide range of compositions. Second-order diversity involves variation among decisionmaking bodies, not within them. It favors interorganizational heterogeneity, not intraorganizational heterogeneity. It fosters diversity without mandating uniformity.

Heather K. Gerken, *Second-Order Diversity*, 118 Harv. L. Rev. 1099, 1102–03 (2005). Prior to Proposal 2, Michigan's universities could be second-order diverse: each was allowed to set its own admissions policies with respect to racial preferences, which meant that different groups might succeed in convincing different university boards of the merits of different positions. Proposal 2 imposed across-the-board(s) uniformity in this regard. The electorate that voted for Proposal 2 may have mirrored the Michigan polity, thus fitting the criteria for first-order diversity, but it took the opportunity to eliminate second-order diversity. Is this a convincing way to read the political process doctrine? If so, does it counsel a different outcome in *Schuette*?

If you are attracted to the second-order-diversity rationale for the political process doctrine, how broadly does it reach? Is a statewide majority ever justified in taking decisionmaking authority away from local institutions to which it had theretofore been entrusted? If so, what rationale would suffice?

The Implementation Problem. Another interaction between direct democracy and representative institutions occurs after an initiative is passed. Once enacted, many initiatives must be implemented by elected and appointed officials—people who often resisted the policy in the first place. After all, the people resort to enacting laws themselves when their representatives have been insufficiently attentive. This leads to the "implementation problem" in direct democracy. For example, a ballot measure might enact sweeping reform of the state's school system, which then must be implemented by the Department of Education, school administrators, and unions. Or the initiative might enact public financing for campaigns, but the legislature has to appropriate the money. Or the initiative might limit judicial power in some way and then be challenged before (and interpreted by) the very courts that it purports to limit.

In *Stealing the Initiative: How State Government Responds to Direct Democracy* (2001), Gerber, Lupia, McCubbins, and Kiewiet identify several conditions that allow government officials to ignore or undermine initiatives more easily. First, substantial technical or political costs will lead to lower levels of compliance because the net value of implementation is reduced. Technical costs might include the effort involved in writing and adopting legislation or regulations to implement the initiative. Political costs might be incurred if legislators have to make promises to enact legislation or take steps that will be opposed by powerful organized interests. Or money to implement the initiative might reduce the resources available for other important legislative goals. Second, if implementers face significant sanctions for noncompliance, they are more likely to work to implement the initiative. Third, and related to the second factor, when it is easier for the public or others who support the initiative to observe compliance, it is more likely that officials will comply. Finally, the more people required for full compliance, the lower the chances of implementation.

One aspect of the implementation problem reached the Supreme Court as part of the litigation surrounding Prop 8, the referendum preventing same-sex marriage in California. When supporters of same-sex marriage attacked Prop 8 in federal District Court, no state official named as a defendant—including the Governor and Attorney General—was willing to defend it. The District Court allowed the proponents of the initiative to intervene and defend the law; ultimately, the judge found Prop 8 to violate the constitutional guarantee of equal protection. *Perry v. Schwarzenegger*, 704 F. Supp. 2d 921 (N.D. Cal. 2010), *aff'd sub nom. Perry v. Brown*, 671 F.3d 1052 (9th Cir. 2012). The Supreme Court did not address the merits of that decision, finding instead that the initiative proponents did not have standing to defend the ballot measure. *Hollingsworth v. Perry*, 570 U.S. 693 (2013). Without some specific authorization from the state that would allow proponents to act as agents of the people of California, these citizens had only a generalized grievance insufficient to confer standing under Article III. As the Supreme Court explained, "Their only interest in having the District Court order reversed was to vindicate the constitutional validity of a generally applicable California law." Their unique role in the initiative process is limited to the enactment phase; once the ballot measure is passed, the proponents become simply what the majority called "concerned bystanders." Four justices dissented and supported the approach of the California Supreme Court, which had concluded that the initiative's primary purpose "is undermined if the very officials the initiative process seeks to circumvent are the only parties who can defend an enacted initiative when it is challenged in a legal proceeding." The dissent noted the irony of the Court's decision that resulted in "litigation conducted by state officials whose preference is to lose the case."

After *Hollingsworth,* can a state enable initiative proponents—or some group other than elected officials who likely do not support the measure—to defend it in court? How would you construct a system that would provide some authority to such groups (and which groups would you choose?), but also provide some oversight of their decisions and actions? See Elizabeth Garrett & Mathew McCubbins, *The Dual Path Initiative Framework*, 80 S. Cal. L. Rev. 299, 332–42 (2007) (proposing an independent Citizens Initiative Implementation Oversight Commission, with members appointed in provisions in successful ballot measures).

Problem 4-4. Consider some of the policies we have already studied that have often been implemented as a result of direct democracy: term limits for legislators, public financing of campaigns, ethics rules, changes in party primaries, supermajority voting requirements for tax increases, and redistricting commissions. Why do groups resort to direct democracy to enact these policies? What hurdles will each face in the effort to gain ballot access? Which interest groups are likely to be active as proponents and opponents, and how successfully can they raise money? Are political candidates likely to align themselves with either side to increase their chances at the polls? Which face significant implementation problems? If you are a proponent of the initiative, how can you minimize the implementation problems when you draft the initiative? See Gerber, Lupia, McCubbins & Kiewiet, *supra* (providing case studies, including term limits and open primaries).

2. STATUTORY INTERPRETATION OF INITIATIVES

In subsequent chapters of this casebook, we will consider at length how courts interpret statutes enacted through traditional means, and we introduced some of these concepts in Chapter 1 in the context of judicial interpretation of provisions of the Civil Rights Act and the Affordable Care Act. Consider what different issues and difficulties might arise when interpreting laws that originate and are adopted outside the normal legislative process. Should interpretive techniques for ballot measures parallel those for legislative enactments, or should the fundamental differences in the two enactment procedures result in differing approaches to interpretation?

In *The Pursuit of "Popular Intent": Interpretive Dilemmas in Direct Democracy*, 105 Yale L.J. 107 (1995), a comprehensive treatment of these issues, Jane Schacter demonstrates that state courts routinely purport to use the same interpretive techniques regardless of statutory enactment process, usually stating that the linchpin of statutory meaning is the "intent" of the enacting authority. Schacter criticizes this approach on empirical grounds. How can the people, at the polls, have some determinate intent about non-obvious issues that could arise under the measure? She suggests that any serious effort to understand voter intent would require an examination of the media coverage and advertising surrounding a ballot campaign, which social science research demonstrates affect the voters much more than formal sources such as the text of the ballot proposition and the official voter pamphlet distributed by the state. Yet state courts routinely refuse to consider the informal materials and counterfactually assume that voter intent coheres with the text of the ballot and pamphlet.

An example of this phenomenon is the Michigan marriage initiative, which added new Article 25, § 11 to the Michigan Constitution in 2004: "To secure and preserve the benefits of marriage for our society and for future generations of children, the union of one man and one woman in marriage shall be the only agreement recognized as a marriage or similar union for any purpose." The Michigan Attorney General and the state's Court of Appeals interpreted that language to bar public employers from giving health care benefits to the "domestic partners" of lesbian and gay employees. *Nat'l Pride at Work, Inc. v. Governor*, 274 Mich. App. 147, 732 N.W. 2d 139 (2007), *aff'd*, 481 Mich. 56, 784 N.W. 2d 524 (2008). The court ruled that the statutory language plainly applied to even the most limited domestic-partnership benefits and refused to consider background materials—which demonstrated that the sponsors repeatedly assured voters that their marriage initiative would *not* affect domestic-partnership benefits. See also Glen Staszewski, *The Bait-and-Switch in Direct Democracy*, 2006 Wis. L. Rev. 17, 21–32 (discussing the proposition and its text). Staszewski argues that initiative proponents should be treated as sponsors accountable for their representations to the electorate, especially ones that appeal to popular prejudices (for purposes of judicial review) or that claim a narrow effect of their proposals if enacted (for purposes of statutory interpretation).

Rejecting the Myth of Popular Sovereignty and Applying an Agency Model to Direct Democracy, 56 Vand. L. Rev. 395 (2003).

Sensitive to the issues Staszewski identifies, Schacter rejects a more capacious judicial consideration of informal materials on the grounds that they are unlikely to assist judges in choosing among the plausible interpretations surrounding ambiguous ballot measures and that judicial receptivity to arguments based on such materials will only encourage interest groups to manipulate media accounts and advertising for post-enactment judicial consumption. Schacter argues that, in place of an illusory search for voter intent, courts should craft principles of statutory interpretation specifically for the context of direct democracy. She proposes that ballot propositions disadvantaging groups subject to the hostility of the majority—such as antigay measures like the Michigan marriage initiative—should be interpreted narrowly. On the other hand, initiatives that break through self-interested legislative gridlocks and seek to enhance the legitimacy of government processes—such as campaign finance restrictions or perhaps term limits—might be interpreted more liberally.

Like Schacter, Philip Frickey argues for a direct-democracy-specific canon of interpretation. *Interpretation on the Borderline: Constitution, Canons, Direct Democracy*, 1996 N.Y.U. Ann. Surv. Am. L. 477 (1996). For him, however, the initial insight is that direct democracy is in tension with the federal constitutional principle of republican government. This will not result in initiatives being struck down (see the discussion in § 1 of this chapter), but for Frickey, it does suggest that ambiguous provisions in initiatives should be interpreted narrowly, to limit their effects in displacing prior law enacted in republican fashion (i.e., by the legislature).

In contrast to Schacter's rejection of voter intent, Michael Gilbert has argued that initiatives should be interpreted to reflect the will of the median voter. *Interpreting Initiatives*, 97 Minn. L. Rev. 1621 (2013). In other words, judges should consider the views of *all* voters—not just those voting for the initiative, and certainly not just the drafters—and should determine the meaning of contested provisions by reference to what the median voter's view on the issue is. Gilbert also posits that elected state judges, often the interpreters in these cases, may be particularly well situated to determine the median voter's likely view.

Keep these different approaches in mind as you read the following case, in which the California Supreme Court divided over the question of whether the interpretation of measures adopted by initiative requires courts to attempt to divine the intent of the voters.

Briggs v. Brown

400 P.3d 29 (Cal. 2017).

In 2016, California voters approved Proposition 66, the Death Penalty Reform and Savings Act. "The measure enacts a series of statutory reforms, which may be grouped into three general categories: (1) provisions to expedite review in capital appeals and habeas corpus proceedings; (2) provisions governing the confinement of prisoners sentenced to death and the administration of the death penalty; and (3) provisions pertaining to California's Habeas Corpus Resource Center." A lawsuit filed in the state supreme court, invoking its original jurisdiction, challenged Proposition 66 on a number of grounds, most of which the court rejected unanimously. However, contention arose over the petitioner's claim that "a variety of time limits and calls for expedited proceedings in Proposition 66 interfere with the courts' inherent power to fairly and effectively address all the matters before them." In particular, one challenged provision "imposes a five-year limit on the completion of the appellate and initial habeas corpus review processes" in capital cases, and another "requires the superior court to resolve an initial petition within one year unless a substantial claim of actual innocence requires a delay, and sets a two-year boundary for the completion of every initial habeas corpus proceeding" in such cases.

Justice Corrigan, for the majority, began with the general principle that the power of the legislature to regulate judicial procedure "is broad, but not unlimited. [T]he legislature may put reasonable restrictions upon constitutional functions of the courts provided they do not defeat or materially impair the exercise of those functions. * * * [T]he mere procedure by which jurisdiction is to be exercised may be prescribed by the Legislature, unless * * * such regulations should be found to substantially impair the constitutional powers of the courts, or practically defeat their exercise. * * * In most matters, the judicial branch must necessarily yield to the legislative power to enact statutes. Only if a legislative regulation truly defeats or *materially impairs* the courts' core functions * * * may a court declare it invalid" (internal quotation marks and citations omitted).

However, "[w]e have long recognized that imposing fixed time limits on the performance of judicial functions raises serious separation of powers concerns." In particular, the time limits in Proposition 66, if rigidly enforced, might well make it impossible for the courts adequately and fairly to perform their adjudicatory roles in at least some capital cases. That is to say, the "courts' core functions" in such cases might be "materially impaired" by strict adherence to those deadlines.

But rather than strike down the time limitations, the majority held that they were "not mandatory," but rather "merely directive." The court recognized that the limits in Proposition 66 were "framed in mandatory terms, and the voters were told in the ballot materials that the five-year limit on the posttrial review process would be binding and enforceable," and even that "the voters intended the * * * limit[s] to be mandatory." Nevertheless, the court invoked a version of the constitutional avoidance canon (see Chapter 6, § 3(B)) to render the limits merely advisory: "Rather than striking down statutes that might unduly interfere with judicial functions, we construe them so as to maintain the courts' discretionary control. * * * [W]e * * * decline to infer that lawmakers intended strict adherence to a fixed deadline that would undermine the courts' authority as a separate branch of government. It is far from certain that the voters contemplated such a result. Nothing in the Proposition 66 suggests that short shrift should be given to the decisionmaking process, or that capital posttrial review proceedings should dominate dockets to the point that other cases would be left to languish. In the absence of clearer indications that this was the voters' intent, we will not presume they meant to hamper the courts in the conduct of their business."

In a partial dissent, **Justice Cuéllar** took issue with this use of the avoidance canon, arguing instead that the meaning of Proposition 66 should be determined by reference to the voters' intent—and that if (as here) that intent indicated an unconstitutional meaning, then the court should strike those provisions down. "What voters most need so they can exercise their constitutionally protected franchise effectively is clarity and candor. Particularly at a time when public discourse dwells on foreign interference in our electoral process, social media bots, and manipulated Facebook news feeds, it is possible—perhaps even easy—to forget how millions of voters endeavor to familiarize themselves with the candidates and issues of the day, and to understand the consequences of their vote. Voters who sought to do so by studying Proposition 66 * * * would not recognize the initiative the majority purports to uphold today. What reasonable voters would have clearly recognized instead—based on the statutory text, the official description by the Legislative Analyst, and the arguments made by the initiative's proponents—is that Proposition 66 contained a genuine, enforceable, five-year deadline for completion of the state court appeal and resolution of the initial habeas corpus petition in death penalty cases."

Justice Cuéllar quoted extensively from the voter information guide prepared by the Secretary of State for Proposition 66 (which Cuéllar described as "the primary means by which voters inform themselves about the policy choices in an election, and * * * a key resource in determining the meaning and validity of the laws enacted by voter initiative"), as well as from campaign materials put forward by Proposition 66's supporters and news stories during the campaign. "When we are trying to determine what the voters enacted, what voters were told matters." And "[e]verything before us—the text and structure of the initiative, its unambiguous purpose, the ballot materials, and the construction endorsed by all of the parties—would lead a reasonable voter to believe that this provision, which had attracted so much attention, constituted a real deadline, and one that could be enforced by a petition for writ of mandate." Because such a hard deadline would be unconstitutional, in Justice Cuéllar's view, "the separation of powers doctrine requires us to strike down th[ese] mandatory * * * deadline[s]."

Justice Cuéllar ended his dissent with an emphatic point about the importance of candor, especially in the initiatives context: "The bait-and-switch undertaken by the proponents of Proposition 66—and countenanced by the majority—will do nothing but breed cynicism in the electorate and supply further kindling to those who doubt the efficacy and workability of constitutional democracy. As an inducement to support this initiative, voters were promised that state court review of death penalty judgments could and would be completed within five years. That promise, as the majority concedes, was a sham. But the way to prevent similar swindles in the future is to be clear about what [the provision containing the time limits] says and why it is unconstitutional. What the majority offers instead—a 'saving construction' to a clearly unconstitutional statute, accompanied by a 'caution' against presenting the voters with 'statutory language that is inconsistent with constitutional norms'—ill-serves the constitutional principles at stake, hinders forthright deliberation, and encourages initiative proponents to repeat the bait-and-switch in the future. * * * When the courts treat voters as adults (i.e., listen to what they are saying and take seriously what they are trying to accomplish), then we will have earned their respect—respect that is sorely needed on those rare occasions when we must explain why a law duly enacted by the voters, but contrary to the Constitution, cannot take effect" (internal citations omitted).

Is Justice Cuéllar right that striking down a provision enacted by the voters treats them more like "adults" than interpreting that provision in such a way that it can be upheld does? Would his argument against the majority's deployment of the constitutional avoidance canon be equally strong if the provision at issue had been passed by the California Legislature rather than by ballot initiative? Or is there something about the nature of direct democracy that makes the intent of the lawmakers especially sacrosanct when it comes to interpreting the law's meaning? And how should a court determine the intent of the mass voting public? Are the sources to which Justice Cuéllar looks—the voter information guide, campaign materials, news accounts, etc.—the right ones? Or is Professor Schacter correct that such materials are more likely to confuse the issue than to clarify it? More generally, how would Professors Schacter, Staszewski, Frickey, and Gilbert decide this case, based upon their different theories? Consider the application of all their theories in the next problem, as well.

PROBLEM INVOLVING POPULAR LAWMAKING AND INTERPRETATION

Problem 4-5. In 1990, California voters adopted Proposition 140, "The Political Reform Act of 1990," which imposed term limits on state elected officials and limited expenditures funding the state legislature. You have been asked to provide advice to several former state legislators who fear that this measure imposes on them a lifetime ban on ever seeking election to the legislature again. They are hoping that you will figure out a persuasive argument for construing the proposition as allowing them to seek office in the future. In addition, they have asked you to investigate whether the proposition might be invalidated as inconsistent with either the federal or state constitution. (Remember that California has a single-subject rule for initiatives.)

Each registered voter in California is mailed an official voter pamphlet. The pamphlet contains the text of each ballot measure, an official summary of it, and arguments for and against it prepared by proponents and opponents. The California pamphlet for the November 1990 election contained the following:[35]

PROPOSITION 140: TEXT OF PROPOSED LAW

This initiative measure expressly amends the Constitution by amending and combining sections thereof; therefore, new provisions proposed to be inserted or added are printed in *italic type* to indicate they are new.

PROPOSED LAW

Section 1.   This measure shall be known and may be cited as "The Political Reform Act of 1990."

Section 2.   Section 1.5 is added to Article IV of the California Constitution, to read:

SEC 1.5. The people find and declare that the Founding Fathers established a system of representative government based upon free, fair and competitive elections. The increased concentration of political power in the hands of incumbent representatives has made our electoral system less free, less competitive and less representative.

The ability of legislators to serve unlimited number of terms, to establish their own retirement system, and to pay for staff and support services at state expense contribute heavily to the extremely high number of incumbents who are elected. These unfair incumbent advantages discourage qualified candidates from seeking public office and create a class of career politicians, instead of the citizen representatives

---

[35]   We thank Einer Elhauge, who served as counsel for the Secretary of State of California, and Thomas Gede, then Special Assistant Attorney General of California, for providing us with these materials.

envisioned by the Founding Fathers. These career politicians become representatives of the bureaucracy, rather than of the people whom they are elected to represent.

To restore a free and democratic system of fair elections, and to encourage qualified candidates to seek public office, the people find and declare that the powers of incumbency must be limited. Retirement benefits must be restricted, state-financed incumbent staff and support services limited, and limitations placed upon the number of terms which may be served.

SEC. 3. Section 2 of Article IV of the California Constitution is amended to read:

SEC. 2. (a) The Senate has a membership of 40 Senators elected for 4-year terms, 20 to begin every 2 years. *No Senator may serve more than 2 terms.* The Assembly has a membership of 80 members elected for 2-year terms. *No member of the Assembly may serve more than 3 terms.* Their terms shall commence on the first Monday in December next following their election.

* * *

SEC. 4. Section 4.5 is added to Article IV of the California Constitution, to read:

SEC. 4.5.   Notwithstanding any other provision of this Constitution or existing law, a person elected to or serving in the Legislature on or after November 1, 1990, shall participate in the Federal Social Security (Retirement, Disability, Health Insurance) Program and the State shall pay only the employer's share of the contribution necessary to such participation. No other pension or retirement benefit shall accrue as a result of service in the Legislature, such service not being intended as a career occupation. This Section shall not be construed to abrogate or diminish any vested pension or retirement benefit which may have accrued under an existing law to a person holding or having held office in the Legislature, but upon adoption of this Act no further entitlement to nor vesting in any existing program shall accrue to any such person, other than Social Security to the extent herein provided.

SEC. 5. Section 7.5 is added to Article IV of the California Constitution to read:

SEC. 7.5.   In the fiscal year immediately following the adoption of this Act, the total aggregate expenditures of the Legislature for the compensation of members and employees of, and the operating expenses and equipment for, the Legislature may not exceed an amount equal to nine hundred fifty thousand dollars ($950,000) per member for that fiscal year or 80 percent of the amount of money expended for those purposes in the preceding fiscal year, whichever is less. For each fiscal year thereafter, the total aggregate expenditures may not exceed an amount equal to that expended for those purposes in the preceding fiscal year, adjusted and compounded by an amount equal to the percentage increase in the appropriations limit for the state established pursuant to Article XIII B.

SEC. 6. Section 2 of Article V of the California Constitution is amended to read:

SEC. 2. The Governor shall be elected every fourth year at the same time and places as members of the Assembly and hold office from the Monday after January 1 following the election until a successor qualifies. The Governor shall be an elector who has been a citizen of the United States and a resident of this State for 5 years immediately preceding the Governor's election. The Governor may not hold other public office. *No Governor may serve more than 2 terms.*

SEC. 7. Section 11 of Article V of the California Constitution is amended to read:

SEC. 11. The Lieutenant Governor, Attorney General, Controller, Secretary of State, and Treasurer shall be elected at the same time and places and for the same term as the Governor. *No Lieutenant Governor, Attorney General, Controller, Secretary of State, or Treasurer may serve in the same office for more than 2 terms.* * * *

Official Title and Summary:

LIMITS ON TERMS OF OFFICE, LEGISLATORS' RETIREMENT, LEGISLATIVE OPERATING COSTS. INITIATIVE CONSTITUTIONAL AMENDMENT

- Persons elected or appointed after November 5, 1990, holding offices of Governor, Lieutenant Governor, Attorney General, Controller, Secretary of State, Treasurer, Superintendent of Public Instruction, Board of Equalization members, and State Senators, limited to two terms; members of the Assembly limited to three terms.

- Requires legislators elected or serving after November 1, 1990, to participate in federal Social Security program; precludes accrual of other pension and retirement benefits resulting from legislative service, except vested rights.

- Limits expenditures of Legislature for compensation and operating costs and equipment, to specified amount.

Summary of Legislative Analyst's Estimate of Net State and Local Government Fiscal Impact:

- The limitation on terms will have no fiscal effect.

- The restrictions on the legislative retirement benefits would reduce state costs by approximately $750,000 a year. * * *

- Legislative expenditures in 1991–92 would be reduced by about 38 percent, or $70 million.

- In subsequent years, the measure would limit growth in these expenditures to the changes in the state's appropriations limit.

Analysis by the Legislative Analyst

Background

There are 132 elected state officials in California. This includes 120 legislators and 12 other state officials, including the Governor, Lieutenant Governor, and Attorney General. Currently, there is no limit on the number of terms that these officials can serve. Proposition 112, passed by the voters in June 1990, requires the annual salaries and benefits (excluding retirement) of these state officials to be set by a commission. Most of these officials participate in the federal Social Security system, and all have the option of participating in the Legislators' Retirement System. The vast majority of the 132 elected state officials participate in this retirement system. The system is supported by contributions from participating officials and the state. * * *

Proposal

This initiative makes three major changes to the California Constitution. First, it limits the number of terms that an elected state official can serve in the *same office* (the new office of Insurance Commissioner is not affected by this measure). Second, it prohibits legislators from earning state retirement benefits from their future service in the Legislature. Third, it limits the total amount of expenditures by the Legislature for salaries and operating expenses.

The specific provisions of this measure are:

Limits on the Terms of Elected State Officials

- The following state elected officials would be limited to no more than two four-year terms in the same office: Governor, Lieutenant Governor, Attorney General, Controller, Secretary of State, Superintendent of Public Instruction, Treasurer, members of the Board of Equalization, and State Senators.

- Members of the State Assembly would be limited to no more than three two-year terms in the same office.

- These limits apply to a state official who is elected on or after November 6, 1990. However, State Senators whose offices are *not* on the November 6, 1990 ballot may serve only one additional term.

Restrictions on Legislative Retirement Benefits

- This measure prohibits current and future legislators from earning state retirement benefits from their service in the Legislature on or after November 7, 1990. This restriction would not eliminate retirement benefits earned prior to that time.

- This measure requires a legislator serving in the Legislature on or after November 7, 1990 to participate in the federal Social Security system. * * *

- This measure does not change the Social Security coverage or the state retirement benefits of other state elected officials such as the Governor, Lieutenant Governor, and Attorney General.

Limits on Expenditures by the Legislature

- This measure limits the amount of expenditures by the Legislature for salaries and operating expenses, beginning in the 1991–92 fiscal year.

- In 1991–92, these expenditures are limited to the *lower* of two amounts: (1) a total of $950,000 per Member or (2) 80 percent of the total amount of money expended in the previous year for these purposes. In future years, the measure limits expenditure growth to an amount equal to the percentage change in the state's appropriations limit.

Fiscal Effect

Limits on the Terms of Elected State Officials. This provision would not have any fiscal effect.

Restrictions on Legislative Retirement Benefits. The provision which prohibits current and future Members of the Legislature from earning state retirement benefits from legislative service on or after November 7, 1990 would reduce state costs by about $750,000 a year. * * *

Limits on Expenditures by the Legislature. In 1991–92, expenditures by the Legislature would be reduced by about 38 percent, or $70 million. In subsequent years, this measure would limit growth in these expenditures to the changes in the state's appropriations limit.

Argument in Favor of Proposition 140

Proposition 140 will for the first time ever place a limit on the number of times a State official may serve in office.

A Yes Vote on Proposition 140 will reform a political system that has created a legislature of career politicians in California. It is a system that has given a tiny elite (only 120 people out of 30 million) almost limitless power over the lives of California's taxpayers and consumers.

Proposition 140 will limit State Senators to two terms (8 years); will limit Assembly members to three terms (6 years); and limit the Governor and other elected constitutional officers to two terms (8 years).

By reducing the amount they can spend on their personal office expenses, Proposition 140, will cut back on the 3,000 political staffers who serve the legislature in Sacramento. In the first year alone, according to the legislative analyst, it will save taxpayers $60 million.

Proposition 140, will end extravagant pensions for legislators. While most Californians have to depend on Social Security and their own savings, the legislative pension system often pays more than the legislator received while in office. In fact, 50 former officials receive $2,000.00 per month or more from the Legislative retirement fund.

Limiting terms will create more competitive elections, so good legislators will always have the opportunity to move up the ladder. Term limitation will end the ingrown, political nature of both houses—to the benefit of every man, woman and child in California.

Proposition 140 will remove the grip that vested interests have over the legislature and remove the huge political slush funds at the disposal of Senate and Assembly leaders.

Proposition 140 will put an end to the life-time legislators, who have developed cozy relationships with special interests. We all remember the saying, "Power corrupts and absolute power corrupts absolutely." But limit the terms of Legislative members, remove the Speaker's cronies, and we will also put an end to the Sacramento web of special favors and patronage.

Proposition 140 will end the reign of the Legislature's powerful officers—the Assembly Speaker (first elected a quarter of a century ago) and the Senate Leader (now into his third decade in the Legislature). Lobbyists and power brokers pay homage to these legislative dictators, for they control the fate of bills, parcel out money to the camp followers and hangers-on, and pull strings behind the scenes to decide election outcomes.

Incumbent legislators seldom lose. In the 1988 election, 100% of incumbent state senators and 96% of incumbent members of the assembly were re-elected. The British House of Lords—even the Soviet Legislature—has a higher turnover rate. Enough is Enough! It's time to put an end to a system that makes incumbents a special class of citizen and pays them a guaranteed annual wage from first election to the grave. Let's restore that form of government of citizens representing their fellow citizens.

VOTE YES ON PROPOSITION 140 TO *LIMIT STATE OFFICIALS TERM OF OFFICE!*

PETER E. SCHABARUM *Chairman, Los Angeles County Board of Supervisors*

LEWIS K. UHLER *President, National Tax-Limitation Committee*

J.G. FORD, JR. *President, Marin United Taxpayers Association*

Rebuttal to Argument in Favor of Proposition 140

Proposition 140 is a proposal by a downtown Los Angeles politician to take away your right to choose your legislators. He has a history of taking away voting rights. He and two political cronies voted to spend $500,000.00 in tax dollars to hire a personal lawyer to defend him against Voting Rights Act violations in Federal Court. Newspapers call it an "outrageous back room deal."

His "Big Bucks" friends, including high-priced lobbyists, have lined his pockets with campaign contributions to help control who *you* can vote for.

- IF 140 PASSES, LOBBYISTS COULD SUBSTITUTE THEIR OWN PAID EMPLOYEES FOR THE INDEPENDENT STAFF RESEARCHERS OF THE LEGISLATURE ELIMINATED BY THIS MEASURE.

- 140 MISLEADS YOU ABOUT THE SO-CALLED "HIGH" COST OF THE LEGISLATURE—THE COST IS LESS THAN ½ PENNY PER TAX DOLLAR.

- THE BIGGEST LIE IS THE FACT THAT THEY DON'T TELL YOU THAT 140 IS A *LIFETIME BAN.*

This is a blatant power grab by Los Angeles contributors and lobbyists who have been wining and dining "Mr. Downtown Los Angeles" in government for SEVEN TERMS—OVER TWENTY YEARS.

Practice what you preach, "Mr. Downtown Los Angeles," Peter Schabarum. Cut *your own* budget and limit *your own* terms. Don't be a piggy and take away the people's rights after you have fully eaten at the table.

There is no need for 140. The vast majority of the Legislature *already* serves less than 10 years.

That's *your* choice. * * *

> ED FOGLIA *President, California Teachers Association*
>
> DAN TERRY *President, California Professional Firefighters*
>
> LINDA M. TANGREN *State Chair, California National Women's Political Caucus*

Argument Against Proposition 140

Proposition 140 claims to mandate term limits. But in fact, it limits our voting rights.

This measure takes away the cherished constitutional right to freely cast a ballot for candidates of our choice.

We are asked to forfeit *our* right to decide *who our* individual representatives will be.

PROPOSITION 140's LIFETIME BAN

140 does *not* limit *consecutive* terms of office. Instead 140 says:

- After serving six years in the Assembly, individuals will be constitutionally *banned for life* from ever serving in the Assembly.

- After serving eight years in the Senate, individuals will be constitutionally *banned for life* from ever serving in the Senate.

- Similar lifetime bans will be imposed on the Superintendent of Public Instruction and other statewide offices.

  There are no exceptions—not for merit, not for statewide emergencies, not for the overwhelming will of the people.

  Once banned, always banned.

PROPOSITION 140 IS UNFAIR

It treats everyone—good and bad, competent and incompetent—the same.

No matter how good a job someone does in office, they will be *banned for life*.

You won't even be able to write-in their names on your ballot. If you do, your vote won't count.

That's just not fair.

LIMITS OUR RIGHT TO CHOOSE

The backers of 140 don't trust us, the people, to choose our elected officials. So instead of promoting thoughtful reforms that help us weed out bad legislators, they impose a lifetime ban that eliminates good legislators and bad ones alike at the expense of our constitutional rights.

No eligible citizen should be *permanently banned* for life from seeking any office in a free society. And we should not be *permanently banned* from voting freely for the candidate of our choice.

Resist the rhetoric. Proposition 140 is not about restricting the powers of incumbency. It's about taking away our powers to choose.

PHONY PENSION REFORM

Proposition 140's retirement provisions are also misdirected and counterproductive.

140 does not eliminate the real abuses: double and triple dipping—the practice of taking multiple pensions.

Instead it raises new barriers to public office by banning our future representatives from earning *any* retirement except their current social security.

140's retirement ban won't hurt rich candidates. It will hurt qualified, ordinary citizens who are not rich and have to work hard to provide economic security for themselves and their families.

PROPOSITION 140 GOES TOO FAR

It upsets our system of constitutional checks and balances, forcing our representatives to become even more dependent on entrenched bureaucrats and shrewd lobbyists.

VOTE NO ON PROPOSITION 140

STOP THIS RADICAL AND DANGEROUS SCHEME! PROTECT OUR CONSTITUTIONAL RIGHTS. VOTE NO ON PROPOSITION 140'S LIFETIME BAN.

DR. REGENE L. MITCHELL *President, Consumer Federation of California*

LUCY BLAKE *Executive Director, California League of Conservation Voters*

DAN TERRY *President, California Professional Firefighters*

Rebuttal to Argument Against Proposition 140

Proposition 140 restores *true* democracy, gives you *real* choices of candidates, protects *your* rights to be represented by someone who knows and cares about *your* wishes. It opens up the political system so *everyone*—not just the entrenched career politicians—can participate.

Proposition 140 will bring new ideas, workable policies and fresh cleansing air to Sacramento. All are needed badly. A stench of greed and vote-selling hangs over Sacramento because lifetime-in-office incumbents think it's *their* government, not yours.

Californians polled by the state's largest newspaper say "most politicians are for sale," and "taking bribes is a relatively common practice" among lawmakers. Proposition 140 cuts the ties between corrupting special interest money and long-term legislators.

Why don't more people vote? Because incumbents have rigged the system in their favor so much, elections are meaningless. Even the worst of legislators get reelected 98% of the time. Honest, ethical, *truly* representative people who want to run for office don't stand a chance.

Who really opposes Proposition 140? It isn't ordinary people who have to work for a living. It's incumbent legislators and their camp followers. * * *

VOTE "YES!" ON PROPOSITION 140. ENOUGH, IS ENOUGH!

> W. BRUCE LEE, II *Executive Director, California Business League*
>
> LEE A. PHELPS *Chairman, Alliance of California Taxpayers*
>
> ART PAGDAN, M.D. *National 1st V.P., Filipino-American Political Association*

A final note from your casebook editors: As is customary in California, the November 1990 ballot did not reprint the text of Proposition 140 or any of the pro and con arguments. Instead, the voters were given this question:

> TERMS OF OFFICE. LEGISLATURE. INITIATIVE CONSTITUTIONAL AMENDMENT. Limits: terms of specified state elected officials, legislators' retirement, pensions. [The text continued to describe briefly the predicted financial impact of the proposal, as required by state law].

Yes ___ No ___

The measure passed by a margin of 52.17% to 47.83%. When you have finished your analysis, compare your conclusions with the published judicial opinions. See *Bates v. Jones*, 131 F.3d 843 (9th Cir. 1997) (en banc); *Legislature v. Eu*, 816 P.2d 1309 (Cal. 1991).

3. RECALL

CHANDLER V. OTTO

Supreme Court of Washington, 1984.
103 Wash. 2d 268, 693 P.2d 71.

[*Editors' note:* In considering this case, the reader may find useful the language of the Washington Constitution governing recall:

Recall of Elective Officers. Every elective public officer in the state of Washington except judges of courts of record is subject to recall and discharge by the legal voters of the state, or of the political subdivision of the state, from which he was elected whenever a petition demanding his recall, reciting that such officer has committed some act or acts of malfeasance or misfeasance while in office, or who has violated his oath of office, stating the matters complained of, signed by the percentages of the qualified electors thereof, hereinafter provided, the percentage required to be computed from the total number of votes cast for all candidates for his said office to which he was elected at the preceding election, is filed with the officer with whom a petition for nomination, or certificate for nomination, to such office must be filed under the laws of this state, and the same officer shall call a special election as provided by the general election laws of this state, and the result determined as therein provided. Wash. Const. Art. I, § 33 (amendment 8).

Same. The legislature shall pass the necessary laws to carry out the provisions of section thirty-three (33) of this article, and to facilitate its operation and effect without delay: Provided, That the authority hereby conferred upon the legislature shall not be construed to grant to the legislature any exclusive power of lawmaking nor in any way limit the initiative and referendum powers reserved by the people. * * * Wash. Const. Art. I, § 34 (also adopted as amendment 8).]

PEARSON, JUSTICE.

This case involves a recall petition filed against members of the Moses Lake City Council. The issue presented is whether the charges propounded in the petition allege sufficient grounds for recall. The trial court, pursuant to RCW 29.82.010, as amended by Laws of 1984, ch. 170, conducted a hearing to determine the sufficiency of the charges and adequacy of the ballot synopsis and concluded that the charges were sufficient. We hold that the recall charges were legally insufficient to serve as the basis for a recall election. Accordingly, we reverse the decision of the trial court.

The salient facts are as follows. In early 1984 the City of Moses Lake invited bids from interested persons desiring to contract with the City for the handling of the City's solid waste. The invitations for bids called for a bid opening on April 27, 1984. The bids were opened on that date and there were seven bidders. Superior Refuse Removal submitted the lowest bid. Shortly after the opening it was discovered that Superior's bid failed to fully comply with the invitation in that some of the pages were not signed as required. Similarly, the second lowest bidder, Western Refuse, had also failed to sign all the pages of its bid. The third lowest bidder was Lakeside Disposal. Lakeside had complied with the invitation and signed each proposal page.

At its regular meeting on May 22, 1984, the City Council considered the seven bids. After some discussion about whether the Council could waive the irregularities in the bids submitted by Superior Refuse and Western Refuse, the Council voted 4–3 not to waive the irregularities and awarded the contract to Lakeside Disposal as the lowest responsible bidder. Thereafter on July 12, 1984, a petition for recall was filed against each of the four councilmen who had voted to award the contract to

Lakeside. The petition alleged the foregoing facts and contended that the actions of the councilmen were an abuse of discretion, done in contravention of the public interest, and would result in increased costs to the citizens of Moses Lake.

* * * On August 9, 1984, a hearing was held in the Superior Court for Grant County wherein the judge determined that the allegations contained in the recall petitions were sufficient to warrant proceeding with the recall election. The councilmen immediately appealed this decision.

Recall is the electoral process by which an elected officer is removed before the expiration of the term of office. Provisions for the recall of public officers did not appear in the Washington Constitution until 1912 when a constitutional recall referendum proposed by the State House of Representatives was passed by the voters. This amendment is the only constitutional recall provision that requires a showing of cause before recall will be allowed. In addition, Washington is one of only a few states that requires a recall petition to allege acts of malfeasance, misfeasance or a violation of the oath of office. These requirements indicate that the drafters of Washington's recall provision wanted to prevent recall elections from reflecting on the popularity of the political decisions made by elected officers.

In 1913 the Legislature passed the necessary laws to carry out the provisions of the new constitutional amendment. *See* RCW 29.82. The Legislature did not, however, define misfeasance, malfeasance, or violation of the oath of office. Nor did the Legislature suggest what might constitute cause. Because of this, interpretation of the unique requirements of Washington's recall provision has been the focus of over half the recall cases at the appellate level. These cases, in trying to interpret the right of recall, developed a narrow scope of review based on the court's traditional role of nonintervention in political controversies. *Cudihee v. Phelps*, 136 P. 367 (Wash. 1913); *McCormick v. Okanogan Cy.*, 578 P.2d 1303 (Wash. 1978). This scope of review has in most instances allowed the court to uphold nearly every recall petition. Such a narrow scope of review, however, disregards the apparent intent of the framers of the recall provision to limit the scope of the recall right to recall for cause. Furthermore, it has encouraged two abuses:

(1)   The charges, though adequate on their face as cause for recall, may lack any factual basis whatsoever,

(2)   The charge may be entirely unrelated to the dispute; the real political issue or dispute between the recall petitioners and the elective officer may be submerged beneath the rhetoric of the charge.

Cohen, [*Recall in Washington: A Time for Reform,*] 50 Wash. L. Rev. [29,] 30 [(1974)].

The narrow scope of review dictated by the vagueness of the enabling legislation has until recently prevented the courts from dealing with these abuses. Recent amendments to RCW 29.82, however, indicate that the Legislature has finally followed the suggestions of members of this court and has provided safeguards to protect an elected official from being subjected to the financial and personal burden of a recall election grounded on false or frivolous charges.

In 1976 * * * the specificity requirements were changed by adding the portions italicized below.

> Whenever any legal voter ... shall desire to demand the recall and discharge of any elective public officer ... under the provisions of sections 33 and 34 of Article 1 of the Constitution, he ... shall prepare a typewritten charge, reciting that such officer ... has committed an act or acts of malfeasance, or an act or acts of misfeasance while in office, or has violated his oath of office ... which charge shall state the act or acts complained of in concise language, *giving a detailed description including the approximate date, location, and nature of each act complained of ...*

(Italics ours.) RCW 29.82.010 (as amended by Laws of 1975, 2d Ex. Sess., ch. 47, § 1, p. 199).

RCW 29.82 was amended for a second time in 1984. First, in addition to believing a charge to be true, a petitioner must now *verify under oath that he or she has knowledge of the alleged facts upon which the stated grounds for recall are based.* (Italics ours.) Laws of 1984, ch. 170, § 1, p. 821. Second, the amendments codify the definitions of misfeasance, malfeasance, or violation of the oath of office in accordance with case law definitions:

> (1) "Misfeasance" or "malfeasance" in office means any wrongful conduct that affects, interrupts, or interferes with the performance of official duty;
>
>> (a) Additionally, "misfeasance" in office means the performance of a duty in an improper manner, and
>>
>> (b) Additionally, "malfeasance" in office means the commission of an unlawful act;
>
> (2) "Violation of the oath of office" means the wilful neglect or failure by an elective public officer to perform faithfully a duty imposed by law.

Laws of 1984, ch. 170, § 1, p. 821. Third, a new section requires the recall petitioner to file the petition with a specified officer who will formulate a ballot synopsis. The preparer shall additionally certify and transmit the charges and the ballot synopsis to the superior court and shall petition the superior court to approve the synopsis and to determine the sufficiency of the charges. Hence, under the new statute the superior courts, rather than the prosecuting attorney, attorney general or Chief Justice of the Supreme Court, are entrusted with initially determining whether the charges are sufficient. A fourth section outlines the duties of the superior court.

> Within fifteen days after receiving the petition, the superior court shall have conducted a hearing on and shall have determined, without cost to any party, (1) whether or not the acts stated in the charge satisfy the criteria for which a recall petition may be filed, and (2) the adequacy of the ballot synopsis. The clerk of the superior court shall notify the person subject to recall and the person demanding recall of the hearing date. Both persons may appear with counsel. The court may hear arguments as to the sufficiency of the charges and the adequacy of the ballot synopsis. *The court shall not consider the truth of the charges, but only their sufficiency.* An appeal of a sufficiency decision shall be filed in the supreme court as specified by RCW 29.82.160. The superior court shall correct any ballot

synopsis it deems inadequate. Any decision regarding the ballot synopsis by the superior court is final. * * *

(Italics ours.) Laws of 1984, ch. 170, § 4, p. 823.

Our obligation in interpreting the foregoing amendments is to ascertain and give effect to the intent of the Legislature. The changes to RCW 29.82 are presumed to indicate a change in the legislative purpose behind recall petitions. We believe the changes indicate a legislative intent to place limits on the recall right, *i.e.,* to allow recall for cause yet free public officials from the harassment of recall elections grounded on frivolous charges or mere insinuations. We perceive the legislative amendments to mean that a recall petition must be both legally and factually sufficient.

Factually sufficient means the petition must comply with the specificity requirements of RCW 29.82.010. As noted [in a previous decision], "these statutory requirements ensure that both the public electorate and the challenged elective official will make informed decisions in the recall process." Factually sufficient indicates that although the charges may contain some conclusions, taken as a whole they do state sufficient facts to identify to the electors and to the official being recalled acts or failure to act which without justification would constitute a prima facie showing of misfeasance, malfeasance, or a violation of the oath of office.

Legally sufficient means that an elected official cannot be recalled for appropriately exercising the discretion granted him or her by law. To be legally sufficient, the petition must state with specificity substantial conduct clearly amounting to misfeasance, malfeasance or violation of the oath of office. 4 E. McQuillin, *Municipal Corporations* § 12.251b, at 334 (3d rev. ed. 1979).

In analyzing the recall petition in the instant case, we conclude that it is not legally sufficient. Pursuant to RCW 35.23.352–.353, members of Moses Lake City Council have the authority to let contracts, such as the one in question here, to the "lowest responsible bidder." This authority is well analyzed in 10 E. McQuillin, *Municipal Corporations* § 29.73, at 398 (3d rev. ed. 1981):

> Concerning the inquiry, how the responsibility is to be determined, "the authorities speak with practically one voice," namely, that the officers in whom the power is vested "must determine the fact, and such determination cannot be set aside unless the action of the tribunal is arbitrary, oppressive or fraudulent. The determination of the question of who is the lowest responsible bidder does not rest in the exercise of an arbitrary and unlimited discretion, but upon a bona fide judgment, based upon facts tending to support the determination." This view has in general been supported by the authorities. The determination of the municipal officials concerning the lowest responsible bidder will not be disturbed by the courts, unless it is shown to have been influenced by fraud, or unless it is an arbitrary, unreasonable misuse of discretion. When the officers have exercised their discretion in the award of the contract, the presumption obtains that such action was regular and lawful, and such presumption can be overcome only by proof that the officers acted without justification or fraudulently.

(Footnotes omitted.)

Respondent's recall petition fails to allege any fraud or arbitrary, unreasonable misuse of discretion. There is no evidence that the appellants exercised their discretion inappropriately. The petition merely attacks the judgment of the councilmen. The exercise of judgment is not grounds for recall. Hence, the petition does not state with specificity substantial conduct clearly amounting to misfeasance, malfeasance, or violation of the oath of office.

Accordingly, we reverse the decision of the trial court and direct a dismissal of the recall charges.

[A concurring opinion is omitted.]

DORE, JUSTICE (dissenting).

The majority affirms the action of the Moses Lake City Council in refusing to award a 5-year garbage contract to the lowest bidder but instead awarded it to the third lowest bidder, at an additional cost to the Moses Lake taxpayers of $3,000 a month, or $180,000 over the life of the contract. It is undisputed that both are competent contractors. The majority affirms the holding that the Council properly exercised its discretion. I disagree and would hold that the Moses Lake Council's actions were a manifest abuse of discretion, and I believe the citizens of Moses Lake, who have to pay the bill, would agree with me.

From the time this court first decided a case dealing with the recall right promulgated in Const. art. 1, §§ 33 and 34, to as recently as last year, we have always interpreted the recall provision broadly so as to allow the people to exercise their right of self-governance.

Only last year, we reaffirmed the principle that

> our constitution establishes a very broad right of the electorate to recall elective public officials. The rights of initiative, referendum, and recall form a weighty triumvirate intended to preserve the people's most basic right of self-governance and any interference with these rights requires strong justification.

Pederson v. Moser, [662 P.2d 866 (Wash. 1983)]. This broad right of recall has manifested itself by providing the foundation for many of the rules which protect this basic right:

> First, in determining the validity of recall charges, courts are limited to examination of the charges stated and cannot inquire into factual matters extraneous to the allegations. Second, courts must assume the truth of the charges in determining whether legally sufficient grounds for recall have been stated. Third, just as there can be no inquiry into the truth or falsity of the charges, there can be no inquiry into the motives of those filing the charges. Fourth, recall charges are sufficiently specific if they are definite enough to allow the charged official to meet them before the tribunal of the people. Finally, any one sufficient charge requires the holding of a recall election.

State ex rel. Citizens Against Mandatory Bussing v. Brooks, [492 P.2d 536 (Wash. 1972)]. The majority now restricts this fundamental right. The majority provides two arguments to justify narrowing the recall right. First, it cites our constitutional requirement that a recall petition allege an act of malfeasance, or a violation of the oath of office. Not once, however, in the past 72 years has this court ever interpreted these requirements to mean that the right of recall should be narrowly construed. Indeed, in the past 72 years this court has always held that the constitution establishes a very broad right of recall. The majority fails to explain what prompted it to decide that over 70 years of case law interpreting the recall provision was wrong. Instead, it meekly states that our constitution requires that cause be shown for a recall election[3] and concludes, without providing any reasoning, that our right of recall has been construed too broadly in the past.

The second justification the majority narrates for its surprising interpretation of the recall provision is that the Legislature, in 1976 and 1984, amended the enabling legislation to the recall provision. The majority asserts that the amendments show that the Legislature intended to narrow the right of recall.[4] As to the 1976 amendment, the majority points to two changes that it asserts show that the Legislature intended to narrow the right of recall. First, it points out that the statute was amended to require that the official who is the subject of the recall receive a copy of the ballot synopsis. RCW 29.82.015. This provision, however, can hardly be characterized as narrowing the recall right. Secondly, the statute was amended to require the petitioner to give a detailed description of the cha[r]ges, including the approximate date, location and nature of each act complained of. RCW 29.82.010. This provision is a procedural clarification and does not restrict the electorate's right of recall. Instead, it merely ensures that both the public and the challenged official will make an informed decision in the recall process.

* * *

The majority asserts that there was no abuse of discretion when the Moses Lake City Council refused to accept the lowest bid and, instead, accepted the third lowest bid. * * * It does not cite any cases to support its position; instead, it cites a treatise on municipal corporations which discusses *judicial review* of bid acceptances. The standard a court uses for reviewing an official's conduct is different from the standard

---

[3]   The majority erroneously asserts that our constitution is the only one in the nation that requires a showing of cause before recall will be allowed. That is simply untrue. West Virginia's constitution provides that

All officers elected or appointed under this Constitution, may, unless in cases herein otherwise provided for, be removed from office for *official misconduct, incompetence, neglect of duty, or gross immorality, in such manner as may be prescribed by general laws, . . .*

(Italics mine.) W.Va. Const. art. 4, § 6. Moreover, while some state constitutions do not explicitly state that cause must be shown, their courts have construed their constitutional recall provisions to require that cause must be shown. *See, e.g., Amberg v. Welsh*, [38 N.W.2d 304 (Mich. 1949)]. Consequently, contrary to what the majority concludes, the drafters of our recall provision did not intend the recall right to be narrowly construed.

[4]   The Legislature's authority to enact enabling legislation is limited and cannot be used to change the scope of recall right.

The legislature shall pass the necessary laws to carry out the provisions of section thirty-three (33) of this article, and to facilitate its operation and effect without delay: *Provided, That the authority hereby conferred upon the legislature shall not be construed to grant to the legislature any exclusive power of lawmaking nor in any way limit the initiative and referendum powers reserved by the people.*

(Italics mine.) Const. art. 1, § 34.

the electorate uses for review. The majority may not feel that accepting a higher bid is an abuse of discretion but the voters of Moses Lake might find that the Council's award of a contract, for an additional windfall of $180,000 to the third bidder, was an abuse of discretion, especially when an equally competent contractor (low bidder) admittedly was available for $180,000 less.

* * *

I believe that the average person in Moses Lake, if allowed to vote, would find that the Council members who voted for the garbage "windfall" abused their discretion. The majority, by depriving such person of his constitutional right to recall public officials, unfortunately prohibits this.

I would affirm the trial court.

NOTES ON CHANDLER V. OTTO

1.   *The Value of Recall.* Consider R. Perry Sentell, Jr., *Remembering Recall in Local Government Law*, 10 Ga. L. Rev. 883, 886 (1976):

> [The value of recall] to the science of local government has been long debated. On the one side, the arguments are that it provides unremitting popular control over persons in public office; it permits the lengthening of terms of elective local officials with the least possible risk; it encourages principles of both responsibility and responsiveness; and it maintains public interest and confidence in the process of government. Alternative contentions are that recall engenders political demoralization; that it can be invoked to displace conscientious officials and thus discourages their participation in government; and that its operation entails prohibitive public expense. That both perspectives are persuasive is manifested by the split of jurisdictions authorizing recall, as well as the varying extent of utilization even where it is authorized.

Although state-level recalls tend to make the most news—including one that elected movie star Arnold Schwarzenegger as Governor of California in 2003—they are much more frequently used at the local level. Recall was first adopted at the municipal level when Los Angeles enacted it in 1903; five years later, the first recall process for state legislators was adopted in Oregon.[36] Nineteen states provide for recall at the state level, and 60% of cities have charters with recall provisions, which is more than provide for local initiative or popular referendum.[37] It is estimated that there have been 4,000 to 5,000 recalls at the local level, with three-fourths of these directed at members of city councils or school boards.[38]

Thus, *Chandler v. Otto* presents a typical recall situation aimed at local officeholders. Are there any characteristics of local politics that make recalls of officials here more necessary than at the state level? If local officials tend to face less competition, or have longer terms of office, could that explain the prevalence of the use of recall by

---

[36]   Floyd Feeney, *The 2003 California Gubernatorial Recall*, 41 Creighton L. Rev. 37, 39–40 (2007).

[37]   See Nat'l Conf. of State Legis., *Recall of State Officials* (Mar. 8, 2016), http://www.ncsl.org/legislatures-elections/elections/recall-of-state-officials.aspx (for state figures); Richard Feiock & Seung-Bum Yang, *Factors Affecting Constitutional Choice: The Case of the Recall in Municipal Charters*, 37 State & Local Gov't Rev. 40, 41 (2005).

[38]   Rachel Weinstein, *You're Fired!: The Voters' Version of "The Apprentice": An Analysis of Local Recall Elections in California*, 15 S. Cal. Interdis. L.J. 131, 138 (2005).

frustrated constituents? Or are local politics more likely to give rise to hot-button issues— like zoning, selection of textbooks, or corruption in contracting—that a dedicated group of opponents can use to trigger a recall? What are the dynamics of a local recall election, in terms of turnout and campaigning, particularly given that they are held at times other than general elections or even broader primary elections?

2.   *Grounds for a Recall.* As the dissent in *Chandler v. Otto* correctly pointed out in a footnote, Washington is not the only state with a recall process that requires certain grounds for recall, although in most states a voter can begin the process for any reason. Michigan's constitution expressly states that "[t]he sufficiency of any statement of reasons or grounds * * * shall be a political rather than a judicial question." Mich. Const., Art. II, § 8. One explanation for the political nature of recall in most states is that there are other methods available to evict state officials from office—for example, removal by impeachment, whereby certain high state officials may be impeached by a majority of the state house of representatives for misconduct, tried by the state senate, and convicted (that is, removed from office and disqualified from holding "any office of honor, trust or profit in the state") by a vote of a supermajority of the senators. In addition, statutory procedures set out provisions for removal for misconduct of officers not subject to impeachment. The Supreme Court of Colorado has explained that these methods of defrocking contemplate removal from office for cause, but that

> [r]ecall, on the other hand, may be used for a purely political reason. The purpose underlying recall of public officials for political reasons is to provide an effective and speedy remedy to remove an official who is unsatisfactory to the public and whom the electors do not want to remain in office, regardless of whether the person is discharging his or her duties consistent with his or her abilities and conscience.

Groditsky v. Pinckney, 661 P.2d 279, 283 (Colo. 1983). The court stated that "the power of recall is a fundamental constitutional right of Colorado citizens and the reservation of this power in the people must be liberally construed," and that "[i]t is not within the purview of courts to pass upon the sufficiency of the grounds in recall petitions." Is the Colorado approach superior to the Washington approach to recall demonstrated in *Chandler*? Would it matter to your answer what percentage of voters is required to initiate a recall election?

Thomas Cronin suggests that the recall petition should contain the names of the persons or groups sponsoring the petition and state why the official should be recalled. *Direct Democracy: The Politics of Initiative, Referendum, and Recall* 245–46 (1999). Moreover, there should be a "high signature requirement" (either the higher of 25% of those voting in the last election for the particular office or 20% of registered voters in general), to deter personal vendettas ending up imposing costly elections upon the public. Furthermore, elected officials should not be subject to recall during their first six months of office; this stops "sour-grapes" attacks on them through the recall process. Finally, if a recall election results in the retention of an official, that official should be immune from another recall effort for six months. Cronin also suggests that some neutral, public body conduct a hearing concerning the merits of the proposed recall.

3.   *Recall and Campaign Finance: Lessons from the California and Wisconsin Gubernatorial Recalls.* Recalls are explicitly hybrid in nature, combining a ballot question about the recall of an official with, sometimes simultaneously, the election of a successor. This frame provides a way to consider the regulation of campaign spending in

candidate and ballot-measure campaigns, and we will explore that briefly in the context of the two recent recall efforts directed at governors.[39] As background, review the material in Chapter 2, § 3, describing the current jurisprudential landscape shaping campaign finance laws.

Historically low approval ratings (21%) and an historically high budget deficit (more than $38 billion) led to the recall of California's Democratic Governor Gray Davis in 2003. The recall was initially backed mostly by anti-tax crusaders who used talk radio and the Internet to make their case. Once the movement began to gain momentum, a Republican member of the U.S. House of Representatives, Darrell Issa, decided to actively support the effort, contributing more than $1 million for the petition drive. Primarily using paid petition circulators, pro-recall forces submitted petitions with 1.36 million signatures, substantially more than the nearly 900,000 signatures required to trigger a recall election.

The recall election in California was historic not only because it was the first gubernatorial recall in California to qualify for a vote, but also because it was only the second time in U.S. history that a governor was successfully recalled.[40] The California recall election received a great deal of media attention throughout the country and the world because it was so unusual, and also because the main contender to succeed Davis was movie star Arnold Schwarzenegger. Under California state law, the names of Davis' potential successors appeared on the same ballot as the recall measure, but Davis could not be listed as a candidate; thus, voters decided whether to recall Davis at the same time that they chose his replacement if the recall passed. Not all states with the recall process structure the election in this way. Some states allow the target of the recall also to appear on the ballot as a candidate in the election for a successor. Some first hold the recall vote, and only if the recall succeeds is a subsequent election held to choose a new governor. In a few states, a successful recall results in a successor being appointed, usually from the same political party as the officeholder who was recalled.

The California recall election was also noteworthy because 135 candidates appeared on the recall ballot in the election to succeed the Governor. Candidates seeking ballot access needed to obtain only 65 signatures and pay $3,500 or obtain 10,000 signatures. That opened the door for the multitude of candidates, the majority of whom ran for reasons other than winning. A few were concerned with publicizing particular political issues or concerns. Some, like former child actor Gary Coleman, porn star Mary Carey, and melon-smashing comedian Gallagher, ran to enhance their visibility in other careers. More importantly for the result of the recall, the wide-open process for getting on the ballot allowed a candidate like Schwarzenegger, who is more liberal than many in his party on some issues, to bypass the usual route to a general election—the Republican Party primary—and proceed directly to a general election.

The two-part ballot and the 135 candidates not only had the potential for a great deal of voter confusion, but they also raised the possibility of a number of troubling election outcomes.[41] For example, because the successor to Davis needed only a plurality

---

[39]   Much of this discussion is drawn from Elizabeth Garrett, *Campaign Finance in the Hybrid Realm of Recall Elections*, 97 Minn. L. Rev. 1654 (2013).

[40]   The first instance occurred in 1921, when North Dakota recalled Governor Lynn Frazier. Arizona Governor Evan Mecham probably would have been recalled in the late 1980s had he not been impeached and removed from office by the legislature, which was reacting to the recall effort.

[41]   For a discussion of the voter confusion that occurred in this recall, see Michael Alvarez, Melanie Goodrich, Thad Hall, Roderick Kiewiet & Sarah Sled, *The Complexity of the California Recall Election*, 37 PS:

to win the office, there was a chance that the recall would barely succeed, and the next Governor would be elected by a relatively small plurality. In such a case, there could be more "no" votes on the recall than votes for the Governor-elect, a possibility that could undermine the legitimacy of the new administration. That scenario did not come to pass in California because Schwarzenegger won decisively with 48.6% of the votes, while only 44.6% of voters cast ballots against the recall (and therefore in support of Davis).

Less than a decade later, in 2012, the country witnessed the third gubernatorial recall election. Wisconsin Governor Scott Walker fought successfully to complete his term in the face of a recall sparked by reaction against his support of state legislation that weakened collective-bargaining rights for government workers. Mounting a successful petition drive in Wisconsin is more difficult than in California: the threshold for signatures is higher (a number equal to 25% of voters in the last election versus 12%) and the period for circulation is shorter (60 days versus 150). It is noteworthy that Walker's foes collected more than 900,000 valid signatures—nearly double the 540,208 required— using volunteer circulators working in the cold Wisconsin winter.

Wisconsin's recall structure is significantly different from California's. A sufficient number of valid signatures on a recall petition in Wisconsin triggers a new election for the office. There is no separate vote on the recall itself; instead, there is a recall election for the office six weeks after the certification of the petitions, and the incumbent automatically appears as a candidate in that election unless he has resigned. If there are more than two candidates for the position, then a partisan recall primary is held six weeks after the certification and the recall election occurs four weeks after that primary. Access to the ballot is governed by the rules that apply in regular elections for the position.

In an election between Walker and Milwaukee Mayor Tom Barrett, the same opponent he defeated to win office in 2010, Walker won with more than 53% of the vote. Although some of the reasons for his victory are peculiar to this election, the Wisconsin system generally favors the incumbent more than the California process because of the automatic inclusion of the incumbent on the ballot and the higher hurdles for qualifying a recall for a vote. Perhaps the most favorable structural advantage stems from the campaign finance rules, however, which allow the incumbent in Wisconsin to raise unlimited amounts of money for particular uses during the campaign, while opponents are limited by the $10,000 cap on campaign contributions throughout the process. Walker used that advantage to raise about $30 million in a record-breaking $63-million campaign. In contrast, all the candidates involved in the California recall had the capacity to raise money through unlimited contributions, and all the major candidates took advantage of that loophole in the $80-million recall campaign there.

Both states have bifurcated campaign rules that apply to recalls because of their hybrid nature. Candidates running for the office are limited by the contribution limits that apply to the office ($21,200 in California in 2003, and $10,000 in Wisconsin) with respect to their campaign committees. However, campaign activities focused only on the recall process are regulated by the rules that apply in ballot-measure campaigns and thus are wholly unaffected by contribution caps, even if the committees are associated with

---

Pol. Sci. & Pol. 23 (Jan. 2004). See also Michael Alvarez, Roderick Kiewiet & Betsy Sinclair, *Rational Voters and the Recall Election*, in *Clicker Politics* 87 (Shawn Bowler & Bruce Cain eds., 2006) (finding that "all but a small number of voters appear able to [make sense of the recall's two-question structure], and that they appear to have cast their ballots in a manner that was consistent with their preferences").

active candidates. To understand how these rules played out, consider their application to three different groups: the target of the recall, candidates during the replacement election, and committees active during the election but independent from the targets or candidates.

First, while Gray Davis was essentially a candidate, seeking to defeat the recall so he could stay in office, he was not listed as a candidate and was active only with respect to the ballot-measure portion of this recall process. California law expressly exempts the target of a recall from regulations on campaign contributions, other than disclosure, and Davis took advantage of that loophole to raise nearly $18.3 million though his anti-recall committee "Californians Against the Costly Recall of the Governor." Could California apply contribution limits to the target of a recall even though the incumbent cannot appear on the second part of the ballot? Isn't there the specter of *quid pro quo* corruption, given the close connection between defeating the recall and retaining office?

The different recall structure in Wisconsin meant that the target of the recall was subject to bifurcated rules. Governor Walker could raise money from unlimited contributions only with respect to expenses related to the recall petition and incurred before the recall election was certified. Once an election is certified, the target—who appears on the ballot as a candidate—is thereafter subject to contribution limits. Of course, many of the pre-certification expenditures play a role in retaining office; Walker spent most of his anti-recall money on broadcast ads and other political communications defending his performance, as well as on setting up campaign infrastructure that he used during the entire campaign. Separating the money he could raise from unlimited contributions and money subject to the gubernatorial limits was difficult because he collected it all in one committee, further blurring the lines.

Second, the candidates running to replace the targets of the recall faced different rules in the two states. In California, the two-part ballot—with simultaneously a vote on the recall and a vote on the replacement—meant that replacement candidates could set up separate committees focused only on the recall itself and spend money from those committees in ways that also helped their campaigns to succeed Davis should he be recalled. While the candidate committees were subject to contribution limits, the candidate-controlled recall committees were governed by ballot-measure campaign rules that did not include any caps. So, for example, Arnold Schwarzenegger had two committees: his candidate committee, which was limited to accepting contributions of $21,200, and his "Total Recall" committee, which supported the recall effort and raised $4.5 million through unrestricted contributions. Both committees ran advertisements that featured the candidate and communicated essentially the same message through slightly different words: Schwarzenegger should be the next Governor of the Golden State.

In Wisconsin, none of the candidates seeking to defeat Walker had the ability to raise money in unlimited amounts during the campaign. While it seems that the rules might have allowed them to do so before any recall was certified, none of them—even those seriously considering a run at that early stage—did so, perhaps because it was uncertain until the very end that the recall effort would succeed in triggering an election.

Could current campaign finance jurisprudence support contribution limits on any campaign-related activities of declared candidates in California, including their recall committees? Isn't there the same possibility of *quid pro quo* corruption with respect to contributions to a pro-recall committee and a candidate committee controlled by the same person? Does your answer suggest that more restrictions are constitutionally possible with respect to candidate-controlled committees involved in more traditional initiative campaigns? If a candidate sees an initiative as beneficial to her electoral success—perhaps by affecting turnout or enacting policy agendas she supports—and a supporter provides substantial financial backing for that ballot measure, is there an appearance of *quid pro quo* corruption sufficient to justify more regulation? Does the Wisconsin system—which essentially restricts all candidates other than the incumbent with respect to contributions—create an unequal playing field? Or should the incumbent enjoy favorable rules, at least to fight off a recall, given the disruption a recall causes in governance?

Third, consider independent committees involved in the recall as well as the election for a replacement: can they be subject to contribution caps? Neither Wisconsin nor California limits contributions to such committees, and there were significant independent expenditures in both states. Independent expenditures in California's recall election exceeded $10.5 million, a figure that would no doubt have been higher had there not been other avenues for all major candidates to raise money through uncapped contributions. In Wisconsin, groups spent more than $30 million in independent expenditures or issue advertisements, with unions providing significant funding to Democratic challenger Tom Barrett. This independent spending arguably counterbalanced Governor Walker's spending from unlimited contributions earlier in the process.

Review the discussion of *Citizens United v. Federal Election Comm'n*, 558 U.S. 310 (2010), in Chapter 2, § 3(B), particularly the holding by the majority that independent expenditures in federal candidate elections "do not give rise to corruption." Is there any way under current constitutional precedent to regulate contributions to independent committees active in recalls, other than through disclosure provisions? The appellate courts have concluded that there is not. See *Wisconsin Right to Life State Political Action Committee v. Barland*, 664 F.3d 139 (7th Cir. 2011) (concluding "after *Citizens United* there is *no* valid governmental interest sufficient to justify imposing limits on fundraising by independent expenditure organizations" in the context of groups active in the recalls mounted against nine Wisconsin state senators); *Farris v. Seabrook*, 677 F.3d 858 (9th Cir. 2012) (drawing a parallel between independent-expenditure-only committees in candidate elections, governed by *Citizens United*, and recall committees unaffiliated with candidates to strike down Washington law that limited contributions to the latter).

As you devise a system of regulation for campaign spending in recall elections, assess the following questions. Is your proposal still bifurcated in ways that give certain candidates or groups substantial advantages? Are there arguments that can be mounted in the context of direct democracy—a governance system devised to attack the disproportionate political influence of monied interests in our representative institutions—that might support more robust regulation in this realm? If not, what are the alternatives for those concerned about the role of money in these elections? And what does your analysis suggest for the local ordinances that apply to recalls in this realm and that often severely restrict contributions not only to the targets of the recall and candidates, but also to independent committees active in petition drives and the campaigns for replacements? Are those ordinances still constitutional after *Citizens United*? See *Citizens for a Clean Gov't v. City of San Diego*, 474 F.3d 647 (9th Cir. 2007) (considering the constitutionality of such sweeping restrictions—still in place but with higher thresholds—in San Diego before *Citizens United*).

4. *Recalls vs. Referendums.* Recalls might be seen as a way to hold elected officials accountable for decisions in office. Cronin describes this as "continuous accountability" because voters do not have to wait until the next election to express their displeasure. *Direct Democracy, supra,* at 133. He also provides another argument in support of the recall: "Recall offers a safety-valve mechanism for intense feelings." *Id.* at 134. The popular referendum is another tool of direct democracy that offers both those features but allows voters to target their disapproval to a particular action by public officials and avoid the disruption of an early election with a potential change of leadership. The issue that sparked the recall against Scott Walker—limiting collective-bargaining rights of public workers—gave rise to a popular referendum in nearby Ohio in November 2011. Like the effort in Wisconsin, proponents of stronger union rights obtained many more signatures than were required to put the referendum on the ballot, and the election was characterized by heavy campaign spending with more than $30 million raised by union supporters.[42] Unlike the case with the Wisconsin recall, however, those opposing reduced collective-bargaining rights won in the Ohio referendum battle: the law was overturned by the people with 62% voting for repeal. Consider these two mechanisms that allow the voters a voice after elected officials make controversial decisions. Which is more effective at expressing displeasure, and in what cases, if any, is each one appropriate? How does each affect the politician—in both of these cases first-term Republican governors—seen as responsible for the action if he remains in power after the vote? As you analyze these different methods of allowing voters a "veto" over policy decisions, the following three aspects of the cases may be relevant:

- The President of the Wisconsin AFL-CIO said during the petition drive to place the Walker recall on the ballot: "Unlike Ohio, Wisconsin workers do not have the opportunity to put a referendum on the ballot. Thankfully we have the right to recall."[43] If Wisconsin had allowed both recall and popular referendum, which one would opponents of the Governor have used? And what would have been the factors they considered as they made their choice? Keep in mind that California has a robust state-level referendum and initiative process, and yet opponents of Governor Davis still used the recall mechanism. Were there relevant differences in the motivations behind the two gubernatorial recalls?

- Exit polls in the Wisconsin gubernatorial election revealed significant voter disapproval of the recall process, which was seen as costly and disruptive. Sixty percent said that a recall was appropriate only in cases of official misconduct, and 10% rejected the recall mechanism entirely. A significant number of people who opposed Walker's actions with regard to public unions also opposed the use of the recall.[44] Does that provide an explanation for the difference between the two outcomes?

---

[42] See John Celock, *Ohio SB 5 Collective Bargaining Law Follows Efforts in Wisconsin and New Jersey,* Huffington Post, Sept. 21, 2011, http://www.huffingtonpost.com/2011/09/20/ohio-sb5–referendum-collective-%1Fbargaining_n_972321.html; Alex Altman, *The Lessons of Issue 2's Defeat in Ohio,* Time, Nov. 15, 2011, http://swampland.time.com/2011/11/15/the-lessons-of-issue-2s-defeat-in-ohio.

[43] David Ariosto, *Ohio Voters Repeal Law Limiting Union Rights, CNN Projects,* CNN.com, Nov. 8, 2011, http://www.cnn.com/2011/11/08/us/ohio-collective-bargaining-vote/index.html.

[44] E.J. Dionne, Jr., *Wisconsin's Lessons for the Left and the Right,* Wash. Post (June 6, 2012), http://articles.washingtonpost.com/2012–06–06/opinions/35460549_1_wisconsin-outcome-three-republican-state-senators-wisconsin-voters.

- Finally, could opponents of laws limiting collective-bargaining rights of public employees use the third tool of direct democracy, the initiative, to obtain their objectives proactively rather than responding to unfavorable legislation through recall or popular referendum? Under what conditions might advocates consider using the initiative, and how are the dynamics of an initiative campaign different from the campaigns surrounding the other mechanisms? For an example of this approach, consider the campaign in fall 2012 in Michigan to pass a ballot measure supported by unions to amend the state constitution to guarantee public and private-sector employees the right to organize and collectively bargain. Proposal 2 was defeated with only 42% of voters supporting the initiative in a state with some of the strongest unions in the country. Moreover, heartened by the result of the initiative, Republican lawmakers led a successful effort to enact "right to work" legislation, long opposed by organized labor, signed into law by Republican Governor Rick Snyder in December 2012.[45] Thus, the Michigan situation, like the statewide recalls in California and Wisconsin and referendum in Ohio, provides yet another example of hybrid democracy.

---

[45] Amanda Terkel, *Rick Snyder: Right to Work Bills Signed Into Law in Michigan*, Huff. Post (Dec. 12, 2012), http://www.huffingtonpost.com/2012/12/11/rick-snyder-right-to-work_n_2280050.html.

CHAPTER 5

THEORIES OF STATUTORY INTERPRETATION

∎ ∎ ∎

Statutes dominate American public law. Therefore, it is a matter of great consequence to know how they are interpreted or should be interpreted. "Hard cases" are inevitable, partly because of the inherent imprecision of language and partly because of the inability of statute drafters to anticipate all problems or circumstances within a statute's ambit. A statute "is not an equation or a formula representing a clearly marked process, nor is it an expression of individual thought to which is imparted the definiteness a single authorship can give. A statute is an instrument of government partaking of its practical purposes but also of its infirmities and limitations, of its awkward and groping efforts." Felix Frankfurter, in *Some Reflections on the Reading of Statutes*, 47 Colum. L. Rev. 527, 528 (1947).

Thus, while Frankfurter, as a professor at Harvard Law School, had developed "his threefold imperative to law students: (1) Read the statute; (2) read the statute; (3) read the statute," Henry Friendly, *Mr. Justice Frankfurter and the Reading of Statutes*, in Friendly, *Benchmarks* 202 (1967), Frankfurter the judge appreciated the difficulty of understanding a statute simply by parsing its language. The following example illustrates this point: A municipal ordinance provides that "all drug shops * * * shall be closed * * * at 10 p.m. on each and every day of the week." Does this require all such shops to remain open until 10 p.m., at which time they must be closed (i.e., is "closed" used as a verb or an adjective)? If a shop is closed at 10 p.m., may it lawfully open ten minutes later? In *Rex v. Liggetts-Findlay Drug-Stores Ltd.*, [1919] 3 W.W.R. 1025, the Supreme Court of Alberta answered the latter of these questions in the negative. The judge delivering the judgment stated:

> I think no one but a lawyer—I mean a person trained in legal technicalities such as a Judge or a lawyer—would ever think of imputing such a meaning to the [ordinance]. Everyone knows what is meant by closing a shop at 10 o'clock p.m. The meaning conveyed by the words used is too obvious for doubt. The rule, of course, is that the grammatical sense must in general be adhered to but with this limitation that if it leads to an absurdity or to something meaningless an effort must be made to give some sensible reading unless the language is absolutely intractable. * * * I think we should take the words to mean what they would quite clearly mean to the ordinary person and that is that shops should be closed not only at the moment of 10 o'clock but for the rest of that day.

Plain Meaning dont over technicalize the 10pm drug store.

Under this decision, could a store lawfully open at one minute after midnight?

For most of this country's history, both the theory and the practice of statutory interpretation have been "eclectic" rather than systematic. After 1900, judges and scholars began to formulate their thoughts more systematically into "theories" (Section 1 of this chapter). An initial impulse was to emphasize legislative intent as the foundational enterprise in statutory cases. In turn, beginning in the 1930s an influential group of skeptics, the legal realists, debunked legislative intent as an indeterminate and incoherent concept for statutory interpretation. During the New Deal, American public law turned toward *purpose*-based approaches as the foundation for statutory meaning (Section 2). Purposivism was in turn criticized for slighting traditional rule-of-law values (e.g., predictability of law, limiting judicial discretion) and for engaging courts in policy analysis for which they are ill-equipped. These critiques revived interest in *ordinary meaning* as the lodestar for statutory interpretation (Section 3). The "new textualism" is a particularly stringent version of the plain meaning rule, although this approach has in turn been criticized as impractical and unrealistic.

Our goal in this theoretical and historical survey is to offer you different theories from which you can learn, even as you criticize each of them. We think you will find the history and the theory useful, both in developing your own analytical skills for interpreting statutes and in appreciating the doctrinal material presented in the remaining chapters.

1. FROM ECLECTICISM TO SYSTEMATIC THEORY, 1789–1938

The early history of statutory interpretation in the United States is a complicated one, with American courts employing a grab-bag variety of approaches. Following English rhetoric and practice,[1] American courts in the eighteenth and early nineteenth centuries generally proclaimed their fidelity to legislative "intent" but would consider as evidence of such intent the statute's text, canons of statutory construction, the common law, the circumstances of enactment, principles of equity, and so forth.[2] Indeed, the big debate at the time of the drafting of the Constitution was how much discretion a court's *equity* powers gave it to ameliorate or extend the letter of the statute.[3]

By most accounts, Chief Justice John Marshall was the first great American statutory interpreter, vigorously exercising equitable powers of construction in pursuit of his nationalist understanding of the Constitution, but under the cover of rigorous and sometimes brilliant analysis of statutory text and structure, the common law, and the law of nations.[4] Consider Marshall's remarkable opinion in *Ex parte Bollman*, 8 U.S. (4 Cranch) 75 (1807). Section 14 of the Judiciary Act of 1789

---

[1] See Samuel Thorne, *A Discourse upon the Exposicion & Understanding of Statutes* (1942) (reprinting a leading early modern English treatise developing intent as the lodestar of statutory interpretation). See also Peter Tiersma, *A Message in a Bottle: Text, Autonomy, and Statutory Interpretation*, 76 Tul. L. Rev. 431 (2001) (medieval English law treated statutes as mere "evidence of law").

[2] See Hans Baade, *"Original Intent" in Historical Perspective: Some Critical Glosses*, 69 Tex. L. Rev. 1001, 1062–1107 (1991); William Eskridge Jr., *Textualism, The Unknown Ideal?*, 96 Mich. L. Rev. 1509, 1523–32 (1998) (book review).

[3] Compare William Eskridge Jr., *All About Words: Early Understandings of the "Judicial Power" in Statutory Interpretation, 1776–1806*, 101 Colum. L. Rev. 990 (2001) (exploring early American deployment of equitable interpretation and its importance for the original public meaning of Article III), with John Manning, *Textualism and the Equity of the Statute*, 101 Colum. L. Rev. 1 (2001) (arguing that the Framers rejected equity-based interpretation through Article I, § 7).

[4] See G. Edward White, *The Marshall Court and Cultural Change, 1815–1835*, in 3 *Oliver Wendell Holmes Devise, History of the Supreme Court of the United States* (1988).

provided, in its first sentence, that the Supreme Court and other federal courts "shall have power to issue writs of *scire facias, habeas corpus*, and all other writs not specially provided for by statute, which may be necessary for the exercise of their respective jurisdictions * * *." The second sentence provided that Supreme Court Justices and district judges, in their chambers, "shall have power to grant writs of *habeas corpus* for the purpose of an inquiry into the cause of commitment." The government maintained that the Supreme Court itself had no jurisdiction to inquire into the legality of Bollman's confinement, as that power was only given to individual judges.

Marshall suggested there was a grammatical objection to this excellent plain meaning argument but declined to rest the decision on linguistic niceties.[5] Instead, "the sound construction, which the court thinks it safer to adopt," was the one consistent with a central goal of the Constitution—to assure "that the privilege of the writ of *habeas corpus* should not be suspended, unless, when in cases of rebellion or invasion, the public safety might require it." *Id.* at 95. "Acting under the immediate influence of this injunction, [Congress in 1789] must have felt, with peculiar force, the obligation of providing efficient means by which this great constitutional privilege should receive life and activity." *Id.* Given the centrality of this writ to the liberty assured by the Constitution as well as the common law, the Chief Justice reasoned "that congress could never intend to give a power of this kind to one of the judges of this court, which is refused to all of them when assembled. * * * This is not consistent with the genius of our legislation, nor with the course of our judicial proceedings." *Id.* at 96. To make sense of this confusing statute, Marshall concluded that "the first sentence vests this power in all courts of the United States; but as those courts are not always in session, the second sentence vests it in every justice or judge of the United States." *Id.* Marshall cemented his argument with precedent: the Court had implicitly resolved the issue of its habeas jurisdiction by granting the writ in *United States v. Hamilton*, 3 U.S. (3 Dall.) 17 (1795).

Note the eclectic mode of argumentation in *Bollman*: Chief Justice Marshall's opinion considered the statutory text, its purpose in light of the constitutional background, and prior precedent. What was most notable about Marshall was not so much his methodology as his vision: he read federal statutes in light of the role they played in the broader fabric of international, constitutional, and common law. At the state level, the first half of the nineteenth century saw judging in the "grand style" by the likes of Nathaniel Chipman of Vermont, William de Saussure of South Carolina, Lemuel Shaw of Massachusetts, and (most important of all) James Kent of New York. Like Marshall, they understood judging as "statecraft," as Farah Peterson puts it.[6]

---

[5]   Marshall noted the rule of the last antecedent: because the limiting language of the first sentence followed "and all other writs etc.," it only modified that item in the list, and not the habeas corpus item. 8 U.S. at 95. As the Chief surely recognized, this was a weak argument, in part because a comma set off the qualifying phrase from the items in the list, see Lawrence Solan, *The Language of Judges* 29–38 (1993) (showing that the last antecedent rule—weak to begin with—does not apply when the modifying phrase is set off from the list by a comma), and in part because the point of the first sentence seems to be the qualification, with no apparent reason for limiting it only to the third catch-all item in the list.

[6]   Farah Peterson, *Interpretation as Statecraft: Chancellor Kent and the Collaborative Era of American Statutory Intepretation*, 77 Md. L. Rev. 712 (2018).

Treatise-writers sought to systematize Anglo-American practice by developing elaborate lists of "canons" of statutory interpretation—most of them borrowed or derived from English treatises.[7] Chancellor Kent was most influential as a treatise writer, but his judicial opinions illustrate twin canons that have resonance even today. "Statutes made for the public good, and for general and beneficent national purposes, are to receive a very liberal construction," while, conversely, statutes for private benefit ought to be read narrowly. Compare *Belknap v. Belknap*, 2 Johns. Ch. 463 (N.Y. Chan. 1817) (Kent read a private water-rights law narrowly), with *Rogers v. Bradshaw*, 20 Johns. 735 (N.Y. 1823) (reading Erie Canal legislation very broadly, consistent with the goal of advancing this great public project).

By the end of the nineteenth century, statutory interpretation was pretty settled in practice, but was theoretically underdeveloped. Consider the sampler of general theoretical approaches, which we have excerpted from the Hart and Sacks "Legal Process" materials, and then consider a leading case that unsettled that practice— *Holy Trinity Church.*

HENRY HART JR. AND ALBERT SACKS, THE LEGAL PROCESS: BASIC PROBLEMS IN THE MAKING AND APPLICATION OF LAW

Pp. 1111–15 (William Eskridge Jr. & Philip Frickey eds., 1994).

A.   *The Mischief Rule*

HEYDON'S CASE
Exchequer, 1584
30 Co. 7a, 76 Eng. Rep. 637.

* * * And it was resolved by them, that for the sure and true interpretation of all statutes in general (be they penal or beneficial, restrictive or enlarging of the common law,) four things are to be discerned and considered:—

1st. What was the common law before the making of the Act.

2nd. What was the mischief and defect for which the common law did not provide.

3rd. What remedy the Parliament hath resolved and appointed to cure the disease of the commonwealth.

And, 4th. The true reason of the remedy; and then the office of all the Judges is always to make such construction as shall suppress the mischief, and advance the remedy, and to suppress subtle inventions and evasions for continuance of the mischief, and *pro privato commodo*, and to add force and life to the cure and remedy, according to the true intent of the makers of the Act, *pro bono publico*.

---

[7]   See, e.g., James Kent, *Commentaries on American Law* (1st ed. 1826) (four volumes); Theodore Sedgwick, *A Treatise on the Rules Which Govern the Interpretation and Application of Statutory and Constitutional Law* (1857); J.G. Sutherland, *Statutes and Statutory Construction* (1st ed. 1891).

B.   *The "Golden" Rule*

Lord Blackburn, in *River Wear Comm'rs v. Adamson*, 2 App. Cas. 743, 764 (House of Lords, 1877):

> * * * But it is to be borne in mind that the office of the Judges is not to legislate, but to declare the expressed intention of the Legislature, even if that intention appears to the Court injudicious; and I believe that it is not disputed that what *Lord Wensleydale* used to call the golden rule is right, viz., that we are to take the whole statute together, and construe it all together, giving the words their ordinary signification, unless when so applied they produce an inconsistency, or an absurdity or inconvenience so great as to convince the Court that the intention could not have been to use them in their ordinary signification, and to justify the Court in putting on them some other signification, which, though less proper, is one which the Court thinks the words will bear.

[handwritten margin note: Judge to declare expressed intention of the leg.]

[handwritten margin note: construe statute all together]

C.   *The Literal Rule*

Lord Atkinson, in *Vacher & Sons, Ltd. v. London Soc'y of Compositers*, [1913] App. Cas. 107, 121–22 (House of Lords):

> If the language of a statute be plain, admitting of only one meaning, the Legislature must be taken to have meant and intended what it has plainly expressed, and whatever it has in clear terms enacted must be enforced though it should lead to absurd or mischievous results. If the language of this subsection be not controlled by some of the other provisions of the statute, it must, since its language is plain and unambiguous, be enforced, and your Lordships' House sitting judicially is not concerned with the question whether the policy it embodies is wise or unwise, or whether it leads to consequences just or unjust, beneficial or mischievous.

[handwritten margin note: enforce plain meaning — regardless!]

Lord Bramwell, in *Hill v. East and West India Dock Co.*, 9 App. Cas. 448, 464–65 (House of Lords, 1884):

> I should like to have a good definition of what is such an absurdity that you are to disregard the plain words of an Act of Parliament. It is to be remembered that what seems absurd to one man does not seem absurd to another. * * * I think it is infinitely better, although an absurdity or an injustice or other objectionable result may be evolved as the consequence of your construction, to adhere to the words of an Act of Parliament and leave the legislature to set it right than to alter those words according to one's notion of an absurdity. * * *

[handwritten margin note: ABSURDITY DEFINITION to disregard plain words?]

F.   *A Second Breath of Fresh Air*

LIEBER, LEGAL AND POLITICAL HERMENEUTICS
(2d ed. St. Louis, 1880) pp. 17–20.

IV.   Let us take an instance of the simplest kind, to show in what degree we are continually obliged to resort to interpretation. By and by we shall find that the same rules which common sense teaches every one to use, in order to understand his neighbor in the most trivial intercourse, are necessary likewise, although not sufficient, for the interpretation of documents or texts of the highest importance, constitutions as well as treaties between the great nations.

Suppose a housekeeper says to a domestic: "fetch some soupmeat," accompanying the act with giving some money to the latter; he will be unable to execute the order without interpretation, however easy and, consequently, rapid the performance of the process may be. Common sense and good faith tell the domestic, that the housekeeper's meaning was this: 1. He should go immediately, or as soon as his other occupations are finished; or, if he be directed to do so in the evening, that he should go next day at the *usual* hour; 2. that the money handed him by the housekeeper is intended to pay for the meat thus ordered, and not as a present to him; 3. that he should buy such meat and of such part of the animal, as, to his knowledge, has commonly been used in the house he stays at, for making soups; 4. that he buy the best meat he can obtain, for a fair price; 5. that he go to that butcher who usually provides the family, with whom the domestic resides, with meat, or to some convenient stall, and not to any unnecessarily distant place; 6. that he return the rest of the money; 7. that he bring home the meat in good faith, neither adding anything disagreeable nor injurious; 8. that he fetch the meat for the use of the family and not for himself. Suppose, on the other hand, the housekeeper, afraid of being misunderstood, had mentioned these eight specifications, she would not have obtained her object, if it were to exclude all *possibility* of misunderstanding. For, the various specifications would have required new ones. Where would be the end? We are constrained then, always, to leave a considerable part of our meaning to be found out by interpretation, which, in many cases must necessarily cause greater or less obscurity with regard to the exact meaning, which our words were intended to convey.

* * * Men have at length found out that little or nothing is gained by attempting to speak with absolute clearness and endless specifications, but that human speech is the clearer, the less we endeavor to supply by words and specifications that interpretation which common sense must give to human words. However minutely we may define, somewhere we [must] trust at last to common sense and good faith. * * *

STATUTORY PREFACE TO THE *HOLY TRINITY* CASE

An act to prohibit the importation and migration of foreigners and aliens under contract or agreement to perform labor in the United States, its Territories and the District of Columbia, Act of February 26, 1885, 23 Stat. 332, c. 164.

Section 1. That from and after the passage of this act it shall be unlawful for any person, company, partnership, or corporation, in any manner whatsoever, to prepay the transportation, or in any way assist or encourage the importation or migration of any alien or aliens, any foreigner or foreigners, into the United States, its Territories, or the District of Columbia, under contract or agreement, parol or special, express or implied, made previous to the importation or migration of such alien or aliens, foreigner or foreigners, to perform labor or service of any kind in the United States, its Territories, or the District of Columbia.

Section 4. That the master of any vessel who shall knowingly bring within the United States on any such vessel * * * any alien, laborer, mechanic or artisan * * * who had entered into contract or agreement * * * to perform labor or service in the United States, shall be guilty of a misdemeanor * * *.

Section 5. * * * [N]or shall the provisions of this act apply to professional actors, artists, lecturers, or singers, nor to persons employed strictly as personal or domestic servants. * * *

RECTOR, HOLY TRINITY CHURCH v. UNITED STATES

Supreme Court of the United States, 1892.
143 U.S. 457, 12 S.Ct. 511, 36 L.Ed. 226.

MR. JUSTICE BREWER delivered the opinion of the Court.

Plaintiff in error is a corporation, duly organized and incorporated as a religious society under the laws of the State of New York. E. Walpole Warren was, prior to September, 1887, an alien residing in England. In that month the plaintiff in error made a contract with him, by which he was to remove to the city of New York and enter into its service as rector and pastor; and in pursuance of such contract, Warren did so remove and enter upon such service. It is claimed by the United States that this contract on the part of the plaintiff in error was forbidden by the act of February 26, 1885, 23 Stat. 332, c. 164, and an action was commenced to recover the penalty prescribed by that act. The Circuit Court held that the contract was within the prohibition of the statute, and rendered judgment accordingly, and the single question presented for our determination is whether it erred in that conclusion.

[Justice Brewer quoted § 1 of the Act.] It must be conceded that the act of the corporation is within the letter of this section, for the relation of rector to his church is one of service, and implies labor on the one side with compensation on the other. Not only are the general words labor and service both used, but also, as it were to guard against any narrow interpretation and emphasize a breadth of meaning, to them is added "of any kind;" and, further, as noticed by the Circuit Judge in his opinion, the fifth section, which makes specific exceptions, among them professional actors, artists, lecturers, singers and domestic servants, strengthens the idea that every other kind of labor and service was intended to be reached by the first section. While there is great force to this reasoning, we cannot think Congress intended to denounce with penalties a transaction like that in the present case. It is a familiar rule, that a thing may be within the letter of the statute and yet not within the statute, because not within its spirit, nor within the intention of its makers. This has been often asserted, and the reports are full of cases illustrating its application. This is not the substitution of the will of the judge for that of the legislator, for frequently words of general meaning are used in a statute, words broad enough to include an act in question, and yet a consideration of the whole legislation, or of the circumstances surrounding its enactment, or of the absurd results which follow from giving such broad meaning to the words, makes it unreasonable to believe that the legislator intended to include the particular act. As said in Plowden, 205: "From which cases, it appears that the sages of the law heretofore have construed statutes quite contrary to the letter in some appearance, and those statutes which comprehend all things in the letter they have expounded to extend to but some things, and those which generally prohibit all people from doing such an act they have interpreted to permit some people to do it, and those which include every person in the letter, they have adjudged to reach to some persons only, which expositions have always been founded upon the intent of the legislature, which they have collected sometimes by considering the cause and necessity of making the act, sometimes by comparing one part of the act with another, and sometimes by foreign circumstances." * * *

* * * [T]he title of this act is, "An act to prohibit the importation and migration of foreigners and aliens under contract or agreement to perform labor in the United States, its Territories and the District of Columbia." Obviously the thought expressed in this reaches only to the work of the manual laborer, as distinguished from that of the professional man. No one reading such a title would suppose that Congress had in its mind any purpose of staying the coming into this country of ministers of the gospel, or, indeed, of any class whose toil is that of the brain. The common understanding of the terms labor and laborers does not include preaching and preachers; and it is to be assumed that words and phrases are used in their ordinary meaning. So whatever of light is thrown upon the statute by the language of the title indicates an exclusion from its penal provisions of all contracts for the employment of ministers, rectors and pastors.

Again, another guide to the meaning of a statute is found in the evil which it is designed to remedy; and for this the court properly looks at contemporaneous events, the situation as it existed, and as it was pressed upon the attention of the legislative body. The situation which called for this statute was briefly but fully stated by Mr. Justice Brown when, as District Judge, he decided the case of *United States v. Craig,* 28 Fed. Rep. 795, 798: "The motives and history of the act are matters of common knowledge. It had become the practice for large capitalists in this country to contract with their agents abroad for the shipment of great numbers of an ignorant and servile class of foreign laborers, under contracts, by which the employer agreed, upon the one hand, to prepay their passage, while, upon the other hand, the laborers agreed to work after their arrival for a certain time at a low rate of wages. The effect of this was to break down the labor market, and to reduce other laborers engaged in like occupations to the level of the assisted immigrant. The evil finally became so flagrant that an appeal was made to Congress for relief by the passage of the act in question, the design of which was to raise the standard of foreign immigrants, and to discountenance the migration of those who had not sufficient means in their own hands, or those of their friends, to pay their passage."

It appears, also, from the petitions, and in the testimony presented before the committees of Congress, that it was this cheap unskilled labor which was making the trouble, and the influx of which Congress sought to prevent. It was never suggested that we had in this country a surplus of brain toilers, and, least of all, that the market for the services of Christian ministers was depressed by foreign competition. Those were matters to which the attention of Congress, or of the people, was not directed.

So far, then, as the evil which was sought to be remedied interprets the statute, it also guides to an exclusion of this contract from the penalties of the act.

A singular circumstance, throwing light upon the intent of Congress, is found in this extract from the report of the Senate Committee on Education and Labor, recommending the passage of the bill: "The general facts and considerations which induce the committee to recommend the passage of this bill are set forth in the Report of the Committee of the House. The committee report the bill back without amendment, although there are certain features thereof which might well be changed or modified, in the hope that the bill may not fail of passage during the present session. Especially would the committee have otherwise recommended amendments, substituting for the expression 'labor and service,' whenever it occurs in the body of the bill, the words 'manual labor' or 'manual service,' as sufficiently broad to accomplish the purposes of the bill, and that such amendments would remove objections which a sharp and perhaps unfriendly criticism may urge to the proposed legislation. The committee, however, believing that the bill in its present form will be construed as including only those whose labor or service is manual in character, and being very desirous that the bill become a law before the adjournment, have reported the bill without change." Page 6059, Congressional Record, 48th Congress. And, referring back to the report of the Committee of the House, there appears this language: "It seeks to restrain and prohibit the immigration or importation of laborers who would have never seen our shores but for the inducements and allurements of men whose only object is to obtain labor at the lowest possible rate, regardless of the social and material well-being of our own citizens and regardless of the evil consequences which result to American laborers from such immigration. This class of immigrants care nothing about our institutions, and in many instances never even heard of them; they are men whose passage is paid by the importers; they come here under contract to labor for a certain number of years; they are ignorant of our social condition, and that they may remain so they are isolated and prevented from coming into contact with Americans. They are generally from the lowest social stratum, and live upon the coarsest food and in hovels of a character before unknown to American workmen. They, as a rule, do not become citizens, and are certainly not a desirable acquisition to the body politic. The inevitable tendency of their presence among us is to degrade American labor, and to reduce it to the level of the imported pauper labor." Page 5359, Congressional Record, 48th Congress.

We find, therefore, that the title of the act, the evil which was intended to be remedied, the circumstances surrounding the appeal to Congress, the reports of the committee of each house, all concur in affirming that the intent of Congress was simply to stay the influx of this cheap unskilled labor.

But beyond all these matters no purpose of action against religion can be imputed to any legislation, state or national, because this is a religious people. This is historically true. From the discovery of this continent to the present hour, there is a single voice making this affirmation. The commission to Christopher Columbus, prior to his sail westward, is from "Ferdinand and Isabella, by the grace of God, King and Queen of Castile," etc., and recites that "it is hoped that by God's assistance some of the continents and islands in the ocean will be discovered," etc. The first colonial grant, that made to Sir Walter Raleigh in 1584, was from "Elizabeth, by the grace of

God, of England, Fraunce and Ireland, queene, defender of the faith," etc.; and the grant authorizing him to enact statutes for the government of the proposed colony provided that "they be not against the true Christian faith nowe professed in the Church of England." * * *

If we examine the constitutions of the various States we find in them a constant recognition of religious obligations. Every constitution of every one of the forty-four States contains language which either directly or by clear implication recognizes a profound reverence for religion and an assumption that its influence in all human affairs is essential to the well being of the community. This recognition may be in the preamble, such as is found in the constitution of Illinois, 1870; "We, the people of the State of Illinois, grateful to Almighty God for the civil, political and religious liberty which He hath so long permitted us to enjoy, and looking to Him for a blessing upon our endeavors to secure and transmit the same unimpaired to succeeding generations," etc. * * *

Even the Constitution of the United States, which is supposed to have little touch upon the private life of the individual, contains in the First Amendment a declaration common to the constitutions of all the States, as follows: "Congress shall make no law respecting an establishment of religion, or prohibiting the free exercise thereof," etc. And also provides in Article 1, section 7, (a provision common to many constitutions,) that the Executive shall have ten days (Sundays excepted) within which to determine whether he will approve or veto a bill. * * *

If we pass beyond these matters to a view of American life as expressed by its laws, its business, its customs and its society, we find everywhere a clear recognition of the same truth. Among other matters note the following: The form of oath universally prevailing, concluding with an appeal to the Almighty; the custom of opening sessions of all deliberative bodies and most conventions with prayer; the prefatory words of all wills, "In the name of God, amen;" the laws respecting the observance of the Sabbath, with the general cessation of all secular business, and the closing of courts, legislatures, and other similar public assemblies on that day; the churches and church organizations which abound in every city, town and hamlet; the multitude of charitable organizations existing everywhere under Christian auspices; the gigantic missionary associations, with general support, and aiming to establish Christian missions in every quarter of the globe. These, and many other matters which might be noticed, add a volume of unofficial declarations to the mass of organic utterances that this is a Christian nation. In the face of all these, shall it be believed that a Congress of the United States intended to make it a misde-meanor for a church of this country to contract for the services of a Christian minister residing in another nation? * * *

NOTES ON HOLY TRINITY AND ECLECTICISM IN STATUTORY INTERPRETATION

1. *The Text of the Statute.* Justice Brewer's opinion seems to adopt something from all the theories introduced at the beginning of this section—except that it seems to violate the "literal rule" of *Vacher & Sons.* Brewer concedes that his interpretation is not "within the letter of the statute." Was this concession too quickly made? One of us has argued

that it was, based on an examination of contemporary dictionaries.[8] The first definition of the term "labor" listed in the 1879 and 1886 editions of *Webster's Dictionary* was "[p]hysical toil or bodily exertion * * * hard muscular effort directed to some useful end, as agriculture, manufactures, and the like." The second definition was "[i]ntellectual exertion, mental effort." Two linguists used a corpus of publications from the *Holy Trinity* era to determine how these terms were actually used. "Specifically, when people spoke of what the clergy do, they rarely used the word 'labor,' and when they used the word 'labor,' they generally did so to describe manual labor, not something typically performed by clergy. Thus, 'labor' and 'clergy' were doubly dissociated." Tammy Gales & Lawrence Solan, "*Holy Trinity Church* Revisited: Corpus Linguistic Analysis of Historic Cases" (draft 2019).

Webster's (1879 and 1886) only relevant definition of "service" was the "act of serving; the occupation of a servant; the performance of labor for the benefit of another, or at another's command; the attendance of an inferior, or hired helper or slave, etc., on a superior employer, master, and the like." Moreover, the term "labor or service" might be a compound term—and so it was in the nineteenth century. Consider Article IV, § 2 of the Constitution, which provides that "[n]o Person held to Service or Labour in one State" shall be discharged from "such Service or Labour" if he escapes to another State. Gales and Solan found nineteenth century usage of this compound term to be most strongly associated with slavery or involuntary servitude, but by the end of the century it was also used to describe wage labor as well.

Is it clear that the letter of the law supported the prosecution?

2. *The Structure of the Statute.* The prohibition is found in § 1 of the 1885 law. (Section 2 voids contracts made in violation of § 1, and § 3 provides for criminal penalties for such alien labor contracts.) Although ignored by the Court, § 4 might be relevant, holding criminally accountable the master of a ship "who shall knowingly bring within the United States * * * any alien *laborer, mechanic or artisan*" who had contracted to perform "labor or service in the United States." Should § 1 be read narrowly, to track the terms in § 4, or does the narrowness of § 4 confirm a broader reading for § 1? The marginal note in the Statutes at Large (not part of the enacted law) describes § 4 as applying to the master of a vessel who knowingly brings "such emigrant laborer" to our shores. 23 Stat. 332 (1885).

Justice Brewer mentions § 5, a list of exemptions to the liabilities imposed by §§ 1–4. Section 5 exempted "professional actors, artists, lecturers, or singers" as well as "personal or domestic servants" from the "provisions of this act." Does the omission of ministers from § 5 demonstrate that they were covered under §§ 1–4? Alternatively, could a minister be included under § 5's exemption for a "lecturer"? The *Oxford English Dictionary* and the 1879 edition of *Webster's* identified "Lecturer" as a religious officer (but not the pastor) in Episcopal churches.

3. *Legislative History as Evidence of Legislative "Intent."* To narrow what he views as the apparent plain meaning of the law, Brewer relies on the evil (or mischief) against which the Act was aimed and the inapplicability to a "brain toiler" of a statute seeking to exclude "laborers." Brewer further cites the Senate committee report saying that the bill was only intended to exclude people engaged in "manual labor" but that it was too late in

---

[8]   See William Eskridge Jr., *Textualism, The Unknown Ideal?*, 96 Mich. L. Rev. 1509, 1517–19, 1533, 1539–40 (1998).

the session to amend the statute to add that precise language. Note the two ways that Brewer deploys the idea of legislative intent: one looks to the general goal of the law and tailors the text to meet the goal ("general intent") and the other asks what the legislators thought they were doing as to the particular issue ("specific intent"). Recall these two levels of intent at work in *Weber*, the affirmative action case in Chapter 1, § 2. The *Weber* majority quoted and followed *Holy Trinity*.

The Supreme Court had essentially rewritten statutes in earlier cases, in order to avoid absurd consequences (the golden rule) or where required by common law or constitutional maxims, but both the Court and commentators followed a rule whereby legislative materials were inadmissible evidence to alter "plain" statutory meanings. *Holy Trinity* seems to be the first case where the Supreme Court "rewrote" the statute based upon evidence from the legislative record. A revised edition of the leading treatise cited it repeatedly and endorsed its proposition that courts could consider legislative records to figure out what the intent of the legislature was on a particular issue. See J.G. Sutherland, *Statutes and Statutory Construction* 879–83 (John Lewis ed., 2d ed. 1904). (The first edition of the Sutherland treatise, published in 1891, followed the English practice of excluding extrinsic legislative materials from consideration in statutory cases.) The federal courts in the twentieth century cited an increasing amount and variety of legislative history, a trend that abated only in the late 1980s.

4. *Legislative History the Court Missed.* Independent examination by modern scholars suggests that Brewer was right about the general intent of Congress and the problem it was addressing, see Carol Chomsky, *Unlocking the Mysteries of* Holy Trinity: *Spirit, Letter, and History in Statutory Interpretation*, 100 Colum. L. Rev. 901 (2000), but missed important evidence bearing on legislators' specific intent. Contrary to Brewer's opinion, the alien contract labor bill was not enacted in 1884, as the Senate committee had hoped, but was brought up in the 1885 session of the 48th Congress, just before the Cleveland Administration took office (see 2011 Documents Supplement 180). The Senate had a lengthy debate about the bill, which was amended in minor ways. Among the amendments were those expanding the exempted classes, but no amendment was proposed to make clear that "labor" referred only to "manual labor." When pressed by an opponent of the bill, who argued that § 5 discriminated against "other classes of professional men" by granting exemptions to singers and lecturers and actors, Senator Blair, the floor manager, engaged in this exchange with the opponent:

> Mr. MORGAN: * * * [If the alien] happens to be a lawyer, an artist, a painter, an engraver, a sculptor, a great author, or what not, and he comes under employment to write for a newspaper, or to write books, or to paint pictures * * * he comes under the general provisions of the bill. * * *

> Mr. BLAIR: *If that class of people are liable to become the subject-matter of such importation, then the bill applies to them. Perhaps the bill ought to be further amended.*

> Mr. MORGAN: * * * I shall propose when we get to it to put an amendment in there. I want to associate with the lecturers and singers and actors, painters, sculptors [etc.], or any person having special skill in any business, art, trade or profession. * * *

16 Cong. Rec. 1633 (1885) (emphasis added). The House floor manager, Representative Hopkins, responded to an inquiry regarding agricultural workers by saying that the bill

"prohibits the importation under contract of all classes with the exceptions named in [§ 5]." 16 Cong. Rec. 2032 (1885). Does this more complete record undermine Brewer's conclusion? See Adrian Vermeule, *Judging Under Uncertainty* 86–117 (2006) (filling in this gap in Brewer's deployment of legislative history and concluding that the judiciary was and remains incompetent to evaluate legislative history).

There is more legislative history that both the Court and subsequent commentators also missed. What is the relationship between § 1, with seemingly broad application to "labor or service of any kind," and § 4, with narrower application only to "labor or service" by "any alien laborer, mechanic, or artisan"? Senator Blair repeatedly assured his colleagues that § 4 was aimed at "the man who knowingly brings an immigrant * * * who comes here under and by virtue of a contract such as is prohibited by [§ 1] of the bill." 16 Cong. Rec. 1630 (1885). We are not aware of any on-the-record statement to the contrary. Should this evidence influence the Court's understanding of the relationship between §§ 1 and 4? See William Eskridge Jr., *No Frills Textualism*, 119 Harv. L. Rev. 2041, 2065–70 (2006).

Similarly, there is potentially relevant legislative history for § 5, which exempted "lecturers" from the statutory coverage (2011 Documents Supplement 175). Senator Morgan, who offered the lecturer exclusion as an amendment to § 5, explained that "[p]eople who can instruct us in morals and *religion* and in every species of elevation by lectures . . . are not prohibited." 16 Cong. Rec. 1633 (1885) (emphasis added). No one spoke against his interpretation. Does this legislative history strike you as relevant? Does it alter your understanding of the statute's meaning?

5. *Subsequent Legislation.* After the federal circuit court in the Southern District of New York construed the statute to apply to Reverend Warren in the *Holy Trinity* litigation, Congress amended the alien contract labor law to exempt ministers and professionals generally. Reversing the lower court, the Supreme Court in *Holy Trinity* did not mention the 1891 statute, which by its terms did not apply to pending proceedings, Act of March 3, 1891, § 12, 26 Stat. 1084, 1086. Does this later statute vindicate, or undermine, the Court's holding? Cf. *United States v. Laws*, 163 U.S. 258, 265 (1896) (discussing the 1891 amendment).

6. *The "Christian Nation" Discussion: Avoiding Absurd Results and Constitutional Issues.* Students might be taken aback by *Holy Trinity*'s invocation of the "Christian nation" analysis to clinch the Court's argument. (Born of Christian missionaries in Asia Minor, David Brewer was an Evangelical jurist.) Was this critical to the Court's opinion? Would Justice Brewer have exempted a doctor from the statute's exclusion, for example? Cf. *Laws*, 163 U.S. 258 (determining whether the 1885 law covered chemists).

A modern version of the Christian nation argument might be the idea that judges should read even clear statutory texts to avoid "absurd results." *Brown v. Plata*, 563 U.S. 493, 550 (2012) (Scalia, J., dissenting) (judges should "bend every effort" to avoid "outrageous" interpretations); Glen Staszewski, *Avoiding Absurdity,* 81 Ind. L. Rev. 1001 (2006). Perhaps, however, the Christian nation discussion suggests how one judge's "absurdity" might be another judge's "public value." See John Manning, *The Absurdity Doctrine,* 116 Harv. L. Rev. 2387 (2003) (strong critique of any absurd results exception to the plain meaning rule).

Another modern rendition of Justice Brewer's concerns would be through the canon that judges should construe ambiguous statutes to avoid serious constitutional difficulties (Chapter 7). Current Supreme Court doctrine says that the First Amendment requires that anti-discrimination statutes permit religions to discriminate on the basis of faith in the hiring and firing of "ministers." *Hosanna-Tabor Evangelical Lutheran Church and School v. EEOC,* 565 U.S. 171 (2012). Might *Holy Trinity* be justified by the Court's inclination to "avoid" a serious constitutional difficulty (even in 1891)?

Caminetti v. United States

242 U.S. 470 (1917).

A federal statute criminalized the transportation of, or the inducement to travel of, "any woman or girl to go from one place to another in interstate or foreign commerce, or in any territory or the District of Columbia, for the purpose of prostitution or debauchery, or for any other immoral purpose * * *." The case concerned a man who brought a woman from Sacramento, California, to Reno, Nevada, to "become his mistress and concubine." The Court, per **Justice Day**, stated that "it is elementary that the meaning of a statute must, in the first instance, be sought in the language in which the act is framed, and if that is plain, and if the law is within the constitutional authority of the lawmaking body which passed it, the sole function of the courts is to enforce it according to its terms." The majority found the statutory meaning plain—the conduct in question was for an "immoral purpose"—and held that Caminetti violated the statute. It refused to consider the title to the Act ("the White Slave Traffic Act") or legislative history suggesting that the purpose of the statute was narrower than its plain meaning (to reach only "commercialized vice").

The majority did not cite *Holy Trinity*, but **Justice McKenna**, joined in dissent by two other Justices, relied on it for the proposition that "the words of the statute should be construed to execute [the statutory purpose], and they may be so construed even if their literal meaning be otherwise." The dissent also argued that the statutory text was not plain: "other immoral purpose" should not be read literally and in isolation, but in light of the limiting words preceding them. As illuminated by the legislative history and by the principle that statutes should be read with "common sense" to avoid absurd applications, the statute should not reach "the occasional immoralities of men and women," but rather the "systematized and mercenary immorality epitomized in the statute's graphic phrase 'white slave traffic.' "

Although the free-wheeling approach of *Holy Trinity* may seem worlds apart from the mechanical approach of *Caminetti*, it appears that unarticulated judicial values played a heavy role in both cases. That is, the Court would stick with literalism (*Caminetti*), or trump literalism with the mischief approach and the golden rule (*Holy Trinity*), in order to reach the interpretation that better matched its sensibilities. In *Caminetti*, for example, Justice McKenna's dissent stated that "[t]here is much in the present case to tempt to a violation of the [mischief] rule. Any measure that protects the purity of women from assault or enticement to degradation finds an instant advocate in our best emotions; but the judicial function cannot yield to emotion * * *."

NOTES ON INTERPRETATION AS "IMAGINATIVE RECONSTRUCTION" OR A SEARCH FOR "LEGISLATIVE INTENT"

1. *Democracy and Statutory Interpretation: The Importance of "Legislative Intent."* The Court that decided *Lochner v. New York*, 198 U.S. 45 (1905) (invoking liberty of contract to strike down a maximum-hours law), of which Justice Brewer was a central figure, not only struck down labor laws but interpreted them stingily (following *Holy*

Trinity)—at the same time it was interpreting morals legislation (such as the Mann Act in *Caminetti*) very broadly. For progressives who favored aggressive legislation supplanting the common law, decisions like *Lochner* and *Holy Trinity* sent the same message of judicial reluctance to accept new statutes.

[handwritten: stingy labor laws + broad moral legislation.]

[handwritten: Judicial Reluctance to Accept New statutes]

Professor Roscoe Pound (later Dean of the Harvard Law School) set forth the baseline most consistent, in his view, with our representative democracy: "The object of genuine interpretation is to discover the rule which the law-maker intended to establish; to discover the intention which the law-maker made the rule, or the sense which he attached to the words wherein the rule is expressed. Its object is to enable others to derive from the language used 'the same idea which the author intended to convey.'" Roscoe Pound, *Spurious Interpretation*, 7 Colum. L. Rev. 379, 381 (1907). On his understanding, textual meaning and authorial intent are not separable concepts: the text has no autonomous significance; it merely consists of signifiers encoding an intended message, however difficult it might be for the interpreter to decode that message. This understanding retains force for some students of interpretation today, both in law and other fields.[9]

[handwritten: "same idea which the author intended to convey"]

[handwritten: text ≠ have an autonomous signif.—consists of signifiers encoded into an intended message.]

Thus, one cannot speak about the "plain meaning" of statutory text in isolation and be engaged in "interpretation" at all. In this way, Pound denied that the "plain meaning" approach to statutory construction constitutes "interpretation"—unless the best textual meaning is simply used as good evidence of legislative intent, to be supplemented by any other evidence of legislative intent available. On this reading, his argument is a remarkable rejection of literalism in statutory interpretation. It also suggests that purposivism is "genuine interpretation," but only so long as the interpreter sticks as closely as possible to the probable purposes that animated the enacting legislature and avoids imposing her own views of appropriate public-policy purposes upon the statute. Anything beyond that is "spurious interpretation," Pound maintained. (Interestingly, he did not claim that "spurious interpretation" is always illegitimate; his point was that it should be called what it actually is—"revising to promote justice" or whatever—and debated on its own merits.)

[handwritten: Rejects literalism in statutory Interpretation]

2. *Ascertaining Legislative Intent: Actual Intent Versus Imaginative Reconstruction.* Pound proposed that interpreters follow legislative "intent," but admitted that this method is frequently difficult to implement. To begin with, if the interpreter has clear evidence of the *actual intent* of the enacting legislature about what the statute should mean in the context under consideration, the interpreter should follow it. Because strong evidence of actual intent will often be absent, the interpreter usually must engage in a second-best inquiry, what we might call the *imaginative reconstruction of legislative intent.* This approach requires the interpreter to put herself in the position of the enacting legislature and, like a historian, examine the available historical evidence against a background of assumptions about the legislature (that it would prefer justice to injustice, for example) that are commonplace to our legal system, but can be rebutted by evidence that this enacting legislature had a different view (for example, that it defined "justice"

[handwritten: Put self in position of enacting legislature]

[handwritten: 2nd best inquiry— b/c Actual Intent often is absent]

[handwritten: interpreters follow leg. intent But Freq. diffic. method to implement.]

---

[9]   Joseph Raz, *Intention in Interpretation*, in *The Autonomy of Law: Essays on Legal Positivism* 249, 258 (Robert George ed., 1996); Lawrence Solan, *The Language of Statutes: Laws and Their Interpretation* (2010). See also Andrei Marmor, *Positive Law and Objective Values* ch. 5 (2001); Paul Campos, *That Obscure Object of Desire: Hermeneutics and the Autonomous Text,* 77 Minn. L. Rev. 1065 (1993).

[handwritten: + historical evidence Against A Background of Assumptions about the Legislature.]

and "injustice" differently than the interpreter would).[10] These remain the two fundamental inquiries of intentionalist interpretation today. Note that, for both, the statutory text is important because it frequently will be the best evidence of legislative intent.

3.   *Federal Courts and Pound's Approach.* After *Holy Trinity*, the Supreme Court grew increasingly interested in what legislators actually expected out of their statutes, e.g., *Johnson v. Southern Pacific Company*, 196 U.S. 1 (1904), though the Court did not always follow legislative history (recall *Caminetti*). Consider *Duplex Printing Press Co. v. Deering*, 254 U.S. 443 (1921), which interpreted the Clayton Act to justify an injunction against a secondary boycott by print workers against an "unfair" employer. Although the Clayton Act contained two broad provisions exempting most labor activity from antitrust regulation, the Court held that it was not the actual intent of Congress to insulate labor boycotts from regulation. The Court relied on a statement by the Clayton Act's House floor manager that neither he nor any member of the reporting committee intended the bill to exempt boycotts from the regulation courts had imposed on them under the older Sherman Act. Justice Brandeis's dissenting opinion railed against this narrowing interpretation, also based upon the actual, subjective expectations of the enacting Congress. (Brandeis was a close adviser of President Wilson, who had proposed the Clayton Act, and hence had an "inside view" of the Act.)

The classic early practitioner of imaginative reconstruction was Judge Learned Hand of the Second Circuit, one of the judges reversed in *Duplex Printing*. See, e.g., *Lehigh Valley Coal Co. v. Yensavage*, 218 F. 547, 553 (2d Cir. 1914); Archibald Cox, *Judge Learned Hand and the Interpretation of Statutes*, 60 Harv. L. Rev. 370 (1947). Consider the following exemplar of Pound's theory.

Fishgold v. Sullivan Drydock & Repair Corporation

154 F.2d 785 (2d Cir.), *aff'd*, 328 U.S. 275 (1946).

Section 8(b)(B) of the Selective Training & Service Act of 1940, 49 Stat. 888, 890, as amended in 1944, provided that the private employer of a person who had left employment for U.S. military service and then sought to return to the same position after discharge from the service "shall restore such person to such position or to a position of like seniority, status, and pay unless the employer's circumstances have so changed as to make it impossible or unreasonable to do so." Section 8(c) provided:

> Any person who is restored to a position in accordance with the provisions of paragraph (A) or (B) of subsection (b) shall be considered as having been on furlough or leave of absence during his period of training and service in the land or naval forces, shall be so restored without loss of seniority * * * and shall not be discharged from such position without cause within one year after such restoration.

Fishgold returned from service in the army during World War II and then was laid off within a year, while non-veteran employees who had more seniority were not laid off. Fishgold challenged the decision to lay him off, relying on § 8(c). **Judge Learned Hand**'s opinion concluded that the layoff was legal. He avoided the thrust of § 8(c)'s protection against "discharge" by noting that its dictionary definition was a permanent termination

---

10   Pound's statement of imaginative reconstruction is taken from the commentary to *Eyston v. Studd*, (1574) 2 Plowden 459, 467, 75 Eng. Rep. 688, 699 (K.B), paraphrasing Aristotle, *The Nicomachean Ethics* bk. V, ch. 10. For a modern exposition, see Richard Posner, *The Federal Courts: Crisis and Reform* 286–93 (1985).

of employment, rather than the temporary termination denoted by "layoff." This reflects the traditional labor law distinction between being terminated or fired (the employment relationship is severed) and being laid off (the employee is not employed but might be recalled to employment). Seniority typically affords virtually absolute protection against discharge or termination but only limited protection against layoffs.

"When we consider the situation at the time that the Act was passed—September, 1940—it is extremely improbable that Congress should have meant to grant any broader privilege than as we are measuring it. * * * The original act limited service to one year, and it was most improbable that within that time we should be called upon to fight upon our own soil; as indeed the event proved, for we were still at peace in September, 1941. Congress was calling young men to the colors to give them an adequate preparation for our defence, but with no forecast of the appalling experiences which they were later to undergo. Against that background it is not likely that a proposal would then have been accepted which gave industrial priority, regardless of their length of employment, to unmarried men—for the most part under thirty—over men in the thirties, forties or fifties, who had wives and children dependent upon them. Today, in the light of what has happened, the privilege then granted may appear an altogether inadequate equivalent for their services; but we have not to decide what is now proper; we are to reconstruct, as best we may, what was the purpose of Congress when it used the words in which § 8(b) and § 8(c) were cast." **Judge Chase** dissented, based upon a broader view of the statute's purpose.

MAX RADIN, STATUTORY INTERPRETATION
43 Harv. L. Rev. 863, 870–71 (1930).

It has frequently been declared that the most approved method is to discover the intent of the legislator. * * * On this transparent and absurd fiction it ought not to be necessary to dwell. It is clearly enough an illegitimate transference to law of concepts proper enough in literature and theology. * * *

That the intention of the legislature is undiscoverable in any real sense is almost an immediate inference from a statement of the proposition. The chances that of several hundred men each will have exactly the same determinate situations in mind as possible reductions of a given [statutory issue], are infinitesimally small. * * * In an extreme case, it might be that we could learn all that was in the mind of the draftsman, or of a committee of half a dozen men who completely approved of every word. But when this draft is submitted to the legislature and at once accepted without a dissentient voice and without debate, what have we then learned of the intentions of the four or five hundred approvers? Even if the contents of the minds of the legislature were uniform, we have no means of knowing that content except by the external utterances or behavior of these hundreds of men, and in almost every case the only external act is the extremely ambiguous one of acquiescence, which may be motivated in literally hundreds of ways, and which by itself indicates little or nothing of the pictures which the statutory descriptions imply. * * *

And if [legislative intent] were discoverable, it would be powerless to bind us. What gives the intention of the legislature obligating force? * * * [I]n law, the specific individuals who make up the legislature are men to whom a specialized function has been temporarily assigned. That function is not to impose their will even within limits on their fellow citizens, but to "pass statutes," which is a fairly precise operation. That is, they make statements in general terms of undesirable and desirable situations, from which flow certain results. * * * When the legislature has uttered the words of a statute, it is *functus officio*, not because of the Montesquieuan separation of powers, but because that is what legislating means. The legislature might also be a court and an executive, but it can never be all three things simultaneously.

And once the words are out, recorded, engrossed, registered, proclaimed, inscribed in bronze, they in turn become instrumentalities which administrators and courts must use in performing their own specialized functions. The principal use is that of "interpretation." Interpretation is an act which requires an existing determinate event—the issue to be litigated—and obviously that determinate event cannot exist until after the statute has come into force. To say that the intent of the legislature decides the interpretation is to say that the legislature interprets in advance * * * a situation which does not exist."

NOTES ON CRITIQUES OF INTENTIONALIST APPROACHES

1. *The Narrow Role of Legislatures.* Radin's last point, that legislatures exist only to pass statutes and not to impose their will on the citizenry, echoed Oliver Wendell Holmes Jr., who insisted that in a "government of laws, not men," legal standards must be external to the decisionmaker. Holmes, *The Common Law* 41, 44 (1881). "[W]e ask, not what this man meant, but what those words would mean in the mouth of a normal speaker of English, using them in the circumstances in which they were used. * * * [T]he normal speaker of English is merely a special variety, a literary form, so to speak, of our old friend the prudent man. He is external to the particular writer, and a reference to him as the criterion is simply another instance of the externality of law. * * * We do not inquire what the legislature meant; we ask only what the statute means." Holmes, *The Theory of Legal Interpretation*, 12 Harv. L. Rev. 417, 417–18, 419 (1899).

But "what the statute means" is not always clear. If the law is ambiguous, should interpreters consider the expectations of the legislators who wrote the statute?[11] If a judge were interpreting a contract, would the judge prefer an interpretation that reconstructs the intent or expectations of the parties to one that the parties did not want? Shouldn't a court pay at least as much attention to the intent of Congress, not only because Congress drafts and enacts statutes, but also because Congress-acting-with-the-President (Article I, § 7) is the "supreme" lawmaking authority in our constitutional democracy?[12]

2. *The Incoherence or Indeterminacy of Collective Intent.* Radin responds that legislative intent is incoherent or undiscoverable. It is incoherent to the extent that a collective body cannot easily be charged with having an "intent." As political scientist Kenneth Shepsle subsequently put it, "Congress is a They, Not an It."[13] Intent is

---

[11]   See Frederick de Sloovère, *Textual Interpretation of Statutes*, 11 N.Y.U. L.Q. Rev. 538 (1934); cf. *Boston Sand & Gravel Co. v. United States*, 278 U.S. 41, 48 (1928) (Holmes, J.) (consulting legislative history to figure out "what the statute means").

[12]   Daniel A. Farber, *Statutory Interpretation and Legislative Supremacy*, 78 Geo. L.J. 281 (1989).

[13]   Kenneth Shepsle, *Congress Is a "They," Not an "It": Legislative Intent as Oxymoron*, 12 Int'l Rev. L. & Econ. 239 (1992). Accord, Ronald Dworkin, *Law's Empire* 314, 335–36 (1986); Jeremy Waldron, *Law and*

undiscoverable because too little evidence of collective understanding finds its way into the public record, and even when reported is hard to interpret. Also, how can the different "intents" of the House, Senate, and President be aggregated?

These are logical quarrels, but there is another way of looking at this matter. If the president or the board of directors of a company negotiates a contract, the president's or the board's representations might be taken to be those of the company itself. As Lawrence Solan has argued, both common sense and the law routinely attribute "intent" to collective bodies based upon the purposive declarations made by subgroups or agents publicly deputized to deliberate for the whole group. Solan, *Private Language, Public Laws: The Central Role of Legislative Intent in Statutory Interpretation*, 93 Geo. L.J. 427, 437–49 (2005).[14] Political scientists make the same point about committees and sponsors in Congress.[15] In the same manner, statements by sponsors and committees might reasonably be thought to represent congressional consensus unless denied by other representatives. Arguably, this is an institutional convention that is reasonable, and that Congress can be expected to adjust to (through better monitoring) if it yields results that systematically fail to reflect legislative bargains or consensuses.[16]

The debates over statutory interpretation took several important turns in the 1930s.[17] The unprecedented degree of statute-making during the New Deal vindicated Pound's claim that the twentieth century would be the age of legislatures rather than courts, but this statutory binge also vindicated Radin's point that there was unlikely to be a clear legislative intent (reconstructed or otherwise) on any but a handful of issues and that interpretive discretion was required. During the New Deal and right before U.S. entry into World War II, an academic consensus found a way to accept both points of view. This approach, whose outlines were clear in the period from 1938–41,[18] blossomed into "legal process" theory after World War II (Section 2).

3.   *Legislative Intent as Deciding.* Contra Radin, Victoria Nourse argues that "Congress has the functional equivalent of intent. Congress's functional equivalent of intent, like that of any group, depends upon sequential procedures. Procedures are how a group plans. The way to look at intent is not to imagine some meaning behind the meaning in an individual's head. Of course, Congress has no mind. Congress's procedures—its way of planning—is its way of having intent. When we consider Congress's intent, we are asking for the context in which Congress has legislated and that includes, most importantly, procedural context." Victoria Nourse, *Elementary*

Disagreement (1999); Frank Easterbrook, *Text, History, and Structure in Statutory Interpretation*, 17 Harv. J.L. & Pub. Pol'y 61 (1994).

[14]   Accord, Stephen Breyer, *Making Our Democracy Work: A Judge's View* (2010); Christian List & Philip Pettit, *Group Agency* (2011).

[15]   Daniel Rodriguez & Barry Weingast, *The Positive Political Theory of Legislative History: New Perspectives on the 1964 Civil Rights Act and Its Interpretation*, 151 U. Pa. L. Rev. 1417 (2003).

[16]   See James Landis, *A Note on "Statutory Interpretation,"* 43 Harv. L. Rev. 886, 888–90 (1930) (responding to Radin's article); McNollgast, *Positive Canons: The Role of Legislative Bargains in Statutory Interpretation*, 80 Geo. L.J. 705 (1992).

[17]   See William Eskridge Jr. & Philip Frickey, "Historical and Critical Introduction," to Henry Hart Jr. & Albert Sacks, *The Legal Process: Basic Problems in the Making and Application of Law* (Eskridge & Frickey eds., 1994); Nicholas Parrillo, *Leviathan and Interpretive Revolution: The Administrative State, the Judiciary, and the Rise of Legislative History, 1890–1950,* 123 Yale L.J. 266 (2014).

[18]   The leading precursors of legal process theory were Lon Fuller, *The Law in Quest of Itself* (1940); Harry Willmer Jones, *Statutory Doubts and Legislative Intention*, 40 Colum. L. Rev. 957 (1940); Frederick de Sloovère, *Extrinsic Aids in the Interpretation of Statutes*, 88 U. Pa. L. Rev. 527 (1940); Lloyd Garrison & Willard Hurst, "Law in Society" (1940 & 1941) (teaching materials at Wisconsin).

Statutory Interpretation: Rethinking Legislative Intent and History, 55 B.C.L. Rev. 1613, 1615 (2014).

Because Radin assumed a "state of mind" view of "intent," Nourse dismisses his objections. In its place, she draws from Christian List & Phillip Pettit, *Group Agency* (2011), a notion of "group intent" that may be inferred from "group action," which occurs because of sequential procedures. "This is how the group plans for the future. If this is correct, then when one looks for 'congressional intent,' one is not looking for any special mental state behind text or action—whether of individuals or groups. Instead, one is looking for crucial context for interpreting group action. Put in other words, one is looking for the public meaning of public acts done according to the rules. Congress has no mind, but it has the functional equivalent of intent—a way to plan for the future." Nourse, *Elementary Statutory Interpretation*, 1640.

Every important procedural step (or vetogate), in the legislative process is an opportunity for expression, aggregation, and revision of legislators' preferences. Contrary to the "mental state" understanding of intent, the procedural understanding takes preferences as evolving and not fixed. Recall our detailed examination of *Weber*, the affirmative action case, in Chapter 1, § 2. None of the Justices understood congressional intent as a function of congressional procedure. Both the majority and the dissent cherry-picked statements from legislators, which as Radin said, can tell you little about what Congress as a body "intended." But an elementary knowledge of congressional procedure suggests that the key moment was when the Mansfield-Dirkson substitute was introduced and passed, adding § 703(j), which would have justified a more detailed examination than the majority and dissenting opinions were willing to engage in.

PROBLEMS APPLYING IMAGINATIVE RECONSTRUCTION TO STATUTES

Problem 5-1. Holy Trinity, *Revisited*. How would Judge Hand and Dean Pound have voted if they were presented with the statutory issue in *Holy Trinity Church*? How about Professor Nourse?

Problem 5-2. Fetch Me Soupmeat. Williams tells her servant to "fetch me some soupmeat" from "Store X" (recall Lieber's hypothetical). The servant goes to Store X and discovers that the store only has one pound of soupmeat left, and it looks old and wormy. The servant knows that Store Y also carries soupmeat and, upon inspection, sees that Store Y's soupmeat looks pretty good. How would the following "servants" interpret the boss' command: Judge Hand? Dean Pound? What do you think the proper interpretation is? Is statutory interpretation similar to this example?

2. LEGAL PROCESS THEORIES OF STATUTORY INTERPRETATION

The intellectual parents of "legal process" theories of the state and of statutory interpretation were Oliver Wendell Holmes Jr., Louis Brandeis, and Felix Frankfurter.[19] Holmes was the great jurist who offered a clear-headed criticism of

---

[19] The exposition that follows is taken from William Eskridge Jr. & Philip Frickey, *A Historical and Critical Introduction*, to Henry Hart Jr. & Albert Sacks, *The Legal Process: Basic Problems in the Making and Application of Law* (Eskridge & Frickey eds., 1994). Other useful sources include Charles Barzun, *The Forgotten Foundations of Hart and Sacks*, 99 Va. L. Rev. 1 (2013); Neil Duxbury, *Faith in Reason: The Process Tradition*

mechanical reasoning that pretended that law was entirely separate from policy. Before joining Holmes on the Supreme Court, Brandeis was the leading intellectual force behind Woodrow Wilson's New Freedom programs for policing market abuses, and Frankfurter and his students played a similar role during the New Deal. While both had substantive theories of regulation, it was their theories of institutional architecture and process that were the more important contribution to American public law.

The difference between Holmes's law-is-policy viewpoint and Brandeis's law-is-policy-but-also-institutional-architecture viewpoint is illustrated in *International News Service v. Associated Press*, 248 U.S. 215 (1918). The issue was whether the Associated Press (AP) held a protected property interest in news stories it generated and was entitled to an injunction against theft of those stories by International News Service (INS), a rival news service. The opinion for the Court was a typical exercise in common law reasoning, deciding that AP was entitled to an injunction because its investment of time, effort, and resources in generating the news stories was analogous to other efforts treated as property (to this day, *INS* is the leading citation for "quasi-property" rights). The Court's assumption of a preexisting concept of property was challenged in Holmes's concurring opinion, which argued that property is a consequence and not an antecedent of law. The issue for him was whether state policy would be advanced by recognizing rights in newsgathering; he decided that it was worth it, in order to encourage this socially productive activity.

Brandeis agreed with Holmes that there is no natural category, "property," and that the decision whether to characterize news stories in this way depends upon a balancing of the consequences of the different positions. But Brandeis dissented on the ground that the policy balancing required by Holmes was best done by the legislature and not the judiciary:

> [W]ith the increasing complexity of society * * * the problems presented by new demands for justice cease to be simple. Then the creation or recognition by courts of a new private right may work serious injury to the general public, unless the boundaries of the right are definitely established and wisely guarded. In order to reconcile the private right with the public interest, it may be necessary to prescribe limitations and rules for its enjoyment; and also to provide administrative machinery for enforcing the rules. It is largely for this reason that, in the effort to meet the many new demands for justice incident to a rapidly changing civilization, resort to legislation has latterly been had with increasing frequency. * * *
>
> Courts are ill-equipped to make the investigations which should precede a determination of the limitations which should be set upon any property right in news or of the circumstances under which news gathered by a private agency should be deemed affected with a public interest. Courts would be powerless to prescribe the detailed regulations essential to full enjoyment of the rights conferred or to introduce the machinery required for enforcement of such regulations. Considerations such as these should lead

in American Jurisprudence, 15 Cardozo L. Rev. 601 (1993); Jan Vetter, *Postwar Legal Scholarship on Judicial Decision Making*, 33 J. Legal Educ. 412 (1983).

us to decline to establish a new rule of law in the effort to redress a newly-disclosed wrong, although the propriety of some remedy appears to be clear.

Thus, Brandeis deepened Holmes's critique of the *Lochner* judiciary: its decisions were not only analytically misleading, poor policy choices, and undemocratic, but also reflected a power grabbiness that was beyond the competence of the judiciary and indeed dangerously debilitating to the entire system of government.

Frankfurter and his colleague James Landis applied this idea of institutional specialization to develop a defense of the key feature of the modern regulatory state: lawmaking by agencies. Frankfurter maintained that the government's aspiration to develop useful policies depended not only upon the enactment of good legislation and judicial deference to those legislative judgments (Holmesian points), but much more upon their elaboration and application by an expert administration. Neither the legislature nor the judiciary was competent to make all the technical, fact-bound judgments necessary for the regulatory process, tasks an agency filled with specially trained experts was particularly competent to fulfill. Expertise not only solved problems, but offered neutral criteria for the solution of problems, which obviated democratic theory concerns with broad legislative delegations to agencies. This is, of course, precisely what happened during the New Deal, which Brandeis defended within the Court, Frankfurter helped craft as an adviser to the President, and Landis (just after his appointment as Dean at Harvard) defended in Yale's 1938 Storrs Lectures on *The Administrative Process*.

A. THE LEGAL PROCESS MATERIALS, 1940s–50s

The consensus about public law issues reached by intellectuals between 1938 and 1941 was reflected in Supreme Court decisions, law review articles, and teaching materials dealing with statutory issues. This consensus gave rise to "legal process theory." Inspired by ideas about statutory interpretation in the context of governance developed by Louis Brandeis and Felix Frankfurter and by the New Deal's expansion in the role of government, a new generation of intellectuals—Willard Hurst (Wisconsin), Henry Hart and Lon Fuller (Harvard), Ernest Gellhorn and Herbert Wechsler (Columbia), Alex Bickel and Harry Wellington (Yale), and Max Radin (Berkeley)—advanced an approach to statutory interpretation that avoided the rigidity of mechanical adherence to the plain meaning rule (*Caminetti*) and the historical ambulance-chasing of legislative intent (*Holy Trinity*).

An early classic, Lon Fuller's *The Case of the Speluncean Explorers*, 62 Harv. L. Rev. 616 (1949), started with a lurid hypothetical: a group of cave explorers were trapped in a cave for 20 days; to survive they drew lots, and the loser (Roger Whetmore) was killed and eaten; the survivors were convicted of murder. Should the murder statute allow such a prosecution? Judge Foster agreed that the killing of Roger Whetmore "violates the literal wording of the statute which declares that he who 'shall willfully take the life of another' is a murderer. But one of the most ancient bits of legal wisdom is the saying that a man may break the letter of the law without breaking the law itself. Every proposition of positive law, whether contained in a statute or a judicial precedent, is to be interpreted reasonably, in the light of its evident purpose." The legal process premise of Foster's judgment was that government (i.e., the New Deal) is and ought to be dedicated to solving social and economic problems. Government is pervasively *purposive,* a premise that was an explicit theme of the Hart and Sacks materials that follow.

"One of the principal objects underlying any criminal legislation is that of deterring men from crime. Now it is apparent that if it were declared to be the law that a killing in self-defense is murder such a rule could not operate in a deterrent manner. A man whose life is threatened will repel his aggressor, whatever the law may say. Looking therefore to the broad purposes of criminal legislation, we may safely declare that this statute was not intended to apply to cases of self-defense. * * * The line of reasoning I have applied above raises no question of fidelity to enacted law, though it may possibly raise a question of the distinction between intelligent and unintelligent fidelity. No superior wants a servant who lacks the capacity to read between the lines," lectured Justice Foster.

In the Case of the Speluncean Explorers, however, Foster was outvoted, 3–2. The primary opinion to uphold the murder conviction was that of Judge Keen. He rejected Foster's conflation of law and morality, based on "the supremacy of the legislative branch of our government. From that principle flows the obligation of the judiciary to enforce faithfully the written law, and to interpret that law in accordance with its plain meaning without reference to our personal desires or our individual conceptions of justice." Keen also sounded a legal process theme, when he questioned the institutional competence of the judiciary to engage in the kind of instrumental (i.e., purpose-means) reasoning called for by his purposive colleague.

At the same time Fuller was publishing his story, his colleague Henry Hart (a protégé of Felix Frankfurter as a student and a law clerk for Louis Brandeis after graduating from Harvard Law) was developing "Legislation" materials that were premised on the same themes of purposive governance, the key role played by process, and institutional competence.[20] In the 1950s, Hart was joined by Albert Sacks (a protégé of Hart as a student and a law clerk for Frankfurter after graduating from Harvard Law), and together they developed "The Legal Process," whose final, but still "tentative," draft came together in 1958.

Hart and Sacks posited a New Deal-inspired theory of society different from traditional liberal (social contract) theory. Central to society is people's recognition of "the fact of their interdependence with other human beings and the community of interest that grows out of it. So recognizing, people form themselves into groups for the protection and advancement of their common interests * * *." Hart & Sacks, *The Legal Process,* 2 (1994 ed.). The state is one of several institutions thus formed, but it is also the "overriding general purpose group" which has the greatest power, and the greatest responsibility, for "establishing, maintaining and perfecting the conditions necessary for community life to perform its role in the complete development of man." *Id.* at 102. In accord with this activist view of the state, Hart and Sacks posited: "Law is a doing of something, a purposive activity, a continuous striving to solve the basic problems of social living." *Id.* at 148.

---

[20]   William Eskridge Jr. & Philip P. Frickey, *The Making of* The Legal Process, 107 Harv. L. Rev. 2031 (1994).

Law's purposiveness generated Hart and Sacks' theory of "reasoned elaboration." *Id.* at 145–52. General directives often do not transparently tell officials and citizens what to do in specific situations, but Hart and Sacks sharply disputed the realist claim that this lack of easy transparency meant that the official simply imposed a political interpretation on the general directive. To the contrary, an official applying a "general directive arrangement" must "elaborate the arrangement in a way which is consistent with the other established applications of it" and "must do so in a way which best serves the principles and policies it expresses." *Id.* at 147. Hart and Sacks extended this idea to legal interpretation. A judge interpreting common law precedents has a responsibility to draw from those precedents some rule, principle, or standard, a responsibility that is only fulfilled if the judge reads the precedents, and the law generally, to figure out what purposes they serve. *Id.* at 397–403. A judge interpreting a statute must first identify the purpose of the statute, what policy or principle it embodies, and then reason toward the interpretation most consistent with that policy or principle. *Id.* at 148–50, 1149–71.

Among the earliest students of these materials were future Justices Ruth Bader Ginsburg, Antonin Scalia, Stephen Breyer, David Souter, and Anthony Kennedy. The Hart and Sacks theory of statutory interpretation is laid out, in detail, in the following excerpt.

HENRY HART JR. AND ALBERT SACKS, THE LEGAL PROCESS: BASIC PROBLEMS IN THE MAKING AND APPLICATION OF LAW

pp. 1374–80 (William Eskridge Jr. & Philip Frickey eds., 1994).[21]

Note on the Rudiments of Statutory Interpretation

A. The General Nature of the Task of Interpretation

The function of the court in interpreting a statute is to decide what meaning ought to be given to the directions of the statute in the respects relevant to the case before it. * * *

B. The Mood in Which the Task Should Be Done

In trying to discharge this function the court should:

1. Respect the position of the legislature as the chief policy-determining agency of the society, subject only to the limitations of the constitution under which it exercises its powers; * * *

5. Be mindful of the nature of law and of the fact that every statute is a part of the law and partakes of the qualities of law, and particularly of the quality of striving for even-handed justice.

C. A Concise Statement of the Task

In interpreting a statute a court should:

1. Decide what purpose ought to be attributed to the statute and to any subordinate provision of it which may be involved; and then

---

21   Reprinted by permission of the editors of the materials.

2.   Interpret the words of the statute immediately in question so as to carry out the purpose as best it can, making sure, however, that it does not give the words either—

(a) a meaning they will not bear, or

(b) a meaning which would violate any established policy of clear statement.

D.   The Double Role of the Words as Guides to Interpretation

* * * When the words fit with all the relevant elements of their context to convey a single meaning, as applied to the matter at hand, the mind of the interpreter moves to a confident conclusion almost instantaneously * * *.

Interpretation requires a conscious effort when the words do not fit with their context to convey any single meaning. It is in such case that the words will be seen to play a double part, first, as a factor together with relevant elements of the context in the formulation of hypotheses about possible purposes, and, second, as a separately limiting factor in checking the hypotheses.

E.   The Meaning the Words Will Bear * * *

The words of the statute are what the legislature has enacted as law, and all that it has the power to enact. Unenacted intentions or wishes cannot be given effect as law.

In deciding whether words will bear a particular meaning, a court needs to be linguistically wise and not naive. It needs to understand, especially, that meaning depends upon context. But language is a social institution. Humpty Dumpty was wrong when he said that you can make words mean whatever you want them to mean.

The language belongs to the whole society and not to the legislature in office for the time being. Courts on occasion can correct mistakes, as by inserting or striking out a negative, when it is completely clear from the context that a mistake has been made. But they cannot permit the legislative process, and all the other processes which depend upon the integrity of language, to be subverted by the misuse of words. * * *

* * * [T]he proposition that words must not be given a meaning they will not bear operates almost wholly to *prevent* rather than to *compel* expansion of the scope of statutes. The meaning of words can almost always be narrowed if the context seems to call for narrowing.

F.   Policies of Clear Statement * * *

Like the first requirement just considered that words must bear the meaning given them, these policies of clear statement may on occasion operate to defeat the actual, consciously held intention of particular legislators, or of the members of the legislature generally. * * * But the requirement should be thought of as constitutionally imposed. The policies have been judicially developed to promote objectives of the legal system which transcend the wishes of any particular session of the legislature. * * *

Two policies of clear statement call for particular mention.

[Handwritten margin note, top right: words marking boundary between crim + non-crim must be extra clear]

The first of these * * * requires that words which mark the boundary between criminal and non-criminal conduct should speak with more than ordinary clearness. This policy has special force when the conduct on the safe side of the line is not, in the general understanding of the community, morally blameworthy.

[Handwritten margin note, left: ② Forbids a court to understand Legi. As Directing a departure from a prevailing principle or policy of the law generally]

The second forbids a court to understand the legislature as directing a departure from a generally prevailing principle or policy of the law unless it does so clearly. This policy has special force when the departure is so great as to raise a serious question of constitutional power. * * *

G. The Attribution of Purpose

[Hart and Sacks emphasize the complexity of the task. A statute may have several purposes, and different purposes may press the interpreter in different directions. Also, the relevant "purpose" includes both the immediate policy objective as well as "a larger and subtler purpose as to how the particular statute is to be fitted into the legal system as a whole."]

[Handwritten margin note: PURPOSE — immediate policy objective + Larger subtler Purpose. statute w/in whole Legal System]

In determining the more immediate purpose which ought to be attributed to a statute * * * a court should try to put itself in imagination in the position of the legislature which enacted the measure.

The court, however, should not do this in the mood of a cynical political observer, taking account of all the short-run currents of political expedience that swirl around any legislative session.

It should assume, unless the contrary unmistakably appears, that the legislature was made up of reasonable persons pursuing reasonable purposes reasonably. * * *

[The court should follow the approach of *Heydon's Case*.] Why would reasonable men, confronted with the law as it was, have enacted this new law to replace it? * * *

The most reliable guides to an answer will be found in the instances of unquestioned application of the statute. Even in the case of a new statute there almost invariably *are* such instances, in which, because of the perfect fit of words and context, the meaning seems unmistakable.

Once these points of reference are established, they throw a double light. The purposes necessarily implied in them illuminate facets of the general purpose. At the same time they provide a basis for reasoning by analogy to the disputed application in hand. * * * What is crucial here is the realization that law is being made, and that law is not supposed to be irrational. * * *

[Hart and Sacks urge that "the whole context of the statute" should be examined, including the "state of the law" both before and after enactment, "general public knowledge" of the mischief to be remedied, and published legislative history as it sheds light on the statute's general purpose.]

The judicial, administrative, and popular construction of a statute, subsequent to its enactment, are all relevant in attributing a purpose to it.

The court's own prior interpretations of a statute in related applications should be accepted, on the principle of *stare decisis*, unless they are manifestly out of accord with other indications of purpose. * * *

H.   Interpreting the Words to Carry Out the Purpose * * *

The main burden of the [interpretive] task should be carried by the institution (court or administrative agency) which has the first-line responsibility for applying the statute authoritatively.

This agency should give sympathetic attention to indications in the legislative history of the lines of contemplated growth, if the history is available. It should give weight to popular construction of self-operating elements of the statute, if that is uniform. Primarily, it should strive to develop a coherent and reasoned pattern of applications intelligibly related to the general purpose. * * *

An interpretation by an administrative agency charged with first-line responsibility for the authoritative application of the statute should be accepted by the court as conclusive, if it is consistent with the purpose properly to be attributed to the statute, and if it has been arrived at with regard to the factors which should be taken into account in elaborating it.

PROBLEMS APPLYING A PURPOSE-BASED APPROACH TO STATUTORY INTERPRETATION

Problem 5-3. Spelunceans and Other Cases Revisited. Antonin Scalia was a star student of Hart and Sacks, and he would have echoed the Keen arguments in *Speluncean Explorers*. How might the young Nino Scalia have justified the Keen result under the premises of "The Legal Process," a course he thoroughly enjoyed? On today's Court, you might substitute Neil Gorsuch, also a Harvard Law graduate and a textualist. Also, how would Hart and Sacks have analyzed the statutory issue in *Holy Trinity*? *Weber*? (Hint: they would certainly have justified their conclusion somewhat differently than Justices Brewer and Brennan did.)

Problem 5-4. The Case of the Personating Voter. A British statute provides criminal penalties for a person who willfully, fraudulently, and with intent to affect the result in an election "personate[s] any person entitled to vote at such election." The defendant, Whiteley, is charged with having "personated" Marston, a person who had been entitled to vote at an election of guardians for the township of Bradford; Marston was a ratepayer listed in the proper book and was authorized to vote at the election. Marston had died before the election, and Whiteley delivered a vote ostensibly signed by Marston to the proper voting personnel. The dictionary defines "personate" as meaning "to act or play the part of a character in a drama or the like." There is no relevant legislative history.

How would Hart and Sacks decide such a case? Before you answer, try their suggestion of figuring out the statute's purpose by posing various situations, starting with the "core" of the statutory policy and radiating out with variations. Compare *The Legal Process* 1116–26 (1994 ed.), with *Whiteley v. Chappel*, [1868] 4 L.R.Q.B. 147.

B. IMPLICATIONS OF AND DEBATES WITHIN LEGAL PROCESS THEORY, 1950s–80s

The legal process methodology was the dominant mode for thinking about statutes for a generation and, in fact, remains highly relevant to issues of statutory interpretation.[22] At the very same time Lon Fuller, Henry Hart, and other scholars were crystallizing their purposive theory, it was being written into the U.S. Reports. Consider the analysis of Justice Stanley Reed in *United States v. American Trucking Associations*, 310 U.S. 534, 543 (1940):

> There is, of course, no more persuasive evidence of the purpose of a statute than the words by which the legislature undertook to give expression to its wishes. Often these words are sufficient in and of themselves to determine the purpose of the legislation. In such cases we have followed their plain meaning. When that meaning has led to absurd or futile results, however, this Court has looked beyond the words to the purpose of the Act. Frequently, however, even when the plain meaning did not produce absurd results but merely an unreasonable one "plainly at variance with the policy of the legislation as a whole" this Court has followed that purpose, rather than the literal words. When aid to construction of the meaning of words, as used in the statute, is available, there certainly can be no "rule of law" which forbids its use, however clear the words may appear on "superficial examination."

The Supreme Court in the 1950s and 1960s generally followed this approach, but not without some debate as to how far to carry out purposive analysis. For example, *Schwegmann Bros. v. Calvert Distillers Corp.*, 341 U.S. 384 (1951), contained a debate among the Justices as to whether the Court's responsibility to apply the statute's purpose (as Justice Douglas' plurality opinion did) could trump the original legislative expectations (Justice Frankfurter's dissenting opinion argued not). Justice Jackson's concurring opinion relied solely on the statutory text: because its meaning was plain, he did not care much about the original legislative intent.

As the debate in *Schwegmann* illustrated, the judges and lawyers who have deployed legal process arguments have followed more than one path. Two contesting strains within legal process thinking have diverged into competing schools of thought.[23] One strain, represented by Judge Foster in Speluncean Explorers, emphasizes statutory purposes and sees judges and agencies as helpful partners as well as normative updaters in the ongoing statutory enterprise. The other strain, represented by Judge Keen, emphasizes the rule-of-law virtues in following statutory plain meanings and the greater institutional competence of the legislature to make and update public policy. See how these legal process debates play out in the

---

[22] On the robustness of legal process thought for current theorizing, see, e.g., Stephen Breyer, *Making Our Democracy Work: A Judge's View* (2010); John Manning, *Justice Ginsburg and the New Legal Process*, 127 Harv. L. Rev. 455 (2013); Nicholas Parrillo, *Leviathan and Interpretive Revolution: The Administrative State, the Judiciary, and the Rise of Legislative History, 1890–1950*, 123 Yale L.J. 266 (2014); Daniel Rodriguez, *The Substance of the New Legal Process*, 77 Calif. L. Rev. 919 (1989) (book review); Edward Rubin, *Legal Reasoning, Legal Process and the Judiciary as an Institution*, 85 Calif. L. Rev. 265 (1997) (book review).

[23] This is the argument of William Eskridge Jr. & Gary Peller, *The New Public Law Movement: Moderation as a Postmodern Cultural Form*, 89 Mich. L. Rev. 707 (1991).

following cases: What role should statutory precedents play in the interpretive enterprise? When should judges overrule erroneous precedents? May judges correct what they consider to be legislative "mistakes"? Can courts "update" statutes or read them "dynamically"? To what extent should judges "bend" statutes in light of larger public values?

1. The Role of Precedent and *Stare Decisis* in Statutory Interpretation

Hart and Sacks understood statutory law as an evolving process of policy elaboration. The legislature determined the institutional roles of other officials. For example, the "reasoned elaboration" of American railroad regulation has been charged to agencies rather than judges. The Affordable Care Act of 2010 is a recent example. In the Sherman Act of 1891 and Title VII of the Civil Rights Act of 1964, in contrast, Congress vested the primary power of reasoned elaboration to judges. For such "common law statutes," judicial precedent will exercise overwhelming influence on how the statute is interpreted in the world. And even where primary authority has been vested with an agency, judicial review of the agency's interpretations will also have precedential effect.

As Hart and Sacks recognized, you cannot have a theory of statutory interpretation without having a theory of judicial and administrative precedent. (Chapter 9 will provide an extensive introduction to the latter.) In the Anglo-American tradition, *stare decisis* exercises a tremendous influence, because a judge is supposed to follow precedent even when she would have decided the issue differently. "Indeed, where there is an authoritative precedent on point, that precedent is more immediately important than the ordinary meaning that today's judge might have otherwise found." William Eskridge Jr., *Interpreting Law: A Primer on How to Interpret Statutes and the Constitution* 141 (2016); see Neil Duxbury, *The Nature and Authority of Precedent* (2008); Michael Gerhardt, *The Power of Precedent* (2008); Frederick Schauer, *Precedent*, 39 Stan. L. Rev. 571 (1987); Lawrence Solan, *Precedent in Statutory Interpretation*, 94 N.C.L. Rev. 1165 (2016).[24]

There are rule of law reasons to follow precedents with which one disagrees. "To the extent that statutory interpretation proceeds through judge-made precedent (a phenomenon that varies from statute to statute), *stare decisis* commits our legal system not only to continuity of legal rules, but also to incrementalism in modifying, narrowing, expanding, or updating them. Relatedly, *stare decisis* promises greater predictability and certainty in the application of law and probably delivers significantly greater predictability, especially in the early stages of a statute's application. Typically, legislators opt for broad terminology whose application is not

---

[24]   For classic treatments of precedent in common law and constitutional adjudication, see Benjamin Cardozo, *The Nature of the Judicial Process* (1921) (the Storrs Lectures); Gary Lawson, *The Constitutional Case Against Precedent*, 17 Harv. J.L. & Pub. Pol'y 23 (1994); Henry Paul Monaghan, *Stare Decisis and Constitutional Adjudication*, 88 Colum. L. Rev. 723 (1988); Christopher Peters, *Foolish Consistency: On Equality, Integrity, and Justice in Stare Decisis*, 105 Yale L.J. 2031 (1996); David Shapiro, *The Role of Precedent in Constitutional Adjudication: An Introspection*, 86 Tex. L. Rev. 929 (2008); David Strauss, *Common Law Constitutional Interpretation,* 63 U. Chi. L. Rev. 877 (1996).

easily predictable—and the passage of time produces more ambiguities as new and unanticipated circumstances present themselves." Eskridge, *Interpreting Law*, 143.[25]

As with the Sherman Act and Title VII, the accumulation of precedent creates a coherent regime of rules that private parties as well as government institutions can rely on when they make plans. From an institutionalist perspective, *stare decisis* constrains judges, who will not only follow precedent, but may be guided by the reasoning as well. Lewis Powell Jr., Stare Decisis *and Judicial Restraint*, 47 Wash. & Lee L. Rev. 281 (1990). "*Stare decisis* also promises to reduce the discretion of the appellate judges who actually decide the first case arising under [a] statute, even if there are no relevant statutory precedents directly constraining them. How is that? The judges deciding [the first case] know that the rule they announce will be binding on lower courts and on themselves for the foreseeable future, and so they have an incentive to be cautious when announcing the rule and suggesting its scope. *Stare decisis* thus motivates appellate judges to announce a rule that is not only grounded in general principles and legislative policy, determinable by any judge, but is also narrowly tailored to resolve the case and reach no further than needed or desirable. This is why appellate judges are, famously, interested in hypotheticals beyond the facts of the case at hand. They want to know what implications for future cases logically follow from each chain of reasoning that they might invoke to decide the case before them." Eskridge, *Interpreting Law*, 144.

Stare decisis in statutory cases also imposes costs on the legal system. The more actors rely on judicial decisions, the less they rely on the text created by the legislature, and there is a danger that common law statutes will become nothing more than common law under the cover of statutory interpretation. Also, fidelity to ancient precedents might introduce ossification into the law. Recall that Hart and Sacks were open to overruling precedents that undermined the purpose of the statute. A theory of statutory interpretation needs to balance the rule of law benefits of stability over time, with the democratic accountability and governance costs of maintaining obsolete judge-made rules.

FLOOD V. KUHN

Supreme Court of the United States, 1972.
407 U.S. 258, 92 S.Ct. 2099, 32 L.Ed.2d 728.

MR. JUSTICE BLACKMUN delivered the opinion of the Court.

[I.   *The* Game] It is a century and a quarter since the New York Nine defeated the Knickerbockers 23 to 1 on Hoboken's Elysian Fields June 19, 1846, with Alexander Jay Cartwright as the instigator and the umpire. The teams were amateur, but the contest marked a significant date in baseball's beginnings. That early game led ultimately to the development of professional baseball and its tightly organized structure.

The Cincinnati Red Stockings came into existence in 1869 upon an outpouring of local pride. With only one Cincinnatian on the payroll, this professional team

---

[25]   Randy Kozel, *Precedent and Reliance*, 62 Emory L.J. 1459, 1481 (2013); Richard Re, *Narrowing Precedents in the Supreme Court*, 114 Colum. L. Rev. 1861 (2014).

traveled over 11,000 miles that summer, winning 56 games and tying one. Shortly thereafter, on St. Patrick's Day in 1871, the National Association of Professional Baseball Players was founded and the professional league was born.

The ensuing colorful days are well known. The ardent follower and the student of baseball know of General Abner Doubleday; the formation of the National League in 1876; Chicago's supremacy in the first year's competition under the leadership of Al Spalding and with Cap Anson at third base; the formation of the American Association and then of the Union Association in the 1880's; the introduction of Sunday baseball; interleague warfare with cut-rate admission prices and player raiding; the development of the reserve "clause"; the emergence in 1885 of the Brotherhood of Professional Ball Players, and in 1890 of the Players League; the appearance of the American League, or "junior circuit," in 1901, rising from the minor Western Association; the first World Series in 1903, disruption in 1904, and the Series' resumption in 1905; the short-lived Federal League on the majors' scene during World War I years; the troublesome and discouraging episode of the 1919 Series; the home run ball; the shifting of franchises; the expansion of the leagues; the installation in 1965 of the major league draft of potential new players; and the formation of the Major League Baseball Players Association in 1966.

Then there are the many names, celebrated for one reason or another, that have sparked the diamond and its environs and that have provided tinder for recaptured thrills, for reminiscence and comparisons, and for conversation and anticipation in-season and off-season: Ty Cobb, Babe Ruth, Tris Speaker, Walter Johnson, Henry Chadwick, Eddie Collins, Lou Gehrig, Grover Cleveland Alexander, Rogers Hornsby, Harry Hooper, Goose Goslin, Jackie Robinson, Honus Wagner, Joe McCarthy, John McGraw, Deacon Phillippe, Rube Marquard, Christy Mathewson, Tommy Leach, Big Ed Delahanty, Davy Jones, Germany Schaefer, King Kelly, Big Dan Brouthers, Wahoo Sam Crawford, Wee Willie Keeler, Big Ed Walsh, Jimmy Austin, Fred Snodgrass, Satchel Paige, Hugh Jennings, Fred Merkle, Iron Man McGinnity, Three-Finger Brown, Harry and Stan Coveleski, Connie Mack, Al Bridwell, Red Ruffing, Amos Rusie, Cy Young, Smokey Joe Wood, Chief Meyers, Chief Bender, Bill Klem, Hans Lobert, Johnny Evers, Joe Tinker, Roy Campanella, Miller Huggins, Rube Bressler, Dazzy Vance, Edd Roush, Bill Wambsganss, Clark Griffith, Branch Rickey, Frank Chance, Cap Anson, Nap Lajoie, Sad Sam Jones, Bob O'Farrell, Lefty O'Doul, Bobby Veach, Willie Kamm, Heinie Groh, Lloyd and Paul Waner, Stuffy McInnis, Charles Comiskey, Roger Bresnahan, Bill Dickey, Zack Wheat, George Sisler, Charlie Gehringer, Eppa Rixey, Harry Heilmann, Fred Clarke, Dizzy Dean, Hank Greenberg, Pie Traynor, Rube Waddell, Bill Terry, Carl Hubbell, Old Hoss Radbourne, Moe Berg, Rabbit Maranville, Jimmie Foxx, Lefty Grove. The list seems endless.

And one recalls the appropriate reference to the "World Serious," attributed to Ring Lardner, Sr.; Ernest L. Thayer's "Casey at the Bat"; the ring of "Tinker to Evers to Chance"; and all the other happenings, habits, and superstitions about and around baseball that made it the "national pastime" or, depending upon the point of view, "the great American tragedy."

[Curt Flood, the petitioner, was a star center fielder with the St. Louis Cardinals. Under the "reserve clause" in his contract he was required to play for the Cardinals, the Cardinals could unilaterally assign his contract to another team, and the Cardinals could annually renew that contract so long as the minimum salary was provided. In October 1969, the Cards traded Flood to the Philadelphia Phillies. Flood refused to report to the Phillies and asked Bowie Kuhn, the Commissioner of Baseball, to be allowed to negotiate a contract with the team of his choice. Kuhn refused. Flood filed a lawsuit claiming, *inter alia*, that the reserve clause violated the antitrust laws because it prevented him from contracting with the team of his choice. Lower courts denied relief based on Supreme Court precedents holding baseball immune from the antitrust laws.]

[IVA. *The Legal Background.*] *Federal Baseball Club v. National League*, 259 U.S. 200 (1922), was a suit for treble damages instituted by a member of the Federal League (Baltimore) against the National and American Leagues and others. The plaintiff obtained a verdict in the trial court, but the Court of Appeals reversed. The main brief filed by the plaintiff with this Court discloses that it was strenuously argued, among other things, that the business in which the defendants were engaged was interstate commerce; that the interstate relationship among the several clubs, located as they were in different States, was predominant; that organized baseball represented an investment of colossal wealth; that it was an engagement in moneymaking; that gate receipts were divided by agreement between the home club and the visiting club; and that the business of baseball was to be distinguished from the mere playing of the game as a sport for physical exercise and diversion.

Mr. Justice Holmes, in speaking succinctly for a unanimous Court, said:

"The business is giving exhibitions of base ball, which are purely state affairs. * * * But the fact that in order to give the exhibitions the Leagues must induce free persons to cross state lines and must arrange and pay for their doing so is not enough to change the character of the business. * * * [T]he transport is a mere incident, not the essential thing. That to which it is incident, the exhibition, although made, for money would not be called trade or commerce in the commonly accepted use of those words. As it is put by the defendant, personal effort, not related to production, is not a subject of commerce. That which in its consummation is not commerce does not become commerce among the States because the transportation that we have mentioned takes place. To repeat the illustrations given by the Court below, a firm of lawyers sending out a member to argue a case, or the Chautauqua lecture bureau sending out lecturers, does not engage in such commerce because the lawyer or lecturer goes to another State.

"If we are right the plaintiff's business is to be described in the same way and the restrictions by contract that prevented the plaintiff from getting players to break their bargains and the other conduct charged against the defendants were not an interference with commerce among the States." 259 U.S., at 208–209. * * *

In the years that followed, baseball continued to be subject to intermittent antitrust attack. The courts, however, rejected these challenges on the authority of

Federal Baseball. In some cases stress was laid, although unsuccessfully, on new factors such as the development of radio and television with their substantial additional revenues to baseball. For the most part, however, the Holmes opinion was generally and necessarily accepted as controlling authority. And in the 1952 Report of the Subcommittee on Study of Monopoly Power of the House Committee on the Judiciary, H.R.Rep. No. 2002, 82d Cong., 2d Sess., 229, it was said, in conclusion:

> "On the other hand the overwhelming preponderance of the evidence established baseball's need for some sort of reserve clause. Baseball's history shows that chaotic conditions prevailed when there was no reserve clause. Experience points to no feasible substitute to protect the integrity of the game or to guarantee a comparatively even competitive struggle. The evidence adduced at the hearings would clearly not justify the enactment of legislation flatly condemning the reserve clause."

C.   The Court granted certiorari in [*Toolson, Kowalski,* and *Corbett*], and, by a short per curiam (Warren, C. J., and Black, Frankfurter, Douglas, Jackson, Clark, and Minton, JJ.), affirmed the judgments of the respective courts of appeals in those three cases. *Toolson v. New York Yankees, Inc.,* 346 U.S. 356 (1953). *Federal Baseball* was cited as holding "that the business of providing public baseball games for profit between clubs of professional baseball players was not within the scope of the federal antitrust laws," and:

> "Congress has had the ruling under consideration but has not seen fit to bring such business under these laws by legislation having prospective effect. The business has thus been left for thirty years to develop, on the understanding that it was not subject to existing antitrust legislation. The present cases ask us to overrule the prior decision and, with retrospective effect, hold the legislation applicable. We think that if there are evils in this field which now warrant application to it of the antitrust laws it should be by legislation. Without re-examination of the underlying issues, the judgments below are affirmed on the authority of *Federal Baseball Club of Baltimore v. National League of Professional Baseball Clubs, supra,* so far as that decision determines that Congress had no intention of including the business of baseball within the scope of the federal antitrust laws."

This quotation reveals four reasons for the Court's affirmance of *Toolson* and its companion cases: (a) Congressional awareness for three decades of the Court's ruling in *Federal Baseball,* coupled with congressional inaction. (b) The fact that baseball was left alone to develop for that period upon the understanding that the reserve system was not subject to existing federal antitrust laws. (c) A reluctance to overrule *Federal Baseball* with consequent retroactive effect. (d) A professed desire that any needed remedy be provided by legislation rather than by court decree. The emphasis in *Toolson* was on the determination, attributed even to *Federal Baseball,* that Congress had no intention to include baseball within the reach of the federal antitrust laws. * * *

[Justice Blackmun discussed three subsequent opinions. In *United States v. Shubert,* 348 U.S. 222 (1955), the Court reversed a dismissal of an antitrust suit against defendants engaged in theatrical attractions across the country, indicating that *Federal Baseball* and *Toolson* gave no general antitrust exemption for businesses built around local exhibitions. Similarly, the Court in *United States v. International Boxing Club*, 348 U.S. 236 (1955), reversed a district court for dismissing the antitrust complaint; the Court denied that *Federal Baseball* gave sports other than baseball an exemption from the antitrust laws. Finally, in *Radovich v. National Football League*, 352 U.S. 445 (1957), the Supreme Court reversed the lower courts for dismissing another antitrust complaint against a football league. Justice Clark's opinion for the Court noted that *Toolson* upheld baseball's immunity, "because it was concluded that more harm would be done in overruling *Federal Base Ball* than in upholding a ruling which at best was of dubious validity." The opinion said:]

> "All this, combined with the flood of litigation that would follow its repudiation, the harassment that would ensue, and the retroactive effect of such a decision, led the Court to the practical result that it should sustain the unequivocal line of authority reaching over many years.

> "[S]ince *Toolson* and *Federal Base Ball* are still cited as controlling authority in antitrust actions involving other fields of business, we now specifically limit the rule there established to the facts there involved, *i.e.*, the business of organized professional baseball. As long as the Congress continues to acquiesce we should adhere to—but not extend—the interpretation of the Act made in those cases. * * *

> "If this ruling is unrealistic, inconsistent, or illogical, it is sufficient to answer, aside from the distinctions between the businesses, that were we considering the question of baseball for the first time upon a clean slate we would have no doubts. But *Federal Base Ball* held the business of baseball outside the scope of the Act. No other business claiming the coverage of those cases has such an adjudication. We therefore, conclude that the orderly way to eliminate error or discrimination, if any there be, is by legislation and not by court decision. Congressional processes are more accommodative, affording the whole industry hearings and an opportunity to assist in the formulation of new legislation. The resulting product is therefore more likely to protect the industry and the public alike. The whole scope of congressional action would be known long in advance and effective dates for the legislation could be set in the future without the injustices of retroactivity and surprise which might follow court action."

Mr. Justice Frankfurter dissented essentially for the reasons stated in his dissent in *International Boxing*. Mr. Justice Harlan, joined by Mr. Justice Brennan, also dissented because he, too, was "unable to distinguish football from baseball." Here again the dissenting Justices did not call for the overruling of the baseball decisions. They merely could not distinguish the two sports and, out of respect for *stare decisis*, voted to affirm.

G.   Finally, in *Haywood v. National Basketball Assn.*, 401 U.S. 1204 (1971), Mr. Justice Douglas, in his capacity as Circuit Justice, reinstated a District Court's injunction *pendente lite* in favor of a professional basketball player and said, "Basketball * * * does not enjoy exemption from the antitrust laws."

H.   This series of decisions understandably spawned extensive commentary, some of it mildly critical and much of it not; nearly all of it looked to Congress for any remedy that might be deemed essential.

I.   Legislative proposals have been numerous and persistent. Since *Toolson* more than 50 bills have been introduced in Congress relative to the applicability or nonapplicability of the antitrust laws to baseball. A few of these passed one house or the other. Those that did would have expanded, not restricted, the reserve system's exemption to other professional league sports. And the Act of Sept. 30, 1961, Pub.L. 87–331, 75 Stat. 732, and the merger addition thereto effected by the Act of Nov. 8, 1966, Pub. L. 89–800, § 6(b), 80 Stat. 1515, 15 U.S.C. §§ 1291–1295, were also expansive rather than restrictive as to antitrust exemption.

[V.] In view of all this, it seems appropriate now to say that:

1.   Professional baseball is a business and it is engaged in interstate commerce.

2.   With its reserve system enjoying exemption from the federal antitrust laws, baseball is, in a very distinct sense, an exception and an anomaly. *Federal Baseball* and *Toolson* have become an aberration confined to baseball.

3.   Even though others might regard this as "unrealistic, inconsistent, or illogical," see *Radovich*, the aberration is an established one, and one that has been recognized not only in *Federal Baseball* and *Toolson*, but in *Shubert, International Boxing*, and *Radovich*, as well, a total of five consecutive cases in this Court. It is an aberration that has been with us now for half a century, one heretofore deemed fully entitled to the benefit of *stare decisis*, and one that has survived the Court's expanding concept of interstate commerce. It rests on a recognition and an acceptance of baseball's unique characteristics and needs.

4.   Other professional sports operating interstate—football, boxing, basketball, and, presumably, hockey and golf—are not so exempt.

5.   The advent of radio and television, with their consequent increased coverage and additional revenues, has not occasioned an overruling of *Federal Baseball* and *Toolson*.

6.   The Court has emphasized that since 1922 baseball, with full and continuing congressional awareness, has been allowed to develop and to expand unhindered by federal legislative action. Remedial legislation has been introduced repeatedly in Congress but none has ever been enacted. The Court, accordingly, has concluded that Congress as yet has had no intention to subject baseball's reserve system to the reach of the antitrust statutes. This, obviously, has been deemed to be something other than mere congressional silence and passivity.

7.   The Court has expressed concern about the confusion and the retroactivity problems that inevitably would result with a judicial overturning of *Federal Baseball*. It has voiced a preference that if any change is to be made, it come by legislative action that, by its nature, is only prospective in operation.

8.   The Court noted in *Radovich* that the slate with respect to baseball is not clean. Indeed, it has not been clean for half a century.

This emphasis and this concern are still with us. We continue to be loath, 50 years after *Federal Baseball* and almost two decades after *Toolson*, to overturn those cases judicially when Congress, by its positive inaction, has allowed those decisions to stand for so long and, far beyond mere inference and implication, has clearly evinced a desire not to disapprove them legislatively.

Accordingly, we adhere once again to *Federal Baseball* and *Toolson* and to their application to professional baseball. We adhere also to *International Boxing* and *Radovich* and to their respective applications to professional boxing and professional football. If there is any inconsistency or illogic in all this, it is an inconsistency and illogic of long standing that is to be remedied by the Congress and not by this Court. If we were to act otherwise, we would be withdrawing from the conclusion as to congressional intent made in *Toolson* and from the concerns as to retrospectivity therein expressed. Under these circumstances, there is merit in consistency even though some might claim that beneath that consistency is a layer of inconsistency.

* * * [W]hat the Court said in *Federal Baseball* in 1922 and what it said in *Toolson* in 1953, we say again here in 1972: the remedy, if any is indicated, is for congressional, and not judicial, action.

MR. JUSTICE WHITE joins in the judgment of the Court, and in all but Part I of the Court's opinion.

MR. JUSTICE POWELL took no part in the consideration or decision of this case.

MR. CHIEF JUSTICE BURGER, concurring.

I concur in all but Part I of the Court's opinion but, like Mr. Justice Douglas, I have grave reservations as to the correctness of *Toolson*; as he notes in his dissent, he joined that holding but has "lived to regret it." The error, if such it be, is one on which the affairs of a great many people have rested for a long time. Courts are not the forum in which this tangled web ought to be unsnarled. I agree with Mr. Justice Douglas that congressional inaction is not a solid base, but the least undesirable course now is to let the matter rest with Congress; it is time the Congress acted to solve this problem.

MR. JUSTICE DOUGLAS, with whom MR. JUSTICE BRENNAN concurs, dissenting.

This Court's decision in *Federal Baseball Club*, made in 1922, is a derelict in the stream of the law that we, its creator, should remove. Only a romantic view[1] of a rather dismal business account over the last 50 years would keep that derelict in midstream.

In 1922 the Court had a narrow, parochial view of commerce. With the demise of the old landmarks of that era, the whole concept of commerce has changed.

Under the modern [Commerce Clause] decisions, the power of Congress was recognized as broad enough to reach all phases of the vast operations of our national industrial system. An industry so dependent on radio and television as is baseball and gleaning vast interstate revenues (see H.R.Rep. No. 2002, 82d Cong., 2d Sess.,

---

[1]   While I joined the Court's opinion in *Toolson*, I have lived to regret it; and I would now correct what I believe to be its fundamental error.

4, 5 (1952)) would be hard put today to say with the Court in the *Federal Baseball Club* case that baseball was only a local exhibition, not trade or commerce.

Baseball is today big business that is packaged with beer, with broadcasting, and with other industries. The beneficiaries of the *Federal Baseball Club* decision are not the Babe Ruths, Ty Cobbs, and Lou Gehrigs.

The owners, whose records many say reveal a proclivity for predatory practices, do not come to us with equities. The equities are with the victims of the reserve clause. I use the word "victims" in the Sherman Act sense, since a contract which forbids anyone to practice his calling is commonly called an unreasonable restraint of trade.

If congressional inaction is our guide, we should rely upon the fact that Congress has refused to enact bills broadly exempting professional sports from antitrust regulation. H.R.Rep. No. 2002, 82nd Cong., 2d Sess. (1952). The only statutory exemption granted by Congress to professional sports concerns broadcasting rights. 15 U.S.C. §§ 1291–1295. I would not ascribe a broader exemption through inaction than Congress has seen fit to grant explicitly.

There can be no doubt "that were we considering the question of baseball for the first time upon a clean slate" we would hold it to be subject to federal antitrust regulation. *Radovich.* The unbroken silence of Congress should not prevent us from correcting our own mistakes.

MR. JUSTICE MARSHALL, with whom MR. JUSTICE BRENNAN joins, dissenting.

This is a difficult case because we are torn between the principle of *stare decisis* and the knowledge that the decisions in *Federal Baseball Club* and *Toolson* are totally at odds with more recent and better reasoned cases. * * * Has Congress acquiesced in our decisions in *Federal Baseball Club* and *Toolson*? I think not. Had the Court been consistent and treated all sports in the same way baseball was treated, Congress might have become concerned enough to take action. But, the Court was inconsistent, and baseball was isolated and distinguished from all other sports. In *Toolson* the Court refused to act because Congress had been silent. But the Court may have read too much into this legislative inaction.

Americans love baseball as they love all sports. Perhaps we become so enamored of athletics that we assume that they are foremost in the minds of legislators as well as fans. We must not forget, however, that there are only some 600 major league baseball players. Whatever muscle they might have been able to muster by combining forces with other athletes has been greatly impaired by the manner in which this Court has isolated them. It is this Court that has made them impotent, and this Court should correct its error.

We do not lightly overrule our prior constructions of federal statutes, but when our errors deny substantial federal rights, like the right to compete freely and effectively to the best of one's ability as guaranteed by the antitrust laws, we must admit our error and correct it. We have done so before and we should do so again here. See, *e.g., Blonder-Tongue Laboratories, Inc. v. University of Illinois Foundation,* 402 U.S. 313 (1971); *Boys Markets, Inc. v. Retail Clerks Union,* 398 U.S. 235, 241 (1970).

To the extent that there is concern over any reliance interests that club owners may assert, they can be satisfied by making our decision prospective only. Baseball should be covered by the antitrust laws beginning with this case and henceforth, unless Congress decides otherwise.

NOTES ON FLOOD AND THE "SUPER-STRONG" PRESUMPTION AGAINST OVERRULING STATUTORY PRECEDENTS

1. *Is There a Rationale for* Flood? It appears that every member of the Court thought that *Federal Baseball* was wrongly decided, yet a majority nevertheless applied the wrongheaded precedent. Is there something to Justice Blackmun's view that this is "an inconsistency and illogic of long standing" which might as well be perpetuated? One's initial reaction to Justice Blackmun's opinion might be that it is simply silly not to overrule discredited precedents. The same argument might have been made to the *Brown* Court not to overrule *Plessy v. Ferguson*, 163 U.S. 537 (1896). Justice Blackmun could respond that he would be more willing to overrule constitutional precedents, because Congress cannot easily correct such decisions. See *Burnet v. Coronado Oil and Gas Co.*, 285 U.S. 393, 406–07 (1932) (Brandeis, J., dissenting). Is this reasoning persuasive?

In strictly respecting *stare decisis*, the *Flood* Court notes "retrospectivity" problems that would inhere if it were to overturn *Toolson* and *Federal Baseball*, suggesting that the Court assumed that the industry had been relying on these precedents in conducting its affairs. Justice Marshall's dissenting opinion suggests the possibility of a "prospective" overruling, to take effect after the industry has time to revamp its rules and practices. Subsequently, the Supreme Court has held that Article III does not allow federal judges to overrule precedents prospectively; what makes adjudication distinctive is the idea that judges are "finding" preexisting law and not, like legislators and sometimes administrators, making new law. *Harper v. Virginia Dep't of Taxation*, 509 U.S. 86 (1993).

Could *Flood v. Kuhn* be an example of *stare nostalgia*? Consider Justice Blackmun's "Ode to Baseball" in Part I of the opinion. Was that an appropriate matter to be included in a judicial opinion? Were Chief Justice Burger and Justice White right in making a point of not joining Part I? (We think this is the only time in history that all of an opinion commanded a Court majority except for its statement of facts!)

The Court never returned to the *Flood* issue (maybe on the ground that, after *Federal Baseball, Toolson*, and *Flood*, three strikes and you're out?). Thwarted on antitrust grounds, the players' union agitated for change through interest arbitration. Five years after *Flood*, an arbitrator awarded free-agent status to two players; the collective bargaining between owners and the players' union that followed, with impasses sometimes resulting in strikes, led to labor agreements that provided players with significant freedom.

In the mid-1990s, following particularly acrimonious labor conflict, management agreed with the union to approach Congress jointly and request legislation effectively overriding *Flood*. Congress responded by enacting the Curt Flood Act of 1998, Pub. L. 105–297, 112 Stat. 2824. The statute subjects any business practices "directly relating to or affecting employment of major league baseball players * * * to the antitrust laws to the same extent such * * * practices * * * would be subject to the antitrust laws if engaged in by persons in any other professional sports business affecting interstate commerce." Drafted to avoid any application of the antitrust laws to such matters as franchise relocation, ticket prices, or the treatment of minor-league players, it is not clear that the statute changed the law in general or, in particular, provided any rights to players that they had not already achieved through collective bargaining. Nor did the override provide solace to Curt Flood, who died of cancer in 1997.[26]

2.   *When Is It Appropriate to Overrule a Statutory Precedent?* As *Flood* suggests, the Supreme Court will not routinely overrule a prior interpretation of a statute. Many state courts are even more emphatic that statutory precedents should rarely, or never (in some states), be overruled, since the legislature can change the statute.[27] Is it ever appropriate to overrule a statutory precedent?

In *Monell v. Department of Social Servs.*, 436 U.S. 658 (1978), the Supreme Court held that municipal corporations were "persons" subject to suit under § 1983 for depriving people of the "rights, privileges, or immunities secured by the Constitution and laws." The Court thereby overruled *Monroe v. Pape*, 365 U.S. 167 (1961), which had inferred that Congress meant to immunize municipalities when it rejected such a provision in the Civil Rights Act of 1871. The proposed provision would have held a municipal corporation liable for damage done to its inhabitants by private persons "riotously and tumultuously assembled" and was rejected (apparently) because the House of Representatives doubted that Congress had the constitutional power to impose that obligation. Justice Brennan argued that the Court misinterpreted the legislative history and that correction was appropriate because *Monroe* was in tension with subsequent decisions of the Court and with Congress's own actions.

Monell might be generalized. "Ultimately, statutory precedents are vulnerable to being overruled if (1) there has been an 'intervening development in the law' that has rendered that precedent 'irreconcilable with competing legal doctrines or policies,' (2) the precedent has become a 'positive detriment to coherence and consistency in the law,' either internally or in relation to policy objectives associated with other laws, and (3) the precedent has been proved outdated and contrary to [modern] understandings of justice and social welfare." Eskridge, *Interpreting Law*, 190; see *Planned Parenthood of Southeastern Pa. v. Casey*, 505 U.S. 833, 854–55 (1992) (joint opinion). Under that approach, why were *Federal Baseball* and *Toolson* not overruled in *Flood*?

3.   Stare Decisis *and the Sherman Act, Revisited.* The debate over the super-strong presumption of correctness for statutory precedents has intensified in the new millennium. Following Hart and Sacks, who strongly disapproved of *Toolson* for some of the reasons developed above, many legal process academics have endorsed a relaxation of the super-strong presumption, so that statutory precedents would be treated more like other precedents.[28] While the super-strong presumption of *stare decisis* for statutory

[26]   For the full story of the case, the arbitral resolution, and the override statute, see Brad Snyder, *A Well Paid Slave: Curt Flood's Fight For Free Agency in Professional Sports* (2007); Stephen Ross, *The Story of* Flood v. Kuhn (1972): *Dynamic Statutory Interpretation, At the Time*, in *Statutory Interpretation Stories* 36–57 (Eskridge, Frickey & Garrett eds., 2011).

[27]   Representative of this approach are *Williams v. Ray*, 246 S.E.2d 387 (Ga. App. 1978); *Williams v. Crickman*, 405 N.E.2d 799 (Ill. 1980); *Land Comm'r v. Hutton*, 307 So.2d 415 (Miss. 1974); *Higby v. Mahoney*, 396 N.E.2d 183 (N.Y. 1979); *Fulton v. Lavallee*, 265 A.2d 655 (R.I. 1970); *James v. Vernon Calhoun Packing Co.*, 498 S.W.2d 160 (Tex. 1973). But see, e.g., *Jepson v. Department of Labor and Indus.*, 573 P.2d 10 (Wash. 1977).

[28]   E.g., Reed Dickerson, *The Interpretation and Application of Statutes* 252–55 (1975); Amy Coney Barrett, *Statutory* Stare Decisis *in the Courts of Appeals,* 73 Geo. Wash. L. Rev. 317 (2005); Frank Easterbrook, *Stability and Reliability in Judicial Decisions*, 73 Corn. L. Rev. 422 (1988); William Eskridge Jr., *Overruling Statutory Precedents*, 76 Geo. L.J. 1361 (1988); Earl Maltz, *The Nature of Precedent*, 66 N.C. L. Rev. 367 (1988).

precedents remains entrenched in Supreme Court doctrine, e.g., *Kimble v. Marvel Entertainment, LLC,* 135 S.Ct. 2401 (2015), the Court does frequently overrule such precedents.

The Court has, for example, relaxed *stare decisis* in antitrust cases. Consider *State Oil Co. v. Khan,* 522 U.S. 3 (1997), where the Court unanimously overruled *Albrecht v. Herald Co.,* 390 U.S. 145 (1968), which had considered vertical maximum price fixing a per se antitrust violation, and replaced that approach with the "rule of reason." The Court dismissed any barrier created by *Toolson* and *Flood,* viewing those cases as having no import outside the peculiar context of baseball. That Congress had not reacted adversely to *Albrecht* "seems neither clearly to support nor to denounce" the holding of that case. The Court also concluded that *stare decisis* has somewhat less force in antitrust law because, "[i]n the area of antitrust law, there is a competing interest, well represented in this Court's decisions, in recognizing and adapting to changed circumstances and the lessons of accumulated experience. Thus, the general presumption that legislative changes should be left to Congress has less force with respect to the Sherman Act in light of the accepted view that Congress 'expected the courts to give shape to the statute's broad mandate by drawing on common-law tradition.' As we have explained, the term 'restraint of trade' * * * also 'invokes the common law itself, and not merely the static content that the common law had assigned to the term in 1890.'" Accord, *Leegin Creative Leather Products, Inc. v. PSKS, Inc.,* 551 U.S. 877 (2007) (invoking the idea that the Sherman Act is a common law statute). Should *Flood* be revisited in an appropriate case, such as a class action by consumers against price-fixing by organized baseball?

Patterson v. McLean Credit Union

491 U.S. 164 (1989).

Brenda Patterson brought a lawsuit against her former employer for workplace racial harassment. She based her claim on 42 U.S.C. § 1981, which prohibits discrimination on the basis of race in the making and enforcement of contracts. Her complaint was dismissed by the lower courts on the ground that it did not state a claim for relief under § 1981. On its own motion after receiving briefs in the case, the Supreme Court requested the parties to brief the issue whether § 1981 affords a remedy against private, as opposed to public, employers. *Runyon v. McCrary,* 427 U.S. 160 (1976), had interpreted § 1981 to provide such a remedy against private schools excluding children on the basis of race, and so the Court invited the parties to address the question whether *Runyon* should be "reconsidered." The Court's request stimulated a firestorm of protest from scholars, the press, and Members of Congress (who took the unusual step of submitting a brief on the issue).

In the end, the Court chose a somewhat more politique path. The opinion for the Court, written by **Justice Kennedy** and joined by the other four justices (Chief Justice Rehnquist and Justices White, Scalia, and O'Connor) who had requested rehearing, declined to overrule *Runyon* but also declined to extend it to workplace harassment claims. "We conclude * * * that no special justification has been shown for overruling *Runyon.* In cases where statutory precedents have been overruled, the primary reason for the Court's shift in position has been the intervening development of the law, through either the growth of judicial doctrine or further action taken by Congress. Where such

But see Lawrence Marshall, *"Let Congress Do It": The Case for an Absolute Rule of Statutory* Stare Decisis, 88 Mich. L. Rev. 177 (1989), who argues for an "absolute" rule of *stare decisis* in statutory cases.

changes have removed or weakened the conceptual underpinnings from the primary decision, or where the law has rendered the decision irreconcilable with competing legal doctrines or policies, the Court has not hesitated to overrule an earlier decision. Our decision in *Runyon* has not been undermined by subsequent changes or developments in the law.

"Another traditional justification for overruling a prior case is that a precedent may be a positive detriment to coherence and consistency in the law, either because of inherent confusion created by an unworkable decision, or because the decision poses a direct obstacle to the realization of important objectives embodied in other laws. In this regard, we do not find *Runyon* to be unworkable or confusing. * * *

"Finally, it has sometimes been said that a precedent becomes more vulnerable as it becomes outdated and after being ' "tested by experience, has been found to be inconsistent with the sense of justice or with the social welfare." ' *Runyon* (Stevens, J., concurring), quoting B. Cardozo, The Nature of the Judicial Process 149 (1921). Whatever the effect of this consideration may be in statutory cases, it offers no support for overruling *Runyon*. In recent decades, state and federal legislation has been enacted to prohibit private racial discrimination in many aspects of our society. Whether *Runyon*'s interpretation of section 1981 as prohibiting racial discrimination in the making and enforcement of private contracts is right or wrong as an original matter, it is certain that it is not inconsistent with the prevailing sense of justice in this country. To the contrary, *Runyon* is entirely consistent with our society's deep commitment to the eradication of discrimination based on a person's race or the color of his or her skin."

Although the Court reaffirmed its prior interpretation applying § 1981 to prohibit racial discrimination in the "mak[ing] and enforce[ment]" of private contracts, the 5–4 majority declined to find that racial harassment on the job is actionable. The majority reasoned that racial harassment did not impair Patterson's ability to "make" or "enforce" the employment contract and, hence, did not fall under § 1981's plain language.

Justice Brennan wrote a separate opinion concurring in the judgment, joined by Justices Marshall, Blackmun, and Stevens. They disagreed with the majority on the *Runyon* issue in three different ways. First, they argued that *Runyon* was correctly decided as an initial matter (a proposition not squarely addressed by the majority). Second, they argued that Congress had "ratified" *Runyon* (a) by failing to overturn the precedent even while Congress was overturning a number of other civil rights precedents in the late 1970s and 1980s, (b) by rejecting an amendment to the Civil Rights Act of 1964 inconsistent with *Runyon*, and (c) by relying on *Runyon* when it enacted an attorney's fees statute in 1976, 42 U.S.C. § 1988.

Third, the concurring Justices argued that the Court's refusal to apply *Runyon* to the instant case was a failure to take the precedent's authority seriously. If the Court really believed in the current policy and other reasons for reaffirming *Runyon*, they argued, the Court would have applied the precedent to Patterson's claims of racial harassment on the job. *Runyon* held that the statute made it illegal for the employer to refuse to contract with a black employee because of her race—but *Patterson* says the employer can then harass or fire her because of her race. Why are both acts not contract violations? The implications of the separate opinion are that the Court was giving lip service to *stare decisis*, while actually departing from the principles and policies it seemingly reaffirmed. The majority might have responded that it was respecting precedent but not expanding it to a new situation.

Postscript. With the support of the Bush Administration, which strongly criticized the Court's decision, Congress codified the *Patterson* holding that employees can assert contract-based claims of racial discrimination against private employers under § 1981 but overrode *Patterson*'s stingy interpretation of what those claims might entail. Civil Rights Act of 1991, Pub. L. No. 102–166, 105 Stat. 1071, discussed in Chapter 1, § 2(C).

2. Statutory Interpreters as Faithful Agents or Cooperative Partners of the Legislature

One important feature of Hart and Sacks' approach to statutory interpretation is that the judge approaches statutory interpretation as a *partner* with legislators. This metaphor might be criticized as inconsistent with the structure of the modern regulatory state: most federal law is now made by Congress (federal courts retain some limited common-law making authority in special areas). On this view, Congress is essentially the only *valid* lawmaking institutions at the federal level, and the role of the judge is to be the *faithful agent* (not the partner) of Congress, to carry out the congressional project and not to impose her own norms and rules.[29] This more limited view of the role of federal judges remains hotly contested. Chief Judge Katzmann, for example, has argued that statutory interpretation by judges must be situated within an institutional context, where courts cooperate with agencies as well as legislatures to create public policy and where courts make substantive contributions to the evolution of statutory policy. Robert Katzmann, *Statutes*, 87 N.Y.U.L. Rev. 637 (2012); cf. Amy Coney Barrett, *Substantive Canons and Faithful Agency,* 90 B.U.L. Rev. 109 (2012).[30] Even assuming that federal judges are required to be "faithful agents" of the enacting Congress, does that metaphor tell you anything about what method courts should deploy when applying statutes to circumstances not contemplated by the "principal" (i.e., Congress)?

The faithful agent versus cooperative partner debate is relevant to a number of doctrinal issues. Should a court "correct" obvious legislative drafting mistakes? Are judges authorized to update statutes? Even if legitimate as a general matter, is judicial updating illegitimate if it goes against the statutory text or the clear expectations of the enacting legislature?

United States v. Locke

471 U.S. 84 (1985).

The Federal Land Policy and Management Act (FLPMA), Pub. L. 94–579, 90 Stat. 2743, codified at 43 U.S.C. §§ 1701–1784 (1982), provided that holders of certain mining claims to federal land must, "prior to December 31" of every year, file certain documents with state officials and the federal Bureau of Land Management (BLM) or lose their claims. § 1744. Simply put, this is the quintessential trap for the unwary, for it seems

---

[29] See, e.g., Thomas Merrill, *The Common Law Powers of Federal Courts,* 52 U. Chi. L. Rev. 1 (1985); John Manning, *What Divides Textualists from Purposivists?,* 106 Colum. L. Rev. 70 (2006).

[30] Accord, Stephen Breyer, *Making Our Democracy Work: A Judge's View* (2010); Richard Posner, *The Problems of Jurisprudence* ch. 7 (1990); William Eskridge Jr. & Philip Frickey, *The Supreme Court, 1993 Term—Foreword: Law as Equilibrium,* 108 Harv. L. Rev. 26 (1994); Daniel Farber, *Legislative Deals and Statutory Bequests,* 75 Minn. L. Rev. 667 (1991); Philip Frickey, *Congressional Intent, Practical Reasoning, and the Dynamic Nature of Federal Indian Law,* 78 Calif. L. Rev. 1137 (1990); Lawrence Lessig, *Fidelity in Translation,* 71 Tex. L. Rev. 1165 (1993).

wholly illogical to require someone to file something, under severe penalty for default, the day *before* the last day of the year. The Locke family had been exercising rights to mine gravel on federal land since the 1950s. Knowing they were required to file papers in order to retain these rights, they sent their daughter to the nearest BLM office, which told her that claims had to be filed by December 31. The Lockes filed on that date, and the BLM rejected the papers on the ground that they were too late.

Justice Marshall, for the Court, agreed with the BLM that the Lockes were out of luck: "While we will not allow a literal reading of a statute to produce a result 'demonstrably at odds with the intentions of its drafters,' with respect to filing deadlines a literal reading of Congress' words is generally the only proper reading of those words. To attempt to decide whether some date other than the one set out in the statute is the date actually 'intended' by Congress is to set sail on an aimless journey, for the purpose of a filing deadline would be just as well served by nearly any date a court might choose as by the date Congress has in fact set out in the statute. * * * [N]othing in the legislative history suggests why Congress chose December 30 over December 31, [b]ut '[d]eadlines are inherently arbitrary,' while fixed dates 'are often essential to accomplish necessary results.'" * * *

Justice Marshall continued: "[W]e are not insensitive to the problems posed by congressional reliance on the words 'prior to December 31.' But the fact that Congress might have acted with greater clarity or foresight does not give courts a *carte blanche* to redraft statutes in an effort to achieve that which Congress is perceived to have failed to do. 'There is a basic difference between filling a gap left by Congress' silence and rewriting rules that Congress has affirmatively and specifically enacted.' *Mobil Oil Corp. v. Higginbotham*, 436 U.S. 618, 625 (1978). * * * [D]eference to the supremacy of the legislature, as well as recognition that congressmen typically vote on the language of a bill, generally requires us to assume that 'the legislative purpose is expressed by the ordinary meaning of the words used.' * * * The phrase 'prior to' may be clumsy, but its meaning is clear."

Justice Stevens, joined by Justice Brennan, dissented. In part, he argued: (1) FLPMA contained obvious drafting errors, which "should cause us to pause before concluding that Congress commanded blind allegiance to the remainder of the literal text" of the statute; (2) the BLM's implementing regulations do not repeat the statutory language, but rather state that filing must be accomplished "on or before December 30 of each year," suggesting that the BLM itself recognized that the statutory language was unclear; (3) indeed, the BLM once made the same mistake as the claimholders in *Locke*, for the agency had issued an information pamphlet that stated that documents must be filed "on or before December 31 of each [year]," demonstrating again that the statutory language is not "plain." Had the BLM issued regulations allowing filings on December 31, the Court surely would have upheld them, which suggests the anomaly that the agency "has more power to interpret an awkwardly drafted statute in an enlightened manner consistent with Congress' intent than does this Court." Justice Stevens continued: "The statutory scheme requires periodic filings on a calendar-year basis. The end of the calendar year is, of course, correctly described either as 'prior to the close of business on December 31,' or 'on or before December 31,' but it is surely understandable that the author of [this statute] might inadvertently use the words 'prior to December 31' when he meant to refer to the end of the calendar year. * * * That it was in fact an error seems rather clear to me because no one has suggested any rational basis for omitting just one day from the period in which an annual filing may be made, and I would not presume that Congress deliberately created a trap for the unwary by such an omission." The dissent concluded: "I have no doubt that Congress would have chosen to adopt a construction of the statute that filing take place by the end of the calendar year if its attention had been focused on this precise issue." Do you agree?

NOTE ON JUDICIAL "CORRECTION" OF STATUTORY SCRIVENER'S ERRORS

Hart and Sacks opined that "[c]ourts on occasion can correct mistakes, as by inserting or striking out a negative, when it is completely clear from the context that a mistake has been made. But they cannot permit the legislative process, and all the other processes which depend upon the integrity of language, to be subverted by the misuse of words." *The Legal Process,* 1375 (1994 ed.).[31] How would Hart and Sacks have decided *Locke*? Can you think of a policy reason for requiring filing before December 31? Think hard, for this is not an impossible task. Suppose that the Lockes had shown up at the BLM at 11:00 p.m. on December 30, "before December 31," but after the BLM had closed for the day. Would they have satisfied the statute as interpreted by the Court? Is this example at all similar to the facts of *Locke*? To the example of the ordinance governing pharmacy closing mentioned at the outset of this chapter?

As omnibus statutes have come to dominate the federal landscape, a somewhat different problem has arisen—what Jesse Cross calls the "staffer's error." Cross, *The Staffer's Error Doctrine,* 56 Harv. J. Legis. 83 (2019). As Cross demonstrates through an empirical analysis, members of Congress rely on a bureaucratic process for statutory drafting, a process they do not monitor carefully. Hence, policy glitches—judgment errors by staff—sometimes slip through and produce results strongly inconsistent with legislative policy. Cross argues for a purposive approach that can correct or ameliorate such drafting snafus. See also Jonathan Siegel, *What Statutory Drafting Errors Teach Us About Statutory Interpretation*, 69 Geo. Wash. L. Rev. 309, 333–44 (2001). An early example of such a "staffer's error" may have been *Holy Trinity* (where the drafting snafu was committed by labor unions that drafted the bill for Congress), and a recent example is *King v. Burwell* (Chapters 1 and 6).

WILLIAM ESKRIDGE JR., DYNAMIC STATUTORY INTERPRETATION
125–28 (1994).[32]

[Interpretation can be viewed as an honest effort by an "agent" to apply the "principal's" directive to unforeseen circumstances. (When circumstances were foreseen and provided for by the principal, it might be said that there is no "interpretive" effort needed.) The dynamic nature of interpretation arises, in large part, out of the agent's need for practical accommodation of the directive to new

---

[31]   Accord, 2A Sutherland, *Statutes and Statutory Construction,* §§ 47.35–.38; *Amalgamated Transit Union Local 1309 v. Laidlaw Transit Servs., Inc.,* 435 F.3d 1140 (9th Cir. 2006); Michael Fried, *A Theory of Scrivener's Error,* 52 Rutgers L. Rev. 589 (2000); John David Ohlendorf, *Textualism and the Problem of Scrivener's Error,* 64 Me. L. Rev. 119 (2011). See also Andrew Gold, *Absurd Results, Scrivener's Errors, and Statutory Interpretation*, 75 U. Cin. L. Rev. 25 (2006); David Sollors, *The Scrivener's Error Doctrine and Textual Criticism: Confronting Errors in Statutes and Literary Texts,* 49 Santa Clara L. Rev. 459 (2009).

[32]   Reprinted by permission of the publishers, Harvard University Press, Copyright © 1994 by the President and Fellows of Harvard College.

circumstances. Consider the following homely example, adapted from Francis Lieber's famous "fetch me the soup meat" hypothetical, excerpted at the beginning of this section. Eskridge invokes a special kind of agent, the "relational agent," who is entrusted with carrying out the principal's directives over a period of time, using his or her "best efforts."]

* * * Williams, the head of the household, retains Diamond as a relational agent to run the household while Williams is away on business. The contract is detailed, setting forth Diamond's duties to care for Williams's two children, maintain the house, prepare the meals, and do the shopping on a weekly basis. One of the more specific directives is that Diamond fetch five pounds of soup meat every Monday (the regular shopping day), so that he can prepare enough soup for the entire week. Diamond knows from talking to Williams that by "soup meat" she means a certain type of nutritious beef that is sold at several local stores. When Williams leaves, Diamond has no doubt as to what he is supposed to do. But over time his interpretation of the directive will change if the social, legal, and constitutional context changes so as to affect important assumptions made in Williams's original directive.

Changes in Social Context. There are a number of changes in the world that would justify Diamond's deviation from the directive that he fetch five pounds of soup meat each Monday. For example, suppose Diamond goes to town one Monday and discovers that none of the stores has the precise kind of soup meat he knows Williams had in mind when she gave the order. Should he drive miles to other towns in search of the proper soup meat? Not necessarily. It might be reasonable for him to purchase a suitable alternative in town, especially if it appears in his judgment to be just as good for the children. One can imagine many practical reasons why, in a given week, Diamond should not follow the apparent command. The reasons for deviating are akin to the interpretive creation of 'exceptions' to a statute's broad mandate based on the interpreter's judgment about the statute's goals and the extent to which other goals should be sacrificed. [Recall Justice Brewer's opinion in *Holy Trinity Church* and Justice Brennan's opinion in *Weber*.]

As the reasons multiply over time, one can imagine changed circumstances that effectively nullify Williams's directive altogether[.] Suppose Diamond discovers that one of the children has an allergy to soup meat. That child can continue to eat soup, but not with meat in it. Because Diamond realizes that one of the reasons Williams directed him to fetch soup meat every Monday was to ensure the good health and nourishment of the children, and because he believes that Williams would not want him to waste money on uneaten soup meat, he henceforth purchases only three pounds of soup meat per week. If both children are allergic to the soup meat, and Diamond does not care for the soup meat himself, he might be justified in entirely forgoing his directive to fetch it. Although he would be violating the original specific intent as well as the plain meaning of Williams's orders, Diamond could argue that his actions are consistent with her general intent that he act to protect the children's health and with her meta-intent that Diamond adapt specific directives to that end.

New Legal Rules and Policies. The agent might receive inconsistent directives over time. Suppose that two months after Williams embarks on her trip, she reads in a "Wellness Letter" that if children do not eat healthy foods, they will have cholesterol problems later in life. She sends Diamond a letter instructing him to place the children on a low-cholesterol diet, which should include Wendy's Bran Muffins and fresh apples. As a faithful relational agent, Diamond complies. He also reads up on the cholesterol literature, including the "Wellness Letter," and discovers that soup meat is high in cholesterol. He discontinues the weekly fetching of soup meat and fetches chicken instead because it is lower in cholesterol. Diamond's action is akin to a court's reconciliation of conflicting statutory mandates, in which one of the statutes often is given a narrowing interpretation to accommodate the policies of a later statute. * * *

Changed circumstances might further alter Diamond's interpretation of Williams's inconsistent directives. Weeks after he has substituted chicken for soup meat, Diamond learns from the "Wellness Letter" that Wendy's Bran Muffins actually do not help lower cholesterol, and that they have been found to cause cancer in rats. Furthermore, Diamond discovers that 50 percent of the apples sold in his region have a dangerous chemical on them. Diamond thereupon switches from Wendy's Bran Muffins to Richard's Bran Muffins, recommended by the "Wellness Letter," and from fresh apples to fresh oranges. Thus, not only has Diamond overthrown Williams's earlier directive on soup meat because of the new policy in her latter directive, but he has also altered her specific choice of low-cholesterol foods in the latter directive!

New Meta-Policies. The relational agent's interpretation of his orders may well be influenced over time by changing meta-policies. The new meta-policies may be endogenous or exogenous. Endogenous meta-policies are those generated from the principal herself and are just a more dramatic form of inconsistent directives. Suppose that, after several months, Williams writes to Diamond that financial reversals impel her to cut back on household expenses. Food costs must thereafter be limited to $100 per week. Although he has long been directed to fetch soup meat every Monday, and there are other ways to economize, Diamond cuts back on soup meat, in part because it is the most expensive item on the shopping list. This is akin to a court's modifying an original statutory policy to take account of supervening statutory policies.

Exogenous meta-policies are those generated from an authority greater than the principal. Suppose that Diamond has an unlimited food budget and no health concerns about soup meat, yet he stops fetching it on a weekly basis because the town is in a crisis period and meat of all sorts is being rationed; hence, Diamond could not lawfully fetch five pounds of soup meat per week. This is akin to a court construing a statute narrowly to avoid constitutional problems based on the legislature's meta-intent not to pass statutes of questionable constitutionality.

In all of these hypotheticals Diamond, our relational agent, has interpreted Williams's soup meat directive dynamically. Quite dynamically, in fact, because in most of the variations Diamond created substantial exceptions to or even negated the original specific meaning of the directive. Notwithstanding his dynamic interpretation of the directive, I believe that Diamond has been nothing but an honest agent.

Query: Consider how Eskridge's theory of the judge as a relational agent could explain (and defend) the result in *Weber* (Chapter 1, § 3). Does it have any bearing on *Holy Trinity*, where the Court was construing a more recent statute? Is it a persuasive justification for dynamic readings of laws in the following case? If so, what "circumstances" have "changed," and why do such changes support interpretations that seem to bend statutory language, perhaps beyond its breaking point?

STATUTORY PREFACE FOR THE *SECOND-PARENT ADOPTION* CASE

New York's Domestic Relations Law (1995)

Section 110. Who May Adopt * * *

An adult unmarried person or an adult husband and his adult wife together may adopt another person. An adult married person who is living separate and apart from his or her spouse pursuant to a decree or judgment of separation or pursuant to a written agreement of separation subscribed by the parties thereto * * * or an adult married person who has been living separate and apart from his or her spouse for at least three years prior to commencing an adoption proceeding may adopt another person; provided, however, that the person so adopted shall not be deemed the child or step-child of the non-adopting spouse for the purposes of inheritance or support rights or obligations or for any other purposes. An adult or minor husband and his adult or minor wife together may adopt a child of either of them born in or out of wedlock and an adult or minor husband or an adult or minor wife may adopt such a child of the other spouse. No person shall hereafter be adopted except in pursuance of this article, and in conformity with section three hundred seventy-three of the social services law. * * *

Adoption is the legal proceeding whereby a person takes another person into the relation of child and thereby acquires the rights and incurs the responsibilities of parent in respect of such other person. * * *

Section 117. Effect of Adoption

1.   (a) After the making of an order of adoption the birth parents of the adoptive child shall be relieved of all parental duties toward and of all responsibilities for and shall have no rights over such adoptive child or to his property by descent or succession, except as hereinafter stated.

(b) The rights of an adoptive child to inheritance and succession from and through his natural parents shall terminate upon the making of the order of adoption except as hereinafter provided.

(c) The adoptive parents or parent and the adoptive child shall sustain toward each other the legal relation of parent and child and shall have all the rights and be subject to all the duties of that relation including the rights of inheritance from and through each other and the natural and adopted kindred of the adoptive parents or parent.

(d) When a natural or adoptive parent, having lawful custody of a child, marries or remarries and consents that the stepparent may adopt such child, such consent shall not relieve the parent so consenting of any parental duty toward such child nor shall such consent or the order of adoption affect the rights of such consenting spouse and such adoptive child to inherit from and through each other and the natural and adopted kindred of such consenting spouse. * * *

(h) The consent of the parent of a child to the adoption of such child by his or her spouse shall operate to vest in the adopting spouse only the rights as distributee of a natural parent and shall leave otherwise unaffected the rights as distributee of the consenting spouse.

(i) This subdivision shall apply only to the intestate descent and distribution of real and personal property. * * *

New York's Social Services Law (1995)

§ 383–c. Guardianship and custody of children in foster care

[This section regulates adoptions through agencies, which enter into "surrender instruments" with a child's birth parent(s). Like § 115–b of the Domestic Relations Law, which regulates private placement adoptions, this section, governing agency adoptions, imposes detailed procedures and notice requirements to assure that birth parents understand their rights and what rights they are giving up.]

2.   Terms. (a) Such guardianship shall be in accordance with the provisions of this article and the instrument shall be upon such terms and subject to such conditions as may be agreed upon by the parties thereto * * *.

(b) If a surrender instrument designates a particular person or persons who will adopt a child, such person or persons, the child's birth parent or parents, the authorized agency having care and custody of the child and the child's attorney, may enter into a written agreement providing for communication or contact between the child and the child's parent or parents on such terms and conditions as may be agreed to by the parties. If a surrender instrument does not designate a particular person or persons who will adopt the child, then the child's birth parent or parents, the authorized agency having care and custody of the child and the child's attorney may enter into a written agreement providing for communication or contact, on such terms and conditions as may be agreed to by the parties. * * * If the court before which the surrender instrument is presented for approval determines that the agreement concerning communication and contact is in the child's best interests, the court shall approve the agreement. If the court does not approve the agreement, the court may nonetheless approve the surrender; provided, however, that the birth parent or parents executing the surrender instrument shall be given the opportunity at that time to withdraw such instrument. * * *

IN THE MATTER OF JACOB, IN THE MATTER OF DANA
New York Court of Appeals, 1995.
86 N.Y.2d 651, 636 N.Y.S.2d 716, 660 N.E.2d 397.

KAYE, C.J. [delivered the opinion for the Court.]

Under the New York adoption statute, a single person can adopt a child (Domestic Relations Law § 110). Equally clear is the right of a single homosexual to adopt (*see,* 18 NYCRR 421.16[h][2] [qualified adoption agencies "shall not . . . reject[ ] [adoption petitions] solely on the basis of homosexuality"]). These appeals call upon us to decide if the unmarried partner of a child's biological mother, whether heterosexual or homosexual, who is raising the child together with the biological parent, can become the child's second parent by means of adoption. [The appeal involved two petitions for adoption. In the *Jacob* case, the cohabiting boyfriend, Stephen T.K., of the child's biological mother, Roseanne M.A., moved to adopt Jacob. In the *Dana* case, the cohabiting female partner, G.M., of the child's biological mother, P.I., petitioned to adopt Dana. In both cases, the family courts denied the petitions as not falling within New York's adoption statute. The Court of Appeals, by a 4–3 vote, reversed.]

[S]ince adoption in this State is "solely the creature of . . . statute," the adoption statute must be strictly construed. What is to be construed strictly and applied rigorously in this sensitive area of the law, however, is legislative purpose as well as legislative language. Thus, the adoption statute must be applied in harmony with the humanitarian principle that adoption is a means of securing the best possible home for a child. * * *

This policy would certainly be advanced in situations like those presented here by allowing the two adults who actually function as a child's parents to become the child's legal parents. The advantages which would result from such an adoption include Social Security and life insurance benefits in the event of a parent's death or disability, the right to sue for the wrongful death of a parent, the right to inherit under rules of intestacy and eligibility for coverage under both parents' health insurance policies. In addition, granting a second parent adoption further ensures that two adults are legally entitled to make medical decisions for the child in case of emergency and are under a legal obligation for the child's economic support *(see,* Domestic Relations Law § 32).

Even more important, however, is the emotional security of knowing that in the event of the biological parent's death or disability, the other parent will have presumptive custody, and the children's relationship with their parents, siblings and other relatives will continue should the coparents separate. Indeed, viewed from the children's perspective, permitting the adoptions allows the children to achieve a measure of permanency with both parent figures * * *.

A second, related point of overriding significance is that the various sections comprising New York's adoption statute today represent a complex and not entirely reconcilable patchwork. Amended innumerable times since its passage in 1873, the adoption statute was last consolidated nearly 60 years ago, in 1938 (L. 1938, ch. 606). Thus, after decades of piecemeal amendment upon amendment, the statute today contains language from the 1870's alongside language from the 1990's. * * *

Despite ambiguity in other sections, one thing is clear: section 110 allows appellants to become adoptive parents. Domestic Relations Law § 110, entitled "Who May Adopt," provides that an "adult unmarried person or an adult husband and his adult wife together may adopt another person" (Domestic Relations Law § 110). Under this language, both appellant G.M. in *Matter of Dana* and appellant Stephen T.K. in *Matter of Jacob,* as adult unmarried persons, have standing to adopt and appellants are correct that the Court's analysis of section 110 could appropriately end here. [Although Jacob's adoption was a joint petition, his mother already enjoyed

454 Theories of Statutory Interpretation Ch. 5

parental rights, and so only Stephen T.K.'s rights were really at stake in the petition. Chief Judge Kaye faulted the dissenting opinion for reading too much into the word "together."]

The conclusion that appellants have standing to adopt is also supported by the history of section 110. The pattern of amendments since the end of World War II evidences a successive expansion of the categories of persons entitled to adopt regardless of their marital status or sexual orientation. [Section 110 was expanded in 1951 to allow adoptions by minors and in 1984 to allow adoptions by adults not yet divorced but living apart from their spouses pursuant to separation agreements.] Supporting [the 1984] amendment was New York's "strong policy of assuring that as many children as possible are adopted into suitable family situations" (Bill Jacket, L. 1984, ch. 218, Mem. of Dept. of Social Services, at 2 [June 19, 1984]). * * *

These amendments reflect some of the fundamental changes that have taken place in the makeup of the family. Today, for example, at least 1.2 of the 3.5 million American households which consist of an unmarried adult couple have children under 15 years old, more than a six-fold increase from 1970. Yet further recognition of this transformation is evidenced by the fact that unlike the States of New Hampshire and Florida (N.H.Rev.Stat.Annot. § 170–B:4; Fla.Stat.Ann. § 63.042[3]), New York does not prohibit adoption by homosexuals. Indeed, as noted earlier, an administrative regulation is in place in this State forbidding the denial of an agency adoption based solely on the petitioner's sexual orientation (18 NYCRR 421.16[h][2]). * * *

Appellants having standing to adopt pursuant to Domestic Relations Law § 110, the other statutory obstacle relied upon by the lower courts in denying the petitions is the provision that "[a]fter the making of an order of adoption the natural parents of the adoptive child shall be relieved of all parental duties toward and of all responsibilities for and shall have no rights over such adoptive child or to his property by descent or succession" (Domestic Relations Law § 117[l][a]). Literal application of this language would effectively prevent these adoptions since it would require the termination of the biological mothers' rights upon adoption thereby placing appellants in the "Catch-22" of having to choose one of two coparents as the child's only legal parent. * * *

Both the title of section 117 ("Effect of adoption") and its opening phrase ("After the making of an order of adoption") suggest that the section has nothing to do with the standing of an individual to adopt, an issue treated exclusively in section 110. Rather, section 117 addresses the legal effect of an adoption on the parties and their property. [This reading of section 117 is directed by the Court's precedents and commentary on the section, as well as the section's textual focus on estate law, § 117(a)(1)(i).]

[Chief Judge Kaye described a 1990 amendment to Social Services Law § 383–c, which now requires agency adoptions to follow detailed procedures to assure that parents explicitly renounce their legal rights when placing a child for adoption. Likewise, a 1986 amendment to Domestic Relations Law § 115–b[1] now requires private placements to follow similar procedures.]

The procedural safeguards contained in Social Services Law § 383–c and Domestic Relations Law § 115–b—safeguards that reflect modern sensitivities as to the level of procedural protection required for waiver of parental rights—further indicate that section 117 does not invariably mandate termination in all circumstances. Under the language of section 117 alone, a biological mother's rights could theoretically be severed unilaterally, without notice as to the consequences or other procedural protections. Though arguably adequate in 1938 when the statute was enacted, such a summary procedure would be unlikely to pass muster today *(see, e.g., Santosky v. Kramer,* 455 US 745, 768–770; *Matter of Sarah K.,* 66 NY2d 223, 237).

[E]ven though the language of section 117 still has the effect of terminating a biological parent's rights in the majority of adoptions between strangers—where there is a need to prevent unwanted intrusion by the child's former biological relatives to promote the stability of the new adoptive family—the cases before us are entirely different. As we recognized in *Matter of Seaman* (78 N.Y.2d 451, 461), "complete severance of the natural relationship is not necessary when the adopted person remains within the natural family unit as a result of an intrafamily adoption." [The Legislature has recognized this principle by amending section 117 to allow adoptions by stepparents and to allow adoptive parents in some circumstances to agree to a continuing relationship between the child and her or his biological parents, though so-called "open adoptions." N.Y. Soc. Servs. Law § 383–c.]

A year prior to the enactment of Social Services Law § 383–c, this Court declined to sanction the concept of "open adoption" because of our belief that it was inconsistent with what we perceived to be section 117's requirement that termination of parental rights was mandatory in all cases *(Matter of Gregory B.,* 74 NY2d 77, 91 [citations omitted]). Significantly, when enacting Social Services Law § 383–c the very next year, the Legislature saw no need to amend Domestic Relations Law § 117. Again, if section 117 automatically terminated parental rights in all circumstances, it would have the practical effect of overriding the conditional surrender/"open adoption" provisions of Social Services Law § 383–c. By passing Social Services Law § 383–c as it did, the Legislature thus necessarily rejected the reading of section 117 articulated in *Matter of Gregory B.*

Given the above, it is plain that an interpretation of section 117 that would limit the number of beneficial intrafamily adoptions cannot be reconciled with the legislative intent to authorize open adoptions and adoptions by minors. The coexistence of the statute's seemingly automatic termination language along with these more recent enactments creates a statutory puzzle not susceptible of ready resolution.

One conclusion that can be drawn, however, is that section 117 does not invariably require termination in the situation where the biological parent, having consented to the adoption, has agreed to retain parental rights and to raise the child together with the second parent. Despite their varying factual circumstances, each of the adoptions described above—stepparent adoptions, adoptions by minor fathers and open adoptions—share such an agreement as a common denominator. Because the facts of the cases before us are directly analogous to these three situations, the half-century-old termination language of section 117 should not be read to preclude the adoptions here. * * *

"Where the language of a statute is susceptible of two constructions, the courts will adopt that which avoids injustice, hardship, constitutional doubts or other objectionable results" *(Kauffman & Sons Saddlery Co. v. Miller,* 298 N.Y. 38, 44 [Fuld, J.]; *see also,* McKinney's Cons. Laws of N.Y., Book 1, Statutes § 150). Given that section 117 is open to two differing interpretations as to whether it automatically terminates parental rights in all cases, a construction of the section that would deny children like Jacob and Dana the opportunity of having their two de facto parents become their legal parents, based solely on their biological mother's sexual orientation or marital status, would not only be unjust under the circumstances, but also might raise constitutional concerns in light of the adoption statute's historically consistent purpose—the best interests of the child. *(See, e.g., Gomez v. Perez,* 409 U.S. 535, 538 [Equal Protection Clause prevents unequal treatment of children whose parents are unmarried]; *Plyler v. Doe,* 457 U.S. 202, 220 [State may not direct the onus of parent's perceived "misconduct against his (or her) children"]; *Matter of Burns v. Miller Constr.,* 55 N.Y.2d 501, 507–510 [New York statute requiring child born out of wedlock to prove "acknowledgment" by deceased parent did not further legitimate State interest].)

These concerns are particularly weighty in *Matter of Dana.* Even if the Court were to rule against him on this appeal, the male petitioner in *Matter of Jacob* could still adopt by marrying Jacob's mother. Dana, however, would be irrevocably deprived of the benefits and entitlements of having as her legal parents the two individuals who have already assumed that role in her life, simply as a consequence of her mother's sexual orientation.

Any proffered justification for rejecting these petitions based on a governmental policy disapproving of homosexuality or encouraging marriage would not apply. * * * New York has not adopted a policy disfavoring adoption by either single persons or homosexuals. In fact, the most recent legislative document relating to the subject urges courts to construe section 117 in precisely the manner we have as it cautions against discrimination against "nonmarital children" and "unwed parents". An interpretation of the statute that avoids such discrimination or hardship is all the more appropriate here where a contrary ruling could jeopardize the legal status of the many New York children whose adoptions by second parents have already taken place. * * *

BELLACOSA, J., dissenting. JUDGES SIMONS, TITONE and I respectfully dissent and vote to affirm in each case. * * *

Although adoption has been practiced since ancient times, the authorization for this unique relationship derives solely from legislation. It has no common-law roots or evolution. Therefore, our Court has approved the proposition that the statutory adoption charter exclusively controls. [Judge Bellacosa also emphasized that the "transcendent societal goal in the field of domestic relations is to stabilize family relationships, particularly parent-child bonds. That State interest promotes permanency planning and provides protection for an adopted child's legally secure familial placement." The state has chosen not to recognize common-law marriages or "lesbian marriages."]

Domestic Relations Law § 110, entitled "Who May Adopt," provides at its outset that *"an adult unmarried person or an adult husband and his adult wife together* may adopt another person" (emphasis added). Married aspirants are directed to apply "together", i.e., jointly, as spouses, except under circumstances not applicable in these cases. [Appellant G.M., the lesbian co-parent in *Dana*, meets this requirement, but appellants Stephen T.K. and Roseanne M.A., the unmarried cohabitants in *Jacob*, do not.]

The legislative history of adoption laws over the last century also reveals a dynamic process with an evolving set of limitations. The original version enacted in 1873 provided: "Any minor child may be adopted *by any adult*" (L. 1873, ch 830 [emphasis added]). In 1896, the Legislature cut back by stating that "[a]n adult unmarried person, or an adult husband or wife, or an adult husband and his adult wife together, may adopt a minor" (L. 1896, ch. 272, § 60; *see also,* L. 1915, ch. 352; L. 1917, ch. 149). This language was further restricted, in 1920, when the Legislature omitted from the statute the language "or an adult husband or wife" *(see,* L. 1920, ch. 433). Since enactment of the 1920 amendment, the statute has provided that "[a]n adult unmarried person or an adult husband and his adult wife *together* may adopt" (Domestic Relations Law § 110 [emphasis added]). The words chosen by the Legislature demonstrate its conclusion that a stable familial entity is provided by either a one-parent family or a two-parent family when the concentric interrelationships enjoy a legal bond. The statute demonstrates that the Legislature, by express will and words, concluded that households that lack legally recognized bonds suffer a relatively greater risk to the stability needed for adopted children and families, because individuals can walk out of these relationships with impunity and unknown legal consequences. * * *

Domestic Relations Law § 117 provides: "After the making of an order of adoption the natural parents of the adoptive child *shall be relieved of all parental duties toward and of all responsibilities for and* shall have no rights over such adoptive child *or* to his [or her] property by descent or succession" (emphasis added). The plain and overarching language and punctuation of section 117 cannot be judicially blinked, repealed or rendered obsolete by interpretation. [Judge Bellacosa cited precedent where the Court of Appeals had refused to read equitable exceptions into the plain language of section 117 to ameliorate its harsh application.]

A careful examination of the Legislature's unaltered intent based on the entire history of the statute reveals the original purpose of section 117 was to enfold adoptees within the exclusive embrace of their new families and to sever all relational aspects with the former family. That goal still applies and especially to the lifetime and lifelong relationships of the affected individuals, not just to the effect of dying intestate.

[Judge Bellacosa faulted the majority's concern that the statute be construed to avoid constitutional problems because (1) that concern had not been briefed or even mentioned by appellants, nor did the Attorney General have an opportunity to present the state's views, (2) the presumption of constitutionality augurs against vague and speculative doubts about a statute's constitutionality, and (3) such a concern could not override the plain meaning of the statute.] Ambiguity cannot directly or indirectly create or substitute for the lack of statutory authorization to adopt. These adoption statutes are luminously clear on one unassailable feature: no express legislative authorization is discernible for what is, nevertheless, permitted by the holdings today. Nor do the statutes anywhere speak of de facto, functional or second parent adoptions. Frankly, if the Legislature had intended to alter the definitions and interplay of its plenary, detailed adoption blueprint to cover the circumstances as presented here, it has had ample and repeated opportunities, means and words to effectuate such purpose plainly and definitively as a matter of notice, guidance, stability and reliability. It has done so before (*see, e.g.*, L. 1984, ch. 218 [permitting adoption by adults not yet divorced]; L. 1951, ch. 211 [permitting adoption by a minor]).

Because the Legislature did not do so here, neither should this Court in this manner. Cobbling law together out of interpretative ambiguity that transforms fundamental, societally recognized relationships and substantive principles is neither sound statutory construction nor justifiable lawmaking. * * *

NOTES ON JACOB/DANA AND DYNAMIC READINGS OF STATE CODES

1.   *Common Law Judges Interpreting State Codes.* One way of understanding the dynamic interpretation in *Jacob* is through the lens of common law judging. In contrast to federal courts, which are courts of strictly limited jurisdiction having little if any traditional common lawmaking authority, see Thomas Merrill, *The Common Law Powers of Federal Courts*, 52 U. Chi. L. Rev. 1, 32–35 (1985), state judiciaries are common law courts, with inherent lawmaking authority. See Peter Strauss, *The Common Law and Statutes*, 70 U. Colo. L. Rev. 225 (1999). Their common law authority to make law may vest state judges with greater legitimacy as well as competence to update statutes to reflect new circumstances. See Judith Kaye, *State Courts at the Dawn of a New Century: Common Law Courts Reading Statutes and Constitutions*, 70 N.Y.U. L. Rev. 1 (1995); Jeffrey Pojanowski, *Statutes in Common Law Courts,* 91 Tex. L. Rev. 479 (2013). Additionally, most state court judges do not serve for life, and many are either initially elected by the voters or subject to retention elections. (New York Court of Appeals judges are appointed for 14-year terms, with mandatory retirement at age of 70.) As a result, such judges are also more democratically accountable, and their accountability might give them greater freedom (a freedom which we should expect such judges to exercise cautiously). See Aaron-Andrew Bruhl & Ethan Leib, *Elected Judges and Statutory Interpretation*, 79 U. Chi. L. Rev. 1215 (2012).

Do these rationales justify Chief Judge Kaye's significant recasting of the adoption statute in *Jacob*? Even by her account, the effect of the Court of Appeals' ruling is that § 117's limitation on property and inheritance rights has been expanded to include cohabiting couples. That is, the Court expanded a relatively clear statutory text that was not a scrivener's error. What is the theoretical basis for such judicial surgery?

2.   *Reversing the Burden of Legislative Inertia as a Justification for Judicial Recognition of Second-Parent Adoptions.* When New York passed its adoption law, the idea of two women raising a child in a "lesbian" household would have been inconceivable. By 1995, lesbian unions with children were not unusual. Like most other states, New

York had amended its adoption law to accommodate "second-parent adoptions" by spouses, but those did not include female couples whose unions were not recognized as "marriages" by the state.[33]

This legislative failure may have been due to ambivalence about lesbian and gay families—and so the New York Court of Appeals' willingness to update the statute may have been a move to *reverse the burden of legislative inertia* in these cases: second parents presumptively can adopt, until the legislature overrides that interpretation. Most state supreme courts in gay-tolerant states followed something like Chief Judge Kaye's dynamic reading of state adoption statutes, e.g., *Adoption of Tammy*, 619 N.E.2d 315 (Mass. 1993); *Adoptions of B.L.V.B. and E.L.V.B.*, 628 A.2d 1271 (Vt. 1993), but several courts ruled the other way, e.g., *Adoption of Baby Z*, 724 A.2d 1035 (Conn. 1999). In 1995, no state allowed lesbian couples to get married, which would have allowed them to use the step-parent adoption process.

Is this kind of political burden-shifting justifiable—or is it yet another example of hated "judicial activism"? Drawing from representation-reinforcing theories of judicial review, William Eskridge Jr., *Dynamic Statutory Interpretation* ch. 5 (1994), argues that reversing the burden of inertia is particularly justified when the political process has traditionally been hostile to a minority group. Not only does this kind of judicial updating level the playing field a little, but it places the burden on political groups that are actually able to attract the legislature's attention. If the will of the people is to deny lesbian and gay parents these rights, a decision granting relief in *Jacob* will probably be overridden in short order. (The converse case will not be: minorities traditionally disadvantaged in the political process find it doubly hard to persuade the legislature to do anything for them, because legislators fear backlash.)

Moreover, reversing the burden of inertia gives the disadvantaged minority an opportunity to falsify stereotypes—in this case, the stereotype of gay people as incapable of forming families or, indeed, as anti-family or even predatory. By allowing lesbian and gay couples to adopt children, Chief Judge Kaye was giving New Yorkers an opportunity to see that lesbian and gay families can be nurturing and productive. The New York Legislature did not rebuke Chief Judge Kaye. Now that New York allows lesbian couples to get married—and hence take advantage of the step-parent allowance in the statutory adoption law—should the Court of Appeals overrule *Jacob* and require marital commitment in order for a "second parent" to adopt? Does this affect your answer: In 2010, the New York Legislature amended § 110 to allow "two unmarried adult intimate partners together" to adopt another person. 2010 N.Y. Laws ch. 509 (S. 1523A).

3.   *The Female Juror Cases, a Classic Example of Judicial Updating.* State statutes have often provided that juries are to be selected from a list of the qualified "electors" (i.e., voters) of the jurisdiction. Both the legislatures of Pennsylvania and Illinois adopted such statutes at a time when women were not allowed to vote in either state. After the ratification of the Nineteenth Amendment, which guaranteed women the right to vote, were women eligible to serve as jurors in these states by virtue of these statutes? In *Commonwealth v. Maxwell*, 114 A. 825, 829 (Pa. 1921), the Supreme Court of Pennsylvania held that women were qualified to serve on juries. Because the statute required jury selection "from the whole qualified electors," and because women were "electors" after the Nineteenth Amendment, women were then eligible to serve on juries.

---

[33]   See Nancy Polikoff, *This Child Does Have Two Mothers: Redefining Parenthood To Meet the Needs of Children in Lesbian-Mother and Other Nontraditional Families*, 78 Geo. L.J. 459 (1990).

"Statutes framed in general terms apply to new cases that arise, and to new subjects that are created from time to time, and which come within their general scope and policy."

But in *People ex rel. Fyfe v. Barnett*, 150 N.E. 290, 292 (Ill. 1925), the Supreme Court of Illinois reached the opposite result. Its jury selection law was adopted under the state's 1870 constitution, which limited the franchise to "male citizen[s]." "The legislative intent that controls in the construction of a statute has reference to the Legislature which passed the given act. * * * The word 'electors,' in the statute here in question, meant male persons, only, to the legislators who used it." Accord *Commonwealth v. Welosky*, 177 N.E. 656 (Mass. 1931).

How would Hart and Sacks analyze these cases? See Hart & Sacks, *The Legal Process*, 1172–85 (1994 ed.). What "purpose" would they "attribute" to the jury selection laws? Should the court avoid an "irrational pattern of particular applications" of the statute? *Id.* at 1125. Does a court have an obligation to enhance law's overall "coherence," rather than recognizing inconsistent rules? Should the court be reluctant to interpret the juror-selection statutes in a way that runs against a fundamental legal principle or policy? Cf. *Hoyt v. Florida*, 368 U.S. 57 (1961) (a system where women but not men could "opt out" of jury service was constitutional in 1961).

NOTE ON OVERRIDES, UNDERWRITES, AND INTERBRANCH DIALOGUE

Legal process theory is deeply interested in institutional interaction—and therefore in legislative responses to judicial decisions. Before the Supreme Court decided *Holy Trinity*, Congress had already amended the alien contract labor law to "override" the lower court decision; that is, Congress abrogated the lower court's point of law and established a new statutory rule. In 1991, Congress "underwrote" (ratified) *Patterson*'s holding that private employers might be sued for contract violations under § 1981 but overrode the Court's stingy understanding of those contract rights. In 2010, the New York Legislature passed an "underwrite" law; that is, the legislature approved and codified the rule set forth in *Jacob* and *Dana*. In 1998, Congress passed a statute responding to *Flood v. Kuhn*, overriding the precedent's narrow result but also implicitly reaffirming its premise that baseball is not subject to the antitrust laws.

Legislative Overrides. The extreme difficulty of amending the Constitution means that the Supreme Court effectively has the final word on constitutional interpretation. That is less true in statutory interpretation, where Congress can alter—and with some frequency has altered—judicial constructions of which it disapproves, by enacting a statutory amendment or *override*. Between 1967 and 1990, Congress enacted nearly 200 statutes overriding 121 Supreme Court decisions and more than 200 lower court decisions. See William Eskridge Jr., *Overriding Supreme Court Statutory Interpretation Decisions*, 101 Yale L.J. 331 (1991). Congress responded relatively quickly when enacting override statutes: almost half the Supreme Court cases were overridden within two years of the decision; two-thirds within five years; and three-fourths within ten years. In terms of subject matter, the number of overrides was highest for criminal law, followed by civil rights, antitrust, bankruptcy, and federal procedure. The article concludes *inter alia* that congressional overrides "are most likely when a Supreme Court interpretation reveals an ideologically fragmented Court, relies on the text's plain meaning and ignores legislative signals, and/or rejects positions taken by federal, state, or local governments."

A subsequent study indicates that the frequency of congressional overrides has declined considerably after the Clinton impeachment in 1998. See Matthew Christiansen & William Eskridge Jr., *Congressional Overrides of Supreme Court Statutory Interpretation Decisions, 1967–2011*, 92 Tex. L. Rev. 1317 (2014); cf. Richard Hasen, *End of the Dialogue? Political Polarization, the Supreme Court, and Congress*, 86 S. Cal. L. Rev. 205 (2013) (situating the decline earlier in the 1990s but emphasizing the dramatic fall-off in the new millennium). The period from 1991–99 was a high point, with 86 Supreme Court decisions overridden—an average of more than 20 per Congress. Two mega-override statutes accounted for 30 percent of this total: the 1991 Civil Rights Act (12 overrides) and the 1996 Antiterrorism and Effective Death Penalty Act (14 overrides). The authors believe that the decline after 1998 was attributable in part to partisanship and paralysis within Congress and its committees. But they view as more significant the changes to Congress's legislative agenda in the new millennium. During the decades prior to 9/11, Congress focused heavily on substantive law reform in areas such as civil rights, workplace rules, criminal law, federal jurisdiction and civil procedure, and other regulatory initiatives—all areas where overrides of judicial decisions were relatively common. Since 2001, however, the agenda has shifted toward the war on terror, health care and insurance, macroeconomic tax and spending policy, and international trade. Why might these newer aspects of Congress's agenda lead to fewer overrides? Because the subject matter is less likely to result in a heavy volume of interpretive litigation? Because the statutes themselves are less likely to have been cobbled together through bipartisan deals that are susceptible to gaps and ambiguities? Because there are simply fewer new statutes in an era characterized by extreme polarization in Congress?

Finally, Christiansen and Eskridge distinguish between overrides that are self-consciously *restorative* like the 1991 Civil Rights Act, and overrides they call *policy-updating*, in that bipartisan majorities in Congress have as their stated goal the routine updating of public law rather than the "correction" of judicial mistakes. Examples of policy-updating overrides have occurred in landmark bipartisan statutes such as the Copyrights Act of 1976, the Bankruptcy Reform Act of 1978, the Judicial Improvements Act of 1990, and the Telecommunications Act of 1996. The authors found that a large majority of overrides occurring between 1967 and 2011 were of the policy-updating nature, and it is this type of override that has declined most dramatically since 1998. In classic legal process mode, the authors lament the decline of such overrides, because they found that the override process in its heyday represented serious legislative deliberation, inputs from a diverse array of groups and government officials, and sensible policy decisions.

Legislative Underwrites. Scholars have paid less attention to situations where a legislature tells the judiciary that its interpretation is *correct*, legislatively endorsing the meaning that the court has conferred. A recent article examined the conditions and justifications for when legislatures do or should *underwrite* the judicial reading of a statute—either by altering or amending statutory text or by being explicit in reliable legislative history that accompanies a statutory amendment. Ethan Leib & James Brudney, *Legislative Underwrites*, 103 Va. L. Rev. 1487 (2017); see also Nancy Staudt et al., *Judicial Decisions as Legislation: Congressional Oversight of Supreme Court Tax Cases, 1954–2005*, 82 N.Y.U.L. Rev. 1340 (2007) (identifying many statutory codifications of judicial decisions in the tax arena). Like their better-known override cousins, legislative underwrites occur with some frequency at both the federal and state levels.

Why would legislatures decide to devote time and resources expressing textual approval for a decision that is already "law"? Leib and Brudney offer several explanations. One is the added value for lower courts, given that very few statutory conflicts reach the Supreme Court or a state's highest court. When the legislature concludes a lower court "got it right," underwriting that decision enables the legislature to minimize the development—or prevent the continuation—of lower court conflicts. This preclusive impact may be especially useful in subject areas where uncertainty can be quite costly to regulated entities and regulators—for instance, securities law or copyright law in the federal context.

A second reason for underwrites is to resolve issues arising from agency non-acquiescence. Executive branch agencies—assigned by Congress to implement national policy through uniform administration of federal laws—may sometimes decline to extend regional court of appeals decisions as properly implementing that national policy. Rather than wait until the Supreme Court enters the fray (which can often take a very long time), congressional underwrites offer a means of resolving such standoffs between agencies and lower courts by restoring legislative supremacy through appropriately elaborated new text.

A third reason for underwrites is that they may reduce some of the confusion and controversy surrounding doctrines of legislative inaction and acquiescence (see *Flood v. Kuhn*). Insofar as underwrites look more like a real option for legislatures, courts may be in a position to rely less often on contestable inferences that legislative silence over time approximates intent. When Congress has the option of either overriding or underwriting a judicial precedent, its failure to respond ought not be viewed as acquiescence or approval of that precedent (if Congress liked it so much, why no underdwrite?). Can you see a counterargument here? Might courts end up using the silence or inaction of *failing to underwrite* to derive statutory meanings?

More broadly, consider the possible interplay between the doctrine of *stare decisis* and legislative underwrites. Under what circumstances, if any, should courts be inclined to discount *stare decisis* and revisit past statutory precedents where legislatures have not underwritten these previous court decisions? One possible response would involve looking at settings in which the doctrine of *stare decisis* itself is less robust. For example, the Supreme Court is not as respectful of *stare decisis* when construing "common law statutes" such as the Sherman Act. See *Kimble v. Marvel Entm't*, 135 S. Ct. 2401, 2412–13 (2015) ("Congress intended the law's reference to 'restraint of trade' to have changing content . . . [hence the Court has] felt relatively free to revise its legal analysis as economic understanding evolves"). In addition, *stare decisis* is not as forceful for appeals court decisions and also for decisions involving elected state court judges.

Might these (and other) situations where *stare decisis* is less robust be attractive candidates for legislative underwrites? If so, should failure to underwrite in one or more of these settings provide further grounds for a court to reject or depart from *stare decisis*?

Interbranch Dialogue? The frequency and self-consciousness of legislative overrides and underwrites invites a further question: To what extent are legislatures and courts engaged in a genuine dialogue about statutory interpretation? There are reasons to be skeptical that such a dialogue exists. Don't courts and legislatures issue commands that signal either approval or disapproval, rather than conversational gambits that invite responsive communication? Aren't courts and legislatures addressing very different audiences? And aren't courts and legislatures unstable institutions (given their constantly changing membership), incapable of forming a collective or coherent dialogic intent?

On the other hand, at least some overrides—of the self-consciously restorative type referred to by Christiansen and Eskridge—can be seen as a form of legislative rebuking a court for not following its earlier legislative instruction. And these overrides may result in judicial replies that contribute to an ongoing if somewhat combative exchange between the branches. For instance, a court may respond to a restorative override in interactive ways such as confining the override's reach, thereby reviving aspects of the court's own overridden interpretation. See Deborah Widiss, *Shadow Precedents and the Separation of Powers: Statutory Interpretation of Congressional Overrides*, 84 Notre Dame L. Rev. 511 (2009). Moreover, as indicated above, legislative underwrites of lower court decisions may be seen as doing more than signaling a seal of approval. They also advise lower courts that conflicting interpretations should be abandoned.

Consider the familiar Supreme Court practice of expressly inviting Congress to override its statutory interpretation. This often occurs when the Court's majority is concerned that its technically correct interpretation may be at odds with Congress's underlying policy preference. See, e.g. *McCarty v. McCarty*, 453 U.S. 210, 235–36 (1981); *John Hancock Mutual Life Ins. Co. v. Harris Trust & Sav. Bank*, 510 U.S. 86, 110 (1993). A leading study by two political scientists found that 7.8 percent of the Court's majority opinions in statutory decisions during the 1986–2000 Terms—more than 70 majorities—included such express invitations. Although not every such invitation results in an override, Congress is more likely to override when the Court has invited such action. Lawrence Baum & Lori Hausegger, *The Supreme Court and Congress: Reconsidering the Relationship*, in *Making Policy Making Law* (Mark Miller & Jeb Barnes eds., 2004). In addition, there are numerous invitations to override issued by justices in dissent, and these too may well be taken up by Congress. State courts also frequently invite legislatures to override their decisions, with affirmative responses.

Are these types of exchanges between courts and legislatures on statutory meaning part of a "dialogue"? And why should we care whether they are or not? For an in-depth examination and analysis of arguments for and against this concept of institutional dialogue, see James Brudney & Ethan Leib, *Statutory Interpretation as "Interbranch Dialogue"?*, 66 UCLA L. Rev. 346 (2019).

3. Coherence with Public Norms

Legal process theory maintains that judges should attribute a purpose to the statute and then apply the statute so as best to achieve the purpose—so long as that does not impose on the words a "meaning they will not bear" *and* does not violate a policy of "clear statement." See Hart & Sacks, *The Legal Process*, excerpted at the beginning of this section. As to the latter point, Hart and Sacks assume that judges operate under a duty to lend greater coherence to the body of law. This duty, they say, "forbids a court to understand the legislature as directing a departure from a generally prevailing principle or policy of the law unless it does so clearly. This policy has special force when the departure is so great as to raise a serious question of constitutional power." What is the source of that duty? And how strong should this interpretive precept operate? Ought judges rewrite clear texts to avoid a conflict between a new statute and deeply rooted principles of law, or even constitutional mandates?

STATUTORY PREFACE FOR THE *BOB JONES* CASE

Internal Revenue Code of 1954 (Tax Advantages for Educational Institutions)

26 U.S.C. § 170. Charitable, etc., contributions and gifts

(a) Allowance of deduction. (1) General rule.—There shall be allowed as a deduction any charitable contribution (as defined in subsection (c)) payment of which is made within the taxable year. A charitable contribution shall be allowable as a deduction only if verified under regulations prescribed by the Secretary. * * *

(c) Charitable contribution defined.—For purposes of this section, the term "charitable contribution" means a contribution or gift to or for the use of * * *

(2) A corporation, trust, or community chest, fund, or foundation * * *

> **(B)** organized and operated exclusively for religious, charitable, scientific, literary, or educational purposes, or to foster national or international amateur sports competition (but only if no part of its activities involve the provision of athletic facilities or equipment), or for the prevention of cruelty to children or animals; * * *

(4) In the case of a contribution or gift by an individual, a domestic fraternal society, order, or association, operating under the lodge system, but only if such contribution or gift is to be used exclusively for religious, charitable, scientific, literary, or educational purposes, or for the prevention of cruelty to children or animals. * * *

26 U.S.C. § 501. Exemption from tax on corporations, certain trusts, etc.

(a) Exemption from taxation.—An organization described in subsection (c) or (d) or section 401(a) shall be exempt from taxation under this subtitle unless such exemption is denied under section 502 or 503. * * *

(c) List of exempt organizations.—The following organizations are referred to in subsection (a): * * *

(3) Corporations, and any community chest, fund, or foundation, organized and operated exclusively for religious, charitable, scientific, testing for public safety, literary, or educational purposes, or to foster national or international amateur sports competition (but only if no part of its activities involve the provision of athletic facilities or equipment), or for the prevention of cruelty to children or animals, no part of the net earnings of which inures to the benefit of any private shareholder or individual, no substantial part of the activities of which is carrying on propaganda, or otherwise attempting, to influence legislation (except as otherwise provided in subsection (h)), and which does not participate in, or intervene in (including the publishing or distributing of statements), any political campaign on behalf of (or in opposition to) any candidate for public office.

[Also listed for exemption were (4) nonprofit "civic leagues or organizations"; (5) "labor, agricultural, or horticultural organizations"; (6) nonprofit "business leagues, chambers of commerce, boards of trade, or professional football leagues"; (7) nonprofit "[c]lubs organized for pleasure, recreation, and other nonprofitable purposes"; and

(8) specified "[f]raternal beneficiary societies, orders, or associations" providing health or life insurance for its members.]

(i)   Prohibition of discrimination by certain social clubs.—Notwithstanding subsection (a), an organization which is described in subsection (c)(7) shall not be exempt from taxation under subsection (a) for any taxable year if, at any time during such taxable year, the charter, bylaws, or other governing instrument, of such organization or any written policy statement of such organization contains a provision which provides for discrimination against any person on the basis of race, color, or religion. The preceding sentence to the extent it relates to discrimination on the basis of religion shall not apply to—

(1)   an auxiliary of a fraternal beneficiary society if such society—

(A)   is described in subsection (c)(8) and exempt from tax under subsection (a), and

(B)   limits its membership to the members of a particular religion, or

(2)   a club which in good faith limits its membership to the members of a particular religion in order to further the teachings or principles of that religion, and not to exclude individuals of a particular race or color. * * *

BOB JONES UNIVERSITY V. UNITED STATES
Supreme Court of the United States, 1983.
461 U.S. 574, 103 S.Ct. 2017, 76 L.Ed.2d 157.

CHIEF JUSTICE BURGER delivered the opinion of the Court.

We granted certiorari to decide whether petitioners, nonprofit private schools that prescribe and enforce racially discriminatory admissions standards on the basis of religious doctrine, qualify as tax-exempt organizations under § 501(c)(3) of the Internal Revenue Code of 1954.

[I]   Until 1970, the Internal Revenue Service granted tax-exempt status to private schools, without regard to their racial admissions policies, under § 501(c)(3) of the Internal Revenue Code, 26 U.S.C. § 501(c)(3), and granted charitable deductions for contributions to such schools under § 170 of the Code, 26 U.S.C. § 170.

On January 12, 1970, a three-judge District Court for the District of Columbia issued a preliminary injunction prohibiting the IRS from according tax-exempt status to private schools in Mississippi that discriminated as to admissions on the basis of race. *Green v. Kennedy*, 309 F. Supp. 1127, *app. dismissed sub nom. Cannon v. Green*, 398 U.S. 956 (1970). Thereafter, in July 1970, the IRS concluded that it could "no longer legally justify allowing tax-exempt status [under § 501(c)(3)] to private schools which practice racial discrimination." IRS News Release July 7, 1970. At the same time, the IRS announced that it could not "treat gifts to such schools as charitable deductions for income tax purposes [under § 170]." By letter dated November 30, 1970, the IRS formally notified private schools, including those involved in this case, of this change in policy, "applicable to all private schools in the United States at all levels of education." [The *Green* court approved the agency's updated interpretation and held that racially discriminatory private schools were not entitled to exemption under § 501(c)(3) and that donors were not entitled to deductions for contributions to such schools under § 170.]

The revised policy on discrimination was formalized in Revenue Ruling 71–447, 1971–2 Cum. Bull. 230:

> "Both the courts and the Internal Revenue Service have long recognized that the statutory requirement of being 'organized and operated exclusively for religious, charitable, . . . or educational purposes' was intended to express the basic common law concept [of 'charity']. . . . All charitable trusts, educational or otherwise, are subject to the requirement that the purpose of the trust may not be illegal or contrary to public policy."

Based on the "national policy to discourage racial discrimination in education," the IRS ruled that "a private school not having a racially nondiscriminatory policy as to students is not 'charitable' within the common law concepts reflected in sections 170 and 501(c)(3) of the Code." * * *

[II.A] In Revenue Ruling 71–447, the IRS formalized the policy, first announced in 1970, that § 170 and § 501(c)(3) embrace the common law "charity" concept. Under that view, to qualify for a tax exemption pursuant to § 501(c)(3), an institution must show, first, that it falls within one of the eight categories expressly set forth in that section, and second, that its activity is not contrary to settled public policy.

Section 501(c)(3) provides that "[c]orporations . . . organized and operated exclusively for religious, charitable . . . or educational purposes" are entitled to tax exemption. Petitioners argue that the plain language of the statute guarantees them tax-exempt status. They emphasize the absence of any language in the statute expressly requiring all exempt organizations to be "charitable" in the common-law sense, and they contend that the disjunctive "or" separating the categories in § 501(c)(3) precludes such a reading. Instead, they argue that if an institution falls within one or more of the specified categories it is automatically entitled to exemption, without regard to whether it also qualifies as "charitable." The Court of Appeals rejected that contention and concluded that petitioners' interpretation of the statute "tears section 501(c)(3) from its roots."

It is a well-established canon of statutory construction that a court should go beyond the literal language of a statute if reliance on that language would defeat the plain purpose of the statute. * * *

Section 501(c)(3) therefore must be analyzed and construed within the framework of the Internal Revenue Code and against the background of the congressional purposes. Such an examination reveals unmistakable evidence that, underlying all relevant parts of the Code, is the intent that entitlement to tax exemption depends on meeting certain common-law standards of charity—namely, that an institution seeking tax-exempt status must serve a public purpose and not be contrary to established public policy.

This "charitable" concept appears explicitly in § 170 of the Code. That section contains a list of organizations virtually identical to that contained in § 501(c)(3). It is apparent that Congress intended that list to have the same meaning in both sections. In § 170, Congress used the list of organizations in defining the term "charitable contributions." On its face, therefore, § 170 reveals that Congress' intention was to provide tax benefits to organizations serving charitable purposes. The form of § 170 simply makes plain what common sense and history tell us: in enacting both § 170 and § 501(c)(3), Congress sought to provide tax benefits to charitable organizations, to encourage the development of private institutions that serve a useful public purpose or supplement or take the place of public institutions of the same kind.

Tax exemptions for certain institutions thought beneficial to the social order of the country as a whole, or to a particular community, are deeply rooted in our history, as in that of England. The origins of such exemptions lie in the special privileges that have long been extended to charitable trusts.[12] * * *

When the Government grants exemptions or allows deductions all taxpayers are affected; the very fact of the exemption or deduction for the donor means that other taxpayers can be said to be indirect and vicarious "donors." Charitable exemptions are justified on the basis that the exempt entity confers a public benefit—a benefit which the society or the community may not itself choose or be able to provide, or which supplements and advances the work of public institutions already supported by tax revenues. History buttresses logic to make clear that, to warrant exemption under § 501(c)(3), an institution must fall within a category specified in that section and must demonstrably serve and be in harmony with the public interest. The institution's purpose must not be so at odds with the common community conscience as to undermine any public benefit that might otherwise be conferred.

[II.B] [A] declaration that a given institution is not "charitable" should be made only where there can be no doubt that the activity involved is contrary to a fundamental public policy. But there can no longer be any doubt that racial discrimination in education violates deeply and widely accepted views of elementary justice. Prior to 1954, public education in many places still was conducted under the pall of *Plessy v. Ferguson*, 163 U.S. 537 (1896); racial segregation in primary and secondary education prevailed in many parts of the country.[20] This Court's decision in *Brown v. Board of Education*, 347 U.S. 483 (1954), signalled an end to that era. Over the past quarter of a century, every pronouncement of this Court and myriad

---

[12]   The form and history of the charitable exemption and deduction sections of the various income tax acts reveal that Congress was guided by the common law of charitable trusts. See Simon, *The Tax-Exempt Status of Racially Discriminatory Religious Schools*, 36 Tax L.Rev. 477, 485–489 (1981). Congress acknowledged as much in 1969. The House Report on the Tax Reform Act of 1969, Pub.L. 91–172, 83 Stat. 487, stated that the § 501(c)(3) exemption was available only to institutions that served "the specified charitable purposes," H.R.Rep. No. 91–413, pt. 1, p. 35 (1969), and described "charitable" as "a term that has been used in the law of trusts for hundreds of years." *Id.*, at 43. We need not consider whether Congress intended to incorporate into the Internal Revenue Code any aspects of charitable trust law other than the requirements of public benefit and a valid public purpose.

[20]   In 1894, when the first charitable exemption provision was enacted, racially segregated educational institutions would not have been regarded as against public policy. Yet contemporary standards must be considered in determining whether given activities provide a public benefit and are entitled to the charitable tax exemption. In *Walz v. Tax Comm'n*, 397 U.S. 664, 673 (1970), we observed: "Qualification for tax exemption is not perpetual or immutable; some tax-exempt groups lose that status when their activities take them outside the classification and new entities can come into being and qualify for exemption." Charitable trust law also makes clear that the definition of "charity" depends upon contemporary standards. See, *e.g.*, Restatement (Second) of Trusts § 374, comment a (1959).

Acts of Congress and Executive Orders attest a firm national policy to prohibit racial segregation and discrimination in public education.

An unbroken line of cases following *Brown v. Board of Education* establishes beyond doubt this Court's view that racial discrimination in education violates a most fundamental national public policy, as well as rights of individuals. * * * In *Norwood v. Harrison*, 413 U.S. 455, 468–469 (1973), we dealt with a nonpublic institution:

> "[A] private school—even one that discriminates—fulfills an important educational function; *however, . . . [that] legitimate educational function cannot be isolated from discriminatory practices . . . [D]iscriminatory treatment exerts a pervasive influence on the entire educational process.*" (Emphasis added.)

Congress, in Titles IV and VI of the Civil Rights Act of 1964, Pub.L. 88–352, 78 Stat. 241, 42 U.S.C. §§ 2000c et seq., 2000c–6, 2000d et seq., clearly expressed its agreement that racial discrimination in education violates a fundamental public policy. Other sections of that Act, and numerous enactments since then, testify to the public policy against racial discrimination. See, *e.g.*, the Voting Rights Act of 1965; Title VIII of the Civil Rights Act of 1968; [the Emergency School Aid Acts of 1972 and 1978].

The Executive Branch has consistently placed its support behind eradication of racial discrimination. Several years before this Court's decision in *Brown v. Board of Education*, President Truman issued Executive Orders prohibiting racial discrimination in federal employment decisions, Exec. Order No. 9980, 3 CFR 720 (1943–1948 Comp.), and in classifications for the Selective Service, Exec. Order No. 9988, 3 CFR 726, 729 (1943–1948 Comp.). In 1957, President Eisenhower employed military forces to ensure compliance with federal standards in school desegregation programs. Exec. Order No. 10730, 3 CFR 389 (1954–1958 Comp.). And in 1962, President Kennedy announced:

> "[T]he granting of Federal assistance for . . . housing and related facilities from which Americans are excluded because of their race, color, creed, or national origin is unfair, unjust, and inconsistent with the public policy of the United States as manifested in its Constitution and laws." Exec. Order No. 11063, 3 CFR 652 (1959–1963 Comp.).

These are but a few of numerous Executive Orders over the past three decades demonstrating the commitment of the Executive Branch to the fundamental policy of eliminating racial discrimination.

Few social or political issues in our history have been more vigorously debated and more extensively ventilated than the issue of racial discrimination, particularly in education. Given the stress and anguish of the history of efforts to escape from the shackles of the "separate but equal" doctrine of *Plessy v. Ferguson*, it cannot be said that educational institutions that, for whatever reasons, practice racial discrimination, are institutions exercising "beneficial and stabilizing influences in community life," *Walz v. Tax Comm'n*, 397 U.S. 664, 673 (1970), or should be encouraged by having all taxpayers share in their support by way of special tax status.

There can thus be no question that the interpretation of § 170 and § 501(c)(3) announced by the IRS in 1970 was correct. That it may be seen as belated does not undermine its soundness. It would be wholly incompatible with the concepts underlying tax exemption to grant the benefit of tax-exempt status to racially discriminatory educational entities, which "exer[t] a pervasive influence on the entire educational process." *Norwood v. Harrison, supra.* Whatever may be the rationale for such private schools' policies, and however sincere the rationale may be, racial discrimination in education is contrary to public policy. Racially discriminatory educational institutions cannot be viewed as conferring a public benefit within the "charitable" concept discussed earlier, or within the Congressional intent underlying § 170 and § 501(c)(3).

[II.C. Chief Justice Burger rejected the argument that the IRS did not have the authority to issue the 1970 rule and that its longstanding prior policy could only be overturned by legislative amendment of the Code. He reasoned that the IRS had been given broad rulemaking power by Congress and, moreover, that the policy adopted by the IRS was fully consistent with national policy since *Brown* and the Civil Rights Act of 1964.]

[II.D] The actions of Congress since 1970 leave no doubt that the IRS reached the correct conclusion in exercising its authority. It is, of course, not unknown for independent agencies or the Executive Branch to misconstrue the intent of a statute; Congress can and often does correct such misconceptions, if the courts have not done so. Yet for a dozen years Congress has been made aware—acutely aware—of the IRS rulings of 1970 and 1971. As we noted earlier, few issues have been the subject of more vigorous and widespread debate and discussion in and out of Congress than those related to racial segregation in education. Sincere adherents advocating contrary views have ventilated the subject for well over three decades. Failure of Congress to modify the IRS rulings of 1970 and 1971, of which Congress was, by its own studies and by public discourse, constantly reminded; and Congress' awareness of the denial of tax-exempt status for racially discriminatory schools when enacting other and related legislation make out an unusually strong case of legislative acquiescence in and ratification by implication of the 1970 and 1971 rulings.

Ordinarily, and quite appropriately, courts are slow to attribute significance to the failure of Congress to act on particular legislation. We have observed that "unsuccessful attempts at legislation are not the best of guides to legislative intent." Here, however, we do not have an ordinary claim of legislative acquiescence. Only one month after the IRS announced its position in 1970, Congress held its first hearings on this precise issue. Exhaustive hearings have been held on the issue at various times since then. These include hearings in February 1982, after we granted review in this case.

Non-action by Congress is not often a useful guide, but the non-action here is significant. During the past 12 years there have been no fewer than 13 bills introduced to overturn the IRS interpretation of § 501(c)(3). Not one of these bills has emerged from any committee, although Congress has enacted numerous other amendments to § 501 during this same period, including an amendment to § 501(c)(3) itself. Tax Reform Act of 1976, Pub.L. 94–455, § 1313(a), 90 Stat. 1730. It is hardly conceivable that Congress—and in this setting, any Member of Congress—was not abundantly aware of what was going on. In view of its prolonged and acute awareness of so important an issue, Congress' failure to act on the bills proposed on this subject provides added support for concluding that Congress acquiesced in the IRS rulings of 1970 and 1971.

The evidence of Congressional approval of the policy embodied in Revenue Ruling 71–447 goes well beyond the failure of Congress to act on legislative proposals. Congress affirmatively manifested its acquiescence in the IRS policy when it enacted the present § 501(i) of the Code, Act of Oct. 20, 1976, Pub.L. 94–568, 90 Stat. 2697 (1976). That provision denies tax-exempt status to social clubs whose charters or policy statements provide for "discrimination against any person on the basis of race, color, or religion." Both the House and Senate Committee Reports on that bill articulated the national policy against granting tax exemptions to racially discriminatory private clubs. S. Rep. No. 94–1318, p. 8 (1976); H.R. Rep. No. 94–1353, p. 8 (1976).

Even more significant is the fact that both reports focus on this Court's affirmance of *Green v. Connally*, 330 F.Supp. 1150 (DC 1971), as having established that "discrimination on account of race is inconsistent with an *educational institution's* tax-exempt status." S. Rep. No. 94–1318 at 7–8, and n. 5; H.R. Rep. No. 94–1353 at 8, and n. 5 (emphasis added). These references in congressional Committee Reports on an enactment denying tax exemptions to racially discriminatory private social clubs cannot be read other than as indicating approval of the standards applied to racially discriminatory private schools by the IRS subsequent to 1970, and specifically of Revenue Ruling 71–447.[27]

[In Part III, Chief Justice Burger rejected the argument that the IRS ruling violated the Free Exercise Clause of the First Amendment, and in Part IV he rejected the argument that the IRS ruling was not properly applied to the petitioners.]

JUSTICE POWELL, concurring in the judgment.

[Justice Powell found much to admire in the dissenting opinion's analysis of the statutory text but agreed with the Court's result, based upon the reasoning in Part II.B-D of the opinion for the Court. He did not agree with the reasoning in Part II.A.] I am unconvinced that the critical question in determining tax-exempt status is

---

[27]   Reliance is placed on scattered statements in floor debate by Congressmen critical of the IRS' adoption of Revenue Ruling 71–447. Those views did not prevail. That several Congressmen, expressing their individual views, argued that the IRS had no authority to take the action in question, is hardly a balance for the overwhelming evidence of Congressional awareness of and acquiescence in the IRS rulings of 1970 and 1971. Petitioners also argue that the Ashbrook and Dornan Amendments to the Treasury, Postal Service, and General Government Appropriations Act of 1980, Pub.L. 96–74, §§ 103, 614, 615, 93 Stat. 559, 562, 576–577 (1979), reflect Congressional opposition to the IRS policy formalized in Revenue Ruling 71–447. Those amendments, however, are directly concerned only with limiting more aggressive enforcement procedures proposed by the IRS in 1978 and 1979 and preventing the adoption of more stringent substantive standards. The Ashbrook Amendment, § 103 of the Act, applies only to procedures, guidelines, or measures adopted after August 22, 1978, and thus in no way affects the status of Revenue Ruling 71–447. In fact, both Congressman Dornan and Congressman Ashbrook explicitly stated that their amendments would have no effect on prior IRS policy, including Revenue Ruling 71–447, see 125 Cong.Rec. H5982 (1979) (Cong. Dornan: "[M]y amendment will not affect existing IRS rules which IRS has used to revoke tax exemptions of white segregated academies under Revenue Ruling 71–447 . . . ."); *id.*, at 18446 (Cong. Ashbrook: "My amendment very clearly indicates on its face that all the regulations in existence as of August 22, 1978, would not be touched"). These amendments therefore do not indicate Congressional rejection of Revenue Ruling 71–447 and the standards contained therein.

whether an individual organization provides a clear "public benefit" as defined by the Court. Over 106,000 organizations filed § 501(c)(3) returns in 1981. I find it impossible to believe that all or even most of those organizations could prove that they "demonstrably serve and [are] in harmony with the public interest" or that they are "beneficial and stabilizing influences in community life." Nor I am prepared to say that petitioners, because of their racially discriminatory policies, necessarily contribute nothing of benefit to the community. It is clear from the substantially secular character of the curricula and degrees offered that petitioners provide educational benefits.

Even more troubling to me is the element of conformity that appears to inform the Court's analysis. The Court asserts that an exempt organization must "demonstrably serve and be in harmony with the public interest," must have a purpose that comports with "the common community conscience," and must not act in a manner "affirmatively at odds with [the] declared position of the whole government." Taken together, these passages suggest that the primary function of a tax-exempt organization is to act on behalf of the Government in carrying out governmentally approved policies. In my opinion, such a view of § 501(c)(3) ignores the important role played by tax exemptions in encouraging diverse, indeed often sharply conflicting, activities and viewpoints. * * * [P]rivate, nonprofit groups receive tax exemptions because "each group contributes to the diversity of association, viewpoint, and enterprise essential to a vigorous, pluralistic society." [*Walz v. Tax Comm'n*, 397 U.S. 664, 689 (1970) (Brennan, J., concurring).] Far from representing an effort to reinforce any perceived "common community conscience," the provision of tax exemptions to nonprofit groups is one indispensable means of limiting the influence of governmental orthodoxy on important areas of community life. Given the importance of our tradition of pluralism, "[t]he interest in preserving an area of untrammeled choice for private philanthropy is very great." *Jackson v. Statler Foundation*, 496 F.2d 623, 639 (CA2 1974) (Friendly, J., dissenting from denial of reconsideration en banc).

[Judgments about whether a class of institutions advances the public interest are best left to Congress, reasoned Justice Powell. The IRS has, by its own admission, no special expertise in making the kind of determinations the Court upholds in this case.] The contours of public policy should be determined by Congress, not by judges or the IRS.

JUSTICE REHNQUIST, dissenting.

The Court points out that there is a strong national policy in this country against racial discrimination. To the extent that the Court states that Congress in furtherance of this policy could deny tax-exempt status to educational institutions that promote racial discrimination, I readily agree. But, unlike the Court, I am convinced that Congress simply has failed to take this action and, as this Court has said over and over again, regardless of our view on the propriety of Congress' failure to legislate we are not constitutionally empowered to act for them.

In approaching this statutory construction question the Court quite adeptly avoids the statute it is construing. This I am sure is no accident, for there is nothing in the language of § 501(c)(3) that supports the result obtained by the Court. * * *

With undeniable clarity, Congress has explicitly defined the requirements for § 501(c)(3) status. An entity must be (1) a corporation, or community chest, fund, or foundation, (2) organized for one of the eight enumerated purposes, (3) operated on a nonprofit basis, and (4) free from involvement in lobbying activities and political campaigns. Nowhere is there to be found some additional, undefined public policy requirement.

The Court first seeks refuge from the obvious reading of § 501(c)(3) by turning to § 170 of the Internal Revenue Code which provides a tax deduction for contributions made to § 501(c)(3) organizations. In setting forth the general rule, § 170 states:

> "There shall be allowed as a deduction any charitable contribution (as defined in subsection (c)) payment of which is made within the taxable year. A charitable contribution shall be allowable as a deduction only if verified under regulations prescribed by the Secretary." 26 U.S.C. § 170(a)(1).

The Court seizes the words "charitable contribution" and with little discussion concludes that "[o]n its face, therefore, § 170 reveals that Congress' intention was to provide tax benefits to organizations serving charitable purposes," intimating that this implies some unspecified common-law charitable trust requirement.

The Court would have been well advised to look to subsection (c) where, as § 170(a)(1) indicates, Congress has defined a "charitable contribution." * * * Plainly, § 170(c) simply tracks the requirements set forth in § 501(c)(3). Since § 170 is no more than a mirror of § 501(c)(3) and, as the Court points out, § 170 followed § 501(c)(3) by more than two decades, it is at best of little usefulness in finding the meaning of § 501(c)(3).

Making a more fruitful inquiry, the Court next turns to the legislative history of § 501(c)(3) and finds that Congress intended in that statute to offer a tax benefit to organizations that Congress believed were providing a public benefit. I certainly agree. But then the Court leaps to the conclusion that this history is proof Congress intended that an organization seeking § 501(c)(3) status "must fall within a category specified in that section *and must demonstrably serve and be in harmony with the public interest.*" (Emphasis added). To the contrary, I think that the legislative history of § 501(c)(3) unmistakably makes clear that *Congress has decided* what organizations are serving a public purpose and providing a public benefit within the meaning of § 501(c)(3) and has clearly set forth in § 501(c)(3) the characteristics of such organizations. In fact, there are few examples which better illustrate Congress' effort to define and redefine the requirements of a legislative act.

The first general income tax law was passed by Congress in the form of the Tariff Act of 1894. A provision of that Act provided an exemption for "corporations, companies, or associations organized and conducted solely for charitable, religious, or educational purposes." The income tax portion of the 1894 Act was held unconstitutional by this Court, see *Pollock v. Farmers' Loan & Trust Co.*, 158 U.S. 601 (1895), but a similar exemption appeared in the Tariff Act of 1909 which imposed a tax on corporate income. The 1909 Act provided an exemption for "any corporation or association organized and operated exclusively for religious, charitable, or educational purposes, no part of the net income of which inures to the benefit of any private stockholder or individual."

With the ratification of the Sixteenth Amendment, Congress again turned its attention to an individual income tax with the Tariff Act of 1913. And again, in the direct predecessor of § 501(c)(3), a tax exemption was provided for "any corporation or association organized and operated exclusively for religious, charitable, scientific, or educational purposes, no part of the net income of which inures to the benefit of any private stockholder or individual." In subsequent Acts Congress continued to broaden the list of exempt purposes. The Revenue Act of 1918 added an exemption for corporations or associations organized "for the prevention of cruelty to children or animals." The Revenue Act of 1921 expanded the groups to which the exemption applied to include "any community chest, fund, or foundation" and added "literary" endeavors to the list of exempt purposes. The exemption remained unchanged in the Revenue Acts of 1924, 1926, 1928, and 1932. In the Revenue Act of 1934 Congress added the requirement that no substantial part of the activities of any exempt organization can involve the carrying on of "propaganda" or "attempting to influence legislation." Again, the exemption was left unchanged by the Revenue Acts of 1936 and 1938.

The tax laws were overhauled by the Internal Revenue Code of 1939, but this exemption was left unchanged. When the 1939 Code was replaced with the Internal Revenue Code of 1954, the exemption was adopted in full in the present § 501(c)(3) with the addition of "testing for public safety" as an exempt purpose and an additional restriction that tax-exempt organizations could not "participate in, or intervene in (including the publishing or distributing of statements), any political campaign on behalf of any candidate for public office." Ch. 1, § 501(c)(3), 68A Stat. 163 (1954). Then in 1976 the statute was again amended adding to the purposes for which an exemption would be authorized, "to foster national or international amateur sports competition," provided the activities did not involve the provision of athletic facilities or equipment. Tax Reform Act of 1976, Pub. L. 94–455, § 1313(a), 90 Stat. 1520, 1730 (1976).

One way to read the opinion handed down by the Court today leads to the conclusion that this long and arduous refining process of § 501(c)(3) was certainly a waste of time, for when enacting the original 1894 statute Congress intended to adopt a common law term of art, and intended that this term of art carry with it all of the common law baggage which defines it. Such a view, however, leads also to the unsupportable idea that Congress has spent almost a century adding illustrations simply to clarify an already defined common law term. * * *

Perhaps recognizing the lack of support in the statute itself, or in its history, for the 1970 IRS change in interpretation, the Court finds that "[t]he actions of Congress since 1970 leave no doubt that the IRS reached the correct conclusion in exercising its authority," concluding that there is "an unusually strong case of legislative acquiescence in and ratification by implication of the 1970 and 1971 rulings." The Court relies first on several bills introduced to overturn the IRS interpretation of § 501(c)(3). But we have said before, and it is equally applicable here, that this type of congressional inaction is of virtually no weight in determining legislative intent.

See *United States v. Wise*, 370 U.S. 405, 411 (1962); *Waterman S.S. Corp. v. United States*, 381 U.S. 252, 269 (1965). These bills and related hearings indicate little more than that a vigorous debate has existed in Congress concerning the new IRS position.

The Court next asserts that "Congress affirmatively manifested its acquiescence in the IRS policy when it enacted the present § 501(i) of the Code," a provision that "denies tax-exempt status to social clubs whose charters or policy statements provide for" racial discrimination. Quite to the contrary, it seems to me that in § 501(i) Congress showed that when it wants to add a requirement prohibiting racial discrimination to one of the tax-benefit provisions, it is fully aware of how to do it.

The Court intimates that the Ashbrook and Dornan Amendments also reflect an intent by Congress to acquiesce in the new IRS position. The amendments were passed to limit certain enforcement procedures proposed by the IRS in 1978 and 1979 for determining whether a school operated in a racially nondiscriminatory fashion. The Court points out that in proposing his amendment, Congressman Ashbrook stated: " 'My amendment very clearly indicates on its face that all the regulations in existence as of August 22, 1978, would not be touched.' " The Court fails to note that Congressman Ashbrook also said:

> "The IRS has no authority to create public policy. . . . So long as the Congress has not acted to set forth a national policy respecting denial of tax exemptions to private schools, it is improper for the IRS or any other branch of the Federal Government to seek denial of tax-exempt status. . . . There exists but a single responsibility which is proper for the Internal Revenue Service: To serve as tax collector." 125 Cong. Rec. H5879–80 (1979).

In the same debate, Congressman Grassley asserted: "Nobody argues that racial discrimination should receive preferred tax status in the United States. However, the IRS should not be making these decisions on the agency's own discretion. Congress should make these decisions." *Id.*, at 5884. The same debates are filled with other similar statements. While on the whole these debates do not show conclusively that Congress believed the IRS had exceeded its authority with the 1970 change in position, they likewise are far less than a showing of acquiescence in and ratification of the new position.

This Court continuously has been hesitant to find ratification through inaction. This is especially true where such a finding "would result in a construction of the statute which not only is at odds with the language of the section in question and the pattern of the statute taken as a whole, but also is extremely far reaching in terms of the virtually untrammeled and unreviewable power it would vest in a regulatory agency." *SEC v. Sloan*, 436 U.S. 103, 121 (1978). Few cases would call for more caution in finding ratification by acquiescence than the present one. The new IRS interpretation is not only far less than a long-standing administrative policy, it is at odds with a position maintained by the IRS, and unquestioned by Congress, for several decades prior to 1970. The interpretation is unsupported by the statutory language, it is unsupported by legislative history, the interpretation has led to considerable controversy in and out of Congress, and the interpretation gives to the IRS a broad power which until now Congress had kept for itself. Where in addition to these circumstances Congress has shown time and time again that it is ready to enact positive legislation to change the Tax Code when it desires, this Court has no business finding that Congress has adopted the new IRS position by failing to enact legislation to reverse it.

I have no disagreement with the Court's finding that there is a strong national policy in this country opposed to racial discrimination. I agree with the Court that Congress has the power to further this policy by denying § 501(c)(3) status to organizations that practice racial discrimination. But as of yet Congress has failed to do so. Whatever the reasons for the failure, this Court should not legislate for Congress. * * *

NOTES ON BOB JONES AND READING STATUTES IN LIGHT OF PUBLIC VALUES

1.   *Was There a Plain Meaning? Why Not Stop with That?* Justice Rehnquist's dissenting opinion argues that § 501(c)(3) had a plain meaning that supported Bob Jones: the statute grants an exemption to any "educational" institution, which clearly includes Bob Jones University. The Chief Justice responds that §§ 501 and 170 should be read together, and the "charitable" requirement of § 170 read into § 501(c)(3)—but § 170 defines "charitable contribution" to include contributions to "educational" institutions, again just like Bob Jones *University*. So why should the Court not apply the statutory plain meaning? The Chief Justice invokes the "charitable" purpose of the exemption—but does he have an answer to Justice Powell's argument that the statutory purpose is to encourage diversity of institutions that offer educational and other services?

2.   *Larger Statutory and Constitutional Policy.* Chief Justice Burger also invokes a wide array of sources—constitutional precedents, statutes, executive orders, etc.—to demonstrate that government subsidies to Bob Jones would violate deeply held public values. Yet none of those sources actually prohibited Bob Jones University's private race discrimination. Is there something anomalous about "expanding" these constitutional and statutory authorities beyond their well-defined ambit? For a critique, see Mayer G. Freed and Daniel D. Polsby, in *Race, Religion & Public Policy*: Bob Jones University v. United States, 1983 Sup. Ct. Rev. 1, 5.

An earlier draft of the Chief Justice's opinion did note that federal law barred private schools from discriminating on the basis of race—but Burger dropped that highly relevant reference in the final opinion. Olatunde Johnson, *The Story of* Bob Jones University v. United States (1983): *Race, Religion, and Congress's Extraordinary Acquiescence*, in *Statutory Interpretation Stories* 126, 151 (Eskridge, Frickey & Garrett eds., 2011). In fact, Bob Jones was violating 42 U.S.C. § 1981, which bars race discrimination in private contracting, and which the Supreme Court had interpreted to bar private schools from discriminating on the basis of race. Does § 1981 provide a cogent response to the Freed and Polsby concerns? Why might the Chief Justice have dropped reference to § 1981 in his opinion for the Court?

3.   *Public Values or Public Hypocrisy? Bob Jones* reads like a very high-minded opinion: How can we as a society subsidize segregated schools? We cannot! That sounds great, a ringing reaffirmation of *Brown v. Board of Education.* But the reality is a great deal less inspiring. See Johnson, *Story of* Bob Jones (detailed account from which we draw). The Carter Administration's IRS issued regulations in 1978–79 placing burdens on schools with low minority percentages to "prove" their nondiscrimination. Congress

reacted with the Dornan and Ashbrook Amendments, which effectively barred the IRS from implementing the new regulations. (Justice Rehnquist relies on these amendments in objecting to the acquiescence argument. Does he have a point?) When *Bob Jones* was decided, IRS enforcement depended heavily on "self-reporting": institutions that admitted to race discrimination were the only ones to lose their tax exemptions. In short, only those institutions that discriminated as a matter of principle—like Bob Jones—lost their tax exemption. Institutions that deceived the IRS (or themselves) did not. Is this a "public value"?

At the same time Bob Jones was suing to recover its tax-exempt status, African-American parents were suing the IRS to enforce the nondiscrimination rule more effectively. Judge Ruth Bader Ginsburg of the D.C. Circuit wrote an opinion favorable to the parents, but the Supreme Court reversed. A year after the Court decided *Bob Jones*, it held (by a 5–4 majority) that these parents lacked "standing" to sue the IRS, thereby failing to satisfy the Court's "case or controversy" requirement. *Allen v. Wright*, 468 U.S. 737 (1984). The grudging approach to standing taken in *Allen* is an ironic contrast to the expansive approach to the antidiscrimination principle taken in *Bob Jones*. The contrast is all the more striking in light of significant justiciability problems in *Bob Jones* itself. While *Bob Jones* was pending on appeal to the Supreme Court, the Reagan Administration switched sides and announced that it agreed with Bob Jones and wanted to change the regulation back to its pre-1970 status. Because the two parties in *Bob Jones University v. United States* both agreed that Bob Jones should be exempt, why was the case not moot? Was there an ongoing "case or controversy" as required by the Court's reading of Article III? As it has done in other cases, the Court kept the appeal alive by appointing William Coleman, a former Secretary of Transportation, "to brief and argue this case, as *amicus curiae*, in support of the judgments below." 456 U.S. 922 (1982) (order of Court). Coleman, who represented neither party, won the case!

After 1984, the IRS was left with few incentives to enforce *Bob Jones*: Congress in the Ashbrook Amendment had signaled that it didn't want vigorous enforcement, President Reagan had formally abandoned the policy until it was forced back upon him by the Supreme Court, and private citizens who might object to the virtual abandonment of the policy were not easily able to get into court, while any segregated school that loses its exemption of course has standing to sue the IRS. Is this a scenario likely to promote "public values"?

Consider a final historical irony. Bob Jones University in the new millennium not only revoked its race-discriminatory admissions policy, but also issued a public apology for the race discrimination it practiced for most of its history. See Johnson, *Story of* Bob Jones, 157.

Public Citizen v. United States Department of Justice

491 U.S. 440 (1989).

The question was whether the Standing Committee on the Federal Judiciary of the American Bar Association (ABA) was subject to the Federal Advisory Committee Act (FACA), 5 U.S.C. § 1 et seq., which imposes disclosure and open meeting requirements on a federal "advisory committee." Section 3(2) of the statute defines "advisory committee" as, among other things, any committee "established or utilized" by the President or by one or more agencies, "in the interest of obtaining advice or recommendations" for the President or an agency. The President, through the Justice

Department, routinely sought the advice of the ABA committee concerning the qualifications of potential federal judicial nominees.

Justice Brennan's majority opinion declined to hold that the ABA committee was within the scope of FACA § 3(2). He started with the proposition that a broad reading of "established or utilized" would impose disclosure and openness requirements on presidential consultation with political consultants, informal advisers, and an indeterminate number of other groups. "FACA was enacted to cure specific ills, above all the wasteful expenditure of public funds for worthless committee meetings and biased proposals; although its reach is extensive, we cannot believe that it was intended to cover every formal and informal consultation between the President or an Executive agency and a group rendering advice. As we said in *Church of the Holy Trinity v. United States*: '[F]requently words of general meaning are used in a statute, words broad enough to include an act in question, and yet a consideration of the whole legislation, or of the circumstances surrounding its enactment, or of the absurd results which follow from giving such broad meaning to the words, makes it unreasonable to believe that the legislator intended to include the particular act.' "

Finding some degree of ambiguity, Justice Brennan examined the background of FACA, starting with President Kennedy's 1962 executive order requiring disclosure of advisory committees; no President considered the ABA committees to fall under that previous, executive department regime. During the Nixon Administration, Congress confirmed and expanded this idea. The original House bill applied to advisory committees "established" by statute or by the Executive, whether by a federal agency or by the President himself. H.R. 4383, 92d Cong., 2d Sess. § 3(2) (1972). The House Committee Report stated that "advisory committees" would include "committees which may have been organized before their advice was sought by the President or any agency, but which are used by the President or any agency in the same way as an advisory committee formed by the President himself or the agency itself," H. R. Rep. No. 92–1017, at 4. This language was aimed at bringing into the disclosure regime quasi-public organizations receiving public funds, such as the National Academy of Sciences. Neither the report nor congressional discussions mentioned anything like these ABA Committees, namely, groups not formed by the executive branch, accepting no public funds, and assisting the President in performing constitutionally specified tasks such as judicial nominations.

The parallel Senate bill defined "advisory committee" as one "established or organized" by statute, the President, or an executive agency. S. 3529, 92d Cong., 2d Sess. §§ 3(1), (2) (1972). The Senate Report stated that the phrase "established or organized" was to be understood in its "most liberal sense, so that when an officer brings together a group by formal or informal means, by contract or other arrangement, and whether or not Federal money is expended, to obtain advice and information, such group is covered by the provisions of this bill." S. Rep. No. 92–1098, at 8 (1972). The Report listed as examples "the Advisory Council on Federal Reports, the National Industrial Pollution Control Council, the National Petroleum Council, advisory councils to the National Institutes of Health, and committees of the national academies where they are utilized and officially recognized as advisory to the President, to an agency, or to a Government official." Justice Brennan characterized these examples as "limited to groups organized by, or closely tied to, the Federal Government, and thus enjoying quasi-public status. Given the prominence of the ABA Committee's role and its familiarity to Members of Congress, its omission from the list of groups formed and maintained by private initiative to offer advice with respect to the President's nomination of Government officials is telling. If the examples offered by the Senate Committee on Government Operations are representative, as seems fair to surmise, then there is little reason to think that there was any support, at least at the committee stage, for going beyond the terms of Executive Order No. 11007 to regulate comprehensively the workings of the ABA Committee."

Of course, the final version of FACA employed the phrase "established or utilized," somewhat broader than the word "established" or the phrase "established or organized." The words "or utilized" were added by the Conference Committee to the definition included in the House bill. See H.R. Conf. Rep. No. 92–1403, p. 2 (1972). The Joint Explanatory Statement, however, said that the definition contained in the House bill was adopted "with modification." *Id.* at 9. Justice Brennan drew this conclusion: "The Conference Report offered no indication that the modification was significant, let alone that it would substantially broaden FACA's application by sweeping within its terms a vast number of private groups, such as the Republican National Committee, not formed at the behest of the Executive or by quasi-public organizations whose opinions the Federal Government sometimes solicits. Indeed, it appears that the House bill's initial restricted focus on advisory committees established by the Federal Government, in an expanded sense of the word 'established,' was retained rather than enlarged by the Conference Committee. In the section dealing with FACA's range of application, the Conference Report stated: 'The Act does not apply to persons or organizations which have contractual relationships with Federal agencies *nor to advisory committees not directly established by or for such agencies.*' *Id.*, at 10 (emphasis added). The phrase 'or utilized' therefore appears to have been added simply to clarify that FACA applies to advisory committees established by the Federal Government in a generous sense of that term, encompassing groups formed indirectly by quasi-public organizations such as the National Academy of Sciences 'for' public agencies as well as 'by' such agencies themselves."

Given the statutory ambiguity revealed by the legislative history, Justice Brennan concluded that the words ought to be given their narrower construction. He added: "[C]onstruing FACA to apply to the Justice Department's consultations with the ABA Committee would present formidable constitutional difficulties," because it might "infring[e] unduly on the President's Article II power to nominate federal judges and violat[e] the doctrine of separation of powers. * * * Where the competing arguments based on FACA's text and legislative history, though both plausible, tend to show that Congress did not desire FACA to apply to the Justice Department's confidential solicitation of the ABA Committee's views on prospective judicial nominees, sound sense counsels adherence to our rule of caution. Our unwillingness to resolve important constitutional questions unnecessarily thus solidifies our conviction that FACA is inapplicable."

Justice Kennedy, joined by Chief Justice Rehnquist and Justice O'Connor, concurred only in the judgment. (**Justice Scalia** did not participate in this case.) "Where the language of a statute is clear in its application, the normal rule is that we are bound by it. There is, of course, a legitimate exception to this rule, which the Court invokes, citing *Holy Trinity Church*, and with which I have no quarrel. Where the plain language of the statute would lead to 'patently absurd consequences' that 'Congress could not *possibly* have intended,' we need not apply the language in such a fashion. When used in a proper manner, this narrow exception to our normal rule of statutory construction does not intrude upon the lawmaking powers of Congress, but rather demonstrates a respect for the coequal Legislative Branch, which we assume would not act in an absurd way."

Justice Kennedy concluded, however, that it would not at all be "absurd" to apply the FACA to ABA committees. "Unable to show that an application of FACA according to the plain meaning of its terms would be absurd, the Court turns instead to the task of demonstrating that a straightforward reading of the statute would be inconsistent with the congressional purposes that lay behind its passage. To the student of statutory construction, this move is a familiar one. It is, as the Court identifies it, the classic *Holy Trinity* argument. '[A] thing may be within the letter of the statute and yet not within the statute, because not within its spirit, nor within the intention of its makers.' *Holy Trinity.* I cannot embrace this principle. Where it is clear that the unambiguous language of a statute embraces certain conduct, and it would not be patently absurd to apply the statute to such conduct, it does not foster a democratic exegesis for this Court to rummage through unauthoritative materials to consult the spirit of the legislation in order to discover an alternative interpretation of the statute with which the Court is more comfortable. It comes as a surprise to no one that the result of the Court's lengthy journey through the legislative history is the discovery of a congressional intent not to include the activities of the ABA Committee within the coverage of FACA. The problem with spirits is that they tend to reflect less the views of the world whence they come than the views of those who seek their advice."

Justice Kennedy sharply criticized *Holy Trinity* for substituting judicial values for rule of law values (as evidenced by the "Christian nation" passage). So the FACA applies, by its plain meaning, to the ABA Committee—but Justice Kennedy also concluded that such an application unconstitutionally infringed on the President's Article II authority to solicit advice. Hence, Justice Kennedy concurred in the result reached by the Court, but in none of its reasoning.

NOTES ON PUBLIC CITIZEN AND COHERENCE-BASED JUSTIFICATIONS FOR "JUDICIAL SURGERY"

1.   *Did the FACA Have a Plain Meaning That Included the ABA Committees?* One wonders whether Hart and Sacks could have gone along with the majority's approach in *Public Citizen.* Has Justice Brennan given the words of FACA § 3(2) a "meaning they will not bear"? Specifically, can you come up with linguistic support for a reading of "established or utilized" by the President or an agency that covers committees advising the National Academy of Sciences, but not the ABA's committees?

Does the legislative history suggest that a narrow reading of "utilized" is possible? Consider these facts: (1) neither the House nor the Senate bill included the broader term "utilized," (2) the term was added by the Conference Committee, and (3) the Rules of both House and Senate say that Conference Committees *cannot expand* any provision beyond the scope set forth in either the House bill or the Senate bill (i.e., the Conference can only *reconcile* the House and Senate bills, not use them as a starting point for crafting new legislation). Do these facts about Congress and its FACA deliberations suggest a defense of the majority's approach? For illumination, consider Victoria Nourse, *A Decision Theory of Statutory Interpretation: Legislative History by the Rules,* 122 Yale L.J. 70, 92–97 (2012) (arguing for a narrow understanding of "utilized" based upon the foregoing Rules of the House and Senate). Before reaching a final conclusion, reread the House and Senate committee report language, discussing or alluding to "established" (the language used in both House and Senate bills). Does this discussion suggest a broader reading of "established" that the Conference Committee might have been trying to capture when it revised the bill language to add "or utilized"?

2. *Can Judicial Surgery Be Defended in* Public Citizen? Assume that Justice Kennedy is right, that the FACA unequivocally includes the ABA's advisory committees, and that Justice Brennan, basically, rewrites the statute. How might the Court's decision be justified? Although a state court judge has analogized this kind of "judicial surgery" to the limited discretion afforded a musician interpreting a piece of music, Stewart Pollock, *The Art of Judging*, 71 N.Y.U. L. Rev. 591, 601–02 (1996), the strong arm given the statutory language makes the case look more like an exercise in "spurious interpretation," to use Roscoe Pound's terminology. Does the Supreme Court even have the constitutional authority (under Article III) to rewrite the statute? As Justice Kennedy observes, the Court clearly has the authority to declare the statute's plain meaning and then invalidate it as inconsistent with the Constitution.

One way to defend Justice Brennan's approach is that congressional purpose, if clear, can justify a narrowing construction of broad statutory text—precisely the holding of *Holy Trinity* and, perhaps, consistent with legal process theory. A problem with such a defense is that the FACA's purpose might be broader than the purpose identified by Justice Brennan. According to the Conference Report, the FACA was aimed at curbing the proliferation of executive branch advisory committees and rendering those committees more transparent to the public. H.R. Conf. Rep. No. 92–1403, at 1–2 (1972). A broader understanding of the statutory purpose, drawn from the same source the majority invoked, might confirm that the statute's apparent plain meaning is exactly what Congress "intended." Note, also, that Justice Kennedy rejects the *Holy Trinity* notion that a narrower congressional purpose can justify judicial constriction of plain statutory text. Would Hart and Sacks disagree?

3. *Coherence-Based Justifications for Judicial Surgery.* Another way to defend Justice Brennan's approach might be institutionally normative: a central role of judges is to make the law relatively coherent and to assure continuity in legal rules. This is the basis for Hart and Sacks' maxim that the legislature ought to be presumed not to "depart[ ] from a generally prevailing principle or policy of the law unless it does so clearly." Hart & Sacks, *The Legal Process*, 1377 (excerpted at the beginning of this section). Professor (now Judge) Amy Coney Barrett defended this perspective, based on the original meaning of Article III, reflecting the founding era practice where courts read even relatively clear texts in light of substantive values reflected in longstanding canons of statutory construction. See Barrett, *Substantive Canons and Faithful Agency,* 90 B.U.L. Rev. 109, 11–12 (2012).

Another institutional way of understanding this issue is that courts should be deliberation-forcing when legislatures are venturing into territory where fundamental values are at stake. See William Eskridge Jr. & Philip Frickey, *Quasi-Constitutional Law: Clear Statement Rules as Constitutional Lawmaking,* 45 Vand. L. Rev. 493, 529–32 (1992); Amanda Tyler, *Continuity, Coherence, and the Canons,* 99 Nw. U. L. Rev. 1389 (2005).[34] Congress is the body that ought to make major policy decisions, but courts ought to be leery of imputing to Congress any intention to alter fundamental rules of the polity,

---

[34] See also Einer Elhauge, *Preference-Eliciting Statutory Default Rules,* 102 Colum. L. Rev. 2162 (2002); Christopher Elmendorf, *Refining the Democracy Canon,* 95 Cornell L. Rev. 1051 (2010). For a critical view of this kind of roving normative authority, see John Manning, *Clear Statement Rules and the Constitution,* 110 Colum. L. Rev. 399 (2010).

without a careful examination of the legislative deliberations as well as the statutory text (precisely the methodology followed by Justice Brennan in *Public Citizen*).

A final way to view these cases is to understand the role of judges as openly critical and normative. This does not sound like a legal process mode of thinking, but leading juris prudes have developed precisely that idea. As you read the following note, consider the separation of powers and majoritarian difficulties with each theory.

NOTE ON LAW AS INTEGRITY AND STATUTORY INTERPRETATION AS A CHAIN NOVEL

In *Law in Quest of Itself* (1940), Lon Fuller contested the positivist claim that fact is wholly independent of value—and interpretation independent of norms:

> If I attempt to retell a funny story which I have heard, the story as I tell it will be the product of two forces: (1) the story as I heard it [and] (2) my conception of the point of the story, in other words, my notion of the story *as it ought to be.* * * * If the story as I heard it was, in my opinion, badly told, I am guided largely by my conception of the story as it ought to be * * *. On the other hand, if I had the story from a master raconteur, I may exert myself to reproduce his exact words. * * * These two forces, then, supplement one another in shaping the story as I tell it. It is the product of the *is* and the *ought* working together. * * * The two are inextricably interwoven, to the point where we can say that "the story" as an entity really embraces both of them. Indeed, if we look at the story across time, its reality becomes even more complex. The "point" of the story, which furnishes its essential unity, may in the course of retelling be changed. As it is brought out more clearly through the skill of successive tellers it becomes a new point; at some indefinable juncture the story has been so improved that it has become a new story. In a sense, then, the thing we call "the story" is not something that is, but something that becomes; it is not a hard chunk of reality, but a fluid process, which is as much directed by men's creative impulses, by their conception of the story as it ought to be, as it is by the original even which unlocked those impulses. The *ought* here is just as real, as a part of human experience, as the *is*, and the line between the two melts away in the common stream of telling and retelling into which they both flow.

"Exactly the same thing may be said of a statute or a decision," Fuller continued. "The statute or decision is not a segment of being, but, like the anecdote, a process of becoming." *Id.* at 9–10.

Fuller maintained that the interconnection between law and morality is a good thing. The main argument was one of coherence. Because the "bulk of human relations find their regulation outside the field of positive law," a continuous interpenetration of law and social morality creates a more seamless web of interconnected rights and duties. *Id.* at 11–12. Fuller emphasized that such interconnection was necessary to the efficacy of law; without a link with changing social mores, law would not be able to achieve its goals or, worse, would lose the respect of the citizenry. See Lon Fuller, *Human Interaction and the Law*, in *The Principles of Social Order: The Selected Essays of Lon L. Fuller* 211–46 (Kenneth Winston ed. 1981).

Following upon Fuller's idea (but without acknowledging the debt), Ronald Dworkin posited that law is an interpretive enterprise that seeks to "show it as the best work of art it can be." *Law as Interpretation*, 60 Tex. L. Rev. 527 (1982). Dworkin explained his vision of interpretation by reference to the idea of a "chain novel," *id.* at 541–43:

> Suppose that a group of novelists is engaged for a particular project and that they draw lots to determine the order of play. The lowest number writes the opening chapter of a novel, which he or she then sends to the next number, with the understanding that he is adding a chapter to that novel rather than beginning a new one, and then sends the two chapters to the next number, and so on. Now every novelist but the first has the dual responsibilities of interpreting and creating because each must read all that has gone before in order to establish, in the interpretivist sense, what the novel so far created is. He or she must decide what the characters are "really" like; what motives in fact guide them; what the point or theme of the developing novel is; how far some literary device or figure, consciously, or unconsciously used, contributes to these, and whether it should be extended or refined or trimmed or dropped in order to send the novel further in one direction rather than another. This must be interpretation in a non-intention-bound style because, at least for all novelists after the second, there is no single author whose intentions any interpreter can, by the rules of the project, regard as decisive. * * *

> Deciding hard cases at law is rather like this strange literary exercise. The similarity is most evident when judges consider and decide common-law cases; that is, when no statute figures centrally in the legal issue, and the argument turns on which rules or principles of law "underlie" the related decisions of other judges in the past. Each judge is then like a novelist in the chain. He or she must read through what other judges in the past have written not simply to discover what these judges have said, or their state of mind when they said it, but to reach an opinion about what these judges have collectively *done*, in the way that each of our novelists formed an opinion about the collective novel so far written.

In *Law's Empire* 313 (1986), Dworkin described how the chain novel tells judges to interpret statutes:

> He will treat Congress as an author earlier than himself in the chain of law, though an author with special powers and responsibilities different from his own [as a judge], and he will see his own role as fundamentally the creative one of a partner continuing to develop, in what he believes is the best way, the statutory scheme Congress began. He will ask himself which reading of the act * * * shows the political history including and surrounding that statute in the better light. His view of how the statute should be read will in part depend on what certain congressmen said when debating it. But it will also depend on the best answer to political questions: how far Congress should defer to public opinion in matters of this sort, for example * * *.

On the application of his theory to *Weber*, see Dworkin, *How to Read the Civil Rights Act*, in Dworkin, *A Matter of Principle* (1985). How would Dworkin's theory apply to *Public Citizen?*[35]

C. CRITIQUES OF LEGAL PROCESS PRECEPTS, 1970s–80s

Legal process theory came into focus around the time of World War II. This was a period of relative consensus in America, sustained economic growth, and burgeoning optimism about government's ability to foster economic growth by solving market failures and creating opportunities. After the mid-1960s, America was a different society, as consensus collapsed on fundamental issues of war, family, and citizenship; economic growth faltered and oil price shocks introduced stagflation; and government came to be perceived as problematic, often even as a drain on society's productivity. These developments raised inevitable questions about statutory methodology, such as the ones that follow.

1. *A More Realistic (or Cynical) View of the Legislative Process?* Public choice and other theories of legislation maintain that legislators are not entirely "reasonable," as Hart and Sacks assume, and are often acting to extract "rents" for their constituents and supportive interest groups. Moreover, even reasonable legislators will disagree, and the resulting statutes may be compromises more than easily understood purposive enactments. Some scholars have argued from such theories that Hart and Sacks' purposive approach should therefore be reined back toward something like Pound's imaginative reconstruction. See Richard Posner, *The Federal Courts: Crisis and Reform* 286–93 (1985).

On the other hand, Hart and Sacks never claimed their "reasonable legislator" approach actually describes the legislature; they only said that courts should "attribute" purposes to the legislature, suggesting that theirs is a normative-based rather than a descriptive-based theory of interpretation. Why should ambiguous interest-group deals be enforced by courts if they do not serve a larger public purpose? See Jonathan Macey, *Promoting Public-Regarding Legislation Through Statutory Interpretation: An Interest Group Model*, 86 Colum. L. Rev. 223 (1986), who argues that the public interest requires that rent-seeking legislators should be held to their stated (public-regarding) justifications.

2. *Does the Hart and Sacks Approach Submerge Substantive Issues?* Both pragmatic and critical scholars criticize legal process theory for suppressing useful substantive discussion. Judge Posner, for example, openly inquires about the practical consequences of different interpretations. See, e.g., Richard Posner, *How Judges Think* ch. 5 (2008), and *The Problems of Jurisprudence* (1990). His practice is to figure out what is the most reasonable statutory interpretation, as applied to the facts before him, and then see if statutory text, history, and precedent foreclose the best option. This sounds a lot like Hart and Sacks, but Posner would say that he adds empirical data and systematic economic thinking that Hart and Sacks did not

---

[35]   For jurisprudential connections between Dworkin's theory of law as integrity and legal process theory, see Vincent Wellman, *Dworkin and the Legal Process Tradition: The Legacy of Hart & Sacks*, 29 Ariz. L. Rev. 413 (1987), as well as William Eskridge Jr., *Nino's Nightmare: Legal Process Theory as a Jurisprudence of Toggling Between Facts and Norms*, 57 St. Louis U.L.J. 865 (2013).

emphasize. Why not introduce rigorous, empirically based economic analysis into decisionmaking?

Critical scholars argue that legal process judges are making unarticulated value choices under the auspices of neutral craft. Allan Hutchinson and Derek Morgan, in *The Semiology of Statutes*, 21 Harv. J. Legis. 583, 593–94 (1984), state:

> Words do not interpret themselves. A sentence will never mean exactly the same thing to any two different people or even the same thing to one person on different occasions. Meaning is shaped by the apperceptive mass of understanding and background that an individual brings to bear on the external fact of a sound or series of marks. As words lack "self-evident reference," purpose and context are ultimately major determinants of meaning. However, as the expression of legislative intent is always more or less incomplete, it is doubtful whether any impartial method of adjudication can be fashioned in a liberal society. * * *

> The necessity of engaging in such invention requires the courts to make substantive political decisions, the very decisions that semantic, historical or counter-factual approaches *claim* to avoid. No one single "construction" is inevitable or natural. Construction means choice. And choice confers power. Of course, this is not to suggest that judicial creativity breeds constitutional anarchy. Communities of interpretation have their own bonding mechanisms, a mixture of moral values and social customs. Interpretation is inextricably bound up with values and it is nowhere seriously suggested the values do not carry ideological underpinnings. The lesson to be gathered from this realization is quite simple. Courts that shield themselves behind descriptions of law as clear, predetermined and objective norms against which they pitch their neutral decisions are worthy of suspicion. * * *

On this understanding, a virtue of Justice Brewer's opinion in *Holy Trinity Church* is that it was candid about the values it was implementing (the Christian nation idea). Hart and Sacks' approach would likely generate the same result in the hands of an Evangelical jurist such as Justice Brewer, but perhaps a less candid discussion.

3.   *The Appeal of Formalism.* Among judges, the most telling criticism of the legal process approach to statutory interpretation is that it neglects the virtues of a more formalist approach. Even contextualists might concede the attractions of the plain meaning rule, defended by Judge Keen in Speluncean Explorers. First, it is arguably more consistent with the structure of the U.S. Constitution (as well as most state constitutions), which vests political power with the legislative and executive branches and only the judicial power with the courts, and which creates formal barriers to lawmaking that are disregarded when courts make new law. See John Manning, *Textualism as a Nondelegation Doctrine*, 97 Colum. L. Rev. 673 (1997). Second, it can be argued that applying statutory plain meanings is more within the "judicial competence" than making policy or even scanning through legislative history to figure out whether the legislature "really meant" the apparent meaning of its statutory words. See Adrian Vermeule, *Legislative History and the Limits of*

Judicial Competence: The Untold Story of Holy Trinity Church, 50 Stan. L. Rev. 1833 (1998).

Third, the ordinary meaning of statutory language is the common understanding of what the "rule of law" is. See Antonin Scalia, *The Rule of Law as a Law of Rules*, 56 U. Chi. L. Rev. 1175 (1989). Citizens ought to be able to open up the statute books and find out what the law requires of them. Once law is understood by the cognoscenti as purposes, spirits, and collective intents, the citizenry might lose faith in the externality of law—the objectivity of legal reasoning which provides us with some assurance that our problems are susceptible of the same rules as those of our neighbor (even if she is a rich and influential neighbor). The changes in American society since the 1960s make an external vision of the rule of law even more important than before. In a society where so many values are open to contest, language may be the main thing we share in common. In a society where "the pie" is not expanding and the economy is stagnant, dividing the pie by an objective criterion becomes ever more critical.

A less complicated approach may also be more democracy-enhancing, because it places responsibility for updating statutes on the shoulders of the people and their legislators, rather than their unelected (federal and some state) or not-often-elected (most state) judges. As potential examples of this phenomenon, consider the following cases.

STATUTORY PREFACE TO *TVA V. HILL* (THE SNAIL DARTER CASE)

The Endangered Species Act of 1973, Public Law 93–205 (codified at 16 U.S.C. § 1531 et seq.)

Section 2, 16 U.S.C. § 1531. Findings, Purposes, and Policy * * *

(b) Purposes.—The purposes of this Act are to provide a means whereby the ecosystems upon which endangered species and threatened species depend may be conserved, to provide a program for the conservation of such endangered species and threatened species, and to take such steps as may be appropriate to achieve the purposes of [various species-protecting] treaties and conventions * * *.

(c) Policy.—It is further declared to be the policy of Congress that all federal departments and agencies shall seek to conserve endangered species and threatened species and shall utilize their authorities in furtherance of the purposes of this Act.

Section 4, 16 U.S.C. § 1533. Determination of Endangered Species and Threatened Species [This section delegates to the Secretary of the Interior the authority, after consultation, to designate species as either endangered or threatened. Private persons and other governmental agencies are bound by the Secretary's determination.]

Section 7, 16 U.S.C. § 1536. Interagency Cooperation

The Secretary [of the Interior] shall review other programs administered by him and utilize such programs in furtherance of the purposes of this Act. All other Federal departments and agencies shall, in consultation with and with the assistance of the

Secretary, utilize their authorities in furtherance of the purposes of this Act by carrying out programs for the conservation of endangered species and threatened species listed pursuant to section 4 of this Act and by taking such action necessary to insure that actions authorized, funded, or carried out by them do not jeopardize the continued existence of such endangered species and threatened species or result in the destruction or modification of habitat of such species which is determined by the Secretary, after consultation as appropriate with the affected States, to be critical.

TENNESSEE VALLEY AUTHORITY V. HILL

United States Supreme Court, 1978.
437 U.S. 153, 98 S.Ct. 2279, 57 L.Ed.2d 117.

CHIEF JUSTICE BURGER delivered the opinion of the Court.

[Pursuant to the statute, the Secretary of the Interior declared the snail darter (*Percina tanasi*) an endangered species and designated a portion of the Little Tennessee River as the only remaining natural habitat of the snail darter. That part of the river, however, would be flooded by operation of the Tellico Dam, a $100 million Tennessee Valley Authority (TVA) project that was under way in 1973 and was almost completed by 1976, when environmentalists sought an injunction against the dam's operation, on the basis of § 7 of the new Act. The district court denied relief. It found that the dam would destroy the snail darter's critical habitat, but it noted that Congress, though fully aware of the snail darter problem, had continued to fund the Tellico Dam after 1973. The court concluded that the Act did not justify an injunction against a project initiated before enactment. The court of appeals reversed and ordered the lower court to enjoin completion of the dam.]

One would be hard pressed to find a statutory provision whose terms were any plainer than those in § 7 of the Endangered Species Act. Its very words affirmatively command all federal agencies "to *insure* that actions *authorized, funded, or carried out* by them do not *jeopardize* the continued existence" of an endangered species or "*result* in the destruction or modification of habitat of such species. . . ." 16 U.S.C. § 1536 (1976 ed.). (Emphasis added.) This language admits of no exception. Nonetheless, petitioner urges, as do the dissenters, that the Act cannot reasonably be interpreted as applying to a federal project which was well under way when Congress passed the Endangered Species Act of 1973. To sustain that position, however, we would be forced to ignore the ordinary meaning of plain language. It has not been shown, for example, how TVA can close the gates of the Tellico Dam without "carrying out" an action that has been "authorized" and "funded" by a federal agency. Nor can we understand how such action will "*insure*" that the snail darter's habitat is not disrupted. * * *

Concededly, this view of the Act will produce results requiring the sacrifice of the anticipated benefits of the project and of many millions of dollars in public funds. But examination of the language, history, and structure of the legislation under review here indicates beyond doubt that Congress intended endangered species to be afforded the highest of priorities.

[Chief Justice Burger examined statutes enacted in 1966 and 1969, which sought to discourage the taking of endangered species. Congressional hearings in 1973 revealed that strategies of encouragement had not abated the "pace of disappearance of species," which appeared to be "accelerating." H.R. Rep. No. 93–412, p. 4 (1973). The dominant theme of the hearings and debates on the 1973 Act was "the overriding need to devote whatever effort and resources were necessary to avoid further diminution of national and worldwide wildlife resources." Congressional committees expressed the "incalculable" value of lost species.]

The legislative proceedings in 1973 are, in fact, replete with expressions of concern over the risk that might lie in the loss of *any* endangered species. Typifying these sentiments is the Report of the House Committee on Merchant Marine and Fisheries on H.R. 37, a bill which contained the essential features of the subsequently enacted Act of 1973; in explaining the need for the legislation, the Report stated:

"As we homogenize the habitats in which these plants and animals evolved, and as we increase the pressure for products that they are in a position to supply (usually unwillingly) we threaten their- and our own-genetic heritage.

"The value of this genetic heritage is, quite literally, incalculable. * * *

"From the most narrow possible point of view, *it is in the best interests of mankind to minimize the losses of genetic variations.* The reason is simple: they are potential resources. They are keys to puzzles which we cannot solve, and may provide answers to questions which we have not yet learned to ask.

"To take a homely, but apt, example: one of the critical chemicals in the regulation of ovulations in humans was found in a common plant. Once discovered, and analyzed, humans could duplicate it synthetically, but had it never existed—or had it been driven out of existence before we knew its potentialities—we would never have tried to synthesize it in the first place.

"Who knows, or can say, what potential cures for <u>cancer</u> or other scourges, present or future, may lie locked up in the structures of plants which may yet be undiscovered, much less analyzed? . . . Sheer self-interest impels us to be cautious.

"*The institutionalization of that caution* lies at the heart of H.R. 37. . . ."

H.R.Rep.No.93–412, pp. 4–5 (1973) (emphasis added). As the examples cited here demonstrate, Congress was concerned about the *unknown uses* that endangered species might have and about the *unforeseeable* place such creatures may have in the chain of life on this planet. * * *

Section 7 of the Act * * * provides a particularly good gauge of congressional intent. As we have seen, this provision had its genesis in the Endangered Species Act of 1966, but that legislation qualified the obligation of federal agencies by stating that they should seek to preserve endangered species only "*insofar as is practicable and consistent with their primary purposes. . . .*" Likewise, every bill introduced in 1973 contained a qualification similar to that found in the earlier statutes. * * * This type of language did not go unnoticed by those advocating strong endangered species legislation. A representative of the Sierra Club, for example, attacked the use of the phrase "consistent with the primary purpose" in proposed H.R. 4758, cautioning that the qualification "could be construed to be a declaration of congressional policy that other agency purposes are necessarily more important than protection of endangered species and would always prevail if conflict were to occur."

What is very significant in this sequence is that the final version of the 1973 Act carefully omitted all of the reservations described above. [The Senate bill contained a practicability reservation; the House bill had no qualifications. The Conference Committee rejected the Senate version of § 7 and adopted the House language. Explaining the Conference action, Representative Dingell pointed out that under existing law the Secretary of Defense has discretion to ignore dangers its bombing missions posed to the near-extinct whooping crane. "[O]nce the bill is enacted, [the Secretary of Defense] *would be required to take the proper steps.*" Another example was the declining population of grizzly bears, whose habitats would have to be protected by the Department of Agriculture. "The purposes of the bill included the conservation of the species and of the ecosystems upon which they depend, and every agency of government is committed to see that those purposes are carried out. The agencies of Government can no longer plead that they can do nothing about it. *They can and they must. The law is clear.*" 119 Cong. Rec. 42913 (emphasis added by the Chief Justice).]

It is against this legislative background that we must measure TVA's claim that the Act was not intended to stop operation of a project which, like Tellico Dam, was near completion when an endangered species was discovered in its path. While there is no discussion of precisely this problem, the totality of congressional action makes it abundantly clear that the result we reach today is wholly in accord with both the words of the statute and the intent of Congress. The plain intent of Congress in enacting this statute was to halt and reverse the trend toward species extinction, whatever the cost. This is reflected not only in the stated provisions of the Act, but in literally every section of the statute. All persons, including federal agencies, are specifically instructed not to "take" endangered species, meaning that no one is "to harass, harm, pursue, hunt, shoot, wound, kill, trap, capture, or collect" such life forms. 16 U.S.C. §§ 1532(14), 1538(a)(1)(B) (1976 ed.). * * *

[TVA also argued that Congress's continued funding of the Dam reflected a congressional judgment, embodied in appropriations statutes, that the Dam not be shut down. Appropriations committees were aware of the effect of the Dam on the snail darter.] There is nothing in the appropriations measures, as passed, which states that the Tellico Project was to be completed irrespective of the requirements of the Endangered Species Act. * * * To find a repeal of the Endangered Species Act under these circumstances would surely do violence to the " 'cardinal rule . . . that repeals by implication are not favored.' " *Morton v. Mancari*, 417 U.S. 535, 549 (1974), quoting *Posadas v. National City Bank*, 296 U.S. 497, 503 (1936). * * *

The doctrine disfavoring repeals by implication "applies with full vigor when . . . the subsequent legislation is an *appropriations* measure." *Committee for Nuclear Responsibility v. Seaborg*, 463 F.2d 783, 785 (D.C. Cir. 1971). This is perhaps an understatement since it would be more accurate to say that the policy applies with even *greater* force when the claimed repeal rests solely with an Appropriations Act. * * * When voting on appropriations measures, legislators are entitled to operate under the assumption that the funds will be devoted to purposes which are lawful and not for any purpose forbidden. [The Chief Justice also pointed to House Rule XXI(2), which forbids amendments to appropriations bills which seeks to "chang[e] existing law." See also Senate Rule 16.4.] Thus, to sustain petitioner's position, we would be obliged to assume that Congress meant to repeal *pro tanto* § 7 of the Act by means of a procedure expressly prohibited under the rules of Congress.

[Chief Justice Burger rejected TVA's urging the Court to balance the harms of shutting down the dam against the dangers to the snail darter. Not only did the Court not consider itself competent to calibrate such a balance, but Congress had already made the judgment that no cost was too high to allow the federal government to imperil a species.] [I]n our constitutional system the commitment to the separation of powers is too fundamental for us to pre-empt congressional action by judicially decreeing what accords with "common sense and the public weal." Our Constitution vests such responsibilities in the political branches.

[JUSTICE POWELL's dissenting opinion, joined by Justice Blackmun, argued that the Court's opinion "disregards 12 years of consistently expressed congressional intent to complete the Tellico Project" and is "an extreme example of a literalist construction, not required by the language of the Act and adopted without regard to its manifest purpose." Citing *Holy Trinity Church*, Justice Powell contended that the Court ought not read the broad language of § 7 so sweepingly and, instead, ought to narrow the language so as to avoid "absurd results." He would have construed the "actions" governed by § 7 to be only those taken *after* 1973, when the statute was enacted.]

[JUSTICE REHNQUIST dissented on the ground that the legitimate debate over the statute's meaning properly informed the district court's decision not to enjoin work on the dam.]

STATUTORY PREFACE TO *GRIFFIN V. OCEANIC*

Rev. Stat. § 4529 (1872), as amended, 46 U.S.C. § 596.

The master or owner of any vessel making coasting voyages shall pay to every seaman his wages within two days after the termination of the agreement under which he was shipped, or at the time such seaman is discharged, whichever first happens; and in case of vessels making foreign voyages, or from a port on the Atlantic to a port on the Pacific, or vice versa, within twenty-four hours after the cargo has been discharged, or within four days after the seaman has been discharged, whichever first happens; and in all cases the seaman shall be entitled to be paid at the time of his discharge on account of wages a sum equal to one-third part of the balance due him. Every master or owner who refuses or neglects to make payment in the manner hereinbefore mentioned without sufficient cause shall pay to the seaman a sum equal to two days' pay for each and every day during which payment is delayed beyond the respective periods, which sum shall be recoverable as wages in any claim made before the court; but this section shall not apply to masters or owners of any vessel the seamen of which are entitled to share in the profits of the cruise or voyage. This section shall not apply to fishing or whaling vessels or yachts.

GRIFFIN V. OCEANIC CONTRACTORS, INC.

Supreme Court of the United States, 1982.
458 U.S. 564, 102 S.Ct. 3245, 73 L.Ed.2d 973.

JUSTICE REHNQUIST delivered the opinion of the Court.

[In February 1976, Danny Griffin contracted to work as a senior pipeline welder on board vessels operated by respondent in the North Sea. The contract specified that petitioner's employment would extend "until December 15, 1976 or until Oceanic's 1976 pipeline committal in the North Sea is fulfilled, whichever shall occur first." The contract also provided that if Griffin quit the job prior to its termination date, or if his services were terminated for cause, he would be charged with the cost of transportation back to the United States. Oceanic reserved the right to withhold $137.50 from each of petitioner's first four paychecks "as a cash deposit for the payment of your return transportation in the event you should become obligated for its payment." On April 1, 1976, Griffin suffered an injury while working on the deck of the vessel readying it for sea. Oceanic refused to take responsibility for the injury or to furnish transportation back to the United States, and continued to retain $412.50 in earned wages that had been deducted from Griffin's first three paychecks for that purpose. He returned to the United States and on May 5, began working as a welder for another company operating in the North Sea.

[In 1978 Griffin brought suit against respondent under the Jones Act, § 20, 38 Stat. 1185, as amended, 46 U.S.C. § 688, and under general maritime law, seeking damages for respondent's failure to pay maintenance, cure, unearned wages, repatriation expenses, and the value of certain personal effects lost on board respondent's vessel. He also sought penalty wages under Rev. Stat. § 4529, as amended, 46 U.S.C. § 596, for respondent's failure to pay over the $412.50 in earned wages allegedly due upon discharge. The District Court found for Griffin and awarded damages totaling $23,670.40.]

In assessing penalty wages under 46 U.S.C. § 596, the court held that "[t]he period during which the penalty runs is to be determined by the sound discretion of the district court and depends on the equities of the case." It determined that the appropriate period for imposition of the penalty was from the date of discharge, April 1, 1976, through the date of petitioner's reemployment, May 5, 1976, a period of 34 days. Applying the statute, it computed a penalty of $6,881.60. Petitioner appealed the award of damages as inadequate. [The Fifth Circuit affirmed the district court judgment. The Supreme Court reversed and ruled that Oceanic owed Griffin more than $302,000 in penalty wages.]

[II.A] The language of the statute first obligates the master or owner of any vessel making coasting or foreign voyages to pay every seaman the balance of his unpaid wages within specified periods after his discharge. It then provides:

"Every master or owner who refuses or neglects to make payments in the manner hereinbefore mentioned without sufficient cause shall pay to the seaman a sum equal to two days' pay for each and every day during which payment is delayed beyond the respective periods * * *."

The statute in straightforward terms provides for the payment of double wages, depending upon the satisfaction of two conditions. First, the master or owner must have refused or failed to pay the seaman his wages within the periods specified. Second, this failure or refusal must be "without sufficient cause." Once these conditions are satisfied, however, the unadorned language of the statute dictates that the master or owner "*shall pay* to the seaman" the sums specified "*for each and every day* during which payment is delayed." The words chosen by Congress, given their plain meaning, leave no room for the exercise of discretion either in deciding whether to exact payment or in choosing the period of days by which the payment is to be calculated. As this Court described the statute many years ago, it "affords a definite and reasonable procedure by which the seaman may establish his right to recover double pay where his wages are unreasonably withheld." Our task is to give effect to the will of Congress, and where its will has been expressed in reasonably plain terms, "that language must ordinarily be regarded as conclusive." *Consumer Product Safety Comm'n v. GTE Sylvania, Inc.*, 447 U.S. 102, 108 (1980).

The District Court found that respondent had refused to pay petitioner the balance of his earned wages promptly after discharge, and that its refusal was "without sufficient cause." Respondent challenges neither of these findings. Although the two statutory conditions were satisfied, however, the District Court obviously did not assess double wages "for each and every day" during which payment was delayed, but instead limited the assessment to the period of petitioner's unemployment. Nothing in the language of the statute vests the courts with the discretion to set such a limitation.

[B] Nevertheless, respondent urges that the legislative purpose of the statute is best served by construing it to permit some choice in determining the length of the penalty period. In respondent's view, the purpose of the statute is essentially remedial and compensatory, and thus it should not be interpreted literally to produce a monetary award that is so far in excess of any equitable remedy as to be punitive.

Respondent, however, is unable to support this view of legislative purpose by reference to the terms of the statute. "There is, of course, no more persuasive evidence of the purpose of a statute than the words by which the legislature undertook to give expression to its wishes." *United States v. American Trucking Assns., Inc.*, 310 U.S. 534, 543 (1940). Nevertheless, in rare cases the literal application of a statute will produce a result demonstrably at odds with the intentions of its drafters, and those intentions must be controlling. We have reserved "some 'scope for adopting a restricted rather than a literal or usual meaning of its words where acceptance of that meaning * * * would thwart the obvious purpose of the statute.'" *Commissioner v. Brown*, 380 U.S. 563, 571 (1965) (quoting *Helvering v. Hammel*, 311 U.S. 504, 510–511 (1941)). This, however, is not the exceptional case.

As the Court recognized in *Collie v. Fergusson*, 281 U.S. 52 (1930), the "evident purpose" of the statute is "to secure prompt payment of seamen's wages * * * and thus to protect them from the harsh consequences of arbitrary and unscrupulous action of their employers, to which, as a class, they are peculiarly exposed." This was to be accomplished "by the imposition of a liability which is not exclusively compensatory, but designed to prevent, by its coercive effect, arbitrary refusals to pay wages, and to induce prompt payment when payment is possible." Thus, although the sure purpose of the statute is remedial, Congress has chosen to secure that purpose through the use of potentially punitive sanctions designed to deter negligent or arbitrary delays in payment.

The legislative history of the statute leaves little if any doubt that this understanding is correct. The law owes its origins to the Act of July 20, 1790, ch. 29, § 6, 1 Stat. 133, passed by the First Congress. Although the statute as originally enacted gave every seaman the right to collect the wages due under his contract "as soon as the voyage is ended," it did not provide for the recovery of additional sums to encourage compliance. Such a provision was added by the Shipping Commissioners Act of 1872, ch. 322, § 35, 17 Stat. 269, which provided for the payment of "a sum not exceeding the amount of two days' pay for each of the days, not exceeding ten days, during which payment is delayed." The Act of 1872 obviously established a ceiling of 10 days on the period during which the penalty could be assessed and, by use of the words "not exceeding," left the courts with discretion to choose an appropriate penalty within that period.

Congress amended the law again in 1898. As amended, it read in relevant part:

> "Every master or owner who refuses or neglects to make payment in manner hereinbefore mentioned without sufficient cause shall pay to the seaman a sum equal to one day's pay for each and every day during which payment is delayed beyond the respective periods." Act of Dec. 21, 1898, ch. 28, § 4, 30 Stat. 756.

The amending legislation thus effected two changes: first, it removed the discretion theretofore existing by which courts might award less than an amount calculated on the basis of each day during which payment was delayed, and, second, it removed the 10-day ceiling which theretofore limited the number of days upon which an award might be calculated. The accompanying Committee Reports identify the purpose of the legislation as "the amelioration of the condition of the American seamen," and characterize the amended wage penalty in particular as "designed to secure the promptest possible payment of wages." H.R.Rep. No. 1657, 55th Cong., 2d Sess., 2, 3 (1898). See also S.Rep. No. 832, 54th Cong., 1st Sess., 2 (1896). Nothing in the legislative history of the 1898 Act suggests that Congress intended to do anything other than what the Act's enacted language plainly demonstrates: to strengthen the deterrent effect of the statute by removing the courts' latitude in assessing the wage penalty.

The statute was amended for the last time in 1915 to increase further the severity of the penalty by doubling the wages due for each day during which payment of earned wages was delayed. Seamen's Act of 1915, ch. 153, § 3, 38 Stat. 1164. There is no suggestion in the Committee Reports or in the floor debates that, in so doing, Congress intended to reinvest the courts with the discretion it had removed in the Act of 1898. Resort to the legislative history, therefore, merely confirms that Congress intended the statute to mean exactly what its plain language says.

[III] Respondent argues, however, that a literal construction of the statute in this case would produce an absurd and unjust result which Congress could not have intended. The District Court found that the daily wage to be used in computing the penalty was $101.20. If the statute is applied literally, petitioner would receive twice this amount for each day after his discharge until September 17, 1980, when respondent satisfied the District Court's judgment.[9] Petitioner would receive over $300,000 simply because respondent improperly withheld $412.50 in wages. In respondent's view, Congress could not have intended seamen to receive windfalls of this nature without regard to the equities of the case.

It is true that interpretations of a statute which would produce absurd results are to be avoided if alternative interpretations consistent with the legislative purpose are available. See *United States v. American Trucking Assns., Inc.*, 310 U.S., at 542–543; *Haggar Co. v. Helvering*, 308 U.S. 389, 394 (1940). In refusing to nullify statutes, however hard or unexpected the particular effect, this Court has said:

> "Laws enacted with good intention, when put to the test, frequently, and to the surprise of the law maker himself, turn out to be mischievous, absurd or otherwise objectionable. But in such case the remedy lies with the law making authority, and not with the courts." *Crooks v. Harrelson*, 282 U.S. 55, 60 (1930).

It is highly probable that respondent is correct in its contention that a recovery in excess of $300,000 in this case greatly exceeds any actual injury suffered by petitioner as a result of respondent's delay in paying his wages. But this Court has previously recognized that awards made under this statute were not intended to be merely compensatory:

> "We think the use of this language indicates a purpose to protect seamen from delayed payments of wages by the imposition of a liability which is not exclusively compensatory, but designed to prevent, by its coercive effect, arbitrary refusals to pay wages, and to induce prompt payment when payment is possible." *Collie v. Fergusson*, 281 U.S., at 55–56.

It is in the nature of punitive remedies to authorize awards that may be out of proportion to actual injury; such remedies typically are established to deter particular conduct, and the legislature not infrequently finds that harsh consequences must be visited upon those whose conduct it would deter. It is probably true that Congress did not precisely envision the grossness of the difference in this case between the actual wages withheld and the amount of the award required by the statute. But it might equally well be said that Congress did not precisely envision the trebled amount of some damages awards in private antitrust actions, see *Reiter v. Sonotone Corp.*, 442 U.S. 330, 344–345 (1979), or that, because it enacted the Endangered Species Act, "the survival of a relatively small number of three-inch fish * * * would require the permanent halting of a virtually completed dam for which

---

[9]   Respondent assumes that the penalty would run until September 17, 1980, since that was the date on which it finally paid petitioner the $412.50. Brief for Respondent 17. Petitioner, on the other hand, apparently assumes that the penalty period expired on May 6, 1980, the date of the District Court's judgment. Brief for Petitioner 19. Under our construction of the statute, the District Court's entry of judgment will not toll the running of the penalty period unless delays beyond that date are explained by sufficient cause. * * *

Congress ha[d] expended more than $1 million," *TVA v. Hill*, 437 U.S. 153, 172 (1978). It is enough that Congress intended that the language it enacted would be applied as we have applied it. The remedy for any dissatisfaction with the results in particular cases lies with Congress and not with this Court. Congress may amend the statute; we may not. * * *

JUSTICE STEVENS, with whom JUSTICE BLACKMUN joins, dissenting.

In final analysis, any question of statutory construction requires the judge to decide how the legislature intended its enactment to apply to the case at hand. The language of the statute is usually sufficient to answer that question, but "the reports are full of cases" in which the will of the legislature is not reflected in a literal reading of the words it has chosen.[1] In my opinion this is such a case. * * *

[II.A] In fixing the amount of the award of double wages, the District Court in this case may have reasoned that respondent had sufficient cause for its delay in paying the earned wages after petitioner obtained employment with another shipmaster, but that there was not sufficient cause for its failure to make payment before that time. Although this reasoning conflicts with a literal reading of § 596, it is perfectly consistent with this Court's contemporary construction of the statute in *Pacific Mail S.S. Co. v. Schmidt*, 241 U.S. 245 (1916). The teaching of Justice Holmes' opinion for the Court in that case is that the wrongful character of the initial refusal to pay does not mean that all subsequent delay in payment is also "without sufficient cause" within the meaning of the statute.

The controversy in *Pacific Mail* arose in 1913, when the statute provided that the sum recoverable as wages was measured by one day's pay, rather than double that amount, for each day that the wages were withheld without sufficient cause; the statute was otherwise exactly as it is today. The seaman was discharged on October 1, 1913, but $30.33 was withheld from his wages because he was believed responsible for the loss of some silverware. He filed an action on October 20, 1913, and on November 5, 1913, obtained a judgment for his wages and an additional sum of $151.59, representing the sum recoverable as wages for the period between October 1 and November 5, 1913. The District Court's decree established the proposition that the vessel owner's defenses did not constitute sufficient cause for refusing to pay the wages and requiring the seaman to sue to recover them.

The vessel owner prosecuted an unsuccessful appeal. The Court of Appeals not only affirmed the decision of the District Court, but also added an additional recovery of daily wages for the period between the entry of the original judgment on November 5 and the actual payment of the disputed wages. The Court of Appeals thus read the statute literally and ordered the result that the District Court's finding seemed to dictate. This Court, however, set aside the additional recovery, reaching a conclusion that cannot be reconciled with a wooden, literal reading of the statute. Concurrent findings of the District Court and the Court of Appeals established that the refusal to make the wage payment when due was without sufficient cause. Justice Holmes and his Brethren accepted that finding for purposes of decision, but reasoned that

---

[1]   It is a familiar rule, that a thing may be within the letter of the statute and yet not within the statute, because not within its spirit, nor within the intention of its makers. This has been often asserted, and the reports are full of cases illustrating its application. * * * *Holy Trinity Church.*

there was sufficient cause for the owner's decision to appeal and his refusal to pay while the appeal was pending.

The curious character of this Court's conclusion that reasons insufficient to justify the refusal to pay before the trial court's decision somehow became sufficient to justify a subsequent refusal to pay is not the most significant point to Justice Holmes' opinion. The case is primarily significant because its holding cannot be squared with a literal reading of the statute. Even though the initial refusal is without sufficient cause, statutory wages are not necessarily recoverable for the entire period until payment is made either to the seaman or to a stakeholder. A subsequent event—even though not expressly mentioned in the statute itself—may foreshorten the recovery period.

In *Pacific Mail* the subsequent event was the vessel owner's decision to appeal. The finding that that event provided sufficient cause for the delay after November 5, 1913, was made *sua sponte* by this Court. In this case the subsequent event was the reemployment of petitioner in a comparable job on May 5, 1976. The finding that that event—coupled with the failure to make any additional demand for almost two years thereafter—was sufficient cause for the delay after May 5, 1976, was made by the District Court. It is true that the judge did not expressly frame his decision in these terms, but his actual decision fits precisely the mold established by *Pacific Mail*. Both cases give a flexible reading to the "sufficient cause" language in the statute. They differ with respect to the nature of the subsequent event but not with respect to their departure from the statutory text. [Justice Stevens also cited *Collie v. Fergusson*, 281 U.S. 52 (1930), in which the Court refused to read the statute to penalize an employer for failing to pay wages because of its financial difficulties. The conclusions reached by Justice Stevens's analysis "dispel any notion that the statute means exactly what it says." Indeed, the same flexibility shown by the Supreme Court in *Collie* also characterized the lower federal courts' treatment of the statute from 1896 to 1966.]

[III] The construction permitting the district court to exercise some discretion in tailoring the double-wage award to the particular equities of the case is just as consistent with the legislative history of § 596 as the Court's new literal approach to this statute. In 1872, when Congress authorized the recovery of additional wages by seamen who were not paid within five days of their discharge, it used the word "shall" to make it clear that such a recovery must be awarded, but it allowed the district courts a limited discretion in setting the amount of such recovery.[17] The judge's discretion as to amount was limited in two ways: (1) the statutory wage rate could not be more than double the amount of the seaman's daily wage; and (2) the period for which the statutory wage could be awarded could not exceed 10 days.

Subsequent amendments to the statute did not remove the requirement that some recovery "shall" be awarded, but did modify both of the limits on the judge's discretion. With respect to the wage rate, Congress first specified that it should equal

---

[17]   The 1872 version of § 596 provided in pertinent part:

"[E]very master or owner who neglects or refuses to make payment [of a seaman's earned wages within five days after the seaman's discharge] without sufficient cause shall pay to the seaman a sum not exceeding the amount of two days' pay for each of the days, not exceeding ten days, during which payment is delayed beyond the [five-day period]; and such sum shall be recoverable as wages in any claim made before the court * * *." Act of June 7, 1872, ch. 322, § 35, 17 Stat. 269.

the daily rate—rather than double the daily rate—and later specified that the rate should be the double rate.[18] With respect to the period for which the statutory wage was payable, the 1898 amendment simply removed the 10-day limit. This amendment is subject to two different interpretations, one that would represent a rather unremarkable change and the other that would be both drastic and dramatic.

The unremarkable change would amount to nothing more than a removal of the narrow 10-day limit on the scope of the judge's discretion. The word "shall" would continue to do nothing more than require some recovery in an amount to be fixed by the judge, but in recognition of the reality that seamen might be stranded for more than 10 days, the recovery period could extend beyond 10 days. This sort of unremarkable change is consistent with the purpose of the statute, as well as with a legislative history that fails to make any comment on its significance. As Justice Rehnquist has perceptively observed in another context, the fact that the dog did not bark can itself be significant.[20]

The Court's construction of the amendment is, however, both drastic and dramatic. Instead of effecting a modest enlargement of the judge's discretion to do justice in these cases, the Court's construction effects a complete prohibition of judicial discretion. Instead of permitting recoveries for a period somewhat longer than 10 days, the amendment is construed as a command that even when the unresolved dispute persists for two or three years without any special hardship to the seaman, an automatic recovery must be ordered for the entire period regardless of the equitable considerations that may arise after the shipmaster's initial mistake has been made. Such a major change in both the potential amount of the statutory recovery and the character of the judge's authority would normally be explained in the committee reports or the debates if it had been intended. * * *

NOTES ON HILL, GRIFFIN, AND THE REVIVAL OF THE PLAIN MEANING RULE

1. *The Legislative Response in* Griffin *and in* TVA v. Hill. As the briefs in the case had suggested would occur, Chief Justice Burger's opinion in *TVA v. Hill* triggered an immediate legislative override. The Endangered Species Act Amendments of 1978, Pub. L. No. 95–632, § 7, 92 Stat. 3751, 3752–60 (1978), established an administrative mechanism for granting exemptions to the Act. When administrators revealed reluctance to apply this process to save the Tellico Dam, that project was specifically exempted by Congress in Pub. L. No. 96–69, tit. IV, 93 Stat. 437, 449 (1979). For an analysis of the complicated politics of the override process in this case, see Elizabeth Garrett, *The Story*

---

[18]   The 1898 version of § 596 provided in pertinent part:

"Every master or owner who refuses or neglects to make payment [of a seaman's earned wages within four days of the seaman's discharge] without sufficient cause shall pay to the seaman a sum equal to one day's pay for each and every day during which payment is delayed beyond the [four-day period], which sum shall be recoverable as wages in any claim made before the court * * *." Act of Dec. 21, 1898, § 4, 30 Stat. 756.

The 1915 amendment substituted "two days' pay" for "one day's pay." See Act of Mar. 4, 1915, § 3, 38 Stat. 1164–1165.

[20]   *Harrison v. PPG Industries, Inc.,* 446 U.S. 578, 602 (1980) (dissenting opinion); cf. A. Conan Doyle, *Silver Blaze,* in The Complete Sherlock Holmes 383 (1938).

of TVA v. Hill, in *Statutory Interpretation Stories* 58–91 (Eskridge, Frickey & Garrett eds. 2011).

Justice Rehnquist's argument for deferring to Congress to change the statute in *Griffin* had a different legislative response—an underwrite more than an override. In 1983, Congress revised much of 46 U.S.C. through Pub. L. No. 98–89. Section 596 was repealed and replaced in part by 46 U.S.C. § 10313(g). The new provision says: "When payment is not made as provided [by the statute] without sufficient cause, the master or owner shall pay to the seaman 2 days' wages for each day payment is delayed." See also *id.* § 10504(c). Obviously, Congress did not change the language important to the Court's result in *Griffin.* Can you speculate why not?

2.   *The Supreme Court's Revival of the Plain Meaning Rule, 1976–86.* Although most commentators of the Burger Court's statutory opinions assumed that the Court was no more interested in the plain meaning rule than the Warren Court had been, one commentator astutely observed that *Griffin's* literalism was more characteristic of the Burger Court's statutory interpretation than the legal process purpose approach was. See Richard Pildes, Note, *Intent, Clear Statements and the Common Law: Statutory Interpretation in the Supreme Court,* 95 Harv. L. Rev. 892 (1982). On the other hand, the Burger Court followed a "soft" version of the plain meaning rule, for it typically (as it did in *Hill* and *Griffin*) attempted to justify harsh results in light of the legislative history and purposes of the statute. See *CPSC v. GTE Sylvania,* 447 U.S. 102 (1980). Indeed, passages in *Griffin* can be read for the proposition that legislative intent controls interpretation, and that the statutory text is given primacy in large part because it provides the best evidence of legislative intent. Moreover, sometimes the Burger Court went beyond even this understanding and interpreted statutes contrary to their apparent plain meaning, but consistent with their purposes and policies. See, e.g., *FDIC v. Philadelphia Gear Corp.,* 476 U.S. 426 (1986); *Midlantic Nat'l Bank v. New Jersey Dept. of Environmental Protection,* 474 U.S. 494 (1986).

3.   *What Is a "Plain Meaning"?* An important issue underlying both *TVA* and *Griffin,* but not seriously examined by the Court's opinions, is what suggests to a judge that there is a "plain meaning" for a statutory provision? One might put it as Hart and Sacks did: There is one plain meaning if any other interpretation would impose on the statutory words a meaning they will not bear. E.g., *Rapanos v. United States,* 547 U.S. 715, 731–32 (2006) (Scalia, J., plurality opinion) (asserting plain meaning in precisely those terms). Do § 7 of the ESA (*TVA*) and § 596 (*Griffin*) both have plain meanings under this formulation? In figuring out whether they have a plain meaning, is it legitimate for the interpreter to consider legislative history and other context? See Brett Kavanaugh, Book Review, *Fixing Statutory Interpretation,* 129 Harv. L. Rev. 2118 (2016) (book review); William Baude & Ryan Doerfler, *The (Not So) Plain Meaning Rule,* 84 U. Chi. L. Rev. 539 (2017).

The dissenting opinions in both cases argued that there is no single plain meaning when the literal meaning was so unreasonable. Thus, if I tell a subordinate to "drop everything and come here immediately," the plain meaning of my command does not require him or her to drop a $100,000 vase or arise immediately from the bathroom. The Court in both *TVA* and *Griffin* seems to concede that possibility, by checking the legislative history to make sure its reading is not unreasonable in light of the statutory purposes. (In both instances, the Court finds evidence that Congress's purpose supported the literal meaning. Why did this not satisfy the dissenters?)

Plain meaning analysis does not necessarily stop with ordinary meaning. See Miranda McGowan, *Do as I Do, Not as I Say: An Empirical Investigation of Justice Scalia's Ordinary Meaning Method of Statutory Interpretation,* 78 Miss. L.J. 129 (2008) (comparing Justice Scalia's textualist approach with that of the Court as a whole). A statute may have a "plain meaning" that would be unavailable to ordinary readers when legal authorities impose a specialized meaning on a term or phrase. Thus, a plain meaning might be different from an ordinary meaning when (a) Congress has defined the term in the statute; (b) the term has been authoritatively construed by the Court, or perhaps even just by the specialized community to which the statute applies (or experts testifying about that); or (c) the ordinary meaning is inconsistent with the whole act or with the way Congress has used the term in other statutes. See *Rapanos* (applying those exceptions).

One of these special exceptions to the presumption in favor of ordinary meaning should have been applied in *Griffin*: the Supreme Court *had* authoritatively construed the statutory terms in *Pacific Mail*, to cut off the running of the double wages ticker when the district court entered judgment. In footnote 9, Justice Rehnquist (or some aggressive law clerk) overruled the holding of *Pacific Mail*, without even mentioning the precedent. This is bizarre as well as anti-textualist, for the *Pacific Mail* cutoff is justified by the law of judgments: all damages are "merged" into a trial court's judgment, hence the cutting of double wages by Justice Holmes. Is there any justification for the Court's footnote? Upon the assumption that the footnote is the judicial equivalent of a "scrivener's error," should a lower court judge still follow *Pacific Mail*?

In *Griffin,* Justice Stevens propounded another source of context: *statutory history*, namely, the formal evolution in the actual terms of the statute, as it is amended over time. Stevens demonstrates that Congress's editing of the double wages law in the two generations after the Civil War rested upon the assumption that there would be a short time between injury (the ship abandons the seaman) and lawsuit and judgment (any judgment for penalty wages would merge with the judgment). See *Pacific Mail,* where the whole matter was wrapped up in months. How would Justice Rehnquist respond to Justice Stevens?

NOTE ON THE PLAIN MEANING RULE IN STATE COURTS

In general, the plain meaning rule had greater staying power at the state level. Through most of the twentieth century, state courts were more likely to resolve issues of statutory interpretation merely by construing the apparent meaning of the statutory language, with attention to textual canons of statutory construction but without *any* examination of the statute's purpose or legislative history. See, e.g., *Bishop v. Linkway Stores, Inc.,* 655 S.W.2d 426 (Ark. 1983). The two most frequently mentioned reasons for state court textualism were the dearth of legislative history materials available for state statutes and a more restrained methodology practiced by many state judges, especially those who are elected by the people or subject to retention elections to remain in office.

This textualist practice changed during the post-World War II era in most states. For example, California courts often eschewed a plain meaning approach. See, e.g., *People v. Hallner,* 277 P.2d 393 (Cal. 1954); *McKeag v. Board of Pension Comm'rs of Los Angeles,* 132 P.2d 198 (Cal. 1942). The California Supreme Court has often used a contextual approach to interpret legislation broadly to promote liberal social policy and fairness. For instance, *County of San Diego v. Muniz,* 583 P.2d 109 (Cal. 1978), involved a statute requiring former or present welfare recipients to reimburse the state if the person "acquires property." The Supreme Court construed "property" *not* to include wages, because deprivation of wages would undermine the overall goal of the welfare law to assist recipients in becoming self-supporting and would be unfair and oppressive.

Other states have looked beyond the plain language of state statutes more and more. Written or published legislative histories of state statutes are now more readily available than at any previous point in American history, and they have wider availability now that more of the materials can be found on the internet. This phenomenon (increased availability) has given rise to a growing body of scholarship analyzing state court use of state legislative history. On the other hand, the Michigan Supreme Court since 1998 has followed a largely textualist approach much more rigorously than that followed by the U.S. Supreme Court, and other state high courts are experimenting with different textualist methodologies. See generally Abbe Gluck, *States as Laboratories of Statutory Interpretation: Methodological Consensus and the New Modified Textualism*, 119 Yale L.J. 1750 (2010).

3. CURRENT DEBATES IN STATUTORY INTERPRETATION

In this final section we survey the debates over appropriate method concerning statutory interpretation that began in the 1980s. The primary debate has involved the challenge of the "new textualism" against more traditional approaches relying on legislative purpose and intent. We introduce the new textualism in Part A. Part B considers the ramifications of economic approaches to statutory interpretation, and Part C does the same for pragmatic approaches.

A. THE NEW TEXTUALISM

In the 1980s, a group of judges and executive officials developed a more constrained version of the plain meaning rule than that followed in cases like *Griffin* and *TVA v. Hill.* For example, Judge Frank Easterbrook's *Statutes' Domains*, 50 U. Chi. L. Rev. 533 (1983), insisted that courts have no authority even to apply a statute to a problem unless the statute's language clearly targets that problem. Judge Easterbrook's *Legal Interpretation and the Power of the Judiciary*, 7 Harv. J.L. & Pub. Pol'y 87 (1984), argued that courts interpreting statutes have no business figuring out legislative intent, which is an incoherent concept, largely for the reasons suggested in 1930 by Professor Radin, but updated to reflect modern public choice theory. Then-Judge Antonin Scalia delivered a series of speeches in 1985–86, urging courts to abandon virtually any reference to legislative history, especially the committee reports referred to in *Griffin* and *TVA v. Hill.* The Department of Justice's Office of Legal Policy endorsed and developed these views in a document drafted by Stephen Markman, *Using and Misusing Legislative History: A Re-Evaluation of the Status of Legislative History in Statutory Interpretation* (1989).

What we call "the new textualism"[36] is an approach to statutory interpretation developed by these judges and scholars. Although its proponents draw from legal

---

[36]   William Eskridge Jr., *The New Textualism*, 37 UCLA L. Rev. 621 (1990); see John Manning, *Second-Generation Textualism*, 98 Calif. L. Rev. 1287 (2010); Jonathan Molot, *The Rise and Fall of Textualism*, 106 Colum. L. Rev. 1 (2006); Nicholas Zeppos, *Justice Scalia's Textualism: The "New" New Legal Process*, 12 Cardozo

process theory for their own purposes, their approach to statutory interpretation differs from that supported by Professors Hart, Sacks, and Fuller. Also, new textualist construction is different from the "soft" plain meaning rule of *TVA v. Hill* and *Griffin*, as suggested by the exchanges in the cases that follow.

STATUTORY PREFACE TO *GREEN V. BOCK LAUNDRY*

The Federal Rules of Evidence (1974)

Rule 102. Purpose and Construction. These rules shall be construed to secure fairness in administration, elimination of unjustifiable expense and delay, and promotion of growth and development of the law of evidence to the end that the truth may be ascertained and proceedings justly determined.

Rule 403. Exclusion of Relevant Evidence on Grounds of Prejudice, Confusion or Waste of Time. The court may exclude relevant evidence if its probative value is substantially outweighed by the danger of unfair prejudice, confusion of the issues, or misleading the jury, or by considerations of undue delay, waste of time, or needless presentation of cumulative evidence.

Rule 609. Impeachment by Evidence of Conviction of Crime. (a) General. For the purpose of attacking the credibility of a witness, evidence that the witness has been convicted of a crime shall be admitted if elicited from the witness or established by public record during cross-examination but only if the crime (1) was punishable by death or imprisonment in excess of one year under the law under which the witness was convicted, and the court determines that the probative value of admitting this evidence outweighs its prejudicial effect to the defendant, or (2) involved dishonesty or false statement, regardless of the punishment.

GREEN V. BOCK LAUNDRY MACHINE CO.

Supreme Court of the United States, 1989.
490 U.S. 504, 109 S.Ct. 1981, 104 L.Ed.2d 557.

JUSTICE STEVENS delivered the opinion of the Court.

[Paul Green, a county prisoner working at a car wash on a work-release program, reached inside a large dryer to stop it and had his arm torn off. At trial in his product liability action against the machine's manufacturer, he testified that he had been inadequately instructed about the machine's operation and dangerousness. Green admitted that he had been convicted of burglary and of conspiracy to commit burglary, both felonies, and those convictions were used by defendant to impeach his credibility. The jury returned a verdict for Bock Laundry. The Court of Appeals affirmed, rejecting Green's argument that the district court erred by denying his pretrial motion to exclude the impeaching evidence.]

[Criticism of automatic admissibility of prior felony convictions to impeach civil witnesses, particularly civil plaintiffs, has been "longstanding and widespread."] Our

---

L. Rev. 1597 (1991). For a short overview placing textualism in context with prior theories, see Philip Frickey, *From the Big Sleep to the Big Heat: The Revival of Theory in Statutory Interpretation*, 77 Minn. L. Rev. 241 (1992).

task in deciding this case, however, is not to fashion the rule we deem desirable but to identify the rule that Congress fashioned. * * *

[I] * * * By its terms [Rule 609(a)] requires a judge to allow impeachment of any witness with prior convictions for felonies not involving dishonesty "only if" the probativeness of the evidence is greater than its prejudice "to the defendant." It follows that impeaching evidence detrimental to the prosecution in a criminal case "shall be admitted" without any such balancing.

The Rule's plain language commands weighing of prejudice to a defendant in a civil trial as well as in a criminal trial. But that literal reading would compel an odd result in a case like this. Assuming that all impeaching evidence has at least minimal probative value, and given that the evidence of plaintiff Green's convictions had some prejudicial effect on his case—but surely none on defendant Bock's—balancing according to the strict language of Rule 609(a)(1) inevitably leads to the conclusion that the evidence was admissible. In fact, under this construction of the Rule, impeachment detrimental to a civil plaintiff always would have to be admitted.

No matter how plain the text of the Rule may be, we cannot accept an interpretation that would deny a civil plaintiff the same right to impeach an adversary's testimony that it grants to a civil defendant. The Sixth Amendment to the Constitution guarantees a criminal defendant certain fair trial rights not enjoyed by the prosecution, while the Fifth Amendment lets the accused choose not to testify at trial. In contrast, civil litigants in federal court share equally the protections of the Fifth Amendment's Due Process Clause. Given liberal federal discovery rules, the inapplicability of the Fifth Amendment's protection against self-incrimination, and the need to prove their case, civil litigants almost always must testify in depositions or at trial. Denomination as a civil defendant or plaintiff, moreover, is often happenstance based on which party filed first or on the nature of the suit. Evidence that a litigant or his witness is a convicted felon tends to shift a jury's focus from the worthiness of the litigant's position to the moral worth of the litigant himself. It is unfathomable why a civil plaintiff—but not a civil defendant—should be subjected to this risk. Thus we agree with the Seventh Circuit that as far as civil trials are concerned, Rule 609(a)(1) "can't mean what it says." *Campbell v. Greer*, 831 F.2d 700, 703 (1987) [Posner, J.].

Out of this agreement flow divergent courses, each turning on the meaning of "defendant." The word might be interpreted to encompass all witnesses, civil and criminal, parties or not. It might be read to connote any party offering a witness, in which event Rule 609(a)(1)'s balance would apply to civil, as well as criminal, cases. Finally, "defendant" may refer only to the defendant in a criminal case. These choices spawn a corollary question: must a judge allow prior felony impeachment of all civil witnesses as well as all criminal prosecution witnesses, or is Rule 609(a)(1) inapplicable to civil cases, in which event Rule 403 would authorize a judge to balance in such cases? Because the plain text does not resolve these issues, we must examine the history leading to enactment of Rule 609 as law.

[II] At common law a person who had been convicted of a felony was not competent to testify as a witness. "[T]he disqualification arose as part of the punishment for the crime, only later being rationalized on the basis that such a person was unworthy of belief." 3 J. Weinstein & M. Berger, Weinstein's Evidence paragraph 609[02], p. 609–58 (1988)[.] As the law evolved, this absolute bar gradually was replaced by a rule that allowed such witnesses to testify in both civil and criminal cases, but also to be impeached by evidence of a prior felony conviction or a *crimen falsi* misdemeanor conviction. In the face of scholarly criticism of automatic admission of such impeaching evidence, some courts moved toward a more flexible approach.

[The American Law Institute's Model Code of Evidence and the ABA's proposed Uniform Rules of Evidence recommended that trial judges be given discretion to exclude evidence of prior convictions in appropriate circumstances. In 1969, however, the Advisory Committee's proposed Rules of Evidence included Rule 6–09, which allowed all *crimen falsi* and felony convictions evidence without mention of judicial discretion. But the Committee's second draft of Rule 609(a)] authorized the judge to exclude either felony or *crimen falsi* evidence upon determination that its probative value was "substantially outweighed by the danger of unfair prejudice." The Committee specified that its primary concern was prejudice to the witness-accused; the "risk of unfair prejudice to a party in the use of [convictions] to impeach the ordinary witness is so minimal as scarcely to be a subject of comment." Yet the text of the proposal was broad enough to allow a judge to protect not only criminal defendants, but also civil litigants and nonparty witnesses, from unfair prejudice.

[T]he Advisory Committee's revision of Rule 609(a) met resistance. The Department of Justice urged that the Committee supplant its proposal with the strict, amended version of the District Code. Senator McClellan objected to the adoption of the *Luck* doctrine and urged reinstatement of the earlier draft.

The Advisory Committee backed off. As Senator McClellan had requested, it submitted as its third and final draft the same strict version it had proposed in March 1969. * * * This Court forwarded the Advisory Committee's final draft to Congress on November 20, 1972.

The House of Representatives did not accept the Advisory Committee's final proposal. A Subcommittee of the Judiciary Committee recommended an amended version similar to the text of the present Rule 609(a), except that it avoided the current rule's ambiguous reference to prejudice to "the defendant." Rather, in prescribing weighing of admissibility of prior felony convictions, it used the same open-ended reference to "unfair prejudice" found in the Advisory Committee's second draft.

The House Judiciary Committee departed even further from the Advisory Committee's final recommendation, preparing a draft that did not allow impeachment by evidence of prior conviction unless the crime involved dishonesty or false statement. Motivating the change were concerns about the deterrent effect upon an accused who might wish to testify and the danger of unfair prejudice, "even upon a witness who was not the accused," from allowing impeachment by prior felony convictions regardless of their relation to the witness' veracity. H.R.Rep. No. 93–650, p. 11 (1973). Although the Committee Report focused on criminal defendants and did not mention civil litigants, its express concerns encompassed all nonaccused witnesses.

Representatives who advocated the automatic admissibility approach of the Advisory Committee's draft and those who favored the intermediate approach proposed by the Subcommittee both opposed the Committee's bill on the House floor. Four Members pointed out that the Rule applied in civil as well as criminal cases. The House voted to adopt the Rule as proposed by its Judiciary Committee.

The Senate Judiciary Committee proposed an intermediate path. For criminal defendants, it would have allowed impeachment only by *crimen falsi* evidence; for other witnesses, it also would have permitted prior felony evidence only if the trial judge found that probative value outweighed "prejudicial effect against the party offering that witness." This language thus required the exercise of discretion before prior felony convictions could be admitted in civil litigation. But the full Senate, prodded by Senator McClellan, reverted to the version that the Advisory Committee had submitted. See 120 Cong. Rec. 37076, 37083 (1974).

Conflict between the House bill, allowing impeachment only by *crimen falsi* evidence, and the Senate bill, embodying the Advisory Committee's automatic admissibility approach, was resolved by a Conference Committee. The conferees' compromise—enacted as Federal Rule of Evidence 609(a)(1)—authorizes impeachment by felony convictions, "but only if" the court determines that probative value outweighs "prejudicial effect to the defendant." The Conference Committee's Report makes it perfectly clear that the balance set forth in this draft, unlike the second Advisory Committee and the Senate Judiciary Committee versions, does not protect all nonparty witnesses:

> "The danger of prejudice to a witness other than the defendant (such as injury to the witness' reputation in his community) was considered and rejected by the Conference as an element to be weighed in determining admissibility. It was the judgment of the Conference that the danger of prejudice to a nondefendant witness is outweighed by the need for the trier of fact to have as much relevant evidence on the issue of credibility as possible." H.R.Conf.Rep. No. 93–1597, pp. 9–10 (1974).

Equally clear is the conferees' intention that the rule shield the accused, but not the prosecution, in a criminal case. Impeachment by convictions, the Committee Report stated, "should only be excluded where it presents a danger of improperly influencing the outcome of the trial by persuading the trier of fact to convict the defendant on the basis of his prior criminal record."

But this emphasis on the criminal context, in the Report's use of terms such as "defendant" and "to convict" and in individual conferees' explanations of the compromise,[26] raises some doubt over the Rule's pertinence to civil litigants. The

---

[26]   Representative Dennis, who had stressed in earlier debates that the Rule would apply to both civil and criminal cases, see 120 Cong. Rec. 2377 (1974), explained the benefits of the Rule for criminal defendants and made no reference to benefits for civil litigants when he said:

> "[Y]ou can ask about all . . . felonies on cross examination, only if you can convince the court, and the burden is on the *government*, which is an important change in the law, that the probative value of the question is greater than the damage to the *defendant*; and that is damage or prejudice *to the defendant alone*." *Id.*, at 40894 (emphases supplied).

In the same debate Representative Hogan manifested awareness of the Rule's broad application. While supporting the compromise, he reiterated his preference for a rule discussions suggest that only two kinds of witnesses risk prejudice—the defendant who elects to testify in a criminal case and witnesses other than the defendant in the same kind of case. Nowhere is it acknowledged that undue prejudice to a civil litigant also may improperly influence a trial's outcome. Although this omission lends support to [an] opinion that "legislative oversight" caused exclusion of civil parties from Rule 609(a)(1)'s balance, a number of considerations persuade us that the Rule was meant to authorize a judge to weigh prejudice against no one other than a criminal defendant.

A party contending that legislative action changed settled law has the burden of showing that the legislature intended such a change. Cf. *Midlantic National Bank v. New Jersey Department of Environmental Protection*, 474 U.S. 494, 502 (1986). The weight of authority before Rule 609's adoption accorded with the Advisory Committee's final draft, admitting all felonies without exercise of judicial discretion in either civil or criminal cases. Departures from this general rule had occurred overtly by judicial interpretation, as in *Luck*, or in evidence codes, such as the Model Code and the Uniform Rules. Rule 609 itself explicitly adds safeguards circumscribing the common-law rule. The unsubstantiated assumption that legislative oversight produced Rule 609(a)(1)'s ambiguity respecting civil trials hardly demonstrates that Congress intended silently to overhaul the law of impeachment in the civil context.

To the extent various drafts of Rule 609 distinguished civil and criminal cases, moreover, they did so only to mitigate prejudice to criminal defendants. Any prejudice that convictions impeachment might cause witnesses other than the accused was deemed "so minimal as scarcely to be a subject of comment." Advisory Committee's Note, 51 F.R.D., at 392. Far from voicing concern lest such impeachment unjustly diminish a civil witness in the eyes of the jury, Representative Hogan declared that this evidence ought to be used to measure a witness' moral value. Furthermore, Representative Dennis—who in advocating a Rule limiting impeachment to *crimen falsi* convictions had recognized the impeachment Rule's applicability to civil trials—not only debated the issue on the House floor, but also took part in the conference out of which Rule 609 emerged. See 120 Cong.Rec. 2377–2380, 39942, 40894–40895 (1974). These factors indicate that Rule 609(a)(1)'s textual limitation of the prejudice balance to criminal defendants resulted from deliberation, not oversight.

Had the conferees desired to protect other parties or witnesses, they could have done so easily. Presumably they had access to all of Rule 609's precursors, particularly the drafts prepared by the House Subcommittee and the Senate Judiciary Committee, both of which protected the civil litigant as well as the criminal defendant. Alternatively, the conferees could have amended their own draft to include other parties. They did not for the simple reason that they intended that only the accused in a criminal case should be protected from unfair prejudice by the balance set out in Rule 609(a)(1).

"that, for the purpose of attacking the credibility of a witness, *even if the witness happens to be the defendant in a criminal case*, evidence that he has been convicted of a crime is admissible and may be used to challenge that witness' credibility if the crime is a felony or is a misdemeanor involving dishonesty of [sic] false statement." *Id.*, at 40895 (emphasis added).

[Finally, the Court concluded that Rule 609, as the specific provision governing the facts of the case, controlled over the general balancing provisions of Rule 403. The Court affirmed the judgment for defendant.]

JUSTICE SCALIA, concurring in the judgment.

We are confronted here with a statute which, if interpreted literally, produces an absurd, and perhaps unconstitutional, result. Our task is to give some alternate meaning to the word "defendant" in Federal Rule of Evidence 609(a)(1) that avoids this consequence; and then to determine whether Rule 609(a)(1) excludes the operation of Federal Rule of Evidence 403.

I think it entirely appropriate to consult all public materials, including the background of Rule 609(a)(1) and the legislative history of its adoption, to verify that what seems to us an unthinkable disposition (civil defendants but not civil plaintiffs receive the benefit of weighing prejudice) was indeed unthought of, and thus to justify a departure from the ordinary meaning of the word "defendant" in the Rule. For that purpose, however, it would suffice to observe that counsel have not provided, nor have we discovered, a shred of evidence that anyone has ever proposed or assumed such a bizarre disposition. The Court's opinion, however, goes well beyond this. Approximately four-fifths of its substantive analysis is devoted to examining the evolution of Federal Rule of Evidence 609 * * * all with the evident purpose, not merely of confirming that the word "defendant" cannot have been meant literally, but of determining what, precisely, the Rule does mean.

I find no reason to believe that any more than a handful of the Members of Congress who enacted Rule 609 were aware of its interesting evolution from the 1942 Model Code; or that any more than a handful of them (if any) voted, with respect to their understanding of the word "defendant" and the relationship between Rule 609 and Rule 403, on the basis of the referenced statements in the Subcommittee, Committee, or Conference Committee Reports, or floor debates—statements so marginally relevant, to such minute details, in such relatively inconsequential legislation. The meaning of terms on the statute books ought to be determined, not on the basis of which meaning can be shown to have been understood by a larger handful of the Members of Congress; but rather on the basis of which meaning is (1) most in accord with context and ordinary usage, and thus most likely to have been understood by the *whole* Congress which voted on the words of the statute (not to mention the citizens subject to it), and (2) most compatible with the surrounding body of law into which the provision must be integrated—a compatibility which, by a benign fiction, we assume Congress always has in mind. I would not permit any of the historical and legislative material discussed by the Court, or all of it combined, to lead me to a result different from the one that these factors suggest.

I would analyze this case, in brief, as follows:

(1) The word "defendant" in Rule 609(a)(1) cannot rationally (or perhaps even constitutionally) mean to provide the benefit of prejudice-weighing to civil defendants and not civil plaintiffs. Since petitioner has not produced, and we have not ourselves discovered, even a snippet of support for this absurd result, we may confidently assume that the word was not used (as it normally would be) to refer to all defendants and only all defendants.

(2) The available alternatives are to interpret "defendant" to mean (a) "civil plaintiff, civil defendant, prosecutor, and criminal defendant," (b) "civil plaintiff and defendant and criminal defendant," or (c) "criminal defendant." Quite obviously, the last does least violence to the text. It adds a qualification that the word "defendant" does not contain but, unlike the others, does not give the word a meaning ("plaintiff" or "prosecutor") it simply will not bear. The qualification it adds, moreover, is one that could understandably have been omitted by inadvertence—and sometimes is omitted in normal conversation ("I believe strongly in defendants' rights"). Finally, this last interpretation is consistent with the policy of the law in general and the Rules of Evidence in particular of providing special protection to defendants in criminal cases.*

(3) As well described by the Court, the "structure of the Rules" makes it clear that Rule 403 is not to be applied in addition to Rule 609(a)(1).

I am frankly not sure that, despite its lengthy discussion of ideological evolution and legislative history, the Court's reasons for both aspects of its decision are much different from mine. I respectfully decline to join that discussion, however, because it is natural for the bar to believe that the juridical importance of such material matches its prominence in our opinions—thus producing a legal culture in which, when counsel arguing before us assert that "Congress has said" something, they now frequently mean, by "Congress," a committee report; and in which it was not beyond the pale for a recent brief to say the following: "Unfortunately, the legislative debates are not helpful. Thus, we turn to the other guidepost in this difficult area, statutory language." * * *

JUSTICE BLACKMUN, with whom JUSTICE BRENNAN and JUSTICE MARSHALL join, dissenting.

* * * The majority concludes that Rule 609(a)(1) cannot mean what it says on its face. I fully agree.

I fail to see, however, why we are required to solve this riddle of statutory interpretation by reading the inadvertent word "defendant" to mean "criminal defendant." I am persuaded that a better interpretation of the Rule would allow the trial court to consider the risk of prejudice faced by any party, not just a criminal defendant. Applying the balancing provisions of Rule 609(a)(1) to all parties would have prevented the admission of unnecessary and inflammatory evidence in this case and will prevent other similar unjust results until Rule 609(a) is repaired, as it must be. The result the Court reaches today, in contrast, endorses "the irrationality and unfairness" of denying the trial court the ability to weigh the risk of prejudice to any party before admitting evidence of a prior felony for purposes of impeachment.

---

*   Acknowledging the statutory ambiguity, the dissent would read "defendant" to mean "any party" because, it says, this interpretation "extend[s] the protection of judicial supervision to a larger class of litigants" than the interpretation the majority and I favor, which "takes protection *away* from litigants." But neither side in this dispute can lay claim to generosity without begging the policy question whether judicial supervision is better than the automatic power to impeach. We could as well say—and with much more support in both prior law and this Court's own recommendation—that our reading "extend[s] the protection of [the right to impeach with prior felony convictions] to a larger class of litigants" than the dissent's interpretation, which "takes protection *away* from litigants."

The majority's lengthy recounting of the legislative history of Rule 609 demonstrates why almost all that history is entitled to very little weight. Because the proposed rule changed so often—and finally was enacted as a compromise between the House and the Senate—much of the commentary cited by the majority concerns versions different from the Rule Congress finally enacted.

The only item of legislative history that focuses on the Rule as enacted is the Report of the Conference Committee. Admittedly, language in the Report supports the majority's position: the Report mirrors the Rule in emphasizing the prejudicial effect on the defendant, and also uses the word "convict" to describe the potential outcome. But the Report's draftsmanship is no better than the Rule's, and the Report's plain language is no more reliable an indicator of Congress' intent than is the plain language of the Rule itself.

Because the slipshod drafting of Rule 609(a)(1) demonstrates that clarity of language was not the Conference's forte, I prefer to rely on the underlying reasoning of the Report, rather than on its unfortunate choice of words, in ascertaining the Rule's proper scope. The Report's treatment of the Rule's discretionary standard consists of a single paragraph. After noting that the Conference was concerned with prejudice to a defendant, the Report states:

> "The danger of prejudice to a witness other than the defendant (such as injury to the witness' reputation in the community) was considered and rejected by the Conference as an element to be weighed in determining admissibility. It was the judgment of the Conference that the danger of prejudice to a nondefendant witness is outweighed by the need for the trier of fact to have as much relevant evidence on the issue of credibility as possible. Such evidence should only be excluded where it presents a danger of improperly influencing the outcome of the trial by persuading the trier of fact to convict the defendant on the basis of his prior criminal record."

The Report indicates that the Conference determined that any felony conviction has sufficient relevance to a witness' credibility to be admitted, even if the felony had nothing directly to do with truthfulness or honesty. In dealing with the question of undue prejudice, however, the Conference drew a line: it distinguished between two types of prejudice, only one of which it permitted the trial court to consider.

As the Conference observed, admitting a prior conviction will always "prejudice" a witness, who, of course, would prefer that the conviction not be revealed to the public. The Report makes clear, however, that this kind of prejudice to the witness' life outside the courtroom is not to be considered in the judicial balancing required by Rule 609(a)(1). Rather, the kind of prejudice the court is instructed to be concerned with is prejudice which "presents a danger of improperly influencing the outcome of the trial." Congress' solution to that kind of prejudice was to require judicial supervision: the conviction may be admitted only if "the court determines that the probative value of admitting this evidence outweighs its prejudicial effect to the defendant." Rule 609(a)(1).

Although the Conference expressed its concern in terms of the effect on a criminal defendant, the potential for prejudice to the outcome at trial exists in any type of litigation, whether criminal or civil, and threatens all parties to the litigation.

The Report and the Rule are best read as expressing Congress' preference for judicial balancing whenever there is a chance that justice shall be denied a party because of the unduly prejudicial nature of a witness' past conviction for a crime that has no direct bearing on the witness' truthfulness. In short, the reasoning of the Report suggests that by "prejudice to the defendant," Congress meant "prejudice to a party," as opposed to the prejudicial effect of the revelation of a prior conviction to the witness' own reputation.

It may be correct, as Justice Scalia notes in his opinion concurring in the judgment, that interpreting "prejudicial effect to the defendant" to include only "prejudicial effect to [a] *criminal* defendant," and not prejudicial effect to other categories of litigants as well, does the "least violence to the text," if what we mean by "violence" is the interpolation of excess words or the deletion of existing words. But the reading endorsed by Justice Scalia and the majority does violence to the logic of the only rationale Members of Congress offered for the Rule they adopted.

Certainly the possibility that admission of a witness' past conviction will improperly determine the outcome at trial is troubling when the witness' testimony is in support of a criminal defendant. The potential, however, is no less real for other litigants. Unlike Justice Scalia, I do not approach the Rules of Evidence, which by their terms govern both civil and criminal proceedings, with the presumption that their general provisions should be read to "provid[e] special protection to defendants in criminal cases." Rather, the Rules themselves specify that they "shall be construed to secure fairness in administration . . . to the end that the truth may be ascertained and proceedings justly determined" in *all* cases. Rule 102. The majority's result does not achieve that end. * * *

As I see it, therefore, our choice is between two interpretations of Rule 609(a)(1), neither of which is completely consistent with the Rule's plain language. The majority's interpretation takes protection *away* from litigants—i.e., civil defendants—who would have every reason to believe themselves entitled to the judicial balancing offered by the Rule. The alternative interpretation—which I favor—also departs somewhat from plain language, but does so by *extending* the protection of judicial supervision to a larger class of litigants—i.e., to all parties. Neither result is compelled by the statutory language or the legislative history, but for me the choice between them is an easy one. I find it proper, as a general matter and under the dictates of Rule 102, to construe the Rule so as to avoid "unnecessary hardship," see *Burnet v. Guggenheim*, 288 U.S. 280, 285 (1933), and to produce a sensible result. * * *

NOTES ON BOCK LAUNDRY AND DIFFERENT THEORIES IN ACTION

1. *Does Textualism Work in* Bock Laundry? Note that, like the other eight Justices, textualist Justice Scalia *also* rewrote the statute, which has a perfectly "plain meaning" in this case: the felony convictions of civil plaintiffs can always be introduced to impeach them, but those of civil defendants are subject to a balancing test. Such a plain meaning is probably unconstitutional, but in that event why doesn't the textualist simply invalidate Rule 609(a)(1) (at least as far as civil cases) and apply the Rule 403 default rule, which would probably exclude Green's conviction from evidence?

Justice Scalia disregarded plain meaning in this case because he believed that Rule 609(a)(1) was absurd as written, that the absurdity was unintended, and that an unintended absurdity justifies departure from plain meaning. This is itself significant. By creating an exception to textualism when a statute requires unintended "absurd" consequences, was Justice Scalia not conceding that following statutory text is not all that is going on in statutory interpretation, and that current interpretive values have a role to play in statutory interpretation? While Justice Scalia surely believed that plain meaning could only be sacrificed in the rare absurd-result case, why not sacrifice plain meaning when it directs an "unreasonable" result that was probably unintended by Congress?

Although Justice Scalia agreed to rewrite the statute in *Bock Laundry*, his opinion dismissed the dissenting opinion's rewrite in favor of the majority's rewrite:

> The available alternatives [for rewriting the rule] are to interpret "defendant" to mean (a) "civil plaintiff, civil defendant, prosecutor and criminal defendant," (b) "civil plaintiff and defendant and criminal defendant," or (c) "criminal defendant." Quite obviously, the last does least violence to the text.

Is that so obvious? In essence, Justice Blackmun's dissent rewrote Rule 609(a)(1) to permit impeaching convictions only when "the court determines that the probative value of admitting this evidence outweighs its prejudicial effect to *a party*" (new language italicized). Does this do more "violence" to the text than Justice Scalia's rewrite to permit impeaching convictions only when "the court determines that the probative value of admitting this evidence outweighs its prejudicial effect to the *criminal* defendant"?

Indeed, Justice Scalia's rewrite leaves the statute as chaotic as it was originally. Rewritten Rule 609(a)(1) still applies in a civil case like *Bock Laundry*, and Justice Scalia's version tells the judge to follow a strange rule: Allow the witness to be impeached by his prior felony convictions, but only if its probative value outweighs its prejudice to the "criminal defendant." What criminal defendant? While the original Rule 609(a)(1) favored civil defendants over civil plaintiffs without apparent justification, it at least set forth a rule that could be applied by the district judge in a civil case. Under the pretense of doing "least violence" to the text, does Justice Scalia's rewrite deprive the judge of an intelligible rule?

In our view, the shortest way to rewrite Rule 609(a)(1) to reflect the understanding of the majority and of Justice Scalia *and* to have it make sense as a rule applicable to civil as well as criminal cases is something like the following: Allow a witness to be impeached by his prior criminal conviction "if the crime (1) was punishable by death or imprisonment in excess of one year under the law under which the witness was convicted, and, *in a criminal case*, the court determines that the probative value of admitting this evidence outweighs its prejudicial effect to the defendant" (new language italicized). Would this flunk Justice Scalia's test of doing "least violence" to the text?

2. *Does Imaginative Reconstruction Work Any Better?* Imaginative reconstruction also may be problematic in *Bock Laundry*, for the reasons suggested by Professor Radin and revived by the new textualists. Who can really tell what the median Member of Congress thought about this issue?

Recall that the House voted for a version of Rule 609(a) that would have given Green the benefit of a balancing test, and a similar version was voted out of the Senate Judiciary Committee. On the floor of the Senate, Senator McClellan proposed an amendment making all felony convictions admissible; his amendment failed by a 35–35 vote. 120 Cong. Rec. 37080 (1974). But on immediate motion for reconsideration, his amendment was adopted, 38–34, because a couple of new senators showed up and a couple changed their votes. *Id.* at 37083. The median senator was Senator Ted Stevens (R-Alaska): He voted against the McClellan amendment, for reconsideration, for the McClellan amendment, and then for the final conference bill, which adopted the ambiguous compromise. Why did he vote this way? What was his "intent"?

In 2006, we posed these questions to Senator Stevens, who was still representing Alaska in the Senate. Senator Stevens told us that the voting pattern for him and several other senators was "confused" as a matter of logic, but not as a matter of political collegiality. "As a former U.S. Attorney I favored the House and Senate Judiciary Committees' version—but McClellan was a friend. He had traveled to Alaska with me— and Jackson and Stennis were sort of mentors. This was my sixth year in the Senate—I voted with McClellan to take his 'compromise' to conference."[37]

In any event, the Senate did vote for a much more limited version of Rule 609(a) than the House, and so the key question for imaginative reconstruction is: What was the conference committee "deal" that was struck on Rule 609(a)? And of course that's completely unclear as well, since the conference report doesn't even mention civil cases, and Senator Stevens did not recall any consensus on the matter when he and other senators passed the conference bill by voice vote. Justice Stevens found great significance in the conference action, but only because of a judicially created canon of statutory construction: If the dog (here, Congress) doesn't bark, assume that "nothing happened"— no radical change was made in the fabric of the law (recall the dog-doesn't-bark canon). Thus, Justice Stevens's imaginative reconstruction boils down to the application of a judicial presumption! And one that seems flimsy at best, because the common law rule was in the process of collapsing—and did collapse within the federal system the year after *Bock Laundry.* See the next note.

3.   *Why Did the Court Go Through This Exercise?* There was a proposed change to Rule 609(a) pending when the Supreme Court interpreted the Rule in *Bock Laundry.*[38] In January 1990 (soon after the decision in *Bock Laundry*), the Supreme Court notified Congress that it had adopted an amendment to Federal Rule of Evidence 609 to take effect on December 1, 1990, unless Congress by statute disapproved it. As explained in the report of the advisory committee, the amendment "does not disturb the special balancing test for the criminal defendant who chooses to testify, but applies the general balancing test of Rule 403 to protect all other litigants against unfair impeachment of witnesses." The report noted that the advisory committee had approved the proposed amendment prior to *Bock Laundry*, but had held it pending the outcome of the case. Congress never disapproved the revised Rule 609(a), and it went into effect on December 1, 1990.

After this amendment, Rule 609 provided:

a.   General rule.—For purposes of attacking the credibility of a witness,

---

[37]   E-mail from Lily Stevens (Senator Stevens's daughter) to Philip Frickey (April 5, 2006) (incorporating an email that Senator Stevens authorized his daughter to forward to Professor Frickey).

[38]   Pursuant to the Federal Rules Enabling Act, amendments to the Federal Rules of Evidence are proposed to the Supreme Court by an advisory committee established by the Judicial Conference of the United States. The Court then notifies Congress of the amendment, including any modifications made by the Court. After a waiting period, the amendment takes effect unless, in the interim, Congress has nullified it by statute.

(1)   evidence that a witness other than an accused has been convicted of a crime shall be admitted, subject to Rule 403, if the crime was punishable by death or imprisonment in excess of one year under the law under which the witness was convicted, and evidence that an accused has been convicted of such a crime shall be admitted if the court determines that the probative value of admitting this evidence outweighs its prejudicial effect to the accused; and

(2)   evidence that any witness has been convicted of a crime shall be admitted if it involved dishonesty or false statement, regardless of the punishment.

This is a unique "Supreme Court override" of its own decision! Under this rule, Paul Green would have gotten a new trial. Why did the Court not reach that result in *Bock Laundry*? If the Court was required to deny Green relief in *Bock Laundry*, why did it have the power to veto Congress's intent a year later?

ANTONIN SCALIA, A MATTER OF INTERPRETATION
Summary and Selected Quotations (1997).[*]

In this published version of his Tanner Lectures delivered at Princeton University, the late Justice Antonin Scalia presented his *textualist* philosophy of legal interpretation. He contended that law students (brainwashed by the first-year indoctrination in common-law methodology) and law professors (who do the brainwashing) tend to approach statutory interpretation as an exercise in applying legal authorities to new factual settings in a manner which yields both a fair result in the case and works toward a just and efficient general rule. Such an equitable common-law approach is not appropriate for construing statutes in a democracy, Justice Scalia argued, because it is fundamentally anti-democratic (pp. 9–14). A theme of the Tanner Lectures is that the common law has its place, but in a democracy it is more important that judges be constrained by, and held to, the legislatively enacted statutory law, than that they do "justice" in the individual case.

Should the lodestar for statutory interpretation, then, be legislative *intent*? Most assuredly not! "It is the *law* that governs, not the intent of the lawgiver. That seems to me the essence of the famous American ideal set forth in the Massachusetts constitution: A government of laws, not of men. Men may intend what they will; but it is only the laws that they enact which bind us" (p. 17). Indeed, Justice Scalia argued that judges following a legislative-intent approach usually end up finding their own preferences in the statute, because "your best shot at figuring out what the legislature meant is to ask yourself what a wise and intelligent person *should* have meant; and that will surely bring you to the conclusion that the law means what you think it *ought* to mean—which is precisely how judges decide things under the common law" (p. 18). Note the implicit criticism of Hart and Sacks' theory.

Justice Scalia then applied this critique to *Holy Trinity Church*. The Court interpreted the alien contract law contrary to its plain meaning because the Justices believed it inconsistent with legislative intent and purpose. Justice Scalia found such an approach no more than invalid judicial lawmaking, although he would allow courts to correct scrivener's errors. "Well of course I think that the act was within the letter of the statute, and was therefore within the statute: end of case" (p. 20). "The text is the law, and it is the text which must be observed" (p. 22), said the author, citing Justice Holmes.

The apparent plain meaning of a statutory text must be the alpha and the omega in a judge's interpretation of a statute. The apparent plain meaning is that which an ordinary speaker of the English language—twin sibling to the common law's reasonable person—would draw from the statutory text. That is what textualism *is*. What it is *not*, according to Justice Scalia, is either "strict constructionism" (p. 23), which gives statutory words their stingiest ambit, nor "nihilism" (p. 24), which reads words to mean anything and everything. "A text should not be construed strictly, and it should not be construed leniently; it should be construed reasonably, to contain all that it fairly means" (p. 23).

Nor is textualism canonical, maintained Justice Scalia. The Tanner Lectures are skeptical of "presumptions and rules of construction that load the dice for or against a particular result" (p. 27), because they "increase the unpredictability, if not the arbitrariness of judicial decisions" (p. 28). "To the honest textualist, all of these preferential rules and presumptions are a lot of trouble," said Scalia (p. 28). On the other hand, canons such as the rule of lenity (ambiguous penal statutes should be construed in favor of the defendant) might have been "validated by sheer antiquity," and other canons (such as the requirement of a clear statement for congressional abrogation of state immunity) might be defensible as rule-of-thumb presumptions about normal meaning (p. 29).

Doctrinally, the most distinctive feature of Justice Scalia's legisprudence was an insistence that judges should almost never consult, and never rely on, the legislative history of a statute (pp. 29–37). Consistent with his concurring opinion in *Bock Laundry*, the Tanner Lectures identify several kinds of reasons for rejecting the relevance of legislative history. First, to the extent that legislative history is mined to determine legislative "intent," it must be rejected as a matter of constitutional principle. Legislative intent is not the proper goal for the statutory interpreter. This is a corollary of the rule of law: law must be objective and impersonal (the "government of laws"), not subjective and intentional ("and not of men"). This reason is related to Professor Radin's critique of legislative intent—and Justice Scalia's second objection to legislative history is very much an elaboration of Professor Radin's criticism two generations earlier.

Even if intent were a proper criterion and it were constitutional to consider the views of legislative subgroups, the debating history preceding statutory enactment would not be reliable evidence of such intent. For most issues, there was no collective understanding; if there were such an understanding, public statements would often point in different directions, as some representatives would find it in their interest to plant misleading evidence. Indeed, the more courts have relied on legislative history, the less reliable it has become! "In earlier days, it was at least genuine and not contrived—a real part of the legislation's *history*, in the sense that it was part of the *development* of the bill, part of the attempt to inform and persuade those who voted. Nowadays, however, when it is universally known and expected that judges will resort to floor debates and (especially) committee reports as authoritative expressions of 'legislative intent,' affecting the courts rather than informing the Congress has become the primary purpose of the exercise" (p. 34).

Justice Scalia also claimed that legislators themselves do not read the committee reports (pp. 32–33). Critics respond that legislators do not read the statutes they enact, either. Justice Scalia replied that the claim to authority of the two sources is different: a committee report's (supposed) authority is bottomed on its being evidence of intent about the law, and so knowledge about its contents would seem critical; the statutory text, on the other hand, is law itself, whether or not anyone read or understood it before enactment (pp. 34–35).

In response to this reply, critics say that committee reports are authoritative evidence because of conventions by which Congress has delegated most of the detail work to committees, with the implication being that the committee product is presumptively the work of Congress. Unconstitutional! opined Justice Scalia.[39] "The legislative power is the power to make laws, not the power to make legislators. It is nondelegable. Congress can no more authorize one committee to 'fill in the details' of a particular law in a binding fashion than it can authorize a committee to enact minor laws. * * * That is the very essence of the separation of powers [and Article I, Section 7, requiring bicameral approval and presentment to the President]. The only conceivable basis for considering committee reports authoritative, therefore, is that they are a genuine indication of the will of the entire house—which, as I have been at pains to explain, they assuredly are not" (p. 35).

Earlier thinkers—like Dean Pound and Professor Landis—had called for courts to consider legislative history, so that judges might be constrained by the legislators' preferences. This was a laudable impulse, Justice Scalia conceded, but it has not worked. Legislative history has augmented rather than ameliorated the discretion of the willful judge, and this was Justice Scalia's third major quarrel with the use of legislative history. "In any major piece of legislation, the legislative history is extensive, and there is something for everybody. As Judge Harold Leventhal used to say, the trick is to look over the heads of the crowd and pick out your friends" (p. 36).

NOTES ON THE NEW TEXTUALISM AS A THEORY OF INTERPRETATION

One might say that the new textualist approach demands that the statutory interpreter consider the text, the whole text, and nothing but the text. This description leaves many important issues unaddressed and may be an oversimplification. Consider the following nuances that have been flagged by scholars and by Justice Scalia himself.

1.   *When Is Meaning Ambiguous?* Surely the obvious question for a textualist theory is this: When is the meaning "plain"? When is there ambiguity? The plain meaning is that which an ordinary speaker of the English language—twin sibling to the common law's reasonable person—would draw from the statutory text. In another context, Justice Scalia said that ordinary meaning requires judges to ask "whether you could use the word in that sense at a cocktail party without having people look at you funny." *Johnson v. United States*, 529 U.S. 694, 718 (2000) (Scalia, J., dissenting). Does a "cocktail party

---

[39]   The following argument is supported and elaborated in detail by John Manning, *Textualism as a Nondelegation Doctrine*, 97 Colum. L. Rev. 673 (1997), and Manning, *Second-Generation Textualism*, 98 Calif. L. Rev. 1287 (2010).

textualism" render statutory meaning too dependent on the perspective of the group a judge parties with? For a suggestion that "plain meaning" is as much a product of interpretation as a reality pre-existing interpretation, see Brett Kavanaugh, *Fixing Statutory Interpretation*, 129 Harv. L. Rev. 2118 (2016) (book review).

Many words, phrases, and sentences can have more than one meaning to the ordinary speaker of the English language (fellow partiers will not "look at you funny"). Often Justice Scalia found a plain meaning, based on statutory context, including the whole act or even the entire U.S. Code. Thus, if Congress has used the same language elsewhere in the statute or even in other statutes, Justice Scalia usually presumed that the same language has the same ordinary meaning. E.g., *United Sav. Ass'n v. Timbers of Inwood Forest Assocs. Ltd.*, 484 U.S. 365, 371 (1988). Consider also his point in *Bock Laundry*, that the ordinary use of "defendant" typically assumes one is talking about a criminal defendant; that takes some edge off of Justice Scalia's willingness to give Rule 609(a)(1) a narrowing construction.

If a statute is genuinely ambiguous, one might wonder what a textualist should do. For Justice Scalia himself, the answer was to follow and reason from Supreme Court precedent construing open-textured laws like the Sherman Act *or* defer to reasonable agency interpretations of statutes *or* attribute a purpose to the statute and construe it according to such purpose. See Miranda McGowan, *Do as I Do, Not as I Say: An Empirical Investigation of Justice Scalia's Ordinary Meaning Method of Statutory Interpretation*, 78 Miss. L.J. 129 (2008). In an empirical analysis of Justice Scalia's dissents, McGowan reports that the Justice followed something other than an "ordinary" or "plain" meaning in most cases and, instead, followed judicial or administrative implications of purpose as the lodestar for construing statutes. Her conclusion is that Justice Scalia's textualism (even in his dissents, less constrained by the process of collecting a majority) contained just as much judicial discretion and judgment as does the approach traditionally followed by the Court.

2. *Should the New Textualists Ever Examine Legislative History?* The new textualists reject the use of legislative history for its *authoritative value*: such materials have no legal authority. This is their strongest point, but it does not preclude consultation of legislative history for other kinds of reasons. Notice that Justice Scalia was willing to have a law clerk examine the legislative history of the 1974 amendment—but simply to confirm that no one in Congress realized that rule 609(a)(1), as written, was going to have possibly unconstitutional consequences in civil cases. This might be the *confirmatory value* of legislative history. See James Brudney, *Confirmatory Legislative History*, 76 Brooklyn L. Rev. 901 (2011). If legislative history can be examined to determine whether Members of Congress "intended" or "thought of" an absurd or probably unconstitutional interpretation, why not look at it to confirm the apparent plain meaning of a statute? See *Carr v. United States*, 560 U.S. 438 (2010), where Justice Sotomayor deployed legislative history in precisely this way—but Justice Scalia refused to join that portion of her opinion.

As a general matter, why shouldn't legislative history be consulted for its *text-illuminating value*—namely, as evidence of how language was used at the time of the statute's enactment? One would expect new textualists who follow "original meaning" to consider legislative history carefully, for the same kinds of reasons they consider *The Federalist Papers* in determining how the public would have understood the "original meaning" of the language used in the Constitution. William Eskridge Jr., *Should the*

Supreme Court Read The Federalist *But Not Statutory Legislative History?*, 66 Geo. Wash. L. Rev. 1301 (1998). Such legislative history would take the edge off of Justice Scalia's blistering critique of *Holy Trinity*. Scholars have reported that the legislative debates used the terms "labor and service" to refer only to manual work, and never to pastoral or brain work, and the term "lecturers" to refer to moral and religious speakers.[40] Justice Scalia responded that he only used *The Federalist* to suggest how "the public" understood the Constitution at the time, and only as confirmatory evidence of original meaning. Antonin Scalia & John Manning, *A Dialogue on Statutory and Constitutional Interpretation,* 80 Geo. Wash. L. Rev. 1610, 1617–18 (2012). So why did he object so strongly to the Court's use of legislative debates to confirm the original public meaning of a statutory text?

Also, should the new textualists ever consider legislative history as a means to understand the structure of a statute? In his analysis of Justice Scalia's critique of *Holy Trinity*, William Eskridge Jr., *No Frills Textualism*, 119 Harv. L. Rev. 2041, 2065–70 (2006), argues that the legislative history indicates that §§ 1 and 4 of the Alien Contract Law were *in pari materia*, namely, they were understood at the time (1885) to cover the same class of aliens. This suggests that the more general terms in § 1 (persons performing labor or service of any kind) might be limited to the more particular ones in § 4 (mechanics, artisans, and laborers). Justice Scalia's book never mentions § 4. Is there a possibility that he would consider legislative materials to reveal statutory structure?

3. *Should the New Textualists Recognize an Absurd Results Rule?* Justice Scalia's concurring opinion in *Bock Laundry* rests on the absurdity of following Rule 609(a)(1) as written. For other examples where Justice Scalia has emphasized absurdity as a guide to statutory text, see *Brown v. Plata*, 563 U.S. 493, 550–52 (2011) (Scalia, J., dissenting in part because the majority's interpretation of the statute is "absurd" and represents a "judicial travesty"); Jane Schacter, *Text or Consequences?*, 76 Brooklyn L. Rev. 1007 (2011) (collecting pre-*Plata* examples from Justice Scalia's opinions).

Recognizing an absurd results exception to the plain meaning rule has its risks: what is absurd to Justice Scalia might be debatable or even reasonable to Justice Kennedy and might be good policy to Justice Ginsburg. (Indeed, that was the case in *Brown v. Plata*, where five Justices approved an injunction requiring a state to reduce its prison population because it created cruel and unusual conditions for mentally and physically disabled inmates. The majority considered the injunction necessary to correct constitutional violations—while the dissenters considered it "absurd" to protect prisoners against probable harm through a "structural" injunction.)

For this reason, leading textualist theorists argue that there should *not* be an "absurd results" exception to the plain meaning rule. See John Nagle, *Textualism's Exceptions,* Issues in Legal Scholarship: Dynamic Statutory Interpretation (2002): Article 15; John Manning, *The Absurdity Doctrine,* 116 Harv. L. Rev. 2387 (2005). Their argument is that the normative rule of law advantages of textualism would be compromised by a subjective absurd-results exception: because "absurdity" is in the mind of the beholder, the law would lose some degree of predictability and objectivity. Should Justice Scalia abandon his support for the absurd results exception? For an argument that normative judgments pervade his statutory jurisprudence, see Schacter, *supra.*

---

[40]   Carol Chomsky, *Unlocking the Mysteries of* Holy Trinity: *Spirit, Letter, and History in Statutory Interpretation*, 100 Colum. L. Rev. 901 (2000); William Eskridge Jr., *Textualism, The Unknown Ideal?*, 96 Mich. L. Rev. 1509 (1998) (reviewing Scalia's book and examining the original meaning of "labor or service" in 1885).

4. *On the Whole, Does the New Textualism "Constrain" Judicial Decisionmaking Better Than Other Methodologies?* Justice Scalia was certain that his method *does* constrain judges and produces more predictable, less ideological decisions. See Antonin Scalia & Bryan Garner, *Reading Law: The Interpretation of Legal Texts* (2012). Legal academics who have studied the matter empirically do not agree, finding either that textualism constrains no more than other methodologies, see Frank Cross, *The Theory and Practice of Statutory Interpretation* 177–79 (2009), or that it actually constrains *less* than methodologies that consider more context. See James Brudney & Corey Ditslear, *Liberal Justices' Reliance on Legislative History: Principle, Strategy, and the Scalia Effect*, 29 Berkeley J. Emp. & Lab. L. 117 (2008). As you read the remaining statutory decisions in this book, you will have an opportunity to decide for yourself whether the new textualism constrains interpreters. Indeed, that is the very puzzle posed in the following Problem.

PROBLEM APPLYING THE NEW TEXTUALISM TO THE VOTING RIGHTS ACT, AS AMENDED 1982

Problem 5-5. Voting Rights and Judicial Elections. From his book, we know that Justice Scalia would have dissented in *Holy Trinity Church*. There is little doubt he would have voted with the majority in *TVA* and *Griffin*—but he would have reached the same result through a different path of reasoning. Now consider the Voting Rights Act of 1965, as amended in 1982, which invalidates state electoral districts or rules that have a disparate impact on racial minorities. For example, in the South, at-large elections were an effective way of excluding candidates of color from elected office, because the majority white electorate would vote against any such candidate. In 1980, the Supreme Court had ruled that § 2 did not police electoral arrangements that were race-neutral and not motivated by racial exclusionary motives (which are hard to prove). To enable minority voters to challenge electoral arrangements, like at-large elections, that were not race-based on their face but that had questionable race-based effects, § 2 was amended in 1982 to provide as follows:

(a) No voting qualification or prerequisite to voting or standard, practice, or procedure shall be imposed or applied by any State or political subdivision in a manner which results in a denial or abridgement of the right of any citizen of the United States to vote on account of race or color, or in contravention of the guarantees set forth in section 4(f)(2), as provided in subsection (b).

(b) A violation of subsection (a) is established if, based on the totality of circumstances, it is shown that the political processes leading to nomination or election in the State or political subdivision are not equally open to participation by members of a class of citizens protected by subsection (a) in that its members have less opportunity than other members of the electorate to participate in the political process and to elect representatives of their choice. The extent to which members of a protected class have been elected to office in the State or political subdivision is one circumstance which may be considered: *Provided,* That nothing in this section establishes a right to have members of a protected class elected in numbers equal to their proportion in the population.

Does § 2 apply to state elections for judges? (Unlike the federal system, judges are popularly elected in many states.) How would a new textualist analyze the foregoing statutory text? Is there a plain meaning? If not, how should ambiguities be resolved?

Would it make a difference to you if you knew that § 2 was applied to judicial elections before the Voting Rights Act was amended in 1982? Jot down your answer now.

Chisom v. Roemer

501 U.S. 380 (1991).

Five of the seven members of the Louisiana Supreme Court are elected from single-member districts, each of which consists of a number of parishes (counties). The other two are elected from one multimember district. In three of the four parishes in this multimember district, more than three-fourths of the registered voters are white. In the fourth parish in the multimember district, Orleans Parish, which contains about half of the population of the multimember district and has about half the registered voters in the district, more than one-half of the registered voters are African American. A class of African American registered voters in Orleans Parish brought this action, contending that the use of the multimember district diluted the voting strength of the minority community in violation of § 2 of the Voting Rights Act, as amended in 1982. Following circuit precedent, the lower court ruled that § 2 was inapplicable to judicial elections.

Section 2 as enacted in 1965 provided: "No voting qualification or prerequisite to voting, or standard, practice, or procedure shall be imposed or applied by any State or political subdivision to deny or abridge the right of any citizen of the United States to vote on account of race or color." In *Mobile v. Bolden*, 446 U.S. 55, 60–61 (1980), the Supreme Court interpreted § 2 to be inapplicable when a jurisdiction's voting rules are race-neutral, even if they have race-based effects. The Voting Rights Act Amendments of 1982 revised § 2, quoted in Problem 6-7, above.

Writing for the Court, **Justice Stevens** ruled that § 2 applied to judicial elections. "Section 2(a) adopts a results test, thus providing that proof of discriminatory intent is no longer necessary to establish *any* violation of the section. Section 2(b) provides guidance about how the results test is to be applied." Louisiana argued that Congress' choice of the word "representatives" in the phrase "have less opportunity than other members of the electorate to participate in the political process and to elect representatives of their choice" in § 2(b) is evidence of congressional intent to exclude vote dilution claims involving judicial elections from the coverage of § 2. The Justices were convinced that "if Congress had such an intent, Congress would have made it explicit in the statute, or at least some of the Members would have identified or mentioned it at some point in the unusually extensive legislative history of the 1982 amendment.[23]

The lower court assumed that § 2 provides two distinct types of protection for minority voters—it protects their opportunity "to participate in the political process" and their opportunity "to elect representatives of their choice." Although the lower court interpreted "representatives" as a word of limitation, it assumed that the word eliminated judicial elections only from the latter protection, without affecting the former. Justice Stevens rejected such a bifurcation: "Any abridgement of the opportunity of members of a protected class to participate in the political process inevitably impairs their ability to influence the outcome of an election. * * * The statute does not create two separate and

---

[23]   [Justice Stevens, for the Court:] Congress' silence in this regard can be likened to the dog that did not bark. See A. Doyle, Silver Blaze, in The Complete Sherlock Holmes 335 (1927). Cf. *Harrison v. PPG Industries, Inc.*, 446 U.S. 578, 602 (1980) (Rehnquist, J., dissenting) ("In a case where the construction of legislative language such as this makes so sweeping and so relatively unorthodox a change as that made here, I think judges as well as detectives may take into consideration the fact that a watchdog did not bark in the night.").

distinct rights. Subsection (a) covers every application of a qualification, standard, practice, or procedure that results in a denial or abridgement of '*the right*' to vote. The singular form is also used in subsection (b) when referring to an injury to members of the protected class who have less 'opportunity' than others 'to participate in the political process *and* to elect representatives of their choice.' 42 U.S.C. § 1973 (emphasis added). It would distort the plain meaning of the sentence to substitute the word 'or' for the word 'and.' Such radical surgery would be required to separate the opportunity to participate from the opportunity to elect."

The lower court ruled that the term "representatives" was used to extend § 2 coverage to executive officials, but not to judges. "We think, however, that the better reading of the word 'representatives' describes the winners of representative, popular elections. If executive officers, such as prosecutors, sheriffs, state attorneys general, and state treasurers, can be considered 'representatives' simply because they are chosen by popular election, then the same reasoning should apply to elected judges.

The lower court reasoned that, ideally, judges are not "representatives" in the way governors and legislators are. The Framers of Article III certainly saw matters that way—but Louisiana has made a different choice. "The fundamental tension between the ideal character of the judicial office and the real world of electoral politics cannot be resolved by crediting judges with total indifference to the popular will while simultaneously requiring them to run for elected office. When each of several members of a court must be a resident of a separate district, and must be elected by the voters of that district, it seems both reasonable and realistic to characterize the winners as representatives of that district. * * * Louisiana could, of course, exclude its judiciary from the coverage of the Voting Rights Act by changing to a system in which judges are appointed, and in that way, it could enable its judges to be indifferent to popular opinion. The reasons why Louisiana has chosen otherwise are precisely the reasons why it is appropriate for § 2, as well as § 5, of the Voting Rights Act to continue to apply to its judicial elections.

"The close connection between § 2 and § 5 further undermines respondents' view that judicial elections should not be covered under § 2. Section 5 requires certain States to submit changes in their voting procedures to the District Court of the District of Columbia or to the Attorney General for preclearance. Section 5 uses language similar to that of § 2 in defining prohibited practices: 'any voting qualification or prerequisite to voting, or standard, practice, or procedure with respect to voting.' This Court has already held that § 5 applies to judicial elections. *Clark v. Roemer*, 500 U.S. 646 (1991). If § 2 did not apply to judicial elections, a State covered by § 5 would be precluded from implementing a new voting procedure having discriminatory effects with respect to judicial elections, whereas a similarly discriminatory system already in place could not be challenged under § 2. It is unlikely that Congress intended such an anomalous result."

Finally, Congress enacted the Voting Rights Act of 1965 for the broad remedial purpose of "rid[ding] the country of racial discrimination in voting." *South Carolina v. Katzenbach*, 383 U.S. 301, 315 (1966). In *Allen v. State Board of Elections*, 393 U.S. 544, 567 (1969), the Court said that the Act should be interpreted in a manner that provides "the broadest possible scope" in combatting racial discrimination. Concluded Justice Stevens: "Congress amended the Act in 1982 in order to relieve plaintiffs of the burden of proving discriminatory intent, after a plurality of this Court had concluded that the original Act, like the Fifteenth Amendment, contained such a requirement. See *Mobile v.*

Bolden. Thus, Congress made clear that a violation of § 2 could be established by proof of discriminatory results alone. It is difficult to believe that Congress, in an express effort to broaden the protection afforded by the Voting Rights Act, withdrew, without comment, an important category of elections from that protection. Today we reject such an anomalous view and hold that state judicial elections are included within the ambit of § 2 as amended."

In dissent, **Justice Scalia** (joined by Chief Justice Rehnquist and Justice Kennedy) started with this: "Section 2 of the Voting Rights Act is not some all-purpose weapon for well-intentioned judges to wield as they please in the battle against discrimination. It is a statute. I thought we had adopted a regular method for interpreting the meaning of language in a statute: first, find the ordinary meaning of the language in its textual context; and second, using established canons of construction, ask whether there is any clear indication that some permissible meaning other than the ordinary one applies. If not—and especially if a good reason for the ordinary meaning appears plain—we apply that ordinary meaning.

"Today, however, the Court adopts a method quite out of accord with that usual practice. It begins not with what the statute says, but with an expectation about what the statute must mean absent particular phenomena ('*we are convinced* that if Congress had . . . an intent [to exclude judges] Congress would have made it explicit in the statute, or at least some of the Members would have identified or mentioned it at some point in the unusually extensive legislative history'); and the Court then interprets the words of the statute to fulfill its expectation. Finding nothing in the legislative history affirming that judges were excluded from the coverage of § 2, the Court gives the phrase 'to elect representatives' the quite extraordinary meaning that covers the election of judges.

"As method, this is just backwards, and however much we may be attracted by the result it produces in a particular case, we should in every case resist it. Our job begins with a text that Congress has passed and the President has signed. We are to read the words of that text as any ordinary Member of Congress would have read them, see Holmes, The Theory of Legal Interpretation, 12 Harv. L. Rev. 417 (1899), and apply the meaning so determined. In my view, that reading reveals that § 2 extends to vote dilution claims for the elections of representatives only, and judges are not representatives."

Although the 1965 VRA applied to all elections, including judicial ones, "[t]he 1982 amendments, however, radically transformed the Act. As currently written, the statute proscribes intentional discrimination only if it has a discriminatory effect, but proscribes practices with discriminatory effect whether or not intentional. This new 'results' criterion provides a powerful, albeit sometimes blunt, weapon with which to attack even the most subtle forms of discrimination. The question we confront here is how broadly the new remedy applies. The foundation of the Court's analysis, the itinerary for its journey in the wrong direction, is the following statement: 'It is difficult to believe that Congress, in an express effort to broaden the protection afforded by the Voting Rights Act, withdrew, without comment, an important category of elections from that protection.' There are two things wrong with this. First is the notion that Congress cannot be credited with having achieved anything of major importance by simply saying it, in ordinary language, in the text of a statute, 'without comment' in the legislative history. As the Court colorfully puts it, if the dog of legislative history has not barked nothing of great significance can have transpired. Apart from the questionable wisdom of assuming that dogs will bark when something important is happening, see 1 T. Livius, The History of Rome 411–413 (1892) (D. Spillan translation), we have forcefully and explicitly rejected the Conan Doyle approach to statutory construction in the past. See *Harrison v. PPG Industries, Inc.*, 446 U.S. 578, 592 (1980) ('In ascertaining the meaning of a statute, a court cannot, in the manner of Sherlock Holmes, pursue the theory of the dog that did not bark'). We are here to apply the statute, not legislative history, and certainly not the absence of legislative history. Statutes are the law though sleeping dogs lie."

Justice Scalia agreed with the lower court that § 2 created two separate rights for protected classes: (1) "to participate in the political process" and (2) "to elect representatives of their choice." On this reading, judicial elections are subject to the first right, but not the second because judges are not "representatives." The Court, petitioners, and petitioners' *amici* have labored mightily to establish that there is *a* meaning of 'representatives' that would include judges, and no doubt there is. But our job is not to scavenge the world of English usage to discover whether there is any possible meaning of 'representatives' which suits our preconception that the statute includes judges; our job is to determine whether the *ordinary* meaning includes them, and if it does not, to ask whether there is any solid indication in the text or structure of the statute that something other than ordinary meaning was intended.

"There is little doubt that the ordinary meaning of 'representatives' does not include judges, see Webster's Second New International Dictionary 2114 (1950). The Court's feeble argument to the contrary is that 'representatives' means those who 'are chosen by popular election.' On that hypothesis, the fan-elected members of the baseball All-Star teams are 'representatives'—hardly a common, if even a permissible, usage. Surely the word 'representative' connotes one who is not only *elected by* the people, but who also, at a minimum, *acts on behalf of* the people. Judges do that in a sense—but not in the ordinary sense. As the captions of the pleadings in some States still display, it is the prosecutor who represents 'the People'; the judge represents the Law—which often requires him to rule against the People. It is precisely because we do not *ordinarily* conceive of judges as representatives that we held judges not within the Fourteenth Amendment's requirement of 'one person, one vote.' *Wells v. Edwards*, 347 F.Supp. 453 (MD La. 1972), aff'd, 409 U.S. 1095 (1973). The point is not that a State could not make judges in some senses representative, or that all judges must be conceived of in the Article III mold, but rather, that giving 'representatives' its ordinary meaning, the ordinary speaker in 1982 would not have applied the word to judges, see Holmes, The Theory of Legal Interpretation, 12 Harv. L. Rev. 417 (1899). It remains only to ask whether there is good indication that ordinary meaning does not apply." Justice Scalia answered "no" to that question.

Justice Scalia also observed that the principle of "one person, one vote" did not apply to the election of judges, *Wells v. Edwards*, 347 F.Supp. 453 (MD La. 1972), aff'd, 409 U.S. 1095 (1973). If Congress was making vote dilution claims available with respect to the election of judges, it was, for the first time, extending that remedy to a context in which "one person, one vote" did not apply. *That* would have been a significant change in the law, and given the need to identify some other baseline for computing "dilution," *that* is a matter which those who believe in barking dogs should be astounded to find unmentioned in the legislative history. If "representatives" is given its normal meaning, on the other hand, there is no change in the law (except elimination of the intent requirement) and the silence is entirely understandable.

"The Court transforms the meaning of § 2, not because the ordinary meaning is irrational, or inconsistent with other parts of the statute, see, *e.g.*, *Green v. Bock Laundry*; *Public Citizen v. Department of Justice* (Kennedy, J., concurring in the judgment), but because it does not fit the Court's conception of what Congress must have had in mind. When we adopt a method that psychoanalyzes Congress rather than reads its laws, when we employ a tinkerer's toolbox, we do great harm. Not only do we reach the wrong result with respect to the statute at hand, but we poison the well of future legislation, depriving legislators of the assurance that ordinary terms, used in an ordinary context, will be given a predictable meaning. Our highest responsibility in the field of statutory construction is to read the laws in a consistent way, giving Congress a sure means by which it may work the people's will. We have ignored that responsibility today."

WEST VIRGINIA UNIVERSITY HOSPITALS V. CASEY

Supreme Court of the United States, 1991.
499 U.S. 83, 111 S.Ct. 1138, 113 L.Ed.2d 68.

[Excerpted in Chapter 6, § 1(C)]

NOTES ON CHISOM, CASEY, AND THE NEW TEXTUALISM IN ACTION

1.   *The Rise of the New Textualism and Its Relationship to the Plain Meaning Rule.* The Court's practice changed after Justice Scalia's appointment. After 1986, the Court's statutory opinions more often found a "plain meaning," much more frequently relied on dictionaries, and much less often examined legislative history to interpret a statute against what the Court felt was its plain meaning.[41] The Justices' opinions also have tended to be more dogmatic about whether there is any ambiguity in statutes; the Court was more likely to find a plain meaning in the 1990s and afterwards than it was before 1986. As in *Casey*, Justice Scalia's own opinions set forth and defended the precepts of the new textualism, often with Justice Stevens in dissent (also as in *Casey*). E.g., *United States v. Nordic Village*, 503 U.S. 30 (1992); *Finley v. United States*, 490 U.S. 545 (1989).

The relationship between the new textualism and the old plain meaning rule is evident, but they are not the same thing. Justice Scalia's formulation of textualism at the beginning of his *Chisom* dissent, as well as his discussion in *A Matter of Interpretation*, stressed the "ordinary meaning" or "reasonable meaning" of statutory text. In his view, legislative history should never trump such ordinary meaning. In contrast, the old plain meaning rule, as exemplified by *Caminetti* (§ 1 of this chapter), operated as an exclusionary rule concerning the use of legislative history: if the statutory text was "plain," one could not consult legislative history; if the statutory text was ambiguous, legislative history was fair game. The softer approach to plain meaning in *TVA v. Hill* and *Griffin* started with the presumption that a statutory plain meaning was probably the correct interpretation, but legislative history could be consulted to confirm that understanding (and in a rare case in which the legislative history conclusively

---

[41]   For empirical examinations of the Supreme Court's relatively textualist methodology, see Frank Cross, *The Theory and Practice of Statutory Interpretation* (2009) (reporting that the Court increasingly relies on textual plain meanings, which do not meaningfully constrain the Justices); James Brudney & Lawrence Baum, *Mirage or Oasis: The Supreme Court's Thirst for Dictionaries in the Rehnquist and Roberts Eras*, 55 Wm. & Mary L. Rev. 483 (2013) (Court's increasing reliance on dictionaries); David Law, *Law versus Ideology: The Supreme Court and the Use of Legislative History*, 51 Wm. & Mary L. Rev. 1653 (2010).

demonstrated that the textual plain meaning was not the appropriate interpretation, the plain meaning could be jettisoned).

In the post-1986 period, "plain meaning" remains an ambiguous term. What we understand Justice Scalia to have meant by "plain meaning" is the best (most coherent) textual understanding that emerges after close textual analysis, which then makes the result in the case plain on his terms—not merely the relatively rare "plain meaning" that leaps off the page to the experienced judge. It is regrettable that in some cases—both federal and state—judges have used the term "plain meaning" loosely, sometimes to mean a textual interpretation that is pretty obvious on the face of the statute (say, 90/10 clear) and sometimes to mean something similar to Justice Scalia's expression of the best textual understanding that emerges from close analysis of statutory provisions that, at the outset, may have seemed ambiguous, confusing, or at least complicated. The former approach to plain meaning is akin to a pretty literal approach to the face of the statute; the latter approach of Justice Scalia sees statutory interpretation to be something like a word puzzle, capable of being solved in almost all cases with a best answer emerging.

Although the Court's practice was influenced by the new textualism in the first few years of Justice Scalia's membership, the Court has never completely accepted its tenets. In *Wisconsin Public Intervenor v. Mortier*, 501 U.S. 597, 610 n.4 (1991), all of the other Justices joined a footnote explicitly rejecting Justice Scalia's insistence that legislative history is irrelevant to proper statutory interpretation. See Charles Tiefer, *The Reconceptualization of Legislative History in the Supreme Court*, 2000 Wis. L. Rev. 205.

In many cases, the Court still considers legislative background to statutes and is open to understanding a statute from the perspective of the legislators who enacted it. E.g., Brudney, *Confirmatory Legislative History, supra.* Often Justice Scalia dissented, as in *Chisom*, or concurred only in the judgment, as in *Bock Laundry*, e.g., *Landgraf v. USI Film Products*, 511 U.S. 244 (1994); *American Red Cross v. S.G.*, 505 U.S. 247 (1992), or concurred in all of the majority opinion except for the portion (sometimes just a footnote) that mentioned legislative history. E.g., *Carr v. United States*, 560 U.S. 438 (2010).

Near the end of his career, Justice Scalia turned to the canons of statutory interpretation, especially those working from statutory text, the whole act, and even the U.S. Code. In *Reading Law: The Interpretation of Legal Texts* (2012), Justice Scalia and his co-author Bryan Garner, listed 57 canons that if religiously followed would make statutory interpretation more predictable, objective, and neutral. Recall his discussion of the canons in *Matter of Interpretation*, where he pronounced them a needless distraction to the textualist. In *Reading Law,* Scalia and Garner focus on textual canons and pronounce them the centerpiece for an even newer textualism. In 2016, Justice Scalia passed away, but debate over his methodology lives on.

2.   *Critiques of the New Textualism in Action: The Elected Judges Case.* Justice Scalia's dissenting opinion in *Chisom* is a crisp statement of his methodology—and also reflects moves that have brought criticism to the application of the new textualism. The main criticism is that text is just as manipulable as legislative history. Victoria Nourse, for example, objects that Scalia and others engage in what she calls *textual gerrymandering*, whereby the judge isolates one relevant text, analyzes that to the hilt, and ignores other text, including language that is more "on point." E.g., Victoria Nourse, *Misreading Law, Misreading Democracy* (2016); Nourse, *Picking and Choosing Text: Lessons for Statutory Interpretation from the Philosophy of Language*, 69 Fla. L. Rev.

1409 (2017). Recall our notes to *Bock Laundry,* where Justice Scalia accused the dissenters of drastically revising the text—but his own slender revision actually made the statute more chaotic than it was before.

In *Chisom*, the governing statutory text is § 2(a), which is quoted in the problem preceding the Court's opinions. It is broadly stated—"*[no]* practice or procedure" imposed "by *any* State * * * in a manner which results in a denial or abridgement of the right of *any* citizen of the United States to vote on account of race or color"—yet Justice Scalia ignored this primary text. Section 2(b) provided a test for how a voter can prove a violation of the "results" standard—and Justice Scalia focused on that provision and gave it an odd gloss, suggesting that there were two separate rights ("participate" and "elect representatives"), and then insisted on an exceedingly narrow reading of "representatives." All of these moves can be questioned, and Scalia gave no grammatical reasons for the two separate rights analysis. (The textual gerrymandering is less blatant in *Casey*, but can you detect some of the same process in that opinion?)

For the meaning of "representatives," Justice Scalia exposes another major criticism of his method—that it shops dictionaries and canons to reach a particular (conservative) result. E.g., James Brudney & Lawrence Baum, *Oasis or Mirage: The Supreme Court's Thirst for Dictionaries in the Rehnquist and Roberts Eras*, 55 Wm. & Mary L. Rev. 483 (2013); James Brudney & Corey Ditslear, *Canons of Construction and the Elusive Quest for Neutral Reasoning*, 58 Vand. L. Rev. 1 (2005). The statute was enacted in 1982—yet Scalia relied, exclusively, on a 1950 dictionary. Even within *Webster's Second,* he shopped around a bit, ignoring that dictionary's general understanding of "representative" as someone who "represents others or another in a special capacity," and lifting the next definition and editing it as well. (Our unabridged version of *Webster's Second* includes as its definition 1b(1), "one who represents a people or community in its legislative or governing capacity.") Dictionary-shopping is a pervasive problem with a textualism that relies on dictionaries to exclude broader definitions. Ellen Aprill, *The Law of the Word: Dictionary Shopping in the Supreme Court*, 30 Ariz. St. L.J. 275 (1998).

At the very least, Justice Scalia needed to defend his principle of selection: Why did he opt for the narrowest understanding of "representative," where an elected sheriff was covered by the VRA but an elected state supreme court judge was not? The statutory purpose is very broad, and supports the majority's approach. By the way, Scalia's one effort at descriptive justification was his claim that no one would call members of baseball's All Star teams, elected by the fans, "representatives" of their teams or cities. Google "All Star Game" and "representatives" and see if he is right about that.

Another criticism of Justice Scalia's legisprudence is that it made loud noises about judicial neutrality, but in practice was less neutral than other approaches. Indeed, the textual canons that Scalia made as the new centerpiece of his approach cannot be applied without normative judgments. William Eskridge Jr., *The New Texualism and Normative Canons*, 113 Colum. L. Rev. 531 (2013) (book review of Scalia & Garner, *Reading Law*). The *Chisom* majority looked to Congress's purpose and deliberations to inform its choices about reading the text. Justice Scalia ignored Congress and denigrates its broad democratic purpose and homed in on a strong normative reading of "representatives" and, more particularly, "judges." Even when they were elected, judges were, in his view, debarred from being mere "representatives" of anything but the rule of law. In our view, this value is what drives everything he says in *Chisom*. Is this neutral, objective textualism?

3. *So Where Is the Court's Methodology, Post-Scalia?* First, and foremost, the text is now, more than it was 30 years ago, the central inquiry at the Supreme Court level and in other courts that are now following the Supreme Court's lead. The last two Supreme Court confirmation hearings heard the nominees—Judges Gorsuch (to the Scalia seat) and Kavanaugh (to the Kennedy seat)—make heartfelt speeches about how they followed the neutral, objective, nonpartisan text-based methodology that Justice Scalia represented. In their early opinions, both have followed the new textualism, albeit without the drama that Justice Scalia usually inserted. "[W]hile it is of course our job to apply faithfully the law Congress has written, it is never our job to rewrite a constitutionally valid statutory text under the banner of speculation about what Congress might have done had it faced a question that, on everyone's account, it never faced." *Henson v. Santander Consumer USA, Inc.,* 137 S. Ct. 1718, 1725 (2017) (Gorsuch); *Apple Inc. v. Pepper,* 139 S. Ct. 1914 (2019) (Kavanaugh); *Artis v. District of Columbia,* 138 S. Ct. 594 (2018) (Gorsuch's dissent).

A brief that starts off with, "the statute means thus-and-so because it says so in the committee report," is asking for trouble. Both advice and advocacy should start with the statutory text: "The statute means thus-and-so because that is its plain meaning," "because that is the meaning the structure of the statute supports," or "because this statute uses more narrow language than Congress purposefully used in other statutes." Because the Court frequently uses the dictionary to provide meaning to key statutory terms, the advocate should incorporate this methodology as well. The lexicon has become a fortress for the effective advocate. Brudney & Baum, *Mirage or Oasis.*

Second, the "contextual" evidence the Court is interested in is now statutory context more than just historical context. Arguments that your position is more consistent with other parts of the same statute are more likely to be winning arguments than those based upon legislative history. E.g., *King v. Burwell,* 135 S.Ct. 2480 (2015); cf. John Manning, *What Divides Textualists from Purposivists?,* 106 Colum. L. Rev 70 (2006) (even purposivist justices hew more closely to text-based analysis than they did pre-Scalia). As *Casey* indicates, the Court sometimes goes beyond the "whole act" rule to something like a "whole code" rule, searching the United States Code for guidance on the usage of key statutory terms and phrases. For an example, consider *Arlington Central School District v. Murphy,* 548 U.S. 291 (2006), where the Court narrowly construed the fee-shifting provision of a 1986 education-rights statute following the same methodology as *Casey,* over strong contrary legislative history and a powerful argument based on the statutory structure (both developed by Justice Breyer's dissenting opinion).

Third, the Court will still look at other kinds of contextual evidence, especially the public law landscape. If a statute seems to require an odd result (as in *Bock Laundry*), the Court will interrogate the background materials to find out why. If a statute overrides judicial or agency decisions (as in *Chisom*), the Court will usually be responsive to Congress's concerns. Compare *Digital Realty Trust v. Somers,* 138 S.Ct. 767 (2018) (Ginsburg opinion for the Court, referencing legislative history), with *id.* at 783–84 (Thomas/Alito/Gorsuch dissenting opinion strongly objecting to any mention of legislative materials), and with *id.* at 782 (Sotomayor/Breyer concurring opinion strongly defending the utility of legislative materials).

When the Justices are themselves divided as to the statute's "plain meaning," at least some of them will examine the statute's background to figure out how the typical legislator would have read the statute—or to confirm the apparent plain meaning derived from the statutory text and structure. See *Carr v. United States,* 560 U.S. 438 (2010) (Sotomayor, J., relying on legislative history to confirm plain meaning, triggering a Scalia, J., concurring opinion rejecting that part of the Court's opinion). For these reasons, it remains important to research and brief the legislative history thoroughly. The effective advocate will appreciate that the presence of such materials in the briefs may influence the outcome more than the opinion in the case will indicate.[42]

B. ECONOMIC THEORIES OF STATUTORY INTERPRETATION

Economic theory assumes that individuals are rational actors who seek to maximize their utilities through actions reasonably designed to do so. Institutions, too, may be rational actors, with their preferences usually determined by the views of the median senator, representative, or judge. Most purely economic theorizing is descriptive, helping us predict the behavior of groups of real people. Consider a simple example of how purely descriptive economic theorizing can enrich your thinking about statutory interpretation.

For most of us, law is a prediction of the rules that interacting government institutions will apply to a set of facts. We ask the IRS, read the newspaper, call a government clerk, note the posted speed limit, or just absorb it by osmosis. Law as prediction also entails evolution through sequential institutional interaction.[43] Congress enacts statutes, agencies interpret and apply those statutes, the judiciary sometimes reviews agency actions and interpretations, and Congress periodically considers legislation updating the law or overriding errant interpretations. A consequence of this sequence is that each institution has trumping power. The agency can undo some legislative bargains by stingy enforcement, the Supreme Court can overturn the agency's application, and Congress can override the Court or the agency. Groups press for changes in the law by working the institution most favorable to their interests and then seeking to protect it against trumping by the next institution down the line.

Most of the time, law is in a *stable equilibrium*: none of the institutions wants to change the rule, in part because if any makes that effort it may be overridden by the next institution in the chain. As a weak political actor ("the least dangerous branch"), the Supreme Court usually locates and applies that political equilibrium on high-visibility issues of public law, as it did in the affirmative action cases (*Weber, Johnson,* and *Ricci*) in Chapter 1, § 3. On the other hand, the equilibrium is often

---

[42]   Consider the comments of Judge Raymond Randolph of the District of Columbia Circuit, in *Dictionaries, Plain Meaning, and Context in Statutory Interpretation,* 17 Harv. J.L. & Pub. Pol'y 71, 76 (1994):

  * * * Nearly every brief I see in cases involving issues of statutory construction contains a discourse on legislative history. This is a wise precaution on the part of appellate advocates. Counsel can never be sure that the court will find the words plain, and stop there. To be safe, in the event the court takes two steps instead of one, counsel must include a backup argument addressing the meaning of the statute in light of the legislative history. Judges read those briefs from cover to cover, or at least they are supposed to. I do. Somewhere during the reading, preliminary views begin to form. When the reading is done and the case has been analyzed and argued, how can it be said that the judge turned to the legislative history only after finding the statutory language ambiguous? The judge himself often cannot identify exactly when his perception of the words actually jelled. * * *

[43]   The model that follows was developed in William Eskridge Jr. & Philip Frickey, *The Supreme Court, 1993 Term—Foreword: Law as Equilibrium,* 108 Harv. L. Rev. 26 (1994).

potentially unstable: one actor may be able to change the rule without being overridden. This is what happened in *Griffin*, where the Supreme Court imposed its rule-of-law values on a statute that apparently was understood for decades to embody a less generous compensation rule—and the issue was too divisive (seafaring unions liking the Court's result, companies not) or not sufficiently troublesome for Congress to override.

Political scientists maintain that judges often read their substantive values into statutes.[44] In politicized areas of law such as workplace discrimination, the Roberts Court gives congressional overrides a narrow reading and expansively follows the Court's own repudiated "shadow precedents."[45] For example, in *Lorance v. AT & T Technologies, Inc.*, 490 U.S. 900 (1989), the Court ruled that women complaining of seniority rules had to file complaints with the EEOC within 180 or 300 days after the rules went into effect. After concluding that the Court should have followed a more liberal line of Title VII limitations precedents, Congress overrode *Lorance* in the 1991 Civil Rights Act, Pub. L. No. 102–166, § 112, which created a more liberal limitations period for seniority claims, 42 U.S.C. § 2000e–5(e)(2). The next case involved female employees who were paid unequal salaries but did not know precisely what male employees were paid—yet the Court imposed a strict limitations period on these plaintiffs in *Ledbetter v. Goodyear Tire & Rubber Co.*, 550 U.S. 618 (2007). The *Ledbetter* majority not only declined to apply the override, as it just covered seniority claims, but followed *Lorance* as binding precedent—and *relied on* the override as evidence that Congress, when it liberalized the limitations period for seniority claims, "intended" to leave strict limitations periods in place everywhere else in Title VII. *Id.* at 627 n.2. Dissenters objected that the Court should have followed its more forgiving precedents and that *Ledbetter*, where the employees were highly unlikely to have known about the pay differentials, was a stronger case than *Lorance* had been. Congress angrily overrode *Ledbetter* with the Lilly Ledbetter Fair Pay Act of 2009, P.L. 111–2, but the Court continues to hand down decisions applying "shadow precedents" and narrowly construing Title VII overrides. E.g., *University of Texas Southwestern Medical Center v. Nassar*, 133 S.Ct. 2517 (2013).

Some of these descriptive points, such as the political science view that judges mainly vote their substantive preferences, are controversial.[46] You might maintain a healthy skepticism about the predictive claims of economics-based theories. In the hands of law-and-economics scholars, however, economics is often harnessed for a normative point. Consider three different kinds of normative contributions law and economics might make to statutory interpretation. They draw from economists' *ex ante* approach to rules, from public choice theory, and from cost-benefit analysis.

---

[44] E.g., Cross, *Practice of Statutory Interpretation*, 159–79; Lee Epstein & Jack Knight, *The Choices Justices Make* (1998); Jeffrey Segal, *Separation-of-Powers Games in the Positive Theory of Congress and Courts*, 91 Am. Pol. Sci. Rev. 28–43 (1997).

[45] See Deborah Widiss, *Shadow Precedents and the Separation of Powers: Statutory Interpretation of Congressional Overrides*, 84 Notre Dame L. Rev. 511 (2009), and Widiss, *Undermining Congressional Overrides: The Hydra Problem in Statutory Interpretation*, 90 Tex. L. Rev. 859 (2012).

[46] E.g., Connor Raso & William Eskridge Jr., *Chevron as a Canon, Not a Precedent: An Empirical Study of What Motivates Justices in Agency Deference Cases*, 110 Colum. L. Rev. 1727 (2010) (evidence that rule of law values motivate the Court at least as much as substantive preferences, even in cases like *Ledbetter*).

1. *Ex Ante* Approaches to the Debate Between Textualists and Contextualists

Most people respond to "hard cases" from an *ex post* point of view: this result is unfair to or imposes needless hardship upon a sympathetic claimant. From an economics point of view, hard cases make bad law because they invite *ex post* decisionmaking, where the judge creates rules and standards that are fair in the particular case—but often have excessive social costs for a society that then has to apply the rule in future interactions and lawsuits.

Economic theory valorizes an *ex ante* perspective: evaluate a rule based on whether it sets up a legal directive that will be good for the average case and provides proper incentives for the citizenry—and not because you like its result in a particular case. *Ex ante* analysis can also apply to general theories. Defending the Hart and Sacks purpose approach from an *ex ante* perspective is Jonathan Macey, *Promoting Public-Regarding Legislation Through Statutory Interpretation: An Interest Group Model*, 86 Colum. L. Rev. 223 (1986): interpreting statutes to carry out their *announced* public-regarding purposes is a good way for judges to maintain a minimal level of honesty in the legislative process; *knowing* that judges will take their public-regarding rhetoric seriously, legislators in the future will be more cautious, and perhaps even more honest, when they defend legislation they want to pass.

William Landes and Richard Posner make an *ex ante* argument for applying original legislative intent in statutory cases, even when such application leads to harsh results. William Landes & Richard Posner, *The Independent Judiciary in an Interest-Group Perspective,* 18 J.L. & Econ. 875 (1976). They argue that judges must be faithful agents reconstructing original deals, not because that is required by the Constitution, but because any other rule would undermine the conditions under which statutes are enacted. *Ex ante*, such an approach gives members of Congress and interest groups sufficient assurance that their deals will be enforced. Accord, Richard Posner, *The Federal Courts: Crisis and Reform* 286–93 (1985).

Frank Easterbrook agrees with Landes and Posner's *ex ante* way of thinking but rejects their approach, on the ground that the best evidence of a statutory deal is the statutory text. See Frank Easterbrook, *The Supreme Court, 1993 Term—Foreword: The Court and the Economic System,* 98 Harv. L. Rev. 4 (1984), and *Statutes' Domains,* 50 Chi. L. Rev. 533 (1983). Treating statutes as contract-like deals is controversial, e.g., Mark Movesian, *Are Statutes Really "Legislative Bargains"? The Failure of the Contract Analogy in Statutory Interpretation*, 76 N.C. L. Rev. 1145 (1998), but assume that this is an apt analogy. Consider how the different "dealist" theories play out in the following case.[47] Note how the approach Judge Posner takes here is different than the theory he developed with Landes.

---

[47] Consistent with descriptive economic theory, Posner and Easterbrook, both law and economics "conservatives" appointed by President Reagan, vote the same way in the large majority of statutory cases, even if for different reasons. See Daniel Farber, *Do Theories of Statutory Interpretation Matter?*, 94 Nw. U. L. Rev. 1409 (2000).

UNITED STATES V. MARSHALL

United States Court of Appeals for the Seventh Circuit (*en banc*), 1990.
908 F.2d 1312, *aff'd sub nom. Chapman v. United States*, 500 U.S. 453 (1991).

EASTERBROOK, CIRCUIT JUDGE.

* * * Stanley J. Marshall was convicted after a bench trial and sentenced to 20 years' imprisonment for conspiring to distribute, and distributing, more than ten grams of LSD, enough for 11,751 doses. Patrick Brumm, Richard L. Chapman, and John M. Schoenecker were convicted by a jury of selling ten sheets (1,000 doses) of paper containing LSD. Because the total weight of the paper and LSD was 5.7 grams, a five-year mandatory minimum applied. The district court sentenced Brumm to 60 months (the minimum), Schoenecker to 63 months, and Chapman to 96 months' imprisonment. All four defendants confine their arguments on appeal to questions concerning their sentences.

The three questions we must resolve are these: (1) Whether 21 U.S.C. § 841(b)(1)(A)(v) and (B)(v), which set mandatory minimum terms of imprisonment—five years for selling more than one gram of a "mixture or substance containing a detectable amount" of LSD, ten years for more than ten grams—exclude the weight of the carrier medium. (2) Whether the weight tables in the sentencing guidelines likewise exclude the weight of any carrier. (3) Whether the statute and the guidelines are unconstitutional to the extent their computations are based on anything other than the weight of the pure drug. * * *

According to the Sentencing Commission, the LSD in an average dose weighs 0.05 milligrams. Twenty thousand pure doses are a gram. But 0.05 mg is almost invisible, so LSD is distributed to retail customers in a carrier. Pure LSD is dissolved in a solvent such as alcohol and sprayed on paper or gelatin; alternatively the paper may be dipped in the solution. After the solvent evaporates, the paper or gel is cut into one-dose squares and sold by the square. Users swallow the squares or may drop them into a beverage, releasing the drug. Although the gelatin and paper are light, they weigh much more than the drug. Marshall's 11,751 doses weighed 113.32 grams; the LSD accounted for only 670.72 mg of this, not enough to activate the five-year mandatory minimum sentence, let alone the ten-year minimum. The ten sheets of blotter paper carrying the 1,000 doses Chapman and confederates sold weighed 5.7 grams; the LSD in the paper did not approach the one-gram threshold for a mandatory minimum sentence. This disparity between the weight of the pure LSD and the weight of LSD-plus-carrier underlies the defendants' arguments.

If the carrier counts in the weight of the "mixture or substance containing a detectable amount" of LSD, some odd things may happen. Weight in the hands of distributors may exceed that of manufacturers and wholesalers. Big fish then could receive paltry sentences or small fish draconian ones. Someone who sold 19, 999 doses of pure LSD (at 0.05 mg per dose) would escape the five-year mandatory minimum of § 841(b)(1)(B)(v) and be covered by § 841(b)(1)(C), which lacks a minimum term and has a maximum of "only" 20 years. Someone who sold a single hit of LSD dissolved in a tumbler of orange juice could be exposed to a ten-year mandatory minimum. Retailers could fall in or out of the mandatory terms depending not on the number of doses but on the medium: sugar cubes weigh more than paper, which weighs more than gelatin. One way to eliminate the possibility of such consequences is to say that the carrier is not a "mixture or substance containing a detectable amount" of the drug. Defendants ask us to do this.

Defendants' submission starts from the premise that the interaction of the statutory phrase "mixture or substance" with the distribution of LSD by the dose in a carrier creates a unique probability of surprise results. The premise may be unwarranted. The paper used to distribute LSD is light stuff, not the kind used to absorb ink. Chapman's 1,000 doses weighed about 0.16 ounces. More than 6,000 doses, even in blotter paper, weigh less than an ounce. Because the LSD in one dose weighs about 0.05 milligrams, the combination of LSD-plus-paper is about 110 times the weight of the LSD. The impregnated paper could be described as "0.9% LSD". * * *

This is by no means an unusual dilution rate for illegal drugs. Heroin sold on the street is 2% to 3% opiate and the rest filler. Sometimes the mixture is even more dilute, approaching the dilution rate for LSD in blotter paper. Heroin and crack cocaine, like LSD, are sold on the streets by the dose, although they are sold by weight higher in the distributional chain. * * *

It is not possible to construe the words of § 841 to make the penalty turn on the net weight of the drug rather than the gross weight of carrier and drug. The statute speaks of "mixture or substance containing a detectable amount" of a drug. "Detectable amount" is the opposite of "pure"; the point of the statute is that the "mixture" is not to be converted to an equivalent amount of pure drug.

The structure of the statute reinforces this conclusion. The 10-year minimum applies to any person who possesses, with intent to distribute, "100 grams or more of phencyclidine (PCP) or 1 kilogram or more of a mixture or substance containing a detectable amount of phencyclidine (PCP)", § 841(b)(1)(A)(iv). Congress distinguished the pure drug from a "mixture or substance containing a detectable amount of" it. All drugs other than PCP are governed exclusively by the "mixture or substance" language. Even brute force cannot turn that language into a reference to pure LSD. Congress used the same "mixture or substance" language to describe heroin, cocaine, amphetamines, and many other drugs that are sold after being cut— sometimes as much as LSD. There is no sound basis on which to treat the words "substance or mixture containing a detectable amount of", repeated verbatim for every drug mentioned in § 841 except PCP, as *different* things for LSD and cocaine although the language is identical, while treating the "mixture or substance" language as meaning the *same* as the reference to pure PCP in 21 U.S.C. § 841(b)(1)(A)(iv) and (B)(iv).

Although the "mixture or substance" language shows that the statute cannot be limited to pure LSD, it does not necessarily follow that blotter paper *is* a "mixture or substance containing" LSD. That phrase cannot include all "carriers". One gram of crystalline LSD in a heavy glass bottle is still only one gram of "statutory LSD". So is a gram of LSD being "carried" in a Boeing 747. How much mingling of the drug with something else is essential to form a "mixture or substance"? The legislative history is silent, but ordinary usage is indicative.

"Substance" may well refer to a chemical compound, or perhaps to a drug in a solvent. LSD does not react chemically with sugar, blotter paper, or gelatin, and none of these is a solvent. "Mixture" is more inclusive. Cocaine often is mixed with mannitol, quinine, or lactose. These white powders do not react, but it is common ground that a cocaine-mannitol mixture is a statutory "mixture".

LSD and blotter paper are not commingled in the same way as cocaine and lactose. What is the nature of their association? The possibility most favorable to defendants is that LSD sits on blotter paper as oil floats on water. Immiscible substances may fall outside the statutory definition of "mixture". The possibility does not assist defendants—not on this record, anyway. LSD is applied to paper in a solvent; after the solvent evaporates, a tiny quantity of LSD remains. Because the fibers absorb the alcohol, the LSD solidifies inside the paper rather than on it. You cannot pick a grain of LSD off the surface of the paper. Ordinary parlance calls the paper containing tiny crystals of LSD a mixture.

United States v. Rose, 881 F.2d 386 (7th Cir. 1989), like every other appellate decision that has addressed the question, concludes that the carrier medium for LSD, like the "cut" for heroin and cocaine, is a "mixture or substance containing a detectable amount" of the drug. Although a chemist might be able to offer evidence bearing on the question whether LSD and blotter paper "mix" any more fully than do oil and water, the record contains no such evidence. Without knowing more of the chemistry than this record reveals, we adhere to the unanimous conclusion of the other courts of appeals that blotter paper treated with LSD is a "mixture or substance containing a detectable quantity of" LSD.

Two reasons have been advanced to support a contrary conclusion: that statutes should be construed to avoid constitutional problems, and that some members of the sitting Congress are dissatisfied with basing penalties on the combined weight of LSD and carrier. Neither is persuasive.

A preference for giving statutes a constitutional meaning is a reason to construe, not to rewrite or "improve". * * * "[S]ubstance or mixture containing a detectable quantity" is not ambiguous. * * * Neither the rule of lenity nor the preference for avoiding constitutional adjudication justifies disregarding unambiguous language.

The canon about avoiding constitutional decisions, in particular, must be used with care, for it is a closer cousin to invalidation than to interpretation. It is a way to enforce the constitutional penumbra, and therefore an aspect of constitutional law proper. Constitutional decisions breed penumbras, which multiply questions. Treating each as justification to construe laws out of existence too greatly enlarges the judicial power. And heroic "construction" is unnecessary, given our conclusion [in discussion omitted here] that Congress possesses the constitutional power to set penalties on the basis of gross weight.

As for the pending legislation: subsequent debates are not a ground for avoiding the import of enactments. Although the views of a subsequent Congress are entitled to respect, ongoing debates do not represent the views of Congress. * * *

CUMMINGS, CIRCUIT JUDGE, with whom BAUER, CHIEF JUDGE, and WOOD, JR., CUDAHY, and POSNER, CIRCUIT JUDGES, join, dissenting.

[T]he United States District Court for the District of Columbia held that blotter paper was not a mixture or substance within the meaning of the statute. *United States v Healy*, 729 F.Supp. 140 (D.D.C. 1990). The court relied not only on ordinary dictionary definitions of the words mixture and substance but also on a November 30, 1988, Sentencing Commission publication, entitled "Questions Most Frequently Asked About the Sentencing Guidelines," which states that the Commission has not taken a position on whether the blotter paper should be weighed. The conclusion that the Commission has not yet resolved this question is further supported by a Sentencing Commission Notice issued on March 3, 1989, which requested public comments on whether the Commission should exclude the weight of the carrier for sentencing purposes in LSD cases.[3]

The *Healy* court also stated that Congress could have intended the words "mixture or substance" to refer to the liquid in which the pure LSD is dissolved. Finally, the *Healy* court relied on a Guidelines table designed to provide a sentencing court with an equivalent weight for sentencing purposes in cases in which the number of doses distributed is known but the actual weight is unknown. The table provides that a dose of LSD weighs .05 milligrams. Guidelines § 2D1.1, Commentary, Drug Equivalency Tables. This weight closely approximates the weight of one dose of LSD without blotter paper, but is not an accurate reflection of one dose with blotter paper. * * *

Two subsequent pieces of legislative history * * * shed some light on this question. In a letter to Senator Joseph R. Biden, Jr., dated April 26, 1989, the Chairman of the Sentencing Commission, William W. Wilkens, Jr., noted the ambiguity in the statute as it is currently written:

> With respect to LSD, it is unclear whether Congress intended the carrier to be considered as a packaging material, or, since it is commonly consumed along with the illicit drug, as a dilutant ingredient in the drug mixture. . . . The Commission suggests that Congress may wish to further consider the LSD carrier issue in order to clarify legislative intent as to whether the weight of the carrier should or should not be considered in determining the quantity of LSD mixture for punishment purposes.

Presumably acting in response to this query, Senator Biden added to the Congressional Record for October 5, 1989, an analysis of one of a series of technical corrections to 21 U.S.C. § 841 that were under consideration by the Senate that day. This analysis states that the purpose of the particular correction at issue was to remove an unintended "inequity" from Section 841 caused by the decisions of some courts to include the weight of the blotter paper for sentencing purposes in LSD cases. According to Senator Biden, the correction "remedie[d] this inequity by removing the weight of the carrier from the calculation of the weight of the mixture or substance." This correction was adopted as part of Amendment No. 976 to S. 1711. 135 Cong.Rec. S12749 (daily ed. Oct. 5, 1989). The amended bill was passed by a

---

[3]   The Commission has recently adopted several amendments and sent them to Congress for approval. Among these is an amendment to Application Note 11 to Guidelines Section 2D1.1. This amendment specifically states that the typical weight per dose of LSD that is given in the Weight Per Dose Table as .05 milligrams is the weight of the LSD alone and not of the LSD combined with any carrier. 55 Fed.Reg. 19197 (May 8, 1990). * * *

unanimous vote of the Senate (*id.* at S12765) and is currently pending before the House.

Comments in more recent issues of the Congressional Record indicate that S. 1711 is not expected to pass the House of Representatives. See 136 Cong.Rec. S943 (daily ed. Feb. 7, 1990). In the meantime, however, a second attempt to clarify Congress' intent in amending 21 U.S.C. § 841 to include the words mixture or substance has now been introduced in the Senate. On April 18, 1990, Senator Kennedy introduced an amendment to S. 1970 (a bill establishing constitutional procedures for the imposition of the death penalty) seeking to clarify the language of 21 U.S.C. § 841. That amendment, Amendment No. 1716, states:

> Section 841(b)(1) of title 21, United States Code, is amended by inserting the following new subsection at the end thereof: "(E) In determining the weight of a 'mixture or substance' under this section, the court shall not include the weight of the carrier upon which the controlled substance is placed, or by which it is transported."

136 Cong.Rec. S7069 (daily ed. May 24, 1990). [Judge Cummings argued from this evidence that the draconian penalty scheme for LSD was simply a mistake never intended by Congress and that the Seventh Circuit should follow *Healy*.]

POSNER, CIRCUIT JUDGE, joined by BAUER, CHIEF JUDGE, and CUMMINGS, WOOD, JR., and CUDAHY, CIRCUIT JUDGES, dissenting.

* * * Based as it is on weight, [the § 841 sentencing scheme] works well for drugs that are sold by weight; and ordinarily the weight quoted to the buyer is the weight of the dilute form, although of course price will vary with purity. The dilute form is the product, and it is as natural to punish its purveyors according to the weight of the product as it is to punish moonshiners by the weight or volume of the moonshine they sell rather than by the weight of the alcohol contained in it. * * *

LSD, however, is sold to the consumer by the dose; it is not cut, diluted, or mixed with something else. Moreover, it is incredibly light. An average dose of LSD weighs .05 milligrams, which is less than two millionths of an ounce. To ingest something that small requires swallowing something much larger. Pure LSD in granular form is first diluted by being dissolved, usually in alcohol, and then a quantity of the solution containing one dose of LSD is sprayed or eyedropped on a sugar cube, or on a cube of gelatin, or, as in the cases before us, on an inch-square section of "blotter" paper. * * * After the solution is applied to the carrier medium, the alcohol or other solvent evaporates, leaving an invisible (and undiluted) spot of pure LSD on the cube or blotter paper. The consumer drops the cube or the piece of paper into a glass of water, or orange juice, or some other beverage, causing the LSD to dissolve in the beverage, which is then drunk. * * * [A] quart of orange juice containing one dose of LSD is not more, in any relevant sense, than a pint of juice containing the same one dose, and it would be loony to punish the purveyor of the quart more heavily than the purveyor of the pint. It would be like basing the punishment for selling cocaine on the combined weight of the cocaine and of the vehicle (plane, boat, automobile, or whatever) used to transport it or the syringe used to inject it or the pipe used to smoke it. The blotter paper, sugar cubes, etc. are the vehicles for conveying LSD to the consumer.

The weight of the carrier is vastly greater than that of the LSD, as well as irrelevant to its potency. There is no comparable disparity between the pure and the mixed form (if that is how we should regard LSD on blotter paper or other carrier medium) with respect to the other drugs in section 841, with the illuminating exception of PCP. There Congress specified alternative weights, for the drug itself and for the substance or mixture containing the drug. For example, the five-year minimum sentence for a seller of PCP requires the sale of either ten grams of the drug itself or one hundred grams of a substance or mixture containing the drug. 21 U.S.C. § 841(b)(1)(B)(iv).

Ten sheets of blotter paper, containing a thousand doses of LSD, weigh almost six grams. The LSD itself weighs less than a hundredth as much. If the thousand doses are on gelatin cubes instead of sheets of blotter paper, the total weight is less, but it is still more than two grams, which is forty times the weight of the LSD. In both cases, if the carrier plus the LSD constitutes the relevant "substance or mixture" (the crucial "if" in this case), the dealer is subject to the minimum mandatory sentence of five years. One of the defendants before us (Marshall) sold almost 12,000 doses of LSD on blotter paper. This subjected him to the ten-year minimum, and the Guidelines then took over and pushed him up to twenty years. Since it takes 20,000 doses of LSD to equal a gram, Marshall would not have been subject to even the five-year mandatory minimum had he sold the LSD in its pure form. And a dealer who sold fifteen times the number of doses as Marshall—180,000—would not be subject to the ten-year mandatory minimum sentence if he sold the drug in its pure form, because 180,000 doses is only nine grams.

At the other extreme, if Marshall were not a dealer at all but dropped a square of blotter paper containing a single dose of LSD into a glass of orange juice and sold it to a friend at cost (perhaps 35 cents), he would be subject to the ten-year minimum. The juice with LSD dissolved in it would be the statutory mixture or substance containing a detectable amount of the illegal drug and it would weigh more than ten grams (one ounce is about 35 grams, and the orange juice in a glass of orange juice weighs several ounces). So a person who sold one dose of LSD might be subject to the ten-year mandatory minimum sentence while a dealer who sold 199,999 doses in pure form would be subject only to the five-year minimum. Defendant Dean sold 198 doses, crowded onto one sheet of blotter paper: this subjected him to the five-year mandatory minimum, too, since the ensemble weighed slightly more than a gram. * * *

All this seems crazy but we must consider whether Congress might have had a reason for wanting to key the severity of punishment for selling LSD to the weight of the carrier rather than to the number of doses or to some reasonable proxy for dosage (as weight is, for many drugs). The only one suggested is that it might be costly to determine the weight of the LSD in the blotter paper, sugar cube, etc., because it is so light! That merely underscores the irrationality of basing the punishment for selling this drug on weight rather than on dosage. But in fact the weight is reported in every case I have seen, so apparently it can be determined readily enough; it *has* to be determined in any event, to permit a purity adjustment under the Guidelines. If the weight of the LSD is difficult to determine, the difficulty is easily overcome by basing punishment on the number of doses, which makes much more sense in any event. To base punishment on the weight of the carrier medium makes about as much sense as basing punishment on the weight of the defendant. * * *

This is a quilt the pattern whereof no one has been able to discern. The legislative history is silent, and since even the Justice Department cannot explain the why of the punishment scheme that it is defending, the most plausible inference is that Congress simply did not realize how LSD is sold. The inference is reinforced by the statutory treatment of PCP. * * *

[The] irrationality is magnified when we compare the sentences for people who sell other drugs prohibited by 21 U.S.C. § 841. Marshall, remember, sold fewer than 12,000 doses and was sentenced to twenty years. Twelve thousand doses sounds like a lot, but to receive a comparable sentence for selling heroin Marshall would have had to sell ten kilograms, which would yield between one and two million doses. To receive a comparable sentence for selling cocaine he would have had to sell fifty kilograms, which would yield anywhere from 325,000 to five million doses. While the corresponding weight is lower for crack—half a kilogram—this still translates into 50,000 doses. * * *

Well, what if anything can we judges do about this mess? The answer lies in the shadow of a jurisprudential disagreement that is not less important by virtue of being unavowed by most judges. It is the disagreement between the severely positivistic view that the content of law is exhausted in clear, explicit, and definite enactments by or under express delegation from legislatures, and the natural lawyer's or legal pragmatist's view that the practice of interpretation and the general terms of the Constitution (such as "equal protection of the laws") authorize judges to enrich positive law with the moral values and practical concerns of civilized society. Judges who in other respects have seemed quite similar, such as Holmes and Cardozo, have taken opposite sides of this issue. Neither approach is entirely satisfactory. The first buys political neutrality and a type of objectivity at the price of substantive injustice, while the second buys justice in the individual case at the price of considerable uncertainty and, not infrequently, judicial willfulness. It is no wonder that our legal system oscillates between the approaches. The positivist view, applied unflinchingly to this case, commands the affirmance of prison sentences that are exceptionally harsh by the standards of the modern Western world, dictated by an accidental, unintended scheme of punishment nevertheless implied by the words (taken one by one) of the relevant enactments. The natural law or pragmatist view leads to a freer interpretation, one influenced by norms of equal treatment; and let us explore the interpretive possibilities here. One is to interpret "mixture or substance containing a detectable amount of [LSD]" to exclude the carrier medium—the blotter paper, sugar or gelatin cubes, and orange juice or other beverage. That is the course we rejected in *United States v Rose, supra*, as have the other circuits. I wrote *Rose*, but I am no longer confident that its literal interpretation of the statute, under which the blotter paper, cubes, etc. are "substances" that "contain" LSD, is inevitable. The blotter paper, etc. are better viewed, I now think, as carriers, like the package in which a kilo of cocaine comes wrapped or the bottle in which a fifth of liquor is sold.

Interpreted to exclude the carrier, the punishment schedule for LSD would make perfectly good sense; it would not warp the statutory design. The comparison with heroin and cocaine is again illuminating. The statute imposes the five-year mandatory minimum sentence on anyone who sells a substance or mixture containing a hundred grams of heroin, equal to 10,000 to 20,000 doses. One gram of pure LSD, which also would trigger the five-year minimum, yields 20,000 doses. The comparable figures for cocaine are 3250 to 50,000 doses, placing LSD in about the middle. So Congress may have wanted to base punishment for the sale of LSD on the weight of the pure drug after all, using one and ten grams of the pure drug to trigger the five-year and ten-year minima (and corresponding maxima—twenty years and forty years). This interpretation leaves "substance or mixture containing" without a referent, so far as LSD is concerned. But we must remember that Congress used the identical term in each subsection that specifies the quantity of a drug that subjects the seller to the designated minimum and maximum punishments. In thus automatically including the same term in each subsection, Congress did not necessarily affirm that, for each and every drug covered by the statute, a substance or mixture containing the drug *must* be found.

The flexible interpretation that I am proposing is decisively strengthened by the constitutional objection to basing punishment of LSD offenders on the weight of the carrier medium rather than on the weight of the LSD. Courts often do interpretive handsprings to avoid having even to *decide* a constitutional question. In doing so they expand, very questionably in my view, the effective scope of the Constitution, creating a constitutional penumbra in which statutes wither, shrink, are deformed. A better case for flexible interpretation is presented when the alternative is to nullify Congress's action: when in other words there is not merely a constitutional question about, but a constitutional barrier to, the statute when interpreted literally. This is such a case.

[Judge Posner then argued that the sentencing scheme for LSD upheld by the majority violates the equal protection guarantee of the Fifth Amendment's due process clause, because of the "unequal treatment of people equally situated." That even the Justice Department cannot formulate a rational basis for the distinctions it has drawn from § 841 in LSD cases is persuasive evidence that Congress has to be sent back to the drawing board.]

The literal interpretation adopted by the majority is not inevitable. All interpretation is contextual. The words of the statute—interpreted against a background that includes a constitutional norm of equal treatment, a (closely related) constitutional commitment to rationality, an evident failure by both Congress and the Sentencing Commission to consider how LSD is actually produced, distributed, and sold, and an equally evident failure by the same two bodies to consider the interaction between heavy mandatory minimum sentences and the Sentencing Guidelines—will bear an interpretation that distinguishes between the carrier vehicle of the illegal drug and the substance or mixture containing a detectable amount of the drug. The punishment of the crack dealer is not determined by the weight of the glass tube in which he sells the crack; we should not lightly attribute to Congress a purpose of punishing the dealer in LSD according to the weight of the LSD carrier. We should not make Congress's handiwork an embarrassment to the members of Congress and to us.

NOTES ON THE LSD CASE AND EX ANTE THINKING

1.   *Review: The New Textualism and Linguistic Meaning.* Judge Easterbrook's opinion in the LSD case is an excellent example of the distinctive features of the new textualism: (a) focus on the text of the statute, including not just the plain meaning of the provision at issue, but also how that provision fits into the "whole statute"; (b) a rejection of, and some contempt for, legislative history as a context for interpreting the statute; and (c) a relatively black-and-white vision of what words mean. Note that judges on the Seventh Circuit were in sharp disagreement about whether LSD on blotter paper is a "mixture." Should the very fact of good-faith disagreement about the law's plain meaning be evidence that the statute has no plain meaning (as Stephen Ross has long suggested)?

In affirming *Marshall*, the Supreme Court was also divided as to what "mixture" meant in the LSD sentencing law. See *Chapman v. United States*, 500 U.S. 453 (1991). While Judge Easterbrook relied on "ordinary usage" to define "mixture," Chief Justice Rehnquist's opinion for the Supreme Court relied on a dictionary definition of mixture as "two substances blended together so that the particles of one are diffused among the particles of the other." Because the LSD "is diffused among the fibers of the paper," the Chief Justice found a statutory plain meaning. This might be called a denotative approach to plain meaning: Apply the dictionary definition and see if it fits.

Professional linguists don't necessarily approach meaning in this way. They are willing to expand and contract meaning beyond its dictionary denotations. Words reflect categories which are fuzzy at the margins; the necessary and sufficient conditions for membership in the category are not completely accessible to us before the fact. Lawrence Solan, a Ph.D. linguist, in *When Judges Use the Dictionary*, 68 Am. Speech 50, 54–55 (1993), analyzes the *Marshall* case in this way:

> Calling the blotter paper impregnated with LSD a mixture seems odd for the same reason that it seems odd to call a pancake soaked with syrup *a pancake-syrup mixture*; or to call a wet towel *a water-cotton mixture*; or to call a towel that one has used to dry one's face during a tennis game *a cotton-sweat mixture*, or later, after the sweat has dried, *a cotton-salt mixture*. The last two I would call *a wet towel* and *a dirty towel*, respectively. In all of these examples, both substances have kept their character in a chemical sense, but one of the substances seems to have kept too much of its character for us to feel natural using the term *mixture*. * * *

Solan criticizes *Chapman* for "taking a concept that is fuzzy at the margins and substituting for it a definition that is subject to more refined application than the concept itself." If the new textualists cannot satisfy professional linguists with their insistence that a statute has a "plain meaning," what legitimacy does their approach offer?

2.   *Liberty Versus* Ex Ante *Thinking?* Judge Easterbrook's first major article on interpretation urged that statutes not be construed beyond the "domain" clearly demarcated by their texts. He defended this approach on the basis of a libertarian presumption akin to the standard Chicago School idea that most things should not be regulated by the state and should be left to the free operation of the market:

> Those who wrote and approved the Constitution thought that most social relations would be governed by private agreements, customs, and

understandings, not resolved in the halls of government. There is still at least a presumption that people's arrangements prevail unless expressly displaced by legal doctrine. * * * It is easier for an agency to justify the revocation of rules (or simple nonregulation) than the creation of new rules.

Easterbrook, *Statutes' Domains*, 50 U. Chi. L. Rev. 533, 549–50 (1983). Note that the libertarian position in *Marshall* is the one taken by Judges Cummings and Posner.

Consider an *ex ante* counterargument: a textualism that yields harsh results, as in the LSD case, sends a signal to judges that they should be careful not to make policy—and to Congress that its statutes will be interpreted "as written," and that any updating or fixing will have to be done by the legislators themselves. If they adopt the "tough love" of the new textualism, courts may enhance democracy and legislative accountability. Everyone will know that Congress, alone, is responsible for statutory applications, and voters can act accordingly.

A problem with the foregoing argument is that there is no evidence that such tough love will have any effect on Congress, for it cannot enact statutes with the degree of specification the new textualists would require. James Brudney, *Congressional Commentary on Judicial Interpretations of Statutes: Idle Chatter or Telling Response?*, 93 Mich. L. Rev. 1 (1994). An implication of Brudney's idea is that the new textualism will sometimes have a likely libertarian effect (by reducing Congress' practical capacity to regulate), bringing us back to Easterbrook's point in *Statute's Domain*. The problem is that legislative paralysis will also sometimes have an anti-libertarian effect—as in the LSD Case, when Congress could not correct what was apparently a drafting error, and Messrs. Marshall, Chapman et al. paid the price with more years in federal prison.

3.   Ex Ante *Arguments for an Approach That Considers Fairness.* Judge Posner is not a bleeding-heart liberal—the classic *ex post* position—yet he voted to overturn the conviction. And he did so for reasons that went well beyond the original legislative intent approach he once championed. Since 1990, Posner has come out of the closet as a flexible pragmatic interpreter of statutes.[48] There are some economic arguments for a more flexible approach than the one followed by the majority in *Marshall*. One argument is that textualism will undermine rather than cultivate the conditions for legislation: because deals will not be reasonably enforced, legislators will be more reluctant to make them; legislators might even lose confidence that the judiciary can be trusted to carry out statutes in a fair way. Another *ex ante* argument is that an unreasonable construction of the LSD law undermines the overall legitimacy of our system of criminal justice (the small fries like Marshall are being treated really unfairly; many of those arrested are people of color), without any discernible offsetting benefit to criminal justice (such as increased deterrence). Congress has not shown enormous wisdom in this area, and if any institution is going to act responsibly it must be the judiciary.

A SEQUEL TO *MARSHALL/CHAPMAN*

Problem 5-6. A New LSD Issue. In 1993, the Sentencing Commission revised the method for calculating the weight of LSD for Sentencing Guideline purposes. Abandoning its former approach of weighing the entire blotter paper containing LSD, the amended Guideline told courts to give each dose of LSD on a carrier medium a presumed weight of

---

[48]   Richard Posner, *The Problems of Jurisprudence* (1990); *Overcoming Law* (1995); and *How Judges Think* (2008).

0.4 mg. U.S. Sentencing Comm'n, U.S. Sentencing Guidelines Manual § 2D1.1(c), n. (H). The new method was retroactive. Meirl Neal was sentenced to 192 months in prison for selling 11,456 doses of LSD on blotter paper. He moved to have his sentence reduced to between 70 and 87 months, the Guideline period for sale of 4.58 grams of LSD (11,456 times 0.4 mg). The Government argued that Neal should serve at least 120 months, because of the mandatory minimum sentence required by 21 U.S.C. § 841(b)(1)(A)(v), as interpreted in *Marshall/Chapman*. Neal argued that the blotter paper should now not be counted for purposes of the mandatory minimum, just as it is now not counted for purposes of setting the ordinary sentence. Should the courts have accepted Neal's argument and reduced his sentence? See *Neal v. United States*, 516 U.S. 284 (1996).

2. Advancing Public-Regarding Goals and Minimizing Rent-Seeking

Public choice theory is the application of economic principles to actions by the state. One conclusion reached by some public choice theorists, developed in Chapter 1, § 2, is that an interest-group-driven legislative process produces too few public-regarding statutes (i.e., those broadly distributing benefits as well as costs) and too many rent-seeking statutes (i.e., those distributing benefits to a small group, at the expense of the general public, and without an efficiency justification).

Echoing a similar approach as that advanced by Chancellor Kent (Section 1), Frank Easterbrook, *The Supreme Court, 1983 Term—Foreword: The Court and the Economic System*, 98 Harv. L. Rev. 4, 14–15 (1984), suggests a general interpretive strategy for the judiciary to respond to this asymmetry:

> * * * There are two basic styles of statutory construction. In one the judge starts with the statute, attributes to it certain purposes (evils to be redressed), and then brings within the statute the class of activities that produce the same or similar objectionable results. The statute's reach goes on expanding so long as there are unredressed objectionable results. The judge interprets omissions and vague terms in the statute as evidence of want of time or foresight and fills in these gaps with more in the same vein. The maxim "Remedial statutes are to be liberally construed" sums up this approach.
>
> In the other approach the judge treats the statute as a contract. He first identifies the contracting parties and then seeks to discover what they resolved and what they left unresolved. * * * A judge then implements the bargain as a faithful agent but without enthusiasm; asked to extend the scope of a back-room deal, he refuses unless the proof of the deal's scope is compelling. Omissions are evidence that no bargain was struck: some issues were left for the future, or perhaps one party was unwilling to pay the price of a resolution in its favor. * * * What the parties did not resolve, the court should not resolve either. The maxim "Statutes in derogation of the common law are to be strictly construed" sums up this approach.
>
> * * * The appropriate treatment of statutes depends on how they come to be and what they are for. * * * If statutes generally are designed to overcome "failures" in markets and to replace the calamities produced by unguided private conduct with the ordered rationality of the public sector,

then it makes sense to use the remedial approach to the construction of statutes—or at least most of them. If, on the other hand, statutes often are designed to replace the outcomes of private transactions with monopolistic ones, to transfer the profits ("rents") of productive activity to a privileged few, then judges should take the beady-eyed contractual approach. The warehouseman does not deliver the grain without seeing the receipt, and so too with goodies dispensed by judges.

Table 5-1 below suggests risks entailed in various kinds of statutes, together with counter-strategies courts could follow in applying those statutes. How would Table 5-1 resolve the LSD Case?

Table 5-1.
Interpretive Strategies for Different Kinds of Laws

[1] Distributed Benefit/ Distributed Cost Laws (General Interest)	**[2] Distributed Benefit/ Concentrated Cost Laws**
Danger: The legislature will often fail to update these public interest statutes.	*Danger*: Regulated groups evade statutory regulation and capture the agency created to administer the law.
Response: Courts can expand the law to new situations in common law fashion, subject to the limits imposed by the statutory text.	*Response*: Courts can press the agency to be faithful to the stated public-regarding goal of the law.
[3] Concentrated Benefit/ Distributed Cost Laws (Rent-Seeking)	**[4] Concentrated Benefit/ Concentrated Cost Laws**
Danger: Rent-seeking by special interest groups at the expense of the general public.	*Danger*: The statutory deal may grow unexpectedly lopsided over time.
Response: Courts ought to construe the law narrowly. Hold the statute to its public-regarding justifications.	*Response*: Enforce statutory compromises, as written, but signal updating needs to legislators.

Source: William Eskridge Jr., *Politics Without Romance: Implications of Public Choice Theory for Statutory Interpretation*, 74 Va. L. Rev. 275, 325 (1988).

3. Institutional Cost-Benefit Analysis

Neil Komesar, *Imperfect Alternatives: Choosing Institutions in Law, Economics, and Public Policy* (1994), argues that allocation of public law decisionmaking duties should be the result of an institutional cost-benefit analysis, much like the Kaldor-Hicks concept of efficiency. (Under Kaldor-Hicks, a move is efficient if the overall benefits to society of such a move outweigh the overall costs.) Thus, he urges courts to reconsider their constitutional activism, in some areas at least, because it is not clear that the system-wide benefits of judge-made rules outweigh their costs. The benefits of judicial activism are limited by the structure of adjudication and the constrained resources of the court system. Costs of judicial activism include third-party expenses incurred in following new judicial rules, as well as the effects of judicial activism on other institutions, such as the legislature. Komesar does not apply his institutional cost-benefit analysis to issues of statutory interpretation, but other scholars have done so.

A Komesarian skepticism about the institutional limits of the judiciary has driven most statutory scholars to endorse the notion that it is agencies, rather than courts, that should do most of the work updating statutes to reflect new circumstances.[49] Professional administrators have the expertise and at least some resources to follow changes in society and to adapt statutory policy so that new developments do not undermine the statutory goals. They are in a position to think about the statutory scheme holistically and to balance competing considerations in the context of the big regulatory picture. Agencies will tend to be much more responsive to current presidential and legislative policy preferences than to those of enacting Congresses. Indeed, agencies will interpret statutes even more dynamically than courts will, and that agency dynamism fuels ever more judicial dynamism in statutory interpretation.

Evaluate the following case, where a closely divided (5–4) Supreme Court was decidedly not deferential to a well-respected agency. Consider the following questions:

(1) The Supreme Court's comparative competence is analysis of legal texts and precedents, the cornerstone of the rule of law. Does the rule of law require the Court's result?

(2) Why does the majority rely so heavily on legislative history? Does the Court reveal surprising competence in analyzing the legislative materials? And why did Justices Scalia and Thomas join every word of that discussion?

(3) Would Easterbrook and Macey consider the FDCA a public-regarding statute? If so, would they apply it liberally here, and vote with the dissenters? If not, why would either vote with the majority?

(4) Tell a descriptive public choice (i.e., interest group) story of the FDA Tobacco Case. Is this an example of the Supreme Court's being "captured" by a special interest, namely, the tobacco lobby, strongly allied with Presidents Reagan and Bush, who appointed all the majority justices?

(5) Tell a strategic story of the case. What features of politics in 2000 gave the Supreme Court leeway to rebuke the agency? Was the majority sending

---

[49] E.g., William Eskridge Jr., *Expanding* Chevron's *Domain: A Comparative Institutional Analysis of the Relative Competence of Courts and Agencies to Interpret Statutes,* 2013 Wis. L. Rev. 411; Edward Rubin, *Dynamic Statutory Interpretation in the Administrative State,* Issues in Legal Scholarship: Dynamic Statutory Interpretation (2002): Article 2, http://www.bepress.com/ils/iss3/art2; Kevin Stack, *Interpreting Regulations,* 111 Mich. L. Rev. 355 (2012) (urging that agency regulations be interpreted purposively, given this characteristic form of agency reasoning). Cf. Adrian Vermeule, *Judging Under Uncertainty: An Institutional Theory of Legal Interpretation* (2006) (maintaining that courts are incompetent to do anything but apply statutory plain meanings—and ought to defer to agencies in statutory interpretation unless the specific statutory language is clearly contrary to the agency's rule of law).

a signal to Congress about its institutional responsibilities? If so, what signal was the Court sending to the executive branch?

(6) Would some of the Justices have expected a congressional override of the Court's interpretation? What would an override accomplish that the Court could not do on its own?

How would you decide this case?

STATUTORY PREFACE TO THE *FDA TOBACCO* CASE

Food, Drug & Cosmetics Act of 1938, P.L. 75–717, codified at various points in 21 U.S.C.

Section 321(g)(1): The term "drug" means (A) articles recognized in the official United States Pharmacopeia, official Homeopathic Pharmacopeia of the United States, or official National Formulary, or any supplement to any of them; and (B) articles intended for use in the diagnosis, cure, mitigation, treatment, or prevention of disease in man or other animals; and (C) articles (other than food) intended to affect the structure or any function of the body of man or other animals; and (D) articles intended for use as a component of any article specified in clause (A), (B), or (C). * * *

Section 321(h): The term "device" * * * means an instrument, apparatus, implement, machine, contrivance, implant, in vitro reagent, or other similar or related article, including any component, part, or accessory, which is—

> **(3)** intended to affect the structure or any function of the body of man or other animals, and which does not achieve its primary intended purposes through chemical action within or on the body of man or other animals and which is not dependent upon being metabolized for the achievement of its primary intended purposes.

Section 321(n): If an article is alleged to be misbranded because the labeling or advertising is misleading, then in determining whether the labeling or advertising is misleading there shall be taken into account (among other things) not only representations made or suggested by statement, word, design, device, or any combination thereof, but also the extent to which the labeling or advertising fails to reveal facts material in the light of such representations or material with respect to consequences which may result from the use of the article to which the labeling or advertising relates under the conditions of use prescribed in the labeling or advertising thereof or under such conditions of use as are customary or usual.

Section 352(f), (j): A drug or device shall be deemed to be misbranded—

> **(f)** Unless its labeling bears (1) adequate directions for use; and (2) such adequate warnings against use in those pathological conditions or by children where its use may be dangerous to health, or against unsafe dosage or methods or duration of administration or application, in such manner and form, as are necessary for the protection of users, * * * [or]

(j) If it is dangerous to health when used in the dosage or manner, or with the frequency or duration prescribed, recommended, or suggested in the labeling thereof.

Section 355(e)(1): The Secretary shall, after due notice and opportunity for hearing to the applicant, withdraw approval of an application with respect to any drug under this section if the Secretary finds (1) that clinical or other experience, tests, or other scientific data show that such drug is unsafe for use under the conditions of use upon the basis of which the application was approved; * * *

Federal Cigarette Labeling and Advertising Act, Pub. L. No. 89–92, 79 Stat. 282 (1965), codified at 15 U.S.C. § 1331 et seq.

Section 1331. It is the policy of the Congress, and the purpose of this chapter, to establish a comprehensive Federal program to deal with cigarette labeling and advertising with respect to any relationship between smoking and health, whereby—

(1) the public may be adequately informed about any adverse health effects of cigarette smoking by inclusion of warning notices on each package of cigarettes and in each advertisement of cigarettes; and

(2) commerce and the national economy may be (A) protected to the maximum extent consistent with this declared policy and (B) not impeded by diverse, nonuniform, and confusing cigarette labeling and advertising regulations with respect to any relationship between smoking and health.

Section 1333: It shall be unlawful for any person to manufacture, import, or package for sale or distribution within the United States any cigarettes the package for which fails to bear the following statement: "Caution: Cigarette Smoking May Be Hazardous to Your Health." Such statement shall be located in a conspicuous place on every cigarette package and shall appear in conspicuous and legible type in contrast by typography, layout, or color with other printed matter on the package.

Comprehensive Smoking Education Act of 1984, P.L. 98–474 (1984), amending 15 U.S.C. § 1331.

Section 1331(a)(1). [Congress revised § 1331 and added new warnings to cigarette packages and, in other revisions to § 1331, advertisements:]

SURGEON GENERAL'S WARNING: Smoking Causes Lung Cancer, Heart Disease, Emphysema, And May Complicate Pregnancy.

SURGEON GENERAL'S WARNING: Quitting Smoking Now Greatly Reduces Serious Risks to Your Health.

SURGEON GENERAL'S WARNING: Smoking By Pregnant Women May Result in Fetal Injury, Premature Birth, And Low Birth Weight.

SURGEON GENERAL'S WARNING: Cigarette Smoke Contains Carbon Monoxide.

FDA v. BROWN & WILLIAMSON TOBACCO CORP.

Supreme Court of the United States, 2000.
529 U.S. 120, 120 S.Ct. 1291, 146 L.Ed.2d 121.

JUSTICE O'CONNOR delivered the opinion of the Court.

[The Food, Drug, and Cosmetic Act (FDCA), 21 U.S.C. § 301 et seq., grants the Food and Drug Administration (FDA) the authority to regulate, among other items, "drugs" and "devices," §§ 321(g)–(h), 393. In 1996, the FDA asserted jurisdiction to regulate tobacco products, concluding that, under the FDCA, nicotine is a "drug" and cigarettes and smokeless tobacco are "devices" that deliver nicotine to the body. Pursuant to this authority, the FDA promulgated regulations governing tobacco products' promotion, labeling, and accessibility to children and adolescents. The FDA found that tobacco use was the nation's leading cause of premature death, resulting in more than 400,000 deaths annually, and that most adult smokers began when they were minors. The regulations therefore aimed to reduce tobacco use by minors so as to substantially reduce the prevalence of addiction in future generations, and thus the incidence of tobacco-related death and disease. Respondents, a group of tobacco manufacturers, retailers, and advertisers, filed this suit challenging the FDA's regulations. The Supreme Court held that Congress had not granted the FDA jurisdiction to regulate tobacco products.]

[II] In determining whether Congress has specifically addressed the question at issue, a reviewing court should not confine itself to examining a particular statutory provision in isolation. The meaning—or ambiguity—of certain words or phrases may only become evident when placed in context. It is a "fundamental canon of statutory construction that the words of a statute must be read in their context and with a view to their place in the overall statutory scheme." *Davis v. Michigan Dept. of Treasury*, 489 U.S. 803, 809 (1989). A court must therefore interpret the statute "as a symmetrical and coherent regulatory scheme," *Gustafson v. Alloyd Co.*, 513 U.S. 561, 569 (1995), and "fit, if possible, all parts into an harmonious whole," *FTC v. Mandel Brothers, Inc.*, 359 U.S. 385, 389 (1959). Similarly, the meaning of one statute may be affected by other Acts, particularly where Congress has spoken subsequently and more specifically to the topic at hand. See *United States v. Estate of Romani*, 523 U.S. 517, 530–31 (1998); *United States v. Fausto*, 484 U.S. 439, 453 (1988). In addition, we must be guided to a degree by common sense as to the manner in which Congress is likely to delegate a policy decision of such economic and political magnitude to an administrative agency. * * *

[In Part II.A, Justice O'Connor concluded that the FDCA rested on the assumption that the FDA would not approve unsafe drugs or devices and would remove them from the market as soon as it determined they were unsafe. E.g., 21 U.S.C. § 355(e)(1)–(3). Congress has enacted six statutes that require disclosure of information regarding tobacco products but do not ban their sale. E.g., 15 U.S.C. § 1331. Given the assumption of the FDCA, these statutes disallowed the agency from finding that tobacco products fell within its health and safety regime. "A fundamental precept of the FDCA is that any product regulated by the FDA—but not banned—must be safe for its intended use. * * * Consequently, if tobacco products were within the FDA's jurisdiction, the Act would require the FDA to remove them from the market entirely. But a ban would contradict Congress' clear intent as expressed in its more recent, tobacco-specific legislation. The inescapable conclusion is that there is no room for tobacco products within the FDCA's regulatory scheme."]

[II.B] In determining whether Congress has spoken directly to the FDA's authority to regulate tobacco, we must also consider in greater detail the tobacco-specific legislation that Congress has enacted over the past 35 years. At the time a statute is enacted, it may have a range of plausible meanings. Over time, however, subsequent acts can shape or focus those meanings. The "classic judicial task of reconciling many laws enacted over time, and getting them to 'make sense' in combination, necessarily assumes that the implications of a statute may be altered by the implications of a later statute." *Fausto.* This is particularly so where the scope of the earlier statute is broad but the subsequent statutes more specifically address the topic at hand. As we recognized recently in *United States v. Estate of Romani*, "a specific policy embodied in a later federal statute should control our construction of the earlier statute, even though it has not been expressly amended."

Congress has enacted six separate pieces of legislation since 1965 addressing the problem of tobacco use and human health. Those statutes, among other things, require that health warnings appear on all packaging and in all print and outdoor advertisements, see 15 U.S.C. §§ 1331, 1333, 4402; prohibit the advertisement of tobacco products through "any medium of electronic communication" subject to regulation by the Federal Communications Commission (FCC), see §§ 1335, 4402(f); require the Secretary of Health and Human Services (HHS) to report every three years to Congress on research findings concerning "the addictive property of tobacco," 42 U.S.C. § 290aa–2(b)(2); and make States' receipt of certain federal block grants contingent on their making it unlawful "for any manufacturer, retailer, or distributor of tobacco products to sell or distribute any such product to any individual under the age of 18," § 300x–26(a)(1).

In adopting each statute, Congress has acted against the backdrop of the FDA's consistent and repeated statements that it lacked authority under the FDCA to regulate tobacco absent claims of therapeutic benefit by the manufacturer. In fact, on several occasions over this period, and after the health consequences of tobacco use and nicotine's pharmacological effects had become well known, Congress considered and rejected bills that would have granted the FDA such jurisdiction. Under these circumstances, it is evident that Congress' tobacco-specific statutes have effectively ratified the FDA's long-held position that it lacks jurisdiction under the FDCA to regulate tobacco products. Congress has created a distinct regulatory scheme to address the problem of tobacco and health, and that scheme, as presently constructed, precludes any role for the FDA.

[In 1964 congressional hearings responding to the Surgeon General's opinion that cigarette smoking is hazardous to one's health, FDA representatives testified that the agency did not have authority to regulate cigarettes or smoking under the FDCA. This was consistent with the position taken by the FDA's predecessor agency, the Bureau of Chemistry under the Pure Food & Drug Act of 1906.] And, as the FDA admits, there is no evidence in the text of the FDCA or its legislative history that Congress in 1938 even considered the applicability of the Act to tobacco products.

Given the economic and political significance of the tobacco industry at the time, it is extremely unlikely that Congress could have intended to place tobacco within the ambit of the FDCA absent any discussion of the matter. * * *

Moreover, before enacting the FCLAA [Federal Cigarette Labeling and Advertising Act] in 1965, Congress considered and rejected several proposals to give the FDA the authority to regulate tobacco. In April 1963, Representative Udall introduced a bill "to amend the Federal Food, Drug, and Cosmetic Act so as to make that Act applicable to smoking products." H. R. 5973, 88th Cong., 1st Sess., 1. Two months later, Senator Moss introduced an identical bill in the Senate. S. 1682, 88th Cong., 1st Sess. (1963). In discussing his proposal on the Senate floor, Senator Moss explained that "this amendment simply places smoking products under FDA jurisdiction, along with foods, drugs, and cosmetics." 109 Cong. Rec. 10322 (1963). In December 1963, Representative Rhodes introduced another bill that would have amended the FDCA "by striking out 'food, drug, device, or cosmetic,' each place where it appears therein and inserting in lieu thereof 'food, drug, device, cosmetic, or smoking product.'" H. R. 9512, 88th Cong., 1st Sess., § 3 (1963). And in January 1965, five months before passage of the FCLAA, Representative Udall again introduced a bill to amend the FDCA "to make that Act applicable to smoking products." H. R. 2248, 89th Cong., 1st Sess., 1. None of these proposals became law.

Congress ultimately decided in 1965 to subject tobacco products to the less extensive regulatory scheme of the FCLAA, which created a "comprehensive Federal program to deal with cigarette labeling and advertising with respect to any relationship between smoking and health." Pub. L. 89–92, § 2, 79 Stat. 282. The FCLAA rejected any regulation of advertising, but it required the warning, "Caution: Cigarette Smoking May Be Hazardous to Your Health," to appear on all cigarette packages. *Id.*, § 4, 79 Stat. 283. In the Act's "Declaration of Policy," Congress stated that its objective was to balance the goals of ensuring that "the public may be adequately informed that cigarette smoking may be hazardous to health" and protecting "commerce and the national economy . . . to the maximum extent." *Id.*, § 2, 79 Stat. 282 (codified at 15 U.S.C. § 1331). * * *

[Justice O'Connor examined in detail each of the six subsequent tobacco-regulating statutes, as well as extensive legislative history supporting those changes and rejecting other legislative proposals: In each instance, the FDA disclaimed jurisdiction over cigarettes and other tobacco products, and Congress expanded upon the disclosure regime that it had adopted in 1965.]

Taken together, these actions by Congress over the past 35 years preclude an interpretation of the FDCA that grants the FDA jurisdiction to regulate tobacco products. We do not rely on Congress' failure to act—its consideration and rejection of bills that would have given the FDA this authority—in reaching this conclusion. Indeed, this is not a case of simple inaction by Congress that purportedly represents its acquiescence in an agency's position. To the contrary, Congress has enacted several statutes addressing the particular subject of tobacco and health, creating a distinct regulatory scheme for cigarettes and smokeless tobacco. In doing so, Congress has been aware of tobacco's health hazards and its pharmacological effects. It has also enacted this legislation against the background of the FDA repeatedly and consistently asserting that it lacks jurisdiction under the FDCA to regulate tobacco products as customarily marketed. Further, Congress has persistently acted to preclude a meaningful role for *any* administrative agency in making policy on the subject of tobacco and health. Moreover, the substance of Congress' regulatory scheme is, in an important respect, incompatible with FDA jurisdiction. Although the supervision of product labeling to protect consumer health is a substantial component of the FDA's regulation of drugs and devices, see 21 U.S.C. § 352 (1994 ed. and Supp. III), the FCLAA and the CSTHEA [Comprehensive Smokeless Tobacco Health Education Act] explicitly prohibit any federal agency from imposing any health-related labeling requirements on cigarettes or smokeless tobacco products, see. 15 U. S C. §§ 1334(a), 4406(a). * * *

[II.C] [W]e are confident that Congress could not have intended to delegate a decision of such economic and political significance to an agency in so cryptic a fashion. To find that the FDA has the authority to regulate tobacco products, one must not only adopt an extremely strained understanding of "safety" as it is used throughout the Act—a concept central to the FDCA's regulatory scheme—but also ignore the plain implication of Congress' subsequent tobacco-specific legislation. It is therefore clear, based on the FDCA's overall regulatory scheme and the subsequent tobacco legislation, that Congress has directly spoken to the question at issue and precluded the FDA from regulating tobacco products. * * *

Justice Breyer, joined by Justice Stevens, Justice Souter, and Justice Ginsburg, dissenting.

The Food and Drug Administration (FDA) has the authority to regulate "articles (other than food) intended to affect the structure or any function of the body. . . ." Federal Food, Drug and Cosmetic Act (FDCA), 21 U.S.C. § 321(g)(1)(C). Unlike the majority, I believe that tobacco products fit within this statutory language.

In its own interpretation, the majority nowhere denies the following two salient points. First, tobacco products (including cigarettes) fall within the scope of this statutory definition, read literally. Cigarettes achieve their mood-stabilizing effects through the interaction of the chemical nicotine and the cells of the central nervous system. Both cigarette manufacturers and smokers alike know of, and desire, that chemically induced result. Hence, cigarettes are "intended to affect" the body's "structure" and "function," in the literal sense of these words.

Second, the statute's basic purpose—the protection of public health—supports the inclusion of cigarettes within its scope. See *United States v. Article of Drug . . . Bacto-Unidisk,* 394 U.S. 784, 798 (1969) (FDCA "is to be given *a liberal construction consistent with [its] overriding purpose to protect the public health*" (emphasis added)). Unregulated tobacco use causes "more than 400,000 people [to] die each year from tobacco-related illnesses, such as cancer, respiratory illnesses, and heart disease." 61 Fed. Reg. 44398 (1996). Indeed, tobacco products kill more people in this country every year "than . . . AIDS, car accidents, alcohol, homicides, illegal drugs, suicides, and fires, *combined.*" *Ibid.* (emphasis added).

Despite the FDCA's literal language and general purpose (both of which support the FDA's finding that cigarettes come within its statutory authority), the majority nonetheless reads the statute as *excluding* tobacco products for two basic reasons:

(1)   the FDCA does not "fit" the case of tobacco because the statute requires the FDA to prohibit dangerous drugs or devices (like cigarettes) outright, and the agency concedes that simply banning the sale of cigarettes is not a proper remedy; and

(2)   Congress has enacted other statutes, which, when viewed in light of the FDA's long history of denying tobacco-related jurisdiction and considered together with Congress' failure explicitly to grant the agency tobacco-specific authority, demonstrate that Congress did not intend for the FDA to exercise jurisdiction over tobacco.

In my view, neither of these propositions is valid. Rather, the FDCA does not significantly limit the FDA's remedial alternatives. And the later statutes do not tell the FDA it cannot exercise jurisdiction, but simply leave FDA jurisdictional law where Congress found it. [C]f. Food and Drug Administration Modernization Act of 1997, 111 Stat. 2380 (codified at note following 21 U.S.C. § 321 (1994 ed., Supp. III)) (statute "shall" *not* "be construed to affect the question of whether" the FDA "has any authority to regulate any tobacco product").

The bulk of the opinion that follows will explain the basis for these latter conclusions. In short, I believe that the most important indicia of statutory meaning—language and purpose—along with the FDCA's legislative history (described briefly in Part I) are sufficient to establish that the FDA has authority to regulate tobacco. The statute-specific arguments against jurisdiction that the tobacco companies and the majority rely upon (discussed in Part II) are based on erroneous assumptions and, thus, do not defeat the jurisdiction-supporting thrust of the FDCA's language and purpose. The inferences that the majority draws from later legislative history are not persuasive, since (as I point out in Part III) one can just as easily infer from the later laws that Congress did not intend to affect the FDA's tobacco-related authority at all. And the fact that the FDA changed its mind about the scope of its own jurisdiction is legally insignificant because (as Part IV establishes) the agency's reasons for changing course are fully justified. [The FDA's stated reasons for not regulating were that it did not have evidence that the cigarette manufacturers "intended" for their product to have a medical effect; by the 1990s, there was ample evidence of such intent.]

In the majority's view, laws enacted since 1965 require us to deny jurisdiction, whatever the FDCA might mean in their absence. But why? Do those laws contain language barring FDA jurisdiction? The majority must concede that they do not. Do they contain provisions that are inconsistent with the FDA's exercise of jurisdiction? With one exception, the majority points to no such provision. Do they somehow repeal the principles of law * * * that otherwise would lead to the conclusion that the FDA has jurisdiction in this area? The companies themselves deny making any such claim. See Tr. of Oral Arg. 27 (denying reliance on doctrine of "partial repeal"). Perhaps the later laws "shape" and "focus" what the 1938 Congress meant a generation earlier. But this Court has warned against using the views of a later Congress to construe a statute enacted many years before. See *Pension Benefit Guaranty Corporation v. LTV Corp.,* 496 U.S. 633, 650 (1990) (later history is " 'a hazardous basis for inferring the intent of an earlier' Congress" (quoting *United States v. Price,* 361 U.S. 304, 313 (1960)). * * * Regardless, the later statutes do not support the majority's conclusion.

That is because, whatever individual Members of Congress after 1964 may have assumed about the FDA's jurisdiction, the laws they enacted did not embody any such "no jurisdiction" assumption. And one cannot automatically *infer* an antijurisdiction intent, as the majority does, for the later statutes are both (and similarly) consistent with quite a different congressional desire, namely, the intent to proceed without interfering with whatever authority the FDA otherwise may have possessed. As I demonstrate below, the subsequent legislative history is critically ambivalent, for it can be read *either* as (a) "ratifying" a no-jurisdiction assumption, *or* as (b) leaving the jurisdictional question just where Congress found it. And the fact that both inferences are "equally tenable," *Pension Benefit Guaranty Corp.*, prevents the majority from drawing from the later statutes the firm, antijurisdiction implication that it needs.

Consider, for example, Congress' failure to provide the FDA with express authority to regulate tobacco—a circumstance that the majority finds significant. In fact, Congress *both* failed to grant express authority to the FDA when the FDA denied it had jurisdiction over tobacco *and* failed to take that authority expressly away when the agency later asserted jurisdiction. See, *e.g.*, S. 1262, 104th Cong., 1st Sess., § 906 (1995) (failed bill seeking to amend FDCA to say that "nothing in this Act or any other Act shall provide the [FDA] with any authority to regulate in any manner tobacco or tobacco products"); [other examples from the 104th Congress, 1995–96]. Consequently, the defeat of various different proposed jurisdictional changes proves nothing. This history shows only that Congress could not muster the votes necessary either to grant or to deny the FDA the relevant authority. It neither favors nor disfavors the majority's position.

[We omit the remainder of Justice Breyer's lengthy opinion, but like Justice O'Connor's opinion it is worth reading in its entirety.]

NOTE ON THE FDA TOBACCO CASE AND THE SUPREME COURT AS A STRATEGIC ACTOR IN OUR POLITY

1.   *Lawmaking as a Sequential Game.* This case might be an example of strategic behavior among legal institutions.[50] For years, the FDA had known that tobacco was a deadly drug; one reason it did not seek to regulate tobacco earlier was that it knew that any regulation would be overridden by Congress, where the tobacco companies were powerfully represented. President Clinton was a relatively anti-tobacco chief executive, who supported the regulatory moves of Dr. David Kessler, the FDA Administrator, to bring tobacco within the agency's health-protective regime. Unlike Presidents Bush and Reagan, Clinton would probably have vetoed a congressional effort to override the agency. Armed with that political knowledge—as well as the medical and "intent" knowledge emphasized in Justice Breyer's dissent—the agency moved to regulate.

The FDA's problem was that the tobacco industry might be able to mobilize the judiciary to override the agency even if Congress-with-the-President would not. Affirming the Fourth Circuit (filled with North Carolina and Virginia tobacco farms as well as GOP judges appointed in the 1980s), the Supreme Court trumped the agency's initiative.

---

[50]   The rich history is recounted and analyzed in Theodore Ruger, *The Story of* FDA v. Brown & Williamson *(2000): The Norm of Agency Continuity*, in *Statutory Interpretation Stories* 334–65 (Eskridge, Frickey & Garrett eds. 2010).

Under the assumptions of rational choice theory, the Court might have been reluctant to act if it were likely to be overridden by Congress—but the Justices knew that would not happen, because relatively pro-tobacco Republicans controlled both houses of Congress in 2000. By reversing the default rule—from the FDA's regulation to the industry's nonregulation—the Court reversed the political outcome, and its resolution stuck until the Democrats secured control of both the Presidency and Congress in 2009.

2.   *The Judiciary as a Part of the Rent-Seeking Process?* The FDA Tobacco Case can be viewed as one kind of caution about economic theories of statutory interpretation, namely, those seeing courts as a remedy for legislative rent-seeking. The courts might be part of the interest-group process. Groups press for the appointment of friendly lawyers or ideologically compatible law professors as judges and then use the judiciary to overturn at least some of their defeats in the political process. This is easier to accomplish by "have" groups, because judges tend to be libertarian, either as a matter of philosophy or practicality (it is much easier for the courts to slow things down than to require the state to act), and "have" groups are usually trying to protect their freedom of action against government regulation.[51] So the FDA Tobacco Case can be viewed, in part, as an expression of the majority Justices' personal aversion to aggressive state regulation of private industry. The five Justices in the majority were the most conservative Republican Justices, the same jurists who formed the majority several months later in *Bush v. Gore,* 531 U.S. 98 (2000), an intervention into the 2000 election that assured the election of the GOP's candidate, Governor George W. Bush; the four dissenters in the FDA Tobacco Case were the four dissenters in *Bush v. Gore.*

3.   *The Rule of Law as a Judicial Preference.* There is another way of looking at the FDA Tobacco Case. Most judges carry or develop strong preferences for rule-of-law values, including predictability in the law, following orderly procedures, and acting within jurisdictional boundaries. The FDA Tobacco Case might be an example of the power of the rule of law: these companies may be morally squalid, but regulation of moral squalor must still follow the proper procedures under the appropriate congressional authorization. As one scholar puts it, the 1965 statute confirmed a longstanding political *deal,* that the FDCA did not regulate tobacco products, which would be subject to warning and disclosure regimes instead (the FCLAA and subsequent laws). Everything Congress did after 1965 reflected and reaffirmed that deal—until the FDA unilaterally abrogated it in 1996. Richard Merrill, *The FDA May Not Regulate Tobacco Products as "Drugs" or "Medical Devices,"* 47 Duke L.J. 1071, 1074–81 (1998).

Consistent with Merrill's argument, Justice O'Connor rested her opinion upon an equilibrium-based idea: the longstanding agreement that the FDA could not regulate smoking without fresh congressional authorization, and the reliance interests it generated, have created a stable "rule of law" not perfectly reflected in the statutory text. This kind of response (supported by lots of legislative history) is inconsistent with Justice Scalia's philosophy—but he swallowed, without a textualist whimper, Justice O'Connor's lengthy recitation of evidence from legislative hearings, reports, and debates. Why would he join that part of the opinion? A further irony: Justice O'Connor (with Justices Scalia and Thomas going along) deploys the kind of "institutional legislative history" that

---

[51]   See also Mark Galanter, *Why the "Haves" Come Out Ahead: Speculations on the Limits of Legal Change,* 9 L. & Soc'y Rev. 95 (1974), which shows how Repeat-Player "Have" groups can deploy the litigation process to advance their goals even if judges are neutral or even hostile.

Justices Breyer and Stevens have championed—with Breyer and Stevens themselves in dissent based in part on the plain meaning rule.

NOTE ON THE 2009 CONGRESSIONAL OVERRIDE OF THE FDA TOBACCO DECISION

Congress ultimately responded to *Brown & Williamson* (the FDA Tobacco Case) with the Family Smoking Prevention & Tobacco Control Act of 2009, Pub. L. No. 111–31, 123 Stat. 1776 (2009). To discourage tobacco use among younger persons, Title I of the Act banned sales of tobacco products to persons under the age of 18 and authorized the FDA to develop an enforcement scheme. Title I also required the FDA to reissue the rules that had been invalidated in *Brown & Williamson*. Other provisions of the 2009 Act gave the FDA authority to set standards for the content of tobacco products (including tar and nicotine levels), to register tobacco companies, and to inspect such companies for compliance with the law. Before tobacco companies can introduce new products, they must secure FDA approval (the FDA has traditionally exercised its approval power aggressively to force changes in products and their marketing). The Act also imposed limitations on the FDA's regulatory authority. Sections 906–907 bar the FDA from banning face-to-face retail sales of tobacco products entirely or from requiring a doctor's prescription to purchase these items.

Title II of the 2009 Act imposed nine new warnings for tobacco products, 15 U.S.C. § 1333, and authorized the FDA to develop the details of these warnings. After notice and comment, the FDA in 2011 announced final rules, with detailed requirements for advertisements of tobacco products. 76 Fed. Reg. 36,628 (June 22, 2011) (final rule, codified in 21 C.F.R. Part 1141, with responses to comments). Among the most controversial were new FDA requirements that packages include not only verbal warnings but also "graphic images" of smokers ravaged by lung cancer and other smoking-related illnesses. Tobacco companies successfully challenged these rules because they forced the companies to spout the government's "ideological" message, contrary to the First Amendment. *R.J. Reynolds Tobacco Co. v. Food & Drug Administration*, 696 F.3d 1205, 1216–17 (D.C. Cir. 2012) (characterizing the FDA-required advertisements as "inflammatory" rather than purely factual disclosures).

Does the congressional override mean that *Brown & Williamson* was wrongly decided? On the one hand, the override vindicates the FDA's original rulemaking. Also relevant is the FDA's finding that the limitations and warnings imposed by its original rules would have saved thousands of lives between 1996 and 2010. On the other hand, the 2009 override statute was not only a more legitimate form of regulation (accomplished after achieving the political consensus required by the vetogate-ridden structure of Congress and bringing the tobacco industry to the table), but also went much further than the FDA had dared go in the 1990s. Congress was able to reconcile the various disclosure statutes with the drug-regulatory statute—and the 2009 override was an occasion for Congress to strengthen required disclosures and to authorize the FDA to create more effective disclosures than the abstract ones Congress had been imposing (with disappointing effects) since 1965. On the legitimating and policy-updating advantages of congressional overrides, see Matthew Christiansen & William Eskridge Jr., *Congressional Overrides of Supreme Court Statutory Interpretation Decisions, 1967–2011*, 92 Tex. L. Rev. 1317 (2014).

C. PRAGMATIC THEORIES OF STATUTORY INTERPRETATION

In *How Judges Think* (2008), Judge Richard Posner distinguishes between "legalistic" and "pragmatic" theories of statutory interpretation. Legalistic theories claim that law is an autonomous discipline that can reach neutral interpretations through application of plain meanings (assisted perhaps with dictionaries and linguists), following precedent, reasoning by analogy, and the like. Pragmatic theories, in contrast, openly admit that law is not (entirely) separate from politics and that interpretation carries with it discretion and policy choice. Hart and Sacks' purpose-based interpretation is, by this reading, pragmatic, and Posner's current approach, well-illustrated in the LSD Case above, is an updated or more sophisticated version of legal process theory. Similarly pragmatic is Justice Stephen Breyer, as illustrated in his dissenting opinion in the FDA Tobacco Case and in his books, *Active Liberty: Interpreting Our Democratic Constitution* (2005), and *Making Our Democracy Work: A Judge's View* (2010).

Another kind of *pragmatic* thinking is philosophical. Inspired by American pragmatic philosophers who rejected "foundationalist" thinking and urged multi-focal theorizing, the following article reflects a practical approach to statutory interpretation that the authors believe best reflects what the Supreme Court (and most state courts) are actually doing in statutory cases.

WILLIAM ESKRIDGE JR. AND PHILIP FRICKEY, STATUTORY INTERPRETATION AS PRACTICAL REASONING
42 Stan. L. Rev. 321, 345–53 (1990).

[Eskridge and Frickey criticize each of the leading "foundationalist" theories of interpretation—textualism, original intent, purpose—and find each wanting in the same ways.] [T]he leading foundationalist theories cannot redeem their claim to follow from the very nature of majoritarian democracy, do not yield objective and determinate answers, and cannot convincingly exclude other values, including current values. *Weber* [Chapter 1, § 2] and *Griffin* illustrate our theoretical critique and suggest that the Supreme Court does not follow any one of the foundationalist theories. We now suggest that these observations form the basis for a positive theory which refuses to privilege intention, purpose, or text as the sole touchstone of interpretation, but which both explains the Supreme Court's practice in statutory interpretation and, at the same time, reflects the insights of modern theories of interpretation.

First, statutory interpretation involves creative policymaking by judges and is not just the Court's figuring out the answer that was put 'in' the statute by the enacting legislature. An essential insight of hermeneutics [the philosophy of interpretation] is that interpretation is a dynamic process, and that the interpreter is inescapably situated historically. 'Every age has to understand a transmitted text in its own way,' says Gadamer [in *Truth and Method* 263 (1965)]. * * *

Hermeneutics suggests that the text lacks meaning *until* it is interpreted. * * * [O]ne does not 'understand' a text in the abstract, without an 'application' of the text to a specific problem. American pragmatism, also influenced by Aristotle, complements this hermeneutic insight. Reasoning in human affairs does not seek abstract answers, but concretely useful results. Theories of reasoning, for [William James, in *Pragmatism* (1907)] are simply "mental modes of *adaptation* to reality, rather than revelations or gnostic answers."

Consider *Weber* in this light. The interpretive process is creative, not mechanical. Viewed in the context of the complex goals of the Civil Rights Act and subsequent difficulties in implementation, making sense of the statute's command not to "discriminate" requires much more than finding a meaning for the term. Even if the interpretive process were viewed as retrieving the answer Congress would have reached in 1964 (had it deliberated on the issue), the inquiry involves "imaginative" work by the judge. These lessons of *Weber* are consistent with the insights of modern literary theory, historiography, and philosophy: There is no interpretation without an interpreter, and the interpreter will interact with the text or historical event. Just as the interpreter learns from the text and history, so too does she speak to it. What was decisive in *Weber,* surely to Justice Blackmun and probably to other Justices in the majority as well, was what the interpreters learned about the statute from considering the facts of the case: More than a decade after the statute was enacted there were only 2 percent blacks in the craft workforce, contrasted with 39 percent blacks in the overall workforce.

Second, because this creation of statutory meaning is not a mechanical operation, it often involves the interpreter's choice among several competing answers. Although the interpreter's range of choices is somewhat constrained by the text, the statute's history, and the circumstances of its application, the actual choice will not be 'objectively' determinable; interpretation will often depend upon political and other assumptions held by judges. Under Gadamer's [analysis], interpretation seeks 'to make the law concrete in each specific case,' and '[t]he creative supplementing of the law that is involved is a task that is reserved to the judge.' As a practical matter, how could it be otherwise? Many statutes leave key terms ambiguous, often intentionally, and thereby delegate rulemaking authority to courts or agencies. Over time, these ambiguities and unanswered questions multiply, as society changes and background legal assumptions change with it. Hermeneutics suggests that as the interpreter's own background context—her 'tradition'—changes, so too will her interpretive choices. * * *

Third, when statutory interpreters make these choices, they are normally not driven by any single value—adhering to majoritarian commands *or* encouraging private reliance on statutory texts *or* finding the best answer according to modern policy—but are instead driven by multiple values. Both hermeneutics and pragmatism emphasize the complex nature of human reasoning. When solving a problem, we tend to test different solutions, evaluating each against a range of values and beliefs we hold as important. The pragmatic idea that captures this concept is the 'web of beliefs' metaphor. We all accept a number of different values and propositions that, taken together, constitute a web of intertwined beliefs about, for example, the role of statutes in our public law. Each of us may accord different weight to the specific values, but almost no one excludes any of the important values altogether. Decisionmaking is, therefore, polycentric, and thus cannot be linear and purely deductive. Instead, it is spiral and inductive: We consider the consistency of the evidence for each value before reaching a final decision, and even then check our decision against the values we esteem the most. Given this web of beliefs and the spiral form of decisionmaking, an individual's reasoning will depend very much on the context of the case at hand, and specifically on the relative strength of each consideration.

Consider *Griffin* from the perspective of the web metaphor. A Justice who is a thoroughgoing textualist would surely agree with the *Griffin* result, given the relative clarity of the statutory language. But so could an intentionalist Justice: Although there is no smoking gun in the legislative history, the legislative context and the strong statutory language suggest that Congress would probably have favored substantial punitive sanctions had it addressed the issue. And so could a purposivist Justice, because surely one major purpose of the statute was to deter employer misconduct, which the $302,000 award in *Griffin* would seem to do. Even a Justice concerned only with fair results might applaud the *Griffin* result. In fact, seven Justices of differing jurisprudential stripes formed the majority in *Griffin,* and Justice Rehnquist's opinion justified the result by arguing from the relatively clear statutory language, the original legislative intent, the overall statutory purpose, and (to some extent) the reasonableness of the interpretation. Whether ultimately correct, the opinion in *Griffin,* by its strategy of cumulative assessment and weighing of factors potentially relevant to interpretation, seems more persuasive than would any foundationalist avenue to the same result. * * *

In addition to the web of beliefs idea, two other metaphors, one drawn from the pragmatist tradition and one drawn from the hermeneutical tradition, suggest more precisely how a practical reasoning approach would work. First, consider [pragmatist philosopher Charles] Peirce's contrast of the chain and the cable. A chain is no stronger than its weakest link, because if any of the singly connected links should break, so too will the chain. In contrast, a cable's strength relies not on that of individual threads, but upon their cumulative strength as they are woven together. Legal arguments are often constructed as chains, but they tend to be more successful when they are cable-like. The Court's opinion in *Griffin* draws its strength from this phenomenon: The text, one probable purpose, some legislative history, and current policy each lend some—even if not unequivocal—support to the result. Each thread standing alone is subject to quarrel and objection; woven together, the threads persuaded both Justice Rehnquist *and* Justice Brennan, a not unimpressive achievement.

In many cases of statutory interpretation, of course, the threads will not all run in the same direction. The cable metaphor suggests that in these cases the result will depend upon the strongest overall combination of threads. That, in turn, depends on which values the decisionmakers find most important, and on the strength of the arguments invoking each value. For most of the Supreme Court Justices, a persuasive textual argument is a stronger thread than an otherwise equally persuasive current policy or fairness argument, because of the reliance and legislative supremacy values implicated in following the clear statutory text. And a clear and convincing textual argument obviously counts more than one beclouded with doubts and ambiguities.

Our model of practical reasoning in statutory interpretation is still not complete, for it lacks a dynamic element that is intrinsic to human reasoning in general, and interpretation in particular. The various arguments (the threads of our cable) do not exist in isolation; they interact with one another. A final metaphor that captures this interaction is the "hermeneutical circle": A part can only be understood in the context of the whole, and the whole cannot be understood without analyzing its various parts. To interpret the statute in *Griffin,* for example, the interpreter will look at the text and the legislative history and the purpose and current values. But to evaluate the text, the interpreter will consider it in light of the whole enterprise, including the history, purpose, and current values. In other words, none of the interpretive threads can be viewed in isolation, and each will be evaluated in its relation to the other threads. * * *

The positive metaphors of our analysis—the web of beliefs idea, the cable-versus-chain contrast, and the hermeneutical circle—suggest the contours of a practical reasoning model of statutory interpretation that roughly captures the Court's practice. Our model holds that an interpreter will look at a broad range of evidence— text, historical evidence, and the text's evolution—and thus form a preliminary view of the statute. The interpreter then develops that preliminary view by testing various possible interpretations against the multiple criteria of fidelity to the text, historical accuracy, and conformity to contemporary circumstances and values. Each criterion is relevant, yet none necessarily trumps the others. Thus while an apparently clear text, for example, will create insuperable doubts for a contrary interpretation if the other evidence reinforces it *(Griffin),* an apparently clear text may yield if other considerations cut against it *(Weber).* As the interpreter comes to accept an interpretation (perhaps a confirmation of her preliminary view), she considers a congeries of supporting arguments, which may buttress her view much "like the legs of a chair and unlike the links of a chain."

[As tweaked by Eskridge in light of pedagogical feedback, the pragmatic method can be diagrammed along the following lines:]

A PRACTICAL REASONING MODEL OF STATUTORY INTERPRETATION

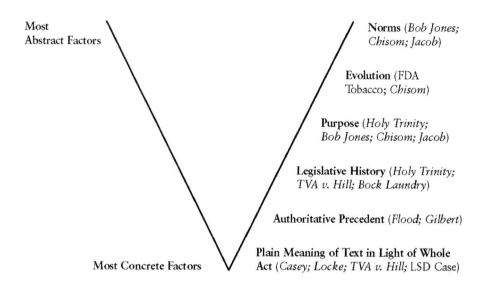

Most
Abstract Factors

Norms (*Bob Jones;*
Chisom; Jacob)

Evolution (FDA
Tobacco; *Chisom*)

Purpose (*Holy Trinity;*
Bob Jones; Chisom; Jacob)

Legislative History (*Holy Trinity;*
TVA v. Hill; Bock Laundry)

Authoritative Precedent (*Flood; Gilbert*)

Most Concrete Factors

Plain Meaning of Text in Light of Whole
Act (*Casey; Locke; TVA v. Hill;* LSD Case)

* * * [T]his model identifies the primary evidentiary inquiries in which the Court will engage. The model is, in crude imagery, a "funnel of abstraction." It is funnel-shaped for three reasons. First, the model suggests the hierarchy of sources that the Court has in fact assumed. For example, in formulating her pre-understanding of the statute *and* in testing it, the interpreter will value more highly a good argument based on the statutory text than a conflicting and equally strong argument based upon the statutory purpose. Second, the model suggests the degree of abstraction at each source. The sources at the bottom of the diagram involve more focused, concrete inquiries, typically with a more limited range of arguments. As the interpreter moves up the diagram, a broader range of arguments is available, partly because the inquiry is less concrete. Third, the model illustrates the pragmatistic and hermeneutical insights explained above: In formulating and testing her understanding of the statute, the interpreter will move up and down the diagram, evaluating and comparing the different considerations represented by each source of argumentation. * * *

NOTE ON THE FUNNEL OF ABSTRACTION

On the whole, the Funnel of Abstraction is a descriptive theory of statutory interpretation: this is how the judicial mind goes about deciding statutory cases, as a practical matter.[52] Its insights derive in large part from an application of American

---

[52]   For evidence suggesting that this diagram accurately displays the factors routinely taken into account in judicial opinions interpreting statutes, see Lawrence Solan, *The Language of Statutes: Laws and Their Interpretation* 50–159 (2010); Nancy Staudt et al., *Judging Statutes: Interpretive Regimes*, 38 Loy. L.A. L. Rev. 1909 (2005) (empirical analysis of tax decisions); Nicholas Zeppos, *The Use of Authority in Statutory Interpretation: An Empirical Analysis*, 70 Tex. L. Rev. 1073 (1992) (earlier and broader analysis of statutory interpretation decisions). See also Frank Cross, *The Theory and Practice of Statutory Interpretation* 24–133 (2009); Robert John Araujo, *Method in Interpretation: Practical Wisdom and the Search for Meaning in Public*

pragmatism to statutory interpretation. See Daniel Farber, *Practical Reason and the Scholarship of Philip P. Frickey,* 98 Calif. L. Rev. 1111 (2010); Francis Mootz III, *Ugly American Hermeneutics,* 10 Nev. L.J. 587 (2010) (fascinating account of the interplay of Americans' "ugly" understanding of hermeneutics, which is redeemed by their pragmatic application of statutes to concrete cases).

The features of the Funnel that are most important are these: **First**, judges will consider a variety of factors, including statutory text and structure, but also statutory purpose, legislative history, authoritative precedents, practical applications of the statute, and current norms. The Funnel theory is distinctive in the formal importance it attributes to *stare decisis* in statutory cases: Supreme Court precedents interpreting a particular statute, or words and phrases borrowed from other statutes (e.g., *Casey*), are always relevant and will be controlling if the statutory text is open-ended or vague. See Peter Tiersma, *The Textualization of Precedent,* 82 Notre Dame L. Rev. 1187 (2007), who describes a process where, over time, Supreme Court statutory precedents will often displace the statutory text as the most concrete authority, unless Congress frequently amends the statute and overrides and modifies those precedents.

Second, the factors have varying legal force. They are hierarchical: a good text-based argument will trump a good legislative history or purpose argument, as in *Casey*. (*Chisom* would be distinguishable on the ground that the statutory text was ambiguous and statutory structure supported the majority.) This feature, by the way, is normative as well as descriptive. The funnel authors are textualists, like Justice Rehnquist in *Griffin*, for they start with the text but do not stop with the text (as Justice Scalia would have done in *Griffin*). See also Lawrence Solan, *The Language of Statutes: Laws and Their Interpretation* (2010), a similarly pragmatic account by a text-loving scholar of linguistics as well as statutory interpretation.

Third, and most unlike more formalist theories, the Funnel of Abstraction posits that the various factors will *interact* with one another. Thus, a textual "plain meaning" will not become firm in the judicial mind until *after* the judge has considered all the evidence; the "authority" of a precedent will not be conclusive until the judge has thought about its consistency with statutory text and purpose; the good judge will not be firm about the relevance of "norms" until she has processed the weight of the textual and historical factors. And so forth.

Think about how the Funnel helps explain the decisions in this chapter, especially *Holy Trinity, Bock Laundry, Jacob,* and *Chisom,* which openly follow the method, but also cases that don't seem to follow the method, like *Casey* and *Marshall.* Although Judge Easterbrook is not a "Funnel judge," the judges who went along with his decision in *Marshall* might well have been—what might have been persuasive to them? Consider the debate among the Justices in *Brown & Williamson* as a debate about how to apply the Funnel. As you read the material that immediately follows, consider the cases from the Funnel perspective, but also rethink the Funnel from a normative perspective. What values should courts be pressing in statutory cases? The Funnel assumes that the rule of law values (text, original intent, precedent) are the weightiest and that process and substantive values are relevant but less weighty. Should the text be as privileged as we

Legal Texts, 68 Miss. L.J. 225 (1998); Morrell Mullins, *Tools Not Rules: The Heuristic Nature of Statutory Interpretation,* 30 J. Legis. 1 (2003). Cf. Miranda McGowan, *Do as I Do, Not as I Say: An Empirical Investigation of Justice Scalia's Ordinary Meaning Method of Statutory Interpretation,* 78 Miss. L.J. 129 (2008) (showing that even Justice Scalia ignores statutory text that he thinks delegates lawmaking authority to federal judges).

assume it to be? Should it be as flexible as hermeneutics suggests? And so on. See how your normative deliberation edits or changes the Funnel or your variation of it.

NOTES ON HOW INSTITUTIONAL ROLE AFFECTS STATUTORY INTERPRETATION

Yet another kind of "pragmatic" consideration in statutory interpretation is *institutional*. How does the operation of an institution affect its interpretation of statutes? This is the kind of inquiry Professors Hart and Sacks (and, before them, Justices Brandeis and Frankfurter) pioneered, and that Justice Breyer represents today. Consider just a few hypotheses that such institutional thinking might generate.

1. *Supreme Court of the United States.* The Supreme Court "administers" a pyramid of lower federal courts, state courts, agencies, and other governmental bodies. As a practical matter, the Court cannot operate as a court of correction, rebuking lower courts for incorrect decisions, and so the Court's approach to cases reflects its institutional incentive to "administer" the rule of law in this country. This institutional role offers a possible argument in favor of any theory that offers more predictability in statutory cases. Thus, if it were true that judges adhering closely to Justice Scalia's new textualism would produce more consistent results, that would be an excellent argument for all the Justices to adopt his approach *and* to impose it on lower courts as a matter of *stare decisis.* See Sydney Foster, *Should Courts Give* Stare Decisis *Effect to Statutory Interpretation Methodology?*, 96 Geo. L.J. 1863 (2008). Unfortunately, there is no evidence that the new textualism constrains interpreters in any manner. E.g., Frank Cross, *The Theory and Practice of Statutory Interpretation* 177–79 (2009); James Brudney & Corey Ditslear, *Canons of Construction and the Elusive Quest for Neutral Reasoning*, 58 Vand. L. Rev. 1, 57–60, 95–105 (2005).

A more modest doctrinal effect of the Court's institutional role is that the Court may follow an *anti-messiness principle.* Given the choice between a complicated multi-factor approach and a simpler bright line rule, the Court prefers the latter, because it is easier to administer. See Anita Krishnakumar, *The Anti-Messiness Principle in Statutory Interpretation*, 87 Notre Dame L. Rev. 1465 (2012). The Supreme Court's decision in *TVA v. Hill* is a classic example: the anti-messiness principle was one strong reason for the Court to *reject* the dissenters' approach, whereby expensive or almost-completed projects could be carried out notwithstanding their effects on endangered species. Likewise, the principle is consistent with the Court's decisions in *Casey, Chisom, Locke,* and *Chapman* (the LSD Case). On the other hand, the points of law emerging from *Holy Trinity* and the FDA Tobacco Case, for examples, are complicated, "messy" precepts, and the Court in each case rejected a simpler bright-line rule.

2. *Lower Federal Courts.* Traditionally, academics have assumed that lower federal courts should behave exactly like the Supreme Court. Surely, a lower federal court, like the Seventh Circuit in *Marshall*, needs to consider the Supreme Court's preferred methodology and its precedents. But there is ample room for divergence, and there is good reason to expect that lower court interpretive practice will differ from that followed by the Supreme Court. See Aaron-Andrew Bruhl, *Hierarchy and Heterogeneity: How to Read a Statute in a Lower Court,* 97 Cornell L. Rev. 433, 442–58 (2012). An obvious difference is that Congress regularly responds to and overrides Supreme Court statutory decisions, especially when the Justices invite overrides, but it rarely overrides lower court decisions, because they are less salient and perhaps less ripe for political

response. Hence, lower courts will be less attentive to institutional dialogue than the Supreme Court is, and they ought to assume that their interpretations will not provoke a political response. *Id.* at 460.

Professor Bruhl also suggests that Supreme Court review will often trigger the creation of new sources of interpretive guidance, especially in the form of *amicus* briefs. *Id.* at 464. The Solicitor General plays a major role in most Supreme Court statutory cases for this reason, and not so big a role among lower courts. Because the Solicitor General mediates, within the executive branch, purposive agency constructions, higher-level presidential policies (sometimes), and coherence and rule of law concerns, her or his advice to the Supreme Court is usually followed. But this deep and public engagement of the Solicitor General and agency inputs into statutory interpretation decisions usually does not occur in lower court cases.

Furthermore, given the resource constraints on lower federal courts (fewer staff, busy dockets, poor briefing, a dearth of helpful *amicus* briefs), Professor Bruhl both predicted and then documented (through a 2018 empirical study) that their constructions of federal statutes are simpler: the lower federal courts, especially the district courts, use fewer interpretive tools (text, precedent, a few canons) and deploy those tools with less methodological complexity, reflecting less capacity for research. Andrew-Aaron Bruhl, *Statutory Interpretation and the Rest of the Iceberg: Divergences Between the Lower Federal Courts and the Supreme Court,* 68 Duke L.J. 1 (2018).

Thus, Bruhl's empirical analysis demonstrates that lower federal courts rely on the plain meaning rule and the primary textual canons—but not as much on the whole act rule and, even less, on comparisons with statutes elsewhere in the U.S. Code. Lower federal courts rely even more heavily than the Supreme Court on precedent, both because the precedential array is thicker (circuit as well as Supreme Court decisions bind them), and because lower courts are absolutely bound by Supreme Court precedent, no questions asked. With less capacity for research, lower courts rely on committee reports—but not rejected proposals, floor debates, committee hearings, and dog-doesn't-bark arguments (*Chisom*).

Bruhl's empirical results are most interesting with regard to the substantive canons (a topic treated in more detail in Chapter 6) and the deference canons (Chapter 9). See generally *id.* at 35–46. Some canons are "bottom-heavy," used extensively in the lower federal courts and rarely in the Supreme Court: narrow construction of federal court jurisdictional laws, a strong presumption against extraterritorial application of federal law, the rule against retroactivity. The Supreme Court endorses all these canons, but does not have to deploy them very often—while lower courts wield them like Jedi lightsabers. Other canons are "top heavy," invoked by the Supreme Court but rarely by the lower courts: the dictionary canon, the rule of lenity, the constitutional avoidance canon, the notion that Congress does not hide elephants in mouseholes, and the common law canon. See *id.* at 50, 52.

How might Professor Bruhl's findings affect Congress's incentives to draft in the shadow of legal rules? Think about the LSD case. You know how the Seventh Circuit (in *Marshall*) and the Supreme Court (in *Chapman,* affirming the Seventh Circuit) handled the issue, and the different methodologies each judge applied. You also know that the Department of Justice, including the Solicitor General, supported the stiff penalty. How do you think the trial court handled the interpretation, compared with the Seventh Circuit? See *United States v. Marshall,* 706 F. Supp. 650 (C.D. Ill. 1989).

3.   *State High Courts, Including Elected Judges.* Recall that Chief Judge Judith Kaye emphasized that state courts are common law courts—and that such a connection to common law methodology generates greater nontextual flexibility for state high courts. Judith Kaye, *State Courts at the Dawn of a New Century: Common Law Courts Reading Statutes and Constitutions,* 70 N.Y.U. L. Rev. 1 (1995); accord, Jeffrey Pojanowski, *Statutes in Common Law Courts,* 91 Tex. L. Rev. 479 (2013). Does this institutional theory support Kaye's decision in *Jacob*—and justify a result that the U.S. Supreme Court might not have reached?

Notwithstanding Justice Scalia's *Chisom* dissent, the election of many state court judges probably undermines those judges' ability to be faithful agents of the legislature in statutory cases. See Aaron-Andrew Bruhl & Ethan Leib, *Elected Judges and Statutory Interpretation,* 79 U. Chi. L. Rev. 1215, 1243–46 (2012); Jed Handelsman Shugerman, *The Twist of Long Terms: Judicial Elections, Role Fidelity, and American Tort Law,* 98 Geo. L.J. 1349 (2010). Instead, elected judges might best be understood as faithful agents of "We the People, with whom judges have the same kind of direct relationship as other "representatives." Bruhl and Leib argue, for example, that the kind of dynamic interpretation Kaye applied in the *Jacob* and *Dana* appeals would have been much more democratically legitimate if the judges of the New York Court of Appeals were elected or were subject to retention votes. Bruhl & Leib, *Elected Judges,* 1262–67.

The foregoing accounts do not exhaust current state court practice. Indeed, as the following case and notes demonstrate, state courts have pioneered newer versions of text-based as well as pragmatic approaches to statutory interpretation and have often imposed such methodologies as a matter of methodological *stare decisis* (consistent with Sydney Foster's article, noted above).

STATUTORY PREFACE TO *PORTLAND GENERAL ELECTRIC*

Oregon Revised Statutes (1992)

Section 659.360

(3) The employee seeking parental leave shall be entitled to utilize any accrued vacation leave, sick leave or other compensatory leave, paid or unpaid, during the parental leave. The employer may require the employee seeking parental leave to utilize any accrued leave during the parental leave unless otherwise provided by an agreement of the employer and the employee, by collective bargaining agreement or by employer policy.

(6) The parental leave required by subsection (1) of this section is not required to be granted with pay unless so specified by agreement of the employer and employee, by collective bargaining agreement or by employer policy.

PORTLAND GENERAL ELECTRIC CO. V. BUREAU OF LABOR AND INDUSTRIES

Supreme Court of Oregon, 1993.
317 Or. 606, 859 P.2d 1143.

VAN HOOMISSEN, J. * * *

[The issue was whether an employee taking family or medical leave could take paid sick leave even if she or he were not sick. Following the opinion of the Bureau of Labor, the Supreme Court of Oregon unanimously ruled that employees had that option, essentially converting much of the unpaid leave time into paid leave. Justice Van Hoomissen's opinion started with a statement of the interpretive approach Oregon courts are supposed to follow.] In interpreting a statute, the court's task is to discern the intent of the legislature. ORS 174.020. To do that, the court examines both the text and context of the statute. That is the first level of our analysis.

In this first level of analysis, the text of the statutory provision itself is the starting point for interpretation and is the best evidence of the legislature's intent. In trying to ascertain the meaning of a statutory provision, and thereby to inform the court's inquiry into legislative intent, the court considers rules of construction of the statutory text that bear directly on how to read the text. Some of those rules are mandated by statute, including, for example, the statutory enjoinder "not to insert what has been omitted, or to omit what has been inserted." ORS 174.010. Others are found in the case law, including, for example, the rule that words of common usage typically should be given their plain, natural, and ordinary meaning.

Also at the first level of analysis, the court considers the context of the statutory provision at issue, which includes other provisions of the same statute and other related statutes. Just as with the court's consideration of the text of a statute, the court utilizes rules of construction that bear directly on the interpretation of the statutory provision in context. Some of those rules are mandated by statute, including, for example, the principles that "where there are several provisions or particulars such construction is, if possible, to be adopted as will give effect to all," ORS 174.010, and that "a particular intent shall control a general one that is inconsistent with it," ORS 174.020. Other such rules of construction are found in case law, including, for example, the rules that use of a term in one section and not in another section of the same statute indicates a purposeful omission, and that use of the same term throughout a statute indicates that the term has the same meaning throughout the statute.

If the legislature's intent is clear from the above-described inquiry into text and context, further inquiry is unnecessary.

If, but only if, the intent of the legislature is not clear from the text and context inquiry, the court will then move to the second level, which is to consider legislative history to inform the court's inquiry into legislative intent. When the court reaches legislative history, it considers it along with text and context to determine whether all of those together make the legislative intent clear. If the legislative intent is clear, then the court's inquiry into legislative intent and the meaning of the statute is at an end and the court interprets the statute to have the meaning so determined.

If, after consideration of text, context, and legislative history, the intent of the legislature remains unclear, then the court may resort to general maxims of statutory construction to aid in resolving the remaining uncertainty. Although some of those maxims of statutory construction may be statutory, *see, e.g.*, ORS 174.030 (natural rights), others more commonly may be found in case law. Those include, for example, the maxim that, where no legislative history exists, the court will attempt to determine how the legislature would have intended the statute to be applied had it considered the issue. * * *

[Applying this structure to the issue on appeal, the Court went no further than level one.] Both of the sentences in ORS 659.360(3) are *empowerment* sentences. The second sentence *empowers* the employer to compel an employee taking parental leave "to utilize any accrued leave." Thus, if an employee has accrued leave, the employer could require the employee to utilize that accrued leave during the parental leave, "unless otherwise provided by an agreement of the employer and the employee, by collective bargaining agreement or by employer policy." ORS 659.360(3).

The reciprocal power, granted to the employee by the first sentence of ORS 659.360(3), permits the employee, at the employee's option, to do what the employer may require the employee to do. The employee may require the employer to let the employee "utilize" any accrued vacation leave, sick leave or other compensatory leave, paid or unpaid, during the parental leave. As noted, the first sentence of the statute does not contain any limitation on the employee's rights imposed under the provisions of a collective bargaining agreement.

In sum, the employer may *require* the employee seeking parental leave to utilize any accrued leave during parental leave, unless otherwise provided by an agreement of the employer and the employee, by collective bargaining agreement, or by employer policy, even if the employee is not on vacation or sick or does not wish to use accrued leave during the parental leave. Similarly, the employee may *require* the employer to let the employee utilize any accrued vacation leave, sick leave, or other compensatory leave, paid or unpaid during the parental leave, even if the employee is not on vacation or sick, and even if the employer does not want to do so. If the legislature had wanted to make the use of accrued leave during parental leave subject to any preconditions in an existing collective bargaining agreement, it easily could have done so by including in the first sentence of ORS 659.360(3) the same qualifying language that presently is found only in the second sentence of that subsection. The legislature knows how to include qualifying language in a statute when it wants to do so. It did not do so here. * * *

STATUTORY POSTSCRIPT TO *PGE*

When the Oregon Legislature recodified its family and medical leave statute in 1995 and 2007, it created a new **Oregon Revised Statutes § 659A.174, "Paid Leave":**

(1) Except as provided in subsection (2) of this section, and unless otherwise provided by the terms of an agreement between the eligible employee and the covered employer, a collective bargaining agreement or an employer policy, family leave is not required to be granted with pay.

(2) An employee taking family leave is entitled to use any paid accrued sick leave or any paid accrued vacation leave during the period of family leave, or to use any other paid leave that is offered by the employer in lieu of vacation leave during the period of family leave.

(3) Subject to the terms of any agreement between the eligible employee and the covered employer or the terms of a collective bargaining agreement, the employer may determine the particular order in which accrued leave is to be used in circumstances in which more than one type of accrued leave is available to the employee.

NOTES ON THE OREGON PGE CASE AND STATES AS LABORATORIES OF STATUTORY INTERPRETATION

1. *A Pragmatic or Modified Textualism? A "Tiered" Funnel of Abstraction?* The Oregon Supreme Court's *PGE* opinion sets forth a pragmatic but largely textualist approach to statutory interpretation—one that rejects the new textualist exclusion of legislative history but gives a formal primacy to textualist analysis that reflects a harder plain meaning rule than the U.S. or Oregon Supreme Court had traditionally applied. In contrast to *TVA v. Hill*, for example, the *PGE* approach does not require judges to check their understanding of plain meaning by reference to legislative history. But the textualism is pragmatic insofar as it invites legislative history and normative analysis when the statute's meaning is not clear.

Note, also, how the *PGE* approach reflects but alters the Funnel of Abstraction. *PGE* retains the Funnel factors but "tiers" them. The most concrete factors in the first tier or level—statutory text, structure, and precedent—are not only primary but are also exclusive when they answer the interpretive question. So, for many cases, the Funnel is foreshortened considerably. The factors in the second tier or level—legislative history and purpose—are considered where the text is ambiguous, but note that, if there is relevant legislative history, it will be briefed by the parties and considered by the judges. So you can never know whether a plain meaning has been found without any reference to legislative history (for the judges have read that part of the brief). Finally, the normative canons, the most abstract considerations, are presented in the third tier or level as a last-resort tiebreaker by the *PGE* Court.

The lower court considered the following legislative history. The original draft of the family leave bill provided that "[t]he leave required by subsection (1) of this Act may be unpaid leave or any other leave the employer and employee agree upon or any leave specified or allowed by any collective bargaining agreement." *Portland Gen. Elec. Co. v. Bureau of Labor & Industries,* 842 P.2d 419, 422 (Or. App. 1992). That language was changed to say: "The leave, with preference given to accumulated sick leave and vacation leave, required by subsection (1) of this section may be paid or unpaid leave or any other leave the employer and employee agree upon or any leave specified or allowed by any collective bargaining agreement." Finally, that subsection was changed and subsection (6) added, to read essentially as it now reads. The House sponsor explained that the final change was to clarify the meaning in the second version: "The second change is * * * to clarify, * * * to make certain that any sick leave, vacation leave, that that will run concurrently with the 12 weeks. And so this 12 weeks is not added on to any vacation time or sick leave that the individual would have." Tape Recording, House Committee on

Labor, March 18, 1987, Tape 61, Side B. Would this legislative history make a difference in your vote if you were a judge?

2.   Stare Decisis *for Methodological Precedents?* Perhaps the most notable feature of *PGE* is that the Oregon Supreme Court made a self-conscious decision to set forth, in clear terms, the methodology it expected lower courts to follow in statutory cases—and that its own justices committed themselves to in subsequent supreme court cases. The House of Lords in the United Kingdom gives *stare decisis* effect to methodological precedents, and Sydney Foster argues that the U.S. Supreme Court should do the same. See Sydney Foster, *Should Courts Give* Stare Decisis *Effect to Statutory Interpretation Methodology?*, 96 Geo. L.J. 1863 (2008). Consider the values of *stare decisis*: judicial economy, predictability, and reliance interests. Foster argues that consistent treatment in matters of methodology would serve those interests—so courts should follow that practice.

On the other hand, are the reliance interests so strong in matters of methodological *stare decisis?* Is *stare decisis* as desirable or even workable for legal *standards* as they are for legal *rules?* Compare Foster, Stare Decisis *Effect*, 1901–05 (on the whole, yes), with Connor Raso & William Eskridge Jr., Chevron *as a Canon, Not a Precedent: An Empirical Analysis of What Motivates Justices in Agency Deference Cases*, 110 Colum. L. Rev. 1727 (2010) (on the whole, no).

Consider Abbe Gluck, *The States as Laboratories of Statutory Interpretation: Methodological Consensus and the New Modified Textualism,* 119 Yale L.J. 1750, 1779–1781 (2010), who embraces the *PGE* experiment: "Three preliminary studies, including one conducted as part of this project, have collected data on how the *PGE* regime has been implemented since its installation. One clearly observable effect of the regime is that it has reduced the number of interpretive tools employed by the Oregon Supreme Court and so made it easier to predict which tools the court will rely on to decide cases. 'The court resolves the vast majority of statutory issues at level one,' i.e., the text-based tier. Between 1993 and 1998, for example, out of 137 statutory interpretation cases, the court looked at legislative history only thirty-three times, finding it 'useless' in one third of those cases. It consequently reached tier three—nontextual canons—only eleven times during the same period. Even more strikingly, between 1999 and 2006, the court applied the *PGE* framework 150 times, and only reached tier two (legislative history) nine times. Not a single case during that period reached the other-maxims tier (tier three). And, in a study conducted as part of this project, across the thirty-five cases in which *PGE* was cited between 2006 and May 2009, legislative history was applied six times and a substantive canon only once.

"Compare the five years before *PGE* was decided. There was no single approach: more than half of the cases resorted immediately to legislative history or policy analysis without prior consideration of text alone, and without the tiered hierarchy of sources that *PGE* later imposed. One justice called the pre-*PGE* period a 'legislative history free-for-all.'

"In contrast, under *PGE*, the court is fairly consistent with respect to which interpretive tools it relies upon. Over the four-and-a-half year period ending in May 2009, the following eight types of textual tools were used in roughly half of the cases: 'plain meaning,' dictionaries, state court precedents, close readings of statutory definition sections, analysis of related statutes, analysis of the contested term's place in the statutory scheme, historical evolution of the statute itself, and textual canons. With respect to the textual canons, the court applied the same eight canons repeatedly throughout the cases in which textual canons were used. The only additional tools used in more than three cases were rules of grammar (ten cases) and legislative history (nine cases), making the list of the eight types of tools described above the fairly complete universe of Oregon statutory interpretation principles. All but six of the opinions over the five-year period were unanimous."

3. *Oregon's Statutory Pushback.* Gluck's study of Oregon's *PGE* experiment noted that, in 2001, the Oregon Legislature enacted a statute in direct response to *PGE*: "A court may limit its consideration of legislative history to the information that the parties provide to the court. A court shall give the weight to the legislative history that the court considers to be appropriate." Although the language of the statute was hortatory, its legislative history suggested that the legislature was reacting negatively to *PGE*. Yet it was not until 2009 that the Oregon Supreme Court acknowledged the legislation. In *State v. Gaines*, 206 P.3d 1042, 1046–51 (Or. 2009), the Oregon Supreme Court held that parties are free to "proffer" legislative history as part of the level one (textual) inquiry, and that the court will consult it regardless of ambiguity, but only "where that legislative history appears useful to the court's analysis."

Gaines may have been the closing curtain for the *PGE* regime of strict tiers or levels. Since *Gaines*, the Oregon Supreme Court has frequently relaxed the first level of the *PGE* approach and has considered legislative history to confirm apparent plain meanings, see, e.g., *Couey v. Atkins*, 355 P.3d 866, 878–81 (Or. 2015); *State v. Swanson*, 266 P.3d 45, 49 (Or. 2011), *In re Marriage of Harris*, 244 P.3d 801, 809–11 (Or. 2010); *State v. Baker-Krofft*, 239 P.3d 226, 231–32 (Or. 2010), or has examined legislative history in detail before rejecting it in favor of statutory plain meanings, see, e.g., *A.G. v. Guitron*, 268 P.3d 589, 592–600 (Or. 2011), or has rested interpretation decisively on legislative history as the best means to fill in the details of a statutory provision, e.g., *Hopkins v. SAIF Corp.*, 245 P.3d 90 (Or. 2010) (seamlessly combining textual and detailed legislative history analysis).

Indeed, the Oregon Supreme Court's decisions after *Gaines* look a lot more like the complicated Funnel of Abstraction (considering text, statutory and legislative history, purpose, case law, and norms) than like the strict tiers/levels announced in *PGE*. See, e.g., *Couey*, 355 P.3d at 878 (citing both *PGE* and *Gaines*, but for the proposition that text, legislative history, and canons are all relevant inquiries); *State v. Glushko*, 266 P.3d 50, 54–60 (Or. 2011) (citing only *Gaines* and not *PGE*); *Arken v. City of Portland*, 263 P.3d 975, 990–92 (Or. 2011) (citing only *Gaines* and examining a wide range of evidence, including a detailed account of the legislative history); *State v. Cloutier*, 261 P.3d 1234 (Or. 2011) (similar). Often, however, the Oregon Supreme Court simply applies statutory text and structure, without any discussion of what method it is applying. E.g., *Malan v. Tipton*, 247 P.3d 1223 (Or. 2011) (citing only *Gaines* but examining just the common law and text to interpret the statute).

What lessons might be drawn from Oregon's experiment? Professor Gluck's article demonstrates that other states have adopted different interpretive regimes, some with rocky histories, and she argues that methodological *stare decisis* is an idea whose time has come for federal courts as well as state courts. For examples of the methodological diversity that still characterizes Supreme Court decisionmaking, see, e.g., *Adoptive Couple v. Baby Girl*, 133 S.Ct. 2552 (2013) (intense debate, where different Justices rely on statutory plain meaning as understood by the enforcing agency, the avoidance of constitutional problems, the common law rights of biological parents, and the statutory structure and congressional purpose); *Brown v. Plata,* 563 U.S. 493 (2011) (majority opinion relying on statutory plain meaning and avoidance of Eighth Amendment problems, contrasted with dissenting views based upon the absurd results canon and avoidance of Article III problems); *Zuni Public School District No. 89 v. Department of Education,* 550 U.S. 81 (2007) (clash between pragmatic and textualist theories, and a debate between concurring and dissenting Justices over the current validity of *Holy Trinity*).

STATUTORY PREFACE FOR *HIVELY*
TITLE VII OF THE CIVIL RIGHTS ACT OF 1964, AS AMENDED

Section 701, 42 U.S.C. § 2000e. Definitions * * *

(k) The terms "because of sex" or "on the basis of sex" include, but are not limited to, because of or on the basis of pregnancy, childbirth, or related medical conditions; and women affected by pregnancy, childbirth, or related medical conditions shall be treated the same for all employment-related purposes, including receipt of benefits under fringe benefit programs, as other persons not so affected but similar in their ability or inability to work * * *. This subsection shall not require an employer to pay for health insurance benefits for abortion, except where the life of the mother would be endangered if the fetus were carried to term, or except where medical complications have arisen from an abortion: Provided, That nothing herein shall preclude an employer from providing abortion benefits or otherwise affect bargaining agreements in regard to abortion. [Added 1978]

Section 703, 42 U.S.C. § 2000e–2. Unlawful Employment Practices.

(a) Employer Practices. It shall be an unlawful employment practice for an employer—

> **(1)** to fail or refuse to hire or to discharge any individual, or otherwise to discriminate against any individual with respect to his compensation, terms, conditions, or privileges of employment, because of such individual's race, color, religion, sex, or national origin; or

> **(2)** to limit, segregate, or classify his employees or applicants for employment in any way which would deprive or tend to deprive any individual of employment opportunities or otherwise adversely affect his status as an employee, because of such individual's race, color, religion, sex, or national origin. * * *

(e) Businesses or enterprises with personnel qualified on basis of religion, sex, or national origin; educational institutions with personnel of particular religion

Notwithstanding any other provision of this subchapter, (1) it shall not be an unlawful employment practice for an employer to hire and employ employees, for an employment agency to classify, or refer for employment any individual, for a labor organization to classify its membership or to classify or refer for employment any individual, or for an employer, labor organization, or joint labor-management committee controlling apprenticeship or other training or retraining programs to admit or employ any individual in any such program, on the basis of his religion, sex, or national origin in those certain instances where religion, sex, or national origin is a bona fide occupational qualification reasonably necessary to the normal operation of that particular business or enterprise * * *.

(m) Impermissible consideration of race, color, religion, sex, or national origin in employment practices

Except as otherwise provided in this subchapter, an unlawful employment practice is established when the complaining party demonstrates that race, color, religion, sex, or national origin was a motivating factor for any employment practice, even though other factors also motivated the practice. [Added 1991]

KIMBERLY HIVELY V. IVY TECH COMMUNITY COLLEGE

United States Court of Appeals for the Seventh Circuit (*en banc*), 2017.
853 F.3d 339.

Before WOOD, CHIEF JUDGE, and BAUER, POSNER, FLAUM, EASTERBROOK, RIPPLE, KANNE, ROVNER, WILLIAMS, SYKES, and HAMILTON, CIRCUIT JUDGES.

WOOD, CHIEF JUDGE.

[Title VII of the Civil Rights Act of 1964 bars employment discrimination "because of * * * sex." A successful part-time teacher at Ivy Tech Community College, Kimberly Hively complained that the college refused to consider her for a permanent job because she is a lesbian. If true, does that constitute discrimination because of sex? Because Title VII does not bar discrimination "because of * * * sexual orientation," federal appeals courts have uniformly said "no" to this question—until the Seventh Circuit, sitting en banc, reconsidered the issue.]

Much ink has been spilled about the proper way to go about the task of statutory interpretation. One can stick, to the greatest extent possible, to the language enacted by the legislature; one could consult the legislative history that led up to the bill that became law; one could examine later actions of the legislature (*i.e.* efforts to amend the law and later enactments) for whatever light they may shed; and one could use a combination of these methods. [Citing various secondary sources.]

Few people would insist that there is a need to delve into secondary sources if the statute is plain on its face. Even if it is not pellucid, the best source for disambiguation is the broader context of the statute that the legislature—in this case, Congress—passed. This is uncontroversial when the reading seems consistent with the conventional wisdom about the reach of the law. It becomes somewhat harder to swallow if the language reveals suspected or actual unintended consequences. It is then that some have thought that legislative history should be used to block a particular reading of a statute. Legislative history, however, is notoriously malleable. Even worse is the temptation to try to divine the significance of unsuccessful legislative efforts to change the law. Those failures can mean almost anything, ranging from the lack of necessity for a proposed change because the law already accomplishes the desired goal, to the undesirability of the change because a majority of the legislature is happy with the way the courts are currently interpreting the law, to the irrelevance of the non-enactment, when it is attributable to nothing more than legislative logrolling or gridlock that had nothing to do with its merits.

Ivy Tech sets great store on the fact that Congress has frequently considered amending Title VII to add the words "sexual orientation" to the list of prohibited characteristics, yet it has never done so. Many of our sister circuits have also noted this fact. In our view, however, it is simply too difficult to draw a reliable inference from these truncated legislative initiatives to rest our opinion on them. The goalposts have been moving over the years, as the Supreme Court has shed more light on the scope of the language that already is in the statute: no *sex* discrimination.

The dissent makes much of the fact that Congresses acting more than thirty years after the passage of Title VII made use of the term "sexual orientation" to prohibit discrimination or violence on that basis in statutes such as the Violence Against Women Act and the federal Hate Crimes Act. But this gets us no closer to answering the question at hand, for Congress may certainly choose to use both a belt and suspenders to achieve its objectives, and the fact that "sex" and "sexual orientation" discrimination may overlap in later statutes is of no help in determining whether sexual orientation discrimination is discrimination on the basis of sex for the purposes of Title VII. * * *

Moreover, the agency most closely associated with this law, the Equal Employment Opportunity Commission, in 2015 announced that it now takes the position that Title VII's prohibition against sex discrimination encompasses discrimination on the basis of sexual orientation. See *Baldwin v. Foxx*, 2015 WL 4397641 (July 15, 2015). Our point here is not that we have a duty to defer to the EEOC's position. We assume for present purposes that no such duty exists. But the Commission's position may have caused some in Congress to think that legislation is needed to carve sexual orientation out of the statute, not to put it in. In the end, we have no idea what inference to draw from congressional inaction or later enactments, because there is no way of knowing what explains each individual member's votes, much less what explains the failure of the body as a whole to change this 1964 statute.

Our interpretive task is guided instead by the Supreme Court's approach in the closely related case of *Oncale v. Sundowner Offshore Servs.*, 523 U.S. 75, 79–80 (1998), where it had this to say as it addressed the question whether Title VII covers sexual harassment inflicted by a man on a male victim:

> We see no justification in the statutory language or our precedents for a categorical rule excluding same-sex harassment claims from the coverage of Title VII. As some courts have observed, male-on-male sexual harassment in the workplace was assuredly not the principal evil Congress was concerned with when it enacted Title VII. But statutory prohibitions often go beyond the principal evil to cover reasonably comparable evils, and it is ultimately the provisions of our laws rather than the principal concerns of our legislators by which we are governed. Title VII prohibits "discriminat[ion] . . . because of . . . sex" in the "terms" or "conditions" of employment. Our holding that this includes sexual harassment must extend to sexual harassment of any kind that meets the statutory requirements.

The Court could not have been clearer: the fact that the enacting Congress may not have anticipated a particular application of the law cannot stand in the way of the provisions of the law that are on the books.

It is therefore neither here nor there that the Congress that enacted the Civil Rights Act in 1964 and chose to include sex as a prohibited basis for employment discrimination (no matter why it did so) may not have realized or understood the full scope of the words it chose. Indeed, in the years since 1964, Title VII has been understood to cover far more than the simple decision of an employer not to hire a woman for Job A, or a man for Job B. The Supreme Court has held that the prohibition against sex discrimination reaches sexual harassment in the workplace, see *Meritor Sav. Bank, FSB v. Vinson*, 477 U.S. 57 (1986), including same-sex workplace harassment, see *Oncale*; it reaches discrimination based on actuarial assumptions about a person's longevity, see *City of Los Angeles, Dep't of Water and Power v. Manhart*, 435 U.S. 702 (1978); and it reaches discrimination based on a person's failure to conform to a certain set of gender stereotypes, see *Price Waterhouse v. Hopkins*, 490 U.S. 228 (1989). It is quite possible that these interpretations may also have surprised some who served in the 88th Congress. Nevertheless, experience with the law has led the Supreme Court to recognize that each of these examples is a covered form of sex discrimination. * * *

Hively alleges that if she had been a man married to a woman (or living with a woman, or dating a woman) and everything else had stayed the same, Ivy Tech would not have refused to promote her and would not have fired her. (We take the facts in the light most favorable to her, because we are here on a Rule 12(b)(6) dismissal; naturally nothing we say will prevent Ivy Tech from contesting these points in later proceedings.) This describes paradigmatic sex discrimination. Ivy Tech is disadvantaging her because she is a woman. Nothing in the complaint hints that Ivy Tech has an anti-marriage policy that extends to heterosexual relationships, or for that matter even an anti-partnership policy that is gender-neutral.

Viewed through the lens of the gender non-conformity line of cases, Hively represents the ultimate case of failure to conform to the female stereotype (at least as understood in a place such as modern America, which views heterosexuality as the norm and other forms of sexuality as exceptional): she is not heterosexual. * * * Hively's claim is no different from the claims brought by women who were rejected for jobs in traditionally male workplaces, such as fire departments, construction, and policing. The employers in those cases were policing the boundaries of what jobs or behaviors they found acceptable for a woman (or in some cases, for a man).

This was the critical point that the Supreme Court was making in [*Price Waterhouse v. Hopkins*, 490 U.S. 228 (1989).] The four justices in the plurality and the two justices concurring in the judgment recognized that Hopkins had alleged that her employer was discriminating only against women who behaved in what the employer viewed as too "masculine" a way—no makeup, no jewelry, no fashion sense. And even before *Hopkins*, courts had found sex discrimination in situations where women were resisting stereotypical roles. As far back as 1971, the Supreme Court held that Title VII does not permit an employer to refuse to hire women with pre-school-age children, but not men. *Phillips v. Martin Marietta Corp.*, 400 U.S. 542

(1971). Around the same time, this court * * * struck down a rule requiring only the female employees to be unmarried. *Sprogis v. United Air Lines, Inc.*, 444 F.2d 1194 (7th Cir. 1971). In both those instances, the employer's rule did not affect every woman in the workforce. Just so here: a policy that discriminates on the basis of sexual orientation does not affect every woman, or every man, but it is based on assumptions about the proper behavior for someone of a given sex. The discriminatory behavior does not exist without taking the victim's biological sex (either as observed at birth or as modified, in the case of transsexuals) into account. Any discomfort, disapproval, or job decision based on the fact that the complainant— woman or man—dresses differently, speaks differently, or dates or marries a same-sex partner, is a reaction purely and simply based on sex. That means that it falls within Title VII's prohibition against sex discrimination, if it affects employment in one of the specified ways. * * *

Hively also has argued that action based on sexual orientation is sex discrimination under the associational theory. It is now accepted that a person who is discriminated against because of the protected characteristic of one with whom she associates is actually being disadvantaged because of her own traits. This line of cases began with [*Loving v. Virginia*, 388 U.S. 1 (1967)], in which the Supreme Court held that "restricting the freedom to marry solely because of racial classifications violates the central meaning of the Equal Protection Clause. The Court rejected the argument that miscegenation statutes do not violate equal protection because they "punish equally both the white and the Negro participants in an interracial marriage." When dealing with a statute containing racial classifications, it wrote, "the fact of equal application does not immunize the statute from the very heavy burden of justification" required by the Fourteenth Amendment for lines drawn by race.

[Circuit courts have all but uniformly applied *Loving* to hold that an employer's discriminating against an employee because of the race of her partner or associates has discriminated "because of race" under Title VII. Chief Judge Wood applied the principle of those race discrimination cases to the sex discrimination claimed by Professor Hively.]

POSNER, CIRCUIT JUDGE, concurring.

It is helpful to note at the outset that the interpretation of statutes comes in three flavors. The first and most conventional is the extraction of the original meaning of the statute—the meaning intended by the legislators—and corresponds to interpretation in ordinary discourse. Knowing English I can usually determine swiftly and straightforwardly the meaning of a statement, oral or written, made to me in English (not always, because the statement may be garbled, grammatically intricate or inaccurate, obtuse, or complex beyond my ability to understand).

The second form of interpretation, illustrated by the commonplace local ordinance which commands "no vehicles in the park," is interpretation by unexpressed intent, whereby we understand that although an ambulance is a vehicle, the ordinance was not intended to include ambulances among the "vehicles" forbidden to enter the park. * * *

Finally and most controversially, interpretation can mean giving a fresh meaning to a statement (which can be a statement found in a constitutional or statutory text)—a meaning that infuses the statement with vitality and significance today. An example of this last form of interpretation—the form that in my mind is most clearly applicable to the present case—is the Sherman Antitrust Act, enacted in 1890, long before there was a sophisticated understanding of the economics of monopoly and competition. Times have changed; and for more than thirty years the Act has been interpreted in conformity to the modern, not the nineteenth-century, understanding of the relevant economics. The Act has thus been updated by, or in the name of, judicial interpretation—the form of interpretation that consists of making old law satisfy modern needs and understandings. And a common form of interpretation it is, despite its flouting "original meaning." Statutes and constitutional provisions frequently are interpreted on the basis of present need and present understanding rather than original meaning—constitutional provisions even more frequently, because most of them are older than most statutes.

Title VII of the Civil Rights Act of 1964, now more than half a century old, invites an interpretation that will update it to the present, a present that differs markedly from the era in which the Act was enacted. But I need to emphasize that this third form of interpretation—call it judicial interpretive updating—presupposes a lengthy interval between enactment and (re)interpretation. A statute when passed has an understood meaning; it takes years, often many years, for a shift in the political and cultural environment to change the understanding of the statute.* * *

It's true that even today if asked what is the sex of plaintiff Hively one would answer that she is female or that she is a woman, not that she is a lesbian. Lesbianism denotes a form of sexual or romantic attraction; it is not a physical sex identifier like masculinity or femininity. A broader understanding of the word "sex" in Title VII than the original understanding is thus required in order to be able to classify the discrimination of which Hively complains as a form of sex discrimination. That broader understanding is essential. Failure to adopt it would make the statute anachronistic, just as interpreting the Sherman Act by reference to its nineteenth-century framers' understanding of competition and monopoly would make the Sherman Act anachronistic.

We now understand that homosexual men and women (and also bisexuals, defined as having both homosexual and heterosexual orientations) are normal in the ways that count, and beyond that have made many outstanding intellectual and cultural contributions to society (think for example of Tchaikovsky, Oscar Wilde, Jane Addams, André Gide, Thomas Mann, Marlene Dietrich, Bayard Rustin, Alan Turing, Alec Guinness, Leonard Bernstein, Van Cliburn, and James Baldwin—a very partial list). We now understand that homosexuals, male and female, play an essential role, in this country at any rate, as adopters of children from foster homes. The compelling social interest in protecting homosexuals (male and female) from discrimination justifies an admittedly loose "interpretation" of the word "sex" in Title VII to embrace homosexuality: an interpretation that cannot be imputed to the framers of the statute but that we are entitled to adopt in light of (to quote Holmes) "*what this country has become,*" or, in Blackstonian terminology, to embrace as a sensible deviation from the literal or original meaning of the statutory language. * * *

The majority opinion states that Congress in 1964 "may not have realized or understood the full scope of the words it chose." This could be understood to imply that the statute forbade discrimination against homosexuals but the framers and ratifiers of the statute were not smart enough to realize that. I would prefer to say that theirs was the then-current understanding of the key word—sex. "Sex" in 1964 meant gender, not sexual orientation. What the framers and ratifiers understandably didn't understand was how attitudes toward homosexuals would change in the following half century. They shouldn't be blamed for that failure of foresight. We understand the words of Title VII differently not because we're smarter than the statute's framers and ratifiers but because we live in a different era, a different culture. * * *

I would prefer to see us acknowledge openly that today we, who are judges rather than members of Congress, are imposing on a half-century-old statute a meaning of "sex discrimination" that the Congress that enacted it would not have accepted. This is something courts do fairly frequently to avoid statutory obsolescence and concomitantly to avoid placing the entire burden of updating old statutes on the legislative branch. We should not leave the impression that we are merely the obedient servants of the 88th Congress (1963–1965), carrying out their wishes. We are not. We are taking advantage of what the last half century has taught.

FLAUM, CIRCUIT JUDGE, joined by RIPPLE, CIRCUIT JUDGE, concurring.

* * * [D]iscrimination against an employee on the basis of their homosexuality is necessarily, in part, discrimination based on their sex. Fundamental to the definition of homosexuality is the sexual attraction to individuals of the "same sex." [Citing various dictionaries.] One cannot consider a person's homosexuality without also accounting for their sex: doing so would render "same" and "own" meaningless. As such, discriminating against that employee because they are homosexual constitutes discriminating against an employee because of (A) the employee's sex, *and* (B) their sexual attraction to individuals of the *same sex*. And "sex," under Title VII, is an enumerated trait.

This raises the question: Does Title VII's text require a plaintiff to show that an employer discriminated against them *solely* "because of" an enumerated trait? Again, I turn to the text, which clearly states:

> Except as otherwise provided in this subchapter, an unlawful employment practice is established when the complaining party demonstrates that . . . sex . . . was *a motivating factor for any employment practice, even though other factors also motivated the practice.*

42 U.S.C. § 2000e–2(m) (emphasis added). Congress added this amendment to Title VII partially in response to the Supreme Court's plurality decision in *Hopkins*, in which the Court stated:

> [S]ince we know that the words "because of" do not mean "*solely* because of," we also know that Title VII meant to condemn even those decisions based on a mixture of legitimate and illegitimate considerations. When, therefore, an employer considers both gender and legitimate factors at the time of making a decision, that decision was "because of" sex and the other,

legitimate considerations. . . . We need not leave our common sense at the doorstep when we interpret a statute. It is difficult for us to imagine that, in the simple words "because of," Congress meant to obligate a plaintiff to identify the precise causal role played by legitimate and illegitimate motivations in the employment decision she challenges. We conclude, instead, that Congress meant to obligate her to prove that the employer relied upon sex-based considerations in coming to its decision.

The Court made clear that "[t]he critical inquiry. . . is whether gender was *a factor* in the employment decision" when it was made. So if discriminating against an employee because she is homosexual is equivalent to discriminating against her because she is (A) a woman who is (B) sexually attracted to women, then it is motivated, in part, by an enumerated trait: the employee's sex. That is all an employee must show to successfully allege a Title VII claim. * * *

SYKES, CIRCUIT JUDGE, with whom BAUER and KANNE, CIRCUIT JUDGES, join, dissenting.

* * * The majority deploys a judge-empowering, common-law decision method that leaves a great deal of room for judicial discretion. So does Judge Posner in his concurrence. Neither is faithful to the statutory text, read fairly, as a reasonable person would have understood it when it was adopted. The result is a statutory amendment courtesy of unelected judges. Judge Posner admits this; he embraces and argues for this conception of judicial power. The majority does not, preferring instead to smuggle in the statutory amendment under cover of an aggressive reading of loosely related Supreme Court precedents. Either way, the result is the same: the circumvention of the legislative process by which the people govern themselves.

Respect for the constraints imposed on the judiciary by a system of written law must begin with fidelity to the traditional first principle of statutory interpretation: When a statute supplies the rule of decision, our role is to give effect to the enacted text, interpreting the statutory language as a reasonable person would have understood it at the time of enactment. We are not authorized to infuse the text with a new or unconventional meaning or to update it to respond to changed social, economic, or political conditions. * * *

Judicial statutory updating, whether overt or covert, cannot be reconciled with the constitutional design. The Constitution establishes a procedure for enacting and amending statutes: bicameralism and presentment. *See* U.S. Const. art. I, § 7. Needless to say, statutory amendments brought to you by the judiciary do not pass through this process. That is why a textualist decision method matters: When we assume the power to alter the original public meaning of a statute through the process of interpretation, we assume a power that is not ours. The Constitution assigns the power to make and amend statutory law to the elected representatives of the people. However welcome today's decision might be as a policy matter, it comes at a great cost to representative self-government. * * *

* * * I agree with my colleagues that the proposed new interpretation is not necessarily incorrect simply because no one in the 1964 Congress that adopted Title VII intended or anticipated its application to sexual-orientation discrimination. The subjective intentions of the legislators do not matter. Statutory interpretation is an

objective inquiry that looks for the meaning the statutory language conveyed to a reasonable person at the time of enactment. The objective meaning of the text is not delimited by what individual lawmakers specifically had in mind when they voted for the statute. The Supreme Court made this point clear in *Oncale* when it said that "statutory prohibitions often go beyond the principal evil to cover reasonably comparable evils, and it is ultimately the provisions of our laws rather than the principal concerns of our legislators by which we are governed." *Oncale v. Sundowner Offshore Servs., Inc.*, 523 U.S. 75, 79 (1998). Broadly worded statutes are regularly applied to circumstances beyond the subjective contemplation of the lawmakers who adopted the text.

But the analysis must begin with the statutory text; it largely ends there too. Is it even remotely plausible that in 1964, when Title VII was adopted, a reasonable person competent in the English language would have understood that a law banning employment discrimination "because of sex" also banned discrimination because of sexual orientation? The answer is no, of course not.

"It is a fundamental canon of statutory construction that, unless otherwise defined, words will be interpreted as taking their ordinary, contemporary, common meaning." *Sandifer v. U.S. Steel Corp.*, 134 S.Ct. 870, 876 (2014). The word "contemporary" as used here means contemporaneous with the statute's enactment, not "contemporary" as in "now." The interpretive inquiry looks to the original public meaning of the statutory text.

Title VII does not define discrimination "because of sex." In common, ordinary usage in 1964—and now, for that matter—the word "sex" means biologically male or female; it does not also refer to sexual orientation. See, e.g., Sex, The American Heritage Dictionary of the English Language (1st ed. 1969) (defining "sex" as "[t]he property or quality by which organisms are classified according to their reproductive functions[;] [e]ither of two divisions, designated male and female, of this classification"); Sex, New Oxford American Dictionary (3d ed. 2010) (defining "sex" as "either of the two main categories (male and female) into which humans and many other living things are divided on the basis of their reproductive functions"); Sex, The American Heritage Desk Dictionary (5th ed. 2013) (defining "sex" as "[e]ither of the two divisions, female and male, by which most organisms are classified on the basis of their reproductive organs and functions[;] [t]he condition or character of being female or male").

To a fluent speaker of the English language—then and now—the ordinary meaning of the word "sex" does not fairly include the concept of "sexual orientation." The two terms are never used interchangeably, and the latter is not subsumed within the former; there is no overlap in meaning. * * * The words plainly describe different traits, and the separate and distinct meaning of each term is easily grasped. More specifically to the point here, discrimination "because of sex" is not reasonably understood to include discrimination based on sexual orientation, a different immutable characteristic. Classifying people by sexual orientation is different than classifying them by sex. The two traits are categorically distinct and widely recognized as such. There is no ambiguity or vagueness here. * * *

This commonsense understanding is confirmed by the language Congress uses when it *does* legislate against sexual-orientation discrimination. For example, the Violence Against Women Act prohibits funded programs and activities from discriminating "on the basis of actual or perceived race, color, religion, national origin, *sex*, gender identity, . . . *sexual orientation*, or disability." 42 U.S.C. § 13925(b)(13)(A) (emphases added). If sex discrimination is commonly understood to encompass sexual-orientation discrimination, then listing the two categories separately, as this statute does, is needless surplusage. The federal Hate Crimes Act is another example. It imposes a heightened punishment for causing or attempting to cause bodily injury "to any person, because of the actual or perceived religion, national origin, *gender*, *sexual orientation*, gender identity, or disability of any person." 18 U.S.C. § 249(a)(2)(A) (emphases added). * * *

As [the majority sees it], even if sex discrimination is understood in the ordinary way, sexual-orientation discrimination is sex discrimination because "it is actually impossible to discriminate on the basis of sexual orientation without discriminating on the basis of sex."

Not true. An employer who refuses to hire homosexuals is not drawing a line based on the job applicant's sex. He is not excluding gay men because they are men and lesbians because they are women. His discriminatory motivation is independent of and unrelated to the applicant's sex. Sexism (misandry and misogyny) and homophobia are separate kinds of prejudice that classify people in distinct ways based on different immutable characteristics. Simply put, sexual-orientation discrimination doesn't classify people by sex; it doesn't draw male/female distinctions but instead targets homosexual men and women for harsher treatment than heterosexual men and women. * * *

The majority also relies on cases involving sex stereotyping, most notably the Supreme Court's decision in *Price Waterhouse v. Hopkins*. More specifically, my colleagues conclude that a claim of sexual-orientation discrimination is indistinguishable from a claim involving sex stereotyping. I disagree. * * * To put the matter plainly, heterosexuality is not a female stereotype; it is not a male stereotype; it is not a sex-specific stereotype at all. An employer who hires only heterosexual employees is neither assuming nor insisting that his female and male employees match a stereotype specific to their sex. He is instead insisting that his employees match the dominant sexual orientation regardless of their sex. Sexual-orientation discrimination does not classify people according to invidious or idiosyncratic male or female stereotypes. It does not spring from a sex-specific bias at all. * * *

The majority also draws on *Loving*, the Supreme Court's iconic decision invalidating Virginia's miscegenation statutes on equal-protection grounds. This case is not a variant of *Loving*. Miscegenation laws plainly employ invidious racial classifications; they are inherently racially discriminatory. In contrast, sexual-orientation discrimination springs from a wholly different kind of bias than sex discrimination. The two forms of discrimination classify people based on different traits and thus are not the same. * * *

As I've explained, a convincing case has not been made. If more is needed, consider for a moment the next step in this litigation. When this case returns to the district court, it will not matter whether the evidence shows that Ivy Tech rejected Hively in favor of male applicants, female applicants, or a combination of men and women. If the facts show that Ivy Tech hired heterosexuals for the six full-time positions, then the community college may be found liable for discriminating against Hively *because of her sex*. That will be so even if *all six positions were filled by women*. Try explaining that to a jury. * * *

Zarda v. Altitude Express, Inc.

883 F.3d 100, 136 (2d Cir. *en banc* 2018).

Also sitting en banc, the Second Circuit took up the same issue as that addressed in *Hively*. A majority of the court, in an opinion by **Chief Judge Katzmann**, agreed with Chief Judge Wood, with different judges emphasizing different arguments. Joined by Judges Livington and Riaggi, **Judge Lynch** wrote a dissenting opinion, arguing that the sex discrimination provisions in Title VII were aimed at helping integrate the workplace for women. "Discrimination against gay women and men, by contrast, was not on the table for public debate. In those dark, pre-Stonewall days, same-sex sexual relations were criminalized in nearly all states," and the federal government officially considered them mentally ill. Almost all gay people quivered in their closets, and even the ACLU (in 1964) accepted the constitutionality of their outlaw status.

"In light of that history, it is perhaps needless to say that there was no discussion of sexual orientation discrimination in the debates on Title VII of the Civil Rights Act. If some sexist legislators considered the inclusion of sex discrimination in the bill something of a joke, or perhaps a poison pill to make civil rights legislation even more controversial, evidently no one thought that adding sexual orientation to the list of forbidden categories was worth using even in that way."

Judge Lynch disavowed any reliance on "legislative history" and claimed only to be discerning the "original public meaning" of Title VII in 1964. "The words used in legislation are used for a reason. Legislation is adopted in response to perceived social problems, and legislators adopt the language that they do to address a social evil or accomplish a desirable goal. The words of the statute take meaning from that purpose, and the principles it adopts must be read in light of the problem it was enacted to address," which was ending job discrimination against women. * * * Simply put, discrimination based on sexual orientation is not the same thing as discrimination based on sex."

The Supreme Court took *Zarda* and two other cases for review and is expected to hand down an authoritative decision by June 2020. How should the Supreme Court resolve this issue? By the way, the Court *also* took review of a case where the lower court ruled that an employee fired on the basis of her transgender status (her presentation as a woman was inconsistent with the sex she was assigned at birth) was discriminated against because of her sex under Title VII. How should the Court rule in that case?

NOTES ON HIVELY, ZARDA, AND THEORIES
OF STATUTORY INTERPRETATION

Broadly speaking, the court of appeals judges started with different methodological approaches. Judges Sykes and Lynch applied what they considered to be Title VII's *original meaning*: the original, objective meaning (to a reasonable speaker) entailed by the statutory text, namely, discrimination "because of * * * sex." Judges Flaum and Ripple applied a *structural* approach: What does that language mean in light of the whole statute?[53] Judge Posner called for judicial *dynamic interpretation* of Title VII, whose original meaning, in his view, has been rendered obsolescent by changed social and workplace norms. Chief Judge Wood followed a *pragmatic approach* that considered statutory text, purpose, and precedents, as well as relevant constitutional norms and directives. As you ponder the cogency of each opinion in the case, consider, too, the cogency of the different theories of statutory interpretation. What follows are some materials not considered by these judges. See William Eskridge Jr., *Title VII's Statutory History and the Sex Discrimination Argument for LGBT Workplace Protections*, 127 Yale L.J. 322 (2017).

    1.   *Original Meaning of "Discriminate Because of * * * Sex."* Start with *Webster's* definition of "sex" on the eve of the 1964 Act:

- "[o]ne of the two divisions of organisms formed on the distinction of male and female," or *sex as biology*;

- "[t]he sphere of behavior dominated by the relations between male and female," or *sex as gender* (man=masculine, woman=feminine);

- "the whole sphere of behavior related even indirectly to the sexual functions and embracing all affectionate and pleasure-seeking conduct," or *sex as sexuality*.

Webster's New International Dictionary of the English Language 2296 (2d unabridged ed. 1961). Other pre-1964 dictionaries were to the same effect (Eskridge, *Title VII's Statutory History*, 338–39). How would Judge Sykes respond?

What does it mean to discriminate "because of" sex? Consistent with the common law, the Supreme Court had ruled that that statute is satisfied if the court finds "treatment of a person in a manner which but for that person's sex would be different." *Los Angeles Dept. of Water & Power v. Manhart*, 435 U.S. 702, 711 (1978), followed in *Univ. of Texas Sw. Med. Ctr. v. Nassar*, 570 U.S. 338, 346–47 (2013); cf. *Burrage v. United States*, 571 U.S. 204, 211–12 (2014). Construct an argument for Hively under this approach. How might the employer respond?

    2.   *Original Meaning: Terms of Art and the* Loving *Analogy.* Handed down shortly after Congress enacted Title VII, *McLaughlin v. Florida,* 379 U.S. 184 (1964) (striking down a state law creating greater penalties for different-race cohabitation), was the leading Supreme Court case on this issue in 1964. *Loving* was the leading case when Congress significantly expanded Title VII in the 1972 Amendments. As a matter of original *legal* meaning, firing a white employee dating a black woman because of prejudice against "racial mixing" would have been discrimination "because of race" in 1964 and in 1972, as the circuit courts have held, almost uniformly. In parallel fashion, why (then) would it not be discrimination "because of sex" to fire a female employee because she is dating a woman?

One response to the race analogy is that *Loving* was all about white supremacy, and so the Virginia law struck at the core of the Fourteenth Amendment—while homophobia

---

[53]   Judge Sykes did not believe Judge Flaum's whole act analysis was persuasive, because in her view there was zero discrimination because of sex. She did, however, consider the whole code—Congress's targeted terminology (barring discrimination because of "sexual orientation") in other statutes.

does not strike at the core of a statute aimed at sexism and patriarchy. Scholars have argued, however, that anti-gay harassment and other forms of discrimination are fundamentally grounded in sex-stereotypes and rigid gender roles. See Andrew Koppelman, *Why Discrimination Against Lesbians and Gay Men Is Sex Discrimination*, 69 N.Y.U.L. Rev. 197, 208 (1994); Brian Soucek, *Perceived Homosexuals: Looking Gay Enough for Title VII*, 63 Am. U.L. Rev. 715 (2014).

The same Congress that enacted the expansive 1972 Amendments to Title VII also passed the Equal Rights Amendment, which would have barred state discrimination "on account of sex." In 1970, Professor Paul Freund told Congress that, by analogy to *Loving,* the ERA would bar states from discriminating against same-sex couples in their marriage laws. In 1972, Senator Ervin argued that the nation's leading constitutional scholars agreed that the ERA would require state toleration of homosexuality and homosexual relationships. See Note, *The Legality of Homosexual Marriage*, 82 Yale L.J. 573, 574 (1973). This argument did not prevent Congress from passing the ERA, but it was persuasive to many state legislators and voters, who prevented the ratification of the ERA. Should the 1972 Amendments and the ERA debate "count" as sources of "original public meaning" (Sykes, Lynch) or an understanding of the text today (Wood, Katzmann)?

3. *Statutory Purpose.* One way of understanding the central purpose of Title VII is to eliminate sex-based stereotypes and other bars to a merit-based workplace for men as well as women. As § 701(k) puts it, Title VII demands that employers treat people who are "similar in their ability or inability to work" the same and bars dissimilar treatment because of the sex of the employee. In thinking about sex stereotypes, a distinction is useful. *Descriptive* stereotypes are assumptions about the different capabilities and limitations supposedly linked with one's sex. If an employer believes most women are emotional and passive and do not have the same commitment to work as men do, this descriptive gender stereotype will disadvantage women applying for supervisory positions requiring initiative and long hours. *Prescriptive* stereotypes are preferences about what roles and attitudes ought to be associated with each sex. If an employer believes that women ought to be passive and compliant to men's initiatives, this prescriptive gender stereotype will disadvantage women applying for supervisory positions. See Zachary Herz, Note, Price's *Progress: Sex Stereotyping and Its Potential for Antidiscrimination Law*, 124 Yale L.J. 396 (2014).

The original (1964) justifications for the sex discrimination provision in Title VII addressed both kinds of stereotyping. Women were disadvantaged in the workplace because employers believed that women's natural inclination was to be mothers and housekeepers (descriptive stereotyping) and that this was what a woman should be doing (prescriptive stereotyping). By its broad text and apparent legislative purpose, Title VII was supposed to make stereotype-based discrimination illegal. See Cary Franklin, *Inventing the "Traditional Concept" of Sex Discrimination*, 125 Harv. L. Rev. 1307 (2012).

During its deliberations in 1972, Congress's committees agreed with this understanding of the statutory purpose. Arguing for an expansion of Title VII to include local, state, and federal government employers and to empower the EEOC, committee reports understood that sex discrimination remained pervasive in the workplace, in large part because of traditional stereotypes that women's best role in life is as a wife and mother in the home. E.g., H.R. Rep. No. 92–238, at 4–5 (1971). In other words, the feminist understanding of Title VII may have been a building block upon which Congress constructed the 1972 Amendments, and was a central justification for exercising its

Fourteenth Amendment power to abrogate state immunity from lawsuits for sex discrimination in government workplaces. *Fitzpatrick v. Bitzer*, 427 U.S. 445, 455 (1976).

4. *Statutory Precedent and the 1991 Amendments. Hopkins* was important for Chief Judge Wood, because the Court in that case held that a purely prescriptive stereotype (this is what a woman should be like) could be the basis for a sex discrimination claim under Title VII. (Price Waterhouse assertedly denied Ann Hopkins partnership, in part because some partners considered her too butch; a friendly partner advised her to dress and act more "feminine," and go to "charm school.") Ivy Tech's discrimination against Professor Hively was, allegedly, grounded in a prescriptive stereotype that proper women date and marry men. *Hopkins* does not squarely control the result in *Hively*, however. Judge Sykes objects that the majority relies on a mere plurality opinion and reads the plurality to be consistent with her view that Title VII only addressed situations where employers separated men from women and treated one (biological) sex more favorably. Justice O'Connor's concurring opinion differed with the majority only with regard to the burden of proof in "mixed motive" cases and explicitly agreed with the plurality that "failure to conform to [sex] stereotypes" constituted discrimination under title VII. *Hopkins*, 490 U.S. at 272–73 (O'Connor).

Relevant to Judges Flaum and Ripple were the 1991 Amendments, which added § 703(m) to Title VII. Section 703(m) overrode the *Hopkins* treatment of "mixed motive" employer decisions with a more liberal burden of proof rule. The Supreme Court ruled that the 1991 Amendments "ratified" the Court's sexual harassment precedents, consistent with the goal of the 1991 Amendments to expand workplace protections. *Faragher v. City of Boca Raton*, 524 U.S. 775, 804 n.4 (1998). In its deliberations, Congress was well-informed about the sex-stereotyping holding of *Hopkins*. Legislators understood *Hopkins* to hold that "evidence of sex-stereotyping is sufficient to prove gender discrimination," H.R. Rep. 101–604, part 1, at 29 note 17 (1990), and thoroughly approved that holding. So the 1991 Amendments were both an "override" and an "underwrite" of *Hopkins*.

5. *Congressional Acquiescence and Rejected Proposals.* The Department of Justice filed an *amicus* brief with the Second Circuit that claimed the 1991 Congress had *acquiesced* in two pre-1991 circuit court decisions holding that employees had no Title VII claim for anti-gay discrimination, one pre-1991 circuit court decision holding that employees had no Title VII claim for gender identity discrimination, and one pre-1991 circuit court decision holding that gay employees had no claims for sex-stereotyping. Section 3(4) of the 1991 Amendments stated that the purpose of the Amendments was "to respond to recent *Supreme Court* [not isolated court of appeals] decisions by *expanding the scope* [not narrowing the scope] of relevant civil rights statutes in order to provide adequate protection to victims of discrimination [not to provide adequate protection to sex-stereotyping employers]." 105 Stat. 1071 (emphasis and brackets supplied).

The Department also claimed that dozens of bills had been proposed in Congress between 1974 and 2016 that would have barred sexual orientation and (after 2007) gender identity discrimination in the workplace. Congress's refusal to enact these proposals was evidence that "discriminate because of sex" does not include sexual orientation discrimination. This was an odd argument to make to a textualist Court. Not only is "subsequent legislative history" an unreliable guide to interpreting prior statutes, e.g., *Bruesewitz v. Wyeth LLC,* 562 U.S. 223, 240–43 (2011); *Pension Ben. Guar. Corp. v. LTV Corp.,* 496 U.S. 633, 650 (1990), but subsequent legislative inaction or, even worse, failure to consider later proposals is all but worthless. *E.g., Wright v. West*, 505 U.S. 277, 295 & n. 9 (1992) (plurality opinion).

Indeed, unknown to the Department, the Court had rejected such an argument in the context of Title VII. In *Oncale v. Sundowner Offshore Servs., Inc.*, 523 U.S. 75 (1998), an employee complained that the employer had ignored homosexual assaults upon him in the all-male workplace. The employer argued that Title VII provides no remedy for same-sex harassment, because it prohibits only sex and not sexual orientation discrimination. The employer's primary evidence was that, between 1974 and 1996, at least 37 bills had been proposed that would have prohibited workplace discrimination because of an employee's "sexual orientation" or "sexual preference" or "affectional orientation" etc., and Congress had acted on none of them. Brief for Respondents, at 5, 21–22, *Oncale*. Writing for a unanimous Court, Justice Scalia rejected that argument out of hand. He conceded that "male-on-male sexual harassment in the workplace was assuredly not the principal evil Congress was concerned with when it enacted Title VII. But statutory prohibitions often go beyond the principal evil to cover reasonably comparable evils, and it is ultimately the provisions of our laws rather than the principal concerns of our legislators by which we are governed." *Oncale*, 523 U.S. at 79.

6.   *Whole Code: Meaningful Variation.* In the last 21 years, as Judge Sykes and the Department argued, Congress has added "sexual orientation" or "gender identity" to several laws that barred discrimination on the basis of sex. For example, the Violence Against Women Reauthorization Act of 2013, P.L. 113–4, § 3(4), 127 Stat. 54, amended the earlier statute to prohibit funded programs and activities from discriminating "on the basis of actual or perceived race, color, religion, national origin, *sex, gender identity* * * *, sexual orientation*, or disability." 42 U.S.C. § 13925(b)(13)(A) (emphasis added). *See also* Patient Protection and Affordable Care Act of 2010, P.L. 111–148, § 5306(a)(3), 124 Stat. 119, 626; Mathew Shepard and James Byrd Hate Crimes Prevention Act of 2009, P.L. 111–84, §§ 4704(a)(1)(C), 4704(a), 123 Stat. 2835, 2837, 2839; Higher Education Amendments of 1998, Pub. L. No. 105–244, § 486(e)(1)(A), 112 Stat. 1581, 1743. This was one of Judge Sykes's strongest arguments.

The Supreme Court has said, however, that drafting inconsistencies, even within a single statute, should not be deployed to undermine the statutory plan. E.g., *Gomez-Perez v. Potter*, 553 U.S. 474, 486 (2008). And an insistence on exact consistency between different statutes enacted by different Congresses in different decades has not been the basis for the Court to decline to follow the plain meaning of a statute that is itself internally consistent. "[N]egative implications raised by disparate provisions" might, at best, be weighed in those instances in which the relevant statutory provisions were "considered simultaneously when the language raising the implication was inserted." *Lindh v. Murphy*, 521 U.S. 320, 330 (1997), followed in *Gomez-Perez*. The Congress that debated and enacted the Civil Rights Act in 1963–64 was the same Congress that enacted the Equal Pay Act of 1963 ("EPA"), P.L. 88–38, 77 Stat. 56. The EPA prohibited employers from discriminating "on the basis of sex" by paying wages to employees "at a rate less than the rate at which he pays wages to *employees of the opposite sex*" for similar work. *Id.* § 3 (emphasis added), codified at 29 U.S.C. § 206(d)(1). The Court has held that employees enjoy a much broader scope of protection under Title VII than under the EPA. *County of Washington v. Gunther*, 452 U.S. 161 (1981).

At the same time Congress was considering amendments to Title VII, it enacted the Americans with Disabilities Act of 1990 (ADA), P.L. 101–336, 104 Stat. 376. Section

511(b) excluded from the ADA's definition of "disability," which triggers the anti-discrimination protections, "homosexuality and bisexuality." 42 U.S.C. § 12211(a). The next year, Congress enacted the 1991 Amendments that significantly revised Title VII. Under the Department of Justice's concept of meaningful variation, is it relevant, or significant, that Congress in 1991 failed to revise its definition of "sex" to specifically exclude "homosexuality and bisexuality," terms that it had just used in the ADA?

On the whole, the new textualism is not as helpful to Judge Sykes and the Department of Justice as one might expect—but perhaps legal process theory would come to their rescue? Construct an argument based upon Hart and Sacks and Komesar that would support the employers in the LGBT rights cases before the Supreme Court.

CHAPTER 6

INTRINSIC DOCTRINES OF STATUTORY INTERPRETATION

■ ■ ■

The previous chapter introduced you to the history of statutory interpretation in the United States and to the major theories that have been debated (textualism old and new, intentionalism and imaginative reconstruction, purposivism and dynamic theories). The next two chapters turn to the doctrines that underlie these theories.

Chapter 6 examines what we call intrinsic doctrines. These are doctrines that derive their authority and persuasiveness from the language, structure, and interpretive presumptions emanating from or accompanying the statutory text. In Chapter 7, we explore doctrines that derive their persuasive authority from sources extrinsic to the statutory text, such as common law, legislative history in its broadest sense, and related statutes.

In this chapter, Section 1 considers two major interpretive resources grounded in statutory text: *ordinary meaning rules*, including reliance on *dictionaries*; and *language canons of statutory construction*, focusing on maxims of word association and also grammar canons. Courts have always examined words for their ordinary meaning, but while judges rarely relied on dictionaries as an interpretive aid before 1980, they now do so on a more regular basis. Language canons have been a bedrock of Anglo-American interpretation for centuries. Although they were de-emphasized in federal courts after the New Deal, the canons remained critically important at the state level and have made a federal comeback since the mid-1980s. Section 1 introduces you to the ordinary meaning approach and to many of the language canons.

Section 2 considers another textually-grounded canonical resource, *structural canons*. Courts often examine statutory terms and phrases in relation to how those terms or phrases are used elsewhere in the same statute, in order to discern coherent or distinctive meanings from the statute taken as a whole. These structural canons include principally the whole act rule and its corollaries, the rule against surplusage, and the presumptions of consistent usage and meaningful variation. Although courts have long relied on these structural canons, it is less clear that legislators and their staffs regard them as sound rules when drafting statutory text. And there has been some recent pushback from judges crediting the virtues of repetition or redundancy, as evidenced in counter-presumptions such as the belt-and-suspenders canon.

Finally, Section 3 addresses canons of interpretation that are based on substantive policy values rather than conventional understandings of language. Unlike their linguistic and structural counterparts, *substantive canons* generally derive from policy positions articulated by courts. Most often, they reflect presumptions regarding how statutory text should be harmonized with judicially perceived constitutional priorities, pre-enactment common law practices, or specific statutorily-based policies. For example, the "rule of lenity" is based in part on principles of fair notice; it presumes that criminal statutes do not outlaw behavior unless the activity clearly comes within the sweep of the statutes. Section 3 focuses on two principal substantive canons: the rule of lenity and constitutional avoidance. Section 3 also examines the rather intense theoretical debates over the textual and substantive canons and provides the perspective of state legislatures that have codified certain canons to guide judicial interpretation for all statutes.

1. ORDINARY MEANING RULES AND LANGUAGE CANONS

There are a good many rules of thumb for interpreting statutes. Typically, courts will assume that the legislature uses words in their ordinary sense: What would the words convey to the "ordinary" or "reasonable" reader? To answer this question, judges have often relied on their own linguistic experience or intuition to decide the most reasonable meaning of the words, given the context in which they are being used and applied. Starting in the 1980s, courts have increasingly identified ordinary meaning by invoking specific interpretive resources, especially dictionaries.[1]

In addition, courts seek to understand statutory text by relying on "maxims," "canons," or "principles" of construction—rules that are said to enable interpreters to draw inferences from the legislature's choice of certain words rather than others, or its configuration of those words in a given statutory provision, or the relationship between those words and text found in other parts of the same statute. Most of the nineteenth century English and American treatises on statutory interpretation were organized around the canons, and the leading doctrinal compilation today (a descendant of an 1891 treatise) is an exhaustive canon-by-canon tour. Sutherland, *Statutes and Statutory Construction* (7th ed., Norman Singer ed.) (hereinafter referred to as Sutherland).[2] Many states have codified the traditional canons in their state codes. See, e.g., Minn. Stat. § 645; Pennsylvania Statutory Construction Act, 1 Pa. Consol. Stat. §§ 1921–28 (hereinafter "Pa. Stat. Constr. Act"). See also 1 U.S.C. §§ 1–8 (codification of word-meaning canons).

Consider the following problem as an introduction.

---

[1]   See Ellen Aprill, *The Law of the Word: Dictionary Shopping in the Supreme Court*, 30 Ariz. St. L.J. 275 (1998); Jeffrey Kirchmeier & Samuel Thumma, *Scaling the Lexicon Fortress: The United States Supreme Court's Use of Dictionaries in the Twenty-First Century*, 94 Marq. L. Rev. 77 (2010); Lawrence Solan, *When Judges Use the Dictionary*, 68 Am. Speech 50 (1993); Samuel Thumma & Jeffrey Kirchmeier, *The Lexicon Has Become a Fortress: The United States Supreme Court's Use of Dictionaries*, 47 Buff. L. Rev. 227 (1999); Note, *Looking It Up: Dictionaries and Statutory Interpretation*, 107 Harv. L. Rev. 1437 (1994).

[2]   Sutherland is the leading American treatise. Also valuable as reference works are leading treatises in the United Kingdom, see D. Bailey & L. Norbury, *Bennion on Statutory Interpretation* (7th ed. 2019), and P. St.J. Langan, *Maxwell on the Interpretation of Statutes* (12th ed. 1969); Canada, see Ruth Sullivan, *Sullivan on the Construction of Statutes* (6th ed. 2014); Ruth Sullivan, *Statutory Interpretation* (3d ed. 2016); Australia, see Donald Gifford, *Statutory Interpretation* (1990), and D.C. Pearce & R.S. Geddes, *Statutory Interpretation in Australia* (8th ed. 2014); New Zealand, see Jim Evans, *Statutory Interpretation: Problems of Communication* (1988); and South Africa, see G.E. Devenish, *Interpretation of Statutes* (1992). For a compendium surveying the practice in civil law countries as well, see *Interpreting Statutes: A Comparative Study* (D. Neil MacCormick & Robert Summers eds., 1991).

PROBLEM: *THE* NO VEHICLES IN THE PARK *STATUTE*

Problem 6-1. In the wake of an accident in which a motorcycle speeding through Pierre Trudeau Park ran over and killed an elderly gentleman, the City Council enacted the following statute in 1980:

> Sec. 1.   The Council finds that vehicles create safety problems when they are operated in parks and further finds that the best solution is to ban any and all vehicles from all municipal parks.

> Sec. 2.   No vehicles of any kind shall be allowed in any municipal park. Any person who brings or drives a vehicle into one of these parks shall be guilty of a misdemeanor, which may be punished by a fine not exceeding $500 or by a two-day incarceration in the municipal jail, or both.

> Sec. 3.   "Vehicle" for purposes of this law means any mechanism for conveying a person from one place to another, including automobiles, trucks, motorcycles, and motor scooters. *Provided that*, bicycles shall be allowed in the park, so long as they are being pushed or carried and not ridden.

After a decade of spotty enforcement, a new constable, Barney Fife, adopts a strict, no-tolerance enforcement policy. In 1996, he arrests (a) a 13-year-old boy riding a skateboard through the park; (b) a mother pushing a baby carriage in the park; and (c) a 6-year-old girl riding her tricycle in the park. All three "perps" (and the parents of the child perps) challenge their arrests, on the ground that the statute does not apply to their conduct. How should the City Magistrate rule?

A. ORDINARY MEANING AND DICTIONARIES

1. Ordinary and Technical Meaning of Words

The starting point of statutory interpretation is to *read* the statute carefully. Judges often rely on their own common sense analysis to determine the ordinary meaning of statutory words. Thus, for example, in *Watson v. United States*, 552 U.S. 74 (2007), the Court held that someone who trades his drugs for a gun does not "use" a firearm "during and in relation to a drug trafficking crime" so as to qualify for a mandatory minimum sentence. 552 U.S. at 83. Justice Souter, writing for the majority, observed that absent a statutory definition, "the meaning of the verb 'use' has to turn on the language as we normally speak it," adding that "[t]he Government may say that a person "uses" a firearm simply by receiving it in a barter transaction, but no one else would." *Id.* at 79. Typically, courts will assume that the legislature uses words in their ordinary sense: What would these words convey to the "ordinary" or "reasonable" reader? Ordinary meaning should be distinguished from literal meaning or strict construction; the latter connotes a narrow understanding of words used, while the former connotes the everyday understanding.

Linguists suggest that the interpreter start with the *prototypical* meaning of statutory words.[3] What is the core idea associated with a word or phrase? For example, this was the approach implicitly followed by Justice Brennan in *Weber*, the

---

[3]   See Lawrence Solan, *Learning Our Limits: The Decline of Textualism in Statutory Cases*, 1997 Wis. L. Rev. 235, 270–75 (explaining linguists' "prototype" theory and applying it to several statutory interpretation cases).

affirmative action case (Chapter 1, § 2(B)): although some dictionaries define "discriminate" broadly enough to include any kind of differentiation, the core or prototypical use of the word requires some invidious intent. Thus, we do not say we "discriminate" against pears if we prefer peaches, nor (according to Brennan) do we say we "discriminate" against a minority if we give him a helping hand to counterbalance what we believe is an inferior starting point because of preexisting prejudice or stereotyping. Ordinary meaning, therefore, might be associated with prototypical meaning. This idea usually supports cautious, or restrictive, readings of statutes. See, e.g., *Holy Trinity Church* (Chapter 5, § 1) (confining "labor or service of any kind" to manual work); *Canada (Attorney General) v. Mossop*, [1991] 1 F.C. 18, 34 (Fed. Ct.), aff'd, [1993] 1 S.C.R. 554 (Can. Sup. Ct.) (applying the "core meaning" of "family" to exclude same-sex partnerships).

What if the statute is an old one? In that event, judges sometimes consult dictionaries and other evidence from the era in which the statute was enacted. For example, the Supreme Court in *St. Francis College v. Al-Khazraji*, 481 U.S. 604 (1987), interpreted the Civil Rights Act of 1866 to apply to discrimination against a person of Arab ancestry. Defendant had argued that any discrimination against an ethnic Arab was not actionable, because the statute only required the same protections as are "enjoyed by white citizens" and Arabs are ethnographically Caucasian. The Court invoked nineteenth-century dictionaries and encyclopedias to demonstrate that defendant's conception of race was not the one held in the nineteenth century, which viewed different ethnic "stock" and family "lineage" as different "races." Thus, these sources referred to Finns, Greeks, Basques, Arabs, Norwegians, Jews, and Hungarians as identifiable "races." For another example, see *Cook County v. United States*, 538 U.S. 119, 132 (2003), interpreting the False Claims Act of 1863.

In addition to special meanings that words may have had historically, words often have meanings limited to parlance in a trade, academic discipline, or technical area. Where the statute itself deals with a technical, specialized subject, courts tend to adopt the specialized meaning of words used in the statute, unless that leads to an absurd result. For a hoary, and perhaps amusing, example of this maxim, see *Nix v. Hedden*, 149 U.S. 304, 306–07 (1893). This was an action to recover back duties on tomatoes, paid under protest by the plaintiff pursuant to the Tariff Act of 1883. The statute imposed a high duty on "[v]egetables in their natural state, or in salt or brine" while exempting "[f]ruits, green, ripe, or dried." At trial, counsel for plaintiff and defendant read into the record multiple dictionary definitions of certain words— including "fruit," "vegetables," "tomato," "eggplant," "pepper," "cucumber," "squash,", "bean," and "pea." Two expert witnesses testified that the terms "fruit" and "vegetables" did not have any special meaning in trade or commerce different from what appeared in dictionaries. The Supreme Court opted for ordinary rather than technical meaning:

> There being no evidence that the words "fruit" and "vegetables" have acquired any special meaning in trade or commerce, they must receive their ordinary meaning. Of that meaning the court is bound to take judicial notice, as it does in regard to all words in our own tongue; and upon such a

question dictionaries are admitted, not as evidence, but only as aids to the memory and understanding of the court.

> Botanically speaking, tomatoes are the fruit of a vine, just as are cucumbers, squashes, beans and peas. But in the common language of the people, whether sellers or consumers of provisions, all these are vegetables, which are grown in kitchen gardens, and which, whether eaten cooked or raw, are, like potatoes, carrots, parsnips, turnips, beets, cauliflower, cabbage, celery and lettuce, usually served at dinner in, with, or after the soup, fish or meats which constitute the principal part of the repast, and not, like fruits generally, as dessert.   *fruits = generally dessert !*

See also *Zuni Pub. Sch. Dist. v. Dep't of Educ.*, 550 U.S. 81, 90–93 (2007) (deferring to the experts when construing technical statutory language for determining whether a state aid program "equalizes expenditures").

A related maxim is this: "Where Congress uses terms that have accumulated settled meaning under either equity or the common law, a court must infer, unless the statute otherwise dictates, that Congress means to incorporate the established meaning of these terms." *NLRB v. Amax Coal Co.*, 453 U.S. 322, 329 (1981); accord *Scheidler v. NOW*, 537 U.S. 393, 402 (2003); *United States v. Wells*, 519 U.S. 482, 491 (1997); *Cmty. for Creative Non-Violence v. Reid*, 490 U.S. 730, 739 (1989). Compare *Jodrey Estate v. Nova Scotia*, [1980] 2 S.C.R. 774 (Can. Sup. Ct.) (reflecting the Canadian preference for following ordinary rather than technical meanings).

2.   The Rising Status of Dictionaries

In recent years, Supreme Court Justices have consulted dictionaries with increased regularity when construing key statutory words or phrases.[4] The Court has relied on dictionary definitions to help determine the meaning of technical legal terms such as "quorum," *New Process Steel L.P. v. NLRB*, 560 U.S. 674 (2010), and "license," *Chamber of Commerce v. Whiting*, 131 S.Ct. 1968 (2011), as well as more ordinary words or phrases like "oppose," *Crawford v. Metro. Gov't of Nashville & Davidson Co.*, 555 U.S. 271 (2009), or "because of," *Gross v. FBL Fin. Servs., Inc.*, 557 U.S. 167 (2009). In these and numerous other decisions, the justices have disagreed over which words need to be defined, which dictionary to use, which definition within a given dictionary is applicable, and whether dictionary definitions are relevant at all.

TANIGUCHI V. KAN PACIFIC SAIPAN, LTD.

Supreme Court of the United States 2012.
566 U.S. 560, 132 S.Ct. 1997, 182 L.Ed.2d 903.

[2012 – SCOTUS] Taniguchi V. Kan Pacific.

ALITO

JUSTICE ALITO delivered the opinion of the Court.

The costs that may be awarded to prevailing parties in lawsuits brought in federal court are set forth in 28 U.S.C. § 1920. The Court Interpreters Act amended that statute to include "compensation of interpreters." § 1920(6). The question presented in this case is whether "compensation of interpreters" covers the cost of

---

4   See sources collected in note 1, *supra*.

costs to prevailing parties. Include compensation of Interpreters

[margin handwritten notes: Cost of interpreters / includes cost translating docs?]

translating documents. Because the ordinary meaning of the word "interpreter" is a person who translates orally from one language to another, we hold that "compensation of interpreters" is limited to the cost of oral translation and does not include the cost of document translation.

[margin handwritten note: Limited to oral ≠ written translation]

[I.　Taniguchi, a professional baseball player in Japan, was injured when his leg broke through a wooden deck during a tour of respondent's resort property. In preparing its defense, respondent paid to have various documents translated from Japanese to English. The District Court granted summary judgment in respondent's favor, and subsequently awarded respondent the costs associated with these written translations under § 1920(6). The court explained that interpreter services cannot be separated into 'translation' and 'interpretation,' and that costs for document translation qualify as compensation of an interpreter.]

[margin handwritten note: interpreter ≠ defined in [relevant] statute]

[II-B.] To determine whether the item "compensation of interpreters" includes costs for document translation, we must look to the meaning of "interpreter." That term is not defined in the Court Interpreters Act or in any other relevant statutory provision. When a term goes undefined in a statute, we give the term its ordinary meaning. The question here is: What is the ordinary meaning of "interpreter"?

[margin handwritten note: 1 Lang → another / translates orally from]

Many dictionaries in use when Congress enacted the Court Interpreters Act in 1978 defined "interpreter" as one who translates spoken, as opposed to written, language. The American Heritage Dictionary, for instance, defined the term as "[o]ne who translates orally from one language into another." American Heritage Dictionary 685 (1978). The Scribner-Bantam English Dictionary defined the related word "interpret" as "to translate orally." Scribner-Bantam English Dictionary 476 (1977). Similarly, the Random House Dictionary defined the intransitive form of "interpret" as "to translate what is *said* in a foreign language." Random House Dictionary of the English Language 744 (1973) (emphasis added). And, notably, the Oxford English Dictionary defined "interpreter" as "[o]ne who translates languages," but then divided that definition into two senses: "a. [a] translator of books or writings," which it designated as obsolete, and "b. [o]ne who translates the communications of persons speaking different languages; *spec.* one whose office it is to do so orally in the presence of the persons; a dragoman." 5 Oxford English Dictionary 416 (1933); see also Concise Oxford Dictionary of Current English 566 (6th ed. 1976) ("One who interprets; one whose office it is to translate the words of persons speaking different languages, esp. orally in their presence"); Chambers Twentieth Century Dictionary 686 (1973) ("one who translates orally for the benefit of two or more parties speaking different languages: . . . a translator (*obs.*)").

Pre-1978 legal dictionaries also generally defined the words "interpreter" and "interpret" in terms of oral translation. The then-current edition of Black's Law Dictionary, for example, defined "interpreter" as "[a] person sworn at a trial to interpret the evidence of a foreigner . . . to the court," and it defined "interpret" in relevant part as "to translate orally from one tongue to another." Black's Law Dictionary 954, 953 (rev. 4th ed. 1968); see also W. Anderson, A Dictionary of Law 565 (1888) ("One who translates the testimony of witnesses speaking a foreign tongue, for the benefit of the court and jury"); 1 B. Abbott, Dictionary of Terms and Phrases Used in American or English Jurisprudence 639 (1878) ("one who restates the testimony of a witness testifying in a foreign tongue, to the court and jury, in their language"). But see Ballentine's Law Dictionary 655, 654 (3d ed. 1969) (defining "interpreter" as "[o]ne who interprets, particularly one who interprets words written or spoken in a foreign language," and "interpret" as "to translate from a foreign language").

Against these authorities, respondent relies almost exclusively on Webster's Third New International Dictionary (hereinafter Webster's Third). The version of that dictionary in print when Congress enacted the Court Interpreters Act defined "interpreter" as "one that translates; *esp*: a person who translates orally for parties conversing in different tongues." Webster's Third 1182 (1976).[2] The sense divider *esp* (for especially) indicates that the most common meaning of the term is one "who translates orally," but that meaning is subsumed within the more general definition "one that translates." See 12,000 Words: A Supplement to Webster's Third 15a (1986) (explaining that *esp* "is used to introduce the most common meaning included in the more general preceding definition"). For respondent, the general definition suffices to establish that the term "interpreter" ordinarily includes persons who translate the written word. Explaining that "the word 'interpreter' can reasonably encompass a 'translator,'" the Court of Appeals reached the same conclusion. We disagree.

That a definition is broad enough to encompass one sense of a word does not establish that the word is *ordinarily* understood in that sense. The fact that the definition of "interpreter" in Webster's Third has a sense divider denoting the most common usage suggests that other usages, although acceptable, might not be common or ordinary. It is telling that all the dictionaries cited above defined "interpreter" at the time of the statute's enactment as including persons who translate orally, but only a handful defined the word broadly enough to encompass translators of written material. Although the Oxford English Dictionary, one of the most authoritative on the English language, recognized that "interpreter" *can* mean one who translates writings, it expressly designated that meaning as obsolete. Were the meaning of "interpreter" that respondent advocates truly common or ordinary, we would expect to see more support for that meaning. We certainly would not expect to see it designated as obsolete in the Oxford English Dictionary. Any definition of a word that is absent from many dictionaries and is deemed obsolete in others is hardly a common or ordinary meaning.

Based on our survey of the relevant dictionaries, we conclude that the ordinary or common meaning of "interpreter" does not include those who translate writings. Instead, we find that an interpreter is normally understood as one who translates orally from one language to another. This sense of the word is far more natural. As the Seventh Circuit put it: "Robert Fagles made famous translations into English of the *Iliad*, the *Odyssey*, and the *Aeneid*, but no one would refer to him as an English-language 'interpreter' of these works."

---

[2]   A handful of other contemporaneous dictionaries used a similar formulation. See Funk & Wagnalls New Comprehensive International Dictionary of the English Language 665 (1977) ("One who interprets or translates; specifically, one who serves as oral translator between people speaking different languages"); 1 World Book Dictionary 1103 (C. Barnhart & R. Barnhart eds. 1977) ("a person whose business is translating, especially orally, from a foreign language"); Cassell's English Dictionary 617 (4th ed. 1969) ("One who interprets, esp. one employed to translate orally to persons speaking a foreign language").

To be sure, the word "interpreter" can encompass persons who translate documents, but because that is not the ordinary meaning of the word, it does not control unless the context in which the word appears indicates that it does. Nothing in the Court Interpreters Act or in § 1920, however, even hints that Congress intended to go beyond the ordinary meaning of "interpreter" and to embrace the broadest possible meaning that the definition of the word can bear. * * *

Because the ordinary meaning of "interpreter" is someone who translates orally from one language to another, we hold that the category "compensation of interpreters" in § 1920(6) does not include costs for document translation. * * *

JUSTICE GINSBURG, with whom JUSTICE BREYER and JUSTICE SOTOMAYOR join, dissenting.

To be comprehended by the parties, the witnesses, and the court, expression in foreign languages must be translated into English. Congress therefore provided, in 28 U.S.C. § 1920(6), that the prevailing party may recoup compensation paid to "interpreters." The word "interpreters," the Court emphasizes, commonly refers to translators of oral speech. But as the Court acknowledges, "interpreters" is more than occasionally used to encompass those who translate written speech as well. See Webster's Third New International Dictionary of the English Language 1182 (1976) (hereinafter Webster's) (defining "interpreter" as "one that translates; *esp*: a person who translates orally for parties conversing in different tongues"); Black's Law Dictionary 895 (9th ed. 2009) (defining "interpreter" as a "person who translates, esp. orally, from one language to another"); Ballentine's Law Dictionary 655 (3d ed. 1969) (defining "interpreter" as "[o]ne who interprets, particularly one who interprets words written or spoken in a foreign language").

In short, employing the word "interpreters" to include translators of written as well as oral speech, if not "the most common usage," is at least an "acceptable" usage. Moreover, the word "interpret" is generally understood to mean "to explain or tell the meaning of: translate into intelligible or familiar language or terms," while "translate" commonly means "to turn into one's own or another language." Webster's 1182, 2429. See also Random House Dictionary of the English Language 744, 1505 (1973) (defining the transitive verb "interpret" as, *inter alia*, "to translate," and "translate" as "to turn (something written or spoken) from one language into another").

Notably, several federal district court decisions refer to translators of written documents as "interpreters." *E.g.*, *United States v. Prado-Cervantez*, 2011 WL 4691934 (D. Kan. 2011) ("Standby counsel should also be prepared to arrange for interpreters to interpret or translate documents when necessary for defendant."); *Mendoza v. Ring*, 2008 WL 2959848 (C.D. Ill. 2008) ("The interpreter is also directed to translate filings by the plaintiff from Spanish to English. The original and translated versions will be docketed."). So do a number of state statutes. *E.g.*, Cal. Gov't. Code Ann. § 26806(a) (West 2008) ("[T]he clerk of the court may employ as many foreign language interpreters as may be necessary . . . to translate documents intended for filing in any civil or criminal action. . . ."). * * *

In practice, federal trial courts have awarded document translation costs in cases spanning several decades. See, *e.g.*, *Raffold Process Corp. v. Castanea Paper*

Co., 25 F. Supp. 593, 594 (W.D. Pa. 1938). Before the Court Interpreters Act added § 1920(6) to the taxation of costs statute in 1978, district courts awarded costs for document translation under § 1920(4), which allowed taxation of "[f]ees for exemplification and copies of papers," or under § 1920's predecessor, 28 U.S.C. § 830 (1925 ed.). Pre-1978, district courts also awarded costs for oral translation of witness testimony. See, *e.g.*, *Kaiser Indus. Corp. v. McLouth Steel Corp.*, 50 F.R.D. 5, 11 (E.D. Mich. 1970). Nothing in the Court Interpreters Act, a measure intended to expand access to interpretation services, indicates a design to eliminate the availability of costs awards for document translation. See S. Rep. No. 95–569, at 4 (1977) (hereinafter S. Rep.) ("The committee . . . feels the time has come to provide by statute for the provision of and access to qualified certified interpreters, for a broader spectrum of people than the present law allows."). Post-1978, rulings awarding document translation costs under § 1920(6) indicate the courts' understanding both that the term "interpreter" can readily encompass oral and written translation, and that Congress did not otherwise instruct. I agree that context should guide the determination whether § 1920(6) is most sensibly read to encompass persons who translate documents. But the context key for me is the practice of federal courts both before and after § 1920(6)'s enactment.

The purpose of translation, after all, is to make relevant foreign-language communication accessible to the litigants and the court. See S. Rep., at 1 (The Court Interpreters Act is intended "to insure that all participants in our Federal courts can meaningfully take part."). Documentary evidence in a foreign language, no less than oral statements, must be translated to equip the parties to present their case clearly and the court to decide the merits intelligently. And it is not extraordinary that what documents say, more than what witnesses testify, may make or break a case. * * *

In short, § 1920(6)'s prescription on "interpreters" is not so clear as to leave no room for interpretation. Given the purpose served by translation and the practice prevailing in district courts, there is no good reason to exclude from taxable costs payments for placing written words within the grasp of parties, jurors, and judges. * * *

NOTE ON DICTIONARY USE IN TANIGUCHI

A relatively recent article examined the Court's use of dictionaries from 1986 to 2011, and found that the justices almost always rely on one or at most two dictionaries to define a particular statutory term. See James Brudney & Lawrence Baum, *Oasis or Mirage: The Supreme Court's Thirst for Dictionaries in the Rehnquist and Roberts Eras*, 55 William & Mary L. Rev. 483 (2013). Justice Alito for the majority in *Taniguchi* surveys fourteen dictionaries to settle on the ordinary meaning of "interpreter." Is this analysis more persuasive than if the majority had looked to only one or two dictionaries? Why or why not?

Consider whether "interpreter" in § 1920(6) is being used in an ordinary meaning sense or instead has a more specialized connotation. If legal dictionaries were deemed more relevant than general dictionaries, would this alter the balance of lexicographic evidence produced by the majority?

Unlike general dictionaries that rely on citation files or electronic corpora to identify word usages, legal dictionaries such as Black's rely on judicial opinions as their primary citation source. See Ellen Aprill, *The Law of the Word: Dictionary Shopping in the Supreme Court*, 30 Ariz. St. L.J. 275, 303–10 (1998) (discussing development of American law dictionaries from mid-nineteenth century to present). Justice Alito invokes the definition of "interpreter" from the fourth edition of Black's Law Dictionary, published in 1968, which referenced exclusively oral translation. The definition in Black's eighth edition (2004) is broader, referencing "a person who translates, esp. orally, from one language to another." Is it appropriate to infer that this broadening reflects an appreciation for developing district court practices, given that Black's derives its definitions from a review of court decisions?

Who is the primary intended audience for the statutory section authorizing costs that is at issue in *Taniguchi*? Is the nature of the statute's intended audience relevant to the type of dictionary a court should use when seeking to understand the ordinary meaning of "interpreter"? Also, what was Congress's evident purpose in enacting the 1978 Court Interpreters Act? How, if at all, should that purpose influence our understanding of the contested term in this case? Assuming Justice Ginsburg's dissent accurately summarizes past federal court practice, does it matter that district court judges had awarded document translation and oral translation costs for many years prior to the 1978 Act?

STATUTORY PREFACE TO THE *COSTELLO* CASE

Immigration Act of February 5, 1917, Pub. L. No. 64–301, ch. 29, § 8, 39 Stat. 874, 880 (repealed).

Section 8.

That any person, including the master, agent, owner, or cosignee of any vessel, who shall bring into or land in the United States, by vessel or otherwise, or shall attempt, by himself or through another, to bring into or land in the United States, by vessel or otherwise, or shall conceal or harbor, or attempt to conceal or harbor, or assist or abet another to conceal or harbor in any place, including any building, vessel, railway car, conveyance, or vehicle, any alien not duly admitted by an immigrant inspector or not lawfully entitled to enter or to reside within the United States under the terms of this Act, shall be deemed guilty of a misdemeanor, and upon conviction therefor shall be punished. . . .

Immigration and Nationality Act of June 27, 1952, Pub. L. No. 82–411, Title IV § 274(a), 66 Stat. 163, 228–29 (codified at 8 U.S.C. § 1324(a)).

Section 1324.   *Bringing in and harboring certain aliens.*

(a) Criminal penalties

(1)(A) Any person who—* * *

(iii) knowing or in reckless disregard of the fact that an alien has come to, entered, or remains in the United States in violation of law, conceals, harbors, or shields from detection, or attempts to conceal, harbor, or shield from detection, such alien in any place, including any building or any means of transportation; * * *

(v)(I) engages in any conspiracy to commit any of the preceding acts, or

(II) aids or abets the commission of any of the preceding acts, shall be punished as provided in subparagraph (B).

UNITED STATES V. COSTELLO

United States Court of Appeals for the Seventh Circuit, 2012.
666 F.3d 1040.

POSNER, CIRCUIT JUDGE:

[The defendant was convicted under a federal law that punishes anyone who "knowing or in reckless disregard of the fact that an alien has come to, entered, or remains in the United States in violation of law, conceals, harbors or shields from detection [or attempts to do any of these things], such alien in any place, including any building or any means of transportation." The Government relied on dictionary definitions of the word "harbors" to argue that the defendant violated the act when she let her boyfriend live with her for seven months after he illegally reentered the United States. Judge Posner was skeptical.]

The government argues that "to harbor" just means to house a person, a meaning that it claims to derive from dictionaries that were in print in 1952 or today; surprisingly the government omits dictionaries that were current in 1917, when concealing and harboring aliens were added to the prohibition of smuggling aliens into this country. Immigration Act of February 5, 1917, Pub. L. No. 64–301, ch. 29, § 8, 39 Stat. 874, 880 (repealed). In the Immigration and Nationality Act of June 27, 1952, Pub. L. No. 82–411, Title IV, § 274(a), 66 Stat. 163, 228–29, Congress added penalties for the concealing and harboring offenses, in response to a Supreme Court decision, *United States v. Evans*, 333 U.S. 483 (1948), that had held that the 1917 Act had somehow failed to specify penalties for those offenses.

The actual definition of "to harbor" that the government has found in these dictionaries and urges us to adopt is "to shelter," which is not synonymous with "to provide a place to stay." "To shelter" has an aura of protectiveness, as in taking "shelter" from a storm. To shelter is to provide a refuge. "Sheltering" doesn't seem the right word for letting your boyfriend live with you. We have not scoured dictionaries current in 1917 or 1952, but note for what it's worth that the 1910 edition of Black's Law Dictionary defines "to harbor" as: "To receive clandestinely and without lawful authority a person for the purpose of so concealing him that another having a right to the lawful custody of such person shall be deprived of the same. A distinction has been taken, in some decisions, between 'harbor' and 'conceal.' A person may be convicted of harboring a slave, although he may not have concealed her." Henry Campbell Black, A Law Dictionary 561 (2d ed. 1910) (citations omitted).

So the government's reliance on the dictionary definition of "harboring" is mistaken, though a point of greater general importance is that dictionaries must be used as sources of statutory meaning only with great caution. "Of course it is true that the words used, even in their literal sense, are the primary, and ordinarily the most reliable, source of interpreting the meaning of any writing: be it a statute, a contract, or anything else. But it is one of the surest indexes of a mature and developed jurisprudence not to make a fortress out of the dictionary; but to remember that statutes always have some purpose or object to accomplish, whose sympathetic and imaginative discovery is the surest guide to their meaning." *Cabell v. Markham*, 148 F.2d 737, 739 (2d Cir. 1945) (L. Hand, J.). "[T]he choice among meanings [of words in statutes] must have a footing more solid than a dictionary—which is a museum of words, an historical catalog rather than a means to decode the work of legislatures." Frank H. Easterbrook, *Text, History, and Structure in Statutory Interpretation*, 17 Harv. J.L. & Public Policy 61, 67 (1994). * * *

Dictionary definitions are acontextual, whereas the meaning of sentences depends critically on context, including all sorts of background understandings. A sign in a park that says "Keep off the grass" is not properly interpreted to forbid the grounds crew to cut the grass. * * * We doubt that the government would argue that a hospital emergency room that takes in a desperately ill person whom the hospital staff knows to be an illegal alien would be guilty of harboring, although it fits the government's definition of the word.

A Google search (conducted on December 13, 2011, rather than in 1952 or 1917, but the government implies by its reliance on current dictionaries that the word means the same today as on the date of the statute's enactment, an implication consistent with Black's Law Dictionary) of several terms in which the word "harboring" appears—a search based on the supposition that the number of hits per term is a rough index of the frequency of its use—reveals the following:

"harboring fugitives": 50,800 hits

"harboring enemies": 4,730 hits

"harboring refugees": 4,820 hits

"harboring victims": 114 hits

"harboring flood victims": 0 hits

"harboring victims of disasters": 0 hits

"harboring victims of persecution": 0 hits

"harboring guests": 184 hits

"harboring friends": 256 hits (but some involve harboring Quakers—"Friends," viewed in colonial New England as dangerous heretics)

"harboring Quakers": 3,870 hits

"harboring Jews": 19,100 hits

It is apparent from these results that "harboring," as the word is actually used, has a connotation—which "sheltering," and *a fortiori* "giving a person a place to stay"—does not, of deliberately safeguarding members of a specified group from the authorities, whether through concealment, movement to a safe location, or physical protection. This connotation enables one to see that the emergency staff at the hospital may not be "harboring" an alien when it renders emergency treatment even if he stays in the emergency room overnight, that giving a lift to a gas station to an alien with a flat tire may not be harboring, that driving an alien to the local office of the Department of Homeland Security to apply for an adjustment of status to that of lawful resident may not be harboring, that inviting an alien for a "one night stand" may not be attempted harboring, that placing an illegal alien in a school may not be harboring (cf. *Plyler v. Doe*, 457 U.S. 202 (1982)), and finally that allowing your boyfriend to live with you may not be harboring, even if you know he shouldn't be in the United States.

The prohibition of concealing, shielding from detection, and harboring known illegal aliens grew out of the prohibition of smuggling aliens into the United States. Immigration Act of 1907, Pub. L. No. 59–96, 34 Stat. 898. Concealing illegal aliens in the United States and shielding them from detection in the United States are closely related to smuggling; they are active efforts to keep illegal aliens in the United States. * * *

To call this harboring would carry section 1324 far beyond smuggling, and a considerable distance as well from concealing and from shielding from detection. That considerable distance identifies a further problem with the use of dictionaries to determine statutory meaning. Legislative prohibitions are often stated in strings of closely related and overlapping terms, to plug loopholes. They do not have identical dictionary definitions (if they did, the use of multiple terms would have no point), but the overlap means that in many applications they will be redundant, so that to pick out of the dictionary, for each statutory term, a definition remote from that of the other terms may be to misunderstand why the legislature included multiple overlapping terms. We have warned that "the fact that a clause is broadly worded to stop up loopholes doesn't justify a literal interpretation that carries far beyond any purpose that can reasonably be imputed to the drafter. 'When a statute is broadly worded in order to prevent loopholes from being drilled in it by ingenious lawyers, there is a danger of its being applied to situations absurdly remote from the concerns of the statute's framers.'" * * *

Rather than contenting themselves with "simple sheltering" or its synonyms as definitions of harboring, some courts struggle for a definition that will avoid the anomalies that we've discussed at such length in this opinion. * * * Some cases, in order to refine the definition of "harboring," adopt the formula "substantial facilitation of" or "substantially to facilitate" the alien's presence. * * * A better gloss than "substantial facilitation" would be providing (or offering—for remember that the statute punishes the attempt as well as the completed act) a known illegal alien a secure haven, a refuge, a place to stay in which the authorities are unlikely to be seeking him—and thus a definition of "harboring" that differentiates it from "simple sheltering" in the sense of just providing a place to stay or just cohabiting, although as we said that is not what sheltering actually means.

Our rejection of equating harboring to providing a place to stay compels the acquittal of the defendant, for on our understanding of the offense no trier of fact could reasonably find that the defendant had "harbored" her boyfriend based on the stipulated facts, or that she had concealed him or shielded him from detection.

[The dissenting opinion of CIRCUIT JUDGE MANION is omitted.]

NOTES ON COSTELLO AND THE ROLE OF DICTIONARIES IN GENERAL

1. *The Google Standard.* Judge Posner concludes that on the stipulated facts of this case, no trier of fact could reasonably find that Costello had "harbored" her boyfriend in the Google-search sense of safeguarding someone from the authorities through concealment or movement to a safe location. The more detailed record discloses that Costello's boyfriend lived with her for a year when he was in the U.S. without having been legally admitted. He then committed drug crimes and was convicted, imprisoned for a period, and deported. In 2006, he re-entered the country in violation of his deportation order. Later that year, Costello picked him up at the Greyhound station in St. Louis and transported him to her home in a southern Illinois town. He lived with her thereafter for extended periods although he also moved out on several occasions and stayed with his uncle or brother elsewhere in Illinois. On this evidence, is there a persuasive argument that Costello's home was a secure haven in which she concealed her boyfriend from the authorities?

2. *Some Broader Context.* In 2010, there were an estimated 10.8 million undocumented immigrants in the United States. The government conceded at oral argument in *Costello* that under its dictionary definition of "harboring" as "sheltering," there might be as many as two million violators of the relevant criminal provision. Should a reviewing court consider this prospect when deciding the meaning of "harboring"? Assume, for instance, that a U.S. citizen couple invites their daughter's immigrant friend and classmate to stay with the family for two weeks in the summer, and that the parents know their young guest is illegally in the country. How likely is it that Congress meant for these parents to be subject to criminal liability for harboring? Even if the invitation is refused, the statute criminalizes attempts: should we infer that Congress meant the criminal prohibition to extend this far? Compare *Costello*, 666 F.3d at 1047 (Posner, J.) with *id.* at 1051 (Manion, J., dissenting).

3. *Dictionaries as an Objective Source.* Is Judge Posner's skepticism about dictionaries warranted? The Supreme Court hardly used dictionaries at all before 1980. What accounts for the enormous increase in usage since that time, and especially in the last 25 years? Might the increase be related to the length or complexity of modern statutes? To the justices' inclination—subconscious or otherwise—to seek out objective and neutral proxies for ordinary meaning? To their desire to deflect or rebut charges of judicial activism? How exactly does reliance on dictionaries contribute to a better understanding of a statutory provision? Dictionaries define words removed from a larger sentence framework, whereas statutory language typically involves some context beyond a particular word or phrase. Should courts adopt any cautionary rules regarding the limitations of dictionaries for interpretive purposes?

In *Oasis or Mirage*, Brudney and Baum examined roughly 700 statutory decisions by the Supreme Court since 1986 in the areas of criminal law, labor and employment law, and commercial and business law. The Court relied on dictionaries in 117 cases, about one-sixth of its decisions. While textualist Justices Scalia, Thomas, and Alito were relatively heavy dictionary users, so too were purposivist Justices Stevens, Souter, and Breyer. See 55 William & Mary L. Rev. at 490.

The authors found that dictionary use overall was strikingly *ad hoc* and subjective, and they concluded that this inconsistent dictionary usage reflected a tendency to cherry-pick definitions in support of results reached largely on other grounds. In addition to the

Court's tendency to rely on only one or two dictionaries, the justices had varied individual brand preferences (*e.g.*, Scalia favored Webster's Second International; O'Connor preferred Webster's Third; Thomas favors Black's Law Dictionary) yet they very often departed from these individual preferences. Further, the justices seemed to use general and legal dictionaries interchangeably: they invoked Black's to define traditional legal terms but also for common words like "use" or "occur"; and in seeking to define more technical law-related terms, the justices sometimes invoked legal dictionaries alone, sometimes general dictionaries alone, and sometimes both. Finally, the authors found that the justices lacked a coherent position on the choice between citing editions from the time of statutory enactment (tailored to meanings presumptively understood by the enacting Congress) or from the time the instant case was filed in court (tailored to meanings presumptively understood by citizens living under the statute today). *Id.* at 488–90, 509–10.

To what extent do these findings undermine the argument that dictionaries are an objective or neutral source for courts to use in determining ordinary meaning? Brudney and Baum contend that the Court should acknowledge it is operating with virtually unbridled discretion in the dictionary domain and take steps to reduce dictionary cherry-picking. Among the options they suggest are (a) identifying one or more dictionaries as presumptive sources and explaining the basis for their selection; (b) consulting a presumptive minimum number of dictionaries for every contested word or phrase, probably at least four; (c) developing a rationale for when it is appropriate to use a general dictionary, a legal dictionary, or both; and (d) similarly, developing a rationale for when to use enactment date, case-filing date, both, or neither. Would you endorse any or all of these suggestions? What else might the Court do to make its now-steady reliance on dictionaries a less subjective enterprise?

B. MAXIMS OF WORD ASSOCIATION

A number of rules—based either on general notions of English composition or syntax—have been stated as guides for finding meaning from the words of the statute and nothing else. These are often called "intrinsic aids," or "language canons" of interpretation. They are normally invoked by courts as conventional benchmarks for discerning the most appropriate use of language. Some judicial rhetoric to the contrary, text-based canons are decidedly not hard-and-fast rules; they are at best presumptions and might be considered most like adages. See Antonin Scalia & Bryan A. Garner, *Reading Law: The Interpretation of Legal Texts* 59–63 (2012) (discussing interrelation of canons and their non-mandatory nature); Lawrence Solan, *The Language of Judges* ch. 2 (1993) (linguistic analysis of several textual canons); Neil MacCormick, *Argumentation and Interpretation in Law*, 6 Ratio Juris 16 (1993) (discussing linguistic arguments as a category of interpretive argument).

1. Noscitur a Sociis

Words are social creatures: they travel in packs. Several canons suggest permissible inferences from the company that words keep. "Noscitur a sociis" translates as "[i]t is known from its associates." Light may be shed on the meaning of an ambiguous word by reference to words associated with it. "Thus, when two or more words are grouped together, and ordinarily have a similar meaning, but are not equally comprehensive, the general word will be limited and qualified by the special word." 2A Sutherland § 47.16; see *Maxwell, supra* note 2, at 289–93 (hereinafter *Maxwell*); *Sullivan* 3d edition *supra* note 2, at 138–41 (hereinafter *Sullivan*). For example, in *Jarecki v. G.D. Searle & Co.*, 367 U.S. 303 (1961), a federal income tax statute allowed allocation to other years of income "resulting from exploration, discovery, or prospecting." A drug manufacturer and a camera manufacturer argued that they should be allowed to take advantage of the allocation statute with respect to income from the sale of patented products because by definition such a product resulted from a "discovery." The Court disagreed. When interpreted in light of the associated words "exploration" and "prospecting," the term "discovery" meant only the discovery of mineral resources. *discovery.*

2. Ejusdem Generis

of the same kind/class/Nature.

A sibling of noscitur a sociis, ejusdem generis translates as "[o]f the same kind, class, or nature." "Where general words follow specific words in a statutory enumeration, the general words are construed to embrace only objects similar in nature to those objects enumerated by the preceding specific words. Where the opposite sequence is found, i.e., specific words following general ones, the doctrine is equally applicable, and restricts application of the general term to things that are similar to those enumerated." 2A Sutherland § 47.17; see *Maxwell* 297–303; *Sullivan* 141–45. The purpose of this rule is to give effect to all the words—the particular words indicate the class and the general words extend the provisions of the statute to everything else in the class (even though not enumerated by the specific words).

Section 1 of the Federal Arbitration Act of 1926 excludes from coverage "contracts of employment of seamen, railroad employees, or any other class of workers engaged in foreign or interstate commerce." 9 U.S.C. § 1. The issue in *Circuit City Stores, Inc. v. Adams*, 532 U.S. 105 (2001), was whether the exclusion was limited to contracts involving *transportation* but not other kinds of employment contracts. Workers suing their employers generally want a court, not an arbitrator, especially for discrimination claims such as those in *Circuit City*. So the plaintiff argued that his job at a retail store, obviously engaged in "interstate commerce," fell within the exclusion: Congress, he argued, meant to exclude employment contracts generally, and used language tied to the jurisdictional basis of the FAA, the Commerce Clause. The Supreme Court rejected that reading, on the ground that ejusdem generis suggested that Congress meant the exclusion to be limited to contracts "like" those involving seamen and railroad workers—namely, transportation contracts.

Noscitur a sociis and ejusdem generis, like the other canons, are just aids to meaning, not ironclad rules. Thus, they have no value if the statute evidences a meaning contrary to their presumptions. See *United States v. Turkette*, 452 U.S. 576, 581 (1981). Dissenting in *Circuit City*, Justice Stevens argued that the legislative purpose and specific history rebutted any presumption created by ejusdem generis. Both the labor unions that had petitioned Congress for the exemption covering contracts of employment and Secretary of Commerce Herbert Hoover, the primary architect of the law, endorsed the broader view of the exclusion. (The Court found the statute sufficiently clear in purely textual terms so that it did not need to assess this evidence of legislative history or purpose.)

[handwritten: what makes the items in the series "similar"]

Deployment of ejusdem generis involves a judgment—often a debatable one—about what it is that makes the items in the series "similar." The *Circuit City* Court found that the common denominator was "transportation contracts," while the dissenters found it to be "employment contracts within Congress's Commerce Clause power." See also *Bilski v. Kappos*, 130 S.Ct. 3218 (2010) (Justice Kennedy for majority declined to apply noscitur a sociis because the assertedly ambiguous term "process" was expressly defined in the patent statute; Justice Stevens, concurring in the judgment, found noscitur useful because the patent statute's definition of "process" included the term "process," leaving residual ambiguity). See generally 2A Sutherland § 47.17–.22 (discussing ejusdem generis and qualifications to its use); *Maxwell* 303–06. For another example of such a debatable judgment, consider the following case.

[handwritten: It's known from its associates]

STATUTORY PREFACE TO *ALI V. FEDERAL BUREAU OF PRISONS*

Federal Tort Claims Act, 28 U.S.C. §§ 1346, 2680.

Section 1346.   *United States as Defendant*

(b)(1)   * * * the district courts * * * shall have exclusive jurisdiction of civil actions on claims against the United States, for money damages * * * for injury or loss of property, or personal injury or death caused by the negligent or wrongful act or omission of any employee of the Government while acting within the scope of his office or employment, under circumstances where the United States, if a private person, would be liable to the claimant in accordance with the law of the place where the act or omission occurred.

Section 2680.   *Exceptions.*

The provisions of this chapter and section 1346(b) of this title shall not apply to—
* * *

(c) Any claim arising in respect of * * * the detention of any goods, merchandise, or other property by any officer of customs or excise or any other law enforcement officer, except that the provisions of this chapter and section 1346(b) of this title apply to any claim based on injury or loss of goods, merchandise, or other property, while in the possession of any officer of customs or excise or any other law enforcement officer, if—

    (1) the property was seized for the purpose of forfeiture under any provision of Federal law providing for the forfeiture of property other than as a sentence imposed upon conviction of a criminal offense;

    (2) the interest of the claimant was not forfeited;

    (3) the interest of the claimant was not remitted or mitigated (if the property was subject to forfeiture); and

    (4) the claimant was not convicted of a crime for which the interest of the claimant in the property was subject to forfeiture under a Federal criminal forfeiture law.

ALI V. FEDERAL BUREAU OF PRISONS

Supreme Court of the United States, 2008.
552 U.S. 214, 128 S.Ct. 831, 169 L.Ed.2d 680.

JUSTICE THOMAS delivered the opinion of the Court.

This case concerns the scope of 28 U.S.C. § 2680, which carves out certain exceptions to the United States' waiver of sovereign immunity for torts committed by federal employees. Section 2680(c) provides that the waiver of sovereign immunity does not apply to claims arising from the detention of property by "any officer of customs or excise or any other law enforcement officer." Petitioner contends that this clause applies only to law enforcement officers enforcing customs or excise laws, and thus does not affect the waiver of sovereign immunity for his property claim against officers of the Federal Bureau of Prisons (BOP). We conclude that the broad phrase "any other law enforcement officer" covers all law enforcement officers. Accordingly, we affirm the judgment of the Court of Appeals upholding the dismissal of petitioner's claim.

[I] [Upon being transferred to a new prison facility, some of petitioner Ali's personal belongings that were of personal and religious significance, such as a Qur'an and prayer rug, went missing. After petitioner's administrative claim failed, he filed a complaint alleging violations of the Federal Tort Claims Act (FTCA), 28 U.S.C. §§ 1346, 2671 et seq. The District Court held, and the Eleventh Circuit agreed, that petitioner's claim was barred by the exception in § 2680(c) for property claims against law enforcement officers.]

[II] As relevant here, the FTCA authorizes "claims against the United States, for money damages . . . for injury or loss of property . . . caused by the negligent or wrongful act or omission of any employee of the Government while acting within the scope of his office or employment." [28 U.S.C. § 1346(b)(1)]. The FTCA exempts from this waiver certain categories of claims [including] "[a]ny claim arising in respect of the assessment or collection of any tax or customs duty, or the detention of any goods, merchandise, or other property by any officer of customs or excise or any other law enforcement officer." § 2680(c).

This case turns on whether the BOP officers who allegedly lost petitioner's property qualify as "other law enforcement officer[s]" within the meaning of § 2680(c). Petitioner argues that they do not because "any other law enforcement officer" includes only law enforcement officers acting in a customs or excise capacity. Noting that Congress referenced customs and excise activities in both the language at issue and the preceding clause in § 2680(c), petitioner argues that the entire subsection is focused on preserving the United States' sovereign immunity only as to officers enforcing those laws.

Petitioner's argument is inconsistent with the statute's language. The phrase "any other law enforcement officer" suggests a broad meaning. * * * Congress' use of "any" to modify "other law enforcement officer" is most naturally read to mean law enforcement officers of whatever kind. The word "any" is repeated four times in the relevant portion of § 2680(c), and two of those instances appear in the particular phrase at issue: "*any* officer of customs or excise or *any* other law enforcement officer." (Emphasis added.) Congress inserted the word "any" immediately before "other law enforcement officer," leaving no doubt that it modifies that phrase. To be sure, the text's references to "tax or customs duty" and "officer[s] of customs or excise" indicate that Congress intended to preserve immunity for claims arising from an officer's enforcement of tax and customs laws. The text also indicates, however, that Congress intended to preserve immunity for claims arising from the detention of property, and there is no indication that Congress intended immunity for those claims to turn on the type of law being enforced.

Petitioner would require Congress to clarify its intent to cover all law enforcement officers by adding phrases such as "performing any official law enforcement function," or "without limitation." But Congress could not have chosen a more all-encompassing phrase than "any other law enforcement officer" to express that intent. We have no reason to demand that Congress write less economically and more repetitiously. * * *

Against this textual and structural evidence that "any other law enforcement officer" does in fact mean any other law enforcement officer, petitioner invokes numerous canons of statutory construction. He relies primarily on ejusdem generis, or the principle that "when a general term follows a specific one, the general term should be understood as a reference to subjects akin to the one with specific enumeration." * * * In petitioner's view, "any officer of customs or excise or any other law enforcement officer" should be read as a three-item list, and the final, catchall phrase "any other law enforcement officer" should be limited to officers of the same nature as the preceding specific phrases.

Petitioner likens his case to two recent cases in which we found the canon useful. In *Washington State Department. of Social and Health Services v. Guardianship Estate of Keffeler*, 537 U.S. 371 (2003), we considered the clause "execution, levy, attachment, garnishment, or other legal process" in 42 U.S.C. § 407(a). Applying ejusdem generis, we concluded that "other legal process" was limited to legal processes of the same nature as the specific items listed. The department's scheme for serving as a representative payee of the benefits due to children under its care, while a "legal process," did not share the common attribute of the listed items, viz., "utilization of some judicial or quasi-judicial mechanism . . . by which control over property passes from one person to another in order to discharge" a debt. Similarly, in *Dolan v. Postal Service*, 546 U.S. 481 (2006), the Court considered whether an exception to the FTCA's waiver of sovereign immunity for claims arising out of the " 'loss, miscarriage, or negligent transmission of letters or postal matter' " barred a claim that mail negligently left on the petitioner's porch caused her to slip and fall. (quoting 28 U.S.C. § 2680(b)). Noting that "loss" and "miscarriage" both addressed "failings in the postal obligation to deliver mail in a timely manner to the right address," the Court concluded that "negligent transmission" must be similarly limited, and rejected the Government's argument that the exception applied to "all torts committed in the course of mail delivery."

Petitioner asserts that § 2680(c), like the clauses at issue in *Keffeler* and *Dolan*, " 'presents a textbook ejusdem generis scenario.' " * * * We disagree. The structure of the phrase "any officer of customs or excise or any other law enforcement officer" does not lend itself to application of the canon. The phrase is disjunctive, with one specific and one general category, not—like the clauses at issue in *Keffeler* and *Dolan*—a list of specific items separated by commas and followed by a general or collective term. The absence of a list of specific items undercuts the inference embodied in ejusdem generis that Congress remained focused on the common attribute when it used the catchall phrase.

Moreover, it is not apparent what common attribute connects the specific items in § 2680(c). Were we to use the canon to limit the meaning of "any other law enforcement officer," we would be required to determine the relevant limiting characteristic of "officer of customs or excise." In *Jarecki v. G.D. Searle & Co.*, 367 U.S. 303 (1961), for example, the Court invoked noscitur a sociis in limiting the scope of the term " 'discovery' " to the common characteristic it shared with " 'exploration' " and " 'prospecting.' " The Court noted that all three words in conjunction "describe[d] income-producing activity in the oil and gas and mining industries." Here, by contrast, no relevant common attribute immediately appears from the phrase "officer of customs or excise." Petitioner suggests that the common attribute is that both types of officers are charged with enforcing the customs and excise laws. But we see no reason why that should be the relevant characteristic as opposed to, for example, that officers of that type are commonly involved in the activities enumerated in the statute: the assessment and collection of taxes and customs duties and the detention of property.

Petitioner's appeals to other interpretive principles are also unconvincing. [Justice Thomas rejected petitioner's argument based on the canon noscitur a sociis because] although customs and excise are mentioned twice in § 2680(c), nothing in the overall statutory context suggests that customs and excise officers were the exclusive focus of the provision. The emphasis in subsection (c) on customs and excise is not inconsistent with the conclusion that "any other law enforcement officer" sweeps as broadly as its language suggests.

Similarly, the rule against superfluities lends petitioner sparse support. The construction we adopt today does not necessarily render "any officer of customs or excise" superfluous; Congress may have simply intended to remove any doubt that officers of customs or excise were included in "law enforcement officers." See *Fort Stewart Schs. v. FLRA*, 495 U.S. 641 (1990) (noting that "technically unnecessary" examples may have been "inserted out of an abundance of caution"). Moreover, petitioner's construction threatens to render "any other law enforcement officer" superfluous because it is not clear when, if ever, "other law enforcement officer[s]" act in a customs or excise capacity. In any event, we do not woodenly apply limiting principles every time Congress includes a specific example along with a general phrase.

In the end, we are unpersuaded by petitioner's attempt to create ambiguity where the statute's text and structure suggest none. Had Congress intended to limit § 2680(c)'s reach as petitioner contends, it easily could have written "any other law enforcement officer acting in a customs or excise capacity." Instead, it used the unmodified, all-encompassing phrase "any other law enforcement officer." * * *

JUSTICE KENNEDY, with whom JUSTICE STEVENS, JUSTICE SOUTER, and JUSTICE BREYER join, dissenting.

Statutory interpretation, from beginning to end, requires respect for the text. The respect is not enhanced, however, by decisions that foreclose consideration of the text within the whole context of the statute as a guide to determining a legislature's intent. To prevent textual analysis from becoming so rarefied that it departs from how a legislator most likely understood the words when he or she voted for the law, courts use certain interpretative rules to consider text within the statutory design. These canons do not demand wooden reliance and are not by themselves dispositive, but they do function as helpful guides in construing ambiguous statutory provisions. Two of these accepted rules are ejusdem generis and noscitur a sociis, which together instruct that words in a series should be interpreted in relation to one another.

Today the Court holds, if my understanding of its opinion is correct, that there is only one possible way to read the statute. Placing implicit reliance upon a comma at the beginning of a clause, the Court says that the two maxims noted, and indeed other helpful and recognized principles of statutory analysis, are not useful as interpretative aids in this case because the clause cannot be understood by what went before. In my respectful submission the Court's approach is incorrect as a general rule and as applied to the statute now before us. * * *

[Justice Kennedy addressed the background of the FTCA, noting that the statute allowed those harmed by the government to seek damages for tortious conduct, with certain exceptions, and he warned that overly generous interpretations of those exceptions could defeat the central purpose of the statute.]

Both on first reading and upon further, close consideration, the plain words of the statute indicate that the exception is concerned only with customs and taxes. The provision begins with a clause dealing exclusively with customs and tax duties. And the provision as a whole contains four express references to customs and tax, making revenue duties and customs and excise officers its most salient features.

This is not to suggest that the Court's reading is wholly impermissible or without some grammatical support. After all, detention of goods is not stated until the outset of the second clause and at the end of the same clause the words "any other law enforcement officer" appear; so it can be argued that the first and second clauses of the provision are so separate that all detentions by all law enforcement officers in whatever capacity they might act are covered. Still, this ought not be the preferred reading; for between the beginning of the second clause and its closing reference to "any other law enforcement officer" appears another reference to "officer[s] of customs or excise," this time in the context of property detention. This is quite sufficient, in my view, to continue the limited scope of the exception. At the very least, the Court errs by adopting a rule which simply bars all consideration of the canons of ejusdem generis and noscitur a sociis. And when those canons are consulted, together with other common principles of interpretation, the case for limiting the exception to customs and tax more than overcomes the position maintained by the Government and adopted by the Court.

The ejusdem generis canon provides that, where a seemingly broad clause constitutes a residual phrase, it must be controlled by, and defined with reference to, the "enumerated categories . . . which are recited just before it," so that the clause encompasses only objects similar in nature. * * * The words "any other law enforcement officer" immediately follow the statute's reference to "officer[s] of customs or excise," as well as the first clause's reference to the assessment of tax and customs duties. 28 U.S.C. § 2680(c).

The Court counters that § 2680(c) "is disjunctive, with one specific and one general category," rendering ejusdem generis inapplicable. The canon's applicability, however, is not limited to those statutes that include a laundry list of items. * * * A proper reading of § 2680(c) thus attributes to the last phrase ("any other law enforcement officer") the discrete characteristic shared by the preceding phrases ("officer[s] of customs or excise" and "assessment or collection of any tax or customs duty"). Had Congress intended otherwise, in all likelihood it would have drafted the section to apply to "any law enforcement officer, including officers of customs and excise," rather than tacking "any other law enforcement officer" on the end of the enumerated categories as it did here.

The common attribute of officers of customs and excise and other law enforcement officers is the performance of functions most often assigned to revenue officers, including, *inter alia*, the enforcement of the United States' revenue laws and the conduct of border searches. Although officers of customs and officers of excise are in most instances the only full-time staff charged with this duty, officers of other federal agencies and general law enforcement officers often will be called upon to act in the traditional capacity of a revenue officer. For example, Drug Enforcement Administration or Federal Bureau of Investigation agents frequently assist customs officials in the execution of border searches. To the extent they detain goods whose possession violates customs laws, the Coast Guard officers while not "officer[s] of customs or excise," 28 U.S.C. § 2680(c)—are without doubt engaging in the enforcement of the United States' revenue laws. * * *

The Court reaches its contrary conclusion by concentrating on the word "any" before the phrase "other law enforcement officer." 28 U.S.C. § 2680(c). It takes this single last phrase to extend the statute so that it covers all detentions of property by any law enforcement officer in whatever capacity he or she acts. There are fundamental problems with this approach, in addition to the ones already mentioned.

First, the Court's analysis cannot be squared with the longstanding recognition that a single word must not be read in isolation but instead defined by reference to its statutory context. As already mentioned, the context of § 2680(c) suggests that, in accordance with these precedents, the statutory provision should be interpreted narrowly to apply only to customs and revenue duties. * * *

Second, the Court's construction of the phrase "any other law enforcement officer" * * * renders "officer[s] of customs or excise" mere surplusage, as there would have been no need for Congress to have specified that officers of customs and officers of excise were immune if they indeed were subsumed within the allegedly all-encompassing "any" officer clause. * * *

[Third, Justice Kennedy pointed to the lack of any reference within the legislative history to a Congressional desire to limit liability to officers beyond customs and excise agents as indicative that Congress did not believe the exception to the waiver applied to officers outside of the customs and excise context. Kennedy maintained that if Congress had meant for the exception to sweep so broadly, it would have spoken more clearly when undermining the Act's general purpose.]

If Congress had intended to give sweeping immunity to all federal law enforcement officials from liability for the detention of property, it would not have dropped this phrase onto the end of the statutory clause so as to appear there as something of an afterthought. The seizure of property by an officer raises serious concerns for the liberty of our people and the Act should not be read to permit appropriation of property without a remedy in tort by language so obscure and indirect.

JUSTICE BREYER, with whom JUSTICE STEVENS joins, dissenting.

* * * I write separately to emphasize, as Justice Kennedy's dissent itself makes clear, that the relevant context extends well beyond Latin canons and other such purely textual devices. * * * As with many questions of statutory interpretation, the issue here is not the meaning of the words. The dictionary meaning of each word is well known. Rather, the issue is the statute's scope. What boundaries did Congress intend to set? To what circumstances did Congress intend the phrase, as used in this statutory provision, to apply? * * *

The word "any" is of no help because all speakers (including writers and legislators) who use general words such as "all," "any," "never," and "none" normally rely upon context to indicate the limits of time and place within which they intend those words to do their linguistic work. And with the possible exception of the assertion of a universal truth, say by a mathematician, scientist, philosopher, or theologian, such limits almost always exist. When I call out to my wife, "There isn't any butter," I do not mean, "There isn't any butter in town." The context makes clear to her that I am talking about the contents of our refrigerator. That is to say, it is context, not a dictionary, that sets the boundaries of time, place, and circumstance within which words such as "any" will apply.

Context, of course, includes the words immediately surrounding the phrase in question. And canons such as ejusdem generis and noscitur a sociis offer help in evaluating the significance of those surrounding words. Yet that help is limited. That is because other contextual features can show that Congress intended a phrase to apply more broadly than the immediately surrounding words by themselves suggest. * * * It is because canons of construction are not "conclusive" and "are often countered . . . by some maxim pointing in a different direction." * * * And it is because these particular canons simply crystallize what English speakers already know, namely, that lists often (but not always) group together items with similar characteristics. * * * In this case, not only the immediately surrounding words but also every other contextual feature supports Justice Kennedy's conclusion. The textual context includes the location of the phrase within a provision that otherwise exclusively concerns customs and revenue duties. And the nontextual context includes several features that, taken together, indicate that Congress intended a narrow tort-liability exception related to customs and excise.

[Justice Breyer relied on the FTCA drafting history to argue that a limited exception made more sense based on what tort remedies were available to those harmed by the government at the time of the statute's drafting, and also on Congress's silence as to any intent that the waiver provision apply more broadly than the customs and excise setting.] [T]he law's history contains much that indicates the provision's scope is limited to customs and excise, [but] it contains nothing at all suggesting an intent to apply the provision more broadly, indeed, to multiply the number of officers to whom it applies by what is likely one or more orders of magnitude. It is thus not the Latin canons, ejusdem generis and noscitur a sociis, that shed light on the application of the statutory phrase but Justice Scalia's more pertinent and easily remembered English-language observation that Congress "does not . . . hide elephants in mouseholes." * * *

NOTES ON ALI AND EJUSDEM GENERIS

1. *What Constitutes the "Common Attribute" of "Words in a Series?"* For Justice Thomas, the meaning of "any" is so clear that ejusdem generis doesn't come into play. But even if it did, Thomas insists the canon would be improperly applied here. In Justice Kennedy's dissent, the fact that "officer[s] of customs or excise" are mentioned immediately before "any other law enforcement officer" narrows the scope of the "law enforcement officer" exception to the waiver of sovereign immunity. Justice Thomas counters by arguing that "customs" and "excise" have no common attribute that would constrain the broad general meaning of "any other law enforcement officer." For the majority, the fact that "any officer of customs or excise" and "any other law enforcement officer" are disjunctive phrases indicates that *ejusdem*—and also *noscitur*—do not apply at all.

If § 2680(6) were phrased "any officer of customs, excise, or any other law enforcement officer," would this change Justice Thomas's position on *ejusdem*'s applicability? What if the phrase read "any officer of customs or excise or border searches or any other law enforcement officer"? How many specific common attributes should be listed before applying the canon to the phrase "any other law enforcement officer"? Should the answer to these questions change depending on other tools used in statutory interpretation, such as the rule against surplusage, the provision's legislative history, or the practical implications of different readings?

Justice Breyer has yet another perspective: both the majority and Justice Kennedy's dissent focus too intensely on close textual readings and textual canons while giving short-shrift to the drafting history and overriding purpose of the Federal Tort Claims Act. Is it appropriate to infer from Congress's failure to discuss a broad reading of the phrase "any other law enforcement officer" that the words were not meant to have that broad an application? The FTCA is itself a statutory waiver of the underlying principle of sovereign immunity: thus one could view § 2680(c) as a specific exception to a more general statutory exception. In this setting, what exactly are the "elephants" and the "mouseholes"? In the end, which approach to construing the contested language do you find most persuasive: The literalist approach taken by Justice Thomas? The canonical position espoused by Justice Kennedy? The purposivist approach utilized by Justice Breyer?

2. *Textual Canons as Constraints on Judicial Activism?* Advocates for the textual canons regularly argue that this canonical approach constrains judges from the tendency "to imbue authoritative texts with their own policy preferences." Antonin Scalia & Bryan A. Garner, *Reading Law: The Interpretation of Legal Texts* xxviii (2012). In Justice

Scalia's view, a canons-based textual approach "will provide greater certainty in the law, and hence greater predictability and greater respect for the rule of law." *Id.* at xxix. More pessimistic observers, from both the academy and the judiciary, suggest that canons tend to disguise the creative elements of statutory construction by presenting the interpretive process as essentially mechanical, and that judges often use the textual canons strategically to justify their own policy preferences or to frustrate clear legislative intent.[5] One of us has argued that far from constraining the imposition of value preferences, these textual canons effectively require judges to engage in normative evaluations—as when textualist judges enforce their understanding of "normal" English-speaking usage on Congress, or decide that the commonality of terms in a list should be specified without regard to the statutory purpose that gave rise to the list itself. See William Eskridge, *The New Textualism and Normative Canons*, 113 Colum. L. Rev. 531, 557–60 (2013) (reviewing *Reading Law*).

Scalia and Garner devote fifteen pages to ejusdem generis, recounting the canon's origins and justifications, and concluding that "it does not always predominate, but neither is it a mere tiebreaker." *Id.* at 213. They assert that ejusdem is generally triggered by the presence of two or more words to establish a genus before the general phrase that follows. Yet they argue that the majority in *Ali* correctly found the canon inapplicable because of the "unexamined but probably correct" premise that the phrase 'officer of customs or excise' reflects a traditional pairing of the two terms as a single type of officer (they cite to Great Britain's Bureau of Customs and Excise) which is not equivalent to 'customs officer or excise officer.' See *id.* at 206–07. Given that in *Ali*, Justices Thomas and Kennedy draw opposing inferences from the presence of two specific words before a general phrase, and that Justice Scalia justifies Justice Thomas's inference based on a premise never articulated in the opinion for the Court, does this case perhaps illustrate how textual canons are unlikely to constrain judicial discretion?

3. *Congressional Drafters' Use of Textual Canons and Dictionaries.* A study by Abbe Gluck and Lisa Schultz Bressman surveyed 137 congressional staffers—drawn from both parties and both chambers—on their knowledge and use of the various interpretive tools in drafting legislation. The study found that the assumptions underlying the ejusdem and noscitur canons were widely used by legislative drafters, although not recognized by their Latin cognates. Over 70 percent of respondents stated that terms in a statutory list often or always relate to one another (when asked by name, two-thirds did not know ejusdem and 85 percent did not know noscitur). Gluck and Bressman found that the 70 percent level of usage was considerably higher than the reliance levels for two other textual canons, discussed below: expressio unius (33 percent) and the rule against superfluities (30 percent). Abbe Gluck & Lisa Schultz Bressman, *Statutory Interpretation From the Inside—An Empirical Study of Congressional Drafting, Delegation, and the Canons: Part I*, 65 Stan. L. Rev. 901, 930–34 (2013). The drafters' reliance on dictionaries was even lower: 15 percent said they often or always used them when drafting whereas more than 50 percent said dictionaries are never or rarely used. The latter finding contrasts starkly with the Court's burgeoning increase in dictionary usage.

---

[5]   See Richard Posner, *The Federal Courts: Crisis and Reform*, 285–86 (1985); T. Alexander Aleinikoff & Theodore Shaw, *The Costs of Incoherence: A Comment on Plain Meaning*, West Virginia Univ. Hospitals, Inc. v. Casey, *and Due Process of Statutory Interpretation*, 45 Vand. L. Rev. 687, 688–89, 696–97 (1992); Stephen Ross, *Where Have You Gone, Karl Llewellyn? Should Congress Turn Its Lonely Eyes to You?*, 45 Vand. L. Rev. 561, 562 (1992).

How relevant is the Gluck and Bressman study when considering what constitutes an appropriate interpretive approach? Their findings on ejusdem and noscitur suggest that textual canons may ultimately be ornate labels describing certain ways in which we process language through context. Should special weight be given to ejusdem and noscitur because the concepts underlying both are readily understood and incorporated by congressional drafters?

Conversely, does it matter whether some textual canons—as well as dictionary definitions—that Justice Scalia and fellow textualists extol as common sense resources are in fact discounted or ignored by those who draft statutory text? Should judges be concerned only with how a "reasonable person" would understand the language that has been enacted? Should those drafting and negotiating the language of the statutes be deemed part of any reasonable person construct? Why might they even be regarded as especially important reference points when deciding which interpretive sources to consult?

3.   Expressio Unius

Words omitted may be just as significant as words set forth. The maxim "expressio [or inclusio] unius est exclusio alterius" means "expression (or inclusion) of one thing indicates exclusion of the other." The notion is one of negative implication: the enumeration of certain things in a statute suggests that the legislature had no intent of including things not listed or embraced. See *Tate v. Ogg*, 195 S.E. 496 (Va. 1938) (statute covering "any horse, mule, cattle, hog, sheep or goat" did not cover turkeys); 2A Sutherland § 47.25 (discussing the limitations of the canon); *Maxwell*, 293–97; *Sullivan*, 153–57.

As *Holy Trinity Church* (Chapter 5, § 1) exemplifies, courts feel free to refuse to apply the maxim when they believe it would lead to a result Congress did not intend.[6] One basic problem is that this canon, like many of the others, assumes that the legislature thinks through statutory language carefully, considering every possible variation. This is clearly not true, for the legislature often omits things because no one thinks about them or everyone assumes that courts will fill in gaps. See Richard Posner, *The Federal Courts: Crisis and Reform* 282 (1985). Some judges have reflected this concern, suggesting that the maxim is unreliable because "it stands on the faulty premise that all possible alternative or supplemental provisions were necessarily considered and rejected by the [legislature]." *Nat'l Petroleum Refiners Ass'n v. FTC*, 482 F.2d 672, 676 (D.C. Cir. 1973).

Another way of looking at this issue is to consider context, including normative context. If Mother tells Sally, "Don't hit, kick, or bite your sister Anne," Sally is *not* authorized by expressio unius to "pinch" her little sister. The reason is that the normative baseline (discerned from prior practice or just family culture) is "no harming sister," and the directive was an expression of that baseline that ought not be narrowly limited. Contrariwise, where the directive in question is a departure from the normative baseline, the canon ought to apply. For example, if Mother tells Sally, "You may have a cookie and a scoop of ice cream," Sally has implicitly been forbidden to snap up that candy bar lying on the kitchen table. For cases where normative statutory baselines augured against

---

[6]   In that case, the statute that prohibited bringing into the United States an alien for employment exempted certain persons such as lecturers and domestic servants. Had the Court followed expressio unius, it would have held that the listed exceptions were the only ones not covered by the prohibition, and therefore that the church had violated the statute.

application of expressio unius, see, e.g., *Marrama v. Citizens Bank of Mass.*, 549 U.S. 365, 373–76 (2007) (Stevens, J.); *Christensen v. Harris Cnty.*, 529 U.S. 576, 583–84 (2000) (Thomas, J.).

But consider *Chan v. Korean Air Lines*, 490 U.S. 122 (1989), where the Supreme Court held that international air carriers do not lose their Warsaw Convention limitation on damages arising out of passenger injury or death when they fail to provide the passenger with the requisite notice of limitation on her ticket. Article 3(1) of the Convention requires such notice, and article 3(2) provides that if the carrier fails to deliver a ticket to the passenger it cannot avail itself of the Convention's liability limits. Although many lower courts had interpreted article 3(2) to include situations where the passenger received a ticket, but without the requisite notice, the Court, in an opinion by Justice Scalia, held to the contrary. Justice Scalia's key argument was that other sections of the Convention provide parallel rules for limiting carrier liability and providing notice thereof, for baggage checks (article 4) and cargo waybills (article 9). The various sections are identical in their notice requirements, but not in their remedies. Article 3 (passenger injury) provides no remedy explicitly covering insufficient notice, while articles 4 and 9 explicitly waive liability limits for the carrier's failure to include the required notice in the documents given to the consumer. By negative implication, Scalia construed article 3 not to have the remedy that had been clearly provided in the other articles.

The dissenting opinion argued from the Convention's negotiating history that the lack of a similar remedy in article 3(2) was probably inadvertent. Justice Scalia considered such evidence inadmissible. If such evidence were admissible, would it persuade you that Justice Scalia's invocation of expressio unius was too hasty? Note that fellow textualist Judge Easterbrook considers expressio unius arguments question-begging and unreliable. See *In re Am. Reserve Corp.*, 840 F.2d 487, 492 (7th Cir. 1988) ("Why should we infer from the list of ways to do something that there are no others? * * * A list of four ways may imply only that Congress has yet to consider whether there should be others. The history and structure of a statute may show that a list is exhaustive, * * * but also may show that Congress has not grappled with the problem.") At the Supreme Court level, though, arguments drawn from the expressio unius concept have had an enduring appeal.[7]

C. GRAMMAR CANONS

1. Punctuation Rules

"The punctuation canon in America * * * has assumed at least three forms: (1) adhering to the strict English rule that punctuation forms no part of the statute; (2) allowing punctuation as an aid in statutory construction; and (3) looking on punctuation as a less-than-desirable, last-ditch alternative aid in statutory construction. The last approach * * * seems to have prevailed as the majority rule." Ray Marcin, *Punctuation and the Interpretation of Statutes*, 9 Conn. L. Rev. 227, 240 (1977). The English rule noted by Marcin was adopted because "[a]t one time * * *

[7]   See, e.g., *Hinck v. United States*, 550 U.S. 501, 506 (2007) (Roberts, C.J.); *TRW, Inc. v. Andrews*, 534 U.S. 19 (2001) (Ginsburg, J.); *Solid Waste Agency v. Army Corps of Eng'rs*, 531 U.S. 159 (2001) (Rehnquist, C.J.); *City of Chicago v. Envtl. Def. Fund*, 511 U.S. 328 (1994) (Scalia, J.,); *Key Tronic Corp. v. United States*, 511 U.S. 809, 818–19 (1994) (Stevens, J.); *United States v. Smith*, 499 U.S. 160 (1991) (Marshall, J.); *Mississippi Band of Choctaw Indians v. Holyfield*, 490 U.S. 30, 46–47 & n.22 (1989) (Brennan, J., who wrote the dissenting opinion in *Chan*).

punctuation [was] inserted by a clerk after the statute had been enacted by Parliament." U.S. legislatures (at both state and federal levels) generally consider and pass bills whose punctuation is not changed after enactment. 2A Sutherland § 47.15, argues that "an act should be read as punctuated unless there is some reason to do otherwise," such as an indication that such a reading would defeat the apparent intent of the legislature. "This is especially true where a statute has been repeatedly reenacted with the same punctuation, or has been the subject of numerous amendments without alteration of punctuation." See also *Sullivan* 170 ("It is very rare for punctuation other than commas to be relied on in interpretation"); Pa. Stat. Constr. Act § 1923(b): "In no case shall the punctuation of a statute control or affect the intention of the General Assembly in the enactment thereof but punctuation may be used in aid in the construction thereof. * * * "

The punctuation canon has *not* played a major role in the legisprudence of the U.S. Supreme Court. The Court found the punctuation rule decisive in *United States v. Ron Pair Enterprises, Inc.*, 489 U.S. 235, 241–42 (1989), but otherwise this canon is rarely controlling. In *United States National Bank v. Independent Insurance Agents*, 508 U.S. 439, 453–62 (1993), the Court in effect repunctuated a statute after concluding that a scrivener's error had occurred.

2. Conjunctive Versus Disjunctive Connectors: The "And" Versus "Or" Rule

The nature of the conjunctions connecting different words or phrases may be significant. Terms connected by the disjunctive "or" are often read to have separate meanings and significance.[8] For instance, 18 U.S.C. § 2114 (1988) prohibits assault with intent to rob "any person having lawful charge, control, or custody of any mail matter or of any money or other property of the United States." The issue in *Garcia v. United States*, 469 U.S. 70 (1984), was whether § 2114 applies to robbery of a Secret Service agent of his "flash money" (to be used to buy counterfeit currency from perpetrators). Petitioners argued that § 2114 only covered robbery of mail carriers, and that may have been the original focus of the statute. But the Court found the plain meaning clear: by separating "mail matter," "money," and "other property" with "or" (rather than "and"), Congress meant to include each of the three as an object of the statute and *not* to limit the statute to robbery of money and property in the custody of postal carriers. Why doesn't the ejusdem generis rule dictate the opposite result in *Garcia*? See *Schreiber v. Burlington Northern, Inc.*, 472 U.S. 1, 7–8 (1985) (interpreting "fraudulent, deceptive, or manipulative" language of Securities Act § 14(e) as all aimed at same thing: failures to disclose).

Linguists complicate the matter with these further observations: (1) The word "or" technically means "and/or" (a locution gaining in popularity). When I say, "I want this or that," I might be saying I want either one item or the other, but I might also be saying I want both items. (2) In ordinary usage, people often use the two conjunctions interchangeably. "I want this and that" might signify that I want both

---

[8] Similarly, as *Chisom v. Roemer* (Chapter 5, § 3(A)) indicates, the use of "and" usually is held to create a conjunctive rather than disjunctive meaning.

items, or that I want only one. (3) De Morgan's Rules state that when preceded by a negative the logic is as follows:

Not (A *and* B) means Not A *or* Not B.

Not (A *or* B) means Not A *and* Not B.

See Solan, *Language of Judges*, 45–49. Professor Solan observes that courts do not always follow this logic, and typically for good reason.

The Comprehensive Crime Control Act of 1984 permits the United States to seize property used to commit crimes related to drug dealing. Under § 881(a)(7) such "real property" cannot be seized if the owner can establish (as an affirmative defense) that the criminal activity was "committed or omitted without the knowledge *or* consent of that owner." Can an owner prevail if he can only show lack of consent? Or does the owner also have to show lack of knowledge? If "without" has a negative connotation (which Solan and we think it does), De Morgan's Rules suggest that the defense requires both lack of knowledge (Not A) and lack of consent (Not B). But the Second Circuit held that the property owner could defend if he or she could show lack of consent, but only if the owner had taken reasonable steps to prevent illicit use of the property once the owner knew of such use. *United States v. 141st Street Corp.*, 911 F.2d 870, 878 (2d Cir. 1990). Solan says that this is an appropriate interpretation, notwithstanding De Morgan's Rules. Do you agree?

3. Mandatory Versus Discretionary Language: The "May" Versus "Shall" Rule

When a statute uses mandatory language ("shall" rather than "may"), courts often interpret the statute to exclude discretion to take account of equitable or policy factors. See *Escondido Mut. Water Co. v. LaJolla Indians*, 466 U.S. 765 (1984); *Dunlop v. Bachowski*, 421 U.S. 560 (1975). On the other hand, ordinary usage does sometimes consider "may" and "shall" interchangeable. "You may help Mother" may be either permissive or directive, depending upon the circumstances.

The statute in *In re Cartmell's Estate*, 138 A.2d 588 (Vt. 1958), provided that probate matters of law are to be tried by a court, and "if a question of fact is to be decided, issue *may* be joined thereon under the direction of the court and a trial had by jury unless waived * * *." The trial court had denied a jury trial, over objections. The appeals court reversed: "The word 'may' can be construed as 'shall' or 'must' when such was the legislative intention." The court, correctly, assumed that "may" applied both to the phrase "be joined * * * court" and to "trial had by jury." Solan, *Language of Judges, supra*, at 46–48. Compare *Lopez v. Davis*, 531 U.S. 230 (2001) (a law providing that the sentence of a nonviolent offender "may be reduced" by the Bureau of Prisons vested discretion with the Bureau not only to deny or grant this benefit to specific nonviolent offenders, but also to create a new category of nonviolent offenders (those whose crime involved a firearm) who could not receive the benefit of its discretion).

4. Singular and Plural Numbers, Male and Female Pronouns

One grammar rule that is *not* often followed by statutory interpreters is the difference between singular and plural nouns. "In determining the meaning of any act or resolution of Congress, unless the context otherwise indicates, words importing the singular include and apply to several persons, parties, or things; words importing the plural include the singular * * *." 1 U.S.C. § 1; accord Interpretation Act of 1889, § 1(1)(b) (U.K.). Many states have analogous provisions.

A grammar rule even less often followed is the pronoun gender rule: He means a male referent, she a female referent. Because most statutes were drafted in eras when the main legal actors who counted were men, the male pronoun includes the female, and vice-versa. 1 U.S.C. § 2; Interpretation Act § 1(1)(a). Most states and the District of Columbia have a similar rule.

5. The Golden Rule (Against Absurdity)—and the Nietzsche Rule

English-speaking jurisdictions have a few catch-all rules providing a mental check for the technical process of word-parsing and grammar-crunching. The *golden rule* is that interpreters should "adhere to the ordinary meaning of the words used, and to the grammatical construction, unless that * * * leads to any manifest absurdity or repugnance, in which case the language may be varied or modified, so as to avoid such inconvenience, but no further." *Becke v. Smith*, 150 Eng. Rep. 724, 726 (U.K. Exch. 1836). See also Hart & Sacks' excerpts from old British cases in Chapter 5, § 1. For example, an early admiralty statute required purchasers of a vessel to register it immediately and barred them from receiving favorable duty treatment until they did so. In *Willing v. United States*, 8 U.S. (4 Cranch) 48 (1807), Chief Justice Marshall allowed favorable duty treatment for purchasers who had bought the vessel at sea and therefore could not have registered the purchase until their return. A strict application of the statute under those circumstances would have been manifestly unreasonable, the Chief Justice reasoned.

The golden rule is, in short, an *absurd results* exception to the plain meaning rule. In *Barnhart v. Thomas*, 540 U.S. 20 (2003), the Social Security Act's disability benefits program was available to a worker whose "physical or mental impairment or impairments are of such severity that he is not only unable to do his previous work but cannot, considering his age, education, and work experience, engage in any other kind of substantial gainful work which exists in the national economy." 42 U.S.C. § 423(d)(2)(A). Pauline Thomas was an elevator operator until that job was eliminated from the economy; she claimed to be disabled from other jobs in the economy. The Third Circuit ruled that she was disabled, rejecting the agency's argument that she could still do "[her] previous work." Then-Judge Alito thought it absurd for the government to consider the applicant not disabled from working her previous job when it no longer existed. Writing for the Supreme Court, Justice Scalia disagreed. A claimant who is concededly able to do her previous job is *probably* able to perform a job *somewhere* in the national economy. Hence, the agency's position was at most stingy, but by no means an absurd proof rule for a program with limited resources.

Relatedly, courts should be willing to revise *scrivener's errors*—obvious mistakes in the transcription of statutes into the law books. See, e.g., *Lamie v. U.S. Trustee*, 540 U.S. 526, 530–31 (2004) (Court rewrites Bankruptcy Act to fix drafting error); *Green v. Bock Laundry* (Chapter 5, § 3(A)) (all Justices agreeing to rewrite statute to correct an absurd provision that must have been the result of a scrivener's error); *Schooner Paulina's Cargo v. United States*, 11 U.S. (7 Cranch) 52, 67–68 (1812) (Marshall, C.J., revising statute to clean up scrivener's error).

The golden rule and its corollaries are now subject to academic debate. Although Justice Scalia recognized an absurd results exception to the plain meaning rule in *Bock Laundry* (concurring opinion), scholars of various persuasions maintain that an absurd results exception to plain meaning is inconsistent with the premises of the new textualism.[9] In *Zuni Public School District v. Department of Education*, 550 U.S. 81, 104–07 (2007), Justice Stevens' concurring opinion rests the absurd result exception upon notions of probable legislative intent: if a plain meaning interpretation is truly absurd, that is prima facie reason to think Congress did not intend it (absent evidence to the contrary, of course). Justice Scalia roundly denounced this approach, in absolute language suggesting that he now agreed with his critics that there should be no absurd result exception to the plain meaning rule. *Id.* at 116–22 (Scalia, J., dissenting).

Friedrich Nietzsche admonished in *Mixed Opinions and Maxims* No. 137 (1879): "The worst readers are those who proceed like plundering soldiers: they pick up a few things they can use, soil and confuse the rest, and blaspheme the whole."[10] All the Justices would agree with this sentiment; indeed, both Stevens and Scalia invoke it in their *Zuni* debate. We read Nietzsche's lesson for the statutory interpreter to include the following: Be humble. Consider how other people use language. Be helpful to the project rather than hypertechnical.

6. Referential and Qualifying Words: The Last Antecedent Rule

Referential and qualifying words or phrases refer only to the last antecedent, unless contrary to the apparent legislative intent derived from the sense of the entire enactment. E.g., *Jama v. Immigration & Customs Enforcement*, 543 U.S. 345 (2005). For example, in a statute providing that "the limitation of an action will not be extended beyond six years of the act or omission of alleged malpractice by a nondiscovery thereof," the "thereof" refers to the "act or omission of alleged malpractice." *Anderson v. Shook*, 333 N.W.2d 708 (N.D. 1983). Similarly, a proviso applies only to the provision, clause, or word immediately preceding it.

---

[9]   E.g., William Eskridge Jr., *Textualism, The Unknown Ideal?*, 96 Mich. L. Rev. 1509 (1998) (criticizing the new textualism for this inconsistency); John Manning, *The Absurdity Doctrine*, 116 Harv. L. Rev. 2387 (2003) (agreeing with Eskridge and urging textualists to abandon the absurd results canon); John Nagle, *Textualism's Exceptions*, Issues in Legal Scholarship (Nov. 2002), www.bepress.com/ils/iss3/art5 (same).

[10]   Friedrich Nietzsche, *On the Genealogy of Morals (and Other Works)* 175 (Walter Kaufman trans. and ed. 1967). David Krentel, Georgetown University Law Center, Class of 1995, brought this maxim to our attention.

LOCKHART V. UNITED STATES

Supreme Court of the United States, 2016.
___ U.S. ___, 136 S.Ct. 958, 194 L.Ed.2d 48.

JUSTICE SOTOMAYOR delivered the opinion of the Court.

Defendants convicted of possessing child pornography in violation of 18 U.S.C. § 2252(a)(4) are subject to a 10-year mandatory minimum sentence and an increased maximum sentence if they have "a prior conviction . . . under the laws of any State relating to aggravated sexual abuse, sexual abuse, or abusive sexual conduct involving a minor or ward." § 2252(b)(2).

The question before us is whether the phrase "involving a minor or ward" modifies all items in the list of predicate crimes ("aggravated sexual abuse," "sexual abuse," and "abusive sexual conduct") or only the one item that immediately precedes it ("abusive sexual conduct"). * * *

[I] In April 2000, Avondale Lockhart was convicted of sexual abuse in the first degree under N.Y. Penal Law Ann. § 130.65(1). The crime involved his then-53-year-old girlfriend. Eleven years later, Lockhart was indicted in the Eastern District of New York for attempting to receive child pornography in violation of 18 U.S.C. § 2252(a)(2) and for possessing child pornography in violation of § 2252(a)(4)(b). Lockhart pleaded guilty to the possession offense and the Government dismissed the receipt offense.

Lockhart's presentence report calculated a guidelines range of 78 to 97 months for the possession offense. But the report also concluded that Lockhart was subject to § 2252(b)(2)'s mandatory minimum because his prior New York abuse conviction related "to aggravated sexual abuse, sexual abuse, or abusive sexual conduct involving a minor or ward."

Lockhart objected, arguing that the statutory phrase "involving a minor or ward" applies to all three listed crimes: "aggravated sexual abuse," "sexual abuse," *and* "abusive sexual conduct." He therefore contended that his prior conviction for sexual abuse involving an adult fell outside the enhancement's ambit. The District Court rejected Lockhart's argument and applied the mandatory minimum. The Second Circuit affirmed his sentence.

[II] Section 2252(b)(2) reads [in relevant part]:

"Whoever violates, or attempts or conspires to violate [§ 2252(a)(4)] shall be fined * * * or imprisoned not more than 10 years, or both, but . . . if such person has a prior conviction under this chapter, chapter 71, chapter 109A * * * or under the laws of any State relating to aggravated sexual abuse, sexual abuse, or abusive sexual conduct involving a minor or ward, * * * such person shall be fined under this title and imprisoned for not less than 10 years nor more than 20 years."

This case concerns that provision's list of state sexual-abuse offenses. * * * We hold that "involving a minor or ward" modifies only "abusive sexual conduct," the antecedent immediately preceding it. Although § 2252(b)(2)'s list of state predicates is awkwardly phrased (to put it charitably), the provision's text and context together reveal a straightforward reading. A timeworn textual canon is confirmed by the structure and internal logic of the statutory scheme.

Consider the text. When this Court has interpreted statutes that include a list of terms or phrases followed by a limiting clause, we have typically applied an interpretive strategy called the "rule of the last antecedent." See *Barnhart v. Thomas*, 540 U.S. 20, 26 (2003). The rule provides that "a limiting clause or phrase . . . should ordinarily be read as modifying only the noun or phrase that it immediately follows." *Ibid*; see also Black's Law Dictionary 1532–1533 (10th ed. 2014) ("[Q]ualifying words or phrases modify the words or phrases immediately preceding them and not words or phrases more remote, unless the extension is necessary from the context or the spirit of the entire writing"); A. Scalia & B. Garner, Reading Law: The Interpretation of Legal Texts 144 (2012). * * *

The rule reflects the basic intuition that when a modifier appears at the end of a list, it is easier to apply that modifier only to the item directly before it. That is particularly true where it takes more than a little mental energy to process the individual entries in the list, making it a heavy lift to carry the modifier across them all. For example, imagine you are the general manager of the Yankees and you are rounding out your 2016 roster. You tell your scouts to find a defensive catcher, a quick-footed shortstop, or a pitcher from last year's World Champion Kansas City Royals. It would be natural for your scouts to confine their search for a pitcher to last year's championship team, but to look more broadly for catchers and shortstops.

Applied here, the last antecedent principle suggests that the phrase "involving a minor or ward" modifies only the phrase that it immediately follows: "abusive sexual conduct." As a corollary, it also suggests that the phrases "aggravated sexual abuse" and "sexual abuse" are not so constrained.

Of course, as with any canon of statutory interpretation, the rule of the last antecedent "is not an absolute and can assuredly be overcome by other indicia of meaning." For instance, take " 'the laws, the treaties, and the constitution of the United States.' " A reader intuitively applies "of the United States" to "the laws," "the treaties" and "the constitution" because (among other things) laws, treaties, and the constitution are often cited together, because readers are used to seeing "of the United States" modify each of them, and because the listed items are simple and parallel without unexpected internal modifiers or structure. Section 2252(b)(2), by contrast, does not contain items that readers are used to seeing listed together or a concluding modifier that readers are accustomed to applying to each of them. And the varied syntax of each item in the list makes it hard for the reader to carry the final modifying clause across all three.

More importantly, here the interpretation urged by the rule of the last antecedent is not overcome by other indicia of meaning. To the contrary, § 2252(b)(2)'s context fortifies the meaning that principle commands. * * *

Section 2252(b)(2) establishes sentencing minimums and maximums for three categories of offenders. The first third of the section imposes a 10-year maximum sentence on offenders with no prior convictions. The second third imposes a 10-year minimum and 20-year maximum on offenders who have previously violated a federal offense listed within various chapters of the Federal Criminal Code. And the last third imposes the same minimum and maximum on offenders who have previously committed state "sexual abuse, aggravated sexual abuse, or abusive sexual conduct involving a minor or ward" as well as a number of state crimes related to the possession and distribution of child pornography.

Among the chapters of the Federal Criminal Code that can trigger § 2252(b)(2)'s recidivist enhancement are crimes "under . . . chapter 109A." Chapter 109A criminalizes a range of sexual-abuse offenses involving adults *or* minors and wards. And it places those federal sexual-abuse crimes under headings that use language nearly identical to the language § 2252(b)(2) uses to enumerate the three categories of state sexual-abuse predicates. The first section in Chapter 109A is titled "Aggravated sexual abuse." 18 U.S.C. § 2241. The second is titled "Sexual abuse." § 2242. And the third is titled "Sexual abuse of a minor or ward." § 2243. Applying the rule of the last antecedent, those sections mirror precisely the order, precisely the divisions, and nearly precisely the words used to describe the three state sexual-abuse predicate crimes in § 2252(b)(2): "aggravated sexual abuse," "sexual abuse," and "abusive sexual conduct involving a minor or ward."

This similarity appears to be more than a coincidence. We cannot state with certainty that Congress used Chapter 109A as a template for the list of state predicates set out in § 2252(b)(2), but we cannot ignore the parallel, particularly because the headings in Chapter 109A were in place when Congress amended the statute to add § 2252(b)(2)'s state sexual-abuse predicates. * * *

The dissent offers a suggestion rooted in its impressions about how people ordinarily speak and write. The problem is that, as even the dissent acknowledges, § 2252(b)(2)'s list of state predicates is hardly intuitive. No one would mistake its odd repetition and inelegant phrasing for a reflection of the accumulated wisdom of everyday speech patterns. It would be as if a friend asked you to get her tart lemons, sour lemons, or sour fruit from Mexico. If you brought back lemons from California, but your friend insisted that she was using customary speech and obviously asked for Mexican fruit only, you would be forgiven for disagreeing on both counts.

Faced with § 2252(b)(2)'s inartful drafting, then, do we interpret the provision by viewing it as a clear, commonsense list best construed as if conversational English? Or do we look around to see if there might be some provenance to its peculiarity? With Chapter 109A so readily at hand, we are unpersuaded by our dissenting colleague's invocation of basic examples from day-to-day life. Whatever the validity of the dissent's broader point, this simply is not a case in which colloquial practice is of much use. * * *

We conclude that the text and structure of § 2252(b)(2) confirm that the provision applies to prior state convictions for "sexual abuse" and "aggravated sexual abuse," whether or not the convictions involved a minor or ward. We therefore hold that Lockhart's prior conviction for sexual abuse of an adult is encompassed by § 2252(b)(2). The judgment of the Court of Appeals, accordingly, is affirmed.

JUSTICE KAGAN, with whom JUSTICE BREYER joins, dissenting.

Imagine a friend told you that she hoped to meet "an actor, director, or producer involved with the new Star Wars movie." You would know immediately that she wanted to meet an actor from the Star Wars cast—not an actor in, for example, the latest Zoolander. Suppose a real estate agent promised to find a client "a house, condo, or apartment in New York." Wouldn't the potential buyer be annoyed if the agent sent him information about condos in Maryland or California? And consider a law imposing a penalty for the "violation of any statute, rule, or regulation relating to insider trading." Surely a person would have cause to protest if punished under that provision for violating a traffic statute. The reason in all three cases is the same: Everyone understands that the modifying phrase—"involved with the new Star Wars movie," "in New York," "relating to insider trading"—applies to each term in the preceding list, not just the last. * * *

Indeed, this Court has made clear that the last-antecedent rule does not generally apply to the grammatical construction present here: when "[t]he modifying clause appear[s] . . . at the end of a single, integrated list." [citation omitted]. * * * A leading treatise puts the point as follows: "When there is a straightforward, parallel construction that involves all nouns or verbs in a series," a modifier at the end of the list "normally applies to the entire series." A. Scalia & B. Garner, Reading Law: The Interpretation of Legal Texts 147 (2012). That interpretive practice of applying the modifier to the whole list boasts a fancy name—the "series-qualifier canon," see Black's Law Dictionary 1574 (10th ed. 2014)—but, as my opening examples show, it reflects the completely ordinary way that people speak and listen, write and read.

Even the exception to the series-qualifier principle is intuitive, emphasizing both its common-sensical basis and its customary usage. When the nouns in a list are so disparate that the modifying clause does not make sense when applied to them all, then the last-antecedent rule takes over. Suppose your friend told you not that she wants to meet "an actor, director, or producer involved with Star Wars," but instead that she hopes someday to meet "a President, Supreme Court Justice, or actor involved with Star Wars." Presumably, you would know that she wants to meet a President or Justice even if that person has no connection to the famed film franchise. But so long as the modifying clause "is applicable as much to the first and other words as to the last," this Court has stated, "the natural construction of the language demands that the clause be read as applicable to all." * * *

The majority responds to all this by claiming that the "inelegant phrasing" of § 2252(b)(2) renders it somehow exempt from a grammatical rule reflecting "how people ordinarily" use the English language. But to begin with, the majority is wrong to suggest that the series-qualifier canon is only about "colloquial" or "conversational" English. In fact, it applies to both speech and writing, in both their informal and their formal varieties. * * * And the majority is wrong too in suggesting that the "odd repetition" in § 2252(b)(2)'s list of state predicates causes the series-qualifier principle to lose its force. The majority's own made-up sentence proves that much. If a friend asked you "to get her tart lemons, sour lemons, or sour fruit from Mexico," you might well think her list of terms perplexing: You might puzzle over the difference between tart and sour lemons, and wonder why she had specifically mentioned lemons when she apparently would be happy with sour fruit of any kind. But of one thing, you would have no doubt: Your friend wants some produce from Mexico; it would not do to get her, say, sour lemons from Vietnam. However weird the way she listed fruits—or the way § 2252(b)(2) lists offenses—the modifying clause still refers to them all. * * *

NOTES ON THE LAST ANTECEDENT RULE

1. *Parallel Versus Disparate Lists.* In a footnote to her dissent omitted from the Casebook, Justice Kagan takes issue with the majority's baseball example involving the Yankees general manager. She contends that the last antecedent rule applies there only because the three terms in the series are *not* parallel. If instead of asking your scouts to find "a defensive catcher, a quick-footed shortstop, or a pitcher from [the Kansas City Royals]," the sentence referred to "a catcher, shortstop, or pitcher from the Kansas City Royals," Kagan maintains that "all three players must [then] come from the Royals—because the three terms (unlike in the majority's sentence) are a parallel series with a modifying clause at the end." Are you persuaded that Justice Kagan has the better of this argument about the search for three new players for the Yankees roster? Is this disagreement relevant or helpful in resolving the application of the Last Antecedent Rule to the three state law crimes listed in section 2252(b)(2)? How else would you seek to distinguish between application of the last antecedent rule and the series qualifier rule?

2. *The Last Antecedent Rule as a Presumption—but How Strong?* Legal writing scholars have established that the rule is being invoked with greater frequency in recent years. Since Justice Scalia's majority opinion in *Barnhart v. Thomas,* 540 U.S. 20, 26 (2003) (relied on by the Court in *Lockhart*), there has been a notable increase in usage in both the Supreme Court and the circuits. See Joseph Kimble, *The Doctrine of the Last Antecedent, the Example in* Barnhart, *Why Both Are Weak, and How Textualism Postures*, 16 Scribes J. of Legal Writing 5 (2014–15) and sources cited therein. The Court in *Lockhart* makes clear that the "rule," like other canons, is a presumption that "can assuredly be overcome by other indicia of meaning." What is less clear is the strength of this presumption. Is it moderately strong, as suggested in *Barnhart* (the modifier "*ordinarily*" refers to the last antecedent)? Scalia and Garner in *Reading Law* suggest it may be a somewhat milder presumption: the modifier "*generally* refers to the nearest *reasonable* antecedent." One scholar has asserted that the rule "contradicts other linguistic principles [and has] created as much confusion and disagreement as the ambiguous modifier its drafter set out to clarify." Terri Le Clercq, *Doctrine of the Last Antecedent: The Mystifying Morass of Ambiguous Modifiers*, 40 Tex. J. Bus. L. 199 (2004). How strong is the presumption in *Lockhart*? Does the majority's reliance on the parallel structure with chapter 109A of the federal criminal code reinforce or diminish the importance of its reliance on the last antecedent rule?

3. *Last Antecedents, Series Qualifiers, and Redundancy.* One argument made by the United States in *Lockhart* was that if the phrases "sexual abuse" and "abusive sexual conduct" are both limited to minors or wards, they say precisely the same thing; thus, in order to avoid pointless redundancy, one of these crimes must be limited in a way that the other is not. Yet, if only "abusive sexual conduct" is limited by the "minor or ward" qualifier, then don't all convictions for abusive sexual conduct involving minors or wards also qualify as "sexual abuse"? Consider whether either side has a better argument based on the rule to avoid redundancy, another oft-invoked language canon discussed in Section 2 below.

4. *Last Antecedents and Context.* The last antecedent rule can be trumped by the punctuation rule. "Evidence that a qualifying phrase is supposed to apply to all

antecedents instead of only to the immediately preceding one may be found in the fact that it is separated from the antecedents by a comma." 2A Sutherland § 47.33. The last antecedent rule can also be negated by other statutory context. Some courts have developed an "across the board rule" which is a special exception to the last antecedent rule: "[W]hen a clause follows several words in a statute and is applicable as much to the first word as to the others in the list, the clause should be applied to all of the words which preceded it." *Bd. of Trustees v. Judge*, 123 Cal. Rptr. 830, 834 (Cal. App. 1975).

2. STRUCTURAL CANONS

Some textually-grounded rules or maxims of statutory interpretation derive not from the association of words or the principles of grammar but instead from the particular language's relationship to the larger structural context of a statute. The Sutherland treatise identifies different approaches that have been used: interpretation of each section in isolation from the others; interpretation of all sections within each part of a statute together; resolution of ambiguities based upon the purposes and goals set forth in the preamble to the statute; and interpretation of each section in the context of the whole enactment. The treatise endorses the "whole act rule" as "the most realistic in view of the fact that a legislature passes judgment upon the act as an entity, not giving one portion of the act any greater authority than another. Thus any attempt to segregate any portion or exclude any other portion from consideration is almost certain to distort the legislative intent." 2A Sutherland § 47.02. See *Maxwell* 47–64 (English background and current application of the whole act rule); *Sullivan* 173–79 (Canadian cases).

A. THE WHOLE ACT RULE

From its earliest cases, the U.S. Supreme Court has followed the whole act rule in construing statutes. E.g., *United States v. Fisher*, 6 U.S. (2 Cranch) 358 (1805); *United States v. Priestman*, 4 U.S. (4 Dall.) 29 (1800) (per curiam). "Statutory interpretation * * * is a holistic endeavor. A provision that may seem ambiguous in isolation is often clarified by the remainder of the statutory scheme—because the same terminology is used elsewhere in a context that makes its meaning clear, or because only one of the permissible meanings produces a substantive effect that is compatible with the rest of the law." *United Savings Ass'n of Texas v. Timbers of Inwood Forest Assocs.*, 484 U.S. 365, 371 (1988). "When 'interpreting a statute, the court will not look merely to a particular clause in which general words may be used, but will take in connection with it the whole statute * * * and the objects and policy of the law, as indicated by its various provisions, and give to it such a construction as will carry into execution the will of the legislature.'" *Kokoszka v. Belford*, 417 U.S. 642, 650 (1974); see also *Doe v. Chao*, 540 U.S. 614 (2004) (considering uncodified parts of the "whole act"). A critical assumption of the whole act approach is *coherence*: the interpreter presumes that the legislature drafted the statute as a document that is internally consistent in its use of language and in the way its provisions work together.[11] Note similarities to interpretation of contracts and sacred texts like the Bible.

---

[11]   See, e.g., *Ledbetter v. Goodyear Tire & Rubber Co.*, 550 U.S. 618 (2007); *Gonzales v. Oregon*, 546 U.S. 243 (2006); *Conroy v. Aniskoff*, 507 U.S. 511 (1993); *King v. St. Vincent's Hosp.*, 502 U.S. 215 (1991). See also

1. Corollaries to the Whole Act Rule

(a) *Titles.* Because Parliament's clerks, rather than Parliament, provided the titles of acts, the traditional English rule has been that the title could not be used for interpretive purposes. Thus, if the statute in Problem 6-1 had the title, "An Act to Prohibit Motorized Vehicles from the Park," English courts would have ignored this evidence of the statute's ambit. (The foregoing, by the way, is the *long title* of the statute; a *short title* would be something like the "The Motor Vehicles in the Park Act.") This is no longer the practice in most English-speaking jurisdictions, for the long title, and often a short title as well, are part of the legislative bill from the very beginning. In the United States, most state constitutions require the legislated enactment to have a title that gives accurate notice of the contents of the law. See also 2A Sutherland § 47.03 (the "title cannot control the plain words of the statute" but "[i]n case of ambiguity the court may consider the title to resolve uncertainty in the purview [the body] of the act or for the correction of obvious errors."); *Maxwell* 3–6 (long title but probably not short title may be used to resolve ambiguities); *Sullivan* 161 (both long and short title may be used "to indicate the purpose or scope of legislation.").

The U.S. Supreme Court in *Holy Trinity Church* (Chapter 5, § 1) considered the statute's long title as cogent evidence of its purpose and indeed reworked the statutory provision to be consistent with it. However, today's Supreme Court generally does not rely on statutory titles as important evidence of statutory meaning, although Justices will sometimes quote the title as marginally relevant context. E.g., *Porter v. Nussle*, 534 U.S. 516, 524 (2002). And see *Yates v. United States*, 135 S.Ct. 1074 (2015), reproduced below, where the majority relies on a section title and caption.

(b) *Preambles and Purpose Clauses.*[12] Statutory preambles typically include a set of Findings followed by a statement of one or more Purposes. The traditional English rule gave great weight to statutory preambles because they were considered the best source for determining statutory purpose. American courts, following the whole act approach, have declined to give the preamble any greater weight than other parts of the statute (the title, purview, individual sections). "[T]he settled principle of law is that the preamble cannot control the enacting part of the statute, in cases where the enacting part is expressed in clear, unambiguous terms" but in instances of ambiguity, "the preamble may be resorted to . . . show the intention of the law maker." 2A Sutherland § 47.4. To the extent that the interpreter is able to find ambiguity and follows the Hart and Sacks purpose/context approach to statutory interpretation (Chapter 5, § 2), the preamble will be a particularly valuable contribution to the interpretive task. The Canadian Supreme Court, for example, vigorously relies on statutory preambles for this reason. See *Rawluk v. Rawluk*,

---

Canada Sugar Refining Co. v. Regina, [1898] A.C. 735, 741 (U.K. House of Lords) (Davey, J.) (every clause of a law should be "construed with reference to the context and other clauses of the Act, so as, so far as possible, to make a consistent enactment of the whole statute"); *Greenshields v. Regina*, [1958] S.C.R. 216, 225 (Can. Sup. Ct.) ("a section or enactment must be construed as a whole, each portion throwing light, if need be, on the rest").

[12]   A *preamble* sets out the important facts or considerations that gave rise to the legislation. A *purpose clause* sets out the objectives the legislation seeks to achieve or the problems it tries to solve. In text, we shall refer to both as preambles.

[1990] 1 S.C.R. 70 (Can. Sup. Ct.) (concluding that because the preamble of Ontario's Family Law Act spoke of marriage as a "form of partnership," the common law remedy of "constructive trust" was authorized under the Act).

A preamble, in the form of congressional findings, played a key interpretive role in *Sutton v. United Airlines, Inc.*, 527 U.S. 471 (1999). The Americans with Disabilities Act (ADA) prohibits job discrimination against people with disabilities. The airline had refused to consider hiring two pilots (they were twin sisters) whose eyesight was severely myopic. The airline argued that because poor eyesight could be completely corrected by eyeglasses, the pilots and other myopics did not have a "physical or mental impairment that substantially limits one or more . . . major life activities." 42 U.S.C. § 12102(2)(C). This was an ironic construction of the ADA, for it would allow the airline to refuse to hire the sisters because of an impairment that the airline conceded was correctable. Yet the Supreme Court agreed, in part because the ADA's preamble found that 43 million people in the U.S. had disabilities, 42 U.S.C. § 12101(a)(1)—a far smaller number than people with poor enough vision to justify eyeglasses. *Id.* at 484–86; see *id.* at 494–95 (Ginsburg, J., concurring especially for this reason).

In a forthcoming article, Jarrod Shobe demonstrates that although findings and purpose statements are part of the enacted text, they have usually been ignored or discounted by courts and are undertheorized by legal scholars. Shobe argues that all of the enacted text should be interpreted as a unified whole with its parts given equal weight, and that findings and purposes offer a text-based path forward that can help bridge the gap between textualists and purposivists. Jarrod Shobe, *Enacted Findings and Purposes*, 86 U. Chi. L. Rev. ___ (2019). Why might textualists regard findings and purposes as "less equal" than the rest of the enacted text? Should these provisions be regarded as more hortatory than prescriptive? Are they less likely to be read or understood by members who vote on the legislation?

(c) *Provisos.* Provisos restrict the effect of statutory provisions or create exceptions to general statutory rules. They typically follow the provision being restricted or excepted, and start with: " * * * *Provided that* * * *." If there is doubt about the interpretation of a proviso, it is supposed to be strictly (narrowly) construed. "This strict construction derives from the idea that an act generally expresses legislative purpose and policy, and only those subjects expressly exempted [by the proviso] should be freed from a statute's operation." 2A Sutherland § 47.8. We do not detect much interest in the proviso rule among recent Supreme Court Justices.

2. Drafting in State Legislatures: Model Bills

The whole act rule is often applied by state courts. In addition, more than 30 states have codified the whole act rule and the presumption of consistent usage, requiring state courts to apply these canons when interpreting state laws. (see § 3(C) of this chapter). At the same time, recent evidence indicates that state legislative drafting may be controlled by private interests in direct ways that could affect the presumption of overarching coherence.

A two-year investigation by USA Today, The Arizona Republic and the Center for Public Integrity revealed the extent to which state lawmakers are relying on so-called "model" bills: fill-in-the-blank legislation written by special interest groups so that nearly identical legislation can be passed in all states. Using a computer algorithm, the investigators found that over 10,000 state bills introduced since 2011 were nearly identical to model legislation. Some 2100 of these bills passed state legislatures and became law. More than 80 percent of the introduced bills and 90 percent of the enacted bills were written by industry and conservative groups like the American Legislative Exchange Council (ALEC) or the Goldwater Institute. The remainder were drafted by liberal groups like the State Innovation Exchange (SIX), or groups with no clear political valence. These model bills are introduced across the country; although the investigation found that introductions are especially heavy in the Southeast and Southwest (Mississippi, Virginia, West Virginia, Missouri, Oklahoma, Arizona), some historically "blue" states also are frequent users (Illinois, New Jersey). *See* Rob O'Dell & Nick Penzenstadler, *Copy, Paste, Legislate* USA Today, Apr. 4, 2019. https://www.usatoday.com/in-depth/news/investigations/2019/04/03/abortion-gun-laws-stand-your-ground-model-bills-conservatives-liberal-corporate-influence-lobbyists/3162173002/.

The drafters of these model bills are referred to by one scholar as Interested Private Lawmakers (IPLs). See Barak Orbach, *Invisible Lawmaking*, 79 U. Chi. L. Rev. Dialogue 1, 2–3 (2012). IPLs bring legislators together with special interest groups. This partnership benefits both parties. Legislators are provided with fully-formed bills they can easily sponsor while also likely gaining new campaign donations from the special interest groups that drafted the model bill. Special interest groups can accomplish their agenda quickly and more efficiently by having state legislators spread these model bills across the country.

The USA Today investigation found that bills copied from model legislation have been used to override positions adopted by local voters and their elected leaders. After cities and counties raised their minimum wage, banned plastic bags, or limited short-term rentals in residential neighborhoods, industry groups that oppose such measures drafted model bills invalidating these local measures, some of which were passed in state legislatures and preempted the local legislation. One example cited was Airbnb's support for the Arizona-based Goldwater Institute, which pushed model bills to strike down local laws limiting short-term rentals in residential neighborhoods in four states. The USA Today investigation also found that legislators passing model bills may not know the impact of the model bill they are sponsoring or even who drafted the bill.

How should reliance on model bills by state legislators impact application of the whole act rule by courts? The idea of thousands of model bills becoming law in multiple states is at least in tension with the presumption of consistency in any given state. And if different IPLs are drafting bills to amend the same chapter of a state's laws, it may be even less likely that these different groups are concerned about creating a uniform body of law. On the other hand, does model legislation written by interest groups really change anything? It is well known that legislation is rarely drafted by legislators, but instead by their staff and legal counsel (see note 3 following the *Casey* decision, § 2(C) below). Legislation written by IPLs may be just as coherent as legislation written by staff or counsel. Perhaps model legislation may even limit certain institutional barriers that obstruct the whole act rule, such as omnibus or conglomerate bills. Are model bills better suited for applying the whole act rule, given that they tend to address only a single topic and thus consistent usage can more naturally be assumed?

Finally, the USA Today investigation highlights the importance of a bill's title and summary. Legislators admitted to agreeing to co-sponsor a model bill after only reading the bill's title and summary. Some legislators decide to co-sponsor a bill without realizing that it is a model bill written by an IPL. Does this mean that courts should be giving more weight to a bill's title and summary? What about model bills that have notoriously misleading titles? For example, ALEC drafted the Asbestos Claims Transparency Act, introduced in at least 17 states and enacted in at least 10 states. While the title may suggest that the bill intends to benefit victims of asbestos exposure, it actually mandates additional procedural hurdles for victims before they can file suit against the responsible parties. ALEC drafted this model bill with support from corporations, like insurance companies, who bear substantial liability for asbestos exposure. If a model bill has a misleading title, should a reviewing court assume the legislator was aware of the substance of the bill? Or should the court account for the discrepancy between the title and the substance? To see the Asbestos Claims Transparency Act model bill, visit https://www.alec.org/model-policy/asbestos-claims-transparency-act/.

B. THE RULE TO AVOID REDUNDANCY (AGAINST SURPLUSAGE)

Under the whole act rule, the presumption is that every word and phrase adds something to the statutory command. Accordingly, it is a "cardinal rule of statutory interpretation that no provision should be construed to be entirely redundant." *Kungys v. United States*, 485 U.S. 759, 778 (1988) (plurality opinion by Scalia, J.); see, e.g., *Circuit City Stores, Inc. v. Adams*, 532 U.S. 105 (2001); *United States v. Alaska*, 521 U.S. 1 (1997); *Walters v. Metro. Educ. Enters., Inc.*, 519 U.S. 202 (1997); *Rake v. Wade*, 508 U.S. 464 (1993); *Colautti v. Franklin*, 439 U.S. 379, 392 (1979). "A construction which would leave without effect any part of the language of a statute will normally be rejected." *Maxwell* 36.

For example, the issue in *Western Union Telegraph Co. v. Lenroot*, 323 U.S. 490 (1945), was whether the Fair Labor Standards Act prohibition against child labor applied to telegraph messengers. The prohibition reached any shipment of "goods" in interstate commerce, and "goods" were defined as "wares, products, commodities, merchandise, and articles or subjects of commerce of any character." The telegraph company argued that its service was intangible and therefore not a "good." Both Judge Learned Hand for the Court of Appeals and Justice Jackson for the Supreme Court held that telegraph services were "subjects of commerce." Hand suggested that if the definition were read to include only tangible things, the term "subjects," which had been added by a special Senate amendment to "articles of commerce of any character," would add nothing to the statute.

No surplusage

The rule against redundancy is more at odds with the legislative drafting process than most of the other whole act rules, as words and phrases are added to important legislation right up to the last minute. Nonetheless, the rule against redundancy plays a more important role in Supreme Court opinions in the new millennium than it did in the old. *Circuit City*, previously discussed in § 1(B)(2) of this chapter, is but one example. Responding to Justice Souter's textual argument in dissent, that "seamen, railroad employees, or any other class of workers engaged in foreign or interstate commerce" included all contract employees, Justice Kennedy's *Circuit City* opinion fell back on the rule against surplusage: "there would be no need for Congress to use the phrases 'seamen' and 'railroad employees' if these same classes of workers were subsumed within the meaning of the 'engaged in . . . commerce' residual clause." 532 U.S. 105, 114 (2001).

BELT-AND-SUSPENDERS

Consider a possible counter-canon to the rule against surplusage. One of us contends that rather than simply being lazy or loquacious, legislatures often include textual features that are "deliberately duplicative, redundant, and/or reinforcing rather than perfectly parsimonious." Ethan J. Leib & James J. Brudney, *The Belt-and-Suspenders Canon*, 105 Iowa L. Rev. ___ (2020). Judicial appreciation for these legislative drafting realities originated with nineteenth and early twentieth century references to *ex abundanti cautela* (out of an abundance of caution) and the Macbeth canon ("make assurance doubly sure"). Leib and Brudney illustrate how Congress and state legislatures today self-consciously adopt belt-and-suspenders strategies to accomplish principled and rational objectives, such as making sure longstanding policy does not get abrogated; avoiding potential conflicts among statutory schemes; responding to concern about impairment of core values; and seeking to build or maintain consensus. Courts have at times credited belt-and-suspenders drafting techniques while framing this credit as a concession to legislative recalcitrance. E.g. *Freeman v. Quicken Loans*, 566 U.S. 624, 635 (2012) (Scalia, J.); *United States v. Bronstein*, 849 F.3d 1101, 1110 (D.C. Cir. 2017). See also Justice Kagan's dissent in *Yates*, below, offering a more positive explanation for redundant drafting.

Legislators may focus on textual redundancy under a caution-based rationale, in order to be sure that agency and judicial implementers get the message. Or they may include repetition for consensus-based reasons, in an effort to attract colleagues who are skeptics or fence-sitters about the bill. Should courts examine the reasons why statutory text is redundant, so as to assess whether redundancy reflects legislative sloth as opposed to something more deliberate and self-conscious? Or should courts simply elevate the judicial value of coherence, which is arguably of primary relevance to citizens living under these laws, and chastise their legislative colleagues to draft in more meticulously clear terms? Leib and Brudney propose that "the belt-and-suspenders canon needs to be foregrounded, not treated as a least-best alternative," and that "one valuable approach to differentiating" between belt-and-suspenders and anti-surplusage is "to look for clues in legislative history." Do you agree? Are there risks involved in encouraging judges to "complexify" their review of the drafting process by inquiring more deeply as to whether redundancy may be deliberate?

Belt + Suspenders   v s.   Anti-surplusage

look @ Leg history clues

C. PRESUMPTIONS OF CONSISTENT USAGE, AND MEANINGFUL VARIATION

Consistent Usage. Under the holistic assumptions of the whole act rule, it is "reasonable to presume that the same meaning is implied by the use of the same expression in every part of the Act." *Maxwell* 278. Similarly, where a statutory word has been used in other statutes dealing with the same subject matter and has a settled meaning in those statutes, interpreters will presumptively follow the settled meaning. Although this is viewed as a weak presumption in most English-speaking countries, it has emerged as a stronger one in the United States, where it is presumed that "identical words used in different parts of the same act are intended to have the same meaning." *Sullivan v. Stroop*, 496 U.S. 478, 484 (1990), followed in, e.g., *Powerex Corp. v. Reliant Energy Servs., Inc.*, 551 U.S. 224 (2007); *Gustafson v. Alloyd Co.*, 513 U.S. 561, 570 (1995). But see *Dewsnup v. Timm*, 502 U.S. 410, 417 & n.3 (1992) (finding such argument unilluminating).

Meaningful Variation. Additionally, "[f]rom the general presumption that the same expression is presumed to be used in the same sense throughout an Act or a series of cognate Acts, there follows the further presumption that a change of wording denotes a change in meaning." *Maxwell* 282; cf. *id.* at 286 (but this is a weak presumption). The leading American case for this presumption of meaningful variation is Chief Justice Marshall's opinion in *United States v. Fisher*, 6 U.S. (2 Cranch) 358, 388–97 (1805). A statute whose first four sections regulated the relationship between the United States and "receivers of public monies" had a fifth section which said that "where any revenue officer, or other person[,] hereafter becoming indebted to the United States . . . shall become insolvent, . . . the debt due to the United States shall be first satisfied." A competing creditor argued that § 5 should have been limited to receivers of public moneys, like §§ 1–4 and the title of the law, but Marshall found no reason to think that Congress intended a narrower ambit for § 5 and so read it without the limitation. Accord *Lawrence v. Florida*, 549 U.S. 327, 333–34 (2007); *Hamdan v. Rumsfeld*, 548 U.S. 557, 577–79 (2006).

Variation in terminology ought to have less force when one statute is adopted at a different time than another. E.g., *Gutierrez v. Ada*, 528 U.S. 250 (2000) (declining to apply a rule of meaningful variation when a later amendment used different terminology from the provision at issue). But if Congress changes a statute when reenacting it, the rule has renewed bite, as in *Osborn v. Bank of the United States*, 22 U.S. (9 Wheat.) 738, 817–18 (1824) (construing a provision to allow for federal jurisdiction because Congress had expanded the provision's language after a previous Supreme Court decision had denied such jurisdiction under the earlier statutory wording).

A wedding of *expressio unius* and consistent usage is the rule that "[w]here Congress includes particular language in one section of a statute but omits it in another . . ., it is generally presumed that Congress acts intentionally and purposely in the disparate inclusion or exclusion." *Keene Corp. v. United States*, 508 U.S. 200, 208 (1993); accord *Arlington Cent. Sch. Dist. Bd. of Educ. v. Murphy*, 548 U.S. 291, 299–304 (2006); *Gozlon-Peretz v. United States*, 498 U.S. 395, 404–05 (1991). The Court refined this canon in *Field v. Mans*, 516 U.S. 59, 67–76 (1995), where it held this negative implication rule was inapplicable when there was a reasonable explanation for the variation. "The more apparently deliberate the contrast, the stronger the inference, as applied, for example, to contrasting statutory sections originally enacted simultaneously in relevant respects. * * * The rule is weakest when it suggests results strangely at odds with other textual pointers, like the common-law language at work in the [bankruptcy] statute here." *Id.* at 75–76. See also *Lindh v. Murphy*, 521 U.S. 320 (1997) (Court vigorously debates use of the canon in interpreting Antiterrorism and Effective Death Penalty Act).

Rule Against Interpreting a Provision in Derogation of Other Provisions. An important corollary of the whole act rule is that one provision of a statute should not be interpreted in such a way as to derogate from other provisions of the statute (to the extent this is possible). An interpretation of provision 1 might derogate from other parts of the statute in one or more of the following ways:

- *operational conflict.* As interpreted, provision 1's operation conflicts with that of provision 2. For example, a citizen cannot obey provision 1 without violating provision 2.

- *philosophical tension.* As interpreted, provision 1 is in tension with an assumption of provision 2. For example, provision 2 might reflect a legislative compromise inconsistent with a broad reading of provision 1.

- *structural derogation.* Sharing elements of both operational conflict and philosophical tension, provision 1's interpretation might be at odds with the overall structure of the statute. Thus, provisions 2 and 3 might reflect a legislative policy that certain kinds of violations be handled administratively rather than judicially, which a broad view of judicially enforceable provision 1 might undermine.

For an example of cross-cutting derogations, see *Robinson v. Shell Oil Co.*, 519 U.S. 337, 345–46 (1997).

WEST VIRGINIA UNIVERSITY HOSPITALS V. CASEY

Supreme Court of the United States, 1991.
499 U.S. 83, 111 S.Ct. 1138, 113 L.Ed.2d 68.

JUSTICE SCALIA delivered the opinion of the Court.

This case presents the question whether fees for [expert] services in civil rights litigation may be shifted to the losing party pursuant to 42 U.S.C. § 1988, which permits the award of "a reasonable attorney's fee."[1]

[I. Petitioner (WVUH) filed suit against the governor of Pennsylvania and other state officials under 42 U.S.C. § 1983, challenging changes made by Pennsylvania to the reimbursement schedule for Medicaid patients. The District Court ruled in favor of petitioner and awarded fees under § 1983, including over $100,000 in fees for expert services. The Court of Appeals affirmed on the merits, but

---

[1]   Title 42 U.S.C. § 1988 provides in relevant part: "In any action or proceeding to enforce a provision of sections 1981, 1982, 1983, 1985, and 1986 of this title, title IX of Public Law 92–318 . . ., or title VI of the Civil Rights Act of 1964 . . ., the court, in its discretion, may allow the prevailing party, other than the United States, a reasonable attorney's fee as part of the costs."

reversed as to the expert fees, disallowing them except to the extent that they fell within the $30-per-day fees for witnesses prescribed by 28 U.S.C. § 1821(b).]

[II] Title 28 U.S.C. § 1920 provides:

"A judge or clerk of any court of the United States may tax as costs the following:

"(1) Fees of the clerk and marshal;

"(2) Fees of the court reporter for all or any part of the stenographic transcript necessarily obtained for use in the case;

"(3) Fees and disbursements for printing and witnesses;

"(4) Fees for exemplification and copies of papers necessarily obtained for use in the case;

"(5) Docket fees under section 1923 of this title;

"(6) Compensation of court appointed experts, compensation of interpreters, and salaries, fees, expenses, and costs of special interpretation services under section 1828 of this title."

Title 28 U.S.C. § 1821(b) limits the witness fees authorized by § 1920(3) as follows: "A witness shall be paid an attendance fee of $30 per day for each day's attendance. A witness shall also be paid the attendance fee for the time necessarily occupied in going to and returning from the place of attendance. . . ." In *Crawford Fitting Co. v. J.T. Gibbons, Inc.*, 482 U.S. 437 (1987), we held that these provisions define the full extent of a federal court's power to shift litigation costs absent express statutory authority to go further. * * * The question before us, then, is—with regard to both testimonial and nontestimonial expert fees—whether the term "attorney's fee" in § 1988 provides the "explicit statutory authority" required by *Crawford Fitting*.

[III] The record of statutory usage demonstrates convincingly that attorney's fees and expert fees are regarded as separate elements of litigation cost. While some fee-shifting provisions, like § 1988, refer only to "attorney's fees," see, *e.g.*, Civil Rights Act of 1964, 42 U.S.C. § 2000e–5(k), many others explicitly shift expert witness fees *as well as* attorney's fees. In 1976, just over a week prior to the enactment of § 1988, Congress passed those provisions of the Toxic Substances Control Act, 15 U.S.C. §§ 2618(d), 2619(c)(2), which provide that a prevailing party may recover "the costs of suit and reasonable fees for attorneys *and expert witnesses.*" (Emphasis added.) Also in 1976, Congress amended the Consumer Product Safety Act, 15 U.S.C. §§ 2060(c), 2072(a), 2073, which as originally enacted in 1972 shifted to the losing party "cost[s] of suit, including a reasonable attorney's fee," see 86 Stat. 1226. In the 1976 amendment, Congress altered the fee-shifting provisions to their present form by adding a phrase shifting expert witness fees *in addition to* attorney's fees. See Pub. L. 94–284, § 10, 90 Stat. 506, 507. Two other significant Acts passed in 1976 contain similar phrasing: the Resource Conservation and Recovery Act of 1976, 42 U.S.C. § 6972(e) ("costs of litigation (including reasonable attorney and expert witness fees)"), and the Natural Gas Pipeline Safety Act Amendments of 1976, 49 U.S.C.A. § 1686(e) ("costs of suit, including reasonable attorney's fees and reasonable expert witnesses fees").

Congress enacted similarly phrased fee-shifting provisions in numerous statutes both before 1976, see, *e.g.*, Endangered Species Act of 1973, 16 U.S.C. § 1540(g)(4) ("costs of litigation (including reasonable attorney and expert witness fees)"), and afterwards, see, *e.g.*, Public Utility Regulatory Policies Act of 1978, 16 U.S.C. § 2632(a)(1) ("reasonable attorneys' fees, expert witness fees, and other reasonable costs incurred in preparation and advocacy of [the litigant's] position"). These statutes encompass diverse categories of legislation, including tax, administrative procedure, environmental protection, consumer protection, admiralty and navigation, utilities regulation, and, significantly, civil rights: The Equal Access to Justice Act (EAJA), the counterpart to § 1988 for violation of federal rights by federal employees, states that " 'fees and other expenses' [as shifted by § 2412(d)(1)(A)] includes the reasonable expenses of expert witnesses . . . and reasonable attorney fees." 28 U.S.C. § 2412(d)(2)(A). At least 34 statutes in 10 different titles of the United States Code explicitly shift attorney's fees *and* expert witness fees.

The laws that refer to fees for nontestimonial expert services are less common, but they establish a similar usage both before and after 1976: Such fees are referred to *in addition to* attorney's fees when a shift is intended [under a] provision of the Criminal Justice Act of 1964, 18 U.S.C. § 3006A(e). * * *

To the same effect is the 1980 EAJA, which provides: " 'fees and other expenses' [as shifted by § 2412(d)(1)(A)] includes the reasonable expenses of expert witnesses, *the reasonable cost of any study, analysis, engineering report, test, or project* which is found by the court to be necessary for the preparation of the party's case, and reasonable attorney fees." 28 U.S.C. § 2412(d)(2)(A) (emphasis added). If the reasonable cost of a "study" or "analysis"—which is but another way of describing nontestimonial expert services—is by common usage already included in the "attorney fees," again a significant and highly detailed part of the statute becomes redundant. The Administrative Procedure Act, 5 U.S.C. § 504(b)(1)(A) (added 1980), and the Tax Equity and Fiscal Responsibility Act of 1982, 26 U.S.C. § 7430(c)(1), contain similar language. Also reflecting the same usage are two railroad regulation statutes, the Regional Rail Reorganization Act of 1973, 45 U.S.C. §§ 726(f)(9) ("costs and expenses (including reasonable fees of accountants, experts, and attorneys) actually incurred"), and the Railroad Revitalization and Regulatory Reform Act of 1976, 45 U.S.C. § 854(g) ("costs and expenses (including fees of accountants, experts, and attorneys) actually and reasonably incurred").[5]

We think this statutory usage shows beyond question that attorney's fees and expert fees are distinct items of expense. If, as WVUH argues, the one includes the other, dozens of statutes referring to the two separately become an inexplicable exercise in redundancy.

---

[5] WVUH cites a House Conference Committee Report from a statute passed in 1986, stating: "The conferees intend that the term 'attorneys' fees as part of the costs' include reasonable expenses and fees of expert witnesses and the reasonable costs of any test or evaluation which is found to be necessary for the preparation of the . . . case." H.R. Conf. Rep. No. 99–687, p. 5 (1986) (discussing the Handicapped Children's Protection Act of 1986, 20 U.S.C. § 1415(e)(4)(B)). In our view this undercuts rather than supports WVUH's position: The specification would have been quite unnecessary if the ordinary meaning of the term included those elements. The statement is an apparent effort to depart from ordinary meaning and to define a term of art.

[IV] WVUH argues that at least in pre-1976 *judicial* usage the phrase "attorney's fees" included the fees of experts. To support this proposition, it relies upon two historical assertions: first, that pre-1976 courts, when exercising traditional equitable discretion in shifting attorney's fees, taxed as an element of such fees the expenses related to expert services; and second, that pre-1976 courts shifting attorney's fees pursuant to statutes identical in phrasing to § 1988 allowed the recovery of expert fees. We disagree with these assertions. The judicial background against which Congress enacted § 1988 mirrored the statutory background: expert fees were regarded not as a subset of attorney's fees, but as a distinct category of litigation expense. * * *

[V] WVUH suggests that a distinctive meaning of "attorney's fees" should be adopted with respect to § 1988 because this statute was meant to overrule our decision in *Alyeska Pipeline Service Co. v. Wilderness Society*, 421 U.S 240 (1975). [P]rior to 1975 many courts awarded expert fees and attorney's fees in certain circumstances pursuant to their equitable discretion. In *Alyeska*, we held that this discretion did not extend beyond a few exceptional circumstances long recognized by common law. [Justice Scalia argued that the text of § 1988 is both broader and narrower than the pre-*Alyeska* regime, notwithstanding statements by the bill's drafters suggesting a goal of repealing the *Alyeska* decision. Accordingly, Justice Scalia saw no reason to depart from the "normal import of the text" by inferring that a repeal of the whole decision was part of the statute.]

WVUH further argues that the congressional purpose in enacting § 1988 must prevail over the ordinary meaning of the statutory terms. It quotes, for example, the House Committee Report to the effect that "the judicial remedy [must be] full and complete," H.R. Rep. No. 94–1558, at 1 (1976), and the Senate Committee Report to the effect that "[c]itizens must have the opportunity to recover what it costs them to vindicate [civil] rights in court," S. Rep. No. 94–1011, *supra*, at 2. As we have observed before, however, the purpose of a statute includes not only what it sets out to change, but also what it resolves to leave alone. The best evidence of that purpose is the statutory text adopted by both Houses of Congress and submitted to the President. Where that contains a phrase that is unambiguous—that has a clearly accepted meaning in both legislative and judicial practice—we do not permit it to be expanded or contracted by the statements of individual legislators or committees during the course of the enactment process. Congress could easily have shifted "attorney's fees and expert witness fees," or "reasonable litigation expenses," as it did in contemporaneous statutes; it chose instead to enact more restrictive language, and we are bound by that restriction.

[Justice Scalia addressed two final arguments of WVUH. First, WVUH argued that the Court's previous decision in *Missouri v. Jenkins*, 491 U.S. 274, 285 (1989), should control. In *Jenkins*, the Court concluded that § 1988 permitted separately billed paralegal and law clerk time to be charged to the losing party. Justice Scalia rebutted WVUH's argument that paralegal fees were analogous to expert fees. He noted that paralegal fees were traditionally included in attorney's fees and only recently had that billing practice been changing. By contrast, the lengthy record in this case illustrated that expert fees and attorney's fees are frequently distinguished within various statutes. Second, WVUH argued that, even if Congress did not expressly include expert fees in the fee-shifting provisions, it would have done so if it had thought about it. Justice Scalia rejected this argument, insisting that to expand unambiguous language to cover what was inadvertently omitted transcends and misunderstands the role of the judiciary.]

JUSTICE STEVENS, with whom JUSTICE MARSHALL and JUSTICE BLACKMUN join, dissenting.

[Justice Stevens began by contending that the Court should look to how this statute, § 1988, has been interpreted in the past, and to its legislative history, instead of analyzing the many other statutes that contain express provisions shifting expert fees.]

[I]   Under either the broad view of "costs" typically assumed in the fee-shifting context or the broad view of "a reasonable attorney's fee" articulated by this Court, expert witness fees are a proper component of an award under § 1988. Because we are not interpreting these words for the first time, they should be evaluated in the context that this and other courts have already created.

The term "costs" has a different and broader meaning in fee-shifting statutes than it has in the cost statutes that apply to ordinary litigation. [Justice Stevens explained that in *Missouri v. Jenkins*, Chief Justice Rehnquist, in a lone dissent, espoused the view that the majority holds in this case, but that the rest of the Court all agreed that fees for the services of paralegals and law clerks, as part of the final work product of the attorneys, were compensable as attorneys fees under the statute. In Justice Stevens' view, this reasoning should apply with equal force to expert fees.] To allow reimbursement of these other categories of expenses, and yet not to include expert witness fees, is both arbitrary and contrary to the broad remedial purpose that inspired the fee-shifting provision of § 1988.

[II]   The Senate Report on the Civil Rights Attorney's Fees Awards Act of 1976 explained that the purpose of the proposed amendment to 42 U.S.C. § 1988 was "to remedy anomalous gaps in our civil rights laws created by the United States Supreme Court's recent decision in *Alyeska Pipeline Service Co. v. Wilderness Society*, 421 U.S. 240 (1975), and to achieve consistency in our civil rights laws." S. Rep. No. 94–1011, at 1 (1976), 1976 U.S. Code Cong. & Admin. News 5909. The Senate Committee on the Judiciary wanted to level the playing field so that private citizens, who might have little or no money, could still serve as "private attorneys general" and afford to bring actions, even against state or local bodies, to enforce the civil rights laws. The Committee acknowledged that "[i]f private citizens are to be able to assert their civil rights, and if those who violate the Nation's fundamental laws are not to proceed with impunity, then citizens must have the opportunity to recover *what it costs them* to vindicate these rights in court." *Id.* at 2 (emphasis added). According to the Committee, the bill would create "no startling new remedy," but would simply provide "the technical requirements" requested by the Supreme Court in *Alyeska*, so that courts could "continue the practice of awarding attorneys' fees which had been going on for years prior to the Court's May decision." *Id.* at 6. * * *

The case before us today is precisely the type of public interest litigation that Congress intended to encourage by amending § 1988 to provide for fee shifting of a "reasonable attorney's fee as part of the costs." Petitioner, a tertiary medical center in West Virginia near the Pennsylvania border, provides services to a large number of Medicaid recipients throughout Pennsylvania. In January 1986, when the Pennsylvania Department of Public Welfare notified petitioner of its new Medicaid payment rates for Pennsylvania Medicaid recipients, petitioner believed them to be below the minimum standards for reimbursement specified by the Social Security Act. Petitioner successfully challenged the adequacy of the State's payment system under 42 U.S.C. § 1983. This Court's determination today that petitioner must assume the cost of $104,133 in expert witness fees is at war with the congressional purpose of making the prevailing party whole. * * *

[III] In recent years the Court has vacillated between a purely literal approach to the task of statutory interpretation and an approach that seeks guidance from historical context, legislative history, and prior cases identifying the purpose that motivated the legislation. Thus, for example, in *Christiansburg Garment Co. v. EEOC*, 434 U.S. 412 (1978), we rejected a "mechanical construction," *id.* at 418, of the fee-shifting provision in § 706(k) of Title VII of the Civil Rights Act of 1964 that the prevailing defendant had urged upon us. Although the text of the statute drew no distinction between different kinds of "prevailing parties," we held that awards to prevailing plaintiffs are governed by a more liberal standard than awards to prevailing defendants. That holding rested entirely on our evaluation of the relevant congressional policy and found no support within the four corners of the statutory text. Nevertheless, the holding was unanimous and, to the best of my knowledge, evoked no adverse criticism or response in Congress.

On those occasions, however, when the Court has put on its thick grammarian's spectacles and ignored the available evidence of congressional purpose and the teaching of prior cases construing a statute, the congressional response has been dramatically different. It is no coincidence that the Court's literal reading of Title VII, which led to the conclusion that disparate treatment of pregnant and nonpregnant persons was not discrimination on the basis of sex, see *General Electric Co. v. Gilbert*, 429 U.S. 125 (1976), was repudiated by the 95th Congress; that its literal reading of the "continuous physical presence" requirement in § 244(a)(1) of the Immigration and Nationality Act, which led to the view that the statute did not permit even temporary or inadvertent absences from this country, see *INS v. Phinpathya*, 464 U.S. 183 (1984), was rebuffed by the 99th Congress; that its literal reading of the word "program" in Title IX of the Education Amendments of 1972, which led to the Court's gratuitous limit on the scope of the antidiscrimination provisions of Title IX, see *Grove City College v. Bell*, 465 U.S. 555 (1984), was rejected by the 100th Congress; or that its refusal to accept the teaching of earlier decisions in *Wards Cove Packing Co. v. Atonio*, 490 U.S. 642 (1989) (reformulating order of proof and weight of parties' burdens in disparate-impact cases), and *Patterson v. McLean Credit Union*, 491 U.S. 164 (1989) (limiting scope of 42 U.S.C. § 1981 to the making and enforcement of contracts), was overwhelmingly rejected by the 101st Congress, and its refusal to accept the widely held view of lower courts about the scope of fraud, see *McNally v. United States*, 483 U.S. 350 (1987) (limiting mail fraud to protection of property), was quickly corrected by the 100th Congress.

In the domain of statutory interpretation, Congress is the master. It obviously has the power to correct our mistakes, but we do the country a disservice when we needlessly ignore persuasive evidence of Congress' actual purpose and require it "to take the time to revisit the matter" and to restate its purpose in more precise English whenever its work product suffers from an omission or inadvertent error. * * *

The fact that Congress has consistently provided for the inclusion of expert witness fees in fee-shifting statutes when it considered the matter is a weak reed on which to rest the conclusion that the omission of such a provision represents a deliberate decision to forbid such awards. Only time will tell whether the Court, with its literal reading of § 1988, has correctly interpreted the will of Congress with respect to the issue it has resolved today.

NOTES ON CASEY AND THE WHOLE ACT RULE

1. *Immediate Override.* When the Supreme Court decided *Casey* in March 1991, Congress was holding hearings on the proposed Civil Rights Act of 1991, which was an effort to modify the vetoed 1990 version enough to secure final enactment. See Chapter 1, § 2(C). The negotiated compromise between a Democratic Congress and President Bush senior focused on whether the language overriding the *Wards Cove* decision would encourage employers to adopt racial quotas. Adding a new provision to override *Casey* was not controversial; it easily became part of the bill that eventually passed by overwhelming margins in both chambers and was signed by the President in November 1991. Does this result vindicate Justice Stevens' position? Read more before you settle on your answer.

The Senate Committee report accompanying § 1988 states that "citizens must have the opportunity to recover what it costs them to vindicate these [civil] rights in court." Assume the report had added that this includes recovering all costs that go into the attorney's preparation and presentation of the case, including the use of paralegals, expert witnesses, and all reasonable non-attorney costs associated with trial preparation. Would that addition change Justice Scalia's analysis or conclusion? Should it?

Justice Stevens in dissent concludes that "we [the Court] do the country a disservice when we needlessly ignore persuasive evidence of Congress' actual purpose and require it 'to take time to revisit the matter.'" What is the disservice to which Stevens refers? Is Congress's override of *Casey* a mere eight months after it was decided an example of such a disservice? Or is it more like an exception that proves the rule? What costs are really involved in requiring Congress to "take time to revisit" a judicial construction of statutory meaning?

2. *Inferences from Text of Other Statutes: Whole Code Rule.* Justice Scalia's majority opinion relies heavily on Congress's use of the terms "attorney's fees" and "expert fees" in other federal statutes. He concludes that "[i]f, as WVUH argues, the one [attorney's fees] includes the other [expert fees], dozens of statutes referring to the two separately become an inexplicable exercise in redundancy." Consider the four statutes with which Justice Scalia begins, all approved by the same Congress that enacted § 1988. Does it matter that these other statutes were drafted and reported to the floor by different committees than the ones that produced the Civil Rights Attorney's Fees Awards Act? Are differences in subject matter among these statutes relevant to Justice Scalia's argument?

In looking to these other statutes, Justice Scalia implicitly invokes another corollary to the whole act rule, the "whole code" rule. The whole code approach looks beyond the

[handwritten margin note at top: whole code rule: looks Beyond the statute in Q to various add. enactments addressing an identical or comparable issue...]

statute in question to various additional enactments addressing an identical or comparable issue, including some laws that may have been enacted decades before or after the text under review. The Court has relied on the whole code approach in a number of decisions since *Casey*. See, e.g., *FDA v. Brown & Williamson Tobacco Corp.*, 529 U.S. 120 (2000) (Justice O'Connor for majority); *Amoco Production Co. v. S. Ute Indian Tribe*, 526 U.S. 865 (1999) (Justice Kennedy for majority); *Bennett v. Spear*, 520 U.S. 154 (1997) (Justice Scalia for majority). This reliance on inter-statutory references has been criticized as prone to judicial manipulation and also likely to unsettle bodies of federal law not before the court. See William W. Buzbee, *The One-Congress Fiction in Statutory Interpretation*, 149 U. Pa. L. Rev. 171, 234–40 (2000). Moreover, a study of congressional overrides documents that decisions like *Casey*, relying heavily on the whole code rule, are disproportionately likely to be overridden by Congress, as indeed are Court decisions that rely heavily on the whole act rule.[13]

[handwritten margin note: inc. laws enacted decades pre/post text in review]

Although the whole act and whole code rules operate under a similar presumption of coherence, there are instances where the two rules conflict. In *Robinson v. Shell Oil Co.*, 519 U.S. 337 (1997), a unanimous Court (per Justice Thomas) determined that the word "employees" in § 704(a) of Title VII, was ambiguous on its face as to whether it encompassed former as well as current employees. Justice Thomas noted that a number of other federal statutes differentiated between "former employees" and "employees," but he viewed this practice in other statutes as simply illustrating that "Congress *can* use the unqualified term 'employees' to refer only to current employees, not that it did so in this particular statute." *Id.* at 341–42. Thomas then focused on a number of other provisions within Title VII to conclude that the term "employees" plainly did encompass former employees.

[handwritten margin note: WHOLE ACT + WHOLE CODE similar pres. of coherence.]

Dissenting in *Casey*, Justice Stevens argued that the legislative history of "*this statute*" and the previous interpretations of "*this statute*" were the proper interpretive tools for determining whether attorney's fees included expert fees. The majority, however (including Justice Thomas, the author of *Robinson v. Shell Oil*) found the argument based on inter-statutory textual references persuasive. Can these two decisions, each interpreting provisions of Title VII, be reconciled?

3.   *The Dubious Presumption of Coherence.* Both *Casey* and *Robinson* suggest that the presumption of overarching coherence may be an unrealistic one. Congress does not usually approach statutory drafting the way God is thought to have dictated the Bible. Instead, statutes are often assembled the way Christmas trees are decorated, with ornaments being added or subtracted willy nilly, and at the last minute, just to satisfy enough interest groups and legislators to gain majorities needed to get through various legislative vetogates (recall Chapter 1 and the history of the 1964 Civil Rights Act). Staff and drafting offices are supposed to clean up legislation to make it appropriate for inclusion in the code, but even the best drafters cannot always meld all the negotiated deals into a coherent whole.

[handwritten margin note: statutes like Christmas trees ornaments added/subtracted willy nilly + @ last minute]

Among the textual canons, the whole act rule and its corollaries have come in for especially harsh criticism from scholars and also some judges—for mistakenly imputing omniscience to the legislature and for assuming that a statute is written as a whole,

---

[13]   See Matthew Christiansen & William Eskridge Jr., *Congressional Overrides of Supreme Court Statutory Interpretation Decisions, 1967–2011*, 92 Tex. L. Rev. 1317, 1405–06 (2014) (reporting that 8 percent of statutory decisions rely heavily on whole code rule yet this rule is a central factor in just under one-fourth of Court decisions that are overridden. Similarly, 10 percent of statutory decisions rely heavily on the whole act rule, but more than four in ten overridden decisions rely centrally on this canon.).

internally coherent document, like a short story. See Richard Posner, *The Federal Courts: Crisis and Reform* 281 (1985) ("The conditions under which legislators work are not conducive to careful, farsighted, and parsimonious drafting. Nor does great care guarantee economy of language; a statute that is the product of compromise may contain redundant language as a by-product of the strains of the negotiating process.").

In recent years, empirical examinations of Congress's approach to legislative drafting have found that the key players from both chambers do not view the whole act rule or its corollaries as important elements when statutory language is being drafted, debated, and enacted. Victoria Nourse and Jane Schacter interviewed a bipartisan group of Senate Judiciary Committee staff as well as lawyers from the Senate Legislative Counsel's office. Those interviewed described drafting as a highly contextual and intensely pressured process, focused on securing collective action through negotiated agreement, often involving a shifting coalition of both invited and late-arriving players. The drafters were generally aware of the whole act rule (and other textual canons), but the promotion of structural coherence and the avoidance of surplus words or phrases were not valued nearly as highly as they are by courts. For those interviewed, successful lawmaking negotiations required achieving sufficient consensus about language, and this tended to result in a fair amount of verbal repetitions, linguistic residues, and incomplete redactions. See Victoria Nourse & Jane Schacter, *The Politics of Legislative Drafting: A Congressional Case Study*, 77 N.Y.U. L. Rev. 575, 590–600, 614–16 (2002).

The results from the Gluck & Bressman study (*Statutory Interpretation From the Inside*, appearing in the Stanford Law Review (see § 1(B)(2) of this chapter) reinforce and expand upon these findings. The authors' 137 congressional staff respondents were aware of the rule against surplusage but over three-fifths stated that it applies either rarely or only sometimes in the drafting process. Gluck and Bressman reported respondents' practical justifications for redundancy, based on a desire "to ensure that the statute covers the intended terrain," and their frequent political preference for redundant wording in order to secure a compromise: "that constituent, that senator, that lobbyist wants to see that word." 65 Stan. L. Rev. at 934. The authors found that the whole act and whole code rules face even greater institutional barriers based on the way Congress is organized. Major statutes are generally amalgamations of work by multiple committees that draft different parts without any focus on internal consistency. Lengthy multidrafter statutes and bundled legislative deals make it highly unlikely that drafters will review a product for consistent word usage even though drafters believe that this should be a goal. And the whole code rule fares worse: it was dismissed as irrelevant to how Congress drafts or even how it attempts to draft. Less than ten percent of respondents indicated that drafters often or always intend to apply terms consistently across statutes that are unrelated by subject matter. *Id.* at 936–37.

In spite of these criticisms, courts around the world continue to operate under the coherence presumption. One common justification, articulated by Justice Scalia in his coauthored book, is that the presumption will encourage Congress to draft with greater care:

> The canons . . . promote better drafting. When it is widely understood in the legal community that, for example, a word used repeatedly in a document will be taken to have the same meaning throughout . . . you can expect those who prepare legal documents competently to draft accordingly. Antonin Scalia & Bryan Garner, *Reading Law: The Interpretation of Legal Texts* 51 (2012).

Do you find this justification persuasive? Gluck and Bressman concluded that, given the range of practical, political, and institutional barriers to drafting coherent and cohesive statutes, Congress is very unlikely to alter its drafting methods in response to the whole act family of canons. Can you think of other justifications for continuing to apply the presumption in favor of coherence? Should courts rely less on the whole act and its corollaries than they do at present?

Recall too the discussion in Chapter 3 § 3(A) on the codification process, where a nonpartisan office within Congress makes judgments about which enacted provisions of a specific law to include in the U.S. Code (only "general and permanent" provisions get codified), whether to include them in the main text of the Code or in notes, where to put them, and whether they repeal or amend preexisting law. As part of the codification process, statutes are often scattered across different sections of the Code. Given that courts, agencies, and lawyers typically encounter and construe enacted text through the U.S. Code, does this provide more support for a whole code approach than for the whole act rule? On the other hand, does the fact that codification involves consequential choices made by unknown bureaucrats raise further doubts about the presumption of coherence?

Although the Supreme Court regularly invokes the whole act rule, several Justices have recognized that the arrangement and phraseology of different statutory provisions is often "the consequence of a legislative *accident*, perhaps caused by nothing more than the unfortunate fact that Congress is too busy to do all of its work as carefully as it should." *Delaware Tribal Business Comm. v. Weeks*, 430 U.S. 73, 97 (1977) (Stevens, J., dissenting) (emphasis in original), quoted in *Mountain States Tel. & Tel. v. Pueblo of Santa Ana*, 472 U.S. 237, 255 (1985) (Brennan, J., dissenting). Note that this latter point is a critique of the textual canons in general. Still, even if Judge Posner, Justice Stevens, and the studies summarized above are descriptively accurate, the whole act rule might be prescriptively correct. Perhaps the virtues of clarity and predictability promoted by the judiciary warrant discounting if not disregarding the realities of the legislative process. Think about both descriptive and prescriptive issues in connection with the case described in the next paragraph.

4.   *A Case of Haphazard Drafting. Sorenson v. Secretary of the Treasury*, 475 U.S. 851 (1986), involved interpretation of the Omnibus Budget Reconciliation Act of 1981 (OBRA), Pub. L. No. 97–35, § 2331, 95 Stat. 860. The Act added provisions to the Social Security Act and the Internal Revenue Code to provide for "interception" of tax refunds for the benefit of state agencies that had been assigned child-support rights. Thus when a taxpayer is in arrears for his or her child support payments, and when the former spouse assigns them to a state (welfare) agency as a condition of receiving public assistance, the state can notify the IRS. The IRS will then give the state's recoupment claim priority over the taxpayer's claim for refunds of overpayment of federal income taxes. The issue in *Sorenson* was whether the "overpayment" which is subject to the recoupment claim includes refunds resulting from an earned-income credit. The Supreme Court held that it does. Section 6402(c), added by OBRA, provides that "*any* overpayment to be refunded * * * shall be reduced by the amount of any past-due support" (emphasis added). Section 6402(b), which was already in the Code, provides that if an earned-income credit exceeds taxpayer's tax liability, the excess amount is "considered an overpayment." Given the whole act rule that terms used in different parts of the statute should presumptively have the same meaning, the result follows.

But Justice Stevens' dissenting opinion pointed out the policy anomalies of the Court's result. The Earned Income Credit Program was created by Congress in 1975 to help keep low-income families off welfare: (1) social security taxes were assessed against earned income but not against welfare payments; (2) as a result, $500 a month in welfare meant more money in the pocket than $500 a month in earned income; (3) to redress this disincentive to work, Congress created a fully refundable credit for low income workers. Applying the OBRA recoupment scheme (one of the obscure goodies given to states in the 1981 reconciliation bill) to penalize low-income families is an accidental consequence of the statute's drafting; nothing in the legislative history supports any legislative desire to curtail the Earned Income Credit Program.

The Court's response to Justice Stevens was that "it defies belief that Congress was unaware" of the impact of the Intercept Program on the Earned Income Credit Program. Justice Stevens riposted: "With all due respect to the Court and to our hard working neighbors in the Congress, I think it 'defies belief' to assume that a substantial number of legislators were sufficiently familiar with OBRA to realize that somewhere in that vast piece of hurriedly enacted legislation there was a provision that changed the 6-year-old Earned Income Credit Program." In footnote 2, Justice Stevens quoted the following passage from N.Y. Times, July 1, 1981, p. A16, col. 1:

> Smoking a big cigar, the Speaker [of the House of Representatives] got angry again over the slap-dash quality of the bill [that became OBRA], with parts of it photocopied from memorandums, other parts handwritten at the last minute, and some final sections hastily crossed out in whorls of pencil marks.
> * * *
>
> But then he smiled, too, noting such cryptic and accidental entries in the bill as a name and phone number—"Ruth Seymour, 225–4844"—standing alone as if it were a special appropriation item.

There is a larger point to be drawn from Justice Stevens' criticisms. In the last generation, Congress has done an increasing amount of its work through gigantic and complex omnibus proposals, as identified in the Gluck and Bressman study. Doesn't the majority's approach in *Sorenson* ignore the realities of drafting and enacting a budget reconciliation bill—often in the days or even hours before congressional recess, with provisions added and dropped at the last minute in the conference room? In light of this new operation of the legislative process, should federal courts rethink the whole act rule and perhaps some other canons of construction? Should there be special canons, or at least practices, for construing omnibus reconciliation legislation like that in *Sorenson*? For a proposal that such omnibus bills be approached cautiously, see Seth Grossman, *Tricameral Legislating: Statutory Interpretation in an Era of Conference Committee Ascendancy*, 9 N.Y.U. J. Leg. & Pub. Pol'y 251 (2006).

5. *The Sherlock Holmes Canon.* Justice Stevens in his *Sorenson* dissent (Note 4) emphasized the unlikelihood that Congress understood it was enacting an important change in the Earned Income Credit Program, because it failed to mention the change at any point in the legislative history of OBRA. Since 1980, the justices have frequently invoked this "silence is telling" canonical approach to argue that ambiguous text ought not be construed to justify significant change in an existing rule of law when the legislative record contains no comment on or reference to any such change. This canon is often referred to as the "Sherlock Holmes" canon or the "dog that did not bark" canon—an homage to the *Silver Blaze* story by Sir Arthur Conan Doyle in which Holmes solves

the mysterious disappearance of the titular race horse by deducing that because the dog guarding the stable had not barked during the horse's disappearance, it must have been an inside job.

In *The Sherlock Holmes Canon*, 84 Geo. Wash. L. Rev. 1 (2016), Anita Krishnakumar finds that the justices have invoked some version of this canon on nearly 30 occasions since 1980, after having used it a mere four times prior to that date (for an example found in the Casebook, see Justice Stevens' dissent in *Griffin v. Oceanic Contractors Inc.*, Chapter 5, § 2(C)). Krishnakumar distinguishes the Holmes canon from another recent Court favorite—the "elephants in mouseholes" canon (an example in the Casebook is Justice Breyer's dissent in *Ali v. Federal Bureau of Prisons* at § 1(B) of this chapter). Both canons "require legislative clarity in order to effect significant 'elephant-sized' changes in the legal regime." For the elephants in mouseholes canon, the Court seeks this clarity in the statutory text, while for the Holmes canon, the Court looks for clarity in the legislative history accompanying the text.

Focusing on the Sherlock Holmes canon, Krishnakumar argues that it rests on dubious assumptions about the legislative process. Given the political and strategic nature of this process, as well as the hurried pace at which statutes are often enacted, she is skeptical that Congress's failure to comment on an important potential legislative change really signals a desire to maintain the status quo. Krishnakumar concludes that the Court's use of the canon constitutes a judicial attempt to impose a default rule on Congress—a form of clear statement rule that guards against legal changes and protects the status quo. Such clear statement rules are traditionally invoked by the Court in relation to constitutional issues (e.g., rules of lenity and constitutional avoidance, discussed in Section 3 of this chapter); Krishnakumar regards the Sherlock Holmes canon as a troubling invitation for judges to implement significant pro-continuity policy biases that are not grounded in constitutional norms. She concludes that the canon should be invoked only in rare cases when there is special reason to expect or require that Congress comment on a change in the law—such as if a contemplated departure from the status quo would upset a longstanding agency interpretation of a statute or would unsettle significant reliance interests.

Are you persuaded by Krishnakumar's characterization of the Sherlock Holmes canon as a burden-shifting clear statement rule in disguise? If so, does this help explain why the canon has become increasingly popular in the past several decades? How does this canon comport or conflict with other trends in the Court's interpretive preferences?

YATES V. UNITED STATES

Supreme Court of the United States, 2015.
RBG, Roberts, U.S. ___, 135 S.Ct 1074, 191 L.Ed.2d 64. *[2015]*
Breyer, Sotomayor.

JUSTICE GINSBURG announced the judgment of the Court and delivered an opinion in which the CHIEF JUSTICE [ROBERTS]. JUSTICE BREYER, and JUSTICE SOTOMAYOR join.

John Yates, a commercial fisherman, caught undersized red grouper in federal waters in the Gulf of Mexico. To prevent federal authorities from confirming that he had harvested undersized fish, Yates ordered a crew member to toss the suspect catch into the sea. For this offense, he was charged with, and convicted of, violating 18 U.S.C. § 1519, which provides:

violated
§§ 1519.

Yates = commercial fisherman caught undersized red grouper in fed waters in Gulf of MX

"Whoever knowingly alters, destroys, mutilates, conceals, covers up, falsifies, or makes a false entry in any record, document, or tangible object with the intent to impede, obstruct, or influence the investigation or proper administration of any matter within the jurisdiction of any department or agency of the United States or any case filed under title 11, or in relation to or contemplation of any such matter or case, shall be fined under this title, imprisoned not more than 20 years, or both." * * *

Yates [contests his conviction on the grounds] that fish are not trapped within the term "tangible object," as that term is used in § 1519.

Section 1519 was enacted as part of the Sarbanes-Oxley Act of 2002, legislation designed to protect investors and restore trust in financial markets following the collapse of Enron Corporation. A fish is no doubt an object that is tangible; fish can be seen, caught, and handled, and a catch, as this case illustrates, is vulnerable to destruction. But it would cut § 1519 loose from its financial-fraud mooring to hold that it encompasses any and all objects, whatever their size or significance, destroyed with obstructive intent. Mindful that in Sarbanes-Oxley, Congress trained its attention on corporate and accounting deception and cover-ups, we conclude that a matching construction of § 1519 is in order: A tangible object captured by § 1519, we hold, must be one used to record or preserve information. * * *

[II] The Sarbanes-Oxley Act, all agree, was prompted by the exposure of Enron's massive accounting fraud and revelations that the company's outside auditor, Arthur Andersen LLP, had systematically destroyed potentially incriminating documents. The Government acknowledges that § 1519 was intended to prohibit, in particular, corporate document-shredding to hide evidence of financial wrongdoing. Prior law made it an offense to "intimidat[e], threate[n], or corruptly persuad[e] *another person*" to shred documents. § 1512(b) (emphasis added). Section 1519 cured a conspicuous omission by imposing liability on a person who destroys records himself. See S.Rep. No. 107–146, p.14 (2002) (describing § 1519 as "a new general anti-shredding provision" and explaining that "certain current provisions make it a crime to persuade another person to destroy documents, but not a crime to actually destroy the same documents yourself"). The new section also expanded prior law by including within the provision's reach "any matter within the jurisdiction of any department or agency of the United States." *Id.*, at 14–15.

In the Government's view, § 1519 extends beyond the principal evil motivating its passage. The words of § 1519, the Government argues, support reading the provision as a general ban on the spoliation of evidence, covering all physical items that might be relevant to any matter under federal investigation.

Yates urges a contextual reading of § 1519, tying "tangible object" to the surrounding words, the placement of the provision within the Sarbanes-Oxley Act, and related provisions enacted at the same time, in particular § 1520 and § 1512(c)(1). Section 1519, he maintains, targets not all manner of evidence, but records, documents, and tangible objects used to preserve them, *e.g.*, computers, servers, and other media on which information is stored.

We agree with Yates and reject the Government's unrestrained reading. "Tangible object" in § 1519, we conclude, is better read to cover only objects one can use to record or preserve information, not all objects in the physical world.

[A] * * * We have several times affirmed that identical language may convey varying content when used in different statutes, sometimes even in different provisions of the same statute. [Justice Ginsburg cited a series of cases]. Although dictionary definitions of the words "tangible" and "object" bear consideration, they are not dispositive as to the meaning of "tangible object" in § 1519. * * *

[B] Familiar interpretive guides aid our construction of the words "tangible object" as they appear in § 1519. We note first § 1519's caption: "Destruction, alteration, or falsification of records in Federal investigations and bankruptcy." That heading conveys no suggestion that the section prohibits spoliation of any and all physical evidence, however remote from records. Neither does the title of the section of the Sarbanes-Oxley Act in which § 1519 was placed, § 802: "Criminal penalties for altering documents." 116 Stat. 800. Furthermore, § 1520, the only other provision passed as part of § 802, is titled "Destruction of corporate audit records" and addresses only that specific subset of records and documents. While these headings are not commanding, they supply cues that Congress did not intend "tangible object" in § 1519 to sweep within its reach physical objects of every kind, including things no one would describe as records, documents, or devices closely associated with them. See *Almendarez-Torres v. United States,* 523 U.S. 224, 234 (1998) ("[T]he title of a statute and the heading of a section are tools available for the resolution of a doubt about the meaning of a statute." (internal quotation marks omitted)). If Congress indeed meant to make § 1519 an all-encompassing ban on the spoliation of evidence, as the dissent believes Congress did, one would have expected a clearer indication of that intent.

Section 1519's position within Chapter 73 of Title 18 further signals that § 1519 was not intended to serve as a cross-the-board ban on the destruction of physical evidence of every kind. Congress placed § 1519 (and its companion provision § 1520) at the end of the chapter, following immediately after the pre-existing § 1516, § 1517, and § 1518, each of them prohibiting obstructive acts in specific contexts. See § 1516 (audits of recipients of federal funds); § 1517 (federal examinations of financial institutions); § 1518 (criminal investigations of federal health care offenses). See also S.Rep. No. 107–146, at 7 (observing that § 1517 and § 1518 "apply to obstruction in certain limited types of cases, such as bankruptcy fraud, examinations of financial institutions, and healthcare fraud").

But Congress did not direct codification of the Sarbanes-Oxley Act's other additions to Chapter 73 adjacent to these specialized provisions. Instead, Congress directed placement of those additions within or alongside retained provisions that address obstructive acts relating broadly to official proceedings and criminal trials: Section 806, "Civil Action to protect against retaliation in fraud cases," was codified as § 1514A and inserted between the pre-existing § 1514, which addresses civil actions to restrain harassment of victims and witnesses in criminal cases, and § 1515, which defines terms used in § 1512 and § 1513. Section 1102, "Tampering with a record or otherwise impeding an official proceeding," was codified as § 1512(c) and inserted within the pre-existing § 1512, which addresses tampering with a victim, witness, or informant to impede any official proceeding. Section 1107, "Retaliation against informants," was codified as § 1513(e) and inserted within the pre-existing § 1513, which addresses retaliation against a victim, witness, or informant in any official proceeding. Congress thus ranked § 1519, not among the broad proscriptions, but together with specialized provisions expressly aimed at corporate fraud and financial audits. This placement accords with the view that Congress' conception of § 1519's coverage was considerably more limited than the Government's. *1519 more limited than Gov.*

The contemporaneous passage of § 1512(c)(1), which was contained in a section of the Sarbanes-Oxley Act discrete from the section embracing § 1519 and § 1520, is also instructive. Section 1512(c)(1) provides:

"(c) Whoever corruptly—

"(1) alters, destroys, mutilates, or conceals a record, document, or other object, or attempts to do so, with the intent to impair the object's integrity or availability for use in an official proceeding

. . .

"shall be fined under this title or imprisoned not more than 20 years, or both."

The legislative history reveals that § 1512(c)(1) was drafted and proposed after § 1519. See 148 Cong. Rec. 12518, 13088–13089 (2002). The Government argues, and Yates does not dispute, that § 1512(c)(1)'s reference to "other object" includes any and every physical object. But if § 1519's reference to "tangible object" already included all physical objects, as the Government and the dissent contend, then Congress had no reason to enact § 1512(c)(1): Virtually any act that would violate § 1512(c)(1) no doubt would violate § 1519 as well, for § 1519 applies to "the investigation or proper administration of any matter within the jurisdiction of any department or agency of the United States . . . or in relation to or contemplation of any such matter," not just to "an official proceeding."

The Government acknowledges that, under its reading, § 1519 and § 1512(c)(1) "significantly overlap." Brief for United States 49. Nowhere does the Government explain what independent function § 1512(c)(1) would serve if the Government is right about the sweeping scope of § 1519. We resist a reading of § 1519 that would render superfluous an entire provision passed in proximity as part of the same Act.

1512(c) have purpose if 1519 is so sweeping

The words immediately surrounding "tangible object" in § 1519—"falsifies, or makes a false entry in any record [or] document"—also cabin the contextual meaning of that term. As explained in *Gustafson v. Alloyd Co.,* 513 U.S. 561, 575 (1995), we rely on the principle of *noscitur a sociis*—a word is known by the company it keeps—to "avoid ascribing to one word a meaning so broad that it is inconsistent with its accompanying words, thus giving unintended breadth to the Acts of Congress." * * * "Tangible object" is the last in a list of terms that begins "any record [or] document." The term is therefore appropriately read to refer, not to any tangible object, but specifically to the subset of tangible objects involving records and documents, *i.e.,* objects used to record or preserve information. See United States Sentencing

Commission, Guidelines Manual § 2J1.2, comment., n. 1 (Nov. 2014) (" 'Records, documents, or tangible objects' includes (A) records, documents, or tangible objects that are stored on, or that are, magnetic, optical, digital, other electronic, or other storage mediums or devices; and (B) wire or electronic communications.").

This moderate interpretation of "tangible object" accords with the list of actions § 1519 proscribes. The section applies to anyone who "alters, destroys, mutilates, conceals, covers up, *falsifies,* or *makes a false entry in* any record, document, or tangible object" with the requisite obstructive intent. (Emphasis added.) The last two verbs, "falsif[y]" and "mak[e] a false entry in," typically take as grammatical objects records, documents, or things used to record or preserve information, such as logbooks or hard drives. See, *e.g.,* Black's Law Dictionary 720 (10th ed. 2014) (defining "falsify" as "[t]o make deceptive; to counterfeit, forge, or misrepresent; esp., to tamper with (a document, record, etc.)"). It would be unnatural, for example, to describe a killer's act of wiping his fingerprints from a gun as "falsifying" the murder weapon. But it would not be strange to refer to "falsifying" data stored on a hard drive as simply "falsifying" a hard drive. Furthermore, Congress did not include on § 1512(c)(1)'s list of prohibited actions "falsifies" or "makes a false entry in." See § 1512(c)(1) (making it unlawful to "alte[r], destro[y], mutilat[e], or concea[l] a record, document, or other object" with the requisite obstructive intent). That contemporaneous omission also suggests that Congress intended "tangible object" in § 1519 to have a narrower scope than "other object" in § 1512(c)(1).

A canon related to *noscitur a sociis, ejusdem generis,* counsels: "Where general words follow specific words in a statutory enumeration, the general words are [usually] construed to embrace only objects similar in nature to those objects enumerated by the preceding specific words." In *Begay v. United States,* 553 U.S. 137, 142–143 (2008), for example, we relied on this principle to determine what crimes were covered by the statutory phrase "any crime . . . that . . . is burglary, arson, or extortion, involves use of explosives, or otherwise involves conduct that presents a serious potential risk of physical injury to another," 18 U.S.C. § 924(e)(2)(B)(ii). The enumeration of specific crimes, we explained, indicates that the "otherwise involves" provision covers "only *similar* crimes, rather than *every* crime that 'presents a serious potential risk of physical injury to another.' " 553 U.S., at 142. Had Congress intended the latter "all encompassing" meaning, we observed, "it is hard to see why it would have needed to include the examples at all." *Ibid.* Just so here. Had Congress intended "tangible object" in § 1519 to be interpreted so generically as to capture physical objects as dissimilar as documents and fish, Congress would have had no reason to refer specifically to "record" or "document." The Government's unbounded reading of "tangible object" would render those words misleading surplusage.

Having used traditional tools of statutory interpretation to examine markers of congressional intent within the Sarbanes-Oxley Act and § 1519 itself, we are persuaded that an aggressive interpretation of "tangible object" must be rejected. It is highly improbable that Congress would have buried a general spoliation statute covering objects of any and every kind in a provision targeting fraud in financial record-keeping. * * *

[C] Finally, if our recourse to traditional tools of statutory construction leaves any doubt about the meaning of "tangible object," as that term is used in § 1519, we would invoke the rule that "ambiguity concerning the ambit of criminal statutes should be resolved in favor of lenity." [The plurality emphasized that the Government's broad reading of "tangible object" in § 1519 "exposes individuals to 20-year prison sentences for tampering with *any* physical object that *might* have evidentiary value in *any* federal investigation into *any* offense," adding "it is appropriate, before we choose the harsher alternative, to require that Congress should have spoken in language that is clear and definite."]

JUSTICE ALITO, concurring in the judgment. [Justice Alito regarded the question as a close one, and he identified reasonable arguments on both sides. But he relied on noscitur a sociis and ejusdem generis, the verb "falsifies," and the inclusion of "records" in § 1519's title to conclude that "tangible object" is best understood to refer to something similar to records or documents, "point[ing] toward filekeeping, not fish."]

JUSTICE KAGAN, with whom JUSTICE SCALIA, JUSTICE KENNEDY, and JUSTICE THOMAS join, dissenting.

* * * This case raises the question whether the term "tangible object" means the same thing in § 1519 as it means in everyday language—any object capable of being touched. The answer should be easy: Yes. The term "tangible object" is broad, but clear. Throughout the U.S. Code and many States' laws, it invariably covers physical objects of all kinds. And in § 1519, context confirms what bare text says: All the words surrounding "tangible object" show that Congress meant the term to have a wide range. That fits with Congress's evident purpose in enacting § 1519: to punish those who alter or destroy physical evidence—*any* physical evidence—with the intent of thwarting federal law enforcement.

The plurality instead interprets "tangible object" to cover "only objects one can use to record or preserve information." The concurring opinion similarly, if more vaguely, contends that "tangible object" should refer to "something similar to records or documents"—and shouldn't include colonial farmhouses, crocodiles, or fish. (Alito, J., concurring in judgment). In my view, conventional tools of statutory construction all lead to a more conventional result: A "tangible object" is an object that's tangible. I would apply the statute that Congress enacted and affirm the judgment below.

[I] While the plurality starts its analysis with § 1519's heading, I would begin with § 1519's text. When Congress has not supplied a definition, we generally give a statutory term its ordinary meaning. As the plurality must acknowledge, the ordinary meaning of "tangible object" is "a discrete thing that possesses physical form." A fish is, of course, a discrete thing that possesses physical form. See generally Dr. Seuss, One Fish Two Fish Red Fish Blue Fish (1960) So the ordinary meaning of the term "tangible object" in § 1519, as no one here disputes, covers fish (including too-small red grouper).

That interpretation accords with endless uses of the term in statute and rule books as construed by courts. Dozens of federal laws and rules of procedure (and hundreds of state enactments) include the term "tangible object" or its first cousin "tangible thing"—some in association with documents, others not. See, *e.g.*, 7 U.S.C.

§ 8302(2) (referring to "any material or tangible object that could harbor a pest or disease"); 15 U.S.C. § 57b–1(c) (authorizing investigative demands for "documentary material or tangible things"); 18 U.S.C. § 668(a)(1)(D) (defining "museum" as entity that owns "tangible objects that are exhibited to the public"); 28 U.S.C. § 2507(b) (allowing discovery of "relevant facts, books, papers, documents or tangible things"). To my knowledge, no court has ever read any such provision to exclude things that don't record or preserve data; rather, all courts have adhered to the statutory language's ordinary (*i.e.,* expansive) meaning. For example, courts have understood the phrases "tangible objects" and "tangible things" in the Federal Rules of Criminal and Civil Procedure to cover everything from guns to drugs to machinery to . . . animals. See, *e.g., United States v. Obiukwu,* 17 F.3d 816, 819 (C.A.6 1994) (*per curiam*) (handgun); *United States v. Acarino,* 270 F.Supp. 526, 527–528 (E.D.N.Y.1967) (heroin); *In re Newman,* 782 F.2d 971, 972–975 (C.A.Fed.1986) (energy generation system); *Martin v. Reynolds Metals Corp.,* 297 F.2d 49, 56–57 (C.A.9 1961) (cattle). No surprise, then, that—until today—courts have uniformly applied the term "tangible object" in § 1519 in the same way. See, *e.g., United States v. McRae,* 702 F.3d 806, 834–838 (C.A.5 2012) (corpse); *United States v. Maury,* 695 F.3d 227, 243–244 (C.A.3 2012) (cement mixer).

That is not necessarily the end of the matter; I agree with the plurality (really, who does not?) that context matters in interpreting statutes. We do not "construe the meaning of statutory terms in a vacuum." Rather, we interpret particular words "in their context and with a view to their place in the overall statutory scheme." And sometimes that means, as the plurality says, that the dictionary definition of a disputed term cannot control. But this is not such an occasion, for here the text and its context point the same way. Stepping back from the words "tangible object" provides only further evidence that Congress said what it meant and meant what it said.

Begin with the way the surrounding words in § 1519 reinforce the breadth of the term at issue. Section 1519 refers to "any" tangible object, thus indicating (in line with *that* word's plain meaning) a tangible object "of whatever kind." Webster's Third New International Dictionary 97 (2002). This Court has time and again recognized that "any" has "an expansive meaning," bringing within a statute's reach *all* types of the item (here, "tangible object") to which the law refers. See, *e.g., Ali v. Federal Bureau of Prisons,* 552 U.S. 214, 219–220 (2008). And the adjacent laundry list of verbs in § 1519 ("alters, destroys, mutilates, conceals, covers up, falsifies, or makes a false entry") further shows that Congress wrote a statute with a wide scope. Those words are supposed to ensure—just as "tangible object" is meant to—that § 1519 covers the whole world of evidence-tampering, in all its prodigious variety. * * *

The words "record, document, or tangible object" in § 1519 also track language in 18 U.S.C. § 1512, the federal witness-tampering law covering (as even the plurality accepts) physical evidence in all its forms. Section 1512, both in its original version (preceding § 1519) and today, repeatedly uses the phrase "record, document, or other object"—most notably, in a provision prohibiting the use of force or threat to induce another person to withhold any of those materials from an official proceeding. § 4(a) of the Victim and Witness Protection Act of 1982, 96 Stat. 1249, as amended, 18 U.S.C. § 1512(b)(2). That language, which itself likely derived from the Model Penal

Code, encompasses no less the bloody knife than the incriminating letter, as all courts have for decades agreed. Context thus again confirms what text indicates.

And legislative history, for those who care about it, puts extra icing on a cake already frosted. Section 1519, as the plurality notes, was enacted after the Enron Corporation's collapse, as part of the Sarbanes-Oxley Act of 2002, 116 Stat. 745. But the provision began its life in a separate bill, and the drafters emphasized that Enron was "only a case study exposing the shortcomings in our current laws" relating to both "corporate and criminal" fraud. S.Rep. No. 107–146, pp. 2, 11 (2002). The primary "loophole[ ]" Congress identified, see *id.,* at 14, arose from limits in the part of § 1512 just described: That provision, as uniformly construed, prohibited a person from inducing another to destroy "record[s], document[s], or other object[s]"—of every type—but not from doing so himself. § 1512(b)(2); see *supra,* at 1093. Congress (as even the plurality agrees) enacted § 1519 to close that yawning gap. But § 1519 could fully achieve that goal only if it covered all the records, documents, and objects § 1512 did, as well as all the means of tampering with them. And so § 1519 was written to do exactly that—"to apply broadly to any acts to destroy or fabricate physical evidence," as long as performed with the requisite intent. S.Rep. No. 107–146, at 14. "When a person destroys evidence," the drafters explained, "overly technical legal distinctions should neither hinder nor prevent prosecution." *Id.,* at 7. Ah well: Congress, meet today's Court, which here invents just such a distinction with just such an effect.

As Congress recognized in using a broad term, giving immunity to those who destroy non-documentary evidence has no sensible basis in penal policy. A person who hides a murder victim's body is no less culpable than one who burns the victim's diary. A fisherman, like John Yates, who dumps undersized fish to avoid a fine is no less blameworthy than one who shreds his vessel's catch log for the same reason. Congress thus treated both offenders in the same way. It understood, in enacting § 1519, that destroying evidence is destroying evidence, whether or not that evidence takes documentary form.

[II-A] The plurality searches far and wide for anything—*anything*—to support its interpretation of § 1519. But its fishing expedition comes up empty.

The plurality's analysis starts with § 1519's title: "Destruction, alteration, or falsification of records in Federal investigations and bankruptcy." That's already a sign something is amiss. I know of no other case in which we have *begun* our interpretation of a statute with the title, or relied on a title to override the law's clear terms. Instead, we have followed "the wise rule that the title of a statute and the heading of a section cannot limit the plain meaning of the text."

The reason for that "wise rule" is easy to see: A title is, almost necessarily, an abridgment. Attempting to mention every term in a statute "would often be ungainly as well as useless"; accordingly, "matters in the text . . . are frequently unreflected in the headings." Just last year, this Court observed that two titles in a nearby section of Sarbanes-Oxley serve as "but a short-hand reference to the general subject matter" of the provision at issue, "not meant to take the place of the detailed provisions of the text." *Lawson v. FMR LLC,* 571 U.S. ___, ___, 134 S.Ct. 1158, 1169 (2014). The "under-inclusiveness" of the headings, we stated, was "apparent." *Lawson,* 571 U.S., at ___, 134 S.Ct., at 1169. So too for § 1519's title, which refers to "destruction, alteration, or falsification" but *not* to mutilation, concealment, or covering up, and likewise mentions "records" but *not* other documents or objects. Presumably, the plurality would not refuse to apply § 1519 when a person only conceals evidence rather than destroying, altering, or falsifying it; instead, the plurality would say that a title is just a title, which cannot "undo or limit" more specific statutory text. *Ibid.* The same holds true when the evidence in question is not a "record" but something else whose destruction, alteration, etc., is intended to obstruct justice.

The plurality next tries to divine meaning from § 1519's "position within Chapter 73 of Title 18." But that move is yet odder than the last. As far as I can tell, this Court has never once suggested that the section number assigned to a law bears upon its meaning. Cf. A. Scalia & B. Garner, Reading Law: The Interpretation of Legal Texts xi–xvi (2012) (listing more than 50 interpretive principles and canons without mentioning the plurality's new number-in-the-Code theory). And even on its own terms, the plurality's argument is hard to fathom. The plurality claims that if § 1519 applied to objects generally, Congress would not have placed it "after the pre-existing § 1516, § 1517, and § 1518" because those are "specialized provisions." But search me if I can find a better place for a broad ban on evidence-tampering. The plurality seems to agree that the law properly goes in Chapter 73—the criminal code's chapter on "obstruction of justice." But the provision does not logically fit into any of that chapter's pre-existing sections. And with the first 18 numbers of the chapter already taken (starting with § 1501 and continuing through § 1518), the law naturally took the 19th place. That is standard operating procedure. Prior to the Sarbanes-Oxley Act of 2002, all of Chapter 73 was ordered chronologically: Section 1518 was later enacted than § 1517, which was later enacted than § 1516, which was . . . well, you get the idea. And after Sarbanes-Oxley, Congress has continued in the same vein. Section 1519 is thus right where you would expect it (as is the contemporaneously passed § 1520)—between § 1518 (added in 1996) and § 1521 (added in 2008).

The plurality's third argument, relying on the surplusage canon, at least invokes a known tool of statutory construction—but it too comes to nothing. Says the plurality: If read naturally, § 1519 "would render superfluous" § 1512(c)(1), which Congress passed "as part of the same act." But that is not so: Although the two provisions significantly overlap, each applies to conduct the other does not. The key difference between the two is that § 1519 protects the integrity of "matter[s] within the jurisdiction of any [federal] department or agency" whereas § 1512(c)(1) safeguards "official proceeding[s]" as defined in § 1515(a)(1)(A). Section 1519's language often applies more broadly than § 1512(c)(1)'s, as the plurality notes. For example, an FBI investigation counts as a matter within a federal department's jurisdiction, but falls outside the statutory definition of "official proceeding" as construed by courts. But conversely, § 1512(c)(1) sometimes reaches more widely than § 1519. For example, because an "official proceeding" includes any "proceeding before a judge or court of the United States," § 1512(c)(1) prohibits tampering with evidence in federal litigation between private parties. See § 1515(a)(1)(A). By contrast, § 1519 wouldn't ordinarily operate in that context because a federal court isn't a "department or agency." So the surplusage canon doesn't come into play.

Overlap—even significant overlap—abounds in the criminal law. This Court has never thought that of such ordinary stuff surplusage is made.

And the legislative history to which the plurality appeals only cuts against it because those materials show that lawmakers knew that § 1519 and § 1512(c)(1) share much common ground. Minority Leader Lott introduced the amendment that included § 1512(c)(1) (along with other criminal and corporate fraud provisions) late in the legislative process, explaining that he did so at the specific request of the President. See 148 Cong. Rec. 12509, 12512 (2002) (remarks of Sen. Lott). Not only Lott but several other Senators noted the overlap between the President's package and provisions already in the bill, most notably § 1519. [Citations omitted.] The presence of both § 1519 and § 1512(c)(1) in the final Act may have reflected belt-and-suspenders caution: If § 1519 contained some flaw, § 1512(c)(1) would serve as a backstop. Or the addition of § 1512(c)(1) may have derived solely from legislators' wish "to satisfy audiences other than courts"—that is, the President and his Justice Department. Gluck & Bressman, Statutory Interpretation from the Inside, 65 Stan. L.Rev. 901, 935 (2013) (emphasis deleted). Whichever the case, Congress's consciousness of overlap between the two provisions removes any conceivable reason to cast aside § 1519's ordinary meaning in service of preventing some statutory repetition. * * *

Getting nowhere with surplusage, the plurality switches canons, hoping that *noscitur a sociis* and *ejusdem generis* will save it. The first of those related canons advises that words grouped in a list be given similar meanings. The second counsels that a general term following specific words embraces only things of a similar kind. According to the plurality, those Latin maxims change the English meaning of "tangible object" to only things, like records and documents, "used to record or preserve information." But understood as this Court always has, the canons have no such transformative effect on the workaday language Congress chose.

As an initial matter, this Court uses *noscitur a sociis* and *ejusdem generis* to resolve ambiguity, not create it. But when words have a clear definition, and all other contextual clues support that meaning, the canons cannot properly defeat Congress's decision to draft broad legislation. See, *e.g., Ali*, 552 U.S., at 227 (rejecting the invocation of these canons as an "attempt to create ambiguity where the statute's text and structure suggest none").

Anyway, assigning "tangible object" its ordinary meaning comports with *noscitur a sociis* and *ejusdem generis* when applied, as they should be, with attention to § 1519's subject and purpose. Those canons require identifying a common trait that links all the words in a statutory phrase. In responding to that demand, the plurality characterizes records and documents as things that preserve information—and so they are. But just as much, they are things that provide information, and thus potentially serve as evidence relevant to matters under review. And in a statute pertaining to obstruction of federal investigations, that evidentiary function comes to the fore. The destruction of records and documents prevents law enforcement agents from gathering facts relevant to official inquiries. And so too does the destruction of tangible objects—of whatever kind. Whether the item is a fisherman's ledger or an undersized fish, throwing it overboard has the identical effect on the administration of justice. For purposes of § 1519, records, documents, and (all) tangible objects are therefore alike. * * *

And the plurality's invocation of § 1519's verbs does nothing to buttress its canon-based argument. The plurality observes that § 1519 prohibits "falsif[ying]" or "mak[ing] a false entry in" a tangible object, and no one can do those things to, say, a murder weapon (or a fish). But of course someone can alter, destroy, mutilate, conceal, or cover up such a tangible object, and § 1519 prohibits those actions too. The Court has never before suggested that all the verbs in a statute need to match up with all the nouns. And for good reason. It is exactly when Congress sets out to draft a statute broadly—to include every imaginable variation on a theme—that such mismatches will arise. To respond by narrowing the law, as the plurality does, is thus to flout both what Congress wrote and what Congress wanted.

Finally, when all else fails, the plurality invokes the rule of lenity. But even in its most robust form, that rule only kicks in when, "after all legitimate tools of interpretation have been exhausted, 'a reasonable doubt persists' regarding whether Congress has made the defendant's conduct a federal crime." No such doubt lingers here. The plurality points to the breadth of § 1519, as though breadth were equivalent to ambiguity. It is not. Section 1519 *is* very broad. It is also very clear. Every traditional tool of statutory interpretation points in the same direction, toward "object" meaning object. Lenity offers no proper refuge from that straightforward (even though capacious) construction. * * *

If none of the traditional tools of statutory interpretation can produce today's result, then what accounts for it? The plurality offers a clue when it emphasizes the disproportionate penalties § 1519 imposes if the law is read broadly. Section 1519, the plurality objects, would then expose individuals to "20-year prison sentences for tampering with *any* physical object that *might* have evidentiary value in *any* federal investigation into *any* offense." That brings to the surface the real issue: overcriminalization and excessive punishment in the U.S. Code.

Now as to this statute, I think the plurality somewhat—though only somewhat—exaggerates the matter. The plurality omits from its description of § 1519 the requirement that a person act "knowingly" and with "the intent to impede, obstruct, or influence" federal law enforcement. And in highlighting § 1519's maximum penalty, the plurality glosses over the absence of any prescribed minimum. (Let's not forget that Yates's sentence was not 20 years, but 30 days.) Congress presumably enacts laws with high maximums and no minimums when it thinks the prohibited conduct may run the gamut from major to minor. That is assuredly true of acts obstructing justice. Still and all, I tend to think, for the reasons the plurality gives, that § 1519 is a bad law—too broad and undifferentiated, with too-high maximum penalties, which give prosecutors too much leverage and sentencers too much discretion. And I'd go further: In those ways, § 1519 is unfortunately not an outlier, but an emblem of a deeper pathology in the federal criminal code.

But whatever the wisdom or folly of § 1519, this Court does not get to rewrite the law. "Resolution of the pros and cons of whether a statute should sweep broadly or narrowly is for Congress." If judges disagree with Congress's choice, we are perfectly entitled to say so—in lectures, in law review articles, and even in dicta. But we are not entitled to replace the statute Congress enacted with an alternative of our own design.

NOTES ON YATES

1. *The Caption and Location of 18 U.S.C. § 1519: Discarded Statutory Directions.* Recall that in *Ali v. Federal Bureau of Prisons*, Justice Thomas and Justice Kennedy disagreed primarily over whether the ejusdem generis canon applied at all to the statute in question. In *Yates*, a more complex dialogue develops between Justice Ginsburg and Justice Kagan, involving which of various interpretive aids have value and which do not, how much weight they deserve in an interpretive dispute, and how to apply them properly to the text of § 1519.

Consider first Justice Ginsburg's substantial reliance on the section's caption and its location within the U.S. Code. As Tobias Dorsey (formerly an assistant counsel in the House Office of the Legislative Counsel) explains, Congress for over a century has often specified that chapter and heading instructions in the U.S. Code are not to be considered when trying to determine the meaning of provisions within a particular title. See Tobias Dorsey, *Some Reflections on* Yates *and the Statutes We Threw Away*, 18 Green Bag 2d 377 (2015). With respect to title 18, Congress back in 1948 enacted the following language: "No inference of a legislative construction is to be drawn by reason of the chapter in Title 18 * * * in which any particular section is placed, nor by reason of the catchlines [section or chapter headings] used in such title." This language still appears at the beginning of Title 18 although it has no official, title 18, section number. Dorsey notes that the Supreme Court used to honor such chapter-and-heading instructions but has not done so since the 1950s; instead courts today "ordinarily view headings and chapter placement as fair game when interpreting statutes."

No justice in *Yates* mentioned the enacted instruction at the start of title 18. Justice Ginsburg relies heavily on section heading and location. Justice Alito too finds that titles are valuable but, he states, "not dispositive" unless further supported by other evidence. Justice Kagan declares that any interpretation that begins with the use of a title is "already a sign something is amiss," because "a title is, almost necessarily, an abridgement," unlikely to capture the full scope of the text. In a similar vein, Ginsburg regards the placement of the section in a particular order in title 18 as intentional and meaningful, whereas Kagan finds the placement to be essentially ministerial and worthy of little evidentiary weight. Even Justice Scalia is silent on the issue, although in his book *Reading Law* (p. 221), he noted that legislative drafters sometimes identify headings as being for convenience only and not affecting interpretation; he added that lawyers should "be sure to check your text or code or compilation for such a disclaimer."

Should these captions and their location be given any weight at all in circumstances when Congress has expressly directed to the contrary? On what basis may courts disregard congressional instructions on how to read statutes? Are enacted instructions about which portions of a text to disregard entitled to more weight than instructions that a statute "is to be construed broadly"? Than a provision that forbids the use of specific pieces of legislative history for interpretive purposes?

2. *Surplusage.* According to Justice Ginsburg, a broad reading of "tangible object" in § 1519 would render § 1512(c)(1), a provision passed after § 1519 that clearly applies to all physical objects, superfluous. If § 1519 already applied to all physical objects, there would have been no need to pass 1512(c)(1). Justice Kagan, however, sees no redundancy

between the two since § 1512 and § 1519 apply to different types of investigations and will each occasionally cover types of investigations that the other will not. Kagan also invokes "belt-and-suspenders caution" to distinguish between overlap and redundancy in the instant drafting process (see Discussion of the belt-and-suspenders canon in § 2(B) of this chapter). What should we make of her assertion that the overlap may derive from legislators' desire to satisfy executive branch players like the Justice Department? Kagan offers no support for this assertion: is it less persuasive for this reason?

3. *Ejusdem and Noscitur.* Finally, the majority and dissent are in sharp disagreement over application of the ejusdem generis and noscitur a sociis language canons. For Justice Ginsburg, these canons dictate that "tangible object" in the statutory phrase "any record, document or tangible object" takes on a meaning similar to the words preceding them, so that the phrase "tangible object" must refer to something that *preserves* information. Justice Kagan, disagrees, arguing that when the canons are applied with a consideration for context, as they should, the common link between the words listed is that they all *provide* information. Because all physical objects, including fish, can *provide* information, even an application of these canons supports a broad reading of "tangible object." Which reading do you regard as more persuasive—be prepared to defend your answer.

Consider the larger goal of all these language-related canons for addressing textual ambiguity. What does it say about the objectivity of such textual interpretive tools if the Justices can disagree at such length over when to use them, how much weight to accord them and how they should be properly applied?

4. *Legislative History.* Justice Ginsburg and Justice Kagan also invoke the legislative history of § 1519. Ginsburg's reference to legislative history is minimal and linked to her reliance on the surplusage canon, which she supports by showing that the two statutory provisions she finds redundant were enacted at the same time. Justice Kagan's reliance is more extensive: she cites statements from the Senate Report for the Sarbanes-Oxley Act, indicating that § 1519 was intended to apply broadly and that prosecutions should not be hindered by technical distinctions such as those made by the majority here. Yet Kagan's review of legislative history comes only at the end of her dissent, with her preface that it is being included "for those who care about it." If the purpose of statutory interpretation is to determine congressional intent, why would Kagan be so reluctant to include such apparently probative evidence?

5. *Interpretation Shaped by Subject Matter.* Noting Justice Ginsburg's mention of the potential for § 1519 to expose a defendant to a 20-year prison sentence, Justice Kagan concludes her dissent by arguing that the real issue for the plurality is a disagreement with "overcriminalization and excessive punishment in the U.S. Code." Kagan emphasizes that only Congress is given the authority to make laws, and she accuses the majority of using meritless statutory interpretation arguments to conceal that it is actually rewriting the law. After reviewing the two opinions, do you find Kagan's accusation persuasive?

Justice Ginsburg is quite explicit about the relevance of statutory subject matter to the Court's conclusion. She states that the Court consistently considers the punitive nature of a criminal law when it interprets ambiguous language narrowly to avoid the harsher of two results. Do you think Yates was confused or in any doubt as to the lawfulness of his conduct when ordering his crew to throw undersized fish into the sea? We have thus far discussed only interpretive guides based on statutory language itself;

should a court ever adopt an assumption about Congress's intent based instead on the subject being legislated? Consider this question as you read the next section.

3. SUBSTANTIVE POLICY CANONS

The canons discussed in Sections 1 and 2 are linguistic or structural guidelines that are policy-neutral on their face. Other canons represent substantive decisions, and hence their application is not policy-neutral. Traditionally, the main substantive canons were directives to interpret different types of statutes "liberally" or "strictly." The old Anglo-American rule was that "remedial" statutes were to be liberally interpreted, while statutes in derogation of the common law were to be strictly interpreted. (But what remedial statute is not in derogation of the common law?)

More modern typologies of the liberal-versus-strict construction canons have emerged. Certain statutes (such as civil rights, securities, and antitrust statutes) are supposed to be liberally construed—in other words, applied expansively to new situations.[14] Appendix B, reporting the Court's deployment of canons from the 1986 through the 2013 Terms, reflects that these liberal construction canons have not been often invoked by the Rehnquist and Roberts Courts. Other statutes are to be strictly construed—in other words, applied stingily. The rule of lenity, requiring strict construction of penal statutes, is the best example and is explored in Part A below. Strict construction of statutes, especially for quasi-constitutional reasons, has been highly popular in the Rehnquist and Roberts Courts.

Consider other canons reflecting substantive judgments about how broadly to read the statute's text:

- *Strict Construction of Statutes in Derogation of Sovereignty.* If a statute is written in general language, it is presumed that it only applies to private parties; governments and their agencies are presumptively not included unless the statute clearly says so. See *Nevada Dep't Human Res. v. Hibbs*, 538 U.S. 721 (2003) (finding such clarity). This canon is based upon the old idea of sovereign immunity: the state cannot be sued or otherwise regulated without its consent. See 3A Sutherland § 62.01.[15]

---

[14]   The Supreme Court has invoked the liberal-construction maxim when interpreting civil rights legislation such as § 1983, *Dennis v. Higgins*, 498 U.S. 439 (1991); statutes providing benefits to seamen, *Cox v. Roth*, 348 U.S. 207 (1955), and to veterans, *King v. St. Vincent's Hosp.*, 502 U.S. 215, 221 n.9 (1991); and safety legislation such as the Occupational Safety and Health Act, *Whirlpool Corp. v. Marshall*, 445 U.S. 1 (1980). See generally William Eskridge Jr. & John Ferejohn, *Super-Statutes*, 50 Duke L.J. 1215, 1234–35, 1239, 1244 (2001) (super-statutes whose policy or principle comes to be entrenched in the public culture over time will be interpreted liberally to advance their policies or principles, and expansively vis-a-vis more ordinary statutes; examples include the Sherman Act of 1890, the Civil Rights Act of 1964, the Endangered Species Act of 1973).

[15]   Since the absolute immunity of the state has eroded substantially in the last thirty years, this presumption has lost much of its original justification. A better rationale for the rule may be that the sovereign needs few constraints upon its freedom of activity as it decides how best to serve the public interest (though this explanation may be a naive view of the way government works). In the United States this rule has quasi-constitutional dimensions, because the states retained their basic immunities when they joined the union, see U.S. Const. amends. X–XI, and the federal government enjoys supremacy over states and their regulation. *Id.* art. VI. In any event, many states have statutes rejecting this rule of strict construction. 3A Sutherland § 62.04. For example: "The term 'person' may be construed to include the United States, this state, or any state or territory or any public or private corporation, as well as an individual." Wash. Rev. Code Ann. § 1.16.080 (West

- *Strict Construction of Public Grants.* Similarly, public grants by the government to private parties are to be construed narrowly, that is, in favor of the government. Sometimes, this precept has been justified on the grounds that such grants were gratuitous or solicited by the grantee, but the canon has been invoked in the whole range of cases—from leases and contracts with the government, to statutes allowing compromise settlements with the government, to pension and compensation laws for public officials.[16]

- *Strict Construction of (Some) Revenue Provisions.* 3 Sutherland § 66.01, announces that "it is a settled rule that tax laws are to be strictly construed against the state and in favor of the taxpayer. Where there is reasonable doubt as to the meaning of a revenue statute, the doubt is resolved in favor of those taxed." See *Gould v. Gould*, 245 U.S. 151 (1917). Generations of taxpayers who have lost lawsuits against the Internal Revenue Service over fine points of statutory interpretation would dispute that generalization. See *United States v. Fior D'Italia*, 536 U.S. 238, 242–43 (2002) (presuming that IRS-generated tax assessments are correct). Courts are turning to more liberal construction because of the necessary public purpose implicated in the system of taxation, "and it is the duty of the courts to see that no one, by mere technicalities which do not affect his substantial rights, shall escape his fair proportion of the public expenses." *Atlantic City Transp. Co. v. Walsh*, 55 A.2d 652 (N.J. 1947); see 3A Sutherland § 66.02. Under this new thinking, the *tax-imposing* provisions would not be strictly construed—but the *tax-exempting* provisions ought to be. See *United States v. Burke*, 504 U.S. 229, 248 (1992) (Souter, J., concurring in judgment).[17]

One way of formulating substantive canons is as presumptions or rules of thumb that cut across different types of statutes and statutory schemes. These represent policies that the Court will "presume" Congress intends to incorporate into statutes, but such presumptions are rebuttable ones. Presumptions will generally not trump contrary statutory text, legislative history, or purpose. See *Astoria Fed. Savings & Loan Ass'n v. Solimino*, 501 U.S. 104, 108 (1991). A presumption or rule of thumb can be treated as a starting point for discussion, a tiebreaker at the end of discussion, or just a balancing factor. The policies underlying interpretive presumptions are derived by courts from the Constitution, federal statutes, and the common law. Some examples of substantive presumptions:

- Presumption against congressional diminishment of American Indian rights. See *Hagen v. Utah*, 510 U.S. 399 (1994); *Montana v. Blackfeet Tribe*, 471 U.S. 759 (1985).

1961). These state rules, of course, are subject to the Supremacy Clause and may be invalid as regards the United States. E.g., *McCulloch v. Maryland*, 17 U.S. (4 Wheat.) 316 (1819).

[16]   3A Sutherland § 63.04, posits that the main reason for this canon is a general tendency "to regard all such grants with extreme distrust, so that in all its dealings the government will not suffer loss." Yet the rule has not generally been applied when the grant is for a great public purpose, such as the land grants to railroads in return for their building the transcontinental railroad in the 1860s. E.g., *Leo Sheep v. United States*, 440 U.S. 668, 682 (1979); *Platt v. Union Pac. R.*, 99 U.S. (9 Otto) 48 (1878).

[17]   Public choice theory (Chapter 1, § 1) lends support to this suggestion. Rent-seeking interest groups can be expected to extract from the legislature special exemptions from the broad taxing provisions. Not only do these exemptions undermine the public fisc, but they tend to do so for already-advantaged groups, thereby making the income tax system much less progressive than it is advertised as being.

- Presumption that Congress does not intend to pass statutes that violate international law. See *Sosa v. Alvarez-Machain*, 542 U.S. 692 (2004); *Murray v. The Schooner Charming Betsy*, 6 U.S. (2 Cranch) 64, 118 (1804).

- Presumption that Congress does not intend to pass statutes that violate treaty obligations. See *Hamdan v. Rumsfeld*, 548 U.S. 557 (2006).

- Presumption that Congress does not intend that statutes have extraterritorial application. See *Foley Brothers v. Filardo*, 336 U.S. 281 (1949).

- Presumption that Congress does not intend that substantive statutes be applied retroactively. See *Landgraf v. USI Film Products*, 511 U.S. 244 (1994).

- Presumption that Congress does not intend that federal regulation unnecessarily intrude into traditional state responsibilities (more than is necessary to subserve national objectives). See *Rush Prudential HMO v. Moran*, 536 U.S. 355 (2002); *Cipollone v. Liggett Group, Inc.*, 505 U.S. 504 (1992).

- Presumption that Congress will not withdraw the courts' traditional equitable discretion. See *Weinberger v. Romero-Barcelo*, 456 U.S. 305, 320 (1982); *Hecht Co. v. Bowles*, 321 U.S. 321, 330 (1944).

- Presumption that Congress will not withdraw all remedies or judicial avenues of relief when it recognizes a statutory right. See *South Carolina v. Regan*, 465 U.S. 367 (1984).

- Presumption of judicial review. See *Demore v. Kim*, 538 U.S. 510 (2003); *Dunlop v. Bachowski*, 421 U.S. 560 (1975); *Abbott Laboratories v. Gardner*, 387 U.S. 136 (1967).

- Presumption against derogation of the President's traditional powers. See *Dep't of Navy v. Egan*, 484 U.S. 518, 527 (1988); *Haig v. Agee*, 453 U.S. 280 (1981).

Another way of formulating substantive canons is as *clear statement rules*, which are presumptions that can be rebutted only by clear language in the text of the statute. See *Solimino*, 501 U.S. at 108–09 (contrasting presumptions and clear statement rules). Clear statement rules have been developed by the Supreme Court as expressions of quasi-constitutional values. For example, Congress cannot impose liability and process directly against the states unless the statutory text clearly says so (Section 2(B) below).

There is some mobility in the Court's articulation of these substantive canons. For example, in *EEOC v. Arabian American Oil Co.*, 499 U.S. 244, 258–59 (1991), a majority of the Court transformed the old *Foley Brothers* presumption against extraterritorial application into a clear statement rule (applied to Title VII in that case), requiring explicit statutory language in order for a law to apply outside the United States. Justice Marshall's dissenting opinion strongly objected to the Court's transformation; he criticized the majority's clear statement approach for sidestepping legislative history evidence reflecting Congress's clear understanding that U.S. employers who operated in foreign lands were within the purview of Title VII. *Id.* at 260–63, 268–69. Note here how the general rule that civil rights laws, like Title VII, should be liberally construed was itself trumped by the more specific (and now fortified) canon against extraterritorial regulation.

As suggested above, substantive canons may vary in their impact upon interpretation, and it is critical to identify how a court is using a canon. By way of review, consider three possibilities alluded to above. First, sometimes courts will treat a substantive canon as merely a *tiebreaker* that affects the outcome only if, at the end of the basic interpretive process, the court is left unable to choose between the two competing interpretations put forward by the parties. Second, courts might treat substantive canons as *presumptions* that, at the beginning of the interpretive process, set up a presumptive outcome, which can be overcome by persuasive support for the contrary interpretation. Typically, the party attempting to overcome the presumption may use any potential evidence of statutory meaning (e.g., statutory text, legislative history, statutory purposes, policy arguments, and so on) to rebut the presumption. On this understanding, a presumption simply adds weight to one side of the balancing process captured by eclectic statutory interpretation. Third, courts may treat substantive canons as *clear statement rules*, which purport to compel a particular interpretive outcome unless there is a clear statement to the contrary. We shall call those canons "clear statement rules" when they may be overcome by clear statutory language and those canons "super-strong clear statement rules" when they may be overcome only by extremely clear statutory text (where the "clear statement" is, in effect, a targeted statement of textual meaning). Keep a sharp eye on which of these approaches is used to implement the canons that are discussed in the remainder of this part.

A. THE RULE OF LENITY IN CRIMINAL CASES

One of the hoariest canons of statutory interpretation states that laws whose purpose is to punish (usually by fine or imprisonment) must be construed strictly. This is called the "rule of lenity" in construing penal statutes: If the punitive statute does not clearly outlaw private conduct, the private actor cannot be penalized. While criminal statutes are the most obvious and common type of penal law, many civil statutes have been so classified by at least some jurisdictions.[18]

What is the purpose of the rule of lenity?[19] In England, courts have long used this canon vigorously for humanitarian reasons "when the number of capital offences was still very large, when it was still punishable with death to cut down a cherry-tree." *Maxwell* 238.[20] Early practice in this country was ambivalent about the rule of lenity: state and federal courts sometimes invoked it, but in early prosecutions for public insurrections and seditious libel, federal judges in particular showed no lenity; the Marshall Court, however, firmly established the rule of lenity in American

---

[18]   Among the statutes to which this canon has been applied are (i) statutes whose penalties include forfeiture; (ii) statutes providing for "extra" damages beyond those needed to make the complainant whole, including punitive damages, treble damages, attorneys' fees, penalty interest (often part of the remedy under usury laws); (iii) statutes permitting revocation of a professional license or disbarment of lawyers; (iv) statutes against extortion or discrimination; (v) statutes declaring certain acts to be per se negligence; and (vi) others. See 3A Sutherland § 59.02.

[19]   For a comprehensive treatment, see Lawrence Solan, *Law, Language, and Lenity*, 40 Wm. & Mary L. Rev. 57 (1998).

[20]   The main line of cases are those construing Parliament's attempted narrowing of the "benefit of clergy" in ways that preserved it as a defense to the death penalty. See J.M. Beattie, *Crime and the Courts in England, 1600–1800* (1986); Livingston Hall, *Strict or Liberal Construction of Penal Statutes*, 48 Harv. L. Rev. 748 (1935).

legisprudence.[21] Especially as penalties have been ameliorated, other kinds of reasons have been invoked to justify the rule of lenity.

For years, the leading justification has been *fair notice*. The state may not impose penalties upon people without clearly warning them about unlawful conduct and its consequences. A classic reference for this rationalization is *McBoyle v. United States*, 283 U.S. 25 (1931). A 1919 federal statute prohibited the transportation of stolen *motor vehicles* in interstate commerce. The law defined motor vehicle to "include an automobile, automobile truck, automobile wagon, motor cycle, or any other self-propelled vehicle not designed for running on rails." The issue in the case was whether defendant's transportation of a stolen airplane fell within the statute. Because *airplane* was not within the popular (or what linguists today call the prototypical) meaning of *motor vehicle*, Justice Holmes' opinion for the Court held that it did not. He justified lenity on grounds of notice:

> Although it is not likely that a criminal will carefully consider the text of the law before he murders or steals, it is reasonable that a fair warning should be given to the world in language that the common world will understand, of what the law intends to do if a certain line is passed. To make the warning fair, so far as possible the line should be clear. When a rule of conduct is laid down in words that evoke in the common mind only the picture of the vehicles moving on land, the statute should not be extended to aircraft, simply because it may seem to us that a similar policy applies, or upon the speculation that if the legislature had thought of it, very likely broader words would have been used.

Accord *United States v. Lanier*, 520 U.S. 259, 265–66 (1997) (excellent elaboration of *McBoyle* and the various fair warning doctrines).

Under a fair warning rationalization, the rule of lenity is most appropriately applied to criminal statutes that create offenses that are *malum prohibitum* (bad only because they are prohibited) rather than *malum in se* (bad by their very nature).[22] Thus, a law criminalizing homicide doesn't have to be as clear in all respects as a law criminalizing hunting and fishing without a license from the state. But can this precept explain *McBoyle*? Or *Regina v. Harris*, 173 Eng. Rep. 198 (Cent. Crim. Ct. 1836), in which an English court held that one who bit off the end of the nose of another was not guilty of violating a statute punishing anyone "who shall unlawfully and maliciously stab, cut, or wound any person" because the statute reached only wounds inflicted by an instrument. In both those cases—and many others—defendants engaging in unquestionably squalid behavior got the benefit of the rule.

A justification related to fair notice might be the Anglo-American emphasis on *mens rea as a presumptive requirement* for criminal penalties. Although ignorance of the law is no defense to a crime, the inability of the reasonable defendant to know

---

[21]   See William Eskridge Jr., *All About Words: Early Understandings of the "Judicial Power" in Statutory Interpretation, 1776–1806*, 101 Colum. L. Rev. 990 (2001).

[22]   Oliver Wendell Holmes, Jr., *The Common Law* 50 (1881) (positing the *malum in se/prohibitum* distinction). See also J. Willard Hurst, *Dealing with Statutes* 64–65 (1982); John Calvin Jeffries, Jr., *Legality, Vagueness, and the Construction of Penal Statutes*, 71 Va. L. Rev. 189 (1985).

that his actions are criminal undermines the justice of inferring a criminal intent in some cases. It also suggests a corollary of the rule of lenity, namely, the presumption that criminal statutes carry with them a mens rea, or intentionality, requirement.

A dramatic illustration of the rule of lenity and its corollary is *Ratzlaf v. United States*, 510 U.S. 135 (1994), which construed the Money Laundering Control Act of 1986. Prior law required banks to report cash transactions in excess of $10,000; to prevent people from "structuring" their transactions to avoid the reports, the 1986 law made it illegal to make lower deposits for the purpose of evading the reporting requirements. The Court interpreted the statute to require *double scienter*: not only must the government prove that defendants Waldemar and Loretta Ratzlaf intended to evade the bank reporting law, but also that they knew about and intended to evade the anti-structuring law as well.[23] Justice Ginsburg's opinion for the Court emphasized that there were many benign reasons people would want to structure their transactions to avoid bank reporting requirements, including fear of burglary and a desire to secrete assets from a spouse or tax inspectors. According to Justice Ginsburg, "structuring is not inevitably nefarious." *Id.* at 144. Four dissenting Justices argued that a double scienter requirement was not justified by the statutory language, would render the statute a nullity, and focused on unduly extreme cases.

A third justification for the rule of lenity was originally suggested by Chief Justice Marshall in *United States v. Wiltberger*, 18 U.S. (5 Wheat.) 76, 92 (1820): *separation of powers*. After much debate, the Marshall Court adopted the proposition that Congress cannot delegate to judges and prosecutors power to make common law crimes, because the moral condemnation inherent in crimes ought only to be delivered by the popularly elected legislature. If the legislature alone has the authority to define crimes, it is inappropriate for judges to elaborate on criminal statutes so as to expand them beyond the clear import of their directive words adopted by the legislature. There is also a separation of powers concern that judicial expansion of criminal statutes, common law style, risks expanding prosecutorial discretion beyond that contemplated by the legislature. See Herbert Packer, *The Limits of the Criminal Sanction* 79–96 (1968).

Notwithstanding the antiquity of and multiple rationales for the rule of lenity, it has fallen into decline since the New Deal. See generally Francis Allen, *The Erosion of Legality in American Criminal Justice: Some Latter-Day Adventures of the* Nulla Poena *Principle*, 29 Ariz. L. Rev. 385 (1987). As of 2013, twenty-eight of the thirty-six states that had codified the rule of lenity have abolished or reversed the rule by statute. Typical is Arizona Penal Code § 13–104, added in 1977: "The general rule that a penal statute is to be strictly construed does not apply to this title, but the provisions herein must be construed according to the fair meaning of their terms to promote justice and effect the objects of the law." The primary explanation for these anti-lenity statutes is that state legislatures in the late twentieth century were prone

---

[23] The Supreme Court similarly read special scienter requirements into a statute making it a crime to possess a "machine gun," *Staples v. United States*, 511 U.S. 600 (1994) (government must prove defendant knew the gun was a machine gun), or to distribute images of minors engaged in sexually explicit conduct, *United States v. X-Citement Video, Inc.*, 513 U.S. 64 (1994) (government must prove defendant knew the performer was actually a minor). See also *Cheek v. United States*, 498 U.S. 192 (1991) (taxpayer's honest but unreasonable belief that he did not have to pay taxes was a valid defense to a charge of willful failure to pay taxes).

to invoke the criminal sanction liberally and did not want judges obstructing such an expansion. If this rationale holds up, does that provide a reason *favoring* the rule of lenity? Do the rule's constitutional overtones trump such statutes under some circumstances? See *State v. Pena*, 683 P.2d 744, 748–49 (Ariz. App.), aff'd, 683 P.2d 743 (Ariz. 1984) (applying rule of lenity notwithstanding the legislative abrogation).

Criticism of the rule of lenity has not been limited to legislators, however. Professor Dan Kahan, *Lenity and Federal Common Law Crimes*, 1994 Sup. Ct. Rev. 345, maintains that the nondelegation reason is the only coherent justification for the rule of lenity, at least for federal criminal statutes, but further argues that the rule of lenity should be abolished as a canon of construction. The polity would be better off without the rule of lenity. Accord John Calvin Jeffries, Jr., *Legality, Vagueness, and the Construction of Penal Statutes*, 71 Va. L. Rev. 189, 189 (1985). Normal interpretation of criminal statutes, without a judicial thumb on either side of the scale, would promote a more orderly and less costly development of criminal law (common law style, the way commercial law has developed, for example), without much in the way of unfairness, especially if the Department of Justice cleared up ambiguities by authoritative interpretations of federal criminal statutes. Consider this thesis in light of the following cases. Is there a coherent rationale for the rule of lenity? Does it serve useful purposes? Or does it impose needless costs on the system?

STATUTORY PREFACE TO THE *MUSCARELLO* CASE

Gun Control Act of 1968, Pub. L. 90–618, 82 Stat. 1213 (as codified in chapter 44 of 18 U.S.C. as of March 1998).

Section 924. * * *

(b) Whoever, with intent to commit therewith an offense punishable by imprisonment for a term exceeding one year, or with knowledge or reasonable cause to believe that an offense punishable by imprisonment for a term exceeding one year is to be committed therewith, ships, transports, or receives a firearm or any ammunition in interstate or foreign commerce shall be fined under this title, or imprisoned not more than ten years, or both.

(c)(1) Whoever, during and in relation to any crime of violence or drug trafficking crime * * * for which the person may be prosecuted in a court of the United States, uses or carries a firearm, shall, in addition to the punishment provided for such crime of violence or drug trafficking crime, be sentenced to imprisonment for five years * * *.

Section 925. * * *

(a)(2) The provisions of this chapter * * * shall not apply with respect to **(A)** the shipment or receipt of firearms or ammunition when sold or issued by the Secretary of the Army pursuant to section 4308 of title 10 before the repeal of such section by section 1624(a) of the Corporation for the Promotion of Rifle Practice and Firearms Safety Act, and **(B)** the transportation of any such firearm or ammunition carried out to enable a person, who lawfully received such firearm or ammunition from the Secretary of the Army, to engage in military training or in competitions.

Section 926A.

Notwithstanding any other provision of any law or any rule or regulation of a State or any political subdivision thereof, any person who is not otherwise prohibited by this chapter from transporting, shipping, or receiving a firearm shall be entitled to transport a firearm for any lawful purpose from any place where he may lawfully possess and carry such firearm to any other place where he may lawfully possess and carry such firearm if, during such transportation the firearm is unloaded, and neither the firearm nor any ammunition being transported is readily accessible or is directly accessible from the passenger compartment of such transporting vehicle: *Provided,* That in the case of a vehicle without a compartment separate from the driver's compartment the firearm or ammunition shall be contained in a locked container other than the glove compartment or console.

MUSCARELLO V. UNITED STATES

Supreme Court of the United States, 1998.
524 U.S. 125, 118 S.Ct. 1911, 141 L.Ed.2d 111.

JUSTICE BREYER delivered the opinion of the Court.

[Section 924(c)(1) of 18 U.S.C. provides that "[w]hoever, during and in relation to any crime of violence or drug trafficking crime * * * uses or carries a firearm, shall, in addition to the punishment provided for such crime of violence or drug trafficking crime, be sentenced to imprisonment for five years[.]" The practical consequence of this provision is that someone who possessed a gun at the time of a drug offense gets a mandatory additional five-year sentence if § 924(c)(1) was violated; if that provision was not violated, the possession of the gun would be taken into account under the federal sentencing guidelines and would add some time to the sentence (perhaps a 30–40% enhancement) unless the gun was clearly not involved in the drug offense. Apparently it is almost always in the interest of the defendant to be subjected to the sentencing guidelines in this way rather than receive the mandatory additional sentence provided by § 924(c)(1). Accordingly, there has been much litigation concerning what the government must show beyond the mere possession of a gun during a drug offense to satisfy § 924(c)(1).

[In *Smith v. United States*, 508 U.S. 223 (1993), the Court held that, when a person traded a gun for drugs, he "used" the gun in violation of § 924(c)(1). Justice Scalia's dissenting opinion contended that the ordinary meaning of § 924(c)(1), read in context, is that "uses a firearm" means "uses the firearm as a weapon," and that in any event the issue was sufficiently doubtful for the rule of lenity to control the outcome in favor of the defendant. In *Bailey v. United States*, 516 U.S. 137 (1995), a unanimous Court held that the "use" element requires active employment of the firearm by the defendant, such that it did not apply to a defendant who had a gun in the trunk of his car in which illegal drugs were found or to a defendant who had a gun locked in a trunk in a closet in a bedroom where illegal drugs were stored.

[Muscarello unlawfully sold marijuana from his truck and confessed that he "carried" a gun in the truck's locked glove compartment " 'for protection in relation' to the drug offense." In a companion case, Donald Cleveland and Enrique Gray-Santana were arrested for stealing and dealing drugs; they had bags of guns in the locked trunk of their car at the scene. The issue was whether these defendants had "carrie[d]" a firearm within the meaning of § 924(c)(1).]

We begin with the statute's language. The parties vigorously contest the ordinary English meaning of the phrase "carries a firearm." Because they essentially agree that Congress intended the phrase to convey its ordinary, and not some special legal, meaning, and because they argue the linguistic point at length, we too have looked into the matter in more than usual depth. Although the word "carry" has many different meanings, only two are relevant here. When one uses the word in the first, or primary, meaning, one can, as a matter of ordinary English, "carry firearms" in a wagon, car, truck, or other vehicle that one accompanies. When one uses the word in a different, rather special, way, to mean, for example, "bearing" or (in slang) "packing" (as in "packing a gun"), the matter is less clear. But, for reasons we shall set out below, we believe Congress intended to use the word in its primary sense and not in this latter, special way.

Consider first the word's primary meaning. The Oxford English Dictionary gives as its *first* definition "convey, originally by cart or wagon, hence in any vehicle, by ship, on horseback, etc." 2 Oxford English Dictionary 919 (2d ed. 1989); see also Webster's Third New International Dictionary 343 (1986) (*first* definition: "move while supporting (*as in a vehicle* or in one's hands or arms)"); The Random House Dictionary of the English Language Unabridged 319 (2d ed. 1987) (*first* definition: "to take or support from one place to another; convey; transport").

The origin of the word "carries" explains why the first, or basic, meaning of the word "carry" includes conveyance in a vehicle. See The Barnhart Dictionary of Etymology 146 (1988) (tracing the word from Latin "carum," which means "car" or "cart"); 2 Oxford English Dictionary, *supra*, at 919 (tracing the word from Old French "carier" and the late Latin "carricare," which meant to "convey in a car") * * *.

The greatest of writers have used the word with this meaning. See, e.g., the King James Bible, 2 Kings 9:28 ("[H]is servants carried him in a chariot to Jerusalem"); *id.*, Isaiah 30:6 ("[T]hey will carry their riches upon the shoulders of young asses"). Robinson Crusoe says, "[w]ith my boat, I carry'd away every Thing." D. Defoe, Robinson Crusoe 174 (J. Crowley ed. 1972). And the owners of Queequeg's ship, Melville writes, "had lent him a [wheelbarrow], in which to carry his heavy chest to his boardinghouse." H. Melville, Moby Dick 43 (U. Chicago 1952). This Court, too, has spoken of the "carrying" of drugs in a car or in its "trunk." [Citations omitted.]

These examples do not speak directly about carrying guns. But there is nothing linguistically special about the fact that weapons, rather than drugs, are being carried. * * * And, to make certain that there is no special ordinary English restriction (unmentioned in dictionaries) upon the use of "carry" in respect to guns, we have surveyed modern press usage, albeit crudely, by searching computerized newspaper databases—both the New York Times data base in Lexis/Nexis, and the "US News" data base in Westlaw. We looked for sentences in which the words "carry," "vehicle," and "weapon" (or variations thereof) all appear. We found thousands of such sentences, and random sampling suggests that many, perhaps more than one third, are sentences used to convey the meaning at issue here, *i.e.*, the carrying of guns in a car. [Justice Breyer gave several examples of such newspaper stories.]

Now consider a different, somewhat special meaning of the word "carry"—a meaning upon which the linguistic arguments of petitioners and the dissent must rest. The Oxford English Dictionary's *twenty-sixth* definition of "carry" is "bear, wear, hold up, or sustain, as one moves about; habitually to bear about with one." Webster's [Third New International Dictionary] defines "carry" as "to move while supporting," not just in a vehicle, but also "in one's hands or arms." And Black's Law Dictionary defines the entire phrase "carry arms or weapons" as "[t]o wear, bear or carry them upon the person or in the clothing or in a pocket, for the purpose of use, or for the purpose of being armed and ready for offensive or defensive action in case of a conflict with another person."

These special definitions, however, do not purport to *limit* the "carrying of arms" to the circumstances they describe. No one doubts that one who bears arms on his person "carries a weapon." But to say that is not to deny that one may also "carry a weapon" tied to the saddle of a horse or placed in a bag in a car.

Nor is there any linguistic reason to think that Congress intended to limit the word "carries" in the statute to any of these special definitions. To the contrary, all these special definitions embody a form of an important, but secondary, meaning of "carry," a meaning that suggests support rather than movement or transportation, as when, for example, a column "carries" the weight of an arch. 2 Oxford English Dictionary, *supra*, at 919, 921. In this sense a gangster might "carry" a gun (in colloquial language, he might "pack a gun") even though he does not move from his chair. It is difficult to believe, however, that Congress intended to limit the statutory word to this definition—imposing special punishment upon the comatose gangster while ignoring drug lords who drive to a sale carrying an arsenal of weapons in their van.

We recognize, as the dissent emphasizes, that the word "carry" has other meanings as well. But those other meanings, (e.g., "carry all he knew," "carries no colours") are not relevant here. And the fact that speakers often do *not* add to the phrase "carry a gun" the words "in a car" is of no greater relevance here than the fact that millions of Americans did *not* see Muscarello carry a gun in his car. The relevant linguistic facts are that the word "carry" in its ordinary sense includes carrying in a car and that the word, used in its ordinary sense, keeps the same meaning whether one carries a gun, a suitcase, or a banana. * * *

We now explore more deeply the purely legal question of whether Congress intended to use the word "carry" in its ordinary sense, or whether it intended to limit the scope of the phrase to instances in which a gun is carried "on the person." We conclude that neither the statute's basic purpose nor its legislative history support circumscribing the scope of the word "carry" by applying an "on the person" limitation.

This Court has described the statute's basic purpose broadly, as an effort to combat the "dangerous combination" of "drugs and guns." *Smith v. United States*, 508 U.S. 223, 240 (1993). And the provision's chief legislative sponsor has said that the provision seeks "to persuade the man who is tempted to commit a Federal felony to leave his gun at home." 114 Cong. Rec. 22231 (1968) (Rep. Poff); see *Busic v. United States*, 446 U.S. 398, 405 (1980) (describing Poff's comments as "crucial material" in interpreting the purpose of § 924(c)); *Simpson v. United States*, 435 U.S. 6, 13–14 (1978) (concluding that Poff's comments are "clearly probative" and "certainly entitled to weight"); see also 114 Cong. Rec. 22243–44 (statutes would apply to "the man who goes out taking a gun to commit a crime") (Rep. Hunt); *id.* at 22244 ("Of course, what we are trying to do by these penalties is to persuade the criminal to leave his gun at home") (Rep. Randall); *id.* at 22236 ("We are concerned . . . with having the criminal leave his gun at home") (Rep. Meskill).

From the perspective of any such purpose (persuading a criminal "to leave his gun at home") what sense would it make for this statute to penalize one who walks with a gun in a bag to the site of a drug sale, but to ignore a similar individual who, like defendant Gray-Santana, travels to a similar site with a similar gun in a similar bag, but instead of walking, drives there with the gun in his car? How persuasive is a punishment that is without effect until a drug dealer who has brought his gun to a sale (indeed has it available for use) actually takes it from the trunk (or unlocks the glove compartment) of his car? It is difficult to say that, considered as a class, those who prepare, say, to sell drugs by placing guns in their cars are less dangerous, or less deserving of punishment, than those who carry handguns on their person.

We have found no significant indication elsewhere in the legislative history of any more narrowly focused relevant purpose. * * * One legislator indicates that the statute responds in part to the concerns of law enforcement personnel, who had urged that "carrying short firearms in motor vehicles be classified as carrying such weapons concealed." *Id.* at 22242 (Rep. May). Another criticizes a version of the proposed statute by suggesting it might apply to drunken driving, and gives as an example a drunken driver who has a "gun in his car." *Id.* at 21792 (Rep. Yates). Others describe the statute as criminalizing gun "possession"—a term that could stretch beyond both the "use" of a gun and the carrying of a gun on the person. See *id.* at 21793 (Rep. Casey); *id.* at 22236 (Rep. Meskill); *id.* at 30584 (Rep. Collier); *id.* at 30585 (Rep. Skubitz).

We are not convinced by petitioners' remaining arguments[.] First, they say that our definition of "carry" makes it the equivalent of "transport." Yet, Congress elsewhere in related statutes used the word "transport" deliberately to signify a different, and broader, statutory coverage. The immediately preceding statutory subsection, for example, imposes a different set of penalties on one who, with an intent to commit a crime, "ships, transports, or receives a firearm" in interstate commerce. 18 U.S.C. § 924(b). Moreover, § 926A specifically "entitle[s]" a person "not otherwise prohibited . . . from transporting, shipping, or receiving a firearm" to "transport a firearm . . . from any place where he may lawfully possess and carry" it to "any other place" where he may do so. Why, petitioners ask, would Congress have used the word "transport," or used both "carry" and "transport" in the same provision, if it had intended to obliterate the distinction between the two?

The short answer is that our definition does not equate "carry" and "transport." "Carry" implies personal agency and some degree of possession, whereas "transport" does not have such a limited connotation and, in addition, implies the movement of goods in bulk over great distances. See Webster's Third New International Dictionary 343 (noting that "carry" means "moving to a location some distance away while supporting or maintaining off the ground" and "is a natural word to use in ref. to cargoes and loads on trucks, wagons, planes, ships, or even beasts of burden," while "transport refers to carriage in bulk or number over an appreciable distance and, typically, by a customary or usual carrier agency"); see also Webster's Dictionary of Synonyms 141 (1942). If Smith, for example, calls a parcel delivery service, which sends a truck to Smith's house to pick up Smith's package and take it to Los Angeles, one might say that Smith has shipped the package and the parcel delivery service has transported the package. But only the truck driver has "carried" the package in the sense of "carry" that we believe Congress intended. Therefore, "transport" is a broader category that includes "carry" but also encompasses other activity.

The dissent refers to § 926A and to another statute where Congress used the word "transport" rather than "carry" to describe the movement of firearms. 18 U.S.C. § 925(a)(2)(B). According to the dissent, had Congress intended "carry" to have the meaning we give it, Congress would not have needed to use a different word in these provisions. But as we have discussed above, we believe the word "transport" is broader than the word "carry."

And, if Congress intended "carry" to have the limited definition the dissent contends, it would have been quite unnecessary to add the proviso in § 926A requiring a person, to be exempt from penalties, to store her firearm in a locked container not immediately accessible. See § 926A (exempting from criminal penalties one who transports a firearm from a place where "he may lawfully possess and carry such firearm" but not exempting the "transportation" of a firearm if it is "readily accessible or is directly accessible from the passenger compartment of transporting vehicle"). The statute simply could have said that such a person may not "carry" a firearm. But, of course, Congress did not say this because that is not what "carry" means.

As we interpret the statutory scheme, it makes sense. Congress has imposed a variable penalty with no mandatory minimum sentence upon a person who "transports" (or "ships" or "receives") a firearm knowing it will be used to commit any "offense punishable by imprisonment for [more than] . . . one year," § 924(b), and it has imposed a 5-year mandatory minimum sentence upon one who "carries" a firearm "during and in relation to" a "drug trafficking crime," § 924(c). The first subsection imposes a less strict sentencing regime upon one who, say, ships firearms by mail for use in a crime elsewhere; the latter subsection imposes a mandatory sentence upon one who, say, brings a weapon with him (on his person or in his car) to the site of a drug sale.

Second, petitioners point out that, in *Bailey v. United States*, we considered the related phrase "uses . . . a firearm" found in the same statutory provision now before us. We construed the term "use" narrowly, limiting its application to the "active employment" of a firearm. Petitioners argue that it would be anomalous to construe broadly the word "carries," its statutory next-door neighbor.

In *Bailey*, however, we limited "use" of a firearm to "active employment" in part because we assumed "that Congress . . . intended each term to have a particular, non-superfluous meaning." A broader interpretation of "use," we said, would have swallowed up the term "carry." But "carry" as we interpret that word does not swallow up the term "use." "Use" retains the same independent meaning we found for it in *Bailey*, where we provided examples involving the displaying or the bartering of a gun. "Carry" also retains an independent meaning, for, under *Bailey*, carrying a gun in a car does not necessarily involve the gun's "active employment." More importantly, having construed "use" narrowly in *Bailey*, we cannot also construe "carry" narrowly without undercutting the statute's basic objective. For the narrow interpretation would remove the act of carrying a gun in a car entirely from the statute's reach, leaving a gap in coverage that we do not believe Congress intended.

Third, petitioners say that our reading of the statute would extend its coverage to passengers on buses, trains, or ships, who have placed a firearm, say, in checked luggage. To extend this statute so far, they argue, is unfair, going well beyond what Congress likely would have thought possible. They add that some lower courts, thinking approximately the same, have limited the scope of "carries" to instances where a gun in a car is immediately accessible, thereby most likely excluding from coverage a gun carried in a car's trunk or locked glove compartment. * * *

In our view, this argument does not take adequate account of other limiting words in the statute—words that make the statute applicable only where a defendant "carries" a gun *both* "during *and* in relation to" a drug crime. § 924(c)(1) (emphasis added). Congress added these words in part to prevent prosecution where guns "played" no part in the crime. See S. Rep. No. 98–225, at 314, n.10.

Once one takes account of the words "during" and "in relation to," it no longer seems beyond Congress' likely intent, or otherwise unfair, to interpret the statute as we have done. If one carries a gun in a car "during" and "in relation to" a drug sale, for example, the fact that the gun is carried in the car's trunk or locked glove compartment seems not only logically difficult to distinguish from the immediately accessible gun, but also beside the point.

At the same time, the narrow interpretation creates its own anomalies. The statute, for example, defines "firearm" to include a "bomb," "grenade," "rocket having a propellant charge of more than four ounces," or "missile having an explosive or incendiary charge of more than one-quarter ounce," where such device is "explosive," "incendiary," or delivers "poison gas." 18 U.S.C. § 921(a)(4)(A). On petitioners' reading, the "carry" provision would not apply to instances where drug lords, engaged in a major transaction, took with them "firearms" such as these, which most likely could not be carried on the person.

Fourth, petitioners argue that we should construe the word "carry" to mean "immediately accessible." * * * That interpretation, however, is difficult to square with the statute's language, for one "carries" a gun in the glove compartment whether or not that glove compartment is locked. Nothing in the statute's history suggests that Congress intended that limitation. And, for reasons pointed out above, we believe that the words "during" and "in relation to" will limit the statute's application to the harms that Congress foresaw.

Finally, petitioners and the dissent invoke the "rule of lenity." The simple existence of some statutory ambiguity, however, is not sufficient to warrant application of that rule, for most statutes are ambiguous to some degree. "The rule of lenity applies only if, 'after seizing everything from which aid can be derived,' . . .

we can make 'no more than a guess as to what Congress intended.' " *United States v. Wells*, 519 U.S. 482, 499 (1997) [quoting earlier cases]. To invoke the rule, we must conclude that there is a " 'grievous ambiguity or uncertainty' in the statute." *Staples v. United States*, 511 U.S. 600, 619 n.17 (1994) (quoting *Chapman v. United States* [Chapter 7, § 3(B)]. Certainly, our decision today is based on much more than a "guess as to what Congress intended," and there is no "grievous ambiguity" here. The problem of statutory interpretation [in this case] is indeed no different from that in many of the criminal cases that confront us. Yet, this Court has never held that the rule of lenity automatically permits a defendant to win. [Affirmed.]

JUSTICE GINSBURG, with whom THE CHIEF JUSTICE [REHNQUIST], JUSTICE SCALIA, and JUSTICE SOUTER join, dissenting.

[Justice Ginsburg explained that defendants' gun possession would have adverse consequences even if § 924(c)(1) were held to be inapplicable. For example, the federal sentencing guidelines provided Muscarello a 6–12 month presumptive sentence for his involvement in the distribution of 3.6 kilograms of marijuana. The "two-level enhancement" under the guidelines for possession of a gun would increase the sentencing range to 10–16 months. If, instead, as the majority held, Muscarello violated § 924(c)(1), his sentence would reflect the underlying drug offense (6–12 months) *plus* the five-year mandatory additional sentence provided by § 924(c)(1).]

* * * Unlike the Court, I do not think dictionaries, surveys of press reports,[3] or the Bible[4] tell us, dispositively, what "carries" means embedded in § 924(c)(1). On definitions, "carry" in legal formulations could mean, *inter alia*, transport, possess, have in stock, prolong (carry over), be infectious, or wear or bear on one's person.[5] At issue here is not "carries" at large but "carries a firearm." The Court's computer search of newspapers is revealing in this light. Carrying guns in a car showed up as the meaning "perhaps more than one third" of the time. One is left to wonder what meaning showed up some two thirds of the time. Surely a most familiar meaning is, as the Constitution's Second Amendment ("keep and *bear* Arms") (emphasis added) and Black's Law Dictionary, at 214, indicate: "wear, bear, or carry . . . upon the person or in the clothing or in a pocket, for the purpose . . . of being armed and ready for offensive or defensive action in a case of conflict with another person."

On lessons from literature, a scan of Bartlett's and other quotation collections shows how highly selective the Court's choices are. If "[t]he greatest of writers" have used "carry" to mean convey or transport in a vehicle, so have they used the hydra-headed word to mean, *inter alia*, carry in one's hand, arms, head, heart, or soul, sans vehicle. [Justice Ginsburg quoted Isaiah 40:11, poems by Oliver Goldsmith and

---

[3] Many newspapers, the New York Times among them, have published stories using "transport," rather than "carry," to describe gun placements resembling petitioners'. [Quoting stories.]

[4] The translator of the Good Book, it appears, bore responsibility for determining whether the servants of Ahaziah "carried" his corpse to Jerusalem. Compare [majority opinion] with, e.g., The New English Bible, 2 Kings 9:28 ("His servants *conveyed* his body to Jerusalem."); Saint Joseph Edition of the New American Bible ("His servants *brought* him in a chariot to Jerusalem."); Tanakh: The Holy Scriptures ("His servants *conveyed* him in a chariot to Jerusalem."); see also *id.*, Isaiah 30:6 ("They *convey* their wealth on the backs of asses."); The New Jerusalem Bible ("[T]hey *bear* their riches on donkeys' backs.") (emphasis added in all quotations).

[5] The dictionary to which this Court referred in *Bailey v. United States* contains 32 discrete definitions of "carry," including "[t]o make good or valid," "to bear the aspect of," and even "[t]o bear (a hawk) on the fist." See Webster's New International Dictionary of English Language 412 (2d ed. 1949).

Rudyard Kipling, and Theodore Roosevelt's famous advice to "[s]peak softly and carry a big stick."]⁶

These and the Court's lexicological sources demonstrate vividly that "carry" is a word commonly used to convey various messages. Such references, given their variety, are not reliable indicators of what Congress meant, in § 924(c)(1), by "carries a firearm."

Noting the paradoxical statement, " 'I *use* a gun to protect my house, but I've never had to *use* it,' " the Court in *Bailey* emphasized the importance of context—the statutory context. Just as "uses" was read to mean not simply "possession," but "active employment," so "carries," correspondingly, is properly read to signal the most dangerous cases—the gun at hand, ready for use as a weapon. It is reasonable to comprehend Congress as having provided mandatory minimums for the most life-jeopardizing gun-connection cases (guns in or at the defendant's hand when committing an offense), leaving other, less imminently threatening, situations for the more flexible guidelines regime. As the Ninth Circuit suggested, it is not apparent why possession of a gun in a drug dealer's moving vehicle would be thought more dangerous than gun possession on premises where drugs are sold: "A drug dealer who packs heat is more likely to hurt someone or provoke someone else to violence. A gun in a bag under a tarp in a truck bed [or in a bedroom closet] poses substantially less risk." *United States v. Foster*, 133 F.3d 704, 707 (1998) (en banc).

For indicators from Congress itself, it is appropriate to consider word usage in other provisions of Title 18's chapter on "Firearms." The Court, however, does not derive from the statutory complex at issue its thesis that " '[c]arry' implies personal agency and some degree of possession, whereas 'transport' does not have such a limited connotation and, in addition, implies the movement of goods in bulk over great distances." [Quoting majority opinion.] Looking to provisions Congress enacted, one finds that the Legislature did not acknowledge or routinely adhere to the distinction the Court advances today; instead, Congress sometimes employed "transports" when, according to the Court, "carries" was the right word to use.

Section 925(a)(2)(B), for example, provides that no criminal sanction shall attend "the transportation of [a] firearm or ammunition carried out to enable a person, who lawfully received such firearm or ammunition from the Secretary of the Army, to engage in military training or in competitions." The full text of § 926A, rather than the truncated version the Court presents, is also telling[.] [Justice Ginsburg quoted the text of 18 U.S.C. § 926A, which is reproduced in the Statutory Preface].

In describing when and how a person may travel in a vehicle that contains his firearm without violating the law, §§ 925(a)(2)(B) and 926A use "transport," not "carry," to "impl[y] personal agency and some degree of possession." [Again quoting majority opinion.]¹⁰

---

⁶   Popular films and television productions provide corroborative illustrations. * * * [I]n the television series "M*A*S*H," Hawkeye Pierce (played by Alan Alda) presciently proclaims: "I will not carry a gun. . . . I'll carry your books, I'll carry a torch, I'll carry a tune, I'll carry on, carry over, carry forward, Cary Grant, cash and carry, carry me back to Old Virginia, I'll even 'hari-kari' if you show me how, but I will not carry a gun!" See http://www.geocities.com/Hollywood/8915/mashquotes.html.

¹⁰   The Court asserts that " 'transport' is a broader category that includes 'carry' but encompasses other activity." "Carry," however, is not merely a subset of "transport." A person seated at a desk with a gun in hand

Reading "carries" in § 924(c)(1) to mean "on or about [one's] person" is fully compatible with these and other "Firearms" statutes.[11] For example, under § 925(a)(2)(B), one could carry his gun to a car, transport it to the shooting competition, and use it to shoot targets. Under the conditions of § 926A, one could transport her gun in a car, but under no circumstances could the gun be readily accessible while she travels in the car. "[C]ourts normally try to read language in different, but related, statutes, so as best to reconcile those statutes, in light of their purposes and of common sense." [*United States v. McFadden*, 13 F.3d 463, 467 (1st Cir. 1994) (Breyer, C.J., dissenting).] So reading the "Firearms" statutes, I would not extend the word "carries" in § 924(c)(1) to mean transports out of hand's reach in a vehicle.[12]

Section 924(c)(1), as the foregoing discussion details, is not decisively clear one way or another. The sharp division in the Court on the proper reading of the measure confirms, "[a]t the very least, . . . that the issue is subject to some doubt. Under these circumstances, we adhere to the familiar rule that, 'where there is ambiguity in a criminal statute, doubts are resolved in favor of the defendant.'" *Adamo Wrecking Co. v. United States*, 434 U.S. 275, 284–285 (1978); see *United States v. Granderson*, 511 U.S. 39, 54 (1994) ("[W]here text, structure, and history fail to establish that the Government's position is unambiguously correct—we apply the rule of lenity and resolve the ambiguity in [the defendant's] favor."). "Carry" bears many meanings, as the Court and the "Firearms" statutes demonstrate.[13] The narrower "on or about

---

or pocket is carrying the gun, but is not transporting it. Yes, the words "carry" and "transport" often can be employed interchangeably, as can the words "carry" and "use." But in *Bailey*, this Court settled on constructions that gave "carry" and "use" independent meanings. Without doubt, Congress is alert to the discrete meanings of "transport" and "carry" in the context of vehicles, as the Legislature's placement of each word in § 926A illustrates. The narrower reading of "carry" preserves discrete meanings for the two words, while in the context of vehicles the Court's interpretation of "carry" is altogether synonymous with "transport." Tellingly, when referring to firearms traveling in vehicles, the "Firearms" statutes routinely use a form of "transport"; they never use a form of "carry."

[11]   The Government points to numerous federal statutes that authorize law enforcement officers to "carry firearms" and notes that, in those authorizing provisions, "carry" of course means "both on the person and in a vehicle." Brief for United States 31–32, and n. 18. Quite right. But as viewers of "Sesame Street" will quickly recognize, "one of these things [a statute *authorizing* conduct] is not like the other [a statute *criminalizing* conduct]." The authorizing statutes in question are properly accorded a construction compatible with the clear purpose of the legislation to aid federal law enforcers in the performance of their official duties. It is fundamental, however, that a penal statute is not to be construed generously in the Government's favor. See, *e.g., United States v. Bass*, 404 U.S. 336, 348 (1971).

[12]   The Court places undue reliance on Representative Poff's statement that § 924(c)(1) seeks "'to persuade the man who is tempted to commit a Federal felony to leave his gun at home.'" See [majority opinion] (quoting 114 Cong. Rec. 22231 (1968)). As the Government argued in its brief to this Court in Bailey:

> In making that statement, Representative Poff was not referring to the "carries" prong of the original Section 924(c). As originally enacted, the "carries" prong of the statute prohibited only the "unlawful" carrying of a firearm while committing an offense. The statute would thus not have applied to an individual who, for instance, had a permit for carrying a gun and carried it with him when committing an offense, and it would have had no force in "persuading" such an individual "to leave his gun at home." Instead, Representative Poff was referring to the "uses" prong of the original Section 924(c). [Quoting U.S. Brief in *Bailey*.]

Representative Poff's next sentence confirms that he was speaking of "uses," not "carries": "Any person should understand that if he *uses* his gun and is caught and convicted, he is going to jail." 114 Cong. Rec., at 22231 (emphasis added).

[13]   Any doubt on that score is dispelled by examining the provisions in the "Firearms" chapter, in addition to § 924(c)(1), that include a form of the word "carry": 18 U.S.C. § 922(a)(5) ("*carry out* a bequest"); §§ 922(s)(6)(B)(ii), (iii) ("*carry out* this subsection"); § 922(u) ("*carry away* [a firearm]"); 18 U.S.C.A. § 924(a)(6)(B)(ii) (Supp.1998) ("*carry* or otherwise possess or discharge or otherwise use [a] handgun"); 18 U.S.C.

[one's] person" interpretation is hardly implausible nor at odds with an accepted meaning of "carries a firearm."

Overlooking that there will be an enhanced sentence for the gun-possessing drug dealer in any event, the Court asks rhetorically: "How persuasive is a punishment that is without effect until a drug dealer who has brought his gun to a sale (indeed has it available for use) actually takes it from the trunk (or unlocks the glove compartment) of his car?" Correspondingly, the Court defines "carries a firearm" to cover "a person who knowingly possesses and conveys firearms [anyplace] in a vehicle . . . which the person accompanies." Congress, however, hardly lacks competence to select the words "possesses" or "conveys" when that is what the Legislature means.[14] Notably in view of the Legislature's capacity to speak plainly, and of overriding concern, the Court's inquiry pays scant attention to a core reason for the rule of lenity: "[B]ecause of the seriousness of criminal penalties, and because criminal punishment usually represents the moral condemnation of the community, legislatures and not courts should define criminal activity. This policy embodies 'the instinctive distaste against men languishing in prison unless the lawmaker has clearly said they should.'" *United States v. Bass* (quoting H. Friendly, Mr. Justice Frankfurter and the Reading of Statutes, in Benchmarks 196, 209 (1967)). * * *

Postscript: Soon after the Court's opinion in *Muscarello*, Congress overrode *Bailey* in Pub. L. No. 105–386, 112 Stat. 3469 (1998). The new law amended 18 U.S.C. § 924(c)(1), to trigger the sentence-enhancement provisions where the defendant possesses a firearm "in furtherance of" one of the predicate offenses. An additional enhancement is triggered if the firearm is "brandished," and a yet-higher one if it is "discharged." Brandish is defined in new § 924(c)(4): "to display all or part of the firearm, or otherwise to make the presence of the firearm known to another person, regardless of whether the firearm is directly visible to that person." Does this new statute lend support to the majority's approach in *Muscarello*?

McNally v. United States

483 U.S. 350 (1987).

The federal mail fraud statute, 18 U.S.C. § 1341, provides that "[w]hoever, having devised or intending to devise any scheme or artifice to defraud, or for obtaining money or property by means of false or fraudulent pretenses, representations, or promises, * * * for the purpose of executing such scheme or artifice or attempting to do so [uses the mails or causes them to be used,] shall be fined not more than $1,000 or imprisoned not more

---

§ 924(e)(2)(B) ("*carrying* of a firearm"); § 925(a)(2) ("*carried out* to enable a person"); § 926(a) ("*carry out* the provisions of this chapter"); § 926A ("lawfully possess and *carry* such firearm to any other place where he may lawfully possess and *carry* such firearm"); § 929(a)(1) ("uses or *carries* a firearm and is in possession of armor piercing ammunition"); § 930(d)(3) ("lawful *carrying* of firearms . . . in a Federal facility incident to hunting or other lawful purposes") (emphasis added in all quotations).

14   See, e.g., 18 U.S.C.A. § 924(a)(6)(B)(ii) (Supp.1998) ("if the person sold . . . a handgun . . . to a juvenile knowing . . . that the juvenile intended to *carry or otherwise possess* . . . the handgun . . . in the commission of a crime of violence"); 18 U.S.C. § 926A ("may lawfully *possess and carry* such firearm to any other place where he may lawfully *possess and carry* such firearm"); § 929(a)(1) ("uses or *carries a firearm and is in possession* of armor piercing ammunition"); § 2277 ("brings, *carries, or possesses* any dangerous weapon") (emphasis added in all quotations).

than five years, or both." The lower courts upheld the convictions of several public officials and one private party activist who made a deal with an insurance company, whereby the state would send business to the company, which in turn would send some of the commissions to other companies designated by the conspirators, including one company they owned. The record apparently did not demonstrate that the state had lost any money by virtue of this kickback scheme. The Court, in an opinion by **Justice White**, reversed the lower courts' interpretation of § 1341, concluding that the statute outlawed only those "frauds on the public" that result in a tangible loss to the public.

"As first enacted in 1872, as part of a recodification of the postal laws, the statute contained a general proscription against using the mails to initiate correspondence in furtherance of 'any scheme or artifice to defraud.' The sponsor of the recodification stated, in apparent reference to the antifraud provision, that measures were needed 'to prevent the frauds which are mostly gotten up in the large cities . . . by thieves, forgers, and rapscallions generally, for the purpose of deceiving and fleecing the innocent people in the country.' Insofar as the sparse legislative history reveals anything, it indicates that the original impetus behind the mail fraud statute was to protect the people from schemes to deprive them of their money or property. * * *

"As the Court long ago stated, * * * the words 'to defraud' commonly refer 'to wronging one in his property rights by dishonest methods or schemes,' and 'usually signify the deprivation of something of value by trick, deceit, chicane or overreaching.' *Hammerschmidt v. United States*, 265 U.S. 182, 188 (1924). [Congress's adding the phrase "or for obtaining money or property" in] 1909 does not indicate that Congress was departing from this common understanding. As we see it, adding the second phrase simply made it unmistakable that the statute reached false promises and misrepresentations as to the future as well as other frauds involving money or property.

"We believe that Congress' intent in passing the mail fraud statute was to prevent the use of the mails in furtherance of such schemes. The Court has often stated that when there are two rational readings of a criminal statute, one harsher than the other, we are to choose the harsher only when Congress has spoken in clear and definite language. * * * Rather than construe the statute in a manner that leaves its outer boundaries ambiguous and involves the Federal Government in setting standards of disclosure and good government for local and state officials, we read § 1341 as limited in scope to the protection of property rights. If Congress desires to go further, it must speak more clearly than it has."

Justice Stevens, in dissent, relied on the plain meaning of the statute, which prohibits the use of the United States mails for the purpose of executing "[1] *any* scheme or artifice to defraud, [2] *or* for obtaining money or property by means of false or fraudulent pretenses, representations, or promises, [3] *or* to sell, dispose of, loan, exchange, alter, give away, distribute, supply, or furnish or procure for unlawful use any counterfeit or spurious coin, obligation, security, or other article, or anything represented to be or intimated or held out to be such counterfeit or spurious article . . ." 18 U.S.C. § 1341 (emphasis and brackets added).

"As the language makes clear, each of these restrictions is independent. One can violate the second clause—obtaining money or property by false pretenses—even though one does not violate the third clause—counterfeiting. Similarly, one can violate the first clause—devising a scheme or artifice to defraud—without violating the counterfeiting provision. Until today it was also obvious that one could violate the first clause by devising a scheme or artifice to defraud, even though one did not violate the second clause by seeking to obtain money or property from his victim through false pretenses. Every court to consider the matter had so held. Yet, today, the Court, for all practical purposes, rejects this longstanding construction of the statute by imposing a requirement that a scheme or artifice to defraud does not violate the statute unless its purpose is to defraud someone of money or property. I am at a loss to understand the source or justification for this holding. Certainly no canon of statutory construction requires us to ignore the plain language of the provision.

"In considering the scope of the mail fraud statute it is essential to remember Congress's purpose in enacting it. Congress sought to protect the integrity of the United States mails by not allowing them to be used as 'instruments of crime.' *United States v. Brewer*, 528 F.2d 492, 498 (4th Cir. 1975). 'The focus of the statute is upon the misuse of the Postal Service, not the regulation of state affairs, and Congress clearly has the authority to regulate such misuse of the mails.' *United States v. States*, 488 F.2d 761, 767 (8th Cir. 1973). Once this purpose is considered, it becomes clear that the construction the Court adopts today is senseless. Can it be that Congress sought to purge the mails of schemes to defraud citizens of money but was willing to tolerate schemes to defraud citizens of their right to an honest government, or to unbiased public officials? Is it at all rational to assume that Congress wanted to ensure that the mails not be used for petty crimes, but did not prohibit election fraud accomplished through mailing fictitious ballots? Given Congress' 'broad purpose,' I 'find it difficult to believe, absent some indication in the statute itself or the legislative history, that Congress would have undercut sharply that purpose by hobbling federal prosecutors in their effort to combat' use of the mails for fraudulent schemes."

Postscript: Justice White's memorandum to the Conference, in which he circulated his opinion, expressed reservations about the broad holding but concluded: "But it is not rare that Opinions of the Court are no more persuasive than an opinion on the other side would have been. Of course, the saving grace in Statutory Construction cases is that Congress may have its way if it does not like the product of our work."[24] In 1988, Congress adopted 18 U.S.C. § 1346, which provides that for purposes of the mail fraud statute " 'scheme or artifice to defraud' includes a scheme or artifice to deprive another of the intangible right of honest services." The statute's legislative history indicates that it was meant to override *McNally* and reinstate the "intangible rights" theory. But see *Skilling v. United States*, 561 U.S. 358 (2010) below, revisiting the meaning of § 1346.

NOTES ON MUSCARELLO, MCNALLY, AND THE SUPREME COURT'S APPROACH TO CRIMINAL STATUTES

1.   *The Rule of Lenity Cuts Across Political Lines.* Note the peculiar—perhaps unprecedented—lineup of Justices on both sides of the issue in *Muscarello*. The lineup in *McNally* is almost as odd, with Justices Scalia and Brennan in the majority and Stevens and O'Connor in dissent. The reason for the odd lineups is that the rule of lenity appeals

---

[24]   The Thurgood Marshall Papers, Library of Congress (Madison Building), Box 423, Folder 3 (Court memoranda regarding *McNally*, Nos. 86–234 & 86–286). Indeed, Congress does often override the Court's statutory decisions, and when the Court applies the rule of lenity to protect federal criminal defendants, the Department of Justice has an especially strong record for obtaining overrides. See generally Matthew Christiansen & William Eskridge Jr., *Congressional Overrides of Supreme Court Statutory Interpretation Decisions, 1967–2011*, 92 Tex. L. Rev. 1317, 1357, 1360–61 (2014). Is this a good justification for writing a weak opinion, though?

to both civil libertarians (like Brennan, Marshall, Ginsburg) and high formalists who are fans of the nondelegation argument (like Scalia and perhaps Ginsburg), while a more expansive application of criminal statutes appeals to both pragmatists who are willing to apply common-law reasoning to statutory cases (like Stevens, O'Connor, Breyer) and hard-liners against criminals (Thomas perhaps). This heterogeneity also makes the rule of lenity cases hard to predict. We were surprised to find Scalia with the nontextualist majority in *McNally* and Rehnquist (usually a hard-liner in criminal cases) with the lenient *Muscarello* dissent.[25]

2. *The Supreme Court's Inconsistency in Applying the Rule of Lenity?* Can *McNally*, where the Court invoked lenity, and *Muscarello*, where it did not, be reconciled? The cases are similar: each involved broadly phrased federal statutes being applied to antisocial conduct. Some possible bases for distinction: (a) the statute was clearer in the firearms case; (b) Supreme Court precedent supported lenity in the mail fraud case but not the firearm case, where *Smith* had already construed "carry" in a broad way; or (c) the mail fraud case involved federal prosecution of state officials and so trenched on federalism values more deeply if broadly construed (as lower courts had been doing).[26] Even if those distinctions work to distinguish *Muscarello* from *McNally*, they do not distinguish it from *Ratzlaf*, where a clear statute that had not been construed by the Court and was not being applied to state officials was nonetheless applied leniently— indeed, in a way that rendered the statute unenforceable.[27] However one resolves the distinction between *Muscarello* and *McNally*, there are plenty of Supreme Court cases going one way or the other.

Although the Supreme Court in *McNally* invoked the rule of lenity, *Muscarello* better reflects Supreme Court practice. Since 1984, the Court has cited the rule of lenity in just over one-fourth of its cases interpreting criminal statutes. In more than 60 percent of the cases, the Court has agreed with the government's interpretation.[28] Although there are still cases where the Court applies the rule of lenity, e.g., *Arthur Andersen LLP v. United States*, 544 U.S. 696 (2005); *Cleveland v. United States*, 531 U.S. 12 (2000), it remains unclear whether the rule has a systematic effect.

3. *Recent Rule of Lenity Developments: Sentencing, Legislative History, Civil Statutes.* For most of American history, the rule of lenity was applied only in the context of substantive criminal law, because sentencing was largely a matter of judicial discretion within well-defined statutory confines. *McNally* is an example. In the last 30 years, the law of sentencing has become more complex and less discretionary with judges—and the Supreme Court applied the rule of lenity to criminal sentencing in *United States v. R.L.C.*, 503 U.S. 291 (1992). See Phillip Spector, *The Sentencing Rule of Lenity*, 33 U. Toledo L.

---

[25] The lineup in *Ratzlaf* was also substantially explicable along lines noted in text. The majority opinion, invoking lenity, was written by Ginsburg, a civil libertarian, and joined by libertarians Souter and Kennedy and by the formalist Scalia, while the dissent was written by the pragmatic Blackmun and joined by Rehnquist and Thomas, both tough on criminals, and by the highly pragmatic O'Connor. An oddity was that the pragmatic Stevens (no fan of the rule of lenity and surely not sympathetic to the Ratzlafs) provided the critical fifth vote for the majority.

[26] In *McCormick v. United States*, 500 U.S. 257 (1991), the Court overturned a Hobbs Act prosecution of a state official who allegedly "extorted" campaign contributions from private parties.

[27] For students tough on crime, don't worry about the lenity in cases like *Ratzlaf*, for it was immediately overridden by Congress. See Pub. L. No. 103–325, § 411, 108 Stat. 2253 (1994). The most frequent legislative overrides come where the government loses criminal law cases. See Christiansen & Eskridge, *supra*.

[28] See William Eskridge Jr. & Lauren Baer, *The Continuum of Deference: Supreme Court Treatment of Agency Statutory Interpretations from* Chevron *to* Hamdan, 96 Geo. L. J. 1083 (2008).

Rev. 511 (2002), who argues against application of the rule to sentencing statutes, on the ground that the notice, prosecutorial discretion, and nondelegation rationales do not apply nearly as strongly to sentencing laws as to those defining substantive crimes.

As in substantive criminal law cases, the Court will not invoke the rule of lenity in sentencing cases where the statutory directive is clear. See *Chapman v. United States*, 500 U.S. 453 (1991) (affirming the Easterbrook decision in *Marshall*, Chapter 5, § 3(B)); *Gozlon-Peretz v. United States*, 498 U.S. 395 (1991). To the extent § 924, an enhancement statute, is viewed as a sentencing law, *Muscarello* illustrates the difficulty of figuring out when sentencing statutes are clear. (*Muscarello* and *Chapman* are also consistent with Spector's argument that the rule of lenity ought not be applied to sentencing statutes.)

As to this point, there is debate within the Court whether legislative history can be considered. In *R.L.C.*, a plurality of Justices stated that the application of the rule of lenity is reserved "for those situations in which a reasonable doubt persists about the statute's intended scope even *after* resort to the language and structure, legislative history, and motivating policies of the statute." 503 U.S. at 305–06. See also *Moskal v. United States*, 498 U.S. 103, 108 (1990). Justice Scalia, joined by Justices Kennedy and Thomas, objected in *R.L.C.* to the presence of legislative history and statutory policies in this inquiry. Note that Kennedy and Thomas joined the Court's opinion in *Muscarello*, which relied on legislative history.

The Court has sometimes ruled that the rule of lenity also applies when a civil-type remedy is applied to a defendant for conduct violating a criminal-type statute. Thus, in *Hughey v. United States*, 495 U.S. 411 (1990), the Court applied the rule of lenity to a statute requiring a criminal defendant to provide restitution. And in *Crandon v. United States*, 494 U.S. 152 (1990), the Court invoked the rule of lenity to protect a civil defendant, where the applicable standard of conduct was found in a criminal statute.

Skilling v. United States

561 U.S. 358 (2010).

Founded in 1985, Enron Corporation swiftly became the seventh highest-revenue-grossing company in America. Jeffrey Skilling was a longtime Enron officer, its chief executive officer for most of 2001. Less than four months after he resigned, Enron crashed into bankruptcy, and its stock plummeted in value. After an investigation uncovered a conspiracy to prop up Enron's stock prices by overstating the company's financial well-being, the federal government prosecuted dozens of Enron employees, culminating in prosecutions of Skilling and two other top executives. The indictment charged that these three defendants violated several federal criminal statutes when they allegedly engaged in a scheme to deceive investors about Enron's true financial performance by manipulating its publicly reported financial results and making false and misleading statements. Count 1 of the indictment charged Skilling with conspiracy to commit "honest-services" wire fraud, 18 U.S.C. §§ 371, 1343, 1346, by depriving Enron and its shareholders of the intangible right of his honest services. Skilling was convicted of these and other charges, and his conviction was upheld on appeal to the Fifth Circuit.

The Supreme Court reversed Skilling's § 1346 conviction. **Justice Ginsburg**'s opinion for the Court on this issue (joined by **Chief Justice Roberts** and **Justices Stevens, Breyer, Alito**, and **Sotomayor**) interpreted § 1346 to be limited to schemes to defraud of honest services only where there have been bribes and kickbacks. Justice Ginsburg started with a review of pre-1987 mail and wire fraud prosecutions under

§§ 1341 and 1343 that expanded "scheme to defraud" crimes to include "honest services" and not just tangible property losses. The leading case was *Shushan* v. *United States*, 117 F.2d 110 (5th Cir. 1941), which upheld the mail-fraud prosecution of a public official who allegedly accepted bribes from entrepreneurs in exchange for urging city action beneficial to the bribe payers. "A scheme to get a public contract on more favorable terms than would likely be got otherwise by bribing a public official," the court observed, "would not only be a plan to commit the crime of bribery, but would also be a scheme to defraud the public." By 1987, every federal court of appeals had accepted the "honest services" interpretation of the wire (§ 1341) and mail (§ 1343) fraud statutes, usually in cases that involved bribes or kickbacks.

In *McNally*, the Supreme Court stopped the lower court development of the intangible rights doctrine "in its tracks"—and Congress "responded swiftly" with new § 1346. Skilling argued that the swift response was too vague to satisfy the Due Process Clause, however. "To satisfy due process, 'a penal statute [must] define the criminal offense [1] with sufficient definiteness that ordinary people can understand what conduct is prohibited and [2] in a manner that does not encourage arbitrary and discriminatory enforcement.' *Kolender* v. *Lawson*, 461 U. S. 352, 357 (1983)." Skilling claimed that § 1346 does not clearly define what behavior it prohibits, and its "standardless sweep allows policemen, prosecutors, and juries to pursue their personal predilections" and sought a judgment invalidating the statute.

"In urging invalidation of § 1346, Skilling swims against our case law's current, which requires us, if we can, to construe, not condemn, Congress' enactments." No court of appeals had ruled that § 1346 was void for vagueness, and the Supreme Court agreed that the better path was a narrowing construction. "First, we look to the doctrine developed in pre-*McNally* cases in an endeavor to ascertain the meaning of the phrase 'the intangible right of honest services.' Second, to preserve what Congress certainly intended the statute to cover, we pare that body of precedent down to its core: In the main, the pre-*McNally* cases involved fraudulent schemes to deprive another of honest services through bribes or kickbacks supplied by a third party who had not been deceived. Confined to these paramount applications, § 1346 presents no vagueness problem."

Based upon constitutional vagueness concerns and the rule of lenity in criminal cases, Justice Ginsburg rejected the government's suggestion that § 1346 also include cases where there is "undisclosed self-dealing by a public official or private employee— *i.e.*, the taking of official action by the employee that furthers his own undisclosed financial interests while purporting to act in the interests of those to whom he owes a fiduciary duty." Because Skilling's alleged misbehavior did not include charges that he received bribes or kickbacks, Justice Ginsburg reversed his § 1346 conviction and remanded to the lower courts to determine whether the other convictions could stand.

Justice Scalia (joined by **Justices Thomas** and **Kennedy**) concurred in the Court's judgment but would have declared § 1346 void for vagueness. He viewed the Court's surgery on § 1346 to be "not interpretation but invention," the equivalent of judicial crafting of a common law crime, which our nation's constitutional culture has long abjured. *E.g.*, *United States* v. *Hudson*, 11 U.S. (7 Cranch) 32, 34 (1812). Additionally, Justice Scalia wondered what rewritten/narrowed § 1346 now covered: Does it apply to private officials, such as Skilling, at all? What would constitute a "bribe" or "kickback" (terms that do not appear in the statute but that are now interpolated into it by the majority) in future cases?

PROBLEM ON RULE OF LENITY

Problem 6-2. The Case of the Fraudulent Insurance Schemers. Alice Adams, the state Commissioner of Insurance, decides which insurance companies will receive contracts to insure certain state activities and buildings. Barbara Bashford heads the Squalid Insurance Company, which wants to secure contracting rights to insure all state buildings associated with public education. Carl Cox is a leader of the Cut-Taxes Party, which has won control of the state legislature and just elected a governor in the state. Adams switches parties to become a Cut-Taxer. In the process, Adams, Bashford, and Cox enter into an agreement whereby Adams would funnel all state education insurance contracts to Squalid Insurance, which would then pay $100,000 per year to a company partly owned by Adams and would contribute $500,000 a year to the Cut-Taxes Party.

Federal prosecutors uncover this scheme and indict Adams, Bashford, and Cox for violating § 1346. Each defendant argues that the statute does not apply to him or her after *Skilling*. Should any of the defendants prevail? Which one(s)?

B. THE RULE OF CONSTITUTIONAL AVOIDANCE

One justification for the rule of lenity arises from the constitutional notion that a legislature cannot penalize people who are wholly passive and unaware of any wrongdoing, based upon a vague criminal prohibition. See *Lambert v. California*, 355 U.S. 225 (1957); *Papachristou v. Jacksonville*, 405 U.S. 156 (1972). Assuming that the legislature is loath to come close to enacting unconstitutional criminal statutes, courts will construe criminal penalties narrowly enough so that there is no question of the statute's constitutionality, as construed. Penal statutes, of course, are not the only ones that may venture close to the precipice beyond which a statute will run afoul of the Constitution, and the Supreme Court from time to time interprets non-penal statutes restrictively to avoid constitutional problems. The Court has invoked this avoidance approach more often in recent years for cases implicating issues of new federalism. Like the rule of lenity, the avoidance canon has both defenders and detractors. Consider the following cases and the notes that follow.

STATUTORY PREFACE TO THE *CATHOLIC BISHOP* CASE

National Labor Relations Act of 1935, as amended in 1947, 1959, 1974 (codified in chapter 7 of 29 U.S.C.).

§ 152.   Definitions

(2) The term "employer" includes any person acting as an agent of an employer, directly or indirectly, but shall not include the United States or any wholly owned Government corporation, or any Federal Reserve Bank, or any State or political subdivision thereof, or any person subject to the Railway Labor Act, * * * or any labor organization (other than when acting as an employer), or anyone acting in the capacity of officer or agent of such labor organization.

§ 169.   Employees with religious convictions; payment of dues and fees

Any employee of a health care institution who is a member of and adheres to established and traditional tenets or teachings of a bona fide religion, body, or sect which has historically held conscientious objections to joining or financially supporting labor organizations shall not be required to join or financially support any labor organization as a condition of employment; except that such employee may be required, in lieu of periodic dues and initiation fees, to pay sums equal to such dues and initiation fees to a nonreligious charitable fund exempt from taxation * * * chosen by such employee from a list of at least three such funds, designated in a contract between such institution and a labor organization, or if the contract fails to designate such funds, then to any such fund chosen by the employee. * * *

NATIONAL LABOR RELATIONS BOARD V. CATHOLIC BISHOP OF CHICAGO

Supreme Court of the United States, 1979.
440 U.S. 490, 99 S.Ct. 1313, 59 L.Ed.2d 533.

THE CHIEF JUSTICE [BURGER] delivered the opinion for the Court.

[The National Labor Relations Board (NLRB) exercised jurisdiction over lay faculty members at two groups of Roman Catholic high schools, certified unions as bargaining agents for the teachers, and ordered the schools to cease and desist their refusals to bargain with these unions. The NLRB asserted jurisdiction based on its policy of declining jurisdiction only when schools are "completely religious," not "religiously associated." The NLRB found that the schools in the instant case were in the latter category, since secular as well as religious topics were taught in the schools.

[The Court of Appeals denied enforcement of the NLRB order, and the Supreme Court affirmed. The Court first held that the NLRB distinction between schools that were "completely religious" and those that were "religiously associated" was not a workable guide for the exercise of the NLRB's discretionary jurisdiction. Recognizing that rejection of this distinction meant that the Board could extend its jurisdiction to all church-operated schools, the Court stated that the Free Exercise and Establishment Clauses of the First Amendment might preclude such an exercise of jurisdiction.]

Although the respondents press their claims under the Religion Clauses, the question we consider first is whether Congress intended the Board to have jurisdiction over teachers in church-operated schools. In a number of cases the Court has heeded the essence of Mr. Chief Justice Marshall's admonition in *Murray v. The Schooner Charming Betsy*, 6 U.S. (2 Cranch) 64, 118 (1804), by holding that an Act of Congress ought not be construed to violate the Constitution if any other possible construction remains available. Moreover, the Court has followed this policy in the interpretation of the Act now before us and related statutes.

In *Machinists v. Street*, 367 U.S. 740 (1961), for example, the Court considered claims that serious First Amendment questions would arise if the Railway Labor Act were construed to allow compulsory union dues to be used to support political candidates or causes not approved by some members. The Court looked to the language of the Act and the legislative history and concluded that they did not permit union dues to be used for such political purposes, thus avoiding "serious doubt of [the Act's] constitutionality." * * *

The values enshrined in the First Amendment plainly rank high "in the scale of our national values." In keeping with the Court's prudential policy it is incumbent on us to determine whether the Board's exercise of its jurisdiction here would give rise to serious constitutional questions. If so, we must first identify "the affirmative intention of the Congress clearly expressed" before concluding that the Act grants jurisdiction. [Quoting *McCulloch v. Sociedad Nacional de Marineros de Honduras*, 372 U.S. 10 (1963).]

In recent decisions involving aid to parochial schools we have recognized the critical and unique role of the teacher in fulfilling the mission of a church-operated school. What was said of the schools in *Lemon v. Kurtzman*, 403 U.S. 602, 617 (1971), is true of the schools in this case: "Religious authority necessarily pervades the school system." The key role played by teachers in such a school system has been the predicate for our conclusions that governmental aid channeled through teachers creates an impermissible risk of excessive governmental entanglement in the affairs of the church-operated schools. * * *

Only recently we again noted the importance of the teacher's function in a church school: "Whether the subject is 'remedial reading,' 'advanced reading,' or simply 'reading,' a teacher remains a teacher, and the danger that religious doctrine will become intertwined with secular instruction persists." *Meek v. Pittenger*, 421 U.S. 349, 370 (1975). Good intentions by government—or third parties—can surely no more avoid entanglement with the religious mission of the school in the setting of mandatory collective bargaining than in the well-motivated legislative efforts consented to by the church-operated schools which we found unacceptable in *Lemon* [and *Meek*.]

The Board argues that it can avoid excessive entanglement since it will resolve only factual issues such as whether an anti-union animus motivated an employer's action. But at this stage of our consideration we are not compelled to determine whether the entanglement is excessive as we would were we considering the constitutional issue. Rather, we make a narrow inquiry whether the exercise of the Board's jurisdiction presents a significant risk that the First Amendment will be infringed.

Moreover, it is already clear that the Board's actions will go beyond resolving factual issues. The Court of Appeals' opinion refers to charges of unfair labor practices filed against religious schools. The court observed that in those cases the schools had responded that their challenged actions were mandated by their religious creeds. The resolution of such charges by the Board, in many instances, will necessarily involve inquiry into the good faith of the position asserted by the clergy-administrators and its relationship to the school's religious mission. It is not only the conclusions that may be reached by the Board which may impinge on rights guaranteed by the Religion Clauses, but also the very process of inquiry leading to findings and conclusions.

The Board's exercise of jurisdiction will have at least one other impact on church-operated schools. The Board will be called upon to decide what are "terms and conditions of employment" and therefore mandatory subjects of bargaining. See 29 U.S.C. § 158(d). Although the Board has not interpreted that phrase as it relates to educational institutions, similar state provisions provide insight into the effect of mandatory bargaining. The Oregon Court of Appeals noted that "nearly everything that goes on in the schools affects teachers and is therefore arguably a 'condition of employment.'" *Springfield Educ. Ass'n. v. Springfield Sch. Dist. No. 19*, 547 P.2d 647, 650 (Or. App. 1976). [The introduction of the mandatory bargaining process itself represents an encroachment by the government into the autonomy of the school's management, which in these cases is pursuing religious purposes that will be compromised.]

The church-teacher relationship in a church-operated school differs from the employment relationship in a public or other nonreligious school. We see no escape from conflicts flowing from the Board's exercise of jurisdiction over teachers in church-operated schools and the consequent serious First Amendment questions that would follow. We therefore turn to an examination of the National Labor Relations Act to decide whether it must be read to confer jurisdiction that would in turn require a decision on the constitutional claims raised by respondents.

There is no clear expression of an affirmative intention of Congress that teachers in church-operated schools should be covered by the Act. Admittedly, Congress defined the Board's jurisdiction in very broad terms; we must therefore examine the legislative history of the Act to determine whether Congress contemplated that the grant of jurisdiction would include teachers in such schools.

In enacting the National Labor Relations Act in 1935, Congress sought to protect the right of American workers to bargain collectively. The concern that was repeated throughout the debates was the need to assure workers the right to organize to counterbalance the collective activities of employers which had been authorized by the National Industrial Recovery Act. But congressional attention focused on employment in private industry and on industrial recovery. See, *e.g.*, 79 Cong. Rec. 7573 (1935) (remarks of Sen. Wagner).

Our examination of the statute and its legislative history indicates that Congress simply gave no consideration to church-operated schools. It is not without significance, however, that the Senate Committee on Education and Labor chose a college professor's dispute with the college as an example of employer-employee relations *not* covered by the Act. S. Rep. No. 573, 74th Cong., 1st Sess., 7 (1935).

Congress' next major consideration of the jurisdiction of the Board came during the passage of the Labor Management Relations Act of 1947—the Taft-Hartley Act. In that Act Congress amended the definition of "employer" in § 2 of the original Act to exclude nonprofit hospitals. 61 Stat. 137, 29 U.S.C. § 152(2) (1970 ed.). There was some discussion of the scope of the Board's jurisdiction but the consensus was that nonprofit institutions in general did not fall within the Board's jurisdiction because they did not affect commerce. [Citing various portions of legislative history.]

The most recent significant amendment to the Act was passed in 1974, removing the exemption of nonprofit hospitals. Pub. L. No. 93–360, 88 Stat. 395. The Board relies upon that amendment as showing that Congress approved the Board's exercise of jurisdiction over church-operated schools. A close examination of that legislative history, however, reveals nothing to indicate an affirmative intention that such schools be within the Board's jurisdiction. Since the Board did not assert jurisdiction over teachers in a church-operated school until after the 1974 amendment, nothing in the history of the amendment can be read as reflecting Congress' tacit approval of the Board's action.

During the debate there were expressions of concern about the effect of the bill on employees of religious hospitals whose religious beliefs would not permit them to join a union. 120 Cong. Rec. 12946, 16914 (1974). The result of those concerns was an amendment which reflects congressional sensitivity to First Amendment guarantees. [Chief Justice Burger quoted the text of 29 U.S.C. § 169, which is reproduced in the Statutory Preface].

The absence of an "affirmative intention of the Congress clearly expressed" fortifies our conclusion that Congress did not contemplate that the Board would require church-operated schools to grant recognition to unions as bargaining agents for their teachers.

The Board relies heavily upon *Associated Press v. NLRB*, 301 U.S. 103 (1937). There the Court held that the First Amendment was no bar to the application of the Act to the Associated Press, an organization engaged in collecting information and news throughout the world and distributing it to its members. Perceiving nothing to suggest that application of the Act would infringe First Amendment guarantees of press freedoms, the Court sustained Board jurisdiction. Here, on the contrary, the record affords abundant evidence that the Board's exercise of jurisdiction over teachers in church-operated schools would implicate the guarantees of the Religion Clauses.

Accordingly, in the absence of a clear expression of Congress' intent to bring teachers in church-operated schools within the jurisdiction of the Board, we decline to construe the Act in a manner that could in turn call upon the Court to resolve difficult and sensitive questions arising out of the guarantees of the First Amendment Religion Clauses. [*Affirmed.*]

MR. JUSTICE BRENNAN, with whom MR. JUSTICE WHITE, MR. JUSTICE MARSHALL, and MR. JUSTICE BLACKMUN join, dissenting.

* * * The general principle of construing statutes to avoid unnecessary constitutional decisions is a well-settled and salutary one. The governing canon, however, is *not* that expressed by the Court today. The Court requires that there be a "clear expression of an affirmative intention of Congress" before it will bring within the coverage of a broadly worded regulatory statute certain persons whose coverage might raise constitutional questions. But those familiar with the legislative process know that explicit expressions of congressional intent in such broadly inclusive statutes are not commonplace. Thus, by strictly or loosely applying its requirement, the Court can virtually remake congressional enactments. * * *

The settled canon for construing statutes wherein constitutional questions may lurk was stated in *Machinists v. Street*, 367 U.S. 740 (1961), cited by the Court, *ante*:

> " 'When the validity of an act of the Congress is drawn in question, and even if a serious doubt of constitutionality is raised, it is a cardinal principle that this Court will first ascertain whether a construction of the statute is *fairly*

possible by which the question may be avoided.' *Crowell v. Benson*, 285 U.S. 22, 62." *Id.*, at 749–750 (emphasis added).

This limitation to constructions that are "fairly possible" and "reasonable" acts as a brake against wholesale judicial dismemberment of congressional enactments. It confines the judiciary to its proper role in construing statutes, which is to interpret them so as to give effect to congressional intention. The Court's new "affirmative expression" rule releases that brake.

The interpretation of the National Labor Relations Act announced by the Court today is not "fairly possible." The Act's wording, its legislative history, and the Court's own precedents leave "the intention of the Congress * * * revealed too distinctly to permit us to ignore it because of mere misgivings as to power." Section 2(2) of the Act, 29 U.S.C. § 152(2), defines "employer" as:

> " * * * any person acting as an agent of an employer, directly or indirectly, *but shall not include* the United States or any wholly owned Government corporation, or any Federal Reserve Bank, or any State or political subdivision thereof, or any person subject to the Railway Labor Act, as amended from time to time, or any labor organization (other than when acting as an employer), or anyone acting in the capacity of officer or agent of such labor organization." (Emphasis added.)

Thus, the Act covers all employers not within the eight express exceptions. The Court today substitutes amendment for construction to insert one more exception—for church-operated schools. This is a particularly transparent violation of the judicial role: The legislative history reveals that Congress itself considered and rejected a very similar amendment.

[The 1935 Act could not have been written more broadly, and the NLRB rejected efforts to except nonprofit employers from its reach.] The Hartley bill, which passed the House of Representatives in 1947, would have provided the exception the Court today writes into the statute:

> "The term 'employer' * * * shall not include * * * any corporation, community chest, fund, or foundation organized and operated exclusively for *religious*, charitable, scientific, literary, or *educational* purposes, * * * no part of the net earnings of which inures to the benefit of any private shareholder or individual * * *." (Emphasis added.) H.R. 3020, 80th Cong., 1st Sess., § 2(2) (Apr. 18, 1947).

But the proposed exception was not enacted. The bill reported by the Senate Committee on Labor and Public Welfare did not contain the Hartley exception. Instead, the Senate proposed an exception limited to nonprofit hospitals, and passed the bill in that form. The Senate version was accepted by the House in conference, thus limiting the exception for nonprofit employers to nonprofit hospitals.

Even that limited exemption was ultimately repealed in 1974. In doing so, Congress confirmed the view of the Act expressed here: that it was intended to cover all employers—including nonprofit employers—unless expressly excluded, and that the 1947 amendment excluded only nonprofit hospitals. See H.R. Rep. No. 93–1051, p. 4 (1974); 120 Cong. Rec. 12938 (1974) (Senator Williams); 120 Cong. Rec. 16900

(1974) (Rep. Ashbrook). Moreover, it is significant that in considering the 1974 amendments, the Senate expressly rejected an amendment proposed by Senator Ervin that was analogous to the one the Court today creates—an amendment to exempt nonprofit hospitals operated by religious groups. Senator Cranston, floor manager of the Senate Committee bill and primary opponent of the proposed religious exception, explained:

> "[S]uch an exception for religiously affiliated hospitals would seriously erode *the existing national policy which holds religiously affiliated institutions generally such as* proprietary nursing homes, residential communities, and *educational facilities to the same standards as their nonsectarian counterparts.*" 120 Cong. Rec. 12957 (1974) (emphasis added).

See also *ibid.* (Sen. Javits); 120 Cong. Rec. 12957 (1974) (Sen. Williams).

In construing the Board's jurisdiction to exclude church-operated schools, therefore, the Court today is faithful to neither the statute's language nor its history. Moreover, it is also untrue to its own precedents. "This Court has consistently declared that in passing the National Labor Relations Act, Congress intended to and did vest in the Board the fullest *jurisdictional* breadth constitutionally permissible under the Commerce Clause." *NLRB v. Reliance Fuel Oil Corp.*, 371 U.S. 224, 226 (1963) (emphasis in original). As long as an employer is within the reach of Congress' power under the Commerce Clause—and no one doubts that respondents are—the Court has held him to be covered by the Act regardless of the nature of his activity. Indeed, *Associated Press v. NLRB*, 301 U.S. 103 (1937), construed the Act to cover editorial employees of a nonprofit news-gathering organization despite a claim—precisely parallel to that made here—that their inclusion rendered the Act in violation of the First Amendment. Today's opinion is simply unable to explain the grounds that distinguish that case from this one.

Thus, the available authority indicates that Congress intended to include—not exclude—lay teachers of church-operated schools. The Court does not counter this with evidence that Congress *did* intend an exception it never stated. Instead, despite the legislative history to the contrary, it construes the Act as excluding lay teachers only because Congress did not state explicitly that they were covered. In Mr. Justice Cardozo's words, this presses "avoidance of a difficulty * * * to the point of disingenuous evasion." *Moore Ice Cream Co. v. Rose*, 289 U.S. at 379.[11]

---

[11]   Not even the Court's redrafting of the statute causes all First Amendment problems to disappear. The Court's opinion implies limitation of its exception to church-operated schools. That limitation is doubtless necessary since this Court has already rejected a more general exception for nonprofit organizations. See *Polish National Alliance v. NLRB*, 322 U.S. 643 (1944). But such an exemption, available only to church-operated schools, generates a possible Establishment Clause *question* of its own. *Walz v. Tax Comm'n*, 397 U.S. 664 (1970), does not put that question to rest, for in upholding the property tax exemption for churches there at issue, we emphasized that New York had "not singled out * * * churches as such; rather, it has granted exemption to all houses of religious worship within a broad class of property owned by nonprofit, quasi-public corporations * * *." Like the Court, "at this stage of [my] consideration [I am] not compelled to determine whether the [Establishment Clause problem] is [as significant] as [I] would were [I] considering the constitutional issue." It is enough to observe that no matter which way the Court turns in interpreting the Act, it cannot avoid constitutional questions.

NOTES ON THE "AVOIDANCE CANON"

1. *Different Ways of Framing the Avoidance Canon.* As the debate in *Catholic Bishop* indicates, there are several ways to express this canon:[29] When one interpretation of an ambiguous statute would be unconstitutional, choose another one that would pass constitutional muster. *Murray v. The Schooner Charming Betsy*, 6 U.S. (2 Cranch) 64 (1804). When one interpretation would raise serious constitutional problems, choose the one that would not. *United States ex rel. Attorney General v. Delaware & Hudson Co.*, 213 U.S. 366 (1909); cf. *Ex parte Bollman*, 8 U.S. (4 Cranch) 75 (1807). When one interpretation presents constitutional difficulties, do not impose it unless there has been an affirmative indication from Congress that it is required. *McCulloch v. Sociedad Nacional de Marineros de Honduras*, 372 U.S. 10 (1963).

The most aggressive way of framing the avoidance canon is *McCulloch*, which Chief Justice Burger invokes in *Catholic Bishop*. The dissenters assail the Chief Justice for this, and the *McCulloch* language is rarely applied today. But neither is the *Charming Betsy* language. Generally, the avoidance canon today follows the *Delaware & Hudson* language.

2. *What Is a "Serious" or "Substantial" Constitutional Problem?* As noted, the *Delaware & Hudson* approach requires courts to interpret a statute in a manner that avoids serious or substantial constitutional problems. How does a court know when a constitutional question is serious or substantial? Does it depend on the fundamental nature of the constitutional provision in question? The First Amendment is implicated in *Catholic Bishops*; would the avoidance canon be presumptively less applicable if a statute implicated the excessive bail provision of the Eighth Amendment?

Alternatively, does the seriousness of a constitutional problem depend on the likelihood that there has been a constitutional violation? What if a court believes a certain interpretation would raise constitutional questions but this interpretation would nonetheless be constitutional? Should a court invoke constitutional avoidance even if it would uphold the challenged interpretation as constitutional anyway?

3. *Values Underlying the Avoidance Canon.* There are a number of values the avoidance doctrine might serve, such as avoiding unnecessary constitutional holdings or advisory opinions by the Court. Consider three potentially important values. First, it may be a *rule of thumb for ascertaining legislative intent*. The avoidance interpreter assumes that the legislature would *not* have wanted to press constitutional limits. Fred Schauer, Ashwander *Revisited*, 1995 Sup. Ct. Rev. 71, finds such an implicit legislative intent theory most implausible. The assumption rests upon no evidence of actual legislative intent. In the average case, why shouldn't the enacting legislature prefer that its work product be given full force—and if it's unconstitutional the Court should say so openly so that there can be a full-blown constitutional controversy? See Jerry Mashaw, *Greed, Chaos, and Governance: Using Public Choice Theory to Improve Public Law* 105 (1997). Consider *Catholic Bishop*: Is it plausible that Congress would have wanted the Court to trim back the statute in the way that it did?

A second value of the avoidance canon is that it might provide a low-salience mechanism for giving effect to what Larry Sager calls "*underenforced constitutional*

---

[29]   For useful introductions, see Trevor Morrison, *Constitutional Avoidance in the Executive Branch*, 106 Colum. L. Rev. 1189 (2006); John Copeland Nagle, Delaware & Hudson *Revisited*, 72 Notre Dame L. Rev. 1495 (1997); Adrian Vermeule, *Saving Constructions*, 85 Geo. L.J. 1945 (1997).

norms."[30] For instance, judges are loath to strike down immigration statutes, because of either the plenary powers idea or institutional competence concerns. But as Hiroshi Motomura has identified, while judges may be unwilling to close off congressional options through constitutional review, they will give effect to due process and free speech norms through narrowing constructions.[31] And so the norm is vindicated—but Congress can (re)assert a broader result after deliberation and debate over a statutory amendment that clearly overrides the norm-adhering interpretation.

Consider ways in which this idea might apply to *Catholic Bishop.* Labor law has been another area where the avoidance canon has been especially active in the Supreme Court's jurisprudence. See the cases discussed in *Catholic Bishop,* as well as more recent cases such as *Edward J. DeBartolo Corp. v. Fla. Gulf Coast Building & Constr. Trades Council,* 485 U.S. 568, 575 (1988). Consider too the possible risks attached to these narrowing constructions, especially in an area like labor law where Congress has long been gridlocked. When a court reframes a statute in service of constitutional avoidance, later courts may amplify the "reframing," incrementally changing both statutory and constitutional doctrine in new contexts. See Charlotte Garden, *Avoidance Creep,* 168 Penn. L. Rev. ___ (forthcoming 2020).

A third value for the avoidance canon is suggested by Professor Bickel's theory of the *passive virtues.*[32] One way that courts conserve their institutional capital is by techniques of avoidance. Standard techniques are for the Court to divest itself of constitutional cases whose resolution is premature by dismissing the complaint on procedural grounds such as standing, ripeness, etc. The avoidance canon represents a middle ground between pure passive virtues and constitutional invalidation. That middle ground allows the Court to slow down a political process that is moving too hastily and overriding human rights, but without incurring the full wrath of a political process that doesn't like to be thwarted. As Philip Frickey has argued, this theory best explains several cases where the Warren Court impeded McCarthy-era initiatives, but without creating a full-blown constitutional crisis.[33] How might this theory apply to *Catholic Bishop,* which was handed down a generation later, and by a more conservative majority?

4.   *Criticisms of the Avoidance Canon.* Perhaps the leading critique of the avoidance canon remains Judge Henry Friendly, *Mr. Justice Frankfurter and the Reading of Statutes,* in *Benchmarks* 211–12 (1967):

> Although questioning the doctrine of construction to avoid constitutional doubts is rather like challenging Holy Writ, the rule has always seemed to me to have almost as many dangers as advantages. For one thing, it is one of those

---

[30]   William Eskridge Jr. & Philip Frickey, *Quasi-Constitutional Law: Clear Statement Rules as Constitutional Lawmaking,* 45 Vand. L. Rev. 593 (1992), drawing from Lawrence Sager, *Fair Measure: The Legal Status of Underenforced Constitutional Norms,* 91 Harv. L. Rev. 1212 (1978). See also Neal Katyal, *Judges as Advicegivers,* 50 Stan. L. Rev. 1709 (1998); Ronald Krotoszynski, Jr., *Constitutional Flares: On Judges, Legislatures, And Dialogue,* 83 Minn. L. Rev. 1 (1998); Ernest Young, *Constitutional Avoidance, Resistance Norms, and the Preservation of Judicial Review,* 78 Tex. L. Rev. 1549, 1585–87 (2000).

[31]   Hiroshi Motomura, *Immigration Law After a Century of Plenary Power: Phantom Constitutional Norms and Statutory Interpretation,* 100 Yale L.J. 545, 561–75 (1990). For good examples of Professor Motomura's thesis, see *Zadvydas v. Davis,* 533 U.S. 678, 696–99 (2001); *INS v. St. Cyr,* 533 U.S. 289 (2001).

[32]   Alexander Bickel, *The Least Dangerous Branch: The Supreme Court at the Bar of Politics* 156–69 (1962). Bickel's ideas about statutory interpretation are set forth in Alexander Bickel & Harry Wellington, *Legislative Purpose and the Judicial Process: The Lincoln Mills Case,* 71 Harv. L. Rev. 1 (1957).

[33]   Philip Frickey, *Getting from Joe to Gene (McCarthy): The Avoidance Canon, Legal Process Theory, and Narrowing Statutory Interpretation in the Early Warren Court,* 93 Cal. L. Rev. 397 (2005).

rules that courts apply when they want and conveniently forget when they don't—some, perhaps, would consider that to be a virtue. * * * Some considerations advanced in its favor, such as the awesome consequences of "a decree of unconstitutionality," overlook that if the Court finds the more likely construction to be unconstitutional, another means of rescue—the principle of construing to avoid unconstitutionality—will be at hand. The strongest basis for the rule is thus that the Supreme Court ought not to indulge in what, if adverse, is likely to be only a constitutional advisory opinion. While there is force in this, the rule of "construing" to avoid constitutional doubts should, in my view, be confined to cases where the doubt is exceedingly real. Otherwise this rule, whether it be denominated one of statutory interpretation or, more accurately, of constitutional adjudication—still more accurately, of constitutional nonadjudication—is likely to become one of evisceration and tergiversation.

Judge Friendly's charge is that the avoidance canon will be an occasion for *stealth judicial activism*, which is both anti-democratic and unhealthy for the judiciary. Accord Judge Richard Posner, *The Federal Courts: Crisis and Reform* 285 (1985); Lisa Kloppenberg, *Avoiding Constitutional Questions*, 35 B.C. L. Rev. 1003 (1994); John Manning, *The Nondelegation Doctrine as a Canon of Avoidance*, 2000 Sup. Ct. Rev. 223; John Nagle, Delaware & Hudson *Revisited*, 72 Notre Dame L. Rev. 1495 (1997).

A corollary to Judge Friendly's charge is that the avoidance canon will be applied unpredictably. Even in the immigration area, where it has made regular appearances in Supreme Court opinions, this charge has much weight. For an example of a case where there were strong constitutional doubts and less than clear statutory language, yet the Court refused to apply this canon (or the rule of lenity, which was also applicable), see *Almendarez-Torres v. United States*, 523 U.S. 224 (1998). See also *Rust v. Sullivan*, 500 U.S. 173 (1991).

5.   *Avoiding Avoidance When Presented with Two Distinct Constitutional Rationales.* In *National Federation of Independent Business v. Sebelius*, 567 U.S. 519 (2012), the Supreme Court reviewed constitutional challenges to the Patient Protection and Affordable Care Act. Chief Justice Roberts authored the pivotal opinion upholding the Act's individual mandate, which required most Americans to maintain minimum essential health care coverage or else make a "shared responsibility" payment to the federal government that is assessed and collected by the Internal Revenue Service.

The Obama Administration sought to sustain the constitutionality of this provision on several different grounds. The Chief Justice concluded first, writing for himself, that the individual mandate was not a valid exercise of Congress's powers under the Commerce Clause or the Necessary and Proper Clause. He then delivered the opinion of the Court upholding the individual mandate as within Congress's power under the Taxing Clause. The Chief Justice concluded, for himself and Justices Ginsburg, Breyer, Sotomayor, and Kagan, that construing the provision as a tax was "fairly possible" even if this was not the "most natural interpretation" of the mandate.

Why was it necessary for Chief Justice Roberts to analyze and reject the Government's commerce power argument—and in doing so add his voice to the conclusion reached by dissenting Justices Scalia, Kennedy, Thomas, and Alito—given that the Court ultimately sustained the individual mandate as constitutional on an independently sufficient ground? The Chief Justice explained his position as follows: "[T]he statute reads more naturally as a command to buy insurance than as a tax, and I would uphold it as a command if the Constitution allowed it. It is only because the Commerce Clause does not authorize such a command that it is necessary to reach the taxing power question. And it is only because we have a duty to construe a statute to save it, if fairly possible, that [the individual mandate] can be interpreted as a tax. Without deciding the Commerce Clause question, I would find no basis for such a saving construction."

Has Chief Justice Roberts added a new dimension to the canon of constitutional avoidance? The Court typically applies the avoidance canon in order to *avoid* expressing a position on the meaning of the Constitution except insofar as is necessary to determine the outcome of the case. That is how the Supreme Court applied the canon in *Catholic Bishop*. Is the traditional approach now qualified when a party offers two or more rationales for sustaining a law against constitutional challenge? Or only when one of the rationales is plainly the most natural one, triggering an "unavoidable" constitutional analysis? Should the parties be asked specifically to address the question of what qualifies as the most natural construction? How much weight should a reviewing court accord to the government's position on this question, as explained in its brief or at oral argument?

PROBLEM ON THE AVOIDANCE CANON

Problem 6-3. Use of Sampling as Part of the Census. Article I, § 2, cl. 3 of the Constitution apportions Representatives among the states "according to their respective Numbers" and requires that there be an "Enumeration" of the "Numbers" of people in the various states every ten years, "in such Manner as they [Congress] shall by Law direct." The Census Act, 13 U.S.C. § 1 et seq., delegates the responsibility for this endeavor to the Commerce Department. Prior to 1976, the Census Bureau's practice, required by statute before that date, was never to use sampling techniques for apportionment purposes.

Congress revised the Census Act in 1976, adding two relevant provisions. Section 141(a), as rewritten in 1976, states: "The Secretary shall * * * take a decennial census of the population * * * in such form and content as he may determine, including the use of sampling procedures and special surveys." Section 195 says: "Except for the determination of population for purposes of apportionment of Representatives in Congress among the several States, the Secretary shall, if he considers it feasible, authorize the use of the statistical method known as 'sampling' in carrying out the provisions of this title." For the 2000 Census, the Commerce Department proposed to supplement its survey with statistical sampling techniques to cure what had been documented as an "undercount" of the population, especially of racial minorities and poor people.

The Department's proposed use of sampling is challenged as unlawful under the 1976 Census Act and the Census Clause of Article I. You are the district court judge deciding the case. Should you (or can you) avoid the constitutional question through a construction of the Census Act? Is there a serious and substantial problem as to whether the "Enumeration" requirement would be satisfied if the Department used statistical sampling as a supplement—not a substitute—for actual counting? See *Dep't of Commerce v. U.S. House of Representatives*, 525 U.S. 316 (1999).

NOTE ON SEVERABILITY

When a provision in a statute is unconstitutional, should the court treat the remainder of the statute as good law, or declare the entire statute invalid? This is a question of *severability*. When the statute contains an express severability clause (instructing courts to save the remainder of the statute) or an express nonseverability clause, the issue would appear to be easy. Nonetheless, because such clauses are sometimes inserted as boilerplate in bills without much thought given to their effects, courts sometimes struggle with whether the clause should be given its full textual meaning if that seems inconsistent with the probable legislative intent concerning the particular severability issue.[34]

Often the statute is silent on the question. In that circumstance, "[u]nless it is evident that the Legislature would not have enacted those provisions which are within its power, independently of that which is not, the invalid part may be dropped if what is left is fully operative as a law." *Alaska Airlines, Inc. v. Brock*, 480 U.S. 678, 684 (1987).

THE NEW FEDERALISM CANONS: A SPECIAL FORM OF "AVOIDANCE"

The Supreme Court starting in the 1980s and early 1990s created or clarified "clear statement rules" that reflect constitutional norms of federalism.[35] See *Pennhurst State Sch. & Hosp. v. Halderman*, 451 U.S. 1 (1981) (conditions attached to federal funding for state programs must be clear); *Atascadero State Hosp. v. Scanlon*, 473 U.S. 234 (1985) (super-strong clear statement rule against congressional abrogation of state Eleventh Amendment immunity from suit in federal courts).[36] The following case is the most dramatic example to date of the Court's activity in protecting state sovereignty through the use of canons.

As background, note that in *Maryland v. Wirtz*, 392 U.S. 183 (1968), the Court upheld the application of the Fair Labor Standards Act's minimum wage provisions to state hospital and school employees, rejecting the claim that the Constitution forbids such direct federal regulation of important state functions. Then, in *National League of Cities v. Usery*, 426 U.S. 833 (1976), by a 5–4 vote, the Court overruled *Wirtz* and refused to apply the FLSA's minimum wage and maximum hours provisions to many state and municipal employees. *National League of Cities* then met its own apparent demise in *Garcia v. San Antonio Metropolitan Transit Authority*, 469 U.S. 528 (1985), another 5–4 case, which explicitly overruled the nine-year-old precedent. As the next case demonstrates, what the Court taketh away as constitutional protection, it can revive as canonical interpretive protection.

---

[34]   For excellent critical analyses of the Court's severability jurisprudence, see Michael Shumsky, *Severability, Inseverability, and the Rule of Law*, 41 Harv. J. Leg. 227 (2004); Comment, Israel Friedman, *Inseverability Clauses in Statutes*, 64 U. Chi. L. Rev. 903 (1997).

[35]   Recall our terminology: a "clear statement rule" requires that a statute be interpreted a certain way unless the contrary interpretation is clearly required by statutory text; a "super-strong clear statement rule" requires that the statutory text targets the issue unmistakably, especially through specific language.

[36]   See generally William Eskridge Jr. & Philip Frickey, *Quasi-Constitutional Law: Clear Statement Rules as Constitutional Lawmaking*, 45 Vand. L. Rev. 593 (1992), surveying and analyzing the Court's aggressive deployment of these federalism-inspired super-strong clear statement rules.

GREGORY V. ASHCROFT
Supreme Court of the United States, 1991.
501 U.S. 452, 111 S.Ct. 2395, 115 L.Ed.2d 410.

JUSTICE O'CONNOR delivered the opinion of the Court.

[It is a prima facie violation of the federal Age Discrimination in Employment Act (ADEA), 29 U.S.C. §§ 621–34, for an "employer" covered by the Act to specify a mandatory retirement age for "employees" over forty years of age who are covered by the Act. State and local governments are "employers" covered by the ADEA. In this case, the Missouri Constitution provided a mandatory retirement age of seventy for most state judges. Petitioners were state judges seeking to obtain a declaration that the mandatory retirement age violates the ADEA. The district court dismissed the action, concluding that the judges were "appointees on the policymaking level," a category of state officials excluded from the definition of "employees" covered by the Act. The Court of Appeals affirmed. What follows is Part II of Justice O'Connor's opinion.]

[II-A] As every schoolchild learns, our Constitution establishes a system of dual sovereignty between the States and the Federal Government. * * * The Constitution created a Federal Government of limited powers. "The powers not delegated to the United States by the Constitution, nor prohibited by it to the States, are reserved to the States respectively, or to the people." U.S. Const. amend. X. The States thus retain substantial sovereign authority under our constitutional system. * * *

This federalist structure of joint sovereigns preserves to the people numerous advantages. It assures a decentralized government that will be more sensitive to the diverse needs of a heterogenous society; it increases opportunity for citizen involvement in democratic processes; it allows for more innovation and experimentation in government; and it makes government more responsive by putting the States in competition for a mobile citizenry.

Perhaps the principal benefit of the federalist system is a check on abuses of government power. "The 'constitutionally mandated balance of power' between the States and the Federal Government was adopted by the Framers to ensure the protection of 'our fundamental liberties.'" *Atascadero State Hosp. v. Scanlon*, 473 U.S. 234, 242 (1985), quoting *Garcia v. San Antonio Metro. Transit Auth.*, 469 U.S. 528, 572 (1985) (Powell, J., dissenting). Just as the separation and independence of the coordinate Branches of the Federal Government serves to prevent the accumulation of excessive power in any one Branch, a healthy balance of power between the States and the Federal Government will reduce the risk of tyranny and abuse from either front. * * *

The Federal Government holds a decided advantage in this delicate balance: the Supremacy Clause. U.S. Const. Art. VI, cl. 2. As long as it is acting within the powers granted it under the Constitution, Congress may impose its will on the States. Congress may legislate in areas traditionally regulated by the States. This is an extraordinary power in a federalist system. It is a power that we must assume Congress does not exercise lightly.

The present case concerns a state constitutional provision through which the people of Missouri establish a qualification for those who sit as their judges. This provision goes beyond an area traditionally regulated by the States; it is a decision of the most fundamental sort for a sovereign entity. Through the structure of its government, and the character of those who exercise government authority, a State defines itself as a sovereign. * * *

Congressional interference with this decision of the people of Missouri, defining their constitutional officers, would upset the usual constitutional balance of federal and state powers. For this reason, "it is incumbent upon the federal courts to be certain of Congress' intent before finding that federal law overrides" this balance. *Atascadero.* We explained recently:

> "[I]f Congress intends to alter the 'usual constitutional balance between the States and the Federal Government,' it must make its intention to do so 'unmistakably clear in the language of the statute.' *Atascadero*; see also *Pennhurst State School and Hosp. v. Halderman*, 465 U.S. 89, 99 (1984). *Atascadero* was an Eleventh Amendment case, but a similar approach is applied in other contexts. Congress should make its intention 'clear and manifest' if it intends to pre-empt the historic powers of the States. *Will v. Mich. Dep't. of State Police*, 491 U.S. 58, 65 (1989).

This plain statement rule is nothing more than an acknowledgment that the States retain substantial sovereign powers under our constitutional scheme, powers with which Congress does not readily interfere.

[Justice O'Connor then referred to a line of cases creating a "political function" exception which allowed states to limit citizens' employment in positions that are "intimately related to the process of democratic self-government."]

We are constrained in our ability to consider the limits that the state-federal balance places on Congress' powers under the Commerce Clause. See *Garcia v. San Antonio Metro. Transit Auth.* (declining to review limitations placed on Congress' Commerce Clause powers by our federal system). But there is no need to do so if we hold that the ADEA does not apply to state judges. Application of the plain statement rule thus may avoid a potential constitutional problem. Indeed, inasmuch as this Court in *Garcia* has left primarily to the political process the protection of the States against intrusive exercises of Congress' Commerce Clause powers, we must be absolutely certain that Congress intended such an exercise. "[T]o give the state-displacing weight of federal law to mere congressional *ambiguity* would evade the very procedure for lawmaking on which *Garcia* relied to protect states' interests." Lawrence Tribe, American Constitutional Law § 6–25, 480 (2d ed. 1988).

[II-B] In 1974, Congress extended the substantive provisions of the ADEA to include the States as employers. At the same time, Congress amended the definition of "employee" to exclude all elected and most high-ranking government officials. Under the Act, as amended:

> "The term 'employee' means an individual employed by any employer except that the term 'employee' shall not include any person elected to public office in any State or political subdivision of any State by the qualified voters

thereof, or any person chosen by such officer to be on such officer's personal staff, or an appointee on the policymaking level or an immediate adviser with respect to the exercise of the constitutional or legal powers of the office." 29 U.S.C. § 630(f).

[Governor Ashcroft made two arguments. First, he argued the state judges were "appointee[s] on the policymaking level" because the judges were appointed by the Governor and are subject to retention election. Alternatively, judges should be considered as making policy because they make common law decisions and exercise supervisory authority over the state bar.

[Petitioners countered by arguing that judges could not be "appointee[s] on the policymaking level" because resolving factual disputes and answering legal questions does not constitute policymaking. Additionally, petitioners relied on noscitur a sociis to argue that all three exceptions in § 630(f) should be limited to appointees with close working relationships with elected officials, as was the common denominator for "personal staff" and "an immediate adviser."]

The Governor stresses judges' policymaking responsibilities, but it is far from plain that the statutory exception requires that judges actually make policy. The statute refers to appointees "on the policymaking level," not to appointees "who make policy." It may be sufficient that the appointee is in a position requiring the exercise of discretion concerning issues of public importance. This certainly describes the bench, regardless of whether judges might be considered policymakers in the same sense as the executive or legislature.

Nonetheless, "appointee at the policymaking level," particularly in the context of the other exceptions that surround it, is an odd way for Congress to exclude judges; a plain statement that judges are not "employees" would seem the most efficient phrasing. But in this case we are not looking for a plain statement that judges are excluded. We will not read the ADEA to cover state judges unless Congress has made it clear that judges are *included*. This does not mean that the Act must mention judges explicitly, though it does not. Rather, it must be plain to anyone reading the Act that it covers judges. In the context of a statute that plainly excludes most important state public officials, "appointee on the policymaking level" is sufficiently broad that we cannot conclude that the statute plainly covers appointed state judges. Therefore, it does not.

The ADEA plainly covers all state employees except those excluded by one of the exceptions. Where it is unambiguous that an employee does not fall within one of the exceptions, the Act states plainly and unequivocally that the employee is included. It is at least ambiguous whether a state judge is an "appointee on the policymaking level." * * *

JUSTICE WHITE, with whom JUSTICE STEVENS joins, concurring in part, dissenting in part, and concurring in the judgment.

[I] While acknowledging [the] principle of federal legislative supremacy, the majority nevertheless imposes upon Congress a "plain statement" requirement. The majority claims to derive this requirement from the plain statement approach developed in our Eleventh Amendment cases, see, *e.g.*, *Atascadero*, and applied two

SEC. 3   SUBSTANTIVE POLICY CANONS   685

Terms ago in *Will*. The issue in those cases, however, was whether Congress intended a particular statute to extend to the States *at all*. * * * In the present case, by contrast, Congress has expressly extended the coverage of the ADEA to the States and their employees. Its intention to regulate age discrimination by States is thus "unmistakably clear in the language of the statute." *Atascadero*. The only dispute is over the precise details of the statute's application. We have never extended the plain statement approach that far, and the majority offers no compelling reason for doing so. * * *

The majority's plain statement rule is not only unprecedented, it directly contravenes our decisions in *Garcia v. San Antonio Metropolitan Transit Authority* and *South Carolina v. Baker*, 485 U.S. 505 (1988). In those cases we made it clear "that States must find their protection from congressional regulation through the national political process, not through judicially defined spheres of unregulable state activity." We also rejected as "unsound in principle and unworkable in practice" any test for state immunity that requires a judicial determination of which state activities are "traditional," "integral," or "necessary." The majority disregards those decisions in its attempt to carve out areas of state activity that will receive special protection from federal legislation.

The majority's approach is also unsound because it will serve only to confuse the law. First, the majority fails to explain the scope of its rule. Is the rule limited to federal regulation of the qualifications of state officials? Or does it apply more broadly to the regulation of any "state governmental functions"? [Quoting majority opinion.] Second, the majority does not explain its requirement that Congress' intent to regulate a particular state activity be "plain to anyone reading [the federal statute]." Does that mean that it is now improper to look to the purpose or history of a federal statute in determining the scope of the statute's limitations on state activities? * * * The vagueness of the majority's rule undoubtedly will lead States to assert that various federal statutes no longer apply to a wide variety of State activities if Congress has not expressly referred to those activities in the statute. Congress, in turn, will be forced to draft long and detailed lists of which particular state functions it meant to regulate. * * *

The majority asserts that its plain statement rule is helpful in avoiding a "potential constitutional problem." It is far from clear, however, why there would be a constitutional problem if the ADEA applied to state judges, in light of our decisions in *Garcia* and *Baker*, discussed above. As long as "the national political *process* did not operate in a defective manner, the Tenth Amendment is not implicated." *Baker*. There is no claim in this case that the political process by which the ADEA was extended to state employees was inadequate to protect the States from being "unduly burden[ed]" by the Federal Government. In any event, as discussed below, a straightforward analysis of the ADEA's definition of "employee" reveals that the ADEA does not apply here. Thus, even if there were potential constitutional problems in extending the ADEA to state judges, the majority's proposed plain statement rule would not be necessary to avoid them in this case. Indeed, because this case can be decided purely on the basis of statutory interpretation, the majority's announcement of its plain statement rule, which purportedly is derived from constitutional principles, *violates* our general practice of avoiding the unnecessary resolution of constitutional issues. * * *

[II] The statute at issue in this case is the ADEA's definition of "employee[.]" [Justice White relied on a dictionary definition of "policy" to conclude that common law judges such as petitioners are engaged in policymaking. He also rejected petitioners' reliance on noscitur a sociis, pointing out that the most obvious similarity among all three exceptions ("personal staff"; "appointee"; "immediate advisor") was that they were in some way connected to an elected official.]

[The dissenting opinion of JUSTICE BLACKMUN, joined by JUSTICE MARSHALL, is omitted.]

NOTES ON GREGORY AND CLEAR STATEMENT RULES

1.   *Contrasting Approaches.* As Justice O'Connor noted, there is a respectable textual argument that the ADEA exceptions do not apply to appointed judges, in part because of the noscitur a sociis canon. But note that every other potential source of statutory meaning points in the other direction. See Philip Frickey, *Lawnet: The Case of the Missing (Tenth) Amendment*, 75 Minn. L. Rev. 755 (1991).

Consider first the absurd-result exception to the plain meaning approach, which even textualists will sometimes apply.[37] On the face of it, the exceptions provision to the ADEA seems to take elected judges completely out of the statute (and thus they can be required to step down at age 70), but protects appointed judges against any retirement requirement. This seems absolutely backwards from any public-policy perspective: if superannuated judges are to remain in authority, presumably that judgment should be made by the voters on a judge-by-judge basis, not as a categorical decision made by Congress. Why would Congress want to hogtie states in this manner? On the other hand, does the "absurdity" here rise to the level called for by Justice Kennedy in his separate opinion in *Public Citizen* (Chapter 5, § 2(B))? Is the apparent distinction between elected and appointed judges so irrational as to raise a serious constitutional question that should be avoided through statutory interpretation (cf. *Catholic Bishop of Chicago*)?

Sources of statutory meaning available to nontextualists strongly cut against the apparent plain meaning of the ADEA exceptions provision as well. The legislative history, irrelevant to Justice O'Connor because of her application of a super-strong clear statement rule, supports excepting these judges from the statute, as explained in a portion of Justice White's separate opinion that we have omitted. The statutory purpose, again irrelevant to Justice O'Connor's approach, seems narrower than the plain meaning of the exception; at least as originally conceived, the ADEA was designed to protect workers from being replaced by younger employees who would accept lower pay, and had little to do with persons who possess guaranteed tenure and who would be replaced by persons receiving the same salary. From the standpoint of public values, as Justice O'Connor suggests, the people of the state ought to be able to choose how to structure important governmental positions. But this need not lead to the creation of a super-strong clear statement rule: any kind of canon (a presumption at the outset, a tiebreaker at the end, a factor to be weighed in the interpretive process) based on federalism would surely

---

[37]   See Justice Kennedy's separate opinion in *Public Citizen* (Chapter 5, § 2(B)) and Justice Scalia's separate opinion in *Bock Laundry* (Chapter 5, § 3(A)).

be sufficient to tip the case to the conclusion Justice O'Connor desired. Why create the canonical equivalent of a nuclear weapon when a fly swatter would have been sufficient?

2. *The Relationship of Textualism and Super-Strong Clear Statement Rules.* Critics could suggest that cases like *Gregory* demonstrate that textualism fails to live up to its promise of providing objective interpretive methods in the face of outcomes judges cannot tolerate. In other words, every human interpretive technique, including textualism, needs a "safety valve" of some sort. For liberals, the *Holy Trinity Church* "purpose trumps plain meaning" approach sometimes serves this purpose, as in *Weber*. For conservative textualists who care about federalism, the safety valve when textualism gets them boxed in, as in *Gregory*, is the creation of a super-strong clear statement rule that trumps the result suggested by ordinary meaning. Is it fair to say that *Gregory* undercuts the textualist principle of constraining judicial discretion in interpretation?

Another concern is whether the use of such super-strong clear statement rules may actually encourage judicial activism because it seems far easier to use them than to do constitutional decisionmaking. Because a decision like *Gregory* is made at the interpretive rather than the constitutional level, the visibility of the decision is lower and the attention paid to it even inside the Court may be less. Contrast the reaction to this kind of stealth constitutionalism in *Gregory* (except in limited academic and states' rights circles, virtually nothing) to the reaction to a hypothetical overruling of *Garcia* and a return to *National League of Cities* (where the Court's disrespect for stare decisis and return to a regime already arguably demonstrated to be unworkable would surely cause considerable controversy). Should the Court be promoting the value of federalism so strongly, or should it defer more to the political process (Congress and the President) to protect the states? Can textualists provide any objective grounding for the values promoted by their super-strong clear statement rules?

3. *The Need for Super-Strong Rules Once the Court Gives Teeth to Previously Underenforced Constitutional Norms?* Does the *Gregory* rule add anything to the rule to avoid constitutional questions? Perhaps as a special application of the avoidance canon, *Gregory* might be defended on the ground that the Tenth Amendment was underenforced by the Supreme Court, which had rarely invalidated federal laws because they intruded into core state functions.[38] (The Court in *National League of Cities* in 1976 had invalidated such a law, but *Garcia* overruled it.) But after *Gregory*, the Court has invalidated several federal statutory provisions on the ground that they commandeered state officials in violation of the Tenth Amendment. See *Printz v. United States*, 521 U.S. 898 (1997); *New York v. United States*, 505 U.S. 144 (1992). If these cases augur an overruling or narrowing of *Garcia*, should the Court trim back its use of the *Gregory* rule? See also *Kimel v. Fla. Bd. of Regents*, 528 U.S. 62 (2000) (Court finds clear statement in ADEA abrogating states' Eleventh Amendment immunity and then rules the abrogation unconstitutional).

4. *The Problem of Congressional Reliance. Bait and Switch?* In Chapter 5, § 3(C), we suggested that one important factor in assessing any theory of statutory interpretation is whether it is compatible with the assumptions about law held by other legal actors (the Congress, the President, attorneys, citizens). One way of criticizing the Court's creation of new super-strong clear statement rules is, then, to focus on the ways in which our political system has relied upon understandings that the Court is now

---

[38]   This was the defense provided *Gregory* in William Eskridge Jr. & Philip Frickey, *Quasi-Constitutional Law: Clear Statement Rules as Constitutional Lawmaking*, 45 Vand. L. Rev. 593 (1992).

unraveling through the use of these rules.[39] The use of reliance arguments in statutory interpretation appeals not just to the traditional conservative idea of legislative supremacy, but also answers the Court's frequent riposte that legislative supremacy is not implicated unless something is clear on the face of the statute. Consider the following example.

The Education of the Handicapped Act (EHA) is a comprehensive statutory scheme to assure that disabled children may receive a free public education appropriate to their needs. The Act guarantees parental rights to participate in state planning of their children's educational needs and to challenge state plans they don't like. The statute imposes pervasive obligations on state and local governments, and it provides that "[a]ny party aggrieved by the findings and decision [made in the state or local administrative process] shall have the right to bring a civil action . . . in any State court of competent jurisdiction or in a district court of the United States without regard to the amount in controversy." 20 U.S.C. § 1415(e)(2). EHA's sponsor made it clear "that a parent or guardian may present a complaint alleging that a State or local educational agency has refused to provide services to which a child may be entitled" and may sue state and local governments in state or federal court. 121 Cong. Rec. 37415 (1975).

When the EHA was enacted in 1975, the above-noted evidence would probably have sufficed to abrogate the states' Eleventh Amendment immunity from suit in federal court, pursuant to *Employees v. Missouri Department of Public Health & Welfare*, 411 U.S. 279 (1973) (general jurisdictional grant plus explicit legislative history would be sufficient to abrogate Eleventh Amendment immunity). In *Atascadero State Hospital v. Scanlon*, 473 U.S. 234 (1985), however, the Court changed the rule for congressional abrogation of Eleventh Amendment immunity: "Congress may abrogate the States' constitutionally secured immunity from suit in federal court only by making its intention unmistakably clear in the language of the statute." The Court held that the Rehabilitation Act of 1973, another statute protecting the disabled, did not abrogate states' immunity, because there was no clear textual indication of such abrogation.

Sensing that the rules had changed, and reacting to the Court's restrictive interpretation of the Rehabilitation Act, Congress in 1986 enacted the following: "A State shall not be immune under the Eleventh Amendment * * * from suit in Federal Court for a violation of [enumerated provisions of the Rehabilitation Act], or the provisions of any other Federal statute prohibiting discrimination by recipients of Federal financial assistance." The latter clause clearly covers the EHA. Then, in *Dellmuth v. Muth*, 491 U.S. 223 (1989), a case that arose before the 1986 amendment, the Court held that the EHA did not abrogate state immunity. The Court pointed to the 1986 statute as a good example of the drafting clarity needed to abrogate immunity, and held that there was no abrogation before 1986.

Poor Congress. It thought it had abrogated state immunity in 1975, and given precedent in 1975 it probably had done so. Then it reiterated its intent in 1986, but the new statute was used by the Court to confirm Congress's failure to abrogate in 1975. This

---

[39]   See Ruth Colker and James Brudney, *Dissing Congress*, 100 Mich. L. Rev. 80, 105–15 (2001) (describing how the Court in *Kimel* and related decisions created "crystal ball" problems for a coequal branch, because the enacting Congress failed to create a legislative record that could satisfy a legal standard announced years or decades later).

might be amusing if important rights were not involved.[40] The matter might become even worse for Congress. Following *Kimel*, the Supreme Court in *Board of Trustees, University of Alabama v. Garrett*, 531 U.S. 356 (2001), ruled that Congress had no power under the Fourteenth Amendment to abrogate the states' Eleventh Amendment immunity in the Americans with Disabilities Act. The Court reasoned that Congress had not found enough of a "history and pattern" of intentional discrimination against people with disabilities by the states themselves to justify the exercise of its enforcement power under the Fourteenth Amendment. Under *Garrett*, Congress's repeated efforts to render the states liable for violations of the EHA might ultimately fail on constitutional grounds.

In assessing the statutory interpretation developments, be certain first that you understand the force of the *Atascadero* clear statement rule: Not only does it require abrogation of state immunity in the statute's text, without regard to legislative history, but the abrogation must be explicit and really clear. E.g., *Hoffman v. Conn. Dep't of Income Maintenance*, 492 U.S. 96 (1989); *Will v. Mich. Dep't of State Police*, 491 U.S. 58 (1989). Thus *Atascadero*, like *Gregory*, fits our definition of a "super-strong clear statement rule." Others that the Court has created include the toughened rule against waivers of federal sovereign immunity, *United States v. Nordic Village*, 503 U.S. 30 (1992); the toughened rule against extraterritorial application of federal statutes, *EEOC v. Arabian Am. Oil Co.*, 499 U.S. 244 (1991); the rule against congressional derogation of traditional presidential powers, *Japan Whaling Ass'n v. Am. Cetacean Soc'y*, 478 U.S. 221 (1986); and the rule created in 1981 that congressional conditions of grants to the states be explicit and clear, *Pennhurst State Sch. and Hosp. v. Halderman*, 451 U.S. 1 (1981).

A more recent bait-and-switch debate occurred under the *Pennhurst* rule. Congress in a 1986 statute provided for "reasonable attorneys' fees as part of the costs" to prevailing litigants (usually parents) in cases arising under the Individuals with Disabilities Education Act. In *Arlington Central School District Board of Education v. Murphy*, 548 U.S. 291 (2006), the Court invoked *Pennhurst* to require a more targeted statement in order to justify recovery of expert fees as part of an attorney's fees award. Dissenting Justices accused the Court of bait-and-switch: when Congress added the fees provision in 1986, it had every reason to believe—and the relevant committees expressed a belief—that the enacted language was sufficient to justify the award of expert witness fees. Such belief was undone by Supreme Court decisions handed down in 1987 and 1991 (*Casey*, see § 2(C) of this chapter)—decisions which Congress immediately overrode in the Civil Rights Act of 1991. The *Murphy* Court not only ignored the 1991 override, but cited the earlier decisions as confirming evidence that there was a plain meaning that trumped Congress's expectations. (Congress's override only extended to job discrimination cases, and not IDEA cases.)

The *Murphy* dissenters had another argument the *Dellmuth* dissenters did not have. It was undisputed that the 1986 statute not only added a provision giving attorneys' fees and other costs to prevailing parents, but also charged the GAO with collecting fee data and analyzing "the range of such *fees, costs and expenses* awarded in the actions and proceedings under such section, * * * and * * * *the number of hours spent by personnel, including attorneys and consultants.*" (Emphasis added.) The legislative history confirmed that this section was written under Congress's assumption that the 1986

---

[40]　　Congress immediately overrode *Dellmuth* in the Education of the Handicapped Act of 1990, Pub. L. No. 101–476, § 103, 104 Stat. 1103, 1106, again with complaints that its expectations had been thwarted. It took Congress three statutes to effectuate a policy it thought had been effectuated in 1975.

authorization included expert witness fees. Thus, the parents had an argument grounded in the whole act, as well as the legislative history. The Court found this whole act evidence insufficient to refute the conventional text-based evidence. The dissenters expressed astonishment that the majority did not concede there was at least ambiguity in the statute, given this dramatic evidence.

5. *Sources for Super-Strong Clear Statements.* According to the new federalism canon relied on in *Gregory*, the Court requires a super-strong clear statement from Congress before it will construe a federal statute as disrupting the traditional dual sovereignty arrangement between the states and the federal government. But what sources should the Court consult to determine whether a super-strong clear statement from Congress exists? Must the Court address only the ordinary meaning of the text? Or is something more permitted, such as statements in the legislative record or contextual evidence? Consider these questions as you read the following case.

BOND V. UNITED STATES
Supreme Court of the United States, 2014.
572 U.S. 844, 134 S.Ct 2077, 189 L.Ed.2d 1.

CHIEF JUSTICE ROBERTS delivered the opinion of the Court.

The horrors of chemical warfare were vividly captured by John Singer Sargent in his 1919 painting Gassed. The nearly life-sized work depicts two lines of soldiers, blinded by mustard gas, clinging single file to orderlies guiding them to an improvised aid station. There they would receive little treatment and no relief; many suffered for weeks only to have the gas claim their lives. The soldiers were shown staggering through piles of comrades too seriously burned to even join the procession.

The painting reflects the devastation that Sargent witnessed in the aftermath of the Second Battle of Arras during World War I. That battle and others like it led to an overwhelming consensus in the international community that toxic chemicals should never again be used as weapons against human beings. Today that objective is reflected in the international Convention on Chemical Weapons, which has been ratified or acceded to by 190 countries. The United States, pursuant to the Federal Government's constitutionally enumerated power to make treaties, ratified the treaty in 1997. To fulfill the United States' obligations under the Convention, Congress enacted the Chemical Weapons Convention Implementation Act of 1998. The Act makes it a federal crime for a person to use or possess any chemical weapon, and it punishes violators with severe penalties. It is a statute that, like the Convention it implements, deals with crimes of deadly seriousness.

The question presented by this case is whether the Implementation Act also reaches a purely local crime: an amateur attempt by a jilted wife to injure her husband's lover, which ended up causing only a minor thumb burn readily treated by rinsing with water. Because our constitutional structure leaves local criminal activity primarily to the States, we have generally declined to read federal law as intruding on that responsibility, unless Congress has clearly indicated that the law should have such reach. The Chemical Weapons Convention Implementation Act contains no such clear indication, and we accordingly conclude that it does not cover the unremarkable local offense at issue here.

[I-A] [The Court provided a brief history of the Chemical Weapons Convention, explaining its genesis as an effort to update the Geneva Protocol's protections and to expand the prohibition on chemical weapons beyond state actors in wartime, encompassing the increasing threat posed by terrorists]. Congress gave the Convention domestic effect in 1998 when it passed the Chemical Weapons Convention Implementation Act. The Act closely tracks the text of the treaty: It forbids any person knowingly "to develop, produce, otherwise acquire, transfer directly or indirectly, receive, stockpile, retain, own, possess, or use, or threaten to use, any chemical weapon." 18 U.S.C. § 229(a)(1). It defines "chemical weapon" in relevant part as "[a] toxic chemical and its precursors, except where intended for a purpose not prohibited under this chapter as long as the type and quantity is consistent with such a purpose." § 229F(1)(A). "Toxic chemical," in turn, is defined in general as "any chemical which through its chemical action on life processes can cause death, temporary incapacitation or permanent harm to humans or animals. The term includes all such chemicals, regardless of their origin or of their method of production, and regardless of whether they are produced in facilities, in munitions or elsewhere." § 229F(8)(A). Finally, "purposes not prohibited by this chapter" is defined as "[a]ny peaceful purpose related to an industrial, agricultural, research, medical, or pharmaceutical activity or other activity," and other specific purposes. § 229F(7). A person who violates section 229 may be subject to severe punishment: imprisonment "for any term of years," or if a victim's death results, the death penalty or imprisonment "for life." § 229A(a).

[I-B] Petitioner Carol Anne Bond is a microbiologist from Lansdale, Pennsylvania. In 2006, Bond's closest friend, Myrlinda Haynes, announced that she was pregnant. When Bond discovered that her husband was the child's father, she sought revenge against Haynes. Bond stole a quantity of 10-chloro-10H-phenoxarsine (an arsenic-based compound) from her employer, a chemical manufacturer. She also ordered a vial of potassium dichromate (a chemical commonly used in printing photographs or cleaning laboratory equipment) on Amazon.com. Both chemicals are toxic to humans and, in high enough doses, potentially lethal. It is undisputed, however, that Bond did not intend to kill Haynes. She instead hoped that Haynes would touch the chemicals and develop an uncomfortable rash.

Between November 2006 and June 2007, Bond went to Haynes's home on at least 24 occasions and spread the chemicals on her car door, mailbox, and door knob. These attempted assaults were almost entirely unsuccessful. The chemicals that Bond used are easy to see, and Haynes was able to avoid them all but once. On that occasion, Haynes suffered a minor chemical burn on her thumb, which she treated by rinsing with water. Haynes repeatedly called the local police to report the suspicious substances, but they took no action. When Haynes found powder on her mailbox, she called the police again, who told her to call the post office. Haynes did so, and postal inspectors placed surveillance cameras around her home. The cameras caught Bond opening Haynes's mailbox, stealing an envelope, and stuffing potassium dichromate inside the muffler of Haynes's car.

Federal prosecutors naturally charged Bond with two counts of mail theft, in violation of 18 U.S.C. § 1708. More surprising, they also charged her with two counts of possessing and using a chemical weapon, in violation of section 229(a). * * *

[Bond ultimately entered a conditional guilty plea, reserving her right to appeal. The Third Circuit rejected both her arguments on appeal. Bond argued first that section 229 did not reach her conduct because that section's exception for the use of chemicals for "peaceful purposes" [see § 229F(7)] should be understood in contradistinction to the "warlike" activities at which the Convention was primarily aimed. She contended that her conduct, while reprehensible, was not at all "warlike." The Third Circuit held that Bond's use of highly toxic chemicals with the intent of harming Haynes could not be characterized as "peaceful" under that word's commonly understood meaning, although the court recognized that the government's broad reading of section 229 would in effect turn every "kitchen cupboard and cleaning cabinet in America into a potential chemical weapons cache." Bond's second argument on appeal was that her conviction violated the Tenth Amendment because the government had acted in excess of the authority that federalism defines. The Third Circuit rejected this challenge as well, holding that section 229 was "necessary and proper to carry the Convention into effect."]

[II] In our federal system, the National Government possesses only limited powers; the States and the people retain the remainder. The States have broad authority to enact legislation for the public good—what we have often called a "police power." *United States v. Lopez,* 514 U.S. 549, 567 (1995). The Federal Government, by contrast, has no such authority and "can exercise only the powers granted to it," *McCulloch v. Maryland,* 4 Wheat. 316, 405 (1819), including the power to make "all Laws which shall be necessary and proper for carrying into Execution" the enumerated powers, U.S. Const., Art. I, § 8, cl. 18. For nearly two centuries it has been "clear" that, lacking a police power, "Congress cannot punish felonies generally." *Cohens v. Virginia,* 6 Wheat. 264, 428 (1821). A criminal act committed wholly within a State "cannot be made an offence against the United States, unless it have some relation to the execution of a power of Congress, or to some matter within the jurisdiction of the United States." *United States v. Fox,* 95 U.S. 670, 672 (1878).

[The Court noted the government's explicit refusal below to defend the instant federal criminal statute as authorized pursuant to Congress's power to regulate interstate commerce. It also reviewed the arguments before the Court as to whether section 229, as applied to Bond's offense, is a necessary and proper means of executing the National Government's power to make treaties under Art. II, § 2, cl. 2 of the Constitution]. Notwithstanding this debate, it is "a well-established principle governing the prudent exercise of this Court's jurisdiction that normally the Court will not decide a constitutional question if there is some other ground upon which to dispose of the case." Bond argues that section 229 does not cover her conduct. So we consider that argument first. * * * Bond was prosecuted under section 229, and the statute must be read consistent with principles of federalism inherent in our constitutional structure.

[III-A] In the Government's view, the conclusion that Bond "knowingly" "use[d]" a "chemical weapon" in violation of section 229(a) is simple: The chemicals that Bond placed on Haynes's home and car are "toxic chemical[s]" as defined by the statute, and Bond's attempt to assault Haynes was not a "peaceful purpose." §§ 229F(1), (8), (7). The problem with this interpretation is that it would "dramatically intrude[ ] upon traditional state criminal jurisdiction," and we avoid reading statutes to have such reach in the absence of a clear indication that they do. *United States v. Bass,* 404 U.S. 336, 350 (1971).

Part of a fair reading of statutory text is recognizing that "Congress legislates against the backdrop" of certain unexpressed presumptions. *EEOC v. Arabian American Oil Co.,* 499 U.S. 244, 248 (1991). * * * Among the background principles of construction that our cases have recognized are those grounded in the relationship between the Federal Government and the States under our Constitution. It has long been settled, for example, that we presume federal statutes do not abrogate state sovereign immunity, *Atascadero State Hospital v. Scanlon,* 473 U.S. 234, 243 (1985), impose obligations on the States pursuant to section 5 of the Fourteenth Amendment, *Pennhurst State School and Hospital v. Halderman,* 451 U.S. 1, 16–17 (1981), or preempt state law, *Rice v. Santa Fe Elevator Corp.,* 331 U.S. 218, 230 (1947).

Closely related to these is the well-established principle that "it is incumbent upon the federal courts to be certain of Congress' intent before finding that federal law overrides" the "usual constitutional balance of federal and state powers." *Gregory v. Ashcroft,* 501 U.S. 452, 460 (1991) (quoting *Atascadero, supra,* at 243). To quote [Justice Frankfurter], if the Federal Government would "radically readjust[ ] the balance of state and national authority, those charged with the duty of legislating [must be] reasonably explicit" about it. * * * Or as explained by Justice Marshall, when legislation "affect[s] the federal balance, the requirement of clear statement assures that the legislature has in fact faced, and intended to bring into issue, the critical matters involved in the judicial decision." *Bass, supra,* at 349. * * *

[III-B] We do not find any such clear indication in section 229. "Chemical weapon" is the key term that defines the statute's reach, and it is defined extremely broadly. But that general definition does not constitute a clear statement that Congress meant the statute to reach local criminal conduct.

In fact, a fair reading of section 229 suggests that it does not have as expansive a scope as might at first appear. To begin, as a matter of natural meaning, an educated user of English would not describe Bond's crime as involving a "chemical weapon." Saying that a person "used a chemical weapon" conveys a very different idea than saying the person "used a chemical in a way that caused some harm." The natural meaning of "chemical weapon" takes account of both the particular chemicals that the defendant used and the circumstances in which she used them.

When used in the manner here, the chemicals in this case are not of the sort that an ordinary person would associate with instruments of chemical warfare. The substances that Bond used bear little resemblance to the deadly toxins that are "of particular danger to the objectives of the Convention." More to the point, the use of something as a "weapon" typically connotes "[a]n instrument of offensive or defensive combat," Webster's Third New International Dictionary 2589 (2002), or "[a]n instrument of attack or defense in combat, as a gun, missile, or sword," American Heritage Dictionary 2022 (3d ed. 1992). But no speaker in natural parlance would describe Bond's feud-driven act of spreading irritating chemicals on Haynes's door knob and mailbox as "combat." Nor do the other circumstances of Bond's offense—an act of revenge born of romantic jealousy, meant to cause discomfort, that produced nothing more than a minor thumb burn—suggest that a chemical weapon was deployed in Norristown, Pennsylvania. Potassium dichromate and 10-chloro-10H-phenoxarsine might be chemical weapons if used, say, to poison a city's water supply. But Bond's crime is worlds apart from such hypotheticals, and covering it would give the statute a reach exceeding the ordinary meaning of the words Congress wrote. * * *

The Government would have us brush aside the ordinary meaning and adopt a reading of section 229 that would sweep in everything from the detergent under the kitchen sink to the stain remover in the laundry room. Yet no one would ordinarily describe those substances as "chemical weapons." The Government responds that because Bond used "specialized, highly toxic" (though legal) chemicals, "this case presents no occasion to address whether Congress intended [section 229] to apply to common household substances." Brief for United States 13, n. 3. That the statute *would* apply so broadly, however, is the inescapable conclusion of the Government's position: Any parent would be guilty of a serious federal offense—possession of a chemical weapon—when, exasperated by the children's repeated failure to clean the goldfish tank, he considers poisoning the fish with a few drops of vinegar. We are reluctant to ignore the ordinary meaning of "chemical weapon" when doing so would transform a statute passed to implement the international Convention on Chemical Weapons into one that also makes it a federal offense to poison goldfish. That would not be a "realistic assessment[ ] of congressional intent." (Scalia J., concurring in judgment).

In light of all of this, it is fully appropriate to apply the background assumption that Congress normally preserves "the constitutional balance between the National Government and the States." That assumption is grounded in the very structure of the Constitution. * * *

The Government's reading of section 229 would " 'alter sensitive federal-state relationships,' " convert an astonishing amount of "traditionally local criminal conduct" into "a matter for federal enforcement," and "involve a substantial extension of federal police resources." [citations omitted]. It would transform the statute from one whose core concerns are acts of war, assassination, and terrorism into a massive federal anti-poisoning regime that reaches the simplest of assaults. * * * Of course Bond's conduct is serious and unacceptable—and against the laws of Pennsylvania. But the background principle that Congress does not normally intrude upon the police power of the States is critically important. In light of that principle, we are reluctant to conclude that Congress meant to punish Bond's crime with a federal prosecution for a chemical weapons attack. * * *

It is also clear that the laws of the Commonwealth of Pennsylvania (and every other State) are sufficient to prosecute Bond. Pennsylvania has several statutes that would likely cover her assault. See 18 Pa. Cons. Stat. §§ 2701 (2012) (simple assault),

2705 (reckless endangerment), 2709 (harassment). And state authorities regularly enforce these laws in poisoning cases. See, *e.g.,* Gamiz, Family Survives Poisoned Burritos, Allentown, Pa., Morning Call, May 18, 2013 (defendant charged with assault, reckless endangerment, and harassment for feeding burritos poisoned with prescription medication to her husband and daughter); Cops: Man Was Poisoned Over 3 Years, Harrisburg, Pa., Patriot News, Aug. 12, 2012, p. A11 (defendant charged with assault and reckless endangerment for poisoning a man with eye drops over three years so that "he would pay more attention to her"). * * *

As we have explained, "Congress has traditionally been reluctant to define as a federal crime conduct readily denounced as criminal by the States." There is no clear indication of a contrary approach here. Section 229 implements the Convention, but Bond's crime could hardly be more unlike the uses of mustard gas on the Western Front or nerve agents in the Iran-Iraq war that form the core concerns of that treaty. There are no life-sized paintings of Bond's rival washing her thumb. And there are no apparent interests of the United States Congress or the community of nations in seeing Bond end up in federal prison, rather than dealt with (like virtually all other criminals in Pennsylvania) by the State. The Solicitor General acknowledged as much at oral argument. See Tr. of Oral Arg. 47 ("I don't think anybody would say [that] whether or not Ms. Bond is prosecuted would give rise to an international incident").

This case is unusual, and our analysis is appropriately limited. Our disagreement with our colleagues reduces to whether section 229 is "utterly clear." (Scalia J., concurring in judgment). We think it is not, given that the definition of "chemical weapon" in a particular case can reach beyond any normal notion of such a weapon, that the context from which the statute arose demonstrates a much more limited prohibition was intended, and that the most sweeping reading of the statute would fundamentally upset the Constitution's balance between national and local power. This exceptional convergence of factors gives us serious reason to doubt the Government's expansive reading of section 229, and calls for us to interpret the statute more narrowly. * * *

JUSTICE SCALIA, with whom JUSTICE THOMAS joins, and with whom JUSTICE ALITO joins as to Part I, concurring in the judgment.

Somewhere in Norristown, Pennsylvania, a husband's paramour suffered a minor thumb burn at the hands of a betrayed wife. The United States Congress— "every where extending the sphere of its activity, and drawing all power into its impetuous vortex" [The Federalist No. 48]—has made a federal case out of it. What are we to do?

It is the responsibility of "the legislature, not the Court, . . . to define a crime, and ordain its punishment." *United States v. Wiltberger,* 5 Wheat. 76, 95 (1820) (Marshall, C.J., for the Court). And it is "emphatically the province and duty of the judicial department to say what the law [including the Constitution] is." *Marbury v. Madison,* 1 Cranch 137, 177 (1803) (same). Today, the Court shirks its job and performs Congress's. As sweeping and unsettling as the Chemical Weapons Convention Implementation Act of 1998 may be, it is clear beyond doubt that it covers what Bond did; and we have no authority to amend it. So we are forced to decide—

there is no way around it—whether the Act's application to what Bond did was constitutional.

I would hold that it was not, and for that reason would reverse the judgment of the Court of Appeals for the Third Circuit.

[I-A] The meaning of the Act is plain. No person may knowingly "develop, produce, otherwise acquire, transfer directly or indirectly, receive, stockpile, retain, own, possess, or use, or threaten to use, any chemical weapon." 18 U.S.C. § 229(a)(1). A "chemical weapon" is "[a] toxic chemical and its precursors, except where intended for a purpose not prohibited under this chapter as long as the type and quantity is consistent with such a purpose." § 229F(1)(A). A "toxic chemical" is "any chemical which through its chemical action on life processes can cause death, temporary incapacitation or permanent harm to humans or animals. The term includes all such chemicals, regardless of their origin or of their method of production, and regardless of whether they are produced in facilities, in munitions or elsewhere." § 229F(8)(A). A "purpose not prohibited" is "[a]ny peaceful purpose related to an industrial, agricultural, research, medical, or pharmaceutical activity or other activity." § 229F(7)(A).

Applying those provisions to this case is hardly complicated. Bond possessed and used "chemical[s] which through [their] chemical action on life processes can cause death, temporary incapacitation or permanent harm." Thus, she possessed "toxic chemicals." And, because they were not possessed or used only for a "purpose not prohibited," § 229F(1)(A), they were "chemical weapons." Ergo, Bond violated the Act. End of statutory analysis, I would have thought.

The Court does not think the interpretive exercise so simple. But that is only because its result-driven antitextualism befogs what is evident.

[I-B] * * * [The Court] *starts* with the federalism-related consequences of the statute's meaning and reasons backwards, holding that, if the statute has what the Court considers a disruptive effect on the "federal-state balance" of criminal jurisdiction, that effect causes the text, even if clear on its face, to be ambiguous. * * * Imagine what future courts can do with that judge-empowering principle: Whatever has improbably broad, deeply serious, and apparently unnecessary consequences . . . *is ambiguous*!

The same skillful use of oh-so-close-to-relevant cases characterizes the Court's *pro forma* attempt to find ambiguity in the text itself, specifically, in the term "[c]hemical weapon." The ordinary meaning of weapon, the Court says, is an instrument of combat, and "no speaker in natural parlance would describe Bond's feud-driven act of spreading irritating chemicals on Haynes's door knob and mailbox as 'combat.'" Undoubtedly so, but undoubtedly beside the point, since the Act supplies its own definition of "chemical weapon," which unquestionably does bring Bond's action within the statutory prohibition. * * *

In this case, the ordinary meaning of the term being defined is irrelevant, because the statute's own definition—however expansive—is utterly clear: any "chemical which through its chemical action on life processes can cause death, temporary incapacitation or permanent harm to humans or animals," § 229F(8)(A), unless the chemical is possessed or used for a "peaceful purpose," § 229F(1)(A), (7)(A). The statute parses itself. There is no opinion of ours, and none written by any court or put forward by any commentator since Aristotle, which says, or even suggests, that "dissonance" between ordinary meaning and the unambiguous words of a definition is to be resolved in favor of ordinary meaning. If that were the case, there would hardly be any use in providing a definition. No, the true rule is entirely clear: "When a statute includes an explicit definition, we must follow that definition, *even if it varies from that term's ordinary meaning*." *Stenberg v. Carhart*, 530 U.S. 914, 942 (2000) (emphasis added). Once again, contemplate the judge-empowering consequences of the new interpretive rule the Court today announces: When there is "dissonance" between the statutory definition and the ordinary meaning of the defined word, the latter may prevail. * * *

[T]here is nothing either (1) realistic or (2) well known about the presumption the Court shoves down the throat of a resisting statute today. Who in the world would have thought that a definition is inoperative if it contradicts ordinary meaning? When this statute was enacted, there was not yet a "*Bond* presumption" to that effect—though presumably Congress will have to take account of the *Bond* presumption in the future, perhaps by adding at the end of all its definitions that depart from ordinary connotation "and we really mean it."

[I-C] I suspect the Act will not survive today's gruesome surgery. A criminal statute must clearly define the conduct it proscribes. If it does not " 'give a person of ordinary intelligence fair notice' " of its scope, *United States v. Batchelder*, 442 U.S. 114 (1979), it denies due process.

The *new § 229(a)(1)* fails that test. Henceforward, a person "shall be fined . . . , imprisoned for any term of years, or both," § 229A(a)(1)—or, if he kills someone, "shall be punished by death or imprisoned for life," § 229A(a)(2)—whenever he "develop[s], produce[s], otherwise acquire[s], transfer[s] directly or indirectly, receive[s], stockpile[s], retain[s], own[s], possess[es], or use[s], or threaten[s] to use," § 229(a)(1), any chemical "*of the sort that an ordinary person would associate with instruments of chemical warfare*," (emphasis added). Whether that test is satisfied, the Court unhelpfully (and also illogically) explains, depends not only on the "particular chemicals that the defendant used" but also on "the circumstances in which she used them." *Ibid.* The "detergent under the kitchen sink" and "the stain remover in the laundry room" are apparently out, but what if they are deployed to poison a neighborhood water fountain? Poisoning a goldfish tank is also apparently out, but what if the fish belongs to a Congressman or Governor and the act is meant as a menacing message, a small-time equivalent of leaving a severed horse head in the bed? See *supra* (using the "concerns" driving the Convention—"acts of war, assassination, and terrorism"—as guideposts of statutory meaning). * * *

No one should have to ponder the totality of the circumstances in order to determine whether his conduct is a felony. Yet that is what the Court will now require of all future handlers of harmful toxins—that is to say, all of us. Thanks to the Court's revisions, the Act, which before was merely broad, is now broad and unintelligible. "[N]o standard of conduct is specified at all." *Coates v. Cincinnati*, 402 U.S. 611, 614 (1971). Before long, I suspect, courts will be required to say so.

[II] Since the Act is clear, the *real* question this case presents is whether the Act is constitutional as applied to petitioner. [Justice Scalia concluded that the statute was unconstitutional as applied to Bond, because Congress's powers to *implement* treaties already made must be exercised consistent with the scope of Congress's enumerated powers under article 1. He argued that unlike appropriating funds to hire treaty negotiators, or empowering the State Department to appoint such negotiators (which would help Congress carry its power to make a treaty), the instant statute *legislating compliance* with U.S. treaty obligations was not a necessary and proper means for "carrying into Execution . . . [the] Power . . . to make Treaties" pursuant to Art.2 § 2, cl.2.]

[The opinion concurring in the judgment of JUSTICE THOMAS, joined by JUSTICE SCALIA and in part by JUSTICE ALITO, is omitted.]

NOTES ON BOND

1. *Statutory Ambiguity and Federalism—Chicken or Egg?* Justice Scalia's disagreement with Chief Justice Roberts in *Bond* is quite contentious, focused on applicability of the clear-statement federalism canon.

For the Chief Justice, the statute in question is ambiguous, in part, because a broad reading of the phrase "chemical weapon" would disrupt the balance between state and federal power. Thus, for the majority, a statute's ambiguity can be derived from considerations *beyond* traditional textual analyses of plain meaning and structure. For Justice Scalia, the process of statutory interpretation is much more formal. Only if the Court first concludes from textual analysis that the statute as written is ambiguous may it then turn to background presumptions of congressional behavior such as the presumption of federalism. Scalia argues that no such ambiguity exists here, because the Act itself defines the term "chemical weapon" and that definition fits squarely with Bond's conduct. Absent textual ambiguity, he believes the Court should never have reached the federalism canon.

Note the precedent that Justice Scalia accuses the Court of establishing. By allowing purpose and context to be incorporated when initially determining statutory ambiguity, the Court is—according to Scalia—opening the door for significant judicial activism. When the Court sees a statute leading to a result that is deemed undesirable, it will declare the text ambiguous and proceed to reconfigure the law, essentially legislating from the bench. Are you persuaded by Justice Scalia's cautionary tale? Think back to the conflicting opinions in cases discussed earlier in this chapter (*Taniguchi*, *Ali*, *Casey*), and our discussion of tensions or inconsistencies that arise even when the Court uses textual tools such as dictionaries and language canons. Without some context, can plain meaning ever be objectively clear? On the other hand, what is the justification for allowing a judicial sense of ordinary meaning to trump an apparently unambiguous statutory definition?

2. *The New Holy Trinity*. Recall the *Holy Trinity* case discussed in Chapter 5, and that Court's willingness to place purpose at the center of its statutory analysis even in the face of arguably clear text to the contrary. *Bond* is not as explicit as *Holy Trinity* in this regard. Instead, the Court in *Bond* insists that its decision is grounded in its own precedent and longstanding preference for interpreting statutes in a manner that preserves the balance between state and federal actors. Yet a deeper look at the majority

opinion may lead one to wonder how different the two cases really are. At the start of his opinion for the Court, the Chief Justice goes into considerable historical and personally-felt detail about the international background leading up to promulgation and widespread ratification of the Chemical Weapons Convention. Why is this initial context relevant when, according to the Court, the question is simply whether Congress provided a clear statement sufficient to overcome the presumption of federalism? Is it possible that the new federalism canon in *Bond* is masking what is actually a return to purposivism?

In *The New Holy Trinity*, 18 Green Bag 2d 407, 417 (2015), Professor Richard Re asserts just that. Analyzing three recent cases from the Supreme Court (*Bond* and *Yates* presented in this chapter and *King v. Burwell* which appears in chapter 7), Re argues that the Supreme Court has embraced an evolved version of purposivism that allows for consideration of non-textual factors when the Court seeks to determine whether a statutory text is ambiguous. He contrasts this with *Holy Trinity* in the following manner:

> Far from eliminating textual considerations or rendering them categorically subordinate to purpose, the New Holy Trinity follows the New Textualism in viewing text as a real constraint on interpretation. If a reading has no textual support, then no amount of pragmatism or purpose can carry the day. Yet the degree of textual support demanded isn't set until other considerations have been identified and accounted for. In other words, purposive and pragmatic considerations help set the Court's interpretive expectations and so inform the Court's textualist judgment.

For Re, the "New Holy Trinity" is in part an outgrowth of the Court's recent creative use of avoidance doctrines—but it expands those doctrines so that the Court utilizes purpose to avoid not only unconstitutional outcomes but also mistaken or inapt textual results. Do you agree that this is what the majority has done in *Bond*?

3. *A Different Aspect of Constitutional Avoidance: Skirting the Treaty Power Issue.* It may seem puzzling to characterize *Bond* as a case that failed to address a core constitutional issue given that constitutional concerns seem to be at the heart of the Court's analysis. Leading up to the Supreme Court's decision, some legal commentators wondered if *Bond* would be the case to resolve longstanding and hotly contested constitutional questions about the scope and limits of Congress's treaty power. Yet although the Court failed to resolve the treaty questions (by reading the statute in a way that does not reach Bond's purely local activity), the majority opinion may provide some small indication of how the future Court would come down on the questions. In *Thoughts on* Bond v. United States, published in the "The Volokh Conspiracy," Professor Ilya Somin finds certain hints in the majority opinion.[41] He explains:

> In this case, the Court concluded that it was plausibly possible to interpret the law narrowly so as to avoid intruding into "local" criminal conduct, such as what Bond did. Notice, however, that Section 229 would not upset "usual constitutional balance" between the states and the federal government if the latter has a power to sign and implement treaties regardless of their subject matter. In that event, a treaty covering "local" conduct would be just constitutional business as usual. Therefore the majority opinion at least suggests that there are serious doubts about whether the treaty power can

---

[41] https://www.washingtonpost.com/news/volokh-conspiracy/wp/2014/06/02/thoughts-on-bond-v-united-states/ (visited June 13, 2016).

reach local crimes like those committed by Bond. That doesn't mean that the majority justices clearly conclude that it does not reach it. They *did* ultimately avoid that issue, after all. But it at least hints in that direction.

Why do you think the Court failed to address the treaty question? The Chief Justice explains that the Supreme Court traditionally will not decide a constitutional issue unless necessary for the resolution of a case. Is that sound policy? Which interested groups or parties benefit when such a central doctrinal issue remains unresolved?

4.   *Reframing the Constitutional Avoidance Canon.* Recall Judge Friendly's critique of the avoidance canon (Notes following *Catholic Bishop*) as an occasion for stealth judicial activism. One scholar has recently proposed that the canon be reconceived so that courts are explicit about their imposition of a constitutional remedy. See Eric Fish, *Constitutional Avoidance as Interpretation and as Remedy*, 114 Mich. L. Rev. 1275 (2016). Fish acknowledges a fundamental contradiction in the doctrine of constitutional avoidance: it is officially characterized as both an interpretive technique to determine legislative intent (because Congress is presumed not to act unconstitutionally, courts construe ambiguous text to avoid constitutional problems) and a tool of constitutional enforcement that subverts this intent (courts reconfigure a statute's meaning to protect a constitutional norm). Fish argues for the second function to be reframed as "remedial reinterpretation": the court should first hold a statute unconstitutional and then creatively reinterpret the text to make it constitutionally valid.

How would Fish's proposed reframing affect the majority's reasoning in *Bond*? Instead of "interpreting" an exception into the Chemical Weapons Convention Implementation Act for Carol Ann Bond's individual acts of poisoning, would the Chief Justice have to decide first whether Congress can criminalize such individual conduct consistent with the Tenth Amendment? Whether Congress can do so through its treaty powers? Are there any disadvantages to inviting the Court to declare a statute unconstitutional before reinterpreting it? Is giving the Court the power to reconfigure a law it has declared unconstitutional any different from giving it the power to strike down the law as a whole? To strike it down as applied in a specific setting?

C.   DEBUNKING AND DEFENDING THE CANONS

KARL LLEWELLYN, *REMARKS ON THE THEORY OF APPELLATE DECISION AND THE RULES OR CANONS ABOUT HOW STATUTES ARE TO BE CONSTRUED*

3 Vand. L. Rev. 395, 401–06 (1950).
Reprinted by permission.

When it comes to presenting a proposed construction in court, there is an accepted conventional vocabulary. As in argument over points of case-law, the accepted convention still, unhappily, requires discussion as if only one single correct meaning could exist. Hence there are two opposing canons on almost every point. An arranged selection is appended. Every lawyer must be familiar with them all: they are still needed tools of argument. At least as early as Fortescue the general picture was clear, on this, to any eye which would see.

Plainly, to make any canon take hold in a particular instance, the construction contended for must be sold, essentially, by means other than the use of the canon;

The good sense of the situation and a *simple* construction of the available language to achieve that sense, *by tenable means, out of the statutory language.*

Canons of Construction

Statutory interpretation still speaks a diplomatic tongue. Here is some of the technical framework for maneuver.

Thrust	**But**	**Parry**
1. A statute cannot go beyond its text.		1. To effect its purpose a statute may be implemented beyond its text.
2. Statutes in derogation of the common law will not be extended by construction.		2. Such acts will be liberally construed if their nature is remedial.
3. Statutes are to be read in the light of the common law and a statute affirming a common law rule is to be construed in accordance with the common law.		3. The common law gives way to a statute which is inconsistent with it and when a statute is designed as a revision of a whole body of law applicable to a given subject it supersedes the common law.
4. Where a foreign statute which has received construction has been adopted, previous construction is adopted too.		4. It may be rejected where there is conflict with the obvious meaning of the statute or where the foreign decisions are unsatisfactory in reasoning or where the foreign interpretation is not in harmony with the spirit or policy of the laws of the adopting state.
5. Where various states have already adopted the statute, the parent state is followed.		5. Where interpretations of other states are inharmonious, there is no such restraint.
6. Statutes in pari materia must be construed together.		6. A statute is not in pari materia if its scope and aim are distinct or where a legislative design to depart from the general purpose or policy of previous enactments may be apparent.
7. A statute imposing a new penalty or forfeiture, or a new liability or disability, or creating a new right of action will not be construed as having a retroactive effect.		7. Remedial statutes are to be liberally construed and if a retroactive interpretation will promote the ends of justice, they should receive such construction.

[handwritten annotation:] new penalty ≠ be construed as having a retroactive effect.

Thrust	**But**	**Parry**

[handwritten: Stub]

[handwritten: Avoid save.]

8. Where design has been distinctly stated no place is left for construction.

8. Courts have the power to inquire into real—as distinct from ostensible—purpose.

9. Definitions and rules of construction contained in an interpretation clause are part of the law and binding.

9. Definitions and rules of construction in a statute will not be extended beyond their necessary import nor allowed to defeat intention otherwise manifested.

10. A statutory provision requiring liberal construction does not mean disregard of unequivocal requirements of the statute.

10. Where a rule of construction is provided within the statute itself the rule should be applied.

11. Titles do not control meaning; preambles do not expand scope; section headings do not change language.

11. The title may be consulted as a guide when there is doubt or obscurity in the body; preambles may be consulted to determine rationale, and thus the true construction of terms; section headings may be looked upon as part of the statute itself.

12. If language is plain and unambiguous it must be given effect.

12. Not when literal interpretation would lead to absurd or mischievous consequences or thwart manifest purpose.

13. Words and phrases which have received judicial construction before enactment are to be understood according to that construction.

13. Not if the statute clearly requires them to have a different meaning.

14. After enactment, judicial decision upon interpretation of particular terms and phrases controls.

14. Practical construction by executive officers is strong evidence of true meaning.

15. Words are to be taken in their ordinary meaning unless they are technical terms or words of art.

15. Popular words may bear a technical meaning and technical words may have a popular signification and they should be so construed as to agree with evident intention or to make the statute operative.

Thrust	**But**	**Parry**

16. Every word and clause must be given effect.

16. If inadvertently inserted or if repugnant to the rest of the statute, they may be rejected as surplusage.

17. The same language used repeatedly in the same connection is presumed to bear the same meaning throughout the statute.

17. This presumption will be disregarded where it is necessary to assign different meanings to make the statute consistent.

18. Words are to be interpreted according to the proper grammatical effect of their arrangement within the statute.

18. Rules of grammar will be disregarded where strict adherence would defeat purpose.

19. Exceptions not made cannot be read.

19. The letter is only the "bark." Whatever is within the reason of the law is within the law itself.

20. Expression of one thing excludes another.

20. The language may fairly comprehend many different cases where some only are expressly mentioned by way of example.

21. General terms are to receive a general construction.

21. They may be limited by specific terms with which they are associated or by the scope and purpose of the statute.

22. It is a general rule of construction that where general words follow an enumeration they are to be held as applying only to persons and things of the same general kind or class specifically mentioned (*ejusdem generis*).

22. General words must operate on something. Further, ejusdem generis is only an aid in getting the meaning and does not warrant confining the operations of a statute within narrower limits than were intended.

23. Qualifying or limiting words or clauses are to be referred to the next preceding antecedent.

23. Not when evident sense and meaning require a different construction.

24. Punctuation will govern when a statute is open to two constructions.

24. Punctuation marks will not control the plain and evident meaning of language.

Thrust	But	Parry
25. It must be assumed that language has been chosen with due regard to grammatical propriety and is not interchangeable on mere conjecture.		25. "And" and "or" may be read interchangeably whenever the change is necessary to give the statute sense and effect.
26. There is a distinction between words of permission and mandatory words.		26. Words imparting permission may be read as mandatory and words imparting command may be read as permissive when such construction is made necessary by evident intention or by the rights of the public.
27. A proviso qualifies the provision immediately preceding.		27. It may clearly be intended to have a wider scope.
28. When the enacting clause is general, a proviso is construed strictly.		28. Not when it is necessary to extend the proviso to persons or cases which come within its equity.

NOTES ON THE INTELLECTUAL WARFARE OVER CANONS OF STATUTORY INTERPRETATION

1. *Assault on the Citadel by Legal Realists and Critical Scholars.* Llewellyn's wonderful *tour de farce* is a justly celebrated exposure of the many faces of the canons of statutory construction, and it is representative of the legal realists' tendency to debunk legal formalisms. Their view was that nothing turned on them. Canons of construction, for example, "are useful only as facades, which for an occasional judge may add luster to an argument persuasive for other reasons." Frank Newman & Stanley Surrey, *Legislation—Cases and Materials* 654 (1955). Critical scholars of the 1970s and 1980s did not focus on the canons, but the perspective of many of them (intellectual heirs to the most skeptical realists) would go one step further. The canons are just part of the mystifying game–that is played with legal logic, which is ultimately indeterminate. Critical scholars argue that legal reasoning can be oppressive by denying its own contingency, i.e., denying that there are other ways of looking at the situation. Perhaps the canons of construction might be deemed similarly oppressive, for they are part of the linguistic and logical pretense that the legislature goes about its work in a methodical, rational way and that judicial interpreters can scientifically discern the proper meaning through simple rules.

2. *Legal Process Defense of the Canons.* Conventional legal process thinkers have tended to defend at least some of the canons against the mockery of the realists. For example, Henry Hart, Jr. & Albert Sacks, *The Legal Process* 1191 (Eskridge & Frickey eds. 1994) (tent. ed. 1958), responded to Llewellyn as follows:

> All this [skepticism], it is ventured, involves a misunderstanding of the function of the canons, and at bottom of the problem of interpretation itself. Of

course, there are pairs of maxims susceptible of being invoked for opposing conclusions. Once it is understood that meaning depends upon context and that contexts vary, how could it be otherwise? Maxims should not be treated, any more than a dictionary, as saying what meaning a word or group of words *must* have in a given context. They simply answer the question whether a particular meaning is linguistically permissible, if the context warrants it. Is this not a useful function?

Professor Dickerson suggests that some of the canons "reflect the probabilities generated by normal usage or legislative behavior. These represent either (1) lexicographical judgments of how legislatures tend to use language and its syntactical patterns, or (2) descriptions of how legislatures tend to behave. They serve as useful presumptions of supposed actual legislative intent and are, therefore, modestly useful in carrying [out] legislative meaning." Reed Dickerson, *The Interpretation and Application of Statutes* 228 (1975).

3. *The Law & Economics Debate over the Canons.* The canons were subjected to sharp criticism by Judge Richard Posner in *Statutory Interpretation—In the Classroom and in the Courtroom*, 50 U. Chi. L. Rev. 800, 806–07 (1983). Judge Posner complains that "most of the canons are just wrong" in that (1) they do not reflect a code by which legislatures draft statutes, (2) they are not even common-sense guides to interpretation, (3) they do not operate to constrain the discretion of judges, and (4) they do not force legislatures to draft statutes with care. Judge Posner blasts one canon after another— from the plain meaning rule to expressio unius to the whole act rule—by showing that the canons erroneously assume legislative omniscience and rest on wholly unrealistic conceptions of the legislative process. For a contrary position, Einer Elhauge, *Statutory Default Rules: How to Interpret Unclear Legislation* (2008), argues that many of the canons reflect preference-eliciting default rules that actually minimize political dissatisfaction with statutory results. These default rules need not correspond either to likely legislative preferences or to sound policy. Their justification is that "the default result is more likely to be corrected [when] it burdens some politically powerful group with ready access to the legislative agenda." *Id.* at 152. Congress, Elhauge suggests, is perfectly happy that the Court smooths over statutory potholes, integrates statutes with the larger legal terrain, and sends some sensitive issues back for more work. Which is the more credible understanding of Congress? Can both be right?

From an economic point of view, it may be better to view the canons ex ante rather than ex post. Under an ex ante perspective, it may not matter whether a canon reflects legislative realities. Instead, the question is this: Does the legal process, including the lawmaking process, work *better* with this set of rules than with another set or with no rules at all? The canons might also be defended from an economic point of view as an *interpretive regime* that affords greater predictability for statutory interpreters. See William Eskridge Jr. & John Ferejohn, *Politics, Interpretation, and the Rule of Law*, in *The Rule of Law* 265, 282–85 (Ian Shapiro ed. 1994), as well as Appendix B to this Casebook (a complex array of more than two hundred canons followed by the Rehnquist-Roberts Court), and Adrian Vermeule, *Interpretive Choice*, 75 NYU L. Rev. 74, 140–43 (2000), who argues that the Court should just pick a set of canons and stick with them. The problem with the canons as an interpretive regime is that the canons are not deployed in a completely predictable manner. (See the Brudney and Ditslear article, excerpted below).

Also from an ex ante point of view, some of the canons can be understood as institutional default rules. The best example is the rule of lenity: when the Court interprets criminal statutes narrowly, Congress typically returns to the issue and often overrides the Court with a better-specified statutory crime. See William Eskridge Jr., *Overriding Supreme Court Statutory Interpretation Decisions*, 101 Yale L.J. 331 (1991), as well as our notes after *Muscarello* and *McNally*. This dovetails perfectly with the best justification for the rule of lenity, the nondelegation idea. Eskridge and Frickey, *Quasi-Constitutional Law*, *supra*, argue that the avoidance canon, the federalism canons, and separation of powers canons can also be understood as requiring Congress—and not agencies or judges—to deliberate and decide to press constitutional envelopes. Accord Elhauge, *Statutory Default Rules*, *supra*.

4.	*Pragmatic Defenses of the Canons.* Geoffrey Miller, *Pragmatics and the Maxims of Interpretation*, 1990 Wis. L. Rev. 1179, presents a defense of many of the linguistic canons, showing them to be consistent with the teachings of (Gricean) philosophical linguistics. Gricean theory understands communication as a purposive, cooperative endeavor, and communicative precepts are means by which cooperation is facilitated. Thus, the canons might be understood as essential to the communicative process and therefore inevitable.

Perhaps the least ambitious defense of the canons is to posit that they are just a checklist of things to think about when approaching a statute. If context will guide interpretation of statutes whose language is ambiguous (and some whose language is not), then the canons may at least be a catalogue of contextual factors which might be investigated. Expressio unius, in this way, will stimulate an investigation into why the legislators did include only one thing and not the other. The rule of lenity will remind interpreters that penal laws require greater clarity and justification in their prohibitions, and that one should be aware of fairness problems in particular. The whole act maxim will suggest that other parts of the statute, including definitional provisions, be read for clues about how the drafters used certain words, phrases, and concepts. And so on.

Professor Mermin says that the canons of construction are similar to folksayings. Samuel Mermin, *Law and the Legal System: An Introduction* 264 (2d ed. 1982). Does "haste make waste" have any validity as a suggestion on how to live? What about "the early bird catches the worm," one obvious "parry" to this "thrust"? Or "nothing ventured, nothing gained" versus "discretion is the better part of valor"? Don't all of those sayings have some truth in them, depending upon the context? Do any of these sayings provide guidance in decisionmaking, or do they simply provide a *post hoc* explanation of why we made a certain decision? Judge Posner believes that the canons never contribute to judicial decisionmaking. Is this a decisive objection to them?

5.	*Openly Normative Visions of the Canons.* David Shapiro, in *Continuity and Change in Statutory Interpretation*, 67 N.Y.U. L. Rev. 921, 925 (1992), has provided a different justification for the canons: they promote legal stability, in that they assume "that close questions of statutory interpretation should be resolved in favor of continuity and against change."[42] A difficulty in assessing this claim is figuring out the relevant status quo: Does it consist of longstanding general assumptions in the legal community (embodied in many canons, particularly the substantive ones), or the specific legislative assumptions surrounding a particular statute, which may be undone if a canon controls

---

[42]	For an extended elaboration of this thesis, see Amanda Tyler, *Continuity, Coherence, and the Canons*, 99 Nw. U. L. Rev. 1389 (2005).

statutory meaning? As the next note indicates, these competing definitions may create widely divergent conclusions about the dynamic or static impact of canons in interpretation. Shapiro concludes that promoting continuity rather than change is more often than not consistent with legislative purposes.

6. *Dynamic Canons and the Problem of Legislative Supremacy. Catholic Bishop* illustrates the way in which the canons can contribute to the dynamic evolution of statutes. The dissenters may have more accurately discerned the expectations of Congress, but the Court majority found that evidence insufficient to require the result which they believed to be constitutionally questionable. The Court's creation of a series of new or strengthened clear statement rules in the last few decades has generated results in many cases that would have surprised the enacting Congresses. Recall *Dellmuth* and *Gregory*. Also compare *EEOC v. Arabian Am. Oil Co. (Aramco)*, 499 U.S. 244 (1991) (Court invokes a clear statement rule as basis for holding that Title VII does not apply extraterritorially, to U.S. company allegedly discriminating against U.S. employees in its foreign offices), with *id.* at 263–64 (Marshall, J., dissenting) (arguing that the Court's clear statement rule was much tougher than the traditional presumption against extraterritoriality).

7. *An Empirical Perspective.* One of us has taken a more systematic approach to the canons, collecting 630 Supreme Court workplace-law decisions between 1969 and 2003 and coding them by result (pro-employee or pro-union liberal and pro-employer conservative) and mode of reasoning. James Brudney and Corey Ditslear, *Canons of Construction and the Elusive Quest for Neutral Reasoning*, 58 Vand. L. Rev. 1 (2005). Using multiple regression analyses that control for other variables, Brudney and Ditslear found that the Rehnquist Court relied on the canons (both textual and substantive canons) much more, and legislative history much less, than the Burger Court had done. *Circuit City, Inc. v. Adams*, 532 U.S. 105 (2001) (analyzed in § 1(B) of this chapter) and *EEOC v. Arabian American Oil Co.*, 499 U.S. 244 (1991) (discussed at the start of § 3), exemplify the Rehnquist Court's (and now the Roberts Court's) approach to workplace law cases.

A troubling though perhaps unsurprising finding was that this methodological development is serving ideological purposes (58 Vand. L. Rev. at 53–69). As summarized at the beginning of the lengthy article:

> "[C]anon usage by justices identified as liberals tends to be linked to liberal outcomes, and canon reliance by conservative justices to be associated with conservative outcomes. We also found that canons are often invoked to justify conservative results in close cases—*i.e.*, those decided by a one-vote or two-vote margin. Indeed, closely divided cases in which the majority relies on substantive canons are more likely to reach conservative results than close cases where those canons are not invoked.

> "In addition, we identified a subset of cases in which the majority relies on canons while the dissent invokes legislative history: these cases, almost all decided since 1988, have yielded overwhelmingly conservative results. Doctrinal analysis of illustrative decisions indicates that conservative members of the Rehnquist Court are using the canons in such contested cases to ignore— and thereby undermine—the demonstrable legislative preferences of Congress. Taken together, the association between canon reliance and outcomes among both conservative and liberal justices, the distinctly conservative influence

associated with substantive canon reliance in close cases, and the recent tensions in contested cases between conservative majority opinions that rely on canons and liberal dissents that invoke legislative history, suggest that the canons are regularly used in an instrumental if not ideologically conscious manner." *Id.* at 6.

Brudney and Ditslear apply their empirical findings to the theoretical debate over the utility of the canons. Their conclusions are as follows. First, the authors are skeptical that the canons form an interpretive regime which can provide an ordering mechanism for legislators and lawyers to make statutory interpretation more predictable. Aside from the fact that legislators do not rely on the canons when drafting statutes (see studies by Nourse & Schacter, and more recently Gluck & Bressman, summarized in §§ 1(B) and 2(C) of this chapter), the canons are unreliable predictors for how statutes will be applied because they are deployed in such an ideological way by both liberal and conservative judges. A neutral observer who just read the statute and the legislative history in *Circuit City*, for example, would have expected the Court to construe the employment-contract exemption to the Arbitration Act much more expansively than the five-Justice majority in fact did. Brudney and Ditslear offer almost two dozen equally dramatic canon surprises from their dataset.

Second, and relatedly, the study lends empirical support to relatively cynical accounts of the canons. Stephen Ross, *Where Have You Gone Karl Llewellyn? Should Congress Turn Its Lonely Eyes to You?*, 45 Vand. L. Rev. 561 (1992), and Edward Rubin, *Modern Canons, Loose Canons, and the Limits of Practical Reason*, 45 Vand. L. Rev. 579 (1992), maintain that Supreme Court Justices, and perhaps other judges, use the canons strategically, to justify judicial policy preferences or to frustrate legislative intent. The malleability noted by Professor Llewellyn not only undermines canonical predictability, but allows the canons to be manipulated by result-oriented jurists. Brudney and Ditslear say their evidence is consistent with, though does not conclusively prove, this claim.

Third, the study found some support for the hypothesis, first advanced by Jonathan Macey and Geoffrey Miller, *The Canons of Construction and Judicial Preferences*, 45 Vand. L. Rev. 647 (1992), that the canons are substitutes for judicial expertise and can reduce error costs in areas (such as ERISA and some procedural complexities of Title VII) where judicial knowledge and preferences are low. E.g., *Adams Fruit Co. v. Barrett*, 494 U.S. 638 (1990) (expressio unius provides the ground for a conservative Court to allow, without dissent, a private right of action under a technical migrant workers' law). Brudney and Ditslear add that such cases may be more strongly influenced by legislative purpose analysis and, most important, agency views than by canon reliance. In short, there is a correlation between canon invocation and certain technical issues but not necessarily any causal link.

These conclusions raise the possibility that in the most technical and nonpartisan areas of law—such as bankruptcy, energy regulation, patents, or taxation—canon usage would be more important and less ideologically slanted than in workplace law. In less technical or more normatively charged areas—such as civil rights, criminal law, and environmental law—canon usage would be less frequent and more ideologically slanted.

8.   *Recent Normative Exchanges.* In *Reading Law*, Justice Scalia and Professor Garner acknowledge that statutory interpretation "is a human enterprise, which cannot be carried out algorithmically by an expert system on a computer." Accepting the inevitability of some judicial discretion, the authors promote the elevation of their 57

"valid canons" or "sound principles of interpretation" as a systematic approach that would minimize or at least reduce problems of unpredictability and judicial policymaking. They argue that their regime of primarily textually-based presumptions and guidelines will constrain judicial discretion because judges will understand they must follow these rules or else risk exposure as willful abusers of power.

One of us has expressed admiration for what Scalia and Garner are attempting to accomplish while concluding that their proposed canons-based regime is plagued by several substantial problems (by now perhaps familiar to readers). See William Eskridge Jr., *The New Textualism and Normative Canons*, 113 Colum. L. Rev. 531 (2013). First, the Scalia and Garner list of 57 approved canons (which they concede may include only one-third of all valid canons), reveals *enormous scope for judicial cherry-picking*. This is due both to the challenge of competing canons (see Llewellyn critique) and to the challenge of deciding what makes a canon canonical in the first instance. The absence of any authoritative hierarchy of canons, along with empirical evidence that their use by judges is ideologically linked (Brudney and Ditslear) deepens this cherry-picking problem. Second, Eskridge discusses the related *norms problem*. Even discounting the risks of cherry-picking, many of Scalia and Garner's valid canons are open-ended and normative. Some reflect non-constitutional values of continuity, fixed-meaning, and presumptions against change; others reflect constitutional values of libertarianism (lenity, respect for property) or federalism (presumptions against federal preemption, against abrogating state sovereign immunity, for respecting state sovereign functions). Judges will have plenty of canons to choose from (subconsciously or otherwise) to support imposing their policy preferences on a contested statutory provision. This is especially troubling because Scalia and Garner disparage a range of purposive guidelines grounded in examination of what Congress communicated during the lawmaking process itself.

This disparagement relates to the final challenge, which Eskridge identifies as a *democracy problem*. Scalia and Garner's canons-based regime enshrines textual canons that legislative drafters tend to dismiss (Gluck and Bressman; Nourse and Schacter). At the same time, Scalia and Garner reject legislative history (exposed in a series of "false notions") as unworthy of interpretive consideration (see § 2 of chapter 7). Their posture ignores the reality, reported dramatically by Gluck and Bressman, that "legislative history was emphatically viewed by almost all of our respondents—Republican and Democrat alike—as the most important drafting and interpretive tool apart from text." In opting for a set of valid canons that isolate them from the legislative (and often legislative-executive) deliberations preceding a statute's enactment, Scalia and Garner exacerbate the countermajoritarian difficulty with judicial interpretation of statutes.

As we turn to chapter 7, addressing extrinsic sources for statutory interpretation, you should keep in mind the tensions between Justice Scalia's canons-based regime and a more purposive approach which is embraced by some of his judicial colleagues. In particular, consider how we should assess the comparative advantages of these two approaches—from the standpoint of predictability, stability, and legitimacy.

NOTE ON LEGISLATED CANONS OF STATUTORY INTERPRETATION

Sometimes the legislature attempts to direct the court in how to approach interpreting a particular statute. For example, a provision of the federal Racketeer Influenced and Corrupt Organizations Act (RICO), 18 U.S.C. § 1961, which contains criminal sanctions, provides that "[t]he provisions of this title shall be liberally construed to effectuate its remedial purposes." There could conceivably be some constitutional objections to such a provision—the most straightforward would be that it violates the separation of powers because it invades the court's power to say what the law is—but leaving that problem aside, what should a court do with it? In *Russello v. United States*, 464 U.S. 16, 26–27 (1983), the Court cited the RICO provision as well as legislative history to support a broad construction of the statute. In contrast, in *Reves v. Ernst & Young*, 507 U.S. 170, 183–84 (1993), the Court said the following about the RICO clause:

> This clause obviously seeks to ensure that Congress' intent is not frustrated by an overly narrow reading of the statute, but it is not an invitation to apply RICO to new purposes that Congress never intended. Nor does the clause help us to determine what purposes Congress had in mind. Those must be gleaned from the statute through the normal means of interpretation. The clause " 'only serves as an aid for resolving an ambiguity; it is not to be used to beget one.' "

Does this approach leave any role for the interpretive clause at all?

Congress has also adopted the Dictionary Act, which codifies a few generic canons of statutory construction, such as the rules that singular terms include the plural, and male pronouns also include females. See 1 U.S.C. § 1 et seq. All fifty states and the District of Columbia have adopted more ambitious model interpretation acts providing legislated canons to guide judicial interpretation for all statutes. Chapter 645 of the Minnesota Statutes, for example, contains the following provisions:

645.16. LEGISLATIVE INTENT CONTROLS

The object of all interpretation and construction of laws is to ascertain and effectuate the intention of the legislature. Every law shall be construed, if possible, to give effect to all its provisions.

When the words of a law in their application to an existing situation are clear and free from all ambiguity, the letter of the law shall not be disregarded under the pretext of pursuing the spirit.

When the words of a law are not explicit, the intention of the legislature may be ascertained by considering, among other matters:

(1) The occasion and necessity for the law;

(2) The circumstances under which it was enacted;

(3) The mischief to be remedied;

(4) The object to be attained;

(5) The former law, if any, including other laws upon the same or similar subjects;

(6) The consequences of a particular interpretation;

(7) The contemporaneous legislative history; and

(8) Legislative and administrative interpretations of the statute.

645.17. PRESUMPTIONS IN ASCERTAINING LEGISLATIVE INTENT

In ascertaining the intention of the legislature the courts may be guided by the following presumptions:

(1) The legislature does not intend a result that is absurd, impossible of execution, or unreasonable;

(2) The legislature intends the entire statute to be effective and certain;

(3) The legislature does not intend to violate the constitution of the United States or of this state;

(4) When a court of last resort has construed the language of a law, the legislature in subsequent laws on the same subject matter intends the same construction to be placed upon such language; and

(5) The legislature intends to favor the public interest as against any private interest.

Notice that Minnesota's legislated canons provide (1) a general theory of statutory interpretation, (2) an indication of the sources judges should consult and when they might consult them, and (3) specific presumptions of statutory meaning.

In an important study, Jacob Scott, *Codified Canons and the Common Law of Interpretation*, 98 Geo. L.J. 341 (2010), collected and categorized the statutory canons for all fifty states and the District of Columbia. Scott then analyzed the patterns he found across the nationwide sample. Among the patterns he reported are the following:

• **Plain Meaning.** Fifteen legislatures, including Minnesota's, have codified the plain meaning rule, but with explicit inclusion of exceptions for "absurd results" and/or "scrivener's errors." Thirty-four legislatures have codified the dictionary canon and the canon that "ordinary usage" should normally be applied. No legislature has codified expressio unius, and only two have codified ejusdem generis or noscitur a sociis.

• **Whole Act.** Thirty legislatures (including Minnesota's) have codified the whole act rule *and* the presumption of consistent usage of terms within a statute. Thirty-one have codified the rule against interpreting one provision in a way that is inconsistent with the structure of the statute. Ten states (including Minnesota) have codified the rule against surplusage.

• **Consistency Across Statutes.** Twenty-six states (including Minnesota) have codified the presumption that the same term should be interpreted consistently across different statutes. Fifteen states have codified the canon against implied repeals.

• **Legislative History.** Eleven states (including Minnesota) have codified the rule that legislative history "may" be considered under various circumstances; no state has legislated against consideration of legislative history. Like Minnesota's codification, most of these codifications require the statute to be ambiguous, but a few states (such as Texas) say legislative history can be consulted under any circumstances.

• **Constitutional Canons.** Minnesota is unusual in not codifying any of the constitutional canons. Five states have codified the avoidance canon, though none has rejected it either. Thirty-five states have codified the presumption of severability. Twenty-four states have codified the presumption against statutory retroactivity.

- **Purposive Canons.** Like Minnesota, twenty-one other states have codified the canon that ambiguous statutes should be interpreted to carry out the legislative purpose. Nineteen state legislatures say that remedial statutes should be liberally construed, and seventeen states say that all statutes should be liberally construed. Eleven states have codified the presumption that the legislature intends "reasonable" results.

Scott argues from this exhaustive survey that there is a "common law" of canons of statutory construction—a common law to which legislatures and not just courts are contributing. He suggests that judges ought to be chary of deploying canons, such as expressio unius, that legislatures have uniformly failed to embrace. If statutory interpretation is supposed to be attentive to legislative intent, as most state legislatures and courts claim, is it not relevant that legislated canons never include expressio unius or ejusdem generis and overwhelmingly endorse the absurd results exception to plain meaning and the importance of legislative purpose in resolving statutory ambiguities?

Moreover, this survey might have some traction for general theories of statutory interpretation. Scott concludes that state legislatures are not friendly to the new textualism's methodology: although legislatures endorse the plain meaning rule, they do so with allowance for an absurd result exception and tend to favor consultation of legislative history and statutory purpose. Conversely, Scott suggests that the pattern of legislative codification lends legislative, and perhaps democratic, support and legitimacy to the pragmatic approach laid out in William Eskridge Jr. and Philip Frickey, *Statutory Interpretation as Practical Reasoning*, 42 Stan. L. Rev. 321 (1990) (Chapter 5, § 3(C)). How would a new textualist respond to this?

For an argument that Congress has and should exercise the authority to enact more ambitious federal rules of statutory interpretation (more like those of Minnesota and other states), see Nicholas Rosenkranz, *Federal Rules of Statutory Interpretation*, 115 Harv. L. Rev. 2085 (2002). For a critique and modification of this approach, see Adam Kiracofe, Note, *The Codified Canons of Statutory Construction: A Response and Proposal to Nicholas Rosenkranz's* Federal Rules of Statutory Interpretation, 84 B.U. L. Rev. 571 (2004). For a critique and counter-proposal suggesting that an organization like the American Law Institute formulate a restatement of statutory interpretation, see Gary O'Connor, *Restatement (First) of Statutory Interpretation*, 7 N.Y.U. J. Legis. & Pub. Pol'y 333 (2003–04). For reservations about either a restatement or federal rules of statutory interpretation, see Lawrence Solan, *Is it Time for a Restatement of Statutory Interpretation?*, 79 Brooklyn L. Rev. 733 (2014) (arguing that it would be misleading to suggest that consensus about statutory interpretation is sufficient to justify a restatement); James J. Brudney & Lawrence Baum, *Protean Statutory Interpretation in the Courts of Appeals*, 58 W. & M. L. Rev. 681 (2017) (showing how federal appeals courts usage patterns for interpretive resources differ substantially from those in the Roberts Court, and contending that certain institutional sources contribute to these interpretive divergences, notably the Justices' interaction with their colleagues in every case and their experience as objects of continuing media and congressional attention).

CHAPTER 7

EXTRINSIC DOCTRINES OF STATUTORY INTERPRETATION

∎ ∎ ∎

This chapter considers sources extrinsic to the statutory text, notably the *common law, legislative background and history,* and *related statutes.* These sources help place the words of the statute in an appropriate larger context, enhancing the interpreter's ability to discern statutory meaning. Legislative history—principally the record of hearings, committee reports, and floor statements preceding a bill's enactment—was not much used before 1892, when the Supreme Court decided *Holy Trinity Church* (Chapter 5, § 1). Since the late 1930s, the Court has often used legislative history, and many state courts will consider it as well. At the same time, canons such as the plain meaning rule, which severely limits the use of extrinsic evidence, especially legislative history, and the rule of deference to agency decisions have made a big comeback since the mid1980s. The revival of the canons and the corresponding decline in reliance on legislative history have generated an unusually rich discussion, and we examine what has become an intense debate over legislative history among judges and scholars. Chapter 7 concludes with the Supreme Court decision in *Babbitt v. Sweet Home Chapter of Communities for a Great Oregon,* 515 U.S. 687 (1995). *Sweet Home* features Justices Stevens (majority) and Scalia (dissent) invoking many of the core interpretive doctrines, from both chapters 6 and 7, in diverse and sophisticated fashion. For this reason, it is an excellent vehicle for review.

Of the key extrinsic sources examined, the chapter devotes principal attention to the legislative background and history of the statute (Section 2), although consideration also is given to the common law (Section 1) and to other statutes and their interpretation (Section 3). The traditional rule was that extrinsic aids should not be considered if the statute had a "plain meaning." But how can we be sure that the statute really has a plain meaning, without considering context? For example, if the legislature uses a term such as "fraud," which had an established common law meaning at the time, we should have to consult extrinsic evidence just to figure out what the plain meaning might be. Or if legislative discussions during the enactment process reveal a specialized use of the term "fraud," shouldn't they be relevant?

The new textualists introduced in Chapter 5, § 3(A) believe that the common law and other statutes are usually admissible extrinsic evidence, but legislative background or history is not. This position is examined more closely in Section 2. It has had some influence on the Supreme Court and the lower federal courts. Ironically, state courts have in the last several decades become more likely to consider legislative history, because documentary legislative materials are more readily available.[359]

1. THE COMMON LAW

The traditional rule in Anglo-American law was that statutes in derogation of the common law should be narrowly construed. This was the philosophy of Blackstone's *Commentaries*, which were pervasively influential at the founding of our constitutional republic, and in the early Supreme Court, especially in admiralty cases.[360] As the Supreme Court later articulated the principle, "[n]o statute is to be construed as altering the common law, farther than its words import." *Shaw v. Railroad Co.*, 101 U.S. (11 Otto) 557, 565 (1879). This canon reflected the foundational character of the common law as a regulatory regime. Any deviation from common-law rules needed special justification.

Such a rule has eroded in the modern regulatory statute, where statutes are the rule and common law the exception. For example, in *Isbrandtsen Co. v. Johnson*, 343 U.S. 779, 783 (1952), the Supreme Court held, in an admiralty proceeding by a seaman for wages earned, that the employer's common-law right to set off damages resulting from the seaman's dereliction of duty had been preempted by federal statute. The Court stated:

> Statutes which invade the common law or the general maritime law are to be read with a presumption favoring the retention of long-established and familiar principles, except when a statutory purpose to the contrary is evident. No rule of construction precludes giving a natural meaning to legislation like this that obviously is of a remedial, beneficial and amendatory character. It should be interpreted so as to effect its purpose. Marine legislation, at least since the Shipping Commissioners Act of June 7, 1872, 17 Stat. 262, should be construed to make effective its design to change the general maritime law so as to improve the lot of seamen.

Isbrandtsen noted, further, that federal statutes regulated virtually every aspect of a seaman's rights and duties, hence negating the force of the common law argument. This suggests another reason for the demise of the common law canon: statutes substantially occupy the field to regulate many areas of human activity, whereas in the nineteenth century (the heyday of the common law canon), statutory regulation was the exception.[361]

---

[359] For a comprehensive overview, see Jos Torres & Steve Windsor, *State Legislative Histories: A Select, Annotated Bibliography*, 85 Law Libr. J. 545 (1993). For an in-depth examination of developments in five states, see Abbe Gluck, *The States as Laboratories of Statutory Interpretation: Methodological Consensus and the New Modified Textualism*, 119 Yale L.J. 1750 (2010).

[360] For early history, see William Eskridge Jr., *All About Words: The Original Understandings of the "Judicial Power" in Statutory Interpretation, 1776–1806*, 101 Colum. L. Rev. 990 (2001). The best historical source for eighteenth century English thinking is David Lieberman, *The Province of Legislation Determined* 16–20, 28, 52–72 (1989) (discussing the proliferation of mangled statutes in eighteenth-century England and Blackstone's disdainful attitude toward them, with judges being the main salvation by protecting the common law against bad statutes).

[361] Compare *United States v. Texas*, 507 U.S. 529 (1993) (applying *Isbrandsten* standard but concluding that federal common law principle was not abrogated by federal statute).

Nonetheless, the common law remains an important extrinsic source for interpreting many statutes. As noted above, when the legislature deploys words with established common law meanings, courts will presume that those meanings are adopted by Congress. E.g., *Wallace v. Kato*, 549 U.S. 384, 388–89 (2007) (§ 1983); *Cmty. for Creative Non-Violence v. Reid*, 490 U.S. 730, 739 (1989). Especially for older, more generally phrased statutes, the common law serves a broader "gap-filling" role: For issues entirely unaddressed by the statute, the interpreter might presume that the legislature intended to adopt the established common law rule. Consider the following problem, and then a leading case, to see how important the common law still is for filling in gaps.

INTRODUCTORY PROBLEM: THE COMMON LAW AS EXTRINSIC EVIDENCE

Problem 7-1. The Civil Rights Act of 1871, 17 Stat. 13, codified as amended at 42 U.S.C. § 1983, provides as follows:

> Every person who, under color of any statute, ordinance, regulation, custom, or usage, of any State or Territory or the District of Columbia, subjects, or causes to be subjected, any citizen of the United States or other person within the jurisdiction thereof to the deprivation of any rights, privileges, or immunities secured by the Constitution and laws, shall be liable to the party injured in an action at law, suit in equity, or other proper proceeding for redress.

This statute was passed in 1871, as part of the Reconstruction effort to ensure newly freed slaves their rights as citizens.

Carl Doe, an official of the NAACP, organizes a boycott of stores in Tylertown, Mississippi, because the stores follow segregated practices. He also organizes a sit-in. The sheriff arrests Doe for breach of the peace, and state Judge Joyce Judicious orders Doe to cease any and all activity meant to disrupt Tylertown businesses. Doe points out that a long line of Supreme Court First Amendment precedents render such an order "lawless," and Judge Judicious holds Doe in contempt and sentences him to a day in jail. When Judge Judicious' order is overturned, Doe sues the sheriff and the judge under § 1983 for violating his First Amendment rights. The sheriff settles the case with Doe, but Judge Judicious argues judicial immunity.

Judge Judicious demonstrates that at common law judges were immune from lawsuits arising out of their judicial duties. The Supreme Court in *Bradley v. Fisher*, 80 U.S. (13 Wall.) 335 (1871), endorsed absolute judicial immunity in order to protect the integrity of judicial decisionmaking, which would be compromised if the judge were worried about being sued by the losers of lawsuits. Because Congress may be assumed not to disturb such a long-established rule of immunity, § 1983 should be interpreted to include this immunity, argues Judicious.

Doe disagrees and cites to the legislative background of § 1983. During Reconstruction, the South was marked by disorder and violence, especially against the newly emancipated black citizens. Often this violence was accomplished under color of state law—through lynchings, rigged trials, and official harassment of freed slaves. The Reconstruction Congress enacted the Civil Rights Act of 1866, 14 Stat. 27, to abate the violence. Section 2 of the 1866 Act provided criminal liability for any person who, under color of any law, deprived another of federal rights by reason of race. Most of the discussion of § 2 recognized that it would apply to state judges, for much of the oppression was conducted through state tribunals. A proposed amendment to exempt state judges from criminal liability failed. President Johnson vetoed the 1866 bill, in part because it would allow prosecution of state court judges. Members of Congress objected to President Johnson's reason. "I answer it is better to invade the judicial power of the State than permit it to invade, strike down, and destroy the civil rights of citizens. A judicial power perverted to such uses should be speedily invaded," argued Representative Lawrence. Congress passed the bill over the President's veto.

Another amendment not adopted in 1866 was Representative Bingham's proposal to substitute a civil action for the criminal penalties of § 2. (The bill's sponsor said the law's beneficiaries could not afford civil suits.) Violence against African Americans continued in the South, and this proposal was renewed in 1871. After President Grant informed Congress of the urgency of attacking the violence of Southern racists against blacks, Congress passed the Civil Rights Act of 1871, § 1 of which is the predecessor of § 1983. Representative Shellabarger, the main House sponsor of the 1871 bill, said on the floor of the House that § 2 of the 1866 Act was "the model" for § 1 of the 1871 bill. "[Section 2] provides a criminal proceeding in identically the same case as [§ 1] provides a civil remedy for, except that the deprivation under color of State law must, under the [1866 Act], have been on account of race, color, or former slavery." The Senate sponsor, Senator Edmunds, stated that § 1 was intended to carry out the principles of the 1866 Act. No one in Congress disputed the analogy.

There was little discussion of § 1 in Congress (most of the discussion focused on the criminal conspiracy provision of the 1871 bill). Opponents of § 1 stressed its invasion of judicial independence and cited to criminal prosecutions of judges under the 1866 Act. "By the first section, in certain cases, the judge of a State court, though acting under oath of office, is made liable to a suit in Federal court and subject to damages for his decision against a suitor," exclaimed Representative Lewis (an opponent of the 1871 bill). Although Representative Shellabarger often corrected opponents' mischaracterizations of his bill, he never disputed opponents' allegations that § 1 would render judges civilly liable. Supporters of the 1871 bill argued that in the South "courts are in many instances under the control of those who are wholly inimical to the impartial administration of law and equity" and that the criminal liability of the 1866 Act was not enough to stop those abuses of justice. The 1871 bill was passed overwhelmingly. This legislative background, argues Doe, shows that the 1871 Congress did *not* expect that § 1 would include the common law's judicial immunity doctrine.

Would the Supreme Court accept Judicious' argument that she is immune from § 1983 in this setting? Is this a case where the Court should follow long-established and familiar common law principles? Alternatively, is there a plainly evident statutory purpose that Congress meant to depart from or abolish common law immunities? Compare *Pierson v. Ray*, 386 U.S. 547 (1967).

Now that you know something about § 1983, evaluate a different kind of issue: For officials who can be sued for damages, what damages might be allowed? Under what circumstances can punitive damages be awarded, for example? Consider the following case.

STATUTORY PREFACE TO *SMITH V. WADE*

42 U.S.C. 1983. *Civil action for deprivation of rights.*

Every person who, under color of any statute, ordinance, regulation, custom, or usage, of any State or Territory or the District of Columbia, subjects, or causes to be subjected, any citizen of the United States or other person within the jurisdiction thereof to the deprivation of any rights, privileges, or immunities secured by the Constitution and laws, shall be liable to the party injured in an action at law, suit in equity, or other proper proceeding for redress * * *.

SMITH V. WADE

Supreme Court of the United States, 1983.
461 U.S. 30, 103 S.Ct. 1625, 75 L.Ed.2d 632.

JUSTICE BRENNAN delivered the opinion of the Court.

[Wade, an inmate of a Missouri state prison, brought a § 1983 suit against Smith and four guards and correction officials. Wade alleged that he was assaulted by cellmates and that defendants did nothing even though they knew or ought to have known that such an assault was likely to occur. The trial judge instructed the jury that Wade could obtain punitive damages if defendants' conduct was in reckless disregard of, or indifferent to, Wade's safety. The jury found Smith liable for both compensatory and punitive damages, and the circuit court affirmed. The issue before the Court was whether punitive damages may be awarded in a § 1983 action based upon a finding of reckless or callous disregard of, or indifference to, plaintiff's rights, or, as Smith contended, only upon a finding that the defendant acted with "actual malicious intent."]

Section 1983 is derived from § 1 of the Civil Rights Act of 1871, 17 Stat. 13. It was intended to create "a species of tort liability" in favor of persons deprived of federally secured rights. *Carey v. Piphus*, 435 U.S. 247, 253 (1978); *Imbler v. Pachtman*, 424 U.S. 409, 417 (1976). We noted in *Carey* that there was little in the section's legislative history concerning the damages recoverable for this tort liability. In the absence of more specific guidance, we looked first to the common law of torts (both modern and as of 1871), with such modification or adaptation as might be necessary to carry out the purpose and policy of the statute. We have done the same in other contexts arising under § 1983, especially the recurring problem of common-law immunities.[2]

---

[2]   [Citing cases, including *Pierson* (See Problem 7-1).]

Justice Rehnquist's dissent faults us for referring to modern tort decisions in construing § 1983. Its argument rests on the unstated and unsupported premise that Congress necessarily intended to freeze into permanent law whatever principles were current in 1871, rather than to incorporate applicable general legal principles as they evolve. [Citing Justice O'Connor's dissent as well]. The dissents are correct, of course, that when the language of the section and its legislative history provide no clear answer, we have found useful guidance in the law prevailing at the time when § 1983 was enacted; but it does not follow that that law is absolutely controlling or that current law is irrelevant. On the contrary, if the prevailing view on some point of general tort law had changed substantially in the intervening century (which is not the case here), we might be highly reluctant to assume that Congress intended to perpetuate a now-obsolete doctrine. See *Carey v. Piphus* ("[O]ver the centuries the common law of torts has developed a set of rules to implement the principle that a person should be compensated fairly for injuries caused by the violation of his legal rights. These rules, defining the elements of damages and the prerequisites for their recovery, provide the appropriate starting point for the

[Smith conceded that punitive damages are available in a "proper" § 1983 action.] Smith argues, nonetheless, that this was not a "proper" case in which to award punitive damages. More particularly, he attacks the instruction that punitive damages could be awarded on a finding of reckless or callous disregard of or indifference to Wade's rights or safety. Instead, he contends that the proper test is one of actual malicious intent—"ill will, spite, or intent to injure." He offers two arguments for this position: first, that actual intent is the proper standard for punitive damages in all cases under § 1983; and second, that even if intent is not always required, it should be required here because the threshold for punitive damages should always be higher than that for liability in the first instance. We address these in turn.

[III] Smith does not argue that the common law, either in 1871 or now, required or requires a showing of actual malicious intent for recovery of punitive damages.

Perhaps not surprisingly, there was significant variation (both terminological and substantive) among American jurisdictions in the latter nineteenth century on the precise standard to be applied in awarding punitive damages—variation that was exacerbated by the ambiguity and slipperiness of such common terms as "malice" and "gross negligence."[8] Most of the confusion, however, seems to have been over the degree of negligence, recklessness, carelessness, or culpable indifference that should be required—not over whether actual intent was essential. On the contrary, the rule in a large majority of jurisdictions was that punitive damages (also called exemplary damages, vindictive damages, or smart money) could be awarded without a showing of actual ill will, spite, or intent to injure.

This Court so stated on several occasions, before and shortly after 1871. In *Philadelphia, W. & B.R. Co. v. Quigley*, 62 U.S. (21 How.) 202 (1859), a diversity libel suit, the Court held erroneous an instruction that authorized the jury to return a punitive award but gave the jury virtually no substantive guidance as to the proper threshold. We described the standard thus:

> "Whenever the injury complained of has been inflicted maliciously or wantonly, and with circumstances of contumely or indignity, the jury are not limited to the ascertainment of a simple compensation for the wrong committed against the aggrieved person. But the malice spoken of in this rule is not merely the doing of an unlawful or injurious act. The word implies that the act complained of was conceived in the spirit of mischief, *or of criminal indifference to civil obligations*." *Id.* at 214. * * *

The large majority of state and lower federal courts were in agreement that punitive damages awards did not require a showing of actual malicious intent; they

---

inquiry under § 1983 as well.") (footnote omitted). Indeed, in *Imbler* we recognized a common-law immunity that first came into existence 25 years after § 1983 was enacted. Under the dissents' view, *Imbler* was wrongly decided.

8   [Footnote 8 is 76 lines of the U.S. Reports, attacking Justice Rehnquist's assumption that in 1871 "malice," "wantonness," and "willfulness" all denoted ill will. Justice Brennan asserted that "[w]ith regard to 'malice' the assumption is dubious at best; with regard to 'wantonness' and 'willfulness,' it is just plain wrong."]

SEC. 1 THE COMMON LAW 719

permitted punitive awards on variously stated standards of negligence, recklessness, or other culpable conduct short of actual malicious intent.[12]

The same rule applies today. The Restatement (Second) of Torts (1977), for example, states: "Punitive damages may be awarded for conduct that is outrageous, because of the defendant's evil motive *or his reckless indifference to the rights of others*." *Id.*, § 908(2) (emphasis added); see also *id.*, Comment *b*. Most cases under state common law, although varying in their precise terminology, have adopted more or less the same rule, recognizing that punitive damages in tort cases may be awarded not only for actual intent to injure or evil motive, but also for recklessness, serious indifference to or disregard for the rights of others, or even gross negligence.[13]

The remaining question is whether the policies and purposes of § 1983 itself require a departure from the rules of tort common law. As a general matter, we discern no reason why a person whose federally guaranteed rights have been violated should be granted a more restrictive remedy than a person asserting an ordinary tort cause of action. Smith offers us no persuasive reason to the contrary.

Smith's argument, which he offers in several forms, is that an actual-intent standard is preferable to a recklessness standard because it is less vague. He points out that punitive damages, by their very nature, are not awarded to compensate the injured party. He concedes, of course, that deterrence of future egregious conduct is a primary purpose of both § 1983 and of punitive damages, see * * * Restatement (Second) of Torts § 908(1) (1979). But deterrence, he contends, cannot be achieved unless the standard of conduct sought to be deterred is stated with sufficient clarity to enable potential defendants to conform to the law and to avoid the proposed sanction. Recklessness or callous indifference, he argues, is too uncertain a standard to achieve deterrence rationally and fairly. A prison guard, for example, can be expected to know whether he is acting with actual ill will or intent to injure, but not whether he is being reckless or callously indifferent.

Smith's argument, if valid, would apply to ordinary tort cases as easily as to § 1983 suits; hence, it hardly presents an argument for adopting a different rule under § 1983. In any event, the argument is unpersuasive. While, *arguendo*, an intent standard may be easier to understand and apply to particular situations than a recklessness standard, we are not persuaded that a recklessness standard is too vague to be fair or useful. In [*Milwaukee & St. Paul R. Co. v. Arms*, 91 U.S. (1 Otto)

---

[12] * * * *Maysville & L.R. Co. v. Herrick*, 76 Ky. 122 (1877), held that the trial court correctly refused to instruct the jury that "willful or intentional wrong" was required to award punitive damages in a railroad accident case, remarking: "The absence of slight care in the management of a railroad station, or in keeping a railroad track in repair, is gross negligence; and to enable a passenger to recover punitive damages, in a case like this, it is not necessary to show the absence of all care, or 'reckless indifference to the safety of * * * passengers,' or 'intentional misconduct' on the part of the agents and officers of the company." *Id.* at 127 (ellipsis in original). [Justice Brennan cited 30 cases in accord with this proposition.]

Justice Rehnquist's assertion that a "solid majority of jurisdictions" required actual malicious intent is simply untrue. In fact, there were fairly few jurisdictions that imposed such a requirement, and fewer yet that adhered to it consistently. Justice Rehnquist's attempt to establish this proposition with case citations does not offer him substantial support. Because the point is not of controlling significance, we will not tarry here to analyze his citations case-by-case or state-by-state, but will only summarize the main themes. [According to Justice Brennan, some of the dissenters' cases support the availability of punitive damages for recklessness, others are too equivocal to categorize, and others support the dissenters' interpretation only if one assumes that terms like "malice," "wantonness," and "criminal" always meant actual intent to injure.]

[13] [Justice Brennan cited 33 recent state cases to support the proposition in text.]

489 (1876),] we adopted a recklessness standard rather than a gross negligence standard precisely because recklessness would better serve the need for adequate clarity and fair application. Almost a century later, in the First Amendment context, we held that punitive damages cannot be assessed for defamation in the absence of proof of "knowledge of falsity or reckless disregard for the truth." [*Gertz v. Robert Welch, Inc.*, 418 U.S. 323, 349 (1974).] Our concern in *Gertz* was that the threat of punitive damages, if not limited to especially egregious cases, might "inhibit the vigorous exercise of First Amendment freedoms"—a concern at least as pressing as any urged by Smith in this case. Yet we did not find it necessary to impose an actual-intent standard there. Just as Smith has not shown why § 1983 should give higher protection from punitive damages than ordinary tort law, he has not explained why it gives higher protection than we have demanded under the First Amendment.

More fundamentally, Smith's argument for certainty in the interest of deterrence overlooks the distinction between a standard for punitive damages and a standard of liability in the first instance. Smith seems to assume that prison guards and other state officials look mainly to the standard for punitive damages in shaping their conduct. We question the premise; we assume, and hope, that most officials are guided primarily by the underlying standards of federal substantive law—both out of devotion to duty, and in the interest of avoiding liability for compensatory damages. At any rate, the conscientious officer who desires clear guidance on how to do his job and avoid lawsuits can and should look to the standard for actionability in the first instance. The need for exceptional clarity in the standard for punitive damages arises only if one assumes that there are substantial numbers of officers who will not be deterred by compensatory damages; only such officers will seek to guide their conduct by the punitive damages standard. The presence of such officers constitutes a powerful argument *against* raising the threshold for punitive damages.

In this case, the jury was instructed to apply a high standard of constitutional right ("physical abuse of such base, inhumane and barbaric proportions as to shock the sensibilities"). It was also instructed, under the principle of qualified immunity, that Smith could not be held liable at all unless he was guilty of "a callous indifference or a thoughtless disregard for the consequences of [his] act or failure to act," or of "a flagrant or remarkably bad failure to protect" Wade. These instructions are not challenged in this Court, nor were they challenged on grounds of vagueness in the lower courts. Smith's contention that this recklessness standard is too vague to provide clear guidance and reasonable deterrence might more properly be reserved for a challenge seeking different standards of liability in the first instance. As for punitive damages, however, in the absence of any persuasive argument to the contrary based on the policies of § 1983, we are content to adopt the policy judgment of the common law—that reckless or callous disregard for the plaintiff's rights, as well as intentional violations of federal law, should be sufficient to trigger a jury's consideration of the appropriateness of punitive damages.

[Justice Brennan, finally, rejected Smith's last argument, that it was error for the court to describe the standard of punitive damages in terms similar to those of the basic liability under § 1983 (indifference to Wade's rights). Primary reliance was placed on the Restatement (Second) of Torts and the modern common law, which generally provide that where the standard for compensatory liability is as high or higher than the usual threshold for punitive damages, such damages may be given without requiring any extra showing.]

JUSTICE REHNQUIST, with whom THE CHIEF JUSTICE [BURGER] and JUSTICE POWELL join, dissenting.

The Court rejects a "wrongful intent" standard, instead requiring a plaintiff to show merely "reckless * * * indifference to the federally protected rights of others." The following justifications are offered by the Court for this result: first, the rule in "[m]ost cases [decided in the last 15 years] under state common law" is "more or less" equivalent to a recklessness standard; second, the Court asserts that a similar rule "prevail[ed] at the time when § 1983 was enacted"; and finally, there is an "absence of any persuasive argument" for not applying existing state tort rules to the federal statutory remedies available against state and local officials under § 1983. In my opinion none of these justifications, taken singly or together, supports the Court's result. First, the decisions of state courts in the last decade or so are all but irrelevant in determining the intent of the 42d Congress, and thus, the meaning of § 1983. Second, the Court's characterization of the common law rules prevailing when § 1983 was enacted is both oversimplified and misleading; in fact, the majority rule in 1871 seems to have been that some sort of "evil intent"—and not mere recklessness—was necessary to justify an award of punitive damages. Third, the Court's inability to distinguish a *state* court's award of punitive damages against a state officer from a *federal* court's analogous action under §§ 1983 and 1988 precludes it from adequately assessing the public policies implicated by its decision. Finally, the Court fails utterly to grapple with the cogent and persuasive criticisms that have been offered of punitive damages generally.

[Part I of Justice Rehnquist's dissenting opinion is a brief consideration of criticism of punitive damages. In light of this criticism, some states do not allow punitive damage awards, and others have required some sort of evil motive to justify punitive awards. This latter proposition is supported by footnote 3, which spends more than 120 lines analyzing nineteenth-century use of the terms "malice," "willfulness," and "wantonness." His overall point is that nineteenth-century thinkers reserved punitive awards for those who "subjectively" visited evil on others, not those whose conduct was deemed to have failed an "objective" or recklessness standard.]

[II] At bottom, this case requires the Court to decide when a particular remedy is available under § 1983. Until today, the Court has adhered, with some fidelity, to the scarcely controversial principle that its proper role in interpreting § 1983 is determining what the 42d Congress intended. That § 1983 is to be interpreted according to this basic principle of statutory construction is clearly demonstrated by our many decisions relying upon the plain language of the section. The Court's opinion purports to pursue an inquiry into legislative intent, yet relies heavily upon state court decisions decided well after the 42d Congress adjourned. I find these cases unilluminating, at least in part because I am unprepared to attribute to the 42d Congress the truly extraordinary foresight that the Court seems to think it had. The reason our earlier decisions interpreting § 1983 have relied upon common law decisions is simple: members of the 42d Congress were lawyers, familiar with the law of their time. In resolving ambiguities in the enactments of that Congress, as with other Congresses, it is useful to consider the legal principles and rules that shaped the thinking of its Members. The decisions of state courts decided well after 1871, while of some academic interest, are largely irrelevant to what Members of the 42d Congress intended by way of a standard for punitive damages.

In an apparent attempt to justify its novel approach to discerning the intent of a body that deliberated more than a century ago, the Court makes passing reference to our decisions relating to common law immunities under § 1983. These decisions provide no support for the Court's analysis, since they all plainly evidence an attempt to discern the intent of the 42d Congress, albeit indirectly, by reference to the common law principles known to members of that body. * * * More recently, in *City of Newport v. Fact Concerts, Inc.*, 453 U.S. 247, 258 (1981), we said:

> It is by now well settled that the tort liability created by § 1983 cannot be understood in a historical vacuum. * * * One important assumption underlying the Court's decisions in this area is that members of the 42d Congress were familiar with common-law principles, including defenses previously recognized in ordinary tort litigation, and that they likely intended these common-law principles to obtain, absent specific provisions to the contrary.

Likewise, our other decisions with respect to common law immunities under § 1983 clearly reveal that our consideration of state common law rules is only a device to facilitate determination of Congressional intent. Decisions from the 1970s, relied on by the Court, are almost completely irrelevant to this inquiry into legislative intent.

[III] The Court also purports to rely on decisions, handed down in the second half of the last century by this Court, in drawing up its rule that mere recklessness will support an award of punitive damages. In fact, these decisions unambiguously support an actual malice standard. The Court rests primarily on *Philadelphia, W. & B.R. Co. v. Quigley*, 62 U.S. (21 How.) 202 (1859), a diversity tort action against a railroad. There, we initially observed that in "certain actions of tort," punitive damages might be awarded, and then described those actions as "[w]henever the injury complained of has been inflicted maliciously or wantonly, and with circumstances of contumely or indignity." *Id.* at 214. * * * [I]t was relatively clear at the time that "malice" required a showing of actual ill will or intent to injure. Perhaps foreseeing future efforts to expand the rule, however, we hastened to specify the type of malice that would warrant punitive damages: "the malice spoken of in this rule is not merely the doing of an unlawful or injurious act. The word implies that the act complained of *was conceived in the spirit of mischief, or of criminal indifference to civil obligations.*" It would have been difficult to have more clearly expressed the "actual malice" standard. We explicitly rejected an "implied malice" formulation, and then mandated inquiry into the "spirit" in which a defendant's act was "conceived."

[Justice Rehnquist analyzed other nineteenth century Supreme Court decisions consistent with his reading of *Quigley*.] In *Lake Shore & Michigan Southern Railway Co. v. Prentice*, 147 U.S. 101 (1893), the Court considered whether punitive damages were properly awarded against a railroad in a diversity action. The Court noted that the law on the subject was "well-settled," and paraphrased the *Quigley* standard: The jury may award punitive damages "if the defendant has acted wantonly, or oppressively, or with such malice as implies a spirit of mischief or criminal indifference to civil obligations." Then, * * * the Court explained this formulation, observing that a "*guilty intention* on the part of the defendant is *required* in order to charge him with exemplary or punitive damages." *Ibid.* (emphasis added). * * *

In addition, the decisions rendered by state courts in the years preceding and immediately following the enactment of § 1983 attest to the fact that a solid majority of jurisdictions took the view that the standard for an award of punitive damages included a requirement of ill will. To be sure, a few jurisdictions followed a broader standard; a careful review of the decisions at the time uncovers a number of decisions that contain some reference to "recklessness." And equally clearly, in more recent years many courts have adopted a standard including "recklessness" as the minimal degree of culpability warranting punitive damages.

Most clear of all, however, is the fact that at about the time § 1983 was enacted a considerable number of the 37 States then belonging to the Union required some showing of wrongful intent before punitive damages could be awarded.[12] As the cases set out in the margin reveal, it is but a statement of the obvious that "evil motive" was the general standard for punitive damages in many states at the time of the 42d Congress. * * *

[IV] Even apart from this historical background, I am persuaded by a variety of additional factors that the 42d Congress intended a "wrongful intent" requirement. As mentioned above, punitive damages are not, and never have been, a favored remedy. In determining whether Congress, not bound by *stare decisis*, would have embraced this often-condemned doctrine, it is worth considering the judgment of one of the most respected commentators in the field regarding the desirability of a legislatively enacted punitive damages remedy: "It is probable that, in the framing of a model code of damages today for use in a country unhampered by legal tradition, the doctrine of exemplary damages would find no place." C. McCormick, *Damages* 276 (1935).

In deciding whether Congress heeded such advice, it is useful to consider the language of § 1983 itself—which should, of course, be the starting point for any inquiry into legislative intent. Section 1983 provides:

---

[12]　See, e.g., *Roberts v. Hiem*, 27 Ala. 678, 683 (1855) ("the law allows [punitive damages] whenever the trespass is committed in a rude, aggravating, or insulting manner, as malice may be inferred from these circumstances"); [citations to 76 state cases followed, most with quotations to illustrate Justice Rehnquist's position].

The Court's treatment of the law prevailing in 1871 relies principally upon state-court decisions from the 1880's and 1890's. These cases are admittedly somewhat more relevant to what the 42d Congress intended than the 20th-century cases cited by the Court; particularly if they explain prior decisions, these cases may reflect a well-settled understanding in a particular jurisdiction of the law regarding punitive damages. Yet, decisions handed down well after 1871 are considerably *less* probative of legislative intent than decisions rendered before or shortly subsequent to the enactment of § 1983: it requires no detailed discussion to demonstrate that a member of the 42d Congress would have been more influenced by a decision from 1870 than by one from the 1890's. Accordingly, the bulk of the cases cited by the Court must be ignored; they simply illustrate the historical shift in legal doctrine, pointed out in text, from an actual-intent standard to a recklessness standard. If the Court is serious in its attention to 19th-century law, analysis must focus on the common law as it stood at the time of the 42d Congress. Here, notwithstanding the Court's numerous attempts to explain why decisions do not mean what they plainly say, it remains clear that in a majority of jurisdictions, actual malice was required in order to recover punitive damages.

"Every person who, under color of any statute, ordinance, regulation, custom, or usage of any State * * * subjects, or causes to be subjected, any citizen of the United States or other person within the jurisdiction thereof to the deprivation of any rights, privileges, or immunities secured by the Constitution and laws, shall be liable to the party *injured* in an action at law, suit in equity, or other proper proceeding *for redress*." (emphasis added).

Plainly, the statutory language itself provides absolutely no support for the cause of action for punitive damages that the Court reads into the provision. Indeed, it merely creates "liab[ility] to the party injured * * * for redress." "Redress" means "[r]eparation of, satisfaction or compensation for, a wrong sustained or the loss resulting from this." 8 Oxford English Dictionary 310 (1933). And, as the Court concedes, punitive damages are not "reparation" or "compensation"; their very purpose is to punish, not to compensate. If Congress meant to create a right to recover punitive damages, then it chose singularly inappropriate words: both the reference to injured parties and to redress suggests compensation, and not punishment.

Other statutes roughly contemporaneous with § 1983 illustrate that if Congress wanted to subject persons to a punitive damages remedy, it did so explicitly. For example, in § 59, 16 Stat. 207, Congress created express punitive damage remedies for various types of commercial misconduct. Likewise, the False Claims Act, § 15, 12 Stat. 698, provided a civil remedy of double damages and a $2,000 civil forfeiture penalty for certain misstatements to the Government. As one Court of Appeals has remarked, "Where Congress has intended [to create a right to punitive damages] it has found no difficulty in using language appropriate to that end." *United Mine Workers v. Patton*, 211 F.2d 742, 749 (4th Cir. 1954). And yet, in § 1983 one searches in vain for some hint of such a remedy.

In the light of the foregoing indications, it is accurate to say that the foundation upon which the right to punitive damages under § 1983 rests is precarious, at the best. * * *

JUSTICE O'CONNOR, dissenting.

[Justice O'Connor found the analysis of the nineteenth century common law by the Court and Justice Rehnquist to be "exhaustive, but ultimately unilluminating" because in her view there was no generally prevailing rule of common law in 1871. Instead, Justice O'Connor relied on the policies underlying § 1983, and concluded that awards of compensatory damages and attorney's fees already provide significant deterrence; accordingly there was not an adequate policy basis for allowing punitive damages as an additional basis for deterring reckless conduct by public officials.]

NOTES ON THE EVOLVING COMMON LAW AS A SOURCE FOR CONSTRUING STATUTES

1.   *Interpretation and the Common Law.* Justice Brennan's opinion for the Court argues that the common law in 1871 supports punitive damages for reckless misconduct. Perhaps, but would the common law have permitted a prisoner to obtain such damages from his or her jailer in the circumstances of *Smith v. Wade*? Certainly not! See, e.g., *Moxley v. Roberts*, 43 S.W. 482 (Ky. 1897) (jailer not liable for beating of one prisoner by

another unless he actually knew of the beating and failed to stop it); *Williams v. Adams*, 85 Mass. (3 Allen) 171 (1861). Why didn't Justice Brennan just rely on the modern common law, which does support his position?

Contrary to Justice Rehnquist's dissent, the Supreme Court sometimes looks to modern common law to fill in the gaps of § 1983. See *Imbler v. Pachtman*, 424 U.S. 409, 421–22 (1976) (rule of prosecutorial immunity, which was first recognized 25 years after § 1983 was enacted); *Carey v. Piphus*, 435 U.S. 247, 257–58 (1978) (modern law is the starting point for determining which injuries are to be compensated under § 1983). Do you suppose the Congress that adopted § 1983 in 1871 intended that the common law of that era was to supply binding answers to questions left open by the statute? Do you think that the Congress intended courts to develop § 1983 law over time by reference to contemporary developments, and thus that § 1983 might mean one thing in 1871 and quite another thing today?

Note this puzzle: Justices Brennan and Rehnquist looked at the same historical evidence yet came up with diametrically opposed conclusions about what the "common law" was in 1871. The initial, and cynical, impulse is to think that they were just manipulating the evidence to support the result each wanted. A less cynical view is that, in this case, each Justice was an amateur historian, but like professional historians the Justices had to figure out which evidence was important, what to make of conflicting signals, and how to assimilate the evidence into an account. In this complicated task, isn't the perspective of the interpreter going to make a difference? Professional historians recognize this. Shouldn't the Justices? Indeed, this is a point suggested by Justice O'Connor's dissent.

2. *Common Law Statutes*. Going one step beyond Justice Brennan's approach, Judge Richard Posner has argued in *The Federal Courts: Crisis and Reform* (1985) that some statutes, such as § 1983 and the Sherman Act, are essentially "common law statutes." That is, briefly phrased statutes addressing an important societal problem may be the occasion for judicial evolution in the common law tradition, especially if the legislature does not amend the statutes. In legal process argot, courts are institutionally competent to fill in the gaps to a statutory scheme when Congress essentially leaves the statute to judicial elaboration. Does this suggest a defense of Justice Brennan's majority opinion?

Classic instances in which the Supreme Court has interpreted a simple and vague federal statute as evidencing a congressional intent that the federal courts are to resolve open questions by use of an essentially common law method include the antitrust prohibitions of the Sherman Act and § 301 of the Taft-Hartley Act, which gives federal district courts jurisdiction to hear suits for violation of collective bargaining agreements. See, e.g., *Textile Workers Union v. Lincoln Mills*, 353 U.S. 448 (1957) ("federal common law" under § 301). More recently, the Foreign Sovereign Immunities Act of 1976 (FSIA), 28 U.S.C. §§ 1331, 1602–1611 et al., sets forth guidelines for federal and state court treatment of the sovereign immunity defense by foreign states. The main exception to immunity is the "commercial activity" exception, *id.* § 1605(a)(2), but the Act gives no precise definition of commercial activity. "The courts would have a great deal of latitude in determining what is a 'commercial activity' for purposes of this bill," said the House Report, and courts have taken that as a charter to apply the most current common law approaches to the issue. For a recent example applying common law property concepts to fill out the details of the FSIA, see *Permanent Mission of India to the United Nations v. City of New York*, 551 U.S. 193 (2007).

One corollary of the common law statute idea is that Supreme Court precedents interpreting them ought to have the normal stare decisis effect of common law precedents—and not the super-strong presumption of correctness that accompanies other statutory precedents (Chapter 5, § 2(B)). See *Leegin Creative Leather Prods., Inc. v. PSKS, Inc.*, 551 U.S. 877 (2007) (precisely this justification for overruling a Sherman Act precedent); *State Oil Co. v. Khan*, 522 U.S. 3 (1997) (same); William Eskridge Jr., *Overruling Statutory Precedents*, 76 Geo. L.J. 1361 (1988). A number of Supreme Court decisions have overruled previous constructions of Section 1983, essentially for common law reasons. E.g., *Monell v. Dep't of Soc. Servs.*, 436 U.S. 658 (1978). It is very likely that a Roberts Court majority would disagree with the *Smith v. Wade* approach to punitive damages. Should the Court feel free to overrule *Smith*? Are there reasons to exercise caution? Jot down your thoughts and read the next note.

3. *More Recent Statutory Treatment of Punitive Damages in Civil Rights Cases.* The Civil Rights Act of 1991 amended Title VII to permit awards of punitive damages in cases of intentional discrimination. New 42 U.S.C. § 1981a(b)(1) allows such an award if the complainant can show that defendant engaged in such discrimination "with malice or with reckless indifference to the federally protected rights of an aggrieved individual." Carole Kolstad sues her employer for allegedly passing over her for promotion on the basis of her sex. She seeks punitive damages because the decisionmaker not only manipulated the rules to deny her the promotion, but also made repeated derogatory references to women. The lower courts refuse Kolstad a charge to the jury for punitive damages; they rule that, to satisfy § 1981a(b)(1), the complainant must show "egregious" misconduct beyond that which would justify a finding of intentional discrimination.

Following *Smith v. Wade*, the Supreme Court reversed the lower courts and interpreted the 1991 Act to allow punitive damages for reckless as well as egregious conduct. See *Kolstad v. Am. Dental Ass'n*, 527 U.S. 526 (1999). Should *Kolstad* augur against overruling *Smith v. Wade* in section 1983 cases—or does it now provide an *additional reason* to overrule? Under the whole code rule of meaningful variation (*Casey*, § 2(C) of chapter 6), when Congress wants liberal punitive damage awards in civil rights statutes, it explicitly provides for such damages (the 1991 Act). Because § 1983 says nothing about punitive damages, should they be available at all?

How should the Court approach the separate issue of when an employer should be liable in punitive damages for unauthorized conduct on the part of its supervisors? What relevance should the common law of agency have in this inquiry? See *Burlington Indus., Inc. v. Ellerth*, 524 U.S. 642 (1998) (standards for employer liability for hostile work environment and quid pro quo sexual harassment by supervisors).

4. *The Remedial Canon Versus the Derogation Canon.* In *CSX Transportation, Inc. v. McBride*, 564 U.S. 685 (2011), the Justices divided on whether the tort principle of proximate cause applies to suits brought by railroad employees against their employers for negligence under the Federal Employers Liability Act (FELA). Justice Ginsburg, writing for the Court (joined by Justices Thomas, Breyer, Sotomayor, and Kagan), reasoned that because FELA sought to achieve broad remedial goals, the Court had long applied a relaxed standard of causation under which it would be inappropriate to import the common-law requirement of proximate cause. In dissent, Chief Justice Roberts (joined by Justices Scalia, Kennedy, and Alito) contended that the Court should apply

proximate cause to FELA because the statute does not expressly abrogate the common law principle although it does abrogate several other common law rules.

Can the remedial canon be reconciled in some neutral way with the presumption favoring retention of longstanding common law principles? Or do they simply create conflicts that enable judges to cloak their own policy preferences? Should courts rely on either canonical presumption if the text or legislative history indicates that Congress intended a statute to be read broadly or narrowly?

ANOTHER PROBLEM ON THE COMMON LAW AND STATUTES

Problem 7-2. A federal statute prohibits the knowing transportation of "falsely made, forged, altered or counterfeited securities" in interstate commerce. Brook and Crook purchased used cars in Pennsylvania, rolled back the cars' odometers, and fraudulently altered the Pennsylvania titles to reflect the reduced mileage. They then sent the titles to Frook, a Virginia resident. Frook took the titles to Virginia authorities, represented that he owned the cars, and was issued Virginia titles to the cars with the false mileage figures. Frook then sent the Virginia titles to Hook, a Maryland resident, where they were used to sell the cars to unsuspecting buyers. Has Hook violated the statute? Hook says "no," arguing that the Virginia titles he received were not "falsely made" by the Virginia authorities, who had no reason to suspect the accuracy of the information contained in the titles they issued. Hook also argues that, at common law, "falsely made" meant "forgery," and that a document genuinely issued by an appropriate official is therefore not "falsely made." Do you agree? What if a sizable minority of the common law decisions existing at the time the statute was enacted treated such a document as "forged" or "falsely made"? Should the rule of lenity provide an easy way out of this problem? See *Moskal v. United States*, 498 U.S. 103 (1990).

2. LEGISLATIVE BACKGROUND (HISTORY)

Statutory history is, in a broad sense, the entire circumstances of a statute's creation and evolution, a point illustrated by the materials in the first subpart that follows. The formal history of a statute's evolution is widely considered relevant to statutory interpretation, even in jurisdictions whose courts will not examine legislative debates. See, e.g., Donald Gifford, *Statutory Interpretation* 91–95 (1990) (Australia). The same is true for the United States, whose courts do generally examine legislative documents and debates. Thus, the Court in *United States v. Wells*, 519 U.S. 482 (1997), interpreted 18 U.S.C. § 1014, criminalizing false statements to federally insured banks, not to have a materiality requirement. Justice Souter's opinion for the Court relied on the <u>formal history of federal criminal provisions regarding such statements.</u> Section 1014 was a synthesis of thirteen different provisions, at least ten of which had no materiality requirements at the time. This background suggested that Congress did not expect § 1014 to have a materiality requirement.

In this country, the term *legislative history* is mostly used in a narrower sense, to refer to the internal legislative pre-history of a statute—the internal institutional progress of a bill to enactment and the deliberation accompanying that progress.[362]

---

[362]   Otto Hetzel, Michael Libonati & Robert Williams, *Legislative Law and Process* 589 (3d ed. 2001), gives an excellent checklist of the materials that will constitute the "legislative history" of a law:

The record of that journey may be quite voluminous and often contains statements by all sorts of people—legislators, bureaucrats, citizens, experts—which support one or another interpretation of the statute. A preliminary issue is how to carry out legal research that will reveal all the components of a statute's legislative history.[363] Once the material is identified, the question turns to what stuff in this internal legislative history "counts" toward interpreting the statute, and how much weight each relevant component should receive. Four parts of this Section (B–E) will explore judicial use (or misuse) of statements made in committee reports, statements in hearings and floor debates, statements by sponsors, and post-enactment statements by legislators and committees. The last part (F) will ask whether interpretive meaning can be derived from things that are *not* said or done in the legislature.

As you read the following materials, consider the suggestion of Judge Patricia Wald, in *Some Observations on the Use of Legislative History in the 1981 Supreme Court Term*, 68 Iowa L. Rev. 195, 214 (1983), that "consistent and uniform rules for statutory construction and use of legislative materials are not being followed today. It sometimes seems that citing legislative history is still, as my late colleague Harold Leventhal once observed, akin to 'looking over a crowd and picking out your friends.' "[364]

---

1. Floor debate.
2. Planned colloquy.
3. Prepared statements on submission of a bill, in committee hearings and at the time of floor debates.
4. Revised and amended statements.
5. Statements in committees by the relevant executive branch administrators.
6. Committee reports.
7. Transcripts of discussions at committee hearings.
8. Statements and submissions by interested persons, both local or state government and private parties.
9. Committee debates on "mark-up" of bills.
10. Conference committee reports.
11. Analysis of bills by legislative counsel.
12. Analysis of bills by relevant executive departments.
13. Amendments accepted or rejected.
14. Actions on and discussions about separate bills on the same topic, offered by each house, or in contrast to a similar composite bill.
15. Executive branch messages and proposals whether from the President, cabinet secretaries or from independent agencies.
16. Prior relevant administrative action or judicial decisions, with or without congressional acknowledgment.
17. Other subsequent or prior legislation, especially conflicting acts.
18. Recorded votes.
19. The status of the person speaking, *i.e.*, a sponsor, committee chairman, floor leader, etc.
20. Actions taken and reports, hearings and debates on prior related legislation.

[363] Many law schools offer advanced legal research courses that deal with legislative history and include excellent reference materials.

[364] Judge Leventhal's quip, in somewhat different form, has now made its way into the Supreme Court reports. Justice Scalia has offered it as a justification for his new textualism: "Judge Harold Leventhal used to describe the use of legislative history as the equivalent of entering a crowded cocktail party and looking over the heads of the guests for one's friends." *Conroy v. Aniskoff*, 507 U.S. 511, 519 (1993) (Scalia, J., concurring in the judgment).

A. CIRCUMSTANCES SURROUNDING THE INTRODUCTION AND CONSIDERATION OF LEGISLATION

STATUTORY PREFACE TO THE *LEO SHEEP* CASE

An Act to aid in the Construction of a Railroad and Telegraph Line from the Missouri River to the Pacific Ocean, and to secure to the Government the Use of the same for Postal, Military, and Other Purposes (Union Pacific Act) of 1862, § 3, 12 Stat. 489.

Section 3.   And be it further enacted, That there be, and is hereby, granted to the said company, for the purpose of aiding in the construction, of said railroad and telegraph line, and to secure the safe and speedy transportation of the mails, troops, munitions of war, and public stores thereon, every alternate section of public land, designated by odd numbers, to the amount of five alternate sections per mile on each side of said railroad, on the line thereof, and within the limits of ten miles on each side of said railroad, not sold, reserved, or otherwise disposed of by the United States, and to which a preemption or homestead claim may not have attached, at the time the line of said road is definitely fixed: Provided, That all mineral lands shall be excepted from the operation of this act; but where the same shall contain timber, the timber thereon is hereby granted to said company. And all such lands, so granted by this section, which shall not be sold or disposed of by said company within three years after the entire road shall have been completed, shall be subject to settlement and preemption, like other lands, at a price not exceeding one dollar and twenty-five cents per acre, to be paid to said company.

LEO SHEEP CO. V. UNITED STATES
Supreme Court of the United States, 1979.
440 U.S. 668, 99 S.Ct. 1403, 59 L.Ed.2d 677.

MR. JUSTICE REHNQUIST delivered the opinion of the Court.

This is one of those rare cases evoking episodes in this country's history that, if not forgotten, are remembered as dry facts and not as adventure. Admittedly the issue is mundane: Whether the Government has an implied easement to build a road across land that was originally granted to the Union Pacific Railroad under the Union Pacific Act of 1862—a grant that was part of a governmental scheme to subsidize the construction of the transcontinental railroad. But that issue is posed against the backdrop of a fascinating chapter in our history. As this Court noted in another case involving the Union Pacific Railroad, "courts, in construing a statute, may with propriety recur to the history of the times when it was passed; and this is frequently necessary, in order to ascertain the reason as well as the meaning of particular provisions in it." *United States v. Union Pac. R. Co.*, 91 U.S. 72, 79 (1875). In this spirit we relate the events underlying passage of the Union Pacific Act of 1862.

[I] The early 19th century—from the Louisiana Purchase in 1803 to the Gadsden Purchase in 1853—saw the acquisition of the territory we now regard as the American West. During those years, however, the area remained a largely untapped resource, for the settlers on the eastern seaboard of the United States did not keep pace with the rapidly expanding western frontier. A vaguely delineated area forbiddingly referred to as the "Great American Desert" can be found on more than one map published before 1850, embracing much of the United States' territory west of the Missouri River. As late as 1860, for example, the entire population of the State of Nebraska was less than 30,000 persons, which represented one person for every five square miles of land area within the State.

With the discovery of gold at Sutter's Mill in California in 1848, the California gold rush began and with it a sharp increase in settlement of the West. Those in the East with visions of instant wealth, however, confronted the unenviable choice among an arduous 4-month overland trek, risking yellow fever on a 35-day voyage via the Isthmus of Panama, and a better than 4-month voyage around Cape Horn. They obviously yearned for another alternative, and interest focused on the transcontinental railroad.

The idea of a transcontinental railroad predated the California gold rush. From the time that Asa Whitney had proposed a relatively practical plan for its construction in 1844, it had, in the words of one of this century's leading historians of the era, "engaged the eager attention of promoters and politicians until dozens of schemes were in the air." The building of the railroad was not to be the unalloyed product of the free-enterprise system. There was indeed the inspiration of men like Thomas Durant and Leland Stanford and the perspiration of a generation of immigrants, but animating it all was the desire of the Federal Government that the West be settled. This desire was intensified by the need to provide a logistical link with California in the heat of the Civil War. That the venture was much too risky and much too expensive for private capital alone was evident in the years of fruitless exhortation; private investors would not move without tangible governmental inducement.

In the mid-19th century there was serious disagreement as to the forms that inducement could take. Mr. Justice Story, in his Commentaries on the Constitution, described one extant school of thought which argued that "internal improvements," such as railroads, were not within the enumerated constitutional powers of Congress. Under such a theory, the direct subsidy of a transcontinental railroad was constitutionally suspect—an uneasiness aggravated by President Andrew Jackson's 1830 veto of a bill appropriating funds to construct a road from Maysville to Lexington within the State of Kentucky.

The response to this constitutional "gray" area, and source of political controversy, was the "checkerboard" land-grant scheme. The Union Pacific Act of 1862 granted public land to the Union Pacific Railroad for each mile of track that it laid. Land surrounding the railway right-of-way was divided into "checkerboard" blocks. Odd-numbered lots were granted to the Union Pacific; even-numbered lots were reserved by the Government. As a result, Union Pacific land in the area of the right-of-way was usually surrounded by public land, and vice versa. The historical explanation for this peculiar disposition is that it was apparently an attempt to disarm the "internal improvement" opponents by establishing a grant scheme with "demonstrable" benefits. As one historian notes in describing an 1827 federal land grant intended to facilitate private construction of a road between Columbus and Sandusky, Ohio:

> "Though awkwardly stated, and not fully developed in the Act of 1827, this was the beginning of a practice to be followed in most future instances of granting land for the construction of specific internal improvements: donating alternate sections or one half of the land within a strip along the line of the project and reserving the other half for sale. . . . In later donations the price of the reserved sections was doubled so that it could be argued, as the *Congressional Globe* shows *ad infinitum*, that by giving half the land away and thereby making possible construction of the road, canal, or railroad, the government would recover from the reserved sections as much as it would have received from the whole." P. Gates, *History of Public Land Law Development* 345–346 (1968).

In 1850 this technique was first explicitly employed for the subsidization of a railroad when the Illinois delegation in Congress, which included Stephen A. Douglas, secured the enactment of a bill that granted public lands to aid the construction of the Illinois Central Railroad. The Illinois Central and proposed connecting lines to the south were granted nearly three million acres along rights of way through Illinois, Mississippi, and Alabama, and by the end of 1854 the main line of the Illinois Central from Chicago to Cairo, Ill., had been put into operation. Before this line was constructed, public lands had gone begging at the Government's minimum price; within a few years after its completion, the railroad had disposed of more than one million acres and was rapidly selling more at prices far above those at which land had been originally offered by the Government.

The "internal improvements" theory was not the only obstacle to a transcontinental railroad. In 1853 Congress had appropriated moneys and authorized Secretary of War Jefferson Davis to undertake surveys of various proposed routes for a transcontinental railroad. Congress was badly split along sectional lines on the appropriate location of the route—so badly split that Stephen A. Douglas, now a Senator from Illinois, in 1854 suggested the construction of a northern, central, and southern route, each with connecting branches in the East. That proposal, however, did not break the impasse.

The necessary impetus was provided by the Civil War. Senators and Representatives from those States which seceded from the Union were no longer present in Congress, and therefore the sectional overtones of the dispute as to routes largely disappeared. Although there were no major engagements during the Civil War in the area between the Missouri River and the west coast which would be covered by any transcontinental railroad, there were two minor engagements which doubtless made some impression upon Congress of the necessity for being able to transport readily men and materials into that area for military purposes. * * *

These engagements gave some immediacy to the comments of Congressman Edwards of New Hampshire during the debate on the Pacific Railroad bill:

> "If this Union is to be preserved, if we are successfully to combat the difficulties around us, if we are to crush out this rebellion against the lawful authority of the Government, and are to have an entire restoration, it

becomes us, with statesmanlike prudence and sagacity, to look carefully into the future, and to guard in advance against all possible considerations which may threaten the dismemberment of the country hereafter." Cong. Globe, 37th Cong., 2d Sess., 1703 (1862).

As is often the case, war spurs technological development, and Congress enacted the Union Pacific Act in May 1862. Perhaps not coincidentally, the Homestead Act was passed the same month.

The Union Pacific Act specified a route west from the 100th meridian, between a site in the Platte River Valley near the cities of Kearney and North Platte, Neb., to California. The original plan was for five eastern terminals located at various points on or near the Missouri River; but in fact Omaha was the only terminal built according to the plan.

The land grants made by the Union Pacific Act included all the odd-numbered lots within 10 miles on either side of the track. When the Union Pacific's original subscription drive for private investment proved a failure, the land grant was doubled by extending the checkerboard grants to 20 miles on either side of the track. Private investment was still sluggish, and construction did not begin until July 1865, three months after the cessation of Civil War hostilities.[13] Thus began a race with the Central Pacific Railroad, which was laying track eastward from Sacramento, for the Government land grants which went with each mile of track laid. The race culminated in the driving of the golden spike at Promontory, Utah, on May 10, 1869.

[II] This case is the modern legacy of these early grants. Petitioners, the Leo Sheep Co. and the Palm Livestock Co., are the Union Pacific Railroad's successors in fee to specific odd-numbered sections of land in Carbon County, Wyo. These sections lie to the east and south of the Seminoe Reservoir, an area that is used by the public for fishing and hunting. Because of the checkerboard configuration, it is physically impossible to enter the Seminoe Reservoir sector from this direction without some minimum physical intrusion upon private land. In the years immediately preceding this litigation, the Government had received complaints that private owners were denying access over their lands to the reservoir area or requiring the payment of access fees. After negotiation with these owners failed, the Government cleared a dirt road extending from a local county road to the reservoir across both public domain

---

[13]   Construction would not have begun then without the Crédit Mobilier, a limited-liability company that was essentially owned by the promoters and investors of the Union Pacific. One of these investors, Oakes Ames, a wealthy New England shovel maker, was a substantial investor in Crédit Mobilier and also a Member of Congress. Crédit Mobilier contracted with the Union Pacific to build portions of the road, and by 1866 several individuals were large investors in both corporations. Allegations of improper use of funds and bribery of Members of the House of Representatives led to the appointment of a special congressional investigatory committee that during 1872 and 1873 looked into the affairs of Crédit Mobilier. These investigations revealed improprieties on the part of more than one Member of Congress, and the committee recommended that Ames be expelled from Congress. The investigation also touched on the career of a future President. See M. Leech & H. Brown, *The Garfield Orbit* (1978).

In 1872 the House of Representatives enacted a resolution condemning the policy of granting subsidies of public lands to railroads. Cong. Globe, 42d Cong., 2d Sess., 1585 (1872); see *Great N. R. Co. v. United States*, 315 U.S. 262, 273–274 (1942). Of course, the reaction of the public or of Congress a decade after the enactment of the Union Pacific Act to the conduct of those associated with the Union Pacific cannot influence our interpretation of that Act today.

lands and fee lands of the Leo Sheep Co. It also erected signs inviting the public to use the road as a route to the reservoir.

Petitioners initiated this action pursuant to 28 U.S.C. § 2409a to quiet title against the United States. The District Court granted petitioners' motion for summary judgment, but was reversed on appeal by the Court of Appeals for the Tenth Circuit. The latter court concluded that when Congress granted land to the Union Pacific Railroad, it implicitly reserved an easement to pass over the odd-numbered sections in order to reach the even-numbered sections that were held by the Government. Because this holding affects property rights in 150 million acres of land in the Western United States, we granted certiorari, and now reverse.

The Government does not claim that there is any express reservation of an easement in the Union Pacific Act that would authorize the construction of a public road on the Leo Sheep Co.'s property. Section 3 of the 1862 Act sets out a few specific reservations to the "checkerboard" grant. The grant was not to include land "sold, reserved, or otherwise disposed of by the United States," such as land to which there were homestead claims. Mineral lands were also excepted from the operation of the Act. Given the existence of such explicit exceptions, this Court has in the past refused to add to this list by divining some "implicit" congressional intent. In *Missouri, K. & T.R. Co. v. Kansas Pac. R. Co.*, 97 U.S. 491, 497 (1878), for example, this Court in an opinion by Mr. Justice Field noted that the intent of Congress in making the Union Pacific grants was clear: "It was to aid in the construction of the road by a gift of lands along its route, without reservation of rights, except such as were specifically mentioned * * *." The Court held that, although a railroad right-of-way under the grant may not have been located until years after 1862, by the clear terms of the Act only claims established prior to 1862 overrode the railroad grant; conflicting claims arising after that time could not be given effect. To overcome the lack of support in the Act itself, the Government here argues that the implicit reservation of the asserted easement is established by "settled rules of property law" and by the Unlawful Inclosures of Public Lands Act of 1885.

Where a private landowner conveys to another individual a portion of his lands in a certain area and retains the rest, it is presumed at common law that the grantor has reserved an easement to pass over the granted property if such passage is necessary to reach the retained property. These rights-of-way are referred to as "easements by necessity." There are two problems with the Government's reliance on that notion in this case. First of all, whatever right of passage a private landowner might have, it is not at all clear that it would include the right to construct a road for public access to a recreational area.[15] More importantly, the easement is not actually a matter of necessity in this case because the Government has the power of eminent

---

[15]   It is very unlikely that Congress in 1862 contemplated this type of intrusion, and it could not reasonably be maintained that failure to provide access to the public at large would render the Seminoe Reservoir land useless. Yet these are precisely the considerations that define the scope of easements by necessity. As one commentator relied on by the Government notes: "As the name implies, these easements are the product of situations where the usefulness of land is at stake. The scope of the resultant easement embodies the best judgment of the court as to what is reasonably essential to the land's use. * * * Changes in the dominant parcel's use exert some, but not a great influence, in determining the scope of such easements." 3 [R. Powell, Real Property ¶ 416 (1978).] See, *e.g.*, *Higbee Fishing Club v. Atlantic City Elec. Co.*, 79 A. 326 (1911) (footpath, not roadway, proper scope of easement where use of dominant estate as clubhouse could not have been contemplated by parties to original grant).

domain. Jurisdictions have generally seen eminent domain and easements by necessity as alternative ways to effect the same result. For example, the State of Wyoming no longer recognizes the common-law easement by necessity in cases involving landlocked estates. It provides instead for a procedure whereby the landlocked owner can have an access route condemned on his behalf upon payment of the necessary compensation to the owner of the servient estate. For similar reasons other state courts have held that the "easement by necessity" doctrine is not available to the sovereign.

The applicability of the doctrine of easement by necessity in this case is, therefore, somewhat strained, and ultimately of little significance. The pertinent inquiry in this case is the intent of Congress when it granted land to the Union Pacific in 1862. The 1862 Act specifically listed reservations to the grant, and we do not find the tenuous relevance of the common-law doctrine of ways of necessity sufficient to overcome the inference prompted by the omission of any reference to the reserved right asserted by the Government in this case. It is possible that Congress gave the problem of access little thought; but it is at least as likely that the thought which was given focused on negotiation, reciprocity considerations, and the power of eminent domain as obvious devices for ameliorating disputes.[18] So both as matter of common-law doctrine and as a matter of construing congressional intent, we are unwilling to imply rights-of-way, with the substantial impact that such implication would have on property rights granted over 100 years ago, in the absence of a stronger case for their implication than the Government makes here.

The Government would have us decide this case on the basis of the familiar canon of construction that, when grants to federal lands are at issue, any doubts "are resolved for the Government not against it." *Andrus v. Charlestone Stone Prods. Co.*, 436 U.S. 604, 617 (1978). But this Court long ago declined to apply this canon in its full vigor to grants under the railroad Acts. In 1885 this Court observed:

> "The solution of [ownership] questions [involving the railroad grants] depends, of course, upon the construction given to the acts making the grants; and they are to receive such a construction as will carry out the

---

[18]   The intimations that can be found in the Congressional Globe are that there was no commonly understood reservation by the Government of the right to enter upon granted lands and construct a public road. Representative Cradlebaugh of Nevada offered an amendment to what became the Union Pacific Act of 1862 that would have reserved the right to the public to enter granted land and prospect for valuable minerals upon the payment of adequate compensation to the owner. The proposed amendment was defeated. The only Representative other than Cradlebaugh who spoke to it, Representative Sargent of California, stated:

"The amendment of the gentleman proposes to allow the public to enter upon the lands of any man, whether they be mineral lands or not, and prospect for gold and silver, and as compensation proposes some loose method of payment for the injuries inflicted. Now, sir, it may turn out that the man who thus commits the injuries may be utterly insolvent, not able to pay a dollar, and how is the owner of the property to be compensated for tearing down his dwellings, rooting up his orchards, and destroying his crops?" Cong. Globe, 37th Cong., 2d Sess., 1910 (1862).

In debates on an earlier Pacific Railroad bill it was explicitly suggested that there be "a reservation in every grant of land that [the Government] shall have a right to go through it, and take it at proper prices to be paid hereafter." The author of this proposal, Senator Simmons of Rhode Island, lamented the lack of such a reservation in the bill under consideration. Cong. Globe, 35th Cong., 2d Sess., 579 (1859). Apparently the intended purpose of this proposed reservation was to permit railroads to obtain rights-of-way through granted property at the Government's behest. Senator Simmons' comments are somewhat confused, but they certainly do not evince any prevailing assumption that the Government implicitly reserved a right-of-way through granted lands.

intent of Congress, however difficult it might be to give full effect to the language used if the grants were by instruments of private conveyance. To ascertain that intent we must look to the condition of the country when the acts were passed, as well as to the purpose declared on their face, and read all parts of them together." *Winona & St. Peter R. Co. v. Barney*, 113 U.S. 618, 625 (1885).

[Justice Rehnquist then discussed the Unlawful Inclosures of Public Lands Act of 1885 and concluded that it was aimed at a different sort of problem: the use of fencing arrangements by cattlemen to deprive sheepherders of access to grazing lands. The Court's opinion concluded with the observation that Congress in 1862 did not anticipate these problems.] The order of the day was the open range—barbed wire had not made its presence felt—and the type of incursions on private property necessary to reach public land was not such an interference that litigation would serve any motive other than spite. Congress obviously believed that when development came, it would occur in a parallel fashion on adjoining public and private lands and that the process of subdivision, organization of a polity, and the ordinary pressures of commercial and social intercourse would work itself into a pattern of access roads. * * * It is some testament to common sense that the present case is virtually unprecedented, and that in the 117 years since the grants were made, litigation over access questions generally has been rare.

Nonetheless, the present times are litigious ones and the 37th Congress did not anticipate our plight. Generations of land patents have issued without any express reservation of the right now claimed by the Government. Nor has a similar right been asserted before. When the Secretary of the Interior has discussed access rights, his discussion has been colored by the assumption that those rights had to be purchased. This Court has traditionally recognized the special need for certainty and predictability where land titles are concerned, and we are unwilling to upset settled expectations to accommodate some ill-defined power to construct public thoroughfares without compensation. * * *

MR. JUSTICE WHITE took no part in the consideration or decision of this case.

NOTES ON LEO SHEEP AND LEGISLATIVE CONTEXT

1. *The Sweep Versus the Reality of History.* Reading Justice Rehnquist's opinion, you can almost feel the wagon train moving you West. The first part of the opinion, the historical saga of the railroad project, strikes us as cogent and useful. The next part, the legal reasoning, strikes us as less so. The unanimous Court is obviously following the "imaginative reconstruction" approach of Judge Hand and Dean Pound—putting oneself in the mindset of the 1862 Congress (see Chapter 5, § 1). But the Court's assertion that "[i]t is possible that Congress gave the problem of access little thought" strikes us as an understatement. Is there any evidence adduced by the Court that the 1862 Congress gave *any* thought to the access issue? And if Congress had given some thought, surely it would have wanted the government to have a reasonable right of access. Is the Court's assumption credible that "the thought which was given focused on negotiation, reciprocity considerations, and the power of eminent domain" as ways of obtaining access? Congress in 1866, for example, enacted a statute giving any person free and unrestricted access over the public domain. Right of Way Act, 14 Stat. 251 (1866). If the

1862 Congress had "assumed" that it could negotiate a trade of railroad access through public lands in return for state access through the railroad's lands, why would Congress have given away that bargaining chip in 1866? Why would Congress in 1862 want to use eminent domain—paying money—for access rights that it could retain by simple statutory fiat? Would the venture capitalists (or robber barons, if you prefer) not have built the transcontinental railroad otherwise?

2. *The Flip Side of* Leo Sheep. Does the private grantee or its successor have an easement by necessity through the government's checkerboard squares? The leading discussion on this question argued that it does. Comment, *Easements by Way of Necessity Across Federal Lands*, 35 Wash. L. Rev. 105, 113–17 (1960). This remarkable student comment correctly anticipated the *Leo Sheep* result and reasoning but argued that the same result (no easement by necessity) should not occur for the converse situation. The common law objections in *Leo Sheep*—that easements by necessity are not created for recreational uses or for government entities which may obtain access through eminent domain—have no force when a private developer demands an easement through the government lands. Nor does the legislative policy argument work against the private grantee's easement, since private access would subserve the Congressional goal of developing the granted land as quickly as possible. Cf. *Utah v. Andrus*, 486 F. Supp. 995, 1002 (D. Utah 1979), *appeal dismissed per stip.*, Nos. 79–2307 & 79–2308 (10th Cir. Jan. 28 & Mar. 28, 1980) (Congress conveyed permanent rights of access to Utah when it granted school trust lands to the State as a means of generating revenue). A contrary position was taken in an Opinion by Attorney General Civiletti. 43 Op. Att'y Gen. 26 (1980). The opinion determined that easements by necessity did not run against the government, unless that was an implied term of the granting statute. "[L]and grants generally are to be strictly construed. This rule must be balanced against the conflicting rule that in some situations certain types of land grants may deserve a more liberal construction because of the circumstances surrounding passage of the statutes in question. [*Leo Sheep*.] Absent express language to the contrary, however, a grant should not be construed to include broad rights to use retained Government property, particularly in the case of gratuitous grants."

Consider this policy argument: not to infer an easement by necessity in the original grant would impel the United States and private grantees holding alternate checkerboard squares to cooperate. That is, if neither holder has an easement, each has an incentive to work out a reasonable deal with the other, or neither will be able to have meaningful access to its land. On the other hand, if the United States has no easement but the grantee does, the grantee has little incentive to reach a "fair" bargain with the United States, forcing the United States to pay a high price or go to the trouble and expense of condemning the easement through eminent domain. Once the Supreme Court has decided that the government does not have an easement, doesn't it make sense then to deny the easement for the private holders as well? (One might argue that the rule which would minimize transactions costs would be to give *both* the government and the private holders an easement, or give them both eminent domain power.)

3. *Subsequent Developments.* In any event, the context in which the *Leo Sheep* problem arose was vastly different from that in which the law was passed. A shift in statutory policy came in the late nineteenth century, to protect the nation's natural resources from the results of what was then perceived as excessively generous land grants earlier. See Roy Robbins, *Our Landed Heritage: The Public Domain, 1776–1970*, at 301–24 (1976). Thus after giving away more than 125 million acres of public land to the

railroads, Congress discontinued the land grant policy in the 1890s. See Paul Gates, *History of Public Land Law Development* (1968). And in 1891, Congress passed a law authorizing the President to reserve forest lands from the public domain (thus taking them out of the coverage of the 1866 access law), Act of March 3, 1891, ch. 561, § 24, 26 Stat. 1103 (the Forest Reserve Act), and 20 million acres were thereby reserved by Presidential proclamation in 1897. Further reservations were made throughout the twentieth century, as federal policy decisively turned toward conserving what was becoming perceived as a scarce resource. The Wilderness Act of 1964, 78 Stat. 890, codified at 16 U.S.C. §§ 1131–1136 (1988), placed even greater restrictions on certain federal lands, and this leading Act was followed in the 1970s and 1980s by more wilderness designations by Congress. In 1976, Congress repealed the access law of 1866 and replaced it with Title V of the Federal Land Policy & Management Act of 1976, 90 Stat. 2744, 2776, codified at 43 U.S.C. §§ 1761–1770 (1988), which authorizes the Department of the Interior to grant rights of access through a discretionary system. Are these subsequent statutes and federal policies relevant to the issue whether private grantees have an absolute right of access across federal checkerboard lands?

KING V. BURWELL

Supreme Court of the United States, 2015.
___ U.S. ___, 135 S.Ct 2480, 192 L.Ed.2d 483.

CHIEF JUSTICE ROBERTS delivered the opinion of the Court.

* * * [I-A] The Patient Protection and Affordable Care Act grew out of a long history of failed health insurance reform. In the 1990s, several States began experimenting with ways to expand people's access to coverage. One common approach was to impose a pair of insurance market regulations—a "guaranteed issue" requirement, which barred insurers from denying coverage to any person because of his health, and a "community rating" requirement, which barred insurers from charging a person higher premiums for the same reason. Together, those requirements were designed to ensure that anyone who wanted to buy health insurance could do so.

The guaranteed issue and community rating requirements achieved that goal, but they had an unintended consequence: They encouraged people to wait until they got sick to buy insurance. * * * This consequence—known as "adverse selection"—led to a second: Insurers were forced to increase premiums to account for the fact that, more and more, it was the sick rather than the healthy who were buying insurance. And that consequence fed back into the first: As the cost of insurance rose, even more people waited until they became ill to buy it.

This led to an economic "death spiral." As premiums rose higher and higher, and the number of people buying insurance sank lower and lower, insurers began to leave the market entirely. As a result, the number of people without insurance increased dramatically.

This cycle happened repeatedly during the 1990s. For example, in 1993, the State of Washington reformed its individual insurance market by adopting the guaranteed issue and community rating requirements. Over the next three years, premiums rose by 78 percent and the number of people enrolled fell by 25 percent.

By 1999, 17 of the State's 19 private insurers had left the market, and the remaining two had announced their intention to do so. * * * In 1996, Massachusetts adopted the guaranteed issue and community rating requirements and experienced similar results. But in 2006, Massachusetts added two more reforms: The Commonwealth required individuals to buy insurance or pay a penalty, and it gave tax credits to certain individuals to ensure that they could afford the insurance they were required to buy. The combination of these three reforms—insurance market regulations, a coverage mandate, and tax credits—reduced the uninsured rate in Massachusetts to 2.6 percent, by far the lowest in the Nation. Hearing on Examining Individual State Experiences with Health Care Reform Coverage Initiatives in the Context of National Reform before the Senate Committee on Health, Education, Labor, and Pensions, 111th Cong., 1st Sess., 9 (2009).

[I-B] The Affordable Care Act adopts a version of the three key reforms that made the Massachusetts system successful. First, the Act adopts the guaranteed issue and community rating requirements. The Act provides that "each health insurance issuer that offers health insurance coverage in the individual . . . market in a State must accept every . . . individual in the State that applies for such coverage." 42 U.S.C. § 300gg–1(a). The Act also bars insurers from charging higher premiums on the basis of a person's health. § 300gg.

Second, the Act generally requires individuals to maintain health insurance coverage or make a payment to the IRS. 26 U.S.C. § 5000A. Congress recognized that, without an incentive, "many individuals would wait to purchase health insurance until they needed care." 42 U.S.C. § 18091(2)(I). So Congress adopted a coverage requirement to "minimize this adverse selection and broaden the health insurance risk pool to include healthy individuals, which will lower health insurance premiums." Ibid. In Congress's view, that coverage requirement was "essential to creating effective health insurance markets." Ibid. Congress also provided an exemption from the coverage requirement for anyone who has to spend more than eight percent of his income on health insurance. 26 U.S.C. §§ 5000A(e)(1)(A), (e)(1)(B)(ii).

Third, the Act seeks to make insurance more affordable by giving refundable tax credits to individuals with household incomes between 100 percent and 400 percent of the federal poverty line. § 36B. Individuals who meet the Act's requirements may purchase insurance with the tax credits, which are provided in advance directly to the individual's insurer. 42 U.S.C. §§ 18081, 18082.

These three reforms are closely intertwined. [Congress found that] the guaranteed issue and community rating requirements would not work without the coverage requirement. And the coverage requirement would not work without the tax credits. The reason is that, without the tax credits, the cost of buying insurance would exceed eight percent of income for a large number of individuals, which would exempt them from the coverage requirement. Given the relationship between these three reforms, the Act provided that they should take effect on the same day—January 1, 2014. See Affordable Care Act, § 1253, redesignated § 1255, 124 Stat. 162, 895; §§ 1401(e), 1501(d), id., at 220, 249.

[I-C] In addition to those three reforms, the Act requires the creation of an "Exchange" in each State where people can shop for insurance, usually online. 42 U.S.C. § 18031(b)(1). An Exchange may be created in one of two ways. First, the Act provides that "[e]ach State shall . . . establish an American Health Benefit Exchange . . . for the State." *Ibid.* Second, if a State nonetheless chooses not to establish its own Exchange, the Act provides that the Secretary of Health and Human Services "shall . . . establish and operate such Exchange within the State." § 18041(c)(1).

The issue in this case is whether the Act's tax credits are available in States that have a Federal Exchange rather than a State Exchange. The Act initially provides that tax credits "shall be allowed" for any "applicable taxpayer." 26 U.S.C. § 36B(a). The Act then provides that the amount of the tax credit depends in part on whether the taxpayer has enrolled in an insurance plan through "an Exchange *established by the State* under section 1311 of the Act [hereinafter 42 U.S.C. § 18031]." 26 U.S.C. §§ 36B(b)–(c) (emphasis added).

The IRS addressed the availability of tax credits by promulgating a rule that made them available on both State and Federal Exchanges. 77 Fed.Reg. 30378 (2012). * * * At this point, 16 States and the District of Columbia have established their own Exchanges; the other 34 States have elected to have HHS do so.

[I-D] Petitioners are four individuals who live in Virginia, which has a Federal Exchange. They do not wish to purchase health insurance. In their view, Virginia's Exchange does not qualify as "an Exchange established by the State under [42 U.S.C. § 18031]," so they should not receive any tax credits. That would make the cost of buying insurance more than eight percent of their income, which would exempt them from the Act's coverage requirement. 26 U.S.C. § 5000A(e)(1).

Under the IRS Rule, however, Virginia's Exchange *would* qualify as "an Exchange established by the State under [42 U.S.C. § 18031]," so petitioners would receive tax credits. That would make the cost of buying insurance *less* than eight percent of petitioners' income, which would subject them to the Act's coverage requirement. The IRS Rule therefore requires petitioners to either buy health insurance they do not want, or make a payment to the IRS.

Petitioners challenged the IRS Rule in Federal District Court. The District Court dismissed the suit, holding that the Act unambiguously made tax credits available to individuals enrolled through a Federal Exchange. *King v. Sebelius,* 997 F.Supp.2d 415 (E.D.Va.2014). The Court of Appeals for the Fourth Circuit affirmed, holding that while the relevant statutory text was ambiguous, the IRS interpretation was a permissible non-arbitrary reading that warranted deference]. 759 F.3d 358 (2014). The same day that the Fourth Circuit issued its decision, the Court of Appeals for the District of Columbia Circuit vacated the IRS Rule in a different case, holding that the Act "unambiguously restricts" the tax credits to State Exchanges. *Halbig v. Burwell,* 758 F.3d 390 (2014). We granted certiorari in the present case. 574 U.S. ___ (2014).

[II] The Affordable Care Act addresses tax credits in what is now Section 36B of the Internal Revenue Code. That section provides: "In the case of an applicable taxpayer, there shall be allowed as a credit against the tax imposed by this subtitle . . . an amount equal to the premium assistance credit amount." 26 U.S.C. § 36B(a).

Section 36B then defines the term "premium assistance credit amount" as "the sum of the *premium assistance amounts* determined under paragraph (2) with respect to all *coverage months* of the taxpayer occurring during the taxable year." § 36B(b)(1) (emphasis added). Section 36B goes on to define the two italicized terms—"premium assistance amount" and "coverage month"—in part by referring to an insurance plan that is enrolled in through "an Exchange established by the State under [42 U.S.C. § 18031]." 26 U.S.C. §§ 36B(b)(2)(A), (c)(2)(A)(i). * * *

It is [ ] our task to determine the correct reading of Section 36B. If the statutory language is plain, we must enforce it according to its terms. But oftentimes the "meaning—or ambiguity—of certain words or phrases may only become evident when placed in context." *FDA v. Brown & Williamson Tobacco Corp.*, 529 U.S. 120, 132 (2000). So when deciding whether the language is plain, we must read the words "in their context and with a view to their place in the overall statutory scheme." *Id.*, at 133. Our duty, after all, is "to construe statutes, not isolated provisions." *Graham County Soil and Water Conservation Dist. v. United States ex rel. Wilson*, 559 U.S. 280, 290 (2010).

[Chief Justice Roberts first analyzed the text itself, and concluded that understood in context, the language was ambiguous. He acknowledged Petitioners' argument, based on the canon of avoiding surplusage, that the words "established by the State" would not be necessary if Congress had meant to extend tax credits to Federal as well as State exchanges. But he proceeded to explain why "rigorous application of the canon" was not appropriate.]

The Affordable Care Act contains more than a few examples of inartful drafting. (To cite just one, the Act creates three separate Section 1563s. See 124 Stat. 270, 911, 912.) Several features of the Act's passage contributed to that unfortunate reality. Congress wrote key parts of the Act behind closed doors, rather than through "the traditional legislative process." Cannan, A Legislative History of the Affordable Care Act: How Legislative Procedure Shapes Legislative History, 105 L. Lib. J. 131, 163 (2013). And Congress passed much of the Act using a complicated budgetary procedure known as "reconciliation," which limited opportunities for debate and amendment, and bypassed the Senate's normal 60-vote filibuster requirement. *Id.*, at 159–167. As a result, the Act does not reflect the type of care and deliberation that one might expect of such significant legislation. Cf. Frankfurter, Some Reflections on the Reading of Statutes, 47 Colum. L. Rev. 527, 545 (1947) (describing a cartoon "in which a senator tells his colleagues 'I admit this new bill is too complicated to understand. We'll just have to pass it to find out what it means.' ").

Anyway, we "must do our best, bearing in mind the fundamental canon of statutory construction that the words of a statute must be read in their context and with a view to their place in the overall statutory scheme." *Utility Air Regulatory Group v. EPA*, 134 S.Ct. 2427, 2441 (2014). After reading Section 36B along with other related provisions in the Act, we cannot conclude that the phrase "an Exchange established by the State under [Section 18031]" is unambiguous.

[II-B] Given that the text is ambiguous, we must turn to the broader structure of the Act to determine the meaning of Section 36B. "A provision that may seem ambiguous in isolation is often clarified by the remainder of the statutory scheme . . .

because only one of the permissible meanings produces a substantive effect that is compatible with the rest of the law." *United Sav. Assn. of Tex. v. Timbers of Inwood Forest Associates, Ltd.,* 484 U.S. 365, 371 (1988). Here, the statutory scheme compels us to reject petitioners' interpretation because it would destabilize the individual insurance market in any State with a Federal Exchange, and likely create the very "death spirals" that Congress designed the Act to avoid. See *New York State Dept. of Social Servs. v. Dublino,* 413 U.S. 405, 419–420, 93 S.Ct. 2507, 37 L.Ed.2d 688 (1973) ("We cannot interpret federal statutes to negate their own stated purposes.").[3]

As discussed above, Congress based the Affordable Care Act on three major reforms: first, the guaranteed issue and community rating requirements; second, a requirement that individuals maintain health insurance coverage or make a payment to the IRS; and third, the tax credits for individuals with household incomes between 100 percent and 400 percent of the federal poverty line. In a State that establishes its own Exchange, these three reforms work together to expand insurance coverage. The guaranteed issue and community rating requirements ensure that anyone can buy insurance; the coverage requirement creates an incentive for people to do so before they get sick; and the tax credits—it is hoped—make insurance more affordable. Together, those reforms "minimize . . . adverse selection and broaden the health insurance risk pool to include healthy individuals, which will lower health insurance premiums." 42 U.S.C. § 18091(2)(I).

Under petitioners' reading, however, the Act would operate quite differently in a State with a Federal Exchange. As they see it, one of the Act's three major reforms—the tax credits—would not apply. And a second major reform—the coverage requirement—would not apply in a meaningful way. As explained earlier, the coverage requirement applies only when the cost of buying health insurance (minus the amount of the tax credits) is less than eight percent of an individual's income. 26 U.S.C. §§ 5000A(e)(1)(A), (e)(1)(B)(ii). So without the tax credits, the coverage requirement would apply to fewer individuals. And it would be a *lot* fewer. In 2014, approximately 87 percent of people who bought insurance on a Federal Exchange did so with tax credits, and virtually all of those people would become exempt. If petitioners are right, therefore, only one of the Act's three major reforms would apply in States with a Federal Exchange.

The combination of no tax credits and an ineffective coverage requirement could well push a State's individual insurance market into a death spiral. One study predicts that premiums would increase by 47 percent and enrollment would decrease by 70 percent. E. Saltzman & C. Eibner, The Effect of Eliminating the Affordable Care Act's Tax Credits in Federally Facilitated Marketplaces (2015). Another study predicts that premiums would increase by 35 percent and enrollment would decrease by 69 percent. L. Blumberg, M. Buettgens, & J. Holahan, The Implications of a Supreme Court Finding for the Plaintiff in King vs. Burwell: 8.2 Million More

---

[3]   The dissent notes that several other provisions in the Act use the phrase "established by the State," and argues that our holding applies to each of those provisions. But "the presumption of consistent usage readily yields to context," and a statutory term may mean different things in different places. *Utility Air Regulatory Group v. EPA,* 134 S.Ct. 2427, 2441–2442 (2014). That is particularly true when, as here, "the Act is far from a *chef d'oeuvre* of legislative draftsmanship." *Ibid.* Because the other provisions cited by the dissent are not at issue here, we do not address them.

Uninsured and 35% Higher Premiums (2015). And those effects would not be limited to individuals who purchase insurance on the Exchanges. Because the Act requires insurers to treat the entire individual market as a single risk pool, 42 U.S.C. § 18032(c)(1), premiums outside the Exchange would rise along with those inside the Exchange.

It is implausible that Congress meant the Act to operate in this manner. See *National Federation of Independent Business v. Sebelius,* 132 S.Ct. 2566, 2674 (2012) (Scalia, Kennedy, Thomas, and Alito, JJ., dissenting) ("Without the federal subsidies . . . the exchanges would not operate as Congress intended and may not operate at all."). Congress made the guaranteed issue and community rating requirements applicable in every State in the Nation. But those requirements only work when combined with the coverage requirement and the tax credits. So it stands to reason that Congress meant for those provisions to apply in every State as well.

Petitioners respond that Congress was not worried about the effects of withholding tax credits from States with Federal Exchanges because "Congress evidently believed it was offering states a deal they would not refuse." Brief for Petitioners 36. Congress may have been wrong about the States' willingness to establish their own Exchanges, petitioners continue, but that does not allow this Court to rewrite the Act to fix that problem. That is particularly true, petitioners conclude, because the States likely *would* have created their own Exchanges in the absence of the IRS Rule, which eliminated any incentive that the States had to do so.

Section 18041 refutes the argument that Congress believed it was offering the States a deal they would not refuse. That section provides that, if a State elects not to establish an Exchange, the Secretary "shall . . . establish and operate such Exchange within the State." 42 U.S.C. § 18041(c)(1)(A). The whole point of that provision is to create a federal fallback in case a State chooses not to establish its own Exchange. Contrary to petitioners' argument, Congress did not believe it was offering States a deal they would not refuse—it expressly addressed what would happen if a State *did* refuse the deal.

[II-C] Finally, the structure of Section 36B itself suggests that tax credits are not limited to State Exchanges. Section 36B(a) initially provides that tax credits "shall be allowed" for any "applicable taxpayer." Section 36B(c)(1) then defines an "applicable taxpayer" as someone who (among other things) has a household income between 100 percent and 400 percent of the federal poverty line. Together, these two provisions appear to make anyone in the specified income range eligible to receive a tax credit.

According to petitioners, however, those provisions are an empty promise in States with a Federal Exchange. In their view, an applicable taxpayer in such a State would be *eligible* for a tax credit—but the *amount* of that tax credit would always be zero. And that is because—diving several layers down into the Tax Code—Section 36B says that the amount of the tax credits shall be "an amount equal to the premium assistance credit amount," § 36B(a); and then says that the term "premium assistance credit amount" means "the sum of the premium assistance amounts determined under paragraph (2) with respect to all coverage months of the taxpayer occurring during the taxable year," § 36B(b)(1); and then says that the term "premium assistance amount" is tied to the amount of the monthly premium for insurance purchased on "an Exchange established by the State under [42 U.S.C. § 18031]," § 36B(b)(2); and then says that the term "coverage month" means any month in which the taxpayer has insurance through "an Exchange established by the State under [42 U.S.C. § 18031]," § 36B(c)(2)(A)(i).

We have held that Congress "does not alter the fundamental details of a regulatory scheme in vague terms or ancillary provisions." *Whitman v. American Trucking Assns., Inc.,* 531 U.S. 457, 468 (2001). But in petitioners' view, Congress made the viability of the entire Affordable Care Act turn on the ultimate ancillary provision: a sub-sub-sub section of the Tax Code. We doubt that is what Congress meant to do. Had Congress meant to limit tax credits to State Exchanges, it likely would have done so in the definition of "applicable taxpayer" or in some other prominent manner. It would not have used such a winding path of connect-the-dots provisions about the amount of the credit.

[II-D] Petitioners' arguments about the plain meaning of Section 36B are strong. But while the meaning of the phrase "an Exchange established by the State under [42 U.S.C. § 18031]" may seem plain "when viewed in isolation," such a reading turns out to be "untenable in light of [the statute] as a whole." *Department of Revenue of Ore. v. ACF Industries, Inc.,* 510 U.S. 332, 343 (1994). In this instance, the context and structure of the Act compel us to depart from what would otherwise be the most natural reading of the pertinent statutory phrase.

Reliance on context and structure in statutory interpretation is a "subtle business, calling for great wariness lest what professes to be mere rendering becomes creation and attempted interpretation of legislation becomes legislation itself." *Palmer v. Massachusetts,* 308 U.S. 79, 83 (1939). For the reasons we have given, however, such reliance is appropriate in this case, and leads us to conclude that Section 36B allows tax credits for insurance purchased on any Exchange created under the Act. Those credits are necessary for the Federal Exchanges to function like their State Exchange counterparts, and to avoid the type of calamitous result that Congress plainly meant to avoid.

In a democracy, the power to make the law rests with those chosen by the people. Our role is more confined—"to say what the law is." *Marbury v. Madison,* 1 Cranch 137, 177 (1803). That is easier in some cases than in others. But in every case we must respect the role of the Legislature, and take care not to undo what it has done. A fair reading of legislation demands a fair understanding of the legislative plan.

Congress passed the Affordable Care Act to improve health insurance markets, not to destroy them. If at all possible, we must interpret the Act in a way that is consistent with the former, and avoids the latter. Section 36B can fairly be read consistent with what we see as Congress's plan, and that is the reading we adopt.

JUSTICE SCALIA, with whom JUSTICE THOMAS and JUSTICE ALITO join, dissenting.

[Justice Scalia began by contesting the majority's conclusion that the text was ambiguous, arguing at length why both the plain meaning of the text and its context clearly indicated that " 'Exchange established by the State' means what it looks like it means." He then addressed Chief Justice Roberts' purposes argument.]

For its next defense of the indefensible, the Court turns to the Affordable Care Act's design and purposes. As relevant here, the Act makes three major reforms. The guaranteed-issue and community-rating requirements prohibit insurers from considering a customer's health when deciding whether to sell insurance and how much to charge; its famous individual mandate requires everyone to maintain insurance coverage or to pay what the Act calls a "penalty," 26 U.S.C. § 5000A(b)(1), and what we have nonetheless called a tax, see *National Federation of Independent Business v. Sebelius,* 132 S.Ct. 2566, 2597–2598 (2012); and its tax credits help make insurance more affordable. The Court reasons that Congress intended these three reforms to "work together to expand insurance coverage"; and because the first two apply in every State, so must the third.

This reasoning suffers from no shortage of flaws. To begin with, "even the most formidable argument concerning the statute's purposes could not overcome the clarity [of] the statute's text." *Kloeckner v. Solis,* 133 S.Ct. 596, 607, n. 4 (2012). Statutory design and purpose matter only to the extent they help clarify an otherwise ambiguous provision. Could anyone maintain with a straight face that § 36B is unclear? To mention just the highlights, the Court's interpretation clashes with a statutory definition, renders words inoperative in at least seven separate provisions of the Act, overlooks the contrast between provisions that say "Exchange" and those that say "Exchange established by the State," gives the same phrase one meaning for purposes of tax credits but an entirely different meaning for other purposes, and (let us not forget) contradicts the ordinary meaning of the words Congress used. On the other side of the ledger, the Court has come up with nothing more than a general provision that turns out to be controlled by a specific one, a handful of clauses that are consistent with either understanding of establishment by the State, and a resemblance between the tax-credit provision and the rest of the Tax Code. If that is all it takes to make something ambiguous, everything is ambiguous.

Having gone wrong in consulting statutory purpose at all, the Court goes wrong again in analyzing it. The purposes of a law must be "collected chiefly from its words," not "from extrinsic circumstances." *Sturges v. Crowninshield,* 4 Wheat. 122, 202 (1819) (Marshall, C.J.). Only by concentrating on the law's terms can a judge hope to uncover the scheme *of the statute,* rather than some other scheme that the judge thinks desirable. Like it or not, the express terms of the Affordable Care Act make only two of the three reforms mentioned by the Court applicable in States that do not establish Exchanges. It is perfectly possible for them to operate independently of tax credits. The guaranteed-issue and community-rating requirements continue to ensure that insurance companies treat all customers the same no matter their health, and the individual mandate continues to encourage people to maintain coverage, lest they be "taxed."

The Court protests that without the tax credits, the number of people covered by the individual mandate shrinks, and without a broadly applicable individual mandate the guaranteed-issue and community-rating requirements "would destabilize the individual insurance market." If true, these projections would show only that the statutory scheme contains a flaw; they would not show that the statute means the opposite of what it says. Moreover, it is a flaw that appeared as well in other parts of the Act. A different title established a long-term-care insurance program with guaranteed-issue and community-rating requirements, but without an individual mandate or subsidies. §§ 8001–8002, 124 Stat. 828–847 (2010). This program never came into effect "only because Congress, in response to actuarial analyses predicting that the [program] would be fiscally unsustainable, repealed the provision in 2013." *Halbig v. Burwell,* 758 F.3d 390, 410 (DC Cir. 2014). How could the Court say that Congress would never dream of combining guaranteed-issue and community-rating requirements with a narrow individual mandate, when it combined those requirements with *no* individual mandate in the context of long-term-care insurance? * * *

Compounding its errors, the Court forgets that it is no more appropriate to consider one of a statute's purposes in isolation than it is to consider one of its words that way. No law pursues just one purpose at all costs, and no statutory scheme encompasses just one element. Most relevant here, the Affordable Care Act displays a congressional preference for state participation in the establishment of Exchanges: Each State gets the first opportunity to set up its Exchange, 42 U.S.C. § 18031(b); States that take up the opportunity receive federal funding for "activities . . . related to establishing" an Exchange, § 18031(a)(3); and the Secretary may establish an Exchange in a State only as a fallback, § 18041(c). But setting up and running an Exchange involve significant burdens—meeting strict deadlines, § 18041(b), implementing requirements related to the offering of insurance plans, § 18031(d)(4), setting up outreach programs, § 18031(i), and ensuring that the Exchange is self-sustaining by 2015, § 18031(d)(5)(A). A State would have much less reason to take on these burdens if its citizens could receive tax credits no matter who establishes its Exchange. (Now that the Internal Revenue Service has interpreted § 36B to authorize tax credits everywhere, by the way, 34 States have failed to set up their own Exchanges.) So even if making credits available on all Exchanges advances the goal of improving healthcare markets, it frustrates the goal of encouraging state involvement in the implementation of the Act. *This* is what justifies going out of our way to read "established by the State" to mean "established by the State or not established by the State"?

Worst of all for the repute of today's decision, the Court's reasoning is largely self-defeating. The Court predicts that making tax credits unavailable in States that do not set up their own Exchanges would cause disastrous economic consequences there. If that is so, however, wouldn't one expect States to react by setting up their own Exchanges? And wouldn't that outcome satisfy two of the Act's goals rather than just one: enabling the Act's reforms to work *and* promoting state involvement in the Act's implementation? The Court protests that the very existence of a federal fallback shows that Congress expected that some States might fail to set up their own Exchanges. So it does. It does not show, however, that Congress expected the number of recalcitrant States to be particularly large. The more accurate the Court's dire economic predictions, the smaller that number is likely to be. That reality destroys the Court's pretense that applying the law as written would imperil "the viability of the entire Affordable Care Act." *Ante,* at 2495. All in all, the Court's arguments about the law's purpose and design are no more convincing than its arguments about context.

[IV] Perhaps sensing the dismal failure of its efforts to show that "established by the State" means "established by the State or the Federal Government," the Court tries to palm off the pertinent statutory phrase as "inartful drafting." This Court, however, has no free-floating power "to rescue Congress from its drafting errors." *Lamie v. United States Trustee,* 540 U.S. 526, 542 (2004). Only when it is patently obvious to a reasonable reader that a drafting mistake has occurred may a court correct the mistake. The occurrence of a misprint may be apparent from the face of the law, as it is where the Act "creates three separate Section 1563s." But the Court does not pretend that there is any such indication of a drafting error on the face of § 36B. The occurrence of a misprint may also be apparent because a provision decrees an absurd result—a consequence "so monstrous, that all mankind would, without hesitation, unite in rejecting the application." *Sturges,* 4 Wheat., at 203. But § 36B does not come remotely close to satisfying that demanding standard. It is entirely plausible that tax credits were restricted to state Exchanges deliberately—for example, in order to encourage States to establish their own Exchanges. We therefore have no authority to dismiss the terms of the law as a drafting fumble. * * * If there was a mistake here, context suggests it was a substantive mistake in designing this part of the law, not a technical mistake in transcribing it.

[V] The Court's decision reflects the philosophy that judges should endure whatever interpretive distortions it takes in order to correct a supposed flaw in the statutory machinery. That philosophy ignores the American people's decision to give *Congress* "[a]ll legislative Powers" enumerated in the Constitution. Art. I, § 1. They made Congress, not this Court, responsible for both making laws and mending them. This Court holds only the judicial power—the power to pronounce the law as Congress has enacted it. We lack the prerogative to repair laws that do not work out in practice, just as the people lack the ability to throw us out of office if they dislike the solutions we concoct. We must always remember, therefore, that "[o]ur task is to apply the text, not to improve upon it." *Pavelic & LeFlore v. Marvel Entertainment Group, Div. of Cadence Industries Corp.,* 493 U.S. 120, 126 (1989). * * *

Even less defensible, if possible, is the Court's claim that its interpretive approach is justified because this Act "does not reflect the type of care and deliberation that one might expect of such significant legislation." It is not our place to judge the quality of the care and deliberation that went into this or any other law. A law enacted by voice vote with no deliberation whatever is fully as binding upon us as one enacted after years of study, months of committee hearings, and weeks of debate. Much less is it our place to make everything come out right when Congress does not do its job properly. It is up to Congress to design its laws with care, and it is up to the people to hold them to account if they fail to carry out that responsibility.

Rather than rewriting the law under the pretense of interpreting it, the Court should have left it to Congress to decide what to do about the Act's limitation of tax credits to state Exchanges. If Congress values above everything else the Act's applicability across the country, it could make tax credits available in every Exchange. If it prizes state involvement in the Act's implementation, it could continue to limit tax credits to state Exchanges while taking other steps to mitigate the economic consequences predicted by the Court. If Congress wants to accommodate both goals, it could make tax credits available everywhere while offering new incentives for States to set up their own Exchanges. And if Congress thinks that the present design of the Act works well enough, it could do nothing. Congress could also do something else altogether, entirely abandoning the structure of the Affordable Care Act. The Court's insistence on making a choice that should be made by Congress both aggrandizes judicial power and encourages congressional lassitude. * * *

NOTES ON KING V. BURWELL

1.   *Context and the Impending Health Insurance Death Spiral.* The Affordable Care Act was signed into law on March 23, 2010. By the time *King* reached the Supreme Court in 2015, millions of Americans had already enrolled in health care plans under the Act, and there were numerous media predictions of serious consequences for the affordability and accessibility of health care nationwide if the Court were to find in favor of the Act's challengers. Studies indicated that over six million Americans were at risk of losing their tax credits, a result which would in turn drastically reduce the number of Americans enrolled in Affordable Care Act exchanges and vastly increase the cost of premiums for those remaining. As Chief Justice Roberts explains in the Court's opinion, excluding those enrolled in federally established exchanges would not only lead to the "death spiral" of state-established exchanges, but would also raise the health care premiums of those with plans purchased outside of the exchanges. To what extent do you think the predicted consequences and accompanying media hype influenced the Court's decision? Should these factors have had an influence?

2.   *Atextualism or Textualism at Its Finest? The Messy Realities of Enacting a Once in a Lifetime Law.* Despite the textual nature of the dispute in *King*, Chief Justice Roberts concludes fairly quickly that the text is ambiguous, and dedicates the bulk of his analysis to the Affordable Care Act's drafting history, broader meaning and general purpose. Roberts justifies this approach in part by relying on "the fundamental canon of statutory interpretation that the words of a statute must be read in their context and with a view to their place in the overall statutory scheme." Roberts seems to believe that this canon is more "fundamental" than other canons such as the rule against surplusage or the presumption of consistent usage. Do you agree? In what way does this "fundamental canon" differ from the language and structural canons presented in sections 1 and 2 of chapter 6?

According to Chief Justice Roberts, the Affordable Care Act was enacted to further three reforms. Because the Petitioners' reading of the Act would eliminate and/or invalidate two of those three reforms, it was "implausible" that Congress meant the Act to operate this way. In reaching this conclusion, Roberts emphasizes that the Act was drafted under circumstances that left it rife with instances of "inartful drafting," including secretive early drafting sessions followed by limited chances for debate and amendment under the budget reconciliation procedure. Does Roberts' conclusion—that "the Act does not reflect the type of care and deliberation that one might expect of such significant legislation"—provide license for the Court to depart from a textualist approach?

In *Imperfect Statutes, Imperfect Courts: Understanding Congress's Plan in the Era of Unorthodox Lawmaking*, 129 Harv. L. Rev. 62, 64, 66 (2015), Abbe Gluck argues that the *King* decision is "the Court's most explicit recognition ever of modern statutory complexity." According to Gluck, the Chief Justice's opinion in *King* reflects not a rejection of textualism, but instead a dramatic shift toward a more sophisticated form of textualism which grounds itself in a quest to utilize the text in order to gain a more holistic understanding of Congress's "plan." Gluck elaborates as follows:

> Justice Scalia's dissent decries [the *King* majority opinion] as an activist departure from "the normal rules of interpretation." But imposing perfection on an imperfect statute, as the canons would have, would itself have been a kind of aggressive judicial legislation. Nor does *King*'s emphasis on the "plan" mean a resort to legislative history or other subjective factors maligned by textualists. The opinion derives its understanding of the ACA's scheme from its text, structure, and the statute's own, codified "stated purposes" (not legislative history). Even *King*'s concept of "plan" has appeared before, both in a long (but perhaps forgotten) tradition in the pre-textualist era and also in textualist opinions themselves. Textualism is chock full of rules that emphasize holistic interpretation—rules that sit in some tension with other textualist rules that advance a laser focus. One way to understand *King* is that the Chief Justice chooses the holistic side of textualism, one that has always shared with purposivism the assumption that Congress legislates rationally, with means to an end.

In what way is the Court's interpretive methodology a move away from the textualism Gluck describes as "laser focus[ed]"? Is it because what the majority calls "the most natural reading" of the contested textual phrase yields to pragmatic considerations? To purposive ones? Or is the Court implying that a textualist judgment ought not to be settled at all until these purposive and pragmatic considerations have been identified and analyzed? See Richard M. Re, *The New Holy Trinity*, 18 Green Bag 2d 407 (2015). Alternatively, is the Court's reasoning best understood as an exceptional approach for an exceptional statute?

3. *Purpose Without Legislative History.* Although the majority opinion does refer once to a Senate hearing when describing the background to the ACA, Professor Gluck is essentially correct that legislative history (as discussed in depth for the remainder of this chapter) is absent from the Court's analysis. When the Court near the end of its opinion states that "[a] fair reading of legislation demands a fair understanding of the legislative plan," it seems to rely on some notion of an institutional purpose. How can that purpose be sufficiently identified in the absence of any commentary from sponsors, supporters, or opponents, as expressed through committee reports and floor debates? Is the Court imputing to Congress as a general matter a "purposive mentality" that influences statutory meaning? Is this reasonable? Is it legitimate?

4. *Realpolitik and* King. Judge Richard Posner, commenting on Professor Gluck's analysis, offers what he calls his own "simpler, cruder" ideas about the majority's statutory interpretation approach. Noting the extraordinary complexity of the legislative process that resulted in the lengthy Affordable Care Act, Posner suggests that the Court acted "in order to avoid a bad consequence" in states that had failed to create their own exchanges. Posner explains that this consequence would be "bad" or "absurd" in political terms:

Professor Gluck suggests that Chief Justice Roberts is struggling to alter the relation of the courts to Congress in statutory cases, but an alternative is that he is struggling to preserve the Supreme Court's, and his own, standing in the public eye. * * * 2015 is the first stage in the next presidential campaign. A decision against the Affordable Care Act * * * would have been a gift to the Democrats in campaigning for the Presidency, because [it] would have created turmoil in the health care market and would have deprived many people of subsidized health benefits, and would have been produced by a majority consisting exclusively of appointees of Republican Presidents.

Richard Posner, *Comment on Professor Gluck's "Imperfect Statutes, Imperfect Courts,"* 129 Harvard Law Review Forum 11, 12–13 (2015). Do you find this explanation persuasive? When, if ever, should the Court's analysis of statutory language be influenced by such electoral considerations?

5. *The Aftermath for State Exchanges.* In Justice Scalia's dissent, he states that even under a purpose-based analysis, the majority's holding is "self-defeating" because it will end up dissuading States from establishing their own exchanges, a result that conflicts with Congress's indisputable preference for State-established exchanges. Prior to *King*, only sixteen states and the District of Columbia had established their own exchanges, with many of them facing significant technical and logistical hurdles. On the day the *King* decision came down, the Pennsylvania governor withdrew his plan to establish a state-based exchange and announced that the State would instead defer to a federal exchange; experts have predicted that others may follow suit.[365] Under a purpose-based analysis, what is a Court to do when facing interpretive alternatives that advance some of Congress's purposes but defeat others? Is it possible that, had the Court held for petitioners, Congress would have intervened to amend the Act in a way that both "saved" healthcare reform and reinforced encouragement for State-based exchanges? Or perhaps if Congress had been able to foresee the complications of establishing state-based exchanges at the time it drafted the Act, it would have changed its preference altogether?

B. COMMITTEE REPORTS (AND AN INTRODUCTION TO THE GREAT LEGISLATIVE HISTORY DEBATE)

Most judges and scholars agree that committee reports should be considered as authoritative legislative history and should be given great weight (i.e., a statement in a committee report will usually count more than a statement by a single legislator). Justice Jackson, concurring in *Schwegmann Bros. v. Calvert Distillers Corp.*, 341 U.S. 384, 395 (1951), objected to the use of legislative materials to interpret statutes, but excepted committee reports from his quarrel. Jorge Carro & Andrew Brann, *The U.S. Supreme Court and the Use of Legislative Histories: A Statistical Analysis*, 22 Jurimeterics J. 294, 304 (1982), report that over a 40-year period, over 60% of the Supreme Court's citations to legislative history were references to committee reports. A more recent study indicates that the qualitative

---

[365] See The Upshot, Obamacare Ruling May Have Just Killed State-Based Exchanges, N.Y. Times, June 25, 2015, available at https://www.nytimes.com/2015/06/26/upshot/obamacare-ruling-may-have-just-killed-state-based-exchanges.html (visited August 21, 2019); Governor Wolf Issues Statement on *King v. Burwell* Supreme Court Ruling: Says Administration Will Withdraw State Based Health Insurance Marketplace Plan, available at https://www.governor.pa.gov/governor-wolf-issues-statement-on-king-v-burwell-supreme-court-ruling/#.VZLLXflViko (visited June 10, 2016).

dominance of committee reports continues: when the Court invoked legislative history in its workplace law and tax law decisions between 1969 and 2008, it relied on House and Senate committee reports from over half the time (workplace law cases) to over two-thirds of the time (tax law cases). See James Brudney and Corey Ditslear, *The Warp and Woof of Statutory Interpretation: Comparing Supreme Court Approaches in Tax Law and Workplace Law*, 58 Duke L.J. 1231, 1262 (2009).

Committee reports appear particularly well-suited for the authoritative role they have played. Most legislation is essentially written in committee or subcommittee, and any collective statement by the members of that subgroup will represent the best-informed thought about what the proposed legislation is doing. Committee reports are also accessible documents, both in the sense of being easily located through legal research and of being easy to comprehend once found. They usually set forth the problem(s) calling forth the proposed legislation, the general solution(s) posited by the bill, and a section-by-section summary of the provisions of the bill. The report of a conference committee (where the two legislative chambers have passed different forms of the same bill and must resolve their differences in conference) typically sets forth, for each provision, the version passed by each chamber and what the conference committee did with the provision (and sometimes also an explanation why it took the action it did).

There are, on the other hand, limitations on the usefulness of committee reports in giving meaning to ambiguous statutes. First, there is sometimes *no* committee report for a particular bill or an important provision in the bill, because it has been added as part of the floor debate. This is especially true of many of the civil rights bills. Recall from Chapter 1, § 1, that the sex discrimination provision in Title VII was added as a floor amendment in the House (and as something of a surprise to the bill's sponsors); hence, there is no discussion of that critical amendment in the House Judiciary Committee report. There was no committee report for the Act in the Senate, because the sponsors avoided sending the House bill to committee, which was Senator Eastland's preserve. Compare *Hishon v. King & Spalding*, 467 U.S. 69, 75 & n.7 (1984) (relying on Senate report for civil rights bill that was similar but never enacted). And there was no conference committee report, because the House rapidly acceded to the Senate's revisions, the sponsors knowing that further delays in the bill's enactment might prove fatal. See also *Local 82, Furniture & Piano Moving Union v. Crowley*, 467 U.S. 526 (1984) (interpreting Landrum-Griffin Act, much of which was written on the House and Senate floor).

Second, the committee report is often as ambiguous as the statute. As a shorter, more compressed form of the statute, the committee report may even be misleading, as it leaves out important qualifications in its discussion of the proposed legislation or particular provisions. (The committee report is probably most useful as a statement of the goals and their relative importance in the statutory scheme, since most statutes do not carry with them statements of purpose.) Indeed, a striking feature of the committee report is that it is the end-product of the committee's consideration, and therefore comes at a stage of consensus. In many instances, the key point in the process is the "mark-up" of the bill in committee or subcommittee, for it is there that the legislators make the critical choices and compromises and specifically reject proposed alternatives. See John Kernochan, *The Legislative*

Process 25 (1981). Traditionally, there was no official record of mark-up sessions, a practice that has been opened up to the public somewhat in the last two decades. As a consequence, what is often the most revealing collection of statements was often not available, or admissible, in the process of statutory interpretation. See Wald, *Legislative History in the 1981 Term*, at 202. In recent decades, however, committee mark-ups, especially of tax bills, have increasingly been made available, either through quasi-official transcripts or unofficial reports in tax journals or online. One might therefore expect to see more references to these sources by judges willing to consider legislative history. E.g., *Regan v. Wald*, 468 U.S. 222 (1984) (both majority and dissenting opinions relying on explanation accompanying House committee mark-up).

Third, when there is a committee report and the report contains relevant statements, one might be suspicious of the usefulness of those statements under some circumstances. Lobbyists and lawyers maneuver endlessly to persuade staff members (who write the committee reports) or their legislative bosses to throw in helpful language in the reports when insertion of similar language would be inappropriate or infeasible for the statute itself. "Smuggling in" helpful language through the legislative history is a time-tested practice.

In state legislatures, committee reports can take a variety of forms, not all of which are published or are readily available to the public: (1) regular reports of standing committees or conference committees, like those produced in the U.S. Congress; (2) staff analysis of a pending bill, which is in many states the main document which is actually distributed to legislators; and (3) reports of special committees created to investigate and to resolve important problems expeditiously or to investigate problems, as well as reports of collections of experts (often "law revision commissions") who have drafted legislation adopted in the state. As described in the lengthy *Note on State Court Reliance on Committee Reports and Other Legislative History Sources* at the end of this section (§ 2(B)), committee reports and similar documents are often used to interpret ambiguous statutes at the state level.

BLANCHARD V. BERGERON

Supreme Court of the United States, 1989.
489 U.S. 87, 109 S.Ct. 939, 105 L.Ed.2d 181.

JUSTICE WHITE delivered the opinion of the Court.

[A jury awarded Blanchard $5,000 in compensatory damages and $5,000 in punitive damages on his civil rights claim, under 42 U.S.C. § 1983, that he had been beaten by a sheriff's deputy. He sought attorney's fees under the 1976 Civil Rights Attorney's Fee Award Act, codified at 42 U.S.C. § 1988. The district court awarded $7,500 in fees. The Fifth Circuit, however, held that under its decision in *Johnson v. Georgia Highway Express, Inc.*, 488 F.2d 714 (5th Cir. 1974), the 40% contingency fee agreement Blanchard had entered into with his attorney set a ceiling on recoverable fees. Thus, the Fifth Circuit limited the fee award to $4,000 (40% of the $10,000 damages awarded).]

Section 1988 provides that the court, "in its discretion, may allow . . . a reasonable attorney's fee. . . ." The section does not provide a specific definition of "reasonable" fee, and the question is whether the award must be limited to the amount provided in a contingent fee agreement. The legislative history of the Act is instructive insofar as it tells us: "In computing the fee, counsel for prevailing parties should be paid, as is traditional with attorneys compensated by a fee-paying client, 'for all time reasonably expended on a matter.'" S. Rep. No. 94–1011, at 6 (1976) (citing *Davis v. County of Los Angeles*, 1974 WL 180 (C.D. Cal. 1974); and *Stanford Daily v. Zurcher*, 64 F.R.D. 680, 684 (N.D. Cal. 1974)).

In many past cases considering the award of attorney's fees under § 1988, we have turned our attention to *Johnson v. Georgia Highway Express, Inc.*, a case decided before the enactment of the Civil Rights Attorney's Fee Award Act of 1976. As we stated in *Hensley v. Eckerhart*, 461 U.S. 424, 429–431 (1983), *Johnson* provides guidance to Congress' intent because both the House and Senate Reports refer to the 12 factors set forth in *Johnson* for assessing the reasonableness of an attorney's fee award. The Senate Report, in particular, refers to three District Court decisions that "correctly applied" the 12 factors laid out in *Johnson*.

In the course of its discussion of the factors to be considered by a court in awarding attorney's fees, the *Johnson* court dealt with fee arrangements:

> "'Whether or not [a litigant] agreed to pay a fee and in what amount is not decisive. Conceivably, a litigant might agree to pay his counsel a fixed dollar fee. This might be even more than the fee eventually allowed by the court. Or he might agree to pay his lawyer a percentage contingent fee that would be greater than the fee the court might ultimately set. Such arrangements should not determine the court's decision. The criterion for the court is not what the parties agree but what is reasonable.'"

Yet in the next sentence, *Johnson* says "In no event, however, should the litigant be awarded a fee greater than he is contractually bound to pay, if indeed the attorneys have contracted as to amount." This latter statement, never disowned in the Circuit, was the basis for the decision below. But we doubt that Congress embraced this aspect of *Johnson*, for it pointed to the three District Court cases in which the factors are "correctly applied." Those cases clarify that the fee arrangement is but a single factor and not determinative. In *Stanford Daily v. Zurcher*, [supra,] for example, the District Court considered a contingent-fee arrangement to be a factor, but not dispositive, in the calculation of a fee award. In *Davis v. County of Los Angeles*, supra, the court permitted a fee award to counsel in a public interest firm which otherwise would have been entitled to no fee. Finally, in *Swann v. Charlotte-Mecklenburg Board of Education*, 66 F.R.D. 483 (W.D. N.C. 1975), the court stated that reasonable fees should be granted regardless of the individual plaintiff's fee obligations. *Johnson*'s "List of 12" thus provides a useful catalog of the many factors to be considered in assessing the reasonableness of an award of attorney's fees; but the one factor at issue here, the attorney's private fee arrangement, standing alone, is not dispositive.

The *Johnson* contingency-fee factor is simply that, a factor. The presence of a pre-existing fee agreement may aid in determining reasonableness. " 'The fee quoted to the client or the percentage of the recovery agreed to is helpful in demonstrating that attorney's fee expectations when he accepted the case.'" *Pennsylvania v. Del. Valley Citizens' Council for Clean Air*, 483 U.S. 711 (1987), quoting *Johnson*. But as we see it, a contingent-fee contract does not impose an automatic ceiling on an award of attorney's fees and to hold otherwise would be inconsistent with the statute and its policy and purpose.

As we understand § 1988's provision for allowing a "reasonable attorney's fee," it contemplates reasonable compensation, in light of all of the circumstances, for the time and effort expended by the attorney for the prevailing plaintiff, no more and no less. Should a fee agreement provide less than a reasonable fee calculated in this manner, the defendant should nevertheless be required to pay the higher amount. The defendant is not, however, required to pay the amount called for in a contingent-fee contract if it is more than a reasonable fee calculated in the usual way. It is true that the purpose of § 1988 was to make sure that competent counsel was available to civil rights plaintiffs, and it is of course arguable that if a plaintiff is able to secure an attorney on the basis of a contingent or other fee agreement, the purpose of the statute is served if the plaintiff is bound by his contract. On that basis, however, the plaintiff should recover nothing from the defendant, which would be plainly contrary to the statute. And Congress implemented its purpose by broadly requiring all defendants to pay a reasonable fee to all prevailing plaintiffs, if ordered to do so by the court. Thus it is that a plaintiff's recovery will not be reduced by what he must pay his counsel. Plaintiffs who can afford to hire their own lawyers, as well as impecunious litigants, may take advantage of this provision. And where there are lawyers or organizations that will take a plaintiff's case without compensation, that fact does not bar the award of a reasonable fee. All of this is consistent with and reflects our decisions in cases involving court-awarded attorney's fees.

Hensley v. Eckerhart, [*supra*,] directed lower courts to make an initial estimate of reasonable attorney's fees by applying prevailing billing rates to the hours reasonably expended on successful claims. And we have said repeatedly that "[t]he initial estimate of a reasonable attorney's fee is properly calculated by multiplying the number of hours reasonably expended on the litigation times a reasonable hourly rate." The courts may then adjust this lodestar calculation by other factors. We have never suggested that a different approach is to be followed in cases where the prevailing party and his (or her) attorney have executed a contingent-fee agreement. To the contrary, * * * we have adopted the lodestar approach as the centerpiece of attorney's fee awards. The *Johnson* factors may be relevant in adjusting the lodestar amount but no one factor is a substitute for multiplying reasonable billing rates by a reasonable estimation of the number of hours expended on the litigation. * * *

If a contingent-fee agreement were to govern as a strict limitation on the award of attorney's fees, an undesirable emphasis might be placed on the importance of the recovery of damages in civil rights litigation. The intention of Congress was to encourage successful civil rights litigation, not to create a special incentive to prove damages and shortchange efforts to seek effective injunctive or declaratory relief. Affirming the decision below would create an artificial disincentive for an attorney who enters into a contingent fee agreement, unsure of whether his client's claim sounded in state tort law or in federal civil rights, from fully exploring all possible avenues of relief. Section 1988 makes no distinction between actions for damages and suits for equitable relief. Congress has elected to encourage meritorious civil rights claims because of the benefits of such litigation for the named plaintiff and for society at large, irrespective of whether the action seeks monetary damages.

It should also be noted that we have not accepted the contention that fee awards in § 1983 damages cases should be modeled upon the contingent-fee arrangements used in personal injury litigation. "[W]e reject the notion that a civil rights action for damages constitutes nothing more than a private tort suit benefiting only the individual plaintiffs whose rights were violated. Unlike most private tort litigants, a civil rights plaintiff seeks to vindicate important civil and constitutional rights that cannot be valued solely in monetary terms."

Respondent cautions us that refusing to limit recovery to the amount of the contingency agreement will result in a "windfall" to attorneys who accept § 1983 actions. Yet the very nature of recovery under § 1988 is designed to prevent any such "windfall." Fee awards are to be reasonable, reasonable as to billing rates and reasonable as to the number of hours spent in advancing the successful claims. Accordingly, fee awards, properly calculated, by definition will represent the reasonable worth of the services rendered in vindication of a plaintiff's civil rights claim. It is central to the awarding of attorney's fees under § 1988 that the district court judge, in his or her good judgment, make the assessment of what is a reasonable fee under the circumstances of the case. The trial judge should not be limited by the contractual fee agreement between plaintiff and counsel. * * *

JUSTICE SCALIA, concurring in part and concurring in the judgment.

I * * * join the opinion of the Court except that portion which rests upon detailed analysis of the Fifth Circuit's opinion in *Johnson* and the District Court decisions in *Swann, Stanford Daily,* and *Davis.* The Court carefully examines those opinions, separating holding from dictum, much as a lower court would study our opinions in order to be faithful to our guidance. The justification for this role reversal is that the Senate and House Committee Reports on the Civil Rights Attorney's Fees Awards Act of 1976 referred approvingly to *Johnson*, and the Senate Report alone referred to the three District Court opinions as having "correctly applied" *Johnson*. The Court resolves the difficulty that *Johnson* contradicts the three District Court opinions on the precise point at issue here by concluding in effect that the analysis in *Johnson* was dictum, whereas in the three District Court opinions it was a holding. Despite the fact that the House Report referred only to *Johnson*, and made no mention of the District Court cases, the Court "doubt[s] that Congress embraced this aspect of *Johnson*, for it pointed to the three District Court cases in which the factors are 'correctly applied.'"

In my view Congress did no such thing. Congress is elected to enact statutes rather than point to cases, and its Members have better uses for their time than poring over District Court opinions. That the Court should refer to the citation of three District Court cases in a document issued by a single committee of a single house as the action *of Congress* displays the level of unreality that our unrestrained use of legislative history has attained. I am confident that only a small proportion of the Members of Congress read either one of the Committee Reports in question, even if (as is not always the case) the Reports happened to have been published before the vote; that very few of those who did read them set off for the nearest law library to check out what was actually said in the four cases at issue (or in the more than 50 other cases cited by the House and Senate Reports); and that *no* Member of Congress came to the judgment that the District Court cases would trump *Johnson* on the point at issue here because the latter was dictum. As anyone familiar with modern-day drafting of congressional committee reports is well aware, the references to the cases were inserted, at best by a committee staff member on his or her own initiative, and at worst by a committee staff member at the suggestion of a lawyer-lobbyist; and the purpose of those references was not primarily to inform the Members of Congress what the bill meant (for that end *Johnson* would not merely have been cited, but its 12 factors would have been described, which they were not), but rather to influence judicial construction. What a heady feeling it must be for a young staffer, to know that his or her citation of obscure district court cases can transform them into the law of the land, thereafter dutifully to be observed by the Supreme Court itself.

I decline to participate in this process. It is neither compatible with our judicial responsibility of assuring reasoned, consistent, and effective application of the statutes of the United States, nor conducive to a genuine effectuation of congressional intent, to give legislative force to each snippet of analysis, and even every case citation, in committee reports that are increasingly unreliable evidence of what the voting Members of Congress actually had in mind. By treating *Johnson* and the District Court trilogy as fully authoritative, the Court today expands what I regard as our cases' excessive preoccupation with them—and with the 12-factor *Johnson* analysis in particular. * * * Except for the few passages to which I object, today's opinion admirably follows our more recent approach of seeking to develop an interpretation of the statute that is reasonable, consistent, and faithful to its apparent purpose, rather than to achieve obedient adherence to cases cited in the committee reports. I therefore join the balance of the opinion.

NOTES ON THE NEW TEXTUALIST CRITIQUE OF COMMITTEE REPORTS

1. *Judge Scalia's Attack on Committee Reports.* Justice Scalia believed that committee reports, in particular, are untrustworthy legislative history. His first effort to explain his position systematically, an unpublished speech delivered at various law schools while he was a judge on the D.C. Circuit, is summarized, quoted, and criticized in Daniel Farber & Philip Frickey, *Legislative Intent and Public Choice*, 74 Va. L. Rev. 423 (1988). Judge Scalia also set forth his doubts in a concurring opinion in *Hirschey v. FERC*, 777 F.2d 1, 7–8 (D.C. Cir. 1985):

> I frankly doubt that it is ever reasonable to assume that the details, as opposed to the broad outlines of purpose, set forth in a committee report come to the attention of, much less are approved by, the house which enacts the committee's bill. And I think it time for courts to become concerned about the fact that routine deference to the detail of committee reports, and the predictable expansion in that detail which routine deference has produced, are converting a system of judicial construction into a system of committee-staff prescription.

Note the similarity to his reason for not joining the Court's opinion in *Bergeron*. In a footnote at the end of the first sentence of the above quotation, Judge Scalia reported the following "illuminating exchange" in the Senate; *id.* at 7–8 n.1. After joining the Supreme Court, Justice Scalia reproduced the identical exchange in his two books addressing statutory interpretation, see Scalia, *A Matter of Interpretation*, 32–34; Scalia & Garner, *Reading Law*, 384–85. We have inserted in bracketed italics a portion of Senator Dole's explanation that Judge Scalia chose to omit from this exchange:

Mr. ARMSTRONG. * * * My question, which may take [the Chairman of the Committee on Finance] by surprise, is this: Is it the intention of the chairman that the Internal Revenue Service and the Tax Court and other courts take guidance as to the intention of Congress from the committee report which accompanies this bill?

Mr. DOLE. I would certainly hope so. * * *

Mr. ARMSTRONG. Mr. President, will the Senator tell me whether or not he wrote the committee report?

Mr. DOLE. Did I write the committee report?

Mr. ARMSTRONG. Yes.

Mr. DOLE. No; the Senator from Kansas did not write the committee report.

Mr. ARMSTRONG. Did any Senator write the committee report?

Mr. DOLE. I have to check.

Mr. ARMSTRONG. Does the Senator know of any Senator who wrote the committee report?

Mr. DOLE. I might be able to identify one, but I would have to search. I was here all during the time it was written, I might say, and worked carefully with the staff as they worked. * * * [*As I recall, during the July 4 recess week, there were about five different working groups of staff from both parties, the Joint Committee, and the Treasury working on different provisions.*]

Mr. ARMSTRONG. Mr. President, has the Senator from Kansas, the chairman of the Finance Committee, read the committee report in its entirety?

Mr. DOLE. I am working on it. It is not a bestseller, but I am working on it.

Mr. ARMSTRONG. Mr. President, did members of the Finance Committee vote on the committee report?

Mr. DOLE. No.

Mr. ARMSTRONG. Mr. President, the reason I raise the issue is not perhaps apparent on the surface, and let me just state it: * * * The report itself is not considered by the Committee on Finance. It was not subject to amendment by the Committee on Finance. It is not subject to amendment now by the Senate. * * *

* * * If there were matter within this report which was disagreed to by the Senator from Colorado or even by a majority of all Senators, there would be no way for us to change the report. I could not offer an amendment tonight to amend the committee report.

* * * [F]or any jurist, administrator, bureaucrat, tax practitioner, or others who might chance upon the written record of this proceeding, let me just make

the point that this is not the law, it was not voted on, it is not subject to amendment, and we should discipline ourselves to the task of expressing congressional intent in the statute.

Consider the different ways in which this Dole-Armstrong colloquy might constitute an "illuminating exchange." For Justice Scalia, focused on what he regarded as the systematic flaws of legislative history, Senator Armstrong (then a first-term Republican from Colorado) has emphasized the fact that members rarely if ever draft committee reports, and they also do not vote on these reports. But members of Congress rarely draft text either—should this matter? To be sure, committee reports (unlike text) are not voted on by committee members, and in this important respect they should not be confused with "the law." On the other hand, there is plenty of anecdotal evidence that legislators facing a vote often pay more attention to the report than to the language of the bill. Senator Arlen Specter, who represented Pennsylvania from 1980 to 2010 and served for decades on the Judiciary Committee, opined that "[M]embers of Congress are more likely to read a committee report than the bill itself. The prose of a report is easier to understand, and, because a bill usually amends an existing statute, it is impossible to follow without referring to the U.S. Code." Joan Biskupic, *Scalia Takes a Narrow View in Seeking Congress' Will*, 48 Cong. Q. 913, 917 (1990) (summarizing Specter's views).[366]

And what about the omitted excerpts from Senator Dole, Chair of the Finance Committee? Dole, who spent over a decade as a chief architect of federal tax legislation, regarded legislative history in this setting as providing valuable guidance to the IRS and the federal courts. The omitted language seems to suggest that Senator Dole was attempting to educate his freshman colleague about how tax legislative history was produced—in deliberative bipartisan fashion and with the cooperative participation of the executive branch. Taken as a whole, does this colloquy indicate that legislative history should be excluded from judicial consideration as a matter of principle? Or that review of such history by courts should be a question of relative weight rather than threshold admissibility?

The co-parent of the new textualism has been Judge Frank Easterbrook of the Seventh Circuit, the author of the textualist en banc opinion in *Marshall* (Chapter 5, § 3(B)(1)). Another of his opinions, *In re Sinclair*, is the next case in this chapter.

2.   *Justice Scalia Updates His Critique of Committee Reports.* After his elevation to the Supreme Court, Justice Scalia developed a more systematic critique of the Court's traditional use of legislative history. See Antonin Scalia, *A Matter of Interpretation* (1997); *Bock Laundry* (Scalia, J., concurring in the judgment) (both excerpted in Chapter 5, § 3(A)).[367] Justice Scalia's more systematic critique goes well beyond the cynicism of

---

[366]   See also Abner Mikva, *Reading and Writing Statutes*, 28 S. Tex. L. Rev. 181, 184 (1986) (Mikva, a House member for five terms who then served on the D.C. Circuit for fifteen years, described the committee report as the "bone structure of the legislation. It is the road map that explains why things are in and things are out of the statute.").

[367]   Some of Justice Scalia's classic criticisms are found in *Zuni Public School District No. 89 v. Department of Education*, 550 U.S. 81, 116–211 (2007) (Scalia, J., dissenting); *Hamdan v. Rumsfeld*, 548 U.S. 557, 665–68 (2006) (Scalia, J., dissenting); *Koons Buick Pontiac GMC, Inc. v. Nigh*, 543 U.S. 50, 70–76 (2004) (Scalia, J., dissenting); *Crosby v. National Foreign Trade Council*, 530 U.S. 363, 388–91 (2000) (Scalia, J., concurring in the judgment); *Thunder Basin Coal Co. v. Reich*, 510 U.S. 200, 219 (1994) (Scalia, J., concurring in part and in the judgment); *Conroy v. Aniskoff*, 507 U.S. 511, 519 (1993) (Scalia, J., concurring in the judgment); *United States v. Thompson/Center Arms Co.*, 504 U.S. 505, 521 (1992) (Scalia, J., concurring in the judgment); *Union Bank v. Wolas*, 502 U.S. 151, 163 (1991) (Scalia, J., concurring); *Wisconsin Public Intervenor v. Mortier*, 501 U.S. 597, 617–23 (1991) (Scalia, J., concurring in the judgment); *Sullivan v. Finkelstein*, 496

Bergeron and rests upon a constitutional interpretation of Article I, § 7. Statutory text is the alpha and the omega of statutory interpretation because it is the only matter that is enacted as authoritative *law* under our constitutional rule of recognition (Article I, § 7).[368] Even if there were a coherent legislative "intent" (a matter Scalia disputes), it would have no authority as law under the Constitution. Like Judge Easterbrook, who developed the structural constitutional features of the new textualism at an earlier stage, Justice Scalia would be willing to examine legislative materials as evidence of how statutory language was used at the time.

3. *Committee Reports and the Constitution.* Notwithstanding Justice Scalia's argument that the Constitution prohibits reliance on legislative history, some scholars have contended that the provisions of Article I, § 5, requiring each chamber to "keep a Journal of its Proceedings, and from time to time publish the same," and authorizing each chamber to "determine the Rules of its Proceedings," create a constitutional framework that allows for the use of legislative history. See generally Adrian Vermeule, *The Constitutional Law of Congressional Procedure*, 71 U. Chi. L. Rev. 361, 411 (2004). One of us has pushed this argument further, maintaining that the Journal Clause and the Rules Clause gave rise to distinctively American legislative design features in the early years of the Republic that effectively invite courts to invoke legislative history in suitable settings. James Brudney, *Canon Shortfalls and the Virtues of Political Branch Interpretive Assets*, 98 Cal. L. Rev. 1199, 1219–24 (2010). The Constitution's insistence on publication under the Journal Clause departed from traditions of secrecy that had prevailed for centuries in the British Parliament and had operated in both the Continental Congress and the Constitutional Convention. Although the House and Senate Journals are summaries of the floor proceedings rather than a record of debates and discussions, Representative Elbridge Gerry (a signer of the Declaration of Independence and later Vice President under James Madison) argued in 1792 that the publication of floor debates would "aid the Executive in administering the Government [and] the Judiciary in expounding the laws." *Id.* at 1220 (quoting from Gerry's proposal for the House to appoint official stenographers who would transcribe and publish its debates). Congressional debates were initially published by commercial journalists admitted to both chambers by 1795. These were collected and published as the *Annals of Congress* beginning in 1834; Congress did not begin printing its own debates until the arrival of the *Congressional Record* in 1873. See Josh Chafetz, *Congress's Constitution: Legislative Authority and the Separation of Powers* 281–82 (2017).

The Rules Clause allowed the House and Senate to create permanent standing committees between 1789 and 1820, in order to shape the priorities and agenda of each chamber. These standing committees—reviewing and reporting bills prior to full chamber consideration—differed dramatically from the temporary select committees relied on by the British Parliament at the time and by Congress during its first few sessions. By the early nineteenth century, first oral and then written committee reports were invoked by members during floor debates and deliberations. Given these foundational developments, Brudney argues that the existence of such constitutionally linked origins "confers upon

U.S. 617, 631–32 (1990) (Scalia, J., concurring in all of the Court's opinion except footnote 8); *Begier v. IRS*, 496 U.S. 53, 67–71 (1990) (Scalia, J., concurring in the judgment).

[368] William Eskridge Jr., *The New Textualism*, 37 UCLA L. Rev. 621 (1990); John Manning, *Textualism as a Nondelegation Doctrine*, 97 Colum. L. Rev. 673 (1997); Jonathan Molot, *The Rise and Fall of Textualism*, 106 Colum. L. Rev. 1, 23–29 (2006).

legislative history an element of authoritative legitimacy that enhances its stature as an interpretive asset." 98 Cal. L. Rev. at 1224.

4. *The Impact of the New Textualism in the Supreme Court.* Justice Scalia's critique has had an impact upon the Court's practice, which is now more cautious in its use of legislative history. The new textualism has had even more of an impact upon the arguments made by the Supreme Court Bar (especially the Solicitor General and others regularly arguing before the Court), who now emphasize and usually lead with their textual arguments and use legislative history to back up these contentions rather than as the touchstone of statutory meaning. The Rehnquist and Roberts Courts (1986 onward) have been less likely to rely heavily upon legislative history today than did the Burger Court (1969–1986). There are more decisions like *Circuit City* (where the majority refused to examine legislative materials) than there have been since the pre-New Deal era.[369]

Nonetheless, the new textualism has not swept the field, and the debate within the Supreme Court continues. Although Justice Scalia picked up a good deal of academic support,[370] the majority of the commentators are unpersuaded.[371] The Supreme Court still relies on committee reports (even if less than before). Moreover, in *Wisconsin Public Intervenor v. Mortier*, 501 U.S. 597, 610 n.4 (1991), all of the other justices joined in a footnote explicitly rejecting Justice Scalia's general position that legislative history is irrelevant to proper statutory interpretation. See also *Bank One Chi. N.A. v. Midwest Bank & Trust*, 516 U.S. 264, 276–79 (1996) (Justice Stevens in concurring opinion, joined by Justice Breyer, objecting strenuously to Justice Scalia's general critique of legislative history). After the appointment of Justice Breyer (a big fan of legislative history), the Supreme Court relied on legislative materials more often in the late 1990s and the early

---

[369] E.g., David Law & David Zaring, *Law versus Ideology: The Supreme Court and the Use of Legislative History*, 51 Wm. & Mary L. Rev. 1653 (2010); James Brudney & Corey Ditslear, *The Decline and Fall of Legislative History? Patterns of Supreme Court Reliance in the Burger and Rehnquist Eras*, 89 Judicature 220 (2006); Michael Koby, *The Supreme Court's Declining Reliance on Legislative History: The Impact of Justice Scalia's Critique*, 36 Harv. J. Legis. 369 (1999). Because Justices Scalia and Thomas routinely refuse to join any majority opinion that relies upon legislative history, in any case in which their votes might be necessary to form a majority the Justice drafting the opinion may strategically avoid reliance upon legislative history. James Brudney and Corey Ditslear, *Liberal Justices' Reliance on Legislative History: Principle, Strategy, and the Scalia Effect*, 29 Berkeley J. Emp. & Lab. L. 117, 160–67 (2008); Thomas Merrill, *Textualism and the Future of the* Chevron *Doctrine*, 72 Wash. U. L.Q. 351 (1994).

[370] E.g. John Manning, *What Divides Textualists from Purposivists?*, 106 Colum. L. Rev. 70 (2006); John Manning, *Justice Scalia and the Legislative Process*, 62 N.Y.U. Ann. Surv. Am. L. 33 (2006); Frank Easterbrook, *Text, History, and Structure in Statutory Interpretation*, 17 Harv. J.L. & Pub. Poly 61 (1994); Kenneth Starr, *Observations About the Use of Legislative History*, 1987 Duke L.J. 371.

[371] Skeptical treatments include Stephen Breyer, *Making Our Democracy Work: A Judge's View* (2010); Stephen Breyer, *On the Uses of Legislative History in Interpreting Statutes*, 65 S. Cal. L. Rev. 845 (1992); George Costello, *Average Voting Members and Other "Benign Fictions": The Relative Reliability of Committee Reports, Floor Debates, and Other Sources of Legislative History*, 1990 Duke L.J. 39; William Eskridge Jr., *Textualism, The Unknown Ideal?*, 96 Mich. L. Rev. 1509 (1998); Daniel Farber & Philip Frickey, *Legislative Intent and Public Choice*, 74 Va. L. Rev. 423 (1988); Philip Frickey, *Revisiting the Revival of Theory in Statutory Interpretation: A Lecture in Honor of Irving Younger*, 84 Minn. L. Rev. 199 (1999); Paul McGreal, *A Constitutional Defense of Legislative History*, 13 Wm. & Mary Bill Rts. J. 1267 (2005); Abner Mikva & Eric Lane, *The Muzak of Justice Scalia's Revolutionary Call To Read Unclear Statutes Narrowly*, 53 SMU L. Rev. 121 (2000); Stephen Ross & Daniel Tranen, *The Modern Parol Evidence Rule and Its Implications for New Textualist Statutory Interpretation*, 87 Geo. L.J. 195 (1998); Peter Strauss, *The Common Law and Statutes*, 70 U. Colo. L. Rev. 225 (1999); Patricia Wald, *The Sizzling Sleeper: The Use of Legislative History in Construing Statutes in the 1988–89 Term of the United States Supreme Court*, 39 Am. U.L. Rev. 277 (1990); Nicholas Zeppos, *Justice Scalia's Textualism: The "New" New Legal Process*, 12 Cardozo L. Rev. 1597 (1991).

part of the new century.[372] In the Roberts Court, new Justices Alito and Gorsuch have aligned themselves with Justice Scalia's position against legislative history while Justices Sotomayor and Kagan have been regular users of that resource. The Court's ongoing internal debates are reflected in *Digital Realty Trust, Inc. v. Somers*, 138 S.Ct. 767 (2018) later in this Section.

As for circuit court approaches, a forthcoming Cornell Law Review article by Stuart Benjamin and Kristen Renberg tested two hypotheses: that Republican appointees to the circuits were more likely to respond to textualist critiques of legislative history than their Democratic counterparts, and that circuit judges appointed after 1985 (when Scalia's forceful critiques began) were more influenced by the critiques than judges appointed before that date. Based on a dataset of all published circuit court majority opinions between 1965 and 2011, the authors concluded that the impact of Scalia's efforts was mixed. Judges projected as legislative history skeptics cited committee hearings and floor debates (traditionally deemed less reliable legislative history sources) less often than did their counterparts. But these same putatively skeptical judges cited committee reports (including conference reports) *more often* than their judicial counterparts. The authors conclude that Scalia's attacks on legislative history pushed skeptical judges (Republican appointees and post-Reagan appointees) not to ignore legislative history altogether as Scalia advocated, but to adjust their reliance toward the more traditional approach of invoking committee reports. See Stuart Minor Benjamin & Kristen M. Renberg, *The Paradoxical Impact of Scalia's Campaign Against Legislative History*, 105 Cornell L. Rev. ___ (2019).

IN RE SINCLAIR

United States Court of Appeals for the Seventh Circuit, 1989.
870 F.2d 1340.

EASTERBROOK, CIRCUIT JUDGE.

This case presents a conflict between a statute and its legislative history. The Sinclairs, who have a family farm, filed a bankruptcy petition in April 1985 under Chapter 11 of the Bankruptcy Act of 1978. In October 1986 Congress added Chapter 12, providing benefits for farmers, and the Sinclairs asked the bankruptcy court to convert their case from Chapter 11 to Chapter 12. The bankruptcy judge declined, and the district court affirmed. Each relied on § 302(c)(1) of the Bankruptcy Judges, United States Trustees, and Family Farmer Bankruptcy Act of 1986, Pub. L. 99–554, 100 Stat. 3088:

> The amendments made by subtitle B of title II shall not apply with respect to cases commenced under title 11 of the United States Code before the effective date of this Act.

The Sinclairs rely on the report of the Conference Committee, which inserted § 302(c)(1) into the bill:

---

[372]   See Jane Schacter, *The Confounding Common Law Originalism in Recent Supreme Court Statutory Interpretation: Implications for the Legislative History Debate and Beyond*, 51 Stan. L. Rev. 1 (1998); Charles Tiefer, *The Reconceptualization of Legislative History in the Supreme Court*, 2000 Wis. L. Rev. 205. For a fairly recent example, featuring a lavish deployment of legislative history by a majority opinion (written by O'Connor but joined without cavil by Scalia and Thomas), see *FDA v. Brown & Williamson Tobacco Co.* (Chapter 5, § 3(B)(3)).

It is not intended that there be routine conversion of Chapter 11 and 13 cases, pending at the time of enactment, to Chapter 12. Instead, it is expected that courts will exercise their sound discretion in each case, in allowing conversions only where it is equitable to do so.

Chief among the factors the court should consider is whether there is a substantial likelihood of successful reorganization under Chapter 12.

Courts should also carefully scrutinize the actions already taken in pending cases in deciding whether, in their equitable discretion, to allow conversion. For example, the court may consider whether the petition was recently filed in another chapter with no further action taken. Such a case may warrant conversion to the new chapter. On the other hand, there may be cases where a reorganization plan has already been filed or confirmed. In cases where the parties have substantially relied on current law, availability [sic] to convert to the new chapter should be limited.

The statute says conversion is impossible; the report says that conversion is possible and describes the circumstances under which it should occur.

Which prevails in the event of conflict, the statute or its legislative history? The statute was enacted, the report just the staff's explanation. Congress votes on the text of the bill, and the President signed that text. Committee reports help courts understand the law, but this report contradicts rather than explains the text. So the statute must prevail. * * *

Statutes are law, not evidence of law. References to "intent" in judicial opinions do not imply that legislators' motives and beliefs, as opposed to their public acts, establish the norms to which all others must conform. "Original meaning" rather than "intent" frequently captures the interpretive task more precisely, reminding us that it is the work of the political branches (the "meaning") rather than of the courts that matters, and that their work acquires its meaning when enacted ("originally"). Revisionist history may be revelatory; revisionist judging is simply unfaithful to the enterprise. Justice Holmes made the point when denouncing a claim that judges should give weight to the intent of a document's authors:

> [A statute] does not disclose one meaning conclusively according to the laws of language. Thereupon we ask, not what this man meant, but what those words would mean in the mouth of a normal speaker of English, using them in the circumstances in which they were used. . . . But the normal speaker of English is merely a special variety, a literary form, so to speak, of our old friend the prudent man. He is external to the particular writer, and a reference to him as the criterion is simply another instance of the externality of the law. . . . We do not inquire what the legislature meant; we ask only what the statute means.

Oliver Wendell Holmes, *The Theory of Legal Interpretation*, 12 Harv. L. Rev. 417, 417–19 (1899), reprinted in Collected Legal Papers 204, 207 (1920). Or as Judge Friendly put things in a variation on Holmes's theme, a court must search for "what Congress meant by what it said, rather than for what it meant *simpliciter*." Henry J.

Friendly, *Mr. Justice Frankfurter and the Reading of Statutes*, in Benchmarks 218–19 (1967).

An opinion poll revealing the wishes of Congress would not translate to legal rules. Desires become rules only after clearing procedural hurdles, designed to encourage deliberation and expose proposals (and arguments) to public view and recorded vote. Resort to "intent" as a device to short-circuit these has no more force than the opinion poll—less, because the legislative history is written by the staff of a single committee and not subject to a vote or veto. The Constitution establishes a complex of procedures, including presidential approval (or support by two-thirds of each house). It would demean the constitutionally prescribed method of legislating to suppose that its elaborate apparatus for deliberation on, amending, and approving a text is just a way to create some *evidence* about the law, while the *real* source of legal rules is the mental processes of legislators. * * *

Concern about the source of law—is the statute law, or is it just evidence of the law?—lies behind statements such as: "[T]he language being plain, and not leading to absurd or wholly impracticable consequences, it is the sole evidence of the ultimate legislative intent." *Caminetti* [v. *United States*, 242 U.S. 470 (1917)]. [Chapter 5, § 1] To treat the text as conclusive evidence of law is to treat it *as* law—which under the constitutional structure it is. Legislative history then may help a court discover but may not change the original meaning. *Pierce v. Underwood*, 487 U.S. 552 (1988). The "plain meaning" rule of *Caminetti* rests not on a silly belief that texts have timeless meanings divorced from their many contexts, not on the assumption that what is plain to one reader must be clear to any other (and identical to the plan of the writer), but on the constitutional allocation of powers. The political branches adopt texts through prescribed procedures; what ensues is the law. Legislative history may show the meaning of the texts—may show, indeed, that a text "plain" at first reading has a strikingly different meaning—but may not be used to show an "intent" at variance with the meaning of the text. * * * This approach also supplies the underpinning for the belief that legislative history is "only admissible to solve doubt and not to create it," which punctuates the U.S. Reports. Legislative history helps us learn what Congress meant by what it said, but it is not a source of legal rules competing with those found in the U.S. Code.

Ours is now an easy case. Section 302(c)(1) of the statute has an ascertainable meaning, a meaning not absurd or inconsistent with the structure of the remaining provisions. It says that Chapter 11 cases pending on the date the law went into force may not be converted to Chapter 12. No legislative history suggests any other meaning. The committee report suggests, at best, a different intent. Perhaps a reader could infer that the committee planned to allow conversion but mistakenly voted for a different text. So two members of the committee have said since, calling § 302(c)(1) an oversight. See 133 Cong. Rec. S2273–76 (daily ed. Feb. 19, 1987) (Sen. Grassley), E544 (daily ed. Feb. 19, 1987) (Rep. Coelho). Not only the committee's remarks on conversion but also the omission of § 302(c)(1) from the section-by-section description of the bill suggest that whoever wrote the report (a staffer, not a Member of Congress) wanted § 302(c)(1) deleted and may have thought that had been accomplished. Still another possibility is that the Conference Committee meant to distinguish Chapter 11 from Chapter 13: to ban conversions from Chapter 11 (covered by § 302(c)(1)) but

[handwritten at top: Maybe allow   Ch 13 → 13]

allow them from Chapter 13. On this reading the gaffe is the failure to delete the reference to Chapter 11 from the report, which could still stand as a treatment of conversions from Chapter 13.

Congress has done nothing to change § 302(c)(1), implying that the statement in the committee report may have been the error. It is easy to imagine opposing forces arriving at the conference armed with their own texts and legislative histories, and in the scramble at the end of session one version slipping into the bill and the other into the report. Whichever was the blunder, we know which one was enacted. What came out of conference, what was voted for by House and Senate, what was signed by the President, says that pending Chapter 11 cases may not be converted. Accordingly, pending Chapter 11 cases may not be converted.

[handwritten margin note: law enacted + voted by House + Senate + signed yes]

NOTES ON SINCLAIR AND THE SEARCH FOR OBJECTIVITY IN STATUTORY INTERPRETATION

1.   *Textual Evidence Judge Easterbrook Missed.* Judge Easterbrook cites § 302 of the 1986 statute, which seems to prevent conversion of the *Sinclair* proceeding. But the legislative history he cites is the Conference Committee language not of § 302, but of § 256(1), which amended 11 U.S.C. § 1112(d). Section 1112 is the provision of Chapter 11 that deals with conversions. As amended, it now reads:

> (d)   The Court may convert a case under this chapter to a case under chapter 12 or 13 of this title only if—
>
> *[handwritten: + Apply to pending proceeding]*
>
>> (1)   the debtor requests such conversion;
>>
>> (2)   the debtor has not been discharged under section 1141(d) of this title; and
>>
>> (3)   if the debtor requests conversion to chapter 12 of this title, such conversion is equitable.

Is the statutory text 100% clear against conversion? It is only if § 256(1) is interpreted not to apply to pending proceedings (see Chapter 5, § 3(C)).

In light of this evidence, construct an argument that *In re Sinclair* is wrongly decided.[373] We have brought this evidence to Judge Easterbrook's attention, and he responded that it would not change his thinking about this case, because the new textual evidence was not briefed by the parties and in any event he was not persuaded that this new evidence created any statutory ambiguity. Does this additional information demonstrate ambiguity? *[handwritten: yes.]*

2.   *Judicial Fears of the Mischievous Staffer.* An enduring image from Justice Scalia's *Bergeron* concurring opinion (and a standard trope in Scalia's speeches deriding legislative history) is the possibility that mischievous staffers will smuggle stuff into committee reports and thereby "trick" judges into bad interpretations that Congress did not "intend." Notice how staffers bent on mischief can do the same thing to statutory text. In *Sinclair*, Judge Easterbrook notes that several Members of Congress later said that a mistake somehow arose with respect to § 302(c)(1), the effective date provision, and that

---

[373]   For an extraordinary discussion concerning broader jurisprudential issues lingering in the *Sinclair* case, see Paul Campos, *The Chaotic Pseudotext*, 94 Mich. L. Rev. 2178 (1996).

the Congress intended to allow conversion of pending farmer bankruptcy proceedings. There are at least three reasons to believe that this is accurate.

First, it is fishy that the Conference Report has no mention of § 302(c)(1). That the "dog didn't bark" in the Conference Report is odd in light of a second factor, the emergency nature of this law. The 1986 act creating Chapter 12 was adopted during the most serious farm economic depression since the 1930s. Farmers had been going under left and right, and Congress decided to ameliorate their debt situation somewhat by adopting Chapter 12, which is more favorable to farmers than is the bankruptcy scheme of Chapter 11, which is available to all debtors. This "help the farmers during this emergency" purpose of the 1986 statute seems in stark conflict with the notion that only future cases could be converted to new Chapter 12. Moreover, § 1112(d) as amended allows conversion only in cases in which it would be equitable, thereby providing some measure of protection to creditors in pending proceedings. Finally, according to prevalent rumors in one segment of the bankruptcy bar, at the behest of lending interests a Senate staff member put § 302 into the bill, contrary to the apparent wishes of the sponsors and supporters of the 1986 statute. It appears that sponsors and supporters of the statute did not even notice § 302 until well after the statute had been adopted. This may shed new light on why § 302 was not discussed in the section-by-section description of the bill in the conference committee report. This rumor seems to turn on its head the complaint by new textualists that *legislative history* is unreliable stuff because of potential shenanigans by legislative staff.[374]

3. *Objectivity in Statutory Interpretation: Empirical Evidence from the Supreme Court's Labor and Employment Cases.* Complementing the image of the mischievous staffer in Justice Scalia's pitch for the new textualism is the result-oriented judge who will look out over the legislative history crowd and pick out his friends. You might review the *big cases* in this Casebook, such as *Weber*, the affirmative action case in Chapter 1; *Holy Trinity* and the FDA Tobacco Case in Chapter 5; and *Sweet Home* at the end of this chapter. In all these cases, Justices (including Scalia, in *Sweet Home*) invoke legislative history to support results that match those Justices' apparent ideologies—but in all the cases except *Holy Trinity* the Justices also invoke textual plain meaning in the same way.

Properly phrased, the inquiry demanded by the new textualism's appeal to objectivity in judging is that a judge who looks at legislative history as well as text is *more likely* to read his or her ideological presuppositions into a statute than a judge who just looks at the text alone. There is no empirical evidence that this is the case—and now some evidence to the contrary. See James Brudney and Corey Ditslear, *Liberal Justices' Reliance on Legislative History: Principle, Strategy, and the Scalia Effect*, 29 Berkeley J. Emp. & Lab. L. 117 (2008). In conducting a deeper empirical analysis of the 578 Supreme Court decisions interpreting basically pro-employee labor and employment statutes (1969–2006), the authors analyzed the voting records of the eight Justices conventionally considered "liberal" and reached the following conclusions:

> [F]or the eight liberals, the relationship between pro-employee outcomes and legislative history usage is not significant. If anything, these Justices' legislative history reliance is associated more often with outcomes to which they would likely be ideologically opposed. When liberal Justices use legislative

---

[374]   On end-of-the-game strategic moves in the legislative process, see William Rodgers, Jr., *The Lesson of the Red Squirrel: Consensus and Betrayal in the Environmental Statutes*, 5 J. Contemp. Health L. & Pol. 161 (1989).

history as part of their majority reasoning, they do so to help justify more than half of their *pro-employer* opinions for the Court but just under one-half of their *pro-employee* outcomes. Further evidence of this moderating association is that majority opinions authored by liberal Justices reach liberal outcomes 30 percent more often than conservative results when *not* relying on legislative history, but the liberal-conservative outcome differential declines to 21 percent when the majority opinion's reasoning includes legislative history. *Id.* at 121.

For the Justices considered "conservative," Brudney and Ditslear found that reliance on legislative history also was correlated with slightly more conservative voting. As for what types of legislative history from pro-employee federal statutes supported so many pro-employer outcomes, the authors identified three distinct categories: (1) legislative history that amplified or unpacked the meaning of employer defenses or exemptions built into the statutes; (2) history that established the existence or details of a compromise on the issue under review; (3) history demonstrating that the legal position identified with employees and their supporters had overreached in its claims. An example of the second category outside of labor law is *Muscarello* in chapter 6, § 3(A), where liberal Justice Breyer relied on legislative history to interpret ambiguous statutory language and impose a harsh sentence on gun-"carrying" defendants. This is preliminary evidence *against* the judicial objectivity argument for textualism.

On the other hand, Brudney and Ditslear also found that this moderating association has waned among the cohort of liberal Justices since Justice Scalia's appointment to the Court. The authors' provisional explanation is that Justice Scalia's hard-hitting style has polarized the Court, leading liberal Justices who wish to secure Scalia's unqualified support for their pro-employer majorities to abandon legislative history even when the prevailing parties have relied heavily on that history in their briefs. See *id.* at 160–67. Has Judge Leventhal's quip become a self-fulfilling prophesy?

NOTE ON LEGISLATIVE HISTORY IN A POST-SCALIA ERA

The unexpected death of Justice Scalia in the middle of the Supreme Court's 2015 Term has left legal observers and scholars wondering how the removal of the most influential textualist justice might impact the Court's approach to legislative history. During the 2010–2014 Terms, other justices invoked legislative history but there was often an undeniable self-consciousness to their usage. See, e.g., *United States v. Kwai Fun Wong*, 135 S.Ct. 1625, 1633 (2015) (Kagan, J.) ("even assuming legislative history alone could provide a clear statement (which we doubt), none does so here."); *Adoptive Couple v. Baby Girl*, 570 U.S. 637, 649 (2013) (Alito, J.) ("And if the legislative history of the [Indian Child Welfare Act] is thought to be relevant, it further underscores . . ."); *Hall v. United States*, 132 S.Ct. 1882, 1888 n.3 (2012) (Sotomayor, J.) ("For those of us for whom it is relevant, the legislative history confirms"). Indeed, five of the eight other justices (all except Justices Kennedy and Thomas and the Chief Justice) made such prefatory qualifying remarks when using legislative history in at least a dozen opinions during this period—opinions that Justice Scalia often joined without criticizing the majority's reliance. See James Brudney & Lawrence Baum, *Protean Statutory Interpretation in the Courts of Appeals*, 58 Wm. & Mary L. Rev. 681, 743–44 (2017).

Given Justice Scalia's well-documented hostility to committee reports and floor debates, other justices apparently decided to accommodate a colleague, and avoid his sharply critical concurring or dissenting remarks, while not abandoning their interest in relying on such legislative record materials for confirmatory purposes. At the same time, the decision by these justices to imply that legislative history is of limited interest or qualified importance to the Court conveys a sense of second-class status in the pantheon of interpretive resources. In Justice Scalia's absence, will we see evidence of a different approach, in which legislative history is invoked more robustly, without diminutive or quasi-apologetic prefatory phrases?

Digital Realty Trust, Inc. v. Somers

138 S.Ct. 767 (2018).

Both the Sarbanes-Oxley Act of 2002, (Sarbanes-Oxley), and the 2010 Dodd-Frank Wall Street Reform and Consumer Protection Act, (Dodd-Frank) protect whistleblowers from retaliation. But while Sarbanes-Oxley applies to all employees reporting misconduct to the Securities and Exchange Commission (SEC or Commission), another federal agency or an internal supervisor, Dodd-Frank protects only individuals reporting misconduct "to the Commission." Under Dodd-Frank, whistleblowers are protected from retaliation for "making disclosures that are required or protected under" Sarbanes-Oxley, certain criminal law provisions, and any law subject to the SEC's jurisdiction.

The Court had to decide whether the anti-retaliation provision of Dodd-Frank extends to an individual who has not reported a violation of the securities laws to the SEC and therefore falls outside the Act's definition of "whistleblower." **Justice Ginsburg** for the Court concluded that the statute did not extend protection for such individuals. She relied on the statutory definition referenced above (specifying a report to the Commission), and on the canon of meaningful variation in that a separate whistleblower-protection provision of Dodd-Frank, applicable to employees of the Consumer Financial Protection Bureau, covered reports to a wide range of state and federal authorities.

In addition, Justice Ginsburg invoked Dodd-Frank's "purpose and design [to] corroborate our comprehension of [the textual] reporting requirement." She relied on discussion in the Senate committee report that the whistleblower program's "core objective [is] to motivate people who know of securities law violations to *tell the SEC*," S. Rep. No. 111–176, at 38 (emphasis added by Court). Justice Ginsburg also cited the legislative history when elaborating on differences between the two statutes' whistleblower provisions; she noted that "[w]hile Sarbanes-Oxley contains an administrative-exhaustion requirement, a 180-day administrative complaint-filing deadline, and a remedial scheme limited to actual damages, Dodd-Frank provides for immediate access to federal court, a generous statute of limitations (at least six years), and the opportunity to recover double backpay. Dodd-Frank's award program and anti-retaliation provision thus work synchronously to motivate individuals with knowledge of illegal activity to 'tell the SEC.' S. Rep. No. 111–176, at 38."

There were no dissenting opinions, but two concurrences drew support from five separate justices. **Justice Thomas**, writing for himself, **Justice Alito**, and **Justice Gorsuch**, concurred only in part and in the judgment.

"I join the Court's opinion only to the extent it relies on the text of the Dodd-Frank Wall Street Reform and Consumer Protection Act. The question in this case is whether the term 'whistleblower' in Dodd-Frank's antiretaliation provision includes a person who does not report information to the Securities and Exchange Commission. * * * As the Court observes, this statutory definition 'resolves the question before us.' The Court goes on, however, to discuss the supposed 'purpose' of the statute, which it primarily derives from a single Senate Report. Even assuming a majority of Congress read the Senate Report, agreed with it, and voted for Dodd-Frank with the same intent, 'we are a government of laws, not of men, and are governed by what Congress enacted rather than by what it intended.' *Lawson v. FMR LLC*, 571 U.S.429, 459–60 (2014) (Scalia, J., concurring in part and concurring in judgment). And 'it would be a strange canon of statutory construction that would require Congress to state in committee reports . . . that which is obvious on the face of a statute.' *Harrison v. PPG Industries, Inc.*, 446 U.S. 578, 592 (1980). For these reasons, I am unable to join the portions of the Court's opinion that venture beyond the statutory text."

Justice Sotomayor, joined by **Justice Breyer**, joined the majority opinion in full but also took aim at the Thomas concurrence.

"I write separately only to note my disagreement with the suggestion in my colleague's concurrence that a Senate Report is not an appropriate source for this Court to consider when interpreting a statute.

"Legislative history is of course not the law, but that does not mean it cannot aid us in our understanding of a law. Just as courts are capable of assessing the reliability and utility of evidence generally, they are capable of assessing the reliability and utility of legislative-history materials.

"Committee reports, like the Senate Report the Court discusses here, are a particularly reliable source to which we can look to ensure our fidelity to Congress' intended meaning. See *Garcia v. United States*, 469 U.S. 70, 76 (1984) ('In surveying legislative history we have repeatedly stated that the authoritative source for finding the Legislature's intent lies in the Committee Reports on the bill, which 'represen[t] the considered and collective understanding of those Congressmen involved in drafting and studying proposed legislation' (quoting *Zuber v. Allen*, 396 U.S. 168, 186 (1969))). Bills presented to Congress for consideration are generally accompanied by a committee report. Such reports are typically circulated at least two days before a bill is to be considered on the floor and provide Members of Congress and their staffs with information about 'a bill's context, purposes, policy implications, and details,' along with information on its supporters and opponents. R. Katzmann, Judging Statutes 20, and n. 62 (2014) (citing A. LaRue, Senate Manual Containing the Standing Rules, Orders, Laws, and Resolutions Affecting the Business of the United States Senate, S. Doc. No. 107–1, p. 17 (2001)). These materials 'have long been important means of informing the whole chamber about proposed legislation,' Katzmann, Judging Statutes, at 19, a point Members themselves have emphasized over the years. It is thus no surprise that legislative staffers view committee and conference reports as the most reliable type of legislative history. See Gluck & Bressman, Statutory Interpretation From the Inside— An Empirical Study of Congressional Drafting, Delegation and the Canons: Part I, 65 Stan. L. Rev. 901, 977 (2013).

"Legislative history can be particularly helpful when a statute is ambiguous or deals with especially complex matters. But even when, as here, a statute's meaning can clearly be discerned from its text, consulting reliable legislative history can still be useful, as it enables us to corroborate and fortify our understanding of the text. See, e.g., *Tapia v. United States*, 564 U.S. 319, 331–332 (2011); *Carr v. United States*, 560 U.S. 438, 457– 458 (2010). Moreover, confirming our construction of a statute by considering reliable legislative history shows respect for and promotes comity with a coequal branch of Government. See Katzmann, Judging Statutes, at 35–36.

"For these reasons, I do not think it wise for judges to close their eyes to reliable legislative history—and the realities of how Members of Congress create and enact laws—when it is available."

NOTES ON DIGITAL REALTY AND ONGOING LEGISLATIVE HISTORY DEBATES

1.   *Drawing Lines on the Post-Scalia Court.* Justice Sotomayor's concurrence argues for the utility of legislative history as a confirming or corroborating resource even when textual meaning seems plain. To what extent does this argument echo the approach taken by Justice Rehnquist in *Griffin v. Oceanic Contractors* (see Chapter 5, § 2(C))? Justice Thomas's concurrence channels the views of the late Justice Scalia. Indeed, in a footnote omitted here, Thomas reproduces the notorious Dole-Armstrong colloquy repeatedly invoked by Scalia, including the material omission identified by the Casebook authors in *Notes* following *Blanchard v. Bergeron* above. Should we attach any significance to the fact that Chief Justice Roberts and Justice Kennedy—both occasional skeptics about the value of legislative history—do not join either concurrence? What about Justice Kagan, who regularly invokes such history?

In *Lamar, Archer, & Cofrin, LLP v. Appling*, 138 S.Ct 1752 (2018), decided three months after *Digital Realty,* Justice Sotomayor for a six-member majority invoked legislative history analysis in her opinion to reinforce her reading of the text. Justices Kennedy, Roberts, and Kagan joined the majority without comment. But once again, Justices Thomas, Gorsuch, and Alito declined to join the legislative history section of the majority opinion.

2.   *Confirmatory Legislative History.* In *Samantar v. Yousuf,* 560 U.S. 305 (2010), Justice Scalia reiterated his particular distaste for legislative history when used simply to confirm a clear statutory text:

> The Court's admirably careful textual analysis demonstrates that the term "foreign state" in the provision "a foreign state shall be immune from the jurisdiction of the courts of the United States and of the States," 28 U.S.C. § 1604, does not include foreign officials. Yet the Court insists on adding legislative history to its analysis. I could understand that (though not agree with it) if, in the absence of supposed legislative-history support, the Court would reach a different result. Or even if there was something in the legislative history that clearly contradicted the Court's result, and had to be explained away. That is not the situation here (or at least the Court's opinion does not think it to be so) * * *.

> The Court's introduction of legislative history serves no purpose except needlessly to inject into the opinion a mode of analysis that not all of the Justices consider valid. And it does so, to boot, in a fashion that does not isolate the superfluous legislative history in a section that those of us who disagree categorically with its use, or at least disagree with its superfluous use, can decline to join. * * * It should be no cause for wonder that, upon careful examination, all of the opinion's excerpts from legislative history turn out to be, at best, nonprobative or entirely duplicative of text. After all, legislative history

is almost never the real reason for the Court's decision—and make-weights do not deserve a lot of the Court's time.

Is Justice Scalia correct that the use of legislative history is particularly troubling and unnecessary when the statutory text is clear? In *Confirmatory Legislative History*, 76 Brooklyn L. Rev. 901 (2011), Brudney notes that confirmatory legislative history has a long historical pedigree motivated by a concern for judicial completeness:

> From the early days of the Supreme Court, justices have observed that when "labour[ing] to discover the design of the legislature, [a judge] seizes everything from which aid can be derived." *United States v. Fisher*, 6 U.S. (2 Cranch) 358, 386 (1805) (Marshall, C.J.). More recently, the Court has explained that in a confirmatory setting 'common sense suggests that inquiry benefits from reviewing additional information rather than ignoring it." *Wis. Pub. Intervenor v. Mortier*, 501 U.S. 597, 611–12 n.4 (1991) (White, J.). This judicial instinct to explore all potentially relevant information is crosscultural if not universal. In Britain, even when the House of Lords prohibited courts from consulting legislative history at all to aid in construing enacted laws, there were distinguished jurists who confessed—in their opinions and on the floor of Parliament—to peeking at the legislative record evidence in search of further enlightenment.

Brudney contends that this quest for completeness when interpreting presumptively clear text reflects in part a desire to avoid error or injustice. Beyond the search for reassurance, confirmatory discussion in judicial opinions may promote other important values. One is judicial accountability: courts considering legislative history arguments in their decisions demonstrate respect for attorneys' efforts in presenting the arguments and thereby attest to the procedural neutrality of our judicial system. Another is transparency: by illuminating all plausible arguments as an essential aspect of their reasoned decision-making, judges avoid succumbing to more conclusory and less deliberative thinking on contested statutory matters. Finally, there is guidance to repeat litigants, especially the executive branch that must construe and apply statutes featuring varying degrees of semantic detail, technical complexity, ideological compromise, and potential for constitutional controversy.

NOTE ON STATE COURT RELIANCE ON COMMITTEE REPORTS AND OTHER LEGISLATIVE HISTORY SOURCES

New Jersey is one of a number of states that have regular reports from standing committees to accompany legislation, and it is one of a smaller number to make committee reports for recent legislation available online. See Adam G. Yoffie, *From Poritz to Rabner: The New Jersey Supreme Court's Statutory Jurisprudence, 2000–2009*, 35 Seton Hall Legis. J. 302, 309–10 (2011). Traditionally, New Jersey state judges have been willing to rely on legislative history to construe statutes. See, e.g., *McClain v. Board of Review, Dep't of Labor*, 206 A.3d 353, 364 n.2 (N.J. 2019) (relying on Senate and Assembly committee statements accompanying bill); *State v. Fleischman*, 917 A.2d 722, 730 n.4 (N.J. 2007) (committee report and whole act creating textual ambiguity, triggering rule of lenity); *Bosland v. Warnock Dodge, Inc.*, 964 A.2d 741, 747 (N.J. 2009). Judges in that state sometimes consider committee reports whether or not the statute's text is ambiguous. See *Pruent-Stevens v. Toms River Twp.*, 206 A.3d 417, 423 (App. Div. 2019) ("Although resort to the legislative history is unnecessary given that the statutory language is clear and unambiguous, and susceptible to only one interpretation," court proceeds to consult sponsors' statements and committee reports.). But compare *State v. Lyons*, 9 A.3d 596, 601 (N.J. App. Div. 2010) ("[i]f the statute is clear and unambiguous on its face and admits of only one interpretation, we need delve no deeper than the act's literal terms to divine the Legislature's intent").

In **Oregon**, the legislature in 2001 provided that the parties may offer legislative history in any case, whether there is ambiguity or not. Ore. Rev. Stat. § 174.020(1)(b) (2001). Although initially cautious following this statutory addition, the Oregon Supreme Court in recent years has regularly consulted legislative history whether or not there is textual ambiguity. See, e.g., *State v. McNally*, 392 P.3d 721, 728 (Or. 2017); *Brown v. SAIF Corp.*, 391 P.3d 773, 792–93 (Or. 2017); *State v. Makin*, 381 P.3d 799, 801 (Or. 2016).

For examples of state appellate courts' reliance on committee reports, see *People v. Berg,* 23 Cal. App. 5th 959, 966 (**California** Ct. App. 2018); *Washington v. United States*, 206 A.3d 864, 868 (**District of Columbia** 2019); *Nakamoto v. Kawauchi*, 418 P.3d 600, 611 (**Hawaii** 2018); *Sallee v. Stewart*, 827 N.W.2d 128, 141 (**Iowa** 2013); *Lang v. State*, 561 S.W.3d 174, 181–82 (**Texas** Crim. App. 2018).

In other states a "bill report" is prepared by the committee staff after a bill is voted out of committee, but it is not necessarily reviewed by the committee or even its chair. The bill report typically contains a background statement, a summary of the bill's provisions, changes made by the committee, a list of the proponents and opponents who testified before the committee, and the pro and con arguments. Courts will sometimes discount such sources. In a number of states, courts consider bill reports as weak but admissible evidence of legislative intent. For example, the Supreme Court of **Florida** has deemed bill reports "one touchstone of the collective legislative will." *White v. State*, 714 So. 2d 440, 443 n.5 (**Florida** 1998), while not always embracing them. See *Kasischke v. State*, 991 So.2d 803, 811 (**Florida** 2008) ("Therefore, even if staff analyses may sometimes help in determining legislative intent, and even if we could expect defendants to review them to determine what conduct was permitted, the Staff Analysis here fails to clarify the Legislature's intent."). See generally *People v. Ramirez*, 201 P.3d 466, 470 (**California** 2009) and *In re Derrick B.*, 139 P.3d 485 (**California** 2006); *Kramer v. Liberty Prop. Trust*, 968 A.2d 120 (**Maryland** 2009); *Fournier v. Elliott*, 966 A.2d 410 (**Maine** 2009); *Mayor of City of Lansing v. Mich. Pub. Serv. Comm'n*, 680 N.W.2d 840, 849 (**Michigan** 2004); *Krupa v. State*, 286 S.W.3d 74 (**Texas** Crim. App. 2009); *Cosmopolitan Engr'g Group, Inc. v. Ondeo Degremont, Inc.*, 149 P.3d 666, 672–73 (**Washington** 2006).

In **New York**, the governor's staff compiles a "bill jacket" (the New York term) to assist the governor in her or his decision whether to veto a bill the legislature has passed. Containing analyses from legislative sponsors as well as interested agencies and private parties, bill jackets are often treasure troves of legislative background materials and legal arguments. See, e.g., *Matter of James Q.*, 120 N.E. 3d 358, 362 (**New York** 2019). Similar reports, called "governor's bills files," can be found in public archives for California, Massachusetts, Oregon, Utah, Washington, and perhaps other states. See generally *Stokes v. Baker*, 35 Cal. App.5th 946 (**California** Ct. App. 2019) (relying on bill author's letter, consented to be printed in Assembly Journal); *Ramirez*, 201 P.3d at 471–72 (relying on sponsor's letter to file compiled for governor in **California**).

In addition to committee reports and bill reports, state legislative history can include a number of other reports compiled by official sources before statutes are enacted. In her dissenting opinion in *State ex rel. Kalal v. Circuit Ct., Dane Cnty.*, 681 N.W.2d 110, 125–26 (**Wisconsin** 2004), Chief Justice Shirley Abrahamson listed other sources her court had traditionally considered, including not just legislative committee reports, but also legislative reference bureau drafting files and prefatory notes for bills, governor's study commission reports, judicial council notes, joint legislative council notes, and governor's veto messages. Wisconsin's Supreme Court still routinely relies on such materials. E.g., *State v. Dorsey,* 906 N.W. 2d 158, 171 (**Wisconsin** 2018) (legislative reference bureau's bill analysis); *State v. Duchow,* 749 N.W.2d 913 (**Wisconsin** 2008) (legislative reference bureau's drafting file). But cf. *State ex rel Dep't of Nat. Res. v. Wisconsin Court of Appeals, Dist. IV,* 909 N.W.2d 114, 126 n.14 (**Wisconsin** 2018) (majority dismisses dissent's reliance on legislative reference bureau bill analysis: "We can assume all legislators received the Bureau's memo. But we have no idea how many read it, or whether the Bureau's use of 'permit' caught their attention or influenced their understanding of the bill, or whether (assuming it did) the Bureau's word-choice influenced their votes, and if it did, whether a majority of each chamber was persuaded to adopt the dissent's understanding of the language they enacted because the Bureau used the word 'permit' in its memo.") See also *Price v. Tens Built Buses, Inc.*, 260 S.W.3d 300, 305–06 (**Arkansas** 2007) (resolving ambiguity by reference to legislative council report); *Jones v. Lodge*, 177 P.3d 232, 240–43 (**California** 2008) (relying on legislative counsel's digest summarizing bills, as well as committee report and agency bill analysis); *People ex. rel. Ryan ex. rel. Shaver v. Cheverko*, 2 N.E.3d 233, 235 (**New York** 2013) (commission staff notes relied on); *McKinney v. Richetelli*, 586 S.E.2d 258, 263 (**North Carolina** 2003) (report of general statutes commission).

In at least one state, there has been serious debate as to what kinds of legislative materials might be admissible. An important decision is *People v. Gardner*, 753 N.W.2d 78, 89 (**Michigan** 2008), where a divided Michigan Supreme Court ruled that legislative materials could only be considered when the statute is ambiguous *and* that only certain legislative materials should be admissible. *Admissible* materials included the statutory history and evidence of proposals rejected by one chamber or the other. *Inadmissible* materials, even when the statute is ambiguous, included committee reports, staff analyses of bills, and floor speeches by sponsors and other legislators. In 2008, the textualist chief justice was turned out of office by the voters, but the court evidently continues to pursue a textualist agenda. See Joseph Kimble, *What the Michigan Supreme Court Wrought in the Name of Textualism and Plain Meaning: A Study of Cases Overruled, 2000–2015*, 62 Wayne L. Rev. 347 (2017).

Consideration of committee and bill reports is hardly a monopoly of large-population states. Practices similar to those in the previous paragraphs can be found in **Alaska**, see, e.g., *Municipality of Anchorage v. Adamson*, 301 P.3d 569, 576–77 (Alaska 2013); **Arizona**, see, e.g., *Haag v. Steinle*, 255 P.3d 1016, 1018 (Ariz. Ct. App. 2011); and **Connecticut**, see, e.g., *Town of Middlebury v. Dep't of Environmental Protection*, 927 A.2d 793, 804 (Conn. 2007). Some states have no high-court authorization for considering committee reports though they may be open to the practice in cases yet to be decided. Judges in these states will discuss "statutory history" (the formal evolution of the statute, as amended over time); see, e.g., **Wyoming**, *McCallister v. State ex rel. Dep't of Workforce Servs., Workers' Comp. Div.*, 440 P.3d 1078, 1086 (Wyo. 2019). Courts in **Missouri** and **Georgia** generally have not cited to legislative history. E.g., *Grange Mut. Casualty Co.*

v. Woodward, 797 S.E.2d 814, 823 (Ga. 2017); *State v. Premium Standard Farms, Inc.*, 100 S.W.3d 157 (Mo. Ct. App. 2003). And some smaller states have no readily available legislative history; there are too few reported decisions to discern a hard-and-fast rule for lawyer use of legislative history. E.g., **Rhode Island**, *Such v. State*, 950 A.2d 1150, 1158–59 (R.I. 2008), relied on in *State Dep't of Corrections v. Rhode Island Bhd. of Corr. Officers*, 64 A.3d 736 n.2 (R.I. 2013).

Finally, legislative history at the state level is more accessible than it was a generation ago. See William Manz, *Guide to State Legislation, Legislative History, and Administrative Materials* (7th ed. 2008). Indeed, judges are sometimes even encouraging counsel to research it. In *Dillehey v. State*, 815 S.W.2d 623 (**Texas** Crim. App. 1991), the appeals court not only relied on legislative history but, in an appendix to the court's opinion, provided counsel in future cases with a roadmap for researching legislative history in Texas. Increasingly, state legislative history is online. Some state supreme courts provide guides to researching legislative history on their websites.[375]

C. STATEMENTS BY SPONSORS OR DRAFTERS OF LEGISLATION

Next to committee reports, the most persuasive legislative materials are explanations of statutory meanings, and compromises reached to achieve enactment, by the sponsors and floor managers of the legislation. Recall that Senator Humphrey and the other primary sponsors of the Civil Rights Act of 1964 were primary sources of legislative history on both sides of the affirmative action debate in *United Steelworkers v. Weber* (Chapter 1, § 2). Because there was no Senate Report for that legislation, the sponsors' statements were most reliable. Even Justice Scalia relied on a sponsor's explanation as key evidence for his dissent in *Sweet Home*, excerpted at the end of this chapter.

As the availability of legislative history for state statutes has dramatically increased, state courts, too, are relying on statements of sponsors to interpret statutes. See, e.g., *Commonwealth v. Ahlborn*, 626 A.2d 1265 (Pa. 1993) (relying on explanation of clarifying amendment, acquiesced in by the committee chair, as useful evidence of legislative intent); *Dillehey v. State*, 815 S.W.2d 623 (Tex. Crim. App. 1991) (relying on colloquy and providing counsel with roadmap for researching legislative history in Texas). On the other hand, statements by ordinary legislators are rarely given much, if any, weight. See *Murphy v. Kenneth Cole Prods., Inc.*, 40 Cal. 4th 1094 (2007) ("we do not consider the motives or understandings of individual legislators, including the bill's author"); *Quelimane Co. v. Stewart Title Guar. Co.*, 960 P.2d 513 (Cal. 1998).

The statements by sponsors are given such deference in part because the sponsors are the most knowledgeable legislators about the proposed bill and in part because their representations about the purposes and effects of the proposal are relied upon by other legislators. This approach is not without its detractors, however. Sponsors or their friends might have incentives to distort the legislative history through "planned colloquies." Congressman William Moorhead, in *A Congressman*

---

[375]   See, e.g., the Washington Supreme Court's website, https://www.courts.wa.gov/library/?fa=library. displayGuides&fileID=rschGuideLeg (viewed June 26, 2019). A good source to find all state legislative history guides is the Indiana University law library: https://law.indiana.libguides.com/c.php?g=19813&p=112411.

Looks at the Planned Colloquy and Its Effect in the Interpretation of Statutes, 45 A.B.A.J. 1314, 1314 (1959), observed that Members of Congress are aware that courts will look to the record of floor debates, especially statements by sponsors of legislation, and that "by the use of the 'friendly colloquy', two [legislators] may be able to legislate more effectively than all of Congress." He continued:

> Many if not most bills are controversial to some degree, and often it may be desirable when drafting a bill to couch provisions in innocuous language in order to minimize possible objections during committee consideration. Naturally, however, the proponents of a particular viewpoint would like to insure that their interpretation be the accepted one. The friendly colloquy on the floor during debate can serve well in this situation. Acquiescence by the committee [chair] in a stated intent will very likely be relied upon by the courts in the absence of objection or other reliable evidence of an opposite intent.

Note the similarity between this bit of realism about colloquies and the Armstrong-Dole exchange about committee reports (Note 1 after *Bergeron*).

Political scientists tend to discount this kind of evidence, because sponsors who distort the deals reached to achieve statutory enactments will not be trusted in future legislative deals. Moreover, judges have shown themselves increasingly sophisticated in handling such evidence. For a recent example, Justice Stevens interpreted the Detainee Treatment Act of 2005 to be not retroactive in *Hamdan v. Rumsfeld*, 548 U.S. 557 (2006). He relied on the statement of Senator Levin, one of the sponsors, and discounted statements by two other sponsors (Senators Kyl and Graham) whose remarks were apparently inserted into the Congressional Record *after the fact*. *Id*. at 580 n.10. Characteristically, Justice Scalia objected that the majority's editing of the legislative history was not only selective, but illustrated the general unreliability of such materials. *Id*. at 665–68 (Scalia, J., dissenting).

Speaking of Justice Scalia, when he was a judge on the D.C. Circuit, one of his arguments against judicial use of legislative history was that the United Kingdom's House of Lords had long excluded its use.[376] He lost that argument in the case that follows—where the House of Lords found the statutory explication by the parliamentary floor manager not only decisive evidence, but evidence that flipped everyone's reading of the statute's "plain meaning."

PEPPER V. HART

House of Lords for the United Kingdom, 1992.
[1993] 1 All E.R. 42, [1992] 3 W.L.R. 1032.

[Malvern College allowed employees to send their children to the school for 20% of the fees paid by other parents. The employees and the tax collector agreed that this kind of fringe benefit was subject to income taxation, but disagreed on how to

---

[376]   This argument was made in then-Judge Scalia's standard speech against legislative history, a copy of which was obtained and distributed by the *Virginia Law Review* and is analyzed in Daniel Farber & Philip Frickey, *Legislative Intent and Public Choice*, 74 Va. L. Rev. 423, 440–43 (1988).

measure the benefit. The statute in question, § 63 of the Finance Act of 1976, defined "cash equivalent of the benefit," which was the measure of taxable benefit, as follows:

> (1) The cash equivalent of any benefit chargeable to tax under section 61 above is an amount equal to the cost of the benefit, less so much (if any) of it as is made good by the employee to those providing the benefit.

> (2) Subject to the following subsections, the cost of a benefit is the amount of any expense incurred in or in connection with its provision, and (here and in those subsections) includes a proper proportion of any expense relating partly to the benefit and partly to other matters.

Because the school in question had not been able to fill all its seats, its marginal costs in providing education to these children were minimal (involving a few items of equipment and food) and amounted to less than the fees paid by the employees. Accordingly, the employees argued that they had received no actual income at all, because the fringe benefit they received, measured as the (marginal) expense incurred by their employer, was less than the fees they had paid. The tax collector disagreed, arguing that the "expense incurred" should be average cost per pupil incurred by the school. When this case made its way to the Law Lords on appeal, they initially voted 4–1 in favor of the tax collector. On rehearing, when they were urged to consider the legislative history, the Law Lords expanded the appellate panel, which then reached the opposite result. In a landmark ruling under English law, the expanded panel abandoned the rule that British courts may not consult legislative history.]

LORD MACKAY OF CLASHFERN [LORD CHANCELLOR].

* * * The benefit which the taxpayers in this case received was the placing of their children in surplus places at the college, if as a matter of discretion the college agreed to do so. * * * They were in a similar position to the person coming along on a standby basis for an airline seat as against the passenger paying a full fare, and without the full rights of a standby passenger, in the sense that the decision whether or not to accommodate them in the college was entirely discretionary. If one regards the benefit in this light I cannot see that the cost incurred in, or in connection with, the provision of the benefit, can properly be held to include the cost incurred, in any event, in providing education to fee-paying pupils at the school who were there as a right in return for the fees paid in respect of them. * * * Although the later words of section 63(2) * * * provide that the expense incurred in, or in connection with, the provision of a benefit includes a proper proportion of any expense relating partly to the benefit and partly to other matters, I consider that the expenses incurred in provision of places for fee-paying pupils were wholly incurred in order to provide those places. * * * I conclude that looking at the matter from the point of view of expense incurred and not from the point of view of loss to the employer no expense could be regarded as having been incurred as a result of the decision of the authorities of the college to provide this particular benefit to the taxpayer.

Notwithstanding the views that have found favour with others I consider this to be a reasonable construction of the statutory provisions and I am comforted in the fact that, apart from an attempt to tax airline employees, which was taken to the Special Commissioners who decided in favour of the taxpayer, this has been the practice of the Inland Revenue in applying the relevant words where they have occurred in the Income Tax Acts for so long as they have been in force, until they initiated the present cases.

At the very least it appears to me that the manner in which I have construed the relevant provisions in their application to the facts in this appeal is a possible construction and that any ambiguity there should be resolved in favour of the taxpayer.

For these reasons I would allow these appeals. I should perhaps add that I was not a member of the committee who heard these appeals in the first hearing * * *.

But much wider issues than the construction of the Finance Act 1976 have been raised in these appeals and for the first time this House has been asked to consider a detailed argument on the extent to which reference can properly be made before a court of law in the United Kingdom to proceedings in Parliament recorded in Hansard.

For the appellant [taxpayers] Mr. Lester submits that it should now be appropriate for the courts to look at Hansard in order to ascertain the intention of the legislators as expressed in the proceedings on the Bill which has then been enacted in the statutory words requiring to be construed. This submission appears to me to suggest a way of making more effective proceedings in Parliament by allowing the court to consider what has been said in Parliament as an aid to resolving an ambiguity which may well have become apparent only as a result of the attempt to apply the enacted words to a particular case. * * *

The principal difficulty I have on this aspect of the case is that in Mr. Lester's submission reference to Parliamentary material as an aid to interpretation of a statutory provision should be allowed only with leave of the court and where the court is satisfied that such a reference is justifiable:

(a) to confirm the meaning of a provision as conveyed by the text, its object and purpose;

(b) to determine a meaning where the provision is ambiguous or obscure; or

(c) to determine the meaning where the ordinary meaning is manifestly absurd or unreasonable.

I believe that practically every question of *statutory* construction that comes before the courts will involve an argument that the case falls under one or more of these three heads. It follows that the parties' legal advisors will require to study Hansard [the official collection of parliamentary debates] in practically every such case to see whether or not there is any help to be gained from it. I believe this is an objection of real substance. It is a practical objection not one of principle * * *. Such an approach appears to me to involve the possibility at least of an immense increase in the cost of litigation in which statutory construction is involved. * * * [T]he Law Commission and the Scottish Law Commission, in their joint report on *The Interpretation of Statutes* (1969) (Law Com. no. 21) (Scot. Law Com. no. 11) and the

Renton Committee Report on *The Preparation of Legislation* ((1975) Cmnd. 6053), advised against a relaxation on the practical grounds to which I have referred. * * *

[We omit the separate opinions of LORD BRIDGE OF HARWICH, LORD GRIFFITHS, LORD OLIVER OF AYLMERTON, LORD KEITH OF KINKEL, and LORD ACKNER. With varying degrees of enthusiasm, all five agreed with the following opinion by LORD BROWNE-WILKINSON. Lords Bridge and Oliver had voted in the first hearing to dismiss the appeal, but the Hansard materials impelled them to change their votes. Finding the statute ambiguous, Lord Griffiths had voted with the taxpayer in the first hearing.]

LORD BROWNE-WILKINSON.

* * * [I]t is necessary first to refer to the legislation affecting the taxation of benefits in kind before 1975. Under the Finance Act 1948, section 39(1), directors and employees of bodies corporate earning more than £2,000 per annum were taxed under Schedule E on certain benefits in kind. The amount charged was the expense incurred by the body corporate "in or in connection with the provision" of the benefit in kind. By section 39(6) it was provided that references to expenses "incurred in or in connection with any matter includes a reference to a proper proportion of any expense incurred partly in or in connection with that matter." Employment by a school or charitable organisation was expressly excluded from the charge: sections 41(5) and 44. These provisions were re-enacted in the Income and Corporation Taxes Act 1970.

Those provisions covered in-house benefits as well as external benefits. We were told that after 1948 the Revenue sought to tax at least two categories of employees in receipt of in-house benefits. Higher-paid employees of the railways enjoy free or concessionary travel on the railways. The Revenue reached an agreement that such employees should be taxed on 20% (later 25%) of the full fare. Airline employees also enjoy concessionary travel. We were told that in the 1960s the Revenue sought to tax such employees on that benefit on the basis of the average cost to the airline of providing a seat, not merely on the marginal cost. The tax commissioners rejected such claim: the Revenue did not appeal. Therefore in practice from 1948 to 1975 the Revenue did not seek to extract tax on the basis of the average cost to the employer of providing in-house benefits. * * *

The Finance Bill 1976 sought to make a general revision of the taxation of benefits in kind. The existing legislation on fringe benefits was to be repealed. Clause 52 of the Bill as introduced eventually became section 61 of the Act of 1976 and imposed a charge to tax on benefits in kind for higher-paid employees, i.e., those paid more than £5,000 per annum. Clause 54 of the Bill eventually became section 63 of the Act of 1976. As introduced, clause 54(1) provided that the cash equivalent of any benefit was to be an amount equal to "the cost of the benefit." Clause 54(2) provided that, except as provided in later subsections "the cost of a benefit is the amount of any expense incurred in or in connection with its provision." Crucially, clause 54(4) of the Bill sought to tax in-house benefits on a different basis from that applicable to external benefits. It provided that the cost of a benefit consisting of the provision of any service or facility which was also provided to the public (i.e., in-house benefits) should be the price which the public paid for such facility or service. Employees of schools were not excluded from the new charge.

Thus if the 1976 Bill had gone through as introduced, railway and airline employees would have been treated as receiving benefits in kind from concessionary travel equal to the open market cost of tickets and schoolmasters would have been taxed for concessionary education on the amount of the normal school fees.

After second reading, clause 52 of the Bill was committed to a committee of the whole House and clause 54 to Standing Committee E. On 17 May 1976, the House considered clause 52 and strong representations were made about the impact of clause 52 on airline and railway employees. At the start of the meeting of Standing Committee E on 17 June 1976 (before clause 54 was being discussed) the Financial Secretary to the Treasury, Mr. Robert Sheldon, made an announcement (Hansard, columns 893–895) in the following terms:

"The next point I wish to make concerns services and deals with the position of employees of organisations, bodies, or firms which provide services, where the employee is in receipt of those services free or at a reduced rate. Under Clause 54(4) the taxable benefit is to be based on the arm's length price of the benefit received. At present the benefit is valued on the cost to the employer. Representations have been made concerning airline travel and railway employees. . . . It was never intended that the benefit received by the airline employee would be the fare paid by the ordinary passenger. The benefit to him would never be as high as that, because of certain disadvantages that the employee has. Similar considerations, although of a different kind, apply to railway employees. I have had many interviews, discussions and meetings on this matter and I have decided to withdraw Clause 54(4). I thought I would mention this at the outset because so many details, which would normally be left until we reached that particular stage, will be discussed with earlier parts of the legislation. I shall give some reasons which weigh heavily in favour of the withdrawal of this provision. The first is the large difference between the cost of providing some services and the amount of benefit which under the Bill would be held to be received. There are a number of cases of this kind, and I would point out that air and rail journeys are only two of a number of service benefits which have a number of problems attached to them. But there is a large difference between the cost of the benefit to the employer and the value of that benefit as assessed. It could lead to unjustifiable situations resulting in a great number of injustices and I do not think we should continue with it. . . .

"The second reason for withdrawing Clause 54(4) is that these services would tend to be much less used. The problem would then arise for those who had advocated the continuation of this legislation that neither the employer nor the employee nor the Revenue would benefit from the lesser use of these services. This factor also weighed with me. The third reason is the difficulty of enforcement and administration which both give rise to certain problems. Finally, it was possible to withdraw this part of the legislation as the services cover not only a more difficult area, but a quite distinct area of these provisions, without having repercussions on some of the other areas. . . .

[His Lordship quoted several further references where the Financial Secretary insisted that the government's intent was not to change the tax treatment previously afforded to railway and airline employees; they would and should be allowed to receive free travel and be assessed only for the extra cost to the employer.]

Simultaneously with the announcement to the standing committee, a press release was issued announcing the withdrawal of clause 54(4). It referred to the same matters as the Financial Secretary had stated to the Committee and concluded:

> "The effect of deleting this subclause will be to continue the present basis of taxation of services, namely the cost to the employer of providing the service."

The point was further debated in committee on 22 June 1976. A member is reported as saying, at column 1013, that

> "Like many others, I welcome the concession that has been made to leave out the airline staff and the railway employees and all the others that are left out by the dropping of clause 54(4)." * * *

The very question which is the subject matter of the present appeal was also raised. A member said, at columns 1091–1092:

> "I should be grateful for the Financial Secretary's guidance on these two points. . . . The second matter applies particularly to private sector, fee-paying schools where, as the Financial Secretary knows, there is often an arrangement for the children of staff in these schools to be taught at less than the commercial fee in other schools. I take it that because of the deletion of Clause 54(4) that is not now caught. Perhaps these examples will help to clarify the extent to which the Government amendment goes."

The Financial Secretary responded to this question as follows:

> "He mentioned the children of teachers. The removal of clause 54(4) will affect the position of a child of one of the teachers at the child's school, because now the benefit will be assessed on the cost to the employer, which would be very small indeed in this case." (Column 1098.)

Thereafter, clause 54 was not the subject of further debate and passed into law as it now stands as section 63 of the Act. * * *

Under present law, there is a general rule that reference to Parliamentary material as an aid to statutory construction is not permissible ("the exclusionary rule") * * *. The exclusionary rule was probably first stated by Willes J. in *Millar v. Taylor* [1769] 4 Burr. 2303, 2332. [Lord Browne-Wilkinson provided a brief history of the exclusionary rule and possible loopholes as well as criticisms that developed over time.]

My Lords, I have come to the conclusion that, as a matter of law, there are sound reasons for making a limited modification to the existing rule (subject to strict safeguards) unless there are constitutional or practical reasons which outweigh them. In my judgment, subject to the questions of the privileges of the House of Commons, reference to Parliamentary material should be permitted as an aid to the construction of legislation which is ambiguous or obscure or the literal meaning of which leads to an absurdity. Even in such cases references in court to Parliamentary material should only be permitted where such material clearly discloses the mischief aimed at or the legislative intention lying behind the ambiguous or obscure words. In the case of statements made in Parliament, as at present advised I cannot foresee that any statement other than the statement of the minister or other promoter of the Bill is likely to meet these criteria.

I accept Mr. Lester's submissions [for the taxpayers], but my main reason for reaching this conclusion is based on principle. Statute law consists of the words that Parliament has enacted. It is for the courts to construe those words and it is the court's duty in so doing to give effect to the intention of Parliament in using those words. It is an inescapable fact that, despite all the care taken in passing legislation, some statutory provisions when applied to the circumstances under consideration in any specific case are found to be ambiguous. One of the reasons for such ambiguity is that the members of the legislature in enacting the statutory provision may have been told what result those words are intended to achieve. Faced with a given set of words which are capable of conveying that meaning it is not surprising if the words are accepted as having that meaning. Parliament never intends to enact an ambiguity. Contrast with that the position of the courts. The courts are faced simply with a set of words which are in fact capable of bearing two meanings. The courts are ignorant of the underlying Parliamentary purpose. Unless something in other parts of the legislation discloses such purpose, the courts are forced to adopt one of the two possible meanings using highly technical rules of construction. In many, I suspect most, cases references to Parliamentary materials will not throw any light on the matter. But in a few cases it may emerge that the very question was considered by Parliament in passing the legislation. Why in such a case should the courts blind themselves to a clear indication of what Parliament intended in using those words? The court cannot attach a meaning to words which they cannot bear, but if the words are capable of bearing more than one meaning why should not Parliament's true intention be enforced rather than thwarted?

A number of other factors support this view. As I have said, the courts can now look at white papers and official reports for the purpose of finding the "mischief" sought to be corrected, although not at draft clauses or proposals for the remedying of such mischief. A ministerial statement made in Parliament is an equally authoritative source of such information: why should the courts be cut off from this source of information as to the mischief aimed at? In any event, the distinction between looking at reports to identify the mischief aimed at but not to find the intention of Parliament in enacting the legislation is highly artificial. Take the normal Law Commission Report which analyses the problem and then annexes a draft Bill to remedy it. It is now permissible to look at the report to find the mischief and at the draft Bill to see that a provision in the draft was *not* included in the legislation enacted. There can be no logical distinction between that case and looking at the draft Bill to see that the statute as enacted reproduced, often in the same words, the provision in the Law Commission's draft. Given the purposive approach to construction now adopted by the courts in order to give effect to the true intentions of the legislature, the fine distinctions between looking for the mischief and looking for the intention in using words to provide the remedy are technical and inappropriate. Clear and unambiguous statements made by ministers in Parliament are as much the background to the enactment of legislation as white papers and Parliamentary reports.

The decision in *Pickstone v. Freemans Plc.* [1989] A.C. 66 which authorises the court to look at ministerial statements made in introducing regulations which could not be amended by Parliament is logically indistinguishable from such statements made in introducing a statutory provision which, though capable of amendment, was not in fact amended. * * *

Text books often include reference to explanations of legislation given by a minister in Parliament, as a result of which lawyers advise their clients taking account of such statements and judges when construing the legislation come to know of them. In addition, a number of distinguished judges have admitted to breaching the exclusionary rule and looking at Hansard in order to seek the intention of Parliament. When this happens, the parties do not know and have no opportunity to address the judge on the matter. A vivid example of this occurred in the *Hadmor* case [1983] 1 A.C. 191 where Lord Denning in the Court of Appeal relied on his own researches into Hansard in reaching his conclusions: in the House of Lords, counsel protested that there were other passages to which he would have wished to draw the court's attention had he known that Lord Denning was looking at Hansard: see the *Hadmor* case at 233. It cannot be right for such information to be available, by a sidewind, for the court but the parties be prevented from presenting their arguments on such material. * * *

It is said that Parliamentary materials are not readily available to, and understandable by, the citizen and his lawyers who should be entitled to rely on the words of Parliament alone to discover his position. It is undoubtedly true that Hansard and particularly records of Committee debates are not widely held by libraries outside London and that the lack of satisfactory indexing of Committee stages makes it difficult to trace the passage of a clause after it is redrafted or renumbered. But such practical difficulties can easily be overstated. It is possible to obtain Parliamentary materials and it is possible to trace the history. The problem is one of expense and effort in doing so, not the availability of the material. In considering the right of the individual to know the law by simply looking at legislation, it is a fallacy to start from the position that all legislation is available in a readily understandable form in any event: the very large number of statutory instruments made every year are not available in an indexed form for well over a year after they have been passed. Yet, the practitioner manages to deal with the problem albeit at considerable expense. Moreover, experience in New Zealand and Australia (where the strict rule has been relaxed for some years) has not shown that the non-availability of materials has raised these practical problems.

Next, it is said that lawyers and judges are not familiar with Parliamentary procedures and will therefore have difficulty in giving proper weight to the Parliamentary materials. Although, of course, lawyers do not have the same experience of these matters as members of the legislature, they are not wholly ignorant of them. If, as I think, significance should only be attached to the clear statements made by a minister or other promoter of the Bill, the difficulty of knowing what weight to attach to such statements is not overwhelming. In the present case, there were numerous statements of view by members in the course of the debate which plainly do not throw any light on the true construction of section 63. What is persuasive in this case is a consistent series of answers given by the minister, after opportunities for taking advice from his officials, all of which point the same way and which were not withdrawn or varied prior to the enactment of the Bill.

Then it is said that court time will be taken up by considering a mass of Parliamentary material and long arguments about its significance, thereby increasing the expense of litigation. In my judgment, though the introduction of further admissible material will inevitably involve some increase in the use of time, this will not be significant as long as courts insist that Parliamentary material should only be introduced in the limited cases I have mentioned and where such material contains a clear indication from the minister of the mischief aimed at, or the nature of the cure intended, by the legislation. Attempts to introduce material which does not satisfy those tests should be met by orders for costs made against those who have improperly introduced the material. Experience in the United States of America, where legislative history has for many years been much more generally admissible than I am now suggesting, shows how important it is to maintain strict control over the use of such material. That position is to be contrasted with what has happened in New Zealand and Australia (which have relaxed the rule to approximately the extent that I favour): there is no evidence of any complaints of this nature coming from those countries.

There is one further practical objection which, in my view, has real substance. If the rule is relaxed legal advisers faced with an ambiguous statutory provision may feel that they have to research the materials to see whether they yield the crock of gold, i.e., a clear indication of Parliament's intentions. In very many cases the crock of gold will not be discovered and the expenditure on the research wasted. This is a real objection to changing the rule. However, again it is easy to overestimate the cost of such research: if a reading of Hansard shows that there is nothing of significance said by the minister in relation to the clause in question, further research will become pointless.

In sum, I do not think that the practical difficulties arising from a limited relaxation of the rule are sufficient to outweigh the basic need for the courts to give effect to the words enacted by Parliament in the sense that they were intended by Parliament to bear. Courts are frequently criticised for their failure to do that. This failure is due not to cussedness but to ignorance of what Parliament intended by the obscure words of the legislation. The courts should not deny themselves the light which Parliamentary materials may shed on the meaning of the words Parliament has used and thereby risk subjecting the individual to a law which Parliament never intended to enact.

[The last section of his Lordship's opinion discussed the "constitutional" issue whether adverting to Hansard is a "questioning" of the freedom of parliamentary speech and debate that is prohibited by article 9 of the Bill of Rights of 1688. His Lordship interpreted article 9 much like the U.S. Constitution's Speech and Debate Clause (see Chapter 3, § 2) and found it inapplicable.]

The Attorney General raised a further constitutional point, namely, that for the court to use Parliamentary material in construing legislation would be to confuse the respective roles of Parliament as the maker of law and the courts as the interpreter. I am not impressed by this argument. The law, as I have said, is to be found in the words in which Parliament has enacted. It is for the courts to interpret those words so as to give effect to that purpose. The question is whether, in addition to other aids to the construction of statutory words, the courts should have regard to a further source. Recourse is already had to white papers and official reports not because they determine the meaning of the statutory words but because they assist the court to make its own determination. I can see no constitutional impropriety in this. * * *

I therefore reach the conclusion, subject to any question of Parliamentary privilege, that the exclusionary rule should be relaxed so as to permit reference to Parliamentary materials where:

(a)   legislation is ambiguous or obscure, or leads to an absurdity;

(b)   the material relied on consists of one or more statements by a minister or other promoter of the Bill together if necessary with such other Parliamentary material as is necessary to understand such statements and their effect;

(c)   the statements relied on are clear.

[In the present case, the statute was ambiguous and the Hansard materials clearly resolved the ambiguity in favor of the taxpayers.]

The question then arises whether it is right to attribute to Parliament as a whole the same intention as that repeatedly voiced by the Financial Secretary. In my judgment it is. It is clear from reading Hansard that the committee was repeatedly asking for guidance as to the effect of the legislation once subclause (4) of clause 54 was abandoned. That Parliament relied on the ministerial statements is shown by the fact that the matter was never raised again after the discussions in committee, that amendments were consequentially withdrawn and that no relevant amendment was made which could affect the correctness of the minister's statement. * * *

NOTES ON PEPPER AND THE DEMISE OF THE EXCLUSIONARY RULE

1.   *The Abandonment of the Exclusionary Rule in English-Speaking Countries.* In the United Kingdom, *Pepper v. Hart* created quite a stir, and unleashed a fair amount of interest in legislative history by lower courts and the House of Lords. See James Brudney, *Below the Surface: Comparative Legislative History Usage by the House of Lords and the Supreme Court*, 85 Wash. U.L. Rev. 1 (2007) (demonstrating that much of the Hansard reliance is to minister (floor manager) explanations and *not* to committee reports, which are not routinely generated in Parliament). On the other hand, Brudney found that during the post-*Pepper* period, the Lords have greatly increased their references to government white papers and commission reports, background documents with some

similarity to our committee reports. In short, the Lords are explicitly considering a lot more background materials than they did twenty years ago.

In October 2009, the House of Lords' jurisdiction was transferred to the new U.K. Supreme Court, and since that date the judges on it are referred to as Justices rather than Law Lords. Although the Justices remained divided over the wisdom of *Pepper*, a majority of them are committed to this new course of action, within limits that have yet to be determined once and for all.[377] In *Regina (Jackson) v. Attorney General*, [2005] All Eng. Law Rep. 1253, for example, the Lords unanimously upheld the famous Hunting Act, which deployed a 1911 statute to override House of Lords opposition to a popular measure. Lord Bingham's lead opinion rejected the relevance of Hansard as authoritative evidence of parliamentary "intent" but relied on the debates (including eight rejected proposals) to confirm the meaning of words Parliament used in the 1911 statute. Lord Nicholls's speech relied even more extensively on Hansard, as confirmation of what he and the other Lords considered the apparent meaning of the text. Lord Steyn objected to any use of Hansard in these circumstances.

The House of Lords' decision in *Pepper v. Hart* has had echoes throughout the Commonwealth countries. The leading Canadian treatise states: "Since the 1980s the [exclusionary] rule has been eroding. Some courts have ignored it while others have carved out significant exceptions and qualifications." *Sullivan* 595. See also David Duff, *Interpreting the Income Tax Act*, 47 Can. Tax. J. 471 & 741 (1999) (two-part article on use of legislative history in tax cases). The exclusionary rule had previously been abandoned in the United States, see *Holy Trinity* (Chapter 5, § 1); Australia, see Commonwealth Acts Interpretation Act § 15ab, discussed in Gifford (Chapter 6, § 1 n.2) and other Commonwealth countries. Many civil-law countries still follow such a rule or practice, however.

2.   *When Should Legislative Materials Be Admissible? The Potato Chip Problem.* The key opinion is that of Lord Browne-Wilkinson, who admits legislative materials, but only in limited circumstances. But how should we characterize the holding of the case? This is more difficult than appears on first glance.

(a)   *Sponsor Statements May Be Consulted When the Statute Is Ambiguous.* This appears to be the holding as articulated by Lord Browne-Wilkinson, and the U.S. Supreme Court sometimes says it follows a like rule. See, e.g., *Director, OWCP v. Greenwich Collieries*, 512 U.S. 267 (1994). But does this precept explain the decision in this case? The first committee of Law Lords found the statute unambiguous against the taxpayer; on the original panel, only Lord Griffith found ambiguity. Lord Chancellor Mackay found ambiguity on rehearing and voted for the taxpayer on that ground, but only Lord Griffith agreed with him. Other Lords, including Browne-Wilkinson, found ambiguity only after they consulted the Hansard materials.

(b)   *Hansard Materials May Be Consulted to Confirm Statutory Plain Meaning.* The narrowest interpretation of *Pepper*, embraced by Lord Steyn and others, is that Hansard

---

[377]   For example, Lord Millett, *Construing Statutes*, 20 Stat. L. Rev. 107 (1999), maintained that *Pepper* was a mistake and that the Lords should return to their previous practice of relying exclusively on statutory text. Lord Hoffman praised *Pepper* for opening up probative evidence of legislative intent (and for discouraging government ministers from making promises to Parliament that they might later renounce) but was skeptical that the costs of extra research were worth these benefits. Hon. Lord Hoffman, *The Intolerable Wrestle With Words and Meanings*, 114 S. Afr. L. J. 656, 669 (1997); see also *Robinson v. Sec'y of State for Northern Ireland*, [2002] N. Ir. L. Rep. 390, 405 (Lord Hoffman, repeating his lament that *Pepper* generated large research costs, with scant benefit).

materials can only be introduced for textualist reasons, namely, to suggest or confirm standard usage of statutory terms and the plain meaning they have to reasonable speakers of the English language.

(c) *Hansard May Be Invoked to Clear up Any Statutory Matters.* In the aftermath of *Pepper*, some Law Lords used the decision as a Magna Carta for browsing parliamentary debates for what they were worth, essentially ignoring Lord Browne-Wilkinson's suggested limits. See David Miers, *Taxing Perks and Interpreting Statutes: Pepper v. Hart*, 56 Mod. L. Rev. 695, 705–06 (1993). Few Lords in the new millennium openly endorse this position, and there are procedural hurdles in place,[378] but there is some indication that some lower court judges are running wild with legislative materials. Should this have been expected?

Aside from the precise limits suggested in this case, consider a *potato chip theory*, suggested by the U.S. history after *Holy Trinity*: once a court starts looking at the "best" legislative history, like committee reports and sponsor statements, other kinds of history will get smuggled in, on the ground that they provide "context" for understanding the committee reports (which of course provide "context" for understanding the text). Before long, everything becomes relevant and might be considered "for what it is worth" (the trend in modern evidence law, by the way). Just as you can never eat just one potato chip, you can never admit just one bit of legislative history. It might take decades for the potato chip process to develop, but the theory is that Hansard reliance will grow by fits and starts until there is some kind of crisis that pushes in the other direction.

3.   *Relevance for the U.S. Debate?* Should *Pepper* suggest to the new textualists that they should adopt a more moderate skepticism about legislative materials?[379] If you were Justice Scalia, how would you have voted in *Pepper*? (Hint: Consider the *evolution* of the treatment of in-house benefits, from 1948 to 1993, nicely laid out in Lord Browne-Wilkinson's opinion. You can be a textualist and consider the formal evolution of the statutory scheme, as the U.S. Supreme Court did in *Leo Sheep*. What argument might a textualist draw from that?)

Brudney, *Below the Surface*, argues that the U.S. Supreme Court should conclude from the Mother Country's post-*Pepper* practice that the most fruitful debates focus not on the tired admissibility debate, but rather on the circumstances under which legislative history would be useful. "[S]hould legislative history be regarded as presumptively more valuable to help resolve textual ambiguities that stem from lack of foresight rather than lack of political consensus? Is legislative history accompanying omnibus bills generally less suitable for judicial use because congressional deals on such a grand scale are simply indecipherable? Should legislative history in certain subject areas be presumed to have less weight where the law is administered primarily by a federal agency rather than

---

[378]   The Lords directed that financial sanctions would be visited upon a party who relied on Hansard in a case that did not meet the three requirements of Lord Browne-Wilkinson's opinion. Also, the Lords issued a Practice Directive in 1994 (reaffirmed in 1999 and 2002) which required parties intending to invoke Hansard to give prior notice, including copies of the pages in Hansard and the argument to be made from it. Brudney, *Below the Surface*.

[379]   See, e.g., John Manning, *Textualism as a Nondelegation Doctrine*, 97 Colum. L. Rev. 673 (1997), which presents a constitutional justification for refusing to consider committee reports "authoritative" (in the way the statute is) but admitting them as evidence of what the statutory words might mean. On *Pepper* and American practice, see Michael Healy, *Legislative Intent and Statutory Interpretation in England and the United States: An Assessment of the Impact of* Pepper v. Hart, 35 Stan. J. Int'l L. 231 (1999).

private parties, or where the statutory text tends to be detailed and technical rather than open-ended and of more general public interest?"

NOTE ON STATE COURT RELIANCE ON SPONSOR'S STATEMENTS

Like the U.K. House of Lords (and now the U.K. Supreme Court), and unlike the U.S. Supreme Court, state supreme courts in this country at times rely more heavily on the statements of legislative sponsors than on committee or bill reports as the sources for illumination about legislative expectations. A large majority of states make available to the public transcripts of legislative floor debates and of committee hearings. See Brian Barnes, "The Transformation of State Statutory Interpretation," at 10–11 (Yale Law School Seminar Paper, May 4, 2010) (33 states offer transcripts or tapes of current legislative floor debates, with 17 offering them on-line as of 2010); *id.* at 12–13 (37 states offer transcripts or tapes of current committee hearings, with 16 offering them on-line as of 2010). Much of the floor debate consists of statements by the sponsor or floor manager presenting the case for the proposed legislation, responding to objections made by opponents, and answering questions posed by colleagues.

Committee chairs (who are usually later the floor managers) play a large role in committee hearings, making speeches, questioning witnesses, and explaining proposed legislation. Because the sponsor/floor manager is usually the most knowledgeable legislator on topics relating to the proposed legislation and usually represents the coalition pushing for the legislation, his or her statements are much more probative than those of other legislators. Recall, for example, the Oregon Court of Appeals decision in *PGE* (Chapter 5, § 3(C)), where the dissenting judges relied on the explanation by the committee chair.

For examples of state supreme court decisions relying on statements by legislative sponsors or floor managers, see *State v. Batts*, 195 P.3d 144, 151–52 (**Alaska** 2008) (sponsor's explanation critical evidence of statutory meaning); *Carter v. Cal. Dep't of Veterans Affairs*, 135 P.3d 637, 646–47 (**California** 2006) (treating sponsor's memo as authoritative but finding that it does not answer the issue before the court); *Hunsaker v. People of the State of Colorado*, 351 P.3d 388, 394 (**Colorado** 2015) (relying on sponsor's statement as "powerful evidence of legislative intent" even if not conclusive); *Nowak v. City of Country Club Hills*, 958 N.E.2d 1021, 1024–25 (**Illinois** 2011) (relying heavily on statements from House and Senate sponsors to demonstrate the purpose of the statute); *State v. Allen*, 708 N.W.2d 361, 366–67 (**Iowa** 2006); *Rural Water Dist. #2 v. City of Louisburg*, 207 P.3d 1055 (**Kansas** 2009) (post-enactment letter from sponsor invoked to support plain meaning); *Stewart Title Guar. Co. v. State Tax Assessor*, 963 A.2d 169, 178–79 (**Maine** 2009) (ambiguity resolved by reference to statutory history as explained by sponsor); *Kramer v. Liberty Prop. Trust*, 968 A.2d 120 (**Maryland** 2009) (sponsor's statement confirms plain meaning); *Lazlo L. v. Commonwealth,* 122 N.E. 2d 532, 541 (**Massachusetts** 2019) (relying on statements from House and Senate committee chairs); *Stockman Bank of Mont. v. Mon-Kota, Inc.*, 180 P.3d 1125 (**Montana** 2008); *Chanos v. Nevada Tax Comm'n*, 181 P.3d 675, 680 & n.17 (**Nevada** 2008); *State v. Mayer*, 186 P.3d 293, 297–98; *Wilson v. City of Jersey City,* 39 A.3d 177, 190–91 (**New Jersey** 2012) (relying on Senate sponsors' statements); *Lawrence Cnty. Educ. Ass'n v. Lawrence Cnty. Bd. of Educ.*, 244 S.W.3d 302, 312 (**Tennessee** 2007); *Dep't of Corr. v. Human Rights Comm'n*, 917 A.2d 451, 453 (**Vermont** 2007).

Like the U.S. Supreme Court, state supreme courts will not credit stray statements by legislators who are probably not speaking for the enacting coalition. See, e.g., *Gillan v. Government Employees Ins. Co.*, 194 P.3d 1071, 1082–83 (**Hawaii** 2008). Likewise, state supreme courts (like federal courts) will not credit post-hoc affidavits by the sponsors or floor managers of enacted bills, because the post-hoc nature of such evidence deprives it of reliability. See, e.g., *Forster v. Town of Henniker*, 118 A.3d 1016, 1024 (**New Hampshire** 2015); *Rhoades v. State of Iowa*, 880 N.W. 2d 431, 447 (**Iowa** 2016); *Entergy Gulf States, Inc. v. Summers*, 282 S.W. 2d 433, 443–44 (**Texas** 2009). Efforts to invoke after-the-fact legislator affidavits often occur (and are usually rebuffed) in states where there is not (at the time) much publicly available legislative material. See, e.g., *Tomei v. Sharp*, 902 A.2d 757, 769 n.41 (**Delaware** Super. 2006); *Utility Ctr., Inc. v. City of Fort Wayne*, 868 N.E.2d 453, 459–60 (**Indiana** 2007); *Direct TV, Inc. v. Levin*, 907 N.E.2d 1242, 1253 (**Ohio** App. 2009); *Catawba Indian Tribe of S.C. v. State*, 642 S.E.2d 751, 754 n.5 (**South Carolina** 2007); *Phillips v. Larry's Drive-In Pharmacy, Inc.*, 647 S.E.2d 920, 924–26 (**West Virginia** 2007).

NOTES ON VIEWS OF NONLEGISLATOR DRAFTERS

1.   *Statements of Nonlegislative Drafters.* In *Kosak v. United States*, 465 U.S. 848 (1984), the Court construed the Federal Tort Claims Act (FTCA) to reject a serviceman's claim for liability after his personal art objects, being shipped from Guam to Philadelphia, were damaged while detained in the custody of the Customs Service. Writing for the majority, Justice Marshall relied in part on an explanation of the contested FTCA text (§ 2680(c), the same exemption at issue in *Ali v. Federal Bureau of Prisons*, see Chapter 6, § 1(B)) that had been offered by Judge Alexander Holtzoff, a major figure in developing the FTCA and the likely author of the precise language in dispute. The Holtzoff Report on the proposed FTCA, prepared while Judge Holtzoff was a Special Assistant to the Attorney General, was submitted to the Justice Department and the GAO in 1931, fifteen years before Congress enacted the law. Justice Marshall agreed with the dissent that, "because the report was never introduced into the public record, the ideas expressed therein should not be given great weight in determining the intent of the legislature. But, in the absence of any direct evidence regarding how members of Congress understood the provision that became § 2680(c), it seems to us senseless to ignore entirely the views of its draftsman." *Id.* at 857, n.13.

The majority opinion in *Kosak* realistically recognized that much legislation is drafted by nonlegislators—mainly executive officials and interest groups. But why should the views of a nonlegislator count—especially if the Court deems its inquiry as a search for the "intent" of *Congress*? Moreover, Holtzoff's memorandum was not "public." Distinguish between the testimony at congressional hearings by Holtzoff, in which Members of Congress could disagree with him (either then or during subsequent floor debate),[380] and his Department of Justice memorandum, which was written before the bill was acted upon even by a committee and which may have represented only his (and not even the Department's) point of view. Why should the latter be entitled to any consideration at all? Are there other ways of thinking about statutory interpretation which make Judge Holtzoff's statement relevant? (Hint: maybe, like a good commentary in a treatise or a law review article, it makes the most sense of the legislation.) See

---

[380]   Ironically, when Holtzoff's public testimony was relevant to an issue of interpretation, the Court ignored it. Compare *Sheridan v. United States*, 487 U.S. 392 (1988) (opinion of the Court), with *id.* at 410 (O'Connor, J., dissenting).

generally Alison Giles, Note, *The Value of Nonlegislators' Contributions to Legislative History*, 79 Geo. L.J. 359 (1991).

Notwithstanding these objections, the Supreme Court or individual Justices have occasionally relied on statements by public, nonlegislative officials who draft or promote statutes. See, e.g., *Circuit City Stores, Inc. v. Adams*, 532 U.S. 105, 128–29 (2001) (Stevens, J., dissenting) (dissenters relying on defense of statute by Secretary of Commerce; majority does not address this argument because of plain meaning rule); *Negonsott v. Samuels*, 507 U.S. 99, 106–09 (1993); *Gollust v. Mendell*, 501 U.S. 115, 125 & n.7 (1991); *Howe v. Smith*, 452 U.S. 473, 485 (1981); *Monroe v. Standard Oil Co.*, 452 U.S. 549, 558–59 (1981). Note, however, that (as in *Kosak*) the Court will not rely on these statements as the most probative—and certainly not the *only*—evidence of statutory meaning. There are very few state cases; almost all of them either reject or denigrate such evidence. E.g., *Hayes v. Continental Ins. Co.*, 872 P.2d 668 (Ariz. 1994).

2.   *Statements of Private Drafters.* At least Holtzoff was a public servant. Should the Court consider authoritative the statements of interest groups which draft and press for legislation? In some instances the Court or some Justices have considered testimony about legislation by private groups or individuals who drafted or commented on the legislation. See, e.g., *Circuit City Stores*, 532 U.S. at 127 (Stevens, J., dissenting) (relying on explanation by ABA committee that originated the statute); *Gustafson v. Alloyd Co.*, 513 U.S. 561 (1995) (relying on statement by Professor Landis, submitted as part of legislative deliberations, as support for Court's text-based interpretation); *Jefferson Cnty. Pharm. Assoc. v. Abbott Labs*, 460 U.S. 150, 159–62 (1983) (relying on explanation of lobbyist who was principal drafter of the statute in question); *NLRB v. Robbins Tire & Rubber Co.*, 437 U.S. 214, 230–32 (1978) (relying on explanation of ABA Administrative Law Division, which had originally proposed the statutory amendment in question during Senate hearings). See also *Grp. Life & Health Inc. Co. v. Royal Drug Co.*, 440 U.S. 205 (1979); *Southland Corp. v. Keating*, 465 U.S. 1, 26–29 (1984) (O'Connor, J., dissenting).

D. HEARINGS, FLOOR DEBATE, REJECTED PROPOSALS, AND DOGS THAT DIDN'T BARK

Compared to statements in committee reports, statements made during committee hearings and floor debates have traditionally received less weight in evaluating legislative intent. If the statement was made by a sponsor or informed supporter of the bill, courts might credit it as a reliable indication of legislative intent—as did the Supreme Court majority and dissenting opinions in *Weber* or as the House of Lords did in *Pepper v. Hart*. The conventional wisdom is that what is said in hearings and floor debates is usually of little value, except for confirmatory purposes. Reed Dickerson, *Statutory Interpretation: Dipping into Legislative History*, 11 Hofstra L. Rev. 1125, 1131–32 (1983).

Reflecting on the Burger Court's practice, Judge Patricia Wald, *Legislative History in the 1981 Term, supra*, 68 Iowa L. Rev. at 202, opined that "[t]he hornbook rule that hearings are relevant only as background to show the purpose of the statute no longer holds. In many cases, the best explanation of what the legislation is about comes from the executive department or outside witnesses at the hearings." Indeed, since proposed legislation is frequently drafted by the executive department or by private interest groups, their statements and explanations at hearings might be the only truly informed explanation of the structure and operation of the statute. E.g., *Gustafson v. Alloyd Co.*, 513 U.S. 561 (1995) (testimony of academic expert commenting on interest group arguments made during congressional deliberations); *Lowe v. SEC*, 472 U.S. 181, 195–99 (1985) (testimony of industry witnesses at hearings); *Trbovich v. United Mine Workers of America*, 404 U.S. 528 (1972) (Senate hearing testimony by Senator John Kennedy, the sponsor, and Professor Archibald Cox, primary drafter of the proposed legislation). Now that many states record committee hearings, and still others provide staff summaries of statements made in them, state courts are coming to rely on statements made in those hearings.[381]

Potentially relevant for similar reasons are presidential statements initiating or issued during congressional deliberations, especially when the President has been a prime mover behind a piece of legislation, as he was with the Civil Rights Act of 1964 and the Voting Rights Act of 1965. Thus, presidential transmittal letters or speeches advocating legislation have sometimes been considered useful legislative history, e.g., *NLRB v. Local 103, Int'l Ass'n of Bridge Workers*, 434 U.S. 335, 347 n.9 (1978); *Connell Constr. Co. v. Plumbers & Steamfitters Local 100*, 421 U.S. 616, 629 n.8 (1975); *W. Union Tel. Co. v. Lenroot*, 323 U.S. 490, 492 (1945). See generally Kathryn Dessayer, Note, *The First Word: The President's Place in "Legislative History,"* 89 Mich. L. Rev. 399 (1990).

In a like spirit, Justices sometimes rely on floor debates, including exchanges between supporters and opponents. Although statements by legislators about bills they oppose are not reliable, see *NLRB v. Fruit & Vegetable Packers*, 377 U.S. 58, 66 (1964), exchanges with supporters may sharpen the precise deals that have been reached. See *BankAmerica v. United States*, 462 U.S. 122 (1983), where the Court relied on a colloquy among two supporters and an opponent at the very end of the legislative debate that spoke directly, and dramatically, to the issue before the Court. In *Weber*, by way of contrast, Justice Brennan's majority opinion responded that all of Justice Rehnquist's parade of quotes critical of racial quotas were uttered before Title VII achieved its final form, laden with compromises, including § 703(j) (which Brennan found critical to his judgment that Congress was tolerant of *voluntary* affirmative action). "To permit what we regard as clear statutory language to be materially altered by such colloquies, which often take place before the bill has achieved its final form, would open the door to the inadvertent, or perhaps even planned, undermining of the language actually voted on by Congress * * *." *Regan v. Wald*, 468 U.S. 222, 237–42 (1984).

---

[381]   For state cases relying on statements in hearings, see, e.g., *Pac. Bell v. Cal. State and Consumer Servs. Agency*, 275 Cal. Rptr. 62, 67–68 (Cal. App. 1990) (testimony in committee hearings); *People v. Luciano*, 662 P.2d 480, 482 n.4 (Colo. 1983) (recordings of Senate and House committee hearings); *In re Sheldon G.*, 583 A.2d 112, 116 & n.6 (Conn. 1990) (testimony in committee hearings); *Jackson v. Kansas City*, 235 Kan. 278 (1984) (statements in committee hearings); *First Nat'l Bank of Deerwood v. Gregg*, 556 N.W.2d 214 (Minn. 1996) (tape-recorded hearings); *Wiseman v. Keller*, 358 N.W.2d 768 (Neb. 1984) (judiciary committee hearing); *Linlee Enters., Inc. v. State*, 445 A.2d 1130, 1131 (N.H. 1982) (House committee hearing and subcommittee report); *Dickinson v. Fund for Support of Free Pub. Schs.*, 469 A.2d 1 (N.J. 1983) (statements made in subcommittee and committee hearings); *Golden v. Koch*, 415 N.Y.S.2d 330 (Sup. Ct. 1979) (committee hearings and report); *Sager v. McClenden*, 672 P.2d 697 (Or. 1983) (minutes of committee hearings). A number of states have ruled that legislator statements during committee hearings cannot be the basis for the court's finding of legislative intent. See *State v. Miranda*, 715 A.2d 680 (Conn. 1998).

Because legislative history has become much more controversial, among federal judges at least, one might expect that references to congressional hearings and floor debates would dry up at the Supreme Court level. This has *not* been the case, as the following opinions and notes will reflect. The first two cases present a recurring issue: what to make of the *rejection* of legislative proposals in committee, on the floor of either chamber, in conference committee, and so forth. The third case brings together a host of legislative sources and the famous "dog that doesn't bark" canon.

FDA v. BROWN & WILLIAMSON TOBACCO CORP.

Supreme Court of the United States, 2000.
529 U.S. 120, 120 S.Ct. 1291, 146 L.Ed.2d 121.

[Excerpted in Chapter 5, § 3(B)(3)]

NOTE ON REJECTED PROPOSALS

Justice O'Connor's opinion in the *FDA Tobacco Case is the* most lavish deployment in the Court's history of what might be called the *rejected proposal rule,* that interpreters should be reluctant to read statutes broadly when a committee, a chamber, or a conference committee rejected language explicitly encoding that broad policy. *United States v. Riverside Bayview Homes, Inc.*, 474 U.S. 121, 137 (1985) reflects this presumption as well. See also, e.g., *Hamdan v. Rumsfeld*, 548 U.S. 557 (2006); *United States v. Yermian*, 468 U.S. 63 (1984) (relying on congressional adoption of broadening language of false swearing statute, 18 U.S.C. § 1001, after earlier bill was vetoed by President). Yet similar rejected proposal arguments were not persuasive to Court majorities in *Rapanos v. United States*, 547 U.S. 715 (2006) and *Solid Waste Agency of Northern Cook County v. U.S. Army Corps of Engineers*, 531 U.S. 159 (2001). How would you distinguish those cases? Or should they be signals that the Supreme Court should no longer follow a rejected proposal rule?

Commentators have been wary, because the range of reasons for rejecting a proposed amendment varies so widely. "It may be rejected by some legislators because they disagree with its substance (but not necessarily the same substance). On the other hand, those who agree with the substance may nevertheless vote against it as a spurious or unnecessary attempt to clarify. Simple non-action, being consistent with many explanations in circumstances not calling for consensus, has no probative value for any purpose." Dickerson, *supra*, at 1133; accord *Solid Waste* (majority opinion's response to the dissenters); *Pattern Makers' League of N. Am. v. NLRB*, 473 U.S. 95 (1985); William Eskridge Jr., *Interpreting Legislative Inaction*, 87 Mich. L. Rev. 67 (1988) (collecting cases using and declining to use the rejected proposal rule); Wald, *supra*, at 202.

A broader point links Justice O'Connor's opinion for the Court in *FDA Tobacco* and Justice Stevens's dissenting opinions in *Solid Waste* and *Rapanos*. Both Justices find in the legislative deliberations evidence that Congress has both accepted and relied upon well-grounded agency policy stances as regards their regulatory mandate. In *FDA Tobacco*, there seems to have been a political consensus that the FDA did not have jurisdiction over tobacco products, and in the *Rapanos* and *Solid Waste* cases there seems to have been a similar consensus that the Corps has broad jurisdiction to protect hydrological ecosystems. Why did one consensus fail to move the Court while the other did move the Court? Consider not only the political preferences of the Justices, but also the Court's traditional role as braking or slowing down political actors.

MONTANA WILDERNESS ASSOCIATION V. UNITED STATES FOREST SERVICE

United States Court of Appeals for the Ninth Circuit, May 14, 1981.
Docket No. 80–3374.

NORRIS, CIRCUIT JUDGE:

This appeal raises fundamental questions concerning the conflict between the ability of the executive branch of the federal government to manage public lands and the access rights of persons whose property is surrounded by those lands. Environmentalists and a neighboring property owner seek to block construction by Burlington Northern of roads over parts of the Gallatin National Forest. They appeal from a partial summary judgment in the district court granting Burlington Northern a right of access to its totally enclosed timber lands. The district court held that Burlington Northern has an easement by necessity or, alternatively, an implied easement under the Northern Pacific Land Grant of 1864. The defendants argue that the Alaska National Interest Lands Act of 1980, passed subsequent to the district court's decision, also grants Burlington Northern assured access to its land. The appellants contend that the doctrine of easement by necessity does not apply to the sovereign, that there was no implied easement conveyed by the 1864 land grant, and that the access provisions of the Alaska Lands Act do not apply to land outside the state of Alaska. We conclude that the appellants are correct on all three issues. We therefore reverse the partial summary judgment and remand the case for further proceedings.

Defendant-appellee Burlington Northern, Inc. owns timber land located within the Gallatin National Forest southwest of Bozeman, Montana. This land was originally acquired by its predecessor, the Northern Pacific Railroad, under the Northern Pacific Land Grant Act of 1864, 13 Stat. 365. The Act granted odd-numbered square sections of land to the railroad, which, with the even-numbered sections retained by the United States, formed a checkerboard pattern.

To harvest its timber, Burlington Northern in 1979 acquired a permit from defendant-appellee United States Forest Service, allowing it to construct an access road across national forest land. The proposed roads would cross the Buck Creek and Yellow Mules drainages, which are protected by the Montana Wilderness Study Act of 1977, Pub. L. 95–150, 91 Stat. 1243, as potential wilderness areas. The proposed logging and road-building will arguably disqualify the areas as wilderness under the Act. * * *

Appellees contend that the recently enacted Alaska National Interest Lands Conservation Act (Alaska Lands Act), Pub. L. No. 96–487, 94 Stat. 2371 (1980), establishes an independent basis for affirming the judgment of the district court. They argue that § 1323(a) of the Act requires that the Secretary of Agriculture provide access to Burlington Northern for its enclosed land. Upon examination of the statute and the legislative history, we do not find this interpretation of the Alaska Lands Act convincing.

Section 1323 is a part of the administrative provisions, Title XIII, of the Alaska Lands Act. Appellees argue that it is the only section of the Act which applies to the entire country; appellants argue that, like the rest of the Act, it applies only to Alaska. Section 1323 reads as follows:

Sec. 1323. (a) Notwithstanding any other provision of law, and subject to such terms and conditions as the Secretary of Agriculture may prescribe, the Secretary shall provide such access to nonfederally owned land within the boundaries of the National Forest System as the Secretary deems adequate to secure to the owner the reasonable use and enjoyment thereof: *Provided*, That such owner comply with rules and regulations applicable to ingress and egress to or from the National Forest System.

(b) Notwithstanding any other provision of law, and subject to such terms and conditions as the Secretary of the Interior may prescribe, the Secretary shall provide such access to nonfederally owned land surrounded by public lands managed by the Secretary under the Federal Land Policy and Management Act of 1976 (43 U.S.C. 1701–82) as the Secretary deems adequate to secure to the owner the responsible use and enjoyment thereof: *Provided*, That such owner comply with rules and regulations applicable to access across public lands.

This section provides for access to nonfederally-owned lands surrounded by certain kinds of federal lands. Subsection (b) deals with access to nonfederal lands "surrounded by public lands managed by the Secretary [of the Interior]." Section 102(3) of the Act defines "public lands" as certain lands "situated in Alaska." Subsection (b) is therefore limited by its terms to Alaska.

Subsection (a) deals with access to nonfederally-owned lands "within the boundaries of the National Forest System." The term "National Forest System" as used in § 1323(a) is to be interpreted as being limited to national forests in Alaska or as including the entire United States.

The parties have not directed us to, nor has our research disclosed, an established or generally accepted meaning for the term "National Forest System." The United States Code contains no statutory definitions for it. We find no record of Congressional use of the term prior to the enactment of the Federal Land Policy and Management Act of 1976. The term "National Forest System" appears in that Act but is nowhere defined; from the context, however, it is apparent that it is used there to refer to national forests anywhere in the United States. See 43 U.S.C. §§ 1701, *et seq.* The same Act also uses the term "public lands" and defines it as meaning lands "owned by the United States within the several States," clearly a definition different from that given the same term in the Alaska Lands Act.

We therefore perceive no basis for assuming that Congress necessarily used the term "National Forest System" in the Alaska Lands Act to refer to national forests in the United States generally. We think that in this context the meaning of the term is ambiguous and therefore look to other indicia.

The Act itself provides some help. Title V of the Act is entitled "National Forest System." Section 501(a) states: "The following units of the National Forest System are hereby expanded * * *." This language shows that Congress used the term "National Forest System" in this Act in a context which refers to and deals with national forests in Alaska. It is not unreasonable to read Section 1323(a) as referring to the "National Forest System" in the context in which it is used in Title V of the Act, rather than to all national forests in the United States.

As the parties agreed at oral argument, moreover, § 1323(b) is *in pari materia* with § 1323(a). The two subsections are placed together in the same section, and use not only a parallel structure but many of the same words and phrases. The natural interpretation is that they were meant to have the same effect, one on lands controlled by the Secretary of Agriculture, the other on lands controlled by the Secretary of the Interior. Since § 1323(b), by the definition of public lands in § 102(3), applies only to Alaskan land, a strong presumption arises that § 1323(a) was meant to apply only to Alaska as well.

That interpretation is confirmed by a review of the entire Act which discloses no other provision having nation-wide application.[4] To attach such a sweeping effect to this obscure and seemingly minor provision of the Act would seem incongruous under the circumstances. We therefore conclude that the language of the Act supports the interpretation that § 1323(a) applies only to national forests in Alaska. Bearing in mind that "[a]bsent a clearly expressed legislative intent to the contrary, [the statutory] language must ordinarily be regarded as conclusive," *Consumer Prod. Safety Comm'n. v. GTE Sylvania*, 447 U.S. 102, 108 (1980), we turn to the legislative history.

Section 1323 was added to the Alaska Lands Bill by the Senate Committee on Energy and Natural Resources in its amendment to H.R. 39, originally passed by the House. S. Rep. No. 96–413, 96th Cong. 1st Sess. (1979). It was incorporated in the Tsongas substitute bill which replaced by amendment the Energy Committee's proposed bill, 126 Cong. Rec. S11099, S11140 (daily ed. Aug. 18, 1980). The Tsongas substitute bill was passed by the Senate, 126 Cong. Rec. S11193 (daily ed. Aug. 19, 1980), and House, 126 Cong. Rec. H10552 (daily ed. Nov. 12, 1980), and became law on December 1, 1980, 94 Stat. 2371.

Section 1323 is mentioned only twice in the Senate materials. The Energy Committee report discussed it in its section-by-section analysis, S. Rep. No. 96–413 at 310, and Senator Melcher, the author of the section, discussed it on the floor of the Senate, 126 Cong. Rec. S14770–71 (daily ed. Nov. 20, 1980). The remarks of Senator Melcher, however, were made on November 20th, eight days after Congress passed

---

[4]   The appellees concede that no other section of the Act applies nationwide. They argue, however, that because another provision of the Act, § 1110(b), gives access rights to all Alaskan inholders, § 1323(a) is superfluous unless it is interpreted to apply to the entire country. Section 1110(b), they argue, like § 1323(b), applies only to Alaska because it uses terms, "public lands" and "conservation system unit," which are defined to include only Alaskan land.

The flaw in appellee's argument is that however § 1323(a) is interpreted, § 1110(b) essentially duplicates the protection given Alaskan lands by § 1323 as a whole. Section 1110(b) overlaps § 1323(b) just as much as it overlaps § 1323(a). If, as appellees claim, § 1110(b) gives access to all Alaskan inholders and § 1323(a) gives access to holders of land surrounded by land administered by the Secretary of Agriculture, the inclusion of § 1323(b) in the Act makes no sense at all. Section 1323(b), after all, gives access to holders of Alaskan land surrounded by land administered by the Secretary of the Interior. Under this view, not only is § 1323(b) superfluous in light of § 1110(b), it is paired with a provision, § 1323(a), of parallel structure but widely different scope. We do not see how the existence of § 1110(b) gives much support to the appellees' position.

[handwritten margin notes: Committee Report, Senate thinking section applies nationwide + Enough]

H.R. 39. His remarks clearly demonstrate that his personal understanding of the section is that it applies nationwide, but because they are the remarks of but one senator made subsequent to the passage of the bill they do not provide a reliable indication of the understanding of the Senate as a whole.

Although the appellees contend that the language of the Energy Committee report makes perfectly clear the Committee's intent that § 1323 apply nationwide, we do not find their interpretation of the report's language persuasive:

> This section is designed to remove the uncertainties surrounding the status of the rights of the owners of non-Federal lands to gain access to such lands across Federal lands. It has been the Committee's understanding that such owners had the right of access to their lands subject to reasonable regulation by either, the Secretary of Agriculture in the case of national forests, or by the Secretary of the Interior in the case of public lands managed by the Bureau of Land Management under the Federal Land Policy and Management Act of 1976. However, a recent District Court decision in Utah (*Utah v. Andrus et al.*, C79–0037, October 1, 1979, D.C. Utah) has cast some doubt over the status of these rights. Furthermore, the Attorney General is currently reviewing the issue because of differing interpretations of the law by the Departments of Agriculture and the Interior. * * *
>
> The Committee amendment is designed to resolve any lingering legal questions by making it clear that non-Federal landowners have a right of access [across] National Forests and public land, subject, of course, to reasonable rules and regulations.

[handwritten margin note: resolve any lingering legal Questions]

S. Rep. No. 96–413 at 310.

While the Committee's intent to guarantee access is clear, it is less than clear whether this provision was meant to guarantee access outside of Alaska. The problem raised in the first paragraph—the differing interpretations of the law of access—is not confined to Alaska, but the scope of the remedy as set forth in the last paragraph could be so confined. As with § 1323 itself, the report uses indiscriminately terms defined in the Act as applying only to Alaskan land ("public land") and terms not so defined ("National Forests").

The absence of any reference to Alaska is not of much import. The report's discussion of other access provisions such as § 1110 and § 1111, which all parties agree apply only to Alaska, fails to mention Alaska and is as ambiguous about whether § 1110 and § 1111 apply nationwide as is the discussion of § 1323. S. Rep. No. 96–413, at 299–300.

[handwritten margin note: Other sections of Report Only Apply to Alaska w/o specifically Stating it!]

What we find most significant in the legislative history in the Senate is the same thing that Sherlock Holmes found to be crucial in solving the case of the Hound of the Baskervilles—the failure of the dog to bark. The Alaska Lands bill was discussed endlessly on the Senate floor. There are numerous occasions when one would expect a change in current laws of access of the magnitude of the appellees' proposed interpretation of § 1323 to be discussed, mentioned or at least alluded to. Yet we have not found in the Senate debates, and appellees have not called to our attention, one single suggestion that anything in the Alaska Land Bill would affect access rights in the rest of the country. In Senator Tsongas' long, detailed comparison of his substitute bill with the Energy Committee bill, § 1323 is not mentioned. 126 Cong. Rec. S11193 (daily ed. Aug. 19, 1980).[6] In discussion about the adequacy of the substitute bill's access provisions (which include § 1323) no mention is made of a change in the law of access for the rest of the country. 126 Cong. Rec. S11061–62 (daily ed. Aug. 18, 1980). We find it difficult to believe that the Senate would have contemplated and effected a profound change in the law of access across government land for the entire country without ever mentioning it.

The legislative history in the House, which considered and passed the Tsongas substitute bill after it was passed by the Senate, also presents an ambiguous picture of § 1323. On October 2, 1980, Representative Udall, chairman of the Committee on Interior and Insular Affairs which had joint responsibility for the bill, introduced an amendment one section of which was to "make clear that [the bill] applies only to Alaska." 127 Cong. Rec. 10376 (daily ed. Oct. 2, 1980). This amendment was never adopted. Representative Udall subsequently declared in prepared remarks inserted into the Congressional Record that although the final version of the bill was "ambiguously drafted and not expressly limited to Alaskan lands, the House believes that, as with all the other provisions of the bill, the language of the section applies only to lands within the State of Alaska." 126 Cong. Rec. H10549 (daily ed. Nov. 12, 1980). Representative Weaver stated that the section granting access rights to inholders on national forest and BLM lands "apparently applies not only to Alaska but also to the entire United States." 126 Cong. Rec. H8638 (daily ed. Sept. 9, 1980). Representative Sieberling inserted into the record a summary of proposed amendments, which refers to Section 1323 as the "nationwide access amendment." 126 Cong. Rec. H10350 (daily ed. Oct. 2, 1980). Representative AuCoin stated that one of the flaws of the final bill is that it "grants private inholders carte blanche access across national forest and public lands nationwide." 126 Cong. Rec. H10529–30 (daily ed. Nov. 12, 1980).

Appellees rely heavily upon an exchange of letters between Representatives Sieberling and Weaver, chairmen of the subcommittees responsible for the bill (Public Lands of the Committee on Interior and Insular Affairs and Forest of the Committee on Agriculture), and the Attorney General's office. In their letter, the representatives express concern over § 1323, which they state applies nationwide, and ask for a clarification of how different the § 1323 access language is from existing access provisions. It is indeed clear from their letter that they believed that § 1323 applies nationwide.

Appellees argue, on the basis of the September 5, 1980 return letter from Assistant Attorney General Alan Parker, that the Department of Justice confirmed this interpretation of § 1323. We interpret the letter differently. As we read the letter, the Assistant Attorney General assumed without analysis that the representatives'

---

6   Neither did Senator Tsongas remark on § 1323 when it was first proposed in the Energy Committee bill, even though in his statement in the Committee report he spends several pages criticizing the bill's overbroad provisions on access. [Citing Senate Report, additional views of Senators Metzenbaum and Tsongas.] Yet the extension of § 1323(a) to the entire country would certainly have a greater impact than the other measures he discusses.

interpretation of § 1323 was correct, and proceeded to discuss in detail the effect of such a change in the law.

The exchanged letters are entitled to little weight. In general, off-the-record views of congressmen are not attributed to Congress as a whole. See *T.V.A. v. Hill*, 437 U.S. 153, 190–91 (1978). This is particularly true where, as here, there is no indication that the House as a whole was aware of the correspondence. *Id.* at 191–92.

In summary, the legislative history concerning § 1323 is surprisingly sparse. The report of the Senate committee which drafted the section is ambiguous. At times when the Senate could have been expected to comment on its intention to make a major change in current law, it did not. The only expression of intent that § 1323 apply nationwide came from a single senator eight days after the Alaska Lands Act was passed by Congress. In the House debates, three representatives suggested that § 1323 did apply nationwide, but the chairman of one of the responsible committees said it did not. Two chairmen of House subcommittees responsible for the bill did state in a letter to the Attorney General that they believed that § 1323 applied nationwide, but there is no indication that the contents of this letter were generally known by members of the House, and so the letter carries little weight in our analysis. We conclude that the ambiguous legislative history gives only slight support at best to the appellees' interpretation that § 1323 applies nationwide. It is not nearly sufficient to overcome the actual language of the statute, which we believe is more naturally read as applying only to Alaska.

Moreover, § 1323 as interpreted by the appellees would repeal by implication a portion of § 5(a) of the Wilderness Act, 16 U.S.C. § 1134(a).[7] "It is, of course, a cardinal principle of statutory construction that repeals by implication are not favored," *Radzanower v. Touche Ross & Co.*, 426 U.S. 148, 154 (1976), and that "the intention of the legislature to repeal must be clear and manifest." *Posadas v. Nat'l. City Bank*, 296 U.S. 497, 503 (1936). Here it is far from clear that the legislature intended that § 1323 apply nationwide. We hold that § 1323 of the Alaska National Interest Lands Conservation Act is limited in its application to the state of Alaska, and so has no relevance to this case. * * *

NOTES ON THE "CHECKERBOARD CASE" AND STATEMENTS DURING LEGISLATIVE DELIBERATION

1. *The Ninth Circuit's Use of Legislative History.* A textualist would likely agree with Judge Norris' analysis of the statutory text, and then would stop. Why should the judge proceed any further? When Judge Norris does, he causes himself some trouble. Note his strategy: Even though the opinion adduces no affirmative support in the legislative history for its view that § 1323(a) only applies to Alaska, Judge Norris isolates all the evidence to the contrary and seeks to neuter each piece of evidence in isolation, either by demonstrating ambiguity or by denigrating the authority of the evidence. This technique—the "piecemeal critique"—is effective advocacy in response to a showing of a

Piecemeal Critique = Effective Advocacy re-showing

---

[7]   16 U.S.C. § 1134(a) gives the Secretary of Agriculture the choice between granting access to state or privately-owned land surrounded by wilderness land and permitting the exchange of the in-held land for federally-owned land of equal value. Section 1323(a), by making access mandatory, renders nugatory the land exchange provision. See generally Op. Att'y Gen. slip at 1, 23–30 (June 23, 1980).

variety of evidence to the contrary, but shouldn't that evidence be allowed to have cumulative weight in assessing overall legislative intent? As you evaluate the following, consider whether an "intentionalist" interpreter would disagree with Judge Norris' outcome.

(a) *Committee Reports.* On first reading, the Senate Report in the Checkerboard Case is ambiguous. But reread the quoted language of the Report. The Senate wants to avoid the problems raised by a federal district court decision in Utah and the Attorney General's consideration (described in Note 2 after *Leo Sheep*). The Utah case (in the Tenth Circuit) is not controlling law in Alaska (in the Ninth Circuit). The Senate Report wants "to resolve *any* lingering legal questions by *making it clear* that non-Federal landowners have a right of access [across] National Forests" (emphasis added). While this Report is not 100% clear that § 1323(a) was meant to apply nationwide, isn't the more probable reading of the Report that it was?

(b) *Statements of Sponsors and Committee Chairs.* Senator Melcher, the sponsor of the amendment adding § 1323(a), explicitly said that it applied nationwide. Judge Norris denigrates this clear evidence by saying that it was uttered after the bill was passed by Congress (but before it had been signed by the President). But he doesn't say that Representative Udall's statements, upon which he relies, were inserted into the Congressional Record *after* the bill was passed. (Udall's remarks are reported in the *Record* for the day the bill was passed, but they are proceeded by a "bullet" [•], which signifies that they were not spoken on the floor of the House but were inserted later.) Indeed, look at the dates of the Udall and Melcher statements. Why might Udall have abandoned any attempt to amend the statute to make it clearly apply only to Alaska and instead simply uttered a comment that the unamended version had the same impact? Why might Melcher have made his comment? Which is the more reliable?

Leaving strategic considerations aside, consider the roles of the key players. Melcher, the sponsor of § 1323(a), and Representatives Seiberling and Weaver, chairs of the relevant House subcommittees, interpreted § 1323(a) to apply nationwide, in statements made to their respective chambers. Udall, chair of the House Committee, interpreted it otherwise, in a statement inserted after the fact. Yet Judge Norris treats Udall's statements as roughly equal to those of Melcher, Seiberling, and Weaver in combination. Isn't this wrong, especially in light of the common view that greater weight should be accorded statements of *supporters* of a provision over statements of *opponents*? See also *Ernst & Ernst v. Hochfelder*, 425 U.S. 185, 204 n.24 (1976).

(c) *Dialogue with Bureaucrats.* The exchange of letters between Seiberling/Weaver and the Justice Department concerning the effect of the Melcher amendment is not unusual in Congress. It is quite common in state legislatures, where assistants to state attorneys general typically advise legislative committees about the probable legal effects of bills. Since Seiberling and Weaver were key House negotiators, and the House accepted the Melcher amendment in negotiations, isn't this exchange of letters more significant than Judge Norris was willing to admit? Compare *Lindahl v. Office of Personnel Management*, 470 U.S. 768, 785 n.17 (1985), where the Supreme Court relied heavily on letters from the OPM Director to the Chairs of the Senate and House Committees to interpret amendments to the Civil Service Retirement Act. Judge Wald, *supra*, at 202–03, noted in the early 1980s an increasing tendency of lawyers to use, and judges to cite, unpublished portions of the legislative history to support their interpretations of statutes. See *Borrell v. U.S. Int'l Commc'n Agency*, 682 F.2d 981, 988 (D.C. Cir. 1982).

2. *Evidence Judge Norris (and Everybody Else) Missed.* Judge Norris makes much of the fact that Senator Melcher's statement that § 1323 applies nationwide was made on the floor of the Senate after the bill was passed. But on July 29, 1980 (well before the bill passed the Senate), Senator Melcher sent a letter to every Senator, explaining that he was opposed to a portion of one of the amendments that would be offered when the Alaska Lands bill came before the Senate. The letter explained that Melcher's amendment was in response to the recent Department of Justice opinion (described in Note 2 following *Leo Sheep, supra*) indicating that private checkerboard landowners did not have an automatic right of access across government land; Melcher considered the Department of Justice view an innovation that disrupted prior understandings among property owners and federal lands administrators. The letter then said:

> In the Alaskan Lands Bill, for Alaska only, specific access to state or private lands was explicitly guaranteed. In order to avoid any change in federal policy on this question, last October [1979] I introduced an amendment to that bill for continuing the historic policy of granting access to property inholders in all the rest of the Bureau of Land Management and National Forest lands. My amendment was accepted by the committee without objection and *it applies to landowners within federal lands (either in national forests or in public lands administered by the Bureau of Land Management) in all the rest of the states where such lands are located.* * * *

The letter warned that Amendment No. 1783, offered by Senators Tsongas and McGovern, would strike this committee amendment, and Melcher urged the other Senators to support his effort to preserve this national right of access provision.[382] Was Judge Norris wrong about the "deal" in Congress?

3. *The Dog That Didn't Bark Canon.* Although Judge Norris cited the wrong Sherlock Holmes story,[383] he is correct to say that the Supreme Court sometimes follows the *dog didn't bark* canon. That is, it may be significant that an intense congressional debate does not even mention an issue—suggesting that the statute contained no unusual departure from the status quo against which Congress was legislating. Thus, in a bill whose title and subject matter are all about Alaska, one would expect some special mention of a provision that adjusted important legal rights in the lower 49 states as well.

We have seen examples of it in *Zuni Public School District No. 89 v. Department of Education*, *Bock Laundry*, and *Chisom v. Roemer* (all in Chapter 5, § 3(A)). In *Chisom*, recall that Justice Scalia lustily assailed this canon on the grounds that it is highly subjective and unreliable (how one characterizes the "status quo" drives the operation of the canon, and that is quite subjective), as well as contrary to Justice Scalia's view (e.g.,

---

[382]   The letter is reproduced in *Oversight on The Montana Wilderness Study Act: Hearing Before the Subcomm. on Public Lands and Reserved Water of the Senate Comm. on Energy and Natural Resources*, 97th Cong., 1st Sess. 53 (May 28, 1981). Senator Melcher represents that the letter was sent to every Senator. *Id.* at 12. One of our students in the Georgetown University Law Center, Class of 1990 came up with this "smoking gun" during class discussion. (Eskridge and Frickey were embarrassed that they didn't find this smoking gun when working on the case in private practice. This is one of the cases they plundered from their experience as attorneys at the old Washington, D.C. law firm of Shea & Gardner (now absorbed into another law firm). It did not occur to them that anything relevant to the Alaska Act would be found in the legislative history of another act, the Montana Wilderness Study Act. *Should* that have occurred to them? Keep this question in mind when you read the next case.)

[383]   In *Silver Blaze*, Sherlock Holmes solves the case of a missing racehorse by observing that the dog guarding the barn had not barked the night before when an intruder entered to get the horse; the deduction (elementary!) was that the culprit was someone the dog knew well. In *The Hound of the Baskervilles*, which Judge Norris cites, the dog barked quite a lot and did not contribute to Holmes's solution of the mystery.

Rapanos) that Congress can proceed *only* through positive legislation adopted under Article I, § 7, and *never* through inaction, etc.

E. POST-ENACTMENT LEGISLATIVE HISTORY

Statutes are often enacted and forgotten by the legislature. Sometimes, though, the legislature—or at least its members and committees—will continue to talk about the statute after enactment. Circumstances for post-enactment discussion include (1) proposals to amend the statute or to enact a new and related statute, including debate and hearings and committee reports on such proposals; (2) oversight hearings in response to agency and/or judicial implementation of the statute; and (3) efforts to "bend" interpretation of the statute. The statutory interpreter is torn between considering relevant evidence and avoiding strategic trickery. One way to set this balance would be to consider only "subsequent legislative history" that is tied to a subsequent statute enacted by the legislature. (The Supreme Court has not always limited itself in this way, as you will see in the notes after the following case.)

In the immediately preceding case, Judge Norris dismissed Senator Melcher's comment as mere subsequent legislative history. The following case is a later opinion on rehearing in the Checkerboard Case. Notice how Judge Norris' interpretation changed when he was confronted with different subsequent legislative history. Should he have changed his mind?

**MONTANA WILDERNESS ASSOCIATION V.
UNITED STATES FOREST SERVICE**

United States Court of Appeals for the Ninth Circuit, 1981.
655 F.2d 951, *cert. denied*, 455 U.S. 989.

[After the May 1981 opinion, *supra*, which held that there was no easement created by the railroad land grant act of 1864 or the Alaska Lands Act of 1980, an intervening party defendant moved for reconsideration based upon yet another new statute, shedding light on the Alaska lands statute construed in the earlier opinion. In light of the new statute, the panel withdrew the May opinion and issued the instant opinion. Judge Norris, the author of the original panel opinion, also wrote the new one.]

The sole issue on appeal is whether Burlington Northern has a right of access across federal land to its inholdings of timberland. Appellees contend that the recently enacted Alaska National Interest Lands Conservation Act (Alaska Lands Act), Pub. L. No. 96–487, 94 Stat. 2371 (1980), establishes an independent basis for affirming the judgment of the district court. They argue that § 1323(a) of the Act requires that the Secretary of Agriculture provide access to Burlington Northern for its enclosed land.

Section 1323 is a part of the administrative provisions, Title XIII, of the Alaska Lands Act. Appellees argue that it is the only section of the Act which applies to the entire country; appellants argue that, like the rest of the Act, it applies only to Alaska. Section 1323 reads as follows:

Sec. 1323.(a) Notwithstanding any other provision of law, and subject to such terms and conditions as the Secretary of Agriculture may prescribe, the Secretary shall provide such access to nonfederally owned land within the boundaries of the National Forest System as the Secretary deems adequate to secure to the owner the reasonable use and enjoyment thereof: *Provided,* That such owner comply with rules and regulations applicable to ingress and egress to or from the National Forest System.

(b) Notwithstanding any other provision of law, and subject to such terms and conditions as the Secretary of the Interior may prescribe, the Secretary shall provide such access to nonfederally owned land surrounded by public lands managed by the Secretary under the Federal Land Policy and Management Act of 1976 (43 U.S.C. 1701–82) as the Secretary deems adequate to secure to the owner the responsible use and enjoyment thereof: *Provided,* That such owner comply with rules and regulations applicable to access across public lands.

This section provides for access to nonfederally-owned lands surrounded by certain kinds of federal lands. Subsection (b) deals with access to nonfederal lands "surrounded by public lands managed by the Secretary [of the Interior]." Section 102(3) of the Act defines "public lands" as certain lands "situated in Alaska." Subsection (b), therefore, is arguably limited by its terms to Alaska, though we do not find it necessary to settle that issue here. Our consideration of the scope of § 1323(a) proceeds under the assumption that § 1323(b) is limited to Alaska.

Subsection (a) deals with access to nonfederally-owned lands "within the boundaries of the National Forest System." The term "National Forest System" is not specifically defined in the Act.

The question before the court is whether the term "National Forest System" as used in § 1323(a) is to be interpreted as being limited to national forests in Alaska or as including the entire United States. We note at the outset that the bare language of § 1323(a) does not, when considered by itself, limit the provision of access to Alaskan land. We must look, however, to the context of the section to determine its meaning.

Elsewhere in the Act, Congress used the term "National Forest System" in a context which refers to and deals with national forests in Alaska. Title V of the Act is entitled "National Forest System." Section 501(a) states: "The following units of the National Forest System are hereby expanded * * *." It is not unreasonable to read Section 1323(a) as referring to the "National Forest System" in the context in which it is used in Title V of the Act, rather than to all national forests in the United States.

Congress did, however, supply us with a general definition of the term in another statute. Pub. Law 93–378, 88 Stat. 480 (1974). 16 U.S.C. § 1609(a) states *inter alia* that:

Congress declares that the National Forest System consists of units of federally owned forest, range, and related lands throughout the United States and its territories, united into a nationally significant system dedicated to the long-term benefit for present and future generations, and that it is the purpose of their section to include all such areas into one integral system. The 'National Forest System' shall include all national forest lands reserved or withdrawn from the public domain of the United States * * *.

No qualification

Application of this definition to § 1323(a) would necessarily yield the conclusion that the section was intended to have nation-wide effect. This seems especially so when Congress uses the term "National Forest System" in § 1323(a) without limitation or qualification.

As the parties agreed at oral argument, however, § 1323(b) is *in pari materia* with § 1323(a). The two subsections are placed together in the same section, and use not only a parallel structure but many of the same words and phrases. The natural interpretation is that they were meant to have the same effect, one on lands controlled by the Secretary of Agriculture, the other on lands controlled by the Secretary of the Interior. Since we assume that § 1323(b), by definition of public lands in § 102(3), applies only to Alaskan land, we face a presumption that § 1323(a) was meant to apply to Alaska as well.

That interpretation is supported by a review of the entire Act which discloses no other provision having nation-wide application. We therefore conclude that the language of the Act provides tentative support for the view that § 1323(a) applies only to national forests in Alaska. Bearing in mind that "[a]bsent a clearly expressed legislative intent to the contrary, [the statutory] language must ordinarily be regarded as conclusive," *Consumer Prod. Safety Comm'n v. GTE Sylvania*, 447 U.S. 102, 108 (1980), we turn to the legislative history.

The legislative history concerning § 1323 is surprisingly sparse. The report of the Senate committee which drafted the section is ambiguous.[7] At times when the Senate could have been expected to comment on its intention to make a major change in current law, it did not. The only expression of intent that § 1323 apply nation-wide

---

[7]   The Energy Committee report discussed it in its section-by-section analysis, S.Rep. No. 96–413 at 310. (The Committee analysis mixes up §§ 1323 and 1324. Thus, the analysis entitled § 1324 is really concerned with § 1323 and vice versa.) Although the appellees contend that the language of the Energy Committee report makes perfectly clear the Committee's intent that § 1323 apply nationwide, we do not find their interpretation of the report's language persuasive:

> This section is designed to remove the uncertainties surrounding the status of the rights of the owners of non-Federal lands to gain access to such lands across Federal lands. It has been the Committee's understanding that such owners had the right of access to their lands subject to reasonable regulation by either, the Secretary of Agriculture in the case of national forests, or by the Secretary of the Interior in the case of public lands managed by the Bureau of Land Management under the Federal Land Policy and Management Act of 1976. However, a recent District Court decision in Utah (*Utah v. Andrus et al.*, C79–0037, October 1, 1979, D.C. Utah) has cast some doubt over the status of these rights. Furthermore, the Attorney General is currently reviewing the issue because of differing interpretations of the law by the Departments of Agriculture and the Interior. * * *

> The Committee amendment is designed to resolve any lingering legal questions by making it clear that non-Federal landowners have a right of access [across] National Forests and public land, subject, of course, to reasonable rules and regulations.

S. Rep. No. 96–413, at 310.

While the Committee's intent to guarantee access is clear, it is less than clear whether this provision was meant to guarantee access outside of Alaska. The problem raised in the first paragraph—the differing interpretations of the law of access—is not confined to Alaska, but the scope of the remedy as set forth in the last paragraph could be so confined. As with § 1323 itself, the report uses indiscriminately terms defined in the Act as applying only to Alaskan land ("public land") and terms not so defined ("National Forests").

came from a single senator eight days after the Alaska Lands Act was passed by Congress.[8] In the House debates, three representatives suggested that § 1323 did apply nation-wide, but the chairman of one of the responsible committees said it did not.[9] Two chairmen of House subcommittees responsible for the bill did state in a letter to the Attorney General that they believed that § 1323 applied nation-wide, but there is no indication that the contents of this letter were generally known by members of the House, and so the letter carries little weight in our analysis. All this gives only slight support at best to the appellees' interpretation that § 1323 applies nation-wide.

The appellees, however, have uncovered subsequent legislative history that, given the closeness of the issue, is decisive. Three weeks after Congress passed the Alaska Lands Act, a House-Senate Conference Committee considering the Colorado Wilderness Act interpreted § 1323 of the Alaska Lands Act as applying nation-wide:

> Section 7 of the Senate amendment contains a provision pertaining to access to non-Federally owned lands within national forest wilderness areas in Colorado. The House bill has no such provision.
>
> *The conferees agreed to delete the section because similar language has already passed Congress in Section 1323 of the Alaska National Interest Lands Conservation Act.*

H.R. Rep. No. 1521, 96th Cong., 2d Sess., 126 Cong. Rec. H11687 (daily ed. Dec. 3, 1980) (emphasis supplied).

This action was explained to both Houses during discussion of the Conference Report. See 126 Cong. Rec. S15571 (daily ed. Dec. 4, 1980) (remarks of Sen. Hart); *id.* at S15573 (remarks of Sen. Armstrong); *id.* at H11705 (daily ed. Dec. 3, 1980) (remarks of Rep. Johnson). Both houses then passed the Colorado Wilderness bill as it was reported by the Conference Committee.

Although a subsequent conference report is not entitled to the great weight given subsequent legislation, *Consumer Prod. Safety Comm'n v. GTE Sylvania*, 477 U.S. 102, 118 n.13 (1980), it is still entitled to significant weight, *Seatrain Shipbuilding Corp. v. Shell Oil Co.*, 444 U.S. 572 (1980), particularly where it is clear that the

---

[8]   Senator Melcher, the author of the section, discussed it on the floor of the Senate, 126 Cong. Rec. S14770–71 (daily ed. Nov. 20, 1980). The remarks of Senator Melcher, however, were made on November 20th, eight days after Congress passed H.R. 39. His remarks clearly demonstrate that his personal understanding of the section is that it applies nation-wide, but because they are the remarks of but one senator made subsequent to the passage of the bill they do not provide a reliable indication of the understanding of the Senate as a whole.

[9]   On October 2, 1980, Representative Udall, chairman of the Committee on Interior and Insular Affairs which had joint responsibility for the bill, introduced an amendment one section of which was to "make clear that [the bill] applies only to Alaska." 127 Cong. Rec. 10376 (daily ed. Oct. 2, 1980). This amendment was never adopted. Representative Udall subsequently declared in prepared remarks inserted into the Congressional Record that although the final version of the bill was "ambiguously drafted and not expressly limited to Alaskan lands, the House believes that, as with all the other provisions of the bill, the language of the section applies only to lands within the State of Alaska." 126 Cong. Rec. H10549 (daily ed. Nov. 12, 1980). Representative Weaver stated that the section granting access rights to inholders on national forest and BLM lands "apparently applies not only to Alaska but also to the entire United States." 126 Cong. Rec. H8638 (daily ed. Sept. 9, 1980). Representative Sieberling inserted into the record a summary of proposed amendments, which refers to Section 1323 as the "nationwide access amendment." 126 Cong. Rec. H10350 (daily ed. Oct. 2, 1980). Representative AuCoin stated that one of the flaws of the final bill is that it "grants private inholders carte blanche access across national forest and public lands nationwide." 126 Cong. Rec. H10529–30 (daily ed. Nov. 12, 1980).

conferees had carefully considered the issue. The conferees, including Representatives Udall and Sieberling and Senator Melcher, had an intimate knowledge of the Alaska Lands Act.[11] Moreover, the Conference Committee's interpretation of § 1323 was the basis for their decision to leave out an access provision passed by one house. In these circumstances, the Conference Committee's interpretation is very persuasive. We conclude that it tips the balance decidedly in favor of the broader interpretation of § 1323.[12] We therefore hold that Burlington Northern has an assured right of access to its land pursuant to the nation-wide grant of access in § 1323. * * *

NOTES ON THE SECOND CHECKERBOARD OPINION AND THE USE OF POST-ENACTMENT STATEMENTS

1.   *The Burger Court's Use of Subsequent Legislative History.* Is Judge Norris' reliance on subsequent legislative history persuasive? While the Supreme Court has said that subsequent statutes should inform interpretation of an earlier one, the Court has professed some skepticism about reliance on subsequent legislative statements. For example, in *Consumer Product Safety Comm'n v. GTE Sylvania*, 447 U.S. 102, 117–18 (1980), petitioners relied upon statements in a conference committee report concerning the 1976 amendments to the Consumer Product Safety Act that purported to interpret a section of the Act enacted in 1972 and not amended in 1976. The Court noted "the oft-repeated warning that 'the views of a subsequent Congress form a hazardous basis for inferring the intent of an earlier one.'" In a footnote, the Court further explained:

> Petitioners invoke the maxim that states: "Subsequent legislation declaring the intent of an earlier statute is entitled to great weight in statutory construction." With respect to subsequent *legislation*, however, Congress has proceeded formally through the legislative process. A mere statement in a conference report of such legislation as to what the Committee believes an earlier statute meant is obviously less weighty.

> The less formal types of subsequent legislative history provide an extremely hazardous basis for inferring the meaning of a congressional enactment.

In *Andrus v. Shell Oil Co.*, 446 U.S. 657 (1980), a case decided the same Term as *GTE Sylvania*, the Court stated: "While arguments predicated upon subsequent

---

[11]   The participation of Representative Udall is particularly noteworthy since he was the one congressman to proclaim in the legislative history of the Alaska Lands Act that Section 1323 applied only to Alaska.

[12]   We recognize a facial problem or tension between § 1323(a) and a portion of § 5(a) of the Wilderness Act, 16 U.S.C. § 1134(a). We need not decide in this case whether there is repeal by implication. In passing, we note only that it is arguable that the two can stand together. § 1134(a) deals specifically with right of access "[i]n any case where State-owned or privately-owned land is completely surrounded by national forest lands *within areas designated by this chapter as wilderness* * * *." (emphasis added). Section 1323(a), on the other hand, deals with "* * * access to non-federally owned land within the boundaries of the National Forest System * * *." Section 1134(a) is addressed specifically to an area designated as "wilderness," while § 1323(a) is addressed to National Forest System lands in general. In cases involving wilderness areas, the Secretary has the option of exchanging land of equal value so that the wilderness area may be preserved. Thus, § 1134(a) could be construed to apply in the specific case of a wilderness area, and § 1323(a) could be construed to apply in all other cases.

Whether or not they are in fact irreconcilable we leave to another case when the issue is squarely presented for review.

congressional actions may be weighed with extreme care, they should not be rejected out of hand as a source that a court may consider in the search for legislative intent." *Id.* at 666 n.8. In a third case decided the same Term, the Court adopted the interpretation of a 1936 statute set forth in a 1971 House committee report based on the theory that, "while the views of subsequent Congresses cannot override the unmistakable intent of the enacting one, * * * such views are entitled to significant weight, * * * and particularly so when the precise intent of the enacting Congress is obscure." *Seatrain Shipbuilding Corp. v. Shell Oil Co.*, 444 U.S. 572, 596 (1980). Later, in *South Carolina v. Regan*, 465 U.S. 367, 378 n.17 (1984), the Court once again "rejected" any suggestion that statutory interpretation can be informed by "the committee reports that accompany subsequent legislation."

2.   *The Checkerboard Problem, Subsequent Legislative History, and the New Textualism.* The policy consequences of Judge Norris' new opinion seem quite malign. The fairest rule for checkerboard cases would be to give a right of reasonable access to both the government and the private holder, but this is precluded by *Leo Sheep, supra.* The second best rule, then, might be to deny rights of access to both parties, for their mutual dependence would probably lead to a deal approximating the best rule (but with more transactions costs). The worst rule is one in which one party has a right of access (*Montana Wilderness*) and the other does not (*Leo Sheep*). This does not create incentives to bargain and may force the government to pay extra money and high transactions costs to take the right of access through eminent domain.

Is this seemingly dysfunctional result compelled by § 1323(a)? Has Judge Norris persuaded you that Congress "intended" to deprive the public fisc of this money, and impair wilderness lands as well? Has Judge Norris even persuaded himself that his first opinion was wrong? Perhaps Judge Norris lost heart when Representative Udall—his bulwark in the first opinion—abandoned his earlier view of § 1323(a). So what? Wasn't Udall posturing in the first place? If Congress is going to create such a dysfunctional rule, shouldn't courts require explicit *statutory* language? If your instinct is "yes," then you need to bring a canon of interpretation into play. Could any established substantive canon apply here?

Subsequent legislative history is surely of no use to the new textualists. If ordinary legislative history is, as Justice Scalia argues, often cooked up by congressional staff and lobbyists to try to slant interpretation after the fact, the possibility for abuse is worse with subsequent legislative history, because there is less congressional monitoring and correction of misleading statements after the statute has been passed. One effect of the new textualism has been to push the current Court toward greater skepticism about the value of subsequent legislative history than the Court had shown in the 1970s and early 1980s. *Rapanos* and *Solid Waste* illustrate this reluctance, as the Court in both cases was extremely reluctant to read the 1972 Water Act in light of proposals rejected by Congress in 1977.[384] But even the skeptical decisions say that the Court will consider subsequent

[384]   See *Massachusetts v. EPA*, 549 U.S. 497, 529–30 (2007) (chapter 8, § 3(C); *Doe v. Chao*, 540 U.S. 614 (2004) (rejecting Privacy Act plaintiff's reliance on statutes in pari materia, when such statutes were enacted after the Privacy Act); *Cent. Bank of Denver N.A. v. First Interstate Bank of Denver N.A.*, 511 U.S. 164, 185–86 (1994) (ignoring congressional interpretations in 1983 and 1988 committee reports in interpreting 1934 statute); *Chapman v. United States*, 500 U.S. 453, 464 n.4 (1991), *aff'g Marshall v. United States* (Chapter 5, § 3(B)(1)) (refusing even to consider subsequent legislative discussion as evidence of statutory ambiguity in criminal sentencing case); *Sullivan v. Finkelstein*, 496 U.S. 617, 628 n.8 (1990) (rejecting arguments based upon subsequent committee print and report; in this case, Scalia, J., concurred but refused to join note 8, because he

legislative history if it is very persuasive and/or accompanied by an amendment to the statute. See *Solid Waste*; *Mackey v. Lanier Collections Agency & Serv.*, 486 U.S. 825, 839–40 (1988).

The Court in *Gozlon-Peretz v. United States*, 498 U.S. 395 (1991), accepted a "public reliance" type of argument similar to the one accepted by Judge Norris in the Second Checkerboard opinion: when a subsequent Congress assumes one interpretation of an earlier statute and acts upon that assumption in enacting a new statute, the Court will consider that as evidence in favor of the assumed interpretation. See also Justice Scalia's opinion concurring in the judgment in *Franklin v. Gwinnett County Public Schools*, 503 U.S. 60 (1992), arguing that the Court should generally be reluctant to imply causes of action to enforce federal statutes, but not when Congress has relied on that understanding in subsequent legislation. Compare *Pub. Emps. Ret. Sys. of Ohio v. Betts*, 492 U.S. 158, 167–68 (1989) (refusing to credit subsequent conference report's understanding of statutory meaning when Congress amended statute). See also the extensive use of such history, including references to discussions pertaining to bills never enacted into law, in *FDA v. Brown & Williamson Tobacco Corp.*

3.   *Post-Enactment Testimony and* Amicus *Briefs by Legislators.* The second Checkerboard Opinion is just one example of how the battle to create legislative meaning can continue after the statute is enacted. Two other techniques have been used. One is the use of affidavits and depositions by legislators, especially at the state level (where legislative history is not always readily available or elaborate enough to provide much guidance). Some states consider such testimony "inadmissible evidence" of "legislative intent" but are, nonetheless, sometimes moved by it. For example, the Washington Supreme Court in *City of Spokane v. State*, 89 P.2d 826 (Wash. 1939), refused to admit affidavits or depositions of the Governor, Speaker of the House, chairs of the relevant committees, 33 Senators and 68 Representatives in one legislature and 33 Senators and 70 Representatives in the next legislature. Nonetheless, the Court overruled its prior interpretation of the statute, effectively conforming to the views pressed in the affidavits and depositions. Compare *Western Air Lines v. Bd. of Equalization*, 480 U.S. 123, 130 n.* (1987) (refusing to consider affidavit from lobbyist involved in the enactment of the law in question).

Another method is a legislator *amicus* brief. The Supreme Court in *Blanchette v. Connecticut General Ins. Corp.*, 419 U.S. 102 (1974), relied on the statements made at oral argument by Representative Brock Adams (D-Wash.), representing 36 Members of Congress, as evidence that the Act did not withdraw a Tucker Act remedy for just compensation. The *Gingles* case, discussed in Chapter 2, § 1(B)(2), reached a result consistent with, and perhaps influenced by, an *amicus* brief filed by a dozen key Members of Congress, opposing the Administration's interpretation of the Voting Rights Act Amendments of 1982.

Nine key legislators (six Democrats, then the majority party in Congress, and three key Republicans) involved in the controlling legislation filed an *amicus* brief in *Rapanos*.[385] Their brief provided a comprehensive examination of the evolution of

---

thought it inappropriate even to discuss subsequent legislative history); *United States v. Monsanto*, 491 U.S. 600, 609–10 (1989) (disregarding postenactment statements of several legislators).

[385]   Brief of the Honorable John Dingell, John Conyers, Jr., Robert Drinan, Gary Hart, Kenneth Hechler, Charles Mathias, Jr., Paul McCloskey, Jr., Charles Rangel, and Richard Schultz Schweiker, as *Amici Curiae* in Support of the Respondent, *Rapanos v. United States*, 547 U.S. 715 (2006).

wetlands regulation, from the Federal Water Pollution Control Act of 1948, through the transformational amendments in 1972 and concluding with the Clean Water Act of 1977. The theme of their brief was that the 1972 law "articulated one of the broadest ecosystem restoration and protection aspirations in all of environmental law." The mandate of the statute was for the EPA and the Army Corps to view the country as a collection of integrated hydrological ecosystems whose integrity was threatened, a threat that had dire consequences for flood control, safe drinking water, and damage to animal populations. The aggressive and comprehensive Corps regulations were affirmatively ratified by the 1977 statute. Although the *Rapanos* plurality rejected this analysis, it was adopted by the four dissenters and may have had an impact on Justice Kennedy, who followed its key points.

4.   *Post-Enactment History from Related Funding Legislation.* In *Bruesewitz v. Wyeth LLC*, 562 U.S. 223 (2011), the Court considered whether the National Childhood Vaccine Injury Act of 1986 (NCVIA) preempted state-law design-defect claims against vaccine manufacturers. The statute states that "No vaccine manufacturer shall be liable in a civil action for damages arising from a vaccine-related injury or death associated with the administration of a vaccine after October 1, 1988, if the injury or death resulted from side effects that were unavoidable even though the vaccine was properly prepared and was accompanied by proper directions and warnings." The majority opinion written by Justice Scalia (joined by Chief Justice Roberts and Justices Kennedy, Thomas, Breyer, and Alito), focused on the text of the statute and held that the statute preempted design-defect claims.

In a dissenting opinion, Justice Sotomayor (joined by Justice Ginsburg) invoked post-enactment legislative history to support her position that Congress intended to incorporate the definition of "unavoidable" found in comment k of the Restatement (Second) of Torts and cases expounding upon this comment. (If the statute incorporated comment k it would not preempt certain design-defect claims.) Justice Sotomayor referred to a committee report accompanying legislation enacted in 1987 that provided funding for the no-fault compensation program established by the NCVIA in 1986. The 1987 committee report clearly stated that the NCVIA codified comment k. Justice Sotomayor argued:

> To be sure, postenactment legislative history created by a subsequent Congress is ordinarily a hazardous basis from which to infer the intent of the enacting Congress. But unlike ordinary postenactment legislative history, which is justifiably given little or no weight, the 1987 Report reflects the intent of the Congress that enacted the funding legislation necessary to give operative effect to the principal provisions of the Vaccine Act * * * Because the tort reforms in the 1986 Act * * * had no operative legal effect unless and until Congress provided funding for the compensation program, the views of the Congress that enacted that funding legislation are a proper and, indeed, authoritative guide to the meaning of [the NCVIA].

Responding to Justice Sotomayor's argument, Justice Scalia rejected her proposed exception to the general rule against post-enactment legislative history:

> Post-enactment legislative history (a contradiction in terms) is not a legitimate tool of statutory interpretation. * * * Real (pre-enactment) legislative history is persuasive to some because it is thought to shed light on what legislators understood an ambiguous statutory text to mean when they voted to enact it

into law. * * * But post-enactment legislative history by definition "could have had no effect on the congressional vote." * * *. Those who voted on the relevant statutory language were not necessarily the same persons who crafted the statements in the later Committee Report; or if they were did not necessarily have the same views at that earlier time; and no one voting at that earlier time could possibly have been informed by those later statements. Permitting the legislative history of subsequent funding legislation to alter the meaning of a statute would set a dangerous precedent. Many provisions of federal law depend on appropriations or include sunset provisions; they cannot be made the device for unenacted statutory revision.

NOTES ON PRESIDENTIAL SIGNING OR VETO STATEMENTS

1.   *Presidents' Use of Signing Statements.* Throughout history, Presidents have made statements about the bills they sign into law, and sometimes those statements have addressed important policy-related issues of statutory meaning, along one of at least three dimensions: (1) discussions highlighting important features of legislation; (2) objections to the constitutionality of some part of a law, usually with an indication that the administration would apply the law more narrowly than it was written; or (3) an intention to apply a law in a particular way, based upon the executive department's interpretation of that statute. See Curtis Bradley & Eric Posner, *Presidential Signing Statements and Executive Power*, 23 Const. Comm. 307 (2006).

The Reagan Administration used the presidential signing statement more aggressively for reasons (2) and (3) than prior administrations had done. In some statements, President Reagan took positions that were apparently inconsistent with congressional deals made in the enactment process. For example, Congress rebuffed Administration attempts to dilute the Safe Drinking Water Act of 1986 by giving the EPA discretion whether to compel local governments to maintain safe water. The bill said EPA "shall" (not "may") issue the safe-water orders. Yet in his signing statement, President Reagan declared that the new law did not "require" EPA to take any enforcement action. Also, the Administration gained wider publication for its signing statements. Such statements ordinarily appear in the Weekly Compilation of Presidential Documents (now succeeded by the Daily Compilation of Presidential Documents) but beginning in 1986 the West Publishing Company has regularly included signing statements in its *United States Code Congressional and Administrative News* (USCCAN), which is the most readily accessible reference work for legislative history. Legal advisers to the President took the position that the President's statements are authoritative on issues of "legislative intent," perhaps trumping contrary statements of Senators and Representatives themselves.[386]

The Bush 41 Administration was similarly aggressive in its use of signing statements, with the Clinton Administration being moderately aggressive. Most aggressive of all was the Bush 43 Administration. In his first five years, President George W. Bush challenged or sought to alter more than 800 statutory provisions, apparently more than the total number of provisions reinterpreted by all three of his immediate

---

[386]   *The New Republic*, 3 Nov. 1986, at 13–14. See also Memorandum from Samuel Alito, Jr., Deputy Assistant Attorney Gen., Office of Legal Counsel, to the Litigation Strategy Working Group (Feb. 5, 1986), available at http://www.archives.gov/news/samuel-alito/accession-060-89-269/Acc060-89-269-box6-SG-LSWG-AlitotoLSWG-Feb1986.pdf.

predecessors in their 20 years of combined service as Presidents. Bradley & Posner, *Presidential Signing Statements*, 324–25.

The Bush 43 signing statements received more publicity, in part because they often rested upon a controversial understanding of the President's Article II powers. For example, the Detainee Treatment Act of 2005 banned cruel, inhuman, or degrading treatment of detainees, such as those at Guantánamo Bay, Cuba. When signing this bill (which his allies had resisted) into law, President Bush 43 stated that the executive branch would construe the ban "in a manner consistent with the constitutional authority of the President to supervise the unitary executive branch and as Commander in Chief and consistent with the constitutional limitations on the judicial power." This language was reminiscent of the language in the controversial memorandum of Bush 43 Administration Justice Department official John Yoo that argued that presidential agents are immune from prosecution for torture of suspects.

Like his predecessors, President Obama regularly issued presidential signing statements. Shortly after taking office, President Obama published a memorandum explaining his approach to signing statements. He noted that "[f]or nearly two centuries, Presidents have issued statements addressing constitutional or other legal questions upon signing bills into law" but "[i]n recent years, there has been considerable public discussion and criticism of the use of signing statements to raise constitutional objections to statutory provisions."

Recognizing the potential for abuse, President Obama articulated four principles to guide his use of signing statements. First, the President will make every effort to communicate his concerns to Congress before enactment of legislation. Second, the President will adopt a presumption of constitutionality and will only conclude that a portion of a bill is unconstitutional if it violates well-founded constitutional principles. Third, the President will articulate his constitutional objections with specificity in order to promote transparency and accountability. Finally, when construing a provision in a manner that is meant to avoid a constitutional problem, the President will only apply legitimate constructions of legislative language. See Memorandum, Presidential Signing Statements, 74 Fed. Reg. 10,669 (Mar. 9, 2009)

Two days after publishing this memorandum, President Obama issued a lengthy signing statement for the Omnibus Appropriations Act of 2009, Pub. L. No. 111–8, 123 Stat. 524, in which he explained that he would refuse to be bound by provisions the White House perceived as congressional encroachments on his constitutional authority in multiple areas, including foreign affairs ("effectively directing the Executive on how to proceed or not proceed in negotiations or discussions with international organizations and foreign governments"), and the Art. II, § 3 Recommendations Clause ("effectively purport[ing] to require me and other executive officers to submit budget requests to the Congress in particular forms").

A student comment addressing this first Obama signing statement argued that the enduring presence of signing statements results from "an inefficient equilibrium" between Congress and the President. Recent Signing Statement, *Omnibus Appropriations Act of 2009, President Obama Issues First Constitutional Signing Statement, Declares Appropriations Bill Provisions Unenforceable.—Statement on Signing the Omnibus Appropriations Act, 2009, Daily Comp. Pres. Doc. No. DCPD200900145 (Mar. 11, 2009)*, 123 Harv. L. Rev. 1051 (2010):

For Congress, the costs of including self-aggrandizing bill provisions are de minimis. The executive, in contrast, must internalize the high costs of an overt, defensive response because the interbranch dialogue occupies two planes: one political, one constitutional. Small political issues, like obscure omnibus provisions, implicate larger constitutional questions. For example, President Obama's objection to budget reporting provisions may seem insignificant, but it reflects a broader concern that Congress might aggrandize its constitutional powers. The executive, it follows, continually fears that the Court and Congress might interpret a political compromise as a constitutional concession in the absence of a signal to the contrary. Concession, it is feared, might foreclose for present and future administrations the ability to invoke executive prerogative when needed. To minimize this risk, the executive adopted a positive system of denial, which, across administrations, entrenched itself as the default practice. But having established this pattern of denial, the executive cannot go back. In this system, silence no longer constitutes an objection; courts and Congress may construe silence as a concession. In effect, executive practice engendered an inefficient equilibrium in which a skewed incentive structure precipitated—and later solidified—Pavlovian signaling practices. Signaling costs might change, but the risk-averse and forward-thinking executive will continue to signal—not because it is efficient, but because the executive has delegitimized silence as an alternative.

Justice Breyer's dissent in *Free Enterprise Fund v. Public Company Accounting Oversight Board*, 561 U.S. 477, 522–23 (2010) (see Chapter 8, § 1(C)) indicates how a president's failure to object to certain provisions of a bill in a signing statement may be construed as tacit approval. The Court struck down statutory provisions that restricted the President in his ability to remove members of the Oversight Board. Justice Breyer contended that the Court should decline to create a separation-of-powers issue when there was apparently no disagreement between Congress and the President at the time of enactment: "The President signed the Act. And, when he did so, he issued a signing statement that critiqued multiple provisions of the Act but did not express any separation-of-powers concerns."

2.   *Should Presidential Signing Statements Be Considered Persuasive of Statutory Meaning?* Reagan Administration Attorney General Edward Meese and some subsequent commentators maintain that presidential signing statements should "count" as evidence of statutory meaning, for the same reasons a committee report or a congressional sponsor's explanation might count. Academic commentators and the ABA have been reluctant to accept the argument that signing statements are authoritative, for the same reasons they are dubious about "subsequent legislative history"—it is unreliable evidence of the expectations of the enacting coalition, and there is too much opportunity for manipulation.[387] If an interpreter is a textualist, she would be suspicious of or uninterested in any such background material, whether originating in the Capitol or the

---

[387]   American Bar Association, Task Force on Presidential Signing Statements and the Separation of Powers Doctrine, Report with Recommendations (2006) (rejecting the Bush 43 Administration's aggressive use of signing statements); Marc Garber & Kurt Wimmer, *Presidential Signing Statements as Interpretations of Legislative Intent: An Executive Aggrandizement of Power*, 24 Harv. J. Legis. 363 (1987); William Popkin, *Judicial Use of Presidential Legislative History: A Critique*, 66 Ind. L.J. 699 (1991). See also Trevor Morrison, *Constitutional Avoidance in the Executive Branch*, 106 Colum. L. Rev. 1189 (2006), who argues against executive department reliance on the avoidance canon, which has been a mainstay of controversial presidential signing statements since the Reagan Administration.

White House. For more contextualist interpreters, problems of reliability are troubling: Congress cannot respond officially to the President's signing statement, whereas a misleading statement by a legislative sponsor can trigger all sorts of counterattacks (amendments to the bill, contrary statements by other Members, and so on). It is probably for these kinds of reasons that federal judges rarely mention presidential signing statements and almost never give them dispositive weight.[388]

On the other hand, for the same reasons that interpreters are usually interested in the views of the congressional sponsors, they might be interested in the views of the President, who effectively sponsors much major legislation and whose veto power (not to mention his status as chief of one of the two major political parties) gives him an important bargaining role in virtually all major legislation.[389] Such views provide useful policy or even linguistic context for understanding the statute, and they can be good evidence of where the political equilibrium lies. While the President might be tempted to negate deals made in Congress, the fact remains that Members can publicly denounce any such interpretation, as they have been doing, with increasing vigor, from the Reagan Administration through the Bush 43 Administration. Because the President is a repeat player on Capitol Hill, he or she has some incentive not to lie about what deals were made.

Finally, from a more formal perspective, in assessing presidential signing statements it may be useful to retreat to a fundamental issue, whether the bill is ambiguous. If it is, and if the congressional history does not clear up the problem, there may be good reason for the President to state that he or she is signing it based on a certain interpretation of it, at least so long as that interpretation is reasonable. In this circumstance, the President is not violating the text or legislative intent, and the President's good-faith interpretation may be a useful guide to courts and administrative agencies.[390] On the other hand, if the bill, as supplemented by the legislative history, is pretty clear on a point, our constitutional system seems to give the President only two options—to acquiesce (by signing it or by allowing it to go into law without presidential signature) or to veto it—and not the option of attempting to skew it in some other direction. Although Congress may formally override a veto, it has no authoritative way to reject a signing statement (if the statute is already clear).

3. *Veto Statements.* Courts will sometimes rely on the President's veto statement. If Congress overrides the President's veto, then an interpreter might infer that Congress rejected the President's preferences. See *McDonald v. Santa Fe Trail Transportation Co.*, 427 U.S. 273, 295 & n.26 (1976); *Kennedy v. Mendoza-Martinez*, 372 U.S. 144, 178 & n.33 (1963); *United States v. CIO*, 335 U.S. 106, 138–39 (1948) (Rutledge, J., concurring in the result). If, instead, the bill is modified and enacted with the President's signature, the veto statement may provide a good understanding of the nature of the new bill. See *United States v. Yermian*, 468 U.S. 63, 72–75 (1984). In assessing whether the 1991 Civil Rights Act was retroactive, the Court in *Landgraf v. USI Film Products*, 511 U.S. 244

[388] Among the few court of appeals decisions giving weight to signing statements, consider *United States v. Perlaza*, 439 F.3d 1149, 1163 (9th Cir. 2006) (Clinton signing statement confirms suggestion in conference report); *United States v. Gonzales*, 311 F.3d 440, 443 & n.2 (1st Cir. 2002) (similar); *United States v. Story*, 891 F.2d 988, 994 (2d Cir. 1989) (relying on a Reagan signing statement, among other factors, to resolve conflicting interpretations in the House and Senate legislative history).

[389] Charles Cameron, *Veto Bargaining: Presidents and the Politics of Negative Power* (2000); William Eskridge Jr. & John Ferejohn, *The Article I, Section 7 Game*, 80 Geo. L.J. 523 (1992).

[390] For a vigorous defense of presidential signing statements as improving the transparency of law enforcement and interpretational debates, see Bradley & Posner, *Presidential Signing Statements*.

(1994) considered President Bush's veto of the 1990 version of that legislation as relevant background.

PROBLEM ON PRESIDENTIAL SIGNING STATEMENTS

Problem 7-3. Congressional outrage at media accounts of torture of non-American prisoners by American guards and interrogators led to the enactment, by large margins, of the Detainee Treatment Act of 2005, Pub. L. No. 109–148, Div. A, tit. X (2005). As noted above, the Act sets limits on torture that President Bush resisted on grounds that they interfered with his executive authority to conduct the war on terror. For war-on-terror prisoners held at Guantanamo Bay, the Act also substitutes for habeas corpus a special summary appeals process to the D.C. Circuit. When the Act was passed, in 2005, numerous Guantanamo detainees were already pursuing habeas relief in the federal courts. The question arose whether the Act applied to (and therefore required dismissal of) habeas cases filed by those detainees and pending on the date of enactment.

Section 1005(e) of the DTA amended 28 U.S.C. § 2241 (the federal habeas law) by adding at the end the following:

(e) Except as provided in section 1005 of the Detainee Treatment Act of 2005, no court, justice, or judge shall have jurisdiction to hear or consider—

(1) an application for a writ of habeas corpus filed by or on behalf of an alien detained by the Department of Defense at Guantanamo Bay, Cuba; or

(2) any other action against the United States or its agents relating to any aspect of the detention by the Department of Defense of an alien at Guantanamo Bay, Cuba, who—

(A) is currently in military custody; or

(B) has been determined by the United States Court of Appeals for the District of Columbia Circuit in accordance with the procedures set forth in section 1005(e) of the Detainee Treatment Act of 2005 to have been properly detained as an enemy combatant.

Section 1005(h)(1) provides that "this section shall take effect upon the date of the enactment of this Act." Section 1005(h)(2) says: "Paragraphs (2) and (3) of subsection (e) shall apply with respect to any claim whose review is governed by one of such paragraphs and that is pending on or after the date of the enactment of this Act."

The government invoked the canon in favor of applying statutes conferring or ousting jurisdiction immediately, *Landgraf v. USI Film Prods.*, 511 U.S. 244, 274 (1994), while the habeas claimants relied on the presumption against retroactive application of new statutes. *Id.* at 280. The claimants relied on statements by Senator Levin, a sponsor, that the DTA would not apply to pending cases and objected to a proposal by Senator Graham, another sponsor, that would have made § 1005(e)(1) applicable to pending cases. The government responded with statements by Senators Graham and Kyl, a third sponsor, that the Act as passed applied to pending Guantanamo cases.

The government also invoked President Bush's signing statement, which said this: "[T]he executive branch shall construe section 1005 to preclude the Federal courts from exercising subject matter jurisdiction over any existing or future action, including applications for writs of habeas corpus, described in section 1005." See Statement on Signing the Department of Defense, Emergency Supplemental Appropriations to Address Hurricanes in the Gulf of Mexico, and Pandemic Influenza Act, 2006, 41 Weekly Comp. Pres. Doc. 1918 (Dec. 30, 2005).

This issue reached the Supreme Court, where the government argued that federal judges no longer had jurisdiction to adjudicate the Guantanamo habeas claims. What role, if any, should the President's signing statement have played in the Court's interpretation? (How should textualist Justices Scalia and Thomas treat the signing statement? Justices Breyer and Stevens?) In your view, what is the right interpretation? Compare *Hamdan v. Rumsfeld*, 548 U.S. 575–84 (2006), with *id.* at 656–68 (dissenting opinion).

F. LEGISLATIVE INACTION

What the legislature doesn't do may be as significant as what it does. Recall the dog didn't bark canon: When no one in the legislative discussions says that an important policy is being changed, a court should presume that no big changes are intended. This canon is related to the *canon of continuity* defended by David Shapiro, *Continuity and Change in Statutory Interpretation*, 67 N.Y.U. L. Rev. 921 (1992). Shapiro maintains that the structure of American government suggests a constitutional bias against discontinuity in legal obligations and rights. Thus, in the absence of clear indications to the contrary, statutes should be construed to maintain established rules and practices.

You have already seen plenty of examples of judicial inferences (or not) from legislative inaction, especially in Chapter 5 and this chapter. There are three specific doctrines that relate to Congress's failure to do something, and it is useful to separate them out.[391]

(1) *The Acquiescence Rule.* If Congress is aware of an authoritative agency or judicial interpretation of a statute and doesn't amend the statute, the Court has sometimes presumed that Congress has "acquiesced" in the interpretation's correctness. The acquiescence rule was followed by the Court to reaffirm its own prior interpretations of statutes in *Johnson v. Transportation Agency* (Chapter 1, § 2(B)) and in *Flood v. Kuhn* (Chapter 5, § 2(B)). But the acquiescence rule can also support implicit congressional ratification of a uniform line of federal appellate interpretations or in a longstanding agency interpretation. E.g., *Zuni Pub. Sch. Dist. No. 89 v. Dep't of Educ.*, 550 U.S. 81 (2007).

This rule is one that the new textualists find particularly abhorrent. E.g., *Johnson* (Scalia, J., dissenting). Absent "overwhelming evidence of acquiescence," the *Solid Waste* Court announced it is "loathe to replace the plain text and original understanding of a statute" with a new construction. Nonetheless, this doctrine is still invoked if there is concrete evidence Congress was aware of the longstanding interpretation and paid attention to the issue, as in the *FDA Tobacco* Case, where

---

[391] This account is drawn from James Brudney, *Congressional Commentary on Judicial Interpretations of Statutes: Idle Chatter or Telling Response?*, 93 Mich. L. Rev. 1 (1994); and William Eskridge Jr., *Interpreting Legislative Inaction*, 87 Mich. L. Rev. 67 (1988), which also contains appendices listing cases following or declining to follow these doctrines.

Justice Scalia himself signed onto dozens of pages of legislative history discussion. See also *Zuni Pub. Sch. District*.[392]

(2) *The Reenactment Rule.* If Congress reenacts a statute without making any material changes in its wording, the Court will often presume that Congress intends to incorporate authoritative agency and judicial interpretations of that language into the reenacted statute. The leading Supreme Court statement of this rule is found in *Lorillard v. Pons* (Section 3(A) of this chapter), which stated: "Congress is presumed to be aware of an administrative or judicial interpretation of a statute and to adopt that interpretation when it reenacts a statute without change." Like the acquiescence rule, the reenactment rule is much more likely to be invoked if the interpretation is a foundational one—that is, the interpretation is authoritative (namely, a leading Supreme Court case or the decision of the chief agency enforcing the law), settled, and likely to have yielded private and public reliance. See *Jama v. Immigration & Customs Enforcement*, 543 U.S. 345 (2005) (application of reenactment rule inappropriate because prior state of the law not well settled); *Fogerty v. Fantasy, Inc.*, 510 U.S. 517, 527–33 (1994) (same, and contrasting the well-settled stature of Creedence Clearwater Revival "as one of the greatest American rock and roll bands of all time").

A dramatic invocation of the reenactment rule came in *Faragher v. City of Boca Raton*, 524 U.S. 775 (1998). The Court ruled that employers can be vicariously liable under Title VII for hostile work environments created or tolerated by supervisors, subject to a reasonableness defense. Justice Souter's opinion for the Court relied on the holding and reasoning in *Meritor Savings Bank FSB v. Vinson*, 477 U.S. 57 (1986), which had greatly elaborated upon the spare language in Title VII that employers cannot "discriminate" because of sex by holding that "hostile environment sexual harassment" was prohibited. Dissenting Justices Thomas and Scalia objected that the Court's opinions were no more than "willful policymaking" in violation of the statute. Justice Souter responded that the holding and reasoning of *Meritor* was binding on the Court not only as a matter of stare decisis, but also because it had been ratified by Congress when it amended Title VII in 1991. See 524 U.S. at 792. Although the 1991 Act overrode a number of Supreme Court interpretations of Title VII, it left *Meritor* intact, which Justice Souter deemed "conspicuous. We thus have to assume that in expanding employers' potential liability under Title VII, Congress relied on our statements in *Meritor* about the limits of employer liability. To disregard those statements now * * * would be not only to disregard *stare decisis* in statutory interpretation, but to substitute our revised judgment about the proper allocation of the costs of harassment for Congress's considered decision on the subject." *Id.* at 804 n.4.

(3) *The Rejected Proposal Rule.* If Congress (in conference committee) or one chamber (on the floor) considers and rejects specific statutory language, the Court

---

[392] See also *Evans v. United States*, 504 U.S. 255, 269 (1992) (assuming Congress had acquiesced in longstanding and highly visible interpretation of statute in lower courts); *United States v. Riverside Bayview Homes, Inc.*, 474 U.S. 121 (1985) (Conference Committee killed House effort to overrule Corps of Engineers' jurisdiction over "wetlands"); *Heckler v. Day*, 467 U.S. 104 (1984) (congressional hearings on disability benefit delays did not produce legislation to hurry agency along); *Guardians Ass'n v. Civil Serv. Comm'n*, 463 U.S. 582, 593 & n.14 (1983) (opinion of White, J.) (acquiescence in Title VI regulations).

has often been reluctant to interpret the statute along lines of the rejected language. The leading case is *Runyon v. McCrary*, 427 U.S. 160 (1976), where the Court reaffirmed a debatable precedent interpreting the Civil Rights Act of 1866, based in large part upon its perception that the Senate in 1971 had rejected attempts to override that interpretation. See also the FDA Tobacco Case.

The *Solid Waste* Court expressed a more skeptical view of this kind of evidence.

" '[F]ailed legislative proposals are "a particularly dangerous ground on which to rest an interpretation of a prior statute.' *Cent. Bank of Denver N.A. v. First Interstate Bank of Denver N.A.*, 511 U.S. 164, 187 (1994). A bill can be proposed for any number of reasons, and it can be rejected for just as many others. The relationship between the actions and inactions of the 95th Congress and the intent of the 92d Congress in passing § 404(a) is also considerably attenuated. Because 'subsequent history is less illuminating than the contemporaneous evidence,' *Hagen v. Utah*, 510 U.S. 399, 420 (1994), respondents face a difficult task in overcoming the plain text and import of § 404(a)."

Consider these various doctrines in connection with the following case, which is excerpted at length in Chapter 5.

BOB JONES UNIVERSITY V. UNITED STATES
Supreme Court of the United States, 1983.
461 U.S. 574, 103 S.Ct. 2017, 76 L.Ed.2d 157.

[Excerpted in Chapter 5, § 2(B)(3)]

NOTES ON POST-ENACTMENT ACQUIESCENCE AND "LAW AS EQUILIBRIUM"

1.   *Criticisms of the Acquiescence Doctrine. Bob Jones* is now a leading citation for the acquiescence rule. That rule has, however, long been subject to criticism. See, e.g., Henry Hart, Jr. & Albert Sacks, *The Legal Process* 1313–70 (Eskridge & Frickey eds. 1994) (tent. ed. 1958); John Grabow, *Congressional Silence and the Search for Legislative Intent: A Venture into "Speculative Unrealities,"* 64 B.U. L. Rev. 737 (1984), and several Justices have strongly objected to it. Dissenting from the Court's reaffirmation of *Weber* in *Johnson* (see Chapter 1, § 2(B)), Justice Scalia rejected the majority's invocation of legislative acquiescence. For him, "vindication by congressional inaction is a canard," because congressional inaction has no formal significance under Article I as interpreted in *INS v. Chadha* (see Chapter 8, § 3(A)), and no functional significance given difficulties in figuring out why Congress did nothing. More recently, the Supreme Court has become much more reluctant to accept legislative acquiescence arguments. See, e.g., *Patterson v. McLean Credit Union* (Chapter 5, § 2(B)), which rejected the dissenting opinion's reliance on legislative inaction (not only the acquiescence rule but also the reenactment and rejected proposal rules) as reason to reaffirm and expand the Court's decision in *Runyon v. McCrary.* Is there any special reason for a skeptic such as Justice Scalia to apply the acquiescence rule in a case like *Bob Jones*, or is this just another "canard"?

Note *Bob Jones*' inconsistent use of congressional inaction. The Court relies on the failure of Congress to overrule the 1971 revenue ruling: Congress, by doing nothing, acquiesced in the agency's action. The Court ignores the failure of Congress to overrule the IRS policy before 1971: that doesn't count, the Court seems to be saying. The Court ignores the repeated failure of Congress to enact statutes penalizing private education discrimination: Congress, by passing statutes which did not cover private schools, nonetheless disapproved of the private action. Is there any good reason to interpret congressional inaction as the Court does?

Justice Rehnquist is critical of the Court's reliance on legislative inaction in *Bob Jones* and, later when he was Chief Justice, in *Solid Waste*. Yet Justice Rehnquist has himself relied upon congressional inaction. See, e.g., *Weinberger v. Rossi*, 456 U.S. 25, 33 (1982) (Rehnquist, J.) (unless Congress says otherwise, Court will presume that it acquiesces in executive agreements). See also *Haig v. Agee*, 453 U.S. 280 (1981) (Burger, C.J.) (absent intent to repudiate executive interpretation of the Passport Act, Congress is presumed to acquiesce in it). Are these foreign-affairs cases more appropriate occasions for relying on legislative inaction than *Bob Jones* is?

2.   *Law as Equilibrium.* In Chapter 5, § 3(B)(3), we suggested that one way to think about law is that it is the result of the equilibrium of institutional forces, rather than the result of formal deduction from first premises. From this perspective, an important issue in *Bob Jones* was how clear the practical equilibrium was in the early 1980s on the question whether the federal government should indirectly support racially segregated schools through tax preferences. Even if the IRS had taken a bold step a decade earlier, the lower courts had ratified it; if by 1980 the Congress and the executive branch were also settled in their support of that policy as well, then that policy is "law" in a very practical way (none of the three federal branches of government would change it) that should be apparent to such schools. When the Reagan Administration switched positions from that taken by the Nixon, Ford, and Carter Administrations, it was, under this perspective, changing the law, not returning the law to its "true" state, and therefore should have been allowed to do that only with the approval of Congress. The Court in *Bob Jones* recognized this practical reality and stabilized the law around its equilibrium point, leaving the Reagan Administration the option of seeking congressional authorization for reviving tax preferences for segregated schools. Is this a persuasive way to justify *Bob Jones*? You might want to apply a similar idea to the *FDA Tobacco* Case and the Court's recent cutbacks on the Army Corps' wetlands regulations in *Solid Waste* and *Rapanos*.[393]

Even if this explains *Bob Jones*, and even if you find it a good justification for the decision, this perspective leaves the Court a lot of room in which to affect the political balance, especially during periods of divided government when it is particularly hard for Congress to override the Court. An example is *Central Bank of Denver N.A. v. First Interstate Bank of Denver N.A.*, 511 U.S. 164 (1994). Justice Kennedy's majority opinion held that an action could not be brought alleging that defendant aided and abetted a violation of § 10(b) of the Securities Exchange Act of 1934, which prohibits securities fraud. In our judgment, this outcome upset a longstanding equilibrium to the contrary. *All* eleven federal courts of appeals that had considered the question had recognized a cause of action against aiders and abettors. Petitioner had asked the Court to address

---

[393]   *Solid Waste* (2001) and *Rapanos* (2006) were both handed down when the Republican Party controlled the Presidency, the House, and the Senate. After *Rapanos*, the Army Corps, under strong pressure from farmers, ranchers, mining companies, and the like, issued new wetlands regulations that cut back on the prior protections.

questions, such as the *mens rea* standard for aider and abettor liability, that also assumed that such a private right of action existed.

The Court *sua sponte* requested the parties to address the question whether the aiding and abetting action existed at all. Justice Kennedy's opinion stressed the plain meaning of § 10(b), which does not mention aiding and abetting liability. In dissent, Justice Stevens argued (1) that the majority had, in effect, engaged in "bait and switch" tactics (our term, not his) by applying the textualist interpretative approach to an old statute adopted by Congress in an era in which courts routinely elaborated upon rights of action, (2) that the majority had rejected a settled interpretation of law in terms of both judicial and administrative construction, which should be the province of Congress, not the Court, and (3) that actions of Congress since 1934 indicated congressional knowledge and approval of the implied right of action. One might add that, in light of this consensus, had a lawyer in the mid-to late-1980s informed Central Bank that it could *not* have been sued as an aider and abettor under § 10(b), that lawyer would have committed malpractice. (Recall that the certiorari petition filed by the lawyers for Central Bank did not even raise the question Justice Kennedy ultimately decided in Central Bank's favor.)

PROBLEM ON LEGISLATIVE INACTION AND LAW AS EQUILIBRIUM

Problem 7-4. The Age Discrimination Act of 1967 (ADEA) prohibits age discrimination by employers in language that is identical to the core antidiscrimination provision of Title VII enacted in the 1964 Civil Rights Act. Each makes it unlawful for an employer "to fail or refuse to hire or to discharge any individual, or otherwise to discriminate against any individual with regard to his compensation, terms, conditions, or privileges of employment, because of such individual's" *age* (ADEA) or *race, color, religion, sex, or national origin* (Title VII). For decades, the Court recognized that its interpretations of this Title VII language applied with equal force in the context of age discrimination. See, e.g., *Trans World Airlines, Inc. v. Thurston*, 469 U.S. 111, 121 (1985) (quoting *Lorillard v. Pons*, 434 U.S. 575, 584 (1978)).

In *Price Waterhouse v. Hopkins*, 490 U.S. 228 (1989), the Court construed the Title VII language above to mean that once a plaintiff proves her membership in the protected class played a motivating part in an employment decision, the defendant may avoid liability if it proves by a preponderance of the evidence that it would have made the same decision even without this factor. Justice Kennedy in dissent argued the proper standard was that a member of the Title VII protected class must prove by a preponderance of the evidence that age was the "but-for" cause of the challenged adverse employment action, and that no burden shifts to the employer simply because the plaintiff showed that race or sex was a motivating factor in that decision.

As part of its 1991 Civil Rights Act, Congress overrode a portion of *Price Waterhouse* by adding two provisions to Title VII. One provides that when a plaintiff establishes that membership in the protected class was a motivating factor for any adverse employment practice, this practice is unlawful even though other lawful factors also motivated the practice. The second provision states that if the employer demonstrates it would have made the same decision anyway, the plaintiff may be entitled to declaratory and injunctive relief and attorney's fees but not to reinstatement or back pay. In other words, the 1991 Act changed the "motivating factor" test into an issue of remedy rather than one of liability. Congress made no similar change to the ADEA in the 1991 Civil Rights Act.

Indeed Congress did not address the ADEA in substantive terms at all in its 1991 statute amending Title VII in numerous places (see discussion of 1991 Act in Chapter 1, § 3(C)).

In 2004, Jack Gross filed an ADEA claim in federal district court alleging that he was demoted by his financial services company employer because of his age. The trial court jury instruction applied the *Price Waterhouse* standard: Gross should prevail if he proved that age was a motivating factor, but the employer should prevail if it proved that it would have demoted him regardless of age.

The case comes to the Supreme Court and there are three options for the applicable standard of proof: (1) *apply Price-Waterhouse as the trial court did*; the ADEA language being construed is the same language the Court construed in 1989 and Congress has not changed it; (2) *apply the 1991 Civil Rights Act standard*; Congress clarified the substantive meaning of the contested Title VII language to assure that proof of "a motivating factor" establishes liability, and Congress's clarification should extend to the exact parallel language of the ADEA; (3) *start afresh with the ADEA*; by amending Title VII in 1991 without making similar changes to the ADEA (then or in the ensuing 13 years), Congress uncoupled the two laws. The Court is free to reinstate the *Price-Waterhouse* majority reasoning, and is also free or to adopt Justice Kennedy's "but-for cause" dissenting position if it believes the ADEA should be construed this way.

How would you rule? See *Gross v. FBL Fin. Servs.*, 557 U.S. 167 (2009).

3. INTERPRETATION IN LIGHT OF OTHER STATUTES

"Statutory interpretation is a holistic endeavor," so that a provision "that may seem ambiguous in isolation is often clarified by" the greater consistency of one interpretation with "the rest of the law." *United Sav. Ass'n of Tex. v. Timbers of Inwood Forest Assocs.*, 484 U.S. 365, 371 (1988). See also *W. Va. Univ. Hosp. v. Casey* (Chapter 6, § 2(C)), (interpreting one statute that authorized prevailing parties to recover attorney's fees by examining the text of many other such statutes.) There are several reasons an interpreter might consider other statutes, and each is associated with a statutory interpretation canon or doctrine:

> • *the in pari materia rule:* other statutes might use the same terminology or address the same issue as the statute being interpreted (Part A);

> • *modeled or borrowed statute rule*: another statute might have been the template from which the statute in issue was designed (Part B);

> • *presumption against implied repeals*: there might be a later statute possibly changing the implications of the statute being interpreted (Part C).

Note that the first two precepts are weaker versions of the rule that a word used several times in a statute is strongly presumed to have the same meaning every time it is used. See § 2(C) of chapter 6, and the cases discussed therein. The third precept is more complex, for it raises the possibility that statutes enacted at different times will be inconsistent with one another. How should interpreters figure out what law to apply when different statutes press in different directions? This conundrum vexed Judge Norris's two opinions in *Montana Wilderness, supra.* Part C will explore several different ways to reconcile apparently clashing statutes.

A. SIMILAR STATUTES (THE *IN PARI MATERIA* RULE)

STATUTORY PREFACE TO *ADEA JURY TRIAL* CASE

Age Discrimination in Employment Act of 1967, 29 U.S.C. § 621 *et seq.* (as of 1978)

Section 626. * * *

(b) The provisions of this Act shall be enforced in accordance with the powers, remedies, and procedures provided in sections 11(b), 16 (except for subsection (a) thereof), and 17 of the Fair Labor Standards Act of 1938, as amended (28 U.S.C. § 211(b), 216, 217), and subsection (c) of this section. * * * Amounts owing to a person as a result of a violation of this Act shall be deemed to be unpaid minimum wages or unpaid overtime compensation for purposes of sections 16 and 17 of the Fair Labor Standards Act of 1938, as amended (28 U.S.C. § 216, 217): *Provided,* That liquidated damages shall be payable only in cases of willful violations of this Act. In any action brought to enforce this Act the court shall have jurisdiction to grant such legal or equitable relief as may be appropriate to effectuate the purposes of this Act, including without limitation judgments compelling employment, reinstatement or promotion, or enforcing the liability for amounts deemed to be unpaid minimum wages or unpaid overtime compensation under this section.

(c) Any person aggrieved may bring a civil action in any court of competent jurisdiction for such legal or equitable relief as will effectuate the purposes of this Act: *Provided,* That the right of any person to bring such action shall terminate upon the commencement of an action by the Secretary to enforce the right of such employee under this Act.

Title VII of the Civil Rights Act of 1964, 42 U.S.C. § 2000e *et seq.* (as of 1978)

Section 2000e–5.

(g) If the court finds that the respondent has intentionally engaged in or is intentionally engaging in an unlawful employment practice charged in the complaint, the court may enjoin the respondent from engaging in such unlawful employment practice, and order such affirmative action as may be appropriate, which may include, but is not limited to, reinstatement or hiring of employees, with or without back pay (payable by the employer, employment agency, or labor organization, as the case may be, responsible for the unlawful employment practice), or any other equitable relief as the court deems appropriate. * * *

LORILLARD V. PONS
Supreme Court of the United States, 1978.
434 U.S. 575, 98 S.Ct. 868, 55 L.Ed.2d 40.

MR. JUSTICE MARSHALL delivered the opinion of the Court.

This case presents the question whether there is a right to a jury trial in private civil actions for lost wages under the Age Discrimination in Employment Act of 1967 (ADEA or Act), 81 Stat. 602, as amended, 88 Stat. 74, 29 U.S.C. § 621 *et seq.* (1970 ed. and Supp. V). * * *

[I] The ADEA broadly prohibits arbitrary discrimination in the workplace based on age. Although the ADEA contains no provision expressly granting a right to jury trial, respondent nonetheless contends that the structure of the Act demonstrates a congressional intent to grant such a right. Alternatively, she argues that the Seventh Amendment requires that in a private action for lost wages under the ADEA, the parties must be given the option of having the case heard by a jury. We turn first to the statutory question since " 'it is a cardinal principle that this Court will first ascertain whether a construction of the statute is fairly possible by which the [constitutional] question may be avoided.' " Because we find the statutory issue dispositive, we need not address the constitutional issue.

The enforcement scheme for the statute is complex—the product of considerable attention during the legislative debates preceding passage of the Act. Several alternative proposals were considered by Congress. The Administration submitted a bill, modeled after §§ 10(c), (e) of the National Labor Relations Act, 29 U.S.C. §§ 160(c), (e), which would have granted power to the Secretary of Labor to issue cease-and-desist orders enforceable in the courts of appeals, but would not have granted a private right of action to aggrieved individuals, S. 830, H.R. 4221, 90th Cong., 1st Sess. (1967). Senator Javits introduced an alternative proposal to make discrimination based on age unlawful under the Fair Labor Standards Act (FLSA), 29 U.S.C. § 201 *et seq.*; the normal enforcement provisions of the FLSA, 29 U.S.C. § 216 *et seq.*, (1970 ed. and Supp. V), then would have been applicable, permitting suits by either the Secretary of Labor or the injured individual, S. 788, 90th Cong., 1st Sess. (1967). A third alternative that was considered would have adopted the statutory pattern of Title VII of the Civil Rights Act of 1964 and utilized the Equal Employment Opportunity Commission.

The bill that was ultimately enacted is something of a hybrid, reflecting, on the one hand, Congress' desire to use an existing statutory scheme and a bureaucracy with which employers and employees would be familiar and, on the other hand, its dissatisfaction with some elements of each of the preexisting schemes. Pursuant to § 7(b) of the Act, 29 U.S.C. § 626(b), violations of the ADEA generally are to be treated as violations of the FLSA. "Amounts owing * * * as a result of a violation" of the ADEA are to be treated as "unpaid minimum wages or unpaid overtime compensation" under the FLSA and the rights created by the ADEA are to be "enforced in accordance with the powers, remedies and procedures" of specified sections of the FLSA.

Following the model of the FLSA, the ADEA establishes two primary enforcement mechanisms. Under the FLSA provisions incorporated in § 7(b) of the ADEA, 29 U.S.C. § 626(b), the Secretary of Labor may bring suit on behalf of an aggrieved individual for injunctive and monetary relief. 29 U.S.C. §§ 216(c), 217 (1970 ed. and Supp. V). The incorporated FLSA provisions together with § 7(c) of the ADEA, 29 U.S.C. § 626(c), in addition, authorize private civil actions for "such legal or equitable relief as will effectuate the purposes of" the ADEA. Although not required by the FLSA, prior to the initiation of any ADEA action, an individual must give notice to the Secretary of Labor of his intention to sue in order that the Secretary can attempt to eliminate the alleged unlawful practice through informal methods. § 7(d), 29 U.S.C. § 626(d). After allowing the Secretary 60 days to conciliate the alleged unlawful practice, the individual may file suit. The right of the individual to sue on his own terminates, however, if the Secretary commences an action on his behalf. § 7(c), 29 U.S.C. § 626(c).

[II] Looking first to the procedural provisions of the statute, we find a significant indication of Congress' intent in its directive that the ADEA be enforced in accordance with the "powers, remedies, and *procedures*" of the FLSA. § 7(b), 29 U.S.C. § 626(b) (emphasis added). Long before Congress enacted the ADEA, it was well established that there was a right to a jury trial in private actions pursuant to the FLSA. Indeed, every court to consider the issue had so held. Congress is presumed to be aware of an administrative or judicial interpretation of a statute and to adopt that interpretation when it reenacts a statute without change. So too, where, as here, Congress adopts a new law incorporating sections of a prior law, Congress normally can be presumed to have had knowledge of the interpretation given to the incorporated law, at least insofar as it affects the new statute.

That presumption is particularly appropriate here since, in enacting the ADEA, Congress exhibited both a detailed knowledge of the FLSA provisions and their judicial interpretation and a willingness to depart from those provisions regarded as undesirable or inappropriate for incorporation. For example, in construing the enforcement sections of the FLSA, the courts had consistently declared that injunctive relief was not available in suits by private individuals but only in suits by the Secretary. Congress made plain its decision to follow a different course in the ADEA by expressly permitting "such * * * equitable relief as may be appropriate to effectuate the purposes of [the ADEA] including without limitation judgments compelling employment, reinstatement or promotion" "in *any* action brought to enforce" the Act. § 7(b), 29 U.S.C. § 626(b) (emphasis added). Similarly, while incorporating into the ADEA the FLSA provisions authorizing awards of liquidated damages, Congress altered the circumstances under which such awards would be available in ADEA actions by mandating that such damages be awarded only where the violation of the ADEA is willful.[8] Finally, Congress expressly declined to incorporate into the ADEA the criminal penalties established for violations of the FLSA.

This selectivity that Congress exhibited in incorporating provisions and in modifying certain FLSA practices strongly suggests that but for those changes Congress expressly made, it intended to incorporate fully the remedies and procedures of the FLSA. Senator Javits, one of the floor managers of the bill, so indicated in describing the enforcement section which became part of the Act: "The enforcement techniques provided by [the ADEA] are directly analogous to those available under the Fair Labor Standards Act; in fact [the ADEA] incorporates by

---

[8]   By its terms, 29 U.S.C. § 216(b) requires that liquidated damages be awarded as a matter of right for violations of the FLSA. However, in response to its dissatisfaction with that judicial interpretation of the provision, Congress enacted the Portal-to-Portal Pay Act of 1947, 61 Stat. 84, which, *inter alia*, grants courts authority to deny or limit liquidated damages where the "employer shows to the satisfaction of the court that the act or omission giving rise to such action was in good faith and that he had reasonable grounds for believing that his act or omission was not a violation of" the FLSA, § 11, 29 U.S.C. § 260 (1970 ed., Supp. V). Although § 7(e) of the ADEA, 29 U.S.C. § 626(e), expressly incorporates §§ 6 and 10 of the Portal-to-Portal Pay Act, 29 U.S.C. §§ 255 and 259 (1970 ed. and Supp. V), the ADEA does not make any reference to § 11, 29 U.S.C. § 260 (1970 ed., Supp. V).

reference, to the greatest extent possible, the provisions of the [FLSA]." 113 Cong. Rec. 31254 (1967).[10] And by directing that actions for lost wages under the ADEA be treated as actions for unpaid minimum wages or overtime compensation under the FLSA, § 7(b), 29 U.S.C. § 626(b), Congress dictated that the jury trial right then available to enforce that FLSA liability would also be available in private actions under the ADEA.

This inference is buttressed by an examination of the language Congress chose to describe the available remedies under the ADEA. Section 7(b), 29 U.S.C. § 626(b), empowers a court to grant "*legal* or equitable relief" and § 7(c), 29 U.S.C. § 626(c), authorizes individuals to bring actions for "*legal* or equitable relief" (emphases added). The word "legal" is a term of art: In cases in which legal relief is available and legal rights are determined, the Seventh Amendment provides a right to jury trial. "[W]here words are employed in a statute which had at the time a well-known meaning at common law or in the law of this country they are presumed to have been used in that sense unless the context compels to the contrary." We can infer, therefore, that by providing specifically for "legal" relief, Congress knew the significance of the term "legal," and intended that there would be a jury trial on demand to "enforc[e] * * * liability for amounts deemed to be unpaid minimum wages or unpaid overtime compensation." § 7(b), 29 U.S.C. § 626(b).

Petitioner strives to find a contrary congressional intent by comparing the ADEA with Title VII of the Civil Rights Act of 1964, 42 U.S.C. § 2000e *et seq.* (1970 ed. and Supp. V), which petitioner maintains does not provide for jury trials. We, of course, intimate no view as to whether a jury trial is available under Title VII as a matter of either statutory or constitutional right. However, after examining the provisions of Title VII, we find petitioner's argument by analogy to Title VII unavailing. There are important similarities between the two statutes, to be sure, both in their aims—the elimination of discrimination from the workplace—and in their substantive prohibitions. In fact, the prohibitions of the ADEA were derived *in haec verba* from Title VII.[12] But in deciding whether a statutory right to jury trial exists, it is the remedial and procedural provisions of the two laws that are crucial and there we find significant differences.

Looking first to the statutory language defining the relief available, we note that Congress specifically provided for both "legal or equitable relief" in the ADEA, but did not authorize "legal" relief in so many words under Title VII. Compare § 7(b), 29 U.S.C. § 626(b), with 42 U.S.C. § 2000e–5(g) (1970 ed., Supp. V). Similarly, the ADEA incorporates the FLSA provision that employers "shall be liable" for amounts deemed

---

[10]   Senator Javits made the only specific reference in the legislative history to a jury trial. He said:

"The whole test is somewhat like the test in an accident case—did the person use reasonable care. A jury will answer yes or no. The question here is: Was the individual discriminated against solely because of his age? The alleged discrimination must be proved and the burden of proof is upon the one who would assert that that was actually the case." 113 Cong. Rec. 31255 (1967).

It is difficult to tell whether Senator Javits was referring to the issue in ADEA cases or in accident cases when he said the jury will say yes or no.

[12]   Title VII with respect to race, color, religion, sex, or national origin, and the ADEA with respect to age make it unlawful for an employer "to fail or refuse to hire or to discharge any individual," or otherwise to "discriminate against any individual with respect to his compensation, terms, conditions, or privileges of employment," on any of those bases. [Citing provisions of each statute.]

unpaid minimum wages or overtime compensation, while under Title VII, the availability of backpay is a matter of equitable discretion. Finally, rather than adopting the procedures of Title VII for ADEA actions, Congress rejected that course in favor of incorporating the FLSA procedures even while adopting Title VII's substantive prohibitions. Thus, even if petitioner is correct that Congress did not intend there to be jury trials under Title VII, that fact sheds no light on congressional intent under the ADEA. Petitioner's reliance on Title VII, therefore, is misplaced. * * * [*Affirmed.*]

NOTES ON LORILLARD *AND* REASONING FROM STATUTES IN PARI MATERIA

1.   *Reasoning from One Statute to Another: What If There Are Several Statutory Analogies?* Justice Marshall in *Lorillard* relies on the interpretational structure of previously enacted statutes to justify his interpretation. Why does he consider this persuasive? Because Congress really and truly "intended" to incorporate all prior interpretations of similarly worded provisions into the newer statute? Because the other interpretations somehow represent "wise" public policy? Because the interpretational history of these other statutes represents a reasoned policy context which ought to affect the application of a related statute, so as to give greater coherence to the law?

Even if justified in general, this approach has its limitations. One is that there may be more than one statute in pari materia, and the statutes may have been interpreted differently. E.g., *Ledbetter v. Goodyear Tire & Rubber Corp.*, 550 U.S. 618 (2007), discussed in Note 2. Or there may be several "similar" statutes, but none quite the same as the statute being interpreted. Thus, in *Lorillard*, the Supreme Court rejected the proposed analogy with Title VII. Are the Court's reasons persuasive? Why should an alleged victim of age discrimination get a jury trial (ADEA), when an alleged victim of race discrimination (Title VII) apparently does not get one? Is there an underlying purposive explanation for why Congress in the 1960s may have intended age discrimination lawsuits to be tried to juries but not race or sex discrimination actions?[394]

In 1974, Congress amended the ADEA to permit age discrimination lawsuits against the federal government. The enforcement provision says: "Any person aggrieved may bring a civil action in any Federal district court of competent jurisdiction for such legal or equitable relief as will effectuate the purposes of this Act." ADEA § 15(c), 29 U.S.C. § 633a(c). The Supreme Court held that § 15(c), unlike § 7, affords no jury trial right, finding the analogy to Title VII closer than the analogy to the FLSA. *Lehman v. Nakshian*, 453 U.S. 156 (1981). Is this consistent with *Lorillard*, upon which the four dissenting Justices relied? The majority responded that *Lorillard* is distinguishable (how?), the federal government is subject to jury trials only if it explicitly permits them (why?), and Congress in 1978 amended § 7(c) explicitly to allow ADEA jury trials but made no comparable amendment to § 15(c) (so what?).

2.   *Different Statutes, Different Policies.* A second limitation on reasoning from one statute to another is that the new statute may embody policies or compromises subtly different from those in the similar statutes—if for no other reason than the different political context of the later statute. For example, the Supreme Court has interpreted

---

[394]   Congress eliminated this disparity when it provided for jury trials in Title VII cases in the Civil Rights Act of 1991.

Title VI of the Civil Rights Act of 1964 (prohibiting discrimination "under any program or activity receiving Federal financial assistance") to reach only instances of intentional discrimination. See *Guardians Ass'n v. Civ. Serv. Comm'n of NYC*, 463 U.S. 582 (1983). Yet the Court in *Alexander v. Choate*, 469 U.S. 287, 294–99 (1985), was unwilling to limit § 504 of the Rehabilitation Act of 1973 (prohibiting discrimination or exclusion of any "qualified handicapped individual" "under any program or activity receiving Federal financial assistance") to instances of intentional discrimination. In dictum, the Court suggested that by 1973 national policy was more concerned with "disparate impact" discrimination than with the "intentional" discrimination that had been a focal point in 1964. *Id.* at 294–95 n.11. Ergo, the Court's interpretation of Title VI was not a helpful guide in its interpretation of § 504. Does this temporal dimension (evolving policy) help explain the result in *Lorillard*? See also *Webb v. Bd. of Ed. of Dyer Cnty.*, 471 U.S. 234 (1985) (rejecting analogy of Title VII attorney's fees provision as guide for interpreting 42 U.S.C. § 1988, because of different statutory schemes).

In *Ledbetter v. Goodyear Tire & Rubber Co.*, 550 U.S. 618 (2007), the Supreme Court strictly enforced the limitations period imposed by Title VII on plaintiffs bringing pay discrimination complaints to the EEOC. Under the Court's approach, an employee subjected to intentional race or sex discrimination in pay has to file a complaint with the EEOC soon after the illegal pay differential first shows up (and before many plaintiffs are even aware of the discrimination, because they do not know how much everyone else is paid). Ledbetter argued that the Court has allowed equitable tolling of Equal Pay Act claims, a statutory analogy the Court rejected because EPA claims do not have to be brought before the EEOC first. The different statutory schemes required different interpretations of the limitations provisions. The Court chose a different statutory analogy in the NLRA, also enforced by an agency. The Court had previously enforced that policy with similar strictness as it applied in *Ledbetter*. Congress, however, disagreed, overruling *Ledbetter* at the start of the Obama administration. See Pub. L. No. 111–2, the Lilly Ledbetter Fair Pay Act of 2009.

3.   *The Possibility of Compromise.* A third limitation on reasoning from one statute to another is that it may undermine deliberative legislative compromises. Consider *Ridgway v. Ridgway*, 454 U.S. 46 (1981). Richard Ridgway, a career sergeant in the U.S. Army, was granted a divorce from his wife April in 1977. The state divorce decree required Richard to keep in force then-existing life insurance policies for the benefit of the three children. Richard remarried and changed the beneficiary to his second wife, Donna, contrary to the divorce decree. When he died, both April and Donna claimed the proceeds to the life insurance—April relying on state law and Donna relying on the Servicemen's Group Life Insurance Act of 1965, 79 Stat. 880, codified as amended at 38 U.S.C. § 765 *et seq.* (1982). The Act provides comprehensive life insurance for members of the armed services, including Richard, and stipulates that the service person can designate the beneficiary, *id.* § 770(a), and that payment of insurance proceeds is not subject to attachment or "any legal or equitable process whatever." *Id.* § 770(g). The Supreme Court held that § 770(a) & (g) preempts state property decrees for support and alimony pursuant to a divorce. The Act's policy that the statutory benefits actually reach the designated beneficiary and that the insurance be operated on a national level clashes with state family law and supersedes it. See also *Hisquierdo v. Hisquierdo*, 439 U.S. 572, 584 (1979).

Three Justices dissented. Justice Stevens' dissenting opinion relied heavily on the equitable argument that Richard's designation of Donna as his beneficiary violated his moral duty to support his children. Surely Congress would not have intended such a scandalous result, argued the dissenters. (What canine metaphor is apt here?) The majority in *Ridgway* responded that "[a] result of this kind, of course, may be avoided if Congress chooses to avoid it," but Congress has not so chosen. Compare *Rose v. Rose*, 481 U.S. 619 (1987).

See also *Cartledge v. Miller*, 457 F. Supp. 1146 (S.D.N.Y. 1978), in which the district court construed the broad and seemingly unambiguous anti-assignment provision of ERISA (the Employee Retirement Income Security Act of 1974) to create an implied exception for family support orders issued pursuant to state law. Judge Weinfeld invoked "an overall congressional purpose not to interfere with the States' power to enforce family support obligations, [which] may be gleaned from judicial interpretation of exemption provisions in other federal statutes" including the Social Security Act, the Veterans Benefits Act, and the Railway Retirement Act. In 1984, Congress amended ERISA to add an explicit statutory exception to the anti-assignment provisions for "qualified domestic orders." Does this codification support or undermine Judge Weinfeld's position? If such an issue arose today, would a more textualist court reason that judges should simply apply the anti-assignment provision as written and leave it to Congress to create exceptions?

4. *The Challenge of Interpreting Legislative Overrides.* When Congress overrides a Supreme Court interpretation, how should the Court apply the override text to other similarly worded provisions in analogous statutes that have not been amended? If the analogous provisions have been construed *in pari materia* in past decisions, does Congress's failure to amend all such provisions justify departure from that approach, on the theory that there is now a meaningful variation between texts? Deborah Widiss criticizes the Court's determination, in *Gross v. FBL Financial Services, Inc.*, 557 U.S. 167 (2009), to reject *in pari materia* considerations in an employment discrimination setting where these considerations had been regularly applied in the past. Deborah Widiss, *Undermining Congressional Overrides: The Hydra Problem in Statutory Interpretation*, 90 Tex. L. Rev. 859 (2012). Widiss argues in favor of applying the *in pari materia* canon to similar employment statutes:

> [T]he practice of interpreting identical or similar language in statutes *in pari materia* to bear consistent meanings will often have the independent virtue of advancing the values served by precedent in a true common law context. That is, it will often promote fairness—in the sense of treating similar issues alike— to interpret distinct statutes that address related subjects (e.g., age discrimination and race discrimination) consistently. The practice will also typically promote efficiency and predictability. This is particularly essential because the Supreme Court and state supreme courts rule on any given statute relatively infrequently. For example, it has been almost fifty years since Title VII was enacted, and many other federal and state statutes have since been enacted that use similar language to prohibit discrimination in employment. In that half century, the Supreme Court has directly addressed the standard of causation that should be applied to claims alleging a mix of legitimate and illegitimate motives just twice: *Price Waterhouse* (interpreting Title VII) and *Gross* (interpreting the ADEA). If lower courts lack an authoritative construction of the statute actually at issue in a given case, they naturally rely on authoritative interpretations of analogous language in related statutes.

Widiss contends that the 1991 Amendments to Title VII should have been interpreted to apply to similar statutes, including the Age Discrimination in Employment Act text at issue in *Gross*. She argues that there should be "a rebuttable presumption that enactment of an override calls for the (re)interpretation of the preexisting language in the statute amended—and analogous provisions in related statutes—consistent with the meaning endorsed by Congress, so long as the preexisting text can reasonably bear that meaning."

B. THE BORROWED STATUTE RULE

Reasoning from statutes in pari materia (similar statutes) generally has greater force when the statutes are all in the same jurisdiction. Indeed, sometimes, as *Lorillard* indicates (though *Gross* does not), such statutes have a familial relationship because the drafting of a newer statute (e.g., the ADEA) was modeled on existing statutes in the same jurisdiction (e.g., the FLSA, Title VII). As *Lorillard* exemplifies, courts routinely assume that, unless there are strong indications to the contrary, the newer statute should be interpreted consistently with the older statutes upon which it was modeled.

Borrowed statutes are those adapted by one jurisdiction from another jurisdiction. For example, if West Virginia were to enact a pension regulation statute, it might "borrow" the language used in ERISA's anti-alienation and assignment provision or that used in a similar statute of another state. See Frank Horack, Jr., *The Common Law of Legislation*, 23 Iowa L. Rev. 41 (1937) (one legislature will copy a successful prior statute from another jurisdiction, following a process Horack calls "stare de statute"). The issues of interpretation for borrowed statutes are subtly different from those concerning modeled statutes, in large part because the policies followed in one jurisdiction may be different from those followed in the original jurisdiction.

Smith v. Bayer Corp.

564 U.S. 299 (2011).

The Supreme Court held that a federal court could not enjoin a plaintiff from litigating a putative class action in state court after a federal district court rejected a previous attempt to certify the class in federal court. Although West Virginia's rule on class certification was nearly textually identical to Federal Rule of Civil Procedure 23, the Court held that it was improper to enjoin the West Virginia lawsuit because West Virginia courts interpreted the state's class certification rule differently from federal courts and thus the state court lawsuit presented a different legal issue. **Justice Kagan** wrote for the unanimous Court.

"The Court of Appeals and Smith offer us two competing ways of deciding whether the West Virginia and Federal Rules differ, but we think the right path lies somewhere in the middle. The Eighth Circuit relied almost exclusively on the near-identity of the two Rules' texts. That was the right place to start, but not to end. Federal and state courts, after all, can and do apply identically worded procedural provisions in widely varying ways. If a State's procedural provision tracks the language of a Federal Rule, but a state court interprets that provision in a manner federal courts have not, then the state court is using a different standard and thus deciding a different issue. See 18 Wright & Miller § 4417, at 454 (stating that preclusion is 'inappropriate' when 'different legal standards . . . masquerad[e] behind similar legal labels'). At the other extreme, Smith contends that the source of law is all that matters: a different sovereign must in each and every case 'have the opportunity, if it chooses, to construe its procedural rule differently.' Brief for Petitioners 22 (quoting ALI, Principles of the Law, Aggregate Litigation § 2.11, Reporters' Notes, *cmt. b*, p. 181 (2010)). But if state courts have made crystal clear that they follow the same approach as the federal court applied, we see no need to ignore that determination; in that event, the issues in the two cases would indeed be the same. So a federal court considering whether the relitigation exception applies should examine whether state law parallels its federal counterpart. But as suggested earlier, * * * the federal court must resolve any uncertainty on that score by leaving the question of preclusion to the state courts.

"Under this approach, the West Virginia Supreme Court has gone some way toward resolving the matter before us by declaring its independence from federal courts' interpretation of the Federal Rules—and particularly of Rule 23. In *In re West Virginia Rezulin Litigation*, 585 S.E.2d 52 (2003) *(In re Rezulin)*, the West Virginia high court considered a plaintiff's motion to certify a class—coincidentally enough, in a suit about an allegedly defective pharmaceutical product. The court made a point of complaining about the parties' and lower court's near-exclusive reliance on federal cases about Federal Rule 23 to decide the certification question. Such cases, the court cautioned, 'may be persuasive, but [they are] not binding or controlling.' *Id.* at 61. And lest anyone mistake the import of this message, the court went on: The aim of this rule is to avoid having our legal analysis of our Rules 'amount to nothing more than Pavlovian responses to federal decisional law.' *Ibid.* (italics omitted). Of course, the state courts might still have adopted an approach to their Rule 23 that tracked the analysis the federal court used in McCollins' case. But absent clear evidence that the state courts had done so, we could not conclude that they would interpret their Rule in the same way. And if that is so, we could not tell whether the certification issues in the state and federal courts were the same. That uncertainty would preclude an injunction."

The Court concluded that federal courts should be influenced "if state courts have made crystal clear that they follow the same approach as the federal court applied." What should constitute a "crystal clear" statement from a state court that it follows federal precedent when interpreting an identical state statute? In *In re Rezulin*, the West Virginia Supreme Court had clearly indicated that it *does not* necessarily follow federal precedent. What if, instead, a state court has consistently followed federal precedent when interpreting its state statute but never affirmatively declared that it would always do so?

C. STATUTORY CLASHES—THE RULE AGAINST IMPLIED REPEALS

Not only similar statutes in the same jurisdiction and statutes copied from other jurisdictions, but also subsequent statutes in the same jurisdiction may be sources of guidance concerning the appropriate interpretation of a statute. The second opinion in *Montana Wilderness* (§ 2(E) of this chapter) is an example of how a similar, subsequently enacted statute may sometimes shed light on a prior statutory provision. In *Babbitt v. Sweet Home* (at end of this chapter), the Court was persuaded to read a provision of the Endangered Species Act of 1973 broadly, in part to assure its consistency with a 1982 amendment to the law.

Both opinions in *Montana Wilderness* point to a clash between the Alaska Lands Act (as applied nationwide in the second opinion) and the Wilderness Act. How do judges resolve apparently conflicting statutes? Obviously, if the more recent statute expressly provides that it controls, the issue is easy. Similarly, if the newer statute contains a savings clause, which states that it does not alter existing law, the older statute controls. Unfortunately, most of the time the more recent statute says nothing on this question. Typically, courts do their best to reconcile the statutes, based on the presumption of whole-code coherence. As the next case demonstrates, there is a longstanding canon in this area, which disfavors *implied repeals*.

MORTON V. MANCARI

Supreme Court of the United States, 1974.
417 U.S. 535, 94 S.Ct. 2474, 41 L.Ed.2d 290.

MR. JUSTICE BLACKMUN delivered the opinion of the Court.

The Indian Reorganization Act of 1934, also known as the Wheeler-Howard Act, 48 Stat. 984, 25 U.S.C. § 461 *et seq.*, accords an employment preference for qualified Indians in the Bureau of Indian Affairs (BIA or Bureau). Appellees, non-Indian BIA employees, challenged this preference as contrary to the anti-discrimination provisions of the Equal Employment Opportunity Act of 1972, 86 Stat. 103, 42 U.S.C. § 2000e *et seq.* (1970 ed., Supp. II), and as violative of the Due Process Clause of the Fifth Amendment. * * *

[I]   Section 12 of the Indian Reorganization Act, 48 Stat. 986, 25 U.S.C. § 472, provides:

> "The Secretary of the Interior is directed to establish standards of health, age, character, experience, knowledge, and ability for Indians who may be appointed, without regard to civil-service laws, to the various positions maintained, now or hereafter, by the Indian Office, in the administration of functions or services affecting any Indian tribe. Such qualified Indians shall hereafter have the preference to appointment to vacancies in any such positions."

In June 1972, pursuant to this provision, the Commissioner of Indian Affairs, with the approval of the Secretary of the Interior, issued a directive (Personnel Management Letter No. 72–12) stating that the BIA's policy would be to grant a preference to qualified Indians not only, as before, in the initial hiring stage, but also in the situation where an Indian and a non-Indian, both already employed by the BIA, were competing for a promotion within the Bureau. The record indicates that this policy was implemented immediately.

Shortly thereafter, appellees, who are non-Indian employees of the BIA at Albuquerque, instituted this class action, on behalf of themselves and other non-Indian employees similarly situated, in the United States District Court for the District of New Mexico, claiming that the "so-called 'Indian Preference Statutes'" were repealed by the 1972 Equal Employment Opportunity Act and deprived them of rights to property without due process of law, in violation of the Fifth Amendment. * * *

After a short trial focusing primarily on how the new policy, in fact, has been implemented, the District Court concluded that the Indian preference was implicitly repealed by § 11 of the Equal Employment Opportunity Act of 1972, Pub. L. 92–261, 86 Stat. 111, 42 U.S.C. § 2000e–16(a) (1970 ed., Supp. II), proscribing discrimination in most federal employment on the basis of race.[6] Having found that Congress repealed the preference, it was unnecessary for the District Court to pass on its constitutionality. The court permanently enjoined appellants "from implementing any policy in the Bureau of Indian Affairs which would hire, promote, or reassign any person in preference to another solely for the reason that such person is an Indian." * * *

[II] The federal policy of according some hiring preference to Indians in the Indian service dates at least as far back as 1834. Since that time, Congress repeatedly has enacted various preferences of the general type here at issue.[8] The purpose of these preferences, as variously expressed in the legislative history, has been to give Indians a greater participation in their own self-government; to further the Government's trust obligation toward the Indian tribes;[9] and to reduce the negative effect of having non-Indians administer matters that affect Indian tribal life.

The preference directly at issue here was enacted as an important part of the sweeping Indian Reorganization Act of 1934. The overriding purpose of that particular Act was to establish machinery whereby Indian tribes would be able to assume a greater degree of self-government, both politically and economically. Congress was seeking to modify the then-existing situation whereby the primarily non-Indian-staffed BIA had plenary control, for all practical purposes, over the lives and destinies of the federally recognized Indian tribes. Initial congressional proposals would have diminished substantially the role of the BIA by turning over to federally chartered self-governing Indian communities many of the functions

---

[6]   Section 2000e–16(a) reads:

"All personnel actions affecting employees or applicants for employment (except with regard to aliens employed outside the limits of the United States) in military departments as defined in section 102 of Title 5, in executive agencies (other than the General Accounting Office) as defined in section 105 of Title 5 (including employees and applicants for employment who are paid from nonappropriated funds), in the United States Postal Service and the Postal Rate Commission, in those units of the Government of the District of Columbia having positions in the competitive service, and in those units of the legislative and judicial branches of the Federal Government having positions in the competitive service, and in the Library of Congress shall be made free from any discrimination based on race, color, religion, sex, or national origin."

[8]   Act of May 17, 1882, § 6, 22 Stat. 88, and Act of July 4, 1884, § 6, 23 Stat. 97, 25 U.S.C. § 46 (employment of clerical, mechanical, and other help on reservations and about agencies); Act of Aug. 15, 1894, § 10, 28 Stat. 313, 25 U.S.C. § 44 (employment of herders, teamsters, and laborers, "and where practicable in all other employments" in the Indian service); Act of June 7, 1897, § 1, 30 Stat. 83, 25 U.S.C. § 274 (employment as matrons, farmers, and industrial teachers in Indian schools); Act of June 25, 1910, § 23, 36 Stat. 861, 25 U.S.C. § 47 (general preference as to Indian labor and products of Indian industry).

[9]   A letter, contained in the House Report to the 1934 Act, from President F. D. Roosevelt to Congressman Howard states:

"We can and should, without further delay, extend to the Indian the fundamental rights of political liberty and local self-government and the opportunities of education and economic assistance that they require in order to attain a wholesome American life. This is but the obligation of honor of a powerful nation toward a people living among us and dependent upon our protection." H.R. Rep. No. 1804, 73d Cong., 2d Sess., 8 (1934).

normally performed by the Bureau.[13] Committee sentiment, however, ran against such a radical change in the role of the BIA. The solution ultimately adopted was to strengthen tribal government while continuing the active role of the BIA, with the understanding that the Bureau would be more responsive to the interests of the people it was created to serve.

One of the primary means by which self-government would be fostered and the Bureau made more responsive was to increase the participation of tribal Indians in the BIA operations. In order to achieve this end, it was recognized that some kind of preference and exemption from otherwise prevailing civil service requirements was necessary.[16] Congressman Howard, the House sponsor, expressed the need for the preference:

"The Indians have not only been thus deprived of civic rights and powers, but they have been largely deprived of the opportunity to enter the more important positions in the service of the very bureau which manages their affairs. Theoretically, the Indians have the right to qualify for the Federal civil service. In actual practice there has been no adequate program of training to qualify Indians to compete in these examinations, especially for technical and higher positions; and even if there were such training, the Indians would have to compete under existing law, on equal terms with multitudes of white applicants. * * * The various services on the Indian reservations are actually local rather than Federal services and are comparable to local municipal and county services, since they are dealing with purely local Indian problems. It should be possible for Indians with the requisite vocational and professional training to enter the service of their own people without the necessity of competing with white applicants for these positions. This bill permits them to do so." 78 Cong. Rec. 11729 (1934).

Congress was well aware that the proposed preference would result in employment disadvantages within the BIA for non-Indians.[17] Not only was this displacement unavoidable if room were to be made for Indians, but it was explicitly determined that gradual replacement of non-Indians with Indians within the Bureau was a desirable feature of the entire program for self-government.[18] Since 1934, the

---

[13]   Hearings on H.R. 7902, Readjustment of Indian Affairs, 73d Cong., 2d Sess., 1–7 (1934) (hereafter House Hearings).

[16]   "The bill admits qualified Indians to the position [sic] in their own service.

"Thirty-four years ago, in 1900, the number of Indians holding regular positions in the Indian Service, in proportion to the total of positions, was greater than it is today." The reason primarily is found in the application of the generalized civil service to the Indian Service, and the consequent exclusion of Indians from their own jobs." House Hearings 19 (memorandum dated Feb. 19, 1934, submitted by Commissioner Collier to the Senate and House Committees on Indian Affairs).

[17]   Congressman Carter, an opponent of the bill, placed in the Congressional Record the following observation by Commissioner Collier at the Committee hearings:

"[W]e must not blind ourselves to the fact that the effect of this bill if worked out would unquestionably be to replace white employees by Indian employees. I do not know how fast, but ultimately it ought to go very far indeed." 78 Cong. Rec. 11737 (1934).

[18]   "It should be possible for Indians to enter the service of their own people without running the gauntlet of competition with whites for these positions. Indian progress and ambition will be enormously strengthened as soon as we adopt the principle that the Indian Service shall gradually become, in fact as well as in name, an Indian service predominantly in the hands of educated and competent Indians." Id. at 11731 (remarks of Cong. Howard).

BIA has implemented the preference with a fair degree of success. The percentage of Indians employed in the Bureau rose from 34% in 1934 to 57% in 1972. This reversed the former downward trend, see n.16, *supra*, and was due, clearly, to the presence of the 1934 Act. The Commissioner's extension of the preference in 1972 to promotions within the BIA was designed to bring more Indians into positions of responsibility and, in that regard, appears to be a logical extension of the congressional intent.

[III] It is against this background that we encounter the first issue in the present case: whether the Indian preference was repealed by the Equal Employment Opportunity Act of 1972. Title VII of the Civil Rights Act of 1964 was the first major piece of federal legislation prohibiting discrimination in *private* employment on the basis of "race, color, religion, sex, or national origin." 42 U.S.C. § 2000e–2(a). Significantly, §§ 701(b) and 703(i) of that Act explicitly exempted from its coverage the preferential employment of Indians by Indian tribes or by industries located on or near Indian reservations. 42 U.S.C. §§ 2000e(b) and 2000e–2(i).[19] This exemption reveals a clear congressional recognition, within the framework of Title VII, of the unique legal status of tribal and reservation-based activities. The Senate sponsor, Senator Humphrey, stated on the floor by way of explanation:

"This exemption is consistent with the Federal Government's policy of encouraging Indian employment and with the special legal position of Indians." 110 Cong. Rec. 12723 (1964).[20]

The 1964 Act did not specifically outlaw employment discrimination by the Federal Government. Yet the mechanism for enforcing longstanding Executive Orders forbidding Government discrimination had proved ineffective for the most part. In order to remedy this, Congress, by the 1972 Act, amended the 1964 Act and proscribed discrimination in most areas of federal employment. See n.6, *supra*. In general, it may be said that the substantive anti-discrimination law embraced in Title VII was carried over and applied to the Federal Government. As stated in the House Report:

"To correct this entrenched discrimination in the Federal service, it is necessary to insure the effective application of uniform, fair and strongly enforced policies. The present law and the proposed statute do not permit industry and labor organizations to be the judges of their own conduct in the area of employment discrimination. There is no reason why government agencies should not be treated similarly. * * * " H.R. Rep. No. 92–238, on H.R. 1746, at 24–25 (1971).

Nowhere in the legislative history of the 1972 Act, however, is there any mention of Indian preference.

---

[19]   Section 701(b) excludes "an Indian Tribe" from the Act's definition of "employer." Section 703(i) states:
"Nothing contained in this subchapter shall apply to any business or enterprise on or near an Indian reservation with respect to any publicly announced employment practice of such business or enterprise under which a preferential treatment is given to any individual because he is an Indian living on or near a reservation."

[20]   Senator Mundt supported these exemptions on the Senate floor by claiming that they would allow Indians "to benefit from Indian preference programs now in operation or later to be instituted." 110 Cong. Rec. 13702 (1964).

Appellees assert * * * that since the 1972 Act proscribed racial discrimination in Government employment, the Act necessarily, albeit *sub silentio*, repealed the provision of the 1934 Act that called for the preference in the BIA of one racial group, Indians, over non-Indians:

> "When a conflict such as in this case, is present, the most recent law or Act should apply and the conflicting Preferences passed some 39 years earlier should be impliedly repealed." Brief for Appellees 7.

We disagree. For several reasons we conclude that Congress did not intend to repeal the Indian preference and that the District Court erred in holding that it was repealed.

First: There are the above-mentioned affirmative provisions in the 1964 Act excluding coverage of tribal employment and of preferential treatment by a business or enterprise on or near a reservation. These 1964 exemptions as to private employment indicate Congress' recognition of the longstanding federal policy of providing a unique legal status to Indians in matters concerning tribal or "on or near" reservation employment. The exemptions reveal a clear congressional sentiment that an Indian preference in the narrow context of tribal or reservation-related employment did not constitute racial discrimination of the type otherwise proscribed. In extending the general anti-discrimination machinery to federal employment in 1972, Congress in no way modified these private employment preferences built into the 1964 Act, and they are still in effect. It would be anomalous to conclude that Congress intended to eliminate the longstanding statutory preferences in BIA employment, as being racially discriminatory, at the very same time it was reaffirming the right of tribal and reservation-related private employers to provide Indian preference. Appellees' assertion that Congress implicitly repealed the preference as racially discriminatory, while retaining the 1964 preferences, attributes to Congress irrationality and arbitrariness, an attribution we do not share.

Second: Three months after Congress passed the 1972 amendments, it enacted two *new* Indian preference laws. These were part of the Education Amendments of 1972, 86 Stat. 235, 20 U.S.C. §§ 887c(a) and (d), and § 1119a (1970 ed., Supp. II). The new laws explicitly require that Indians be given preference in Government programs for training teachers of Indian children. It is improbable, to say the least, that the same Congress which affirmatively approved and enacted these additional and similar Indian preferences was, at the same time, condemning the BIA preference as racially discriminatory. In the total absence of any manifestation of supportive intent, we are loathe to imply this improbable result.

Third: Indian preferences, for many years, have been treated as exceptions to Executive Orders forbidding Government employment discrimination. The 1972 extension of the Civil Rights Act to Government employment is in large part merely a codification of prior anti-discrimination Executive Orders that had proved ineffective because of inadequate enforcement machinery. There certainly was no indication that the substantive proscription against discrimination was intended to be any broader than that which previously existed. By codifying the existing anti-discrimination provisions, and by providing enforcement machinery for them, there is no reason to presume that Congress affirmatively intended to erase the preferences that previously had co-existed with broad anti-discrimination provisions in Executive Orders.

Fourth: Appellees encounter head-on the "cardinal rule * * * that repeals by implication are not favored." *Posadas v. Nat'l City Bank*, 296 U.S. 497, 503 (1936). They and the District Court read the congressional silence as effectuating a repeal by implication. There is nothing in the legislative history, however, that indicates affirmatively any congressional intent to repeal the 1934 preference. Indeed, as explained above, there is ample independent evidence that the legislative intent was to the contrary.

This is a prototypical case where an adjudication of repeal by implication is not appropriate. The preference is a longstanding, important component of the Government's Indian program. The anti-discrimination provision, aimed at alleviating minority discrimination in employment, obviously is designed to deal with an entirely different and, indeed, opposite problem. Any perceived conflict is thus more apparent than real.

In the absence of some affirmative showing of an intention to repeal, the only permissible justification for a repeal by implication is when the earlier and later statutes are irreconcilable. *Georgia v. Pennsylvania R. Co.*, 324 U.S. 439, 456–457 (1945). Clearly, this is not the case here. A provision aimed at furthering Indian self-government by according an employment preference within the BIA for qualified members of the governed group can readily coexist with a general rule prohibiting employment discrimination on the basis of race. Any other conclusion can be reached only by formalistic reasoning that ignores both the history and purposes of the preference and the unique legal relationship between the Federal Government and tribal Indians.

Furthermore, the Indian preference statute is a specific provision applying to a very specific situation. The 1972 Act, on the other hand, is of general application. Where there is no clear intention otherwise, a specific statute will not be controlled or nullified by a general one, regardless of the priority of enactment. See, *e.g.*, *Bulova Watch Co. v. United States*, 365 U.S. 753, 758 (1961); *Rodgers v. United States*, 185 U.S. 83, 87–89 (1902).

The courts are not at liberty to pick and choose among congressional enactments, and when two statutes are capable of co-existence, it is the duty of the courts, absent a clearly expressed congressional intention to the contrary, to regard each as effective. "When there are two acts upon the same subject, the rule is to give effect to both if possible * * *. The intention of the legislature to repeal 'must be clear and manifest.'" *United States v. Borden Co.*, 308 U.S. 188, 198 (1939). In light of the factors indicating no repeal, we simply cannot conclude that Congress consciously abandoned its policy of furthering Indian self-government when it passed the 1972 amendments.

We therefore hold that the District Court erred in ruling that the Indian preference was repealed by the 1972 Act. * * *

NOTES ON MANCARI AND INTERPRETATION IN LIGHT OF SUBSEQUENT STATUTES

1.   *Repeals by Implication. Mancari* introduces you to a canon of statutory interpretation not mentioned in § 2 of chapter 6: repeals by implication are not favored.[395] This canon is subject to the criticism that it naively assumes legislative omniscience—legislators and their staff members do not search the statute books to ensure that new legislation will interfere minimally with established legislation. And why should they? Shouldn't new legislative policy be applied to full effect, liberally supplanting outdated prior statutes? On the other hand, the canon against implied repeals might be defended, "not only to avoid misconstruction of the law effecting the putative repeal, but also to preserve the intent of later Congresses that have already enacted laws that are dependent on the continued applicability of the law whose implicit repeal is in question." *Smith v. Robinson*, 468 U.S. 992, 1026 (1984) (Brennan, J., dissenting).

As Judge Norris recognized, *Mancari* is in tension with the Ninth Circuit's ultimate position in the Checkerboard Case: the Alaska Lands Act's access provision was found to repeal huge chunks of wilderness protection acts passed by Congress in the 1960s and 1970s. Why isn't the Checkerboard Case a much better case for *refusing* to allow repeals by implication?

2.   *Applying the Canon in* Mancari. Figure out the best arguments against Justice Blackmun's reasons why no repeal by implication occurred in *Mancari*. (Hint: As to the first, Congress showed itself able to exempt Indians from the operation of antidiscrimination laws in 1964; the absence of any express exemption in the 1972 Act, then, gives a strong *expressio unius* argument to plaintiffs. In addition, sticking to the first argument made by Justice Blackmun, isn't it quite different to exempt an Indian tribe or a private employer from the coverage of an employment discrimination statute, on the one hand, and to exempt the federal government, on the other?) We think that the best arguments against Justice Blackmun's first three points are strong ones. If we are right, then the "repeal by implication" canon is crucial to the outcome of the case. As note 1 above suggests, that canon has some theoretical problems when it is stated broadly, as saying that repeals of *statutes* by implication are disfavored. Can the Blackmun result be saved by narrowing the canon to "repeals of *longstanding policies* are disfavored, especially where there is no collateral evidence (in other statutes, regulations, executive orders, authoritative committee reports, and the like) supporting the notion that the longstanding policy has been repudiated"? Does narrowing the canon in this way alleviate the general objections to it suggested in note 1 as well?

3.   *Policy Behind Overcoming the Presumption.* Unlike the presumption against federal preemption of state law, the *Mancari* presumption against implied repeals is one that is rarely overcome. In an excellent analysis of this canon, Karen Petroski determined that of 42 Supreme Court decisions addressing implied repeals from 1981 to 2003, the Court ruled against implied repeals in 41. Comment, *Retheorizing the Presumption Against Implied Repeals*, 92 Cal. L. Rev. 487, 539–40 (2004). The presumption has usually been litigated, and occasionally rebutted, in antitrust cases. Antitrust defendants often argue that post-1890 regulatory statutes create implicit exceptions to the Sherman

---

[395]   See also *Hamdan v. Rumsfeld*, 548 U.S. 557, 594–95 (2006); *Granholm v. Heald*, 544 U.S. 460 (2005); *Cnty. of Yakima v. Confederated Tribes & Bands of Yakima Indian Nation*, 502 U.S. 251 (1992); *St. Martin Evangelical Lutheran Church v. South Dakota*, 451 U.S. 772, 788 (1981); *Watt v. Alaska*, 451 U.S. 259 (1981); *Radzanower v. Touche Ross & Co.*, 426 U.S. 148, 154 (1976).

Act. They generally lose with such arguments but have at times prevailed. E.g., *United States v. Nat'l Ass'n of Sec. Dealers*, 422 U.S. 694 (1975). Outside of the antitrust context, it is almost unheard of for federal judges to declare that a recent federal law has implicitly repealed a previous one. One reason why courts may overcome the presumption involves a perceived duty to harmonize the law when two statutes are capable of co-existence; judges will usually strain to reconcile federal statutes seemingly at odds. Should we be concerned that such efforts at reconciliation amount to "judicial legislation"? Compare Judge Norris's effort to reconcile his interpretation of the Alaska Lands Act with the Wilderness Act in the published opinion in the Checkerboard Case.

4.   *Repeal of Treaties by Implication.* Treaties, like statutes, are the law of the land under the Supremacy Clause, U.S. Const. Art. VI, and the Supreme Court has stated that "[a] treaty," like a statute, "will not be deemed to have been abrogated or modified by a later statute unless such purpose on the part of Congress has been clearly expressed." *Cook v. United States*, 288 U.S. 102, 120 (1933); see *Weinberger v. Rossi*, 456 U.S. 25 (1982). Consider the following problem. The United States in 1934 ratified the Warsaw Convention, which sets forth uniform rules governing air transportation. Article 22 sets a limit on carrier liability for lost cargo; the liability is expressed in terms of gold, a uniform international standard of value when the Convention was drafted in the 1920s. The United States suspended convertibility of the dollar for gold in 1971 and in 1978 passed a statute implementing an international agreement creating a new regime for international monetary cooperation. The CAB, charged with implementing the Warsaw Convention in the U.S., set the liability limits in 1978 at $9.07 per pound of lost cargo— the last figure it had used under the gold conversion approach before the 1978 statute. The Supreme Court in *TWA v. Franklin Mint Corp.*, 466 U.S. 243 (1984), rejected the Second Circuit's determination that the Warsaw Convention's liability limits were unenforceable as implicitly nullified by the 1978 statute, based upon the presumption against implied repeals. The Court noted that the presumption is potentially stronger in the case of treaties, because they usually have provisions requiring the U.S. to notify the other country (or countries) party to the treaty if the U.S. is withdrawing from it.

PROBLEM ON THE RULE AGAINST IMPLIED REPEALS

Problem 7-5. The 2000 census caused Mississippi to lose one congressional seat. The state legislature failed to pass a new redistricting plan after the decennial census results were published in 2001. A number of state residents filed suit in Mississippi state court, seeking a redistricting plan for the 2002 congressional elections. Article I, § 4, cl. 1, of the Constitution provides that the "Times, Places and Manner of holding Elections for Senators and Representatives, shall be prescribed in each State by the Legislature thereof. . . ." It reserves to Congress, however, the power "at any time by Law [to] make or alter such Regulations, except as to the Places of chusing Senators." Pursuant to this authority, Congress in 1929 enacted the current statutory scheme governing apportionment of the House of Representatives. 2 U.S.C. §§ 2a(a), (b). In 1941, Congress added to those provisions a subsection addressing what is to be done pending redistricting:

> "Until a State is redistricted in the manner provided by the law thereof after
> any apportionment, the Representatives to which such State is entitled under
> such apportionment shall be elected in the following manner: * * * (5) if there is
> a decrease in the number of Representatives and the number of districts in such

State exceeds such decreased number of Representatives, they shall be elected from the State at large." § 2a(c).

In 1967, 26 years after § 2a(c) was enacted, Congress adopted § 2c, which provides, as relevant here:

> "In each State entitled in the Ninety-first Congress or in any subsequent Congress thereafter to more than one Representative under an apportionment made pursuant to the provisions of section 2a(a) of this title, there shall be established by law a number of districts equal to the number of Representatives to which such State is so entitled, and Representatives shall be elected only from districts so established, no district to elect more than one Representative. . . ."

There is a clear tension between these two provisions. Section 2c apparently requires States entitled to more than one Representative to elect their Representatives from single-member districts, rather than from the State at large. Section 2a(c)(5) seems to require at-large elections in certain situations, such as where Mississippi, by reason of the 2000 census, lost a congressional seat.

One way to reconcile the two provisions is by interpreting the introductory phrase of § 2a(c) ("Until a State is redistricted in the manner provided by the law thereof after any apportionment"), and the phrase "established by law" in § 2c to refer exclusively to *legislative* redistricting—so that § 2c tells the legislatures what to do (single-member districting) and § 2a(c) provides what will happen *absent* legislative action—in the present cases, the mandating of at-large elections.

The clause in § 2c "there shall be established by law a number of districts equal to the number of Representatives to which such State is so entitled" could be construed so that the phrase "by law" refers only to legislative action. But its more common meaning encompasses judicial decisions as well. In addition, the limited role that a narrow construction would assign to § 2c (governing legislative apportionment but not judicial apportionment) is contradicted by the historical context of § 2c's enactment. When Congress adopted § 2c in 1967, the immediate issue was precisely the involvement of the courts in fashioning electoral plans. The Voting Rights Act of 1965 had recently been enacted, assigning to the federal courts jurisdiction to involve themselves in elections. In addition, the Court's decisions in a series of one-person, one-vote cases had ushered in a new era in which federal courts were overseeing efforts by badly malapportioned States to conform their congressional electoral districts to the constitutionally required one-person, one-vote standards. In a world in which the role of federal courts in redistricting disputes had been transformed from spectating to directing, there was a risk that judges forced to fashion remedies would simply order at-large elections.

Assuming that in enacting 2 U.S.C. § 2c, Congress mandated that States are to provide for the election of their Representatives from single-member districts, and that this mandate applies equally to courts remedying a state legislature's failure to redistrict constitutionally, the key remaining question is what to make of § 2a(c)? Representatives cannot be "elected only from districts," § 2c, while being elected "at large," § 2a(c). Some lower courts confronted with this conflict have concluded that § 2c repeals § 2a(c) by implication. Yet the Supreme Court has repeatedly stated that absent "a clearly expressed congressional intention," *Morton v. Mancari*, "repeals by implication are not favored." An implied repeal will only be found where provisions in two statutes are in "irreconcilable conflict," or where the latter act covers the whole subject of the earlier one and "is clearly intended as a substitute." What is the better answer: that § 2c was a substitute for § 2a(c), or that § 2a(c) continues to apply in this setting? See *Branch v. Smith*, 538 U.S. 254 (2003).

REVIEW CASE FOR DOCTRINES OF INTERPRETATION

Now that you have studied a full range of interpretive resources, we offer the case below as an unusually rich example of how those resources can be marshaled by two Justices operating at the top of their respective games. *Sweet Home* involves judicial review of an agency rule interpreting a statutory provision, and federal courts typically approach review of agency interpretations with a certain degree of deference (the topic of agency deference is addressed at length in chapter 9). In this instance, however, Justice Stevens for the majority and Justice Scalia in dissent engage in what effectively amounts to de novo review; each invokes a range of arguments based on word meaning, various canons, and appeals to legislative history and purpose. For this reason, we believe the decision provides an excellent opportunity for you to review many of the issues raised in this chapter as well as chapter 6.

STATUTORY PREFACE TO THE *SWEET HOME* CASE

Endangered Species Act of 1973, 16 U.S.C. § 1531 *et seq.*

Section 1532.   Definitions.

(19) The term "take" means to harass, harm, pursue, hunt, shoot, wound, kill, trap, capture, or collect, or to attempt to engage in any such conduct.

Section 1536.   Interagency Cooperation

(a) * * * **(2)** Each Federal agency shall, in consultation with and with the assistance of the Secretary, insure that any action authorized, funded, or carried out by such agency * * * is not likely to jeopardize the continued existence of any endangered species or threatened species or result in the destruction or adverse modification of habitat of such species which is determined by the Secretary * * * to be critical, * * *. In fulfilling the requirements of this paragraph each agency shall use the best scientific and commercial data available.

Section 1538.   Prohibited Acts

(a) Generally

    (1) Except as provided in sections 1535(g)(2) and 1529 of this title, with respect to any endangered species of fish or wildlife listed pursuant to section 1533 of this title it is unlawful for any person subject to the jurisdiction of the United States to—* * *

        (B) take any such species within the United States or the territorial sea of the United States;

Section 1539.   Exceptions

(a) Permits.

(1) The Secretary may permit, under such terms and conditions as he shall prescribe—* * *

(B) any taking otherwise prohibited by section 1538(a)(1)(B) of this title if such taking is incidental to, and not the purpose of, the carrying out of an otherwise lawful activity.

(2)(A)   No permit may be issued by the Secretary authorizing any taking referred to in paragraph (1)(B) unless the applicant therefor submits to the Secretary a conservation plan that specifies—

(i) the impact which will likely result from such taking;

(ii) what steps the applicant will take to minimize and mitigate such impacts, and the funding that will be available to implement such steps;

(iii) what alternative actions to such taking the applicant considered and the reasons why such alternatives are not being utilized; and

(iv) such other measures that the Secretary may require as being necessary or appropriate for purposes of the plan. * * *

Section 1540.   Penalties and Enforcement

(b) Criminal violations

(1) Any person who knowingly violates any provision of this chapter, of any permit or certificate issued hereunder, or of any regulation issued in order to implement * * * shall, upon conviction, be fined not more than $50,000 or imprisoned for not more than one year, or both. * * *

(e) enforcement

* * * (4)

(B) All guns, traps, nets, and other equipment, vessels, vehicles, aircraft, and other means of transportation used to aid the taking, possessing, selling, purchasing, offering for sale or purchase, transporting, delivering, receiving, carrying, shipping, exporting, or importing of any fish or wildlife or plants in violation of this chapter, any regulation made pursuant thereto, or any permit or certificate issued thereunder shall be subject to forfeiture to the United States upon conviction of a criminal violation pursuant to subsection (b)(1) of this section.

BABBITT v. SWEET HOME CHAPTER OF COMMUNITIES
FOR A GREAT OREGON

Supreme Court of the United States, 1995.
515 U.S. 687, 115 S.Ct. 2407, 132 L.Ed.2d 597.

(1995)

JUSTICE STEVENS delivered the opinion of the Court.

The Endangered Species Act of 1973 (ESA or Act), 87 Stat. 884, 16 U.S.C. § 1531 (1988 ed. and Supp. V), contains a variety of protections designed to save from extinction species that the Secretary of the Interior designates as endangered or threatened. Section 9 of the Act makes it unlawful for any person to "take" any endangered or threatened species. The Secretary has promulgated a regulation that defines the statute's prohibition on takings to include "significant habitat modification or degradation where it actually kills or injures wildlife." This case presents the question whether the Secretary exceeded his authority under the Act by promulgating that regulation.

Section 9(a)(1) of the Act provides the following protection for endangered species:

> Except as provided in sections 1535(g)(2) and 1539 of this title, with respect to any endangered species of fish or wildlife listed pursuant to section 1533 of this title it is unlawful for any person subject to the jurisdiction of the United States to—
>
> . . .
>
> (B) take any such species within the United States or the territorial sea of the United States. [16 U.S.C. § 1538(a)(1).]

Section 3(19) of the Act defines the statutory term "take":

> The term "take" means to harass, harm, pursue, hunt, shoot, wound, kill, trap, capture, or collect, or to attempt to engage in any such conduct. [16 U.S.C. § 1532(19).]

The Act does not further define the terms it uses to define "take." The Interior Department regulations that implement the statute, however, define the statutory term "harm":

> *Harm* in the definition of "take" in the Act means an act which actually kills or injures wildlife. Such act may include significant habitat modification or degradation where it actually kills or injures wildlife by significantly impairing essential behavioral patterns, including breeding, feeding, or sheltering. [50 CFR § 17.3 (1994).]

This regulation has been in place since 1975.

A limitation on the § 9 "take" prohibition appears in § 10(a)(1)(B) of the Act, which Congress added by amendment in 1982. That section authorizes the Secretary to grant a permit for any taking otherwise prohibited by § 9(a)(1)(B) "if such taking is incidental to, and not the purpose of, the carrying out of an otherwise lawful activity." 16 U.S.C. § 1539(a)(1)(B).

In addition to the prohibition on takings, the Act provides several other protections for endangered species. Section 4, 16 U.S.C. § 1533, commands the Secretary to identify species of fish or wildlife that are in danger of extinction and to publish from time to time lists of all species he determines to be endangered or threatened. Section 5, 16 U.S.C. § 1534, authorizes the Secretary, in cooperation with the States, see § 1535, to acquire land to aid in preserving such species. Section 7 requires federal agencies to ensure that none of their activities, including the granting of licenses and permits, will jeopardize the continued existence of endangered species "or result in the destruction or adverse modification of habitat of such species which is determined by the Secretary . . . to be critical." 16 U.S.C. § 1536(a)(2).

[A group of small landowners, logging companies, and families dependent on the forest products industries and organizations that represent their interests brought this action to challenge the Secretary's definition of *harm* to include habitat modification and degradation. They specifically objected to the application of the regulation to protect the red-cockaded woodpecker and the spotted owl by prohibiting changes in their natural habitat that would have the effect of injuring or killing those animals. The court of appeals agreed with respondents' challenge, but the Supreme Court reversed.]

The text of the Act provides three reasons for concluding that the Secretary's interpretation is reasonable. First, an ordinary understanding of the word "harm" supports it. The dictionary definition of the verb form of "harm" is "to cause hurt or damage to: injure." Webster's Third New International Dictionary 1034 (1966). In the context of the ESA, that definition naturally encompasses habitat modification that results in actual injury or death to members of an endangered or threatened species.

Respondents argue that the Secretary should have limited the purview of "harm" to direct applications of force against protected species, but the dictionary definition does not include the word "directly" or suggest in any way that only direct or willful action that leads to injury constitutes "harm." Moreover, unless the statutory term "harm" encompasses indirect as well as direct injuries, the word has no meaning that does not duplicate the meaning of other words that § 3 uses to define "take." A reluctance to treat statutory terms as surplusage supports the reasonableness of the Secretary's interpretation.

Second, the broad purpose of the ESA supports the Secretary's decision to extend protection against activities that cause the precise harms Congress enacted the statute to avoid. In *TVA v. Hill*, 437 U.S. 153 (1978) [Chapter 5, § 2(C)], we described the Act as "the most comprehensive legislation for the preservation of endangered species ever enacted by any nation." Whereas predecessor statutes enacted in 1966 and 1969 had not contained any sweeping prohibition against the taking of endangered species except on federal lands, the 1973 Act applied to all land in the United States and to the Nation's territorial seas. As stated in § 2 of the Act, among its central purposes is "to provide a means whereby the ecosystems upon which endangered species and threatened species depend may be conserved. . . ."

In *Hill*, we construed § 7 as precluding the completion of the Tellico Dam because of its predicted impact on the survival of the snail darter. Both our holding and the language in our opinion stressed the importance of the statutory policy. "The plain intent of Congress in enacting this statute," we recognized, "was to halt and reverse the trend toward species extinction, whatever the cost. This is reflected not only in the stated policies of the Act, but in literally every section of the statute." Although the § 9 "take" prohibition was not at issue in *Hill*, we took note of that prohibition, placing particular emphasis on the Secretary's inclusion of habitat modification in his definition of "harm." In light of that provision for habitat protection, we could "not understand how TVA intends to operate Tellico Dam without 'harming' the snail darter." Congress' intent to provide comprehensive protection for endangered and threatened species supports the permissibility of the Secretary's "harm" regulation. * * *

(3)   Third, the fact that Congress in 1982 authorized the Secretary to issue permits for takings that § 9(a)(1)(B) would otherwise prohibit, "if such taking is incidental to, and not the purpose of, the carrying out of an otherwise lawful activity," 16 U.S.C. § 1539(a)(1)(B), strongly suggests that Congress understood § 9(a)(1)(B) to prohibit indirect as well as deliberate takings. The permit process requires the applicant to prepare a "conservation plan" that specifies how he intends to "minimize and mitigate" the "impact" of his activity on endangered and threatened species, 16 U.S.C. § 1539(a)(2)(A), making clear that Congress had in mind foreseeable rather than merely accidental effects on listed species. No one could seriously request an "incidental" take permit to avert § 9 liability for direct, deliberate action against a member of an endangered or threatened species, but respondents would read "harm" so narrowly that the permit procedure would have little more than that absurd purpose. "When Congress acts to amend a statute, we presume it intends its amendment to have real and substantial effect." Congress' addition of the § 10 permit provision supports the Secretary's conclusion that activities not intended to harm an endangered species, such as habitat modification, may constitute unlawful takings under the ESA unless the Secretary permits them.

[The court of appeals had come to a contrary conclusion on the basis of the *noscitur a sociis* canon: the surrounding words—such as pursue, hunt, shoot—connoted application of force directed at a particular animal. But other words, such as harass, do not so connote, and the lower court's construction would effectively write *harm* out of the statute entirely.]

We need not decide whether the statutory definition of "take" compels the Secretary's interpretation of "harm," because our conclusions that Congress did not unambiguously manifest its intent to adopt respondents' view, and that the Secretary's interpretation is reasonable suffice to decide this case. See generally *Chevron, U.S.A., Inc. v. Nat. Res. Defense Council* [Chapter 9, § 1]. The latitude the ESA gives the Secretary in enforcing the statute, together with the degree of regulatory expertise necessary to its enforcement, establishes that we owe some degree of deference to the Secretary's reasonable interpretation. See Breyer, *Judicial Review of Questions of Law and Policy*, 38 Admin. L. Rev. 363, 373 (1986). [Justice Stevens also rejected application of the rule of lenity. Although there is a separate criminal sanction for "knowing" violations of the ESA, the Court has never applied the rule of lenity to review agency rules implementing a civil statute that has parallel criminal sanctions.]

Our conclusion that the Secretary's definition of "harm" rests on a permissible construction of the ESA gains further support from the legislative history of the statute. The Committee Reports accompanying the bills that became the ESA do not specifically discuss the meaning of "harm," but they make clear that Congress intended "take" to apply broadly to cover indirect as well as purposeful actions. The Senate Report stressed that " "[t]ake' is defined . . . in the broadest possible manner to include every conceivable way in which a person can 'take' or attempt to 'take' any fish or wildlife." S. Rep. No. 93–307, at 7 (1973). The House Report stated that "the broadest possible terms" were used to define restrictions on takings. H.R. Rep. No. 93–412, at 15 (1973). The House Report underscored the breadth of the "take" definition by noting that it included "harassment, *whether intentional or not.*" *Id.* at 11 (emphasis added). The Report explained that the definition "would allow, for example, the Secretary to regulate or prohibit the activities of birdwatchers where the effect of those activities might disturb the birds and make it difficult for them to hatch or raise their young." *Ibid.* * * *

The definition of "take" that originally appeared in S. 1983 differed from the definition as ultimately enacted in [this] significant respect: It included "the destruction, modification, or curtailment of [the] habitat or range" of fish and wildlife. Respondents make much of the fact that the Commerce Committee removed this phrase from the "take" definition before S. 1983 went to the floor. See 119 Cong. Rec. 25663 (1973). We do not find that fact especially significant. The legislative materials contain no indication why the habitat protection provision was deleted. That provision differed greatly from the regulation at issue today. Most notably, the habitat protection in S. 1983 would have applied far more broadly than the regulation does because it made adverse habitat modification a categorical violation of the "take" prohibition, unbounded by the regulation's limitation to habitat modifications that actually kill or injure wildlife. The S. 1983 language also failed to qualify "modification" with the regulation's limiting adjective "significant." We do not believe the Senate's unelaborated disavowal of the provision in S. 1983 undermines the reasonableness of the more moderate habitat protection in the Secretary's "harm" regulation. [In footnote 19, Justice Stevens rejected the argument that statements by Senate and House sponsors supported the idea that the § 5 land acquisition provision and not § 9 was expected to be the ESA's remedy for habitat modification.]

The history of the 1982 amendment that gave the Secretary authority to grant permits for "incidental" takings provides further support for his reading of the Act. The House Report expressly states that "[b]y use of the word 'incidental' the Committee intends to cover situations in which it is known that a taking will occur if the other activity is engaged in but such taking is incidental to, and not the purpose of, the activity." H.R. Rep. No. 97–567, p. 31 (1982). This reference to the foreseeability of incidental takings undermines respondents' argument that the 1982 amendment covered only accidental killings of endangered and threatened animals that might occur in the course of hunting or trapping other animals. Indeed, Congress had habitat modification directly in mind: Both the Senate Report and the House Conference Report identified as the model for the permit process a cooperative state-federal response to a case in California where a development project threatened incidental harm to a species of endangered butterfly by modification of its habitat. See S. Rep. No. 97–418, at 10 (1982); H.R. Conf. Rep. No. 97–835, at 30–32 (1982). Thus, Congress in 1982 focused squarely on the aspect of the "harm" regulation at issue in this litigation. Congress' implementation of a permit program is consistent with the Secretary's interpretation of the term "harm." * * *

JUSTICE SCALIA, with whom THE CHIEF JUSTICE [REHNQUIST] and JUSTICE THOMAS join, dissenting.

I think it unmistakably clear that the legislation at issue here (1) forbade the hunting and killing of endangered animals, and (2) provided federal lands and federal funds for the acquisition of private lands, to preserve the habitat of endangered animals. The Court's holding that the hunting and killing prohibition incidentally preserves habitat on private lands imposes unfairness to the point of financial ruin—not just upon the rich, but upon the simplest farmer who finds his land conscripted to national zoological use. I respectfully dissent.

[Justice Scalia objected to three features of the regulation, which, as he saw it, (1) failed to consider whether death or injury to wildlife is an intentional or even foreseeable effect of a habitat modification; (2) covered omissions as well as acts; and (3) considered injuries to future as well as present animal populations, and not just specific animals.] *None* of these three features of the regulation can be found in the statutory provisions supposed to authorize it. The term "harm" in § 1532(19) has no legal force of its own. An indictment or civil complaint that charged the defendant with "harming" an animal protected under the Act would be dismissed as defective, for the only *operative* term in the statute is to "take." If "take" were not elsewhere defined in the Act, none could dispute what it means, for the term is as old as the law itself. To "take," when applied to wild animals, means to reduce those animals, by killing or capturing, to human control. [Citing dictionaries, cases, and Blackstone.] This is just the sense in which "take" is used elsewhere in federal legislation and treaty. See, e.g., Migratory Bird Treaty Act, 16 U.S.C. § 703 (1988 ed., Supp. V) (no person may "pursue, hunt, take, capture, kill, [or] attempt to take, capture, or kill" any migratory bird); Agreement on the Conservation of Polar Bears, Nov. 15, 1973, Art. I, 27 U.S.T. 3918, 3921, T.I.A.S. No. 8409 (defining "taking" as "hunting, killing and capturing"). And that meaning fits neatly with the rest of § 1538(a)(1), which makes it unlawful not only to take protected species, but also to import or export them (§ 1538(a)(1)(A)); to possess, sell, deliver, carry, transport, or ship any taken species (§ 1538(a)(1)(D)); and to transport, sell, or offer to sell them in interstate or foreign commerce (§§ 1538(a)(1)(E), (F)). The taking prohibition, in other words, is only part of the regulatory plan of § 1538(a)(1), which covers all the stages of the process by which protected wildlife is reduced to man's dominion and made the object of profit. It is obvious that "take" in this sense—a term of art deeply embedded in the statutory and common law concerning wildlife—describes a class of acts (not omissions) done directly and intentionally (not indirectly and by accident) to particular animals (not populations of animals).

[Although "harm" has a range of meaning, the most likely in this statutory context is one that focuses on specific and intentional harming.] "Harm" is merely one of 10 prohibitory words in § 1532(19), and the other 9 fit the ordinary meaning of "take" perfectly. To "harass, pursue, hunt, shoot, wound, kill, trap, capture, or collect" are all affirmative acts (the provision itself describes them as "conduct," see § 1532(19)) which are directed immediately and intentionally against a particular animal—not acts or omissions that indirectly and accidentally cause injury to a population of animals. * * * What the nine other words in § 1532(19) have in common—and share with the narrower meaning of "harm" described above, but not with the Secretary's ruthless dilation of the word—is the sense of affirmative conduct intentionally directed against a particular animal or animals.

I am not the first to notice this fact, or to draw the conclusion that it compels. In 1981 the Solicitor of the Fish and Wildlife Service delivered a legal opinion on § 1532(19) that is in complete agreement with my reading:

> The Act's definition of "take" contains a list of actions that illustrate the intended scope of the term. . . . With the possible exception of "harm," these terms all represent forms of conduct that are directed against and likely to injure or kill *individual* wildlife. Under the principle of statutory construction, *ejusdem generis*, . . . the term "harm" should be interpreted to include only those actions that are directed against, and likely to injure or kill, individual wildlife. [Memorandum of April 17, 1981 (emphasis in original).]

I would call it *noscitur a sociis*, but the principle is much the same: The fact that "several items in a list share an attribute counsels in favor of interpreting the other items as possessing that attribute as well." * * * [Moreover,] the Court's contention that "harm" in the narrow sense adds nothing to the other words underestimates the ingenuity of our own species in a way that Congress did not. To feed an animal poison, to spray it with mace, to chop down the very tree in which it is nesting, or even to destroy its entire habitat in order to take it (as by draining a pond to get at a turtle), might neither wound nor kill, but would directly and intentionally harm.

The penalty provisions of the Act counsel this interpretation as well. Any person who "knowingly" violates § 1538(a)(1)(B) is, subject to criminal penalties under § 1540(b)(1) and civil penalties under § 1540(a)(1); moreover, under the latter section, any person "who otherwise violates" the taking prohibition (i.e., violates it unknowingly) may be assessed a civil penalty of $500 for each violation, with the stricture that "[e]ach such violation shall be a separate offense." This last provision should be clear warning that the regulation is in error, for when combined with the regulation it produces a result that no legislature could reasonably be thought to have intended: A large number of routine private activities—for example, farming, ranching, roadbuilding, construction and logging—are subjected to strict-liability penalties when they fortuitously injure protected wildlife, no matter how remote the chain of causation and no matter how difficult to foresee (or to disprove) the "injury" may be (e.g., an "impairment" of breeding). * * *

So far I have discussed only the immediate statutory text bearing on the regulation. But the definition of "take" in § 1532(19) applies "[f]or the purposes of this chapter," that is, it governs the meaning of the word *as used everywhere in the Act*. Thus, the Secretary's interpretation of "harm" is wrong if it does not fit with the use of "take" throughout the Act. And it does not. In § 1540(e)(4)(B), for example, Congress provided for the forfeiture of "[a]ll guns, traps, nets, and other equipment . . . used to aid the taking, possessing, selling, [etc.]" of protected animals. This listing plainly relates to "taking" in the ordinary sense. If environmental modification were part (and necessarily a major part) of taking, as the Secretary maintains, one would have expected the list to include "plows, bulldozers, and backhoes." * * * The Act is full of like examples. See, e.g., § 1538(a)(1)(D) (prohibiting possession, sale, and transport of "species taken in violation" of the Act). "[I]f the Act is to be interpreted as a symmetrical and coherent regulatory scheme, one in which the operative words have a consistent meaning throughout," *Gustafson v. Alloyd Co.*, 513 U.S. 561, 569 (1995), the regulation must fall.

The broader structure of the Act confirms the unreasonableness of the regulation. Section 1536 provides:

> Each Federal agency shall . . . insure that any action authorized, funded, or carried out by such agency . . . is not likely to jeopardize the continued existence of any endangered species or threatened species or *result in the destruction or adverse modification of habitat* of such species which is determined by the Secretary . . . to be critical. [16 U.S.C. § 1536(a)(2) (emphasis added).]

The Act defines "critical habitat" as habitat that is "essential to the conservation of the species," §§ 1532(5)(A)(i), (A)(ii), with "conservation" in turn defined as the use of methods necessary to bring listed species "to the point at which the measures provided pursuant to this chapter are no longer necessary." § 1532(3).

Critical habitat = habitat essential to conservation of the species

These provisions have a double significance. Even if §§ 1536(a)(2) and 1538(a)(1)(B) were totally independent prohibitions—the former applying only to federal agencies and their licensees, the latter only to private parties—Congress's explicit prohibition of habitat modification in the one section would bar the inference of an implicit prohibition of habitat modification in the other section. "[W]here Congress includes particular language in one section of a statute but omits it in another . . ., it is generally presumed that Congress acts intentionally and purposely in the disparate inclusion or exclusion." *Keene Corp. v. United States*, 508 U.S. 200, 208 (1993). And that presumption against implicit prohibition would be even stronger where the one section which uses the language carefully defines and limits its application. That is to say, it would be passing strange for Congress carefully to define "critical habitat" as used in § 1536(a)(2), but leave it to the Secretary to evaluate, willynilly, impermissible "habitat modification" (under the guise of "harm") in § 1538(a)(1)(B).

intentionally purposely in disparate Inclusion/exclusion

In fact, however, §§ 1536(a)(2) and 1538(a)(1)(B) do *not* operate in separate realms; federal agencies are subject to *both*, because the "person[s]" forbidden to take protected species under § 1538 include agencies and departments of the Federal Government. See § 1532(13). This means that the "harm" regulation also contradicts another principle of interpretation: that statutes should be read so far as possible to give independent effect to all their provisions. See *Ratzlaf v. United States*, 510 U.S. 135, 140–41 (1994). By defining "harm" in the definition of "take" in § 1538(a)(1)(B) to include significant habitat modification that injures populations of wildlife, the regulation makes the habitat-modification restriction in § 1536(a)(2) almost wholly superfluous. As "critical habitat" is habitat "essential to the conservation of the species," adverse modification of "critical" habitat by a federal agency would also constitute habitat modification that injures a population of wildlife.

The Court makes * * * other arguments. First, "the broad purpose of the [Act] supports the Secretary's decision to extend protection against activities that cause the precise harms Congress enacted the statute to avoid." I thought we had renounced the vice of "simplistically . . . assum[ing] that *whatever* furthers the statute's primary objective must be the law." *Rodriguez v. United States*, 480 U.S. 522, 526 (1987) (*per curiam*) (emphasis in original). Deduction from the "broad purpose" of a statute begs the question if it is used to decide by what *means* (and hence to what *length*) Congress pursued that purpose; to get the right answer to that question there is no substitute for the hard job (or in this case, the quite simple one) of reading the whole text. "The Act must do everything necessary to achieve its broad purpose" is the slogan of the enthusiast, not the analytical tool of the arbiter.

Second, the Court maintains that the legislative history of the 1973 Act supports the Secretary's definition. Even if legislative history were a legitimate and reliable tool of interpretation (which I shall assume in order to rebut the Court's claim); and even if it could appropriately be resorted to when the enacted text is as clear as this, but see *Chicago v. Environmental Defense Fund*, 511 U.S. 328, 337 (1994); here it shows quite the opposite of what the Court says. I shall not pause to discuss the Court's reliance on such statements in the Committee Reports as " '[t]ake' is defined . . . in the broadest possible manner to include every conceivable way in which a person can 'take' or attempt to 'take' any fish or wildlife." [S. Rep. No. 93–307, at 7 (1973)]. This sort of empty flourish—to the effect that "this statute means what it means all the way"—counts for little even when enacted into the law itself. See *Reves v. Ernst & Young*, 507 U.S. 170, 183–84 (1993).

Much of the Court's discussion of legislative history is devoted to two items: first, the Senate floor manager's introduction of an amendment that added the word "harm" to the definition of "take," with the observation that (along with other amendments) it would " 'help to achieve the purposes of the bill' "; second, the relevant Committee's removal from the definition of a provision stating that "take" includes " 'the destruction, modification or curtailment of [the] habitat or range' " of fish and wildlife. The Court inflates the first and belittles the second, even though the second is on its face far more pertinent. But this elaborate inference from various pre-enactment actions and inactions is quite unnecessary, since we have direct evidence of what those who brought the legislation to the floor thought it meant—evidence as solid as any ever to be found in legislative history, but which the Court banishes to a footnote.

Both the Senate and House floor managers of the bill explained it in terms which leave no doubt that the problem of habitat destruction on private lands was to be solved principally by the land acquisition program of § 1534, while § 1538 solved a different problem altogether—the problem of takings. Senator Tunney stated:

> Through [the] land acquisition provisions, we will be able to conserve habitats necessary to protect fish and wildlife from further destruction.

Although most endangered species are threatened primarily by the destruction of their natural habitats, a significant portion of these animals are subject to *predation by man for commercial, sport, consumption, or other purposes.* The provisions of [the bill] would prohibit the commerce in or the importation, exportation, or taking of endangered species. . . . [119 Cong. Rec. 25669 (1973) (emphasis added).]

The House floor manager, Representative Sullivan, put the same thought in this way:

[T]he principal threat to animals stems from destruction of their habitat. . . . *[The bill] will meet this problem by providing funds for acquisition of critical habitat. . . .* It will also enable the Department of Agriculture to cooperate with willing landowners who desire to assist in the protection of endangered species, *but who are understandably unwilling to do so at excessive cost to themselves.* Another hazard to endangered species arises from those who would *capture or kill them for pleasure or profit.* There is no way that the Congress can make it less pleasurable for a person to take an animal, but we can certainly make it less profitable for them to do so. [*Id.* at 30162 (emphasis added).]

Habitat modification and takings, in other words, were viewed as different problems, addressed by different provisions of the Act. [Justice Scalia argued that these statements destroy the Court's legislative history case and that the Court has no response.]

Third, the Court seeks support from a provision that was added to the Act in 1982, the year after the Secretary promulgated the current regulation. The provision states:

[T]he Secretary may permit, under such terms and conditions as he shall prescribe—

. . .

any taking otherwise prohibited by section 1538(a)(1)(B) . . . if such taking is incidental to, and not the purpose of, the carrying out of an otherwise lawful activity. [16 U.S.C. § 1539(a)(1)(B).]

This provision does not, of course, implicate our doctrine that reenactment of a statutory provision ratifies an extant judicial or administrative interpretation, for neither the taking prohibition in § 1538(a)(1)(B) nor the definition in § 1532(19) was reenacted. The Court claims, however, that the provision "strongly suggests that Congress understood [§ 1538(a)(1)(B)] to prohibit indirect as well as deliberate takings." That would be a valid inference if habitat modification were the only substantial "otherwise lawful activity" that might incidentally and nonpurposefully cause a prohibited "taking." Of course it is not. This provision applies to the many otherwise lawful takings that incidentally take a protected species—as when fishing for unprotected salmon also takes an endangered species of salmon. * * *

This is enough to show, in my view, that the 1982 permit provision does not support the regulation. I must acknowledge that the Senate Committee Report on this provision, and the House Conference Committee Report, clearly contemplate

that it will enable the Secretary to permit environmental modification. But the *text* of the amendment cannot possibly bear that asserted meaning, when placed within the context of an Act that must be interpreted (as we have seen) not to prohibit private environmental modification. The neutral language of the amendment cannot possibly alter that interpretation, nor can its legislative history be summoned forth to contradict, rather than clarify, what is in its totality an unambiguous statutory text. There is little fear, of course, that giving no effect to the relevant portions of the Committee Reports will frustrate the real-life expectations of a majority of the Members of Congress. If they read and relied on such tedious detail on such an obscure point (it was not, after all, presented as a revision of the statute's prohibitory scope, but as a discretionary-waiver provision) the Republic would be in grave peril.
* * *

[JUSTICE O'CONNOR wrote a separate concurring opinion, responding to some of Justice Scalia's concerns. "[T]he regulation's application is limited by ordinary principles of proximate causation, which introduce notions of foreseeability." For example, she disapproved of an application of the statute where the grazing of sheep was found to be a "taking" of palila birds, as the sheep destroyed seedlings which would have grown into trees needed by the bird for nesting. The chain of causation is simply too attenuated, Justice O'Connor concluded. Justice Scalia responded that this was Justice O'Connor's gloss on the statute, not the agency's. He chided his colleague for trying to have it both ways—deferring to the agency under *Chevron* (see Chapter 9, § 1) but then rewriting the regulation to suit her fancy. Justice Scalia concluded: "We defer to reasonable agency interpretations of ambiguous statutes precisely in order that agencies, rather than courts, may exercise policymaking discretion in the interstices of statutes. See *Chevron*, 467 U.S. at 843–45. Just as courts may not exercise an agency's power to adjudicate, and so may not affirm an agency order on discretionary grounds the agency has not advanced, so also this Court may not exercise the Secretary's power to regulate, and so may not uphold a regulation by adding to it even the most reasonable of elements it does not contain."]

NOTES ON SWEET HOME

1. *The Canons Debate.* Notice, first, how many of the canons are relevant to the Justices' deliberations about the plain meaning of the text in this case: the ordinary meaning rule, and its corollaries regarding dictionaries and technical meaning; noscitur a sociis and (possibly) ejusdem generis; expressio (or inclusio) unius and other rules of negative implication; the rule against redundancy; the rule of consistent usage and of significant variation; and the anti-derogation rule. Notice also how the anti-derogation rule figures centrally in both majority and dissenting opinions. Justice Scalia emphasizes the structural conflict between Congress' asserted allocation of responsibilities in §§ 5 and 7 and the majority's broad interpretation of § 9; Justice Stevens emphasizes the philosophical and structural conflict between a narrow reading of § 9 and the statutory scheme established in § 10.

A problem sharply illustrated by *Sweet Home* is that different canons cut in different directions. How can one resolve conflicting canonical signals? One way to resolve the conflict is resort to the statutory purpose, but that may only generalize the disagreement. The dissenters' sarcasm suggests the possibility that they were not sympathetic to the statutory goals of biodiversity: note their alarm that the "simplest farmer" finds his land "conscripted to national zoological use." Does this reflect a neutral interpretation of the law? Is the Nietzsche rule possibly applicable here?

2.   *Bringing in Legislative History.* In assessing the relative strengths of the majority and dissent, consider too their deployment of non-canonical resources. If the canons skirmish is a wash (or maybe even if it favors one side but not conclusively?), do the legislative history arguments cut clearly in favor of the majority or dissent? Is your response the same for the 1973 history and the 1982 history?

The verb "harm" was added to the text on the Senate floor by Senator Tunney (Dem., California), the Senate manager of the 1973 Act. Tunney added "harm" to the nine-verb definition of "take" that appeared in the text of the bill reported by the Senate committee. The change was part of a series of "technical and clarifying" amendments approved unanimously by the Senate. See 119 Cong. Rec. 25682–83. Senator Tunney referred to the amendments as "technical in nature" but also "important." Does this addition clarify the Senate committee report explanation of "take" that appears in the Court's decision? In what way is the addition "important"?

According to Justice Scalia, Rep. Sullivan's floor statement signifies that the law addresses habitat destruction through its land acquisition program rather than through its prohibition on takings. Is this the only inference one can draw from Rep. Sullivan's statement? Can you offer any alternative reading?

3.   *The Bottom Line.* Which side is able to create a more complete—or more elegant—case for its interpretation? We are particularly impressed with the dissenters' ability to weave together a wide array of canons to support their position. Should this assure their triumph? If so, why did their usual ally, Justice O'Connor, jump ship? She might have been influenced by the fact that the *political equilibrium* favored the agency (remember that she authored the Court's opinion in the *FDA Tobacco* Case, Chapter 5, § 3(B)). Indeed, the agency itself reflected the prevailing political consensus in this case, perhaps justifying the Court's deferring to its rule. (See Chapter 9).

CHAPTER 8

IMPLEMENTATION OF STATUTES IN THE ADMINISTRATIVE STATE

■ ■ ■

Under the system of mutually encroaching government powers described in *Federalist* #51 (Madison), the legislature shares lawmaking power with the executive and the judiciary. By now, it should be clear that statutes are not the end of lawmaking; indeed, they are often only the beginning. Earlier chapters have explored how courts may construe statutory text narrowly while discounting evidence of legislative history or purpose; expand statutes beyond their literal terms by reference to that same historical and purposive evidence; and update statutes in appropriate circumstances. In the next two chapters, we focus on the parallel and often primary role played by agencies in the implementation and interpretation of statutes. This chapter considers implementation issues; chapter 9 addresses the methods courts apply when reviewing agency interpretation of statutory provisions—methods that may involve varying levels of judicial deference.

There are several implementation choices available to the legislature when drafting statutes. First, the legislature can authorize public enforcers to prosecute violators of the statute and exact some penalty from them (e.g., criminal laws). Second, the legislature can authorize victims of conduct violating the statute to sue the violators for damages and/or injunctive relief (e.g., the Uniform Commercial Code and most tort statutes). In these first two implementation choices, the legislature is authorizing courts to adjudicate the enforcement lawsuits and to develop the standards and rules of the statute. Third, the legislature can delegate the development of standards, the adjudication of violations, and the promulgation of guidance to a public administrative agency or a private group (e.g., the federal securities laws, state licensing regulations). This last choice has been increasingly characteristic of the modern administrative state, at both the federal and state levels.

Section 1 traces the history of the modern federal administrative state during the twentieth century. It then presents a Case Study addressing commercial airplane safety in the modern age of terrorism that introduces some of the challenges agencies face when seeking to fulfill their mission. Section 1 also considers two core constitutional issues related to implementation choices: the limits on agency authority and the tenure of agency officials. First, is it legitimate for Congress to delegate so much of its authority to agencies? At what point does delegation of *law implementing* power essentially become abdication of *lawmaking* power? Why might this question be answered differently in state legislatures than in Congress? Second, does the President's authority to appoint inferior officers include *unlimited power to remove them from office*? To what extent does Congress's authority to restrict presidential removal powers differ based on the two types of agencies created by Congress—executive branch agencies and independent agencies? Assuming

Congress may exercise greater control over the tenure of certain agency officials, are there constitutional limits on this ability to restrict presidential power?

Section 2 explores agency implementation under the Administrative Procedure Act (APA), the statute that has shaped agency procedural approaches since 1946. It begins with an overview of the APA, including a look at its extensive legislative history and some core definitional issues. Section 2 then examines the major procedures by which agencies exercise their statutorily assigned policymaking responsibilities pursuant to the APA: (1) *rulemaking*—both formal rulemaking "on the record after opportunity for an agency hearing," and the more prevalent informal or notice-and-comment rulemaking; (2) *adjudication*; and (3) *interpretive rules* and *policy statements*. Congress and the courts help determine which options agencies may pursue in a given set of circumstances, although agencies retain a degree of flexibility in this regard. Under rulemaking and adjudication, agencies must conform to certain APA procedural requirements, subject to judicial review that can be searching.

Section 3 addresses efforts by all three branches to monitor and control day-to-day aspects of agency implementation. It examines congressional monitoring mechanisms, including legislative oversight and investigation of agency enforcement, and the appropriations power. These mechanisms are somewhat indirect and often not terribly effective means of congressional control. Other congressional monitoring approaches—such as the legislative veto, use of Senate confirmation authority, and overruling regulations under the Congressional Review Act—raise more troubling questions which we discuss. Section 3 next explores efforts by the President to monitor and influence agency policymaking conduct. It focuses on the formal role played by the Office of Management and Budget (OMB), including the Office of Information and Regulatory Affairs (OIRA), as well as limits imposed on the "administrative state" by political appointees and also the White House. These monitoring approaches tend to be less headline-grabbing than many congressional efforts, but they may also be more effective. Finally, Section 3 examines judicial review of agency action under the APA. Like congressional oversight and investigation (and unlike cost-benefit analysis and OIRA review), litigation typically comes into play only after an agency has engaged in some form of implementation. Consider in this setting whether judicial review is more effective than Congress's *ex post* approaches, and perhaps also more influential than the *ex ante* approaches that tend to characterize executive branch monitoring efforts.

1. IMPLEMENTATION CHOICES AND THE SEPARATION OF POWERS

State and federal criminal laws are typically enforced exclusively by official prosecution of offenders. Many other statutes provide for both civil and criminal penalties that may be enforced by official actions filed in court. For example, the Justice Department may bring a civil lawsuit for an injunction under the Sherman Act to prevent or terminate violations of the Act, or it may refer discovered violations to a U.S. Attorney's Office for criminal prosecution, or both.

Since 1875, however, public enforcement has gradually been transformed from such *a prosecutorial model*, in which a government agency or department brings lawsuits against statutory violators and the adjudication and development of rules is accomplished by courts, to a *bureaucratic model*. Under the bureaucratic model, the government agency or department itself adjudicates the individual prosecutions or makes the rules, and the only role for courts is limited judicial review of what the administrators have done. In this section, we present a short history of the modern administrative state, and the main constitutional problems that it presents.

A. A BRIEF HISTORY OF THE MODERN ADMINISTRATIVE STATE[1]

1. *Origins: Regulatory Police.* Wherever there is government there is bureaucracy. At the national level, the conventional historical account is that from the ratification of the Constitution through most of the nineteenth century, very little policy creation was done through the federal bureaucracy. Jerry Mashaw has done much to challenge this conventional story, excavating and analyzing a rich pre-history of the modern administrative state in which Congress at various times conferred broad authority on administrators, including extra-judicial coercive powers and the authority to engage in rulemaking and adjudication. See Jerry L. Mashaw, *Creating the Administrative Constitution: The Lost One Hundred Years of American Administrative Law* (2012).

Still, the most visible administrative activity was on the state level, in the form of rate regulation of natural monopolies, such as grain elevators, utilities, and railroads. There were 25 state railroad commissions in 1886, for example. The Supreme Court invalidated state railroad regulation under the Commerce Clause in *Wabash, St. Louis and Pacific Railway v. Illinois*, 118 U.S. 557 (1886), which stimulated Congress to create the first major federal regulatory agency, the Interstate Commerce Commission (ICC), in 1887. 24 Stat. 379.[2] Congress established the Federal Trade Commission (FTC) in 1914 to enforce some of the antitrust laws and regulate unfair competition, the United States Shipping Board in 1916, the Federal Power Commission in 1920, and the Federal Radio Commission (predecessor to the Federal Communications Commission) in 1927. These commissions and the ICC were the first modern *independent federal agencies*, bureaucracies set up outside of the formal departments of the Executive Branch and with their own adjudicatory and rulemaking responsibilities. See generally Geoffrey Miller, *Independent Agencies*, 1986 Sup. Ct. Rev. 41.[3]

---

[1]   This history is drawn, in substantial part, from Robert Rabin, *Federal Regulation in Historical Perspective*, 38 Stan. L. Rev. 1189 (1986). See also Joseph Kearney & Thomas Merrill, *The Great Transformation of Regulated Industries Law*, 98 Colum. L. Rev. 1323 (1998).

[2]   Ironically, or perhaps appropriately, the ICC was also one of the first major regulatory agencies to be abolished by the Republican Congresses in the late 1990s that sought to reduce the federal bureaucracy. See also Jerry Mashaw, *Federal Administration and Administrative Law in the Gilded Age*, 119 Yale L.J. 1362 (2010) (demonstrating, *contra* the more familiar narrative, that Congress created multiple departments, bureaus, and programs in the post-Reconstruction period, and federal civilian employment grew more rapidly than the population as a whole).

[3]   At the same time Congress was creating independent agencies, it gave bureaus or divisions within the existing executive departments similar duties. The Patent Office had existed within the executive department since 1790, and the Secretary of Agriculture accumulated a great amount of adjudicatory

police the
excesses of
business

The philosophy behind the establishment of these agencies and bureaus by Populist reformers in the 1880s and 1890s and Progressives in the 1900s and 1910s was to police the excesses of businesses. Many laws were responses to scandals exposed during the Progressive Era. For example, the Pure Food and Drug Act of 1906 and the Meat Inspection Act of 1906–07 were triggered by the publication of Upton Sinclair's *The Jungle*, which exposed horrid meat processing practices. Both the Populists, who favored draconian measures against the enemies of the farmer (especially railroads), and the Progressives, who favored marginal change, generally accepted the existing market mechanisms as the norm. They envisioned the work of the ICC and FTC and the Bureau of Chemistry (which administered the Pure Food and Drug Act) as merely facilitating the "natural" operation of the competitive market by preventing the intrusion of "unnatural" practices—fraud, price-fixing, and discrimination.[4]

The reformist approach in this early policing period was, therefore, ambivalent. The judiciary's attitude was often openly hostile, as judges treated determinations by the ICC and FTC with little deference and refused to enforce well-justified agency requests. On the other hand, the ICC managed to increase its statutory power in 1906 and 1910, when Congress granted the agency authority to regulate rates. Courts gradually came to defer to the agency, though they also required it to follow essential procedural safeguards (a trial-type hearing) in order to develop an administrative record that could be the basis for meaningful judicial review. See, e.g., *ICC v. Louisville & Nashville Ry. Co.*, 227 U.S. 88, 93 (1913).

The evolution of the ICC brought to light a problem with viewing agencies merely as policing institutions. World War I was to underscore the problem, as lawmakers and the public began to perceive government boards as necessary to compel the private sector to meet the needs of the war effort. An immediate result of the war effort was the Transportation Act of 1920, 41 Stat. 456, which greatly expanded the powers of the ICC beyond the policing of price discrimination against shippers. During the war, the government ran the railroads, and the Act gave the ICC authority to do the same—by regulating rates, mergers and consolidations, and service schedules comprehensively (and, presumably, efficiently).

2.   *The New Deal: Regulatory Planning and Market Management.* The Great Depression suggested to many that the "natural" operation of the market was not necessarily a good thing at all, and that much more government direction was needed. FDR's New Deal was a cluster of experiments proceeding in many different directions—from the aspirations of comprehensive industrial planning in the National Industrial Recovery Act (NIRA) to the ambitious subsidy program of the Agricultural Adjustment Act. Most of these regulatory initiatives rejected the

---

responsibility as a result of the Pure Food and Drug Act of 1906, 34 Stat. 768; the Meat Inspection Act of 1906–07, 34 Stat. 674, 1260; the Cotton Futures Act and the Warehouse Act of 1916, 39 Stat. 453 & 486; and later statutes. For an argument that the differences between independent agencies and executive departments rest on something less than a well-defined legal distinction, see Kirti Datla & Richard Revesz, *Deconstructing Independent Agencies (and Executive Agencies)* 98 Cornell L. Rev. 769 (2013), discussed in § 1(C) of this chapter.

[4]   See 3 Robert Himmelberg, *Growth of the Regulatory State, 1900–1917: State and Federal Regulation of Railroads and Other Enterprises* (1994). For an argument that most of these early statutes represented rent-seeking by regulated interests, see Gabriel Kolko, *The Triumph of Conservatism: A Reinterpretation of American History* (1963).

policing approach of the Populists and Progressives. The New Deal measures were more comprehensive and affirmative (and sometimes managerial) approaches to a market that was seen to be structurally unfair and unreliable. The distinction between public and private spheres of American life became more blurred.

The New Deal created an unprecedented array of new independent agencies and departmental bureaus. Some of them had brief lives. The NIRA, representing the New Deal's most ambitious effort at economic planning, did little to help the economy and was declared unconstitutional by the Supreme Court in *A.L.A. Schechter Poultry Corp. v. United States*, 295 U.S. 495 (1935). Other New Deal agencies have become part of our federal governance. The National Labor Relations Board (NLRB) was established as an independent agency outside the Labor Department to alleviate inequality in the labor market and to head off labor strife by adjudicating the existence of "unfair labor practices" by management and labor unions. It had the authority to enforce its determinations through "cease-and-desist" orders. The Securities and Exchange Commission (SEC) was established to prevent unstable capital markets by registering and regulating securities offerings according to the commands provided in the applicable statutes and SEC rules. The Federal Deposit Insurance Corporation (FDIC) was a response to the disastrous bank runs of the Great Depression and sought to improve confidence in the system by insuring small depositors. By 1941, there were, by one count, 19 separate lawmaking bureaus within the executive branch and 22 independent agencies. *Final Report of the Attorney General's Committee on Administrative Procedure* (1941).

As administrative agencies and bureaus proliferated, so did criticisms of them. But given the New Deal's transformation of attitudes about across-the-board federal structural intervention in the market, most criticisms did not focus on the appropriate field of administrative activity. Instead, critics targeted the inadequacies of agency procedure and judicial review: important property rights were being stripped away without proper procedural safeguards, such as trial-type hearing procedures and/or meaningful judicial review of the bureaucratic decision. In 1945, the Attorney General endorsed legislation standardizing administrative procedure, and the Administrative Procedure Act (APA), 60 Stat. 237, codified as amended at 5 U.S.C. §§ 551–559, 701–706 *et al.*, was enacted in 1946. The APA legislative history and purpose are addressed in detail in Section 2 below.

The APA compromise was essentially designed to recognize the legislative and adjudicative roles of independent agencies and departmental bureaus (both of which are included in the APA definition of "agency," *id.* § 551(1)), but also to "rein in" the bureaucratic state with procedural safeguards and judicial review to prevent arbitrary or unlawful action. The APA's enactment broadly validated the bureaucratic revolution of the New Deal and ushered in a period of relative consensus in favor of agency lawmaking in the 1950s.

3.   *The Public Interest Era: New Kinds of Regulation.* As early as the 1950s, some scholars raised concerns that bureaucratic regulation of the economy is subject to bias and debilitation over time. Marver Bernstein, *Regulating Business by Independent Commission* (1955), for example, argued that agencies, like human beings, typically go through a "life cycle." The agency's *youth* is characterized by a

crusading spirit engendered by its statutory mandate, but also by the agency's struggle to devise a regulatory strategy to deal with the better organized and often savvy industry to be regulated. The agency's *maturity* comes after it has lost much of the political support and enthusiasm that spawned its enabling statute; the agency "understands" the industry better but often takes a less aggressive approach to regulating it, becoming a "captive" of the regulated industry and even a pawn in the industry's own plans. *Senescence* comes when the agency grows not only less vital but also inflexible, a condition that may lead to some form of euthanasia. Later public choice scholars have been even less charitable in thinking about the typical agency biography than Bernstein was, characterizing agencies as captured from childhood by rent-seeking special interests.[5] The 1950s also saw the true beginnings of noneconomic regulatory activities stimulated first by the civil rights revolution, followed in the 1960s by the environmental movement.

These two developments inspired a new period of administrative law in the 1960s and the 1970s. Bureaucracy became both more distrusted and better integrated into the great public interest movements of those decades. The regulatory emphasis shifted from comprehensive direction of the economy to *command-and-control* statutes aimed at specific problems not traditionally thought of in market terms.

The Great Society was the linchpin of this shift. The Civil Rights Act of 1964, 78 Stat. 241, established an impressive range of bureaucratic sanctions for civil rights violations. For example, Titles III and IV of the Act authorized the Attorney General to file public lawsuits to desegregate public facilities and public education. Title VI provided for nondiscrimination in federally assisted programs. It was to be implemented by rules that made federal grants, loans, or other financial assistance contingent upon the recipient following nondiscriminatory policies.

Chapter 1 describes Title VII of the 1964 Act, which established the Equal Employment Opportunity Commission (EEOC) and charged it with rulemaking and adjudication of the very broad prohibition of employment discrimination. Although troubled with administrative problems over time, the EEOC served as a model for a new bureaucracy of conscience. Its intrusion into the affairs of corporations and state and local institutions helped broaden the concept of regulation. The Government's agenda extended beyond the economic marketplace and toward concern for the creation of a "great society" in which racial, sexual, and ethnic equality would be recognized. Even many of the economic initiatives of the 1960s—the War on Poverty, Medicare, the Food Stamp Program—were aimed at different targets from traditional New Deal regulation. These programs, like Title VII, sought to help the poor and the disadvantaged, often without any attempted justification based on systemic or isolated market failure.

The 1970s saw the societal transformation approach to regulation expand to include consumer rights, public health and safety, and environmental purity as important agenda items. Just as the regulatory *agenda* was changing, so was the

---

[5]   See, e.g., Anthony Downs, *Inside Bureaucracy* (1967); William Niskanen, *Bureaucracy and Representative Government* (1971); Sam Peltzman, *Toward a More General Theory of Regulation*, 19 J.L. & Econ. 211 (1976); George Stigler, *The Theory of Economic Regulation*, 2 Bell J. Econ. & Mgmt. Sci. 3 (1971).

regulatory *mechanism*. Both authorized and encouraged by the new generation of regulatory statutes, United States agencies in the 1970s showed unprecedented interest in *rulemaking* rather than adjudication and less formal mechanisms.

The National Traffic and Motor Vehicle Safety Act of 1966 exemplified the new approach. The Vehicle Safety Act and other regulatory statutes of this period tended to have more specific mandates, to focus authority in a single administrator (rather than a multi-member commission), to open up agencies to public input, and to focus agency action on the establishment of mandatory policy through general rules.[6] The agency rules themselves were different from what came before: rather than command-and-control models, agencies emphasized goals and limits, and left regulated institutions with choices about how to reach those goals and limits.

Closely following this new model was a wave of pollution control legislation, mainly the Clean Air Act Amendments of 1970 (CAA), 84 Stat. 1676, and the Federal Water Pollution Control Act Amendments of 1972 (FWPCA), 86 Stat. 816. Congress established ambitious mandates to clean up our environment. Most of the directives were very general, with the details filled in by the Environmental Protection Agency (EPA). The National Environmental Policy Act of 1969 (NEPA), 83 Stat. 852, and other statutes directed all federal departments and agencies to consider environmental effects when decisions are made. The Occupational Health and Safety Act of 1970, 84 Stat. 1590, created the Occupational Health and Safety Administration and directed it to enforce more stringent standards of safety in the workplace. Several pieces of landmark legislation worked to redistribute resources to the less well-off in society; Congress enacted the Food Stamp Act, 1 U.S.C. § 2011 et seq., Head Start programs, Medicare, and Medicaid, and it expanded welfare programs substantially.

These statutes marked a significant change in economic regulation as well. First, they redefined market imperfection. The New Deal approach defined costs rather mechanically in terms of lost output and distorted flows of resources. Things like pollution and injuries were treated as *externalities* borne for the most part by those receiving them. Regulation in the 1970s compelled businesses to consider these social costs and to do something about them. Second, the public interest legislation of the 1970s at least implicitly recognized and built upon perceived biases in the federal bureaucracy. Many reformers argued that even the few agencies and bureaus that were not essentially captured by their regulated interests were limited by their statutory mandate to consider only a few policy concerns, usually of a material and tangible nature. The regulatory structures created in the 1970s insisted that quality of life concerns be factored into the bureaucratic calculus (NEPA) and often provided very specific substantive guidelines and time deadlines for agencies to accomplish their regulatory goals (CAA).

Other developments have sought to open up agency decisionmaking. For example, the Freedom of Information Act, 5 U.S.C. § 552, was passed in 1966, 80 Stat. 250, and significantly amended in 1974, 88 Stat. 1561, to require federal

---

[6]   Jerry Mashaw, *The Story of Motor Vehicle Manufacturers Association etc: Law, Science, and Politics in the Administrative State*, in *Administrative Law Stories* 334, 339–42 (Peter Strauss ed., 2006); David Shapiro, *The Choice of Rulemaking or Adjudication in the Development of Administrative Policy*, 78 Harv. L. Rev. 921 (1965).

agencies and departments to disclose documents and information to persons requesting them, subject to specific exemptions in the Act. The purpose of the Act was to encourage citizens to monitor government performance and publicize problems. See also Privacy Act of 1974, 88 Stat. 1896, codified at 5 U.S.C. § 552a (protecting personal information from disclosure). The Government in the Sunshine Act of 1976, 90 Stat. 1241, codified at 5 U.S.C. § 552b, requires agencies headed by collegial bodies (e.g., FTC, SEC) to conduct their official business in public meetings, again subject to specific exemptions. Like the APA, these statutes were enacted to assure structures of agency decisionmaking that are responsive to the reasoned public interest. Indeed, this statutory liberalization in the 1970s was accompanied by more aggressive APA judicial review of agency decisions and procedures in the 1970s and 1980s, a phenomenon explored in Section 3.

4. *1980 to the Present: Deregulation Revived, Criticized, and Re-Energized.* During the 1970s, the American economy experienced an extended period of slow economic growth and high inflation (stagflation) combined with rising unemployment, leading many politicians and scholars to argue for diminished regulation of the economy.[7] The real sea change for the American administrative state came with the election of President Reagan in 1980. Reagan and the conservative wing of the Republican Party made "supply-side economics" a household phrase during the 1980 campaign. Sometimes cynically labeled "trickle-down economics," supply-side economics argues that lower barriers to the production or supply of goods and services are the most effective path to economic growth. The Reagan Administration implemented the supply-side approach, advocating successfully for reductions in income tax and capital gains tax rates and for rolling back regulatory controls on various industries. During the 1980s, extensive deregulation was implemented by means of Executive Order,[8] separate agency efforts,[9] and legislative change.[10]

In the 1990s, President Clinton, embodying a different vision for the Democratic Party that earlier in the century had enacted New Deal and Great Society legislation, continued this deregulatory movement. Clinton famously declared in his 1996 State of the Union address that "the era of big government is over." The Clinton Administration oversaw deregulation of credit-default swaps through the Commodity Futures Modernization Act of 2000, loosening of housing rules through the Community Reinvestment Act of 1995, and—most notably—repeal of the Glass-Steagall Act, a central component in New Deal regulation of the banking industry that had restricted the securities-related activities of commercial banks. Many economists and commentators have argued that the erosion and repeal of these

---

[7]	Major legislative responses during the Carter Administration included the Airline Deregulation Act of 1978 (deregulating the commercial airline industry) and the Motor Carrier Reform Act of 1980 (deregulating the trucking industry).

[8]	See, e.g., Exec. Order 12,287, 46 Fed. Reg. 9909 (Jan. 28, 1981) (removing controls on crude oil and refined petroleum products).

[9]	See, e.g., *In re Deregulation of Radio*, 84 F.C.C. 2d 968 (1981) (deregulating controls on radio); *Syracuse Peace Council*, 2 FCC Rcd. 5043 (1987) (eliminating fairness doctrine).

[10]	See, e.g., 1982 Bus Regulatory Reform Act; 1982 Garn-St. Germain Depository Institutions Act (deregulating savings and loan associations); 1984 Cable Television Deregulation Act; 1989 Natural Gas Wellhead Decontrol Act. For an overview of deregulatory efforts from the 1970s through the 1990s, see John E. Kwoka, *Twenty-Five Years of Deregulation: Lessons for Electric Power*, 33 Loy. U. Chi. L.J. 885 (2001–02).

banking restrictions contributed in important ways to the financial crisis that began in 2007.[11]

In the new millennium, some of this deregulatory spirit remained evident, as with President George W. Bush's public campaign, following his 2004 re-election, to privatize Social Security.[12] However, a growing chorus of deregulation critics contended that some regulation is important in allowing companies to remain competitive, to create level playing fields, to maintain quality control over the provision of services (through licensing and other qualification requirements), and to protect the public from risks like environmental degradation and excessive risk-taking by banks.

Moreover, from 2001 to 2016 there was a surge of renewed regulatory interest on the part of Congress and the President. In response to the attacks of September 11 on the World Trade Center and the Pentagon, Congress passed the Homeland Security Act of 2002, 116 Stat. 2135, conferring vast regulatory powers on a new Department of Homeland Security. Also in response to 9/11, Congress enacted the Aviation and Transportation Security Act, which is discussed in the Case Study that follows this history. Then, following the financial crisis that began in 2007, Congress enacted the Dodd-Frank Wall Street Reform and Consumer Protection Act of 2010, 124 Stat. 1376–2223. Dodd-Frank imposed additional regulatory controls on the finance industry and created the Consumer Financial Protection Bureau (CFPB), an agency designed to protect the interests of consumers with respect to financial products and services. Finally, Congress enacted, with President Obama's crucial support, the Patient Protection and Affordable Care Act (PPACA) of 2010, 124 Stat. 119–1025. Unlike the Dodd-Frank and Homeland Security legislation, the PPACA was not a response to a particular crisis of the moment. Also unlike those two other laws, the PPACA carved out a sizable role for private industry as part of its regulatory efforts. Although there was debate over the possibility of including a public option or single-payer health insurance, Congress enacted legislation mandating that individuals purchase health insurance from private companies on regulated exchanges. Indeed, without the support of the private insurance industry, the PPACA might never have become law at all.

In 2016, Donald Trump was elected President on an anti-Washington platform. A key Administration official at the time, Steve Bannon, proclaimed early in 2017 that the "deconstruction of the administrative state" was one of Trump's major objectives. Upon taking office, the President appointed agency heads, like Scott Pruitt of the Environmental Protection Agency, who worked to dismantle the administrative state from the inside (see § 3(B)(3) of this chapter). Additionally, the Republican Congress began using the Congressional Review Act in unprecedented ways, overturning more than a dozen Obama-era regulations (see § 3(A)(6) of this chapter). And an increasingly conservative Supreme Court, reinforced by the arrival of two justices appointed by President Trump, has raised new questions about the

---

[11]   See, e.g., Joseph E. Stiglitz, *Capitalist Fools*, Vanity Fair, January 2009 at 52; Robert Kuttner, *The Alarming Parallels Between 1929 and 2007*, (testimony before House Committee on Financial Services, available at The American Prospect, October 2, 2007).

[12]   See Jeanne Sahadi, *Bush's Plan for Social Security*, CNN Money, March 4, 2005, available at http://money.cnn.com/2005/02/02/retirement/stofunion_socsec/.

*administrative state as a threat to liberty and democracy. Some of these changes are addressed by Gillian E. Metzger, *The Supreme Court 2016 Term, Foreword: 1930s Redux: The Administrative State Under Siege*, 131 Harv. L. Rev. 1 (2017).

Partisan debates continue to rage over whether the administrative state is having an intrusive, stultifying, or even unconstitutional impact on the American economy, or instead has been seriously weakened by decades of deregulatory efforts, to the detriment of consumers, the public, and our environment. It remains to be seen if developments such as the three major statutes from the Bush and Obama years augur the beginning of a new regulatory era of agency strength, or are simply a pause in the ongoing deregulatory movement.

A PRELIMINARY TAXONOMY OF FEDERAL AGENCIES

As this brief history illustrates, federal agencies are units of government, created by Congress through statutes and given considerable powers to implement public policy that Congress has set forth in legislation—policy often expressed in general or expansive terms. The chart below presents the fifteen cabinet departments and when they began operating at cabinet-level status, as well as a sample of other important federal agencies.[13] The total number of agencies listed (42) is less than half the number that exist today. See, e.g. listing at end of § 1(C), excerpted from Kirti Datla & Richard Revesz, *Deconstructing Independent Agencies (and Executive Agencies)*, 98 Cornell L. Rev. 769, 825 (2013). Even our abbreviated list conveys a sense of how federal agencies affect so many aspects of everyday life for all of us as individuals and as a nation. Notice too how Congress has created agencies in response to evolving perceptions of national policy priorities. When did Congress first mandate cabinet-level attention on issues of war and peace? On matters of workplace protection? On the need to respond to the energy crisis? On the threat of global terrorism?

Cabinet Departments*

Department of State (1789)	Department of the Treasury (1789)	Department of Defense (1789)†
Department of the Interior (1849)	Department of Justice (1870)	Department of Agriculture (1889)
Department of Commerce (1903)	Department of Labor (1913)	Department of Health and Human Services (1953)+
Department of Housing and Urban Development (1966)	Dept. of Transportation (1967) (Fed. Aviation Admin. located within DOT)	Department of Energy (1977)
Department of Education (1979)	Department of Veterans Affairs (1989)	Department of Homeland Security (2002)

---

[13]   We are indebted for the excellent idea to include such a chart to the work of Lisa Schultz Bressman, Edward Rubin, and Kevin Stack, *The Regulatory State*, 3–4 (2010).

* Dates of initial operation in parentheses

† 1789 War Department, 1798 Navy Department, 1949 Unified Defense Department

+ Began as Department of Health, Education and Welfare

Some Prominent Other Agencies*

Central Intelligence Agency	Commodity Futures Trading Commission	Consumer Product Safety Commission
Environmental Protection Agency	Equal Employment Opportunity Commission	**Export-Import Bank of the United States**
Federal Communications Commission	**Federal Deposit Insurance Corporation**	Federal Election Commission
Federal Maritime Commission	**Federal Reserve System**	**Federal Trade Commission**
General Services Administration	**National Aeronautics and Space Administration**	National Archives and Records Administration
National Labor Relations Board	National Transportation Safety Board	Nuclear Regulatory Commission
Occupational Safety and Health Review Commission	Office of Personnel Management	Pension Benefit Guaranty Corporation
Railroad Retirement Board	**Securities and Exchange Commission**	**Social Security Administration**
Small Business Administration	United States International Trade Commission	**United States Postal Service**

* Agencies in **bold** were established before 1960.

A CASE STUDY: THE FEDERAL AVIATION ADMINISTRATION AND AIRPLANE COCKPIT SECURITY

FAA r Airplane cockpit Security

The Administrator of the Federal Aviation Administration (FAA) has long had authority for aviation safety under laws codified at title 49. Section 44701(a) confers on the FAA authority to "prescribe minimum standards required in the interest of safety * * * for the design, material, construction, quality of work, and performance of aircraft." From the mid-1970s through late 2001, the FAA issued several rules and notices of proposed rulemaking and undertook assessments pursuant to this authority in response to the presence of terrorist acts abroad.

Starting in the 1960s and continuing into the late 1980s, commercial airplanes around the world experienced a series of bombings and also hijackings in which planes were diverted to different locations.[14] The International Civil Aviation Organization (ICAO), a non-government organization under the United Nations comprised of 189 member countries, began considering proposals to incorporate security safeguards into the design of new airplanes. On December 21, 1988, a terrorist placed a bomb on an airplane, causing the plane to explode over Lockerbie, Scotland, killing all 259 people on board and 11 people on the ground. As a result, ICAO intensified its efforts. Within several months, ICAO formed the Incorporation of Security into Aircraft Design study group, with representatives from the airworthiness authorities of the United States, the United Kingdom, France, Germany, Brazil, and Russia, as well as various trade association members. The study group was charged with reviewing the existing proposals and recommending standards for security in airplane design. The study group considered, among other things, the "protection of [the] pilot compartment from penetration by small arms fire or shrapnel."

On March 12, 1997, ICAO adopted new standards with respect to many safety concerns, including protection of pilot compartments from penetration by small arms fire or shrapnel, standards that the member countries subsequently approved. Normally, ICAO standards do not apply directly to the design of an airplane; they are implemented by adoption into the airworthiness codes of ICAO member countries. The 1997 standard sought compliance within three years. Once implemented, airplane certification by a member country implies compliance with the standard. As a signatory, the United States was required to implement ICAO's standards into its aviation regulations and statutes to the extent practicable. However, a signatory may file differences with ICAO if it is unable to implement the ICAO standards in the timeframe adopted, an action the United States took (along with all other signatories of manufacture). The United States did not disagree with the ICAO standards or believe a permanent difference was warranted or required, but the FAA needed time to promulgate rulemaking and implement the ICAO standards into its own airworthiness standards (at Title 14 of the Code of Federal Regulations). Accordingly, the U.S. filed a temporary difference with the ICAO standards while the FAA tasked certain working groups with proposing ways to incorporate the ICAO standards.

In 1991, during the period when the U.S. was working on international standards with ICAO, the FAA chartered the creation of the Aviation Rulemaking Advisory Committee (ARAC), in order to maintain harmonized security standards between the United States and Europe. Composed of 76 member organizations reflecting a range of interests in the aviation community, ARAC provided the FAA with firsthand information regarding proposed rules. On October 27, 1999, the FAA tasked ARAC to propose harmonized regulations incorporating security measures into airplane design, including "Pilot Compartment—Penetration Resistance." 64 Fed. Reg. 57,921–02. The FAA specifically asked ARAC to develop regulations incorporating the ICAO security design provisions that had been adopted on March 12, 1997, and that would have been effective

---

[14] This history is drawn principally from two sources produced after the 9/11 attacks. *Security Related Considerations in the Design and Operation of Transport Category Airplanes*, 72 Fed. Reg. 630–01, 631–33 (proposed Jan. 5, 2007); National Commission on Terrorist Attacks Upon the United States, *The 9/11 Commission Report* 82–85 (2004).

on March 12, 2000. The task was assigned to the Design for Security Harmonization Working Group (DSHWG), which included members from the aviation industry and the governments of Europe, the United States, Brazil, and Canada. ARAC was given until February 1, 2000, to submit the first part of its report and until the end of 2001 to submit the second part. *Id.*

As subsequently described in the 9/11 Commission Report, the FAA's efforts took place in the context of its "sometimes conflicting mandate [from Congress] of regulating the safety and security of U.S. civil aviation while also promoting the aviation industry." National Commission on Terrorist Attacks Upon the United States, *The 9/11 Commission Report* 82 (2004). In the late 1990s, the FAA perceived sabotage as posing a higher safety risk than hijacking, given that no domestic hijacking had occurred in a decade and the commercial aviation system was viewed as more vulnerable to explosives than to weapons such as firearms. *Id.* Further, the air carriers played a major role in the pre-9/11 security system. The Inspector General for the Department of Transportation emphasized the pressures these carriers exerted to control security costs, and to "limit the impact of security requirements on aviation operations, so that the industry could concentrate on its primary mission of moving passengers and aircraft." *Id.* at 85.

It is perhaps not surprising that security efforts on board commercial aircraft were not designed to counter suicide hijackings.

> "The FAA-approved 'Common Strategy' had been elaborated over decades of experience with scores of hijackings, beginning in the 1960s. It taught flight crews that the best way to deal with hijackers was to accommodate their demands, get the plane to land safely, and then let law enforcement or the military handle the situation. * * * The strategy operated on the fundamental assumption that hijackers issue negotiable demands (most often for asylum or the release of prisoners), and that, as one FAA official put it, 'suicide wasn't in the game plan of hijackers. FAA training material provided no guidance for flight crews should violence occur.' " *Id.*

On June 11, 2001, after several airlines reported incidents of flightdeck intrusion by aggressive passengers, the FAA further tasked the DSHWG to propose harmonized regulations to improve the intrusion resistance of the flightdeck. 66 Fed. Reg. 31,273–01. FAA regulations already mandated that the cockpit door remain closed and locked in flight, but this requirement was not always observed or vigorously enforced. Indeed, some interested parties responded skeptically to the proposed rulemaking to install reinforced cockpit doors. A pilots association representative observed that "even if you make a vault out of the door, if they have a noose around my flight attendant's neck, I'm going to open the door." The June 11, 2001 Notice of New Task Assignment indicated completion was due no later than December 31, 2001.

On September 11, 2001, nineteen hijackers gained access to the flightdeck of four commercial airplanes, crashing two of the airplanes into the North and South Towers of the World Trade Center and crashing a third into the Pentagon. The fourth plane crashed outside of Shanksville, Pennsylvania.

Following these terrorist acts, Congress moved to pass legislation. On October 11, 2001, the Senate passed a version of an aviation security bill; on November 1, 2001, the House passed a significantly different bill. After a conference, President Bush signed the Aviation and Transportation Security Act (ATSA) on November 19, 2001. Pub. L. 107–

71, 115 Stat. 597 (codified as amended in scattered sections of 49 U.S.C.). ATSA directed the FAA to take action to improve airplane security both immediately and in the long-term, giving the FAA the authority to carry out the ATSA's directives. As soon as possible, ATSA required that the FAA prohibit unauthorized access to the airplane cockpit, control authorized access to the cockpit, require strengthening of the cockpit door and door locks to ensure that the door cannot be forced open from the passenger cabin, require that flight deck doors remain locked during flight, and prohibit the possession of a key to the cockpit door by anyone not assigned to the cockpit. Section 104 of ATSA directed the FAA to issue final rules, without seeking public comment prior to adoption, normally a requirement for any rulemaking, in order to accomplish the goals of cockpit door reinforcement.

In response to this law, and to President Bush's call for increased aircraft security during a speech at Chicago O'Hare International Airport, the FAA issued a series of Special Federal Aviation Regulations (SFARs) and four final rules without notice. On October 9, 2001, the FAA published the first SFAR, which expedited the immediate modification of cockpit doors in the U.S. as a first phase short-term fix. 66 Fed. Reg. 51,546. The major U.S. airlines voluntarily modified the cockpit doors on 4,000 airplanes within the first 45 days of the SFAR. By January 2002, 98 percent of the airlines had voluntarily installed this fix. By March 1, 2002, the major U.S. airlines completed installation of cockpit door modifications on all U.S. airplanes. *FAA Fact Sheet on Aircraft Security Accomplishments Since Sept. 11*, released September 5, 2002.

On January 15, 2002, as a permanent measure, the FAA published an amendment requiring the flightdeck door to be strengthened to resist forcible intrusion by unauthorized persons or penetration by small arms fire and fragmentation devices. This amendment required compliance by April 9, 2003, for all U.S. operators. 67 Fed. Reg. 2,118. This measure was published without prior notice or prior comment. On June 21, 2002, the FAA published a final rule requiring foreign airlines to install reinforced cockpit doors on aircrafts serving the United States by April 9, 2003, the same deadline as U.S. carriers. This measure also was published without prior notice or prior comment.

In both its January 15, 2002 and June 21, 2002 measures, the FAA noted that federal regulations must undergo several economic analyses. First, and most importantly, agencies must conduct a cost-benefit analysis pursuant to Executive Order 12,866, which directs each federal agency proposing or adopting a regulation to show that the benefits of the intended regulation justify its costs (see Appendix D of the Casebook). With respect to the domestically affected aircraft, the January 15, 2002 rule estimated that the retrofitted cockpit door costs would range between $79.6 million and $112.7 million (the cost of the new doors would range between $12,000 and $17,000 and over 6,600 airplanes were affected). In addition, the FAA estimated that the additional 50 pounds resulting from a heavier door would result in additional fuel requirement costs of $27.5 million over ten years. Therefore, the FAA determined that the total cost was expected to range from a base of $107.1 million to $140.2 million over the ten-year period.

With respect to foreign aircraft affected by the June 21, 2002 rule, the FAA estimated that the retrofitted cockpit door costs would be approximately $32.7 million; the cost of the doors was about $17,000 each and the number of affected aircraft was 1,921. The FAA noted that because the air carriers might have to have their doors installed by the original manufacturer, the cost would increase to about $27,500 per door for narrowbody aircraft and $39,900 for widebody aircraft. Accordingly, the cost to foreign air carriers to purchase and install the compliant doors could be as high as $72.0 million. The FAA also estimated that the additional 50 pounds would result in an additional $11.2 million fuel requirement cost over the next decade. In explaining both rules, the FAA determined that the benefits—to ensure the safety and security of the flying public; to prevent the reoccurrence of an event like September 11, 2001, in terms of averted loss of life and property; and to avoid damage to the economy—justified the costs. Although the FAA could not provide a reasonable quantitative estimate of benefits, the agency noted that the benefit would most likely be in the tens of billions of dollars, clearly justifying any cost associated with the rules.[15]

On September 28, 2001, the President had already announced an FAA federal grant program to help U.S. airlines finance reinforced cockpit doors, and Congress appropriated $100 million to fund the initiatives. The FAA distributed approximately $97 million to air carriers to strengthen their cockpit doors, leaving $3 million to fund other pilot programs aimed at cabin surveillance and alert systems.

Although the January 15, 2002 and June 21, 2002 measures were final rules, the FAA also requested comments, inviting interested parties to submit written data, views, or arguments. While expressing general support for the requirements of the rulemaking, the trade association representing U.S. domestic carriers commented that the agency had significantly underestimated the cost of replacement doors. The association attached a letter indicating that one major domestic airline was spending $49,000 per flight deck door ($39,000 for the door plus $10,000 for installation), not the $17,000 upper bound identified by the FAA on January 15, 2002. The trade association requested that "the rule be modified as necessary" to take account of this issue.

ATSA also established a new agency, the Transportation Security Administration (TSA), to assume responsibility for most civil aviation security functions from the FAA. However, the statute gave FAA immediate authority to change airplane design, and that continues to be an FAA responsibility. 115 Stat. 597, § 104.

In addition to enacting ATSA, Congress addressed the issue of liability in the aftermath of the September 11 attacks. On September 22, 2001, after two hours of debate and less than two days of hearings, both the House and the Senate passed the Air Transportation Safety and System Stabilization Act (ATSSSA), Pub. L. 107–42, 115 Stat. 230 (2001) (codified at 49 U.S.C. § 40101 note). This was an attempt to stabilize the airline industry, which had lost billions of dollars as a result of the attacks and faced even greater losses in litigation that threatened to bankrupt the entire industry.[16] ATSSSA capped "liability for all claims . . . arising from . . . September 11, 2001 against any air carrier" not to exceed "the limits of the liability coverage maintained by the air carrier." Pub. L. No. 107–42, at § 408(a). The Act provided for a federally-funded Victim Compensation Fund (VCF), offering victims a no-fault alternative to tort litigation by compensating "any individual (or relatives of a deceased individual) who was physically

---

[15]   The second means of economic analysis the FAA undertook was pursuant to the Regulatory Flexibility Act of 1980, requiring agencies to analyze the economic impact of regulatory changes on small entities. The FAA determined that both rules would not have a significant impact on a substantial number of small entities. Third, the Trade Agreements Act prohibits agencies from setting standards that create unnecessary obstacles to the foreign commerce of the United States. The FAA determined that both rules would have no effect on trade-sensitive activity. Finally, the Unfunded Mandates Act of 1995 requires agencies to prepare a written assessment of the costs and benefits, and other effects of proposed and final rules, where the rule imposes on state, local, or tribal governments, or on the private sector, a mandate likely to result in a total expenditure of $100 million or more in any one year. The FAA determined that these rules did not impose an unfunded mandate on state, local, or tribal governments, or on the private sector.

[16]   United Airlines, American Airlines, and U.S. Airways subsequently filed for Chapter 11 bankruptcy.

injured or killed as a result of the terrorist-related aircraft crashes of September 11, 2001." *Id.* § 405.

The Attorney General was to administer the VCF, acting through a Special Master charged with promulgating all procedural and substantive rules for the administration of the statute. On November 26, 2001, Attorney General John Ashcroft appointed mediator Kenneth Feinberg as Special Master of the VCF. About 97 percent of those eligible chose to opt for recovery through the VCF, not through the court system. Six billion dollars was distributed to the families of the 2,880 deceased victims and one billion dollars was distributed to 2,680 injury victims. *See* Kenneth Feinberg et al., U.S. Dept. of Justice, *Final Report of the Special Master for the September 11th Victim Compensation Fund of 2001.*

In order to receive compensation from the VCF, victims or their representatives were required to waive all rights to file a civil suit for damages against the aviation industry. For those victims that did not opt in to the VCF, ATSSSA created an exclusive cause of action for all claims "arising out of the hijacking and subsequent crashes" of September 11, 2001, providing for federal jurisdiction in the United States District Court for the Southern District of New York. *Id.* at § 408(b)(3). Further, the United States had not waived its sovereign immunity under the Federal Tort Claims Act, 18 U.S.C. § 2671 et seq., with respect to being sued for damages arising from the attacks.

Some ninety-five of the injured and representatives of those who died plus twenty-one entities that sustained property damage chose to file lawsuits against defendants they claimed were legally responsible to compensate them: the airlines, the airport security companies, the airport operators, the airplane manufacturer, and the operators and owners of the World Trade Center. Early on, the defendants moved to dismiss the claims, and the judge held each of the defendants owed a duty of care to the plaintiffs who sued. *In re September 11 Litig.*, 280 F. Supp. 2d 279, 286–87 (S.D.N.Y. 2003); see also *In re September 11 Litig.*, 600 F. Supp. 2d 549, 550 (S.D.N.Y. 2009). By the end of 2013, all ninety-five personal injury or wrongful death claims and nineteen of the twenty-one property damage claims had settled. See Docket, *In re September 11 Litig.*, No. 21 MC 101 (AKH) (S.D.N.Y); *Cantor Fitzgerald Settles 9/11 Suit Against American Airlines for $135 Million*, N.Y. Times, Dec. 18, 2013, at A1. All property loss claims have now been resolved, and the case has been closed. *In re September 11 Litig.*, 328 F. Supp. 2d 178, 188 (S.D.N.Y. 2018).

As we consider various aspects of agency implementation procedures and agency oversight by all three branches, you should keep this Case Study in mind. Did the agency initiate and proceed with rulemaking in a responsible and diligent fashion prior to the 9/11 attacks?

PROBLEMS ON THE FAA CASE STUDY

Problem 8-1. Assume you are the FAA policymaker responsible for coordinating the agency's anti-hijacking flight deck security measures as of June 10, 2001. In addition to the facts presented in the Case Study, you are aware that there were a handful of hijackings on Europe-originating flights during the 1990s, all of which ended without casualties. You also know that on December 24, 1994, an Air France flight destined for Paris was hijacked at its originating point of Algiers, Algeria by four hijackers, armed with Kalashnikov assault rifles, Uzi submachine guns, pistols, homemade hand grenades, and two 10-stick dynamite packs. The hijackers planned to crash the plane into the Eiffel Tower in Paris. They murdered three passengers before departing Algiers, but when they were forced to land in Marseilles to refuel, French law enforcement stormed the plane, killing all hijackers and freeing the remaining passengers.

What actions (rulemakings, policy statements, studies) would you recommend the agency undertake to strengthen flight deck security, *other than* requesting—as the Case Study shows FAA did at the time—that the Design for Security Harmonization Working Group (DSHWG) propose harmonized regulations? Is your proposed action something the agency is authorized to initiate under 49 U.S.C. § 44701(a)? Assuming there is some action you deem worth taking, with whom would you consult before proposing it: The White House? Relevant congressional committee chairs? Federal law enforcement officials? Foreign governments? The domestic airlines or their trade association? The airline pilots union?

Problem 8-2. It is still June 10, 2001 and the same additional facts as in Problem 8-1 are known to you, but now you are the FAA General Counsel heading an agency task force to coordinate passenger safety for all domestic flights. How foreseeable is the risk of suicide hijackings on U.S. domestic flights in June 2001? Is the risk substantially greater than it was in 1988 before Lockerbie? In 1994 before Air France? How should you determine the foreseeable risk of such hijackings in this setting? Is the idea of foreseeable risk even something the agency should be thinking about or acting on? If your answer is yes, is weighing costs associated with new security measures a relevant consideration? Why or why not?

The data on hijackings establish that almost all attempts involve the use of firearms or explosives. Assume it would cost $300 million for the domestic airlines to install reinforced cockpit doors on all their planes, and would cost $900 million to install and staff metal detectors and x-ray machines for passenger and luggage security screening at every major U.S. airport. Would these costs lead you to prefer one approach to the other? What if the airlines bring you a valid scientific study indicating that the public will take 15 percent fewer airplane trips annually if they are required to go through the metal detector/x-ray machine screening process (they will take buses, trains, or cars, or else not travel as much); would this affect the safety measures you recommend in June 2001?

B.   THE NONDELEGATION DOCTRINE

1.   Federal Nondelegation Doctrine

The nondelegation doctrine posits that the legislature may not delegate its inherent lawmaking powers to agencies without providing specific standards for the bureaucracy to apply in administering the delegation—in the Supreme Court's words, laying down "an intelligible principle" to which administrators must conform. *J.W. Hampton, Jr. & Co. v. United States*, 276 U.S. 394, 409 (1928). The doctrine was highly controversial during the New Deal when it was used by the Supreme Court to strike down major provisions of the National Industrial Recovery Act. See *Panama Refining v. Ryan*, 293 U.S. 388 (1935); *A.L.A. Schechter Poultry Corp. v. United States*, 295 U.S. 495 (1935).

After President Franklin Roosevelt made several new appointments to the Supreme Court and the administrative state became an accepted part of our democracy, the nondelegation doctrine fell into constitutional disuse. In *Yakus v.*

United States, 321 U.S. 414 (1944), the Court upheld a broad delegation of price control authority to the Office of Price Administration during World War II. The only "intelligible principle" in the statute was that prices be "fair and equitable" but the court sustained the delegation. "Only if we could say that there is an absence of standards for the guidance of the Administrator's action, so that it would be impossible in a proper proceeding to ascertain whether the will of Congress has been obeyed, would we be justified in overriding its choice of means for effecting its declared purpose of preventing inflation."

The Economic Stabilization Act of 1970, 84 Stat. 799, codified at 12 U.S.C. § 1904 note, did not even have a "fair and equitable" standard when it authorized the President "to issue such orders and regulations as he may deem appropriate to stabilize prices, rents, wages, and salaries at levels not less than those prevailing on May 25, 1970." Nonetheless, when President Nixon exercised that power to freeze prices and wages in Executive Order 11,615, 36 Fed. Reg. 15,727 (1971), a special three-judge court rejected a nondelegation doctrine challenge. See *Amalgamated Meat Cutters and Butcher Workmen of N. Am. v. Connolly*, 337 F. Supp. 737 (D.D.C. 1971) (three-judge court). Judge Leventhal constructed standards to guide presidential implementation of the Act from (1) its legislative history, which revealed the purposes of the law; (2) prior price control statutes, such as the one upheld in *Yakus;* and (3) judicial power to elaborate on implicit statutory terms, such as a "fairness and equitable" standard, enforceable through judicial review of the executive implementation decisions. In addition, the court found that the agency's ability to act arbitrarily was blunted by a requirement that it promulgate additional standards to guide its actions taken under the statute. "This requirement, inherent in the Rule of Law and implicit in the Act, means that however broad the discretion of the Executive at the outset, the standard once developed limits the latitude of subsequent Executive action." *Id.* at 759. This period was the nadir of the nondelegation doctrine. Cf. *Mistretta v. United States*, 488 U.S. 361 (1989) (Court unanimously rejects nondelegation challenge to Sentencing Commission; majority opinion suggests that doctrine might be limited to "giving narrow constructions to statutory delegations that might otherwise be thought to be unconstitutional").

WHITMAN V. AMERICAN TRUCKING ASSOCIATIONS, INC.

Supreme Court of the United States, 2001.
531 U.S. 457, 121 S.Ct. 903, 149 L.Ed.2d 1.

JUSTICE SCALIA delivered the opinion of the Court.

These cases present the following questions: (1) Whether § 109(b)(1) of the Clean Air Act (CAA) delegates legislative power to the Administrator of the Environmental Protection Agency (EPA) * * *.

[I] Section 109(a) of the CAA, as added, 84 Stat. 1679, and amended, 42 U.S.C. § 7409(a), requires the Administrator of the EPA to promulgate [National Ambient Air Quality Standards] NAAQS for each air pollutant for which "air quality criteria" have been issued under § 108, 42 U.S.C. § 7408. Once a NAAQS has been promulgated, the Administrator must review the standard (and the criteria on which it is based) "at five-year intervals" and make "such revisions . . . as may be appropriate." CAA § 109(d)(1), 42 U.S.C. § 7409(d)(1). These cases arose when, on July 18, 1997, the Administrator revised the NAAQS for particulate matter and ozone. American Trucking Associations, Inc., and its co-respondents * * * challenged the new standards in the Court of Appeals for the District of Columbia Circuit, pursuant to 42 U.S.C. § 7607(b)(1).

The District of Columbia Circuit accepted some of the challenges and rejected others. It agreed with the respondents that § 109(b)(1) delegated legislative power to the Administrator in contravention of the United States Constitution, Art. I, § 1, because it found that the EPA had interpreted the statute to provide no "intelligible principle" to guide the agency's exercise of authority. The court thought, however, that the EPA could perhaps avoid the unconstitutional delegation by adopting a restrictive construction of § 109(b)(1), so instead of declaring the section unconstitutional the court remanded the NAAQS to the agency. * * *

[III] Section 109(b)(1) of the CAA instructs the EPA to set "ambient air quality standards the attainment and maintenance of which in the judgment of the Administrator, based on [the] criteria [documents of § 108] and allowing an adequate margin of safety, are requisite to protect the public health." 42 U.S.C. § 7409(b)(1). The Court of Appeals held that this section as interpreted by the Administrator did not provide an "intelligible principle" to guide the EPA's exercise of authority in setting NAAQS. "[The] EPA," it said, "lack[ed] any determinate criteria for drawing lines. It has failed to state intelligibly how much is too much." The court hence found that the EPA's interpretation (but not the statute itself) violated the nondelegation doctrine. We disagree.

In a delegation challenge, the constitutional question is whether the statute has delegated legislative power to the agency. Article I, § 1, of the Constitution vests "[a]ll legislative Powers herein granted . . . in a Congress of the United States." This text permits no delegation of those powers, and so we repeatedly have said that when Congress confers decisionmaking authority upon agencies Congress must "lay down by legislative act an intelligible principle to which the person or body authorized to [act] is directed to conform." *J.W. Hampton, Jr. & Co. v. United States*, 276 U.S. 394, 409 (1928). We have never suggested that an agency can cure an unlawful delegation of legislative power by adopting in its discretion a limiting construction of the statute. Both *Fahey v. Mallonee*, 332 U.S. 245, 252–253 (1947), and *Lichter v. United States*, 334 U.S. 742, 783 (1948), mention agency regulations in the course of their nondelegation discussions, but *Lichter* did so because a subsequent Congress had incorporated the regulations into a revised version of the statute, *ibid.*, and *Fahey* because the customary practices in the area, implicitly incorporated into the statute, were reflected in the regulations, 332 U.S. at 250. The idea that an agency can cure an unconstitutionally standardless delegation of power by declining to exercise some of that power seems to us internally contradictory. The very choice of which portion of the power to exercise—that is to say, the prescription of the standard that Congress had omitted—would *itself* be an exercise of the forbidden legislative authority. Whether the statute delegates legislative power is a question for the courts, and an agency's voluntary self-denial has no bearing upon the answer.

We agree with the Solicitor General that the text of § 109(b)(1) of the CAA at a minimum requires that "[f]or a discrete set of pollutants and based on published air quality criteria that reflect the latest scientific knowledge, [the] EPA must establish uniform national standards at a level that is requisite to protect public health from the adverse effects of the pollutant in the ambient air." Tr. of Oral Arg. in No. 99–1257, p. 5. Requisite, in turn, "mean[s] sufficient, but not more than necessary." *Id.*, at 7. These limits on the EPA's discretion are strikingly similar to the ones we approved in *Touby v. United States*, 500 U.S. 160 (1991), which permitted the Attorney General to designate a drug as a controlled substance for purposes of criminal drug enforcement if doing so was " 'necessary to avoid an imminent hazard to the public safety.' " *Id.* at 163. They also resemble the Occupational Safety and Health Act of 1970 provision requiring the agency to " 'set the standard which most adequately assures, to the extent feasible, on the basis of the best available evidence, that no employee will suffer any impairment of health' "—which the Court upheld in *Indust. Union Dep't., AFL-CIO v. Am. Petroleum Inst.*, 448 U.S. 607, 646 (1980), and which even then-Justice Rehnquist, who alone in that case thought the statute violated the nondelegation doctrine, see *Id.* at 671 (opinion concurring in judgment), would have upheld if, like the statute here, it did not permit economic costs to be considered. See *Am. Textile Mfrs. Inst., Inc. v. Donovan*, 452 U.S. 490, 545 (1981) (Rehnquist, J., dissenting).

The scope of discretion § 109(b)(1) allows is in fact well within the outer limits of our nondelegation precedents. In the history of the Court we have found the requisite "intelligible principle" lacking in only two statutes, one of which provided literally no guidance for the exercise of discretion, and the other of which conferred authority to regulate the entire economy on the basis of no more precise a standard than stimulating the economy by assuring "fair competition." See *Panama Refining Co. v. Ryan*, 293 U.S. 388 (1935); *A.L.A. Schechter Poultry Corp. v. United States*, 295 U.S. 495 (1935). We have, on the other hand, upheld the validity of § 11(b)(2) of the Public Utility Holding Company Act of 1935, 49 Stat. 821, which gave the Securities and Exchange Commission authority to modify the structure of holding company systems so as to ensure that they are not "unduly or unnecessarily complicate[d]" and do not "unfairly or inequitably distribute voting power among security holders." *Am. Power & Light Co. v. SEC*, 329 U.S. 90, 104 (1946). We have approved the wartime conferral of agency power to fix the prices of commodities at a level that " 'will be generally fair and equitable and will effectuate the [in some respects conflicting] purposes of th[e] Act.' " *Yakus v. United States*, 321 U.S. 414, 420, 423–426 (1944). And we have found an "intelligible principle" in various statutes authorizing regulation in the "public interest." See, e.g., *Nat'l Broad. Co. v. United States*, 319 U.S. 190, 225–226 (1943) (Federal Communications Commission's power to regulate airwaves); *N.Y. Cent. Sec. Corp. v. United States*, 287 U.S. 12, 24–25 (1932) (Interstate Commerce Commission's power to approve railroad consolidations). In short, we have "almost never felt qualified to second-guess Congress regarding the permissible degree of policy judgment that can be left to those executing or applying the law." *Mistretta v. United States*, 488 U.S. 361, 416 (1989) (Scalia, J., dissenting); see *id.* at 373 (majority opinion).

It is true enough that the degree of agency discretion that is acceptable varies according to the scope of the power congressionally conferred. While Congress need not provide any direction to the EPA regarding the manner in which it is to define "country elevators," which are to be exempt from new-stationary-source regulations governing grain elevators, see 42 U.S.C. § 7411(i), it must provide substantial guidance on setting air standards that affect the entire national economy. But even in sweeping regulatory schemes we have never demanded, as the Court of Appeals did here, that statutes provide a "determinate criterion" for saying "how much [of the regulated harm] is too much." In *Touby*, for example, we did not require the statute to decree how "imminent" was too imminent, or how "necessary" was necessary enough, or even—most relevant here—how "hazardous" was too hazardous. Similarly, the statute at issue in *Lichter* authorized agencies to recoup "excess profits" paid under wartime Government contracts, yet we did not insist that Congress specify how much profit was too much. It is therefore not conclusive for delegation purposes that, as respondents argue, ozone and particulate matter are "nonthreshold" pollutants that inflict a continuum of adverse health effects at any airborne concentration greater than zero, and hence require the EPA to make judgments of degree. "[A] certain degree of discretion, and thus of lawmaking, inheres in most executive or judicial action." *Mistretta v. United States, supra*, at 417 (Scalia, J., dissenting) (emphasis deleted); see 488 U.S. at 378–379 (majority opinion). Section 109(b)(1) of the CAA, which to repeat we interpret as requiring the EPA to set air quality standards at the level that is "requisite" that is, not lower or higher than is necessary—to protect the public health with an adequate margin of safety, fits comfortably within the scope of discretion permitted by our precedent.

We therefore reverse the judgment of the Court of Appeals remanding for reinterpretation that would avoid a supposed delegation of legislative power. It will remain for the Court of Appeals—on the remand that we direct for other reasons— to dispose of any other preserved challenge to the NAAQS under the judicial-review provisions contained in 42 U.S.C. § 7607(d)(9).

[The concurring opinion of JUSTICE THOMAS is omitted.]

JUSTICE STEVENS, with whom JUSTICE SOUTER joins, concurring in part and concurring in the judgment.

Section 109(b)(1) delegates to the Administrator of the Environmental Protection Agency (EPA) the authority to promulgate national ambient air quality standards (NAAQS). In Part III of its opinion, the Court convincingly explains why the Court of Appeals erred when it concluded that § 109 effected "an unconstitutional delegation of legislative power." I wholeheartedly endorse the Court's result and endorse its explanation of its reasons, albeit with the following caveat.

The Court has two choices. We could choose to articulate our ultimate disposition of this issue by frankly acknowledging that the power delegated to the EPA is "legislative" but nevertheless conclude that the delegation is constitutional because adequately limited by the terms of the authorizing statute. Alternatively, we could pretend, as the Court does, that the authority delegated to the EPA is somehow not "legislative power." Despite the fact that there is language in our opinions that supports the Court's articulation of our holding, I am persuaded that it would be both wiser and more faithful to what we have actually done in delegation cases to admit that agency rulemaking authority is "legislative power."[2]

The proper characterization of governmental power should generally depend on the nature of the power, not on the identity of the person exercising it. See Black's Law Dictionary 899 (6th ed. 1990) (defining "legislation" as, *inter alia*, "[f]ormulation of rule[s] for the future"); 1 K. Davis & R. Pierce, Administrative Law Treatise § 2.3, p. 37 (3d ed. 1994) ("If legislative power means the power to make rules of conduct that bind everyone based on resolution of major policy issues, scores of agencies exercise legislative power routinely by promulgating what are candidly called 'legislative rules' "). If the NAAQS that the EPA promulgated had been prescribed by Congress, everyone would agree that those rules would be the product of an exercise of "legislative power." The same characterization is appropriate when an agency exercises rulemaking authority pursuant to a permissible delegation from Congress.

My view is not only more faithful to normal English usage, but is also fully consistent with the text of the Constitution. In Article I, the Framers vested "All legislative Powers" in the Congress, Art. I, § 1, just as in Article II they vested the "executive Power" in the President, Art. II, § 1. Those provisions do not purport to limit the authority of either recipient of power to delegate authority to others. See *Bowsher v. Synar*, 478 U.S. 714, 752 (1986) (Stevens, J., concurring in judgment) ("Despite the statement in Article I of the Constitution that 'All legislative powers herein granted shall be vested in a Congress of the United States,' it is far from novel to acknowledge that independent agencies do indeed exercise legislative powers"); *INS v. Chadha*, 462 U.S. 919, 985–986 (1983) (White, J., dissenting) ("[L]egislative power can be exercised by independent agencies and Executive departments . . ."); 1 Davis & Pierce, Administrative Law Treatise § 2.6, at 66 ("The Court was probably mistaken from the outset in interpreting Article I's grant of power to Congress as an implicit limit on Congress' authority to delegate legislative power"). Surely the authority granted to members of the Cabinet and federal law enforcement agents is properly characterized as "Executive" even though not exercised by the President. Cf. *Morrison v. Olson*, 487 U.S. 654, 705–706 (1988) (Scalia, J., dissenting) (arguing that the independent counsel exercised "executive power" unconstrained by the President).

It seems clear that an executive agency's exercise of rulemaking authority pursuant to a valid delegation from Congress is "legislative." As long as the delegation provides a sufficiently intelligible principle, there is nothing inherently unconstitutional about it. Accordingly, while I join Parts I, II, and IV of the Court's opinion, and agree with almost everything said in Part III, I would hold that when Congress enacted § 109, it effected a constitutional delegation of legislative power to the EPA.

---

[2]   See *Mistretta v. United States*, 488 U.S. 361, 372 (1989) ("[O]ur jurisprudence has been driven by a practical understanding that in our increasingly complex society . . . Congress simply cannot do its job absent an ability to delegate power . . ."). See also *Loving v. United States*, 517 U.S. 748, 758 (1996) ("[The nondelegation] principle does not mean . . . that only Congress can make a rule of prospective force"); 1 K. Davis & R. Pierce, *Administrative Law Treatise* § 2.6, at 66 (3d ed. 1994) ("Except for two 1935 cases, the Court has never enforced its frequently announced prohibition on congressional delegation of legislative power").

[The opinion of JUSTICE BREYER, who concurred in part and concurred in the judgment, is omitted.]

NOTES ON THE FEDERAL NONDELEGATION DOCTRINE

1.   *Judicial Manageability.* Justice Scalia reiterates a statement he made twelve years earlier (dissenting in *Mistretta*) that the Court "has almost never felt qualified to second guess Congress" regarding how much policy discretion may be left in the hands of agency officials. Is this prudential consideration related simply to the Court's sense of its own competence? Is the Court perhaps worried, as Cass Sunstein has suggested, that given the vagueness of the "intelligible principle" standard, any delegation the Court invalidates is "likely to suffer from the appearance, and perhaps the reality, of judicial hostility to the particular program at issue"? See Cass Sunstein, *Nondelegation Canons*, 67 U. Chi. L. Rev. 315, 327 (2000). Should the Court's concerns about its own perceived legitimacy justify a virtual abandonment of the nondelegation doctrine?

2.   *Continuing Vitality?* Although no federal statute has been invalidated by the Supreme Court pursuant to the nondelegation doctrine since the 1930s, individual Justices have occasionally invoked the doctrine. See, e.g., *Zemel v. Rusk*, 381 U.S. 1, 20 (1965) (Black, J., dissenting); *Indus. Union Dep't, AFL-CIO v. Am. Petroleum Inst.*, 448 U.S. 607, 685–86 (1980) (Rehnquist, J., dissenting); *American Textile Mfrs. Inst., Inc. v. Donovan*, 452 U.S. 490, 543 (1981) (Rehnquist, J., dissenting). Moreover, some state courts still enforce a nondelegation doctrine (see § 1(B)(2) of this chapter).

Notwithstanding the apparent demise of the nondelegation doctrine after *Schechter Poultry*, some scholars find the doctrine to be a useful concept and argue for its resurrection. Political scientist Theodore Lowi, in *The End of Liberalism: The Second Republic of the United States* (2d ed. 1979), argues that legislatures tend to avoid hard political choices by delegating virtually blanket authority to bureaucrats. Public choice theory, discussed in Chapter 1, § 1, reinforces Lowi's point. Public choice theorists posit that legislators' chief motivation is to achieve reelection. One effective method for achieving reelection is for legislators to spend most of their time doing things which their constituents find uncontroversial, such as casework helping constituents wind their way through the bureaucracy and pork barrel projects benefitting their districts. As to substantive legislation, the best strategy is usually to avoid positions that offend important electoral groups in the legislator's district. This can be done through ducking the issue entirely or, if that is impossible, delegating resolution of the most divisive issues to agencies. With Lowi, one can argue from a public choice perspective that the temptation to pass the substantive buck to agencies is as tempting as it is undemocratic (bureaucrats rather than legislators are making important policy choices) and counterproductive (the choices may be biased if the agency is captured and timid if the agency is not). See David Schoenbrod, *Power Without Responsibility: How Congress Abuses the People Through Delegation* (1993).

Jerry Mashaw disputes the pessimistic public choice perspective on the nondelegation doctrine, and he argues instead that broad delegations to administrative agencies can sometimes ensure better policymaking. *Greed, Chaos, and Governance: Using Public Choice to Improve Public Law* (1997). He demonstrates that broad delegations may actually reduce rent-seeking by interest groups because they inhibit vote-trading and deal-making. Once power has been delegated to an agency, lawmakers find it more difficult to offer bargains in that issue arena, and administrators cannot make tradeoffs on issues outside their jurisdiction. In fact, some laws that result from the most questionable interest group activity are often very specifically worded to guarantee that bargainers get the deals they struck. Mashaw also argues that voters can often hold members of Congress accountable for broad delegations more easily than they can learn of specific deals found in the details of omnibus legislation. "No one has been able to demonstrate any systematic relationship between improving accountability, or enhancing the public welfare, or respecting the rule of law, and the specificity of legislation." Mashaw goes on to make the affirmative case for broad delegations, arguing that they take advantage of administrative expertise and flexibility. Furthermore, agencies may be more responsive to public desires, because they can often act more quickly than Congress can enact legislation, and they benefit from the President's accountability to a national electorate.[17]

In recent years, the nondelegation doctrine has also enjoyed an indirect revival at the Supreme Court level. As one of us noted in 1992, although "the Court has not invalidated a statute on [nondelegation] grounds since the 1930s," the Court now "refers to the nondelegation idea as a canon of statutory interpretation rather than as an enforceable constitutional doctrine."[18] When agencies aggressively assert a broad jurisdiction not supported by a congressional authorization, clearly expressed in the statute, the Court ought to overrule the agency and insist on a more targeted statutory authorization.[19] This thesis is supported by the Court's decision in *Whitman*, which rejected a constitutional nondelegation challenge to the Clean Air Act but construed the Act narrowly in light of the apparent limiting principle, and in *MCI v. AT&T* (Chapter 9), which narrowly construed a telecommunications law on the ground that the broad revisionary authority claimed by the FCC had to be more clearly stated on the face of the statute for the Court to give it effect. See also *FDA v. Brown & Williamson Tobacco Co.* (Chapter 5, § 3(B)(3)). If a court is faced with an extremely broad delegation that might implicate constitutional concerns, it uses the canon to adopt a narrow interpretation that would restrain agency discretion. This approach is similar to the one used in *Yakus* or *Amalgamated Meat Cutters*, discussed above, where the courts poured meaning into general statutory language to find intelligible guidelines and procedural requirements to limit agency discretion.

On the other hand, the Court in *Whitman* rejected the D.C. Circuit's reasoning that an agency can avoid an unlawful delegation by adopting in its discretion a limiting construction of the statute. What is the justification for allowing *courts*, but not *agencies*, to invoke this form of the avoidance canon? From a pragmatic standpoint, is it that the Court trusts the judiciary to constrain the powers exercised by an agency but does not

---

[17]   See also Edward Rubin, *Law and Legislation in the Administrative State*, 89 Colum. L. Rev. 369 (1989) (offering a pragmatic justification for broad delegations); David Spence & Frank Cross, *A Public Choice Case for the Administrative State*, 89 Geo. L.J. 97 (2000) (using public choice theory to defend broad delegations). See generally *Symposium: The Phoenix Rises Again: The Nondelegation Doctrine from Constitutional and Policy Perspectives*, 20 Cardozo L. Rev. 731–1018 (1999) (providing various scholarly perspectives on the nondelegation doctrine).

[18]   William Eskridge Jr. & Philip Frickey, *Quasi-Constitutional Law: Clear Statement Rules as Constitutional Lawmaking*, 45 Vand. L. Rev. 593, 607 (1992). See also Lisa Schultz Bressman, *Schechter Poultry at the Millennium: A Delegation Doctrine for the Administrative State*, 109 Yale L.J. 1399 (2000) (making a similar argument that the doctrine survives in the judicial requirement that an agency rule include standards limiting its own discretion). For support in the cases, see, e.g., *Mistretta*, 488 U.S. at 373 n.7; *Indust. Union Dep't, AFL-CIO v. Am Petroleum Inst.*, 448 U.S. 607 (1980).

[19]   See William Eskridge Jr. & John Ferejohn, *The Article I, Section 7 Game*, 80 Geo. L.J. 523, 561–62 (1992).

trust agencies to narrow their own powers? Alternatively, from an institutional perspective, perhaps courts are authorized under Article III to help Congress act constitutionally but agencies—as subordinate extensions of Congress—lack this authority?

3.   *Nondelegation and the FAA Case Study.* Review the language of 49 U.S.C. § 44701(a), conferring certain safety-related authority on the FAA. Also consider section 104(a) of the Aviation and Transportation Security Act of 2001 (115 Stat. 597), which directs the FAA Administrator to strengthen flight deck doors and locks, and "take such other action, including modification of safety and security procedures and flight deck redesign, as may be necessary to ensure the safety and security of the aircraft."

El Al Israel Airlines, which has long been a prime target for terrorists, requires that all cockpits have locked double doors to prevent access by unauthorized persons. Each door has a separate access code, and the second door can be opened only after the first has been closed and the person seeking entry has been identified by the captain or first officer. In addition, undercover agents carrying concealed firearms sit among the passengers on every international El Al flight. Would one or both of the two statutory provisions cited above authorize the FAA to require double doors with coded access on every U.S. passenger plane? To direct that federal sky marshals with concealed firearms travel on all international flights to and from the U.S.?

A NEW ERA FOR THE NONDELEGATION DOCTRINE?

The decision in *Whitman* suggested that the Court had little interest in using the nondelegation doctrine to invalidate federal laws. But the arrival of Justices Gorsuch and Kavanaugh may lead to the doctrine's resurrection. Is the following case the first step in that direction?

Gundy v. United States

139 S.Ct. 2116 (2019).

In 2006, Congress passed the Sex Offender Registration and Notification Act, 34 U.S.C. § 20901 et seq. (SORNA), creating a national registration system for sex offenders. SORNA provides that offenders convicted after enactment must register before completing their prison sentence or (if not sentenced to prison) within three days after being sentenced. But the statute is less clear on its treatment of offenders convicted prior to enactment. Section 20913(d) provides that "[t]he Attorney General shall have the authority to specify the applicability of the requirements of this subchapter to sex offenders convicted before the enactment of this chapter." Herman Gundy pleaded guilty to sexual assault of a minor prior to SORNA's enactment. After serving his time in prison, Gundy was arrested for failing to register under SORNA. He appealed his conviction, arguing that § 20913(d) was an unconstitutional delegation of power from Congress to the Attorney General.

Writing for a plurality, **Justice Kagan** (joined by **Justices Ginsburg**, **Breyer**, and **Sotomayor**) found the case straightforward, inasmuch as the issue had been largely settled by the Court in *Reynolds v. United States*, 565 U.S. 432 (2012). In *Reynolds*, the Court interpreted § 20913(d) as obligating pre-SORNA sex offenders to register but given various practical difficulties leading to implementation delays, registration should occur as soon as the Attorney General determined they needed to register. The Court made clear that while the Attorney General had flexibility as to timing, his authority was limited. Because *Reynolds* was apparently not sufficiently detailed in this regard, Justice Kagan analyzed SORNA's purpose, definition of "sex offender," and legislative history to reach what she believed was the "intelligible principle" Congress had bestowed on the Attorney General in § 20913(d): to apply registration requirements to pre-SORNA offenders as soon as he thought it feasible to do so. Justice Kagan concluded that "[s]ection 20913(d)'s delegation falls well within permissible bounds" of the intelligible principle requirement when the section's text is considered alongside its context, purpose, and history. In her view, "if SORNA's delegation is unconstitutional, then most of Government is unconstitutional—dependent as Congress is on the need to give discretion to executive officials to implement its programs."

In a lengthy dissent, **Justice Gorsuch** (joined by **Chief Justice Roberts** and **Justice Thomas**) painted a very different picture. Justice Gorsuch did more than take issue with the delegation of authority under § 20913(d); he attacked the Court's "intelligible principle" jurisprudence. Gorsuch charted the history of the nondelegation doctrine, beginning with the Founding Fathers' understanding of the separation of powers, moving through the doctrine's use in 19th and early 20th century caselaw, followed by the doctrine's steep decline, simultaneous with the rise of a "mutated version" of the intelligible principle doctrine. This history recognized Congress's ability and need to delegate some of its lawmaking duties. However, the intelligible principle doctrine used by the Court today "has no basis in the original meaning of the Constitution, in history, or even in the [1928 *J.W. Hampton*] decision from which it was plucked." Instead, the Court should return to the three original principles through which Congress is able to delegate authority. First, Congress may allow another branch to "fill up the details" of legislation so long as Congress makes the policy decisions when regulating private conduct. Second, Congress may prescribe rules governing private conduct that are applicable based on executive fact-finding. Third, Congress may assign the other branches certain non-legislative responsibilities. These three areas are rooted both in the Constitution and the history of the nondelegation doctrine.

Turning to SORNA's delegation of authority, Justice Gorsuch did not regard § 20913(d) as an instance of Congress permitting the Attorney General to fill in the gaps. Instead, Congress "gave the Attorney General unfettered discretion to decide which requirements to impose on which pre-Act offenders." The Attorney General, not Congress, will decide whether 500,000 pre-SORNA offenders will be criminally liable for failing to register. This, Justice Gorsuch asserted, is exactly what the Framers feared. "It would be easy enough to let this case go. After all, sex offenders are one of the most disfavored groups in our society. But the rule that prevents Congress from giving the executive *carte blanche* to write laws for sex offenders is the same rule that protects everyone else. Nor is it hard to imagine how the power at issue in this case—the power of a prosecutor to require a group to register with the government on pain of weighty criminal penalties—could be abused in other settings. To allow the nation's chief law enforcement officer to write the criminal laws he is charged with enforcing * * * would be to mark the end of any meaningful enforcement of our separation of powers and invite the tyranny of the majority that follows when lawmaking and law enforcement responsibilities are united in the same hands."

In a one-paragraph opinion concurring in the judgment, **Justice Alito** noted the unbroken string of decisions since 1935 in which the Court "has upheld provisions that authorized agencies to adopt important rules pursuant to extraordinarily capacious standards." While voting to affirm the judgment based on the Court's longstanding approach, Justice Alito added that "[i]f a majority of this Court were willing to reconsider the approach taken for the past 84 years, I would support that effort."

Gundy was argued on October 2, 2018, one week before Justice Kavanaugh began his tenure on the Supreme Court. If the lines are truly drawn, Justice Kavanaugh may have the deciding vote on whether to revitalize the nondelegation doctrine.

Assessing the dissent. Are Justice Gorsuch's concerns persuasive with respect to abusive prosecutorial powers delegated under SORNA? Justice Kagan in her plurality points to Congress's clear directive for registration to occur, to the rule promulgated within seven months of enactment that SORNA apply immediately to pre-Act offenders, and to the fact that no Attorney General has sought to use § 20913(d) in the expansive ways asserted by the dissent. Is that a convincing rebuttal? What about Justice Gorsuch's broader attack on the doctrine? In his dissent, he discusses other ways the Court has policed improper Congressional delegation during the "intelligible principle" years, including the major questions doctrine (discussed in *King v. Burwell,* see ch.9, § 2(B)) and striking down vague laws. Should these options be enough to alleviate Gorsuch's concerns?

Assuming his concerns remain valid, are Justice Gorsuch's three principles for delegable legislative authority a sound replacement for the intelligible principle doctrine? Would these three broad categories change how Congress currently delegates authority?

2.   The Nondelegation Doctrine and the States

While the nondelegation doctrine has been essentially dormant at the federal level, it is alive and well in a number of states. The following decision from the New York Court of Appeals illustrates this heightened receptivity to the doctrine.

Boreali v. Axelrod

71 N.Y.2d 1, 517 N.E. 2d 1350 (1987).

In 1987, the New York state Public Health Council (PHC) promulgated regulations banning smoking in a wide variety of indoor areas open to the public, such as schools, hospitals, auditoriums, banks, and stores. Several affected businesses challenged the regulations, which also required nonsmoking sections in restaurants with seating available to 50 or more customers. The regulations permitted exemptions for certain businesses (like bars and small restaurants) as well as waivers for businesses based on a showing of financial hardship.

Writing for the majority, **Judge Titone** raised two questions: (1) whether the legislature's delegated authority to PHC was valid; and if so, (2) whether the PHC exceeded the scope of its delegated authority? To answer the first question, Judge Titone looked to Section 225(5)(a) of the New York Public Health Law in which the state legislation authorized the PHC to "deal with any matters affecting the * * * public health." While acknowledging that this was a broad delegation of power, Judge Titone found the legislature's grant of authority to be within the confines of permissible delegation to the administrative agency.

Judge Titone then turned to whether the PHC had exceeded the scope of its delegated authority, by considering whether the regulations were administrative rule-making as opposed to legislative policy-making. Policy-making should be left to elected representatives who can be held accountable for their decisions. Judge Titone relied on four "coalescing circumstances" to decide that "the difficult-to-define line between administrative rule-making and legislative policy-making has been transgressed."

First, the court considered whether the PHC in promulgating the regulations considered factors not related to the specific purpose of the regulation. Judge Titone noted that carving out exemptions and waivers has "no foundation in considerations of public health. Rather, they demonstrate the agency's own efforts to weigh the goal of promoting health against its social costs and to reach a suitable compromise." This particular cost-benefit analysis was not authorized by the PHC's statutory authority and was an inherently legislative concern. "Thus, to the extent that the agency has built a regulatory scheme on its own conclusions about the appropriate balance of trade-offs between health and cost to particular industries in the private sector, it was 'acting solely on [its] own ideas of sound public policy' and was therefore operating outside of its proper sphere of authority."

Second, Judge Titone determined that the antismoking regulations "did not merely fill in the details of broad legislation describing the over-all policies to be implemented. Instead, the PHC wrote on a clean slate, creating its own comprehensive set of rules without benefit of legislative guidance." Third, Judge Titone considered the history of the legislature's failed attempts to pass broad smoking prohibitions. When there is evidence of legislative inaction (and more specifically, trying and failing to reach agreement), the PHC is not permitted to "take it upon itself to fill the vacuum and impose a solution of its own." Instead, it is the elected representatives who should be deciding how to resolve difficult social problems. Fourth and finally, the court considered whether the antismoking regulations required special expertise or technical competency to develop. Judge Titone opined that although the effects of smoking are a health issue, the regulation simply determined which locales smoking should be prohibited in, and thus did not require any technical or medical knowledge.

Thus, Judge Titone concluded that while Public Health Law § 225(5)(a) was a valid delegation of regulatory authority, the four circumstances, taken together, "paint a portrait of an agency that has improperly assumed for itself 'the open-ended discretion to choose ends', which characterizes the elected Legislature's role in our system of government."

NOTES ON BOREALI

1. It is possible to view the four-factor test in *Boreali* as being "*Whitman* with bite." *Whitman* only requires the authorizing statute to have "an intelligible principle" to which the agency must conform. By contrast, *Boreali* expects that even if the authorizing statute is broad, an agency should not act "solely on its own ideas of sound public policy" and especially should not do so in the face of the legislature's failed attempts to address the difficult social problem. Does the *Boreali* test adequately address concerns that expert agencies are necessary so that the legislature is not forced to address or revisit specific aspects of its statutory mandate? Does *Boreali* successfully strike the balance between separation of powers/accountability concerns and the practical necessity of having agencies?

2. Consider two subsequent cases applying *Boreali*. In *New York Statewide Coalition of Hispanic Chambers of Commerce v. the New York City Department of Health and Mental Hygiene*, 23 N.Y.3d 681, 16 N.E.3d 538 (2014), the Court of Appeals reviewed the New York City Board of Health's (BOH) attempt to regulate serving sizes of sugary

beverages in restaurants and movie theaters (but not convenience stores or supermarkets). Inaccurately deemed "the soda ban," these regulations became the center of a media storm, fueled by beverage industry claims that the portion cap was an attack on consumer freedom. In reviewing the regulations, the Court of Appeals found that the focus of any *Boreali* analysis "must be on whether the challenged regulation attempts to resolve difficult social problems in this manner. That task, policy-making, is reserved to the legislative branch." After analyzing the first three *Boreali* factors, the Court of Appeals invalidated the portion cap regulations as usurping the legislature's policymaking role. The following year, in *Greater New York Taxi Assn. v. New York City Taxi and Limousine Commission*, 25 N.Y.3d 600, 36 N.E.3d 632 (2015), the Court of Appeals accepted a legislative delegation. The Taxi and Limousine Commission (TLC) had promulgated a regulation to identify a Taxi of Tomorrow that would create uniformity and modernize its taxi fleet. The regulation was challenged on the grounds that the TLC had intruded on the City Council's legislative domain by requiring use of a particular make and model of taxi. Reviewing the regulation based on the *Boreali* factors, the court noted that "these factors are not mandatory, need not be weighed evenly, and are essentially guidelines for conducting an analysis of an agency's exercise of power." Citing to its previous decisions on smoking and sugary beverages, the court focused on "whether the challenged regulation attempted to resolve difficult social problems concerning matters of personal autonomy by interfering with commonplace daily activities preferred by large numbers of people" and concluded that the Taxi of Tomorrow rules "do not involve difficult social problems of any nature." Do these decisions applying *Boreali*'s four factors yield a coherent approach to the nondelegation doctrine? Is the New York approach preferable to the Supreme Court's virtual abandonment of the doctrine? Why or why not?

3.   Some public health officials have argued that *Boreali* and *Statewide Coalition* prohibit agencies from regulating any issue that is considered controversial. If an issue such as smoking in public facilities, which has serious public health implications and also involves "matters of personal autonomy," is politically difficult and/or controversial, must it be resolved only by elected legislators? What about regulations that require young children in day care centers or preschools to be vaccinated against influenza or measles? Vaccination is politically controversial; is this a workable standard? Are there fields such as public health, where agency expertise should outweigh concerns about individual autonomy or institutional accountability? *See* Thomas G. Merrill, Wilfredo Lopez, Sarah B. Perl, Mary T. Bassett, *The Judicial Threat to Public Health Innovation—The Sword of* Boreali, 378 N. Engl. J. Med. 499 (2018).

4.   New York is not the only state where courts have used nondelegation doctrine to restrict health departments and also zoning boards. See, for example *T.A.B.E. v. Toledo-Lucas County Board of Health*, 773 N.E.2d 536 (Ohio 2002). In *T.A.B.E.*, the Ohio Supreme Court held that the relevant state statute did not delegate to a local board of health the authority to prohibit smoking in indoor public places. See also *Kosalka v. Town of Georgetown*, 752 A.2d 183 (Me. 2000) (invalidating local zoning determination). On the other hand, the Massachusetts Supreme Judicial Court held that a local board of health regulation imposing an absolute ban on smoking in all food service establishments, lounges, and bars did not exceed the authority granted under a state statute authorizing local boards of health to make reasonable health regulations. *Tri-Nel Management, Inc. v. Board of Health of Barnstable*, 741 N.E.2d 37 (Mass. 2001). Nestor Davidson suggests that the nondelegation doctrine may be more alive at the local level because local boards

are more influenced by possibilities of private capture or volunteer activism, thereby "rais[ng] judicial anxiety about authority given to local residents." But Davidson cautions that "nondelegation should reflect the advantages as well as the risks that public involvement, knowledge, and accountability bring to local agencies." Nestor M. Davidson, *Localist Administrative Law*, 126 Yale L. J. 564, 622–24 (2017). How would you assess these advantages and risks? Do they come out differently with respect to health factors than zoning considerations?

C. APPOINTMENT AND REMOVAL OF AGENCY OFFICIALS

In order to understand the constitutional basis for administrative agencies, it is worth reviewing the language of Article II, section 2, found in Appendix A of the Casebook. Several references indicate that the Framers anticipated the national government would need departments or agencies in order to function. The President is authorized to require written opinions from "*the principal Officer in each of the executive Departments*"; he is further authorized to appoint "Ambassadors, other public Ministers and Consuls, Judges of the supreme Court, and *all other [impliedly inferior] Officers* of the United States, whose Appointments are not herein otherwise provided for"; finally, Congress is authorized to "vest the Appointment *of such inferior Officers* in the President alone, in the Courts of Law, or *in the Heads of Departments.*" (emphases added). The Constitution does not elaborate further as to the structure or organization of departments, or the distinction between principal and inferior officers within those departments. The Framers evidently decided to leave determinations about how agencies would be created, what powers they would exercise, and what procedures they would follow, to the new national government.

As for what qualifies as an "agency," Congress has developed more than one statutory definition. In the Paperwork Reduction Act of 1980, which imposed various procedural requirements on agencies seeking to collect information from the public, the term 'agency' means:

> "any executive department, military department, Government corporation, Government controlled corporation, or other establishment in the executive branch of the Government (including the Executive Office of the President), or any independent regulatory agency,"

but excluding two specifically named government entities and also excluding governments of the District of Columbia and U.S. territories as well as facilities that are government-owned and contractor-operated. 44 U.S.C. § 3502(1). Compare this definition with an earlier one from the APA, enacted in 1946 and set forth in Appendix C, 5 U.S.C. § 551(1). Are there any important differences? Is the President an agency under the APA? Is the military treated identically under the two statutes?

The Paperwork Reduction Act also defines the term "independent regulatory agency" as encompassing 19 specific agencies plus "any other similar agency designated by statute as a Federal independent regulatory agency or commission." 44 U.S.C. § 3502(5). If an independent regulatory agency is not within the executive branch, where precisely does it reside? Does it occupy a different constitutional status from executive branch agencies? Consider these questions as you read the next two cases.

MYERS V. UNITED STATES

Supreme Court of the United States 1926.
272 U.S. 52, 47 S.Ct. 21, 71 L.Ed. 160.

MR. CHIEF JUSTICE TAFT delivered the opinion of the Court.

This case presents the question whether under the Constitution the President has the exclusive power of removing executive officers of the United States whom he has appointed by and with the advice and consent of the Senate.

[In 1917, Myers was appointed by President Wilson, with the advice and consent of the Senate, to be a postmaster of the first class in Portland, Oregon, for a term of four years. On January 20, 1920, Myers' resignation was demanded. He refused the demand, and two weeks later he was removed from office by order of the Postmaster General, acting at the direction of the President. Myers protested against his removal and continued to do so until the end of his term. On April 21, 1921, he brought suit in the Court of Claims for his salary from the date of his removal.]

By the sixth section of the Act of Congress of July 12, 1876, 19 Stat. 80, 81, c. 179 (Comp. St. § 7190), under which Myers was appointed with the advice and consent of the Senate as a first-class postmaster, it is provided that: "Postmasters of the first, second, and third classes shall be appointed and may be removed by the President by and with the advice and consent of the Senate, and shall hold their offices for four years unless sooner removed or suspended according to law."

The Senate did not consent to the President's removal of Myers during his term. If this statute in its requirement that his term should be four years unless sooner removed by the President by and with the consent of the Senate is valid, the appellant, Myers' administratrix, is entitled to recover his unpaid salary for his full term. * * * The government maintains that the requirement is invalid, for the reason that under article 2 of the Constitution the President's power of removal of executive officers appointed by him with the advice and consent of the Senate is full and complete without consent of the Senate. If this view is sound, the removal of Myers by the President without the Senate's consent was legal. * * *

The question where the power of removal of executive officers appointed by the President by and with the advice and consent of the Senate was vested, was presented early in the first session of the First Congress. There is no express provision respecting removals in the Constitution, except as section 4 of article 2, above quoted, provides for removal from office by impeachment. The subject was not discussed in the Constitutional Convention. Under the Articles of Confederation, Congress was given the power of appointing certain executive officers of the Confederation, and during the Revolution and while the articles were given effect, Congress exercised the power of removal.

[The Court reviewed the Constitutional Convention's consideration of the shape and scope of executive power, and the First Congress's establishment of a

Department of Foreign Affairs whose Secretary was to be appointed by the President with the advice and consent of the Senate, and removable by the President.]

The debates in the Constitutional Convention indicated an intention to create a strong executive, and after a controversial discussion the executive power of the government was vested in one person and many of his important functions were specified so as to avoid the humiliating weakness of the Congress during the Revolution and under the Articles of Confederation. Mr. Madison and his associates in the discussion in the House dwelt at length upon the necessity there was for construing article 2 to give the President the sole power of removal in his responsibility for the conduct of the executive branch, and enforced this by emphasizing his duty expressly declared in the third section of the article to "take care that the laws be faithfully executed."

The vesting of the executive power in the President was essentially a grant of the power to execute the laws. But the President alone and unaided could not execute the laws. He must execute them by the assistance of subordinates. This view has since been repeatedly affirmed by this court. As he is charged specifically to take care that they be faithfully executed, the reasonable implication, even in the absence of express words, was that as part of his executive power he should select those who were to act for him under his direction in the execution of the laws. The further implication must be, in the absence of any express limitation respecting removals, that as his selection of administrative officers is essential to the execution of the laws by him, so must be his power of removing those for whom he cannot continue to be responsible. It was urged that the natural meaning of the term "executive power" granted the President included the appointment and removal of executive subordinates. If such appointments and removals were not an exercise of the executive power, what were they? They certainly were not the exercise of legislative or judicial power in government as usually understood. * * *

The power to prevent the removal of an officer who has served under the President is different from the authority to consent to or reject his appointment. When a nomination is made, it may be presumed that the Senate is, or may become, as well advised as to the fitness of the nominee as the President, but in the nature of things the defects in ability or intelligence or loyalty in the administration of the laws of one who has served as an officer under the President are facts as to which the President, or his trusted subordinates, must be better informed than the Senate, and the power to remove him may therefor be regarded as confined for very sound and practical reasons, to the governmental authority which has administrative control. The power of removal is incident to the power of appointment, not to the power of advising and consenting to appointment, and when the grant of the executive power is enforced by the express mandate to take care that the laws be faithfully executed, it emphasizes the necessity for including within the executive power as conferred the exclusive power of removal.* * *

The constitutional construction that excludes Congress from legislative power to provide for the removal of superior officers finds support in the second section of article 2. By it the appointment of all officers, whether superior or inferior, by the President is declared to be subject to the advice and consent of the Senate. In the absence of any specific provision to the contrary, the power of appointment to executive office carries with it, as a necessary incident, the power of removal. Whether the Senate must concur in the removal is aside from the point we now are considering. That point is that by the specific constitutional provision for appointment of executive officers with its necessary incident of removal, the power of appointment and removal is clearly provided for by the Constitution, and the legislative power of Congress in respect to both is excluded save by the specific exception as to inferior offices in the clause that follows. This is "but the Congress may by law vest the appointment of such inferior officers, as they think proper, in the President alone, in the Courts of Law, or in the Heads of Departments." * * *

It is reasonable to suppose also that had it been intended to give to Congress power to regulate or control removals in the manner suggested, it would have been included among the specifically enumerated legislative powers in article 1, or in the specified limitations on the executive power in article 2. The difference between the grant of legislative power under article 1 to Congress which is limited to powers therein enumerated, and the more general grant of the executive power to the President under article 2 is significant. The fact that the executive power is given in general terms strengthened by specific terms where emphasis is appropriate, and limited by direct expressions where limitation is needed, and that no express limit is placed on the power of removal by the executive is a convincing indication that none was intended. * * *

Mr. Madison and his associates pointed out with great force the unreasonable character of the view that the convention intended, without express provision, to give to Congress or the Senate, in case of political or other differences, the means of thwarting the executive in the exercise of his great powers and in the bearing of his great responsibility by fastening upon him, as subordinate executive officers, men who by their inefficient service under him, by their lack of loyalty to the service, or by their different views of policy might make his taking care that the laws be faithfully executed most difficult or impossible. As Mr. Madison said in the debate in the First Congress: "Vest this power in the Senate jointly with the President, and you abolish at once the great principle of unity and responsibility in the executive department, which was intended for the security of liberty and the public good. If the President should possess alone the power of removal from office, those who are employed in the execution of the law will be in their proper situation, and the chain of dependence will be preserved: the lowest officers, the middle grade, and the highest will depend, as they ought, on the President, and the President on the community." * * *

Made responsible under the Constitution for the effective enforcement of the law, the President needs as an indispensable aid to meet it the disciplinary influence upon those who act under him of a reserve power of removal. But it is contended that executive officers appointed by the President with the consent of the Senate are bound by the statutory law, and are not his servants to do his will, and that his obligation to care for the faithful execution of the laws does not authorize him to treat them as such. The degree of guidance in the discharge of their duties that the President may exercise over executive officers varies with the character of their service as prescribed in the law under which they act. The highest and most important duties which his subordinates perform are those in which they act for him. In such cases they are exercising not their own but his discretion. This field is a very large one. It is sometimes described as political. Each head of a department is and must be the President's alter ego in the matters of that department where the President is required by law to exercise authority. * * *

The ordinary duties of officers prescribed by statute come under the general administrative control of the President by virtue of the general grant to him of the executive power, and he may properly supervise and guide their construction of the statutes under which they act in order to secure that unitary and uniform execution of the laws which article 2 of the Constitution evidently contemplated in vesting general executive power in the President alone. Laws are often passed with specific provision for adoption of regulations by a department or bureau head to make the law workable and effective. The ability and judgment manifested by the official thus empowered, as well as his energy and stimulation of his subordinates, are subjects which the President must consider and supervise in his administrative control. Finding such officers to be negligent and inefficient, the President should have the power to remove them. Of course there may be duties so peculiarly and specifically committed to the discretion of a particular officer as to raise a question whether the President may overrule or revise the officer's interpretation of his statutory duty in a particular instance. Then there may be duties of a quasi-judicial character imposed on executive officers and members of executive tribunals whose decisions after hearing affect interests of individuals, the discharge of which the President cannot in a particular case properly influence or control. But even in such a case he may consider the decision after its rendition as a reason for removing the officer, on the ground that the discretion regularly entrusted to that officer by statute has not been on the whole intelligently or wisely exercised. Otherwise he does not discharge his own constitutional duty of seeing that the laws be faithfully executed.

We have devoted much space to this discussion and decision of the question of the presidential power of removal in the First Congress, not because a congressional conclusion on the constitutional issue is conclusive, but first because of our agreement with the reasons upon which it was avowedly based, second because this was the decision of the First Congress on a question of primary importance in the organization of the government made within two years after the Constitutional Convention and within a much shorter time after its ratification, and third because that Congress numbered among its leaders those who had been members of the convention. * * *

[The Court reviewed in detail legislation enacted through the Civil War and concluded that Congress had consistently supported its initial understanding as to the President's power of removal. The Court then recounted how Congress's position changed when the 1867 Tenure of Office Act, enacted over President Johnson's veto, specified that executive officers appointed with the advice and consent of the Senate could only be removed with the Senate's concurrence. The Court added that in the nearly sixty years since the Tenure of Office Act, several presidents had stated that Congress lacked constitutional authority to limit their removal powers, and the Court had not resolved the issue. Chief Justice Taft concluded that instead of relying on the actions of a post-Civil War, intensely politicized Congress, the Court should follow the construction of the Constitution agreed upon by the first Congress, that the President has plenary power to remove executive officials.]

* * *

For the reasons given, we must therefore hold that the provision of the law of 1876 by which the unrestricted power of removal of first-class postmasters is denied to the President is in violation of the Constitution and invalid.

[The dissenting opinions of MR. JUSTICE MCREYNOLDS and MR. JUSTICE HOLMES are omitted.]

MR. JUSTICE BRANDEIS, dissenting.

* * * The contention that Congress is powerless to make consent of the Senate a condition of removal by the President from an executive office rests mainly upon the clause in section 1 of article 2 which declares that "the executive Power shall be vested in a President." The argument is that appointment and removal of officials are executive prerogatives; that the grant to the President of "the executive power" confers upon him, as inherent in the office, the power to exercise these two functions without restriction by Congress, except in so far as the power to restrict his exercise of them is expressly conferred upon Congress by the Constitution; that in respect to appointment certain restrictions of the executive power are so provided for; but that in respect to removal there is no express grant to Congress of any power to limit the President's prerogative. The simple answer to the argument is this: The ability to remove a subordinate executive officer, being an essential of effective government, will, in the absence of express constitutional provision to the contrary, be deemed to have been vested in some person or body. But it is not a power inherent in a chief executive. The President's power of removal from statutory civil inferior offices, like the power of appointment to them, comes immediately from the Congress. It is true that the exercise of the power of removal is said to be an executive act, and that when the Senate grants or withholds consent to a removal by the President, it participates in an executive act. But the Constitution has confessedly granted to Congress the legislative power to create offices, and to prescribe the tenure thereof; and it has not in terms denied to Congress the power to control removals. To prescribe the tenure involves prescribing the conditions under which incumbency shall cease. For the possibility of removal is a condition or qualification of the tenure. When Congress provides that the incumbent shall hold office for four years unless sooner removed with the consent of the Senate, it prescribes the term of the tenure. * * *

The end to which the President's efforts are to be directed is not the most efficient civil service conceivable, but the faithful execution of the laws consistent with the provisions therefor made by Congress. * * * Power to remove, as well as to suspend, a high political officer, might conceivably be deemed indispensable to democratic government and, hence, inherent in the President. But power to remove an inferior administrative officer appointed for a fixed term cannot conceivably be deemed an essential of government. To imply a grant to the President of the uncontrollable power of removal from statutory inferior executive offices involves an unnecessary and indefensible limitation upon the constitutional power of Congress to fix the tenure of the inferior statutory offices. That such a limitation cannot be justified on the ground of necessity is demonstrated by the practice of our governments, state and national. In none of the original 13 states did the chief executive possess such power at the time of the adoption of the federal Constitution. In none of the 48 states has such power been conferred at any time since by a state Constitution, with a single possible exception. * * *

The practice of Congress to control the exercise of the executive power of removal from inferior offices is evidenced by many statutes which restrict it in many ways besides the removal clause here in question. Each of these restrictive statutes became law with the approval of the President. Every President who has held office since 1861, except President Garfield, approved one or more of such statutes. Some of these statutes, prescribing a fixed term, provide that removal shall be made only for one of several specified causes. Some provide a fixed term, subject generally to removal for cause. Some provide for removal only after a hearing. Some provide a fixed term, subject to removal for reasons to be communicated by the President to the Senate. Some impose the restriction in still other ways.

The practical disadvantage to the public service of denying to the President the uncontrollable power of removal from inferior civil offices would seem to have been exaggerated. Upon the service, the immediate effect would ordinarily be the same, whether the President, acting alone, has or has not the power of removal. For he can, at any time, exercise his constitutional right to suspend an officer and designate some other person to act temporarily in his stead; and he cannot while the Senate is in session, appoint a successor without its consent. On the other hand, to the individual in the public service, and to the maintenance of its morale, the existence of a power in Congress to impose upon the Senate a duty to share in the responsibility for a removal is of paramount importance. The Senate's consideration of a proposed removal may be necessary to protect reputation and emoluments of office from arbitrary executive action. * * *

The historical data submitted present a legislative practice, established by concurrent affirmative action of Congress and the President, to make consent of the Senate a condition of removal from statutory inferior, civil, executive offices to which appointment is made for a fixed term by the President with such consent. They show that the practice has existed, without interruption, continuously for the last 58 years; that throughout this period it has governed a great majority of all such offices; that the legislation applying the removal clause specifically to the office of the postmaster was enacted more than half a century ago; and that recently the practice has, with the President's approval, been extended to several newly created offices. * * * A persistent legislative practice which involves a delimitation of the respective powers of Congress and the President, and which has been so established and maintained, should be tantamount to judicial construction, in the absence of any decision by the court to the contrary. * * *

The action taken by Congress in 1789 * * * does not present an instance [of recognizing uncontrollable executive power to remove an inferior civil officer]. The vote then taken * * * involved merely the decision that the Senate does not, in the absence of legislative grant thereof, have the right to share in the removal of an officer appointed with its consent, and that the President has, in the absence of restrictive legislation, the constitutional power of removal without such consent.

Moreover * * * the debate and the decision related to a high political office, not to inferior ones. Nor does the [congressional] debate show that the majority of those then in Congress thought that the President had the uncontrollable power of removal. The Senators divided equally in their votes. As to their individual views we lack knowledge; for the debate was secret. In the House only 24 of the 54 members voting took part in the debate. Of the 24, only 6 appear to have held the opinion that the President possessed the uncontrollable power of removal. * * *

The separation of the powers of government did not make each branch completely autonomous. It left each in some measure, dependent upon the others, as it left to each power to exercise, in some respects, functions in their nature executive, legislative and judicial. Obviously the President cannot secure full execution of the laws, if Congress denies to him adequate means of doing so. * * * If, in any such way, adequate means are denied to the President, the fault will lie with Congress. The President performs his full constitutional duty, if, with the means and instruments provided by Congress and within the limitations prescribed by it, he uses his best endeavors to secure the faithful execution of the laws enacted.

Checks and balances were established in order that this should be "a government of laws and not of men." * * * The doctrine of the separation of powers was adopted by the convention of 1787 not to promote efficiency but to preclude the exercise of arbitrary power. * * * Nothing in support of the claim of uncontrollable power can be inferred from the silence of the convention of 1787 on the subject of removal. For the outstanding fact remains that every specific proposal to confer such uncontrollable power upon the President was rejected. In America, as in England, the conviction prevailed then that the people must look to representative assemblies for the protection of their liberties. And protection of the individual, even if he be an official, from the arbitrary or capricious exercise of power was then believed to be an essential of free government.

NOTES ON MYERS

1. *Original Congressional Intent Versus Consistent Congressional Practice.* In interpreting the President's removal powers under Article II, Chief Justice Taft relied heavily on the discussion and decision by the First Congress, emphasizing that congressional leaders, who had been members of the Constitutional Convention, were deciding a key question of government organization less than two years after the Convention. By contrast, Justice Brandeis invoked a continuous practice of nearly sixty years, in place since 1876 and continued through concurrent action of Congress and every President except Garfield since that time. Assuming arguendo that each argument is historically accurate, is one interpretive foundation more legitimate or convincing than the other with respect to the tenure of inferior officers such as Myers? Would your answer be different if Article II were a legislative provision rather than a constitutional one?

2. *The Meaning of Silence.* The Chief Justice ascribes conclusive weight to the President's constitutional duty to take care that the laws be faithfully executed, noting that unlike the appointment power, there is no express limitation on this general duty with respect to removal of administrative officers. Justice Brandeis responds that the ability to remove such inferior officers is not an inherent executive power; rather, absent an express constitutional provision to the contrary, removal power like appointment

power comes immediately from Congress. Which inference from constitutional silence do you find more persuasive? Is Taft correct that in this context, "[t]he difference between the grant of legislative power under article 1 to Congress which is limited to powers therein enumerated, and the more general grant of the executive power to the President under article 2 is significant"? Does Congress have any general or unenumerated powers under Article I? If so, are they relevant here?

3.   *Policy Considerations.* What substantive reasons does the Chief Justice offer to explain why the President alone is in the right position to evaluate the performance of his subordinates? What substantive concerns does Justice Brandeis express regarding the consequences if the President alone retains removal power over administrative officers? Who has the better of this policy-based disagreement? Can you argue that the disagreement should be resolved differently for high political officers as opposed to inferior officials?

Humphrey's Executor v. United States

295 U.S. 602 (1935).

In 1931, President Hoover reappointed William E. Humphrey to another seven-year term as a member of the Federal Trade Commission (FTC). After taking office in March 1933, President Roosevelt sought to remove Humphrey for not supporting the President's New Deal policies, and eventually did remove him in October 1933. Humphrey, and after his death, his executor, brought suit against the United States to recover the salary he would have earned as a Commissioner had President Roosevelt not removed him. Section 1 of the Federal Trade Commission Act states that "[a]ny commissioner may be removed by the President for inefficiency, neglect of duty, or malfeasance in office." Humphrey's executor argued that by removing Humphrey for political differences, President Roosevelt violated the Act and exceeded his Article II powers.

Writing for a unanimous court, **Justice Sutherland** set out to determine whether this statutory language restricted or limited the President's power to remove to the specific causes enumerated, and if so, whether that limitation is constitutional. After reviewing the Act's text, legislative history, and general purpose, Justice Sutherland concluded the Act intended "to create a body of experts who shall gain experience by length of service [which is] free to exercise its judgment without the leave or hindrance of any other official or any department of the government." To achieve this, Congress intended to limit the executive's power of removal. To permit the President to remove the Commissioner for any other reason than those listed would thwart Congress's intent.

The government relied on *Myers* to argue that any limitation on the executive's removal power is unconstitutional. Justice Sutherland clarified that in *Myers* "the narrow point actually decided was only that the President had power to remove a postmaster of the first class, without the advice and consent of the Senate as required by act of Congress" and therefore stare decisis was inapplicable. Justice Sutherland then distinguished the postmaster in *Myers* from the Commissioner in the case at bar. First, the actual role in question is different: "[a] postmaster is an executive officer restricted to the performance of executive functions. He is charged with no duty at all related to either the legislative or judicial power." By contrast, "[t]he Federal Trade Commission is an administrative body created by Congress to carry into effect legislative policies embodied in the statute in accordance with the legislative standard therein prescribed, and to perform other specified duties as a legislative or as a judicial aid. Such a body cannot in any proper sense be characterized as an arm or an eye of the executive. Its duties are performed without executive leave and, in the contemplation of the statute, must be free from executive control."

The Court found that with regard to the FTC as a quasi-judicial and quasi-legislative body, the President does not have an unlimited power of removal. Justice Sutherland stressed that Congress must retain the power to fix the terms of agency heads and forbid their removal except for cause so as to not threaten the separation of powers. Accordingly, "[w]hether the power of the President to remove an officer shall prevail over the authority of Congress to condition the power by fixing a definite term and precluding a removal except for cause will depend upon the character of the office; the *Myers* decision, affirming the power of the President alone to make the removal, is confined to purely executive officers; and as to officers of the kind here under consideration, we hold that no removal can be made during the prescribed term for which the officer is appointed, except for one or more of the causes named in the applicable statute."

NOTES ON THE TENSION BETWEEN MYERS AND HUMPHREY'S EXECUTOR

1.   *Two Kinds of Agencies.* The decision in *Myers* seems to suggest that Congress may not place any limits on the President's Article II power to remove executive officers. By contrast, *Humphrey's Executor* makes clear that Congress has the Article I power to create federal offices, charge them with implementing congressional statutes, and assure their independence by specifying that occupants of these offices may not be dismissed except for cause. The Court in *Humphrey's* insists that *Myers* decided only a "narrow point" about the power to remove a postmaster of the first class, although Chief Justice Taft's in-depth historical analysis in *Myers* (occupying 117 pages in the U.S. Reports) suggests otherwise. Is the *Humphrey's* Court persuasive in reconciling these two holdings by reference to whether an officer (and presumably the agency she helps direct) performs purely executive functions versus effectuating legislative policies? The FTC has congressional authority to investigate and report to Congress in aid of legislative power, and to issue adjudicative orders. But what about an executive-branch agency like the Department of Labor (DOL), created by Congress in 1913? Over the past century, Congress has given various DOL offices authority to investigate and report as a means of legislative assistance, and to dispense statutory benefits or penalties through the application of adjudicative processes. Yet the Secretary of Labor, as well as DOL bureau chiefs appointed by the President, are subject to removal at the President's whim. Are there really two different types of agencies, as Justice Sutherland concluded in *Humphrey's Executor?*

2.   *Brandeis Vindicated?* Another possibility is that Brandeis was right all along. There is only one kind of agency, created by Congress pursuant to its powers under Article I, § 8, with agency offices structured by Congress pursuant to its "necessary and proper" authority under Article I, § 10. The President controls many (perhaps most) aspects of agencies' operations, and he can remove appointed federal officials. But Congress retains authority to define and constrain the conditions for removal, just as Congress defines other features of these agency offices such as single versus multimember heads, the length of terms to be served, and any requirements for partisan balance among multi-member agency heads. Are you persuaded by this argument? Does it help explain the Court's decision in *Morrison v. Olson*, discussed below in "More Recent

Separation of Powers Developments"? Might it help support the idea from the Datla and Revesz article (see below) that the executive-independent agency distinction is fundamentally misguided?

MORE RECENT SEPARATION OF POWERS DEVELOPMENTS

In *Humphrey's Executor*, the Supreme Court characterized the FTC as performing both adjudicative and quasi-legislative duties, and reasoned that Congress could restrict presidential removal power in such agencies in ways it could not do with respect to officials in purely executive agencies. *Humphrey's Executor* suggested that Congress might have some room within the constitutional scheme to exercise direct control over officials implementing quasi-legislative duties. This hypothesis was tested in a series of decisions beginning 50 years later.

Bowsher v. Synar

478 U.S. 714 (1986).

This litigation arose out of the 1985 balanced budget law. The Graham-Rudman-Hollings Act (GRH), 99 Stat. 1038, codified at 2 U.S.C. § 901 et seq., was designed to eliminate the budget deficit through adherence to a set of deficit targets. If Congress failed to make spending and taxing changes in any year sufficient to meet the target, then a sequester would take place to implement pro rata spending reductions in all eligible programs. The key to accomplishing these automatic reductions was the Comptroller General (CG) of the General Accounting Office (GAO), who is an agent of Congress (appointed by the President but removable by Congress). The CG reviewed deficit projections and possible program spending reductions calculated and reported to him by the executive Office of Management and Budget (OMB) and the legislative Congressional Budget Office (CBO), and then made his own report to the President. The Act required the President to issue a "sequestration order" to implement the spending reductions specified by the CG. Congress had an opportunity to alter or implement the reductions by legislation, but if nothing were done the sequestration order automatically became effective.

The Supreme Court invalidated the enforcement provision of GRH. **Chief Justice Burger**'s opinion for the Court accepted Congress's characterization of sequestration as executive in nature; in other words, the CG was merely implementing a congressional policy decision. Executive actions can be delegated to executive branch entities or to independent agencies without raising constitutional concerns. Further, the GRH sequestration provisions constrained the CG's discretion in numerous ways—specifying which programs were eligible for cuts and which were exempt; demanding uniformity; and requiring pro rata cuts at the program, project, and activity level. Nonetheless, the Chief Justice concluded that the GRH "usurped" executive power by giving an officer of Congress the authority to execute the laws. Such power can be unproblematically delegated to an executive entity; it cannot be retained by a direct agent of Congress.

Burger's analysis is subject to several objections. **Justices White** and **Blackmun** (dissenting) and **Justices Marshall** and **Stevens** (concurring in the judgment) found unrealistic the Court's suggestion that the CG would be "subservient" to Congress. The CG enjoys a 15-year term and may only be removed by Congress for (i) permanent disability; (ii) inefficiency; (iii) neglect of duty; (iv) malfeasance; or (v) felony or conduct involving moral turpitude. 31 U.S.C. § 703(e)(1)(B). A Comptroller General has never been removed for policy reasons. Is there *any* reason to believe that official might kowtow to Congress under GRH, especially given that the CG's duties under the Act are substantially limited by the OMB and CBO projections? Justices Marshall and Stevens also argued that if the Court's opinion were taken literally—that Congress may not "control" an official who performs "executive" rather than "legislative" powers—it would be an absurdity. The Capitol Police who arrest lawbreakers, the Sergeant-at-Arms who manages the congressional payroll, and the Capitol Architect who maintains the grounds are all agents of Congress who "execute" laws. Do these positions violate the Constitution?

One might read *Bowsher* as suggesting a broad principle against *excessive* congressional control over statutory implementation. The vice in *Bowsher* was handing over statutory implementation to a congressional agent, but what if Congress hands over statutory implementation to an "independent" agency that Congress bullies into policy shifts because of *ex parte* pressure by Members of Congress, threats of funding cutoffs, or brutal accusations during oversight hearings? As discussed in Section 3, none of these mechanisms of congressional control is per se unconstitutional. Still, perhaps there is a *Bowsher* line that Congress would cross if it went "too far." How might you define that line?

Since *Bowsher*, the Court has addressed two other federal statutes that creatively insulated the tenure of agency officials—including purely executive officials—from presidential control. The Ethics in Government Act of 1978, codified at 28 U.S.C. §§ 591–599 (EGA), established a special court and empowered the Attorney General to recommend to that court the appointment of an independent counsel to investigate, and, if necessary, prosecute government officials for certain violations of federal criminal laws. In 1986, Alexia Morrison was appointed to investigate charges that former Assistant Attorney General Theodore Olson and two other DOJ officials had obstructed a House Judiciary Committee investigation into alleged mismanagement of the "Superfund Law" by the Environmental Protection Agency. Olson challenged the constitutionality of the independent counsel provision, arguing that it deprived the President of executive powers and created a hybrid fourth branch of government ultimately not answerable to anyone.

Morrison v. Olson

487 U.S. 654 (1988).

Chief Justice Rehnquist, writing for seven of the eight sitting justices (**Justice Kennedy** took no part), held that the EGA did not violate the Appointments Clause or the separation of powers doctrine. With respect to the Appointments Clause, Morrison possessed some independent discretion to exercise the powers delegated to her, but the statute authorized her removal by the Attorney General for misconduct, indicating her "inferior" rank and authority. The Court pointed to further evidence of inferior office status: the independent counsel was empowered to perform only limited duties (investigation and prosecution but not administration or policy formulation); the counsel could act only within the scope of jurisdiction granted by the Attorney General; and the position was "temporary" in that appointment was to perform only a single task.

With respect to separation of powers, the Court acknowledged that its earlier decisions had distinguished between limits on presidential removal authority for "purely executive" officers and "quasi-legislative" or "quasi-judicial" officials. It concluded, however, that Congress may in appropriate circumstances create good-cause type protections even for independent agencies that exercise purely executive powers because "faithful execution of the laws" under Article II does not require at-will removability. In this instance, Congress had properly walked the line between respecting the President's removal authority and establishing the necessary independence of the office. Importantly, the EGA did not include any attempt by Congress to increase its own powers at the expense of the Executive Branch. Congress' role was limited to receiving reports or other information and to overseeing the independent counsel's activities—both functions that are incidental to the legislative power of Congress. Although the independent counsel was free from Executive Branch supervision to a greater degree than other federal prosecutors, the EGA gave the Executive sufficient control to ensure that the President was able to perform his constitutionally assigned duties. (The Court further held that the EGA did not violate Article III; that article does not prevent Congress from vesting certain miscellaneous powers in a special court, and the special court's powers were not inherently "executive," but rather analogous to functions that federal judges perform in other contexts)

Justice Scalia, the lone dissenter, argued that criminal law enforcement is a "quintessentially executive activity" under the Constitution, and the EGA deprived the President of exclusive control over that activity. In doing so, the statute substantially altered the balance of power between the two political branches. Scalia further predicted that the law would be abused in practice: "If Congress is controlled by the party other than the one to which the President belongs, it has little incentive to repeal [the EGA]; if [Congress] is controlled by the same party, it dare not. By its shortsighted action today, I fear the Court has permanently encumbered the Republic with an institution that will do it great harm."

Republicans began to echo Scalia's pragmatic concern when, shortly before the 1992 Presidential election, independent counsel Lawrence Walsh announced the re-indictment of former Reagan Administration defense secretary Caspar Weinberger on charges related to the Iran-Contra affair. Democrats in turn became concerned when independent counsel Kenneth Starr spent four years in the mid 1990s investigating President Clinton's land deals and extramarital affairs. With legislators on both sides of the aisle believing that these investigations had become intensely partisan, Congress allowed the independent counsel provision to expire in 1999.

The Sarbanes-Oxley Act of 2002, 116 Stat. 745, created the Public Company Accounting Oversight Board (PCAOB), codified at 15 U.S.C. §§ 7211 et seq.). The Board was composed of five members serving for staggered five-year terms; it was appointed by the SEC and modeled on private self-regulatory organizations in the securities industry such as the New York Stock Exchange. Sarbanes-Oxley gave the PCAOB expansive powers to govern the accounting industry: every accounting firm that audits public companies under the securities laws must register with the PCAOB, pay it an annual fee, and comply with its rules and oversight. While the SEC had oversight of the PCAOB, it could not remove Board members at will, but only "for good cause shown" and in accordance with specified procedures. An accounting firm being investigated by the PCAOB challenged the Board's constitutional status.

Free Enterprise Fund v. Public Co. Accounting Oversight Board

561 U.S. 477 (2010).

The Court by a 5–4 vote held that the dual for-cause limitations on the removal of Board members contravened the separation of powers doctrine. **Chief Justice Roberts** for the majority reasoned that because the Act vested removal power in SEC Commissioners, who are not subject to the President's direct control, and because the SEC could not remove a PCAOB member at will, the President was unable to hold the SEC fully accountable for the PCAOB's conduct. The President's power was limited to reviewing SEC determinations, and where the President disagreed, he was unable to intervene. The Court concluded that the Board's lack of accountability to the President violated Article II, which gives the President ultimate responsibility for the actions of the executive branch. The Chief Justice observed that the Act "shelter[s] the bureaucracy behind two layers of good-cause tenure," and he warned that this would allow Congress to create agencies with three or even five layers of insulation. "The officers of such an agency—safely encased within a Matryoshka doll of tenure protections—would be immune from Presidential oversight, even as they exercised power in the people's name."

In dissent, **Justice Breyer** emphasized the intersection of two constitutional principles: separation of powers and the Necessary and Proper Clause, which gives Congress broad authority to create and structure government offices "as it chooses." He argued that neither principle is absolute when applied to removal cases. "The Necessary and Proper Clause does not grant Congress power to free *all* Executive Branch officials from dismissal at the will of the President. Nor does the separation-of-powers principle grant the President an absolute authority to remove *any and all* Executive Branch officials at will." Absent clear constitutional guidance on the removal issue, the Court should resolve the constitutional issue based on considerations of function and context while taking account of the judicial branch's comparative lack of expertise. Breyer noted that Board members perform complex technical roles as well as adjudicative functions, adding that the subject matter of financial regulation "historically . . . has been thought to exhibit a particular need for independence." The dissent concluded that Congress and the President "could reasonably have thought it prudent to insulate . . . Board members from fear of purely politically based removal" and that the Court should defer to the "two comparatively more expert branches" that had supported the Act's removal provisions.

PHH Corp. v. Consumer Financial Protection Bureau

881 F.3d 75 (D.C. Cir. *en banc* 2018).

After the 2008 financial crisis, Congress "determined that the financial services industry had pushed consumers into unsustainable forms of debt and that federal regulators had failed to prevent mounting risks to the economy, in part because those regulators were overly responsive to the industry they purported to police." In response, Congress—as part of the Dodd-Frank Wall Street Reform and Consumer Protection Act (Dodd-Frank)—established the Consumer Financial Protection Bureau (CFPB) to restore the public's confidence in the market. The CFPB was structured to be led by a single Director who could only be removed by the President "for cause." Sitting en banc, ten judges of the D.C. Circuit considered whether this design was unconstitutional under the *Humphrey's Executor* standard. The challengers argued that the *Humphrey's Executor* precedent only excepted multi-member commissions, like the FTC, from the *Myers* rule, not singly-headed agencies, like the CFPB. Speaking for a majority of six judges, **Judge**

Pillard authored the opinion for the Court. She rejected the petitioners' argument, finding the CFPB constitutionally indistinguishable from the FTC, whose "for cause" removal provision was upheld in *Humphrey's Executor*.

Judge Pillard determined that Supreme Court precedent (including *Humphrey's Executor* and *Morrison*) and a long history of independent financial regulators established sufficient authority to support the structure of the CFPB. The CFPB Director's for cause removal is verbatim the words that the Supreme Court sustained in *Humphrey's Executor* ("inefficiency, neglect of duty, or malfeasance in office"). Further, in Judge Pillard's view, the CFPB has a remarkably similar function to the FTC. And unlike the structures in *Myers* and *Bowsher*, the for-cause removal of the CFPB Director does not give Congress any powers that could be seen as intruding into the President's removal authority. Additionally, the CFPB's structure does not impose any additional obstacles in the President's ability to remove the Director, as was the issue in *Free Enterprise*. Judge Pillard concluded that the CFPB's structure was fully in line with the removal power cases that the Supreme Court had previously approved.

PHH Corp. and the dissent argued that the single-director structure made the CFPB for-cause removal requirement unconstitutional. As historical precedents for "sole-headed financial regulators," Judge Pillard cited "the Comptroller of the Treasury, dating back to [1789]; and the Office of the Comptroller of the Currency, established in [1863]. Other examples of single-headed independent agencies include the Social Security Administration, which was placed under a single director in 1994, and the Office of Special Counsel established under a sole director in 1978, the same year as the Office of Independent Counsel upheld in *Morrison*. Congress established the sole-headed, for-cause-protected Federal Housing Finance Agency in 2008, in response to similar concerns as gave rise to the CFPB. This longstanding tradition provides historical pedigree to the CFPB, and refutes the contention that the CFPB's single director structure is anything new." Because this history exists, courts should not question why Congress chose an individual versus a board to head the agency. Instead, the courts should only decide "whether the removal restrictions are of such a nature that they impede the President's ability to perform his constitutional duty." *Morrison*.

In short, Judge Pillard found "nothing constitutionally suspect about the CFPB's leadership structure. *Morrison* and *Humphrey's Executor* stand in the way of any holding to the contrary. And there is no reason to assume an agency headed by an individual will be less responsive to presidential supervision than one headed by a group. It is surely more difficult to fire and replace several people than one. And, if anything, the Bureau's consolidation of regulatory authority . . . allows the President more efficiently to oversee the faithful execution of consumer protection laws. Decisional responsibility is clear now that there is one, publicly identifiable face of the CFPB who stands to account—to the President, the Congress, and the people—for all its consumer protection actions. The fact that the Director stands alone atop the agency means he cannot avoid scrutiny through finger-pointing, buck-passing, or sheer anonymity. What is more, in choosing a replacement, the President is unhampered by partisan balance or *ex-officio* requirements; the successor replaces the agency's leadership wholesale. Nothing about the CFPB stands out to give us pause that it—distinct from other financial regulators or independent agencies more generally—is constitutionally defective."

Judge Griffith concurred in the judgment of the en banc Court. Although believing that *Humphrey's Executor* and *Morrison* are inconsistent with the text and original meaning of Article II, he acknowledged that only the Supreme Court can overrule those precedents. In any event, Judge Griffith determined the issue should be resolved by asking the following antecedent question: "How difficult is it for the President to remove the Director? The President may remove the CFPB Director for 'inefficiency, neglect of duty, or malfeasance in office.' After reviewing these removal grounds, I conclude they provide only a minimal restriction on the President's removal power, even permitting him to remove the Director for ineffective policy choices. Therefore, I agree that the CFPB's structure does not impermissibly interfere with the President's ability to perform his constitutional duties."

Filing the principal dissent, then-**Judge Kavanaugh** began by declaring "[t]his is a case about executive power and individual liberty." Judge Kavanaugh relied on the Framers' reasoning behind employing separation of powers to conclude that the executive power was vested solely in the President, who is elected and accountable to all the people, " 'not merely to assure effective government but to preserve individual freedom.' *Morrison v. Olson* (Scalia, J., dissenting)." While *Myers* supported the Framers' intent, the Supreme Court's exception in *Humphrey's Executor*, permitting Congress to create independent agencies by limiting the President's removal power over the agency's leadership, threatened individual freedom. "The independent agencies collectively constitute, in effect, a headless fourth branch of the U.S. Government. They hold enormous power over the economic and social life of the United States. Because of their massive power and the absence of Presidential supervision and direction, independent agencies pose a significant threat to individual liberty and to the constitutional system of separation of powers and checks and balances.

"To mitigate the risk to individual liberty, the independent agencies historically have been headed by *multiple* commissioners or board members. In the Supreme Court's words, each independent agency has traditionally been established as a 'body of experts appointed by law and informed by experience.' *Humphrey's Executor*. * * * In other words, the heads of *executive* agencies are accountable to and checked by the President; and the heads of *independent* agencies, although not accountable to or checked by the President, are at least accountable to and checked by their fellow commissioners or board members. No independent agency exercising substantial executive authority has ever been headed by *a single person*."

Judge Kavanaugh provided an historical analysis of the structure of independent agencies, noting that all but three independent agencies have been headed by multi-member boards. The three independent agencies headed by single directors (the Social Security Administration, the Office of Special Counsel, and the Federal Housing Finance Agency) differ from the CFPB in that those directors did not have nearly the same amount of authority as the CFPB Director.

Additionally, Supreme Court precedents like *Humphrey's Executor* and *Morrison* do not support the constitutionality of the CFPB's structure. According to Judge Kavanaugh, *Morrison* is inapplicable because it was not concerned with the constitutionality of the head of an independent agency, but instead about the constitutionality of an inferior officer. Similarly, *Humphrey's Executor* is inapplicable because the Court repeatedly emphasized the FTC's multi-member structure, thus leaving open the question about the status of single-director boards or agencies.

Instead, *Free Enterprise* should control, which held that an independent agency's structure is unconstitutional "when it causes an *additional* diminution of Presidential control beyond that caused by a traditional independent agency." Judge Kavanaugh argued that the CFPB's single director with a five-year fixed term caused the additional diminution, because a President may be stuck with a CFPB Director who was appointed by a previous administration for his entire four-year term. This is significantly less control than the President has over chairs of multi-member independent agencies, who the President can replace within days of taking office.

NOTES ON RECENT APPOINTMENT-AND-REMOVAL DECISIONS

1. *The Debate in* PHH Corp. Is Judge Pillard persuasive in citing to other single-headed independent agencies? Does the subject matter of these agencies matter for purposes of Article II removal? Judge Pillard also distinguished the CFPB director from Cabinet officers who answer directly to the President's will. She analogized the CFPB instead to other federal financial regulators, including the Federal Reserve and the FDIC as well as the FTC, that have "long been permissibly afforded a degree of independence." By contrast, Judge Kavanaugh is deeply troubled by the authority of the CFPB Director in comparison to chairs of independent agencies with multi-member structures. Is he persuasive in relying on *Myers* and *Free Enterprise* instead of the *Morrison* test? On the other hand, did Judge Kavanaugh overstep the judicial boundary and interfere with Congress's judgment on how best to deal with the 2008 financial crisis? Scholars have disagreed over whether his dissent fails to recognize the threat to separation of powers from giving the president too much control. *See* Opinion, What Does Kavanaugh's Paper Trail Say? Let's Ask the Experts., Wash. Post, Aug. 31, 2018 (contrasting views of Ilya Somin and Akhil Amar) https://www.washingtonpost.com/opinions/what-does-kavanaughs-paper-trail-say-lets-ask-the-experts/2018/08/31/beffd014-ad33-11e8-a8d7-0f63ab8b1370_story.html?utm_term=.420975ec89ba.

2. *Aftermath of* PHH Corp. Following the D.C. Circuit's decision, the Ninth Circuit held that the CFPB's structure was constitutional; the Fifth Circuit will decide the same issue soon. *Consumer Financial Protection Bureau v. Seila Law,* 923 F.3d 680 (9th Cir. 2019); *Consumer Financial Protection Bureau v. All American Check Cashing, Inc.,* No. 18–60302 (5th Cir. 2019). Judge Kavanaugh's dissent was adopted by the Southern District of New York, which found the CFPB's structure unconstitutional. *See CFPB v. RD Legal Funding, LLC,* 332 F.Supp.3d 729 (S.D.N.Y. 2018), *appeal docketed,* No. 18–3156 (2d Cir. Oct. 23, 2018). If a circuit split ensues, the Supreme Court, including Justice Kavanaugh, may decide this question.

A bill was introduced in the House in March of 2018 (only weeks after the D.C. Circuit's decision in *PHH Corp.*) to change the structure of the CFPB so that it is headed by a five-person commission, with each member appointed by the President but with staggered terms, and with the President's removal power limited to for-cause situations. H.R. 5266, 115th Cong. (2018). By the time Congress adjourned in December of 2018, the bill had garnered 19 cosponsors but no action was taken in the Committee on Financial Services. Does the bill's failure to get a hearing, even in a Republican House, suggest that Congress is not ready to hand over all the power Judge Kavanaugh believes it should? Can House inaction in this setting be read as tacit approval of the court's holding?

On November 24, 2017, Richard Cordray named Leandra English CFPB's Deputy Director as his replacement before resigning later that day as CFPB's Director. On the same day, President Trump appointed John Mulvaney as acting Director of the CFPB, instead of English. A lawsuit followed, and the D.C. District Court denied English injunctive relief. The court held that the Federal Vacancies Reform Act (FVRA) authorized the President to appoint a CFPB Acting Director, and Dodd-Frank's requirement that the Deputy Director "shall" serve as acting Director can be overridden by the President's authority under the FVRA. *English v. Trump*, 279 F. Supp. 3d 307, 317–19 (D.D.C. 2018), appeal voluntarily dismissed, 2018 WL 3526296 (D.C. Cir. 2018). Does Trump's triumph in installing Mulvaney suggest that Judge Kavanaugh's concerns may be exaggerated?

3. *Executive Versus Independent Agencies in Practice.* *Myers* and *Humphrey's Executor* establish a constitutional distinction involving the leadership status of executive and independent agencies. But in an important article examining agencies from a functional standpoint, Peter Strauss argues that executive branch agencies and independent commissions are more similar than different when viewed below the highest levels. See Peter Strauss, *The Place of Agencies in Government: Separation of Powers and the Fourth Branch*, 84 Colum. L. Rev. 573, 584–90 (1984). Strauss discusses how the two types of agencies follow the same principles of bureaucratic organization: they have the same reliance on civil service-protected staff; they perform the same basic functions of legislating (rules), investigating (compliance) and adjudicating (complaints); and they use the same public procedures for rules and adjudications that are governed by the APA. Strauss recognizes that bipartisan membership requirements for independent agencies may help lower the political temperature, and that independent agencies have somewhat more control when making budget submissions to Congress or conducting litigation, but he views these differences as relatively modest.

Is there any basis to push back against Strauss's argument for overriding functional similarity? To what extent does the deeper reach of presidential appointments in executive agencies—not just the Secretary but deputy and assistant secretaries, who in turn control some appointments themselves—encourage or even assure greater political influence over daily operations? Can the President and his "minions" influence mid-level bureaucrats at the Department of Labor more easily than at the National Labor Relations Board? At the Justice Department more readily than the SEC? Further, with respect to the *Free Enterprise* decision, isn't the President's influence over SEC Commissioners greater than over the PCOAB?

Even when comparing independent agencies, certain differences may have functional consequences. Some independent agencies serve a relatively dispersed and unorganized public—think of the SEC, which has a basic mission to protect investors who depend on accurate information and the integrity of securities markets. Other independent agencies perform more as a traffic cop—think of the National Labor Relations Board, which historically has overseen relations between unions and management in the private sector. How might this difference in mission affect the likelihood of agency capture? How might it affect the risk of agency ossification?

One apparent lesson of *Myers* and *Humphrey's Executor* is that for-cause tenure protection is the crucial element when determining agency independence. But Adrian Vermeule has recently argued that such protection from presidential removal does not capture the observable practices shaping agency independence in the administrative state. See *Conventions of Agency Independence*, 113 Colum. L. Rev. 1163, 1165–81 (2013). A number of features—including staggered terms, multimember boards at the top level, bipartisan composition, and independent budgetary or litigating authority—distinguish many independent agencies, but for-cause tenure protection is typically viewed as necessary for independence, even if not sufficient. Vermeule agrees that judicial doctrine accords a crucial role to for-cause protections against removal, citing the Supreme Court's post-*Humphrey's Executor* decisions in *Bowsher*, *Morrison*, and *Free Enterprise* (discussed above).

Despite these Supreme Court holdings, Vermeule maintains that as a practical matter, executive and legislative officials, agency personnel, administrative law commentators and practitioners, and regulated parties create and follow observable norms of agency independence—unwritten conventions—that are not derived from the judicial doctrine and in some cases cannot be squared with it. Thus, for instance, *for-cause tenure protection is not necessary to agency independence.* Commissioners of the Securities and Exchange Commission (SEC), the Federal Communications Commission (FCC), and the Federal Election Commission (FEC), as well as the Chair and two Vice Chairs of the Federal Reserve, are conventionally considered "independent." Indeed, Congress included the SEC and FCC in a list of independent agencies under the Paperwork Reduction Act although these officials do *not* have for-cause tenure protections written into their statutes. *Nor is for-cause protection sufficient to create an independent agency.* The National Labor Relations Board (NLRB) statute expressly provides the reasons for removal of Board members, and the NLRB itself was designed to be independent, but, Vermeule argues that the NLRB is one of the "most politicized agencies" and that Board members vote reliably in accordance with the party of the appointing President and their own partisan affiliation.

4.   *The Agency Continuum.* Another recent law review article questions the binary view of agencies as either executive or independent. The authors contend instead that agencies are best understood from a continuum perspective: all agencies should be regarded as executive but seen as falling on a spectrum from more independent to less independent. Kirti Datla & Richard Revesz, *Deconstructing Independent Agencies (and Executive Agencies)*, 98 Cornell L. Rev. 769 (2013). Datla and Revesz identify seven indicia of independence: (1) for-cause removal protection, (2) set term tenure, (3) multimember structure, (4) partisan balance requirements, (5) budget and congressional communication authority, (6) litigation authority, and (7) adjudication authority. Using these seven factors, Datla and Revesz create the following continuum of agency independence, with the "more independent" agencies possessing a higher number of indicia. *Id.* at 825 (reprinted by permission).

Agencies by Number of Indicia of Independence

Number of Indicia	Agencies
7	Consumer Product Safety Commission; Federal Energy Regulatory Commission; Surface Transportation Board; U.S. Postal Service
6	Commodity Futures Trading Commission; Federal Election Commission; Securities & Exchange Commission; Federal Reserve; Federal Labor Relations Authority; Federal Maritime Commission; Federal Trade Commission; Merit Systems Protection Board; National Transportation Safety Board; Postal Regulatory Commission

5	Consumer Financial Protection Bureau; Federal Housing Finance Authority; National Labor Relations Board; Nuclear Regulatory Commission; Defense Nuclear Facilities Safety Board; Equal Employment Opportunity Commission; Farm Credit Administration; Federal Deposit Insurance Corporation; U.S. International Trade Commission; National Credit Union Administration
4	National Mediation Board; Chemical Safety and Hazard Investigation Board; Commission on Civil Rights; Independent Payment Advisory Board; Mine Safety and Health Review Commission; Occupational Safety & Health Review Commission; Social Security Administration; Advisory Council on Historic Preservation; Department of Transportation; Election Assistance Commission; Export-Import Bank; Federal Communications Commission
3	Office of Special Counsel; African Development Foundation; Federal Retirement Thrift Investment Board; Millennium Challenge Corporation; Overseas Private Investment Corporation; Railroad Retirement Board; Small Business Administration; Tennessee Valley Authority
2	Administrative Conference of the United States; Corporation for National and Community Service; Department of Labor; Department of Defense; Department of Education; Department of Justice; Environmental Protection Agency; National Capital Planning Commission; National Council on Disability; Department of Veterans Affairs
1	Department of Agriculture; Department of State; Department of the Interior; Department of the Treasury; Department of Homeland Security; Department of Health and Human Services; Nuclear Energy Agency; National Endowment for the Humanities; National Science Foundation; Office of Government Ethics; Office of Personnel Management; Panama Canal Commission; Pension Benefit Guaranty Corporation; Selective Service
0	Central Intelligence Agency; Department of Commerce; Department of Education; Federal Mediation and Conciliation Service; General Services Administration; Department of Housing and Urban Development; International Broadcasting Bureau; National Archives and Record Administration; National Aeronautics and Space Administration; Office of the Director of National Intelligence; Peace Corps; U. S. Trade and Development Agency; U.S. Agency for International Development

Datla and Revesz classify the NLRB as more independent than the FCC, a conclusion disputed under Vermeule's less formally doctrinal analysis and presumably questioned under Strauss's functional approach as well. Do you think one of these approaches best captures the reality of agency operations? Should they be considered together? Are there any agencies traditionally regarded as "independent" that Datla and Revesz list towards the less-independent end of the spectrum? Conversely, are there any traditionally "executive" agencies that appear toward the more-independent end of the spectrum? Although SEC Commissioners do not have for-cause removal protection, they still appear toward the more-independent end of the table because they possess six of the seven indicia. Does this seven-factor continuum approach reflect the genuine status of agencies more accurately than the constitutional distinctions identified and developed by the Supreme Court?

2. AGENCY IMPLEMENTATION UNDER THE ADMINISTRATIVE PROCEDURE ACT

Federal bureaucrats have existed since the dawn of the Republic, when Congress in 1789 established agencies charged with collecting import duties and providing military pensions to wounded veterans. There are sound policy reasons why Congress regularly opts for administrative processes to complement both statutory and judicial decisionmaking. When addressing scientific or technical subjects such as pollution, broadcast licensing, or taxes, neither Congress nor the federal courts can acquire the same *expertise* as civil servants trained in these areas. Moreover, from an *efficiency* standpoint, Congress lacks the time to resolve innumerable first-order implementation questions, like what qualifies as a valid job-specific performance criterion under an anti-discrimination provision, or how many portable toilets should be available for seasonal farmworkers under an occupational health and safety law. And in terms of *flexibility,* statutes create rules and standards that are meant to apply over many decades; agencies may be in the best position to update these policies in modest yet important respects by taking account of post-enactment changes in technological, scientific, or social circumstances.

On the other hand, the proliferation of administrative processes, particularly when developed separately for each agency, carries attendant risks—the public may not understand how laws are being implemented; agencies may be captured by the interests they are meant to regulate; agencies may become rigidly self-serving and unresponsive to new developments; or agencies may simply engage in arbitrary decisionmaking. A partial antidote to these risks is for Congress to develop a framework of fair procedures and to insist that agencies adhere to them. The APA, the end-product of more than a decade of legislative consideration, is a framework statute. It sets forth an array of process-related steps agencies must follow, and related determinations they must make, when acting to implement their statutory directives.

A. ORIGINS AND BASIC PROVISIONS OF THE APA

1. Legislative Origins

As noted in Section 1(A) of this chapter, federal agencies were created long before the passage of the Administrative Procedure Act of 1946. But with the enormous expansion of executive branch and independent agencies during the New Deal, some private sector observers voiced increasing alarm about the bureaucracy's authority and influence over the actions of individuals and entities. The American Bar

Association (ABA) was an early and persistent critic. In 1933, the ABA appointed a special committee on administrative law, which in turn began issuing annual reports. In 1938, the ABA committee, chaired by former Dean Roscoe Pound of Harvard Law School, scathingly denounced the new bureaucracy for malign "tendencies" to decide without a hearing, to consider matters not in the record, and to conflate the legislative, prosecutorial, and adjudicative functions—all to the detriment of hapless regulated interests. Between 1938 and 1945, the ABA had legislation introduced in every session of Congress that urged the adoption of a "Code of Standards of Fair Procedure." The ABA's efforts met with regular opposition from administrative agencies.

In 1939, the Walter-Logan administrative procedure bill, intended to limit the burgeoning power of the agencies, was favorably reported to the Senate. A passage from the Senate Judiciary Committee report, included in the House committee report accompanying the APA seven years later, captures the mischief at which that bill was aimed:

> "Unfortunately, the statutes providing for hearings before the so-called independent agencies of the Federal Government as well as those providing for the conduct of the affairs of the single-headed agencies, *do not provide for uniform procedure for * * * hearings or for a uniform method and scope of judicial review.* * * * The results of the lack of uniform procedure * * * have been at least threefold: (1) The respective administrative agencies give little heed to, and are little assisted by, the decisions of other administrative agencies or by the decisions of the courts applicable to such agencies; (2) the courts are placed at considerable disadvantage because they must verify the basic statutes of all decisions relating to other administrative agencies which are cited to them * * *; (3) individuals and their attorneys are at a disadvantage in the presentation of their administrative appeals.* * * *" H.R. Rep. No. 79–1980, at 9 (1946) (emphasis added).

Congress passed the Walter-Logan bill in 1940, but President Roosevelt vetoed it, noting his desire to await recommendations from the Attorney General's Committee on Administrative Procedure before approving any administrative law measure. In 1941, the committee issued its final report along with 27 separate studies of 33 administrative agencies. Subsequently, the United States' entry into World War II interrupted the process.

In early 1945, the chairmen of the two Judiciary Committees introduced revised bills and requested that the administrative agencies submit their further views and suggestions in writing. In October 1945, the Attorney General favorably recommended enactment. In November 1945 and May 1946, the Judiciary Committees of both Houses unanimously reported the bill. After further changes, the bill was approved by both House and Senate in May 1946. President Truman signed the APA into law on June 11, 1946, and it became effective on September 11, 1946.

The following excerpts from the House Judiciary Committee report convey a sense of what Congress expected from its new legislation:

> "The present bill must be distinguished from the Walter-Logan bill in several essential respects. Unlike that bill it differentiates the several types

of rules. It requires no agency hearings in connection with either regulations or adjudications unless statutes already do so in particular cases. Where statutory hearings are already provided, it fills in some of the essential requirements; and it provides for a special class of semi-independent hearing officers. * * * The bill is an outline of minimum essential rights and procedures. Agencies may fill in details so long as they publish them. It affords private parties a means of knowing what their rights are and how they may protect them, while administrators are given a simple framework upon which to base such operations as are subject to the provisions of the bill. What the bill does in substance may be summarized under four headings: 1. It provides that agencies must issue as rules certain specified information as to their organization and procedure, and also make available other materials of administrative law. 2. It states the essentials of the several forms of administrative proceedings and the general limitations on administrative powers. 3. It provides in more detail the requirements for administrative hearing and decisions in cases in which statutes require such hearings. 4. It sets forth a simplified statement of judicial review designed to afford a remedy for every legal wrong." H.R. Rep. No. 79–1980, at 10, 16–17 (1946).

Over the years, scholars have identified the APA's goals variously as (1) the codification of administrative procedure, (2) the achievement of uniformity, standardization, and simplification, (3) the curbing of arbitrary administrative excesses, and (4) the publicizing of administrative acts. But while Congress acted to limit the arbitrary exercise of power by agencies and to provide for judicial review by affected individuals and entities, the APA did not reduce the number of agencies or prevent their growth. In examining the APA text and the ways it has been construed and applied in judicial decisions, consider the meaning of this "compromise" statute. Does the Act subject agencies to uniformity of procedures as recommended by the ABA and the earlier Walter-Logan bill? To what extent does the statute standardize agencies' procedural choices with regard to implementation of policy? More broadly, do the cases in this Section suggest that the APA has succeeded in balancing agency accountability and discretion while providing for public participation that is both procedurally inclusive and substantively meaningful?

2. Basic Statutory Requirements and Definitions

The key provisions of the APA are reproduced in Appendix C. On its face, the Act divides administrative decisions according to a *bipolar model*, to use Dean Ronald Cass's term. Administrative decisions are treated as either *rules* or *orders.* Rules are like statutes, for they are agency statements "of general or particular applicability and future effect [that are] designed to implement, interpret, or prescribe law or policy." 5 U.S.C. § 551(4). Most rules are *informal*, but the procedure generating most informal rules is the more formal-sounding *notice-and-comment rulemaking.* In this process, the agency must publish notice of proposed rules in the Federal Register, followed by the opportunity for interested persons to submit comments, usually written, on the proposed rules. *Id.* § 553. See Cornelius Kerwin, *Rulemaking: How Government Agencies Write Law and Policy* (2d ed. 1999) (comprehensive description and analysis of notice-and-comment rulemaking); Peter Strauss, *The Rulemaking Continuum*, 41 Duke L.J. 1463 (1992) (the variety of rulemaking options).

Orders are like judicial decisions in that they constitute the "final disposition" of a controversy involving the statutory or agency rules. 5 U.S.C. § 551(6). The typical procedure for formal adjudicative orders is similar to trial in a court. If the enabling statute calls for decision "on the record after opportunity for an agency hearing," *Id.* §§ 554(a) and 556(a), the agency must not only provide particularized notice to the affected person, but it must also allow him or her "to present his [or her] case or defense by oral or documentary evidence, to submit rebuttal evidence, and to conduct such cross-examination as may be required for a full and true disclosure of the facts." *Id.* § 556(d). The agency's decision must be based on the trial-type record and supported by reliable, probative, and substantial evidence. *Id.* § 557.[20] Sections 554 and 556–557 mandate at least a partial separation of functions between the prosecutorial staff and agency decisionmakers, particularly in formal adjudications. For example, formal adjudications are usually handled by *administrative law judges* (§ 3105), who have their own staff and are monitored and rewarded by the Civil Service Commission and not by the agency itself.

Agency communications may require a less conventional structure than either notice-and-comment rules or orders that result from formal adjudications. The APA recognizes *interpretive rules* and *general policy statements* as more flexible modes of agency transmission; the Act exempts them from notice-and-comment requirements (§ 553(b)(A)) but requires that they be separately published in the Federal Register when they are of "general applicability" (§ 552(a)(1)(D)). In addition, agencies may merely "make available" (without publication in the Federal Register) guidance documents that are not of general applicability. (§ 552(a)(2)).

Sections 701–706 provide for judicial review of agency rules and orders. "A[ny] person suffering legal wrong because of agency action, or adversely affected or aggrieved by agency action within the meaning of a relevant statute, is entitled to judicial review thereof," *id.* § 702, unless "(1) statutes preclude judicial review; or (2) agency action is committed to agency discretion by law." *Id.* § 701(a). In an action for judicial review, the court "shall" under § 706:

(1) compel agency action unlawfully withheld or unreasonably delayed; and

(2) hold unlawful and set aside agency action, findings, and conclusions found to be—

(A) arbitrary, capricious, an abuse of discretion, or otherwise not in accordance with law;

(B) contrary to constitutional right, power, privilege, or immunity;

(C) in excess of statutory jurisdiction, authority, or limitations, or short of statutory right;

---

[20]   The text sets forth the typical procedures for formal rulemaking, informal rulemaking, and adjudication. The APA has alternate procedures in each instance. See *United States v. Fla. E. Coast Ry.*, 410 U.S. 224 (1973) (presented and discussed below). The vast amount of agency work is done through informal initiatives or communications, covering actions that do not fall into one of the other three categories.

(D) without observance of procedure required by law;

(E) unsupported by substantial evidence in a case subject to sections 556 and 557 of this title or otherwise reviewed on the record of an agency hearing provided by statute; or

(F) unwarranted by the facts to the extent that the facts are subject to trial de novo by the reviewing court.

3. Formal Rulemaking

Before enactment of the APA, federal agencies that engaged in rulemaking proceeded largely as they saw fit. Statutes enabling an agency to issue rules may have specified that a "hearing" be provided as part of rulemaking procedures. The Court, however, often construed such "hearing" requirements to mean not trial-type adversarial proceedings but something more akin to public meetings where arguments take place. See *Norwegian Nitrogen Prods. Co. v. United States*, 288 U.S. 294, 299–301, 306–08 (1933).

The APA in section 553(c) set forth procedures to be followed in notice-and-comment rulemaking, and prescribed more formal trial-type procedures "when rules are required by statute to be made on the record after opportunity for an agency hearing." The scope of this provision for trial-type formal rulemaking was initially considered and narrowly construed by the Supreme Court in *United States v. Allegheny-Ludlum Steel Corp.*, 406 U.S. 742 (1972). The *Florida East Coast* decision came down the following Term.

United States v. Florida East Coast Railway Co.

410 U.S. 224 (1973).

In 1966, Congress enlarged the Interstate Commerce Commission's authority under § 1(14)(a)[1] of the Interstate Commerce Act, 24 Stat. 379, as amended, 49 U.S.C. § 1(14)(a). Congress did so out of concerns for chronic freight car shortages that had become more frequent and were affecting the national transportation market. Acting pursuant to its new authority, the Commission began by requiring that railroads compile and report information about freight-car supply and demand during 12 four-week periods. After the affected railroads voiced concerns about the study, the Commission held an informal conference where the objections and proposed modifications to the study were discussed.

As Congress expressed more concerns with the Commission's slow progress, the Commission released an interim report, announcing plans to adopt a rule requiring railroads to pay a charge for the use of a freight-car owned by another railroad. These 'incentive' per diem charges were more expansive than the per diem charges the Commission had required before the amendment to § 1(14)(a). The interim report permitted interested parties to submit written comments to the Commission; the parties could also request oral hearings to present evidence. Appellees and numerous other

---

[1] Section 1(14)(a) provides:

"The Commission may, *after hearing*, on a complaint or upon its own initiative without complaint, establish reasonable rules, regulations, and practices with respect to car service by common carriers by railroad subject to this chapter, including the compensation to be paid and other terms of any contract, agreement, or arrangement for the use of any locomotive, car, or other vehicle not owned by the carrier using it (and whether or not owned by another carrier), and the penalties or other sanctions for nonobservance of such rules, regulations, or practices. * * * "[emphasis added] railroads submitted comments and requested hearings, but the Commission issued a final rule without holding any hearings.

The District Court concluded that the language of § 1(14)(a) required the Commission in a proceeding such as this to act in accordance with § 556(d) of the APA. By limiting submissions from the railroads to written form, the Commission had violated the companies' presumptive right to a trial-type hearing and left them 'prejudiced' within the meaning of § 556(d) of the APA.

Justice Rehnquist began his opinion by reviewing the Court's recent decision in *Allegheny-Ludlum Steel Corp.* In that case, the Court determined that § 1(14)(a)'s "after hearing" language was not equivalent to the requirement under § 553(c) of the APA that a rule be made "on the record after opportunity for an agency hearing." Thus, the holding in *Allegheny-Ludlum* would still apply unless the 1966 amendment changed the language sufficiently to trigger the stricter requirements of §§ 556 and 557.

The District Court had found it "hard to believe" that Congress intended the exception in § 553(c) to apply only "to the few legislative spots where the words 'on the record' or their equivalent found their way into the statute book." The Court, however, reiterated its observation from *Allegheny-Ludlum* that several statutes enacted after the APA used this language, and concluded that Congress understood the importance of the words. *Allegheny-Ludlum* had held that the "after hearing" language in § 1(14)(a) did not have the same effect as the language in § 553(c). Justice Rehnquist determined that this conclusion still applied after the 1966 amendment.

There remained the question of what meaning to give to the language "after hearing" in § 1(14)(a) itself. Justice Rehnquist noted that the word "hearing" has various meanings based on the legal context in which it is used; the term could refer to rulemaking-type proceedings or to adjudications. As guidance for determining the meaning of "hearing" in § 1(14)(a), Justice Rehnquist looked at how Congress intended the term to be used in the APA "in which Congress devoted itself exclusively to questions such as the nature and scope of hearings." He concluded that in the APA setting, "hearing" does not necessarily mean the right to oral testimony or arguments. He pointed out that although some types of agency actions are excepted from the requirements of § 553 (such as interpretive rules and general statements of policy), that section does not except actions "when notice or hearing is required by statute." Because (as the Court had held in *Allegheny-Ludlum*) these § 553 requirements do not themselves mandate oral presentation, it follows that statutes requiring a "hearing" may sometimes be satisfied by procedures that meet no more than the notice-and-comment standards of § 553.

The railroads had cited a number of Supreme Court cases that required hearings in administrative proceedings. Justice Rehnquist focused on two of these cases, *Londoner v. Denver*, 210 U.S. 373 (1908), and *Bi-Metallic Investment Co. v. State Board of Equalization*, 239 U.S. 441 (1915). In *Londoner*, the Court held that when a landowner wanted to object to an assessment of the value of his land, a local rule that only permitted submissions of written complaints deprived the landowner of due process. However, the Court in *Bi-Metallic Investment Co.* did not find a hearing was constitutionally necessary before state action that would raise the valuation of all taxable property in a city.

The difference in these holdings, in Justice Rehnquist's view, was analogous to the difference between administrative rulemaking ("proceedings for the purpose of promulgating policy-type rules") and adjudication ("proceedings designed to adjudicate disputed facts in particular cases"). The action objected to by the railroads was more akin to the agency rulemaking in *Bi-Metallic Investment Co.* because the Commission's order was applicable to all railroads subject to the Interstate Commerce Act. The Commission did not "single out any particular railroad for special consideration based on its own peculiar circumstances" (as was the case in the adjudicative action in *Londoner*). Even though the Commission relied on factual inferences as a basis for its rule, the difference is how those facts are used. Because the Commission relied on the facts to formulate "a basically legislative-type judgement, for prospective application only," the action satisfied the requirements of § 553 and § 1(14)(a). The railroads were not guaranteed a hearing.

In dissent, **Justice Douglas** contended that the decision was "a sharp break [from] traditional concepts of procedural due process," to allow an agency to "saddle anyone with a new rate, charge, or fee without a full hearing that includes the right to present oral testimony, cross-examine witnesses, and present oral argument," as called for under §§ 556(d) and 553(c) of the APA.

NOTES ON FLORIDA EAST COAST RAILWAY

1. *The Demise of Formal Rulemaking?* In Judge Friendly's words, *Florida East Coast* "seems to say that 'hearing' provisions in regulatory statutes, which had long been regarded as requiring trial-type hearings, have been modified by the Administrative Procedure Act so that nothing more than notice and written comment is required if the action falls within the APA's expansive definition of rulemaking." Henry J. Friendly, *"Some Kind of Hearing"*, 123 U. Pa. L. Rev. 1267, 1308 (1975). Does anything in the APA text allow it to preempt earlier statutes that agencies previously determined to require formal rulemaking? Does *Florida East Coast* foreclose Congress from mandating trial-type hearings as part of rulemaking in future statutes? Congress has enacted very few provisions since 1974 requiring rules to be made "on the record after opportunity for a hearing."[21] Perhaps this reflects Congress's belief that "too much process" will simply paralyze agency rulemaking. On the other hand, perhaps regulated entities and the public are left with inadequate procedural protections under section 553. Should we expect lower courts reviewing agency rulemaking to strengthen the meaning of notice-and-comment procedures once the Supreme Court has made clear that trial-type procedures are truly exceptional? In that regard, consider the Second Circuit's decision that follows in *United States v. Nova Scotia Food Products Corp.*

2. *Constitutional Aspects of the Hearing Requirement.* The Court in *Florida East Coast* relied on two early twentieth century decisions, each involving taxes levied by Colorado authorities, to explain why agency action requires a "hearing" under the Due Process Clause for adjudication but not rulemaking. In *Londoner v. Denver*, 210 U.S. 373 (1908), the city of Denver imposed a special assessment on a small group of property-owners based on their individual circumstances, without allowing them an opportunity to be heard in person and present evidence. The Court held that the failure to provide an

---

[21]   We identified two such post-1974 enacted provisions. In the Deep Seabed Hard Mineral Resources Act, 94 Stat. 553 (1980) (codified at 30 U.S.C. §§ 1401–1473), Congress required *amendments to a regulation* to be "on the record after opportunity for an agency hearing." In the Consolidated Appropriations Act, 2000, 113 Stat.1501 (Pub. L. No. 106–113), Congress required the Secretary of Agriculture to "conduct rulemaking, on the record after an opportunity for an agency hearing, to reconsider the Class III and Class IV milk pricing formulas included in the final rule for the consolidation and reform of Federal milk marketing orders that was published in the Federal Register on September 1, 1999." Other introduced bills have included this phrase or some permutation of it, but we found none that have become law.

oral hearing violated the Due Process Clause of the Fourteenth Amendment. But in *Bi-Metallic Investment Co. v. State Board of Equalization*, 239 U.S. 441 (1915), the Court rejected a similar due process challenge to a general increase in property taxes. Writing for the Court, Justice Holmes distinguished *Londoner*, where a relatively small number of persons "were exceptionally affected, in each case upon individual grounds," from *Bi-Metallic*, where the taxpayers of Denver were affected equally and in large numbers. Holmes then famously observed: "Where a rule of conduct applies to more than a few people, it is impracticable that everyone should have a direct voice in its adoption. * * *There must be a limit to individual argument in such matters if government is to go on." *Id.* at 445. Should the due process distinction between rulemaking and adjudication depend more on the small number of persons affected or on whether there has been an individualized fact-bound agency determination?

Even for adjudicative orders that require a "hearing" under the Due Process clause, the nature and timing of the hearing may vary depending on the interests at stake. In *Mathews v. Eldridge*, 424 U.S. 319, 335 (1976), the Court stated that

> "identification of the specific dictates of due process generally requires consideration of three distinct factors: First, the private interest that will be affected by the official action; second, the risk of an erroneous deprivation of such interest through the procedures used, and the probable value, if any, of additional or substitute procedural safeguards; and finally, the Government's interest, including the function involved and the fiscal and administrative burdens that the additional or substitute procedural requirement would entail."

Establishing a proper balance among these three factors may determine the timing of a hearing as well as the extent of trial-type rights accorded to the private interest affected by government action. For example, should an untenured university professor be entitled to an oral hearing before a state university may terminate her employment? Should a middle school student be entitled to an oral hearing before the school implements his planned three-day suspension? In either instance, should any such hearing include the right to present evidence on one's own behalf? To cross-examine university or school administrators? Is the case for a pre-deprivation hearing stronger in one instance than the other? Compare *Board of Regents v. Roth*, 408 U.S. 564 (1972) with *Goss v. Lopez*, 419 U.S. 565 (1975).

B. NOTICE AND COMMENT RULEMAKING

The Supreme Court's *Florida East Coast* decision signaled the ascendancy of the notice and comment approach for rulemaking. At the same time, the comparative "informality" of notice and comment does not mean an absence of predictable procedures. Consider for a moment the analogy to Congress, which enacts laws based on sequential consideration within each chamber—notice to the public and members through bill introduction and referral; development and explanation of the proposal through standing committee hearings and reports; full chamber consideration through floor debate including amendments; and final resolution through conference and presentment to the President.

Notice and comment rulemaking follows a comparably predictable process. An agency typically issues a notice in the Federal Register, proposing to take certain action, providing background data and information, and establishing a period in which interested members of the public may respond with comments. The agency's final published rule includes discussion of the comments received and how they have been treated, including identification of revisions made by the agency, and also an explanation of the basis for the most salient policy decisions embedded in the rule itself. Within these broad stages of notice and comment rulemaking, procedural issues arise regarding the adequacy of the record, the treatment of public comments, and the agency's justification for its final work product. The leading case addressing these issues is *Nova Scotia.*

UNITED STATES V. NOVA SCOTIA FOOD PRODUCTS CORP.

United States Court of Appeals for the Second Circuit, 1977.
568 F.2d 240.

GURFEIN, CIRCUIT JUDGE:

This appeal involving a regulation of the Food and Drug Administration is not here upon a direct review of agency action. It is an appeal from a judgment of the District Court for the Eastern District of New York enjoining the appellants, after a hearing, from processing hot smoked whitefish except in accordance with time-temperature-salinity (T-T-S) regulations contained in 21 C.F.R. Part 122 (1977). * * * The injunction was sought and granted on the ground that smoked whitefish which has been processed in violation of the T-T-S regulation is "adulterated." Food, Drug and Cosmetics Act ("the Act") §§ 302(a) and 301(k), 21 U.S.C. §§ 332(a), 331(k).

Appellant Nova Scotia receives frozen or iced whitefish in interstate commerce which it processes by brining, smoking and cooking. The fish are then sold as smoked whitefish.

The regulations cited above require that hot-process smoked fish be heated by a controlled heat process that provides a monitoring system positioned in as many strategic locations in the oven as necessary to assure a continuous temperature through each fish of not less than 180° F. for a minimum of 30 minutes for fish which have been brined to contain 3.5% Water phase salt or at 150° F. for a minimum of 30 minutes if the salinity was at 5% Water phase. Since each fish must meet these requirements, it is necessary to heat an entire batch of fish to even higher temperatures so that the lowest temperature for any fish will meet the minimum requirements.

Government inspection of appellants' plant established without question that the minimum T-T-S requirements were not being met. There is no substantial claim that the plant was processing whitefish under "insanitary conditions" in any other material respect. Appellants, on their part, do not defend on the ground that they were in compliance, but rather that the requirements could not be met if a marketable whitefish was to be produced. They defend upon the grounds that the regulation is invalid (1) because it is beyond the authority delegated by the statute; (2) because the FDA improperly relied upon undisclosed evidence in promulgating the regulation and because it is not supported by the administrative record; and (3) because there was no adequate statement setting forth the basis of the regulation. We reject the contention that the regulation is beyond the authority delegated by the statute, but we find serious inadequacies in the procedure followed in the

promulgation of the regulation, and hold it to be invalid as appli[...]
herein.

The hazard which the FDA sought to minimize was the o[...] formation of Clostridium botulinum Type E spores of the bacteri[...] inhabit fish. There had been an occurrence of several cases of [...] consumption of fish from inland waters in 1960 and 1963 [...] considerable bacteriological research. These bacteria can be present in the soil and water of various regions. They can invade fish in their natural habitat and can be further disseminated in the course of evisceration and preparation of the fish for cooking. A failure to destroy such spores through an adequate brining, thermal, and refrigeration process was found to be dangerous to public health.

The Commissioner of Food and Drugs ("Commissioner"), employing informal "notice-and-comment" procedures under 21 U.S.C. § 371(a), issued a proposal for the control of C. botulinum bacteria Type E in fish. 34 Fed. Reg. 17,176 (Oct. 23, 1969). For his statutory authority to promulgate the regulations, the Commissioner specifically relied only upon § 342(a)(4) of the Act which provides:

"A food shall be deemed to be adulterated

"(4) if it has been prepared, packed, or held under insanitary conditions whereby it may have become contaminated with filth, or whereby it may have been rendered injurious to health;"

* * * Responding to the Commissioner's invitation in the notice of proposed rulemaking, members of the industry, including appellants and the intervenor-appellant, submitted comments on the proposed regulation.

The Commissioner thereafter issued the final regulations in which he adopted certain suggestions made in the comments, including a suggestion by the National Fisheries Institute, Inc. ("the Institute"), the intervenor herein. 35 Fed. Reg. 17,401 (Nov. 13, 1970). The original proposal provided that the fish would have to be cooked to a temperature of 180° F. for at least 30 minutes, if the fish have been brined to contain 3.5% Water phase salt, with no alternative. In the final regulation, an alternative suggested by the intervenor "that the parameter of 150° F. for 30 minutes and 5% Salt in the water phase be established as an alternate procedure to that stated in the proposed regulation for an interim period until specific parameters can be established" was accepted, but as a permanent part of the regulation rather than for an interim period.

The intervenor suggested that "specific parameters" be established. This referred to particular processing parameters for different species of fish on a "species by species" basis. Such "species by species" determination was proposed not only by the intervenor but also by the Bureau of Commercial Fisheries of the Department of the Interior. That Bureau objected to the general application of the T-T-S requirement proposed by the FDA on the ground that application of the regulation to all species of fish being smoked was not commercially feasible, and that the regulation should therefore specify time-temperature-salinity requirements, as developed by research and study, on a species-by-species basis. The Bureau suggested that "wholesomeness considerations could be more practically and adequately realized by reducing processing temperature and using suitable concentrations of nitrite and salt." The Commissioner took cognizance of the suggestion, but decided, nevertheless, to impose the T-T-S requirement on all species of fish (except chub, which were regulated by 21 C.F.R. 172.177 (1977) (dealing with food additives)).

He did acknowledge, however, in his "basis and purpose" statement required by the Administrative Procedure Act ("APA"), 5 U.S.C. § 553(c), that "adequate times, temperatures and salt concentrations have not been demonstrated for each individual species of fish presently smoked". 35 Fed. Reg. 17,401 (Nov. 13, 1970). The Commissioner concluded, nevertheless, that "the processing requirements of the proposed regulations are the safest now known to prevent the outgrowth and toxin formation of C. botulinum Type E". He determined that "the conditions of current good manufacturing practice for this industry should be established without further delay." *Id.*

The Commissioner did not answer the suggestion by the Bureau of Fisheries that nitrite and salt as additives could safely lower the high temperature otherwise required, a solution which the FDA had accepted in the case of chub. Nor did the Commissioner respond to the claim of Nova Scotia through its trade association, the Association of Smoked Fish Processors, Inc., Technical Center that "(t)he proposed process requirements suggested by the FDA for hot processed smoked fish are neither commercially feasible nor based on sound scientific evidence obtained with the variety of smoked fish products to be included under this regulation."

Nova Scotia, in its own comment, wrote to the Commissioner that "the heating of certain types of fish to high temperatures will completely destroy the product". * * * We have noted above that the response given by the Commissioner was in general terms. He did not specifically aver that the T-T-S requirements as applied to whitefish were, in fact, commercially feasible.

When, after several inspections and warnings, Nova Scotia failed to comply with the regulation, an action by the United States Attorney for injunctive relief was filed on April 7, 1976, six years later, and resulted in the judgment here on appeal. * * *

[I] [The court rejected Nova Scotia's contention that the FDA lacked statutory authority to promulgate the challenged T-T-S regulation.]

[II] Appellants contend that there is an inadequate administrative record upon which to predicate judicial review, and that the failure to disclose to interested persons the factual material upon which the agency was relying vitiates the element of fairness which is essential to any kind of administrative action. Moreover, they argue that the "concise general statement of . . . . basis and purpose" by the Commissioner was inadequate.

The question of what is an adequate "record" in informal rulemaking has engaged the attention of commentators for several years. The extent of the administrative record required for judicial review of informal rulemaking is largely a function of the scope of judicial review. Even when the standard of review is whether the promulgation of the rule was "arbitrary, capricious, an abuse of discretion, or otherwise not in accordance with law," as specified in 5 U.S.C.

§ 706(2)(A), judicial review must nevertheless, be based on the "whole record" (Id.). Adequate review of a determination requires an adequate record, if the review is to be meaningful. What will constitute an adequate record for meaningful review may vary with the nature of the administrative action to be reviewed. Review must be based on the whole record even when the judgment is one of policy, except that findings of fact such as would be required in an adjudicatory proceeding or in a formal "on the record" hearing for rulemaking need not be made. Though the action was informal, without an evidentiary record, the review must be "thorough, probing, [and] in depth".

This raises several questions regarding the informal rulemaking procedure followed here: (1) What record does a reviewing court look to? (2) How much of what the agency relied on should have been disclosed to interested persons? (3) To what extent must the agency respond to criticism that is material?

[A] With respect to the content of the administrative "record," the Supreme Court has told us that in informal rulemaking, "the focal point for judicial review should be the administrative record already in existence, not some new record made initially in the reviewing court." See *Camp v. Pitts*, 411 U.S. 138 (1973).

No contemporaneous record was made or certified.[13] When, during the enforcement action, the basis for the regulation was sought through pretrial discovery, the record was created by searching the files of the FDA and the memories of those who participated in the process of rulemaking. This resulted in what became Exhibit D at the trial of the injunction action. Exhibit D consists of (1) Tab A containing the comments received from outside parties during the administrative "notice-and-comment" proceeding and (2) Tabs B through L consisting of scientific data and the like upon which the Commissioner now says he relied but which were not made known to the interested parties.

Appellants object to the exclusion of evidence in the District Court "aimed directly at showing that the scientific evidence relied upon by the FDA was inaccurate and not based upon a realistic appraisal of the true facts. Appellants attempted to introduce scientific evidence to demonstrate that in fixing the processing parameters FDA relied upon tests in which ground fish were injected with many millions of botulism (sic) spores and then tested for outgrowth at various processing levels whereas the spore levels in nature are far less and outgrowth would have been prevented by far less stringent processing parameters." The District Court properly excluded the evidence.

In an enforcement action, we must rely exclusively on the record made before the agency to determine the validity of the regulation. The exception to the exclusivity of that record is that "there may be independent judicial fact-finding when issues that were not before the agency are raised in a proceeding to *enforce* non-

---

[13] A practice developed in the early years of the APA of not making a formal contemporaneous record, but rather, when challenged, to put together a historical record of what had been available for agency consideration at the time the regulation was promulgated. "One can conclude that 'record' now means whatever the agency produces on review." Verkuil, *supra*, 60 Va. L. Rev. at 204. Professor Davis in a balanced review, has stated: "When the facts are of central importance and might be challenged, parties adversely affected by them should have a chance to respond to them. Clearly, whatever "factual information the agency has considered should be a part of the record for judicial review." K. Davis, *supra*, § 29.01–6, pp. 672–73.

adjudicatory agency action." *Overton Park*, 401 U.S. at 415, (1971). (Emphasis added.)

Though this is an enforcement proceeding and the question is close, we think that the "issues" were fairly before the agency and hence that de novo evidence was properly excluded. *Camp v. Pitts*. Our concern is, rather, with the manner in which the agency treated the issues tendered.

[B] The key issues were (1) whether, in the light of the rather scant history of botulism in whitefish, that species should have been considered separately rather than included in a general regulation which failed to distinguish species from species; (2) whether the application of the proposed T-T-S requirements to smoked whitefish made the whitefish commercially unsaleable; and (3) whether the agency recognized that prospect, but nevertheless decided that the public health needs should prevail even if that meant commercial death for the whitefish industry. The procedural issues were whether, in the light of these key questions, the agency procedure was inadequate because (i) it failed to disclose to interested parties the scientific data and the methodology upon which it relied; and (ii) because it failed utterly to address itself to the pertinent question of commercial feasibility.

The history of botulism occurrence in whitefish, as established in the trial record, which we must assume was available to the FDA in 1970, is as follows. Between 1899 and 1964 there were only eight cases of botulism reported as attributable to hot-smoked whitefish. In all eight instances, vacuum-packed whitefish was involved. All of the eight cases occurred in 1960 and 1963. The industry has abandoned vacuum-packing, and there has not been a single case of botulism associated with commercially prepared whitefish since 1963, though 2,750,000 pounds of whitefish are processed annually. Thus, in the seven-year period from 1964 through 1970, 17.25 million pounds of whitefish have been commercially processed in the United States without a single reported case of botulism. The evidence also disclosed that defendant Nova Scotia has been in business some 56 years, and that there has never been a case of botulism illness from the whitefish processed by it.

Interested parties were not informed of the scientific data, or at least of a selection of such data deemed important by the agency, so that comments could be addressed to the data. Appellants argue that unless the scientific data relied upon by the agency are spread upon the public records, criticism of the methodology used or the meaning to be inferred from the data is rendered impossible.

We agree with appellants in this case, for although we recognize that an agency may resort to its own expertise outside the record in an informal rulemaking procedure, we do not believe that when the pertinent research material is readily available and the agency has no special expertise on the precise parameters involved, there is any reason to conceal the scientific data relied upon from the interested parties. As Judge Leventhal said in *Portland Cement Ass'n v. Ruckelshaus*, 486 F.2d 375, 393 (1973): "It is not consonant with the purpose of a rulemaking proceeding to promulgate rules on the basis of inadequate data, or on data that (in) critical degree, is known only to the agency." This is not a case where the agency methodology was based on material supplied by the interested parties themselves. Cf. *Int'l Harvester Co. v. Ruckelshaus*, 478 F.2d 615, 632 (1973). Here all the scientific research was collected by the agency, and none of it was disclosed to interested parties as the material upon which the proposed rule would be fashioned.[14] Nor was an articulate effort made to connect the scientific requirements to available technology that would make commercial survival possible, though the burden of proof was on the agency. This required it to "bear a burden of adducing a reasoned presentation supporting the reliability of its methodology." *Int'l Harvester*, 478 F.2d at 643.

Though a reviewing court will not match submission against counter-submission to decide whether the agency was correct in its conclusion on scientific matters (unless that conclusion is arbitrary), it will consider whether the agency has taken account of all "relevant factors and whether there has been a clear error of judgment." *Overton Park, supra*, 401 U.S. at 415–16. * * *

If the failure to notify interested persons of the scientific research upon which the agency was relying actually prevented the presentation of relevant comment, the agency may be held not to have considered all "the relevant factors." We can think of no sound reasons for secrecy or reluctance to expose to public view (with an exception for trade secrets or national security) the ingredients of the deliberative process. Indeed, the FDA's own regulations now specifically require that every notice of proposed rulemaking contain "references to all data and information on which the Commissioner relies for the proposal (copies or a full list of which shall be a part of the administrative file on the matter . . .)." 21 C.F.R. § 10.40(b) (1) (1977). And this is, undoubtedly, the trend.[15]

We think that the scientific data should have been disclosed to focus on the proper interpretation of "insanitary conditions." When the basis for a proposed rule is a scientific decision, the scientific material which is believed to support the rule should be exposed to the view of interested parties for their comment. One cannot ask for comment on a scientific paper without allowing the participants to read the paper. Scientific research is sometimes rejected for diverse inadequacies of methodology; and statistical results are sometimes rebutted because of a lack of adequate gathering technique or of supportable extrapolation. Such is the stuff of scientific debate. To suppress meaningful comment by failure to disclose the basic data relied upon is akin to rejecting comment altogether. For unless there is common ground, the comments are unlikely to be of a quality that might impress a careful agency. The inadequacy of comment in turn leads in the direction of arbitrary decision-making. We do not speak of findings of fact, for such are not technically required in the informal rulemaking procedures. We speak rather of what the agency should make known so as to elicit comments that probe the fundamentals. Informal rulemaking does not lend itself to a rigid pattern. Especially, in the circumstance of our broad reading of statutory authority in support of the agency, we conclude that the failure to disclose to interested persons the scientific data upon which the FDA relied was procedurally erroneous. Moreover, the burden was upon the agency to

---

[14] We recognize the problem posed by Judge Leventhal in *International Harvester*, that a proceeding might never end if such submission required a reply ad infinitum, *ibid.* Here the exposure of the scientific research relied on simply would have required a single round of comment addressed thereto.

[15] And see Judge Friendly's discussion of recent developments in rulemaking and judicial review in Friendly, *"Some Kind of Hearing,"* 123 U. Pa. L. Rev. 1267, 1305–15 (1975).

articulate rationally why the rule should apply to a large and diverse class, with the same T-T-S parameters made applicable to all species.

[C] Appellants additionally attack the "concise general statement" required by APA, 5 U.S.C. § 553, as inadequate. We think that, in the circumstances, it was less than adequate. It is not in keeping with the rational process to leave vital questions, raised by comments which are of cogent materiality, completely unanswered. The agencies certainly have a good deal of discretion in expressing the basis of a rule, but the agencies do not have quite the prerogative of obscurantism reserved to legislatures. "Congress did not purport to transfer its legislative power to the unbounded discretion of the regulatory body." *F.C.C. v. RCA Commc'ns, Inc.*, 346 U.S. 86, 90 (1953) (Frankfurter, J.). * * *

The test of adequacy of the "concise general statement" was expressed by Judge McGowan in the following terms:

"We do not expect the agency to discuss every item of fact or opinion included in the submissions made to it in informal rulemaking. We do expect that, if the judicial review which Congress has thought it important to provide is to be meaningful, the 'concise general statement of . . . basis and purpose' mandated by Section 4 will enable us to see what major issues of policy were ventilated by the informal proceedings and why the agency reacted to them as it did." *Auto. Parts & Accessories Ass'n v. Boyd*, 407 F.2d 330, 338 (1968).

* * * The Secretary was squarely faced with the question whether it was necessary to formulate a rule with specific parameters that applied to all species of fish, and particularly whether lower temperatures with the addition of nitrite and salt would not be sufficient. Though this alternative was suggested by an agency of the federal government, its suggestion, though acknowledged, was never answered.

Moreover, the comment that to apply the proposed T-T-S requirements to whitefish would destroy the commercial product was neither discussed nor answered. We think that to sanction silence in the face of such vital questions would be to make the statutory requirement of a "concise general statement" less than an adequate safeguard against arbitrary decision-making.

We cannot improve on the statement of the District of Columbia Circuit in *Industrial Union Dep't, AFL-CIO v. Hodgson*, 499 F.2d 467, 475 (1974).

"What we are entitled to at all events is a careful identification by the Secretary, when his proposed standards are challenged, of the reasons why he chooses to follow one course rather than another. Where that choice purports to be based on the existence of certain determinable facts, the Secretary must, in form as well as in substance, find those facts from evidence in the record. By the same token, when the Secretary is obliged to make policy judgments where no factual certainties exist or where facts alone do not provide the answer, he should so state and go on to identify the considerations he found to be persuasive."

One may recognize that even commercial infeasibility cannot stand in the way of an overwhelming public interest. Yet the administrative process should disclose, at least, whether the proposed regulation is considered to be commercially feasible, or whether other considerations prevail even if commercial infeasibility is acknowledged. This kind of forthright disclosure and basic statement was lacking in the formulation of the T-T-S standard made applicable to whitefish. It is easy enough for an administrator to ban everything. In the regulation of food processing, the worldwide need for food also must be taken into account in formulating measures taken for the protection of health. In the light of the history of smoked whitefish to which we have referred, we find no articulate balancing here sufficient to make the procedure followed less than arbitrary.

[handwritten margin note: No Articulate Balancing sufficient to make procedure less than arbitrary]

After seven years of relative inaction, the FDA has apparently not reviewed the T-T-S regulations in the light of present scientific knowledge and experience. In the absence of a new statutory directive by Congress regarding control of microorganisms, which we hope will be worthy of its consideration, we think that the T-T-S standards should be reviewed again by the FDA.

We cannot, on this appeal, remand to the agency to allow further comments by interested parties, addressed to the scientific data now disclosed at the trial below. We hold in this enforcement proceeding, therefore, that the regulation, as it affects non-vacuum-packed hot-smoked whitefish, was promulgated in an arbitrary manner and is invalid. * * *

[handwritten note: Arbitrary Regulation]

[handwritten note: here]

NOTES ON NOVA SCOTIA *AND THE* NOTICE-AND-COMMENT *RULEMAKING PROCESS*

1.   *Contents of the* Nova Scotia *Administrative Record.* The "record" in *Nova Scotia* was constructed after the fact by searching agency files and the memories of agency participants. As Judge Gurfein observes, agencies no longer rely on such informal post-hoc techniques; instead, notices of proposed rulemaking typically include references to all data and information on which the agency is relying for its proposal. The court criticizes the FDA for failing to disclose in its original notice the scientific studies on which it based its proposed T-T-S regulation. At the time it issued its notice, did the agency need to disclose every scientific study of which it was aware regarding the risks of botulism and methods of preventing it? Or only those on which it actually relied when formulating its proposal? On what basis did the Second Circuit decide that certain scientific evidence was properly excluded by the district court?

2.   *The Record as Described in the APA.* The APA text is not terribly precise with respect to what should be part of the rulemaking record. Under section 553(b)(3), the notice of proposed rulemaking that appears in the Federal Register "shall include . . . either the terms or substance of the proposed rule or a description of the subjects and issues involved." After this notice, section 553(c) accords interested persons "an opportunity to participate in the rule making through submission of written data, views, or arguments. . . ." Notwithstanding the statute's failure to require inclusion of an evidentiary basis for proposed rules, reviewing courts have devoted considerable attention to the adequacy of informal rulemaking records pursuant to the Supreme Court's holding that under section 706, judicial review of agency action must be based on the "whole record" compiled by the agency. *Citizens to Preserve Overton Park v. Volpe*, 401 U.S. 402, 419 (1971).

Richard McMillan Jr. and Todd Peterson argue that courts have created five guidelines for determining the proper scope of what constitutes a whole or complete record: (1) the record should include all documents the agency considers, not just those on which the agency relies; (2) the record should include all documents considered or relied on by agency personnel whose work and recommendations reached the agency decisionmaker; (3) bona fide confidential business information ordinarily need not be included in the record; (4) deliberative intra-agency memoranda and staff reports should ordinarily be excluded from the record, although a court may require their inclusion to supply a contemporaneous explanation for the decision if the agency has made no findings to explain its decision or its findings are incomplete; (5) materials that provide factual support for materials in the record need not be part of the record unless they were reviewed or considered by the agency personnel involved in the decision. Richard McMillan, Jr. and Todd Peterson, *The Permissible Scope of Hearings, Discovery, and Additional Factfinding During Judicial Review of Informal Agency Action*, 1982 Duke L.J. 333, 341–43 (1982). To what extent do these five guidelines reflect the concerns Judge Gurfein raises in his opinion? Why do courts want the record to include documents *considered*, rather than simply *relied on*, by the agency? How onerous might it be for a record to include all documents considered by agency employees whose work contributed to the final decision? What about the guidelines that presumptively exclude certain materials—what is the basis for such limitations?

3.   *Scope and Timing of Disclosure Requirement.* Quoting Judge Harold Leventhal, Judge Gurfein emphasized that "it is not consonant with the purpose of a rulemaking proceeding to promulgate rules [based on] data that [in] critical degree is known only to the agency." We have discussed whether this disclosure requirement covers only information or data the agency relied on, or also information the agency considered or even information of which it was aware. Another aspect of scope involves what constitutes *publicly available information*. Suppose the agency has relied on an enormous number of well-settled scientific studies, information that is clearly *not* "known only to the agency." Do agency officials need to list hundreds of studies and explain how each study contributes to their proposal? Isn't it likely that some publicly available information will be so plainly relevant that it would neither promote fairness to interested parties nor improve the quality of judicial review to have it listed as part of the record? Alternatively, should such exclusions be limited to studies that are truly background sources rather than any information on which the agency relies as central to its proposal? See *Chamber of Commerce v. SEC*, 443 F.3d 890, 906 (D.C. Cir. 2006).

Then there is the matter of the *timing of the disclosure requirement*. In *Nova Scotia*, the agency's failure occurred during the period before the FDA began soliciting comments. What are the agency's disclosure obligations with respect to information or data received during the comment period or after the period ends? If the APA requires the agency to disclose all new material by issuing an amended notice of proposed rulemaking setting a further period for comments, what problems might result? On the other hand, if the agency is permitted to issue a final rule relying primarily or exclusively on material received once the comment period began, is such discretion consistent with the language and purposes of the APA? In responding to these questions, is it relevant whether the after-acquired information was generated by the agency itself or by a potentially affected party? If the latter, does it matter whether the information was produced at the party's initiative or in response to an agency request or invitation? Should it make a difference whether the information contributes genuinely new evidence as opposed to supporting or confirming data already in the record?

Consider two decisions from the Ninth Circuit that address an agency's obligations to disclose material after the close of the comment period. In *Rybachek v. EPA*, 904 F.2d 1276 (9th Cir. 1990), plaintiffs alleged that the EPA's addition of over 6,000 pages to the administrative record following the comment period on a proposed Clean Water Act regulation had deprived them of their rights as interested parties to comment on the record. The court held that no right to meaningful public participation was violated:

> "The additional material was the EPA's response to comments made during a public-comment period. Nothing prohibits the Agency from adding supporting documentation for a final rule in response to public comments. In fact, adherence to the [plaintiffs'] view might result in the EPA's never being able to issue a final rule capable of standing up to review: every time the Agency responded to public comments, such as those in this rulemaking, it would trigger a new comment period. Thus, either the comment period would continue in a never-ending circle, or, if the EPA chose not to respond to the last set of public comments, any final rule could be struck down for lack of support in the record. The [plaintiffs'] unviolated right was to comment on the proposed regulations, not to comment in a never-ending way on the EPA's responses to their comments." *Id.* at 1286.

In *Ober v. EPA*, 84 F.3d 304 (9th Cir. 1996), plaintiffs complained that the EPA had violated their rights to notice and an opportunity to comment on pending air quality standards when the agency requested additional material from the state of Arizona after the time period for comments had closed and then relied on this additional information in its final plan. This time the court reached a different result, and in doing so limited the reach of *Rybachek*:

> "In *Rybachek*, the added materials were the EPA's *own* responses to comments received during the public comment period. Here, in contrast, the additional documentation was submitted by the State in response to the EPA's request for further information. * * * Thus, the additional materials in *Rybachek* involved the EPA's internal assessment of comments from the public; whereas, here, the new information was solicited by the EPA from an interested party. Furthermore, in *Rybachek*, * * * [t]he additional information was not relied on or critical to the EPA's decision. Instead, the EPA decided not to alter the regulation based on the additional information it developed in response to the comments. Here, on the other hand, the added material related to the Implementation Plan's compliance with a critical statutory provision. * * * Although there is merit to EPA's argument that agencies are not required to review an endless cycle of comments from interested parties, the nature and extent of the additional information in this case required another round of comment and review." *Id.* at 314–15.

Is the court in *Ober* persuasive in distinguishing its *Rybachek* holding? Why should it matter whether EPA solicited new information from an interested party? Assuming that the new information was merely confirmatory and not "related to . . . compliance with a critical statutory provision," would the court even have invoked this factor? If the different results really hinge on the importance of the after-acquired information, what is the risk that courts will wield undue discretion in making such judgments?

4.   *Agency Responses to Criticism.* Judge McGowan in the D.C. Circuit's *Automotive Parts* decision (quoted by Judge Gurfein) explained that an agency is not "expect[ed] to

discuss every item of fact or opinion included in the submissions made to it in informal rulemaking," but at the same time the statement should "enable [courts] to see what major issues of policy were ventilated by the informal proceedings and why the agency reacted to them as it did." *Auto. Parts & Accessories Ass'n v. Boyd*, 407 F.2d 330, 338 (1968). In Judge Gurfein's words, "[i]t is not in keeping with the rational process to leave vital questions, raised by comments which are of cogent materiality, completely unanswered."

The court in *Nova Scotia* views the general statement requirement as a critical safeguard against arbitrary decisionmaking. But how does an agency determine which questions raised by the comments are "vital," thus requiring a response? Does vital encompass every non-frivolous comment or is the universe more limited? If an agency receives hundreds of non-frivolous comments, should it anticipate having to respond to a substantial number in order to establish its bona fides for a reviewing court? For example, assume the Federal Aviation Administration issues a notice and proposed rule to close air traffic control towers at 150 regional airports across the country. All 150 airports respond with comments explaining why their tower should not be closed—for reasons of safety, fairness, or convenience. Is every comment vital? Judge Gurfein's quote mentions responding to comments of "cogent materiality" but this seems rather open-ended: is there any reason to view safety as more cogent than fairness, or fairness as more material than convenience? Alternatively, should the meaning of vitality relate to some more quantifiable factor, such as the number of parties affected? The extent to which scientific data is implicated? Whether a comment is predominantly or substantially repetitive of points raised by others? Is the test for vitality likely to differ between agencies?

Once it has determined which questions are vital, how expansive must an agency be in discussing each question? Should the agency be obligated to dispel the criticism in full or simply say enough to show that it considered the comment? Many questions may raise complex factual issues related to cost, safety, or efficiency; must the agency always provide individualized responses or may it rely in part on boilerplate approaches? One can imagine a menu of agency responses: some aimed at establishing the correctness of the agency's position, others indicating that reasonable minds can disagree on the issue raised, and still others suggesting that the question is best addressed with more information collected in some subsequent notice and comment proceeding. Won't agencies inevitably consider a version of this blended response as they anticipate how to survive judicial review? Does this type of strategic thinking serve the goals underlying the concise general statement requirement?

Should the standard of judicial review be influenced at all by whether an agency receives little or no public input, as opposed to responding to hundreds or thousands of individualized comments and suggestions? David Fontana proposes that the APA require agencies to include as part of their general statement a "democratic participation statement (DPS) . . . indicat[ing] the number of relevant and non-repetitive comments received during rulemaking, and break[ing] down by category and by individual or institutional interest who precisely submitted these comments." Comments that are unresponsive or that duplicate other comments would not be counted. Courts would have jurisdiction to review the DPS (under a flexible standard) to make sure it is truthful. Fontana contends that the number of relevant and non-repetitive comments submitted should form the basis for determining whether the agency rule is entitled to special deference from a reviewing court. He recognizes various criticisms, but argues that individual counting of comments would be relatively objective while screening out repetitive comments would minimize the risks of agency capture from organized interest group campaigns. David Fontana, *Reforming the Administrative Procedure Act: Democracy Index Rulemaking*, 74 Fordham L. Rev. 81, 89–90, 99, 120–21 (2005). Does Fontana's proposal seem like an improvement on the current judicial review process? Does it adequately account for considerations of equality or for public choice-related concerns?

5.   *Agency Versus Legislative Rulemaking.* With respect to the "concise general statement of basis and purpose" required under section 553(c), Judge Gurfein observed that "agencies do not have quite the prerogative of obscurantism reserved to legislatures." Why not? What explains the fact that an agency must respond to material questions or concerns about its proposed rule when Congress need not do so as part of its lawmaking process? More generally, the language of section 553(c) does not require that agencies compile a complete documentary record, or furnish rational explanations in writing for their final rules that include responses to significant critical comments. Yet Judge Gurfein, Judge McGowan, and other circuit court judges have essentially read these requirements into the APA. To what extent have reviewing courts undermined the idea of agencies as experts in the subject matter delegated to them by Congress? Or have they simply replaced the expertise model of agency decisionmaking with a different one? See Lisa Schultz Bressman, *Beyond Accountability: Arbitrariness and Legitimacy in the Administrative State*, 78 N.Y.U. L. Rev. 461, 473–74 (2003).

Assume that concerns about botulism and smoked fish had been taken up by Congress instead of the FDA, and that following committee consideration and floor debate, Congress had adopted the same approach in statutory form—a single provision applicable to all forms of smoked or salted fish without reference to the particular species. What procedural objections could Nova Scotia raise before a reviewing court? Would you expect Nova Scotia to prevail in challenging such a statute? If not, how can you justify the company's success in contesting the FDA rulemaking effort under the APA? Is the different result due to considerations of political accountability? To differences in the level of generality between laws and regulations? Are there other reasons?

C. ADJUDICATION

The APA provides for rulemaking and adjudication as the two main procedural channels for agencies implementing statutory policies. From APA enactment in 1946 until the late 1960s, most agencies relied on case-by-case adjudication to develop policies. See M. Elizabeth Magill, *Agency Choice of Policymaking Form*, 71 U. Chi. L. Rev. 1383, 1398 (2004) (citing sources). In the course of adjudicating a particular controversy, an agency may develop detailed rules to which it subsequently ascribes precedential status. These adjudicatory rules will affect if not control the resolution of future cases presenting identical or comparable issues. The agency may, for example, amplify the meaning of crucial yet ambiguous statutory terms (see *Town & Country Elec. Co.*, 309 N.L.R.B. 1250 (1992)), or it may set forth burdens of proof with respect to certain statutorily protected activities (see *Levitz Furniture Co.*, 333 N.L.R.B. 717 (2001)). These types of adjudicatory rules effectively make policy, facilitating resolution of similar issues in later cases.

Between the late 1960s and late 1970s, many agencies shifted from adjudication to rulemaking as their primary policymaking approach. Multiple factors contributed to this shift. An important element was Congress, which created new health and safety agencies such as EPA, OSHA, and the National Highway Traffic Safety Administration, and required that these agencies pursue rulemaking in specified contexts. In addition, existing agencies acted from efficiency considerations, responding to increasingly onerous caseloads and to criticism for lack of predictability or rationality in explaining their policies. See Reuel Schiller, *Rulemaking's Promise: Administrative Law and Legal Culture in the 1960s and 1970s*, 53 Admin. L. Rev. 1139, 1148–51 (2001). Not all agencies followed this trend: the NLRB and the FTC, among others, continued to rely heavily on adjudication as a mode of policy implementation. And Magill observes that we may now be experiencing another sea change in agency behavior: "making policy through [strategic agency-initiated] litigation, negotiated settlements, or the waiver of rules in individual contexts can be seen as a shift back" to the case-by-case approach. 71 U. Chi. L. Rev. at 1399.

In reading the two cases that follow, consider the benefits and costs of adjudication versus rulemaking from the standpoint of agencies and also regulated entities. Does one approach offer a better prospect for developing and implementing policies that are predictable? Consistent? Flexible? What role does Congress play in shaping agency choice of procedural approach? What about the role of reviewing courts: does the extent of judicial scrutiny, and an agency's related ability to survive judicial challenge, exert influence in a particular direction?

SECURITIES AND EXCHANGE COMMISSION
V. CHENERY CORPORATION

Supreme Court of the United States, 1947.
332 U.S. 194, 67 S.Ct. 1575, 91 L.Ed. 1995.

MR. JUSTICE MURPHY delivered the opinion of the Court.

This case is here for the second time. In *S.E.C. v. Chenery Corporation*, 318 U.S. 80, we held that an order of the Securities and Exchange Commission could not be sustained on the grounds upon which that agency acted. We therefore directed that the case be remanded to the Commission for such further proceedings as might be appropriate. On remand, the Commission reexamined the problem, recast its rationale and reached the same result. The issue now is whether the Commission's action is proper in light of the principles established in our prior decision.

When the case was first here, we emphasized a simple but fundamental rule of administrative law. That rule is to the effect that a reviewing court, in dealing with a determination or judgment which an administrative agency alone is authorized to make, must judge the propriety of such action solely by the grounds invoked by the agency. If those grounds are inadequate or improper, the court is powerless to affirm the administrative action by substituting what it considers to be a more adequate or proper basis. To do so would propel the court into the domain which Congress has set aside exclusively for the administrative agency.

We also emphasized in our prior decision an important corollary of the foregoing rule. If the administrative action is to be tested by the basis upon which it purports to rest, that basis must be set forth with such clarity as to be understandable. It will not do for a court to be compelled to guess at the theory underlying the agency's action; nor can a court be expected to chisel that which must be precise from what the agency has left vague and indecisive. In other words, "We must know what a decision means before the duty becomes ours to say whether it is right or wrong."

Applying this rule and its corollary, the Court was unable to sustain the Commission's original action.

[The case involved a complicated reorganization of the Federal Water Service Corporation (Federal), a holding company registered under the Public Utility Holding Company Act of 1935. Company shareholders with "preferred" stock lacked voting rights to elect corporate directors. Chenery and his group (respondents) owned a controlling block of "common" stock that gave them the power to select corporate management. In rejecting numerous consecutive reorganization plans submitted by Federal, the SEC insisted initially that an acceptable plan must convert the non-voting preferred stock into common stock in order to insure adequate distribution of shareholder voting power; and subsequently that respondents' purchases of preferred shares in contemplation of this conversion (although fully disclosed and at a fair market price) improperly conferred the same voting rights as were given to other converted preferred shares. In the end, the agency amended Federal's plan, over respondents' objections, to provide that respondents' preferred stock was to be surrendered at cost plus any accumulated dividends.

The SEC justified its decision based on its understanding of judicial precedent, which was that corporate management occupied a fiduciary position toward all shareholders during a reorganization, and that pursuant to applicable judge-made equitable principles, management's duty of fair dealing would be violated if it traded in the corporation's stock during this period, even at a fair price and without fraud. The Supreme Court held against the SEC, concluding that the agency's decision was based on a misreading of principles of equity derived from judicial decisions; the courts had not imposed upon corporate officers and directors any fiduciary duty to stockholders that precluded them from buying and selling the corporation's stock simply because they were officers and directors.]

The latest order of the Commission definitely avoids the fatal error of relying on judicial precedents which do not sustain it. This time, after a thorough reexamination of the problem in light of the purposes and standards of the Holding Company Act, the Commission has concluded that the proposed transaction is inconsistent with the standards of §§ 7 and 11 of the Act. It has drawn heavily upon its accumulated experience in dealing with utility reorganizations. And it has expressed its reasons with a clarity and thoroughness that admit of no doubt as to the underlying basis of its order.

The argument is pressed upon us, however, that the Commission was foreclosed from taking such a step following our prior decision. It is said that, in the absence of findings of conscious wrongdoing on the part of Federal's management, the Commission could not determine by an order in this particular case that it was inconsistent with the statutory standards to permit Federal's management to realize a profit through the reorganization purchases. All that it could do was to enter an order allowing an amendment to the plan so that the proposed transaction could be

[Handwritten margin notes: "Before deciding(?) What does a decision mean"; "reorg Federal Water Service corporation"; "nonvoting preferred stock into common stock"; "preferred stock surrender"; "self dealing?"; "Allowing An Amendment to the plan so the proposed transaction could Be consummated"]

consummated. Under this view, the Commission would be free only to promulgate a general rule outlawing such profits in future utility reorganizations; but such a rule would have to be prospective in nature and have no retroactive effect upon the instant situation.

We reject this contention, for it grows out of a misapprehension of our prior decision and of the Commission's statutory duties. We held no more and no less than that the Commission's first order was unsupportable for the reasons supplied by that agency. * * * Still unsettled, however, was the answer the Commission might give were it to bring to bear on the facts the proper administrative and statutory considerations, a function which belongs exclusively to the Commission in the first instance. The administrative process had taken an erroneous rather than a final turn. Hence we carefully refrained from expressing any views as to the propriety of an order rooted in the proper and relevant considerations. * * * After the remand was made, therefore, the Commission was bound to deal with the problem afresh, performing the function delegated to it by Congress. It was again charged with the duty of measuring the proposed treatment of the management's preferred stock holdings by relevant and proper standards. Only in that way could the legislative policies embodied in the Act be effectuated.

The absence of a general rule or regulation governing management trading during reorganization did not affect the Commission's duties in relation to the particular proposal before it. The Commission was asked to grant or deny effectiveness to a proposed amendment to Federal's reorganization plan whereby the management would be accorded parity treatment on its holdings. It could do that only in the form of an order, entered after a due consideration of the particular facts in light of the relevant and proper standards. That was true regardless of whether those standards previously had been spelled out in a general rule or regulation. Indeed, if the Commission rightly felt that the proposed amendment was inconsistent with those standards, an order giving effect to the amendment merely because there was no general rule or regulation covering the matter would be unjustified.

It is true that our prior decision explicitly recognized the possibility that the Commission might have promulgated a general rule dealing with this problem under its statutory rule-making powers, in which case the issue for our consideration would have been entirely different from that which did confront us. But we did not mean to imply thereby that the failure of the Commission to anticipate this problem and to promulgate a general rule withdrew all power from that agency to perform its statutory duty in this case. To hold that the Commission had no alternative in this proceeding but to approve the proposed transaction, while formulating any general rules it might desire for use in future cases of this nature, would be to stultify the administrative process. That we refuse to do.

Since the Commission, unlike a court, does have the ability to make new law prospectively through the exercise of its rule-making powers, it has less reason to rely upon ad hoc adjudication to formulate new standards of conduct within the framework of the Holding Company Act. The function of filling in the interstices of the Act should be performed, as much as possible, through this quasi-legislative promulgation of rules to be applied in the future. But any rigid requirement to that effect would make the administrative process inflexible and incapable of dealing with many of the specialized problems which arise. See Report of the Attorney General's Committee on Administrative Procedure in Government Agencies, S. Doc. No. 8, 77th Cong., 1st Sess., at 29. Not every principle essential to the effective administration of a statute can or should be cast immediately into the mold of a general rule. Some principles must await their own development, while others must be adjusted to meet particular, unforeseeable situations. In performing its important functions in these respects, therefore, an administrative agency must be equipped to act either by general rule or by individual order. To insist upon one form of action to the exclusion of the other is to exalt form over necessity.

In other words, problems may arise in a case which the administrative agency could not reasonably foresee, problems which must be solved despite the absence of a relevant general rule. Or the agency may not have had sufficient experience with a particular problem to warrant rigidifying its tentative judgment into a hard and fast rule. Or the problem may be so specialized and varying in nature as to be impossible of capture within the boundaries of a general rule. In those situations, the agency must retain power to deal with the problems on a case-to-case basis if the administrative process is to be effective. There is thus a very definite place for the case-by-case evolution of statutory standards. And the choice made between proceeding by general rule or by individual, ad hoc litigation is one that lies primarily in the informed discretion of the administrative agency.

Hence we refuse to say that the Commission, which had not previously been confronted with the problem of management trading during reorganization, was forbidden from utilizing this particular proceeding for announcing and applying a new standard of conduct. That such action might have a retroactive effect was not necessarily fatal to its validity. Every case of first impression has a retroactive effect, whether the new principle is announced by a court or by an administrative agency. But such retroactivity must be balanced against the mischief of producing a result which is contrary to a statutory design or to legal and equitable principles. If that mischief is greater than the ill effect of the retroactive application of a new standard, it is not the type of retroactivity which is condemned by law. * * *

The Commission concluded that it could not find that the reorganization plan, if amended as proposed, would be "fair and equitable to the persons affected (thereby)" within the meaning of § 11(e) of the Act, under which the reorganization was taking place. Its view was that the amended plan would involve the issuance of securities on terms 'detrimental to the public interest or the interest of investors' contrary to §§ 7(d)(6) and 7(e), and would result in an 'unfair or inequitable distribution of voting power' among the Federal security holders within the meaning of § 7(e). It was led to this result "not by proof that the interveners (Federal's management) committed acts of conscious wrongdoing but by the character of the conflicting interests created by the interveners program of stock purchases carried out while plans for reorganization were under consideration."

* * * Drawing upon its experience, the Commission indicated that [the broad range of] normal and special powers [wielded by] holding company management during the course of a § 11(e) reorganization placed in the management's command

"a formidable battery of devices that would enable it, if it should choose to use them selfishly, to affect in material degree the ultimate allocation of new securities among the various existing classes, to influence the market for its own gain and to manipulate or obstruct the reorganization required by the mandate of the statute." In that setting, the Commission felt that a management program of stock purchase would give rise to the temptation and the opportunity to shape the reorganization proceeding so as to encourage public selling on the market at low prices. No management could engage in such a program without raising serious questions as to whether its personal interests had not opposed its duties "to exercise disinterested judgment in matters pertaining to subsidiaries' accounting, budgetary and dividend policies, to present publicly an unprejudiced financial picture of the enterprise, and to effectuate a fair and feasible plan expeditiously." * * *

Turning to the facts in this case, the Commission noted the salient fact that the primary object of Federal's management in buying the preferred stock was admittedly to obtain the voting power that was accruing to that stock through the reorganization and to profit from the investment therein. That stock had been purchased in the market at prices that were depressed in relation to what the management anticipated would be, and what in fact was, the earning and asset value of its reorganization equivalent. The Commission admitted that the good faith and personal integrity of this management were not in question; but as to the management's justification of its motives, the Commission concluded that it was merely trying to "deny that they made selfish use of their powers during the period when their conflict of interest, vis-a-vis public investors was in existence owing to their purchase program." Federal's management had thus placed itself in a position where it was 'peculiarly susceptible to temptation to conduct the reorganization for personal gain rather than the public good' and where its desire to make advantageous purchases of stock could have an important influence, even though subconsciously, upon many of the decisions to be made in the course of the reorganization. Accordingly, the Commission felt that all of its general considerations of the problem were applicable to this case.

The scope of our review of an administrative order wherein a new principle is announced and applied is no different from that which pertains to ordinary administrative action. The wisdom of the principle adopted is none of our concern. Our duty is at an end when it becomes evident that the Commission's action is based upon substantial evidence and is consistent with the authority granted by Congress. We are unable to say in this case that the Commission erred in reaching the result it did. The facts being undisputed, we are free to disturb the Commission's conclusion only if it lacks any rational and statutory foundation. In that connection, the Commission has made a thorough examination of the problem, utilizing statutory standards and its own accumulated experience with reorganization matters. In essence, it has made what we indicated in our prior opinion would be an informed, expert judgment on the problem. * * *

The "fair and equitable" rule of § 11(e) and the standard of what is "detrimental to the public interest or the interest of investors or consumers" under § 7(d)(6) and § 7(e) were inserted by the framers of the Act in order that the Commission might have broad powers to protect the various interests at stake. The application of those criteria, whether in the form of a particular order or a general regulation, necessarily requires the use of informal discretion by the Commission. The very breath of the statutory language precludes a reversal of the Commission's judgment save where it has plainly abused its discretion in these matters. Such an abuse is not present in this case.

The purchase by a holding company management of that company's securities during the course of a reorganization may well be thought to be so fraught with danger as to warrant a denial of the benefits and profits accruing to the management. The possibility that such a stock purchase program will result in detriment to the public investors is not a fanciful one. The influence that program may have upon the important decisions to be made by the management during reorganization is not inconsequential. Since the officers and directors occupy fiduciary positions during this period, their actions are to be held to a higher standard than that imposed upon the general investing public. There is thus a reasonable basis for a value judgment that the benefits and profits accruing to the management from the stock purchases should be prohibited, regardless of the good faith involved. And it is a judgment that can justifiably be reached in terms of fairness and equitableness, to the end that the interests of the public, the investors and the consumers might be protected. But it is a judgment based upon public policy, a judgment which Congress has indicated is of the type for the Commission to make.

The Commission's conclusion here rests squarely in that area where administrative judgments are entitled to the greatest amount of weight by appellate courts. It is the product of administrative experience, appreciation of the complexities of the problem, realization of the statutory policies, and responsible treatment of the uncontested facts. It is the type of judgment which administrative agencies are best equipped to make and which justifies the use of the administrative process. Whether we agree or disagree with the result reached, it is an allowable judgment which we cannot disturb.

MR. JUSTICE BURTON concurs in the result.

THE CHIEF JUSTICE [VINSON] and MR. JUSTICE DOUGLAS took no part in the consideration or decision of this case.

MR. JUSTICE JACKSON, dissenting.

* * * The difference between the first and the latest decision of the Court is simply the difference between holding that administrative orders must have a basis in law and a holding that absence of a legal basis is no ground on which courts may annul them.

* * * The Court's reasoning adds up to this: The Commission must be sustained because of its accumulated experience in solving a problem which it had never before confronted! Of course, thus to uphold the Commission by professing to find that it has enunciated a "new standard of conduct" brings the Court squarely against the invalidity of retroactive law-making. But the Court does not falter: "That such action might have a retroactive effect was not necessarily fatal to its validity." "But such retroactivity must be balanced against the mischief of producing a result which is contrary to a statutory design or to legal or equitable principles." Of course, if what

these parties did really was condemned by "statutory design" or "legal and equitable principles," it could be stopped without resort to a new rule and there would be no retroactivity to condone. * * * I give up. Now I realize what Mark Twain meant when he said, "The more you explain it, the more I don't understand it."

* * * This administrative authoritarianism, this power to decide without law, is what the Court seems to approve in so many words. "The absence of a general rule or regulation governing management trading during reorganization did not affect the Commission's duties * * *. " This seems to me to undervalue and to belittle the place of law, even in the system of administrative justice. * * *

MR. JUSTICE FRANKFURTER joins in this opinion.

NOTES ON CHENERY II

1.   *Post-Hoc Justifications.* Justice Murphy explains that the Court's first *Chenery* decision announced a fundamental rule of administrative law. Agency action can be upheld by a court solely on the grounds invoked by the agency when taking the action under review, not based on some "more adequate or proper" rationale offered after the fact by the agency or a reviewing court. From the standpoint of administrative law, what justifies a ban on making use of post-hoc rationalizations? Does it derive from the non-delegation doctrine, in that agencies as politically accountable actors must state the grounds for their exercise of delegated authority? See *Kevin Stack, The Constitutional Foundations of* Chenery, 116 Yale L.J. 952, 958–59 (2007). Alternatively, perhaps separation of powers is not implicated; rather, the agency's legal authority to act is conceded but the ban on post-hoc justifications stems from the core nature of reasoned decisionmaking. See Elizabeth Magill and Adrian Vermeule, *Allocating Power Within Agencies*, 120 Yale L.J. 1032, 1043 (2011). However it is justified, one practical effect of the ban may be to allocate power horizontally within agencies. The argument is that allowing post-hoc rationalizations would elevate the role of lawyers within an agency, especially appellate lawyers, whereas the ban on such rationalizations privileges agency personnel who formulate policy before it is challenged in court. These policy-formulators may include lawyers but they will also include other agency professionals—notably scientists, technical experts, civil servants, and political appointees. See Magill and Vermeule, 120 Yale L.J. at 1043–44.

2.   *The Adjudication "Exceptions"?* Justice Murphy opines that "filling in the interstices of the Act should be performed, as much as possible, through" rulemaking. He then sets forth three settings in which case-by-case adjudication is more likely to be warranted. Are these three settings genuinely limiting exceptions? To what extent do lack of reasonably foreseeable circumstances, insufficient agency experience, and specialized problems invite the exercise of broad agency discretion? Justice Jackson in dissent contends that the Court has approved "administrative authoritarianism, th[e] power to decide without law." Do you find his argument persuasive?

Is it the Court's position that an agency is permitted to proceed by adjudication only in one of the three specified settings identified in the opinion? If not, are there *any* limits on the agency's choice of implementation options? What sources of institutional authority besides reviewing courts might create such limits? *See* Magill, *supra*, 71 U. Chi. L. Rev. at 1409.

NATIONAL LABOR RELATIONS BOARD V.
BELL AEROSPACE COMPANY

Supreme Court of the United States, 1974.
416 U.S. 267, 94 S.Ct. 1757, 40 L.Ed.2d 134.

MR. JUSTICE POWELL delivered the opinion of the Court.

This case presents two questions: first, whether the National Labor Relations Board properly determined that all "managerial employees," except those whose participation in a labor organization would create a conflict of interest with their job responsibilities, are covered by the National Labor Relations Act; and second, whether the Board must proceed by rulemaking rather than by adjudication in determining whether certain buyers are "managerial employees." We answer both questions in the negative. * * *

[In answering the first question, the Court rejected the Board's recent re-interpretation of the NLRA to establish protections for some managerial employees. The majority held that the Board's early decisions on this issue, the purpose and legislative history of the Act's 1947 amendments, subsequent and consistent agency interpretations over two decades, and the decisions of the courts of appeals, "all point unmistakably to the conclusion that 'managerial employees' are not covered by the Act." The Court observed that "the Board is not now free to read a new and more restrictive meaning into the Act," and added that "in view of our conclusion, the case must be remanded to permit the Board to apply the proper legal standard in determining the status of these buyers. *SEC v. Chenery Corp.*, 318 U.S. 80, 85 (1943)."]

The Court of Appeals also held that, although the Board was not precluded from determining that buyers or some types of buyers were not 'managerial employees,' it could do so only by invoking its rulemaking procedures under § 6 of the Act, 29 U.S.C. § 156. We disagree.

At the outset, the precise nature of the present issue must be noted. The question is not whether the Board should have resorted to rulemaking, or in fact improperly promulgated a 'rule,' when in the context of the prior representation proceeding it held that the Act covers all 'managerial employees' except those meeting the new 'conflict of interest in labor relations' touchstone. Our conclusion that the Board applied the wrong legal standard makes consideration of that issue unnecessary. Rather, the present question is whether on remand the Board must invoke its rulemaking procedures if it determines, in light of our opinion, that these buyers are not 'managerial employees' under the Act. The Court of Appeals thought that rulemaking was required because any Board finding that the company's buyers are not 'managerial' would be contrary to its prior decisions and would presumably be in the nature of a general rule designed 'to fit all cases at all times.'

A similar issue was presented to this Court in its second decision in *SEC v. Chenery Corp.*, 332 U.S. 194 (1947) *(Chenery II)*. There, the respondent corporation argued that in an adjudicative proceeding the Commission could not apply a general standard that it had formulated for the first time in that proceeding. Rather, the Commission was required to resort instead to its rulemaking procedures if it desired to promulgate a new standard that would govern future conduct. In rejecting this contention, the Court first noted that the Commission had a statutory duty to decide the issue at hand in light of the proper standards and that this duty remained 'regardless of whether those standards previously had been spelled out in a general rule or regulation.' *Id.* at 201. The Court continued:

> "The function of filling in the interstices of the (Securities) Act should be performed, as much as possible, through this quasi-legislative promulgation of rules to be applied in the future. But any rigid requirement to that effect would make the administrative process inflexible and incapable of dealing with many of the specialized problems which arise. . . . Not every principle essential to the effective administration of a statute can or should be cast immediately into the mold of a general rule. Some principles must await their own development, while others must be adjusted to meet particular, unforeseeable situations. *In performing its important functions in these respects, therefore, an administrative agency must be equipped to act either by general rule or by individual order. To insist upon one form of action to the exclusion of the other is to exalt form over necessity.*"

(Emphasis added.)

The Court concluded that 'the choice made between proceeding by general rule or by individual, ad hoc litigation is one that lies primarily in the informed discretion of the administrative agency.' *Id.* at 203.

And in *NLRB v. Wyman-Gordon Co.*, 394 U.S. 759 (1969), the Court upheld a Board order enforcing an election list requirement first promulgated in an earlier adjudicative proceeding in *Excelsior Underwear Inc.*, 156 N.L.R.B. 1236 (1966). The plurality opinion of Mr. Justice Fortas, joined by The Chief Justice, Mr. Justice Stewart, and Mr. Justice White, recognized that "[a]djudicated cases may and do . . . serve as vehicles for the formulation of agency policies, which are applied and announced therein," and that such cases "generally provide a guide to action that the agency may be expected to take in future cases." *NLRB v. Wyman-Gordon Co.*, at 765–766. The concurring opinion of Mr. Justice Black, joined by Mr. Justice Brennan and Mr. Justice Marshall, also noted that the Board had both adjudicative and rulemaking powers and that the choice between the two was "within its informed discretion." *Id.* at 772.

The views expressed in *Chenery II* and *Wyman-Gordon* make plain that the Board is not precluded from announcing new principles in an adjudicative proceeding and that the choice between rulemaking and adjudication lies in the first instance within the Board's discretion. Although there may be situations where the Board's reliance on adjudication would amount to an abuse of discretion or a violation of the Act, nothing in the present case would justify such a conclusion. Indeed, there is ample indication that adjudication is especially appropriate in the instant context. As the Court of Appeals noted, "(t)here must be tens of thousands of manufacturing, wholesale and retail units which employ buyers, and hundreds of thousands of the latter." 475 F.2d at 496. Moreover, duties of buyers vary widely depending on the company or industry. It is doubtful whether any generalized standard could be framed which would have more than marginal utility. The Board thus has reason to proceed with caution, developing its standards in a case-by-case manner with attention to the specific character of the buyers' authority and duties in each company. The Board's judgment that adjudication best serves this purpose is entitled to great weight.

The possible reliance of industry on the Board's past decisions with respect to buyers does not require a different result. It has not been shown that the adverse consequences ensuing from such reliance are so substantial that the Board should be precluded from reconsidering the issue in an adjudicative proceeding. Furthermore, this is not a case in which some new liability is sought to be imposed on individuals for past actions which were taken in good-faith reliance on Board pronouncements. Nor are fines or damages involved here. In any event, concern about such consequences is largely speculative, for the Board has not yet finally determined whether these buyers are "managerial."

It is true, of course, that rulemaking would provide the Board with a forum for soliciting the informed views of those affected in industry and labor before embarking on a new course. But surely the Board has discretion to decide that the adjudicative procedures in this case may also produce the relevant information necessary to mature and fair consideration of the issues. Those most immediately affected, the buyers and the company in the particular case, are accorded a full opportunity to be heard before the Board makes its determination.

Judgment of the Court of Appeals affirmed in part and reversed in part, and cause remanded.

[The opinion of MR. JUSTICE WHITE, with whom MR. JUSTICE BRENNAN, MR. JUSTICE STEWART, and MR. JUSTICE MARSHALL join, dissenting in part, is omitted.]

NOTES ON RULEMAKING V. ADJUDICATION

1. *Adjudication to Revise a Longstanding Policy?* Justice Powell near the end of his opinion in *Bell Aerospace* dismisses as unpersuasive the fact that the NLRB had changed its position from prior orders in which it had determined that similar buyers were not entitled to the Act's protections for collective bargaining. Is there a salient difference between adjudicatory policymaking in the first instance and adjudicatory policymaking reversing a prior agency adjudication? Judge Friendly, who authored the Second Circuit opinion reversed by the Supreme Court, suggested that "the argument for rulemaking is especially strong when the Board is proposing to reverse a long-standing and oft-repeated policy on which industry and labor have relied." *Bell Aerospace Co. v. NLRB*, 475 F.2d 485, 496–97 (2d Cir. 1973). Justice Powell concedes that "there may be situations where the Board's reliance on adjudication would amount to an abuse of discretion." When, if ever, might it be an "abuse of discretion" under section 706(2) of the APA for the NLRB to reverse a heavily-relied-upon adjudicatory ruling without going through notice-and-comment rulemaking? Courts reverse longstanding statutory precedents from time to time, because the precedent is deemed irreconcilable with competing legal doctrines or even inconsistent with the sense of justice or social welfare. See *Patterson v. McLean Credit Union*, 491 U.S. 164, 173–74 (1989) (discussed in Chapter 5, § 2(B)(1)). Is there any reason why an agency's policy precedents should not be similarly revisited? Why regard reliance interests differently in agency adjudicatory settings? See Problem 8-3 following these Notes.

2.   *The Advantages of Rulemaking?* In his classic article, *The Choice of Rulemaking or Adjudication in the Development of Administrative Policy*, 78 Harv. L. Rev. 921, 929–42 (1965), David Shapiro sets forth a number of potential advantages to rulemaking over adjudication in the development of administrative policies: (a) *fairness:* the requirement for notice and comment facilitates general participation in the deliberative process by all parties who may be affected; (b) *advance planning:* an agency is better able to allocate its limited resources in a rational manner, as opposed to litigating a possibly voluminous number of fact-specific cases; (c) *prospectivity:* rulemaking is more likely to be limited to determining the status of future conduct and therefore less likely to defeat justifiable expectations based on prior agency policy; (d) *uniformity:* rulemaking's uniform application to all regulated entities minimizes the chance that competitors will pursue or gain an unfair advantage; (e) *flexibility:* rulemaking leaves agencies relatively free to consult experts on their staffs, to receive far-ranging submissions of data, and to pursue information unconstrained by rules of evidence or other formalities of a trial-type proceeding; (f) *accessibility and clarity of formulation*: rulemaking requires the development and articulation of policies over time and through processes that are both formal and relatively transparent, making it likely that the rules or standards finally enunciated are easier to locate, decipher and understand; and (g) *judicial review:* rulemaking allows affected parties to test agency positions in the courts on a readily available and timely basis when compared to post-hoc review of adjudications or even to the deterrent effect of threatened agency sanctions that secure changes in private conduct without an adjudicatory decision.

Shapiro is nuanced and judicious in presenting these advantages, but there are counterarguments. Indeed, agencies as well as regulated entities often prefer adjudication to rulemaking, although perhaps for different reasons. In what ways are the advantages for rulemaking overstated? For each of the benefits set forth above, can you think of possible rebuttals in defense of adjudication as a policymaking option?

3.   *Judicial Review of Agency Choice of Procedures.* Under section 706(2)(A) of the APA, courts may review agency adjudicatory and rulemaking decisions under the arbitrary and capricious standard. But what about the predicate agency decision to choose between rulemaking and adjudication? Magill contends that this predicate agency choice has been regarded as essentially unreviewable by courts: "an agency does not feel obligated to explain, much less defend, why it chose a particular policymaking tool; and the agency is not asked to do so by parties or courts. An agency's choice of procedure is not in doctrinal terms "unreviewable," but it might as well be." 71 U. Chi. L. Rev. at 1414. Magill is critical of the absence of any reason-giving requirement; she contends that the arbitrary and capricious standard can and should apply to the review of an agency's choice between rulemaking and adjudication. Specifically, she maintains that the agency should be required to provide an explanation for its choice and that the agency's rationale should be sufficient to persuade the court that the agency exercised its discretion in a reasoned way, i.e. that the agency considered the important alternatives and settled on its course of action for sensible reasons.

What factors might have lead courts not to review an agency's choice between rulemaking and adjudication? Based on the text and plain meaning of the APA, should courts be conducting reviews of these agency determinations? If the courts were to undertake such reviews, should they be based on the arbitrary and capricious standard as Magill suggests? Or is there a third option, other than arbitrary-and-capricious and non-review?

4. *Adjudication and Presidential Review.* Jennifer Nou suggests that agencies may prefer adjudication to rulemaking as a means of insulating themselves from presidential review. Jennifer Nou, *Agency Self-Insulation Under Presidential Review*, 126 Harv. L. Rev. 1755 (2013). Under the current structure of presidential oversight (discussed in section 3(B) of this chapter), review generally focuses on actions that are "economically significant" and that are expected to lead to the promulgation of a rule or regulation. [*economically significant*] Accordingly, agencies can choose adjudication (as well as other strategies like guidance documents, non-significant rules or simple inaction) as an instrument that is likely to escape presidential review. Agencies issue thousands of adjudications annually, and "[b]ecause adjudication, unlike rulemaking, proceeds on a case-by-case basis, each adjudication's policy impacts are limited and aggregate policy change is developed only incrementally." *Id.* at 1783–84 (2013). Should insulation from presidential review through adjudication be added to Shapiro's list of reasons why rulemaking is more advantageous? Or are there certain benefits to this insulation through the use of adjudication?

5. *Power Allocation and the Choice Between Adjudication and Rulemaking.* In *Allocating Power Within Agencies*, 120 Yale L.J. 1032 (2011), Elizabeth Magill and Adrian Vermeule hypothesize that allocation of power within an agency can influence the choice between rulemaking and adjudication. Lawyer-dominated agencies will tend to prefer adjudication whereas agencies more dominated by scientists, or other non-lawyer professionals will tend to favor rulemaking. [*Adjudication favored by lawyer*] This is in part because empowering particular types of professionals within agencies can have spillover effects: "Once lawyers, scientists, or economists—or any other professionals—are employed to cope with a particular issue, they become major stakeholders within agencies, and their influence can seep out laterally to encompass issues other than the one for which they were originally conscripted." The authors concede, however, that their hypothesis, "is fragile because it depends upon the proposition that lawyers, qua lawyers, are more likely to favor case-specific modes of agency policymaking." *Id.* at 1080–81.

Magill and Vermeule then provide the following example, based on a previous account by Jerry Mashaw and David Harfst.[22] In the early 1970s, safety engineers dominated the National Highway Transportation Safety Administration's (NHTSA's) [*Rulemaking favored by scientists + others*] culture, and the agency made extensive use of *ex ante* rulemaking. When the courts rejected these standards in a series of 1972 decisions, this resulted in the engineers' efforts being delegitimized. The medium-term impact was to bend agency strategy toward litigation, specifically a large number of *ex post* recalls that were successful in the courts. This shift led to increased power being allocated to lawyers and economists over engineers in the NHTSA; a further result was "to bias systematically the agency's choice of policymaking away from rulemaking and toward adjudication." *Id.* at 1083. What lessons, if any, might other agencies draw from this episode? Assuming that the judges reviewing NHTSA rules did not anticipate the reshaping of internal agency decisionmaking, should courts today be more sensitive to such possibly dynamic effects of judicial review?

---

[22]   See Jerry Mashaw & David Harfst, *Inside the National Highway Traffic Safety Administration: Legal Determinants of Bureaucratic Organization and Performance*, 57 U. Chi. L. Rev. 443 (1990).

PROBLEM ON AGENCY CHOICE OF PROCEDURES

Problem 8-3. In *Excelsior Underwear Inc.*, 156 N.L.R.B. 1236 (1966), employees asked their employer for a list of names and addresses of all employees eligible to vote in an upcoming union representation election. The employer refused to provide the list, the union lost the election, and employees then filed a charge with the agency alleging unlawful conduct under the National Labor Relations Act (NLRA). The National Labor Relations Board (Board), which usually resolves such adjudicatory disputes based on written submission from the parties, took the unusual step of inviting interested groups to submit amicus briefs and make oral arguments. The Board's subsequent decision included its so-called "Excelsior Rule": within one week after a union representation election has been ordered or agreed upon, the employer is required to submit to the Board, for transmittal to the union, the names and addresses of all employees eligible to vote. In reaching this decision, the Board considered and rejected employer arguments that sharing addresses would raise important problems of employee privacy. The *Excelsior* decision was not appealed and remains the relevant legal standard under the NLRA.

Recently, another dispute has arisen in which employees seek the phone numbers and email addresses of all employees eligible to vote in an upcoming union election. The employees contend that mailing addresses no longer provide timely or even adequate access to contact voters given the typically short time period (21–30 days) for an election campaign and the fact that employees often live great distances from their workplace. The employer refuses to provide this information; she maintains that requiring disclosure of employee phone numbers and email addresses raises a novel set of privacy issues, and that disclosure of company-issued email addresses is also highly problematic. The employees have filed a charge with the Board alleging unlawful employer conduct.

You are a Board attorney in the General Counsel's office; your boss wants your advice as to *how the Board should handle this dispute as a procedural matter*. Some colleagues have recommended the dispute be treated as a garden-variety adjudicatory matter, to be resolved based on written submissions from the parties. Others argue that the dispute calls for *Excelsior*-type treatment: the Board should invite amicus submissions and oral argument. A third group contends that any change from the *Excelsior* standard should be implemented only through notice-and-comment rulemaking. What is your recommendation on the appropriate process to follow, and why? Regardless of which process you propose the agency should follow, what weight should be given to the reliance interests of the parties—or of any regulated entities that will be affected by a change in the Board's substantive approach?

D. INTERPRETIVE RULES AND POLICY STATEMENTS

Agencies often implement statutory provisions through processes that are less prescribed or conventional than formal rulemaking, notice-and-comment rulemaking, and adjudication. Indeed, most federal agencies issue hundreds of communications each year that never appear in the Federal Register yet are designed to guide the conduct of private parties as well as agency employees. Examples include benefit or eligibility forms and instructions for completing them; inspection reports; staff training manuals; press releases; responses to frequently asked questions (FAQs); and speeches given by bureaucrats at varying levels of authority.

Two additional types of less conventional agency communication specifically addressed in the APA are interpretive rules and general statements of policy. Although section 553(b)(A) exempts them from notice-and-comment requirements, section 552(a)(1)(D) requires that they be "separately state[d] and currently publish[ed] in the Federal Register for the guidance of the public" when they are "of general applicability." Interpretive rules and policy statements may be thought of as "rule-like" in applying broadly to potentially affected individuals and entities, but as "non-legislative" in that they do not express new substantive rights or responsibilities.

Interpretive rules and policy statements also differ from one another. The Attorney General's Manual on the APA, drafted in 1947, describes *interpretive rules* as "rules or statements issued by an agency to advise the public of the agency's construction of the statutes and rules which it administers," and *general statements of policy* as "statements issued by an agency to advise the public prospectively of the manner in which the agency proposes to exercise a discretionary power." This distinction may be difficult to apply when considering ways in which an agency exercises its interpretive discretion to address ambiguous statutory or regulatory language. Think about the difference between interpretive rules and policy statements as you consider the cases that follow.

1. Interpretive Rules

PEREZ V. MORTGAGE BANKERS ASS'N

Supreme Court of the United States, 2015.
___ U.S. ___, 135 S.Ct 1199, 191 L.Ed.2d 186.

JUSTICE SOTOMAYOR delivered the opinion of the Court.

When a federal administrative agency first issues a rule interpreting one of its regulations, it is generally not required to follow the notice-and-comment rulemaking procedures of the Administrative Procedure Act (APA or Act). See 5 U.S.C. § 553(b)(A). The United States Court of Appeals for the District of Columbia Circuit has nevertheless held, in a line of cases beginning with *Paralyzed Veterans of Am. v. D.C. Arena L.P.*, 117 F.3d 579 (1997), that an agency must use the APA's notice-and-comment procedures when it wishes to issue a new interpretation of a regulation that deviates significantly from one the agency has previously adopted. The question in these cases is whether the rule announced in *Paralyzed Veterans* is consistent with the APA. We hold that it is not. * * *

[II] The *Paralyzed Veterans* doctrine is contrary to the clear text of the APA's rulemaking provisions, and it improperly imposes on agencies an obligation beyond the "maximum procedural requirements" specified in the APA, *Vermont Yankee Nuclear Power Corp. v. Natural Resources Defense Council, Inc.*, 435 U.S. 519, 524 (1978).

[II-A] The text of the APA answers the question presented. Section 4 of the APA provides that "notice of proposed rule making shall be published in the Federal Register." 5 U.S.C. § 553(b). When such notice is required by the APA, "the agency shall give interested persons an opportunity to participate in the rule making."

§ 553(c). But § 4 further states that unless "notice or hearing is required by statute," the Act's notice-and-comment requirement "does not apply . . . to interpretative rules." § 553(b)(A). This exemption of interpretive rules from the notice-and-comment process is categorical, and it is fatal to the rule announced in *Paralyzed Veterans*.

Rather than examining the exemption for interpretive rules contained in § 4(b)(A) of the APA, the D.C. Circuit in *Paralyzed Veterans* focused its attention on § 1 of the Act. That section defines "rule making" to include not only the initial issuance of new rules, but also "repeal[s]" or "amend[ments]" of existing rules. See § 551(5). Because notice-and-comment requirements may apply even to these later agency actions, the court reasoned, "allow[ing] an agency to make a fundamental change in its interpretation of a substantive regulation without notice and comment" would undermine the APA's procedural framework.

This reading of the APA conflates the differing purposes of §§ 1 and 4 of the Act. Section 1 defines what a rulemaking is. It does not, however, say what procedures an agency must use when it engages in rulemaking. That is the purpose of § 4. And § 4 specifically exempts interpretive rules from the notice-and-comment requirements that apply to legislative rules. So, the D.C. Circuit correctly read § 1 of the APA to mandate that agencies use the same procedures when they amend or repeal a rule as they used to issue the rule in the first instance. Where the court went wrong was in failing to apply that accurate understanding of § 1 to the exemption for interpretive rules contained in § 4: Because an agency is not required to use notice-and-comment procedures to issue an initial interpretive rule, it is also not required to use those procedures when it amends or repeals that interpretive rule.

[II-B] The straightforward reading of the APA we now adopt harmonizes with longstanding principles of our administrative law jurisprudence. Time and again, we have reiterated that the APA "sets forth the full extent of judicial authority to review executive agency action for procedural correctness." *Fox Television Stations, Inc.*, 556 U.S. 502, 513 (2009). Beyond the APA's minimum requirements, courts lack authority "to impose upon [an] agency its own notion of which procedures are 'best' or most likely to further some vague, undefined public good." *Vermont Yankee*, 435 U.S., at 549. To do otherwise would violate "the very basic tenet of administrative law that agencies should be free to fashion their own rules of procedure." *Id.*, at 544.

These foundational principles apply with equal force to the APA's procedures for rulemaking. We explained in *Vermont Yankee* that § 4 of the Act "established the maximum procedural requirements which Congress was willing to have the courts impose upon agencies in conducting rulemaking procedures." *Id.*, at 524. * * *

The *Paralyzed Veterans* doctrine creates just such a judge-made procedural right: the right to notice and an opportunity to comment when an agency changes its interpretation of one of the regulations it enforces. That requirement may be wise policy. Or it may not. Regardless, imposing such an obligation is the responsibility of Congress or the administrative agencies, not the courts. * * * In the end, Congress decided to adopt standards that permit agencies to promulgate freely such rules— whether or not they are consistent with earlier interpretations. That the D.C. Circuit would have struck the balance differently does not permit that court or this one to overturn Congress' contrary judgment.

[III-A] MBA begins its defense of the *Paralyzed Veterans* doctrine by attempting to bolster the D.C. Circuit's reading of the APA. *"Paralyzed Veterans,"* MBA contends, "simply acknowledges the reality that where an agency significantly alters a prior, definitive interpretation of a regulation, it has effectively amended the regulation itself," something that under the APA requires use of notice-and-comment procedures.

The act of "amending," however, in both ordinary parlance and legal usage, has its own meaning separate and apart from the act of "interpreting." Compare Black's Law Dictionary 98 (10th ed. 2014) (defining "amend" as "[t]o change the wording of" or "formally alter . . . by striking out, inserting, or substituting words"), with *id.,* at 943 (defining "interpret" as "[t]o ascertain the meaning and significance of thoughts expressed in words"). One would not normally say that a court "amends" a statute when it interprets its text. So too can an agency "interpret" a regulation without "effectively amend[ing]" the underlying source of law. MBA does not explain *how* precisely an interpretive rule changes the regulation it interprets, and its assertion is impossible to reconcile with the longstanding recognition that interpretive rules do not have the force and effect of law.

MBA's "interpretation-as-amendment" theory is particularly odd in light of the limitations of the *Paralyzed Veterans* doctrine. Recall that the rule of *Paralyzed Veterans* applies only when an agency has previously adopted an interpretation of its regulation. Yet in that initial interpretation as much as all that come after, the agency is giving a definite meaning to an ambiguous text—the very act MBA insists requires notice and comment. MBA is unable to say why its arguments regarding revised interpretations should not also extend to the agency's first interpretation. * * *

[III-B] In the main, MBA attempts to justify the *Paralyzed Veterans* doctrine on practical and policy grounds. MBA contends that the doctrine reinforces the APA's goal of "procedural fairness" by preventing agencies from unilaterally and unexpectedly altering their interpretation of important regulations. There may be times when an agency's decision to issue an interpretive rule, rather than a legislative rule, is driven primarily by a desire to skirt notice-and-comment provisions. But regulated entities are not without recourse in such situations. Quite the opposite. The APA contains a variety of constraints on agency decisionmaking— the arbitrary and capricious standard being among the most notable. As we held in *Fox Television Stations,* and underscore again today, the APA requires an agency to provide more substantial justification when "its new policy rests upon factual findings that contradict those which underlay its prior policy; or when its prior policy has engendered serious reliance interests that must be taken into account. It would be arbitrary and capricious to ignore such matters." 556 U.S., at 515 (citation omitted); see also *id.,* at 535, (Kennedy, J., concurring in part and concurring in judgment).

In addition, Congress is aware that agencies sometimes alter their views in ways that upset settled reliance interests. For that reason, Congress sometimes includes in the statutes it drafts safe-harbor provisions that shelter regulated entities from liability when they act in conformance with previous agency interpretations. * * * These safe harbors will often protect parties from liability when an agency adopts an interpretation that conflicts with its previous position. * * *

JUSTICE ALITO, concurring in part and concurring in the judgment.

I join the opinion of the Court except for Part III-B. I agree that the doctrine of *Paralyzed Veterans of America v. D.C. Arena L.P.* is incompatible with the Administrative Procedure Act. The creation of that doctrine may have been prompted by an understandable concern about the aggrandizement of the power of administrative agencies as a result of the combined effect of (1) the effective delegation to agencies by Congress of huge swaths of lawmaking authority, (2) the exploitation by agencies of the uncertain boundary between legislative and interpretive rules, and (3) this Court's cases holding that courts must ordinarily defer to an agency's interpretation of its own ambiguous regulations. See *Bowles v. Seminole Rock & Sand Co.,* 325 U.S. 410 (1945). I do not dismiss these concerns, but the *Paralyzed Veterans* doctrine is not a viable cure for these problems. At least one of the three factors noted above, however, concerns a matter that can be addressed by this Court. The opinions of JUSTICE SCALIA and JUSTICE THOMAS offer substantial reasons why the *Seminole Rock* doctrine may be incorrect. I await a case in which the validity of *Seminole Rock* may be explored through full briefing and argument. * * *

[The opinions of JUSTICE SCALIA and JUSTICE THOMAS, concurring in the judgment, are omitted; the *Seminole Rock* doctrine is more fully addressed in Chapter 9, § 2(C).]

NOTE ON PEREZ V. MORTGAGE BANKERS ASS'N

Writing for the majority, Justice Sotomayor rapidly concludes that the *Paralyzed Veterans* doctrine is inconsistent with a "straightforward reading of the APA." Why then does she go on to demonstrate at greater length how this holding is consistent with the Court's precedent and also with sound policy? Do you agree that the interpretation of the APA is as "straightforward" as Sotomayor finds it to be? If so, why does she proceed to justify the Court's interpretation on policy grounds?

In *Pixelating Administrative Common Law in* Perez v. Mortgage Bankers Association, Kathryn Kovacs argues that the Court's discussion of policy in *Mortgage Bankers* actually does more harm than good. 125 Yale L.J. Forum 31 (2015). By considering the merits of the case on practical and policy grounds, the Court engages in exactly the type of "administrative common law" creation that led the D.C. Circuit to its erroneous decision in the first place and that exceeds the role of the courts under the APA. Avoiding the creation of judge-made doctrine, Kovacs asserts, is particularly important for the APA as a "superstatute" that emerged after deep public deliberation and that carries extraordinary normative weight given its impact on so many different agencies. (See William Eskridge & John Ferejohn, *A Republic of Statutes: The New American Constitution* (2010), explaining the concept of "superstatutes"; § 2(A)(1) of this chapter, summarizing the lengthy legislative history of the 1946 APA).

Professor Kovacs contends that because no single agency has control over the APA or its interpretive processes, all public deliberation shaping this statute should continue to occur in Congress rather than through "judges deliberating behind closed doors" while reading party briefs. When the Court discussed policy in *Mortgage Bankers*, it "invited the lower courts to continue to use administrative common law as a sort of constitutional avoidance doctrine unmoored from the public deliberation inherent in the APA." Do you agree that the Court should be particularly deferential to Congress's text when interpreting the APA? Beyond affecting more than one agency, are there other aspects of the APA that make it a candidate for strict judicial interpretation? Are there aspects that support a more functional approach?

In Justice Alito's concurring opinion, he articulates sympathy for the D.C. Circuit, noting that the *Paralyzed Veterans* doctrine likely stems from an "understandable concern" about the increasing power of agencies. Yet he still signs onto the Court's opinion, agreeing that *Paralyzed Veterans* is "not a viable cure." Is it true that even in the face of what Justice Alito terms an "aggrandizement of the power of administrative agencies," the Court is completely helpless to obey the clear text of the APA? Or, as Alito suggests, is there more the Court can do to rein in agencies even within the powers granted to it under the APA?

AMERICAN MINING CONGRESS V. MINE SAFETY & HEALTH ADMINISTRATION

United States Court of Appeals for the District of Columbia Circuit, 1993.
995 F.2d 1106.

STEPHEN F. WILLIAMS, CIRCUIT JUDGE:

This case presents a single issue: whether Program Policy Letters of the Mine Safety and Health Administration, stating the agency's position that certain x-ray readings qualify as "diagnose[s]" of lung disease within the meaning of agency reporting regulations, are interpretive rules under the Administrative Procedure Act. We hold that they are.

The Federal Mine Safety and Health Act, 30 U.S.C. § 801 *et seq.*, extensively regulates health and safety conditions in the nation's mines and empowers the Secretary of Labor to enforce the statute and relevant regulations. See *Id.* at §§ 811, 813–14. In addition, the Act requires "every operator of a . . . mine . . . [to] establish and maintain such records, make such reports, and provide such information, as the Secretary . . . may reasonably require from time to time to enable him to perform his functions." *Id.* at § 813(h). The Act makes a general grant of authority to the Secretary to issue "such regulations as . . . [he] deems appropriate to carry out" any of its provisions. *Id.* at § 957.

Pursuant to its statutory authority, the Mine Safety and Health Administration (acting on behalf of the Secretary of Labor) maintains regulations known as "Part 50" regulations, which cover the "Notification, Investigation, Reports and Records of Accidents, Injuries, Illnesses, Employment, and Coal Production in Mines." See 30 CFR Part 50. These were adopted via notice-and-comment rulemaking. See 42 Fed. Reg. 55,568 (1977) (notice of proposed rulemaking); 42 Fed. Reg. 65,534 (1977) (adopted rules). Subpart C deals with the "Reporting of Accidents, Injuries, and

[handwritten margin: operator report - w/ 10 days]

[handwritten margin left: dx if illness diagnosed → must report it! notice comm]

[handwritten top: Mine Saf Health Adm]

Illnesses" and requires mine operators to report to the MSHA within ten days "each accident, occupational injury, or occupational illness" that occurs at a mine. See 30 CFR § 50.20(a). Of central importance here, the regulation also says that whenever any of certain occupational illnesses are "*diagnosed*," the operator must similarly report the diagnosis within ten days. *Id.* (emphasis added). Among the occupational illnesses covered are "[s]ilicosis, asbestosis, coal worker's pneumoconiosis, and other pneumoconioses." *Id.* at § 50.20–6(b)(7)(ii). An operator's failure to report may lead to citation and penalty. See 30 U.S.C. §§ 814(a), 815(a) & (d), 816(a).

As the statute and formal regulations contain ambiguities, the MSHA from time to time issues Program Policy Letters ("PPLs") intended to coordinate and convey agency policies, guidelines, and interpretations to agency employees and interested members of the public. See *MSHA Administrative Policy and Procedures Manual*, Volume II, paragraph 112 (July 17, 1990); *MSHA Program Information Bulletin No. 88–03* (August 19, 1988). One subject on which it has done so—apparently in response to inquiries from mine operators about whether certain x-ray results needed to be reported as "diagnos[es]"—has been the meaning of the term diagnosis for purposes of Part 50.

[handwritten: What Are the Rules]

[handwritten margin: PPL 1]

The first of the PPLs at issue here, PPL No. 91–III–2 (effective September 6, 1991), stated that any chest x-ray of a miner who had a history of exposure to pneumonoconiosis-causing dust that rated 1/0 or higher on the International Labor Office (ILO) classification system would be considered a "diagnosis that the x-rayed miner has silicosis or one of the other pneumonoconioses" for the purposes of the Part 50 reporting requirements. (The ILO classification system uses a 12-step scale to measure the concentration of opacities (i.e., areas of darkness or shading) on chest x-rays. A 1/0 rating is the fourth most severe of the ratings.) The 1991 PPL also set up a procedure whereby, if a mine operator had a chest x-ray initially evaluated by a relatively unskilled reader, the operator could seek a reading by a more skilled one; if the latter rated the x-ray below 1/0, the MSHA would delete the "diagnosis" from its files. We explain the multiple-reader rules further in the context of the third PPL, where they took their final form (so far).

[handwritten margin: opacities / procedure multiple reader rule]

[handwritten: took place of]

[handwritten circle: PPL 2]

The second letter, PPL No. P92–III–2 (effective May 6, 1992), superseded the 1991 PPL but largely repeated its view about a Part 50 diagnosis. In addition, the May 1992 PPL stated the MSHA's position that mere diagnosis of an occupational disease or illness within the meaning of Part 50 did not automatically entitle a miner to benefits for disability or impairment under a workers' compensation scheme. The PPL also said that the MSHA did not intend for an operator's mandatory reporting of an x-ray reading to be equated with an admission of liability for the reported disease.

[handwritten heart: PPL 3]

The final PPL under dispute, PPL No. P92–III–2 (effective August 1, 1992), replaced the May 1992 PPL and again restated the MSHA's basic view that a chest x-ray rating above 1/0 on the ILO scale constituted a "diagnosis" of silicosis or some other pneumoconiosis. The August 1992 PPL also modified the MSHA's position on additional readings. Specifically, when the first reader is not a "B" reader (i.e., one certified by the National Institute of Occupational Safety and Health to perform ILO ratings), and the operator seeks a reading from a "B" reader, the MSHA will stay

[handwritten bottom: 1st reader ≠ certified → operator seeks certified reader]

enforcement for failure to report the first reading. If the "B" reader concurs with the initial determination that the x-ray should be scored a 1/0 or higher, the mine operator must report the "diagnosis". If the "B" reader scores the x-ray below 1/0, the MSHA will continue to stay enforcement if the operator gets a third reading, again from a "B" reader; the MSHA then will accept the majority opinion of the three readers.

The MSHA did not follow the notice and comment requirements of 5 U.S.C. § 553 in issuing any of the three PPLs. In defending its omission of notice and comment, the agency relies solely on the interpretive rule exemption of § 553(b)(3)(A). * * *

The distinction between those agency pronouncements subject to APA notice-and-comment requirements and those that are exempt has been aptly described as "enshrouded in considerable smog." Given the confusion, it makes some sense to go back to the origins of the distinction in the legislative history of the Administrative Procedure Act. Here the key document is the *Attorney General's Manual on the Administrative Procedure Act* (1947), which offers "the following working definitions":

> *Substantive rules*—rules, other than organizational or procedural under section 3(a)(1) and (2), issued by an agency pursuant to statutory authority and which implement the statute, as, for example, the proxy rules issued by the Securities and Exchange Commission pursuant to section 14 of the Securities Exchange Act of 1934 (15 U.S.C. § 78n). Such rules have the force and effect of law.

> *Interpretative rules*—rules or statements issued by an agency to advise the public of the agency's construction of the statutes and rules which it administers. . . .

> *General statements of policy*—statements issued by an agency to advise the public prospectively of the manner in which the agency proposes to exercise a discretionary power.

* * * Our own decisions have often used similar language, inquiring whether the disputed rule has "the force of law". We have said that a rule has such force only if Congress has delegated legislative power to the agency and if the agency intended to exercise that power in promulgating the rule.

On its face, the "intent to exercise" language may seem to lead only to more smog, but in fact there are a substantial number of instances where such "intent" can be found with some confidence. The first and clearest case is where, in the absence of a legislative rule by the agency, the legislative basis for agency enforcement would be inadequate. The example used by the Attorney General's Manual fits exactly—the SEC's proxy authority under § 14 of the Securities Exchange Act of 1934, 15 U.S.C. § 78n. Section 14(b), for example, forbids certain persons, "to give, or to refrain from giving a proxy" "in contravention of such rules and regulations as the Commission may prescribe." 15 U.S.C. § 78n(b). The statute itself forbids *nothing* except acts or omissions to be spelled out by the Commission in "rules or regulations." The present case is similar, as to Part 50 itself, in that § 813(h) merely requires an operator to maintain "such records . . . as the Secretary . . . may reasonably require from time to time." 30 U.S.C. § 813(h). Although the Secretary might conceivably create some "require[ments]" ad hoc, clearly some agency creation of a duty is a necessary predicate to any enforcement against an operator for failure to keep records. Analogous cases may exist in which an agency may offer a government benefit only after it formalizes the prerequisites.

Second, an agency seems likely to have intended a rule to be legislative if it has the rule published in the Code of Federal Regulations; 44 U.S.C. § 1510 limits publication in that code to rules "having general applicability and legal effect." Third, "'[i]f a second rule repudiates or is irreconcilable with [a prior legislative rule], the second rule must be an amendment of the first; and, of course, an amendment to a legislative rule must itself be legislative.'" * * *

In *United States v. Picciotto*, 875 F.2d 345 (D.C. Cir. 1989), the Park Service had issued an indisputably legislative rule containing an "open-ended" provision stating that a "permit may contain additional reasonable conditions". Then, in a rule issued without notice and comment, it established some such conditions. We struck down the disputed condition, as it was not an interpretation of the prior regulation but an exercise of the legislative authority reserved by the prior legislative rule.

Th[e] focus on whether the agency *needs* to exercise legislative power (to provide a basis for enforcement actions or agency decisions conferring benefits) helps explain some distinctions that may, out of context, appear rather metaphysical. For example, * * * we drew a distinction between instances where an agency merely "declare[s] its understanding of what a statute requires" (interpretive), and ones where an agency "go[es] beyond the text of a statute" (legislative). The difficulty with the distinction is that almost every rule may seem to do both. But if the dividing line is the necessity for agency legislative action, then a rule supplying that action will be legislative no matter how grounded in the agency's "understanding of what the statute requires," and an interpretation that spells out the scope of an agency's or regulated entity's pre-existing duty will be interpretive, even if * * * it widens that duty even beyond the scope allowed to the agency under *Chevron U.S.A., Inc. v. NRDC*, 467 U.S. 837 (1984).

Similarly, we have distinguished between cases where a rule is "based on specific statutory provisions" (interpretive), and where one is instead "based on an agency's power to exercise its judgment as to how best to implement a general statutory mandate" (legislative). A statute or legislative rule that actually establishes a duty or a right is likely to be relatively specific (and the agency's refinement will be interpretive), whereas an agency's authority to create rights and duties will typically be relatively broad (and the agency's actual establishment of rights and duties will be legislative). But the legislative or interpretive status of the agency rules turns not in some general sense on the narrowness or breadth of the statutory (or regulatory) term in question, but on the prior existence or non-existence of legal duties and rights.

* * * Nor is there much explanatory power in any distinction that looks to the use of mandatory as opposed to permissive language. While an agency's decision to use "will" instead of "may" may be of use when drawing a line between *policy statements* and legislative rules, the endeavor miscarries in the

[handwritten: Interpretation = chameleon that gets color from context]

interpretive/legislative rule context. Interpretation is a chameleon that takes its color from its context; therefore, an interpretation will use imperative language—or at least have imperative meaning—if the interpreted term is part of a command; it will use permissive language—or at least have a permissive meaning—if the interpreted term is in a permissive provision.

A non-legislative rule's capacity to have a binding effect is limited in practice by the fact that agency personnel at every level act under the shadow of judicial review. If they believe that courts may fault them for brushing aside the arguments of persons who contest the rule or statement, they are obviously far more likely to entertain those arguments. And, as failure to provide notice-and-comment rulemaking will usually mean that affected parties have had no prior formal opportunity to present their contentions, judicial review for want of reasoned decisionmaking is likely, in effect, to take place in review of specific agency actions implementing the rule. * * * Because the threat of judicial review provides a spur to the agency to pay attention to facts and arguments submitted in derogation of any rule not supported by notice and comment, even as late as the enforcement stage, *any* agency statement not subjected to notice-and-comment rulemaking will be more vulnerable to attack not only in court but also within the agency itself.

[handwritten: Not Notice + comment → more subject to attack]

Not only does an agency have an incentive to entertain objections to an interpretive rule, but the ability to promulgate such rules, without notice and comment, does not appear more hazardous to affected parties than the likely alternative. Where a statute or legislative rule has created a legal basis for enforcement, an agency can simply let its interpretation evolve ad hoc in the process of enforcement or other applications (e.g., grants). The protection that Congress sought to secure by requiring notice and comment for legislative rules is not advanced by reading the exemption for "interpretive rule" so narrowly as to drive agencies into pure ad hocery—an ad hocery, moreover, that affords less notice, or less convenient notice, to affected parties.

Accordingly, insofar as our cases can be reconciled at all, we think it almost exclusively on the basis of whether the purported interpretive rule has "legal effect", which in turn is best ascertained by asking (1) whether in the absence of the rule there would not be an adequate legislative basis for enforcement action or other agency action to confer benefits or ensure the performance of duties, (2) whether the agency has published the rule in the Code of Federal Regulations, (3) whether the agency has explicitly invoked its general legislative authority, or (4) whether the rule effectively amends a prior legislative rule. If the answer to any of these questions is affirmative, we have a legislative, not an interpretive rule.

[handwritten: Leg rule if Yes to Any]

Here we conclude that the August 1992 PPL is an interpretive rule. The Part 50 regulations themselves require the reporting of diagnoses of the specified diseases, so there is no legislative gap that required the PPL as a predicate to enforcement action. Nor did the agency purport to act legislatively, either by including the letter in the Code of Federal Regulations, or by invoking its general legislative authority under 30 U.S.C. § 811(a). See *MSHA Program Information Bulletin No. 88–03* (August 19, 1988) (characterizing PPLs generally as "[i]nterpretation"). The

[handwritten: Aug PPL = Interpret. rule]

[handwritten margin notes: "Aug 1992 = de facto amendment of prior leg rules"]

remaining possibility therefore is that the August 1992 PPL is a de facto amendment of prior legislative rules, namely the Part 50 regulations.

A rule does not, in this inquiry, become an amendment merely because it supplies crisper and more detailed lines than the authority being interpreted. If that were so, no rule could pass as an interpretation of a legislative rule unless it were confined to parroting the rule or replacing the original vagueness with another. * * *

[handwritten margin note: "diagnosis def"]

Although petitioners cite some definitions of "diagnosis" suggesting that with pneumoconiosis and silicosis, a diagnosis requires more than a chest x-ray—specifically, additional diagnostic tools as tissue examination or at least an occupational history, * * * MSHA points to some administrative rules that make x-rays at the level specified here the basis for a finding of pneumoconiosis. * * * A finding of a disease is surely equivalent, in normal terminology, to a diagnosis, and thus the PPLs certainly offer no interpretation that repudiates or is irreconcilable with an existing legislative rule.

[handwritten margin note: "X-ray = Basis"]

We stress that deciding whether an interpretation is an amendment of a legislative rule is different from deciding the substantive validity of that interpretation. An interpretive rule may be sufficiently within the language of a legislative rule to be a genuine interpretation and not an amendment, while at the same time being an incorrect interpretation of the agency's statutory authority. Here, petitioners have made no attack on the PPLs' substantive validity. Nothing that we say upholding the agency's decision to act without notice and comment bars any such substantive claims.

NOTE ON INTERPRETIVE RULES

[handwritten margin notes: "Interpretive Rules clarify An Agency's Interpretation of An Existing Leg Rule w/o Substantive Changes"]

Legislative Versus Interpretive. Interpretive rules clarify an agency's interpretation of an existing legislative rule or statute without imposing substantive changes. Although they do not carry the force of law, interpretive rules may, nonetheless, have the effect of altering conduct. In *American Mining Congress*, couldn't you argue that the rule in question—defining "diagnosis" based on a certain x-ray rating—does more than simply interpret the legislative rule requiring mine operators to report diagnosed instances of occupational disease? MSHA relied on the fourth most severe rating out of twelve under the ILO classification system. What if the agency's definition of diagnosis relied on the least severe of the twelve ILO ratings? What if MSHA devised its own rating system for measuring the concentration of opacities on chest x-rays? Is there some point at which the agency's x-ray rating approach would constitute a distinctly stronger (or weaker) safety standard, requiring notice-and-comment?

Courts have employed different approaches to determine whether a rule is legislative or interpretive. Prominent among them is Judge Williams' four-part test, set forth in *American Mining Congress*. For many decisions invoking this test, the final factor—whether the rule effectively amends a prior rule—receives particular emphasis. See e.g., *Hemp Indus. Ass'n v. DEA*, 333 F.3d 1082, 1088–91 (9th Cir. 2003). Why do you think the fourth factor has received greater attention from reviewing courts? If the first three factors suggest that a rule is interpretive but the fourth factor suggests legislative, how should a court resolve the matter?

2. Policy Statements

GENERAL ELECTRIC COMPANY V. E.P.A.

United States Court of Appeals, District of Columbia Circuit, 2002.
290 F.3d 377.

GINSBURG, CHIEF JUDGE:

General Electric Co. petitions for review of the "PCB Risk Assessment Review Guidance Document" issued by the Environmental Protection Agency. The parties dispute * * * whether the Document is a "rule" within the meaning of § 19(a) of the Toxic Substances Control Act (TSCA), and hence whether the court has jurisdiction to review its promulgation; and whether the Agency should have followed the procedures required for rulemaking in the TSCA and in the Administrative Procedure Act when it promulgated the Document. We conclude that * * * the Guidance Document is a legislative rule such that the court does have jurisdiction to entertain GE's petition and the Document should not have been issued without prior notice and an opportunity for public comment.

[I] [The TSCA prohibits the manufacturing and use of polychlorinated biphenyls (PCBs) unless the EPA determines that the activity will not result in unreasonable risks to human or environmental health. The Guidance Document governs the application of two regulations involving the cleanup and disposal of PCBs. A regulated entity may apply to the EPA to use a cleanup or disposal method other than one specified in the regulations, and the EPA will approve an application if the alternative method poses no "unreasonable risk of injury to health or the environment." The regulations do not tell applicants how to conduct the necessary risk assessment to submit with their application, although the Guidance Document provides an overview of risk assessment techniques.]

* * * Of particular relevance to this case, in the Guidance Document the EPA explains that an applicant seeking to use an alternative method under [the regulation] may take either of two approaches to risk assessment. Guidance Document at 21, 42. [The first approach is to calculate separately cancer and non-cancer risks, using a cancer potency factor recognized by the EPA and taking account of certain specified non-cancer risks. The second approach is to use a "total toxicity factor" of 4.0 $(\text{mg/kg/day})^{-1}$ to account for cancer and non-cancer risks together. The EPA's brief argued that this approach "provides the applicant an opportunity to reduce the time and expense associated with the risk assessment" because the Agency is willing "to accept this 'default' toxicity value of 4.0 $(\text{mg/kg/day})^{-1}$[ ] without requiring further justification."]

[II] GE's primary argument is that the Guidance Document is a legislative rule and therefore should have been promulgated only after public notice and an opportunity for comment. * * *

[Chief Judge Ginsburg first rejected the EPA's arguments that the case was not yet ripe for review.]

[II-B] * * * GE argues that the Guidance Document is a legislative rule rather than a statement of policy or an interpretive rule because it gives substance to the vague language of 40 C.F.R. § 761.61(c) ("unreasonable risk of injury to health or the environment"), does so in an obligatory fashion, and is treated by the EPA as "controlling in the field." *See Community Nutrition Inst. v. Young,* 818 F.2d 943, 946 (D.C.Cir.1987); *McLouth Steel Prods. Corp. v. Thomas,* 838 F.2d 1317, 1320–22 (D.C.Cir.1988); *Appalachian Power,* 208 F.3d at 1021. The EPA argues that under the three-part test applied in *Molycorp, Inc. v. EPA,* 197 F.3d 543, 545 (D.C.Cir.1999), the Guidance Document is not a legislative rule. Although it is not entirely clear what in the EPA's view the Document is, the EPA comes closest to characterizing it as a statement of policy; thus:

> [T]he portion of the guidance at issue here is simply an expression of EPA's policy judgment, based on the available scientific data and analysis, that when the "total toxicity" analysis is used, the 4.0 (mg/kg/day)$^{-1}$ toxicity value is appropriate to avoid an unreasonable risk to health or the environment.

With the Agency's argument so understood, the question before us can be framed as whether the Guidance Document is a legislative rule or a statement of policy.

As GE argues, in cases where we have attempted to draw the line between legislative rules and statements of policy, we have considered whether the agency action (1) "impose[s] any rights and obligations" or (2) "genuinely leaves the agency and its decisionmakers free to exercise discretion." *Community Nutrition Inst.,* 818 F.2d at 946; *Chamber of Commerce v. Dep't of Labor,* 174 F.3d 206, 212 (D.C.Cir.1999). In *McLouth,* we recognized that "[i]n practice, there appears some overlap in the Community Nutrition criteria" because "[i]f a statement denies the decisionmaker discretion in the area of its coverage, so that [the agency] will automatically decline to entertain challenges to the statement's position, then the statement is binding, and creates rights or obligations." 838 F.2d at 1320. * * *

The EPA urges the court to consider three factors: "(1) the Agency's own characterization of its action; (2) whether the action was published in the Federal Register or the Code of Federal Regulations; and (3) whether the action has binding effects on private parties or on the agency." *Molycorp, Inc.,* 197 F.3d at 545. As the EPA concedes, however, the third factor is the most important: "[T]he ultimate focus of the inquiry is whether the agency action partakes of the fundamental characteristic of a regulation, i.e., that it has the force of law." *Molycorp, Inc.,* 197 F.3d at 545.

The two tests overlap at step three of the *Molycorp* formulation—in which the court determines whether the agency action binds private parties or the agency itself with the "force of law." This common standard has been well stated as follows:

> If a document expresses a change in substantive law or policy (that is not an interpretation) which the agency intends to make binding, or administers with binding effect, the agency may not rely upon the statutory exemption for policy statements, but must observe the APA's legislative rulemaking procedures.

Robert A. Anthony, *Interpretive Rules, Policy Statements, Guidances, Manuals, and the Like—Should Federal Agencies Use Them to Bind the Public?,* 41 Duke L.J. 1311, 1355 (1992).

Our cases likewise make clear that an agency pronouncement will be considered binding as a practical matter if it either appears on its face to be binding, *Appalachian Power,* 208 F.3d at 1023 ("[T]he entire Guidance, from beginning to end . . . reads like a ukase. It commands, it requires, it orders, it dictates."), or is applied by the agency in a way that indicates it is binding, *McLouth,* 838 F.2d at 1321. As Professor Anthony cogently comments, the mandatory language of a document alone can be sufficient to render it binding:

> A document will have practical binding effect before it is actually applied if the affected private parties are reasonably led to believe that failure to conform will bring adverse consequences, such as . . . denial of an application. If the document is couched in mandatory language, or in terms indicating that it will be regularly applied, a binding intent is strongly evidenced. In some circumstances, if the language of the document is such that private parties can rely on it as a norm or safe harbor by which to shape their actions, it can be binding as a practical matter.

Interpretive Rules, 41 Duke L.J. at 1328–29.

GE argues that the Guidance Document is binding both because it facially requires an applicant for a risk-based variance to calculate toxicity by one of two methods—either use a total toxicity factor of 4.0 (mg/kg/day)$^{-1}$ or use a cancer potency factor and account for the specified non-cancer health risks—and because, considering the cost, delay, and uncertainty entailed in the latter course, "[f]or all practical purposes, the Guidance is a rule that directs PCB toxicity to be measured by a 4.0 (mg/kg/day)$^{-1}$ CPF."

The EPA counters that the Guidance Document lacks the force of law because it does not purport to be binding and because it has not been applied as though it were binding. First, we are told, the Document "allows great flexibility" because it not only "recognizes two broad approaches to risk assessment," but also acknowledges that

> some risk assessments may have components that require the use of non-standard reference materials, unique exposure scenarios or assumptions, or require the use of unconventional methods for estimating risks. These risk assessments will need to be addressed on a case-by-case basis.

Second, the EPA says that it has not in practice "applied the guidance document inflexibly, as if it were a rule or regulation." By this, however, the EPA means only that it has received and approved applications based upon the use of the total toxicity factor and upon a separate analysis of cancer and non-cancer risks—and even this limited assertion is disputed by GE. Finally, the Agency contends that the Guidance Document is "an expression of EPA's judgment on values to be used in conducting risk assessments," much like the data in the Agency's Integrated Risk Information System (IRIS), which this court held are not subject to the requirements of notice and comment rulemaking. *See Chemical Mfrs. Ass'n v. EPA,* 28 F.3d 1259, 1263 (1994).

We think it clear that the Guidance Document does purport to bind applicants for approval of a risk-based cleanup plan under 40 C.F.R. § 761.61(c). Consider the principal directives: "When developing a risk-based cleanup application . . . both the cancer and non-cancer endpoints must be addressed. . . ." Guidance Document at 21. If an applicant chooses not to use the 4.0 total toxicity factor, then it "must, at a minimum account for the risk from non-cancer endpoints for neurotoxicity, reproductive and developmental toxicity, immune system suppression, liver damage, skin irritation, and endocrine disruption for each of the commercial mixtures found at the cleanup site." *Id.* Although the Guidance Document does, as noted, anticipate and acknowledge that "some risk assessments may have components that require the use of non-standard . . . unique . . . or unconventional methods for estimating risk," *id.* at 44, that does not undermine the binding force of the Guidance Document in standard cases. *See McLouth,* 838 F.2d at 1321 ("such a provision for exceptions . . . does not push it much in the direction of a policy statement"). Furthermore, even though the Guidance Document gives applicants the option of calculating risk in either of two ways (assuming both are practical) it still requires them to conform to one or the other, that is, not to submit an application based upon a third way. And if an applicant does choose to calculate cancer and non-cancer risks separately, then it must consider the non-cancer risks specified in the Guidance Document. To the applicant reading the Guidance Document the message is clear: in reviewing applications the Agency will not be open to considering approaches other than those prescribed in the Document.

The Guidance Document also appears to bind the Agency to accept applications using a total toxicity factor of 4.0 (mg/kg/day)$^{-1}$ to calculate the risk from both cancer and non-cancer endpoints. Guidance Document at 21. [Judge Ginsburg pointed to a contradiction between the EPA's claim in its principal brief, that a total toxicity value of 4.0 (mg/kg/day)$^{-1}$ would be accepted without detailed justification, and its supplemental brief, which claimed the EPA was not bound to accept an application using this factor.] How can this be? According to the Agency, its position with respect to the total toxicity factor "is a matter of policy" that "can be changed at any time to respond to, *inter alia,* advances in scientific knowledge." But the Guidance Document itself says nothing of the sort. * * * Stating without qualification that an applicant may use a total toxicity factor of 4.0 (mg/kg/day)$^{-1}$ strongly implies that use of that value will not be questioned; an applicant reasonably could rely upon that implication.

The EPA argues that the Guidance Document "neither adds to EPA's prior position nor imposes any further obligations on EPA or the regulated community" because the Agency had used the toxicity factor of 4.0 (mg/kg/day)$^{-1}$ when it "establish[ed] the generic cleanup standards in the 1998 [PCB] regulations." In its supplemental brief, however, the Agency explicitly states that it does not think its use of 4.0 (kg/mg/day)$^{-1}$ in the 1998 regulations requires it to approve use of that factor in an application under § 761.61(c). Because we conclude that the Guidance Document does bind the Agency to accept use of 4.0 (kg/mg/day)$^{-1}$, it follows that the Document does indeed impose a "further obligation[ ] on the EPA." * * *

Furthermore, the EPA does not contend that in practice it has not treated the Guidance Document as binding in the ways described above. The EPA does not claim, for example, that it has accepted any applications that (1) use neither of the two methods of risk assessment approved in the Guidance Document; or (2) calculate risk separately for cancer and non-cancer endpoints, but fail to calculate endpoints for all the non-cancer risks required by the Guidance Document to be addressed. Nor does the EPA contend that it has ever rejected an applicant's use of 4.0 (mg/kg/day)$^{-1}$. Whether an applicant has successfully used the second method of risk assessment set out in the Guidance Document—as the EPA asserts and GE disputes—is immaterial because, even if both methods are practically available, the Document nonetheless binds applicants and the Agency in the ways described above.

In sum, the commands of the Guidance Document indicate that it has the force of law. On its face the Guidance Document imposes binding obligations upon applicants to submit applications that conform to the Document and upon the Agency not to question an applicant's use of the 4.0 (mg/kg/day)$^{-1}$ total toxicity factor. This is sufficient to render it a legislative rule. Furthermore, the Agency's application of the Document does nothing to demonstrate that the Document has any lesser effect in practice. Consequently, we conclude that the Guidance Document is a legislative rule. The Guidance Document is therefore undisputedly a "rule" for purposes of § 19(a)(1)(A) of the TSCA, and the manner of its promulgation is subject to review.

[The Court determined that because the Guidance Document was a "rule," it did not need to reach GE's alternative arguments on the merits]. GE's petition for review is granted because the EPA promulgated a legislative rule without following the procedures required by the TSCA and the APA. The Guidance Document is accordingly *Vacated*.

NOTES ON POLICY GUIDANCE MATERIALS
AND AGENCY CHOICES

1. *An Overview of Policy Guidance Materials.* Policy guidance may be found in an array of agency communications, including advice documents, manuals, circulars, memoranda and bulletins. All are aimed at providing the public with a sense of how the agency intends to implement a particular statutory or regulatory provision pursuant to a relatively broad grant of authority. As previously noted, section 552(a)(1)(D) of the APA requires agencies to publish interpretive rules and policy statements of general applicability in the Federal Register. (Other guidance materials are exempt from this publication requirement, although § 552(a)(2)(B) requires that additional guidance materials be made available to the general public). Failure to publish documents that are required to appear in the Federal Register precludes the agency from using the documents in a way that adversely affects any parties. § 552(a)(1). Policy statements are nonbinding on both private parties and the issuing agency. Nonetheless, determining if an agency has exceeded the limits of what it may advise in a policy statement, straying into legislative rule territory, can raise difficult questions.

The court in *General Electric* cites to a law review article by Robert Anthony; in that same article, Professor Anthony also contends that some nonlegislative rules "have the purpose or effect of binding the public *as a practical matter*" because they "are intended to impose mandatory standards or obligations, or [that] as a practical matter are given that effect." Robert Anthony, *Interpretive Rules, Policy Statements, Guidances, Manuals, and the Like—Should Federal Agencies Use Them to Bind the Public?*, 41 Duke L.J. 1311, 1328 (1992) (emphasis in original). How can it be determined whether a policy statement is meant to bind the public? What factors does the court look to in the *General Electric* decision to determine that the document has crossed over from mere guidance to a legislative rule? Are certain factors more influential than others? For instance, what about the document's recognition that non-standard methods for estimating risk are permissible? Alternatively, consider what would have happened if the EPA had identified instances where it had accepted applications that did not use either of the risk assessment methods approved in the Guidance Document. Would that have changed the outcome? Should it?

2. *Legal Effect of Policy Statements.* The courts generally agree that policy statements are nonbinding and that they are meant to inform rather than to control. In *Colwell v. Department of Health and Human Services*, 558 F.3d 1112, 1124 (9th Cir. 2009), the Ninth Circuit reiterated that the "critical factor" in determining whether "a directive announcing a new policy constitutes a rule or a general statement of policy is the extent to which the challenged [directive] leaves the agency, or its implementing official free to exercise discretion to follow, or not to follow, the [announced] policy in an individual case." What factors must a reviewing court consider when deciding if a challenged policy statement is meant to bind the public, as opposed to "merely provid[ing] guidance to agency officials in exercising their discretionary power while preserving their flexibility and their opportunity to make individualized determinations"? *Id.* Judge Williams in *American Mining Congress* suggested in passing that an agency's use of permissive instead of mandatory language may aid in linedrawing between policy statements and legislative rules. Should judicial inquiry focus primarily on such language? How important are non-mandatory terms, as when a Policy Guidance describes conduct that *may* constitute a violation of law, or identifies practices that are *encouraged*, or lists steps that *may be helpful* in attaining compliance, or *clarifies* that failure to act in a certain way does not necessarily amount to non-compliance? See *Colwell, supra*, at 1125–26. Is this permissive language sufficient, or must courts look to more contextual factors to determine whether a policy statement is meant to bind? Conversely, what if the agency announces that it will *refrain* from instituting enforcement proceedings based on criteria set forth in a policy statement? Does the presence of such safe harbors in a policy statement establish or imply that there are certain obligations for which compliance is mandatory? See *id.* at 1126–27.

Should courts distinguish between policy statements meant to bind the public and those meant to bind agency employees? Agencies often use policy guidance to control the conduct of their employees. Is this type of guidance material permissible without notice-and-comment if it effectively controls how an agency conducts policy-related business? Consider, for example, a policy statement that determines aspects of how agency employees must evaluate eligibility for benefits? What sort of problems, if any, do such policy statements raise?

3. *Interpretive Rules and Policy Statements Versus Rulemaking.* Agencies may have both practical and strategic reasons to opt for interpretive rules or policy statements rather than notice-and-comment rulemaking. As Nina Mendelson explains, issuing a guidance document is inexpensive compared to the costs of rulemaking; the agency retains flexibility to modify the guidance cheaply and quickly; avoiding notice-and-comment publication in the Federal Register means that guidance documents are less likely to attract media attention or congressional oversight; and these documents also are less likely to provoke costly and time-consuming litigation on substantive or procedural grounds. "In short, by issuing a guidance document, an agency can obtain a rule-like effect while minimizing political oversight and avoiding the procedural discipline, public participation, and judicial accountability required by the APA." *Regulatory Beneficiaries*

and Informal Agency Policymaking, 92 Cornell L. Rev. 397, 408 (2007). Does Mendelson's analysis suggest that courts are the only potentially effective means of oversight with respect to agency guidance? Concerned that agencies were using guidance documents to formulate policy outside the rulemaking process, the Bush Administration in 2007 issued an executive order that subjected these documents to a standardized review process focused especially on "significant guidance documents" that may reasonably be expected to have a material budgetary impact or a sizable effect on the economy, to interfere with actions by other agencies, or to raise novel legal or policy issues. See Executive Order No. 13,422, 72 Fed. Reg. 2763.

Bush executive order

In *Strategic or Sincere? Analyzing Agency Use of Guidance Documents*, 119 Yale L.J. 782 (2010), Connor Raso recognized the concerns expressed by the Bush Administration and others regarding agency preferences for guidance documents over legislative rules. But based on his empirical study of agency behavior, Raso concluded that agencies rarely abuse guidance documents to avoid issuing legislative rules. In testing for possible strategic use by agencies, Raso found that (i) agency leaders do not use guidance to implement a flurry of policies at the end of their terms of office, nor do they revise guidance to reflect the ideological preferences of a new president; (ii) agencies issue guidance slightly more often under divided government but the difference was not statistically significant; (iii) agencies do not rely more heavily on guidance documents in the face of congressional disapproval (measured by the number of oversight hearings); (iv) agencies do not use significant guidance documents on a wide scale relative to significant legislative rules (see chart below); and (v) agencies that issue guidance documents at a substantially high rate do so when acting under a mandated time constraint (Homeland Security) or primarily to clarify technical details (EPA, OSHA, and Transportation). Raso concludes that while there are instances of egregious abuse, agencies overall are not using guidance documents to circumvent APA processes. Absent a strong empirical case for change, Raso warns that restrictions on the use of these documents could increase the cost to agencies of clarifying their legislative rules (thus encouraging agencies to substitute adjudication for rulemaking) and undermine ability of agency leaders to manage their own organizations.

agencies that issue guidance documents @ a subst. high rate do so when acting under a mandated time constraint.

undermine ability of Agency Leaders to Manage their Own Organiz.

Use of Guidance Documents by Agency

AGENCY	NUMBER OF SIGNIFICANT GUIDANCE DOCUMENTS IN EFFECT IN AUGUST 2008	NUMBER OF SIGNIFICANT LEGISLATIVE RULES ISSUED, 1993–2008	RATIO OF SIGNIFICANT GUIDANCE DOCUMENTS TO LEGISLATIVE RULES
Agriculture	25	1327	0.02
Defense	0	199	0.00
Education	127	405	0.31
Energy	1	108	0.01

Environmental Protection Agency	204	1095	0.19
Health and Human Services	46	1792	0.03
Homeland Security	67	170	0.39
Housing and Urban Development	2	607	0.00
Interior	2	570	0.00
Justice	43	432	0.10
Labor	80	405	0.20
State	0	61	0.00
Transportation	124	853	0.15
Treasury	2	853	0.00
Veterans Affairs	0	461	0.00
TOTAL:	723	9338	0.08

Raso, 119 Yale L.J. at 813 table 3.

Why do you think the empirical evidence contradicts the traditional hypothesis regarding agencies' preference for guidance documents? What factors might explain why presidents do not engage in the revision of previous administrations' guidance? If agencies have more latitude to issue agency guidance and are subject to less oversight through this channel, why would agencies so overwhelmingly choose to issue legislative rules? What makes agency guidance less appealing to agencies as a policymaking option?

PROBLEM ON POLICY STATEMENTS

Problem 8-4. Broadcast Indecency.[23] In 2001, the FCC issued a 22-page Policy Statement intended "to provide guidance to the broadcast industry regarding our case law *** and enforcement policies with respect to broadcast indecency." The Commission's administrative enforcement responsibility (conferred by statute) authorizes it to revoke a station license, impose a monetary forfeiture, or issue a warning for broadcast of indecent material. The Policy Statement reviewed and discussed the Commission's analytical approach when making indecency determinations pursuant to 18 U.S.C. § 1464, which prohibits the utterance of "any obscene, indecent, or profane language by means of radio communication."

---

[23] In addition to the agency's 2001 Policy Statement and its 2004 Memorandum Opinion and Order, this problem draws on Michael Botein & Darius Adamski, *The FCC's New Indecency Enforcement Policy and its European Counterparts: A Cautionary Tale*, 15 Media L. & Pol'y 7 (Fall 2005), and Clay Calvert, *Bono, The Culture Wars, and a Profane Decision: The FCC's Reversal of Course on Decency Determinations and its New Path on Profanity*, 28 Seattle U. L. Rev. 61 (2004).

The Statement explained that under the agency's enforcement policy, shaped by a number of Supreme Court and congressional decisions, obscene speech may not be broadcast at any time; *indecent speech*, which enjoys some First Amendment protection, may be prohibited between 6am and 10pm based on concern for the welfare of children and support for parental supervision of children. The Commission's definition of "indecency" had been upheld against constitutional challenge in the D.C. Circuit and quoted "with apparent approval" by the Supreme Court in 1978; it was substantially unchanged since the late 1970s: "language or material that, in context, depicts or describes, in terms *patently offensive* as measured by contemporary community standards for the broadcast medium, sexual or excretory activities or organs." (Emphasis added).

Elaborating on the meaning of "patently offensive" (as exemplified in over 30 Commission determinations cited and described), the Policy Statement emphasized the importance of full context. When reviewing for indecency, the Commission had considered whether the broadcast material dwells on or repeats at length descriptions of sexual organs or activities, and whether the material is used to titillate or for shock value. Finally, the Policy Statement cited various examples to demonstrate that "fleeting and isolated references" to sexual organs or activities had regularly been found not to be indecent.

In November 2003, NBC broadcast the Golden Globes Awards program during evening prime time, prior to 10pm. The artist Bono won an award for "Best Original Song"; in receiving his award on stage, he said "This is really, really fucking brilliant. Really great." The Commission received hundreds of complaints from individuals associated with the Parents Television Council (PTC), a public interest group with a strong anti-indecency agenda. The FTC Enforcement Bureau concluded that the material was not indecent, because Bono's utterance was fleeting and isolated, and it did not describe sexual activity in any context.

The full Commission reversed the Bureau in March 2004, making a number of changes in the settled law summarized in its 2001 Policy Statement. First, the Commission rejected the string of cases holding that isolated, fleeting, and otherwise unanticipated uses of "fuck" were not indecent. Second, the FCC ruling relied for the first time on technological advances as a factor in indecency determinations, specifically the ease with which broadcasters today can bleep out even fleeting words during a live broadcast. Third, the ruling deemed it irrelevant whether broadcast or use of the word "fuck" was unintentional. Finally, the Commission held that use of the F-word was also unlawfully profane under § 1464, departing from FCC and judicial precedent that had long understood "profane" as focused on blasphemy or divine imprecation.

The Commission's abandonment of its Policy Statement position occurred in the midst of intense congressional pressure and apparent public outcry. The agency's recorded complaints alleging "indecent" broadcasting had grown from 111 in 2000 to 346 in 2002, 13,922 in 2003, and 1,068,802 in 2004. And in March 2004, one week before the FCC released its *Golden Globe* ruling, the House had passed (by 391–22) an anti-indecency bill that *inter alia* raised the cap on fines for indecent broadcasts from $32,500 to $500,000, and authorized the FCC to fine performers who utter indecencies, not just broadcast station licensees.[24]

---

[24]   The bill did not pass the Senate before Congress adjourned.

The FCC Policy Statement is a reasoned in-depth review of decades of agency practice, taking account of constitutional as well as policy factors. If you are a reviewing court, what weight would you give this Statement in considering the agency's decision to adopt a wholly new indecency policy? Assuming that NBC appeals the *Golden Globe* decision, should the Policy Statement be any more persuasive or probative to a reviewing court than the sum total of the 30-plus agency precedents it analyzes? Is there any problem with the Commission abandoning a policy guidance that is based on 20 years of settled analysis by means of a single adjudicatory order? Is abandonment based on consideration of a heretofore unexamined factor (technology) particularly troubling? Or is it perhaps especially justifiable?

Assume that virtually all of the one million indecency complaints filed in 2004 were orchestrated by the PTC and other "family values" interest groups. How seriously should the agency take this showing of public concern? How seriously should it take the passage of House legislation, imposing severe new penalties for indecency in broadcasting, while the case is *sub judice*?

Assume the FCC in *Golden Globe* ruled that although its reasoning on indecency was a departure from precedent, the agency was levying a $30,000 fine against NBC and each affiliate that broadcast the Awards show, because these stations should be held to know the F-word is both inherently indecent and prohibited profanity. Should the Policy Statement be relevant to a reviewing court in determining whether the agency may impose such fines?

NOTE ON THE TRUMP ADMINISTRATION'S
WAR ON POLICY GUIDANCE

Starting in 2017, President Trump's executive agencies have expressed growing skepticism about the administrative state's use of Policy Guidances. These critiques have responded to particular guidance documents from prior administrations, and in broader terms to the use of these guidances as part of any civil enforcement effort.

In September 2017, the Department of Education's Office of Civil Rights published a Dear Colleague letter announcing its withdrawal of two prior statements of policy and guidance that addressed issues pertaining to Sexual Violence and Title IX: a 2011 Dear Colleague letter and a 2014 set of Questions-and Answers. See U.S. Dep't Education, *Department of Education Issues New Interim Guidance on Campus Sexual Misconduct* (Sept. 22, 2017), https://www.ed.gov/news/press-releases/department-education-issues-new-interim-guidance-campus-sexual-misconduct. The interim guidance document stated that the prior guidances had imposed "regulatory burdens" on educational institutions without affording the opportunity for public comment. These burdens included *inter alia* (a) requiring schools to adopt a minimal standard of proof (preponderance of the evidence) when administering student discipline although many schools had previously used a higher clear-and-convincing evidence standard; (b) requiring schools to allow complainants to appeal not-guilty findings although many schools had reserved appeals rights for accused students; and (c) providing that any due process protections given to accused students should not "unnecessarily delay" resolving the charges against them. The Dear Colleague letter announced that new policies would be promulgated in this area through a rulemaking process. In the interim, the Department issued a new Q-and-A document reversing the positions set forth in the 2011 and 2014 documents with respect to mandatory burden of proof and appeal rights, while emphasizing that there is no fixed time frame under which a school must complete its Title IX investigation. *No time frame*

In December 2017, the Justice Department announced that it had rescinded 25 guidance documents covering over 200 pages and dating back to 1975. *See* Charlie Savage, *Justice Dept. Revokes 25 Legal Guidance Documents Dating to 1975*, N.Y. Times, Dec. 21, 2017, https://www.nytimes.com/2017/12/21/us/politics/justice-dept-guidance-documents.html. The revoked documents included a Reagan-era "industry circular" stating it was illegal to ship certain guns to buyers across state lines and an Obama-era letter urging state and local judges not to impose fines and fees in a way that locks poor people into cycles of debt and prison. Attorney General Sessions justified the revocations as "good government [that] prevents confusing the public with improper or wrong advice," adding that "any guidance that is outdated, used to circumvent the regulatory process or that improperly goes beyond what is provided for in statutes or regulation should not be given effect." The announcement followed Sessions' appointment in November of Associate AG Rachel Brand to lead a regulatory reform task force charged with identifying (in Brand's words) "existing guidance documents that go too far." *Id. existing guidance docs that go too FAR*

In January 2018, Brand issued a Memorandum stating that effective immediately for all affirmative civil enforcement (ACE) cases, "the Department may not use its enforcement authority to effectively convert agency guidance documents into binding rules. Likewise, Department litigators may not use noncompliance with guidance documents as a basis for proving violations of applicable law in ACE cases. . . . [T]he Department should not treat a party's noncompliance with an agency guidance document as presumptively or conclusively establishing that the party violated the applicable statute or regulation." *Dept litigators ≠ use noncompliance w/ Guidance doc as a basis for proving violation of Appl:*

Based on these positions (and others) adopted since late 2017, it appears that the Trump Administration views guidance documents as a genuine threat to the rule of law, and at times a deliberate effort to circumvent, if not undermine, APA processes. This view is at odds with the result of Conor Raso's empirical study of agency behavior, published in the Yale Law Journal in 2010 (see above). In light of the Trump Administration's aggressive pushback against guidances, should we expect to see agencies use adjudication or some other means to clarify their legislative rules? Alternatively, if agencies become more cautious about applying those rules, and their underlying statutory powers, should this invite any responses from Congress? From the courts? *congressional Responses?*

The Administration's pushback against guidance documents raises additional questions in light of conclusions reached in a report to the Administrative Conference of the United States by Nicholas R. Parrillo, *Federal Agency Guidance: An Institutional Perspective* (Oct. 12, 2017), available at https://www.acus.gov/sites/default/files/documents/parrillo-agency-guidance-final-report.pdf. Parrillo interviewed 135 individuals for the ACUS study in 2016–17: 26% were agency career officials; 48% came from industry; 19% from NGOs or unions; and 7% "other." Parrillo drew three basic conclusions from his interviews that are relevant here: (1) regulated entities often face strong practical pressure to follow what a guidance document "suggests," and agencies are at times not open to entities' arguments seeking an individual dispensation; (2) while this pressure and inflexibility are real, they are not universal but instead can be predicted based on certain organizational and legal factors present in some regulatory schemes but not others; and (3) two such factors are (a) officials face competing pressures from other

1) regulated entities often Face strong pressure to follow suggestion

stakeholders to behave in consistent and predictable ways, resulting from rule-of-law values that agencies can hardly ignore; (b) officials succumb to unconscious organizational tendencies favoring rigidity that cannot be altered without undertaking costly reforms in terms of resources and managerial energy. In what ways are Parrillo's conclusions consistent with the Trump Administration strategy? In what ways do they perhaps suggest a different perspective?

3. OVERSIGHT BY THE THREE BRANCHES

You should appreciate by this point why administrative agencies are routinely called the fourth branch of government. Although Article I vests lawmaking powers in Congress, much of the federal "law" that affects our daily lives is enacted not as statutes but as agency regulations and orders. Article II empowers the President to hold federal officers accountable, but in practice the federal bureaucracy operates with considerable independence when engaged in regulatory activity. Article III authorizes the judiciary to resolve cases or controversies arising under federal law, but today "a citizen is ten times more likely to be tried by an agency than by an actual court."[25]

Given the accumulation by agencies of what Chief Justice Roberts has referred to, with regret, as "a potent brew of executive, legislative, and judicial power,"[26] it is not surprising that the three other branches devote considerable attention to oversight of agency performance. *Congress* invests in the oversight function to determine whether its laws are being properly applied, its funds well-spent, and its powers respected. The *President* exerts a measure of control in an effort to assure that agencies minimize overlapping jurisdictions and conflicting missions, weigh costs as well as benefits before taking action, and defer to the White House as necessary for faithful execution of the laws. Finally, *Federal Courts* review administrative decision-making in an attempt to monitor whether agencies are adhering to Congress's original substantive directives, and whether agencies are complying with the APA's procedural requirements—to consider all relevant evidence, provide well-reasoned explanations for their decisions, and avoid acting (or refusing to act) in an arbitrary fashion.

In this Section, we present and analyze principal methods of oversight employed by each branch. In doing so, we emphasize the practical and constitutional questions raised by these efforts to control or even monitor the growing federal bureaucracy.

A. CONGRESSIONAL MONITORING

1. Oversight Hearings and Investigations

A Congress that has delegated much of its lawmaking authority to agencies would rationally seek to monitor those agencies to assure their continued adherence to the original legislative delegation. Before 1933, there were few agencies to oversee, and Congress devoted little effort to monitoring. Agencies proliferated during the

---

[25] See Jonathan Turley, *The Rise of the Fourth Branch of Government*, Washington Post, May 24, 2013, at B-01 (reporting that federal judges conduct 95,000 adjudicatory proceedings, including trials, in a given year, whereas federal agencies complete more than 939,000).

[26] *City of Arlington, Texas v. FCC*, 133 S.Ct. 1863, 1886 (2013) (Roberts, C.J., dissenting).

New Deal. Congress responded with the Legislative Reorganization Act of 1946, 60 Stat. 812, codified at 2 U.S.C. § 31 *et al.*, which signaled a new commitment to oversight and started a process by which Congress and its committees added legislative staff to accomplish this goal. The conventional wisdom of the 1950s was that oversight could effectively assure majoritarian control of policy.

Some political scientists suggest that the conventional wisdom was too optimistic because structural problems impede effective legislative oversight.[27] Thus, legislative oversight committees may become captured by the same forces that capture agencies—interested persons and firms, who provide information, ideas, and encouragement. Also, motivations of legislators are more important in determining oversight activity than is the availability of resources. "Unless [oversight] reveals a scandalous situation with possibilities for favorable publicity for the legislators, the work is considered dull and potentially troublesome."[28] There are opportunity costs for oversight; time spent monitoring agencies is time away from fundraising, casework, and enacting new programs to benefit constituents. The latter are activities that often mean more to a legislator's reelection chances than tedious oversight. Finally, and most important, partisan politics can eviscerate oversight: in periods where Congress is controlled by the same political party as the President (1993–95, 2003–07, 2009–11), one would expect little critical oversight. On the other hand, when at least one branch of Congress and the President are controlled by different parties, as has been the recent norm (1981–93, 1995–2001, May 2001–03, 2007–09, 2011–14), one would expect to see more aggressive oversight.

Whatever the partisan make-up of the federal government, positive political theorists argue that Congress can be expected to protect its institutional interests relatively vigorously. It is helpful to distinguish among the various forms of oversight because some actions that occur steadily are less public and thus may be overlooked. We tend to think first of formal committee hearings as the main mechanism to monitor agencies, but in fact, much of the oversight done by legislators is informal. Lawmakers jawbone agency officials as policy is formulated, or they intervene on behalf of constituents to present arguments and perspectives. Although rules prohibit some forms of *ex parte* communications, particularly during formal adjudication, there are numerous ways for members of Congress to communicate with bureaucrats as rules are being considered. Mark Moran and Barry Weingast, for example, argue that the FTC is strongly influenced by subtle messages sent outside the formal oversight process and that this influence is statistically significant for both enforcement and policymaking initiatives by the FTC.[29] See also Joel

[27]   For leading surveys of congressional oversight, and its problems, see, e.g., Martin James, *Congressional Oversight* (2002); Kathleen Bawn, *Choosing Strategies to Control the Bureaucracy: Statutory Constraints, Oversight, and the Committee System*, 13 J.L. Econ. & Org. 101 (1997); Morris Ogul, *Congressional Oversight: Structures and Incentives*, in Congress Reconsidered 317 (Lawrence Dodd & Bruce Oppenheimer eds. 2d ed. 1981); Charles Shipan, *Regulatory Regimes, Agency Actions, and the Conditional Nature of Congressional Influence*, 98 Am. Pol. Sci. Rev. 467 (2004).

[28]   Bernard Rosen, *Holding Government Bureaucracies Accountable* 21 (1982).

[29]   Barry Weingast & Mark Moran, *Bureaucratic Discretion or Congressional Control? Regulatory Policymaker at the Federal Trade Commission*, 91 J. Pol. Econ. 765 (1983); Weingast & Moran, *The Myth of the Runaway Bureaucracy; The Case of the FTC*, Regulation, May/June 1982, at 33. To the same effect is John Ferejohn's study of communications policy. See John Ferejohn & Charles Shipan, *Congressional Influence on Bureaucracy*, 6 J. L. Econ. & Org. 1 (1990) (special issue).

Auerbach, *Keeping A Watchful Eye: The Politics of Congressional Oversight* (1990), arguing that vigorous congressional oversight is responsive to public demands for greater government accountability.

Various mechanisms exist to provide members of Congress with information that alerts them to the need for aggressive oversight or that supports them as they engage in monitoring. Mathew McCubbins and Thomas Schwartz describe two kinds of monitoring strategies. *Congressional Oversight Overlooked: Police Patrols Versus Fire Alarms*, 28 Am. J. Pol. Sci. 165 (1984). A *police patrol* strategy is time-consuming as legislators and their staffs regularly monitor to discover bureaucratic drift. In contrast, employing *a fire alarm* strategy saves congressional resources as members wait to hear the alarm raised by interested parties upset about agency policy. Once the alarm has been sounded, members can begin aggressive oversight, and they can ignore areas where no discontent is evident. In this way, lawmakers externalize some of the costs of oversight, perhaps engaging in police patrols only in arenas without much interest group activity and thus with less possibility of alarms. After they sound the alarm, lobbyists and interest groups continue to provide supporters with information and expertise to further reduce legislative monitoring costs.

Congress engages in more oversight than it once did. Unfortunately, there is evidence that oversight has many problems.

Regulatory Priorities and Efficacy. Oversight hearings, controlled by a congressional subgroup, may push agencies away from their public-regarding agendas. With their scarce resources, committed agencies have their hands full devising workable strategies and fighting off industry attacks. If an oversight committee is controlled or even influenced by the regulated industry, it can thwart agency regulation by pressuring the agency toward less intrusive (and often less efficacious) modes of regulation. Even well-intended oversight might undermine agency efficacy if it adds more to the agency's plate, as illustrated in the auto safety area.[30] A major regulatory initiative undertaken by the National Highway Traffic Safety Administration (NHTSA) was Standard 208, which required automakers to produce cars that would protect passengers against injury under specified performance criteria. Manufacturers could meet the standard with airbags, automatic seatbelts, and other mechanisms. For various institutional reasons, after 1971, the only way to comply with the standard was an "ignition interlock" system, whereby the car would not start until all passengers engaged their seatbelts. The public was not pleased. Drivers disengaged their interlocks (which were mandatory for the 1974 auto market) and wrote their members of Congress against this intrusion into their "freedom to drive."

Responding to public outrage, Congress held several oversight hearings, and the result was a massive disruption in the agency's regulatory program. On the one hand, the auto industry and elected representatives alike had a field day deriding the interlock system. Senator Norris Cotton joked, to great laughter, that his car would not start when he placed groceries in the passenger's seat. Instead of placing them

---

[30]   See Jerry Mashaw, *The Story of* Motor Vehicle Manufacturers Association etc: *Law, Science, and Politics in the Administrative State*, in *Administrative Law Stories* 334, 357–67 Peter Strauss ed., 2006). See also Steven Balla & John Wright, *Interest Groups, Advisory Committees, and Congressional Control of the Bureaucracy*, 45 Am. J. Pol. Sci. 799 (2001).

on the floor (duh!), the New Hampshire legislator belted "a pound of cheese and a loaf of bread" to satisfy the system. Although the experts maintained that ignition interlocks saved lives, popular resentment about inconveniences and infringements on their freedom to drive overwhelmed the theoretical safety gains.

On the other hand, oversight focused on a decidedly minor problem: schoolbus design. Of the 54,000+ annual death toll as a result of auto accidents, the agency found only a few dozen where an expensive schoolbus redesign might have saved the lives of schoolchildren. (As many as 80% of child deaths from schoolbus accidents occur *outside* of the bus.) Even sympathetic Members of Congress were appalled by the agency's failure to focus on *children's deaths* because of schoolbus accidents. Representative Les Aspin, a liberal, berated the agency for "misusing the concept of cost-benefit analysis" (Mashaw, *Law, Science, and Politics*, 363–65). *misusing cost-benefit analysis.*

The upshot of all this oversight was the Motor Vehicle and Schoolbus Safety Amendments of 1974. These amendments forbade imposition of the ignition interlock (which saved hundreds and probably thousands of lives each year) and required the agency to impose stringent new design requirements on schoolbuses (which might save a life or three each year, at much greater expense). As Jerry Mashaw wearily concludes, "[i]f Congress had wanted to protect the lives of children, it would have done better to re-energize NHTSA's lagging standard-setting enterprise as it applied to the passenger car" (*Id.* at 367). *Forbade ignition interlock. Req. Agency to imp. of stringent new design.*

Congressional Oversight and Individual Rights. When Congress or its committees exercise vigorous oversight power, there may be problems involving overreaching or violation of individual rights. In the 1950s, several congressional committees engaged in what many regard as a "witch hunt" for Communists and "homosexuals" in American government and society. The legislative investigations often seemed bent on ruining peoples' reputations rather than on serving valid legislative goals, and courts through the 1950s and 1960s sometimes overturned contempt citations against uncooperative witnesses.[31] *Congressional oversight witchhunts*

The leading case was *Watkins v. United States*, 354 U.S. 178 (1957), in which the Supreme Court overturned a contempt conviction based upon its finding that the House Un-American Activities Committee had ventured far beyond its House-authorized arena of investigation. See also Judge Weinfeld's earlier decision in *United States v. Lamont*, 18 F.R.D. 27 (S.D.N.Y. 1955), *aff'd*, 236 F.2d 312 (2d Cir. 1956), which made similar findings for the Senate's Permanent Subcommittee on Investigations (chaired by Joseph McCarthy (R-Wis.)). Chief Justice Warren's opinion in *Watkins* suggested, moreover, that legislative investigations are limited to building a factual record for proposed legislation and providing information for the exercise of legislative insight. "We have no doubt that there is no congressional power to expose for the sake of exposure," concluded Warren. 354 U.S. at 200.

The holding in *Watkins* was based on lack of "pertinency" of the questions asked to the mission Congress had delegated to its committee, see *Barenblatt v. United States*, 360 U.S. 109 (1959) (upholding contempt and distinguishing *Watkins*), but

---

[31]   Witnesses refusing to answer questions posed by these committees or to produce documents requested by the committees were subject to criminal prosecution under 2 U.S.C. § 192.

Chief Justice Warren's concerns included the process's threat to First Amendment freedoms (354 U.S. at 197):

> Abuses of the investigative process may imperceptibly lead to abridgment of protected freedoms. The mere summoning of a witness and compelling him to testify, against his will, about his beliefs, expressions or associations is a measure of governmental interference. And when those forced revelations concern matters that are unorthodox, unpopular, or even hateful to the general public, the reaction in the life of the witness may be disastrous. This effect is even more harsh when it is past beliefs, expressions or associations that are disclosed and judged by current standards rather than those contemporary with the matters exposed. * * *

Interference with Agency Adjudication of Pending Cases. Effective legislative oversight often requires congressional committees to challenge executive branch officials in ways that are tough and even intimidating. Relatively recent examples include committee hearings on Watergate (1973–74), the Iran-Contra affair (1987), China's acquisition of U.S. nuclear weapon secrets (1998–2000), and the administration of TARP, the Troubled Assets Relief Program (2009–11). Recognizing Congress's constitutional responsibility to monitor what the Executive Branch is doing right or wrong, courts traditionally give Congress broad leeway to engage in aggressive oversight activity.

This oversight power may be subject to certain limitations, however, when Congress investigates an ongoing adjudicatory proceeding. Agency officials acting in the midst of an adjudicatory dispute are analogous to prosecutors or judges, and appellate courts have held that extreme political pressures might influence—or appear to influence—the agency's decisions, undermining basic notions of fairness or due process. The leading case is *Pillsbury Co. v. Federal Trade Commission*, 354 F.2d 952 (5th Cir. 1966), where Senator Kefauver and other members of a Senate Judiciary subcommittee interrogated the FTC Chair and several of his staff with respect to a pending injunctive proceeding that involved Pillsbury. The senators expressed strong views on how the case should be decided, and the FTC subsequently ruled as the senators had wanted. The Fifth Circuit reversed on the ground that the agency's decisionmaking process was impermissibly biased by congressional pressure. Chief Judge Tuttle explained:

> "when [a congressional] investigation focuses directly and substantially upon the mental decisional processes of a Commission in a case which is pending before it, Congress is no longer intervening in the agency's legislative function, but rather, in its judicial function. At this latter point, we become concerned with the right of private litigants to a fair trial and, equally important, with their right to the appearance of impartiality, which cannot be maintained unless those who exercise the judicial function are free from powerful external influences." *Id.* at 964.[32]

---

[32]   See also *Koniag v. Kleppe*, 405 F. Supp. 1360 (D.D.C. 1975), *modified sub nom Koniag v. Andrus*, 580 F.2d 601 (D.C. Cir 1978) (setting aside adjudicatory decisions of Secretary of Interior under Alaska Native Claims Settlement Act based at least partially on improper congressional subcommittee pressure during oversight hearings).

A PROBLEM ON OVERSIGHT AND ADJUDICATION

Problem 8-5. On April 20, 2011, the Acting General Counsel (GC) of the National Labor Relations Board, Lafe Solomon, who had been nominated by the President for the permanent position, issued a complaint against the Boeing Company. The complaint alleged that top managers and executives from Boeing had repeatedly announced that the company was moving the manufacture of its second 737-Dreamliner airplane from the state of Washington to South Carolina because of past lawful strikes engaged in by the Machinists Union. Acting GC Solomon's complaint asserted that Boeing was relocating work for illegal discriminatory reasons. Boeing responded that the move was based on a lawful business judgment to avoid future disruptions in the production process. The complaint was scheduled to be heard by an Administrative Law Judge (ALJ) in Seattle on June 14.

In early May, ten Republican Senators wrote to Solomon expressing dismay over the Boeing complaint and suggesting that his prospects for confirmation were linked to his position on the Boeing case. The next day, 19 Republican senators wrote to President Obama urging that he immediately withdraw Solomon's nomination to become GC, due to the Boeing case. On May 12, a number of Republican Senators introduced a bill amending the NLRA to immunize the conduct that was allegedly unlawful as set forth in the Boeing complaint.

In mid-May, the chairmen of the House committees on Education and Workforce, and Oversight and Government Reform sent separate letters to Acting GC Solomon demanding that he turn over all internal Board documents addressing the Boeing complaint and all documents relating in any way to the GC Office's investigation of Boeing, and do so in advance of the June 14 ALJ hearing. Solomon declined to provide these documents in an explanatory letter, citing the pending litigation. House Oversight Committee chair Darrell Issa then announced that his committee would hold a hearing in South Carolina to address the Boeing complaint on June 17, three days after the ALJ hearing. Issa requested that Solomon attend his committee hearing. Solomon declined Chair Issa's invitation on the ground that his appearance could threaten the rights of the parties to a fair trial. Chair Issa wrote to Solomon asking him to reconsider or else face a subpoena compelling his attendance. Solomon responded on June 10, offering as alternatives either to submit written testimony or to provide the Associate General Counsel, who did not have a direct role in the case. Chair Issa rejected those offers and insisted on Solomon's presence at the oversight hearing. Ultimately, Solomon attended the June 17 hearing.

Assume that the ALJ hearing took place as scheduled on June 14, and the ALJ subsequently ruled in favor of Boeing, dismissing the Labor Board complaint. Did any actions taken by members of Congress impermissibly taint the ALJ proceeding? Would you evaluate the oversight actions of the Senators differently from the actions taken in the House? If so, on what basis?

Agency Defiance and Executive Privilege. A final concern about legislative oversight is that even when it is vigorous and public-seeking—and respectful of individual rights—it may face frustrating obstacles to obtaining information from the agency, particularly one located in the executive branch. Some of the recent oversight hearings during the Clinton and Bush 43 Administrations demonstrate that difficulty, as well as the political aspects of oversight.

A CASE STUDY: THE DISMISSAL OF U.S. ATTORNEYS DURING THE GEORGE W. BUSH ADMINISTRATION

1. *Background.* In late 2006, the Justice Department under President George W. Bush dismissed eight United States Attorneys. United States Attorneys are federal prosecutors appointed to four-year terms by the President with the advice and consent of the Senate. Although the nature of the position is non-partisan, the Bush Administration allegedly dismissed several U.S. Attorneys for investigating or prosecuting Republican politicians and declining to investigate or prosecute Democratic politicians. At least one U.S. Attorney was terminated because the White House wanted to fill the position with a Bush loyalist who had political ambitions.

During the months preceding the dismissals, Bush Administration officials considered removing all ninety-three U.S. Attorneys but ultimately decided to replace about one-fifth. As Administration officials planned the removals, the Senate Judiciary Committee, at the request of the Department of Justice, inserted language into the 2005 Patriot Act reauthorization allowing the Attorney General to appoint new U.S. Attorneys in the event of a vacancy for an indefinite term and without the advice and consent of the Senate. Thus the dismissals potentially gave the Attorney General unchecked authority to install the Administration's cronies as U.S. Attorneys.

2. *Congressional Oversight of the Justice Department.* In January 2007, Senators Patrick Leahy and Dianne Feinstein of the Senate Judiciary Committee responded to the firings and the newly enacted appointment procedures. On January 18, Attorney General Alberto Gonzales testified before the Senate Judiciary Committee:

> **Senator FEINSTEIN.** You and I talked on Tuesday about what is happening with U.S. Attorneys. It spurred me to do a little research, and let me begin. Title 28, Section 541 states, "Each U.S. Attorney shall be appointed for a term of 4 years. On the expiration of his term, a U.S. Attorney shall continue to perform the duties of his office until his successor is appointed and qualified." Now, I understand that there is a pleasure aspect to it, but I also understand what practice has been in the past. We have 13 vacancies. Yesterday you sent up two nominees for the 13 existing vacancies.

> **Attorney General GONZALES.** There have been 11 vacancies created since the law was changed, 11 vacancies in the U.S. Attorney's offices. The President has now nominated as to six of those. As to the remaining five, we are in discussion with home-State Senators. So let me publicly sort of preempt, perhaps, a question you are going to ask me. That is, I am fully committed, as the administration is fully committed, to ensure that with respect to every U.S. Attorney position in this country, we will have a Presidentially appointed, Senate-confirmed U.S. Attorney. I think a U.S. Attorney, who I view as the leader, law enforcement leader, my representative in the community, has greater imprimatur of authority if in fact that person has been confirmed by the Senate.

> **Senator FEINSTEIN.** All right.

> Now, let me get at where I am going. How many U.S. Attorneys have been asked to resign in the past year?

Attorney General GONZALES. Senator, you are asking me to get into a public discussion about personnel.

Senator FEINSTEIN. No. I am just asking you to give me a number, that is all.

Attorney General GONZALES. I do not know the answer.

Senator FEINSTEIN. I am just asking you to give me a number.

Attorney General GONZALES. I do not know the answer to that question. But we have been very forthcoming—

Senator FEINSTEIN. You did not know it on Tuesday when I spoke with you. You said you would find out and tell me.

Attorney General GONZALES. I am not sure I said that.

Senator FEINSTEIN. Yes, you did, Mr. Attorney General.

Attorney General GONZALES. Well, if that is what I said, that is what I will do. But we did provide to you a letter where we gave you a lot of information about—

Senator FEINSTEIN. I read the letter.

Attorney General GONZALES. All right.

Senator FEINSTEIN. It does not answer the questions that I have. I know of at least six that have been asked to resign. I know that we amended the law in the Patriot Act and we amended it because if there were a national security problem the Attorney General would have the ability to move into the gap. We did not amend it to prevent the confirmation process from taking place. I am very concerned. I have had two of them ask[ed] to resign in my State from major jurisdictions with major cases ongoing, with substantially good records as prosecutors. I am very concerned because, technically, under the Patriot Act, you can appoint someone without confirmation for the remainder of the President's term. I do not believe you should do that. We are going to try to change the law back.

Attorney General GONZALES. Senator, may I just say that I do not think there is any evidence that that is what I am trying to do? In fact, to the contrary. The evidence is quite clear that what we are trying to do is ensure that, for the people in each of these respective districts, we have the very best possible representative for the Department of Justice and that we are working to nominate people, and that we are working with home-State Senators to get U.S. Attorneys nominated. So the evidence is just quite contrary to what you are possibly suggesting. Let me just say—

Senator FEINSTEIN. Do you deny that you have asked, your office has asked, U.S. Attorneys to resign in the past year, yes or no?

Attorney General GONZALES. Yes. No, I do not deny that. What I am saying is, that happens during every administration, during different periods for different reasons. So the fact that that has happened, quite frankly, some people should view that as a sign of good management.

What we do, is we make an evaluation about the performance of individuals. I have a responsibility to the people in your district that we have the best possible people in these positions. That is the reason why changes sometimes have to be made, although there are a number of reasons why changes get made and why people leave on their own.

I think I would never, ever make a change in a U.S. Attorney position for political reasons or if it would in any way jeopardize an ongoing serious investigation. I just would not do it.

Senator FEINSTEIN. Well, let me just say one thing. I believe very strongly that these positions should come to this committee for confirmation.

Attorney General GONZALES. They are, Senator.

Senator FEINSTEIN. I believe very strongly we should have the opportunity to answer questions about it.

Attorney General GONZALES. I agree with you.

In February 2007, Deputy Attorney General Paul McNulty testified that the dismissals were performance related, in spite of the fact that all but one of the fired U.S. Attorneys had positive performance reviews. McNulty's claim prompted the dismissed U.S. Attorneys to testify on March 6, 2007 where they claimed that they had favorable performance reviews and that the Justice Department never expressed concerns about their performance. In spite of this testimony, Gonzales penned an op-ed in USA Today on March 6, in which he insisted that "To be clear, it was for reasons related to policy, priorities and management—what have been referred to broadly as 'performance-related' reasons—that seven U.S. attorneys were asked to resign last December." He further stated that "While I am grateful for the public service of these seven U.S. attorneys, they simply lost my confidence. I hope that this episode ultimately will be recognized for what it is: an overblown personnel matter."[33]

In the following weeks, the Justice Department released documents showing extensive communications between the White House and Justice Department officials relating to the removal of U.S. Attorneys. These revelations led Gonzales to acknowledge that "mistakes were made. I accept the responsibility." Nonetheless, he stood by the decision to dismiss the U.S. Attorneys, contending that "it was a right decision."[34]

On April 19, 2007, Attorney General Gonzales appeared again before the Senate Judiciary Committee where he continued to express regret for "mistakes" at the Department of Justice but insisted that the dismissals were appropriate.

Attorney General GONZALES. I acknowledge the mistakes that I have made here. I've identified the mistakes. I know what I would do differently. I think it was still a good idea.

Senator GRAHAM. What kind of damage do you believe needs to be repaired on your part with the Congress or the Senate in particular?

Attorney General GONZALES. Senator, I think I need to continue to have dialog with the Congress, to try to be as forthcoming as I can be to reassure the Congress. I've tried to inform the Congress that I don't have anything to hide. I

---

[33] Alberto Gonzales, *They Lost My Confidence*, USA Today, Mar. 6, 2007.

[34] Dan Eggen & Paul Kane, *Gonzales: 'Mistakes Were Made'*, Wash. Post, Mar. 14, 2007.

didn't say no, to the document request. I didn't say "no, you can't interview" to my internal staff.

You know, I asked OPR [Office of Professional Responsibility] to get involved. I've done—everything I've done has been consistent with the principle of pursuing truth and accountability.

Senator GRAHAM. Finally, you are situationally aware that you have a tremendous credibility problem with many Members of the Congress, and you are intent on trying to fix that. Today is a start, right?

Attorney General GONZALES. Absolutely, Senator.

Although Gonzales expressed a willingness to mend relations with Congress, his inability to recall various meetings and conversations frustrated the senators, a growing number of whom called for his resignation. Senator Leahy and Senator Arlen Specter (the ranking Republican on the Senate Judiciary Committee) wrote to Gonzales, requesting that he supplement his testimony:

> You spent weeks preparing for the April 19th hearing. Yet during your testimony, in response to questions from Senators on both sides of the aisle, you often responded that you could not recall. By some counts you failed to answer more than 100 questions, by other counts more than 70, but the most conservative count had you failing to provide answers well over 60 times. As a result, the Committee's efforts to learn the truth of why and how these dismissals took place, and the role you and other Department and White House officials had in them, has been hampered.

> The questions asked by Senators should not have been a surprise. You were alerted in letters to you well in advance of last Thursday's hearing. By letter sent April 4, you were asked to include in your written testimony a "full and complete account of the development of the plan to replace Untied States Attorneys, and all the specifics of your role in connection with that matter." That account was not included in your written testimony nor in your answers to questions at the hearing. You were also alerted in advance of the hearing, by a letter sent on April 13, that you would be asked about information derived from the staff interviews of your senior aides. You were, nevertheless, unprepared to answer those questions.[35]

During the following months Gonzales testified again before the Senate Judiciary Committee as well as before the House Judiciary Committee but calls for his resignation only intensified. On August 27, 2007, Gonzales announced his resignation.

3. *Congressional Oversight of the White House.* As House and Senate Committees wrote letters, issued subpoenas, and held hearings to learn about the Justice Department officials' involvement in the dismissals, they also sought documents and testimony from White House officials. On March 20, **White House Counsel Fred Fielding** responded to congressional requests with an offer to provide documents and testimony subject to certain conditions:

> In keeping with the President's commitment to ensure that Congress and the American people understand the resignations of the U.S. Attorneys, the

---

[35]   Letter from Sens. Leahy & Specter to Attorney General Alberto Gonzales (Apr. 25, 2007).

Department of Justice has produced more than 3,000 pages of documents relating to this matter. These documents do not reflect that any U.S. Attorney was replaced to interfere with a pending or future criminal investigation or for any other improper reason. These documents, together with the interviews to be provided by Department officials, will provide extensive background on the decisions in question, including an account of communications between the Department and senior White House officials. Congress, in short, is receiving a virtually unprecedented window into personnel decision-making within the Executive Branch.

In the midst of this current debate, the President must remain faithful to the fundamental interests of the Presidency and the requirements of the constitutional separation of powers. We wish to reach a reasonable accommodation so as to provide your Committees the information they are seeking in a way that will allow this President, and future Presidents, to continue to discharge their constitutional responsibilities effectively.

In response to the invitations for interviews extended by the Committees, I am prepared to make available for interviews the President's former Counsel [Harriet Miers]; current Deputy Chief of Staff and Senior Advisor [Karl Rove]; Deputy Counsel [William Kelley]; and a Special Assistant in the Office of Political Affairs [Scott Jennings]. We are prepared to agree to the following terms, which, considering applicable constitutional principles relating to the Presidency and your Committee's interests, we believe are fair, reasonable, and respectful. We believe that such interviews should be a last resort, and should be conducted, if needed, only after Congress has heard from Department of Justice officials about the decision to request the resignations of the U.S. Attorneys.

Such interviews may cover, and would be limited to, the subject of a) communications between the White House and persons outside the White House concerning the request for resignations of the U.S. Attorneys in question; and b) communications between the White House and Members of Congress concerning those requests. Those interviews should be conducted by both Committees jointly. Questioning of White House officials would be conducted by a Member or limited number of Members, who would be accompanied by committee staff. Such interviews would be private and conducted without the need for an oath, transcript, subsequent testimony, or the subsequent issuance of subpoenas. A representative of the Office of the Counsel to the President would attend these interviews and personal counsel to the invited officials may be present at their election.

As an additional accommodation, and as part of this proposal, we are prepared to provide to your Committee copies of two categories of documents: a) communications between the White House and the Department of Justice concerning the request for resignation of the U.S. Attorneys in question; and b) communications on the same subject between White House staff and third parties, including Members of Congress or their staffs on the subject.

We trust and believe that the accommodation we offer here, in addition to what the Department of Justice has provided, should satisfy the Committee's interests.[36]

Senator Patrick Leahy, Chairman of the Senate Judiciary Committee and **Representative John Conyers**, Chairman of the House Judiciary Committee, responded by insisting that the White House make available internal communications. They also suggested that a compromise might be possible:

> We do believe your willingness to provide documents is worth pursuing. We hope that you will reconsider your "all or nothing" approach with respect to documents you identified that you would be willing to provide. We urge you to provide all relevant documents without delay. The White House documents to and from the Department of Justice and with third parties, such as Republican state party officials, should be provided without delay. You have acknowledged your willingness to provide those to us previously.
>
> That would narrow the dispute over White House documents to those you refer to as "internal". We believe that these are important to our investigation, as well. For example, if there is a memorandum or an e-mail from Karl Rove to Harriet Miers initiating consideration of firing some United States attorneys in order to impede an investigation, that would be very important for the Committees to know. Thus, while we do not agree with you that what you describe as "internal" White House documents should be off limits, we recognize that you view them as a separate category and you disagree whether those should be shared with the Committees. Recognizing we have a dispute over those documents should not delay the Committees receiving the other documents that you indicate you are willing to provide.
>
> If we can narrow our dispute, we may then be able to work through it by agreeing, for example, that we initially designate as "Committee Confidential" what you refer to as "internal" White House documents. We could then consider a process by which we would consult with you prior to making them public.[37]

Fielding rejected this proposal and stated that the White House's initial offer of interviews and documents already "reflect[ed] a series of balanced compromises designed to respect and accommodate your interests in obtaining information while also protecting the institution of the Presidency."[38]

Unable to negotiate a mutually agreeable arrangement, the House and Senate Judiciary Committees issued subpoenas on June 13, 2007 to several White House officials including President Bush's Chief of Staff Joshua Bolten (for documents) and former White House Counsel Harriet Miers (for testimony and documents). On June 28, after receiving legal advice from Solicitor General and Acting Attorney General Paul Clement, Fielding informed Chairmen Conyers and Leahy that "the President has decided to assert Executive Privilege and therefore the White House will not be making any production in response to these subpoenas for documents."[39] The House and Senate Committees

---

[36]   Letter from Fred Fielding, Counsel to the President, to Sen. Leahy, Rep. Conyers, Sen. Specter, Rep. Smith & Rep. Sánchez (Mar. 20, 2007).

[37]   Letter from Sen. Leahy and Rep. Conyers to Fred Fielding (Mar. 28, 2007).

[38]   Letter from Fred Fielding to Sen. Leahy and Rep. Conyers (Apr. 12, 2007).

[39]   Letter from Fred Fielding to Sen. Leahy and Rep. Conyers (June 28, 2007).

rejected the White House's basis for executive privilege and on July 25, 2007 the House Judiciary Committee recommended that the full House cite Miers and Bolten for contempt of Congress. On February 14, 2008, after further fruitless attempts to negotiate a settlement, the full House of Representatives voted to hold Miers and Bolten in contempt by a vote of 223–32.

The House's contempt citation consisted of two resolutions. The first called on the Attorney General and the U.S. Attorney for the District of Columbia to prosecute Miers and Bolten for criminal contempt. This approach was unsuccessful because the Attorney General determined that Miers and Bolten had properly invoked executive privilege and thus no prosecution was authorized. The House's second resolution authorized the Chairman of the House Judiciary Committee to bring a declaratory action against Miers and Bolten in federal court requiring them to comply with the subpoenas. The D.C. district court held that the House Judiciary Committee had standing to bring a civil action to enforce congressional subpoenas issued to senior presidential aides. It further held that the judiciary was the "ultimate arbiter" of executive privilege and concluded that Miers and Bolten lacked absolute executive privilege, although they could make specific claims when appearing before the Committee to provide testimony.[40]

The parties eventually reached a settlement in March 2009 whereby the Bush White House agreed to provide internal documents, and Miers and former Bush senior advisor Karl Rove agreed to testify under oath in a closed-door hearing. For further discussion of the U.S. Attorneys controversy see, e.g., John McKay, *Train Wreck at the Justice Department: An Eyewitness Account*, 31 Seattle U. L. Rev. 265 (2008); David C. Weiss, *Note, Nothing Improper? Examining Constitutional Limits, Congressional Action, Partisan Motivation, and Pretextual Justification in the U.S. Attorney Removals*, 107 Mich. L. Rev. 317 (2008). For the Department of Justice report on the matter see U.S. Department of Justice, *An Investigation Into the Removal of Nine U.S. Attorneys in 2006* (Sept. 2008).

NOTES ON THE U.S. ATTORNEYS DISMISSAL CAPER

1.   *Antiseptic Sunbeams.* Justice Brandeis famously remarked that "sunlight is said to be the best of disinfectants." By shedding substantial light on the controversial new appointment procedures for U.S. Attorneys, the Senate Judiciary Committee was able to force Attorney General Gonzales to promise to submit future appointments to the Senate for confirmation. This congressional ability to draw attention to controversial executive department practices may be viewed as similar to the role of the press. Unlike the press, however, Congress has the power to compel executive officials to answer questions and offer justifications for controversial policies. Should the Senate interrogation of Attorney General Gonzales, eventually leading to his resignation, be understood as an example of effective investigatory oversight? Or is it better viewed as an instance of the Senate redressing its own earlier mistake in the 2005 Patriot Act reauthorization?

2.   *Removal Power Under* Myers. Aren't U.S. Attorneys executive branch officials who serve at the President's pleasure? Under *Myers v. United States* (§ 1(C) above), could President Bush have removed all 93 sitting U.S. Attorneys without regard to Congress conferring appointment authority on the Attorney General in the 2005 Patriot Act

---

[40]   *Committee on the Judiciary, U.S. House of Representatives v. Miers*, 558 F. Supp. 2d 53 (D.D.C. 2008).

reauthorization? If so, why do you think Bush did not pursue this course? Is this, perhaps, an instance when informal norms trumped constitutionally permissible options?

3. *Executive Agencies Versus the White House.* Congress obtained considerable access to Justice Department documents and testimony from the Attorney General and several lower-level officials. The White House was also willing to provide documents related to communications between the White House and the Department of Justice, but not internal White House communications. Are there constitutional justifications for drawing a distinction between Congress's oversight power over White House officials and Justice Department officials? In a letter of June 28, 2007, White House Counsel Fielding contended that congressional discovery of internal White House communications would unconstitutionally encroach upon presidential authority. Should White House officials be considered agents of the President or should they instead be treated like officials in executive agencies such as the Department of Justice or Department of State? Does it matter that, unlike the Attorney General, the President's Chief of Staff and White House Counsel are appointed without the advice and consent of the Senate?

4. *Congressional Contempt.* Josh Chafetz has noted that the Miers-Bolten episode constituted "only the second time in the nation's history [that] a house of Congress sued high-ranking executive branch officials in an attempt to enforce a subpoena for their testimony in the face of the officials' claims of executive privilege," adding that "[u]nlike the previous suit, in which the defendant was none other than the president of the United States, the 2008 suit was successful." Josh Chafetz, *Executive Branch Contempt of Congress*, 76 U. Chi. L. Rev. 1083 (2009). Chafetz argues that in the Miers-Bolten contempt proceedings "all three branches—including, and perhaps most significantly, Congress itself—have acted improperly in this case so as to diminish Congress's constitutional powers." After reviewing the history of the English parliament, pre-Revolutionary colonial legislatures, and earlier congresses, Chafetz concludes that Congress has an independent authority to punish executive officials for contempt of Congress without the cooperation of the executive (through a prosecution) or the judiciary (through a court order). Is it troubling that in the Miers-Bolten affair, Congress could not vindicate its authority without the assistance of other branches of government? Is this predicament any different from that of the executive which must rely on Congress for the laws it enforces, or the judiciary which cannot pass judgment on a criminal matter unless the executive initiates a prosecution? As summarized above, the D.C. district court insisted that the judiciary was the "ultimate arbiter" of privilege claims. Does the Constitution require this role for the courts or is it simply motivated by a desire to subject disputes between Congress and the Executive to an ostensibly neutral arbiter?

2. Budget and Appropriations

Under Article I, § 8, clauses 1 and 18 and § 9, clause 7, Congress has virtually plenary power to determine how the United States' money will be spent. This power of the purse gives Congress an ongoing substantive power as well—notably, Congress's power of the purse and legislative oversight activities are related. Much oversight occurs when programs are reauthorized or receive appropriations, not only in primary-purpose oversight hearings. Auerbach, *Keeping a Watchful Eye*, 130–33. The use of spending control to influence executive branch actions works in several different ways.

The statute establishing a program or agency typically does not also appropriate money to fund its activities. With regard to discretionary spending programs, the authorization process is separate from the appropriations process. What one Congress establishes as a statutory scheme can be negated entirely by a subsequent Congress's failure to fund that scheme or the agency administering it. More commonly, Congress will fund a statutory scheme and the agency, but the level of funding will depend upon Congress's attitude toward the scheme and the agency. An agency might have a strong incentive to move statutory policy close to the House or Senate position even though the agency's preferred policy would be protected by a presidential veto, if the agency fears that Congress will fail to fund it adequately in retaliation for the agency's policy position. This reveals the great advantage the appropriations power gives Congress: because the agency needs each Congress to act affirmatively to give it money, Congress has something of a backdoor "legislative veto" if it chooses to exercise it through the appropriations process. Moreover, because most appropriations of discretionary money must be renewed annually, the process provides Congress continuing influence.

It is impossible to tell how important the appropriations power is in this respect. The main limitation involves a coordination problem: the oversight (sub)committee cannot routinely pressure the agency to adopt new substantive policies by threatening to cut off funds, because separate appropriations subcommittees control funding. Unless the two different congressional entities share the same political preferences *and* can coordinate their activities, the funding weapon will be hard to deploy. Moreover, the preferences of the two (sub)committees can be expected to diverge most of the time. Because of the requirements of the congressional budget process, the appropriations committees are usually required to operate under a zero-sum mentality more often than the corresponding substantive committees: the primary goal of the former is to meet certain budget needs, while the primary goal of the latter is to solve social or economic problems. The NHTSA was caught in this bind. It received ample funding in the 1960s but suffered budget cuts as a consequence of general belt-tightening during the Nixon Administration and beyond. Even though the substantive committees were still quite keen on auto safety, the President and the appropriations committees were much more concerned with other budgetary priorities. Moreover, when Congress does bestir itself to focus on auto safety concerns, as during the interlock controversy in 1973–74, it may well make the agency's job more difficult (with diminishing funds) by curtailing unpopular regulatory options and adding low priority issues (school-bus safety) to the already-crowded agency agenda.

Congress's spending power can be used as a mechanism of control in less direct ways than not funding or underfunding a particular agency. For example, committee reports accompanying appropriations bills include directives to agencies about how the money should be spent. Reports contain line items with specific instructions to fund particular projects, usually in the districts of key congressional players. Although language in committee reports is not legally binding, agencies usually follow the mandates in order to retain the good will of the appropriators whom they will face again next year. Not infrequently, Congress will include substantive restrictions in appropriations measures, which are legally binding because they meet the constitutional requirements for laws. This occurs even though congressional rules often forbid riders or other substantive legislation on an appropriations bill. Although such provisions obviously subject the appropriations bill to a possible veto, the President will sometimes swallow them because of the need to fund the government.

The Supreme Court has taken a balanced approach to substantive provisions in appropriations measures. On the one hand, repeals by implication are especially disfavored in the appropriations context. E.g., *TVA v. Hill*, 437 U.S. 153, 190 (1978), where the Court refused to credit continued congressional funding of the Tellico Dam as an amendment to the Endangered Species Act (ESA). On the other hand, Congress may amend substantive law in an appropriations statute, as long as it does so clearly. E.g., *Robertson v. Seattle Audubon Society*, 503 U.S. 429 (1992), where the Court applied an appropriations rider to allow timber-cutting that threatened the habitat of an endangered species (the spotted owl), which would otherwise have been a violation of the ESA.

3.   The Legislative Veto of Agency Rules

Another response to the tension between administrative lawmaking and majoritarian government has been the development of the *legislative veto*. The legislative veto is generally any statutory mechanism that renders the implementation of agency decisions or actions subject to some further form of legislative review or control, usually for a specified time period. The purpose of the legislative veto is to provide a quick mechanism to slow down or overturn administrative actions that are unresponsive to the legislature's aims in the original authorizing statute, without going through the obstacle course of the full legislative process. Hence, the power to nullify an administrative decision has been vested in joint action of both chambers of the legislature, action by only one house, or action by a legislative committee. (At the state level, there have been mechanisms for suspension, rather than veto, of agency decisions by joint legislative committees.) Any of these procedures is more streamlined than the normal legislative process; even a two-house legislative veto avoids the presentment clause. Getting around the President is important because he would presumably veto most legislative nullifications of regulations passed by agencies in his government, thereby requiring a supermajority in each house to implement congressional preferences.

The form of the veto can be either negative or positive. A *negative veto provision* (the typical one) stipulates that administrative decisions will be effective, unless the legislature or its designated subgroup actually disapproves the decisions. A *positive veto provision* requires legislative approval of the administrative decision before it becomes effective.

The legislative veto idea was used sporadically in the early part of the previous century, but it was only in the 1970s that it became a popular mechanism for legislative oversight of the administrative process. A Library of Congress study for the period 1932 to 1975 found 295 congressional review provisions in 196 federal statutes; for the year 1975 alone, there were 58 provisions in 21 statutes.[41] Legislative veto provisions were attached to important legislation involving defense and foreign policy (e.g., the War Powers Resolution, 87 Stat. 555); energy and environmental policy (e.g., the Energy Policy and Conservation Act, 89 Stat. 871); consumer welfare policy (e.g., the Employee Retirement Income Security Act of 1974, 88 Stat. 829); and transportation policy (e.g., the Regional Rail Reorganization Act of 1973, 87 Stat. 985).[42] When Congress revisited the Motor Vehicle Safety Act in 1974, it required that any future regulation of passive restraints be subject to a two-house legislative veto. State legislatures in the 1970s adopted a variety of legislative veto devices as well. The tendency at the state level was to create a committee, consisting either of legislators or bureaucrats or experts, to advise the legislature and, in some cases, to suspend operation of agency rules until the legislature could study them.

The concept of the legislative veto drew criticisms from political scientists, who argued that they created as many problems for popular government as they solved, and from legal scholars, who argued that they were hard to reconcile with the concept of separation of powers. These constitutional and political concerns generated a series of challenges to legislative vetoes at both the state and federal level.

Immigration & Naturalization Service v. Chadha

462 U.S. 919 (1983).

Section 244(c)(2) of the Immigration and Nationality Act (8 U.S.C. § 1254(c)(2)) authorized one chamber of Congress, by resolution, to invalidate a decision by the executive to allow a deportable alien to remain in the United States. Chadha, an East Indian born in Kenya and holding a British passport, was able to obtain a suspension of his deportation pursuant to the Act. He had been deportable because he remained in the United States after the expiration of his nonimmigrant student visa. At the behest of Representative Eilberg, Chair of the Judiciary Committee Subcommittee on Immigration, the House overrode the suspension of Chadha's deportation. After the House action, the immigration judge reopened Chadha's case and ordered him deported. Chadha appealed the order through the Department of Justice, and then to the federal courts. The Ninth Circuit declared § 244(c)(2) unconstitutional. The Supreme Court affirmed.

Chief Justice Burger's opinion for the Court relied on Article I, § 7, the bicameralism and presentment requirements for congressional statutes and resolutions having the force of law. "The decision to provide the President with a limited and qualified power to nullify proposed legislation by veto was based on the profound conviction of the Framers that the powers conferred on Congress were the powers to be most carefully circumscribed. It is beyond doubt that lawmaking was a power to be shared by both Houses and the President."

The Court's opinion relied extensively on statements from the Federalist Papers, the Constitutional Convention debates, and Story's Commentaries on the Constitution. Chief

---

[41]   Clark Norton, *Congressional Review, Deferral and Disapproval of Executive Actions: A Summary and Inventory of Statutory Authority* 8–12 (1976).

[42]   See Louis Fisher, *Constitutional Conflicts Between Congress and the President* 134–143 (3d rev. ed. 1991).

Justice Burger concluded that the Court must strictly enforce both the presentment and the bicameralism requirements whenever Congress was seeking to exercise its *legislative* power. The House resolution abrogating the suspension of Chadha's deportation was such an action, because it "had the purpose and effect of altering the legal rights, duties and relations of persons, including the Attorney General, Executive Branch officials and Chadha, all outside the legislative branch. Section 244(c)(2) purports to authorize one House of Congress to require the Attorney General to deport an individual alien whose deportation otherwise would be cancelled under § 244. The one-House veto operated in this case to overrule the Attorney General and mandate Chadha's deportation; absent the House action, Chadha would remain in the United States. Congress has *acted* and its action has altered Chadha's status."

The Chief Justice recognized that "[t]he veto authorized by § 244(c)(2) doubtless has been in many respects a convenient shortcut; the 'sharing' with the Executive by Congress of its authority over aliens in this manner is, on its face, an appealing compromise. In purely practical terms, it is obviously easier for action to be taken by one House without submission to the President; but it is crystal clear from the records of the Convention, contemporaneous writings and debates, that the Framers ranked other values higher than efficiency."

Framers ranked other powers higher than efficiency

Justice Powell concurred only in the Court's judgment. He was unwilling to strike down the hundreds of legislative veto provisions that Congress had included in laws since the New Deal. "One reasonably may disagree with Congress' assessment of the veto's utility, but the respect due its judgment as a coordinate branch of Government cautions that our holding should be no more extensive than necessary to decide those cases. In my view, the case may be decided on a narrower ground. When Congress finds that a particular person does not satisfy the statutory criteria for permanent residence in this country it has assumed a judicial function in violation of the principle of separation of powers."

Justice White was the only dissenter. He characterized the legislative veto as "an important if not indispensable political invention that allows the President and Congress to resolve major constitutional and policy differences, assures the accountability of independent regulatory agencies, and preserves Congress' control over lawmaking. Perhaps there are other means of accommodation and accountability, but the increasing reliance of Congress upon the legislative veto suggests that the alternatives to which Congress must now turn are not entirely satisfactory.

"The history of the legislative veto also makes clear that it has not been a sword with which Congress has struck out to aggrandize itself at the expense of the other branches— the concerns of Madison and Hamilton. Rather, the veto has been a means of defense, a reservation of ultimate authority necessary if Congress is to fulfill its designated role under Article I as the Nation's lawmaker."

Justice White also emphasized the tensions between the Court's holding and the realities of agency rulemaking. "The Court's holding today that all legislative-type action must be enacted through the lawmaking process ignores that legislative authority is routinely delegated to the Executive Branch, to the independent regulatory agencies, and to private individuals and groups. * * * There is no question but that agency rulemaking is lawmaking in any functional or realistic sense of the term. The Administrative Procedure Act, 5 U.S.C. § 551(4) provides that a rule is an agency statement 'designed to implement, interpret, or prescribe law or policy.' When agencies are authorized to prescribe law through substantive rulemaking, the administrator's regulation is not only due deference, but is accorded 'legislative effect.' These regulations bind courts and officers of the federal government, may pre-empt state law, and grant rights to and impose obligations on the public. In sum, they have the force of law.

"If Congress may delegate lawmaking power to independent and executive agencies, it is most difficult to understand Article I as prohibiting Congress from also reserving a check on legislative power for itself. Absent the veto, the agencies receiving delegations of legislative or quasi-legislative power may issue regulations having the force of law without bicameral approval and without the President's signature. It is thus not apparent why the reservation of a veto over the exercise of that legislative power must be subject to a more exacting test. In both cases, it is enough that the initial statutory authorizations comply with the Article I requirements."

NOTES ON CHADHA

1.   *Different Visions of the Structure of the Constitution.* The three *Chadha* opinions offer strikingly different visions of the structures of constitutional law. The opinions of Justices Powell and White (who would allow legislative vetoes in many instances) take a functional approach to the separation of powers concept. Their main concern is that Congress should not usurp duties given to the executive (Justice White) or judicial (Justice Powell) powers. See Articles I–III of the Constitution.[43]

The Chief Justice's opinion seems to focus on a distinct but related issue of the circumstances under which Congress can legislate, under Article I, § 7. Because the Framers considered the lawmaking branch the most dangerous arm of government, they limited the instances in which Congress could act decisively by erecting anti-majoritarian barriers within the legislative process—bicameralism and presentment to the President. If Congress can make "law" without going through both Houses of Congress and the President, then there is a greater danger of abuse of legislative power, Chief Justice Burger contends. Is the Chief Justice right in focusing on this feature of the Constitution, and treating it so strictly? His approach has been termed a formalist one, in contrast to the more functional approach reflected in the other opinions. How do Justices Powell and White justify their different focus?

2.   *Policy Arguments.* Underlying the different constitutional visions of the various opinions in *Chadha* are probably different attitudes about the necessity or usefulness of the legislative veto. See generally Stanley Brubaker, *Slouching Toward Constitutional Duty: The Legislative Veto and the Delegation of Authority*, 1 Const. Comm. 81 (1984).

The chief argument for the legislative veto is that once the Court has allowed Congress to delegate enormous lawmaking power to agencies, with virtually no enforceable guidelines, Congress ought to be allowed to attach "strings" to that delegation, especially strings that allow the democratic process (Congress) to provide agencies with feedback having greater bite than oversight hearings. Moreover, the legislative veto provides flexibility in the conduct of public affairs in situations that could not have been foreseen by the Framers. Congress does not have the capacity to oversee the complicated regulatory state, and if it attempted to do so, the machinery of

---

[43]   See Martin Redish, *The Constitution as Political Structure* 113–125 (1995) (arguing in favor of a pragmatic formalism in this area); E. Donald Elliott, INS v. Chadha: *The Administrative Constitution, the Constitution, and the Legislative Veto,* 1983 Sup. Ct. Rev. 125 (distinguishing between formalist and functionalist approaches to separation of powers issues).

government would grind to a halt. "By delegating a qualified authority, Congress can maintain the system's energy, while by reserving authority to review proposed rules and acts, it can restore balance and accountability." *Id.* at 85.

Brubaker surveys several policy arguments against the legislative veto. First, the legislative veto distorts the legislative process. Legislation that would otherwise fail will pass if key legislators know that later they will have the opportunity to block offending provisions through the use of the legislative veto. This allows Congress to appear to be addressing hard questions, when in fact the legislative veto will thwart any substantial action by an administrative agency to address those questions.

Second, the legislative veto makes agencies vitally concerned with the views of entities other than the enacting Congress, which may be problematic. For example, because interest in the legislation will be lower when, months or years after its passage, the agency proposes implementing regulations, the task of reviewing those regulations will fall upon the congressional committees and subcommittees. "Thus a likely and apparently common occurrence is a significant skewing of the original legislative intent towards the interest of the congressmen on the overseeing committee or subcommittee and the groups and people most responsible for their re-election." *Id.* at 92. If committees are comprised of members with preferences more extreme than that of the body, a one-committee legislative veto may produce regulations far away from the preferences of the median legislator. In addition, the legislative veto allows subsequent Congresses a great deal of influence over the implementation of statutes enacted in the past. This may allow for substantial shifts from the original intent of the enactors. Consider how a committee in a conservative Republican Congress might influence policies enacted by more liberal Democratic Congresses with very different ideological commitments. Is that legitimate?[44]

Third, the legislative veto may have encouraged very broad delegations because Congress could exert continuing and effective control over the agencies as they exercised their delegated authority. In other words, the incentive to constrain agency discretion *ex ante* by enacting detailed and precise statutes is less compelling if Congress has *ex post* tools to constrain agencies. For those who object to broad delegations, perhaps on the ground that they reduce political accountability, this possibility is disturbing. An excellent empirical study of the legislative veto suggests that it had some effect on the breadth of congressional delegations. See Jessica Korn, *The Power of Separation: American Constitutionalism and the Myth of the Legislative Veto* (1996). For example, after *Chadha* invalidated the legislative veto, members of Congress rescinded broad authority given to the Secretary of Education with respect to Pell Grants and enacted their policy preferences more precisely. But other forces, practical and political, continue to discourage legislators from using specific and detailed statutory directives to reduce agency discretion, so the effect of *Chadha* in this area has not been substantial.

3. *Constitutionality of State Legislative Vetoes.* As an interpretation of Article I of the U.S. Constitution, *Chadha* does not control the validity of state legislative vetoes. Most states have followed *Chadha*, e.g., *Blank v. Department of Corrections*, 564 N.W.2d 130 (Mich. 1997), but there are some interesting variations.

---

[44]　　See Michael Herz, *The Legislative Veto in Times of Political Reversal: Chadha and the 104th Congress*, 14 Const. Comm. 319 (1997) (using game theory to demonstrate how legislative vetoes could radically shift regulatory outcomes when the partisan makeup of Congress changes). See also Eskridge & Ferejohn, *The Article I, Section 7 Game, supra.*

In *Opinion of the Justices*, 431 A.2d 783 (N.H. 1981), the New Hampshire Supreme Court advised the legislature that a legislative committee veto is not valid under the New Hampshire Constitution but that other legislative veto arrangements were valid. "The objectives of the proposed legislation could be met and the constitutional objections minimized, if the statute were to provide for approval or rejection of the rules to be determined by a majority of a quorum of both houses, possibly acting pursuant to the recommendations of significantly representative committees, and then presented to the Governor for his approval. In such an instance, if any rule was rejected by either house or the Governor, its resubmission as a law would have to await enactment by the General Court and would be subject to a veto as with bills."

The Idaho Supreme Court in *Mead v. Arnell*, 791 P.2d 410 (Idaho 1990), upheld a statute allowing the legislature to override agency rules by a concurrent resolution passed by both chambers but not submitted to the governor for veto. The court explicitly relied on Justice White's dissenting opinion in *Chadha.* Iowa's voters added a new article III, § 40 to that state's constitution in 1984: "The general assembly may nullify an adopted administrative rule of a state agency by the passage of a resolution by a majority of all the members of each house of the general assembly." New Jersey similarly amended its constitution in 1992.

Would these state developments violate the U.S. Constitution's requirement, Art. IV, § 4, that states have a "Republican form of Government"? See *Van Sickle v. Shanahan*, 511 P.2d 223 (Kan. 1973) (provision in state constitution authorizing governor to reorganize state legislature, subject to one-house veto, does not violate Article IV, § 4).

4.   *The Impact of* Chadha. Law professors tend to read great import into constitutional decisions; political scientists tend to see them gobbled up by larger structural features of American governance. So it has been with *Chadha.* Several scholars maintain that this decision had relatively little effect on congressional practice or on Congress-agency relations. On the one hand, congressional scholar Louis Fisher reports that many statutes enacted after *Chadha* continue to include legislative vetoes, and administrative agencies regularly attend to them as though they were the "law," seeking committee permission for certain decisions. See Louis Fisher, *The Legislative Veto: Invalidated, It Survives*, 56 Law & Contemp. Probs. 273 (1993).

On the other hand, Jessica Korn argues that other mechanisms, constitutional under *Chadha*, can and do work just as well as the legislative veto. Korn's comprehensive study leads her to conclude that the practice was never a particularly important weapon in the arsenal of congressional oversight. "Members did not need the legislative shortcut to force executive branch officials to attend to congressional concerns, because the most useful sources of congressional oversight power—the power to make laws, and the power to require that executive branch and independent agency officials report [to committees] proposed actions before implementation—are well nestled in the authorities granted to members by Article I of the Constitution." Korn, *Power of Separation*, at 116. Of fourteen potential oversight mechanisms, some of which we discuss in this section, the legislative veto ranked last in terms of frequency of use and ninth in terms of effectiveness, according to Joel Auerbach, *Keeping a Watchful Eye: The Politics of Congressional Oversight* 132 (Table 6-1), 135 (Table 6-2) (1990).

Does it make sense to think that *Chadha* has had *no* effect, as these scholars seem to maintain? Doesn't the *threat* of a one-House veto change the bargaining game between Congress and the President or an agency?

5. *The Line Item Veto Case.* In 1995, Congress enacted the Line Item Veto Act, 110 Stat. 1200, which authorized the President to "cancel" statutory items relating to discretionary spending or tax benefits. See Chapter 3, § 2(B), discussing the Act and its invalidation in *Clinton v. City of New York*, 524 U.S. 417 (1997). *Query:* If Congress really wants the President to have something like a line item veto authority, as a way of restraining Congress's tendency to undertax and overspend, is there a way to do that after *Clinton?*

4. Congressional Design of Agency Structure and Procedures

Oversight, appropriations pressure, and the legislative veto are all *ex post* methods for Congress to control the agencies to which it has delegated power. That is, these methods are after-the-fact: the agency does something Congress doesn't like, and Congress responds. Another way to control agency policy is *ex ante:* by careful design of the agency's procedure, jurisdiction, and composition, the enacting coalition can press agency policy in desired directions. McNollgast[45] have called this "hardwiring" the agency.

By the design of the agency's procedures and jurisdiction, the enacting Congress can create a powerful or a weak agency. We saw an example of the latter in Chapter 1. When Congress created the EEOC in the Civil Rights Act of 1964, it created procedural complexities and denied substantive rulemaking authority to the agency as part of the deal with conservative Senator Dirksen, who wanted to protect small businesses against too much federal meddling in their affairs.[46] Dirksen correctly believed that the agency would be captive of pro-civil rights super-regulatory activists, although the EEOC has been a more successful policy entrepreneur than Dirksen probably would have wanted.

Congressional Restrictions Apart from the APA. One mechanism Congress has deployed in the last generation has been to impose statutory restrictions on agency rulemaking beyond what is provided for under the APA. These statutes have been systematically examined in Connor Raso, *Procedural Constraints on Agency Rulemaking* (Ph. D. Diss., Stanford University, Political Science Dep't, 2010). Raso explores the many ways that Congress tries to build *ex ante* controls on the administrative process by imposing various requirements on agency rulemaking. Among the statutes following such a strategy are the following:

National Environmental Policy Act, 1969, 42 U.S.C. § 4321 et seq., which requires environmental impact statements before federal projects can proceed;

Consumer Products Safety Act Amendments, 1981, 15 U.S.C. § 2058, which imposes new requirements before the Consumer Product Safety Commission (CPSC) issues new regulations, including a major curtailment

---

[45]   Matthew McCubbins, Roger Noll, and Barry Weingast have combined their names and efforts to create McNollgast. The hardwiring concept is developed in McNollgast, *Administrative Procedures as Instruments of Political Control*, 3 J.L. Econ. & Org. 243 (1987). See also Jonathan Macey, *Separated Powers and Positive Political Theory: The Tug of War Over Administrative Agencies*, 80 Geo. L.J. 671 (1992).

[46]   For one in depth perspective on the complex "deal" with Dirksen, see Daniel Rodriguez & Barry Weingast, *The Positive Political Theory of Legislative History: New Perspectives on the 1964 Civil Rights Act and Its Interpretation*, 151 U. Pa. L. Rev. 1417 (2003).

in the role of consumer groups and the accountability of the CPSC to such groups;

> Regulatory Flexibility Act, 1980, 5 U.S.C. § 601 et seq., which requires a "regulatory flexibility" analysis for agency action imposing significant costs on small businesses;

> Congressional Review Act, 1995, 5 U.S.C. § 801, which requires agencies to report new rules to Congress and prevents their taking effect for 60 days so that Congress can overturn them, through a resolution that must be adopted by both chambers and presented to the President but is not subject to the Senate filibuster;

> Unfunded Mandates Reform Act, 1995, 2 U.S.C. § 658 et al., which requires agencies to disclose new costs its rules will impose on private parties or state/local governments and to consider alternatives to those "unfunded" costs.

Raso evaluates the efficacy of these structural restrictions, determining whether agencies actually follow the new rules and whether the restrictions have had the effect desired by their sponsors. The evidence is clear that the first two statutes have been reasonably effective, while the latter three have had no discernible effect on agency rulemaking.

NEPA has been a model of effectiveness because (1) the statute sets forth a broad and easily understood directive, with few exemptions; (2) empowers environmental groups to participate early in the process of creating and responding to environmental impact statements; and assures compliance through (3) judicial review and (4) executive branch monitoring (NEPA created a Council on Environmental Quality within the White House). In contrast, the Regulatory Flexibility Act (RFA), even as strengthened in 1996, has been ineffective because the statute (1) contains big loopholes that can easily be exploited by agencies; (2) does not empower interested groups to have much influence early in the process; and (3) has no effective monitoring (the 1996 amendment added limited judicial review, but to little effect).

The Consumer Financial Protection Bureau. In response to the financial crisis of 2008, rooted in the default of subprime mortgages, Congress passed the Consumer Financial Protection Act as part of the Dodd-Frank Wall Street Reform and Consumer Protection Act of 2010 (the "Act"). The Act created the Consumer Financial Protection Bureau (CFPB) with the mandate of regulating "the offering and provision of consumer financial products or services under the federal consumer financial laws."

The CFPB has a number of features that give it unusual power and independence. First, the CFPB is granted exclusive authority to promulgate regulations and orders administering federal consumer financial laws. This includes exclusive authority over all existing consumer protection laws such as the Fair Debt Collection Practices Act, the Equal Credit Opportunity Act, and the Home Mortgage Disclosure Act. Second, unlike other independent agencies such as the SEC and FEC that have multi-member boards, the CFPB has a single director who serves a term of five years and is appointed by the President with the advice and consent of the Senate. Third, the CFPB is insulated from the executive branch because the President may only remove the director for cause. Finally, and perhaps most uniquely, the CFPB is insulated from congressional budgetary control. The CPFB relies for its funding not on Congress but, rather, on the Federal Reserve within which it is technically housed. At the same time, the Federal Reserve does not control the CFPB budget. The CFPB is entitled to request each year, and the Federal Reserve must transfer, an amount "reasonably necessary" from the earnings of the Federal Reserve, up to a statutory cap.

Does this structure raise constitutional concerns? Do *Free Enterprise* and the en banc opinions in *PHH Corp* (discussed in § 1(C) of this chapter), suggest that the Supreme Court might be willing to intervene in this kind of case? What could be the doctrinal basis for a Supreme Court intervention?

5. The Confirmation Process[47]

Policy Debates and Political Pressures. Presidents traditionally use their appointment authority to help control the administrative state by creating a bureaucracy that is supportive of the presidential agenda. The Constitution's formal barrier to unlimited presidential control over appointments is the Senate's advice and consent role under Article II. Through its confirmation power, the Senate may conduct a serious review of nominees' professional, ethical, or personal qualifications and prevent unqualified nominees from taking office. Senators may also use confirmation hearings to raise questions about administration policies linked to the nominee's agency, or to develop a record against which nominees can later be measured. During the 1983 confirmation hearings for Reagan nominee Kenneth Adelman to head the Arms Control and Development Agency, Senate Democrats used the process to stimulate a high-profile debate on arms control while also "hoping to obtain answers that affect future actions," noting that nominees "with extreme views often come in and soften them." See Steven V. Roberts, *A Lesson in Advising and Consenting*, N.Y. Times, Apr. 14, 1983.

For most of our history, the Senate's role in confirming appointments has been fairly deferential. Political scientists Nolan McCarty and Rose Razaghian reviewed more than 3500 executive branch nominations from 1885 to 1996, and found a nominations failure rate (Senate rejections or presidential withdrawals) of only 4.4%. The rate was somewhat higher (7%) during periods of divided party control of White House and Senate than in periods of same-party control (3%). Still, although "the conventional wisdom [was] that when it [came] to appointees to the executive branch the confirmation process [was] little more than a technicality, formality, or perhaps nuisance," McCarty and Razaghian determined that successful confirmations often take substantially longer during periods of divided government and in periods when the Senate is ideologically polarized. One of us has argued that confirmation politics is importantly related to a nominating president's popularity when he submits a nominee: higher presidential approval levels usually translate to easier confirmation

---

[47]   Background is drawn in large part from Nolan McCarty and Rose Razaghian, *Advice and Consent: Senate Responses to Executive Branch Nominations 1885–1996*, 43 Am. J. Pol. Sci. 122–43 (1999) and *Developments in the Law—Presidential Authority: Executive Appointments*, 125 Harv. L. Rev. 2135–55 (2012).

for a president's nominees. Josh Chafetz, *Congress's Constitution: Legislative Authority and the Separation of Powers* 124–29 (2017). A president's relative popularity tends to correlate more strongly with partisanship during polarized political periods, but one can understand the two factors as making separate contributions.

McCarty and Razaghian found that the average duration of confirmation processes has been climbing since the 1970s, which coincided with the growth in other types of Senate obstruction such as filibusters. Starting in the 1990s, the confirmation process has grown even more contentious as levels of partisan polarization intensified and both parties have perceived increased policy stakes associated with executive appointments. In the past 15 years, the Senate has blocked up-or-down votes for "qualified" candidates based on their ideological beliefs.[48] More recently, the Senate has prevented up-or-down votes as a bargaining chip to modify agency authority or even to frustrate agency operations. From July 2011 to July 2013, Senate Republicans refused to allow an up-or-down vote on President Obama's nomination of Richard Cordray to head the Consumer Financial Protection Bureau (CFPB) unless the President agreed to weaken the agency's statutory powers.[49] And between April 2009 and July 2013, Republicans similarly blocked up-or-down votes on four Obama nominees to the National Labor Relations Board (NLRB), knowing that failure to confirm at least three individuals to the five-member Board would have meant the agency lacked a quorum to function.

The *internal* response to these Senate tactics was for majority party senators to threaten the obstructionist minority with the so-called "nuclear option," a Senate rule change allowing a simple majority—rather than the current supermajority of 60 Senators—to invoke cloture and vote to confirm executive branch nominees. Democrat Majority Leader Harry Reid was on the brink of imposing the nuclear option in July 2013, following years of delay on Cordray and various NLRB nominees. Instead, Reid and the Democrats secured an agreement from a group of more moderate Republicans to allow up or down votes on these nominees and several others; all were confirmed prior to the Senate's August 2013 recess. In assessing their own conduct, Republican Senator Lindsey Graham, who helped negotiate the agreement after vigorously opposing Cordray, stated, "Cordray was being filibustered because we don't like the law [that created the CPFB]. That's not a reason to deny someone their appointment. We were wrong." Jonathan Weisman & Jennifer Steinhauer, *Senators Reach Agreement to Avert Fight Over Filibuster*, N.Y. Times, July 17, 2013. Was it wrong for Senator Graham and his Republican colleagues to withhold their consent power in order to extract policy concessions from the President? Is there some principled or pragmatic basis for limiting the consent power in this regard?

Constitutional Considerations—Recess Appointments. The response of Presidents George W. Bush and Barack Obama to the Senate's obstructionism was

---

[48]   Among well-qualified executive branch candidates (in professional terms) who never received an up-or-down-vote are Obama nominee Dawn Johnsen to head the Office of Legal Counsel in the Justice Department and George W. Bush nominee John Bolton to serve as U.S. Ambassador to the United Nations.

[49]   The Republicans hoped to force an amendment that would alter the CFPB's budgetary insulation from congressional accountability and also convert the agency into a multi-member commission.

to begin using their recess appointment powers to bypass the Senate. The Recess Appointments Clause grants the President "Power to fill up all Vacancies that *may happen during the Recess* of the Senate, by granting Commissions which shall expire at the End of their next Session." Art. II, § 2, cl. 3 (emphasis added). In 2006 President Bush made 40 appointments of executive officials during Senate recesses.[50] The Senate in turn began conducting pro forma sessions to prevent recess appointments. In 2007, Democrat Senate Majority Leader Reid enlisted senators to return to the empty Senate chamber every few days during the Thanksgiving holiday to conduct pro forma sessions, typically lasting under one minute. This tactic prevented Bush from making any recess appointments in his final twenty-one months as President.[51] In late 2010, Republican Senators deployed the pro forma sessions to prevent President Obama from using his recess appointment power.

President Bush did not challenge the opposition party's pro forma tactic, but President Obama did. On January 4, 2012, during a pro forma session, Obama announced the recess appointments of three NLRB members and Richard Cordray. President Obama relied on advice from the Justice Department Office of Legal Counsel (OLC) that the pro forma sessions do not sufficiently interrupt a recess for purposes of the Recess Appointments Clause. The OLC's January 2012 memorandum invoked a 1921 Attorney General opinion prepared for President Harding, which in turn had relied on a 1905 Senate committee report.[52] The Senate committee report asserted "The word 'recess' is one of ordinary, not technical signification, and it is evidently used in the constitutional provision in its common and popular sense"; the report described the Senate as being in recess when "its members have no duty of attendance; when its Chamber is empty; when, because of its absence, it cannot receive communications from the president or participate as a body in making appointments." The Justice Department memorandum observed that the Senate's 2011 and 2012 pro forma sessions were conducted pursuant to a unanimous consent resolution providing that there would be "no business conducted" during those sessions.

Subsequently, Noel Canning (a Pepsi-Cola bottling firm in Yakima, Wash.) appealed from an adverse ruling by the NLRB, alleging that the three recess appointments were invalid and the Board therefore lacked a three-member quorum. In January 2013, a D.C. Circuit panel agreed. The court reasoned that the phrase "the recess" in the Recess Appointments Clause would have been understood by the Framers to refer only to the period of adjournment between two sessions of Congress, and the challenged appointments were made after the second session of the 112th Congress had commenced on January 3, 2013. Two members of the D.C. Circuit panel went further, concluding that the original meaning of "happen" in the Clause requires the vacancies to occur during a recess between sessions of Congress as well as being filled during that period. Few if any of the more than 1300 presidential recess appointments made since 1933 would satisfy this latter requirement.

---

[50]　Henry Hogue & Maureen Bearden, Cong. Research Serv., RL33310, *Recess Appointments Made by President George W. Bush, January 20, 2001–October 31, 2008*, at 2 (2008).

[51]　*Id.* at 15, 19.

[52]　This legal background is set forth by Peter Shane in *The Future of Recess Appointments in Light of Noel Canning v. NLRB*, 27 Lab. Relations Week 1078–85 (June 5, 2013)

The Supreme Court, interpreting the Recess Clause for the very first time, affirmed the D.C. Circuit's holding but not its reasoning. In *NLRB v. Noel Canning*, 573 U.S. 513 (2014), Justice Breyer (joined by Justices Kennedy, Ginsburg, Sotomayor, and Kagan) relied on the purpose of the Clause and the long historical practice of recess appointments by Presidents of both parties, rather than a close reading of the text. The Court observed that Presidents for two centuries had made recess appointments during breaks that occur both between sessions of Congress and within those sessions, and it held they may constitutionally do so provided the break is of sufficient length. At times, a congressional recess can be too short to make a recess appointment necessary. Noting that under Art. I, § 5, the House must consent to any Senate recess of more than three days, Justice Breyer concluded that a recess of three days or less is automatically too short. A recess of four to nine days will ordinarily be too short except for "some very unusual circumstance—a national catastrophe, for instance, that renders the Senate unavailable but calls for an urgent response."

The Court further held that the President may fill any vacancies that happen to exist during a recess, as opposed to only vacancies created during that recess. Justice Breyer invoked the Clause's purpose: the President, who is always acting to execute the law, must be able to obtain the assistance of subordinate officers while the Senate is unavailable to confirm those officers. A narrower reading would prevent Presidents from filling vacancies that arise before a recess, "no matter who the official, * * * how dire the need, * * * how uncontroversial the appointment, and * * * how late in the session the office fell vacant." Justice Breyer also again pointed to historical practice: presidents had made recess appointments to preexisting vacancies for 200 years and the Senate as a body had not objected for at least three-quarters of a century.

Finally, however, the Court held that the Senate can prevent the President from making recess appointments by conducting "pro forma" sessions every three days, even in the midst of longer recesses. The Court rejected the Justice Department's argument that these pro forma sessions are simply a sham to thwart the President's appointment powers. All that matters, said Justice Breyer, is whether the Senate says it is in session and "under its own rules, it retains the capacity to transact Senate business"; the latter is possible even if unlikely during pro forma sessions.

Applying its newly articulated standard, the Court held the Senate was in session during the pro forma sessions scheduled intermittently in December 2011 and early January 2012. The challenged NLRB appointments were made during a three day recess between two such pro forma sessions in early January, and three days was too short a time to bring a recess within the scope of the Clause. Justice Scalia (joined by the Chief Justice and Justices Thomas and Alito) concurred in the judgment, substantially following the D.C. Circuit's text-based analysis, and insisting that the Clause applies only during the single recess between two formal congressional sessions and only for offices that become vacant during that intermission.

Practical Implications? The majority decision in *Noel Canning* may be viewed as a victory for the Senate, as both parties (at different times since 2007) have pursued the strategy of enlisting members to help conduct pro forma sessions that prevent a recess from taking place. But consider whether political actors will now seek creative ways to prevent a recess the Senate wants, or to impose a recess the Senate resists. On the one hand, because the House under Art. I, § 5 can prevent a recess of more than three days, it may be able to undermine the President's recess appointments power when both the White House and the Senate are controlled by the opposite party. What if the Senate votes to adjourn, initiating a recess period, but the House disagrees and objects? Under Art. II, § 3, "in Case of Disagreement between the [chambers], with Respect to the Time of Adjournment, [the President] may adjourn them to such a time as he shall think proper." This power has never been exercised. Could a President order a recess in the setting described here?

On the other hand, Justice Breyer's conclusion about the validity of pro forma sessions presumes that the Senate retains power to conduct business in such sessions even when it passes a resolution that it will not do so. The Senate's capacity to conduct business during a pro forma session rests in turn on its ability to act by unanimous consent agreement, because Senate rules presume the existence of a quorum for action unless a Senator who is present questions the quorum. See *Noel Canning*, 134 S.Ct. at 2575. Given that any Senator can suggest the absence of a quorum under Senate rules, what if a Senator from the President's party comes to the floor and repeatedly makes this suggestion during a pro forma session? Would the Senator's stance activate the Recess Clause by establishing that in this particular pro forma session the Senate is, in Justice Breyer's terms, "[without] the capacity to transact Senate business"?

6. Congressional Review Act

Energized by President Trump's 2016 campaign promise to "dismantle the Administrative state," Congress in 2017 began making extensive use of the Congressional Review Act ("CRA"), 5 U.S.C. § 801. The CRA was enacted in 1996 pursuant to the GOP's 1994 "Contract with America." The Act authorizes Congress to review new regulations by means of an expedited legislative process, and to overrule a regulation by passage of a joint resolution. Once a rule is thus "overruled" or repealed, the CRA prohibits the agency from issuing "a new rule that is substantially the same . . . unless . . . specifically authorized" by Congress in a later enactment. 5 U.S.C. § 801(b)(2). Under this scorched earth provision, a CRA repeal has a more lasting effect than an APA rescission via notice and comment because the repeal effectively precludes the agency from taking the same action in the future. See Paul J. Larkin, Jr., *Reawakening the Congressional Review Act*, 41 Harv. J.L. & Pub. Pol'y 187, 250 (2018). One unexplored question is how different a later agency action must be in order to avoid being labeled "substantially the same" as the repealed rule.

Once the agency promulgating a rule has published it in the Federal Register and submitted it to Congress, lawmakers in each chamber have 60 *legislative days* (i.e. days that Congress is actually in session, rather than simply calendar days) to disapprove the rule by simple majority vote. Because the 114th Congress (2015–16) had relatively short legislative sessions, the 115th Congress (2017–18) was able to target rules issued by the Obama administration going back as far as May 2016.

The CRA requires either presidential approval or a veto-proof Congressional super-majority for use. Not surprisingly, the Act finds its most natural use during transitions between Presidential administrations. Before President Trump took office, the CRA had only been used to repeal an agency regulation once. That was in 2001, when incoming President Bush signed a repeal of OSHA's major ergonomics rule, a rule the Clinton administration had issued following years of agency study, including ten weeks of hearings as part of extensive notice and comment. See Note, *The Mysteries of the Congressional Review Act*, 122 Harv. L. Rev. 2162, 2171–74 (2009).

However, in 2017 Congressional Republicans used the CRA to repeal a total of 16 agency actions, including 15 legislative rules and one policy guidance. The rules disapproved by the CRA in 2017 include some notable examples:

- The Office of Surface Mining's 'stream protection' rule would have prohibited certain types of coal surface mining that damage water supplies and forced regulated entities engaging in such practices to clean up polluted waterways. See Stream Protection Rule, 81 Fed. Reg. 93,066 (Dec. 20, 2016).

- The FCC data privacy rule would have required broadband and telecom companies to protect their customers' data by taking specific required actions, such as explicitly requesting permission to use or share such data with others and reporting harmful data breaches. See 81 Fed. Reg. 87,274 (Dec. 2, 2016).

- An SSA rule on disability recipients and gun use would have required disclosure of social security disability recipients who are receiving that benefit because of a mental illness to the National Instant Criminal background System (NICS), the Federal gun sale background check database. See 81 Fed. Reg. 91,702 (Dec. 19, 2016).

- An SEC rule would have clarified that compliance with a requirement in § 1504 of the 2010 Dodd-Frank Wall Street reform bill, requiring gas, oil, and mining companies to disclose payments made to foreign governments and the Federal government, can be met by adopting standards used by either the EU or Canada. See 81 Fed. Reg. 49,163 (July 27, 2016).

Labor (4) and Interior (3) were particular targets of the sixteen successful repeals. See Geo. Wash. U. Reg. Stud. Ctr., *Congressional Review Act Tracker—* [hereinafter Tracker] 115th Congress (last updated May 16, 2018), https://regulatorystudies.columbian.gwu.edu/congressional-review-act; Tamara Keith, *Trump Signed 96 Laws In 2017. Here Is What They Do And How They Measure Up,* NPR (Dec. 27, 2017), https://www.npr.org/2017/12/27/573546883/trump-signed-96-laws-in-2017-here-is-what-they-do-and-how-they-measure-up. Moreover, the CRA legislative process was generally successful: only a single repeal attempt that came to the floor failed during the 60 legislative calendar day carryover period in 2017, a BLM surface emissions rule. See Tracker, *supra.*

Following this powerful use of the CRA by the GOP, some Democrats have called for the law's repeal. See Sunset the CRA and Restore American Protection Act of 2017, H.R. 2449 and S.1140, 115th Cong. (1st Sess. 2017). In addition, however, all Senate Democrats, joined by several Republicans, recently used the CRA to try and overturn the controversial net neutrality rule issued by the FCC last year. See S.J. Res. 52, 115th Cong. (2d Sess. 2018) (passed Senate by 52–47, May 15, 2018). The effort failed as Democratic members of the House of Representatives could not collect enough signatures for the discharge petition necessary to consider the joint resolution. See H.J. Res. 129, 115th Cong. (2d Sess. 2018).

Finally, because of their informal nature, policy guidances often are not subject to the protocol of being sent to Congress. As a result, the CRA's 60-day window period never begins running even if the guidance was published in the Federal Register. Using this strategy, the Republican majority successfully repealed CFPB policy guidances addressing auto-lending forced arbitration and discriminatory markup disparities by auto dealers. See Pub. L. No. 115–74; Pub. L. No. 115–172; Tracker *supra*. In April 2019, OMB issued a Memorandum providing guidance on compliance with the CRA. (OMB Memo M-19-14, April 11, 2019). The Memorandum explicitly includes policy guidances as defined under "rules" and requires executive and independent agencies to submit these proposed rules to OIRA.

Given that rescinding a policy guidance does not ordinarily require compliance with APA procedures, what are the advantages of using the CRA to repeal policy guidances in this manner? Does it perhaps reflect an effort by both the President and Congress to assert greater control over the perceived proliferation of policy guidances by agencies? (see Trump Administration's War on Policy Guidance at § 2(D)(2) of this chapter). Additionally (or alternatively) might it be indicative of a desire to preclude the agency from ever re-issuing the repealed guidance, based on the CRA's special 'scorched earth' provision discussed above?

B. PRESIDENTIAL MONITORING AND OVERSIGHT

1. OMB and Cost-Benefit Analysis

Historical Development of OMB Involvement. Although the Constitution does not expressly provide for presidential involvement in agency decision-making, the president has come to exercise considerable influence through monitoring and oversight of agency actions. The legal authority for presidential involvement may be located in Article II of the Constitution, which directs the President to "take Care that the Laws be faithfully executed." In pragmatic terms, the president is "uniquely capable of assuming a role that is distinct from other forms of oversight." Harold Bruff, *Presidential Power and Administrative Rulemaking*, 88 Yale L.J. 451, 461–63 (1979). Bruff identifies certain features of the Presidency that create special oversight advantages. One is the President's national constituency, a characteristic not shared by individual legislators or the congressional committees that oversee federal agencies. Even more important is the President's "unique responsibility to superintend the execution of many statutes at once." Bruff invokes Chief Justice Vinson's observation in a 1952 dissenting opinion that "[u]nlike an administrative commission confined to the enforcement of the statute under which it was created,

Pres' make sur of legislation Be Executed

or the head of a department when administering a particular statute, the President is a constitutional officer charged with taking care that a 'mass of legislation' be executed," *Youngstown Sheet & Tube Co. v. Sawyer*, 343 U.S. 579, 702 (1952) (Vinson, C.J., dissenting). Bruff argues for the President's implied authority "to harmonize the welter of statutes, or to act interstitially at times," because "legislation necessarily distributes power in a somewhat fragmented fashion" to agencies, and it "cannot resolve all the future problems of coordinating policy under separate statutes." Thus, the President "has a unique vantage point from which he can focus on a vital issue that falls within the jurisdiction of a variety of executive and independent agencies, each having power to deal with only part of the problem." 88 Yale L.J. at 462.

Notwithstanding arguments based on Article II, the absence of explicit constitutional delegation led presidents to defer to agency decisionmaking through much of the last century.[53] President Nixon became more involved in agency policymaking. He created the *Office of Management and Budget* (OMB) from the existing Bureau of the Budget, see Executive Order 11,541, and directed OMB to perform "Quality of Life" review, which involved circulating an agency's proposed rules related to environmental quality, consumer protection, and certain matters of public health to other agencies for comment and subsequent feedback. This coordinated review rarely involved OMB exerting substantive influence, but the review process initiated an enhanced presidential role in agency decisionmaking. While Presidents Ford and Carter added incrementally to the centralizing process, there was a general belief that decisionmaking authority remained with the agency. And because agencies viewed the presidential representatives' roles as primarily consultative, they tended to regard these initiatives as more of a paperwork obligation than a meaningful constraint.

President Reagan altered the playing field in substantial ways. He signed Executive Order 12,291 (46 Fed. Reg. 13,193, Feb. 17, 1981), which required executive—but not independent—agencies to submit "major rules" to the *Office of Information and Regulatory Affairs (OIRA)*, an office within OMB that had been created initially in 1980 by the Paperwork Reduction Act, Pub. L. No. 96–511, 94 Stat. 2812 (1980) (codified as amended at 44 U.S.C. §§ 3501–21). Major rules were basically regulations likely to have an annual effect on the economy of at least $100 million, or to result in a "major increase" in costs or prices or in "significant adverse effects" on competition, employment, or productivity. The agency submissions to OMB were for the purpose of prepublication review, and agencies were required to accompany their submissions with "regulatory impact analyses" and cost-benefit analyses "to the extent permitted by law." The Reagan Executive Order further charged OMB with responsibility to review and approve, or decline to approve, federal rules from executive agencies. Agencies could regulate only if "the potential benefits to society outweigh the potential costs to society," and the choice among alternatives "involv[ed] the least net cost to society." This Order effectively gave OMB a form of substantive control over executive agencies, because OMB's authority to determine the adequacy of agency impact analyses allowed it to delay or even

---

[53]   The account of historical developments through the Clinton Administration is drawn substantially from Elena Kagan, *Presidential Administration*, 114 Harv. L. Rev. 2245, 2275–2300 (2001).

prevent the publication of a rule. During the Reagan era, an average of 85 rules per year were either withdrawn by agencies in the course of OMB review or returned to the agencies for reconsideration.

President Clinton increased presidential involvement in several respects. Clinton signed Executive Order 12,866 (58 Fed. Reg. 51,735, Sept. 30, 1993), modifying the Reagan approach; major excerpts from the Clinton Executive Order are reproduced in Appendix D. The Order required that OMB review for "significant regulatory action" (comparable to Reagan's "major rule") take place during a specified window of time; it increased the number of factors that agencies should consider in their mandatory cost-benefit analyses; and it required OIRA to disclose its communications with the agency and with persons outside of the executive branch. Should these changes be viewed as expansions of OIRA authority or as constraints on that authority? With respect to cost-benefit analysis, the Executive Order directed that "[e]ach agency shall assess both the costs and the benefits of the intended regulation and, recognizing that some costs and benefits are difficult to quantify, propose or adopt a regulation only upon a reasoned determination that the benefits of the intended regulation justify its costs." Does this formulation differ meaningfully from the Reagan Executive Order requirement that the benefits to society must *outweigh* the costs?

The Executive Order reiterated that OMB was to carry out the regulatory review function, and that within OMB, OIRA was the repository of expertise concerning regulatory issues, including methodologies and procedures that affect more than one agency and more broadly the President's regulatory policies. President Clinton expanded the role of OIRA by (1) requiring executive agencies to designate Regulatory Policy Officers (RPOs) to serve as OIRA point-persons, (2) subjecting independent agencies to the regulatory planning process administered by OMB and overseen by the Vice President, although not requiring them to submit individual rules for review, and (3) stipulating that the President would resolve agency-OMB disputes "to the extent permitted by law."

President George W. Bush further increased the level of presidential involvement by issuing an executive order requiring that agency RPOs be presidential appointees and that "unless specifically authorized by the head of the agency," no rulemaking may commence without RPO consent. This effectively meant that an RPO need not report to an agency head and may not even have to be Senate-confirmed. See Peter Strauss, *Overseer, or "The Decider"? The President in Administrative Law*, 75 Geo. Wash. L. Rev. 696, 701 (2007). Upon taking office, President Obama revoked the Bush era changes and returned to the original Clinton executive order. See Executive Order 13,497 (74 Fed. Reg. 6,113, Jan. 30, 2009). The current cost-benefit analysis requirements for agencies largely reflect the Clinton directive with some clarifications from President Obama, who introduced some additional principles and requirements involving public participation, integration and coordination, flexibility, and scientific integrity to the cost-benefit analysis. See Executive Order 13,563 (76 Fed. Reg. 3,821, Jan. 18, 2011), reproduced in Appendix D. In 2017, President Trump issued Executive Orders 13771 and 13777, seeking to manage and control the private costs of compliance imposed by new regulations. These executive orders are discussed in § 3(B)(3) of this chapter.

Cost-Benefit Analysis; Economic Issues.[54] Cost-benefit analysis requires agencies to assign a monetary value to both the benefits and costs associated with their proposed regulation. With respect to benefits, one key challenge is determining how much a human life is worth in dollars. As explained by the OIRA Administrator for the second President Bush, "administrative law saves lives by reducing small probabilities of premature death, injury, or illness among large numbers of anonymous workers, consumers, travelers, and residents. The names of those whose lives will be saved are unknown when the rule is adopted and may never be known. They are sometimes called 'statistical lives.'" John Graham, *Saving Lives Through Administrative Law and Economics*, 157 U. Pa. L. Rev. 395, 398 (2008). The valuation methodology for statistical lives—based on amounts we are willing to pay (to secure a benefit) or willing to accept (to bear a risk)—can seem straightforward. Viscusi analogizes establishing the value of risk reduction to assessing benefits in other contexts. Just as we measure benefits from construction of a new public parking garage by estimating the sum of community residents' willingness to pay, so when assessing the benefits of reducing the risk of death or disease, we estimate the amount of tax dollars we are willing to spend to reduce incrementally the probability of an adverse health outcome that might otherwise affect one or more random members of the community. *Fatal Tradeoffs* at 19. For example, suppose a regulation is expected to prevent fifty premature deaths. If the agency uses $7 million as the value of a statistical life (VSL), the estimated benefits would be $350 million.[55]

The approach an agency takes to VSL raises a number of issues. In terms of valuation methodology, agencies vary considerably in the dollar amount they assign to a statistical life; OMB has at times recommended a range of between $1 million and $10 million. Agencies also may adjust their VSL over time. In 2008, EPA lowered its VSL by almost $1 million (11%) although EPA's valuation was still higher than all other federal agencies, including the Department of Transportation which had twice raised its VSL in the same time period.[56] And in 2002, EPA decided the VSL for elderly persons was 38 percent less than that of persons under age 70; the agency reversed itself after the move became public.[57] It is not surprising that skeptics claim the valuation process is heavily tainted by political considerations.

Another valuation issue involves how an agency should discount future gains and losses. Assuming that a certain adjustment in permissible exposure levels to a hazardous substance would reduce the risk of a fatal disease occurring in 50 years time, how should the agency value that reduced risk in today's dollars? Sunstein observes that if an agency values human life at $8 million and selects a 10% discount rate, a life saved 100 years from now is worth only $581. OMB guidelines, which

---

[54]   What follows on the economics of cost-benefit analysis is drawn substantially from W. Kip Viscusi, *Fatal Tradeoffs* (1972); Cass Sunstein, *The Real World of Cost-Benefit Analysis: Thirty-Six Questions (and Almost as Many Answers)*, 114 Colum. L. Rev. 167 (2014); and Cass Sunstein, *Cost-Benefit Default Principles*, 99 Mich. L. Rev. 1651 (2001).

[55]   In Sunstein's words, "the government is not actually 'valuing life' [but instead] valuing the reduction of mortality risks—typically by eliminating low-level risks, for example risks of 1 in 100,000. When it is said that a life is 'worth' $7 million in such cases, what is really meant is that people are willing to pay, or ask to be paid, $70, on average, to eliminate a risk of 1 in 100,000." *Thirty-Six Questions (and Almost as Many Answers)*, 114 Colum. L. Rev. at 182.

[56]   See Seth Borenstein, *American Life Worth Less Today*, Huffington Post, July 10, 2008.

[57]   See *id.*

suggest a 7% discount rate (departing from its 10% rate in the 1980s), are not mandatory. Even within a single agency, discount rates vary widely: EPA at one point chose a 3% rate for regulation of lead-based paint, a 7% rate for regulation of drinking water, and a 10% rate for regulating emissions from locomotives. *Cost-Benefit Default Principles* at 1711–12.

Further, Viscusi notes that "economic valuations of risk tend to be distorted by underlying misweighting of risks." For example, we tolerate voluntarily assumed risks more than environmental hazards over which we have no control; we tend to regulate new technologies more strictly than familiar risks; and we scrutinize man-made carcinogens while often accepting much higher levels of natural carcinogens. *Fatal Tradeoffs* at 151–52. The weighting of risks also can have serious equity consequences. With respect to locating an environmental hazard like a toxic dump site or a landfill facility, wealthy communities may be seen as willing to pay far more than poor communities can afford to pay for the benefit of avoidance. The "net benefit" to society as a whole is therefore maximized by putting the facility in a low-income area.[58]

When assessing an agency's estimates of both costs and benefits, OIRA must assure that there has been consideration of alternative options in order to evaluate whether the agency has chosen the approach that maximizes net benefits. This requirement too raises various questions, for the agencies and OIRA. How many alternative options must an agency consider? How serious and detailed must this consideration be? Do the alternatives considered have to meet some benchmark of reasonableness? What if the agency concludes there are no reasonable alternatives?

When the benefits do not appear to justify the costs, OIRA will raise questions about whether the agency should proceed with the rule at all. In practical terms, the monetized benefits exceed the monetized costs for the great majority of recent, economically significant rules where the agency submitted monetized costs and benefits. (If an agency determines that the monetized costs are larger than the monetized benefits, the agency may simply choose not to submit a draft rule to OIRA.) In addition, there are certain situations where an agency cannot provide monetized benefits but the agency may be able to show the kinds and breadth of benefits a certain rule will achieve. For example, a regulation limiting workers' exposure to a carcinogenic substance may prevent only a small number of cancers but also prevent a much larger number of painful non-fatal illnesses that are not as readily quantified. A regulation that would increase water quality may have no quantifiable beneficial effects on human health yet produce various aesthetic or recreational benefits. In the latter instance, OIRA would focus on questions like: how many water bodies will experience improved quality? What kind of improvements, and what would they actually achieve? Would there be any benefits for humans and if so, what kind? Would there be other kinds of beneficiaries, such as fish and wildlife, or the environment? Is the number of such beneficiaries large? Is it large relative to the total number? How much would they be helped—in a substantial or a marginal

---

[58]   See Frank Ackerman & Lisa Heinzerling, *Pricing the Priceless: Cost-Benefit Analysis of Environmental Protection*, 150 U. Pa. L. Rev. 1553, 1574 (2002) (discussing *inter alia* the 1991 memo from Larry Summers, then chief economist at World Bank, that explained the economic logic behind migration of "dirty industries" to developing countries).

way? *Thirty-Six Questions* at 196–97. By addressing such questions, the agency is seeking to justify the monetized costs with information relating to the breadth of the benefits rather than to monetized figures, which it cannot provide.

Suppose that a proposed rule's monetized benefits are outweighed by the monetized costs or that the analysis yields no net monetized benefit. Would OIRA decline to approve it? The answer is not necessarily for two reasons. First, if Congress through a statute requires the agency to proceed with a certain task, the rule may still proceed even if the monetized benefits are lower than the costs. A well-known illustration is the 1958 Delaney Clause amendment to the Food, Drugs, and Cosmetic Act, which effectively banned consideration of costs by prohibiting the use in food of any chemical additives that had been found to induce cancer in man or animals. Second, the current cost-benefit analysis framework requires agencies to show that the benefits *justify* the costs, not that they *outweigh* the costs. This distinction clearly recognizes that hard numbers are not the only determinative factor. Executive Order 13,563 expressly states that "each agency may consider (and discuss qualitatively) values that are difficult or impossible to quantify, including equity, human dignity, fairness, and distributive impacts."

One recent example involves a 2010 Justice Department regulation increasing building access for disabled persons, which included a requirement that new bathrooms contain sufficient space for wheelchair users to transfer onto toilets from the side. The Department acknowledged that the monetized costs (which were relatively high) substantially exceeded the monetized benefits, but the Department offered several non-monetary counterarguments: "the additional benefits that persons with disabilities will derive from greater safety, enhanced independence, and the avoidance of stigma and humiliation" were also likely to be quite high. Returning war veterans confined to wheelchairs are taught to use side-transfers because they are safe, efficient, and independence-producing; and the Americans With Disabilities Act "is intended to provide important benefits [such as these water closet clearance provisions] that are distributional and equitable in character."[59]

Cost-benefit analyses are not simple undertakings. Agencies may spend hundreds of thousands of dollars collecting data, conducting studies surveying consumer preferences, and analyzing all relevant information. Think back to the FAA's cost-benefit analysis in the Case Study at the start of this chapter. In its January 15, 2002 final rule, the FAA estimated that the cost per fortified cockpit door ranged from $12,000 to $17,000. At the time, the fleet of American airplanes numbered just under 7,000. A letter from a major domestic air carrier responded that the FAA's estimation was low, and that the actual cost per fortified door was $49,000. Is a substantial change in cost, from $84 million to $343 million, justified? Would other options—such as modestly improving the current intense airport security screening of passengers—yield the same or comparable benefits at far less additional cost? If not, how would you quantify the distinct benefits of reinforced cockpit doors? Are the benefits the same for a small regional airline flying 10-passenger planes as for an international airline flying planes that carry 200 or more passengers?

---

[59]   *Nondiscrimination on the Basis of Disability in State and Local Government Services*, 75 Fed. Reg. 56,164, 56,170 (Sept. 15, 2010).

Cost-Benefit Analysis; Legal Issues. OMB is not the only institutional player shaping the cost-benefit approach. Congress plays an important *ex ante* role, in that cost-benefit analysis may be prohibited, permitted, or required under approaches set forth in statutes that regulate health, safety, and the environment. Thus, for example, the Clean Air Act provisions defining national ambient air quality standards as those "requisite to protect public health" have been recognized as requiring a cost-blind judgment based on "public health" alone. See *Whitman v. Am. Trucking Associations*, 531 U.S. 457 (2001), in § 1(B) of this chapter. And the Occupational Safety and Health Act (OSHA) provisions authorizing promulgation of workplace health and safety standards have been understood as requiring the agency to make a threshold finding that "significant risks" are present and can be reduced by a change in practices. See *Indus. Union Dep't, AFL-CIO v. Am. Petroleum Inst.*, 448 U.S. 607, 642–43 (1980). This approach suggests that OSHA regulation is permissible once risk-reduction benefits rise above the threshold, regardless of what costs accompany the benefits. At the same time, the fact that an agency is not *required* to engage in cost-benefit analysis may not mean the agency isn't *permitted* to do so. See *Entergy Corp. v. Riverkeeper, Inc.*, 556 U.S. 208, 223 (2009). What if a statute prohibits an executive branch agency from engaging in cost-benefit analysis when promulgating its health and safety rules, but a proposed rule constitutes a "significant regulatory action" under Executive Order 12,866. May OIRA require the agency to assess the proposed rule's costs and benefits? Is the agency justified in refusing to do so based on its congressional directive? How is this situation likely to be resolved?

Assume instead that Congress requires an agency to undertake safety or health regulation "to the extent feasible"? Does this refer to technical feasibility: regulation should proceed as long as the relevant control technology exists? Is it better understood to mean economic feasibility: regulation should go forward unless the regulated entities cannot bear the cost without experiencing business failures across significant portions of the industry? What if the two feasibility concepts inevitably overlap—does this suggest that feasibility requirements in a statute implicate only analysis of the cost-side of the equation? Or is cost-benefit analysis also permitted?

In addition to Congress's input, courts can play an influential *ex post* role when asked to review agency cost-benefit analyses. Consider whether the economic concerns raised in this part (valuation of statistical lives, discount rates, misweighting of risks, equity, politicization) might be exacerbated by judicial review of an agency's cost-benefit determinations. Should we assume that federal judges have levels of expertise comparable to agency regulators when applying highly technical economic models and assumptions? If a reviewing court concludes that the agency chose wrongly from among complex conflicting studies about economic costs or benefits, what are the chances the court is simply aligning with the opposite side of a politically charged debate? Is close judicial oversight of an agency's cost-benefit analysis especially suspect when the statute that authorized the regulation reflects strongly pro-regulatory intent? For a recent example of aggressive judicial review on cost-benefit matters, see *Business Roundtable v. SEC*, 647 F.3d 1144 (D.C. Cir. 2011), addressed in § 3(C) of this chapter. For sharp criticism of the decision, see *Recent Cases: D.C. Circuit Finds SEC Proxy Access Rule Arbitrary and Capricious for Inadequate Economic Analysis*, 125 Harv. L. Rev. 1088 (2011).

2. OIRA: Aggregating Information and Coordinating Among Agencies

Created by Congress in 1980, OIRA has in a short time become a central actor in the agency review process. Executive Order 12,866 (1993) describes OIRA as "the repository of expertise concerning regulatory issues, including methodologies and procedures that affect more than one agency, this Executive Order, and the President's regulatory policies." President Clinton's Order adds that the OIRA Administrator initiates centralized review of all planned "significant regulatory actions,"[60] and has the power to investigate—and if necessary reject—agency actions that he believes "may be inconsistent with the President's priorities or the principles set forth in this Executive Order or may be in conflict with any policy or action taken or planned by another agency." Between January 21, 2009 and August 10, 2012, OIRA reviewed just over 2300 regulatory actions. During this period, it approved 320 actions (14%) without change, and approved 1758 actions (76%) "consistent with change" meaning that the published rule differed from the submitted version in either minor or substantial respects. An additional 161 regulatory actions (7%) were withdrawn following OIRA intervention.[61]

The OIRA Administrator is appointed by the President, subject to being confirmed by the Senate. Under Executive Order 12866, he is a "regulatory policy advisor" to the President; in this respect he shares status with the Director of OMB (also a Senate-confirmed position) as well as various other Assistants to the President who are lodged within the White House but are not subject to confirmation (see § 3(B)(3) below).

From September 2009 to August 2012, Harvard law professor Cass Sunstein served as the Administrator of OIRA. Sunstein's *Commentary*, published in 2013 in the Harvard Law Review, provides a unique insider's perspective on OIRA's operations, priorities, and challenges. In an effort to dispel misunderstandings about how OIRA functions, Sunstein highlights four central propositions:

- (1) *Oversight of a genuinely interagency process.* Sunstein emphasizes that OIRA often functions as a conveyer and convener, identifying and sharing interagency views and striving to develop a reasonable consensus, rather than insisting on its own positions.

- (2) *Delays in OIRA review.* Often, a rule is delayed even though there is consensus that it should ultimately be promulgated, because matters such as legal complexity or language precision deserve more attention to avoid publishing anything that could generate needless confusion or apprehension. Even a proposed rule containing such technical issues may well alter behavior, and thus create difficulties, if the public or regulated entities believe that it is likely to be finalized in the same form.

---

[60]   As referenced in § 3(B)(1), a "significant regulatory action" is a broad category, encompassing actions that have an annual effect on the economy of at least $100 million; have a material adverse effect on the economy, the environment, or public health or safety; create a serious inconsistency with action by another agency; or raise novel legal or policy issues arising out of legal mandates or presidential priorities. See Exec. Order 12,866, § 3(f).

[61]   See Cass Sunstein, *Commentary, The Office of Information and Regulatory Affairs: Myths and Realities,* 126 Harv. L. Rev. 1838, 1847 (2013).

● (3) *Cost-benefit analysis important but not usually dominant.* For economically significant rules, the cost-benefit analysis required under the applicable executive orders receives careful attention. But most of OIRA's day-to-day work involves addressing interagency concerns, ensuring adequate discussion of alternatives, and promoting the receipt and consideration of public comments.

● (4) *OIRA review process often highly technical.* This relates to point (2) above. OIRA may seek the Justice Department's position on a legal issue, or the U.S. Trade Representative's input on an issue involving international trade, or the Energy Department's views as to a rule's effects on the energy supply. Because career officials with technical expertise are frequently the central actors, delays result as these technical specialists work through the technical questions to arrive at solid answers. 126 Harv. L. Rev. at 1841–43.

Sunstein's emphasis on the OIRA role as a convenor and facilitator between agencies and an aggregator of information, and his downplaying of cost-benefit analysis, are somewhat at odds with popular conceptions of how OIRA operates to monitor executive agencies. Later in his *Commentary*, Sunstein identifies the two chief criticisms directed at OIRA: (a) meddling beyond its competence with agencies that are more specialized and expert about the relevant facts and law; and (b) unduly politicizing the regulatory review process because of its intimate ties to a White House staffed by political actors. Sunstein responds by reiterating that most of the OIRA process is technical, not political. This technical focus is appropriately coordinated in that it combines OIRA's own expertise with a convening of outside agency officials who bring scientific, economic, and legal expertise to the table. And politics—in the sense of electoral factors and broader public reactions—is not a significant part of OIRA's role although it may be important for other offices within the White House. *Id.* at 1871–73.

The concerns that OIRA may be overly meddlesome and unduly politicized deserve some separate attention.

OIRA and Meddling. Sunstein notes the existence of litigation about whether agencies have used interpretive rules and guidance documents to reach decisions that are the functional equivalent of rules (see related discussion in § 2(D) above). Even if such agency documents fall within proper legal bounds, they may still have substantial effects on the private sector—whether or not they amount to significant regulatory actions. Sunstein contends that OIRA is interested in promoting public comment in such situations, "not because such comment is required as a matter of law, * * * but because when the stakes are high and the issues novel, obtaining public comment is good practice as a way of avoiding mistakes." *Id.* at 1854.

Sunstein concedes that the APA exempts interpretive rules and guidance documents from notice and comment requirements. Does OIRA's promotion of public comment on such proposed agency actions undermine Congress's explicit understanding of a limited public role? Does it improperly interfere with an agency's internal choices on what procedural strategies or tactics to follow? Will the mere threat of OIRA mandating a public comment period for policy guidances issued by the SEC or FAA make those agencies less willing to pursue more efficient and flexible approaches? Alternatively, is it proper for OIRA to insist that agencies invite public input and response whenever they might be engaged in regulatory conduct that involves "high stakes" or "novel issues"?

OIRA and Politicization. In elaborating on his four core propositions, Sunstein discusses OIRA's open-door policy of meeting upon their request with representatives of affected companies, public interest groups, state and local governments, and congressional staffs. He acknowledges that businesses and others subject to regulation arrange the great majority of these meetings, in which they seek to scale back or oppose planned agency actions. But while recognizing the attendant risk of "epistemic capture"—that OIRA or others within the President's Office "will ultimately form a view that matches what those around them are telling them"— Sunstein discounts this risk. He contends that meetings are only one aspect of a complex OIRA review process and their sheer numbers reveal little of value, given that often the meeting initiators present no new information or repeat well-known arguments or speak in unhelpfully general terms. For these and other reasons, Sunstein argues that the role of meetings tends to be greatly exaggerated; the review process relies more on interagency comments and written comments from the public. *Id.* at 1860–62.

Some others are less convinced. Based on its detailed 2011 study of OIRA operations, the Center for Progressive Reform (CPF) claimed that "[n]early three years into the Obama Administration, * * * the regulatory process is every bit as political as it was during the Bush years, while being no more transparent; and vigorous enforcement of the nation's health, safety, and environmental laws has suffered as a result."[62] The CPF study, covering OIRA meetings from October 2001 to June 2011, concluded *inter alia* that not only does industry dominate the meetings process (on this point Sunstein agrees), but (1) rules that were the subject of OIRA meetings were 29% more likely to be changed than those that were not; and (2) EPA is a special OIRA target—its rules made up only 11% of all OIRA reviews but 41% of OIRA meetings, and EPA rules were changed at a significantly higher rate (84%) than those of other agencies (65%) during the ten-year period.[63] Do you find persuasive Sunstein's view that the risk of capture in these settings is largely illusory? Assuming the accuracy of the CPF findings on OIRA meeting participation—65% of attendees represented industry groups while 12% represented public interest groups—is this pattern likely to have only minimal or cosmetic effects?

A high-profile illustration of CPF's concerns involved OIRA deliberations in the summer of 2011, ending with White House refusal to approve the draft final rule on ozone pollution submitted by President Obama's EPA Administrator, Lisa Jackson.[64]

---

[62] *Politicizing the Regulatory Process,* available at http://www.progressivereform.org/OIRASpec Interests.cfm.

[63] Center for Progressive Reform, *Behind Closed Doors at the White House: How Politics Trumps Protection of Public Health, Worker Safety, and the Environment,* available at http://www.progressivereform. org/articles/OIRA_Meetings_1111.pdf.

[64] The following account is drawn from John M. Broder, *Re-election Strategy is Tied to a Shift on Smog,* New York Times, Nov. 16, 2011, at A1.

The ozone standard had been set in 2008 by the Bush Administration at a level of 75 parts per billion (ppb); this was above the range of 60 to 70 ppb recommended by the EPA scientific advisory panel at the time. Environmental and public health groups challenged the Bush standard in court, arguing that it would endanger human health and had been tainted by political interference. Administrator Jackson asked the groups to hold their lawsuit in abeyance while she reconsidered the ozone standard, a reconsideration she expected would be complete by summer 2010.

After several delays that carried into spring 2011, EPA determined the standard should be set at 65 ppb to meet Clean Air Act requirements; the agency calculated this new level would avoid up to 7,200 deaths, 11,000 emergency room visits, and 38,000 acute cases of asthma each year. Jackson understood that the costs of compliance with this new standard would be highly controversial with businesses and local governments. Before submitting the draft final rule to OIRA, she met several times with White House chief of staff William M. Daley, listened to his sharp questioning about costs, burdens, and timing, and eventually offered Daley a somewhat weaker standard as well as measures to allow for substantial flexibility in compliance. In early July, Jackson was convinced she and Daley had a deal, and she sent the White House a 500-page package that included a detailed cost-benefit analysis.

The business community, however, remained adamantly opposed to the proposal, as did Republicans in Congress. In a campaign that featured intense lobbying, letter-writing, and advertising, business representatives claimed the rule would cost $90 billion a year—far more than EPA cost estimates—and would result in massive economic retrenchment in the Midwest. Local and state government officials weighed in, complaining to the White House that they lacked the resources to enforce the new rule. And some Democratic lawmakers warned the White House that the regulation would damage their re-election prospects. Listening closely to these concerns was Daley, whose mission as recently appointed chief of staff was in part to help repair relations with the business community and Congress. Business executives met with Jackson at EPA in mid-July to argue their case. They emphasized that the rule would result in massive local government non-compliance with the Clean Air Act, and they urged that she wait until the next review in 2013. Jackson listened politely and demurred; the business executives left the meeting frustrated.

OIRA Administrator Sunstein was not overly enthused about the proposed ozone rule. He knew the rule was subject to revision again in 2013 and was also aware that nearly half the EPA's own case studies found the cost of the new rule outweighed its benefits. Sunstein and Daley agreed to meet with the business lobbyists on August 16, the same day they were meeting with the environmental and public health groups. Business representatives brought a map showing how many midwestern and east coast states that Obama had won in 2008 would be out of compliance with the proposed regulation. Several governors also attended this meeting; North Carolina governor Bev Perdue (a Democrat) argued against the new rule and her air quality director sent a letter to EPA pleading for a delay and citing the health effects to North Carolina citizens from lack of employment and loss of health care. Several hours after meeting with business interests, Sunstein and Daley met with the environmental and public health groups. These groups explained why the proposed standard would reduce smog levels, and the consequent impact in terms of fewer deaths and incidents of lung disease including for children. Daley listened and then asked, "What are the health impacts of unemployment?"

Following two weeks of silence, the President met with Jackson on September 1, and informed her of his decision to return the ozone rule to EPA for reconsideration. The next day, Sunstein sent a letter to Jackson offering three related reasons for the President's decision: (1) the Clean Air Act's current five-year cycle for review of this air quality standard began in 2008 and was to end in 2013; accordingly, issuing a final rule in late 2011 right before having to develop a new assessment and potentially a new standard would not promote predictability and reduce uncertainty, as called for in Executive Order 13,563; (2) the agency had relied on its review of scientific literature as of 2006; this scientific assessment was no longer current, raising concerns in light of the Executive Order's requirement that rules must be based on the best available science; (3) the EPA under Jackson had already promulgated groundbreaking air quality standards (addressed to heavy-duty trucks and cross-state air pollution) projected to reduce ozone pollution as well as other toxic pollutants; reconsideration would enable the agency to assess operation of these rules and in doing so avoid duplicative or inconsistent efforts.

When the White House publicly announced the decision on September 3, environmental and public health advocates were furious. The New York Times reported their characterization of the OIRA action as "a bald surrender to business pressure, an act of political pandering and, most galling, a cold-blooded betrayal of a loyal constituency." Interviewed by the Times, Sunstein said "the decision was made on the merits and not on politics. There isn't an agreement to do things until the process runs its course. There is sometimes a surprise."

The Center for Progressive Reform study described OIRA's actions on the ozone standard as disturbingly secretive and politically motivated. Sunstein rejected that position, insisting the decision was based on judgments about the merits. *What do you think?* To what extent does Chief of Staff Daley's direct continuing involvement compromise the integrity of the OIRA review process? In his *Commentary*, Sunstein emphasized that "the Office of the Chief of Staff has an important role insofar as it works to advise on and help coordinate executive branch activity with close reference to the President's own commitments." 126 Harv. L. Rev. at 1874. In instances where congressional lawmakers and governors have expressed strong views to the White House, shouldn't politics have some role? At this elevated level, does politics become part of "the merits"? On the other hand, should an agency's scientific conclusions, reached after years of public dialogue and deliberations, be overridden by considerations of presidential politics? Or is this simply a rare instance where politics plays an influential or determining part in the OIRA review process?

Postscript on Ozone. In July 2013, the D.C. Circuit issued a decision in the lawsuit challenging the 2008 standard, which earlier had been held in abeyance pursuant to EPA Administrator Jackson's request. The appellate court concluded that although the ozone standard of 75 ppb was weaker than recommended unanimously by EPA's science advisors, the agency had not acted arbitrarily in 2008 when it determined to adopt this weaker standard.

Meanwhile, the five-year cycle for review of the 2008 standard ended in 2013, with no new notice of proposed rulemaking. In February 2014, the EPA released a draft policy statement that contained an EPA staff suggestion of lowering the current ozone standard to 60 ppb based on the available scientific evidence, as well as two draft risk and exposure documents. The EPA made the documents available for public comment. On April 30, 2014, a federal judge in the Northern District of California ordered the EPA to finish its ozone review and update the national standards, directing the agency to issue a proposal by December 1, 2014, and a final rule by October 1, 2015. *Sierra Club v. EPA*, 13-CV-2809-YGR, slip opinion (N.D. Cal. Apr. 30, 2014).

3. Trump Administration Executive Orders: A Cost-Focused Regulatory Budget

Like his recent White House predecessors, President Trump issued a number of executive orders (EO) and agency policy changes immediately upon taking office. Two Executive Orders in particular, EO 13771 and 13777, targeted the administrative rulemaking process.

On January 30, 2017, Trump promulgated Executive Order 13771, *Reducing Regulation and Controlling Regulatory Costs* ("EO 13771") which OMB later accompanied with two guidance documents. The Order's stated purpose is "to manage the costs associated with the governmental imposition of private expenditures required to comply with Federal regulations." It requires (unless otherwise prohibited by law) that agencies identify two regulations to be repealed whenever they publicly propose or promulgate a single new regulatory action. Relatedly, EO 13771 requires agencies to offset the private costs of compliance posed by new regulations by eliminating existing costs associated with at least two prior regulations.

Under the principal OMB guidance for EO 13771 (OMB Memo M-17-21, issued April 5, 2017), OIRA substantially controls this new process. The OMB Guidance Memo set a September 30, 2017 deadline for compliance in the initial fiscal year under the Trump administration. The Memo explains that a "new regulatory action" pertains to legislative-style rulemakings or significant guidance documents (such as interpretive guidance) that "impose[ ] total costs greater than zero."

The range of what qualifies as a "deregulatory action" that can provide cost offsets under EO 13771 is actually greater than what is considered a regulatory action. In addition to including legislative rulemakings and "guidance and interpretative documents," the OMB guidance also refers to "actions related to international regulatory cooperation" and "information collection requests" that reduce the cost of "recordkeeping, reporting, or disclosure requirements." This greater scope of deregulatory actions presumably reflects an effort to improve agency flexibility when seeking to comply with the mandate.

The OMB guidance also mentions that agencies can "bank" cost savings from prior fiscal years for use in subsequent ones so long as they comply with the eliminate-two-to-create-one mandate. The Memo also makes no distinction between internal departments at the same agency: any of them can participate in either the regulatory or deregulatory actions and it will all factor into the agency's overall single calculation.

Moreover, there are exemptions set out in the OMB guidance and EO 13,771 itself. Independent agencies, as defined by statute, are exempt from this mandate. The EO exempts regulations "issued with respect to a military, national security, or foreign affairs function . . . [or] related to agency organization, management, or personnel." Exec. Order No. 13,771. The OMB guidance identifies additional exemptions, including for "routine hunting and fishing regulatory actions," for regulations arising in cases of emergency, and for those that impose only de minimis costs.

Indep Agencies Are Exempt

In assigning significant control to OIRA for this cost-focused regulatory budget process, EO 13771 also defers to EO 12866 (1993) which created OIRA's general regulatory oversight process. (See Appendix D). If an agency is unable to comply with this new mandate, the OMB guidance clarifies that—within 30 days of the end of a fiscal year—the agency must explain to OIRA the reasons for its failure and set forth a plan for coming into full compliance.

On February 24, 2017, President Trump issued EO 13777, *Enforcing the Regulatory Reform Agenda,* ("EO 13777"). This Order directs the head of each agency to appoint a "Regulatory Reform Officer (RRO)" and to "establish a Regulatory Reform Task Force" that will implement the mandates of EO 13771 and other regulatory reform initiatives. Under the OMB guidance on EO 13777 (OMB Memo M-17-23, issued April 28, 2017), independent agencies are not required to participate although they "are still encouraged to comply."

In order to help the task force and RROs decide which types of regulations should be eliminated, EO 13777 provides specific categories, including regulations that (i) "eliminate jobs or inhibit job creation"; (ii) "are outdated, unnecessary, or ineffective"; (iii) "impose costs that exceed benefits"; (iv) "rely in whole or in part on data, information, or methods that are not publicly available or that are insufficiently transparent to meet the standard for reproducibility."

NOTES ON THE TRUMP EXECUTIVE ORDERS

1.   Perhaps because they deal mostly with coordination and planning processes, these two executive orders have met with little resistance from the courts thus far. A group of organizational plaintiffs mounted a challenge to EO 13771 and the OMB Guidance Memo, alleging that the restrictions imposed on the administrative process violated the APA and also the President's constitutional duty to execute legislation under Article II's Take Care Clause. The District Court dismissed the action based on its conclusion that the plaintiffs lacked standing to challenge the President's action. *See Public Citizen, Inc. et al. v. Trump,* 297 F. Supp.3d 6 (D.D.C. 2018). However, the court accepted an amended complaint and held that plaintiffs provided sufficient plausibility to survive a motion to dismiss on the standing issue. See *Public Citizen, Inc. et al. v. Trump,* 361 F.Supp.3d 60 (D.D.C. 2019). If this claim (or some other action alleging concrete injury under a specific regulation that has been repealed pursuant to EO 13771)

reaches the merits, how would you argue that plaintiffs have a valid claim under the APA? How might the Trump Administration defend against such a claim?

2.   At least since President Reagan, presidential administrations of both parties have argued that regulatory policymaking should involve an effort to balance benefits against costs, to the extent not otherwise prohibited by law. By essentially ignoring the role of benefits, President Trump's cost-focused regulatory budget would seem to represent a departure from decades of bipartisan regulatory philosophy. In *Evaluating the Trump Administration's Regulatory Reform Program* (October 2017), the Brookings Institution Center on Regulation and Markets summarized pros and cons related to this departure (emphasis in original):

> *At least as far as economic theory is concerned, any new regulation that offers more benefits than costs should be undertaken, regardless of its contribution to the aggregate regulatory costs to society.* The justification for a regulatory budget, however, is that the real-world political economy of the regulatory policymaking process deviates from the conceptual idea of maximizing net social benefits, leading to an inefficiently high burden from regulations.

To what extent should courts take account of these policy-related arguments when asked to review the legality of the new regulatory approach in a future case? Does the APA itself provide support for either traditional cost-benefit analysis or the newer regulatory budget approach?

EPA AND RESISTANCE TO THE ADMINISTRATIVE STATE

One of President Trump's earliest appointments to direct an agency was Scott Pruitt as Administrator of the Environmental Protection Agency (EPA). Pruitt had previously made a name for himself by opposing numerous EPA actions as Oklahoma's attorney general. During his tenure at EPA, which ended when he resigned in early July 2018, Pruitt's initiatives were viewed by some observers as part of a Trump Administration effort to dismantle the administrative state. The following case, decided in July of 2017 during Pruitt's first year in office, is one of many in which EPA actions have been challenged as violating agency duties or responsibilities under the Clean Air Act.

Clean Air Council v. Pruitt

862 F. 3d 1 (D.C. Cir. 2017) *(per curiam)*.

In June 2016, EPA administrator Gina McCarthy issued a final rule establishing "new source performance standards" for fugitive emissions of methane and other pollutants by the oil and natural gas industries. After final publication of the rule, several oil and gas industry groups filed administrative petitions seeking reconsideration of the final rule under § 307(d)(7)(B) of the Clean Air Act ("CAA") on grounds that they had inadequate opportunity to comment on certain portions of the final rule during the notice period. Despite these petitions, the rule went into effect on August 2, 2016 and required regulated entities to conduct an initial monitoring survey to identify leaks by June 3, 2017.

In April 2017, new Administrator Pruitt announced his agreement with the industry groups that the rule should be reconsidered. In June 2017, EPA published a "notice of reconsideration and partial stay," relying on CAA § 307(d)(7)(B) to grant reconsideration. Later in June, EPA published a notice of proposed rulemaking ("NPRM") announcing its intention to extend the stay "for two years" and "to look broadly at the entire 2016 Rule" during its reconsideration proceeding.

Environmental groups then filed an emergency motion in the D.C. Circuit for a judicial stay of EPA's administrative stay. They argued that the agency stay violated section 307 (d)(7)(B) because "all of the issues Administrator Pruitt identified could have been, *and actually were*, raised and extensively deliberated during the comment period."

The D.C. Circuit (Judge Brown dissenting) held that the stay was "arbitrary, capricious, [and] in excess of statutory authority" under the CAA. The majority dealt first with the argument that the court lacked jurisdiction because the agency's stay was temporary and thus not a final agency action under the CAA or APA. The majority noted that imposition of the stay suspended the rule's compliance deadlines, and that the agency had proposed to extend the stay for years. Accordingly, the stay had a binding effect on legal obligations of regulated entities by relieving them of the otherwise-imminent need to comply with the new rule, and was "sufficiently final to warrant review" (quoting *Friedman v. FAA*, 841 F.3d 537, 542 (D.C. Cir. 2016)).

On the merits, the court dismissed EPA's assertion that it has "broad discretion" to reconsider its own rules. Invoking both the APA and the Supreme Court discussion in *Perez v. Mortgage Bankers Association* (see § 2(D)(1) of this chapter), the court emphasized that an agency issuing a legislative rule is itself bound by the rule until the rule is amended or revoked, and it may not alter such a rule without notice and comment. The court added that when EPA granted reconsideration and imposed the stay, it had not relied on its so-called inherent authority, but rather on § 307(d)(7)(B). Under *SEC v. Chenery* (see § 2(C) of this chapter), agency action is judged by a reviewing court based only on the grounds the agency relied on when it acted.

Turning to section 307(d)(7)(B) of the CAA, which sets forth circumstances under which EPA *must* reconsider a rule, the court noted that such mandatory reconsideration may occur only if a petitioner demonstrates (1) that it was *impracticable* to raise such objection within the notice and comment period, and (2) that the objection is of *central relevance* to the outcome of the rule. The court decided the case solely on the impracticability factor, which depends on "whether the final rule was a logical outgrowth of the NPRM." The court explained that "a final rule is the logical outgrowth of a proposed rule if interested parties should have anticipated that the change was possible and thus reasonably should have filed their comments on the subject during the notice-and-comment period."

The EPA had reconsidered the fugitive emissions rule and stayed its implementation on the grounds that industry groups had no opportunity to object to four aspects of the final rule: (1) the determination not to exempt low-production wells from its mandate; (2) the presentation of a process for demonstrating "alternate means of compliance" in the NPRM; (3) the requirement that a professional engineer certify proper design of closed vent systems; and (4) the conditioning of exemption from regulation for well-site pneumatic pumps based on certification that it was technically infeasible to route the pneumatic pump to a control device or a process.

The court examined at length the administrative record with respect to each of these four grounds. It concluded that industry groups had ample opportunity to comment on all four issues, and that "in several instances the agency incorporated those comments into the final rule." Because it was not "impracticable" for industry groups to have raised their objections during the notice and comment period, the EPA's contentions to the contrary were "inaccurate and . . . unreasonable" and its decision to stay the rule was "arbitrary and capricious."

In conclusion, the D.C. Circuit emphasized that although the agency had no statutory *obligation* to reconsider the methane leaks rule, nothing in the court's opinion limits EPA's authority to reconsider that rule and to proceed with its June 2017 NPRM as long as "the new policy is permissible under the statute, there are good reasons for it, and the agency *believes* it to be better." (quoting *FCC v. Fox Television Stations, Inc*, 556 U.S. 502, 515 (2009)).

NOTES ON CLEAN AIR COUNCIL *AND* EPA *EFFORTS TO ROLL BACK REGULATIONS*

1.   In April 2018, nine months after the Clean Air Council decision rejecting a stay of the agency rule to control methane leaks, fourteen states filed suit against the EPA for its failure to issue regulations establishing methane-control measures for existing wells, pipelines, storage tanks, pumping stations, and other facilities. The lawsuit responded to the agency's decision in March 2017 to cease collecting data from fossil fuel operations in connection with preparing relevant performance standards. See Steve Gorman, *EPA Sued by Fourteen States Over Delay in Methane Emission Standards,* Reuters, April 5, 2018, https://www.reuters.com/article/us-usa-epa-methane/epa-sued-by-14-states-over-delay-in-methane-emission-standards-idUSKCN1HC2X9.

2.   One of EPA's arguments in *Clean Air Council* was that it has "inherent authority to issue a brief stay of a final rule—that is not to issue a lawfully issued final rule—while it reconsiders it." The DC Circuit rejected this position on delegation grounds, concluding that agencies may act only pursuant to statutorily delegated authority and neither the CAA nor the APA grants authority to stay a duly promulgated legislative rule. What about 5 U.S.C. § 705? In that section, the APA states that "When an agency finds that justice so requires, it may postpone the effective date of action taken by it, pending judicial review." Requests for courts to stay agency action are essentially petitions for temporary injunctions aimed at preserving the status quo. Under traditional equitable principles, a reviewing court would assess the costs of moving from the status quo and the prospect of success in challenging the agency action, as well as the balance of harms and the effect of a stay on public interests. Should these same factors apply when an agency seeks to stay its own rule? If not, what should the agency have to show in order to meet the "justice so requires" standard?

In February 2016, the Supreme Court by a 5–4 vote stayed the EPA's "Clean Power Plan" (establishing emission guidelines for states to follow in regulating carbon dioxide from existing power plants). See *West Virginia v. Environmental Protection Agency*, 136 S.Ct. 1000 (2016) (mem). This was the first time the Court has stayed an agency rule that had not been reviewed by any lower court. Lisa Heinzerling maintained that the Court "has opened a new world of opportunity for those disappointed with agency regulations." *The Supreme Court's Clean-Power Power Grab*, 28 Geo. Envtl. L. Rev. 425, 439 (2016). Under what circumstances should that "world of opportunity" extend to agencies postponing implementation of their own duly promulgated rules?

3.   The decision in *Clean Air Council* is hardly the only instance in which federal courts rebuffed EPA Administrator Pruitt's efforts to reverse or stay prior court decisions or agency actions. The courts have struck down at least six efforts by the EPA to delay or

roll back Obama-era regulations. See Coral Davenport and Lisa Friedman, *In His Haste to Roll Back Rules, Scott Pruitt, EPA Chief, Risks His Agenda*, NY Times, April 7, 2018; https://www.nytimes.com/2018/04/07/climate/scott-pruitt-epa-rollbacks.html. In one further example, *In re Ozone Designation Litigation*, 286 F. Supp.3d 1082 (N.D.Cal 2018), the court granted summary judgment for environmental and health organization plaintiffs against the EPA. The district court concluded that the agency "failed to perform a non-discretionary duty" imposed by the CAA under the 2015 NAAQS (National Ambient Air Quality Standards) for ozone by letting the deadline for action pass without promulgating the final designation for each area of the country; the court ordered the EPA to comply within a six week period.

The agency also has proposed new rules that change the types of scientific data on which the EPA can base its rulemaking and the way it conducts cost-benefit analyses. See 83 Fed. Reg. 18768 (April 30, 2018). The proposal has been criticized by scientists and public health groups for its likely impact blocking agency use of landmark studies on the harmful effects of air pollution and pesticide exposure. See Juliet Eilperin & Brady Dennis, *Pruitt Unveils Controversial "Transparency" Rule Limiting What Research EPA Can Use*, Wash. Post, April 24, 2018, https://www.washingtonpost.com/news/energy-environment/wp/2018/04/24/pruitt-to-unveil-controversial-transparency-rule-limiting-what-research-epa-can-use/?noredirect=on&utm_term=.83c107881be5.

Assume arguendo that EPA is pursuing an agenda that seeks to stay or roll back prior agency rules, or to refuse to act when required to do so by statute. Should this consciously deregulatory agenda be viewed as an extension of presidential oversight of agency action, comparable to activities undertaken by OMB or OIRA? Why or why not? How likely is Congress to become more active in overseeing agency actions such as those identified?

C. JUDICIAL REVIEW OF AGENCY RULES AND ORDERS

Section 2 of this chapter approached agency-court relations under the APA from the standpoint of how agencies implement legislative policy. We examined the requirements agencies face and the procedural strategies and tactics they adopt to regulate or guide the conduct of private parties and the general public. We now focus on court-agency relations under the APA as a primary form of judicial monitoring and oversight.

Judicial review of *agency action* under the APA is separate from judicial review of whether *agency statutory interpretation* is persuasive or reasonable. See chapter 9 § 2(E) (Notes to *Brand X*). Although both forms of review seek to assure that an agency's decision is sufficiently attentive to applicable congressional text and purposes, APA review focuses more on whether the agency's action includes an adequate response in *procedural terms* to material questions raised by commenters, and whether that response has a plausible *factual basis*. In short, courts reviewing agency action face a distinct set of challenges as they seek to assure that agencies have followed through on legislative policies, complied with procedural requirements, and adequately protected the interests of the affected public.

If the federal courts can use their review powers under the APA to enforce Congress's original directives upon the agency, then Congress presumably could feel more comfortable about delegating lawmaking authority to those agencies.

Consistent with this idea and with the further idea that judicial review can counteract "capture" of the agency by "special interests," appellate judges in the 1960s and 1970s grew more aggressive, especially in the Court of Appeals for the District of Columbia Circuit. The main developments were (1) the establishment of a strong presumption in favor of judicial review of agency action or inaction, and the enlargement of the class of interests which can invoke judicial review; (2) more searching judicial review based upon a detailed agency justification for its decision, including an indication that reasonable alternatives were considered; and (3) judicial policing of informal lobbying of agency officials by special interests. See Richard Stewart, *The Reformation of American Administrative Law*, 88 Harv. L. Rev. 1669, 1716 (1975). As you examine these developments, consider the drawbacks of expanded judicial review.

1. *Expanding Judicial Review: The "Hard Look Doctrine."* The APA explicitly provides for judicial review of discretionary agency action under §§ 702–06. Formal adjudication and rulemaking must be supported by "substantial evidence"; informal action, including notice and comment rulemaking, must not be "arbitrary and capricious." In *Citizens to Preserve Overton Park, Inc. v. Volpe*, 401 U.S. 402 (1971), the Supreme Court applied the arbitrary and capricious standard in the context of an informal adjudication, where there was a written record and only a few public hearings, none of which rose to the level of a judicial proceeding. The Department of Transportation Act of 1966, 80 Stat. 931, codified at 49 U.S.C. § 1653(f) (1964, Supp. V, 1969), and the Federal-Aid Highway Act of 1966, 80 Stat. 771, codified at 23 U.S.C. § 138 (1964, Supp. V, 1969), prohibited the Secretary of Transportation from authorizing the use of federal funds to finance construction of highways through public parks if a "feasible and prudent" alternative route existed. Proposed Interstate 40 would have cut across Overton Park, a 342-acre park in Memphis, Tennessee. Pursuant to the above statutes, the Secretary approved the highway project in 1968; concerned citizens and a national environmental group sued the Secretary, on the ground that it would be "feasible and prudent" to route I-40 around Overton Park.

The Supreme Court, in an opinion by Justice Marshall, determined that review should address whether the Secretary's action was "arbitrary or capricious" under APA § 706(2)(A). To determine this, the reviewing court should conduct a review that is "thorough, probing, in-depth" and "must consider whether the [agency] decision was based on a consideration of the relevant factors and whether there has been a clear error of judgment. * * * Although this inquiry into the facts is to be searching and careful, the ultimate standard of review is a narrow one. The court is not empowered to substitute its judgment for that of the agency." On remand, the Secretary was ultimately unable to justify his decision and so declined to approve the parkland route. See *Citizens to Preserve Overton Park, Inc. v. Brinegar*, 494 F.2d 1212 (6th Cir. 1974), cert. denied, 421 U.S. 991 (1975).

The judicial scrutiny in *Overton Park* become known as the *hard look doctrine*, because courts scrutinize agency rationales and justifications so closely. See Harold Leventhal, *Environmental Decisionmaking and the Role of the Courts*, 122 U. Pa. L. Rev. 509 (1973); *Ethyl Corp. v. EPA*, 541 F.2d 1, 68–69 (D.C. Cir. 1976) (Leventhal, J., concurring). Hard-look review requires that the agency examine all relevant evidence, explain its decisions in detail, justify departures from past practices, and consider all reasonable alternatives before reaching a final policy decision. Courts in most cases do not pass on the merits of the decision, merely the support the agency provides. In some cases, a rule remanded to the agency for further consideration is adopted again in similar form, but the agency provides a better explanation.

The hard look doctrine is not without its critics. Peter Strauss has reassessed *Overton Park*[65] and found Justice Marshall's interpretation of the statutory directive to be in conflict with the statute's legislative history which assumed that the Secretary would consider the importance of the parkland, along with cost, community disruption, and other factors. The Secretary did consider park values, and plans were changed several times in response to park concerns, but this was not enough for Justice Marshall. Strauss argues that by requiring that parklands be given paramount rather than ordinary consideration, the Court was imposing values by judicial dictate on the Secretary that were not clearly those Congress had put into the statute. Strauss maintains that the political balance between park values and efficient roadbuilding values was disrupted by the Court's hurried, blunderbuss decision.

The Supreme Court struck a different balance regarding review of agency enforcement decisions. In *Heckler v. Chaney*, 470 U.S. 821 (1985), the Court upheld the refusal by the Food and Drug Administration (FDA) to investigate the applicability of the federal food and drug standards to the use of lethal injections in some states as their means of imposing the death penalty. Justice Rehnquist's opinion for the Court stated that an agency's decision not to prosecute or enforce, whether through civil or criminal process, is a decision generally committed to an agency's absolute discretion. "[A]n agency decision not to enforce often involves a complicated balancing of a number of factors which are peculiarly within its expertise. Thus, the agency must not only assess whether a violation has occurred, but whether agency resources are best spent on this violation or another, whether the agency is likely to succeed if it acts, whether the particular enforcement action requested best fits the agency's overall policies, and indeed, whether the agency has enough resources to undertake the action at all." Additionally, when an agency refuses to prosecute, "it generally does not exercise its *coercive* power over an individual's liberty or property rights, and thus does not infringe upon areas that courts often are called upon to protect." (emphasis in original).

2.   *Softening "Hard Look."* Courts began to soften the hard look doctrine out of concerns that aggressive review of agency policy would lead to ossification because second guessing by nonexpert courts undermined the agencies' ability to act decisively on important new policies. See e.g., *Syracuse Peace Council v. FCC*, 867 F.2d 654 (D.C. Cir. 1989). In one example of a soft-glance rather than hard-look analysis, Judge Posner upheld regulations adopted by OSHA regulating occupational exposure to blood-borne pathogens, a rule designed to protect health care workers from hepatitis and AIDS. See *Am. Dental Ass'n v. Martin*, 984 F.2d 823 (7th Cir. 1993), cert. denied, 510 U.S. 859 (1993). Posner stated that much regulation occurs

---

[65]   See Peter Strauss, *Revisiting* Overton Park: *Political and Judicial Controls over Administrative Actions Affecting the Community*, 39 U.C.L.A. L. Rev. 1251 (1992), deepened in Strauss, Citizens to Preserve Overton Park v. Volpe—*Of Politics and Law, Young Lawyers and the Highway Goliath*, in *Administrative Law Stories* 258–332 (Peter Strauss ed., 2006).

under conditions of uncertainty, and in such cases, the conclusions of experts on technical issues "are entitled to respect by the nonspecialist, biomedically unsophisticated Article III judiciary, at least in the absence of a more systematic showing of harms" by the challengers.

3.   *Procedural Requirements in Rulemaking Proceedings.* When an agency engages in informal rulemaking, it is acting like a legislature (APA § 553) and so does not have to follow the formal procedures of adjudication (APA § 554), where the agency is acting like a court. Under a benign view of agency decisionmaking, this makes perfect sense. But there are also concerns that the agency may be captured by special interests, "corrupting" the informal rulemaking process. In the 1970s, the D.C. Circuit considered procedural ways to open up such rulemaking, a process ostensibly halted by the Supreme Court in 1978. See Gillian Metzger, *The Story of* Vermont Yankee: *A Cautionary Tale of Judicial Review and Nuclear Waste*, in *Administrative Law Stories* 124–67 (Peter Strauss ed., 2006).

Take for example the D.C. Circuit's decision in *Home Box Office, Inc. v. FCC*, 567 F.2d 9 (D.C. Cir. 1977). The Court overturned the FCC's rules because of evidence that the public docket for the proposed rules was "a sham" and the "real" deliberations had been conducted privately between the Commissioners and industry representatives. The Court read *Overton Park* to require that agency decisions be rendered upon a record that discloses all relevant evidence and argumentation that the agency considered. Hence, a decision in which there were undisclosed *ex parte* communications was invalid. Yet, the Court ignored considerations that the dialogue between administrators and the private sector is a necessary part of regulation, which led to much of the decision's criticisms.

Unlike the D.C. Circuit, the Supreme Court was hostile to "judicializing" rulemaking proceedings. See, for example, *United States v. Fla. E. Coast Ry. Co.*, 410 U.S. 224 (1973), discussed at length in § 2(A)(3) of this chapter. And in *Vermont Yankee Nuclear Power Corp. v. Natural Resources Defense Council, Inc.*, 435 U.S. 519 (1978), the Court expressed serious misgivings about these judicially imposed hybrid procedures. See Metzger, *The Story of* Vermont Yankee, for a comprehensive analysis.

In reviewing a rule promulgated by the Atomic Energy Commission, the D.C. Circuit in *Vermont Yankee* found that although the Commission had followed all the § 553 procedures for informal rulemaking, the procedures were inadequate overall; the court remanded for the agency to follow procedures permitting greater public scrutiny of information upon which the Commission relied. The Supreme Court, in an opinion by Justice Rehnquist, reversed the D.C. Circuit and pointedly criticized its "Monday morning quarterbacking" of the agency's procedures. Rehnquist cited *Florida East Coast Railway* for the proposition that § 553 of the APA "established the maximum procedural requirements which Congress was willing to have the courts impose upon agencies in conducting rulemaking procedures." Moreover, apart from the APA, "this Court has for more than four decades emphasized that the formulation of procedures was basically to be left within the discretion of the agencies to which Congress had confided the responsibility for substantive judgments." The Court reversed the D.C. Circuit's invalidation of the procedures used in the agency's informal rulemaking and remanded to the D.C. Circuit to review the rule on the merits.

Notwithstanding *Vermont Yankee*, federal courts of appeals have continued to impose procedural requirements on "informal" rulemaking. They have done so, however, under cover of liberally "interpreting" the notice-and-comment requirements of § 553, rather than imposing them as a matter of administrative common law. See Gary Lawson, *Federal Administrative Law* 240–83 (4th ed. 2007) (disapproving); Metzger, *Story of* Vermont Yankee (acquiescent).

MOTOR VEHICLE MANUFACTURERS ASS'N V. STATE FARM MUTUAL AUTOMOBILE INS. CO.

Supreme Court of the United States, 1983.
463 U.S. 29, 103 S.Ct. 2856, 77 L. Ed. 2d 443.

JUSTICE WHITE delivered the opinion of the Court.

The development of the automobile gave Americans unprecedented freedom to travel, but exacted a high price for enhanced mobility. Since 1929, motor vehicles have been the leading cause of accidental deaths and injuries in the United States. * * * Congress responded by enacting the National Traffic and Motor Vehicle Safety Act of 1966. The Act, created for the purpose of "reduc[ing] traffic accidents and deaths and injuries to persons resulting from traffic accidents," 15 U.S.C. § 1381, directs the Secretary of Transportation or his delegate to issue motor vehicle safety standards that "shall be practicable, shall meet the need for motor vehicle safety, and shall be stated in objective terms." 15 U.S.C. § 1392(a). In issuing these standards, the Secretary is directed to consider "relevant available motor vehicle safety data," whether the proposed standard "is reasonable, practicable and appropriate" for the particular type of motor vehicle, and the "extent to which such standards will contribute to carrying out the purposes" of the Act. 15 U.S.C. § 1392(f)(1), (3), (4).

The Act also authorizes judicial review under the provisions of the Administrative Procedure Act (APA), 5 U.S.C. § 706, of all "orders establishing, amending, or revoking a Federal motor vehicle safety standard," 15 U.S.C. § 1392(b). Under this authority, we review today whether NHTSA acted arbitrarily and capriciously in revoking the requirement in Motor Vehicle Safety Standard 208 that new motor vehicles produced after September 1982 be equipped with passive restraints to protect the safety of the occupants of the vehicle in the event of a collision. Briefly summarized, we hold that the agency failed to present an adequate basis and explanation for rescinding the passive restraint requirement and that the agency must either consider the matter further or adhere to or amend Standard 208 along lines which its analysis supports.

[I]   As originally issued by the Department of Transportation in 1967, Standard 208 simply required the installation of seatbelts in all automobiles. 32 Fed. Reg. 2408, 2415 (Feb. 3, 1967). It soon became apparent that the level of seatbelt use was too low to reduce traffic injuries to an acceptable level. The Department therefore began consideration of "passive occupant restraint systems"—devices that do not depend for their effectiveness upon any action taken by the occupant except that necessary to operate the vehicle. Two types of automatic crash protection emerged:

automatic seatbelts and airbags. The automatic seatbelt is a traditional safety belt, which when fastened to the interior of the door remains attached without impeding entry or exit from the vehicle, and deploys automatically without any action on the part of the passenger. The airbag is an inflatable device concealed in the dashboard and steering column. It automatically inflates when a sensor indicates that deceleration forces from an accident have exceeded a preset minimum, then rapidly deflates to dissipate those forces. The life-saving potential of these devices was immediately recognized, and in 1977, after substantial on-the-road experience with both devices, it was estimated by NHTSA that passive restraints could prevent approximately 12,000 deaths and over 100,000 serious injuries annually, 42 Fed. Reg. 34,298.

In 1969, the Department formally proposed a standard requiring the installation of passive restraints, 34 Fed. Reg. 11,148 (July 2, 1969), thereby commencing a lengthy series of proceedings. In 1970, the agency revised Standard 208 to include passive protection requirements, 35 Fed. Reg. 16,927 (Nov. 3, 1970), and in 1972, the agency amended the standard to require full passive protection for all front seat occupants of vehicles manufactured after August 15, 1975. 37 Fed. Reg. 3911 (Feb. 24, 1972). In the interim, vehicles built between August 1973 and August 1975 were to carry either passive restraints or lap and shoulder belts coupled with an "ignition interlock" that would prevent starting the vehicle if the belts were not connected. On review, the agency's decision to require passive restraints was found to be supported by "substantial evidence" and upheld. *Chrysler Corp. v. Dep't of Transp.*, 472 F.2d 659 (6th Cir. 1972).

In preparing for the upcoming model year, most car makers chose the "ignition interlock" option, a decision which was highly unpopular, and led Congress to amend the Act to prohibit a motor vehicle safety standard from requiring or permitting compliance by means of an ignition interlock or a continuous buzzer designed to indicate that safety belts were not in use. Motor Vehicle and Schoolbus Safety Amendments of 1974, Pub. L. 93–492, § 109, 88 Stat. 1482, 15 U.S.C. § 1410b(b). The 1974 Amendments also provided that any safety standard that could be satisfied by a system other than seatbelts would have to be submitted to Congress where it could be vetoed by concurrent resolution of both houses. 15 U.S.C. § 1410b(b)(2).

The effective date for mandatory passive restraint systems was extended for a year until August 31, 1976. 40 Fed. Reg. 16,217 (April 10, 1975); *id.* at 33,977 (Aug. 13, 1975). But in June 1976, Secretary of Transportation William T. Coleman, Jr., initiated a new rulemaking on the issue, 41 Fed. Reg. 24,070 (June 9, 1976). After hearing testimony and reviewing written comments, Coleman extended the optional alternatives indefinitely and suspended the passive restraint requirement. Although he found passive restraints technologically and economically feasible, the Secretary based his decision on the expectation that there would be widespread public resistance to the new systems. He instead proposed a demonstration project involving up to 500,000 cars installed with passive restraints, in order to smooth the way for public acceptance of mandatory passive restraints at a later date. Department of Transportation, *The Secretary's Decision Concerning Motor Vehicle Occupant Crash Protection* (December 6, 1976).

Coleman's successor as Secretary of Transportation disagreed. Within months of assuming office, Secretary Brock Adams decided that the demonstration project was unnecessary. He issued a new mandatory passive restraint regulation, known as Modified Standard 208. 42 Fed. Reg. 34,289 (July 5, 1977); 42 CFR § 571.208 (1978). The Modified Standard mandated the phasing in of passive restraints beginning with large cars in model year 1982 and extending to all cars by model year 1984. The two principal systems that would satisfy the Standard were airbags and passive belts; the choice of which system to install was left to the manufacturers. In *Pacific Legal Foundation v. Department of Transportation*, 593 F.2d 1338 (D.C. Cir.), cert. denied, 444 U.S. 830 (1979), the Court of Appeals upheld Modified Standard 208 as a rational, nonarbitrary regulation consistent with the agency's mandate under the Act. The standard also survived scrutiny by Congress, which did not exercise its authority under the legislative veto provision of the 1974 Amendments.

Over the next several years, the automobile industry geared up to comply with Modified Standard 208. As late as July, 1980, NHTSA reported:

> "On the road experience in thousands of vehicles equipped with airbags and automatic safety belts has confirmed agency estimates of the life-saving and injury-preventing benefits of such systems. When all cars are equipped with automatic crash protection systems, each year an estimated 9,000 more lives will be saved and tens of thousands of serious injuries will be prevented."

NHTSA, Automobile Occupant Crash Protection, Progress Report No. 3, p. 4. In February 1981, however, Secretary of Transportation Andrew Lewis reopened the rulemaking due to changed economic circumstances and, in particular, the difficulties of the automobile industry. 46 Fed. Reg. 12,033 (Feb. 12, 1981). Two months later, the agency ordered a one-year delay in the application of the standard to large cars, extending the deadline to September 1982, 46 Fed. Reg. 21,172 (April 9, 1981) and at the same time, proposed the possible rescission of the entire standard. 46 Fed. Reg. 21,205 (April 9, 1981). After receiving written comments and holding public hearings, NHTSA issued a final rule (Notice 25) that rescinded the passive restraint requirement contained in Modified Standard 208.

[II] In a statement explaining the rescission, NHTSA maintained that it was no longer able to find, as it had in 1977, that the automatic restraint requirement would produce significant safety benefits. Notice 25, 46 Fed. Reg. 53,419 (Oct. 29, 1981). This judgment reflected not a change of opinion on the effectiveness of the technology, but a change in plans by the automobile industry. In 1977, the agency had assumed that airbags would be installed in 60% of all new cars and automatic seatbelts in 40%. By 1981 it became apparent that automobile manufacturers planned to install the automatic seatbelts in approximately 99% of the new cars. For this reason, the life-saving potential of airbags would not be realized. Moreover, it now appeared that the overwhelming majority of passive belts planned to be installed by manufacturers could be detached easily and left that way permanently. Passive belts, once detached, then required "the same type of affirmative action that is the stumbling block to obtaining high usage levels of manual belts." 46 Fed. Reg., at 53,421. For this reason, the agency concluded that there was no longer a basis for reliably predicting that the standard would lead to any significant increased usage of restraints at all.

In view of the possibly minimal safety benefits, the automatic restraint requirement no longer was reasonable or practicable in the agency's view. The requirement would require approximately $1 billion to implement and the agency did not believe it would be reasonable to impose such substantial costs on manufacturers and consumers without more adequate assurance that sufficient safety benefits would accrue. In addition, NHTSA concluded that automatic restraints might have an adverse effect on the public's attitude toward safety. Given the high expense and limited benefits of detachable belts, NHTSA feared that many consumers would regard the standard as an instance of ineffective regulation, adversely affecting the public's view of safety regulation and, in particular, "poisoning . . . popular sentiment toward efforts to improve occupant restraint systems in the future." 46 Fed. Reg., at 53424.

[The United States Court of Appeals for the District of Columbia Circuit invalidated the agency's rule rescinding the passive restraint requirement, on the ground that it was arbitrary and capricious and therefore in violation of the APA. 680 F.2d 206 (1982).] *invalid. agency rule rescinding passive restraint req.*

[III] The Court held that the APA fully applied to NHTSA's rulemaking proceeding, and that a reviewing court has an obligation to set aside any rule found to be "arbitrary, capricious, an abuse of discretion, or otherwise not in accordance with law." 5 U.S.C. § 706(2)(A); see *Overton Park*. The Court rejected Motor Vehicle's argument that an agency's rescission of a rule should be governed by the same narrow standard as the agency's refusal to issue a rule in the first place.]

[Justice White explained the "arbitrary and capricious" standard of review.] [T]he agency must examine the relevant data and articulate a satisfactory explanation for its action including a "rational connection between the facts found and the choice made." *Burlington Truck Lines Inc. v. United States*, 371 U.S. 156, 168 (1962). In reviewing that explanation, we must "consider whether the decision was based on a consideration of the relevant factors and whether there has been a clear error of judgment." *Bowman Transp. Inc. v. Arkansas-Best Freight System*, [419 U.S. 281, 285 (1974)]. Normally, an agency rule would be arbitrary and capricious if the agency has relied on factors which Congress has not intended it to consider, entirely failed to consider an important aspect of the problem, offered an explanation for its decision that runs counter to the evidence before the agency, or is so implausible that it could not be ascribed to a difference in view or the product of agency expertise. The reviewing court should not attempt itself to make up for such deficiencies; we may not supply a reasoned basis for the agency's action that the agency itself has not given. * * * For purposes of these cases, it is also relevant that Congress required a record of the rulemaking proceedings to be compiled and submitted to a reviewing court, 15 U.S.C. § 1394, and intended that agency findings under the Motor Vehicle Safety Act would be supported by "substantial evidence on the record considered as a whole," S. Rep. No. 1301, 89th Cong., 2d Sess. 8 (1966); H.R. Rep. No. 1776, 89th Cong., 2d Sess. 21 (1966).

[In Part IV, Justice White rejected the lower court's requirement that NHTSA was obligated to provide "increasingly clear and convincing reasons" for its action. The Court of Appeals relied on post-1974 congressional signals (such as Congress's failure to override the Carter-era NHTSA initiatives) to infer a "congressional commitment to the concept of automatic crash protection devices for vehicle occupants." Justice White found the lower court's reading of the materials misguided. Also, "this Court has never suggested that the *standard* of review is enlarged or diminished by subsequent congressional action. While an agency's interpretation of a statute may be confirmed or ratified by subsequent congressional failure to change that interpretation, *Bob Jones University* [Chapters 5, § 3(B) and 7, § 5(F)], in the cases before us, even an unequivocal ratification—short of statutory incorporation— of the passive restraint standard would not connote approval or disapproval of an agency's later decision to rescind the regulation. That decision remains subject to the arbitrary and capricious standard."]

[V] The ultimate question before us is whether NHTSA's rescission of the passive restraint requirement of Standard 208 was arbitrary and capricious. We conclude, as did the Court of Appeals, that it was. We also conclude, but for somewhat different reasons, that further consideration of the issue by the agency is therefore required. * * *

[A] The first and most obvious reason for finding the rescission arbitrary and capricious is that NHTSA apparently gave no consideration whatever to modifying the Standard to require that airbag technology be utilized. Standard 208 sought to achieve automatic crash protection by requiring automobile manufacturers to install either of two passive restraint devices: airbags or automatic seatbelts. There was no suggestion in the long rulemaking process that led to Standard 208 that if only one of these options were feasible, no passive restraint standard should be promulgated. Indeed, the agency's original proposed Standard contemplated the installation of inflatable restraints in all cars. Automatic belts were added as a means of complying with the standard because they were believed to be as effective as airbags in achieving the goal of occupant crash protection. 36 Fed. Reg. 12,858, 12,859 (July 8, 1971). At that time, the passive belt approved by the agency could not be detached. Only later, at a manufacturer's behest, did the agency approve of the detachability feature—and only after assurances that the feature would not compromise the safety benefits of the restraint. Although it was then foreseen that 60% of the new cars would contain airbags and 40% would have automatic seatbelts, the ratio between the two was not significant as long as the passive belt would also assure greater passenger safety.

The agency has now determined that the detachable automatic belts will not attain anticipated safety benefits because so many individuals will detach the mechanism. Even if this conclusion were acceptable in its entirety, standing alone it would not justify any more than an amendment of Standard 208 to disallow compliance by means of the one technology which will not provide effective passenger protection. It does not cast doubt on the need for a passive restraint standard or upon the efficacy of airbag technology. In its most recent rulemaking, the agency again acknowledged the lifesaving potential of the airbag:

"The agency has no basis at this time for changing its earlier conclusions in 1976 and 1977 that basic airbag technology is sound and has been sufficiently demonstrated to be effective in those vehicles in current use. . . ."

NHTSA Final Regulatory Impact Analysis (RIA) at XI-4 (Oct. 1981). Given the effectiveness ascribed to airbag technology by the agency, the mandate of the Act to achieve traffic safety would suggest that the logical response to the faults of detachable seatbelts would be to require the installation of airbags. At the very least this alternative way of achieving the objectives of the Act should have been addressed and adequate reasons given for its abandonment. But the agency not only did not require compliance through airbags, it also did not even consider the possibility in its 1981 rulemaking. Not one sentence of its rulemaking statement discusses the airbags-only option. * * * [W]hat we said in *Burlington Truck Lines v. United States* is apropos here:

"There are no findings and no analysis here to justify the choice made, no indication of the basis on which the [agency] exercised its expert discretion. We are not prepared to and the Administrative Procedure Act will not permit us to accept such . . . practice. . . . Expert discretion is the lifeblood of the administrative process, but 'unless we make the requirements for administrative action strict and demanding, *expertise*, the strength of modern government, can become a monster which rules with no practical limits on its discretion."

We have frequently reiterated that an agency must cogently explain why it has exercised its discretion in a given manner, and we reaffirm this principle again today.

The automobile industry has opted for the passive belt over the airbag, but surely it is not enough that the regulated industry has eschewed a given safety device. For nearly a decade, the automobile industry waged the regulatory equivalent of war against the airbag and lost—the inflatable restraint was proved sufficiently effective. Now the automobile industry has decided to employ a seatbelt system which will not meet the safety objectives of Standard 208. This hardly constitutes cause to revoke the Standard itself. Indeed, the Motor Vehicle Safety Act was necessary because the industry was not sufficiently responsive to safety concerns. The Act intended that safety standards not depend on current technology and could be "technology-forcing" in the sense of inducing the development of superior safety design. If, under the statute, the agency should not defer to the industry's failure to develop safer cars, which it surely should not do, *a fortiori* it may not revoke a safety standard which can be satisfied by current technology simply because the industry has opted for an ineffective seatbelt design. * * *

[In Part V-B, Justice White ruled that NHTSA was "too quick to dismiss the safety benefits of automatic seatbelts." Although an agency may decline to issue and may revoke a safety standard on the basis of serious uncertainties about its efficacy, those uncertainties must be supported in the administrative record and reasonably explained. In this case, there was no direct evidence in the record supporting NHTSA's finding that detachable automatic belts cannot be predicted to yield a substantial increase in usage. Evidence in the record revealed more than a doubling of seat belt use under those circumstances. For one example, Volkswagen between 1975 and 1980 sold 350,000 Rabbits equipped with passive seatbelts guarded by an ignition interlock. NHTSA found that seatbelt use in Rabbits averaged 34% where the cars had regular manual belts, and 84% for the detachable passive belts. Although Justice White maintained that the agency had discretion to refuse to generalize from studies of Rabbit drivers to the general population of drivers, the agency was required to consider a fact that it neglected but that critically distinguishes detachable automatic belts and ordinary manual ones: A detachable passive belt requires an affirmative act to detach it, while a manual belt can be safely ignored. "Thus, inertia—a factor which the agency's own studies have found significant in explaining the current low usage rates for seatbelts—works in *favor* of, not *against*, use of the protective device." This would suggest that seatbelt use by occasional users would be substantially increased by detachable passive belts. "Whether this is in fact the case is a matter for the agency to decide, but it must bring its expertise to bear on the question."]

The agency is correct to look at the costs as well as the benefits of Standard 208. The agency's conclusion that the incremental costs of the requirements were no longer reasonable was predicated on its prediction that the safety benefits of the regulation might be minimal. Specifically, the agency's fears that the public may resent paying more for the automatic belt systems is expressly dependent on the assumption that detachable automatic belts will not produce more than "negligible safety benefits." 46 Fed. Reg., at 53,424. When the agency reexamines its findings as to the likely increase in seatbelt usage, it must also reconsider its judgment of the reasonableness of the monetary and other costs associated with the Standard. In reaching its judgment, NHTSA should bear in mind that Congress intended safety to be the preeminent factor under the Motor Vehicle Safety Act. [Quoting committee reports for the Safety Act.] * * *

JUSTICE REHNQUIST, with whom THE CHIEF JUSTICE [BURGER], JUSTICE POWELL, and JUSTICE O'CONNOR join, concurring in part and dissenting in part.

I join Parts I, II, III, IV, and V-A of the Court's opinion. In particular, I agree that, since the airbag and continuous spool automatic seatbelt were explicitly approved in the standard the agency was rescinding, the agency should explain why it declined to leave those requirements intact. In this case, the agency gave no explanation at all. Of course, if the agency can provide a rational explanation, it may adhere to its decision to rescind the entire standard.

I do not believe, however, that NHTSA's view of detachable automatic seatbelts was arbitrary and capricious. The agency adequately explained its decision to rescind the standard insofar as it was satisfied by detachable belts.

The statute that requires the Secretary of Transportation to issue motor vehicle safety standards also requires that "[e]ach such ... standard shall be practicable [and] shall meet the need for motor vehicle safety." 15 U.S.C. § 1392(a). The Court rejects the agency's explanation for its conclusion that there is substantial uncertainty whether requiring installation of detachable automatic belts would substantially increase seatbelt usage. The agency chose not to rely on a study showing a substantial increase in seatbelt usage in cars equipped with automatic seatbelts and an ignition interlock to prevent the car from being operated when the belts were not in place *and* which were voluntarily purchased with this equipment by consumers. It is reasonable for the agency to decide that this study does not support any conclusion concerning the effect of automatic seatbelts that are installed in all cars whether the consumer wants them or not and are not linked to an ignition interlock system.

The Court rejects this explanation because "there would seem to be grounds to believe that seatbelt use by occasional users will be substantially increased by the detachable passive belts," and the agency did not adequately explain its rejection of these grounds. It seems to me that the agency's explanation, while by no means a model, is adequate. The agency acknowledged that there would probably be some increase in belt usage, but concluded that the increase would be small and not worth the cost of mandatory detachable automatic belts. 46 Fed. Reg. 53,421–54,323 (1981). The agency's obligation is to articulate a " 'rational connection between the facts found and the choice made.' " I believe it has met this standard. * * *

cost / benefit?

The agency's changed view of the standard seems to be related to the election of a new President of a different political party. It is readily apparent that the responsible members of one administration may consider public resistance and uncertainties to be more important than do their counterparts in a previous administration. A change in administration brought about by the people casting their votes is a perfectly reasonable basis for an executive agency's reappraisal of the costs and benefits of its programs and regulations. As long as the agency remains within the bounds established by Congress, it is entitled to assess administrative records and evaluate priorities in light of the philosophy of the administration.

NOTES ON STATE FARM

1.   *Right or Wrong?* Did the Court do the right thing in this case—either from the Court's point of view, or the nation's? Write down your answer in the margin, and read on.

No! add belt seat belt

2.   *The Proper Role of the Judiciary in the Implementation of Public Policy?* In light of the national experience with implementation of the Safety Act, what do you think the role of the Court should be: (1) Agent of Congress? If so, which Congress—the enacting one, the amending one, or the current one? (2) Independent principal, imposing the Court's own values, thwarting agencies implementing bad policies, and rewarding agencies that protect the Court's conception of the public interest? (3) Independent principal, imposing rule of law values? If so, what does the rule of law require in *State Farm?*

In chapter 11 of Jerry Mashaw & David Harfst, *The Struggle for Auto Safety* (1990), the authors ask this question: Does the participation of the judiciary in the statutory implementation game advance the public interest? Their analysis suggests some doubt that the Court performs a useful role. The judiciary is the forum of choice whenever the government tries to upset traditional ways of doing things (ways easily translated into "rights"). Thus, the courts were a forum for the auto industry to harass the agency and delay implementation of its rules. The proceduralization of the rulemaking process rendered it less decisive and more vulnerable to shifts in public opinion and presidential leadership. Recall the wild shifts in Standard 208 from the Johnson Administration to the Nixon-Ford Administration to the Carter Administration to the Reagan Administration.

Adverse judicial decisions in the 1970s (the hard look decade) directly contributed to the interlock debacle and contributed less directly to an increasingly cautious attitude toward regulation. For example, *Chrysler* required "objective" testing standards that the agency's "dummy" regulations did not meet. This requirement discouraged the agency from imposing rules before it had "objective" scientific evidence well in hand, and thereby prevented the sort of experimentation and technology-forcing rules that the early experts thought were necessary to make genuine advances to reduce auto injuries and fatalities. More generally, the adverse judicial decisions discouraged NHTSA from proceeding by rulemaking, which had been the agency's original mandate and was probably its only hope for regulatory success. Favorable judicial decisions in response to NHTSA's recall campaigns, on the other hand, encouraged the agency to rely more and more heavily on that less effective regulatory mechanism. Like a Pavlovian dog, NHTSA was trained by the judiciary to quail at the thought of rules and salivate at the prospect of recalls.

Mashaw and Harfst are pessimistic about the role of the "legal culture" and of multiple principals in our administrative state of separated powers. "[T]he combination of congressional oversight and appropriations, Executive Office intervention and monitoring, and judicial review, has sharply limited the degree to which NHTSA could translate [its regulatory] aspirations into concrete technological requirements." *The Struggle for Auto Safety* 228. Do you find this level of pessimism persuasive? Jot down your initial thoughts in the margin, and then read the next note.

3. *The Aftermath of* State Farm. Transportation Secretary Elizabeth Dole initiated rulemaking to answer the Court's inquiries, and 7,800 comments were filed. On July 17, 1984, Dole issued the final rule, which (1) dropped mandatory airbags like a lead balloon and (2) required phasing in "automatic occupant restraints" (including airbags as an option for the manufacturer) between 1986 and 1989, unless (3) before April 1, 1989, two-thirds of the U.S. population are covered by state mandatory seat belt use laws meeting NHTSA's conditions. 49 Fed. Reg. 28,962–63 (1984).

With the support of the auto industry as well as new groups such as Mothers Against Drunk Driving (MADD), almost all the states adopted mandatory seatbelt laws—although most were careful *not* to satisfy the requirements of the Dole rule. "As a consequence, the American public got both airbags and mandatory use laws." Mashaw, *Law, Science, and Politics*, in *Administrative Law Stories* 385. Most surprisingly, *both* kinds of regulations captured the imagination of Americans. We the People started buckling up in record numbers *and* demanded more airbags from manufacturers than the law required. Professor Mashaw reports these results with no dimming of his customary pessimism, but do they suggest that the judiciary might play a productive role in the evolution of statutory policy?

Presumably in response (at least partly) to the public's persisting appetite, Congress and NHTSA have remained active on both airbags and seatbelts. The Intermodal Surface Transportation Efficiency Act of 1991 (ISTEA) ordered NHTSA to require both driver's side and passenger air-bags in all new vehicles by 1998 while subsequent legislation also ordered NHTSA to issue a rule that would minimize the risks to children and other occupants from injuries or deaths caused by airbags. NHTSA's 2000 regulation specified a range of design requirements to diminish the risk of serious airbag-induced injuries.

On seatbelts, ISTEA required equipping the driver and passenger side front seats with a lap/shoulder seat belt. In its 2002 Conference Report accompanying the DOT Appropriations Act, Congress requested that NHTSA study seat belt reminder technologies with a goal of further increasing seat belt use. Current federal standards require all new vehicles to be equipped with a "basic" seat belt reminder system, consisting of an audible signal and warning light that are activated immediately after the vehicle is started: the signal continues for four to eight seconds and the light for at least 60 seconds if the driver is not belted. Studies conducted by NHTSA in 2013 indicate that most vehicle manufacturers equip their vehicles with enhanced safety belt reminder systems.

Contrast all this congressional and agency involvement with Kevin McDonald's more skeptical account. Looking back on decades of expensive federal regulation of auto safety, he argues that NHTSA's focus on passive standards has reduced occupant fatality risk by only 15–20%, not an impressive amount given the tens of billions of dollars in cost and the much greater traffic safety achieved in Canada, Europe, and Australia, which focus on seat belts and driver error. *Shifting Out of Park: Moving Auto Safety from Recalls to Reason*, 18–19 (2006). See also Leonard Evans, *Traffic Safety* 117 (2004). Indeed, in the United States, reducing the speed limit has had greater safety effects than all the design changes posed by NHTSA. *Shifting Out of Park* 42 n.65.

FCC v. Fox Television Stations, Inc.

556 U.S. 502 (2009).

Federal law prohibits the broadcasting of "any . . . indecent . . . language," 18 U.S.C. § 1464, which includes expletives referring to sexual or excretory activity or organs, see *FCC v. Pacifica Foundation*, 438 U.S. 726 (1978). For many years, the FCC followed an announced regulatory approach that banned sexual or excretory "expletives" only if their use was "deliberate and repetitive"; mere "fleeting" expletives would generally be allowed. Even as the FCC expanded its indecency standard to encompass ever more words and phrases, it preserved this approach—until a 2006 FCC ruling against Fox. In that ruling, the FCC rejected its longstanding distinction between "expletive" and "literal" uses of terms like "fuck" as "artificial." Also, the FCC ended its tolerance for "fleeting" expletives, finding that they have the power to offend parents and children and that permitting them gives broadcasters too much freedom to be offensive.

Invoking the Supreme Court's decision in *State Farm*, the Second Circuit overturned the agency's order against Fox, on the ground that the FCC had not adequately explained why it was jettisoning its longstanding rule. The Supreme Court reversed in a 5–4 vote, in an opinion by **Justice Scalia**. "We find no basis in the Administrative Procedure Act or in our opinions for a requirement that all agency [action that changes prior policy] be subjected to more searching review. The Act mentions no such heightened standard. And our opinion in *State Farm* neither held nor implied that every agency action representing a policy change must be justified by reasons more substantial than those required to adopt a policy in the first instance. That case, which involved the rescission of a prior regulation, said only that such action requires 'a reasoned analysis for the change beyond that which may be required when an agency *does not act* in the first instance.' ([E]mphasis added). Treating failures to act and rescissions of prior action differently for purposes of the standard of review makes good sense, and has basis in the text of the [APA], which likewise treats the two separately. It instructs a reviewing court to 'compel agency action unlawfully withheld or unreasonably delayed,' 5 U.S.C. § 706(1), and to 'hold unlawful and set aside agency action, findings, and conclusions found to be [among other things] . . . arbitrary [or] capricious,' § 706(2)(A). The statute makes no distinction, however, between initial agency action and subsequent agency action undoing or revising that action.

"To be sure, the requirement that an agency provide reasoned explanation for its action would ordinarily demand that it display awareness that it *is* changing position. An agency may not, for example, depart from a prior policy *sub silentio* or simply disregard rules that are still on the books. And of course the agency must show that there are good reasons for the new policy. But it need not demonstrate to a court's satisfaction that the reasons for the new policy are *better* than the reasons for the old one; it suffices that the new policy is permissible under the statute, that there are good reasons for it, and that the agency *believes* it to be better, which the conscious change of course adequately indicates. This means that the agency need not always provide a more detailed justification than what would suffice for a new policy created on a blank slate. Sometimes it must—when, for example, its new policy rests upon factual findings that contradict those which underlay its prior policy; or when its prior policy has engendered serious reliance interests that must be taken into account. It would be arbitrary or capricious to ignore such matters. In such cases it is not that further justification is demanded by the mere fact of policy change; but that a reasoned explanation is needed for disregarding facts and circumstances that underlay or were engendered by the prior policy."

Under this understanding of the law, Justice Scalia ruled that the FCC's order was not "arbitrary and capricious." The FCC had "forthrightly acknowledged" that it was creating new policy and repudiating inconsistent prior actions taken by the Commission and staff. Also, the FCC's reasons for its decision were "entirely rational." It was reasonable for the FCC to conclude that the literal-expletive distinction was nonsensical given that both kinds of uses could cause offense and subject children to a harmful "first blow" of indecency; given technological advances, it was reasonable for the FCC to expect broadcasters to "bleep out" even fleeting expletives.

Justice Kennedy, whose vote was needed to obtain a majority, joined Justice Scalia's opinion as to all of the foregoing matters but issued a concurring opinion that adopted a more situation-specific approach. "Where there is a policy change the record may be much more developed because the agency based its prior policy on factual findings. In that instance, an agency's decision to change course may be arbitrary and capricious if the agency ignores or countermands its earlier factual findings without reasoned explanation for doing so. An agency cannot simply disregard contrary or inconvenient factual determinations that it made in the past, any more than it can ignore inconvenient facts when it writes on a blank slate." This is the lesson Justice Kennedy drew from *State Farm*. "The present case does not raise the concerns addressed in *State Farm*" because the FCC had based its prior policy not on factual findings, but on its interpretation of the Court's *Pacifica* ruling, and had given appropriate reasons for changing its policy.

Justice Stevens dissented in an opinion emphasizing the FCC's status as an independent agency, which, he believed, should be relatively free from political influence. He referred to "a strong presumption that the FCC's initial views, reflecting the informed judgment of independent commissioners with expertise in the regulated area, also reflect the views of the Congress that delegated the Commission authority to flesh out details not fully defined in the enacting statute." Justice Stevens also pointed to that fact that the rules adopted after *Pacifica* had been in effect for decades. "[B]roadcasters have a substantial interest in regulatory stability; the threat of crippling financial penalties looms large over these entities. The FCC's shifting and impermissibly vague indecency policy only imperils these broadcasters and muddles the regulatory landscape. It therefore makes eminent sense to require the Commission to justify why its prior policy is no longer sound before allowing it to change course."

Justice Breyer (joined by **Justices Stevens**, **Souter**, and **Ginsburg**) dissented. He started with the premise that, as an independent agency, the FCC was relatively insulated from political oversight. "That insulation helps to secure important governmental objectives, such as the constitutionally related objective of maintaining broadcast regulation that does not bend too readily before the political winds. But that agency's comparative freedom from ballot-box control makes it all the more important that courts review its decisionmaking to assure compliance with applicable provisions of the law—including law requiring that major policy decisions be based upon articulable reasons." Additionally, the agency must act consistently, and when it changes its own rules the agency must focus on the fact of change and explain the basis for that change.

"To explain a change requires more than setting forth reasons why the new policy is a good one. It also requires the agency to answer the question, 'Why did you change?' And a rational answer to this question typically requires a more complete explanation than would prove satisfactory were change itself not at issue." *State Farm* "requires the agency here to focus upon the reasons that led the agency to adopt the initial policy, and to explain why it now comes to a new judgment.

"I recognize that *sometimes* the ultimate explanation for a change may have to be, 'We now weigh the relevant considerations differently.' But at other times, an agency can and should say more. Where, for example, the agency rested its previous policy on particular factual findings; or where an agency rested its prior policy on its view of the governing law; or where an agency rested its previous policy on, say, a special need to coordinate with another agency, one would normally expect the agency to focus upon those earlier views of fact, of law, or of policy and explain why they are no longer controlling. Regardless, to say that the agency here must answer the question 'why change' is not to require the agency to provide a justification that is '*better* than the reasons for the old [policy].' It is only to recognize the obvious fact that *change* is sometimes (not always) a relevant background feature that sometimes (not always) requires focus (upon prior justifications) and explanation lest the adoption of the new policy (in that circumstance) be 'arbitrary, capricious, an abuse of discretion.'"

Like the Second Circuit, Justice Breyer concluded that the FCC's decision violated the *State Farm* requirement that an agency making a policy change "consider . . . important aspect[s] of the problem." In particular, he faulted the FCC for failing adequately to consider its new policy's First Amendment implications and potential impact on local broadcasters, many of whom might not be able to afford the technology necessary to "bleep out" fleeting expletives. Justice Breyer dismissed as inadequate the various reasons the FCC had adduced for its policy change—in particular, the claim that the literal-expletive distinction was nonsensical and the claim that the new policy better protects children against "the first blow" of broadcast indecency. Neither of these claims, Justice Breyer argued, could justify the FCC's policy *change* since both claims remained conclusory, failing to address the rationales underlying the prior policy.

NOTES ON STATE FARM V. FOX TELEVISION: WHEN ARE AGENCY POLICY SHIFTS "ARBITRARY"?

State Farm can be read as trying to strike a balance between two kinds of risks attending judicial review of agency policy changes. On the one hand, if courts are too deferential, there is the "yo-yo" risk that agency policies will fluctuate too frequently. On the other hand, if courts are too scrutinizing, there is the "ossification" risk that agencies will become too loath to change their policies. While the *State Farm* Court and the *Fox* dissenters seem to be more troubled by the yo-yo risk than the ossification risk, the *Fox* Court seems to have the opposite concern. Is *Fox* therefore inconsistent with *State Farm*? If so, can the inconsistency be justified?

1. *Independent Versus Executive Agencies?* The agency in *State Farm* was an executive department directly accountable to the President, while the agency in *Fox* was an independent agency. The dissenters, of course, argue that, because of the relative insulation of independent agencies from political pressures, policy changes made by independent agencies should be subject to *more* stringent judicial scrutiny than those made by executive agencies and, consequently, that *State Farm* applies a fortiori to *Fox*. But might the opposite be true? Might the relative insulation of independent agencies from political pressures lead one to expect their decisions to be generally *more* reasoned than the decisions of executive agencies and thus to merit *more* deference from courts?

Writing for a plurality of Justices (Part III-E of his opinion, which Justice Kennedy did not join), Justice Scalia argues that independent agencies like the FCC are subject to significant political pressures exerted by Congress through its oversight authority. Thus, "independent" agencies are not necessarily free from politics; the political pressure just comes from different branches of government. (In fact, Justice Scalia argues that the FCC's new policy in *Fox Television* was a direct consequence of congressional complaints that families were being subjected to inappropriate language during prime-time television.) But once again, might the opposite be true? Might the political accountability of independent agencies lead one to expect their decisions to be *as poorly* reasoned as those of executive agencies and thus to merit *as much* scrutiny from courts?

Should APA judicial review distinguish between the kinds of agency promulgating the evolving policy that is being reviewed?

2. *Facts Versus Law.* Rather than trying to distinguish *State Farm* and *Fox* based on the different kinds of *agencies* involved in each, one might try to distinguish them based on the different kinds of *policies* involved in each: whereas the policy in *State Farm* seemed to be based on a relatively technical cost-benefit factual analysis, the policy in *Fox* seemed to be based more on a social or moral judgment.

This difference might help to explain Justice Scalia's observation about the difficulty of obtaining data about the harmfulness of fleeting expletives in broadcasts and the comparative ease of obtaining data about the benefits of passive restraints in automobiles. Perhaps the FCC's policy change rested on the judgment that, whatever the tangible harm caused by fleeting expletives, it was simply *wrong* or *immoral* to expose the public—and especially children—to such indecency. If this was in fact the nature of the FCC's judgment, should courts be more willing to defer to it than they would be to defer to a more technical cost-benefit analysis?

Consider the historical analysis developed in Thomas Merrill, *Article III, Agency Adjudication, and the Origins of the Appellate Review Model in Administrative Law*, 111

Colum. L. Rev. 939 (2011). Professor Merrill demonstrates that the Supreme Court's twentieth century doctrines of administrative law were grounded in the model of judge-jury interaction: judges declared the law, and agencies (like juries) found facts, subject to lenient rational basis review. Under this model, which is the conceptual foundation for the APA, *Fox Television* might be a better candidate for hard look judicial review, because the key issues did not rest upon factual findings by the agency. As Professor Merrill notes, judicial review of informal rulemaking fits uneasily in the Supreme Court's classic model of administrative law. Perhaps *State Farm* might be defended on the ground that the Court was not "finding" facts but was merely sending the factfinders back to explain why they had rejected obvious alternatives.

Note also that the moral judgment represented in *Fox* raises important First Amendment concerns not present in the cost-benefit judgment represented in *State Farm*: Isn't a "fleeting expletive" a classic example of free expression? Cf. *Cohen v. California*, 403 U.S. 15 (1971) (invalidating state censorship of a young man with "Fuck the Draft" on his jacket). As *Pacifica* held, Congress has greater leeway to regulate indecent speech on the radio and television than in newspapers and the print media—but the regulatory authority is not unlimited. Shouldn't there be more specific guidance from Congress as to such important matters—or is Justice Scalia probably right, that Congress was behind the FCC's tighter rule?

Postscript. On remand, the Second Circuit ruled that the FCC's fleeting expletive policy, no longer confined to the earlier seven dirty words, violated the First Amendment. *Fox Television Stations, Inc. v. FCC*, 613 F.3d 317 (2d Cir. 2010). The Supreme Court reviewed the Second Circuit's decision and held, more narrowly, that the Commission's standards as applied were impermissibly vague, because it had failed to give Fox fair notice prior to the broadcasts that fleeting expletives and momentary nudity could be found actionably indecent. *FCC v. Fox Television Stations, Inc.*, 567 U.S. 239 (2012). The Court therefore did not reach the First Amendment implications of the indecency policy or reconsider its ruling in *Pacifica*.

3. *The Difference Process Might Make?* Should process distinguish *State Farm* from *Fox Television*? The obvious process difference is that the former was a rulemaking proceeding, while the latter was an agency adjudication—but that difference might just as easily cut the other way. That is, a shift in agency policy might be more legitimate in the kind of rulemaking that *State Farm* overturned than in an adjudication that *Fox Television* sanctioned. In notice-and-comment rulemaking, for example, a greater variety of interests will submit formal analyses, and the agency must consider them—in contrast to adjudication, where the agency must only respond to the parties' presentations.

Another possible process distinction is that the DOT's auto safety policy had been a political football through several administrations, and the *State Farm* Court might have felt that the agency needed to buckle down and take its law work more seriously. In contrast, perhaps, the FCC's policy was more stable over several administrations. Although the FCC was moving policy toward greater regulation in *Fox Television*, it was making a small step (expanding the longstanding policy to include "fleeting" expletives), and a step that was arguably justified by proliferation of fleeting expletives during prime time (when more children are watching TV) and by technology allowing networks to bleep out fleeting expletives.

Are any of these distinctions persuasive—or is *Fox Television* simply a precedent-narrowing reading of *State Farm*? Should *State Farm* be reframed, or even overruled?

Business Roundtable v. Securities and Exchange Commission

647 F.3d 1144 (D.C. Cir. 2011).

The "proxy process" is the means through which shareholders of a publicly traded corporation elect the company's board of directors at the annual meeting. Director nominations are placed on "proxy statements," documents that are mailed to investors before a shareholder meeting. Because most shareholders will vote by proxy (by submitting a vote electronically or in the mail instead of attending and voting at the actual meeting), anyone hoping to be elected to the board needs to be on the proxy statement. Typically, the nominees described on the proxy statements are chosen by the incumbent directors with little input from shareholders. A shareholder who wishes to nominate someone for the board may separately file his own proxy statement and solicit votes from all shareholders, thereby initiating a "proxy contest."

"Proxy access" provides an easier way for shareholders to gain seats on the company's board. This process grants shareholders the right to include their own nominees in the proxy statement, thereby avoiding the expensive project of circulating their own proxy statements. The SEC attempted to require proxy access by promulgating Rule 14a–11 after a notice and comment period. Facilitating Shareholder Director Nominations, 74 Fed. Reg. 29,024, 29,025–26 (2009). Rule 14a–11 requires that the nominating shareholder must have at least 3% of the voting power of the company's securities for at least three years prior to the nomination. Business Roundtable argued that Rule 14a–11 was inconsistent with both the APA and the governing statute, the Exchange Act.

Writing for the D.C. Circuit, **Judge Douglas Ginsburg** reviewed Rule 14a–11 according to *State Farm*'s interpretation of the arbitrary and capricious standard per APA § 706(2)(1). Further, the Exchange Act required the Commission to consider the rule's effect on "efficiency, competition, and capital formation" or else the rule is considered arbitrary and capricious. Judge Ginsburg found Rule 14a–11 to be arbitrary and capricious for a laundry list of reasons: "the Commission inconsistently and opportunistically framed the costs and benefits of the rule; failed adequately to quantify the certain costs or to explain why those costs could not be quantified; neglected to support its predictive judgments; contradicted itself; and failed to respond to substantial problems raised by commenters."

The court held first that the Commission underestimated the costs of Rule 14a–11. The Commission recognized that the Rule would impose significant costs on the companies as they would have to expend resources to oppose shareholder director nominees. Instead of quantifying those costs, the Commission instead concluded that the costs would be limited by the companies' fiduciary duty to shareholders not to use company resources to oppose shareholder nominees without a corporate purpose. Additionally, the Commission said that Rule 14a–11's requisite ownership threshold and holding period would limit the number of nominations the company would have to contest. Judge Ginsburg was unconvinced: "[a]lthough it is possible that a board, consistent with its fiduciary duties, might forgo expending resources to oppose a shareholder nominee—for example, if it believes the cost of opposition would exceed the cost to the company of the board's preferred candidate losing the election, discounted by the probability of that happening—the Commission has presented no evidence that such forbearance is ever seen in practice."

For Judge Ginsburg, the Commission's acknowledgment of possible costs to companies was not enough. "Although the Commission acknowledged that companies may expend resources to oppose shareholder nominees, it did nothing to estimate and quantify the costs it expected companies to incur; nor did it claim estimating those costs was not possible, for empirical evidence about expenditures in traditional proxy contests was readily available. Because the agency failed to 'make tough choices about which of the competing estimates is most plausible, [or] to hazard a guess as to which is correct,' we believe it neglected its statutory obligation to assess the economic consequences of its rule."

Second, Judge Ginsburg found that the Commission overestimated expected benefits with regard to the impact of Rule 14a–11 resulting from more dissident-sponsored directors being elected to the board. The Commission relied on two "relatively unpersuasive" studies to show performance improvements and increased shareholder value, and instead discounted studies submitted by commenters that reached opposite conclusions "because of questions raised by subsequent studies, limitations acknowledged by the studies' authors, or [its] own concerns about the studies' methodology or scope." This, according to Judge Ginsburg, was insufficient to support the Commission's conclusions.

Lastly, Judge Ginsburg found that the Commission acted arbitrarily and capriciously by "fail[ing] to consider an important aspect of the problem." *State Farm.* Specifically, the Commission failed to address how shareholders with special interests (like unions or pension funds) might use and abuse Rule 14a–11. Business Roundtable argued that shareholders with special interests would use the proxy access rule as leverage to gain benefits only for some, not all, of the shareholders. The Commission claimed that it did consider this problem when it concluded that "the totality of the evidence and economic theory" indicate the rule "has the potential of creating the benefit of improved board performance and enhanced shareholder value." Again, Judge Ginsburg was unimpressed: "The Commission did not completely ignore these potential costs, but neither did it adequately address them."

NOTES ON BUSINESS ROUNDTABLE

1.   *Business Roundtable* has been criticized by numerous scholars. Some argue that Judge Ginsburg applied a stricter standard than what is required by *State Farm*, abandoning any semblance of deference to the agency's expertise by requiring it to demonstrate the sufficiency and persuasiveness of the empirical data it used, *see* Bruce R. Kraus & Connor Raso, *Rational Boundaries to SEC Cost-Benefit Analysis*, 30 Yale J. Reg. 289, 314–16 (2013), while itself engaging in an "extremely cursory" analysis of the data "particularly in contrast to that of the Commission." Grant M. Hayden & Matthew T. Bodie, *The Bizarre Law & Economics of* Business Roundtable v. SEC, 38 J. Corp. L. 1, 25 (2012). See also James D. Cox & Benjamin J.C. Baucom, *The Emperor Has No Clothes: Confronting the D.C. Circuit's Usurpation of SEC Rulemaking Authority*, 90 Tex. L. Rev. 1811 (2012); Michael E. Murphy, *The SEC and the District of Columbia Circuit: The Emergency of a Distinct Standard of Judicial Review*, 7 Va. L. & Bus. Rev. 125 (2012). Kraus and Raso asserted that the court's summary dismissal of the agency's extensive review of empirical evidence was also somewhat deceptive: "The court singled out "[o]ne commenter, for example, [who] submitted an empirical study showing that when dissident directors win board seats, those firms underperform peers by 19 to 40%." The

opinion failed to inform readers of the opinion that the "commenter" in question was none other than petitioner Business Roundtable itself. The opinion also inaccurately referred to the National Economic Research Associates (NERA) Report as an "empirical study" without noting that NERA was the Business Roundtable's paid consultant." 30 Yale J. Reg. at 314. Yet, Kraus and Raso did not place all the blame on Judge Ginsburg. They encouraged the SEC to affirm its expertise going forward by relying on greater collaboration between policymakers and economists in the rulemaking process, which they viewed as a substantial change in the culture of the agency. Id. at 325–29.

2.   Other scholars have argued that even if the level of review used by Judge Ginsburg was stricter than *State Farm*, this heightened review incentivized the SEC to provide better cost-benefit analyses moving forward. For this reason, some law and economics theorists tend to view the decision favorably. See, e.g., Jonathan S. Masur & Eric A. Posner, *Cost-Benefit Analysis and the Judicial Role*, 85 U. Chi. L. Rev. 935, 967–70 (2018). Does the SEC's role as a financial regulator justify a less deferential standard of review when it issues rules directly impacting the economy?

3.   By requiring the SEC to consider "efficiency, competition, and capital formation," Congress apparently intended for the SEC to undertake some form of cost-benefit analysis even though—as an independent agency—it is not required to do so by OIRA. Perhaps Judge Ginsburg's opinion was meant to remind the SEC and other agencies that cost-benefit analyses should not be influenced by the agency's desired results. This may be an issue at other agencies as well. Reeve Bull and Jerry Ellig undertook an extensive analysis of agencies' cost-benefit analyses and how courts have reviewed them. After analyzing 42 cases, Bull and Ellig conclude that courts are capable of reviewing these complex matters but do so inconsistently because the "arbitrary and capricious" standard of review is too vague and leads to highly inconsistent decisions. They propose an amendment to the APA regarding judicial review of cost-benefit analyses that would not require courts to determine if the agency's conclusion was correct, but rather whether the agency used the best evidence available to assess the nature and cause of the regulatory problem and to discuss reasonable alternative solutions. Would this solution lead to better regulations? Reeve Bull & Jerry Ellig, *Judicial Review of Regulatory Impact Analysis: Why Not the Best?*, 69 Admin. L. Rev. 725 (2017).

4.   In the Dodd-Frank Act of 2010, Congress amended the Exchange Act, explicitly authorizing the SEC to adopt rules ensuring that shareholders can use the proxy process to nominate potential directors. Pub. L. No. 111–203, § 971, 124 Stat. 1376 (2010). Judge Ginsburg's opinion does not address this express congressional authority. How, if at all, is this legislative change relevant to the case?

MASSACHUSETTS V. ENVIRONMENTAL PROTECTION AGENCY

Supreme Court of the United States, 2007.
549 U.S. 497, 127 S.Ct. 1438, 167 L.Ed.2d 248.

JUSTICE STEVENS delivered the opinion of the Court.

[In 1999, a group of private organizations filed a rulemaking petition asking the Environmental Protection Agency (EPA) to regulate the emissions of four greenhouse gases, including carbon dioxide, pursuant to its responsibility under the Clean Air Act. EPA denied the petition in 2003. Petitioners, joined by Massachusetts and other state and local governments sought review in the D.C. Circuit. The appeals court ruled that the agency's denial was a proper exercise of its discretion. The Supreme Court agreed to review that decision. In a part of its decision omitted here, the Court held that Massachusetts and other governments had standing to challenge EPA's denial, because the agency's decision not to regulate greenhouse gases "contributes" to Massachusetts' injuries related to global warming.]

[I]   Section 202(a)(1) of the Clean Air Act, as added by Pub. L. 89–272, § 101(8), 79 Stat. 992, and as amended by, *inter alia*, 84 Stat. 1690 and 91 Stat. 791, 42 U.S.C. § 7521(a)(1), provides:

> "The [EPA] Administrator shall by regulation prescribe (and from time to time revise) in accordance with the provisions of this section, standards applicable to the emission of any air pollutant from any class or classes of new motor vehicles or new motor vehicle engines, which in his judgment cause, or contribute to, air pollution which may reasonably be anticipated to endanger public health or welfare. . . ."

The Act defines "air pollutant" to include "any air pollution agent or combination of such agents, including any physical, chemical, biological, radioactive . . . substance or matter which is emitted into or otherwise enters the ambient air." § 7602(g). "Welfare" is also defined broadly: among other things, it includes "effects on . . . weather . . . and climate." § 7602(h).

When Congress enacted these provisions, the study of climate change was in its infancy. [By the time Congress enacted § 202(a)(1) in 1970, carbon dioxide levels had reached 325 parts per million, up from a recorded mean level of 316 parts per million in 1959. In 1978, Congress enacted the National Climate Program Act, requiring the President to establish a program to "assist the Nation and the world to understand and respond to natural and man-induced climate processes and their implications." President Carter asked the National Research Council, the working arm of the National Academy of Sciences, to investigate the subject. Congress in 1987 enacted the Global Climate Protection Act, directing EPA to propose to Congress a "coordinated national policy on global climate change," and ordering the Secretary of State to work "through the channels of multilateral diplomacy" and coordinate diplomatic efforts to combat global warming.

In 1990, the Intergovernmental Panel on Climate Change (IPCC), a multinational scientific body organized under the United Nations, published its first comprehensive report on the topic, concluding that greenhouse gases will increase the warming of the Earth's surface. In response, the United Nations convened the "Earth Summit" in 1992 in Rio de Janeiro, and the first President Bush attended and signed the United Nations Framework Convention on Climate Change (UNFCCC), a nonbinding agreement among 154 nations to reduce atmospheric concentrations of carbon dioxide and other greenhouse gases, which the Senate unanimously ratified. In 1997, after the IPCC's second comprehensive report concluded that there was a discernible human influence on global climate, the UNFCCC signatories adopted the Kyoto protocol assigning mandatory targets for industrialized nations to reduce greenhouse gas emissions. Because those targets did not apply to China, India, and other developing countries that were heavy polluters, the Senate passed a resolution expressing its sense that the United States should not enter into the protocol. President Clinton did not submit the protocol to the Senate for ratification.]

[II] On October 20, 1999, a group of 19 private organizations filed a rulemaking petition asking EPA to regulate "greenhouse gas emissions from new motor vehicles under § 202 of the Clean Air Act." Petitioners maintained that 1998 was the "warmest year on record"; that carbon dioxide, methane, nitrous oxide, and hydrofluorocarbons are "heat trapping greenhouse gases"; that greenhouse gas emissions have significantly accelerated climate change; and that the IPCC's 1995 report warned that "carbon dioxide remains the most important contributor to [manmade] forcing of climate change." The petition further alleged that climate change will have serious adverse effects on human health and the environment. As to EPA's statutory authority, the petition observed that the Agency itself had already confirmed that it had the power to regulate carbon dioxide. In 1998, Jonathan Z. Cannon, then EPA's general counsel, prepared a legal opinion concluding that "CO_2 emissions are within the scope of EPA's authority to regulate," even as he recognized that EPA had so far declined to exercise that authority. Cannon's successor, Gary S. Guzy, reiterated that opinion before a congressional committee just two weeks before the rulemaking petition was filed.

Fifteen months after the petition's submission, EPA requested public comment on "all the issues raised in [the] petition," adding a "particular" request for comments on "any scientific, technical, legal, economic or other aspect of these issues that may be relevant to EPA's consideration of this petition." 66 Fed. Reg. 7,486, 7,487 (2001). EPA received more than 50,000 comments over the next five months.

Before the close of the comment period, the White House sought "assistance in identifying the areas in the science of climate change where there are the greatest certainties and uncertainties" from the National Research Council, asking for a response "as soon as possible." The result was a 2001 report titled Climate Change Science: An Analysis of Some Key Questions (NRC Report), which, drawing heavily on the 1995 IPCC report, concluded that "[g]reenhouse gases are accumulating in Earth's atmosphere as a result of human activities, causing surface air temperatures and subsurface ocean temperatures to rise. Temperatures are, in fact, rising."

On September 8, 2003, EPA entered an order denying the rulemaking petition. The Agency gave two reasons for its decision: (1) that contrary to the opinions of its former general counsels, the Clean Air Act does not authorize EPA to issue mandatory regulations to address global climate change; and (2) that even if the Agency had the authority to set greenhouse gas emission standards, it would be unwise to do so at this time.

In concluding that it lacked statutory authority over greenhouse gases, EPA observed that Congress was well aware of the global climate change issue when it last comprehensively amended the Clean Air Act in 1990, yet it declined to adopt a proposed amendment establishing binding emissions limitations. Congress instead chose to authorize further investigation into climate change. EPA further reasoned that Congress' specially tailored solutions to global atmospheric issues—in particular, its 1990 enactment of a comprehensive scheme to regulate pollutants that depleted the ozone layer, see 42 U.S.C. §§ 7671–7671q—counseled against reading the general authorization of § 202(a)(1) to confer regulatory authority over greenhouse gases.

EPA stated that it was urged on in this view by this Court's decision in *FDA v. Brown & Williamson Tobacco Corp.*, 529 U.S. 120 (2000). In that case, relying on "tobacco['s] unique political history," we invalidated the Food and Drug Administration's reliance on its general authority to regulate drugs as a basis for asserting jurisdiction over an "industry constituting a significant portion of the American economy." *Id.* at 159.

EPA reasoned that climate change had its own "political history": Congress designed the original Clean Air Act to address *local* air pollutants rather than a substance that "is fairly consistent in its concentration throughout the *world's* atmosphere"; declined in 1990 to enact proposed amendments to force EPA to set carbon dioxide emission standards for motor vehicles; and addressed global climate change in other legislation. Because of this political history, and because imposing emission limitations on greenhouse gases would have even greater economic and political repercussions than regulating tobacco, EPA was persuaded that it lacked the power to do so. In essence, EPA concluded that climate change was so important that unless Congress spoke with exacting specificity, it could not have meant the Agency to address it.

Having reached that conclusion, EPA believed it followed that greenhouse gases cannot be "air pollutants" within the meaning of the Act. * * * The Agency bolstered this conclusion by explaining that if carbon dioxide were an air pollutant, the only feasible method of reducing tailpipe emissions would be to improve fuel economy. But because Congress has already created detailed mandatory fuel economy standards subject to Department of Transportation (DOT) administration, the Agency concluded that EPA regulation would either conflict with those standards or be superfluous.

Even assuming that it had authority over greenhouse gases, EPA explained in detail why it would refuse to exercise that authority. The Agency began by recognizing that the concentration of greenhouse gases has dramatically increased as a result of human activities, and acknowledged the attendant increase in global surface air temperatures. EPA nevertheless gave controlling importance to the NRC Report's statement that a causal link between the two cannot be unequivocally established. Given that residual uncertainty, EPA concluded that regulating greenhouse gas emissions would be unwise.

The Agency furthermore characterized any EPA regulation of motor-vehicle emissions as a "piecemeal approach" to climate change, and stated that such regulation would conflict with the President's "comprehensive approach" to the problem. That approach involves additional support for technological innovation, the creation of nonregulatory programs to encourage voluntary private-sector reductions in greenhouse gas emissions, and further research on climate change—not actual regulation. According to EPA, unilateral EPA regulation of motor-vehicle greenhouse gas emissions might also hamper the President's ability to persuade key developing countries to reduce greenhouse gas emissions.

[III] Petitioners, now joined by intervenor States and local governments, sought review of EPA's order in the United States Court of Appeals for the District of Columbia Circuit. Although each of the three judges on the panel wrote a separate opinion, two judges agreed that the EPA Administrator properly exercised his discretion under § 202(a)(1) in denying the petition for rule making. The court therefore denied the petition for review. * * * [The Supreme Court granted certiorari regarding the following two questions concerning the meaning of § 202(a)(1) of the Act: whether EPA has the statutory authority to regulate greenhouse gas emissions from new motor vehicles; and if so, whether its stated reasons for refusing to do so are consistent with the statute.]

In Part IV, the EPA argued that the Supreme Court should not address the questions raised unless at least one petitioner has standing to invoke jurisdiction under Article III of the Constitution. The majority found that it had jurisdiction, emphasizing Massachusetts' status as a sovereign with the ability to litigate as *parens patriae* to protect quasi-sovereign interests as distinct from private litigants.]

[V] The scope of our review of the merits of the statutory issues is narrow. As we have repeated time and again, an agency has broad discretion to choose how best to marshal its limited resources and personnel to carry out its delegated responsibilities. See *Chevron U.S.A. Inc. v. Natural Resources Defense Council, Inc.*, 467 U.S. 837, 842–845 (1984). That discretion is at its height when the agency decides not to bring an enforcement action. Therefore, in *Heckler v. Chaney*, 470 U.S. 821 (1985), we held that an agency's refusal to initiate enforcement proceedings is not ordinarily subject to judicial review. Some debate remains, however, as to the rigor with which we review an agency's denial of a petition for rulemaking.

There are key differences between a denial of a petition for rulemaking and an agency's decision not to initiate an enforcement action. See *Am. Horse Protection Ass'n., Inc. v. Lyng*, 812 F.2d 1, 3–4 (D.C. Cir. 1987). In contrast to nonenforcement decisions, agency refusals to initiate rulemaking "are less frequent, more apt to involve legal as opposed to factual analysis, and subject to special formalities, including a public explanation." *Id.* at 4; see also 5 U.S.C. § 555(e). They moreover arise out of denials of petitions for rulemaking which (at least in the circumstances here) the affected party had an undoubted procedural right to file in the first instance. Refusals to promulgate rules are thus susceptible to judicial review, though such review is "extremely limited" and "highly deferential." *Nat'l Customs Brokers & Forwarders Ass'n. of America, Inc. v. United States*, 883 F.2d 93, 96 (D.C. Cir. 1989).

EPA concluded in its denial of the petition for rulemaking that it lacked authority under 42 U.S.C. § 7521(a)(1) to regulate new vehicle emissions because carbon dioxide is not an "air pollutant" as that term is defined in § 7602. In the alternative, it concluded that even if it possessed authority, it would decline to do so because regulation would conflict with other administration priorities. As discussed earlier, the Clean Air Act expressly permits review of such an action. § 7607(b)(1). We therefore "may reverse any such action found to be . . . arbitrary, capricious, an abuse of discretion, or otherwise not in accordance with law." § 7607(d)(9).

[VI] On the merits, the first question is whether § 202(a)(1) of the Clean Air Act authorizes EPA to regulate greenhouse gas emissions from new motor vehicles in the event that it forms a "judgment" that such emissions contribute to climate change. We have little trouble concluding that it does. In relevant part, § 202(a)(1) provides that EPA "shall by regulation prescribe . . . standards applicable to the emission of any air pollutant from any class or classes of new motor vehicles or new motor vehicle engines, which in [the Administrator's] judgment cause, or contribute to, air pollution which may reasonably be anticipated to endanger public health or welfare." 42 U.S.C. § 7521(a)(1). Because EPA believes that Congress did not intend it to regulate substances that contribute to climate change, the agency maintains that carbon dioxide is not an "air pollutant" within the meaning of the provision.

The statutory text forecloses EPA's reading. The Clean Air Act's sweeping definition of "air pollutant" includes "*any* air pollution agent or combination of such agents, including *any* physical, chemical . . . substance or matter which is emitted into or otherwise enters the ambient air. . . ." § 7602(g) (emphasis added). On its face, the definition embraces all airborne compounds of whatever stripe, and underscores that intent through the repeated use of the word "any." Carbon dioxide, methane, nitrous oxide, and hydrofluorocarbons are without a doubt "physical [and] chemical . . . substance [s] which [are] emitted into . . . the ambient air." The statute is unambiguous.

Rather than relying on statutory text, EPA invokes postenactment congressional actions and deliberations it views as tantamount to a congressional command to refrain from regulating greenhouse gas emissions. Even if such postenactment legislative history could shed light on the meaning of an otherwise-unambiguous statute, EPA never identifies any action remotely suggesting that Congress meant to curtail its power to treat greenhouse gases as air pollutants. That subsequent Congresses have eschewed enacting binding emissions limitations to combat global warming tells us nothing about what Congress meant when it amended § 202(a)(1) in 1970 and 1977. And unlike EPA, we have no difficulty reconciling Congress' various efforts to promote interagency collaboration and research to better understand climate change with the Agency's pre-existing mandate to regulate "any air pollutant" that may endanger the public welfare. Collaboration and research do not conflict with any thoughtful regulatory effort; they complement it.

EPA's reliance on *Brown & Williamson Tobacco Corp.*, is similarly misplaced. In holding that tobacco products are not "drugs" or "devices" subject to Food and Drug Administration (FDA) regulation pursuant to the Food, Drug and Cosmetic Act (FDCA), we found critical at least two considerations that have no counterpart in this case.

First, we thought it unlikely that Congress meant to ban tobacco products, which the FDCA would have required had such products been classified as "drugs" or "devices." *Id.* at 135–137. Here, in contrast, EPA jurisdiction would lead to no such extreme measures. EPA would only *regulate* emissions, and even then, it would have to delay any action "to permit the development and application of the requisite technology, giving appropriate consideration to the cost of compliance," § 7521(a)(2). However much a ban on tobacco products clashed with the "common sense" intuition that Congress never meant to remove those products from circulation, *Brown &*

Williamson, 529 U.S. at 133, there is nothing counterintuitive to the notion that EPA can curtail the emission of substances that are putting the global climate out of kilter.

Second, in *Brown & Williamson*, we pointed to an unbroken series of congressional enactments that made sense only if adopted "against the backdrop of the FDA's consistent and repeated statements that it lacked authority under the FDCA to regulate tobacco." *Id.* at 144. We can point to no such enactments here: EPA has not identified any congressional action that conflicts in any way with the regulation of greenhouse gases from new motor vehicles. Even if it had, Congress could not have acted against a regulatory "backdrop" of disclaimers of regulatory authority. Prior to the order that provoked this litigation, EPA had never disavowed the authority to regulate greenhouse gases, and in 1998 it in fact affirmed that it *had* such authority. There is no reason, much less a compelling reason, to accept EPA's invitation to read ambiguity into a clear statute.

EPA finally argues that it cannot regulate carbon dioxide emissions from motor vehicles because doing so would require it to tighten mileage standards, a job (according to EPA) that Congress has assigned to DOT. But that DOT sets mileage standards in no way licenses EPA to shirk its environmental responsibilities. EPA has been charged with protecting the public's "health" and "welfare," 42 U.S.C. § 7521(a)(1), a statutory obligation wholly independent of DOT's mandate to promote energy efficiency. See Energy Policy and Conservation Act, § 2(5), 89 Stat. 874, 42 U.S.C. § 6201(5). The two obligations may overlap, but there is no reason to think the two agencies cannot both administer their obligations and yet avoid inconsistency.

While the Congresses that drafted § 202(a)(1) might not have appreciated the possibility that burning fossil fuels could lead to global warming, they did understand that without regulatory flexibility, changing circumstances and scientific developments would soon render the Clean Air Act obsolete. The broad language of § 202(a)(1) reflects an intentional effort to confer the flexibility necessary to forestall such obsolescence. See *Pa. Dep't. of Corr. v. Yeskey*, 524 U.S. 206, 212 (1998) ("[T]he fact that a statute can be applied in situations not expressly anticipated by Congress does not demonstrate ambiguity. It demonstrates breadth" (internal quotation marks omitted)). Because greenhouse gases fit well within the Clean Air Act's capacious definition of "air pollutant," we hold that EPA has the statutory authority to regulate the emission of such gases from new motor vehicles.

[VII] The alternative basis for EPA's decision—that even if it does have statutory authority to regulate greenhouse gases, it would be unwise to do so at this time—rests on reasoning divorced from the statutory text. While the statute does condition the exercise of EPA's authority on its formation of a "judgment," 42 U.S.C. § 7521(a)(1), that judgment must relate to whether an air pollutant "cause[s], or contribute[s] to, air pollution which may reasonably be anticipated to endanger public health or welfare," *ibid.* Put another way, the use of the word "judgment" is not a roving license to ignore the statutory text. It is but a direction to exercise discretion within defined statutory limits.

If EPA makes a finding of endangerment, the Clean Air Act requires the Agency to regulate emissions of the deleterious pollutant from new motor vehicles. *Ibid* (stating that "[EPA] shall by regulation prescribe . . . standards applicable to the emission of any air pollutant from any class or classes of new motor vehicles"). EPA no doubt has significant latitude as to the manner, timing, content, and coordination of its regulations with those of other agencies. But once EPA has responded to a petition for rulemaking, its reasons for action or inaction must conform to the authorizing statute. Under the clear terms of the Clean Air Act, EPA can avoid taking further action only if it determines that greenhouse gases do not contribute to climate change or if it provides some reasonable explanation as to why it cannot or will not exercise its discretion to determine whether they do. *Ibid.* To the extent that this constrains agency discretion to pursue other priorities of the Administrator or the President, this is the congressional design.

EPA has refused to comply with this clear statutory command. Instead, it has offered a laundry list of reasons not to regulate. For example, EPA said that a number of voluntary Executive Branch programs already provide an effective response to the threat of global warming, that regulating greenhouse gases might impair the President's ability to negotiate with "key developing nations" to reduce emissions, and that curtailing motor-vehicle emissions would reflect "an inefficient, piecemeal approach to address the climate change issue."

Although we have neither the expertise nor the authority to evaluate these policy judgments, it is evident they have nothing to do with whether greenhouse gas emissions contribute to climate change. Still less do they amount to a reasoned justification for declining to form a scientific judgment. * * *

Nor can EPA avoid its statutory obligation by noting the uncertainty surrounding various features of climate change and concluding that it would therefore be better not to regulate at this time. If the scientific uncertainty is so profound that it precludes EPA from making a reasoned judgment as to whether greenhouse gases contribute to global warming, EPA must say so. That EPA would prefer not to regulate greenhouse gases because of some residual uncertainty— which, contrary to Justice Scalia's apparent belief, is in fact all that it said—is irrelevant. The statutory question is whether sufficient information exists to make an endangerment finding.

In short, EPA has offered no reasoned explanation for its refusal to decide whether greenhouse gases cause or contribute to climate change. Its action was therefore "arbitrary, capricious, . . . or otherwise not in accordance with law." 42 U.S.C. § 7607(d)(9)(A). We need not and do not reach the question whether on remand EPA must make an endangerment finding, or whether policy concerns can inform EPA's actions in the event that it makes such a finding. Cf. Chevron, 467 U.S. at 843–844. We hold only that EPA must ground its reasons for action or inaction in the statute. * * *

[CHIEF JUSTICE ROBERTS' dissenting opinion, joined by JUSTICES SCALIA, THOMAS, and ALITO, is omitted. The Chief Justice argued that the Court lacked jurisdiction because none of the petitioners had standing under Article III.]

JUSTICE SCALIA, with whom the CHIEF JUSTICE, JUSTICE THOMAS, and JUSTICE ALITO join, dissenting.

I join the Chief Justice's opinion in full, and would hold that this Court has no jurisdiction to decide this case because petitioners lack standing. The Court having decided otherwise, it is appropriate for me to note my dissent on the merits.

[I-A] The provision of law at the heart of this case is § 202(a)(1) of the Clean Air Act (CAA or Act), which provides that the Administrator of the Environmental Protection Agency (EPA) "shall by regulation prescribe . . . standards applicable to the emission of any air pollutant from any class or classes of new motor vehicles or new motor vehicle engines, which *in his judgment* cause, or contribute to, air pollution which may reasonably be anticipated to endanger public health or welfare." 42 U.S.C. § 7521(a)(1) (emphasis added). As the Court recognizes, the statute "condition[s] the exercise of EPA's authority on its formation of a 'judgment.' " There is no dispute that the Administrator has made no such judgment in this case.

The question thus arises: Does anything *require* the Administrator to make a "judgment" whenever a petition for rulemaking is filed? Without citation of the statute or any other authority, the Court says yes. Why is that so? When Congress wishes to make private action force an agency's hand, it knows how to do so. See, e.g., *Brock v. Pierce County*, 476 U.S. 253, 254–255 (1986) (discussing the Comprehensive Employment and Training Act (CETA), 92 Stat. 1926, 29 U.S.C. § 816(b) (1976 ed., Supp. V), which "provide[d] that the Secretary of Labor 'shall' issue a final determination as to the misuse of CETA funds by a grant recipient within 120 days after receiving a complaint alleging such misuse"). Where does the CAA say that the EPA Administrator is required to come to a decision on this question whenever a rulemaking petition is filed? The Court points to no such provision because none exists.

Instead, the Court invents a multiple-choice question that the EPA Administrator must answer when a petition for rulemaking is filed. The Administrator must exercise his judgment in one of three ways: (a) by concluding that the pollutant *does* cause, or contribute to, air pollution that endangers public welfare (in which case EPA is required to regulate); (b) by concluding that the pollutant *does not* cause, or contribute to, air pollution that endangers public welfare (in which case EPA is *not* required to regulate); or (c) by "provid[ing] some reasonable explanation as to why it cannot or will not exercise its discretion to determine whether" greenhouse gases endanger public welfare, (in which case EPA is *not* required to regulate). * * *

The Court, with no basis in text or precedent, rejects all of EPA's stated "policy judgments" as not "amount[ing] to a reasoned justification," effectively narrowing the universe of potential reasonable bases to a single one: Judgment can be delayed *only* if the Administrator concludes that "the scientific uncertainty is [too] profound." The Administrator is precluded from concluding *for other reasons* "that it would . . . be better not to regulate at this time."[9] Such other reasons—perfectly valid reasons— were set forth in the Agency's statement.

---

9   The Court's way of putting it is, of course, not quite accurate. The issue is whether it would be better *to defer the decision about whether to exercise judgment*. This has the *effect* of deferring regulation but is quite a different determination.

The Court dismisses this analysis as "rest[ing] on reasoning divorced from the statutory text." "While the statute does condition the exercise of EPA's authority on its formation of a 'judgment,' . . . that judgment must relate to whether an air pollutant 'cause[s], or contribute[s] to, air pollution which may reasonably be anticipated to endanger public health or welfare.' " True but irrelevant. When the Administrator *makes* a judgment whether to regulate greenhouse gases, that judgment must relate to whether they are air pollutants that "cause, or contribute to, air pollution which may reasonably be anticipated to endanger public health or welfare." 42 U.S.C. § 7521(a)(1). But the statute says *nothing at all* about the reasons for which the Administrator may *defer* making a judgment—the permissible reasons for deciding not to grapple with the issue at the present time. Thus, the various "policy" rationales that the Court criticizes are not "divorced from the statutory text," except in the sense that the statutory text is silent, as texts are often silent about permissible reasons for the exercise of agency discretion. The reasons EPA gave are surely considerations executive agencies *regularly* take into account (and *ought* to take into account) when deciding whether to consider entering a new field: the impact such entry would have on other Executive Branch programs and on foreign policy. There is no basis in law for the Court's imposed limitation. * * * As the Administrator acted within the law in declining to make a "judgment" for the policy reasons above set forth, I would uphold the decision to deny the rulemaking petition on that ground alone.

[I-B] Even on the Court's own terms, however, the same conclusion follows. As mentioned above, the Court gives EPA the option of determining that the science is too uncertain to allow it to form a "judgment" as to whether greenhouse gases endanger public welfare. Attached to this option (on what basis is unclear) is an essay requirement: "If," the Court says, "the scientific uncertainty is so profound that it precludes EPA from making a reasoned judgment as to whether greenhouse gases contribute to global warming, EPA must say so." But EPA *has* said precisely that— and at great length, based on information contained in a 2001 report by the National Research Council (NRC) entitled Climate Change Science: An Analysis of Some Key Questions[.] [Justice Scalia notes several excerpts from the report that highlighted the complexity of climate change, the continued evolution of the scientific study, the substantial scientific uncertainties that limit NRC's ability to assess climate change, and NRC's infant study of the relationships between climate and human health.]

[II-A] Even before reaching its discussion of the word "judgment," the Court makes another significant error when it concludes that "§ 202(a)(1) of the Clean Air Act *authorizes* EPA to regulate greenhouse gas emissions from new motor vehicles in the event that it forms a 'judgment' that such emissions contribute to climate change." * * * The Court's analysis faithfully follows the argument advanced by petitioners, which focuses on the word "including" in the statutory definition of "air pollutant." As that argument goes, anything that *follows* the word "including" must necessarily be a subset of whatever *precedes* it. * * *

That is certainly one possible interpretation of the statutory definition. The word "including" can indeed indicate that what follows will be an "illustrative" sampling of the general category that precedes the word. [But] the word "including" does not require the Court's (or the petitioners') result. It is perfectly reasonable to view the definition of "air pollutant" in its entirety: An air pollutant *can* be "any physical, chemical, . . . substance or matter which is emitted into or otherwise enters the ambient air," but only if it retains the general characteristic of being an "air pollution agent or combination of such agents." This is precisely the conclusion EPA reached: "[A] substance does not meet the CAA definition of 'air pollutant' simply because it is a 'physical, chemical, . . . substance or matter which is emitted into or otherwise enters the ambient air.' It must also be an 'air pollution agent.' * * * Evidently, the Court defers only to those reasonable interpretations that it favors. * * *

The Court's alarm over global warming may or may not be justified, but it ought not distort the outcome of this litigation. This is a straightforward administrative-law case, in which Congress has passed a malleable statute giving broad discretion, not to us but to an executive agency. No matter how important the underlying policy issues at stake, this Court has no business substituting its own desired outcome for the reasoned judgment of the responsible agency.

NOTES ON MASS. V. EPA AND AGENCY REFUSALS TO ACT

1.   *Perverse Incentives.* In Massachusetts v. EPA: *Breaking New Ground on Issues Other Than Global Warming*, 102 Nw. U. L. Rev. Colloquy 1, 16 (2007), Kathryn Watts and Amy Wildermuth suggest that the Court's rigorous standard for review of agency inaction "will create perverse incentives for agencies." Although the Court made clear that EPA was not required to act on the rulemaking petition within a certain time frame, once the agency decided to act it effectively invited a challenge to its reasons for denying the petition, reasons that had to conform to the authorizing statute. Accordingly, the authors continue, a key lesson that agencies may well take away from *Massachusetts* is that "whatever discretion [exists] prior to taking action on a rulemaking petition may well disappear once [the agency] affirmatively rules on a petition." *Id.* What recourse, if any, does a private party have when an agency has simply ignored a petition for rulemaking? How should a court assess agency discretion not to respond at all in light of the Court's reasoning?

2.   *Reasonableness.* Relatedly, what will qualify as a reasonable explanation when an agency denies a rulemaking petition? The Court's opinion dismisses policy-driven considerations as divorced from the statutory text but "does not even hint at a general line between permissible and impermissible reasons to regulate." *Id.* at 15. If policy considerations will not be a basis, what else may an agency invoke for exercising its discretion to deny a petition? Will courts only entertain reliance on scientific or technical data? If so, what options will agencies like the Securities & Exchange Commission, whose rulemaking is necessarily tethered to policy considerations, offer as reasonable explanations?

3.   *Aftermath of* Massachusetts v. EPA. Following the Supreme Court decision, the Bush EPA announced that it would promulgate greenhouse gas (GHG) regulations for cars and trucks. Before the agency could act, however, Congress in 2007 passed the Energy Independence and Security Act, 121 Stat. 1492, amending the Clean Air Act to require that EPA and the Department of Transportation (DOT) jointly establish fuel economy and GHG vehicle emission standards.

Between 2009 and 2010, the Obama EPA promulgated a series of GHG-related rules. An Endangerment Finding concluded that GHGs may reasonably be anticipated to endanger public health or welfare and that emissions from motor vehicles contribute to this pollution. 74 Fed. Reg. 66,496 (Dec. 15, 2009). A Tailpipe Rule, promulgated with DOT, set GHG emission standards for cars and light trucks. 75 Fed. Reg. 25,324 (May 7, 2010). Finally, Timing and Tailoring Rules required *major stationary sources of greenhouse gases* to obtain construction and operating permits but limited initial permitting requirements to the largest GHG emitters. 75 Fed. Reg. 31,514 (June 3, 2010). More than 35 petitioners filed some 80 lawsuits challenging these agency actions. In July 2012, the D.C. Circuit ruled on the consolidated lawsuits, upholding the agency's positions—EPA's Endangerment Finding and Tailpipe Rules were not arbitrary or capricious, and EPA's determination to extend permitting programs to major emitters was an unambiguously correct interpretation of the applicable CAA provisions.

In *Utility Air Regulatory Group v. EPA*, 573 U.S. 302 (2014), the Supreme Court affirmed in part and reversed in part. Writing for the Court, Justice Scalia ruled that the CAA does not *compel* EPA to adopt an interpretation requiring a source to obtain a permit on the sole basis of its potential greenhouse-gas emissions. The majority reasoned that while the Court in *Massachusetts v. EPA* had held the Act-wide definition of "air pollutant" includes greenhouse gases, the agency has routinely given that term a narrower context-appropriate meaning in the Act's specific operative provisions governing permitting requirements. In addition, Justice Scalia concluded that the statute does not *permit* the EPA's "Tailoring Rule" interpretation focusing on the largest GHG emitters. Because the CAA specifies particular threshold amounts of greenhouse gas pollution that EPA may regulate, the agency has no power to rewrite those limits, even though it was doing so to make regulation more manageable by precluding agency efforts to control GHG emissions beyond major sources like power plants. If the text as written cannot be implemented without bringing "millions of small sources" such as schools or apartment buildings under EPA supervision, then it falls on Congress, not the agency, to narrow the statutory terms.

Justice Scalia also concluded, though, that the EPA had reasonably interpreted the CAA to allow for the regulation of greenhouse-gas emissions from sources already emitting other kinds of pollution and thus subject to regulation pursuant to established CAA permitting programs. And the Court held the agency may require those sources to use the best available technology to control greenhouse gases.

In announcing his majority opinion from the bench, Justice Scalia stated that the result of the Court's decision was to leave the agency with authority to cut back on greenhouse-gas pollution at eighty-three percent of sources across the country while denying it that authority for an additional three percent. What are we to make of this ongoing saga of rulemaking, resistance, and litigation? Do you regard the decision in *Utility Air Regulatory Group* as a "win" for EPA? What are the future implications of the Court's analysis, largely vindicating the agency's bottom line position while sharply criticizing much of its regulatory approach? Is twelve years (and counting) since *Massachusetts v. EPA* an appropriate period of time for national debate and disagreement over regulatory action of this magnitude?

4.   *Failure to Act.* The APA authorizes suit by "[a] person suffering legal wrong because of agency action, or adversely affected or aggrieved by agency action within the meaning of a relevant statute," 5 U.S.C. § 702, where an " 'agency action' " includes "the whole or a part of an agency rule, order, license, sanction, relief, or the equivalent or denial thereof, or failure to act," § 551(13). Under § 706(1), the APA provides the following

relief: "The reviewing court shall . . . compel agency action unlawfully withheld or unreasonably delayed." At first blush, this appears to provide an answer to the question of how a court can compel an agency to respond to a petition for rulemaking rather than indefinitely ignore the petition. However, the Supreme Court in 2004 handed down a unanimous opinion in *Norton v. Southern Utah Wilderness Alliance*, 542 U.S. 55, that limited a "failure to act" claim under § 706(1) to proceedings where plaintiff can assert that an agency failed to take a discrete agency action that it is required to take. The opinion, authored by *Massachusetts* dissenter Justice Scalia, stated that "a failure to act" was "properly understood to be limited, as are the other items in § 551(13), to a discrete action." 542 U.S. at 63. Justice Scalia wrote that the phrase, "or the equivalent or denial thereof," which appears after the list of examples of specific affirmative agency actions, "must also be discrete (or it would not be equivalent)," so a "denial thereof" must be the denial of a discrete agency action. *Id.* Next, he moved to the final term in the definition in § 551(13), "failure to act," which the Court understood as a failure to take an agency action; and moreover, the canon of ejusdem generis would attribute to the last item, "failure to act," the same characteristic of discreteness shared by all the preceding items even if the Court did not tether "act" to "agency action." *Id.* at 64. Is responding to a petition for rulemaking a discrete agency action under *Norton*? By reading § 706(1)'s authorization for courts to "compel agency action *unlawfully* withheld," the opinion holds that only agency action that can be compelled under the APA is action legally required. Is an agency required to take action in response to a petition for rulemaking? Where would a potential litigant look to find out whether a particular agency must respond to petitions?

In *The Federal Inaction Commission*, 59 Emory L.J. 369 (2009), Glen Staszewski proposes the establishment of a new, independent federal administrative agency that would be charged with "(1) identifying policy areas in which Executive Branch agencies have declined to exercise their delegated statutory authority; (2) directing agencies to adopt sensible enforcement guidelines for implementing their existing programs; (3) investigating and resolving complaints regarding particular non-enforcement decisions; (4) securing reasoned explanations from Executive Branch agencies for any perceived deficiencies in the foregoing areas; (5) reporting to elected officials and the public on the nature and scope of regulatory inaction by Executive Branch agencies; and (6) making recommendations regarding budgetary matters and substantive legislation that could alleviate perceived deficiencies." In light of *Massachusetts*, *Norton*, and *Heckler v. Chaney*, 470 U.S. 821 (1985) (discussed at start of this part; Court held that agency non-enforcement decisions are presumptively nonreviewable), would such an agency serve a useful purpose? Or is adding to the alphabet soup of American national bureaucracy only likely to create further problems? If a Federal Inaction Commission were to assume oversight of other agencies, what entity would be responsible for oversight of this Commission?

TIMING OF AGENCY CONSIDERATION OF COSTS WHEN DECIDING TO REGULATE

When an agency decides to regulate, it will at some point address associated cost factors (see § 3(B)(1) of his chapter). In providing statutory direction, Congress can decide to require, permit, or prohibit an agency's consideration of costs, and it may vary its statutory approaches to the same agency for different regulatory delegations. One aspect of Congress's consideration of costs is timing: at what stage of the regulatory process should—or must—an agency take cost into account? The next case squarely presents this issue.

Michigan v. E.P.A.

135 S.Ct. 2699 (2015).

The Clean Air Act directs the Environmental Protection Agency (EPA) to regulate power plant emissions of hazardous air pollutants wherever it "finds such regulation is appropriate and necessary." 42 U.S.C. § 7412(n)(1)(A). In 2012, EPA issued emission floor standards for power plants, determining that such regulation was "appropriate and necessary" because these emissions had been shown to create a substantial risk of harm to both humans and the environment and they could be controlled. In making this determination, however, EPA explicitly declined to consider cost. When the rule came under review in the DC Circuit, the Court of Appeals upheld the EPA's determination not to consider cost.

The Court by a 5–4 vote reversed the decision of the DC Circuit. In a decision authored by **Justice Scalia**, the Court held that the EPA's failure to consider costs as part of its initial decision to regulate was an unreasonable interpretation of § 7412(n)(1)(A).

Under § 7412(n)(1)(A), EPA is directed to perform a study of the hazards to public health reasonably anticipated to occur as a result of emissions by power plants of hazardous air pollutants, and to regulate power plants if the Agency determines that regulation is "appropriate and necessary after considering the results of the study." EPA completed the study in 1998, and concluded that regulation of coal- and oil-fired power plants was "appropriate and necessary" in 2000. In 2012, the Agency reaffirmed the appropriate-and-necessary finding and promulgated floor standards. The Agency found regulation was "appropriate" because (1) power plants' emissions of mercury and other hazardous air pollutants posed risks to human health and the environment and (2) controls were available to reduce these emissions. It found regulation was "necessary" because imposition of the Act's other requirements did not eliminate these risks. EPA concluded that "costs should not be considered" when deciding whether power plants should be regulated under § 7412.

The Court invoked its *State Farm* decision when noting that the requirement for reasoned decisionmaking by federal agencies includes adhering to a logical and rational process that rests on a consideration of the relevant factors. Justice Scalia recognized that "EPA's decision to regulate power plants under § 7412 allowed the Agency to reduce power plants' emissions of hazardous air pollutants and thus to improve public health and the environment." At the same time, "the decision also ultimately cost power plants, according to the Agency's own estimate, nearly $10 billion a year."

The Court concluded that "there are undoubtedly settings in which the phrase 'appropriate and necessary' does not encompass cost. But this is not one of them. Section 7412(n)(1)(A) directs EPA to determine whether '*regulation* is appropriate and necessary.' (Emphasis added.) Agencies have long treated cost as a centrally relevant factor when deciding whether to regulate. Consideration of cost reflects the understanding that reasonable regulation ordinarily requires paying attention to the advantages *and* the disadvantages of agency decisions." It also reflects the reality that excessive and wasteful expenditure devoted to one problem may well result in considerably fewer resources being available to deal effectively with other problems that may be more serious. Given such established administrative practice, the Court held that it was unreasonable to read an instruction to an administrative agency to determine whether "regulation is appropriate and necessary" as an invitation to ignore cost.

In rejecting EPA's various reasons for construing § 7412(n)(1)(A) to mean that cost is irrelevant to the initial decision to regulate, the Court turned aside the agency's argument that it need not consider cost when first deciding *whether* to regulate power plants because it can consider cost later when deciding *how much* to regulate them. "The question before us, however, is the meaning of the 'appropriate and necessary' standard that governs the initial decision to regulate. And as we have discussed, context establishes that this expansive standard encompasses cost. Cost may become relevant again at a later stage of the regulatory process, but that possibility does not establish its irrelevance at *this* stage. In addition, once the Agency decides to regulate power plants, it must promulgate certain minimum or floor standards no matter the cost (here, nearly $10 billion a year); the Agency may consider cost only when imposing regulations *beyond* these minimum standards. By EPA's logic, someone could decide whether it is 'appropriate' to buy a Ferrari without thinking about cost, because he plans to think about cost later when deciding whether to upgrade the sound system."

Justice Scalia emphasized that by requiring a preliminary estimate of cost, including especially cost of compliance, the Court was not requiring EPA to conduct a formal cost-benefit analysis. "It will be up to the Agency to decide (as always, within the limits of reasonable interpretation) how to account for cost."

Justice Kagan, joined by **Justices Ginsburg**, **Breyer**, and **Sotomayor**, dissented on the grounds that while cost was undoubtedly a relevant and important factor, the EPA had actually given cost "exhaustive consideration" during its lengthy regulatory process, including "conducting a formal cost-benefit study which found that the quantifiable benefits of its regulation would exceed the costs up to nine times over—by as much as $80 billion each year."

Kagan reasoned that while cost is almost always a relevant—and usually, a highly important—factor in regulation, that proposition does not resolve the issue before us because the "appropriate and necessary" finding was only the start. EPA knew that a lengthy rulemaking process lay ahead of it, and that the determination of emissions limits was years in the future. And the Agency, in making its initial finding, explicitly noted in multiple portions of the Federal Register that consideration of costs and exploration of least-cost solutions would follow. Accordingly, Kagan contended that when making its "appropriate and necessary" finding, EPA did not decline to consider costs as part of the regulatory process; it simply "declined to consider costs at a single stage of that process, knowing that they would come in later on."

The dissent framed the issue as not whether EPA can reasonably find it "appropriate" to regulate without thinking about costs, but whether the Agency can reasonably find it "appropriate" to trigger the regulatory process based on harms and technological feasibility alone, given that costs will come into play in multiple ways before any emission limit goes into effect.

"In considering that question, the very nature of the word 'appropriate' matters. * * * [Determining whether the EPA acted reasonably] demands taking account of the entire regulatory process in thinking about what is 'appropriate' in its first phase. The statutory language, in other words, is a directive to remove one's blinders and view things whole—

to consider what it is fitting to do at the threshold stage given what will happen at every other. * * *

"Suppose you were in charge of designing a regulatory process. The subject matter—an industry's emissions of hazardous material—was highly complex, involving multivarious factors demanding years of study. Would you necessarily try to do everything at once? Or might you try to break down this lengthy and complicated process into discrete stages? And might you consider different factors, in different ways, at each of those junctures? I think you might. You know that everything must get done in the end—every relevant factor considered. But you tend to think that 'in the end' does not mean 'in the beginning.' And you structure your rulemaking process accordingly * * * .

"[Justice Scalia's Ferrari] comparison is witty but wholly inapt. To begin with, emissions limits are not a luxury good: They are a safety measure, designed to curtail the significant health and environmental harms caused by power plants spewing hazardous pollutants. And more: EPA knows from past experience and expertise alike that it will have the opportunity to purchase that good in a cost-effective way. A better analogy might be to a car owner who decides without first checking prices that it is 'appropriate and necessary' to replace her worn-out brake-pads, aware from prior experience that she has ample time to comparison-shop and bring that purchase within her budget. Faced with a serious hazard and an available remedy, EPA moved forward like that sensible car owner, with a promise that it would, and well-grounded confidence that it could, take costs into account down the line. * * *

"Costs matter in regulation. But when Congress does not say how to take costs into account, agencies have broad discretion to make that judgment. * * * Far more than courts, agencies have the expertise and experience necessary to design regulatory processes suited to 'a technical and complex arena.' And in any event, Congress has entrusted such matters to them, not to us."

Justice Thomas joined the majority but concurred separately to raise constitutional concerns about the longstanding Court practice of deferring to agency interpretations of federal laws.

NOTES ON MICHIGAN V. EPA

1. *The Aftermath of* Michigan v. EPA. The Court's decision came down at the end of June 2015. In December of that year, the D.C. Circuit, in an unpublished order, remanded the matter to the EPA without vacating the EPA's rule. The opinion noted that the EPA had represented to the court that it was on track to issue a final finding by April 2016. The petitioners sought Supreme Court review, arguing that the Court's decision meant that the EPA had acted without statutory authority, and this required that the D.C. Circuit vacate the rule. While the cert. petition was pending, the EPA did, indeed, issue a final finding: "consideration of cost does not cause [the EPA] to alter the previous conclusion that . . . [the regulations are] appropriate and necessary." Supplemental Finding that it is Appropriate and Necessary to Regulate Hazardous Air Pollutants from Coal- and Oil-Fired Electric Utility Steam Generating Units, 81 Fed. Reg. 24420 (Apr. 25, 2016). Less than three weeks later, the Supreme Court denied the cert. petition. *Michigan v. EPA*, 136 S.Ct. 2463 (2016). (Justice Scalia, who authored the initial decision, had passed away by this point. None of the other justices from the *Michigan v. EPA* majority dissented from the denial of cert.)

2.   *The Decision to Regulate Versus the Regulatory Process.* Note that in *Michigan v. EPA*, Justice Scalia and Justice Kagan agree about the issue as framed by Scalia—whether the EPA must consider cost when it issues regulations. They differ, however, on the question of timing. For Justice Scalia, because the Clean Air Act authorized the EPA to regulate whenever "appropriate and necessary," it is the decision to regulate, and not what comes later, that must be reviewed for reasonableness based on Congress's directive. For Justice Kagan, the EPA's failure to consider costs at the initial stage may still be reasonable under § 7412(n)(1)(A) so long as the Agency carefully considered cost before issuing the regulations.

Is Scalia correct in asserting that the distinction between an initial decision to regulate and the ultimate issuance of a regulation is an important one? Or, as Kagan suggests, is it more important to focus on the reasonableness of the regulatory process as a whole, regardless of the steps at which certain factors were considered? What is the harm in scrutinizing decisions about whether to regulate less strictly than scrutinizing the process by which those regulations are subsequently determined? Justice Scalia responds to this question; is his argument persuasive? And how does the subsequent history, described in the previous Note, bear on this question? If, as seemed likely from the beginning, EPA would find on remand that, after considering costs, regulation remained "appropriate and necessary," then was there a point to this drawn-out process?

3.   *Implying Consideration of Cost Under the Clean Air Act.* In *Whitman v. American Trucking Ass'ns, Inc*, 531 U.S. 457 (2001) (Section 1(B)(1) of this chapter), Justice Scalia, writing for the Court, addressed § 7409(b)(1) of the Clean Air Act, requiring EPA to set ambient air quality standards at levels "requisite to protect the public health" with an "adequate margin of safety." In a portion of the majority opinion omitted from the Casebook, the Court refused to read that provision as containing an implicit authorization to consider cost, in part because "authority to consider cost had elsewhere and so often been expressly granted [under the Act]." On what basis would you argue that "appropriate and necessary" as used in § 7412(n)(1)(A) impliedly encompasses cost considerations when "requisite to protect the public health" in § 7409(b) does not? Is this based on a fair reading of text? On consideration of larger context?

4.   *The Relevance of* SEC v. Chenery? EPA eschewed reliance on cost considerations when it deemed regulation of power plants appropriate and necessary. Should the Court then ignore EPA's arguments that it in fact conducted cost-benefit analysis before promulgating its regulation, because of the foundational administrative law principle that a court may uphold agency action only on the grounds invoked by the agency for taking its action? See *SEC v. Chenery*, 318 U.S. 80, 87 (1943) (see § 2(C) of this chapter, *Notes on* Chenery II). Alternatively, how relevant to the Chenery principle is EPA's express recognition when making its initial finding that consideration of costs would follow as part of developing a regulation? How relevant is the fact that the Agency knew when initiating the rulemaking process that any regulation would need to undergo cost-benefit review pursuant to Executive Order No. 12,866 (Appendix D)?

OVERVIEW ON JUDICIAL REVIEW OF AGENCY ACTION

As should be clear by now, judicial review of agency action can be complex and controversial. Courts at times must consider whether the action is even reviewable by the judiciary, what evidence to consider as part of their review, and then the contours and limits of deference to be given to the agency's decision. The Court's recent decision in

Department of Commerce v. New York confronted all of these questions, in an opinion authored by Chief Justice Roberts. Each answer provided by the Chief Justice was greeted with sharp disagreement from one or more of his colleagues.

Department of Commerce et al. v. New York et al.

139 S.Ct. 2551 (2019).

In March 2018, Secretary of Commerce Wilbur Ross announced that the 2020 census would include a question about citizenship status. Previous censuses had included questions about citizenship, but since 1950, the question was only sent to a fraction of all households (one-fourth to one-sixth until 2000; less than three percent in 2010). Lawsuits challenged the Secretary's decision, including a lawsuit brought by 18 states, the District of Columbia, and various cities and counties. These plaintiffs argued that the citizenship question would lead to less accurate results regarding population because substantial numbers of noncitizens and Hispanics would not respond to the census. With fewer responses, states with higher populations that included these groups could lose federal funds and even seats in the House of Representatives. Secretary Ross explained that his decision to include the question was based on collecting data the Department of Justice (DOJ) needed to better enforce the Voting Rights Act. However, in a supplemental memo presented to the district court at the DOJ's urging, it became clear that Secretary Ross had started considering addition of the citizenship question a year earlier than the administrative record suggested, and that he had approached the DOJ asking if it would support the need for the citizenship question. In an unusual turn of events, the district judge required the Department of Commerce to supplement the administrative record with materials including intra-agency communications and depositions of department officials.

After a bench trial, the district court ruled that Secretary Ross's decision was judicially reviewable, and that his decision had been arbitrary and capricious, and also based on a pretextual rationale. The district court enjoined the Department of Commerce from placing the citizenship question on the census until these legal errors were cured. The Department of Commerce appealed.

Chief Justice Roberts determined that at least some of the plaintiffs had standing, and that the Secretary's decision was not unconstitutional under the Enumeration Clause (which vests in Congress the authority to conduct a census, authority Congress had delegated to the Secretary). The Chief Justice then asked and answered three questions involving judicial review under the APA in order to reach his ultimate conclusions. First, was the Secretary's decision reviewable by the Court? If so, then second, was the decision arbitrary and capricious? And third, should the decision be set aside and remanded to the agency because the Secretary's reasoning was pretextual?

On the first question (reviewability) Chief Justice Roberts was joined by **Justices Thomas, Ginsburg, Breyer, Sotomayor, Kagan,** and **Kavanaugh.** Under the APA, judicial review of an agency action is not permitted to the extent that a relevant statute precludes judicial review (§ 701(a)(1)) or the action is "committed to agency discretion by law" (§ 701(a)(2)). The Court had read these judicial review exceptions narrowly, applying them only to actions that are traditionally committed to agency discretion (the Court here referred to *Heckler v. Chaney*, discussed at the start of § 3(C) of this chapter) or in cases where the relevant substantive statute fails to confer a meaningful standard of review.

This narrow exception was not applicable here. The Census Act tasked the Secretary of Commerce to conduct the census "in such form and content as he may determine." 13 U.S.C. § 141(a). Though clearly a broad delegation of authority, the provision does not mean the Secretary's discretion is unfettered. Chief Justice Roberts pointed to several provisions of the Act constraining the Secretary's decision-making in some way, and he reasoned that the Court was able to review whether the Secretary's action complies with his authority under the Act. Further, it was evident that questions about census-related decision-making were not traditionally committed to the agency's discretion, given that the Court has previously reviewed various challenges to these agency determinations, such as the use of statistical sampling (see Problem 6-3 in chapter 6). Accordingly, Chief Justice Roberts affirmed the district court's decision that the Secretary's action was judicially reviewable.

On the second question (arbitrary and capricious agency action), the Chief Justice was joined by **Justices Thomas, Alito, Gorsuch,** and **Kavanaugh**. The district court found that the Secretary's decision was arbitrary and capricious because it was not supported by the evidence presented to him. Secretary Ross had been given two options: include the citizenship question on the census or rely on administrative records to address the Department of Justice's concerns. The Census Bureau urged Secretary Ross to use the administrative records alone; it maintained that adding the citizenship question would lead to less accurate enumeration of the population because many noncitizens and Hispanics would choose not to participate. Secretary Ross, however, chose to implement the citizenship question in order to fill in gaps left in the administrative record. Respondents argued, and the district court agreed, that the Secretary had ignored the evidence presented by the Bureau and thus acted arbitrarily and capriciously in deciding to include the citizenship question.

Chief Justice Roberts disagreed, concluding that the evidence in the record supported the Secretary's decision to add the citizenship question to the census. Each choice before the Secretary had its own tradeoffs between accuracy and completeness of information. The Secretary was justified in finding the Bureau's decision inconclusive because the Bureau's analysis (involving projections and estimates) was incapable of determining that the citizenship question would cause a decline in responsiveness. Therefore, "the choice between reasonable policy alternatives in the face of uncertainty was the Secretary's to make. He considered the relevant factors, weighed risks and benefits, and articulated a satisfactory explanation for his decision. In overriding that reasonable exercise of discretion, the [district] court improperly substituted its judgment for that of the agency."

Finally, on the third question (pretext), the Chief Justice was joined by **Justices Ginsburg, Breyer, Sotomayor,** and **Kagan**. The Court initially had to determine which record to consider: the original administrative record or the expanded record ordered by the district court. While an agency must disclose the basis for its action, judicial review is "ordinarily limited to evaluating the agency's contemporaneous explanation in light of the existing administrative record." Indeed, "further judicial inquiry into 'executive motivation' represents 'a substantial intrusion' into the workings of another branch of Government." Further, "a court may not reject an agency's stated reasons simply because the agency might also have unstated reasons."

Nonetheless, the Chief Justice recognized a narrow exception to these settled APA principles: a reviewing court is permitted to order an expanded record to inquire into the mental processes of an agency decision-maker based on a "strong showing of bad faith or improper behavior." The district court's decision to expand the record here was premature but it was ultimately justified; thus, the Court reviewed the district court's finding of pretext in light of the expanded record. The Court noted that it was not improper for an agency head to come into office with his own policy preferences and ideas. At the same time, the Chief Justice added: "viewing the evidence as a whole, we share the District Court's conviction that the decision to reinstate a citizenship question cannot be adequately explained in terms of DOJ's request for improved citizenship data to better enforce the [Voting Rights Act]." The record showed that the Secretary wanted to reinstate the citizenship question and tasked his agency "to find the best rationale" to do so. The letter from the DOJ asking for the citizenship question to promote Voting Rights Act enforcement "was proposed by Commerce staff along the way and eventually pursued." The record further demonstrated at various points that DOJ lacked any real interest in this approach. While an agency is permitted to have both stated and unstated reasons for its decisions, an agency's decision will be considered pretextual if the sole stated reason (in this case, enforcement of the Voting Rights Act) "seems to have been contrived."

Chief Justice Roberts noted that the court's review should be deferential to the agency, but quoting an opinion from Judge Friendly on the Second Circuit, Roberts emphasized that "we are 'not required to exhibit a naiveté from which ordinary citizens are free.' The reasoned explanation requirement of administrative law, after all, is meant to ensure that agencies offer genuine justifications for important decisions, reasons that can be scrutinized by the courts and the interested public. Accepting contrived reasons would defeat the purpose of the enterprise. If judicial review is to be more than an empty ritual, it must demand something better than the explanation offered for the action taken in this case."

NOTES ON DEPARTMENT OF COMMERCE V. NEW YORK

The Court's decision issued on June 27, 2019. President Trump initially stated that he would ask for a delay in the 2020 Census "no matter how long" to continue the fight for inclusion of a question on citizenship. Subsequently, the Administration announced that it would proceed to conduct the census without a citizenship question, but then quickly changed back to state that it would seek a new permissible reason for keeping such a question. Finally on July 11, President Trump abandoned his quest to place a question about citizenship on the 2020 census; instead, he instructed the government to compile citizenship data from existing federal records.

1.   *Reviewability.* Was Chief Justice Roberts correct in determining that Secretary Ross's decision could be reviewed by the courts? Justice Alito dissented on this issue, insisting that the language of the Census Act (13 U.S.C. § 141(a): "[The Secretary shall] take a decennial census of population . . . in such form and content as he may determine") precluded judicial review under § 701(a)(2) of the APA. Additionally, judicial review was not necessary according to Justice Alito because Secretary Ross is held accountable by Congress, which must review the census questions according to the Census Act, and by the president, who is in turn accountable to the People. Are these arguments sufficient to overcome the Court's position that Congress did not delegate this much authority to agencies without the safeguard of judicial review?

2. *Arbitrary and Capricious.* Why did Chief Justice Roberts not find Secretary Ross's decision to be arbitrary and capricious given the contradictions between his decision and the record? Dissenting on this issue, Justice Breyer, joined by Justices Ginsburg, Sotomayor, and Kagan, provided ample evidence that Secretary Ross ignored, without reason, findings provided by the Census Bureau that asking the citizenship question on the census would lead to more inaccurate population data than would reliance on the administrative records. Breyer sums up his argument by asking "[h]ow can an agency support the decision to add a question to the short form [of the census], thereby risking a significant undercount of the population, on the grounds that it will *improve* the accuracy of citizenship data, when in fact the evidence indicates that adding the question will *harm* the accuracy of citizenship data?"

When writing his opinion, Justice Breyer may have had an answer to this question in mind. A month after oral argument in the case, and several weeks before the decision issued, the justices were made aware of new evidence that Thomas Hofeller, a Republican redistricting strategist, had played a large role in advocating for the citizenship question to be added to the 2020 census. Hofeller (who had died in the summer of 2018 but whose computer hard drives were made available by his daughter) had conducted a study in 2015 which found that adding such a question would make it possible to draw district boundaries that "would be advantageous to Republicans and non-Hispanic whites." Respondents alleged that Hofeller contributed to drafting the letter from the DOJ detailing the need for the citizenship question. None of the four opinions by the justices addresses Hofeller's role, although, if true, it would be damning proof that Secretary Ross's decision was made based on animus towards Hispanic voters. Might this newfound evidence help explain Chief Justice Roberts' choice to take the "pretext" route rather than the "arbitrary and capricious" route?

3. *Pretext.* Is Chief Justice Roberts' analysis that Secretary Ross's decision was pretextual supported by the APA? He seems to reach his conclusion in part out of concern for a lack of transparency and accountability that are essential to a democratic system. Criticism comes from Justice Thomas, joined by Justices Gorsuch and Kavanaugh. Justice Thomas goes through the administrative record in detail, pointing out that all the evidence relied upon by the Court supporting pretext shows "at most that the Secretary had other unstated reasons for reinstating the citizenship question." This, as Chief Justice Roberts agrees, is not cause for a finding of abuse of agency discretion. Justice Thomas opines that the Court's decision, unsupported by the APA, will create a new legal precedent through which anyone opposed to an agency action will be able to go on a witch hunt to find pretext. The Court's decision "could even implicate separation-of-powers concerns insofar as it enables judicial interference with the enforcement of laws."

Are the risks that Justice Thomas foresees worth the benefit of guarding against pretext in agency decisionmaking? Jennifer Nou contends that pretext has always been a part of the administrative system, as a way for agency officials to reconcile politics and expertise. This pretext, Nou argues, is not inherently bad in that it sometimes provides agencies with public legitimacy that leads to overall better results. Focusing on the Court's quote from Judge Friendly, Nou suggests that Chief Justice Roberts may have introduced a new principle: "the idea that such pretext must at least be plausible." Nou adds that lower courts should limit the Court's decision to rare instances because "allowing litigants to pounce at any hint of substantive or procedural bad faith threatens ossification and delay." Jennifer Nou, *Census symposium: A place for pretext in administrative law?* ScotusBlog (June 28, 2019), https://www.scotusblog.com/2019/06/

census-symposium-a-place-for-pretext-in-administrative-law/. Others are less sanguine about the use of pretext, contending that the Executive Branch has for years relied on pretext in the form of stealth "science" to advance deregulatory goals. A recent study by Thomas McGarity and Wendy Wagner found that agencies have a tendency to manipulate scientific findings as a way to advance their pre-determined political goals. This trend, seen across several administrations, undermines agency legitimacy and can have real-world consequences. Thomas O. McGarity & Wendy E. Wagner, *Deregulation Using Stealth "Science" Strategies*, 68 Duke L. J. 1719 (2019). Did Chief Justice Roberts strike the right balance between permitting agencies to make political decisions and preventing decisions where lack of transparency involves pretext?

CHAPTER 9

JUDICIAL DEFERENCE TO AGENCY INTERPRETATIONS

■ ■ ■

This chapter builds from the basic issues of statutory interpretation covered in Chapters 6 and 7 and from the introduction to administrative law in Chapter 8. Jerry Mashaw argues that agencies will and *ought to* follow different approaches to statutory interpretation than courts will and *ought to* follow, because of their different institutional competences and responsibilities.

Table 9-1.
Comparison of Statutory Interpretation by Agencies & Courts

Canon for Statutory Interpretation	Appropriate for Agencies?	Appropriate for Courts?
1. *Follow presidential directives unless clearly outside your authority*	Yes	No
2. *Interpret to avoid raising constitutional questions*	No	Yes
3. *Use legislative history as a primary interpretive guide*	Yes	No
4. *Interpret to give energy and breadth to all legislative programs within your jurisdiction*	Yes	No
5. *Engage in activist lawmaking*	Yes	No
6. *Respect all judicial precedent*	No	Yes
7. *Interpret to lend coherence to the overall legal order*	No	Yes
8. *Pay particular attention to the strategic parameters of interpretive efficiency*	Yes	No
9. *Interpret to secure hierarchical control over subordinates*	Yes	No
10. *Pay constant attention to your contemporary political milieu*	Yes	No
* Source: Jerry Mashaw, *Agency Statutory Interpretation*, Issues in Legal Scholarship, Issue 3: Dynamic Statutory Interpretation (2002): Article 9, *available at* www.bepress.com/ils/iss3/art9.		

Some items in Mashaw's table might be questioned. For example, item 5 strikes us as meaningless without a careful definition of "activist." Trevor Morrison,

Constitutional Avoidance in the Executive Branch, 106 Colum. L. Rev. 1189 (2006), argues, contra Mashaw, that agencies should consider the avoidance canon when they interpret statutes.

Overall, agencies are more instrumental, or purposive, in their application of statutes than courts tend to be. Kevin Stack, *Interpreting Regulations*, 111 Mich. L. Rev. 355 (2012); Christopher Walker, *Inside Agency Statutory Interpretation*, 67 Stan. L. Rev. 999, 1038–42 (2015). Conversely, courts are more text-focused and holistic (whole statute and other provisions in the code) than agencies. Given these different philosophies and competences, one might expect a great deal of conflict when judges review agency interpretations. Yet the dominant theme is "deference," with courts usually going along with agency interpretations. Around this basic insight has developed an increasingly complex body of Supreme Court doctrine.

1. THE BASIC FRAMEWORK: *SKIDMORE* AND *CHEVRON*

The New Deal approach to deference was founded on the comparative expertise of courts and agencies: the former should defer to the experts who worked with the statute day-in and day-out and developed wisdom about what worked and what did not. The leading case was *Skidmore v. Swift & Co.*, 323 U.S. 134 (1944). The case arose out of claims by Jim Skidmore and six other employees to recover overtime pay withheld allegedly in violation of the Fair Labor Standards Act of 1938 (FLSA). The men worked at the Fort Worth, Texas packing plant of Swift & Co. Two were engaged in general fire hall duties and maintenance of fire-fighting equipment of the plant. The others operated elevators or acted as relief men in fire duties. They worked from 7:00 a.m. to 3:30 p.m., with a half-hour lunch period, five days a week. Under an agreement with Swift, however, the workers agreed to stay in the fire hall on the company premises, or within hailing distance, three to four nights a week. This involved no task except to answer alarms, either because of fire or because the sprinkler was set off for some other reason. The employees claimed overtime pay under the FLSA. Swift refused, on the ground that the evening "on-call time" did not constitute "hours worked" for purposes of the statute.

Skidmore and his colleagues lost in the lower courts—but on appeal the Administrator of the Wage and Hour Division of the Department of Labor filed an *amicus* brief with the Supreme Court that described the flexible approach he had taken to the issue in a bulletin issued soon after the law was enacted. The Administrator distinguished situations where the employee carries on his normal life activities, subject to being called to solve a problem (such as a mechanic on-call to address problems with a company pump when they arise), from situations where the employee must stay in the office or close by (such as a company chauffeur). In the first situation, the employer was not required to pay workers for time spent sleeping and eating, but was required to pay for their "waiting around" time; in the second situation, the employer would usually be required to pay for "on call" time.

In the Administrator's view, the on-call time Skidmore spent sleeping and eating should not have been included in "hours worked," but the remainder of the on-call time should have been included. Justice Jackson's opinion for the *Skidmore* Court observed that the Administrator's practices and his recommendation in this case did not constitute a "binding" interpretation of the statute, but they were entitled to "respect," because they "constituted a body of experience and informed judgment" regarding workplace practices. "The weight of such a judgment in a particular case will depend upon the thoroughness evident in its consideration, the validity of its reasoning, its consistency with earlier and later pronouncements, and all those factors which give it power to persuade, if lacking power to control." The Court followed the Administrator's judgment.

Soon after the adoption of the Administrative Procedure Act of 1946 (APA), Louis Jaffe explained how the modern administrative state fit into the traditional statutory interpretation framework, while at the same time altering it subtly. Louis Jaffe, *Judicial Review: Question of Law*, 69 Harv. L. Rev. 239 (1955). Consistent with *Marbury* and APA § 706, the Supreme Court remained the expositor of what the law is, but in carrying out that duty the Court was and ought to be open to agency inputs. Sometimes the Court found that the statute was relatively clear, but other times statutory vagueness suggested a range of possible meanings and the Court was willing to accept the agency's interpretation if it were within that range, as in *Skidmore* and later decisions such as *Udall v. Tallman*, 380 U.S. 1, 16 (1965).

Jaffe also maintained that the New Deal had regularized a different kind of agency role. In many statutes, Congress had delegated to agencies the authority to create enforceable "law," usually through binding adjudications and legislative rules. Under those circumstances, Jaffe argued that the role of the Court was more like the deferential judicial review that the New Deal Court applied to social and economic legislation. Likewise, when reviewing agency *lawmaking*, the Court should give the agency's rule the benefit of the doubt and overturn it only if it was *unreasonable*, in light of the statutory text and purposes. Jaffe, *Judicial Review*, 243–44. This idea was the germ for what would become the famous "*Chevron* Doctrine," below.

Title VII was an important situs for debates about how deferential federal courts should be to agency interpretations of statutes Congress had charged them with implementing. Recall, from Chapter 1, the EEOC's aggressive interpretation of Title VII to prohibit employer policies having a disparate impact on racial minorities (unless the policy was required by business necessity). One of the reasons the Supreme Court gave for following that interpretation was strong deference to the EEOC's views. *Griggs v. Duke Power Co.*, 401 U.S. 424, 433–34 (1971).

Contrast the Supreme Court's attitude in *General Electric Co. v. Gilbert*, 429 U.S. 125 (1976). General Electric Co. provided for all of its employees a disability plan which paid weekly nonoccupational sickness and accident benefits. Excluded from the plan's coverage were disabilities arising from pregnancy. Female employees challenged this plan as sex discrimination in violation of Title VII. The Supreme Court, in an opinion by Justice Rehnquist, held that the exclusion of pregnancy was, technically, not sex discrimination, as the exclusion did not affect most female employees. More important, because there was "no proof that the package is in fact worth more to men than to women, it is impossible to find any gender-based discrimination in the scheme simply because women disabled as a result of pregnancy do not receive benefits * * *."

The employees relied on a 1972 guideline issued by the EEOC and urged the Court to defer to it. Because Congress did not give the EEOC authority to promulgate legislative rules to implement Title VII, Justice Rehnquist evaluated the agency's views under the *Skidmore* standard. Unlike the Administrator's bulletin in *Skidmore,* the EEOC's guideline in *Gilbert* was promulgated almost a decade after the statute was enacted, was at odds with advice the agency had been giving companies before 1972, and was inconsistent with the Department of Labor's interpretation of the Equal Pay Act of 1963. (Section 703(h) of Title VII explicitly permits practices allowed under § 6 of the Equal Pay Act.)

The dissenting Justices responded that "the final EEOC determination followed thorough and well-informed consideration. Indeed, realistically viewed, this extended evaluation of an admittedly complex problem and an unwillingness to impose additional, potentially premature costs on employers during the decision-making stages ought to be perceived as a practice to be commended. It is bitter irony that the care that preceded promulgation of the 1972 guideline is today condemned by the Court as tardy indecisiveness, its unwillingness irresponsibly to challenge employers' practices during the formative period is labeled as evidence of inconsistency, and this indecisiveness and inconsistency are bootstrapped into reasons for denying the Commission's interpretation its due deference." (Congress overrode *Gilbert* in the Pregnancy Discrimination Act of 1978, 42 U.S.C. § 2000e(k).)

The Supreme Court's *Skidmore* jurisprudence was very complicated by the time *Gilbert* was decided. The level of deference the Court accorded an agency interpretation depended on whether Congress had delegated the agency lawmaking authority, whether the agency interpretation was contemporaneous with the statute, whether the agency had consistently interpreted the statute, whether public or private institutions had relied on the agency's interpretation, and so forth. Colin Diver, *Statutory Interpretation in the Administrative State*, 133 U. Pa. L. Rev. 549, 562 n.95 (1985). The Court generally followed agency views, as in *Skidmore*, but lacked a general doctrinal approach to agency deference.

CHEVRON, U.S.A., INC. V. NATURAL RESOURCES DEFENSE COUNCIL

(1984)

Supreme Court of the United States, 1984.
467 U.S. 837, 104 S.Ct. 2778, 81 L.Ed.2d 694.

JUSTICE STEVENS delivered the opinion of the Court.

In the Clean Air Act Amendments of 1977, Pub. L. 95–95, 91 Stat. 685, Congress enacted certain requirements applicable to States that had not achieved the national air quality standards established by the Environmental Protection Agency (EPA) pursuant to earlier legislation. The amended Clean Air Act required these "nonattainment" States to establish a permit program regulating "new or modified major stationary sources" of air pollution. Generally, a permit may not be issued for a new or modified major stationary source unless several stringent conditions are met.[1] The EPA regulation promulgated to implement this permit requirement allows

---

[1]   Section 172(b)(6), 42 U.S.C. § 7502(b)(6), provides:

"The plan provisions required by subsection (a) shall— * * *

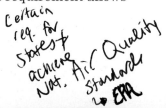

a State to adopt a plantwide definition of the term "stationary source." Under this definition, an existing plant that contains several pollution-emitting devices may install or modify one piece of equipment without meeting the permit conditions if the alteration will not increase the total emissions from the plant. The question presented by these cases is whether EPA's decision to allow States to treat all of the pollution-emitting devices within the same industrial grouping as though they were encased within a single "bubble" is based on a reasonable construction of the statutory term "stationary source." * * *

[II] When a court reviews an agency's construction of the statute which it administers, it is confronted with two questions. First, always, is the question whether Congress has directly spoken to the precise question at issue. If the intent of Congress is clear, that is the end of the matter, for the court, as well as the agency, must give effect to the unambiguously expressed intent of Congress.[9] If, however, the court determines Congress has not directly addressed the precise question at issue, the court does not simply impose its own construction on the statute, as would be necessary in the absence of an administrative interpretation. Rather, if the statute is silent or ambiguous with respect to the specific issue, the question for the court is whether the agency's answer is based on a permissible construction of the statute.[11]

"The power of an administrative agency to administer a congressionally created . . . program necessarily requires the formulation of policy and the making of rules to fill any gap left, implicitly or explicitly, by Congress." If Congress has explicitly left a gap for the agency to fill, there is an express delegation of authority to the agency to elucidate a specific provision of the statute by regulation. Such legislative regulations are given controlling weight unless they are arbitrary, capricious, or manifestly contrary to the statute. Sometimes the legislative delegation to an agency on a particular question is implicit rather than explicit. In such a case, a court may not substitute its own construction of a statutory provision for a reasonable interpretation made by the administrator of an agency.

We have long recognized that considerable weight should be accorded to an executive department's construction of a statutory scheme it is entrusted to administer, and the principle of deference to administrative interpretations

"has been consistently followed by this Court whenever decision as to the meaning or reach of a statute has involved reconciling conflicting policies,

"(6) require permits for the construction and operation of new or modified major stationary sources in accordance with section 173 (relating to permit requirements)." 91 Stat. 747.

[2] "(i) 'Stationary source' means any building, structure, facility, or installation which emits or may emit any air pollutant subject to regulation under the Act.

"(ii) 'Building, structure, facility, or installation' means all of the pollutant-emitting activities which belong to the same industrial grouping, are located on one or more contiguous or adjacent properties, and are under the control of the same person (or persons under common control) except the activities of any vessel." 40 CFR §§ 51.18(j)(1)(i) and (ii) (1983).

[9] The judiciary is the final authority on issues of statutory construction and must reject administrative constructions which are contrary to clear congressional intent. If a court, employing traditional tools of statutory construction, ascertains that Congress had an intention on the precise question at issue, that intention is the law and must be given effect.

[11] The court need not conclude that the agency construction was the only one it permissibly could have adopted to uphold the construction, or even the reading the court would have reached if the question initially had arisen in a judicial proceeding. * * *

and a full understanding of the force of the statutory policy in the given situation has depended upon more than ordinary knowledge respecting the matters subjected to agency regulations.

". . . If this choice represents a reasonable accommodation of conflicting policies that were committed to the agency's care by the statute, we should not disturb it unless it appears from the statute or its legislative history that the accommodation is not one that Congress would have sanctioned." *United States v. Shimer*, 367 U.S. 374, 382, 383 (1961).

In light of these well-settled principles it is clear that the Court of Appeals misconceived the nature of its role in reviewing the regulations at issue. Once it determined, after its own examination of the legislation, that Congress did not actually have an intent regarding the applicability of the bubble concept to the permit program, the question before it was not whether in its view the concept is "inappropriate" in the general context of a program designed to improve air quality, but whether the Administrator's view that it is appropriate in the context of this particular program is a reasonable one. Based on the examination of the legislation and its history which follows, we agree with the Court of Appeals that Congress did not have a specific intention on the applicability of the bubble concept in these cases, and conclude that the EPA's use of that concept here is a reasonable policy choice for the agency to make.

[The 1977 Amendments added a definition of "major stationary source," as "any stationary facility or source of air pollutants which directly emits, or has the potential to emit, one hundred tons per year or more of any air pollutant." Justice Stevens found this definition ambiguous. Examining the legislative history, he found only that Congress sought to accommodate both the "economic interest in permitting capital improvements to continue and the environmental interest in improving air quality." There was no clear evidence as to how Congress expected this balance to be carried out with regard to stationary sources.]

In these cases the Administrator's interpretation represents a reasonable accommodation of manifestly competing interests and is entitled to deference: the regulatory scheme is technical and complex, the agency considered the matter in a detailed and reasoned fashion, and the decision involves reconciling conflicting policies. Congress intended to accommodate both interests, but did not do so itself on the level of specificity presented by these cases. Perhaps that body consciously desired the Administrator to strike the balance at this level, thinking that those with great expertise and charged with responsibility for administering the provision would be in a better position to do so; perhaps it simply did not consider the question at this level; and perhaps Congress was unable to forge a coalition on either side of the question, and those on each side decided to take their chances with the scheme devised by the agency. For judicial purposes, it matters not which of these things occurred.

Judges are not experts in the field, and are not part of either political branch of the Government. Courts must, in some cases, reconcile competing political interests, but not on the basis of the judges' personal policy preferences. In contrast, an agency to which Congress has delegated policymaking responsibilities may, within the limits of that delegation, properly rely upon the incumbent administration's views of wise policy to inform its judgments. While agencies are not directly accountable to the people, the Chief Executive is, and it is entirely appropriate for this political branch of the Government to make such policy choices—resolving the competing interests which Congress itself either inadvertently did not resolve, or intentionally left to be resolved by the agency charged with the administration of the statute in light of everyday realities.

When a challenge to an agency construction of a statutory provision, fairly conceptualized, really centers on the wisdom of the agency's policy, rather than whether it is a reasonable choice within a gap left open by Congress, the challenge must fail. In such a case, federal judges—who have no constituency—have a duty to respect legitimate policy choices made by those who do. The responsibilities for assessing the wisdom of such policy choices and resolving the struggle between competing views of the public interest are not judicial ones: "Our Constitution vests such responsibilities in the political branches." *TVA v. Hill*, 437 U.S. 153, 195 (1978). * * *

JUSTICE MARSHALL and JUSTICE REHNQUIST did not participate in the consideration or decision of these cases.

JUSTICE O'CONNOR did not participate in the decision of these cases.

NOTES ON CHEVRON *DEFERENCE*

1. *The Accidental Birth of a New Regime.* The "bubble concept" adopted by the EPA was twice rebuffed in the D.C. Circuit, but the Department of Justice pressed it before the Supreme Court in an effort to reduce judicial interference with its deregulatory agency initiatives. Representing the EPA, Deputy Solicitor General Paul Bator argued that Congress's purpose was complex—to clean up the nation's air (the lower court's focus), but at a reasonable cost to industry (the EPA's focus). Because the statute was fairly open-ended, the EPA had considerable discretion in setting this policy balance, and federal judges should not upset that balance unless the EPA's view was clearly contrary to the statute.[1]

Penned by the first "political" deputy within the SG's Office, Bator's brief was a roadmap for relief from excessive regulatory burdens that was a hallmark of the Reagan Administration (1981–89). Liberal Justice William Brennan was suspicious of Bator's framework, but the Administration caught some lucky breaks as Justices dropped out of the case like flies in a hailstorm.[2] Their biggest break, though, was that the legality of the bubble concept was impossibly complicated for the Court. Apparently, the shakiest voice in the original 4–3 conference vote to reverse the D.C. Circuit, Justice Stevens explained his tentative willingness to side with the EPA: "When I am so confused, I go with the agency." (Conference Notes by Justice Blackmun.) Encouraged by Justice White,

---

[1] On the Bator brief and its background, see Thomas Merrill, *The Story of* Chevron USA Inc. v. Natural Resources Defense Council, Inc.: *Sometimes Great Cases Are Made, Not Born*, in *Statutory Interpretation Stories* 164, 177–80 (Eskridge, Frickey & Garrett eds., 2011).

[2] Although liberal Justice Brennan voted to affirm the D.C. Circuit, his liberal colleague Thurgood Marshall was absent due to illness. After voting with Brennan to affirm, Justice O'Connor also dropped out of the case because of a potential conflict of interest after her father died. See Memorandum from O'Connor to the Conference, June 14, 1984, in the Papers of Harry A. Blackmun, Library of Congress, Madison Building, Box 397, Folder 7. Also out of the case was Justice Rehnquist, who would probably have been a voice for deference.

the assigning Justice in the case, Justice Stevens not only accepted Bator's argument from complex statutory purpose, but went further to write an opinion that was analytically quite innovative.

2. *The Different Approach of* Chevron. *Chevron* reflects a different analytical approach to deference issues than *Gilbert* or *Skidmore* does. To begin with, the new approach is more formal and much simplified: Step One asks whether Congress specifically addressed the interpretive question. Justice Stevens's opinion says this is an issue Congress fudged. In that event, the Court moved to Step Two, which asks whether the agency's interpretation is "reasonable." If so, the Court has an obligation to defer. "Where an agency acts pursuant to delegated legislative authority, the task of interpretation is merely to define the boundaries" of what Peter Strauss calls the "zone of indeterminacy" within which Congress has authorized the agency to act.[3]

Chevron is also an important recognition of dynamic statutory interpretation in the modern administrative state, because it recognizes that first-order statutory interpretation will usually be accomplished by politically accountable—and therefore politically protean—agencies; because it further recognizes that under general statutory language that does not target the interpretive issue (Step One) there may be several "reasonable" agency interpretations, any of which must be upheld (Step Two); and because it recognizes that agency interpretations may themselves change over time. "An initial agency interpretation is not carved in stone. On the contrary, the agency, to engage in informal rulemaking, must consider varying interpretations and the wisdom of its policy on a continuing basis." *Chevron,* 467 U.S. at 863–64.

Finally, *Chevron* rests the idea of deference, at least in part, to the greater democratic legitimacy that agencies enjoy over courts in making policy choices that have been left open by Congress. This reflects the legal realist insight that the law will often be indeterminate, susceptible of more than one reading, but reconciles the realist insight with democratic accountability by insisting that unelected judges ratify the "reasonable" alternative adopted by the agency. Note that agencies may be accountable to Congress as well as the President, which gives them a double dose of greater policymaking legitimacy than federal courts have.

3. *Critical Reception. Chevron* was controversial from the very beginning. Then-Judge Breyer objected that a broad reading of *Chevron* is inconsistent with the judicial role articulated in both *Marbury* and in the APA. Both require courts to exercise independent judgment to declare what the law of the land is. Stephen Breyer, *Judicial Review of Questions of Law and Policy,* 38 Admin. L. Rev. 363, 370 (1986); see Cynthia Farina, *Statutory Interpretation and the Balance of Power in the Administrative State,* 89 Colum. L. Rev. 452 (1989) (developing this objection in detail). "[T]he present law of judicial review of administrative decisionmaking, the heart of administrative law, contains an important anomaly," Breyer said. "The law (1) requires courts to defer to agency judgments about *matters of law,* but (2) it also suggests that courts conduct independent, 'in-depth' reviews of agency judgments about *matters of policy.* Is this not the exact opposite of a rational system? Would one not expect courts to conduct a stricter

---

[3]   Peter Strauss, *One Hundred and Fifty Cases Per Year: Some Implications of the Supreme Court's Limited Resources for Judicial Review of Agency Action,* 87 Colum. L. Rev. 1093, 1124 (1987); see also Michael E. Herz, *Deference Running Riot: Separating Interpretation and Lawmaking under* Chevron, 6 Admin. L.J. Am. U. 187, 199 (1992); Peter Strauss, *"Deference" Is too Confusing—Let's Call Them "Chevron Space" and "Skidmore Weight,"* 112 Colum. L. Rev. 1143 (2012).

review of matters of law, where courts are more expert, but more lenient review of matters of policy, where agencies are more expert?" Breyer, *Judicial Review*, 397.

John Duffy suggested that the APA and *Chevron* could be reconciled only by understanding that regulatory statutes delegate to agencies the power to interpret ambiguous statutory commands, so long as the agencies' decisions do not conflict with other provisions of law. "Thus, *Chevron* is primarily a case about delegation, not deference." Duffy, *Administrative Common Law in Judicial Review*, 77 Tex. L. Rev. 113, 202 (1998). How consistent is Duffy's conclusion with the reasoning in *Chevron*? Or with the actual ruling of the case (upholding the agency)?

4. *Was There a* Chevron *Revolution? Preliminary Soundings.* The conventional wisdom in administrative law has been that *Chevron* was a revolutionary decision ushering in a new period of greater deference to agency interpretations of statutes agencies are charged with enforcing. This might be questioned or qualified. On the one hand, deference to agencies was a trend long preceding *Chevron*. Peter Schuck & E. Donald Elliott, *To the* Chevron *Station: An Empirical Study of Federal Administrative Law*, 1990 Duke L.J. 984, conclude from a lengthy historical study of federal appellate review of agency determinations that long before *Chevron* agency affirmance rates were on the rise in the federal courts—especially during the 1970s, even though that was the heyday of hard look review in the D.C. Circuit (which supposedly subjected administrative decisions to a greater degree of review).

On the other hand, it is not clear how much *Chevron* changed the prevailing Supreme Court practice. Since the New Deal, the Court has been deferential to agency decisions, sometimes with language presaging *Chevron*. In *Batterton v. Francis*, 432 U.S. 416 (1977), the Court held that when Congress delegates lawmaking authority to an agency, "Congress entrusts to the [agency], rather than to the courts, the primary responsibility for interpreting the statutory term." Once the agency has authoritatively construed the statute through legislative rules, the reviewing court "is not free to set aside the [agency] regulation simply because it would have interpreted the statute in a different manner."

Just as the Court was often highly deferential before *Chevron*, it was often pretty scrutinizing after *Chevron*. For example, in *INS v. Cardoza-Fonseca*, 480 U.S. 421 (1987), the Court not only rejected the INS's interpretation of its obligations not to deport noncitizens who have a "well-founded fear" of political persecution, 8 U.S.C. § 1158(a), but laid out a detailed legal regime for the INS to follow. Moreover, the Court in *Christensen v. Harris County*, 529 U.S. 576, 586–88 (2000), *id.* at 596–97 (Breyer, J., dissenting on other grounds), reaffirmed the *Skidmore* standard for weighing the views of an agency when expressed through informal opinions and letters. In both cases, Justice Scalia objected that the *Chevron* theory for deference (the superior legitimacy agencies had in filling in genuine statutory gaps) should apply to the EEOC and to informal but public rulings by the agency, but agreed that the EEOC's interpretations should be set aside because they were inconsistent with the statute.

Many well-informed judges and scholars believe that *Chevron* has had a bigger impact among federal courts of appeals than at the Supreme Court itself.[4] One reason for

---

[4]   Kent Barnett & Christopher Walker, Chevron *in the Circuits*, 116 Mich. L. Rev. 1 (2017) (empirical survey of court of appeals decisions citing *Chevron*, 2003–13); Schuck & Elliott, Chevron *Station*. See also Kristin Hickman & Mathew Krueger, *In Search of the Modern* Skidmore *Standard*, 107 Colum. L. Rev. 1235 (2007), finding a statistically significant amount of *Skidmore* deference among the courts of appeals.

this phenomenon may be the Supreme Court's discretionary jurisdiction. Courts of appeals must rule on all legitimate appeals, and *Chevron* gives them an easy way to dispatch many routine regulatory issues. The Supreme Court, in contrast, usually takes only the hardest issues that divide the lower courts, and the Justices may be reluctant just to go along with agency constructions that raise complicated normative as well as doctrinal issues.

MCI TELECOMMUNICATIONS CORP. V. AT&T

Supreme Court of the United States, 1994.
512 U.S. 218, 114 S.Ct. 2223, 129 L.Ed.2d 182.

JUSTICE SCALIA delivered the opinion for the Court.

Section 203(a) of Title 47 of the United States Code requires communications common carriers to file tariffs with the Federal Communications Commission, and § 203(b) authorizes the Commission to "modify" any requirement of § 203. These cases present the question whether the Commission's decision to make tariff filing optional for all nondominant long-distance carriers is a valid exercise of its modification authority.

[The Communications Act of 1934, 48 Stat. 1064, as amended, authorized the Federal Communication Commission (FCC) to regulate the rates charged for communication services to ensure that they were reasonable and nondiscriminatory. The requirements of § 203 that common carriers file their rates with the Commission and charge only the filed rate were the centerpiece of the Act's regulatory scheme. For decades, AT&T had a virtual monopoly over the nation's telephone service, but in the 1970s new competitors emerged. During the 1980s, the Commission allowed, and briefly required, nondominant carriers an exemption from the tariff requirements. The Supreme Court accepted AT&T's challenge to the agency rule.]

The dispute between the parties turns on the meaning of the phrase "modify any requirement" in § 203(b)(2). Petitioners [MCI and the FCC] argue that it gives the Commission authority to make even basic and fundamental changes in the scheme created by that section. We disagree. The word "modify"—like a number of other English words employing the root "mod-" (deriving from the Latin word for "measure") such as "moderate," "modulate," "modest," and "modicum"—has a connotation of increment or limitation. Virtually every dictionary we are aware of says that "to modify" means to change moderately or in minor fashion. See, e.g., Random House Dictionary of the English Language 1236 (2d ed. 1987) ("to change somewhat the form or qualities of; alter partially; amend"); [similar references from Webster's Third New International Dictionary, Oxford English Dictionary, and Black's Law Dictionary].

In support of their position, petitioners cite dictionary definitions contained in, or derived from, a single source, Webster's Third New International Dictionary 1452 (1981) (Webster's Third), which includes among the meanings of "modify," "to make a basic or important change in." Petitioners contend that this establishes sufficient ambiguity to entitle the Commission to deference in its acceptance of the broader meaning, which in turn requires approval of its permissive detariffing policy. See

Chevron. In short, they contend that the courts must defer to the agency's choice among available dictionary definitions. * * *

Most cases of verbal ambiguity in statutes involve * * * a selection between accepted alternative meanings shown as such by many dictionaries. One can envision (though a court case does not immediately come to mind) having to choose between accepted alternative meanings, one of which is so newly accepted that it has only been recorded by a single lexicographer. (Some dictionary must have been the very first to record the widespread use of "projection," for example, to mean "forecast.") But what petitioners demand that we accept as creating an ambiguity here is a rarity even rarer than that: a meaning set forth in a single dictionary (and, as we say, its progeny) which not only *supplements* the meaning contained in all other dictionaries, but *contradicts* one of the meanings contained in virtually all other dictionaries. Indeed, contradicts one of the alternative meanings contained in the out-of-step dictionary itself—for * * * Webster's Third itself defines "modify" to connote *both* (specifically) major change *and* (specifically) minor change. It is hard to see how that can be. When the word "modify" has come to mean *both* "to change in some respects" *and* "to change fundamentally" it will in fact mean *neither* of those things. It will simply mean "to change," and some adverb will have to be called into service to indicate the great or small degree of the change.

If that is what the peculiar Webster's Third definition means to suggest has happened—and what petitioners suggest by appealing to Webster's Third—we simply disagree. "Modify," in our view, connotes moderate change. It might be good English to say that the French Revolution "modified" the status of the French nobility—but only because there is a figure of speech called understatement and a literary device known as sarcasm. And it might be unsurprising to discover a 1972 White House press release saying that "the Administration is modifying its position with regard to prosecution of the war in Vietnam"—but only because press agents tend to impart what is nowadays called "spin." Such intentional distortions, or simply careless or ignorant misuse, must have formed the basis for the usage that Webster's Third, and Webster's Third alone, reported.[3] It is perhaps gilding the lily to add this: In 1934, when the Communications Act became law—the most relevant time for determining a statutory term's meaning, see *Perrin v. United States*, 444 U.S. 37, 42–45 (1979)—Webster's Third was not yet even contemplated. To our knowledge *all* English dictionaries provided the narrow definition of "modify," including those published by G. & C. Merriam Company. We have not the slightest doubt that is the meaning the statute intended. * * *

Since an agency's interpretation of a statute is not entitled to deference when it goes beyond the meaning that the statute can bear, *Chevron*, the Commission's permissive detariffing policy can be justified only if it makes a less than radical or fundamental change in the Act's tariff-filing requirement. The Commission's attempt to establish that no more than that is involved greatly understates the extent to

---

[3]   That is not an unlikely hypothesis. Upon its long-awaited appearance in 1961, Webster's Third was widely criticized for its portrayal of common error as proper usage. See, e.g., Follett, Sabotage in Springfield, 209 Atlantic 73 (Jan. 1962); Barzun, What is a Dictionary? 32 The American Scholar 176, 181 (spring 1963); Macdonald, The String Unwound, 38 The New Yorker 130, 156–157 (Mar. 1962). An example is its approval (without qualification) of the use of "infer" to mean "imply". * * *

which its policy deviates from the filing requirement, and greatly undervalues the importance of the filing requirement itself. [Tariff-filing is at the heart of the regulatory scheme, because it provides the data by which the FCC can police rate-discrimination and unreasonableness in charges.]

Bearing in mind, then, the enormous importance to the statutory scheme of the tariff-filing provision, we turn to whether what has occurred here can be considered a mere "modification." The Commission stresses that its detariffing policy applies only to nondominant carriers, so that the rates charged to over half of all consumers in the long-distance market are on file with the Commission. It is not clear to us that the proportion of customers affected, rather than the proportion of carriers affected, is the proper measure of the extent of the exemption (of course *all* carriers in the long-distance market are exempted, except AT&T). But even assuming it is, we think an elimination of the crucial provision of the statute for 40% of a major sector of the industry is much too extensive to be considered a "modification." What we have here, in reality, is a fundamental revision of the statute, changing it from a scheme of rate regulation in long-distance common-carrier communications to a scheme of rate regulation only where effective competition does not exist. That may be a good idea, but it was not the idea Congress enacted into law in 1934. * * *

[JUSTICE O'CONNOR took no part in the consideration or decision of these cases.]

JUSTICE STEVENS, with whom JUSTICE BLACKMUN and JUSTICE SOUTER join, dissenting. * * *

Although the majority observes that further relaxation of tariff-filing requirements might more effectively enhance competition, it does not take issue with the Commission's conclusions that mandatory filing of tariff schedules serves no useful purpose and is actually counterproductive in the case of carriers who lack market power. As the Commission had noted in its prior detariffing orders, if a nondominant carrier sought to charge inflated rates, "customers would simply move to other carriers." Moreover, an absence of market power will ordinarily preclude firms of any kind from engaging in price discrimination. The Commission plausibly concluded that any slight enforcement benefits a tariff-filing requirement might offer were outweighed by the burdens it would put on new entrants and consumers. Thus, the sole question for us is whether the FCC's policy, however sensible, is nonetheless inconsistent with the Act.

In my view, each of the Commission's detariffing orders was squarely within its power to "modify any requirement" of § 203. Section 203(b)(2) plainly confers at least some discretion to modify the general rule that carriers file tariffs, for it speaks of "*any* requirement." Section 203(c) of the Act, ignored by the Court, squarely supports the FCC's position; it prohibits carriers from providing service without a tariff "*unless otherwise provided by or under authority of this Act.*" Section 203(b)(2) is plainly one provision that "otherwise provides," and thereby authorizes, service without a filed schedule. The FCC's authority to modify § 203's requirements in "particular instances" or by "general order applicable to special circumstances or conditions" emphasizes the expansive character of the Commission's authority: modifications may be narrow or broad, depending upon the Commission's appraisal of current conditions. From the vantage of a Congress seeking to regulate an almost completely monopolized industry, the advent of competition is surely a "special circumstance or condition" that might legitimately call for different regulatory treatment. * * *

According to the Court, the term "modify," as explicated in all but the most unreliable dictionaries, rules out the Commission's claimed authority to relieve nondominant carriers of the basic obligation to file tariffs. Dictionaries can be useful aids in statutory interpretation, but they are no substitute for close analysis of what words mean as used in a particular statutory context. Even if the sole possible meaning of "modify" were to make "minor" changes,[3] further elaboration is needed to show why the detariffing policy should fail. The Commission came to its present policy through a series of rulings that gradually relaxed the filing requirements for nondominant carriers. Whether the current policy should count as a cataclysmic or merely an incremental departure from the § 203(a) baseline depends on whether one focuses on particular carriers' obligations to file (in which case the Commission's policy arguably works a major shift) or on the statutory policies behind the tariff-filing requirement (which remain satisfied because market constraints on nondominant carriers obviate the need for rate filing). When § 203 is viewed as part of a statute whose aim is to constrain monopoly power, the Commission's decision to exempt nondominant carriers is a rational and "measured" adjustment to novel circumstances—one that remains faithful to the core purpose of the tariff-filing section. See Black's Law Dictionary 1198 (3d ed. 1933) (defining "modification" as "A change; an alteration which introduces new elements into the details, or cancels some of them, but leaves *the general purpose and effect of the subject-matter* intact").

The Court seizes upon a particular sense of the word "modify" at the expense of another, long-established meaning that fully supports the Commission's position. That word is first defined in Webster's Collegiate Dictionary 628 (4th ed. 1934) as meaning "to limit or reduce in extent or degree." The Commission's permissive detariffing policy fits comfortably within this common understanding of the term. The FCC has in effect adopted a general rule stating that "if you are dominant you must file, but if you are nondominant you need not." The Commission's partial detariffing policy—which excuses nondominant carriers from filing *on condition that* they remain nondominant—is simply a relaxation of a costly regulatory requirement that recent developments had rendered pointless and counterproductive in a certain class of cases. * *

A modification pursuant to § 203(b)(1), like any other order issued under the Act, must of course be consistent with the purposes of the statute. On this point, the Court asserts that the Act's prohibition against unreasonable and discriminatory rates "would not be susceptible of effective enforcement if rates were not publicly filed." That determination, of course, is for the Commission to make in the first instance. But the Commission has repeatedly explained that (1) a carrier that lacks market power is entirely unlikely to charge unreasonable or discriminatory rates, (2) the statutory bans on unreasonable charges and price discrimination apply with full force regardless of whether carriers have to file tariffs, (3) any suspected violations by nondominant carriers can be addressed on the Commission's own motion or on a

---

[3]   As petitioner MCI points out, the revolutionary consent decree providing for the breakup of the Bell System was, per AT&T's own proposal, entitled "Modification of Final Judgment." See *United States v. American Telephone & Telegraph Co.*, 552 F. Supp. 131 (D.C. 1982), aff'd, 460 U.S. 1001 (1983).

damages complaint filed pursuant to § 206, and (4) the FCC can reimpose a tariff requirement should violations occur. The Court does not adequately respond to the FCC's explanations, and gives no reason whatsoever to doubt the Commission's considered judgment that tariff filing is altogether unnecessary in the case of competitive carriers; the majority's ineffective enforcement argument lacks any evidentiary or historical support. * * *

The filed tariff provisions of the Communications Act are not ends in themselves, but are merely one of several procedural *means* for the Commission to ensure that carriers do not charge unreasonable or discriminatory rates. The Commission has reasonably concluded that this particular means of enforcing the statute's substantive mandates will prove counterproductive in the case of nondominant long-distance carriers. Even if the 1934 Congress did not define the scope of the Commission's modification authority with perfect scholarly precision, this is surely a paradigm case for judicial deference to the agency's interpretation, particularly in a statutory regime so obviously meant to maximize administrative flexibility. Whatever the best reading of § 203(b)(2), the Commission's reading cannot in my view be termed unreasonable. It is informed (as ours is not) by a practical understanding of the role (or lack thereof) that filed tariffs play in the modern regulatory climate and in the telecommunications industry. Since 1979, the FCC has sought to adapt measures originally designed to control monopoly power to new market conditions. It has carefully and consistently explained that mandatory tariff-filing rules frustrate the core statutory interest in rate reasonableness. The Commission's use of the "discretion" expressly conferred by § 203(b)(2) reflects "a reasonable accommodation of manifestly competing interests and is entitled to deference: the regulatory scheme is technical and complex, the agency considered the matter in a detailed and reasoned fashion, and the decision involves reconciling conflicting policies." *Chevron.* The FCC has permissibly interpreted its § 203(b)(2) authority in service of the goals Congress set forth in the Act. We should sustain its eminently sound, experience-tested, and uncommonly well-explained judgment.

NOTES ON MCI, THE NEW TEXTUALISM, AND "EXCESSIVE" LEGISLATIVE DELEGATIONS TO AGENCIES

1. *The New Textualism and* Chevron: *Should the Court Consider Legislative History?* In *INS v. Cardoza-Fonseca*, 480 U.S. 421 (1987), Justice Scalia alone adhered to the view that *Chevron* permits overturning agency action only when the agency view clashes with a clear statutory text. All other Justices consulted the legislative history to determine the validity of the agency view under *Chevron*. Justice Scalia continued to press his view that statutory text and structure are the only relevant inquiries in Step One of the *Chevron* analysis (has Congress specifically addressed the issue?). Justice Stevens's approach, that other traditional tools such as legislative history and purpose are also relevant in Step One, seemed to lose ground on the Court after *Cardoza-Fonseca*. E.g., *Sutton v. United Air Lines, Inc.*, 527 U.S. 471, 482 (1999); *City of Chicago v. Environmental Defense Fund*, 511 U.S. 328 (1994).

However, there were many post-*MCI* decisions in which the Court considered legislative history and other nontextual arguments when doing a *Chevron* analysis. E.g., *FDA v. Brown & Williamson Tobacco Corp.* (Chapter 5, § 3(B)); *Babbitt v. Sweet Home* (the last case in Chapter 6). In *Wisconsin Public Intervenor v. Mortier,* 501 U.S. 597, 610 n.4 (1991), the Court *Chevron*-deferred to an agency interpretation that the federal pesticide law did not preempt state law. In determining whether Congress had directly addressed this question (Step One), the 8–1 Court examined the legislative history as well as the statutory text. Justice White's opinion marshaling legislative history won over the votes of Chief Justice Rehnquist and Justice O'Connor, who had originally thought that the statutory scheme "occupied the field" and therefore preempted state law (according to Justice Blackmun's conference notes). In dissent, Justice Scalia mounted a full-scale assault on the Court's reliance on legislative history—an assault that drew no support from any other Justice. See also William Eskridge Jr. & Lauren Baer, *The Continuum of Deference: Supreme Court Treatment of Agency Statutory Interpretations from* Chevron *to* Hamdan, 96 Geo. L.J. 1083, 1135–36 (2008) (empirical study of Supreme Court decisions, 1984-2006, finding that the Court relies on legislative history *more* often in *Chevron* cases than in other statutory interpretation cases).

Consider a suggestion made by the Seventh Circuit in *Bankers Life & Cas. Co. v. United States,* 142 F.3d 973 (1998). "While this circuit has examined legislative history during the first step of *Chevron,* we now seem to lean toward reserving consideration of legislative history and other appropriate factors until the second *Chevron* step." Consider how this might have applied to *Sweet Home,* the spotted owl case. If the statutory text were found ambiguous as to whether destruction of habitat constituted a taking of endangered animals, the Justices would have evaluated the agency's position under Step Two of *Chevron.* The legislative discussions surrounding the 1973 statute (relied on by dissenting Justice Scalia) and its 1982 amendment (relied on by Justice Stevens's opinion for the Court) would then have been relevant to the reasonableness of the agency's choice.

2. *The Implications of the New Textualism for Deference, More Generally.* If Justice Scalia's position on *Chevron* were adopted by the Court, agency rules might be *more* prone to reversal. Justice Scalia explains why this might be so in *Judicial Deference to Administrative Interpretation of Law,* 1989 Duke L.J. 511, 521:

> * * * One who finds *more* often (as I do) that the meaning of a statute is apparent from its text and from its relationship with other laws, thereby finds *less* often that the triggering requirement for *Chevron* deference exists. It is thus relatively rare that *Chevron* will require me to accept an interpretation which, though reasonable, I would not personally adopt. Contrariwise, one who abhors a "plain meaning" rule, and is willing to permit the apparent meaning of a statute to be impeached by legislative history, will more frequently find agency-liberating ambiguity. * * *

Accord, *Thomas Merrill, Textualism and the Future of the* Chevron *Doctrine,* 72 Wash. U.L.Q. 351, 372 (1994).[5] After the appointments of Justices Gorsuch and Kavanaugh, the

---

[5] Professor Merrill speculates that textualism may lead to a "permanent subordination of the *Chevron* doctrine." 72 Wash. U.L.Q. at 372. He explains:

> This has to do with the style of judging associated with textualism. Intentionalism mandates an "archeological" excavation of the past, producing opinions written in the style of the dry archivist sifting through countless documents in search of the tell-tale smoking gun of congressional intent. Textualism, in contrast, seems to transform statutory interpretation into a kind of exercise in judicial ingenuity. The textualist judge treats questions of interpretation like a puzzle to which it is assumed there is one right answer. The task is to assemble the various pieces of linguistic data, dictionary definitions, and canons into the best (most coherent, most explanatory) account of the meaning of the statute. This exercise places a great premium on cleverness. In one case the outcome turns on the place of a comma, in another on the inconsistency between a comma and rules of grammar, in a third on the

Court has remained willing to trump or confirm agency views with purely text-based arguments and without deferring *à la Chevron*. E.g., *Epic Sys. Corp. v. Lewis*, 138 S.Ct. 1612 (2018).

Textualists are more likely to resolve cases at Step One of *Chevron* (the agency is either right or wrong) and are less likely to get to Step Two, which is where deference really kicks in (the law is unclear, so the agency can make a choice the judges would not have otherwise made). Others are skeptical that methodology *per se* is decisive. See Eskridge & Baer, *Continuum of Deference*, 96 Geo. L.J. at 1153–56 (reporting relatively low agency agreement rates for textualist Justices Scalia and Thomas, but even lower rates for Justice Stevens, who relies on legislative history). Indeed, there are plenty of cases where new textualists were more lenient toward agency interpretations than they were in *MCI* or *Sweet Home*. E.g., *Massachusetts v. EPA*, 549 U.S. 497 (2007) (Scalia, J., dissenting) (deferring to EPA interpretation narrowly construing its broad statutory authority over greenhouse gases allegedly contributing to global warming).

3. *MCI, Dictionaries, and Excessive Delegations. MCI* is a leading case for the Court's well-honed deployment of dictionaries. See Chapter 6, § 1(A); James Brudney & Lawrence Baum, *Oasis or Mirage: The Supreme Court's Thirst for Dictionaries in the Rehnquist and Roberts Eras*, 55 Wm & Mary L. Rev. 483 (2013). The Court faults *Webster's Third* for too readily incorporating ordinary usage—which would seem to be most desirable for discerning the meaning an ordinary reader would draw from the statute. One might argue, however, that legislative drafters use language more formally, and thus more consistently with the prescriptive approach of *Webster's Second. MCI* also involves a methodological debate over the extent to which policy context matters.

One reading of *MCI* is that it supports a rule or presumption against excessive delegations. The Supreme Court will not enforce the nondelegation doctrine anymore— it will not strike down, as a constitutional violation, even extremely broad legislative delegations of lawmaking authority to administrative agencies. The Court can still give this "underenforced constitutional norm" some teeth, however, by "canonizing" it. Thus, the Court will be reluctant to read statutory delegations broadly, for fear that this will encourage the legislature to make excessive delegations. Does this reading make *MCI* a more persuasive opinion? How can this be reconciled with *Chevron*?

This reading of *MCI* reappeared in *FDA v. Brown & Williamson* (Chapter 5, § 3(B)), where the Court said: "Deference under *Chevron* to an agency's construction of a statute that it administers is premised on the theory that a statute's ambiguity constitutes an implicit delegation from Congress to the agency to fill in the statutory gaps. In extraordinary cases, however, there may be reason to hesitate before concluding that Congress has intended such an implicit delegation." The Court then noted the "unique place" tobacco has in American history and the "distinct regulatory scheme" Congress created for tobacco products. "Given this history and the breadth of the authority that the FDA has asserted, we are obliged to defer not to the agency's expansive construction of the statute, but to Congress' consistent judgment to deny the FDA this power. * * * As

---

conflict between quotation marks and the language of the text. One day arguments must be advanced in support of broad dictionary definitions; the next day in support of narrow dictionary definitions. New canons of construction and clear statement rules must be invented and old ones reinterpreted.

This active, creative approach to interpretation is subtly incompatible with an attitude of deference toward other institutions—whether the other institution is Congress or an administrative agency. In effect, the textualist interpreter does not *find* the meaning of the statute so much as *construct* the meaning. Such a person will very likely experience some difficulty in deferring to the meanings that other institutions have developed.

in *MCI*, we are confident that Congress could not have intended to delegate a decision of such economic and political significance to an agency in so cryptic a fashion." *Brown & Williamson*, 529 U.S. at 159–60. Is this a persuasive deployment of *MCI*? Should this precept have counseled a different result in some of the other cases where the Court has deferred to agencies, such as *Sweet Home* (end of Chapter 6)? *Bob Jones* (Chapter 5, § 2)?

UNITED STATES V. MEAD CORP.

Supreme Court of the United States, 2001.
533 U.S. 218, 121 S.Ct. 2164, 150 L.Ed.2d 292.

JUSTICE SOUTER delivered the opinion of the Court.

[Imports are taxed under the Harmonized Tariff Schedule of the United States, 19 U.S.C. § 1202. Title 19 further provides that the Customs Service "shall, under rules and regulations prescribed by the Secretary (of the Treasury), fix the final classification and rate of duty applicable to merchandise" under the Harmonized Schedule. The Secretary's regulations authorize "ruling letters" which set tariff classifications for particular imports. Such letters represent the official position of the Customs Service (USCS) with respect to a particular transaction or issue described therein, and they are binding on USCS personnel until modified or revoked.

[Mead Corporation imports three-ring bound "day planners." A USCS ruling letter set the tariff at 4% for "diaries, notebooks and address books, bound; memorandum pads . . . and similar articles," and at 0% for "Other items" in a general category that included registers, account books, and receipt books. From 1989 to 1993, USCS repeatedly treated day planners under the "Other" category. Then in 1993, USCS changed its position and issued a ruling letter classifying Mead's day planners as "Diaries . . . bound" subject to a 4% tariff.]

The question is whether a tariff classification ruling by the United States Customs Service deserves judicial deference. The Federal Circuit rejected Customs's invocation of *Chevron* in support of such a ruling, to which it gave no deference. We agree that a tariff classification has no claim to judicial deference under *Chevron*; there being no indication that Congress intended such a ruling to carry the force of law, but we hold that under *Skidmore*, the ruling is eligible to claim respect according to its persuasiveness. * * *

[II.A] When Congress has "explicitly left a gap for an agency to fill, there is an express delegation of authority to the agency to elucidate a specific provision of the statute by regulation," *Chevron*, and any ensuing regulation is binding in the courts unless procedurally defective, arbitrary or capricious in substance, or manifestly contrary to the statute. See APA, 5 U.S.C. § 706(2)(A), (D). But whether or not they enjoy any express delegation of authority on a particular question, agencies charged with applying a statute necessarily make all sorts of interpretive choices, and while not all of those choices bind judges to follow them, they certainly may influence courts facing questions the agencies have already answered. "[T]he well-reasoned views of the agencies implementing a statute 'constitute a body of experience and informed judgment to which courts and litigants may properly resort for guidance,'" *Bragdon v. Abbott*, 524 U.S. 624, 642 (1998) (quoting *Skidmore*), and "[w]e have long recognized that considerable weight should be accorded to an executive department's construction of a statutory scheme it is entrusted to administer. . . ." *Chevron.*

The fair measure of deference to an agency administering its own statute has been understood to vary with circumstances, and courts have looked to the degree of the agency's care, its consistency, formality, and relative expertise, and to the persuasiveness of the agency's position, see *Skidmore.* * * *

Since 1984, we have identified a category of interpretive choices distinguished by an additional reason for judicial deference. This Court in *Chevron* recognized that Congress not only engages in express delegation of specific interpretive authority, but that "[s]ometimes the legislative delegation to an agency on a particular question is implicit." Congress, that is, may not have expressly delegated authority or responsibility to implement a particular provision or fill a particular gap. Yet it can still be apparent from the agency's generally conferred authority and other statutory circumstances that Congress would expect the agency to be able to speak with the force of law when it addresses ambiguity in the statute or fills a space in the enacted law, even one about which "Congress did not actually have an intent" as to a particular result. When circumstances implying such an expectation exist, a reviewing court has no business rejecting an agency's exercise of its generally conferred authority to resolve a particular statutory ambiguity simply because the agency's chosen resolution seems unwise, but is obliged to accept the agency's position if Congress has not previously spoken to the point at issue and the agency's interpretation is reasonable; *cf.* 5 U.S.C. § § 706(2) (a reviewing court shall set aside agency action, findings, and conclusions found to be "arbitrary, capricious, an abuse of discretion, or otherwise not in accordance with law").

We have recognized a very good indicator of delegation meriting *Chevron* treatment in express congressional authorizations to engage in the process of rulemaking or adjudication that produces regulations or rulings for which deference is claimed. [Citing cases, including *Gilbert*, that applied only *Skidmore* deference to EEOC interpretations.] It is fair to assume generally that Congress contemplates administrative action with the effect of law when it provides for a relatively formal administrative procedure tending to foster the fairness and deliberation that should underlie a pronouncement of such force. Thus, the overwhelming number of our cases applying *Chevron* deference have reviewed the fruits of notice-and-comment rulemaking or formal adjudication. That said, and as significant as notice-and-comment is in pointing to *Chevron* authority, the want of that procedure here does not decide the case, for we have sometimes found reasons for *Chevron* deference even when no such administrative formality was required and none was afforded, see, e.g., *NationsBank of N.C., N.A.* v. *Variable Annuity Life Ins. Co.*, 513 U.S. 251, 256–257, 263 (1995). The fact that the tariff classification here was not a product of such formal process does not alone, therefore, bar the application of *Chevron.*

There are, nonetheless, ample reasons to deny *Chevron* deference here. The authorization for classification rulings, and Customs's practice in making them, present a case far removed not only from notice-and-comment process, but from any other circumstances reasonably suggesting that Congress ever thought of classification rulings as deserving the deference claimed for them here.

[II.B] No matter which angle we choose for viewing the Customs ruling letter in this case, it fails to qualify under *Chevron*. On the face of the statute, to begin with, the terms of the congressional delegation give no indication that Congress meant to delegate authority to Customs to issue classification rulings with the force of law. We are not, of course, here making any global statement about Customs's authority, for it is true that the general rulemaking power conferred on Customs authorizes some regulation with the force of law, or "legal norms" * * *. It is true as well that Congress had classification rulings in mind when it explicitly authorized, in a parenthetical, the issuance of "regulations establishing procedures for the issuance of binding rulings prior to the entry of the merchandise concerned," 19 U.S.C. § 1502(a). The reference to binding classifications does not, however, bespeak the legislative type of activity that would naturally bind more than the parties to the ruling, once the goods classified are admitted into this country. And though the statute's direction to disseminate "information" necessary to "secure" uniformity, *ibid.*, seems to assume that a ruling may be precedent in later transactions, precedential value alone does not add up to *Chevron* entitlement; interpretive rules may sometimes function as precedents, see Strauss, *The Rulemaking Continuum*, 41 Duke L.J. 1463, 1472–1473 (1992), and they enjoy no *Chevron* status as a class. In any event, any precedential claim of a classification ruling is counterbalanced by the provision for independent review of Customs classifications by the CIT [Court of International Trade]; the scheme for CIT review includes a provision that treats classification rulings on par with the Secretary's rulings on "valuation, rate of duty, marking, restricted merchandise, entry requirements, drawbacks, vessel repairs, or similar matters," § 1581(h). It is hard to imagine a congressional understanding more at odds with the *Chevron* regime. [Indeed, the Customs Service itself did not act as though its letter rulings were lawmaking. The agency did not follow the notice-and-comment process when issuing such documents—10,000 to 15,000 letter rulings a year churned out by 46 different Customs offices. Hence, the Court treated them the same way it treats agency guidances or policy documents, as "beyond the *Chevron* pale."]

[II.C] To agree with the Court of Appeals that Customs ruling letters do not fall within *Chevron* is not, however, to place them outside the pale of any deference whatever. *Chevron* did nothing to eliminate *Skidmore*'s holding that an agency's interpretation may merit some deference whatever its form, given the "specialized experience and broader investigations and information" available to the agency, and given the value of uniformity in its administrative and judicial understandings of what a national law requires.

There is room at least to raise a *Skidmore* claim here, where the regulatory scheme is highly detailed, and Customs can bring the benefit of specialized experience to bear on the subtle questions in this case: whether the daily planner with room for brief daily entries falls under "diaries," when diaries are grouped with "notebooks and address books, bound; memorandum pads, letter pads and similar articles"; and whether a planner with a ring binding should qualify as "bound," when a binding may be typified by a book, but also may have "reinforcements or fittings of metal, plastics, etc." A classification ruling in this situation may therefore at least seek a respect proportional to its "power to persuade," *Skidmore*. Such a ruling may surely claim the merit of its writer's thoroughness, logic and expertness, its fit with prior interpretations, and any other sources of weight.

[II.D] Underlying the position we take here, like the position expressed by Justice Scalia in dissent, is a choice about the best way to deal with an inescapable feature of the body of congressional legislation authorizing administrative action. That feature is the great variety of ways in which the laws invest the Government's administrative arms with discretion, and with procedures for exercising it, in giving meaning to Acts of Congress. Implementation of a statute may occur in formal adjudication or the choice to defend against judicial challenge; it may occur in a central board or office or in dozens of enforcement agencies dotted across the country; its institutional lawmaking may be confined to the resolution of minute detail or extend to legislative rulemaking on matters intentionally left by Congress to be worked out at the agency level.

Although we all accept the position that the Judiciary should defer to at least some of this multifarious administrative action, we have to decide how to take account of the great range of its variety. If the primary objective is to simplify the judicial process of giving or withholding deference, then the diversity of statutes authorizing discretionary administrative action must be declared irrelevant or minimized. If, on the other hand, it is simply implausible that Congress intended such a broad range of statutory authority to produce only two varieties of administrative action, demanding either *Chevron* deference or none at all, then the breadth of the spectrum of possible agency action must be taken into account. Justice Scalia's first priority over the years has been to limit and simplify. The Court's choice has been to tailor deference to variety. This acceptance of the range of statutory variation has led the Court to recognize more than one variety of judicial deference, just as the Court has recognized a variety of indicators that Congress would expect *Chevron* deference. * * *

Since the *Skidmore* assessment called for here ought to be made in the first instance by the Court of Appeals for the Federal Circuit or the CIT, we go no further than to vacate the judgment and remand the case for further proceedings consistent with this opinion.

JUSTICE SCALIA, dissenting.

Today's opinion makes an avulsive change in judicial review of federal administrative action. Whereas previously a reasonable agency application of an ambiguous statutory provision had to be sustained so long as it represented the agency's authoritative interpretation, henceforth such an application can be set aside unless "it appears that Congress delegated authority to the agency generally to make rules carrying the force of law," as by giving an agency "power to engage in adjudication or notice-and-comment rulemaking, or . . . some other [procedure] indicati[ng] comparable congressional intent," and "the agency interpretation claiming deference was promulgated in the exercise of that authority." What was previously a general presumption of authority in agencies to resolve ambiguity in the statutes they have been authorized to enforce has been changed to a presumption of no such authority, which must be overcome by affirmative legislative intent to the contrary. And whereas previously, when agency authority to resolve ambiguity did not exist the court was free to give the statute what it considered the best interpretation, henceforth the court must supposedly give the agency view some indeterminate amount of so-called *Skidmore* deference. We will be sorting out the consequences of the *Mead* doctrine, which has today replaced the *Chevron* doctrine, for years to come. I would adhere to our established jurisprudence, defer to the reasonable interpretation the Customs Service has given to the statute it is charged with enforcing, and reverse the judgment of the Court of Appeals.

[I.A] As to principle: The doctrine of *Chevron*—that all *authoritative* agency interpretations of statutes they are charged with administering deserve deference— was rooted in a legal presumption of congressional intent, important to the division of powers between the Second and Third Branches. When, *Chevron* said, Congress leaves an ambiguity in a statute that is to be administered by an executive agency, it is presumed that Congress meant to give the agency discretion, within the limits of reasonable interpretation, as to how the ambiguity is to be resolved. By committing enforcement of the statute to an agency rather than the courts, Congress committed its initial and primary interpretation to that branch as well.

There is some question whether *Chevron* was faithful to the text of the Administrative Procedure Act (APA), which it did not even bother to cite. But it was in accord with the origins of federal-court judicial review. Judicial control of federal executive officers was principally exercised through the prerogative writ of mandamus. That writ generally would not issue unless the executive officer was acting plainly beyond the scope of his authority. [Quoting *Wilbur v. United States ex rel. Kadrie*, 281 U.S. 206, 221–222 (1930).] Statutory ambiguities, in other words, were left to reasonable resolution by the Executive.

The basis in principle for today's new doctrine can be described as follows: The background rule is that ambiguity in legislative instructions to agencies is to be resolved not by the agencies but by the judges. Specific congressional intent to depart from this rule must be found—and while there is no single touchstone for such intent it can generally be found when Congress has authorized the agency to act through (what the Court says is) relatively formal procedures such as informal rulemaking and formal (and informal?) adjudication, and when the agency in fact employs such procedures. The Court's background rule is contradicted by the origins of judicial review of administrative action. But in addition, the Court's principal criterion of congressional intent to supplant its background rule seems to me quite implausible. There is no necessary connection between the formality of procedure and the power of the entity administering the procedure to resolve authoritatively questions of law. The most formal of the procedures the Court refers to—formal adjudication—is modeled after the process used in trial courts, which of course are not generally accorded deference on questions of law. The purpose of such a procedure is to produce a closed record for determination and review of the facts—which implies nothing about the power of the agency subjected to the procedure to resolve authoritatively questions of law. * * *

[In Part II.B, Justice Scalia lamented the terrible "practical effects" of the Court's new rule.] (1) The principal effect will be protracted confusion. As noted above, the one test for *Chevron* deference that the Court enunciates is wonderfully imprecise: whether "Congress delegated authority to the agency generally to make rules carrying the force of law, . . . as by . . . adjudication[,] notice-and-comment rulemaking, or . . . some other [procedure] indicati[ng] comparable congressional intent." But even this description does not do justice to the utter flabbiness of the Court's criterion, since, in order to maintain the fiction that the new test is really just the old one, applied consistently throughout our case law, the Court must make a virtually open-ended exception to its already imprecise guidance: In the present case, it tells us, the absence of notice-and-comment rulemaking (and "[who knows?] [of] some other [procedure] indicati[ng] comparable congressional intent") is not enough to decide the question of *Chevron* deference, "for we have sometimes found reasons for *Chevron* deference even when no such administrative formality was required and none was afforded." The opinion then goes on to consider a grab bag of other factors—including the factor that used to be the sole criterion for *Chevron* deference: whether the interpretation represented the *authoritative* position of the agency. It is hard to know what the lower courts are to make of today's guidance.

(2) Another practical effect of today's opinion will be an artificially induced increase in informal rulemaking. Buy stock in the GPO. Since informal rulemaking and formal adjudication are the only more-or-less safe harbors from the storm that the Court has unleashed; and since formal adjudication is not an option but must be mandated by statute or constitutional command; informal rulemaking—which the Court was once careful to make voluntary unless required by statute—will now become a virtual necessity. As I have described, the Court's safe harbor requires not merely that the agency have been given rulemaking authority, but also that the agency have *employed* rulemaking as the means of resolving the statutory ambiguity. (It is hard to understand why that should be so. Surely the mere *conferral* of rulemaking authority demonstrates—if one accepts the Court's logic—a congressional intent to allow the agency to resolve ambiguities. And given that intent, what difference does it make that the agency chooses instead to use another perfectly permissible means for that purpose?) Moreover, the majority's approach will have a perverse effect on the rules that do emerge, given the principle (which the Court leaves untouched today) that judges must defer to reasonable agency interpretations of their own regulations. Agencies will now have high incentive to rush out barebones, ambiguous rules construing statutory ambiguities, which they can then in turn further clarify through informal rulings entitled to judicial respect.

(3) Worst of all, the majority's approach will lead to the ossification of large portions of our statutory law. Where *Chevron* applies, statutory ambiguities remain ambiguities subject to the agency's ongoing clarification. They create a space, so to speak, for the exercise of continuing agency discretion. As *Chevron* itself held, the Environmental Protection Agency can interpret "stationary source" to mean a single smokestack, can later replace that interpretation with the "bubble concept" embracing an entire plant, and if that proves undesirable can return again to the original interpretation. For the indeterminately large number of statutes taken out of *Chevron* by today's decision, however, ambiguity (and hence flexibility) will cease with the first judicial resolution. *Skidmore* deference gives the agency's current position some vague and uncertain amount of respect, but it does not, like *Chevron*, *leave* the matter within the control of the Executive Branch for the future. Once the

court has spoken, it becomes *unlawful* for the agency to take a contradictory position; the statute now *says* what the court has prescribed. It will be bad enough when this ossification occurs as a result of judicial determination (under today's new principles) that there is no affirmative indication of congressional intent to "delegate"; but it will be positively bizarre when it occurs simply because of an agency's failure to act by rulemaking (rather than informal adjudication) before the issue is presented to the courts.

One might respond that such ossification would not result if the agency were simply to readopt its interpretation, after a court reviewing it under *Skidmore* had rejected it, by repromulgating it through one of the *Chevron*-eligible procedural formats approved by the Court today. Approving this procedure would be a landmark abdication of judicial power. It is worlds apart from *Chevron* proper, where the court does not *purport* to give the statute a judicial interpretation—except in identifying the scope of the statutory ambiguity, as to which the court's judgment is final and irreversible. (Under *Chevron* proper, when the agency's authoritative interpretation comes within the scope of that ambiguity—and the court therefore approves it—the agency will not be "overruling" the court's decision when it later decides that a different interpretation (still within the scope of the ambiguity) is preferable.) By contrast, under this view, the reviewing court will not be holding the agency's authoritative interpretation within the scope of the ambiguity; but will be holding that the agency has not used the "delegation-conferring" procedures, and that the court must therefore *interpret the statute on its own*—but subject to reversal if and when the agency uses the proper procedures.

*** I know of no case, in the entire history of the federal courts, in which we have allowed a judicial interpretation of a statute to be set aside by an agency—or have allowed a lower court to render an interpretation of a statute subject to correction by an agency. As recently as 1996, we rejected an attempt to do *precisely that.* In *Chapman* v. *United States*, 500 U.S. 453 (1991) [affirming *Marshall* v. *United States*, excerpted and discussed in Chapter 7, § 3], we had held that the weight of the blotter paper bearing the lysergic acid diethylamide (LSD) must be counted for purposes of determining whether the quantity crossed the 10-gram threshold of 21 U.S.C. § 841(b)(1)(A)(v) imposing a minimum sentence of 10 years. At that time the United States Sentencing Commission applied a similar approach under the Sentencing Guidelines, but had taken no position regarding the meaning of the statutory provision. The Commission later changed its Guidelines approach, and, according to the petitioner in *Neal* v. *United States*, 516 U.S. 284 (1996), made clear its view that the statute bore that meaning as well. The petitioner argued that we should defer to that new approach. We would have none of it.

"Were we, for argument's sake, to adopt petitioner's view that the Commission intended the commentary as an interpretation of § § 841(b)(1), and that the last sentence of the commentary states the Commission's view that the dose-based method is consistent with the term 'mixture or substance' in the statute, he still would not prevail. The Commission's dose-based method cannot be squared with *Chapman*. . . . In these circumstances, we need not decide what, if any, deference is owed the Commission in order to reject its alleged contrary interpretation. Once we have determined a statute's meaning, we adhere to our ruling under the doctrine of *stare decisis*, and we assess an agency's later interpretation of the statute against that settled law."

There is, in short, no way to avoid the ossification of federal law that today's opinion sets in motion. What a court says is the law after according *Skidmore* deference will be the law forever, beyond the power of the agency to change even through rulemaking.

(4) And finally, the majority's approach compounds the confusion it creates by breathing new life into the anachronism of *Skidmore*, which sets forth a sliding scale of deference owed an agency's interpretation of a statute that is dependent "upon the thoroughness evident in [the agency's] consideration, the validity of its reasoning, its consistency with earlier and later pronouncements, and all those factors which give it power to persuade, if lacking power to control"; in this way, the appropriate measure of deference will be accorded the "body of experience and informed judgment" that such interpretations often embody. Justice Jackson's eloquence notwithstanding, the rule of *Skidmore* deference is an empty truism and a trifling statement of the obvious: A judge should take into account the well-considered views of expert observers.

It was possible to live with the indeterminacy of *Skidmore* deference in earlier times. But in an era when federal statutory law administered by federal agencies is pervasive, and when the ambiguities (intended or unintended) that those statutes contain are innumerable, totality-of-the-circumstances *Skidmore* deference is a recipe for uncertainty, unpredictability, and endless litigation. To condemn a vast body of agency action to that regime (all except rulemaking, formal (and informal?) adjudication, and whatever else might now and then be included within today's intentionally vague formulation of affirmative congressional intent to "delegate") is irresponsible.

[In Part II, Justice Scalia criticized the majority's approach as an important departure from the Court's post-*Chevron* precedents as well as *Chevron* itself. In Part III, Justice Scalia explained why *Chevron*, properly understood, required deference to the Customs Service. "*Chevron* sets forth an across-the-board presumption, which operates as a background rule of law against which Congress legislates: Ambiguity means Congress intended agency discretion. Any resolution of the ambiguity by the administering agency that is authoritative—that represents the official position of the agency—must be accepted by the courts if it is reasonable." Given that precept as his starting point, Justice Scalia found nothing in the customs statute to rebut the presumptive discretion Congress gave the Service to draw lines as to tariff categories. In Part IV, Justice Scalia maintained that deference was required by *NationsBank of N.C., N.A. v. Variable Annuity Life Ins. Co.*, 513 U. S. 251 (1995), which the Court acknowledged as an instance in which *Chevron* deference was warranted notwithstanding the absence of formal adjudication, notice-and-comment rulemaking, or comparable administrative formality.]

NOTES ON MEAD AND THE "CHEVRON REVOLUTION"

1.   *The Grounding of* Chevron *on the Notion of Delegated Authority to Issue Orders or Rules Having the Force of Law.* The Court's decision in *Mead* makes clear that the normative basis for *Chevron*'s deference regime is congressional intent to delegate *lawmaking* authority to agencies. See Thomas Merrill & Kristin Hickman, Chevron's *Domain*, 89 Geo. L.J. 833 (2001), as well as Merrill, *Rethinking Article I, Section 1: From Nondelegation to Exclusive Delegation*, 104 Colum. L. Rev. 2097 (2004). Again over the dissents of Justice Scalia, the Court reaffirmed this understanding in *National Cable & Telecommunications Ass'n v. Brand X Internet Services*, 545 U.S. 967 (2005), and *Gonzales v. Oregon*, 546 U.S. 243 (2006) (both excerpted below).

Although this is the Court's official test, it is one that the post-*Chevron* Court has applied unevenly. On the one hand, the Court does not seem to have a clear idea of when Congress has vested agencies with authority to create rules or orders having the "force of law." Thus, the Court often treats National Labor Relations Board (NLRB) orders as having the force of law, even though that is clearly incorrect as a technical or historical matter: The NLRA says that the agency's orders should *not* have legal effect unless the agency or a party goes to court and obtains an order to that effect. See Thomas Merrill & Kathryn Tongue Watts, *Agency Rules with the Force of Law: The Original Convention*, 116 Harv. L. Rev. 467 (2002). Indeed, the EPA rule in *Chevron* was not, in 1984, a rule having the force of law. *Id.* at 587. The Court's approach is further complicated in *Mead*, where the Court says that Congress might implicitly delegate lawmaking authority to an agency. It is far from clear what kinds of statutory schemes would amount to an "implicit" delegation, and the lower courts have shown evidence of increased confusion since *Mead*.[6]

On the other hand, the Court's deployment of *Chevron* has been underwhelming in those cases where there has been an explicit grant of lawmaking authority. The Eskridge and Baer study surveyed 1014 post-*Chevron* Supreme Court decisions between 1984 and 2006 where an agency statutory interpretation was presented to the Court. In 8.3% of those cases, the Court majority applied the *Chevron* framework—but almost 27% of the cases involved agency decisions pursuant to grants of adjudicatory or legislative rulemaking authority. About 10% of the *Chevron* cases involved very informal agency action clearly not derived from lawmaking grants—agency letters, interpretive guidances, and even opinions voiced in *amicus* briefs. See William Eskridge Jr. & Lauren Baer, *The Continuum of Deference: Supreme Court Treatment of Agency Statutory Interpretations from* Chevron *to* Hamdan, 96 Geo. L.J. 1083, 1125 (2008) (Table 4).

The Eskridge and Baer study also found that, for the period 1984–2006, the Court followed pre-*Chevron* deference-plus (i.e., more deferential than *Skidmore*) regimes in 4.8% of its cases. *Id.* at 1099–1100 (Table 1). The conceptual basis for these cases falls somewhere between *Chevron* and *Skidmore*: Congress has vested such-and-such agency with authority to carry out the statutory purpose; to carry out the congressional purpose, the agency needs interpretational breathing room; hence, courts ought to defer to reasonable agency readings of the statute. E.g., *Beth Israel Hospital v. NLRB*, 437 U.S. 483 (1978) (NLRB); *National Muffler Dealers v. United States*, 440 U.S. 472 (1979), overruled in *Mayo Foundation v. United States*, 131 S.Ct. 704 (2011) (*Chevron* replacing *National Muffler* in tax cases).

---

6   See Lisa Schultz Bressman, *How* Mead *Has Muddled Judicial Review of Agency Action*, 58 Vand. L. Rev. 1443 (2005) (yes, *Mead* has muddled judicial review of agency action).

2. *The Survival—Indeed, Flourishing—of* Skidmore. *Mead* confirmed the survival of *Skidmore* as the default deference regime. The Eskridge and Baer study identified 6.7% of the cases in their database as ones where the Court explicitly applied *Skidmore* deference, almost as many cases as where the Court applied *Chevron* during their time period (1984–2006). See Eskridge & Baer, *Continuum of Deference,* 96 Geo. L.J. at 1099–1100 (Table 1). Moreover, in 17.8% of the cases Eskridge and Baer collected, the Court relied on or was clearly influenced by an agency rule or *amicus* brief, but without citation of *Skidmore* or an announcement that the Court was "deferring."

A different picture emerges from a study of the courts of appeals. Kent Barnett & Christopher Walker, Chevron *in the Circuits,* 116 Mich. L. Rev. 1 (2017). The authors collected circuit court decisions citing *Chevron* between 2003 and 2013. Among the decisions applying the *Chevron* framework, the agency prevailed 77.4% of the time, compared with a 56.0% win rate when those courts applied *Skidmore* and 38.5% when those courts engaged in *de novo* review. Barnett and Walker believe that *Chevron* exercises a much greater influence among the courts of appeals than within the Supreme Court itself.

3. *Evidence of Ideological Voting by the Justices in Agency Deference Cases.* In the wake of *Mead,* a number of academic studies found evidence of ideological voting in agency deference cases. Consider the results of the Eskridge and Baer study:

Table 9-2.
Justices' Agreement with Agency Interpretations, 1984–2006

Supreme Court Justice (Tenure)	Agreement with Agency Overall	Agreement with Liberal Agency Interpretations	Agreement with Conservative Agency Interpretations
Warren Burger (1969–86)	82.3%	75.9%	87.0%
Byron White (1962–93)	74.0%	71.9%	76.3%
Lewis Powell (1971–87)	72.7%	73.9%	73.0%
Stephen Breyer (1994–)	72.0%	79.5%	64.9%
William Rehnquist (1971–2006)	70.6%	59.4%	79.1%
Ruth Bader Ginsburg (1993–)	69.5%	77.1%	61.9%
Anthony Kennedy (1986–)	69.3%	61.8%	74.0%
David Souter (1990–2009)	68.7%	75.6%	62.5%
Sandra Day O'Connor (1981–2007)	68.6%	61.5%	73.7%
Harry Blackmun (1970–93)	65.1%	80.6%	55.3%
Antonin Scalia (1986–2016)	64.5%	53.8%	71.6%
Clarence Thomas (1991–)	63.1%	46.8%	75.8%
John Paul Stevens (1975–2010)	60.9%	79.2%	49.6%
Thurgood Marshall (1967–91)	55.6%	84.8%	38.8%
William Brennan (1956–90)	52.6%	81.6%	36.7%
Source: Eskridge & Baer, *Continuum of Deference,* 96 Geo. L.J. at 1154 (Table 20).			

These data reveal a wide variance of judicial willingness to go along with agency interpretations: Warren Burger, Byron White, and Lewis Powell were quite deferential, while William Brennan and Thurgood Marshall went against agency views almost half of the time. Surprisingly, John Paul Stevens, the author of *Chevron*, was one of the less deferential in practice, as was Antonin Scalia.

Eskridge and Baer found pretty much the same pattern when they limited their analysis to the *Chevron* cases in their database or to the 267 cases involving agency interpretations pursuant to delegated lawmaking authority. The Justices had slightly higher deference rates, but the ideological pattern remained the same. Accord, Thomas Miles & Cass Sunstein, *Do Judges Make Regulatory Policy? An Empirical Investigation of* Chevron, 73 U. Chi. L. Rev. 823 (2006).

PROBLEM INVOLVING AN AGENCY'S DYNAMIC INTERPRETATION OF AN OLD STATUTE

Problem 9-1. Is a Late-Payment Fee Statutory "Interest"? Section 30 of the National Bank Act of 1864, Rev. Stat. § 5197, as amended, 12 U.S.C. § 85, provides that a national bank may charge its loan customers "interest at the rate allowed by the laws of the State * * * where the bank is located." In *Marquette Nat. Bank of Minneapolis v. First of Omaha Service Corp.,* 439 U.S. 299 (1978), the Supreme Court held that this provision authorizes a national bank to charge out-of-state credit-card customers an interest rate allowed by the bank's home state, even when that rate is higher than what is permitted by the states in which the cardholders reside. Citibank is a national bank, and it starts to charge *late-payment fees* that are lawful in its home state but prohibited in many states where cardholders reside. Can Citibank lawfully charge the late-payment fees? Are such fees *interest* authorized by the Bank Act, as Citibank claims?

(A) How would a judge decide this issue? A judge would start with the statutory language and the Supreme Court's *Marquette National Bank* precedent. Is a late-payment fee "interest" as that term is used in ordinary or regulatory parlance? You might consult modern dictionaries as well as dictionaries of the era in which the statute was enacted. For example, 1 J. Bouvier, *A Law Dictionary* 652 (6th ed. 1856), defined "interest" as "compensation which is paid by the borrower to the lender or by the debtor to the creditor for * * * use [of money]." The Supreme Court said this in *Brown v. Hiatts,* 15 Wall. 177, 185 (1873): "Interest is the compensation allowed by law, or fixed by the parties, for the use or forbearance of money or as damages for its detention." More recently, *Webster's Ninth New Collegiate* defines interest as "a charge for borrowed money, generally a percentage of the amount borrowed." And the Oxford English Dictionary (2d edition) defined it this way in 1989: "Money paid for the use of money lent (the principal), or for forbearance of a debt, according to a fixed ratio."

Is there a statutory plain meaning here? If you were a lower court judge obligated to follow the Supreme Court's guidance, would you also consult legislative history and the purpose of the National Bank Act? If you think you should, read the Court's decision in *Marquette National Bank*, which has an excellent discussion of the legislative history and goals of the 1864 Act. Is it relevant that the Federal Reserve Board does not consider late-payment fees to be "finance charges" that must be disclosed to mortgage borrowers as an annual percentage interest rate under the Truth in Lending Act of 1967? Federal Reserve Board, Regulation Z, § 226.4(c)(2).

Ultimately, how would you rule on the late-payments issue: Interest? Or not?

(B) Does an agency interpretation make a difference? The issue of late-payment fees was not a salient one in 1864, when the statute was enacted. But once late-payment fees became an important consumer issue and many states prohibited the practice, the Comptroller of the Currency started to address the issue. "The Comptroller of the Currency is charged with the enforcement of banking laws to an extent that warrants the invocation of [judicial deference] with respect to his deliberative conclusions as to the meaning of these laws." *NationsBank of N.C., N.A. v. Variable Annuity Life Ins. Co.,* 513 U.S. 251, 256–257 (1995).

In 1996, more than a century after the statute's enactment, the Comptroller, after notice-and-comment, adopted the following rule:

> The term "interest" as used in 12 U.S.C. § 85 includes any payment compensating a creditor or prospective creditor for an extension of credit, making available of a line of credit, or any default or breach by a borrower of a condition upon which credit was extended. It includes, among other things, the following fees connected with credit extension or availability: numerical periodic rates, late fees, not sufficient funds (NSF) fees, overlimit fees, annual fees, cash advance fees, and membership fees. It does not ordinarily include appraisal fees, premiums and commissions attributable to insurance guaranteeing repayment of any extension of credit, finders' fees, fees for document preparation or notarization, or fees incurred to obtain credit reports."

61 Fed. Reg. 4862 (codified at 12 CFR § 7.4001(a)). Is this regulation entitled to *Chevron* deference, even though it was adopted more than a century after the statute was enacted? Does this regulation change the answer you gave to Problem 9-1(A)?

(C) Does the agency's change of position make a difference? Consider, further, that the 1996 regulation was not the first occasion for the Comptroller's Office to address the issue of late-payment fees. In June 1964, the Comptroller wrote a letter to the President's Committee on Consumer Interests, which states that "[c]harges for late payments, credit life insurance, recording fees, documentary stamp are illustrations of charges which are made by some banks which would not properly be characterized as interest." In a 1988 opinion letter, the Deputy Chief Counsel of the OCC stated that "it is my position that [under § 85] the laws of the states where the banks are located * * * determine whether or not the banks can impose the foregoing fees and charges [including late fees] on Iowa residents," OCC Interpretive Letter No. 452, reprinted in 1988–1989 Transfer Binder, CCH Fed. Banking L. Rep. ¶ 85,676, p. 78,064 (1988).

Do these earlier interpretations change your answer to Problem 9-2(B)? In other words, do they undermine the deference you might otherwise accord the 1996 rule? Cf. *Gilbert v. General Electric Co.,* above. Is *Gilbert* distinguishable? Should the Court treat an agency interpretation modified from one opinion letter to the next differently from a changed interpretation that is expressed through notice and comment rulemaking?

For the U.S. Supreme Court's analysis of the foregoing issues, see *Smiley v. Citibank (South Dakota), N.A.,* 517 U.S. 735 (1996). Would a similar issue (namely, the meaning of a statutory term) be handled the same by a state supreme court? Do state courts follow something like the *Chevron* regime? If so, would they handle issues like this the same way the U.S. Supreme Court does? Consider the following case and the Note following it.

Seeton v. Pennsylvania Game Commission

594 Pa. 563, 937 A.2d 1028 (2007).

Johnna Seeton sued to require the Pennsylvania Game Commission to assume authority over the Tioga Boar Hunt Preserve's alleged violations of the Pennsylvania Game and Wildlife Code, 34 Pa.C.S. §§ 101, *et seq.* Tioga was in the business of selling "canned hunts," in which customers paid a fee to shoot and kill an animal in an enclosed area which limited the ability of the animal to escape and the amount of pursuit in which the customer might engage. Seeton alleged that "[a]nimals used in canned hunts are often drugged, tied to stakes or lured to feeding stations in order to further assure that the 'hunter' will get the guaranteed kill that has been promised by the hunting preserve's proprietor." Complaint in Mandamus ¶ 6.

The Commission's Chief Counsel rejected Seeton's contention that the animals hunted at the Preserve, including wild boar (as well as elk, rams, and buffalo), were "protected mammals" pursuant to the Commission's regulations promulgated under the Game and Wildlife Code. *See* 58 Pa. Code § 133.1. Among the mammals protected under the Commission's regulations were "wild mammals," but that term was defined nowhere in the Game and Wildlife Code or in the Commission's regulations. Relying on a dictionary, the Chief Counsel opined that "wild mammals" must apply only to "mammals that are currently living in a state of nature," thus excluding "mammals that are currently living in a state of captivity, either in pens or within enclosures." Because the animals at the Preserve were kept within enclosures, the Commission concluded that they are not "wild" for purposes of the Game and Wildlife Code and regulations issued thereunder; rather, they are "the personal property of their owners." *Id.*

The Declaration of Policy in the Game & Wildlife Code referred to the Commission's "proprietary ownership, jurisdiction and control of game or wildlife living free in nature," which the same provision identifies as "a renewable natural resource of this Commonwealth." 34 Pa.C.S. § 2161(a). The Code empowered and directed the Commission "to protect, propagate, manage, and preserve the game or wildlife of this Commonwealth and to enforce, by proper actions and proceedings, the laws of this Commonwealth relating thereto." 34 Pa.C.S. § 322(a). The Code also conferred discretion upon the Commission to regulate hunting, *id.* §§ 322(c)(1)–(7), classify wild birds and animals, *id.* § 322(c)(8), manage and develop game lands, *id.* § 322(c)(10); and to promulgate necessary and appropriate regulations concerning hunting and fur-taking in the Commonwealth, *id.* § 2102(a).

The Commission's main argument on appeal was that the Court should defer to its interpretation, so long as it was a reasonable one, even if not the only reasonable reading of the Game & Wildlife Code. Writing for the majority, **Justice Baer** agreed that judges should defer to agency interpretations of statutes it is charged with implementing, but not when the General Assembly has directly addressed the issue.

"While an agency's interpretation of an ambiguous statute it is charged with enforcing is entitled to deference, courts' deference never comes into play when the statute is clear. Notably, the United States Supreme Court, in its extensive precedent concerning judicial deference to administrative interpretations of ambiguous enabling statutes, *see, e.g., Chevron*, has recognized the dangers of deferring to interpretations developed in anticipation of litigation. *See Bowen v. Georgetown Univ. Hosp.*, 488 U.S. 204 (1988) (declining to defer to agency interpretations forwarded for the first time in connection with litigation)." In footnote 12, Justice Baer said this: "[W]e appear never to have explicitly adopted even *Chevron*'s general rule in the context of state administrative law. The *Chevron* approach to such cases at the federal level, however, is indistinguishable from our own approach to agency interpretations of Commonwealth statutes."

The Court decided the case at what the U.S. Supreme Court would consider *Chevron* Step One. "Wildlife," the court noted, "is defined by the Game and Wildlife Code as, *inter alia,* 'wild birds' and 'wild mammals.' 34 Pa.C.S. § 102. Thus, while the Commission is correct that the term 'wild mammals' is not itself defined by either the Game and Wildlife Code or the Commission's regulations, it is not wholly undetermined within the statutory scheme. Rather, 'wild mammals' plainly are a subset of the term 'wildlife.' Thus, whatever is true of 'wildlife' must also be true of 'wild mammals,' barring an explicit statutory exception. Interestingly, 34 Pa.C.S. § 2163(b) prohibits, *inter alia,* the release within the Commonwealth of 'imported game or wildlife *or game or wildlife reared in captivity*' (emphasis added). This provision undermines the Commission's claims regarding the meaning of the word 'wild' in at least two dimensions. First, insofar as 'wildlife' is defined to include 'wild animals' and 'wild mammals,' as explained above, the notion of 'wildlife reared in captivity' (which posits the prospect of 'wild animals' and 'wild mammals' reared in captivity), is wholly antithetical to the Commission's attempt to tie the word 'wild' to the degree of freedom enjoyed by a given animal. Similarly, it is impossible to 'release' 'wildlife' (and hence 'wild animals' and 'wild mammals'), the activity proscribed in the abovementioned section, if the animal's liberty is a necessary condition to its status as 'wild,' since one cannot release an animal from a non-captive state.

"Notably, the Commission does not dispute [Seeton's] assertion that Tioga drugs or otherwise disables wild boar to facilitate easier kills, nor does it argue that, were it bound to enforce the law against Tioga, the alleged conduct would be permissible. The Game and Wildlife Code makes it illegal to hunt through use of poison or chemical of any kind. 34 Pa.C.S. § 2308(9). Thus, the Commission effectively argues that the hunting of captive animals on fenced, private property may be undertaken by means such as drugs or restraint that violate, at a minimum, the spirit of the Game and Wildlife Code. This is an untenably narrow interpretation of its statutory mandate.

"Interestingly, the Commission does not in all instances espouse such a restrained view of its authority. In *Commonwealth v. Gosselin,* 861 A.2d 996 (Pa. Super. 2004), appellants rescued and effectively domesticated an injured squirrel, [they named] Nutkin, while residing in South Carolina, where to do so was legal. Later, however, appellants moved to Pennsylvania, where they had some dealings with the Commission. Specifically, a Wildlife Officer, while investigating an unrelated tip lodged by appellants, observed Nutkin in the house, explained that appellants were barred by Pennsylvania law from housing a squirrel, and cited them for a violation when they refused to surrender custody of Nutkin to the officer. In resolving the case, the Commission agreed that Nutkin was a 'wild animal' under the Game and Wildlife Code."

The Court ruled that mandamus should have been granted to require the Commission to accept authority over Tioga. Retiring **Justices Nigro** (turned out in a retention election) and **Newman** (winning her retention election but then retiring voluntarily) did not participate in the case.

Dissenting, **Justice Eakin** maintained that the controversy was not justiciable and that the Court should have deferred to the Commission's interpretation. "The majority does not afford due deference to [the agency's] determination that boars are not protected wild animals under the Game Code. An administrative interpretation receives controlling weight unless the interpretation is plainly erroneous or inconsistent with the agency's regulation. *Department of Public Welfare v. Forbes Health System*, 492 Pa. 77, 422 A.2d 480, 482 (1980). [Seeton] argues the term wild animals is defined as all non-domestic mammals; therefore, wild animals and wild mammals are the same. Although the Game Code defines wild animals as all non-domestic mammals, it does not formally define the term wild mammal or the term wild. The boars at Tioga Boar Hunt Preserve are living in a state of captivity; thus, they are not living in a state of nature. The Game Code's policy declaration regarding actions for damages to game or wildlife provides:

> The Commonwealth has sufficient interest in *game or wildlife living in a free state* to give it standing, through its authorized agents, to recover compensatory and punitive damages in a civil action against any person who kills any game or wildlife or who damages any game or wildlife habitat. The proprietary ownership, jurisdiction and control of *game or wildlife living free in nature* is vested in the Commonwealth by virtue of the continued expenditure of its funds and its efforts to protect, propagate, manage and preserve the game or wildlife population as a renewable natural resource of this Commonwealth.

34 Pa.C.S. § 2161(a) (emphasis added). Considering the legislative expression of Pennsylvania's inherent interest in preserving wildlife living free in nature, the Commission's interpretation that the Preserve's boars are not wild animals is not plainly erroneous or inconsistent with the Game Code."

NOTE ON DEFERENCE TO AGENCY INTERPRETATIONS BY STATE COURTS

Chevron has received a mixed reception in the states. For decades, the dominant view among state supreme courts was to give strong deference (akin to *Chevron* Step Two) to agency interpretations only in limited circumstances, such as where the interpretation was longstanding or was the product of the agency's particular expertise. Otherwise, state courts hewed to their traditional prerogative to review agency interpretations of law *de novo*. E.g., *Tesoro Alaska Petroleum v. Kenai Pipe Line*, 796 P.2d 896, 903 (Alaska 1987); Eric Lane, *How to Read a Statute in New York: A Response to Judge Kaye and Some More*, 28 Hofstra L. Rev. 85, 123–24 (1999). In the new millennium, however, a growing number of states have adopted the *Chevron* deference regime (or something akin to it), see Michael Pappas, *No Two-Stepping in the Laboratories: State Deference Standards and Their Implications for Improving the* Chevron *Doctrine*, 39 McGeorge L. Rev. 977 (2008), while a small but also growing number of states have rejected deference to agency interpretations. E.g., *Tetra Tech EC, Inc. v. Wisconsin Dep't of Revenue*, 914 N.W.2d 21 (Wis. 2018).

States that have adopted a *Chevron*-like approach include **Alabama**, see *Ex parte State Health Planning & Dev. Agency*, 855 So. 2d 1098, 1102 (Ala. 2002); **Colorado**, see *North Colorado Medical Center, Inc. v. Committee on Anticompetitive Conduct*, 914 P.2d 902, 907 (Colo. 1996) (citing *Chevron*); **Florida**, see *Donato v. AT&T*, 767 So.2d 1146, 1153 (Fla. 2000) (adopting a two-step, *Chevron*-style analysis, but see our further discussion below); **Georgia**, see *Tibbles v. Teachers Retirement*, 775 So.E.2d 527 (Ga. 2015); **Hawaii**, see *Del Monte Fresh Produce (Haw.), Inc. v. Int'l Longshore & Warehouse Union, Local 142, AFL-CIO*, 146 P.3d 1066, 1076–77 (Haw. 2006); **Maine**, see *Cobb v.*

Bd. of Counseling Prof'ls Licensure, 896 A.2d 271, 275 (Me. 2006); **Massachusetts**, see *Commerce Ins. Co. v. Comm'r of Ins.*, 852 N.E.2d 1061, 1064 (Mass. 2006); *Protective Life Ins. Co. v. Sullivan*, 682 N.E.2d 624, 627–28 (Mass. 1997); **Nebraska**, see *Reed v. State Dep't of Labor*, 717 N.W.2d 899 (Neb. 2006); **Nevada**, see *Cable v. State ex rel. ITS Employers Ins. Co. of Nev.*, 127 P.3d 528, 532 (Nev. 2006); **South Carolina**, see *Brown v. Bi-Lo, Inc.*, 581 S.E.2d 836, 838 (S.C. 2003); **Texas**, *Railroad Comm'n of Texas v. Texas Citizens for a Safe Future and Clean Water*, 336 S.W.3d 619 (2011); and **Wyoming**, see *Qwest Corp. v. State ex rel. Wyo. Dep't of Revenue*, 130 P.3d 507, 511 (Wyo. 2006).

States that have explicitly adopted *Chevron* itself for reviewing points of law announced in legislative rulemaking and adjudications by agencies include **Kentucky**, see *Board of Trustees of Judicial Form Retirement System v. Attorney General of the Commonwealth*, 132 S.W.3d 770, 786–87 (Ky. 2003); **Mississippi**, see *Parkerson v. Smith*, 817 So.2d 529, 534 (Miss. 2002); **Montana**, see *Thompson v. J.C. Billion, Inc.*, 294 P.3d 397 (Mont. 2013); and **West Virginia**, see *Maikotter v. University of West Virginia Bd. of Trustees*, 527 S.E.2d 802 (W.Va. 1999). The Montana Supreme Court's decision in *Billion* suggested that the trend in the state cases was in the direction of *Chevron* or its equivalent, at least when agency interpretations are generated by legislative rulemaking or agency adjudications.

As reflected in *Seeton*, **Pennsylvania** follows something like the *Chevron* approach, but without the elaborate doctrinal trappings that the U.S. Supreme Court has associated with *Chevron*. E.g., *Harmon v. Unemployment Compensation Bd. of Rev.*, 207 A.3d 292 (Pa. 2019). As *Seeton* also reflects, it is not clear that the Pennsylvania Supreme Court is actually more deferential to agency interpretations than other state high courts. While Justice Baer makes out a very good case for Seeton's view, doesn't Justice Eakins make out an equally good case for the Commission's view? Were the Pennsylvania judges deferential in fact? Was there really a plain meaning that defeated the agency's views? How would the U.S. Supreme Court have decided the Case of the Wild Boars?

An indeterminate number of states, such as **Washington**, have articulated a formal *Chevron*-like approach, but have not applied it with regularity. Compare *Sebastian v. Department of Labor and Industries*, 12 P.3d 594 (Wash. 2000) (refusing to defer to the agency construction of an ambiguous statute and applying substantive canons instead), with *Durant v. State Farm Mut. Automobile Ins. Co.*, 419 P.3d 400, 206 (Wash. 2018) (deferring to agency explanation in an *amicus* brief). The Eskridge and Baer study found that the U.S. Supreme Court did not apply *Chevron* with regularity either.

Similar ambiguity also characterizes the situation in **California**. The state supreme court's basic approach is deferential to administrative agencies. *Yamaha Corp. of Am. v. State Bd. of Equalization*, 960 P.2d 1031 (Cal. 1998); *People ex rel. Lungren v. Superior Court*, 926 P.2d 1042, 1051 (Cal. 1996). However, California state courts tend to discuss deference in terms of expertise and longstanding agency interpretations—which sounds more like *Skidmore* than *Chevron*. See *Hoechst Celanese Corp. v. Franchise Tax Bd.*, 22 P.3d 324, 335 (Cal. 2001); *Henning v. Industrial Welfare Comm'n*, 762 P.2d 442, 451 (Cal. 1988).

A number of state supreme courts have not adopted the *Chevron* deference regime and defer to agency interpretations only in a limited range of cases. This position is illustrated by *Connecticut State Medical Society v. Connecticut Board of Examiners in Podiatry*, 546 A.2d 830 (Conn. 1988). There, the state's podiatry board had interpreted the statutory term "foot" to include the ankle. The **Connecticut** Supreme Court overturned this construction, holding that the dictionary definition of the word, rather than the agency's understanding of the legislature's intent, provided the proper resolution of the interpretation question. The court's approach to the *Chevron* issue was instructive. First, the court described statutory interpretation as "purely a question of law," requiring less deference to the agency than would normally be shown in judicial review of administrative action. The court then suggested that only when the statute has previously been subjected to judicial scrutiny or to "time-tested agency interpretations" should a court afford the agency's interpretation any "special deference." Here, the court held that because "neither the board nor the courts have previously ruled on the issue presented . . . such deference is not due."

Also representative of a narrower deference approach, more like *Skimore* than like *Chevron*, are decisions in **Idaho**, see *J.R. Simplot Co. v. Tax Comm'n,* 820 P.2d 1206 (Idaho 1991); **Iowa**, see *Lee v. Iowa Dep't of Transp., Motor Vehicle Div.,* 693 N.W.2d 342, 344 (Iowa 2005); **Michigan**, see *In re Complaint of Rovas against SBC Michigan,* 754 N.W.2d 259 (Mich. 2008) (explicitly rejecting *Chevron*); **New Jersey**, see *In re Distribution of Liquid Assets,* 773 A.2d 6 (N.J. 2001) (citing *Chevron*, but concluding that courts are "in no way bound" by agency interpretations and do not sit to "rubber stamp" agency determinations); **New Mexico**, see *Dona Ana Mut. Domestic Water Consumers Ass'n v. N.M. Pub. Regulation Comm'n,* 139 P.3d 166, 169–70 (N.M. 2006); **New York**, see *Lorillard Tobacco Co. v. Roth,* 786 N.E.2d 7, 10 (N.Y. 2003); and **Ohio**, see *Ohio Consumers' Counsel v. Pub. Util. Comm'n,* 856 N.E.2d 940, 950 (Ohio 2006).

An example of a no-deference-whatsoever state is **Delaware**, which has explicitly declined to adopt *Chevron.* See *Public Water Supply Co. v. DiPasquale,* 735 A.2d 378, 382–83 (Del. 1999): "A reviewing court may accord due weight, but not defer, to an agency interpretation of a statute administered by it. A reviewing court will not defer to such an interpretation as correct merely because it is rational or not clearly erroneous."

In the last five years, there has been a concerted movement to press state as well as federal courts to reject deference regimes anything like *Chevron*, and that movement is seeing results. In 2018, **Wisconsin** called into question its complicated, *Chevron*-like deference doctrine, and a majority of the judges on the Wisconsin Supreme Court cited the recent criticisms made by Justices Scalia, Thomas, and Gorsuch to announce that state judges would review agency determinations of law *de novo*, the same standard applied to lower court conclusions of law. *Tetra Tech EC, Inc. v. Wisconsin Dep't of Revenue,* 914 N.W.2d 21 (Wis. 2018). A majority of the justices seemed willing to abrogate the court's previous deference precedents based upon strict separation of powers and the *Marbury* responsibility of judges to say what the law is. Because there was no majority opinion, the matter may remain unsettled in Wisconsin, as we go to press in 2019.

On April 11, 2018, **Arizona** House Bill 2238 was signed into law, amending Ariz. Rev. Stats. § 12–910. The new law instructs courts handling proceedings between an agency and regulated party to decide all questions of law without deference to government agencies, including on matters of constitutional, statutory, and regulatory interpretation. (Similar proposals have been made in Congress but have not had political traction as of 2019.) There are two exceptions to the no-deference rule: First, for healthcare-related appeals arising from a specific article of Arizona law, courts are instructed to defer to agencies unless they find that the agency action in question "is not supported by substantial evidence, is contrary to law, is arbitrary and capricious or is an abuse of discretion." Second, agencies created pursuant to the Arizona Corporation Commission (the state's utility regulator) are exempt from the no-deference rule.

In November 2018, Florida voters adopted Amendment 6, which (among a number of changes) added a new § 21 to Article V of the Florida Constitution:

> **Judicial interpretation of statutes and rules.**—In interpreting a state statute or rule, a state court or an officer hearing an administrative action pursuant to general law may not defer to an administrative agency's interpretation of such statute or rule, and must instead interpret such statute or rule *de novo*.

We do not know what the Florida courts will make of this constitutional amendment, nor do we know what the Arizona courts will do in response to its statutory directive. Might deference regimes survive in those states?

2. IMPORTANT ISSUES OF DEFERENCE DOCTRINE

So long as the Supreme Court sticks with the *Mead* understanding of *Chevron*, the linchpin is whether the agency interpretation is pursuant to a congressional delegation of authority to issue orders or rules having the force of law. Many of the implications of this conceptual basis for *Chevron* are spelled out in Thomas Merrill & Kristin Hickman, Chevron's *Domain*, 89 Geo. L.J. 833 (2001), which the Court cited and drew from in *Mead*. Consider some of these issues as the Supreme Court has wrestled with them.

A. IS THE AGENCY ACTING WITHIN ITS DELEGATED AUTHORITY?

If the *Chevron* deference boost rests upon congressional delegation of lawmaking authority, then the Court should make sure that Congress has delegated such authority to the agency in general *and* as applied. Professors Merrill and Hickman call this *Chevron* Step Zero. See Chevron's *Domain*, 89 Geo. L.J. at 873. Although written as a Step One opinion, *MCI v. AT&T* may be read as an early example of Step Zero. Consider the following case, which is clearly Step Zero and illustrates the complexity that Step Zero inquiries might have.

GONZALES V. OREGON
Supreme Court of the United States, 2006.
546 U.S. 243, 126 S.Ct. 904, 163 L.Ed.2d 748.

JUSTICE KENNEDY delivered the opinion of the Court.

In 1994, Oregon became the first State to legalize assisted suicide when voters approved a ballot measure enacting the Oregon Death With Dignity Act (ODWDA). ODWDA, which survived a 1997 ballot measure seeking its repeal, exempts from civil or criminal liability state-licensed physicians who, in compliance with the specific safeguards in ODWDA, dispense or prescribe a lethal dose of drugs upon the request of a terminally ill patient.

The drugs Oregon physicians prescribe under ODWDA are regulated under a federal statute, the Controlled Substances Act (CSA or Act). 84 Stat. 1242, as amended, 21 U.S.C. § 801 et seq. The CSA allows these particular drugs to be available only by a written prescription from a registered physician. In the ordinary course the same drugs are prescribed in smaller doses for pain alleviation.

A November 9, 2001 Interpretive Rule issued by the Attorney General addresses the implementation and enforcement of the CSA with respect to ODWDA. It determines that using controlled substances to assist suicide is not a legitimate medical practice and that dispensing or prescribing them for this purpose is unlawful under the CSA. The Interpretive Rule's validity under the CSA is the issue before us.

[I]   We turn first to the text and structure of the CSA. Enacted in 1970 with the main objectives of combating drug abuse and controlling the legitimate and illegitimate traffic in controlled substances, the CSA creates a comprehensive, closed regulatory regime criminalizing the unauthorized manufacture, distribution, dispensing, and possession of substances classified in any of the Act's five schedules. 21 U.S.C. § 841; 21 U.S.C. § 844. The Act places substances in one of five schedules based on their potential for abuse or dependence, their accepted medical use, and their accepted safety for use under medical supervision. Schedule I contains the most severe restrictions on access and use, and Schedule V the least. 21 U.S.C. § 812. Congress classified a host of substances when it enacted the CSA, but the statute permits the Attorney General to add, remove, or reschedule substances. He may do so, however, only after making particular findings, and on scientific and medical matters he is required to accept the findings of the Secretary of Health and Human Services (Secretary). These proceedings must be on the record after an opportunity for comment. See 21 U.S.C. § 811.

The present dispute involves controlled substances listed in Schedule II, substances generally available only pursuant to a written, nonrefillable prescription by a physician. 21 U.S.C. § 829(a). A 1971 regulation promulgated by the Attorney General requires that every prescription for a controlled substance "be issued for a legitimate medical purpose by an individual practitioner acting in the usual course of his professional practice." 21 CFR § 1306.04(a) (2005).

To prevent diversion of controlled substances with medical uses, the CSA regulates the activity of physicians. To issue lawful prescriptions of Schedule II drugs, physicians must "obtain from the Attorney General a registration issued in accordance with the rules and regulations promulgated by him." 21 U.S.C. § 822(a)(2). The Attorney General may deny, suspend, or revoke this registration if, as relevant here, the physician's registration would be "inconsistent with the public interest." § 824(a)(4); § 822(a)(2). When deciding whether a practitioner's registration is in the public interest, the Attorney General "shall" consider:

"(1) The recommendation of the appropriate State licensing board or professional disciplinary authority.

"(2) The applicant's experience in dispensing, or conducting research with respect to controlled substances.

"(3) The applicant's conviction record under Federal or State laws relating to the manufacture, distribution, or dispensing of controlled substances.

"(4) Compliance with applicable State, Federal, or local laws relating to controlled substances.

"(5) Such other conduct which may threaten the public health and safety." § 823(f).

The CSA explicitly contemplates a role for the States in regulating controlled substances, as evidenced by its pre-emption provision.

"No provision of this subchapter shall be construed as indicating an intent on the part of the Congress to occupy the field in which that provision operates . . . to the exclusion of any State law on the same subject matter which would otherwise be within the authority of the State, unless there is a positive conflict between that provision . . . and that State law so that the two cannot consistently stand together." § 903.

[After Oregon voters adopted its Death With Dignity Act in 1994 and reaffirmed it in a 1997 referendum, several senators, including John Ashcroft of Missouri, petitioned Attorney General Janet Reno to override the Oregon law through an interpretation of the CSA declaring that use of controlled substances for "assisted suicide" was a federal crime. Reno declined, but when Ashcroft himself became Attorney General, he issued the Directive. The Ninth Circuit rejected his interpretation, and the Attorney General appealed. He argued that his Interpretive Rule was entitled to *Chevron* deference. Because Congress had not directly addressed the issue of "assisted suicide," the Court should defer to his interpretation. (The government also argued that Ashcroft was entitled to *"Auer"* deference, analyzed below, because he was interpreting the 1971 regulation.)]

[II   After rejecting the Attorney General's argument for *Auer* deference because he was construing a Department rule, the Court considered his *Chevron* deference argument and posed the *Mead* question: Had Congress delegated lawmaking authority to the Attorney General to preempt this kind of state law?] The Attorney General has rulemaking power to fulfill his duties under the CSA. The specific respects in which he is authorized to make rules, however, instruct us that he is not authorized to make a rule declaring illegitimate a medical standard for care and treatment of patients that is specifically authorized under state law. * * *

The CSA gives the Attorney General limited powers, to be exercised in specific ways. His rulemaking authority under the CSA is described in two provisions: (1) "The Attorney General is authorized to promulgate rules and regulations and to charge reasonable fees relating to the registration and control of the manufacture, distribution, and dispensing of controlled substances and to listed chemicals," 21 U.S.C. § 821; and (2) "The Attorney General may promulgate and enforce any rules, regulations, and procedures which he may deem necessary and appropriate for the efficient execution of his functions under this subchapter," 21 U.S.C. § 871(b). As is evident from these sections, Congress did not delegate to the Attorney General authority to carry out or effect all provisions of the CSA. Rather, he can promulgate rules relating only to "registration" and "control," and "for the efficient execution of his functions" under the statute.

Turning first to the Attorney General's authority to make regulations for the "control" of drugs, this delegation cannot sustain the Interpretive Rule's attempt to define standards of medical practice. Control is a term of art in the CSA. "As used in this subchapter," § 802—the subchapter that includes § 821—

> "The term 'control' means to add a drug or other substance, or immediate precursor, to a schedule under part B of this subchapter, whether by transfer from another schedule or otherwise." § 802(5).

To exercise his scheduling power, the Attorney General must follow a detailed set of procedures, including requesting a scientific and medical evaluation from the Secretary. See 21 U.S.C. §§ 811, 812. The statute is also specific as to the manner in which the Attorney General must exercise this authority: "Rules of the Attorney General under this subsection [regarding scheduling] shall be made on the record after opportunity for a hearing pursuant to the rulemaking procedures prescribed by [the Administrative Procedure Act, 5 U.S.C. § 553]." 21 U.S.C. § 811(a). The Interpretive Rule now under consideration does not concern the scheduling of substances and was not issued after the required procedures for rules regarding scheduling, so it cannot fall under the Attorney General's "control" authority. * * *

We turn, next, to the registration provisions of the CSA. Before 1984, the Attorney General was required to register any physician who was authorized by his State. The Attorney General could only deregister a physician who falsified his application, was convicted of a felony relating to controlled substances, or had his state license or registration revoked. The CSA was amended in 1984 to allow the Attorney General to deny registration to an applicant "if he determines that the issuance of such registration would be inconsistent with the public interest." 21 U.S.C. § 823(f). Registration may also be revoked or suspended by the Attorney General on the same grounds. § 824(a)(4). In determining consistency with the public interest, the Attorney General must * * * consider five factors, including: the State's recommendation; compliance with state, federal, and local laws regarding controlled substances; and public health and safety. § 823(f).

The Interpretive Rule cannot be justified under this part of the statute. It does not undertake the five-factor analysis and concerns much more than registration. Nor does the Interpretive Rule on its face purport to be an application of the registration provision in § 823(f). It is, instead, an interpretation of the substantive federal law requirements (under 21 CFR § 1306.04 (2005)) for a valid prescription. It begins by announcing that assisting suicide is not a "legitimate medical purpose" under § 1306.04, and that dispensing controlled substances to assist a suicide violates the CSA. 66 Fed. Reg. 56608 (2001). Violation is a criminal offense, and often a felony, under 21 U.S.C. § 841. The Interpretive Rule thus purports to declare that using controlled substances for physician-assisted suicide is a crime, an authority that goes well beyond the Attorney General's statutory power to register or deregister.

The Attorney General's deregistration power, of course, may carry implications for criminal enforcement because if a physician dispenses a controlled substance after he is deregistered, he violates § 841. The Interpretive Rule works in the opposite direction, however: it declares certain conduct criminal, placing in jeopardy the registration of any physician who engages in that conduct. To the extent the Interpretive Rule concerns registration, it simply states the obvious because one of the five factors the Attorney General must consider in deciding the "public interest" is "[c]ompliance with applicable State, Federal, or local laws relating to controlled substances." 21 U.S.C. § 823(f)(4). The problem with the design of the Interpretive Rule is that it cannot, and does not, explain why the Attorney General has the authority to decide what constitutes an underlying violation of the CSA in the first place. The explanation the Government seems to advance is that the Attorney General's authority to decide whether a physician's actions are inconsistent with the "public interest" provides the basis for the Interpretive Rule.

By this logic, however, the Attorney General claims extraordinary authority. If the Attorney General's argument were correct, his power to deregister necessarily would include the greater power to criminalize even the actions of registered physicians, whenever they engage in conduct he deems illegitimate. This power to criminalize—unlike his power over registration, which must be exercised only after considering five express statutory factors—would be unrestrained. It would be anomalous for Congress to have so painstakingly described the Attorney General's limited authority to deregister a single physician or schedule a single drug, but to have given him, just by implication, authority to declare an entire class of activity outside "the course of professional practice," and therefore a criminal violation of the CSA. * * * See also *Adams Fruit Co. v. Barrett,* 494 U.S. 638, 649–50 (1990) (holding that a delegation of authority to promulgate motor vehicle safety "*standards*" did not include the authority to decide the pre-emptive scope of the federal statute because "[n]o such delegation regarding [the statute's] enforcement provisions is evident in the statute").

The same principle controls here. It is not enough that the terms "public interest," "public health and safety," and "Federal law" are used in the part of the statute over which the Attorney General has authority. The statutory terms "public interest" and "public health" do not call on the Attorney General, or any other Executive official, to make an independent assessment of the meaning of federal law. The Attorney General did not base the Interpretive Rule on an application of the five-factor test generally, or the "public health and safety" factor specifically. Even if he had, it is doubtful the Attorney General could cite the "public interest" or "public health" to deregister a physician simply because he deemed a controversial practice permitted by state law to have an illegitimate medical purpose. * * *

The authority desired by the Government is inconsistent with the design of the statute in other fundamental respects. The Attorney General does not have the sole delegated authority under the CSA. He must instead share it with, and in some respects defer to, the Secretary [of the Department of Health and Human Services], whose functions are likewise delineated and confined by the statute. The CSA allocates decisionmaking powers among statutory actors so that medical judgments, if they are to be decided at the federal level and for the limited objects of the statute, are placed in the hands of the Secretary. In the scheduling context, for example, the Secretary's recommendations on scientific and medical matters bind the Attorney General. The Attorney General cannot control a substance if the Secretary disagrees. 21 U.S.C. § 811(b). See H.R. Rep. No. 91–1444, pt. 1, p. 33 (1970) (the section "is not intended to authorize the Attorney General to undertake or support medical and scientific research [for the purpose of scheduling], which is within the competence of the Department of Health, Education, and Welfare").

In a similar vein the 1970 Act's regulation of medical practice with respect to drug rehabilitation gives the Attorney General a limited role; for it is the Secretary who, after consultation with the Attorney General and national medical groups, "determine[s] the appropriate methods of professional practice in the medical treatment of . . . narcotic addiction." 42 U.S.C. § 290bb–2a; see 21 U.S.C. § 823(g) (2000 ed. and Supp. II) (stating that the Attorney General shall register practitioners who dispense drugs for narcotics treatment when the Secretary has determined the applicant is qualified to treat addicts and the Attorney General has concluded the applicant will comply with record keeping and security regulations); H.R. Rep. No. 93–884, p 6 (1974) ("This section preserves the distinctions found in the [CSA] between the functions of the Attorney General and the Secretary. . . . All decisions of a medical nature are to be made by the Secretary. . . . Law enforcement decisions respecting the security of stocks of narcotics drugs and the maintenance of records on such drugs are to be made by the Attorney General"). * * *

The structure of the CSA, then, conveys unwillingness to cede medical judgments to an Executive official who lacks medical expertise. In interpreting statutes that divide authority, the Court has recognized: "Because historical familiarity and policymaking expertise account in the first instance for the presumption that Congress delegates interpretive lawmaking power to the agency rather than to the reviewing court, we presume here that Congress intended to invest interpretive power in the administrative actor in the best position to develop these attributes." *Martin v. OSHRC*, 499 U.S. 144, 153 (1991). This presumption works against a conclusion that the Attorney General has authority to make quintessentially medical judgments. * * *

The idea that Congress gave the Attorney General such broad and unusual authority through an implicit delegation in the CSA's registration provision is not sustainable. "Congress, we have held, does not alter the fundamental details of a regulatory scheme in vague terms or ancillary provisions—it does not, one might say, hide elephants in mouseholes." *Whitman v. American Trucking Assns., Inc.*, 531 U.S. 457, 468 (2001); see *FDA v. Brown & Williamson* ("[W]e are confident that Congress could not have intended to delegate a decision of such economic and political significance to an agency in so cryptic a fashion").

The importance of the issue of physician-assisted suicide, which has been the subject of an "earnest and profound debate" across the country, [*Washington v. Glucksberg*, 521 U.S., 702, 735 (1997), which upheld a state prohibition on physician-assisted suicide, in part on the argument that the states should have discretion to decide such issues for themselves], makes the oblique form of the claimed delegation all the more suspect. Under the Government's theory, moreover, the medical judgments the Attorney General could make are not limited to physician-assisted suicide. Were this argument accepted, he could decide whether any particular drug may be used for any particular purpose, or indeed whether a physician who administers any controversial treatment could be deregistered. This would occur, under the Government's view, despite the statute's express limitation of the Attorney General's authority to registration and control, with attendant restrictions on each of those functions, and despite the statutory purposes to combat drug abuse and prevent illicit drug trafficking.

[III. Finding no delegation, and therefore no *Chevron* deference, the Court considered the Attorney General's facts and arguments under *Skidmore*.] The statute and our case law amply support the conclusion that Congress regulates medical practice insofar as it bars doctors from using their prescription-writing powers as a means to engage in illicit drug dealing and trafficking as conventionally understood. Beyond this, however, the statute manifests no intent to regulate the practice of medicine generally. The silence is understandable given the structure and limitations of federalism, which allow the States " 'great latitude under their police powers to legislate as to the protection of the lives, limbs, health, comfort, and quiet of all persons.' " *Medtronic, Inc. v. Lohr*, 518 U.S. 470, 475 (1996).

* * * [W]e find only one area in which Congress set general, uniform standards of medical practice. Title I of the Comprehensive Drug Abuse Prevention and Control Act of 1970, of which the CSA was Title II, provides that

> "[The Secretary], after consultation with the Attorney General and with national organizations representative of persons with knowledge and experience in the treatment of narcotic addicts, shall determine the appropriate methods of professional practice in the medical treatment of the narcotic addiction of various classes of narcotic addicts, and shall report thereon from time to time to the Congress." § 4, 84 Stat. 1241, codified at 42 U.S.C. § 290bb–2a.

This provision strengthens the understanding of the CSA as a statute combating recreational drug abuse, and also indicates that when Congress wants to regulate medical practice in the given scheme, it does so by explicit language in the statute [and with consultation involving the medical experts in HHS]. * * *

JUSTICE SCALIA, joined by CHIEF JUSTICE ROBERTS and JUSTICE THOMAS, dissenting. * * *

Even if the Directive were entitled to no deference whatever, the most reasonable interpretation of the Regulation and of the statute would produce the same result. Virtually every relevant source of authoritative meaning confirms that the phrase "legitimate medical purpose" does not include intentionally assisting suicide. "Medicine" refers to "[t]he science and art dealing with the prevention, cure, or alleviation of disease." Webster's Second 1527. The use of the word "legitimate" connotes an *objective* standard of "medicine," and our presumption that the CSA creates a uniform federal law regulating the dispensation of controlled substances means that this objective standard must be a federal one. As recounted in detail in the memorandum for the Attorney General that is attached as an appendix to the Directive (OLC Memo), virtually every medical authority from Hippocrates to the current American Medical Association (AMA) confirms that assisting suicide has seldom or never been viewed as a form of "prevention, cure, or alleviation of disease," and (even more so) that assisting suicide is not a "legitimate" branch of that "science and art." Indeed, the AMA has determined that " '[p]hysician-assisted suicide is fundamentally incompatible with the physician's role as a healer.'" *Glucksberg.* "[T]he overwhelming weight of authority in judicial decisions, the past and present policies of nearly all of the States and of the Federal Government, and the clear, firm and unequivocal views of the leading associations within the American medical and nursing professions, establish that assisting in suicide . . . is not a legitimate medical purpose." OLC Memo. See also *Glucksberg* (prohibitions or condemnations of assisted suicide in 50 jurisdictions, including 47 States, the District of Columbia, and 2 Territories). * * *

Even if the Regulation did not exist and "prescription" in § 829 could not be interpreted to require a "legitimate medical purpose," the Directive's conclusion that "prescribing, dispensing, or administering federally controlled substances . . . by a physician . . . may 'render his registration . . . inconsistent with the public interest' and therefore subject to possible suspension or revocation under 21 U.S.C. [§] 824(a)(4)," 66 Fed. Reg. 56608, would nevertheless be unassailable in this Court.

Sections 823(f) and 824(a) explicitly grant the Attorney General the authority to register and deregister physicians, and his discretion in exercising that authority is spelled out in very broad terms. He may refuse to register or deregister if he determines that registration is "inconsistent with the public interest," 21 U.S.C. § 823(f), after considering five factors, the fifth of which is "[s]uch other conduct which may threaten the public health and safety," § 823(f)(5). As the Court points out, these broad standards were enacted in the 1984 amendments for the specific purpose of *freeing* the Attorney General's discretion over registration from the decisions of state authorities.

The fact that assisted-suicide prescriptions are issued in violation of § 829 is of course sufficient to support the Directive's conclusion that issuing them may be cause for deregistration: such prescriptions would violate the fourth factor of § 823(f), namely "[c]ompliance with applicable . . . Federal . . . laws relating to controlled substances," 21 U.S.C. § 823(f)(4). But the Attorney General did not rely solely on subsection (f)(4) in reaching his conclusion that registration would be "inconsistent with the public interest"; nothing in the text of the Directive indicates that. Subsection (f)(5) ("[s]uch other conduct which may threaten the public health and safety") provides an independent, alternative basis for the Directive's conclusion regarding deregistration—provided that the Attorney General has authority to interpret "public interest" and "public health and safety" in § 823(f) to exclude assisted suicide.

Three considerations make it perfectly clear that the statute confers authority to interpret these phrases upon the Attorney General. First, the Attorney General is solely and explicitly charged with administering the registration and deregistration provisions. See §§ 823(f), 824(a). By making the criteria for such registration and deregistration such obviously ambiguous factors as "public interest" and "public health and safety," Congress implicitly (but clearly) gave the Attorney General authority to interpret those criteria—*whether or not* there is any explicit delegation provision in the statute. "Sometimes the legislative delegation to an agency on a particular question is implicit rather than explicit. In such a case, a court may not substitute its own construction of a statutory provision for a reasonable interpretation made by the administrator of an agency." *Chevron.* The Court's exclusive focus on the *explicit* delegation provisions is, at best, a fossil of our pre-*Chevron* era; at least since *Chevron,* we have not conditioned our deferral to agency interpretations upon the existence of explicit delegation provisions. *Mead* left this principle of implicit delegation intact.

Second, even if explicit delegation were required, Congress provided it in § 821, which authorizes the Attorney General to "promulgate rules and regulations . . . relating to the *registration and control* of the manufacture, distribution, and dispensing of controlled substances. . . ." (Emphasis added.) Because "dispensing" refers to the delivery of a controlled substance "pursuant to the lawful order of a practitioner," 21 U.S.C. § 802(10), the deregistration of such practitioners for writing impermissible orders "relat[es] to the registration . . . of the . . . dispensing" of controlled substances, 21 U.S.C.A. § 821 (Supp. 2005).

Third, § 821 also gives the Attorney General authority to promulgate rules and regulations "relating to the . . . control of the . . . dispensing of controlled substances." As discussed earlier, it is plain that the *ordinary* meaning of "control" must apply to § 821, so that the plain import of the provision is to grant the Attorney General rulemaking authority over all the provisions of part C of the CSA, 21 U.S.C. §§ 821–830. Registering and deregistering the practitioners who issue the prescriptions necessary for lawful dispensation of controlled substances plainly "relat[es] to the . . . control of the . . . dispensing of controlled substances." § 821.

The Attorney General is thus authorized to promulgate regulations interpreting §§ 823(f) and 824(a), both by implicit delegation in § 823(f) and by two grounds of explicit delegation in § 821. The Court nevertheless holds that this triply unambiguous delegation cannot be given full effect because "the design of the statute" evinces the intent to grant the Secretary of Health and Human Services exclusive authority over scientific and medical determinations. This proposition is not remotely plausible. The Court cites as authority for the Secretary's exclusive authority two specific areas in which his medical determinations are said to be binding on the Attorney General—with regard to the "scientific and medical evaluation" of a drug's effects that precedes its scheduling, § 811(b), and with regard to "the appropriate methods of professional practice in the medical treatment of the narcotic addiction of various classes of narcotic addicts," 42 U.S.C. § 290bb–2a. Far from establishing a general principle of Secretary supremacy with regard to all scientific and medical determinations, the fact that Congress granted the Secretary specifically defined authority in the areas of scheduling and addiction treatment, *without otherwise mentioning him* in the registration provisions, suggests, to the contrary, that Congress envisioned *no* role for the Secretary in that area—where, as we have said, interpretive authority was both implicitly and explicitly conferred upon the Attorney General.

Even if we could rewrite statutes to accord with sensible "design," it is far from a certainty that the Secretary, rather than the Attorney General, ought to control the registration of physicians. Though registration decisions sometimes require judgments about the legitimacy of medical practices, the Department of Justice has seemingly had no difficulty making them. But unlike decisions about whether a substance should be scheduled or whether a narcotics addiction treatment is legitimate, registration decisions are not exclusively, or even primarily, concerned with "medical [and] scientific" factors. See 21 U.S.C. § 823(f). Rather, the decision to register, or to bring an action to deregister, an individual *physician* implicates all the policy goals and competing enforcement priorities that attend any exercise of prosecutorial discretion. It is entirely reasonable to think (as Congress evidently did) that it would be easier for the Attorney General occasionally to make judgments about the legitimacy of medical practices than it would be for the Secretary to get into the business of law enforcement. It is, in other words, perfectly consistent with an intelligent "design of the statute" to give the Nation's chief law enforcement official, not its chief health official, broad discretion over the substantive standards that govern registration and deregistration. That is *especially* true where the contested "scientific and medical" judgment at issue has to do with the legitimacy of physician-assisted suicide, which ultimately rests, not on "science" or "medicine," but on a naked value judgment. It no more depends upon a "quintessentially medical judgmen[t]" than does the legitimacy of polygamy or eugenic infanticide. And it requires no particular *medical* training to undertake the objective inquiry into how the continuing traditions of Western medicine have consistently treated this subject. The Secretary's supposedly superior "medical expertise" to make "medical judgments" is strikingly irrelevant to the case at hand. * * *

It follows from what we have said that the Attorney General's authoritative interpretations of "public interest" and "public health and safety" in § 823(f) are subject to *Chevron* deference. As noted earlier, the Court does not [contend] that the absence of notice-and-comment procedures for the Directive renders *Chevron* inapplicable. And there is no serious argument that "Congress has directly spoken to the precise question at issue," or that the Directive's interpretations of "public health and safety" and "inconsistent with the public interest" are not "permissible." *Chevron.* On the latter point, in fact, the condemnation of assisted suicide by 50 American jurisdictions supports the Attorney General's view. The Attorney General may therefore weigh a physician's participation in assisted suicide as a factor counseling against his registration, or in favor of deregistration, under § 823(f). * * *

NOTES ON THE OREGON AID-IN-DYING CASE
AND CHEVRON STEP ZERO

The take-no-prisoners debate between Justices Kennedy and Scalia provides an occasion for students to practice their skills with the statutory interpretation rules and practices covered in this casebook. Note especially the dissent's integration of dictionary meanings, grammatical analyses, and structural points. Justice Scalia had excellent arguments for the proposition that the Ashcroft Directive was literally within at least one of the CSA delegations, maybe several of them. Such a reading may also fit with the CSA's purpose, which was to create a federal regulatory regime for the dispensation of drugs by doctors. Yet this deft wedding of Reagan Era textualism and New Deal purposivism was not persuasive to Justices Kennedy and O'Connor, Reagan conservatives who were probably not great friends to the death-with-dignity movement. Why were they not persuaded?

Here's one way of understanding why some pretty conservative jurists rejected Justice Scalia's legal arguments. Consider this: Parents A and B retain babysitter C to look after their beloved child while they attend the opera. Their instructions to C: "You are in charge; we delegate you all decisions regarding his care while we are gone." In a tragic twist of fate, the baby has a terrible accident, and C rushes him to the hospital. The hospital asks C who has authority to make decisions about treatment options, risk assessment, and even possible termination of life support. Can C legitimately respond that she is "authorized" to make those decisions? A strict reading of the instructions might suggest "yes," but common sense makes us sure the answer is "no."

This is probably the point of the Court's invocation of the idea that Congress does not hide elephants in mouseholes. Assuming this point, however, why would Justices O'Connor and Kennedy consider the "assisted suicide" rule an "elephant" and not a "mouse"? If the CSA represented a federalization of drug regulation, why wasn't the Ashcroft Directive simply the routine agency decision suggested by the dissenters? Does a negative answer to that question rest upon a reservation of a special judicial role for aid-in-dying issues?

1.   *Deference in Matters of Criminal Law.* The *Oregon* majority was troubled that Ashcroft was expansively interpreting a statute imposing serious criminal liability. Recall, from Chapter 6, that the rule of lenity theoretically requires anti-deference— presumptive rejection of the agency's interpretation—when a criminal statute is ambiguous. Indeed, Justice Scalia was one of the few Justices who seemed to apply the rule of lenity with rigor and even enthusiasm—but not in *Oregon.* Why not? Apparently, Justice Scalia viewed the notice and nondelegation policies underlying the rule of lenity to be satisfied by an open rule promulgated by the Attorney General pursuant to congressional authorization. Accord, Dan Kahan, *Is* Chevron *Relevant to Federal Criminal Law?*, 110 Harv. L. Rev. 469 (1996) (arguing that criminal law should move in precisely this direction).

Note that *Chevron* might apply in federal criminal sentencing law. Congress has vested the Sentencing Commission with substantive rulemaking authority as regards sentencing, and the Court sometimes gave *Chevron* deference to the Sentencing Guidelines before they were partially nullified. See *Stinson v. United States*, 508 U.S. 36 (1993). Should *Stinson* make us more willing to defer in cases like *Oregon*?

2.   *Ideological Voting in* Chevron *Cases.* Commentators are finding that ideology is a better predictor than doctrine with respect to Supreme Court voting patterns in agency deference cases. The Oregon Aid-in-Dying Case helps us see how this works. Notice the completely different linguistic as well as normative attitudes in the majority and chief dissenting opinions. Thus, the majority cited *Glucksberg* (the constitutional "right to die" case) and its treatment of aid-in-dying as a matter for serious national debate. These and other bits of textual evidence suggest that the majority understood the matter as a possible privacy right of persons to choose "death with dignity." Was it for this *normative* reason that the majority thought that aid-in-dying was an "elephant" that could not hide in a normative "mousehole"? Consider, in addition, the federalism argument that Oregon ought to have authority to decide the question of aid in dying without federal intervention.

The dissenters, in contrast, rhetorically agreed with Ashcroft that this was "assisted suicide," a half step away from murder. Because the matter has long been settled by religious doctrine, state law, and national policy, this was no "elephant," but was instead a mouse hiding in the mousehole. It is for this *normative* reason that the dissenters believed it outrageous for the majority to treat Oregon's law as a great matter for state experimentation and deviance from settled national policy.

The process by which the Justices vote their norms more than their dictionaries is probably unconscious. Social scientists would explain this phenomenon as an example of framing effects and cognitive dissonance: the way an interpreter frames the issue drives her thinking, and indeed she will filter evidence through the lens of this frame. Philosophers would cite this as an example of how interpretation is an activity by which we come to be who we are.

3.   *Process Matters: Deliberative Agency Actions May Trigger More Deference.* Another way to read the Oregon Aid-in-Dying Case emphasizes the agency's public process and justifications. One of us argues that the Court was reluctant to defer in the case because the agency had tackled a big normative issue without the public process of information-gathering and deliberation that usually accompanies agency rulemaking. See William Eskridge Jr., *The Story of* Gonzales v. Oregon: *Death, Deference, Deliberation,* in *Statutory Interpretation Stories* 366–98 (Eskridge, Frickey & Garrett eds., 2011). Eskridge endorses "deliberation-rewarding" canons of statutory interpretation, such as the Oregon Case, where the Court rewards public deliberation with greater deference. Is this a sensible canon? Does such a canon create too much complexity in an already complicated regime of rules and principles? Consider the following case.

Encino Motorcars, LLC v. United States

136 S.Ct. 2117 (2016).

As we saw in *Skidmore,* the Fair Labor Standards Act of 1938 (FLSA) assures that covered employees are paid extra if they work overtime; the statute vests informal rulemaking authority with the Department of Labor. Five current and former service advisors claimed the automobile dealership where they were employed was required by the FLSA to pay them overtime wages. The dealership contended that the position and duties of a service advisor bring these employees within § 213(b)(10)(A), which establishes an exemption from the FLSA overtime provisions for any "salesman, partsman, or mechanic primarily engaged in selling or servicing automobiles, trucks, or farm implements." The plaintiffs responded that they did not sell automobiles, nor did they service (fix) them but, instead, provided customers with professional advice and assistance; hence, they did not fall within the exemption.

Before 1987, the Department had interpreted the exemption not to include service advisors, because they were not "salesmen" or "partsmen" or "mechanics." That interpretation met resistance from some courts; some judges felt that service advisors were "salesmen" who provided "servicing" (broadly understood) for auto repairs. After 1987, the Department informally went along with those courts and included service advisors. In 2008, the Department issued a proposed rule to formalize the 1987 interpretation. Comments were received, but the rule was not adopted. Instead, the Department in 2011 completed its 2008 notice-and-comment rulemaking by issuing a final rule that took the opposite position from the proposed rule. The new final rule followed the original 1970 regulation and interpreted the statutory term "salesman" to mean only an employee who sells automobiles, trucks, or farm implements. Therefore, service advisors did not fall within the exemption, as interpreted.

The Ninth Circuit *Chevron*-deferred to the Department's 2011 rule, but the Supreme Court reversed, in an opinion by **Justice Kennedy**. "A premise of *Chevron* is that when Congress grants an agency the authority to administer a statute by issuing regulations with the force of law, it presumes the agency will use that authority to resolve ambiguities in the statutory scheme. See *Chevron; Mead.* When Congress authorizes an agency to proceed through notice-and-comment rulemaking, that 'relatively formal administrative procedure' is a 'very good indicator' that Congress intended the regulation to carry the force of law, so *Chevron* should apply. *Mead.* But *Chevron* deference is not warranted where the regulation is 'procedurally defective'—that is, where the agency errs by failing to follow the correct procedures in issuing the regulation."

Justice Kennedy found such a procedural defect here, based upon the APA requirements, as interpreted in *State Farm.* "When an agency changes its existing position, it 'need not always provide a more detailed justification than what would suffice for a new policy created on a blank slate.' *FCC v. Fox Television Stations, Inc.,* 556 U.S. 502, 515 (2009). But the agency must at least 'display awareness that it is changing position' and 'show that there are good reasons for the new policy.' *Ibid.* (emphasis deleted). In explaining its changed position, an agency must also be cognizant that longstanding policies may have 'engendered serious reliance interests that must be taken into account.' *Ibid.* 'In such cases it is not that further justification is demanded by the mere fact of policy change; but that a reasoned explanation is needed for disregarding facts and circumstances that underlay or were engendered by the prior policy.' *Fox Television Stations.* It follows that an '[u]nexplained inconsistency' in agency policy is 'a reason for holding an interpretation to be an arbitrary and capricious change from agency practice.' *Brand X.* An arbitrary and capricious regulation of this sort is itself unlawful and receives no *Chevron* deference. See *Mead.*"

Since 1978, the retail automobile and truck industry had relied on the Department's earlier, informal interpretation. Because the agency did not provide a sufficient explanation for why it was changing course (as the agency had not in *State Farm*), the Court found its rulemaking record procedurally deficient and therefore not entitled to *Chevron* deference. There was no dissent from that holding.

On remand, the Ninth Circuit agreed with the Department on the merits, and the Supreme Court reversed in *Encino Motorcars LLC v. Navarro,* 138 S.Ct. 1134 (2018). The Court found the statute 100% clear: service advisors are "salesmen * * * primarily engaged in * * * servicing automobiles." Are you persuaded that the statutory exemption can only be read that way? Specifically, the Court read "servicing" broadly—but in the context of cars might "servicing" have a narrower interpretation?

NOTE ON DEFERENCE WHEN CONGRESS HAS DELEGATED RESPONSIBILITIES TO MORE THAN ONE AGENCY

The Oregon Aid-in-Dying Case is an example of a growing range of controversies involving several possibly relevant agencies. One reason the *Gilbert* Court rejected the EEOC's understanding of pregnancy exclusions as being sex discrimination was that another body had reached a different interpretation. In addition to inter-agency *conflict* is the problem of *primacy* among agencies. As Justice Kennedy was in *Oregon*, the Court is usually pretty particular about matching the most apparently authorized agency with an award of deference. E.g., *Martin v. OSHRC*, 499 U.S. 144 (1991), where the Court ruled that in OSHA cases deference was owed to the Department of Labor, which issues substantive rules, rather than the Commission which adjudicates controversies by applying rules to facts.

Sometimes, the Court has been very picky about this matching game. For example, in *Sutton v. United Air Lines, Inc.*, 527 U.S. 471 (1999), the Court interpreted the ADA's definition of "disability" to exclude conditions easily corrected for. (The plaintiffs lost their jobs as airline pilots because they had poor vision; the Court held that this was not a disability, because it could be corrected by eyeglasses. The employer's policy was that corrected vision was still disqualifying. Catch-22.) Although the EEOC had been given rulemaking authority for implementing the jobs title of the Act, which was the basis for Sutton's claims, the Court ruled that the EEOC was *not* delegated authority to determine the scope of the ADA's coverage of "disability," which was defined in a different title to the Act (as to which there was no agency with delegated lawmaking authority).

A recent example is *Epic Systems Corp. v. Lewis,* 138 S.Ct. 1612 (2018). The National Labor Relations Board is charged with interpreting and implementing the National Labor Relations Act of 1935, which protects workers' rights to organize and bargain collectively. Section 7 provides:

> Employees shall have the right to self-organization, to form, join, or assist labor organizations, to bargain collectively through representatives of their own choosing, and to engage in other concerted activities for the purpose of collective bargaining or other mutual aid or protection, and shall also have the right to refrain from any or all of such activities * * *.

Section 8(a)(1) of the Act makes it an unfair labor practice for an employer "to interfere with, restrain, or coerce employees in the exercise of the rights guaranteed in Section 7." The NLRB had applied these provisions to bar employers from securing employee agreements that any claims under the Fair Labor Standards Act (FLSA) would be brought only through arbitration and not through judicial or administrative processes.

The FLSA gives employees a federal claim for overtime pay. Section 7 of the FLSA allows employees to file a group lawsuit (not exactly a class action, but a statutory variant that allows similarly situated employees to "opt into" the lawsuit) to enforce violations of the statutory overtime-payment rules. The Department of Labor, not the NLRB, has delegated authority to interpret the FLSA. A final statute is the Federal Arbitration Act of 1925 (FAA), which the Supreme Court has interpreted to channel disputes into arbitration—and not court or agency procedures—if parties have contractually agreed to arbitration. The courts are the primary implementers of the FAA.

To reach its result, the NLRB had to interpret its own statute *plus* the FLSA *plus* the FAA, including Supreme Court precedents imposing a clear statement rule—namely, that a federal statute will not be understood to override the preference for arbitration unless it clearly does so. Hence, the NLRB had to demonstrate that the NLRA and/or the FLSA overrode the FAA under these circumstances. In all likelihood, *Chevron* will usually not enable an agency to get around a strong substantive canon like the super-strong presumption of arbitration canon. (Neither the NLRA nor the FLSA specifically mentions arbitration in this context.) None of the nine Justices argued that the *Chevron* regime applied here, and the NLRB lost the case, 5–4.

City of Arlington, Texas v. FCC

569 U.S. 290 (2013).

The Communications Act of 1934 is the super-statute regulating electronic communications; § 201(b) of the 1934 Act empowers the Federal Communications Commission (FCC) to "prescribe such rules and regulations as may be necessary in the public interest to carry out [its] provisions." One substantive provision, added to the law in 1996, requires state or local governments to act on wireless siting applications "within a reasonable period of time after the request is duly filed." 47 U.S.C. § 332(c)(7)(B)(ii). In 2009, the FCC issued a rule providing that a "reasonable period of time" for purposes of § 332(c)(7)(B)(ii) is presumptively (and therefore rebuttably) 90 days to process an application to place a new antenna on an existing tower and 150 days to process all other applications.

State and local governments challenged the rule as inconsistent with the statute. They maintained that the FCC has no authority to narrow § 332(c)(7)(B)(ii). Section 332(c)(7)(A) provides that nothing in § 332 "shall limit or affect the authority of a State or local government" over siting decisions. Section 332(c)(7)(B)(v), moreover, authorizes a person who believes a state or local government's wireless-siting decision to be inconsistent with any of the limitations in § 332(c)(7)(B) to "commence an action in any court of competent jurisdiction." Rejecting the challenge, the Ninth Circuit held that the FCC was acting pursuant to delegated lawmaking authority and therefore was entitled to *Chevron* deference, given the reasonableness of its rule and the vagueness of § 332(c)(7)(B)(ii).

Affirming the Ninth Circuit, **Justice Scalia** wrote a majority opinion joined by Justices Thomas, Ginsburg, Sotomayor, and Kagan (an unusual majority coalition). The key issue, as the majority framed it, was whether *Chevron* applied to agency interpretations of its own "jurisdiction." Justice Scalia said yes, in large part because there is no way to separate jurisdictional issues and merits issues. For agencies, unlike for courts, "[b]oth their power to act and how they are to act is authoritatively prescribed by Congress, so that when they act improperly, no less than when they act beyond their jurisdiction, what they do is ultra vires. Because the question—whether framed as an incorrect application of agency authority or an assertion of authority not conferred—is always whether the agency has gone beyond what Congress has permitted it to do, there is no principled basis for carving out some arbitrary subset of such claims as 'jurisdictional.'"

Justice Scalia provided a hypothetical pair of statutes to illustrate his point. The first "Common Carrier Act" read this way:

> Section 1. The Agency shall have jurisdiction to prohibit any common carrier from imposing an unreasonable condition upon access to its facilities.

An interpretation of § 1's terms is "jurisdictional." But the statute could just as easily have been drafted in another way:

> Section 1. No common carrier shall impose an unreasonable condition upon access to its facilities.

> Section 2. The Agency may prescribe rules and regulations necessary in the public interest to effectuate Section 1 of this Act.

Justice Scalia continued: "Now imagine that the Agency, invoking its Section 2 authority, promulgates this Rule: '(1) The term "common carrier" in Section 1 includes Internet Service Providers. (2) The term "unreasonable condition" in Section 1 includes unreasonably high prices. (3) A monthly fee greater than $25 is an unreasonable condition on access to Internet service.' By this Rule, the Agency has claimed for itself jurisdiction that is doubly questionable: Does its authority extend to Internet Service Providers? And does it extend to setting prices? Yet Section 2 makes clear that Congress, in petitioners' words, 'conferred interpretive power on the agency' with respect to Section 1. Even under petitioners' theory, then, a court should defer to the Agency's interpretation of the terms 'common carrier' and 'unreasonable condition'—that is to say, its assertion that its 'jurisdiction' extends to regulating Internet Service Providers and setting prices.

"In the first case, by contrast, petitioners' theory would accord the agency no deference. The trouble with this is that in both cases, the underlying question is *exactly the same*: Does the statute give the agency authority to regulate Internet Service Providers and cap prices, or not? The reality, laid bare, is that there is *no difference,* insofar as the validity of agency action is concerned, between an agency's exceeding the scope of its authority (its 'jurisdiction') and its exceeding authorized application of authority that it unquestionably has. 'To exceed authorized application is to exceed authority. Virtually any administrative action can be characterized as either the one or the other, depending on how generally one wishes to describe the authority.' *Mississippi Power & Light Co. v. Mississippi ex rel. Moore,* 487 U.S. 354, 381 (1988) (Scalia, J., concurring in judgment).

"In sum, judges should not waste their time in the mental acrobatics needed to decide whether an agency's interpretation of a statutory provision is 'jurisdictional' or 'nonjurisdictional.' Once those labels are sheared away, it becomes clear that the question in every case is, simply, whether the statutory text forecloses the agency's assertion of authority, or not. The federal judge as haruspex, sifting the entrails of vast statutory schemes to divine whether a particular agency interpretation qualifies as 'jurisdictional,' is not engaged in reasoned decisionmaking."

Justice Scalia said that the Court has "consistently" held that *Chevron* applies to agency interpretations of their own jurisdiction. His "prime example" was *Commodity Futures Trading Comm'n v. Schor,* 478 U.S. 833 (1986). The CFTC interpreted 7 U.S.C. § 18(c), which provides that before the Commission takes action on a complaint, the complainant must file a bond to cover "any reparation award that may be issued by the Commission against the complainant *on any counterclaim* by respondent." (Emphasis added.) Pursuant to rulemaking authority, the CFTC claimed "the power to take jurisdiction over" not just federal-law counterclaims, but state-law counterclaims as well. The Court deferred under *Chevron* to the Commission's "eminently reasonable . . . interpretation of the statute it is entrusted to administer," and also chided the Court of Appeals for declining to afford deference because of the putatively " 'statutory interpretation-jurisdictional' nature of the question at issue." Justice Scalia also invoked the FDA Tobacco Case and *MCI v. AT&T.* Although the agency was rebuked in both cases, the Court applied the *Chevron* framework to issues that were allegedly "jurisdictional."

Under *Chevron,* the agency's interpretation of the vague statutory provision was eminently reasonable, and so the Court sustained it. Concurring in part and in the judgment, **Justice Breyer** rejected any special rule for "jurisdictional" questions but also applied a more contextual *Mead*-like approach to the question whether Congress intended the agency to fill in the details of § 332(c)(7)(B)(ii). He felt there was no good reason not to defer to the general rulemaking authority the FCC had been given over the entire statute, even as amended.

Writing also for Justices Kennedy and Alito, **Chief Justice Roberts** dissented. "A court should not defer to an agency until the court decides, on its own, that the agency is entitled to deference. Courts defer to an agency's interpretation of law when and because Congress has conferred on the agency interpretive authority over the question at issue. An agency cannot exercise interpretive authority until it has it; the question whether an agency enjoys that authority must be decided by a court, without deference to the agency." Because *Mead* held that *Chevron* rests upon Congress's delegation of lawmaking authority to the agency, courts ought to take care that there actually *has been such a delegation.* For this reason, the Chief Justice rejected the Court's articulation of the issue. The issue is *not* whether an agency enjoys *Chevron* deference to its assertion of "jurisdiction." Instead, the issue is whether an agency's interpretation has been issued pursuant to a congressional authorization to make rules with the force of law (the *Mead* inquiry).

Indeed, the Chief Justice maintained, the judicial role under *Marbury* demands that a court, before it abdicates its authority to declare the law, be certain that *Congress* has authorized an agency to create rules with the force of law for this kind of issue. Of course, this was the precise holding of *Chevron.* Recall that *Chevron* rested upon the notion that, because Congress had not answered the specific question at issue, judges had no business providing their own resolution on the basis of their "personal policy preferences." Instead, the "agency to which Congress ha[d] delegated policymaking responsibilities" was the appropriate political actor to resolve the competing interests at stake, "within the limits of that delegation." As the Chief Justice emphasized, "the Court did not ask simply whether Congress had delegated to the EPA the authority to administer the Clean Air Act generally. We asked whether Congress had 'delegat[ed] authority to the agency to elucidate a *specific provision* of the statute by regulation.' *Chevron* (emphasis added); see *id.* (discussing 'the legislative delegation to an agency on a *particular question*' (emphasis added)). We deferred to the EPA's interpretation of 'stationary sources' based on our conclusion that the agency had been 'charged with responsibility for administering *the provision.*' *Id.* (emphasis added)."

The Chief Justice claimed that the Court had "never faltered" in refusing deference on the question of lawmaking authorization. In *Adams Fruit Co. v. Barrett,* 494 U.S. 638 (1990), for example, the Court did not defer to the Department of Labor's interpretation of the scope of the private right of action provided by the Migrant and Seasonal Agriculture Worker Protection Act, 29 U.S.C. § 1854, against employers who intentionally violated the Act's motor vehicle safety provisions. "A precondition to deference under *Chevron* is a congressional delegation of administrative authority." Although "Congress clearly envisioned, indeed expressly mandated, a role for the Department of Labor in administering the statute by requiring the Secretary to promulgate *standards* implementing AWPA's motor vehicle provisions," the Court found "[n]o such delegation regarding AWPA's enforcement provisions."

The dissenters concluded: "*Adams Fruit, Mead,* and *Gonzales* thus confirm that *Chevron* deference is based on, and finds legitimacy as, a congressional delegation of interpretive authority. An agency interpretation warrants such deference only if Congress has delegated authority to definitively interpret a particular ambiguity in a particular manner. Whether Congress has done so must be determined by the court on its own before *Chevron* can apply."

NOTE ON CHEVRON *DEFERENCE TO AGENCY ASSERTIONS* *OF JURISDICTIONAL AUTHORITY*

City of Arlington seems to settle the thorny issue of whether *Chevron* applies to an agency's interpretation of its own authority or jurisdiction. Most scholars agreed with the Chief Justice on this point,[7] but six Justices, embracing different theories about *Chevron*, have rejected the point. It is especially notable that Justice Breyer, an early critic of *Chevron* as inconsistent with *Marbury* (the key point made by the Chief Justice), agreed with Justice Scalia's critique (though Breyer went his own way to decide the case). Consider how *City of Arlington* plays into the Court's ongoing debate about how to apply *Chevron*. For example, can *Gonzales v. Oregon* be reconciled with *City of Arlington*? Notice that Justice Kennedy, the author of *Oregon,* was in dissent for *City of Arlington*. And Justice Scalia, dissenting in *Oregon*, wrote a very different opinion for the Court in *City of Arlington*.

B. SHOULD COURTS DEFER WHEN THE AGENCY TACKLES "MAJOR QUESTIONS"?

Another way to understand *Gonzales v. Oregon* is to see it as a case where the Justices felt that the *Chevron/Mead* deference regime should not apply to major questions of federal policy, especially questions that implicated constitutional concerns such as the rule of lenity and the right of privacy in some circumstance. We start with the leading case on the "major questions doctrine," followed by notes on earlier cases supporting that *Chevron* exception. We also refer to scholarship criticizing the doctrine.

King v. Burwell

135 S.Ct. 2480 (2015).

This is a leading case excerpted in Chapter 6. Recall that the issue in this case was whether the Affordable Care Act's tax credits are available in states that have a Federal Exchange rather than a State Exchange. The Act provides that tax credits "shall be allowed" for any "applicable taxpayer." 26 U.S.C. § 36B(a). The Act then directs that the amount of the tax credit depends in part on whether the taxpayer has enrolled in an insurance plan through "an Exchange *established by the State* under section 1311" of the Act, [i.e., 42 U.S.C. § 18031], 26 U.S.C. §§ 36B(b)–(c) (emphasis added).

Implementing the ACA, the IRS, after notice-and-comment, promulgated a rule that made the subsidies available on both State and Federal Exchanges. 77 Fed. Reg. 30378 (2012). The rule provides that a taxpayer is eligible for a tax credit if he or she enrolled in an insurance plan through "an Exchange," 26 CFR § 1.36B–2 (2013), which is defined

---

[7]   See Ernest Gellhorn & Paul Verkuil, *Controlling Chevron-Based Delegations*, 20 Cardozo L. Rev. 989, 1006–17 (1999); Merrill & Hickman, Chevron's *Domain*, 89 Geo. L.J. 833; see also Bressman, *How* Mead *Has Muddled*, 1469–74 (after *Mead,* lower courts have tended to avoid applying *Chevron* deference to issues of agency jurisdiction or authority); Eskridge & Baer, *Continuum of Deference,* 96 Geo. L.J. at 1131–32 (Tables 8– 9) (finding lower agency win rates for issues where the agency was interpreting its own jurisdiction or authority). But see Kevin M. Stack, *The Statutory President,* 90 Iowa L. Rev. 539, 594–95 (2005) (agreeing with the Scalia position).

as "an Exchange serving the individual market . . . regardless of whether the Exchange is established and operated by a State . . . or by HHS," 45 CFR § 155.20 (2014). At this point, 16 States and the District of Columbia had established their own Exchanges; the other 34 States had elected to have HHS do so.

The issue before the Court was whether Section 36B authorized tax credits for individuals who enrolled in an insurance plan through a Federal Exchange. The challengers argued that a Federal Exchange was not "an Exchange established by the State under [42 U.S.C. § 18031]," and that the IRS Rule therefore contradicted Section 36B. The Government responded that the IRS Rule was lawful because the phrase "an Exchange established by the State under [42 U.S.C. § 18031]" should be read to include Federal Exchanges and that, in any event, the ACA was ambiguous on this score and the Court's *Chevron* jurisprudence was applicable to sustain the agency rule.

The opinion for the Court, by **Chief Justice Roberts**, started with the framework for judicial review. The Fourth Circuit, below, had found the statute ambiguous and had deferred to the IRS pursuant to *Chevron*. The Court rejected that approach. "When analyzing an agency's interpretation of a statute, we often apply the two-step framework announced in *Chevron*. Under that framework, we ask whether the statute is ambiguous and, if so, whether the agency's interpretation is reasonable. This approach 'is premised on the theory that a statute's ambiguity constitutes an implicit delegation from Congress to the agency to fill in the statutory gaps.' *FDA v. Brown & Williamson Tobacco Corp.* 'In extraordinary cases, however, there may be reason to hesitate before concluding that Congress has intended such an implicit delegation.' *Ibid.*

"This is one of those cases. The tax credits are among the Act's key reforms, involving billions of dollars in spending each year and affecting the price of health insurance for millions of people. Whether those credits are available on Federal Exchanges is thus a question of deep 'economic and political significance' that is central to this statutory scheme; had Congress wished to assign that question to an agency, it surely would have done so expressly. *Utility Air Regulatory Group v. EPA,* 134 S.Ct. 2427, 2444 (2014) (quoting *Brown & Williamson*). It is especially unlikely that Congress would have delegated this decision to the *IRS,* which has no expertise in crafting health insurance policy of this sort. See *Gonzales v. Oregon*. This is not a case for the IRS."

The Chief Justice's opinion for the Court then interpreted the ACA without deference to the IRS. Finding the specific language ambiguous, the Court resolved the ambiguity not by deferring to the agency, but by considering the statutory plan. (The agency's view prevailed.) Writing for the three dissenters, **Justice Scalia** strongly disagreed with the Court's finding of ambiguity and its application of the statutory plan and design but followed the Court in not applying the *Chevron* framework.

NOTE ON THE "MAJOR QUESTIONS DOCTRINE"

King v. Burwell confirms the following structure for the Supreme Court's *Chevron* jurisprudence: The Court will defer to agency rules and orders promulgated pursuant to delegated lawmaking authority (*Mead*) and following the required procedures of the APA (*Encino Motors*). That the agency is interpreting its own jurisdiction or authority does not bar *Chevron* deference (*City of Arlington*)—but the Court will not defer if the agency is resolving an issue of "deep economic or political significance" (*Utility Air, Brown & Williamson, Gonzales v. Oregon*). As in *King*, the agency view might still prevail, but only because the Court's independent interpretation of the statute is the same as the agency's view. (We think it goes without saying that the agency's views will still receive *Skidmore* deference, whether the Court says so or not, because the Justices will read the Solicitor General's brief with great attention to its account of the regulatory history, facts in the world, and the statutory language and plan.)

So that is the doctrine. Is the major questions exception to *Chevron* justified? The major questions canon is a potentially elastic loophole to *Chevron*'s broad commitment of judicial deference to agency interpretations pursuant to congressional delegations of lawmaking authority, because many issues can be understood as either "major questions" or "routine applications." Indeed, the Supreme Court has applied the doctrine erratically, at best. Sometimes, when the agency is making a big move, the Court ignores the doctrine, as it did, for example, in *Babbitt v. Sweet Home* (end of Chapter 6). See also Abigail Moncrieff, *Reincarnating the "Major Questions" Exception to Chevron Deference as a Doctrine of Non-Interference (Or Why* Massachusetts v. EPA *Got it Wrong)*, 60 Admin. L. Rev. 593 (2008).

When the Court does invoke the doctrine, it does so in a variety of ways. In *King,* the Chief Justice invoked the major questions doctrine at Step Zero: *Chevron*'s framework did not apply at all. In *MCI v. ATT,* the Court seemed to invoke major questions as support for its conclusion that the FCC failed Step One (Congress directly addressed the issue). In *Utility Air Regulatory Group*, the Court invoked the doctrine at Step Two. The issue was whether the Clean Air Act authorized EPA to regulate the emission of greenhouse gases for all stationary sources, including those not otherwise regulated by the Act. As in *Chevron* itself, the Court applied the two-step *Chevron* deference regime, hence ruling that Step Zero was satisfied. As in *Chevron*, the Court at Step One found the statute ambiguous and therefore ruled that Congress has not directly addressed the issue. But at Step Two, which had been perfunctory in *Chevron*, the *Utility Air Regulatory Group* Court held that the EPA's interpretation was unreasonable. Citing *Brown and Williamson*, the Court held that Congress did not intend EPA to regulate this broadly.

In short, major questions concerns can show up at any stage of the *Chevron* analysis—and in some cases it is not clear even where the major questions doctrine is having force. E.g., *Gonzales v. Oregon*. Notice, also, the tension between the major questions doctrine in Step Zero and the Court's holding in *City of Arlington,* which says that *Chevron* applies to agency interpretation of its own jurisdiction. The Chief Justice dissented in *City of Arlington* but wrote for the Court in *King v. Burwell.*

On the other hand, the major questions canon might be defensible along precisely the same lines as *Chevron* itself. The key reason is the strong presumption of continuity for major policies unless and until Congress has deliberated about and enacted a change in those major policies. David Shapiro, *Continuity and Change in Statutory Interpretation,* 67 N.Y.U. L. Rev. 921 (1992); accord, William Eskridge Jr., *Interpreting Law: A Primer on How to Read Statutes and the Constitution* 287–90 (2016); John Manning, *Continuity and the Legal Design,* 79 Notre Dame L. Rev. 1863 (2004). On the other hand, in an era of congressional gridlock, the major questions doctrine empowers judges who block regulatory initiatives, rather than Congress, which is usually powerless to respond with a statute of any sort. Josh Chafetz, *Gridlock?*, 130 Harv. L. Rev. F. 51, 55–58 (2016).

Additionally, one might say that a major policy change should be made by the most democratically accountable process—Article I, Section 7 legislation. Thus, the major questions doctrine might be consistent with democratic values. See Theodore Ruger, *The*

Story of FDA *v.* Brown & Williamson*: The Norm of Agency Continuity*, in *Statutory Interpretation Stories* 334 (Eskridge, Frickey & Garrett eds., 2011). Although Congress is sometimes criticized for booting controversial issues to agencies to avoid political accountability, congressional drafting staff support the premise of the major questions canon, because they do not view lawmaking delegations as reaching policy shifts not explicitly made by statute. Abbe Gluck & Lisa Schultz Bressman, *Statutory Interpretation from the Inside: An Empirical Study of Congressional Drafting, Delegation and the Canons: Part I,* 65 Stan. L. Rev. 901, 994, 1003–04 (2014).

Lisa Heinzerling, however, offers a different account. Like the federalism canons, the major questions doctrine is an example of a "power canon" that a libertarian Court deploys to limit (or undermine, depending on your point of view) the activist regulatory state. Specifically, she maintains that this key power canon is wielded to require "clear congressional language to enable a regulatory agenda, but not to disable one." Heinzerling, *The Power Canons*, 58 Wm. & Mary L. Rev. 1933 (2017). This kind of theory fits reasonably well with *MCC v. AT&T*, *Gonzalez v. Oregon*, the FDA Tobacco Case (*Brown & Williamson*), and *Utility Air*—but not so well with *King v. Burwell*, where the Court's approach hard-wired the Obama Administration's view of subsidies into the ACA, impervious to administrative change by, for example, a subsequent presidency hostile to the ACA.

NOTE ON DEFERENCE WHEN THE AGENCY INTERPRETATION CREATES "SERIOUS CONSTITUTIONAL DIFFICULTIES"

Yet another way to read the Oregon Aid-in-Dying Case is through a constitutional lens. Five Justices (O'Connor, Stevens, Souter, Ginsburg, Breyer), all in the *Oregon* majority, had opined in separate concurring opinions in *Washington v. Glucksberg*, 521 U.S. 702 (1997), that they were open to recognizing a "constitutionally cognizable interest in controlling the circumstances of his or her imminent death," in at least some instances. Without any constitutional nuance or case-by-case reservation, the Ashcroft Directive made medical assistance with aid-in-dying a crime. Justice Kennedy's opinion mentioned the "earnest and profound debate" over the constitutionality of state efforts to ban all forms of "euthanasia" as one reason the Court was reluctant to find a congressional delegation to the Attorney General on this issue. Some and perhaps all of the majority Justices—and none of the dissenters—found the Ashcroft Directive constitutionally problematic in the breadth of its intrusion into private decisionmaking and state policymaking. See Eskridge, *Story of* Gonzales v. Oregon, 366–75, 384–94.

Does the existence of potential constitutional problems make a difference in the Court's overall willingness to defer? Recall, for example, that our lead avoidance case in Chapter 6, § 3 was *NLRB v. Catholic Bishop of Chicago*. Although a pre-*Chevron* case, the Court had created a special deference regime for NLRB decisions but didn't even mention it, perhaps because the First Amendment difficulties trumped deference. The Eskridge and Baer study generalized that insight. In the 75 cases where at least one Justice flagged a constitutional concern with the agency's interpretation, the agency view prevailed only 45.3 percent of the time, while the agency view won in 70.7 percent of the cases where no Justice raised constitutional concerns. Eskridge & Baer, *Continuum of Deference.* This is the most dramatic differential in their study and strongly suggests that agencies do *not* get nearly as much deference when there are constitutional concerns with their interpretations.

What would be the theoretical basis for that? One might presume that Congress does not normally delegate to agencies the authority to press constitutional limits, and so constitutional concerns would show up at Step Zero, as in the *Oregon* case. Or one might invoke the avoidance canon in Step One: when there are two possible meanings of statutory language, the Court should, for institutional process reasons, follow the one that does not raise constitutional problems. In that event, the avoidance canon would trump *Chevron*. The Court has in fact gone that route in some *Chevron*-eligible cases. E.g., *Department of Commerce v. U.S. House of Representatives* (Chapter 6, § 3). One can even imagine the constitutional analysis coming in *Chevron* Step Two: an agency interpretation is not "reasonable" if it raises constitutional concerns when a more cautious interpretation would just as easily serve congressional goals.

PROBLEM WHEN AGENCY INTERPRETATIONS RAISE CONSTITUTIONAL CONCERNS

Problem 9-2. Abortion Counseling. In 1970, Congress enacted Title X of the Public Health Service Act, 84 Stat. 1499, 1504, which provides federal funding for family-planning services. The purposes of the Act expressed in § 2 are:

(1) to assist in making comprehensive voluntary family planning services readily available to all persons desiring such services; * * *

(5) to develop and make readily available information (including educational materials) on family planning and population growth to all persons desiring such information.

The Act authorizes the provision of federal funds to support the establishment and operation of voluntary family planning projects and empowers the Secretary of Health and Human Services to promulgate regulations imposing conditions on grant recipients to ensure that "grants will be effectively utilized for the purposes for which made."

Section 1 of the Act authorizes the Secretary to "make grants to and enter into contracts with public or nonprofit private entities to assist in the establishment and operation of voluntary family planning projects which shall offer a broad range of acceptable and effective family planning methods and services." Section 1008 provides: "None of the funds appropriated under this Act shall be used in programs where abortion is a method of family planning." According to the conference report for the Act, the § 1008 restriction was to ensure that Title X funds would "be used only to support preventive family planning services, population research, infertility services, and other related medical, informational, and educational opportunities."

The Secretary's 1971 regulations implementing the Act described the kind of services that grant recipients had to provide in order to be eligible for federal funding. Pursuant to § 1008, the regulations stipulated that "the project will not provide abortions as a method of family planning." The 1971 regulations, even as revised in 1986, did not regulate the form of counseling or the distribution of information at federally funded projects.

In 1988, the Secretary promulgated new regulations to clarify the "family planning" services that Title X funds may be used to assist. Section 59.2 of the new regulations limited Title X services to "preconceptual counseling, education, and general reproductive health care (including obstetric or prenatal care)." Section 59.8(a)(1) specified that henceforth a "Title X project may not provide counseling concerning the use of abortion as a method of family planning or provide referral for abortion as a method of family planning." Section 59.8(a)(2)–(3) made clear that Title X programs would have to refer pregnant women to other services, but doctors in the program could not "steer" expectant mothers to health care providers who perform abortions. Even if the client specifically requested referral to an abortion provider, the Title X program could not do so, nor could doctors associated with the program. According to § 59.8(b)(5), the appropriate response was that "the project does not consider abortion an appropriate method of family planning and therefore does not counsel or refer for abortion."

Grantees and doctors immediately challenged the new regulations. What arguments could they invoke against the Secretary's interpretation of § 1008? What arguments should the Secretary make in response? How would the Supreme Court analyze and decide this issue? Compare *Rust v. Sullivan*, 500 U.S. 173 (1991).

C. DOES THE AGENCY HAVE BROADER FREEDOM TO INTERPRET ITS OWN RULES AND REGULATIONS?

Since the New Deal, the Supreme Court has sometimes given special deference to agency interpretations of their own regulations. Such interpretations are "controlling unless plainly erroneous or inconsistent with the regulation." *Bowles v. Seminole Rock & Sand Co.*, 325 U.S. 410, 414 (1945). The *Seminole Rock* rule survived *Chevron* and was sometimes key to the Court's willingness to sustain agency views, as illustrated by *Auer v. Robbins*, 519 U.S. 452 (1997), and *Coeur Alaska, Inc. v. Southeast Alaska Conservation Council*, 557 U.S. 261 (2009).

This very issue was the first claim by the Attorney General in *Gonzales v. Oregon*, 546 U.S. 243 (2006). Under the Controlled Substances Act (CSA), Schedule II substances are generally available only pursuant to a written, nonrefillable prescription by a physician. 21 U.S.C. § 829(a). A 1971 regulation promulgated by the Department of Justice requires that every prescription for a controlled substance "be issued for a legitimate medical purpose by an individual practitioner acting in the usual course of his professional practice." 21 C.F.R. § 1306.04(a). Attorney General Ashcroft presented his Directive, preempting the Oregon Death With Dignity Act, as an interpretation of the Department's 1971 regulation and therefore entitled to *Seminole Rock-Auer* deference. In his opinion for the Court, Justice Kennedy rejected this assertion of deference, because the regulation simply "parroted" (repeated) the statute. In dissent, Justice Scalia questioned whether there was any authority creating a "parroting" exception to *Auer* and insisted that the regulation did more than "parrot" the statute.

NOTE ON AN AGENCY'S INTERPRETATIONS OF ITS OWN REGULATIONS

An agency's interpretation of its own regulations can come in a variety of formats— *amicus* briefs (as in *Auer*), directives or interpretive rules/guidances (as in *Oregon*), opinion letters (SEC and IRS especially), and so forth. Generally, agency interpretations in these formats are entitled to *Skidmore* deference, as in the Oregon Aid-in-Dying Case—but if the agency can relate them somehow to an existing *Chevron*-eligible rule, then it can not only jump *Skidmore*, but also jump *Chevron*, all the way to *Seminole-Auer*. This concern with "agency bootstrapping" is probably what worried Justice Kennedy in the Oregon Aid-in-Dying Case, and it has certainly worried other Justices, e.g., *Thomas Jefferson Univ. v. Shalala*, 512 U.S. 504, 525 (1994) (Thomas, J., dissenting), and commentators, e.g., John Manning, *Constitutional Structure and Judicial Deference to Agency Interpretations of Agency Rules*, 96 Colum. L. Rev. 612 (1996).

The Eskridge and Baer survey of 1014 Supreme Court cases between *Chevron* and *Hamdan* identified 155 cases where an agency said it was interpreting its own prior rules—yet the Court applied *Seminole-Auer* deference in only 12 of those cases, a surprisingly low number. See Eskridge & Baer, *Continuum of Deference,* 96 Geo. L.J. at 1104–05 (Table 2). Perhaps *Seminole Rock* is most relevant under the circumstances identified in *Auer*: the regulatory concept in play is one that the agency itself created (pursuant to a valid congressional delegation) and is now interpreting. As argued in Kevin Stack, *Interpreting Regulations*, 111 Mich. L. Rev. 355 (2012), agencies interpret their own regulations purposively. Hence, *Auer* deference might also offer the advantage of enabling agencies to develop appropriate regulatory regimes.

State supreme courts have been reluctant to create a special rule for agency interpretations of its own regulations. Recall the Pennsylvania Supreme Court's decision in *Seeton*. That Court's deference jurisprudence parallels *Chevron*, but none of the judges in *Seeton* mentioned that the agency was interpreting its own regulations. The majority was, if anything, not very deferential to the agency—nor did dissenting Justice Eakins rely on anything like *Auer* as a reason for going along with the agency.

Although Justice Scalia authored *Auer* and relied on that precedent in his dissent in the Oregon Aid-in-Dying Case, within a decade he had changed his mind. In a concurring opinion in *Decker v. Northwest Environmental Defense Center,* 568 U.S. 597, 616–21 (2013), Justice Scalia urged the Court to jettison *Auer* as a special category of deference, because it encouraged agencies to issue "vague" regulations and then elaborate on them through aggressive interpretations. "*Auer* is not a logical corollary to *Chevron* but a dangerous permission slip for the arrogation of power." In *Perez v. Mortgage Bankers Ass'n,* 135 S.Ct. 1199 (2015), Justices Scalia, Thomas, and Alito wrote special concurring opinions signaling their interest in revisiting and (for Scalia and Thomas) overruling *Seminole Rock/Auer*. Justice Gorsuch, who succeeded Justice Scalia in 2017, had, as a Tenth Circuit judge, criticized the Supreme Court's deference regimes in *Gutierrez-Brizuela v. Lynch*, 834 F.3d 1142 (10th Cir. 2016) (concurring opinion).

KISOR V. WILKIE
Supreme Court of the United States, 2019.
___ U.S. ___, 139 S.Ct. 2400

JUSTICE KAGAN delivered the judgment of the Court and the opinion for the Court in Parts I, II.B, III.B, and IV, [joined by CHIEF JUSTICE ROBERTS and JUSTICES GINSBURG, BREYER, and SOTOMAYOR.]

[Kisor was a Marine denied benefits for post-traumatic stress disorder, based upon an interpretation by the Department of Veterans Affairs of its own regulations. The lower court *Auer*-deferred, and the Supreme Court granted review to determine whether courts should continue to afford *Auer* deference to agency interpretations of its own regulations.]

[In Part II.A, of her opinion, joined only by Justices Ginsburg, Breyer, and Sotomayor, Justice Kagan set forth the practical as well as doctrinal background. Since 1945 (*Seminole Rock*), and perhaps earlier, the Court had given special deference to an agency's interpretations of its own regulations. In *Auer*, the agency had to] decide whether police captains are eligible for overtime under the Fair Labor Standards Act. According to the agency's regulations, employees could not receive overtime if they were paid on a "salary basis." 29 C.F.R. § 541.118(a) (1996). And in deciding whether an employee was salaried, one question was whether his pay was "subject to reduction" based on performance. *Ibid.* A police department's manual informed its officers that their pay might be docked if they committed a disciplinary infraction. Did that fact alone make them "subject to" pay deductions? Or must the department have a practice of docking officer pay, so that the possibility of that happening is more than theoretical?

[The *Seminole Rock/Auer* rule is that the agency's answer to that question should presumptively be accepted by courts. This rule makes sense, because it is presumably what Congress would want, produces better answers given the agency's knowledge of its own rules and practices as well as policy expertise, and yields an answer that is immediately applicable nationwide, in contrast to case-by-case, circuit-by-circuit litigation.]

[In Part II.B, Justice Kagan spoke for the Court, as she laid out the limitations of *Auer* deference.] First and foremost, a court should not afford *Auer* deference unless the regulation is genuinely ambiguous. * * * [I]f the law gives an answer—if there is only one reasonable construction of a regulation—then a court has no business deferring to any other reading, no matter how much the agency insists it would make more sense. Deference in that circumstance would "permit the agency, under the guise of interpreting a regulation, to create de facto a new regulation." *Auer* does not, and indeed could not, go that far.

And before concluding that a rule is genuinely ambiguous, a court must exhaust all the "traditional tools" of construction. *Chevron* (adopting the same approach for ambiguous statutes). * * * [A] court must "carefully consider[ ]" the text, structure, history, and purpose of a regulation, in all the ways it would if it had no agency to fall back on. Doing so will resolve many seeming ambiguities out of the box, without resort to *Auer* deference.

If genuine ambiguity remains, moreover, the agency's reading must still be "reasonable." *Thomas Jefferson*. In other words, it must come within the zone of ambiguity the court has identified after employing all its interpretive tools. (Note that serious application of those tools therefore has use even when a regulation turns out to be truly ambiguous. The text, structure, history, and so forth at least establish the outer bounds of permissible interpretation.) Some courts have thought (perhaps because of *Seminole Rock*'s "plainly erroneous" formulation) that at this stage of the analysis, agency constructions of rules receive greater deference than agency constructions of statutes. But that is not so. Under *Auer*, as under *Chevron*, the agency's reading must fall "within the bounds of reasonable interpretation." *Arlington v. FCC*. And let there be no mistake: That is a requirement an agency can fail.

Still, we are not done—for not every reasonable agency reading of a genuinely ambiguous rule should receive *Auer* deference. We have recognized in applying *Auer* that a court must make an independent inquiry into whether the character and context of the agency interpretation entitles it to controlling weight. As explained above, we give *Auer* deference because we presume, for a set of reasons relating to the comparative attributes of courts and agencies, that Congress would have wanted us to. But the administrative realm is vast and varied, and we have understood that such a presumption cannot always hold. Cf. *Mead* ("tailor[ing] deference to [the] variety" of administrative action). The inquiry on this dimension does not reduce to any exhaustive test. But we have laid out some especially important markers for identifying when *Auer* deference is and is not appropriate.

To begin with, the regulatory interpretation must be one actually made by the agency. In other words, it must be the agency's "authoritative" or "official position," rather than any more ad hoc statement not reflecting the agency's views. *Mead* (Scalia, J., dissenting). * * * Of course, the requirement of "authoritative" action must recognize a reality of bureaucratic life: Not everything the agency does comes from, or is even in the name of, the Secretary or his chief advisers. So, for example, we have deferred to "official staff memoranda" that were "published in the Federal Register," even though never approved by the agency head. But there are limits. The interpretation must at the least emanate from those actors, using those vehicles, understood to make authoritative policy in the relevant context. [Examples included a "speech of a mid-level official," an "informal memorandum" recounting a telephone conversation between employees, and "regulatory guides" the agency itself had "disclaimed."] If the interpretation does not do so, a court may not defer.

Next, the agency's interpretation must in some way implicate its substantive expertise. Administrative knowledge and experience largely "account [for] the presumption that Congress delegates interpretive lawmaking power to the agency." *Martin.* So the basis for deference ebbs when "[t]he subject matter of the [dispute is] distan[t] from the agency's ordinary" duties or "fall[s] within the scope of another agency's authority." *Arlington.* * * * "Generally, agencies have a nuanced understanding of the regulations they administer." Brief for Respondent 33. That point is most obvious when a rule is technical * * *. But more prosaic-seeming questions also commonly implicate policy expertise; consider the TSA assessing the security risks of pâté or a disabilities office weighing the costs and benefits of an accommodation. Once again, though, there are limits. Some interpretive issues may fall more naturally into a judge's bailiwick. Take one requiring the elucidation of a simple common-law property term, or one concerning the award of an attorney's fee. When the agency has no comparative expertise in resolving a regulatory ambiguity, Congress presumably would not grant it that authority.

Finally, an agency's reading of a rule must reflect "fair and considered judgment" to receive *Auer* deference. [*Christopher v. SmithKline Beecham Corp.*, 567 U.S. 142 (2012).] That means, we have stated, that a court should decline to defer to a merely "convenient litigating position" or "post hoc rationalizatio[n] advanced" to "defend past agency action against attack." *Christopher.* And a court may not defer to a new interpretation, whether or not introduced in litigation, that creates "unfair surprise" to regulated parties. That disruption of expectations may occur when an agency substitutes one view of a rule for another. We have therefore only rarely given *Auer* deference to an agency construction "conflict[ing] with a prior" one. *Thomas Jefferson.* Or the upending of reliance may happen without such an explicit interpretive change. This Court, for example, recently refused to defer to an interpretation that would have imposed retroactive liability on parties for longstanding conduct that the agency had never before addressed. See *Christopher.* Here too the lack of "fair warning" outweighed the reasons to apply *Auer*.

[In Part III, Justice Kagan rejected Kisor's argument that the *Seminole Rock/Auer* line of cases ought to be overruled. Speaking for the plurality in Part III.A, she was unpersuaded that *Auer* was incorrectly decided. Kisor's main argument was that it was consistent with the APA's availability of judicial review of agency rules, 5 U.S.C. § 706, and its procedures for informal rulemaking, *id.* § 553. As the Court held in *Mortgage Bankers* [Chapter 8], agency interpretations of legislative rules do not have the force of law and so do not have to go through the notice-and-comment rulemaking process. As explained in Part II.B, *Auer* did not eliminate or even significantly limit the legitimate role of judicial review; § 706 does not tell courts how to conduct their review, and *Auer* structured it in a way that is faithful to congressional expectations.]

[Speaking for the Court in Part III.B, Justice Kagan found no good reason to overrule the many precedents that have been entrenched in federal law since 1945. Even if *Seminole Rock/Auer* were wrongly decided, reliance on those precedents, including by Congress, would present a big obstacle to overruling them, and Kisor offered no reason to think that *Seminole Rock/Auer* were unworkable, inconsistent with the fabric of law, or pernicious. In Part IV, the Court remanded the case to the Federal Circuit to determine whether the interpretation of the applicable regulation qualified as an action of the agency, a point raised by the Solicitor General.]

[CHIEF JUSTICE ROBERTS concurred in the judgment and joined Parts I, IIB, IIIB, and IV of Justice Kagan's opinion. He opined that the carefully defined limits of *Auer* set forth in Part II.B of the opinion for the Court were not so different from the *Skidmore* reasons that can persuade a court to adopt agency interpretations as their own. Thus, "the cases in which *Auer* deference is warranted largely overlap with the cases in which it would be unreasonable for a court not to be persuaded by an agency's interpretation of its own regulation." In his separate dissenting opinion, JUSTICE KAVANAUGH (joined by JUSTICE ALITO) agreed with the Chief Justice on this point.]

JUSTICE GORSUCH, joined by JUSTICES THOMAS, ALITO [Parts I–III], and KAVANAUGH [Parts I–V], dissenting.

It should have been easy for the Court to say goodbye to *Auer v. Robbins*. In disputes involving the relationship between the government and the people, *Auer* requires judges to accept an executive agency's interpretation of its own regulations even when that interpretation doesn't represent the best and fairest reading. This rule creates a "systematic judicial bias in favor of the federal government, the most powerful of parties, and against everyone else." Nor is *Auer*'s biased rule the product of some congressional mandate we are powerless to correct: This Court invented it, almost by accident and without any meaningful effort to reconcile it with the Administrative Procedure Act or the Constitution. A legion of academics, lower court judges, and Members of this Court—even *Auer*'s author—has called on us to abandon *Auer*. Yet today a bare majority flinches, and *Auer* lives on.

Still, today's decision is more a stay of execution than a pardon. The Court cannot muster even five votes to say that *Auer* is lawful or wise. Instead, a majority retains *Auer* only because of *stare decisis*. And yet, far from standing by that precedent, the majority proceeds to impose so many new and nebulous qualifications and limitations on *Auer* that the Chief Justice claims to see little practical difference between keeping it on life support in this way and overruling it entirely. So the doctrine emerges maimed and enfeebled—in truth, zombified. * * *

Consider this case. Mr. Kisor is a Marine who lost out on benefits for post-traumatic stress disorder when the court of appeals deferred to a regulatory interpretation advanced by the Department of Veterans Affairs. The court of appeals was guilty of nothing more than faithfully following *Auer*. But the majority today invokes *stare decisis*, of all things, to vacate that judgment and tell the court of appeals to try again using its newly retooled, multi-factored, and far less determinate version of *Auer*. Respectfully, I would stop this business of making up excuses for judges to abdicate their job of interpreting the law, and simply allow the court of appeals to afford Mr. Kisor its best independent judgment of the law's meaning.

[In Part I, Justice Gorsuch argued that the baseline New Deal precedent was *Skidmore*, which involved an agency interpretation of its own regulation. The Court gave the agency inputs due weight but assumed responsibility for interpreting the statute. By his account, *Seminole Rock* was not considered much different from *Skidmore*—until the 1960s, when a more aggressive doctrine took shape, culminating in *Auer*.]

[In Part II, Justice Gorsuch argued that *Auer* is inconsistent with the APA, starting with § 706's requirement of judicial review.] [T]he APA further directs courts to "determine the meaning" of any relevant "agency action," including any rule issued by the agency. The APA thus requires a reviewing court to resolve for itself any dispute over the proper interpretation of an agency regulation. A court that, in deference to an agency, adopts something other than the best reading of a regulation isn't "decid[ing]" the relevant "questio[n] of law" or "determin[ing] the meaning" of the regulation. Instead, it's allowing the agency to dictate the answer to that question. In doing so, the court is abdicating the duty Congress assigned to it in the APA.

* * * [C]onsider a statute that tells a court to "determin[e]" an appropriate sentence in a criminal case. If the judge said he was sending a defendant to prison for longer than he believed appropriate only in deference to the government's "reasonable" sentencing recommendation, would anyone really think that complied with the law? Or take a statute that instructs a court to "determine" whether a consent judgment proposed by the government in a civil antitrust case "is in the public interest." If a court thought the proposed judgment harmful to the public but decided to defer to the government's "reasonable" contrary view anyway, would anyone suggest the court had complied with Congress's instruction?

Nor does Justice Kagan's reading of § 706 offer any logical stopping point. If courts can "determine the meaning" of a regulation by deferring to any "reasonable" agency reading, then why not by deferring to any agency reading? If it were really true that the APA has nothing to say about how courts decide what regulations mean, then it would follow that the APA tolerates a rule that "the agency is always right." And if you find yourself in a place as absurd as that, you might want to consider whether you've taken a wrong turn along the way.

[Justice Gorsuch also argued that *Auer* was inconsistent with the notice-and-comment process for informal rulemaking.] We've held that the Constitution's specification of a "single, finely wrought" procedure for the enactment of statutes (bicameralism and presentment) necessarily implies that Congress cannot amend an enacted statute without following that procedure—say, by allowing a single House to change what the law requires. By the same logic, Congress's specification in the APA of procedures for the creation of new substantive rules (like notice and comment) necessarily implies that an agency cannot amend a substantive rule without following those procedures. To hold otherwise, as *Auer* demands, subverts the APA's design.

[Likewise, in Part III, Justice Gorsuch maintained that *Auer* was inconsistent with the "judicial Power" vested in federal courts by Article III. Speaking only for himself and Justices Thomas and Kavanaugh in Part IV (as well as Part V below), Justice Gorsuch argued that Justice Kagan's "policy" props lent zero support for *Auer*: far from reflecting the expectations of Congress (which has never ratified or endorsed *Auer*) or advancing national uniformity, *Auer* encourages executive branch usurpation of both legislative and judicial duties and different administrations to waffle back and forth in their politics-driven interpretations of previous agency rules.]

[V] * * * While pretending to bow to *stare decisis*, the majority goes about reshaping our precedent in new and experimental ways. True, the majority admits, this Court has in the past accorded *Auer* deference " 'reflexive[ly],' " "without significant analysis of the underlying regulation" or "careful attention to [its] nature and context," and encouraged lower courts to do the same. But no more. From now on, the majority says, not only must judges "exhaust all the 'traditional tools' of construction" to decide whether the agency's interpretation is "reasonable," they must also make "an independent inquiry into whether the character and context of the agency interpretation" justifies deference. The majority candidly admits that it finds it impossible to "reduce" this new inquiry "to any exhaustive test," so it settles for laying out some "markers." What are the markers? We are told that courts should often—but not always—withhold deference from an interpretation offered by mid-level agency staff; often—but not always—withhold deference from a nontechnical, "prosaic-seeming" interpretation; often—but not always—withhold deference from an interpretation advanced for the first time in an amicus brief; and often—but not always—withhold deference from an interpretation that conflicts with an earlier one. The only certainty in all this is that the majority isn't really much moved by *stare decisis*; everyone recognizes, to one degree or another, that *Auer* cannot stand. And between our remaining choices—continuing to make up new deference rules, or returning to the text of the APA and the approach to judicial review that prevailed for most of our history—the answer should have been easy.

[And why, by the way, Justice Gorsuch wondered, ought *stare decisis* even attach to a statement of methodology?] We are not dealing with a precedent that purported to settle the meaning of a single statute or regulation or resolve a particular case. The *Auer* doctrine claims to do much more than that—to prescribe an interpretive methodology governing every future dispute over the meaning of every regulation. In other contexts, we do not regard statements in our opinions about such generally applicable interpretive methods, like the proper weight to afford historical practice in constitutional cases or legislative history in statutory cases, as binding future Justices with the full force of horizontal stare decisis. Why, then, should we regard as binding *Auer*'s statements about the weight to afford agencies' interpretations in regulatory cases? To the extent *Auer* purports to dictate "the interpretive inferences that future Justices must draw in construing statutes and regulations that the Court has never engaged," it may well "exceed the limits of *stare decisis*."

[Even if entitled to any *stare decisis* consideration, Justice Gorsuch urged an overruling, because *Auer* was wrongly decided and at war with the APA, its standard is so unworkable that he majority has completely recast it, thus there are no reliance interests involved, and the doctrine promises to work more mischief n the future, given the vast expansion of the modern regulatory state. He concluded his dissenting opinion with a passage joined only by Justice Thomas:]

Overruling *Auer* would have taken us directly back to *Skidmore*, liberating courts to decide cases based on their independent judgment and "follow [the] agency's [view] only to the extent it is persuasive." By contrast, the majority's attempt to remodel *Auer*'s rule into a multi-step, multi-factor inquiry guarantees more uncertainty and much litigation. Proceeding in this convoluted way burdens our colleagues on the lower courts, who will have to spend time debating deference that they could have spent interpreting disputed regulations. It also continues to deny the people who come before us the neutral forum for their disputes that they rightly expect and deserve.

But this cloud may have a silver lining: The majority leaves *Auer* so riddled with holes that, when all is said and done, courts may find that it does not constrain their independent judgment any more than *Skidmore*. As reengineered, *Auer* requires courts to "exhaust all the 'traditional tools' of construction" before they even consider deferring to an agency. And those tools include all sorts of tie-breaking rules for resolving ambiguity even in the closest cases. Courts manage to make do with these tools in many other areas of the law, so one might hope they will hardly ever find them inadequate here. And if they do, they will now have to conduct a further inquiry that includes so few firm guides and so many cryptic "markers" that they will rarely, if ever, have to defer to an agency regulatory interpretation that differs from what they believe is the best and fairest reading.

But whatever happens, this case hardly promises to be this Court's last word on *Auer*. If today's opinion ends up reducing *Auer* to the role of a tin god—officious, but ultimately powerless—then a future Court should candidly admit as much and stop requiring litigants and lower courts to pay token homage to it. Alternatively, if *Auer* proves more resilient, this Court should reassert its responsibility to say what the law is and afford the people the neutral forum for their disputes that they expect and deserve.

NOTE ON THE REAFFIRMATION AND REVISION OF AUER

1. Stare Decisis *for Methodological Precedents?* A majority of the Court holds that *stare decisis* attaches to a methodological decision, at least as regards deference. Most academic commentary went the other way, in part because the Court generally has not given *stare decisis* effect to methodological decisions or reasoning, such as the weight to be afforded legislative history.[8] One consequence of the Court's holding is that *Chevron* is entitled to *stare decisis* effect. (Does *Kisor* itself bind Gorsuch and the other dissenters? Are they required, by *stare decisis*, to accept the proposition that deference decisions are protected by *stare decisis*?) How about the canons of statutory interpretation surveyed in Chapter 6? The legislative history rules examined in Chapter 7?

The dissenters make sport of Justice Kagan's transformation of *Auer* at the same time she was reaffirming it, but notice the similarities in the Court's leading decision on constitutional *stare decisis*—namely, *Planned Parenthood of Southeastern Pa. v. Casey*,

---

[8]   E.g., Evan Criddle & Glen Staszewski, *Against Methodological* Stare Decisis, 102 Geo. L. J. 1573 (2014); Randy Kozel, *Statutory Interpretation, Administrative Deference, and the Law of* Stare Decisis, 97 Texas L. Rev. 1125, 1159 (2019); Connor Raso & William Eskridge Jr., Chevron *as a Canon, Not a Precedent: An Empirical Study of What Motivates Justices in Agency Deference Cases*, 110 Colum. L. Rev. 1727, 1765–1766 (2010).

505 U.S. 833 (1992) (joint opinion, reaffirming *Roe v. Wade* but completely recasting its constitutional restrictions).

2.   *The Ongoing Revival of* Skidmore. Not so long ago, Justice Scalia declared that *Skidmore* was dead, rendered obsolete by *Chevron*—but the Court rejected that idea in *Mead*. The Eskridge and Baer study of Supreme Court deference decisions found that *Skidmore* (including what they called "*Skidmore* Lite") was the dominant deference regime at the Supreme Court level even before *Mead*, and that the agency win rate was just as impressive under that regime as under *Chevron*. In *Kisor*, all nine Justices seem to agree that *Auer* deference should look much more like *Skidmore* than anyone thought before 2019. Why shouldn't the Court simply announce *Skidmore* deference for all agency interpretations? That would preserve the Court's *Marbury* role and respond to the APA critique of *Chevron* and *Auer*, while bringing practical wisdom to bear.

3.   *Stepification of* Auer. The Kagan opinion looks like the Court is bringing the same kind of "stepification" (Mitchell Johnston's delightfully awful term) to *Auer* that the commentators and the Court brought to *Chevron*.[9] After *Kisor,* there is an *Auer* Step 0: Is the interpretation sufficiently "by the agency" to qualify for the deference regime? If yes, then Step 1: Drawing on all the tools of interpretation available to judges— dictionaries, grammar, common usage, statutory and regulatory structure, precedent, canons, legislative history, purpose, and so much more—is the regulation ambiguous? If yes, then Step 2: Is the agency's interpretation of its own regulation "reasonable"? What is going on with this relentless process of stepification? Why does this appeal to the Justices at this point in our history?

D. SHOULD COURTS DEFER TO AGENCIES ON WHETHER FEDERAL LAW PREEMPTS STATE REGULATION?

The Supremacy Clause of Article VI requires that federal statutes be the supreme law of the land and that state courts enforce them rather than state law when they are inconsistent, or "preempted." There are three different circumstances when state law, such as the Oregon Death With Dignity Act, might be preempted by federal law. First, a valid federal statute can stipulate that it preempts state law, and the Court will follow that statutory directive (unless there is a constitutional problem). E.g., *Shaw v. Delta Airlines*, 463 U.S. 85 (1983). Of course, Congress can also write a "non-preemption" *saving clause* into legislation, which will direct courts not to read the legislation to preempt state law.

Second, a federal statute will preempt state law whose operation is inconsistent with that of the federal statutory scheme. This applies not only "where compliance with both federal and state regulations is a physical impossibility," *Florida Lime & Avocado Growers, Inc. v. Paul*, 373 U.S. 132, 142–43 (1963), but also where the state law "stands as an obstacle to the accomplishment and execution of the full purposes and objectives of Congress." *Hines v. Davidowitz*, 312 U.S. 52, 67 (1941).

Third is "field" preemption. "The scheme of federal regulations may be so pervasive as to make reasonable the inference that Congress left no room for the States to supplement it. Or the Act of Congress may touch a field in which the federal

---

9   Mitchell Johnston, "Stepification" (Yale Law School Seminar Paper, May 2019).

interest is so dominant that the federal system will be assumed to preclude enforcement of state laws of the same subject." *Rice v. Santa Fe Elevator Corp.*, 331 U.S. 218, 230 (1947). Areas such as immigration, naturalization, and regulation of noncitizens are examples of fields where federal legislation is likely to be preemptive. E.g., *Toll v. Moreno*, 458 U.S. 1 (1982).

Assume you have a federal statute, such as the Motor Vehicle Safety Act of 1966, which delegates lawmaking and other authority to an agency within the Department of Transportation. The agency might have important input into a court's determination of the scope of federal preemption. First, Congress might give the agency direct authority to preempt state law through notice-and-comment rulemaking. Such rules would, theoretically, be subject to *Chevron* deference. Second, Congress might delegate to the agency the authority to adopt substantive rules which could then be the basis for federal preemption the same as explicit statutory rules would. The validity of such rules might be evaluated under *Chevron*, but the agency's understanding of their preemptive force would probably entail only *Skidmore* deference. Third, the agency might, on its own, present its views, usually through interpretive guidances or in *amicus* briefs. What level of deference should that entail?

As you ponder that question, recall that the Supreme Court has recognized a substantive canon that is relevant: "The historic police powers of the States [are] not to be superseded by . . . a Federal Act unless that [is] the clear and manifest purpose of Congress." *Cipollone v. Liggett Group, Inc.*, 505 U.S. 504, 516 (1992). How does this canon relate to the three different kinds of preemption *and* to the three kinds of agency inputs? Consider the following case.

GEIER V. AMERICAN HONDA MOTOR CO., INC.

United States Supreme Court, 2000.
529 U.S. 861, 120 S.Ct. 1913, 146 L.Ed.2d 914.

JUSTICE BREYER delivered the opinion of the Court.

[In 1992, petitioner Alexis Geier, driving a 1987 Honda Accord, collided with a tree and was seriously injured. The car was equipped with manual shoulder and lap belts which Geier had buckled up at the time. The car was not equipped with airbags or other passive restraint devices. Geier and her parents, also petitioners, sued the car's manufacturer, American Honda, under District of Columbia tort law. They claimed that American Honda had designed its car negligently and defectively because it lacked a driver's side airbag. The District Court dismissed the lawsuit on grounds of preemption. Because Geier's lawsuit sought to establish a stricter safety standard (an airbag requirement) than FMVSS 208 (which then permitted choice between airbags and passive restraints), the asserted tort claim was pre-empted by a provision of the Safety Act of 1966 which pre-empts "any safety standard" that is not identical to a federal safety standard applicable to the same aspect of performance, 15 U.S.C. § 1392(d).

[Disagreeing, the Supreme Court held that the preemption provision was inapplicable because of a saving provision, which says that "compliance with" a federal safety standard "does not exempt any person from any liability under common law." 15 U.S.C. § 1397(k). The saving clause assumes that there are some significant number of common-law liability cases to save. Justice Breyer did not, however, agree that the saving clause precluded the Court's application of ordinary pre-emption principles. See *Freightliner Corp. v. Myrick*, 514 U.S. 280 (1995).]

The basic question, then, is whether a common-law "no airbag" action like the one before us actually conflicts with FMVSS 208. We hold that it does.

In petitioners' and the dissent's view, FMVSS 208 sets a minimum airbag standard. As far as FMVSS 208 is concerned, the more airbags, and the sooner, the better. But that was not the Secretary's view. [Department of Transportation (DOT)] comments, which accompanied the promulgation of FMVSS 208, make clear that the standard deliberately provided the manufacturer with a range of choices among different passive restraint devices. Those choices would bring about a mix of different devices introduced gradually over time; and FMVSS 208 would thereby lower costs, overcome technical safety problems, encourage technological development, and win widespread consumer acceptance—all of which would promote FMVSS 208's safety objectives. See generally 49 Fed. Reg. 28962 (1984).

* * * Read in light of this history, DOT's own contemporaneous explanation of FMVSS 208 makes clear that the 1984 version of FMVSS 208 reflected the following significant considerations. First, buckled up seatbelts are a vital ingredient of automobile safety. Second, despite the enormous and unnecessary risks that a passenger runs by not buckling up manual lap and shoulder belts, more than 80% of front seat passengers would leave their manual seatbelts unbuckled. Third, airbags could make up for the dangers caused by unbuckled manual belts, but they could not make up for them entirely.

Fourth, passive restraint systems had their own disadvantages, for example, the dangers associated with, intrusiveness of, and corresponding public dislike for, nondetachable automatic belts. Fifth, airbags brought with them their own special risks to safety, such as the risk of danger to out-of-position occupants (usually children) in small cars.

Sixth, airbags were expected to be significantly more expensive than other passive restraint devices, raising the average cost of a vehicle price $320 for full frontal airbags over the cost of a car with manual lap and shoulder seatbelts (and potentially much more if production volumes were low). And the agency worried that the high replacement cost—estimated to be $800—could lead car owners to refuse to replace them after deployment. Seventh, the public, for reasons of cost, fear, or physical intrusiveness, might resist installation or use of any of the then-available passive restraint devices—a particular concern with respect to airbags.

FMVSS 208 reflected these considerations in several ways. Most importantly, that standard deliberately sought variety—a mix of several different passive restraint systems. It did so by setting a performance requirement for passive restraint devices and allowing manufacturers to choose among different passive restraint mechanisms, such as airbags, automatic belts, or other passive restraint technologies to satisfy that requirement. And DOT explained why FMVSS 208 sought the mix of devices that it expected its performance standard to produce. DOT wrote that it had *rejected* a proposed FMVSS 208 "all airbag" standard because of safety concerns (perceived or real) associated with airbags, which concerns threatened a "backlash" more easily overcome "if airbags" were "not the only way of complying." [In order to give manufacturers more time to develop airbags or other passive restraint systems, the 1984 FMVSS 208 standard entailed a *gradual* phase-in of passive restraints, over a three-year period (1986–89).]

In effect, petitioners' tort action depends upon its claim that manufacturers had a duty to install an airbag when they manufactured the 1987 Honda Accord. Such a state law—*i.e.*, a rule of state tort law imposing such a duty—by its terms would have required manufacturers of all similar cars to install airbags rather than other passive restraint systems, such as automatic belts or passive interiors. It thereby would have presented an obstacle to the variety and mix of devices that the federal regulation sought. It would have required all manufacturers to have installed airbags in respect to the entire District-of-Columbia-related portion of their 1987 new car fleet, even though FMVSS 208 at that time required only that 10% of a manufacturer's nationwide fleet be equipped with any passive restraint device at all. It thereby also would have stood as an obstacle to the gradual passive restraint phase-in that the federal regulation deliberately imposed. In addition, it could have made less likely the adoption of a state mandatory buckle-up law. Because the rule of law for which petitioners contend would have stood "as an obstacle to the accomplishment and execution of" the important means-related federal objectives that we have just discussed, it is pre-empted. * * *

One final point: We place some weight upon DOT's interpretation of FMVSS 208's objectives and its conclusion, as set forth in the Government's brief, that a tort suit such as this one would " 'stand as an obstacle to the accomplishment and execution' " of those objectives. Brief for United States as *Amicus Curiae* 25–26 (quoting *Hines v. Davidowitz*, 312 U.S. 52, 67 (1941)). Congress has delegated to DOT authority to implement the statute; the subject matter is technical; and the relevant history and background are complex and extensive. The agency is likely to have a thorough understanding of its own regulation and its objectives and is "uniquely qualified" to comprehend the likely impact of state requirements. And DOT has explained FMVSS 208's objectives, and the interference that "no airbag" suits pose thereto, consistently over time. In these circumstances, the agency's own views should make a difference. * * *

[We omit the dissenting opinion of JUSTICE STEVENS, joined by JUSTICES SOUTER, THOMAS, and GINSBURG. Most of the dissenters' arguments are mentioned in the notes following the decision.]

NOTES ON GEIER AND FEDERAL PREEMPTION OF STATE LAW

1.   *The Debate Among the Justices.* Key to Justice Breyer's opinion is the Court's belief that allowing state courts to find that airbags are sometimes required to satisfy the manufacturer's duty of care would undermine the federal statute's compromise, whereby manufacturers would have choices. Justice Stevens's dissent objected that case-by-case adjudications would not establish a hard-and-fast rule that airbags were required; not only could different juries reach different results, but manufacturers could win all the cases if they showed airbags to be ineffective or other methods just as effective. See Peter Strauss, *The Story of* Geier v. American Honda Motor Co.: *Statutes, Regulation, and the*

Common Law, in *Statutory Interpretation Stories* 294, 320–32 (Eskridge, Frickey & Garrett eds., 2011).

The dissenters also argued that the Court ignored the *Cipollone* presumption and was too willing to preempt the state tort suit. Was it clear that preemption was required by the "clear and manifest purpose of Congress"? Justice Stevens also insisted that the majority's holding was in tension with the saving clause: "The saving clause in the Safety Act unambiguously expresses a decision by Congress that compliance with a federal safety standard does not exempt a manufacturer from *any* common-law liability. In light of this reference to common-law liability in the saving clause, Congress surely would have included a similar reference in § 1392(d) if it had intended to pre-empt such liability." Should the Court be especially chary of preempting state common law under "inconsistent application" preemption when there is a saving clause? Note, also, that state law is essentially preempted by an agency rule and not by a statutory provision. Although the agency had authority to issue the rule, the Court ought to think twice before giving the rule preemptive authority to displace state law, especially in light of the federalism presumption of *Cipollone*.

2.   *Titanic Concerns: Underenforcement Versus Overenforcement of Safety Norms?* Addressing this issue, Ralph Nader and Joe Page had argued in *Automobile-Design Liability and Compliance with Federal Standards*, 64 Geo. Wash. L. Rev. 415, 419 (1996), that the statutory minimum should not preclude state regulation that raised the floor. In addition to the saving clause, which seemed to embody this philosophy, Nader and Page invoked the *Titanic* precedent. That famous vessel had fully "complied with British governmental regulations setting minimum requirements for lifeboats when it left port on its final, fateful voyage with boats capable of carrying only about [half] of the people on board," W. Wade, The *Titanic*: End of a Dream 68 (1986), yet one might reasonably conclude that the *Titanic* had not satisfied its duty of care to the other half of the passengers who lost their lives when the ship sunk in ice-cold waters. Because people's lives are at stake just as much in auto safety regulation, Nader and Page maintained that states ought to be able to raise the floor. The dissenting Justices agreed and cited their article and its *Titanic* analogy. Their position was that the majority was standing in the way of permissible enforcement of the safety norm. The Court may have even been seen as pandering to the auto industry's determination to *underenforce* safety norms.

The majority did not respond but might have said that the regulatory scheme sought a balance of safety and cost. The National Highway Traffic Safety Administration (NHTSA) was willing to trade off human lives (more people would die in accidents) for cost savings by manufacturers. This may seem terrible, but don't forget that the nation's decision to allow automobiles on the road and to travel 65 miles per hour has predictable costs in human lives each year—lives that could be saved if all of us suffered the inconvenience of not being able to drive (or drive so fast) on the open road. The majority's view was that Congress had authorized the agency to make these kinds of trade-offs (recall Justice White's opinion in *State Farm*, not to mention Justice Stevens's opinion in *Chevron*). Hence, the dissenters' position would have *overenforced* safety norms.

3.   *Should the Court Defer to the Agency in Preemption Cases?* How should *Chevron/Skidmore* interact with *Cipollone* in these cases? Justice Thomas has suggested that the Court should be *less* deferential if the federal agency is pushing for preemption and *more* deferential when the agency is arguing against preemption, especially in conflict or field preemption cases. *Pharmacological Res. & Mfrs. v. Walsh*, 538 U.S. 644,

675–83 (2003) (Thomas, J., concurring in the judgment); accord, William Eskridge Jr., *Vetogates,* Chevron, *Preemption,* 83 Notre Dame L. Rev. 1441 (2008) (between 1984 and 2006, the Supreme Court agreed with the agency in 85% of the cases where it argued against preemption, much higher than its agreement when the agency was, more predictably, urging preemption).

Nina Mendelson, Chevron *and Preemption,* 102 Mich. L. Rev. 737 (2004), argues against *Chevron* deference for agency views regarding preemption. Although she demonstrates that agencies are more accountable to state interests than the Court or (surprisingly) Congress, she cautions against *Chevron* deference because courts continue to have some comparative advantages in evaluating preemption claims and because agencies will often tend to expand their own authority at the expense of the states. Mendelson believes that agencies often have useful contributions and so favors *Skidmore* deference as appropriate—the same accommodation reached by Justice Breyer in *Geier* and Justice Kennedy in *Oregon.*

The Supreme Court seemed to follow something like Mendelson's suggestion in *Wyeth v. Levine,* 555 U.S. 555 (2009), which held that the Food Drug & Cosmetic Act of 1938 (FDCA) did not preempt a tort suit for a drug company's failure to warn consumers of the risks associated with Phenergan. Invoking the *Cipollone* presumption against preemption, Justice Stevens's opinion for the Court rejected the FDA's argument (in an *amicus* brief) that Wyeth's compliance with its labeling rules insulated it from tort liability. Federal law then allowed Wyeth to amend its label without FDA approval based on safety concerns of the sort raised by the state tort suit. Thus, it was *not* impossible for Wyeth to comply with both federal law and state law. Moreover, the FDCA vested primary responsibility for labeling with drug companies, not the FDA, which is merely a monitor. The Court also found the FDA's opinion that liability would upset its regulatory balance was not entitled to deference because it (1) was inconsistent with the FDA's own longstanding position to the contrary, (2) was not subject to comments from the public, and (3) was not supported by new evidence or cogent reasoning.

In *Wyeth,* Justice Thomas expressed reluctance, for constitutional reasons, to apply obstacle or impossibility preemption to state common law—yet he wrote for a 5–4 Court finding obstacle preemption in *Pliva, Inc. v. Mensing,* 131 S.Ct. 2567 (2011). Cf. Eskridge, *Vetogates,* Chevron, *Preemption*(agency win rate 72.2% for 97 express preemption cases, versus 72.4% win rate for 29 conflict or obstacle preemption cases). As in *Wyeth,* a drug company had complied with FDA labeling requirements that failed to disclose potentially fatal side effects. As before, the FDA agreed with the manufacturer, but this time the FDA also maintained that the manufacturer had an obligation, under the FDCA as amended in 1984, to request from the FDA authority to change the drug labeling once it knew about the deadly side effects. Citing *Auer* (a precedent he has recently considered unconstitutional), Justice Thomas deferred to the FDA's interpretation of its own regulations and found impossibility preemption.

Since 2011, the Supreme Court has not directly addressed this issue. In *Coventry Health Care of Missouri, Inc. v. Nevils,* 137 S.Ct. 1190 (2017), the issue was briefed but the Court found preemption without addressing the deference issue.

PROBLEM REVISITING THE COURT'S DECISION IN GEIER

Problem 9-3. Another Issue of Preemption and Auto Safety. Some lower courts interpreted *Geier* to allow preemption of state tort law when claims arose out of choices auto manufacturers were allowed to make under Standard 208. One case arose out of an accident where Thanh Williamson, a passenger in the middle back row of a Mazda van, died. Williamson's estate claimed that she would have survived if she had been wearing a seatbelt that covered both her lap and shoulder—but Standard 208 allowed auto manufacturers to use just lap belts for the inner seat belts for the back seats of automobiles, a less expensive choice that manufacturers overwhelmingly used in their recent models.

The Williamson case reaches the Supreme Court, which decides whether Standard 208 preempts the state tort lawsuit. Unless it overrules *Geier,* the Court would rule that the express preemption clause of the statute would apply to the lawsuit—but that the savings clause takes "common law" tort lawsuits out of the preemption clause. Hence, the key issue would be whether ordinary principles of conflict/obstacle preemption would suggest negation of state law in this case. Unlike the government's position in *Geier*, the Solicitor General tells the Court that the agency left manufacturers this limited choice of regular seatbelts and lap-and-shoulder seatbelts primarily for cost-benefit reasons, but expected the costs and the benefits to evolve over time. Hence, the agency did not believe that state common law actions such as Williamson's stood as an obstacle to the agency's achievement of its statutory mission. How should the Court decide Williamson's case? Should the Court overrule *Geier*? If the Court declines to revisit *Geier,* is the different posture of the agency sufficient to decide the case differently? See *Williamson v. Mazda Motor of America, Inc.*, 131 S.Ct. 1131 (2011).

E. DEFERENCE AND *STARE DECISIS*

National Cable & Telecommunications Association v. Brand X Internet Services

545 U.S. 967 (2005).

Title II of the Communications Act of 1934, 48 Stat. 1064, as amended, 47 U.S.C. § 151 *et seq.,* subjects all providers of "telecommunications servic[e]" to mandatory common-carrier regulation. An FCC order concluded that cable companies selling broadband Internet service do not provide "telecommunications servic[e]" as the 1934 Act defined the term, and hence were exempt from mandatory common-carrier regulation under Title II.

The traditional means by which consumers in the United States access the network of interconnected computers that make up the Internet had been through "dial-up" connections provided over local telephone facilities. These "narrow-band" connections were relatively slow by modern standards and have been superseded by "broadband" Internet service, which transmits data at much higher speeds. There are two principal kinds of broadband Internet service: cable modem service and Digital Subscriber Line (DSL) service. Cable modem service transmits data between the Internet and users' computers via the network of television cable lines owned by cable companies. DSL service provides high-speed access using the local telephone wires owned by local telephone companies. Cable companies and telephone companies can either provide Internet access directly to consumers, thus acting as [Information Service Providers, or ISPs] themselves, or can lease their transmission facilities to independent ISPs that then use the facilities to provide consumers with Internet access.

As amended in 1996, the Communications Act of 1934 distinguishes between telecommunications carriers and information-service providers. The Act regulates telecommunications carriers as common carriers that must charge just and reasonable, nondiscriminatory rates to their customers, 47 U.S.C. §§ 201–209, and must design their systems so that other carriers can interconnect with their communications networks, § 251(a)(1). These provisions are mandatory, but the FCC must forbear from applying them if it determines that the public interest requires it. § 160(a), (b). Information-service providers are not subject to mandatory common-carrier regulation under Title II, though the FCC has jurisdiction to impose regulatory obligations under its Title I ancillary jurisdiction to regulate interstate and foreign communications, see §§ 151–161.

These two statutory classifications originated in the late 1970s, in FCC rules that were essentially adopted by Congress in the 1996 Amendments. "Telecommunications service" is "the offering of telecommunications for a fee directly to the public . . . regardless of the facilities used." 47 U.S.C. § 153(46). "Telecommunications" is "the transmission, between or among points specified by the user, of information of the user's choosing, without change in the form or content of the information as sent and received." § 153(43). "Telecommunications carrier[s]"—those subjected to mandatory Title II common-carrier regulation—are defined as "provider[s] of telecommunications services." § 153(44). And "information service" is "the offering of a capability for generating, acquiring, storing, transforming, processing, retrieving, utilizing, or making available information via telecommunications." § 153(20).

In 2002, after notice-and-comment rulemaking, the FCC concluded that broadband Internet service provided by cable companies was an "information service" but not a "telecommunications service" under the Act, and therefore not subject to mandatory Title II common-carrier regulation. On appeal, the Ninth Circuit vacated the ruling and held that the FCC could not construe the Communications Act to exempt cable companies providing Internet service from Title II regulation. The Court of Appeals grounded its holding in the *stare decisis* effect of *AT&T Corp. v. Portland,* 216 F.3d 871 (9th Cir. 2000), where a panel of the Ninth Circuit held that cable modem service was a "telecommunications service." In an opinion by **Justice Thomas**, the Supreme Court reversed the Ninth Circuit and upheld the FCC's order.

Justice Thomas rebuked the lower court for applying its precedent rather than *Chevron*-deferring to the FCC: "A court's prior judicial construction of a statute trumps an agency construction otherwise entitled to *Chevron* deference only if the prior court decision holds that its construction follows from the unambiguous terms of the statute and thus leaves no room for agency discretion. This principle follows from *Chevron* itself. *Chevron* established a 'presumption that Congress, when it left ambiguity in a statute meant for implementation by an agency, understood that the ambiguity would be resolved, first and foremost, by the agency, and desired the agency (rather than the courts) to possess whatever degree of discretion the ambiguity allows.' Yet allowing a judicial precedent to foreclose an agency from interpreting an ambiguous statute, as the Court of Appeals assumed it could, would allow a court's interpretation to override an agency's. *Chevron's* premise is that it is for agencies, not courts, to fill statutory gaps. The better rule is to hold judicial interpretations contained in precedents to the same demanding *Chevron* step one standard that applies if the court is reviewing the agency's construction on a blank slate: Only a judicial precedent holding that the statute unambiguously forecloses the agency's interpretation, and therefore contains no gap for the agency to fill, displaces a conflicting agency construction.

"A contrary rule * * * would mean that whether an agency's interpretation of an ambiguous statute is entitled to *Chevron* deference would turn on the order in which the interpretations issue: If the court's construction came first, its construction would prevail, whereas if the agency's came first, the agency's construction would command *Chevron* deference. Yet whether Congress has delegated to an agency the authority to interpret a statute does not depend on the order in which the judicial and administrative constructions occur. The Court of Appeals' rule, moreover, would 'lead to the ossification of large portions of our statutory law,' *Mead* (Scalia, J., dissenting), by precluding agencies from revising unwise judicial constructions of ambiguous statutes. Neither *Chevron* nor the doctrine of *stare decisis* requires these haphazard results."

Was the statute unambiguous? Is a cable modem service a "telecommunications service"? Recall that "telecommunications" is defined as "the transmission, between or among points specified by the user, of information of the user's choosing, without change in the form or content of the information as sent and received." § 153(43). The FCC conceded that, like all information-service providers, cable companies use "telecommunications" to provide consumers with Internet service; cable companies provide such service via the high-speed wire that transmits signals to and from an end user's computer. For the Commission, however, the question whether cable broadband Internet providers "offer" telecommunications involved more than whether telecommunications was one necessary component of cable modem service. Instead, whether that service also includes a telecommunications offering "turn[ed] on the nature of the functions the *end user* is offered," for the statutory definition of "telecommunications service" does not "res[t] on the particular types of facilities used." See § 153(46) (definition of "telecommunications service" applies "regardless of the facilities used").

Understood from the consumer's point of view, the Commission concluded, cable modem service is not a telecommunications offering, because the consumer uses the high-speed wire always in connection with the information-processing capabilities provided by Internet access, and because the transmission is a necessary component of Internet access: "As provided to the end user the telecommunications is part and parcel of cable modem service and is integral to its other capabilities." The wire is used, in other words, to access the World Wide Web, newsgroups, and so forth, rather than "transparently" to transmit and receive ordinary-language messages without computer processing or storage of the message. The integrated character of this offering led the Commission to conclude that cable modem service is not a "stand-alone," transparent offering of telecommunications.

Justice Thomas ruled that the FCC's reading was a plausible understanding of the statutory text. "Cable companies in the broadband Internet service business 'offe[r]' consumers an information service in the form of Internet access and they do so 'via telecommunications,' § 153(20), but it does not inexorably follow as a matter of ordinary language that they also 'offe[r]' consumers the high-speed data transmission (telecommunications) that is an input used to provide this service, § 153(46). * * * It is common usage to describe what a company 'offers' to a consumer as what the consumer perceives to be the integrated finished product, even to the exclusion of discrete components that compose the product, as the dissent concedes. One might well say that a car dealership 'offers' cars, but does not 'offer' the integrated major inputs that make purchasing the car valuable, such as the engine or the chassis. It would, in fact, be odd to describe a car dealership as 'offering' consumers the car's components in addition to the car itself. Even if it is linguistically permissible to say that the car dealership 'offers' engines when it offers cars, that shows, at most, that the term 'offer,' when applied to a commercial transaction, is ambiguous about whether it describes only the offered finished product, or the product's discrete components as well. It does not show that no other usage is permitted. * * *

"The question, then, is whether the transmission component of cable modem service is sufficiently integrated with the finished service to make it reasonable to describe the two as a single, integrated offering. We think that they are sufficiently integrated, because '[a] consumer uses the high-speed wire always in connection with the information-processing capabilities provided by Internet access, and because the transmission is a necessary component of Internet access.' In the telecommunications context, it is at least reasonable to describe companies as not 'offering' to consumers each discrete input that is necessary to providing, and is always used in connection with, a finished service."

Justice Thomas also ruled that the FCC's interpretation was "reasonable," the *Chevron* Step Two inquiry. The challengers argued that the FCC's rule was unreasonable because it allowed communications providers to "evade" mandatory Title II (common-carrier) regulation by bundling information services with telecommunications. The Court was not persuaded that companies could easily escape regulation in this way, however. For example, a local telephone company could not escape Title II by bundling its service with voice mail, because the information transmission is not integrated with the voice mail, and hence subject to FCC regulation under the 2002 rule. "Equally, were a telephone company to add a time-of-day announcement that played every time the user picked up his telephone, the 'transparent' information transmitted in the ensuing call would be only trivially dependent on the information service the announcement provides. By contrast, the high-speed transmission used to provide cable modem service is a functionally integrated component of that service because it transmits data only in connection with the further processing of information and is necessary to provide Internet service. The Commission's construction therefore was more limited than respondents assume."

Finally, Justice Thomas ruled that the FCC's rule was not "arbitrary and capricious" in violation of APA § 706(2)(A). MCI claimed that the FCC's treatment of cable modem service was inconsistent with its treatment of DSL service and therefore was an arbitrary and capricious deviation from agency policy. When local telephone companies began to offer Internet access through DSL technology in addition to telephone service, the FCC invoked Title II to require them to make the telephone lines used to transmit DSL service available to competing ISPs on nondiscriminatory, common-carrier terms. The Court rejected that claim, on the ground that the agency had a reasonable explanation for the different treatment. The FCC's treatment of DSL providers was dictated by its earlier ruling that applied Title II to regulate any Internet providers where a telephone network was the primary or exclusive means through which information service providers can gain access to their customers.

The 2002 rule, in contrast, addressed new market conditions, with a range of competitive substitutes. The Commission concluded that "broadband services should exist in a minimal regulatory environment that promotes investment and innovation in a competitive market." This, the Commission reasoned, warranted treating cable companies unlike the facilities-based enhanced-service providers of the past. "We find nothing arbitrary about the Commission's providing a fresh analysis of the problem as applied to the cable industry, which it has never subjected to these rules," concluded Justice Thomas. "The questions the Commission resolved in the order under review involve a 'subject matter [that] is technical, complex, and dynamic.' The Commission is in a far better position to address these questions than we are. Nothing in the Communications Act or the Administrative Procedure Act makes unlawful the Commission's use of its expert policy judgment to resolve these difficult questions."

Dissenting **Justice Scalia** (joined by Justices Souter and Ginsburg) objected that the FCC was doing the same thing in this case that the Court rejected in *MCI,* namely, substantially deregulating an industry without proper statutory authority. He maintained that the statute was clear: DSL providers "offer * * * telecommunications for a fee directly to the public," and hence the FCC must regulate such companies under Title II. "The Court concludes that the word 'offer' is ambiguous in the sense that it has 'alternative dictionary definitions' that might be relevant. It seems to me, however, that the analytic problem pertains not really to the meaning of 'offer,' but to the identity of what is offered. The relevant question is whether the individual components in a package being offered still possess sufficient identity to be described as separate objects of the offer, or whether they have been so changed by their combination with the other components that it is no longer reasonable to describe them in that way.

"Thus, I agree (to adapt the Court's example) that it would be odd to say that a car dealer is in the business of selling steel or carpets because the cars he sells include both steel frames and carpeting. Nor does the water company sell hydrogen, nor the pet store water (though dogs and cats are largely water at the molecular level). But what is sometimes true is not, as the Court seems to assume, *always* true. There are instances in which it is ridiculous to deny that one part of a joint offering is being offered merely because it is not offered on a 'stand-alone' basis.

"If, for example, I call up a pizzeria and ask whether they offer delivery, both common sense and common 'usage,' would prevent them from answering: 'No, we do not offer delivery—but if you order a pizza from us, we'll bake it for you and then bring it to your house.' The logical response to this would be something on the order of, 'so, you *do* offer delivery.' But our pizza-man may continue to deny the obvious and explain, paraphrasing the FCC and the Court: 'No, even though we bring the pizza to your house, we are not actually 'offering' you delivery, because the delivery that we provide to our end users is 'part and parcel' of our pizzeria-pizza-at-home service and is 'integral to its other capabilities.' Any reasonable customer would conclude at that point that his interlocutor was either crazy or following some too-clever-by-half legal advice."

From the consumer's point of view, Justice Scalia argued, the question is what other products a cable-modem service substitutes for in the marketplace. For dial-up and DSL access, the two competing products, the physical transmission pathway to the Internet is sold separately from the Internet functionality. (The pathway is a regulated telecommunications service but the enhanced Internet functionality is not.) The typical consumer will view cable-modem service in the same way, as offering both computing functionality (the pizza) *and* the physical pathway (pizza delivery).

Finally, Justice Scalia observed that the FCC might, in the future, require cable companies to offer other ISPs access to their facilities on common-carrier terms, based upon the FCC's Title I discretionary authority. "In other words, what the Commission hath given, the Commission may well take away—unless it doesn't. This is a wonderful illustration of how an experienced agency can (with some assistance from credulous courts) turn statutory constraints into bureaucratic discretions. The main source of the Commission's regulatory authority over common carriers is Title II, but the Commission has rendered that inapplicable in this instance by concluding that the definition of 'telecommunications service' is ambiguous and does not (in its current view) apply to cable-modem service. It contemplates, however, altering that (unnecessary) outcome, not by changing the law (*i.e.,* its construction of the Title II definitions), but by reserving the right to change the facts. Under its undefined and sparingly used 'ancillary' powers, the Commission might conclude that it can order cable companies to 'unbundle' the telecommunications component of cable-modem service. And presto, Title II will then apply to them, because they will finally be 'offering' telecommunications service! Of course, the Commission will still have the statutory power to forbear from regulating them under § 160 (which it has already tentatively concluded it would do). Such Möbius-strip reasoning mocks the principle that the statute constrains the agency in any meaningful way."

In a portion of his dissent not joined by Justices Souter and Ginsburg, Justice Scalia continued his *Kulturkampf* against *Mead*. As he characterized it, *Brand X* was the Court's response to his own objection in *Mead* that agency law would be "ossified" by incessant judicial review; under *Brand X,* that would not be a problem, because agencies would not be bound by precedents giving them discretion under *Chevron-Mead*. Indeed, according to Justice Scalia, *Brand X* violated Article III by allowing agencies to disregard judicial precedent.

Justice Thomas responded: "Since *Chevron* teaches that a court's opinion as to the best reading of an ambiguous statute an agency is charged with administering is not authoritative, the agency's decision to construe that statute differently from a court does not say that the court's holding was legally wrong. Instead, the agency may, consistent with the court's holding, choose a different construction, since the agency remains the authoritative interpreter (within the limits of reason) of such statutes. In all other respects, the court's prior ruling remains binding law (for example, as to agency interpretations to which *Chevron* is inapplicable). The precedent has not been 'reversed' by the agency, any more than a federal court's interpretation of a State's law can be said to have been 'reversed' by a state court that adopts a conflicting (yet authoritative) interpretation of state law."

NOTES ON BRAND X

1. *What Does It Mean to "Defer" to an Agency Interpretation? Chevron* suggests a spatial metaphor: the Court sets the goalposts, the statutory parameters within which the agency sets policy, subject to a "reasonableness" requirement:

Court	Agency	Court

Skidmore suggests a gravity metaphor: in figuring out how to interpret statutory language, judges weigh the views and policy reasons advanced by the agency having greater experience with the statutory area. Peter Strauss, *"Deference" Is too Confusing— Let's Call Them "Chevron Space" and "Skidmore Weight,"* 112 Colum. L. Rev. 1143 (2012).

Brand X is a case where the majority Justices not only "defer" to the FCC's decision within the policy "space" not occupied by a congressional judgment, but also seem to "defer" to the FCC's views about how to define the parameters of the statute (i.e., what is a "telecommunications service"). Even in *Chevron* cases, shouldn't judges give *Skidmore* deference to an agency's views about whether Congress has answered the interpretive question in the statute itself?

Skidmore	*Chevron*	*Skidmore*
Court, with Agency Inputs	**Agency, with Court Check**	**Court, with Agency Inputs**

Ever a critic of *Mead*, Justice Scalia would have none of this in his *Brand X* dissent. Even as he insisted that agencies ought to have great discretion within the parameters set by Congress, Justice Scalia jealously guarded the Court's primacy in determining precisely what those parameters are. In *Brand X*, he accused the FCC of pulling a "fast one" on the gullible ("credulous") majority.

2. *The Relationship Between* Chevron *Step Two and* State Farm *Arbitrariness Review.* Justice Thomas's opinion sets forth the different analytical hurdles the FCC must surmount:

> *Chevron* Step One: Did Congress decide this issue? No. Hence, the agency's interpretation fell with the agency's reasoned discretion.

> *Chevron* Step Two: Was the agency's interpretation "reasonable"? Yes. Hence, the agency's interpretation passed *Chevron*.

> *State Farm*: Was the agency's rule arbitrary or capricious? No. Hence, the rule passed APA § 706(2)(A) review as well.

So one larger doctrinal question is this: What is the difference between *Chevron* Step Two and APA § 706(2)(A), as applied in *State Farm*? On the one hand, both standards assume a range of agency choices and discretion as to which choice the agency must make. Also, both standards ask whether the agency's decision is supported by reasons that are cognizant of and attentive to the congressional purpose(s). On the other hand, the *State Farm* inquiry is more fact-based and procedural. It is procedural in the sense that the agency needs to respond to material questions and problems raised by commenters; it is factual in the sense that the agency's responses need a plausible basis in fact.

3. *The Role of* Stare Decisis *and Deference.* Another bone of contention between the majority and the dissent is what role judicial precedent ought to play in the *Chevron* inquiry. As a precedent, *Chevron* itself allows the agency to shift environmental policy within the parameters set by the statute. But the Ninth Circuit thought its decision fixed a statutory parameter that the agency traversed. What did the majority believe was wrong with that? After *Brand X*, under what circumstances is an agency bound by a much earlier (pre-*Chevron*) Supreme Court decision interpreting a statute?

In *United States v. Home Concrete & Supply, LLC*, 566 U.S. 478 (2012), the Supreme Court had to figure out whether a 1958 precedent of the Court precluded judges from *Chevron*-deferring to a recent IRS regulation to the contrary. Although the 1958 decision had conceded that the relevant statutory language was "not unambiguous," the Court found that the Justices in the earlier case "thought that Congress had 'directly spoken to the question at hand,' and thus left '[no] gap for the agency to fill.' *Chevron*." The statutory precedent rested upon a preference for the taxpayer's reading of the statutory language, strongly confirmed by legislative history and the statutory scheme. Four Justices dissented, on the ground that somewhat revised statutory language gave the IRS enough *Chevron* space to reach a different result. Both Scalia and Thomas were with the majority, the former still complaining about *Brand X* and *Mead*.

NOTE ON ADMINISTRATIVE OVERRIDES OF SUPREME COURT STATUTORY INTERPRETATION DECISIONS

In this casebook, you have seen a number of examples of congressional overrides of Supreme Court statutory interpretation decisions, such as *Flood v. Kuhn* (Chapter 5, § 2), and *TVA v. Hill* (Chapter 5, § 3(A)). Since 1998, congressional overrides have fallen off substantially, but that has brought to light the policy punch line of *Brand X*—namely, the possibility of *administrative overrides* of Supreme Court statutory interpretation decisions. Matthew Christiansen & William Eskridge Jr., *Congressional Overrides of Supreme Court Statutory Interpretation Decisions, 1967–2011*, 92 Tex. L. Rev. 1317 (2014). *Brand X* can be understood to vest the executive branch with formal override authority for a limited subset of cases. This is most commonly understood in the context *Brand X* presented, namely, where a court upholds one interpretation as reasonable under *Chevron* Step Two. Subsequently, the agency (often after a change in presidential administration) decides to change its interpretation. *Brand X* thus gives administrators the authority to make such changes when the rule is made pursuant to an ambiguous statute. Because many cases are resolved at *Chevron* Step Two, *Brand X* has the potential to counteract statutory ossification in a number of important areas—especially the FCC's regulation of the Internet, which has evolved rapidly in the new millennium.

Administrative "overrides" or "workarounds" (a gentler term) might be even broader than suggested by *Brand X*, however. Note that the main difference between *Wyeth* and *Pliva* was the FDA's stronger stance: by requiring drug companies to secure federal approval for their labels, the agency was giving them a free pass for state tort liability. The federal government's shift between *Geier* (preemption of airbag claim) and *Williamson* (seatbelt preemption of seatbelt claim) also drove different results in those two cases: in the first, there was obstacle preemption because the agency represented the manufacturer's choice as essential to a cost-benefit regulatory policy, while in the second case the agency represented manufacturer's choice as an experiment allowing manufacturers to find out what would be the best balance between safety and cost.

F. DEFERENCE IN NATIONAL SECURITY AND FOREIGN AFFAIRS

In *United States v. Curtiss-Wright Export Co.*, 299 U.S. 304 (1936), the Court said that "congressional legislation * * * within the international field must often accord to the President a degree of discretion and freedom from statutory restriction which would not be admissible were domestic affairs alone involved." The source of this discretion in statutory enforcement was Article II, namely, the inherent powers of the President to represent the nation in foreign matters and to protect America's security interests.

Curtiss-Wright deference is theoretically distinguishable from *Chevron* deference. Because it rests upon the President's Article II powers, rather than nothing more than Congress's Article I authority, *Curtiss-Wright* deference does not necessarily depend upon a statutory delegation of lawmaking responsibilities, although the power of its presumption might be augmented by such delegation. Moreover, the *Curtiss-Wright* rule is a more deferential standard than *Chevron*: the executive department interpretation prevails not only in cases of statutory ambiguity, but also in cases where Congress has not clearly trumped the agency or presidential construction.

For example, the Court in *Department of Navy v. Egan*, 484 U.S. 518 (1988), ruled against judicial review of presidential revocation of security clearances. Given the President's broad powers to protect national security and conduct foreign policy, the Court reasoned that, "unless Congress specifically has provided otherwise, courts traditionally [should be] * * * reluctant to intrude upon the authority of the Executive in military and national security affairs." *Egan* is a strong post-*Chevron* statement of *Curtiss-Wright* deference, but is a rare instance where the Court actually discusses such deference. See Eskridge & Baer, *Deference Continuum*, 96 Geo. L.J. at 1100–02 (reporting that the Court invoked *Curtiss-Wright* deference in fewer than 10% of its foreign affairs and national security docket).

On the other hand, the executive branch does sometimes lose cases involving interpretation of military, foreign affairs, and immigration cases. For example, the Supreme Court in *Hamdan v. Rumsfeld,* 548 U.S. 557 (2006) ruled that presidential military commissions dispensing summary justice could not legally try Salim Ahmed Hamdan, a Yemeni national apprehended by American allies in Afghanistan. Writing for the Court, Justice Stevens refused to defer to the President's executive order creating military commissions, because it clashed with the Uniform Code of Military Justice and the Geneva Conventions. Stevens emphasized Congress's primacy in regulating the armed forces and the procedures for military justice.

Following a *Curtiss-Wright* approach strongly deferential to presidential authority, Justice Thomas and two other dissenters argued that application of that framework in military matters required *expansive* interpretation of congressional authorizations to meet the unpredictable demands of war. See also *Dames & Moore v. Regan*, 453 U.S. 654, 678 (1981).

TRUMP V. HAWAII

Supreme Court of the United States, 2018.
___ U.S. ___, 138 S.Ct 2392, 201 L.Ed.2d 775.

CHIEF JUSTICE ROBERTS delivered the opinion of the Court.

[In September 2017, the President issued Proclamation No. 9645, seeking to improve vetting procedures for foreign nationals traveling to the United States by identifying ongoing deficiencies in the information needed to assess whether nationals of particular countries present a security threat. The Proclamation placed entry restrictions on the nationals of eight foreign states whose systems for managing and sharing information about their nationals the President deemed inadequate. Foreign states were selected for inclusion based on a review undertaken pursuant to one of the President's earlier Executive Orders. As part of that review, the Department of Homeland Security (DHS), in consultation with the State

Department and intelligence agencies, developed an information and risk assessment "baseline." DHS then identified countries having deficient information-sharing practices and presenting national security concerns. After a 50-day period during which the State Department made diplomatic efforts to encourage foreign governments to improve their practices, the Acting Secretary of Homeland Security concluded that eight countries—Chad, Iran, Iraq, Libya, North Korea, Syria, Venezuela, and Yemen—remained deficient. She recommended entry restrictions for certain nationals from all of those countries but Iraq, which had a close cooperative relationship with the U.S. She also recommended including Somalia.

[After consulting with multiple Cabinet members, the President adopted the recommendations and issued the Proclamation. Invoking his authority under 8 U.S.C. §§ 1182(f) and 1185(a), he determined that certain restrictions were necessary to "prevent the entry of those foreign nationals about whom the United States Government lacks sufficient information" and "elicit improved identity-management and information-sharing protocols and practices from foreign governments." The Proclamation imposed a range of entry restrictions that varied based on the "distinct circumstances" in each of the eight countries. It exempted lawful permanent residents and provides case-by-case waivers under certain circumstances. It also directed DHS to assess on a continuing basis whether the restrictions should be modified or continued, and to report to the President every 180 days. At the completion of the first such review period, the President determined that Chad had sufficiently improved its practices and so lifted restrictions on its nationals.]

Plaintiffs—the State of Hawaii, three individuals with foreign relatives affected by the entry suspension, and the Muslim Association of Hawaii—argue that the Proclamation violates the Immigration and Nationality Act (INA) and the Establishment Clause. The District Court granted a nationwide preliminary injunction barring enforcement of the restrictions. The Ninth Circuit affirmed, concluding that the Proclamation contravened two provisions of the INA: § 1182(f), which authorizes the President to "suspend the entry of all aliens or any class of aliens" whenever he "finds" that their entry "would be detrimental to the interests of the United States," and § 1152(a)(1)(A), which provides that "no person shall . . . be discriminated against in the issuance of an immigrant visa because of the person's race, sex, nationality, place of birth, or place of residence."

The text of § 1182(f) states:

"Whenever the President finds that the entry of any aliens or of any class of aliens into the United States would be detrimental to the interests of the United States, he may by proclamation, and for such period as he shall deem necessary, suspend the entry of all aliens or any class of aliens as immigrants or nonimmigrants, or impose on the entry of aliens any restrictions he may deem to be appropriate."

By its terms, § 1182(f) exudes deference to the President in every clause. It entrusts to the President the decisions whether and when to suspend entry ("[w]henever [he] finds that the entry" of aliens "would be detrimental" to the national interest); whose entry to suspend ("all aliens or any class of aliens"); for how long ("for such period as he shall deem necessary"); and on what conditions ("any restrictions he may deem to be appropriate"). It is therefore unsurprising that we have previously observed that § 1182(f) vests the President with "ample power" to impose entry restrictions in addition to those elsewhere enumerated in the INA. [*Sale v. Haitian Centers Council, Inc.,* 509 U.S. 155, 187 (1993)] (finding it "perfectly clear" that the President could "establish a naval blockade" to prevent illegal migrants from entering the United States).

The Proclamation falls well within this comprehensive delegation. The sole prerequisite set forth in § 1182(f) is that the President "find[ ]" that the entry of the covered aliens "would be detrimental to the interests of the United States." The President has undoubtedly fulfilled that requirement here. He first ordered DHS and other agencies to conduct a comprehensive evaluation of every single country's compliance with the information and risk assessment baseline. The President then issued a Proclamation setting forth extensive findings describing how deficiencies in the practices of select foreign governments—several of which are state sponsors of terrorism—deprive the Government of "sufficient information to assess the risks [those countries' nationals] pose to the United States." Based on that review, the President found that it was in the national interest to restrict entry of aliens who could not be vetted with adequate information—both to protect national security and public safety, and to induce improvement by their home countries. The Proclamation therefore "craft[ed] . . . country-specific restrictions that would be most likely to encourage cooperation given each country's distinct circumstances," while securing the Nation "until such time as improvements occur."

Plaintiffs believe that these findings are insufficient. They argue, as an initial matter, that the Proclamation fails to provide a persuasive rationale for why nationality alone renders the covered foreign nationals a security risk. And they further discount the President's stated concern about deficient vetting because the Proclamation allows many aliens from the designated countries to enter on nonimmigrant visas.

Such arguments are grounded on the premise that § 1182(f) not only requires the President to *make* a finding that entry "would be detrimental to the interests of the United States," but also to explain that finding with sufficient detail to enable judicial review. That premise is questionable. See *Webster v. Doe,* 486 U.S. 592, 600 (1988) (concluding that a statute authorizing the CIA Director to terminate an employee when the Director "shall deem such termination necessary or advisable in the interests of the United States" forecloses "any meaningful judicial standard of review"). But even assuming that some form of review is appropriate, plaintiffs' attacks on the sufficiency of the President's findings cannot be sustained. The 12-page Proclamation—which thoroughly describes the process, agency evaluations, and recommendations underlying the President's chosen restrictions—is more detailed than any prior order a President has issued under § 1182(f).

Moreover, plaintiffs' request for a searching inquiry into the persuasiveness of the President's justifications is inconsistent with the broad statutory text and the deference traditionally accorded the President in this sphere. "Whether the President's chosen method" of addressing perceived risks is justified from a policy perspective is "irrelevant to the scope of his [§ 1182(f)] authority." *Sale,* 509 U.S., at

187–188. And when the President adopts "a preventive measure . . . in the context of international affairs and national security," he is "not required to conclusively link all of the pieces in the puzzle before [courts] grant weight to [his] empirical conclusions." *Holder v. Humanitarian Law Project,* 561 U.S. 1, 35 (2010). * * *

For more than a century, this Court has recognized that the admission and exclusion of foreign nationals is a "fundamental sovereign attribute exercised by the Government's political departments largely immune from judicial control." *Fiallo v. Bell,* 430 U.S. 787, 792 (1977). Because decisions in these matters may implicate "relations with foreign powers," or involve "classifications defined in the light of changing political and economic circumstances," such judgments "are frequently of a character more appropriate to either the Legislature or the Executive." *Mathews v. Diaz,* 426 U.S. 67, 81 (1976).

Nonetheless, although foreign nationals seeking admission have no constitutional right to entry, this Court has engaged in a circumscribed judicial inquiry when the denial of a visa allegedly burdens the constitutional rights of a U.S. citizen. In *Kleindienst v. Mandel,* the Attorney General denied admission to a Belgian journalist and self-described "revolutionary Marxist," Ernest Mandel, who had been invited to speak at a conference at Stanford University. The professors who wished to hear Mandel speak challenged that decision under the First Amendment, and we acknowledged that their constitutional "right to receive information" was implicated. But we limited our review to whether the Executive gave a "facially legitimate and bona fide" reason for its action. Given the authority of the political branches over admission, we held that "when the Executive exercises this [delegated] power negatively on the basis of a facially legitimate and bona fide reason, the courts will neither look behind the exercise of that discretion, nor test it by balancing its justification" against the asserted constitutional interests of U.S. citizens.

The upshot of our cases in this context is clear: "Any rule of constitutional law that would inhibit the flexibility" of the President "to respond to changing world conditions should be adopted only with the greatest caution," and our inquiry into matters of entry and national security is highly constrained. *Mathews.* We need not define the precise contours of that inquiry in this case. A conventional application of *Mandel,* asking only whether the policy is facially legitimate and bona fide, would put an end to our review. But the Government has suggested that it may be appropriate here for the inquiry to extend beyond the facial neutrality of the order. For our purposes today, we assume that we may look behind the face of the Proclamation to the extent of applying rational basis review. That standard of review considers whether the entry policy is plausibly related to the Government's stated objective to protect the country and improve vetting processes. As a result, we may consider plaintiffs' extrinsic evidence, but will uphold the policy so long as it can reasonably be understood to result from a justification independent of unconstitutional grounds. * * *

The Proclamation is expressly premised on legitimate purposes: preventing entry of nationals who cannot be adequately vetted and inducing other nations to improve their practices. The text says nothing about religion. Plaintiffs and the dissent nonetheless emphasize that five of the seven nations currently included in the Proclamation have Muslim-majority populations. Yet that fact alone does not support an inference of religious hostility, given that the policy covers just 8% of the world's Muslim population and is limited to countries that were previously designated by Congress or prior administrations as posing national security risks. See 8 U.S.C. § 1187(a)(12)(A) (identifying Syria and state sponsors of terrorism such as Iran as "countr[ies] or area[s] of concern" for purposes of administering the Visa Waiver Program); Dept. of Homeland Security, DHS Announces Further Travel Restrictions for the Visa Waiver Program (Feb. 18, 2016) (designating Libya, Somalia, and Yemen as additional countries of concern). * * *

[We omit the concurring opinions of JUSTICE KENNEDY and JUSTICE THOMAS, as well as the dissenting opinions of JUSTICE BREYER (joined by JUSTICE KAGAN) and JUSTICE SOTOMAYOR (joined by JUSTICE GINSBURG).]

Queries: Although the Court did not cite *Curtiss-Wright,* the majority opinion did rely on *Webster,* which is a *Curtisss-Wright* super-deference precedent. How did the President's inherent Article II powers help him in this case? None of the Justices dissented from the Chief Justice's statutory analysis, though Justices Breyer and Kagan would have remanded for a trial court hearing to determine whether the Trump Administration was actually applying a context-specific approach, which they believed was consistent with the statutory scheme. Two of the Justices (Sotomayor and Ginsburg) explicitly dissented from the constitutional analysis; the President's many statements in 2015–17 indicated that the Proclamation was advertised to the public as a Muslim Travel Ban. How did "deference" help the President on the statutory and constitutional issues? Was the deference boost justified? At least two, and probably four, Justices believed it was not justified here.

3.   QUO VADIS THE *"CHEVRON* REVOLUTION"?

Commentators and judges agree there has been a "*Chevron* Revolution" of some sort. Most judges and commentators believe that the *Chevron* framework has transformed federal judicial treatment of agency interpretations among circuit courts. Kent Barnett & Christopher Walker, Chevron *in the Circuits,* 116 Mich. L. Rev. 1 (2017); Orin Kerr, *Shedding Light on* Chevron: *An Empirical Study of the* Chevron *Doctrine in the U.S. Courts of Appeals*, 15 Yale J. on Reg. 1 (1998). Some agencies have internalized the new *Chevron* regime as freeing them up to make more decisions on policy or political lines rather than legal ones. E.g., E. Donald Elliot, Chevron *Matters: How the Chevron Doctrine Redefined the Roles of Congress, Courts, and Agencies in Environmental Law*, 16 Vill. Envtl. L.J. 1, 11–12 (2005). Ironically, the effect of *Chevron* is most equivocal at the Supreme Court itself. The Court was highly deferential to agency rules and interpretations before *Chevron* and has continued to be highly deferential after *Chevron.*

As we have seen earlier, *Chevron* is not the main deference precedent at the Supreme Court. Notwithstanding its dismissal by Justice Scalia, *Skidmore* flourished at the high court during this period, as well as the federal district and circuit courts. Kristin Hickman & Mathew Krueger, *In Search of the Modern* Skidmore *Standard*, 107 Colum. L. Rev. 1235 (2007). Overall, the Supreme Court has announced a more elaborate set of deference doctrines—creating a *deference continuum* than goes beyond the simple *Chevron-Skidmore* dichotomy. Table 9-3 summarizes the deference regimes found by Eskridge and Baer in the 1014 Supreme Court they examined where there was an agency interpretation.

Table 9-3. Supreme Court Deference Regimes, 1984–2006

Deference Regime (% Cases)	Deference Accorded	Legal Basis for Deference	Subject Areas
Curtiss-Wright (0.9%)	Super-strong deference in national security cases	Article II + Congressional Delegation	Foreign Affairs; National Security; Military; Immigration
Seminole Rock/Auer (1.1%)	Strong deference for agency interpretations of own regulations	Congressional Delegation + Agency Expertise	Entitlements; Labor; Telecommunications
Chevron (8.3%)	Defer to reasonable interpretations unless Congress has directly addressed the issue	Congressional Delegation	Energy; Environmental; Entitlements; Immigration; Labor; Securities; Transportation
Diaz/Beth Israel (4.8%)	Defer to reasonable interpretations if consistent with statute	Congressional Purposes	Health; Immigration; Labor; Taxation
Skidmore (6.7%)	Consider agency views for persuasive value (e.g., policy expertise, statutory scheme, reliance interests)	Agency Expertise and Experience	Civil Rights; Education; Energy; Environmental; Transportation
Skidmore-Lite (17.8%)	Consider agency-generated factual materials + background rules	Agency Expertise and Experience	Antitrust; Bankruptcy; Civil Rights; Energy; Intellectual Property; Indian Law; Pensions
No Deference (53.6%)	Court follows ordinary, ad hoc judicial reasoning	No Basis for Deference	All areas of Supreme Court practice are dominated by this category
Anti-Deference (6.8%)	Presumption *against* agency interpretation	Constitutional Values	Criminal Law; Cases raising constitutional issues

Source: William Eskridge Jr. & Lauren Baer, *The Continuum of Deference: Supreme Court Treatment of Agency Statutory Interpretations from* Chevron *to* Hamdan, 96 Geo. L.J. 1083, 1100 (2008) (Table 1).

Eskridge and Baer also report that when the Court applies the *Chevron* framework the agency wins 76.2% of the time, a very high agreement rate. But the agency win rate is also very high when the Court invokes other deference regimes: 73.5% when the Court invokes *Skidmore*; 73.5% when it invokes *Beth Israel*; 90.9% when it invokes *Seminole Rock*; and 100.0% when it invokes *Curtiss-Wright* deference. Eskridge & Baer, *Continuum of Deference,* 96 Geo. L.J. at 1100 (Table 1). All these figures are inflated by the fact that the Court probably cites these deference regimes primarily when it is inclined to decide in favor of the agency. Thus, the Court follows *Chevron, Auer,* and *Curtiss-Wright* in only a fraction of the cases where each is potentially applicable. If *Kisor* is right that all these Supreme Court deference decisions—from *Seminole Rock, Skidmore,* and *Curtiss-Wright* to the more recent ones in *Chevron* and *Auer*—enjoy *stare decisis* respect, then there is a lot of slippage in the Court's actual practice. (If *Chevron* were a binding precedent, protected by *stare decisis,* one would expect the Court to cite and follow it more regularly.)

What a mess.

Surely this elaborate continuum can be simplified, and if simplified maybe the Justices would follow it more faithfully. But how should the continuum be simplified? Different Justices and commentators have come up with an array of proposed simplifications—which cut in all sorts of different directions. In concluding this chapter, we offer you several clusters of theories, and you are responsible for developing the approach that makes the best legal sense.

A. SHARPEN *CHEVRON* AND *SKIDMORE* WITHIN THE *MEAD* FRAMEWORK

The dominant impulse among judges and law professors has been to work within the assumptions of *Mead* and to formulate and consistently apply *Chevron* and *Skidmore* accordingly. Like Eskridge and Baer, most of these commentators would be happy to absorb *Beth Israel* and *Seminole Rock* into *Chevron.* See Kristin Hickman, *The Need for* Mead: *Rejecting Tax Exceptionalism in Judicial Deference,* 90 Minn. L. Rev. 1537 (2006), proposing that the Supreme Court jettison the special deference regime the Court long applied to IRS revenue rulings and just apply *Chevron,* and adopted in *Mayo Foundation v. United States,* 131 S.Ct. 704 (2011).

Many commentators would reject *Mead*'s notion that Congress can delegate lawmaking authority *implicitly.* This notion has created confusion among lower courts. E.g., Lisa Schultz Bressman, *How* Mead *Has Muddled Judicial Review of Agency Action,* 58 Vand. L. Rev. 1443 (2005). Different authors, of course, have come up with somewhat different prescriptions. More important, different authors have emphasized different normative underpinnings of *Mead.*

1. *Legislative Supremacy.* Probably the most important normative assumption of *Mead* is legislative supremacy: both judges and administrators are faithful agents of congressional directives embodied in statutes. Congress's intent as to who decides is just as important as its intent as to what the decision ought to be.[10]

---

[10]   For an excellent constitutional analysis of Congress's power to delegate lawmaking authority to agencies, see Thomas Merrill, *Rethinking Article I, Section 1: From Nondelegation to Exclusive Delegation,* 104 Colum. L. Rev. 2097 (2004).

Thomas Merrill and Kristin Hickman anticipated *Mead's* holding that an agency interpretation is entitled to *Chevron* deference *only* when it is pursuant to congressional delegation of lawmaking authority to the agency. See Merrill & Hickman, Chevron's *Domain*, 89 Geo. L.J. 833 (2001). They lay out the doctrinal consequences for this foundation, including the notion that courts should *not* *Chevron*-defer to an agency's interpretation of its own jurisdiction or authority, a precept the Court recently rejected in *City of Arlington v. FCC.* Thus, for them, *Chevron* Step Zero is critical, and the Oregon Aid-in-Dying Case exemplifies the kind of inquiry the Court should be making.

Thomas Merrill and Kathryn Tongue Watts complicate the implications of *Mead* in *Agency Rules with the Force of Law: The Original Convention,* 116 Harv. L. Rev. 467 (2002). They demonstrate that the longstanding legislative tradition for delegating "lawmaking" authority required an expression of direct sanctions for violation of an agency rule or order. Many of the cases where the Court has applied *Chevron* deference—including *Chevron* itself—did not meet this conventional test. Because they require a court order to be enforceable, NLRB orders are not properly considered "lawmaking" delegations for this reason. The authors discuss various ways their discoveries could push the *Chevron* line of cases but come to no firm conclusions.

2.   *Democratic Legitimacy.* In our democracy, the legitimacy of legislation (the moral reason we accept and obey its commands) rests in part on popular participation or, at least, the accountability of elected representatives to We the People for the laws they adopt. In the modern administrative state, most of the actual rules are developed by unelected agencies, and so there is a potential democracy deficit.

Henry Richardson, *Democratic Autonomy: Public Reasoning About the Ends of Policy* (2003), argues that agencies can contribute to rather than derogate from democratic decisionmaking when they engage in notice-and-comment rulemaking which replicates the legislative process (proposal, popular feedback, deliberated decision, with opportunity for people to object). Richardson's focus, therefore, would not be the fact of legislative *delegation,* but instead the manner in which delegated *lawmaking* is accomplished. Thus, the executive department decisions in *Mead, Oregon,* and *Trump* (administrative or presidential fiat) do not deserve as much deference as the decision in *Chevron* itself (notice-and-comment rulemaking) does.

Complementing Richardson's analysis, Lisa Schultz Bressman, *Beyond Accountability: Arbitrariness and Legitimacy in the Administrative State,* 78 N.Y.U. L. Rev. 461 (2003), argues that we ought to be even more concerned about administrative arbitrariness than political accountability. Bressman's prescription is that notice-and-comment rulemaking is most likely to produce decisions that reflect reasoned judgment and not arbitrary fiat.[11]

Abbe Gluck & Lisa Schultz Bressman, *Statutory Interpretation from the Inside— An Empirical Study of Congressional Drafting, Delegation, and the Canons: Part I,* 65 Stan. L. Rev. 901 (2013), engaged a large sample of congressional drafting and

---

[11]   Accord, William Eskridge Jr. & John Ferejohn, *A Republic of Statutes: Our New American Constitution* ch. 6 (2010); Mark Seidenfeld, *A Syncopated* Chevron*: Emphasizing Reasoned Decisionmaking in Reviewing Agency Interpretations of Statutes,* 73 Tex. L. Rev. 83 (1994).

committee staff to determine how much they knew about the Supreme Court's statutory interpretation rules, practices, and doctrine. Gluck and Bressman found that an overwhelming majority of congressional drafters were aware of and understood *Chevron,* more than any other doctrine apart from the plain meaning rule. *Id.* at 995–96. Although the drafters did not know all the ins and outs of the Court's *Chevron* legisprudence, they did draft statutes with *Chevron* in mind and believed that congressional enacting coalitions routinely expected judicial deference to agency interpretations when the drafters did not nail down points of law through specific statutory text. *Id.* at 996; see *id.* at 997–1006 (detailed discussion of other fascinating findings along these lines). Gluck and Bressman offer evidence that *Chevron* is a doctrine that implements presumed legislative preferences.

      3.   *Institutional Competence.* Few scholars have focused on *Skidmore,* which is not only the default regime under the *Chevron* jurisprudence, but is a default regime that both dominates *Chevron* and generates high agency win rates. In recent empirical articles, one focusing on the Supreme Court and the other on lower courts, scholars have sought to clarify *Skidmore* with a focus on *institutional competence.* Competence is the old New Deal theme: agencies are better qualified than judges to make certain kinds of policies. The Eskridge and Baer study found that the Justices' uncertainty about technical issues in the fields of intellectual property, telecommunications, taxation, pensions, and bankruptcy generated high levels of win rates for agency interpretations in those areas, whatever the deference regime the Court invoked. In contrast, more normative arenas such as criminal, Indian affairs, civil rights, and labor law found the Justices agreeing less often, again regardless of the deference regime invoked or applicable. Eskridge & Baer, *Continuum of Deference*, 96 Geo. L.J. at 1144 (Table 16). An implication of their empirical study is that *Skidmore* factors like institutional competence show up in *Chevron* cases as well.

      Applying *Skidmore* as the critical regime, Eskridge and Baer urge the Court to focus on three factors: (1) the rule of law, including agency consistency and public reliance on agency interpretations; (2) comparative institutional competence, with technical issues, matters of regulatory tradeoffs, and uncertainty better handled by agencies and bigger normative issues as those where courts should be more scrutinizing; and (3) legitimacy, with open processes and public participation being pluses for the agency. *Id.* at 1180–83. The Gluck and Bressman study found that congressional drafters were alert to these kind of functional criteria as well. See Gluck & Bressman, *Statutory Interpretation from the Inside: Part I,* 65 Stan. L. Rev. at 998–1004 (also announcing that *Mead* best reflected the assumptions in the congressional drafting process).

B. REJECT *MEAD* IN FAVOR OF GREATER DEFERENCE TO AGENCY INTERPRETATIONS

      Some commentators reject or would go beyond *Mead* and would read *Chevron* much more expansively than the Supreme Court has thus far been willing to do. These scholars are broadly critical of judicial "interference" in the ongoing administration of statutory schemes and urge that agency monitoring is better left to the political than the judicial process. Most of these scholars favor an expanded reading of *Chevron*, a vigorous revival of *Curtiss-Wright*, or perhaps even a diminished role for *Skidmore*. As before, there are several theoretical ways to reach this conclusion.

1. *Agencies Rather than Courts as the Preferred Congressional Agents.* A respected administrative law scholar before his appointment as a judge, Justice Scalia found no inconsistency between congressional supremacy and a broad reading of *Chevron* that defers to any interpretation adopted by the head of an agency that is not a litigating position. His argument was that any ambiguity or gap that Congress leaves in a statute is an implicit delegation of lawmaking authority to the agency Congress has charged with enforcing the statute. *Mead*, 533 U.S. at 256–57 (Scalia, J., dissenting); Antonin Scalia, *Judicial Deference to Administrative Interpretations of Law*, 1989 Duke L.J. 511, 516.

John Duffy responded that such a broad reading of *Chevron* is inconsistent with the text, structure, and original meaning of the Administrative Procedure Act, especially 5 U.S.C. §§ 558(b) (limits on agency sanctions) and 706(2) (judicial review of agency action), which codify a *Marbury* model of judicial review for agency decisions (under which it is the responsibility of the judiciary to say what the law is). Duffy, *Administrative Common Law in Judicial Review*, 77 Tex. L. Rev. 113, 193–99 (1998). Other scholars have taken a broader view of the APA and the Constitution.

Jack Goldsmith and John Manning have argued for a "completion power" in Article II, namely "the President's authority to prescribe incidental details needed to carry into execution a legislative scheme, even in the absence of any congressional authorization to complete that scheme." Goldsmith & Manning, *The President's Completion Power*, 115 Yale L.J. 2280 (2006). They invoked historical practice, where the President has exercised a completion power with the acquiescence of both Congress and the Court. E.g., *Dames & Moore v. Regan*, 453 U.S. 654 (1981); Proposed Executive Order Entitled "Federal Regulation," 5 Op. O.L.C. 59 (1981) (defending presidential cost-benefit review of proposed agency rules).

Such a completion power might justify *Chevron*: "[W]hile Congress can legitimately give either courts or agencies ultimate authority to resolve statutory ambiguities or fill up statutory interstices, it is more consistent with the background premises of our constitutional democracy to embrace a default rule that Congress prefers to leave such completion power in the hands of the more accountable executive." *Completion Power*, 115 Yale L.J. at 2299. This constitutional default rule would inform one's reading of the APA as well as *Chevron* and would provide an argument for the broad Article II reading of *Chevron*, namely, that statutory ambiguities represent an implicit delegation of lawmaking authority to agencies, but not courts.

2. *Democratic Legitimacy.* Recall that *Chevron* emphasized the relatively greater accountability of agencies (responsible to the nationally elected President) compared with federal courts (responsible to the unelected Supreme Court). When the President has taken a role in an agency interpretation *or* an interpretation has been adopted by the President's appointee (the agency head), see David Barron & Elena Kagan, Chevron's *Nondelegation Doctrine*, 2001 Sup. Ct. Rev. 201, 234–57 (amending the suggestions of the earlier article), then federal judges ought to

Chevron-defer. According to Elena Kagan, the main advantage of this approach would be *national transparency*. The buck stops with the President, and any policy option he or she chooses will be subject to national examination and critique—much more legitimate checks than those offered by judicial review. Kagan, *Presidential Administration*, 114 Harv. L. Rev. 2245, 2332–33 (2001).

Lisa Schultz Bressman questions whether presidential interventions are either transparent or public-regarding. Bressman, *Beyond Accountability,* 78 N.Y.U. L. Rev. at 503–13. A lot of presidential interventions are either behind-the-scenes or below the media radar, but can easily be trumpeted by the Solicitor General if needed to give an agency interpretation a boost. Moreover, many presidential interventions represent the worst sort of rent-seeking politics. It is not clear that the balance of rent-seeking and public-regarding presidential interventions weighs in favor of the latter.[12]

A more modest proposal was that made in Kevin Stack, *The Statutory President*, 90 Iowa L. Rev. 539 (2005). Stack argued that *Chevron* deference ought to apply to congressionally authorized lawmaking by the President. Other scholars would go much further in situations where the President is acting to protect national security or engage in matters touching foreign affairs. For example, Curtis Bradley & Jack Goldsmith, *Congressional Authorization and the War on Terrorism*, 118 Harv. L. Rev. 2047, 2100–06 (2005), maintain that congressional authorizations for the President's use of force against foreign enemies should be interpreted to include previous presidential practices *and* should be interpreted not to interfere with the President's inherent powers to respond to international emergencies and threats.

3. *Comparative Institutional Competence.* Neil Komesar argues in *Imperfect Alternatives: Choosing Institutions in Law, Economics, and Public Policy* (1994), that the structural limitations of the judiciary create significant costs for statutory as well as constitutional judicial review. Although he does not address *Chevron,* some of the most judge-critical voices have relied on his framework. Because agencies are more both more knowledgeable about statutory policy (*Skidmore*) and more democratically legitimate policymakers (*Chevron*), most commentators applying institutional cost-benefit analysis have concluded that agency interpretations should be the baseline, with courts in a monitoring role, whether or not Congress has delegated lawmaking authority.[13] Unsurprisingly, scholars are divided as to how aggressively courts ought to engage in "monitoring."

Other commentators maintain that judicial review of agency rulemaking has been counterproductive, because judges are not sufficiently knowledgeable, because

---

[12]   See also Jide Nzelibe, *The Fable of the Nationalist President and the Parochial Congress*, 53 UCLA L. Rev. 1217 (2006), arguing that the President does not necessarily represent a national majoritarian constituency any better than Congress does.

[13]   William Eskridge Jr., *Dynamic Statutory Interpretation* ch. 5 (1994) (applying legal process theory to argue for agency primacy in statutory interpretation, with judges as second-order interpreters). See also Adrian Vermeule, *Judging Under Uncertainty* (2006) (following something like Komesar's comparative institutional analysis to argue for a much more marginal role for judges and much greater role for agencies in statutory interpretation); William Eskridge Jr., *Expanding* Chevron's *Domain: A Comparative Institutional Analysis of the Relative Competence of Courts and Agencies to Interpret Statutes,* 2013 Wis. L. Rev. 411 (applying Komesar's analysis to argue for an expanded *Chevron,* along Scalia-Kagan lines); David Spence & Frank Cross, *A Public Choice Case for the Administrative State*, 89 Geo. L.J. 97 (2000).

judicial interventions tend to be legalistic and thereby derogate from the agency's purposive activities, and because even well-considered judicial interventions may have counterproductive side effects. These problems are illustrated by Jerry Mashaw & David Harfst, *The Struggle for Auto Safety* (1990). Mashaw, in general, has urged courts to be more deferential in the sense that judges need to leave agencies alone so that they can do the jobs Congress has given them. For this reason, he supports a broad reading of *Chevron*. See Jerry Mashaw, *Prodelegation: Why Administrators Should Make Political Decisions*, 1 J.L. Econ. & Org. 81, 91–99 (1985).

C. OVERRULE *CHEVRON*? UNIVERSAL *SKIDMORE*?

Justice Breyer has long been a critic of *Chevron* deference as inconsistent with the judicial role.[14] Rather than seeking to overrule *Chevron*, Breyer seems to apply *Chevron* as a special case of general *Skidmore* (Article III) deference, and the *Mead* notion of congressionally delegated lawmaking authority as a big "plus" in the *Skidmore* scale. For example, in *Barnhart v. Walton*, 535 U.S. 212 (2002), Justice Breyer wrote for the Court in affirming a rule adopted by the Social Security Administration. *Chevron* was applicable because Congress had delegated lawmaking authority to the agency. But Breyer continued the threshold analysis with the further observations that *Chevron*'s applicability was confirmed by the agency's expertise and its longstanding adherence to that interpretation for years before the rule was adopted—classic *Skidmore* considerations. *Id.* at 219–22.

The upshot of Breyer's point of view would be that *Skidmore* is the baseline, with pluses awarded for congressional delegation (*Chevron*), agency expertise (*Geier*) or foreign affairs subject matter (*Curtiss-Wright*), and minuses subtracted for agency wishy-washiness, secret processes, or lack of obvious expertise (*Gonzales v. Oregon*). By the way, Breyer is the judge on the current Court who is most willing to go along with agency interpretations, including those at odds with his overall political philosophy, according to the Eskridge and Baer study.

Although Breyer's approach sounds kind of radical after almost a quarter century of *Chevron*, it is not so dissimilar from what the Supreme Court has actually been doing. According to Eskridge & Baer, *Continuum of Deference*, 96 Geo. L.J. at 1142–51, agency success rates do not have a strong correlation with announced deference regimes but do enjoy strong correlation with perceived agency expertise and consistency of the agency's position over time (the same *Skidmore* factors Breyer emphasized in *Barnhart*). Moreover, Congress seems to be operating under the kinds of assumptions reflected in *Barnhart,* a point documented by Gluck & Bressman, *Statutory Interpretation from the Inside: Part I,* 65 Stan. L. Rev. at 1000–03.

Consider a more radical approach to *Chevron-Mead-Brand X* and all the rest. Read the following lower court opinion in light of the dissenting opinions in *Kisor v. Wilkie* (above) and *Gundy v. United States*, 139 S.Ct. 2116 (2019) (discussed in Chapter 8)

---

[14]   E.g., Stephen Breyer, *Judicial Review of Questions of Law and Policy*, 38 Admin. L. Rev. 363 (1986); accord. Cynthia Farina, *Statutory Interpretation and the Balance of Power in the Administrative State,* 89 Colum. L. Rev. 452 (1989).

Gutierrez-Brizuela v. Lynch

834 F.3d 1142 (10th Cir. 2016).

The case involved an application of *Brand X*. The Board of Immigration Appeals had exercised its *Chevron* Step Two authority to override a Tenth Circuit decision interpreting the immigration laws allow the Attorney General to "adjust the status" of an illegal immigrant. The issue in this case was whether the agency could apply the new interpretation retroactively. Writing for a unanimous Tenth Circuit panel, **Judge Gorsuch** overruled the agency. The court's primary reasoning rested upon the premises that judges presume Congress does not legislate retroactively and that retroactive agency action involving liberty interests raised due process concerns. Hence, the panel ruled that the agency's new rule should not apply retroactively.

Concurring in his own panel opinion, Judge Gorsuch wrote a lengthy essay questioning the *Chevron-Brand X* interpretive regime announced by the Supreme Court. "*Chevron* and *Brand X* permit executive bureaucracies to swallow huge amounts of core judicial and legislative power and concentrate federal power in a way that seems more than a little difficult to square with the Constitution of the framers' design. Maybe the time has come to face the behemoth.

"In enlightenment theory and hard won experience under a tyrannical king the founders found proof of the wisdom of a government of separated powers. In the avowedly political legislature, the framers endowed the people's representatives with the authority to prescribe new rules of general applicability prospectively. In the executive, they placed the task of ensuring the legislature's rules are faithfully executed in the hands of a single person also responsive to the people. And in the judiciary, they charged individuals insulated from political pressures with the job of interpreting the law and applying it retroactively to resolve past disputes. This allocation of different sorts of power to different sorts of decisionmakers was no accident. To adapt the law to changing circumstances, the founders thought, the collective wisdom of the people's representatives is needed. To faithfully execute the laws often demands the sort of vigor hard to find in management-by-committee. And to resolve cases and controversies over past events calls for neutral decisionmakers who will apply the law as it is, not as they wish it to be.

"Even more importantly, the founders considered the separation of powers a vital guard against governmental encroachment on the people's liberties, including all those later enumerated in the Bill of Rights. What would happen, for example, if the political majorities who run the legislative and executive branches could decide cases and controversies over past facts? They might be tempted to bend existing laws, to reinterpret and apply them retroactively in novel ways and without advance notice. Effectively leaving parties who cannot alter their past conduct to the mercy of majoritarian politics and risking the possibility that unpopular groups might be singled out for this sort of mistreatment—and raising along the way, too, grave due process (fair notice) and equal protection problems. Conversely, what would happen if politically unresponsive and life-tenured judges were permitted to decide policy questions for the future or try to execute those policies? The very idea of self-government would soon be at risk of withering to the point of pointlessness. It was to avoid dangers like these, dangers the founders had studied and seen realized in their own time, that they pursued the separation of powers. A government of diffused powers, they knew, is a government less capable of invading the liberties of the people.

"Founders meet *Brand X*. Precisely to avoid the possibility of allowing politicized decisionmakers to decide cases and controversies about the meaning of existing laws, the framers sought to ensure that judicial judgments 'may not lawfully be revised, overturned or refused faith and credit by' the elected branches of government. *Chi. & S. Air Lines v. Waterman S.S. Corp.*, 333 U.S. 103, 113 (1948). Yet this deliberate design, this separation of functions aimed to ensure a neutral decisionmaker for the people's disputes, faces more than a little pressure from *Brand X*. Under *Brand X*'s terms, after all, courts are required to overrule their own declarations about the meaning of existing law in favor of interpretations dictated by executive agencies. By *Brand X*'s own telling, this means a judicial declaration of the law's meaning in a case or controversy before it is not 'authoritative,' but is instead subject to revision by a politically accountable branch of government.* * *

"When the political branches disagree with a judicial interpretation of existing law, the Constitution prescribes the appropriate remedial process. It's called legislation. Admittedly, the legislative process can be an arduous one. But that's no bug in the constitutional design: it is the very point of the design. The framers sought to ensure that the people may rely on judicial precedent about the meaning of existing law until and unless that precedent is overruled or the purposefully painful process of bicameralism and presentment can be cleared. Indeed, the principle of *stare decisis* was one 'entrenched and revered by the framers' precisely because they knew its importance 'as a weapon against . . . tyranny.' Michael B.W. Sinclair, *Anastasoff Versus Hart: The Constitutionality and Wisdom of Denying Precedential Authority to Circuit Court Decisions*, 64 U. Pitt. L. Rev. 695, 707 (2003). Yet even as now semi-tamed (at least in this circuit), *Brand X* still risks trampling the constitutional design by affording executive agencies license to overrule a judicial declaration of the law's meaning prospectively, just as legislation might—and all without the inconvenience of having to engage the legislative processes the Constitution prescribes. A form of Lawmaking Made Easy, one that permits all too easy intrusions on the liberty of the people.

"Of course, *Brand X* asserts that its rule about judicial deference to executive revisions follows logically 'from *Chevron* itself.' And that assessment seems fair enough as far as it goes. If you accept *Chevron*'s claim that legislative ambiguity represents a license to executive agencies to render authoritative judgments about what a statute means, *Brand X*'s rule requiring courts to overturn their own contrary judgments does seem to follow pretty naturally.

"But acknowledging this much only brings the colossus now fully into view. In the Administrative Procedure Act (APA), Congress vested the courts with the power to 'interpret . . . statutory provisions' and overturn agency action inconsistent with those interpretations. 5 U.S.C. § 706. Congress assigned the courts much the same job in the immigration field where we happen to find ourselves today. 8 U.S.C. § 1252(a)(2)(D). And there's good reason to think that legislative assignments like these are often constitutionally compelled. After all, the question whether Congress has or hasn't vested a private legal right in an individual 'is, in its nature, judicial, and must be tried by the judicial authority.' *Marbury v. Madison*, 5 U.S. (1 Cranch) 137, 167 (1803). Yet, rather than completing the task expressly assigned to us, rather than 'interpret[ing] . . . statutory provisions,' declaring what the law is, and overturning inconsistent agency action, *Chevron* step two tells us we must allow an executive agency to resolve the meaning of any ambiguous statutory provision. In this way, *Chevron* seems no less than a judge-made doctrine for the abdication of the judicial duty. Of course, *some* role remains for judges even under *Chevron*. At *Chevron* step one, judges decide whether the statute is 'ambiguous,' and at step two they decide whether the agency's view is 'reasonable.' But where in all this does a court *interpret* the law and say what it *is*? When does a court independently decide what the statute means and whether it has or has not vested a legal right in a person? Where *Chevron* applies that job seems to have gone extinct."

Can Congress, consistent with Article I, really delegate so much lawmaking authority in this vague and unguided manner? The Supreme Court has not stringently enforced the nondelegation doctrine, and it has allowed massive delegations so long as they are accompanied by an "intelligible principle." (Hence, Judge Gorsuch anticipates his 2019 dissenting opinion in *Gundy*.)

"But even taking the forgiving intelligible principle test as a given, it's no small question whether *Chevron* can clear it. For if an agency can enact a new rule of general applicability affecting huge swaths of the national economy one day and reverse itself the next (and that is exactly what *Chevron* permits), you might be forgiven for asking: where's the 'substantial guidance' in that? And if an agency can interpret the scope of its statutory jurisdiction one way one day and reverse itself the next (and that is exactly what *City of Arlington*'s application of *Chevron* says it can), you might well wonder: where are the promised 'clearly delineated boundaries' of agency authority? The Supreme Court once unanimously declared that a statute affording the executive the power to write an industrial code of competition for the poultry industry violated the separation of powers. *A.L.A. Schechter Poultry Corp. v. United States*, 295 U.S. 495, 537–42 (1935). And if that's the case, you might ask how is it that *Chevron*—a rule that invests agencies with pretty unfettered power to regulate a lot more than chicken—can evade the chopping block.

"Even under the most relaxed or functionalist view of our separated powers some concern has to arise, too, when so much power is concentrated in the hands of a single branch of government. *See* The Federalist No. 47 (James Madison) ('The accumulation of all powers, legislative, executive, and judiciary, in the same hands . . . may justly be pronounced the very definition of tyranny.'). After all, *Chevron* invests the power to decide the meaning of the law, and to do so with legislative policy goals in mind, in the very entity charged with enforcing the law. Under its terms, an administrative agency may set and revise policy (legislative), override adverse judicial determinations (judicial), and exercise enforcement discretion (executive). Add to this the fact that today many administrative agencies 'wield[ ] vast power' and are overseen by political appointees (but often receive little effective oversight from the chief executive to whom they nominally report), and you have a pretty potent mix. Under any conception of our separation of powers, I would have thought powerful and centralized authorities like today's administrative agencies would have warranted less deference from other branches, not more. None of this is to suggest that *Chevron* is 'the very definition of tyranny.' But on any account it certainly seems to have added prodigious new powers to an already titanic administrative state—and spawned along the way more than a few due process and equal protection problems of the sort documented in the court's opinion today."

Judge Gorsuch continued: "*Chevron* has presented its fair share of practical problems in its administration. By way of illustration, consider just two examples. First, we once thought *Chevron*'s presumption of delegation for ambiguous statutes applied uniformly to Congress's work. Then we learned it doesn't apply to criminal statutes. Now we know it doesn't always apply even when it comes to purely civil statutes. In *Mead*, the Court added a 'step zero' to the *Chevron* sequence, one that requires courts to employ a multi-factor balancing test to decide whether to proceed to apply *Chevron* to a civil statute. So today courts will only *sometimes* apply *Chevron* deference to ambiguous civil statutes. Neither, respectfully, does looking to the Supreme Court's case law supply a great deal of guidance on how to apply *Mead*'s balancing test. In recent years, the Court has declined to apply *Chevron* deference to arguably ambiguous civil statutes but it has only sometimes cited the *Mead* balancing test as the reason, leaving more than a few litigants and lower courts to wonder how they are supposed to proceed. *See, e.g., PGA Tour, Inc. v. Martin*, 532 U.S. 661 (2001); *see also* William Eskridge, Jr. & Lauren Baer, *The Continuum of Deference: Supreme Court Treatment of Agency Statutory Interpretations from Chevron to Hamdan*, 96 Geo. L.J. 1083, 1097–1120 (2008).

"Second, long lingering questions linger still about just how rigorous *Chevron* step one is supposed to be. In deciding whether Congress has 'directly spoken' to a question or left it 'ambiguous,' what materials are we to consult? The narrow language of the statute alone? Its structure and history? Canons of interpretation? Committee reports? Every scrap of legislative history we can dig up? Some claim to have identified at least three potential variants of *Chevron* jurisprudence governing the line between step one and step two in the Supreme Court's case law. * * *

"All of which raises this question: what would happen in a world without *Chevron*? If this goliath of modern administrative law were to fall? Surely Congress could and would continue to pass statutes for executive agencies to enforce. And just as surely agencies could and would continue to offer guidance on how they intend to enforce those statutes. The only difference would be that courts would then fulfill their duty to exercise their independent judgment about what the law *is*. Of course, courts could and would consult agency views and apply the agency's interpretation when it accords with the best reading of a statute. But *de novo* judicial review of the law's meaning would limit the ability of an agency to alter and amend existing law. It would avoid the due process and equal protection problems of the kind documented in our decisions. It would promote reliance interests by allowing citizens to organize their affairs with some assurance that the rug will not be pulled from under them tomorrow, the next day, or after the next election. And an agency's recourse for a judicial declaration of the law's meaning that it dislikes would be precisely the recourse the Constitution prescribes—an appeal to higher judicial authority or a new law enacted consistent with bicameralism and presentment. We managed to live with the administrative state before *Chevron*. We could do it again. Put simply, it seems to me that in a world without *Chevron* very little would change— except perhaps the most important things."

NOTE ON A WORLD WITHOUT CHEVRON

Judge Gorsuch now sits on the Supreme Court. Thus far, he has been notably reluctant to apply that precedent's deference regime. For example, in *Wisconsin Central, Ltd. v. United States,* 138 S.Ct. 2067 (2018), the lower court judges *Chevron*-deferred to the IRS's interpretation that the Railroad Retirement Tax Act includes stock options as taxable "compensation." Reversing, Justice Gorsuch found *Chevron* inapplicable, because the Act defined compensation as "any form of money remuneration," and so the law could not plausibly include stock options that five Justices felt were not "monetary." He rejected the views held by the lower courts and four Justices that there was sufficient ambiguity to justify *Chevron* deference.

In *Pereira v. Sessions,* 138 S.Ct. 2105 (2018), the Court declined to defer to the Board of Immigration Appeals, on the ground that the statute was clear (notwithstanding an extensive analysis to the contrary by Justice Alito, in dissent). Concurring Justice Kennedy expressed concern that the courts of appeals rallied around the Board's interpretation without careful analysis of the statute. "The type of reflexive deference exhibited in some of these cases is troubling. And when deference is applied to other questions of statutory interpretation, such as an agency's interpretation of the statutory provisions that concern the scope of its own authority, it is more troubling still. See *Arlington v. FCC,* 569 U.S. 290, 327 (2013) (Roberts, C.J., dissenting). Given the concerns raised by some Members of this Court, see, e.g., * * * *Gutierrez-Brizuela* (Gorsuch, J., concurring), it seems necessary and appropriate to reconsider, in an appropriate case, the premises that underlie *Chevron* and how courts have implemented that decision. The proper rules for interpreting statutes and determining agency jurisdiction and substantive agency powers should accord with constitutional separation-of-powers principles and the function and province of the Judiciary."

Notice how Justices Kennedy and Gorsuch associated their concerns about *Chevron* with separation of powers theory, as well as a *Marbury* theory of Article III that motivated Judge Breyer's criticism, cited above. Is the Gorsuch reading of *Chevron* a fair one? Can *Chevron* be more narrowly understood? Or has the whole *Chevron* assembly of rules, exceptions, caveats, and inconsistent applications become a Jenga stack that is on the verge of falling down? (Jenga is a game where players start with a tower of interlocked wood blocks; each player removes one block from the tower, until it comes crashing down.)

And what would statutory interpretation look like if *Chevron* were abrogated? Universal *Skidmore*? The hodge-podge regime that preceded *Chevron*? The Eskridge and Baer study suggests that, at the Supreme Court level—where the Justices are not bashful about trumping agency interpretations with their own reading of the statutory text and structure and where agencies have the highest win rates when their expertise gives them a strong comparative advantage over courts, when they have followed a deliberative process, and/or when they have offered an interpretation that accords with the Justices' understanding of sound statutory policy—the disappearance of *Chevron* would not have a big effect on the results or even the reasoning of the Court's decisions.

But the 2017 Barnett and Walker study reports that *Chevron* has a more significant effect in the courts of appeals. How much weight should that have? Like the 2008 Eskridge and Baer study, theirs does not evaluate the merits of the agency deference cases, so we don't really know whether agencies do a better job when judges defer to their views. (Some experienced administrative law professors have informed views on this; Jerry Mashaw, for example, believes agencies usually do a better job than judges.)

APPENDIX A

THE CONSTITUTION OF THE UNITED STATES

• • •

We the People of the United States, in Order to form a more perfect Union, establish Justice, insure domestic Tranquility, provide for the common defence, promote the general Welfare, and secure the Blessings of Liberty to ourselves and our Posterity, do ordain and establish this Constitution for the United States of America.

ARTICLE I

Section 1. All legislative Powers herein granted shall be vested in a Congress of the United States, which shall consist of a Senate and House of Representatives.

Section 2. [1] The House of Representatives shall be composed of Members chosen every second Year by the People of the several States, and the Electors in each State shall have the Qualifications requisite for Electors of the most numerous Branch of the State Legislature.

[2] No Person shall be a Representative who shall not have attained to the Age of twenty five Years, and been seven Years a Citizen of the United States, and who shall not, when elected, be an Inhabitant of that State in which he shall be chosen.

[3] Representatives and direct Taxes shall be apportioned among the several States which may be included within this Union, according to their respective Numbers, which shall be determined by adding to the whole Number of free Persons, including those bound to Service for a Term of Years, and excluding Indians not taxed, three fifths of all other Persons. The actual Enumeration shall be made within three Years after the first Meeting of the Congress of the United States, and within every subsequent Term of ten Years, in such Manner as they shall by Law direct. The Number of Representatives shall not exceed one for every thirty Thousand, but each State shall have at Least one Representative; and until such enumeration shall be made, the State of New Hampshire shall be entitled to chuse three, Massachusetts eight, Rhode Island and Providence Plantations one, Connecticut five, New York six, New Jersey four, Pennsylvania eight, Delaware one, Maryland six, Virginia ten, North Carolina five, South Carolina five, and Georgia three.

[4] When vacancies happen in the Representation from any State, the Executive Authority thereof shall issue Writs of Election to fill such Vacancies.

[5] The House of Representatives shall chuse their Speaker and other Officers; and shall have the sole Power of impeachment.

Section 3. [1] The Senate of the United States shall be composed of two Senators from each State, chosen by the Legislature thereof, for six Years; and each Senator shall have one Vote.

[2] Immediately after they shall be assembled in Consequence of the first Election, they shall be divided as equally as may be into three Classes. The Seats of the Senators of the first Class shall be vacated at the Expiration of the second Year, of the second Class at the Expiration of the fourth Year, and of the third Class at the Expiration of the sixth Year, so that one third may be chosen every second Year; and if Vacancies happen by Resignation, or otherwise, during the Recess of the Legislature of any State, the Executive thereof may make temporary Appointments until the next Meeting of the Legislature, which shall then fill such Vacancies.

[3] No Person shall be a Senator who shall not have attained to the Age of thirty Years, and been nine Years a Citizen of the United States, and who shall not, when elected, be an Inhabitant of that State for which he shall be chosen.

[4] The Vice President of the United States shall be President of the Senate, but shall have no Vote, unless they be equally divided.

[5] The Senate shall chuse their other Officers, and also a President pro tempore, in the Absence of the Vice President, or when he shall exercise the Office of President of the United States.

[6] The Senate shall have the sole Power to try all Impeachments. When sitting for that Purpose, they shall be on Oath or Affirmation. When the President of the United States is tried, the Chief Justice shall preside: And no Person shall be convicted without the Concurrence of two thirds of the Members present.

[7] Judgment in Cases of Impeachment shall not extend further than to removal from Office, and disqualification to hold and enjoy any Office of honor, Trust, or Profit under the United States: but the Party convicted shall nevertheless be liable and subject to Indictment, Trial, Judgment, and Punishment, according to Law.

Section 4. [1] The Times, Places and Manner of holding Elections for Senators and Representatives, shall be prescribed in each State by the Legislature thereof; but the Congress may at any time by Law make or alter such Regulations, except as to the Places of chusing Senators.

[2] The Congress shall assemble at least once in every Year, and such Meeting shall be on the first Monday in December, unless they shall by Law appoint a different Day.

Section 5. [1] Each House shall be the Judge of the Elections, Returns, and Qualifications of its own Members, and a Majority of each shall constitute a Quorum to do Business; but a smaller Number may adjourn from day to day, and may be authorized to compel the Attendance of absent Members, in such Manner, and under such Penalties as each House may provide.

[2] Each House may determine the Rules of its Proceedings, punish its Members for disorderly Behaviour, and, with the Concurrence of two thirds, expel a Member.

[3] Each House shall keep a Journal of its Proceedings, and from time to time publish the same, excepting such Parts as may in their Judgment require Secrecy; and the Yeas and Nays of the Members of either House on any question shall, at the Desire of one fifth of those Present, be entered on the Journal.

[4] Neither House, during the Session of Congress, shall without the Consent of the other, adjourn for more than three days, nor to any other Place than that in which the two Houses shall be sitting.

Section 6. [1] The Senators and Representatives shall receive a Compensation for their Services, to be ascertained by Law, and paid out of the Treasury of the United States. They shall in all Cases, except Treason, Felony, and Breach of the Peace, be privileged from Arrest during their Attendance at the Session of their respective Houses, and in going to and returning from the same; and for any Speech or Debate in either House, they shall not be questioned in any other Place.

[2] No Senator or Representative shall, during the Time for which he was elected, be appointed to any civil Office under the Authority of the United States, which shall have been created, or the Emoluments whereof shall have been encreased during such time; and no Person holding any Office under the United States, shall be a Member of either House during his Continuance in Office.

Section 7. [1] All Bills for raising Revenue shall originate in the House of Representatives; but the Senate may propose or concur with Amendments as on other Bills.

[2] Every Bill which shall have passed the House of Representatives and the Senate, shall, before it become a Law, be presented to the President of the United States; If he approve he shall sign it, but if not he shall return it, with his Objections to that House in which it shall have originated, who shall enter the Objections at large on their Journal, and proceed to reconsider it. If after such Reconsideration two thirds of that House shall agree to pass the Bill, it shall be sent, together with the Objections, to the other House, by which it shall likewise be reconsidered, and if approved by two thirds of that House, it shall become a Law. But in all such Cases the Votes of both Houses shall be determined by Yeas and Nays, and the Names of the Persons voting for and against the Bill shall be entered on the Journal of each House respectively. If any Bill shall not be returned by the President within ten Days (Sundays excepted) after it shall have been presented to him, the Same shall be a Law, in like Manner as if he had signed it, unless the Congress by their Adjournment prevent its Return, in which Case it shall not be a Law.

[3] Every Order, Resolution, or Vote to which the Concurrence of the Senate and House of Representatives may be necessary (except on a question of Adjournment) shall be presented to the President of the United States; and before the Same shall take Effect, shall be approved by him, or being disapproved by him, shall be repassed by two thirds of the Senate and House of Representatives, according to the Rules and Limitations prescribed in the Case of a Bill.

Section 8. [1] The Congress shall have Power To lay and collect Taxes, Duties, Imposts and Excises, to pay the Debts and provide for the common Defence and general Welfare of the United States; but all Duties, Imposts and Excises shall be uniform throughout the United States;

[2] To borrow Money on the credit of the United States;

[3] To regulate Commerce with foreign Nations, and among the several States, and with the Indian Tribes;

[4] To establish an uniform Rule of Naturalization, and uniform Laws on the subject of Bankruptcies throughout the United States;

[5] To coin Money, regulate the Value thereof, and of foreign Coin, and fix the Standard of Weights and Measures;

[6] To provide for the Punishment of counterfeiting the Securities and current Coin of the United States;

[7] To establish Post Offices and Post Roads;

[8] To promote the Progress of Science and useful Arts, by securing for limited Times to Authors and Inventors the exclusive Right to their respective Writings and Discoveries;

[9] To constitute Tribunals inferior to the supreme Court;

[10] To define and punish Piracies and Felonies committed on the high Seas, and Offences against the Law of Nations;

[11] To declare War, grant Letters of Marque and Reprisal, and make Rules concerning Captures on Land and Water;

[12] To raise and support Armies, but no Appropriation of Money to that Use shall be for a longer Term than two Years;

[13] To provide and maintain a Navy;

[14] To make Rules for the Government and Regulation of the land and naval Forces;

[15] To provide for calling forth the Militia to execute the Laws of the Union, suppress Insurrections and repel Invasions;

[16] To provide for organizing, arming, and disciplining, the Militia, and for governing such Part of them as may be employed in the Service of the United States, reserving to the States respectively, the Appointment of the Officers, and the Authority of training the Militia according to the discipline prescribed by Congress;

[17] To exercise exclusive Legislation in all Cases whatsoever, over such District (not exceeding ten Miles square) as may, by Cession of particular States and the Acceptance of Congress, become the Seat of the Government of the United States, and to exercise like Authority over all Places purchased by the Consent of the Legislature of the State in which the Same shall be, for the Erection of Forts, Magazines, Arsenals, dock-Yards, and other needful Buildings;—And

[18] To make all Laws which shall be necessary and proper for carrying into Execution the foregoing Powers, and all other Powers vested by this Constitution in the Government of the United States, or in any Department or Officer thereof.

Section 9. [1] The Migration or Importation of such Persons as any of the States now existing shall think proper to admit, shall not be prohibited by the Congress prior to the Year one thousand eight hundred and eight, but a Tax or duty may be imposed on such Importation, not exceeding ten dollars for each Person.

[2] The Privilege of the Writ of Habeas Corpus shall not be suspended, unless when in Cases of Rebellion or Invasion the public Safety may require it.

No act of Leg declaring someone guilty w/o Trial

[3] No Bill of Attainder or ex post facto Law shall be passed.

[4] No Capitation, or other direct, Tax shall be laid, unless in Proportion to the Census or Enumeration herein before directed to be taken.

[5] No Tax or Duty shall be laid on Articles exported from any State. *no state tax/duty*

[6] No Preference shall be given by any Regulation of Commerce or Revenue to the Ports of one State over those of another: nor shall Vessels bound to, or from, one State, be obliged to enter, clear, or pay Duties in another.

[7] No Money shall be drawn from the Treasury, but in Consequence of Appropriations made by Law; and a regular Statement and Account of the Receipts and Expenditures of all public Money shall be published from time to time.

[8] No Title of Nobility shall be granted by the United States: And no Person holding any Office of Profit or Trust under them, shall, without the Consent of the Congress, accept of any present, Emolument, Office, or Title, of any kind whatever, from any King, Prince, or foreign State.

Section 10. [1] No State shall enter into any Treaty, Alliance, or Confederation; grant Letters of Marque and Reprisal; coin Money; emit Bills of Credit; make any Thing but gold and silver Coin a Tender in Payment of Debts; pass any Bill of Attainder, ex post facto Law, or Law impairing the Obligation of Contracts, or grant any Title of Nobility.

[2] No State shall, without the Consent of the Congress, lay any Imposts or Duties on Imports or Exports, except what may be absolutely necessary for executing its inspection Laws: and the net Produce of all Duties and Imposts, laid by any State on Imports or Exports, shall be for the Use of the Treasury of the United States; and all such Laws shall be subject to the Revision and Controul of the Congress.

[3] No State shall, without the Consent of Congress, lay any Duty of Tonnage, keep Troops, or Ships of War in time of Peace, enter into any Agreement or Compact with another State, or with a foreign Power, or engage in War, unless actually invaded, or in such imminent Danger as will not admit of delay.

ARTICLE II

exec powers

Section 1. [1] The executive Power shall be vested in a President of the United States of America. He shall hold his Office during the Term of four Years, and, together with the Vice President, chosen for the same Term, be elected, as follows:

[2] Each State shall appoint, in such Manner as the Legislature thereof may direct, a Number of Electors, equal to the whole Number of Senators and Representatives to which the State may be entitled in the Congress: but no Senator or Representative, or Person holding an Office of Trust or Profit under the United States, shall be appointed an Elector. *senators + Rep* *# of electors =*

[3] The electors shall meet in their respective States, and vote by ballot for two Persons, of whom one at least shall not be an Inhabitant of the same State with themselves. And they shall make a List of all the Persons voted for, and of the Number of Votes for each; which List they shall sign and certify, and transmit sealed to the Seat of the Government of the United States, directed to the President of the

sign+ seal Ballots | # be inhab of same state — electors meet in state + vote for 2 people

Senate. The President of the Senate shall, in the Presence of the Senate and House of Representatives, open all the Certificates, and the Votes shall then be counted. The Person having the greatest Number of Votes shall be the President, if such Number be a Majority of the whole Number of Electors appointed; and if there be more than one who have such Majority, and have an equal Number of Votes, then the House of Representatives shall immediately chuse by Ballot one of them for President; and if no Person have a Majority, then from the five highest on the List the said House shall in like Manner chuse the President. But in chusing the President, the Votes shall be taken by States, the Representation from each State having one Vote; A quorum for this Purpose shall consist of a Member or Members from two thirds of the States, and a Majority of all the States shall be necessary to a Choice. In every Case, after the Choice of the President, the Person having the greatest Number of Votes of the Electors shall be the Vice President. But if there should remain two or more who have equal Votes, the Senate shall chuse from them by Ballot the Vice-President.

[4] The Congress may determine the Time of chusing the Electors, and the Day on which they shall give their Votes; which Day shall be the same throughout the United States.

[5] No Person except a natural born Citizen, or a Citizen of the United States, at the time of the Adoption of this Constitution, shall be eligible to the Office of President; neither shall any Person be eligible to that Office who shall not have attained to the Age of thirty five Years, and been fourteen Years a Resident within the United States.

[6] In Case of the Removal of the President from Office, or of his Death, Resignation, or Inability to discharge the Powers and Duties of the said Office, the Same shall devolve on the Vice President, and the Congress may by Law provide for the Case of Removal, Death, Resignation or Inability, both of the President and Vice President, declaring what Officer shall then act as President, and such Officer shall act accordingly, until the Disability be removed, or a President shall be elected.

[7] The President shall, at stated Times, receive for his Services, a Compensation, which shall neither be encreased nor diminished during the Period for which he shall have been elected, and he shall not receive within that Period any other Emolument from the United States, or any of them. [8] Before he enter on the Execution of his Office, he shall take the following Oath or Affirmation: "I do solemnly swear (or affirm) that I will faithfully execute the Office of President of the United States, and will to the best of my Ability, preserve, protect and defend the Constitution of the United States."

Section 2. [1] The President shall be Commander in Chief of the Army and Navy of the United States, and of the Militia of the several States, when called into the actual Service of the United States; he may require the Opinion, in writing, of the principal Officer in each of the executive Departments, upon any Subject relating to the Duties of their respective Offices, and he shall have Power to grant Reprieves and Pardons for Offenses against the United States, except in Cases of Impeachment.

[2] He shall have Power, by and with the Advice and Consent of the Senate, to make Treaties, provided two thirds of the Senators present concur; and he shall

nominate, and by and with the Advice and Consent of the Senate, shall appoint Ambassadors, other public Ministers and Consuls, Judges of the supreme Court, and all other Officers of the United States, whose Appointments are not herein otherwise provided for, and which shall be established by Law: but the Congress may by Law vest the Appointment of such inferior Officers, as they think proper, in the President alone, in the Courts of Law, or in the Heads of Departments.

[3] The President shall have Power to fill up all Vacancies that may happen during the Recess of the Senate, by granting Commissions which shall expire at the End of their next Session.

Section 3. He shall from time to time give to the Congress Information of the State of the Union, and recommend to their Consideration such Measures as he shall judge necessary and expedient; he may, on extraordinary Occasions, convene both Houses, or either of them, and in Case of Disagreement between them, with Respect to the Time of Adjournment, he may adjourn them to such Time as he shall think proper; he shall receive Ambassadors and other public Ministers; he shall take Care that the Laws be faithfully executed, and shall Commission. all the Officers of the United States.

Section 4. The President, Vice President and all civil Officers of the United States, shall be removed from Office on Impeachment for, and Conviction of, Treason, Bribery, or other high Crimes and Misdemeanors.

ARTICLE III

Section 1. The judicial Power of the United States, shall be vested in one supreme Court, and in such inferior Courts as the Congress may from time to time ordain and establish. The Judges, both of the supreme and inferior Courts, shall hold their Offices during good Behaviour, and shall, at stated Times, receive for their Services, a Compensation, which shall not be diminished during their Continuance in Office.

Section 2. [1] The judicial Power shall extend to all Cases, in Law and Equity, arising under this Constitution, the Laws of the United States, and Treaties made, or which shall be made, under their Authority;—to all Cases affecting Ambassadors, other public Ministers and Consuls;—to all Cases of admiralty and maritime Jurisdiction;—to Controversies to which the United States shall be a Party;—to Controversies between two or more States;—between a State and Citizens of another State;—between Citizens of different States;—between Citizens of the same State claiming Lands under Grants of different States, and between a State, or the Citizens thereof, and foreign States, Citizens or Subjects.

[2] In all Cases affecting Ambassadors, other public Ministers and Consuls, and those in which a State shall be Party, the supreme Court shall have original Jurisdiction. In all the other Cases before mentioned, the supreme Court shall have appellate Jurisdiction, both as to Law and Fact, with such Exceptions, and under such Regulations as the Congress shall make.

[3] The Trial of all Crimes, except in Cases of Impeachment, shall be by Jury; and such Trial shall be held in the State where the said Crimes shall have been

committed; but when not committed within any State, the Trial shall be at such Place or Places as the Congress may by Law have directed.

Section 3. [1] Treason against the United States, shall consist only in levying War against them, or in adhering to their Enemies, giving them Aid and Comfort. No Person shall be convicted of Treason unless on the Testimony of two Witnesses to the same overt Act, or on Confession in open Court.

[2] The Congress shall have Power to declare the Punishment of Treason, but no Attainder of Treason shall work Corruption of Blood, or Forfeiture except during the Life of the Person attainted.

ARTICLE IV

Section 1. Full Faith and Credit shall be given in each State to the public Acts, Records, and judicial Proceedings of every other State. And the Congress may by general Laws prescribe the Manner in which such Acts, Records and Proceedings shall be proved, and the Effect thereof.

Section 2. [1] The Citizens of each State shall be entitled to all Privileges and Immunities of Citizens in the several States.

[2] A person charged in any State with Treason, Felony, or other Crime, who shall flee from Justice, and be found in another State, shall on Demand of the executive Authority of the State from which he fled, be delivered up, to be removed to the State having Jurisdiction of the Crime.

[3] No Person held to Service or Labour in one State, under the Laws thereof, escaping into another, shall, in Consequence of any Law or Regulation therein, be discharged from such Service or Labour, but shall be delivered up on Claim of the Party; to whom such Service or Labour may be due.

Section 3. [1] New States may be admitted by the Congress into this Union; but no new State shall be formed or erected within the Jurisdiction of any other State; nor any State be formed by the Junction of two or more States, or Parts of States, without the Consent of the Legislatures of the States concerned as well as of the Congress.

[2] The Congress shall have Power to dispose of and make all needful Rules and Regulations respecting the Territory or other Property belonging to the United States; and nothing in this Constitution shall be so construed as to Prejudice any Claims of the United States, or of any particular State.

Section 4. The United States shall guarantee to every State in this Union a Republican Form of Government, and shall protect each of them against Invasion; and on Application of the Legislature, or of the Executive (when the Legislature cannot be convened) against domestic Violence.

ARTICLE V

The Congress, whenever two thirds of both Houses shall deem it necessary, shall propose Amendments to this Constitution, or on the Application of the Legislatures of two thirds of the several States, shall call a Convention for proposing Amendments, which, in either Case, shall be valid to all Intents and Purposes, as

Part of this Constitution, when ratified by the Legislatures of three fourths of the several States, or by Conventions in three fourths thereof, as the one or the other Mode of Ratification may be proposed by the Congress; Provided that no Amendment which may be made prior to the Year One thousand eight hundred and eight shall in any Manner affect the first and fourth Clauses in the Ninth Section of the first Article; and that no State, without its Consent, shall be deprived of its equal Suffrage in the Senate.

ARTICLE VI

[1] All Debts contracted and Engagements entered into, before the Adoption of this Constitution, shall be as valid against the United States under this Constitution, as under the Confederation.

[2] This Constitution, and the Laws of the United States which shall be made in Pursuance thereof; and all Treaties made, or which shall be made, under the Authority of the United States, shall be the supreme Law of the Land; and the Judges in every State shall be bound thereby, any Thing in the Constitution or Laws of any State to the Contrary notwithstanding.

[3] The Senators and Representatives before mentioned, and the Members of the several State Legislatures, and all executive and judicial Officers, both of the United States and of the several States, shall be bound by Oath or Affirmation, to support this Constitution; but no religious Test shall ever be required as a Qualification to any Office or public Trust under the United States.

ARTICLE VII

The Ratification of the Conventions of nine States, shall be sufficient for the Establishment of this Constitution between the States so ratifying the Same.

ARTICLES IN ADDITION TO, AND AMENDMENT OF, THE CONSTITUTION OF THE UNITED STATES OF AMERICA, PROPOSED BY CONGRESS, AND RATIFIED BY THE LEGISLATURES OF THE SEVERAL STATES, PURSUANT TO THE FIFTH ARTICLE OF THE ORIGINAL CONSTITUTION.

AMENDMENT I [1791]

Congress shall make no law respecting an establishment of religion, or prohibiting the free exercise thereof; or abridging the freedom of speech, or of the press; or the right of the people peaceably to assemble, and to petition the Government for a redress of grievances.

AMENDMENT II [1791]

A well regulated Militia, being necessary to the security of a free State, the right of the people to keep and bear Arms, shall not be infringed.

AMENDMENT III [1791]

No Soldier shall, in time of peace be quartered in any house, without the consent of the Owner, nor in time of war, but in a manner to be prescribed by law.

AMENDMENT IV [1791]

The right of the people to be secure in their persons, houses, papers, and effects, against unreasonable searches and seizures, shall not be violated, and no Warrants shall issue, but upon probable cause, supported by Oath or affirmation, and particularly describing the place to be searched, and the persons or things to be seized.

AMENDMENT V [1791]

No person shall be held to answer for a capital, or otherwise infamous crime, unless on a presentment or indictment of a Grand Jury, except in cases arising in the land or naval forces, or in the Militia, when in actual service in time of War or public danger; nor shall any person be subject for the same offence to be twice put in jeopardy of life or limb; nor shall be compelled in any criminal case to be a witness against himself, nor be deprived of life, liberty, or property, without due process of law; nor shall private property be taken for public use, without just compensation.

AMENDMENT VI [1791]

In all criminal prosecutions, the accused shall enjoy the right to a speedy and public trial, by an impartial jury of the State and district wherein the crime shall have been committed, which district shall have been previously ascertained by law, and to be informed of the nature and cause of the accusation; to be confronted with the witnesses against him; to have compulsory process for obtaining witnesses in his favor, and to have the Assistance of Counsel for his defence.

AMENDMENT VII [1791]

In Suits at common law, where the value in controversy shall exceed twenty dollars, the right of trial by jury shall be preserved, and no fact tried by a jury, shall be otherwise re-examined in any Court of the United States, than according to the rules of the common law.

AMENDMENT VIII [1791]

Excessive bail shall not be required, nor excessive fines imposed, nor cruel and unusual punishments inflicted.

AMENDMENT IX [1791]

The enumeration in the Constitution, of certain rights, shall not be construed to deny or disparage others retained by the people.

AMENDMENT X [1791]

The powers not delegated to the United States by the Constitution, nor prohibited by it to the States, are reserved to the States respectively, or to the people.

AMENDMENT XI [1798]

The Judicial power of the United States shall not be construed to extend to any suit in law or equity, commenced or prosecuted against one of the United States by Citizens of another State, or by Citizens or Subjects of any Foreign State.

AMENDMENT XII [1804]

The Electors shall meet in their respective states and vote by ballot for President and Vice-President, one of whom, at least, shall not be an inhabitant of the same state with themselves; they shall name in their ballots the person voted for as President, and in distinct ballots the person voted for as Vice-President, and they shall make distinct lists of all persons voted for as President, and of all persons voted for as Vice-President, and of the number of votes for each, which lists they shall sign and certify, and transmit sealed to the seat of the government of the United States, directed to the President of the Senate;-The President of the Senate shall, in the presence of the Senate and House of Representatives, open all the certificates and the votes shall then be counted;-The person having the greatest number of votes for President, shall be the President, if such number be a majority of the whole number of Electors appointed; and if no person have such majority, then from the persons having the highest numbers not exceeding three on the list of those voted for as President, the House of Representatives shall choose immediately, by ballot, the President. But in choosing the President, the votes shall be taken by states, the representation from each state having one vote; a quorum for this purpose shall consist of a member or members from two-thirds of the states, and a majority of all the states shall be necessary to a choice. And if the House of Representatives shall not choose a President whenever the right of choice shall devolve upon them, before the fourth day of March next following, then the Vice-President shall act as President, as in the case of the death or other constitutional disability of the President. The person having the greatest number of votes as Vice-President, shall be the Vice-President, if such number be a majority of the whole number of Electors appointed, and if no person have a majority, then from the two highest numbers on the list, the Senate shall choose the Vice-President; a quorum for the purpose shall consist of two-thirds of the whole number of Senators, and a majority of the whole number shall be necessary to a choice. But no person constitutionally ineligible to the office of President shall be eligible to that of Vice-President of the United States.

AMENDMENT XIII [1865]

Section 1. Neither slavery nor involuntary servitude, except as a punishment for crime whereof the party shall have been duly convicted, shall exist within the United States, or any place subject to their jurisdiction.

Section 2. Congress shall have power to enforce this article by appropriate legislation.

AMENDMENT XIV [1868]

Section 1. All persons born or naturalized in the United States, and subject to the jurisdiction thereof, are citizens of the United States and of the State wherein they reside. No State shall make or enforce any law which shall abridge the privileges or immunities of citizens of the United States; nor shall any State deprive any person of life, liberty, or property, without due process of law; nor deny to any person within its jurisdiction the equal protection of the laws.

Section 2. Representatives shall be apportioned among the several States according to their respective numbers, counting the whole number of persons in each

State, excluding Indians not taxed. But when the right to vote at any election for the choice of electors for President and Vice President of the United States, Representatives in Congress, the Executive and Judicial officers of a State, or the members of the Legislature thereof, is denied to any of the male inhabitants of such State, being twenty-one years of age, and citizens of the United States, or in any way abridged, except for participation in rebellion, or other crime, the basis of representation therein shall be reduced in the proportion which the number of such male citizens shall bear to the whole number of male citizens twenty-one years of age in such State.

Section 3. No person shall be a Senator or Representative in Congress, or elector of President and Vice President, or hold any office, civil or military, under the United States, or under any State, who, having previously taken an oath, as a member of Congress, or as an officer of the United States, or as a member of any State legislature, or as an executive or judicial officer of any State, to support the Constitution of the United States, shall have engaged in insurrection or rebellion against the same, or given aid or comfort to the enemies thereof. But Congress may by a vote of two-thirds of each House, remove such disability.

Section 4. The validity of the public debt of the United States, authorized by law, including debts incurred for payment of pensions and bounties for services in suppressing insurrection or rebellion, shall not be questioned. But neither the United States nor any State shall assume or pay any debt or obligation incurred in aid of insurrection or rebellion against the United States, or any claim for the loss or emancipation of any slave; but all such debts, obligations and claims shall be held illegal and void.

Section 5. The Congress shall have power to enforce, by appropriate legislation, the provisions of this article.

AMENDMENT XV [1870]

Section 1. The right of citizens of the United States to vote shall not be denied or abridged by the United States or by any State on account of race, color, or previous condition of servitude.

Section 2. The Congress shall have power to enforce this article by appropriate legislation.

AMENDMENT XVI [1913]

The Congress shall have power to lay and collect taxes on incomes, from whatever source derived, without apportionment among the several States, and without regard to any census or enumeration.

AMENDMENT XVII [1913]

[1] The Senate of the United States shall be composed of two Senators from each State, elected by the people thereof, for six years; and each Senator shall have one vote. The electors in each State shall have the qualifications requisite for electors of the most numerous branch of the State legislatures.

[2] When vacancies happen in the representation of any State in the Senate, the executive authority of such State shall issue writs of election to fill such vacancies:

Provided, That the legislature of any State may empower the executive thereof to make temporary appointments until the people fill the vacancies by election as the legislature may direct.

[3] This amendment shall not be so construed as to affect the election or term of any Senator chosen before it becomes valid as part of the Constitution.

AMENDMENT XVIII [1919]

Section 1. After one year from the ratification of this article the manufacture, sale, or transportation of intoxicating liquors within, the importation thereof into, or the exportation thereof from the United States and all territory subject to the jurisdiction thereof for beverage purposes is hereby prohibited.

Section 2. The Congress and the several States shall have concurrent power to enforce this article by appropriate legislation.

Section 3. This article shall be inoperative unless it shall have been ratified as an amendment to the Constitution by the legislatures of the several States, as provided in the Constitution, within seven years from the date of the submission hereof to the States by the Congress.

AMENDMENT XIX [1920]

[1] The right of citizens of the United States to vote shall not be denied or abridged by the United States or by any State on account of sex.

[2] Congress shall have power to enforce this article by appropriate legislation.

AMENDMENT XX [1933]

Section 1. The terms of the President and Vice President shall end at noon on the 20th day of January, and the terms of Senators and Representatives at noon on the 3d day of January, of the years in which such terms would have ended if this article had not been ratified; and the terms of their successors shall then begin.

Section 2. The Congress shall assemble at least once in every year, and such meeting shall begin at noon on the 3d day of January, unless they shall by law appoint a different day.

Section 3. If, at the time fixed for the beginning of the term of the President, the President elect shall have died, the Vice President elect shall become President. If a President shall not have been chosen before the time fixed for the beginning of his term, or if the President elect shall have failed to qualify, then the Vice President elect shall act as President until a President shall have qualified; and the Congress may by law provide for the case wherein neither a President elect nor a Vice President elect shall have qualified, declaring who shall then act as President, or the manner in which one who is to act shall be selected, and such person shall act accordingly until a President or Vice President shall have qualified.

Section 4. The Congress may by law provide for the case of the death of any of the persons from whom the House of Representatives may choose a President whenever the right of choice shall have devolved upon them, and for the case of the death of any of the persons from whom the Senate may choose a Vice President whenever the right of choice shall have devolved upon them.

Section 5. Sections I and 2 shall take effect on the 15th day of October following the ratification of this article.

Section 6. This article shall be inoperative unless it shall have been ratified as an amendment to the Constitution by the legislatures of three-fourths of the several States within seven years from the date of its submission.

AMENDMENT XXI [1933]

Section 1. The eighteenth article of amendment to the Constitution of the United States is hereby repealed.

Section 2. The transportation or importation into any State, Territory, or possession of the United States for delivery or use therein of intoxicating liquors, in violation of the laws thereof, is hereby prohibited.

Section 3. This article shall be inoperative unless it shall have been ratified as an amendment to the Constitution by conventions in the several States, as provided in the Constitution, within seven years from the date of the submission hereof to the States by the Congress.

AMENDMENT XXII [1951]

Section 1. No person shall be elected to the office of the President more than twice, and no person who has held the office of President, or acted as President, for more than two years of a term to which some other person was elected President shall be elected to the office of the President more than once. But this Article shall not apply to any person holding the office of President when this Article was proposed by the Congress, and shall not prevent any person who may be holding the office of President, or acting as President, during the term within which this Article becomes operative from holding the office of President or acting as President during the remainder of such term.

Section 2. This article shall be inoperative unless it shall have been ratified as an amendment to the Constitution by the legislatures of three-fourths of the several States within seven years from the date of its submission to the States by the Congress.

AMENDMENT XXIII [1961]

Section 1. The District constituting the seat of Government of the United States shall appoint in such manner as the Congress may direct:

A number of electors of President and Vice President equal to the whole number of Senators and Representatives in Congress to which the District would be entitled if it were a State, but in no event more than the least populous State; they shall be in addition to those appointed by the States, but they shall be considered, for the purposes of the election of President and Vice President, to be electors appointed by a State; and they shall meet in the District and perform such duties as provided by the twelfth article of amendment.

Section 2. The Congress shall have power to enforce this article by appropriate legislation.

AMENDMENT XXIV [1964]

Section 1. The right of citizens of the United States to vote in any primary or other election for President or Vice President, for electors for President or Vice President, or for Senator or Representative in Congress, shall not be denied or abridged by the United States or any State by reason of failure to pay any poll tax or other tax.

Section 2. The Congress shall have power to enforce this article by appropriate legislation.

AMENDMENT XXV [1967]

Section 1. In case of the removal of the President from office or of his death or resignation, the Vice President shall become President.

Section 2. Whenever there is a vacancy in the office of the Vice President, the President shall nominate a Vice President who shall take office upon confirmation by a majority vote of both Houses of Congress.

Section 3. Whenever the President transmits to the President pro tempore of the Senate and the Speaker of the House of Representatives his written declaration that he is unable to discharge the powers and duties of his office, and until he transmits to them a written declaration to the contrary, such powers and duties shall be discharged by the Vice President as Acting President.

Section 4. Whenever the Vice President and a majority of either the principal officers of the executive departments or of such other body as Congress may by law provide, transmit to the President pro tempore of the Senate and the Speaker of the House of Representatives their written declaration that the President is unable to discharge the powers and duties of his office, the Vice President shall immediately assume the powers and duties of the office as Acting President.

Thereafter, when the President transmits to the President pro temp ore of the Senate and the Speaker of the House of Representatives his written declaration that no inability exists, he shall resume the powers and duties of his office unless the Vice President and a majority of either the principal officers of the executive department or of such other body as Congress may by law provide, transmit within four days to the President pro tempore of the Senate and the Speaker of the House of Representatives their written declaration that the President is unable to discharge the powers and duties of his office. Thereupon Congress shall decide the issue, assembling within forty-eight hours for that purpose if not in session. If the Congress, within twenty-one days after receipt of the latter written declaration, or, if Congress is not in session, within twenty-one days after Congress is required to assemble, determines by two-thirds vote of both Houses that the President is unable to discharge the powers and duties of his office, the Vice President shall continue to discharge the same as Acting President; otherwise, the President shall resume the powers and duties of his office.

AMENDMENT XXVI [1971]

Section 1. The right of citizens of the United States, who are eighteen years of age or older, to vote shall not be denied or abridged by the United States or by any State on account of age.

Section 2. The Congress shall have power to enforce this article by appropriate legislation.

AMENDMENT XXVII [1992]

No law, varying the compensation for the services of the Senators and Representatives, shall take effect, until an election of Representatives shall have intervened.

APPENDIX B

THE SUPREME COURT'S CANONS OF STATUTORY INTERPRETATION

■ ■ ■

This is a collection of canons invoked by the Rehnquist and Roberts Courts (1986–2014) and divided into categories that parallel the typology provided in Chapters 5, 6 and 7.[*]

TEXTUAL CANONS

- Plain meaning rule: follow the plain meaning of the statutory text,[1] except when textual plain meaning requires an absurd result[2] or suggests a scrivener's error.[3]

LINGUISTIC INFERENCES

- *Expressio* (or *inclusio*) *unius*: expression of one thing suggests the exclusion of others.[4] Inapplicable if context suggests listing is not comprehensive.[5]

- *Noscitur a sociis*: interpret a general term to be similar to more specific terms in a series.[6] *Noscitur* is often not helpful when applied to a technical statute whose details were hammered out through a complex process.[7]

---

[*] Diana Rusk, Yale Law School Class of 2009, provided invaluable assistance in the preparation of this appendix.

[1] Mohamad v. Palestinian Auth., 132 S.Ct. 1702 (2012); Pacific Operators Offshire, LLC v. Valladolid, 132 S.Ct. 680 (2012); Massachusetts v. EPA, 549 U.S. 497 (2007); Arlington Cent. Sch. Dist. Bd. of Educ. v. Murphy, 548 U.S. 291, 296 (2006); Barnhart v. Thomas, 540 U.S. 20, 26–29 (2003); West Virginia Univ. Hosps. v. Casey, 499 U.S. 83 (1991); United States v. Providence Journal Co., 485 U.S. 693, 700–01 (1988).

[2] Utility Air Regulatory Group v. EPA, 134 S.Ct. 2427 (2014) (plurality and concurring opinions); Brown v. Plata, 131 S.Ct. 1910, 1950–51 (2011) (Scalia, J., dissenting); Zuni Pub. Sch. Dist. No. 89 v. Department of Educ., 550 U.S. 81, 104–07 (2007) (Stevens, J., concurring); United States v. Wilson, 503 U.S. 329, 334 (1992); Green v. Bock Laundry Mach. Co., 490 U.S. 504, 509–11 (1989).

[3] Lamie v. United States Trustee, 540 U.S. 526, 530–31 (2004); United States Nat'l Bank v. Independent Ins. Agents, 508 U.S. 439, 462 (1993).

[4] POM Wonderful LLC v. Coca-Cola Co., 134 S.Ct. 2228, 2237–38 (2014); Hinck v. United States, 550 U.S. 501 (2007); TRW, Inc. v. Andrews, 534 U.S. 19 (2001); City of Chicago v. Environmental Def. Fund, 511 U.S. 328 (1994); United States v. Smith, 499 U.S. 160 (1991); Mississippi Band of Choctaw Indians v. Holyfield, 490 U.S. 30, 46–47 & n.22 (1989); Chan v. Korean Air Lines, Ltd., 490 U.S. 122, 133–34 (1989).

[5] Marrama v. Citizens Bank of Mass., 549 U.S. 365 (2007); Christensen v. Harris County, 529 U.S. 576, 583–84 (2000); Burns v. United States, 501 U.S. 129, 136 (1991); Sullivan v. Hudson, 490 U.S. 877, 891–92 (1989).

[6] Entergy Corp. v. Riverkeeper, Inc., 556 U.S. 208, 222 (2009); Circuit City Stores, Inc. v. Adams, 532 U.S. 105 (2001); Gustafson v. Alloyd Co., 513 U.S. 561, 575 (1995); Dole v. United Steelworkers of Am., 494 U.S. 26, 36 (1990); Massachusetts v. Morash, 490 U.S. 107, 114–15 (1989).

[7] Bilski v. Kappos, 561 U.S. 593 (2010); S.D. Warren Co. v. Maine Bd. of Envtl. Prot., 547 U.S. 370 (2006).

- *Ejusdem generis*: interpret a general term to reflect the class of objects reflected in more specific terms accompanying it.[8] *Ejusdem* might be trumped by other canons, such as the rule against redundancy.[9]

- Follow ordinary usage of terms, unless Congress gives them a specified or technical meaning.[10]

- Where Congress uses terms that have settled meaning, either by common usage or through the common law, interpreters should apply that settled meaning.[11]

- Defer to experts, including agencies, regarding the meaning of technical terminology.[12]

- Follow dictionary definitions of terms,[13] unless Congress has provided a specific definition.[14] Consider dictionaries of the era in which the statute was enacted.[15] For technical terms, consult specialized dictionaries.[16] Do not credit nonstandard, "idiosyncratic" dictionary definitions.[17]

- Rules of Construction Act (Dictionary Act), 1 U.S.C. § 1 et seq., contains default definitions that apply if Congress fails to define a particular term.[18]

- A statute has a plain meaning if you'd use its terminology at a cocktail party, and "no one would look at you funny."[19]

---

[8]   James v. United States, 550 U.S. 192 (2007); Circuit City Stores, Inc. v. Adams, 532 U.S. 105 (2001); Hughey v. United States, 495 U.S. 411, 419 (1990); Norfolk & Western Ry. Co. v. American Train Dispatchers' Ass'n, 499 U.S. 117, 129 (1991).

[9]   Ali v. Federal Bur. of Prisons, 552 U.S. 214 (2008); Babbitt v. Sweet Home Chapter of Communities for a Great Oregon, 515 U.S. 687 (1995).

[10]   Octane Fitness, LLC v. Icon Health & Fitness, Inc., 134 S.Ct. 1749 (2014); Lopez v. Gonzales, 549 U.S. 47 (2006); Pasquantino v. United States, 544 U.S. 349, 355 (2005); Will v. Michigan Dep't of State Police, 491 U.S. 58, 64 (1989).

[11]   CTS Corp. v. Waldburger, 134 S.Ct. 2175 (2014); Merck & Co. v. Reynolds, 559 U.S. 633 (2010); Stewart v. Dutra Constr. Co., 543 U.S. 481, 487 (2005); Scheidler v. NOW, Inc., 537 U.S. 393, 402 (2003); United States v. Wells, 519 U.S. 482, 491 (1997); Community for Creative Non-Violence v. Reid, 490 U.S. 730, 739 (1989).

[12]   Zuni Pub. Sch. Dist. No. 89 v. Department of Educ., 550 U.S. 81 (2007).

[13]   CTS Corp. v. Waldburger, 134 S.Ct. 2175 (2014) (Black's); Taniguchi v. Kan Pacific Saipan, Ltd., 132 S.Ct. 1997 (2012) (many dictionaries); Rapanos v. United States, 547 U.S. 715 (2006) (plurality opinion.) (Webster's Second); Muscarello v. United States, 524 U.S. 125 (1998) (Oxford English); Pittston Coal Group v. Sebben, 488 U.S. 105, 113 (1988) (Webster's Third).

[14]   Burwell v. Hobby Lobby Stores, Inc., 134 S.Ct. 2751 (June 30, 2014); Babbitt v. Sweet Home Chapter of Communities for a Great Oregon, 515 U.S. 687 (1995).

[15]   Bilski v. Kappos, 561 U.S. 593 (2010); Permanent Mission of India to the United Nations v. City of New York, 551 U.S. 193 (2007); Cook County v. United States ex rel. Chandler, 538 U.S. 119, 125–27 (2003); St. Francis College v. Al-Khazraji, 481 U.S. 604 (1987).

[16]   Zuni Pub. Sch. Dist. No. 89 v. Department of Educ., 550 U.S. 81 (2007).

[17]   MCI v. AT&T, 512 U.S. 218 (1994) (disrespecting Webster's Third for including colloquial as well as standard definitions).

[18]   Burwell v. Hobby Lobby Stores, Inc., 134 S.Ct. 2751 (June 30, 2014) (definition of "person" presumptively includes corporations); Stewart v. Dutra Constr. Co., 543 U.S. 481 (2005).

[19]   Johnson v. United States, 529 U.S. 694, 718 (2000) (Scalia, J., dissenting).

GRAMMAR AND SYNTAX

- Punctuation rule: Congress is presumed to follow accepted punctuation standards, so that placements of commas and other punctuation are assumed to be meaningful.[20]

- Grammar rule: Congress is presumed to follow accepted standards of grammar.[21]

- Rule of the last antecedent: referential and qualifying words or phrases refer only to the last antecedent, unless contrary to the apparent legislative intent derived from the sense of the entire enactment.[22] Do not have to apply this rule if not practical.[23]

- "May" is usually precatory and connotes decisionmaking discretion,[24] while "shall" is usually mandatory and suggests less discretion.[25]

- "Or" means in the alternative.[26]

TEXTUAL INTEGRITY (WHOLE ACT RULE)

- Each statutory provision should be read by reference to the whole act.[27] Statutory interpretation is a "holistic" endeavor.[28]

- The statute's preamble may provide clues to statutory meaning,[29] as may the title.[30]

- Presumption against redundancy: avoid interpreting a provision in a way that would render other provisions of the statute superfluous or unnecessary.[31] This

---

[20]   Jama v. Immigration & Customs Enforcement, 543 U.S. 335, 344 (2005) (significance of periods); United States v. Ron Pair Enters., 489 U.S. 235, 241–42 (1989) (comma placement); San Francisco Arts & Athletics, Inc. v. United States Olympic Comm'n, 483 U.S. 522, 528–29 (1987).

[21]   Carr v. United States, 560 U.S. 438 (2010); Limtiaco v. Camacho, 549 U.S. 483 (2007); Rapanos v. United States, 547 U.S. 715 (2006) (plurality opinion); Jama v. Immigration & Customs Enforcement, 543 U.S. 335. (2005).

[22]   Jama v. Immigration & Customs Enforcement, 543 U.S. 335 (2005); Barnhart v. Thomas, 540 U.S. 20, 26 (2003); Nobelman v. American Savs. Bank, 508 U.S. 324, 330 (1993).

[23]   Nobelman v. American Sav. Bank, 508 U.S. 324, 330–31 (1993).

[24]   Jama v. Immigration & Customs Enforcement, 543 U.S. 335 (2005); Lopez v. Davis, 531 U.S. 230 (2001) ("may" vests wide discretion in agency).

[25]   Mallard v. United States Dist. Ct., 490 U.S. 296, 302 (1989).

[26]   Loughrin v. United States, 134 S.Ct. 2384, 2389–90 (2014); Hawaiian Airlines v. Norris, 512 U.S. 246, 253–54 (1994).

[27]   Samantar v. Yousuf, 560 U.S. 305 (2010); Ricci v. DeStefano, 557 U.S. 557 (2009); Ledbetter v. Goodyear Tire & Rubber Co., 550 U.S. 618 (2007); Gonzales v. Oregon, 546 U.S. 243, 273–74 (2006); Doe v. Chao, 540 U.S. 614 (2004) (considering uncodified parts of the "whole act"); Clark v. Martinez, 543 U.S. 371 (2005); Babbitt v. Sweet Home Chapter of Communities for a Great Oregon, 515 U.S. 687 (1995); Pavelic & Leflore v. Marvel Entm't Group, 493 U.S. 120, 123–24 (1989); Massachusetts v. Morash, 490 U.S. 107, 114–15 (1989).

[28]   Burwell v. Hobby Lobby Stores, Inc., 134 S.Ct. 2751 (2014); United Sav. Ass'n v. Timbers of Inwood Forest Assocs., Ltd., 484 U.S. 365, 371 (1988).

[29]   Sutton v. United Airlines, Inc., 527 U.S. 471 (1999) (majority and concurring opinions)).

[30]   Almendarez-Torres v. United States, 523 U.S. 224, 234 (1998).

[31]   Fifth Third Bancorp v. Didenhoeffer, 134 S.Ct. 2459 (2014); Ricci v. DeStefano, 557 U.S. 557 (2009); Circuit City Stores, Inc. v. Adams, 532 U.S. 105 (2001); United States v. Alaska, 521 U.S. 1 (1997); Walters v. Metropolitan Educ. Enters., Inc., 519 U.S. 202 (1997); Rake v. Wade, 508 U.S. 464 (1993); Kungys v. United States, 485 U.S. 759, 778 (1988) (plurality opinion by Scalia, J.).

presumption must give way when offset by other evidence of statutory meaning, however.[32]

- Presumption of statutory consistency: interpret the same or similar terms in a statute the same way.[33] Presumption rebutted when other evidence suggests Congress was using the same term in different ways.[34]

- Presumption of meaningful variation: different statutory wording suggests different statutory meaning,[35] especially when Congress considered and rejected the alternate wording.[36] Presumption inapplicable when there is a reasonable explanation for variation (e.g., different provisions are enacted at different times).[37]

- Avoid interpreting a provision in a way that is inconsistent with the overall structure of the statute[38] *or* with another provision[39] *or* with a subsequent amendment to the statute[40] *or* with another statute enacted by a Congress relying on a particular interpretation.[41]

- Presumption of purposive amendment: statutory amendments are meant to have real and substantial effect.[42]

- Avoid the implication of broad congressional delegation of agency authority when statute carefully limits agency authority in particular matters.[43]

- Avoid broad readings of statutory provisions if Congress has specifically provided for the broader policy in more specific language elsewhere.[44]

---

[32]   United States v. Home Concrete & Supply, LLC, 132 S.Ct. 1836 (2012); Gutierrez v. Ada, 528 U.S. 250 (2000); Landgraf v. USI Film Prods., 511 U.S. 240, 259–60 (1994).

[33]   Robers v. United States, 134 S.Ct. 1854 (2014); Powerex Corp. v. Reliant Energy Servs., Inc., 551 U.S. 224 (2007); IBP, Inc. v. Alvarez, 546 U.S. 21, 34 (2005); Commissioner v. Lundy, 516 U.S. 235, 249–50 (1996); Gustafson v. Alloyd Co., 513 U.S. 561, 570 (1995); Sullivan v. Stroop, 496 U.S. 478, 484 (1990); United Sav. Ass'n v. Timbers of Inwood Forest Assocs., Ltd., 484 U.S. 365, 371 (1988).

[34]   Utility Air Regulatory Group v. EPA, 134 S.Ct. 2427 (2014); Environmental Defense v. Duke Energy Corp., 549 U.S. 561 (2007); Robinson v. Shell Oil Co., 519 U.S. 337, 343–44 (1997); Dewsnup v. Timm, 502 U.S. 410, 417 & n.3 (1992).

[35]   Burwell v. Hobby Lobby Stores, Inc., 134 S.Ct. 2751, 2772–74 (2014); Loughrin v. United States, 134 S.Ct. 2384, 2390–92 (2014); Lawrence v. Florida, 549 U.S. 327 (2007); Lopez v. Gonzales, 549 U.S. 47 (2006); Lindh v. Murphy, 521 U.S. 320 (1997); Keene Corp. v. United States, 508 U.S. 200, 208 (1993); Gozlon-Peretz v. United States, 498 U.S. 395, 404–05 (1991). The leading case is Russello v. United States, 464 U.S. 16, 23 (1983).

[36]   Hamdan v. Rumsfeld, 548 U.S. 557 (2006).

[37]   Gutierrez v. Ada, 528 U.S. 250 (2000); Field v. Mans, 516 U.S. 59, 67–69 (1995).

[38]   Abramski v. United States, 134 S.Ct. 2259 (2014); Samantar v. Yousuf, 560 U.S. 305 (2010); Ledbetter v. Goodyear Tire & Rubber Co., 550 U.S. 618 (2007); Beck v. PACE Int'l Union, 551 U.S. 96 (2007).

[39]   Petrella v. MGM, Inc., 134 S.Ct. 1962 (2014); Ricci v. DeStefano, 557 U.S. 557 (2009); Babbitt v. Sweet Home Chapter of Communities for a Great Oregon, 515 U.S. 687 (1995); Gade v. National Solid Waste Management Ass'n, 505 U.S. 88, 100–01 (1992); United Sav. Ass'n v. Timbers of Inwood Forest Assocs., Ltd., 484 U.S. 365, 371 (1988).

[40]   Gonzales v. Oregon, 546 U.S. 243, 257–58 (2006).

[41]   FDA v. Brown & Williamson Tobacco Corp., 529 U.S. 120, 144 (2000).

[42]   Rumsfeld v. Forum for Academic & Institutional Rights, Inc., 547 U.S. 47 (2006); Babbitt v. Sweet Home Chapter of Communities for a Great Oregon, 515 U.S. 687 (1995).

[43]   Gonzales v. Oregon, 547 U.S. 243, 262–63 (2006).

[44]   Arlington Cent. Sch. Dist. Bd. of Educ. v. Murphy, 548 U.S. 291 (2006); Jama v. Immigration & Customs Enforcement, 543 U.S. 335 (2005); Custis v. United States, 511 U.S. 485, 491 (1994); West Virginia Univ. Hosps. v. Casey, 499 U.S. 83, 99 (1991).

- Broad term is presumptively ambiguous if Congress has elsewhere used more targeted terminology.[45]

- Specific provisions targeting a particular issue apply instead of provisions more generally covering the issue.[46]

- Provisos and statutory exceptions should be read narrowly.[47]

- Do not create exceptions in addition to those specified by Congress.[48]

EXTRINSIC SOURCE CANONS

AGENCY INTERPRETATIONS

- *Skidmore* deference. Agency interpretations are entitled to respect to the extent that they have "power to persuade" based upon consistency, factual basis, and expertise.[49] Contrariwise, agency views that are shifting or insufficiently developed have little or no persuasive value.[50]

- Even informal and unsettled agency interpretations (such as those embodied in handbooks or litigation briefs) may be useful confirmations for the interpreter's interpretation of statutory language.[51]

- *Chevron* deference. "Reasonable" agency interpretations pursuant to congressional delegation of lawmaking authority are binding on courts unless Congress has directly addressed the issue.[52] *Chevron* might also apply to notice-and-comment rules filling statutory gaps that the agency reasonably treats as binding on itself and the public.[53] The agency's discretion is at its height when the agency decides not to enforce a statute.[54]

- For *Chevron* purposes, whether Congress has delegated the agency lawmaking authority is itself a matter of statutory interpretation.[55] Presumption against

---

[45]   Zuni Pub. Sch. Dist. No. 89 v. Department of Educ., 550 U.S. 81 (2007).

[46]   Green v. Bock Laundry Mach. Co., 490 U.S. 504, 524–26 (1989); Crawford Fitting Co. v. J.T. Gibbons, Inc., 482 U.S. 437, 444–45 (1987).

[47]   Maracich v. Spears, 133 S.Ct. 2191, 2200 (2013); Cherokee Nation of Oklahoma v. Leavitt, 543 U.S. 631 (2005); City of Edmonds v. Oxford House, Inc., 514 U.S. 725, 732 (1995). The leading case is Commissioner v. Clark, 489 U.S. 726, 739–40 (1989). But see Republic of Iraq v. Beaty, 556 U.S. 848, 857–58 (2009) (relaxing this presumption in foreign affairs context).

[48]   Argentina v. NML Capital, Ltd., 134 S.Ct. 2250 (2014); United States v. Smith, 499 U.S. 160, 166–67 (1991).

[49]   Beck v. PACE Int'l Union, 551 U.S. 96 (2007); Gonzales v. Oregon, 546 U.S. 243, 255–56 (2006); United States v. Mead Corp., 533 U.S. 218, 226–27 (2001); EEOC v. Arabian Am. Oil Co., 499 U.S. 244 (1991). The leading case is Skidmore v. Swift & Co., 323 U.S. 134, 140 (1944).

[50]   Burlington Northern & Santa Fe Ry. v. White, 548 U.S. 53 (2006).

[51]   S.D. Warren Co. v. Maine Bd. of Envtl. Prot., 547 U.S. 370 (2006).

[52]   Utility Air Regulatory Group v. EPA, 134 S.Ct. 2427 (2014) (plurality and concurring opinions); Scialabba v. Cuellar de Osorio, 134 S.Ct. 2191 (2014) (plurality and concurring opinions); Zuni Pub. Sch. Dist. No. 89 v. Department of Educ., 550 U.S. 81 (2007) (majority and concurring opinions); National Cable & Telecommunications Ass'n v. Brand X Internet Servs., 545 U.S. 967 (2005); ABF Freight Sys., Inc. v. NLRB, 510 U.S. 317, 324 (1994); Sullivan v. Everhart, 494 U.S. 83, 88–89 (1990); K Mart Corp. v. Cartier, Inc., 486 U.S. 281, 291–92 (1988). The leading case is Chevron U.S.A., Inc. v. Natural Resources Defense Council, 467 U.S. 837 (1984).

[53]   Long Island Care at Home, Ltd. v. Coke, 551 U.S. 158 (2007).

[54]   Massachusetts v. EPA, 549 U.S. 497 (2007).

[55]   City of Arlington, Texas v. FCC, 133 S.Ct. 1863 (2013) (deferential on this issue); Gonzales v. Oregon, 546 U.S. 243 (2006) (not so deferential).

congressional delegation of authority for agency to make fundamental changes in the statute.[56] The Court demands a clear statement authorizing agency constructions that press the envelope of constitutional validity.[57]

- *Seminole Rock* deference. Agency interpretation of its own regulations is controlling unless "plainly erroneous or inconsistent with the regulation."[58] Rule does not apply when agency rule merely "parrots" the statute,[59] or where agency interpretation has been unstable over time.[60]

- *Curtiss-Wright* deference. In matters of foreign affairs and national security, presidential or executive statutory interpretations enjoy a super-strong presumption of correctness.[61] (The executive is still bound by statutory and treaty directives.[62]) Similar deference for executive branch views of federal jurisdiction over foreign states.[63]

- Courts accord great weight to executive department interpretation of treaties.[64]

CONTINUITY IN LAW

- Super-strong presumption of correctness for statutory precedents,[65] sometimes including statutory precedents whose narrow holding has been overridden by

---

[56]   Utility Air Regulatory Group v. EPA, 134 S.Ct. 2427 (2104) (plurality and concurring opinions); Gonzales v. Oregon, 546 U.S. 243 (2006); FDA v. Brown & Williamson Tobacco Corp., 529 U.S. 120 (2000); MCI v. AT&T, 512 U.S. 218 (1994).

[57]   Bond v. United States, 134 S.Ct. 2077 (2014); Wyeth v. Levine, 555 U.S. 555, 576 (2009); Rapanos v. United States, 547 U.S. 715 (2006) (plurality opinion); Edward J. DeBartolo Corp. v. Florida Gulf Coast Building & Constr. Trades Council, 485 U.S. 568, 575 (1988).

[58]   Pliva, Inc. v. Mensing, 131 S.Ct. 2567, 2575–76 (2011); Chase Bank NA v. McCoy, 131 S.Ct. 871, 880 (2011); Coeur Alaska, Inc. v. Southeastern Alaska Conserv. Coun., 557 U.S. 261 (2009); Auer v. Robbins, 519 U.S. 452, 461–63 (1997); Thomas Jefferson Univ. v. Shalala, 512 U.S. 504, 512 (1994); Mullins Coal Co. v. Director, Office of Workers' Compensation Programs, 484 U.S. 135, 159 (1987). The leading case is Bowles v. Seminole Rock & Sand Co., 325 U.S. 410, 414 (1945). This canon has been questioned in Decker v. Northwest Envir. Def. Center, 133 S.Ct. 1326, 1339 (2013) (Scalia, J., concurring).

[59]   Gonzales v. Oregon, 546 U.S. 243, 257 (2006).

[60]   Commissioner v. Schleier, 515 U.S. 323 (1995); Bowen v. Georgetown Univ. Hosp., 488 U.S. 204 (1988).

[61]   Hamdi v. Rumsfeld, 542 U.S. 507, 518 (2004) (plurality opinion of O'Connor, J.); id. at 580–81 (Thomas, J., concurring in part); Cheney v. U.S. Dist. Court, 542 U.S. 367 (2004); Crosby v. National Foreign Trade Council, 530 U.S. 363 (2000); Department of Navy v. Egan, 484 U.S. 518 (1988). The leading case is United States v. Curtiss-Wright Export Corp., 299 U.S. 304 (1936).

[62]   Hamdan v. Rumsfeld, 548 U.S. 557 (2006).

[63]   Republic of Austria v. Altmann, 541 U.S. 677, 689–90 (2004). But see Argentina v. NML Capital, 134 S.Ct. 2250 (2014) (ignoring this canon).

[64]   Medellin v. Texas, 552 U.S. 491 (2008); Sanchez-Llamas v. Oregon, 548 U.S. 331 (2006); El Al Israel Airlines v. Tsui Yuan Tseng, 525 U.S. 155 (1999).

[65]   Halliburton Co. v. Erica P. John Fund, Inc., 134 S.Ct. 2398 (2014); Michigan v. Bay Mills Indian Community, 134 S.Ct. 2024 (2014); CSX Transp., Inc. v. McBride, 131 S.Ct. 2630, 2641 (2011); John R. Sand & Gravel Co. v. United States, 552 U.S. 130 (2007); Hohn v. United States, 524 U.S. 236, 251 (1998); Neal v. United States, 516 U.S. 284 (1996); California v. FERC, 495 U.S. 490, 498–99 (1990); Patterson v. McLean Credit Union, 491 U.S. 164 (1989).

Congress.[66] The super-strong rule against overruling statutory precedents is less applicable to the Sherman Act, which is a common law statute.[67]

- Wrongly decided precedents that are also inconsistent with recent legal developments can be overruled.[68]

- Where a court decision follows an agency interpretation filling a gap in the law left by Congress *(Chevron),* a revised agency interpretation through rulemaking is not barred by *stare decisis.*[69]

- Presumption of continuity: Congress does not create discontinuities in legal rights and obligations without some clear statement.[70]

- Presumption against repeals by implication.[71] But where there is a clear repugnancy between a more recent statutory scheme and an earlier one, partial repeal will be inferred.[72]

- Presumption against hiding elephants in mouseholes: Congress usually does not alter the fundamental details of a regulatory scheme in vague or ancillary provisions.[73]

- Presumption that Congress uses same term consistently in different statutes.[74]

- Presumption that statutes be interpreted consistent with international law and treaties.[75] But international agreements do not trump the plain meaning of federal statutes.[76]

---

[66]   Ledbetter v. Goodyear Tire & Rubber Co., 550 U.S. 618 (2007); Arlington Cent. Sch. Dist. Bd. of Educ. v. Murphy, 548 U.S. 291 (2006); Public Emp. Ret. Sys. of Ohio v. Betts, 492 U.S. 158 (1989). This canon is controversial within the Court, see *Ledbetter,* 550 U.S. at 652–54 (Ginsburg, J., dissenting), and, even more, within Congress, which angrily overrode both *Betts* and *Ledbetter.*

[67]   Leegin Creative Leather Prods. v. PSKS, Inc., 551 U.S. 877 (2007); State Oil Co. v. Khan, 522 U.S. 3 (1997).

[68]   Leegin Creative Leather Prods. v. PSKS, Inc., 551 U.S. 877 (2007); Bowles v. Russell, 127 S.Ct. 2360 (2007); Rodriguez de Quijas v. Shearson/American Express, Inc., 490 U.S. 477, 480–81 (1989).

[69]   National Cable & Telecomm. Serv. v. Brand X Internet Servs., 545 U.S. 967 (2005); Christensen v. Harris County, 529 U.S. 576, 589 (2000) (Souter, J., concurring); United States v. Watts, 519 U.S. 148 (1997) (Breyer, J., concurring). This canon does not apply when it appears that a court has closed off agency discretion. United States v. Home Concrete & Supply, LLC, 132 S.Ct. 1836 (2012)

[70]   POM Wonderful LLC v. Coca-Cola Co., 134 S.Ct. 2228 (2014); Pacific Operators Offshire, LLC v. Valladolid, 132 S.Ct. 680 (2012) (concurring opinion); Green v. Bock Laundry Mach. Co., 490 U.S. 504, 521–22 (1989); Finley v. United States, 490 U.S. 545, 554 (1989).

[71]   POM Wonderful LLC v. Coca-Cola Co., 134 S.Ct. 2228 (2014); Hamdan v. Rumsfeld, 548 U.S. 557 (2006); Granholm v. Heald, 544 U.S. 460 (2005); Branch v. Smith, 538 U.S. 254, 273 (2003); Pittsburgh & Lake Erie R.R. v. Railway Labor Executives' Ass'n, 491 U.S. 490, 509 (1989); Traynor v. Turnage, 485 U.S. 535, 547–48 (1988). The leading case is Morton v. Mancari, 417 U.S. 535 (1974).

[72]   Credit Suisse Securities (USA) LLC v. Billing, 551 U.S. 264 (2007).

[73]   Gonzales v. Oregon, 546 U.S. 243, 267 (2006); Whitman v. American Trucking Ass'ns, Inc., 531 U.S. 457, 468 (2001); FDA v. Brown & Williamson Tobacco Corp., 529 U.S. 120, 160 (2000).

[74]   Hawaiian Airlines v. Norris, 512 U.S. 246, 254 (1994); Smith v. United States, 508 U.S. 223, 234–35 (1993); Pierce v. Underwood, 487 U.S. 552 (1988).

[75]   Spector v. Norwegian Cruise Line Ltd., 545 U.S. 119 (2005) (majority and concurring opinions); Hamdi v. Rumsfeld, 542 U.S. 507 (2004) (plurality opinion); INS v. Cardoza-Fonseca, 480 U.S. 421 (1987) (strong presumption when statute is implementing an international agreement).

[76]   Société Nationale Industrielle Aerospatialle v. U.S. Dist. Ct., 482 U.S. 522, 538–39 (1987).

- Borrowed statute rule: when Congress borrows a statute, it adopts by implication interpretations placed on that statute,[77] absent indication to the contrary.[78]

- *In pari materia* rule: when similar statutory provisions are found in comparable statutory schemes, interpreters should presumptively apply them the same way.[79]

- Re-enactment rule: when Congress re-enacts a statute, it incorporates settled interpretations of the re-enacted statute.[80] The rule is inapplicable when there is no settled standard Congress could have known.[81]

- Acquiescence rules: consistent agency or Supreme Court interpretation known to Congress is presumed correct.[82] Also, consider unbroken line of lower court decisions interpreting statute, but do not give them decisive weight.[83]

EXTRINSIC LEGISLATIVE SOURCES

- Statutory history (the formal evolution of a statute, as Congress amends it over the years) is always potentially relevant.[84]

- Consider legislative history (the internal evolution of a statute before enactment) if the statute is ambiguous.[85] Legislative history may also be useful to confirm statutory plain meaning.[86]

- Committee reports (especially conference committee reports reflecting the understanding of both House and Senate) are the most authoritative legislative

---

[77] Molzof v. United States, 502 U.S. 301, 307 (1992); Metropolitan Life Ins. Co. v. Taylor, 481 U.S. 58, 65–66 (1987).

[78] Shannon v. United States, 512 U.S. 573, 581 (1994).

[79] Hardt v. Reliance Standard Life Ins. Co., 560 U.S. 242 (2010); Ledbetter v. Goodyear Tire & Rubber Co., 550 U.S. 618 (2007) (finding NLRA but not EPA analogous to Title VII for limitations purposes).

[80] Merck & Co. v. Reynolds, 559 U.S. 633 (2010); Davis v. United States, 495 U.S. 472, 482 (1990); Pierce v. Underwood, 487 U.S. 552 (1988).

[81] Jama v. Immigration & Customs Enforcement, 543 U.S. 335 (2005).

[82] Michigan v. Bay Mills Indian Community, 134 S.Ct. 2024 (2014); Zuni Pub. Sch. Dist. No. 89 v. Department of Educ., 550 U.S. 81 (2007) (agency interpretation); FDA v. Brown & Williamson Tobacco Corp., 529 U.S. 120 (2000) (agency).

[83] Gonzalez v. Crosby, 545 U.S. 524 (2005); General Dynamics Land Sys., Inc. v. Cline, 540 U.S. 581 (2004); National Archives & Records Admin. v. Favish, 541 U.S. 157 (2004); Monessen Sw. Ry. Co. v. Morgan, 486 U.S. 330, 338–39 (1988).

[84] Burwell v. Hobby Lobby Stores, Inc., 134 S.Ct. 2751 (2014); Powerex Corp. v. Reliant Energy Servs., Inc., 551 U.S. 224 (2007); Ballard v. Commissioner, 544 U.S. 40 (2005). Unlike reference to internal legislative materials, this canon is *not* controversial within the Court.

[85] Bond v. United States, 134 S.Ct. 2077 (2014); Safeco Ins. Co. of Am. v. Burr, 551 U.S. 47 (2007); Zuni Pub. Sch. Dist. No. 89 v. Department of Educ., 550 U.S. 81 (2007); Gonzales v. Oregon, 546 U.S. 243, 257–58 (2006); Rumsfeld v. Forum for Academic & Institutional Rights, 547 U.S. 47 (2006); Koons Buick Pontiac GMC, Inc. v. Nigh, 543 U.S. 50, 62–64 (2004); id. at 65–66 (Stevens, J., concurring); FDA v. Brown & Williamson Tobacco Corp., 529 U.S. 120 (2000); Babbitt v. Sweet Home Chapter of Communities for a Great Oregon, 515 U.S. 687 (1995); Wisconsin Pub. Intervenor v. Mortier, 501 U.S. 597, 610 n.4 (1991). This canon is controversial within the Court. See id. at 616–17 (Scalia, J., concurring in the judgment). Cf. James v. United States, 127 S.Ct. 1586, 1593 (2007) (legislative history not useful if provision is obsolete).

[86] Loughrin v. United States, 134 S.Ct. 2384 (2014); Carr v. United States, 560 U.S. 438 (2010); Samantar v. Yousuf, 560 U.S. 305 (2010); Shinseki v. Sanders, 556 U.S. 396, 406–07 (2009); United States v. Ressam, 553 U.S. 272, 275–76 (2008).

history,[87] but cannot trump a textual plain meaning,[88] and should not be relied on if they are themselves ambiguous or imprecise.[89]

- Committee report language that cannot be tied to a specific statutory provision cannot be credited.[90] House and Senate reports inconsistent with one another should be discounted.[91]

- Caution against interpretation considered and rejected by floor vote of a chamber of Congress or committee.[92] Cautionary principle inapplicable when it is not clear why Congress rejected the proposal.[93]

- Floor statements, especially by statutory sponsors, can be used to confirm apparent meaning.[94]

- Public give-and-take between Members of Congress and executive department drafters or sponsors during committee hearings are relevant if they illuminate a shared meaning of statutory language by the participants closest to the process.[95]

- The "dog didn't bark" canon: presumption that prior legal rule should be retained if no one in legislative deliberations even mentioned the rule or discussed any changes in the rule.[96]

---

[87] Brown v. Plata, 131 S.Ct. 1910, 1937 (2011); Tellabs, Inc. v. Makor Issues & Rights, Ltd., 551 U.S. 308 (2007); Rumsfeld v. Forum for Academic & Institutional Rights, 547 U.S. 47 (2006); Cherokee Nation of Oklahoma v. Leavitt, 543 U.S. 631 (2005); Intel Corp. v. Advanced Micro Devices, Inc., 542 U.S. 241 (2004); Jones v. R.R. Donnelley & Sons Co., 541 U.S. 369 (2004); Boeing Co. v. United States, 537 U.S. 437 (2003); Johnson v. DeGrandy, 512 U.S. 997, 1010–11 & n.9 (1994).

[88] Arlington Cent. Sch. Dist. Bd. of Educ. v. Murphy, 548 U.S. 291 (2006) (majority and concurring opinions); City of Chicago v. Environmental Def. Fund, 511 U.S. 328, 337 (1994); American Hosp. Ass'n v. NLRB, 499 U.S. 606, 613 (1991). This canon is controversial within the Court. See *Murphy,* 126 S.Ct. at 2466–68 (Breyer, J., dissenting).

[89] Marrama v. Citizens Bank of Mass., 549 U.S. 365 (2007); Small v. United States, 544 U.S. 385 (2005).

[90] Shannon v. United States, 512 U.S. 573, 583 (1994).

[91] Moreau v. Klevenhagen, 508 U.S. 22, 26 (1993).

[92] Mohamad v. Palestinian Auth., 132 S.Ct. 1702 (2012); Hamdan v. Rumsfeld, 548 U.S. 557 (2006); Doe v. Chao, 540 U.S. 614 (2004); F. Hoffmann-LaRoche, Ltd. v. Empagran S.A., 540 U.S. 1088 (2004); FDA v. Brown & Williamson Tobacco Corp., 529 U.S. 120, 144 (2000); Department of Revenue v. ACF Indus., 510 U.S. 332, 345–36 (1994).

[93] Safeco Ins. Co. of Am. v. Burr, 551 U.S. 47 (2007); Rapanos v. United States, 547 U.S. 715 (2006) (plurality opinion); Solid Waste Agency v. Army Corps of Eng'rs, 531 U.S. 159, 169 (2001).

[94] Entergy Corp. v. Riverkeeper, Inc., 556 U.S. 208, 230–35 (2009) (Breyer, J., concurring); Hamdan v. Rumsfeld, 548 U.S. 557 (2006); Department of Revenue v. ACF Indus., Inc., 510 U.S. 332, 345–46 (1994).

[95] General Dynamics Land Sys., Inc. v. Cline, 540 U.S. 581 (2004); FDA v. Brown & Williamson Tobacco Corp., 529 U.S. 120 (2000); Hagen v. Utah, 510 U.S. 399, 418 (1994); Darby v. Cisneros, 509 U.S. 137, 147–51 (1993).

[96] Zuni Pub. Sch. Dist. No. 89 v. Department of Educ., 550 U.S. 81 (2007); Chisom v. Roemer, 501 U.S. 380, 396 & n.23 (1991).

- Views of a subsequent Congress are a hazardous basis for inferring the intent of an earlier one,[97] but are sometimes relevant.[98] Subsequent legislation clearly incorporating these views is relevant and persuasive.[99]

SUBSTANTIVE POLICY CANONS

CONSTITUTION-BASED CANONS

- Avoidance canon: avoid interpretations that would render a statute unconstitutional *or* that would raise serious constitutional difficulties.[100] Inapplicable if statute would clearly survive constitutional attack, or if statutory text is clear.[101]

1. *Separation of Powers*

- Super-strong rule against congressional interference with President's inherent powers, his executive authority.[102] Avoid interpretations whereby judges would interfere with foreign affairs.[103]

- Rule against review of President's core executive actions for "abuse of discretion. "[104]

- Where Congress appropriates money without specific textual restrictions, the executive has leeway as to its expenditure, unlimited by more informal signals.[105]

- Rule of special treatment of President and Vice-President as litigants, affording them special privileges so as not to interfere with their official duties.[106]

- Rule against congressional curtailment of the judiciary' s "inherent powers" or its· "equity" powers.[107]

---

[97] Bruesewitz v. Wyeth LLC, 131 S.Ct. 1068, 1081–82 (2011); Massachusetts v. EPA, 549 U.S. 497 (2007); Doe v. Chao, 540 U.S. 614 (2004); Solid Waste Agency v. Army Corps of Eng'rs, 531 U.S. 159, 170 (2001); Sullivan v. Finkelstein, 496 U.S. 617, 628 n.8 (1990).

[98] Musick, Peeler & Garrett v. Employers Ins. of Wassau, 508 U.S. 286, 293 (1993). This canon is controversial within the Court. Sullivan v. Finkelstein, 496 U.S. 617, 631–32 (1990) (Scalia, J., concurring in part).

[99] FDA v. Brown & Williamson Tobacco Corp., 529 U.S. 120, 144 (2000); Babbitt v. Sweet Home Chapter of Communities for a Great Oregon, 515 U.S. 687 (1995); Franklin v. Gwinnett County Pub. Sch., 503 U.S. 60 (1990); id. at 77–78 (Scalia, J., concurring in the judgment); Bowen v. Yuckert, 482 U.S. 137, 149–51 (1987).

[100] Bond v. United States, 134 S.Ct. 2077 (2014); Brown v. Plata, 131 S.Ct. 1910, 1928–29, 1937 (2011); Northwest Austin Mun. Utility Dist. No. 1 v. Holder, 557 U.S. 193 (2010); Rapanos v. United States, 547 U.S. 715 (2006) (plurality opinion); Cherokee Nation of Oklahoma v. Leavitt, 543 U.S. 631 (2005); Zadvydas v. Davis, 533 U.S. 678, 696–99 (2001); Public Citizen v. United States Dep't of Justice, 491 U.S. 440, 465–66 (1989); Edward J. Debartolo Corp. v. Florida Gulf Coast Building & Constr. Trades Council, 485 U.S. 568, 575 (1988).

[101] Stern v. Marshall, 131 S.Ct. 2594, 2607–08 (2011); Peretz v. United States, 501 U.S. 923, 932 (1991); Rust v. Sullivan, 500 U.S. 173, 182 (1991).

[102] Department of Navy v. Egan, 484 U.S. 518, 527 (1988); Morrison v. Olson, 487 U.S. 654, 682–83 (1988); Carlucci v. Doe, 488 U.S. 93, 99 (1988); United States v. Johnson, 481 U.S. 681, 690–91 (1987).

[103] Sosa v. Alvarez-Machain, 542 U.S. 692 (2004).

[104] Franklin v. Massachusetts, 505 U.S. 788, 800–01 (1991).

[105] Cherokee Nation of Oklahoma v. Leavitt, 543 U.S. 631 (2005); Lincoln v. Vigil, 508 U.S. 182, 191 (1993).

[106] Cheney v. U.S. Dist. Court, 542 U.S. 367 (2004).

[107] Brown v. Plata, 131 S.Ct. 1910, 1928–29, 1936–37 (2011); Chambers v. Nasco, Inc., 501 U.S. 32, 43–44 (1991).

- Rule against congressional expansion of Article III injury in fact to include intangible and procedural injuries.[108]

- Presumption that Congress does not delegate authority without sufficient guidelines.[109]

- Presumption against "implying" causes of action into federal statutes.[110]

- Presumption that U.S. law conforms to U.S. international obligations.[111] Presumption that Congress takes account of the legitimate sovereign interests of other nations when it writes American laws.[112]

- Rule against congressional abrogation of Indian treaty rights.[113]

- Presumption favoring severability of unconstitutional provisions.[114]

2. *Federalism*

- Super-strong rule against federal invasion of "core state functions."[115] Strong presumption against statutory interpretations that would alter the federal-state balance.[116]

- Super-strong rule against federal abrogation of states' Eleventh Amendment immunity from lawsuits in federal courts.[117] Eleventh Amendment rules does not apply to municipalities and counties.[118]

- Super-strong rule against inferring conditions on federal grants to the states under the Spending Clause; conditions must be expressed clearly and unambiguously.[119] Sometimes the Court will require less than targeted statutory

---

[108]   Lujan v. Defenders of Wildlife, 504 U.S. 555, 557–61 (1992); id. at 579–80 (Kennedy, J., concurring in part).

[109]   Mistretta v. United States, 488 U.S. 361, 373 n.7 (1989).

[110]   Virginia Bancshares, Inc. v. Sandberg, 501 U.S. 1083, 1102–05 (1991); Thompson v. Thompson, 484 U.S. 174, 179 (1988).

[111]   Hamdan v. Rumsfeld, 548 U.S. 557 (2006) (majority and concurring opinions); Sale v. Haitian Centers Council, 509 U.S. 155, 173–74 (1993).

[112]   Samantar v. Yousuf, 560 U.S. 305 (2010); Microsoft Corp. v. AT&T, 550 U.S. 437 (2007); F. Hoffmann-LaRoche, Ltd. v. Empagran S.A., 542 U.S. 155, 164 (2004).

[113]   Michigan v. Bay Mills Indian Community, 134 S.Ct. 2024 (2014); South Dakota v. Bourland, 508 U.S. 679, 687 (1993).

[114]   Executive Benefits Ins. Agency v. Arkison, 134 S.Ct. 2165 (2014); National Fed. Indep. Business v. Sebelius, 132 S.Ct. 2566 (2012) (plurality and concurring opinions). The leading case is Alaska Airlines, Inc. v. Brock, 480 U.S. 678, 684 (1987).

[115]   Rapanos v. United States, 548 U.S. 715 (2006) (plurality opinion); Nixon v. Missouri Municipal League, 541 U.S. 125 (2004); BFP v. Resolution Trust Corp., 511 U.S. 531, 544 (1994); Gregory v. Ashcroft, 501 U.S. 452, 461–64 (1991).

[116]   Bond v. United States, 134 S.Ct. 2077 (2014); Gonzales v. Oregon, 546 U.S. 243 (2006); Owasso Indep. Sch. Dist. v. Falvo, 534 U.S. 426 (2002); Raygor v. Regents of the Univ. of Minn., 534 U.S. 533 (2002); BFP v. Resolution Trust Corp., 511 U.S. 531, 544 (1994); Gregory v. Ashcroft, 501 U.S. 452, 461–64 (1991); Will v. Michigan Dep't of State Police, 491 U.S. 58, 65 (1989).

[117]   Nevada Dep't of Human Resources v. Hibbs, 538 U.S. 721 (2003) (finding abrogation); Raygor v. Regents of the Univ. of Minn., 534 U.S. 533 (2001); Blatchford v. Native Village of Noatak, 501 U.S. 775, 779 (1991); Dellmuth v. Muth, 491 U.S. 223, 227–28 (1989); Pennsylvania v. Union Gas, 491 U.S. 1, 7 (1989) (finding abrogation). The leading case is Atascadero State Hosp. v. Scanlon, 473 U.S. 234, 241 (1985).

[118]   Jinks v. Richland County, 538 U.S. 456 (2003).

[119]   Arlington Cent. Sch. Dist. Bd. of Educ. v. Murphy, 548 U.S. 291 (2006); Barnes v. Gorman, 536 U.S. 181 (2002); Gonzaga Univ. v. Doe, 536 U.S. 273 (2002); Blessing v. Freestone, 520 U.S. 329 (1997); Suter v.

language, so long as states are reasonably on notice of conditions, as through agency guidances to that effect.[120]

- Presumption against federal preemption of traditional state regulation.[121]

- Presumption trumped if clear statutory language or the statutory purpose requires preemption.[122]

- Presumption against federal regulation of intergovernmental taxation by the states.[123]

- Presumption against application of federal statutes to state and local political processes,[124] except when statutory plain meaning or other factors counsel in favor of such application.[125]

- Presumption against congressional derogation from state's land claims based upon its entry into Union on an "equal footing" with all other states.[126] Presumption that upon statehood, the new state acquires title to the land under navigable rivers.[127]

- Rule against federal habeas review of state criminal convictions unless prisoner has properly exhausted state remedies.[128] Rule against federal habeas review of state criminal convictions supported by independent state ground.[129] Presumption of finality of state convictions for purposes of habeas review.[130]

- Narrow construction of federal court jurisdictional grants that would siphon cases away from state courts.[131]

- Rule against reading an ambiguous federal statute to authorize states to engage in activities that would violate the dormant commerce clause.[132]

Artist M., 503 U.S. 347 (1991). The leading case is Pennhurst State Sch. & Hosp. v. Halderman, 451 U.S. 1 (1981).

[120] Davis v. Monroe County Bd. of Educ., 526 U.S. 629 (1999); Franklin v. Gwinnett County Pub. Sch., 503 U.S. 60 (1992).

[121] CTS Corp. v. Waldburger, 134 S.Ct. 2175, 2188–89 (2014); Wyeth v. Levine, 555 U.S. 555 (2008); Altria Group, Inc. v. Good, 555 U.S. 70, 77 (2008); Bates v. Dow Agrosciences LLC, 544 U.S. 431 (2005); Rush Prudential HMO v. Moran, 536 U.S. 355 (2002); Medtronic, Inc. v. Lohr, 518 U.S. 470 (1996); Hawaiian Airlines v. Norris, 512 U.S. 246, 252 (1994); BFP v. Resolution Trust Corp., 511 U.S. 531, 544 (1994); Cipollone v. Liggett Group, Inc., 505 U.S. 504 (1992); California v. ARC Am. Corp., 490 U.S. 93, 100–01 (1989); Rose v. Rose, 481 U.S. 619, 635–36 (1987) (O'Connor, J., concurring in part).

[122] FTC v. Phoebe Putney Health Sys., Inc., 133 S.Ct. 1003 (2013); National Meat Ass'n v. Harris, 132 S.Ct. 965 (2012); Riegel v. Medtronic, Inc., 552 U.S. 312 (2008); Geier v. Honda Motor Co., 529 U.S. 861 (2000).

[123] Davis v. Michigan Dep't of Treasury, 489 U.S. 803, 810 (1989).

[124] City of Columbia v. Omni Outdoor Advertising, Inc., 499 U.S. 365, 373 (1991); McCormick v. United States, 500 U.S. 257, 269 n.6 (1988); McNally v. United States, 483 U.S. 350, 361 n.9 (1987).

[125] Evans v. United States, 504 U.S. 255, 270–71 (1992).

[126] Utah Div'n of State Lands v. United States, 482 U.S. 193, 196 (1987).

[127] Idaho v. United States, 533 U.S. 262 (2001).

[128] O'Sullivan v. Boerckel, 526 U.S. 838, 845 (1999).

[129] Sanchez-Llamas v. Oregon, 548 U.S. 331 (2006); Massaro v. United States, 538 U.S. 500, 504 (2003); Wright v. West, 505 U.S. 277, 289 (1992); Coleman v. Thompson, 501 U.S. 722, 729 (1991).

[130] Felkner v. Jackson, 132 S.Ct. 1305 (2011); Hardy v. Cross, 132 S.Ct. 490 (2011); Brecht v. Abrahamson, 507 U.S. 619, 635–38 (1993).

[131] Smith v. Bayer Corp., 131 S.Ct. 2368 (2011); Kokkonen v. Guardian Life Ins. Co. of Am., 511 U.S. 375, 377 (1994); Finely v. United States, 490 U.S. 545, 552–54 (1989).

[132] Granholm v. Heald, 544 U.S. 460 (2005); Wyoming v. Oklahoma, 502 U.S. 437, 458 (1992).

- Rule favoring concurrent state and federal court jurisdiction over federal claims.[133]

- Super-strong rule that Indian tribes retain their sovereign immunity, unless Congress has unequivocally negated it.[134]

- Presumption that states can tax activities within their borders, including Indian tribal activities,[135] but also presumption that states cannot tax on Indian lands.[136]

- Principle that federal equitable remedies must consider interests of state and local authorities.[137]

- Presumption that Congress borrows state statutes of limitations for federal statutory schemes.[138]

3. *Due Process*

- Rule of lenity: rule against applying punitive sanctions if there is ambiguity as to underlying criminal liability or criminal penalty.[139] Rule is trumped when Congress clearly intended to criminalize the conduct in question.[140]

- Rule of lenity may apply to civil sanction that is punitive or when underlying liability is criminal.[141]

- Rule against criminal penalties imposed without showing of specific intent.[142] But willfulness requirement in civil sanction cases typically includes to reckless conduct as well.[143]

---

[133] Mims v. Arrow Financial Serv., LLC, 132 S.Ct. 740 (2012); Tafflin v. Levitt, 493 U.S. 455, 458 (1990); Yellow Freight Sys., Inc. v. Donnelly, 494 U.S. 820, 823 (1990).

[134] Michigan v. Bay Mills Indian Community, 134 S.Ct. 2024 (2014); Kiowa Tribe of Oklahoma v. Manufacturing Technologies, Inc., 523 U.S. 751 (1998).

[135] Atkinson Trading Co. v. Shirley, 532 U.S. 645 (2001); Cotton Petroleum Corp. v. New Mexico, 490 U.S. 163, 174 (1989).

[136] Oklahoma Tax Comm'n v. Sac and Fox Nation, 508 U.S. 114 (1993); County of Yakima v. Confederated Tribes & Bands of the Yakima Indian Nation, 502 U.S. 251, 268 (1992).

[137] Raygor v. Regents of the Univ. of Minn., 534 U.S. 533 (2002); Spallone v. United States, 493 U.S. 265, 276 (1990).

[138] Wallace v. Kato, 549 U.S. 384 (2007); Lampf, Pleva, Lipkind, Prupis & Petigrow v. Gilbertson, 501 U.S. 350, 355–56 (1991).

[139] Burrage v. United States, 134 S.Ct. 881 (2014) (majority and concurring opinions); Skilling v. United States, 561 U.S. 358 (2010); Arthur Andersen LLP v. United States, 544 U.S. 696 (2005); Cleveland v. United States, 531 U.S. 12 (2000) (explaining both notice and nondelegation rationales); United States v. Aguilar, 515 U.S. 593 (1995); United States v. Granderson, 511 U.S. 39 (1994); United States v. Kozminski, 487 U.S. 931, 939 (1988). The leading case is United States v. Bass, 404 U.S. 336, 347–49 (1971).

[140] Abramski v. United States, 134 S.Ct. 2259 (2014); Robers v. United States, 134 S.Ct. 1854 (2014); Muscarello v. United States, 524 U.S. 125 (1998); Chapman v. United States, 500 U.S. 453, 463–64 (1991).

[141] Crandon v. United States, 494 U.S. 152, 158 (1990). The Court applies this canon very unevenly. E.g., Babbitt v. Sweet Home Chapter of Communities for a Great Oregon, 515 U.S. 687 (1995).

[142] Arthur Andersen LLP v. United States, 544 U.S. 696 (2005); Bryan v. United States, 524 U.S. 184, 191–92 (1998); Ratzlaf v. United States, 510 U.S. 135, 137 (1994); Cheek v. United States, 498 U.S. 192, 200–01 (1991).

[143] Safeco Ins. Co. of Am. v. Burr, 551 U.S. 47 (2007); McLaughlin v. Richland Shoe Co., 486 U.S. 128, 132–33 (1988).

- Super-strong rule against implied congressional abrogation or repeal of habeas corpus.[144]

- Rule against interpreting statutes to be retroactive,[145] even if statute is curative or restorative.[146]

- Rule against interpreting statutes to deny a right to jury trial.[147]

- Presumption in favor of judicial review.[148]

- Presumption against pre-enforcement challenges to implementation.[149]

- Presumption against exhaustion of remedies requirement for lawsuit to enforce constitutional rights.[150]

- Presumption that judgments will not be binding upon persons not party to adjudication.[151]

- Presumption against national service of process unless authorized by Congress.[152]

- Presumption against foreclosure of private enforcement of important federal rights.[153]

- Presumption that preponderance of the evidence standard applies in civil cases.[154]

COMMON LAW-BASED CANONS

- Presumption in favor of following common law usage and rules where Congress has employed words or concepts with well-settled common law traditions.[155]

---

[144]   Demore v. Kim, 538 U.S. 510 (2003); INS v. St. Cyr, 533 U.S. 289 (2001).

[145]   Vartelas v. Holder, 132 S.Ct. 1479 (2012); Fernandez-Vargas v. Gonzales, 548 U.S. 30 (2006). The leading case is Landgraf v. USI Film Prods., 51 I U.S. 244 (1994).

[146]   Rivers v. Roadway Express, 511 U.S. 298 (1994).

[147]   Gomez v. United States, 490 U.S. 858, 863 (1989).

[148]   Sackett v. EPA, 132 S.Ct. 1367 (2012); Demore v. Kim, 538 U.S. 510 (2003); Webster v. Doe, 486 U.S. 592 (1988).

[149]   Thunder Basin Coal Co. v. Reich, 510 U.S. 200, 208–10 (1994).

[150]   McCarthy. v. Madigan, 503 U.S. 140, 146–49 (1992).

[151]   Martin v. Wilks, 490 U.S. 755, 761–62 (1989).

[152]   Omni Capital Int'l v. Rudolf Wolff & Co., 484 U.S. 97, 107–08 (1987).

[153]   Wilder v. Virginia Hosp. Ass'n, 496 U.S. 498, 520–21 (1990). This presumption is probably no longer viable. See Gonzaga Univ. v. Doe, 536 U.S. 273 (2002).

[154]   Grogan v. Garner, 498 U.S. 279, 286 (1991).

[155]   CTS Corp. v. Waldburger, 134 S.Ct. 2175 (2014) (CERCLA); Wal-Mart Stores v. Dukes, 131 S.Ct. 2541, 2557–58 (2011) (FRCP); Permanent Mission of India to the United Nations v. City of New York, 551 U.S. 193 (2007) (FSIA); Wallace v. Kato, 549 U.S. 384 (2007) (§ 1983); Dura Pharmaceuticals, Inc. v. Broudo, 544 U.S. 336 (2005) (§ 10(b)); Stewart v. Dutra Constr. Co., 543 U.S. 481, 487 (2005) (LWHCA); United States v. Texas, 507 U.S. 529, 534 (1993) (Debt Collection Act); Nationwide Mut. Ins. Co. v. Darden, 503 U.S. 318 (1992) (ERISA); Kamen v. Kemper Fin. Servs., Inc., 500 U.S. 90, 98–99 (1991) (Investment Company Act); Community for Creative Nonviolence v. Reid, 490 U.S. 730, 739–40 (1989) (Copyright Act). See also Pacific Operators Offshore, LLC v. Valladolid, 132 S.Ct. 680, 691–94 (2012) (Scalia, J., concurring in the judgment) (presuming that Congress intended an easy-to-apply common law standard rather than a novel standard that would be harder to administer).

Presumption inapplicable when Congress has directly addressed the issue[156] or when common law usage is inconsistent with statutory purpose.[157]

- Rule against extraterritorial application of U.S. law.[158] Presumption that Congress legislates with domestic concerns in mind.[159]

- American laws apply to foreign-flag ships in U.S. territory and affecting Americans, but will not apply to the "internal affairs" of a foreign-flag ship unless there is a clear statutory statement to that effect.[160]

- Super-strong rule against waivers of United States sovereign immunity.[161] Even if there is a waiver of immunity from suit, the scope of the immunity will be narrowly read.[162]

- Super-strong rule against congressional abrogation of state immunity from suit.[163] Common law rule does not apply to counties and other subdivisions created by the states.[164]

- Rule that debts to the United States shall bear interest.[165]

- Presumption against conveyance of U.S. public lands to private parties.[166]

- Rule presuming against attorney fee-shifting in federal courts and federal statutes,[167] and narrow construction of fee-shifting statutes to exclude costs that are not explicitly identified.[168]

- Presumption that jury finds facts, judge declares law.[169]

- Rule presuming that law takes effect on date of enactment.[170]

---

[156] Pasquantino v. United States, 544 U.S. 349, 356 (2005).

[157] CSX Transp., Inc. v. McBride, 131 S.Ct. 2630 (2011); Taylor v. United States, 495 U.S. 575, 593–95 (1990).

[158] Morrison v. National Australia National Bank Ltd., 561 U.S. 247 (2010); Microsoft Corp. v. AT&T, 550 U.S. 437 (2007); F. Hoffman-LaRoche, Ltd. v. Empangran S.A., 540 U.S. 1088 (2004); Sale v. Haitian Centers Council, 509 U.S. 155 (1993); EEOC v. Arabian Am. Oil Co., 499 U.S. 244, 248 (1991); Argentine Republic v. Amerada Hess Shipping Corp., 488 U.S. 428, 440 (1989).

[159] Morrison v. National Australia National Bank Ltd., 561 U.S. 247 (2010); Small v. United States, 544 U.S. 385 (2005); Smith v. United States, 507 U.S. 197, 204 n.5 (1993).

[160] Spector v. Norwegian Cruise Line Ltd., 545 U.S. 119 (2005).

[161] Richlin Security Serv. Co. v. Chertoff, 553 U.S. 571, 589 (2008); United States v. White Mt. Apache Tribe, 537 U.S. 465, 472–73 (2003); United States v. Nordic Village, Inc., 503 U.S. 30 (1992); Ardestani v. INS, 502 U.S. 129 (1991); United States v. Dalm, 494 U.S. 596, 608 (1990).

[162] FAA v. Cooper, 132 S.Ct. 1441 (2012).

[163] Alden v. Maine, 527 U.S. 706, 713 (1999) (announcing that state immunity from suit was based on common law, not just Eleventh Amendment). This canon is controversial within the Court. See id. at 760 (Souter, J., dissenting).

[164] Northern Ins. Co. of N.Y. v. Chatham County, 547 U.S. 189 (2006).

[165] United States v. Texas, 507 U.S. 529 (1993).

[166] Utah Div. of State Lands v. United States, 482 U.S. 193, 197–98 (1987).

[167] Key Tronic Corp. v. United States, 511 U.S. 809 (1994). The leading case is Alyeska Pipeline Serv. Co. v. Wilderness Society, 421 U.S. 240 (1975).

[168] Arlington Cent. Sch. Dist. Bd. of Educ. v. Murphy, 548 U.S. 291 (2006); West Virginia Univ. Hosps., Inc. v. Casey, 499 U.S. 83 (1991). But cf. Octane Fitness, LLC v. Icon Health & Fitness, Inc., 134 S.Ct. 1749 (2014) (presuming that fee-shifting statutes reach beyond common law bases for fee shifting, such as bad faith or contempt).

[169] Shannon v. United States, 512 U.S. 573 (1994).

[170] Gozlon-Peretz v. United States, 498 U.S. 395 (1991).

- Presumption that public (government) interest not be prejudiced by negligence of federal officials.[171]

- Presumption that federal agencies launched into commercial world with power to "sue and be sued" are not entitled to sovereign immunity.[172] Presumption favoring enforcement of forum selection clauses.[173] Presumption that federal judgment has preclusive effect in state administrative proceedings.[174]

- Presumption importing common law immunities into federal civil rights statutes.[175]

STATUTE-BASED CANONS

- Purposive construction: interpret ambiguous statutes so as best to carry out their statutory purposes.[176] Caution: no law pursues its purpose at all costs, and text-based limits on a law's scope are part of its "purpose.[177]

- Anti-Messiness Rule: avoid interpretations that create "messy" (vague, obscure, muddy) rules of law that will be hard to implement.[178]

1. *General canons*

- Presumption against repeals by implication.[179] But where there is a clear repugnancy between a more recent statutory scheme and an earlier one, partial repeal will be inferred.[180]

- *In pari materia:* similar statutes should be interpreted similarly,[181] unless legislative history or purpose suggests material differences.[182]

---

[171] United States v. Montalvo-Murillo, 495 U.S. 711, 717–18 (1990).

[172] Loeffler v. Frank, 486 U.S. 549, 554–55 (1988).

[173] Carnival Cruise Lines v. Shute, 499 U.S. 585, 589 (1991); Stewart Org. v. Ricoh Corp., 487 U.S. 22, 33 (1988) (Kennedy, J., concurring).

[174] Astoria Fed. Sav. & Loan Ass'n v. Solimino, 501 U.S. 104, 108 (1991).

[175] Rehberg v. Paulk, 132 S.Ct. 1497 (2012); Burns v. Reed, 500 U.S. 478, 484–85 (1991); Forrester v. White, 484 U.S. 219, 225–26 (1988).

[176] ABC, Inc. v. Aereo, Inc., 134 S.Ct. 2498 (2014); Clark v. Rameker, 134 S.Ct. 2242 (2014); Abramski, v. United States, 134 S.Ct. 2259 (2014); CSX Transp., Inc. v. McBride, 131 S.Ct. 2630, 2641 (2011); Zuni Pub. Sch. Dist. No. 89 v. Department of Educ., 550 U.S. 81 (2007); Burlington Northern & Santa Fe Ry. v. White, 126 S.Ct. 2405, 2412–14 (2006); Jones v. R.R. Donnelley & Sons Co., 541 U.S. 369 (2004); PGA Tour, Inc. v. Martin, 532 U.S. 661 (2001); Reves v. Ernst & Young, 494 U.S. 56, 60–61 (1990). See also POM Wonderful LLC v. Coca-Cola Co., 134 S.Ct. 2228 (2014) (applying different statutory schemes so that each carries out its mission).

[177] Utility Air Regulatory Group v. EPA, 134 S.Ct. 2427 (June 23, 2014) (plurality opinion); Rapanos v. United States, 547 U.S. 715 (2006) (plurality opinion).

[178] Limelight Networks Inc. v. Akamai Technologies, Inc., 134 S.Ct. 2111 (2014); Robers v. United States, 134 S.Ct. 1854 (2014).

[179] See sources in note 71, *supra*.

[180] Credit Suisse Securities (USA) LLC v. Billing, 551 U.S. 264 (2007).

[181] Powerex Corp. v. Reliant Energy Servs., Inc., 551 U.S. 224 (2007); Ledbetter v. Goodyear Tire & Rubber Co., 550 U.S. 618 (2007); John Hancock Mut. Life Ins. Co. v. Harris Trust & Sav. Bank, 510 U.S. 86, 101–06 (1993); Morales v. TWA, Inc., v. 504 U.S. 374 (1992); Communications Workers v. Beck, 487 U.S. 735, 750–52 (1988); Wimberly v. Labor & Indus. Relations Comm'n, 479 U.S. 511, 517 (1987).

[182] Ledbetter v. Goodyear Tire & Rubber Co., 550 U.S. 618 (2007); Fogerty v. Fantasy, Inc., 510 U.S. 517 (1994).

- Presumption *against* private right of action unless statute expressly provides one,[183] [183] but once recognized a private right of action carries with it all traditional remedies.[184] Regulations cannot create a private cause of action not authorized by the statute.[185]

- A precisely drawn, detailed statute preempts or governs a more general statute or remedies.[186]

- When Congress enacts a specific remedy when no remedy was clearly recognized previously, the new remedy is regarded as exclusive.[187]

- Presumption against creating exemptions in a statute that has none.[188] Narrow interpretation of explicit exemptions.[189]

- Allow *de minimis* exceptions to statutory rules, so long as they do not undermine statutory policy.[190]

2. *Process Canons*

- Presumption that adjudicative bodies are vested with inherent authority to sanction abusive litigation practices.[191] Judges presumptively have discretion to raise procedural errors sua sponte.[192]

- Presumption that statutory exhaustion requirements entail implicit requirements that the petitioner follow the proper procedures; failing that, the petitioner has not met statutory exhaustion requirements.[193]

- Strict construction of statutes authorizing appeals.[194] Rule that Court of Claims is proper forum for Tucker Act claims against federal government.[195]

- Rule that "sue and be sued" clauses waive sovereign immunity and should be liberally construed.[196] Presumption that statute creating agency and authorizing

---

[183]   Gonzaga Univ. v. Doe, 536 U.S. 273 (2002); Blessing v. Freestone, 520 U.S. 329 (1997); Suter v. Artist M., 503 U.S. 347 (1992).

[184]   Franklin v. Gwinnett County Pub. Sch., 503 U.S. 60 (1992).

[185]   Alexander v. Sandoval, 532 U.S. 275 (2001).

[186]   Credit Suisse Securities (USA) LLC v. Billing, 551 U.S. 264 (2007); EC Term of Years Trust v. United States, 550 U.S. 429 (2007). The leading case is Brown v. General Serv. Admin., 425 U.S. 820, 834 (1976).

[187]   Hinck v. United States, 550 U.S. 501 (2007).

[188]   Burwell v. Hobby Lobby Stores, Inc., 134 S.Ct. 2751 (June 30, 2014); City of Chicago v. Environmental Def. Fund, 511 U.S. 328, 33 7 (1994).

[189]   John Hancock Mut. Life Ins. Co. v. Harris Trust & Sav. Bank, 510 U.S. 86, 96–97 (1994); United States Dep't of Justice v. Landano, 508 U.S. 165 (1993); Citicorp Indus. Credit, Inc. v. Brock, 483 U.S. 27, 33–35 (1987).

[190]   Wisconsin Dep't of Revenue v. William Wrigley, Jr., Co., 505 U.S. 214 (1992).

[191]   Marrama v. Citizens Bank of Mass., 549 U.S. 365 (2007).

[192]   Day v. McDonough, 547 U.S. 198 (2006).

[193]   Woodford v. Ngo, 548 U.S. 181 (2006); see also O'Sullivan v. Boerckel, 526 U.S. 838, 845 (1999) (similar rule in habeas corpus law).

[194]   Bowles v. Russell, 551 U.S. 205 (2007); Hohn v. United States, 524 U.S. 236, 24 7 (1998); California Coastal Comm'n v. Granite Rock Co., 480 U.S. 572, 579 (1987).

[195]   Preseault v. ICC, 494 U.S. 1, 11–12 (1990).

[196]   FDIC v. Meyer, 510 U.S. 471 (1994).

it to "sue and be sued" also creates federal subject matter jurisdiction for lawsuits by and against the agency.[197]

- American rule: strong presumption that each side bears its own costs in adjudications.[198] Super-strong rule against finding statutory authorization of witness fees as costs unless the statute refers explicitly to witness fees.[199]

- Rule that the burden of proof is on the party requesting benefits or entitlements from the state.[200]

- Rule that nonjurisdictional process objections (e.g., exhaustion of remedies, venue) are waived if not timely raised.[201]

3. *Specific statutory subject areas*

- **Antitrust.** Sherman Act should be applied in light of its overall purpose of benefitting consumers.[202]

- Presumption against application of Sherman Act to activities authorized by states.[203]

- Exemption from antitrust liability should not be lightly inferred.[204] Principle that statutes should not be interpreted to create anti-competitive effects.[205]

- **Arbitration.** Federal court deference to arbitral awards, even where the Federal Arbitration Act is not by its terms applicable.[206]

- Strong presumption in favor of arbitration and of enforcing labor arbitration agreements.[207]

- Rule favoring arbitration of federal statutory claims.[208]

- **Banking.** National Bank Act (NBA) policy shielding national banks from "burdensome" state regulation.[209] But national banks are subject to state laws not conflicting with the NBA's purposes.[210]

---

[197]   American Nat'l Red Cross v. S.G., 505 U.S. 247 (1992).

[198]   Buckhannon Bd. & Care Home, Inc. v. West Virginia Dep't Health & Human Resources, 532 U.S. 598 (2001). The leading case is Alyeska Pipeline Serv. Co. v. Wilderness Soc'y, 421 U.S. 240 (1975).

[199]   Arlington Cent. Sch. Dist. Bd. of Educ. v. Murphy, 548 U.S. 291 (2006); Crawford Fitting Co. v. J.T. Gibbons, Inc., 482 U.S. 437, 445 (1987).

[200]   NLRB v. Kentucky River Community Care, Inc., 532 U.S. 706 (2001).

[201]   Kontrick v. Ryan, 540 U.S. 443 (2004).

[202]   Weyerhauser v. Ross-Simmons Hardwood Lumber, 549 U.S. 312 (2007).

[203]   City of Columbia v. Omni Outdoor Advertising, Inc., 499 U.S. 365, 370 (1991).

[204]   Credit Suisse Securities (USA) LLC v. Billing, 551 U.S. 264 (2007).

[205]   Nautilus, Inc. v. Biosig Instruments, Inc., 134 S.Ct. 2120 (2014); Two Pesos, Inc. v. Taco Cabana, Inc., 505 U.S. 763 (1992).

[206]   United Paperworkers Int'l Union v. Misco, Inc., 484 U.S. 29, 36–37 (1987).

[207]   Howsam v. Dean Witter Reynolds, Inc., 537 U.S. 79, 83 (2002); Groves v. Ring Screw Works, Ferndale Fastener Div'n, 498 U.S. 168, 173 (1990).

[208]   CompuCredit Corp. v. Greenwood, 132 S.Ct. 665 (2012); Circuit City Stores, Inc. v. Adams, 532 U.S. 105 (2001); Gilmer v. Interstate/Johnson Lane Corp., 500 U.S. 20, 26 (1991); Shearson/American Express, Inc. v. McMahon, 482 U.S. 220, 226–27 (1987).

[209]   Watters v. Wachovia Bank, 550 U.S. 1 (2007); Beneficial Nat'l Bank v. Anderson, 539 U.S. 1, 10 (2003); Barnett Bank of Marion County, N.A. v. Nelson, 517 U.S. 25, 32–34 (1996).

[210]   Atherton v. FDIC, 519 U.S. 213, 221–22 (1997).

- **Bankruptcy.** Bankruptcy Act of 1978 (BRA) should be construed in light of its overall purpose, to give a fresh start to the class of "honest but unfortunate debtors."[211]

- Presumption that the BRA preserved prior bankruptcy doctrines.[212]

- Where statute is ambiguous, courts should create gapfilling rules that are familiar, objective, and less expensive to administer.[213]

- **Civil Procedure & Jurisdiction.** Subject-matter jurisdictional rules will be strictly enforced and applied.[214]

- Jurisdictional provisions will not be inferred.[215] Article III baseline is that litigation involves claims by individuals (and not groups of people) aggrieved by a defendant's actions and presenting enough facts to warrant a plausible claim for legal relief.[216]

- Federal Rules of Civil Procedure apply in habeas cases, except to the extent they are inconsistent with the Habeas Corpus Rules.[217]

- Presumption that time-limitation periods, venue, and other nonjurisdictional requirements are waivable.[218]

- **Civil Rights.** Aspects of section 1983 not governed by state law are governed by federal rules conforming to common law tort principles.[219]

- Title VII of the Civil Rights Act should be interpreted to effectuate its goal of a workplace where individuals are not discriminated against because of their racial, ethnic, religious, or gender-based status.[220] But Title VII does not set forth a general code of workplace civility.[221]

- Voting Rights Act should be interpreted in light of its core purpose of preventing race discrimination in voting and fostering a transformation of America into a society no longer fixated on race.[222]

---

[211] Marrama v. Citizens Bank of Mass., 549 U.S. 365 (2007).

[212] Dewsnup v. Timm, 502 U.S. 410 (1992).

[213] Till v. CSC Credit Corp., 541 U.S. 465 (2004) (plurality opinion of Stevens, J.).

[214] Bowles v. Russell, 551 U.S. 205 (2007). Relatedly, courts will interpret even long-established jurisdictional exceptions narrowly. Marshall v. Marshall, 547 U.S. 293 (2006) (narrow interpretation of "probate exception"); Ankenbrandt v. Richards, 504 U.S. 689 (1992) (narrow interpretation of "domestic relations exception").

[215] Stern v. Marshall, 131 S.Ct. 2594, 2606–07 (2011); Henderson v. Shinseki, 131 S.Ct. 1197 (2011); Arbaugh v. Y&H Corp., 546 U.S. 500, 516 (2006).

[216] Wal-Mart Stores, Inc. v. Dukes, 131 S.Ct. 2541, 2550 (2011); Ashcroft v. Iqbal, 556 U.S. 662 (2009). Compare the majority and dissenting opinions in Brown v. Plata, 131 S.Ct. 1910 (2011).

[217] Woofard v. Garceau, 538 U.S. 202, 208 (2003).

[218] Eberhart v. United States, 546 U.S. 12, 17–18 (2006) (per curiam).

[219] Wallace v. Kato, 549 U.S. 381 (2007).

[220] Burlington Northern & Santa Fe Ry. v. White, 548 U.S. 53 (2006).

[221] Oncale v. Sundowner Offshore Servs., Inc., 523 U.S. 75, 80 (1998); Faragher v. Boca Raton, 524 U.S. 775, 788 (1998).

[222] League of United Latin Am. Citizens v. Perry, 548 U.S. 399 (2006); Georgia v. Ashcroft, 539 U.S. 461, 490 (2003).

- **Criminal Law and Sentencing.** Rule of lenity: ambiguities in criminal statutes shall be decided in favor of the accused.[223] Likewise, ambiguous sentencing provisions should be interpreted against the government.[224]

- Failure of U.S. Attorneys to initiate criminal prosecutions in the past is evidence that the Attorney General's current reading of the statute is too broad.[225]

- Even when courts are not bound by Sentencing Commission interpretations, such interpretations may be considered.[226]

- **Environmental Law.** Environmental laws should be applied in light of their overall purpose of cleaning up the environment at a reasonable cost.[227]

- NEPA contains an implicit "rule of reason," relieving agencies of filing environmental impact statements that would serve no statutory purpose.[228]

- **Immigration.** Construe ambiguities in deportation statutes in favor of aliens.[229]

- **Indian Law.** Rule against state taxation of Indian tribes and reservation activities.[230]

- Presumption against national "diminishment" of Indian lands.[231]

- Longstanding assertion of state jurisdiction over Indian lands creates justifiable expectations of sovereign authority.[232]

- Presumption against criminal jurisdiction by an Indian tribe over a nonmember.[233]

- Presumption that party cannot invoke federal jurisdiction until she has exhausted her remedies in Indian tribal courts.[234]

- **Labor Law.** Rule against statutory interference in labor-management discipline disputes.[235]

---

[223]   See sources in note 138, supra.

[224]   United States v. R.L.C., 503 U.S. 291 (1992).

[225]   Lopez v. Gonzales, 549 U.S. 47 (2006).

[226]   James v. United States, 550 U.S. 192 (2007).

[227]   Massachusetts v. EPA, 549 U.S. 497 (2007).

[228]   Department of Transportation v. Public Citizen, 541 U.S. 752 (2004); Marsh v. Oregon Natural Resources Council, 490 U.S. 360, 373–74 (1989).

[229]   INS v. St. Cyr, 533 U.S. 289, 320 (2001); INS v. Cardoza-Fonseca, 480 U.S. 421, 449 (1987). This canon is applied with an unusual level of unpredictability. Compare, e.g., INS v. Elias-Zacarias, 502 U.S. 478 (1992).

[230]   California v. Cabazon Band of Mission Indians, 480 U.S. 202, 208 (1987).

[231]   Hagen v. Utah, 510 U.S. 399 (1994).

[232]   City of Sherrill v. Oneida Indian Nation of N.Y., 544 U.S. 197 (2005); Hagen v. Utah, 510 U.S. 399, 421 (1994).

[233]   Duro v. Reina, 495 U.S. 676, 693–94 (1990).

[234]   Iowa Mut. Ins. Co. v. LaPlante, 480 U.S. 9, 15–17 (1987).

[235]   Eastern Associated Coal Corp. v. UMW Dist. 17, 531 U.S. 57 (2000).

- **Patent Law.** Practice and precedent of Patent Office are particularly persuasive evidence of statutory meaning in this area, given the much greater competence of that Office.[236]

- Strong presumption that abstract ideas and laws of nature are not patentable.[237]

- **Taxation.** Presumption that IRS tax assessments are correct.[238]

- Narrow interpretation of exemptions from federal taxation.[239] Presumption against taxpayer claiming income tax deduction.[240]

- Presumption that tax valuation statutes follow majority approach, and that departures from the majority approach would be signaled with clear statutory language.[241]

- **Veterans Benefits.** Principle that veterans' benefits statutes be construed liberally for their beneficiaries.[242]

---

[236]   Festo Corp. v. Shoketsu Kinzoku Kogyo Kabushiki Co., 535 U.S. 722 (2002). This canon seems to be exceedingly weak in practice. E.g.,

[237]   Alice Corp. Pty. Ltd. v. CLS Bank Int'l, 134 S.Ct. 2347 (2014); Mayo Collaborative Servs. v. Prometheus Labs., Inc., 132 S.Ct. 1289 (2012).

[238]   United States v. Fior D'Italia, 536 U.S. 238, 242–43 (2002).

[239]   United States v. Burke, 504 U.S. 229 (1992) (Souter, J., concurring in the judgment); United States v. Wells Fargo Bank, 485 U.S. 351, 357 (1988).

[240]   INDOPCO, Inc. v. Commissioner, 503 U.S. 79 (1992).

[241]   Limtiaco v. Camacho, 549 U.S. 483 (2007).

[242]   King v. St. Vincent's Hosp., 502 U.S. 215 (1991).

APPENDIX C

ADMINISTRATIVE PROCEDURE ACT
(SELECTED PROVISIONS)

■ ■ ■

5 U.S.C. § 551. Definitions

For the purpose of this subchapter—

(1) "agency" means each authority of the Government of the United States, whether or not it is within or subject to review by another agency, but does not include—

(A) the Congress;

(B) the courts of the United States;

(C) the governments of the territories or possessions of the United States;

(D) the government of the District of Columbia; or except as to the requirements of section 552 of this title—

(E) agencies composed of representatives of the parties or of representatives of organizations of the parties to the disputes determined by them;

(F) courts martial and military commissions;

(G) military authority exercised in the field in time of war or in occupied territory; or

(H) functions conferred by sections 1738, 1739, 1743, and 1744 of title 12; subchapter II of chapter 471 of title 49; or sections 1884, 1891–1902, and former section 1641(b)(2), of title 50, appendix;

(2) "person" includes an individual, partnership, corporation, association, or public or private organization other than an agency;

(3) "party" includes a person or agency named or admitted as a party, or properly seeking and entitled as of right to be admitted as a party, in an agency proceeding, and a person or agency admitted by an agency as a party for limited purposes;

(4) "rule" means the whole or a part of an agency statement of general or particular applicability and future effect designed to implement, interpret, or prescribe law or policy or describing the organization, procedure, or practice requirements of an agency and includes the approval or prescription for the future of rates, wages, corporate or financial structures or reorganizations thereof, prices, facilities, appliances, services or allowances therefore or of valuations, costs, or accounting, or practices bearing on any of the foregoing;

1173

(5) "rule making" means agency process for formulating, amending, or repealing a rule;

(6) "order" means the whole or a part of a final disposition, whether affirmative, negative, injunctive, or declaratory in form, of an agency in a matter other than rule making but including licensing;

(7) "adjudication" means agency process for the formulation of an order;

(8) "license" includes the whole or a part of an agency permit, certificate, approval, registration, charter, membership, statutory exemption or other form of permission;

(9) "licensing" includes agency process respecting the grant, renewal, denial, revocation, suspension, annulment, withdrawal, limitation, amendment, modification, or conditioning of a license;

(10) "sanction" includes the whole or a part of an agency—

(A) prohibition, requirement, limitation, or other condition affecting the freedom of a person;

(B) withholding of relief;

(C) imposition of penalty or fine;

(D) destruction, taking, seizure, or withholding of property;

(E) assessment of damages, reimbursement, restitution, compensation, costs, charges, or fees;

(F) requirement, revocation, or suspension of a license; or

(G) taking other compulsory or restrictive action;

(11) "relief" includes the whole or a part of an agency—

(A) grant of money, assistance, license, authority, exemption, exception, privilege, or remedy;

(B) recognition of a claim, right, immunity, privilege, exemption, or exception; or

(C) taking of other action on the application or petition of, and beneficial to, a person;

(12) "agency proceeding" means an agency process as defined by paragraphs (5), (7), and (9) of this section;

(13) "agency action" includes the whole or a part of an agency rule, order, license, sanction, relief, or the equivalent or denial thereof, or failure to act; and

(14) "ex parte communication" means an oral or written communication not on the public record with respect to which reasonable prior notice to all parties is not given, but it shall not include requests for status reports on any matter or proceeding covered by this subchapter.

5 U.S.C. § 552.   Public information; agency rules, opinions, orders, records, and proceedings

(a)   Each agency shall make available to the public information as follows:

(1)   Each agency shall separately state and currently publish in the Federal Register for the guidance of the public—

(A)   descriptions of its central and field organization and the established places at which, the employees (and in the case of a uniformed service, the members) from whom, and the methods whereby, the public may obtain information, make submittals or requests, or obtain decisions;

(B)   statements of the general course and method by which its functions are channeled and determined, including the nature and requirements of all formal and informal procedures available;

(C)   rules of procedure, descriptions of forms available or the places at which forms may be obtained, and instructions as to the scope and contents of all papers, reports, or examinations;

(D)   substantive rules of general applicability adopted as authorized by law, and statements of general policy or interpretations of general applicability formulated and adopted by the agency; and

(E)   each amendment, revision, or repeal of the foregoing.

Except to the extent that a person has actual and timely notice of the terms thereof, a person may not in any manner be required to resort to, or be adversely affected by, a matter required to be published in the Federal Register and not so published. For the purpose of this paragraph, matter reasonably available to the class of persons affected thereby is deemed published in the Federal Register when incorporated by reference therein with the approval of the Director of the Federal Register.

(2)   Each agency, in accordance with published rules, shall make available for public inspection and copying—

(A)   final opinions, including concurring and dissenting opinions, as well as orders, made in the adjudication of cases;

(B)   those statements of policy and interpretations which have been adopted by the agency and are not published in the Federal Register;

(C)   administrative staff manuals and instructions to staff that affect a member of the public;

(D)   copies of all records, regardless of form or format, which have been released to any person under paragraph (3) and which, because of the nature of their subject matter, the agency determines have become or are likely to become the subject of subsequent requests for substantially the same records; and

(E)   a general index of the records referred to under subparagraph (D);

unless the materials are promptly published and copies offered for sale. * * * To the extent required to prevent a clearly unwarranted invasion of personal privacy, an agency may delete identifying details when it makes available or publishes an opinion, statement of policy, interpretation, staff manual, instruction, or copies of records referred to in subparagraph (D). However, in each case the justification for the deletion shall be explained fully in writing, and the extent of such deletion shall be indicated on the portion of the record which is made available or published, unless including that indication would harm an interest protected by the exemption in subsection (b) under which the deletion is made. If technically feasible, the extent of the deletion shall be indicated at the place in the record where the deletion was made. Each agency shall also maintain and make available for public inspection and copying current indexes providing identifying information for the public as to any matter issued, adopted, or promulgated after July 4, 1967, and required by this paragraph to be made available or published. Each agency shall promptly publish, quarterly or more frequently, and distribute (by sale or otherwise) copies of each index or supplements thereto unless it determines by order published in the Federal Register that the publication would be unnecessary and impracticable, in which case the agency shall nonetheless provide copies of such index on request at a cost not to exceed the direct cost of duplication. Each agency shall make the index referred to in subparagraph (E) available by computer telecommunications by December 31, 1999. A final order, opinion, statement of policy, interpretation, or staff manual or instruction that affects a member of the public may be relied on, used, or cited as precedent by an agency against a party other than an agency only if—

> (i)   it has been indexed and either made available or published as provided by this paragraph; or

> (ii) the party has actual and timely notice of the terms thereof.

(3)(A)   Except with respect to the records made available under paragraphs (1) and (2) of this subsection, and except as provided in subparagraph (E), each agency, upon any request for records which (i) reasonably describes such records and (ii) is made in accordance with published rules stating the time, place, fees (if any), and procedures to be followed, shall make the records promptly available to any person.

(B) In making any record available to a person under this paragraph, an agency shall provide the record in any form or format requested by the person if the record is readily reproducible by the agency in that form or format. Each agency shall make reasonable efforts to maintain its records in forms or formats that are reproducible for purposes of this section.

(C) In responding under this paragraph to a request for records, an agency shall make reasonable efforts to search for the records in electronic form or format, except when such efforts would significantly interfere with the operation of the agency's automated information system.

(D) For purposes of this paragraph, the term "search" means to review, manually or by automated means, agency records for the purpose of locating those records which are responsive to a request. * * *

(4)(A)(i) In order to carry out the provisions of this section, each agency shall promulgate regulations, pursuant to notice and receipt of public comment, specifying the schedule of fees applicable to the processing of requests under this section and establishing procedures and guidelines for determining when such fees should be waived or reduced. Such schedule shall conform to the guidelines which shall be promulgated, pursuant to notice and receipt of public comment, by the Director of the Office of Management and Budget and which shall provide for a uniform schedule of fees for all agencies.

(ii) Such agency regulations shall provide that—

(I) fees shall be limited to reasonable standard charges for document search, duplication, and review, when records are requested for commercial use;

(II) fees shall be limited to reasonable standard charges for document duplication when records are not sought for commercial use and the request is made by an educational or noncommercial scientific institution, whose purpose is scholarly or scientific research; or a representative of the news media; and

(III) for any request not described in (I) or (II), fees shall be limited to reasonable standard charges for document search and duplication.

* * *

(iii) Documents shall be furnished without any charge or at a charge reduced below the fees established under clause (ii) if disclosure of the information is in the public interest because it is likely to contribute significantly to public understanding of the operations or activities of the government and is not primarily in the commercial interest of the requester. * * *

(b) This section does not apply to matters that are—

(1)(A) specifically authorized under criteria established by an Executive order to be kept secret in the interest of national defense or foreign policy and (B) are in fact properly classified pursuant to such Executive order;

(2) related solely to the internal personnel rules and practices of an agency;

(3) specifically exempted from disclosure by statute (other than section 552b of this title), if that statute—

(A)(i) requires that the matters be withheld from the public in such a manner as to leave no discretion on the issue; or

(ii) establishes particular criteria for withholding or refers to particular types of matters to be withheld; and

(B) if enacted after the date of enactment of the OPEN FOIA Act of 2009, specifically cites to this paragraph.

(4) trade secrets and commercial or financial information obtained from a person and privileged or confidential;

(5) inter-agency or intra-agency memorandums or letters which would not be available by law to a party other than an agency in litigation with the agency;

(6) personnel and medical files and similar files the disclosure of which would constitute a clearly unwarranted invasion of personal privacy;

(7) records or information compiled for law enforcement purposes, but only to the extent that the production of such law enforcement records or information (A) could reasonably be expected to interfere with enforcement proceedings, (B) would deprive a person of a right to a fair trial or an impartial adjudication, (C) could reasonably be expected to constitute an unwarranted invasion of personal privacy, (D) could reasonably be expected to disclose the identity of a confidential source,

* * *

5 U.S.C. § 553. Rule making

(a) This section applies, according to the provisions thereof, except to the extent that there is involved—

(1) a military or foreign affairs function of the United States; or

(2) a matter relating to agency management or personnel or to public property, loans, grants, benefits, or contracts.

(b) General notice of proposed rule making shall be published in the Federal Register, unless persons subject thereto are named and either personally served or otherwise have actual notice thereof in accordance with law. The notice shall include—

(1) a statement of the time, place, and nature of public rule making proceedings;

(2) reference to the legal authority under which the rule is proposed; and

(3) either the terms or substance of the proposed rule or a description of the subjects and issues involved.

Except when notice or hearing is required by statute, this subsection does not apply—

(A) to interpretative rules, general statements of policy, or rules of agency organization, procedure, or practice; or

(B) when the agency for good cause finds (and incorporates the finding and a brief statement of reasons therefor in the rules issued) that notice and public procedure thereon are impracticable, unnecessary, or contrary to the public interest.

(c) After notice required by this section, the agency shall give interested persons an opportunity to participate in the rule making through submission of written data, views, or arguments with or without opportunity for oral presentation. After consideration of the relevant matter presented, the agency shall incorporate in the rules adopted a concise general statement of their basis and purpose. When rules are required by statute to be made on the record after opportunity for an agency hearing, sections 556 and 557 of this title apply instead of this subsection.

concise general statement of basis / purpose

(d) The required publication or service of a substantive rule shall be made not less than 30 days before its effective date, except—

> (1) a substantive rule which grants or recognizes an exemption or relieves a restriction;

> (2) interpretative rules and statements of policy; or

> (3) as otherwise provided by the agency for good cause found and published with the rule.

(e) Each agency shall give an interested person the right to petition for the issuance, amendment, or repeal of a rule.

5 U.S.C. § 554. Adjudications

(a) This section applies, according to the provisions thereof, in every case of adjudication required by statute to be determined on the record after opportunity for an agency hearing, except to the extent that there is involved—

> (1) a matter subject to a subsequent trial of the law and the facts de novo in a court;

> (2) the selection or tenure of an employee, except a[n] administrative law judge appointed under section 3105 of this title;

> (3) proceedings in which decisions rest solely on inspections, tests, or elections;

> (4) the conduct of military or foreign affairs functions;

> (5) cases in which an agency is acting as an agent for a court; or

> (6) the certification of worker representatives.

(b) Persons entitled to notice of an agency hearing shall be timely informed of—

> (1) the time, place, and nature of the hearing;

> (2) the legal authority and jurisdiction under which the hearing is to be held; and

> (3) the matters of fact and law asserted.

When private persons are the moving parties, other parties to the proceeding shall give prompt notice of issues controverted in fact or law; and in other instances agencies may by rule require responsive pleading. In fixing the time and place for hearings, due regard shall be had for the convenience and necessity of the parties or their representatives.

(c) The agency shall give all interested parties opportunity for—

(1) the submission and consideration of facts, arguments, offers of settlement, or proposals of adjustment when time, the nature of the proceeding, and the public interest permit; and

(2) to the extent that the parties are unable so to determine a controversy by consent, hearing and decision on notice and in accordance with sections 556 and 557 of this title.

(d) The employee who presides at the reception of evidence pursuant to section 556 of this title shall make the recommended decision or initial decision required by section 557 of this title, unless he becomes unavailable to the agency. Except to the extent required for the disposition of ex parte matters as authorized by law, such an employee may not—

(1) consult a person or party on a fact in issue, unless on notice and opportunity for all parties to participate; or

(2) be responsible to or subject to the supervision or direction of an employee or agent engaged in the performance of investigative or prosecuting functions for an agency.

An employee or agent engaged in the performance of investigative or prosecuting functions for an agency in a case may not, in that or a factually related case, participate or advise in the decision, recommended decision, or agency review pursuant to section 557 of this title, except as witness or counsel in public proceedings. This subsection does not apply—

(A) in determining applications for initial licenses;

(B) to proceedings involving the validity or application of rates, facilities, or practices of public utilities or carriers; or

(C) to the agency or a member or members of the body comprising the agency.

(e) The agency, with like effect as in the case of other orders, and in its sound discretion, may issue a declaratory order to terminate a controversy or remove uncertainty.

5 U.S.C. § 555. Ancillary matters

(a) This section applies, according to the provisions thereof, except as otherwise provided by this subchapter.

(b) A person compelled to appear in person before an agency or representative thereof is entitled to be accompanied, represented, and advised by counsel or, if permitted by the agency, by other qualified representative. A party is entitled to appear in person or by or with counsel or other duly qualified representative in an agency proceeding. So far as the orderly conduct of public business permits, an interested person may appear before an agency or its responsible employees for the presentation, adjustment, or determination of an issue, request, or controversy in a proceeding, whether interlocutory, summary, or otherwise, or in connection with an agency function. With due regard for the convenience and necessity of the parties or their representatives and within a reasonable time, each agency shall proceed to conclude a matter presented to it. This subsection does not grant or deny a person who is not a lawyer the right to appear for or represent others before an agency or in an agency proceeding.

(c)   Process, requirement of a report, inspection, or other investigative act or demand may not be issued, made, or enforced except as authorized by law. A person compelled to submit data or evidence is entitled to retain or, on payment of lawfully prescribed costs, procure a copy or transcript thereof, except that in a nonpublic investigatory proceeding the witness may for good cause be limited to inspection of the official transcript of his testimony.

(d)   Agency subpoenas authorized by law shall be issued to a party on request and, when required by rules of procedure, on a statement or showing of general relevance and reasonable scope of the evidence sought. On contest, the court shall sustain the subpoena or similar process or demand to the extent that it is found to be in accordance with law. In a proceeding for enforcement, the court shall issue an order requiring the appearance of the witness or the production of the evidence or data within a reasonable time under penalty of punishment for contempt in case of contumacious failure to comply.

(e)   Prompt notice shall be given of the denial in whole or in part of a written application, petition, or other request of an interested person made in connection with any agency proceeding. Except in affirming a prior denial or when the denial is self-explanatory, the notice shall be accompanied by a brief statement of the grounds for denial.

5 U.S.C. § 556.   Hearings; presiding employees; powers and duties; burden of proof; evidence; record as basis of decision

(a)   This section applies, according to the provisions thereof, to hearings required by section 553 or 554 of this title to be conducted in accordance with this section.

(b)   There shall preside at the taking of evidence—

   (1)   the agency;

   (2)   one or more members of the body which comprises the agency; or

   (3)   one or more administrative law judges appointed under section 3105 of this title.

This subchapter does not supersede the conduct of specified classes of proceedings, in whole or in part, by or before boards or other employees specially provided for by or designated under statute. The functions of presiding employees and of employees participating in decisions in accordance with section 557 of this title shall be conducted in an impartial manner. A presiding or participating employee may at any time disqualify himself. On the filing in good faith of a timely and sufficient affidavit of personal bias or other disqualification of a presiding or participating employee, the agency shall determine the matter as a part of the record and decision in the case.

(c)   Subject to published rules of the agency and within its powers, employees presiding at hearings may—

   (1)   administer oaths and affirmations;

(2)   issue subpoenas authorized by law;

(3)   rule on offers of proof and receive relevant evidence;

(4)   take depositions or have depositions taken when the ends of justice would be served;

(5)   regulate the course of the hearing;

(6)   hold conferences for the settlement or simplification of the issues by consent of the parties or by the use of alternative means of dispute resolution as provided in subchapter IV of this chapter;

(7)   inform the parties as to the availability of one or more alternative means of dispute resolution, and encourage use of such methods;

(8)   require the attendance at any conference held pursuant to paragraph (6) of at least one representative of each party who has authority to negotiate concerning resolution of issues in controversy;

(9)   dispose of procedural requests or similar matters;

(10) make or recommend decisions in accordance with section 557 of this title; and

(11) take other action authorized by agency rule consistent with this subchapter.

(d)   Except as otherwise provided by statute, the proponent of a rule or order has the burden of proof. Any oral or documentary evidence may be received, but the agency as a matter of policy shall provide for the exclusion of irrelevant, immaterial, or unduly repetitious evidence. A sanction may not be imposed or rule or order issued except on consideration of the whole record or those parts thereof cited by a party and supported by and in accordance with the reliable, probative, and substantial evidence. The agency may, to the extent consistent with the interests of justice and the policy of the underlying statutes administered by the agency, consider a violation of section 557(d) of this title sufficient grounds for a decision adverse to a party who has knowingly committed such violation or knowingly caused such violation to occur. A party is entitled to present his case or defense by oral or documentary evidence, to submit rebuttal evidence, and to conduct such cross-examination as may be required for a full and true disclosure of the facts. In rule making or determining claims for money or benefits or applications for initial licenses an agency may, when a party will not be prejudiced thereby, adopt procedures for the submission of all or part of the evidence in written form.

(e)   The transcript of testimony and exhibits, together with all papers and requests filed in the proceeding, constitutes the exclusive record for decision in accordance with section 557 of this title and, on payment of lawfully prescribed costs, shall be made available to the parties. When an agency decision rests on official notice of a material fact not appearing in the evidence in the record, a party is entitled, on timely request, to an opportunity to show the contrary.

5 U.S.C. § 557. Initial decisions; conclusiveness; review by agency; submissions by parties; contents of decisions; record

(a) This section applies, according to the provisions thereof, when a hearing is required to be conducted in accordance with section 556 of this title.

(b) When the agency did not preside at the reception of the evidence, the presiding employee or, in cases not subject to section 554(d) of this title, an employee qualified to preside at hearings pursuant to section 556 of this title, shall initially decide the case unless the agency requires, either in specific cases or by general rule, the entire record to be certified to it for decision. When the presiding employee makes an initial decision, that decision then becomes the decision of the agency without further proceedings unless there is an appeal to, or review on motion of, the agency within time provided by rule. On appeal from or review of the initial decision, the agency has all the powers which it would have in making the initial decision except as it may limit the issues on notice or by rule. When the agency makes the decision without having presided at the reception of the evidence, the presiding employee or an employee qualified to preside at hearings pursuant to section 556 of this title shall first recommend a decision, except that in rule making or determining applications for initial licenses—

> (1) instead thereof the agency may issue a tentative decision or one of its responsible employees may recommend a decision; or

> (2) this procedure may be omitted in a case in which the agency finds on the record that due and timely execution of its functions imperatively and unavoidably so requires.

(c) Before a recommended, initial, or tentative decision, or a decision on agency review of the decision of subordinate employees, the parties are entitled to a reasonable opportunity to submit for the consideration of the employees participating in the decisions—

> (1) proposed findings and conclusions; or

> (2) exceptions to the decisions or recommended decisions of subordinate employees or to tentative agency decisions; and

> (3) supporting reasons for the exceptions or proposed findings or conclusions.

The record shall show the ruling on each finding, conclusion, or exception presented. All decisions, including initial, recommended, and tentative decisions, are a part of the record and shall include a statement of—

> (A) findings and conclusions, and the reasons or basis therefor, on all the material issues of fact, law, or discretion presented on the record; and

> (B) the appropriate rule, order, sanction, relief, or denial thereof.

(d)(1) In any agency proceeding which is subject to subsection (a) of this section, except to the extent required for the disposition of ex parte matters as authorized by law—

> (A) no interested person outside the agency shall make or knowingly cause to be made to any member of the body comprising the agency,

administrative law judge, or other employee who is or may reasonably be expected to be involved in the decisional process of the proceeding, an ex parte communication relevant to the merits of the proceeding;

(B) no member of the body comprising the agency, administrative law judge, or other employee who is or may reasonably be expected to be involved in the decisional process of the proceeding, shall make or knowingly cause to be made to any interested person outside the agency an ex parte communication relevant to the merits of the proceeding;

(C) a member of the body comprising the agency, administrative law judge, or other employee who is or may reasonably be expected to be involved in the decisional process of such proceeding who receives, or who makes or knowingly causes to be made, a communication prohibited by this subsection shall place on the public record of the proceeding:

(i) all such written communications;

(ii) memoranda stating the substance of all such oral communications; and

(iii) all written responses, and memoranda stating the substance of all oral responses, to the materials described in clauses (i) and (ii) of this subparagraph;

(D) upon receipt of a communication knowingly made or knowingly caused to be made by a party in violation of this subsection, the agency, administrative law judge, or other employee presiding at the hearing may, to the extent consistent with the interests of justice and the policy of the underlying statutes, require the party to show cause why his claim or interest in the proceeding should not be dismissed, denied, disregarded, or otherwise adversely affected on account of such violation; and

(E) the prohibitions of this subsection shall apply beginning at such time as the agency may designate, but in no case shall they begin to apply later than the time at which a proceeding is noticed for hearing unless the person responsible for the communication has knowledge that it will be noticed, in which case the prohibitions shall apply beginning at the time of his acquisition of such knowledge.

(2) This subsection does not constitute authority to withhold information from Congress.

5 U.S.C. § 558.   Imposition of sanctions; determination of applications for licenses; suspension, revocation, and expiration of licenses

(a) This section applies, according to the provisions thereof, to the exercise of a power or authority.

(b) A sanction may not be imposed or a substantive rule or order issued except within jurisdiction delegated to the agency and as authorized by law.

(c) When application is made for a license required by law, the agency, with due regard for the rights and privileges of all the interested parties or adversely affected persons and within a reasonable time, shall set and complete proceedings required to be conducted in accordance with sections 556 and 557 of this title or other proceedings required by law and shall make its decision. Except in cases of willfulness or those in which public health, interest, or safety requires otherwise, the withdrawal, suspension, revocation, or annulment of a license is lawful only if, before the institution of agency proceedings therefor, the licensee has been given—

(1) notice by the agency in writing of the facts or conduct which may warrant the action; and

(2) opportunity to demonstrate or achieve compliance with all lawful requirements. When the licensee has made timely and sufficient application for a renewal or a new license in accordance with agency rules, a license with reference to an activity of a continuing nature does not expire until the application has been finally determined by the agency.

* * *

5 U.S.C. § 701.   Application; Definitions

(a) This chapter applies, according to the provisions thereof, except to the extent that—

(1) statutes preclude judicial review; or

(2) agency action is committed to agency discretion by law.

(b) For the purpose of this chapter—

(1) "agency" means each authority of the Government of the United States, whether or not it is within or subject to review by another agency, but does not include—

(A) the Congress;

(B) the courts of the United States;

(C) the governments of the territories or possessions of the United States;

(D) the government of the District of Columbia;

(E) agencies composed of representatives of the parties or of representatives of organizations of the parties to the disputes determined by them;

(F) courts martial and military commissions;

(G) military authority exercised in the field in time of war or in occupied territory; or

(H) functions conferred by sections 1738, 1739, 1743, and 1744 of title 12; subchapter II of chapter 471 of title 49; or sections 1884, 1891–1902, and former section 1641(b)(2), of title 50, appendix; and

(2) "person", "rule", "order", "license", "sanction", "relief", and "agency action" have the meanings given them by section 551 of this title.

5 U.S.C. § 702.   Right of review

A person suffering legal wrong because of agency action, or adversely affected or aggrieved by agency action within the meaning of a relevant statute, is entitled to judicial review thereof. An action in a court of the United States seeking relief other than money damages and stating a claim that an agency or an officer or employee thereof acted or failed to act in an official capacity or under color of legal authority shall not be dismissed nor relief therein be denied on the ground that it is against the United States or that the United States is an indispensable party. The United States may be named as a defendant in any such action, and a judgment or decree may be entered against the United States: *Provided,* That any mandatory or injunctive decree shall specify the Federal officer or officers (by name or by title), and their successors in office, personally responsible for compliance. Nothing herein (1) affects other limitations on judicial review or the power or duty of the court to dismiss any action or deny relief on any other appropriate legal or equitable ground; or (2) confers authority to grant relief if any other statute that grants consent to suit expressly or impliedly forbids the relief which is sought.

5 U.S.C. § 703.   Form and venue of proceeding

The form of proceeding for judicial review is the special statutory review proceeding relevant to the subject matter in a court specified by statute or, in the absence or inadequacy thereof, any applicable form of legal action, including actions for declaratory judgments or writs of prohibitory or mandatory injunction or habeas corpus, in a court of competent jurisdiction. If no special statutory review proceeding is applicable, the action for judicial review may be brought against the United States, the agency by its official title, or the appropriate officer. Except to the extent that prior, adequate, and exclusive opportunity for judicial review is provided by law, agency action is subject to judicial review in civil or criminal proceedings for judicial enforcement.

5 U.S.C. § 704.   Actions reviewable

Agency action made reviewable by statute and final agency action for which there is no other adequate remedy in a court are subject to judicial review. A preliminary, procedural, or intermediate agency action or ruling not directly reviewable is subject to review on the review of the final agency action. Except as otherwise expressly required by statute, agency action otherwise final is final for the purposes of this section whether or not there has been presented or determined an application for a declaratory order, for any form of reconsideration, or, unless the agency otherwise requires by rule and provides that the action meanwhile is inoperative, for an appeal to superior agency authority.

5 U.S.C. § 705.   Relief pending review

When an agency finds that justice so requires, it may postpone the effective date of action taken by it, pending judicial review. On such conditions as may be required and to the extent necessary to prevent irreparable injury, the reviewing court, including the court to which a case may be taken on appeal from or on application for certiorari or other writ to a reviewing court, may issue all necessary and appropriate process to postpone the effective date of an agency action or to preserve status or rights pending conclusion of the review proceedings.

5 U.S.C. § 706.   Scope of review

To the extent necessary to decision and when presented, the reviewing court shall decide all relevant questions of law, interpret constitutional and statutory provisions, and determine the meaning or applicability of the terms of an agency action. The reviewing court shall—

(1)   compel agency action unlawfully withheld or unreasonably delayed; and

(2)   hold unlawful and set aside agency action, findings, and conclusions found to be—

(A)   arbitrary, capricious, an abuse of discretion, or otherwise not in accordance with law;

(B)   contrary to constitutional right, power, privilege, or immunity;

(C)   in excess of statutory jurisdiction, authority, or limitations, or short of statutory right;

(D)   without observance of procedure required by law;

(E)   unsupported by substantial evidence in a case subject to sections 556 and 557 of this title or otherwise reviewed on the record of an agency hearing provided by statute; or

(F)   unwarranted by the facts to the extent that the facts are subject to trial de novo by the reviewing court.

In making the foregoing determinations, the court shall review the whole record or those parts of it cited by a party, and due account shall be taken of the rule of prejudicial error.

* * *

5 U.S.C. § 3105.   Appointment of administrative law judges

Each agency shall appoint as many administrative law judges as are necessary for proceedings required to be conducted in accordance with sections 556 and 557 of this title. Administrative law judges shall be assigned to cases in rotation so far as practicable, and may not perform duties inconsistent with their duties and responsibilities as administrative law judges.

APPENDIX D

EXECUTIVE ORDERS ADDRESSING REGULATORY PLANNING AND REVIEW

■ ■ ■

Executive Order 12866; 58 Fed. Reg. 51735, October 4, 1993

The American people deserve a regulatory system that works for them, not against them: a regulatory system that protects and improves their health, safety, environment, and well-being and improves the performance of the economy without imposing unacceptable or unreasonable costs on society; regulatory policies that recognize that the private sector and private markets are the best engine for economic growth; regulatory approaches that respect the role of State, local, and tribal governments; and regulations that are effective, consistent, sensible, and understandable. We do not have such a regulatory system today.

With this Executive order, the Federal Government begins a program to reform and make more efficient the regulatory process. The objectives of this Executive order are to enhance planning and coordination with respect to both new and existing regulations; to reaffirm the primacy of Federal agencies in the regulatory decision-making process; to restore the integrity and legitimacy of regulatory review and oversight; and to make the process more accessible and open to the public. In pursuing these objectives, the regulatory process shall be conducted so as to meet applicable statutory requirements and with due regard to the discretion that has been entrusted to the Federal agencies.

Accordingly, by the authority vested in me as President by the Constitution and the laws of the United States of America, it is hereby ordered as follows:

Section 1. *Statement of Regulatory Philosophy and Principles.*

(a) *The Regulatory Philosophy.* Federal agencies should promulgate only such regulations as are required by law, are necessary to interpret the law, or are made necessary by compelling public need, such as material failures of private markets to protect or improve the health and safety of the public, the environment, or the well-being of the American people. In deciding whether and how to regulate, agencies should assess all costs and benefits of available regulatory alternatives, including the alternative of not regulating. Costs and benefits shall be understood to include both quantifiable measures (to the fullest extent that these can be usefully estimated) and qualitative measures of costs and benefits that are difficult to quantify, but nevertheless essential to consider. Further, in choosing among alternative regulatory approaches, agencies should select those approaches that maximize net benefits (including potential economic, environmental, public health and safety, and other advantages; distributive impacts; and equity), unless a statute requires another regulatory approach.

(b) *The Principles of Regulation.* To ensure that the agencies' regulatory programs are consistent with the philosophy set forth above, agencies should adhere to the following principles, to the extent permitted by law and where applicable:

(1) Each agency shall identify the problem that it intends to address (including, where applicable, the failures of private markets or public institutions that warrant new agency action) as well as assess the significance of that problem.

(2) Each agency shall examine whether existing regulations (or other law) have created, or contributed to, the problem that a new regulation is intended to correct and whether those regulations (or other law) should be modified to achieve the intended goal of regulation more effectively.

(3) Each agency shall identify and assess available alternatives to direct regulation, including providing economic incentives to encourage the desired behavior, such as user fees or marketable permits, or providing information upon which choices can be made by the public.

(4) In setting regulatory priorities, each agency shall consider, to the extent reasonable, the degree and nature of the risks posed by various substances or activities within its jurisdiction.

(5) When an agency determines that a regulation is the best available method of achieving the regulatory objective, it shall design its regulations in the most cost-effective manner to achieve the regulatory objective. In doing so, each agency shall consider incentives for innovation, consistency, predictability, the costs of enforcement and compliance (to the government, regulated entities, and the public), flexibility, distributive impacts, and equity.

(6) Each agency shall assess both the costs and the benefits of the intended regulation and, recognizing that some costs and benefits are difficult to quantify, propose or adopt a regulation only upon a reasoned determination that the benefits of the intended regulation justify its costs.

(7) Each agency shall base its decisions on the best reasonably obtainable scientific, technical, economic, and other information concerning the need for, and consequences of, the intended regulation.

(8) Each agency shall identify and assess alternative forms of regulation and shall, to the extent feasible, specify performance objectives, rather than specifying the behavior or manner of compliance that regulated entities must adopt.

(9) Wherever feasible, agencies shall seek views of appropriate State, local, and tribal officials before imposing regulatory requirements that might significantly or uniquely affect those governmental entities. Each agency shall assess the effects of Federal regulations on State, local, and tribal governments, including specifically the availability of resources to carry out those mandates, and seek to minimize those burdens that uniquely or significantly affect such governmental entities, consistent with achieving regulatory objectives. In addition, as appropriate, agencies shall seek to harmonize Federal regulatory

actions with related State, local, and tribal regulatory and other governmental functions.

(10) Each agency shall avoid regulations that are inconsistent, incompatible, or duplicative with its other regulations or those of other Federal agencies.

(11) Each agency shall tailor its regulations to impose the least burden on society, including individuals, businesses of differing sizes, and other entities (including small communities and governmental entities), consistent with obtaining the regulatory objectives, taking into account, among other things, and to the extent practicable, the costs of cumulative regulations.

(12) Each agency shall draft its regulations to be simple and easy to understand, with the goal of minimizing the potential for uncertainty and litigation arising from such uncertainty.

Section 2. *Organization.* An efficient regulatory planning and review process is vital to ensure that the Federal Government's regulatory system best serves the American people.

(a) *The Agencies.* Because Federal agencies are the repositories of significant substantive expertise and experience, they are responsible for developing regulations and assuring that the regulations are consistent with applicable law, the President's priorities, and the principles set forth in this Executive order.

(b) *The Office of Management and Budget.* Coordinated review of agency rulemaking is necessary to ensure that regulations are consistent with applicable law, the President's priorities, and the principles set forth in this Executive order, and that decisions made by one agency do not conflict with the policies or actions taken or planned by another agency. The Office of Management and Budget (OMB) shall carry out that review function. Within OMB, the Office of Information and Regulatory Affairs (OIRA) is the repository of expertise concerning regulatory issues, including methodologies and procedures that affect more than one agency, this Executive order, and the President's regulatory policies. To the extent permitted by law, OMB shall provide guidance to agencies and assist the President, the Vice President, and other regulatory policy advisors to the President in regulatory planning and shall be the entity that reviews individual regulations, as provided by this Executive order.

(c) *The Vice President.* The Vice President is the principal advisor to the President on, and shall coordinate the development and presentation of recommendations concerning, regulatory policy, planning, and review, as set forth in this Executive order. In fulfilling their responsibilities under this Executive order, the President and the Vice President shall be assisted by the regulatory policy advisors within the Executive Office of the President and by such agency officials and personnel as the President and the Vice President may, from time to time, consult.

Section 3. *Definitions.* For purposes of this Executive order:

(a) "Advisors" refers to such regulatory policy advisors to the President as the President and Vice President may from time to time consult, including, among others: (1) the Director of OMB; (2) the Chair (or another member) of the Council of

Economic Advisers; (3) the Assistant to the President for Economic Policy; (4) the Assistant to the President for Domestic Policy; (5) the Assistant to the President for National Security Affairs; (6) the Assistant to the President for Science and Technology; (7) the Assistant to the President for Intergovernmental Affairs; (8) the Assistant to the President and Staff Secretary; (9) the Assistant to the President and Chief of Staff to the Vice President; (10) the Assistant to the President and Counsel to the President; (11) the Deputy Assistant to the President and Director of the White House Office on Environmental Policy; and (12) the Administrator of OIRA, who also shall coordinate communications relating to this Executive order among the agencies, OMB, the other Advisors, and the Office of the Vice President.

(b) "Agency," unless otherwise indicated, means any authority of the United States that is an "agency" under 44 U.S.C. 3502(1), other than those considered to be independent regulatory agencies, as defined in 44 U.S.C. 3502(10).

(c) "Director" means the Director of OMB.

(d) "Regulation" or "rule" means an agency statement of general applicability and future effect, which the agency intends to have the force and effect of law, that is designed to implement, interpret, or prescribe law or policy or to describe the procedure or practice requirements of an agency. It does not, however, include:

(1) Regulations or rules issued in accordance with the formal rulemaking provisions of 5 U.S.C. 556, 557;

(2) Regulations or rules that pertain to a military or foreign affairs function of the United States, other than procurement regulations and regulations involving the import or export of non-defense articles and services;

(3) Regulations or rules that are limited to agency organization, management, or personnel matters; or

(4) Any other category of regulations exempted by the Administrator of OIRA.

(e) "Regulatory action" means any substantive action by an agency (normally published in the Federal Register) that promulgates or is expected to lead to the promulgation of a final rule or regulation, including notices of inquiry, advance notices of proposed rulemaking, and notices of proposed rulemaking.

(f) "Significant regulatory action" means any regulatory action that is likely to result in a rule that may:

(1) Have an annual effect on the economy of $100 million or more or adversely affect in a material way the economy, a sector of the economy, productivity, competition, jobs, the environment, public health or safety, or State, local, or tribal governments or communities;

(2) Create a serious inconsistency or otherwise interfere with an action taken or planned by another agency;

(3) Materially alter the budgetary impact of entitlements, grants, user fees, or loan programs or the rights and obligations of recipients thereof; or

(4) Raise novel legal or policy issues arising out of legal mandates, the President's priorities, or the principles set forth in this Executive order.

Section 4. *Planning Mechanism.* In order to have an effective regulatory program, to provide for coordination of regulations, to maximize consultation and the resolution of potential conflicts at an early stage, to involve the public and its State, local, and tribal officials in regulatory planning, and to ensure that new or revised regulations promote the President's priorities and the principles set forth in this Executive order, these procedures shall be followed, to the extent permitted by law:

(a) *Agencies' Policy Meeting.* Early in each year's planning cycle, the Vice President shall convene a meeting of the Advisors and the heads of agencies to seek a common understanding of priorities and to coordinate regulatory efforts to be accomplished in the upcoming year.

(b) *Unified Regulatory Agenda.* For purposes of this subsection, the term "agency" or "agencies" shall also include those considered to be independent regulatory agencies, as defined in 44 U.S.C. 3502(10). Each agency shall prepare an agenda of all regulations under development or review, at a time and in a manner specified by the Administrator of OIRA. The description of each regulatory action shall contain, at a minimum, a regulation identifier number, a brief summary of the action, the legal authority for the action, any legal deadline for the action, and the name and telephone number of a knowledgeable agency official. Agencies may incorporate the information required under 5 U.S.C. 602 and 41 U.S.C. 402 into these agendas.

(c) *The Regulatory Plan.* For purposes of this subsection, the term "agency" or "agencies" shall also include those considered to be independent regulatory agencies, as defined in 44 U.S.C. 3502(10).

(1) As part of the Unified Regulatory Agenda, beginning in 1994, each agency shall prepare a Regulatory Plan (Plan) of the most important significant regulatory actions that the agency reasonably expects to issue in proposed or final form in that fiscal year or thereafter. The Plan shall be approved personally by the agency head and shall contain at a minimum:

(A) A statement of the agency's regulatory objectives and priorities and how they relate to the President's priorities;

(B) A summary of each planned significant regulatory action including, to the extent possible, alternatives to be considered and preliminary estimates of the anticipated costs and benefits;

(C) A summary of the legal basis for each such action, including whether any aspect of the action is required by statute or court order;

(D) A statement of the need for each such action and, if applicable, how the action will reduce risks to public health, safety, or the environment, as well as how the magnitude of the risk addressed by the action relates to other risks within the jurisdiction of the agency;

(E) The agency's schedule for action, including a statement of any applicable statutory or judicial deadlines; and

(F) The name, address, and telephone number of a person the public may contact for additional information about the planned regulatory action.

(2) Each agency shall forward its Plan to OIRA by June 1st of each year.

(3) Within 10 calendar days after OIRA has received an agency's Plan, OIRA shall circulate it to other affected agencies, the Advisors, and the Vice President.

(4) An agency head who believes that a planned regulatory action of another agency may conflict with its own policy or action taken or planned shall promptly notify, in writing, the Administrator of OIRA, who shall forward that communication to the issuing agency, the Advisors, and the Vice President.

(5) If the Administrator of OIRA believes that a planned regulatory action of an agency may be inconsistent with the President's priorities or the principles set forth in this Executive order or may be in conflict with any policy or action taken or planned by another agency, the Administrator of OIRA shall promptly notify, in writing, the affected agencies, the Advisors, and the Vice President.

(6) The Vice President, with the Advisors' assistance, may consult with the heads of agencies with respect to their Plans and, in appropriate instances, request further consideration or inter-agency coordination.

(7) The Plans developed by the issuing agency shall be published annually in the October publication of the Unified Regulatory Agenda. This publication shall be made available to the Congress; State, local, and tribal governments; and the public. Any views on any aspect of any agency Plan, including whether any planned regulatory action might conflict with any other planned or existing regulation, impose any unintended consequences on the public, or confer any unclaimed benefits on the public, should be directed to the issuing agency, with a copy to OIRA.

(d) *Regulatory Working Group.* Within 30 days of the date of this Executive order, the Administrator of OIRA shall convene a Regulatory Working Group ("Working Group"), which shall consist of representatives of the heads of each agency that the Administrator determines to have significant domestic regulatory responsibility, the Advisors, and the Vice President. The Administrator of OIRA shall chair the Working Group and shall periodically advise the Vice President on the activities of the Working Group. The Working Group shall serve as a forum to assist agencies in identifying and analyzing important regulatory issues (including, among others (1) the development of innovative regulatory techniques, (2) the methods, efficacy, and utility of comparative risk assessment in regulatory decision-making, and (3) the development of short forms and other streamlined regulatory approaches for small businesses and other entities). The Working Group shall meet at least quarterly and may meet as a whole or in subgroups of agencies with an interest in particular issues or subject areas. To inform its discussions, the Working Group may commission analytical studies and reports by OIRA, the Administrative Conference of the United States, or any other agency.

(e) *Conferences.* The Administrator of OIRA shall meet quarterly with representatives of State, local, and tribal governments to identify both existing and proposed regulations that may uniquely or significantly affect those governmental entities. The Administrator of OIRA shall also convene, from time to time, conferences with representatives of businesses, nongovernmental organizations, and the public to discuss regulatory issues of common concern.

Section 5. *Existing Regulations.* * * *

Section 6. *Centralized Review of Regulations.* The guidelines set forth below shall apply to all regulatory actions, for both new and existing regulations, by agencies other than those agencies specifically exempted by the Administrator of OIRA:

(a) *Agency Responsibilities.* (1) Each agency shall (consistent with its own rules, regulations, or procedures) provide the public with meaningful participation in the regulatory process. In particular, before issuing a notice of proposed rulemaking, each agency should, where appropriate, seek the involvement of those who are intended to benefit from and those expected to be burdened by any regulation (including, specifically, State, local, and tribal officials). In addition, each agency should afford the public a meaningful opportunity to comment on any proposed regulation, which in most cases should include a comment period of not less than 60 days. Each agency also is directed to explore and, where appropriate, use consensual mechanisms for developing regulations, including negotiated rulemaking.

(2) Within 60 days of the date of this Executive order, each agency head shall designate a Regulatory Policy Officer who shall report to the agency head. The Regulatory Policy Officer shall be involved at each stage of the regulatory process to foster the development of effective, innovative, and least burdensome regulations and to further the principles set forth in this Executive order.

(3) In addition to adhering to its own rules and procedures and to the requirements of the Administrative Procedure Act, the Regulatory Flexibility Act, the Paperwork Reduction Act, and other applicable law, each agency shall develop its regulatory actions in a timely fashion and adhere to the following procedures with respect to a regulatory action:

(A) Each agency shall provide OIRA, at such times and in the manner specified by the Administrator of OIRA, with a list of its planned regulatory actions, indicating those which the agency believes are significant regulatory actions within the meaning of this Executive order. Absent a material change in the development of the planned regulatory action, those not designated as significant will not be subject to review under this section unless, within 10 working days of receipt of the list, the Administrator of OIRA notifies the agency that OIRA has determined that a planned regulation is a significant regulatory action within the meaning of this Executive order. The Administrator of OIRA may waive review of any planned regulatory action designated by the agency as significant, in which case the agency need not further comply with subsection (a)(3)(B) or subsection (a)(3)(C) of this section.

(B) For each matter identified as, or determined by the Administrator of OIRA to be, a significant regulatory action, the issuing agency shall provide to OIRA:

(i) The text of the draft regulatory action, together with a reasonably detailed description of the need for the regulatory action and an explanation of how the regulatory action will meet that need; and

(ii) An assessment of the potential costs and benefits of the regulatory action, including an explanation of the manner in which the regulatory action is consistent with a statutory mandate and, to the extent permitted by law, promotes the President's priorities and avoids undue interference with State, local, and tribal governments in the exercise of their governmental functions.

(C) For those matters identified as, or determined by the Administrator of OIRA to be, a significant regulatory action within the scope of section 3(f)(1), the agency shall also provide to OIRA the following additional information developed as part of the agency's decision-making process (unless prohibited by law):

(i) An assessment, including the underlying analysis, of benefits anticipated from the regulatory action (such as, but not limited to, the promotion of the efficient functioning of the economy and private markets, the enhancement of health and safety, the protection of the natural environment, and the elimination or reduction of discrimination or bias) together with, to the extent feasible, a quantification of those benefits;

(ii) An assessment, including the underlying analysis, of costs anticipated from the regulatory action (such as, but not limited to, the direct cost both to the government in administering the regulation and to businesses and others in complying with the regulation, and any adverse effects on the efficient functioning of the economy, private markets (including productivity, employment, and competitiveness), health, safety, and the natural environment), together with, to the extent feasible, a quantification of those costs; and

(iii) An assessment, including the underlying analysis, of costs and benefits of potentially effective and reasonably feasible alternatives to the planned regulation, identified by the agencies or the public (including improving the current regulation and reasonably viable nonregulatory actions), and an explanation why the planned regulatory action is preferable to the identified potential alternatives.

(D) In emergency situations or when an agency is obligated by law to act more quickly than normal review procedures allow, the agency shall notify OIRA as soon as possible and, to the extent practicable, comply with subsections (a)(3)(B) and (C) of this section. For those regulatory actions that are governed by a statutory or court-imposed deadline, the agency shall, to the extent practicable, schedule rulemaking proceedings so as to permit sufficient time for OIRA to conduct its review, as set forth below in subsection (b)(2) through (4) of this section.

(E) After the regulatory action has been published in the **Federal Register** or otherwise issued to the public, the agency shall:

(i) Make available to the public the information set forth in subsections (a)(3)(B) and (C);

(ii) Identify for the public, in a complete, clear, and simple manner, the substantive changes between the draft submitted to OIRA for review and the action subsequently announced; and

(iii) Identify for the public those changes in the regulatory action that were made at the suggestion or recommendation of OIRA.

(F) All information provided to the public by the agency shall be in plain, understandable language.

(b) *OIRA Responsibilities.* The Administrator of OIRA shall provide meaningful guidance and oversight so that each agency's regulatory actions are consistent with applicable law, the President's priorities, and the principles set forth in this Executive order and do not conflict with the policies or actions of another agency. OIRA shall, to the extent permitted by law, adhere to the following guidelines:

(1) OIRA may review only actions identified by the agency or by OIRA as significant regulatory actions under subsection (a)(3)(A) of this section.

(2) OIRA shall waive review or notify the agency in writing of the results of its review within the following time periods:

(A) For any notices of inquiry, advance notices of proposed rulemaking, or other preliminary regulatory actions prior to a Notice of Proposed Rulemaking, within 10 working days after the date of submission of the draft action to OIRA;

(B) For all other regulatory actions, within 90 calendar days after the date of submission of the information set forth in subsections (a)(3)(B) and (C) of this section, unless OIRA has previously reviewed this information and, since that review, there has been no material change in the facts and circumstances upon which the regulatory action is based, in which case, OIRA shall complete its review within 45 days; and

(C) The review process may be extended (1) once by no more than 30 calendar days upon the written approval of the Director and (2) at the request of the agency head.

(3) For each regulatory action that the Administrator of OIRA returns to an agency for further consideration of some or all of its provisions, the Administrator of OIRA shall provide the issuing agency a written explanation for such return, setting forth the pertinent provision of this Executive order on which OIRA is relying. If the agency head disagrees with some or all of the bases for the return, the agency head shall so inform the Administrator of OIRA in writing.

(4) Except as otherwise provided by law or required by a Court, in order to ensure greater openness, accessibility, and accountability in the regulatory review process, OIRA shall be governed by the following disclosure requirements:

(A) Only the Administrator of OIRA (or a particular designee) shall receive oral communications initiated by persons not employed by the executive branch of the Federal Government regarding the substance of a regulatory action under OIRA review;

(B) All substantive communications between OIRA personnel and persons not employed by the executive branch of the Federal Government regarding a regulatory action under review shall be governed by the following guidelines:

　(i) A representative from the issuing agency shall be invited to any meeting between OIRA personnel and such person(s);

　(ii) OIRA shall forward to the issuing agency, within 10 working days of receipt of the communication(s), all written communications, regardless of format, between OIRA personnel and any person who is not employed by the executive branch of the Federal Government, and the dates and names of individuals involved in all substantive oral communications (including meetings to which an agency representative was invited, but did not attend, and telephone conversations between OIRA personnel and any such persons); and

　(iii) OIRA shall publicly disclose relevant information about such communication(s), as set forth below in subsection (b)(4)(C) of this section.

(C) OIRA shall maintain a publicly available log that shall contain, at a minimum, the following information pertinent to regulatory actions under review:

　(i) The status of all regulatory actions, including if (and if so, when and by whom) Vice Presidential and Presidential consideration was requested;

　(ii) A notation of all written communications forwarded to an issuing agency under subsection (b)(4)(B)(ii) of this section; and

　(iii) The dates and names of individuals involved in all substantive oral communications, including meetings and telephone conversations, between OIRA personnel and any person not employed by the executive branch of the Federal Government, and the subject matter discussed during such communications

(D) After the regulatory action has been published in the **Federal Register** or otherwise issued to the public, or after the agency has announced its decision not to publish or issue the regulatory action, OIRA shall make available to the public all documents exchanged between OIRA and the agency during the review by OIRA under this section.

(5) All information provided to the public by OIRA shall be in plain, understandable language.

Section 7. *Resolution of Conflicts.* To the extent permitted by law, disagreements or conflicts between or among agency heads or between OMB and any agency that cannot be resolved by the Administrator of OIRA shall be resolved by the President, or by the Vice President acting at the request of the President, with the relevant agency head (and, as appropriate, other interested government officials). Vice Presidential and Presidential consideration of such disagreements may be initiated only by the Director, by the head of the issuing agency, or by the head of an agency that has a significant interest in the regulatory action at issue. Such review will not be undertaken at the request of other persons, entities, or their agents.

Resolution of such conflicts shall be informed by recommendations developed by the Vice President, after consultation with the Advisors (and other executive branch officials or personnel whose responsibilities to the President include the subject matter at issue). The development of these recommendations shall be concluded within 60 days after review has been requested.

During the Vice Presidential and Presidential review period, communications with any person not employed by the Federal Government relating to the substance of the regulatory action under review and directed to the Advisors or their staffs or to the staff of the Vice President shall be in writing and shall be forwarded by the recipient to the affected agency(ies) for inclusion in the public docket(s). When the communication is not in writing, such Advisors or staff members shall inform the outside party that the matter is under review and that any comments should be submitted in writing.

At the end of this review process, the President, or the Vice President acting at the request of the President, shall notify the affected agency and the Administrator of OIRA of the President's decision with respect to the matter.

Section 8. *Publication.* * * *

Section 9. *Agency Authority.* Nothing in this order shall be construed as displacing the agencies' authority or responsibilities, as authorized by law.

Section 10. *Judicial Review.* Nothing in this Executive order shall affect any otherwise available judicial review of agency action. This Executive order is intended only to improve the internal management of the Federal Government and does not create any right or benefit, substantive or procedural, enforceable at law or equity by a party against the United States, its agencies or instrumentalities, its officers or employees, or any other person.

Section 11. *Revocations.* Executive Orders Nos. 12291 and 12498; all amendments to those Executive orders; all guidelines issued under those orders; and any exemptions from those orders heretofore granted for any category of rule are revoked.

WILLIAM CLINTON

THE WHITE HOUSE

SEPTEMBER 30, 1993.

Executive Order 13563; 76 Fed. Reg. 3821, January 21, 2011

By the authority vested in me as President by the Constitution and the laws of the United States of America, and in order to improve regulation and regulatory review, it is hereby ordered as follows:

Section 1. *General Principles of Regulation.* (a) Our regulatory system must protect public health, welfare, safety, and our environment while promoting economic growth, innovation, competitiveness, and job creation. It must be based on the best available science. It must allow for public participation and an open exchange of ideas. It must promote predictability and reduce uncertainty. It must identify and use the best, most innovative, and least burdensome tools for achieving regulatory ends. It must take into account benefits and costs, both quantitative and qualitative. It must ensure that regulations are accessible, consistent, written in plain language, and easy to understand. It must measure, and seek to improve, the actual results of regulatory requirements.

(b) This order is supplemental to and reaffirms the principles, structures, and definitions governing contemporary regulatory review that were established in Executive Order 12866 of September 30, 1993. As stated in that Executive Order and to the extent permitted by law, each agency must, among other things: (1) propose or adopt a regulation only upon a reasoned determination that its benefits justify its costs (recognizing that some benefits and costs are difficult to quantify); (2) tailor its regulations to impose the least burden on society, consistent with obtaining regulatory objectives, taking into account, among other things, and to the extent practicable, the costs of cumulative regulations; (3) select, in choosing among alternative regulatory approaches, those approaches that maximize net benefits (including potential economic, environmental, public health and safety, and other advantages; distributive impacts; and equity); (4) to the extent feasible, specify performance objectives, rather than specifying the behavior or manner of compliance that regulated entities must adopt; and (5) identify and assess available alternatives to direct regulation, including providing economic incentives to encourage the desired behavior, such as user fees or marketable permits, or providing information upon which choices can be made by the public.

(c) In applying these principles, each agency is directed to use the best available techniques to quantify anticipated present and future benefits and costs as accurately as possible. Where appropriate and permitted by law, each agency may consider (and discuss qualitatively) values that are difficult or impossible to quantify, including equity, human dignity, fairness, and distributive impacts.

Section 2. *Public Participation.* (a) Regulations shall be adopted through a process that involves public participation. To that end, regulations shall be based, to the extent feasible and consistent with law, on the open exchange of information and perspectives among State, local, and tribal officials, experts in relevant disciplines, affected stakeholders in the private sector, and the public as a whole.

(b) To promote that open exchange, each agency, consistent with Executive Order 12866 and other applicable legal requirements, shall endeavor to provide the public with an opportunity to participate in the regulatory process. To the extent feasible and permitted by law, each agency shall afford the public a meaningful opportunity to comment through the Internet on any proposed regulation, with a comment period that should generally be at least 60 days. To the extent feasible and permitted by law, each agency shall also provide, for both proposed and final rules, timely online access to the rulemaking docket on regulations.gov, including relevant scientific and technical findings, in an open format that can be easily searched and downloaded. For proposed rules, such access shall include, to the extent feasible and permitted by law, an opportunity for public comment on all pertinent parts of the rulemaking docket, including relevant scientific and technical findings.

(c) Before issuing a notice of proposed rulemaking, each agency, where feasible and appropriate, shall seek the views of those who are likely to be affected, including those who are likely to benefit from and those who are potentially subject to such rulemaking.

Section 3. *Integration and Innovation.* Some sectors and industries face a significant number of regulatory requirements, some of which may be redundant, inconsistent, or overlapping. Greater coordination across agencies could reduce these requirements, thus reducing costs and simplifying and harmonizing rules. In developing regulatory actions and identifying appropriate approaches, each agency shall attempt to promote such coordination, simplification, and harmonization. Each agency shall also seek to identify, as appropriate, means to achieve regulatory goals that are designed to promote innovation.

Section 4. *Flexible Approaches.* Where relevant, feasible, and consistent with regulatory objectives, and to the extent permitted by law, each agency shall identify and consider regulatory approaches that reduce burdens and maintain flexibility and freedom of choice for the public. These approaches include warnings, appropriate default rules, and disclosure requirements as well as provision of information to the public in a form that is clear and intelligible.

Section 5. *Science.* Consistent with the President's Memorandum for the Heads of Executive Departments and Agencies, "Scientific Integrity" (March 9, 2009), and its implementing guidance, each agency shall ensure the objectivity of any scientific and technological information and processes used to support the agency's regulatory actions.

Section 6. *Retrospective Analyses of Existing Rules.* (a) To facilitate the periodic review of existing significant regulations, agencies shall consider how best to promote retrospective analysis of rules that may be outmoded, ineffective, insufficient, or excessively burdensome, and to modify, streamline, expand, or repeal them in accordance with what has been learned. Such retrospective analyses, including supporting data, should be released online whenever possible.

(b) Within 120 days of the date of this order, each agency shall develop and submit to the Office of Information and Regulatory Affairs a preliminary plan, consistent with law and its resources and regulatory priorities, under which the agency will periodically review its existing significant regulations to determine whether any such regulations should be modified, streamlined, expanded, or repealed so as to make the agency's regulatory program more effective or less burdensome in achieving the regulatory objectives.

Section 7. *General Provisions.* (a) For purposes of this order, "agency" shall have the meaning set forth in section 3(b) of Executive Order 12866.

(b) Nothing in this order shall be construed to impair or otherwise affect:

(i)   authority granted by law to a department or agency, or the head thereof; or

(ii) functions of the Director of the Office of Management and Budget relating to budgetary, administrative, or legislative proposals.

(c) This order shall be implemented consistent with applicable law and subject to the availability of appropriations.

(d) This order is not intended to, and does not, create any right or benefit, substantive or procedural, enforceable at law or in equity by any party against the United States, its departments, agencies, or entities, its officers, employees, or agents, or any other person.

BARACK OBAMA

THE WHITE HOUSE

JANUARY 18, 2011.

INDEX

References are to Pages